The Charles F. Stanley
LIFE PRINCIPLES
DAILY BIBLE

Charles F. Stanley

General Editor

New American Standard Bible

THOMAS NELSON

Since 1798

www.ThomasNelsonBibles.com

TABLE OF CONTENTS

THE NEW TESTAMENT

Symbols

➤ A pointer next to the Bible text indicates that there is a corresponding Life Lesson on the page.

✳ An asterisk next to highlighted Bible text indicates a Bible promise.

WELCOME TO *THE CHARLES F. STANLEY LIFE PRINCIPLES DAILY BIBLE*

Dear Friend,

*A*s I look back on my 50 years of ministry, I can say with assurance that the Holy Spirit has used God's Word to teach, encourage, strengthen, convict, and comfort me in ways too profound to express with words. Of all the books in the world, there is none more powerful, wonderful, precious, or instructive than the Word of God. That's because only the Bible is completely inspired by our heavenly Father and utterly indispensable in our pursuit of knowing Him.

When I think about how to celebrate all that God has done in my life, I realize the best thing I can do is encourage you to walk with Him day by day as I have— by reading and meditating upon Scripture. That's why I have developed the *Life Principles Daily Bible* . . . to help you read through the entire Bible in a year and grow closer to your heavenly Father.

Each day, you and I will study the Bible together through the 365 devotions I've compiled to teach you and bless your life. No doubt, you will recognize the 30 Life Principles I've included from the *Life Principles Bible*. These 30 principles are central to my relationship with God, and I pray that as you study them over the course of the year, they will help you live a life of obedience and joy in Christ.

I cannot fully express the joy it gives me to know that you will be in God's Word every day. Although you may face some very difficult times and challenges, I am confident that the Father will show Himself absolutely trustworthy. It is my prayer that as you kneel before Him and submit yourself to Him daily, you will experience His intimate presence, amazing strength, and overwhelming love more powerfully than you ever have before.

Thank you for celebrating this milestone of ministry and for being part of God's awesome work with me. I eagerly anticipate all the wonderful things He is going to do through us in the future, and I am thankful that the best is yet to come.

Prayerfully yours,

Charles F. Stanley

How to Use the
Life Principles Daily Bible

Throughout this resource, you'll find several features designed to help you get the most out of your time in God's Word:

- **Daily Bible readings** provide a portion of the Old Testament, a bit from Psalms and Proverbs, and a portion of the New Testament, from the trusted NASB. It's all in Bible order: In each day's readings, you pick up where you left off the day before. If you stay in this *Daily Bible* every day for a year, you will have read through the entire Bible!

- **Life Principles** articles highlight thirty of the Bible's most critical principles for successful Christian living. They focus on such crucial topics as building intimacy with God, prayer, obedience, dealing with adversity, and more.

- **What the Bible Says About** articles bring scriptural insight to bear on a wide variety of topics of special concern to all believers in Christ: the Holy Spirit's guidance, the process of spiritual growth, experiencing forgiveness, listening to God, and much more.

- **Answers to Life's Questions** focus on the many challenges we face in our Christian faith as we try to live for God in a world often hostile to our growth in grace. How do we deal with jealousy or bitterness, or how do we gain God's mind in a tough situation? You'll find those kinds of questions answered here.

- **Life Lessons** offer insights into individual Bible verses and passages, emphasizing the practical and personal nature of God's Word to us.

  ➤ **Pointers** in the margins indicate corresponding Life Lessons verses.

- **God's Promises** highlight hundreds of the Lord's promises to His people—promises meant to encourage, strengthen, and fill us with hope.

  ✳ **Asterisks** next to highlighted Bible text denote a Bible promise.

LIFE PRINCIPLES

FOREWORD TO THE NEW AMERICAN STANDARD BIBLE®

Scriptural Promise

"The grass withers, the flower fades, but the word of our God stands forever."
ISAIAH 40:8

*T*he New American Standard Bible has been produced with the conviction that the words of Scripture as originally penned in the Hebrew, Aramaic, and Greek were inspired by God. Since they are the eternal Word of God, the Holy Scriptures speak with fresh power to each generation, to give wisdom that leads to salvation, that men may serve Christ to the glory of God.

The purpose of the Editorial Board in making this translation was to adhere as closely as possible to the original languages of the Holy Scriptures, and to make the translation in a fluent and readable style according to current English usage.

The Fourfold Aim of the Lockman Foundation

1. These publications shall be true to the original Hebrew, Aramaic, and Greek.
2. They shall be grammatically correct.
3. They shall be understandable.
4. They shall give the Lord Jesus Christ His proper place, the place which the Word gives Him; therefore, no work will ever be personalized.

Preface to the New American Standard Bible

In the history of English Bible translations, the King James Version is the most prestigious. This time-honored version of 1611, itself a revision of the Bishops' Bible of 1568, became the basis for the English Revised Version appearing in 1881 (New Testament) and 1885 (Old Testament). The American counterpart of this last work was published in 1901 as the American Standard Version. The ASV, a product of both British and American scholarship, has been highly regarded for its scholarship and accuracy. Recognizing the values of the American Standard Version, The Lockman Foundation felt an urgency to preserve these and other lasting values of the ASV by incorporating recent discoveries of Hebrew and Greek textual sources and by rendering it into more current English. Therefore, in 1959 a new translation project was launched, based on the time-honored principles of translation of the ASV and KJV. The result is the New American Standard Bible.

Translation work for the NASB was begun in 1959. In the preparation of this work numerous other translations have been consulted along with the linguistic tools and literature of biblical scholarship. Decisions about English renderings were made by consensus of a team composed of educators and pastors. Subsequently, review and evaluation by other Hebrew and Greek scholars outside the Editorial Board were sought and carefully considered.

The Editorial Board has continued to function since publication of the complete

Bible in 1971. This edition of the NASB represents revisions and refinements recommended over the last several years as well as thorough research based on modern English usage.

Principles of Translation

MODERN ENGLISH USAGE: The attempt has been made to render the grammar and terminology in contemporary English. When it was felt that the word-for-word literalness was unacceptable to the modern reader, a change was made in the direction of a more current English idiom. There are a few exceptions to this procedure. In particular, frequently "And" is not translated at the beginning of sentences because of differences in style between ancient and modern writing. Punctuation is a relatively modern invention, and ancient writers often linked most of their sentences with "and" or other connectives. Also, the Hebrew idiom "answered and said" is sometimes reduced to "answered" or "said" as demanded by the context. For current English the idiom "it came about that" has not been translated in the New Testament except when a major transition is needed.

ALTERNATIVE READINGS: In addition to the more literal renderings, only such notations have been used as have been felt justified in assisting the reader's comprehension of the terms used by the original author.

HEBREW TEXT: In the present translation the latest edition of Rudolf Kittel's *Biblia Hebraica* has been employed together with the most recent light from lexicography, cognate languages, and the Dead Sea Scrolls.

HEBREW TENSES: Consecution of tenses in Hebrew remains a puzzling factor in translation. The translators have been guided by the requirements of a literal translation, the sequence of tenses, and the immediate and broad contexts.

THE PROPER NAME OF GOD IN THE OLD TESTAMENT: In the Scriptures, the name of God is most significant and understandably so. It is inconceivable to think of spiritual matters without a proper designation for the Supreme Deity. Thus the most common name for the Deity is God, a translation of the original *Elohim*. One of the titles for God is Lord, a translation of *Adonai*. There is yet another name which is particularly assigned to God as His special or proper name, that is, the four letters YHWH (Exodus 3:14 and Isaiah 42:8). This name has not been pronounced by the Jews because of reverence for the great sacredness of the divine name. Therefore, it has been consistently translated LORD. The only exception to this translation of YHWH is when it occurs in immediate proximity to the word Lord, that is, *Adonai*. In that case it is regularly translated GOD in order to avoid confusion.

It is known that for many years YHWH has been transliterated as Yahweh, however no complete certainty attaches to this pronunciation.

GREEK TEXT: Consideration was given to the latest available manuscripts with a view to determining the best Greek text. In most instances the 26th edition of Eberhard Nestle's *Novum Testamentum Graece* was followed.

GREEK TENSES: A careful distinction has been made in the treatment of the Greek aorist tense (usually translated as the English past, "He did") and the Greek imperfect tense (normally rendered either as English past progressive, "He was doing"; or, if inceptive, as "He began to do" or "He started to do"; or else if customary past, as "He used to do"). "Began" is italicized if it renders an imperfect tense, in order to distinguish it from the Greek verb for "begin." In some contexts the difference between the Greek imperfect and the English past is conveyed better by the choice of vocabulary or by other words in the context, and in such cases the Greek imperfect may be rendered as a simple past tense (e.g. "had an illness for many years" would be preferable to "was having an illness for many years" and would be understood in the same way).

On the other hand, not all aorists have been rendered as English pasts ("He did"), for some of them are clearly to be rendered as English perfects ("He has done"), or even as past perfects ("He had done"), judging from the context in which they occur. Such aorists have been rendered as perfects or past perfects in this translation.

As for the distinction between aorist and present imperatives, the translators have usually rendered these imperatives in the customary manner, rather than attempting any such fine distinction as "Begin to do!" (for the aorist imperative), or, "Continually do!" (for the present imperative).

As for sequence of tenses, the translators took care to follow English rules rather than Greek in translating Greek presents, imperfects and aorists. Thus, where English says, "We knew that he was doing," Greek puts it, "We knew that he does"; similarly, "We knew that he had done" is the Greek, "We knew that he did." Likewise, the English, "When he had come, they met him," is represented in Greek by, "When he came, they met him." In all cases a consistent transfer has been made from the Greek tense in the subordinate clause to the appropriate tense in English.

In the rendering of negative questions introduced by the particle *mē* (which always expects the answer "No") the wording has been altered from a mere, "Will he not do this?" to a more accurate, "He will not do this, will he?"

The Format

- **Small Caps** in the New Testament are used in the text to indicate Old Testament quotations or obvious references to Old Testament texts. Variations of Old Testament wording are found in New Testament citations depending on whether the New Testament writer translated from a Hebrew text, used existing Greek or Aramaic translations, or paraphrased the material. It should be noted that modern rules for the indication of direct quotation were not used in biblical times; thus, the ancient writer would use exact quotations or references to quotation without specific indication of such.
- **Italics** are used in the text to indicate words which are not found in the original Hebrew, Aramaic, or Greek but implied by it.
- **Asterisks** are used to mark verbs that are historical presents in the Greek which have been translated with an English past tense in order to conform to modern usage. The translators recognized that in some contexts the present tense seems more unexpected and unjustified to the English reader than a past tense would have been. But Greek authors frequently used the present tense for the sake of heightened vividness, thereby transporting their readers in imagination to the actual scene at the time of occurrence. However, the translators felt that it would be wise to change these historical presents to English past tenses.
- **Personal pronouns** are capitalized when pertaining to Deity.
- **Quotation marks** are used in the text in accordance with modern English usage.
- **"Thou," "Thee" and "Thy"** are not used in this edition and have been rendered as "You" and "Your."

THE LOCKMAN FOUNDATION

Genesis 1:1—2:25

1 IN the beginning God created the heavens and the earth.

2 The earth was formless and void, and darkness was over the surface of the deep, and the Spirit of God was moving over the surface of the waters.

3 Then God said, "Let there be light"; and there was light.

4 God saw that the light was good; and God separated the light from the darkness.

5 God called the light day, and the darkness He called night. And there was evening and there was morning, one day.

6 Then God said, "Let there be an expanse in the midst of the waters, and let it separate the waters from the waters."

7 God made the expanse, and separated the waters which were below the expanse from the waters which were above the expanse; and it was so.

8 God called the expanse heaven. And there was evening and there was morning, a second day.

9 Then God said, "Let the waters below the heavens be gathered into one place, and let the dry land appear"; and it was so.

10 God called the dry land earth, and the gathering of the waters He called seas; and God saw that it was good.

11 Then God said, "Let the earth sprout vegetation, plants yielding seed, *and* fruit trees on the earth bearing fruit after their kind with seed in them"; and it was so.

12 The earth brought forth vegetation, plants yielding seed after their kind, and trees bearing fruit with seed in them, after their kind; and God saw that it was good.

13 There was evening and there was morning, a third day.

14 Then God said, "Let there be lights in the expanse of the heavens to separate the day from the night, and let them be for signs and for seasons and for days and years;

15 and let them be for lights in the expanse of the heavens to give light on the earth"; and it was so.

16 God made the two great lights, the greater light to govern the day, and the lesser light to govern the night; *He made* the stars also.

17 God placed them in the expanse of the heavens to give light on the earth,

18 and to govern the day and the night, and to separate the light from the darkness; and God saw that it was good.

19 There was evening and there was morning, a fourth day.

20 Then God said, "Let the waters teem with swarms of living creatures, and let birds fly above the earth in the open expanse of the heavens."

21 God created the great sea monsters and every living creature that moves, with which the waters swarmed after their kind, and every winged bird after its kind; and God saw that it was good.

22 God blessed them, saying, "Be fruitful and multiply, and fill the waters in the seas, and let birds multiply on the earth."

23 There was evening and there was morning, a fifth day.

24 Then God said, "Let the earth bring forth living creatures after their kind: cattle and creeping things and beasts of the earth after their kind"; and it was so.

25 God made the beasts of the earth after their kind, and the cattle after their kind, and everything that creeps on the ground after its kind; and God saw that it was good.

26 Then God said, "Let Us make man ⊰ in Our image, according to Our likeness; and let them rule over the fish of the sea and over the birds of the sky and over ✳ the cattle and over all the earth, and over every creeping thing that creeps on the earth."

27 God created man in His own image, in the image of God He created him; male and female He created them.

28 God blessed them; and God said to them, "Be fruitful and multiply, and fill the earth, and subdue it; and rule over the fish of the sea and over the birds

LIFE LESSONS

➤ **Genesis 1:26 —** *God said, "Let Us make man in Our image."*

*W*hen God created us, He made us like Himself; therefore we have the capacity for close, personal fellowship with Him. We can count on Him to meet our need for deep personal connection.

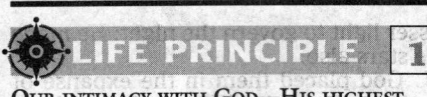
LIFE PRINCIPLE 1

OUR INTIMACY WITH GOD—HIS HIGHEST
PRIORITY FOR OUR LIVES—DETERMINES THE
IMPACT OF OUR LIVES.

GENESIS 1:26

*O*ne of our greatest needs is to know we
are loved. Each of us has to feel certain,
deep down in our hearts, that someone loves
us, cares for us, and has our best interests at
heart.

That is how God designed us. He wants us
to know He loves us with a passionate intensity too deep for words.

God created human beings with fellowship
in mind—first with Himself, then with others.
But we cannot fully love one another until we
have ourselves experienced the love of God.
We experience His love when we willingly
surrender to His call to be our Savior, Lord,
and Friend.

There are at least three reasons God seeks
our surrender:
• *He loves us and desires our fellowship and
worship.*
As long as we hold something back from
God, we cannot know Him completely or
fully experience His love. When we surrender
to Him, we get all of Him.
• *He wants our service for Him to be effective and fruitful.*
The more we know and love Jesus, the
more effective our service will be. The closer
we draw to God, the more impact our lives
will have. The more energetically we nurture
our relationship with the Lord, the greater
the positive mark we will leave behind.
• *He waits for the freedom to bless us.*
God is omnipotent, but He will not violate
His own principles. He draws us to Himself
so we can experience His love and forgiveness.
He asks for our willing surrender so He can
give us the best blessings He has to offer.
So why do we resist? With all this in
mind, why does anyone resist surrendering
to God?
Pride is the key reason most people resist
surrender. They think they know better than
God and that they can handle their lives
better than He can, so they keep Him at a
distance.

Others do not surrender because they fear
what God will do (or not do) for them. They
think that if they give Him control, He'll
make them do exactly what will make them
most miserable.

Still others refuse to surrender to Christ
because they believe Satan's lie, which tells
them God is judgmental and will punish them
for their mistakes.

All of this is completely false! God *always*
has our best in mind. He will refuse us no
good thing when we gladly submit to His will
(Rom. 8:32). He tells us, "'I know the plans
that I have for you,' declares the LORD, 'plans
for welfare and not for calamity to give you a
future and a hope'" (Jer. 29:11).

It only makes sense to surrender to God,
because when we do, we grow close to
Him—His highest priority for us—and we
begin to have an impact on our world.

Fulfill your destiny. Anne Graham Lotz
once told an interviewer about the many trials
she had faced in previous years, including her
parents' serious illnesses and her son's battle
with cancer. She finally came to the point
where all she wanted was Jesus. "Just give me
Jesus," she declared.

Anne realized that if she had a personal,
intimate relationship with the Savior of this
universe, then whatever problems she faced,
He would face them with her. He would
bring sweet resolve and peace to her heart.

Is this the cry of *your* heart? Do you want
to know the Savior and live in the fullness of
His blessing each day? You can. David wrote,
"They who seek the LORD shall not be in
want of any good thing" (Ps. 34:10).

When you accepted Jesus Christ as your
Savior, He not only forgave you but also
made you into a new creature. You were no
longer standing at a distance from God but
then were able to draw near to Him.

If you have drifted in your devotion to the
Savior and feel as though you grow more distant each day in your relationship to Him,
then pray He will draw you near once more.
He knows your weaknesses, and if you will tell
Him you want Him to take control of your
life, He will come to you in a mighty way and
bring hope and light to your situation, no
matter how dark and hopeless it may feel
(Is. 55:6, 7). ❖

of the sky and over every living thing that moves on the earth."

29 Then God said, "Behold, I have given you every plant yielding seed that is on the surface of all the earth, and every tree which has fruit yielding seed; it shall be food for you;

30 and to every beast of the earth and to every bird of the sky and to every thing that moves on the earth which has life, *I have given* every green plant for food"; and it was so.

31 God saw all that He had made, and behold, it was very good. And there was evening and there was morning, the sixth day.

2 THUS the heavens and the earth were completed, and all their hosts.

2 By the seventh day God completed His work which He had done, and He rested on the seventh day from all His work which He had done.

3 Then God blessed the seventh day and sanctified it, because in it He rested from all His work which God had created and made.

4 This is the account of the heavens and the earth when they were created, in the day that the LORD God made earth and heaven.

5 Now no shrub of the field was yet in the earth, and no plant of the field had yet sprouted, for the LORD God had not sent rain upon the earth, and there was no man to cultivate the ground.

6 But a mist used to rise from the earth and water the whole surface of the ground.

7 Then the LORD God formed man of dust from the ground, and breathed into his nostrils the breath of life; and man became a living being.

8 The LORD God planted a garden toward the east, in Eden; and there He placed the man whom He had formed.

9 Out of the ground the LORD God caused to grow every tree that is pleasing to the sight and good for food; the tree of life also in the midst of the garden, and the tree of the knowledge of good and evil.

10 Now a river flowed out of Eden to water the garden; and from there it divided and became four rivers.

11 The name of the first is Pishon; it flows around the whole land of Havilah, where there is gold.

12 The gold of that land is good; the bdellium and the onyx stone are there.

13 The name of the second river is Gihon; it flows around the whole land of Cush.

14 The name of the third river is Tigris; it flows east of Assyria. And the fourth river is the Euphrates.

15 Then the LORD God took the man and put him into the garden of Eden to cultivate it and keep it.

16 The LORD God commanded the man, saying, "From any tree of the garden you may eat freely;

17 but from the tree of the knowledge of good and evil you shall not eat, for in the day that you eat from it you will surely die."

18 Then the LORD God said, "It is not good for the man to be alone; I will make him a helper suitable for him."

19 Out of the ground the LORD God formed every beast of the field and every bird of the sky, and brought *them* to the man to see what he would call them; and whatever the man called a living creature, that was its name.

20 The man gave names to all the cattle, and to the birds of the sky, and to every beast of the field, but for Adam there was not found a helper suitable for him.

21 So the LORD God caused a deep sleep to fall upon the man, and he slept; then He took one of his ribs and closed up the flesh at that place.

22 The LORD God fashioned into a woman the rib which He had taken from the man, and brought her to the man.

23 The man said,
"This is now bone of my bones,
And flesh of my flesh;
She shall be called Woman,
Because she was taken out of Man."

24 For this reason a man shall leave his father and his mother, and be joined

---

LIFE LESSONS

➤ **Genesis 2:25 —** *And the man and his wife were both naked and were not ashamed.*

God's intention for us has always been a deep, unrestricted intimacy with Him, with no walls between us. Sin has destroyed that intimacy, but Jesus reconciles us to God and makes a relationship with Him possible (1 John 3:2).

to his wife; and they shall become one flesh.

➤ 25 And the man and his wife were both naked and were not ashamed.

Psalm 1:1–6

1 How blessed is the man who
does not walk in the counsel of
the wicked,
Nor stand in the path of sinners,
Nor sit in the seat of scoffers!
2 But his delight is in the law of the
LORD,
And in His law he meditates day
and night.
3 He will be like a tree *firmly* planted
by streams of water,
Which yields its fruit in its season
And its leaf does not wither;
And in whatever he does, he
prospers.
4 The wicked are not so,
But they are like chaff which the
wind drives away.
5 Therefore the wicked will not stand
in the judgment,
Nor sinners in the assembly of the
righteous.
6 For the LORD knows the way of the
righteous,
But the way of the wicked will
perish.

Proverbs 1:1–7

1 THE proverbs of Solomon the son of
David, king of Israel:
2 To know wisdom and instruction,
To discern the sayings of
understanding,
3 To receive instruction in wise
behavior,
Righteousness, justice and equity;
4 To give prudence to the naive,
To the youth knowledge and
discretion,
5 A wise man will hear and increase
in learning,
And a man of understanding will
acquire wise counsel,
6 To understand a proverb and a
figure,

The words of the wise and their
riddles.
7 The fear of the LORD is the
beginning of knowledge;
Fools despise wisdom and
instruction.

Matthew 1:1–25

1 THE record of the genealogy of Jesus
the Messiah, the son of David, the son
of Abraham:
2 Abraham was the father of Isaac,
Isaac the father of Jacob, and Jacob the
father of Judah and his brothers.
3 Judah was the father of Perez and
Zerah by Tamar, Perez was the father of
Hezron, and Hezron the father of Ram.
4 Ram was the father of Amminadab,
Amminadab the father of Nahshon, and
Nahshon the father of Salmon.
5 Salmon was the father of Boaz by
Rahab, Boaz was the father of Obed by
Ruth, and Obed the father of Jesse.
6 Jesse was the father of David the
king.
David was the father of Solomon
by Bathsheba who had been the wife of
Uriah.
7 Solomon was the father of Rehoboam, Rehoboam the father of Abijah,
and Abijah the father of Asa.

LIFE LESSONS

➤ **Psalm 1:3 — *He will be like a tree
firmly planted by streams of water,
which yields its fruit in its season***

God provides whatever you need when
you live in submission to Him. He
loves to bless His obedient children—
moving out ahead of us, preparing the
way, bringing us into good and pleasant
places. He doesn't promise lack of trials
but does promise eventual victory.

➤ **Proverbs 1:7 — *The fear of the LORD is
the beginning of knowledge.***

When we base our lives on the
truth of God—His holiness, power,
love, wisdom, goodness, and salvation—we build on the only solid, eternal,
unchanging foundation for life (Luke
6:47-49).

8   Asa was the father of Jehoshaphat, Jehoshaphat the father of Joram, and Joram the father of Uzziah.
9   Uzziah was the father of Jotham, Jotham the father of Ahaz, and Ahaz the father of Hezekiah.
10 Hezekiah was the father of Manasseh, Manasseh the father of Amon, and Amon the father of Josiah.
11 Josiah became the father of Jeconiah and his brothers, at the time of the deportation to Babylon.
12 After the deportation to Babylon: Jeconiah became the father of Shealtiel, and Shealtiel the father of Zerubbabel.
13 Zerubbabel was the father of Abihud, Abihud the father of Eliakim, and Eliakim the father of Azor.
14 Azor was the father of Zadok, Zadok the father of Achim, and Achim the father of Eliud.
15 Eliud was the father of Eleazar, Eleazar the father of Matthan, and Matthan the father of Jacob.
16 Jacob was the father of Joseph the husband of Mary, by whom Jesus was born, who is called the Messiah.
17 So all the generations from Abraham to David are fourteen generations; from David to the deportation to Babylon, fourteen generations; and from the deportation to Babylon to the Messiah, fourteen generations.
➤ 18 Now the birth of Jesus Christ was as follows: when His mother Mary had been betrothed to Joseph, before they came together she was found to be with child by the Holy Spirit.
19 And Joseph her husband, being a righteous man and not wanting to disgrace her, planned to send her away secretly.
➤ 20 But when he had considered this, behold, an angel of the Lord appeared to him in a dream, saying, "Joseph,

son of David, do not be afraid to take Mary as your wife; for the Child who has been conceived in her is of the Holy Spirit.
21 "She will bear a Son; and you shall call His name Jesus, for He will save His people from their sins."
22 Now all this took place to fulfill what was spoken by the Lord through the prophet:
23 "BEHOLD, THE VIRGIN SHALL BE WITH CHILD AND SHALL BEAR A SON, AND THEY SHALL CALL HIS NAME IMMANUEL," which translated means, "GOD WITH US."
24 And Joseph awoke from his sleep and did as the angel of the Lord commanded him, and took *Mary* as his wife, 25 but kept her a virgin until she gave birth to a Son; and he called His name Jesus.

LIFE LESSONS

➤ **Matthew 1:18** — *Now the birth of Jesus Christ was as follows: when His mother Mary had been betrothed to Joseph, before they came together she was found to be with child by the Holy Spirit.*

*J*esus Christ alone can be our sinless Sin-Bearer because only He was born in this miraculous manner. Through the virgin birth, He was unstained by sin and demonstrated His nature as both fully human *and* fully God.

➤ **Matthew 1:20** — *But when he had considered this, behold, an angel of the Lord appeared to him in a dream*

*W*hy didn't the angel Gabriel appear to Joseph when he appeared to Mary? We're not told. But God always reveals His will to us at just the right moment.

Genesis 3:1—4:26

➤ **3**NOW the serpent was more crafty than any beast of the field which

the LORD God had made. And he said to the woman, "Indeed, has God said, 'You shall not eat from any tree of the garden'?"
2   The woman said to the serpent,

"From the fruit of the trees of the garden we may eat;
3   but from the fruit of the tree which is in the middle of the garden, God has said, 'You shall not eat from it or touch it, or you will die.'"
4   The serpent said to the woman, "You surely will not die!
5   "For God knows that in the day you eat from it your eyes will be opened, and you will be like God, knowing good and evil."
6   When the woman saw that the tree was good for food, and that it was a delight to the eyes, and that the tree was desirable to make one wise, she took from its fruit and ate; and she gave also to her husband with her, and he ate.
7   Then the eyes of both of them were opened, and they knew that they were naked; and they sewed fig leaves together and made themselves loin coverings.
➤ 8   They heard the sound of the LORD God walking in the garden in the cool of the day, and the man and his wife hid themselves from the presence of the LORD God among the trees of the garden.
9   Then the LORD God called to the man, and said to him, "Where are you?"
10   He said, "I heard the sound of You in the garden, and I was afraid because I was naked; so I hid myself."
11   And He said, "Who told you that you were naked? Have you eaten from the tree of which I commanded you not to eat?"
12   The man said, "The woman whom You gave to be with me, she gave me from the tree, and I ate."
13   Then the LORD God said to the woman, "What is this you have done?" And the woman said, "The serpent deceived me, and I ate."
14   The LORD God said to the serpent,
"Because you have done this,
Cursed are you more than all cattle,
And more than every beast of the field;
On your belly you will go,
And dust you will eat
All the days of your life;
➤ 15   And I will put enmity
Between you and the woman,
And between your seed and her seed;
✳ He shall bruise you on the head,

And you shall bruise him on the heel."
16   To the woman He said,
"I will greatly multiply
Your pain in childbirth,
In pain you will bring forth children;
Yet your desire will be for your husband,
And he will rule over you."
17   Then to Adam He said, "Because you have listened to the voice of your wife, and have eaten from the tree about which I commanded you, saying, 'You shall not eat from it';

LIFE LESSONS

➤ **Genesis 3:1** — *He said to the woman, "Indeed, has God said, 'You shall not eat from any tree of the garden'?"*

*S*atan often begins his temptations by questioning God's commands and suggesting that obedience is not really necessary. Don't fall for his trap! We do ourselves great harm when we believe we will find greater blessing in doing our own thing than in obeying God. Obedience is necessary and always results in blessings.

➤ **Genesis 3:8** — *They heard the sound of the LORD God walking in the garden in the cool of the day, and the man and his wife hid themselves from the presence of the LORD God among the trees of the garden.*

*S*in fractures our relationships with God and with others. It creates a painful emotional distance and destroys the close fellowship the Lord intended for us to enjoy. Yet God created us to interact with Him and have an intimate relationship with Him. He desires for us to walk with Him daily, enjoying the rich fellowship He offers.

➤ **Genesis 3:15** — *"I will put enmity between you and the woman, and between your seed and her seed; He shall bruise you on the head, and you shall bruise him on the heel."*

*G*od has a plan. From the very beginning of time, He moved history toward the Cross where Christ would restore humans like us to rich fellowship with Himself (Rom. 5:15; 1 Cor. 15:22).

Cursed is the ground because of
    you;
In toil you will eat of it
All the days of your life.
18 "Both thorns and thistles it shall
    grow for you;
And you will eat the plants of the
    field;
19 By the sweat of your face
You will eat bread,
Till you return to the ground,
Because from it you were taken;
For you are dust,
And to dust you shall return."
20 Now the man called his wife's name
Eve, because she was the mother of all
the living.
21 The LORD God made garments of
skin for Adam and his wife, and clothed
them.
22 Then the LORD God said, "Behold,
the man has become like one of Us,
knowing good and evil; and now, he
might stretch out his hand, and take also
from the tree of life, and eat, and live
forever"—
23 therefore the LORD God sent him out
from the garden of Eden, to cultivate the
ground from which he was taken.
24 So He drove the man out; and at the
east of the garden of Eden He stationed
the cherubim and the flaming sword
which turned every direction to guard
the way to the tree of life.
4 NOW the man had relations with his
wife Eve, and she conceived and gave
birth to Cain, and she said, "I have gotten
a manchild with *the help of* the LORD."
2 Again, she gave birth to his brother
Abel. And Abel was a keeper of flocks,
but Cain was a tiller of the ground.
3 So it came about in the course of
time that Cain brought an offering to the
LORD of the fruit of the ground.
4 Abel, on his part also brought of the
firstlings of his flock and of their fat portions. And the LORD had regard for Abel
and for his offering;
5 but for Cain and for his offering He
had no regard. So Cain became very
angry and his countenance fell.
6 Then the LORD said to Cain, "Why
are you angry? And why has your countenance fallen?
7 "If you do well, will not *your countenance* be lifted up? And if you do not do
well, sin is crouching at the door; and its

desire is for you, but you must master it."
8 Cain told Abel his brother. And
it came about when they were in the
field, that Cain rose up against Abel his
brother and killed him.
9 Then the LORD said to Cain, "Where
is Abel your brother?" And he said, "I do
not know. Am I my brother's keeper?"
10 He said, "What have you done? The
voice of your brother's blood is crying to
Me from the ground.
11 "Now you are cursed from the ground,
which has opened its mouth to receive
your brother's blood from your hand.
12 "When you cultivate the ground, it
will no longer yield its strength to you;
you will be a vagrant and a wanderer on
the earth."
13 Cain said to the LORD, "My punishment is too great to bear!
14 "Behold, You have driven me this day
from the face of the ground; and from
Your face I will be hidden, and I will be
a vagrant and a wanderer on the earth,
and whoever finds me will kill me."
15 So the LORD said to him, "Therefore
whoever kills Cain, vengeance will be
taken on him sevenfold." And the LORD
appointed a sign for Cain, so that no one
finding him would slay him.
16 Then Cain went out from the presence of the LORD, and settled in the land
of Nod, east of Eden.
17 Cain had relations with his wife and
she conceived, and gave birth to Enoch;
and he built a city, and called the name
of the city Enoch, after the name of his
son.
18 Now to Enoch was born Irad, and
Irad became the father of Mehujael, and
Mehujael became the father of Methushael, and Methushael became the father
of Lamech.
19 Lamech took to himself two wives:
the name of the one was Adah, and the
name of the other, Zillah.
20 Adah gave birth to Jabal; he was the
father of those who dwell in tents and
have livestock.
21 His brother's name was Jubal; he
was the father of all those who play the
lyre and pipe.
22 As for Zillah, she also gave birth to
Tubal-cain, the forger of all implements
of bronze and iron; and the sister of
Tubal-cain was Naamah.
23 Lamech said to his wives,

"Adah and Zillah,
Listen to my voice,
You wives of Lamech,
Give heed to my speech,
For I have killed a man for
    wounding me;
And a boy for striking me;
24 If Cain is avenged sevenfold,
Then Lamech seventy-sevenfold."
25 Adam had relations with his wife
again; and she gave birth to a son, and
named him Seth, for, *she said,* "God has
appointed me another offspring in place
of Abel, for Cain killed him."
26 To Seth, to him also a son was born;
and he called his name Enosh. Then *men*
began to call upon the name of the LORD.

Psalm 2:1–6

2 WHY are the nations in an uproar
And the peoples devising a vain
    thing?
2 The kings of the earth take their
    stand
And the rulers take counsel together
Against the LORD and against His
    Anointed, saying,
3 "Let us tear their fetters apart
And cast away their cords from us!"
4 He who sits in the heavens laughs,
The Lord scoffs at them.
5 Then He will speak to them in His
    anger
And terrify them in His fury, saying,
6 "But as for Me, I have installed My
    King
Upon Zion, My holy mountain."

Proverbs 1:8–9

8 Hear, my son, your father's
    instruction
And do not forsake your mother's
    teaching;
9 Indeed, they are a graceful wreath
    to your head
And ornaments about your neck.

Matthew 2:1–23

2 NOW after Jesus was born in Bethlehem of Judea in the days of Herod
the king, magi from the east arrived in
Jerusalem, saying,
2 "Where is He who has been born
King of the Jews? For we saw His star in
the east and have come to worship Him."
3 When Herod the king heard *this*,
he was troubled, and all Jerusalem with
him.
4 Gathering together all the chief
priests and scribes of the people, he inquired of them where the Messiah was to
be born.
5 They said to him, "In Bethlehem of
Judea; for this is what has been written
by the prophet:
6 'AND YOU, BETHLEHEM, LAND OF
    JUDAH,
    ARE BY NO MEANS LEAST AMONG THE
    LEADERS OF JUDAH;
    FOR OUT OF YOU SHALL COME FORTH A
    RULER
    WHO WILL SHEPHERD MY PEOPLE
    ISRAEL.'"

Life Examples:

THE WISE MEN: Giving Passionate Praise

MATTHEW 2:1–12

*T*he wise men eagerly journeyed to
Bethlehem to give a royal welcome
to the baby Jesus—God's promised gift of
salvation to mankind. They packed gold,
frankincense, and myrrh so they could join
in the heavenly worship of the infant King.
These men formed an important part of the
celebration surrounding Christ's birth. In fact,
they represented *you* in God's great plan.
They came to worship the Lord of lords and
the King of kings, and their visit to the Christ
child symbolizes the thousands of men and
women who have humbly sought the Messiah
through history.

Through your own seeking and serving,
you become part of the heavenly symphony
giving passionate praise to the Savior. Allow
your heart to burst into song at the thought
of Him. Permit the tune of your being to swell
with the joy of who He is. Just like the wise
men, you have joined the great multitude in
never-ending worship. Seek Him and sing, for
surely He is worthy.

7 Then Herod secretly called the magi and determined from them the exact time the star appeared.

8 And he sent them to Bethlehem and said, "Go and search carefully for the Child; and when you have found *Him,* report to me, so that I too may come and worship Him."

9 After hearing the king, they went their way; and the star, which they had seen in the east, went on before them until it came and stood over *the place* where the Child was.

10 When they saw the star, they rejoiced exceedingly with great joy.

➤ **11** After coming into the house they saw the Child with Mary His mother; and they fell to the ground and worshiped Him. Then, opening their treasures, they presented to Him gifts of gold, frankincense, and myrrh.

12 And having been warned *by God* in a dream not to return to Herod, the magi left for their own country by another way.

13 Now when they had gone, behold, an angel of the Lord *appeared to Joseph in a dream and said, "Get up! Take the Child and His mother and flee to Egypt, and remain there until I tell you; for Herod is going to search for the Child to destroy Him."

14 So Joseph got up and took the Child and His mother while it was still night, and left for Egypt.

15 He remained there until the death of Herod. *This was* to fulfill what had been spoken by the Lord through the prophet: "OUT OF EGYPT I CALLED MY SON."

16 Then when Herod saw that he had been tricked by the magi, he became very enraged, and sent and slew all the male children who were in Bethlehem and all its vicinity, from two years old and under, according to the time which he had determined from the magi.

17 Then what had been spoken through Jeremiah the prophet was fulfilled:

18 "A VOICE WAS HEARD IN RAMAH,
WEEPING AND GREAT MOURNING,
RACHEL WEEPING FOR HER CHILDREN;
AND SHE REFUSED TO BE COMFORTED,
BECAUSE THEY WERE NO MORE."

19 But when Herod died, behold, an angel of the Lord *appeared in a dream to Joseph in Egypt, and said,

20 "Get up, take the Child and His mother, and go into the land of Israel; for those who sought the Child's life are dead."

21 So Joseph got up, took the Child and His mother, and came into the land of Israel.

22 But when he heard that Archelaus ◄ was reigning over Judea in place of his father Herod, he was afraid to go there. Then after being warned *by God* in a dream, he left for the regions of Galilee,

23 and came and lived in a city called Nazareth. *This was* to fulfill what was spoken through the prophets: "He shall be called a Nazarene."

LIFE LESSONS

➤ **Matthew 2:4 —** *Gathering together all the chief priests and scribes of the people, he inquired of them where the Messiah was to be born.*

*H*erod believed enough in the prophecies to inquire where the Messiah would be born, but his intentions were not to know the Son of God. Herod wanted to kill Jesus. Compromise and sin are very dangerous. Greed and the desire for power can be deadly. This ruler wanted to ensure his stronghold on the Jewish people. Therefore, he looked for a way to prevent the fulfillment of this prophecy.

➤ **Matthew 2:11 —** *After coming into the house they saw the Child with Mary His mother; and they fell to the ground and worshiped Him.*

*T*he wise men probably visited Jesus when He was about two years old. They came to a house instead of a stable and saw the Child rather than an infant. Regardless of His age, they worshiped Him and acknowledged Him as the Messiah (Matt. 2:6).

➤ **Matthew 2:22 —** *Then after being warned by God in a dream, he left for the regions of Galilee.*

*F*our times in this short narrative, Joseph received divine instructions through dreams. The wise men also received God's message of warning and guidance through a dream they had. The Lord uses many methods to communicate His will to us (Matt. 27:19).

Genesis 5:1—6:22

5 THIS is the book of the generations of Adam. In the day when God created man, He made him in the likeness of God.

2 He created them male and female, and He blessed them and named them Man in the day when they were created.

3 When Adam had lived one hundred and thirty years, he became the father of *a son* in his own likeness, according to his image, and named him Seth.

4 Then the days of Adam after he became the father of Seth were eight hundred years, and he had *other* sons and daughters.

5 So all the days that Adam lived were nine hundred and thirty years, and he died.

6 Seth lived one hundred and five years, and became the father of Enosh.

7 Then Seth lived eight hundred and seven years after he became the father of Enosh, and he had *other* sons and daughters.

8 So all the days of Seth were nine hundred and twelve years, and he died.

9 Enosh lived ninety years, and became the father of Kenan.

10 Then Enosh lived eight hundred and fifteen years after he became the father of Kenan, and he had *other* sons and daughters.

11 So all the days of Enosh were nine hundred and five years, and he died.

12 Kenan lived seventy years, and became the father of Mahalalel.

13 Then Kenan lived eight hundred and forty years after he became the father of Mahalalel, and he had *other* sons and daughters.

14 So all the days of Kenan were nine hundred and ten years, and he died.

15 Mahalalel lived sixty-five years, and became the father of Jared.

16 Then Mahalalel lived eight hundred and thirty years after he became the father of Jared, and he had *other* sons and daughters.

17 So all the days of Mahalalel were eight hundred and ninety-five years, and he died.

18 Jared lived one hundred and sixty-two years, and became the father of Enoch.

19 Then Jared lived eight hundred years after he became the father of Enoch, and he had *other* sons and daughters.

20 So all the days of Jared were nine hundred and sixty-two years, and he died.

21 Enoch lived sixty-five years, and became the father of Methuselah.

22 Then Enoch walked with God three hundred years after he became the father of Methuselah, and he had *other* sons and daughters.

23 So all the days of Enoch were three hundred and sixty-five years.

24 Enoch walked with God; and he was not, for God took him.

25 Methuselah lived one hundred and eighty-seven years, and became the father of Lamech.

26 Then Methuselah lived seven hundred and eighty-two years after he became the father of Lamech, and he had *other* sons and daughters.

27 So all the days of Methuselah were nine hundred and sixty-nine years, and he died.

28 Lamech lived one hundred and eighty-two years, and became the father of a son.

29 Now he called his name Noah, saying, "This one will give us rest from our work and from the toil of our hands *arising* from the ground which the LORD has cursed."

30 Then Lamech lived five hundred and ninety-five years after he became the father of Noah, and he had *other* sons and daughters.

31 So all the days of Lamech were seven hundred and seventy-seven years, and he died.

32 Noah was five hundred years old, and Noah became the father of Shem, Ham, and Japheth.

6 NOW it came about, when men began to multiply on the face of the land, and daughters were born to them,

2 that the sons of God saw that the daughters of men were beautiful; and they took wives for themselves, whomever they chose.

3 Then the LORD said, "My Spirit shall not strive with man forever, because he also is flesh; nevertheless his

days shall be one hundred and twenty years."

4   The Nephilim were on the earth in those days, and also afterward, when the sons of God came in to the daughters of men, and they bore *children* to them. Those were the mighty men who *were* of old, men of renown.

5   Then the LORD saw that the wickedness of man was great on the earth, and that every intent of the thoughts of his heart was only evil continually.

➤ 6   The LORD was sorry that He had made man on the earth, and He was grieved in His heart.

7   The LORD said, "I will blot out man whom I have created from the face of the land, from man to animals to creeping things and to birds of the sky; for I am sorry that I have made them."

8   But Noah found favor in the eyes of the LORD.

9   These are *the records of* the generations of Noah. Noah was a righteous man, blameless in his time; Noah walked with God.

10   Noah became the father of three sons: Shem, Ham, and Japheth.

11   Now the earth was corrupt in the sight of God, and the earth was filled with violence.

12   God looked on the earth, and behold, it was corrupt; for all flesh had corrupted their way upon the earth.

13   Then God said to Noah, "The end of all flesh has come before Me; for the earth is filled with violence because of them; and behold, I am about to destroy them with the earth.

14   "Make for yourself an ark of gopher wood; you shall make the ark with rooms, and shall cover it inside and out with pitch.

15   "This is how you shall make it: the length of the ark three hundred cubits, its breadth fifty cubits, and its height thirty cubits.

16   "You shall make a window for the ark, and finish it to a cubit from the top; and set the door of the ark in the side of it; you shall make it with lower, second, and third decks.

17   "Behold, I, even I am bringing the flood of water upon the earth, to destroy all flesh in which is the breath of life, from under heaven; everything that is on the earth shall perish.

18   "But I will establish My covenant with you; and you shall enter the ark—you and your sons and your wife, and your ✳ sons' wives with you.

19   "And of every living thing of all flesh, you shall bring two of every *kind* into the ark, to keep *them* alive with you; they shall be male and female.

20   "Of the birds after their kind, and of the animals after their kind, of every creeping thing of the ground after its kind, two of every *kind* will come to you to keep *them* alive.

21   "As for you, take for yourself some of all food which is edible, and gather *it* to yourself; and it shall be for food for you and for them."

22   Thus Noah did; according to all that ◄ God had commanded him, so he did.

LIFE LESSONS

➤ **Genesis 6:6 —** *The LORD was sorry that He had made man on the earth, and He was grieved in His heart.*

*O*ur sin grieves the Creator who made us because it stands against His very nature. God will always judge sin; He cannot merely ignore it.

➤ **Genesis 6:22 —** *Thus Noah did; according to all that God had commanded him, so he did.*

*N*oah displayed his righteous character by doing exactly as God had commanded him, even though building the ark must have seemed ridiculous to his neighbors. Because Noah was obedient, God spared his life.

✦ Psalm 2:7–12

7   "I will surely tell of the decree of the ◄
        LORD:
    He said to Me, 'You are My Son,
    Today I have begotten You.

8   'Ask of Me, and I will surely give the
        nations as Your inheritance,
    And the *very* ends of the earth as
        Your possession.

9   'You shall break them with a rod of
        iron,
    You shall shatter them like
        earthenware.'"

NOAH: Obedient and Dry

GENESIS 6:22

*N*othing indicated an approaching storm. Still, since Noah believed God, he prepared for the downpour God promised. His friends must have mocked him, but he built an ark (Gen. 6).

Obedience is the cornerstone to our faith in God. While Noah's obedience led to God's blessing and reward, the disobedience of his contemporaries led to their destruction. At the time of the flood, the physical salvation of mankind fell to Noah and his willingness to be used by God.

The ark merely foreshadowed the eternal salvation from sin that is ours through Jesus Christ. Just as Noah's faith saved him and his family, so our faith saves us today. We are saved by grace through faith and not by good deeds (Eph. 2:8, 9). Building the ark did not bring Noah any closer to the Lord—but his obedience and faith in God did. The minor point was that it kept him safe and dry.

10 Now therefore, O kings, show
discernment;
Take warning, O judges of the earth.
11 Worship the LORD with reverence
And rejoice with trembling.
12 Do homage to the Son, that He not
become angry, and you perish *in*
the way,
For His wrath may soon be
kindled.
How blessed are all who take refuge
in Him!

⊕ Proverbs 1:10–19

10 My son, if sinners entice you,
Do not consent.
11 If they say, "Come with us,
Let us lie in wait for blood,
Let us ambush the innocent without
cause;
12 Let us swallow them alive like Sheol,
Even whole, as those who go down
to the pit;
13 We will find all *kinds* of precious
wealth,
We will fill our houses with spoil;

14 Throw in your lot with us,
We shall all have one purse,"
15 My son, do not walk in the way
with them.
Keep your feet from their path,
16 For their feet run to evil
And they hasten to shed blood.
17 Indeed, it is useless to spread the
baited net
In the sight of any bird;
18 But they lie in wait for their own
blood;
They ambush their own lives.
19 So are the ways of everyone who
gains by violence;
It takes away the life of its
possessors.

⊕ Matthew 3:1–17

3 NOW in those days John the Baptist
*came, preaching in the wilderness of
Judea, saying,
2 "Repent, for the kingdom of heaven is
at hand."
3 For this is the one referred to by
Isaiah the prophet when he said,
"THE VOICE OF ONE CRYING IN THE
WILDERNESS,
'MAKE READY THE WAY OF THE LORD,
MAKE HIS PATHS STRAIGHT!'"

4 Now John himself had a garment of
camel's hair and a leather belt around
his waist; and his food was locusts and
wild honey.
5 Then Jerusalem was going out to
him, and all Judea and all the district
around the Jordan;
6 and they were being baptized by him

LIFE LESSONS

➤ **Psalm 2:7 — "I will surely tell of the decree of the LORD: He said to Me, 'You are My Son, today I have begotten You.'"**

*T*he writer of Hebrews quotes this verse to show how far superior Jesus is to angels (Heb. 1:5). Our Savior is fully one of us, even as He is fully God. We can trust Him completely (Heb. 2:14-18; 4:14-16).

in the Jordan River, as they confessed their sins.

7   But when he saw many of the Pharisees and Sadducees coming for baptism, he said to them, "You brood of vipers, who warned you to flee from the wrath to come?

8   "Therefore bear fruit in keeping with repentance;

9   and do not suppose that you can say to yourselves, 'We have Abraham for our father'; for I say to you that from these stones God is able to raise up children to Abraham.

10 "The axe is already laid at the root of the trees; therefore every tree that does not bear good fruit is cut down and thrown into the fire.

11 "As for me, I baptize you with water for repentance, but He who is coming after me is mightier than I, and I am not fit to remove His sandals; He will baptize you with the Holy Spirit and fire.

12 "His winnowing fork is in His hand, and He will thoroughly clear His threshing floor; and He will gather His wheat into the barn, but He will burn up the chaff with unquenchable fire."

13 Then Jesus *arrived from Galilee at the Jordan *coming* to John, to be baptized by him.

14 But John tried to prevent Him, saying, "I have need to be baptized by You, and do You come to me?"

15 But Jesus answering said to him, "Permit *it* at this time; for in this way it is fitting for us to fulfill all righteousness." Then he *permitted Him.

16 After being baptized, Jesus came up immediately from the water; and behold, the heavens were opened, and he saw the Spirit of God descending as a dove *and* lighting on Him,

17 and behold, a voice out of the heavens said, "This is My beloved Son, in whom I am well-pleased."

LIFE LESSONS

➤ **Matthew 3:8 —** *"Therefore bear fruit in keeping with repentance."*

*G*enuine repentance leads not only to a change in attitude, but also to a change in behavior. Merely feeling sorry for some wrong action does not constitute repentance.

➤ **Matthew 3:15 —** *Jesus answering said to him, "Permit it at this time; for in this way it is fitting for us to fulfill all righteousness."*

*I*n His holiness, Jesus submitted Himself to John's baptism to provide a perfect example to us of how to live in righteousness and obedience to the Father (Rom. 6:3-4).

➤ **Matthew 3:17 —** *A voice out of the heavens said, "This is My beloved Son, in whom I am well-pleased."*

*G*od the Father loves Jesus the Son and publicly stated His pleasure in Christ's righteous manner of living. Yet it also pleased God to send His Son to the Cross on our behalf (Is. 53:10).

 Genesis 7:1—8:22

7 THEN the LORD said to Noah, "Enter the ark, you and all your household, for you *alone* I have seen *to be* righteous before Me in this time.

2   "You shall take with you of every clean animal by sevens, a male and his female; and of the animals that are not clean two, a male and his female;

3   also of the birds of the sky, by sev-

ens, male and female, to keep offspring alive on the face of all the earth.

4   "For after seven more days, I will send rain on the earth forty days and forty nights; and I will blot out from the face of the land every living thing that I have made."

5   Noah did according to all that the LORD had commanded him.

6   Now Noah was six hundred years old when the flood of water came upon the earth.

7   Then Noah and his sons and his wife

and his sons' wives with him entered the ark because of the water of the flood.

8   Of clean animals and animals that are not clean and birds and everything that creeps on the ground,

9   there went into the ark to Noah by twos, male and female, as God had commanded Noah.

10   It came about after the seven days, that the water of the flood came upon the earth.

11   In the six hundredth year of Noah's life, in the second month, on the seventeenth day of the month, on the same day all the fountains of the great deep burst open, and the floodgates of the sky were opened.

12   The rain fell upon the earth for forty days and forty nights.

13   On the very same day Noah and Shem and Ham and Japheth, the sons of Noah, and Noah's wife and the three wives of his sons with them, entered the ark,

14   they and every beast after its kind, and all the cattle after their kind, and every creeping thing that creeps on the earth after its kind, and every bird after its kind, all sorts of birds.

15   So they went into the ark to Noah, by twos of all flesh in which was the breath of life.

16   Those that entered, male and female of all flesh, entered as God had commanded him; and the LORD closed *it* behind him.

17   Then the flood came upon the earth for forty days, and the water increased and lifted up the ark, so that it rose above the earth.

18   The water prevailed and increased greatly upon the earth, and the ark floated on the surface of the water.

19   The water prevailed more and more upon the earth, so that all the high mountains everywhere under the heavens were covered.

20   The water prevailed fifteen cubits higher, and the mountains were covered.

21   All flesh that moved on the earth perished, birds and cattle and beasts and every swarming thing that swarms upon the earth, and all mankind;

22   of all that was on the dry land, all in whose nostrils was the breath of the spirit of life, died.

23   Thus He blotted out every living thing that was upon the face of the land, from man to animals to creeping things and to birds of the sky, and they were blotted out from the earth; and only Noah was left, together with those that were with him in the ark.

24   The water prevailed upon the earth one hundred and fifty days.

8 BUT God remembered Noah and all the beasts and all the cattle that were with him in the ark; and God caused a wind to pass over the earth, and the water subsided.

2   Also the fountains of the deep and the floodgates of the sky were closed, and the rain from the sky was restrained;

3   and the water receded steadily from the earth, and at the end of one hundred and fifty days the water decreased.

4   In the seventh month, on the seventeenth day of the month, the ark rested upon the mountains of Ararat.

5   The water decreased steadily until the tenth month; in the tenth month, on the first day of the month, the tops of the mountains became visible.

6   Then it came about at the end of forty days, that Noah opened the window of the ark which he had made;

7   and he sent out a raven, and it flew here and there until the water was dried up from the earth.

8   Then he sent out a dove from him, to see if the water was abated from the face of the land;

9   but the dove found no resting place for the sole of her foot, so she returned to him into the ark, for the water was on the surface of all the earth. Then he put out his hand and took her, and brought her into the ark to himself.

10   So he waited yet another seven days; and again he sent out the dove from the ark.

11   The dove came to him toward eve-

LIFE LESSONS

➣ **Genesis 8:1 — *God remembered Noah and all the beasts and all the cattle that were with him in the ark.***

*G*od always remembers His people, not merely to recall their existence or names, but to act in grace toward them—even if they must wait for Him to act.

ning, and behold, in her beak was a freshly picked olive leaf. So Noah knew that the water was abated from the earth.

12 Then he waited yet another seven days, and sent out the dove; but she did not return to him again.

13 Now it came about in the six hundred and first year, in the first *month,* on the first of the month, the water was dried up from the earth. Then Noah removed the covering of the ark, and looked, and behold, the surface of the ground was dried up.

14 In the second month, on the twenty-seventh day of the month, the earth was dry.

15 Then God spoke to Noah, saying,

16 "Go out of the ark, you and your wife and your sons and your sons' wives with you.

17 "Bring out with you every living thing of all flesh that is with you, birds and animals and every creeping thing that creeps on the earth, that they may breed abundantly on the earth, and be fruitful and multiply on the earth."

18 So Noah went out, and his sons and his wife and his sons' wives with him.

19 Every beast, every creeping thing, and every bird, everything that moves on the earth, went out by their families from the ark.

20 Then Noah built an altar to the LORD, and took of every clean animal and of every clean bird and offered burnt offerings on the altar.

21 The LORD smelled the soothing aroma; and the LORD said to Himself, "I will never again curse the ground on account of man, for the intent of man's heart is evil from his youth; and I will never again destroy every living thing, as I have done.

22 "While the earth remains,
Seedtime and harvest,
And cold and heat,
And summer and winter,
And day and night
Shall not cease."

Psalm 3:1–4

A Psalm of David, when he fled from Absalom his son.

3 O LORD, how my adversaries have increased!
Many are rising up against me.

2 Many are saying of my soul,
"There is no deliverance for him in God."   Selah.

3 But You, O LORD, are a shield about me,
My glory, and the One who lifts my head.

4 I was crying to the LORD with my voice,
And He answered me from His holy mountain.   Selah.

Proverbs 1:20–22

20 Wisdom shouts in the street,
She lifts her voice in the square;

21 At the head of the noisy *streets* she cries out;
At the entrance of the gates in the city she utters her sayings:

22 "How long, O naive ones, will you love being simple-minded?
And scoffers delight themselves in scoffing
And fools hate knowledge?

LIFE LESSONS

➤ **Genesis 8:22 — *"While the earth remains, seedtime and harvest, and cold and heat, and summer and winter, and day and night shall not cease."***

*G*od's promises mean the difference between life and death. Even when things look darkest, we can rely on His trustworthy Word.

➤ **Psalm 3:2 — *Many are saying of my soul, "There is no deliverance for him in God."***

*T*o succeed in the Christian life, we must surround ourselves with other believers who love the Lord and who love us. Doubters and skeptics we can find anywhere; in the church, we should find encouragement.

◈ Matthew 4:1–25

4 THEN Jesus was led up by the Spirit into the wilderness to be tempted by the devil.
2 And after He had fasted forty days and forty nights, He then became hungry.
3 And the tempter came and said to Him, "If You are the Son of God, command that these stones become bread."
4 But He answered and said, "It is written, 'MAN SHALL NOT LIVE ON BREAD ALONE, BUT ON EVERY WORD THAT PROCEEDS OUT OF THE MOUTH OF GOD.'"
5 Then the devil *took Him into the holy city and had Him stand on the pinnacle of the temple,
6 and *said to Him, "If You are the Son of God, throw Yourself down; for it is written,

'HE WILL COMMAND HIS ANGELS
CONCERNING YOU';
and
'ON *their* HANDS THEY WILL BEAR YOU
UP,
SO THAT YOU WILL NOT STRIKE YOUR
FOOT AGAINST A STONE.'"

7 Jesus said to him, "On the other hand, it is written, 'YOU SHALL NOT PUT THE LORD YOUR GOD TO THE TEST.'"
8 Again, the devil *took Him to a very high mountain and *showed Him all the kingdoms of the world and their glory;
9 and he said to Him, "All these things I will give You, if You fall down and worship me."
10 Then Jesus *said to him, "Go, Satan! For it is written, 'YOU SHALL WORSHIP THE LORD YOUR GOD, AND SERVE HIM ONLY.'"
11 Then the devil *left Him; and behold, angels came and *began* to minister to Him.
12 Now when Jesus heard that John had been taken into custody, He withdrew into Galilee;
13 and leaving Nazareth, He came and settled in Capernaum, which is by the sea, in the region of Zebulun and Naphtali.
14 *This was* to fulfill what was spoken through Isaiah the prophet:
15 "THE LAND OF ZEBULUN AND THE LAND
OF NAPHTALI,
BY THE WAY OF THE SEA, BEYOND
THE JORDAN, GALILEE OF THE
GENTILES—
16 "THE PEOPLE WHO WERE SITTING IN
DARKNESS SAW A GREAT LIGHT,
AND THOSE WHO WERE SITTING IN THE
LAND AND SHADOW OF DEATH,
UPON THEM A LIGHT DAWNED."
17 From that time Jesus began to preach and say, "Repent, for the kingdom of heaven is at hand."
18 Now as Jesus was walking by the Sea of Galilee, He saw two brothers, Simon who was called Peter, and Andrew his brother, casting a net into the sea; for they were fishermen.
19 And He *said to them, "Follow Me, and I will make you fishers of men."
20 Immediately they left their nets and followed Him.

LIFE LESSONS

➤ **Matthew 4:1 —** *Jesus was led up by the Spirit into the wilderness to be tempted by the devil.*

*T*he Holy Spirit led Jesus to a barren place where the devil waited to tempt Him. We should never doubt God's leading just because we run into temptation. Though God will never tempt us (James 1:13), He will test our faith to see if we will stay on the course He has set for us to follow. He will answer whenever you pray and request His guidance.

➤ **Matthew 4:3 —** *And the tempter came and said to Him, "If You are the Son of God, command that these stones become bread."*

*S*atan is a relentless foe. He will stop at nothing to tempt us into doubting the Word of God and His promises. He will whisper words of doubt saying the Lord cannot be trusted or that what He has said is not the whole truth.

➤ **Matthew 4:4, 7, 10 —** *"It is written . . . It is written . . . it is written."*

*J*esus responded to each of Satan's three temptations by appealing to the unchanging Word of God: "It is written!" If we want to successfully overcome temptation, we *must* do the same—using God's Word as our offensive weapon against an inferior foe.

ANSWERS TO LIFE'S QUESTIONS

How do I handle nagging doubt?

MATTHEW 4:1–11

Satan loves to use fear and doubt to discourage believers. He knows if he can get you to question God, then maybe you will give up and abandon His will for your life. Feelings of fear often accompany feelings of doubt and uncertainty. If left unattended, these runaway emotions can tempt you to stop trusting the Lord and His ability to provide for you.

The first step to turning away from doubt and discouragement is to proclaim your faith in Jesus Christ. When trouble strikes, He is your omniscient help. He also is the only One who truly understands you completely. He knows your weaknesses and strengths. He also knows exactly what is needed to encourage you and lift you up so you can continue walking forward in faith.

Second, set a goal to read God's Word each day. This is the best way to combat fear and doubt. The Lord uses a daily reading program to train your mind and to teach you how to handle doubt. The Book of Psalms highlights many personal battles over emotions such as fear, doubt, loneliness, and discouragement. David and others made a conscious decision to trust the Lord through tremendously difficult circumstances and found that God never once failed them.

Third, prayer is essential in fighting fear and doubt. In essence, prayer is faith in action. When we pray, regardless of whether we feel like it, we make a statement of faith. We pray because we see God as the solution to what we face. If you are facing a difficult situation, don't hesitate to ask Him to show you the best way to handle it. If your level of trust seems low, don't worry. The Lord is wise and kind. He wants to teach you more about Himself, not frighten you away. Your faith will increase as you get to know Him better.

Even if you don't feel you have the emotional strength to trust God, don't worry. The Lord is your strength (Psalm 18). A. B. Simpson often told those who found themselves in a difficult spot, "When God tests you, it is a good time for you to test Him by putting His promises to the proof, and claiming from Him just as much as your trials have rendered necessary."

The last thing Satan wants you to do is to go to God in prayer and tell Him you feel doubtful. Always be honest with Him; He knows it all. Honesty breaks the pattern of doubt and provides the right atmosphere for God to work mightily in your life. Remember: He loves you with an eternal love, and He will provide for your every need.

21 Going on from there He saw two other brothers, James the *son* of Zebedee, and John his brother, in the boat with Zebedee their father, mending their nets; and He called them.
22 Immediately they left the boat and their father, and followed Him.
23 Jesus was going throughout all Galilee, teaching in their synagogues and proclaiming the gospel of the kingdom, and healing every kind of disease and every kind of sickness among the people.
24 The news about Him spread throughout all Syria; and they brought to Him all who were ill, those suffering with various diseases and pains, demoniacs, epileptics, paralytics; and He healed them.
25 Large crowds followed Him from Galilee and *the* Decapolis and Jerusalem and Judea and *from* beyond the Jordan.

 Genesis 9:1—10:32

9 AND God blessed Noah and his sons and said to them, "Be fruitful and multiply, and fill the earth.
2 "The fear of you and the terror of you will be on every beast of the earth and on every bird of the sky; with everything that creeps on the ground, and all the fish of the sea, into your hand they are given.
3 "Every moving thing that is alive shall be food for you; I give all to you, as *I gave* the green plant.
4 "Only you shall not eat flesh with its life, *that is*, its blood.
5 "Surely I will require your lifeblood;

from every beast I will require it. And from *every* man, from every man's brother I will require the life of man.

6 "Whoever sheds man's blood,
     By man his blood shall be shed,
     For in the image of God
     He made man.

7 "As for you, be fruitful and multiply;
     Populate the earth abundantly and
        multiply in it."

8 Then God spoke to Noah and to his sons with him, saying,

9 "Now behold, I Myself do establish My covenant with you, and with your descendants after you;

10 and with every living creature that is with you, the birds, the cattle, and every beast of the earth with you; of all that comes out of the ark, even every beast of the earth.

11 "I establish My covenant with you; and all flesh shall never again be cut off by the water of the flood, neither shall there again be a flood to destroy the earth."

12 God said, "This is the sign of the covenant which I am making between Me and you and every living creature that is with you, for all successive generations;

13 I set My bow in the cloud, and it shall be for a sign of a covenant between Me and the earth.

14 "It shall come about, when I bring a cloud over the earth, that the bow will be seen in the cloud,

15 and I will remember My covenant, which is between Me and you and every living creature of all flesh; and never again shall the water become a flood to destroy all flesh.

16 "When the bow is in the cloud, then I will look upon it, to remember the everlasting covenant between God and every living creature of all flesh that is on the earth."

17 And God said to Noah, "This is the sign of the covenant which I have established between Me and all flesh that is on the earth."

18 Now the sons of Noah who came out of the ark were Shem and Ham and Japheth; and Ham was the father of Canaan.

19 These three *were* the sons of Noah, and from these the whole earth was populated.

20 Then Noah began farming and planted a vineyard.

21 He drank of the wine and became drunk, and uncovered himself inside his tent.

22 Ham, the father of Canaan, saw the nakedness of his father, and told his two brothers outside.

23 But Shem and Japheth took a garment and laid it upon both their shoulders and walked backward and covered the nakedness of their father; and their faces were turned away, so that they did not see their father's nakedness.

24 When Noah awoke from his wine, he knew what his youngest son had done to him.

25 So he said,
     "Cursed be Canaan;
     A servant of servants
     He shall be to his brothers."

26 He also said,
     "Blessed be the LORD,
     The God of Shem;
     And let Canaan be his servant.

27 "May God enlarge Japheth,
     And let him dwell in the tents of
        Shem;
     And let Canaan be his servant."

LIFE LESSONS

➤ **Genesis 9:12** — *"This is the sign of the covenant I am making between Me and you and every living creature."*

When God makes a promise, He does not want us to forget it. Therefore, He often gives us some tangible sign or pledge to memorialize His promise.

➤ **Genesis 9:21** — *He drank of the wine and became drunk, and uncovered himself inside his tent.*

Even righteous and blameless people like Noah do foolish things and fall into sin. But God is so gracious that He calls us to repentance so we might once more enjoy the fullness of His blessing.

28 Noah lived three hundred and fifty years after the flood.

29 So all the days of Noah were nine hundred and fifty years, and he died.

10 NOW these are *the records of* the generations of Shem, Ham, and Japheth, the sons of Noah; and sons were born to them after the flood.

2 The sons of Japheth *were* Gomer and Magog and Madai and Javan and Tubal and Meshech and Tiras.

3 The sons of Gomer *were* Ashkenaz and Riphath and Togarmah.

4 The sons of Javan *were* Elishah and Tarshish, Kittim and Dodanim.

5 From these the coastlands of the nations were separated into their lands, every one according to his language, according to their families, into their nations.

6 The sons of Ham *were* Cush and Mizraim and Put and Canaan.

7 The sons of Cush *were* Seba and Havilah and Sabtah and Raamah and Sabteca; and the sons of Raamah *were* Sheba and Dedan.

8 Now Cush became the father of Nimrod; he became a mighty one on the earth.

9 He was a mighty hunter before the LORD; therefore it is said, "Like Nimrod a mighty hunter before the LORD."

10 The beginning of his kingdom was Babel and Erech and Accad and Calneh, in the land of Shinar.

11 From that land he went forth into Assyria, and built Nineveh and Rehoboth-Ir and Calah,

12 and Resen between Nineveh and Calah; that is the great city.

13 Mizraim became the father of Ludim and Anamim and Lehabim and Naphtuhim

14 and Pathrusim and Casluhim (from which came the Philistines) and Caphtorim.

15 Canaan became the father of Sidon, his firstborn, and Heth

16 and the Jebusite and the Amorite and the Girgashite

17 and the Hivite and the Arkite and the Sinite

18 and the Arvadite and the Zemarite and the Hamathite; and afterward the families of the Canaanite were spread abroad.

19 The territory of the Canaanite extended from Sidon as you go toward Gerar, as far as Gaza; as you go toward Sodom and Gomorrah and Admah and Zeboiim, as far as Lasha.

20 These are the sons of Ham, according to their families, according to their languages, by their lands, by their nations.

21 Also to Shem, the father of all the children of Eber, *and* the older brother of Japheth, children were born.

22 The sons of Shem *were* Elam and Asshur and Arpachshad and Lud and Aram.

23 The sons of Aram *were* Uz and Hul and Gether and Mash.

24 Arpachshad became the father of Shelah; and Shelah became the father of Eber.

25 Two sons were born to Eber; the name of the one *was* Peleg, for in his days the earth was divided; and his brother's name *was* Joktan.

26 Joktan became the father of Almodad and Sheleph and Hazarmaveth and Jerah

27 and Hadoram and Uzal and Diklah

28 and Obal and Abimael and Sheba

29 and Ophir and Havilah and Jobab; all these were the sons of Joktan.

30 Now their settlement extended from Mesha as you go toward Sephar, the hill country of the east.

31 These are the sons of Shem, according to their families, according to their languages, by their lands, according to their nations.

32 These are the families of the sons of Noah, according to their genealogies, by their nations; and out of these the nations were separated on the earth after the flood.

◈ Psalm 3:5–8

5 I lay down and slept;
I awoke, for the LORD sustains
   me.

6 I will not be afraid of ten thousands
   of people
Who have set themselves against
   me round about.

7 Arise, O LORD; save me, O my
   God!

For You have smitten all my enemies
  on the cheek;
You have shattered the teeth of the
  wicked.
8 Salvation belongs to the LORD;
Your blessing *be* upon Your
  people!   Selah.

Proverbs 1:23–27

23 "Turn to my reproof,
Behold, I will pour out my spirit on
  you;
I will make my words known to
  you.
24 "Because I called and you refused,
I stretched out my hand and no one
  paid attention;
25 And you neglected all my counsel
And did not want my reproof;
26 I will also laugh at your calamity;
I will mock when your dread
  comes,
27 When your dread comes like a
  storm
And your calamity comes like a
  whirlwind,
When distress and anguish come
  upon you.

Matthew 5:1–26

5 WHEN Jesus saw the crowds, He
went up on the mountain; and after
He sat down, His disciples came to
Him.
2 He opened His mouth and *began* to
teach them, saying,
3 "Blessed are the poor in spirit, for
theirs is the kingdom of heaven.
4 "Blessed are those who mourn, for
they shall be comforted.
5 "Blessed are the gentle, for they shall
inherit the earth.
6 "Blessed are those who hunger and
thirst for righteousness, for they shall be
satisfied.
7 "Blessed are the merciful, for they
shall receive mercy.
8 "Blessed are the pure in heart, for
they shall see God.
9 "Blessed are the peacemakers, for
they shall be called sons of God.

10 "Blessed are those who have been
persecuted for the sake of righteousness,
for theirs is the kingdom of heaven.
11 "Blessed are you when *people* insult
you and persecute you, and falsely say
all kinds of evil against you because of
Me.
12 "Rejoice and be glad, for your
reward in heaven is great; for in the
same way they persecuted the prophets
who were before you.
13 "You are the salt of the earth; but if
the salt has become tasteless, how can it
be made salty *again*? It is no longer good
for anything, except to be thrown out
and trampled under foot by men.
14 "You are the light of the world. A
city set on a hill cannot be hidden;

LIFE LESSONS

➤ **Matthew 5:6** — *"Blessed are those
who hunger and thirst for righteousness,
for they shall be satisfied."*

To hunger and thirst for righteousness
ultimately means that one hungers
and thirsts for God. And those who long
for the Lord—the true King of kings, not
a false deity of their own imagination—
will find Him and be filled to overflowing with joy, peace, happiness, and true
contentment.

➤ **Matthew 5:13** — *"You are the salt of
the earth."*

Jesus wants us to take our roles as salt
seriously—both as a preservative and
as a seasoning. Through us, the lost are
to be drawn to the Lord—preserved for
eternal life. They also "taste and see that
the LORD is good" (Ps. 34:8) and see that
following Him is life at its very best.

➤ **Matthew 5:17** — *"Do not think that I
came to abolish the Law or the Prophets;
I did not come to abolish but to fulfill."*

Some people mistakenly think Jesus'
revelation of God is totally different
from the Old Testament, but this is completely false. Jesus is the "exact representation of His nature" (Heb. 1:3)—as He
always was in time past and as He will
always be. He came as the fulfillment of
the Law and the promise of salvation to
this lost world.

ANSWERS TO LIFE'S QUESTIONS

How can I rid myself of guilt?

MATTHEW 5:23, 24

Consider several key steps required to be free from guilt, all under the banner of forgiveness:

1. *Admit the sin that created your guilt.* Repent of your sin to God. If you have sinned against another person, confess to that person. Remember that our society is quick to accept some sinful behaviors as normal. The Bible presents a very clear picture of what is iniquity and what isn't. If you have any doubt about whether or not you have sinned, consult Scripture. God will show you what is a violation of His Word and what isn't.

When you confess to God that you have sinned, don't try to justify what you did. Simply state your transgression. Then ask God to forgive you.

2. *Make amends.* If you have wronged another person, don't try to substitute a request for forgiveness by doing kind deeds for that person. This same principle holds for your relationship with God—don't try to substitute works for genuine repentance.

In seeking to make amends for a wrong committed against another person, you may be wise to ask what he or she would consider fair payment for the hurt or injury, or you may want to offer remuneration of some type. The best repayment may be a genuine change in your life (which may involve counseling, professional help, or therapy). Ask God to give you wisdom in identifying an appropriate way for you to respond. Also ask Him to give you the courage and the fortitude to follow through on your commitment to the offended person.

3. *Accept forgiveness.* If you have sinned against God and have repented, you can be assured He has forgiven you. His Word promises He will pardon you (1 John 1:9)—and God always keeps His Word. If you have sinned against another person and he forgives you, accept his words of forgiveness at face value. Don't try to second-guess his sincerity or motives.

What happens if you confess a sin against another person and the person refuses to forgive you? That person bears the responsibility for failing to forgive; you don't. You have done what the Lord requires of you, and you stand clean before the Lord.

---

15 nor does *anyone* light a lamp and put it under a basket, but on the lampstand, and it gives light to all who are in the house.

16 "Let your light shine before men in such a way that they may see your good works, and glorify your Father who is in heaven.

➤ 17 "Do not think that I came to abolish the Law or the Prophets; I did not come to abolish but to fulfill.

18 "For truly I say to you, until heaven and earth pass away, not the smallest letter or stroke shall pass from the Law until all is accomplished.

19 "Whoever then annuls one of the least of these commandments, and teaches others *to do* the same, shall be called least in the kingdom of heaven; but whoever keeps and teaches *them,* he shall be called great in the kingdom of heaven.

20 "For I say to you that unless your righteousness surpasses *that* of the scribes and Pharisees, you will not enter the kingdom of heaven.

21 "You have heard that the ancients were told, 'YOU SHALL NOT COMMIT MURDER' and 'Whoever commits murder shall be liable to the court.'

22 "But I say to you that everyone who is angry with his brother shall be guilty before the court; and whoever says to his brother, 'You good-for-nothing,' shall be guilty before the supreme court; and whoever says, 'You fool,' shall be guilty *enough to go* into the fiery hell.

23 "Therefore if you are presenting your offering at the altar, and there remember that your brother has something against you,

24 leave your offering there before the altar and go; first be reconciled to your brother, and then come and present your offering.

25 "Make friends quickly with your opponent at law while you are with him on the way, so that your opponent may not hand you over to the judge, and the judge to the officer, and you be thrown into prison.

26 "Truly I say to you, you will not come out of there until you have paid up the last cent.

11 NOW the whole earth used the same language and the same words.

2 It came about as they journeyed east, that they found a plain in the land of Shinar and settled there.

3 They said to one another, "Come, let us make bricks and burn *them* thoroughly." And they used brick for stone, and they used tar for mortar.

4 They said, "Come, let us build for ourselves a city, and a tower whose top *will reach* into heaven, and let us make for ourselves a name, otherwise we will be scattered abroad over the face of the whole earth."

5 The LORD came down to see the city and the tower which the sons of men had built.

6 The LORD said, "Behold, they are one people, and they all have the same language. And this is what they began to do, and now nothing which they purpose to do will be impossible for them.

7 "Come, let Us go down and there confuse their language, so that they will not understand one another's speech."

8 So the LORD scattered them abroad from there over the face of the whole earth; and they stopped building the city.

9 Therefore its name was called Babel, because there the LORD confused the language of the whole earth; and from there the LORD scattered them abroad over the face of the whole earth.

10 These are *the records of* the generations of Shem. Shem was one hundred years old, and became the father of Arpachshad two years after the flood;

11 and Shem lived five hundred years after he became the father of Arpachshad, and he had *other* sons and daughters.

ANSWERS TO LIFE'S QUESTIONS

How can I become a more obedient child of God?

GENESIS 12:1

*O*bedience is a major characteristic of a person who is mighty in spirit. Generally speaking, obedience characterized the faith of Abraham from his first encounter with God until his death.

1. *We grow in obedience by having faith in the sovereignty of God.*

If we fail to believe in God's sovereignty, we will find it difficult to obey Him. Abraham based his relationship with God on his confidence that God would do what He had promised (Rom. 4:20, 21). Faith comes by hearing the Word of God and responding in confident trust (Rom. 10:17). We will learn to trust Him as we study and meditate on His Word.

2. *We grow in obedience by waiting for God's timing.*

God is very time conscious—not in terms of minutes and seconds, but in regard to our acting in obedience according to His schedule. Throughout Scripture, we find Him moving in "the fullness of the time" (Gal. 4:4). He is neither early nor late. He is always right on time.

3. *We continue to grow in obedience by refusing to subject God's plan to "common sense" or the reasoning of the world.*

Some things God requires may look ridiculous from a human perspective. He told Abraham he would have a son through whom He would bless the entire world. Yet the Lord allowed Abraham's obedience to be severely tested—first by requiring him to wait nearly a quarter of a century before providing the promised provision, and later by requiring him to offer Isaac as a sacrifice. God knew the motive of Abraham's heart. It was one of obedience. When it came time to complete the sacrifice, the Lord was the one who provided a ram to be used in Isaac's place.

4. *We grow in obedience by promptly responding in obedience.*

If you long to obey God, you will not hesitate when He tells you to do something. Many times we fail to obey God because we fear the consequences. Yet He never requires us to do anything outside His will for our lives. Our only responsibility is to obey; God's responsibility is to take care of the consequences of our obedience.

Our sensitivity to God's will increases as we obey Him. Along the way, He provides glimpses of the blessings waiting for us. God *always* blesses obedience. You can trust Him, obey Him, and be blessed. Or you can disobey Him and spend the rest of your life wondering what He would have done had you obeyed Him. Once you glimpse the blessings of obedience, however, the consequences no longer matter.

12 Arpachshad lived thirty-five years, and became the father of Shelah;

13 and Arpachshad lived four hundred and three years after he became the father of Shelah, and he had *other* sons and daughters.

14 Shelah lived thirty years, and became the father of Eber;

15 and Shelah lived four hundred and three years after he became the father of Eber, and he had *other* sons and daughters.

16 Eber lived thirty-four years, and became the father of Peleg;

17 and Eber lived four hundred and thirty years after he became the father of Peleg, and he had *other* sons and daughters.

18 Peleg lived thirty years, and became the father of Reu;

19 and Peleg lived two hundred and nine years after he became the father of Reu, and he had *other* sons and daughters.

20 Reu lived thirty-two years, and became the father of Serug;

21 and Reu lived two hundred and seven years after he became the father of Serug, and he had *other* sons and daughters.

22 Serug lived thirty years, and became the father of Nahor;

23 and Serug lived two hundred years after he became the father of Nahor, and he had *other* sons and daughters.

24 Nahor lived twenty-nine years, and became the father of Terah;

25 and Nahor lived one hundred and nineteen years after he became the father of Terah, and he had *other* sons and daughters.

26 Terah lived seventy years, and became the father of Abram, Nahor and Haran.

27 Now these are *the records of* the generations of Terah. Terah became the father of Abram, Nahor and Haran; and Haran became the father of Lot.

28 Haran died in the presence of his father Terah in the land of his birth, in Ur of the Chaldeans.

29 Abram and Nahor took wives for themselves. The name of Abram's wife was Sarai; and the name of Nahor's wife was Milcah, the daughter of Haran, the father of Milcah and Iscah.

30 Sarai was barren; she had no child.

31 Terah took Abram his son, and Lot the son of Haran, his grandson, and Sarai his daughter-in-law, his son Abram's wife; and they went out together from Ur of the Chaldeans in order to enter the land of Canaan; and they went as far as Haran, and settled there.

32 The days of Terah were two hundred and five years; and Terah died in Haran.

12 NOW the LORD said to Abram, ◄
"Go forth from your country,
And from your relatives
And from your father's house,
To the land which I will show you;
2 And I will make you a great nation,
And I will bless you,
And make your name great;
And so you shall be a blessing;
3 And I will bless those who bless you, ✳
And the one who curses you I will curse.
And in you all the families of the earth will be blessed."

4 So Abram went forth as the LORD had spoken to him; and Lot went with him. Now Abram was seventy-five years old when he departed from Haran.

5 Abram took Sarai his wife and Lot his nephew, and all their possessions which they had accumulated, and the persons which they had acquired in Haran, and they set out for the land of Canaan; thus they came to the land of Canaan.

6 Abram passed through the land as far as the site of Shechem, to the oak of Moreh. Now the Canaanite *was* then in the land.

7 The LORD appeared to Abram and ◄ said, "To your descendants I will give this land." So he built an altar there to the LORD who had appeared to him.

LIFE LESSONS

➤ **Genesis 12:1 — *"Go forth from your country, And from your relatives and from your father's house, to the land which I will show you."***

*G*od always connects obedience with blessing, even when He does not sketch out the full details of what that blessing may be.

> **Genesis 12:7** — *The LORD appeared to Abram and said, "To your descendants I will give this land."*

*T*he Lord appeared to Abram only after he obeyed His voice by leaving Ur and traveling to Canaan. As Abram's faith grew, so did the details of God's promise to him.

8 Then he proceeded from there to the mountain on the east of Bethel, and pitched his tent, with Bethel on the west and Ai on the east; and there he built an altar to the LORD and called upon the name of the LORD.
9 Abram journeyed on, continuing toward the Negev.
> 10 Now there was a famine in the land; so Abram went down to Egypt to sojourn there, for the famine was severe in the land.
11 It came about when he came near to Egypt, that he said to Sarai his wife, "See now, I know that you are a beautiful woman;
12 and when the Egyptians see you, they will say, 'This is his wife'; and they will kill me, but they will let you live.
13 "Please say that you are my sister so that it may go well with me because of you, and that I may live on account of you."
14 It came about when Abram came into Egypt, the Egyptians saw that the woman was very beautiful.
15 Pharaoh's officials saw her and praised her to Pharaoh; and the woman was taken into Pharaoh's house.
16 Therefore he treated Abram well for her sake; and gave him sheep and oxen and donkeys and male and female servants and female donkeys and camels.

> **Genesis 12:10** — *Now there was a famine in the land, and Abram went down to Egypt to live there for a while because the famine was severe.*

*M*en and women of faith must endure hardship, just like anyone else. But if we will trust Him, God will use our adversity to deepen and strengthen our relationships with Him.

17 But the LORD struck Pharaoh and his house with great plagues because of Sarai, Abram's wife.
18 Then Pharaoh called Abram and said, "What is this you have done to me? Why did you not tell me that she was your wife?
19 "Why did you say, 'She is my sister,' so that I took her for my wife? Now then, here is your wife, take her and go."
20 Pharaoh commanded *his* men concerning him; and they escorted him away, with his wife and all that belonged to him.

Psalm 4:1–3

For the choir director; on stringed instruments. A Psalm of David.

4 ANSWER me when I call, O God of my righteousness!
You have relieved me in my distress; Be gracious to me and hear my prayer.
2 O sons of men, how long will my honor become a reproach?
How long will you love what is worthless and aim at deception?
Selah.
3 But know that the LORD has set apart the godly man for Himself; The LORD hears when I call to Him. ✳

Proverbs 1:28–33

28 "Then they will call on me, but I will not answer;
They will seek me diligently but they will not find me,
29 Because they hated knowledge And did not choose the fear of the LORD.
30 "They would not accept my counsel, They spurned all my reproof.
31 "So they shall eat of the fruit of their own way
And be satiated with their own devices.
32 "For the waywardness of the naive will kill them,
And the complacency of fools will destroy them.

33 "But he who listens to me shall live
securely
And will be at ease from the dread
of evil."

◈ Matthew 5:27–48

27 "You have heard that it was said,
'YOU SHALL NOT COMMIT ADULTERY';
28 but I say to you that everyone who
looks at a woman with lust for her has
already committed adultery with her in
his heart.
29 "If your right eye makes you stumble, tear it out and throw it from you; for
it is better for you to lose one of the parts
of your body, than for your whole body
to be thrown into hell.
30 "If your right hand makes you stumble, cut it off and throw it from you; for it
is better for you to lose one of the parts
of your body, than for your whole body
to go into hell.
31 "It was said, 'WHOEVER SENDS HIS
WIFE AWAY, LET HIM GIVE HER A CERTIFICATE
OF DIVORCE';
32 but I say to you that everyone who
divorces his wife, except for the reason
of unchastity, makes her commit adultery; and whoever marries a divorced
woman commits adultery.
33 "Again, you have heard that the
ancients were told, 'YOU SHALL NOT MAKE
FALSE VOWS, BUT SHALL FULFILL YOUR VOWS
TO THE LORD.'
34 "But I say to you, make no oath at
all, either by heaven, for it is the throne
of God,
35 or by the earth, for it is the footstool
of His feet, or by Jerusalem, for it is THE
CITY OF THE GREAT KING.
36 "Nor shall you make an oath by
your head, for you cannot make one hair
white or black.
37 "But let your statement be, 'Yes, yes'
or 'No, no'; anything beyond these is of
evil.
38 "You have heard that it was said, 'AN
EYE FOR AN EYE, AND A TOOTH FOR A TOOTH.'
39 "But I say to you, do not resist an evil
person; but whoever slaps you on your
right cheek, turn the other to him also.
40 "If anyone wants to sue you and take
your shirt, let him have your coat also.

41 "Whoever forces you to go one mile,
go with him two.
42 "Give to him who asks of you, and
do not turn away from him who wants to
borrow from you.
43 "You have heard that it was said,
'YOU SHALL LOVE YOUR NEIGHBOR and hate
your enemy.'
44 "But I say to you, love your enemies
and pray for those who persecute you,
45 so that you may be sons of your
Father who is in heaven; for He causes
His sun to rise on the evil and the good,
and sends rain on the righteous and the
unrighteous.
46 "For if you love those who love you,
what reward do you have? Do not even
the tax collectors do the same?
47 "If you greet only your brothers,
what more are you doing than others?
Do not even the Gentiles do the same?
48 "Therefore you are to be perfect, as
your heavenly Father is perfect.

LIFE LESSONS

➤ **Matthew 5:28** — *"But I say to you
that everyone who looks at a woman
with lust for her has already committed
adultery with her in his heart."*

*J*esus made it clear God is not after
outward compliance but inward
change. He doesn't want religious fanat-
ics but spiritually transformed men and
women whose lives are completely
devoted to Him. He wants people who
love to do His will.

➤ **Matthew 5:37** — *"But let your statement be, 'Yes, yes' or 'No, no'; anything
beyond these is of evil."*

*J*esus frowned on taking an oath
because this amounted to nothing
more than human works. When we
break our oaths, it reflects negatively
on our godly characters and on the Lord
Jesus. As believers, our word should be
just as trustworthy as an vow.

➤ **Matthew 5:48** — *"Therefore you are
to be perfect, as your heavenly Father is
perfect."*

*T*he only way to be perfect as the
Father is to be clothed, through
faith, with the righteousness of Christ.
This is necessary, for without holiness
"no one will see the Lord" (Heb. 12:14).

Genesis 13:1—14:24

13 SO Abram went up from Egypt to the Negev, he and his wife and all that belonged to him, and Lot with him.
2 Now Abram was very rich in livestock, in silver and in gold.
3 He went on his journeys from the Negev as far as Bethel, to the place where his tent had been at the beginning, between Bethel and Ai,
➤ 4 to the place of the altar which he had made there formerly; and there Abram called on the name of the LORD.
5 Now Lot, who went with Abram, also had flocks and herds and tents.
6 And the land could not sustain them while dwelling together, for their possessions were so great that they were not able to remain together.
7 And there was strife between the herdsmen of Abram's livestock and the herdsmen of Lot's livestock. Now the Canaanite and the Perizzite were dwelling then in the land.
8 So Abram said to Lot, "Please let there be no strife between you and me, nor between my herdsmen and your herdsmen, for we are brothers.
9 "Is not the whole land before you? Please separate from me; if *to* the left, then I will go to the right; or if *to* the right, then I will go to the left."
10 Lot lifted up his eyes and saw all the valley of the Jordan, that it was well watered everywhere—*this was* before the LORD destroyed Sodom and Gomorrah—like the garden of the LORD, like the land of Egypt as you go to Zoar.
11 So Lot chose for himself all the valley of the Jordan, and Lot journeyed eastward. Thus they separated from each other.

12 Abram settled in the land of Canaan, while Lot settled in the cities of the valley, and moved his tents as far as Sodom.
13 Now the men of Sodom were wicked exceedingly and sinners against the LORD.
14 The LORD said to Abram, after Lot had separated from him, "Now lift up your eyes and look from the place where you are, northward and southward and eastward and westward;
15 for all the land which you see, I will give it to you and to your descendants forever.
16 "I will make your descendants as the dust of the earth, so that if anyone can number the dust of the earth, then your descendants can also be numbered.
17 "Arise, walk about the land through its length and breadth; for I will give it to you."
18 Then Abram moved his tent and came and dwelt by the oaks of Mamre, which are in Hebron, and there he built an altar to the LORD.

14 AND it came about in the days of Amraphel king of Shinar, Arioch king of Ellasar, Chedorlaomer king of Elam, and Tidal king of Goiim,
2 *that* they made war with Bera king of Sodom, and with Birsha king of Gomorrah, Shinab king of Admah, and Shemeber king of Zeboiim, and the king of Bela (that is, Zoar).
3 All these came as allies to the valley of Siddim (that is, the Salt Sea).
4 Twelve years they had served Chedorlaomer, but the thirteenth year they rebelled.
5 In the fourteenth year Chedorlaomer and the kings that were with him, came and defeated the Rephaim in Ashteroth-karnaim and the Zuzim in Ham and the Emim in Shaveh-kiriathaim,
6 and the Horites in their Mount Seir, as far as El-paran, which is by the wilderness.
7 Then they turned back and came to En-mishpat (that is, Kadesh), and conquered all the country of the Amalekites, and also the Amorites, who lived in Hazazon-tamar.
8 And the king of Sodom and the king of Gomorrah and the king of Admah and the king of Zeboiim and the king of

---

· L I F E   L E S S O N S ·

➤ **Genesis 13:4 —** *There Abram called on the name of the LORD.*

*W*e have no record Abram "called on the name of the Lord" while in Egypt, where he got into trouble. How much better off we would be if we would learn prayer is life's greatest time saver!

Bela (that is, Zoar) came out; and they arrayed for battle against them in the valley of Siddim,
9   against Chedorlaomer king of Elam and Tidal king of Goiim and Amraphel king of Shinar and Arioch king of Ellasar—four kings against five.
10 Now the valley of Siddim was full of tar pits; and the kings of Sodom and Gomorrah fled, and they fell into them. But those who survived fled to the hill country.
11 Then they took all the goods of Sodom and Gomorrah and all their food supply, and departed.
12 They also took Lot, Abram's nephew, and his possessions and departed, for he was living in Sodom.
13 Then a fugitive came and told Abram the Hebrew. Now he was living by the oaks of Mamre the Amorite, brother of Eshcol and brother of Aner, and these were allies with Abram.
14 When Abram heard that his relative had been taken captive, he led out his trained men, born in his house, three hundred and eighteen, and went in pursuit as far as Dan.
15 He divided his forces against them by night, he and his servants, and defeated them, and pursued them as far as Hobah, which is north of Damascus.
16 He brought back all the goods, and also brought back his relative Lot with his possessions, and also the women, and the people.
17 Then after his return from the defeat of Chedorlaomer and the kings who were with him, the king of Sodom went out to meet him at the valley of Shaveh (that is, the King's Valley).
18 And Melchizedek king of Salem brought out bread and wine; now he was a priest of God Most High.
19 He blessed him and said,
   "Blessed be Abram of God Most
      High,
   Possessor of heaven and earth;
20 And blessed be God Most High,   ◄
   Who has delivered your enemies
      into your hand."
He gave him a tenth of all.
21 The king of Sodom said to Abram, "Give the people to me and take the goods for yourself."
22 Abram said to the king of Sodom, "I have sworn to the Lord God Most High, possessor of heaven and earth,
23 that I will not take a thread or a sandal thong or anything that is yours, for fear you would say, 'I have made Abram rich.'
24 "I will take nothing except what the young men have eaten, and the share of the men who went with me, Aner, Eshcol, and Mamre; let them take their share."

Psalm 4:4–8

4   Tremble, and do not sin;
   Meditate in your heart upon your
      bed, and be still.   Selah.
5   Offer the sacrifices of righteousness,
   And trust in the Lord.
6   Many are saying, "Who will show us
      any good?"
   Lift up the light of Your countenance
      upon us, O Lord!
7   You have put gladness in my heart,   ◄
   More than when their grain and
      new wine abound.

LIFE LESSONS

➤ **Genesis 14:20 — *"Blessed be God Most High, who has delivered your enemies into your hand."***

*T*he mysterious priest Melchizedek reminded Abram that God had delivered Abram's enemies into his hand, even though it was Abram's men who did the fighting. God is the author of all blessings.

➤ **Psalm 4:7 — *You have put gladness in my heart, more than when their grain and new wine abound.***

*T*he joy of the Lord is a supernatural thing. It is deeper, stronger, tougher, and more resilient than any joy derived from mere circumstances. Those without it cannot understand it, so we need to lead them to the Lord so that they can experience it for themselves.

LIFE PRINCIPLE 12

PEACE WITH GOD IS THE FRUIT OF ONENESS WITH GOD.

PSALM 4:8

*E*very now and then we do well to take stock of our situations, so I'd like to ask you to look around. What's happening in your life and in your family?

You may not be experiencing a difficult time. From your perspective, everything may seem sunny and clear. Storms come, however. At times, they roll into our lives with bounding blows. How do we maintain a sense of peace and spiritual balance when trials strike?

The answer is found in a close, abiding relationship with Jesus Christ. The words of Helen Lemmel's classic hymn, "Turn Your Eyes Upon Jesus," contain a vital and exciting truth: an unshakable peace is available to all who turn the eyes of their hearts to Jesus.

Chances are when adversity strikes, one of the first things you do is to wonder why. Then you may question what kind of impact it will have on your life. While reactions such as these are normal, we also need another response—and that is to turn to the One who holds all comfort and security firmly within His grasp.

No one, outside of God, is equipped to handle our problems. He never meant for us to be strong on our own. He wants us to find courage, hope, and strength in Him and His Word.

Many wonder what they can do to change the feelings of anxiety they feel when they come under pressure. One of the first steps is to recognize anxiety for what it is—the opposite of peace. It is the fan that flames the fires of doubt and confusion, and it has the ability to leave us helplessly bundled up in worry and fear. When we cave into thoughts of anxiety, we lose our spiritual focus and mindset. The key to overcoming anxiety is found only in the presence of God.

Paul admonishes us: "Be anxious for nothing, but in everything by prayer and supplication with thanksgiving let your requests be made known to God. And the peace of God, which surpasses all comprehension, will guard your hearts and your minds in Christ Jesus" (Phil. 4:6, 7).

Accepting God's timetable and the limitations He places on a given situation help to dispel rising anxiety. Therefore, let Him provide for you in His timing. When you accept life as a gift from the hand of God, then you will do what Helen Lemmel's song says—you will turn your eyes toward Jesus. You will look full into His glorious face and there find mercy and grace, forgiveness and hope, peace and everlasting security.

What would you give to experience the peace of God? Are you willing to lay down the anger that haunts your soul because someone has done something to wound you? God knows the hurt you have experienced. Will you trust Him in quietness, knowing He has not forgotten you but stands ready to heal you?

God's peace is unshakable because there has never been a time or an event when He has felt disturbed. His peace and presence are sure. They are immovable. You will accomplish many things—great and mighty—when you keep your focus on God.

At one of the most difficult points in his life, David wrote Psalm 57, which begins: "Be gracious to me, O God, be gracious to me, for my soul takes refuge in You; and in the shadow of Your wings I will take refuge until destruction passes by. I will cry to God Most High, to God who accomplishes all things for me. He will send from heaven and save me; He reproaches him who tramples upon me. God will send forth His lovingkindness and His truth" (vv. 1–3).

How could David write such trusting words, especially with King Saul trying to kill him? David had a divine, unshakable peace within his heart that God would protect his life and fulfill His promises to him.

The safest place for you when trials come is in the everlasting arms of Jesus. After His resurrection, Jesus appeared to His disciples and said to them, "Peace be with you" (John 20:19). This was not a trite greeting; the Lord had a specific purpose in mind. He spoke of God's peace, immovable and eternal—the peace He had paid for on the Cross (John 14:27; Rom. 5:1; Eph. 2:13–16)—The peace you need today.

Does something trouble you? Has a conflict, sorrow, or situation escalated beyond your control? Hear His word to you: "Peace be with you."

Let His peace invade your heart. Tell Him all you are feeling. He understands and knows life can be difficult—but He has a solution. Our peace resides in our Savior, who loves us unconditionally. He has promised to keep us and deliver us into the Father's loving arms.

➤ 8 In peace I will both lie down and
sleep,
For You alone, O LORD, make me to
dwell in safety.

◈ Proverbs 2:1–5

2 MY son, if you will receive my words
And treasure my commandments
within you,
2 Make your ear attentive to
wisdom,
Incline your heart to understanding;
3 For if you cry for discernment,
Lift your voice for understanding;
4 If you seek her as silver
And search for her as for hidden
treasures;
5 Then you will discern the fear of the
LORD
And discover the knowledge of God.

◈ Matthew 6:1–18

6 "BEWARE of practicing your righteousness before men to be noticed
by them; otherwise you have no reward
with your Father who is in heaven.
2 "So when you give to the poor, do
not sound a trumpet before you, as the
hypocrites do in the synagogues and in
the streets, so that they may be honored
by men. Truly I say to you, they have
their reward in full.
3 "But when you give to the poor, do
not let your left hand know what your
right hand is doing,
➤ 4 so that your giving will be in secret;
and your Father who sees *what is done*
in secret will reward you.
5 "When you pray, you are not to be
like the hypocrites; for they love to stand
and pray in the synagogues and on the
street corners so that they may be seen
by men. Truly I say to you, they have
their reward in full.
6 "But you, when you pray, go into
your inner room, close your door and
✳ pray to your Father who is in secret, and
your Father who sees *what is done* in
secret will reward you.
➤ 7 "And when you are praying, do not
use meaningless repetition as the Gen-

tiles do, for they suppose that they will
be heard for their many words.
8 "So do not be like them; for your
Father knows what you need before you
ask Him.
9 "Pray, then, in this way:
'Our Father who is in heaven,
Hallowed be Your name.
10 'Your kingdom come.
Your will be done,
On earth as it is in heaven.
11 'Give us this day our daily bread.
12 'And forgive us our debts, as we
also have forgiven our debtors.
13 'And do not lead us into temptation,
but deliver us from evil. [For
Yours is the kingdom and the
power and the glory forever.
Amen.']

LIFE LESSONS

➤ **Psalm 4:8 —** *In peace I will both lie
down and sleep, for You alone, O LORD,
make me to dwell in safety.*

*D*avid wrote this psalm during a time
of great distress—possibly while Saul
was pursuing him (1 Sam. 18—26), after
Absalom's betrayal (2 Sam. 15—18), or
during the rebellion of Sheba (2 Sam.
20). The stress could have caused David
to be restless and wakeful. Yet he was
able to sleep well because he knew the
Lord would keep him safe. God wants
this same kind of confidence and peace
to take root in us.

➤ **Matthew 6:4 —** *"Your Father who sees
what is done in secret will reward you."*

*W*e do not need to boast about our
Spirit-led good deeds or advertise
the kind things we do that might otherwise be overlooked. God gives the only
rewards that matter, and He keeps careful tally.

➤ **Matthew 6:7 —** *"When you are praying, do not use meaningless repetition as
the Gentiles do."*

*E*ffective prayer is not magic; it's not
about speaking the right string of
words or using the correct formula so
God will move on our behalf. Instead,
it's about communicating on a heart-to-
heart level with the Lord of the universe.
We have an awesome opportunity to
draw near to Him and learn His ways.

14 "For if you forgive others for their transgressions, your heavenly Father will also forgive you.
15 "But if you do not forgive others, then your Father will not forgive your transgressions.
16 "Whenever you fast, do not put on a gloomy face as the hypocrites *do,* for they neglect their appearance so that

they will be noticed by men when they are fasting. Truly I say to you, they have their reward in full.
17 "But you, when you fast, anoint your head and wash your face
18 so that your fasting will not be noticed by men, but by your Father who is in secret; and your Father who sees *what is done* in secret will reward you.

◈ Genesis 15:1—16:16

15 AFTER these things the word of the LORD came to Abram in a vision, saying,

> "Do not fear, Abram,
> I am a shield to you;
> Your reward shall be very great."

2 Abram said, "O Lord GOD, what will You give me, since I am childless, and the heir of my house is Eliezer of Damascus?"
3 And Abram said, "Since You have given no offspring to me, one born in my house is my heir."
4 Then behold, the word of the LORD came to him, saying, "This man will not be your heir; but one who will come forth from your own body, he shall be your heir."
5 And He took him outside and said, "Now look toward the heavens, and count the stars, if you are able to count them." And He said to him, "So shall your descendants be."
6 Then he believed in the LORD; and He reckoned it to him as righteousness.
7 And He said to him, "I am the LORD who brought you out of Ur of the Chaldeans, to give you this land to possess it."
8 He said, "O Lord GOD, how may I know that I will possess it?"
9 So He said to him, "Bring Me a three year old heifer, and a three year old female goat, and a three year old ram, and a turtledove, and a young pigeon."
10 Then he brought all these to Him and cut them in two, and laid each half opposite the other; but he did not cut the birds.

11 The birds of prey came down upon the carcasses, and Abram drove them away.
12 Now when the sun was going down, a deep sleep fell upon Abram; and behold, terror *and* great darkness fell upon him.
13 *God* said to Abram, "Know for certain that your descendants will be strangers in a land that is not theirs, where they will be enslaved and oppressed four hundred years.
14 "But I will also judge the nation whom they will serve, and afterward they will come out with many possessions.
15 "As for you, you shall go to your fathers in peace; you will be buried at a good old age.
16 "Then in the fourth generation they

LIFE LESSONS

➤ **Genesis 15:6 —** *Then he believed in the LORD; and He reckoned it to him for righteousness.*

*E*ven when Abram did not see how God could fulfill His gracious promise to him regarding an heir, he trusted the Lord anyway. He looked beyond what he could see to what God could see.

➤ **Genesis 15:16 —** *"Then in the fourth generation they will return here, for the iniquity of the Amorite is not yet complete."*

*G*od is more patient than we can imagine. He would wait over 400 years to give the land of promise to His people because the wicked Canaanites had not yet reached the point of no return (2 Pet. 3:9).

will return here, for the iniquity of the Amorite is not yet complete."

17 It came about when the sun had set, that it was very dark, and behold, *there appeared* a smoking oven and a flaming torch which passed between these pieces.

18 On that day the Lord made a covenant with Abram, saying,

"To your descendants I have given this land,

From the river of Egypt as far as the great river, the river Euphrates:

19 the Kenite and the Kenizzite and the Kadmonite

20 and the Hittite and the Perizzite and the Rephaim

21 and the Amorite and the Canaanite and the Girgashite and the Jebusite."

16 NOW Sarai, Abram's wife had borne him no *children,* and she had an Egyptian maid whose name was Hagar.

2 So Sarai said to Abram, "Now behold, the Lord has prevented me from bearing *children.* Please go in to my maid; perhaps I will obtain children through her." And Abram listened to the voice of Sarai.

3 After Abram had lived ten years in the land of Canaan, Abram's wife Sarai took Hagar the Egyptian, her maid, and gave her to her husband Abram as his wife.

4 He went in to Hagar, and she conceived; and when she saw that she had conceived, her mistress was despised in her sight.

5 And Sarai said to Abram, "May the wrong done me be upon you. I gave my maid into your arms, but when she saw that she had conceived, I was despised in her sight. May the Lord judge between you and me."

6 But Abram said to Sarai, "Behold, your maid is in your power; do to her what is good in your sight." So Sarai treated her harshly, and she fled from her presence.

7 Now the angel of the Lord found her by a spring of water in the wilderness, by the spring on the way to Shur.

8 He said, "Hagar, Sarai's maid, where have you come from and where are you going?" And she said, "I am fleeing from the presence of my mistress Sarai."

9 Then the angel of the Lord said to her, "Return to your mistress, and submit yourself to her authority."

10 Moreover, the angel of the Lord said to her, "I will greatly multiply your descendants so that they will be too many to count."

11 The angel of the Lord said to her further,

"Behold, you are with child,
And you will bear a son;
And you shall call his name Ishmael,
Because the Lord has given heed to your affliction.

12 "He will be a wild donkey of a man,
His hand *will be* against everyone,
And everyone's hand *will be* against him;
And he will live to the east of all his brothers."

13 Then she called the name of the Lord who spoke to her, "You are a God who sees"; for she said, "Have I even remained alive here after seeing Him?"

14 Therefore the well was called Beer-lahai-roi; behold, it is between Kadesh and Bered.

15 So Hagar bore Abram a son; and Abram called the name of his son, whom Hagar bore, Ishmael.

16 Abram was eighty-six years old when Hagar bore Ishmael to him.

Psalm 5:1–7

For the choir director; for flute accompaniment. A Psalm of David.

5 GIVE ear to my words, O Lord,
Consider my groaning.

2 Heed the sound of my cry for help,
my King and my God,
For to You I pray.

3 In the morning, O Lord, You will hear my voice;
In the morning I will order *my prayer* to You and *eagerly* watch.

4 For You are not a God who takes pleasure in wickedness;
No evil dwells with You.

5 The boastful shall not stand before Your eyes;
You hate all who do iniquity.

LIFE LESSONS

➤ **Psalm 5:4** — *For you are not a God who takes pleasure in wickedness; No evil dwells with You.*

*M*any today think grace means they can sin without consequence—that God loves them and forgives them, so they can do whatever they want. But grace never changes the way God feels about sin. He hates it because it is destructive and harmful to those He loves (1 Cor. 6:12).

6 You destroy those who speak falsehood;
 The LORD abhors the man of bloodshed and deceit.

7 But as for me, by Your abundant lovingkindness I will enter Your house,
 At Your holy temple I will bow in reverence for You.

Proverbs 2:6–9

6 For the LORD gives wisdom;
 From His mouth *come* knowledge and understanding.
7 He stores up sound wisdom for the upright;
 He is a shield to those who walk in integrity,
8 Guarding the paths of justice,
 And He preserves the way of His godly ones.
9 Then you will discern righteousness and justice
 And equity *and* every good course.

Matthew 6:19–34

19 "Do not store up for yourselves treasures on earth, where moth and rust

---

ANSWERS TO LIFE'S QUESTIONS

How can I overcome anxiety?

MATTHEW 6:25–34

*G*od did not design you to be anxious or nervous. In His Sermon on the Mount, Jesus told the crowds, "Do not worry then, saying, 'What will we eat?' or 'What will we drink?' or 'What will we wear for clothing?' . . . Do not worry about tomorrow" (Matt. 6:31, 34).

At some point, all of us have worried about the basics of life. Most of our anxieties involve fundamental things: where to live, what food to buy, what clothes to wear, what friends to have, and what others think about us. In all these concerns, the issue is one of faith and trust in God. Do we really believe He will do what He has promised to do in His Word?

If you assume you are the one who is in charge of your life, then you will battle anxiety and fear. However, if you understand the ways of the Lord, then you will know He is in charge and the sovereign God of the universe cares for you. If you worry and doubt His goodness, you will never have the peace He wants you to experience. Do you take time to acknowledge Him as your Provider? Your answer has everything to do with your anxiety level.

Have you ever watched a mouse running inside a wheel? The faster he runs, the faster the wheel moves—but he doesn't make the slightest progress. He does not even have the sense to get off the wheel. This is exactly what anxiety does to you. As fearful thoughts fill your mind, you begin to run faster, trying harder to meet the demands of others or to prevent an uncertain disaster. But you will never gain complete control over your circumstances because God is the One who is solely in control of all things.

There is only one way to step off the wheel: by acknowledging the Lord's ability to take care of every need you have. God created you. He knows your needs and the deepest desires of your heart (Ps. 37:4). He longs for you to end the anxiety cycle and let Him lead (Matt. 11:28). First Peter 5:6, 7 says, "Therefore humble yourselves under the mighty hand of God, that He may exalt you at the proper time, casting all your anxiety on Him, because He cares for you." The word "casting" is related to the Greek verb used in Luke 19:35, when on Palm Sunday the people of Jerusalem threw their garments onto a colt for Jesus to ride. The word describes the same motion: a deliberate action of setting something down and leaving it there.

Jesus wants you to give your cares over to Him *and leave them with Him.* You depend on Him for life itself, and you acknowledge this by saying, "Here, Jesus. Take my problems. You have the answers! I trust You to show me what to do and to take care of the consequences."

destroy, and where thieves break in and steal.

20 "But store up for yourselves treasures in heaven, where neither moth nor rust destroys, and where thieves do not break in or steal;

➤ 21 for where your treasure is, there your heart will be also.

22 "The eye is the lamp of the body; so then if your eye is clear, your whole body will be full of light.

23 "But if your eye is bad, your whole body will be full of darkness. If then the light that is in you is darkness, how great is the darkness!

➤ 24 "No one can serve two masters; for either he will hate the one and love the other, or he will be devoted to one and despise the other. You cannot serve God and wealth.

25 "For this reason I say to you, do not be worried about your life, *as to* what you will eat or what you will drink; nor for your body, *as to* what you will put on. Is not life more than food, and the body more than clothing?

26 "Look at the birds of the air, that they do not sow, nor reap nor gather into barns, and *yet* your heavenly Father feeds them. Are you not worth much more than they?

27 "And who of you by being worried can add a *single* hour to his life?

28 "And why are you worried about clothing? Observe how the lilies of the field grow; they do not toil nor do they spin,

29 yet I say to you that not even Solomon in all his glory clothed himself like one of these.

30 "But if God so clothes the grass of the field, which is *alive* today and tomorrow is thrown into the furnace, *will He* not much more *clothe* you? You of little faith!

31 "Do not worry then, saying, 'What will we eat?' or 'What will we drink?' or 'What will we wear for clothing?'

32 "For the Gentiles eagerly seek all ◄ these things; for your heavenly Father knows that you need all these things.

33 "But seek first His kingdom and His righteousness, and all these things will be added to you.

34 "So do not worry about tomorrow; ✳ for tomorrow will care for itself. Each day has enough trouble of its own.

LIFE LESSONS

➤ **Matthew 6:21 — *"For where your treasure is, there your heart will be also."***

*W*hat do you think about most throughout the day? What gets your heart beating faster and louder? What do you think you couldn't live without? Whatever "it" is, it's your treasure—and nothing but God is worthy of it.

➤ **Matthew 6:24 — *"No one can serve two masters."***

*T*oo many of us try to serve two masters: God *and* work, or God *and* bank accounts, or God *and* family. But Jesus says this is impossible, for two masters inevitably give contradictory demands. Who will *you* serve?

➤ **Matthew 6:32 — *"Your heavenly Father knows that you need all these things."***

*G*od doesn't tell us to stop worrying over food, shelter, and clothing because we don't really need them. He *knows* we need them. We can stop worrying because He has promised to take care of the essentials.

 Genesis 17:1—18:33

17 NOW when Abram was ninety-nine years old, the LORD appeared to Abram and said to him,

"I am God Almighty;
Walk before Me, and be blameless.

2 "I will establish My covenant between Me and you,
And I will multiply you exceedingly."

3   Abram fell on his face, and God talked with him, saying,

4   "As for Me, behold, My covenant is with you,
And you will be the father of a multitude of nations.

5   "No longer shall your name be called Abram,
But your name shall be Abraham;
For I have made you the father of a multitude of nations.

6   "I will make you exceedingly fruitful, and I will make nations of you, and kings will come forth from you.

7   "I will establish My covenant between Me and you and your descendants after you throughout their generations for an everlasting covenant, to be God to you and to your descendants after you.

8   "I will give to you and to your descendants after you, the land of your sojournings, all the land of Canaan, for an everlasting possession; and I will be their God."

9   God said further to Abraham, "Now as for you, you shall keep My covenant, you and your descendants after you throughout their generations.

10   "This is My covenant, which you shall keep, between Me and you and your descendants after you: every male among you shall be circumcised.

11   "And you shall be circumcised in the flesh of your foreskin, and it shall be the sign of the covenant between Me and you.

12   "And every male among you who is eight days old shall be circumcised throughout your generations, a *servant* who is born in the house or who is bought with money from any foreigner, who is not of your descendants.

13   "A *servant* who is born in your house

---

or who is bought with your money shall surely be circumcised; thus shall My covenant be in your flesh for an everlasting covenant.

14   "But an uncircumcised male who is not circumcised in the flesh of his foreskin, that person shall be cut off from his people; he has broken My covenant."

15   Then God said to Abraham, "As for Sarai your wife, you shall not call her name Sarai, but Sarah *shall be* her name.

16   "I will bless her, and indeed I will give you a son by her. Then I will bless her, and she shall be *a mother of* nations; kings of peoples will come from her."

17   Then Abraham fell on his face and laughed, and said in his heart, "Will a child be born to a man one hundred years old? And will Sarah, who is ninety years old, bear *a child?*"

18   And Abraham said to God, "Oh that Ishmael might live before You!"

19   But God said, "No, but Sarah your wife will bear you a son, and you shall call his name Isaac; and I will establish My covenant with him for an everlasting covenant for his descendants after him.

20   "As for Ishmael, I have heard you; behold, I will bless him, and will make him fruitful and will multiply him exceedingly. He shall become the father of twelve princes, and I will make him a great nation.

21   "But My covenant I will establish with Isaac, whom Sarah will bear to you at this season next year."

22   When He finished talking with him, God went up from Abraham.

23   Then Abraham took Ishmael his son, and all *the servants* who were born in his house and all who were bought with his money, every male among the men of Abraham's household, and circumcised the flesh of their foreskin in the very same day, as God had said to him.

24   Now Abraham was ninety-nine years old when he was circumcised in the flesh of his foreskin.

25   And Ishmael his son was thirteen years old when he was circumcised in the flesh of his foreskin.

26   In the very same day Abraham was circumcised, and Ishmael his son.

27   All the men of his household, who were born in the house or bought with money from a foreigner, were circumcised with him.

LIFE LESSONS

➤ **Genesis 17:5** — *"No longer shall your name be called Abram, but your name shall be Abraham; for I have made you the father of a multitude of nations."*

*E*ven before God fulfilled His promise to Abraham to give him a son through Sarai, He said, "I *have made* you a father of many nations." God's promises are so solid He can speak of their future fulfillment in the past tense!

18 NOW the LORD appeared to him by the oaks of Mamre, while he was sitting at the tent door in the heat of the day.

2 When he lifted up his eyes and looked, behold, three men were standing opposite him; and when he saw *them,* he ran from the tent door to meet them and bowed himself to the earth,

3 and said, "My Lord, if now I have found favor in Your sight, please do not pass Your servant by.

4 "Please let a little water be brought and wash your feet, and rest yourselves under the tree;

5 and I will bring a piece of bread, that you may refresh yourselves; after that you may go on, since you have visited your servant." And they said, "So do, as you have said."

6 So Abraham hurried into the tent to Sarah, and said, "Quickly, prepare three measures of fine flour, knead *it* and make bread cakes."

7 Abraham also ran to the herd, and took a tender and choice calf and gave *it* to the servant, and he hurried to prepare it.

8 He took curds and milk and the calf which he had prepared, and placed *it* before them; and he was standing by them under the tree as they ate.

9 Then they said to him, "Where is Sarah your wife?" And he said, "There, in the tent."

10 He said, "I will surely return to you at this time next year; and behold, Sarah your wife will have a son." And Sarah was listening at the tent door, which was behind him.

LIFE LESSONS

➤ **Genesis 18:14 — *"Is anything too difficult for the LORD? At the appointed time I will return to you . . . and Sarah will have a son."***

Things we find difficult to do, God finds very easy. That is why we can trust all of His promises. We do not have to understand how He will fulfill them; we have only to believe He will.

---

11 Now Abraham and Sarah were old, advanced in age; Sarah was past childbearing.

12 Sarah laughed to herself, saying, "After I have become old, shall I have pleasure, my lord being old also?"

13 And the LORD said to Abraham, "Why did Sarah laugh, saying, 'Shall I indeed bear *a child,* when I am *so* old?'

14 "Is anything too difficult for the ◄ LORD? At the appointed time I will return to you, at this time next year, and Sarah will have a son."

15 Sarah denied *it* however, saying, "I did not laugh"; for she was afraid. And He said, "No, but you did laugh."

16 Then the men rose up from there, and looked down toward Sodom; and Abraham was walking with them to send them off.

17 The LORD said, "Shall I hide from Abraham what I am about to do,

18 since Abraham will surely become a great and mighty nation, and in him all the nations of the earth will be blessed?

19 "For I have chosen him, so that he may command his children and his household

---

Life Examples:

SARAH: Laughing All the Way to the Crib

GENESIS 18:9–15

Sarah probably smiled to herself as the words of her husband rang in her ears. How could she believe the outlandish story? "God spoke to me!" he had said. "He promised to make me the head of many nations—*me*! A man of 99 years! And He is going to do it through you!"

Sarah's reaction to the news her husband had given may have been similar to something we have felt. She laughed. "I am 90 years old; I am no longer capable of giving you children. There must be some mistake!"

But there had been no mistake. God challenged her with the words, "Is anything too difficult for the LORD?" (Gen. 18:14). Nine months later, the birth of a baby boy provided the answer. God loves doing the impossible. And the only requirement for Him to work in our lives is faith in line with the truth of His Word.

Sarah's story represents something much greater than one woman's experience. It demonstrates God's unrelenting pursuit of each of us. Despite her faults and persistent lack of faith, Sarah witnessed God turn the "impossible" into reality—and so can you.

after him to keep the way of the LORD by doing righteousness and justice, so that the LORD may bring upon Abraham what He has spoken about him."

20 And the LORD said, "The outcry of Sodom and Gomorrah is indeed great, and their sin is exceedingly grave.

21 "I will go down now, and see if they have done entirely according to its outcry, which has come to Me; and if not, I will know."

22 Then the men turned away from there and went toward Sodom, while Abraham was still standing before the LORD.

23 Abraham came near and said, "Will You indeed sweep away the righteous with the wicked?

24 "Suppose there are fifty righteous within the city; will You indeed sweep it away and not spare the place for the sake of the fifty righteous who are in it?

➤ 25 "Far be it from You to do such a thing, to slay the righteous with the wicked, so that the righteous and the wicked are treated alike. Far be it from You! Shall not the Judge of all the earth deal justly?"

26 So the LORD said, "If I find in Sodom fifty righteous within the city, then I will spare the whole place on their account."

27 And Abraham replied, "Now behold, I have ventured to speak to the Lord, although I am but dust and ashes.

28 "Suppose the fifty righteous are lacking five, will You destroy the whole city because of five?" And He said, "I will not destroy it if I find forty-five there."

29 He spoke to Him yet again and said, "Suppose forty are found there?" And He said, "I will not do it on account of the forty."

30 Then he said, "Oh may the Lord not be angry, and I shall speak; suppose thirty are found there?" And He said, "I will not do it if I find thirty there."

31 And he said, "Now behold, I have ventured to speak to the Lord; suppose twenty are found there?" And He said, "I will not destroy it on account of the twenty."

32 Then he said, "Oh may the Lord not be angry, and I shall speak only this once; suppose ten are found there?" And He said, "I will not destroy it on account of the ten."

33 As soon as He had finished speaking to Abraham the LORD departed, and Abraham returned to his place.

◈ Psalm 5:8–12

8 O LORD, lead me in Your
      righteousness because of my foes;
   Make Your way straight before me.
9 There is nothing reliable in what
      they say;
   Their inward part is destruction
      itself.
   Their throat is an open grave;
   They flatter with their tongue.
10 Hold them guilty, O God;
   By their own devices let them fall!
   In the multitude of their
      transgressions thrust them out,
   For they are rebellious against You.
11 But let all who take refuge in You be
      glad,
   Let them ever sing for joy;
   And may You shelter them,
   That those who love Your name may   ✳
      exult in You.
12 For it is You who blesses the
      righteous man, O LORD,
   You surround him with favor as
      with a shield.

◈ Proverbs 2:10–22

10 For wisdom will enter your heart
   And knowledge will be pleasant to
      your soul;
11 Discretion will guard you,
   Understanding will watch over you,
12 To deliver you from the way of evil,
   From the man who speaks perverse
      things;
13 From those who leave the paths of
      uprightness
   To walk in the ways of darkness;

LIFE LESSONS

➤ **Genesis 18:25 — *"Shall not the Judge of all the earth deal justly?"***

We can rest assured God, "the Judge of all the earth," will always do exactly what is right. We never have to fear He will make a mistake or suffer a lapse in judgment.

14 Who delight in doing evil
   And rejoice in the perversity of evil;
15 Whose paths are crooked,
   And who are devious in their ways;
16 To deliver you from the strange
      woman,
   From the adulteress who flatters
      with her words;
17 That leaves the companion of her
      youth
   And forgets the covenant of her God;
18 For her house sinks down to death
   And her tracks *lead* to the dead;
19 None who go to her return again,
   Nor do they reach the paths of life.
20 So you will walk in the way of good
      men
   And keep to the paths of the
      righteous.
21 For the upright will live in the land
   And the blameless will remain in it;
22 But the wicked will be cut off from
      the land
   And the treacherous will be
      uprooted from it.

◈ Matthew 7:1–29

7 "DO not judge so that you will not be
  judged.
2 "For in the way you judge, you will
be judged; and by your standard of measure, it will be measured to you.
3 "Why do you look at the speck that
is in your brother's eye, but do not notice
the log that is in your own eye?
4 "Or how can you say to your brother,
'Let me take the speck out of your eye,'
and behold, the log is in your own eye?
5 "You hypocrite, first take the log
out of your own eye, and then you will
see clearly to take the speck out of your
brother's eye.

6 "Do not give what is holy to dogs,
and do not throw your pearls before
swine, or they will trample them under
their feet, and turn and tear you to pieces.
7 "Ask, and it will be given to you;
seek, and you will find; knock, and it will
be opened to you.
8 "For everyone who asks receives,
and he who seeks finds, and to him who
knocks it will be opened.
9 "Or what man is there among you
who, when his son asks for a loaf, will
give him a stone?
10 "Or if he asks for a fish, he will not
give him a snake, will he?
11 "If you then, being evil, know how
to give good gifts to your children, how
much more will your Father who is in
heaven give what is good to those who
ask Him!
12 "In everything, therefore, treat people the same way you want them to treat
you, for this is the Law and the Prophets.
13 "Enter through the narrow gate; for
the gate is wide and the way is broad that
leads to destruction, and there are many
who enter through it.
14 "For the gate is small and the way is
narrow that leads to life, and there are
few who find it.
15 "Beware of the false prophets, who
come to you in sheep's clothing, but inwardly are ravenous wolves.
16 "You will know them by their fruits.
Grapes are not gathered from thorn
bushes nor figs from thistles, are they?
17 "So every good tree bears good fruit,
but the bad tree bears bad fruit.
18 "A good tree cannot produce bad
fruit, nor can a bad tree produce good
fruit.
19 "Every tree that does not bear good
fruit is cut down and thrown into the fire.
20 "So then, you will know them by
their fruits.

LIFE LESSONS

➤ **Matthew 7:2 — *"For in the way you
judge, you will be judged."***

Living by this simple guideline would
eliminate the vast majority of squab-
bles and conflicts we endure. Would we
want to be judged by the standards we
judge others? Do we demand grace but
never give mercy?

➤ **Matthew 7:7 — *"Ask, and it will be
given to you; seek, and you will find;
knock, and it will be opened to you."***

We must stop believing God is stingy,
miserly, or tight-fisted with His
grace and goodness. He delights in show-
ering us with good things—but we have
to present Him with our requests.

➤ 21 "Not everyone who says to Me, 'Lord, Lord,' will enter the kingdom of heaven, but he who does the will of My Father who is in heaven *will enter.*
22 "Many will say to Me on that day, 'Lord, Lord, did we not prophesy in Your name, and in Your name cast out demons, and in Your name perform many miracles?'

LIFE LESSONS

➤ **Matthew 7:21** — *"Not everyone who says to Me, 'Lord, Lord,' will enter the kingdom of heaven, but he who does the will of My Father who is in heaven will enter."*

*W*illing and eager obedience is the hallmark of someone who has truly come to faith in Jesus Christ. We obey, not because we want to earn God's favor, but because we feel delighted to have already received it.

---

23 "And then I will declare to them, 'I never knew you; DEPART FROM ME, YOU WHO PRACTICE LAWLESSNESS.'
24 "Therefore everyone who hears these words of Mine and acts on them, may be compared to a wise man who built his house on the rock.
25 "And the rain fell, and the floods came, and the winds blew and slammed against that house; and *yet* it did not fall, for it had been founded on the rock.
26 "Everyone who hears these words of Mine and does not act on them, will be like a foolish man who built his house on the sand.
27 "The rain fell, and the floods came, and the winds blew and slammed against that house; and it fell—and great was its fall."
28 When Jesus had finished these words, the crowds were amazed at His teaching;
29 for He was teaching them as *one* having authority, and not as their scribes.

JANUARY 10

◈ Genesis 19:1—20:18

19NOW the two angels came to Sodom in the evening as Lot was sitting in the gate of Sodom. When Lot saw *them,* he rose to meet them and bowed down *with his* face to the ground.
2 And he said, "Now behold, my lords, please turn aside into your servant's house, and spend the night, and wash your feet; then you may rise early and go on your way." They said however, "No, but we shall spend the night in the square."
3 Yet he urged them strongly, so they turned aside to him and entered his house; and he prepared a feast for them, and baked unleavened bread, and they ate.
4 Before they lay down, the men of the city, the men of Sodom, surrounded the house, both young and old, all the people from every quarter;
5 and they called to Lot and said to him, "Where are the men who came to you tonight? Bring them out to us that we may have relations with them."
6 But Lot went out to them at the doorway, and shut the door behind him,
7 and said, "Please, my brothers, do not act wickedly.
8 "Now behold, I have two daughters who have not had relations with man; please let me bring them out to you, and do to them whatever you like; only do nothing to these men, inasmuch as they have come under the shelter of my roof."
9 But they said, "Stand aside." Furthermore, they said, "This one came in as an alien, and already he is acting like a judge; now we will treat you worse than them." So they pressed hard against Lot and came near to break the door.
10 But the men reached out their hands and brought Lot into the house with them, and shut the door.
11 They struck the men who were at the doorway of the house with blindness, both small and great, so that they wearied *themselves trying* to find the doorway.

12 Then the *two* men said to Lot, "Whom else have you here? A son-in-law, and your sons, and your daughters, and whomever you have in the city, bring *them* out of the place;

13 for we are about to destroy this place, because their outcry has become so great before the Lord that the Lord has sent us to destroy it."

14 Lot went out and spoke to his sons-in-law, who were to marry his daughters, and said, "Up, get out of this place, for the Lord will destroy the city." But he appeared to his sons-in-law to be jesting.

15 When morning dawned, the angels urged Lot, saying, "Up, take your wife and your two daughters who are here, or you will be swept away in the punishment of the city."

16 But he hesitated. So the men seized his hand and the hand of his wife and the hands of his two daughters, for the compassion of the Lord *was* upon him; and they brought him out, and put him outside the city.

17 When they had brought them outside, one said, "Escape for your life! Do not look behind you, and do not stay anywhere in the valley; escape to the mountains, or you will be swept away."

18 But Lot said to them, "Oh no, my lords!

19 "Now behold, your servant has found favor in your sight, and you have magnified your lovingkindness, which you have shown me by saving my life; but I cannot escape to the mountains, for the disaster will overtake me and I will die;

20 now behold, this town is near *enough* to flee to, and it is small. Please, let me escape there (is it not small?) that my life may be saved."

21 He said to him, "Behold, I grant you this request also, not to overthrow the town of which you have spoken.

22 "Hurry, escape there, for I cannot do anything until you arrive there." Therefore the name of the town was called Zoar.

23 The sun had risen over the earth when Lot came to Zoar.

24 Then the Lord rained on Sodom and Gomorrah brimstone and fire from the Lord out of heaven,

25 and He overthrew those cities, and all the valley, and all the inhabitants of the cities, and what grew on the ground.

26 But his wife, from behind him, looked *back,* and she became a pillar of salt.

27 Now Abraham arose early in the morning *and went* to the place where he had stood before the Lord;

28 and he looked down toward Sodom and Gomorrah, and toward all the land of the valley, and he saw, and behold, the smoke of the land ascended like the smoke of a furnace.

29 Thus it came about, when God destroyed the cities of the valley, that God remembered Abraham, and sent Lot out of the midst of the overthrow, when He overthrew the cities in which Lot lived.

30 Lot went up from Zoar, and stayed in the mountains, and his two daughters with him; for he was afraid to stay in Zoar; and he stayed in a cave, he and his two daughters.

31 Then the firstborn said to the younger, "Our father is old, and there is not a man on earth to come in to us after the manner of the earth.

32 "Come, let us make our father drink wine, and let us lie with him that we may preserve our family through our father."

33 So they made their father drink wine that night, and the firstborn went in and lay with her father; and he did not know when she lay down or when she arose.

34 On the following day, the firstborn said to the younger, "Behold, I lay last night with my father; let us make him drink wine tonight also; then you go in and lie with him, that we may preserve our family through our father."

35 So they made their father drink wine that night also, and the younger arose and lay with him; and he did not know when she lay down or when she arose.

LIFE LESSONS

➤ **Genesis 19:29 —** *God remembered Abraham, and sent Lot out of the midst of the overthrow.*

*E*verything Lot had gained during his time in Sodom, he lost in an instant. What we gain outside of God's blessing is not worth having, and eventually goes up in smoke (Gen. 19:24). Yet God spared Lot's life because of the request of righteous Abraham. Our prayers bring mightier results than we will ever know.

36 Thus both the daughters of Lot were with child by their father.

37 The firstborn bore a son, and called his name Moab; he is the father of the Moabites to this day.

38 As for the younger, she also bore a son, and called his name Ben-ammi; he is the father of the sons of Ammon to this day.

20 NOW Abraham journeyed from there toward the land of the Negev, and settled between Kadesh and Shur; then he sojourned in Gerar.

2 Abraham said of Sarah his wife, "She is my sister." So Abimelech king of Gerar sent and took Sarah.

3 But God came to Abimelech in a dream of the night, and said to him, "Behold, you are a dead man because of the woman whom you have taken, for she is married."

4 Now Abimelech had not come near her; and he said, "Lord, will You slay a nation, even *though* blameless?

5 "Did he not himself say to me, 'She is my sister'? And she herself said, 'He is my brother.' In the integrity of my heart and the innocence of my hands I have done this."

6 Then God said to him in the dream, "Yes, I know that in the integrity of your heart you have done this, and I also kept you from sinning against Me; therefore I did not let you touch her.

7 "Now therefore, restore the man's wife, for he is a prophet, and he will pray for you and you will live. But if you do not restore *her,* know that you shall surely die, you and all who are yours."

8 So Abimelech arose early in the morning and called all his servants and told all these things in their hearing; and the men were greatly frightened.

➤ 9 Then Abimelech called Abraham and said to him, "What have you done to

us? And how have I sinned against you, that you have brought on me and on my kingdom a great sin? You have done to me things that ought not to be done."

10 And Abimelech said to Abraham, "What have you encountered, that you have done this thing?"

11 Abraham said, "Because I thought, surely there is no fear of God in this place, and they will kill me because of my wife.

12 "Besides, she actually is my sister, the daughter of my father, but not the daughter of my mother, and she became my wife;

13 and it came about, when God caused me to wander from my father's house, that I said to her, 'This is the kindness which you will show to me: everywhere we go, say of me, "He is my brother."'"

14 Abimelech then took sheep and oxen and male and female servants, and gave them to Abraham, and restored his wife Sarah to him.

15 Abimelech said, "Behold, my land is before you; settle wherever you please."

16 To Sarah he said, "Behold, I have given your brother a thousand pieces of silver; behold, it is your vindication before all who are with you, and before all men you are cleared."

17 Abraham prayed to God, and God healed Abimelech and his wife and his maids, so that they bore *children.*

18 For the LORD had closed fast all the wombs of the household of Abimelech because of Sarah, Abraham's wife.

✦ Psalm 6:1–5

For the choir director; with stringed instruments, upon an eight-string lyre. A Psalm of David.

6 O LORD, do not rebuke me in Your anger,
Nor chasten me in Your wrath.

2 Be gracious to me, O LORD, for I *am* pining away;
Heal me, O LORD, for my bones are dismayed. ✳

3 And my soul is greatly dismayed;
But You, O LORD—how long?

4 Return, O LORD, rescue my soul; ◄
Save me because of Your lovingkindness.

LIFE LESSONS

➤ **Genesis 20:9 — *"You have done to me things that ought not to be done."***

Sometimes God uses the ungodly to rebuke and correct His own people. He does so to remind us we can trust Him in all circumstances, however dangerous they may seem.

L I F E   L E S S O N S

➤ **Psalm 6:4** — *Return, O L*ORD*, rescue my soul; Save me because of Your lovingkindness.*

*W*e do not ask God to rescue and deliver us because we deserve His help. We ask Him to come to our aid because He loves to show mercy to His humble, obedient children.

➤ **Proverbs 3:3, 4** — *Do not let kindness and truth leave you; bind them around your neck.*

*M*ercy without truth can lead to ungodly compromise; truth without mercy can lead to unfeeling legalism. When we pursue both equally and simultaneously, we reflect the heart of God and bring Him great pleasure.

5   For there is no mention of You in death;
      In Sheol who will give You thanks?

◈ Proverbs 3:1–4

3MY son, do not forget my teaching,
    But let your heart keep my commandments;
2   For length of days and years of life
    And peace they will add to you.
➤ 3   Do not let kindness and truth leave you;

      Bind them around your neck,
      Write them on the tablet of your heart.
4   So you will find favor and good repute
      In the sight of God and man.

◈ Matthew 8:1–17

8WHEN Jesus came down from the mountain, large crowds followed Him.
2   And a leper came to Him and bowed

Life Examples:

The Admirable Quality of Kindness

PROVERBS 3:1-4

*W*hat does it mean to bind kindness around our neck and write it on the tablet of our hearts? It means kindness should be a deep, central part of our lives. Unfortunately, kindness doesn't automatically become one of our characteristics when we accept Christ as our Savior. We have to work at it—we must deliberately take responsibility for our actions and attitudes toward others and choose to act compassionately toward others. What are some things we should do to develop kindness?

- *First, we should realize even though we don't immediately become kind at salvation, we do have the potential to exhibit kindness because of the indwelling of the Holy Spirit.* The Holy Spirit develops the quality of kindness in us (Gal. 5:22).
- *Second, we must eliminate those characteristics, actions, and attitudes within us that stop us from being loving, tenderhearted, and useful.* We cannot be selfish. Rather, we must lay aside the characteristics that do not fit who we are as believers in order for kindness to flow out of our lives (Eph. 4:31, 32).
- *Third, we must focus on the needs of other people.* As long as we are focused on ourselves—our needs, wants, desires, and plans—we are not going to be very kind. Yet when we focus on others, we will become sensitive to who they are and what they need in life (Col. 3:12, 13).
- *Fourth, we must ask God to teach us to be kind.* We must look to God to make us sensitive to the situations that need a special touch of kindness and to express His kindness through us. We do so with the hope that people will be attracted to Jesus Christ as their Savior (Matt. 5:16).
- *Fifth, if we want to learn to be kind, we must practice kindness.* Every day, we should ask the Lord, "Father, please show me at least one person I can be kind to today." We should look for opportunities to be kind and praise God whenever we find them, knowing God is working through us whenever we show kindness to others.

down before Him, and said, "Lord, if You are willing, You can make me clean."

3 Jesus stretched out His hand and touched him, saying, "I am willing; be cleansed." And immediately his leprosy was cleansed.

4 And Jesus *said to him, "See that you tell no one; but go, show yourself to the priest and present the offering that Moses commanded, as a testimony to them."

5 And when Jesus entered Capernaum, a centurion came to Him, imploring Him,

6 and saying, "Lord, my servant is lying paralyzed at home, fearfully tormented."

7 Jesus *said to him, "I will come and heal him."

8 But the centurion said, "Lord, I am not worthy for You to come under my roof, but just say the word, and my servant will be healed.

9 "For I also am a man under authority, with soldiers under me; and I say to this one, 'Go!' and he goes, and to another, 'Come!' and he comes, and to my slave, 'Do this!' and he does it."

10 Now when Jesus heard this, He marveled and said to those who were following, "Truly I say to you, I have not found such great faith with anyone in Israel.

11 "I say to you that many will come from east and west, and recline at the table with Abraham, Isaac and Jacob in the kingdom of heaven;

12 but the sons of the kingdom will be cast out into the outer darkness; in that place there will be weeping and gnashing of teeth."

13 And Jesus said to the centurion, "Go; it shall be done for you as you have believed." And the servant was healed that very moment.

14 When Jesus came into Peter's home, He saw his mother-in-law lying sick in bed with a fever.

15 He touched her hand, and the fever left her; and she got up and waited on Him.

16 When evening came, they brought to Him many who were demon-possessed; and He cast out the spirits with a word, and healed all who were ill.

17 This was to fulfill what was spoken through Isaiah the prophet: "HE HIMSELF TOOK OUR INFIRMITIES AND CARRIED AWAY OUR DISEASES."

Genesis 21:1—22:24

21 THEN the LORD took note of Sarah as He had said, and the LORD did for Sarah as He had promised.

2 So Sarah conceived and bore a son to Abraham in his old age, at the appointed time of which God had spoken to him.

3 Abraham called the name of his son who was born to him, whom Sarah bore to him, Isaac.

4 Then Abraham circumcised his son Isaac when he was eight days old, as God had commanded him.

5 Now Abraham was one hundred years old when his son Isaac was born to him.

6 Sarah said, "God has made laughter for me; everyone who hears will laugh with me."

Life Examples:

ABRAHAM: The Man of Endurance

GENESIS 21:1–3

*C*all Abraham not only a man of faith (Gal. 3:9) but a man of endurance.

It is as if the starting gun sounded in his life when God promised him he would have a son in his old age. But year after year came and went, and Abraham and Sarah still did not have the answer to God's promise. Yet the Bible tells us Abraham "believed in the LORD" (Gen. 15:5, 6).

Abraham kept the eyes of his heart firmly set on the Lord.

Two years flashed by, and still no child. Still he continued to trust God.

Despite a stumble at mid-race (Gen. 16), Abraham ran a faithful race. For 25 *years* he kept in step with God, until at last, at age 100, he and his wife, age 90, had a son (Gen. 21:1–3).

Why the long wait? Apparently, God wanted Abraham (and us!) to learn the connection between waiting, trust, and hope (Ps. 33:20). And that hope, the apostle Paul reminds us, prompts us to wait on God "with perseverance" (Rom. 8:25).

Even if that means running the longest marathon of our lives.

---

7   And she said, "Who would have said to Abraham that Sarah would nurse children? Yet I have borne him a son in his old age."

8   The child grew and was weaned, and Abraham made a great feast on the day that Isaac was weaned.

9   Now Sarah saw the son of Hagar the Egyptian, whom she had borne to Abraham, mocking.

10   Therefore she said to Abraham, "Drive out this maid and her son, for the son of this maid shall not be an heir with my son Isaac."

11   The matter distressed Abraham greatly because of his son.

12   But God said to Abraham, "Do not be distressed because of the lad and your maid; whatever Sarah tells you, listen to her, for through Isaac your descendants shall be named.

13   "And of the son of the maid I will make a nation also, because he is your descendant."

14   So Abraham rose early in the morning and took bread and a skin of water and gave *them* to Hagar, putting *them* on her shoulder, and *gave her* the boy, and sent her away. And she departed and wandered about in the wilderness of Beersheba.

15   When the water in the skin was used up, she left the boy under one of the bushes.

16   Then she went and sat down opposite him, about a bowshot away, for she said, "Do not let me see the boy die." And she sat opposite him, and lifted up her voice and wept.

17   God heard the lad crying; and the angel of God called to Hagar from heaven and said to her, "What is the matter with you, Hagar? Do not fear, for God has heard the voice of the lad where he is.

18   "Arise, lift up the lad, and hold him by the hand, for I will make a great nation of him."

19   Then God opened her eyes and she saw a well of water; and she went and filled the skin with water and gave the lad a drink.

20   God was with the lad, and he grew; and he lived in the wilderness and became an archer.

21   He lived in the wilderness of Paran, and his mother took a wife for him from the land of Egypt.

22   Now it came about at that time that Abimelech and Phicol, the commander of his army, spoke to Abraham, saying, "God is with you in all that you do;

23   now therefore, swear to me here by God that you will not deal falsely with me or with my offspring or with my posterity, but according to the kindness that I have

LIFE LESSONS

➤ **Genesis 21:16 — *For she said, "Do not let me see the boy die."***

*H*agar discovered we learn more in our valley experiences than on our mountaintops. Only when it seemed as though all hope was lost did she find her ultimate hope in the Lord.

shown to you, you shall show to me and to the land in which you have sojourned."

24 Abraham said, "I swear it."

25 But Abraham complained to Abimelech because of the well of water which the servants of Abimelech had seized.

26 And Abimelech said, "I do not know who has done this thing; you did not tell me, nor did I hear of it until today."

27 Abraham took sheep and oxen and gave them to Abimelech, and the two of them made a covenant.

28 Then Abraham set seven ewe lambs of the flock by themselves.

29 Abimelech said to Abraham, "What do these seven ewe lambs mean, which you have set by themselves?"

30 He said, "You shall take these seven ewe lambs from my hand so that it may be a witness to me, that I dug this well."

31 Therefore he called that place Beersheba, because there the two of them took an oath.

32 So they made a covenant at Beersheba; and Abimelech and Phicol, the commander of his army, arose and returned to the land of the Philistines.

33 *Abraham* planted a tamarisk tree at Beersheba, and there he called on the name of the LORD, the Everlasting God.

34 And Abraham sojourned in the land of the Philistines for many days.

➤ **22** NOW it came about after these things, that God tested Abraham, and said to him, "Abraham!" And he said, "Here I am."

2 He said, "Take now your son, your only son, whom you love, Isaac, and go to the land of Moriah, and offer him there as a burnt offering on one of the mountains of which I will tell you."

3 So Abraham rose early in the morning and saddled his donkey, and took two of his young men with him and Isaac his son; and he split wood for the burnt offering, and arose and went to the place of which God had told him.

4 On the third day Abraham raised his eyes and saw the place from a distance.

➤ 5 Abraham said to his young men, "Stay here with the donkey, and I and the lad will go over there; and we will worship and return to you."

6 Abraham took the wood of the burnt offering and laid it on Isaac his son, and he took in his hand the fire and the

knife. So the two of them walked on together.

7 Isaac spoke to Abraham his father and said, "My father!" And he said, "Here I am, my son." And he said, "Behold, the fire and the wood, but where is the lamb for the burnt offering?"

8 Abraham said, "God will provide for Himself the lamb for the burnt offering, my son." So the two of them walked on together.

9 Then they came to the place of which God had told him; and Abraham built the altar there and arranged the wood, and bound his son Isaac and laid him on the altar, on top of the wood.

10 Abraham stretched out his hand and took the knife to slay his son.

11 But the angel of the LORD called to him from heaven and said, "Abraham, Abraham!" And he said, "Here I am."

12 He said, "Do not stretch out your hand against the lad, and do nothing to him; for now I know that you fear God, since you have not withheld your son, your only son, from Me."

13 Then Abraham raised his eyes and looked, and behold, behind *him* a ram caught in the thicket by his horns; and Abraham went and took the ram and offered him up for a burnt offering in the place of his son.

LIFE LESSONS

➤ **Genesis 22:1 — *Now it came about after these things, that God tested Abraham.***

*G*od permits testing for all of His children, including His own Son, Jesus Christ (Matt. 4:1). For Abraham, this had to be a dark time—but it lasted only so long as was necessary for God to accomplish His purpose in Abraham's life.

➤ **Genesis 22:5 — *"Stay here with the donkey, and I and the lad will go over there; and we will worship and return to you."***

*A*braham expressed confidence to the servants that both he and Isaac would return alive, even though he intended to obey God's command to sacrifice his son. Abraham obeyed and trusted, though he did not understand (Heb. 11:17–19).

14 Abraham called the name of that place The LORD Will Provide, as it is said to this day, "In the mount of the LORD it will be provided."
15 Then the angel of the LORD called to Abraham a second time from heaven,
16 and said, "By Myself I have sworn, declares the LORD, because you have done this thing and have not withheld your son, your only son,
17 indeed I will greatly bless you, and I will greatly multiply your seed as the stars of the heavens and as the sand which is on the seashore; and your seed shall possess the gate of their enemies.
18 "In your seed all the nations of the earth shall be blessed, because you have obeyed My voice."
19 So Abraham returned to his young men, and they arose and went together to Beersheba; and Abraham lived at Beersheba.
20 Now it came about after these things, that it was told Abraham, saying, "Behold, Milcah also has borne children to your brother Nahor:
21 Uz his firstborn and Buz his brother and Kemuel the father of Aram
22 and Chesed and Hazo and Pildash and Jidlaph and Bethuel."
23 Bethuel became the father of Rebekah; these eight Milcah bore to Nahor, Abraham's brother.
24 His concubine, whose name was Reumah, also bore Tebah and Gaham and Tahash and Maacah.

LIFE LESSONS

> Genesis 22:14 — *"In the mount of the LORD it will be provided."*

The Lord will provide—*always.* He may surprise us, He may perplex us, He may make us wait. But He will *always* provide exactly what we need, when we need it.

> Psalm 6:9 — *The LORD has heard my supplication, the LORD receives my prayer.*

How did the psalmist know God had heard his prayer? How could he express such confidence in the Lord answering his request? Through faith. He prayed in faith, and he expected an answer by faith—just like us.

Psalm 6:6–10

6 I am weary with my sighing;
  Every night I make my bed swim,
  I dissolve my couch with my tears.
7 My eye has wasted away with grief;
  It has become old because of all my adversaries.
8 Depart from me, all you who do iniquity,
  For the LORD has heard the voice of my weeping.
9 The LORD has heard my supplication,
  The LORD receives my prayer.
10 All my enemies will be ashamed and greatly dismayed;
  They shall turn back, they will suddenly be ashamed.

Proverbs 3:5–6

5 Trust in the LORD with all your heart
  And do not lean on your own understanding.
6 In all your ways acknowledge Him,
  And He will make your paths straight.

Matthew 8:18–34

18 Now when Jesus saw a crowd around Him, He gave orders to depart to the other side of *the sea.*
19 Then a scribe came and said to Him, "Teacher, I will follow You wherever You go."
20 Jesus *said to him, "The foxes have holes and the birds of the air *have* nests, but the Son of Man has nowhere to lay His head."
21 Another of the disciples said to Him, "Lord, permit me first to go and bury my father."
22 But Jesus *said to him, "Follow Me, and allow the dead to bury their own dead."
23 When He got into the boat, His disciples followed Him.
24 And behold, there arose a great storm on the sea, so that the boat was

being covered with the waves; but Jesus Himself was asleep.

25 And they came to *Him* and woke Him, saying, "Save *us*, Lord; we are perishing!"

➤ 26 He *said to them, "Why are you afraid, you men of little faith?" Then He got up and rebuked the winds and the sea, and it became perfectly calm.

✳ 27 The men were amazed, and said, "What kind of a man is this, that even the winds and the sea obey Him?"

28 When He came to the other side into the country of the Gadarenes, two men who were demon-possessed met Him as they were coming out of the tombs. *They were* so extremely violent that no one could pass by that way.

29 And they cried out, saying, "What business do we have with each other, Son of God? Have You come here to torment us before the time?"

30 Now there was a herd of many swine feeding at a distance from them.

31 The demons *began* to entreat Him, saying, "If You *are going to* cast us out, send us into the herd of swine."

32 And He said to them, "Go!" And they came out and went into the swine, and the whole herd rushed down the steep bank into the sea and perished in the waters.

33 The herdsmen ran away, and went to the city and reported everything, including what had happened to the demoniacs.

34 And behold, the whole city came out to meet Jesus; and when they saw Him, they implored Him to leave their region.

LIFE LESSONS

➤ **Matthew 8:26 — *"Why are you afraid, you men of little faith?" Then He got up and rebuked the winds and the sea, and it became perfectly calm.***

*T*he storm terrified the disciples, but it did not cause the Lord to so much as raise an eyebrow. Why the difference? Because Jesus trusted in God and believed He would get them to the other side.

◈ Genesis 23:1—24:67

23 NOW Sarah lived one hundred and twenty-seven years; *these were* the years of the life of Sarah.

2 Sarah died in Kiriath-arba (that is, Hebron) in the land of Canaan; and Abraham went in to mourn for Sarah and to weep for her.

3 Then Abraham rose from before his dead, and spoke to the sons of Heth, saying,

4 "I am a stranger and a sojourner among you; give me a burial site among you that I may bury my dead out of my sight."

5 The sons of Heth answered Abraham, saying to him,

6 "Hear us, my lord, you are a mighty prince among us; bury your dead in the choicest of our graves; none of us will refuse you his grave for burying your dead."

7 So Abraham rose and bowed to the people of the land, the sons of Heth.

8 And he spoke with them, saying, "If it is your wish *for me* to bury my dead out of my sight, hear me, and approach Ephron the son of Zohar for me,

9 that he may give me the cave of Machpelah which he owns, which is at the end of his field; for the full price let him give it to me in your presence for a burial site."

10 Now Ephron was sitting among the sons of Heth; and Ephron the Hittite

---

LIFE LESSONS

➤ **Genesis 24:7 — *"The LORD, the God of heaven . . . will send His angel before you."***

*W*hen we walk in faith and obedience, God sends His angels ahead of us to make sure we arrive at a place of blessing.

answered Abraham in the hearing of the sons of Heth; *even* of all who went in at the gate of his city, saying,

11 "No, my lord, hear me; I give you the field, and I give you the cave that is in it. In the presence of the sons of my people I give it to you; bury your dead."

12 And Abraham bowed before the people of the land.

13 He spoke to Ephron in the hearing of the people of the land, saying, "If you will only please listen to me; I will give the price of the field, accept *it* from me that I may bury my dead there."

14 Then Ephron answered Abraham, saying to him,

15 "My lord, listen to me; a piece of land worth four hundred shekels of silver, what is that between me and you? So bury your dead."

16 Abraham listened to Ephron; and Abraham weighed out for Ephron the silver which he had named in the hearing of the sons of Heth, four hundred shekels of silver, commercial standard.

17 So Ephron's field, which was in Machpelah, which faced Mamre, the field and cave which was in it, and all the trees which were in the field, that were within all the confines of its border, were deeded over

18 to Abraham for a possession in the presence of the sons of Heth, before all who went in at the gate of his city.

19 After this, Abraham buried Sarah his wife in the cave of the field at Machpelah facing Mamre (that is, Hebron) in the land of Canaan.

20 So the field and the cave that is in it, were deeded over to Abraham for a burial site by the sons of Heth.

24 NOW Abraham was old, advanced in age; and the LORD had blessed Abraham in every way.

2 Abraham said to his servant, the oldest of his household, who had charge of all that he owned, "Please place your hand under my thigh,

3 and I will make you swear by the LORD, the God of heaven and the God of earth, that you shall not take a wife for my son from the daughters of the Canaanites, among whom I live,

4 but you will go to my country and to my relatives, and take a wife for my son Isaac."

5 The servant said to him, "Suppose the woman is not willing to follow me to this land; should I take your son back to the land from where you came?"

6 Then Abraham said to him, "Beware that you do not take my son back there!

7 "The LORD, the God of heaven, who took me from my father's house and from the land of my birth, and who spoke to me and who swore to me, saying, 'To your descendants I will give this land,' He will send His angel before you, and you will take a wife for my son from there.

8 "But if the woman is not willing to follow you, then you will be free from this my oath; only do not take my son back there."

9 So the servant placed his hand under the thigh of Abraham his master, and swore to him concerning this matter.

10 Then the servant took ten camels from the camels of his master, and set out with a variety of good things of his master's in his hand; and he arose and went to Mesopotamia, to the city of Nahor.

11 He made the camels kneel down outside the city by the well of water at evening time, the time when women go out to draw water.

12 He said, "O LORD, the God of my master Abraham, please grant me success today, and show lovingkindness to my master Abraham.

13 "Behold, I am standing by the spring, and the daughters of the men of the city are coming out to draw water;

14 now may it be that the girl to whom I say, 'Please let down your jar so that I may drink,' and who answers, 'Drink, and I will water your camels also'—*may* she *be the one* whom You have appointed for Your servant Isaac; and by

---

LIFE LESSONS

➣ **Genesis 24:12 —** *"O LORD, the God of my master Abraham, please grant me success today, and show lovingkindness to my master Abraham."*

The servant of Abraham fought his greatest battle on his knees, and in doing so he won a great victory—even before he opened his eyes. God loves to answer the selfless prayers of His people!

this I will know that You have shown lovingkindness to my master."

15 Before he had finished speaking, behold, Rebekah who was born to Bethuel the son of Milcah, the wife of Abraham's brother Nahor, came out with her jar on her shoulder.

16 The girl was very beautiful, a virgin, and no man had had relations with her; and she went down to the spring and filled her jar and came up.

17 Then the servant ran to meet her, and said, "Please let me drink a little water from your jar."

18 She said, "Drink, my lord"; and she quickly lowered her jar to her hand, and gave him a drink.

19 Now when she had finished giving him a drink, she said, "I will draw also for your camels until they have finished drinking."

20 So she quickly emptied her jar into the trough, and ran back to the well to draw, and she drew for all his camels.

21 Meanwhile, the man was gazing at her in silence, to know whether the LORD had made his journey successful or not.

22 When the camels had finished drinking, the man took a gold ring weighing a half-shekel and two bracelets for her wrists weighing ten shekels in gold,

23 and said, "Whose daughter are you? Please tell me, is there room for us to lodge in your father's house?"

24 She said to him, "I am the daughter of Bethuel, the son of Milcah, whom she bore to Nahor."

25 Again she said to him, "We have plenty of both straw and feed, and room to lodge in."

➤ 26 Then the man bowed low and worshiped the LORD.

✳ 27 He said, "Blessed be the LORD, the God of my master Abraham, who has not forsaken His lovingkindness and His truth toward my master; as for me, the LORD has guided me in the way to the house of my master's brothers."

LIFE LESSONS

➤ **Genesis 24:26 —** *Then the man bowed low and worshiped the LORD.*

*W*hen God answers our prayers, worship is the only proper response.

---

28 Then the girl ran and told her mother's household about these things.

29 Now Rebekah had a brother whose name was Laban; and Laban ran outside to the man at the spring.

30 When he saw the ring and the bracelets on his sister's wrists, and when he heard the words of Rebekah his sister, saying, "This is what the man said to me," he went to the man; and behold, he was standing by the camels at the spring.

31 And he said, "Come in, blessed of the LORD! Why do you stand outside since I have prepared the house, and a place for the camels?"

32 So the man entered the house. Then Laban unloaded the camels, and he gave straw and feed to the camels, and water to wash his feet and the feet of the men who were with him.

33 But when *food* was set before him to eat, he said, "I will not eat until I have told my business." And he said, "Speak on."

34 So he said, "I am Abraham's servant.

35 "The LORD has greatly blessed my master, so that he has become rich; and He has given him flocks and herds, and silver and gold, and servants and maids, and camels and donkeys.

36 "Now Sarah my master's wife bore a son to my master in her old age, and he has given him all that he has.

37 "My master made me swear, saying, 'You shall not take a wife for my son from the daughters of the Canaanites, in whose land I live;

38 but you shall go to my father's house and to my relatives, and take a wife for my son.'

39 "I said to my master, 'Suppose the woman does not follow me.'

40 "He said to me, 'The LORD, before whom I have walked, will send His angel with you to make your journey successful, and you will take a wife for my son from my relatives and from my father's house;

41 then you will be free from my oath, when you come to my relatives; and if they do not give her to you, you will be free from my oath.'

42 "So I came today to the spring, and said, 'O LORD, the God of my master Abraham, if now You will make my journey on which I go successful;

43 behold, I am standing by the spring,

and may it be that the maiden who comes out to draw, and to whom I say, "Please let me drink a little water from your jar";

44 and she will say to me, "You drink, and I will draw for your camels also"; let her be the woman whom the Lord has appointed for my master's son.'

45 "Before I had finished speaking in my heart, behold, Rebekah came out with her jar on her shoulder, and went down to the spring and drew, and I said to her, 'Please let me drink.'

46 "She quickly lowered her jar from her *shoulder*, and said, 'Drink, and I will water your camels also'; so I drank, and she watered the camels also.

47 "Then I asked her, and said, 'Whose daughter are you?' And she said, 'The daughter of Bethuel, Nahor's son, whom Milcah bore to him'; and I put the ring on her nose, and the bracelets on her wrists.

48 "And I bowed low and worshiped the Lord, and blessed the Lord, the God of my master Abraham, who had guided me in the right way to take the daughter of my master's kinsman for his son.

49 "So now if you are going to deal kindly and truly with my master, tell me; and if not, let me know, that I may turn to the right hand or the left."

50 Then Laban and Bethuel replied, "The matter comes from the Lord; *so* we cannot speak to you bad or good.

51 "Here is Rebekah before you, take *her* and go, and let her be the wife of your master's son, as the Lord has spoken."

52 When Abraham's servant heard their words, he bowed himself to the ground before the Lord.

53 The servant brought out articles of silver and articles of gold, and garments, and gave them to Rebekah; he also gave precious things to her brother and to her mother.

54 Then he and the men who were with him ate and drank and spent the night. When they arose in the morning, he said, "Send me away to my master."

55 But her brother and her mother said, "Let the girl stay with us *a few* days, say ten; afterward she may go."

56 He said to them, "Do not delay me, since the Lord has prospered my way. Send me away that I may go to my master."

57 And they said, "We will call the girl and consult her wishes."

58 Then they called Rebekah and said to her, "Will you go with this man?" And she said, "I will go."

59 Thus they sent away their sister Rebekah and her nurse with Abraham's servant and his men.

60 They blessed Rebekah and said to her,

  "May you, our sister,
    Become thousands of ten
      thousands,
    And may your descendants
      possess
    The gate of those who hate
      them."

61 Then Rebekah arose with her maids, and they mounted the camels and followed the man. So the servant took Rebekah and departed.

62 Now Isaac had come from going to Beer-lahai-roi; for he was living in the Negev.

63 Isaac went out to meditate in the ◁ field toward evening; and he lifted up his eyes and looked, and behold, camels were coming.

64 Rebekah lifted up her eyes, and when she saw Isaac she dismounted from the camel.

65 She said to the servant, "Who is that man walking in the field to meet us?" And the servant said, "He is my master." Then she took her veil and covered herself.

66 The servant told Isaac all the things that he had done.

67 Then Isaac brought her into his mother Sarah's tent, and he took Rebekah, and she became his wife, and he loved her; thus Isaac was comforted after his mother's death.

LIFE LESSONS

➤ **Genesis 24:63 — *Isaac went out to meditate in the field toward evening; and he lifted up his eyes and looked, and behold, camels were coming.***

*I*saac must have learned the value of meditation from his godly father, Abraham, who clearly taught his son that intimacy with God was life's highest priority.

Psalm 7:1–5

A Shiggaion of David, which he sang to the LORD concerning Cush, a Benjamite.

7 O LORD my God, in You I have
  taken refuge;
  Save me from all those who pursue
  me, and deliver me,

2 Or he will tear my soul like a lion,
  Dragging me away, while there is
  none to deliver.

3 O LORD my God, if I have done this,
  If there is injustice in my hands,

4 If I have rewarded evil to my friend,
  Or have plundered him who without
  cause was my adversary,

5 Let the enemy pursue my soul and
  overtake it;
  And let him trample my life down to
  the ground
  And lay my glory in the dust. Selah.

Proverbs 3:7–8

7 Do not be wise in your own eyes;
  Fear the LORD and turn away from
  evil.

8 It will be healing to your body
  And refreshment to your bones.

Matthew 9:1–17

9 GETTING into a boat, Jesus crossed over the sea and came to His own city.
2 And they brought to Him a paralytic

LIFE LESSONS

➤ **Matthew 9:2 —** *When Jesus saw their faith.*

*I*t would be hard to "see" faith if it never worked its way out in meaningful action. If our faith does not affect the way we live or ever get noticed by others, then perhaps it is not genuine faith at all.

lying on a bed. Seeing their faith, Jesus said to the paralytic, "Take courage, son; your sins are forgiven."
3 And some of the scribes said to themselves, "This *fellow* blasphemes."
4 And Jesus knowing their thoughts said, "Why are you thinking evil in your hearts?
5 "Which is easier, to say, 'Your sins are forgiven,' or to say, 'Get up, and walk'?
6 "But so that you may know that the Son of Man has authority on earth to forgive sins"—then He *said to the paralytic, "Get up, pick up your bed and go home."
7 And he got up and went home.
8 But when the crowds saw *this*, they were awestruck, and glorified God, who had given such authority to men.
9 As Jesus went on from there, He saw a man called Matthew, sitting in the tax collector's booth; and He *said to him, "Follow Me!" And he got up and followed Him.
10 Then it happened that as Jesus was reclining *at the table* in the house, behold, many tax collectors and sinners

Life Examples:

MATTHEW: Leaving It All Behind

MATTHEW 9:9–12

*A*fter years of counting out coins, writing out customs receipts, and collecting Roman taxes from his Jewish countrymen, Matthew finally heard an offer he could not refuse. "Follow Me," Jesus said to him. At the sound of those words, Matthew "left everything behind, and got up and began to follow Him" (Luke 5:27, 28).
  Notice the words he uses to emphasize his call into ministry. He tells us he *left everything*—the money, his connections within the Roman government, and the powerful position he held. He left it all—except his gift for accurate recordkeeping! Before his conversion, his name had been Levi, the son of Alphaeus (Mark 2:14). But after he accepted Christ's call to ministry, Jesus gave him a new name, *Matthew* ("Gift of the Lord"). When Luke and Mark refer to Matthew, they identify him as Levi. But in Matthew 10:3, he refers to himself as "Matthew the tax collector"—a pointed reminder of the past he had given up.
  What "old life" did you leave behind in order to fully follow the Son of God?

came and were dining with Jesus and His disciples.

11 When the Pharisees saw *this*, they said to His disciples, "Why is your Teacher eating with the tax collectors and sinners?"

12 But when Jesus heard *this*, He said, "*It is* not those who are healthy who need a physician, but those who are sick.

13 "But go and learn what this means: 'I DESIRE COMPASSION, AND NOT SACRIFICE,' for I did not come to call the righteous, but sinners."

14 Then the disciples of John *came to Him, asking, "Why do we and the Pharisees fast, but Your disciples do not fast?"

15 And Jesus said to them, "The attendants of the bridegroom cannot mourn as long as the bridegroom is with them, can they? But the days will come when the bridegroom is taken away from them, and then they will fast.

16 "But no one puts a patch of unshrunk cloth on an old garment; for the patch pulls away from the garment, and a worse tear results.

17 "Nor do *people* put new wine into old wineskins; otherwise the wineskins burst; and the wine pours out and the wineskins are ruined; but they put new wine into fresh wineskins, and both are preserved."

LIFE LESSONS

➤ **Matthew 9:13 — "Go and learn what this means: 'I DESIRE COMPASSION, AND NOT SACRIFICE.'"**

Throughout the Bible, God makes it clear He wants our hearts, not merely our lips. He wants genuine devotion to Him resulting in beneficial action toward others. Dutiful religious activity means nothing without devotion to God and a real concern for others.

Genesis 25:1—26:35

25 NOW Abraham took another wife, whose name was Keturah.

2 She bore to him Zimran and Jokshan and Medan and Midian and Ishbak and Shuah.

3 Jokshan became the father of Sheba and Dedan. And the sons of Dedan were Asshurim and Letushim and Leummim.

4 The sons of Midian *were* Ephah and Epher and Hanoch and Abida and Eldaah. All these *were* the sons of Keturah.

5 Now Abraham gave all that he had to Isaac;

6 but to the sons of his concubines, Abraham gave gifts while he was still living, and sent them away from his son Isaac eastward, to the land of the east.

7 These are all the years of Abraham's life that he lived, one hundred and seventy-five years.

8 Abraham breathed his last and died in a ripe old age, an old man and satisfied *with life*; and he was gathered to his people.

9 Then his sons Isaac and Ishmael buried him in the cave of Machpelah, in the field of Ephron the son of Zohar the Hittite, facing Mamre,

10 the field which Abraham purchased from the sons of Heth; there Abraham was buried with Sarah his wife.

11 It came about after the death of Abraham, that God blessed his son Isaac; and Isaac lived by Beer-lahai-roi.

12 Now these are *the records of* the generations of Ishmael, Abraham's son, whom Hagar the Egyptian, Sarah's maid, bore to Abraham;

13 and these are the names of the sons of Ishmael, by their names, in the order of their birth: Nebaioth, the firstborn of Ishmael, and Kedar and Adbeel and Mibsam

14 and Mishma and Dumah and Massa,

15 Hadad and Tema, Jetur, Naphish and Kedemah.

16 These are the sons of Ishmael and these are their names, by their villages, and by their camps; twelve princes according to their tribes.

17 These are the years of the life of Ishmael, one hundred and thirty-seven

years; and he breathed his last and died, and was gathered to his people.

18 They settled from Havilah to Shur which is east of Egypt as one goes toward Assyria; he settled in defiance of all his relatives.

19 Now these are *the records of* the generations of Isaac, Abraham's son: Abraham became the father of Isaac;

20 and Isaac was forty years old when he took Rebekah, the daughter of Bethuel the Aramean of Paddan-aram, the sister of Laban the Aramean, to be his wife.

➤ 21 Isaac prayed to the LORD on behalf of his wife, because she was barren; and the LORD answered him and Rebekah his wife conceived.

22 But the children struggled together within her; and she said, "If it is so, why then am I *this way?*" So she went to inquire of the LORD.

23 The LORD said to her,
"Two nations are in your womb;
And two peoples will be separated
from your body;
And one people shall be stronger
than the other;
And the older shall serve the
younger."

24 When her days to be delivered were fulfilled, behold, there were twins in her womb.

25 Now the first came forth red, all over like a hairy garment; and they named him Esau.

26 Afterward his brother came forth with his hand holding on to Esau's heel, so his name was called Jacob; and Isaac was sixty years old when she gave birth to them.

27 When the boys grew up, Esau became a skillful hunter, a man of the field, but Jacob was a peaceful man, living in tents.

28 Now Isaac loved Esau, because he had a taste for game, but Rebekah loved Jacob.

29 When Jacob had cooked stew, Esau came in from the field and he was famished;

30 and Esau said to Jacob, "Please let me have a swallow of that red stuff there, for I am famished." Therefore his name was called Edom.

31 But Jacob said, "First sell me your birthright."

32 Esau said, "Behold, I am about to die; so of what *use* then is the birthright to me?"

33 And Jacob said, "First swear to me"; so he swore to him, and sold his birthright to Jacob.

34 Then Jacob gave Esau bread and ◄ lentil stew; and he ate and drank, and rose and went on his way. Thus Esau despised his birthright.

26 NOW there was a famine in the land, besides the previous famine that had occurred in the days of Abraham. So Isaac went to Gerar, to Abimelech king of the Philistines.

2 The LORD appeared to him and said, "Do not go down to Egypt; stay in the land of which I shall tell you.

3 "Sojourn in this land and I will be with you and bless you, for to you and to your descendants I will give all these lands, and I will establish the oath which I swore to your father Abraham.

4 "I will multiply your descendants as the stars of heaven, and will give your descendants all these lands; and by your

---

LIFE LESSONS

➤ **Genesis 25:21 — *Isaac prayed to the LORD on behalf of his wife, because she was barren; and the LORD answered him and Rebekah his wife conceived.***

*A*t many key points in Scripture, God grants a childless woman a family, often in response to prayer. Why saddle His people with such a difficult burden? Perhaps because brokenness is God's requirement for maximum usefulness.

➤ **Genesis 25:34 — *Esau despised his birthright.***

*I*n "despising" his birthright, Esau proved himself "godless" (Heb. 12:16) because he considered filling his empty stomach more important than the spiritual promises of God to Abraham.

➤ **Genesis 26:5 — *"Abraham obeyed Me and kept My charge, My commandments, My statutes and My laws."***

*G*od remembered Abraham as one who obeyed Him—and therefore Abraham provided his descendants with the greatest possible legacy.

descendants all the nations of the earth shall be blessed;

➤ 5   because Abraham obeyed Me and kept My charge, My commandments, My statutes and My laws."

6   So Isaac lived in Gerar.

7   When the men of the place asked about his wife, he said, "She is my sister," for he was afraid to say, "my wife," *thinking,* "the men of the place might kill me on account of Rebekah, for she is beautiful."

8   It came about, when he had been there a long time, that Abimelech king of the Philistines looked out through a window, and saw, and behold, Isaac was caressing his wife Rebekah.

9   Then Abimelech called Isaac and said, "Behold, certainly she is your wife! How then did you say, 'She is my sister'?" And Isaac said to him, "Because I said, 'I might die on account of her.'"

10   Abimelech said, "What is this you have done to us? One of the people might easily have lain with your wife, and you would have brought guilt upon us."

11   So Abimelech charged all the people, saying, "He who touches this man or his wife shall surely be put to death."

12   Now Isaac sowed in that land and reaped in the same year a hundredfold. And the LORD blessed him,

13   and the man became rich, and continued to grow richer until he became very wealthy;

14   for he had possessions of flocks and herds and a great household, so that the Philistines envied him.

15   Now all the wells which his father's servants had dug in the days of Abraham his father, the Philistines stopped up by filling them with earth.

16   Then Abimelech said to Isaac, "Go away from us, for you are too powerful for us."

17   And Isaac departed from there and camped in the valley of Gerar, and settled there.

18   Then Isaac dug again the wells of water which had been dug in the days of his father Abraham, for the Philistines had stopped them up after the death of Abraham; and he gave them the same names which his father had given them.

19   But when Isaac's servants dug in the valley and found there a well of flowing water,

20   the herdsmen of Gerar quarreled with the herdsmen of Isaac, saying, "The water is ours!" So he named the well Esek, because they contended with him.

21   Then they dug another well, and they quarreled over it too, so he named it Sitnah.

22   He moved away from there and dug another well, and they did not quarrel over it; so he named it Rehoboth, for he said, "At last the LORD has made room for us, and we will be fruitful in the land."

23   Then he went up from there to Beersheba.

24   The LORD appeared to him the same night and said,

"I am the God of your father
    Abraham;
Do not fear, for I am with you.
I will bless you, and multiply your
    descendants,
For the sake of My servant
    Abraham."

✳

25   So he built an altar there and called upon the name of the LORD, and pitched his tent there; and there Isaac's servants dug a well.

26   Then Abimelech came to him from Gerar with his adviser Ahuzzath and Phicol the commander of his army.

27   Isaac said to them, "Why have you come to me, since you hate me and have sent me away from you?"

28   They said, "We see plainly that the ◄ LORD has been with you; so we said, 'Let there now be an oath between us, *even* between you and us, and let us make a covenant with you,

29   that you will do us no harm, just as we have not touched you and have done to you nothing but good and have sent you away in peace. You are now the blessed of the LORD.'"

30   Then he made them a feast, and they ate and drank.

31   In the morning they arose early and

LIFE LESSONS

➤ **Genesis 26:28 — *"We see plainly that the LORD has been with you."***

*W*hen God blesses His children, sometimes even the ungodly can clearly see it (Prov. 16:7). When we live in a way that invites the blessing of the Lord, that blessing can spill over to our neighbors.

exchanged oaths; then Isaac sent them away and they departed from him in peace.

32 Now it came about on the same day, that Isaac's servants came in and told him about the well which they had dug, and said to him, "We have found water."

33 So he called it Shibah; therefore the name of the city is Beersheba to this day.

34 When Esau was forty years old he married Judith the daughter of Beeri the Hittite, and Basemath the daughter of Elon the Hittite;

35 and they brought grief to Isaac and Rebekah.

WHAT THE BIBLE SAYS ABOUT ⊚

God's Best for Your Life

Proverbs 3:5–10

*P*roverbs 3:5–10 is a godly compass for your life. It does not make any difference who you are, what you do, where you live, or what your vocation is—this concise, trustworthy compass will help you find God's best for your life.

- *The first point of this spiritual compass is centered upon your trusting God* (Prov. 3:5).

Friend, here is the most important key to finding God's best for you: You must have faith in the Lord God for every area of your life. He is omniscient (knows all things), omnipotent (all powerful), and He loves you perfectly, which means He can and will arrange every circumstance of your life to work out for your best if you'll trust Him with all your heart. It all begins with centering your trust in Him.

- *The second point of this spiritual compass helps you to understand God's three requirements for you* (Prov. 3:5–7).

1. *You are to rely upon God only—and not upon your own wisdom or understanding*. You see, there are some things you will never be able to understand with your limited knowledge. Therefore, you must rely upon God's profound wisdom for your life.

2. *You are to respect Him as your God*. You should stand in awe before Him, worship Him, and obey Him. Friend, if you do not respect and honor God, you cannot expect to be wise. You see, wisdom starts with fearing Him (Prov.

⊚ Psalm 7:6–8

6   Arise, O LORD, in Your anger;
Lift up Yourself against the rage of
my adversaries,
And arouse Yourself for me; You
have appointed judgment.

7   Let the assembly of the peoples
encompass You,
And over them return on high.

8   The LORD judges the peoples;
Vindicate me, O LORD, according
to my righteousness and my
integrity that is in me.

9:10). He is the only one who has the authority to govern every area of your life.

3. *You are to reject evil*. Everyone faces evil at one point or another, and you are going to be tempted to sin. God will not eliminate your temptations, trials, heartaches, burdens, or defeats. Rather, you must trust Him to help you flee from all evil.

- *The third point of this spiritual compass is everything that God promises you* (Prov. 3:6–10).

1. *God will make your path straight*. In other words, God will guide you and make your life easier. That doesn't mean you won't have any obstacles along the way; rather, it means God will either remove them or enable you to overcome them.

2. *God will bring health to your body*. Now, not everyone who is sick is living in sin. However, most of us would admit sometimes we disobey God by using our body unwisely—which often results in sickness. Therefore, trust His clear guidance to lead you to better health.

3. *God will bless you with plenty*. You must obey Him in every area of your life—even with your finances. God is your source, and He wants to bless you with plenty. However, first you must honor Him with what you have.

Friend, if you want your life to be the very best it can be, you must put your full trust in God, you must honor Him as your Lord, and you must obey Him in every area of your life. This is what godly living is all about—the heart of living life at its best. As you put your full trust in Him with all your heart, you can anticipate God's direction, better health, and financial blessing. So trust Him. He has the answer to your every need. ⊚

Proverbs 3:9–10

9   Honor the LORD from your
    wealth
    And from the first of all your
    produce;
10 So your barns will be filled with
    plenty
    And your vats will overflow with
    new wine.

Matthew 9:18–38

18   While He was saying these things
to them, a *synagogue* official came and
bowed down before Him, and said, "My
daughter has just died; but come and lay
Your hand on her, and she will live."
19   Jesus got up and *began* to follow
him, and *so did* His disciples.
20   And a woman who had been suffering from a hemorrhage for twelve years,
came up behind Him and touched the
fringe of His cloak;
21   for she was saying to herself, "If I
only touch His garment, I will get well."
22   But Jesus turning and seeing her
said, "Daughter, take courage; your faith
has made you well." At once the woman
was made well.
23   When Jesus came into the official's
house, and saw the flute-players and the
crowd in noisy disorder,
24   He said, "Leave; for the girl has not
died, but is asleep." And they *began*
laughing at Him.
25   But when the crowd had been sent
out, He entered and took her by the
hand, and the girl got up.

26   This news spread throughout all that
land.
27   As Jesus went on from there, two
blind men followed Him, crying out,
"Have mercy on us, Son of David!"
28   When He entered the house, the
blind men came up to Him, and Jesus
*said to them, "Do you believe that I am
able to do this?" They *said to Him, "Yes,
Lord."
29   Then He touched their eyes, saying,
"It shall be done to you according to your
faith."
30   And their eyes were opened. And
Jesus sternly warned them: "See that no
one knows *about this!*"
31   But they went out and spread the
news about Him throughout all that land.
32   As they were going out, a mute,
demon-possessed man was brought to
Him.
33   After the demon was cast out, the
mute man spoke; and the crowds were
amazed, *and were* saying, "Nothing like
this has ever been seen in Israel."
34   But the Pharisees were saying, "He
casts out the demons by the ruler of the
demons."
35   Jesus was going through all the cities and villages, teaching in their synagogues and proclaiming the gospel of
the kingdom, and healing every kind of
disease and every kind of sickness.
36   Seeing the people, He felt compassion for them, because they were distressed and dispirited like sheep without
a shepherd.
37   Then He *said to His disciples, "The
harvest is plentiful, but the workers are
few.
38   "Therefore beseech the Lord of the
harvest to send out workers into His harvest."

LIFE LESSONS

➤ **Matthew 9:24** — *"Leave; for the girl
has not died, but is asleep." And they
began laughing at Him.*

*B*ecause Jesus looked beyond what
people could see to what God sees,
they ridiculed Him. Faith often looks
ridiculous to those who don't have it. But
God does what no one else can.

➤ **Matthew 9:36** — *Seeing the people, He
felt compassion for them.*

*B*y this point in the story, Jesus and
His men were tired and needed rest.
But when Jesus saw the haggard masses,
He couldn't help but feel compassion
for them, so He continued to minister to
them. He is the Good Shepherd.

27 NOW it came about, when Isaac was old and his eyes were too dim to see, that he called his older son Esau and said to him, "My son." And he said to him, "Here I am."

2 Isaac said, "Behold now, I am old *and* I do not know the day of my death.

3 "Now then, please take your gear, your quiver and your bow, and go out to the field and hunt game for me;

4 and prepare a savory dish for me such as I love, and bring it to me that I may eat, so that my soul may bless you before I die."

5 Rebekah was listening while Isaac spoke to his son Esau. So when Esau went to the field to hunt for game to bring *home*,

6 Rebekah said to her son Jacob, "Behold, I heard your father speak to your brother Esau, saying,

7 'Bring me *some* game and prepare a savory dish for me, that I may eat, and bless you in the presence of the LORD before my death.'

8 "Now therefore, my son, listen to me as I command you.

9 "Go now to the flock and bring me two choice young goats from there, that I may prepare them *as* a savory dish for your father, such as he loves.

10 "Then you shall bring *it* to your father, that he may eat, so that he may bless you before his death."

11 Jacob answered his mother Rebekah, "Behold, Esau my brother is a hairy man and I am a smooth man.

12 "Perhaps my father will feel me, then I will be as a deceiver in his sight, and I will bring upon myself a curse and not a blessing."

13 But his mother said to him, "Your curse be on me, my son; only obey my voice, and go, get *them* for me."

14 So he went and got *them*, and brought *them* to his mother; and his mother made savory food such as his father loved.

15 Then Rebekah took the best garments of Esau her elder son, which were with her in the house, and put them on Jacob her younger son.

16 And she put the skins of the young goats on his hands and on the smooth part of his neck.

17 She also gave the savory food and the bread, which she had made, to her son Jacob.

18 Then he came to his father and said, "My father." And he said, "Here I am. Who are you, my son?"

19 Jacob said to his father, "I am Esau your firstborn; I have done as you told me. Get up, please, sit and eat of my game, that you may bless me."

20 Isaac said to his son, "How is it that you have *it* so quickly, my son?" And he said, "Because the LORD your God caused *it* to happen to me."

21 Then Isaac said to Jacob, "Please come close, that I may feel you, my son, whether you are really my son Esau or not."

22 So Jacob came close to Isaac his father, and he felt him and said, "The voice is the voice of Jacob, but the hands are the hands of Esau."

23 He did not recognize him, because his hands were hairy like his brother Esau's hands; so he blessed him.

24 And he said, "Are you really my son Esau?" And he said, "I am."

25 So he said, "Bring *it* to me, and I will eat of my son's game, that I may bless you." And he brought *it* to him, and he ate; he also brought him wine and he drank.

26 Then his father Isaac said to him, "Please come close and kiss me, my son."

27 So he came close and kissed him; and when he smelled the smell of his garments, he blessed him and said,

"See, the smell of my son
Is like the smell of a field which the
LORD has blessed;
28 Now may God give you of the dew
of heaven,
And of the fatness of the earth,
And an abundance of grain and
new wine;
29 May peoples serve you,
And nations bow down to you;
Be master of your brothers,
And may your mother's sons bow
down to you.
Cursed be those who curse you,
And blessed be those who bless
you."

30 Now it came about, as soon as Isaac

had finished blessing Jacob, and Jacob had hardly gone out from the presence of Isaac his father, that Esau his brother came in from his hunting.

31 Then he also made savory food, and brought it to his father; and he said to his father, "Let my father arise and eat of his son's game, that you may bless me."

32 Isaac his father said to him, "Who are you?" And he said, "I am your son, your firstborn, Esau."

33 Then Isaac trembled violently, and said, "Who was he then that hunted game and brought *it* to me, so that I ate of all *of it* before you came, and blessed him? Yes, and he shall be blessed."

34 When Esau heard the words of his father, he cried out with an exceedingly great and bitter cry, and said to his father, "Bless me, *even* me also, O my father!"

35 And he said, "Your brother came deceitfully and has taken away your blessing."

36 Then he said, "Is he not rightly named Jacob, for he has supplanted me these two times? He took away my birthright, and behold, now he has taken away my blessing." And he said, "Have you not reserved a blessing for me?"

37 But Isaac replied to Esau, "Behold, I have made him your master, and all his relatives I have given to him as servants; and with grain and new wine I have sustained him. Now as for you then, what can I do, my son?"

38 Esau said to his father, "Do you have only one blessing, my father? Bless me, *even* me also, O my father." So Esau lifted his voice and wept.

39 Then Isaac his father answered and said to him,

"Behold, away from the fertility of
    the earth shall be your dwelling,
And away from the dew of heaven
    from above.

40 "By your sword you shall live,
And your brother you shall serve;
But it shall come about when you
    become restless,
That you will break his yoke from
    your neck."

➤ **41** So Esau bore a grudge against Jacob because of the blessing with which his father had blessed him; and Esau said to himself, "The days of mourning for

---

my father are near; then I will kill my brother Jacob."

42 Now when the words of her elder son Esau were reported to Rebekah, she sent and called her younger son Jacob, and said to him, "Behold your brother Esau is consoling himself concerning you *by planning* to kill you.

43 "Now therefore, my son, obey my voice, and arise, flee to Haran, to my brother Laban!

44 "Stay with him a few days, until your brother's fury subsides,

45 until your brother's anger against you subsides and he forgets what you did to him. Then I will send and get you from there. Why should I be bereaved of you both in one day?"

46 Rebekah said to Isaac, "I am tired of living because of the daughters of Heth; if Jacob takes a wife from the daughters of Heth, like these, from the daughters of the land, what good will my life be to me?"

28 SO Isaac called Jacob and blessed him and charged him, and said to him, "You shall not take a wife from the daughters of Canaan.

2 "Arise, go to Paddan-aram, to the house of Bethuel your mother's father; and from there take to yourself a wife from the daughters of Laban your mother's brother.

3 "May God Almighty bless you and make you fruitful and multiply you, that you may become a company of peoples.

4 "May He also give you the blessing of Abraham, to you and to your descendants with you, that you may possess the land of your sojournings, which God gave to Abraham."

5 Then Isaac sent Jacob away, and he went to Paddan-aram to Laban, son of Bethuel the Aramean, the brother of Rebekah, the mother of Jacob and Esau.

6   Now Esau saw that Isaac had blessed Jacob and sent him away to Paddan-aram to take to himself a wife from there, *and that* when he blessed him he charged him, saying, "You shall not take a wife from the daughters of Canaan,"
7   and that Jacob had obeyed his father and his mother and had gone to Paddan-aram.
8   So Esau saw that the daughters of Canaan displeased his father Isaac;
9   and Esau went to Ishmael, and married, besides the wives that he had, Mahalath the daughter of Ishmael, Abraham's son, the sister of Nebaioth.
10   Then Jacob departed from Beer-sheba and went toward Haran.
11   He came to a certain place and spent the night there, because the sun had set; and he took one of the stones of the place and put it under his head, and lay down in that place.
12   He had a dream, and behold, a ladder was set on the earth with its top reaching to heaven; and behold, the angels of God were ascending and descending on it.
13   And behold, the LORD stood above it and said, "I am the LORD, the God of your father Abraham and the God of Isaac; the land on which you lie, I will give it to you and to your descendants.
14   "Your descendants will also be like the dust of the earth, and you will spread out to the west and to the east and to the north and to the south; and in you and in your descendants shall all the families of the earth be blessed.
15   "Behold, I am with you and will keep you wherever you go, and will bring you back to this land; for I will not leave you until I have done what I have promised you."
16   Then Jacob awoke from his sleep and said, "Surely the LORD is in this place, and I did not know it."
17   He was afraid and said, "How awesome is this place! This is none other than the house of God, and this is the gate of heaven."
18   So Jacob rose early in the morning, and took the stone that he had put under his head and set it up as a pillar and poured oil on its top.
19   He called the name of that place Bethel; however, previously the name of the city had been Luz.

20   Then Jacob made a vow, saying, "If God will be with me and will keep me on this journey that I take, and will give me food to eat and garments to wear,
21   and I return to my father's house in safety, then the LORD will be my God.
22   "This stone, which I have set up as a pillar, will be God's house, and of all that You give me I will surely give a tenth to You."

Psalm 7:9–17

9   O let the evil of the wicked come
        to an end, but establish the
        righteous;
    For the righteous God tries the
        hearts and minds.
10   My shield is with God,
        Who saves the upright in heart.
11   God is a righteous judge,
        And a God who has indignation
        every day.
12   If a man does not repent, He will
        sharpen His sword;
    He has bent His bow and made it
        ready.
13   He has also prepared for Himself
        deadly weapons;
    He makes His arrows fiery shafts.
14   Behold, he travails with wickedness,
    And he conceives mischief and
        brings forth falsehood.
15   He has dug a pit and hollowed it
        out,
    And has fallen into the hole which
        he made.
16   His mischief will return upon his
        own head,
    And his violence will descend upon
        his own pate.
17   I will give thanks to the LORD
        according to His righteousness

LIFE LESSONS

➤ **Psalm 7:11 — *God is a righteous judge, and a God who has indignation every day.***

God loves the world and sent His Son to die for undeserving sinners (John 3:16), yet He remains a holy God and will certainly judge all who reject His Son (John 3:36).

Life Examples:

Closer to You, Lord

PROVERBS 3:11, 12

*E*arly in his life, John Donne, one of England's great poets, was known for his controversial poetry and satirical criticism of religious denominations. However, Donne did not remain antagonistic toward God.

After joining the Church of England and marrying Anne More, Donne experienced immense suffering. He and Anne lost five of their 12 children and lived in despondent poverty. Donne continually struggled with depression and physical affliction. One would think the suffering would have driven Donne farther from God.

However, the exact opposite is true. During this time, Donne studied God's ways with fervor. Donne wrote: "Batter my heart, three person'd God; for you / As yet but knock, breathe, shine and seek to mend . . . / Take me to you, imprison me, for I / Except you enthrall me, never shall be free."

Donne understood all his trials brought him closer to God. As Proverbs 3:12 says, "For whom the Lord loves He reproves, even as a father corrects the son in whom he delights."

If you are suffering greatly, do not think God has abandoned you. Rather, like Donne, God is making your life into a sweet sonnet. Donne was not only one of England's great poets, but also one of its greatest preachers. God is making something phenomenal of your life, too. As W. L. Watkinson wrote, "The rarest souls have been tested with high pressures and temperatures, but Heaven will not desert them."

And will sing praise to the name of the LORD Most High.

Proverbs 3:11–12

11 My son, do not reject the discipline
of the LORD
Or loathe His reproof,
12 For whom the LORD loves He
reproves,
Even as a father *corrects* the son in
whom he delights.

Matthew 10:1–20

10 JESUS summoned His twelve disciples and gave them authority over unclean spirits, to cast them out, and to heal every kind of disease and every kind of sickness.
2 Now the names of the twelve apostles are these: The first, Simon, who is called Peter, and Andrew his brother; and James the son of Zebedee, and John his brother;
3 Philip and Bartholomew; Thomas and Matthew the tax collector; James the son of Alphaeus, and Thaddaeus;
4 Simon the Zealot, and Judas Iscariot, the one who betrayed Him.
5 These twelve Jesus sent out after instructing them: "Do not go in *the* way of *the* Gentiles, and do not enter *any* city of the Samaritans;
6 but rather go to the lost sheep of the house of Israel.
7 "And as you go, preach, saying, 'The kingdom of heaven is at hand.'
8 "Heal *the* sick, raise *the* dead, cleanse *the* lepers, cast out demons. Freely you received, freely give.
9 "Do not acquire gold, or silver, or copper for your money belts,
10 or a bag for *your* journey, or even two coats, or sandals, or a staff; for the worker is worthy of his support.
11 "And whatever city or village you enter, inquire who is worthy in it, and stay at his house until you leave *that city.*

LIFE LESSONS

➤ **Psalm 7:17 — *I will give thanks to the Lord according to His righteousness and will sing praise to the name of the Lord Most High.***

*E*verything God does, He does right. There will never come a time when someone can say, "Lord, I'm afraid You messed up here." Even when we don't understand what He does, we can be sure He acts in righteousness.

➤ **Matthew 10:8 — *"Freely you received, freely give."***

*G*od blesses us so we can bless others.

12 "As you enter the house, give it your greeting.
13 "If the house is worthy, give it your *blessing of* peace. But if it is not worthy, take back your *blessing of* peace.
14 "Whoever does not receive you, nor heed your words, as you go out of that house or that city, shake the dust off your feet.
15 "Truly I say to you, it will be more tolerable for *the* land of Sodom and Gomorrah in the day of judgment than for that city.
16 "Behold, I send you out as sheep in the midst of wolves; so be shrewd as serpents and innocent as doves.
17 "But beware of men, for they will hand you over to *the* courts and scourge you in their synagogues;
18 and you will even be brought before

governors and kings for My sake, as a testimony to them and to the Gentiles.
19 "But when they hand you over, do not worry about how or what you are to say; for it will be given you in that hour what you are to say.
20 "For it is not you who speak, but *it is* the Spirit of your Father who speaks in you.

JANUARY 15

◈ Genesis 29:1—30:43

29 THEN Jacob went on his journey, and came to the land of the sons of the east.
2 He looked, and saw a well in the field, and behold, three flocks of sheep were lying there beside it, for from that well they watered the flocks. Now the stone on the mouth of the well was large.
3 When all the flocks were gathered there, they would then roll the stone from the mouth of the well and water the sheep, and put the stone back in its place on the mouth of the well.
4 Jacob said to them, "My brothers, where are you from?" And they said, "We are from Haran."
5 He said to them, "Do you know Laban the son of Nahor?" And they said, "We know *him.*"
6 And he said to them, "Is it well with him?" And they said, "It is well, and here is Rachel his daughter coming with the sheep."
7 He said, "Behold, it is still high day; it is not time for the livestock to be gathered. Water the sheep, and go, pasture them."
8 But they said, "We cannot, until all

the flocks are gathered, and they roll the stone from the mouth of the well; then we water the sheep."
9 While he was still speaking with them, Rachel came with her father's sheep, for she was a shepherdess.
10 When Jacob saw Rachel the daughter of Laban his mother's brother, and the sheep of Laban his mother's brother, Jacob went up and rolled the stone from the mouth of the well and watered the flock of Laban his mother's brother.
11 Then Jacob kissed Rachel, and lifted his voice and wept.
12 Jacob told Rachel that he was a relative of her father and that he was Rebekah's son, and she ran and told her father.
13 So when Laban heard the news of Jacob his sister's son, he ran to meet him, and embraced him and kissed him and brought him to his house. Then he related to Laban all these things.
14 Laban said to him, "Surely you are my bone and my flesh." And he stayed with him a month.
15 Then Laban said to Jacob, "Because you are my relative, should you therefore serve me for nothing? Tell me, what shall your wages be?"

16 Now Laban had two daughters; the name of the older was Leah, and the name of the younger was Rachel.

17 And Leah's eyes were weak, but Rachel was beautiful of form and face.

18 Now Jacob loved Rachel, so he said, "I will serve you seven years for your younger daughter Rachel."

19 Laban said, "It is better that I give her to you than to give her to another man; stay with me."

20 So Jacob served seven years for Rachel and they seemed to him but a few days because of his love for her.

21 Then Jacob said to Laban, "Give me my wife, for my time is completed, that I may go in to her."

22 Laban gathered all the men of the place and made a feast.

23 Now in the evening he took his daughter Leah, and brought her to him; and Jacob went in to her.

24 Laban also gave his maid Zilpah to his daughter Leah as a maid.

25 So it came about in the morning that, behold, it was Leah! And he said to Laban, "What is this you have done to me? Was it not for Rachel that I served with you? Why then have you deceived me?"

26 But Laban said, "It is not the practice in our place to marry off the younger before the firstborn.

27 "Complete the week of this one, and we will give you the other also for the service which you shall serve with me for another seven years."

28 Jacob did so and completed her week, and he gave him his daughter Rachel as his wife.

29 Laban also gave his maid Bilhah to his daughter Rachel as her maid.

30 So Jacob went in to Rachel also, and indeed he loved Rachel more than Leah, and he served with Laban for another seven years.

31 Now the LORD saw that Leah was unloved, and He opened her womb, but Rachel was barren.

32 Leah conceived and bore a son and named him Reuben, for she said, "Because the LORD has seen my affliction; surely now my husband will love me."

33 Then she conceived again and bore a son and said, "Because the LORD has heard that I am unloved, He has therefore given me this son also." So she named him Simeon.

34 She conceived again and bore a son and said, "Now this time my husband will become attached to me, because I have borne him three sons." Therefore he was named Levi.

35 And she conceived again and bore a ◄ son and said, "This time I will praise the LORD." Therefore she named him Judah. Then she stopped bearing.

Life Examples:

Detours

GENESIS 29:15–30

It happens just as you are within sight of your goal—something puts the object of your pursuit even further away from your grasp. It is a detour that makes you doubt whether you will ever succeed in your efforts.

For Jacob, it was the moment he realized he had married Leah instead of Rachel (Gen. 29:25–27). For the disciples, it was when the Messiah they hoped would restore the kingdom of Israel was crucified (Luke 24:13–21).

What was it for you? Did your company reorganize and let you go just as you were up for a promotion? Has some illness or financial problem impeded your progress? It can be any number of setbacks that break your heart and crush your spirit.

Yet understand this—God has not failed you. He has a better plan than you realize. Though the detour is difficult, you will see it was definitely worth it.

Remember, God had a greater plan for Jacob. From Leah's womb came six of the 12 tribes of Israel (Gen. 29:32–35; 30:17–20); and from her maid Zilpah came two more of the tribes (Gen. 30:9–13).

For the disciples, three days after the crucifixion they discovered the kingdom the Messiah was ushering in was greater and more powerful than they could ever imagine—because it was the eternal kingdom of God (Luke 24:44–49).

But you must ask yourself as you wait: *Is this goal I have been pursuing more important than my relationship with God?* Will you still trust Him, even though you cannot see how to reach your goal? Trust Him, friend. Surely, "the LORD will accomplish what concerns [you]" (Ps. 138:8).

30 NOW when Rachel saw that she bore Jacob no children, she became jealous of her sister; and she said to Jacob, "Give me children, or else I die."

2   Then Jacob's anger burned against Rachel, and he said, "Am I in the place of God, who has withheld from you the fruit of the womb?"

3   She said, "Here is my maid Bilhah, go in to her that she may bear on my knees, that through her I too may have children."

4   So she gave him her maid Bilhah as a wife, and Jacob went in to her.

5   Bilhah conceived and bore Jacob a son.

6   Then Rachel said, "God has vindicated me, and has indeed heard my voice and has given me a son." Therefore she named him Dan.

7   Rachel's maid Bilhah conceived again and bore Jacob a second son.

8   So Rachel said, "With mighty wrestlings I have wrestled with my sister, *and* I have indeed prevailed." And she named him Naphtali.

9   When Leah saw that she had stopped bearing, she took her maid Zilpah and gave her to Jacob as a wife.

10   Leah's maid Zilpah bore Jacob a son.

11   Then Leah said, "How fortunate!" So she named him Gad.

12   Leah's maid Zilpah bore Jacob a second son.

13   Then Leah said, "Happy am I! For women will call me happy." So she named him Asher.

14   Now in the days of wheat harvest Reuben went and found mandrakes in the field, and brought them to his mother Leah. Then Rachel said to Leah, "Please give me some of your son's mandrakes."

15   But she said to her, "Is it a small matter for you to take my husband? And would you take my son's mandrakes also?" So Rachel said, "Therefore he may lie with you tonight in return for your son's mandrakes."

16   When Jacob came in from the field in the evening, then Leah went out to meet him and said, "You must come in to me, for I have surely hired you with my son's mandrakes." So he lay with her that night.

17   God gave heed to Leah, and she conceived and bore Jacob a fifth son.

18   Then Leah said, "God has given me my wages because I gave my maid to my husband." So she named him Issachar.

19   Leah conceived again and bore a sixth son to Jacob.

20   Then Leah said, "God has endowed me with a good gift; now my husband will dwell with me, because I have borne him six sons." So she named him Zebulun.

21   Afterward she bore a daughter and named her Dinah.

22   Then God remembered Rachel, and God gave heed to her and opened her womb.

23   So she conceived and bore a son and said, "God has taken away my reproach."

24   She named him Joseph, saying, "May the LORD give me another son."

25   Now it came about when Rachel had borne Joseph, that Jacob said to Laban, "Send me away, that I may go to my own place and to my own country.

26   "Give *me* my wives and my children for whom I have served you, and let me depart; for you yourself know my service which I have rendered you."

27   But Laban said to him, "If now it pleases you, *stay with me;* I have divined that the LORD has blessed me on your account."

28   He continued, "Name me your wages, and I will give it."

29   But he said to him, "You yourself know how I have served you and how your cattle have fared with me.

30   "For you had little before I came and it has increased to a multitude, and the

---

LIFE LESSONS

> Genesis 29:35 — *"I will praise the LORD." Therefore she named him Judah.*

*L*eah hoped to find happiness, first in the love of her husband, then in the blessing of sons. But in the end she began to see that lasting contentment can be found only in an intimate relationship with God.

> Genesis 30:2 — *"Am I in the place of God, who has withheld from you the fruit of the womb?"*

*W*hen Rebekah tried and failed to have children, her husband, Isaac, prayed for her (Gen. 25:21). Abraham had done the same for Abimelech's household (Gen. 20:17). But Jacob had not yet learned the power of kneeling in prayer.

LORD has blessed you wherever I turned. But now, when shall I provide for my own household also?"
31 So he said, "What shall I give you?" And Jacob said, "You shall not give me anything. If you will do this *one* thing for me, I will again pasture *and* keep your flock:
32 let me pass through your entire flock today, removing from there every speckled and spotted sheep and every black one among the lambs and the spotted and speckled among the goats; and *such* shall be my wages.
33 "So my honesty will answer for me later, when you come concerning my wages. Every one that is not speckled and spotted among the goats and black among the lambs, *if found* with me, will be considered stolen."
34 Laban said, "Good, let it be according to your word."
35 So he removed on that day the striped and spotted male goats and all the speckled and spotted female goats, every one with white in it, and all the black ones among the sheep, and gave them into the care of his sons.
36 And he put *a distance of* three days' journey between himself and Jacob, and Jacob fed the rest of Laban's flocks.
37 Then Jacob took fresh rods of poplar and almond and plane trees, and peeled white stripes in them, exposing the white which *was* in the rods.
38 He set the rods which he had peeled in front of the flocks in the gutters, *even* in the watering troughs, where the flocks came to drink; and they mated when they came to drink.
39 So the flocks mated by the rods, and the flocks brought forth striped, speckled, and spotted.
40 Jacob separated the lambs, and made the flocks face toward the striped and all the black in the flock of Laban; and he put his own herds apart, and did not put them with Laban's flock.
41 Moreover, whenever the stronger of the flock were mating, Jacob would place the rods in the sight of the flock in the gutters, so that they might mate by the rods;
42 but when the flock was feeble, he did not put *them* in; so the feebler were Laban's and the stronger Jacob's.
43 So the man became exceedingly prosperous, and had large flocks and female and male servants and camels and donkeys.

Psalm 8:1–5

For the choir director; on the Gittith. A Psalm of David.

8 O LORD, our Lord,
How majestic is Your name in all the earth,
Who have displayed Your splendor above the heavens!
2 From the mouth of infants and nursing babes You have established strength
Because of Your adversaries,
To make the enemy and the revengeful cease.
3 When I consider Your heavens, the work of Your fingers,
The moon and the stars, which You have ordained;
4 What is man that You take thought of him,
And the son of man that You care for him?
5 Yet You have made him a little lower than God,
And You crown him with glory and majesty!

Proverbs 3:13–18

13 How blessed is the man who finds wisdom
And the man who gains understanding.
14 For her profit is better than the profit of silver
And her gain better than fine gold.
15 She is more precious than jewels;
And nothing you desire compares with her.
16 Long life is in her right hand;
In her left hand are riches and honor.

LIFE LESSONS

➤ **Psalm 8:4 — *What is man that You take thought of him, and the son of man that You care for him?***

The more we learn about the vastness of the universe, the more powerful this question becomes. Although we are but a speck drifting in the immensity of the cosmos, God places His love and unwavering attention on us.

17 Her ways are pleasant ways
   And all her paths are peace.
18 She is a tree of life to those who
   take hold of her,
   And happy are all who hold her fast.

Matthew 10:21–42

21 "Brother will betray brother to death, and a father *his* child; and children will rise up against parents and cause them to be put to death.
22 "You will be hated by all because of My name, but it is the one who has endured to the end who will be saved.
23 "But whenever they persecute you in one city, flee to the next; for truly I say to you, you will not finish *going through* the cities of Israel until the Son of Man comes.
24 "A disciple is not above his teacher, nor a slave above his master.
25 "It is enough for the disciple that he become like his teacher, and the slave like his master. If they have called the head of the house Beelzebul, how much more *will they malign* the members of his household!
26 "Therefore do not fear them, for there is nothing concealed that will not be revealed, or hidden that will not be known.
27 "What I tell you in the darkness, speak in the light; and what you hear *whispered* in *your* ear, proclaim upon the housetops.
28 "Do not fear those who kill the body but are unable to kill the soul; but rather fear Him who is able to destroy both soul and body in hell.
29 "Are not two sparrows sold for a cent? And *yet* not one of them will fall to the ground apart from your Father.
30 "But the very hairs of your head are all numbered.
31 "So do not fear; you are more valuable than many sparrows.
32 "Therefore everyone who confesses Me before men, I will also confess him before My Father who is in heaven.
33 "But whoever denies Me before men, I will also deny him before My Father who is in heaven.
34 "Do not think that I came to bring peace on the earth; I did not come to bring peace, but a sword.
35 "For I came to SET A MAN AGAINST HIS FATHER, AND A DAUGHTER AGAINST HER MOTHER, AND A DAUGHTER-IN-LAW AGAINST HER MOTHER-IN-LAW;
36 and A MAN'S ENEMIES WILL BE THE MEMBERS OF HIS HOUSEHOLD.
37 "He who loves father or mother more than Me is not worthy of Me; and he who loves son or daughter more than Me is not worthy of Me.
38 "And he who does not take his cross and follow after Me is not worthy of Me.
39 "He who has found his life will lose it, and he who has lost his life for My sake will find it.
40 "He who receives you receives Me, and he who receives Me receives Him who sent Me.
41 "He who receives a prophet in *the* name of a prophet shall receive a prophet's reward; and he who receives a righteous man in the name of a righteous man shall receive a righteous man's reward.
42 "And whoever in the name of a disciple gives to one of these little ones even a cup of cold water to drink, truly I say to you, he shall not lose his reward."

LIFE LESSONS

➤ **Matthew 10:28** — *"Do not fear those who kill the body but are unable to kill the soul; but rather fear Him who is able to destroy both soul and body in hell."*

*J*ust before His execution, Jesus told Pilate, the Roman governor: "You would have no authority over Me unless it had been given you from above" (John 19:11). He didn't fear Pilate because God was in control.

➤ **Matthew 10:42** — *"Whoever in the name of a disciple gives to one of these little ones even a cup of cold water to drink, truly I say to you, he shall not lose his reward."*

*G*od doesn't reward only big jobs and important works. He loves to give and He loves to reward obedience, no matter how small or insignificant it may seem to us.

Genesis 31:1—32:32

31 NOW Jacob heard the words of Laban's sons, saying, "Jacob has taken away all that was our father's, and from what belonged to our father he has made all this wealth."

2 Jacob saw the attitude of Laban, and behold, it was not *friendly* toward him as formerly.

3 Then the LORD said to Jacob, "Return to the land of your fathers and to your relatives, and I will be with you."

4 So Jacob sent and called Rachel and Leah to his flock in the field,

5 and said to them, "I see your father's attitude, that it is not *friendly* toward me as formerly, but the God of my father has been with me.

6 "You know that I have served your father with all my strength.

7 "Yet your father has cheated me and changed my wages ten times; however, God did not allow him to hurt me.

8 "If he spoke thus, 'The speckled shall be your wages,' then all the flock brought forth speckled; and if he spoke thus, 'The striped shall be your wages,' then all the flock brought forth striped.

9 "Thus God has taken away your father's livestock and given *them* to me.

10 "And it came about at the time when the flock were mating that I lifted up my eyes and saw in a dream, and behold, the male goats which were mating *were* striped, speckled, and mottled.

11 "Then the angel of God said to me in the dream, 'Jacob,' and I said, 'Here I am.'

12 "He said, 'Lift up now your eyes and see *that* all the male goats which are mating are striped, speckled, and mottled; for I have seen all that Laban has been doing to you.

13 'I am the God *of* Bethel, where you anointed a pillar, where you made a vow to Me; now arise, leave this land, and return to the land of your birth.'"

14 Rachel and Leah said to him, "Do we still have any portion or inheritance in our father's house?

15 "Are we not reckoned by him as foreigners? For he has sold us, and has also entirely consumed our purchase price.

16 "Surely all the wealth which God has taken away from our father belongs to us and our children; now then, do whatever God has said to you."

17 Then Jacob arose and put his children and his wives upon camels;

18 and he drove away all his livestock and all his property which he had gathered, his acquired livestock which he had gathered in Paddan-aram, to go to the land of Canaan to his father Isaac.

19 When Laban had gone to shear his flock, then Rachel stole the household idols that were her father's.

20 And Jacob deceived Laban the Aramean by not telling him that he was fleeing.

21 So he fled with all that he had; and he arose and crossed the *Euphrates* River, and set his face toward the hill country of Gilead.

22 When it was told Laban on the third day that Jacob had fled,

23 then he took his kinsmen with him and pursued him *a distance of* seven days' journey, and he overtook him in the hill country of Gilead.

24 God came to Laban the Aramean in a dream of the night and said to him, "Be careful that you do not speak to Jacob either good or bad."

25 Laban caught up with Jacob. Now Jacob had pitched his tent in the hill country, and Laban with his kinsmen camped in the hill country of Gilead.

26 Then Laban said to Jacob, "What have you done by deceiving me and carrying away my daughters like captives of the sword?

27 "Why did you flee secretly and deceive me, and did not tell me so that I might have sent you away with joy and with songs, with timbrel and with lyre;

28 and did not allow me to kiss my sons and my daughters? Now you have done foolishly.

29 "It is in my power to do you harm, but the God of your father spoke to me last night, saying, 'Be careful not to speak either good or bad to Jacob.'

30 "Now you have indeed gone away because you longed greatly for your father's house; *but* why did you steal my gods?"

31 Then Jacob replied to Laban, "Because I was afraid, for I thought that you would take your daughters from me by force.

32 "The one with whom you find your gods shall not live; in the presence of our kinsmen point out what is yours among my belongings and take *it* for yourself." For Jacob did not know that Rachel had stolen them.

33 So Laban went into Jacob's tent and into Leah's tent and into the tent of the two maids, but he did not find *them.* Then he went out of Leah's tent and entered Rachel's tent.

34 Now Rachel had taken the household idols and put them in the camel's saddle, and she sat on them. And Laban felt through all the tent but did not find *them.*

35 She said to her father, "Let not my lord be angry that I cannot rise before you, for the manner of women is upon me." So he searched but did not find the household idols.

36 Then Jacob became angry and contended with Laban; and Jacob said to Laban, "What is my transgression? What is my sin that you have hotly pursued me?

37 "Though you have felt through all my goods, what have you found of all your household goods? Set *it* here before my kinsmen and your kinsmen, that they may decide between us two.

38 "These twenty years I *have been* with you; your ewes and your female goats have not miscarried, nor have I eaten the rams of your flocks.

39 "That which was torn *of beasts* I did not bring to you; I bore the loss of it myself. You required it of my hand *whether* stolen by day or stolen by night.

40 "*Thus* I was: by day the heat consumed me and the frost by night, and my sleep fled from my eyes.

41 "These twenty years I have been in your house; I served you fourteen years for your two daughters and six years for your flock, and you changed my wages ten times.

➤ 42 "If the God of my father, the God of Abraham, and the fear of Isaac, had not been for me, surely now you would have sent me away empty-handed. God has seen my affliction and the toil of my hands, so He rendered judgment last night."

43 Then Laban replied to Jacob, "The daughters are my daughters, and the children are my children, and the flocks are my flocks, and all that you see is mine. But what can I do this day to these my daughters or to their children whom they have borne?

44 "So now come, let us make a covenant, you and I, and let it be a witness between you and me."

45 Then Jacob took a stone and set it up *as* a pillar.

46 Jacob said to his kinsmen, "Gather stones." So they took stones and made a heap, and they ate there by the heap.

47 Now Laban called it Jegarsahadutha, but Jacob called it Galeed.

48 Laban said, "This heap is a witness between you and me this day." Therefore it was named Galeed,

49 and Mizpah, for he said, "May the LORD watch between you and me when we are absent one from the other.

50 "If you mistreat my daughters, or if you take wives besides my daughters, *although* no man is with us, see, God is witness between you and me."

51 Laban said to Jacob, "Behold this heap and behold the pillar which I have set between you and me.

52 "This heap is a witness, and the pillar is a witness, that I will not pass by this heap to you for harm, and you will not pass by this heap and this pillar to me, for harm.

53 "The God of Abraham and the God ◄ of Nahor, the God of their father, judge between us." So Jacob swore by the fear of his father Isaac.

54 Then Jacob offered a sacrifice on the

LIFE LESSONS

➤ **Genesis 31:42 — *"If the God of my father . . . had not been for me, surely now you would have sent me away empty-handed."***

*J*acob was finally beginning to understand that scheming for blessings cannot compete with God-given blessings.

➤ **Genesis 31:53 — *Jacob swore by the fear of his father Isaac.***

*W*hen the passage calls God "the fear of Isaac" (Gen. 31:42), it declares God is not only loving, but just; not only gentle, but strong—what Romans 11:22 calls the "kindness and severity" of God.

mountain, and called his kinsmen to the meal; and they ate the meal and spent the night on the mountain.

55 Early in the morning Laban arose, and kissed his sons and his daughters and blessed them. Then Laban departed and returned to his place.

32 NOW as Jacob went on his way, the angels of God met him.

2 Jacob said when he saw them, "This is God's camp." So he named that place Mahanaim.

3 Then Jacob sent messengers before him to his brother Esau in the land of Seir, the country of Edom.

4 He also commanded them saying, "Thus you shall say to my lord Esau: 'Thus says your servant Jacob, "I have sojourned with Laban, and stayed until now;

5 I have oxen and donkeys *and* flocks and male and female servants; and I have sent to tell my lord, that I may find favor in your sight." '"

6 The messengers returned to Jacob, saying, "We came to your brother Esau, and furthermore he is coming to meet you, and four hundred men are with him."

7 Then Jacob was greatly afraid and distressed; and he divided the people who were with him, and the flocks and the herds and the camels, into two companies;

8 for he said, "If Esau comes to the one company and attacks it, then the company which is left will escape."

9 Jacob said, "O God of my father Abraham and God of my father Isaac, O Lord, who said to me, 'Return to your country and to your relatives, and I will prosper you,'

10 I am unworthy of all the lovingkindness and of all the faithfulness which You have shown to Your servant; for with my staff *only* I crossed this Jordan, and now I have become two companies.

11 "Deliver me, I pray, from the hand of my brother, from the hand of Esau; for I fear him, that he will come and attack me *and* the mothers with the children.

12 "For You said, 'I will surely prosper you and make your descendants as the sand of the sea, which is too great to be numbered.'"

13 So he spent the night there. Then he selected from what he had with him a present for his brother Esau:

14 two hundred female goats and twenty male goats, two hundred ewes and twenty rams,

15 thirty milking camels and their colts, forty cows and ten bulls, twenty female donkeys and ten male donkeys.

16 He delivered *them* into the hand of his servants, every drove by itself, and said to his servants, "Pass on before me, and put a space between droves."

17 He commanded the one in front, saying, "When my brother Esau meets you and asks you, saying, 'To whom do you belong, and where are you going, and to whom do these *animals* in front of you belong?'

18 then you shall say, '*These* belong to your servant Jacob; it is a present sent to my lord Esau. And behold, he also is behind us.'"

19 Then he commanded also the second and the third, and all those who followed the droves, saying, "After this manner you shall speak to Esau when you find him;

20 and you shall say, 'Behold, your servant Jacob also is behind us.'" For he said, "I will appease him with the present that goes before me. Then afterward I will see his face; perhaps he will accept me."

21 So the present passed on before him, while he himself spent that night in the camp.

22 Now he arose that same night and took his two wives and his two maids and his eleven children, and crossed the ford of the Jabbok.

23 He took them and sent them across the stream. And he sent across whatever he had.

24 Then Jacob was left alone, and a man wrestled with him until daybreak.

25 When he saw that he had not prevailed against him, he touched the socket of his thigh; so the socket of Jacob's thigh was dislocated while he wrestled with him.

26 Then he said, "Let me go, for the dawn is breaking." But he said, "I will not let you go unless you bless me."

27 So he said to him, "What is your name?" And he said, "Jacob."

28 He said, "Your name shall no longer be Jacob, but Israel; for you have striven with God and with men and have prevailed."

Life Examples:

JACOB: Wrestling with God

GENESIS 32:24–32

*T*he story of Jacob alternately comforts and confounds. For while we could look upon many of his decisions with contempt—and even wonder why God would so favor such a man—it equally reassures us to realize the God who extended grace to Jacob also extends it to us.

In a famous episode described in Genesis 32, Jacob wrestles with a powerful stranger whom he later concludes is God. Some scholars believe Jacob wrestled with the pre-incarnate Christ; others consider the opponent an angel. Still others suggest Jacob wrangled with God only in prayer. In any event, the nation Israel received its name from Jacob, whom God renamed "Israel," meaning, "he struggles with God."

Despite his many failings, weaknesses, and subsequent sorrows, God loved Jacob. And through his strange wrestling match, he provides us with a model of the effort required for effective prayer (Col. 4:12).

29 Then Jacob asked him and said, "Please tell me your name." But he said, "Why is it that you ask my name?" And he blessed him there.
30 So Jacob named the place Peniel, for *he said,* "I have seen God face to face, yet my life has been preserved."
31 Now has the sun rose upon him just as he crossed over Penuel, and he was limping on his thigh.
32 Therefore, to this day the sons of Israel do not eat the sinew of the hip which is on the socket of the thigh, because he touched the socket of Jacob's thigh in the sinew of the hip.

Psalm 8:6–9

6 You make him to rule over the works of Your hands;
You have put all things under his feet,
7 All sheep and oxen,
And also the beasts of the field,
8 The birds of the heavens and the fish of the sea,
Whatever passes through the paths of the seas.
9 O Lord, our Lord,
How majestic is Your name in all the earth!

Proverbs 3:19–20

19 The Lord by wisdom founded the earth,
By understanding He established the heavens.
20 By His knowledge the deeps were broken up
And the skies drip with dew.

Matthew 11:1–30

11 WHEN Jesus had finished giving instructions to His twelve disciples, He departed from there to teach and preach in their cities.
2 Now when John, while imprisoned,

LIFE LESSONS

> **Genesis 32:31 — *Just as he crossed over Penuel, and he was limping on his thigh.***

*J*acob's wrestling match left him with a painful limp, but also with a better understanding of God. God renamed him Israel, meaning "He struggles with God," or perhaps "a prince with God." Because of this painful encounter, Jacob took a great spiritual leap forward.

> **Psalm 8:9 — *O Lord, our Lord, how majestic is Your name in all the earth!***

*W*hen we say God's name is excellent, we mean everything about Him— His character, His actions, His thoughts, His desires, His plans, His words—is excellent, praiseworthy, and perfect.

heard of the works of Christ, he sent *word* by his disciples

3   and said to Him, "Are You the Expected One, or shall we look for someone else?"

4   Jesus answered and said to them, "Go and report to John what you hear and see:

5   *the* BLIND RECEIVE SIGHT and *the* lame walk, *the* lepers are cleansed and *the* deaf hear, *the* dead are raised up, and *the* POOR HAVE THE GOSPEL PREACHED TO THEM.

6   "And blessed is he who does not take offense at Me."

7   As these men were going *away*, Jesus began to speak to the crowds about John, "What did you go out into the wilderness to see? A reed shaken by the wind?

8   "But what did you go out to see? A man dressed in soft *clothing*? Those who wear soft *clothing* are in kings' palaces!

9   "But what did you go out to see? A prophet? Yes, I tell you, and one who is more than a prophet.

10   "This is the one about whom it is written,

'BEHOLD, I SEND MY MESSENGER AHEAD
       OF YOU,
WHO WILL PREPARE YOUR WAY BEFORE
       YOU.'

➤ 11   "Truly I say to you, among those born of women there has not arisen *anyone* greater than John the Baptist! Yet the one who is least in the kingdom of heaven is greater than he.

12   "From the days of John the Baptist until now the kingdom of heaven suffers violence, and violent men take it by force.

13   "For all the prophets and the Law prophesied until John.

14   "And if you are willing to accept *it*, John himself is Elijah who was to come.

15   "He who has ears to hear, let him hear.

16   "But to what shall I compare this generation? It is like children sitting in the market places, who call out to the other *children*,

17   and say, 'We played the flute for you, and you did not dance; we sang a dirge, and you did not mourn.'

18   "For John came neither eating nor drinking, and they say, 'He has a demon!'

19   "The Son of Man came eating and drinking, and they say, 'Behold, a gluttonous man and a drunkard, a friend of tax collectors and sinners!' Yet wisdom is vindicated by her deeds."

20   Then He began to denounce the cities in which most of His miracles were done, because they did not repent.

21   "Woe to you, Chorazin! Woe to you, Bethsaida! For if the miracles had occurred in Tyre and Sidon which occurred in you, they would have repented long ago in sackcloth and ashes.

22   "Nevertheless I say to you, it will be more tolerable for Tyre and Sidon in *the* day of judgment than for you.

23   "And you, Capernaum, will not be exalted to heaven, will you? You will descend to Hades; for if the miracles had occurred in Sodom which occurred in you, it would have remained to this day.

24   "Nevertheless I say to you that it will be more tolerable for the land of Sodom in *the* day of judgment, than for you."

25   At that time Jesus said, "I praise You, Father, Lord of heaven and earth, that You have hidden these things from *the* wise and intelligent and have revealed them to infants.

LIFE LESSONS

➤ **Matthew 11:11** — *"Among those born of women there has not risen anyone greater than John the Baptist! Yet the one who is least in the kingdom of heaven is greater than he."*

*T*oday, believers have something unknown to believers in Old Testament times: the indwelling and permanent presence of the Holy Spirit. We are the temple of the Holy Spirit, and that makes us "great" in God's eyes.

➤ **Matthew 11:29** — *"Take My yoke upon you and learn from Me, for I am gentle and lowly in heart, and YOU WILL FIND REST FOR YOUR SOULS."*

*A*ll of us need rest, and Jesus promises to give it to us when we find our rest in Him. He will not scold us for being weak or scorn us for being foolish. He promises to gently and humbly refresh our weary souls.

26 "Yes, Father, for this way was well-pleasing in Your sight.
27 "All things have been handed over to Me by My Father; and no one knows the Son except the Father; nor does anyone know the Father except the Son, and anyone to whom the Son wills to reveal *Him*.

28 "Come to Me, all who are weary and heavy-laden, and I will give you rest.
29 "Take My yoke upon you and learn from Me, for I am gentle and humble in heart, and YOU WILL FIND REST FOR YOUR SOULS.
30 "For My yoke is easy and My burden is light."

JANUARY 17

Genesis 33:1—34:31

33 THEN Jacob lifted his eyes and looked, and behold, Esau was coming, and four hundred men with him. So he divided the children among Leah and Rachel and the two maids.
2 He put the maids and their children in front, and Leah and her children next, and Rachel and Joseph last.
3 But he himself passed on ahead of them and bowed down to the ground seven times, until he came near to his brother.
4 Then Esau ran to meet him and embraced him, and fell on his neck and kissed him, and they wept.
5 He lifted his eyes and saw the women and the children, and said, "Who are these with you?" So he said, "The children whom God has graciously given your servant."
6 Then the maids came near with their children, and they bowed down.
7 Leah likewise came near with her children, and they bowed down; and afterward Joseph came near with Rachel, and they bowed down.
8 And he said, "What do you mean by all this company which I have met?" And he said, "To find favor in the sight of my lord."
9 But Esau said, "I have plenty, my brother; let what you have be your own."
10 Jacob said, "No, please, if now I have found favor in your sight, then take my present from my hand, for I see your face as one sees the face of God, and you have received me favorably.
11 "Please take my gift which has been brought to you, because God has dealt

graciously with me and because I have plenty." Thus he urged him and he took *it*.
12 Then Esau said, "Let us take our journey and go, and I will go before you."
13 But he said to him, "My lord knows that the children are frail and that the flocks and herds which are nursing are a care to me. And if they are driven hard one day, all the flocks will die.
14 "Please let my lord pass on before his servant, and I will proceed at my leisure, according to the pace of the cattle that are before me and according to the pace of the children, until I come to my lord at Seir."
15 Esau said, "Please let me leave with you some of the people who are with me." But he said, "What need is there? Let me find favor in the sight of my lord."
16 So Esau returned that day on his way to Seir.
17 Jacob journeyed to Succoth, and built for himself a house and made booths for his livestock; therefore the place is named Succoth.
18 Now Jacob came safely to the city of Shechem, which is in the land of Canaan, when he came from Paddan-aram, and camped before the city.

LIFE LESSONS

➢ Genesis 33:11 — *"Please take my gift which has been brought to you, because God has dealt graciously with me."*

W e should be glad God does not deal with us on the basis of our own righteousness but on the basis of His boundless grace. He blesses us because of who He is, not who we are.

19 He bought the piece of land where he had pitched his tent from the hand of the sons of Hamor, Shechem's father, for one hundred pieces of money.

20 Then he erected there an altar and called it El-Elohe-Israel.

34 NOW Dinah the daughter of Leah, whom she had borne to Jacob, went out to visit the daughters of the land.

2 When Shechem the son of Hamor the Hivite, the prince of the land, saw her, he took her and lay with her by force.

3 He was deeply attracted to Dinah the daughter of Jacob, and he loved the girl and spoke tenderly to her.

4 So Shechem spoke to his father Hamor, saying, "Get me this young girl for a wife."

5 Now Jacob heard that he had defiled Dinah his daughter; but his sons were with his livestock in the field, so Jacob kept silent until they came in.

6 Then Hamor the father of Shechem went out to Jacob to speak with him.

7 Now the sons of Jacob came in from the field when they heard it; and the men were grieved, and they were very angry because he had done a disgraceful thing in Israel by lying with Jacob's daughter, for such a thing ought not to be done.

8 But Hamor spoke with them, saying, "The soul of my son Shechem longs for your daughter; please give her to him in marriage.

9 "Intermarry with us; give your daughters to us and take our daughters for yourselves.

10 "Thus you shall live with us, and the land shall be open before you; live and trade in it and acquire property in it."

11 Shechem also said to her father and to her brothers, "If I find favor in your sight, then I will give whatever you say to me.

12 "Ask me ever so much bridal payment and gift, and I will give according as you say to me; but give me the girl in marriage."

13 But Jacob's sons answered Shechem and his father Hamor with deceit, because he had defiled Dinah their sister.

14 They said to them, "We cannot do this thing, to give our sister to one who is uncircumcised, for that would be a disgrace to us.

15 "Only on this condition will we consent to you: if you will become like us, in that every male of you be circumcised,

16 then we will give our daughters to you, and we will take your daughters for ourselves, and we will live with you and become one people.

17 "But if you will not listen to us to be circumcised, then we will take our daughter and go."

18 Now their words seemed reasonable to Hamor and Shechem, Hamor's son.

19 The young man did not delay to do the thing, because he was delighted with Jacob's daughter. Now he was more respected than all the household of his father.

20 So Hamor and his son Shechem came to the gate of their city and spoke to the men of their city, saying,

21 "These men are friendly with us; therefore let them live in the land and trade in it, for behold, the land is large enough for them. Let us take their daughters in marriage, and give our daughters to them.

22 "Only on this condition will the men consent to us to live with us, to become one people: that every male among us be circumcised as they are circumcised.

23 "Will not their livestock and their property and all their animals be ours? Only let us consent to them, and they will live with us."

24 All who went out of the gate of his city listened to Hamor and to his son Shechem, and every male was circumcised, all who went out of the gate of his city.

25 Now it came about on the third day, when they were in pain, that two of Jacob's sons, Simeon and Levi, Dinah's brothers, each took his sword and came upon the city unawares, and killed every male.

26 They killed Hamor and his son Shechem with the edge of the sword, and took Dinah from Shechem's house, and went forth.

27 Jacob's sons came upon the slain and looted the city, because they had defiled their sister.

28 They took their flocks and their

herds and their donkeys, and that which was in the city and that which was in the field;

29 and they captured and looted all their wealth and all their little ones and their wives, even all that *was* in the houses.

30 Then Jacob said to Simeon and Levi, "You have brought trouble on me by making me odious among the inhabitants of the land, among the Canaanites and the Perizzites; and my men being few in number, they will gather together against me and attack me and I will be destroyed, I and my household."

31 But they said, "Should he treat our sister as a harlot?"

◈ Psalm 9:1–5

For the choir director; on Muth-labben. A Psalm of David.

9 I WILL give thanks to the LORD with all my heart;
I will tell of all Your wonders.

2 I will be glad and exult in You;

I will sing praise to Your name, O Most High.

3 When my enemies turn back, They stumble and perish before You.

4 For You have maintained my just cause;
You have sat on the throne judging righteously.

5 You have rebuked the nations, You have destroyed the wicked;
You have blotted out their name forever and ever.

◈ Proverbs 3:21–26

21 My son, let them not vanish from your sight;
Keep sound wisdom and discretion,

22 So they will be life to your soul And adornment to your neck.

23 Then you will walk in your way securely
And your foot will not stumble.

24 When you lie down, you will not be afraid;
When you lie down, your sleep will be sweet.

WHAT THE BIBLE SAYS ABOUT ◈

His Worthy, Eternal Name

Psalm 9:1, 2

*P*salm 9:1, 2 says, "I will give thanks to the LORD with all my heart; I will tell of all Your wonders. I will be glad and exult in You; I will sing praise to Your name, O Most High." Truly, we can agree God is worthy of praise, but why is His name written in such a unique way? What does it mean when we see God's name—LORD—in all capitals?

Whenever we see LORD presented in this way, it is because the original Hebrew text said "YHWH." These four letters are known as the *Tetragrammaton*—and they signify the personal name of God. Because YHWH does not have any vowels, we do not know exactly how to pronounce God's name. Most often, we hear His name pronounced as *Yahweh* or *Jehovah*.

However, what is really important is this wondrous name reflects God's character. *YHWH* means He is the existing one—the "I AM." God told Moses in Exodus 3:14, "I AM WHO I AM." Because the Hebrew language does not indicate time here, another way we could translate this is, "I WILL ALWAYS BE WHO I HAVE ALWAYS BEEN," or "I WILL FOREVER BE WHO I AM NOW."

God never changes. As faithful and loving as He was yesterday, He will also be today, and He will continue to be for all eternity (Heb. 13:8). That is why God is so worthy of our praise and adoration—because we are certain He will help us with the same wisdom, love, and power as He's helped all those before us.

Therefore, whenever you see LORD in all capitals, give Him the praise He deserves. Echo the words of the prophet Jeremiah, "There is none like You, O LORD; You are great, and great is Your name in might" (Jer. 10:6). ◈

LIFE LESSONS

➤ **Proverbs 3:26** — *The LORD will be your confidence and will keep your foot from being caught.*

*W*hen we listen to God and obey His commands, He gives us the wisdom we need to avoid dishonest schemes. As Psalm 119:110 says, "The wicked have laid a snare for me, yet I have not gone astray from Your precepts." God protects us when we obey Him by giving us wisdom.

➤ **Matthew 12:8** — *"The Son of Man is Lord of the Sabbath."*

*A*s the Creator of heaven and earth, Jesus was far greater than the Sabbath, a day instituted to remember His work of creation. Jesus is Lord of all, and the Sabbath is intended to honor Him.

25 Do not be afraid of sudden fear
    Nor of the onslaught of the wicked
        when it comes;
26 For the LORD will be your
        confidence
    And will keep your foot from being
        caught.

Matthew 12:1–21

12 AT that time Jesus went through the grainfields on the Sabbath, and His disciples became hungry and began to pick the heads of grain and eat.
2   But when the Pharisees saw *this*, they said to Him, "Look, Your disciples do what is not lawful to do on a Sabbath."
3   But He said to them, "Have you not read what David did when he became hungry, he and his companions,
4   how he entered the house of God, and they ate the consecrated bread, which was not lawful for him to eat nor for those with him, but for the priests alone?
5   "Or have you not read in the Law, that on the Sabbath the priests in the temple break the Sabbath and are innocent?

6   "But I say to you that something greater than the temple is here.
7   "But if you had known what this means, 'I DESIRE COMPASSION, AND NOT A SACRIFICE,' you would not have condemned the innocent.
8   "For the Son of Man is Lord of the Sabbath."
9   Departing from there, He went into their synagogue.
10 And a man *was there* whose hand was withered. And they questioned Jesus, asking, "Is it lawful to heal on the Sabbath?"—so that they might accuse Him.
11 And He said to them, "What man is there among you who has a sheep, and if it falls into a pit on the Sabbath, will he not take hold of it and lift it out?
12 "How much more valuable then is a man than a sheep! So then, it is lawful to do good on the Sabbath."
13 Then He *said to the man, "Stretch out your hand!" He stretched it out, and it was restored to normal, like the other.
14 But the Pharisees went out and conspired against Him, *as to* how they might destroy Him.
15 But Jesus, aware of *this*, withdrew from there. Many followed Him, and He healed them all,
16 and warned them not to tell who He was.
17 *This was* to fulfill what was spoken through Isaiah the prophet:
18 "BEHOLD, MY SERVANT WHOM I HAVE CHOSEN;
        MY BELOVED IN WHOM MY SOUL is
            WELL-PLEASED;
        I WILL PUT MY SPIRIT UPON HIM,
        AND HE SHALL PROCLAIM JUSTICE TO
            THE GENTILES.
19 "HE WILL NOT QUARREL, NOR CRY
            OUT;
        NOR WILL ANYONE HEAR HIS VOICE
            IN THE STREETS.
20 "A BATTERED REED HE WILL NOT
            BREAK OFF,
        AND A SMOLDERING WICK HE WILL
            NOT PUT OUT,
        UNTIL HE LEADS JUSTICE TO
            VICTORY.
21 "AND IN HIS NAME THE GENTILES
            WILL HOPE."

Genesis 35:1—36:43

35 THEN God said to Jacob, "Arise, go up to Bethel and live there, and make an altar there to God, who appeared to you when you fled from your brother Esau."

2 So Jacob said to his household and to all who were with him, "Put away the foreign gods which are among you, and purify yourselves and change your garments;

3 and let us arise and go up to Bethel, and I will make an altar there to God, who answered me in the day of my distress and has been with me wherever I have gone."

4 So they gave to Jacob all the foreign gods which they had and the rings which were in their ears, and Jacob hid them under the oak which was near Shechem.

5 As they journeyed, there was a great terror upon the cities which were around them, and they did not pursue the sons of Jacob.

6 So Jacob came to Luz (that is, Bethel), which is in the land of Canaan, he and all the people who were with him.

7 He built an altar there, and called the place El-bethel, because there God had revealed Himself to him when he fled from his brother.

8 Now Deborah, Rebekah's nurse, died, and she was buried below Bethel under the oak; it was named Allon-bacuth.

9 Then God appeared to Jacob again when he came from Paddan-aram, and He blessed him.

10 God said to him,
"Your name is Jacob;
You shall no longer be called Jacob,
But Israel shall be your name."

Thus He called him Israel.

11 God also said to him,
"I am God Almighty;
Be fruitful and multiply;
A nation and a company of nations
shall come from you,
And kings shall come forth from
you.

12 "The land which I gave to Abraham
and Isaac,
I will give it to you,
And I will give the land to your
descendants after you."

13 Then God went up from him in the place where He had spoken with him.

14 Jacob set up a pillar in the place where He had spoken with him, a pillar of stone, and he poured out a drink offering on it; he also poured oil on it.

15 So Jacob named the place where God had spoken with him, Bethel.

16 Then they journeyed from Bethel; and when there was still some distance to go to Ephrath, Rachel began to give birth and she suffered severe labor.

17 When she was in severe labor the midwife said to her, "Do not fear, for now you have another son."

18 It came about as her soul was departing (for she died), that she named him Ben-oni; but his father called him Benjamin.

19 So Rachel died and was buried on the way to Ephrath (that is, Bethlehem).

20 Jacob set up a pillar over her grave; that is the pillar of Rachel's grave to this day.

21 Then Israel journeyed on and pitched his tent beyond the tower of Eder.

22 It came about while Israel was dwelling in that land, that Reuben went and lay with Bilhah his father's concubine, and Israel heard of it.

Now there were twelve sons of Jacob—

23 the sons of Leah: Reuben, Jacob's firstborn, then Simeon and Levi and Judah and Issachar and Zebulun;

24 the sons of Rachel: Joseph and Benjamin;

25 and the sons of Bilhah, Rachel's maid: Dan and Naphtali;

26 and the sons of Zilpah, Leah's maid: Gad and Asher. These are the sons of Jacob who were born to him in Paddan-aram.

LIFE LESSONS

➤ Genesis 35:2 — "Put away the foreign gods which are among you."

God calls for our exclusive allegiance—not allegiance to God *and* something or someone else, but allegiance to God alone. He will accept no other kind of loyalty.

27 Jacob came to his father Isaac at Mamre of Kiriath-arba (that is, Hebron), where Abraham and Isaac had sojourned.
28 Now the days of Isaac were one hundred and eighty years.
29 Isaac breathed his last and died and was gathered to his people, an old man of ripe age; and his sons Esau and Jacob buried him.

36 NOW these are *the records of* the generations of Esau (that is, Edom).
2 Esau took his wives from the daughters of Canaan: Adah the daughter of Elon the Hittite, and Oholibamah the daughter of Anah and the granddaughter of Zibeon the Hivite;
3 also Basemath, Ishmael's daughter, the sister of Nebaioth.
4 Adah bore Eliphaz to Esau, and Basemath bore Reuel,
5 and Oholibamah bore Jeush and Jalam and Korah. These are the sons of Esau who were born to him in the land of Canaan.
6 Then Esau took his wives and his sons and his daughters and all his household, and his livestock and all his cattle and all his goods which he had acquired in the land of Canaan, and went to *another* land away from his brother Jacob.
7 For their property had become too great for them to live together, and the land where they sojourned could not sustain them because of their livestock.
8 So Esau lived in the hill country of Seir; Esau is Edom.
9 These then are *the records of* the generations of Esau the father of the Edomites in the hill country of Seir.
10 These are the names of Esau's sons: Eliphaz the son of Esau's wife Adah, Reuel the son of Esau's wife Basemath.
11 The sons of Eliphaz were Teman, Omar, Zepho and Gatam and Kenaz.
12 Timna was a concubine of Esau's son Eliphaz and she bore Amalek to Eliphaz. These are the sons of Esau's wife Adah.
13 These are the sons of Reuel: Nahath and Zerah, Shammah and Mizzah. These were the sons of Esau's wife Basemath.
14 These were the sons of Esau's wife Oholibamah, the daughter of Anah and the granddaughter of Zibeon: she bore to Esau, Jeush and Jalam and Korah.
15 These are the chiefs of the sons of Esau. The sons of Eliphaz, the firstborn of Esau, are chief Teman, chief Omar, chief Zepho, chief Kenaz,
16 chief Korah, chief Gatam, chief Amalek. These are the chiefs descended from Eliphaz in the land of Edom; these are the sons of Adah.
17 These are the sons of Reuel, Esau's son: chief Nahath, chief Zerah, chief Shammah, chief Mizzah. These are the chiefs descended from Reuel in the land of Edom; these are the sons of Esau's wife Basemath.
18 These are the sons of Esau's wife Oholibamah: chief Jeush, chief Jalam, chief Korah. These are the chiefs descended from Esau's wife Oholibamah, the daughter of Anah.
19 These are the sons of Esau (that is, Edom), and these are their chiefs.
20 These are the sons of Seir the Horite, the inhabitants of the land: Lotan and Shobal and Zibeon and Anah,
21 and Dishon and Ezer and Dishan. These are the chiefs descended from the Horites, the sons of Seir in the land of Edom.
22 The sons of Lotan were Hori and Hemam; and Lotan's sister was Timna.
23 These are the sons of Shobal: Alvan and Manahath and Ebal, Shepho and Onam.
24 These are the sons of Zibeon: Aiah and Anah—he is the Anah who found the hot springs in the wilderness when he was pasturing the donkeys of his father Zibeon.
25 These are the children of Anah: Dishon, and Oholibamah, the daughter of Anah.
26 These are the sons of Dishon: Hemdan and Eshban and Ithran and Cheran.
27 These are the sons of Ezer: Bilhan and Zaavan and Akan.
28 These are the sons of Dishan: Uz and Aran.
29 These are the chiefs descended from the Horites: chief Lotan, chief Shobal, chief Zibeon, chief Anah,
30 chief Dishon, chief Ezer, chief Dishan. These are the chiefs descended from the Horites, according to their *various* chiefs in the land of Seir.

31 Now these are the kings who reigned in the land of Edom before any king reigned over the sons of Israel.

32 Bela the son of Beor reigned in Edom, and the name of his city was Dinhabah.

33 Then Bela died, and Jobab the son of Zerah of Bozrah became king in his place.

34 Then Jobab died, and Husham of the land of the Temanites became king in his place.

35 Then Husham died, and Hadad the son of Bedad, who defeated Midian in the field of Moab, became king in his place; and the name of his city was Avith.

36 Then Hadad died, and Samlah of Masrekah became king in his place.

37 Then Samlah died, and Shaul of Rehoboth on the *Euphrates* River became king in his place.

38 Then Shaul died, and Baal-hanan the son of Achbor became king in his place.

39 Then Baal-hanan the son of Achbor died, and Hadar became king in his place; and the name of his city was Pau; and his wife's name was Mehetabel, the daughter of Matred, daughter of Mezahab.

40 Now these are the names of the chiefs descended from Esau, according to their families *and* their localities, by their names: chief Timna, chief Alvah, chief Jetheth,

41 chief Oholibamah, chief Elah, chief Pinon,

42 chief Kenaz, chief Teman, chief Mibzar,

43 chief Magdiel, chief Iram. These are the chiefs of Edom (that is, Esau, the father of the Edomites), according to their habitations in the land of their possession.

Psalm 9:6–10

6 The enemy has come to an end in perpetual ruins,
And You have uprooted the cities;
The very memory of them has perished.

7 But the LORD abides forever;

He has established His throne for judgment,

8 And He will judge the world in righteousness;
He will execute judgment for the peoples with equity.

9 The LORD also will be a stronghold for the oppressed,
A stronghold in times of trouble;

10 And those who know Your name will put their trust in You,
For You, O LORD, have not forsaken those who seek You.

Proverbs 3:27–30

27 Do not withhold good from those to whom it is due,
When it is in your power to do *it.*

28 Do not say to your neighbor, "Go, and come back,
And tomorrow I will give *it*,"
When you have it with you.

29 Do not devise harm against your neighbor,
While he lives securely beside you.

30 Do not contend with a man without cause,
If he has done you no harm.

LIFE LESSONS

➤ **Psalm 9:7 —** *The* LORD *abides forever; He has established His throne for judgment.*

God never had a beginning, and He will never have an end. That makes Him the perfect judge, for He knows all the causes leading up to an event and all the consequences leading from it. He judges perfectly.

➤ **Psalm 9:10 —** *Those who know Your name will put their trust in You, for You, O* LORD, *have not forsaken those who seek You.*

God never forsakes any man or woman who places his or her trust in Him. He may allow them to wade through some very deep and cold waters, but He will never abandon them. When everyone else flees, He remains.

Matthew 12:22–50

22 Then a demon-possessed man *who was* blind and mute was brought to Jesus, and He healed him, so that the mute man spoke and saw.
23 All the crowds were amazed, and were saying, "This man cannot be the Son of David, can he?"
24 But when the Pharisees heard *this,* they said, "This man casts out demons only by Beelzebul the ruler of the demons."
➤ 25 And knowing their thoughts Jesus said to them, "Any kingdom divided against itself is laid waste; and any city or house divided against itself will not stand.
26 "If Satan casts out Satan, he is divided against himself; how then will his kingdom stand?
27 "If I by Beelzebul cast out demons,

WHAT THE BIBLE SAYS ABOUT

Binding Satan

Matthew 12:22–29

*J*esus triumphed over Satan at the Cross—a victory that contained absolutely no hint of defeat. You also can claim victory over the enemy in daily battles because, as a believer, you are indwelt with the triumphant power of Jesus Christ through the presence of the Holy Spirit. You have the privilege of calling upon the divine power of God, which ultimately means you have authority over Satan and all his demons (1 John 4:4).

How does one bind the enemy by the power of the Holy Spirit and experience the Lord's release and restoration? There are three steps you must take:
1. *Claim the name of Jesus.*
The Bible tells us to pray in Jesus' name (John 16:23). Throughout the New Testament, the apostles healed and performed the works of the Lord in Jesus' name (Acts 3:6). You and I transact spiritual business, so to speak, by using the name of the Lord Jesus Christ. When we use the name of Jesus, we are doing what He has called us to do: act with authority over the enemy by demonstrating who we are in

LIFE LESSONS

➤ **Matthew 12:25 — *And knowing their thoughts Jesus said to them . . .***

*T*he Book of Hebrews says, "all things are open and laid bare to the eyes of Him with whom we have to do" (4:13). And Paul says the Lord will "disclose the motives of men's hearts" (1 Cor. 4:5).

by whom do your sons cast *them* out? For this reason they will be your judges.
28 "But if I cast out demons by the Spirit of God, then the kingdom of God has come upon you.
29 "Or how can anyone enter the strong man's house and carry off his property, unless he first binds the strong *man?* And then he will plunder his house.

Christ. Can you imagine what would happen to the church if believers took God at His Word and appropriated the power of the Holy Spirit?
2. *Claim the blood of Jesus.*
We dare not come boldly into battle with Satan without the protection of the shed blood of Jesus Christ. Throughout Scripture, we learn His blood is our protection and the basis of our redemption (Ex. 12; Matt. 26:28; Eph. 1:7; Heb. 9:11–28). The blood of Christ's sacrifice paid the price of sin and eternally broke the power of Satan over us.
3. *Claim the Word of God.*
Jesus put an end to Satan's words of temptation by quoting Scripture. He confronted the enemy with the Word of God, and we must do the same. Never argue with Satan. Notice Jesus did not get into a battle of words. He spoke the truth of God's Word, and it stopped the enemy in his tracks.

The power to defeat Satan is available to every believer. Every one of us has the ability to deal with the enemy by the almighty, supernatural power of God. We have the right to declare Satan bound, his work restricted, and the prisoner set free. Allow God to show you the victory and work though you to the maximum every day. ❖

LIFE LESSONS

➤ **Matthew 12:31** — *"Therefore I say to you, any sin and blasphemy shall be forgiven people, but blasphemy against the Spirit shall not be forgiven."*

*B*lasphemy against the Spirit is unforgivable because it prevents repentance. Some worry they have committed the unforgivable sin, but God will *never* reject anyone who is truly repentant.

➤ **Matthew 12:50** — *"Whoever does the will of My Father who is in heaven, he is My brother and sister and mother."*

*J*esus came to earth to do the will of His Father, so anyone who has the same goal is one in spirit with Him. A genuine desire to please God creates a stronger bond than anything else in the universe.

30 "He who is not with Me is against Me; and he who does not gather with Me scatters.

➤ 31 "Therefore I say to you, any sin and blasphemy shall be forgiven people, but blasphemy against the Spirit shall not be forgiven.

32 "Whoever speaks a word against the Son of Man, it shall be forgiven him; but whoever speaks against the Holy Spirit, it shall not be forgiven him, either in this age or in the *age* to come.

33 "Either make the tree good and its fruit good, or make the tree bad and its fruit bad; for the tree is known by its fruit.

34 "You brood of vipers, how can you, being evil, speak what is good? For the mouth speaks out of that which fills the heart.

✳ 35 "The good man brings out of *his* good treasure what is good; and the evil man brings out of *his* evil treasure what is evil.

36 "But I tell you that every careless word that people speak, they shall give an accounting for it in the day of judgment.

37 "For by your words you will be justified, and by your words you will be condemned."

38 Then some of the scribes and Pharisees said to Him, "Teacher, we want to see a sign from You."

39 But He answered and said to them, "An evil and adulterous generation craves for a sign; and *yet* no sign will be given to it but the sign of Jonah the prophet;

40 for just as JONAH WAS THREE DAYS AND THREE NIGHTS IN THE BELLY OF THE SEA MONSTER, so will the Son of Man be three days and three nights in the heart of the earth.

41 "The men of Nineveh will stand up with this generation at the judgment, and will condemn it because they repented at the preaching of Jonah; and behold, something greater than Jonah is here.

42 "*The* Queen of *the* South will rise up with this generation at the judgment and will condemn it, because she came from the ends of the earth to hear the wisdom of Solomon; and behold, something greater than Solomon is here.

43 "Now when the unclean spirit goes out of a man, it passes through waterless places seeking rest, and does not find *it*.

44 "Then it says, 'I will return to my house from which I came'; and when it comes, it finds *it* unoccupied, swept, and put in order.

45 "Then it goes and takes along with it seven other spirits more wicked than itself, and they go in and live there; and the last state of that man becomes worse than the first. That is the way it will also be with this evil generation."

46 While He was still speaking to the crowds, behold, His mother and brothers were standing outside, seeking to speak to Him.

47 Someone said to Him, "Behold, Your mother and Your brothers are standing outside seeking to speak to You."

48 But Jesus answered the one who was telling Him and said, "Who is My mother and who are My brothers?"

49 And stretching out His hand toward His disciples, He said, "Behold My mother and My brothers!

50 "For whoever does the will of My Father who is in heaven, he is My brother and sister and mother." ➤

---

37 NOW Jacob lived in the land where his father had sojourned, in the land of Canaan.

2 These are *the records of* the generations of Jacob.

Joseph, when seventeen years of age, was pasturing the flock with his brothers while he was *still* a youth, along with the sons of Bilhah and the sons of Zilpah, his father's wives. And Joseph brought back a bad report about them to their father.

3 Now Israel loved Joseph more than all his sons, because he was the son of his old age; and he made him a varicolored tunic.

4 His brothers saw that their father loved him more than all his brothers; and so they hated him and could not speak to him on friendly terms.

5 Then Joseph had a dream, and when he told it to his brothers, they hated him even more.

6 He said to them, "Please listen to this dream which I have had;

7 for behold, we were binding sheaves in the field, and lo, my sheaf rose up and also stood erect; and behold, your sheaves gathered around and bowed down to my sheaf."

8 Then his brothers said to him, "Are you actually going to reign over us? Or are you really going to rule over us?" So they hated him even more for his dreams and for his words.

9 Now he had still another dream, and related it to his brothers, and said, "Lo, I have had still another dream; and behold, the sun and the moon and eleven stars were bowing down to me."

10 He related *it* to his father and to his brothers; and his father rebuked him and said to him, "What is this dream that you have had? Shall I and your mother and

---

ANSWERS TO LIFE'S QUESTIONS

How can I deal effectively with jealousy?

GENESIS 37

*H*ave you ever felt jealous of someone else's success? Maybe your neighbor has a brand new car, or perhaps someone at work got the promotion you desired. When situations like these stir up unexpected reactions within us, we just might have a problem.

Jealousy is the emotion of extreme displeasure upon seeing someone else's good fortune—and it can poison good relationships, ruin our witness, and keep us from experiencing God's blessings. The Bible calls jealousy a work of the flesh (Gal. 5:19, 20).

Is it possible to take control of a jealous attitude? Yes! Since God wants His children to take charge over these volatile emotions, let's examine some specific things you can do to gain victory.

1. *Confess your jealousy.* This emotion will always—*always*—take your eyes off the Lord and fix them on some other person or object. That, at its heart, is idolatry. Whenever you place a higher value on some "thing" than you place on God,

you put yourself under divine judgment. Repent of that sin immediately!

2. *Realize you disagree with God.* If the Lord chooses to bring some specific blessing into another person's life, then that is His prerogative. Your jealousy merely declares you think you deserve the blessing more than the other person. Bring this disagreement honestly before the Lord, and ask Him to restore a godly perspective to you.

3. *Thank God for what He's doing in that person's life.* You may not like this point. But when you praise God—even if you do not feel like it—you put yourself in a position to receive His blessings by showing you fully trust His judgment.

4. *Ask God to place love in your heart for the other person.* So often in Scripture the word *anger* follows the word *jealous.* Do not allow jealousy to stir up malice and hate. Instead, learn how to rejoice when others receive blessings, even when you believe you should have received those blessings instead.

5. *Keep your focus on God alone.* Delight in Him, knowing He's promised to give you the desires of your heart. Focus first and foremost on what He's done for you and on the promises He's made to you through His Word. Always remember God is God, and it is His prerogative to bless each one of us in exactly the way He sees fit.

your brothers actually come to bow our-selves down before you to the ground?"
11 His brothers were jealous of him, but his father kept the saying in mind.
12 Then his brothers went to pasture their father's flock in Shechem.
13 Israel said to Joseph, "Are not your brothers pasturing the flock in Shechem? Come, and I will send you to them." And he said to him, "I will go."
14 Then he said to him, "Go now and see about the welfare of your brothers and the welfare of the flock, and bring word back to me." So he sent him from the valley of Hebron, and he came to Shechem.
15 A man found him, and behold, he was wandering in the field; and the man asked him, "What are you looking for?"
16 He said, "I am looking for my broth-ers; please tell me where they are pastur-ing the flock."
17 Then the man said, "They have moved from here; for I heard them say, 'Let us go to Dothan.'" So Joseph went after his brothers and found them at Do-than.
18 When they saw him from a distance and before he came close to them, they plotted against him to put him to death.
19 They said to one another, "Here comes this dreamer!
20 "Now then, come and let us kill him and throw him into one of the pits; and we will say, 'A wild beast devoured him.' Then let us see what will become of his dreams!"
21 But Reuben heard this and rescued him out of their hands and said, "Let us not take his life."
22 Reuben further said to them, "Shed no blood. Throw him into this pit that is in the wilderness, but do not lay hands on him"—that he might rescue him out of their hands, to restore him to his father.
23 So it came about, when Joseph reached his brothers, that they stripped Joseph of his tunic, the varicolored tunic that was on him;
24 and they took him and threw him into the pit. Now the pit was empty, with-out any water in it.
25 Then they sat down to eat a meal. And as they raised their eyes and looked, behold, a caravan of Ishmaelites was coming from Gilead, with their camels bearing aromatic gum and balm and

myrrh, on their way to bring them down to Egypt.
26 Judah said to his brothers, "What profit is it for us to kill our brother and cover up his blood?
27 "Come and let us sell him to the Ish-maelites and not lay our hands on him, for he is our brother, our own flesh." And his brothers listened to him.
28 Then some Midianite traders passed by, so they pulled him up and lifted Joseph out of the pit, and sold him to the Ishmaelites for twenty shekels of silver. Thus they brought Joseph into Egypt.
29 Now Reuben returned to the pit, and behold, Joseph was not in the pit; so he tore his garments.
30 He returned to his brothers and said, "The boy is not there; as for me, where am I to go?"
31 So they took Joseph's tunic, and slaughtered a male goat and dipped the tunic in the blood;
32 and they sent the varicolored tunic and brought it to their father and said, "We found this; please examine it to see whether it is your son's tunic or not."
33 Then he examined it and said, "It is my son's tunic. A wild beast has de-voured him; Joseph has surely been torn to pieces!"
34 So Jacob tore his clothes, and put sackcloth on his loins and mourned for his son many days.
35 Then all his sons and all his daugh-ters arose to comfort him, but he refused to be comforted. And he said, "Surely I will go down to Sheol in mourning for my son." So his father wept for him.
36 Meanwhile, the Midianites sold him in Egypt to Potiphar, Pharaoh's officer, the captain of the bodyguard.

38 AND it came about at that time, that Judah departed from his brothers and visited a certain Adullamite, whose name was Hirah.
2 Judah saw there a daughter of a cer-tain Canaanite whose name was Shua; and he took her and went in to her.
3 So she conceived and bore a son and he named him Er.
4 Then she conceived again and bore a son and named him Onan.
5 She bore still another son and named him Shelah; and it was at Chezib that she bore him.

6 Now Judah took a wife for Er his firstborn, and her name *was* Tamar.

7 But Er, Judah's firstborn, was evil in the sight of the LORD, so the LORD took his life.

8 Then Judah said to Onan, "Go in to your brother's wife, and perform your duty as a brother-in-law to her, and raise up offspring for your brother."

9 Onan knew that the offspring would not be his; so when he went in to his brother's wife, he wasted his seed on the ground in order not to give offspring to his brother.

➢ **10** But what he did was displeasing in the sight of the LORD; so He took his life also.

11 Then Judah said to his daughter-in-law Tamar, "Remain a widow in your father's house until my son Shelah grows up"; for he thought, "*I am afraid* that he too may die like his brothers." So Tamar went and lived in her father's house.

12 Now after a considerable time Shua's daughter, the wife of Judah, died; and when the time of mourning was ended, Judah went up to his sheepshearers at Timnah, he and his friend Hirah the Adullamite.

13 It was told to Tamar, "Behold, your father-in-law is going up to Timnah to shear his sheep."

14 So she removed her widow's garments and covered *herself* with a veil, and wrapped herself, and sat in the gateway of Enaim, which is on the road to Timnah; for she saw that Shelah had grown up, and she had not been given to him as a wife.

15 When Judah saw her, he thought she *was* a harlot, for she had covered her face.

16 So he turned aside to her by the road, and said, "Here now, let me come in to you"; for he did not know that she

was his daughter-in-law. And she said, "What will you give me, that you may come in to me?"

17 He said, therefore, "I will send you a young goat from the flock." She said, moreover, "Will you give a pledge until you send *it?*"

18 He said, "What pledge shall I give you?" And she said, "Your seal and your cord, and your staff that is in your hand." So he gave *them* to her and went in to her, and she conceived by him.

19 Then she arose and departed, and removed her veil and put on her widow's garments.

20 When Judah sent the young goat by his friend the Adullamite, to receive the pledge from the woman's hand, he did not find her.

21 He asked the men of her place, saying, "Where is the temple prostitute who was by the road at Enaim?" But they said, "There has been no temple prostitute here."

22 So he returned to Judah, and said, "I did not find her; and furthermore, the men of the place said, 'There has been no temple prostitute here.'"

23 Then Judah said, "Let her keep them, otherwise we will become a laughingstock. After all, I sent this young goat, but you did not find her."

24 Now it was about three months later that Judah was informed, "Your daughter-in-law Tamar has played the harlot, and behold, she is also with child by harlotry." Then Judah said, "Bring her out and let her be burned!"

25 It was while she was being brought out that she sent to her father-in-law, saying, "I am with child by the man to whom these things belong." And she said, "Please examine and see, whose signet ring and cords and staff are these?"

26 Judah recognized *them*, and said, "She is more righteous than I, inasmuch as I did not give her to my son Shelah." And he did not have relations with her again.

27 It came about at the time she was giving birth, that behold, there were twins in her womb.

28 Moreover, it took place while she was giving birth, one put out a hand, and the midwife took and tied a scarlet

---

LIFE LESSONS

➢ **Genesis 38:10 — *But what he did was displeasing in the sight of the LORD; so He took his life also.***

*I*f we ever doubt we serve a holy and righteous God who hates sin, we should remember Er and Onan, the wicked sons of Judah (Gen. 38:6–9).

thread on his hand, saying, "This one came out first."

29 But it came about as he drew back his hand, that behold, his brother came out. Then she said, "What a breach you have made for yourself!" So he was named Perez.

30 Afterward his brother came out who had the scarlet *thread* on his hand; and he was named Zerah.

Psalm 9:11–20

11 Sing praises to the LORD, who dwells in Zion;
   Declare among the peoples His deeds.

12 For He who requires blood remembers them;
   He does not forget the cry of the afflicted.

13 Be gracious to me, O LORD;
   See my affliction from those who hate me,
   You who lift me up from the gates of death,

14 That I may tell of all Your praises,
   That in the gates of the daughter of Zion
   I may rejoice in Your salvation.

15 The nations have sunk down in the pit which they have made;
   In the net which they hid, their own foot has been caught.

16 The LORD has made Himself known;
   He has executed judgment.
   In the work of his own hands the wicked is snared.
                    Higgaion Selah.

17 The wicked will return to Sheol,
   Even all the nations who forget God.

18 For the needy will not always be forgotten,
   Nor the hope of the afflicted perish forever.

19 Arise, O LORD, do not let man prevail;
   Let the nations be judged before You.

20 Put them in fear, O LORD;
   Let the nations know that they are but men.   Selah.

Proverbs 3:31–35

31 Do not envy a man of violence
   And do not choose any of his ways.

32 For the devious are an abomination to the LORD;
   But He is intimate with the upright.

33 The curse of the LORD is on the house of the wicked,
   But He blesses the dwelling of the righteous.

34 Though He scoffs at the scoffers,
   Yet He gives grace to the afflicted.

35 The wise will inherit honor,
   But fools display dishonor.

Matthew 13:1–30

13 THAT day Jesus went out of the house and was sitting by the sea.

2 And large crowds gathered to Him, so He got into a boat and sat down, and the whole crowd was standing on the beach.

3 And He spoke many things to them in parables, saying, "Behold, the sower went out to sow;

4 and as he sowed, some *seeds* fell beside the road, and the birds came and ate them up.

5 "Others fell on the rocky places, where they did not have much soil; and immediately they sprang up, because they had no depth of soil.

6 "But when the sun had risen, they were scorched; and because they had no root, they withered away.

7 "Others fell among the thorns, and the thorns came up and choked them out.

8 "And others fell on the good soil and *yielded a crop, some a hundredfold, some sixty, and some thirty.

9 "He who has ears, let him hear."

10 And the disciples came and said to Him, "Why do You speak to them in parables?"

11 Jesus answered them, "To you it has been granted to know the mysteries of the kingdom of heaven, but to them it has not been granted.

12 "For whoever has, to him *more* shall be given, and he will have an abundance;

but whoever does not have, even what he has shall be taken away from him.

13 "Therefore I speak to them in parables; because while seeing they do not see, and while hearing they do not hear, nor do they understand.

14 "In their case the prophecy of Isaiah is being fulfilled, which says,

'YOU WILL KEEP ON HEARING, BUT WILL
    NOT UNDERSTAND;
YOU WILL KEEP ON SEEING, BUT WILL
    NOT PERCEIVE;

15 FOR THE HEART OF THIS PEOPLE HAS
    BECOME DULL,
WITH THEIR EARS THEY SCARCELY
    HEAR,
AND THEY HAVE CLOSED THEIR EYES,
OTHERWISE THEY WOULD SEE WITH
    THEIR EYES,
HEAR WITH THEIR EARS,
AND UNDERSTAND WITH THEIR HEART
    AND RETURN,
AND I WOULD HEAL THEM.'

16 "But blessed are your eyes, because they see; and your ears, because they hear.

17 "For truly I say to you that many prophets and righteous men desired to see what you see, and did not see *it*, and to hear what you hear, and did not hear *it*.

18 "Hear then the parable of the sower.

19 "When anyone hears the word of the kingdom and does not understand it, the evil *one* comes and snatches away what has been sown in his heart. This is the one on whom seed was sown beside the road.

20 "The one on whom seed was sown on the rocky places, this is the man who hears the word and immediately receives it with joy;

21 yet he has no *firm* root in himself, but is *only* temporary, and when affliction or persecution arises because of the word, immediately he falls away.

22 "And the one on whom seed was sown among the thorns, this is the man who hears the word, and the worry of the world and the deceitfulness of wealth choke the word, and it becomes unfruitful.

23 "And the one on whom seed was sown on the good soil, this is the man who hears the word and understands it; who indeed bears fruit and brings forth, some a hundredfold, some sixty, and some thirty."

24 Jesus presented another parable to them, saying, "The kingdom of heaven may be compared to a man who sowed good seed in his field.

25 "But while his men were sleeping, his enemy came and sowed tares among the wheat, and went away.

26 "But when the wheat sprouted and bore grain, then the tares became evident also.

27 "The slaves of the landowner came and said to him, 'Sir, did you not sow good seed in your field? How then does it have tares?'

28 "And he said to them, 'An enemy has done this!' The slaves *said to him, 'Do you want us, then, to go and gather them up?'

29 "But he *said, 'No; for while you are gathering up the tares, you may uproot the wheat with them.

30 'Allow both to grow together until the harvest; and in the time of the harvest I will say to the reapers, "First gather up the tares and bind them in bundles to burn them up; but gather the wheat into my barn."'"

LIFE LESSONS

➤ **Matthew 13:12** — *"For whoever has, to him more shall be given, and he will have an abundance; but whoever does not have, even what he has shall be taken away from him."*

This combination of promise and warning typifies a great deal of God's instruction in His Word. He motivates us to experience life through both offers of blessing and declarations of caution.

➤ **Matthew 13:23** — *"And the one on whom seed was sown on the good soil, this is the man who hears the word and understands it; who indeed bears fruit."*

God wants us to hear, understand, and put into practice His counsel and instruction. He doesn't see us as vaults into which He hides His Word, but rather as gardens in which His Word can sprout and grow.

Genesis 39:1—40:23

39 NOW Joseph had been taken down to Egypt; and Potiphar, an Egyptian officer of Pharaoh, the captain of the bodyguard, bought him from the Ishmaelites, who had taken him down there.
2   The LORD was with Joseph, so he became a successful man. And he was in the house of his master, the Egyptian.
3   Now his master saw that the LORD was with him and *how* the LORD caused all that he did to prosper in his hand.
4   So Joseph found favor in his sight and became his personal servant; and he made him overseer over his house, and all that he owned he put in his charge.
5   It came about that from the time he made him overseer in his house and over all that he owned, the LORD blessed the Egyptian's house on account of Joseph; thus the LORD'S blessing was upon all that he owned, in the house and in the field.
6   So he left everything he owned in Joseph's charge; and with him *there* he

LIFE LESSONS

> **Genesis 39:2 —** *The* LORD *was with Joseph, so he became a successful man.*

Joseph is a prime illustration of the truth that adversity is a setback from which we take our greatest leaps forward.

did not concern himself with anything except the food which he ate.
    Now Joseph was handsome in form and appearance.
7   It came about after these events that his master's wife looked with desire at Joseph, and she said, "Lie with me."
8   But he refused and said to his master's wife, "Behold, with me *here*, my master does not concern himself with anything in the house, and he has put all that he owns in my charge.
9   "There is no one greater in this house than I, and he has withheld nothing from me except you, because you are his wife. How then could I do this great evil and sin against God?"

WHAT THE BIBLE SAYS ABOUT

The Value of Hard Work

Genesis 39:2

While God requires us to work, at the same time, He leads others to pay us a fair wage for the work we do. We find a marvelous example of good compensation for hard work in the life of Joseph, the eleventh son of Jacob. Joseph's spiteful brothers sold him into slavery to some passing merchants, and eventually the young man ended up the property of a powerful Egyptian official. Yet despite Joseph's slavery, "The LORD was with Joseph, so he became a successful man . . . Now his master saw that the LORD was with him and how the LORD caused all that he did to prosper in his hand. So Joseph found favor in his sight and became his personal servant; and he made him overseer over his house, and all that he owned he put in his charge . . . the LORD blessed the Egyptian's house on account of Joseph . . . So he left everything he owned in Joseph's charge" (Gen. 39:2–6).

Joseph did not own the large Egyptian estate he managed. Yet he had full run of it. Even though he was in a difficult place, God was using Him and he was fully in charge of his master's property. He lived well, ate well, and dressed well. He had all of his material needs met. Why? Because the Lord caused his master to deal with him favorably. The same can be true of your life.

If you are giving your best effort at work and are trusting God to give you wisdom in all of your endeavors, then watch for the ways in which the Lord will cause others to bless you.

Second, the Egyptian received blessing in return. He had no worries or concerns while Joseph managed his household. Joseph had proven himself worthy of his trust.

God calls you to give maximum effort in your work and to do all you can to earn the trust of those who work with you or who supervise you. How can you motivate yourself to reach this high standard? The best way is to consciously acknowledge God's presence in every area of your work. The knowledge God is with you as you work will energize you every day! ◈

LIFE LESSONS

➤ **Genesis 39:9 — *"How then could I do this great evil and sin against God?"***

*J*oseph understood any sin we commit is really an offense against God. Our sins may harm and defraud others, but God is always the one most aggrieved.

10 As she spoke to Joseph day after day, he did not listen to her to lie beside her *or* be with her.

11 Now it happened one day that he went into the house to do his work, and none of the men of the household was there inside.

12 She caught him by his garment, saying, "Lie with me!" And he left his garment in her hand and fled, and went outside.

13 When she saw that he had left his garment in her hand and had fled outside,

14 she called to the men of her household and said to them, "See, he has brought in a Hebrew to us to make sport of us; he came in to me to lie with me, and I screamed.

15 "When he heard that I raised my voice and screamed, he left his garment beside me and fled and went outside."

16 So she left his garment beside her until his master came home.

17 Then she spoke to him with these words, "The Hebrew slave, whom you brought to us, came in to me to make sport of me;

18 and as I raised my voice and screamed, he left his garment beside me and fled outside."

19 Now when his master heard the words of his wife, which she spoke to him, saying, "This is what your slave did to me," his anger burned.

20 So Joseph's master took him and put him into the jail, the place where the king's prisoners were confined; and he was there in the jail.

➤ 21 But the LORD was with Joseph and extended kindness to him, and gave him favor in the sight of the chief jailer.

22 The chief jailer committed to Joseph's charge all the prisoners who were in the jail; so that whatever was done there, he was responsible *for it.*

23 The chief jailer did not supervise anything under Joseph's charge because the LORD was with him; and whatever he did, the LORD made to prosper.

40 THEN it came about after these things, the cupbearer and the baker for the king of Egypt offended their lord, the king of Egypt.

2 Pharaoh was furious with his two officials, the chief cupbearer and the chief baker.

3 So he put them in confinement in the house of the captain of the bodyguard, in the jail, the *same* place where Joseph was imprisoned.

4 The captain of the bodyguard put Joseph in charge of them, and he took care of them; and they were in confinement for some time.

5 Then the cupbearer and the baker for the king of Egypt, who were confined in jail, both had a dream the same night, each man with his *own* dream *and* each dream with its *own* interpretation.

6 When Joseph came to them in the morning and observed them, behold, they were dejected.

7 He asked Pharaoh's officials who were with him in confinement in his master's house, "Why are your faces so sad today?"

8 Then they said to him, "We have had a dream and there is no one to interpret it." Then Joseph said to them, "Do not interpretations belong to God? Tell *it* to me, please."

9 So the chief cupbearer told his dream to Joseph, and said to him, "In my dream, behold, *there was* a vine in front of me;

10 and on the vine *were* three branches. And as it was budding, its blossoms came out, *and* its clusters produced ripe grapes.

LIFE LESSONS

➤ **Genesis 39:21 — *The LORD was with Joseph and extended kindness to him, and gave him favor in the sight of the chief jailer.***

*E*ven when Joseph was thrown into prison for doing nothing wrong, God was with him and blessed him—even in that dark place. The young man learned not to think of himself as a victim, but as a child of God.

11 "Now Pharaoh's cup was in my hand; so I took the grapes and squeezed them into Pharaoh's cup, and I put the cup into Pharaoh's hand."

12 Then Joseph said to him, "This is the interpretation of it: the three branches are three days;

13 within three more days Pharaoh will lift up your head and restore you to your office; and you will put Pharaoh's cup into his hand according to your former custom when you were his cupbearer.

14 "Only keep me in mind when it goes well with you, and please do me a kindness by mentioning me to Pharaoh and get me out of this house.

15 "For I was in fact kidnapped from the land of the Hebrews, and even here I have done nothing that they should have put me into the dungeon."

16 When the chief baker saw that he had interpreted favorably, he said to Joseph, "I also *saw* in my dream, and behold, *there were* three baskets of white bread on my head;

17 and in the top basket *there were* some of all sorts of baked food for Pharaoh, and the birds were eating them out of the basket on my head."

18 Then Joseph answered and said, "This is its interpretation: the three baskets are three days;

19 within three more days Pharaoh will lift up your head from you and will hang you on a tree, and the birds will eat your flesh off you."

20 Thus it came about on the third day, *which was* Pharaoh's birthday, that he made a feast for all his servants; and he lifted up the head of the chief cupbearer and the head of the chief baker among his servants.

21 He restored the chief cupbearer to his office, and he put the cup into Pharaoh's hand;

22 but he hanged the chief baker, just as Joseph had interpreted to them.

23 Yet the chief cupbearer did not remember Joseph, but forgot him.

◈ Psalm 10:1–11

> **10** WHY do You stand afar off, O LORD?

LIFE LESSONS

> ➤ **Psalm 10:1 — *Why do You stand afar off, O LORD? Why do You hide Yourself in times of trouble?***

*D*uring hard times in the desert, the Israelites thought God had abandoned them. But Moses told them, "In the wilderness where you saw how the LORD your God carried you, just as a man carries his son" (Deut. 1:31).

Why do You hide *Yourself* in times of trouble?

2 In pride the wicked hotly pursue the afflicted;
Let them be caught in the plots which they have devised.

3 For the wicked boasts of his heart's desire,
And the greedy man curses *and* spurns the LORD.

4 The wicked, in the haughtiness of his countenance, does not seek *Him.*
All his thoughts are, "There is no God."

5 His ways prosper at all times;
Your judgments are on high, out of his sight;
As for all his adversaries, he snorts at them.

6 He says to himself, "I will not be moved;
Throughout all generations I will not be in adversity."

7 His mouth is full of curses and deceit and oppression;
Under his tongue is mischief and wickedness.

8 He sits in the lurking places of the villages;
In the hiding places he kills the innocent;
His eyes stealthily watch for the unfortunate.

9 He lurks in a hiding place as a lion in his lair;
He lurks to catch the afflicted;
He catches the afflicted when he draws him into his net.

10 He crouches, he bows down,
And the unfortunate fall by his mighty ones.

11 He says to himself, "God has forgotten;

He has hidden His face; He will
never see it."

✦ Proverbs 4:1–6

4 HEAR, O sons, the instruction of a
father,
And give attention that you may
gain understanding,
2 For I give you sound teaching;
Do not abandon my instruction.
3 When I was a son to my father,
Tender and the only son in the sight
of my mother,
4 Then he taught me and said to me,
"Let your heart hold fast my words;
Keep my commandments and live;
5 Acquire wisdom! Acquire
understanding!
Do not forget nor turn away from
the words of my mouth.
6 "Do not forsake her, and she will
guard you;
Love her, and she will watch over
you.

✦ Matthew 13:31–58

31 He presented another parable to
them, saying, "The kingdom of heaven
is like a mustard seed, which a man took
and sowed in his field;
32 and this is smaller than all *other*
seeds, but when it is full grown, it is
larger than the garden plants and becomes a tree, so that THE BIRDS OF THE AIR
come and NEST IN ITS BRANCHES."
33 He spoke another parable to them,
"The kingdom of heaven is like leaven,
which a woman took and hid in three
pecks of flour until it was all leavened."
34 All these things Jesus spoke to the
crowds in parables, and He did not speak
to them without a parable.
35 *This was* to fulfill what was spoken
through the prophet:
"I WILL OPEN MY MOUTH IN PARABLES;
I WILL UTTER THINGS HIDDEN SINCE THE
FOUNDATION OF THE WORLD."
36 Then He left the crowds and went
into the house. And His disciples came to
Him and said, "Explain to us the parable
of the tares of the field."

37 And He said, "The one who sows the
good seed is the Son of Man,
38 and the field is the world; and *as for*
the good seed, these are the sons of the
kingdom; and the tares are the sons of
the evil *one;*
39 and the enemy who sowed them is
the devil, and the harvest is the end of
the age; and the reapers are angels.
40 "So just as the tares are gathered up
and burned with fire, so shall it be at the
end of the age.
41 "The Son of Man will send forth His
angels, and they will gather out of His
kingdom all stumbling blocks, and those
who commit lawlessness,
42 and will throw them into the furnace
of fire; in that place there will be weeping
and gnashing of teeth.
43 "Then THE RIGHTEOUS WILL SHINE
FORTH AS THE SUN in the kingdom of their
Father. He who has ears, let him hear.
44 "The kingdom of heaven is like a
treasure hidden in the field, which a man
found and hid *again;* and from joy over it
he goes and sells all that he has and buys
that field.
45 "Again, the kingdom of heaven is
like a merchant seeking fine pearls,
46 and upon finding one pearl of great
value, he went and sold all that he had
and bought it.
47 "Again, the kingdom of heaven is
like a dragnet cast into the sea, and gathering *fish* of every kind;
48 and when it was filled, they drew it
up on the beach; and they sat down and
gathered the good *fish* into containers,
but the bad they threw away.
49 "So it will be at the end of the age;
the angels will come forth and take out
the wicked from among the righteous,
50 and will throw them into the furnace

LIFE LESSONS

➤ **Matthew 13:38 —** *"The field is the
world; and as for the good seed, these
are the sons of the kingdom; and the
tares are the sons of the evil one."*

*W*e may not like it, but God allows
the righteous and the wicked to
live alongside one another. The situation
will change one day, but for now, we
must remember, "not all have faith"
(1 Thess. 3:2).

of fire; in that place there will be weeping and gnashing of teeth.

51 "Have you understood all these things?" They *said to Him, "Yes."

52 And Jesus said to them, "Therefore every scribe who has become a disciple of the kingdom of heaven is like a head of a household, who brings out of his treasure things new and old."

53 When Jesus had finished these parables, He departed from there.

54 He came to His hometown and *began* teaching them in their synagogue, so that they were astonished, and said, "Where *did* this man *get* this wisdom and *these* miraculous powers?

55 "Is not this the carpenter's son? Is not His mother called Mary, and His brothers, James and Joseph and Simon and Judas?

56 "And His sisters, are they not all with us? Where then *did* this man *get* all these things?"

57 And they took offense at Him. But Jesus said to them, "A prophet is not without honor except in his hometown and in his *own* household."

58 And He did not do many miracles ◄ there because of their unbelief.

LIFE LESSONS

➤ **Matthew 13:58 —** *He did not do many mighty works there because of their unbelief.*

*U*nbelief acts like a wet blanket on a smoldering fire, discouraging anything from really getting started. It does not prevent God from acting—as though we had the power to stop Him—but it does dampen the possibility.

◈ Genesis 41:1–42:38

➤ **41** NOW it happened at the end of two full years that Pharaoh had a dream, and behold, he was standing by the Nile.

2 And lo, from the Nile there came up seven cows, sleek and fat; and they grazed in the marsh grass.

3 Then behold, seven other cows came

LIFE LESSONS

➤ **Genesis 41:1 —** *Now it happened at the end of two full years that Pharaoh had a dream.*

*J*oseph languished in prison for two full years before he gained his freedom. Yet he did not blame God, but continued to serve Him. He learned, as we must, that God acts on behalf of those who wait for Him.

Life Examples:

JOSEPH: Waiting and Trusting

GENESIS 41

*G*od doesn't always meet our needs immediately or in a way we expect. Why not? Often He is redirecting us or preparing us for something new. The life of Joseph in the Old Testament provides a perfect example of this.

Although Joseph had visions that he would one day be a great ruler (Gen. 37:6–10), the accomplishment of those dreams took a very long time. In fact, before God raised Joseph up, He brought him to the lowest

point imaginable—locked away in prison for years on false charges.

Why did God delay so long before freeing Joseph from his chains and putting him in the seat of power? Answer: So that a greater purpose might be accomplished, namely so that Joseph could learn to depend upon the Lord no matter what his circumstances were. Because of his faithful obedience and trust during the darkest times, God was able to deliver Joseph's entire family and the nation of Egypt from terrible famine (Gen 45:5–8).

In a similar way, while God is in the process of redirecting our lives, sometimes He delays meeting certain needs. Why? So His greater plan for us—and for others—might be accomplished.

up after them from the Nile, ugly and gaunt, and they stood by the *other* cows on the bank of the Nile.

4   The ugly and gaunt cows ate up the seven sleek and fat cows. Then Pharaoh awoke.

5   He fell asleep and dreamed a second time; and behold, seven ears of grain came up on a single stalk, plump and good.

6   Then behold, seven ears, thin and scorched by the east wind, sprouted up after them.

7   The thin ears swallowed up the seven plump and full ears. Then Pharaoh awoke, and behold, *it was* a dream.

8   Now in the morning his spirit was troubled, so he sent and called for all the magicians of Egypt, and all its wise men. And Pharaoh told them his dreams, but there was no one who could interpret them to Pharaoh.

9   Then the chief cupbearer spoke to Pharaoh, saying, "I would make mention today of my *own* offenses.

10 "Pharaoh was furious with his servants, and he put me in confinement in the house of the captain of the bodyguard, *both* me and the chief baker.

11 "We had a dream on the same night, he and I; each of us dreamed according to the interpretation of his *own* dream.

12 "Now a Hebrew youth *was* with us there, a servant of the captain of the bodyguard, and we related *them* to him, and he interpreted our dreams for us. To each one he interpreted according to his *own* dream.

13 "And just as he interpreted for us, so it happened; he restored me in my office, but he hanged him."

14   Then Pharaoh sent and called for Joseph, and they hurriedly brought him out of the dungeon; and when he had shaved himself and changed his clothes, he came to Pharaoh.

15   Pharaoh said to Joseph, "I have had a dream, but no one can interpret it; and I have heard it said about you, that when you hear a dream you can interpret it."

➤ 16   Joseph then answered Pharaoh, saying, "It is not in me; God will give Pharaoh a favorable answer."

17   So Pharaoh spoke to Joseph, "In my dream, behold, I was standing on the bank of the Nile;

18   and behold, seven cows, fat and sleek came up out of the Nile, and they grazed in the marsh grass.

19 "Lo, seven other cows came up after them, poor and very ugly and gaunt, such as I had never seen for ugliness in all the land of Egypt;

20   and the lean and ugly cows ate up the first seven fat cows.

21 "Yet when they had devoured them, it could not be detected that they had devoured them, for they were just as ugly as before. Then I awoke.

22 "I saw also in my dream, and behold, seven ears, full and good, came up on a single stalk;

23   and lo, seven ears, withered, thin, *and* scorched by the east wind, sprouted up after them;

24   and the thin ears swallowed the seven good ears. Then I told it to the magicians, but there was no one who could explain it to me."

25   Now Joseph said to Pharaoh, "Pharaoh's dreams are one *and the same*; God has told to Pharaoh what He is about to do.

26 "The seven good cows are seven years; and the seven good ears are seven years; the dreams are one *and the same*.

27 "The seven lean and ugly cows that came up after them are seven years, and the seven thin ears scorched by the east wind will be seven years of famine.

28 "It is as I have spoken to Pharaoh: God has shown to Pharaoh what He is about to do.

29 "Behold, seven years of great abundance are coming in all the land of Egypt;

30   and after them seven years of famine will come, and all the abundance will be forgotten in the land of Egypt, and the famine will ravage the land.

31 "So the abundance will be unknown

LIFE LESSONS

➤ **Genesis 41:16 —** *Joseph then answered Pharaoh, saying, "It is not in me; God will give Pharaoh a favorable answer."*

*W*e never truly advance our interests by shining the spotlight on ourselves. Godly men and women realize and eagerly declare God is the true source of all wisdom.

in the land because of that subsequent famine; for it *will be* very severe.
32 "Now as for the repeating of the dream to Pharaoh twice, *it means* that the matter is determined by God, and God will quickly bring it about.
33 "Now let Pharaoh look for a man discerning and wise, and set him over the land of Egypt.
34 "Let Pharaoh take action to appoint overseers in charge of the land, and let him exact a fifth *of the produce* of the land of Egypt in the seven years of abundance.
35 "Then let them gather all the food of these good years that are coming, and store up the grain for food in the cities under Pharaoh's authority, and let them guard *it*.
36 "Let the food become as a reserve for the land for the seven years of famine which will occur in the land of Egypt, so that the land will not perish during the famine."
37 Now the proposal seemed good to Pharaoh and to all his servants.
38 Then Pharaoh said to his servants, "Can we find a man like this, in whom is a divine spirit?"
39 So Pharaoh said to Joseph, "Since God has informed you of all this, there is no one so discerning and wise as you are.
40 "You shall be over my house, and according to your command all my people shall do homage; only in the throne I will be greater than you."
41 Pharaoh said to Joseph, "See, I have set you over all the land of Egypt."
42 Then Pharaoh took off his signet ring from his hand and put it on Joseph's hand, and clothed him in garments of fine linen and put the gold necklace around his neck.
43 He had him ride in his second chariot; and they proclaimed before him, "Bow the knee!" And he set him over all the land of Egypt.
44 Moreover, Pharaoh said to Joseph, "*Though* I am Pharaoh, yet without your permission no one shall raise his hand or foot in all the land of Egypt."
45 Then Pharaoh named Joseph Zaphenath-paneah; and he gave him Asenath, the daughter of Potiphera priest of On, as his wife. And Joseph went forth over the land of Egypt.
46 Now Joseph was thirty years old when he stood before Pharaoh, king of

---

> ### LIFE LESSONS
>
> ➤ **Genesis 41:46** — *Joseph was thirty years old when he stood before Pharaoh.*
>
> *B*y the time Joseph rose to power in Egypt, he was 30 years old—perhaps a dozen or more years after his brothers sold him into slavery. No doubt he felt disappointed during those years, but he never chose to feel discouraged.

Egypt. And Joseph went out from the presence of Pharaoh and went through all the land of Egypt.
47 During the seven years of plenty the land brought forth abundantly.
48 So he gathered all the food of *these* seven years which occurred in the land of Egypt and placed the food in the cities; he placed in every city the food from its own surrounding fields.
49 Thus Joseph stored up grain in great abundance like the sand of the sea, until he stopped measuring *it*, for it was beyond measure.
50 Now before the year of famine came, two sons were born to Joseph, whom Asenath, the daughter of Potiphera priest of On, bore to him.
51 Joseph named the firstborn Manasseh, "For," *he said*, "God has made me forget all my trouble and all my father's household."
52 He named the second Ephraim, "For," *he said*, "God has made me fruitful in the land of my affliction."
53 When the seven years of plenty which had been in the land of Egypt came to an end,
54 and the seven years of famine began to come, just as Joseph had said, then there was famine in all the lands, but in all the land of Egypt there was bread.
55 So when all the land of Egypt was famished, the people cried out to Pharaoh for bread; and Pharaoh said to all the Egyptians, "Go to Joseph; whatever he says to you, you shall do."
56 When the famine was *spread* over all the face of the earth, then Joseph opened all the storehouses, and sold to the Egyptians; and the famine was severe in the land of Egypt.
57 *The people of* all the earth came to Egypt to buy grain from Joseph, because the famine was severe in all the earth.

42 NOW Jacob saw that there was grain in Egypt, and Jacob said to his sons, "Why are you staring at one another?"

2 He said, "Behold, I have heard that there is grain in Egypt; go down there and buy *some* for us from that place, so that we may live and not die."

3 Then ten brothers of Joseph went down to buy grain from Egypt.

4 But Jacob did not send Joseph's brother Benjamin with his brothers, for he said, "I am afraid that harm may befall him."

➤ 5 So the sons of Israel came to buy grain among those who were coming, for the famine was in the land of Canaan *also*.

6 Now Joseph was the ruler over the land; he was the one who sold to all the people of the land. And Joseph's brothers came and bowed down to him with *their* faces to the ground.

7 When Joseph saw his brothers he recognized them, but he disguised himself to them and spoke to them harshly. And he said to them, "Where have you come from?" And they said, "From the land of Canaan, to buy food."

8 But Joseph had recognized his brothers, although they did not recognize him.

9 Joseph remembered the dreams which he had about them, and said to them, "You are spies; you have come to look at the undefended parts of our land."

10 Then they said to him, "No, my lord, but your servants have come to buy food.

11 "We are all sons of one man; we are honest men, your servants are not spies."

12 Yet he said to them, "No, but you have come to look at the undefended parts of our land!"

13 But they said, "Your servants are twelve brothers *in all*, the sons of one man in the land of Canaan; and behold, the youngest is with our father today, and one is no longer alive."

14 Joseph said to them, "It is as I said to you, you are spies;

15 by this you will be tested: by the life of Pharaoh, you shall not go from this place unless your youngest brother comes here!

16 "Send one of you that he may get your brother, while you remain confined, that your words may be tested, whether there is truth in you. But if not, by the life of Pharaoh, surely you are spies."

17 So he put them all together in prison for three days.

18 Now Joseph said to them on the third day, "Do this and live, for I fear God:

19 if you are honest men, let one of your brothers be confined in your prison; but as for *the rest of* you, go, carry grain for the famine of your households,

20 and bring your youngest brother to me, so your words may be verified, and you will not die." And they did so.

21 Then they said to one another, "Truly we are guilty concerning our brother, because we saw the distress of his soul when he pleaded with us, yet we would not listen; therefore this distress has come upon us."

22 Reuben answered them, saying, "Did I not tell you, 'Do not sin against the boy'; and you would not listen? Now comes the reckoning for his blood."

23 They did not know, however, that Joseph understood, for there was an interpreter between them.

24 He turned away from them and wept. But when he returned to them and spoke to them, he took Simeon from them and bound him before their eyes.

25 Then Joseph gave orders to fill their bags with grain and to restore every man's money in his sack, and to give them provisions for the journey. And thus it was done for them.

26 So they loaded their donkeys with their grain and departed from there.

27 As one *of them* opened his sack to give his donkey fodder at the lodging place, he saw his money; and behold, it was in the mouth of his sack.

28 Then he said to his brothers, "My money has been returned, and behold, it is even in my sack." And their hearts

---

LIFE LESSONS

➤ **Genesis 42:5 —** *So the sons of Israel came to buy grain among those who were coming, for the famine was in the land of Canaan also.*

*G*od used a famine to bring together the fractured family of Jacob. What we see as disasters, God can use for good.

sank, and they *turned* trembling to one another, saying, "What is this that God has done to us?"

29 When they came to their father Jacob in the land of Canaan, they told him all that had happened to them, saying,

30 "The man, the lord of the land, spoke harshly with us, and took us for spies of the country.

31 "But we said to him, 'We are honest men; we are not spies.

32 'We are twelve brothers, sons of our father; one is no longer alive, and the youngest is with our father today in the land of Canaan.'

33 "The man, the lord of the land, said to us, 'By this I will know that you are honest men: leave one of your brothers with me and take *grain for* the famine of your households, and go.

34 'But bring your youngest brother to me that I may know that you are not spies, but honest men. I will give your brother to you, and you may trade in the land.'"

35 Now it came about as they were emptying their sacks, that behold, every man's bundle of money *was* in his sack; and when they and their father saw their bundles of money, they were dismayed.

36 Their father Jacob said to them, "You have bereaved me of my children: Joseph is no more, and Simeon is no more, and you would take Benjamin; all these things are against me."

37 Then Reuben spoke to his father, saying, "You may put my two sons to death if I do not bring him *back* to you; put him in my care, and I will return him to you."

38 But Jacob said, "My son shall not go down with you; for his brother is dead, and he alone is left. If harm should befall him on the journey you are taking, then you will bring my gray hair down to Sheol in sorrow."

✦ Psalm 10:12–18

12 Arise, O LORD; O God, lift up Your hand.
   Do not forget the afflicted.
13 Why has the wicked spurned God?
   He has said to himself, "You will not require *it*."

14 You have seen *it*, for You have beheld mischief and vexation to take it into Your hand.
   The unfortunate commits *himself* to You;
   You have been the helper of the orphan.
15 Break the arm of the wicked and the evildoer,
   Seek out his wickedness until You find none.
16 The LORD is King forever and ever;
   Nations have perished from His land.
17 O LORD, You have heard the desire of the humble;
   You will strengthen their heart, You will incline Your ear
18 To vindicate the orphan and the oppressed,
   So that man who is of the earth will no longer cause terror.

✦ Proverbs 4:7–9

7 "The beginning of wisdom *is*:
   Acquire wisdom;
   And with all your acquiring, get understanding.
8 "Prize her, and she will exalt you;
   She will honor you if you embrace her.
9 "She will place on your head a garland of grace;
   She will present you with a crown of beauty."

✦ Matthew 14:1–21

14 AT that time Herod the tetrarch heard the news about Jesus,

2   and said to his servants, "This is John the Baptist; he has risen from the dead, and that is why miraculous powers are at work in him."
3   For when Herod had John arrested, he bound him and put him in prison because of Herodias, the wife of his brother Philip.
4   For John had been saying to him, "It is not lawful for you to have her."
5   Although Herod wanted to put him to death, he feared the crowd, because they regarded John as a prophet.
6   But when Herod's birthday came, the daughter of Herodias danced before *them* and pleased Herod,
7   so *much* that he promised with an oath to give her whatever she asked.
8   Having been prompted by her mother, she *said, "Give me here on a platter the head of John the Baptist."
9   Although he was grieved, the king commanded *it* to be given because of his oaths, and because of his dinner guests.
10   He sent and had John beheaded in the prison.
11   And his head was brought on a platter and given to the girl, and she brought it to her mother.
12   His disciples came and took away the body and buried it; and they went and reported to Jesus.
13   Now when Jesus heard *about John*, He withdrew from there in a boat to a secluded place by Himself; and when the people heard *of this*, they followed Him on foot from the cities.
➤ 14   When He went ashore, He saw a

large crowd, and felt compassion for them and healed their sick.
15   When it was evening, the disciples came to Him and said, "This place is desolate and the hour is already late; so send the crowds away, that they may go into the villages and buy food for themselves."
16   But Jesus said to them, "They do not need to go away; you give them *something* to eat!"
17   They *said to Him, "We have here only five loaves and two fish."
18   And He said, "Bring them here to Me."
19   Ordering the people to sit down on the grass, He took the five loaves and the two fish, and looking up toward heaven, He blessed *the food*, and breaking the loaves He gave them to the disciples, and the disciples *gave them* to the crowds,
20   and they all ate and were satisfied. They picked up what was left over of the broken pieces, twelve full baskets.
21   There were about five thousand men who ate, besides women and children.

Genesis 43:1—44:34

43 NOW the famine was severe in the land.
2   So it came about when they had finished eating the grain which they had brought from Egypt, that their father said to them, "Go back, buy us a little food."
3   Judah spoke to him, however, saying, "The man solemnly warned us, 'You shall not see my face unless your brother is with you.'

4   "If you send our brother with us, we will go down and buy you food.
5   "But if you do not send *him*, we will not go down; for the man said to us, 'You will not see my face unless your brother is with you.'"
6   Then Israel said, "Why did you treat me so badly by telling the man whether you still had *another* brother?"
7   But they said, "The man questioned particularly about us and our relatives, saying, 'Is your father still alive? Have you *another* brother?' So we answered

his questions. Could we possibly know that he would say, 'Bring your brother down'?"

8 Judah said to his father Israel, "Send the lad with me and we will arise and go, that we may live and not die, we as well as you and our little ones.

9 "I myself will be surety for him; you may hold me responsible for him. If I do not bring him *back* to you and set him before you, then let me bear the blame before you forever.

10 "For if we had not delayed, surely by now we could have returned twice."

11 Then their father Israel said to them, "If *it must be* so, then do this: take some of the best products of the land in your bags, and carry down to the man as a present, a little balm and a little honey, aromatic gum and myrrh, pistachio nuts and almonds.

12 "Take double *the* money in your hand, and take back in your hand the money that was returned in the mouth of your sacks; perhaps it was a mistake.

13 "Take your brother also, and arise, return to the man;

14 and may God Almighty grant you compassion in the sight of the man, so that he will release to you your other brother and Benjamin. And as for me, if I am bereaved of my children, I am bereaved."

15 So the men took this present, and they took double *the* money in their hand, and Benjamin; then they arose and went down to Egypt and stood before Joseph.

16 When Joseph saw Benjamin with them, he said to his house steward, "Bring the men into the house, and slay an animal and make ready; for the men are to dine with me at noon."

17 So the man did as Joseph said, and brought the men to Joseph's house.

18 Now the men were afraid, because they were brought to Joseph's house; and they said, "It *is* because of the money that was returned in our sacks the first time that we are being brought in, that he may seek occasion against us and fall upon us, and take us for slaves with our donkeys."

19 So they came near to Joseph's house steward, and spoke to him at the entrance of the house,

20 and said, "Oh, my lord, we indeed came down the first time to buy food,

21 and it came about when we came to the lodging place, that we opened our sacks, and behold, each man's money was in the mouth of his sack, our money in full. So we have brought it back in our hand.

22 "We have also brought down other money in our hand to buy food; we do not know who put our money in our sacks."

23 He said, "Be at ease, do not be afraid. Your God and the God of your father has given you treasure in your sacks; I had your money." Then he brought Simeon out to them.

24 Then the man brought the men into Joseph's house and gave them water, and they washed their feet; and he gave their donkeys fodder.

25 So they prepared the present for Joseph's coming at noon; for they had heard that they were to eat a meal there.

26 When Joseph came home, they brought into the house to him the present which was in their hand and bowed to the ground before him.

27 Then he asked them about their welfare, and said, "Is your old father well, of whom you spoke? Is he still alive?"

28 They said, "Your servant our father is well; he is still alive." They bowed down in homage.

29 As he lifted his eyes and saw his brother Benjamin, his mother's son, he said, "Is this your youngest brother, of whom you spoke to me?" And he said, "May God be gracious to you, my son."

30 Joseph hurried *out* for he was deeply stirred over his brother, and he sought *a place* to weep; and he entered his chamber and wept there.

31 Then he washed his face and came out; and he controlled himself and said, "Serve the meal."

32 So they served him by himself, and them by themselves, and the Egyptians who ate with him by themselves, because the Egyptians could not eat bread with the Hebrews, for that is loathsome to the Egyptians.

33 Now they were seated before him, the firstborn according to his birthright and the youngest according to his youth, and the men looked at one another in astonishment.

34 He took portions to them from his own table, but Benjamin's portion was five times as much as any of theirs. So they feasted and drank freely with him.

44 THEN he commanded his house steward, saying, "Fill the men's sacks with food, as much as they can carry, and put each man's money in the mouth of his sack.

2 "Put my cup, the silver cup, in the mouth of the sack of the youngest, and his money for the grain." And he did as Joseph had told *him*.

3 As soon as it was light, the men were sent away, they with their donkeys.

4 They had *just* gone out of the city, *and* were not far off, when Joseph said to his house steward, "Up, follow the men; and when you overtake them, say to them, 'Why have you repaid evil for good?

5 'Is not this the one from which my lord drinks and which he indeed uses for divination? You have done wrong in doing this.'"

6 So he overtook them and spoke these words to them.

7 They said to him, "Why does my lord speak such words as these? Far be it from your servants to do such a thing.

8 "Behold, the money which we found in the mouth of our sacks we have brought back to you from the land of Canaan. How then could we steal silver or gold from your lord's house?

9 "With whomever of your servants it is found, let him die, and we also will be my lord's slaves."

10 So he said, "Now let it also be according to your words; he with whom it is found shall be my slave, and *the rest of* you shall be innocent."

11 Then they hurried, each man lowered his sack to the ground, and each man opened his sack.

12 He searched, beginning with the oldest and ending with the youngest, and the cup was found in Benjamin's sack.

13 Then they tore their clothes, and when each man loaded his donkey, they returned to the city.

14 When Judah and his brothers came to Joseph's house, he was still there, and they fell to the ground before him.

15 Joseph said to them, "What is this deed that you have done? Do you not know that such a man as I can indeed practice divination?"

16 So Judah said, "What can we say to my lord? What can we speak? And how can we justify ourselves? God has found out the iniquity of your servants; behold, we are my lord's slaves, both we and the one in whose possession the cup has been found."

17 But he said, "Far be it from me to do this. The man in whose possession the cup has been found, he shall be my slave; but as for you, go up in peace to your father."

18 Then Judah approached him, and said, "Oh my lord, may your servant please speak a word in my lord's ears, and do not be angry with your servant; for you are equal to Pharaoh.

19 "My lord asked his servants, saying, 'Have you a father or a brother?'

20 "We said to my lord, 'We have an old father and a little child of *his* old age. Now his brother is dead, so he alone is left of his mother, and his father loves him.'

21 "Then you said to your servants, 'Bring him down to me that I may set my eyes on him.'

22 "But we said to my lord, 'The lad cannot leave his father, for if he should leave his father, his father would die.'

23 "You said to your servants, however, 'Unless your youngest brother comes down with you, you will not see my face again.'

24 "Thus it came about when we went up to your servant my father, we told him the words of my lord.

25 "Our father said, 'Go back, buy us a little food.'

26 "But we said, 'We cannot go down. If our youngest brother is with us, then we will go down; for we cannot see the man's face unless our youngest brother is with us.'

27 "Your servant my father said to us, 'You know that my wife bore me two sons;

28 and the one went out from me, and I said, "Surely he is torn in pieces," and I have not seen him since.

29 'If you take this one also from me, and harm befalls him, you will bring my gray hair down to Sheol in sorrow.'

30 "Now, therefore, when I come to your servant my father, and the lad is not with us, since his life is bound up in the lad's life,

31 when he sees that the lad is not *with*

us, he will die. Thus your servants will bring the gray hair of your servant our father down to Sheol in sorrow.

32 "For your servant became surety for the lad to my father, saying, 'If I do not bring him *back* to you, then let me bear the blame before my father forever.'

33 "Now, therefore, please let your servant remain instead of the lad a slave to my lord, and let the lad go up with his brothers.

34 "For how shall I go up to my father if the lad is not with me—for fear that I see the evil that would overtake my father?"

Psalm 11:1–7

For the choir director. *A Psalm* of David.

➤ **11** IN the LORD I take refuge;
How can you say to my soul,
"Flee *as* a bird to your mountain;

2 For, behold, the wicked bend the bow,
They make ready their arrow upon the string
To shoot in darkness at the upright in heart.

3 If the foundations are destroyed,
What can the righteous do?"

4 The LORD is in His holy temple; the LORD'S throne is in heaven;
His eyes behold, His eyelids test the sons of men.

5 The LORD tests the righteous and the wicked,
And the one who loves violence His soul hates.

6 Upon the wicked He will rain snares;
Fire and brimstone and burning wind will be the portion of their cup.

➤ 7 For the LORD is righteous, He loves righteousness;
The upright will behold His face.

Proverbs 4:10–13

10 Hear, my son, and accept my sayings
And the years of your life will be many.

11 I have directed you in the way of wisdom;
I have led you in upright paths.

12 When you walk, your steps will not be impeded;
And if you run, you will not stumble.

13 Take hold of instruction; do not let go.
Guard her, for she is your life.

Matthew 14:22–36

22 Immediately He made the disciples get into the boat and go ahead of Him to the other side, while He sent the crowds away.

23 After He had sent the crowds away, He went up on the mountain by Himself to pray; and when it was evening, He was there alone.

24 But the boat was already a long distance from the land, battered by the waves; for the wind was contrary.

LIFE LESSONS

➤ **Psalm 11:1 — *In the LORD I take refuge; how can you say to my soul, "Flee as a bird to your mountain"?***

*W*hen foes urged Nehemiah to run from trouble, he replied, "Should such a man as I flee?" He realized his enemies wanted to make him "afraid" and "sin" by fleeing instead of trusting God (Neh. 6:11, 13).

➤ **Psalm 11:7 — *For the LORD is righteous, He loves righteousness; The upright will behold His face.***

*G*od made us in His image to reflect who He is and to bring Him glory. Since the Lord is righteous, He wants us to act in righteous ways. Through His Spirit He gives us the power we need.

➤ **Matthew 14:23 — *He went up on the mountain by Himself to pray.***

*J*esus spent a good deal of His time alone with God in prayer. He made this a practice not only to make requests of His Father, but even more to stay in close fellowship with Him.

Growing in Our Faith

MATTHEW 14:31

*I*n Matthew 14, we read how the disciples were caught in a frightening situation. A storm swept in suddenly, and the threat of physical harm became very real. Just as they became convinced they were about to be swamped by the raging sea, Peter looked out and saw what he thought was a ghost walking toward their boat. But it was no ghost. It was Jesus. So the overzealous disciple called out to Him asking the Lord to bid him to come to Him.

Thus began a vital chapter in Peter's chronicle of faith. He climbed out of the boat and started walking toward the Savior. Unfortunately, before the disciple reached his destination, the thunderous, buffeting waves took his attention away from the Savior. He froze in fear and immediately began to sink.

There are a couple of positive things we can say about Peter's quest. First, he got out of the boat and began walking to Jesus while the others stayed put. Second, when he began to sink, he cried out to the Lord. Peter immediately understood the situation was too grave for him and he needed Jesus.

So the Lord reached out to him and pulled him to safety. Then He asked Peter, "You of little faith, why did you doubt?" (Matt.

14:31). Jesus was not scolding Peter as much as He was reminding him faith and trust in Him were all he needed to reach His goal. The same is true for us.

Have you ever thought about the fact that the way you grow in your faith is by facing challenges and trials? The fact is: this is probably when we grow the most in our walk with Christ. A need arises and there is no way we can fill the void, solve the problem, or decrease the pain. We struggle, fight, and finally call out to the one Person who knows us fully and loves us unconditionally.

We also grow in faith when we learn to listen to and submit to God's voice. As long as we are chattering and proclaiming our ability, we will never be able to discern His words of hope, direction, correction, and encouragement. The Lord is always speaking to us, but if we aren't hearing from and obeying Him, it's impossible for us to grow in faith.

Peter did the right things: He saw Jesus and he got out of the boat. He wanted to trust the Savior, but his faith was not sufficiently developed. For faith to increase requires our consistency, endurance, and watchfulness. We must continue to stand firm in what we believe. When we do, God will provide the strength and hope to continue on.

Therefore, persevere in believing what He says to you. Obey and endure because you will certainly see the fulfillment of all His promises.

---

25 And in the fourth watch of the night He came to them, walking on the sea.
26 When the disciples saw Him walking on the sea, they were terrified, and said, "It is a ghost!" And they cried out in fear.
27 But immediately Jesus spoke to them, saying, "Take courage, it is I; do not be afraid."
28 Peter said to Him, "Lord, if it is You, command me to come to You on the water."

LIFE LESSONS

➤ **Matthew 14:27** — *Jesus spoke to them, saying, "Take courage, it is I; do not be afraid."*

*T*he unexpected way God often does things may startle us or even frighten us. We may not understand why He works in a certain way. That is why He continually tells us, "It is I; do not be afraid."

29 And He said, "Come!" And Peter got out of the boat, and walked on the water and came toward Jesus.
30 But seeing the wind, he became frightened, and beginning to sink, he cried out, "Lord, save me!"
31 Immediately Jesus stretched out His hand and took hold of him, and *said to him, "You of little faith, why did you doubt?"
32 When they got into the boat, the wind stopped.
33 And those who were in the boat worshiped Him, saying, "You are certainly God's Son!"
34 When they had crossed over, they came to land at Gennesaret.
35 And when the men of that place recognized Him, they sent *word* into all that surrounding district and brought to Him all who were sick;
36 and they implored Him that they might just touch the fringe of His cloak; and as many as touched *it* were cured.

Genesis 45:1—46:34

45THEN Joseph could not control himself before all those who stood by him, and he cried, "Have everyone go out from me." So there was no man with him when Joseph made himself known to his brothers.

2   He wept so loudly that the Egyptians heard *it*, and the household of Pharaoh heard *of it*.

3   Then Joseph said to his brothers, "I am Joseph! Is my father still alive?" But his brothers could not answer him, for they were dismayed at his presence.

4   Then Joseph said to his brothers, "Please come closer to me." And they came closer. And he said, "I am your brother Joseph, whom you sold into Egypt.

5   "Now do not be grieved or angry with yourselves, because you sold me here, for God sent me before you to preserve life.

6   "For the famine *has been* in the land these two years, and there are still five years in which there will be neither plowing nor harvesting.

7   "God sent me before you to preserve for you a remnant in the earth, and to keep you alive by a great deliverance.

8   "Now, therefore, it was not you who sent me here, but God; and He has made me a father to Pharaoh and lord of all his household and ruler over all the land of Egypt.

9   "Hurry and go up to my father, and say to him, 'Thus says your son Joseph, "God has made me lord of all Egypt; come down to me, do not delay.

10 "You shall live in the land of Goshen, and you shall be near me, you and your children and your children's children and your flocks and your herds and all that you have.

11 "There I will also provide for you, for there are still five years of famine *to come*, and you and your household and all that you have would be impoverished."'

12 "Behold, your eyes see, and the eyes of my brother Benjamin *see*, that it is my mouth which is speaking to you.

13 "Now you must tell my father of all my splendor in Egypt, and all that you have seen; and you must hurry and bring my father down here."

14 Then he fell on his brother Benjamin's neck and wept, and Benjamin wept on his neck.

15 He kissed all his brothers and wept on them, and afterward his brothers talked with him.

16 Now when the news was heard in Pharaoh's house that Joseph's brothers had come, it pleased Pharaoh and his servants.

17 Then Pharaoh said to Joseph, "Say to your brothers, 'Do this: load your beasts and go to the land of Canaan,

18 and take your father and your households and come to me, and I will give you the best of the land of Egypt and you will eat the fat of the land.'

19 "Now you are ordered, 'Do this: take wagons from the land of Egypt for your little ones and for your wives, and bring your father and come.

20 'Do not concern yourselves with your goods, for the best of all the land of Egypt is yours.'"

21 Then the sons of Israel did so; and Joseph gave them wagons according to the command of Pharaoh, and gave them provisions for the journey.

22 To each of them he gave changes of garments, but to Benjamin he gave three hundred *pieces of* silver and five changes of garments.

23 To his father he sent as follows: ten donkeys loaded with the best things of Egypt, and ten female donkeys loaded with grain and bread and sustenance for his father on the journey.

24 So he sent his brothers away, and as they departed, he said to them, "Do not quarrel on the journey."

LIFE LESSONS

Genesis 45:5 — *"Now do not be grieved or angry with yourselves, because you sold me here, for God sent me before you to preserve life."*

*G*od calls us to have a forgiving spirit. Knowing God remains in control of all that happens to us releases us to forgive others. He also asks us to trust and obey Him day by day and to learn the lessons He sets before us.

ANSWERS TO LIFE'S QUESTIONS

Why doesn't God answer my prayers sooner?

GENESIS 45:25—46:4

*I*f God hears our requests and loves us so much He sent His own Son, Jesus Christ, to die for us, then why does it appear to take Him so long to respond to some of our most urgent requests? Carefully consider the following eight reasons. The delay may be caused by:

1. *Our doubt*

God wants us to trust Him—to go to Him with our needs without doubting His love, power, and provision for us (James 1:5–8). Always remember, with faith, all things are possible (Mark 9:23).

2. *Our attempts at manipulation*

If we try to control or manipulate God, we should not expect answers to our prayers (1 Sam. 13:9–14). He is the Master; we are the servants.

3. *Wrong motivation*

Neither self-centered requests nor those tinged with evil intent will receive an answer (James 4:3). God refuses to partner with our lusts or our schemes.

4. *Our disobedience*

Our sin can prompt God to withhold His gracious hand (Ps. 81:10–12). When we disobey His commands and refuse to repent, He will give us over to the stubbornness of our hearts. He will withdraw His favor and wait to answer us until we are willing to deal with our sin.

5. *Our lack of responsibility*

God cannot be expected to compensate for a lazy or negligent person (Prov. 19:15). The Lord has His work to do; we have ours.

6. *Rejecting God's method*

Don't turn away God's means of supplying your need merely because it doesn't fit your expectations or criteria (Josh. 6). A man named Naaman almost made this mistake—and it would have cost him his health (2 Kin. 5:8–14).

7. *God's redirection*

Sometimes God is in the process of redirecting us or preparing us for something new (Gen. 37; 39–50). God loves to do fresh, exciting things with His people (Is. 43:19).

8. *God's desire to teach us*

God may want us to focus on our spiritual and eternal needs so we will learn to trust Him in all things and for all things (Is. 48:18).

Even when God delays His answers, He instructs us to keep on praying (Luke 18:1–8). He also wants us to trust Him at every turn in life. Prayer is an act of faith because when we pray, we are essentially saying, "Lord, You know all things and I need Your wisdom, strength, ability, and peace. Without fail, God answers when we call to Him.

---

25 Then they went up from Egypt, and came to the land of Canaan to their father Jacob.
26 They told him, saying, "Joseph is still alive, and indeed he is ruler over all the land of Egypt." But he was stunned, for he did not believe them.
27 When they told him all the words of Joseph that he had spoken to them, and when he saw the wagons that Joseph had sent to carry him, the spirit of their father Jacob revived.
28 Then Israel said, "It is enough; my son Joseph is still alive. I will go and see him before I die."

46 SO Israel set out with all that he had, and came to Beersheba, and offered sacrifices to the God of his father Isaac.
2 God spoke to Israel in visions of the night and said, "Jacob, Jacob." And he said, "Here I am."
3 He said, "I am God, the God of your father; do not be afraid to go down to Egypt, for I will make you a great nation there.
4 "I will go down with you to Egypt, and I will also surely bring you up again; and Joseph will close your eyes."
5 Then Jacob arose from Beersheba; and the sons of Israel carried their father Jacob and their little ones and their wives in the wagons which Pharaoh had sent to carry him.
6 They took their livestock and their

LIFE LESSONS

➤ **Genesis 46:4** — *"I will go down with you to Egypt, and I will also surely bring you up again."*

*I*srael found strength to do a difficult thing once he heard God's promise, for God's Word is an immovable anchor in times of storm.

property, which they had acquired in the land of Canaan, and came to Egypt, Jacob and all his descendants with him:
7   his sons and his grandsons with him, his daughters and his granddaughters, and all his descendants he brought with him to Egypt.
8   Now these are the names of the sons of Israel, Jacob and his sons, who went to Egypt: Reuben, Jacob's firstborn.
9   The sons of Reuben: Hanoch and Pallu and Hezron and Carmi.
10 The sons of Simeon: Jemuel and Jamin and Ohad and Jachin and Zohar and Shaul the son of a Canaanite woman.
11 The sons of Levi: Gershon, Kohath, and Merari.
12 The sons of Judah: Er and Onan and Shelah and Perez and Zerah (but Er and Onan died in the land of Canaan). And the sons of Perez were Hezron and Hamul.
13 The sons of Issachar: Tola and Puvvah and Iob and Shimron.
14 The sons of Zebulun: Sered and Elon and Jahleel.
15 These are the sons of Leah, whom she bore to Jacob in Paddan-aram, with his daughter Dinah; all his sons and his daughters *numbered* thirty-three.
16 The sons of Gad: Ziphion and Haggi, Shuni and Ezbon, Eri and Arodi and Areli.
17 The sons of Asher: Imnah and Ishvah and Ishvi and Beriah and their sister Serah. And the sons of Beriah: Heber and Malchiel.
18 These are the sons of Zilpah, whom Laban gave to his daughter Leah; and she bore to Jacob these sixteen persons.
19 The sons of Jacob's wife Rachel: Joseph and Benjamin.
20 Now to Joseph in the land of Egypt were born Manasseh and Ephraim, whom Asenath, the daughter of Potiphera, priest of On, bore to him.
21 The sons of Benjamin: Bela and Becher and Ashbel, Gera and Naaman, Ehi and Rosh, Muppim and Huppim and Ard.
22 These are the sons of Rachel, who were born to Jacob; *there were* fourteen persons in all.
23 The sons of Dan: Hushim.
24 The sons of Naphtali: Jahzeel and Guni and Jezer and Shillem.
25 These are the sons of Bilhah, whom Laban gave to his daughter Rachel, and she bore these to Jacob; *there were* seven persons in all.

26 All the persons belonging to Jacob, who came to Egypt, his direct descendants, not including the wives of Jacob's sons, *were* sixty-six persons in all,
27 and the sons of Joseph, who were born to him in Egypt were two; all the persons of the house of Jacob, who came to Egypt, *were* seventy.
28 Now he sent Judah before him to Joseph, to point out *the way* before him to Goshen; and they came into the land of Goshen.
29 Joseph prepared his chariot and went up to Goshen to meet his father Israel; as soon as he appeared before him, he fell on his neck and wept on his neck a long time.
30 Then Israel said to Joseph, "Now let me die, since I have seen your face, that you are still alive."
31 Joseph said to his brothers and to his father's household, "I will go up and tell Pharaoh, and will say to him, 'My brothers and my father's household, who *were* in the land of Canaan, have come to me;
32 and the men are shepherds, for they have been keepers of livestock; and they have brought their flocks and their herds and all that they have.'
33 "When Pharaoh calls you and says, 'What is your occupation?'
34 you shall say, 'Your servants have been keepers of livestock from our youth even until now, both we and our fathers,' that you may live in the land of Goshen; for every shepherd is loathsome to the Egyptians."

✦ Psalm 12:1–8

For the choir director; upon an eight-stringed lyre. A Psalm of David.

12 HELP, Lord, for the godly man
     ceases to be,
   For the faithful disappear from
        among the sons of men.
2   They speak falsehood to one another;
     With flattering lips and with a
        double heart they speak.
3   May the Lord cut off all flattering
     lips,
     The tongue that speaks great things;
4   Who have said, "With our tongue
        we will prevail;
     Our lips are our own; who is lord
        over us?"

➤ 5　"Because of the devastation of the afflicted, because of the groaning of the needy,
Now I will arise," says the LORD; "I will set him in the safety for which he longs."

➤ 6　The words of the LORD are pure words;
As silver tried in a furnace on the earth, refined seven times.

7　You, O LORD, will keep them;
You will preserve him from this generation forever.

8　The wicked strut about on every side
When vileness is exalted among the sons of men.

✦ Proverbs 4:14–17

14　Do not enter the path of the wicked
And do not proceed in the way of evil men.

15　Avoid it, do not pass by it;
Turn away from it and pass on.

16　For they cannot sleep unless they do evil;
And they are robbed of sleep unless they make *someone* stumble.

17　For they eat the bread of wickedness
And drink the wine of violence.

✦ Matthew 15:1–20

15THEN some Pharisees and scribes *came to Jesus from Jerusalem and said,

2　"Why do Your disciples break the tradition of the elders? For they do not wash their hands when they eat bread."

3　And He answered and said to them, "Why do you yourselves transgress the commandment of God for the sake of your tradition?

4　"For God said, 'HONOR YOUR FATHER AND MOTHER,' and, 'HE WHO SPEAKS EVIL OF FATHER OR MOTHER IS TO BE PUT TO DEATH.'

5　"But you say, 'Whoever says to *his* father or mother, "Whatever I have that would help you has been given *to God*,"

6　he is not to honor his father or his mother.' And *by this* you invalidated the word of God for the sake of your tradition.

7　"You hypocrites, rightly did Isaiah prophesy of you:

8　'THIS PEOPLE HONORS ME WITH THEIR LIPS,
BUT THEIR HEART IS FAR AWAY FROM ME.

9　'BUT IN VAIN DO THEY WORSHIP ME,
TEACHING AS DOCTRINES THE PRECEPTS OF MEN.'"

10 After Jesus called the crowd to Him, He said to them, "Hear and understand.

11 "*It is* not what enters into the mouth *that* defiles the man, but what proceeds out of the mouth, this defiles the man."

12 Then the disciples *came and *said to Him, "Do You know that the Pharisees were offended when they heard this statement?"

13 But He answered and said, "Every plant which My heavenly Father did not plant shall be uprooted.

14 "Let them alone; they are blind guides of the blind. And if a blind man guides a blind man, both will fall into a pit."

15 Peter said to Him, "Explain the parable to us."

16 Jesus said, "Are you still lacking in understanding also?

17 "Do you not understand that everything that goes into the mouth passes into the stomach, and is eliminated?

18 "But the things that proceed out of the mouth come from the heart, and those defile the man.

19 "For out of the heart come evil thoughts, murders, adulteries, fornications, thefts, false witness, slanders.

20 "These are the things which defile the man; but to eat with unwashed hands does not defile the man."

JANUARY 24

Genesis 47:1—48:22

47 THEN Joseph went in and told Pharaoh, and said, "My father and my brothers and their flocks and their herds and all that they have, have come out of the land of Canaan; and behold, they are in the land of Goshen."

2 He took five men from among his brothers and presented them to Pharaoh.

3 Then Pharaoh said to his brothers, "What is your occupation?" So they said to Pharaoh, "Your servants are shepherds, both we and our fathers."

4 They said to Pharaoh, "We have come to sojourn in the land, for there is no pasture for your servants' flocks, for the famine is severe in the land of Canaan. Now, therefore, please let your servants live in the land of Goshen."

5 Then Pharaoh said to Joseph, "Your father and your brothers have come to you.

6 "The land of Egypt is at your disposal; settle your father and your brothers in the best of the land, let them live in the land of Goshen; and if you know any capable men among them, then put them in charge of my livestock."

7 Then Joseph brought his father Jacob and presented him to Pharaoh; and Jacob blessed Pharaoh.

8 Pharaoh said to Jacob, "How many years have you lived?"

9 So Jacob said to Pharaoh, "The years of my sojourning are one hundred and thirty; few and unpleasant have been the years of my life, nor have they attained the years that my fathers lived during the days of their sojourning."

10 And Jacob blessed Pharaoh, and went out from his presence.

11 So Joseph settled his father and his brothers and gave them a possession in the land of Egypt, in the best of the land, in the land of Rameses, as Pharaoh had ordered.

12 Joseph provided his father and his brothers and all his father's household with food, according to their little ones.

13 Now there was no food in all the land, because the famine was very severe, so that the land of Egypt and the land of Canaan languished because of the famine.

14 Joseph gathered all the money that was found in the land of Egypt and in the land of Canaan for the grain which they bought, and Joseph brought the money into Pharaoh's house.

15 When the money was all spent in the land of Egypt and in the land of Canaan, all the Egyptians came to Joseph and said, "Give us food, for why should we die in your presence? For *our* money is gone."

16 Then Joseph said, "Give up your livestock, and I will give you *food* for your livestock, since *your* money is gone."

17 So they brought their livestock to Joseph, and Joseph gave them food in exchange for the horses and the flocks and the herds and the donkeys; and he fed them with food in exchange for all their livestock that year.
18 When that year was ended, they came to him the next year and said to him, "We will not hide from my lord that our money is all spent, and the cattle are my lord's. There is nothing left for my lord except our bodies and our lands.
19 "Why should we die before your eyes, both we and our land? Buy us and our land for food, and we and our land will be slaves to Pharaoh. So give us seed, that we may live and not die, and that the land may not be desolate."
20 So Joseph bought all the land of Egypt for Pharaoh, for every Egyptian sold his field, because the famine was severe upon them. Thus the land became Pharaoh's.
21 As for the people, he removed them to the cities from one end of Egypt's border to the other.
22 Only the land of the priests he did not buy, for the priests had an allotment from Pharaoh, and they lived off the allotment which Pharaoh gave them. Therefore, they did not sell their land.
23 Then Joseph said to the people, "Behold, I have today bought you and your land for Pharaoh; now, *here* is seed for you, and you may sow the land.
24 "At the harvest you shall give a fifth to Pharaoh, and four-fifths shall be your own for seed of the field and for your food and for those of your households and as food for your little ones."
25 So they said, "You have saved our lives! Let us find favor in the sight of my lord, and we will be Pharaoh's slaves."
26 Joseph made it a statute concerning the land of Egypt *valid* to this day, that Pharaoh should have the fifth; only the land of the priests did not become Pharaoh's.
27 Now Israel lived in the land of Egypt, in Goshen, and they acquired property in it and were fruitful and became very numerous.
28 Jacob lived in the land of Egypt seventeen years; so the length of Jacob's life was one hundred and forty-seven years.
29 When the time for Israel to die drew near, he called his son Joseph and said

to him, "Please, if I have found favor in your sight, place now your hand under my thigh and deal with me in kindness and faithfulness. Please do not bury me in Egypt,
30 but when I lie down with my fathers, you shall carry me out of Egypt and bury me in their burial place." And he said, "I will do as you have said."
31 He said, "Swear to me." So he swore to him. Then Israel bowed *in worship* at the head of the bed.

48 NOW it came about after these things that Joseph was told, "Behold, your father is sick." So he took his two sons Manasseh and Ephraim with him.
2 When it was told to Jacob, "Behold, your son Joseph has come to you," Israel collected his strength and sat up in the bed.
3 Then Jacob said to Joseph, "God Almighty appeared to me at Luz in the land of Canaan and blessed me,
4 and He said to me, 'Behold, I will make you fruitful and numerous, and I will make you a company of peoples, and will give this land to your descendants after you for an everlasting possession.'
5 "Now your two sons, who were born to you in the land of Egypt before I came to you in Egypt, are mine; Ephraim and Manasseh shall be mine, as Reuben and Simeon are.
6 "But your offspring that have been born after them shall be yours; they shall be called by the names of their brothers in their inheritance.
7 "Now as for me, when I came from Paddan, Rachel died, to my sorrow, in the land of Canaan on the journey, when there was still some distance to go to Ephrath; and I buried her there on the way to Ephrath (that is, Bethlehem)."
8 When Israel saw Joseph's sons, he said, "Who are these?"
9 Joseph said to his father, "They are my sons, whom God has given me here." So he said, "Bring them to me, please, that I may bless them."
10 Now the eyes of Israel were *so* dim from age *that* he could not see. Then Joseph brought them close to him, and he kissed them and embraced them.
11 Israel said to Joseph, "I never ◄ expected to see your face, and behold,

God has let me see your children as well."

12 Then Joseph took them from his knees, and bowed with his face to the ground.

13 Joseph took them both, Ephraim with his right hand toward Israel's left, and Manasseh with his left hand toward Israel's right, and brought them close to him.

14 But Israel stretched out his right hand and laid it on the head of Ephraim, who was the younger, and his left hand on Manasseh's head, crossing his hands, although Manasseh was the firstborn.

➤ 15 He blessed Joseph, and said,
"The God before whom my fathers
   Abraham and Isaac walked,
The God who has been my
   shepherd all my life to this day,

16 The angel who has redeemed me
   from all evil,
Bless the lads;
And may my name live on in
   them,

And the names of my fathers
   Abraham and Isaac;
And may they grow into a multitude
   in the midst of the earth."

17 When Joseph saw that his father laid his right hand on Ephraim's head, it displeased him; and he grasped his father's hand to remove it from Ephraim's head to Manasseh's head.

18 Joseph said to his father, "Not so, my father, for this one is the firstborn. Place your right hand on his head."

19 But his father refused and said, "I know, my son, I know; he also will become a people and he also will be great. However, his younger brother shall be greater than he, and his descendants shall become a multitude of nations."

20 He blessed them that day, saying,
"By you Israel will pronounce
   blessing, saying,
'May God make you like Ephraim
   and Manasseh!'"
Thus he put Ephraim before Manasseh.

21 Then Israel said to Joseph, "Behold, I am about to die, but God will be with you, and bring you back to the land of your fathers.

22 "I give you one portion more than your brothers, which I took from the hand of the Amorite with my sword and my bow."

◈ **Psalm 13:1–6**

For the choir director. A Psalm of David.

13 HOW long, O LORD? Will You forget me forever?
   How long will You hide Your face from me?

2 How long shall I take counsel in my soul,
   Having sorrow in my heart all the day?
   How long will my enemy be exalted over me?

3 Consider *and* answer me, O LORD my God;
   Enlighten my eyes, or I will sleep the *sleep of* death,

4 And my enemy will say, "I have overcome him,"
   And my adversaries will rejoice when I am shaken.

LIFE LESSONS

➤ **Psalm 13:5 —** *I have trusted in Your lovingkindness; my heart shall rejoice in Your salvation.*

The Christian life thrives on both memory and hope. We remember how God has shown us mercy in the past, and so we look forward to how He will save us in the future.

5 But I have trusted in Your
    lovingkindness;
  My heart shall rejoice in Your
    salvation.
6 I will sing to the LORD,
  Because He has dealt bountifully
    with me.

Proverbs 4:18–19

18 But the path of the righteous is like
    the light of dawn,
  That shines brighter and brighter
    until the full day.
19 The way of the wicked is like
    darkness;
  They do not know over what they
    stumble.

Matthew 15:21–39

21 Jesus went away from there, and withdrew into the district of Tyre and Sidon.
22 And a Canaanite woman from that region came out and *began* to cry out, saying, "Have mercy on me, Lord, Son of David; my daughter is cruelly demon-possessed."
23 But He did not answer her a word. And His disciples came and implored Him, saying, "Send her away, because she keeps shouting at us."
24 But He answered and said, "I was sent only to the lost sheep of the house of Israel."
25 But she came and *began* to bow down before Him, saying, "Lord, help me!"
26 And He answered and said, "It is not good to take the children's bread and throw it to the dogs."
27 But she said, "Yes, Lord; but even the dogs feed on the crumbs which fall from their masters' table."
28 Then Jesus said to her, "O woman, your faith is great; it shall be done for you as you wish." And her daughter was healed at once.
29 Departing from there, Jesus went along by the Sea of Galilee, and having gone up on the mountain, He was sitting there.
30 And large crowds came to Him, bringing with them *those who were* lame, crippled, blind, mute, and many others, and they laid them down at His feet; and He healed them.
31 So the crowd marveled as they saw the mute speaking, the crippled restored, and the lame walking, and the blind seeing; and they glorified the God of Israel.
32 And Jesus called His disciples to Him, and said, "I feel compassion for the people, because they have remained with Me now three days and have nothing to eat; and I do not want to send them away hungry, for they might faint on the way."
33 The disciples *said to Him, "Where would we get so many loaves in *this* desolate place to satisfy such a large crowd?"
34 And Jesus *said to them, "How many loaves do you have?" And they said, "Seven, and a few small fish."
35 And He directed the people to sit down on the ground;
36 and He took the seven loaves and the fish; and giving thanks, He broke them and started giving them to the disciples, and the disciples *gave them* to the people.
37 And they all ate and were satisfied, and they picked up what was left over of the broken pieces, seven large baskets full.
38 And those who ate were four thousand men, besides women and children.
39 And sending away the crowds, Jesus got into the boat and came to the region of Magadan.

LIFE LESSONS

➤ **Matthew 15:28 —** *Then Jesus said to her, "O woman, your faith is great."*

Only two people in the Gospels are said to have great faith, and both of them were Gentiles (the other was a Roman centurion, see Matt. 8:10). Great faith does not depend on background or position, but on the heart.

WHAT THE BIBLE SAYS ABOUT

Provision

Matthew 15:29–38

The service you do for God may be demanding and draining. You may come to the point where the only thing that can help you is His intervention because all other resources have been used up. Good! This is the perfect opportunity for God to remind you that He fuels the ministry done in His name.

Be encouraged by the testimony of Matthew 15. The people had been on the mountainside with Jesus for three days—listening to His words and hoping for healing. Jesus saw they were tired and hungry and said, "I feel compassion for the people, because they have remained with Me now three days and have nothing to eat; and I do not want to send them away hungry, for they might faint on the way" (v. 32).

Unfortunately, the disciples could not look past the barrenness of their surroundings. They asked, "Where would we get so many loaves in this desolate place to satisfy such a large crowd?" (v. 33).

Where, indeed? The disciples trusted Christ enough to drop their nets and follow Him (Matt. 4:18–22), but they still did not understand that the Lord God would care for all of their needs—and the needs of anyone who follows Him (Phil. 4:19).

God knows when you have run out of resources. In fact, in Matthew 6:8, Jesus tells us, "Your Father knows what you need before you ask Him." You've trusted Jesus to provide for your salvation. Can't you also trust Him to provide for the other things you need?

God will always provide for your needs above and beyond your expectations when you are obeying Him—so trust Him. He will have compassion on you and will not send you away hungry. ◈

JANUARY 25

Genesis 49:1—50:26

49 THEN Jacob summoned his sons and said, "Assemble yourselves that I may tell you what will befall you in the days to come.

2 "Gather together and hear, O sons of Jacob;
   And listen to Israel your father.

3 "Reuben, you are my firstborn;
   My might and the beginning of my strength,
   Preeminent in dignity and preeminent in power.

4 "Uncontrolled as water, you shall not have preeminence,
   Because you went up to your father's bed;
   Then you defiled *it*—he went up to my couch.

5 "Simeon and Levi are brothers;
   Their swords are implements of violence.

6 "Let my soul not enter into their council;

Let not my glory be united with their assembly;
   Because in their anger they slew men,
   And in their self-will they lamed oxen.

7 "Cursed be their anger, for it is fierce;
   And their wrath, for it is cruel.
   I will disperse them in Jacob,
   And scatter them in Israel.

8 "Judah, your brothers shall praise you;
   Your hand shall be on the neck of your enemies;
   Your father's sons shall bow down to you.

9 "Judah is a lion's whelp;
   From the prey, my son, you have gone up.
   He couches, he lies down as a lion,
   And as a lion, who dares rouse him up?

10 "The scepter shall not depart from Judah,

LIFE LESSONS

➤ **Genesis 49:10 —** *"The scepter shall not depart from Judah, nor the ruler's staff from between his feet."*

Israel foresaw that the Messiah, Jesus, would come through the line of Judah, and He would be both the King and the Judge of the entire earth.

Nor the ruler's staff from between
   his feet,
Until Shiloh comes,
And to him *shall be* the obedience
   of the peoples.

11 "He ties *his* foal to the vine,
   And his donkey's colt to the choice
    vine;
   He washes his garments in wine,
   And his robes in the blood of
    grapes.

12 "His eyes are dull from wine,
   And his teeth white from milk.

13 "Zebulun will dwell at the seashore;
   And he *shall be* a haven for ships,
   And his flank *shall be* toward
    Sidon.

14 "Issachar is a strong donkey,
   Lying down between the
    sheepfolds.

15 "When he saw that a resting place
    was good
   And that the land was pleasant,
   He bowed his shoulder to bear
    burdens,
   And became a slave at forced labor.

16 "Dan shall judge his people,
   As one of the tribes of Israel.

17 "Dan shall be a serpent in the way,
   A horned snake in the path,
   That bites the horse's heels,
   So that his rider falls backward.

18 "For Your salvation I wait, O LORD.

19 "As for Gad, raiders shall raid him,
   But he will raid *at* their heels.

20 "As for Asher, his food shall be rich,
   And he will yield royal dainties.

21 "Naphtali is a doe let loose,
   He gives beautiful words.

22 "Joseph is a fruitful bough,
   A fruitful bough by a spring;
   Its branches run over a wall.

23 "The archers bitterly attacked him,
   And shot *at him* and harassed him;

24 But his bow remained firm,
   And his arms were agile,

From the hands of the Mighty One
   of Jacob
(From there is the Shepherd, the
   Stone of Israel),

25 From the God of your father who
   helps you,
   And by the Almighty who blesses
    you
   With blessings of heaven above,
   Blessings of the deep that lies
    beneath,
   Blessings of the breasts and of the
    womb.

26 "The blessings of your father
   Have surpassed the blessings of my
    ancestors
   Up to the utmost bound of the
    everlasting hills;
   May they be on the head of
    Joseph,
   And on the crown of the head of
    the one distinguished among his
    brothers.

27 "Benjamin is a ravenous wolf;
   In the morning he devours the prey,
   And in the evening he divides the
    spoil."

28 All these are the twelve tribes of Israel, and this is what their father said to them when he blessed them. He blessed them, every one with the blessing appropriate to him.

29 Then he charged them and said to them, "I am about to be gathered to my people; bury me with my fathers in the cave that is in the field of Ephron the Hittite,

30 in the cave that is in the field of Machpelah, which is before Mamre, in the land of Canaan, which Abraham bought along with the field from Ephron the Hittite for a burial site.

31 "There they buried Abraham and his wife Sarah, there they buried Isaac and his wife Rebekah, and there I buried Leah—

32 the field and the cave that is in it, purchased from the sons of Heth."

33 When Jacob finished charging his sons, he drew his feet into the bed and breathed his last, and was gathered to his people.

50 THEN Joseph fell on his father's face, and wept over him and kissed him.

2 Joseph commanded his servants the

physicians to embalm his father. So the physicians embalmed Israel.

3   Now forty days were required for it, for such is the period required for embalming. And the Egyptians wept for him seventy days.

4   When the days of mourning for him were past, Joseph spoke to the household of Pharaoh, saying, "If now I have found favor in your sight, please speak to Pharaoh, saying,

5   'My father made me swear, saying, "Behold, I am about to die; in my grave which I dug for myself in the land of Canaan, there you shall bury me." Now therefore, please let me go up and bury my father; then I will return.'"

6   Pharaoh said, "Go up and bury your father, as he made you swear."

7   So Joseph went up to bury his father, and with him went up all the servants of Pharaoh, the elders of his household and all the elders of the land of Egypt,

8   and all the household of Joseph and his brothers and his father's household; they left only their little ones and their flocks and their herds in the land of Goshen.

9   There also went up with him both chariots and horsemen; and it was a very great company.

10   When they came to the threshing floor of Atad, which is beyond the Jordan, they lamented there with a very great and sorrowful lamentation; and he observed seven days mourning for his father.

11   Now when the inhabitants of the land, the Canaanites, saw the mourning at the threshing floor of Atad, they said, "This is a grievous mourning for the Egyptians." Therefore it was named Abel-mizraim, which is beyond the Jordan.

12   Thus his sons did for him as he had charged them;

13   for his sons carried him to the land of Canaan and buried him in the cave of the field of Machpelah before Mamre, which Abraham had bought along with the field for a burial site from Ephron the Hittite.

14   After he had buried his father, Joseph returned to Egypt, he and his brothers, and all who had gone up with him to bury his father.

15   When Joseph's brothers saw that their father was dead, they said, "What if Joseph bears a grudge against us and pays us back in full for all the wrong which we did to him!"

16   So they sent *a message* to Joseph, saying, "Your father charged before he died, saying,

17   'Thus you shall say to Joseph, "Please forgive, I beg you, the transgression of your brothers and their sin, for they did you wrong."' And now, please forgive the transgression of the servants of the God of your father." And Joseph wept when they spoke to him.

18   Then his brothers also came and fell down before him and said, "Behold, we are your servants."

19   But Joseph said to them, "Do not be afraid, for am I in God's place?

20   "As for you, you meant evil against me, *but* God meant it for good in order to bring about this present result, to preserve many people alive.

21   "So therefore, do not be afraid; I will provide for you and your little ones." So he comforted them and spoke kindly to them.

22   Now Joseph stayed in Egypt, he and his father's household, and Joseph lived one hundred and ten years.

23   Joseph saw the third generation of Ephraim's sons; also the sons of Machir, the son of Manasseh, were born on Joseph's knees.

24   Joseph said to his brothers, "I am about to die, but God will surely take care of you and bring you up from this land to the land which He promised on oath to Abraham, to Isaac and to Jacob."

25   Then Joseph made the sons of Israel swear, saying, "God will surely take care of you, and you shall carry my bones up from here."

26   So Joseph died at the age of one hundred and ten years; and he was embalmed and placed in a coffin in Egypt.

LIFE LESSONS

➤ **Genesis 50:20 —** *"You meant evil against me, but God meant it for good."*

Sometimes God allows us to go through difficult times, even as a result of the wicked actions of others. Yet whatever we have to endure, no matter how unfair or unjust, we can be sure God will use it for good (Rom. 8:28).

ANSWERS TO LIFE'S QUESTIONS

Does God bring us adversity?

GENESIS 50:19, 20

*T*he life story of Joseph clearly illustrates God sometimes grants permission for adversity to enter our lives so He might accomplish an ultimate good.

Jacob didn't try to hide his lopsided love for Joseph, his son by his favorite wife, Rachel. So when Joseph shared two dreams with his brothers—dreams in which Joseph took center stage and his brothers bowed low to serve him—they started looking for a way to destroy him.

One day, Joseph's brothers secretly sold him into slavery. Eventually, he became the slave of Potiphar, an officer of Pharaoh. Joseph quickly rose to prominence in his new position, but when Potiphar's wife falsely accused him of rape, Joseph found himself being imprisoned for a crime he did not commit.

Even there, in total confinement, he rose to a position of leadership. When he correctly interpreted the dream of a royal servant, Joseph hoped his fortunes were about to change. But the man promptly forgot him for two long years. Not until Pharaoh himself needed someone to interpret a troubling dream did the man mention Joseph (Gen. 39–40).

At the right time, God reversed Joseph's adversity.

After he had correctly interpreted the dream, Pharaoh ordered him released and placed in charge of Egypt's granaries. Later, Joseph used his new authority as prime minister to help his family through a severe famine.

After Jacob's death, Joseph's brothers feared he might try to pay them back. "But Joseph said to them, 'Do not be afraid, for am I in God's place? As for you, you meant evil against me, but God meant it for good in order to bring about this present result, to preserve many people alive'" (Gen. 50:19, 20).

In looking back over his life—even the dark and painful events—Joseph realized God had been in charge the entire time. Nothing had happened to him apart from His will and divine plan.

In the same way, when you belong to the Lord, any adversity you experience remains subject to the Lord's power and grace. He never stops being in charge of your life. He never loses authority over you or over the circumstances affecting you. God is *always* in control.

Therefore, you must realize, on occasion, the Lord permits adversity to enter your life. But He always uses adversity to fulfill His purposes in your life.

Psalm 14:1–7

For the choir director. *A Psalm* of David.

14 THE fool has said in his heart, "There is no God."
They are corrupt, they have committed abominable deeds;
There is no one who does good.

2 The LORD has looked down from heaven upon the sons of men

To see if there are any who understand,
Who seek after God.

3 They have all turned aside, together they have become corrupt;
There is no one who does good, not even one.

4 Do all the workers of wickedness not know,
Who eat up my people *as* they eat bread,
And do not call upon the Lord?

5 There they are in great dread,
For God is with the righteous generation.

6 You would put to shame the counsel of the afflicted,
But the LORD is his refuge.

7 Oh, that the salvation of Israel would come out of Zion!
When the LORD restores His captive people,
Jacob will rejoice, Israel will be glad.

LIFE LESSONS

➤ **Psalm 14:1 — *The fool has said in his heart, "There is no God."***

*O*ur society has a lot more "practical atheists" than it does self-proclaimed atheists. A practical atheist acts as though God does not exist, whatever he or she may proclaim to believe. Both views of God are foolish and self-destructive

Proverbs 4:20–24

20 My son, give attention to my words;
    Incline your ear to my sayings.
21 Do not let them depart from your
        sight;
    Keep them in the midst of your
        heart.
22 For they are life to those who find
        them
    And health to all their body.
23 Watch over your heart with all
        diligence,
    For from it *flow* the springs of life.
24 Put away from you a deceitful
        mouth
    And put devious speech far from
        you.

Matthew 16:1–28

16THE Pharisees and Sadducees
    came up, and testing Jesus, they
asked Him to show them a sign from
heaven.
2 But He replied to them, "When it is
evening, you say, '*It will be* fair weather,
for the sky is red.'
3 "And in the morning, '*There will
be* a storm today, for the sky is red and
threatening.' Do you know how to discern the appearance of the sky, but cannot *discern* the signs of the times?
4 "An evil and adulterous generation
seeks after a sign; and a sign will not be
given it, except the sign of Jonah." And
He left them and went away.
5 And the disciples came to the other
side *of the sea,* but they had forgotten to
bring *any* bread.
6 And Jesus said to them, "Watch out

and beware of the leaven of the Pharisees and Sadducees."
7 They began to discuss *this* among
themselves, saying, "*He said that* because we did not bring *any* bread."
8 But Jesus, aware of this, said, "You
men of little faith, why do you discuss among yourselves that you have no
bread?
9 "Do you not yet understand or remember the five loaves of the five thousand, and how many baskets *full* you
picked up?
10 "Or the seven loaves of the four
thousand, and how many large baskets
full you picked up?
11 "How is it that you do not understand that I did not speak to you concerning bread? But beware of the leaven
of the Pharisees and Sadducees."
12 Then they understood that He did
not say to beware of the leaven of bread,
but of the teaching of the Pharisees and
Sadducees.
13 Now when Jesus came into the district of Caesarea Philippi, He was asking
His disciples, "Who do people say that
the Son of Man is?"
14 And they said, "Some *say* John the
Baptist; and others, Elijah; but still others, Jeremiah, or one of the prophets."
15 He *said to them, "But who do you
say that I am?"
16 Simon Peter answered, "You are the
Christ, the Son of the living God."
17 And Jesus said to him, "Blessed are
you, Simon Barjona, because flesh and
blood did not reveal *this* to you, but My
Father who is in heaven.
18 "I also say to you that you are
Peter, and upon this rock I will build My
church; and the gates of Hades will not
overpower it.
19 "I will give you the keys of the

LIFE LESSONS

➤ **Matthew 16:4 — "A sign will not be
given it, except the sign of Jonah."**

*O*nce before, Jesus had spoken of the
"sign of the prophet Jonah" (Matt.
12:39–41). As Jonah had spent three days
in the belly of the great fish, so Jesus
would spend three days "in the heart of
the earth" before His resurrection (Matt.
12:40).

➤ **Matthew 16:15 — "Who do you say
that I am?"**

*J*esus has no interest in dispassionate,
hypothetical views regarding His life
and work. Instead, He wanted to know
what His followers and disciples thought
about Him. His question to you today is,
"Who do *you* say I am?"

kingdom of heaven; and whatever you bind on earth shall have been bound in heaven, and whatever you loose on earth shall have been loosed in heaven."
20 Then He warned the disciples that they should tell no one that He was the Christ.
21 From that time Jesus began to show His disciples that He must go to Jerusalem, and suffer many things from the elders and chief priests and scribes, and be killed, and be raised up on the third day.
22 Peter took Him aside and began to rebuke Him, saying, "God forbid *it*, Lord! This shall never happen to You."
23 But He turned and said to Peter, "Get behind Me, Satan! You are a stumbling block to Me; for you are not setting your mind on God's interests, but man's."
24 Then Jesus said to His disciples, "If anyone wishes to come after Me, he must deny himself, and take up his cross and follow Me.
25 "For whoever wishes to save his life will lose it; but whoever loses his life for My sake will find it.

LIFE LESSONS

➢ **Matthew 16:23 — *"Get behind Me, Satan! You are a stumbling block to Me; for you are not setting your mind on God's interests, but man's."***

The "gentle Jesus" could be very stern when He had to be. He knows when to show us compassion, and He knows when we need correction or rebuke. He always gives us what we need, not necessarily what we want.

26 "For what will it profit a man if he gains the whole world and forfeits his soul? Or what will a man give in exchange for his soul?
27 "FOR THE SON OF MAN IS GOING TO COME IN THE GLORY OF HIS FATHER WITH HIS ANGELS, AND WILL THEN REPAY EVERY MAN ACCORDING TO HIS DEEDS.
28 "Truly I say to you, there are some of those who are standing here who will not taste death until they see the Son of Man coming in His kingdom."

✤ Exodus 1:1—2:25

1 NOW these are the names of the sons of Israel who came to Egypt with Jacob; they came each one with his household:
2 Reuben, Simeon, Levi and Judah;
3 Issachar, Zebulun and Benjamin;
4 Dan and Naphtali, Gad and Asher.
5 All the persons who came from the loins of Jacob were seventy in number, but Joseph was *already* in Egypt.
6 Joseph died, and all his brothers and all that generation.
7 But the sons of Israel were fruitful and increased greatly, and multiplied, and became exceedingly mighty, so that the land was filled with them.
8 Now a new king arose over Egypt, who did not know Joseph.
9 He said to his people, "Behold, the people of the sons of Israel are more and mightier than we.

10 "Come, let us deal wisely with them, or else they will multiply and in the event of war, they will also join themselves to those who hate us, and fight against us and depart from the land."
11 So they appointed taskmasters over them to afflict them with hard labor. And they built for Pharaoh storage cities, Pithom and Raamses.
12 But the more they afflicted them, the more they multiplied and the more they spread out, so that they were in dread of the sons of Israel.
13 The Egyptians compelled the sons of Israel to labor rigorously;
14 and they made their lives bitter with hard labor in mortar and bricks and at all *kinds* of labor in the field, all their labors which they rigorously imposed on them.
15 Then the king of Egypt spoke to the Hebrew midwives, one of whom was named Shiphrah and the other was named Puah;
16 and he said, "When you are helping

the Hebrew women to give birth and see *them* upon the birthstool, if it is a son, then you shall put him to death; but if it is a daughter, then she shall live."

➤ 17 But the midwives feared God, and did not do as the king of Egypt had commanded them, but let the boys live.

18 So the king of Egypt called for the midwives and said to them, "Why have you done this thing, and let the boys live?"

19 The midwives said to Pharaoh, "Because the Hebrew women are not as the Egyptian women; for they are vigorous and give birth before the midwife can get to them."

20 So God was good to the midwives, and the people multiplied, and became very mighty.

21 Because the midwives feared God, He established households for them.

22 Then Pharaoh commanded all his people, saying, "Every son who is born you are to cast into the Nile, and every daughter you are to keep alive."

2 NOW a man from the house of Levi went and married a daughter of Levi.

2 The woman conceived and bore a son; and when she saw that he was beautiful, she hid him for three months.

3 But when she could hide him no longer, she got him a wicker basket and covered it over with tar and pitch. Then she put the child into it and set *it* among the reeds by the bank of the Nile.

4 His sister stood at a distance to find out what would happen to him.

5 The daughter of Pharaoh came down

to bathe at the Nile, with her maidens walking alongside the Nile; and she saw the basket among the reeds and sent her maid, and she brought it *to her*.

6 When she opened *it*, she saw the child, and behold, *the* boy was crying. And she had pity on him and said, "This is one of the Hebrews' children."

7 Then his sister said to Pharaoh's daughter, "Shall I go and call a nurse for you from the Hebrew women that she may nurse the child for you?"

8 Pharaoh's daughter said to her, "Go ahead." So the girl went and called the child's mother.

9 Then Pharaoh's daughter said to her, "Take this child away and nurse him for me and I will give *you* your wages." So the woman took the child and nursed him.

10 The child grew, and she brought him ◄ to Pharaoh's daughter and he became her son. And she named him Moses, and said, "Because I drew him out of the water."

Life Examples:

MOSES: God's Pattern for Success

EXODUS 1:22—2:25

*O*ne of the greatest differences between the world's message about success and God's is this: The world seeks a single formula to produce one set of results for all people, while God's plan is far more creative, far more individualized, and far more personal.

Moses did not have a vision for success early in his life, although as an adopted son of Pharaoh's daughter he enjoyed a certain degree of privilege. After taking the life of an Egyptian, however, he left Egypt in fear that his heinous act would be exposed. Moses spent forty years in the wilderness tending sheep. But these years were not wasted. The Lord was in the process of preparing him for service. When Moses was ready—when brokenness had reached its goal—God called to him from the midst of a burning bush and gave him a specific set of instructions and life mission.

Many of us go through difficult and even devastating experiences, and then one day come face-to-face with the reality and calling of God. Is this the pattern that God seems to be implementing in your life? If so, stick with His plan, regardless of how extraordinary it may seem—the Promised Land lies in that direction!

LIFE LESSONS

➤ **Exodus 2:10 — *She brought him to Pharaoh's daughter and he became her son.***

*T*he Lord can take the evil of men and use it for immense good. Here, God took an Egyptian edict meant to kill Hebrew boys and used it to rear a Hebrew deliverer in Pharaoh's own household!

➤ **Exodus 2:23 — *They cried out; and their cry for help because of their bondage rose up to God.***

*G*od heard the cries and groans of the enslaved Hebrews and moved to act for their deliverance long before they understood His plan. God is at work on our behalf, even when He appears silent. He will always keep His promises.

11 Now it came about in those days, when Moses had grown up, that he went out to his brethren and looked on their hard labors; and he saw an Egyptian beating a Hebrew, one of his brethren.
12 So he looked this way and that, and when he saw there was no one *around,* he struck down the Egyptian and hid him in the sand.
13 He went out the next day, and behold, two Hebrews were fighting with each other; and he said to the offender, "Why are you striking your companion?"
14 But he said, "Who made you a prince or a judge over us? Are you intending to kill me as you killed the Egyptian?" Then Moses was afraid and said, "Surely the matter has become known."
15 When Pharaoh heard of this matter, he tried to kill Moses. But Moses fled from the presence of Pharaoh and settled in the land of Midian, and he sat down by a well.
16 Now the priest of Midian had seven daughters; and they came to draw water and filled the troughs to water their father's flock.
17 Then the shepherds came and drove them away, but Moses stood up and helped them and watered their flock.
18 When they came to Reuel their father, he said, "Why have you come *back* so soon today?"
19 So they said, "An Egyptian delivered us from the hand of the shepherds, and what is more, he even drew the water for us and watered the flock."
20 He said to his daughters, "Where is he then? Why is it that you have left the man behind? Invite him to have something to eat."
21 Moses was willing to dwell with the man, and he gave his daughter Zipporah to Moses.

22 Then she gave birth to a son, and he named him Gershom, for he said, "I have been a sojourner in a foreign land."
23 Now it came about in *the course of* those many days that the king of Egypt died. And the sons of Israel sighed because of the bondage, and they cried out; and their cry for help because of *their* bondage rose up to God.
24 So God heard their groaning; and God remembered His covenant with Abraham, Isaac, and Jacob.
25 God saw the sons of Israel, and God took notice *of them.*

Psalm 15:1–5

A Psalm of David.

15 O LORD, who may abide in Your tent?
Who may dwell on Your holy hill?
2 He who walks with integrity, and works righteousness,
And speaks truth in his heart.
3 He does not slander with his tongue,
Nor does evil to his neighbor,
Nor takes up a reproach against his friend;
4 In whose eyes a reprobate is despised,
But who honors those who fear the LORD;
He swears to his own hurt and does not change;
5 He does not put out his money at interest,
Nor does he take a bribe against the innocent.
He who does these things will never be shaken.

Proverbs 4:25–27

25 Let your eyes look directly ahead
    And let your gaze be fixed straight
       in front of you.
26 Watch the path of your feet
    And all your ways will be
       established.
27 Do not turn to the right nor to the
       left;
    Turn your foot from evil.

Matthew 17:1–27

17 SIX days later Jesus *took with Him Peter and James and John his brother, and *led them up on a high mountain by themselves.
2 And He was transfigured before them; and His face shone like the sun, and His garments became as white as light.
3 And behold, Moses and Elijah appeared to them, talking with Him.
4 Peter said to Jesus, "Lord, it is good for us to be here; if You wish, I will make three tabernacles here, one for You, and one for Moses, and one for Elijah."
5 While he was still speaking, a bright cloud overshadowed them, and behold, a voice out of the cloud said, "This is My beloved Son, with whom I am well-pleased; listen to Him!"
6 When the disciples heard *this*, they fell face down to the ground and were terrified.
7 And Jesus came to *them* and touched them and said, "Get up, and do not be afraid."
8 And lifting up their eyes, they saw no one except Jesus Himself alone.

9 As they were coming down from the mountain, Jesus commanded them, saying, "Tell the vision to no one until the Son of Man has risen from the dead."
10 And His disciples asked Him, "Why then do the scribes say that Elijah must come first?"
11 And He answered and said, "Elijah is coming and will restore all things;
12 but I say to you that Elijah already came, and they did not recognize him, but did to him whatever they wished. So also the Son of Man is going to suffer at their hands."
13 Then the disciples understood that He had spoken to them about John the Baptist.
14 When they came to the crowd, a man came up to Jesus, falling on his knees before Him and saying,
15 "Lord, have mercy on my son, for he is a lunatic and is very ill; for he often falls into the fire and often into the water.
16 "I brought him to Your disciples, and they could not cure him."
17 And Jesus answered and said, "You unbelieving and perverted generation, how long shall I be with you? How long shall I put up with you? Bring him here to Me."
18 And Jesus rebuked him, and the demon came out of him, and the boy was cured at once.

19 Then the disciples came to Jesus privately and said, "Why could we not drive it out?"
20 And He *said to them, "Because of the littleness of your faith; for truly I say to you, if you have faith the size of a mustard seed, you will say to this mountain, 'Move from here to there,' and it will move; and nothing will be impossible to you.
21 ["But this kind does not go out except by prayer and fasting."]
22 And while they were gathering together in Galilee, Jesus said to them, "The Son of Man is going to be delivered into the hands of men;
23 and they will kill Him, and He will be raised on the third day." And they were deeply grieved.

24 When they came to Capernaum, those who collected the two-drachma *tax* came to Peter and said, "Does your teacher not pay the two-drachma *tax*?"
25 He *said, "Yes." And when he came into the house, Jesus spoke to him first, saying, "What do you think, Simon? From whom do the kings of the earth collect customs or poll-tax, from their sons or from strangers?"
26 When Peter said, "From strangers," Jesus said to him, "Then the sons are exempt.
27 "However, so that we do not offend them, go to the sea and throw in a hook, and take the first fish that comes up; and when you open its mouth, you will find a shekel. Take that and give it to them for you and Me."

◈ Exodus 3:1—4:31

3 NOW Moses was pasturing the flock of Jethro his father-in-law, the priest of Midian; and he led the flock to the west side of the wilderness and came to Horeb, the mountain of God.
2 The angel of the LORD appeared to him in a blazing fire from the midst of a bush; and he looked, and behold, the bush was burning with fire, yet the bush was not consumed.
3 So Moses said, "I must turn aside now and see this marvelous sight, why the bush is not burned up."
4 When the LORD saw that he turned aside to look, God called to him from the midst of the bush and said, "Moses, Moses!" And he said, "Here I am."

LIFE LESSONS

➤ **Exodus 3:2 — *And he looked, and behold, the bush was burning with fire, yet the bush was not consumed.***

God often speaks to us through unusual circumstances. When we find ourselves in the midst of confusing times that we don't understand, we should slow down and listen. God just might be trying to tell us something.

5 Then He said, "Do not come near here; remove your sandals from your feet, for the place on which you are standing is holy ground."
6 He said also, "I am the God of your father, the God of Abraham, the God of Isaac, and the God of Jacob." Then Moses hid his face, for he was afraid to look at God.
7 The LORD said, "I have surely seen the affliction of My people who are in Egypt, and have given heed to their cry because of their taskmasters, for I am aware of their sufferings.
8 "So I have come down to deliver them from the power of the Egyptians, and to bring them up from that land to a good and spacious land, to a land flowing with milk and honey, to the place of the Canaanite and the Hittite and the Amorite and the Perizzite and the Hivite and the Jebusite.
9 "Now, behold, the cry of the sons of Israel has come to Me; furthermore, I have seen the oppression with which the Egyptians are oppressing them.
10 "Therefore, come now, and I will send you to Pharaoh, so that you may bring My people, the sons of Israel, out of Egypt."
11 But Moses said to God, "Who am I, that I should go to Pharaoh, and that

What can I do to earn a more spiritually responsible role?

EXODUS 3:3–9

Few men ever had a greater responsibility placed on their shoulders than Moses, whom God tasked with leading the nation of Israel out of Egyptian bondage and into the Promised Land.

Responsibility requires a spirit of faithfulness, dependability, and the refusal to give up when times get tough. Moses had these qualities, and God chose him as His special human representative.

It took years, however, to prepare Moses for the enormous job. He began life as an impetuous, hotheaded, and stubborn young man. When he witnessed the suffering of God's people in Egypt, immediately he sought to deliver them through his own human strength—and neither he nor his people benefited from his hasty actions.

The Father always clarifies our responsibility so we can respond in obedience. He never leaves us alone; He promises to shoulder the burden with us. If He didn't, we would become easily discouraged and would fail to understand the significance of our callings.

He uses various events and circumstances to prepare us for increasing levels of spiritual responsibility. He used a burning bush to gain Moses' attention (Ex. 3:3–9): This was the man's moment of calling. By this time, Moses' heart had become receptive and his spirit primed for greater spiritual responsibility.

God always equips us for the work He gives us to do. He provided Aaron as a brother, friend, and spokesman for Moses. Even the staff He gave Moses was amazingly useful as a symbol of His power.

He also always prepares us for the role He assigns us. Throughout Moses' life, God had been preparing him to lead the nation of Israel.

Anytime the Lord calls us to fulfill a certain responsibility, we enter a period of waiting. Moses tried to take a shortcut but failed, and he spent forty years in the desert as a result. Yet in these times of waiting, God molds and shapes us. The *only* way to meet the challenge of responsibility is to be willing to wait on God's timing in every situation.

Three words characterize a responsible person: *confidence* in God's calling and ability; the *courage* to obey regardless of the cost; and a *commitment* to Jesus Christ.

God gives us limitless opportunities, but we must assume responsibility and obey His call. As you pray, ask God to expand your world of opportunities and give you the desire to become responsible, like Moses, and willing to obey regardless of the cost.

I should bring the sons of Israel out of Egypt?"

12 And He said, "Certainly I will be with you, and this shall be the sign to you that it is I who have sent you: when you have brought the people out of Egypt, you shall worship God at this mountain."

13 Then Moses said to God, "Behold, I am going to the sons of Israel, and I will say to them, 'The God of your fathers has sent me to you.' Now they may say to me, 'What is His name?' What shall I say to them?"

14 God said to Moses, "I AM WHO I AM"; and He said, "Thus you shall say to the sons of Israel, 'I AM has sent me to you.'"

15 God, furthermore, said to Moses, "Thus you shall say to the sons of Israel, 'The LORD, the God of your fathers, the God of Abraham, the God of Isaac, and the God of Jacob, has sent me to you.'

This is My name forever, and this is My memorial-name to all generations.

16 "Go and gather the elders of Israel together and say to them, 'The LORD, the God of your fathers, the God of Abraham, Isaac and Jacob, has appeared to me, saying, "I am indeed concerned about you and what has been done to you in Egypt.

17 "So I said, I will bring you up out

LIFE LESSONS

➤ **Exodus 3:14 — "I AM WHO I AM"; and He said, "Thus you shall say to the sons of Israel, 'I AM has sent me to you.'"**

We serve the God who is alive, who is present, who is here right now, and who gives life and breath to everything that lives (Acts 17:25). He IS, whether anything else remains or not.

of the affliction of Egypt to the land of the Canaanite and the Hittite and the Amorite and the Perizzite and the Hivite and the Jebusite, to a land flowing with milk and honey."'

18 "They will pay heed to what you say; and you with the elders of Israel will come to the king of Egypt and you will say to him, 'The LORD, the God of the Hebrews, has met with us. So now, please, let us go a three days' journey into the wilderness, that we may sacrifice to the LORD our God.'

19 "But I know that the king of Egypt will not permit you to go, except under compulsion.

20 "So I will stretch out My hand and strike Egypt with all My miracles which I shall do in the midst of it; and after that he will let you go.

21 "I will grant this people favor in the sight of the Egyptians; and it shall be that when you go, you will not go empty-handed.

22 "But every woman shall ask of her neighbor and the woman who lives in her house, articles of silver and articles of gold, and clothing; and you will put them on your sons and daughters. Thus you will plunder the Egyptians."

4 THEN Moses said, "What if they will not believe me or listen to what I say? For they may say, 'The LORD has not appeared to you.'"

2 The LORD said to him, "What is that in your hand?" And he said, "A staff."

3 Then He said, "Throw it on the ground." So he threw it on the ground, and it became a serpent; and Moses fled from it.

4 But the LORD said to Moses, "Stretch out your hand and grasp *it* by its tail"—so he stretched out his hand and caught it, and it became a staff in his hand—

5 "that they may believe that the LORD, the God of their fathers, the God of Abraham, the God of Isaac, and the God of Jacob, has appeared to you."

6 The LORD furthermore said to him, "Now put your hand into your bosom." So he put his hand into his bosom, and when he took it out, behold, his hand was leprous like snow.

7 Then He said, "Put your hand into your bosom again." So he put his hand into his bosom again, and when he took

it out of his bosom, behold, it was restored like *the rest of* his flesh.

8 "If they will not believe you or heed the witness of the first sign, they may believe the witness of the last sign.

9 "But if they will not believe even these two signs or heed what you say, then you shall take some water from the Nile and pour it on the dry ground; and the water which you take from the Nile will become blood on the dry ground."

10 Then Moses said to the LORD, "Please, Lord, I have never been eloquent, neither recently nor in time past, nor since You have spoken to Your servant; for I am slow of speech and slow of tongue."

11 The LORD said to him, "Who has made man's mouth? Or who makes *him* mute or deaf, or seeing or blind? Is it not I, the LORD?

12 "Now then go, and I, even I, will be with your mouth, and teach you what you are to say."

13 But he said, "Please, Lord, now send *the message* by whomever You will."

14 Then the anger of the LORD burned against Moses, and He said, "Is there not your brother Aaron the Levite? I know that he speaks fluently. And moreover, behold, he is coming out to meet you; when he sees you, he will be glad in his heart.

15 "You are to speak to him and put the words in his mouth; and I, even I, will be with your mouth and his mouth, and I will teach you what you are to do.

16 "Moreover, he shall speak for you to the people; and he will be as a mouth for you and you will be as God to him.

17 "You shall take in your hand this staff, with which you shall perform the signs."

18 Then Moses departed and returned

---

to Jethro his father-in-law and said to him, "Please, let me go, that I may return to my brethren who are in Egypt, and see if they are still alive." And Jethro said to Moses, "Go in peace."

19 Now the LORD said to Moses in Midian, "Go back to Egypt, for all the men who were seeking your life are dead."

20 So Moses took his wife and his sons and mounted them on a donkey, and returned to the land of Egypt. Moses also took the staff of God in his hand.

21 The LORD said to Moses, "When you go back to Egypt see that you perform before Pharaoh all the wonders which I have put in your power; but I will harden his heart so that he will not let the people go.

22 "Then you shall say to Pharaoh, 'Thus says the LORD, "Israel is My son, My firstborn.

23 "So I said to you, 'Let My son go that he may serve Me'; but you have refused to let him go. Behold, I will kill your son, your firstborn."'"

24 Now it came about at the lodging place on the way that the LORD met him and sought to put him to death.

25 Then Zipporah took a flint and cut off her son's foreskin and threw it at Moses' feet, and she said, "You are indeed a bridegroom of blood to me."

26 So He let him alone. At that time she said, "*You are* a bridegroom of blood"—because of the circumcision.

27 Now the LORD said to Aaron, "Go to meet Moses in the wilderness." So he went and met him at the mountain of God and kissed him.

28 Moses told Aaron all the words of the LORD with which He had sent him, and all the signs that He had commanded him *to do*.

29 Then Moses and Aaron went and assembled all the elders of the sons of Israel;

30 and Aaron spoke all the words which the LORD had spoken to Moses. He then performed the signs in the sight of the people.

31 So the people believed; and when they heard that the LORD was concerned about the sons of Israel and that He had seen their affliction, then they bowed low and worshiped.

✦ Psalm 16:1–6

A Mikhtam of David.

16 PRESERVE me, O God, for I take refuge in You.

2 I said to the LORD, "You are my Lord; I have no good besides You."

3 As for the saints who are in the earth, They are the majestic ones in whom is all my delight.

4 The sorrows of those who have bartered for another *god* will be multiplied; I shall not pour out their drink offerings of blood, Nor will I take their names upon my lips.

5 The LORD is the portion of my inheritance and my cup; You support my lot.

6 The lines have fallen to me in pleasant places; Indeed, my heritage is beautiful to me.

✦ Proverbs 5:1–6

5 MY son, give attention to my wisdom, Incline your ear to my understanding;

2 That you may observe discretion And your lips may reserve knowledge.

3 For the lips of an adulteress drip honey And smoother than oil is her speech;

4 But in the end she is bitter as wormwood, Sharp as a two-edged sword.

5 Her feet go down to death, Her steps take hold of Sheol.

6 She does not ponder the path of life; Her ways are unstable, she does not know *it*.

✦ Matthew 18:1–20

18 AT that time the disciples came to Jesus and said, "Who then is greatest in the kingdom of heaven?"

LIFE LESSONS

➤ **Matthew 18:3 —** *"Truly I say to you, unless you are converted and become like children, you will not enter the kingdom of heaven."*

*J*esus has in mind the humility of little children and their unconcern for social status or public opinion. He encourages us to place childlike trust in Him, regardless of what others may think.

---

2   And He called a child to Himself and set him before them,

➤ 3   and said, "Truly I say to you, unless you are converted and become like children, you will not enter the kingdom of heaven.

4   "Whoever then humbles himself as this child, he is the greatest in the kingdom of heaven.

5   "And whoever receives one such child in My name receives Me;

6   but whoever causes one of these little ones who believe in Me to stumble, it would be better for him to have a heavy millstone hung around his neck, and to be drowned in the depth of the sea.

7   "Woe to the world because of *its* stumbling blocks! For it is inevitable that stumbling blocks come; but woe to that man through whom the stumbling block comes!

8   "If your hand or your foot causes you to stumble, cut it off and throw it from you; it is better for you to enter life crippled or lame, than to have two hands or two feet and be cast into the eternal fire.

9   "If your eye causes you to stumble, pluck it out and throw it from you. It is better for you to enter life with one eye, than to have two eyes and be cast into the fiery hell.

10   "See that you do not despise one of these little ones, for I say to you that their angels in heaven continually see the face of My Father who is in heaven.

11   ["For the Son of Man has come to ✳ save that which was lost.]

12   "What do you think? If any man has a hundred sheep, and one of them has gone astray, does he not leave the ninety-nine on the mountains and go and search for the one that is straying?

13   "If it turns out that he finds it, truly I say to you, he rejoices over it more than over the ninety-nine which have not gone astray.

14   "So it is not *the* will of your Father ◄ who is in heaven that one of these little ones perish.

15   "If your brother sins, go and show him his fault in private; if he listens to you, you have won your brother.

16   "But if he does not listen *to you*, take one or two more with you, so that BY THE MOUTH OF TWO OR THREE WITNESSES EVERY FACT MAY BE CONFIRMED.

17   "If he refuses to listen to them, tell it to the church; and if he refuses to listen even to the church, let him be to you as a Gentile and a tax collector.

18   "Truly I say to you, whatever you bind on earth shall have been bound in heaven; and whatever you loose on earth shall have been loosed in heaven.

19   "Again I say to you, that if two of you agree on earth about anything that they may ask, it shall be done for them by My Father who is in heaven.

20   "For where two or three have gath- ◄ ered together in My name, I am there in their midst."

LIFE LESSONS

➤ **Matthew 18:14 —** *"It is not the will of your Father who is in heaven that one of these little ones perish."*

*G*od wants "all men to be saved and to come to the knowledge of the truth" (1 Tim. 2:4). He is "not willing that any should perish but that all should come to repentance" (2 Pet. 3:9). That includes children.

➤ **Matthew 18:20 —** *"For where two or three have gathered together in My name, I am there in their midst."*

*T*he Spirit of Jesus lives in each indi- vidual Christian, but He promises to be with them in a unique and special way when they gather "in His name" for wor- ship, service, and mutual encouragement.

Exodus 5:1—6:30

5 AND afterward Moses and Aaron came and said to Pharaoh, "Thus says the LORD, the God of Israel, 'Let My people go that they may celebrate a feast to Me in the wilderness.'"
2 But Pharaoh said, "Who is the LORD that I should obey His voice to let Israel go? I do not know the LORD, and besides, I will not let Israel go."
3 Then they said, "The God of the Hebrews has met with us. Please, let us go a three days' journey into the wilderness that we may sacrifice to the LORD our God, otherwise He will fall upon us with pestilence or with the sword."
4 But the king of Egypt said to them, "Moses and Aaron, why do you draw the people away from their work? Get *back* to your labors!"
5 Again Pharaoh said, "Look, the people of the land are now many, and you would have them cease from their labors!"
6 So the same day Pharaoh commanded the taskmasters over the people and their foremen, saying,
7 "You are no longer to give the people straw to make brick as previously; let them go and gather straw for themselves.
8 "But the quota of bricks which they were making previously, you shall impose on them; you are not to reduce any of it. Because they are lazy, therefore they cry out, 'Let us go and sacrifice to our God.'
➤ 9 "Let the labor be heavier on the men,

and let them work at it so that they will pay no attention to false words."
10 So the taskmasters of the people and their foremen went out and spoke to the people, saying, "Thus says Pharaoh, 'I am not going to give you *any* straw.
11 'You go *and* get straw for yourselves wherever you can find *it*, but none of your labor will be reduced.'"
12 So the people scattered through all the land of Egypt to gather stubble for straw.
13 The taskmasters pressed them, saying, "Complete your work quota, *your* daily amount, just as when you had straw."
14 Moreover, the foremen of the sons of Israel, whom Pharaoh's taskmasters had set over them, were beaten and were asked, "Why have you not completed your required amount either yesterday or today in making brick as previously?"
15 Then the foremen of the sons of Israel came and cried out to Pharaoh, saying, "Why do you deal this way with your servants?
16 "There is no straw given to your

Life Examples:

PHARAOH: A Bad Case of a Hard Heart

EXODUS 5

*P*haraoh is probably the best illustration in the Bible of a person with a hard heart. He thus provides a blueprint for what happens when a person refuses to accept and bend his or her will to the truth of God.
   Pharaoh received overwhelming evidence of God's authority over him—plague after

plague, sign after sign, miracle after miracle—and still, he refused to let the Israelites go. Even when faced with undeniable evidence of his error, Pharaoh refused to acknowledge the Lord God was greater than he. In the end, his pride and hard-heartedness cost him his firstborn son, his army, and almost his kingdom.
   All of us have stubbornly desired to have things the way we want them, even when our way opposes God's way. However, if we repeatedly say no to God, then like Pharaoh we may develop a hard heart that leads to destruction.

servants, yet they keep saying to us, 'Make bricks!' And behold, your servants are being beaten; but it is the fault of your *own* people."

17　But he said, "You are lazy, *very* lazy; therefore you say, 'Let us go *and* sacrifice to the LORD.'

18　"So go now *and* work; for you will be given no straw, yet you must deliver the quota of bricks."

19　The foremen of the sons of Israel saw that they were in trouble because they were told, "You must not reduce *your* daily amount of bricks."

20　When they left Pharaoh's presence, they met Moses and Aaron as they were waiting for them.

21　They said to them, "May the LORD look upon you and judge *you*, for you have made us odious in Pharaoh's sight and in the sight of his servants, to put a sword in their hand to kill us."

22　Then Moses returned to the LORD and said, "O Lord, why have You brought harm to this people? Why did You ever send me?

23　"Ever since I came to Pharaoh to speak in Your name, he has done harm to this people, and You have not delivered Your people at all."

6 THEN the LORD said to Moses, "Now you shall see what I will do to Pharaoh; for under compulsion he will let them go, and under compulsion he will drive them out of his land."

2　God spoke further to Moses and said to him, "I am the LORD;

3　and I appeared to Abraham, Isaac, and Jacob, as God Almighty, but *by* My name, LORD, I did not make Myself known to them.

4　"I also established My covenant with them, to give them the land of Canaan, the land in which they sojourned.

5　"Furthermore I have heard the groaning of the sons of Israel, because the Egyptians are holding them in bondage, and I have remembered My covenant.

6　"Say, therefore, to the sons of Israel, 'I am the LORD, and I will bring you out from under the burdens of the Egyptians, and I will deliver you from their bondage. I will also redeem you with an outstretched arm and with great judgments.

7　'Then I will take you for My people, and I will be your God; and you shall know that I am the LORD your God, who brought you out from under the burdens of the Egyptians.

8　'I will bring you to the land which I swore to give to Abraham, Isaac, and Jacob, and I will give it to you *for* a possession; I am the LORD.'"

9　So Moses spoke thus to the sons of Israel, but they did not listen to Moses on account of *their* despondency and cruel bondage.

10　Now the LORD spoke to Moses, saying,

11　"Go, tell Pharaoh king of Egypt to let the sons of Israel go out of his land."

12　But Moses spoke before the LORD, saying, "Behold, the sons of Israel have not listened to me; how then will Pharaoh listen to me, for I am unskilled in speech?"

13　Then the LORD spoke to Moses and to Aaron, and gave them a charge to the sons of Israel and to Pharaoh king of Egypt, to bring the sons of Israel out of the land of Egypt.

14　These are the heads of their fathers' households. The sons of Reuben, Israel's firstborn: Hanoch and Pallu, Hezron and Carmi; these are the families of Reuben.

15　The sons of Simeon: Jemuel and Jamin and Ohad and Jachin and Zohar and Shaul the son of a Canaanite woman; these are the families of Simeon.

16　These are the names of the sons of Levi according to their generations: Gershon and Kohath and Merari; and

---

LIFE LESSONS

➤ **Exodus 5:22 — *"O Lord, why have You brought harm to this people?"***

Sometimes we obey God, expecting a certain result—and the opposite happens. Then we wonder if God has made a mistake. But He never does; we simply have to wait until He finishes the story.

➤ **Exodus 6:9 — *Moses spoke thus to the sons of Israel, but they did not listen to Moses on account of their despondency and cruel bondage.***

When we feel oppressed and our spirit groans, it is difficult for us to believe the good promises of God regarding our welfare. But disappointments are inevitable; discouragement is a choice.

the length of Levi's life was one hundred and thirty-seven years.

17 The sons of Gershon: Libni and Shimei, according to their families.

18 The sons of Kohath: Amram and Izhar and Hebron and Uzziel; and the length of Kohath's life was one hundred and thirty-three years.

19 The sons of Merari: Mahli and Mushi. These are the families of the Levites according to their generations.

20 Amram married his father's sister Jochebed, and she bore him Aaron and Moses; and the length of Amram's life was one hundred and thirty-seven years.

21 The sons of Izhar: Korah and Nepheg and Zichri.

22 The sons of Uzziel: Mishael and Elzaphan and Sithri.

23 Aaron married Elisheba, the daughter of Amminadab, the sister of Nahshon, and she bore him Nadab and Abihu, Eleazar and Ithamar.

24 The sons of Korah: Assir and Elkanah and Abiasaph; these are the families of the Korahites.

25 Aaron's son Eleazar married one of the daughters of Putiel, and she bore him Phinehas. These are the heads of the fathers' *households* of the Levites according to their families.

26 It was *the same* Aaron and Moses to whom the LORD said, "Bring out the sons of Israel from the land of Egypt according to their hosts."

27 They were the ones who spoke to Pharaoh king of Egypt about bringing out the sons of Israel from Egypt; it was *the same* Moses and Aaron.

28 Now it came about on the day when the LORD spoke to Moses in the land of Egypt,

29 that the LORD spoke to Moses, saying, "I am the LORD; speak to Pharaoh king of Egypt all that I speak to you."

30 But Moses said before the LORD, "Behold, I am unskilled in speech; how then will Pharaoh listen to me?"

Psalm 16:7–11

7 I will bless the LORD who has
      counseled me;
   Indeed, my mind instructs me in the
      night.

8 I have set the LORD continually
      before me;
   Because He is at my right hand, I
      will not be shaken.

9 Therefore my heart is glad and my
      glory rejoices;
   My flesh also will dwell securely.

10 For You will not abandon my soul
      to Sheol;
   Nor will You allow Your Holy One to
      undergo decay.

11 You will make known to me the
      path of life;
   In Your presence is fullness of joy;
   In Your right hand there are
      pleasures forever.

Proverbs 5:7–14

7 Now then, *my* sons, listen to me
   And do not depart from the words
      of my mouth.

LIFE LESSONS

➤ **Psalm 16:7 — *I will bless the LORD who has counseled me; indeed, my mind instructs me in the night.***

*G*od often gives us His counsel when we grow quiet enough to listen to Him while in bed or getting ready for sleep. We must be ready to listen at all times, because He may be ready to speak at any time.

➤ **Psalm 16:10 — *For You will not abandon my soul to Sheol; nor will You allow Your Holy One to undergo decay.***

*T*his verse is an important prophecy about the resurrection of Jesus Christ, quoted by Peter in Acts 2:27. Peter argued that since David had died and his body decayed, the verse had to apply to the Messiah, Jesus.

➤ **Proverbs 5:8 — *Keep your way far from her and do not go near the door of her house.***

*G*od's Word tells us to "flee immorality" (1 Cor. 6:18), not to test our spiritual maturity by seeing how close we can get to it without falling into it. If you know something tempts you, stay away from it.

➤ 8   Keep your way far from her
     And do not go near the door of her
     house,
9   Or you will give your vigor to
     others
     And your years to the cruel one;
10   And strangers will be filled with
     your strength
     And your hard-earned goods *will go*
     to the house of an alien;
11   And you groan at your final end,
     When your flesh and your body are
     consumed;
12   And you say, "How I have hated
     instruction!
     And my heart spurned reproof!
13   "I have not listened to the voice of
     my teachers,
     Nor inclined my ear to my
     instructors!
14   "I was almost in utter ruin
     In the midst of the assembly and
     congregation."

✦ Matthew 18:21–35

21 Then Peter came and said to Him, "Lord, how often shall my brother sin against me and I forgive him? Up to seven times?"
22 Jesus *said to him, "I do not say to you, up to seven times, but up to seventy times seven.
23 "For this reason the kingdom of heaven may be compared to a king who wished to settle accounts with his slaves.
24 "When he had begun to settle *them,* one who owed him ten thousand talents was brought to him.
25 "But since he did not have *the means* to repay, his lord commanded him to be sold, along with his wife and children and all that he had, and repayment to be made.
26 "So the slave fell *to the ground* and prostrated himself before him, saying, 'Have patience with me and I will repay you everything.'
27 "And the lord of that slave felt compassion and released him and forgave him the debt.
28 "But that slave went out and found one of his fellow slaves who owed him a hundred denarii; and he seized him and *began* to choke *him,* saying, 'Pay back what you owe.'
29 "So his fellow slave fell *to the ground* and *began* to plead with him, saying, 'Have patience with me and I will repay you.'
30 "But he was unwilling and went and threw him in prison until he should pay back what was owed.
31 "So when his fellow slaves saw what had happened, they were deeply grieved and came and reported to their lord all that had happened.
32 "Then summoning him, his lord *said to him, 'You wicked slave, I forgave you all that debt because you pleaded with me.
33 'Should you not also have had mercy on your fellow slave, in the same way that I had mercy on you?'
34 "And his lord, moved with anger, handed him over to the torturers until he should repay all that was owed him.
35 "My heavenly Father will also do the same to you, if each of you does not forgive his brother from your heart."

✦ Exodus 7:1—8:32

7 THEN the Lord said to Moses, "See, I make you *as* God to Pharaoh, and your brother Aaron shall be your prophet.
2 "You shall speak all that I command you, and your brother Aaron shall speak to Pharaoh that he let the sons of Israel go out of his land.
3 "But I will harden Pharaoh's heart that I may multiply My signs and My wonders in the land of Egypt.
4 "When Pharaoh does not listen to you, then I will lay My hand on Egypt and bring out My hosts, My people the sons of Israel, from the land of Egypt by ✳ great judgments.
5 "The Egyptians shall know that I am ◄ the Lord, when I stretch out My hand on

Egypt and bring out the sons of Israel from their midst.''

6   So Moses and Aaron did it; as the LORD commanded them, thus they did.

7   Moses was eighty years old and Aaron eighty-three, when they spoke to Pharaoh.

8   Now the LORD spoke to Moses and Aaron, saying,

9   "When Pharaoh speaks to you, saying, 'Work a miracle,' then you shall say to Aaron, 'Take your staff and throw it down before Pharaoh, that it may become a serpent.'''

10   So Moses and Aaron came to Pharaoh, and thus they did just as the LORD had commanded; and Aaron threw his staff down before Pharaoh and his servants, and it became a serpent.

➤ 11   Then Pharaoh also called for the wise men and the sorcerers, and they also, the magicians of Egypt, did the same with their secret arts.

12   For each one threw down his staff and they turned into serpents. But Aaron's staff swallowed up their staffs.

13   Yet Pharaoh's heart was hardened, and he did not listen to them, as the LORD had said.

14   Then the LORD said to Moses, "Pharaoh's heart is stubborn; he refuses to let the people go.

15   "Go to Pharaoh in the morning as he is going out to the water, and station yourself to meet him on the bank of the Nile; and you shall take in your hand the staff that was turned into a serpent.

16   "You shall say to him, 'The LORD, the God of the Hebrews, sent me to you, saying, "Let My people go, that they may serve Me in the wilderness. But behold, you have not listened until now."

17   'Thus says the LORD, "By this you shall know that I am the LORD: behold, I will strike the water that is in the Nile with the staff that is in my hand, and it will be turned to blood.

18   "The fish that are in the Nile will die, and the Nile will become foul, and the Egyptians will find difficulty in drinking water from the Nile."''

19   Then the LORD said to Moses, "Say to Aaron, 'Take your staff and stretch out your hand over the waters of Egypt, over their rivers, over their streams, and over their pools, and over all their reservoirs of water, that they may become blood; and there will be blood throughout all the land of Egypt, both in vessels of wood and in vessels of stone.'"

20   So Moses and Aaron did even as the LORD had commanded. And he lifted up the staff and struck the water that was in the Nile, in the sight of Pharaoh and in the sight of his servants, and all the water that was in the Nile was turned to blood.

21   The fish that were in the Nile died, and the Nile became foul, so that the Egyptians could not drink water from the Nile. And the blood was through all the land of Egypt.

22   But the magicians of Egypt did the same with their secret arts; and Pharaoh's heart was hardened, and he did not listen to them, as the LORD had said.

23   Then Pharaoh turned and went into his house with no concern even for this.

24   So all the Egyptians dug around the Nile for water to drink, for they could not drink of the water of the Nile.

25   Seven days passed after the LORD had struck the Nile.

8 THEN the LORD said to Moses, "Go to Pharaoh and say to him, 'Thus says the LORD, "Let My people go, that they may serve Me.

2   "But if you refuse to let them go, behold, I will smite your whole territory with frogs.

3   "The Nile will swarm with frogs, which will come up and go into your

---

LIFE LESSONS

➤ **Exodus 7:5 — "The Egyptians shall know that I am the LORD."**

*T*he Lord wants all the peoples of the earth to know Him—His power, glory, love, grace, and justice. And He wants to show the world who He is through what He does in our lives.

➤ **Exodus 7:11 — Then Pharaoh also called for the wise men and the sorcerers, and they also, the magicians of Egypt, did the same with their secret arts.**

*T*he devil is fully capable of counterfeiting some of God's miraculous works and thus blinds many people to the truth (Matt. 24:24). This is why we must stay alert (2 Cor. 2:11; 1 Pet. 5:8).

house and into your bedroom and on your bed, and into the houses of your servants and on your people, and into your ovens and into your kneading bowls.
4 "So the frogs will come up on you and your people and all your servants."'"
5 Then the LORD said to Moses, "Say to Aaron, 'Stretch out your hand with your staff over the rivers, over the streams and over the pools, and make frogs come up on the land of Egypt.'"
6 So Aaron stretched out his hand over the waters of Egypt, and the frogs came up and covered the land of Egypt.
7 The magicians did the same with their secret arts, making frogs come up on the land of Egypt.
8 Then Pharaoh called for Moses and Aaron and said, "Entreat the LORD that He remove the frogs from me and from my people; and I will let the people go, that they may sacrifice to the LORD."
9 Moses said to Pharaoh, "The honor is yours to tell me: when shall I entreat for you and your servants and your people, that the frogs be destroyed from you and your houses, *that* they may be left only in the Nile?"
10 Then he said, "Tomorrow." So he said, "*May it be* according to your word, that you may know that there is no one like the LORD our God.
11 "The frogs will depart from you and your houses and your servants and your people; they will be left only in the Nile."
12 Then Moses and Aaron went out from Pharaoh, and Moses cried to the LORD concerning the frogs which He had inflicted upon Pharaoh.
13 The LORD did according to the word of Moses, and the frogs died out of the houses, the courts, and the fields.
14 So they piled them in heaps, and the land became foul.
15 But when Pharaoh saw that there was relief, he hardened his heart and did not listen to them, as the LORD had said.
16 Then the LORD said to Moses, "Say to Aaron, 'Stretch out your staff and strike the dust of the earth, that it may become gnats through all the land of Egypt.'"
17 They did so; and Aaron stretched out his hand with his staff, and struck the dust of the earth, and there were gnats on man and beast. All the dust of the earth became gnats through all the land of Egypt.

18 The magicians tried with their secret arts to bring forth gnats, but they could not; so there were gnats on man and beast.
19 Then the magicians said to Pharaoh, "This is the finger of God." But Pharaoh's heart was hardened, and he did not listen to them, as the LORD had said.
20 Now the LORD said to Moses, "Rise early in the morning and present yourself before Pharaoh, as he comes out to the water, and say to him, 'Thus says the LORD, "Let My people go, that they may serve Me.
21 "For if you do not let My people go, behold, I will send swarms of flies on you and on your servants and on your people and into your houses; and the houses of the Egyptians will be full of swarms of flies, and also the ground on which they *dwell.*
22 "But on that day I will set apart the land of Goshen, where My people are living, so that no swarms of flies will be there, in order that you may know that I, the LORD, am in the midst of the land.
23 "I will put a division between My ◄ people and your people. Tomorrow this sign will occur."'"
24 Then the LORD did so. And there came great swarms of flies into the house of Pharaoh and the houses of his servants and the land was laid waste because of the swarms of flies in all the land of Egypt.
25 Pharaoh called for Moses and Aaron and said, "Go, sacrifice to your God within the land."
26 But Moses said, "It is not right to do so, for we will sacrifice to the LORD our God what is an abomination to the Egyptians. If we sacrifice what is an abomination to the Egyptians before their eyes, will they not then stone us?
27 "We must go a three days' journey

LIFE LESSONS

➤ **Exodus 8:23 —** *"I will put a division between My people and your people."*

*A*lthough Christians suffer troubles and hardships like anyone else, the Lord does make a difference between His people and those who do not believe. We may have to wait to see it, but it will come.

into the wilderness and sacrifice to the LORD our God as He commands us."

28 Pharaoh said, "I will let you go, that you may sacrifice to the LORD your God in the wilderness; only you shall not go very far away. Make supplication for me."

29 Then Moses said, "Behold, I am going out from you, and I shall make supplication to the LORD that the swarms of flies may depart from Pharaoh, from his servants, and from his people tomorrow; only do not let Pharaoh deal deceitfully again in not letting the people go to sacrifice to the LORD."

30 So Moses went out from Pharaoh and made supplication to the LORD.

31 The LORD did as Moses asked, and removed the swarms of flies from Pharaoh, from his servants and from his people; not one remained.

32 But Pharaoh hardened his heart this time also, and he did not let the people go.

Psalm 17:1–7

A Prayer of David.

17 HEAR a just cause, O LORD, give heed to my cry;
Give ear to my prayer, which is not from deceitful lips.

2 Let my judgment come forth from Your presence;
Let Your eyes look with equity.

3 You have tried my heart;
You have visited *me* by night;
You have tested me and You find nothing;
I have purposed that my mouth will not transgress.

4 As for the deeds of men, by the word of Your lips
I have kept from the paths of the violent.

5 My steps have held fast to Your paths.
My feet have not slipped.

6 I have called upon You, for You will answer me, O God;
Incline Your ear to me, hear my speech.

7 Wondrously show Your lovingkindness,

O Savior of those who take refuge at Your right hand
From those who rise up *against them*.

Proverbs 5:15–20

15 Drink water from your own cistern
And fresh water from your own well.

16 Should your springs be dispersed abroad,
Streams of water in the streets?

17 Let them be yours alone
And not for strangers with you.

18 Let your fountain be blessed,
And rejoice in the wife of your youth.

19 As a loving hind and a graceful doe,
Let her breasts satisfy you at all times;
Be exhilarated always with her love.

20 For why should you, my son, be exhilarated with an adulteress
And embrace the bosom of a foreigner?

Matthew 19:1–30

19 WHEN Jesus had finished these words, He departed from Galilee and came into the region of Judea beyond the Jordan;

2 and large crowds followed Him, and He healed them there.

3 *Some* Pharisees came to Jesus, testing Him and asking, "Is it lawful *for a man* to divorce his wife for any reason at all?"

4 And He answered and said, "Have you not read that He who created *them* from the beginning MADE THEM MALE AND FEMALE,

5 and said, 'FOR THIS REASON A MAN SHALL LEAVE HIS FATHER AND MOTHER AND BE JOINED TO HIS WIFE, AND THE TWO SHALL BECOME ONE FLESH'?

6 "So they are no longer two, but one flesh. What therefore God has joined together, let no man separate."

7 They *said to Him, "Why then did Moses command to GIVE HER A CERTIFICATE OF DIVORCE AND SEND *her* AWAY?"

8 He *said to them, "Because of your

➤ **Matthew 19:6 — *"What therefore God has joined together, let no man separate."***

*M*arriage is not merely a social convention, as many declare today. It is far more than a piece of paper. In marriage, *God* joins a man and a woman into a single family unit. This is what makes divorce such a tragedy.

hardness of heart Moses permitted you to divorce your wives; but from the beginning it has not been this way.

9 "And I say to you, whoever divorces his wife, except for immorality, and marries another woman commits adultery."

10 The disciples *said to Him, "If the relationship of the man with his wife is like this, it is better not to marry."

11 But He said to them, "Not all men *can* accept this statement, but *only* those to whom it has been given.

12 "For there are eunuchs who were born that way from their mother's womb; and there are eunuchs who were made eunuchs by men; and there are *also* eunuchs who made themselves eunuchs for the sake of the kingdom of heaven. He who is able to accept *this,* let him accept *it.*"

13 Then *some* children were brought to Him so that He might lay His hands on them and pray; and the disciples rebuked them.

14 But Jesus said, "Let the children alone, and do not hinder them from coming to Me; for the kingdom of heaven belongs to such as these."

15 After laying His hands on them, He departed from there.

16 And someone came to Him and said, "Teacher, what good thing shall I do that I may obtain eternal life?"

17 And He said to him, "Why are you asking Me about what is good? There is *only* One who is good; but if you wish to enter into life, keep the commandments."

Life Examples:

Good, But Not Good Enough

MATTHEW 19:16–26

*I*n Matthew 19:16, a rich young ruler went to Jesus and asked, "Teacher, what good thing shall I do that I may obtain eternal life?" What he was really asking Jesus was, "I've done so many good things—haven't I done enough to earn eternal life?" Like so many people, the rich young ruler was asking the wrong question.

Remember, eternal life is more than just life without end—eternal life is also a *quality* of life. It is the life of God. When you receive the Lord Jesus Christ as your personal Savior, you receive Him by faith. You believe Jesus Christ is the Son of God who went to the Cross and died for your sins in order to reconcile you to God (Col. 1:20). Then, the Holy Spirit comes to live in you—and He is the life of God in you (Rom. 8:9–11).

You see, the rich young ruler's emphasis was on what he could do to *earn* salvation. Unfortunately, this is the great deception. Eternal life cannot be earned (Gal. 2:16; Eph. 2:8, 9; 2 Tim. 1:9). We'll never perform in a manner so good that God will see what we've done, approve of us, and give us eternal life. Sadly, that's the way most people approach God.

Of course, the real problem with that idea is that it ignores our sinful nature. We are naturally disobedient to God (Rom. 7:14–24). We cannot do the things God created us to do or fulfill the purposes He wants us to fulfill apart from the life of Christ in us. Therefore we disobey God and break His law—we sin. And as James 2:10 tells us, "Whoever keeps the whole law and yet stumbles in one point, he has become guilty of all."

So when people think, "If I do better in a few areas of my life, surely God will accept me"; they don't realize that "doing better" does not take care of the real problem. What is the real problem? Even one sin earns us a penalty of death (Rom. 6:23).

Good works cannot erase sin. That's why good works can't save us; they can't erase the sin-debt we already owe. Only the shed blood of Jesus Christ on the Cross can do that. It is Jesus' crucifixion that makes it possible for us to be forgiven of our sin-debt. There will never be anything else that can eliminate our death penalty.

Of course, the rich, young ruler believed that there was something that he could do to earn eternal life. And the great tragedy is that he walked away from the one person who could give it to him—Jesus. It's the tragic decision that so many people make in life. Friend, don't make that same mistake.

18　*Then* he *said to Him, "Which ones?" And Jesus said, "YOU SHALL NOT COMMIT MURDER; YOU SHALL NOT COMMIT ADULTERY; YOU SHALL NOT STEAL; YOU SHALL NOT BEAR FALSE WITNESS;
19　HONOR YOUR FATHER AND MOTHER; and YOU SHALL LOVE YOUR NEIGHBOR AS YOURSELF."
20　The young man *said to Him, "All these things I have kept; what am I still lacking?"
21　Jesus said to him, "If you wish to be complete, go *and* sell your possessions and give to *the* poor, and you will have treasure in heaven; and come, follow Me."
22　But when the young man heard this statement, he went away grieving; for he was one who owned much property.
23　And Jesus said to His disciples, "Truly I say to you, it is hard for a rich man to enter the kingdom of heaven.
24　"Again I say to you, it is easier for a camel to go through the eye of a needle, than for a rich man to enter the kingdom of God."
25　When the disciples heard *this*, they were very astonished and said, "Then who can be saved?"
26　And looking at *them* Jesus said to them, "With people this is impossible, but with God all things are possible."
27　Then Peter said to Him, "Behold, we have left everything and followed You; what then will there be for us?"
28　And Jesus said to them, "Truly I say to you, that you who have followed Me, in the regeneration when the Son of Man will sit on His glorious throne, you also shall sit upon twelve thrones, judging the twelve tribes of Israel.
29　"And everyone who has left houses or brothers or sisters or father or mother or children or farms for My name's sake, will receive many times as much, and will inherit eternal life.
30　"But many *who are* first will be last; and *the* last, first.

LIFE LESSONS

> **Matthew 19:23 —** *"Truly I say to you, it is hard for a rich man to enter the kingdom of heaven."*

*W*hy is it hard for the rich to enter heaven? For the same reason it's hard for the strong, or the bright, or the politically connected. They tend to rely on their own resources; pride keeps them from trusting God's resources.

> **Matthew 19:30 —** *"Many who are first will be last; and the last, first."*

*G*od loves to exalt the humble and humble the proud. So Paul says, "Not many wise according to the flesh, not many mighty, not many noble" and "LET HIM WHO BOASTS, BOAST IN THE LORD" (1 Cor. 1:26, 31).

JANUARY 30

 Exodus 9:1—10:29

9 THEN the LORD said to Moses, "Go to Pharaoh and speak to him, 'Thus says the LORD, the God of the Hebrews, "Let My people go, that they may serve Me.
2　"For if you refuse to let *them* go and continue to hold them,
3　behold, the hand of the LORD will come *with* a very severe pestilence on your livestock which are in the field, on the horses, on the donkeys, on the camels, on the herds, and on the flocks.
4　"But the LORD will make a distinction between the livestock of Israel and the livestock of Egypt, so that nothing will die of all that belongs to the sons of Israel."'"
5　The LORD set a definite time, saying, "Tomorrow the LORD will do this thing in the land."
6　So the LORD did this thing on the next day, and all the livestock of Egypt died; but of the livestock of the sons of Israel, not one died.
7　Pharaoh sent, and behold, there was not even one of the livestock of Israel

dead. But the heart of Pharaoh was hardened, and he did not let the people go.

8 Then the LORD said to Moses and Aaron, "Take for yourselves handfuls of soot from a kiln, and let Moses throw it toward the sky in the sight of Pharaoh.

9 "It will become fine dust over all the land of Egypt, and will become boils breaking out with sores on man and beast through all the land of Egypt."

10 So they took soot from a kiln, and stood before Pharaoh; and Moses threw it toward the sky, and it became boils breaking out with sores on man and beast.

11 The magicians could not stand before Moses because of the boils, for the boils were on the magicians as well as on all the Egyptians.

12 And the LORD hardened Pharaoh's heart, and he did not listen to them, just as the LORD had spoken to Moses.

13 Then the LORD said to Moses, "Rise up early in the morning and stand before Pharaoh and say to him, 'Thus says the LORD, the God of the Hebrews, "Let My people go, that they may serve Me.

14 "For this time I will send all My plagues on you and your servants and your people, so that you may know that there is no one like Me in all the earth.

---

15 "For if by now I had put forth My hand and struck you and your people with pestilence, you would then have been cut off from the earth.

16 "But, indeed, for this reason I have allowed you to remain, in order to show you My power and in order to proclaim My name through all the earth.

17 "Still you exalt yourself against My people by not letting them go.

18 "Behold, about this time tomorrow, I will send a very heavy hail, such as has not been seen in Egypt from the day it was founded until now.

19 "Now therefore send, bring your livestock and whatever you have in the field to safety. Every man and beast that is found in the field and is not brought home, when the hail comes down on them, will die."'"

Life Examples:

A Plan of Plagues

EXODUS 7:4—12:33

When God freed the Israelites from slavery, He realized He would need to convince Pharaoh to let them go. After all, the Israelites were central to the Egyptian economy. So God showed His power to Pharaoh through the plagues and struck everything the Egyptian nation relied upon.

The Nile was seen as a god to the Egyptians because it sustained their civilization (Ex. 7:14–24). When God turned it to blood, He cut off their lifeline and showed He was stronger than their main deity. The frogs were thought to represent the deity of fertility, but when they invaded the Egyptian's homes and beds, those annoying, croaking creatures disgusted the people (Ex. 8:1–15).

The lice irritated them to no end (Ex. 8:16–19). The flies not only disfigured their bodies, but ruined their plants as well (Ex. 8:20–32). Disease destroyed their livestock (Ex. 9:1–7), and boils burned their skin (Ex. 9:8–12). Hail (Ex. 9:13–35) and locusts (Ex. 10:1–20)

decimated the remainder of their animals and finished off their crops. The plague of darkness showed that the Egyptian sun deity, Ra, was completely powerless before the one true God (10:21–29).

Finally, the death of the firstborn in every Egyptian household showed that their hope was completely cut off (Ex. 11:1—12:33). There was nothing the Egyptians could turn to help them against the almighty God of Israel. Everything they knew was ruined.

What was the result? Exodus 12 tells us, "The Egyptians urged the people, to send them out of the land in haste. . . . Now the sons of Israel . . . requested from the Egyptians articles of silver and articles of gold, and clothing; and the LORD had given the people favor in the sight of the Egyptians, so that they let them have their request. Thus they plundered the Egyptians" (vv. 33, 35, 36). Not only did the Egyptians ask them to leave, but they also gave the Israelites their possessions!

We may not understand what God is doing in a given situation, but we can always trust His plan. He knows exactly what to do to deliver us from our bondage.

➤ Exodus 9:16 — *"But, indeed, for this reason I have allowed you to remain, in order to show you My power and in order to proclaim My name through all the earth."*

*G*od rules with such a mighty hand that He even raises up adversaries in order to demonstrate His glory and might to the world. He works His wonders not only so that unbelievers might see His power and repent and believe, but also so that His own people might remember His glory and so remain loyal to Him (Ex. 10:2).

20 The one among the servants of Pharaoh who feared the word of the LORD made his servants and his livestock flee into the houses;
21 but he who paid no regard to the word of the LORD left his servants and his livestock in the field.
22 Now the LORD said to Moses, "Stretch out your hand toward the sky, that hail may fall on all the land of Egypt, on man and on beast and on every plant of the field, throughout the land of Egypt."
23 Moses stretched out his staff toward the sky, and the LORD sent thunder and hail, and fire ran down to the earth. And the LORD rained hail on the land of Egypt.
24 So there was hail, and fire flashing continually in the midst of the hail, very severe, such as had not been in all the land of Egypt since it became a nation.
25 The hail struck all that was in the field through all the land of Egypt, both man and beast; the hail also struck every plant of the field and shattered every tree of the field.
26 Only in the land of Goshen, where the sons of Israel *were*, there was no hail.
27 Then Pharaoh sent for Moses and Aaron, and said to them, "I have sinned this time; the LORD is the righteous one, and I and my people are the wicked ones.
28 "Make supplication to the LORD, for there has been enough of God's thunder and hail; and I will let you go, and you shall stay no longer."
29 Moses said to him, "As soon as I go out of the city, I will spread out my hands to the LORD; the thunder will cease and there will be hail no longer, that you may know that the earth is the LORD's.

30 "But as for you and your servants, I know that you do not yet fear the LORD God."
31 (Now the flax and the barley were ruined, for the barley was in the ear and the flax was in bud.
32 But the wheat and the spelt were not ruined, for they *ripen* late.)
33 So Moses went out of the city from Pharaoh, and spread out his hands to the LORD; and the thunder and the hail ceased, and rain no longer poured on the earth.
34 But when Pharaoh saw that the rain and the hail and the thunder had ceased, he sinned again and hardened his heart, he and his servants.
35 Pharaoh's heart was hardened, and he did not let the sons of Israel go, just as the LORD had spoken through Moses.

10 THEN the LORD said to Moses, "Go to Pharaoh, for I have hardened his heart and the heart of his servants, that I may perform these signs of Mine among them,
2 and that you may tell in the hearing of your son, and of your grandson, how I made a mockery of the Egyptians and how I performed My signs among them, that you may know that I am the LORD."
3 Moses and Aaron went to Pharaoh and said to him, "Thus says the LORD, the God of the Hebrews, 'How long will you refuse to humble yourself before Me? Let My people go, that they may serve Me.
4 'For if you refuse to let My people go, behold, tomorrow I will bring locusts into your territory.
5 'They shall cover the surface of the land, so that no one will be able to see the land. They will also eat the rest of what has escaped—what is left to you from the hail—and they will eat every tree which sprouts for you out of the field.
6 'Then your houses shall be filled and the houses of all your servants and the houses of all the Egyptians, *something* which neither your fathers nor your grandfathers have seen, from the day that they came upon the earth until this day.'" And he turned and went out from Pharaoh.
7 Pharaoh's servants said to him, "How long will this man be a snare to us? Let the men go, that they may serve

the LORD their God. Do you not realize that Egypt is destroyed?"

8 So Moses and Aaron were brought back to Pharaoh, and he said to them, "Go, serve the LORD your God! Who are the ones that are going?"

9 Moses said, "We shall go with our young and our old; with our sons and our daughters, with our flocks and our herds we shall go, for we must hold a feast to the LORD."

10 Then he said to them, "Thus may the LORD be with you, if ever I let you and your little ones go! Take heed, for evil is in your mind.

11 "Not so! Go now, the men *among you*, and serve the LORD, for that is what you desire." So they were driven out from Pharaoh's presence.

12 Then the LORD said to Moses, "Stretch out your hand over the land of Egypt for the locusts, that they may come up on the land of Egypt and eat every plant of the land, *even* all that the hail has left."

13 So Moses stretched out his staff over the land of Egypt, and the LORD directed an east wind on the land all that day and all that night; and when it was morning, the east wind brought the locusts.

14 The locusts came up over all the land of Egypt and settled in all the territory of Egypt; *they were* very numerous. There had never been so *many* locusts, nor would there be so *many* again.

15 For they covered the surface of the whole land, so that the land was darkened; and they ate every plant of the land and all the fruit of the trees that the hail had left. Thus nothing green was left on tree or plant of the field through all the land of Egypt.

16 Then Pharaoh hurriedly called for Moses and Aaron, and he said, "I have sinned against the LORD your God and against you.

17 "Now therefore, please forgive my sin only this once, and make supplication to the LORD your God, that He would only remove this death from me."

18 He went out from Pharaoh and made supplication to the LORD.

19 So the LORD shifted *the wind* to a very strong west wind which took up the locusts and drove them into the Red Sea; not one locust was left in all the territory of Egypt.

20 But the LORD hardened Pharaoh's

heart, and he did not let the sons of Israel go.

21 Then the LORD said to Moses, "Stretch out your hand toward the sky, that there may be darkness over the land of Egypt, even a darkness which may be felt."

22 So Moses stretched out his hand toward the sky, and there was thick darkness in all the land of Egypt for three days.

23 They did not see one another, nor did anyone rise from his place for three days, but all the sons of Israel had light in their dwellings.

24 Then Pharaoh called to Moses, and said, "Go, serve the LORD; only let your flocks and your herds be detained. Even your little ones may go with you."

25 But Moses said, "You must also let us have sacrifices and burnt offerings, that we may sacrifice *them* to the LORD our God.

26 "Therefore, our livestock too shall go with us; not a hoof shall be left behind, for we shall take some of them to serve the LORD our God. And until we arrive there, we ourselves do not know with what we shall serve the LORD."

27 But the LORD hardened Pharaoh's heart, and he was not willing to let them go.

28 Then Pharaoh said to him, "Get away from me! Beware, do not see my face again, for in the day you see my face you shall die!"

29 Moses said, "You are right; I shall never see your face again!"

Psalm 17:8–15

8 Keep me as the apple of the eye;
   Hide me in the shadow of Your
      wings

LIFE LESSONS

➤ **Psalm 17:8 —** *Keep me as the apple of the eye; hide me in the shadow of Your wings.*

God delights in all those who place their trust in Him. He considers each one the apple of His eye, the object of His special devotion. They find both protection and shelter in His loving presence.

9   From the wicked who despoil me,
    My deadly enemies who surround
       me.
10 They have closed their unfeeling
       heart,
    With their mouth they speak proudly.
11 They have now surrounded us in
       our steps;
    They set their eyes to cast *us* down
       to the ground.
12 He is like a lion that is eager to tear,
    And as a young lion lurking in
       hiding places.
13 Arise, O LORD, confront him, bring
       him low;
    Deliver my soul from the wicked
       with Your sword,
14 From men with Your hand, O LORD,
    From men of the world, whose
       portion is in *this* life,
    And whose belly You fill with Your
       treasure;
    They are satisfied with children,
    And leave their abundance to their
       babes.
➤ 15 As for me, I shall behold Your face
       in righteousness;
    I will be satisfied with Your likeness
       when I awake.

◈ Proverbs 5:21–23

➤ 21 For the ways of a man are before
          the eyes of the LORD,
✳   And He watches all his paths.
22 His own iniquities will capture the
       wicked,
    And he will be held with the cords
       of his sin.
23 He will die for lack of instruction,
    And in the greatness of his folly he
       will go astray.

◈ Matthew 20:1–16

20 "FOR the kingdom of heaven is like
    a landowner who went out early
in the morning to hire laborers for his
vineyard.
2   "When he had agreed with the laborers for a denarius for the day, he sent
them into his vineyard.
3   "And he went out about the third
hour and saw others standing idle in the
market place;
4   and to those he said, 'You also go
into the vineyard, and whatever is right I
will give you.' And *so* they went.
5   "Again he went out about the sixth
and the ninth hour, and did the same
thing.
6   "And about the eleventh *hour* he
went out and found others standing
around; and he *said to them, 'Why
have you been standing here idle all day
long?'
7   "They *said to him, 'Because no one
hired us.' He *said to them, 'You go into
the vineyard too.'
8   "When evening came, the owner of
the vineyard *said to his foreman, 'Call
the laborers and pay them their wages,
beginning with the last *group* to the first.'
9   "When those *hired* about the eleventh hour came, each one received a
denarius.
10 "When those *hired* first came, they
thought that they would receive more;
but each of them also received a denarius.
11 "When they received it, they grumbled at the landowner,
12 saying, 'These last men have worked
only one hour, and you have made them
equal to us who have borne the burden
and the scorching heat of the day.'

LIFE LESSONS

➤ **Psalm 17:15** — *I shall behold Your face in righteousness; I will be satisfied with Your likeness when I awake.*

*W*e look forward to that great day when we will see Jesus as He is, when we will be transformed into His glorious image (1 John 3:2). It will be like waking from a deep sleep into a stunningly beautiful new day.

➤ **Proverbs 5:21** — *For the ways of a man are before the eyes of the LORD, and He watches all his paths.*

*G*od is constantly watching over us, noticing our decisions, pondering our plans, observing our behavior—not primarily for judgment, but for blessing. He knows exactly what we need, and so He invites us to ask Him for His counsel.

13 "But he answered and said to one of them, 'Friend, I am doing you no wrong; did you not agree with me for a denarius?

14 'Take what is yours and go, but I wish to give to this last man the same as to you.

➤ 15 'Is it not lawful for me to do what I wish with what is my own? Or is your eye envious because I am generous?'

✳ 16 "So the last shall be first, and the first last."

JANUARY 31

Exodus 11:1—12:51

11 NOW the LORD said to Moses, "One more plague I will bring on Pharaoh and on Egypt; after that he will let you go from here. When he lets you go, he will surely drive you out from here completely.

2 "Speak now in the hearing of the people that each man ask from his neighbor and each woman from her neighbor for articles of silver and articles of gold."

➤ 3 The LORD gave the people favor in the sight of the Egyptians. Furthermore, the man Moses *himself* was greatly esteemed in the land of Egypt, *both* in the sight of Pharaoh's servants and in the sight of the people.

4 Moses said, "Thus says the LORD, 'About midnight I am going out into the midst of Egypt,

5 and all the firstborn in the land of Egypt shall die, from the firstborn of the Pharaoh who sits on his throne, even to the firstborn of the slave girl who is behind the millstones; all the firstborn of the cattle as well.

6 'Moreover, there shall be a great cry

in all the land of Egypt, such as there has not been *before* and such as shall never be again.

7 'But against any of the sons of Israel a dog will not *even* bark, whether against man or beast, that you may understand how the LORD makes a distinction between Egypt and Israel.'

8 "All these your servants will come down to me and bow themselves before me, saying, 'Go out, you and all the people who follow you,' and after that I will go out." And he went out from Pharaoh in hot anger.

9 Then the LORD said to Moses, "Pharaoh will not listen to you, so that My wonders will be multiplied in the land of Egypt."

10 Moses and Aaron performed all these wonders before Pharaoh; yet the LORD hardened Pharaoh's heart, and he did not let the sons of Israel go out of his land.

12 NOW the LORD said to Moses and Aaron in the land of Egypt,

2 "This month shall be the beginning of months for you; it is to be the first month of the year to you.

3 "Speak to all the congregation of Israel, saying, 'On the tenth of this month they are each one to take a lamb for themselves, according to their fathers' households, a lamb for each household.

4 'Now if the household is too small for a lamb, then he and his neighbor nearest to his house are to take one according to the number of persons *in them*; according to what each man should eat, you are to divide the lamb.

5 'Your lamb shall be an unblemished male a year old; you may take it from the sheep or from the goats.

6 'You shall keep it until the fourteenth day of the same month, then the whole assembly of the congregation of Israel is to kill it at twilight.

7 'Moreover, they shall take some of the blood and put it on the two doorposts and on the lintel of the houses in which they eat it.

8 'They shall eat the flesh that *same* night, roasted with fire, and they shall eat it with unleavened bread and bitter herbs.

9 'Do not eat any of it raw or boiled at all with water, but rather roasted with fire, *both* its head and its legs along with its entrails.

10 'And you shall not leave any of it over until morning, but whatever is left of it until morning, you shall burn with fire.

11 'Now you shall eat it in this manner: *with* your loins girded, your sandals on your feet, and your staff in your hand; and you shall eat it in haste—it is the LORD's Passover.

12 'For I will go through the land of Egypt on that night, and will strike down all the firstborn in the land of Egypt, both man and beast; and against all the gods of Egypt I will execute judgments—I am the LORD.

13 'The blood shall be a sign for you on the houses where you live; and when I see the blood I will pass over you, and no plague will befall you to destroy *you* when I strike the land of Egypt.

14 'Now this day will be a memorial to you, and you shall celebrate it *as* a feast to the LORD; throughout your generations you are to celebrate it *as* a permanent ordinance.

15 'Seven days you shall eat unleavened bread, but on the first day you shall remove leaven from your houses; for whoever eats anything leavened from the first day until the seventh day, that person shall be cut off from Israel.

16 'On the first day you shall have a holy assembly, and *another* holy assembly on the seventh day; no work at all shall be done on them, except what must be eaten by every person, that alone may be prepared by you.

17 'You shall also observe the *Feast of Unleavened Bread*, for on this very day I brought your hosts out of the land of Egypt; therefore you shall observe this day throughout your generations as a permanent ordinance.

18 'In the first *month*, on the fourteenth day of the month at evening, you shall eat unleavened bread, until the twenty-first day of the month at evening.

19 'Seven days there shall be no leaven found in your houses; for whoever eats what is leavened, that person shall be cut off from the congregation of Israel, whether *he is* an alien or a native of the land.

20 'You shall not eat anything leavened; in all your dwellings you shall eat unleavened bread.'"

21 Then Moses called for all the elders of Israel and said to them, "Go and take for yourselves lambs according to your families, and slay the Passover *lamb*.

22 "You shall take a bunch of hyssop and dip it in the blood which is in the basin, and apply some of the blood that is in the basin to the lintel and the two doorposts; and none of you shall go outside the door of his house until morning.

23 "For the LORD will pass through to smite the Egyptians; and when He sees the blood on the lintel and on the two doorposts, the LORD will pass over the door and will not allow the destroyer to come in to your houses to smite *you*.

24 "And you shall observe this event as an ordinance for you and your children forever.

25 "When you enter the land which the LORD will give you, as He has promised, you shall observe this rite.

26 "And when your children say to you, 'What does this rite mean to you?'

27 you shall say, 'It is a Passover sacrifice to the LORD who passed over the houses of the sons of Israel in Egypt when He smote the Egyptians, but spared

---

LIFE LESSONS

➤ **Exodus 12:11 —** *"It is the LORD's Passover."*

*T*he Passover lamb symbolized the work that Jesus Christ would finish in His death on the Cross and resurrection from the grave. This is why the apostle Paul wrote, "Christ our Passover also has been sacrificed" (1 Cor. 5:7).

our homes.'" And the people bowed low and worshiped.

28 Then the sons of Israel went and did so; just as the LORD had commanded Moses and Aaron, so they did.

29 Now it came about at midnight that the LORD struck all the firstborn in the land of Egypt, from the firstborn of Pharaoh who sat on his throne to the firstborn of the captive who was in the dungeon, and all the firstborn of cattle.

30 Pharaoh arose in the night, he and all his servants and all the Egyptians, and there was a great cry in Egypt, for there was no home where there was not someone dead.

31 Then he called for Moses and Aaron at night and said, "Rise up, get out from among my people, both you and the sons of Israel; and go, worship the LORD, as you have said.

32 "Take both your flocks and your herds, as you have said, and go, and bless me also."

33 The Egyptians urged the people, to send them out of the land in haste, for they said, "We will all be dead."

34 So the people took their dough before it was leavened, with their kneading bowls bound up in the clothes on their shoulders.

35 Now the sons of Israel had done according to the word of Moses, for they had requested from the Egyptians articles of silver and articles of gold, and clothing;

36 and the LORD had given the people favor in the sight of the Egyptians, so that they let them have their request. Thus they plundered the Egyptians.

37 Now the sons of Israel journeyed from Rameses to Succoth, about six hundred thousand men on foot, aside from children.

38 A mixed multitude also went up with them, along with flocks and herds, a very large number of livestock.

39 They baked the dough which they had brought out of Egypt into cakes of unleavened bread. For it had not become leavened, since they were driven out of Egypt and could not delay, nor had they prepared any provisions for themselves.

40 Now the time that the sons of Israel lived in Egypt was four hundred and thirty years.

41 And at the end of four hundred and thirty years, to the very day, all the hosts of the LORD went out from the land of Egypt.

42 It is a night to be observed for the LORD for having brought them out from the land of Egypt; this night is for the LORD, to be observed by all the sons of Israel throughout their generations.

43 The LORD said to Moses and Aaron, "This is the ordinance of the Passover: no foreigner is to eat of it;

44 but every man's slave purchased with money, after you have circumcised him, then he may eat of it.

45 "A sojourner or a hired servant shall not eat of it.

46 "It is to be eaten in a single house; you are not to bring forth any of the flesh outside of the house, nor are you to break any bone of it.

47 "All the congregation of Israel are to celebrate this.

48 "But if a stranger sojourns with you, and celebrates the Passover to the LORD, let all his males be circumcised, and then let him come near to celebrate it; and he shall be like a native of the land. But no uncircumcised person may eat of it.

49 "The same law shall apply to the native as to the stranger who sojourns among you."

50 Then all the sons of Israel did so; they did just as the LORD had commanded Moses and Aaron.

51 And on that same day the LORD brought the sons of Israel out of the land of Egypt by their hosts.

Psalm 18:1–12

For the choir director. A *Psalm* of David the servant of the LORD, who spoke to the LORD the words of this song in the day that the LORD delivered him from the hand of all his enemies and from the hand of Saul. And he said,

18 "I LOVE You, O LORD, my strength."

2 The LORD is my rock and my fortress and my deliverer,
My God, my rock, in whom I take refuge;
My shield and the horn of my salvation, my stronghold.

3 I call upon the LORD, who is worthy to be praised,
And I am saved from my enemies.

ANSWERS TO LIFE'S QUESTIONS

What can I do when my feelings go from discouraged to hopeless?

PSALM 18:1–6

*I*f you feel hopeless, helpless, or power-less—unable to deal with people or problems and on the verge of exhaustion—take heart in the prophet Habakkuk's stirring conclusion to his short book.

Knowing that a savage army of Babylonians would soon plunder his homeland, Habakkuk was discouraged. Surely, the coming destruction would be absolutely unbearable. Yet despite the disheartening scenario, Habakkuk penned an amazing response: "I will rejoice in the God of my salvation. The Lord GOD is my strength, and He has made my feet like hinds' feet, and makes me walk on my high places" (Hab. 3:18, 19). Even if the crops all failed, the livestock died, and everything he had learned to depend on was ruined, Habakkuk would still trust the Lord (Hab. 3:17).

Where did the prophet find such hope in the face of such terrible calamity? For one thing, God's Word had strengthened him. His expression of faith closely echoes the words of David, uttered centuries before: "The LORD is my rock and my fortress and my deliverer, my God, my rock, in whom I take refuge; my

shield and the horn of my salvation, my stronghold. I call upon the LORD, who is worthy to be praised, and I am saved from my enemies" (Ps. 18:2, 3).

Also, Habakkuk had spent a great deal of time alone with the Lord. In fact, the book that bears his name is a record of his extended conversation with God concerning His ways and plans. While Habakkuk did not understand (or particularly like) what he heard from God, he acknowledged the fact that His ways are best. He trusted the Lord for the future of Israel and for his own life. Regardless of the circumstances, the prophet knew the Lord was at work and would bring good out of what seemed to be horrendous circumstances. This is God's promise to us. He is always at work in our lives to bring good out of the darkest of situations (Rom. 8:28).

When the outlook looks grim, Christ is your strength. When the circumstances seem volatile, Christ is your stability. When the future appears foreboding, Christ remains your hope. The strength of Christ is both inexhaustible and immeasurable—and it is yours to receive.

God delights in upholding the weary and reviving the fainthearted (Is. 40:29–31). Your reservoir of emotional and physical energy may feel nearly drained, but God's supply of spiritual stamina never runs out. Come to Him and His Word for the strength to carry on, and He will supply the power you need to traverse the rough terrain ahead. That's His promise, and God always keeps His promises.

---

4 The cords of death encompassed me,
 And the torrents of ungodliness
  terrified me.
5 The cords of Sheol surrounded me;
 The snares of death confronted me.
6 In my distress I called upon the
  LORD,
 And cried to my God for help;
 He heard my voice out of His
  temple,
 And my cry for help before Him
  came into His ears.

LIFE LESSONS

➤ **Psalm 18:2** — *The LORD is my rock and my fortress and my deliverer.*

*W*e are wise if we fill our minds with many graphic images of who God is for us: our Rock, our Fortress, our Shield, our Stronghold. How do you best like to think of Him? What is He to you?

7 Then the earth shook and quaked;
 And the foundations of the
  mountains were trembling
 And were shaken, because He was
  angry.
8 Smoke went up out of His nostrils,
 And fire from His mouth
  devoured;
 Coals were kindled by it.
9 He bowed the heavens also, and
  came down
 With thick darkness under His
  feet.
10 He rode upon a cherub and flew;
 And He sped upon the wings of the
  wind.
11 He made darkness His hiding place,
  His canopy around Him,
 Darkness of waters, thick clouds of
  the skies.
12 From the brightness before Him
  passed His thick clouds,
 Hailstones and coals of fire.

⬧ **Proverbs 6:1–5**

6 MY son, if you have become surety
for your neighbor,
Have given a pledge for a
stranger,
2   If you have been snared with the
words of your mouth,
Have been caught with the words of
your mouth,
3   Do this then, my son, and deliver
yourself;
Since you have come into the hand
of your neighbor,
Go, humble yourself, and importune
your neighbor.
4   Give no sleep to your eyes,
Nor slumber to your eyelids;
5   Deliver yourself like a gazelle from
the hunter's hand
And like a bird from the hand of
the fowler.

⬧ **Matthew 20:17–34**

17 As Jesus was about to go up to Jerusalem, He took the twelve *disciples* aside
by themselves, and on the way He said
to them,
18 "Behold, we are going up to Jerusalem; and the Son of Man will be delivered to the chief priests and scribes, and
they will condemn Him to death,
19 and will hand Him over to the Gentiles to mock and scourge and crucify
Him, and on the third day He will be
raised up."
20 Then the mother of the sons of Zebedee came to Jesus with her sons, bowing
down and making a request of Him.
21 And He said to her, "What do you
wish?" She *said to Him, "Command
that in Your kingdom these two sons of
mine may sit one on Your right and one
on Your left."
22 But Jesus answered, "You do not
know what you are asking. Are you
able to drink the cup that I am about
to drink?" They *said to Him, "We are
able."
23 He *said to them, "My cup you shall
drink; but to sit on My right and on *My*
left, this is not Mine to give, but it is for

those for whom it has been prepared by
My Father."
24 And hearing *this,* the ten became
indignant with the two brothers.
25 But Jesus called them to Himself
and said, "You know that the rulers of
the Gentiles lord it over them, and *their*
great men exercise authority over them.
26 "It is not this way among you, but
whoever wishes to become great among
you shall be your servant,
27 and whoever wishes to be first
among you shall be your slave;
28 just as the Son of Man did not come
to be served, but to serve, and to give His
life a ransom for many."
29 As they were leaving Jericho, a
large crowd followed Him.
30 And two blind men sitting by the
road, hearing that Jesus was passing by,
cried out, "Lord, have mercy on us, Son
of David!"
31 The crowd sternly told them to be
quiet, but they cried out all the more,
"Lord, Son of David, have mercy on us!"
32 And Jesus stopped and called them,
and said, "What do you want Me to do
for you?"
33 They *said to Him, "Lord, *we want*
our eyes to be opened."
34 Moved with compassion, Jesus
touched their eyes; and immediately
they regained their sight and followed
Him.

LIFE LESSONS

➤ **Matthew 20:26 —** *"Whoever wishes
to become great among you shall be
your servant."*

*C*hristian leadership is never about
exercising power over someone or
putting someone in his or her place;
whenever it comes to that, the "Christian" element has vanished. Christian
leaders are always servants first.

➤ **Matthew 20:28 —** *"The Son of Man
did not come to be served, but to serve,
and to give His life a ransom for many."*

*N*o one ever mistook Jesus for anything but a leader, and yet He came
to serve, right up to the time He performed the ultimate service by giving His
life so that we might not have to die.

Exodus 13:1—14:31

13 THEN the LORD spoke to Moses, saying,

2 "Sanctify to Me every firstborn, the first offspring of every womb among the sons of Israel, both of man and beast; it belongs to Me."

3 Moses said to the people, "Remember this day in which you went out from Egypt, from the house of slavery; for by a powerful hand the LORD brought you out from this place. And nothing leavened shall be eaten.

4 "On this day in the month of Abib, you are about to go forth.

5 "It shall be when the LORD brings you to the land of the Canaanite, the Hittite, the Amorite, the Hivite and the Jebusite, which He swore to your fathers to give you, a land flowing with milk and honey, that you shall observe this rite in this month.

6 "For seven days you shall eat unleavened bread, and on the seventh day there shall be a feast to the LORD.

7 "Unleavened bread shall be eaten throughout the seven days; and nothing leavened shall be seen among you, nor shall any leaven be seen among you in all your borders.

8 "You shall tell your son on that day, saying, 'It is because of what the LORD did for me when I came out of Egypt.'

9 "And it shall serve as a sign to you on your hand, and as a reminder on your forehead, that the law of the LORD may be in your mouth; for with a powerful hand the LORD brought you out of Egypt.

10 "Therefore, you shall keep this ordinance at its appointed time from year to year.

11 "Now when the LORD brings you to the land of the Canaanite, as He swore to you and to your fathers, and gives it to you,

12 you shall devote to the LORD the first offspring of every womb, and the first offspring of every beast that you own; the males belong to the LORD.

13 "But every first offspring of a donkey you shall redeem with a lamb, but if you do not redeem *it*, then you shall break its neck; and every firstborn of man among your sons you shall redeem.

14 "And it shall be when your son asks you in time to come, saying, 'What is this?' then you shall say to him, 'With a powerful hand the LORD brought us out of Egypt, from the house of slavery.

15 'It came about, when Pharaoh was stubborn about letting us go, that the LORD killed every firstborn in the land of Egypt, both the firstborn of man and the firstborn of beast. Therefore, I sacrifice to the LORD the males, the first offspring of every womb, but every firstborn of my sons I redeem.'

16 "So it shall serve as a sign on your hand and as phylacteries on your forehead, for with a powerful hand the LORD brought us out of Egypt."

17 Now when Pharaoh had let the people go, God did not lead them by the way of the land of the Philistines, even though it was near; for God said, "The people might change their minds when they see war, and return to Egypt."

18 Hence God led the people around by the way of the wilderness to the Red Sea; and the sons of Israel went up in martial array from the land of Egypt.

19 Moses took the bones of Joseph with him, for he had made the sons of Israel solemnly swear, saying, "God will surely take care of you, and you shall carry my bones from here with you."

20 Then they set out from Succoth and camped in Etham on the edge of the wilderness.

21 The LORD was going before them in a

LIFE LESSONS

➤ **Exodus 13:17** — *"The people might change their minds when they see war, and return to Egypt."*

*O*ur God is a practical God, and He deals with us according to our nature. He will always lead us in a way that is appropriate to us.

➤ **Exodus 13:21** — *The LORD was going before them in a pillar of cloud by day to lead them on the way, and in a pillar of fire by night to give them light.*

*W*hen we personally know the Lord, we never need to feel "in the dark" in how we follow Him. God provides everything we need for life, and that includes illumination of the path before us.

pillar of cloud by day to lead them on the way, and in a pillar of fire by night to give them light, that they might travel by day and by night.

22 He did not take away the pillar of cloud by day, nor the pillar of fire by night, from before the people.

14 NOW the LORD spoke to Moses, saying,

2 "Tell the sons of Israel to turn back and camp before Pi-hahiroth, between Migdol and the sea; you shall camp in front of Baal-zephon, opposite it, by the sea.

3 "For Pharaoh will say of the sons of Israel, 'They are wandering aimlessly in the land; the wilderness has shut them in.'

4 "Thus I will harden Pharaoh's heart, and he will chase after them; and I will be honored through Pharaoh and all his army, and the Egyptians will know that I am the LORD." And they did so.

5 When the king of Egypt was told that the people had fled, Pharaoh and his servants had a change of heart toward the people, and they said, "What is this we have done, that we have let Israel go from serving us?"

6 So he made his chariot ready and took his people with him;

7 and he took six hundred select chariots, and all the *other* chariots of Egypt with officers over all of them.

8 The LORD hardened the heart of Pharaoh, king of Egypt, and he chased after the sons of Israel as the sons of Israel were going out boldly.

9 Then the Egyptians chased after them *with* all the horses *and* chariots of Pharaoh, his horsemen and his army, and they overtook them camping by the sea, beside Pi-hahiroth, in front of Baal-zephon.

10 As Pharaoh drew near, the sons of Israel looked, and behold, the Egyptians were marching after them, and they became very frightened; so the sons of Israel cried out to the LORD.

11 Then they said to Moses, "Is it because there were no graves in Egypt that you have taken us away to die in the wilderness? Why have you dealt with us in this way, bringing us out of Egypt?

12 "Is this not the word that we spoke to you in Egypt, saying, 'Leave us alone that we may serve the Egyptians'? For it would have been better for us to serve the Egyptians than to die in the wilderness."

13 But Moses said to the people, "Do not fear! Stand by and see the salvation of the LORD which He will accomplish for you today; for the Egyptians whom you have seen today, you will never see them again forever.

14 "The LORD will fight for you while you keep silent."

15 Then the LORD said to Moses, "Why are you crying out to Me? Tell the sons of Israel to go forward.

16 "As for you, lift up your staff and stretch out your hand over the sea and divide it, and the sons of Israel shall go through the midst of the sea on dry land.

17 "As for Me, behold, I will harden the hearts of the Egyptians so that they will go in after them; and I will be honored through Pharaoh and all his army, through his chariots and his horsemen.

18 "Then the Egyptians will know that I am the LORD, when I am honored through Pharaoh, through his chariots and his horsemen."

19 The angel of God, who had been going before the camp of Israel, moved and went behind them; and the pillar of cloud moved from before them and stood behind them.

20 So it came between the camp of

Exodus 14:2 — *"Tell the sons of Israel to turn back and camp . . . by the sea."*

Sometimes the Lord purposefully leads us into situations that look like dead-ends, not only to test our faith, but also to show His power in and complete control over all situations. Wherever He leads, we must follow.

Exodus 14:13 — *"Do not fear! Stand by and see the salvation of the LORD which He will accomplish for you today."*

Throughout Scripture, we read the phrase, "Do not fear." It is God's refrain to His people, whatever their circumstances, for He has promised to save and deliver us.

Egypt and the camp of Israel; and there was the cloud along with the darkness, yet it gave light at night. Thus the one did not come near the other all night.

21 Then Moses stretched out his hand over the sea; and the LORD swept the sea *back* by a strong east wind all night and turned the sea into dry land, so the waters were divided.

22 The sons of Israel went through the midst of the sea on the dry land, and the waters *were like* a wall to them on their right hand and on their left.

23 Then the Egyptians took up the pursuit, and all Pharaoh's horses, his chariots and his horsemen went in after them into the midst of the sea.

24 At the morning watch, the LORD looked down on the army of the Egyptians through the pillar of fire and cloud and brought the army of the Egyptians into confusion.

25 He caused their chariot wheels to swerve, and He made them drive with difficulty; so the Egyptians said, "Let us flee from Israel, for the LORD is fighting for them against the Egyptians."

26 Then the LORD said to Moses, "Stretch out your hand over the sea so that the waters may come back over the Egyptians, over their chariots and their horsemen."

27 So Moses stretched out his hand over the sea, and the sea returned to its normal state at daybreak, while the Egyptians were fleeing right into it; then the LORD overthrew the Egyptians in the midst of the sea.

28 The waters returned and covered the chariots and the horsemen, even Pharaoh's entire army that had gone into the sea after them; not even one of them remained.

29 But the sons of Israel walked on dry land through the midst of the sea, and the waters *were like* a wall to them on their right hand and on their left.

30 Thus the LORD saved Israel that day from the hand of the Egyptians, and Israel saw the Egyptians dead on the seashore.

31 When Israel saw the great power which the LORD had used against the Egyptians, the people feared the LORD, and they believed in the LORD and in His servant Moses.

Psalm 18:13–19

13 The LORD also thundered in the heavens,
And the Most High uttered His voice,
Hailstones and coals of fire.

14 He sent out His arrows, and scattered them,
And lightning flashes in abundance, and routed them.

15 Then the channels of water appeared,
And the foundations of the world were laid bare
At Your rebuke, O LORD,
At the blast of the breath of Your nostrils.

16 He sent from on high, He took me;
He drew me out of many waters.

17 He delivered me from my strong enemy,
And from those who hated me, for they were too mighty for me.

18 They confronted me in the day of my calamity,
But the LORD was my stay.

19 He brought me forth also into a broad place;
He rescued me, because He delighted in me.

Proverbs 6:6–11

6 Go to the ant, O sluggard,
Observe her ways and be wise,

7 Which, having no chief,
Officer or ruler,

8 Prepares her food in the summer
And gathers her provision in the harvest.

9 How long will you lie down, O sluggard?
When will you arise from your sleep?

10 "A little sleep, a little slumber,
A little folding of the hands to rest"—

11 Your poverty will come in like a vagabond
And your need like an armed man.

Matthew 21:1–22

21 WHEN they had approached Jerusalem and had come to Bethphage, at the Mount of Olives, then Jesus sent two disciples,

2 saying to them, "Go into the village opposite you, and immediately you will find a donkey tied *there* and a colt with her; untie them and bring them to Me.

3 "If anyone says anything to you, you shall say, 'The Lord has need of them,' and immediately he will send them."

4 This took place to fulfill what was spoken through the prophet:

5 "SAY TO THE DAUGHTER OF ZION,
'BEHOLD YOUR KING IS COMING TO YOU,
GENTLE, AND MOUNTED ON A DONKEY,
EVEN ON A COLT, THE FOAL OF A BEAST
OF BURDEN.'"

6 The disciples went and did just as Jesus had instructed them,

7 and brought the donkey and the colt, and laid their coats on them; and He sat on the coats.

8 Most of the crowd spread their coats in the road, and others were cutting branches from the trees and spreading them in the road.

9 The crowds going ahead of Him, and those who followed, were shouting,
"Hosanna to the Son of David;
BLESSED IS HE WHO COMES IN THE
NAME OF THE LORD;
Hosanna in the highest!"

10 When He had entered Jerusalem, all the city was stirred, saying, "Who is this?"

11 And the crowds were saying, "This is the prophet Jesus, from Nazareth in Galilee."

12 And Jesus entered the temple and drove out all those who were buying and selling in the temple, and overturned the tables of the money changers and the seats of those who were selling doves.

13 And He *said to them, "It is written, 'MY HOUSE SHALL BE CALLED A HOUSE OF PRAYER'; but you are making it a ROBBERS' DEN."

14 And *the* blind and *the* lame came to Him in the temple, and He healed them.

15 But when the chief priests and the scribes saw the wonderful things that He had done, and the children who were shouting in the temple, "Hosanna to the Son of David," they became indignant

16 and said to Him, "Do You hear what these *children* are saying?" And Jesus *said to them, "Yes; have you never read, 'OUT OF THE MOUTH OF INFANTS AND NURSING BABIES YOU HAVE PREPARED PRAISE FOR YOURSELF'?"

17 And He left them and went out of the city to Bethany, and spent the night there.

18 Now in the morning, when He was returning to the city, He became hungry.

19 Seeing a lone fig tree by the road, He came to it and found nothing on it except leaves only; and He *said to it, "No longer shall there ever be *any* fruit from you." And at once the fig tree withered.

20 Seeing *this,* the disciples were amazed and asked, "How did the fig tree wither *all* at once?"

21 And Jesus answered and said to them, "Truly I say to you, if you have faith and do not doubt, you will not only do what was done to the fig tree, but even if you say to this mountain, 'Be taken up and cast into the sea,' it will happen.

22 "And all things you ask in prayer, believing, you will receive."

LIFE LESSONS

➤ **Matthew 21:4** — *This took place to fulfill what was spoken through the prophet.*

*G*od is serious about fulfilling His Word. If He makes sure that even "little" prophesied details take place (Matt. 2:15; 13:35; John 19:24, 28), then we can expect He will surely fulfill all the "big" ones.

➤ **Matthew 21:12** — *Jesus entered the temple and drove out all those who were buying and selling in the temple.*

*T*he Lord is passionate about His name being honored and His people being treated well. His silence may unnerve us at times, but He overlooks nothing and lets nothing "slide." The day of His justice is coming.

ANSWERS TO LIFE'S QUESTIONS

How can God use an imperfect person like me?

MATTHEW 21:22

*I*n John 14:12, Jesus made this amazing statement: "He who believes in Me, the works that I do, he will do also; and greater works than these he will do." Astounding isn't it? We as believers will do works *greater* than He—the Savior of the world—has done. If it is a difficult thing for you to believe, you are not alone. This truth seems impossible when we consider it in light of our faults, sins, and weaknesses.

Maybe you have been sitting on the sidelines because you have yielded to sin, and shame has completely discouraged you. You feel as though God cannot use you because of mistakes you've made or wrongs you've committed. Perhaps you feel so broken in spirit that you don't believe you will ever be useful to Him again. This is absolutely not true! When we confess our sins, God forgives and restores us.

The problem isn't your inadequacies or imperfections—it is that you have allowed your feelings to overshadow the truth of God's Word. The Lord is able to use you to show His love to others (1 John 1:9; 2 Cor. 1:3–7).

Once you have confessed and turned from your sins, you are cleansed—*permanently* (Ps. 103:12; Is. 43:25; Jer. 31:43). The Lord purifies you and equips you for His service. The questions are not "Do I deserve to serve Him?" or

"Am I talented enough to represent Him?" These questions no longer matter because the Lord takes care of those issues completely. Rather, the question is: "Will I obey God and trust Him to show His love to others through me?"

Once we accept Jesus Christ as our Lord and Savior, His Holy Spirit lives in us. He empowers us to do *everything* He asks of us, making the possibilities for service limitless. When Jesus said we would do greater things than He has done, it is because *He* would be working through us in a powerful manner—enabling us to be mighty witnesses for His name. *He* is our adequacy. And He works through us to show others His love.

The apostle John explains, "God has sent His only begotten Son into the world so that we might live through Him. In this is love, not that we loved God, but that He loved us and sent His Son to be the propitiation for our sins. Beloved, if God so loved us, we also ought to love one another" (1 John 4:10, 11).

We don't serve the Lord because we are perfect—we do it because we are thankful for what He has done for us. And the work we do is greater because every time we show His everlasting love to another person, it multiplies and grows.

Do not worry about your weaknesses, imperfections, faults, or inadequacies. The Lord will work through them (1 Cor. 1:27; 2 Cor. 12:9, 10). Confess your sins, receive God's love, and allow Him to display His wonderful grace and forgiveness through you. Share His saving love with others, and embrace the great things He wants to do through you.

FEBRUARY 2

Exodus 15:1—16:36

15 THEN Moses and the sons of Israel sang this song to the LORD, and said,

"I will sing to the LORD, for He is highly exalted;
The horse and its rider He has hurled into the sea.

2 "The LORD is my strength and song,
And He has become my salvation;
This is my God, and I will praise Him;

My father's God, and I will extol Him.

3 "The LORD is a warrior;
The LORD is His name.

4 "Pharaoh's chariots and his army He has cast into the sea;
And the choicest of his officers are drowned in the Red Sea.

5 "The deeps cover them;
They went down into the depths like a stone.

6 "Your right hand, O LORD, is majestic in power,
Your right hand, O LORD, shatters the enemy.

7 "And in the greatness of Your
excellence You overthrow those
who rise up against You;
You send forth Your burning anger,
and it consumes them as chaff.
8 "At the blast of Your nostrils the
waters were piled up,
The flowing waters stood up like a
heap;
The deeps were congealed in the
heart of the sea.
9 "The enemy said, 'I will pursue, I will
overtake, I will divide the spoil;
My desire shall be gratified against
them;
I will draw out my sword, my hand
will destroy them.'
10 "You blew with Your wind, the sea
covered them;
They sank like lead in the mighty
waters.
11 "Who is like You among the gods,
O LORD?
Who is like You, majestic in
holiness,
Awesome in praises, working
wonders?
12 "You stretched out Your right hand,
The earth swallowed them.
13 "In Your lovingkindness You have
led the people whom You have
redeemed;
In Your strength You have guided
them to Your holy habitation.
14 "The peoples have heard, they
tremble;
Anguish has gripped the inhabitants
of Philistia.
15 "Then the chiefs of Edom were
dismayed;
The leaders of Moab, trembling
grips them;
All the inhabitants of Canaan have
melted away.
16 "Terror and dread fall upon them;
By the greatness of Your arm they
are motionless as stone;
Until Your people pass over, O LORD,
Until the people pass over whom
You have purchased.
17 "You will bring them and plant
them in the mountain of Your
inheritance,
The place, O LORD, which You have
made for Your dwelling,
The sanctuary, O Lord, which Your
hands have established.

18 "The LORD shall reign forever and
ever." ⤠
19 For the horses of Pharaoh with his
chariots and his horsemen went into
the sea, and the LORD brought back the
waters of the sea on them, but the sons
of Israel walked on dry land through the
midst of the sea.
20 Miriam the prophetess, Aaron's sister, took the timbrel in her hand, and
all the women went out after her with
timbrels and with dancing.
21 Miriam answered them,
"Sing to the LORD, for He is highly
exalted;
The horse and his rider He has
hurled into the sea."
22 Then Moses led Israel from the Red
Sea, and they went out into the wilderness of Shur; and they went three days
in the wilderness and found no water.
23 When they came to Marah, they could ⤠
not drink the waters of Marah, for they
were bitter; therefore it was named Marah.
24 So the people grumbled at Moses,
saying, "What shall we drink?"
25 Then he cried out to the LORD, and
the LORD showed him a tree; and he
threw *it* into the waters, and the waters
became sweet.
There He made for them a statute
and regulation, and there He tested them.
26 And He said, "If you will give earnest
heed to the voice of the LORD your God,
and do what is right in His sight, and give

LIFE LESSONS

➤ **Exodus 15:18 —** *"The LORD shall reign
forever and ever."*

*W*e can find great comfort during
times of difficulty in knowing God
has promised that He was, is, and always
will be in control—not only over world
events, but also over everything in our
own lives.

➤ **Exodus 15:23 —** *They could not drink
the waters of Marah, for they were bitter.*

*I*mmediately after the miraculous
triumph at the Red Sea, God led
Israel for three days on a route devoid of
water. Why? The Lord trains us to trust
Him by letting us experience both need
and abundance.

ear to His commandments, and keep all His statutes, I will put none of the diseases on you which I have put on the Egyptians; for I, the LORD, am your healer."

27 Then they came to Elim where there *were* twelve springs of water and seventy date palms, and they camped there beside the waters.

16 THEN they set out from Elim, and all the congregation of the sons of Israel came to the wilderness of Sin, which is between Elim and Sinai, on the fifteenth day of the second month after their departure from the land of Egypt.

2 The whole congregation of the sons of Israel grumbled against Moses and Aaron in the wilderness.

3 The sons of Israel said to them, "Would that we had died by the LORD's

hand in the land of Egypt, when we sat by the pots of meat, when we ate bread to the full; for you have brought us out into this wilderness to kill this whole assembly with hunger."

4 Then the LORD said to Moses, "Behold, I will rain bread from heaven for

ANSWERS TO LIFE'S QUESTIONS

Can I really trust God to provide what I need?

EXODUS 16:1–3

*F*rom cover to cover, the Bible is full of God's promises to provide for our needs. Our heavenly Father always gives, always loves, always remains generous toward His children.

In the first few chapters of Genesis, the Lord gives the first man and woman a perfect garden. In Revelation, we read about our ultimate home—the perfect and eternal heaven He's created for us. In all the books between, we read how God delights in blessing His people. At the very outset of the New Testament, we read how God sent His Son, Jesus Christ, as His ultimate gift of blessing to provide what we need most of all: forgiveness of sin and restored fellowship with Himself.

When you limit yourself to your own abilities and resources, you run out of both commodities very quickly. But when you focus your faith on what God can do, you discover an infinite supply that cannot be measured or depleted. God's resources are 100 percent inflation-proof and recession-proof.

The very nature of God gives you assurance of His abundant provision. God is:

- *Omniscient*—the Lord knows your need. He knows it even better than you do and before you do (Matt. 6:8).

- *Omnipotent*—the Lord has all power to supply to you whatever you need (Phil. 4:19).
- *Omnipresent*—the Lord is at work even now to meet your needs (Ps. 34:7, 8).
- *Omni-benevolent*—because of the Lord's perfect, unconditional love, you can be sure He will always provide the very best for you (Eph. 2:4–7).

Not only do you have the character of God as your assurance that He is going to provide for you, but you also have the testimony of God's past performance in providing for His people. Scripture repeatedly points to Him as the faithful source of all life and goodness (Heb. 5:9; James 1:17). Consider just a few examples from the Book of Exodus:

- He made a way for His people to cross the Red Sea and find deliverance from their enemies (Ex. 14).
- He provided manna for the people to eat in the wilderness (Ex. 16:1–21).
- He caused water to gush forth from a rock to quench the people's thirst (Ex. 17:1–6).
- He gave His commandments to His people, even when they lacked moral fiber Ex. 20—31).
- He provided all they needed to construct the tabernacle (Ex. 12:35, 36; 35:21–29).

As the Israelites left behind the only home they had ever known in Egypt, God provided for all their needs. He provided for their protection, their basic physical necessities (food and water), spiritual instruction, and healing. He does the same for us today!

you; and the people shall go out and gather a day's portion every day, that I may test them, whether or not they will walk in My instruction.

5 "On the sixth day, when they prepare what they bring in, it will be twice as much as they gather daily."

6 So Moses and Aaron said to all the sons of Israel, "At evening you will know that the LORD has brought you out of the land of Egypt;

7 and in the morning you will see the glory of the LORD, for He hears your grumblings against the LORD; and what are we, that you grumble against us?"

➤ 8 Moses said, *"This will happen* when the LORD gives you meat to eat in the evening, and bread to the full in the morning; for the LORD hears your grumblings which you grumble against Him. And what are we? Your grumblings are not against us but against the LORD."

9 Then Moses said to Aaron, "Say to all the congregation of the sons of Israel, 'Come near before the LORD, for He has heard your grumblings.'"

10 It came about as Aaron spoke to the whole congregation of the sons of Israel, that they looked toward the wilderness, and behold, the glory of the LORD appeared in the cloud.

11 And the LORD spoke to Moses, saying,

12 "I have heard the grumblings of the sons of Israel; speak to them, saying, 'At twilight you shall eat meat, and in the morning you shall be filled with bread; and you shall know that I am the LORD your God.'"

13 So it came about at evening that the quails came up and covered the camp, and in the morning there was a layer of dew around the camp.

14 When the layer of dew evaporated, behold, on the surface of the wilderness there was a fine flake-like thing, fine as the frost on the ground.

15 When the sons of Israel saw *it,* they said to one another, "What is it?" For they did not know what it was. And Moses said to them, "It is the bread which the LORD has given you to eat.

16 "This is what the LORD has commanded, 'Gather of it every man as much as he should eat; you shall take an omer apiece according to the number of persons each of you has in his tent.'"

17 The sons of Israel did so, and *some* gathered much and *some* little.

18 When they measured it with an omer, he who had gathered much had no excess, and he who had gathered little had no lack; every man gathered as much as he should eat.

19 Moses said to them, "Let no man leave any of it until morning."

20 But they did not listen to Moses, and some left part of it until morning, and it bred worms and became foul; and Moses was angry with them.

21 They gathered it morning by morning, every man as much as he should eat; but when the sun grew hot, it would melt.

22 Now on the sixth day they gathered twice as much bread, two omers for each one. When all the leaders of the congregation came and told Moses,

23 then he said to them, "This is what the LORD meant: Tomorrow is a sabbath observance, a holy sabbath to the LORD. Bake what you will bake and boil what you will boil, and all that is left over put aside to be kept until morning."

24 So they put it aside until morning, as Moses had ordered, and it did not become foul nor was there any worm in it.

25 Moses said, "Eat it today, for today is a sabbath to the LORD; today you will not find it in the field.

26 "Six days you shall gather it, but on the seventh day, *the* sabbath, there will be none."

27 It came about on the seventh day that some of the people went out to gather, but they found none.

28 Then the LORD said to Moses, "How long do you refuse to keep My commandments and My instructions?

29 "See, the LORD has given you the sabbath; therefore He gives you bread for two days on the sixth day. Remain every

---

LIFE LESSONS

➤ **Exodus 16:8 —** *"Your grumblings are not against us but against the LORD."*

*W*hen we complain about our circumstances and blame others, we are in fact complaining against the Lord, who exercises complete control over our circumstances.

man in his place; let no man go out of his place on the seventh day."

30 So the people rested on the seventh day.

31 The house of Israel named it manna, and it was like coriander seed, white, and its taste was like wafers with honey.

32 Then Moses said, "This is what the LORD has commanded, 'Let an omerful of it be kept throughout your generations, that they may see the bread that I fed you in the wilderness, when I brought you out of the land of Egypt.'"

33 Moses said to Aaron, "Take a jar and put an omerful of manna in it, and place it before the LORD to be kept throughout your generations."

34 As the LORD commanded Moses, so Aaron placed it before the Testimony, to be kept.

35 The sons of Israel ate the manna forty years, until they came to an inhabited land; they ate the manna until they came to the border of the land of Canaan.

36 (Now an omer is a tenth of an ephah.)

Psalm 18:20–27

20 The LORD has rewarded me
according to my righteousness;
According to the cleanness of my
hands He has recompensed me.

21 For I have kept the ways of the
LORD,
And have not wickedly departed
from my God.

22 For all His ordinances were before
me,
And I did not put away His statutes
from me.

23 I was also blameless with Him,
And I kept myself from my iniquity.

24 Therefore the LORD has
recompensed me according to my
righteousness,
According to the cleanness of my
hands in His eyes.

25 With the kind You show Yourself
kind;
With the blameless You show
Yourself blameless;

26 With the pure You show Yourself
pure,

And with the crooked You show
Yourself astute.

27 For You save an afflicted people,
But haughty eyes You abase.

Proverbs 6:12–15

12 A worthless person, a wicked man,
Is the one who walks with a
perverse mouth,

13 Who winks with his eyes, who
signals with his feet,
Who points with his fingers;

14 Who with perversity in his heart
continually devises evil,
Who spreads strife.

15 Therefore his calamity will come
suddenly;
Instantly he will be broken and
there will be no healing.

Matthew 21:23–46

23 When He entered the temple, the chief priests and the elders of the people came to Him while He was teaching, and said, "By what authority are You doing these things, and who gave You this authority?"

24 Jesus said to them, "I will also ask you one thing, which if you tell Me, I will also tell you by what authority I do these things.

25 "The baptism of John was from what source, from heaven or from men?" And they began reasoning among themselves, saying, "If we say, 'From heaven,' He will say to us, 'Then why did you not believe him?'

26 "But if we say, 'From men,' we fear the people; for they all regard John as a prophet."

27 And answering Jesus, they said, "We do not know." He also said to them, "Neither will I tell you by what authority I do these things.

28 "But what do you think? A man had two sons, and he came to the first and said, 'Son, go work today in the vineyard.'

29 "And he answered, 'I will not'; but afterward he regretted it and went.

30 "The man came to the second and

said the same thing; and he answered, 'I *will*, sir'; but he did not go.

31 "Which of the two did the will of his father?" They *said, "The first." Jesus *said to them, "Truly I say to you that the tax collectors and prostitutes will get into the kingdom of God before you.

32 "For John came to you in the way of righteousness and you did not believe him; but the tax collectors and prostitutes did believe him; and you, seeing *this*, did not even feel remorse afterward so as to believe him.

33 "Listen to another parable. There was a landowner who PLANTED A VINE-YARD AND PUT A WALL AROUND IT AND DUG A WINE PRESS IN IT, AND BUILT A TOWER, and rented it out to vine-growers and went on a journey.

34 "When the harvest time approached, he sent his slaves to the vine-growers to receive his produce.

35 "The vine-growers took his slaves and beat one, and killed another, and stoned a third.

36 "Again he sent another group of slaves larger than the first; and they did the same thing to them.

37 "But afterward he sent his son to them, saying, 'They will respect my son.'

38 "But when the vine-growers saw the son, they said among themselves, 'This is the heir; come, let us kill him and seize his inheritance.'

39 "They took him, and threw him out of the vineyard and killed him.

40 "Therefore when the owner of the vineyard comes, what will he do to those vine-growers?"

41 They *said to Him, "He will bring those wretches to a wretched end, and will rent out the vineyard to other vine-growers who will pay him the proceeds at the *proper* seasons."

42 Jesus *said to them, "Did you never read in the Scriptures,

'THE STONE WHICH THE BUILDERS REJECTED,
THIS BECAME THE CHIEF CORNER *stone*;
THIS CAME ABOUT FROM THE LORD,
AND IT IS MARVELOUS IN OUR EYES'?

43 "Therefore I say to you, the kingdom of God will be taken away from you and given to a people, producing the fruit of it.

44 "And he who falls on this stone will be broken to pieces; but on whomever it falls, it will scatter him like dust."

45 When the chief priests and the Pharisees heard His parables, they understood that He was speaking about them.

46 When they sought to seize Him, they feared the people, because they considered Him to be a prophet.

Exodus 17:1—18:27

17 THEN all the congregation of the sons of Israel journeyed by stages from the wilderness of Sin, according to the command of the LORD, and camped at Rephidim, and there was no water for the people to drink.

2 Therefore the people quarreled with Moses and said, "Give us water that we may drink." And Moses said to them, "Why do you quarrel with me? Why do you test the LORD?"

3 But the people thirsted there for water; and they grumbled against Moses and said, "Why, now, have you brought us up from Egypt, to kill us and our children and our livestock with thirst?"

4 So Moses cried out to the LORD, saying, "What shall I do to this people? A little more and they will stone me."

5 Then the LORD said to Moses, "Pass before the people and take with you some of the elders of Israel; and take in your hand your staff with which you struck the Nile, and go.

6 "Behold, I will stand before you there on the rock at Horeb; and you shall strike the rock, and water will come out of it, that the people may drink." And Moses did so in the sight of the elders of Israel.

7 He named the place Massah and Meribah because of the quarrel of the sons of Israel, and because they tested the LORD, saying, "Is the LORD among us, or not?"

8 Then Amalek came and fought against Israel at Rephidim.

LIFE LESSONS

➤ **Exodus 17:7 — "Is the LORD among us, or not?"**

*I*n times of difficulty, it is easy to start wondering, "Is the LORD among us, or not?" If we have placed our faith in Him, however, He has promised to be with us— so the question actually casts doubt on His truthfulness.

➤ **Exodus 17:12 — Moses' hands were heavy . . . Aaron and Hur supported his hands.**

*I*n order to succeed in the Christian life, we need the help and support of others. No believer has ever been called to "go it alone" in his or her walk of faith.

---

9 So Moses said to Joshua, "Choose men for us and go out, fight against Amalek. Tomorrow I will station myself on the top of the hill with the staff of God in my hand."
10 Joshua did as Moses told him, and fought against Amalek; and Moses, Aaron, and Hur went up to the top of the hill.
11 So it came about when Moses held his hand up, that Israel prevailed, and when he let his hand down, Amalek prevailed.
➤ 12 But Moses' hands were heavy. Then they took a stone and put it under him, and he sat on it; and Aaron and Hur supported his hands, one on one side and

one on the other. Thus his hands were steady until the sun set.
13 So Joshua overwhelmed Amalek and his people with the edge of the sword.
14 Then the LORD said to Moses, "Write this in a book as a memorial and recite it to Joshua, that I will utterly blot out the memory of Amalek from under heaven."
15 Moses built an altar and named it The LORD is My Banner;
16 and he said, "The LORD has sworn; the LORD will have war against Amalek from generation to generation."

18 NOW Jethro, the priest of Midian, Moses' father-in-law, heard of all that God had done for Moses and for

---

Life Examples:

Good Advice

EXODUS 18

*I*t's the attitude that has defeated so many servants of God: "If I want it done right, I've got to do it myself!" Instead of revealing godly commitment and skill, this attitude exposes our pride and need for control—destructive characteristics that do not honor God.

It was this attitude Moses unknowingly struggled with when his father-in-law Jethro came to confront him. When Jethro learned that Moses was judging all the people of Israel by himself, Jethro said, "The thing that you are doing is not good. You will surely wear out, both yourself and these people who are with you, for the task is too heavy for you; you cannot do it alone" (Ex. 18:17, 18).

Moses probably realized there was a problem, but what could he do about it? Only he knew the statutes and laws of God.

If we are honest, we'll admit there have been times when we've said the same thing about ourselves:

"I'm the only one who knows how that program works."

"There's no one else who knows how to put this event together."

"If I don't do it, they're just going to make a mess of it."

Can you see the prideful nature of those statements? We do ourselves no favors when we wear ourselves out with activities because we cannot let them go—when we will not trust anyone else with them.

We, like Moses, must take Jethro's advice. In Exodus 18:20, Jethro counseled, "Teach them the statutes and the laws, and make known to them the way in which they are to walk and the work they are to do." We must choose trustworthy, godly people to follow in our footsteps. We must teach them what we know so that they can serve the Lord. (See 2 Tim. 2:2.)

In doing so, we may eventually work ourselves out of a job—but that's good! This will ensure the work will carry on, even when we are gone—and that is absolutely essential when doing ministry (Matt. 28:19, 20).

Israel His people, how the Lord had brought Israel out of Egypt.

2 Jethro, Moses' father-in-law, took Moses' wife Zipporah, after he had sent her away,

3 and her two sons, of whom one was named Gershom, for Moses said, "I have been a sojourner in a foreign land."

4 The other was named Eliezer, for *he said,* "The God of my father was my help, and delivered me from the sword of Pharaoh."

5 Then Jethro, Moses' father-in-law, came with his sons and his wife to Moses in the wilderness where he was camped, at the mount of God.

6 He sent word to Moses, "I, your father-in-law Jethro, am coming to you with your wife and her two sons with her."

7 Then Moses went out to meet his father-in-law, and he bowed down and kissed him; and they asked each other of their welfare and went into the tent.

➤ 8 Moses told his father-in-law all that the Lord had done to Pharaoh and to the Egyptians for Israel's sake, all the hardship that had befallen them on the journey, and *how* the Lord had delivered them.

9 Jethro rejoiced over all the goodness which the Lord had done to Israel, in delivering them from the hand of the Egyptians.

10 So Jethro said, "Blessed be the Lord who delivered you from the hand of the Egyptians and from the hand of Pharaoh, *and* who delivered the people from under the hand of the Egyptians.

✳ 11 "Now I know that the Lord is greater than all the gods; indeed, it was proven when they dealt proudly against the people."

12 Then Jethro, Moses' father-in-law, took a burnt offering and sacrifices for

God, and Aaron came with all the elders of Israel to eat a meal with Moses' father-in-law before God.

13 It came about the next day that Moses sat to judge the people, and the people stood about Moses from the morning until the evening.

14 Now when Moses' father-in-law saw all that he was doing for the people, he said, "What is this thing that you are doing for the people? Why do you alone sit *as judge* and all the people stand about you from morning until evening?"

15 Moses said to his father-in-law, "Because the people come to me to inquire of God.

16 "When they have a dispute, it comes to me, and I judge between a man and his neighbor and make known the statutes of God and His laws."

17 Moses' father-in-law said to him, "The thing that you are doing is not good.

18 "You will surely wear out, both yourself and these people who are with you, for the task is too heavy for you; you cannot do it alone.

19 "Now listen to me: I will give you counsel, and God be with you. You be the people's representative before God, and you bring the disputes to God,

20 then teach them the statutes and the laws, and make known to them the way in which they are to walk and the work they are to do.

21 "Furthermore, you shall select out of all the people able men who fear God, men of truth, those who hate dishonest gain; and you shall place *these* over them *as* leaders of thousands, of hundreds, of fifties and of tens.

22 "Let them judge the people at all times; and let it be that every major dispute they will bring to you, but every minor dispute they themselves will judge. So it will be easier for you, and they will bear *the burden* with you.

23 "If you do this thing and God *so* commands you, then you will be able to endure, and all these people also will go to their place in peace." ◄

24 So Moses listened to his father-in-law and did all that he had said.

25 Moses chose able men out of all Israel and made them heads over the people, leaders of thousands, of hundreds, of fifties and of tens.

26 They judged the people at all times;

LIFE LESSONS

➤ Exodus 18:23 — *"If you do this thing and God so commands you, then you will be able to endure."*

God often uses the advice of wise counselors to help us find His will for our lives. Of course, any helpful counsel has to line up with the Word of God and will be confirmed by the Holy Spirit. When we follow godly, Spirit-led counsel, it will lead us to peace.

the difficult dispute they would bring to Moses, but every minor dispute they themselves would judge.
27 Then Moses bade his father-in-law farewell, and he went his way into his own land.

Psalm 18:28–36

28 For You light my lamp;
The LORD my God illumines my darkness.
29 For by You I can run upon a troop;
And by my God I can leap over a wall.
30 As for God, His way is blameless;
The word of the LORD is tried;
He is a shield to all who take refuge in Him.
31 For who is God, but the LORD?
And who is a rock, except our God,
32 The God who girds me with strength
And makes my way blameless?
33 He makes my feet like hinds' *feet*,
And sets me upon my high places.
34 He trains my hands for battle,
So that my arms can bend a bow of bronze.
35 You have also given me the shield of Your salvation,
And Your right hand upholds me;
And Your gentleness makes me great.
36 You enlarge my steps under me,
And my feet have not slipped.

Proverbs 6:16–19

16 There are six things which the LORD hates,

Yes, seven which are an abomination to Him:
17 Haughty eyes, a lying tongue,
And hands that shed innocent blood,
18 A heart that devises wicked plans,
Feet that run rapidly to evil,
19 A false witness *who* utters lies,
And one who spreads strife among brothers.

Matthew 22:1–22

22 JESUS spoke to them again in parables, saying,
2 "The kingdom of heaven may be compared to a king who gave a wedding feast for his son.
3 "And he sent out his slaves to call those who had been invited to the wedding feast, and they were unwilling to come.
4 "Again he sent out other slaves saying, 'Tell those who have been invited, "Behold, I have prepared my dinner; my oxen and my fattened livestock are *all* butchered and everything is ready; come to the wedding feast."'
5 "But they paid no attention and went their way, one to his own farm, another to his business,
6 and the rest seized his slaves and mistreated them and killed them.
7 "But the king was enraged, and he sent his armies and destroyed those murderers and set their city on fire.
8 "Then he *said to his slaves, 'The wedding is ready, but those who were invited were not worthy.
9 'Go therefore to the main highways, and as many as you find *there,* invite to the wedding feast.'
10 "Those slaves went out into the streets and gathered together all they found, both evil and good; and the wedding hall was filled with dinner guests.
11 "But when the king came in to look over the dinner guests, he saw a man there who was not dressed in wedding clothes,
12 and he *said to him, 'Friend, how did you come in here without wedding clothes?' And the man was speechless.
13 "Then the king said to the servants, 'Bind him hand and foot, and throw him

into the outer darkness; in that place there will be weeping and gnashing of teeth.'

➤ 14 "For many are called, but few *are* chosen."

15 Then the Pharisees went and plotted together how they might trap Him in what He said.

16 And they *sent their disciples to

LIFE LESSONS

➤ **Matthew 22:14 — *"For many are called, but few are chosen."***

*G*od instructs us to share the gospel with anyone who will listen. Since we do not know who will respond and who will not (the most unlikely candidates often come to faith), we are to make our appeals to everyone we can.

Him, along with the Herodians, saying, "Teacher, we know that You are truthful and teach the way of God in truth, and defer to no one; for You are not partial to any.

17 "Tell us then, what do You think? Is it lawful to give a poll-tax to Caesar, or not?"

18 But Jesus perceived their malice, and said, "Why are you testing Me, you hypocrites?

19 "Show Me the coin *used* for the poll-tax." And they brought Him a denarius.

20 And He *said to them, "Whose likeness and inscription is this?"

21 They *said to Him, "Caesar's." Then He *said to them, "Then render to Caesar the things that are Caesar's; and to God the things that are God's."

22 And hearing *this*, they were amazed, and leaving Him, they went away.

✦ Exodus 19:1—20:26

19 IN the third month after the sons of Israel had gone out of the land of Egypt, on that very day they came into the wilderness of Sinai.

2 When they set out from Rephidim, they came to the wilderness of Sinai and camped in the wilderness; and there Israel camped in front of the mountain.

3 Moses went up to God, and the LORD called to him from the mountain, saying, "Thus you shall say to the house of Jacob and tell the sons of Israel:

4 'You yourselves have seen what I did to the Egyptians, and *how* I bore you on eagles' wings, and brought you to Myself.

5 'Now then, if you will indeed obey My voice and keep My covenant, then you shall be My own possession among all the peoples, for all the earth is Mine;

6 and you shall be to Me a kingdom of priests and a holy nation.' These are the words that you shall speak to the sons of Israel."

7 So Moses came and called the elders of the people, and set before them all these words which the LORD had commanded him.

8 All the people answered together and said, "All that the LORD has spoken we will do!" And Moses brought back the words of the people to the LORD.

9 The LORD said to Moses, "Behold, I will come to you in a thick cloud, so that the people may hear when I speak with you and may also believe in you forever." Then Moses told the words of the people to the LORD.

10 The LORD also said to Moses, "Go to the people and consecrate them today and tomorrow, and let them wash their garments;

11 and let them be ready for the third day, for on the third day the LORD will come down on Mount Sinai in the sight of all the people.

12 "You shall set bounds for the people all around, saying, 'Beware that you do not go up on the mountain or touch the border of it; whoever touches the mountain shall surely be put to death.

13 'No hand shall touch him, but he shall surely be stoned or shot through; whether beast or man, he shall not live.' When the ram's horn sounds a long blast, they shall come up to the mountain."

14 So Moses went down from the mountain to the people and consecrated

LIFE PRINCIPLE 2

OBEY GOD AND LEAVE ALL THE CONSE-
QUENCES TO HIM.

EXODUS 19:5

*O*bedience can be a challenge, especially
when we feel tempted to believe that
we stand to lose more through our obedience
than we might gain. However, obeying God
is essential to pleasing Him—not just in times
of temptation, but at all times.

When God commands us to obey Him, He
is giving us a principle by which to live. He is
also setting a framework around our lives that
forms a hedge of protection from evil.

Can you remember the last time you felt
tempted to do the opposite of what you knew
God desired you to do? Most likely, a struggle
erupted within your heart. The question arose:
*Will obeying God cost me more than disobeying
Him? Can I experience greater happiness by committing this sin than I would by obeying God?*

When we choose to obey God, we take the
way of wisdom. His promises of blessing for
obedience far outweigh any possible consequences. He asks us to submit ourselves to Him
and leave whatever happens to His loving care.

As we grow in our walks with the Lord,
obedience becomes the avenue by which we
know Him better. When we obey Him, He
pulls us closer to Himself and teaches us more
about His precepts and His love.

Disobedience sends a message to the Lord,
declaring that we know better than He does
when it comes to our lives and the circumstances surrounding them.

God loves us and is committed to us. He
commands our obedience, not because He is
a strict taskmaster, but because He knows the
devastating effect disobedience and sin will
have on our lives.

Satan, however, has another goal in mind.
He seeks to tempt believers to disobey God,
usually by telling them the Lord's promises
cannot be trusted and we can enjoy life more if
we ignore His commands.

Remember, disobedience always has fierce
repercussions—feelings of guilt, shame, and
worthlessness, broken lives, destroyed marriages, and bitter disputes, among them. While
sin can never change God's eternal love for
His children, it certainly disrupts our fellowship with the Savior and alienates us from His
blessings. In times of disobedience, we become
spiritually weak and unable to discern right

from wrong. We sink deeper into sin's grasp
and find it impossible to reverse our sinfulness
on our own.

As we apply the following principles to our
lives, we will begin to obey God with confidence and joy, knowing He can be fully trusted
to keep all His promises:

• *Trust God with your life and all that concerns you.*

There is no way to go wrong if you
place your hope and trust in God. He
created you and He loves you with an
eternal love. Therefore, He will always
lead you in the best way possible.

• *Wait on the Lord for an answer to your
problem or situation.*

When in doubt, refuse to move ahead
unless you know God is leading you.

• *Meditate on God's Word.*

When you saturate your mind with the
Word of God, you gain His viewpoint.
When a temptation comes, you will know
right from wrong and can act accordingly.

• *Listen to the Holy Spirit.*

God continues to speak to His people
today. He speaks to us through His Word,
the Holy Spirit, and through the words
of a pastor or trusted Christian friend. We
become sensitive to the Spirit of God by
spending time with Him—praying and
studying the principles in Scripture.

• *Be willing to wait or walk away when the
way before you is unclear.*

If you desire to please God above all
others, obedience to Him will require you
to remain firm. If you do not sense clear
guidance in your situation, ask God to
confirm His will to you in His Word. He
will never contradict Scripture. His will
for your life always lines up perfectly with
what the Bible says.

• *Be willing to endure conflict.*

When the nation of Israel entered the
Promised Land at God's direction, she
had to face strong enemy opposition. God
rarely empties our lives of trouble and
conflict. If He did, we would have no reason to depend on Him. He allows enough
difficulty to keep us turned toward Him.

• *Leave the consequences to God.*

Obedience may not be easy—you may
receive criticism from others or face fierce
obstacles and opposition—but it will
always put you in a favorable position
before God. He will take care of all that
concerns you. Stay on the path of obedience, and leave the rest to Him. ◈

the people, and they washed their garments.

15 He said to the people, "Be ready for the third day; do not go near a woman."

➤ 16 So it came about on the third day, when it was morning, that there were thunder and lightning flashes and a thick cloud upon the mountain and a very loud trumpet sound, so that all the people who *were* in the camp trembled.

17 And Moses brought the people out of the camp to meet God, and they stood at the foot of the mountain.

18 Now Mount Sinai *was* all in smoke because the LORD descended upon it in fire; and its smoke ascended like the smoke of a furnace, and the whole mountain quaked violently.

19 When the sound of the trumpet grew louder and louder, Moses spoke and God answered him with thunder.

20 The LORD came down on Mount Sinai, to the top of the mountain; and the LORD called Moses to the top of the mountain, and Moses went up.

21 Then the LORD spoke to Moses, "Go down, warn the people, so that they do not break through to the LORD to gaze, and many of them perish.

22 "Also let the priests who come near to the LORD consecrate themselves, or else the LORD will break out against them."

23 Moses said to the LORD, "The people cannot come up to Mount Sinai, for You warned us, saying, 'Set bounds about the mountain and consecrate it.'"

24 Then the LORD said to him, "Go down and come up *again,* you and Aaron with you; but do not let the priests and the people break through to come up to the LORD, or He will break forth upon them."

25 So Moses went down to the people and told them.

20 THEN God spoke all these words, saying,

2 "I am the LORD your God, who brought you out of the land of Egypt, out of the house of slavery.

➤ 3 "You shall have no other gods before Me.

4 "You shall not make for yourself an idol, or any likeness of what is in heaven above or on the earth beneath or in the water under the earth.

5 "You shall not worship them or serve them; for I, the LORD your God, am a jeal-

ous God, visiting the iniquity of the fathers on the children, on the third and the fourth generations of those who hate Me,

6 but showing lovingkindness to thousands, to those who love Me and keep My commandments.

7 "You shall not take the name of the LORD your God in vain, for the LORD will not leave him unpunished who takes His name in vain.

8 "Remember the sabbath day, to keep it holy.

9 "Six days you shall labor and do all your work,

10 but the seventh day is a sabbath of the LORD your God; *in it* you shall not do any work, you or your son or your daughter, your male or your female servant or your cattle or your sojourner who stays with you.

11 "For in six days the LORD made the heavens and the earth, the sea and all that is in them, and rested on the seventh day; therefore the LORD blessed the sabbath day and made it holy.

12 "Honor your father and your mother, ◄ that your days may be prolonged in the land which the LORD your God gives you.

13 "You shall not murder.

14 "You shall not commit adultery.

15 "You shall not steal.

16 "You shall not bear false witness against your neighbor.

17 "You shall not covet your neighbor's house; you shall not covet your neighbor's wife or his male servant or his

---

LIFE LESSONS

➤ **Exodus 19:16 —** *There were thunder and lightning flashes and a thick cloud upon the mountain . . . all the people who were in the camp trembled.*

The people trembled at the manifested presence of God on Mount Sinai—and for good reason. The Bible reminds us we must serve God "with reverence and awe" since "our God is a consuming fire" (Heb. 12:28, 29).

➤ **Exodus 20:3 —** *"You shall have no other gods before Me."*

The first commandment is first for a reason. God must be first in everything we do, for intimacy with God is His highest priority for our lives.

LIFE LESSONS

➤ **Exodus 20:12** — *"Honor your father and your mother, that your days may be prolonged in the land which the LORD your God gives you."*

*W*ith every divine commandment comes not merely a curse for disobedience, but a blessing for obedience. God does not give us commandments because He wants to control us; His commandments prepare us for His blessings.

female servant or his ox or his donkey or anything that belongs to your neighbor."
18 All the people perceived the thunder and the lightning flashes and the sound of the trumpet and the mountain smoking; and when the people saw *it,* they trembled and stood at a distance.
19 Then they said to Moses, "Speak to us yourself and we will listen; but let not God speak to us, or we will die."
20 Moses said to the people, "Do not be afraid; for God has come in order to test you, and in order that the fear of Him may remain with you, so that you may not sin."
21 So the people stood at a distance, while Moses approached the thick cloud where God *was.*
22 Then the LORD said to Moses, "Thus you shall say to the sons of Israel, 'You yourselves have seen that I have spoken to you from heaven.
23 'You shall not make *other gods* besides Me; gods of silver or gods of gold, you shall not make for yourselves.
24 'You shall make an altar of earth for Me, and you shall sacrifice on it your burnt offerings and your peace offerings, your sheep and your oxen; in every place where I cause My name to be remembered, I will come to you and bless you.
25 'If you make an altar of stone for Me, you shall not build it of cut stones, for if you wield your tool on it, you will profane it.
26 'And you shall not go up by steps to My altar, so that your nakedness will not be exposed on it.'

Psalm 18:37–45

37 I pursued my enemies and overtook them,

And I did not turn back until they were consumed.
38 I shattered them, so that they were not able to rise;
They fell under my feet.
39 For You have girded me with strength for battle;
You have subdued under me those who rose up against me.
40 You have also made my enemies turn their backs to me,
And I destroyed those who hated me.
41 They cried for help, but there was none to save,
Even to the LORD, but He did not answer them.
42 Then I beat them fine as the dust before the wind;
I emptied them out as the mire of the streets.
43 You have delivered me from the contentions of the people;
You have placed me as head of the nations;
A people whom I have not known serve me.
44 As soon as they hear, they obey me;
Foreigners submit to me.
45 Foreigners fade away,
And come trembling out of their fortresses.

Proverbs 6:20–25

20 My son, observe the commandment of your father
And do not forsake the teaching of your mother;
21 Bind them continually on your heart;
Tie them around your neck.
22 When you walk about, they will guide you;
When you sleep, they will watch over you;
And when you awake, they will talk to you.
23 For the commandment is a lamp and the teaching is light;
And reproofs for discipline are the way of life
24 To keep you from the evil woman,

From the smooth tongue of the
adulteress.
25 Do not desire her beauty in your
heart,
Nor let her capture you with her
eyelids.

Matthew 22:23–46

23 On that day *some* Sadducees (who say there is no resurrection) came to Jesus and questioned Him,
24 asking, "Teacher, Moses said, 'IF A MAN DIES HAVING NO CHILDREN, HIS BROTHER AS NEXT OF KIN SHALL MARRY HIS WIFE, AND RAISE UP CHILDREN FOR HIS BROTHER.'
25 "Now there were seven brothers with us; and the first married and died, and having no children left his wife to his brother;
26 so also the second, and the third, down to the seventh.
27 "Last of all, the woman died.
28 "In the resurrection, therefore, whose wife of the seven will she be? For they all had *married* her."
➤ **29** But Jesus answered and said to them, "You are mistaken, not understanding the Scriptures nor the power of God.
30 "For in the resurrection they neither marry nor are given in marriage, but are like angels in heaven.

31 "But regarding the resurrection of the dead, have you not read what was spoken to you by God:
32 'I AM THE GOD OF ABRAHAM, AND THE GOD OF ISAAC, AND THE GOD OF JACOB'? He is not the God of the dead but of the living."
33 When the crowds heard *this*, they were astonished at His teaching.
34 But when the Pharisees heard that Jesus had silenced the Sadducees, they gathered themselves together.
35 One of them, a lawyer, asked Him *a question*, testing Him,
36 "Teacher, which is the great commandment in the Law?"
37 And He said to him, "'YOU SHALL LOVE THE LORD YOUR GOD WITH ALL YOUR HEART, AND WITH ALL YOUR SOUL, AND WITH ALL YOUR MIND.'
38 "This is the great and foremost commandment.
39 "The second is like it, 'YOU SHALL LOVE YOUR NEIGHBOR AS YOURSELF.'
40 "On these two commandments depend the whole Law and the Prophets."
41 Now while the Pharisees were gathered together, Jesus asked them a question:
42 "What do you think about the Christ, whose son is He?" They *said to Him, "The son of David."
43 He *said to them, "Then how does David in the Spirit call Him 'Lord,' saying,
44 'THE LORD SAID TO MY LORD,
"SIT AT MY RIGHT HAND,
UNTIL I PUT YOUR ENEMIES BENEATH YOUR FEET"'?
45 "If David then calls Him 'Lord,' how is He his son?"
46 No one was able to answer Him a word, nor did anyone dare from that day on to ask Him another question.

21 "NOW these are the ordinances which you are to set before them:
2 "If you buy a Hebrew slave, he shall serve for six years; but on the seventh he shall go out as a free man without payment.
3 "If he comes alone, he shall go out alone; if he is the husband of a wife, then his wife shall go out with him.
4 "If his master gives him a wife, and she bears him sons or daughters, the wife and her children shall belong to her master, and he shall go out alone.
5 "But if the slave plainly says, 'I love my master, my wife and my children; I will not go out as a free man,'
6 then his master shall bring him to God, then he shall bring him to the door or the doorpost. And his master shall pierce his ear with an awl; and he shall serve him permanently.
7 "If a man sells his daughter as a female slave, she is not to go free as the male slaves do.
8 "If she is displeasing in the eyes of her master who designated her for himself, then he shall let her be redeemed. He does not have authority to sell her to a foreign people because of his unfairness to her.
9 "If he designates her for his son, he shall deal with her according to the custom of daughters.
10 "If he takes to himself another woman, he may not reduce her food, her clothing, or her conjugal rights.
11 "If he will not do these three things for her, then she shall go out for nothing, without payment of money.
12 "He who strikes a man so that he dies shall surely be put to death.
13 "But if he did not lie in wait for him, but God let him fall into his hand, then I will appoint you a place to which he may flee.
14 "If, however, a man acts presumptuously toward his neighbor, so as to kill him craftily, you are to take him even from My altar, that he may die.
15 "He who strikes his father or his mother shall surely be put to death.
16 "He who kidnaps a man, whether he sells him or he is found in his possession, shall surely be put to death.

17 "He who curses his father or his mother shall surely be put to death.
18 "If men have a quarrel and one strikes the other with a stone or with his fist, and he does not die but remains in bed,
19 if he gets up and walks around outside on his staff, then he who struck him shall go unpunished; he shall only pay for his loss of time, and shall take care of him until he is completely healed.
20 "If a man strikes his male or female slave with a rod and he dies at his hand, he shall be punished.
21 "If, however, he survives a day or two, no vengeance shall be taken; for he is his property.
22 "If men struggle with each other and strike a woman with child so that she gives birth prematurely, yet there is no injury, he shall surely be fined as the woman's husband may demand of him, and he shall pay as the judges decide.
23 "But if there is any further injury, then you shall appoint as a penalty life for life,
24 eye for eye, tooth for tooth, hand for hand, foot for foot,
25 burn for burn, wound for wound, bruise for bruise.
26 "If a man strikes the eye of his male or female slave, and destroys it, he shall let him go free on account of his eye.
27 "And if he knocks out a tooth of his male or female slave, he shall let him go free on account of his tooth.
28 "If an ox gores a man or a woman to death, the ox shall surely be stoned and its flesh shall not be eaten; but the owner of the ox shall go unpunished.
29 "If, however, an ox was previously in the habit of goring and its owner has been warned, yet he does not confine it and it kills a man or a woman, the ox shall be stoned and its owner also shall be put to death.
30 "If a ransom is demanded of him, then he shall give for the redemption of his life whatever is demanded of him.
31 "Whether it gores a son or a daughter, it shall be done to him according to the same rule.
32 "If the ox gores a male or female slave, the owner shall give his or her master thirty shekels of silver, and the ox shall be stoned.

➤ **33** "If a man opens a pit, or digs a pit and does not cover it over, and an ox or a donkey falls into it,

34 the owner of the pit shall make restitution; he shall give money to its owner, and the dead *animal* shall become his.

35 "If one man's ox hurts another's so that it dies, then they shall sell the live ox and divide its price equally; and also they shall divide the dead ox.

➤ **36** "Or *if* it is known that the ox was previously in the habit of goring, yet its owner has not confined it, he shall surely pay ox for ox, and the dead *animal* shall become his.

22 "IF a man steals an ox or a sheep and slaughters it or sells it, he shall pay five oxen for the ox and four sheep for the sheep.

2 "If the thief is caught while breaking in and is struck so that he dies, there will be no bloodguiltiness on his account.

3 "*But* if the sun has risen on him, there will be bloodguiltiness on his account. He shall surely make restitution; if he owns nothing, then he shall be sold for his theft.

4 "If what he stole is actually found alive in his possession, whether an ox or a donkey or a sheep, he shall pay double.

5 "If a man lets a field or vineyard be grazed *bare* and lets his animal loose so that it grazes in another man's field, he shall make restitution from the best of his own field and the best of his own vineyard.

6 "If a fire breaks out and spreads to thorn bushes, so that stacked grain or the standing grain or the field *itself* is consumed, he who started the fire shall surely make restitution.

7 "If a man gives his neighbor money or goods to keep *for him* and it is stolen from the man's house, if the thief is caught, he shall pay double.

8 "If the thief is not caught, then the owner of the house shall appear before the judges, *to* determine whether he laid his hands on his neighbor's property.

9 "For every breach of trust, *whether it is* for ox, for donkey, for sheep, for clothing, *or* for any lost thing about which one says, 'This is it,' the case of both parties shall come before the judges; he whom the judges condemn shall pay double to his neighbor.

10 "If a man gives his neighbor a donkey, an ox, a sheep, or any animal to keep *for him*, and it dies or is hurt or is driven away while no one is looking,

11 an oath before the LORD shall be made by the two of them that he has not laid hands on his neighbor's property; and its owner shall accept *it*, and he shall not make restitution.

12 "But if it is actually stolen from him, he shall make restitution to its owner.

13 "If it is all torn to pieces, let him bring it as evidence; he shall not make restitution for what has been torn to pieces.

14 "If a man borrows *anything* from his neighbor, and it is injured or dies while its owner is not with it, he shall make full restitution.

15 "If its owner is with it, he shall not make restitution; if it is hired, it came for its hire.

16 "If a man seduces a virgin who is not engaged, and lies with her, he must pay a dowry for her *to be* his wife.

17 "If her father absolutely refuses to give her to him, he shall pay money equal to the dowry for virgins.

18 "You shall not allow a sorceress to live.

19 "Whoever lies with an animal shall surely be put to death.

20 "He who sacrifices to any god, other than to the LORD alone, shall be utterly destroyed.

21 "You shall not wrong a stranger or

LIFE LESSONS

➤ **Exodus 21:33** — *"If a man opens a pit, or digs a pit and does not cover it over, and an ox or a donkey falls into it."*

*W*e live in a fallen world, and although God has the power to prevent every accident, He does not. Instead, He asks us to trust Him—no matter what happens.

➤ **Exodus 21:36** — *"If it is known that the ox was previously in the habit of goring, yet its owner has not confined it, he shall surely pay ox for ox."*

*G*od expects His people to act in a responsible manner and to use sound judgment in the way they conduct their affairs. He holds us accountable for our inaction as well as for our actions.

oppress him, for you were strangers in the land of Egypt.

22 "You shall not afflict any widow or orphan.

23 "If you afflict him at all, *and* if he does cry out to Me, I will surely hear his cry;

24 and My anger will be kindled, and I will kill you with the sword, and your wives shall become widows and your children fatherless.

25 "If you lend money to My people, to the poor among you, you are not to act as a creditor to him; you shall not charge him interest.

26 "If you ever take your neighbor's cloak as a pledge, you are to return it to him before the sun sets,

27 for that is his only covering; it is his cloak for his body. What else shall he sleep in? And it shall come about that when he cries out to Me, I will hear *him*, for I am gracious.

➤ 28 "You shall not curse God, nor curse a ruler of your people.

29 "You shall not delay *the offering from* your harvest and your vintage. The firstborn of your sons you shall give to Me.

30 "You shall do the same with your oxen *and* with your sheep. It shall be with its mother seven days; on the eighth day you shall give it to Me.

31 "You shall be holy men to Me, therefore you shall not eat *any* flesh torn to pieces in the field; you shall throw it to the dogs.

Psalm 18:46–50

✳ 46 The LORD lives, and blessed be my rock;
    And exalted be the God of my salvation,

---

47 The God who executes vengeance for me,
    And subdues peoples under me.

48 He delivers me from my enemies;
    Surely You lift me above those who rise up against me;
    You rescue me from the violent man.

49 Therefore I will give thanks to You among the nations, O LORD,
    And I will sing praises to Your name.

50 He gives great deliverance to His king,
    And shows lovingkindness to His anointed,
    To David and his descendants forever.

Proverbs 6:26–29

26 For on account of a harlot *one is reduced* to a loaf of bread,
    And an adulteress hunts for the precious life.

27 Can a man take fire in his bosom
    And his clothes not be burned?

28 Or can a man walk on hot coals
    And his feet not be scorched?

29 So is the one who goes in to his neighbor's wife;
    Whoever touches her will not go unpunished.

Matthew 23:1–22

23 THEN Jesus spoke to the crowds and to His disciples,

2 saying: "The scribes and the Pharisees have seated themselves in the chair of Moses;

3 therefore all that they tell you, do and observe, but do not do according to their deeds; for they say *things* and do not do *them*.

4 "They tie up heavy burdens and lay them on men's shoulders, but they themselves are unwilling to move them with *so much as* a finger.

5 "But they do all their deeds to be noticed by men; for they broaden their phylacteries and lengthen the tassels *of their garments*.

LIFE LESSONS

➤ **Exodus 22:28 — *"You shall not curse God, nor curse a ruler of your people."***

Followers of Christ are to honor their leaders, regardless of whether or not they agree with their politics. God places leaders in their roles (Dan. 4:17) and calls us to pray for them, not revile them (1 Tim. 2:1, 2).

WHAT THE BIBLE SAYS ABOUT ◉

God, Our Father

Matthew 23:9

*W*hat do you think of when you hear the word "father"? Do you recall a man who gave you love, wisdom, and support? Or does the word stir negative memories of a man who treated you badly? It's unfortunate that so many people are disappointed when they think about their fathers.

However, God wants to show you what a godly father should be. That's why He tells us to address Him as our Father. He desires to have a close, personal relationship with us. Jesus says in Matthew 23:9, "One is your Father, He who is in heaven."

The freedom of calling God, "my Father," is an awesome privilege. What is God like as a father?

1. *God desires to have a close, personal relationship with you* (Is. 49:15, 16).

God isn't a distant father. Rather, He wants to reveal His presence to you. He wants to be close to you. God loves you enough to meet with you whenever you call upon Him. Whether you want companionship, need some wisdom, yearn for a sense of belonging, or just want someone to talk to, God is always available to you.

2. *God desires to communicate with you* (Jer. 33:3; Matt. 6:6).

The only way you are truly going to embrace God as your Father is if you are open and honest with Him. You must open your heart to Him and invite Him into your situation. He wants to communicate with you and lead you in the way you should go. He wants to reveal Himself to you and share His wisdom with you.

3. *God loves you unconditionally* (Rom. 5:8; 1 John 3:1).

God is wise and knows everything about you. There is nothing you have to do to earn His love—and nothing you can do that will ever lose it. God loves you. Period.

4. *God already knows all of your needs before you ask Him* (Matt 6:8; Phil. 4:19).

As your Provider, God always gives to you perfectly. He knows your needs, even before you do. Whereas earthly fathers often

fail to provide for their children—whether because of their characters or unavoidable circumstances—your heavenly Father will always grant whatever you need without fail.

5. *God will always be with you* (Deut. 31:6, 8).

Unlike earthly fathers, God will never leave you. He will always be with you—not only preparing you for eternity, but also leading you into it.

6. *God is a Father who disciplines* (Heb. 12:5–10).

Sometimes His discipline will hurt and you won't like it. However, the fact that God disciplines you is evidence you are His child. He corrects you in order to protect you from evil and so you will be conformed into the likeness of Christ. He disciplines you so you will learn to be obedient, becoming everything He created you to be.

7. *God holds you accountable for your life* (Gal 6:7, 8).

You are accountable to God for your life, behavior, attitude, and actions. However, God helps you stay obedient to Him by giving you His Holy Spirit. This accountability protects you from many dangerous, destructive things.

8. *God will always help you do the right thing* (Prov. 3:5, 6).

God is the best example you can have, and He will always give you the best counsel. Because of His omnipotence, omniscience, and perfect love for you, he will not only lead you to do the right thing, but He will also show you the best way to do it and will empower you to accomplish it.

You have a wonderful, loving Father who wants you to know Him. No matter how your earthly father succeeded in raising you or utterly failed you, God is the Father who will never let you down. He understands your weaknesses, forgives the things you've done wrong, calms your fears, and helps you become all you were created to be.

Friend, you can have an intimate relationship with God—communicating with Him, experiencing His unconditional love, and enjoying His extraordinary presence. Won't you give Him a chance? ◉

6 "They love the place of honor at banquets and the chief seats in the synagogues,

7 and respectful greetings in the market places, and being called Rabbi by men.

8 "But do not be called Rabbi; for One is your Teacher, and you are all brothers.

9 "Do not call *anyone* on earth your father; for One is your Father, He who is in heaven.

10 "Do not be called leaders; for One is your Leader, *that is*, Christ.

11 "But the greatest among you shall be your servant.

12 "Whoever exalts himself shall be humbled; and whoever humbles himself shall be exalted.

➤ 13 "But woe to you, scribes and Pharisees, hypocrites, because you shut off the kingdom of heaven from people; for you do not enter in yourselves, nor do you allow those who are entering to go in.

14 ["Woe to you, scribes and Pharisees, hypocrites, because you devour widows' houses, and for a pretense you make long prayers; therefore you will receive greater condemnation.]

15 "Woe to you, scribes and Pharisees, hypocrites, because you travel around on sea and land to make one proselyte; and when he becomes one, you make him twice as much a son of hell as yourselves.

16 "Woe to you, blind guides, who say, 'Whoever swears by the temple, *that* is nothing; but whoever swears by the gold of the temple is obligated.'

17 "You fools and blind men! Which is more important, the gold or the temple that sanctified the gold?

18 "And, 'Whoever swears by the altar, *that* is nothing, but whoever swears by the offering on it, he is obligated.'

19 "You blind men, which is more important, the offering, or the altar that sanctifies the offering?

20 "Therefore, whoever swears by the altar, swears *both* by the altar and by everything on it.

21 "And whoever swears by the temple, swears *both* by the temple and by Him who dwells within it.

22 "And whoever swears by heaven, swears *both* by the throne of God and by Him who sits upon it.

LIFE LESSONS

➤ **Matthew 23:13 — *"Woe to you, scribes and Pharisees, hypocrites."***

*E*ight times in Matthew 23, Jesus pronounces "woes" upon those He calls "hypocrites", "fools", "blind", and "serpents." When love speaks harshly, it does so because no other language has a chance of breaking through.

FEBRUARY 6

Exodus 23:1—24:18

23 "YOU shall not bear a false report; do not join your hand with a wicked man to be a malicious witness.

2 "You shall not follow the masses in doing evil, nor shall you testify in a dispute so as to turn aside after a multitude in order to pervert *justice;*

3 nor shall you be partial to a poor man in his dispute.

4 "If you meet your enemy's ox or his donkey wandering away, you shall surely return it to him.

5 "If you see the donkey of one who hates you lying *helpless* under its load, you shall refrain from leaving it to him, you shall surely release *it* with him.

6 "You shall not pervert the justice *due* to your needy *brother* in his dispute.

7 "Keep far from a false charge, and do not kill the innocent or the righteous, for I will not acquit the guilty.

8 "You shall not take a bribe, for a bribe blinds the clear-sighted and subverts the cause of the just.

9 "You shall not oppress a stranger, since you yourselves know the feelings of a stranger, for you *also* were strangers in the land of Egypt.

10 "You shall sow your land for six years and gather in its yield,

11 but *on* the seventh year you shall let it rest and lie fallow, so that the needy of your people may eat; and whatever they leave the beast of the field may eat. You are to do the same with your vineyard *and* your olive grove.

12 "Six days you are to do your work, but on the seventh day you shall cease *from labor* so that your ox and your donkey may rest, and the son of your female slave, as well as your stranger, may refresh themselves.

13 "Now concerning everything which I have said to you, be on your guard; and do not mention the name of other gods, nor let *them* be heard from your mouth.

14 "Three times a year you shall celebrate a feast to Me.

15 "You shall observe the Feast of Unleavened Bread; for seven days you are to eat unleavened bread, as I commanded you, at the appointed time in the month Abib, for in it you came out of Egypt. And none shall appear before Me empty-handed.

16 "Also *you shall observe* the Feast of the Harvest *of* the first fruits of your labors *from* what you sow in the field; also the Feast of the Ingathering at the end of the year when you gather in *the fruit of* your labors from the field.

17 "Three times a year all your males shall appear before the Lord GOD.

18 "You shall not offer the blood of My sacrifice with leavened bread; nor is the fat of My feast to remain overnight until morning.

19 "You shall bring the choice first fruits of your soil into the house of the LORD your God.

"You are not to boil a young goat in the milk of its mother.

20 "Behold, I am going to send an angel before you to guard you along the way and to bring you into the place which I have prepared.

21 "Be on your guard before him and obey his voice; do not be rebellious toward him, for he will not pardon your transgression, since My name is in him.

22 "But if you truly obey his voice and do all that I say, then I will be an enemy to your enemies and an adversary to your adversaries.

---

23 "For My angel will go before you and bring you in to *the land of* the Amorites, the Hittites, the Perizzites, the Canaanites, the Hivites and the Jebusites; and I will completely destroy them.

24 "You shall not worship their gods, nor serve them, nor do according to their deeds; but you shall utterly overthrow them and break their *sacred* pillars in pieces.

25 "But you shall serve the LORD your God, and He will bless your bread and your water; and I will remove sickness from your midst.

26 "There shall be no one miscarrying or barren in your land; I will fulfill the number of your days.

27 "I will send My terror ahead of you, and throw into confusion all the people among whom you come, and I will make all your enemies turn *their* backs to you.

28 "I will send hornets ahead of you so that they will drive out the Hivites, the Canaanites, and the Hittites before you.

29 "I will not drive them out before you in a single year, that the land may not become desolate and the beasts of the field become too numerous for you.

30 "I will drive them out before you little by little, until you become fruitful and take possession of the land.

31 "I will fix your boundary from the Red Sea to the sea of the Philistines, and from the wilderness to the River *Euphrates;* for I will deliver the inhabitants of the land into your hand, and you will drive them out before you.

32 "You shall make no covenant with them or with their gods.

33 "They shall not live in your land, because they will make you sin against Me; for *if* you serve their gods, it will surely be a snare to you."

24 THEN He said to Moses, "Come up to the LORD, you and Aaron, Nadab and Abihu and seventy of the elders of Israel, and you shall worship at a distance.

2 "Moses alone, however, shall come near to the LORD, but they shall not come near, nor shall the people come up with him."

3 Then Moses came and recounted to the people all the words of the LORD and all the ordinances; and all the people answered with one voice and said, "All the words which the LORD has spoken we will do!"

4 Moses wrote down all the words of the LORD. Then he arose early in the morning, and built an altar at the foot of the mountain with twelve pillars for the twelve tribes of Israel.

5 He sent young men of the sons of Israel, and they offered burnt offerings and sacrificed young bulls as peace offerings to the LORD.

6 Moses took half of the blood and put *it* in basins, and the *other* half of the blood he sprinkled on the altar.

7 Then he took the book of the covenant and read *it* in the hearing of the people; and they said, "All that the LORD has spoken we will do, and we will be obedient!"

8 So Moses took the blood and sprinkled *it* on the people, and said, "Behold the blood of the covenant, which the LORD has made with you in accordance with all these words."

9 Then Moses went up with Aaron, Nadab and Abihu, and seventy of the elders of Israel,

10 and they saw the God of Israel; and under His feet there appeared to be a pavement of sapphire, as clear as the sky itself.

11 Yet He did not stretch out His hand against the nobles of the sons of Israel; and they saw God, and they ate and drank.

12 Now the LORD said to Moses, "Come up to Me on the mountain and remain there, and I will give you the stone tablets with the law and the commandment which I have written for their instruction."

13 So Moses arose with Joshua his servant, and Moses went up to the mountain of God.

14 But to the elders he said, "Wait here for us until we return to you. And behold, Aaron and Hur are with you; whoever has a legal matter, let him approach them."

15 Then Moses went up to the mountain, and the cloud covered the mountain.

16 The glory of the LORD rested on Mount Sinai, and the cloud covered it for six days; and on the seventh day He called to Moses from the midst of the cloud.

17 And to the eyes of the sons of Israel the appearance of the glory of the LORD was like a consuming fire on the mountain top.

18 Moses entered the midst of the cloud as he went up to the mountain; and Moses was on the mountain forty days and forty nights.

Psalm 19:1–6

For the choir director. A Psalm of David.

19 THE heavens are telling of the glory of God;
And their expanse is declaring the work of His hands.

2 Day to day pours forth speech,
And night to night reveals knowledge.

LIFE LESSONS

➤ **Exodus 24:10** — *They saw the God of Israel; and under His feet there appeared to be a pavement of sapphire, as clear as the sky itself.*

*B*iblical descriptions of God tend to focus more on the surroundings of God than on the Lord Himself, primarily because He is beyond description. What a wonder this majestic God calls us His own!

➤ **Psalm 19:1** — *The heavens are telling of the glory of God; and their expanse is declaring the work of His hands.*

*G*o outside on a clear night and look into the sky for several minutes. Soak in the grandeur, majesty, and vastness of the starry host—and then reflect: *My God made all this.*

WHAT THE BIBLE SAYS ABOUT ◈

The Praise of the Heavens

Psalm 19:1

How do the heavens declare God's glory? Can they sing? Do the stars and planets tell tales of God's splendor? You shouldn't be surprised the answer is yes. The heavens reflect the brilliance of almighty God. And though the trillions of stars in the universe together are dim in comparison to the magnificence of God, through them we begin to understand His glory (Rom. 1:20).

Look at what else displays the handiwork and praise of God: Ephesians 2:10 tells us, "We are His workmanship, created in Christ Jesus for good works, which God prepared beforehand so that we would walk in them."

We show the world God's glory when we obey Him—when we do what He has planned for us.

However, what we must always remember as we serve Him is that we reflect *His* glory. Just as a sculpture exhibits the ability of the artist or a poem reveals the skill of a writer, we are merely the vessels through which His splendor shines (2 Cor. 4:7). We praise Him best when we are simply doing as He says—and when we are not trying to steal the credit for ourselves.

That is why it is so important for us to heed Jesus' instruction in Matthew 5:16, "Let your light shine before men in such a way that they may see your good works, and glorify your Father who is in heaven." That means the next time God does wonderful things through us, we should direct all the glory, honor, and praise to Him. He alone deserves it. ◈

3 There is no speech, nor are there words;
Their voice is not heard.
4 Their line has gone out through all the earth,
And their utterances to the end of the world.
In them He has placed a tent for the sun,
5 Which is as a bridegroom coming out of his chamber;
It rejoices as a strong man to run his course.
6 Its rising is from one end of the heavens,
And its circuit to the other end of them;
And there is nothing hidden from its heat.

◈ Proverbs 6:30, 31

30 Men do not despise a thief if he steals
To satisfy himself when he is hungry;
31 But when he is found, he must repay sevenfold;
He must give all the substance of his house.

◈ Matthew 23:23–39

23 "Woe to you, scribes and Pharisees, hypocrites! For you tithe mint and dill and cummin, and have neglected the weightier provisions of the law: justice and mercy and faithfulness; but these are the things you should have done without neglecting the others.
24 "You blind guides, who strain out a gnat and swallow a camel!
25 "Woe to you, scribes and Pharisees, hypocrites! For you clean the outside of the cup and of the dish, but inside they are full of robbery and self-indulgence.
26 "You blind Pharisee, first clean the inside of the cup and of the dish, so that the outside of it may become clean also.

LIFE LESSONS

➤ **Matthew 23:28 — *"So you, too, outwardly appear righteous to men, but inwardly you are full of hypocrisy and lawlessness."***

God despises disobedience of any kind, but He seems to have a special hatred for religious pretense. Why? Perhaps because those who only pretend to love God do a great job of keeping others away from God.

27 "Woe to you, scribes and Pharisees, hypocrites! For you are like whitewashed tombs which on the outside appear beautiful, but inside they are full of dead men's bones and all uncleanness.

➤ **28** "So you, too, outwardly appear righteous to men, but inwardly you are full of hypocrisy and lawlessness.

29 "Woe to you, scribes and Pharisees, hypocrites! For you build the tombs of the prophets and adorn the monuments of the righteous,

30 and say, 'If we had been *living* in the days of our fathers, we would not have been partners with them in *shedding* the blood of the prophets.'

31 "So you testify against yourselves, that you are sons of those who murdered the prophets.

32 "Fill up, then, the measure *of the guilt* of your fathers.

33 "You serpents, you brood of vipers, how will you escape the sentence of hell?

34 "Therefore, behold, I am sending you prophets and wise men and scribes; some of them you will kill and crucify, and some of them you will scourge in your synagogues, and persecute from city to city,

35 so that upon you may fall *the guilt of* all the righteous blood shed on earth, from the blood of righteous Abel to the blood of Zechariah, the son of Berechiah, whom you murdered between the temple and the altar.

36 "Truly I say to you, all these things will come upon this generation.

37 "Jerusalem, Jerusalem, who kills the ⊲ prophets and stones those who are sent to her! How often I wanted to gather your children together, the way a hen gathers her chicks under her wings, and you were unwilling.

38 "Behold, your house is being left to you desolate!

39 "For I say to you, from now on you will not see Me until you say, 'BLESSED IS HE WHO COMES IN THE NAME OF THE LORD!'"

LIFE LESSONS

➤ **Matthew 23:37 — *"How often I wanted to gather your children together, the way a hen gathers her chicks under her wings."***

God's greatest desire for us is always to develop and nurture a growing, satisfying relationship with Him. He created us for deep fellowship with Himself, but we make the choice whether we will fulfill our purpose and love Him in return.

⊛ Exodus 25:1—26:37

25 THEN the LORD spoke to Moses, saying,

➤ **2** "Tell the sons of Israel to raise a contribution for Me; from every man whose heart moves him you shall raise My contribution.

3 "This is the contribution which you are to raise from them: gold, silver and bronze,

4 blue, purple and scarlet *material*, fine linen, goat *hair*,

5 rams' skins dyed red, porpoise skins, acacia wood,

6 oil for lighting, spices for the anointing oil and for the fragrant incense,

7 onyx stones and setting stones for the ephod and for the breastpiece.

8 "Let them construct a sanctuary for Me, that I may dwell among them.

9 "According to all that I am going to show you, *as* the pattern of the tabernacle and the pattern of all its furniture, just so you shall construct *it.*

10 "They shall construct an ark of acacia wood two and a half cubits long, and

---

LIFE LESSONS

➤ **Exodus 25:2 — *"From every man whose heart moves him you shall raise My contribution."***

The kind of offering God most desires from us is a willing one given out of a grateful heart. But even when we give in this joyful way, we can never out give God.

one and a half cubits wide, and one and a half cubits high.

11 "You shall overlay it with pure gold, inside and out you shall overlay it, and you shall make a gold molding around it.

12 "You shall cast four gold rings for it and fasten them on its four feet, and two rings shall be on one side of it and two rings on the other side of it.

13 "You shall make poles of acacia wood and overlay them with gold.

14 "You shall put the poles into the rings on the sides of the ark, to carry the ark with them.

15 "The poles shall remain in the rings of the ark; they shall not be removed from it.

16 "You shall put into the ark the testimony which I shall give you.

17 "You shall make a mercy seat of pure gold, two and a half cubits long and one and a half cubits wide.

18 "You shall make two cherubim of gold, make them of hammered work at the two ends of the mercy seat.

19 "Make one cherub at one end and one cherub at the other end; you shall make the cherubim *of one piece* with the mercy seat at its two ends.

20 "The cherubim shall have *their* wings spread upward, covering the mercy seat with their wings and facing one another; the faces of the cherubim are to be *turned* toward the mercy seat.

21 "You shall put the mercy seat on top of the ark, and in the ark you shall put the testimony which I will give to you.

22 "There I will meet with you; and from above the mercy seat, from between the two cherubim which are upon the ark of the testimony, I will speak to you about all that I will give you in commandment for the sons of Israel.

23 "You shall make a table of acacia wood, two cubits long and one cubit wide and one and a half cubits high.

24 "You shall overlay it with pure gold and make a gold border around it.

25 "You shall make for it a rim of a handbreadth around *it*; and you shall make a gold border for the rim around it.

26 "You shall make four gold rings for it and put rings on the four corners which are on its four feet.

27 "The rings shall be close to the rim as holders for the poles to carry the table.

28 "You shall make the poles of acacia wood and overlay them with gold, so that with them the table may be carried.

29 "You shall make its dishes and its pans and its jars and its bowls with which to pour drink offerings; you shall make them of pure gold.

30 "You shall set the bread of the Presence on the table before Me at all times.

31 "Then you shall make a lampstand of pure gold. The lampstand *and* its base and its shaft are to be made of hammered work; its cups, its bulbs and its flowers shall be *of one piece* with it.

32 "Six branches shall go out from its sides; three branches of the lampstand from its one side and three branches of the lampstand from its other side.

33 "Three cups *shall be* shaped like almond *blossoms* in the one branch, a bulb and a flower, and three cups shaped like almond *blossoms* in the other branch, a bulb and a flower—so for six branches going out from the lampstand;

34 and in the lampstand four cups shaped like almond *blossoms*, its bulbs and its flowers.

35 "A bulb shall be under the *first* pair of branches *coming* out of it, and a bulb under the *second* pair of branches *coming* out of it, and a bulb under the *third* pair of branches *coming* out of it, for the six branches coming out of the lampstand.

36 "Their bulbs and their branches *shall be of one piece* with it; all of it shall be one piece of hammered work of pure gold.

37 "Then you shall make its lamps seven *in number*; and they shall mount its lamps so as to shed light on the space in front of it.

38 "Its snuffers and their trays *shall be* of pure gold.

39 "It shall be made from a talent of pure gold, with all these utensils.

40 "See that you make *them* after the pattern for them, which was shown to you on the mountain.

26 "MOREOVER you shall make the tabernacle with ten curtains of fine twisted linen and blue and purple and scarlet *material;* you shall make them with cherubim, the work of a skillful workman.

2 "The length of each curtain shall be twenty-eight cubits, and the width of

WHAT THE BIBLE SAYS ABOUT

The Mercy Seat

Exodus 25:22

*O*nce a year on the Day of Atonement, the high priest would enter in behind the veil of the Holy of Holies and stand before God. On that day, he would sprinkle blood on the mercy seat in order to receive forgiveness for the sins of the community. It was there that the *shekinah* glory—or presence of God—would rest between the golden figures of two cherubim, which were a kind of angel.

Only one man could be in the presence of God and on only one day a year. One man, once a year—and by the time Jesus walked on the earth, it had been hundreds of years since the *shekinah* glory of God had been seen in the temple. The average Israelite was not accustomed to being in the presence of God.

However, imagine the excitement and glory on the Day of Atonement when God's presence would dwell between the two angels. In Exodus 25:22, God says, "There I will meet with you; and from above the mercy seat, from between the two cherubim which are upon the ark of the testimony, I will speak to you about all that I will give you in commandment for the sons of Israel."

It was there on the mercy seat—between the two angels, above the ark of the covenant—that God showed Himself merciful in forgiving sin. God met with the high priest and spoke with him. And the high priest had the privilege of worshiping God and finding guidance.

Now, fast forward to three days after the crucifixion. It was very early in the morning when Mary Magdalene and some other women traveled to Jesus' tomb out of love and devotion. John 20:11, 12 tells us, "Mary was standing outside the tomb weeping; and so, as she wept, she stooped and looked into the tomb; and she saw two angels in white sitting, one at the head and one at the feet, where the body of Jesus had been lying."

Though Mary did not realize it at the time, what she was seeing was the wondrous fulfillment of the Old Testament mercy seat—the glory of God shone between those two angels. But this time, God's *shekinah* glory was not being revealed to a priest with an offering; rather, it was being shown to a woman with a broken heart.

Why would God put the mercy seat in the tomb? The interesting thing is that the mercy seat was the cover of the ark of the covenant. The word for "ark" in the Hebrew is *arown*, which means "coffin." God's glory appeared in the Old Testament above a coffin. And now, through Christ, God's great victory had likewise appeared over the tomb—to signify His victory over death.

You see, Jesus had already become our High Priest, and He had already made our atonement offering (Heb. 9:23–28). The veil of the Holy of Holies had been torn in two, and we were no longer separated from the presence of God (Heb. 10:19–23). The forgiveness, guidance, and very presence of God—that had previously been accessible to only one man on one day a year—had been made available to all of us for all eternity.

No matter what you've done, no matter what sin you've committed—the mercy seat is available for your forgiveness.

No matter what counsel you need, no matter why you need direction—the mercy seat is available to give you guidance.

No matter what the tomb, no matter what hope or promise has died in you—the mercy seat is available to you, and the glory of God will shine on your situation.

You may not see it yet, but the victory is yours. Jesus Christ has become your mercy seat—He has opened the way so that the *shekinah* glory of God can illuminate your life in every circumstance.

So what do you do with this great access to the mercy seat? Hebrews 4:16 says, "Let us draw near with confidence to the throne of grace, so that we may receive mercy and find grace to help in time of need."

Enter in, friend, and rejoice in the glory of God.

---

each curtain four cubits; all the curtains shall have the same measurements.
3 "Five curtains shall be joined to one another, and *the other* five curtains *shall be* joined to one another.

4 "You shall make loops of blue on the edge of the outermost curtain in the *first* set, and likewise you shall make *them* on the edge of the curtain that is outermost in the second set.

5 "You shall make fifty loops in the one curtain, and you shall make fifty loops on the edge of the curtain that is in the second set; the loops shall be opposite each other.
6 "You shall make fifty clasps of gold, and join the curtains to one another with the clasps so that the tabernacle will be a unit.
7 "Then you shall make curtains of goats' *hair* for a tent over the tabernacle; you shall make eleven curtains in all.
8 "The length of each curtain *shall be* thirty cubits, and the width of each curtain four cubits; the eleven curtains shall have the same measurements.
9 "You shall join five curtains by themselves and the *other* six curtains by themselves, and you shall double over the sixth curtain at the front of the tent.
10 "You shall make fifty loops on the edge of the curtain that is outermost in the *first* set, and fifty loops on the edge of the curtain *that is outermost in* the second set.
11 "You shall make fifty clasps of bronze, and you shall put the clasps into the loops and join the tent together so that it will be a unit.
12 "The overlapping part that is left over in the curtains of the tent, the half curtain that is left over, shall lap over the back of the tabernacle.
13 "The cubit on one side and the cubit on the other, of what is left over in the length of the curtains of the tent, shall lap over the sides of the tabernacle on one side and on the other, to cover it.
14 "You shall make a covering for the tent of rams' skins dyed red and a covering of porpoise skins above.
15 "Then you shall make the boards for the tabernacle of acacia wood, standing upright.
16 "Ten cubits *shall be* the length of each board and one and a half cubits the width of each board.
17 "*There shall be* two tenons for each board, fitted to one another; thus you shall do for all the boards of the tabernacle.
18 "You shall make the boards for the tabernacle: twenty boards for the south side.
19 "You shall make forty sockets of silver under the twenty boards, two sockets under one board for its two tenons and

two sockets under another board for its two tenons;
20 and for the second side of the tabernacle, on the north side, twenty boards,
21 and their forty sockets of silver; two sockets under one board and two sockets under another board.
22 "For the rear of the tabernacle, to the west, you shall make six boards.
23 "You shall make two boards for the corners of the tabernacle at the rear.
24 "They shall be double beneath, and together they shall be complete to its top to the first ring; thus it shall be with both of them: they shall form the two corners.
25 "There shall be eight boards with their sockets of silver, sixteen sockets; two sockets under one board and two sockets under another board.
26 "Then you shall make bars of acacia wood, five for the boards of one side of the tabernacle,
27 and five bars for the boards of the other side of the tabernacle, and five bars for the boards of the side of the tabernacle for the rear *side* to the west.
28 "The middle bar in the center of the boards shall pass through from end to end.
29 "You shall overlay the boards with gold and make their rings of gold *as* holders for the bars; and you shall overlay the bars with gold.
30 "Then you shall erect the tabernacle according to its plan which you have been shown in the mountain.
31 "You shall make a veil of blue and purple and scarlet *material* and fine twisted linen; it shall be made with cherubim, the work of a skillful workman.
32 "You shall hang it on four pillars of acacia overlaid with gold, their hooks *also being of* gold, on four sockets of silver.
33 "You shall hang up the veil under the clasps, and shall bring in the ark of the testimony there within the veil; and the veil shall serve for you as a partition between the holy place and the holy of holies.
34 "You shall put the mercy seat on the ark of the testimony in the holy of holies.
35 "You shall set the table outside the veil, and the lampstand opposite the table on the side of the tabernacle toward the south; and you shall put the table on the north side.

36 "You shall make a screen for the doorway of the tent of blue and purple and scarlet *material* and fine twisted linen, the work of a weaver.

37 "You shall make five pillars of acacia for the screen and overlay them with gold, their hooks *also being of* gold; and you shall cast five sockets of bronze for them.

Psalm 19:7–14

7 The law of the LORD is perfect,
     restoring the soul;
     The testimony of the LORD is sure,
     making wise the simple.

8 The precepts of the LORD are right,
     rejoicing the heart;
     The commandment of the LORD is
     pure, enlightening the eyes.

9 The fear of the LORD is clean,
     enduring forever;
     The judgments of the LORD are true;
     they are righteous altogether.

10 They are more desirable than gold,
     yes, than much fine gold;
     Sweeter also than honey and the
     drippings of the honeycomb.

11 Moreover, by them Your servant is
     warned;
     In keeping them there is great
     reward.

12 Who can discern *his* errors? Acquit
     me of hidden *faults*.

13 Also keep back Your servant from
     presumptuous *sins*;
     Let them not rule over me;
     Then I will be blameless,
     And I shall be acquitted of great
     transgression.

14 Let the words of my mouth and the
     meditation of my heart

Be acceptable in Your sight,
O LORD, my rock and my Redeemer.

Proverbs 6:32–35

32 The one who commits adultery with
     a woman is lacking sense;
     He who would destroy himself does it.

33 Wounds and disgrace he will find,
     And his reproach will not be blotted
     out.

34 For jealousy enrages a man,
     And he will not spare in the day of
     vengeance.

35 He will not accept any ransom,
     Nor will he be satisfied though you
     give many gifts.

Matthew 24:1–28

24 JESUS came out from the temple and was going away when His disciples came up to point out the temple buildings to Him.

2 And He said to them, "Do you not see all these things? Truly I say to you, not one stone here will be left upon another, which will not be torn down."

3 As He was sitting on the Mount of Olives, the disciples came to Him privately, saying, "Tell us, when will these things happen, and what *will be* the sign of Your coming, and of the end of the age?"

4 And Jesus answered and said to them, "See to it that no one misleads you.

5 "For many will come in My name, saying, 'I am the Christ,' and will mislead many.

LIFE LESSONS

➢ **Psalm 19:14 —** *Let the words of my mouth and the meditation of my heart be acceptable in Your sight, O LORD, my rock and my Redeemer.*

*T*he God who made the universe by His almighty power offers to exercise that same power on our behalf to help us speak and think in a way that honors Him. He wants to be involved in every aspect of our lives.

➢ **Matthew 24:5 —** *"Many will come in My name, saying, 'I am the Christ,' and will mislead many."*

*T*here have always been deceivers in the church, leading people away from a relationship with Christ and into religious bondage. But Jesus says as the time nears for His return, such deception will markedly increase.

6 "You will be hearing of wars and rumors of wars. See that you are not frightened, for *those things* must take place, but *that* is not yet the end.
7 "For nation will rise against nation, and kingdom against kingdom, and in various places there will be famines and earthquakes.
8 "But all these things are *merely* the beginning of birth pangs.
9 "Then they will deliver you to tribulation, and will kill you, and you will be hated by all nations because of My name.
10 "At that time many will fall away and will betray one another and hate one another.
11 "Many false prophets will arise and will mislead many.
12 "Because lawlessness is increased, most people's love will grow cold.
✳ 13 "But the one who endures to the end, he will be saved.
➤ 14 "This gospel of the kingdom shall be preached in the whole world as a testimony to all the nations, and then the end will come.
15 "Therefore when you see the ABOMINATION OF DESOLATION which was spoken of through Daniel the prophet, standing in the holy place (let the reader understand),
16 then those who are in Judea must flee to the mountains.
17 "Whoever is on the housetop must not go down to get the things out that are in his house.
18 "Whoever is in the field must not turn back to get his cloak.
19 "But woe to those who are pregnant and to those who are nursing babies in those days!

LIFE LESSONS

➤ **Matthew 24:14 — *"This gospel of the kingdom shall be preached in the whole world as a testimony to all the nations, and then the end will come."***

God will not wind down human history until the entire world has had the opportunity to hear the good news about Jesus Christ. His amazing patience leads to our rich salvation.

---

20 "But pray that your flight will not be in the winter, or on a Sabbath.
21 "For then there will be a great tribulation, such as has not occurred since the beginning of the world until now, nor ever will.
22 "Unless those days had been cut short, no life would have been saved; but for the sake of the elect those days will be cut short.
23 "Then if anyone says to you, 'Behold, here is the Christ,' or 'There *He is,*' do not believe *him.*
24 "For false Christs and false prophets will arise and will show great signs and wonders, so as to mislead, if possible, even the elect.
25 "Behold, I have told you in advance.
26 "So if they say to you, 'Behold, He is in the wilderness,' do not go out, *or,* 'Behold, He is in the inner rooms,' do not believe *them.*
27 "For just as the lightning comes from the east and flashes even to the west, so will the coming of the Son of Man be.
28 "Wherever the corpse is, there the vultures will gather.

◈ Exodus 27:1—28:43

27 "AND you shall make the altar of acacia wood, five cubits long and five cubits wide; the altar shall be square, and its height shall be three cubits.
2 "You shall make its horns on its four corners; its horns shall be of one piece with it, and you shall overlay it with bronze.
3 "You shall make its pails for removing its ashes, and its shovels and its basins and its forks and its firepans; you shall make all its utensils of bronze.
4 "You shall make for it a grating of network of bronze, and on the net you shall make four bronze rings at its four corners.
5 "You shall put it beneath, under the ledge of the altar, so that the net will reach halfway up the altar.
6 "You shall make poles for the altar,

poles of acacia wood, and overlay them with bronze.

7 "Its poles shall be inserted into the rings, so that the poles shall be on the two sides of the altar when it is carried.

8 "You shall make it hollow with planks; as it was shown to you in the mountain, so they shall make *it*.

9 "You shall make the court of the tabernacle. On the south side *there shall be* hangings for the court of fine twisted linen one hundred cubits long for one side;

10 and its pillars *shall be* twenty, with their twenty sockets of bronze; the hooks of the pillars and their bands *shall be* of silver.

11 "Likewise for the north side in length *there shall be* hangings one hundred *cubits* long, and its twenty pillars with their twenty sockets of bronze; the hooks of the pillars and their bands *shall be* of silver.

12 "*For* the width of the court on the west side *shall be* hangings of fifty cubits *with* their ten pillars and their ten sockets.

13 "The width of the court on the east side *shall be* fifty cubits.

14 "The hangings for the *one* side *of the gate shall be* fifteen cubits *with* their three pillars and their three sockets.

15 "And for the other side *shall be* hangings of fifteen cubits *with* their three pillars and their three sockets.

16 "For the gate of the court *there shall be* a screen of twenty cubits, of blue and purple and scarlet *material* and fine twisted linen, the work of a weaver, *with* their four pillars and their four sockets.

17 "All the pillars around the court shall be furnished with silver bands *with* their hooks of silver and their sockets of bronze.

18 "The length of the court *shall be* one hundred cubits, and the width fifty throughout, and the height five cubits of fine twisted linen, and their sockets of bronze.

19 "All the utensils of the tabernacle *used* in all its service, and all its pegs, and all the pegs of the court, *shall be* of bronze.

20 "You shall charge the sons of Israel, that they bring you clear oil of beaten olives for the light, to make a lamp burn continually.

21 "In the tent of meeting, outside the veil which is before the testimony, Aaron and his sons shall keep it in order from evening to morning before the Lord; *it shall be* a perpetual statute throughout their generations for the sons of Israel.

28 "THEN bring near to yourself Aaron your brother, and his sons with him, from among the sons of Israel, to minister as priest to Me—Aaron, Nadab and Abihu, Eleazar and Ithamar, Aaron's sons.

2 "You shall make holy garments for Aaron your brother, for glory and for beauty.

3 "You shall speak to all the skillful ◄ persons whom I have endowed with the spirit of wisdom, that they make Aaron's garments to consecrate him, that he may minister as priest to Me.

4 "These are the garments which they shall make: a breastpiece and an ephod and a robe and a tunic of checkered work, a turban and a sash, and they shall make holy garments for Aaron your brother and his sons, that he may minister as priest to Me.

5 "They shall take the gold and the blue and the purple and the scarlet *material* and the fine linen.

6 "They shall also make the ephod of gold, of blue and purple *and* scarlet *material* and fine twisted linen, the work of the skillful workman.

7 "It shall have two shoulder pieces joined to its two ends, that it may be joined.

8 "The skillfully woven band, which is on it, shall be like its workmanship, of the same material: of gold, of blue and purple and scarlet *material* and fine twisted linen.

9 "You shall take two onyx stones and

engrave on them the names of the sons of Israel,

10 six of their names on the one stone and the names of the remaining six on the other stone, according to their birth.

11 "As a jeweler engraves a signet, you shall engrave the two stones according to the names of the sons of Israel; you shall set them in filigree *settings* of gold.

12 "You shall put the two stones on the shoulder pieces of the ephod, *as* stones of memorial for the sons of Israel, and Aaron shall bear their names before the LORD on his two shoulders for a memorial.

13 "You shall make filigree *settings* of gold,

14 and two chains of pure gold; you shall make them of twisted cordage work, and you shall put the corded chains on the filigree *settings*.

15 "You shall make a breastpiece of judgment, the work of a skillful workman; like the work of the ephod you shall make it: of gold, of blue and purple and scarlet *material* and fine twisted linen you shall make it.

16 "It shall be square *and* folded double, a span in length and a span in width.

17 "You shall mount on it four rows of stones; the first row *shall be* a row of ruby, topaz and emerald;

18 and the second row a turquoise, a sapphire and a diamond;

19 and the third row a jacinth, an agate and an amethyst;

20 and the fourth row a beryl and an onyx and a jasper; they shall be set in gold filigree.

21 "The stones shall be according to the names of the sons of Israel: twelve, according to their names; they shall be *like* the engravings of a seal, each according to his name for the twelve tribes.

22 "You shall make on the breastpiece chains of twisted cordage work in pure gold.

23 "You shall make on the breastpiece two rings of gold, and shall put the two rings on the two ends of the breastpiece.

24 "You shall put the two cords of gold on the two rings at the ends of the breastpiece.

25 "You shall put the *other* two ends of the two cords on the two filigree *settings*, and put them on the shoulder pieces of the ephod, at the front of it.

26 "You shall make two rings of gold and shall place them on the two ends of the breastpiece, on the edge of it, which is toward the inner side of the ephod.

27 "You shall make two rings of gold and put them on the bottom of the two shoulder pieces of the ephod, on the front of it close to the place where it is joined, above the skillfully woven band of the ephod.

28 "They shall bind the breastpiece by its rings to the rings of the ephod with a blue cord, so that it will be on the skillfully woven band of the ephod, and that the breastpiece will not come loose from the ephod.

29 "Aaron shall carry the names of the sons of Israel in the breastpiece of judgment over his heart when he enters the holy place, for a memorial before the LORD continually.

30 "You shall put in the breastpiece of judgment the Urim and the Thummim, and they shall be over Aaron's heart when he goes in before the LORD; and Aaron shall carry the judgment of the sons of Israel over his heart before the LORD continually.

31 "You shall make the robe of the ephod all of blue.

32 "There shall be an opening at its top in the middle of it; around its opening there shall be a binding of woven work, like the opening of a coat of mail, so that it will not be torn.

33 "You shall make on its hem pomegranates of blue and purple and scarlet *material,* all around on its hem, and bells of gold between them all around:

34 a golden bell and a pomegranate, a golden bell and a pomegranate, all around on the hem of the robe.

35 "It shall be on Aaron when he ministers; and its tinkling shall be heard when he enters and leaves the holy place before the LORD, so that he will not die.

36 "You shall also make a plate of pure gold and shall engrave on it, like the engravings of a seal, 'Holy to the LORD.'

37 "You shall fasten it on a blue cord, and it shall be on the turban; it shall be at the front of the turban.

38 "It shall be on Aaron's forehead, and Aaron shall take away the iniquity of the holy things which the sons of Israel consecrate, with regard to all their holy gifts; and it shall always be on his forehead,

ANSWERS TO LIFE'S QUESTIONS

How can I feel secure in the Lord during troubled times?

PSALM 20:1–5

*W*hen you know Jesus Christ as your Lord and Savior, you can be certain of one thing in times of trouble, suffering, hardship, difficulty, pain, or tragedy: The Lord is with you! Time and again in His Word, He assures you of His presence:

- "The LORD is with you when you are with Him. And if you seek Him, He will let you find Him" (2 Chr. 15:2).
- "Stand and see the salvation of the LORD on your behalf . . . Do not fear or be dismayed" (2 Chr. 20:17).
- "Do not be afraid of him," declares the LORD, "for I am with you to save you and deliver you from his hand" (Jer. 42:11).
- "All you people of the land take courage," declares the LORD, "and work; for I am with you" (Hag. 2:4).

Jesus said the same thing to His disciples: "I am with you always" (Matt. 28:20).

The apostle Paul considered this truth and asked, "If God is for us, who is against us?" (Rom. 8:31). Don't answer his question too quickly. The truth is, many people can rise up against us. They can cheat us, harass us, persecute us, insult us, mock us, and even physically injure us. But here's the point: *In the end, they cannot win.*

That is why Jesus said, "You will be betrayed . . . and they will put some of you to death, and you will be hated by all because of My name. Yet not a hair of your head will perish" (Luke 21:16–18). If you belong to God, He gives you the eternal victory. Period. No one can take away what He has so freely provided for you.

When rough times come, immerse yourself in God's Word. Read His promises to you, His beloved child. Read about His power, His strength, His wisdom, and His love. Read how He has helped countless men and women through the ages as they trusted in Him. Read about His saving, delivering, and restoring power.

The more you read and study God's Word, the stronger your faith will grow.

The more you trust God, the more you will grow in your understanding that He is trustworthy in all things, at all times.

The more you take courage in the Lord's presence with you, the more secure you will feel—even in the most troubling of times and the most trying of circumstances. The Lord alone is your security, every moment of your life.

---

that they may be accepted before the LORD. 39 "You shall weave the tunic of checkered work of fine linen, and shall make a turban of fine linen, and you shall make a sash, the work of a weaver. 40 "For Aaron's sons you shall make tunics; you shall also make sashes for them, and you shall make caps for them, for glory and for beauty. 41 "You shall put them on Aaron your brother and on his sons with him; and you shall anoint them and ordain them and consecrate them, that they may serve Me as priests. 42 "You shall make for them linen breeches to cover *their* bare flesh; they shall reach from the loins even to the thighs. 43 "They shall be on Aaron and on his sons when they enter the tent of meeting, or when they approach the altar to minister in the holy place, so that they do not incur guilt and die. It *shall be* a statute forever to him and to his descendants after him.

Psalm 20:1–5

For the choir director. A Psalm of David.

20 MAY the LORD answer you in the day of trouble!
May the name of the God of Jacob set you *securely* on high!

2   May He send you help from the sanctuary
And support you from Zion!

3   May He remember all your meal offerings
And find your burnt offering acceptable!   Selah.

4   May He grant you your heart's desire
And fulfill all your counsel!

5   We will sing for joy over your victory,
And in the name of our God we will set up our banners.
May the LORD fulfill all your petitions.

Proverbs 7:1–5

7 MY son, keep my words
And treasure my commandments
within you.

2 Keep my commandments and live,
And my teaching as the apple of
your eye.

3 Bind them on your fingers;
Write them on the tablet of your
heart.

4 Say to wisdom, "You are my sister,"
And call understanding *your*
intimate friend;

5 That they may keep you from an
adulteress,
From the foreigner who flatters with
her words.

Matthew 24:29–51

29 "But immediately after the tribulation of those days THE SUN WILL BE DARK-
ENED, AND THE MOON WILL NOT GIVE ITS
LIGHT, AND THE STARS WILL FALL from the
sky, and the powers of the heavens will
be shaken.

30 "And then the sign of the Son of Man
will appear in the sky, and then all the
tribes of the earth will mourn, and they
will see the SON OF MAN COMING ON THE
CLOUDS OF THE SKY with power and great
glory.

31 "And He will send forth His angels
with A GREAT TRUMPET and THEY WILL
GATHER TOGETHER His elect from the four
winds, from one end of the sky to the
other.

32 "Now learn the parable from the
fig tree: when its branch has already
become tender and puts forth its leaves,
you know that summer is near;

33 so, you too, when you see all these
things, recognize that He is near, *right* at
the door.

34 "Truly I say to you, this generation
will not pass away until all these things
take place.

35 "Heaven and earth will pass away,
but My words will not pass away.

36 "But of that day and hour no one
knows, not even the angels of heaven,
nor the Son, but the Father alone.

37 "For the coming of the Son of Man
will be just like the days of Noah.

38 "For as in those days before the flood
they were eating and drinking, marrying
and giving in marriage, until the day that
Noah entered the ark,

39 and they did not understand until the
flood came and took them all away; so
will the coming of the Son of Man be.

40 "Then there will be two men in the
field; one will be taken and one will be left.

41 "Two women *will be* grinding at the
mill; one will be taken and one will be
left.

42 "Therefore be on the alert, for you do
not know which day your Lord is coming.

43 "But be sure of this, that if the head
of the house had known at what time of
the night the thief was coming, he would
have been on the alert and would not
have allowed his house to be broken
into.

44 "For this reason you also must be
ready; for the Son of Man is coming at
an hour when you do not think *He will.*

45 "Who then is the faithful and sensible slave whom his master put in charge
of his household to give them their food
at the proper time?

46 "Blessed is that slave whom his master finds so doing when he comes.

47 "Truly I say to you that he will put
him in charge of all his possessions.

LIFE LESSONS

➤ **Proverbs 7:2 —** *Keep my commandments and live, and my teaching as the
apple of your eye.*

*H*ow do we approach our time in
God's Word—as a grinding duty to
be completed as quickly as possible? Or as
a delightful opportunity to get to know
God? David exclaimed, "Oh how I love
Your law!" (Ps. 119:97).

➤ **Matthew 24:44 —** *"You also must be
ready; for the Son of Man is coming at an
hour when you do not think He will."*

*D*espite many attempts over the centuries to pinpoint the time of Jesus'
return, God's Word stands: He will come
"at an hour when you do not think He
will." We are to remain in a perpetual
state of readiness.

48 "But if that evil slave says in his heart, 'My master is not coming for a long time,'

49 and begins to beat his fellow slaves and eat and drink with drunkards;

50 the master of that slave will come on a day when he does not expect *him* and at an hour which he does not know,

51 and will cut him in pieces and assign him a place with the hypocrites; in that place there will be weeping and gnashing of teeth.

FEBRUARY 9

☉ Exodus 29:1—30:38

29 "NOW this is what you shall do to them to consecrate them to minister as priests to Me: take one young bull and two rams without blemish,

2 and unleavened bread and unleavened cakes mixed with oil, and unleavened wafers spread with oil; you shall make them of fine wheat flour.

3 "You shall put them in one basket, and present them in the basket along with the bull and the two rams.

➤ 4 "Then you shall bring Aaron and his sons to the doorway of the tent of meeting and wash them with water.

5 "You shall take the garments, and put on Aaron the tunic and the robe of the ephod and the ephod and the breastpiece, and gird him with the skillfully woven band of the ephod;

6 and you shall set the turban on his head and put the holy crown on the turban.

7 "Then you shall take the anointing oil and pour it on his head and anoint him.

8 "You shall bring his sons and put tunics on them.

9 "You shall gird them with sashes, Aaron and his sons, and bind caps on them, and they shall have the priesthood by a perpetual statute. So you shall ordain Aaron and his sons.

10 "Then you shall bring the bull before the tent of meeting, and Aaron and his sons shall lay their hands on the head of the bull.

11 "You shall slaughter the bull before the LORD at the doorway of the tent of meeting.

12 "You shall take some of the blood of the bull and put *it* on the horns of the altar with your finger; and you shall pour out all the blood at the base of the altar.

13 "You shall take all the fat that covers the entrails and the lobe of the liver, and the two kidneys and the fat that is on them, and offer them up in smoke on the altar.

14 "But the flesh of the bull and its hide and its refuse, you shall burn with fire outside the camp; it is a sin offering.

15 "You shall also take the one ram, and Aaron and his sons shall lay their hands on the head of the ram;

16 and you shall slaughter the ram and shall take its blood and sprinkle it around on the altar.

17 "Then you shall cut the ram into its pieces, and wash its entrails and its legs, and put *them* with its pieces and its head.

18 "You shall offer up in smoke the whole ram on the altar; it is a burnt offering to the LORD: it is a soothing aroma, an offering by fire to the LORD.

19 "Then you shall take the other ram, and Aaron and his sons shall lay their hands on the head of the ram.

20 "You shall slaughter the ram, and take some of its blood and put *it* on the lobe of Aaron's right ear and on the lobes of his sons' right ears and on the thumbs of their right hands and on the big toes of their right feet, and sprinkle the *rest of the* blood around on the altar.

21 "Then you shall take some of the blood that is on the altar and some of the

---

LIFE LESSONS

➤ **Exodus 29:4 — "Aaron and his sons to the doorway of the tent of meeting and wash them with water."**

*W*e must be clean to come before the Holy One of Israel. Under the new covenant, we do this by making sure we have "a sincere heart in full assurance of faith" (Heb. 10:22).

anointing oil, and sprinkle *it* on Aaron and on his garments and on his sons and on his sons' garments with him; so he and his garments shall be consecrated, as well as his sons and his sons' garments with him.

22 "You shall also take the fat from the ram and the fat tail, and the fat that covers the entrails and the lobe of the liver, and the two kidneys and the fat that is on them and the right thigh (for it is a ram of ordination),

23 and one cake of bread and one cake of bread *mixed with* oil and one wafer from the basket of unleavened bread which is *set* before the LORD;

24 and you shall put all these in the hands of Aaron and in the hands of his sons, and shall wave them as a wave offering before the LORD.

25 "You shall take them from their hands, and offer them up in smoke on the altar on the burnt offering for a soothing aroma before the LORD; it is an offering by fire to the LORD.

26 "Then you shall take the breast of Aaron's ram of ordination, and wave it as a wave offering before the LORD; and it shall be your portion.

27 "You shall consecrate the breast of the wave offering and the thigh of the heave offering which was waved and which was offered from the ram of ordination, from the one which was for Aaron and from the one which was for his sons.

28 "It shall be for Aaron and his sons as *their* portion forever from the sons of Israel, for it is a heave offering; and it shall be a heave offering from the sons of Israel from the sacrifices of their peace offerings, *even* their heave offering to the LORD.

29 "The holy garments of Aaron shall be for his sons after him, that in them they may be anointed and ordained.

30 "For seven days the one of his sons who is priest in his stead shall put them on when he enters the tent of meeting to minister in the holy place.

31 "You shall take the ram of ordination and boil its flesh in a holy place.

32 "Aaron and his sons shall eat the flesh of the ram and the bread that is in the basket, at the doorway of the tent of meeting.

33 "Thus they shall eat those things by which atonement was made at their ordination *and* consecration; but a layman shall not eat *them*, because they are holy.

34 "If any of the flesh of ordination or any of the bread remains until morning, then you shall burn the remainder with fire; it shall not be eaten, because it is holy.

35 "Thus you shall do to Aaron and to his sons, according to all that I have commanded you; you shall ordain them through seven days.

36 "Each day you shall offer a bull as a sin offering for atonement, and you shall purify the altar when you make atonement for it, and you shall anoint it to consecrate it.

37 "For seven days you shall make atonement for the altar and consecrate it; then the altar shall be most holy, *and* whatever touches the altar shall be holy.

38 "Now this is what you shall offer on the altar: two one year old lambs each day, continuously.

39 "The one lamb you shall offer in the morning and the other lamb you shall offer at twilight;

40 and there *shall be* one-tenth *of an ephah* of fine flour mixed with one-fourth of a hin of beaten oil, and one-fourth of a hin of wine for a drink offering with one lamb.

41 "The other lamb you shall offer at twilight, and shall offer with it the same grain offering and the same drink offering as in the morning, for a soothing aroma, an offering by fire to the LORD.

42 "It shall be a continual burnt offering throughout your generations at the doorway of the tent of meeting before the LORD, where I will meet with you, to speak to you there.

43 "I will meet there with the sons of Israel, and it shall be consecrated by My glory.

44 "I will consecrate the tent of meeting and the altar; I will also consecrate Aaron and his sons to minister as priests to Me.

45 "I will dwell among the sons of Israel and will be their God.

46 "They shall know that I am the LORD their God who brought them out of the land of Egypt, that I might dwell among them; I am the LORD their God.

✳

30 "MOREOVER, you shall make an altar as a place for burning incense; you shall make it of acacia wood.

2 "Its length *shall be* a cubit, and its width a cubit, it shall be square, and its height *shall be* two cubits; its horns *shall be* of one piece with it.

3 "You shall overlay it with pure gold, its top and its sides all around, and its horns; and you shall make a gold molding all around for it.

4 "You shall make two gold rings for it under its molding; you shall make *them* on its two side walls—on opposite sides—and they shall be holders for poles with which to carry it.

5 "You shall make the poles of acacia wood and overlay them with gold.

6 "You shall put this altar in front of the veil that is near the ark of the testimony, in front of the mercy seat that is over *the ark of* the testimony, where I will meet with you.

7 "Aaron shall burn fragrant incense on it; he shall burn it every morning when he trims the lamps.

8 "When Aaron trims the lamps at twilight, he shall burn incense. *There shall be* perpetual incense before the LORD throughout your generations.

➤ 9 "You shall not offer any strange incense on this altar, or burnt offering or meal offering; and you shall not pour out a drink offering on it.

10 "Aaron shall make atonement on its horns once a year; he shall make atonement on it with the blood of the sin offering of atonement once a year throughout your generations. It is most holy to the LORD."

11 The LORD also spoke to Moses, saying,

12 "When you take a census of the sons of Israel to number them, then each one of them shall give a ransom for himself to the LORD, when you number them, so that there will be no plague among them when you number them.

13 "This is what everyone who is numbered shall give: half a shekel according to the shekel of the sanctuary (the shekel is twenty gerahs), half a shekel as a contribution to the LORD.

14 "Everyone who is numbered, from twenty years old and over, shall give the contribution to the LORD.

15 "The rich shall not pay more and the poor shall not pay less than the half shekel, when you give the contribution to the LORD to make atonement for yourselves.

16 "You shall take the atonement money from the sons of Israel and shall give it for the service of the tent of meeting, that it may be a memorial for the sons of Israel before the LORD, to make atonement for yourselves."

17 The LORD spoke to Moses, saying,

18 "You shall also make a laver of bronze, with its base of bronze, for washing; and you shall put it between the tent of meeting and the altar, and you shall put water in it.

19 "Aaron and his sons shall wash their hands and their feet from it;

20 when they enter the tent of meeting, they shall wash with water, so that they will not die; or when they approach the altar to minister, by offering up in smoke a fire *sacrifice* to the LORD.

21 "So they shall wash their hands and their feet, so that they will not die; and it shall be a perpetual statute for them, for Aaron and his descendants throughout their generations."

22 Moreover, the LORD spoke to Moses, saying,

23 "Take also for yourself the finest of spices: of flowing myrrh five hundred *shekels*, and of fragrant cinnamon half as much, two hundred and fifty, and of fragrant cane two hundred and fifty,

24 and of cassia five hundred, according to the shekel of the sanctuary, and of olive oil a hin.

25 "You shall make of these a holy anointing oil, a perfume mixture, the work of a perfumer; it shall be a holy anointing oil.

LIFE LESSONS

➤ **Exodus 30:9** — *"You shall not offer any strange incense on this altar, or burnt offering or meal offering; and you shall not pour out a drink offering on it."*

*W*hen Aaron's sons, Nadab and Abihu, transgressed this command, the Lord destroyed them in fire (Lev. 10:1, 2). God does not require us to understand His will, just obey it, even if it seems unreasonable.

26 "With it you shall anoint the tent of meeting and the ark of the testimony,

27 and the table and all its utensils, and the lampstand and its utensils, and the altar of incense,

28 and the altar of burnt offering and all its utensils, and the laver and its stand.

29 "You shall also consecrate them, that they may be most holy; whatever touches them shall be holy.

30 "You shall anoint Aaron and his sons, and consecrate them, that they may minister as priests to Me.

31 "You shall speak to the sons of Israel, saying, 'This shall be a holy anointing oil to Me throughout your generations.

32 'It shall not be poured on anyone's body, nor shall you make *any* like it in the same proportions; it is holy, *and* it shall be holy to you.

33 'Whoever shall mix *any* like it or whoever puts any of it on a layman shall be cut off from his people.'"

34 Then the LORD said to Moses, "Take for yourself spices, stacte and onycha and galbanum, spices with pure frankincense; there shall be an equal part of each.

35 "With it you shall make incense, a perfume, the work of a perfumer, salted, pure, *and* holy.

36 "You shall beat some of it very fine, and put part of it before the testimony in the tent of meeting where I will meet with you; it shall be most holy to you.

37 "The incense which you shall make, you shall not make in the same proportions for yourselves; it shall be holy to you for the LORD.

38 "Whoever shall make *any* like it, to use as perfume, shall be cut off from his people."

Psalm 20:6–9

6 Now I know that the LORD saves His anointed;
He will answer him from His holy heaven
With the saving strength of His right hand.

7 Some *boast* in chariots and some in horses,

But we will boast in the name of the LORD, our God.

8 They have bowed down and fallen,
But we have risen and stood upright.

9 Save, O LORD;
May the King answer us in the day we call.

Proverbs 7:6–23

6 For at the window of my house
I looked out through my lattice,

7 And I saw among the naive,
And discerned among the youths
A young man lacking sense,

8 Passing through the street near her corner;
And he takes the way to her house,

9 In the twilight, in the evening,
In the middle of the night and *in* the darkness.

10 And behold, a woman *comes* to meet him,
Dressed as a harlot and cunning of heart.

11 She is boisterous and rebellious,
Her feet do not remain at home;

12 *She is* now in the streets, now in the squares,
And lurks by every corner.

13 So she seizes him and kisses him

LIFE LESSONS

➤ **Psalm 20:7** — *Some boast in chariots and some in horses, but we will boast in the name of the LORD, our God.*

We could change this verse to say, "Some trust in tanks and some in missiles; but we will put our hope in the God and Father of our Lord Jesus Christ." Armaments throughout history have changed, but God always remains the same.

➤ **Proverbs 7:14** — *"I was due to offer peace offerings; today I have paid my vows."*

People have long used religious language to entice naïve believers into sin. Others confuse religious practices with genuine godliness. We should never confuse sentiment with true spirituality.

And with a brazen face she says to him:

14 "I was due to offer peace offerings;
Today I have paid my vows.

15 "Therefore I have come out to meet you,
To seek your presence earnestly,
and I have found you.

16 "I have spread my couch with coverings,
With colored linens of Egypt.

17 "I have sprinkled my bed
With myrrh, aloes and cinnamon.

18 "Come, let us drink our fill of love until morning;
Let us delight ourselves with caresses.

19 "For my husband is not at home,
He has gone on a long journey;

20 He has taken a bag of money with him,
At the full moon he will come home."

21 With her many persuasions she entices him;
With her flattering lips she seduces him.

22 Suddenly he follows her
As an ox goes to the slaughter,
Or as *one in* fetters to the discipline of a fool,

23 Until an arrow pierces through his liver;
As a bird hastens to the snare,
So he does not know that it *will cost him* his life.

Matthew 25:1–30

25 "THEN the kingdom of heaven will be comparable to ten virgins, who took their lamps and went out to meet the bridegroom.

2 "Five of them were foolish, and five were prudent.

3 "For when the foolish took their lamps, they took no oil with them,

4 but the prudent took oil in flasks along with their lamps.

5 "Now while the bridegroom was delaying, they all got drowsy and *began* to sleep.

6 "But at midnight there was a shout, 'Behold, the bridegroom! Come out to meet *him.*'

7 "Then all those virgins rose and trimmed their lamps.

8 "The foolish said to the prudent, 'Give us some of your oil, for our lamps are going out.'

9 "But the prudent answered, 'No, there will not be enough for us and you *too;* go instead to the dealers and buy *some* for yourselves.'

10 "And while they were going away to make the purchase, the bridegroom came, and those who were ready went in with him to the wedding feast; and the door was shut.

11 "Later the other virgins also came, saying, 'Lord, lord, open up for us.'

12 "But he answered, 'Truly I say to you, I do not know you.'

13 "Be on the alert then, for you do not know the day nor the hour.

14 "For *it is* just like a man *about* to go on a journey, who called his own slaves and entrusted his possessions to them.

15 "To one he gave five talents, to another, two, and to another, one, each according to his own ability; and he went on his journey.

16 "Immediately the one who had received the five talents went and traded with them, and gained five more talents.

17 "In the same manner the one who *had received* the two *talents* gained two more.

18 "But he who received the one *talent* went away, and dug *a hole* in the ground and hid his master's money.

19 "Now after a long time the master of those slaves *came and *settled accounts with them.

20 "The one who had received the five talents came up and brought five more talents, saying, 'Master, you entrusted five talents to me. See, I have gained five more talents.'

21 "His master said to him, 'Well done, good and faithful slave. You were faithful with a few things, I will put you in

LIFE LESSONS

➤ **Matthew 25:13 —** *"Be on the alert then, for you do not know the day nor the hour."*

Some people have claimed to know the season of Christ's return, even though the Bible says no one can determine the day or hour. All such speculation is useless. The point is to continually watch for His coming.

charge of many things; enter into the joy of your master.'

22 "Also the one who *had received* the two talents came up and said, 'Master, you entrusted two talents to me. See, I have gained two more talents.'

23 "His master said to him, 'Well done, good and faithful slave. You were faithful with a few things, I will put you in charge of many things; enter into the joy of your master.'

24 "And the one also who had received the one talent came up and said, 'Master, I knew you to be a hard man, reaping where you did not sow and gathering where you scattered no *seed*.

25 'And I was afraid, and went away and hid your talent in the ground. See, you have what is yours.'

26 "But his master answered and said to him, 'You wicked, lazy slave, you knew that I reap where I did not sow and gather where I scattered no *seed*.

27 'Then you ought to have put my money in the bank, and on my arrival I would have received my *money* back with interest.

28 'Therefore take away the talent from him, and give it to the one who has the ten talents.'

29 "For to everyone who has, *more* shall be given, and he will have an abundance; but from the one who does not have, even what he does have shall be taken away.

30 "Throw out the worthless slave into the outer darkness; in that place there will be weeping and gnashing of teeth."

Life Examples:

A Warning Against Slothfulness

MATTHEW 25:19–30

*I*n Matthew 25, Jesus called the lazy servant "wicked" (v. 26) and "worthless" (v. 30). That was a very strong rebuke, and we must take heed that Jesus considers slothfulness evil. So what is God's description of a person who is slothful? What does a lazy person look like?

- *The first word that describes slothfulness is rebellion* (Eph. 2:8–10).

Though we do not serve God in order to earn our salvation, our service to God shows our thankfulness and obedience to Him. It is the will of God that His children live a productive life. If we refuse to carry out the works God has called us to do, then we are rebelling against God. Slothfulness is a sin of rebellion.

- *The second word that describes slothfulness is wastefulness* (1 Cor. 12:7).

God gifts us in many ways, and He calls us to do certain jobs. It is our personal responsibility—as good stewards of those spiritual gifts—to use them for His glory. Rather than serve our own interests, we help one another. Unfortunately, slothful people are very self-centered and waste their gifts on mundane things that have no real value for the kingdom of God.

- *The third word that describes slothfulness is selfishness* (Phil. 2:3, 4).

People who are lazy are not concerned with the needs of others—they only care about their own desires. They prefer to steal and take advantage of others in order to get

what they want, instead of working for it honestly. However, to honor God, we must deal honorably with others.

- *The fourth word that describes slothfulness is violation* (Col. 3:23, 24).

We are to honor God with everything we do. We have a responsibility to do our work with diligence, integrity, creativity, and energy because we are representing our Lord and Savior Jesus Christ. Therefore, let us serve conscientiously with the knowledge that we are pleasing God. Even if our employer does not reward us in the way we would like, God will.

Proverbs 26:16 tells us that, "The sluggard is wiser in his own eyes than seven men who can give a discreet answer." This is the main problem with the slothful person—he thinks he has all the answers. He thinks he can handle everything, but he really cannot handle anything. Slothful people are always deceiving themselves about their own abilities and wisdom.

In reality, slothful people are foolish and very shortsighted. Instead of preparing for the future, they only worry about today. They have no sense of direction, and they do not try to accomplish anything—not even for their own survival. They do not try to do the will of God because they believe it takes too much energy to serve God. They are just doing whatever it takes to get them through life.

Therefore, avoid being slothful and serve the Lord with humility and enthusiasm. Then, you will hear the Master say to you, "Well done, good and faithful slave. You were faithful with a few things, I will put you in charge of many things; enter into the joy of your master" (Matt. 25:23). That is certainly better than the alternative!

Exodus 31:1—32:35

31 NOW the LORD spoke to Moses, saying,

2 "See, I have called by name Bezalel, the son of Uri, the son of Hur, of the tribe of Judah.

3 "I have filled him with the Spirit of God in wisdom, in understanding, in knowledge, and in all *kinds of* craftsmanship,

4 to make artistic designs for work in gold, in silver, and in bronze,

5 and in the cutting of stones for settings, and in the carving of wood, that he may work in all *kinds of* craftsmanship.

6 "And behold, I Myself have appointed with him Oholiab, the son of Ahisamach, of the tribe of Dan; and in the hearts of all who are skillful I have put skill, that they may make all that I have commanded you:

7 the tent of meeting, and the ark of testimony, and the mercy seat upon it, and all the furniture of the tent,

8 the table also and its utensils, and the pure *gold* lampstand with all its utensils, and the altar of incense,

9 the altar of burnt offering also with all its utensils, and the laver and its stand,

10 the woven garments as well, and the holy garments for Aaron the priest, and the garments of his sons, *with which* to carry on their priesthood;

11 the anointing oil also, and the fragrant incense for the holy place, they are to make *them* according to all that I have commanded you."

12 The LORD spoke to Moses, saying,

13 "But as for you, speak to the sons of Israel, saying, 'You shall surely observe My sabbaths; for *this* is a sign between Me and you throughout your generations, that you may know that I am the LORD who sanctifies you.

14 'Therefore you are to observe the sabbath, for it is holy to you. Everyone who profanes it shall surely be put to death; for whoever does any work on it, that person shall be cut off from among his people.

15 'For six days work may be done, but on the seventh day there is a sabbath of complete rest, holy to the LORD; whoever does any work on the sabbath day shall surely be put to death.

16 'So the sons of Israel shall observe the sabbath, to celebrate the sabbath throughout their generations as a perpetual covenant.'

17 "It is a sign between Me and the sons of Israel forever; for in six days the LORD made heaven and earth, but on the seventh day He ceased *from labor,* and was refreshed."

18 When He had finished speaking with him upon Mount Sinai, He gave Moses the two tablets of the testimony, tablets of stone, written by the finger of God.

32 NOW when the people saw that Moses delayed to come down from the mountain, the people assembled about Aaron and said to him, "Come, make us a god who will go before us; as for this Moses, the man who brought us up from the land of Egypt, we do not know what has become of him."

2 Aaron said to them, "Tear off the gold rings which are in the ears of your wives, your sons, and your daughters, and bring *them* to me."

3 Then all the people tore off the gold rings which were in their ears and brought *them* to Aaron.

4 He took *this* from their hand, and fashioned it with a graving tool and made it into a molten calf; and they said, "This is your god, O Israel, who brought you up from the land of Egypt."

5 Now when Aaron saw *this,* he built an altar before it; and Aaron made a proclamation and said, "Tomorrow *shall be* a feast to the LORD."

6 So the next day they rose early and offered burnt offerings, and brought peace offerings; and the people sat down to eat and to drink, and rose up to play.

7 Then the LORD spoke to Moses, "Go down at once, for your people, whom you brought up from the land of Egypt, have corrupted *themselves.*

LIFE LESSONS

➤ **Exodus 31:18 —** *He gave Moses the two tablets of the testimony, tablets of stone, written by the finger of God.*

Since God does not want His people to wonder what He has said, He has committed His words to written form. We can depend upon His Word, no matter what happens around us.

WHAT THE BIBLE SAYS ABOUT ◉

How God Speaks to Us

Exodus 31:18

*T*hrough the ages, God has used a variety of ways to speak to His people. He spoke directly with Adam and Eve in the Garden of Eden, meeting them in the cool of the day (Gen. 3:8). But after they were expelled from the garden because of their disobedience, He turned to other forms of communication. These forms have included direct revelation, dreams and visions, the words of prophets, and others. Today, God's primary (though not only) form of communication with His people is His written Word, the Bible. However, He will also use the circumstances of life to teach us His principles, as well as the wise and godly counsel of men and women whose lives are committed to Him. He also speaks to us through the presence of His Spirit within us: The Holy Spirit bears witness to God's truth.

We read in Exodus 31:18: "When He had finished speaking with him upon Mount Sinai, He gave Moses the two tablets of the testimony, tablets of stone, written by the finger of God."

God has always placed great value on the written Word. In fact, the Hebrew people were among the first on earth to have an alphabet that allowed them to record documents. The reading of the Torah (the first five books of the Old Testament) has remained a mainstay in synagogue services through the centuries.

The early church received God's counsel through both spoken and written means. The Gospel accounts document the life and words of Jesus, while much of the rest of the New Testament consists of letters from the apostles to various groups of believers.

Why such confidence in the Bible? Because the Word of God is His inspired, living, and active message to His people (Heb. 4:12). We read in 2 Timothy 3:16, 17: "All Scripture is inspired by God and profitable for teaching, for reproof, for correction, for training in righteousness; so that ??the man of God may be adequate, equipped for every good work."

The psalmist acknowledged the importance of knowing and obeying the Word of God when he wrote, "Your word is a lamp to my feet and a light to my path" (Ps. 119:105). Centuries later, the apostle Paul referred to the written Word as a weapon to be used in spiritual battle: "Take the . . . sword of the Spirit, which is the word of God" (Eph. 6:17). God's Word really is an immovable anchor in times of storm—and it's through the inspiration of His Spirit and Scripture that He actively communicates with us today. ◉

---

8 "They have quickly turned aside from the way which I commanded them. They have made for themselves a molten calf, and have worshiped it and have sacrificed to it and said, 'This is your god, O Israel, who brought you up from the land of Egypt!'"

9 The LORD said to Moses, "I have seen this people, and behold, they are an obstinate people.

10 "Now then let Me alone, that My anger may burn against them and that I may destroy them; and I will make of you a great nation."

11 Then Moses entreated the LORD his God, and said, "O LORD, why does Your anger burn against Your people whom You have brought out from the land of Egypt with great power and with a mighty hand?

12 "Why should the Egyptians speak, saying, 'With evil *intent* He brought them out to kill them in the mountains and to destroy them from the face of the earth'? Turn from Your burning anger and change Your mind about *doing* harm to Your people.

13 "Remember Abraham, Isaac, and Israel, Your servants to whom You swore by Yourself, and said to them, 'I will

---

LIFE LESSONS

➤ **Exodus 32:13** — *"Remember Abraham, Isaac, and Israel, Your servants to whom You swore by Yourself."*

*P*owerful prayer finds its support in the promises of God. When we base our prayers on what God has pledged Himself to do, we stand on unshakable ground.

multiply your descendants as the stars of the heavens, and all this land of which I have spoken I will give to your descendants, and they shall inherit *it* forever.'"

14 So the LORD changed His mind about the harm which He said He would do to His people.

15 Then Moses turned and went down from the mountain with the two tablets of the testimony in his hand, tablets which were written on both sides; they were written on one *side* and the other.

16 The tablets were God's work, and the writing was God's writing engraved on the tablets.

17 Now when Joshua heard the sound of the people as they shouted, he said to Moses, "There is a sound of war in the camp."

18 But he said,

"It is not the sound of the cry of
　　triumph,
Nor is it the sound of the cry of
　　defeat;
But the sound of singing I hear."

19 It came about, as soon as Moses came near the camp, that he saw the calf and *the* dancing; and Moses' anger burned, and he threw the tablets from his hands and shattered them at the foot of the mountain.

20 He took the calf which they had made and burned *it* with fire, and ground it to powder, and scattered it over the surface of the water and made the sons of Israel drink *it*.

21 Then Moses said to Aaron, "What did this people do to you, that you have brought *such* great sin upon them?"

22 Aaron said, "Do not let the anger of my lord burn; you know the people yourself, that they are prone to evil.

23 "For they said to me, 'Make a god for us who will go before us; for this Moses, the man who brought us up from the land of Egypt, we do not know what has become of him.'

24 "I said to them, 'Whoever has any gold, let them tear it off.' So they gave *it* to me, and I threw it into the fire, and out came this calf."

25 Now when Moses saw that the people were out of control—for Aaron had let them get out of control to be a derision among their enemies—

26 then Moses stood in the gate of the camp, and said, "Whoever is for the LORD, *come* to me!" And all the sons of Levi gathered together to him.

27 He said to them, "Thus says the LORD, the God of Israel, 'Every man *of* you put his sword upon his thigh, and go back and forth from gate to gate in the camp, and kill every man his brother, and every man his friend, and every man his neighbor.'"

28 So the sons of Levi did as Moses instructed, and about three thousand men of the people fell that day.

29 Then Moses said, "Dedicate yourselves today to the LORD—for every man has been against his son and against his brother—in order that He may bestow a blessing upon you today."

30 On the next day Moses said to the people, "You yourselves have committed a great sin; and now I am going up to the LORD, perhaps I can make atonement for your sin."

31 Then Moses returned to the LORD, and said, "Alas, this people has committed a great sin, and they have made a god of gold for themselves!

32 "But now, if You will, forgive their sin—and if not, please blot me out from Your book which You have written!"

33 The LORD said to Moses, "Whoever has sinned against Me, I will blot him out of My book.

34 "But go now, lead the people where I told you. Behold, My angel shall go before you; nevertheless in the day when I punish, I will punish them for their sin."

35 Then the LORD smote the people, because of what they did with the calf which Aaron had made.

LIFE LESSONS

➤ **Exodus 32:34 — *"I will punish them for their sin."***

*G*od forgives sin and wickedness when we repent and come to Him in faith, but He does not always prevent us from experiencing the consequences of our wicked behavior.

◈　**Psalm 21:1–7**

For the choir director. A Psalm of David.

21 O LORD, in Your strength the king
　　will be glad,

And in Your salvation how greatly
he will rejoice!

2 You have given him his heart's
desire,
And You have not withheld the
request of his lips.   Selah.

3 For You meet him with the
blessings of good things;
You set a crown of fine gold on his
head.

4 He asked life of You,
You gave it to him,
Length of days forever and ever.

5 His glory is great through Your
salvation,
Splendor and majesty You place
upon him.

➤ 6 For You make him most blessed
forever;
✳ You make him joyful with gladness
in Your presence.

7 For the king trusts in the LORD,
And through the lovingkindness
of the Most High he will not be
shaken.

◉ Proverbs 7:24–27

24 Now therefore, *my* sons, listen to
me,
And pay attention to the words of
my mouth.

25 Do not let your heart turn aside to
her ways,
Do not stray into her paths.

26 For many are the victims she has
cast down,
And numerous are all her slain.

27 Her house is the way to Sheol,
Descending to the chambers of
death.

◉ Matthew 25:31–46

31 "But when the Son of Man comes in
His glory, and all the angels with Him,
then He will sit on His glorious throne.

32 "All the nations will be gathered
before Him; and He will separate them
from one another, as the shepherd separates the sheep from the goats;

33 and He will put the sheep on His
right, and the goats on the left.

34 "Then the King will say to those on ⊰
His right, 'Come, you who are blessed of ✳
My Father, inherit the kingdom prepared
for you from the foundation of the world.

35 'For I was hungry, and you gave Me
something to eat; I was thirsty, and you
gave Me *something* to drink; I was a
stranger, and you invited Me in;

36 naked, and you clothed Me; I was
sick, and you visited Me; I was in prison,
and you came to Me.'

37 "Then the righteous will answer
Him, 'Lord, when did we see You hun-
gry, and feed You, or thirsty, and give
You *something* to drink?

38 'And when did we see You a stranger,
and invite You in, or naked, and clothe
You?

39 'When did we see You sick, or in
prison, and come to You?'

40 "The King will answer and say to
them, 'Truly I say to you, to the extent
that you did it to one of these brothers of
Mine, *even* the least *of them*, you did it to
Me.'

41 "Then He will also say to those on
His left, 'Depart from Me, accursed ones,
into the eternal fire which has been prepared for the devil and his angels;

42 for I was hungry, and you gave Me
nothing to eat; I was thirsty, and you
gave Me nothing to drink;

LIFE LESSONS

➤ **Psalm 21:6 —** *You make him most
blessed forever; you make him joyful with
gladness in Your presence.*

*G*od invites us to ask Him for things, but
even the things He gives us will never
make us happy; only His presence can do
that. The deepest delights are found only
in Him, not in any of His gifts.

➤ **Matthew 25:34 —** *"Come, you who are
blessed of My Father, inherit the kingdom
prepared for you from the foundation of
the world."*

*J*ust as Jesus is "the Lamb who has
been slain" (Rev. 13:8), so has the
coming kingdom been prepared for God's
people "from the foundation of the
world". His plan is as ancient as it is sure.

43 I was a stranger, and you did not invite Me in; naked, and you did not clothe Me; sick, and in prison, and you did not visit Me.'

44 "Then they themselves also will answer, 'Lord, when did we see You hungry, or thirsty, or a stranger, or naked, or sick, or in prison, and did not take care of You?'

45 "Then He will answer them, 'Truly I say to you, to the extent that you did not do it to one of the least of these, you did not do it to Me.'

➤ 46 "These will go away into eternal punishment, but the righteous into eternal life."

LIFE LESSONS

➤ **Matthew 25:46 — *"These will go away into eternal punishment, but the righteous into eternal life."***

*W*hat we do with the good news of Christ has enormous consequences. The punishment of those who reject Jesus is just as eternal as the reward of those who serve Him.

FEBRUARY 11

◈ Exodus 33:1—34:35

33 THEN the LORD spoke to Moses, "Depart, go up from here, you and the people whom you have brought up from the land of Egypt, to the land of which I swore to Abraham, Isaac, and Jacob, saying, 'To your descendants I will give it.'

2 "I will send an angel before you and I will drive out the Canaanite, the Amorite, the Hittite, the Perizzite, the Hivite and the Jebusite.

3 *"Go up* to a land flowing with milk and honey; for I will not go up in your midst, because you are an obstinate people, and I might destroy you on the way."

4 When the people heard this sad word, they went into mourning, and none of them put on his ornaments.

5 For the LORD had said to Moses, "Say to the sons of Israel, 'You are an obstinate people; should I go up in your midst for one moment, I would destroy you. Now therefore, put off your ornaments from you, that I may know what I shall do with you.'"

6 So the sons of Israel stripped themselves of their ornaments, from Mount Horeb *onward.*

7 Now Moses used to take the tent and pitch it outside the camp, a good distance from the camp, and he called it the tent of meeting. And everyone who sought the LORD would go out to the tent of meeting which was outside the camp.

8 And it came about, whenever Moses went out to the tent, that all the people would arise and stand, each at the entrance of his tent, and gaze after Moses until he entered the tent.

9 Whenever Moses entered the tent, the pillar of cloud would descend and stand at the entrance of the tent; and the LORD would speak with Moses.

10 When all the people saw the pillar of cloud standing at the entrance of the tent, all the people would arise and worship, each at the entrance of his tent.

11 Thus the LORD used to speak to Moses face to face, just as a man speaks to his friend. When Moses returned to the camp, his servant Joshua, the son of Nun, a young man, would not depart from the tent.

12 Then Moses said to the LORD, "See, You say to me, 'Bring up this people!' But You Yourself have not let me know whom You will send with me. Moreover, You have said, 'I have known you by name, and you have also found favor in My sight.'

13 "Now therefore, I pray You, if I have found favor in Your sight, let me know Your ways that I may know You, so that I may find favor in Your sight. Consider too, that this nation is Your people."

14 And He said, "My presence shall go *with you,* and I will give you rest."

15 Then he said to Him, "If Your presence does not go *with us,* do not lead us up from here.

Life Examples:

Intimacy Through Obedience

EXODUS 33:7–11

*M*oses was one of the few people known for his intimacy with God. His pathway to knowing God was his extraordinary obedience. Moses risked everything to follow God's commands. He left the safe life of a Midianite farmer to face the dangers of freeing the people of Israel.

Yet Moses trusted God and was able to witness His almighty hand in action. As Moses obeyed God's will, he beheld the ten plagues, parted sea, escape from Egypt, manna from heaven, water from a stone, and God's presence in the tabernacle. Through every act, he knew God more intimately.

Exodus 33:11 teaches, "The Lord used to speak to Moses face to face, just as a man speaks to his friend." Through his obedience, Moses learned to trust the heart of the Creator. He learned to talk to God as a friend because he saw God in a way few ever see Him.

Ugolino of Montegiorgio wrote, "Let no man deem himself the perfect friend of God until he has passed through many temptations and tribulations . . . I am ready to endure patiently all things that my Lord would do with me."

When you obey God, He is able to reveal Himself to you in a more personal way. He is able to prepare you to know Him and experience deep intimacy with Him. Are you willing to endure patiently all things that your Lord would do with you? Will you be His friend?

---

16 "For how then can it be known that I have found favor in Your sight, I and Your people? Is it not by Your going with us, so that we, I and Your people, may be distinguished from all the *other* people who are upon the face of the earth?"

17 The LORD said to Moses, "I will also do this thing of which you have spoken; for you have found favor in My sight and I have known you by name."

18 Then Moses said, "I pray You, show me Your glory!"

➤ 19 And He said, "I Myself will make all My goodness pass before you, and will proclaim the name of the LORD before you; and I will be gracious to whom I will be gracious, and will show compassion on whom I will show compassion."

20 But He said, "You cannot see My face, for no man can see Me and live!"

21 Then the LORD said, "Behold, there is a place by Me, and you shall stand *there* on the rock;

22 and it will come about, while My glory is passing by, that I will put you in the cleft of the rock and cover you with My hand until I have passed by.

23 "Then I will take My hand away and you shall see My back, but My face shall not be seen."

34 NOW the LORD said to Moses, "Cut out for yourself two stone tablets like the former ones, and I will write on the tablets the words that were on the former tablets which you shattered.

LIFE LESSONS

➤ **Exodus 33:13 — "If I have found favor in Your sight, let me know Your ways that I may know You."**

*A*s children of God, we have received the Lord's unmerited and unending favor. But as we get to know Him better through such things as prayer, fasting, and study of His Word, He extends us even more favor! Nothing comforts and empowers us more than knowing God promises to grant our requests—and He knows each of us personally and by name.

➤ **Exodus 33:19 — "I will be gracious to whom I will be gracious, and will show compassion on whom I will show compassion."**

*T*he Father consistently reveals Himself as a God of grace and compassion—something that greatly comforts us during difficult times or when we sin or make errors in judgment. It's a promise we can always count on.

2 "So be ready by morning, and come up in the morning to Mount Sinai, and present yourself there to Me on the top of the mountain.

3 "No man is to come up with you, nor let any man be seen anywhere on the mountain; even the flocks and the herds may not graze in front of that mountain."

4 So he cut out two stone tablets like the former ones, and Moses rose up early in the morning and went up to Mount Sinai, as the LORD had commanded him, and he took two stone tablets in his hand.

5 The LORD descended in the cloud and stood there with him as he called upon the name of the LORD.

6 Then the LORD passed by in front of him and proclaimed, "The LORD, the LORD God, compassionate and gracious, slow to anger, and abounding in lovingkindness and truth;

7 who keeps lovingkindness for thousands, who forgives iniquity, transgression and sin; yet He will by no means leave the guilty unpunished, visiting the iniquity of fathers on the children and on the grandchildren to the third and fourth generations."

8 Moses made haste to bow low toward the earth and worship.

➤ 9 He said, "If now I have found favor in Your sight, O Lord, I pray, let the Lord go along in our midst, even though the people are so obstinate, and pardon our iniquity and our sin, and take us as Your own possession."

10 Then God said, "Behold, I am going to make a covenant. Before all your people I will perform miracles which have not been produced in all the earth nor among any of the nations; and all the people among whom you live will see the working of the LORD, for it is a fearful thing that I am going to perform with you.

11 "Be sure to observe what I am commanding you this day: behold, I am going to drive out the Amorite before you, and the Canaanite, the Hittite, the Perizzite, the Hivite and the Jebusite.

12 "Watch yourself that you make no covenant with the inhabitants of the land into which you are going, or it will become a snare in your midst.

13 "But rather, you are to tear down their altars and smash their sacred pillars and cut down their Asherim

14 —for you shall not worship any ◄ other god, for the LORD, whose name is Jealous, is a jealous God—

15 otherwise you might make a covenant with the inhabitants of the land and they would play the harlot with their gods and sacrifice to their gods, and someone might invite you to eat of his sacrifice,

16 and you might take some of his daughters for your sons, and his daughters might play the harlot with their gods and cause your sons also to play the harlot with their gods.

17 "You shall make for yourself no molten gods.

18 "You shall observe the Feast of Unleavened Bread. For seven days you are to eat unleavened bread, as I commanded you, at the appointed time in the month of Abib, for in the month of Abib you came out of Egypt.

19 "The first offspring from every womb belongs to Me, and all your male livestock, the first offspring from cattle and sheep.

LIFE LESSONS

➤ **Exodus 34:9** — *"Lord, I pray, let the Lord go along in our midst, even though the people are so obstinate, and pardon our iniquity and our sin, and take us as Your own possession."*

*O*nly by grace has anyone ever been able to establish, develop, and enjoy an intimate relationship with the God of glory. Moses and his people could not earn His favor, and we cannot either. All of our efforts will always fall short. Thankfully, we don't have to work for God's acceptance; He gives His love freely to us (Eph. 2:8, 9).

➤ **Exodus 34:14** — *"For you shall not worship any other god, for the LORD, whose name is Jealous, is a jealous God."*

*T*he Lord made us for a relationship with Himself, and He will never stand idly by while a rival tries to replace Him in our hearts. Giving our hearts to anyone else arouses His jealousy—a dangerous proposition (1 Cor. 10:22).

20 "You shall redeem with a lamb the first offspring from a donkey; and if you do not redeem *it*, then you shall break its neck. You shall redeem all the firstborn of your sons. None shall appear before Me empty-handed.
21 "You shall work six days, but on the seventh day you shall rest; *even* during plowing time and harvest you shall rest.
22 "You shall celebrate the Feast of Weeks, *that is*, the first fruits of the wheat harvest, and the Feast of Ingathering at the turn of the year.
23 "Three times a year all your males are to appear before the Lord God, the God of Israel.
24 "For I will drive out nations before you and enlarge your borders, and no man shall covet your land when you go up three times a year to appear before the Lord your God.
25 "You shall not offer the blood of My sacrifice with leavened bread, nor is the sacrifice of the Feast of the Passover to be left over until morning.
26 "You shall bring the very first of the first fruits of your soil into the house of the Lord your God.
"You shall not boil a young goat in its mother's milk."
27 Then the Lord said to Moses, "Write down these words, for in accordance with these words I have made a covenant with you and with Israel."
28 So he was there with the Lord forty days and forty nights; he did not eat bread or drink water. And he wrote on the tablets the words of the covenant, the Ten Commandments.
29 It came about when Moses was coming down from Mount Sinai (and the two tablets of the testimony *were* in Moses' hand as he was coming down from the mountain), that Moses did not know that the skin of his face shone because of his speaking with Him.
30 So when Aaron and all the sons of Israel saw Moses, behold, the skin of his face shone, and they were afraid to come near him.
31 Then Moses called to them, and Aaron and all the rulers in the congregation returned to him; and Moses spoke to them.
32 Afterward all the sons of Israel came near, and he commanded them *to do*

everything that the Lord had spoken to him on Mount Sinai.
33 When Moses had finished speaking with them, he put a veil over his face.
34 But whenever Moses went in before the Lord to speak with Him, he would take off the veil until he came out; and whenever he came out and spoke to the sons of Israel what he had been commanded,
35 the sons of Israel would see the face of Moses, that the skin of Moses' face shone. So Moses would replace the veil over his face until he went in to speak with Him.

Psalm 21:8–13

8   Your hand will find out all your
        enemies;
    Your right hand will find out those
        who hate you.
9   You will make them as a fiery oven
        in the time of your anger;
    The Lord will swallow them up in
        His wrath,
    And fire will devour them.
10 Their offspring You will destroy
        from the earth,
    And their descendants from among
        the sons of men.
11 Though they intended evil against
        You
    And devised a plot,
    They will not succeed.
12 For You will make them turn their
        back;
    You will aim with Your bowstrings
        at their faces.
13 Be exalted, O Lord, in Your
        strength;
    We will sing and praise Your
        power.

LIFE LESSONS

➤ **Psalm 21:8** — *Your hand will find out all your enemies; your right hand will find out those who hate you.*

*W*e can come to God in faith and receive His pardon and grace, or we can reject His offer of life and become His enemy. Those are the options.

✦ Proverbs 8:1–5

8 DOES not wisdom call,
And understanding lift up her
voice?
2 On top of the heights beside the
way,
Where the paths meet, she takes her
stand;
3 Beside the gates, at the opening to
the city,
At the entrance of the doors, she
cries out:
4 "To you, O men, I call,
And my voice is to the sons of men.
5 "O naive ones, understand
prudence;
And, O fools, understand wisdom.

✦ Matthew 26:1–25

26 WHEN Jesus had finished all these
words, He said to His disciples,
2 "You know that after two days the
Passover is coming, and the Son of Man
is to be handed over for crucifixion."
3 Then the chief priests and the elders
of the people were gathered together in
the court of the high priest, named Caiaphas;
4 and they plotted together to seize
Jesus by stealth and kill Him.
5 But they were saying, "Not during
the festival, otherwise a riot might occur
among the people."
6 Now when Jesus was in Bethany, at
the home of Simon the leper,
7 a woman came to Him with an alabaster vial of very costly perfume, and
she poured it on His head as He reclined
at the table.

LIFE LESSONS

➤ Matthew 26:13 — "Wherever this gospel is preached . . . what this woman has
done will also be spoken of in memory
of her."

The woman could not have known
what she did that day would be
memorialized in God's Word and distributed to the ends of the earth. God loves
to reward faithful devotion to Him.

---

8 But the disciples were indignant
when they saw this, and said, "Why this
waste?
9 "For this perfume might have been
sold for a high price and the money
given to the poor."
10 But Jesus, aware of this, said to
them, "Why do you bother the woman?
For she has done a good deed to Me.
11 "For you always have the poor with
you; but you do not always have Me.
12 "For when she poured this perfume
on My body, she did it to prepare Me for
burial.
13 "Truly I say to you, wherever this ◄
gospel is preached in the whole world,
what this woman has done will also be
spoken of in memory of her."
14 Then one of the twelve, named Judas
Iscariot, went to the chief priests
15 and said, "What are you willing to
give me to betray Him to you?" And they
weighed out thirty pieces of silver to him.
16 From then on he began looking for a
good opportunity to betray Jesus.
17 Now on the first day of Unleavened
Bread the disciples came to Jesus and
asked, "Where do You want us to prepare for You to eat the Passover?"
18 And He said, "Go into the city to
a certain man, and say to him, 'The
Teacher says, "My time is near; I am to
keep the Passover at your house with My
disciples."'"
19 The disciples did as Jesus had directed them; and they prepared the Passover.
20 Now when evening came, Jesus was
reclining at the table with the twelve
disciples.
21 As they were eating, He said, "Truly
I say to you that one of you will betray
Me."
22 Being deeply grieved, they each one
began to say to Him, "Surely not I,
Lord?"
23 And He answered, "He who dipped
his hand with Me in the bowl is the one
who will betray Me.
24 "The Son of Man is to go, just as it
is written of Him; but woe to that man
by whom the Son of Man is betrayed! It
would have been good for that man if he
had not been born."
25 And Judas, who was betraying Him,
said, "Surely it is not I, Rabbi?" Jesus
*said to him, "You have said it yourself."

Exodus 35:1—36:38

35 THEN Moses assembled all the congregation of the sons of Israel, and said to them, "These are the things that the LORD has commanded you to do:
2 "For six days work may be done, but on the seventh day you shall have a holy day, a sabbath of complete rest to the LORD; whoever does any work on it shall be put to death.
3 "You shall not kindle a fire in any of your dwellings on the sabbath day."
4 Moses spoke to all the congregation of the sons of Israel, saying, "This is the thing which the LORD has commanded, saying,
5 'Take from among you a contribution to the LORD; whoever is of a willing heart, let him bring it as the LORD's contribution: gold, silver, and bronze,
6 and blue, purple and scarlet material, fine linen, goats' hair,
7 and rams' skins dyed red, and porpoise skins, and acacia wood,
8 and oil for lighting, and spices for the anointing oil, and for the fragrant incense,
9 and onyx stones and setting stones for the ephod and for the breastpiece.
10 'Let every skillful man among you come, and make all that the LORD has commanded:
11 the tabernacle, its tent and its covering, its hooks and its boards, its bars, its pillars, and its sockets;
12 the ark and its poles, the mercy seat, and the curtain of the screen;
13 the table and its poles, and all its utensils, and the bread of the Presence;
14 the lampstand also for the light and its utensils and its lamps and the oil for the light;
15 and the altar of incense and its poles, and the anointing oil and the fragrant incense, and the screen for the doorway at the entrance of the tabernacle;
16 the altar of burnt offering with its bronze grating, its poles, and all its utensils, the basin and its stand;
17 the hangings of the court, its pillars and its sockets, and the screen for the gate of the court;
18 the pegs of the tabernacle and the pegs of the court and their cords;
19 the woven garments for ministering in the holy place, the holy garments for Aaron the priest and the garments of his sons, to minister as priests.'"
20 Then all the congregation of the sons of Israel departed from Moses' presence.
21 Everyone whose heart stirred him and everyone whose spirit moved him came and brought the LORD's contribution for the work of the tent of meeting and for all its service and for the holy garments.
22 Then all whose hearts moved them, both men and women, came and brought brooches and earrings and signet rings and bracelets, all articles of gold; so did every man who presented an offering of gold to the LORD.
23 Every man, who had in his possession blue and purple and scarlet material and fine linen and goats' hair and rams' skins dyed red and porpoise skins, brought them.
24 Everyone who could make a contribution of silver and bronze brought the LORD's contribution; and every man who had in his possession acacia wood for any work of the service brought it.
25 All the skilled women spun with their hands, and brought what they had spun, in blue and purple and scarlet material and in fine linen.
26 All the women whose heart stirred with a skill spun the goats' hair.
27 The rulers brought the onyx stones and the stones for setting for the ephod and for the breastpiece;
28 and the spice and the oil for the light and for the anointing oil and for the fragrant incense.
29 The Israelites, all the men and women, whose heart moved them to bring material for all the work, which the LORD had commanded through Moses to be done, brought a freewill offering to the LORD.

LIFE LESSONS

➤ **Exodus 35:21 — *Everyone whose heart stirred him and everyone whose spirit moved him came and brought the Lord's contribution.***

*G*od loves cheerful, willing, and self-motivated giving because it demonstrates a genuine devotion to and a vibrant connection with Him. Regular giving breaks money's hold over us and deepens our devotion to the Lord.

30 Then Moses said to the sons of Israel, "See, the LORD has called by name Bezalel the son of Uri, the son of Hur, of the tribe of Judah.
31 "And He has filled him with the Spirit of God, in wisdom, in understanding and in knowledge and in all craftsmanship;
32 to make designs for working in gold and in silver and in bronze,
33 and in the cutting of stones for settings and in the carving of wood, so as to perform in every inventive work.
34 "He also has put in his heart to teach, both he and Oholiab, the son of Ahisamach, of the tribe of Dan.
35 "He has filled them with skill to perform every work of an engraver and of a designer and of an embroiderer, in blue and in purple *and* in scarlet *material*, and in fine linen, and of a weaver, as performers of every work and makers of designs.

➤ **36** "NOW Bezalel and Oholiab, and every skillful person in whom the LORD has put skill and understanding to know how to perform all the work in the construction of the sanctuary, shall perform in accordance with all that the LORD has commanded."
2 Then Moses called Bezalel and Oholiab and every skillful person in whom the LORD had put skill, everyone whose heart stirred him, to come to the work to perform it.
3 They received from Moses all the contributions which the sons of Israel had brought to perform the work in the construction of the sanctuary. And they still *continued* bringing to him freewill offerings every morning.
4 And all the skillful men who were performing all the work of the sanctuary

came, each from the work which he was performing,
5 and they said to Moses, "The people are bringing much more than enough for the construction work which the LORD commanded *us* to perform."
6 So Moses issued a command, and a proclamation was circulated throughout the camp, saying, "Let no man or woman any longer perform work for the contributions of the sanctuary." Thus the people were restrained from bringing *any more.*
7 For the material they had was sufficient and more than enough for all the work, to perform it.
8 All the skillful men among those who were performing the work made the tabernacle with ten curtains; of fine twisted linen and blue and purple and scarlet *material*, with cherubim, the work of a skillful workman, Bezalel made them.
9 The length of each curtain was twenty-eight cubits and the width of each curtain four cubits; all the curtains had the same measurements.
10 He joined five curtains to one another and *the other* five curtains he joined to one another.
11 He made loops of blue on the edge of the outermost curtain in the first set; he did likewise on the edge of the curtain that was outermost in the second set.
12 He made fifty loops in the one curtain and he made fifty loops on the edge of the curtain that was in the second set; the loops were opposite each other.
13 He made fifty clasps of gold and joined the curtains to one another with the clasps, so the tabernacle was a unit.
14 Then he made curtains of goats' *hair* for a tent over the tabernacle; he made eleven curtains in all.
15 The length of each curtain *was* thirty cubits and four cubits the width of each curtain; the eleven curtains had the same measurements.
16 He joined five curtains by themselves and *the other* six curtains by themselves.
17 Moreover, he made fifty loops on the edge of the curtain that was outermost in the *first* set, and he made fifty loops on the edge of the curtain *that was outermost in* the second set.
18 He made fifty clasps of bronze to

---

join the tent together so that it would be a unit.
19 He made a covering for the tent of rams' skins dyed red, and a covering of porpoise skins above.
20 Then he made the boards for the tabernacle of acacia wood, standing upright.
21 Ten cubits *was* the length of each board and one and a half cubits the width of each board.
22 *There were* two tenons for each board, fitted to one another; thus he did for all the boards of the tabernacle.
23 He made the boards for the tabernacle: twenty boards for the south side;
24 and he made forty sockets of silver under the twenty boards; two sockets under one board for its two tenons and two sockets under another board for its two tenons.
25 Then for the second side of the tabernacle, on the north side, he made twenty boards,
26 and their forty sockets of silver; two sockets under one board and two sockets under another board.
27 For the rear of the tabernacle, to the west, he made six boards.
28 He made two boards for the corners of the tabernacle at the rear.
29 They were double beneath, and together they were complete to its top to the first ring; thus he did with both of them for the two corners.
30 There were eight boards with their sockets of silver, sixteen sockets, two under every board.
31 Then he made bars of acacia wood, five for the boards of one side of the tabernacle,
32 and five bars for the boards of the other side of the tabernacle, and five bars for the boards of the tabernacle for the rear *side* to the west.
33 He made the middle bar to pass through in the center of the boards from end to end.
34 He overlaid the boards with gold and made their rings of gold *as* holders for the bars, and overlaid the bars with gold.
35 Moreover, he made the veil of blue and purple and scarlet *material*, and fine twisted linen; he made it with cherubim, the work of a skillful workman.
36 He made four pillars of acacia for it, and overlaid them with gold, with their

hooks of gold; and he cast four sockets of silver for them.
37 He made a screen for the doorway of the tent, of blue and purple and scarlet *material*, and fine twisted linen, the work of a weaver;
38 and *he made* its five pillars with their hooks, and he overlaid their tops and their bands with gold; but their five sockets were of bronze.

Psalm 22:1–8

For the choir director; upon Aijeleth Hashshahar. A Psalm of David.

22 MY God, my God, why have You forsaken me?
     Far from my deliverance are the words of my groaning.
2   O my God, I cry by day, but You do not answer;
     And by night, but I have no rest.
3   Yet You are holy,
     O You who are enthroned upon the praises of Israel.
4   In You our fathers trusted;
     They trusted and You delivered them.
5   To You they cried out and were delivered;
     In You they trusted and were not disappointed.
6   But I am a worm and not a man,
     A reproach of men and despised by the people.
7   All who see me sneer at me;
     They separate with the lip, they wag the head, *saying,*
8   "Commit *yourself* to the LORD; let Him deliver him;
     Let Him rescue him, because He delights in him."

LIFE LESSONS

➢ **Psalm 22:1 —** *My God, my God, why have You forsaken me? Far from my deliverance are the words of my groaning.*

*J*esus Christ knew more about feeling abandoned by God than we ever will—but in His case, it was more than a feeling. For a moment, God turned His back on His Son when He became sin for us (Matt. 27:46).

Proverbs 8:6–11

6 "Listen, for I will speak noble things;
    And the opening of my lips *will
    reveal* right things.

7 "For my mouth will utter truth;
    And wickedness is an abomination
    to my lips.

8 "All the utterances of my mouth are
    in righteousness;
    There is nothing crooked or
    perverted in them.

9 "They are all straightforward to him
    who understands,
    And right to those who find
    knowledge.

10 "Take my instruction and not silver,
    And knowledge rather than choicest
    gold.

11 "For wisdom is better than jewels;
    And all desirable things cannot
    compare with her.

Matthew 26:26–50

26 While they were eating, Jesus took *some* bread, and after a blessing, He broke *it* and gave *it* to the disciples, and said, "Take, eat; this is My body."
27 And when He had taken a cup and given thanks, He gave *it* to them, saying, "Drink from it, all of you;
28 for this is My blood of the covenant, which is poured out for many for forgiveness of sins.
29 "But I say to you, I will not drink of this fruit of the vine from now on until that day when I drink it new with you in My Father's kingdom."
30 After singing a hymn, they went out to the Mount of Olives.

31 Then Jesus *said to them, "You will all fall away because of Me this night, for it is written, 'I WILL STRIKE DOWN THE SHEPHERD, AND THE SHEEP OF THE FLOCK SHALL BE SCATTERED.'
32 "But after I have been raised, I will go ahead of you to Galilee."
33 But Peter said to Him, "*Even* though all may fall away because of You, I will never fall away."
34 Jesus said to him, "Truly I say to you that this *very* night, before a rooster crows, you will deny Me three times."
35 Peter *said to Him, "Even if I have to die with You, I will not deny You." All the disciples said the same thing too.
36 Then Jesus *came with them to a place called Gethsemane, and *said to His disciples, "Sit here while I go over there and pray."
37 And He took with Him Peter and the two sons of Zebedee, and began to be grieved and distressed.
38 Then He *said to them, "My soul is deeply grieved, to the point of death; remain here and keep watch with Me."
39 And He went a little beyond *them*, and fell on His face and prayed, saying, "My Father, if it is possible, let this cup pass from Me; yet not as I will, but as You will."
40 And He *came to the disciples and *found them sleeping, and *said to Peter, "So, you *men* could not keep watch with Me for one hour?
41 "Keep watching and praying that you may not enter into temptation; the spirit is willing, but the flesh is weak."
42 He went away again a second time and prayed, saying, "My Father, if this cannot pass away unless I drink it, Your will be done."
43 Again He came and found them sleeping, for their eyes were heavy.

LIFE LESSONS

➤ **Matthew 26:29 —** *"I will not drink of this fruit of the vine from now on until that day when I drink it new with you in My Father's kingdom."*

The Lord's Supper not only looks back to the sacrifice of Christ's death, it also looks ahead to His glorious reign. It both memorializes and anticipates the work of Christ and invites us to remember and celebrate.

➤ **Matthew 26:37 —** *He began to be grieved and distressed.*

Isaiah called the coming Messiah "a Man of sorrows and acquainted with grief" (Is. 53:3), and in the garden of Gethsemane, Jesus faced sorrow like He had never known. Truly, He "has been tempted in all things as we are" (Heb. 4:15).

Life Examples:

JESUS: Example or Sacrifice?

MATTHEW 26:39

Some believe Jesus came to show us how to live a good life—and to be sure, He *is* our example of righteousness. We are to become like Him. But that isn't the reason Jesus came. He came to earth so He could die a sacrificial, substitutionary, all-sufficient atoning death for your sins.

If Jesus had not come, there would be no crucifixion or resurrection. The New Testament consistently confronts us with this message: *Christ died for us.* Jesus came so you and I might have eternal life through the forgiveness He provides. But we must come to Him and confess our transgressions. When we do,

He saves us and removes the burden of our guilt and shame.

Accepting Him as your Savior is an act of faith and not of works. There is nothing you can do to earn salvation. It is a free gift He gives to those who come to Him seeking His mercy.

If you are looking for forgiveness on the basis of your pleas, promises, and performance, then you will remain in your sins. Only if you accept His sacrifice will you open yourself to receiving the fullness of God's life-giving Spirit. Take time right now to tell Him you need Him and you want to be set free from every sin preventing you from experiencing His best. When you do, your life will change. The burden of your heart will lift, and you will be free to experience the fullness of God's unconditional love.

---

44 And He left them again, and went away and prayed a third time, saying the same thing once more.
45 Then He *came to the disciples and *said to them, "Are you still sleeping and resting? Behold, the hour is at hand and the Son of Man is being betrayed into the hands of sinners.
46 "Get up, let us be going; behold, the one who betrays Me is at hand!"
47 While He was still speaking, behold, Judas, one of the twelve, came up accompanied by a large crowd with swords and clubs, *who came* from the chief priests and elders of the people.
48 Now he who was betraying Him gave them a sign, saying, "Whomever I kiss, He is the one; seize Him."
49 Immediately Judas went to Jesus and said, "Hail, Rabbi!" and kissed Him.
50 And Jesus said to him, "Friend, *do* what you have come for." Then they came and laid hands on Jesus and seized Him.

Exodus 37:1—38:31

37 NOW Bezalel made the ark of acacia wood; its length was two and a half cubits, and its width one and a half cubits, and its height one and a half cubits;
2 and he overlaid it with pure gold inside and out, and made a gold molding for it all around.
3 He cast four rings of gold for it on its four feet; even two rings on one side of it, and two rings on the other side of it.
4 He made poles of acacia wood and overlaid them with gold.
5 He put the poles into the rings on the sides of the ark, to carry it.

6 He made a mercy seat of pure gold, two and a half cubits long and one and a half cubits wide.
7 He made two cherubim of gold; he made them of hammered work at the two ends of the mercy seat;

LIFE LESSONS

➤ **Exodus 37:1 — *Now Bezalel made the ark of acacia wood.***

The ark of the covenant was essentially a wooden chest, covered with pure gold, containing the law of God. It disappears from the biblical record before the Babylonian captivity. Whether it was hidden or destroyed is not generally known.

8   one cherub at the one end and one cherub at the other end; he made the cherubim *of one piece* with the mercy seat at the two ends.

9   The cherubim had *their* wings spread upward, covering the mercy seat with their wings, with their faces toward each other; the faces of the cherubim were toward the mercy seat.

10   Then he made the table of acacia wood, two cubits long and a cubit wide and one and a half cubits high.

11   He overlaid it with pure gold, and made a gold molding for it all around.

12   He made a rim for it of a handbreadth all around, and made a gold molding for its rim all around.

13   He cast four gold rings for it and put the rings on the four corners that were on its four feet.

14   Close by the rim were the rings, the holders for the poles to carry the table.

15   He made the poles of acacia wood and overlaid them with gold, to carry the table.

16   He made the utensils which were on the table, its dishes and its pans and its bowls and its jars, with which to pour out drink offerings, of pure gold.

17   Then he made the lampstand of pure gold. He made the lampstand of hammered work, its base and its shaft; its cups, its bulbs and its flowers were *of one piece* with it.

18   There were six branches going out of its sides; three branches of the lampstand from the one side of it and three branches of the lampstand from the other side of it;

19   three cups shaped like almond *blossoms*, a bulb and a flower in one branch, and three cups shaped like almond *blossoms*, a bulb and a flower in the other branch—so for the six branches going out of the lampstand.

20   In the lampstand *there were* four cups shaped like almond *blossoms*, its bulbs and its flowers;

21   and a bulb was under the *first* pair of branches *coming* out of it, and a bulb under the *second* pair of branches *coming* out of it, and a bulb under the *third* pair of branches *coming* out of it, for the six branches coming out of the lampstand.

22   Their bulbs and their branches were *of one piece* with it; the whole of it *was* a single hammered work of pure gold.

23   He made its seven lamps with its snuffers and its trays of pure gold.

24   He made it and all its utensils from a talent of pure gold.

25   Then he made the altar of incense of acacia wood: a cubit long and a cubit wide, square, and two cubits high; its horns were *of one piece* with it.

26   He overlaid it with pure gold, its top and its sides all around, and its horns; and he made a gold molding for it all around.

27   He made two golden rings for it under its molding, on its two sides—on opposite sides—as holders for poles with which to carry it.

28   He made the poles of acacia wood and overlaid them with gold.

29   And he made the holy anointing oil and the pure, fragrant incense of spices, the work of a perfumer.

38 THEN he made the altar of burnt offering of acacia wood, five cubits long, and five cubits wide, square, and three cubits high.

2   He made its horns on its four corners, its horns being *of one piece* with it, and he overlaid it with bronze.

3   He made all the utensils of the altar, the pails and the shovels and the basins, the flesh hooks and the firepans; he made all its utensils of bronze.

4   He made for the altar a grating of bronze network beneath, under its ledge, reaching halfway up.

5   He cast four rings on the four ends of the bronze grating *as* holders for the poles.

6   He made the poles of acacia wood and overlaid them with bronze.

7   He inserted the poles into the rings on the sides of the altar, with which to carry it. He made it hollow with planks.

8   Moreover, he made the laver of bronze with its base of bronze, from the mirrors of the serving women who served at the doorway of the tent of meeting.

9   Then he made the court: for the south side the hangings of the court were of fine twisted linen, one hundred cubits;

10   their twenty pillars, and their twenty sockets, *made* of bronze; the hooks of the pillars and their bands *were* of silver.

11 For the north side *there were* one hundred cubits; their twenty pillars and their twenty sockets *were* of bronze, the hooks of the pillars and their bands *were* of silver.

12 For the west side *there were* hangings of fifty cubits *with* their ten pillars and their ten sockets; the hooks of the pillars and their bands *were* of silver.

13 For the east side fifty cubits.

14 The hangings for the *one* side *of the gate were* fifteen cubits, *with* their three pillars and their three sockets,

15 and so for the other side. On both sides of the gate of the court *were* hangings of fifteen cubits, *with* their three pillars and their three sockets.

16 All the hangings of the court all around *were* of fine twisted linen.

17 The sockets for the pillars *were* of bronze, the hooks of the pillars and their bands, of silver; and the overlaying of their tops, of silver, and all the pillars of the court were furnished with silver bands.

18 The screen of the gate of the court was the work of the weaver, of blue and purple and scarlet *material* and fine twisted linen. And the length *was* twenty cubits and the height *was* five cubits, corresponding to the hangings of the court.

19 Their four pillars and their four sockets *were* of bronze; their hooks *were* of silver, and the overlaying of their tops and their bands *were* of silver.

20 All the pegs of the tabernacle and of the court all around *were* of bronze.

➤ 21 This is the number of the things for the tabernacle, the tabernacle of the testimony, as they were numbered according to the command of Moses, for the service of the Levites, by the hand of Ithamar the son of Aaron the priest.

22 Now Bezalel the son of Uri, the son of Hur, of the tribe of Judah, made all that the LORD had commanded Moses.

23 With him *was* Oholiab the son of Ahisamach, of the tribe of Dan, an engraver and a skillful workman and a weaver in blue and in purple and in scarlet *material*, and fine linen.

24 All the gold that was used for the work, in all the work of the sanctuary, even the gold of the wave offering, was 29 talents and 730 shekels, according to the shekel of the sanctuary.

25 The silver of those of the congregation who were numbered was 100 talents and 1,775 shekels, according to the shekel of the sanctuary;

26 a beka a head (*that is,* half a shekel according to the shekel of the sanctuary), for each one who passed over to those who were numbered, from twenty years old and upward, for 603,550 men.

27 The hundred talents of silver were for casting the sockets of the sanctuary and the sockets of the veil; one hundred sockets for the hundred talents, a talent for a socket.

28 Of the 1,775 *shekels,* he made hooks for the pillars and overlaid their tops and made bands for them.

29 The bronze of the wave offering was 70 talents and 2,400 shekels.

30 With it he made the sockets to the doorway of the tent of meeting, and the bronze altar and its bronze grating, and all the utensils of the altar,

31 and the sockets of the court all around and the sockets of the gate of the court, and all the pegs of the tabernacle and all the pegs of the court all around.

Psalm 22:9–15

9   Yet You are He who brought me
        forth from the womb;
     You made me trust *when* upon my
        mother's breasts.
10   Upon You I was cast from birth;
     You have been my God from my
        mother's womb.
11   Be not far from me, for trouble is
        near;
     For there is none to help.
12   Many bulls have surrounded me;

LIFE LESSONS

➤ **Exodus 38:21 — *This is the number of the things for the tabernacle, the tabernacle of the testimony, as they were numbered according to the command of Moses.***

*G*od has always taken an acute interest in the offerings, gifts, and items of material worth that help His people to effectively worship in a corporate setting. Jesus carefully observed what went into the temple treasury (Mark 12:41).

Strong *bulls* of Bashan have encircled me.

13 They open wide their mouth at me,
As a ravening and a roaring lion.

14 I am poured out like water,
And all my bones are out of joint;
My heart is like wax;
It is melted within me.

15 My strength is dried up like a potsherd,
And my tongue cleaves to my jaws;
And You lay me in the dust of death.

Proverbs 8:12–21

12 "I, wisdom, dwell with prudence,
And I find knowledge *and* discretion.

13 "The fear of the LORD is to hate evil;
Pride and arrogance and the evil way
And the perverted mouth, I hate.

14 "Counsel is mine and sound wisdom;
I am understanding, power is mine.

15 "By me kings reign,
And rulers decree justice.

16 "By me princes rule, and nobles,
All who judge rightly.

17 "I love those who love me;
And those who diligently seek me will find me.

18 "Riches and honor are with me,
Enduring wealth and righteousness.

19 "My fruit is better than gold, even pure gold,
And my yield *better* than choicest silver.

20 "I walk in the way of righteousness,
In the midst of the paths of justice,

21 To endow those who love me with wealth,
That I may fill their treasuries.

LIFE LESSONS

➤ **Proverbs 8:13 — *The fear of the LORD is to hate evil.***

*A*s we grow spiritually, we gradually change our reaction to sin. At first, we struggle to stop ourselves from engaging in the evil behavior we enjoy. However, we eventually grow to the point where we actually hate the evil behavior and no longer want to do it.

Matthew 26:51–75

51 And behold, one of those who were with Jesus reached and drew out his sword, and struck the slave of the high priest and cut off his ear.

52 Then Jesus *said to him, "Put your sword back into its place; for all those who take up the sword shall perish by the sword.

53 "Or do you think that I cannot appeal to My Father, and He will at once put at My disposal more than twelve legions of angels?

54 "How then will the Scriptures be fulfilled, *which say* that it must happen this way?"

55 At that time Jesus said to the crowds, "Have you come out with swords and clubs to arrest Me as *you would* against a robber? Every day I used to sit in the temple teaching and you did not seize Me.

56 "But all this has taken place to fulfill the Scriptures of the prophets." Then all the disciples left Him and fled.

57 Those who had seized Jesus led Him away to Caiaphas, the high priest, where the scribes and the elders were gathered together.

58 But Peter was following Him at a distance as far as the courtyard of the high priest, and entered in, and sat down with the officers to see the outcome.

59 Now the chief priests and the whole Council kept trying to obtain false testimony against Jesus, so that they might put Him to death.

60 They did not find *any*, even though many false witnesses came forward. But later on two came forward,

61 and said, "This man stated, 'I am able to destroy the temple of God and to rebuild it in three days.'"

62 The high priest stood up and said to Him, "Do You not answer? What is it that these men are testifying against You?"

63 But Jesus kept silent. And the high priest said to Him, "I adjure You by the living God, that You tell us whether You are the Christ, the Son of God."

64 Jesus *said to him, "You have said it *yourself*; nevertheless I tell you, hereafter you will see THE SON OF MAN SITTING AT THE RIGHT HAND OF POWER, and COMING ON THE CLOUDS OF HEAVEN."

65 Then the high priest tore his robes

and said, "He has blasphemed! What further need do we have of witnesses? Behold, you have now heard the blasphemy;
66 what do you think?" They answered, "He deserves death!"
67 Then they spat in His face and beat Him with their fists; and others slapped Him,
68 and said, "Prophesy to us, You Christ; who is the one who hit You?"
69 Now Peter was sitting outside in the courtyard, and a servant-girl came to him and said, "You too were with Jesus the Galilean."
70 But he denied it before them all, saying, "I do not know what you are talking about."

71 When he had gone out to the gateway, another *servant-girl* saw him and *said to those who were there, "This man was with Jesus of Nazareth."
72 And again he denied it with an oath, "I do not know the man."
73 A little later the bystanders came up and said to Peter, "Surely you too are *one* of them; for even the way you talk gives you away."
74 Then he began to curse and swear, "I do not know the man!" And immediately a rooster crowed.
75 And Peter remembered the word which Jesus had said, "Before a rooster crows, you will deny Me three times." And he went out and wept bitterly.

Life Examples:

Denying Christ

MATTHEW 26:69–75

*W*hen we read about Peter's denials of Christ, we may be tempted to feel a little self-righteous. After all, Peter walked with Christ for three years. How could he possibly refuse his Friend and Rabbi? How could he turn away from the one he called "the Christ, the Son of the living God" (Matt. 16:16)? True, the situation was very tense, and we can understand why Peter would be fearful. Yet he completely disavowed knowing the Lord Jesus. His denial strikes us as wrong to the very core of our being. We're sure we would never deny our Savior in such a terrible way.

Before we condemn Peter's actions, we must take a long look at ourselves. How often do we doubt God will help us in a difficult situation? How often do we avoid the subject of religion so we will not have to tell people we're Christians? How often do we indulge in sins that are clearly prohibited in God's Word? Though Peter denied Christ in a way that was loud and public, we may deny Christ in hundreds of smaller ways every day. We must ask ourselves: How often do I deny Christ's existence in my own life?

We know Peter was devastated by his actions (Matt. 26:75). We also know that later he would completely change his attitude about being Christ's representative. In 1 Peter 4:14, 16 he tells us, "If you are reviled for the name of Christ, you are blessed, because the Spirit of glory and of God rests on you . . . If anyone suffers as a Christian, he is not to be ashamed, but is to glorify God in this name." Peter rejoiced that he was "considered worthy to suffer shame for His name" (Acts 5:41).

We must also allow the Holy Spirit to make that change in us. We must come to the place where Christ comes first in every area of our lives—no matter what the consequences.

Are you there, friend? Or will you continue to deny Christ with your actions? Like Peter, you must make your choice. The Savior is waiting.

Exodus 39:1—40:38

39 MOREOVER, from the blue and purple and scarlet *material*, they made finely woven garments for ministering in the holy place as well as the holy garments which were for Aaron, just as the LORD had commanded Moses.

2 He made the ephod of gold, *and* of blue and purple and scarlet *material*, and fine twisted linen.
3 Then they hammered out gold sheets and cut *them* into threads to be woven in *with* the blue and the purple and the scarlet *material*, and the fine linen, the work of a skillful workman.
4 They made attaching shoulder pieces

for the ephod; it was attached at its two *upper* ends.

5   The skillfully woven band which was on it was like its workmanship, of the same material: of gold *and* of blue and purple and scarlet *material*, and fine twisted linen, just as the LORD had commanded Moses.

6   They made the onyx stones, set in gold filigree *settings;* they were engraved *like* the engravings of a signet, according to the names of the sons of Israel.

7   And he placed them on the shoulder pieces of the ephod, *as* memorial stones for the sons of Israel, just as the LORD had commanded Moses.

8   He made the breastpiece, the work of a skillful workman, like the workmanship of the ephod: of gold *and* of blue and purple and scarlet *material* and fine twisted linen.

9   It was square; they made the breastpiece folded double, a span long and a span wide when folded double.

10   And they mounted four rows of stones on it. The first row *was* a row of ruby, topaz, and emerald;

11   and the second row, a turquoise, a sapphire and a diamond;

12   and the third row, a jacinth, an agate, and an amethyst;

13   and the fourth row, a beryl, an onyx, and a jasper. They were set in gold filigree *settings* when they were mounted.

14   The stones were corresponding to the names of the sons of Israel; they were twelve, corresponding to their names, *engraved with* the engravings of a signet, each with its name for the twelve tribes.

15   They made on the breastpiece chains like cords, of twisted cordage work in pure gold.

16   They made two gold filigree *settings* and two gold rings, and put the two rings on the two ends of the breastpiece.

17   Then they put the two gold cords in the two rings at the ends of the breastpiece.

18   They put the *other* two ends of the two cords on the two filigree *settings*, and put them on the shoulder pieces of the ephod at the front of it.

19   They made two gold rings and placed *them* on the two ends of the breastpiece, on its inner edge which was next to the ephod.

20   Furthermore, they made two gold rings and placed them on the bottom of the two shoulder pieces of the ephod, on the front of it, close to the place where it joined, above the woven band of the ephod.

21   They bound the breastpiece by its rings to the rings of the ephod with a blue cord, so that it would be on the woven band of the ephod, and that the breastpiece would not come loose from the ephod, just as the LORD had commanded Moses.

22   Then he made the robe of the ephod of woven work, all of blue;

23   and the opening of the robe was *at the top* in the center, as the opening of a coat of mail, with a binding all around its opening, so that it would not be torn.

24   They made pomegranates of blue and purple and scarlet *material and* twisted *linen* on the hem of the robe.

25   They also made bells of pure gold, and put the bells between the pomegranates all around on the hem of the robe,

26   alternating a bell and a pomegranate all around on the hem of the robe for the service, just as the LORD had commanded Moses.

27   They made the tunics of finely woven linen for Aaron and his sons,

28   and the turban of fine linen, and the decorated caps of fine linen, and the linen breeches of fine twisted linen,

29   and the sash of fine twisted linen, and blue and purple and scarlet *material*, the work of the weaver, just as the LORD had commanded Moses.

30   They made the plate of the holy crown of pure gold, and inscribed it like the engravings of a signet, "Holy to the LORD."

31   They fastened a blue cord to it, to fasten it on the turban above, just as the LORD had commanded Moses.

32   Thus all the work of the tabernacle of the tent of meeting was completed; and the sons of Israel did according to all that the LORD had commanded Moses; so they did.

33   They brought the tabernacle to Moses, the tent and all its furnishings: its clasps, its boards, its bars, and its pillars and its sockets;

34   and the covering of rams' skins dyed red, and the covering of porpoise skins, and the screening veil;

35   the ark of the testimony and its poles and the mercy seat;

36 the table, all its utensils, and the bread of the Presence;

37 the pure *gold* lampstand, with its arrangement of lamps and all its utensils, and the oil for the light;

38 and the gold altar, and the anointing oil and the fragrant incense, and the veil for the doorway of the tent;

39 the bronze altar and its bronze grating, its poles and all its utensils, the laver and its stand;

40 the hangings for the court, its pillars and its sockets, and the screen for the gate of the court, its cords and its pegs and all the equipment for the service of the tabernacle, for the tent of meeting;

41 the woven garments for ministering in the holy place and the holy garments for Aaron the priest and the garments of his sons, to minister as priests.

➤ 42 So the sons of Israel did all the work according to all that the LORD had commanded Moses.

43 And Moses examined all the work and behold, they had done it; just as the LORD had commanded, this they had done. So Moses blessed them.

40 THEN the LORD spoke to Moses, saying,

2 "On the first day of the first month you shall set up the tabernacle of the tent of meeting.

3 "You shall place the ark of the testimony there, and you shall screen the ark with the veil.

4 "You shall bring in the table and arrange what belongs on it; and you shall bring in the lampstand and mount its lamps.

5 "Moreover, you shall set the gold altar of incense before the ark of the testimony, and set up the veil for the doorway to the tabernacle.

6 "You shall set the altar of burnt offering

in front of the doorway of the tabernacle of the tent of meeting.

7 "You shall set the laver between the tent of meeting and the altar and put water in it.

8 "You shall set up the court all around and hang up the veil for the gateway of the court.

9 "Then you shall take the anointing oil and anoint the tabernacle and all that is in it, and shall consecrate it and all its furnishings; and it shall be holy.

10 "You shall anoint the altar of burnt offering and all its utensils, and consecrate the altar, and the altar shall be most holy.

11 "You shall anoint the laver and its stand, and consecrate it.

12 "Then you shall bring Aaron and his sons to the doorway of the tent of meeting and wash them with water.

13 "You shall put the holy garments on Aaron and anoint him and consecrate him, that he may minister as a priest to Me.

14 "You shall bring his sons and put tunics on them;

15 and you shall anoint them even as you have anointed their father, that they may minister as priests to Me; and their anointing will qualify them for a perpetual priesthood throughout their generations."

16 Thus Moses did; according to all that the LORD had commanded him, so he did.

17 Now in the first month of the second year, on the first *day* of the month, the tabernacle was erected.

18 Moses erected the tabernacle and laid its sockets, and set up its boards, and inserted its bars and erected its pillars.

19 He spread the tent over the tabernacle and put the covering of the tent on top of it, just as the LORD had commanded Moses.

20 Then he took the testimony and put *it* into the ark, and attached the poles to the ark, and put the mercy seat on top of the ark.

21 He brought the ark into the tabernacle, and set up a veil for the screen, and screened off the ark of the testimony, just as the LORD had commanded Moses.

22 Then he put the table in the tent of meeting on the north side of the tabernacle, outside the veil.

23 He set the arrangement of bread in

LIFE LESSONS

➤ **Exodus 39:42 — *So the sons of Israel did all the work according to all that the LORD had commanded Moses.***

*G*od calls us to obey Him in all things, whether we understand all of His commands or not. The people carefully carried out all of Moses' instructions, even down to little details that might not have seemed crucial to them.

order on it before the LORD, just as the LORD had commanded Moses.

24　Then he placed the lampstand in the tent of meeting, opposite the table, on the south side of the tabernacle.

25　He lighted the lamps before the LORD, just as the LORD had commanded Moses.

26　Then he placed the gold altar in the tent of meeting in front of the veil;

27　and he burned fragrant incense on it, just as the LORD had commanded Moses.

28　Then he set up the veil for the doorway of the tabernacle.

29　He set the altar of burnt offering *before* the doorway of the tabernacle of the tent of meeting, and offered on it the burnt offering and the meal offering, just as the LORD had commanded Moses.

30　He placed the laver between the tent of meeting and the altar and put water in it for washing.

31　From it Moses and Aaron and his sons washed their hands and their feet.

32　When they entered the tent of meeting, and when they approached the altar, they washed, just as the LORD had commanded Moses.

33　He erected the court all around the tabernacle and the altar, and hung up the veil for the gateway of the court. Thus Moses finished the work.

34　Then the cloud covered the tent of meeting, and the glory of the LORD filled the tabernacle.

➤ 35　Moses was not able to enter the tent of meeting because the cloud had settled on it, and the glory of the LORD filled the tabernacle.

36　Throughout all their journeys whenever the cloud was taken up from over the tabernacle, the sons of Israel would set out;

✷ 37　but if the cloud was not taken up, then they did not set out until the day when it was taken up.

38　For throughout all their journeys, the ◄ cloud of the LORD was on the tabernacle by day, and there was fire in it by night, in the sight of all the house of Israel.

❋ Psalm 22:16–21

16　For dogs have surrounded me;
　　A band of evildoers has encompassed
　　me;
　　They pierced my hands and my feet.

17　I can count all my bones.
　　They look, they stare at me;

18　They divide my garments among
　　them,
　　And for my clothing they cast lots.

19　But You, O LORD, be not far off;
　　O You my help, hasten to my
　　assistance.

20　Deliver my soul from the sword,
　　My only *life* from the power of the
　　dog.

21　Save me from the lion's mouth;
　　From the horns of the wild oxen You
　　answer me.

❋ Proverbs 8:22–31

22　"The LORD possessed me at the
　　beginning of His way,
　　Before His works of old.

23　"From everlasting I was established,
　　From the beginning, from the
　　earliest times of the earth.

24　"When there were no depths I was
　　brought forth,
　　When there were no springs
　　abounding with water.

25　"Before the mountains were settled,
　　Before the hills I was brought forth;

LIFE LESSONS

➤ **Exodus 40:35** — *The glory of the LORD filled the tabernacle.*

*A*similar phenomenon occurred when Solomon dedicated the temple in Jerusalem (1 Kin. 8:10, 11). God wanted to leave no doubt among His people that He would be with them as promised (Is. 6:4; Rev. 8:4).

➤ **Exodus 40:38** — *The cloud of the LORD was on the tabernacle by day, and there was fire in it by night.*

*W*ith such a continuous and obvious sign of the Lord's guiding presence, we might wonder why the Israelites ever doubted His leading. Yet we have His Spirit within us, and how many of us doubt His guidance?

26 While He had not yet made the earth
and the fields,
Nor the first dust of the world.
27 "When He established the heavens, I
was there,
When He inscribed a circle on the
face of the deep,
28 When He made firm the skies above,
When the springs of the deep
became fixed,
29 When He set for the sea its boundary
So that the water would not
transgress His command,
When He marked out the
foundations of the earth;
30 Then I was beside Him, *as* a master
workman;
And I was daily *His* delight,
Rejoicing always before Him,
31 Rejoicing in the world, His earth,
And *having* my delight in the sons of
men.

✦ Matthew 27:1–26

27 NOW when morning came, all the
chief priests and the elders of the
people conferred together against Jesus
to put Him to death;
2 and they bound Him, and led Him
away and delivered Him to Pilate the
governor.
3 Then when Judas, who had betrayed
Him, saw that He had been condemned,
he felt remorse and returned the thirty
pieces of silver to the chief priests and
elders,
4 saying, "I have sinned by betraying
innocent blood." But they said, "What is
that to us? See *to that* yourself!"
5 And he threw the pieces of silver
into the temple sanctuary and departed;
and he went away and hanged himself.
6 The chief priests took the pieces of
silver and said, "It is not lawful to put
them into the temple treasury, since it is
the price of blood."
7 And they conferred together and
with the money bought the Potter's Field
as a burial place for strangers.
8 For this reason that field has been
called the Field of Blood to this day.
9 Then that which was spoken through
Jeremiah the prophet was fulfilled: "And
THEY TOOK THE THIRTY PIECES OF SILVER,
THE PRICE OF THE ONE WHOSE PRICE HAD
BEEN SET by the sons of Israel;
10 AND THEY GAVE THEM FOR THE POT-
TER'S FIELD, AS THE LORD DIRECTED ME."
11 Now Jesus stood before the governor, and the governor questioned Him,
saying, "Are You the King of the Jews?"
And Jesus said to him, "*It is as* you say."
12 And while He was being accused by
the chief priests and elders, He did not
answer.
13 Then Pilate *said to Him, "Do You
not hear how many things they testify
against You?"
14 And He did not answer him with ≺
regard to even a *single* charge, so the
governor was quite amazed.
15 Now at *the* feast the governor was
accustomed to release for the people *any*
one prisoner whom they wanted.
16 At that time they were holding a no-
torious prisoner, called Barabbas.
17 So when the people gathered together, Pilate said to them, "Whom do
you want me to release for you? Barabbas, or Jesus who is called Christ?"
18 For he knew that because of envy
they had handed Him over.
19 While he was sitting on the judg- ≺
ment seat, his wife sent him *a message*,
saying, "Have nothing to do with that
righteous Man; for last night I suffered
greatly in a dream because of Him."
20 But the chief priests and the elders
persuaded the crowds to ask for Barabbas and to put Jesus to death.
21 But the governor said to them,
"Which of the two do you want me to
release for you?" And they said, "Barabbas."
22 Pilate *said to them, "Then what
shall I do with Jesus who is called
Christ?" They all *said, "Crucify Him!"
23 And he said, "Why, what evil has

LIFE LESSONS

➤ **Matthew 27:14** — *He did not answer
him with regard to even a single charge,
so the governor was quite amazed.*

*P*ilate was used to prisoners cower-
ing in his presence. This one did
not, and it unnerved him. Isaiah had
predicted the Messiah would keep silent
before His accusers, and Jesus did exactly
that (Is. 53:7).

Life Examples:

In His Thoughts

MATTHEW 27:12

*T*here is no doubt that as Jesus stood trial in front of Pilate, He was completely focused. Matthew 27:12 tells us, "While He was being accused by the chief priests and elders, He did not answer." Think about that. As the false accusations were being flung at Him, the Son of God didn't call a battalion of angels to His aide. He didn't curse the priests and elders as He had the fig tree that didn't bear fruit (Matt. 21:19). He did not do anything to defend Himself.

He answered nothing.

Hebrews 12:2 helps us understand Christ's mindset, "Jesus, the author and perfecter of faith, who for the joy set before Him endured the cross, despising the shame."

Jesus endured it all for the joy set before Him. It was enough to stop Him from answering His accusers. It was sufficient to keep Him focused.

What was this overwhelming joy? It was doing the Father's will. But it was also you and I.

Ephesians 5:2 admonishes, "Walk in love, just as Christ also loved you and gave Himself up for us." Galatians 2:20 says, "The Son of God . . . loved me and gave Himself up for me."

Think about that as you celebrate St. Valentine's Day. Love is not simply red hearts, bouquets of flowers, and chocolates. True love is unconditional. True love reaches out. True love gives itself sacrificially.

Perhaps you have a special loved one with which to celebrate today. Or perhaps today is one of the loneliest days of the year for you. Perhaps you are wondering if anyone is thinking about you. The answer is yes: Jesus is. He's thinking about you today, and He thought about you back then. He thought about you as He stood trial, and His love for you kept Him focused on the goal: to reconcile you to God. To show you His love—eternally.

Today, remember you are Christ's joy—His beloved. And have a very happy Valentine's Day.

He done?" But they kept shouting all the more, saying, "Crucify Him!"
24 When Pilate saw that he was accomplishing nothing, but rather that a riot was starting, he took water and washed his hands in front of the crowd, saying, "I am innocent of this Man's blood; see *to that* yourselves."
25 And all the people said, "His blood shall be on us and on our children!"
26 Then he released Barabbas for them; but after having Jesus scourged, he handed Him over to be crucified.

LIFE LESSONS

➤ **Matthew 27:19** — *"Have nothing to do with that righteous Man; for last night I suffered greatly in a dream because of Him."*

*W*hat did God tell Pilate's wife in this dream? What did He intend to accomplish through it? How should the dream have influenced events? We don't know—but we do know God speaks to those with open ears.

FEBRUARY 15

 Leviticus 1:1—2:16

1 THEN the LORD called to Moses and spoke to him from the tent of meeting, saying,
2 "Speak to the sons of Israel and say to them, 'When any man of you brings an offering to the LORD, you shall bring your offering of animals from the herd or the flock.
➤ 3 'If his offering is a burnt offering from the herd, he shall offer it, a male without defect; he shall offer it at the doorway of

LIFE LESSONS

➤ **Leviticus 1:3** — *"He shall offer it at the doorway of the tent of meeting, that he may be accepted before the LORD."*

*W*illing offerings to the Lord demonstrate where the desires of our hearts truly lie.

the tent of meeting, that he may be accepted before the LORD.

4 'He shall lay his hand on the head of the burnt offering, that it may be accepted for him to make atonement on his behalf.

5 'He shall slay the young bull before the LORD; and Aaron's sons the priests shall offer up the blood and sprinkle the blood around on the altar that is at the doorway of the tent of meeting.

6 'He shall then skin the burnt offering and cut it into its pieces.

7 'The sons of Aaron the priest shall put fire on the altar and arrange wood on the fire.

8 'Then Aaron's sons the priests shall arrange the pieces, the head and the suet over the wood which is on the fire that is on the altar.

9 'Its entrails, however, and its legs he shall wash with water. And the priest shall offer up in smoke all of it on the altar for a burnt offering, an offering by fire of a soothing aroma to the LORD.

10 'But if his offering is from the flock, of the sheep or of the goats, for a burnt offering, he shall offer it a male without defect.

11 'He shall slay it on the side of the altar northward before the LORD, and Aaron's sons the priests shall sprinkle its blood around on the altar.

12 'He shall then cut it into its pieces with its head and its suet, and the priest shall arrange them on the wood which is on the fire that is on the altar.

13 'The entrails, however, and the legs he shall wash with water. And the priest shall offer all of it, and offer it up in smoke on the altar; it is a burnt offering, an offering by fire of a soothing aroma to the LORD.

14 'But if his offering to the LORD is a burnt offering of birds, then he shall bring his offering from the turtledoves or from young pigeons.

15 'The priest shall bring it to the altar, and wring off its head and offer it up in smoke on the altar; and its blood is to be drained out on the side of the altar.

16 'He shall also take away its crop with its feathers and cast it beside the altar eastward, to the place of the ashes.

17 'Then he shall tear it by its wings, *but* shall not sever *it*. And the priest shall offer it up in smoke on the altar on the wood which is on the fire; it is a burnt

---

LIFE LESSONS

➤ **Leviticus 1:17 —** *"It is a burnt offering, an offering by fire of a soothing aroma to the LORD."*

*E*ager obedience is a sweet aroma to the Lord. Christ lived to obey His Father, and when we follow His example, we too become a sweet aroma to the Lord—the aroma of Christ Himself (2 Cor. 2:15).

---

offering, an offering by fire of a soothing aroma to the LORD.

2 'NOW when anyone presents a grain offering as an offering to the LORD, his offering shall be of fine flour, and he shall pour oil on it and put frankincense on it.

2 'He shall then bring it to Aaron's sons the priests; and shall take from it his handful of its fine flour and of its oil with all of its frankincense. And the priest shall offer *it* up in smoke *as* its memorial portion on the altar, an offering by fire of a soothing aroma to the LORD.

3 'The remainder of the grain offering belongs to Aaron and his sons: a thing most holy, of the offerings to the LORD by fire.

4 'Now when you bring an offering of a grain offering baked in an oven, *it shall be* unleavened cakes of fine flour mixed with oil, or unleavened wafers spread with oil.

5 'If your offering is a grain offering *made* on the griddle, *it shall be* of fine flour, unleavened, mixed with oil;

6 you shall break it into bits and pour oil on it; it is a grain offering.

7 'Now if your offering is a grain offering *made* in a pan, it shall be made of fine flour with oil.

8 'When you bring in the grain offering which is made of these things to the LORD, it shall be presented to the priest and he shall bring it to the altar.

9 'The priest then shall take up from the grain offering its memorial portion, and shall offer *it* up in smoke on the altar *as* an offering by fire of a soothing aroma to the LORD.

10 'The remainder of the grain offering belongs to Aaron and his sons: a thing

LIFE LESSONS

➤ **Leviticus 2:11 — "No grain offering, which you bring to the LORD, shall be made with leaven."**

*T*he Bible often uses "leaven" or "yeast" as a picture of sin (Matt. 16:6). It was not to be offered on the altar, just as sin is not to be allowed to dominate the life of the believer.

➤ **Leviticus 2:13 — "You shall season with salt, so that the salt of the covenant of your God shall not be lacking from your grain offering."**

*S*alt here is used to symbolize God's covenant with His people. Just as salt is necessary to sustain life, so is His continual relationship with us necessary to sustain and enjoy life everlasting.

---

most holy of the offerings to the LORD by fire.

➤ 11 'No grain offering, which you bring to the LORD, shall be made with leaven, for you shall not offer up in smoke any leaven or any honey as an offering by fire to the LORD.

12 'As an offering of first fruits you shall bring them to the LORD, but they shall not ascend for a soothing aroma on the altar.

➤ 13 'Every grain offering of yours, moreover, you shall season with salt, so that the salt of the covenant of your God shall not be lacking from your grain offering; with all your offerings you shall offer salt.

14 'Also if you bring a grain offering of early ripened things to the LORD, you shall bring fresh heads of grain roasted in the fire, grits of new growth, for the grain offering of your early ripened things.

15 'You shall then put oil on it and lay incense on it; it is a grain offering.

16 'The priest shall offer up in smoke its memorial portion, part of its grits and its oil with all its incense as an offering by fire to the LORD.

✦ Psalm 22:22–31

22 I will tell of Your name to my brethren;

In the midst of the assembly I will praise You.

23 You who fear the LORD, praise Him;
All you descendants of Jacob, glorify Him,
And stand in awe of Him, all you descendants of Israel.

24 For He has not despised nor abhorred the affliction of the afflicted;
Nor has He hidden His face from him;
But when he cried to Him for help, He heard.

25 From You *comes* my praise in the great assembly;
I shall pay my vows before those who fear Him.

26 The afflicted will eat and be satisfied;
Those who seek Him will praise the LORD.
Let your heart live forever!

27 All the ends of the earth will remember and turn to the LORD,
And all the families of the nations will worship before You.

28 For the kingdom is the LORD'S
And He rules over the nations.

29 All the prosperous of the earth will eat and worship,
All those who go down to the dust will bow before Him,
Even he who cannot keep his soul alive.

30 Posterity will serve Him;
It will be told of the Lord to the *coming* generation.

31 They will come and will declare His righteousness
To a people who will be born, that He has performed *it*.

LIFE LESSONS

➤ **Psalm 22:24 — He has not despised nor abhorred the affliction of the afflicted; nor has He hidden His face from him; but when he cried to Him for help, He heard.**

*J*esus clearly had this psalm on His mind as He hung from the Cross, so He must also have taken great comfort from this part of the psalm. He knew that God heard His cries and would cause Him to triumph.

◈ Proverbs 8:32–36

32 "Now therefore, *O* sons, listen to me,
For blessed are they who keep my ways.
33 "Heed instruction and be wise,
And do not neglect *it.*
34 "Blessed is the man who listens to me,
Watching daily at my gates,
Waiting at my doorposts.
35 "For he who finds me finds life
And obtains favor from the LORD.
36 "But he who sins against me injures himself;
All those who hate me love death."

◈ Matthew 27:27–54

27 Then the soldiers of the governor took Jesus into the Praetorium and gathered the whole *Roman* cohort around Him.
28 They stripped Him and put a scarlet robe on Him.
29 And after twisting together a crown of thorns, they put it on His head, and a reed in His right hand; and they knelt down before Him and mocked Him, saying, "Hail, King of the Jews!"
30 They spat on Him, and took the reed and *began* to beat Him on the head.
31 After they had mocked Him, they took the *scarlet* robe off Him and put His *own* garments back on Him, and led Him away to crucify Him.
32 As they were coming out, they found a man of Cyrene named Simon, whom they pressed into service to bear His cross.
33 And when they came to a place called Golgotha, which means Place of a Skull,
34 they gave Him wine to drink mixed with gall; and after tasting *it,* He was unwilling to drink.
35 And when they had crucified Him, they divided up His garments among themselves by casting lots.
36 And sitting down, they *began* to keep watch over Him there.
37 And above His head they put up the charge against Him which read, "THIS IS JESUS THE KING OF THE JEWS."
38 At that time two robbers *were crucified with Him, one on the right and one on the left.
39 And those passing by were hurling abuse at Him, wagging their heads
40 and saying, "You who *are going to* destroy the temple and rebuild it in three days, save Yourself! If You are the Son of God, come down from the cross."
41 In the same way the chief priests also, along with the scribes and elders, were mocking *Him* and saying,
42 "He saved others; He cannot save Himself. He is the King of Israel; let Him now come down from the cross, and we will believe in Him.
43 "HE TRUSTS IN GOD; LET GOD RESCUE *Him* now, IF HE DELIGHTS IN HIM; for He said, 'I am the Son of God.'"
44 The robbers who had been crucified with Him were also insulting Him with the same words.
45 Now from the sixth hour darkness fell upon all the land until the ninth hour.
46 About the ninth hour Jesus cried out with a loud voice, saying, "ELI, ELI, LAMA SABACHTHANI?" that is, "MY GOD, MY GOD, WHY HAVE YOU FORSAKEN ME?"
47 And some of those who were standing there, when they heard it, *began* saying, "This man is calling for Elijah."
48 Immediately one of them ran, and taking a sponge, he filled it with sour wine and put it on a reed, and gave Him a drink.
49 But the rest *of them* said, "Let us see whether Elijah will come to save Him."
50 And Jesus cried out again with a loud voice, and yielded up His spirit.
51 And behold, the veil of the temple was torn in two from top to bottom; and the earth shook and the rocks were split.

LIFE LESSONS

➤ **Matthew 27:44 — *The robbers who had been crucified with Him were also insulting Him with the same words.***

*A*t the beginning of the crucifixion, both robbers jeered Jesus. But when one criminal saw how Jesus reacted to the angry mob with grace and forgiveness, he was struck to the heart and came to faith (Luke 23:40–43).

Forsaken?

MATTHEW 27:46

*W*e have all at least thought it: *My God, why have You forsaken me*? We've all come to the point where we feel like God has left us to despair in our bad situations. Whether it's because of medical problems, relational difficulties, or financial setbacks—we know what it's like to feel abandoned.

Yet for some reason, it's disturbing that Jesus said it on the Cross. Matthew 27:46 tells us, "About the ninth hour Jesus cried out with a loud voice, saying, 'ELI, ELI, LAMA SABACHTHANI?' that is, 'MY GOD, MY GOD, WHY HAVE YOU FORSAKEN ME?'"

The word *forsaken* means *to abandon* or *leave helpless*. Generally, we are accustomed to hearing it in terms of God's promise to never desert us. As Deuteronomy 31:6 says, "The LORD your God, is the one who goes with you. He will not fail you or forsake you."

Therefore, because we know God honors His promises, we are convinced He is never going to forsake us. And even when it feels like the Lord is nowhere to be found, we claim the promise and have confidence He is still with us.

However, when we read that Jesus said it on the Cross, it's somewhat disconcerting. Of course, we understand Jesus had to be crucified in order to forgive us of our sins (Heb. 9:22); and we know it was excruciating for Him. Still, the outburst seems strange coming from Jesus.

Think about it: Jesus had been on the Cross almost six hours. Why did He say this just as He was about to die—when He was almost through with the mission? After all, Jesus knew the Father would keep His promise to resurrect Him from the grave (Ps. 16:10). Knowing the promise, and knowing the suffering would be over soon—why did Jesus say that God had forsaken Him? We know it couldn't be from a lack of faith.

Sometimes in the immensity of all that happened at the Cross, we lose the small details of God's astounding plan. However, it's important to note the exact moment when Jesus cried out.

The Mishnah, which is the oral law of the Jewish people, reports, "The slaughter of the Passover Lamb was performed during the ninth hour." The ninth hour. We learn that at the exact moment when the lambs were being sacrificed in the temple, Jesus was crying out about being forsaken.

If you've ever wondered when exactly Jesus became our sin offering—understand it was in that one awful, horrifying, redeeming moment when He cried out. It was in that moment He became sin for us. As Paul teaches us in 2 Corinthians 5:21, "He made Him who knew no sin to be sin on our behalf, so that we might become the righteousness of God in Him." In 1 Corinthians 5:7 Paul confirmed, "For Christ our Passover also has been sacrificed."

In that moment, Jesus knew what it meant to be separated from God. For the first time since before the beginning of time—Jesus didn't feel God's presence. This doesn't mean the Godhead was breached—Jesus was still fully God. Rather, it means the Son understood the poverty of being separated from the Father. The hopelessness of it. The loneliness of it. It was the most heart-wrenching, awful moment of His life—worse than any scourging, beating, or crucifixion.

Perhaps this was the way Jesus best experienced what it's like to be us—what it feels like to be a sinner—without actually being one (Heb. 2:14).

Jesus felt every fear that you and I feel in that moment. He felt the consequences of sin. He felt what it means to be forsaken—what it means to be without God's perfect love. Perhaps that's what is at the core of every time we feel forsaken, abandoned, enraged, offended, and hurt: It all comes from fear. We're afraid of being left with nothing. We're scared of being unloved and rejected. We're terrified of dying alone. However, at the core of it all is the fear that comes from not feeling God's perfect love.

First, 1 John 4:18 says, "There is no fear in love; but perfect love casts out fear, because fear involves punishment, and the one who fears is not perfected in love."

Friend, perfect love doesn't abandon you. When you experience God's perfect love and are obedient to His will, it doesn't matter what happens—you are fully convinced of God's provision and protection.

Therefore, whenever you feel forsaken, remember the resurrected Christ knows exactly how you feel. He knows the depth of your pain. And He did not leave you helpless to face your fears—He did not abandon you to a life without the perfect love of God.

The next time you read the profound words, "My God, My God, why have You forsaken Me?", thank Jesus for identifying with you in such a deep way. Realize you can always count on Him. Friend, there's no situation you will face that He will not face with you.

52 The tombs were opened, and many bodies of the saints who had fallen asleep were raised;
53 and coming out of the tombs after His resurrection they entered the holy city and appeared to many.

54 Now the centurion, and those who were with him keeping guard over Jesus, when they saw the earthquake and the things that were happening, became very frightened and said, "Truly this was the Son of God!"

FEBRUARY 16

Leviticus 3:1—4:35

3 'NOW if his offering is a sacrifice of peace offerings, if he is going to offer out of the herd, whether male or female, he shall offer it without defect before the LORD.
2 'He shall lay his hand on the head of his offering and slay it at the doorway of the tent of meeting, and Aaron's sons the priests shall sprinkle the blood around on the altar.
3 'From the sacrifice of the peace offerings he shall present an offering by fire to the LORD, the fat that covers the entrails and all the fat that is on the entrails,
4 and the two kidneys with the fat that is on them, which is on the loins, and the lobe of the liver, which he shall remove with the kidneys.
5 'Then Aaron's sons shall offer it up in smoke on the altar on the burnt offering, which is on the wood that is on the fire; it is an offering by fire of a soothing aroma to the LORD.
6 'But if his offering for a sacrifice of peace offerings to the LORD is from the flock, he shall offer it, male or female, without defect.
7 'If he is going to offer a lamb for his offering, then he shall offer it before the LORD,
8 and he shall lay his hand on the head of his offering and slay it before the tent of meeting, and Aaron's sons shall sprinkle its blood around on the altar.
9 'From the sacrifice of peace offerings he shall bring as an offering by fire to the LORD, its fat, the entire fat tail which he shall remove close to the backbone, and the fat that covers the entrails and all the fat that is on the entrails,

10 and the two kidneys with the fat that is on them, which is on the loins, and the lobe of the liver, which he shall remove with the kidneys.
11 'Then the priest shall offer it up in smoke on the altar as food, an offering by fire to the LORD.
12 'Moreover, if his offering is a goat, then he shall offer it before the LORD,
13 and he shall lay his hand on its head and slay it before the tent of meeting, and the sons of Aaron shall sprinkle its blood around on the altar.
14 'From it he shall present his offering as an offering by fire to the LORD, the fat that covers the entrails and all the fat that is on the entrails,
15 and the two kidneys with the fat that is on them, which is on the loins, and the lobe of the liver, which he shall remove with the kidneys.
16 'The priest shall offer them up in smoke on the altar as food, an offering by fire for a soothing aroma; all fat is the LORD'S.
17 'It is a perpetual statute throughout your generations in all your dwellings: you shall not eat any fat or any blood.'"

4 THEN the LORD spoke to Moses, saying,
2 "Speak to the sons of Israel, saying, 'If a person sins unintentionally in any of the things which the LORD has commanded not to be done, and commits any of them,
3 if the anointed priest sins so as to bring guilt on the people, then let him offer to the LORD a bull without defect as a sin offering for the sin he has committed.
4 'He shall bring the bull to the doorway of the tent of meeting before the LORD, and he shall lay his hand on the head of the bull and slay the bull before the LORD.

➢ **Leviticus 4:2, 3 — "If a person sins unintentionally in any of the things which the LORD has commanded . . . then let him offer to the LORD a bull without defect as a sin offering for the sin he has committed."**

To sin unintentionally is better understood as to sin unthinkingly—something we all do. Yet God is gracious; He not only reveals our sin to us, but He also offers us His forgiveness.

5 'Then the anointed priest is to take some of the blood of the bull and bring it to the tent of meeting,
6   and the priest shall dip his finger in the blood and sprinkle some of the blood seven times before the LORD, in front of the veil of the sanctuary.
7   'The priest shall also put some of the blood on the horns of the altar of fragrant incense which is before the LORD in the tent of meeting; and all the blood of the bull he shall pour out at the base of the altar of burnt offering which is at the doorway of the tent of meeting.
8   'He shall remove from it all the fat of the bull of the sin offering: the fat that covers the entrails, and all the fat which is on the entrails,
9   and the two kidneys with the fat that is on them, which is on the loins, and the lobe of the liver, which he shall remove with the kidneys
10   (just as it is removed from the ox of the sacrifice of peace offerings), and the priest is to offer them up in smoke on the altar of burnt offering.
11 'But the hide of the bull and all its flesh with its head and its legs and its entrails and its refuse,
12   that is, all *the rest of* the bull, he is to bring out to a clean place outside the camp where the ashes are poured out, and burn it on wood with fire; where the ashes are poured out it shall be burned.
13 'Now if the whole congregation of Israel commits error and the matter escapes the notice of the assembly, and they commit any of the things which the LORD has commanded not to be done, and they become guilty;
14   when the sin which they have committed becomes known, then the assem-

bly shall offer a bull of the herd for a sin offering and bring it before the tent of meeting.
15 'Then the elders of the congregation shall lay their hands on the head of the bull before the LORD, and the bull shall be slain before the LORD.
16 'Then the anointed priest is to bring some of the blood of the bull to the tent of meeting;
17   and the priest shall dip his finger in the blood and sprinkle *it* seven times before the LORD, in front of the veil.
18 'He shall put some of the blood on the horns of the altar which is before the LORD in the tent of meeting; and all the blood he shall pour out at the base of the altar of burnt offering which is at the doorway of the tent of meeting.
19 'He shall remove all its fat from it and offer it up in smoke on the altar.
20 'He shall also do with the bull just as he did with the bull of the sin offering; thus he shall do with it. So the priest shall make atonement for them, and they will be forgiven.
21 'Then he is to bring out the bull to *a place* outside the camp and burn it as he burned the first bull; it is the sin offering for the assembly.
22   'When a leader sins and unintentionally does any one of all the things which the LORD his God has commanded not to be done, and he becomes guilty,
23   if his sin which he has committed is made known to him, he shall bring for his offering a goat, a male without defect.
24 'He shall lay his hand on the head of the male goat and slay it in the place where they slay the burnt offering before the LORD; it is a sin offering.
25 'Then the priest is to take some of the blood of the sin offering with his finger and put it on the horns of the altar of burnt offering; and *the rest of* its blood he shall pour out at the base of the altar of burnt offering.
26 'All its fat he shall offer up in smoke on the altar as *in the case of* the fat of the sacrifice of peace offerings. Thus the priest shall make atonement for him in regard to his sin, and he will be forgiven.
27 'Now if anyone of the common people sins unintentionally in doing any of the things which the LORD has com-

manded not to be done, and becomes guilty,

28 if his sin which he has committed is made known to him, then he shall bring for his offering a goat, a female without defect, for his sin which he has committed.

29 'He shall lay his hand on the head of the sin offering and slay the sin offering at the place of the burnt offering.

30 'The priest shall take some of its blood with his finger and put it on the horns of the altar of burnt offering; and all *the rest of* its blood he shall pour out at the base of the altar.

31 'Then he shall remove all its fat, just as the fat was removed from the sacrifice of peace offerings; and the priest shall offer it up in smoke on the altar for a soothing aroma to the LORD. Thus the priest shall make atonement for him, and he will be forgiven.

32 'But if he brings a lamb as his offering for a sin offering, he shall bring it, a female without defect.

33 'He shall lay his hand on the head of the sin offering and slay it for a sin offering in the place where they slay the burnt offering.

34 'The priest is to take some of the blood of the sin offering with his finger and put it on the horns of the altar of burnt offering, and all *the rest of* its blood he shall pour out at the base of the altar.

35 'Then he shall remove all its fat, just as the fat of the lamb is removed from the sacrifice of the peace offerings, and the priest shall offer them up in smoke on the altar, on the offerings by fire to the LORD. Thus the priest shall make atonement for him in regard to his sin which he has committed, and he will be forgiven.

Psalm 23:1–6

A Psalm of David.

23 THE LORD is my shepherd,
I shall not want.

2 He makes me lie down in green
pastures;
He leads me beside quiet waters.

3 He restores my soul;

He guides me in the paths of
righteousness
For His name's sake.

4 Even though I walk through the
valley of the shadow of death,
I fear no evil, for You are with me;
Your rod and Your staff, they
comfort me.

5 You prepare a table before me in
the presence of my enemies;
You have anointed my head with
oil;
My cup overflows.

6 Surely goodness and lovingkindness
will follow me all the days of my
life,
And I will dwell in the house of the
LORD forever.

Proverbs 9:1–6

9 WISDOM has built her house,
She has hewn out her seven
pillars;

2 She has prepared her food, she has
mixed her wine;
She has also set her table;

3 She has sent out her maidens, she
calls

ANSWERS TO LIFE'S QUESTIONS

How can I find renewal and restoration?

PSALM 23:2-4

"*He* leads me beside quiet waters. He restores my soul" (Ps. 23:2, 3). More than likely you have heard this passage quoted more times than you can count. No matter how often this much-loved psalm is recited, however, we still seem to miss the full impact of the message: *God restores our souls.*

How does He do this? He restores our souls through fellowship with Himself. Even though at times we stray far from Him, He remains the Good Shepherd. Though we wander, He receives us back gladly and willingly pardons His wayward sheep.

Why would we ever leave such a loving Guide? Most likely you have never made a conscious decision to forsake the Father. Instead, you may have slipped away slowly and subtly as a result of wandering desires and selfish attempts to meet your own needs. But when you strive to attain comfort and safety apart from God, you stray farther and farther away from Him.

Luke 15 presents a wonderful picture of the warm reception awaiting a lost "sheep."

Did the shepherd scold or punish the wayward lamb? No. Instead, all of heaven celebrated because the lost had been found. Likewise, heaven rejoices when a wandering child of God returns "to the fold." Jesus tells us, "There will be more joy in heaven over one sinner who repents than over ninety-nine righteous persons who need no repentance" (Luke 15:7).

In restoring our souls, God is more than a *pardoning* Shepherd. He is also a *providing* Shepherd. He knows what we need before we even ask, and He delights in meeting our needs (Matt. 7:9–11). This means He knows what you need physically, emotionally, and spiritually, right now. In fact, He is already at work, accomplishing and providing the things you need, even though you may not have thought of them yet.

Finally, God is our *protecting* Shepherd. What comforts the psalmist in Psalm 23:4? It is the Lord's rod and staff. Ancient shepherds used these tools to defend their sheep from vicious animals seeking a quick meal. In the same way, God moves before us, clearing the way of the enemy's snares.

Have you experienced God's provision, only to fall into subsequent doubt and fear because of loss or hardship? God has not left you. He remains your Good Shepherd, leading you through the darkness and into the light. It is there in His presence that He will pardon, provide for, and protect you. Always.

From the tops of the heights of
　　the city:
4　"Whoever is naive, let him turn in
　　　here!"
　　To him who lacks understanding
　　　she says,
5　"Come, eat of my food
　　And drink of the wine I have mixed.
✳ 6　"Forsake *your* folly and live,
　　And proceed in the way of
　　　understanding."

◈ Matthew 27:55–66

55 Many women were there looking on from a distance, who had followed Jesus from Galilee while ministering to Him.
56 Among them was Mary Magdalene, and Mary the mother of James and Joseph, and the mother of the sons of Zebedee.

57 When it was evening, there came a rich man from Arimathea, named Joseph, who himself had also become a disciple of Jesus.
58 This man went to Pilate and asked for the body of Jesus. Then Pilate ordered it to be given *to him*.
59 And Joseph took the body and wrapped it in a clean linen cloth,
60 and laid it in his own new tomb, which he had hewn out in the rock; and he rolled a large stone against the entrance of the tomb and went away.
61 And Mary Magdalene was there, and the other Mary, sitting opposite the grave.
62 Now on the next day, the day after the preparation, the chief priests and the Pharisees gathered together with Pilate,
63 and said, "Sir, we remember that ◄ when He was still alive that deceiver said, 'After three days I *am* to rise again.'

64 "Therefore, give orders for the grave to be made secure until the third day, otherwise His disciples may come and steal Him away and say to the people, 'He has risen from the dead,' and the last deception will be worse than the first."
65 Pilate said to them, "You have a guard; go, make it *as* secure as you know how."
66 And they went and made the grave secure, and along with the guard they set a seal on the stone.

LIFE LESSONS

➤ **Matthew 27:63 — *"We remember that when He was still alive that deceiver said, 'After three days I am to rise again.'"***

*T*he enemies of Jesus often understood Him better than His friends and followers did. The disciples did not grasp until some time after the resurrection that Jesus would actually rise from the dead (John 20:9).

Leviticus 5:1—6:30

5 'NOW if a person sins after he hears a public adjuration *to testify* when he is a witness, whether he has seen or *otherwise* known, if he does not tell *it*, then he will bear his guilt.
2 'Or if a person touches any unclean thing, whether a carcass of an unclean beast or the carcass of unclean cattle or a carcass of unclean swarming things, though it is hidden from him and he is unclean, then he will be guilty.
3 'Or if he touches human uncleanness, of whatever *sort* his uncleanness *may* be with which he becomes unclean, and it is hidden from him, and then he comes to know *it*, he will be guilty.
4 'Or if a person swears thoughtlessly with his lips to do evil or to do good, in whatever matter a man may speak thoughtlessly with an oath, and it is hidden from him, and then he comes to know *it*, he will be guilty in one of these.
5 'So it shall be when he becomes guilty in one of these, that he shall confess that in which he has sinned.
6 'He shall also bring his guilt offering to the LORD for his sin which he has committed, a female from the flock, a lamb or a goat as a sin offering. So the priest shall make atonement on his behalf for his sin.
7 'But if he cannot afford a lamb, then he shall bring to the LORD his guilt offering for that in which he has sinned, two turtledoves or two young pigeons, one for a sin offering and the other for a burnt offering.

8 'He shall bring them to the priest, who shall offer first that which is for the sin offering and shall nip its head at the front of its neck, but he shall not sever *it*.
9 'He shall also sprinkle some of the blood of the sin offering on the side of the altar, while the rest of the blood shall be drained out at the base of the altar: it is a sin offering.
10 'The second he shall then prepare as a burnt offering according to the ordinance. So the priest shall make atonement on his behalf for his sin which he has committed, and it will be forgiven him.
11 'But if his means are insufficient for two turtledoves or two young pigeons, then for his offering for that which he has sinned, he shall bring the tenth of an ephah of fine flour for a sin offering; he shall not put oil on it or place incense on it, for it is a sin offering.
12 'He shall bring it to the priest, and the priest shall take his handful of it as its memorial portion and offer *it* up in smoke on the altar, with the offerings of the LORD by fire: it is a sin offering.
13 'So the priest shall make atonement for him concerning his sin which he has committed from one of these, and it will be forgiven him; then *the rest* shall become the priest's, like the grain offering.'"
14 Then the LORD spoke to Moses, saying,
15 "If a person acts unfaithfully and sins unintentionally against the LORD's holy things, then he shall bring his guilt offering to the LORD: a ram without defect

from the flock, according to your valuation in silver by shekels, in *terms of* the shekel of the sanctuary, for a guilt offering.

16 "He shall make restitution for that which he has sinned against the holy thing, and shall add to it a fifth part of it and give it to the priest. The priest shall then make atonement for him with the ram of the guilt offering, and it will be forgiven him.

➤ 17 "Now if a person sins and does any of the things which the LORD has commanded not to be done, though he was unaware, still he is guilty and shall bear his punishment.

18 "He is then to bring to the priest a ram without defect from the flock, according to your valuation, for a guilt offering. So the priest shall make atonement for him concerning his error in which he sinned unintentionally and did not know *it*, and it will be forgiven him.

19 "It is a guilt offering; he was certainly guilty before the LORD."

6 THEN the LORD spoke to Moses, saying,

2 "When a person sins and acts unfaithfully against the LORD, and deceives his companion in regard to a deposit or a security entrusted *to him*, or through robbery, or *if* he has extorted from his companion,

3 or has found what was lost and lied about it and sworn falsely, so that he sins in regard to any one of the things a man may do;

4 then it shall be, when he sins and becomes guilty, that he shall restore what he took by robbery or what he got by extortion, or the deposit which was entrusted to him or the lost thing which he found,

5 or anything about which he swore ◄ falsely; he shall make restitution for it in full and add to it one-fifth more. He shall give it to the one to whom it belongs on the day *he presents* his guilt offering.

6 "Then he shall bring to the priest his guilt offering to the LORD, a ram without defect from the flock, according to your valuation, for a guilt offering,

7 and the priest shall make atonement for him before the LORD, and he will be forgiven for any one of the things which he may have done to incur guilt."

8 Then the LORD spoke to Moses, saying,

9 "Command Aaron and his sons, saying, 'This is the law for the burnt offering: the burnt offering itself *shall remain* on the hearth on the altar all night until the morning, and the fire on the altar is to be kept burning on it.

10 'The priest is to put on his linen robe, and he shall put on undergarments next to his flesh; and he shall take up the ashes *to* which the fire reduces the burnt offering on the altar and place them beside the altar.

11 'Then he shall take off his garments and put on other garments, and carry the ashes outside the camp to a clean place.

12 'The fire on the altar shall be kept burning on it. It shall not go out, but the priest shall burn wood on it every morning; and he shall lay out the burnt offering on it, and offer up in smoke the fat portions of the peace offerings on it.

13 'Fire shall be kept burning continually on the altar; it is not to go out.

14 'Now this is the law of the grain offering: the sons of Aaron shall present it before the LORD in front of the altar.

15 'Then one *of them* shall lift up from it a handful of the fine flour of the grain

offering, with its oil and all the incense that is on the grain offering, and he shall offer *it* up in smoke on the altar, a soothing aroma, as its memorial offering to the Lord.

16 'What is left of it Aaron and his sons are to eat. It shall be eaten as unleavened cakes in a holy place; they are to eat it in the court of the tent of meeting.

17 'It shall not be baked with leaven. I have given it as their share from My offerings by fire; it is most holy, like the sin offering and the guilt offering.

18 'Every male among the sons of Aaron may eat it; it is a permanent ordinance throughout your generations, from the offerings by fire to the Lord. Whoever touches them will become consecrated.'"

19 Then the Lord spoke to Moses, saying,

20 "This is the offering which Aaron and his sons are to present to the Lord on the day when he is anointed; the tenth of an ephah of fine flour as a regular grain offering, half of it in the morning and half of it in the evening.

21 "It shall be prepared with oil on a griddle. When it is *well* stirred, you shall bring it. You shall present the grain offering in baked pieces as a soothing aroma to the Lord.

22 "The anointed priest who will be in his place among his sons shall offer it. By a permanent ordinance it shall be entirely offered up in smoke to the Lord.

23 "So every grain offering of the priest shall be burned entirely. It shall not be eaten."

24 Then the Lord spoke to Moses, saying,

25 "Speak to Aaron and to his sons, saying, 'This is the law of the sin offering: in the place where the burnt offering is slain the sin offering shall be slain before the Lord; it is most holy.

26 'The priest who offers it for sin shall eat it. It shall be eaten in a holy place, in the court of the tent of meeting.

27 'Anyone who touches its flesh will become consecrated; and when any of its blood splashes on a garment, in a holy place you shall wash what was splashed on.

28 'Also the earthenware vessel in which it was boiled shall be broken; and if it was boiled in a bronze vessel, then it shall be scoured and rinsed in water.

29 'Every male among the priests may eat of it; it is most holy.

30 'But no sin offering of which any of the blood is brought into the tent of meeting to make atonement in the holy place shall be eaten; it shall be burned with fire.

Psalm 24:1–6

A Psalm of David.

24 THE earth is the Lord's, and all it contains,
The world, and those who dwell in it.

2 For He has founded it upon the seas
And established it upon the rivers.

3 Who may ascend into the hill of the Lord?
And who may stand in His holy place?

4 He who has clean hands and a pure heart,
Who has not lifted up his soul to falsehood
And has not sworn deceitfully.

5 He shall receive a blessing from the Lord
And righteousness from the God of his salvation.

6 This is the generation of those who seek Him,
Who seek Your face—*even* Jacob.
Selah.

Proverbs 9:7–9

7 He who corrects a scoffer gets dishonor for himself,
And he who reproves a wicked man *gets* insults for himself.

LIFE LESSONS

➤ **Psalm 24:1 — *The earth is the Lord's, and all it contains, the world, and those who dwell in it.***

Occasionally you may hear a teaching that claims this world is the legal property of Satan, obtained in the Fall. Don't believe it. This world always has been and always will be God's. He hands His sovereignty over to no one.

8   Do not reprove a scoffer, or he will
     hate you,
     Reprove a wise man and he will
     love you.
9   Give *instruction* to a wise man and
     he will be still wiser,
     Teach a righteous man and he will
     increase *his* learning.

Matthew 28:1–20

28 NOW after the Sabbath, as it began
to dawn toward the first *day* of the
week, Mary Magdalene and the other
Mary came to look at the grave.
2   And behold, a severe earthquake
had occurred, for an angel of the Lord
descended from heaven and came and
rolled away the stone and sat upon it.
3   And his appearance was like lightning, and his clothing as white as snow.
4   The guards shook for fear of him
and became like dead men.
5   The angel said to the women, "Do
not be afraid; for I know that you are
looking for Jesus who has been crucified.
6   "He is not here, for He has risen, just
as He said. Come, see the place where He
was lying.
7   "Go quickly and tell His disciples that
He has risen from the dead; and behold,
He is going ahead of you into Galilee,
there you will see Him; behold, I have
told you."

LIFE LESSONS

➤ **Matthew 28:4, 5 — *The guards shook
for fear of him . . . The angel said to the
women.***

*T*he angel ignored the tough male
guards—he even sat silently on
the stone covering the entrance to the
tomb—but he did speak to the startled
women. God speaks to those who want
to listen.

➤ **Matthew 28:6 — *"He is not here, for
He has risen, just as He said."***

*J*esus did exactly what He had repeatedly said He would do. We can count
on His promises and build our lives on
them, for He always does just what He
says.

---

8   And they left the tomb quickly with
fear and great joy and ran to report it to
His disciples.
9   And behold, Jesus met them and
greeted them. And they came up and
took hold of His feet and worshiped
Him.
10   Then Jesus *said to them, "Do not be
afraid; go and take word to My brethren
to leave for Galilee, and there they will
see Me."
11   Now while they were on their way,
some of the guard came into the city and
reported to the chief priests all that had
happened.
12   And when they had assembled with
the elders and consulted together, they
gave a large sum of money to the soldiers,
13   and said, "You are to say, 'His disciples came by night and stole Him away
while we were asleep.'
14   "And if this should come to the governor's ears, we will win him over and
keep you out of trouble."
15   And they took the money and did as
they had been instructed; and this story
was widely spread among the Jews, *and
is* to this day.
16   But the eleven disciples proceeded to
Galilee, to the mountain which Jesus had
designated.
17   When they saw Him, they worshiped
Him; but some were doubtful.
18   And Jesus came up and spoke to
them, saying, "All authority has been
given to Me in heaven and on earth.
19   "Go therefore and make disciples
of all the nations, baptizing them in the
name of the Father and the Son and the
Holy Spirit,
20   teaching them to observe all that I
commanded you; and lo, I am with you
always, even to the end of the age."

LIFE LESSONS

➤ **Matthew 28:18, 19 — *"All authority
has been given to Me in heaven and on
earth. Go therefore and make disciples of
all the nations."***

*W*e can confidently bring the truth of
Jesus to the world because we have
Jesus' divine authority to back it up. Our
job is to be His faithful messengers.

Do I have a role to play in communicating God's truth to others?

MATTHEW 28:19, 20

*G*od never wants us to keep what He teaches us to ourselves. Whether it is money, insight, or truth, He wants us to share it with others. There is a tremendous blessing to be gained by opening our hearts and lives to those who need to know about the unconditional love and forgiveness of Jesus Christ.

The truth is Jesus commands us to "make disciples of all the nations . . . teaching them to observe all that I commanded you" (Matt. 28:19, 20). Just before He ascended to heaven, He told His disciples, "You shall be My witnesses both in Jerusalem, and in all Judea and Samaria, and even to the remotest part of the earth" (Acts 1:8). He never intended for the disciples to keep the truth of His Word stored away in personal reservoirs of knowledge. Instead, He instructed them to give away all they received from Him. He commands us to do the same.

Paul also admonished Timothy, his young protégé, to communicate the truth he had learned to others who would, in turn, pass it along (2 Tim. 2:2). Elsewhere he noted, "We are ambassadors for Christ" (2 Cor. 5:20). The sole purpose of an ambassador is to relay the policies and decisions of their superiors to the people of the countries where they serve. Likewise, we have an obligation to declare the divine plan and scriptural policies of our Master.

Each of us communicates something by what we say and don't say, by what we do and fail to do. A father who never reads the Bible is essentially telling his family he does not care enough about the Lord to study His Word. His lack of desire in this area sends the message he believes he is smart enough to make his own decisions apart from God's input. The child who never sees her parents praying mistakenly learns trials and tribulations can be handled without any direction from the Lord. This assumption is totally wrong. On the other hand, a father who tells his family, "We are going to trust the Lord to provide us with what we need," declares God can be trusted in every facet of life. When children hear their parents praying, they quickly learn to trust God for every detail. They grow up viewing Him as very loving—the God who has the very best in mind for their lives.

Even when we remain silent, we subtly state something. Although the apostle Peter recognized the Gentiles as rightful recipients of God's grace, he developed the bad habit of withdrawing from them during meals. His fellow Jews soon picked up on his prideful practice, with the result "that even Barnabas was carried away by their hypocrisy" (Gal. 2:13). Without a word, Peter had effectively sent a message that the Gentiles were inferior.

We must honestly evaluate our response to the Lord's commands. Are we deliberately and daily applying what He has taught us over the years? When we comprehend the truth, are we conforming ourselves to the image of Christ? Are we then communicating this truth to others?

Leviticus 7:1—8:36

7 'NOW this is the law of the guilt offering; it is most holy.
2 'In the place where they slay the burnt offering they are to slay the guilt offering, and he shall sprinkle its blood around on the altar.
3 'Then he shall offer from it all its fat: the fat tail and the fat that covers the entrails,
4 and the two kidneys with the fat that is on them, which is on the loins, and the lobe on the liver he shall remove with the kidneys.
5 'The priest shall offer them up in smoke on the altar as an offering by fire to the LORD; it is a guilt offering.
6 'Every male among the priests may eat of it. It shall be eaten in a holy place; it is most holy.
7 'The guilt offering is like the sin offering, there is one law for them; the priest who makes atonement with it shall have it.
8 'Also the priest who presents any man's burnt offering, that priest shall

have for himself the skin of the burnt offering which he has presented.

9 'Likewise, every grain offering that is baked in the oven and everything prepared in a pan or on a griddle shall belong to the priest who presents it.

10 'Every grain offering, mixed with oil or dry, shall belong to all the sons of Aaron, to all alike.

11 'Now this is the law of the sacrifice of peace offerings which shall be presented to the LORD.

12 'If he offers it by way of thanksgiving, then along with the sacrifice of thanksgiving he shall offer unleavened cakes mixed with oil, and unleavened wafers spread with oil, and cakes of *well* stirred fine flour mixed with oil.

13 'With the sacrifice of his peace offerings for thanksgiving, he shall present his offering with cakes of leavened bread.

14 'Of this he shall present one of every offering as a contribution to the LORD; it shall belong to the priest who sprinkles the blood of the peace offerings.

15 'Now *as for* the flesh of the sacrifice of his thanksgiving peace offerings, it shall be eaten on the day of his offering; he shall not leave any of it over until morning.

16 'But if the sacrifice of his offering is a votive or a freewill offering, it shall be eaten on the day that he offers his sacrifice, and on the next day what is left of it may be eaten;

17 but what is left over from the flesh of the sacrifice on the third day shall be burned with fire.

18 'So if any of the flesh of the sacrifice of his peace offerings should *ever* be eaten on the third day, he who offers it will not be accepted, *and* it will not be reckoned to his *benefit.* It shall be an offensive thing, and the person who eats of it will bear his *own* iniquity.

19 'Also the flesh that touches anything unclean shall not be eaten; it shall be burned with fire. As for *other* flesh, anyone who is clean may eat *such* flesh.

20 'But the person who eats the flesh of the sacrifice of peace offerings which belong to the LORD, in his uncleanness, that person shall be cut off from his people.

21 'When anyone touches anything unclean, whether human uncleanness, or an unclean animal, or any unclean de-testable thing, and eats of the flesh of the sacrifice of peace offerings which belong to the LORD, that person shall be cut off from his people.'"

22 Then the LORD spoke to Moses, saying,

23 "Speak to the sons of Israel, saying, 'You shall not eat any fat *from* an ox, a sheep or a goat.

24 'Also the fat of *an animal* which dies and the fat of an animal torn *by beasts* may be put to any other use, but you must certainly not eat it.

25 'For whoever eats the fat of the animal from which an offering by fire is offered to the LORD, even the person who eats shall be cut off from his people.

26 'You are not to eat any blood, either of bird or animal, in any of your dwellings.

27 'Any person who eats any blood, even that person shall be cut off from his people.'"

28 Then the LORD spoke to Moses, saying,

29 "Speak to the sons of Israel, saying, 'He who offers the sacrifice of his peace offerings to the LORD shall bring his offering to the LORD from the sacrifice of his peace offerings.

30 'His own hands are to bring offerings by fire to the LORD. He shall bring the fat with the breast, that the breast may be presented as a wave offering before the LORD.

31 'The priest shall offer up the fat in smoke on the altar, but the breast shall belong to Aaron and his sons.

32 'You shall give the right thigh to the priest as a contribution from the sacrifices of your peace offerings.

33 'The one among the sons of Aaron who offers the blood of the peace offerings and the fat, the right thigh shall be his as *his* portion.

34 'For I have taken the breast of the wave offering and the thigh of the contribution from the sons of Israel from the sacrifices of their peace offerings, and have given them to Aaron the priest and to his sons as *their* due forever from the sons of Israel.

35 'This is that which is consecrated to Aaron and that which is consecrated to his sons from the offerings by fire to the LORD, in that day when he presented them to serve as priests to the LORD.

36 'These the LORD had commanded to be given them from the sons of Israel in the day that He anointed them. It is *their* due forever throughout their generations.'"

37 This is the law of the burnt offering, the grain offering and the sin offering and the guilt offering and the ordination offering and the sacrifice of peace offerings,

38 which the LORD commanded Moses at Mount Sinai in the day that He commanded the sons of Israel to present their offerings to the LORD in the wilderness of Sinai.

8 THEN the LORD spoke to Moses, saying,

2 "Take Aaron and his sons with him, and the garments and the anointing oil and the bull of the sin offering, and the two rams and the basket of unleavened bread,

3 and assemble all the congregation at the doorway of the tent of meeting."

4 So Moses did just as the LORD commanded him. When the congregation was assembled at the doorway of the tent of meeting,

5 Moses said to the congregation, "This is the thing which the LORD has commanded to do."

6 Then Moses had Aaron and his sons come near and washed them with water.

7 He put the tunic on him and girded him with the sash, and clothed him with the robe and put the ephod on him; and he girded him with the artistic band of the ephod, with which he tied *it* to him.

8 He then placed the breastpiece on him, and in the breastpiece he put the Urim and the Thummim.

9 He also placed the turban on his head, and on the turban, at its front, he placed the golden plate, the holy crown, just as the LORD had commanded Moses.

10 Moses then took the anointing oil and anointed the tabernacle and all that was in it, and consecrated them.

11 He sprinkled some of it on the altar seven times and anointed the altar and all its utensils, and the basin and its stand, to consecrate them.

12 Then he poured some of the anointing oil on Aaron's head and anointed him, to consecrate him.

13 Next Moses had Aaron's sons come near and clothed them with tunics, and girded them with sashes and bound caps on them, just as the LORD had commanded Moses.

14 Then he brought the bull of the sin offering, and Aaron and his sons laid their hands on the head of the bull of the sin offering.

15 Next Moses slaughtered *it* and took the blood and with his finger put *some of it* around on the horns of the altar, and purified the altar. Then he poured out *the rest of* the blood at the base of the altar and consecrated it, to make atonement for it.

16 He also took all the fat that was on the entrails and the lobe of the liver, and the two kidneys and their fat; and Moses offered it up in smoke on the altar.

17 But the bull and its hide and its flesh and its refuse he burned in the fire outside the camp, just as the LORD had commanded Moses.

18 Then he presented the ram of the burnt offering, and Aaron and his sons laid their hands on the head of the ram.

19 Moses slaughtered *it* and sprinkled the blood around on the altar.

Life Examples:

AARON: A Fatal Compromise

LEVITICUS 8:2, 3

*A*aron—Moses' older brother, right-hand man, and spokesman during the time of the exodus—received a very high divine calling: to serve as priest for the liberated nation (Lev. 8:1–36). Because this enormous task also carried great responsibility, such a man had to live in a manner beyond reproach.

Unfortunately, Aaron had a weakness for unwise compromise. At a crucial time when Moses and his people needed him to stand strong, he gave in to the clamoring of the Israelites and forged a golden calf for them to worship. Through his failure he missed out on the Father's very best for himself and doomed a number of Israelites to a fatal encounter with holy God. Aaron's compromise led to the deaths of three thousand of his fellow Hebrews (Ex. 32:28).

Aaron reminds us that God requires full obedience to His Word, no matter how tempting it may feel to compromise.

20 When he had cut the ram into its pieces, Moses offered up the head and the pieces and the suet in smoke.

21 After he had washed the entrails and the legs with water, Moses offered up the whole ram in smoke on the altar. It was a burnt offering for a soothing aroma; it was an offering by fire to the LORD, just as the LORD had commanded Moses.

22 Then he presented the second ram, the ram of ordination, and Aaron and his sons laid their hands on the head of the ram.

23 Moses slaughtered *it* and took some of its blood and put it on the lobe of Aaron's right ear, and on the thumb of his right hand and on the big toe of his right foot.

24 He also had Aaron's sons come near; and Moses put some of the blood on the lobe of their right ear, and on the thumb of their right hand and on the big toe of their right foot. Moses then sprinkled *the rest of* the blood around on the altar.

25 He took the fat, and the fat tail, and all the fat that was on the entrails, and the lobe of the liver and the two kidneys and their fat and the right thigh.

26 From the basket of unleavened bread that was before the LORD, he took one unleavened cake and one cake of bread *mixed with* oil and one wafer, and placed *them* on the portions of fat and on the right thigh.

27 He then put all *these* on the hands of Aaron and on the hands of his sons and presented them as a wave offering before the LORD.

28 Then Moses took them from their hands and offered them up in smoke on the altar with the burnt offering. They were an ordination offering for a soothing aroma; it was an offering by fire to the LORD.

29 Moses also took the breast and presented it for a wave offering before the LORD; it was Moses' portion of the ram of ordination, just as the LORD had commanded Moses.

30 So Moses took some of the anointing oil and some of the blood which was on the altar and sprinkled it on Aaron, on his garments, on his sons, and on the garments of his sons with him; and he consecrated Aaron, his garments, and his sons, and the garments of his sons with him.

31 Then Moses said to Aaron and to his sons, "Boil the flesh at the doorway of the tent of meeting, and eat it there together with the bread which is in the basket of the ordination offering, just as I commanded, saying, 'Aaron and his sons shall eat it.'

32 "The remainder of the flesh and of the bread you shall burn in the fire.

33 "You shall not go outside the doorway of the tent of meeting for seven days, until the day that the period of your ordination is fulfilled; for he will ordain you through seven days.

34 "The LORD has commanded to do as has been done this day, to make atonement on your behalf.

35 "At the doorway of the tent of meeting, moreover, you shall remain day and night for seven days and keep the charge of the LORD, so that you will not die, for so I have been commanded."

36 Thus Aaron and his sons did all the things which the LORD had commanded through Moses.

Psalm 24:7–10

7   Lift up your heads, O gates,
     And be lifted up, O ancient doors,
     That the King of glory may come in!
8   Who is the King of glory?
     The LORD strong and mighty,
     The LORD mighty in battle.

LIFE LESSONS

➤ **Leviticus 8:35 —** *"So I have been commanded."*

*E*ven in worship, Moses did only what God had commanded him. God takes the lead; we are to follow. God's greatest servants understood this, and so should we if we want to serve Him.

➤ **Psalm 24:8 —** *Who is the King of glory? The LORD strong and mighty, the LORD mighty in battle.*

*T*he Lord is not only glorious; He is *the King* of glory. He is the greatest in glory, the pinnacle of excellence, the mountaintop of majesty, the summit of splendor. He is "over all, God blessed forever" (Rom. 9:5).

9 Lift up your heads, O gates,
    And lift *them* up, O ancient doors,
    That the King of glory may come
      in!
10 Who is this King of glory?
    The LORD of hosts,
    He is the King of glory.   Selah.

Proverbs 9:10–12

10 The fear of the LORD is the
    beginning of wisdom,
    And the knowledge of the Holy One
    is understanding.
11 For by me your days will be
    multiplied,
    And years of life will be added to
    you.
12 If you are wise, you are wise for
    yourself,
    And if you scoff, you alone will bear
    it.

Mark 1:1–22

1 THE beginning of the gospel of Jesus Christ, the Son of God.
2 As it is written in Isaiah the prophet:
"BEHOLD, I SEND MY MESSENGER
    AHEAD OF YOU,
WHO WILL PREPARE YOUR WAY;
3 THE VOICE OF ONE CRYING IN THE
    WILDERNESS,
'MAKE READY THE WAY OF THE LORD,
MAKE HIS PATHS STRAIGHT.'"
4 John the Baptist appeared in the wilderness preaching a baptism of repentance for the forgiveness of sins.
5 And all the country of Judea was going out to him, and all the people of Jerusalem; and they were being baptized by him in the Jordan River, confessing their sins.
6 John was clothed with camel's hair and *wore* a leather belt around his waist, and his diet was locusts and wild honey.
7 And he was preaching, and saying, "After me One is coming who is mightier than I, and I am not fit to stoop down and untie the thong of His sandals.
8 "I baptized you with water; but He will baptize you with the Holy Spirit."
9 In those days Jesus came from Nazareth in Galilee and was baptized by John in the Jordan.
10 Immediately coming up out of the water, He saw the heavens opening, and the Spirit like a dove descending upon Him;
11 and a voice came out of the heavens: "You are My beloved Son, in You I am well-pleased."
12 Immediately the Spirit *impelled Him to go* out into the wilderness.
13 And He was in the wilderness forty days being tempted by Satan; and He was with the wild beasts, and the angels were ministering to Him.
14 Now after John had been taken into custody, Jesus came into Galilee, preaching the gospel of God,
15 and saying, "The time is fulfilled, and the kingdom of God is at hand; repent and believe in the gospel."
16 As He was going along by the Sea of Galilee, He saw Simon and Andrew, the brother of Simon, casting a net in the sea; for they were fishermen.
17 And Jesus said to them, "Follow Me, and I will make you become fishers of men."
18 Immediately they left their nets and followed Him.
19 Going on a little farther, He saw James the son of Zebedee, and John his brother, who were also in the boat mending the nets.
20 Immediately He called them; and they left their father Zebedee in the boat with the hired servants, and went away to follow Him.
21 They *went into Capernaum; and immediately on the Sabbath He entered the synagogue and *began* to teach.
22 They were amazed at His teaching; for He was teaching them as *one* having authority, and not as the scribes.

LIFE LESSONS

➤ **Mark 1:5** — *And all the country of Judea was going out to him . . . and they were being baptized by him in the Jordan River, confessing their sins.*

*C*onfessing our sins reminds us of our guilt and inability to make ourselves right, even as it points us to the grace of God who alone can give us spiritual life.

9 NOW it came about on the eighth day that Moses called Aaron and his sons and the elders of Israel;

2 and he said to Aaron, "Take for yourself a calf, a bull, for a sin offering and a ram for a burnt offering, *both* without defect, and offer *them* before the LORD.

3 "Then to the sons of Israel you shall speak, saying, 'Take a male goat for a sin offering, and a calf and a lamb, both one year old, without defect, for a burnt offering,

4 and an ox and a ram for peace offerings, to sacrifice before the LORD, and a grain offering mixed with oil; for today the LORD will appear to you.'"

5 So they took what Moses had commanded to the front of the tent of meeting, and the whole congregation came near and stood before the LORD.

6 Moses said, "This is the thing which the LORD has commanded you to do, that the glory of the LORD may appear to you."

7 Moses then said to Aaron, "Come near to the altar and offer your sin offering and your burnt offering, that you may make atonement for yourself and for the people; then make the offering for the people, that you may make atonement for them, just as the LORD has commanded."

8 So Aaron came near to the altar and slaughtered the calf of the sin offering which was for himself.

9 Aaron's sons presented the blood to him; and he dipped his finger in the blood and put *some* on the horns of the altar, and poured out *the rest of* the blood at the base of the altar.

10 The fat and the kidneys and the lobe of the liver of the sin offering, he then offered up in smoke on the altar just as the LORD had commanded Moses.

11 The flesh and the skin, however, he burned with fire outside the camp.

12 Then he slaughtered the burnt offering; and Aaron's sons handed the blood to him and he sprinkled it around on the altar.

13 They handed the burnt offering to him in pieces, with the head, and he offered *them* up in smoke on the altar.

14 He also washed the entrails and the legs, and offered *them* up in smoke with the burnt offering on the altar.

15 Then he presented the people's offering, and took the goat of the sin offering which was for the people, and slaughtered it and offered it for sin, like the first.

16 He also presented the burnt offering, and offered it according to the ordinance.

17 Next he presented the grain offering, and filled his hand with some of it and offered *it* up in smoke on the altar, besides the burnt offering of the morning.

18 Then he slaughtered the ox and the ram, the sacrifice of peace offerings which was for the people; and Aaron's sons handed the blood to him and he sprinkled it around on the altar.

19 As for the portions of fat from the ox and from the ram, the fat tail, and the *fat* covering, and the kidneys and the lobe of the liver,

20 they now placed the portions of fat on the breasts; and he offered them up in smoke on the altar.

21 But the breasts and the right thigh Aaron presented as a wave offering before the LORD, just as Moses had commanded.

22 Then Aaron lifted up his hands toward the people and blessed them, and he stepped down after making the sin offering and the burnt offering and the peace offerings.

23 Moses and Aaron went into the tent of meeting. When they came out and blessed the people, the glory of the LORD appeared to all the people.

24 Then fire came out from before the LORD and consumed the burnt offering and the portions of fat on the altar; and when all the people saw *it*, they shouted and fell on their faces.

10 NOW Nadab and Abihu, the sons of Aaron, took their respective firepans, and after putting fire in them, placed incense on it and offered strange fire before the LORD, which He had not commanded them.

2 And fire came out from the presence of the LORD and consumed them, and they died before the LORD.

3 Then Moses said to Aaron, "It is ◄ what the LORD spoke, saying,

   'By those who come near Me I will
     be treated as holy,

LIFE LESSONS

➤ **Leviticus 10:3 — *"By those who come near Me I will be treated as holy."***

*W*hile we no longer live under the Mosaic law, God's nature has not changed. We can never forget that we serve a holy God, who insists on being treated as holy.

And before all the people I will be honored.'"
So Aaron, therefore, kept silent.
4 Moses called also to Mishael and Elzaphan, the sons of Aaron's uncle Uzziel, and said to them, "Come forward, carry your relatives away from the front of the sanctuary to the outside of the camp."
5 So they came forward and carried them still in their tunics to the outside of the camp, as Moses had said.
6 Then Moses said to Aaron and to his sons Eleazar and Ithamar, "Do not uncover your heads nor tear your clothes, so that you will not die and that He will not become wrathful against all the congregation. But your kinsmen, the whole house of Israel, shall bewail the burning which the LORD has brought about.
7 "You shall not even go out from the doorway of the tent of meeting, or you will die; for the LORD's anointing oil is upon you." So they did according to the word of Moses.
8 The LORD then spoke to Aaron, saying,
9 "Do not drink wine or strong drink, neither you nor your sons with you, when you come into the tent of meeting, so that you will not die—it is a perpetual statute throughout your generations—
10 and so as to make a distinction between the holy and the profane, and between the unclean and the clean,
11 and so as to teach the sons of Israel all the statutes which the LORD has spoken to them through Moses."
12 Then Moses spoke to Aaron, and to his surviving sons, Eleazar and Ithamar, "Take the grain offering that is left over from the LORD's offerings by fire and eat it unleavened beside the altar, for it is most holy.
13 "You shall eat it, moreover, in a holy place, because it is your due and your sons' due out of the LORD's offerings by fire; for thus I have been commanded.
14 "The breast of the wave offering, however, and the thigh of the offering you may eat in a clean place, you and your sons and your daughters with you; for they have been given as your due and your sons' due out of the sacrifices of the peace offerings of the sons of Israel.
15 "The thigh offered by lifting up and the breast offered by waving they shall bring along with the offerings by fire of the portions of fat, to present as a wave offering before the LORD; so it shall be a thing perpetually due you and your sons with you, just as the LORD has commanded."
16 But Moses searched carefully for the goat of the sin offering, and behold, it had been burned up! So he was angry with Aaron's surviving sons Eleazar and Ithamar, saying,
17 "Why did you not eat the sin offering at the holy place? For it is most holy, and He gave it to you to bear away the guilt of the congregation, to make atonement for them before the LORD.
18 "Behold, since its blood had not been brought inside, into the sanctuary, you should certainly have eaten it in the sanctuary, just as I commanded."
19 But Aaron spoke to Moses, "Behold, this very day they presented their sin offering and their burnt offering before the LORD. When things like these happened to me, if I had eaten a sin offering today, would it have been good in the sight of the LORD?"
20 When Moses heard *that*, it seemed good in his sight.

Psalm 25:1–7

A Psalm of David.

25 TO You, O LORD, I lift up my soul.
2 O my God, in You I trust,

LIFE LESSONS

➤ **Leviticus 10:19 — *"If I had eaten a sin offering today, would it have been good in the sight of the LORD?"***

*G*od is holy, and yet He is also merciful. We should never forget His holiness, and never take for granted His mercy.

ANSWERS TO LIFE'S QUESTIONS

Why should we know the ways of God?

PSALM 25:4, 5

*I*n order to know someone intimately, you can't just know what they do—you must know his character and his heart. You have to know what motivates him.

The same is true for God. Unfortunately, sometimes we know *about* God, but we really don't know *Him*. Even more unfortunate is that we're satisfied just knowing a few facts about Him. Yet God wants us to truly know and love Him.

Here are six reasons we should know God's ways.

1. *We should know the ways of God because they are essential in knowing Him.*

Why should we learn the ways of God? Because we can get to know God's heart by learning about His ways. Life's greatest pleasure is knowing Him personally and intimately.

2. *We should know the ways of God because He requires that we know them.*

God commands us to know His ways. Deuteronomy 10:12 tells us God requires us to fear Him, walk in all His ways, and love Him. And since God requires us to know His ways,

He will certainly help us to understand them. We will learn His ways one at a time as we ask Him to show us.

3. *We should know the ways of God because they are the yearning of His heart.*

God deeply desires our fellowship. This fact alone should motivate us to seek Him more passionately. He wants us to know Him in a deep, meaningful way.

4. *We should know the ways of God because He loves us.*

God offers us His way—which is the wisest way—because He's an all-knowing God who loves us and desires the best for us. He wants each of us to realize that His way is so much better than our own, and it's the only way we'll be truly happy.

5. *We should know the ways of God because they are the best way.*

No matter what situation we face—no matter how difficult a choice it may be—we can be certain that God's way is the best way, even if it is a difficult and painful one. God will guide us and will give us the strength and wisdom to face our circumstances in a godly manner.

6. *We should know the ways of God because they are the pathway to success.*

God's way offers the true path to success. What is real success? The world's definition involves wealth and power, but true success is godly living. When we imitate His ways, He blesses us above and beyond our imaginations.

Do not let me be ashamed;
Do not let my enemies exult over me.
3 Indeed, none of those who wait for
You will be ashamed;
Those who deal treacherously
without cause will be ashamed.
4 Make me know Your ways, O LORD;
Teach me Your paths.
5 Lead me in Your truth and teach
me,
For You are the God of my salvation;
For You I wait all the day.

6 Remember, O LORD, Your
compassion and Your
lovingkindnesses,
For they have been from of old.
7 Do not remember the sins of my
youth or my transgressions;
According to Your lovingkindness
remember me,
For Your goodness' sake, O LORD.

Proverbs 9:13–18

13 The woman of folly is boisterous,
She is naive and knows nothing.
14 She sits at the doorway of her
house,
On a seat by the high places of the
city,
15 Calling to those who pass by,
Who are making their paths
straight:
16 "Whoever is naive, let him turn in
here,"

LIFE LESSONS

Psalm 25:4, 5 — *Make me know Your ways, O LORD . . . for You are the God of my salvation; for You I wait all the day.*

*W*e learn God's ways and His truth over time; we do not become experts in the things of God overnight. He takes years to mold His servants into the likeness of His Son, so we must beware of growing impatient.

And to him who lacks
understanding she says,
17 "Stolen water is sweet;
And bread *eaten* in secret is
pleasant."
18 But he does not know that the dead
are there,
That her guests are in the depths of
Sheol.

◈ Mark 1:23–45

23 Just then there was a man in their synagogue with an unclean spirit; and he cried out,
24 saying, "What business do we have with each other, Jesus of Nazareth? Have You come to destroy us? I know who You are—the Holy One of God!"
25 And Jesus rebuked him, saying, "Be quiet, and come out of him!"
26 Throwing him into convulsions, the unclean spirit cried out with a loud voice and came out of him.
27 They were all amazed, so that they debated among themselves, saying, "What is this? A new teaching with authority! He commands even the unclean spirits, and they obey Him."
28 Immediately the news about Him spread everywhere into all the surrounding district of Galilee.
29 And immediately after they came out of the synagogue, they came into the house of Simon and Andrew, with James and John.
30 Now Simon's mother-in-law was lying sick with a fever; and immediately they *spoke to Jesus about her.
31 And He came to her and raised her up, taking her by the hand, and the fever left her, and she waited on them.
32 When evening came, after the sun had set, they *began* bringing to Him all who were ill and those who were demon-possessed.
33 And the whole city had gathered at the door.
34 And He healed many who were ill with various diseases, and cast out many demons; and He was not permitting the demons to speak, because they knew who He was.
35 In the early morning, while it was

still dark, Jesus got up, left *the house,* and went away to a secluded place, and was praying there.
36 Simon and his companions searched for Him;
37 they found Him, and *said to Him, "Everyone is looking for You."
38 He *said to them, "Let us go somewhere else to the towns nearby, so that I may preach there also; for that is what I came for."
39 And He went into their synagogues throughout all Galilee, preaching and casting out the demons.
40 And a leper *came to Jesus, beseeching Him and falling on his knees before Him, and saying, "If You are willing, You can make me clean."
41 Moved with compassion, Jesus stretched out His hand and touched him, and *said to him, "I am willing; be cleansed."
42 Immediately the leprosy left him and he was cleansed.

LIFE LESSONS

➤ **Mark 1:27 —** *"A new teaching with authority! He commands even the unclean spirits, and they obey Him."*

*J*esus closely connected His teaching with His miracles. The miracles were designed to point to the validity of both His teachings and His personal claims.

➤ **Mark 1:34 —** *He healed many who were ill with various diseases, and cast out many demons; and He was not permitting the demons to speak, because they knew who He was.*

*J*esus does not need the testimony of evil spirits to corroborate His identity or to vouch for His holy character. We might be impressed with such supernatural witnesses, but Jesus dismissed them.

➤ **Mark 1:35 —** *In the early morning, while it was still dark, Jesus got up, left the house, and went away to a secluded place, and was praying there.*

*J*esus was never too busy to pray. If He had to get up before sunrise to pray, that's what He did. He valued His time alone with His Father and pursued it His entire life.

43 And He sternly warned him and immediately sent him away,
44 and He *said to him, "See that you say nothing to anyone; but go, show yourself to the priest and offer for your cleansing what Moses commanded, as a testimony to them."

45 But he went out and began to proclaim it freely and to spread the news around, to such an extent that Jesus could no longer publicly enter a city, but stayed out in unpopulated areas; and they were coming to Him from everywhere.

Leviticus 11:1—12:8

11 THE LORD spoke again to Moses and to Aaron, saying to them,
2 "Speak to the sons of Israel, saying, 'These are the creatures which you may eat from all the animals that are on the earth.
3 'Whatever divides a hoof, thus making split hoofs, *and* chews the cud, among the animals, that you may eat.
4 'Nevertheless, you are not to eat of these, among those which chew the cud, or among those which divide the hoof: the camel, for though it chews cud, it does not divide the hoof, it is unclean to you.
5 'Likewise, the shaphan, for though it chews cud, it does not divide the hoof, it is unclean to you;
6 the rabbit also, for though it chews cud, it does not divide the hoof, it is unclean to you;
7 and the pig, for though it divides the hoof, thus making a split hoof, it does not chew cud, it is unclean to you.
8 'You shall not eat of their flesh nor touch their carcasses; they are unclean to you.
9 'These you may eat, whatever is in the water: all that have fins and scales, those in the water, in the seas or in the rivers, you may eat.
10 'But whatever is in the seas and in the rivers that does not have fins and scales among all the teeming life of the water, and among all the living creatures that are in the water, they are detestable things to you,
11 and they shall be abhorrent to you; you may not eat of their flesh, and their carcasses you shall detest.

12 'Whatever in the water does not have fins and scales is abhorrent to you.
13 'These, moreover, you shall detest among the birds; they are abhorrent, not to be eaten: the eagle and the vulture and the buzzard,
14 and the kite and the falcon in its kind,
15 every raven in its kind,
16 and the ostrich and the owl and the sea gull and the hawk in its kind,
17 and the little owl and the cormorant and the great owl,
18 and the white owl and the pelican and the carrion vulture,
19 and the stork, the heron in its kinds, and the hoopoe, and the bat.
20 'All the winged insects that walk on *all* fours are detestable to you.
21 'Yet these you may eat among all the winged insects which walk on *all* fours: those which have above their feet jointed legs with which to jump on the earth.
22 'These of them you may eat: the locust in its kinds, and the devastating locust in its kinds, and the cricket in its kinds, and the grasshopper in its kinds.
23 'But all other winged insects which are four-footed are detestable to you.
24 'By these, moreover, you will be made unclean: whoever touches their carcasses becomes unclean until evening,
25 and whoever picks up any of their carcasses shall wash his clothes and be unclean until evening.
26 'Concerning all the animals which divide the hoof but do not make a split *hoof*, or which do not chew cud, they are unclean to you: whoever touches them becomes unclean.
27 'Also whatever walks on its paws, among all the creatures that walk on

all fours, are unclean to you; whoever touches their carcasses becomes unclean until evening,

28 and the one who picks up their carcasses shall wash his clothes and be unclean until evening; they are unclean to you.

29 'Now these are to you the unclean among the swarming things which swarm on the earth: the mole, and the mouse, and the great lizard in its kinds,

30 and the gecko, and the crocodile, and the lizard, and the sand reptile, and the chameleon.

31 'These are to you the unclean among all the swarming things; whoever touches them when they are dead becomes unclean until evening.

32 'Also anything on which one of them may fall when they are dead becomes unclean, including any wooden article, or clothing, or a skin, or a sack—any article of which use is made—it shall be put in the water and be unclean until evening, then it becomes clean.

33 'As for any earthenware vessel into which one of them may fall, whatever is in it becomes unclean and you shall break the vessel.

34 'Any of the food which may be eaten, on which water comes, shall become unclean, and any liquid which may be drunk in every vessel shall become unclean.

35 'Everything, moreover, on which part of their carcass may fall becomes unclean; an oven or a stove shall be smashed; they are unclean and shall continue as unclean to you.

36 'Nevertheless a spring or a cistern collecting water shall be clean, though the one who touches their carcass shall be unclean.

37 'If a part of their carcass falls on any seed for sowing which is to be sown, it is clean.

38 'Though if water is put on the seed and a part of their carcass falls on it, it is unclean to you.

39 'Also if one of the animals dies which you have for food, the one who touches its carcass becomes unclean until evening.

40 'He too, who eats some of its carcass shall wash his clothes and be unclean until evening, and the one who picks up its carcass shall wash his clothes and be unclean until evening.

41 'Now every swarming thing that swarms on the earth is detestable, not to be eaten.

42 'Whatever crawls on its belly, and whatever walks on *all* fours, whatever has many feet, in respect to every swarming thing that swarms on the earth, you shall not eat them, for they are detestable.

43 'Do not render yourselves detestable through any of the swarming things that swarm; and you shall not make yourselves unclean with them so that you become unclean.

44 'For I am the LORD your God. Consecrate yourselves therefore, and be holy, for I am holy. And you shall not make yourselves unclean with any of the swarming things that swarm on the earth.

45 'For I am the LORD who brought you up from the land of Egypt to be your God; thus you shall be holy, for I am holy.'"

46 This is the law regarding the animal and the bird, and every living thing that moves in the waters and everything that swarms on the earth,

47 to make a distinction between the unclean and the clean, and between the edible creature and the creature which is not to be eaten.

12 THEN the LORD spoke to Moses, saying,

2 "Speak to the sons of Israel, saying: 'When a woman gives birth and bears a male *child,* then she shall be unclean for seven days, as in the days of her menstruation she shall be unclean.

3 'On the eighth day the flesh of his foreskin shall be circumcised.

4 'Then she shall remain in the blood of *her* purification for thirty-three days;

LIFE LESSONS

➤ **Leviticus 11:45 —** *"You shall be holy, for I am holy."*

God created us to be holy as He is holy. He makes us holy when we place our faith in Christ, and we live out that holiness when we are led by the power of His Spirit and when we obey God.

WHAT THE BIBLE SAYS ABOUT ◈

Interesting Commands

Leviticus 12:1–8

*A*ll of God's commands are for our good and well-being. Of course, it is easier to understand some of them more than others. We agree that we should not murder anyone (Ex. 20:13) or steal (Ex. 20:15); however, we might wonder how the commands of Leviticus 12 are still essential for our lives.

Certainly, Leviticus 12 is not very "politically correct"—especially in declaring women who have just given birth as "unclean" (vv. 2, 5). To be unclean meant that a person was morally or ceremonially defiled because they had come in contact with blood; a disease such as leprosy; food specifically forbidden by God; or a dead person or animal. As a result, the unclean person was not permitted to—as Leviticus 12:4 says—"touch any consecrated thing, nor enter the sanctuary until the days of her purification are completed." For the new mother, the purification time was to last forty days for a boy, and eighty days for a girl.

One may wonder why God would order such a law. After all, aren't children supposed to be a blessing? We read in Psalm 127:3, "Children are a gift of the LORD, the fruit of the womb is a reward."

Yet to understand the significance of God's command, we must realize the majority of ancient cultures required women to return to their daily chores immediately after childbirth. Those societies took no notice of the needs of the mother or of the child—to their great detriment.

However, the Hebrew culture was different because of the commands of God found in Leviticus 12:1–8. Jewish women were able to recuperate during their time of purification—regaining their strength and bonding with the baby. Instead of an unimportant afterthought, the babies would not only have the undivided attentions of their mothers, but the entire household would pull together to care for them because the mothers could not do any cooking or cleaning. So, as you can see, the time of purification—God's command—was actually a blessing.

As with all of God's Word, we must look deeply to the underlying spiritual principle in order to understand God's profound wisdom in it. That is why Psalm 111:10 declares, "The fear of the LORD is the beginning of wisdom; a good understanding have all those who do His commandments; His praise endures forever."

God's Word is always good and trustworthy. Therefore, don't pick and choose what commands you want to follow. Instead, understand the wisdom of the entire counsel of God. ◈

---

she shall not touch any consecrated thing, nor enter the sanctuary until the days of her purification are completed.

5 'But if she bears a female *child*, then she shall be unclean for two weeks, as in her menstruation; and she shall remain in the blood of *her* purification for sixty-six days.

6 'When the days of her purification are completed, for a son or for a daughter, she shall bring to the priest at the doorway of the tent of meeting a one year old lamb for a burnt offering and a young pigeon or a turtledove for a sin offering.

7 'Then he shall offer it before the LORD and make atonement for her, and she shall be cleansed from the flow of her blood. This is the law for her who bears *a child, whether* a male or a female.

8 'But if she cannot afford a lamb, then she shall take two turtledoves or two young pigeons, the one for a burnt offering and the other for a sin offering; and the priest shall make atonement for her, and she will be clean.'"

◈   Psalm 25:8–15

8   Good and upright is the LORD;
    Therefore He instructs sinners in the way.
9   He leads the humble in justice,
    And He teaches the humble His way.
10 All the paths of the LORD are lovingkindness and truth
    To those who keep His covenant and His testimonies.
11 For Your name's sake, O LORD,
    Pardon my iniquity, for it is great.

12 Who is the man who fears the LORD?
   He will instruct him in the way he
      should choose.
13 His soul will abide in prosperity,
   And his descendants will inherit the
      land.
14 The secret of the LORD is for those
      who fear Him,
   And He will make them know His
      covenant.
15 My eyes are continually toward the
      LORD,
   For He will pluck my feet out of the
      net.

Proverbs 10:1–3

10 THE proverbs of Solomon.
   A wise son makes a father glad,
   But a foolish son is a grief to his
      mother.
2 Ill-gotten gains do not profit,
   But righteousness delivers from
      death.
3 The LORD will not allow the
      righteous to hunger,
   But He will reject the craving of the
      wicked.

Mark 2:1–28

2 WHEN He had come back to Capernaum several days afterward, it was
heard that He was at home.

LIFE LESSONS

➤ **Psalm 25:11 — *For Your name's sake,
O LORD, pardon my iniquity, for it is great.***

*G*od saves us, not because He thinks
we're smart or worthy of His Son's
work on our behalf, but because of His
own nature and goodness. He saves us
for His name's sake and for His glory.

➤ **Proverbs 10:2 — *Ill-gotten gains do
not profit.***

*T*he Bible never tries to hide the fact
that the wicked can indeed amass
"treasures" through their wicked deeds.
But it also insists those ill-gotten treasures
will not benefit them at all in the end.

---

2 And many were gathered together,
so that there was no longer room, not
even near the door; and He was speaking
the word to them.
3 And they *came, bringing to Him a
paralytic, carried by four men.
4 Being unable to get to Him because
of the crowd, they removed the roof
above Him; and when they had dug an
opening, they let down the pallet on
which the paralytic was lying.
5 And Jesus seeing their faith *said
to the paralytic, "Son, your sins are forgiven."
6 But some of the scribes were sitting
there and reasoning in their hearts,
7 "Why does this man speak that way?
He is blaspheming; who can forgive sins
but God alone?"
8 Immediately Jesus, aware in His
spirit that they were reasoning that way
within themselves, *said to them, "Why
are you reasoning about these things in
your hearts?
9 "Which is easier, to say to the paralytic, 'Your sins are forgiven'; or to say,
'Get up, and pick up your pallet and
walk'?
10 "But so that you may know that the
Son of Man has authority on earth to
forgive sins"—He *said to the paralytic,
11 "I say to you, get up, pick up your
pallet and go home."
12 And he got up and immediately
picked up the pallet and went out in the
sight of everyone, so that they were all
amazed and were glorifying God, saying,
"We have never seen anything like this."
13 And He went out again by the seashore; and all the people were coming to
Him, and He was teaching them.
14 As He passed by, He saw Levi the
son of Alphaeus sitting in the tax booth,
and He *said to him, "Follow Me!" And
he got up and followed Him.
15 And it *happened that He was reclining *at the table* in his house, and many
tax collectors and sinners were dining
with Jesus and His disciples; for there
were many of them, and they were following Him.
16 When the scribes of the Pharisees
saw that He was eating with the sinners
and tax collectors, they said to His disciples, "Why is He eating and drinking
with tax collectors and sinners?"
17 And hearing *this*, Jesus *said to

LIFE LESSONS

➤ **Mark 2:17 —** *"I did not come to call the righteous, but sinners."*

Sometimes we feel as if we need to be perfect to seek God, but the opposite is true. Jesus came to help all of us in our deepest, most desperate need—the need for a Savior. If you feel weary, discouraged, and hopeless, then Jesus is the physician you need. He offers Himself to you right now.

➤ **Mark 2:22 —** *"No one puts new wine into old wineskins."*

All of us tend to resist change, but God's Spirit continually moves in new ways and in new directions. If we want to keep in step with the Spirit, we need to be willing to change the way we do things.

them, "*It is* not those who are healthy who need a physician, but those who are sick; I did not come to call the righteous, but sinners."
18 John's disciples and the Pharisees were fasting; and they *came and *said to Him, "Why do John's disciples and the disciples of the Pharisees fast, but Your disciples do not fast?"
19 And Jesus said to them, "While the bridegroom is with them, the attendants of the bridegroom cannot fast, can they? So long as they have the bridegroom with them, they cannot fast.
20 "But the days will come when the bridegroom is taken away from them, and then they will fast in that day.
21 "No one sews a patch of unshrunk cloth on an old garment; otherwise the

patch pulls away from it, the new from the old, and a worse tear results.
22 "No one puts new wine into old wineskins; otherwise the wine will burst the skins, and the wine is lost and the skins *as well*; but *one puts* new wine into fresh wineskins."
23 And it happened that He was passing through the grainfields on the Sabbath, and His disciples began to make their way along while picking the heads *of grain*.
24 The Pharisees were saying to Him, "Look, why are they doing what is not lawful on the Sabbath?"
25 And He *said to them, "Have you never read what David did when he was in need and he and his companions became hungry;
26 how he entered the house of God in the time of Abiathar *the* high priest, and ate the consecrated bread, which is not lawful for *anyone* to eat except the priests, and he also gave it to those who were with him?"
27 Jesus said to them, "The Sabbath was made for man, and not man for the Sabbath.
28 "So the Son of Man is Lord even of the Sabbath."

LIFE LESSONS

➤ **Mark 2:27 —** *"The Sabbath was made for man, and not man for the Sabbath."*

God created the Sabbath to bless humankind, to give men and women a much-needed opportunity to rest, relax, and regain strength. The Sabbath was not meant to be a burden but a blessing.

Leviticus 13:1–59

13 THEN the LORD spoke to Moses and to Aaron, saying,
2 "When a man has on the skin of his body a swelling or a scab or a bright spot, and it becomes an infection of leprosy on the skin of his body, then he

shall be brought to Aaron the priest or to one of his sons the priests.
3 "The priest shall look at the mark on the skin of the body, and if the hair in the infection has turned white and the infection appears to be deeper than the skin of his body, it is an infection of leprosy; when the priest has looked at him, he shall pronounce him unclean.
4 "But if the bright spot is white on the

skin of his body, and it does not appear to be deeper than the skin, and the hair on it has not turned white, then the priest shall isolate *him who has* the infection for seven days.

5 "The priest shall look at him on the seventh day, and if in his eyes the infection has not changed *and* the infection has not spread on the skin, then the priest shall isolate him for seven more days.

6 "The priest shall look at him again on the seventh day, and if the infection has faded and the mark has not spread on the skin, then the priest shall pronounce him clean; it is *only* a scab. And he shall wash his clothes and be clean.

7 "But if the scab spreads farther on the skin after he has shown himself to the priest for his cleansing, he shall appear again to the priest.

8 "The priest shall look, and if the scab has spread on the skin, then the priest shall pronounce him unclean; it is leprosy.

9 "When the infection of leprosy is on a man, then he shall be brought to the priest.

10 "The priest shall then look, and if there is a white swelling in the skin, and it has turned the hair white, and there is quick raw flesh in the swelling,

11 it is a chronic leprosy on the skin of his body, and the priest shall pronounce him unclean; he shall not isolate him, for he is unclean.

12 "If the leprosy breaks out farther on the skin, and the leprosy covers all the skin of *him who has* the infection from his head even to his feet, as far as the priest can see,

13 then the priest shall look, and behold, *if* the leprosy has covered all his body, he shall pronounce clean *him who has* the infection; it has all turned white *and* he is clean.

14 "But whenever raw flesh appears on him, he shall be unclean.

15 "The priest shall look at the raw flesh, and he shall pronounce him unclean; the raw flesh is unclean, it is leprosy.

16 "Or if the raw flesh turns again and is changed to white, then he shall come to the priest,

17 and the priest shall look at him, and behold, *if* the infection has turned to white, then the priest shall pronounce clean *him who has* the infection; he is clean.

18 "When the body has a boil on its skin and it is healed,

19 and in the place of the boil there is a white swelling or a reddish-white, bright spot, then it shall be shown to the priest;

20 and the priest shall look, and behold, *if* it appears to be lower than the skin, and the hair on it has turned white, then the priest shall pronounce him unclean; it is the infection of leprosy, it has broken out in the boil.

21 "But if the priest looks at it, and behold, there are no white hairs in it and it is not lower than the skin and is faded, then the priest shall isolate him for seven days;

22 and if it spreads farther on the skin, then the priest shall pronounce him unclean; it is an infection.

23 "But if the bright spot remains in its place and does not spread, it is *only* the scar of the boil; and the priest shall pronounce him clean.

24 "Or if the body sustains in its skin a burn by fire, and the raw *flesh* of the burn becomes a bright spot, reddish-white, or white,

25 then the priest shall look at it. And if the hair in the bright spot has turned white and it appears to be deeper than the skin, it is leprosy; it has broken out in the burn. Therefore, the priest shall pronounce him unclean; it is an infection of leprosy.

26 "But if the priest looks at it, and indeed, there is no white hair in the bright spot and it is no deeper than the skin, but is dim, then the priest shall isolate him for seven days;

27 and the priest shall look at him on the seventh day. If it spreads farther in the skin, then the priest shall pronounce him unclean; it is an infection of leprosy.

28 "But if the bright spot remains in its place and has not spread in the skin, but is dim, it is the swelling from the burn; and the priest shall pronounce him clean, for it is *only* the scar of the burn.

29 "Now if a man or woman has an infection on the head or on the beard,

30 then the priest shall look at the infection, and if it appears to be deeper than the skin and there is thin yellowish hair in it, then the priest shall pronounce him unclean; it is a scale, it is leprosy of the head or of the beard.

31 "But if the priest looks at the infection

of the scale, and indeed, it appears to be no deeper than the skin and there is no black hair in it, then the priest shall isolate *the person* with the scaly infection for seven days.

32 "On the seventh day the priest shall look at the infection, and if the scale has not spread and no yellowish hair has grown in it, and the appearance of the scale is no deeper than the skin,

33 then he shall shave himself, but he shall not shave the scale; and the priest shall isolate *the person* with the scale seven more days.

34 "Then on the seventh day the priest shall look at the scale, and if the scale has not spread in the skin and it appears to be no deeper than the skin, the priest shall pronounce him clean; and he shall wash his clothes and be clean.

35 "But if the scale spreads farther in the skin after his cleansing,

36 then the priest shall look at him, and if the scale has spread in the skin, the priest need not seek for the yellowish hair; he is unclean.

37 "If in his sight the scale has remained, however, and black hair has grown in it, the scale has healed, he is clean; and the priest shall pronounce him clean.

38 "When a man or a woman has bright spots on the skin of the body, *even* white bright spots,

39 then the priest shall look, and if the bright spots on the skin of their bodies are a faint white, it is eczema that has broken out on the skin; he is clean.

40 "Now if a man loses the hair of his head, he is bald; he is clean.

41 "If his head becomes bald at the front and sides, he is bald on the forehead; he is clean.

42 "But if on the bald head or the bald forehead, there occurs a reddish-white infection, it is leprosy breaking out on his bald head or on his bald forehead.

43 "Then the priest shall look at him; and if the swelling of the infection is reddish-white on his bald head or on his bald forehead, like the appearance of leprosy in the skin of the body,

44 he is a leprous man, he is unclean. The priest shall surely pronounce him unclean; his infection is on his head.

45 "As for the leper who has the infection, his clothes shall be torn, and the hair of his head shall be uncovered, and he shall cover his mustache and cry, 'Unclean! Unclean!'

46 "He shall remain unclean all the days during which he has the infection; he is unclean. He shall live alone; his dwelling shall be outside the camp.

47 "When a garment has a mark of leprosy in it, whether it is a wool garment or a linen garment,

48 whether in warp or woof, of linen or of wool, whether in leather or in any article made of leather,

49 if the mark is greenish or reddish in the garment or in the leather, or in the warp or in the woof, or in any article of leather, it is a leprous mark and shall be shown to the priest.

50 "Then the priest shall look at the mark and shall quarantine the article with the mark for seven days.

51 "He shall then look at the mark on the seventh day; if the mark has spread in the garment, whether in the warp or in the woof, or in the leather, whatever the purpose for which the leather is used, the mark is a leprous malignancy, it is unclean.

52 "So he shall burn the garment, whether the warp or the woof, in wool or in linen, or any article of leather in which the mark occurs, for it is a leprous malignancy; it shall be burned in the fire.

53 "But if the priest shall look, and indeed the mark has not spread in the garment, either in the warp or in the woof, or in any article of leather,

54 then the priest shall order them to wash the thing in which the mark occurs and he shall quarantine it for seven more days.

55 "After the article with the mark has been washed, the priest shall again look, and if the mark has not changed its appearance, even though the mark has not spread, it is unclean; you shall burn it in the fire, whether an eating away has produced bareness on the top or on the front of it.

56 "Then if the priest looks, and if the mark has faded after it has been washed, then he shall tear it out of the garment or out of the leather, whether from the warp or from the woof;

57 and if it appears again in the garment, whether in the warp or in the

woof, or in any article of leather, it is an outbreak; the article with the mark shall be burned in the fire.
58 "The garment, whether the warp or the woof, or any article of leather from which the mark has departed when you washed it, it shall then be washed a second time and will be clean."
59 This is the law for the mark of leprosy in a garment of wool or linen, whether in the warp or in the woof, or in any article of leather, for pronouncing it clean or unclean.

Psalm 25:16–22

16 Turn to me and be gracious to me,
For I am lonely and afflicted.
17 The troubles of my heart are enlarged;
Bring me out of my distresses.
18 Look upon my affliction and my trouble,
And forgive all my sins.
19 Look upon my enemies, for they are many,

ANSWERS TO LIFE'S QUESTIONS

What are the consequences of slothful living?

PROVERBS 10:4, 5

We know that the Lord is displeased with laziness because it hurts us. Idleness stops us from becoming everything He created us to be, and it prevents us from receiving God's best blessings. In fact, Proverbs 10:4, 5 tells us, "Poor is he who works with a negligent hand . . . He who sleeps in harvest is a son who acts shamefully."

People often don't realize that slothfulness during their youth costs them dearly when they are older because they learn to function in a destructive pattern. As lazy people get older, they notice they don't have the same comforts and achievements as other people their age, so they begin to question why they haven't received the same opportunities others have gotten. However, the reason they lack those things is because they've been lazy—they haven't made the effort to achieve them. They've chosen the kind of life they're living.

So what are the actual consequences of slothful living?

• *The first consequence of slothful living is problems.*

When we're slothful, we're going to have problems with ourselves, with our relationships, and with our vocations. We are going to fail to follow God's will for our lives—because we'll be too lazy to do what God calls us to do.

• *The second consequence of slothful living is pressure.*

We will feel pressure from the people who work with us because we won't be doing our share. We will feel financial pressures because when we aren't performing our jobs properly, we're either going to lose it or not be promoted.

• *The third consequence of slothful living is pain.*

We will experience pain because we won't listen to God. We won't take care of our families or our own health. Then, when problems come, we'll have no one to blame but ourselves, and that will affect us psychologically.

• *The fourth consequence of slothful living is poverty.*

Some people can never find the right job. More than likely, it is because they've never proven themselves trustworthy in any of their jobs. They would eventually have a better career if they'd put some effort into it.

• *The fifth word that describes the effects of slothful living is penalty.*

There are penalties both now and later for laziness—there are both earthly and eternal consequences. First Corinthians 3:13 says, "Each man's work will become evident; for the day will show it because it is to be revealed with fire, and the fire itself will test the quality of each man's work." Whatever we've done in this life that's selfish, lazy, or wicked will burn up; whatever we've done that honors God will remain forever.

This is why we must be obedient to God every day. If we are accustomed to doing our best to honor Him in every situation, we'll react in a way that pleases Him, no matter the situation. However, if we are lazy and selfish, we'll eventually find ourselves facing terrible penalties.

Therefore, we should heed the instruction of Proverbs 6:6–8. "Go to the ant . . . which, having no chief, officer or ruler, prepares her food in the summer and gathers her provision in the harvest."

Let us be like the ant: working, preparing, and providing for the future. If we're as diligent in obeying God as the ant is in gathering food, God will teach us what we need to know for every situation, and all we do will honor Him.

And they hate me with violent
hatred.
20 Guard my soul and deliver me;
Do not let me be ashamed, for I take
refuge in You.
21 Let integrity and uprightness
preserve me,
For I wait for You.
22 Redeem Israel, O God,
Out of all his troubles.

Proverbs 10:4, 5

4 Poor is he who works with a
negligent hand,
But the hand of the diligent makes
rich.
5 He who gathers in summer is a son
who acts wisely,
But he who sleeps in harvest is a
son who acts shamefully.

Mark 3:1–19

3HE entered again into a synagogue;
and a man was there whose hand was
withered.
2 They were watching Him *to see* if He
would heal him on the Sabbath, so that
they might accuse Him.
3 He *said to the man with the withered hand, "Get up and come forward!"
4 And He *said to them, "Is it lawful to
do good or to do harm on the Sabbath,
to save a life or to kill?" But they kept
silent.
5 After looking around at them with
anger, grieved at their hardness of heart,
He *said to the man, "Stretch out your
hand." And he stretched it out, and his
hand was restored.

LIFE LESSONS

➤ **Mark 3:2 — *They were watching Him
to see if He would heal him on the Sabbath, so that they might accuse Him.***

*W*hen we exchange the freedom of
the Spirit for the straightjacket
of legalism, the rules become far more
important than the life the rules were
meant to guard. Legalism saps the life
out of everyone it touches.

6 The Pharisees went out and immediately *began* conspiring with the Herodians against Him, *as to* how they might
destroy Him.
7 Jesus withdrew to the sea with His
disciples; and a great multitude from
Galilee followed; and *also* from Judea,
8 and from Jerusalem, and from Idu-
mea, and beyond the Jordan, and the vicinity of Tyre and Sidon, a great number
of people heard of all that He was doing
and came to Him.
9 And He told His disciples that a boat
should stand ready for Him because of
the crowd, so that they would not crowd
Him;
10 for He had healed many, with the
result that all those who had afflictions
pressed around Him in order to touch
Him.
11 Whenever the unclean spirits saw
Him, they would fall down before Him
and shout, "You are the Son of God!"
12 And He earnestly warned them not
to tell who He was.
13 And He *went up on the mountain
and *summoned those whom He Himself
wanted, and they came to Him.
14 And He appointed twelve, so that
they would be with Him and that He
could send them out to preach,
15 and to have authority to cast out the
demons.
16 And He appointed the twelve: Simon
(to whom He gave the name Peter),

LIFE LESSONS

➤ **Mark 3:5 — *After looking around at
them with anger, grieved at their hardness of heart.***

*D*o you ever picture Jesus as angry,
as grieved over hard hearts? As the
perfect reflection of His heavenly Father,
He is both angered by sin and grieved
by unrepentant hearts. He takes sin seriously.

➤ **Mark 3:14 — *And He appointed
twelve, so that they would be with Him.***

*J*esus trained His disciples primarily
by being *with* them—walking with
them, talking with them, eating with
them, observing them, asking them
questions. There is no substitute for
investing time with others.

17 and James, the son of Zebedee, and John the brother of James (to them He gave the name Boanerges, which means, "Sons of Thunder");
18 and Andrew, and Philip, and Bar-

tholomew, and Matthew, and Thomas, and James the son of Alphaeus, and Thaddaeus, and Simon the Zealot;
19 and Judas Iscariot, who betrayed Him.

Leviticus 14:1–57

14 THEN the LORD spoke to Moses, saying,
2 "This shall be the law of the leper in the day of his cleansing. Now he shall be brought to the priest,
3 and the priest shall go out to the outside of the camp. Thus the priest shall look, and if the infection of leprosy has been healed in the leper,
4 then the priest shall give orders to take two live clean birds and cedar wood and a scarlet string and hyssop for the one who is to be cleansed.
5 "The priest shall also give orders to slay the one bird in an earthenware vessel over running water.
6 "As for the live bird, he shall take it together with the cedar wood and the scarlet string and the hyssop, and shall dip them and the live bird in the blood of the bird that was slain over the running water.
7 "He shall then sprinkle seven times the one who is to be cleansed from the leprosy and shall pronounce him clean, and shall let the live bird go free over the open field.
8 "The one to be cleansed shall then wash his clothes and shave off all his hair and bathe in water and be clean. Now afterward, he may enter the camp, but he shall stay outside his tent for seven days.
9 "It will be on the seventh day that he shall shave off all his hair: he shall shave his head and his beard and his eyebrows, even all his hair. He shall then wash his clothes and bathe his body in water and be clean.
10 "Now on the eighth day he is to take two male lambs without defect, and a yearling ewe lamb without defect, and

three-tenths of an ephah of fine flour mixed with oil for a grain offering, and one log of oil;
11 and the priest who pronounces him clean shall present the man to be cleansed and the aforesaid before the LORD at the doorway of the tent of meeting.
12 "Then the priest shall take the one male lamb and bring it for a guilt offering, with the log of oil, and present them as a wave offering before the LORD.
13 "Next he shall slaughter the male lamb in the place where they slaughter the sin offering and the burnt offering, at the place of the sanctuary—for the guilt offering, like the sin offering, belongs to the priest; it is most holy.
14 "The priest shall then take some of the blood of the guilt offering, and the priest shall put it on the lobe of the right ear of the one to be cleansed, and on the thumb of his right hand and on the big toe of his right foot.
15 "The priest shall also take some of the log of oil, and pour it into his left palm;
16 the priest shall then dip his right-hand finger into the oil that is in his left palm, and with his finger sprinkle some of the oil seven times before the LORD.
17 "Of the remaining oil which is in his palm, the priest shall put some on the right ear lobe of the one to be cleansed, and on the thumb of his right hand, and on the big toe of his right foot, on the blood of the guilt offering;
18 while the rest of the oil that is in the priest's palm, he shall put on the head of the one to be cleansed. So the priest shall make atonement on his behalf before the LORD.
19 "The priest shall next offer the sin offering and make atonement for the one to be cleansed from his uncleanness. Then afterward, he shall slaughter the burnt offering.

20 "The priest shall offer up the burnt offering and the grain offering on the altar. Thus the priest shall make atonement for him, and he will be clean.

21 "But if he is poor and his means are insufficient, then he is to take one male lamb for a guilt offering as a wave offering to make atonement for him, and one-tenth *of an ephah* of fine flour mixed with oil for a grain offering, and a log of oil,

22 and two turtledoves or two young pigeons which are within his means, the one shall be a sin offering and the other a burnt offering.

23 "Then the eighth day he shall bring them for his cleansing to the priest, at the doorway of the tent of meeting, before the Lord.

24 "The priest shall take the lamb of the guilt offering and the log of oil, and the priest shall offer them for a wave offering before the Lord.

25 "Next he shall slaughter the lamb of the guilt offering; and the priest is to take some of the blood of the guilt offering and put *it* on the lobe of the right ear of the one to be cleansed and on the thumb of his right hand and on the big toe of his right foot.

26 "The priest shall also pour some of the oil into his left palm;

27 and with his right-hand finger the priest shall sprinkle some of the oil that is in his left palm seven times before the Lord.

28 "The priest shall then put some of the oil that is in his palm on the lobe of the right ear of the one to be cleansed, and on the thumb of his right hand and on the big toe of his right foot, on the place of the blood of the guilt offering.

29 "Moreover, the rest of the oil that is in the priest's palm he shall put on the head of the one to be cleansed, to make atonement on his behalf before the Lord.

30 "He shall then offer one of the turtledoves or young pigeons, which are within his means.

31 "*He shall offer* what he can afford, the one for a sin offering and the other for a burnt offering, together with the grain offering. So the priest shall make atonement before the Lord on behalf of the one to be cleansed.

32 "This is the law *for him* in whom there

is an infection of leprosy, whose means are limited for his cleansing."

33 The Lord further spoke to Moses and to Aaron, saying:

34 "When you enter the land of Canaan, which I give you for a possession, and I put a mark of leprosy on a house in the land of your possession,

35 then the one who owns the house shall come and tell the priest, saying, '*Something* like a mark *of leprosy* has become visible to me in the house.'

36 "The priest shall then command that they empty the house before the priest goes in to look at the mark, so that everything in the house need not become unclean; and afterward the priest shall go in to look at the house.

37 "So he shall look at the mark, and if the mark on the walls of the house has greenish or reddish depressions and appears deeper than the surface,

38 then the priest shall come out of the house, to the doorway, and quarantine the house for seven days.

39 "The priest shall return on the seventh day and make an inspection. If the mark has indeed spread in the walls of the house,

40 then the priest shall order them to tear out the stones with the mark in them and throw them away at an unclean place outside the city.

41 "He shall have the house scraped all around inside, and they shall dump the plaster that they scrape off at an unclean place outside the city.

42 "Then they shall take other stones and replace *those* stones, and he shall take other plaster and replaster the house.

43 "If, however, the mark breaks out again in the house after he has torn out

---

LIFE LESSONS

➤ **Leviticus 14:33, 34 — "*I put a mark of leprosy on a house in the land of your possession.*"**

*G*od is sovereign. Just as the Lord would bring His people into the Promised Land, so would He afflict some houses in the land with mildew and mold. Why? So that through their example, we might learn to trust Him regardless.

the stones and scraped the house, and after it has been replastered,

44 then the priest shall come in and make an inspection. If he sees that the mark has indeed spread in the house, it is a malignant mark in the house; it is unclean.

45 "He shall therefore tear down the house, its stones, and its timbers, and all the plaster of the house, and he shall take *them* outside the city to an unclean place.

46 "Moreover, whoever goes into the house during the time that he has quarantined it, becomes unclean until evening.

47 "Likewise, whoever lies down in the house shall wash his clothes, and whoever eats in the house shall wash his clothes.

48 "If, on the other hand, the priest comes in and makes an inspection and the mark has not indeed spread in the house after the house has been replastered, then the priest shall pronounce the house clean because the mark has not reappeared.

49 "To cleanse the house then, he shall take two birds and cedar wood and a scarlet string and hyssop,

50 and he shall slaughter the one bird in an earthenware vessel over running water.

51 "Then he shall take the cedar wood and the hyssop and the scarlet string, with the live bird, and dip them in the blood of the slain bird as well as in the running water, and sprinkle the house seven times.

52 "He shall thus cleanse the house with the blood of the bird and with the running water, along with the live bird and with the cedar wood and with the hyssop and with the scarlet string.

53 "However, he shall let the live bird go free outside the city into the open field. So he shall make atonement for the house, and it will be clean."

54 This is the law for any mark of leprosy—even for a scale,

55 and for the leprous garment or house,

56 and for a swelling, and for a scab, and for a bright spot—

57 to teach when they are unclean and when they are clean. This is the law of leprosy.

Psalm 26:1–5

A Psalm of David.

26 VINDICATE me, O LORD, for I have walked in my integrity,
And I have trusted in the LORD without wavering.

2 Examine me, O LORD, and try me;
Test my mind and my heart.

3 For Your lovingkindness is before my eyes, ✳
And I have walked in Your truth.

4 I do not sit with deceitful men,
Nor will I go with pretenders.

5 I hate the assembly of evildoers,
And I will not sit with the wicked.

Proverbs 10:6–7

6 Blessings are on the head of the righteous,
But the mouth of the wicked conceals violence.

7 The memory of the righteous is ◄ blessed,
But the name of the wicked will rot.

Mark 3:20–35

20 And He *came home, and the crowd *gathered again, to such an extent that they could not even eat a meal.

21 When His own people heard *of this,* ◄ they went out to take custody of Him; for they were saying, "He has lost His senses."

22 The scribes who came down from

LIFE LESSONS

➤ **Proverbs 10:7 —** *The memory of the righteous is blessed, but the name of the wicked will rot.*

*T*ime will show the quality of all our works and deeds. People who were scorned because they honored God will be vindicated. People who rose to places of prominence through wicked means will eventually be revealed for who they really are (Ps. 73:12–19; Matt. 5:11, 12; 1 Cor. 3:13; Gal. 6:7, 8).

WHAT THE BIBLE SAYS ABOUT

The Unpardonable Sin

Mark 3:28–30

*T*his sin against the Holy Spirit is called *the unpardonable sin*, and many people have written to me because they're afraid they have committed it. However, people are usually wrong about what they think the unpardonable sin really is.

Jesus says in Mark 3:28, 29, "Truly I say to you, all sins shall be forgiven the sons of men, and whatever blasphemies they utter; but whoever blasphemes against the Holy Spirit never has forgiveness, but is guilty of an eternal sin."

So what did Jesus mean? Understand that the Pharisees had been accusing Jesus of using Satan's power to cast out demons (Mark 3:22). Can you imagine that? They were saying Jesus was acting as an enemy of God by setting people free of their satanic strongholds. However, we know Jesus carried out His ministry completely by God's power—by the power of God's Spirit (Mark 1:10–11).

We must remember the Pharisees, who knew the Law and were supposed to protect the truth, were very jealous as they watched Jesus heal people. They knew Jesus was operating under the power of God, but they were angry because Jesus was threatening their positions of honor and control. If they admitted that Jesus' power was from God, they would have to give up all their authority to Him—and that was the last thing they wanted to do. For the sake of their reign, they lied about the source of Jesus' power.

That is the essence of the unpardonable sin. The Pharisees chose to reject the work of the Holy Spirit for their own greedy purposes. They lied by saying that what Jesus had done was the work of Satan. That is defiant irreverence toward the work of God—and it's completely inexcusable. These Pharisees were supposed to lead the people to God. However, what they really did was deliberately impede God's work.

You may be wondering, "How can I know if I've ever committed the unpardonable sin?" Let me explain it to you in this way: While Jesus was here on earth in His earthly body,

the unpardonable sin was different than it is today. This is because Jesus Christ's crucifixion and resurrection changed everything.

Before Jesus went to the Cross, people were required to keep the Law. Whenever they committed sins against God, they would make sacrifices to cover them. These sacrifices were very costly. Unfortunately for the Pharisees, there was no provision for being deceitful about the work of God. There was absolutely no sacrifice that could cover that—not under the Law.

Of course, when Jesus died on the Cross, He forgave all of our sins. First John 2:1, 2 says, "If anyone sins, we have an Advocate with the Father, Jesus Christ the righteous; and He Himself is the propitiation for our sins; and not for ours only, but also for those of the whole world." We no longer have to offer a sacrifice each time we sin because Christ's death on the Cross was sufficient to forgive any and every act of sin. Anyone who wants to be forgiven can call upon Jesus Christ to be his Lord and Savior.

Jesus is our ultimate, final, and complete sacrifice. Today, salvation is open to every person. When Jesus is your Savior, you cannot commit the unpardonable sin as the Pharisees did. Their situation cannot repeat itself because of what Jesus provided for us on the Cross.

However, understand there is still a way for a person to sin against the Holy Spirit in such a way that is unpardonable. Instead of the unpardonable *sin*, I call it the *unpardoned state*.

Hebrews 10:26, 27 tells us, "For if we go on sinning willfully after receiving the knowledge of the truth, there no longer remains a sacrifice for sins, but a terrifying expectation of judgment." The unpardonable state is when people deliberately choose to reject the Lord Jesus after hearing the good news of salvation. They completely turn away from God and willfully choose not to believe in Christ as their Savior under any condition. What have they done? They have chosen to remain without forgiveness for their sin (John 3:17, 18).

Friend, if you've never received Jesus as your Savior, do not remain in the unpardoned state. Turn to Him, ask Him to forgive your sins, and trust Him to save you. It's the best decision you'll ever make. ◈

Jerusalem were saying, "He is possessed by Beelzebul," and "He casts out the demons by the ruler of the demons."
23 And He called them to Himself and began speaking to them in parables, "How can Satan cast out Satan?
24 "If a kingdom is divided against itself, that kingdom cannot stand.
25 "If a house is divided against itself, that house will not be able to stand.
26 "If Satan has risen up against himself and is divided, he cannot stand, but he is finished!

27 "But no one can enter the strong man's house and plunder his property unless he first binds the strong man, and then he will plunder his house.
28 "Truly I say to you, all sins shall be forgiven the sons of men, and whatever blasphemies they utter;
29 but whoever blasphemes against the Holy Spirit never has forgiveness, but is guilty of an eternal sin"—
30 because they were saying, "He has an unclean spirit."
31 Then His mother and His brothers *arrived, and standing outside they sent *word* to Him and called Him.
32 A crowd was sitting around Him, and they *said to Him, "Behold, Your mother and Your brothers are outside looking for You."
33 Answering them, He *said, "Who are My mother and My brothers?"
34 Looking about at those who were sitting around Him, He *said, "Behold My mother and My brothers!
35 "For whoever does the will of God, ✳ he is My brother and sister and mother."

Leviticus 15:1—16:34

15 THE LORD also spoke to Moses and to Aaron, saying,
2 "Speak to the sons of Israel, and say to them, 'When any man has a discharge from his body, his discharge is unclean.
3 'This, moreover, shall be his uncleanness in his discharge: it is his uncleanness whether his body allows its discharge to flow or whether his body obstructs its discharge.
4 'Every bed on which the person with the discharge lies becomes unclean, and everything on which he sits becomes unclean.
5 'Anyone, moreover, who touches his bed shall wash his clothes and bathe in water and be unclean until evening;
6 and whoever sits on the thing on which the man with the discharge has been sitting, shall wash his clothes and bathe in water and be unclean until evening.

7 'Also whoever touches the person with the discharge shall wash his clothes and bathe in water and be unclean until evening.
8 'Or if the man with the discharge spits on one who is clean, he too shall wash his clothes and bathe in water and be unclean until evening.
9 'Every saddle on which the person with the discharge rides becomes unclean.
10 'Whoever then touches any of the things which were under him shall be unclean until evening, and he who carries them shall wash his clothes and bathe in water and be unclean until evening.
11 'Likewise, whomever the one with the discharge touches without having rinsed his hands in water shall wash his clothes and bathe in water and be unclean until evening.
12 'However, an earthenware vessel which the person with the discharge touches shall be broken, and every wooden vessel shall be rinsed in water.

13 'Now when the man with the discharge becomes cleansed from his discharge, then he shall count off for himself seven days for his cleansing; he shall then wash his clothes and bathe his body in running water and will become clean.

14 'Then on the eighth day he shall take for himself two turtledoves or two young pigeons, and come before the LORD to the doorway of the tent of meeting and give them to the priest;

15 and the priest shall offer them, one for a sin offering and the other for a burnt offering. So the priest shall make atonement on his behalf before the LORD because of his discharge.

16 'Now if a man has a seminal emission, he shall bathe all his body in water and be unclean until evening.

17 'As for any garment or any leather on which there is seminal emission, it shall be washed with water and be unclean until evening.

18 'If a man lies with a woman *so that* there is a seminal emission, they shall both bathe in water and be unclean until evening.

19 'When a woman has a discharge, *if* her discharge in her body is blood, she shall continue in her menstrual impurity for seven days; and whoever touches her shall be unclean until evening.

20 'Everything also on which she lies during her menstrual impurity shall be unclean, and everything on which she sits shall be unclean.

21 'Anyone who touches her bed shall wash his clothes and bathe in water and be unclean until evening.

22 'Whoever touches any thing on which she sits shall wash his clothes and bathe in water and be unclean until evening.

23 'Whether it be on the bed or on the thing on which she is sitting, when he touches it, he shall be unclean until evening.

24 'If a man actually lies with her so that her menstrual impurity is on him, he shall be unclean seven days, and every bed on which he lies shall be unclean.

25 'Now if a woman has a discharge of her blood many days, not at the period of her menstrual impurity, or if she has a discharge beyond that period, all the days of her impure discharge she shall continue as though in her menstrual impurity; she is unclean.

26 'Any bed on which she lies all the days of her discharge shall be to her like her bed at menstruation; and every thing on which she sits shall be unclean, like her uncleanness at that time.

27 'Likewise, whoever touches them shall be unclean and shall wash his clothes and bathe in water and be unclean until evening.

28 'When she becomes clean from her discharge, she shall count off for herself seven days; and afterward she will be clean.

29 'Then on the eighth day she shall take for herself two turtledoves or two young pigeons and bring them in to the priest, to the doorway of the tent of meeting.

30 'The priest shall offer the one for a sin offering and the other for a burnt offering. So the priest shall make atonement on her behalf before the LORD because of her impure discharge.'

31 "Thus you shall keep the sons of Israel separated from their uncleanness, so that they will not die in their uncleanness by their defiling My tabernacle that is among them."

32 This is the law for the one with a discharge, and for the man who has a seminal emission so that he is unclean by it,

33 and for the woman who is ill because of menstrual impurity, and for the one who has a discharge, whether a male or a female, or a man who lies with an unclean woman.

16NOW the LORD spoke to Moses after the death of the two sons of Aaron, when they had approached the presence of the LORD and died.

2 The LORD said to Moses: "Tell your brother Aaron that he shall

---

LIFE LESSONS

➤ **Leviticus 15:31** — *"You shall keep the sons of Israel separated from their uncleanness."*

*W*e may wonder at all of the rules and regulations given to Moses, but it comes down to this: Will we trust that God knows best, even when something makes no sense to us?

WHAT THE BIBLE SAYS ABOUT

The Cover-Up

Leviticus 16

The Old Testament uses an interesting word, *atonement*, in connection with the forgiveness of God. Leviticus tells sinful Hebrews to bring a guilt offering to the priest, who "shall make atonement for him before the LORD, and he will be forgiven for any one of the things which he may have done to incur guilt" (Lev. 6:7). It also describes the "Day of Atonement" known today as *Yom Kippur*. God told the Hebrews, "On this day that atonement shall be made for you to cleanse you; you will be clean from all your sins before the LORD" (16:30).

Atonement means "to cover." It is the same Hebrew word translated "to coat" in Genesis 6:14, where God instructs Noah how to build the ark: "Make for yourself an ark of gopher wood; you shall make the ark with rooms, and shall cover it inside and out with pitch."

While the sacrificial system functioned adequately for a time, it was temporary in nature. The sins of those living under the Levitical system were *covered* but not *forgiven* in the absolute sense. Why? Because the blood of animals can never pay the entire debt incurred by sinners: "But in those sacrifices there is a reminder of sins every year. For it is impossible for the blood of bulls and goats to take away sins" (Heb. 10:3, 4).

In God's economy, sin creates a deficit. Whenever sin occurs, something is taken or demanded from the sinner. Ultimately, God requires death as payment for sin. So Paul writes, "Through one man sin entered into the world, and death through sin, and so death spread to all men, because all sinned" (Rom. 5:12).

So if the penalty for sin is death, then why did God not immediately snuff out the lives of Adam and Eve? Did He not say that on the "day" they sinned, they would "surely die" (Gen. 2:17)? Why does He not do the same for all sinners? Why provide a system through which fellowship could be restored if sin ultimately results in death?

The answer is simple, yet life-changing. God wants something more than retribution. He desires something more than getting paid back for the disrespect shown Him. *God wants fellowship with us.* And He willingly put His own system of justice on hold while He made final provision for the rescue of sinful men and women.

---

not enter at any time into the holy place inside the veil, before the mercy seat which is on the ark, or he will die; for I will appear in the cloud over the mercy seat.
3 "Aaron shall enter the holy place with this: with a bull for a sin offering and a ram for a burnt offering.
4 "He shall put on the holy linen tunic, and the linen undergarments shall be next to his body, and he shall be girded with the linen sash and attired with the linen turban (these are holy garments). Then he shall bathe his body in water and put them on.
5 "He shall take from the congregation of the sons of Israel two male goats for a sin offering and one ram for a burnt offering.
6 "Then Aaron shall offer the bull for the sin offering which is for himself, that he may make atonement for himself and for his household.
7 "He shall take the two goats and present them before the LORD at the doorway of the tent of meeting.
8 "Aaron shall cast lots for the two goats, one lot for the LORD and the other lot for the scapegoat.
9 "Then Aaron shall offer the goat on which the lot for the LORD fell, and make it a sin offering.
10 "But the goat on which the lot for the scapegoat fell shall be presented alive before the LORD, to make atonement upon it, to send it into the wilderness as the scapegoat.

LIFE LESSONS

➤ Leviticus 16:2 — *"Tell your brother Aaron that he shall not enter at any time into the holy place inside the veil, before the mercy seat . . . or he will die."*

It is a holy thing to come into the presence of the Lord. We should never treat it casually or flippantly, as Aaron learned.

11 "Then Aaron shall offer the bull of the sin offering which is for himself and make atonement for himself and for his household, and he shall slaughter the bull of the sin offering which is for himself.

12 "He shall take a firepan full of coals of fire from upon the altar before the LORD and two handfuls of finely ground sweet incense, and bring *it* inside the veil.

13 "He shall put the incense on the fire before the LORD, that the cloud of incense may cover the mercy seat that is on *the ark of* the testimony, otherwise he will die.

14 "Moreover, he shall take some of the blood of the bull and sprinkle *it* with his finger on the mercy seat on the east *side;* also in front of the mercy seat he shall sprinkle some of the blood with his finger seven times.

15 "Then he shall slaughter the goat of the sin offering which is for the people, and bring its blood inside the veil and do with its blood as he did with the blood of the bull, and sprinkle it on the mercy seat and in front of the mercy seat.

16 "He shall make atonement for the holy place, because of the impurities of the sons of Israel and because of their transgressions in regard to all their sins; and thus he shall do for the tent of meeting which abides with them in the midst of their impurities.

17 "When he goes in to make atonement in the holy place, no one shall be in the tent of meeting until he comes out, that he may make atonement for himself and for his household and for all the assembly of Israel.

18 "Then he shall go out to the altar that is before the LORD and make atonement for it, and shall take some of the blood of the bull and of the blood of the goat and put it on the horns of the altar on all sides.

19 "With his finger he shall sprinkle some of the blood on it seven times and cleanse it, and from the impurities of the sons of Israel consecrate it.

20 "When he finishes atoning for the holy place and the tent of meeting and the altar, he shall offer the live goat.

21 "Then Aaron shall lay both of his hands on the head of the live goat, and confess over it all the iniquities of the sons of Israel and all their transgressions in regard to all their sins; and he shall lay them on the head of the goat and send *it* away into the wilderness by the hand of a man who *stands* in readiness.

22 "The goat shall bear on itself all their iniquities to a solitary land; and he shall release the goat in the wilderness.

23 "Then Aaron shall come into the tent of meeting and take off the linen garments which he put on when he went into the holy place, and shall leave them there.

24 "He shall bathe his body with water in a holy place and put on his clothes, and come forth and offer his burnt offering and the burnt offering of the people and make atonement for himself and for the people.

25 "Then he shall offer up in smoke the fat of the sin offering on the altar.

26 "The one who released the goat as the scapegoat shall wash his clothes and bathe his body with water; then afterward he shall come into the camp.

27 "But the bull of the sin offering and the goat of the sin offering, whose blood was brought in to make atonement in the holy place, shall be taken outside the camp, and they shall burn their hides, their flesh, and their refuse in the fire.

28 "Then the one who burns them shall wash his clothes and bathe his body with water, then afterward he shall come into the camp.

29 "*This* shall be a permanent statute ◄ for you: in the seventh month, on the tenth day of the month, you shall humble your souls and not do any work, whether the native, or the alien who sojourns among you;

30 for it is on this day that atonement shall be made for you to cleanse you; you will be clean from all your sins before the LORD.

31 "It is to be a sabbath of solemn rest

---

for you, that you may humble your souls; it is a permanent statute.

32 "So the priest who is anointed and ordained to serve as priest in his father's place shall make atonement: he shall thus put on the linen garments, the holy garments,

33 and make atonement for the holy sanctuary, and he shall make atonement for the tent of meeting and for the altar. He shall also make atonement for the priests and for all the people of the assembly.

34 "Now you shall have this as a permanent statute, to make atonement for the sons of Israel for all their sins once every year." And just as the LORD had commanded Moses, so he did.

Psalm 26:6–12

6   I shall wash my hands in innocence,
    And I will go about Your altar,
       O LORD,
7   That I may proclaim with the voice
       of thanksgiving
    And declare all Your wonders.
8   O LORD, I love the habitation of Your
       house
    And the place where Your glory
       dwells.
9   Do not take my soul away along
       with sinners,
    Nor my life with men of bloodshed,
10 In whose hands is a wicked scheme,
    And whose right hand is full of
       bribes.
11 But as for me, I shall walk in my
       integrity;
    Redeem me, and be gracious to me.
12 My foot stands on a level place;
    In the congregations I shall bless
       the LORD.

Proverbs 10:8

8   The wise of heart will receive
       commands,
    But a babbling fool will be ruined.

Mark 4:1–20

4 HE began to teach again by the sea. And such a very large crowd gathered to Him that He got into a boat in the sea and sat down; and the whole crowd was by the sea on the land.

2   And He was teaching them many things in parables, and was saying to them in His teaching,

3   "Listen to this! Behold, the sower went out to sow;

4   as he was sowing, some seed fell beside the road, and the birds came and ate it up.

5   "Other seed fell on the rocky ground where it did not have much soil; and immediately it sprang up because it had no depth of soil.

6   "And after the sun had risen, it was scorched; and because it had no root, it withered away.

7   "Other seed fell among the thorns, and the thorns came up and choked it, and it yielded no crop.

8   "Other seeds fell into the good soil, and as they grew up and increased, they yielded a crop and produced thirty, sixty, and a hundredfold."

9   And He was saying, "He who has ears to hear, let him hear."

10 As soon as He was alone, His followers, along with the twelve, began asking Him about the parables.

11 And He was saying to them, "To you has been given the mystery of the

---

LIFE LESSONS

➤ Psalm 26:12 — *In the congregations I shall bless the LORD.*

Some believers say, "I don't need to go to church; Jesus and I get along just fine on our own." But the Bible never endorses such a spirit. It always pictures believers coming together for worship and mutual encouragement.

➤ Mark 4:9 — *"He who has ears to hear, let him hear."*

God does not force any of us to hear His words or listen to His counsel. He may employ a series of uncomfortable situations to try to get our attention, but whether we choose to hear is entirely up to us.

kingdom of God, but those who are outside get everything in parables,

12 so that WHILE SEEING, THEY MAY SEE AND NOT PERCEIVE, AND WHILE HEARING, THEY MAY HEAR AND NOT UNDERSTAND, OTHERWISE THEY MIGHT RETURN AND BE FORGIVEN."

13 And He *said to them, "Do you not understand this parable? How will you understand all the parables?

14 "The sower sows the word.

15 "These are the ones who are beside the road where the word is sown; and when they hear, immediately Satan comes and takes away the word which has been sown in them.

16 "In a similar way these are the ones on whom seed was sown on the rocky *places*, who, when they hear the word, immediately receive it with joy;

➤ 17 and they have no *firm* root in themselves, but are *only* temporary; then, when affliction or persecution arises because of the word, immediately they fall away.

LIFE LESSONS

➤ **Mark 4:17 —** *"When affliction or persecution arises because of the word, immediately they fall away."*

*A*ll of us need the help and encouragement of others to grow in our faith and send our roots deep into the soil of God's grace. We cannot endure on our own; we need each other to advance in our faith.

---

18 "And others are the ones on whom seed was sown among the thorns; these are the ones who have heard the word,

19 but the worries of the world, and the deceitfulness of riches, and the desires for other things enter in and choke the word, and it becomes unfruitful.

20 "And those are the ones on whom seed was sown on the good soil; and they hear the word and accept it and bear fruit, thirty, sixty, and a hundredfold." ✳

FEBRUARY 24

✦ Leviticus 17:1—18:30

17 THEN the LORD spoke to Moses, saying,

2 "Speak to Aaron and to his sons and to all the sons of Israel and say to them, 'This is what the LORD has commanded, saying,

3 "Any man from the house of Israel who slaughters an ox or a lamb or a goat in the camp, or who slaughters it outside the camp,

4 and has not brought it to the doorway of the tent of meeting to present *it* as an offering to the LORD before the tabernacle of the LORD, bloodguiltiness is to be reckoned to that man. He has shed blood and that man shall be cut off from among his people.

5 "The reason is so that the sons of Israel may bring their sacrifices which they were sacrificing in the open field, that they may bring them in to the LORD, at the doorway of the tent of meeting to the priest, and sacrifice them as sacrifices of peace offerings to the LORD.

6 "The priest shall sprinkle the blood on the altar of the LORD at the doorway of the tent of meeting, and offer up the fat in smoke as a soothing aroma to the LORD.

7 "They shall no longer sacrifice their ◁ sacrifices to the goat demons with which they play the harlot. This shall be a permanent statute to them throughout their generations."'

8 "Then you shall say to them, 'Any man from the house of Israel, or from the aliens who sojourn among them, who offers a burnt offering or sacrifice,

---

LIFE LESSONS

➤ **Leviticus 17:7 —** *"They shall no longer sacrifice their sacrifices to the goat demons."*

*T*o serve and worship other gods is described as spiritual adultery—a detestable unfaithfulness both then and now. As adultery rouses an offended spouse's wrath, so idolatry rouses the anger of God.

9   and does not bring it to the doorway of the tent of meeting to offer it to the LORD, that man also shall be cut off from his people.

10   'And any man from the house of Israel, or from the aliens who sojourn among them, who eats any blood, I will set My face against that person who eats blood and will cut him off from among his people.

11   'For the life of the flesh is in the blood, and I have given it to you on the altar to make atonement for your souls; for it is the blood by reason of the life that makes atonement.'

12   "Therefore I said to the sons of Israel, 'No person among you may eat blood, nor may any alien who sojourns among you eat blood.'

13   "So when any man from the sons of Israel, or from the aliens who sojourn among them, in hunting catches a beast or a bird which may be eaten, he shall pour out its blood and cover it with earth.

14   "For *as for the* life of all flesh, its blood is *identified* with its life. Therefore I said to the sons of Israel, 'You are not to eat the blood of any flesh, for the life of all flesh is its blood; whoever eats it shall be cut off.'

15   "When any person eats *an animal* which dies or is torn *by beasts,* whether he is a native or an alien, he shall wash his clothes and bathe in water, and remain unclean until evening; then he will become clean.

16   "But if he does not wash *them* or bathe his body, then he shall bear his guilt.

18 THEN the LORD spoke to Moses, saying,

2   "Speak to the sons of Israel and say to them, 'I am the LORD your God.

3   'You shall not do what is done in the land of Egypt where you lived, nor are you to do what is done in the land of Canaan where I am bringing you; you shall not walk in their statutes.

4   'You are to perform My judgments and keep My statutes, to live in accord with them; I am the LORD your God.

5   'So you shall keep My statutes and My judgments, by which a man may live if he does them; I am the LORD.

6   'None of you shall approach any blood relative of his to uncover nakedness; I am the LORD.

7   'You shall not uncover the nakedness of your father, that is, the nakedness of your mother. She is your mother; you are not to uncover her nakedness.

8   'You shall not uncover the nakedness of your father's wife; it is your father's nakedness.

9   'The nakedness of your sister, *either* your father's daughter or your mother's daughter, whether born at home or born outside, their nakedness you shall not uncover.

10   'The nakedness of your son's daughter or your daughter's daughter, their nakedness you shall not uncover; for their nakedness is yours.

11   'The nakedness of your father's wife's daughter, born to your father, she is your sister, you shall not uncover her nakedness.

12   'You shall not uncover the nakedness of your father's sister; she is your father's blood relative.

13   'You shall not uncover the nakedness of your mother's sister, for she is your mother's blood relative.

14   'You shall not uncover the nakedness of your father's brother; you shall not approach his wife, she is your aunt.

15   'You shall not uncover the nakedness of your daughter-in-law; she is your son's wife, you shall not uncover her nakedness.

16   'You shall not uncover the nakedness of your brother's wife; it is your brother's nakedness.

LIFE LESSONS

➤ **Leviticus 17:11** — *"It is the blood by reason of the life that makes atonement."*

*B*lood was sacred, since it stood for the life of human beings made in God's image. So Christ's blood had to be shed for the salvation of the world (Rom. 3:25; 5:9; Eph. 1:7; Heb. 9:22).

➤ **Leviticus 18:4** — *"You are to perform My judgments and keep My statutes, to live in accord with them; I am the LORD your God."*

*W*e are to be a distinct people who follow the ways of God rather than the ways of the ungodly. When we allow Jesus to live His life through us, we live in the holy way God requires.

17 'You shall not uncover the nakedness of a woman and of her daughter, nor shall you take her son's daughter or her daughter's daughter, to uncover her nakedness; they are blood relatives. It is lewdness.
18 'You shall not marry a woman in addition to her sister as a rival while she is alive, to uncover her nakedness.
19 'Also you shall not approach a woman to uncover her nakedness during her menstrual impurity.
20 'You shall not have intercourse with your neighbor's wife, to be defiled with her.
21 'You shall not give any of your offspring to offer them to Molech, nor shall you profane the name of your God; I am the LORD.
22 'You shall not lie with a male as one lies with a female; it is an abomination.
23 'Also you shall not have intercourse with any animal to be defiled with it, nor shall any woman stand before an animal to mate with it; it is a perversion.
24 'Do not defile yourselves by any of these things; for by all these the nations which I am casting out before you have become defiled.
25 'For the land has become defiled, therefore I have brought its punishment upon it, so the land has spewed out its inhabitants.
26 'But as for you, you are to keep My statutes and My judgments and shall not do any of these abominations, *neither* the native, nor the alien who sojourns among you
27 (for the men of the land who have been before you have done all these abominations, and the land has become defiled);
28 so that the land will not spew you out, should you defile it, as it has spewed out the nation which has been before you.
29 'For whoever does any of these abominations, those persons who do *so* shall be cut off from among their people.
30 'Thus you are to keep My charge, that you do not practice any of the abominable customs which have been practiced before you, so as not to defile yourselves with them; I am the LORD your God.'"

Psalm 27:1–3

A Psalm of David.

27 THE LORD is my light and my salvation;
Whom shall I fear?
The LORD is the defense of my life;
Whom shall I dread?
2 When evildoers came upon me to devour my flesh,
My adversaries and my enemies, they stumbled and fell.
3 Though a host encamp against me,
My heart will not fear;
Though war arise against me,
In *spite of* this I shall be confident.

Proverbs 10:9

9 He who walks in integrity walks securely,
But he who perverts his ways will be found out.

Mark 4:21–41

21 And He was saying to them, "A lamp is not brought to be put under a basket, is it, or under a bed? Is it not *brought* to be put on the lampstand?
22 "For nothing is hidden, except to be revealed; nor has *anything* been secret, but that it would come to light.
23 "If anyone has ears to hear, let him hear."

LIFE LESSONS

➤ **Psalm 27:1 —** *The LORD is my light and my salvation; whom shall I fear?*

*W*e don't need to be afraid of the dark when the Lord gives us His light. We don't need to fear the power of enemies when we walk in the power of God's Spirit. "Perfect love casts out fear" (1 John 4:18). That means we are secure because we know God's perfect love protects us no matter what our circumstances may be.

WHAT THE BIBLE SAYS ABOUT ◉

How Adversity Reveals Our Level of Faith

Mark 4:35–41

*W*hen hardships come our way, do we respond, "God, I trust You to bring me through this"? Or do we tend to say, "I'm doomed, and there's nothing anybody can do"?

At one point, Jesus allowed His disciples to sail straight into the path of a horrific storm. These men were seasoned fishermen, but the intensity of the waves and the wind caused them to believe they would die on the Sea of Galilee. Yet Jesus had a plan, and it did not include their destruction.

Instead, the Lord taught them a tremendous lesson of faith. He had instructed them, "Go over to the other side" (Mark 4:35). They should have taken His statement as assurance they would have a safe trip. He certainly was not worried. In fact, He was fast asleep in the stern of the boat. When the wind picked up and the waves threatened to sink their tiny ship, they panicked and cried out, "Teacher, do You not care that we are perishing?"

How many times have you felt the same way? Life turns stormy, and no matter what you do, it seems as though you will perish. You cry out: "Don't You care, Lord, that this is happening to me? God, don't You love me enough to do something about this hardship?"

The disciples woke Jesus, and immediately He rebuked the wind and a great calm settled on the lake. Then He turned to His disciples and said, "Why are you afraid? Do you still have no faith?" (Mark 4:40).

God has given each of us the ability to trust Him, and He expects us to use this to overcome doubt, fear, and anxiety. Many times, these feelings accompany adversity. Our trials tempt us to think the worst and wonder if we will ever recover. Satan loves to tell us that all hope is lost and that we will never achieve our goals. But his words are pure folly.

As we see in Scripture, Jesus has authority over all things. He is in control and will cause "all things to work together for good" for us (Rom. 8:28). Therefore, we must stay the course, continue to trust, and know that because Christ is with us, we will make it to the other side. No matter how serious the difficulty, we *will* recover and our final state *will* be better than anything we have experienced.

Allow adversity to spur your faith to action rather than into question. When you do, you will find that it reveals areas in which you need to act in confidence rather than fear. When hard times come, instead of running for cover, make a commitment to trust God. The more you depend upon Him, the greater your faith will grow. ◉

---

24 And He was saying to them, "Take care what you listen to. By your standard of measure it will be measured to you; and more will be given you besides.
25 "For whoever has, to him *more* shall be given; and whoever does not have, even what he has shall be taken away from him."
26 And He was saying, "The kingdom of God is like a man who casts seed upon the soil;
27 and he goes to bed at night and gets up by day, and the seed sprouts and grows—how, he himself does not know.
28 "The soil produces crops by itself; first the blade, then the head, then the mature grain in the head.
29 "But when the crop permits, he immediately puts in the sickle, because the harvest has come."

30 And He said, "How shall we picture the kingdom of God, or by what parable shall we present it?
31 "*It is* like a mustard seed, which, when sown upon the soil, though it is smaller than all the seeds that are upon the soil,
32 yet when it is sown, it grows up and becomes larger than all the garden plants and forms large branches; so that THE BIRDS OF THE AIR can NEST UNDER ITS SHADE."
33 With many such parables He was speaking the word to them, so far as they were able to hear it;
34 and He did not speak to them without a parable; but He was explaining everything privately to His own disciples.
35 On that day, when evening came, He

*said to them, "Let us go over to the other side."

36 Leaving the crowd, they *took Him along with them in the boat, just as He was; and other boats were with Him.

37 And there *arose a fierce gale of wind, and the waves were breaking over the boat so much that the boat was already filling up.

➤ 38 Jesus Himself was in the stern, asleep on the cushion; and they *woke Him and *said to Him, "Teacher, do You not care that we are perishing?"

39 And He got up and rebuked the wind and said to the sea, "Hush, be still." And the wind died down and it became perfectly calm.

40 And He said to them, "Why are you afraid? Do you still have no faith?"

41 They became very much afraid and ✳ said to one another, "Who then is this, that even the wind and the sea obey Him?"

LIFE LESSONS

➤ **Mark 4:38 — "Teacher, do You not care that we are perishing?"**

*H*ow often do we say things like this to our Lord? When we get into trouble, we question His love, not His ability. Yet despite our lack of faith, He reaches out His hand and saves us.

✦ Leviticus 19:1—20:27

19 THEN the LORD spoke to Moses, saying:

2 "Speak to all the congregation of the sons of Israel and say to them, 'You shall be holy, for I the LORD your God am holy.

3 'Every one of you shall reverence his mother and his father, and you shall keep My sabbaths; I am the LORD your God.

4 'Do not turn to idols or make for yourselves molten gods; I am the LORD your God.

5 'Now when you offer a sacrifice of peace offerings to the LORD, you shall offer it so that you may be accepted.

6 'It shall be eaten the same day you offer it, and the next day; but what remains until the third day shall be burned with fire.

7 'So if it is eaten at all on the third day, it is an offense; it will not be accepted.

8 'Everyone who eats it will bear his iniquity, for he has profaned the holy thing of the LORD; and that person shall be cut off from his people.

9 'Now when you reap the harvest of your land, you shall not reap to the very corners of your field, nor shall you gather the gleanings of your harvest.

➤ 10 'Nor shall you glean your vineyard, nor shall you gather the fallen fruit of

your vineyard; you shall leave them for the needy and for the stranger. I am the LORD your God.

11 'You shall not steal, nor deal falsely, nor lie to one another.

12 'You shall not swear falsely by My name, so as to profane the name of your God; I am the LORD.

13 'You shall not oppress your neighbor, nor rob *him*. The wages of a hired man are not to remain with you all night until morning.

14 'You shall not curse a deaf man, nor place a stumbling block before the blind, but you shall revere your God; I am the LORD.

15 'You shall do no injustice in judgment; you shall not be partial to the poor nor defer to the great, but you are to judge your neighbor fairly.

16 'You shall not go about as a slanderer among your people, and you are not to act

LIFE LESSONS

➤ **Leviticus 19:10 — "Nor shall you glean your vineyard . . . you shall leave them for the needy and for the stranger."**

*G*od has a special concern for the poor and the disadvantaged, and His people are to share His concern for them. The more we become like God, the more we share His concerns.

against the life of your neighbor; I am the LORD.

17 'You shall not hate your fellow countryman in your heart; you may surely reprove your neighbor, but shall not incur sin because of him.

18 'You shall not take vengeance, nor bear any grudge against the sons of your people, but you shall love your neighbor as yourself; I am the LORD.

19 'You are to keep My statutes. You shall not breed together two kinds of your cattle; you shall not sow your field with two kinds of seed, nor wear a garment upon you of two kinds of material mixed together.

20 'Now if a man lies carnally with a woman who is a slave acquired for *another* man, but who has in no way been redeemed nor given her freedom, there shall be punishment; they shall not, *however*, be put to death, because she was not free.

21 'He shall bring his guilt offering to the LORD to the doorway of the tent of meeting, a ram for a guilt offering.

22 'The priest shall also make atonement for him with the ram of the guilt offering before the LORD for his sin which he has committed, and the sin which he has committed will be forgiven him.

23 'When you enter the land and plant all kinds of trees for food, then you shall count their fruit as forbidden. Three years it shall be forbidden to you; *it* shall not be eaten.

24 'But in the fourth year all its fruit shall be holy, an offering of praise to the LORD.

25 'In the fifth year you are to eat of its fruit, that its yield may increase for you; I am the LORD your God.

26 'You shall not eat *anything* with the blood, nor practice divination or soothsaying.

27 'You shall not round off the sidegrowth of your heads nor harm the edges of your beard.

28 'You shall not make any cuts in your body for the dead nor make any tattoo marks on yourselves: I am the LORD.

29 'Do not profane your daughter by making her a harlot, so that the land will not fall to harlotry and the land become full of lewdness.

30 'You shall keep My sabbaths and revere My sanctuary; I am the LORD.

31 'Do not turn to mediums or spiritists; do not seek them out to be defiled by them. I am the LORD your God.

32 'You shall rise up before the gray-headed and honor the aged, and you shall revere your God; I am the LORD.

33 'When a stranger resides with you in your land, you shall not do him wrong.

34 'The stranger who resides with you shall be to you as the native among you, and you shall love him as yourself, for you were aliens in the land of Egypt; I am the LORD your God.

35 'You shall do no wrong in judgment, in measurement of weight, or capacity.

36 'You shall have just balances, just weights, a just ephah, and a just hin; I am the LORD your God, who brought you out from the land of Egypt.

37 'You shall thus observe all My statutes and all My ordinances and do them; I am the LORD.'"

20 THEN the LORD spoke to Moses, saying,

2 "You shall also say to the sons of Israel:

'Any man from the sons of Israel or from the aliens sojourning in Israel who gives any of his offspring to Molech, shall surely be put to death; the people of the land shall stone him with stones.

3 'I will also set My face against that man and will cut him off from among his people, because he has given some of his offspring to Molech, so as to defile My sanctuary and to profane My holy name.

4 'If the people of the land, however, should ever disregard that man when he gives any of his offspring to Molech, so as not to put him to death,

5 then I Myself will set My face against that man and against his family, and I will cut off from among their people both him and all those who play the harlot after him, by playing the harlot after Molech.

LIFE LESSONS

➤ **Leviticus 19:32 —** *"You shall . . . honor the aged, and you shall revere your God."*

God connects fear of the Lord with honoring the elderly. Those who disrespect the aged in fact slander the Lord.

6 'As for the person who turns to mediums and to spiritists, to play the harlot after them, I will also set My face against that person and will cut him off from among his people.
7 'You shall consecrate yourselves therefore and be holy, for I am the LORD your God.
8 'You shall keep My statutes and practice them; I am the LORD who sanctifies you.
9 'If *there is* anyone who curses his father or his mother, he shall surely be put to death; he has cursed his father or his mother, his bloodguiltiness is upon him.
10 'If *there is* a man who commits adultery with another man's wife, one who commits adultery with his friend's wife, the adulterer and the adulteress shall surely be put to death.
11 'If *there is* a man who lies with his father's wife, he has uncovered his father's nakedness; both of them shall surely be put to death, their bloodguiltiness is upon them.
12 'If *there is* a man who lies with his daughter-in-law, both of them shall surely be put to death; they have committed incest, their bloodguiltiness is upon them.
13 'If *there is* a man who lies with a male as those who lie with a woman, both of them have committed a detestable act; they shall surely be put to death. Their bloodguiltiness is upon them.
14 'If *there is* a man who marries a woman and her mother, it is immorality; both he and they shall be burned with fire, so that there will be no immorality in your midst.
15 'If *there is* a man who lies with an animal, he shall surely be put to death; you shall also kill the animal.
16 'If *there is* a woman who approaches any animal to mate with it, you shall kill the woman and the animal; they shall surely be put to death. Their bloodguiltiness is upon them.
17 'If *there is* a man who takes his sister, his father's daughter or his mother's daughter, so that he sees her nakedness and she sees his nakedness, it is a disgrace; and they shall be cut off in the sight of the sons of their people. He has uncovered his sister's nakedness; he bears his guilt.
18 'If *there is* a man who lies with a men-struous woman and uncovers her nakedness, he has laid bare her flow, and she has exposed the flow of her blood; thus both of them shall be cut off from among their people.
19 'You shall also not uncover the nakedness of your mother's sister or of your father's sister, for such a one has made naked his blood relative; they will bear their guilt.
20 'If *there is* a man who lies with his uncle's wife he has uncovered his uncle's nakedness; they will bear their sin. They will die childless.
21 'If *there is* a man who takes his brother's wife, it is abhorrent; he has uncovered his brother's nakedness. They will be childless.
22 'You are therefore to keep all My statutes and all My ordinances and do them, so that the land to which I am bringing you to live will not spew you out.
23 'Moreover, you shall not follow the customs of the nation which I will drive out before you, for they did all these things, and therefore I have abhorred them.
24 'Hence I have said to you, "You are to possess their land, and I Myself will give it to you to possess it, a land flowing with milk and honey." I am the LORD your God, who has separated you from the peoples.
25 'You are therefore to make a distinction between the clean animal and the unclean, and between the unclean bird and the clean; and you shall not make yourselves detestable by animal or by bird or by anything that creeps on the ground, which I have separated for you as unclean.
26 'Thus you are to be holy to Me, for I the LORD am holy; and I have set you apart from the peoples to be Mine.

LIFE LESSONS

➤ **Leviticus 20:26 —** *"You are to be holy to Me, for I the LORD am holy; and I have set you apart from the peoples to be Mine."*

*I*t is both a great privilege and an enormous responsibility to belong to the Lord. We cannot have an intimate relationship with God without reflecting His holiness, and intimacy with Him is our highest calling.

27 'Now a man or a woman who is a medium or a spiritist shall surely be put to death. They shall be stoned with stones, their bloodguiltiness is upon them.'"

Psalm 27:4–10

4 One thing I have asked from the
    LORD, that I shall seek:
    That I may dwell in the house of the
    LORD all the days of my life,
    To behold the beauty of the LORD
    And to meditate in His temple.
5 For in the day of trouble He will
    conceal me in His tabernacle;
    In the secret place of His tent He
    will hide me;
    He will lift me up on a rock.

6 And now my head will be lifted up
    above my enemies around me,
    And I will offer in His tent sacrifices
    with shouts of joy;
    I will sing, yes, I will sing praises to
    the LORD.
7 Hear, O LORD, when I cry with my
    voice,
    And be gracious to me and answer
    me.
8 *When You said*, "Seek My face," my
    heart said to You,
    "Your face, O LORD, I shall seek."
9 Do not hide Your face from me,
    Do not turn Your servant away in
    anger;
    You have been my help;
    Do not abandon me nor forsake
    me,
    O God of my salvation!

ANSWERS TO LIFE'S QUESTIONS

How can I get to really know God?

PSALM 27:4, 8

Did you know God wants to show you more of Himself every day? Are you seeking after God with all your strength? Does your time with the Lord revitalize you, or does it feel more like a ritualistic experience?

Contrast the experience of Gomer with that of an earlier Israelite, Hannah (1 Sam. 1–2). Gomer did not care to know God. Yet Hannah sought after God with all her heart. What made the difference? Knowing God.

In Hosea 6:6, God is clear: "I delight in loyalty rather than sacrifice, and in the knowledge of God rather than burnt offerings." In order to deepen your relationship with the Lord and remain devoted to Him:

- *You must come to Him honestly.*
  Confessing your sins and inviting Jesus Christ into your heart requires you to be vulnerable. Although such humility and repentance may be intimidating, accepting Christ is the best decision anyone can make.
- *You must understand your reliance upon Him.* Hannah saw God as her only source of comfort and power: "She, greatly distressed, prayed to the LORD and wept bitterly" (1 Sam. 1:10). And because she did, He looked upon her with compassion and grace (1 Sam. 1:19, 20).

- *You must become interested in what interests Him.* Has your desire for spiritual insight and godly wisdom declined? If so, ask the Lord to restore your longing for Him and for the things that most concern Him.
- *You must know His Word.* By reading the Bible, you open your heart to Him. He has given you the Holy Spirit to help you understand His Word, and He wants you to meditate on it so you can apply it to your life.
- *You must observe His characteristics and ways.* Read the promises God makes in His Word. Ask Him to remind you of how He has already worked in your life—with all the wisdom, love, and power you will ever need for any challenge you will ever face.
- *You must accept His invitation and follow His commands.* God is constantly inviting you to walk with Him. Give the Lord total control of your decisions, time, talents, and possessions—walking in complete submission to Him. Your obedience will certainly bring great blessings.

Your knowledge of God grows as you increasingly recognize His love for you. God delights in your joyful praise and worship of Him. Psalm 46:10 says, "Cease striving and know that I am God; I will be exalted among the nations, I will be exalted in the earth." As you get to know God on deeper levels, your ability to trust and obey Him will increase. You will find your life's fulfillment when you come to know and exalt the Lord of all creation.

10 For my father and my mother have
     forsaken me,
    But the LORD will take me up.

✸ Proverbs 10:10–12

10 He who winks the eye causes
     trouble,
    And a babbling fool will be ruined.
11 The mouth of the righteous is a
     fountain of life,
    But the mouth of the wicked
     conceals violence.
➤ 12 Hatred stirs up strife,
    But love covers all transgressions.

✸ Mark 5:1–20

5 THEY came to the other side of the
sea, into the country of the Gerasenes.
2 When He got out of the boat, immediately a man from the tombs with an unclean spirit met Him,
3 and he had his dwelling among the tombs. And no one was able to bind him anymore, even with a chain;
4 because he had often been bound with shackles and chains, and the chains had been torn apart by him and the shackles broken in pieces, and no one was strong enough to subdue him.
5 Constantly, night and day, he was screaming among the tombs and in the mountains, and gashing himself with stones.
6 Seeing Jesus from a distance, he ran up and bowed down before Him;
7 and shouting with a loud voice, he *said, "What business do we have with each other, Jesus, Son of the Most High God? I implore You by God, do not torment me!"
8 For He had been saying to him, "Come out of the man, you unclean spirit!"
9 And He was asking him, "What is your name?" And he *said to Him, "My name is Legion; for we are many."
10 And he *began* to implore Him earnestly not to send them out of the country.
11 Now there was a large herd of swine feeding nearby on the mountain.
12 *The demons* implored Him, saying,

"Send us into the swine so that we may enter them."
13 Jesus gave them permission. And coming out, the unclean spirits entered the swine; and the herd rushed down the steep bank into the sea, about two thousand *of them*; and they were drowned in the sea.
14 Their herdsmen ran away and reported it in the city and in the country. And *the people* came to see what it was that had happened.
15 They *came to Jesus and *observed the man who had been demon-possessed sitting down, clothed and in his right mind, the very man who had had the "legion"; and they became frightened.
16 Those who had seen it described to them how it had happened to the demon-possessed man, and *all* about the swine.
17 And they began to implore Him to leave their region.
18 As He was getting into the boat, the man who had been demon-possessed was imploring Him that he might accompany Him.
19 And He did not let him, but He *said to him, "Go home to your people and report to them what great things the Lord has done for you, and *how* He had mercy on you."
20 And he went away and began to proclaim in Decapolis what great things Jesus had done for him; and everyone was amazed.

LIFE LESSONS

➤ **Proverbs 10:12 —** *Hatred stirs up strife, but love covers all transgressions.*

*W*e all make mistakes in our relationships, and the natural reaction to an offense is anger. But if we want our relationships to work, we must learn to apply love, not bitterness, to the wounds we suffer.

➤ **Mark 5:19 —** *"Go home to your people and report to them what great things the Lord has done for you."*

*T*he former demoniac really wanted to go with Jesus; he probably did not think it very compassionate that Jesus refused to let him do so. But Jesus' compassion is much more than merely being nice.

21 THEN the LORD said to Moses, "Speak to the priests, the sons of Aaron, and say to them:

'No one shall defile himself for a *dead* person among his people,

2 except for his relatives who are nearest to him, his mother and his father and his son and his daughter and his brother,

3 also for his virgin sister, who is near to him because she has had no husband; for her he may defile himself.

4 'He shall not defile himself as a relative by marriage among his people, and so profane himself.

5 'They shall not make any baldness on their heads, nor shave off the edges of their beards, nor make any cuts in their flesh.

6 'They shall be holy to their God and not profane the name of their God, for they present the offerings by fire to the LORD, the food of their God; so they shall be holy.

7 'They shall not take a woman who is profaned by harlotry, nor shall they take a woman divorced from her husband; for he is holy to his God.

8 'You shall consecrate him, therefore, for he offers the food of your God; he shall be holy to you; for I the LORD, who sanctifies you, am holy.

9 'Also the daughter of any priest, if she profanes herself by harlotry, she profanes her father; she shall be burned with fire.

10 'The priest who is the highest among his brothers, on whose head the anointing oil has been poured and who has been consecrated to wear the garments, shall not uncover his head nor tear his clothes;

11 nor shall he approach any dead person, nor defile himself *even* for his father or his mother;

12 nor shall he go out of the sanctuary nor profane the sanctuary of his God, for the consecration of the anointing oil of his God is on him; I am the LORD.

13 'He shall take a wife in her virginity.

14 'A widow, or a divorced woman, or one who is profaned by harlotry, these he may not take; but rather he is to marry a virgin of his own people,

15 so that he will not profane his offspring among his people; for I am the LORD who sanctifies him.'"

16 Then the LORD spoke to Moses, saying,

17 "Speak to Aaron, saying, 'No man of your offspring throughout their generations who has a defect shall approach to offer the food of his God.

18 'For no one who has a defect shall approach: a blind man, or a lame man, or he who has a disfigured *face*, or any deformed *limb*,

19 or a man who has a broken foot or broken hand,

20 or a hunchback or a dwarf, or *one who has* a defect in his eye or eczema or scabs or crushed testicles.

21 'No man among the descendants of Aaron the priest who has a defect is to come near to offer the LORD's offerings by fire; *since* he has a defect, he shall not come near to offer the food of his God.

22 'He may eat the food of his God, *both* of the most holy and of the holy,

23 only he shall not go in to the veil or come near the altar because he has a defect, so that he will not profane My sanctuaries. For I am the LORD who sanctifies them.'"

24 So Moses spoke to Aaron and to his sons and to all the sons of Israel.

22 THEN the LORD spoke to Moses, saying,

2 "Tell Aaron and his sons to be careful with the holy *gifts* of the sons of Israel, which they dedicate to Me, so as not to profane My holy name; I am the LORD.

3 "Say to them, 'If any man among all your descendants throughout your generations approaches the holy *gifts* which the sons of Israel dedicate to the LORD, while he has an uncleanness, that person shall be cut off from before Me; I am the LORD.

4 'No man of the descendants of Aaron, who is a leper or who has a discharge, may eat of the holy *gifts* until he is clean. And if one touches anything made unclean by a corpse or if a man has a seminal emission,

5 or if a man touches any teeming things by which he is made unclean, or any man by whom he is made unclean, whatever his uncleanness;

6 a person who touches any such shall be unclean until evening, and shall not eat of the holy *gifts* unless he has bathed his body in water.

7 'But when the sun sets, he will be

clean, and afterward he shall eat of the holy *gifts*, for it is his food.

8 'He shall not eat *an animal* which dies or is torn *by beasts*, becoming unclean by it; I am the LORD.

9 'They shall therefore keep My charge, so that they will not bear sin because of it and die thereby because they profane it; I am the LORD who sanctifies them.

10 'No layman, however, is to eat the holy *gift*; a sojourner with the priest or a hired man shall not eat of the holy *gift*.

11 'But if a priest buys a slave as *his* property with his money, that one may eat of it, and those who are born in his house may eat of his food.

12 'If a priest's daughter is married to a layman, she shall not eat of the offering of the *gifts*.

13 'But if a priest's daughter becomes a widow or divorced, and has no child and returns to her father's house as in her youth, she shall eat of her father's food; but no layman shall eat of it.

14 'But if a man eats a holy *gift* unintentionally, then he shall add to it a fifth of it and shall give the holy *gift* to the priest.

15 'They shall not profane the holy *gifts* of the sons of Israel which they offer to the LORD,

16 and *so* cause them to bear punishment for guilt by eating their holy *gifts*; for I am the LORD who sanctifies them.'"

17 Then the LORD spoke to Moses, saying,

18 "Speak to Aaron and to his sons and to all the sons of Israel and say to them, 'Any man of the house of Israel or of the aliens in Israel who presents his offering, whether it is any of their votive or any of their freewill offerings, which they present to the LORD for a burnt offering—

19 for you to be accepted—*it must be* a male without defect from the cattle, the sheep, or the goats.

20 'Whatever has a defect, you shall not offer, for it will not be accepted for you.

➤ 21 'When a man offers a sacrifice of peace offerings to the LORD to fulfill a special vow or for a freewill offering, of the herd or of the flock, it must be perfect to be accepted; there shall be no defect in it.

22 'Those *that are* blind or fractured or maimed or having a running sore or eczema or scabs, you shall not offer to the LORD, nor make of them an offering by fire on the altar to the LORD.

23 'In respect to an ox or a lamb which has an overgrown or stunted *member*, you may present it for a freewill offering, but for a vow it will not be accepted.

24 'Also anything *with its testicles* bruised or crushed or torn or cut, you shall not offer to the LORD, or sacrifice in your land,

25 nor shall you accept any such from the hand of a foreigner for offering as the food of your God; for their corruption is in them, they have a defect, they shall not be accepted for you.'"

26 Then the LORD spoke to Moses, saying,

27 "When an ox or a sheep or a goat is born, it shall remain seven days with its mother, and from the eighth day on it shall be accepted as a sacrifice of an offering by fire to the LORD.

28 "But, *whether* it is an ox or a sheep, you shall not kill *both* it and its young in one day.

29 "When you sacrifice a sacrifice of thanksgiving to the LORD, you shall sacrifice it so that you may be accepted.

30 "It shall be eaten on the same day, you shall leave none of it until morning; I am the LORD.

31 "So you shall keep My commandments, and do them; I am the LORD.

32 "You shall not profane My holy name, but I will be sanctified among the sons of ✳ Israel; I am the LORD who sanctifies you,

33 who brought you out from the land of Egypt, to be your God; I am the LORD."

❖ Psalm 27:11–14

11 Teach me Your way, O LORD,
And lead me in a level path
Because of my foes.

LIFE LESSONS

➤ **Leviticus 22:21** — *"It must be perfect to be accepted; there shall be no defect in it."*

*W*e are to give our best to the Lord, not our leftovers. We reveal what the Lord means to us by what we freely offer to Him. Most of all, He wants our hearts—and in return, He gives us Himself.

12 Do not deliver me over to the desire
of my adversaries,
For false witnesses have risen
against me,
And such as breathe out violence.
13 *I would have despaired* unless I
had believed that I would see the
goodness of the LORD
In the land of the living.
14 Wait for the LORD;
Be strong and let your heart take
courage;
Yes, wait for the LORD.

Proverbs 10:13–16

13 On the lips of the discerning,
wisdom is found,
But a rod is for the back of him who
lacks understanding.

WHAT THE BIBLE SAYS ABOUT

Seeking God's Guidance

Psalm 27:14

Life is full of decisions, and if we want to make the right choices—those that glorify God and benefit us and others—we need God's guidance. The following seven words will help us in seeking His direction:
1. *Cleansing.* We need to ask, "Is anything in my life hindering me from hearing what You are saying? If so, what is it?" Cleansing comes by confession (1 John 1:9).
2. *Surrendering.* We must submit to whatever God instructs us to do. Sometimes we find it difficult to move ahead because we want to know step two before we complete step one of God's will. However, we must surrender ourselves to His timing and guidance. Obeying the will of God is both a humbling and an uplifting experience (1 Pet. 5:6).
3. *Asking.* James 4:2 reports, "You do not have because you do not ask." God promises that when we ask according to His will, He hears us. And when we know He hears us, we know He will answer (1 John 5:14, 15)—even though the answer may come over a long period of time.

14 Wise men store up knowledge,
But with the mouth of the foolish,
ruin is at hand.
15 The rich man's wealth is his
fortress,
The ruin of the poor is their poverty.
16 The wages of the righteous is life,
The income of the wicked,
punishment.

LIFE LESSONS

➤ **Psalm 27:13** — *I would have despaired unless I had believed that I would see the goodness of the LORD in the land of the living.*

Christians do not merely hope for "pie in the sky in the great by-and-by." We can expect and trust to receive God's help and salvation right now, in the heat of the battle.

---

4. *Meditating.* God promises that His Word will be a light to our path (Ps. 119:105). The more we think about His Word, the clearer our path will become.
5. *Believing.* In Mark's Gospel, we learn that when we ask, we must believe He is going to give us what we have requested (Mark 11:22–24). Therefore, trust that He will show you what to do.
6. *Waiting.* God promises that He acts on our behalf when we wait for Him (Is. 64:4). If we run ahead of Him and try to fix things on our own or manipulate circumstances, we will most certainly be disappointed. However, if we wait on the Lord, then our sovereign, divine, omnipotent God will act on our behalf. It's our choice.
7. *Receiving.* When we obediently seek the will of God, we can be sure He will hear us and give us the wisdom we need to make the right choices (Matt. 7:7, 8; James 1:5). Once we know His will, we have a responsibility to embrace His direction and obey Him completely.

You will find great peace and confidence in knowing that you are making choices based on God's guidance. Perhaps no one else will understand or agree with your decision—but you will have heard from the One who matters most. ◈

Mark 5:21-43

21 When Jesus had crossed over again in the boat to the other side, a large crowd gathered around Him; and so He stayed by the seashore.
22 One of the synagogue officials named Jairus *came up, and on seeing Him, *fell at His feet
23 and *implored Him earnestly, saying, "My little daughter is at the point of death; *please* come and lay Your hands on her, so that she will get well and live."
24 And He went off with him; and a large crowd was following Him and pressing in on Him.
25 A woman who had had a hemorrhage for twelve years,
26 and had endured much at the hands of many physicians, and had spent all that she had and was not helped at all, but rather had grown worse—
27 after hearing about Jesus, she came up in the crowd behind *Him* and touched His cloak.
28 For she thought, "If I just touch His garments, I will get well."
29 Immediately the flow of her blood was dried up; and she felt in her body that she was healed of her affliction.
30 Immediately Jesus, perceiving in Himself that the power *proceeding* from Him had gone forth, turned around in the crowd and said, "Who touched My garments?"
31 And His disciples said to Him, "You see the crowd pressing in on You, and You say, 'Who touched Me?'"
32 And He looked around to see the woman who had done this.
33 But the woman fearing and trembling, aware of what had happened to her, came and fell down before Him and told Him the whole truth.
34 And He said to her, "Daughter, your faith has made you well; go in peace and be healed of your affliction." ✳
35 While He was still speaking, they *came from the *house of* the synagogue official, saying, "Your daughter has died; why trouble the Teacher anymore?"
36 But Jesus, overhearing what was being spoken, *said to the synagogue official, "Do not be afraid *any longer,* only believe." ◄
37 And He allowed no one to accompany Him, except Peter and James and John the brother of James.
38 They *came to the house of the synagogue official; and He *saw a commotion, and *people* loudly weeping and wailing.
39 And entering in, He *said to them, "Why make a commotion and weep? The child has not died, but is asleep."
40 They *began* laughing at Him. But putting them all out, He *took along the child's father and mother and His own companions, and *entered *the room* where the child was.
41 Taking the child by the hand, He *said to her, "Talitha kum!" (which translated means, "Little girl, I say to you, get up!").
42 Immediately the girl got up and *began* to walk, for she was twelve years old. And immediately they were completely astounded.
43 And He gave them strict orders that no one should know about this, and He said that *something* should be given her to eat. ◄

LIFE LESSONS

➤ **Mark 5:36 — *"Do not be afraid any longer, only believe."***

Jesus did not comfort the man upon hearing the news of his daughter's death; he challenged him to faith instead. Regardless of our circumstances, God always urges us on to faith and away from fear.

➤ **Mark 5:43 — *He said that something should be given her to eat.***

If Jesus brought the little girl back to life, why didn't He also put something in her empty stomach? God does what only He can do; He instructs us to do what He equips us to do.

⚜ **Leviticus 23:1—24:23**

23THE LORD spoke again to Moses, saying,

➤ 2 "Speak to the sons of Israel and say to them, 'The LORD'S appointed times which you shall proclaim as holy convocations—My appointed times are these:

✳ **3** 'For six days work may be done, but on the seventh day there is a sabbath of complete rest, a holy convocation. You shall not do any work; it is a sabbath to the LORD in all your dwellings.

4 'These are the appointed times of the LORD, holy convocations which you shall proclaim at the times appointed for them.

5 'In the first month, on the fourteenth day of the month at twilight is the LORD'S Passover.

6 'Then on the fifteenth day of the same month there is the Feast of Unleavened Bread to the LORD; for seven days you shall eat unleavened bread.

7 'On the first day you shall have a holy convocation; you shall not do any laborious work.

8 'But for seven days you shall present an offering by fire to the LORD. On the seventh day is a holy convocation; you shall not do any laborious work.'"

9 Then the LORD spoke to Moses, saying,

10 "Speak to the sons of Israel and say to them, 'When you enter the land which I am going to give to you and reap its harvest, then you shall bring in the sheaf of the first fruits of your harvest to the priest.

11 'He shall wave the sheaf before the LORD for you to be accepted; on the day after the sabbath the priest shall wave it.

12 'Now on the day when you wave the sheaf, you shall offer a male lamb one year old without defect for a burnt offering to the LORD.

13 'Its grain offering shall then be two-tenths *of an ephah* of fine flour mixed with oil, an offering by fire to the LORD *for* a soothing aroma, with its drink offering, a fourth of a hin of wine.

14 'Until this same day, until you have brought in the offering of your God, you shall eat neither bread nor roasted grain nor new growth. It is to be a perpetual statute throughout your generations in all your dwelling places.

15 'You shall also count for yourselves from the day after the sabbath, from the day when you brought in the sheaf of the wave offering; there shall be seven complete sabbaths.

16 'You shall count fifty days to the day after the seventh sabbath; then you shall present a new grain offering to the LORD.

17 'You shall bring in from your dwelling places two *loaves* of bread for a wave offering, made of two-tenths *of an ephah*; they shall be of a fine flour, baked with leaven as first fruits to the LORD.

18 'Along with the bread you shall present seven one year old male lambs without defect, and a bull of the herd and two rams; they are to be a burnt offering to the LORD, with their grain offering and their drink offerings, an offering by fire of a soothing aroma to the LORD.

19 'You shall also offer one male goat for a sin offering and two male lambs one year old for a sacrifice of peace offerings.

20 'The priest shall then wave them with the bread of the first fruits for a wave offering with two lambs before the LORD; they are to be holy to the LORD for the priest.

21 'On this same day you shall make a proclamation as well; you are to have a holy convocation. You shall do no laborious work. It is to be a perpetual statute in all your dwelling places throughout your generations.

22 'When you reap the harvest of your land, moreover, you shall not reap to the very corners of your field nor gather the gleaning of your harvest; you are to leave them for the needy and the alien. I am the LORD your God.'"

23 Again the LORD spoke to Moses, saying,

24 "Speak to the sons of Israel, saying,

LIFE LESSONS

➤ **Leviticus 23:2 —** *"The LORD'S appointed times which you shall proclaim as holy convocations."*

*I*t is important to God that His people regularly come together to celebrate His goodness and provision. Something happens in community that cannot happen in solitude.

'In the seventh month on the first of the month you shall have a rest, a reminder by blowing *of trumpets,* a holy convocation.

25 'You shall not do any laborious work, but you shall present an offering by fire to the LORD.'"

26 The LORD spoke to Moses, saying,

27 "On exactly the tenth day of this seventh month is the day of atonement; it shall be a holy convocation for you, and you shall humble your souls and present an offering by fire to the LORD.

28 "You shall not do any work on this same day, for it is a day of atonement, to make atonement on your behalf before the LORD your God.

29 "If there is any person who will not humble himself on this same day, he shall be cut off from his people.

30 "As for any person who does any work on this same day, that person I will destroy from among his people.

31 "You shall do no work at all. It is to be a perpetual statute throughout your generations in all your dwelling places.

32 "It is to be a sabbath of complete rest to you, and you shall humble your souls; on the ninth of the month at evening, from evening until evening you shall keep your sabbath."

33 Again the LORD spoke to Moses, saying,

34 "Speak to the sons of Israel, saying, 'On the fifteenth of this seventh month is the Feast of Booths for seven days to the LORD.

35 'On the first day is a holy convocation; you shall do no laborious work of any kind.

36 'For seven days you shall present an offering by fire to the LORD. On the eighth day you shall have a holy convocation and present an offering by fire to the LORD; it is an assembly. You shall do no laborious work.

37 'These are the appointed times of the LORD which you shall proclaim as holy convocations, to present offerings by fire to the LORD—burnt offerings and grain offerings, sacrifices and drink offerings, *each* day's matter on its own day—

38 besides *those of* the sabbaths of the LORD, and besides your gifts and besides all your votive and freewill offerings, which you give to the LORD.

39 'On exactly the fifteenth day of the seventh month, when you have gath-

ered in the crops of the land, you shall celebrate the feast of the LORD for seven days, with a rest on the first day and a rest on the eighth day.

40 'Now on the first day you shall take for yourselves the foliage of beautiful trees, palm branches and boughs of leafy trees and willows of the brook, and you shall rejoice before the LORD your God for seven days.

41 'You shall thus celebrate it *as* a feast to the LORD for seven days in the year. It *shall be* a perpetual statute throughout your generations; you shall celebrate it in the seventh month.

42 'You shall live in booths for seven days; all the native-born in Israel shall live in booths,

43 so that your generations may know that I had the sons of Israel live in booths when I brought them out from the land of Egypt. I am the LORD your God.'"

44 So Moses declared to the sons of Israel the appointed times of the LORD.

24 THEN the LORD spoke to Moses, saying,

2 "Command the sons of Israel that they bring to you clear oil from beaten olives for the light, to make a lamp burn continually.

3 "Outside the veil of testimony in the tent of meeting, Aaron shall keep it in order from evening to morning before the LORD continually; *it shall be* a perpetual statute throughout your generations.

4 "He shall keep the lamps in order on the pure *gold* lampstand before the LORD continually.

5 "Then you shall take fine flour and bake twelve cakes with it; two-tenths *of an ephah* shall be *in* each cake.

6 "You shall set them *in* two rows, six to a row, on the pure *gold* table before the LORD.

7 "You shall put pure frankincense on each row that it may be a memorial portion for the bread, *even* an offering by fire to the LORD.

8 "Every sabbath day he shall set it in order before the LORD continually; it is an everlasting covenant for the sons of Israel.

9 "It shall be for Aaron and his sons, and they shall eat it in a holy place; for it is most holy to him from the LORD's offerings by fire, *his* portion forever."

10 Now the son of an Israelite woman, whose father was an Egyptian, went out among the sons of Israel; and the Israelite woman's son and a man of Israel struggled with each other in the camp. **11** The son of the Israelite woman blasphemed the Name and cursed. So they brought him to Moses. (Now his mother's name was Shelomith, the daughter of Dibri, of the tribe of Dan.) **12** They put him in custody so that the command of the LORD might be made clear to them. **13** Then the LORD spoke to Moses, saying, **14** "Bring the one who has cursed outside the camp, and let all who heard him lay their hands on his head; then let all the congregation stone him. **15** "You shall speak to the sons of Israel, saying, 'If anyone curses his God, then he will bear his sin. **16** 'Moreover, the one who blasphemes the name of the LORD shall surely be put to death; all the congregation shall certainly stone him. The alien as well as the native, when he blasphemes the Name, shall be put to death. **17** 'If a man takes the life of any human being, he shall surely be put to death. **18** 'The one who takes the life of an animal shall make it good, life for life. **19** 'If a man injures his neighbor, just as he has done, so it shall be done to him: **20** fracture for fracture, eye for eye, tooth for tooth; just as he has injured a man, so it shall be inflicted on him. **21** 'Thus the one who kills an animal shall make it good, but the one who kills a man shall be put to death. **22** 'There shall be one standard for you; it shall be for the stranger as well as the native, for I am the LORD your God.'" **23** Then Moses spoke to the sons of Israel, and they brought the one who had cursed outside the camp and stoned him with stones. Thus the sons of Israel did, just as the LORD had commanded Moses.

Psalm 28:1–5

A Psalm of David.

28 TO You, O LORD, I call;
My rock, do not be deaf to me,
For if You are silent to me,
I will become like those who go
down to the pit.
2 Hear the voice of my supplications
when I cry to You for help,
When I lift up my hands toward
Your holy sanctuary.
3 Do not drag me away with the
wicked
And with those who work iniquity,
Who speak peace with their
neighbors,
While evil is in their hearts.
4 Requite them according to their
work and according to the evil of
their practices;
Requite them according to the deeds
of their hands;
Repay them their recompense.
5 Because they do not regard the
works of the LORD
Nor the deeds of His hands,
He will tear them down and not
build them up.

Proverbs 10:17, 18

17 He is *on* the path of life who heeds
instruction,
But he who ignores reproof goes
astray.
18 He who conceals hatred *has* lying
lips,
And he who spreads slander is a
fool.

Mark 6:1–29

6 JESUS went out from there and *came into His hometown; and His disciples *followed Him.

LIFE LESSONS

➤ **Leviticus 24:12 — *They put him in custody so that the command of the LORD might be made clear to them.***

*I*t is always wise to wait to act until we can learn the mind of the Lord. If we truly want to know God's will, He will move heaven and earth to show it to us.

2   When the Sabbath came, He began to teach in the synagogue; and the many listeners were astonished, saying, "Where did this man *get* these things, and what is *this* wisdom given to Him, and such miracles as these performed by His hands?

3   "Is not this the carpenter, the son of Mary, and brother of James and Joses and Judas and Simon? Are not His sisters here with us?" And they took offense at Him.

4   Jesus said to them, "A prophet is not without honor except in his hometown and among his *own* relatives and in his *own* household."

5   And He could do no miracle there except that He laid His hands on a few sick people and healed them.

➤ 6   And He wondered at their unbelief.
     And He was going around the villages teaching.

✴ **7**   And He *summoned the twelve and began to send them out in pairs, and gave them authority over the unclean spirits;

8   and He instructed them that they should take nothing for *their* journey, except a mere staff—no bread, no bag, no money in their belt;

9   but *to* wear sandals; and *He added,* "Do not put on two tunics."

10   And He said to them, "Wherever you enter a house, stay there until you leave town.

11   "Any place that does not receive you or listen to you, as you go out from there, shake the dust off the soles of your feet for a testimony against them."

12   They went out and preached that *men* should repent.

13   And they were casting out many de-

LIFE LESSONS

➤ **Mark 6:6** — *He wondered at their unbelief.*

*U*nbelief always causes Jesus to marvel because He knows that the God who asks us to trust Him is almighty, all-wise, all-present, and all-loving. Why would someone *not* trust God? The very idea is beyond understanding.

mons and were anointing with oil many sick people and healing them.

14   And King Herod heard *of it,* for His name had become well known; and *people* were saying, "John the Baptist has risen from the dead, and that is why these miraculous powers are at work in Him."

15   But others were saying, "He is Elijah." And others were saying, "*He is* a prophet, like one of the prophets *of old.*"

16   But when Herod heard *of it,* he kept saying, "John, whom I beheaded, has risen!"

17   For Herod himself had sent and had John arrested and bound in prison on account of Herodias, the wife of his brother Philip, because he had married her.

18   For John had been saying to Herod, "It is not lawful for you to have your brother's wife."

19   Herodias had a grudge against him and wanted to put him to death and could not *do so;*

20   for Herod was afraid of John, knowing that he was a righteous and holy man, and he kept him safe. And when he heard him, he was very perplexed; but he used to enjoy listening to him.

21   A strategic day came when Herod on

Life Examples:

JOHN THE BAPTIST:
A Man of Discernment

MARK 6:14–29

*W*hat would you think of a man who lived alone in the desert, wore camel skins, and ate wild honey and locusts? Now, how would you feel if this man said you needed to let God change your life?
     You can see why many people who heard about John the Baptist went to see him out

of sheer curiosity. But John was no lunatic, nor was his message his own. For almost thirty years, God prepared John to announce the coming of Jesus Christ, the Messiah. John was a man of great spiritual discernment who knew the difference between those who came with humble, repentant hearts, and those who came to mock or criticize.
     When you ask God for discernment, He gives it to you freely. For those who truly seek His face and His direction for their lives, the Lord brings a wisdom that comes only from Him.

his birthday gave a banquet for his lords and military commanders and the leading men of Galilee;

22 and when the daughter of Herodias herself came in and danced, she pleased Herod and his dinner guests; and the king said to the girl, "Ask me for whatever you want and I will give it to you."

23 And he swore to her, "Whatever you ask of me, I will give it to you; up to half of my kingdom."

24 And she went out and said to her mother, "What shall I ask for?" And she said, "The head of John the Baptist."

25 Immediately she came in a hurry to the king and asked, saying, "I want you to give me at once the head of John the Baptist on a platter."

26 And although the king was very sorry, *yet* because of his oaths and because of his dinner guests, he was unwilling to refuse her.

27 Immediately the king sent an executioner and commanded *him* to bring *back* his head. And he went and had him beheaded in the prison,

28 and brought his head on a platter, and gave it to the girl; and the girl gave it to her mother.

29 When his disciples heard *about this*, they came and took away his body and laid it in a tomb.

Leviticus 25:1–55

25 THE LORD then spoke to Moses at Mount Sinai, saying,

2 "Speak to the sons of Israel and say to them, 'When you come into the land which I shall give you, then the land shall have a sabbath to the LORD.

3 'Six years you shall sow your field, and six years you shall prune your vineyard and gather in its crop,

4 but during the seventh year the land shall have a sabbath rest, a sabbath to the LORD; you shall not sow your field nor prune your vineyard.

5 'Your harvest's aftergrowth you shall not reap, and your grapes of untrimmed vines you shall not gather; the land shall have a sabbatical year.

6 'All of you shall have the sabbath *products* of the land for food; yourself, and your male and female slaves, and your hired man and your foreign resident, those who live as aliens with you.

7 'Even your cattle and the animals that are in your land shall have all its crops to eat.

8 'You are also to count off seven sabbaths of years for yourself, seven times seven years, so that you have the time of the seven sabbaths of years, *namely*, forty-nine years.

9 'You shall then sound a ram's horn abroad on the tenth day of the seventh month; on the day of atonement you shall sound a horn all through your land.

10 'You shall thus consecrate the fiftieth year and proclaim a release through the land to all its inhabitants. It shall be a jubilee for you, and each of you shall return to his own property, and each of you shall return to his family.

11 'You shall have the fiftieth year as a jubilee; you shall not sow, nor reap its aftergrowth, nor gather in *from* its untrimmed vines.

12 'For it is a jubilee; it shall be holy to you. You shall eat its crops out of the field.

13 'On this year of jubilee each of you shall return to his own property.

14 'If you make a sale, moreover, to your friend or buy from your friend's hand, you shall not wrong one another.

15 'Corresponding to the number of years after the jubilee, you shall buy from your friend; he is to sell to you according to the number of years of crops.

16 'In proportion to the extent of the years you shall increase its price, and in proportion to the fewness of the years you shall diminish its price, for *it is* a number of crops he is selling to you.

17 'So you shall not wrong one another, but you shall fear your God; for I am the LORD your God.

18 'You shall thus observe My statutes and keep My judgments, so as to carry

them out, that you may live securely on the land.

19 'Then the land will yield its produce, so that you can eat your fill and live securely on it.

20 'But if you say, "What are we going to eat on the seventh year if we do not sow or gather in our crops?"

➤ 21 then I will so order My blessing for you in the sixth year that it will bring forth the crop for three years.

22 'When you are sowing the eighth year, you can still eat old things from the crop, eating *the old* until the ninth year when its crop comes in.

23 'The land, moreover, shall not be sold permanently, for the land is Mine; for you are *but* aliens and sojourners with Me.

24 'Thus for every piece of your property, you are to provide for the redemption of the land.

25 'If a fellow countryman of yours becomes so poor he has to sell part of his property, then his nearest kinsman is to come and buy back what his relative has sold.

26 'Or in case a man has no kinsman, but so recovers his means as to find sufficient for its redemption,

27 then he shall calculate the years since its sale and refund the balance to the man to whom he sold it, and so return to his property.

28 'But if he has not found sufficient means to get it back for himself, then what he has sold shall remain in the hands of its purchaser until the year of jubilee; but at the jubilee it shall revert, that he may return to his property.

29 'Likewise, if a man sells a dwelling house in a walled city, then his redemption right remains valid until a full year from its sale; his right of redemption lasts a full year.

30 'But if it is not bought back for him within the space of a full year, then the house that is in the walled city passes

permanently to its purchaser throughout his generations; it does not revert in the jubilee.

31 'The houses of the villages, however, which have no surrounding wall shall be considered as open fields; they have redemption rights and revert in the jubilee.

32 'As for cities of the Levites, the Levites have a permanent right of redemption for the houses of the cities which are their possession.

33 'What, therefore, belongs to the Levites may be redeemed and a house sale in the city of this possession reverts in the jubilee, for the houses of the cities of the Levites are their possession among the sons of Israel.

34 'But pasture fields of their cities shall not be sold, for that is their perpetual possession.

35 'Now in case a countryman of yours becomes poor and his means with regard to you falter, then you are to sustain him, like a stranger or a sojourner, that he may live with you.

36 'Do not take usurious interest from him, but revere your God, that your countryman may live with you.

37 'You shall not give him your silver at interest, nor your food for gain.

38 'I am the LORD your God, who brought you out of the land of Egypt to give you the land of Canaan *and* to be your God.

39 'If a countryman of yours becomes so poor with regard to you that he sells himself to you, you shall not subject him to a slave's service.

40 'He shall be with you as a hired man, as if he were a sojourner; he shall serve with you until the year of jubilee.

41 'He shall then go out from you, he and his sons with him, and shall go back to his family, that he may return to the property of his forefathers.

42 'For they are My servants whom I brought out from the land of Egypt; they are not to be sold *in* a slave sale.

43 'You shall not rule over him with severity, but are to revere your God.

44 'As for your male and female slaves whom you may have—you may acquire male and female slaves from the pagan nations that are around you.

45 'Then, too, *it is* out of the sons of the sojourners who live as aliens among you that you may gain acquisition, and out of their families who are with you, whom

ANSWERS TO LIFE'S QUESTIONS

What does it mean to live in "the fear of the Lord"?

LEVITICUS 25:36

*T*here are several practical indications of a life lived in the fear of the Lord.

1. *Obedience to God's commandments*

The Lord has given us very specific commandments in His Word, and He expects us to obey Him *without regard to circumstances or situations*. No matter what others may say in offering us an alluring, good-sounding "alternative plan" to God's commands, we must never choose to follow their advice. Schemes of man's design may seem to make sense, but the Lord tells us, "There is a way which seems right to a man, but its end is the way of death" (Prov. 14:12). God's Word is very clear. The problem most Christians encounter is their lack of understanding when it comes to His standards for right and wrong. They may know what is right and God's will for their lives, but they choose to *disobey* Him—and this always leads to disappointment, frustration, and heartache.

2. *A desire to be like Jesus*

Those who truly love Jesus as their Savior and Lord will want to be like Him. How did Jesus live? Jesus lived in complete obedience to His Father. He did only what the Father instructed Him to do and He spoke only what the Father prompted Him to say. What Jesus did, we are to do—not to the best of our *abilities*, but in *submission* to the Holy Spirit within us. The Spirit empowers us to live as Jesus lived, and it is our responsibility to ask Him to guide, help, counsel, and empower us to obey. The more we allow the Holy Spirit to work in us and through us, the more we gain the ability to live like Jesus.

3. *A life of courage*

Those who fear mankind and natural disaster suffer a panic that paralyzes. Those who fear the Lord with a holy awe, on the other hand, find a courage that mobilizes them to act. God challenges His people to live in confidence and to respond boldly and courageously to life. Such "heroes of the faith" as Moses, Joshua, and the apostles Peter and Paul faced incredible challenges, yet they succeeded because of their God-given courage. They learned the same lesson that emboldened Ezra to say, "Thus I was strengthened according to the hand of the LORD my God upon me" (Ezra 7:28).

---

they will have produced in your land; they also may become your possession.

46 'You may even bequeath them to your sons after you, to receive as a possession; you can use them as permanent slaves. But in respect to your countrymen, the sons of Israel, you shall not rule with severity over one another.

47 'Now if the means of a stranger or of a sojourner with you becomes sufficient, and a countryman of yours becomes so poor with regard to him as to sell himself to a stranger who is sojourning with you, or to the descendants of a stranger's family,

48 then he shall have redemption right after he has been sold. One of his brothers may redeem him,

49 or his uncle, or his uncle's son, may redeem him, or one of his blood relatives from his family may redeem him; or if he prospers, he may redeem himself.

50 'He then with his purchaser shall calculate from the year when he sold himself to him up to the year of jubilee; and the price of his sale shall correspond to the number of years. *It is* like the days of a hired man *that* he shall be with him.

51 'If there are still many years, he shall refund part of his purchase price in proportion to them for his own redemption;

52 and if few years remain until the year of jubilee, he shall so calculate with him. In proportion to his years he is to refund *the amount for* his redemption.

53 'Like a man hired year by year he shall be with him; he shall not rule over him with severity in your sight.

54 'Even if he is not redeemed by these *means*, he shall still go out in the year of jubilee, he and his sons with him.

55 'For the sons of Israel are My servants; they are My servants whom I brought out

LIFE LESSONS

➤ **Leviticus 25:55 —** *"For the sons of Israel are My servants."*

*W*e are not only children of God, we are His servants. The one speaks of privilege, the other of duty. Both are ours in Christ.

from the land of Egypt. I am the LORD your God.

✦ Psalm 28:6–9

6 Blessed be the LORD,
    Because He has heard the voice of
      my supplication.
7 The LORD is my strength and my
      shield;
    My heart trusts in Him, and I am
      helped;
    Therefore my heart exults,
    And with my song I shall thank
      Him.
8 The LORD is their strength,
    And He is a saving defense to His
      anointed.
9 Save Your people and bless Your
      inheritance;
    Be their shepherd also, and carry
      them forever.

✦ Proverbs 10:19–21

19 When there are many words,
      transgression is unavoidable,
    But he who restrains his lips is wise.
20 The tongue of the righteous is as
      choice silver,
    The heart of the wicked is worth little.
21 The lips of the righteous feed many,
    But fools die for lack of
      understanding.

✦ Mark 6:30–56

30 The apostles *gathered together with
Jesus; and they reported to Him all that
they had done and taught.

31 And He *said to them, "Come away
by yourselves to a secluded place and
rest a while." (For there were many
people coming and going, and they did
not even have time to eat.)
32 They went away in the boat to a secluded place by themselves.
33 The people saw them going, and
many recognized them and ran there
together on foot from all the cities, and
got there ahead of them.
34 When Jesus went ashore, He saw a
large crowd, and He felt compassion for
them because they were like sheep without a shepherd; and He began to teach
them many things.
35 When it was already quite late, His
disciples came to Him and said, "This
place is desolate and it is already quite
late;
36 send them away so that they may
go into the surrounding countryside and
villages and buy themselves something
to eat."
37 But He answered them, "You give
them something to eat!" And they *said
to Him, "Shall we go and spend two
hundred denarii on bread and give them
something to eat?"
38 And He *said to them, "How many
loaves do you have? Go look!" And when
they found out, they *said, "Five, and two
fish."
39 And He commanded them all to sit
down by groups on the green grass.
40 They sat down in groups of hundreds and of fifties.
41 And He took the five loaves and the
two fish, and looking up toward heaven,
He blessed the food and broke the loaves
and He kept giving them to the disciples
to set before them; and He divided up the
two fish among them all.
42 They all ate and were satisfied,
43 and they picked up twelve full

LIFE LESSONS

➤ **Psalm 28:9 — Save Your people and bless Your inheritance.**

*G*od gives us His hand of salvation right now, not just in heaven. He blesses us right now, not just in eternity. He leads us and sustains us every day on earth. Heaven merely completes our relationship with Him.

➤ **Mark 6:31 — "Come away by your-selves to a secluded place and rest a while."**

*J*esus and His disciples worked hard, but they did not drive themselves to exhaustion. Jesus made sure that His men took care of themselves, not only spiritu-ally, but physically as well.

baskets of the broken pieces, and also of the fish.

44 There were five thousand men who ate the loaves.

45 Immediately Jesus made His disciples get into the boat and go ahead of *Him* to the other side to Bethsaida, while He Himself was sending the crowd away.

➤ 46 After bidding them farewell, He left for the mountain to pray.

47 When it was evening, the boat was in the middle of the sea, and He was alone on the land.

48 Seeing them straining at the oars, for the wind was against them, at about the fourth watch of the night He *came to them, walking on the sea; and He intended to pass by them.

49 But when they saw Him walking on the sea, they supposed that it was a ghost, and cried out;

✳ 50 for they all saw Him and were terrified. But immediately He spoke with them and *said to them, "Take courage; it is I, do not be afraid."

51 Then He got into the boat with them, and the wind stopped; and they were utterly astonished,

➤ 52 for they had not gained any insight from the *incident of* the loaves, but their heart was hardened.

53 When they had crossed over they came to land at Gennesaret, and moored to the shore.

54 When they got out of the boat, immediately *the people* recognized Him,

55 and ran about that whole country and began to carry here and there on their pallets those who were sick, to the place they heard He was.

56 Wherever He entered villages, or cities, or countryside, they were laying the sick in the market places, and imploring Him that they might just touch the fringe of His cloak; and as many as touched it were being cured.

LIFE LESSONS

➤ **Mark 6:46 — *After bidding them farewell, He left for the mountain to pray.***

Throughout the Gospels, we find Jesus getting alone with God to pray. During these times of intimate fellowship, He found renewed strength, direction, and a deep love for His Father.

➤ **Mark 6:52 — *They had not gained any insight from the incident of the loaves, but their heart was hardened.***

Had Jesus' disciples understood the meaning behind His first miracles (that they revealed Him as the Messiah, the Son of God) His other miracles would not have surprised them. They saw, but they did not understand.

Leviticus 26:1—27:34

26 'YOU shall not make for yourselves idols, nor shall you set up for yourselves an image or a *sacred* pillar, nor shall you place a figured stone in your land to bow down to it; for I am the LORD your God.

2 'You shall keep My sabbaths and reverence My sanctuary; I am the LORD.

3 'If you walk in My statutes and keep My commandments so as to carry them out,

4 then I shall give you rains in their season, so that the land will yield its produce and the trees of the field will bear their fruit.

5 'Indeed, your threshing will last for you until grape gathering, and grape gathering will last until sowing time. You will thus eat your food to the full and live securely in your land.

6 'I shall also grant peace in the land, so that you may lie down with no one making *you* tremble. I shall also eliminate harmful beasts from the land, and no sword will pass through your land.

7 'But you will chase your enemies and they will fall before you by the sword;

8 five of you will chase a hundred, and a hundred of you will chase ten thousand, and your enemies will fall before you by the sword.

9 'So I will turn toward you and make you fruitful and multiply you, and I will confirm My covenant with you.

10 'You will eat the old supply and clear out the old because of the new.

11 'Moreover, I will make My dwelling among you, and My soul will not reject you.

12 'I will also walk among you and be your God, and you shall be My people.

13 'I am the LORD your God, who brought you out of the land of Egypt so that *you* would not be their slaves, and I broke the bars of your yoke and made you walk erect.

14 'But if you do not obey Me and do not carry out all these commandments,

15 if, instead, you reject My statutes, and if your soul abhors My ordinances so as not to carry out all My commandments, *and* so break My covenant,

16 I, in turn, will do this to you: I will appoint over you a sudden terror, consumption and fever that will waste away the eyes and cause the soul to pine away; also, you will sow your seed uselessly, for your enemies will eat it up.

17 'I will set My face against you so that you will be struck down before your enemies; and those who hate you will rule over you, and you will flee when no one is pursuing you.

18 'If also after these things you do not obey Me, then I will punish you seven times more for your sins.

19 'I will also break down your pride of power; I will also make your sky like iron and your earth like bronze.

20 'Your strength will be spent uselessly, for your land will not yield its produce and the trees of the land will not yield their fruit.

21 'If then, you act with hostility against Me and are unwilling to obey Me, I will increase the plague on you seven times according to your sins.

22 'I will let loose among you the beasts of the field, which will bereave you of your children and destroy your cattle and reduce your number so that your roads lie deserted.

23 'And if by these things you are not turned to Me, but act with hostility against Me,

24 then I will act with hostility against you; and I, even I, will strike you seven times for your sins.

25 'I will also bring upon you a sword which will execute vengeance for the covenant; and when you gather together into your cities, I will send pestilence

---

LIFE LESSONS

➤ **Leviticus 26:12** — *"I will also walk among you and be your God, and you shall be My people."*

Peace with God is the fruit of oneness with Him. The Lord's greatest desire since the beginning of creation is to be with us, His people, to display His glory through us, and to bless us. God not only desires to be in the closest, most intimate relationship possible with His people, but He has provided everything necessary for that relationship through Jesus Christ.

among you, so that you shall be delivered into enemy hands.
26 'When I break your staff of bread, ten women will bake your bread in one oven, and they will bring back your bread in rationed amounts, so that you will eat and not be satisfied.
27 'Yet if in spite of this you do not obey Me, but act with hostility against Me,
28 then I will act with wrathful hostility against you, and I, even I, will punish you seven times for your sins.
29 'Further, you will eat the flesh of your sons and the flesh of your daughters you will eat.
30 'I then will destroy your high places, and cut down your incense altars, and heap your remains on the remains of your idols, for My soul shall abhor you.
31 'I will lay waste your cities as well and will make your sanctuaries desolate, and I will not smell your soothing aromas.
32 'I will make the land desolate so that your enemies who settle in it will be appalled over it.
33 'You, however, I will scatter among the nations and will draw out a sword after you, as your land becomes desolate and your cities become waste.
34 'Then the land will enjoy its sabbaths all the days of the desolation, while you are in your enemies' land; then the land will rest and enjoy its sabbaths.
35 'All the days of *its* desolation it will observe the rest which it did not observe on your sabbaths, while you were living on it.
36 'As for those of you who may be left, I will also bring weakness into their hearts in the lands of their enemies. And the sound of a driven leaf will chase them, and even when no one is pursuing they will flee as though from the sword, and they will fall.
37 'They will therefore stumble over each other as if *running* from the sword, although no one is pursuing; and you will have *no strength* to stand up before your enemies.
38 'But you will perish among the nations, and your enemies' land will consume you.
39 'So those of you who may be left will rot away because of their iniquity in the lands of your enemies; and also because of the iniquities of their forefathers they will rot away with them.

40 'If they confess their iniquity and the iniquity of their forefathers, in their unfaithfulness which they committed against Me, and also in their acting with hostility against Me—
41 I also was acting with hostility against them, to bring them into the land of their enemies—or if their uncircumcised heart becomes humbled so that they then make amends for their iniquity,
42 then I will remember My covenant with Jacob, and I will remember also My covenant with Isaac, and My covenant with Abraham as well, and I will remember the land.
43 'For the land will be abandoned by them, and will make up for its sabbaths while it is made desolate without them. They, meanwhile, will be making amends for their iniquity, because they rejected My ordinances and their soul abhorred My statutes.
44 'Yet in spite of this, when they are in the land of their enemies, I will not reject them, nor will I so abhor them as to destroy them, breaking My covenant with them; for I am the LORD their God.
45 'But I will remember for them the covenant with their ancestors, whom I brought out of the land of Egypt in the sight of the nations, that I might be their God. I am the LORD.'"
46 These are the statutes and ordinances and laws which the LORD established between Himself and the sons of Israel through Moses at Mount Sinai.

27 AGAIN, the LORD spoke to Moses, saying,
2 "Speak to the sons of Israel and say to them, 'When a man makes a difficult vow, he *shall be valued* according to your valuation of persons belonging to the LORD.
3 'If your valuation is of the male from twenty years even to sixty years old, then your valuation shall be fifty shekels of silver, after the shekel of the sanctuary.
4 'Or if it is a female, then your valuation shall be thirty shekels.
5 'If it be from five years even to twenty years old then your valuation for the male shall be twenty shekels and for the female ten shekels.
6 'But if *they are* from a month even up to five years old, then your valuation

shall be five shekels of silver for the male, and for the female your valuation shall be three shekels of silver.

7 'If *they are* from sixty years old and upward, if it is a male, then your valuation shall be fifteen shekels, and for the female ten shekels.

8 'But if he is poorer than your valuation, then he shall be placed before the priest and the priest shall value him; according to the means of the one who vowed, the priest shall value him.

9 'Now if it is an animal of the kind which men can present as an offering to the LORD, any such that one gives to the LORD shall be holy.

10 'He shall not replace it or exchange it, a good for a bad, or a bad for a good; or if he does exchange animal for animal, then both it and its substitute shall become holy.

11 'If, however, it is any unclean animal of the kind which men do not present as an offering to the LORD, then he shall place the animal before the priest.

12 'The priest shall value it as either good or bad; as you, the priest, value it, so it shall be.

13 'But if he should ever *wish to* redeem it, then he shall add one-fifth of it to your valuation.

14 'Now if a man consecrates his house as holy to the LORD, then the priest shall value it as either good or bad; as the priest values it, so it shall stand.

15 'Yet if the one who consecrates it should *wish to* redeem his house, then he shall add one-fifth of your valuation price to it, so that it may be his.

16 'Again, if a man consecrates to the LORD part of the fields of his own property, then your valuation shall be proportionate to the seed needed for it: a homer of barley seed at fifty shekels of silver.

17 'If he consecrates his field as of the year of jubilee, according to your valuation it shall stand.

18 'If he consecrates his field after the jubilee, however, then the priest shall calculate the price for him proportionate to the years that are left until the year of jubilee; and it shall be deducted from your valuation.

19 'If the one who consecrates it should ever wish to redeem the field, then he shall add one-fifth of your valuation price to it, so that it may pass to him.

20 'Yet if he will not redeem the field, but has sold the field to another man, it may no longer be redeemed;

21 and when it reverts in the jubilee, the field shall be holy to the LORD, like a field set apart; it shall be for the priest as his property.

22 'Or if he consecrates to the LORD a field which he has bought, which is not a part of the field of his own property,

23 then the priest shall calculate for him the amount of your valuation up to the year of jubilee; and he shall on that day give your valuation as holy to the LORD.

24 'In the year of jubilee the field shall return to the one from whom he bought it, to whom the possession of the land belongs.

25 'Every valuation of yours, moreover, shall be after the shekel of the sanctuary. The shekel shall be twenty gerahs.

26 'However, a firstborn among animals, which as a firstborn belongs to the LORD, no man may consecrate it; whether ox or sheep, it is the LORD'S.

27 'But if *it is* among the unclean animals, then he shall redeem it according to your valuation and add to it one-fifth of it; and if it is not redeemed, then it shall be sold according to your valuation.

28 'Nevertheless, anything which a man sets apart to the LORD out of all that he has, of man or animal or of the fields of his own property, shall not be sold or redeemed. Anything devoted to destruction is most holy to the LORD.

29 'No one who may have been set apart among men shall be ransomed; he shall surely be put to death.

30 'Thus all the tithe of the land, of the seed of the land or of the fruit of the tree, is the LORD'S; it is holy to the LORD.

31 'If, therefore, a man wishes to redeem part of his tithe, he shall add to it one-fifth of it.

32 'For every tenth part of herd or flock, whatever passes under the rod, the tenth one shall be holy to the LORD.

33 'He is not to be concerned whether *it is* good or bad, nor shall he exchange it; or if he does exchange it, then both it and its substitute shall become holy. It shall not be redeemed.'"

34 These are the commandments which the LORD commanded Moses for the sons of Israel at Mount Sinai.

WHAT THE BIBLE SAYS ABOUT ◉

Tithing and Giving

Leviticus 27:30–33

God has set forth very specific directives about what He expects us to give back to Him (Lev. 27:30; Deut. 14:22, 23). Malachi 3:8–12 clearly teaches we are to give Him a tithe, which is ten percent of what we produce or earn (the word *tithe* is based on the number ten in Hebrew).

Offerings were gifts, often of material goods, given above and beyond the tithe. People normally made offerings for specific reasons. In this case, it was a requirement of the Law, such as their sacrifice on the Passover; and sometimes voluntarily to meet a special need or as thanksgiving for a special blessing (Lev. 1:1—7:21; 23). The children of Israel gave such a generous offering at the time they built the tabernacle that Moses actually had to tell them to stop giving (Ex. 35:4—36:7)! The tithe is given to God *from* our increase and *for* our increase. It is our acknowledgement that all we have and all we are able to achieve comes directly from the hand of God (Mark 12:41–44). It is also the way we open the door of our finances to give and then to receive His blessing. When we give the first tenth of our earnings back to the Lord, we return to Him what was His in the first place, and what He asks us to give to Him so that He will remain our first priority (Matt. 6:19–24).

The Lord is very specific in the ways we are to give our tithes and offerings.

First, we are to bring them into His storehouse. Generally that meant His tabernacle or temple in the Old Testament, and the church in the New Testament. We are to give our tithes wherever we regularly worship the Lord—not only to care for the church building and those who work there, but to support the expansion of His kingdom by spreading the gospel and ministering to the community for His name's sake (2 Cor. 9:7–14).

Second, we are to make our gifts on a regular basis. Paul advised the Corinthians, "On the first day of every week each one of you is to put aside and save, as he may prosper, so that no collections be made when I come" (1 Cor. 16:2). In this way, we make our obedience to God a consistent practice and have a constant reminder of His Lordship and provision in our lives.

Third, choosing to obey God by tithing our income indicates the level of our faith in Him. When we obey Him, we are essentially saying, "Lord, I trust You for every need I have." We not only honor Him through our giving, we also demonstrate our faith in His ability to provide for us. There is no way we can out give God. Therefore, we need to give with a willing heart, knowing that He has given more to us than we could ever give back to Him.

Fourth, we are to make our gifts joyfully. People who give grudgingly, solely from a sense of duty, do not truly open up their lives to God's purpose and blessings for them (Matt. 6:1–4; 2 Cor. 8:1–15). The joy in our hearts about giving is a direct expression of our trust in God to meet our needs (Phil. 4:19). ◉

◉ Psalm 29:1–6

A Psalm of David.

29 ASCRIBE to the LORD, O sons of the mighty,
Ascribe to the LORD glory and strength.
2 Ascribe to the LORD the glory due to His name;
Worship the LORD in holy array.
3 The voice of the LORD is upon the waters;
The God of glory thunders,
The LORD is over many waters.

4 The voice of the LORD is powerful,
The voice of the LORD is majestic.
5 The voice of the LORD breaks the cedars;

LIFE LESSONS

➤ **Psalm 29:2 — *Worship the LORD in holy array.***

We should never think of God's holiness as cold or cruel. Although God's holiness sets Him apart as the only one worthy of our worship, it should never drive us away from Him. Rather, God's holiness is our guarantee that God will always act in a loving, trustworthy, and honorable way toward us.

Yes, the LORD breaks in pieces the
cedars of Lebanon.
6   He makes Lebanon skip like a calf,
And Sirion like a young wild ox.

Proverbs 10:22–25

22   It is the blessing of the LORD that
makes rich,
And He adds no sorrow to it.
23   Doing wickedness is like sport to a
fool,
And so is wisdom to a man of
understanding.
24   What the wicked fears will come
upon him,
But the desire of the righteous will
be granted.
25   When the whirlwind passes, the
wicked is no more,
But the righteous has an everlasting
foundation.

Mark 7:1–13

7 THE Pharisees and some of the scribes
gathered around Him when they had
come from Jerusalem,
2   and had seen that some of His disciples were eating their bread with impure
hands, that is, unwashed.
3   (For the Pharisees and all the Jews
do not eat unless they carefully wash
their hands, thus observing the traditions of the elders;
4   and when they come from the market place, they do not eat unless they
cleanse themselves; and there are many
other things which they have received in
order to observe, such as the washing of
cups and pitchers and copper pots.)
5   The Pharisees and the scribes *asked

LIFE LESSONS

➤ **Mark 7:6** — *"This people honors me
with their lips, but their heart is far away
from me."*

Beware of Christian leaders who
appear to be very religious by their
actions, but who are really glorifying
themselves rather than God. We should
never honor anyone above God. Only He
is truly worthy of our praise.

Him, "Why do Your disciples not walk
according to the tradition of the elders,
but eat their bread with impure hands?"
6   And He said to them, "Rightly did
Isaiah prophesy of you hypocrites, as it
is written:
'THIS PEOPLE HONORS ME WITH THEIR
LIPS,
BUT THEIR HEART IS FAR AWAY FROM
ME.
7   'BUT IN VAIN DO THEY WORSHIP ME,
TEACHING AS DOCTRINES THE PRECEPTS
OF MEN.'
8   "Neglecting the commandment of
God, you hold to the tradition of men."
9   He was also saying to them, "You
are experts at setting aside the commandment of God in order to keep your
tradition.
10   "For Moses said, 'HONOR YOUR FA-
THER AND YOUR MOTHER'; and, 'HE WHO
SPEAKS EVIL OF FATHER OR MOTHER, IS TO BE
PUT TO DEATH';
11   but you say, 'If a man says to his father or his mother, whatever I have that
would help you is Corban (that is to say,
given to God),'
12   you no longer permit him to do anything for his father or his mother;
13   thus invalidating the word of God by
your tradition which you have handed
down; and you do many things such as
that."

Numbers 1:1—2:34

1 THEN the LORD spoke to Moses in
the wilderness of Sinai, in the tent

of meeting, on the first of the second
month, in the second year after they had
come out of the land of Egypt, saying,
2   "Take a census of all the congregation
of the sons of Israel, by their families, by

their fathers' households, according to the number of names, every male, head by head

3 from twenty years old and upward, whoever *is able to* go out to war in Israel, you and Aaron shall number them by their armies.

4 "With you, moreover, there shall be a man of each tribe, each one head of his father's household.

5 "These then are the names of the men who shall stand with you: of Reuben, Elizur the son of Shedeur;

6 of Simeon, Shelumiel the son of Zurishaddai;

7 of Judah, Nahshon the son of Amminadab;

8 of Issachar, Nethanel the son of Zuar;

9 of Zebulun, Eliab the son of Helon;

10 of the sons of Joseph: of Ephraim, Elishama the son of Ammihud; of Manasseh, Gamaliel the son of Pedahzur;

11 of Benjamin, Abidan the son of Gideoni;

12 of Dan, Ahiezer the son of Ammishaddai;

13 of Asher, Pagiel the son of Ochran;

14 of Gad, Eliasaph the son of Deuel;

15 of Naphtali, Ahira the son of Enan.

16 "These are they who were called of the congregation, the leaders of their fathers' tribes; they were the heads of divisions of Israel."

17 So Moses and Aaron took these men who had been designated by name,

18 and they assembled all the congregation together on the first of the second month. Then they registered by ances-

---

LIFE LESSONS

➤ **Numbers 1:1 — *Then the LORD spoke to Moses in the wilderness of Sinai.***

*G*od speaks to us at specific times, in specific places, about specific things. Listening to what He says is essential to walking with Him.

➤ **Numbers 1:17 — *So Moses and Aaron took these men who had been designated by name.***

*G*od calls us *by name* into His service. He knows the gifts, abilities, and backgrounds of each one of us, and by His Spirit He places us in exactly the right spots to serve Him best.

---

try in their families, by their fathers' households, according to the number of names, from twenty years old and upward, head by head,

19 just as the LORD had commanded Moses. So he numbered them in the wilderness of Sinai.

20 Now the sons of Reuben, Israel's firstborn, their genealogical registration by their families, by their fathers' households, according to the number of names, head by head, every male from twenty years old and upward, whoever *was able to* go out to war,

21 their numbered men of the tribe of Reuben *were* 46,500.

22 Of the sons of Simeon, their genealogical registration by their families, by their fathers' households, their numbered men, according to the number of names, head by head, every male from twenty years old and upward, whoever *was able to* go out to war,

23 their numbered men of the tribe of Simeon *were* 59,300.

24 Of the sons of Gad, their genealogical registration by their families, by their fathers' households, according to the number of names, from twenty years old and upward, whoever *was able to* go out to war,

25 their numbered men of the tribe of Gad *were* 45,650.

26 Of the sons of Judah, their genealogical registration by their families, by their fathers' households, according to the number of names, from twenty years old and upward, whoever *was able to* go out to war,

27 their numbered men of the tribe of Judah *were* 74,600.

28 Of the sons of Issachar, their genealogical registration by their families, by their fathers' households, according to the number of names, from twenty years old and upward, whoever *was able to* go out to war,

29 their numbered men of the tribe of Issachar *were* 54,400.

30 Of the sons of Zebulun, their genealogical registration by their families, by their fathers' households, according to the number of names, from twenty years old and upward, whoever *was able to* go out to war,

31 their numbered men of the tribe of Zebulun *were* 57,400.

32 Of the sons of Joseph, *namely*, of the sons of Ephraim, their genealogical registration by their families, by their fathers' households, according to the number of names, from twenty years old and upward, whoever *was able to* go out to war,
33 their numbered men of the tribe of Ephraim *were* 40,500.
34 Of the sons of Manasseh, their genealogical registration by their families, by their fathers' households, according to the number of names, from twenty years old and upward, whoever *was able to* go out to war,
35 their numbered men of the tribe of Manasseh *were* 32,200.
36 Of the sons of Benjamin, their genealogical registration by their families, by their fathers' households, according to the number of names, from twenty years old and upward, whoever *was able to* go out to war,
37 their numbered men of the tribe of Benjamin *were* 35,400.
38 Of the sons of Dan, their genealogical registration by their families, by their fathers' households, according to the number of names, from twenty years old and upward, whoever *was able to* go out to war,
39 their numbered men of the tribe of Dan *were* 62,700.
40 Of the sons of Asher, their genealogical registration by their families, by their fathers' households, according to the number of names, from twenty years old and upward, whoever *was able to* go out to war,
41 their numbered men of the tribe of Asher *were* 41,500.
42 Of the sons of Naphtali, their genealogical registration by their families, by their fathers' households, according to the number of names, from twenty years old and upward, whoever *was able to* go out to war,
43 their numbered men of the tribe of Naphtali *were* 53,400.
44 These are the ones who were numbered, whom Moses and Aaron numbered, with the leaders of Israel, twelve men, each of whom was of his father's household.
45 So all the numbered men of the sons of Israel by their fathers' households, from twenty years old and upward, whoever *was able to* go out to war in Israel,

46 even all the numbered men were 603,550.
47 The Levites, however, were not numbered among them by their fathers' tribe.
48 For the LORD had spoken to Moses, saying,
49 "Only the tribe of Levi you shall not number, nor shall you take their census among the sons of Israel.
50 "But you shall appoint the Levites over the tabernacle of the testimony, and over all its furnishings and over all that belongs to it. They shall carry the tabernacle and all its furnishings, and they shall take care of it; they shall also camp around the tabernacle.
51 "So when the tabernacle is to set out, the Levites shall take it down; and when the tabernacle encamps, the Levites shall set it up. But the layman who comes near shall be put to death.
52 "The sons of Israel shall camp, each man by his own camp, and each man by his own standard, according to their armies.
53 "But the Levites shall camp around the tabernacle of the testimony, so that there will be no wrath on the congregation of the sons of Israel. So the Levites shall keep charge of the tabernacle of the testimony."
54 Thus the sons of Israel did; according to all which the LORD had commanded Moses, so they did.

2 NOW the LORD spoke to Moses and to Aaron, saying,
2 "The sons of Israel shall camp, each by his own standard, with the banners of their fathers' households; they shall camp around the tent of meeting at a distance.
3 "Now those who camp on the east side toward the sunrise *shall be* of the standard of the camp of Judah, by their armies, and the leader of the sons of Judah: Nahshon the son of Amminadab,
4 and his army, even their numbered men, 74,600.
5 "Those who camp next to him *shall be* the tribe of Issachar, and the leader of the sons of Issachar: Nethanel the son of Zuar,
6 and his army, even their numbered men, 54,400.
7 "*Then comes* the tribe of Zebulun, and the leader of the sons of Zebulun: Eliab the son of Helon,

8   and his army, even his numbered men, 57,400.

9   "The total of the numbered men of the camp of Judah: 186,400, by their armies. They shall set out first.

10 "On the south side *shall be* the standard of the camp of Reuben by their armies, and the leader of the sons of Reuben: Elizur the son of Shedeur,

11 and his army, even their numbered men, 46,500.

12 "Those who camp next to him *shall be* the tribe of Simeon, and the leader of the sons of Simeon: Shelumiel the son of Zurishaddai,

13 and his army, even their numbered men, 59,300.

14 "Then *comes* the tribe of Gad, and the leader of the sons of Gad: Eliasaph the son of Deuel,

15 and his army, even their numbered men, 45,650.

16 "The total of the numbered men of the camp of Reuben: 151,450 by their armies. And they shall set out second.

17 "Then the tent of meeting shall set out *with* the camp of the Levites in the midst of the camps; just as they camp, so they shall set out, every man in his place by their standards.

18 "On the west side *shall be* the standard of the camp of Ephraim by their armies, and the leader of the sons of Ephraim *shall be* Elishama the son of Ammihud,

19 and his army, even their numbered men, 40,500.

20 "Next to him *shall be* the tribe of Manasseh, and the leader of the sons of Manasseh: Gamaliel the son of Pedahzur,

21 and his army, even their numbered men, 32,200.

22 "Then *comes* the tribe of Benjamin, and the leader of the sons of Benjamin: Abidan the son of Gideoni,

23 and his army, even their numbered men, 35,400.

24 "The total of the numbered men of the camp of Ephraim: 108,100, by their armies. And they shall set out third.

25 "On the north side *shall be* the standard of the camp of Dan by their armies, and the leader of the sons of Dan: Ahiezer the son of Ammishaddai,

26 and his army, even their numbered men, 62,700.

27 "Those who camp next to him *shall be* the tribe of Asher, and the leader of the sons of Asher: Pagiel the son of Ochran,

28 and his army, even their numbered men, 41,500.

29 "Then *comes* the tribe of Naphtali, and the leader of the sons of Naphtali: Ahira the son of Enan,

30 and his army, even their numbered men, 53,400.

31 "The total of the numbered men of the camp of Dan *was* 157,600. They shall set out last by their standards."

32 These are the numbered men of the sons of Israel by their fathers' households; the total of the numbered men of the camps by their armies, 603,550.

33 The Levites, however, were not numbered among the sons of Israel, just as the LORD had commanded Moses.

34 Thus the sons of Israel did; according to all that the LORD commanded Moses, so they camped by their standards, and so they set out, every one by his family according to his father's household.

Psalm 29:7–11

7   The voice of the LORD hews out
        flames of fire.
8   The voice of the LORD shakes the
        wilderness;
    The LORD shakes the wilderness of
        Kadesh.
9   The voice of the LORD makes the
        deer to calve
    And strips the forests bare;
    And in His temple everything says,
        "Glory!"
10 The LORD sat *as King* at the flood;
    Yes, the LORD sits as King forever.
11 The LORD will give strength to His
        people;
    The LORD will bless His people with
        peace.

Proverbs 10:26–29

26 Like vinegar to the teeth and smoke
        to the eyes,
    So is the lazy one to those who send
        him.
27 The fear of the LORD prolongs life,

WHAT THE BIBLE SAYS ABOUT

The Voice of God

Psalm 29:7–9

*T*he voice of God is mighty, inventive, and wonderful. In the beginning, when God spoke, the worlds were created—as were all the stars and other phenomena in the sky. His words formed the multitudes of different animals, fishes, and birds, as well as all the crops, trees, and flowers that cover the earth (Gen. 1).

He opened His mouth and man and woman were created in His image—as was the plan that would save all of humanity (Gen. 2–3).

When the Word of God came to dwell with us—the *Logos*, our Savior—He brought us life and light (John 1:4). When He said, "Hush, be still," the winds and the waves obeyed Him and were calmed (Mark 4:39). At His command, "Be opened!" the mute could speak (Mark 7:34). At the sound of His voice, the deaf could hear, the lame could walk, and all manner of sicknesses were healed.

Through His Word, we were taught the new covenant. He said, "I will put My law within them and on their heart I will write it; and I will be their God, and they shall be My people. They will not teach again, each man his neighbor and each man his brother, saying, 'Know the LORD,' for they will all know Me, from the least of them to the greatest of them," declares the LORD, "for I will forgive their iniquity, and their sin I will remember no more" (Jer. 31:33, 34).

So it was that God's voice changed our hearts.

And one day, when He calls—when He shouts out in victory—we will recognize the voice of our Savior and meet Him in the air (1 Thess. 4:16, 17).

Friend, if God's voice is so powerful, creative, and wise, why don't you listen for it more? He can heal your pain, open your understanding, and lead you to triumph.

Therefore, listen to Him. His voice is certainly the best thing you'll hear all day. ◈

But the years of the wicked will be shortened.
28 The hope of the righteous is gladness, But the expectation of the wicked perishes.
✳ 29 The way of the LORD is a stronghold to the upright, But ruin to the workers of iniquity.

◈ Mark 7:14–37

14 After He called the crowd to Him again, He *began* saying to them, "Listen to Me, all of you, and understand:
➤ 15 there is nothing outside the man
✳ which can defile him if it goes into him; but the things which proceed out of the man are what defile the man.
16 ["If anyone has ears to hear, let him hear."]
17 When he had left the crowd *and* entered the house, His disciples questioned Him about the parable.
18 And He *said to them, "Are you so lacking in understanding also? Do you not understand that whatever goes into the man from outside cannot defile him,
19 because it does not go into his heart, but into his stomach, and is eliminated?" (*Thus He* declared all foods clean.)
20 And He was saying, "That which proceeds out of the man, that is what defiles the man.
21 "For from within, out of the heart of men, proceed the evil thoughts, fornications, thefts, murders, adulteries,
22 deeds of coveting *and* wickedness, as *well as* deceit, sensuality, envy, slander, pride *and* foolishness.
23 "All these evil things proceed from within and defile the man."
24 Jesus got up and went away from

LIFE LESSONS

➤ **Mark 7:15** — *"There is nothing outside the man which can defile him if it goes into him; but the things which proceed out of the man are what defile the man."*

*W*hat a person eats and drinks cannot "defile" him, but what comes out of him—ungodly words and actions— certainly can. Jesus wanted His disciples to see the core issue always comes down to the heart (1 Sam. 16:7; 1 Chr. 28:9).

there to the region of Tyre. And when He had entered a house, He wanted no one to know of it; yet He could not escape notice.
25 But after hearing of Him, a woman whose little daughter had an unclean spirit immediately came and fell at His feet.
26 Now the woman was a Gentile, of the Syrophoenician race. And she kept asking Him to cast the demon out of her daughter.
27 And He was saying to her, "Let the children be satisfied first, for it is not good to take the children's bread and throw it to the dogs."
28 But she answered and *said to Him, "Yes, Lord, but even the dogs under the table feed on the children's crumbs."
29 And He said to her, "Because of this answer go; the demon has gone out of your daughter."
30 And going back to her home, she found the child lying on the bed, the demon having left.
31 Again He went out from the region of Tyre, and came through Sidon to the Sea of Galilee, within the region of Decapolis.
32 They *brought to Him one who was deaf and spoke with difficulty, and they *implored Him to lay His hand on him.

33 Jesus took him aside from the crowd, by himself, and put His fingers into his ears, and after spitting, He touched his tongue with the saliva;
34 and looking up to heaven with a deep sigh, He *said to him, "Ephphatha!" that is, "Be opened!"
35 And his ears were opened, and the impediment of his tongue was removed, and he began speaking plainly.
36 And He gave them orders not to tell anyone; but the more He ordered them, the more widely they continued to proclaim it.
37 They were utterly astonished, saying, "He has done all things well; He makes even the deaf to hear and the mute to speak." ◄

LIFE LESSONS

➤ **Mark 7:37 — They were utterly astonished, saying, "He has done all things well."**

*J*esus does all things well, but He also usually does them in unexpected ways. He astonishes us, not only by the mighty works He performs, but also because He so often catches us off guard.

Numbers 3:1—4:49

3 NOW these are the records of the generations of Aaron and Moses at the time when the LORD spoke with Moses on Mount Sinai.
2 These then are the names of the sons of Aaron: Nadab the firstborn, and Abihu, Eleazar and Ithamar.
3 These are the names of the sons of Aaron, the anointed priests, whom he ordained to serve as priests.
4 But Nadab and Abihu died before the LORD when they offered strange fire before the LORD in the wilderness of Sinai; and they had no children. So Eleazar and Ithamar served as priests in the lifetime of their father Aaron.
5 Then the LORD spoke to Moses, saying,

6 "Bring the tribe of Levi near and set them before Aaron the priest, that they may serve him.
7 "They shall perform the duties for him and for the whole congregation before the tent of meeting, to do the service of the tabernacle.
8 "They shall also keep all the furnishings of the tent of meeting, along with the duties of the sons of Israel, to do the service of the tabernacle.
9 "You shall thus give the Levites to Aaron and to his sons; they are wholly given to him from among the sons of Israel.
10 "So you shall appoint Aaron and his ◄ sons that they may keep their priesthood, but the layman who comes near shall be put to death."
11 Again the LORD spoke to Moses, saying,

12 "Now, behold, I have taken the Levites from among the sons of Israel instead of every firstborn, the first issue of the womb among the sons of Israel. So the Levites shall be Mine.

13 "For all the firstborn are Mine; on the day that I struck down all the firstborn in the land of Egypt, I sanctified to Myself all the firstborn in Israel, from man to beast. They shall be Mine; I am the LORD."

14 Then the LORD spoke to Moses in the wilderness of Sinai, saying,

15 "Number the sons of Levi by their fathers' households, by their families; every male from a month old and upward you shall number."

16 So Moses numbered them according to the word of the LORD, just as he had been commanded.

17 These then are the sons of Levi by their names: Gershon and Kohath and Merari.

18 These are the names of the sons of Gershon by their families: Libni and Shimei;

19 and the sons of Kohath by their families: Amram and Izhar, Hebron and Uzziel;

20 and the sons of Merari by their families: Mahli and Mushi. These are the families of the Levites according to their fathers' households.

21 Of Gershon *was* the family of the Libnites and the family of the Shimeites; these *were* the families of the Gershonites.

22 Their numbered men, in the numbering of every male from a month old and upward, *even* their numbered men *were* 7,500.

23 The families of the Gershonites were to camp behind the tabernacle westward,

24 and the leader of the fathers' households of the Gershonites *was* Eliasaph the son of Lael.

25 Now the duties of the sons of Gershon in the tent of meeting *involved* the tabernacle and the tent, its covering, and the screen for the doorway of the tent of meeting,

26 and the hangings of the court, and the screen for the doorway of the court which is around the tabernacle and the altar, and its cords, according to all the service concerning them.

27 Of Kohath *was* the family of the Amramites and the family of the Izharites and the family of the Hebronites and the family of the Uzzielites; these were the families of the Kohathites.

28 In the numbering of every male from a month old and upward, *there were* 8,600, performing the duties of the sanctuary.

29 The families of the sons of Kohath were to camp on the southward side of the tabernacle,

30 and the leader of the fathers' households of the Kohathite families was Elizaphan the son of Uzziel.

31 Now their duties *involved* the ark, the table, the lampstand, the altars, and the utensils of the sanctuary with which they minister, and the screen, and all the service concerning them;

32 and Eleazar the son of Aaron the priest *was* the chief of the leaders of Levi, *and had* the oversight of those who perform the duties of the sanctuary.

33 Of Merari *was* the family of the Mahlites and the family of the Mushites; these *were* the families of Merari.

34 Their numbered men in the numbering of every male from a month old and upward, *were* 6,200.

35 The leader of the fathers' households of the families of Merari *was* Zuriel the son of Abihail. They *were* to camp on the northward side of the tabernacle.

36 Now the appointed duties of the sons of Merari *involved* the frames of the tabernacle, its bars, its pillars, its sockets, all its equipment, and the service concerning them,

37 and the pillars around the court with their sockets and their pegs and their cords.

38 Now those who were to camp before the tabernacle eastward, before the tent of meeting toward the sunrise, are Moses and Aaron and his sons, performing the duties of the sanctuary for the obligation

of the sons of Israel; but the layman coming near was to be put to death.

39 All the numbered men of the Levites, whom Moses and Aaron numbered at the command of the LORD by their families, every male from a month old and upward, *were* 22,000.

40 Then the LORD said to Moses, "Number every firstborn male of the sons of Israel from a month old and upward, and make a list of their names.

41 "You shall take the Levites for Me, I am the LORD, instead of all the firstborn among the sons of Israel, and the cattle of the Levites instead of all the firstborn among the cattle of the sons of Israel."

42 So Moses numbered all the firstborn among the sons of Israel, just as the LORD had commanded him;

43 and all the firstborn males by the number of names from a month old and upward, for their numbered men were 22,273.

44 Then the LORD spoke to Moses, saying,

45 "Take the Levites instead of all the firstborn among the sons of Israel and the cattle of the Levites. And the Levites shall be Mine; I am the LORD.

46 "For the ransom of the 273 of the firstborn of the sons of Israel who are in excess beyond the Levites,

47 you shall take five shekels apiece, per head; you shall take *them* in terms of the shekel of the sanctuary (the shekel is twenty gerahs),

48 and give the money, the ransom of those who are in excess among them, to Aaron and to his sons."

49 So Moses took the ransom money from those who were in excess, beyond those ransomed by the Levites;

50 from the firstborn of the sons of Israel he took the money in terms of the shekel of the sanctuary, 1,365.

51 Then Moses gave the ransom money to Aaron and to his sons, at the command of the LORD, just as the LORD had commanded Moses.

4 THEN the LORD spoke to Moses and to Aaron, saying,

2 "Take a census of the descendants of Kohath from among the sons of Levi, by their families, by their fathers' households,

3 from thirty years and upward, even

to fifty years old, all who enter the service to do the work in the tent of meeting.

4 "This is the work of the descendants of Kohath in the tent of meeting, *concerning* the most holy things.

5 "When the camp sets out, Aaron and his sons shall go in and they shall take down the veil of the screen and cover the ark of the testimony with it;

6 and they shall lay a covering of porpoise skin on it, and shall spread over *it* a cloth of pure blue, and shall insert its poles.

7 "Over the table of the bread of the Presence they shall also spread a cloth of blue and put on it the dishes and the pans and the sacrificial bowls and the jars for the drink offering, and the continual bread shall be on it.

8 "They shall spread over them a cloth of scarlet *material,* and cover the same with a covering of porpoise skin, and they shall insert its poles.

9 "Then they shall take a blue cloth and cover the lampstand for the light, along with its lamps and its snuffers, and its trays and all its oil vessels, by which they serve it;

10 and they shall put it and all its utensils in a covering of porpoise skin, and shall put it on the carrying bars.

11 "Over the golden altar they shall spread a blue cloth and cover it with a covering of porpoise skin, and shall insert its poles;

12 and they shall take all the utensils of service, with which they serve in the sanctuary, and put them in a blue cloth and cover them with a covering of porpoise skin, and put them on the carrying bars.

13 "Then they shall take away the ashes from the altar, and spread a purple cloth over it.

14 "They shall also put on it all its utensils by which they serve in connection with it: the firepans, the forks and shovels and the basins, all the utensils of the altar; and they shall spread a cover of porpoise skin over it and insert its poles.

15 "When Aaron and his sons have finished covering the holy *objects* and all the furnishings of the sanctuary, when the camp is to set out, after that the sons of Kohath shall come to carry *them,* so that they will not touch the holy *objects* and die. These are the things in the tent

of meeting which the sons of Kohath are to carry.

16 "The responsibility of Eleazar the son of Aaron the priest is the oil for the light and the fragrant incense and the continual grain offering and the anointing oil—the responsibility of all the tabernacle and of all that is in it, with the sanctuary and its furnishings."

17 Then the LORD spoke to Moses and to Aaron, saying,

18 "Do not let the tribe of the families of the Kohathites be cut off from among the Levites.

19 "But do this to them that they may live and not die when they approach the most holy *objects:* Aaron and his sons shall go in and assign each of them to his work and to his load;

20 but they shall not go in to see the holy *objects* even for a moment, or they will die."

21 Then the LORD spoke to Moses, saying,

22 "Take a census of the sons of Gershon also, by their fathers' households, by their families;

23 from thirty years and upward to fifty years old, you shall number them; all who enter to perform the service to do the work in the tent of meeting.

24 "This is the service of the families of the Gershonites, in serving and in carrying:

25 they shall carry the curtains of the tabernacle and the tent of meeting *with* its covering and the covering of porpoise skin that is on top of it, and the screen for the doorway of the tent of meeting,

26 and the hangings of the court, and the screen for the doorway of the gate of the court which is around the tabernacle and the altar, and their cords and all the equipment for their service; and all that is to be done, they shall perform.

27 "All the service of the sons of the Gershonites, in all their loads and in all their work, shall be *performed* at the command of Aaron and his sons; and you shall assign to them as a duty all their loads.

28 "This is the service of the families of the sons of the Gershonites in the tent of meeting, and their duties *shall be* under the direction of Ithamar the son of Aaron the priest.

29 "*As for* the sons of Merari, you shall number them by their families, by their fathers' households;

30 from thirty years and upward even to fifty years old, you shall number them, everyone who enters the service to do the work of the tent of meeting.

31 "Now this is the duty of their loads, for all their service in the tent of meeting: the boards of the tabernacle and its bars and its pillars and its sockets,

32 and the pillars around the court and ◀ their sockets and their pegs and their cords, with all their equipment and with all their service; and you shall assign *each man* by name the items he is to carry.

33 "This is the service of the families of the sons of Merari, according to all their service in the tent of meeting, under the direction of Ithamar the son of Aaron the priest."

34 So Moses and Aaron and the leaders of the congregation numbered the sons of the Kohathites by their families and by their fathers' households,

35 from thirty years and upward even to fifty years old, everyone who entered the service for work in the tent of meeting.

36 Their numbered men by their families were 2,750.

37 These are the numbered men of the Kohathite families, everyone who was serving in the tent of meeting, whom Moses and Aaron numbered according to the commandment of the LORD through Moses.

38 The numbered men of the sons of Gershon by their families and by their fathers' households,

39 from thirty years and upward even to fifty years old, everyone who entered the service for work in the tent of meeting.

40 Their numbered men by their families, by their fathers' households, were 2,630.

41 These are the numbered men of the families of the sons of Gershon, everyone who was serving in the tent of meeting, whom Moses and Aaron numbered according to the commandment of the LORD.

LIFE LESSONS

➤ **Numbers 4:32** — *"You shall assign each man by name the items he is to carry."*

*O*ur service is important to God, regardless of what that service is. He calls us individually to particular ministries and kinds of service. And He knows us by name!

42 The numbered men of the families of the sons of Merari by their families, by their fathers' households,

43 from thirty years and upward even to fifty years old, everyone who entered the service for work in the tent of meeting.

44 Their numbered men by their families were 3,200.

45 These are the numbered men of the families of the sons of Merari, whom Moses and Aaron numbered according to the commandment of the LORD through Moses.

46 All the numbered men of the Levites, whom Moses and Aaron and the leaders of Israel numbered, by their families and by their fathers' households,

47 from thirty years and upward even to fifty years old, everyone who could enter to do the work of service and the work of carrying in the tent of meeting.

48 Their numbered men were 8,580.

49 According to the commandment of the LORD through Moses, they were numbered, everyone by his serving or carrying; thus *these were* his numbered men, just as the LORD had commanded Moses.

◈ Psalm 30:1–7

A Psalm; a Song at the Dedication of the House. A Psalm of David.

30 I WILL extol You, O LORD, for
    You have lifted me up,
And have not let my enemies rejoice
    over me.

LIFE LESSONS

➤ **Psalm 30:5 —** *His anger is but for a moment, His favor is for a lifetime; weeping may last for the night, but a shout of joy comes in the morning.*

*W*hen darkness covers your heart, you may think you have no hope. But just as the sun disperses the nighttime at daybreak, your circumstances will change at the Lord's command. So wait in hope and trust Him. His joyous triumph is surely on its way.

---

2   O LORD my God,
        I cried to You for help, and You
            healed me.
3   O LORD, You have brought up my
            soul from Sheol;
        You have kept me alive, that I
            would not go down to the pit.
4   Sing praise to the LORD, you His
            godly ones,
        And give thanks to His holy
            name.
5   For His anger is but for a moment,
        His favor is for a lifetime;
        Weeping may last for the night,
        But a shout of joy *comes* in the
            morning.
6   Now as for me, I said in my
            prosperity,
        "I will never be moved."
7   O LORD, by Your favor You have
            made my mountain to stand
            strong;
        You hid Your face, I was dismayed.

Life Examples:

Night and Day

PSALM 30:5

*F*riend, be encouraged. Though difficult circumstances may weigh on your heart, there is great hope for you because God is your help and deliverer.

Psalm 30:5 says, "Weeping may last for the night, but a shout of joy comes in the morning."

And it's true.

The issues that seem so insurmountable at night—after you've had a long, difficult day and are tired—are not so unsolvable in the morning. Your situation will always appear gloomier at night when it reflects the darkness of the midnight sky.

Yet when the sun rises and you spend time in God's powerful presence, you will feel a renewal of God's strength and will receive His fresh wisdom for the day.

God will bring you joy. As swiftly as God changes night into day—He can transform your cries of sorrow into a reason for praise. Though He may not remove the situation, He will certainly show you His powerful hand at work in it.

Therefore, trust Him. Remember that "nothing will be impossible with God" (Luke 1:37). Sing His praises with faith that as the sun makes its appearance on the horizon, God will show His faithfulness in your situation.

Proverbs 10:30-32

30　The righteous will never be
　　shaken,
　　But the wicked will not dwell in the
　　land.
31　The mouth of the righteous flows
　　with wisdom,
　　But the perverted tongue will be cut
　　out.
32　The lips of the righteous bring forth
　　what is acceptable,
　　But the mouth of the wicked what is
　　perverted.

Mark 8:1–21

8 IN those days, when there was again
　a large crowd and they had nothing to
eat, Jesus called His disciples and *said
to them,
2　"I feel compassion for the people because they have remained with Me now
three days and have nothing to eat.
3　"If I send them away hungry to their
homes, they will faint on the way; and
some of them have come from a great
distance."
4　And His disciples answered Him,
"Where will anyone be able *to find*
enough bread here in *this* desolate place
to satisfy these people?"
5　And He was asking them, "How
many loaves do you have?" And they
said, "Seven."
6　And He *directed the people to sit
down on the ground; and taking the
seven loaves, He gave thanks and broke
them, and started giving them to His disciples to serve to them, and they served
them to the people.
7　They also had a few small fish; and
after He had blessed them, He ordered
these to be served as well.
8　And they ate and were satisfied; and
they picked up seven large baskets full of
what was left over of the broken pieces.
9　About four thousand were *there;* and
He sent them away.
10　And immediately He entered the
boat with His disciples and came to the
district of Dalmanutha.
11　The Pharisees came out and began to

argue with Him, seeking from Him a sign
from heaven, to test Him.
12　Sighing deeply in His spirit, He *said,
"Why does this generation seek for a
sign? Truly I say to you, no sign will be
given to this generation."
13　Leaving them, He again embarked
and went away to the other side.
14　And they had forgotten to take bread,
and did not have more than one loaf in
the boat with them.
15　And He was giving orders to them,
saying, "Watch out! Beware of the leaven
of the Pharisees and the leaven of Herod."
16　They *began* to discuss with one another *the fact* that they had no bread.
17　And Jesus, aware of this, *said to
them, "Why do you discuss *the fact* that
you have no bread? Do you not yet see
or understand? Do you have a hardened
heart?
18　"HAVING EYES, DO YOU NOT SEE? AND
HAVING EARS, DO YOU NOT HEAR? And do
you not remember,
19　when I broke the five loaves for the
five thousand, how many baskets full of
broken pieces you picked up?" They *said
to Him, "Twelve."
20　"When *I broke* the seven for the four
thousand, how many large baskets full of
broken pieces did you pick up?" And they
*said to Him, "Seven."
21　And He was saying to them, "Do you
not yet understand?"

LIFE LESSONS

➢ **Mark 8:12 —** *Sighing deeply in His*
spirit.

*J*esus demonstrated disillusionment
with the spiritual leaders of His day.
Since He knew their hearts, He had no
expectations of them. Still, He expressed
His disappointment with their lack of
desire for God's truth.

➢ **Mark 8:21 —** *"Do you not yet under-*
stand?"

*S*ometimes we mistakenly think grace
excuses us from the hard work of
growing spiritually. It doesn't. The Bible
says that "because of practice" we have
our "senses trained to discern good and
evil" (Heb. 5:14). We grow by allowing
the Holy Spirit to direct us, by obeying
God, and by making godly decisions.

5 THEN the LORD spoke to Moses, saying,

2 "Command the sons of Israel that they send away from the camp every leper and everyone having a discharge and everyone who is unclean because of a *dead* person.

3 "You shall send away both male and female; you shall send them outside the camp so that they will not defile their camp where I dwell in their midst."

4 The sons of Israel did so and sent them outside the camp; just as the LORD had spoken to Moses, thus the sons of Israel did.

5 Then the LORD spoke to Moses, saying,

6 "Speak to the sons of Israel, 'When a man or woman commits any of the sins of mankind, acting unfaithfully against the LORD, and that person is guilty,

➤ 7 then he shall confess his sins which he has committed, and he shall make restitution in full for his wrong and add to it one-fifth of it, and give *it* to him whom he has wronged.

8 'But if the man has no relative to whom restitution may be made for the wrong, the restitution which is made for the wrong *must go* to the LORD for the priest, besides the ram of atonement, by which atonement is made for him.

9 'Also every contribution pertaining to all the holy *gifts* of the sons of Israel, which they offer to the priest, shall be his.

10 'So every man's holy *gifts* shall be his; whatever any man gives to the priest, it becomes his.'"

11 Then the LORD spoke to Moses, saying,

LIFE LESSONS

➤ **Numbers 5:7 —** *"Then he shall confess his sins which he has committed, and he shall make restitution in full for his wrong."*

Confession of sin is a prerequisite for re-establishing close fellowship with the Lord. Since all sin is unfaithfulness to God, we must admit to Him how we have been disloyal and turn from our ways in obedience to Him.

---

12 "Speak to the sons of Israel and say to them, 'If any man's wife goes astray and is unfaithful to him,

13 and a man has intercourse with her and it is hidden from the eyes of her husband and she is undetected, although she has defiled herself, and there is no witness against her and she has not been caught in the act,

14 if a spirit of jealousy comes over him and he is jealous of his wife when she has defiled herself, or if a spirit of jealousy comes over him and he is jealous of his wife when she has not defiled herself,

15 the man shall then bring his wife to the priest, and shall bring *as* an offering for her one-tenth of an ephah of barley meal; he shall not pour oil on it nor put frankincense on it, for it is a grain offering of jealousy, a grain offering of memorial, a reminder of iniquity.

16 'Then the priest shall bring her near and have her stand before the LORD,

17 and the priest shall take holy water in an earthenware vessel; and he shall take some of the dust that is on the floor of the tabernacle and put *it* into the water.

18 'The priest shall then have the woman stand before the LORD and let *the hair of* the woman's head go loose, and place the grain offering of memorial in her hands, which is the grain offering of jealousy, and in the hand of the priest is to be the water of bitterness that brings a curse.

19 'The priest shall have her take an oath and shall say to the woman, "If no man has lain with you and if you have not gone astray into uncleanness, *being* under *the authority of* your husband, be immune to this water of bitterness that brings a curse;

20 if you, however, have gone astray, *being* under *the authority of* your husband, and if you have defiled yourself and a man other than your husband has had intercourse with you"

21 (then the priest shall have the woman swear with the oath of the curse, and the priest shall say to the woman), "the LORD make you a curse and an oath among your people by the LORD'S making your thigh waste away and your abdomen swell;

22 and this water that brings a curse shall go into your stomach, and make

your abdomen swell and your thigh waste away." And the woman shall say, "Amen. Amen."

23 'The priest shall then write these curses on a scroll, and he shall wash them off into the water of bitterness.

24 'Then he shall make the woman drink the water of bitterness that brings a curse, so that the water which brings a curse will go into her and *cause* bitterness.

25 'The priest shall take the grain offering of jealousy from the woman's hand, and he shall wave the grain offering before the LORD and bring it to the altar;

26 and the priest shall take a handful of the grain offering as its memorial offering and offer *it* up in smoke on the altar, and afterward he shall make the woman drink the water.

27 'When he has made her drink the water, then it shall come about, if she has defiled herself and has been unfaithful to her husband, that the water which brings a curse will go into her and *cause* bitterness, and her abdomen will swell and her thigh will waste away, and the woman will become a curse among her people.

28 'But if the woman has not defiled herself and is clean, she will then be free and conceive children.

29 'This is the law of jealousy: when a wife, *being* under *the authority of* her husband, goes astray and defiles herself,

30 or when a spirit of jealousy comes over a man and he is jealous of his wife, he shall then make the woman stand before the LORD, and the priest shall apply all this law to her.

31 'Moreover, the man will be free from guilt, but that woman shall bear her guilt.'"

6 AGAIN the LORD spoke to Moses, saying,

2 "Speak to the sons of Israel and say to them, 'When a man or woman makes a special vow, the vow of a Nazirite, to dedicate himself to the LORD,

3 he shall abstain from wine and strong drink; he shall drink no vinegar, whether made from wine or strong drink, nor shall he drink any grape juice nor eat fresh or dried grapes.

4 'All the days of his separation he shall not eat anything that is produced by the grape vine, from *the* seeds even to *the* skin.

5 'All the days of his vow of separation no razor shall pass over his head. He shall be holy until the days are fulfilled for which he separated himself to the LORD; he shall let the locks of hair on his head grow long.

6 'All the days of his separation to the LORD he shall not go near to a dead person.

7 'He shall not make himself unclean for his father or for his mother, for his brother or for his sister, when they die, because his separation to God is on his head.

8 'All the days of his separation he is holy to the LORD.

9 'But if a man dies very suddenly beside him and he defiles his dedicated head *of hair,* then he shall shave his head on the day when he becomes clean; he shall shave it on the seventh day.

10 'Then on the eighth day he shall bring two turtledoves or two young pigeons to the priest, to the doorway of the tent of meeting.

11 'The priest shall offer one for a sin offering and *the* other for a burnt offering, and make atonement for him concerning his sin because of the *dead* person. And that same day he shall consecrate his head,

12 and shall dedicate to the LORD his days as a Nazirite, and shall bring a male lamb a year old for a guilt offering; but the former days will be void because his separation was defiled.

13 'Now this is the law of the Nazirite when the days of his separation are fulfilled, he shall bring the offering to the doorway of the tent of meeting.

14 'He shall present his offering to the LORD: one male lamb a year old without defect for a burnt offering and one ewe-lamb a year old without defect for a sin offering and one ram without defect for a peace offering,

15 and a basket of unleavened cakes of fine flour mixed with oil and unleavened wafers spread with oil, along with their grain offering and their drink offering.

16 'Then the priest shall present *them* before the LORD and shall offer his sin offering and his burnt offering.

17 'He shall also offer the ram for a sacrifice of peace offerings to the LORD, together with the basket of unleavened cakes; the priest shall likewise offer its grain offering and its drink offering.

18 'The Nazirite shall then shave his dedicated head *of hair* at the doorway of the tent of meeting, and take the dedicated hair of his head and put *it* on the fire which is under the sacrifice of peace offerings.

19 'The priest shall take the ram's shoulder *when it has been* boiled, and one unleavened cake out of the basket and one unleavened wafer, and shall put *them* on the hands of the Nazirite after he has shaved his dedicated *hair.*

20 'Then the priest shall wave them for a wave offering before the LORD. It is holy for the priest, together with the breast offered by waving and the thigh offered by lifting up; and afterward the Nazirite may drink wine.'

21 "This is the law of the Nazirite who vows his offering to the LORD according to his separation, in addition to what *else* he can afford; according to his vow which he takes, so he shall do according to the law of his separation."

22 Then the LORD spoke to Moses, saying,

23 "Speak to Aaron and to his sons, saying, 'Thus you shall bless the sons of Israel. You shall say to them:

24 The LORD bless you, and keep you;

25 The LORD make His face shine on you,
And be gracious to you;

26 The LORD lift up His countenance on you,
And give you peace.'

27 "So they shall invoke My name on the sons of Israel, and I *then* will bless them."

◈ Psalm 30:8–12

8 To You, O LORD, I called,
And to the Lord I made supplication:

9 "What profit is there in my blood, if I go down to the pit?
Will the dust praise You? Will it declare Your faithfulness?

10 "Hear, O LORD, and be gracious to me;
O LORD, be my helper."

11 You have turned for me my mourning into dancing;

You have loosed my sackcloth and girded me with gladness,

12 That *my* soul may sing praise to You and not be silent.
O LORD my God, I will give thanks to You forever.

◈ Proverbs 11:1–3

11 A FALSE balance is an abomination to the LORD,
But a just weight is His delight.

2 When pride comes, then comes dishonor,
But with the humble is wisdom.

3 The integrity of the upright will guide them,
But the crookedness of the treacherous will destroy them.

LIFE LESSONS

➤ **Numbers 6:26 — *"The LORD lift up His countenance on you, and give you peace."***

*G*od loves to bless His people—to show us grace, favor, and peace. And the greatest blessing of all is that He blesses us with His presence.

➤ **Psalm 30:11 — *You have turned for me my mourning into dancing.***

*T*here are hardships we endure that are extremely difficult to overcome. But God has promised to cause *"all things* to work together for good" (Rom. 8:28)—and that includes the major heartbreaks of life. We may not understand how, but we can be confident the Lord will use the experience as a springboard of praise—turning our mourning into dancing.

➤ **Proverbs 11:1 — *A false balance is an abomination to the LORD, but a just weight is His delight.***

*D*ishonesty is "an abomination to the LORD," because it violates the holy character His children should demonstrate. God is as concerned that His people conduct fair and honest business practice as He is that their sexual lives honor Him (Lev. 19:35-37; Prov. 20:23). He delights in a "just weight" because it reflects His righteousness.

Mark 8:22–38

22 And they *came to Bethsaida. And they *brought a blind man to Jesus and *implored Him to touch him.

23 Taking the blind man by the hand, He brought him out of the village; and after spitting on his eyes and laying His hands on him, He asked him, "Do you see anything?"

24 And he looked up and said, "I see men, for I see *them* like trees, walking around."

25 Then again He laid His hands on his eyes; and he looked intently and was restored, and *began* to see everything clearly.

26 And He sent him to his home, saying, "Do not even enter the village."

27 Jesus went out, along with His disciples, to the villages of Caesarea Philippi; and on the way He questioned His disciples, saying to them, "Who do people say that I am?"

28 They told Him, saying, "John the Baptist; and others *say* Elijah; but others, one of the prophets."

29 And He *continued* by questioning them, "But who do you say that I am?" Peter *answered and *said to Him, "You are the Christ."

30 And He warned them to tell no one about Him.

31 And He began to teach them that the Son of Man must suffer many things and be rejected by the elders and the chief priests and the scribes, and be killed, and after three days rise again.

32 And He was stating the matter plainly. And Peter took Him aside and began to rebuke Him.

33 But turning around and seeing His disciples, He rebuked Peter and *said, "Get behind Me, Satan; for you are not setting your mind on God's interests, but man's."

34 And He summoned the crowd with His disciples, and said to them, "If anyone wishes to come after Me, he must

---

ANSWERS TO LIFE'S QUESTIONS

Should I tithe when I am struggling financially?

MARK 8:34–36

*F*rom the human perspective, the Bible may seem to be a book of paradoxes. It says, for example, that if we really want to have life, we must first lose it (Matt. 10:39). If we want to understand authority, we must first become a servant (Matt. 20:26, 27). If we want to be exalted, we must first humble ourselves (1 Pet. 5:6).

And giving to God is the first step toward financial freedom.

You may ask, "How can I give God *any-thing* when I can't even pay my bills? Doesn't God expect me to take care of my debts first?"

At first glance, such a concern sounds reasonable. The problem is it disregards God's authority and perspective. He insists that if we don't give, we are robbing Him—and we will end up in worse financial shape than ever (Mal. 3:8, 9).

We should always keep in mind everything we have is from God, and it's all His in the first place (1 Chr. 29:14). Therefore, what God asks of us is not unreasonable. He instructs, "You shall surely tithe all the produce from what you sow . . . so that you may learn to fear the Lord your God always" (Deut. 14:22, 23). This tithe is merely ten percent of all He has provided for us, and He asks us to give it back to Him as an acknowledgement of His provision and evidence of our trust in Him. Also, when we place our trust in Him, He rewards us with His many blessings. As He promises in Malachi 3:10, "'Bring the whole tithe into the storehouse, so that there may be food in My house, and test Me now in this,' says the Lord of hosts, 'if I will not open for you the windows of heaven and pour out for you a blessing until it overflows.'" As we know, God's promises have been tried and proven; so we can trust that when we obey Him, He will pour out His blessings upon us, just as He has promised.

You may wonder, *Should I tithe when I am struggling financially? Should I devote a tenth of my income to the Lord, when I already find it impossible to make ends meet?* The answer is unequivocally yes!

Since God owns it all, you can trust Him with all you have. He can bless your 90 percent and make it stretch further than you ever imagined (1 Kin. 17:8–16; 2 Kin. 4:1–7; Matt. 14:15–21; 15:32–38). This is not an exercise of fiscal ingenuity, but of faith. God doesn't need your money; rather, He wants you to discover the rewards of obedience. Submitting to Him in the area of finances is the prerequisite for enjoying true freedom. It is only when you truly trust and obey Him that you see all He can do in and through you. Therefore, trust God and watch Him work in your life.

deny himself, and take up his cross and follow Me.

35 "For whoever wishes to save his life will lose it, but whoever loses his life for My sake and the gospel's will save it.

36 "For what does it profit a man to gain the whole world, and forfeit his soul?

37 "For what will a man give in exchange for his soul?

38 "For whoever is ashamed of Me and My words in this adulterous and sinful generation, the Son of Man will also be ashamed of him when He comes in the glory of His Father with the holy angels."

Numbers 7:1—8:26

7 NOW on the day that Moses had finished setting up the tabernacle, he anointed it and consecrated it with all its furnishings and the altar and all its utensils; he anointed them and consecrated them also.

2 Then the leaders of Israel, the heads of their fathers' households, made an offering (they were the leaders of the tribes; they were the ones who were over the numbered men).

3 When they brought their offering before the LORD, six covered carts and twelve oxen, a cart for *every* two of the leaders and an ox for each one, then they presented them before the tabernacle.

4 Then the LORD spoke to Moses, saying,

5 "Accept *these things* from them, that they may be used in the service of the tent of meeting, and you shall give them to the Levites, *to* each man according to his service."

6 So Moses took the carts and the oxen and gave them to the Levites.

7 Two carts and four oxen he gave to the sons of Gershon, according to their service,

8 and four carts and eight oxen he gave to the sons of Merari, according to their service, under the direction of Ithamar the son of Aaron the priest.

9 But he did not give *any* to the sons of Kohath because theirs *was* the service of the holy *objects, which* they carried on the shoulder.

10 The leaders offered the dedication *offering* for the altar when it was anointed, so the leaders offered their offering before the altar.

11 Then the LORD said to Moses, "Let them present their offering, one leader each day, for the dedication of the altar."

12 Now the one who presented his offering on the first day was Nahshon the son of Amminadab, of the tribe of Judah;

13 and his offering *was* one silver dish whose weight *was* one hundred and thirty *shekels,* one silver bowl of seventy shekels, according to the shekel of the sanctuary, both of them full of fine flour mixed with oil for a grain offering;

14 one gold pan of ten *shekels,* full of incense;

15 one bull, one ram, one male lamb one year old, for a burnt offering;

16 one male goat for a sin offering;

17 and for the sacrifice of peace offerings, two oxen, five rams, five male goats, five male lambs one year old. This *was* the offering of Nahshon the son of Amminadab.

18 On the second day Nethanel the son of Zuar, leader of Issachar, presented *an offering;*

19 he presented as his offering one silver dish whose weight *was* one hundred and thirty *shekels,* one silver bowl of seventy shekels, according to the shekel of the sanctuary, both of them full of fine flour mixed with oil for a grain offering;

20 one gold pan of ten *shekels*, full of incense;
21 one bull, one ram, one male lamb one year old, for a burnt offering;
22 one male goat for a sin offering;
23 and for the sacrifice of peace offerings, two oxen, five rams, five male goats, five male lambs one year old. This *was* the offering of Nethanel the son of Zuar.
24 On the third day *it was* Eliab the son of Helon, leader of the sons of Zebulun;
25 his offering *was* one silver dish whose weight *was* one hundred and thirty *shekels*, one silver bowl of seventy shekels, according to the shekel of the sanctuary, both of them full of fine flour mixed with oil for a grain offering;
26 one gold pan of ten *shekels*, full of incense;
27 one young bull, one ram, one male lamb one year old, for a burnt offering;
28 one male goat for a sin offering;
29 and for the sacrifice of peace offerings, two oxen, five rams, five male goats, five male lambs one year old. This *was* the offering of Eliab the son of Helon.
30 On the fourth day *it was* Elizur the son of Shedeur, leader of the sons of Reuben;
31 his offering *was* one silver dish whose weight *was* one hundred and thirty *shekels*, one silver bowl of seventy shekels, according to the shekel of the sanctuary, both of them full of fine flour mixed with oil for a grain offering;
32 one gold pan of ten *shekels*, full of incense;
33 one bull, one ram, one male lamb one year old, for a burnt offering;
34 one male goat for a sin offering;
35 and for the sacrifice of peace offerings, two oxen, five rams, five male goats, five male lambs one year old. This *was* the offering of Elizur the son of Shedeur.
36 On the fifth day *it was* Shelumiel the son of Zurishaddai, leader of the children of Simeon;
37 his offering *was* one silver dish whose weight *was* one hundred and thirty *shekels*, one silver bowl of seventy shekels, according to the shekel of the sanctuary, both of them full of fine flour mixed with oil for a grain offering;
38 one gold pan of ten *shekels*, full of incense;
39 one bull, one ram, one male lamb one year old, for a burnt offering;

40 one male goat for a sin offering;
41 and for the sacrifice of peace offerings, two oxen, five rams, five male goats, five male lambs one year old. This *was* the offering of Shelumiel the son of Zurishaddai.
42 On the sixth day *it was* Eliasaph the son of Deuel, leader of the sons of Gad;
43 his offering *was* one silver dish whose weight *was* one hundred and thirty *shekels*, one silver bowl of seventy shekels, according to the shekel of the sanctuary, both of them full of fine flour mixed with oil for a grain offering;
44 one gold pan of ten *shekels*, full of incense;
45 one bull, one ram, one male lamb one year old, for a burnt offering;
46 one male goat for a sin offering;
47 and for the sacrifice of peace offerings, two oxen, five rams, five male goats, five male lambs one year old. This *was* the offering of Eliasaph the son of Deuel.
48 On the seventh day *it was* Elishama the son of Ammihud, leader of the sons of Ephraim;
49 his offering *was* one silver dish whose weight *was* one hundred and thirty *shekels*, one silver bowl of seventy shekels, according to the shekel of the sanctuary, both of them full of fine flour mixed with oil for a grain offering;
50 one gold pan of ten *shekels*, full of incense;
51 one bull, one ram, one male lamb one year old, for a burnt offering;
52 one male goat for a sin offering;
53 and for the sacrifice of peace offerings, two oxen, five rams, five male goats, five male lambs one year old. This *was* the offering of Elishama the son of Ammihud.
54 On the eighth day *it was* Gamaliel the son of Pedahzur, leader of the sons of Manasseh;
55 his offering *was* one silver dish whose weight *was* one hundred and thirty *shekels*, one silver bowl of seventy shekels, according to the shekel of the sanctuary, both of them full of fine flour mixed with oil for a grain offering;
56 one gold pan of ten *shekels*, full of incense;
57 one bull, one ram, one male lamb one year old, for a burnt offering;
58 one male goat for a sin offering;

59 and for the sacrifice of peace offerings, two oxen, five rams, five male
goats, five male lambs one year old. This
was the offering of Gamaliel the son of
Pedahzur.
60 On the ninth day *it was* Abidan the
son of Gideoni, leader of the sons of Benjamin;
61 his offering *was* one silver dish
whose weight *was* one hundred and
thirty *shekels*, one silver bowl of seventy
shekels, according to the shekel of the
sanctuary, both of them full of fine flour
mixed with oil for a grain offering;
62 one gold pan of ten *shekels*, full of
incense;
63 one bull, one ram, one male lamb
one year old, for a burnt offering;
64 one male goat for a sin offering;
65 and for the sacrifice of peace offerings, two oxen, five rams, five male
goats, five male lambs one year old. This
was the offering of Abidan the son of
Gideoni.
66 On the tenth day *it was* Ahiezer the
son of Ammishaddai, leader of the sons
of Dan;
67 his offering *was* one silver dish
whose weight *was* one hundred and
thirty *shekels*, one silver bowl of seventy
shekels, according to the shekel of the
sanctuary, both of them full of fine flour
mixed with oil for a grain offering;
68 one gold pan of ten *shekels*, full of
incense;
69 one bull, one ram, one male lamb
one year old, for a burnt offering;
70 one male goat for a sin offering;
71 and for the sacrifice of peace offerings, two oxen, five rams, five male
goats, five male lambs one year old. This
was the offering of Ahiezer the son of
Ammishaddai.
72 On the eleventh day *it was* Pagiel
the son of Ochran, leader of the sons of
Asher;
73 his offering *was* one silver dish
whose weight *was* one hundred and
thirty *shekels*, one silver bowl of seventy
shekels, according to the shekel of the
sanctuary, both of them full of fine flour
mixed with oil for a grain offering;
74 one gold pan of ten *shekels*, full of
incense;
75 one bull, one ram, one male lamb
one year old, for a burnt offering;
76 one male goat for a sin offering;

77 and for the sacrifice of peace offerings, two oxen, five rams, five male
goats, five male lambs one year old. This
was the offering of Pagiel the son of
Ochran.
78 On the twelfth day *it was* Ahira the
son of Enan, leader of the sons of Naphtali;
79 his offering *was* one silver dish
whose weight *was* one hundred and
thirty *shekels*, one silver bowl of seventy
shekels, according to the shekel of the
sanctuary, both of them full of fine flour
mixed with oil for a grain offering;
80 one gold pan of ten *shekels*, full of
incense;
81 one bull, one ram, one male lamb
one year old, for a burnt offering;
82 one male goat for a sin offering;
83 and for the sacrifice of peace offerings, two oxen, five rams, five male
goats, five male lambs one year old.
This *was* the offering of Ahira the son of
Enan.
84 This *was* the dedication *offering* for
the altar from the leaders of Israel when
it was anointed: twelve silver dishes,
twelve silver bowls, twelve gold pans,
85 each silver dish *weighing* one hundred and thirty *shekels* and each bowl
seventy; all the silver of the utensils *was*
2,400 *shekels*, according to the shekel of
the sanctuary;
86 the twelve gold pans, full of incense,
weighing ten *shekels* apiece, according
to the shekel of the sanctuary, all the
gold of the pans 120 *shekels*;
87 all the oxen for the burnt offering
twelve bulls, *all* the rams twelve, the
male lambs one year old with their grain
offering twelve, and the male goats for a
sin offering twelve;
88 and all the oxen for the sacrifice of
peace offerings 24 bulls, *all* the rams 60,
the male goats 60, the male lambs one
year old 60. This *was* the dedication *offering* for the altar after it was anointed.
89 Now when Moses went into the tent
of meeting to speak with Him, he heard
the voice speaking to him from above the
mercy seat that was on the ark of the testimony, from between the two cherubim,
so He spoke to him.
8 THEN the Lord spoke to Moses, saying,
2 "Speak to Aaron and say to him,
'When you mount the lamps, the seven

lamps will give light in the front of the lampstand.'"

3   Aaron therefore did so; he mounted its lamps at the front of the lampstand, just as the LORD had commanded Moses.

4   Now this was the workmanship of the lampstand, hammered work of gold; from its base to its flowers it was hammered work; according to the pattern which the LORD had shown Moses, so he made the lampstand.

5   Again the LORD spoke to Moses, saying,

6   "Take the Levites from among the sons of Israel and cleanse them.

7   "Thus you shall do to them, for their cleansing: *sprinkle* purifying water on them, and let them use a razor over their whole body and wash their clothes, and they will be clean.

8   "Then let them take a bull with its grain offering, fine flour mixed with oil; and a second bull you shall take for a sin offering.

9   "So you shall present the Levites before the tent of meeting. You shall also assemble the whole congregation of the sons of Israel,

10   and present the Levites before the LORD; and the sons of Israel shall lay their hands on the Levites.

11   "Aaron then shall present the Levites before the LORD as a wave offering from the sons of Israel, that they may qualify to perform the service of the LORD.

12   "Now the Levites shall lay their hands on the heads of the bulls; then offer the one for a sin offering and the other for a burnt offering to the LORD, to make atonement for the Levites.

13   "You shall have the Levites stand before Aaron and before his sons so as to present them as a wave offering to the LORD.

14   "Thus you shall separate the Levites from among the sons of Israel, and the Levites shall be Mine.

15   "Then after that the Levites may go in to serve the tent of meeting. But you shall cleanse them and present them as a wave offering;

16   for they are wholly given to Me from among the sons of Israel. I have taken them for Myself instead of every first issue of the womb, the firstborn of all the sons of Israel.

17   "For every firstborn among the sons of Israel is Mine, among the men and among the animals; on the day that I struck down all the firstborn in the land of Egypt I sanctified them for Myself.

18   "But I have taken the Levites instead of every firstborn among the sons of Israel.

19   "I have given the Levites as a gift to Aaron and to his sons from among the sons of Israel, to perform the service of the sons of Israel at the tent of meeting and to make atonement on behalf of the sons of Israel, so that there will be no plague among the sons of Israel by their coming near to the sanctuary."

20   Thus did Moses and Aaron and all the congregation of the sons of Israel to the Levites; according to all that the LORD had commanded Moses concerning the Levites, so the sons of Israel did to them.

21   The Levites, too, purified themselves from sin and washed their clothes; and Aaron presented them as a wave offering

---

LIFE LESSONS

> **Numbers 7:89 —** *Now when Moses went into the tent of meeting to speak with Him, he heard the voice speaking to him from above the mercy seat.*

*M*oses heard the voice of the Lord speaking to him from above the ark of the covenant but did not see His face. Like Moses, we listen for God's voice and follow His Word, looking forward to the day when we see God face-to-face (Rev. 22:3, 4).

> **Numbers 8:4 —** *According to the pattern which the LORD had shown Moses, so he made the lampstand.*

*T*he Lord had shown Moses a particular pattern that needed to be followed—the lampstand needed to have seven branches, which is the Hebrew number of completion or perfection (Ex. 25:31-40). As the Levites were readied to become the priests of Israel, the illuminated lampstand within the tabernacle would remind them of the perfect light and leadership of the Lord. Today, every believer is part of the holy priesthood (1 Pet. 2:5, 9), and we have the Light of the World—the Lord Jesus—to guide us (John 1:4-9; 8:12, 9:5).

before the LORD. Aaron also made atonement for them to cleanse them.

22 Then after that the Levites went in to perform their service in the tent of meeting before Aaron and before his sons; just as the LORD had commanded Moses concerning the Levites, so they did to them.

23 Now the LORD spoke to Moses, saying,

24 "This is what *applies* to the Levites: from twenty-five years old and upward they shall enter to perform service in the work of the tent of meeting.

25 "But at the age of fifty years they shall retire from service in the work and not work any more.

26 "They may, however, assist their brothers in the tent of meeting, to keep an obligation, but they *themselves* shall do no work. Thus you shall deal with the Levites concerning their obligations."

Psalm 31:1–5

For the choir director. A Psalm of David.

31 IN You, O LORD, I have taken refuge;
Let me never be ashamed;
In Your righteousness deliver me.

2 Incline Your ear to me, rescue me quickly;
Be to me a rock of strength,
A stronghold to save me.

➢ 3 For You are my rock and my fortress;
For Your name's sake You will lead me and guide me.

4 You will pull me out of the net which they have secretly laid for me,
For You are my strength.

✳ 5 Into Your hand I commit my spirit;
You have ransomed me, O LORD, God of truth.

Proverbs 11:4–6

4 Riches do not profit in the day of wrath,
✳ But righteousness delivers from death.

5 The righteousness of the blameless will smooth his way,
But the wicked will fall by his own wickedness.

6 The righteousness of the upright will deliver them,
But the treacherous will be caught by *their own* greed.

Mark 9:1–29

9 AND Jesus was saying to them, "Truly I say to you, there are some of those who are standing here who will not taste death until they see the kingdom of God after it has come with power."

2 Six days later, Jesus *took with Him Peter and James and John, and *brought them up on a high mountain by themselves. And He was transfigured before them;

3 and His garments became radiant and exceedingly white, as no launderer on earth can whiten them.

4 Elijah appeared to them along with ◄ Moses; and they were talking with Jesus.

5 Peter *said to Jesus, "Rabbi, it is

LIFE LESSONS

➢ **Psalm 31:3 —** *For Your name's sake You will lead me and guide me.*

*W*hen we place our trust in Christ, He becomes our stronghold and identifies us with Himself forever (Rom. 8:14-23; Gal. 4:4-7). Our futures are bound with His, which is why we can confidently ask for His guidance (2 Tim. 2:11-13).

➢ **Mark 9:4 —** *Elijah appeared to them along with Moses; and they were talking with Jesus.*

*H*ow did Peter and the others instantly recognize Moses and Elijah, men they'd never met and who had died centuries before? In the Transfiguration, we get a brief foretaste of heaven and its wonders. They understood who was with Jesus because He revealed it to them. Likewise, when we as believers go to be with the Lord, He will reveal great things to us (1 Cor. 13:12).

good for us to be here; let us make three tabernacles, one for You, and one for Moses, and one for Elijah."

6   For he did not know what to answer; for they became terrified.

7   Then a cloud formed, overshadowing them, and a voice came out of the cloud, "This is My beloved Son, listen to Him!"

8   All at once they looked around and saw no one with them anymore, except Jesus alone.

9   As they were coming down from the mountain, He gave them orders not to relate to anyone what they had seen, until the Son of Man rose from the dead.

10   They seized upon that statement, discussing with one another what rising from the dead meant.

11   They asked Him, saying, "Why is it that the scribes say that Elijah must come first?"

12   And He said to them, "Elijah does first come and restore all things. And yet how is it written of the Son of Man that He will suffer many things and be treated with contempt?

13   "But I say to you that Elijah has indeed come, and they did to him whatever they wished, just as it is written of him."

14   When they came back to the disciples, they saw a large crowd around them, and some scribes arguing with them.

15   Immediately, when the entire crowd saw Him, they were amazed and began running up to greet Him.

16   And He asked them, "What are you discussing with them?"

17   And one of the crowd answered Him, "Teacher, I brought You my son, possessed with a spirit which makes him mute;

18   and whenever it seizes him, it slams him to the ground and he foams at the mouth, and grinds his teeth and stiffens out. I told Your disciples to cast it out, and they could not do it."

19   And He *answered them and *said, "O unbelieving generation, how long shall I be with you? How long shall I put up with you? Bring him to Me!"

20   They brought the boy to Him. When he saw Him, immediately the spirit threw him into a convulsion, and falling to the ground, he began rolling around and foaming at the mouth.

21   And He asked his father, "How long has this been happening to him?" And he said, "From childhood.

22   "It has often thrown him both into the fire and into the water to destroy him. But if You can do anything, take pity on us and help us!"

23   And Jesus said to him, "'If You can?' All things are possible to him who believes."

24   Immediately the boy's father cried out and said, "I do believe; help my unbelief."

25   When Jesus saw that a crowd was rapidly gathering, He rebuked the unclean spirit, saying to it, "You deaf and mute spirit, I command you, come out of him and do not enter him again."

26   After crying out and throwing him into terrible convulsions, it came out; and the boy became so much like a corpse that most of them said, "He is dead!"

27   But Jesus took him by the hand and raised him; and he got up.

28   When He came into the house, His disciples began questioning Him privately, "Why could we not drive it out?"

29   And He said to them, "This kind cannot come out by anything but prayer."

LIFE LESSONS

> Mark 9:10 — *They seized upon that statement, discussing with one another what rising from the dead meant.*

*J*esus sometimes did speak figuratively, so perhaps we can sympathize with the disciples' failure to grasp the Lord's meaning (Mark 9:32). However, if we want to understand the Word of God and embrace His principles, we must surrender our hearts to Him and ask Him to reveal His truth to us through His Holy Spirit. We may receive instant insight, or the Lord may choose to teach us His vital lessons over time.

> Mark 9:24 — *"I do believe; help my unbelief!"*

*T*he Lord does not demand that we have mountains of trust before He acts on our behalf; a little mustard seed of genuine faith is all He requires. Then He steps in and supplies what we lack.

Life Examples:

No In-Between

MARK 9:17-29

*H*e wanted to believe—really, he did. After seeing his son suffer terribly, all this desperate father wanted was for his boy to be healed. So many other things had failed—even Jesus' own disciples could not rid his son of the demon that tormented him so cruelly. Could Jesus really heal the boy? Or would he be disappointed again?

The father pleaded with Jesus, voicing the only hope he had left, "But if You can do anything, take pity on us and help us!" (Mark 9:22).

Have you been there? You see no possible way out of your situation. You've tried everything, but it was all in vain. The issue continues to eat away at you, and you know that if you don't get help soon, it will destroy you. Your only hope is that Jesus will help you. However, after so many things have failed, you have only a half-hearted faith that Jesus can really do anything for you.

Like the father in Mark 9, you are trapped between belief and unbelief. Though you believe in Jesus for your salvation and know that the miracles He did in the New Testament are real, it's a different story trusting Him to deal with your problem.

First, you may be questioning whether He will help you because you doubt you are worth helping. This is especially true when your situation is due to your own mistakes. However, understand that Christ's love for you is unconditional, and He wants to help you. Yet He also calls you to repent of your sins and obey Him. Therefore, in order to receive Christ's aid, confess your sins to Him and begin obeying Him immediately.

Second, you may be wondering if Jesus is able to deal with your modern-day problem. Most assuredly, the God who created the universe can deal with any situation that arises in it. Jesus assures you, "'If You can?' All things are possible to him who believes" (Mark 9:23). God can do it. Can you believe it?

Friend, you may have to pray like the father in Mark 9 did: "I do believe; help my unbelief" (Mark 9:24). As He teaches you, be deliberate about relinquishing your doubts. Your willingness to trust Him is key. Have faith that He will do the impossible in your situation—and truly believe.

⊕ Numbers 9:1—10:36

9THUS the LORD spoke to Moses in the wilderness of Sinai, in the first month of the second year after they had come out of the land of Egypt, saying,

2 "Now, let the sons of Israel observe the Passover at its appointed time.

3 "On the fourteenth day of this month, at twilight, you shall observe it at its appointed time; you shall observe it according to all its statutes and according to all its ordinances."

4 So Moses told the sons of Israel to observe the Passover.

5 They observed the Passover in the first *month*, on the fourteenth day of the month, at twilight, in the wilderness of Sinai; according to all that the LORD had commanded Moses, so the sons of Israel did.

6 But there were *some* men who were unclean because of *the* dead person, so that they could not observe Passover on that day; so they came before Moses and Aaron on that day.

7 Those men said to him, "*Though* we are unclean because of *the* dead person, why are we restrained from presenting the offering of the LORD at its appointed time among the sons of Israel?"

8 Moses therefore said to them, "Wait, ◄ and I will listen to what the LORD will command concerning you."

LIFE LESSONS

➤ **Numbers 9:8 —** *"Wait, and I will listen to what the LORD will command concerning you."*

*D*espite his exalted leadership position, Moses did not presume to speak for the Lord when the Lord had not spoken to him. He, like all of us, must continually listen for the voice of God.

9 Then the LORD spoke to Moses, saying,

10 "Speak to the sons of Israel, saying, 'If any one of you or of your generations becomes unclean because of a *dead* person, or is on a distant journey, he may, however, observe the Passover to the LORD.

11 'In the second month on the fourteenth day at twilight, they shall observe it; they shall eat it with unleavened bread and bitter herbs.

12 'They shall leave none of it until morning, nor break a bone of it; according to all the statute of the Passover they shall observe it.

13 'But the man who is clean and is not on a journey, and yet neglects to observe the Passover, that person shall then be cut off from his people, for he did not present the offering of the LORD at its appointed time. That man will bear his sin.

14 'If an alien sojourns among you and observes the Passover to the LORD, according to the statute of the Passover and according to its ordinance, so he shall do; you shall have one statute, both for the alien and for the native of the land.'"

15 Now on the day that the tabernacle was erected the cloud covered the tabernacle, the tent of the testimony, and in the evening it was like the appearance of fire over the tabernacle, until morning.

16 So it was continuously; the cloud would cover it *by day*, and the appearance of fire by night.

17 Whenever the cloud was lifted from over the tent, afterward the sons of Israel would then set out; and in the place where the cloud settled down, there the sons of Israel would camp.

18 At the command of the LORD the sons of Israel would set out, and at the command of the LORD they would camp; as long as the cloud settled over the tabernacle, they remained camped.

19 Even when the cloud lingered over the tabernacle for many days, the sons of Israel would keep the LORD's charge and not set out.

20 If sometimes the cloud remained a few days over the tabernacle, according to the command of the LORD they remained camped. Then according to the command of the LORD they set out.

21 If sometimes the cloud remained from evening until morning, when the cloud was lifted in the morning, they would move out; or *if it remained* in the daytime and at night, whenever the cloud was lifted, they would set out.

22 Whether it was two days or a month or a year that the cloud lingered over the tabernacle, staying above it, the sons of Israel remained camped and did not set out; but when it was lifted, they did set out.

23 At the command of the LORD they ◄ camped, and at the command of the LORD they set out; they kept the LORD's charge, according to the command of the LORD through Moses.

10 THE LORD spoke further to Moses, saying,

2 "Make yourself two trumpets of silver, of hammered work you shall make them; and you shall use them for summoning the congregation and for having the camps set out.

3 "When both are blown, all the congregation shall gather themselves to you at the doorway of the tent of meeting.

4 "Yet if *only* one is blown, then the leaders, the heads of the divisions of Israel, shall assemble before you.

5 "But when you blow an alarm, the camps that are pitched on the east side shall set out.

6 "When you blow an alarm the second time, the camps that are pitched on the south side shall set out; an alarm is to be blown for them to set out.

7 "When convening the assembly, however, you shall blow without sounding an alarm.

8 "The priestly sons of Aaron, moreover, shall blow the trumpets; and this shall be for you a perpetual statute throughout your generations.

LIFE LESSONS

➤ **Numbers 9:23 —** *At the command of the LORD they camped, and at the command of the LORD they set out.*

*H*ow blessed we would be if we would go when the Lord told us to go and stay when the Lord told us to stay! Obedience is always essential to everything we do in life, and a close relationship with God always brings gladness.

9 "When you go to war in your land against the adversary who attacks you, then you shall sound an alarm with the trumpets, that you may be remembered before the LORD your God, and be saved from your enemies.

10 "Also in the day of your gladness and in your appointed feasts, and on the first *days* of your months, you shall blow the trumpets over your burnt offerings, and over the sacrifices of your peace offerings; and they shall be as a reminder of you before your God. I am the LORD your God."

11 Now in the second year, in the second month, on the twentieth of the month, the cloud was lifted from over the tabernacle of the testimony;

12 and the sons of Israel set out on their journeys from the wilderness of Sinai. Then the cloud settled down in the wilderness of Paran.

13 So they moved out for the first time according to the commandment of the LORD through Moses.

14 The standard of the camp of the sons of Judah, according to their armies, set out first, with Nahshon the son of Amminadab, over its army,

15 and Nethanel the son of Zuar, over the tribal army of the sons of Issachar;

16 and Eliab the son of Helon over the tribal army of the sons of Zebulun.

17 Then the tabernacle was taken down; and the sons of Gershon and the sons of Merari, who were carrying the tabernacle, set out.

18 Next the standard of the camp of Reuben, according to their armies, set out with Elizur the son of Shedeur, over its army,

19 and Shelumiel the son of Zurishaddai over the tribal army of the sons of Simeon,

20 and Eliasaph the son of Deuel was over the tribal army of the sons of Gad.

21 Then the Kohathites set out, carrying the holy *objects;* and the tabernacle was set up before their arrival.

22 Next the standard of the camp of the sons of Ephraim, according to their armies, was set out, with Elishama the son of Ammihud over its army,

23 and Gamaliel the son of Pedahzur over the tribal army of the sons of Manasseh;

24 and Abidan the son of Gideoni over the tribal army of the sons of Benjamin.

25 Then the standard of the camp of the sons of Dan, according to their armies, *which formed* the rear guard for all the camps, set out, with Ahiezer the son of Ammishaddai over its army,

26 and Pagiel the son of Ochran over the tribal army of the sons of Asher;

27 and Ahira the son of Enan over the tribal army of the sons of Naphtali.

28 This was the order of march of the sons of Israel by their armies as they set out.

29 Then Moses said to Hobab the son ◁ of Reuel the Midianite, Moses' father-in-law, "We are setting out to the place of which the LORD said, 'I will give it to you'; come with us and we will do you good, for the LORD has promised good concerning Israel."

30 But he said to him, "I will not come, but rather will go to my *own* land and relatives."

31 Then he said, "Please do not leave us, inasmuch as you know where we should camp in the wilderness, and you will be as eyes for us.

32 "So it will be, if you go with us, that whatever good the LORD does for us, we will do for you."

33 Thus they set out from the mount of the LORD three days' journey, with the ark of the covenant of the LORD journeying in front of them for the three days, to seek out a resting place for them.

34 The cloud of the LORD was over them by day when they set out from the camp.

35 Then it came about when the ark set out that Moses said,
"Rise up, O LORD!
And let Your enemies be scattered,
And let those who hate You flee ✳
before You."

36 When it came to rest, he said,
"Return, O LORD,
To the myriad thousands of Israel."

LIFE LESSONS

➤ **Numbers 10:29 —** *"Come with us and we will do you good, for the LORD has promised good concerning Israel."*

*G*enerosity of spirit always accompanies a mature saint of God. Godly believers understand that God blesses them so that they might bless others (2 Cor. 9:11).

Psalm 31:6–10

6   I hate those who regard vain idols,
But I trust in the LORD.

7   I will rejoice and be glad in Your
lovingkindness,
Because You have seen my affliction;
You have known the troubles of my
soul,

8   And You have not given me over
into the hand of the enemy;
You have set my feet in a large
place.

9   Be gracious to me, O LORD, for I am
in distress;
My eye is wasted away from grief,
my soul and my body *also*.

10   For my life is spent with sorrow
And my years with sighing;
My strength has failed because of
my iniquity,
And my body has wasted away.

Proverbs 11:7–11

7   When a wicked man dies, *his*
expectation will perish,
And the hope of strong men
perishes.

8   The righteous is delivered from
trouble,
But the wicked takes his place.

9   With *his* mouth the godless man
destroys his neighbor,
But through knowledge the
righteous will be delivered.

10   When it goes well with the
righteous, the city rejoices,
And when the wicked perish, there
is joyful shouting.

11   By the blessing of the upright a city
is exalted,
But by the mouth of the wicked it is
torn down.

Mark 9:30–50

30   From there they went out and *began*
to go through Galilee, and He did not
want anyone to know *about it*.

31   For He was teaching His disciples
and telling them, "The Son of Man is to
be delivered into the hands of men, and
they will kill Him; and when He has been
killed, He will rise three days later."

32   But they did not understand *this*
statement, and they were afraid to ask
Him.

33   They came to Capernaum; and when
He was in the house, He *began* to question them, "What were you discussing on
the way?"

34   But they kept silent, for on the way
they had discussed with one another
which *of them was* the greatest.

35   Sitting down, He called the twelve
and *said to them, "If anyone wants to be
first, he shall be last of all and servant of
all."

36   Taking a child, He set him before
them, and taking him in His arms, He
said to them,

37   "Whoever receives one child like this
in My name receives Me; and whoever
receives Me does not receive Me, but Him
who sent Me."

38   John said to Him, "Teacher, we saw
someone casting out demons in Your
name, and we tried to prevent him because he was not following us."

39   But Jesus said, "Do not hinder him,
for there is no one who will perform a
miracle in My name, and be able soon
afterward to speak evil of Me.

40   "For he who is not against us is for
us.

41   "For whoever gives you a cup of
water to drink because of your name as
followers of Christ, truly I say to you, he
will not lose his reward.

42   "Whoever causes one of these little
ones who believe to stumble, it would be
better for him if, with a heavy millstone
hung around his neck, he had been cast
into the sea.

43   "If your hand causes you to stumble,
cut it off; it is better for you to enter life
crippled, than, having your two hands, to
go into hell, into the unquenchable fire,

44   [where THEIR WORM DOES NOT DIE, AND
THE FIRE IS NOT QUENCHED.]

45   "If your foot causes you to stumble,
cut it off; it is better for you to enter life
lame, than, having your two feet, to be
cast into hell,

46   [where THEIR WORM DOES NOT DIE, AND
THE FIRE IS NOT QUENCHED.]

ANSWERS TO LIFE'S QUESTIONS

Who's First?

MARK 9:33–41

*D*o you serve for the good of others? Or do you serve for yourself? Are you doing what you do because God assigned you the task? Or are you doing it because it makes you look good?

This may seem like a strange line of questioning—but this is something that will confront every Christian at one point or another. Even the disciples struggled with their desires to be the greatest in the kingdom (Mark 9:34). But Jesus was always quick to remind them, "If anyone wants to be first, he shall be last of all and servant of all" (Mark 9:35).

Unfortunately, we sometimes fall into the trap of thinking that we can measure the success of what we're doing the same way the world measures achievement. We mistakenly believe that if God receives glory from our service, then it should be glorious for us as well.

Yet when we remember some of God's faithful servants from the Bible, we realize their situations were far from easy or glamorous.

- God allowed Job to suffer the loss of his children, his health, and everything he owned (Job 1–2).
- God told Isaiah to be barefoot and naked for three years as a judgment against Egypt and Ethiopia (Is. 20).
- God commanded Ezekiel to lie on his side a day for every year of iniquity found in Israel and Judah. He was also to prepare his food using cow dung as fuel (Ezek. 4).
- God instructed Hosea to marry a prostitute (Hos. 1:2).
- God sent His only Son to die naked on the Cross for our sins (Matt. 27; Mark 15; Luke 23; John 19).

Of course, most often, God will call us to do those mundane things that seem so unimportant—that don't benefit us in any way. As Jesus said in Mark 9:41, "For whoever gives you a cup of water to drink because of your name as followers of Christ, truly I say to you, he will not lose his reward." These are the simple acts that show compassion towards other people—and which display the character of Christ. They are not done for any personal gain; rather, they are done out of an overflow of Christ's love in us.

Friend, the reason you serve God is not for the sake of your name, reputation, or even your income. The reason you serve God is to be obedient to God—to show His love to a lost world. Whenever you go to do something in His name, check your motives. Are you doing it for His kingdom or for yours? Are you putting yourself first or last?

---

47 "If your eye causes you to stumble, throw it out; it is better for you to enter the kingdom of God with one eye, than, having two eyes, to be cast into hell, 48 where THEIR WORM DOES NOT DIE, AND THE FIRE IS NOT QUENCHED.

49 "For everyone will be salted with fire. 50 "Salt is good; but if the salt becomes unsalty, with what will you make it salty *again*? Have salt in yourselves, and be at peace with one another."

Numbers 11:1—12:16

11 NOW the people became like those who complain of adversity in the hearing of the LORD; and when the LORD heard *it*, His anger was kindled, and the fire of the LORD burned among them and consumed *some* of the outskirts of the camp.
2 The people therefore cried out to Moses, and Moses prayed to the LORD and the fire died out.

LIFE LESSONS

➤ **Numbers 11:1 — *Now the people became like those who complain of adversity in the hearing of the LORD; and when the LORD heard it, His anger was kindled.***

*J*ust as God always blesses an obedient spirit, so He always judges a complaining spirit (1 Cor. 10:10). No one can grumble and honor God at the same time.

3   So the name of that place was called Taberah, because the fire of the LORD burned among them.

4   The rabble who were among them had greedy desires; and also the sons of Israel wept again and said, "Who will give us meat to eat?

5   "We remember the fish which we used to eat free in Egypt, the cucumbers and the melons and the leeks and the onions and the garlic,

6   but now our appetite is gone. There is nothing at all to look at except this manna."

7   Now the manna was like coriander seed, and its appearance like that of bdellium.

8   The people would go about and gather it and grind it between two millstones or beat it in the mortar, and boil it in the pot and make cakes with it; and its taste was as the taste of cakes baked with oil.

9   When the dew fell on the camp at night, the manna would fall with it.

10   Now Moses heard the people weeping throughout their families, each man at the doorway of his tent; and the anger of the LORD was kindled greatly, and Moses was displeased.

11   So Moses said to the LORD, "Why have You been so hard on Your servant? And why have I not found favor in Your sight, that You have laid the burden of all this people on me?

12   "Was it I who conceived all this people? Was it I who brought them forth, that You should say to me, 'Carry them in your bosom as a nurse carries a nursing infant, to the land which You swore to their fathers'?

13   "Where am I to get meat to give to all this people? For they weep before me, saying, 'Give us meat that we may eat!'

14   "I alone am not able to carry all this people, because it is too burdensome for me.

15   "So if You are going to deal thus with me, please kill me at once, if I have found favor in Your sight, and do not let me see my wretchedness."

16   The LORD therefore said to Moses, "Gather for Me seventy men from the elders of Israel, whom you know to be the elders of the people and their officers and bring them to the tent of meeting, and let them take their stand there with you.

17   "Then I will come down and speak with you there, and I will take of the Spirit who is upon you, and will put *Him* upon them; and they shall bear the burden of the people with you, so that you will not bear *it* all alone.

18   "Say to the people, 'Consecrate yourselves for tomorrow, and you shall eat meat; for you have wept in the ears of the LORD, saying, "Oh that someone would give us meat to eat! For we were well-off in Egypt." Therefore the LORD will give you meat and you shall eat.

19   'You shall eat, not one day, nor two days, nor five days, nor ten days, nor twenty days,

20   but a whole month, until it comes out of your nostrils and becomes loathsome to you; because you have rejected the LORD who is among you and have wept before Him, saying, "Why did we ever leave Egypt?"'"

21   But Moses said, "The people, among whom I am, are 600,000 on foot; yet You have said, 'I will give them meat, so that they may eat for a whole month.'

22   "Should flocks and herds be slaughtered for them, to be sufficient for them? Or should all the fish of the sea be gathered together for them, to be sufficient for them?"

23   The LORD said to Moses, "Is the LORD's power limited? Now you shall see whether My word will come true for you or not."

24   So Moses went out and told the people the words of the LORD. Also, he gathered seventy men of the elders of the people, and stationed them around the tent.

25   Then the LORD came down in the cloud and spoke to him; and He took of the Spirit who was upon him and placed

---

LIFE LESSONS

➤ **Numbers 11:20 —** *"You have rejected the LORD who is among you."*

We reject the Lord, who lives among us, when we declare His provision insufficient and His plan defective. How much better to praise the Lord for who He is than to complain about what we don't have!

Him upon the seventy elders. And when the Spirit rested upon them, they prophesied. But they did not do *it* again.
26 But two men had remained in the camp; the name of one was Eldad and the name of the other Medad. And the Spirit rested upon them (now they were among those who had been registered, but had not gone out to the tent), and they prophesied in the camp.
27 So a young man ran and told Moses and said, "Eldad and Medad are prophesying in the camp."
28 Then Joshua the son of Nun, the attendant of Moses from his youth, said, "Moses, my lord, restrain them."
29 But Moses said to him, "Are you jealous for my sake? Would that all the LORD's people were prophets, that the LORD would put His Spirit upon them!"
30 Then Moses returned to the camp, *both* he and the elders of Israel.
31 Now there went forth a wind from the LORD and it brought quail from the sea, and let *them* fall beside the camp, about a day's journey on this side and a day's journey on the other side, all around the camp and about two cubits *deep* on the surface of the ground.
32 The people spent all day and all night and all the next day, and gathered the quail (he who gathered least gathered ten homers) and they spread *them* out for themselves all around the camp.
33 While the meat was still between their teeth, before it was chewed, the anger of the LORD was kindled against the people, and the LORD struck the people with a very severe plague.
34 So the name of that place was called Kibroth-hattaavah, because there they buried the people who had been greedy.
35 From Kibroth-hattaavah the people set out for Hazeroth, and they remained at Hazeroth.

12 THEN Miriam and Aaron spoke against Moses because of the Cushite woman whom he had married (for he had married a Cushite woman);
2 and they said, "Has the LORD indeed spoken only through Moses? Has He not spoken through us as well?" And the LORD heard it.
3 (Now the man Moses was very humble, more than any man who was on the face of the earth.)

4 Suddenly the LORD said to Moses and to Aaron and to Miriam, "You three come out to the tent of meeting." So the three of them came out.
5 Then the LORD came down in a pillar of cloud and stood at the doorway of the tent, and He called Aaron and Miriam. When they had both come forward,
6 He said,
"Hear now My words:
If there is a prophet among you,
I, the LORD, shall make Myself
   known to him in a vision.
I shall speak with him in a dream.
7 "Not so, with My servant Moses,
He is faithful in all My household;
8 With him I speak mouth to mouth,
Even openly, and not in dark
   sayings,
And he beholds the form of the
   LORD.
Why then were you not afraid
To speak against My servant,
   against Moses?"
9 So the anger of the LORD burned against them and He departed.
10 But when the cloud had withdrawn from over the tent, behold, Miriam *was* leprous, as *white as* snow. As Aaron turned toward Miriam, behold, she *was* leprous.
11 Then Aaron said to Moses, "Oh, my lord, I beg you, do not account *this* sin to us, in which we have acted foolishly and in which we have sinned.
12 "Oh, do not let her be like one dead, whose flesh is half eaten away when he comes from his mother's womb!"
13 Moses cried out to the LORD, saying, "O God, heal her, I pray!"
14 But the LORD said to Moses, "If her ◄ father had but spit in her face, would she not bear her shame for seven days? Let her be shut up for seven days outside

---

the camp, and afterward she may be received again."

15 So Miriam was shut up outside the camp for seven days, and the people did not move on until Miriam was received again.

16 Afterward, however, the people moved out from Hazeroth and camped in the wilderness of Paran.

Psalm 31:11–18

11 Because of all my adversaries, I
       have become a reproach,
    Especially to my neighbors,
    And an object of dread to my
       acquaintances;
    Those who see me in the street flee
       from me.
12 I am forgotten as a dead man, out of
       mind;
    I am like a broken vessel.
13 For I have heard the slander of
       many,
    Terror is on every side;

While they took counsel together
    against me,
They schemed to take away my
    life.
14 But as for me, I trust in You,
       O LORD,
    I say, "You are my God."
15 My times are in Your hand;
    Deliver me from the hand of my
       enemies and from those who
       persecute me.
16 Make Your face to shine upon
       Your servant;
    Save me in Your lovingkindness.

LIFE LESSONS

➤ **Psalm 31:15** — *My times are in Your hand; deliver me from the hand of my enemies and from those who persecute me.*

*P*eople can oppose and harass us, but as children of a sovereign God, we are never victims of our circumstances. Our lives are in the Lord's hands, and no one else's.

ANSWERS TO LIFE'S QUESTIONS

What should I do during times of adversity?

PSALMS 31:13–15

*P*art of life is facing adversity, even the kind of adversity that challenges our faith. King David provides us some great advice when it comes to facing times of adversity.

As part of his final blessing to his son, Solomon, David said to him: "You will prosper, if you are careful to observe the statutes and the ordinances which the LORD commanded Moses concerning Israel. Be strong and courageous, do not fear nor be dismayed" (1 Chr. 22:13).

That's good advice for us today, too. It's still true that obedience always brings blessing.

Time and again in the Law of Moses, we find the word *keep*. The children of Israel were commanded to keep the feasts, to keep the law and commandments, to keep the Sabbath day holy, to keep their oaths to God, and to keep themselves from evil. Moses said to the children of Israel as he led them into a covenant relationship with God, "So keep the words of this covenant to do them, that you may prosper in all that you do" (Deut. 29:9).

To *keep* means to hold fast and to cherish at the same time. When adversity strikes, that should be our mind-set: above all else, we need to hold fast to the Lord and cherish our relationships with Him. Rather than blame God or turn from God, we need to turn to God and rely on His help. Obeying God in the face of adversity actually leads us toward prosperity— a better state of being.

When adversity hits, those around you may criticize you for clinging to faith or reaffirming your belief that God is your good and benevolent heavenly Father. They may mock you or scorn you. Don't feel dismayed if that happens. Continue to keep God's Word and remain faithful in your relationship with the Lord. Remember what David said: "I have heard the slander of many, terror is on every side; while they took counsel together against me, they schemed to take away my life. But as for me, I trust in You, O LORD, I say, 'You are my God.' My times are in Your hand; deliver me from the hand of my enemies" (Ps. 31:13–15).

Ask the Lord to give you courage to withstand the hurtful comments of others and to be able to give a bold witness about God's power and presence, even in your time of trouble.

17　Let me not be put to shame, O LORD,
　　for I call upon You;
　　Let the wicked be put to shame, let
　　them be silent in Sheol.
18　Let the lying lips be mute,
　　Which speak arrogantly against the
　　righteous
　　With pride and contempt.

Proverbs 11:12–14

12　He who despises his neighbor lacks
　　sense,
　　But a man of understanding keeps
　　silent.
13　He who goes about as a talebearer
　　reveals secrets,
　　But he who is trustworthy conceals
　　a matter.
14　Where there is no guidance the
　　people fall,
　　But in abundance of counselors
　　there is victory.

Mark 10:1–31

10 GETTING up, He *went from there
to the region of Judea and beyond
the Jordan; crowds *gathered around
Him again, and, according to His custom,
He once more *began* to teach them.
2　*Some* Pharisees came up to Jesus,
testing Him, and *began* to question Him
whether it was lawful for a man to divorce a wife.
3　And He answered and said to them,
"What did Moses command you?"
4　They said, "Moses permitted *a man*
TO WRITE A CERTIFICATE OF DIVORCE AND
SEND *her* AWAY."
5　But Jesus said to them, "Because of
your hardness of heart he wrote you this
commandment.
6　"But from the beginning of creation,
God MADE THEM MALE AND FEMALE.
7　"FOR THIS REASON A MAN SHALL LEAVE
HIS FATHER AND MOTHER,
8　AND THE TWO SHALL BECOME ONE
FLESH; so they are no longer two, but one
flesh.
9　"What therefore God has joined together, let no man separate."

10　In the house the disciples *began*
questioning Him about this again.
11　And He *said to them, "Whoever
divorces his wife and marries another
woman commits adultery against her;
12　and if she herself divorces her husband and marries another man, she is
committing adultery."
13　And they were bringing children to
Him so that He might touch them; but the
disciples rebuked them.
14　But when Jesus saw this, He was
indignant and said to them, "Permit the
children to come to Me; do not hinder
them; for the kingdom of God belongs to
such as these.
15　"Truly I say to you, whoever does
not receive the kingdom of God like a
child will not enter it *at all.*"
16　And He took them in His arms and
began blessing them, laying His hands
on them.
17　As He was setting out on a journey, a
man ran up to Him and knelt before Him,
and asked Him, "Good Teacher, what
shall I do to inherit eternal life?"
18　And Jesus said to him, "Why do you
call Me good? No one is good except God
alone.
19　"You know the commandments, 'Do

LIFE LESSONS

➤ **Mark 10:5 —** *Jesus said to them,
"Because of your hardness of heart he
wrote you this commandment."*

G od is realistic about our faults. He
gives us a high standard to shoot
for, but since "He is mindful that we are
but dust" (Ps. 103:14), He also keeps our
weaknesses in mind when dealing with
us. Yet that is not an excuse for us to
sin—He always calls us to obey Him and
refuse to compromise what we know is
right. And when we honor Him with our
conduct, He blesses us with an abundant
sense of peace, joy, and goodness.

➤ **Mark 10:18 —** *Jesus said to him, "Why
do you call Me good? No one is good
except God alone."*

J esus did not contradict the man's
description of Him as good. He
merely asked him why he used the term.
As God in the flesh, Jesus is truly good—
but He wanted the man to see it for
himself.

NOT MURDER, DO NOT COMMIT ADULTERY, DO NOT STEAL, DO NOT BEAR FALSE WITNESS, Do not defraud, HONOR YOUR FATHER AND MOTHER.'"

20 And he said to Him, "Teacher, I have kept all these things from my youth up."

21 Looking at him, Jesus felt a love for him and said to him, "One thing you lack: go and sell all you possess and give to the poor, and you will have treasure in heaven; and come, follow Me."

22 But at these words he was saddened, and he went away grieving, for he was one who owned much property.

23 And Jesus, looking around, *said to His disciples, "How hard it will be for those who are wealthy to enter the kingdom of God!"

24 The disciples were amazed at His words. But Jesus *answered again and *said to them, "Children, how hard it is to enter the kingdom of God!

25 "It is easier for a camel to go through the eye of a needle than for a rich man to enter the kingdom of God."

26 They were even more astonished and said to Him, "Then who can be saved?"

27 Looking at them, Jesus *said, "With people it is impossible, but not with God; ✳ for all things are possible with God."

28 Peter began to say to Him, "Behold, we have left everything and followed You."

29 Jesus said, "Truly I say to you, there is no one who has left house or brothers or sisters or mother or father or children or farms, for My sake and for the gospel's sake,

30 but that he will receive a hundred times as much now in the present age, houses and brothers and sisters and mothers and children and farms, along with persecutions; and in the age to come, eternal life.

31 "But many who are first will be last, and the last, first."

Numbers 13:1—14:45

13 THEN the LORD spoke to Moses saying,

➤ 2 "Send out for yourself men so that they may spy out the land of Canaan, which I am going to give to the sons of Israel; you shall send a man from each of their fathers' tribes, every one a leader among them."

LIFE LESSONS

➤ **Numbers 13:2 — "Send out for yourself men so that they may spy out the land of Canaan, which I am going to give to the sons of Israel."**

The Lord had said He was sending His people into a good land, and now He directed them to send one leader from each tribe to spy out the land and confirm His words. He could have sent them in blindly, but instead graciously gave them a preview. Unfortunately for them, this blessing turned into a test that exposed their faithlessness.

---

3 So Moses sent them from the wilderness of Paran at the command of the LORD, all of them men who were heads of the sons of Israel.

4 These then were their names: from the tribe of Reuben, Shammua the son of Zaccur;

5 from the tribe of Simeon, Shaphat the son of Hori;

6 from the tribe of Judah, Caleb the son of Jephunneh;

7 from the tribe of Issachar, Igal the son of Joseph;

8 from the tribe of Ephraim, Hoshea the son of Nun;

9 from the tribe of Benjamin, Palti the son of Raphu;

10 from the tribe of Zebulun, Gaddiel the son of Sodi;

11 from the tribe of Joseph, from the tribe of Manasseh, Gaddi the son of Susi;

12 from the tribe of Dan, Ammiel the son of Gemalli;

13 from the tribe of Asher, Sethur the son of Michael;

14 from the tribe of Naphtali, Nahbi the son of Vophsi;

15 from the tribe of Gad, Geuel the son of Machi.
16 These are the names of the men whom Moses sent to spy out the land; but Moses called Hoshea the son of Nun, Joshua.
17 When Moses sent them to spy out the land of Canaan, he said to them, "Go up there into the Negev; then go up into the hill country.
18 "See what the land is like, and whether the people who live in it are strong or weak, whether they are few or many.
19 "How is the land in which they live, is it good or bad? And how are the cities in which they live, are they like open camps or with fortifications?
20 "How is the land, is it fat or lean? Are there trees in it or not? Make an effort then to get some of the fruit of the land." Now the time was the time of the first ripe grapes.
21 So they went up and spied out the land from the wilderness of Zin as far as Rehob, at Lebo-hamath.
22 When they had gone up into the Negev, they came to Hebron where Ahiman, Sheshai and Talmai, the descendants of Anak were. (Now Hebron was built seven years before Zoan in Egypt.)
23 Then they came to the valley of Eshcol and from there cut down a branch with a single cluster of grapes; and they carried it on a pole between two men, with some of the pomegranates and the figs.
24 That place was called the valley of Eshcol, because of the cluster which the sons of Israel cut down from there.
25 When they returned from spying out the land, at the end of forty days,
26 they proceeded to come to Moses and Aaron and to all the congregation of the sons of Israel in the wilderness of Paran, at Kadesh; and they brought back word to them and to all the congregation and showed them the fruit of the land.
27 Thus they told him, and said, "We went in to the land where you sent us; and it certainly does flow with milk and honey, and this is its fruit.
28 "Nevertheless, the people who live in the land are strong, and the cities are fortified and very large; and moreover, we saw the descendants of Anak there.
29 "Amalek is living in the land of the Negev and the Hittites and the Jebusites and the Amorites are living in the hill country, and the Canaanites are living by the sea and by the side of the Jordan."
30 Then Caleb quieted the people before Moses and said, "We should by all means go up and take possession of it, for we will surely overcome it."
31 But the men who had gone up with him said, "We are not able to go up against the people, for they are too strong for us."
32 So they gave out to the sons of Israel a bad report of the land which they had spied out, saying, "The land through which we have gone, in spying it out, is a land that devours its inhabitants; and all the people whom we saw in it are men of great size.
33 "There also we saw the Nephilim (the sons of Anak are part of the Nephilim); and we became like grasshoppers in our own sight, and so we were in their sight."

14 THEN all the congregation lifted up their voices and cried, and the people wept that night.
2 All the sons of Israel grumbled against Moses and Aaron; and the whole congregation said to them, "Would that we had died in the land of Egypt! Or would that we had died in this wilderness!
3 "Why is the LORD bringing us into this land, to fall by the sword? Our wives and our little ones will become plunder; would it not be better for us to return to Egypt?"
4 So they said to one another, "Let us appoint a leader and return to Egypt."

LIFE LESSONS

➤ **Numbers 13:28 — "Nevertheless, the people who live in the land are strong, and the cities are fortified and very large."**

It is always spiritually foolish to focus our attention on the things the Lord ignores. He had emphasized the goodness of the land, while ten of the spies focused on the strength of the opposition. The point is never whether our spiritual opponents will be stronger than us—most often, they are! But they are never stronger than the Lord, and that's the fact we must never forget.

5   Then Moses and Aaron fell on their faces in the presence of all the assembly of the congregation of the sons of Israel.
6   Joshua the son of Nun and Caleb the son of Jephunneh, of those who had spied out the land, tore their clothes;
7   and they spoke to all the congregation of the sons of Israel, saying, "The land which we passed through to spy out is an exceedingly good land.
8   "If the LORD is pleased with us, then He will bring us into this land and give it to us—a land which flows with milk and honey.
9   "Only do not rebel against the LORD; and do not fear the people of the land, for they will be our prey. Their protection has been removed from them, and the LORD is with us; do not fear them."
10   But all the congregation said to stone them with stones. Then the glory of the LORD appeared in the tent of meeting to all the sons of Israel.
11   The LORD said to Moses, "How long will this people spurn Me? And how long

LIFE LESSONS

➤ **Numbers 14:3 — "Would it not be better for us to return to Egypt?"**

*A*t times it might seem easier to return to a place of spiritual bondage, but we will never move toward blessing by returning to slavery. God told Israel to move forward, not back.

➤ **Numbers 14:11 — "How long will they not believe in Me, despite all the signs which I have performed in their midst?"**

*H*ow easily we forget the many "signs" of God's love and protection! One great way to drive out unbelief from our hearts is to regularly count the blessings God has showered upon us. When did you last do this?

will they not believe in Me, despite all the signs which I have performed in their midst?
12   "I will smite them with pestilence and

ANSWERS TO LIFE'S QUESTIONS

How do I keep my focus on God and not on the obstacles in my life?

NUMBERS 14:8, 9

*T*here are times when fear can paralyze the bravest of hearts. When we perceive a threat to our well-being or an obstacle standing between us and our goals, we often fear that the overall plan for our lives is in serious jeopardy.

In those times we need to remember the promises of God.

When the Israelite spies set out on a reconnaissance mission to assess the land of Canaan, they had no idea what they would encounter. It was a great honor to be chosen by Moses for such an assignment, and Moses selected the top leader from each of the twelve tribes for the job.

Yet all of their training and leadership experience did not prepare them for something so overwhelming. Who had ever heard of a grape cluster so huge that it had to be carried on a pole lifted by two men (Num. 13:23)? Who could possibly be prepared for Canaanite warriors so massive they dwarfed the best of Israel's army (Num. 13:33)? It is no wonder

these spies felt a whirling mix of emotions as they headed back to their commander-in-chief to give a full report.

You can imagine the scene. Moses and Aaron (Moses' brother) gathered the people to hear the news. The spies confirmed the Promised Land was indeed everything God said it was—but they focused on what they saw as the obstacles to their taking the land, namely the giants who lived there. They gave an accurate report, but they failed to give the entire story. Only Joshua and Caleb spoke the truth.

These faithful men recounted what they had seen and then reiterated, in their own words, the promises of God that had brought them to this point: "If the LORD is pleased with us, then He will bring us into this land and give it to us—a land which flows with milk and honey. Only do not rebel against the LORD; and do not fear the people of the land, for they will be our prey. Their protection has been removed from them, and the LORD is with us; do not fear them" (Num. 14:8, 9). Joshua and Caleb lived to see the Promised Land, but only because they focused on the goal God had laid out for them and not on the obstacles standing in the way (Num. 14:30; 26:64, 65; 32:11, 12).

The many blessings God has in store for you are just as rich! Never allow shortsighted vision—especially one focused on obstacles—to block the far-reaching plan of the Lord.

dispossess them, and I will make you into a nation greater and mightier than they."

13 But Moses said to the LORD, "Then the Egyptians will hear of it, for by Your strength You brought up this people from their midst,

14 and they will tell *it* to the inhabitants of this land. They have heard that You, O LORD, are in the midst of this people, for You, O LORD, are seen eye to eye, while Your cloud stands over them; and You go before them in a pillar of cloud by day and in a pillar of fire by night.

15 "Now if You slay this people as one man, then the nations who have heard of Your fame will say,

16 'Because the LORD could not bring this people into the land which He promised them by oath, therefore He slaughtered them in the wilderness.'

17 "But now, I pray, let the power of the Lord be great, just as You have declared,

18 'The LORD is slow to anger and abundant in lovingkindness, forgiving iniquity and transgression; but He will by no means clear *the guilty,* visiting the iniquity of the fathers on the children to the third and the fourth *generations.'*

19 "Pardon, I pray, the iniquity of this people according to the greatness of Your lovingkindness, just as You also have forgiven this people, from Egypt even until now."

20 So the LORD said, "I have pardoned *them* according to your word;

21 but indeed, as I live, all the earth will be filled with the glory of the LORD.

22 "Surely all the men who have seen My glory and My signs which I performed in Egypt and in the wilderness, yet have put Me to the test these ten times and have not listened to My voice,

23 shall by no means see the land which I swore to their fathers, nor shall any of those who spurned Me see it.

24 "But My servant Caleb, because he has had a different spirit and has followed Me fully, I will bring into the land which he entered, and his descendants shall take possession of it.

25 "Now the Amalekites and the Canaanites live in the valleys; turn tomorrow and set out to the wilderness by the way of the Red Sea."

26 The LORD spoke to Moses and Aaron, saying,

27 "How long *shall I bear* with this evil congregation who are grumbling against Me? I have heard the complaints of the sons of Israel, which they are making against Me.

28 "Say to them, 'As I live,' says the LORD, 'just as you have spoken in My hearing, so I will surely do to you;

29 your corpses will fall in this wilderness, even all your numbered men, according to your complete number from twenty years old and upward, who have grumbled against Me.

30 'Surely you shall not come into the land in which I swore to settle you, except Caleb the son of Jephunneh and Joshua the son of Nun.

31 'Your children, however, whom you said would become a prey—I will bring them in, and they will know the land which you have rejected.

32 'But as for you, your corpses will fall in this wilderness.

33 'Your sons shall be shepherds for forty years in the wilderness, and they will suffer *for* your unfaithfulness, until your corpses lie in the wilderness.

34 'According to the number of days which you spied out the land, forty days,

---

LIFE LESSONS

> Numbers 14:19 — *"Pardon, I pray, the iniquity of this people according to the greatness of Your lovingkindness, just as You also have forgiven this people, from Egypt even until now."*

*M*oses appeals to the Lord on behalf of His people on the basis of God's reputation, attributes, and character. Moses won this battle on behalf of God's people because he fought it on his knees.

> Numbers 14:24 — *"My servant Caleb, because he . . . has followed Me fully, I will bring into the land."*

*G*od promised to do for Caleb what He refused to do for the rebels. Why? Because Caleb followed his Lord unconditionally, with complete faith and trust. God assumes full responsibility for our needs when we obey Him wholeheartedly.

for every day you shall bear your guilt a year, *even* forty years, and you will know My opposition.

35 'I, the LORD, have spoken, surely this I will do to all this evil congregation who are gathered together against Me. In this wilderness they shall be destroyed, and there they will die.'"

36 As for the men whom Moses sent to spy out the land and who returned and made all the congregation grumble against him by bringing out a bad report concerning the land,

37 even those men who brought out the very bad report of the land died by a plague before the LORD.

38 But Joshua the son of Nun and Caleb the son of Jephunneh remained alive out of those men who went to spy out the land.

39 When Moses spoke these words to all the sons of Israel, the people mourned greatly.

40 In the morning, however, they rose up early and went up to the ridge of the hill country, saying, "Here we are; we have indeed sinned, but we will go up to the place which the LORD has promised."

41 But Moses said, "Why then are you transgressing the commandment of the LORD, when it will not succeed?

42 "Do not go up, or you will be struck down before your enemies, for the LORD is not among you.

43 "For the Amalekites and the Canaanites will be there in front of you, and you will fall by the sword, inasmuch as you have turned back from following the LORD. And the LORD will not be with you."

44 But they went up heedlessly to the ridge of the hill country; neither the ark of the covenant of the LORD nor Moses left the camp.

45 Then the Amalekites and the Canaanites who lived in that hill country came down, and struck them and beat them down as far as Hormah.

Psalm 31:19–24

19 How great is Your goodness,
   Which You have stored up for those
      who fear You,

Which You have wrought for those
   who take refuge in You,
Before the sons of men!

20 You hide them in the secret place
      of Your presence from the
      conspiracies of man;
   You keep them secretly in a shelter
      from the strife of tongues.

21 Blessed be the LORD,
   For He has made marvelous His
      lovingkindness to me in a
      besieged city.

22 As for me, I said in my alarm,
   "I am cut off from before Your
      eyes";
   Nevertheless You heard the voice of
      my supplications
   When I cried to You.

23 O love the LORD, all you His godly
      ones!
   The LORD preserves the faithful
   And fully recompenses the proud
      doer.

24 Be strong and let your heart take
      courage,
   All you who hope in the LORD.

Proverbs 11:15

15 He who is guarantor for a stranger
      will surely suffer for it,
   But he who hates being a guarantor
      is secure.

Mark 10:32–52

32 They were on the road going up to Jerusalem, and Jesus was walking on ahead of them; and they were amazed; and those who followed were fearful. And again He took the twelve aside and began to tell them what was going to happen to Him,

33 *saying,* "Behold, we are going up to Jerusalem, and the Son of Man will be delivered to the chief priests and the scribes; and they will condemn Him to death and will hand Him over to the Gentiles.

34 "They will mock Him and spit on Him, and scourge Him and kill *Him,* and three days later He will rise again."

35 James and John, the two sons of

Zebedee, *came up to Jesus, saying, "Teacher, we want You to do for us whatever we ask of You."

36 And He said to them, "What do you want Me to do for you?"

37 They said to Him, "Grant that we may sit, one on Your right and one on *Your* left, in Your glory."

38 But Jesus said to them, "You do not know what you are asking. Are you able to drink the cup that I drink, or to be baptized with the baptism with which I am baptized?"

39 They said to Him, "We are able." And Jesus said to them, "The cup that I drink you shall drink; and you shall be baptized with the baptism with which I am baptized.

40 "But to sit on My right or on *My* left, this is not Mine to give; but it is for those for whom it has been prepared."

41 Hearing *this*, the ten began to feel indignant with James and John.

42 Calling them to Himself, Jesus *said to them, "You know that those who are recognized as rulers of the Gentiles lord it over them; and their great men exercise authority over them.

✻ 43 "But it is not this way among you, but whoever wishes to become great among you shall be your servant;

44 and whoever wishes to be first among you shall be slave of all.

45 "For even the Son of Man did not come to be served, but to serve, and to give His life a ransom for many."

46 Then they *came to Jericho. And as He was leaving Jericho with His disciples and a large crowd, a blind beggar *named* Bartimaeus, the son of Timaeus, was sitting by the road.

47 When he heard that it was Jesus the Nazarene, he began to cry out and say, "Jesus, Son of David, have mercy on me!"

48 Many were sternly telling him to be quiet, but he kept crying out all the more, "Son of David, have mercy on me!"

49 And Jesus stopped and said, "Call him *here*." So they *called the blind man, saying to him, "Take courage, stand up! He is calling for you."

50 Throwing aside his cloak, he jumped up and came to Jesus.

51 And answering him, Jesus said, "What do you want Me to do for you?" And the blind man said to Him, "Rabboni, *I want* to regain my sight!"

52 And Jesus said to him, "Go; your faith has made you well." Immediately he regained his sight and *began* following Him on the road.

Numbers 15:1—16:50

15 NOW the LORD spoke to Moses, saying,

2 "Speak to the sons of Israel and say to them, 'When you enter the land where you are to live, which I am giving you,

3 then make an offering by fire to the LORD, a burnt offering or a sacrifice to fulfill a special vow, or as a freewill offering or in your appointed times, to make a soothing aroma to the LORD, from the herd or from the flock.

4 'The one who presents his offering shall present to the LORD a grain offering of one-tenth *of an ephah* of fine flour mixed with one-fourth of a hin of oil,

5 and you shall prepare wine for the drink offering, one-fourth of a hin, with

the burnt offering or for the sacrifice, for each lamb.

6 'Or for a ram you shall prepare as a grain offering two-tenths *of an ephah* of fine flour mixed with one-third of a hin of oil;

7 and for the drink offering you shall offer one-third of a hin of wine as a soothing aroma to the LORD.

8 'When you prepare a bull as a burnt offering or a sacrifice, to fulfill a special vow, or for peace offerings to the LORD,

9 then you shall offer with the bull a grain offering of three-tenths *of an ephah* of fine flour mixed with one-half of a hin of oil;

10 and you shall offer as the drink offering one-half a hin of wine as an offering by fire, as a soothing aroma to the LORD.

11 'Thus it shall be done for each ox, or for each ram, or for each of the male lambs, or of the goats.

12 'According to the number that you prepare, so you shall do for everyone according to their number.

13 'All who are native shall do these things in this manner, in presenting an offering by fire, as a soothing aroma to the LORD.

14 'If an alien sojourns with you, or one who may be among you throughout your generations, and he *wishes to* make an offering by fire, as a soothing aroma to the LORD, just as you do so he shall do.

15 'As for the assembly, there shall be one statute for you and for the alien who sojourns *with you,* a perpetual statute throughout your generations; as you are, so shall the alien be before the LORD.

16 'There is to be one law and one ordinance for you and for the alien who sojourns with you.'"

17 Then the LORD spoke to Moses, saying,

18 "Speak to the sons of Israel and say to them, 'When you enter the land where I bring you,

19 then it shall be, that when you eat of the food of the land, you shall lift up an offering to the LORD.

20 'Of the first of your dough you shall lift up a cake as an offering; as the offering of the threshing floor, so you shall lift it up.

21 'From the first of your dough you shall give to the LORD an offering throughout your generations.

22 'But when you unwittingly fail and do not observe all these commandments, which the LORD has spoken to Moses,

23 *even* all that the LORD has commanded you through Moses, from the day when the LORD gave commandment and onward throughout your generations,

24 then it shall be, if it is done unintentionally, without the knowledge of the congregation, that all the congregation shall offer one bull for a burnt offering, as a soothing aroma to the LORD, with its grain offering and its drink offering, according to the ordinance, and one male goat for a sin offering.

25 'Then the priest shall make atonement for all the congregation of the sons of Israel, and they will be forgiven; for it was an error, and they have brought their offering, an offering by fire to the LORD, and their sin offering before the LORD, for their error.

26 'So all the congregation of the sons of Israel will be forgiven, with the alien who sojourns among them, for *it happened* to all the people through error.

27 'Also if one person sins unintentionally, then he shall offer a one year old female goat for a sin offering.

28 'The priest shall make atonement before the LORD for the person who goes astray when he sins unintentionally, making atonement for him that he may be forgiven.

29 'You shall have one law for him who does *anything* unintentionally, for him who is native among the sons of Israel and for the alien who sojourns among them.

30 'But the person who does *anything* ≺ defiantly, whether he is native or an alien, that one is blaspheming the LORD; and that person shall be cut off from among his people.

31 'Because he has despised the word of the LORD and has broken His commandment, that person shall be completely cut off; his guilt *will be* on him.'"

32 Now while the sons of Israel were in the wilderness, they found a man gathering wood on the sabbath day.

33 Those who found him gathering wood brought him to Moses and Aaron and to all the congregation;

34 and they put him in custody because it had not been declared what should be done to him.

35 Then the LORD said to Moses, "The

LIFE LESSONS

≻ **Numbers 15:30 —** *"But the person who does anything defiantly . . . is blaspheming the LORD; and that person shall be cut off from among his people."*

*A*ll sin separates us from God, but some sins bring harsher consequences than others. Presumptuous sins—brazen, knowing, defiant, arrogant, premeditated sins—carry a heavy penalty. Only fools plan to sin and ask forgiveness later.

man shall surely be put to death; all the congregation shall stone him with stones outside the camp."

36 So all the congregation brought him outside the camp and stoned him to death with stones, just as the LORD had commanded Moses.

37 The LORD also spoke to Moses, saying,

38 "Speak to the sons of Israel, and tell them that they shall make for themselves tassels on the corners of their garments throughout their generations, and that they shall put on the tassel of each corner a cord of blue.

39 "It shall be a tassel for you to look at and remember all the commandments of the LORD, so as to do them and not follow after your own heart and your own eyes, after which you played the harlot,

40 so that you may remember to do all My commandments and be holy to your God.

41 "I am the LORD your God who brought you out from the land of Egypt to be your God; I am the LORD your God."

16 NOW Korah the son of Izhar, the son of Kohath, the son of Levi, with Dathan and Abiram, the sons of Eliab, and On the son of Peleth, sons of Reuben, took *action,*

2 and they rose up before Moses, together with some of the sons of Israel, two hundred and fifty leaders of the congregation, chosen in the assembly, men of renown.

3 They assembled together against Moses and Aaron, and said to them, "You have gone far enough, for all the congregation are holy, every one of them, and the LORD is in their midst; so why do you exalt yourselves above the assembly of the LORD?"

4 When Moses heard *this,* he fell on his face;

5 and he spoke to Korah and all his company, saying, "Tomorrow morning the LORD will show who is His, and who is holy, and will bring *him* near to Himself; even the one whom He will choose, He will bring near to Himself.

6 "Do this: take censers for yourselves, Korah and all your company,

7 and put fire in them, and lay incense upon them in the presence of the LORD tomorrow; and the man whom the LORD

chooses *shall be* the one who is holy. You have gone far enough, you sons of Levi!"

8 Then Moses said to Korah, "Hear now, you sons of Levi,

9 is it not enough for you that the God of Israel has separated you from the *rest of* the congregation of Israel, to bring you near to Himself, to do the service of the tabernacle of the LORD, and to stand before the congregation to minister to them;

10 and that He has brought you near, *Korah,* and all your brothers, sons of Levi, with you? And are you seeking for the priesthood also?

11 "Therefore you and all your company are gathered together against the LORD; but as for Aaron, who is he that you grumble against him?"

12 Then Moses sent a summons to Dathan and Abiram, the sons of Eliab; but they said, "We will not come up.

13 "Is it not enough that you have brought us up out of a land flowing with milk and honey to have us die in the wilderness, but you would also lord it over us?

14 "Indeed, you have not brought us into a land flowing with milk and honey, nor have you given us an inheritance of fields and vineyards. Would you put out the eyes of these men? We will not come up!"

15 Then Moses became very angry and said to the LORD, "Do not regard their offering! I have not taken a single donkey from them, nor have I done harm to any of them."

16 Moses said to Korah, "You and all your company be present before the LORD tomorrow, both you and they along with Aaron.

17 "Each of you take his firepan and put incense on it, and each of you bring his censer before the LORD, two hundred and fifty firepans; also you and Aaron *shall bring* his firepan."

18 So they each took his *own* censer and put fire on it, and laid incense on it; and they stood at the doorway of the tent of meeting, with Moses and Aaron.

19 Thus Korah assembled all the congregation against them at the doorway of the tent of meeting. And the glory of the LORD appeared to all the congregation.

20 Then the LORD spoke to Moses and Aaron, saying,

21 "Separate yourselves from among this congregation, that I may consume them instantly."

22 But they fell on their faces and said, "O God, God of the spirits of all flesh, when one man sins, will You be angry with the entire congregation?"

23 Then the LORD spoke to Moses, saying,

24 "Speak to the congregation, saying, 'Get back from around the dwellings of Korah, Dathan and Abiram.'"

25 Then Moses arose and went to Dathan and Abiram, with the elders of Israel following him,

26 and he spoke to the congregation, saying, "Depart now from the tents of these wicked men, and touch nothing that belongs to them, or you will be swept away in all their sin."

27 So they got back from around the dwellings of Korah, Dathan and Abiram; and Dathan and Abiram came out and stood at the doorway of their tents, along with their wives and their sons and their little ones.

➤ 28 Moses said, "By this you shall know that the LORD has sent me to do all these deeds; for this is not my doing.

29 "If these men die the death of all men or if they suffer the fate of all men, then the LORD has not sent me.

30 "But if the LORD brings about an entirely new thing and the ground opens its mouth and swallows them up with all that is theirs, and they descend alive into Sheol, then you will understand that these men have spurned the LORD."

31 As he finished speaking all these words, the ground that was under them split open;

32 and the earth opened its mouth and swallowed them up, and their households, and all the men who belonged to Korah with their possessions.

33 So they and all that belonged to them went down alive to Sheol; and the earth closed over them, and they perished from the midst of the assembly.

34 All Israel who were around them fled at their outcry, for they said, "The earth may swallow us up!"

35 Fire also came forth from the LORD and consumed the two hundred and fifty men who were offering the incense.

36 Then the LORD spoke to Moses, saying,

37 "Say to Eleazar, the son of Aaron the priest, that he shall take up the censers out of the midst of the blaze, for they are holy; and you scatter the burning coals abroad.

38 "As for the censers of these men who have sinned at the cost of their lives, let them be made into hammered sheets for a plating of the altar, since they did present them before the LORD and they are holy; and they shall be for a sign to the sons of Israel."

39 So Eleazar the priest took the bronze censers which the men who were burned had offered, and they hammered them out as a plating for the altar,

40 as a reminder to the sons of Israel that no layman who is not of the descendants of Aaron should come near to burn incense before the LORD; so that he will not become like Korah and his company—just as the LORD had spoken to him through Moses.

41 But on the next day all the congregation of the sons of Israel grumbled against Moses and Aaron, saying, "You are the ones who have caused the death of the LORD's people."

42 It came about, however, when the congregation had assembled against Moses and Aaron, that they turned toward the tent of meeting, and behold, the cloud covered it and the glory of the LORD appeared.

43 Then Moses and Aaron came to the front of the tent of meeting,

---

LIFE LESSONS

➤ **Numbers 16:28 — Moses said, "By this you shall know that the LORD has sent me to do all these deeds; for this is not my doing."**

God is wise—He knows the consequences of rebellion are chaos and destruction. Moses did only what God sent him to do, and because he obeyed the Lord, God gave him success. Obedience always brings blessing. Centuries later, Jesus said, "I do nothing on My own initiative, but I speak these things as the Father taught Me. And He who sent Me is with Me; He has not left Me alone, for I always do the things that are pleasing to Him" (John 8:28, 29).

44 and the LORD spoke to Moses, saying,
45 "Get away from among this congregation, that I may consume them instantly." Then they fell on their faces.
46 Moses said to Aaron, "Take your censer and put in it fire from the altar, and lay incense *on it*; then bring it quickly to the congregation and make atonement for them, for wrath has gone forth from the LORD, the plague has begun!"
47 Then Aaron took *it* as Moses had spoken, and ran into the midst of the assembly, for behold, the plague had begun among the people. So he put *on* the incense and made atonement for the people.
48 He took his stand between the dead and the living, so that the plague was checked.
49 But those who died by the plague were 14,700, besides those who died on account of Korah.
50 Then Aaron returned to Moses at the doorway of the tent of meeting, for the plague had been checked.

✦ Psalm 32:1–5

A Psalm of David. A Maskil.

32 HOW blessed is he whose transgression is forgiven, Whose sin is covered!
2 How blessed is the man to whom the LORD does not impute iniquity, And in whose spirit there is no deceit!

3 When I kept silent *about my sin,* my body wasted away Through my groaning all day long.
4 For day and night Your hand was heavy upon me; My vitality was drained away *as* with the fever heat of summer. Selah.
5 I acknowledged my sin to You, And my iniquity I did not hide; I said, "I will confess my transgressions to the LORD"; And You forgave the guilt of my sin. Selah.

✦ Proverbs 11:16–18

16 A gracious woman attains honor, And ruthless men attain riches.
17 The merciful man does himself good, But the cruel man does himself harm.

Life Examples:

DAVID: The Joy of Forgiveness

PSALM 32:1–11

*P*salm 32 is David's confession of his sin with Bathsheba. He wrote it after his encounter with the prophet Nathan and probably after he had spent time alone with God in prayer and repentance.

If we were to give this psalm a title, a good one would be *The Joy of Forgiveness.* David writes: "How blessed is he whose trans-gression is forgiven, whose sin is covered!" (v. 1). "How blessed" can be translated, "How happy!"

Sin blocks our fellowship with the Lord. It also keeps us from experiencing God's goodness. David could not enjoy the sweetness of God's presence so long as he had not repented of his sin.

When you find yourself discouraged because you have repeated a certain sin, turn to God in prayer. Ask Him to apply His forgiveness to your life and receive His mercy. He loves you and wants to enjoy your fellowship once again.

LIFE LESSONS

➤ **Proverbs 11:17 —** *The merciful man does himself good, but the cruel man does himself harm.*

*T*he Lord calls us to do what is good and right, not only because godly living reflects His own holy character, but also because it benefits and blesses us. Living by God's Word and according to His will is life at its very best.

18 The wicked earns deceptive
    wages,
    But he who sows righteousness
    gets a true reward.

◈   **Mark 11:1–19**

11AS they *approached Jerusalem, at Bethphage and Bethany, near the Mount of Olives, He *sent two of His disciples,
2   and *said to them, "Go into the village opposite you, and immediately as you enter it, you will find a colt tied *there*, on which no one yet has ever sat; untie it and bring it *here*.
3   "If anyone says to you, 'Why are you doing this?' you say, 'The Lord has need of it'; and immediately he will send it back here."
4   They went away and found a colt tied at the door, outside in the street; and they *untied it.
5   Some of the bystanders were saying to them, "What are you doing, untying the colt?"
6   They spoke to them just as Jesus had told *them*, and they gave them permission.
7   They *brought the colt to Jesus and put their coats on it; and He sat on it.
8   And many spread their coats in the road, and others *spread* leafy branches which they had cut from the fields.
9   Those who went in front and those who followed were shouting:
    "Hosanna!
      BLESSED IS HE WHO COMES IN THE
        NAME OF THE LORD;
10 Blessed *is* the coming kingdom of
      our father David;
      Hosanna in the highest!"

11 Jesus entered Jerusalem *and came* into the temple; and after looking around at everything, He left for Bethany with the twelve, since it was already late.
12 On the next day, when they had left Bethany, He became hungry.
13 Seeing at a distance a fig tree in leaf, He went *to see* if perhaps He would find anything on it; and when He came to it, He found nothing but leaves, for it was not the season for figs.
14 He said to it, "May no one ever eat fruit from you again!" And His disciples were listening.
15 Then they *came to Jerusalem. And He entered the temple and began to drive out those who were buying and selling in the temple, and overturned the tables of the money changers and the seats of those who were selling doves;
16 and He would not permit anyone to carry merchandise through the temple.
17 And He *began* to teach and say to them, "Is it not written, 'MY HOUSE SHALL BE CALLED A HOUSE OF PRAYER FOR ALL THE NATIONS'? But you have made it a ROBBERS' DEN."
18 The chief priests and the scribes heard *this*, and *began* seeking how to destroy Him; for they were afraid of Him, for the whole crowd was astonished at His teaching.
19 When evening came, they would go out of the city.

LIFE LESSONS

➤ **Mark 11:10 —** *"Blessed is the coming kingdom of our father David; Hosanna in the highest!"*

"*H*osanna" means "Save now!" Many in the crowd recognized Jesus as the Son of David who would come to reign (Zech 9:9), but they misunderstood the timing and the nature of His kingdom.

➤ **Mark 11:14 —** *"May no one ever eat fruit from you again!"*

*T*his is the only destructive miracle reported in the Gospels. Jesus meant it to picture God's displeasure with a people who appeared religious, but whose lives remained barren of the fruits of godliness (Gal. 5:22, 23).

17 THEN the LORD spoke to Moses, saying,

2 "Speak to the sons of Israel, and get from them a rod for each father's household; twelve rods, from all their leaders according to their fathers' households. You shall write each name on his rod,

3 and write Aaron's name on the rod of Levi; for there is one rod for the head of each of their fathers' households.

4 "You shall then deposit them in the tent of meeting in front of the testimony, where I meet with you.

5 "It will come about that the rod of the man whom I choose will sprout. Thus I will lessen from upon Myself the grumblings of the sons of Israel, who are grumbling against you."

6 Moses therefore spoke to the sons of Israel, and all their leaders gave him a rod apiece, for each leader according to their fathers' households, twelve rods, with the rod of Aaron among their rods.

7 So Moses deposited the rods before the LORD in the tent of the testimony.

➤ 8 Now on the next day Moses went into the tent of the testimony; and behold, the rod of Aaron for the house of Levi had sprouted and put forth buds and produced blossoms, and it bore ripe almonds.

9 Moses then brought out all the rods from the presence of the LORD to all the sons of Israel; and they looked, and each man took his rod.

10 But the LORD said to Moses, "Put back the rod of Aaron before the testi-mony to be kept as a sign against the rebels, that you may put an end to their grumblings against Me, so that they will not die."

11 Thus Moses did; just as the LORD had commanded him, so he did.

12 Then the sons of Israel spoke to Moses, saying, "Behold, we perish, we are dying, we are all dying!

13 "Everyone who comes near, who comes near to the tabernacle of the LORD, must die. Are we to perish completely?"

18 SO the LORD said to Aaron, "You and your sons and your father's household with you shall bear the guilt in connection with the sanctuary, and you and your sons with you shall bear the guilt in connection with your priest-hood.

2 "But bring with you also your broth-ers, the tribe of Levi, the tribe of your father, that they may be joined with you and serve you, while you and your sons with you are before the tent of the testi-mony.

3 "And they shall thus attend to your obligation and the obligation of all the tent, but they shall not come near to the furnishings of the sanctuary and the altar, or both they and you will die.

4 "They shall be joined with you and attend to the obligations of the tent of meeting, for all the service of the tent; but an outsider may not come near you.

5 "So you shall attend to the obligations of the sanctuary and the obligations of the altar, so that there will no longer be wrath on the sons of Israel.

6 "Behold, I Myself have taken your fellow Levites from among the sons of Israel; they are a gift to you, dedicated to the LORD, to perform the service for the tent of meeting.

7 "But you and your sons with you shall attend to your priesthood for everything concerning the altar and inside the veil, and you are to perform service. I am giving you the priesthood as a bestowed service, but the outsider who comes near shall be put to death."

8 Then the LORD spoke to Aaron, "Now behold, I Myself have given you charge of My offerings, even all the holy gifts of the sons of Israel I have given them to you as a portion and to your sons as a perpetual allotment.

LIFE LESSONS

➤ **Numbers 17:8 —** *Behold, the rod of Aaron . . . had sprouted and put forth buds and produced blossoms, and it bore ripe almonds.*

*T*he Lord will go to great lengths to show us and confirm to us His perfect will. Not only did Aaron's rod show signs of growth but it showed the complete cycle of the almond tree—from bud to blossom to fruit. Interestingly, the almond was a symbol for haste and vigi-lance (Jer. 1:11, 12)—two qualities the high priest would need to exhibit.

9 "This shall be yours from the most holy *gifts reserved* from the fire; every offering of theirs, even every grain offering and every sin offering and every guilt offering, which they shall render to Me, shall be most holy for you and for your sons.

10 "As the most holy *gifts* you shall eat it; every male shall eat it. It shall be holy to you.

11 "This also is yours, the offering of their gift, even all the wave offerings of the sons of Israel; I have given them to you and to your sons and daughters with you as a perpetual allotment. Everyone of your household who is clean may eat it.

12 "All the best of the fresh oil and all the best of the fresh wine and of the grain, the first fruits of those which they give to the LORD, I give them to you.

13 "The first ripe fruits of all that is in their land, which they bring to the LORD, shall be yours; everyone of your household who is clean may eat it.

14 "Every devoted thing in Israel shall be yours.

15 "Every first issue of the womb of all flesh, whether man or animal, which they offer to the LORD, shall be yours; nevertheless the firstborn of man you shall surely redeem, and the firstborn of unclean animals you shall redeem.

16 "As to their redemption price, from a month old you shall redeem them, by your valuation, five shekels in silver, according to the shekel of the sanctuary, which is twenty gerahs.

17 "But the firstborn of an ox or the firstborn of a sheep or the firstborn of a goat, you shall not redeem; they are holy. You shall sprinkle their blood on the altar and shall offer up their fat in smoke *as* an offering by fire, for a soothing aroma to the LORD.

18 "Their meat shall be yours; it shall be yours like the breast of a wave offering and like the right thigh.

19 "All the offerings of the holy *gifts*, which the sons of Israel offer to the LORD, I have given to you and your sons and your daughters with you, as a perpetual allotment. It is an everlasting covenant of salt before the LORD to you and your descendants with you."

➤ 20 Then the LORD said to Aaron, "You shall have no inheritance in their land nor own any portion among them; I

am your portion and your inheritance among the sons of Israel.

21 "To the sons of Levi, behold, I have given all the tithe in Israel for an inheritance, in return for their service which they perform, the service of the tent of meeting.

22 "The sons of Israel shall not come near the tent of meeting again, or they will bear sin and die.

23 "Only the Levites shall perform the service of the tent of meeting, and they shall bear their iniquity; it shall be a perpetual statute throughout your generations, and among the sons of Israel they shall have no inheritance.

24 "For the tithe of the sons of Israel, which they offer as an offering to the LORD, I have given to the Levites for an inheritance; therefore I have said concerning them, 'They shall have no inheritance among the sons of Israel.'"

25 Then the LORD spoke to Moses, saying,

26 "Moreover, you shall speak to the Levites and say to them, 'When you take from the sons of Israel the tithe which I have given you from them for your inheritance, then you shall present an offering from it to the LORD, a tithe of the tithe.

27 'Your offering shall be reckoned to you as the grain from the threshing floor or the full produce from the wine vat.

28 'So you shall also present an offering to the LORD from your tithes, which you receive from the sons of Israel; and from it you shall give the LORD's offering to Aaron the priest.

29 'Out of all your gifts you shall present every offering due to the LORD, from all the best of them, the sacred part from them.'

30 "You shall say to them, 'When you have offered from it the best of it, then *the rest* shall be reckoned to the Levites

as the product of the threshing floor, and as the product of the wine vat.

31 'You may eat it anywhere, you and your households, for it is your compensation in return for your service in the tent of meeting.

32 'You will bear no sin by reason of it when you have offered the best of it. But you shall not profane the sacred gifts of the sons of Israel, or you will die.'"

Psalm 32:6–11

6 Therefore, let everyone who is
      godly pray to You in a time when
      You may be found;
   Surely in a flood of great waters
      they will not reach him.
7 You are my hiding place; You
      preserve me from trouble;
   You surround me with songs of
      deliverance.   Selah.
8 I will instruct you and teach you in
      the way which you should go;
   I will counsel you with My eye upon
      you.
9 Do not be as the horse or as the mule
      which have no understanding,
   Whose trappings include bit and
      bridle to hold them in check,
   Otherwise they will not come near
      to you.
10 Many are the sorrows of the wicked,
   But he who trusts in the LORD,
      lovingkindness shall surround
      him.
11 Be glad in the LORD and rejoice, you
      righteous ones;

LIFE LESSONS

➤ **Psalm 32:9 — Do not be as the horse or as the mule which have no understanding, whose trappings include bit and bridle to hold them in check.**

Stubborn, untrained horses must be guided with bits and bridles because they fight against the direction of their masters. In the same way, whenever we refuse to submit to the Lord's commands, He may choose to guide us to do His will through the reigns of adversity. As believers, He wants us to delight in drawing near to Him, not fight against His perfect will.

And shout for joy, all you who are
   upright in heart.

Proverbs 11:19–21

19 He who is steadfast in righteousness
      will attain to life,
   And he who pursues evil will bring
      about his own death.
20 The perverse in heart are an
      abomination to the LORD,
   But the blameless in their walk are
      His delight.
21 Assuredly, the evil man will not go
      unpunished,
   But the descendants of the righteous
      will be delivered.

Mark 11:20–33

20 As they were passing by in the morning, they saw the fig tree withered from the roots up.

21 Being reminded, Peter *said to Him, "Rabbi, look, the fig tree which You cursed has withered."

22 And Jesus *answered saying to them, "Have faith in God.

23 "Truly I say to you, whoever says to this mountain, 'Be taken up and cast into the sea,' and does not doubt in his heart, but believes that what he says is going to happen, it will be granted him.

24 "Therefore I say to you, all things for which you pray and ask, believe that you have received them, and they will be granted you.

25 "Whenever you stand praying, forgive, if you have anything against anyone, so that your Father who is in heaven will also forgive you your transgressions.

26 ["But if you do not forgive, neither will your Father who is in heaven forgive your transgressions."]

27 They *came again to Jerusalem. And as He was walking in the temple, the chief priests and the scribes and the elders *came to Him,

28 and began saying to Him, "By what authority are You doing these things, or who gave You this authority to do these things?"

29 And Jesus said to them, "I will ask you one question, and you answer Me,

Why is it so important to forgive others?

MARK 11:25, 26

*A*ll of us at some point have to deal with the issue of unforgiveness. When we allow a bitter spirit to lodge in our souls where it can grow and fester, it becomes both painful and destructive. Unforgiveness lies at the root of many of the physical, emotional, psychological, and spiritual problems we see today.

The apostle Paul wrote, "Let all bitterness and wrath and anger and clamor and slander be put away from you, along with all malice. Be kind to one another, tender-hearted, forgiving each other, just as God in Christ also has forgiven you" (Eph. 4:31, 32). When Paul spoke of bitterness, wrath, anger, clamor, and evil speaking (slander), he was describing the ugly manifestations of a "spirit of unforgiveness."

A spirit of unforgiveness goes beyond a temporary unwillingness to forgive—the period between the time a person gets hurt and the time he forgives the one who hurt him. A spirit of unforgiveness develops when the one hurt chooses to remain in that unforgiving state.

People who develop this unrelenting spirit often say, "I just don't think I could ever forgive *that*." They make the statement when they feel they have been treated in such an unjust,

unfair, and harmful way that they simply can't let go of the pain.

At some point, every one of us has been hurt. Some who are reading these words are hurting now, or they may face hurt from a friend soon. The question is what will you do when someone speaks an unkind word or does something deliberate to injure you? Do you know how to extend forgiveness the same way Christ has extended it to you?

Hurt is unavoidable, but we can learn how to deal with it. No pain is too deep or too widespread to be beyond the power of God's forgiveness, working in and through us. Forgiveness and unforgiveness are both choices we make with the will. Refusing to forgive another, no matter how serious the crime, is always a devastating choice because it puts us in bondage to our offender.

Someone may say, "But you don't know what has happened to me." God knows and He admonishes us to allow Him to avenge the wrongs that have been done against us. Our forgiveness does not mean the person who hurt us was right or "off the hook." It means we are willing to trust God to deal with the problems and with those who hurt us in His time and in His way.

We shouldn't forget that it was our loving Savior, Jesus Christ, who ended a story on the necessity of forgiveness with these words: "And his lord, moved with anger, handed him over to the torturers until he should repay all that was owed him. My heavenly Father will also do the same to you, if each of you does not forgive his brother from your heart" (Matt. 18:34, 35).

---

and *then* I will tell you by what authority I do these things.
30 "Was the baptism of John from heaven, or from men? Answer Me."
31 They *began* reasoning among themselves, saying, "If we say, 'From heaven,' He will say, 'Then why did you not believe him?'

32 "But shall we say, 'From men'?"— they were afraid of the people, for everyone considered John to have been a real prophet.
33 Answering Jesus, they *said, "We do not know." And Jesus *said to them, "Nor will I tell you by what authority I do these things."

 Numbers 19:1—20:29

19 THEN the LORD spoke to Moses and Aaron, saying,
2 "This is the statute of the law which the LORD has commanded, saying, 'Speak

to the sons of Israel that they bring you an unblemished red heifer in which is no defect *and* on which a yoke has never been placed.
3 'You shall give it to Eleazar the priest, and it shall be brought outside the camp and be slaughtered in his presence.

4 'Next Eleazar the priest shall take some of its blood with his finger and sprinkle some of its blood toward the front of the tent of meeting seven times.
5 'Then the heifer shall be burned in his sight; its hide and its flesh and its blood, with its refuse, shall be burned.
6 'The priest shall take cedar wood and hyssop and scarlet *material* and cast it into the midst of the burning heifer.
7 'The priest shall then wash his clothes and bathe his body in water, and afterward come into the camp, but the priest shall be unclean until evening.
8 'The one who burns it shall also wash his clothes in water and bathe his body in water, and shall be unclean until evening.
9 'Now a man who is clean shall gather up the ashes of the heifer and deposit them outside the camp in a clean place, and the congregation of the sons of Israel shall keep it as water to remove impurity; it is purification from sin.
10 'The one who gathers the ashes of the heifer shall wash his clothes and be unclean until evening; and it shall be a perpetual statute to the sons of Israel and to the alien who sojourns among them.
11 'The one who touches the corpse of any person shall be unclean for seven days.
12 'That one shall purify himself from uncleanness with the water on the third day and on the seventh day, *and then* he will be clean; but if he does not purify himself on the third day and on the seventh day, he will not be clean.
13 'Anyone who touches a corpse, the body of a man who has died, and does not purify himself, defiles the tabernacle of the LORD; and that person shall be cut off from Israel. Because the water for impurity was not sprinkled on him, he shall be unclean; his uncleanness is still on him.
14 'This is the law when a man dies in a tent: everyone who comes into the tent and everyone who is in the tent shall be unclean for seven days.
15 'Every open vessel, which has no covering tied down on it, shall be unclean.
16 'Also, anyone who in the open field touches one who has been slain with a sword or who has died *naturally*, or a human bone or a grave, shall be unclean for seven days.

17 'Then for the unclean *person* they shall take some of the ashes of the burnt purification from sin and flowing water shall be added to them in a vessel.
18 'A clean person shall take hyssop and dip *it* in the water, and sprinkle *it* on the tent and on all the furnishings and on the persons who were there, and on the one who touched the bone or the one slain or the one dying *naturally* or the grave.
19 'Then the clean *person* shall sprinkle on the unclean on the third day and on the seventh day; and on the seventh day he shall purify him from uncleanness, and he shall wash his clothes and bathe *himself* in water and shall be clean by evening.
20 'But the man who is unclean and does not purify himself from uncleanness, that person shall be cut off from the midst of the assembly, because he has defiled the sanctuary of the LORD; the water for impurity has not been sprinkled on him, he is unclean.
21 'So it shall be a perpetual statute for them. And he who sprinkles the water for impurity shall wash his clothes, and he who touches the water for impurity shall be unclean until evening.
22 'Furthermore, anything that the unclean *person* touches shall be unclean; and the person who touches *it* shall be unclean until evening.'"

20 THEN the sons of Israel, the whole congregation, came to the wilderness of Zin in the first month; and the people stayed at Kadesh. Now Miriam died there and was buried there.
2 There was no water for the congregation, and they assembled themselves against Moses and Aaron.
3 The people thus contended with Moses and spoke, saying, "If only we had perished when our brothers perished before the LORD!
4 "Why then have you brought the LORD'S assembly into this wilderness, for us and our beasts to die here?
5 "Why have you made us come up from Egypt, to bring us in to this wretched place? It is not a place of grain or figs or vines or pomegranates, nor is there water to drink."
6 Then Moses and Aaron came in from the presence of the assembly to the doorway of the tent of meeting and fell

on their faces. Then the glory of the LORD appeared to them;

7 and the LORD spoke to Moses, saying,

8 "Take the rod; and you and your brother Aaron assemble the congregation and speak to the rock before their eyes, that it may yield its water. You shall thus bring forth water for them out of the rock and let the congregation and their beasts drink."

9 So Moses took the rod from before the LORD, just as He had commanded him;

10 and Moses and Aaron gathered the assembly before the rock. And he said to them, "Listen now, you rebels; shall we bring forth water for you out of this rock?"

11 Then Moses lifted up his hand and struck the rock twice with his rod; and water came forth abundantly, and the congregation and their beasts drank.

➤ 12 But the LORD said to Moses and Aaron, "Because you have not believed Me, to treat Me as holy in the sight of the sons of Israel, therefore you shall not bring this assembly into the land which I have given them."

13 Those *were* the waters of Meribah, because the sons of Israel contended with the LORD, and He proved Himself holy among them.

14 From Kadesh Moses then sent messengers to the king of Edom: "Thus your brother Israel has said, 'You know all the hardship that has befallen us;

15 that our fathers went down to Egypt, and we stayed in Egypt a long time, and the Egyptians treated us and our fathers badly.

16 'But when we cried out to the LORD, He heard our voice and sent an angel and brought us out from Egypt; now behold, we are at Kadesh, a town on the edge of your territory.

17 'Please let us pass through your land. We will not pass through field or through vineyard; we will not even drink water from a well. We will go along the king's highway, not turning to the right or left, until we pass through your territory.'"

18 Edom, however, said to him, "You shall not pass through us, or I will come out with the sword against you."

19 Again, the sons of Israel said to him, "We will go up by the highway, and if I

and my livestock do drink any of your water, then I will pay its price. Let me only pass through on my feet, nothing *else*."

20 But he said, "You shall not pass through." And Edom came out against him with a heavy force and with a strong hand.

21 Thus Edom refused to allow Israel ◄ to pass through his territory; so Israel turned away from him.

22 Now when they set out from Kadesh, the sons of Israel, the whole congregation, came to Mount Hor.

23 Then the LORD spoke to Moses and Aaron at Mount Hor by the border of the land of Edom, saying,

24 "Aaron will be gathered to his people; for he shall not enter the land which I have given to the sons of Israel, because you rebelled against My command at the waters of Meribah.

25 "Take Aaron and his son Eleazar and bring them up to Mount Hor;

26 and strip Aaron of his garments and

LIFE LESSONS

➤ **Numbers 20:12 —** *"Because you have not believed Me . . . you shall not bring this assembly into the land which I have given them."*

*M*oses acted presumptuously when he struck the rock twice because God had instructed him to only speak to it (Num. 20:8). Instead, he allowed his anger and frustration to provoke him into an ugly display of the flesh. Yet God is no respecter of persons—He did not make allowances for Moses because of his position as leader of the Israelites. On the contrary, because of his influence with the people, it was even more important for Moses to honor the Lord in everything (James 3:1). Obedience always brings blessing, just as disobedience always brings consequences. For Moses, the consequence of such blatant disrespect for God was that he would never live in the Land of Promise.

➤ **Numbers 20:21 —** *Thus Edom refused to allow Israel to pass through his territory; so Israel turned away from him.*

*I*t may have confused Israel why the Lord allowed the Edomites to refuse them passage. But as children of a sovereign God, we are never victims of our circumstances.

put them on his son Eleazar. So Aaron will be gathered *to his people*, and will die there."

27 So Moses did just as the LORD had commanded, and they went up to Mount Hor in the sight of all the congregation.

28 After Moses had stripped Aaron of his garments and put them on his son Eleazar, Aaron died there on the mountain top. Then Moses and Eleazar came down from the mountain.

29 When all the congregation saw that

Aaron had died, all the house of Israel wept for Aaron thirty days.

 Psalm 33:1–9

33 SING for joy in the LORD, O you righteous ones;
Praise is becoming to the upright.
2 Give thanks to the LORD with the lyre;

WHAT THE BIBLE SAYS ABOUT

The Source of Our Joy

Psalm 33:1, 2

Throughout the Bible, we are told to rejoice in the Lord (Ps. 33:1; 97:12; Is. 41:16; Joel 2:23; Phil. 3:1; 4:4). Though we know that those who know the Lord God should be joyful, what exactly is joy? And why should joy flow forth from us?

The first thing we need to understand is there is a difference between *joy* and *happiness*. Happiness generally has an external cause. People are happy when things go their way—when they have enough of what they need and can do as they please. We can have moments or seasons of happiness. However, the most important thing to understand about happiness is that it is based on external circumstances.

Joy, however, is the result of something that goes on within us; it has an internal cause. Joy is an abiding emotion that God gives to His children through the work of the Holy Spirit (Gal. 5:22, 23). A person who has not accepted Christ as his Savior—and therefore does not have the Holy Spirit indwelling him—may have seasons of happiness, but he cannot have the joy of the Lord because the Holy Spirit is not there to produce it within him.

Therefore, the source of our joy is a personal relationship with Jesus Christ. It is the result of the indwelling presence of the Holy Spirit.

When the Spirit of God comes to live in you, the Spirit will produce—as Galatians 5:22, 23 says, "love, joy, peace, patience, kindness, goodness, faithfulness, gentleness, self-control." The Holy Spirit produces joy within us by conforming us to the likeness of Christ, teaching us how to exhibit the characteristics of Christ in our lives (Rom. 8:29; 12:2).

When we are walking in submission to the Holy Spirit, it is natural for us to experience joy no matter what is going on in our lives. Even when we go through difficulties and trials, we will still have joy because the Holy Spirit will remind us of God's promises.

As Jesus says in John 14:26, 27, "The Helper, the Holy Spirit . . . will teach you all things, and bring to your remembrance all that I said to you. Peace I leave with you; My peace I give to you; not as the world gives do I give to you. Do not let your heart be troubled, nor let it be fearful." When we suffer, the Holy Spirit will remind us of all Christ has given us—and He will fill us with peace.

Still, that means we have to believe God's promises. If we don't trust God's assurances to us, then it won't help us when the Holy Spirit reminds us of them. Therefore, to have the joy of the Lord, we must have faith in the Bible—we must obey the Word of God. There is no such thing as doubting God's promises and having the joy of the Lord.

Friend, have you lost your joy? You can lose your joy when you sin against God or refuse to believe His Word. To regain your joy, you must immediately confess your sin to God and repent of it.

God intends for His people to rejoice, which is why He's given us the awesome gift of joy. Therefore, trust God, believe His Word, and allow the Holy Spirit to express the joy of the Lord through you. My prayer for you will be the one found in Romans 15:13, "May the God of hope fill you with all joy and peace in believing, so that you will abound in hope by the power of the Holy Spirit." Amen. ◈

Sing praises to Him with a harp of
ten strings.

3 Sing to Him a new song;
Play skillfully with a shout of joy.

4 For the word of the LORD is upright,
And all His work is *done* in
faithfulness.

5 He loves righteousness and justice;
The earth is full of the
lovingkindness of the LORD.

6 By the word of the LORD the
heavens were made,
And by the breath of His mouth all
their host.

7 He gathers the waters of the sea
together as a heap;
He lays up the deeps in storehouses.

8 Let all the earth fear the LORD;
Let all the inhabitants of the world
stand in awe of Him.

9 For He spoke, and it was done;
He commanded, and it stood fast.

Proverbs 11:22–24

22 *As* a ring of gold in a swine's snout
So is a beautiful woman who lacks
discretion.

23 The desire of the righteous is only
good,
But the expectation of the wicked is
wrath.

24 There is one who scatters, and *yet*
increases all the more,
And there is one who withholds
what is justly due, *and yet it
results* only in want.

Mark 12:1–27

12 AND He began to speak to them in
parables: "A man PLANTED A VINE-
YARD AND PUT A WALL AROUND IT, AND DUG
A VAT UNDER THE WINE PRESS AND BUILT A
TOWER, and rented it out to vine-growers
and went on a journey.

2 "At the *harvest* time he sent a slave
to the vine-growers, in order to receive
some of the produce of the vineyard from
the vine-growers.

3 "They took him, and beat him and
sent him away empty-handed.

4 "Again he sent them another slave,

and they wounded him in the head, and
treated him shamefully.

5 "And he sent another, and that one
they killed; and *so with* many others,
beating some and killing others.

6 "He had one more *to send,* a beloved
son; he sent him last *of all* to them, saying, 'They will respect my son.'

7 "But those vine-growers said to one
another, 'This is the heir; come, let us kill
him, and the inheritance will be ours!'

8 "They took him, and killed him and
threw him out of the vineyard.

9 "What will the owner of the vineyard
do? He will come and destroy the vine-
growers, and will give the vineyard to
others.

10 "Have you not even read this Scripture:

'THE STONE WHICH THE BUILDERS
REJECTED,
THIS BECAME THE CHIEF CORNER *stone;*

11 THIS CAME ABOUT FROM THE LORD,
AND IT IS MARVELOUS IN OUR EYES'?"

12 And they were seeking to seize Him,
and *yet* they feared the people, for they
understood that He spoke the parable
against them. And *so* they left Him and
went away.

13 Then they *sent some of the Pharisees and Herodians to Him in order to
trap Him in a statement.

14 They *came and *said to Him,
"Teacher, we know that You are truthful and defer to no one; for You are not
partial to any, but teach the way of God
in truth. Is it lawful to pay a poll-tax to
Caesar, or not?

15 "Shall we pay or shall we not pay?"
But He, knowing their hypocrisy, said to
them, "Why are you testing Me? Bring
Me a denarius to look at."

16 They brought *one.* And He *said to
them, "Whose likeness and inscription is
this?" And they said to Him, "Caesar's."

17 And Jesus said to them, "Render to
Caesar the things that are Caesar's, and
to God the things that are God's." And
they were amazed at Him.

18 *Some* Sadducees (who say that there
is no resurrection) *came to Jesus, and
began questioning Him, saying,

19 "Teacher, Moses wrote for us that IF
A MAN'S BROTHER DIES and leaves behind
a wife AND LEAVES NO CHILD, HIS BROTHER
SHOULD MARRY THE WIFE AND RAISE UP
CHILDREN TO HIS BROTHER.

20 "There were seven brothers; and the first took a wife, and died leaving no children.

21 "The second one married her, and died leaving behind no children; and the third likewise;

22 and *so* all seven left no children. Last of all the woman died also.

23 "In the resurrection, when they rise again, which one's wife will she be? For all seven had married her."

24 Jesus said to them, "Is this not the reason you are mistaken, that you do not understand the Scriptures or the power of God?

25 "For when they rise from the dead, they neither marry nor are given in marriage, but are like angels in heaven.

26 "But regarding the fact that the dead rise again, have you not read in the book of Moses, in the *passage* about *the burning* bush, how God spoke to him, saying, 'I AM THE GOD OF ABRAHAM, AND THE GOD OF ISAAC, and the God of Jacob'?

27 "He is not the God of the dead, but of the living; you are greatly mistaken."

LIFE LESSONS

➤ **Mark 12:17 —** *Jesus said to them, "Render to Caesar the things that are Caesar's, and to God the things that are God's."*

*W*e have duties and responsibilities to civil authorities that our faith does not negate. Jesus never advocated rebellion against the occupying Romans, despite their brutality and godlessness.

➤ **Mark 12:27 —** *"He is not the God of the dead, but of the living; you are greatly mistaken."*

*L*uke 20:38 adds, "He is not the God of the dead but of the living; *for all live* to Him." Abraham may be physically dead to us, but he is alive to God. One day we will join the patriarchs and stand in God's glorious presence together.

◈ Numbers 21:1—22:41

21 WHEN the Canaanite, the king of Arad, who lived in the Negev, heard that Israel was coming by the way of Atharim, then he fought against Israel and took some of them captive.

2 So Israel made a vow to the LORD and said, "If You will indeed deliver this people into my hand, then I will utterly destroy their cities."

LIFE LESSONS

➤ **Numbers 21:2 —** *"If You will indeed deliver this people into my hand, then I will utterly destroy their cities."*

*G*od allowed a pagan king to take some Israelites captive in battle. But when we serve the Lord, momentary defeats give way to ultimate victory. Adversity is always a bridge to a deeper relationship with God and an opportunity for us to take our greatest leaps forward spiritually.

---

3 The LORD heard the voice of Israel and delivered up the Canaanites; then they utterly destroyed them and their cities. Thus the name of the place was called Hormah.

4 Then they set out from Mount Hor by the way of the Red Sea, to go around the land of Edom; and the people became impatient because of the journey.

5 The people spoke against God and Moses, "Why have you brought us up out of Egypt to die in the wilderness? For there is no food and no water, and we loathe this miserable food."

6 The LORD sent fiery serpents among the people and they bit the people, so that many people of Israel died.

7 So the people came to Moses and said, "We have sinned, because we have spoken against the LORD and you; intercede with the LORD, that He may remove the serpents from us." And Moses interceded for the people.

8 Then the LORD said to Moses, "Make a fiery *serpent,* and set it on a standard; and it shall come about, that everyone

who is bitten, when he looks at it, he will live."

➤ 9 And Moses made a bronze serpent and set it on the standard; and it came about, that if a serpent bit any man, when he looked to the bronze serpent, he lived.

10 Now the sons of Israel moved out and camped in Oboth.

11 They journeyed from Oboth and camped at Iye-abarim, in the wilderness which is opposite Moab, to the east.

12 From there they set out and camped in Wadi Zered.

13 From there they journeyed and camped on the other side of the Arnon, which is in the wilderness that comes out of the border of the Amorites, for the Arnon is the border of Moab, between Moab and the Amorites.

14 Therefore it is said in the Book of the Wars of the LORD,

"Waheb in Suphah,
And the wadis of the Arnon,

15 And the slope of the wadis
That extends to the site of Ar,
And leans to the border of Moab."

16 From there *they continued* to Beer, that is the well where the LORD said to Moses, "Assemble the people, that I may give them water."

17 Then Israel sang this song:
"Spring up, O well! Sing to it!

18 "The well, which the leaders sank,
Which the nobles of the people dug,
With the scepter *and* with their
staffs."

And from the wilderness *they continued* to Mattanah,

19 and from Mattanah to Nahaliel, and from Nahaliel to Bamoth,

20 and from Bamoth to the valley that is in the land of Moab, at the top of Pisgah which overlooks the wasteland.

21 Then Israel sent messengers to Sihon, king of the Amorites, saying,

22 "Let me pass through your land. We will not turn off into field or vineyard; we will not drink water from wells. We will go by the king's highway until we have passed through your border."

23 But Sihon would not permit Israel to pass through his border. So Sihon gathered all his people and went out against Israel in the wilderness, and came to Jahaz and fought against Israel.

24 Then Israel struck him with the edge of the sword, and took possession of his land from the Arnon to the Jabbok, as far as the sons of Ammon; for the border of the sons of Ammon *was* Jazer.

25 Israel took all these cities and Israel lived in all the cities of the Amorites, in Heshbon, and in all her villages.

26 For Heshbon was the city of Sihon, king of the Amorites, who had fought against the former king of Moab and had taken all his land out of his hand, as far as the Arnon.

27 Therefore those who use proverbs say,

"Come to Heshbon! Let it be built!
So let the city of Sihon be established.

28 "For a fire went forth from Heshbon,
A flame from the town of Sihon;
It devoured Ar of Moab,
The dominant heights of the Arnon.

29 "Woe to you, O Moab!
You are ruined, O people of
Chemosh!
He has given his sons as fugitives,
And his daughters into captivity,
To an Amorite king, Sihon.

30 "But we have cast them down,
Heshbon is ruined as far as Dibon,
Then we have laid waste even to
Nophah,
Which *reaches* to Medeba."

LIFE LESSONS

➤ **Numbers 21:9** — *And Moses made a bronze serpent and set it on the standard; and it came about, that if a serpent bit any man, when he looked to the bronze serpent, he lived.*

The bronze serpent Moses made in the desert foreshadowed the ultimate work of salvation that Jesus accomplished for us on the Cross (John 3:14–16).

➤ **Numbers 21:24** — *Then Israel struck him with the edge of the sword, and took possession of his land from the Arnon to the Jabbok.*

In years to come, Israel often remembered the victories God had given them over Sihon and Og (Deut. 31:4; Josh. 2:10; Judg. 11:21; Ps. 135:10, 11; Neh. 9:22). It helps us move forward when we commemorate spiritual victories!

31 Thus Israel lived in the land of the Amorites.
32 Moses sent to spy out Jazer, and they captured its villages and dispossessed the Amorites who *were* there.
33 Then they turned and went up by the way of Bashan, and Og the king of Bashan went out with all his people, for battle at Edrei.
34 But the LORD said to Moses, "Do not fear him, for I have given him into your hand, and all his people and his land; and you shall do to him as you did to Sihon, king of the Amorites, who lived at Heshbon."
35 So they killed him and his sons and all his people, until there was no remnant left him; and they possessed his land.

22 THEN the sons of Israel journeyed, and camped in the plains of Moab beyond the Jordan *opposite* Jericho.
2 Now Balak the son of Zippor saw all that Israel had done to the Amorites.
3 So Moab was in great fear because of the people, for they were numerous; and Moab was in dread of the sons of Israel.
4 Moab said to the elders of Midian, "Now this horde will lick up all that is around us, as the ox licks up the grass of the field." And Balak the son of Zippor was king of Moab at that time.
5 So he sent messengers to Balaam the son of Beor, at Pethor, which is near the River, *in* the land of the sons of his people, to call him, saying, "Behold, a people came out of Egypt; behold, they cover the surface of the land, and they are living opposite me.
6 "Now, therefore, please come, curse this people for me since they are too mighty for me; perhaps I may be able to defeat them and drive them out of the land. For I know that he whom you bless is blessed, and he whom you curse is cursed."
7 So the elders of Moab and the elders of Midian departed with the *fees for* divination in their hand; and they came to Balaam and repeated Balak's words to him.
8 He said to them, "Spend the night here, and I will bring word back to you as the LORD may speak to me." And the leaders of Moab stayed with Balaam.

9 Then God came to Balaam and said, "Who are these men with you?"
10 Balaam said to God, "Balak the son of Zippor, king of Moab, has sent *word* to me,
11 'Behold, there is a people who came out of Egypt and they cover the surface of the land; now come, curse them for me; perhaps I may be able to fight against them and drive them out.'"
12 God said to Balaam, "Do not go with them; you shall not curse the people, for they are blessed."
13 So Balaam arose in the morning and said to Balak's leaders, "Go back to your land, for the LORD has refused to let me go with you."
14 The leaders of Moab arose and went to Balak and said, "Balaam refused to come with us."
15 Then Balak again sent leaders, more numerous and more distinguished than the former.
16 They came to Balaam and said to him, "Thus says Balak the son of Zippor, 'Let nothing, I beg you, hinder you from coming to me;
17 for I will indeed honor you richly, and I will do whatever you say to me. Please come then, curse this people for me.'"
18 Balaam replied to the servants of Balak, "Though Balak were to give me his house full of silver and gold, I could not do anything, either small or great, contrary to the command of the LORD my God.
19 "Now please, you also stay here tonight, and I will find out what else the LORD will speak to me."
20 God came to Balaam at night and said to him, "If the men have come to call you, rise up *and* go with them; but only the word which I speak to you shall you do."
21 So Balaam arose in the morning, and saddled his donkey and went with the leaders of Moab.
22 But God was angry because he was going, and the angel of the LORD took his stand in the way as an adversary against him. Now he was riding on his donkey and his two servants were with him.
23 When the donkey saw the angel of the LORD standing in the way with his drawn sword in his hand, the donkey turned off from the way and went into

the field; but Balaam struck the donkey to turn her back into the way.

24 Then the angel of the LORD stood in a narrow path of the vineyards, *with* a wall on this side and a wall on that side.

25 When the donkey saw the angel of the LORD, she pressed herself to the wall and pressed Balaam's foot against the wall, so he struck her again.

26 The angel of the LORD went further, and stood in a narrow place where there was no way to turn to the right hand or the left.

27 When the donkey saw the angel of the LORD, she lay down under Balaam; so Balaam was angry and struck the donkey with his stick.

28 And the LORD opened the mouth of the donkey, and she said to Balaam, "What have I done to you, that you have struck me these three times?"

29 Then Balaam said to the donkey, "Because you have made a mockery of me! If there had been a sword in my hand, I would have killed you by now."

30 The donkey said to Balaam, "Am I not your donkey on which you have ridden all your life to this day? Have I ever been accustomed to do so to you?" And he said, "No."

31 Then the LORD opened the eyes of Balaam, and he saw the angel of the LORD standing in the way with his drawn sword in his hand; and he bowed all the way to the ground.

➤ 32 The angel of the LORD said to him, "Why have you struck your donkey these three times? Behold, I have come out as an adversary, because your way was contrary to me.

33 "But the donkey saw me and turned aside from me these three times. If she had not turned aside from me, I would

---

LIFE LESSONS

➤ **Numbers 22:32 —** *"Your way was contrary to me."*

*W*hy was Balaam's way "contrary" before God? Because despite his good words, he harbored ill will against God's people—and eventually he died because of it (Num. 31:8). Those whom the Lord blesses will not be cursed—and woe to any who try. God wants a right heart, not nice words.

---

surely have killed you just now, and let her live."

34 Balaam said to the angel of the LORD, "I have sinned, for I did not know that you were standing in the way against me. Now then, if it is displeasing to you, I will turn back."

35 But the angel of the LORD said to Balaam, "Go with the men, but you shall speak only the word which I tell you." So Balaam went along with the leaders of Balak.

36 When Balak heard that Balaam was coming, he went out to meet him at the city of Moab, which is on the Arnon border, at the extreme end of the border.

37 Then Balak said to Balaam, "Did I not urgently send to you to call you? Why did you not come to me? Am I really unable to honor you?"

38 So Balaam said to Balak, "Behold, I have come now to you! Am I able to speak anything at all? The word that God puts in my mouth, that I shall speak."

39 And Balaam went with Balak, and they came to Kiriath-huzoth.

40 Balak sacrificed oxen and sheep, and sent *some* to Balaam and the leaders who were with him.

41 Then it came about in the morning that Balak took Balaam and brought him up to the high places of Baal, and he saw from there a portion of the people.

✦ Psalm 33:10–17

10 The LORD nullifies the counsel of the nations;
   He frustrates the plans of the peoples.
11 The counsel of the LORD stands forever,
   The plans of His heart from generation to generation.
12 Blessed is the nation whose God is the LORD,
   The people whom He has chosen for His own inheritance.
13 The LORD looks from heaven;
   He sees all the sons of men;
14 From His dwelling place He looks out
   On all the inhabitants of the earth,
15 He who fashions the hearts of them all,
   He who understands all their works.

16 The king is not saved by a mighty
   army;
   A warrior is not delivered by great
   strength.
➤ 17 A horse is a false hope for victory;
   Nor does it deliver anyone by its
   great strength.

✦ Proverbs 11:25–26

25 The generous man will be
   prosperous,
   And he who waters will himself be
   watered.
26 He who withholds grain, the people
   will curse him,
   But blessing will be on the head of
   him who sells *it*.

✦ Mark 12:28–44

28 One of the scribes came and heard
them arguing, and recognizing that He
had answered them well, asked Him,
"What commandment is the foremost of
all?"
29 Jesus answered, "The foremost is,
'HEAR, O ISRAEL! THE LORD OUR GOD IS
ONE LORD;
30 AND YOU SHALL LOVE THE LORD YOUR
GOD WITH ALL YOUR HEART, AND WITH ALL
YOUR SOUL, AND WITH ALL YOUR MIND, AND
WITH ALL YOUR STRENGTH.'
31 "The second is this, 'YOU SHALL LOVE
YOUR NEIGHBOR AS YOURSELF.' There is no
other commandment greater than these."
32 The scribe said to Him, "Right,
Teacher; You have truly stated that HE
IS ONE, AND THERE IS NO ONE ELSE BESIDES
HIM;
33 AND TO LOVE HIM WITH ALL THE HEART
AND WITH ALL THE UNDERSTANDING AND
WITH ALL THE STRENGTH, AND TO LOVE
ONE'S NEIGHBOR AS HIMSELF, is much more
than all burnt offerings and sacrifices."
➤ 34 When Jesus saw that he had answered intelligently, He said to him, "You
are not far from the kingdom of God."
After that, no one would venture to ask
Him any more questions.
35 And Jesus *began* to say, as He taught
in the temple, "How *is it that* the scribes
say that the Christ is the son of David?

36 "David himself said in the Holy
Spirit,
   'THE LORD SAID TO MY LORD,
   "SIT AT MY RIGHT HAND,
   UNTIL I PUT YOUR ENEMIES BENEATH
      YOUR FEET."'
37 "David himself calls Him 'Lord'; so
in what sense is He his son?" And the
large crowd enjoyed listening to Him.
38 In His teaching He was saying: "Beware of the scribes who like to walk
around in long robes, and *like* respectful
greetings in the market places,
39 and chief seats in the synagogues
and places of honor at banquets,
40 who devour widows' houses, and for
appearance's sake offer long prayers;
these will receive greater condemnation."
41 And He sat down opposite the treasury, and *began* observing how the
people were putting money into the treasury; and many rich people were putting
in large sums.
42 A poor widow came and put in two
small copper coins, which amount to a
cent.
43 Calling His disciples to Him, He said
to them, "Truly I say to you, this poor
widow put in more than all the contributors to the treasury;
44 for they all put in out of their surplus, but she, out of her poverty, put in
all she owned, all she had to live on."

LIFE LESSONS

➤ **Psalm 33:17 —** *A horse is a false hope
for victory; nor does it deliver anyone by
its great strength.*

A horse is much stronger and faster
than a man, but no wise person
puts his hope in the animal for deliverance. There is no real safety outside of a
close walk with God.

➤ **Mark 12:34 —** *After that, no one
would venture to ask Him any more
questions.*

*J*esus' opponents never succeeded in
trapping Him with their questions.
But when the Lord asked a question of
His own—not a trick question, but a serious one—they fell silent. It's always foolish to think oneself wiser than God. He is
Lord of all!

How can I know if my worship pleases God?

MARK 12:43, 44

*H*ave you ever wondered if your worship pleases God? Perhaps you've read about the Old Testament regulations for the Mosaic sacrificial system and have wondered what you're required to do now that Jesus has fulfilled the Law. It's important to remember that whenever you worship, God's priority is your heart (1 Chr. 28:9; Ps. 51:17; Joel 2:13).

But what exactly does that mean? What characterizes a heart that is lovely to the Lord? Jesus tells us, "True worshipers will worship the Father in spirit and truth; for such people the Father seeks to be His worshipers. God is Spirit, and those who worship Him must worship in spirit and truth" (John 4:23, 24). The heart that is led by God's Spirit and filled with His truth is pleasing to Him—and the only one actually equipped to really adore Him.

Jesus was unimpressed by those who displayed their "devotion" in a pompous, attention-getting manner. Their worship was not characterized by love for Him and the desire to do His will; rather, they were motivated by their own fleshly agendas and goals. Therefore, He instructed us, "When you pray, you are not to be like the hypocrites; for they love to stand and pray in the synagogues and on the street corners so that they may be seen by men. Truly I say to you, they have their reward in full. But you, when you pray, go into your inner room, close your door and pray to your Father who is in secret, and your Father who sees what is done in secret will reward you" (Matt. 6:5, 6).

Authentic service to God begins with the wholehearted trust that nothing escapes His loving and sovereign eye (Heb. 6:10; 11:6), and that He assumes full responsibility for our needs when we obey Him. This was illustrated one day when, sitting in the temple, Jesus watched the people who presented their offerings. Some rich people put large amounts into the treasury, making quite a scene. Then a poor widow put in what amounted to one cent. Jesus told His disciples. "Truly I say to you, this poor widow put in more than all the contributors to the treasury; for they all put in out of their surplus, but she, out of her poverty, put in all she owned, all she had to live on'" (Mark 12:43, 44).

Are you noticing what is important to the Lord? It's not the size of your offering that matters; it is the trust of your heart to give everything you are and dedicate everything you have to Him. It is not the beauty of your praising, giving thanks, singing, praying, or giving financially that moves Him; it's your motivation—your true feelings of love and adoration for the Lord.

As you prepare to worship God in spirit and in truth, examine the reason you are approaching His throne. Is it to further your goals or to experience His loving presence? Is it to get something you want or to give Him your utmost devotion? As Philippians 3:3 instructs, "Worship in the Spirit of God and glory in Christ Jesus and put no confidence in the flesh." It will not only satisfy your being, but will build intimacy in your relationship with Him.

MARCH 13

 Numbers 23:1—24:25

23 THEN Balaam said to Balak, "Build seven altars for me here, and prepare seven bulls and seven rams for me here."

2   Balak did just as Balaam had spoken, and Balak and Balaam offered up a bull and a ram on each altar.

3   Then Balaam said to Balak, "Stand beside your burnt offering, and I will go; perhaps the LORD will come to meet me, and whatever He shows me I will tell you." So he went to a bare hill.

4   Now God met Balaam, and he said to Him, "I have set up the seven altars, and I have offered up a bull and a ram on each altar."

5   Then the LORD put a word in Balaam's mouth and said, "Return to Balak, and you shall speak thus."

6   So he returned to him, and behold, he was standing beside his burnt offering, he and all the leaders of Moab.

7   He took up his discourse and said,

"From Aram Balak has brought me,
Moab's king from the mountains of
the East,
'Come curse Jacob for me,
And come, denounce Israel!'
8 "How shall I curse whom God has
not cursed?
And how can I denounce whom the
LORD has not denounced?
9 "As I see him from the top of the
rocks,
And I look at him from the hills;
Behold, a people *who* dwells apart,
And will not be reckoned among
the nations.
10 "Who can count the dust of Jacob,
Or number the fourth part of Israel?
Let me die the death of the upright,
And let my end be like his!"

11 Then Balak said to Balaam, "What
have you done to me? I took you to curse
my enemies, but behold, you have actually blessed them!"
12 He replied, "Must I not be careful to
speak what the LORD puts in my mouth?"
13 Then Balak said to him, "Please
come with me to another place from
where you may see them, although you
will only see the extreme end of them
and will not see all of them; and curse
them for me from there."
14 So he took him to the field of Zo-
phim, to the top of Pisgah, and built
seven altars and offered a bull and a ram
on *each* altar.
15 And he said to Balak, "Stand here
beside your burnt offering while I myself
meet *the* LORD over there."
16 Then the LORD met Balaam and put
a word in his mouth and said, "Return to
Balak, and thus you shall speak."
17 He came to him, and behold, he
was standing beside his burnt offering,
and the leaders of Moab with him. And
Balak said to him, "What has the LORD
spoken?"
18 Then he took up his discourse and
said,
"Arise, O Balak, and hear;
Give ear to me, O son of Zippor!
19 "God is not a man, that He should
lie,
Nor a son of man, that He should
repent;
Has He said, and will He not do it?
Or has He spoken, and will He not
make it good?

20 "Behold, I have received *a command*
to bless;
When He has blessed, then I cannot
revoke it.
21 "He has not observed misfortune in
Jacob;
Nor has He seen trouble in Israel;
The LORD his God is with him,
And the shout of a king is among
them.
22 "God brings them out of Egypt,
He is for them like the horns of the
wild ox.
23 "For there is no omen against
Jacob,
Nor is there any divination against
Israel;
At the proper time it shall be said to
Jacob
And to Israel, what God has done!
24 "Behold, a people rises like a lioness,
And as a lion it lifts itself;
It will not lie down until it devours
the prey,
And drinks the blood of the slain."

25 Then Balak said to Balaam, "Do not
curse them at all nor bless them at all!"
26 But Balaam replied to Balak, "Did I
not tell you, 'Whatever the LORD speaks,
that I must do'?"
27 Then Balak said to Balaam, "Please
come, I will take you to another place;
perhaps it will be agreeable with God
that you curse them for me from there."
28 So Balak took Balaam to the top of
Peor which overlooks the wasteland.
29 Balaam said to Balak, "Build seven
altars for me here and prepare seven
bulls and seven rams for me here."
30 Balak did just as Balaam had said,
and offered up a bull and a ram on *each*
altar.

24 WHEN Balaam saw that it pleased
the LORD to bless Israel, he did not
go as at other times to seek omens but he
set his face toward the wilderness.
2 And Balaam lifted up his eyes and
saw Israel camping tribe by tribe; and
the Spirit of God came upon him.
3 He took up his discourse and said,
"The oracle of Balaam the son of
Beor,
And the oracle of the man whose
eye is opened;
4 The oracle of him who hears the
words of God,
Who sees the vision of the Almighty,

Falling down, yet having his eyes
uncovered,

5 How fair are your tents, O Jacob,
Your dwellings, O Israel!

6 "Like valleys that stretch out,
Like gardens beside the river,
Like aloes planted by the LORD,
Like cedars beside the waters.

7 "Water will flow from his buckets,
And his seed *will be* by many
waters,
And his king shall be higher than
Agag,
And his kingdom shall be exalted.

8 "God brings him out of Egypt,
He is for him like the horns of the
wild ox.
He will devour the nations *who are*
his adversaries,
And will crush their bones in pieces,
And shatter *them* with his arrows.

9 "He couches, he lies down as a lion,
And as a lion, who dares rouse him?
Blessed is everyone who blesses
you,
And cursed is everyone who curses
you."

10 Then Balak's anger burned against
Balaam, and he struck his hands together; and Balak said to Balaam, "I
called you to curse my enemies, but behold, you have persisted in blessing them
these three times!
11 "Therefore, flee to your place now. I
said I would honor you greatly, but behold, the LORD has held you back from
honor."
12 Balaam said to Balak, "Did I not tell
your messengers whom you had sent to
me, saying,
13 'Though Balak were to give me his
house full of silver and gold, I could not
do anything contrary to the command of
the LORD, either good or bad, of my own
accord. What the LORD speaks, that I will
speak'?
14 "And now, behold, I am going to my
people; come, *and* I will advise you what
this people will do to your people in the
days to come."
15 He took up his discourse and said,
"The oracle of Balaam the son of
Beor,
And the oracle of the man whose
eye is opened,
16 The oracle of him who hears the
words of God,

And knows the knowledge of the
Most High,
Who sees the vision of the
Almighty,
Falling down, yet having his eyes
uncovered.

17 "I see him, but not now;
I behold him, but not near;
A star shall come forth from Jacob,
A scepter shall rise from Israel,
And shall crush through the
forehead of Moab,
And tear down all the sons of
Sheth.

18 "Edom shall be a possession,
Seir, its enemies, also will be a
possession,
While Israel performs valiantly.

19 "One from Jacob shall have
dominion,
And will destroy the remnant from
the city."

20 And he looked at Amalek and took
up his discourse and said,
"Amalek was the first of the nations,
But his end *shall be* destruction."

21 And he looked at the Kenite, and
took up his discourse and said,
"Your dwelling place is enduring,
And your nest is set in the cliff.

22 "Nevertheless Kain will be
consumed;
How long will Asshur keep you
captive?"

23 Then he took up his discourse and
said,
"Alas, who can live except God has
ordained it?

24 "But ships *shall come* from the coast
of Kittim,
And they shall afflict Asshur and
will afflict Eber;
So they also *will come* to
destruction."

25 Then Balaam arose and departed

LIFE PRINCIPLE [3]

GOD'S WORD IS AN IMMOVABLE ANCHOR IN
TIMES OF STORM.

NUMBERS 23:19

*T*he words of King Darius echoed
through Daniel's mind as servants
lowered him into the lion's den. "Your God
whom you constantly serve will Himself deliver
you" (Dan. 6:16). Workers then laid a heavy
stone over the opening to the underground
chamber.

Even after assessing his dire situation, Daniel
did not waver in his faith. The next morning,
King Darius found Daniel untouched and proclaiming, "O king, live forever! My God sent
His angel and shut the lions' mouths and they
have not harmed me" (vv. 21, 22).

How did Daniel survive? Were the lions
not hungry? Historians tell us animals used
for such planned executions went unfed for
days in an effort to ensure the death of the
accused. But Daniel's fate was never in the
hands of men. His life belonged to God, and
therein lies the victory. Daniel survived by
placing his trust in God and his faith in the
Lord's promises.

Each of us can remember times when we
wished we had a sure word from God—something we could cling to when doubts and fears
arose. God knows when we need encouragement, guidance, and hope. This is why He
provides specific promises in His Word, that
we might understand His nature and trust
Him. In emotionally devastating times, God's
promises are essential to our spiritual welfare.

His Word is therefore a compass, a guide,
and an instruction book to life. Just as we use
instruction manuals at work or in the kitchen,
we are to use God's Word as our resource
for wisdom and truth. No one would think
of baking a cake without a recipe, nor would
a mechanic rebuild a car engine without a
manual.

Some of God's promises are conditional,
but we can stand in faith on all of them. It's
not a matter of naming and claiming a promise, however; promises should be coupled with
prayer and an earnestness to know God's will
for our lives. While God wants each of us to
experience His best, He also wants us to know
and enjoy His presence in a personal way
that best expresses His sufficiency. Claiming
a promise without leadership from His Holy
Spirit will lead to disappointment, disillusionment, and frustration.

At times God brings a specific Scripture to
mind that ministers His hope and reassurance
to our hearts. At other times, He challenges us
to pray and seek His wisdom on a certain issue.
When we look to God in faith, He will lead
us according to His will. Of course, this may
not happen overnight. Many times God wants
us to meditate on a certain Scripture over a
period of time before He gives His guidance.

When King David sought God's heart
regarding his desire to build the temple, the
Bible says: "Then David the king went in and
sat before the LORD" (2 Sam. 7:18). David
didn't order his men to begin construction.
He *waited* for God's leadership—and it was a
good thing he did, because the Lord wanted
David's son Solomon to do the job instead.

God honored David's attitude, however,
and gave him a wonderful promise: "Your
house and your kingdom shall endure before
Me forever; your throne shall be established
forever" (2 Sam. 7:16). The Lord always honors our desire to seek His guidance and wisdom. If we will come to God expecting Him
to answer, He will never disappoint us.

In Daniel's day, God spoke through visions,
dreams, and sometimes audibly. Today, He
speaks primarily through His Word, since He
never wants us involved in anything that contradicts Scripture. Any verse can be taken out
of context and twisted. But if we are true to
God's Word and understand Scripture within
its context, then we will realize how to apply
His principles and promises to our lives—and
find strength to cling to the Lord in the most
difficult situations. Instead of being emotionally blown one way and then another, we learn
to stand firm in our commitment and trust in
Christ.

Therefore, consider God's promises your
spiritual anchors. Once you learn to follow
Him, pursue His lead wherever He goes
because He never fails to keep His promises.
Rather, He is teaching you to depend upon
Him through meditating on His Word and
listening for His voice.

Are you willing to patiently wait for Him to
fulfill everything He has promised you and rescue you as He did Daniel? Never try putting
God on your time schedule. Instead, cling to
Him, anchor your heart to His Word, and
leave room for Him to bring everything
together according to His plan and timing.
You'll be glad you did. ❖

and returned to his place, and Balak also went his way.

Psalm 33:18–22

18 Behold, the eye of the LORD is on
     those who fear Him,
    On those who hope for His
     lovingkindness,
19 To deliver their soul from death
    And to keep them alive in famine.
✷ 20 Our soul waits for the LORD;
    He is our help and our shield.
21 For our heart rejoices in Him,
    Because we trust in His holy name.
22 Let Your lovingkindness, O LORD,
     be upon us,
    According as we have hoped in You.

Proverbs 11:27

✷ 27 He who diligently seeks good seeks
     favor,
    But he who seeks evil, evil will
     come to him.

Mark 13:1–20

13 AS He was going out of the temple, one of His disciples *said to Him, "Teacher, behold what wonderful stones and what wonderful buildings!"
➤ 2 And Jesus said to him, "Do you see these great buildings? Not one stone will be left upon another which will not be torn down."
3 As He was sitting on the Mount of Olives opposite the temple, Peter and James and John and Andrew were questioning Him privately,
4 "Tell us, when will these things be, and what *will be* the sign when all these things are going to be fulfilled?"
5 And Jesus began to say to them, "See to it that no one misleads you.
6 "Many will come in My name, saying, 'I am *He!'* and will mislead many.
7 "When you hear of wars and rumors of wars, do not be frightened; *those things* must take place; but *that is* not yet the end.

8 "For nation will rise up against nation, and kingdom against kingdom; there will be earthquakes in various places; there will *also* be famines. These things are *merely* the beginning of birth pangs.
9 "But be on your guard; for they will deliver you to *the* courts, and you will be flogged in *the* synagogues, and you will stand before governors and kings for My sake, as a testimony to them.
10 "The gospel must first be preached to all the nations.
11 "When they arrest you and hand you over, do not worry beforehand about ✷ what you are to say, but say whatever is given you in that hour; for it is not you who speak, but *it is* the Holy Spirit.
12 "Brother will betray brother to death, and a father *his* child; and children will rise up against parents and have them put to death.
13 "You will be hated by all because of ◄ My name, but the one who endures to the end, he will be saved.
14 "But when you see the ABOMINATION OF DESOLATION standing where it should not be (let the reader understand), then

---

LIFE LESSONS

➤ **Mark 13:2 — *"Not one stone will be left upon another which will not be torn down."***

*W*e know the stones used to build Herod's temple were immense and appeared impenetrable, which is why the people were shocked when Jesus said it would be destroyed. However, we also know that Jesus' prophesy came true in A.D. 70, when Titus' Roman armies destroyed the temple. Remember, no matter how large the obstacles, God's Word always remains true.

➤ **Mark 13:13 — *"You will be hated by all because of My name."***

*M*illions of people have died throughout history for their faith in Jesus Christ. In fact, the intensity of persecution continues to grow in modern times, and more believers will die this year than did in the early church. We must be willing to suffer abuse for our connection to Christ because eternity is more important than our present sufferings (Rom 8:18; 2 Cor. 4:17, 18).

those who are in Judea must flee to the mountains.

15 "The one who is on the housetop must not go down, or go in to get anything out of his house;

16 and the one who is in the field must not turn back to get his coat.

17 "But woe to those who are pregnant and to those who are nursing babies in those days!

18 "But pray that it may not happen in the winter.

19 "For those days will be a *time of* tribulation such as has not occurred since the beginning of the creation which God created until now, and never will.

20 "Unless the Lord had shortened *those* days, no life would have been saved; but for the sake of the elect, whom He chose, He shortened the days.

Numbers 25:1—26:65

25 WHILE Israel remained at Shittim, the people began to play the harlot with the daughters of Moab.

2 For they invited the people to the sacrifices of their gods, and the people ate and bowed down to their gods.

3 So Israel joined themselves to Baal of Peor, and the LORD was angry against Israel.

4 The LORD said to Moses, "Take all the leaders of the people and execute them in broad daylight before the LORD, so that the fierce anger of the LORD may turn away from Israel."

5 So Moses said to the judges of Israel, "Each of you slay his men who have joined themselves to Baal of Peor."

6 Then behold, one of the sons of Israel came and brought to his relatives a Midianite woman, in the sight of Moses and in the sight of all the congregation of the sons of Israel, while they were weeping at the doorway of the tent of meeting.

7 When Phinehas the son of Eleazar, the son of Aaron the priest, saw it, he

arose from the midst of the congregation and took a spear in his hand,

8 and he went after the man of Israel into the tent and pierced both of them through, the man of Israel and the woman, through the body. So the plague on the sons of Israel was checked.

9 Those who died by the plague were 24,000.

10 Then the LORD spoke to Moses, saying,

11 "Phinehas the son of Eleazar, the son of Aaron the priest, has turned away My wrath from the sons of Israel in that he was jealous with My jealousy among them, so that I did not destroy the sons of Israel in My jealousy.

12 "Therefore say, 'Behold, I give him My covenant of peace;

13 and it shall be for him and his descendants after him, a covenant of a perpetual priesthood, because he was jealous for his God and made atonement for the sons of Israel.'"

14 Now the name of the slain man of Israel who was slain with the Midianite woman, was Zimri the son of Salu, a leader of a father's household among the Simeonites.

15 The name of the Midianite woman who was slain was Cozbi the daughter of Zur, who was head of the people of a father's household in Midian.

16 Then the LORD spoke to Moses, saying,

17 "Be hostile to the Midianites and strike them;

18 for they have been hostile to you with their tricks, with which they have deceived you in the affair of Peor and in the affair of Cozbi, the daughter of the leader

---

LIFE LESSONS

➤ **Numbers 25:2 —** *For they invited the people to the sacrifices of their gods, and the people ate and bowed down to their gods.*

*E*ven a polite invitation to worship any god other than the Lord ought to be immediately and firmly rejected. We are to serve God alone—no exceptions.

PHINEHAS: A Man with a Zeal for God

NUMBERS 25:12, 13

*P*hinehas, the son of Eleazar and the grandson of the high priest Aaron, was a man noted by God for his zeal. God highly esteemed him and gave him a remarkable promise because of his passion (Num. 25:12, 13).

And how did Phinehas earn such favor? He took a javelin in hand and executed a wicked Israelite who had brazenly committed adultery with a pagan woman in full sight of the nation. The quick action of Phinehas stopped a divine plague that took the lives of 24,000 sinning Israelites. And the Lord lauded him for his godly zeal.

As believers, we are to have a passion for God. Today, the word *passion* often carries a sexual connotation, but the true meaning of the word is "an overwhelming, strong desire," which can be a strong desire for matters of the spirit. Like Phinehas, believers are to have an urgency, a fervor, a zealous desire for the Lord and everything related to Him.

---

of Midian, their sister who was slain on the day of the plague because of Peor."

26 THEN it came about after the plague, that the LORD spoke to Moses and to Eleazar the son of Aaron the priest, saying,

2 "Take a census of all the congregation of the sons of Israel from twenty years old and upward, by their fathers' households, whoever is able to go out to war in Israel."

3 So Moses and Eleazar the priest spoke with them in the plains of Moab by the Jordan at Jericho, saying,

4 "Take a census of the people from twenty years old and upward, as the LORD has commanded Moses."

Now the sons of Israel who came out of the land of Egypt *were:*

5 Reuben, Israel's firstborn, the sons of Reuben: *of* Hanoch, the family of the Hanochites; of Pallu, the family of the Palluites;

6 of Hezron, the family of the Hezronites; of Carmi, the family of the Carmites.

7 These are the families of the Reubenites, and those who were numbered of them were 43,730.

8 The son of Pallu: Eliab.

9 The sons of Eliab: Nemuel and Dathan and Abiram. These are the Dathan and Abiram who were called by the congregation, who contended against Moses and against Aaron in the company of Korah, when they contended against the LORD,

10 and the earth opened its mouth and swallowed them up along with Korah, when that company died, when the fire devoured 250 men, so that they became a warning.

11 The sons of Korah, however, did not die.

12 The sons of Simeon according to their families: of Nemuel, the family of the Nemuelites; of Jamin, the family of the Jaminites; of Jachin, the family of the Jachinites;

13 of Zerah, the family of the Zerahites; of Shaul, the family of the Shaulites.

14 These are the families of the Simeonites, 22,200.

15 The sons of Gad according to their families: of Zephon, the family of the Zephonites; of Haggi, the family of the Haggites; of Shuni, the family of the Shunites;

16 of Ozni, the family of the Oznites; of Eri, the family of the Erites;

17 of Arod, the family of the Arodites; of Areli, the family of the Arelites.

18 These are the families of the sons of Gad according to those who were numbered of them, 40,500.

19 The sons of Judah *were* Er and Onan, but Er and Onan died in the land of Canaan.

20 The sons of Judah according to their families were: of Shelah, the family of the Shelanites; of Perez, the family of

the Perezites; of Zerah, the family of the Zerahites.

21 The sons of Perez were: of Hezron, the family of the Hezronites; of Hamul, the family of the Hamulites.

22 These are the families of Judah according to those who were numbered of them, 76,500.

23 The sons of Issachar according to their families: of Tola, the family of the Tolaites; of Puvah, the family of the Punites;

24 of Jashub, the family of the Jashubites; of Shimron, the family of the Shimronites.

25 These are the families of Issachar according to those who were numbered of them, 64,300.

26 The sons of Zebulun according to their families: of Sered, the family of the Seredites; of Elon, the family of the Elonites; of Jahleel, the family of the Jahleelites.

27 These are the families of the Zebulunites according to those who were numbered of them, 60,500.

28 The sons of Joseph according to their families: Manasseh and Ephraim.

29 The sons of Manasseh: of Machir, the family of the Machirites; and Machir became the father of Gilead: of Gilead, the family of the Gileadites.

30 These are the sons of Gilead: of Iezer, the family of the Iezerites; of Helek, the family of the Helekites;

31 and of Asriel, the family of the Asrielites; and of Shechem, the family of the Shechemites;

32 and of Shemida, the family of the Shemidaites; and of Hepher, the family of the Hepherites.

33 Now Zelophehad the son of Hepher had no sons, but only daughters; and the names of the daughters of Zelophehad were Mahlah, Noah, Hoglah, Milcah and Tirzah.

34 These are the families of Manasseh; and those who were numbered of them were 52,700.

35 These are the sons of Ephraim according to their families: of Shuthelah, the family of the Shuthelahites; of Becher, the family of the Becherites; of Tahan, the family of the Tahanites.

36 These are the sons of Shuthelah: of Eran, the family of the Eranites.

37 These are the families of the sons of Ephraim according to those who were

numbered of them, 32,500. These are the sons of Joseph according to their families.

38 The sons of Benjamin according to their families: of Bela, the family of the Belaites; of Ashbel, the family of the Ashbelites; of Ahiram, the family of the Ahiramites;

39 of Shephupham, the family of the Shuphamites; of Hupham, the family of the Huphamites.

40 The sons of Bela were Ard and Naaman: of Ard, the family of the Ardites; of Naaman, the family of the Naamites.

41 These are the sons of Benjamin according to their families; and those who were numbered of them were 45,600.

42 These are the sons of Dan according to their families: of Shuham, the family of the Shuhamites. These are the families of Dan according to their families.

43 All the families of the Shuhamites, according to those who were numbered of them, were 64,400.

44 The sons of Asher according to their families: of Imnah, the family of the Imnites; of Ishvi, the family of the Ishvites; of Beriah, the family of the Beriites.

45 Of the sons of Beriah: of Heber, the family of the Heberites; of Malchiel, the family of the Malchielites.

46 The name of the daughter of Asher was Serah.

47 These are the families of the sons of Asher according to those who were numbered of them, 53,400.

48 The sons of Naphtali according to their families: of Jahzeel, the family of the Jahzeelites; of Guni, the family of the Gunites;

49 of Jezer, the family of the Jezerites; of Shillem, the family of the Shillemites.

50 These are the families of Naphtali according to their families; and those who were numbered of them were 45,400.

51 These are those who were numbered of the sons of Israel, 601,730.

52 Then the LORD spoke to Moses, saying,

53 "Among these the land shall be divided for an inheritance according to the number of names.

54 "To the larger group you shall increase their inheritance, and to the smaller group you shall diminish their inheritance; each shall be given their inheritance according to those who were numbered of them.

55 "But the land shall be divided by lot. They shall receive their inheritance according to the names of the tribes of their fathers.

56 "According to the selection by lot, their inheritance shall be divided between the larger and the smaller *groups*."

57 These are those who were numbered of the Levites according to their families: of Gershon, the family of the Gershonites; of Kohath, the family of the Kohathites; of Merari, the family of the Merarites.

58 These are the families of Levi: the family of the Libnites, the family of the Hebronites, the family of the Mahlites, the family of the Mushites, the family of the Korahites. Kohath became the father of Amram.

59 The name of Amram's wife was Jochebed, the daughter of Levi, who was born to Levi in Egypt; and she bore to Amram: Aaron and Moses and their sister Miriam.

60 To Aaron were born Nadab and Abihu, Eleazar and Ithamar.

61 But Nadab and Abihu died when they offered strange fire before the LORD.

62 Those who were numbered of them were 23,000, every male from a month old and upward, for they were not numbered among the sons of Israel since no inheritance was given to them among the sons of Israel.

63 These are those who were numbered by Moses and Eleazar the priest, who numbered the sons of Israel in the plains of Moab by the Jordan at Jericho.

64 But among these there was not a man of those who were numbered by Moses and Aaron the priest, who numbered the sons of Israel in the wilderness of Sinai.

➤ 65 For the LORD had said of them, "They shall surely die in the wilderness." And not a man was left of them, except Caleb the son of Jephunneh and Joshua the son of Nun.

Psalm 34:1–7

A Psalm of David when he feigned madness before Abimelech, who drove him away and he departed.

➤ **34** I WILL bless the LORD at all times;

His praise shall continually be in my mouth.

2 My soul will make its boast in the LORD;
The humble will hear it and rejoice.

3 O magnify the LORD with me,
And let us exalt His name together.

4 I sought the LORD, and He answered me,
And delivered me from all my fears.

5 They looked to Him and were radiant,
And their faces will never be ashamed.

6 This poor man cried, and the LORD heard him
And saved him out of all his troubles.

7 The angel of the LORD encamps around those who fear Him,
And rescues them.

Proverbs 11:28

28 He who trusts in his riches will fall,
But the righteous will flourish like the *green* leaf.

LIFE LESSONS

➤ **Numbers 26:65** — *And not a man was left of them, except Caleb the son of Jephunneh and Joshua the son of Nun.*

God had said all those who had accepted the spies' report and refused to enter Canaan would die in the wilderness, and His word came true. It always does.

➤ **Psalm 34:1** — *I will bless the LORD at all times; His praise shall continually be in my mouth.*

If it's not already your practice, praise God throughout the day. Exalt Him when you wake up, when you eat, when you leave the house, and when you return. An attitude of adoring trust in the Lord will make an amazing difference in your life.

Mark 13:21–37

21 "And then if anyone says to you, 'Behold, here is the Christ'; or, 'Behold, He is there'; do not believe him;
22 for false Christs and false prophets will arise, and will show signs and wonders, in order to lead astray, if possible, the elect.
➤ 23 "But take heed; behold, I have told you everything in advance.
24 "But in those days, after that tribulation, THE SUN WILL BE DARKENED AND THE MOON WILL NOT GIVE ITS LIGHT,
25 AND THE STARS WILL BE FALLING from heaven, and the powers that are in the heavens will be shaken.
26 "Then they will see THE SON OF MAN COMING IN CLOUDS with great power and glory.
✳ 27 "And then He will send forth the angels, and will gather together His elect from the four winds, from the farthest end of the earth to the farthest end of heaven.
28 "Now learn the parable from the fig tree: when its branch has already become tender and puts forth its leaves, you know that summer is near.
29 "Even so, you too, when you see these things happening, recognize that He is near, right at the door.
30 "Truly I say to you, this generation will not pass away until all these things take place.
31 "Heaven and earth will pass away, but My words will not pass away.
32 "But of that day or hour no one knows, not even the angels in heaven, nor the Son, but the Father alone.
33 "Take heed, keep on the alert; for

you do not know when the appointed time will come.
34 "It is like a man away on a journey, ◄ who upon leaving his house and putting his slaves in charge, assigning to each one his task, also commanded the doorkeeper to stay on the alert.
35 "Therefore, be on the alert—for you do not know when the master of the house is coming, whether in the evening, at midnight, or when the rooster crows, or in the morning—
36 in case he should come suddenly and find you asleep.
37 "What I say to you I say to all, 'Be on the alert!'"

Numbers 27:1—28:31

27 THEN the daughters of Zelophehad, the son of Hepher, the son of Gilead, the son of Machir, the son of Manasseh, of the families of Manasseh the son of Joseph, came near; and these

are the names of his daughters: Mahlah, Noah and Hoglah and Milcah and Tirzah.
2 They stood before Moses and before Eleazar the priest and before the leaders and all the congregation, at the doorway of the tent of meeting, saying,
3 "Our father died in the wilderness, yet he was not among the company of

those who gathered themselves together against the LORD in the company of Korah; but he died in his own sin, and he had no sons.

4 "Why should the name of our father be withdrawn from among his family because he had no son? Give us a possession among our father's brothers."

5 So Moses brought their case before the LORD.

6 Then the LORD spoke to Moses, saying,

7 "The daughters of Zelophehad are right in *their* statements. You shall surely give them a hereditary possession among their father's brothers, and you shall transfer the inheritance of their father to them.

8 "Further, you shall speak to the sons of Israel, saying, 'If a man dies and has no son, then you shall transfer his inheritance to his daughter.

9 'If he has no daughter, then you shall give his inheritance to his brothers.

10 'If he has no brothers, then you shall give his inheritance to his father's brothers.

11 'If his father has no brothers, then you shall give his inheritance to his nearest relative in his own family, and he shall possess it; and it shall be a statutory ordinance to the sons of Israel, just as the LORD commanded Moses.'"

➤ 12 Then the LORD said to Moses, "Go up to this mountain of Abarim, and see the land which I have given to the sons of Israel.

13 "When you have seen it, you too will be gathered to your people, as Aaron your brother was;

14 for in the wilderness of Zin, during the strife of the congregation, you rebelled against My command to treat Me as holy before their eyes at the water." (These are the waters of Meribah of Kadesh in the wilderness of Zin.)

15 Then Moses spoke to the LORD, saying,

16 "May the LORD, the God of the spirits of all flesh, appoint a man over the congregation,

17 who will go out and come in before them, and who will lead them out and bring them in, so that the congregation of the LORD will not be like sheep which have no shepherd."

18 So the LORD said to Moses, "Take ◄ Joshua the son of Nun, a man in whom is the Spirit, and lay your hand on him;

19 and have him stand before Eleazar

LIFE LESSONS

➤ **Numbers 27:12 —** *"Go up to this mountain of Abarim, and see the land which I have given to the sons of Israel."*

*G*od would not allow Moses to enter the Promised Land because of his public disobedience at the waters of Meribah. But in His grace, God did allow him to view the land from a distance. Even in judgment, God is merciful.

➤ **Numbers 27:18 —** *"Take Joshua the son of Nun, a man in whom is the Spirit, and lay your hand on him."*

*G*od authorized Moses to make Joshua, "a man in whom is the Spirit," the next leader of Israel. Spirit-filled leadership is the only kind of leadership worth following. The best leaders know to follow God's example and direction.

Life Examples:

JOSHUA: The Need for Courage

NUMBERS 27:15–23

*A*ny time you take a risk for God, you are going to need courage. Joshua certainly understood this requirement.

The Lord challenged Joshua with the mission of leading the nation of Israel across the Jordan River so they might claim the Land of Promise. Before allowing the people to proceed, the Lord exhorted Joshua three times to have courage, telling him to remember the promises He had made to his forefathers, reminding him to obey the Law of Moses, and promising Joshua He would be with him every step of the way.

Fear and discouragement are subject to your will, especially when you are walking in step with God. Through faith in Him, you can rule over them, not them over you. Remind yourself daily of what you heard the Lord say in His Word, stay close to Him, and refuse to allow yourself to give in to fear and discouragement.

the priest and before all the congregation, and commission him in their sight.
20 "You shall put some of your authority
on him, in order that all the congregation
of the sons of Israel may obey *him*.
21 "Moreover, he shall stand before Eleazar the priest, who shall inquire for
him by the judgment of the Urim before
the LORD. At his command they shall go
out and at his command they shall come
in, *both* he and the sons of Israel with
him, even all the congregation."
22 Moses did just as the LORD commanded him; and he took Joshua and set
him before Eleazar the priest and before
all the congregation.
23 Then he laid his hands on him and
commissioned him, just as the LORD had
spoken through Moses.

28 THEN the LORD spoke to Moses,
saying,
2 "Command the sons of Israel and say
to them, 'You shall be careful to present
My offering, My food for My offerings by
fire, of a soothing aroma to Me, at their
appointed time.'
3 "You shall say to them, 'This is the
offering by fire which you shall offer to
the LORD: two male lambs one year old
without defect *as* a continual burnt offering every day.
4 'You shall offer the one lamb in the
morning and the other lamb you shall
offer at twilight;
5 also a tenth of an ephah of fine flour
for a grain offering, mixed with a fourth
of a hin of beaten oil.
6 'It is a continual burnt offering which
was ordained in Mount Sinai as a soothing aroma, an offering by fire to the
LORD.
7 'Then the drink offering with it *shall
be* a fourth of a hin for each lamb, in the
holy place you shall pour out a drink offering of strong drink to the LORD.
8 'The other lamb you shall offer at
twilight; as the grain offering of the
morning and as its drink offering, you
shall offer it, an offering by fire, a soothing aroma to the LORD.
9 'Then on the sabbath day two male
lambs one year old without defect, and
two-tenths *of an ephah* of fine flour
mixed with oil as a grain offering, and its
drink offering:
10 'This *is* the burnt offering of every

sabbath in addition to the continual
burnt offering and its drink offering.
11 'Then at the beginning of each of
your months you shall present a burnt
offering to the LORD: two bulls and one
ram, seven male lambs one year old
without defect;
12 and three-tenths *of an ephah* of fine
flour mixed with oil for a grain offering,
for each bull; and two-tenths of fine flour
mixed with oil for a grain offering, for
the one ram;
13 and a tenth *of an ephah* of fine flour
mixed with oil for a grain offering for
each lamb, for a burnt offering of a
soothing aroma, an offering by fire to the
LORD.
14 'Their drink offerings shall be half
a hin of wine for a bull and a third of a
hin for the ram and a fourth of a hin for
a lamb; this is the burnt offering of each
month throughout the months of the
year.
15 'And one male goat for a sin offering
to the LORD; it shall be offered with its
drink offering in addition to the continual burnt offering.
16 'Then on the fourteenth day of the
first month shall be the LORD's Passover.
17 'On the fifteenth day of this month
shall be a feast, unleavened bread *shall
be* eaten for seven days.
18 'On the first day *shall be* a holy convocation; you shall do no laborious work.
19 'You shall present an offering by fire,
a burnt offering to the LORD: two bulls
and one ram and seven male lambs one
year old, having them without defect.
20 'For their grain offering, you shall
offer fine flour mixed with oil: three-
tenths *of an ephah* for a bull and two-
tenths for the ram.
21 'A tenth *of an ephah* you shall offer
for each of the seven lambs;
22 and one male goat for a sin offering
to make atonement for you.
23 'You shall present these besides the
burnt offering of the morning, which is
for a continual burnt offering.
24 'After this manner you shall present
daily, for seven days, the food of the
offering by fire, of a soothing aroma to
the LORD; it shall be presented with its
drink offering in addition to the continual burnt offering.
25 'On the seventh day you shall have a

holy convocation; you shall do no laborious work.

26 'Also on the day of the first fruits, when you present a new grain offering to the LORD in your *Feast of* Weeks, you shall have a holy convocation; you shall do no laborious work.

27 'You shall offer a burnt offering for a soothing aroma to the LORD: two young bulls, one ram, seven male lambs one year old;

28 and their grain offering, fine flour mixed with oil: three-tenths *of an ephah* for each bull, two-tenths for the one ram,

29 a tenth for each of the seven lambs;

30 *also* one male goat to make atonement for you.

31 'Besides the continual burnt offering and its grain offering, you shall present *them* with their drink offerings. They shall be without defect.

Psalm 34:8–14

8   O taste and see that the LORD is
  good;
  How blessed is the man who takes
  refuge in Him!

9   O fear the LORD, you His saints;
  For to those who fear Him there is
  no want.

10 The young lions do lack and suffer
  hunger;
  But they who seek the LORD shall
  not be in want of any good thing.

11 Come, you children, listen to me;
  I will teach you the fear of the
  LORD.

12 Who is the man who desires life
  And loves *length of* days that he
  may see good?

13 Keep your tongue from evil
  And your lips from speaking
  deceit.

14 Depart from evil and do good;
  Seek peace and pursue it.

Proverbs 11:29

29 He who troubles his own house will
  inherit wind,
  And the foolish will be servant to
  the wisehearted.

Mark 14:1–26

14 NOW the Passover and Unleavened Bread were two days away; and the chief priests and the scribes were seeking how to seize Him by stealth and kill *Him;*

2   for they were saying, "Not during the festival, otherwise there might be a riot of the people."

3   While He was in Bethany at the home of Simon the leper, and reclining *at the table,* there came a woman with an alabaster vial of very costly perfume of pure nard; *and* she broke the vial and poured it over His head.

4   But some were indignantly *remarking* to one another, "Why has this perfume been wasted?

5   "For this perfume might have been sold for over three hundred denarii, and *the money* given to the poor." And they were scolding her.

6   But Jesus said, "Let her alone; why do you bother her? She has done a good deed to Me.

7   "For you always have the poor with you, and whenever you wish you can do good to them; but you do not always have Me.

8   "She has done what she could; she has anointed My body beforehand for the burial.

9   "Truly I say to you, wherever the gospel is preached in the whole world, what this woman has done will also be spoken of in memory of her."

10 Then Judas Iscariot, who was one of the twelve, went off to the chief priests in order to betray Him to them.

11 They were glad when they heard *this,* and promised to give him money.

LIFE LESSONS

➤ **Mark 14:10 —** *Then Judas Iscariot, who was one of the twelve, went off to the chief priests in order to betray Him to them.*

*J*udas went to the religious authorities with his offer to betray Jesus immediately after Jesus rebuked him for criticizing a woman who had honored the Lord with an expensive gift (John 12:6).

And he *began* seeking how to betray Him at an opportune time.

12 On the first day of Unleavened Bread, when the Passover *lamb* was being sacrificed, His disciples *said to Him, "Where do You want us to go and prepare for You to eat the Passover?"

13 And He *sent two of His disciples and *said to them, "Go into the city, and a man will meet you carrying a pitcher of water; follow him;

14 and wherever he enters, say to the owner of the house, 'The Teacher says, "Where is My guest room in which I may eat the Passover with My disciples?"'

15 "And he himself will show you a large upper room furnished *and* ready; prepare for us there."

➤ 16 The disciples went out and came to the city, and found *it* just as He had

---

LIFE LESSONS

➤ **Mark 14:16 — *The disciples went out and came to the city, and found it just as He had told them.***

*J*ust as the disciples found the Passover preparations as Jesus had told them, so we will find life to be just as He tells us. We will always find our smoothest life path by carefully following Jesus' instructions.

---

told them; and they prepared the Passover.

17 When it was evening He *came with the twelve.

18 As they were reclining *at the table* and eating, Jesus said, "Truly I say to you that one of you will betray Me—one who is eating with Me."

19 They began to be grieved and to say to Him one by one, "Surely not I?"

20 And He said to them, "*It is* one of the twelve, one who dips with Me in the bowl.

21 "For the Son of Man *is to* go just as it is written of Him; but woe to that man by whom the Son of Man is betrayed! *It would have been* good for that man if he had not been born."

22 While they were eating, He took *some* bread, and after a blessing He broke *it*, and gave *it* to them, and said, "Take *it*; this is My body."

23 And when He had taken a cup *and* given thanks, He gave *it* to them, and they all drank from it.

24 And He said to them, "This is My ✳ blood of the covenant, which is poured out for many.

25 "Truly I say to you, I will never again drink of the fruit of the vine until that day when I drink it new in the kingdom of God."

26 After singing a hymn, they went out to the Mount of Olives.

✦ Numbers 29:1—30:16

29'NOW in the seventh month, on the first day of the month, you shall also have a holy convocation; you shall do no laborious work. It will be to you a day for blowing trumpets.

2 'You shall offer a burnt offering as a soothing aroma to the LORD: one bull, one ram, *and* seven male lambs one year old without defect;

3 also their grain offering, fine flour mixed with oil: three-tenths *of an ephah* for the bull, two-tenths for the ram,

4 and one-tenth for each of the seven lambs.

5 'Offer one male goat for a sin offering, to make atonement for you,

6 besides the burnt offering of the new moon and its grain offering, and the continual burnt offering and its grain offering, and their drink offerings, according to their ordinance, for a soothing aroma, an offering by fire to the LORD.

7 'Then on the tenth day of this seventh month you shall have a holy convocation, and you shall humble yourselves; you shall not do any work.

8 'You shall present a burnt offering to the LORD *as* a soothing aroma: one bull, one ram, seven male lambs one year old, having them without defect;

9 and their grain offering, fine flour

mixed with oil: three-tenths *of an ephah* for the bull, two-tenths for the one ram, 10 a tenth for each of the seven lambs; 11 one male goat for a sin offering, besides the sin offering of atonement and the continual burnt offering and its grain offering, and their drink offerings.

12 'Then on the fifteenth day of the seventh month you shall have a holy convocation; you shall do no laborious work, and you shall observe a feast to the LORD for seven days.

13 'You shall present a burnt offering, an offering by fire as a soothing aroma to the LORD: thirteen bulls, two rams, fourteen male lambs one year old, which are without defect;

14 and their grain offering, fine flour mixed with oil: three-tenths *of an ephah* for each of the thirteen bulls, two-tenths for each of the two rams,

15 and a tenth for each of the fourteen lambs;

16 and one male goat for a sin offering, besides the continual burnt offering, its grain offering and its drink offering.

17 'Then on the second day: twelve bulls, two rams, fourteen male lambs one year old without defect;

18 and their grain offering and their drink offerings for the bulls, for the rams and for the lambs, by their number according to the ordinance;

19 and one male goat for a sin offering, besides the continual burnt offering and its grain offering, and their drink offerings.

20 'Then on the third day: eleven bulls, two rams, fourteen male lambs one year old without defect;

21 and their grain offering and their drink offerings for the bulls, for the rams and for the lambs, by their number according to the ordinance;

22 and one male goat for a sin offering, besides the continual burnt offering and its grain offering and its drink offering.

23 'Then on the fourth day: ten bulls, two rams, fourteen male lambs one year old without defect;

24 their grain offering and their drink offerings for the bulls, for the rams and for the lambs, by their number according to the ordinance;

25 and one male goat for a sin offering, besides the continual burnt offering, its grain offering and its drink offering.

26 'Then on the fifth day: nine bulls, two rams, fourteen male lambs one year old without defect;

27 and their grain offering and their drink offerings for the bulls, for the rams and for the lambs, by their number according to the ordinance;

28 and one male goat for a sin offering, besides the continual burnt offering and its grain offering and its drink offering.

29 'Then on the sixth day: eight bulls, two rams, fourteen male lambs one year old without defect;

30 and their grain offering and their drink offerings for the bulls, for the rams and for the lambs, by their number according to the ordinance;

31 and one male goat for a sin offering, besides the continual burnt offering, its grain offering and its drink offerings.

32 'Then on the seventh day: seven bulls, two rams, fourteen male lambs one year old without defect;

33 and their grain offering and their drink offerings for the bulls, for the rams and for the lambs, by their number according to the ordinance;

34 and one male goat for a sin offering, besides the continual burnt offering, its grain offering and its drink offering.

35 'On the eighth day you shall have a solemn assembly; you shall do no laborious work.

36 'But you shall present a burnt offering, an offering by fire, as a soothing aroma to the LORD: one bull, one ram, seven male lambs one year old without defect;

37 their grain offering and their drink offerings for the bull, for the ram and for the lambs, by their number according to the ordinance;

38 and one male goat for a sin offering, besides the continual burnt offering and its grain offering and its drink offering.

39 'You shall present these to the LORD at your appointed times, besides your votive offerings and your freewill offerings, for your burnt offerings and for your grain offerings and for your drink offerings and for your peace offerings.'"

40 Moses spoke to the sons of Israel in accordance with all that the LORD had commanded Moses.

30 THEN Moses spoke to the heads of the tribes of the sons of Israel,

saying, "This is the word which the LORD has commanded.

➤ 2 "If a man makes a vow to the LORD, or takes an oath to bind himself with a binding obligation, he shall not violate his word; he shall do according to all that proceeds out of his mouth.

3 "Also if a woman makes a vow to the LORD, and binds herself by an obligation in her father's house in her youth,

4 and her father hears her vow and her obligation by which she has bound herself, and her father says nothing to her, then all her vows shall stand and every obligation by which she has bound herself shall stand.

5 "But if her father should forbid her on the day he hears of it, none of her vows or her obligations by which she has bound herself shall stand; and the LORD will forgive her because her father had forbidden her.

6 "However, if she should marry while under her vows or the rash statement of her lips by which she has bound herself,

7 and her husband hears of it and says nothing to her on the day he hears it, then her vows shall stand and her obligations by which she has bound herself shall stand.

8 "But if on the day her husband hears of it, he forbids her, then he shall annul her vow which she is under and the rash statement of her lips by which she has bound herself; and the LORD will forgive her.

9 "But the vow of a widow or of a divorced woman, everything by which she has bound herself, shall stand against her.

10 "However, if she vowed in her husband's house, or bound herself by an obligation with an oath,

11 and her husband heard it, but said nothing to her and did not forbid her, then all her vows shall stand and every obligation by which she bound herself shall stand.

12 "But if her husband indeed annuls them on the day he hears them, then whatever proceeds out of her lips concerning her vows or concerning the obligation of herself shall not stand; her husband has annulled them, and the LORD will forgive her.

13 "Every vow and every binding oath to humble herself, her husband may confirm it or her husband may annul it.

14 "But if her husband indeed says nothing to her from day to day, then he confirms all her vows or all her obligations which are on her; he has confirmed them, because he said nothing to her on the day he heard them.

15 "But if he indeed annuls them after he has heard them, then he shall bear her guilt."

16 These are the statutes which the LORD commanded Moses, as between a man and his wife, and as between a father and his daughter, while she is in her youth in her father's house.

✦ Psalm 34:15–22

15 The eyes of the LORD are toward the righteous
   And His ears are open to their cry.

16 The face of the LORD is against evildoers,
   To cut off the memory of them from the earth.

17 The righteous cry, and the LORD hears
   And delivers them out of all their troubles.

LIFE LESSONS

➤ **Numbers 30:2** — *"If a man makes a vow to the LORD . . . he shall not violate his word; he shall do according to all that proceeds out of his mouth."*

If we make a vow to God, we are not to violate it or "take it back." However, Jesus tells us that it is better not to make a vow at all, but rather to always speak forthrightly (Matt. 5:33–37).

➤ **Psalm 34:18** — *The LORD is near to the brokenhearted.*

*D*o you avoid God when you're feeling down because you feel like you're useless to Him? Friend, He knows this is when you need Him the most, and He rushes in to comfort you. He will give you His strength and courage, so turn to Him.

➤ 18 The LORD is near to the
      brokenhearted
      And saves those who are crushed in
      spirit.
19   Many are the afflictions of the
      righteous,
      But the LORD delivers him out of
      them all.
20   He keeps all his bones,
      Not one of them is broken.
21   Evil shall slay the wicked,
      And those who hate the righteous
      will be condemned.
22   The LORD redeems the soul of His
      servants,
      And none of those who take refuge
      in Him will be condemned.

◈ Proverbs 11:30, 31

✳ 30 The fruit of the righteous is a tree of
      life,
      And he who is wise wins souls.
31   If the righteous will be rewarded in
      the earth,
      How much more the wicked and the
      sinner!

◈ Mark 14:27–54

27   And Jesus *said to them, "You will
all fall away, because it is written, 'I
WILL STRIKE DOWN THE SHEPHERD, AND THE
SHEEP SHALL BE SCATTERED.'

Life Examples:

Courage by Clinging

MARK 14:32–50

*H*ow did Jesus face the Cross with
such courage, while the disciples "all
left Him and fled" (Mark 14:50)? The garden
of Gethsemane holds the answer for us. As
the disciples slept, Jesus prayed. While the disciples were giving in to the weakness of their
bodies, Jesus was drawing strength by obeying the will of God.
   When your body is tired and everything
is falling apart, you must cling to courage by
communing with God. You must pray and
draw your hope from Him.

28   "But after I have been raised, I will
go ahead of you to Galilee."
29   But Peter said to Him, "*Even* though
all may fall away, yet I will not."
30   And Jesus *said to him, "Truly I
say to you, that this very night, before
a rooster crows twice, you yourself will
deny Me three times."
31   But *Peter* kept saying insistently,
"*Even* if I have to die with You, I will not
deny You!" And they all were saying the
same thing also.
32   They *came to a place named Gethsemane; and He *said to His disciples,
"Sit here until I have prayed."
33   And He *took with Him Peter and
James and John, and began to be very
distressed and troubled.
34   And He *said to them, "My soul is
deeply grieved to the point of death; remain here and keep watch."
35   And He went a little beyond *them*, ◄
and fell to the ground and *began* to pray
that if it were possible, the hour might
pass Him by.
36   And He was saying, "Abba! Father!

LIFE LESSONS

➤ **Mark 14:35 — He . . . fell to the
ground and began to pray that if it were
possible, the hour might pass Him by.**

*I*n the garden of Gethsemane, the
will of Jesus regarding the will of
His Father was tested—yet Jesus did not
sin. He willingly submitted Himself to
His Father's will, even though He desired
something else.

   Jesus warned, "Keep watching and praying that you may not come into temptation;
the spirit is willing, but the flesh is weak"
(Mark 14:38). Fear will grip you unless you
are tuned in to what God is doing—unless
you are aware of His will and are committed to doing it. This is doubly true when you
are physically weak—when you are weary,
hungry, or sick.
   Friend, are you facing a situation that
overwhelms and frightens you? Then, pray.
Not only will God give you the wisdom to deal
with the circumstances according to His will,
but He will give you His strength to face them
with courage.

All things are possible for You; remove this cup from Me; yet not what I will, but what You will."

37 And He *came and *found them sleeping, and *said to Peter, "Simon, are you asleep? Could you not keep watch for one hour?

38 "Keep watching and praying that you may not come into temptation; the spirit is willing, but the flesh is weak."

39 Again He went away and prayed, saying the same words.

40 And again He came and found them sleeping, for their eyes were very heavy; and they did not know what to answer Him.

41 And He *came the third time, and *said to them, "Are you still sleeping and resting? It is enough; the hour has come; behold, the Son of Man is being betrayed into the hands of sinners.

42 "Get up, let us be going; behold, the one who betrays Me is at hand!"

43 Immediately while He was still speaking, Judas, one of the twelve, *came up accompanied by a crowd with swords and clubs, who were from the chief priests and the scribes and the elders.

44 Now he who was betraying Him had given them a signal, saying, "Whomever I kiss, He is the one; seize Him and lead Him away under guard."

45 After coming, Judas immediately went to Him, saying, "Rabbi!" and kissed Him.

46 They laid hands on Him and seized Him.

47 But one of those who stood by drew his sword, and struck the slave of the high priest and cut off his ear.

48 And Jesus said to them, "Have you come out with swords and clubs to arrest Me, as you would against a robber?

49 "Every day I was with you in the temple teaching, and you did not seize Me; but this has taken place to fulfill the Scriptures."

50 And they all left Him and fled.

51 A young man was following Him, wearing nothing but a linen sheet over his naked body; and they *seized him.

52 But he pulled free of the linen sheet and escaped naked.

53 They led Jesus away to the high priest; and all the chief priests and the elders and the scribes *gathered together.

54 Peter had followed Him at a distance, right into the courtyard of the high priest; and he was sitting with the officers and warming himself at the fire.

Numbers 31:1—32:42

31 THEN the LORD spoke to Moses, saying,

2 "Take full vengeance for the sons of Israel on the Midianites; afterward you will be gathered to your people."

3 Moses spoke to the people, saying, "Arm men from among you for the war, that they may go against Midian to execute the LORD'S vengeance on Midian.

4 "A thousand from each tribe of all the tribes of Israel you shall send to the war."

5 So there were furnished from the thousands of Israel, a thousand from each tribe, twelve thousand armed for war.

6 Moses sent them, a thousand from each tribe, to the war, and Phinehas the son of Eleazar the priest, to the war with them, and the holy vessels and the trumpets for the alarm in his hand.

7 So they made war against Midian, just as the LORD had commanded Moses, and they killed every male.

8 They killed the kings of Midian along with the rest of their slain: Evi and Rekem and Zur and Hur and Reba, the five kings of Midian; they also killed Balaam the son of Beor with the sword.

9 The sons of Israel captured the women of Midian and their little ones; and all their cattle and all their flocks and all their goods they plundered.

10 Then they burned all their cities where they lived and all their camps with fire.

11 They took all the spoil and all the prey, both of man and of beast.

12 They brought the captives and the prey and the spoil to Moses, and to

Eleazar the priest and to the congregation of the sons of Israel, to the camp at the plains of Moab, which are by the Jordan *opposite* Jericho.

13 Moses and Eleazar the priest and all the leaders of the congregation went out to meet them outside the camp.

14 Moses was angry with the officers of the army, the captains of thousands and the captains of hundreds, who had come from service in the war.

15 And Moses said to them, "Have you spared all the women?

16 "Behold, these caused the sons of Israel, through the counsel of Balaam, to trespass against the LORD in the matter of Peor, so the plague was among the congregation of the LORD.

17 "Now therefore, kill every male among the little ones, and kill every woman who has known man intimately.

18 "But all the girls who have not known man intimately, spare for yourselves.

19 "And you, camp outside the camp seven days; whoever has killed any person and whoever has touched any slain, purify yourselves, you and your captives, on the third day and on the seventh day.

20 "You shall purify for yourselves every garment and every article of leather and all the work of goats' *hair,* and all articles of wood."

21 Then Eleazar the priest said to the men of war who had gone to battle, "This is the statute of the law which the LORD has commanded Moses:

22 only the gold and the silver, the bronze, the iron, the tin and the lead,

23 everything that can stand the fire, you shall pass through the fire, and it shall be clean, but it shall be purified with water for impurity. But whatever cannot stand the fire you shall pass through the water.

24 "And you shall wash your clothes on the seventh day and be clean, and afterward you may enter the camp."

25 Then the LORD spoke to Moses, saying,

26 "You and Eleazar the priest and the heads of the fathers' *households* of the congregation take a count of the booty that was captured, both of man and of animal;

27 and divide the booty between the warriors who went out to battle and all the congregation.

28 "Levy a tax for the LORD from the men of war who went out to battle, one in five hundred of the persons and of the cattle and of the donkeys and of the sheep;

29 take it from their half and give it to Eleazar the priest, as an offering to the LORD.

30 "From the sons of Israel's half, you shall take one drawn out of every fifty of the persons, of the cattle, of the donkeys and of the sheep, from all the animals, and give them to the Levites who keep charge of the tabernacle of the LORD."

31 Moses and Eleazar the priest did just as the LORD had commanded Moses.

32 Now the booty that remained from the spoil which the men of war had plundered was 675,000 sheep,

33 and 72,000 cattle,

34 and 61,000 donkeys,

35 and of human beings, of the women who had not known man intimately, all the persons were 32,000.

36 The half, the portion of those who went out to war, was *as follows:* the number of sheep was 337,500,

37 and the LORD's levy of the sheep was 675;

38 and the cattle were 36,000, from which the LORD's levy was 72;

39 and the donkeys were 30,500, from which the LORD's levy was 61;

40 and the human beings were 16,000, from whom the LORD's levy was 32 persons.

41 Moses gave the levy *which was* the LORD's offering to Eleazar the priest, just as the LORD had commanded Moses.

42 As for the sons of Israel's half, which Moses separated from the men who had gone to war—

43 now the congregation's half was 337,500 sheep,

44 and 36,000 cattle,

45 and 30,500 donkeys,

46 and the human beings were 16,000—

47 and from the sons of Israel's half, Moses took one drawn out of every fifty, both of man and of animals, and gave them to the Levites, who kept charge of the tabernacle of the LORD, just as the LORD had commanded Moses.

48 Then the officers who were over the thousands of the army, the captains of thousands and the captains of hundreds, approached Moses,

49 and they said to Moses, "Your ser-

vants have taken a census of men of war who are in our charge, and no man of us is missing.

50 "So we have brought as an offering to the LORD what each man found, articles of gold, armlets and bracelets, signet rings, earrings and necklaces, to make atonement for ourselves before the LORD."

51 Moses and Eleazar the priest took the gold from them, all kinds of wrought articles.

52 All the gold of the offering which they offered up to the LORD, from the captains of thousands and the captains of hundreds, was 16,750 shekels.

53 The men of war had taken booty, every man for himself.

54 So Moses and Eleazar the priest took the gold from the captains of thousands and of hundreds, and brought it to the tent of meeting as a memorial for the sons of Israel before the LORD.

32 NOW the sons of Reuben and the sons of Gad had an exceedingly large number of livestock. So when they saw the land of Jazer and the land of Gilead, that it was indeed a place suitable for livestock,

2 the sons of Gad and the sons of Reuben came and spoke to Moses and to Eleazar the priest and to the leaders of the congregation, saying,

3 "Ataroth, Dibon, Jazer, Nimrah, Heshbon, Elealeh, Sebam, Nebo and Beon,

4 the land which the LORD conquered before the congregation of Israel, is a land for livestock, and your servants have livestock."

5 They said, "If we have found favor in your sight, let this land be given to your servants as a possession; do not take us across the Jordan."

6 But Moses said to the sons of Gad and to the sons of Reuben, "Shall your brothers go to war while you yourselves sit here?

7 "Now why are you discouraging the sons of Israel from crossing over into the land which the LORD has given them?

8 "This is what your fathers did when I sent them from Kadesh-barnea to see the land.

9 "For when they went up to the valley of Eshcol and saw the land, they discouraged the sons of Israel so that they did not go into the land which the LORD had given them.

10 "So the LORD's anger burned in that day, and He swore, saying,

11 'None of the men who came up from Egypt, from twenty years old and upward, shall see the land which I swore to Abraham, to Isaac and to Jacob; for they did not follow Me fully,

12 except Caleb the son of Jephunneh the Kenizzite and Joshua the son of Nun, for they have followed the LORD fully.'

13 "So the LORD's anger burned against Israel, and He made them wander in the wilderness forty years, until the entire generation of those who had done evil in the sight of the LORD was destroyed.

14 "Now behold, you have risen up in your fathers' place, a brood of sinful men, to add still more to the burning anger of the LORD against Israel.

15 "For if you turn away from following ◄ Him, He will once more abandon them in the wilderness, and you will destroy all these people."

16 Then they came near to him and said, "We will build here sheepfolds for our livestock and cities for our little ones;

17 but we ourselves will be armed ready *to go* before the sons of Israel, until we have brought them to their place, while our little ones live in the fortified cities because of the inhabitants of the land.

18 "We will not return to our homes until every one of the sons of Israel has possessed his inheritance.

19 "For we will not have an inheritance with them on the other side of the Jordan and beyond, because our inheritance has fallen to us on this side of the Jordan toward the east."

20 So Moses said to them, "If you will do this, if you will arm yourselves before the LORD for the war,

---

LIFE LESSONS

➤ **Numbers 32:15** — *"For if you turn away from following Him, He will once more abandon them in the wilderness, and you will destroy all these people."*

*A*s believers, we must always take our responsibilities seriously. When we try to take the easy way out of a difficult situation, we may hurt others—even if it is unintentional.

21 and all of you armed men cross over the Jordan before the LORD until He has driven His enemies out from before Him,
22 and the land is subdued before the LORD, then afterward you shall return and be free of obligation toward the LORD and toward Israel, and this land shall be yours for a possession before the LORD.
23 "But if you will not do so, behold, you have sinned against the LORD, and be sure your sin will find you out.
24 "Build yourselves cities for your little ones, and sheepfolds for your sheep, and do what you have promised."
25 The sons of Gad and the sons of Reuben spoke to Moses, saying, "Your servants will do just as my lord commands.
26 "Our little ones, our wives, our livestock and all our cattle shall remain there in the cities of Gilead;
27 while your servants, everyone who is armed for war, will cross over in the presence of the LORD to battle, just as my lord says."
28 So Moses gave command concerning them to Eleazar the priest, and to Joshua the son of Nun, and to the heads of the fathers' *households* of the tribes of the sons of Israel.
29 Moses said to them, "If the sons of Gad and the sons of Reuben, everyone who is armed for battle, will cross with you over the Jordan in the presence of the LORD, and the land is subdued before you, then you shall give them the land of Gilead for a possession;
30 but if they will not cross over with you armed, they shall have possessions among you in the land of Canaan."
31 The sons of Gad and the sons of Reuben answered, saying, "As the LORD has said to your servants, so we will do.
32 "We ourselves will cross over armed in the presence of the LORD into the land of Canaan, and the possession of our inheritance *shall remain* with us across the Jordan."
33 So Moses gave to them, to the sons of Gad and to the sons of Reuben and to the half-tribe of Joseph's son Manasseh, the kingdom of Sihon, king of the Amorites and the kingdom of Og, the king of Bashan, the land with its cities with *their* territories, the cities of the surrounding land.

34 The sons of Gad built Dibon and Ataroth and Aroer,
35 and Atroth-shophan and Jazer and Jogbehah,
36 and Beth-nimrah and Beth-haran as fortified cities, and sheepfolds for sheep.
37 The sons of Reuben built Heshbon and Elealeh and Kiriathaim,
38 and Nebo and Baal-meon—*their* names being changed—and Sibmah, and they gave *other* names to the cities which they built.
39 The sons of Machir the son of Manasseh went to Gilead and took it, and dispossessed the Amorites who were in it.
40 So Moses gave Gilead to Machir the son of Manasseh, and he lived in it.
41 Jair the son of Manasseh went and took its towns, and called them Havvoth-jair.
42 Nobah went and took Kenath and its villages, and called it Nobah after his own name.

Psalm 35:1–8

A Psalm of David.

35 CONTEND, O LORD, with those who contend with me;
Fight against those who fight against me.
2 Take hold of buckler and shield
And rise up for my help.
3 Draw also the spear and the battle-axe
to meet those who pursue me;
Say to my soul, "I am your salvation."
4 Let those be ashamed and dishonored who seek my life;
Let those be turned back and humiliated who devise evil against me.
5 Let them be like chaff before the wind,
With the angel of the LORD driving *them* on.
6 Let their way be dark and slippery,
With the angel of the LORD pursuing them.
7 For without cause they hid their net for me;
Without cause they dug a pit for my soul.

Life Examples:

He Pleads Your Case

PSALM 35:1–4

Sometimes people will tell lies about you, and you will not be able to defend yourself. Their fabrications will endanger everything you care about—your job, reputation, family, even your future. Because Satan "is a liar and the father of lies" (John 8:44), he will often concoct untruths about God's children in order to hurt them or damage their credibility.

This certainly happened to Jesus. Mark 14:56 tells us, "For many were giving false testimony against Him." This was the only way the Jewish religious leaders could send Jesus to be crucified—by lying about what He had done.

After they had crucified Jesus, the chief priests and Pharisees went even further. They said to Pilate, "Sir, we remember that when He was still alive that deceiver said, 'After three days I am to rise again.' Therefore, give orders for the grave to be made secure until the third day, otherwise His disciples may come and steal Him away and say to the people, 'He has risen from the dead,' and the last deception will be worse than the first" (Matt. 27:63, 64).

Finally, after Christ fulfilled His promise to rise from the dead, the religious leaders bribed the guards to say the disciples had stolen Jesus' body (Matt. 28:11–15).

Lie after lie was told, yet Proverbs 19:5 promises, "A false witness will not go unpunished, and he who tells lies will not escape."

The falsehoods of the priests and Pharisees were soon dismissed. Jesus confirmed His resurrection by appearing to many witnesses (Acts 13:30, 31). In fact, it's been reported that there were more than 500 eyewitnesses to Christ's resurrection! Because of the people who saw Jesus risen from the grave, the gospel spread like wildfire. No lie or clever deception could stop the truth from prevailing.

The point is, God is a good and able defender—He will bring the truth to light (Matt. 10:26). Therefore, ask Him as Psalm 35:1 instructs, "Contend, O LORD, with those who contend with me; fight against those who fight against me."

Surely, as you serve Him, He will show the justice of your actions and show your accusers for who they really are (Ps. 37:6). Therefore, don't fear their falsehoods. God's truth will prevail, and you will, too.

---

8   Let destruction come upon him
         unawares,
     And let the net which he hid catch
         himself;
     Into that very destruction let him
         fall.

◈ Proverbs 12:1

12 WHOEVER loves discipline loves knowledge,
     But he who hates reproof is stupid.

LIFE LESSONS

➢ **Proverbs 12:1 — *Whoever loves discipline loves knowledge, but he who hates reproof is stupid.***

Criticism is often difficult to listen to. However, the best way to handle it is to ask God if there is truth in it. He may be using someone else's words to reveal blind spots in your character that need work. Correction is always an opportunity for growth.

◈ Mark 14:55–72

55 Now the chief priests and the whole Council kept trying to obtain testimony against Jesus to put Him to death, and they were not finding any.
56 For many were giving false testimony against Him, but their testimony was not consistent.
57 Some stood up and *began* to give false testimony against Him, saying,
58 "We heard Him say, 'I will destroy this temple made with hands, and in three days I will build another made without hands.'"
59 Not even in this respect was their testimony consistent.
60 The high priest stood up and *came* forward and questioned Jesus, saying, "Do You not answer? What is it that these men are testifying against You?"
61 But He kept silent and did not answer. Again the high priest was questioning Him, and saying to Him, "Are You the Christ, the Son of the Blessed One?"
62 And Jesus said, "I am; and you shall

see THE SON OF MAN SITTING AT THE RIGHT HAND OF POWER, and COMING WITH THE CLOUDS OF HEAVEN."

63 Tearing his clothes, the high priest *said, "What further need do we have of witnesses?

64 "You have heard the blasphemy; how does it seem to you?" And they all condemned Him to be deserving of death.

65 Some began to spit at Him, and to blindfold Him, and to beat Him with their fists, and to say to Him, "Prophesy!" And the officers received Him with slaps in the face.

66 As Peter was below in the courtyard, one of the servant-girls of the high priest *came,

67 and seeing Peter warming himself, she looked at him and *said, "You also were with Jesus the Nazarene."

68 But he denied it, saying, "I neither know nor understand what you are talking about." And he went out onto the porch.

69 The servant-girl saw him, and began once more to say to the bystanders, "This is one of them!"

70 But again he denied it. And after a little while the bystanders were again saying to Peter, "Surely you are one of them, for you are a Galilean too."

71 But he began to curse and swear, "I do not know this man you are talking about!"

72 Immediately a rooster crowed a second time. And Peter remembered how Jesus had made the remark to him, "Before a rooster crows twice, you will deny Me three times." And he began to weep.

LIFE LESSONS

➤ **Mark 14:72 — And Peter remembered how Jesus had made the remark to him . . . and he began to weep.**

*P*eter immediately understood the seriousness of his sin, which is a good thing. Second Corinthians 7:10 tells us, "For the sorrow that is according to the will of God produces a repentance without regret, leading to salvation, but the sorrow of the world produces death." Peter was no longer belligerent, as he was in the garden (John 18:10). Rather, he was repentant, which is just what he needed to be to receive the risen Christ.

MARCH 18

 Numbers 33:1—34:29

33 THESE are the journeys of the sons of Israel, by which they came out from the land of Egypt by their armies, under the leadership of Moses and Aaron.

2 Moses recorded their starting places according to their journeys by the command of the LORD, and these are their journeys according to their starting places.

3 They journeyed from Rameses in the first month, on the fifteenth day of the first month; on the next day after the Passover the sons of Israel started out boldly in the sight of all the Egyptians,

4 while the Egyptians were burying all their firstborn whom the LORD had struck down among them. The LORD had also executed judgments on their gods.

5 Then the sons of Israel journeyed from Rameses and camped in Succoth.

6 They journeyed from Succoth and camped in Etham, which is on the edge of the wilderness.

7 They journeyed from Etham and turned back to Pi-hahiroth, which faces Baal-zephon, and they camped before Migdol.

8 They journeyed from before Hahiroth and passed through the midst of the sea into the wilderness; and they went three days' journey in the wilderness of Etham and camped at Marah.

9 They journeyed from Marah and came to Elim; and in Elim there were twelve springs of water and seventy palm trees, and they camped there.

10 They journeyed from Elim and camped by the Red Sea.

11 They journeyed from the Red Sea and camped in the wilderness of Sin.

12 They journeyed from the wilderness of Sin and camped at Dophkah.
13 They journeyed from Dophkah and camped at Alush.
14 They journeyed from Alush and camped at Rephidim; now it was there that the people had no water to drink.
15 They journeyed from Rephidim and camped in the wilderness of Sinai.
16 They journeyed from the wilderness of Sinai and camped at Kibroth-hattaavah.
17 They journeyed from Kibroth-hattaavah and camped at Hazeroth.
18 They journeyed from Hazeroth and camped at Rithmah.
19 They journeyed from Rithmah and camped at Rimmon-perez.
20 They journeyed from Rimmon-perez and camped at Libnah.
21 They journeyed from Libnah and camped at Rissah.
22 They journeyed from Rissah and camped in Kehelathah.
23 They journeyed from Kehelathah and camped at Mount Shepher.
24 They journeyed from Mount She-pher and camped at Haradah.
25 They journeyed from Haradah and camped at Makheloth.
26 They journeyed from Makheloth and camped at Tahath.
27 They journeyed from Tahath and camped at Terah.
28 They journeyed from Terah and camped at Mithkah.
29 They journeyed from Mithkah and camped at Hashmonah.
30 They journeyed from Hashmonah and camped at Moseroth.
31 They journeyed from Moseroth and camped at Bene-jaakan.
32 They journeyed from Bene-jaakan and camped at Hor-haggidgad.
33 They journeyed from Hor-haggidgad and camped at Jotbathah.
34 They journeyed from Jotbathah and camped at Abronah.
35 They journeyed from Abronah and camped at Ezion-geber.
36 They journeyed from Ezion-geber and camped in the wilderness of Zin, that is, Kadesh.
37 They journeyed from Kadesh and camped at Mount Hor, at the edge of the land of Edom.
38 Then Aaron the priest went up to Mount Hor at the command of the LORD, and died there in the fortieth year after the sons of Israel had come from the land of Egypt, on the first *day* in the fifth month.
39 Aaron was one hundred twenty-three years old when he died on Mount Hor.
40 Now the Canaanite, the king of Arad who lived in the Negev in the land of Canaan, heard of the coming of the sons of Israel.
41 Then they journeyed from Mount Hor and camped at Zalmonah.
42 They journeyed from Zalmonah and camped at Punon.
43 They journeyed from Punon and camped at Oboth.
44 They journeyed from Oboth and camped at Iye-abarim, at the border of Moab.
45 They journeyed from Iyim and camped at Dibon-gad.
46 They journeyed from Dibon-gad and camped at Almon-diblathaim.
47 They journeyed from Almon-diblathaim and camped in the mountains of Abarim, before Nebo.
48 They journeyed from the mountains of Abarim and camped in the plains of Moab by the Jordan *opposite* Jericho.
49 They camped by the Jordan, from Beth-jeshimoth as far as Abel-shittim in the plains of Moab.
50 Then the LORD spoke to Moses in the plains of Moab by the Jordan *opposite* Jericho, saying,
51 "Speak to the sons of Israel and say to them, 'When you cross over the Jordan into the land of Canaan,
52 then you shall drive out all the inhabitants of the land from before you, and destroy all their figured stones, and destroy all their molten images and demolish all their high places;
53 and you shall take possession of the land and live in it, for I have given the land to you to possess it.
54 'You shall inherit the land by lot according to your families; to the larger you shall give more inheritance, and to the smaller you shall give less inheritance. Wherever the lot falls to anyone, that shall be his. You shall inherit according to the tribes of your fathers.
55 'But if you do not drive out the inhabitants of the land from before you, then

LIFE LESSONS

➤ **Numbers 33:55 —** *"If you do not drive out the inhabitants of the land . . . they will trouble you."*

*T*he Lord warned Israel what would happen if they failed to drive out *all* the inhabitants of the land, as He had commanded. In this too, His Word proved true (Judg. 2:11, 12).

it shall come about that those whom you let remain of them *will become* as pricks in your eyes and as thorns in your sides, and they will trouble you in the land in which you live.

56 'And as I plan to do to them, so I will do to you.'"

34 THEN the LORD spoke to Moses, saying,

➤ 2 "Command the sons of Israel and say to them, 'When you enter the land of Canaan, this is the land that shall fall to you as an inheritance, *even the* land of Canaan according to its borders.

3 'Your southern sector shall extend from the wilderness of Zin along the side of Edom, and your southern border shall extend from the end of the Salt Sea eastward.

4 'Then your border shall turn *direction* from the south to the ascent of Akrabbim and continue to Zin, and its termination shall be to the south of Kadesh-barnea; and it shall reach Hazaraddar and continue to Azmon.

5 'The border shall turn *direction* from

LIFE LESSONS

➤ **Numbers 34:2 —** *This is the land that shall fall to you as an inheritance, even the land of Canaan according to its borders."*

*G*od was always giving the Israelites boundaries—and for good reason. By establishing defendable borders, the Israelites knew what land they were responsible to manage and what was dangerous enemy territory. In the same way, God's commands show us what we're accountable to Him for, and they also safeguard us from the "enemy territory" of sin. God's boundaries always protect us.

Azmon to the brook of Egypt, and its termination shall be at the sea.

6 'As for the western border, you shall have the Great Sea, that is, *its* coastline; this shall be your west border.

7 'And this shall be your north border: you shall draw your *border* line from the Great Sea to Mount Hor.

8 'You shall draw a line from Mount Hor to the Lebo-hamath, and the termination of the border shall be at Zedad;

9 and the border shall proceed to Ziphron, and its termination shall be at Hazar-enan. This shall be your north border.

10 'For your eastern border you shall also draw a line from Hazar-enan to Shepham,

11 and the border shall go down from Shepham to Riblah on the east side of Ain; and the border shall go down and reach to the slope on the east side of the Sea of Chinnereth.

12 'And the border shall go down to the Jordan and its termination shall be at the Salt Sea. This shall be your land according to its borders all around.'"

13 So Moses commanded the sons of Israel, saying, "This is the land that you are to apportion by lot among you as a possession, which the LORD has commanded to give to the nine and a half tribes.

14 "For the tribe of the sons of Reuben have received *theirs* according to their fathers' households, and the tribe of the sons of Gad according to their fathers' households, and the half-tribe of Manasseh have received their possession.

15 "The two and a half tribes have received their possession across the Jordan opposite Jericho, eastward toward the sunrising."

16 Then the LORD spoke to Moses, saying,

17 "These are the names of the men who shall apportion the land to you for inheritance: Eleazar the priest and Joshua the son of Nun.

18 "You shall take one leader of every tribe to apportion the land for inheritance.

19 "These are the names of the men: of the tribe of Judah, Caleb the son of Jephunneh.

20 "Of the tribe of the sons of Simeon, Samuel the son of Ammihud.
21 "Of the tribe of Benjamin, Elidad the son of Chislon.
22 "Of the tribe of the sons of Dan a leader, Bukki the son of Jogli.
23 "Of the sons of Joseph: of the tribe of the sons of Manasseh a leader, Hanniel the son of Ephod.
24 "Of the tribe of the sons of Ephraim a leader, Kemuel the son of Shiphtan.
25 "Of the tribe of the sons of Zebulun a leader, Elizaphan the son of Parnach.
26 "Of the tribe of the sons of Issachar a leader, Paltiel the son of Azzan.
27 "Of the tribe of the sons of Asher a leader, Ahihud the son of Shelomi.
28 "Of the tribe of the sons of Naphtali a leader, Pedahel the son of Ammihud."
29 These are those whom the LORD commanded to apportion the inheritance to the sons of Israel in the land of Canaan.

Psalm 35:9–16

9 And my soul shall rejoice in the LORD;
It shall exult in His salvation.
10 All my bones will say, "LORD, who is like You,
Who delivers the afflicted from him who is too strong for him,
And the afflicted and the needy from him who robs him?"
11 Malicious witnesses rise up;
They ask me of things that I do not know.
12 They repay me evil for good,
To the bereavement of my soul.
13 But as for me, when they were sick, my clothing was sackcloth;
I humbled my soul with fasting,
And my prayer kept returning to my bosom.
14 I went about as though it were my friend or brother;
I bowed down mourning, as one who sorrows for a mother.
15 But at my stumbling they rejoiced and gathered themselves together;
The smiters whom I did not know gathered together against me,
They slandered me without ceasing.

16 Like godless jesters at a feast,
They gnashed at me with their teeth.

Proverbs 12:2

2 A good man will obtain favor from the LORD,
But He will condemn a man who devises evil.

Mark 15:1–24

15 EARLY in the morning the chief priests with the elders and scribes and the whole Council, immediately held a consultation; and binding Jesus, they led Him away and delivered Him to Pilate.
2 Pilate questioned Him, "Are You the King of the Jews?" And He *answered him, "It is as you say."
3 The chief priests began to accuse Him harshly.
4 Then Pilate questioned Him again, saying, "Do You not answer? See how many charges they bring against You!"
5 But Jesus made no further answer; so Pilate was amazed.
6 Now at the feast he used to release for them any one prisoner whom they requested.
7 The man named Barabbas had been imprisoned with the insurrectionists who had committed murder in the insurrection.
8 The crowd went up and began asking him to do as he had been accustomed to do for them.
9 Pilate answered them, saying, "Do you want me to release for you the King of the Jews?"
10 For he was aware that the chief priests had handed Him over because of envy.
11 But the chief priests stirred up the crowd to ask him to release Barabbas for them instead.
12 Answering again, Pilate said to them, "Then what shall I do with Him whom you call the King of the Jews?"
13 They shouted back, "Crucify Him!"
14 But Pilate said to them, "Why, what

evil has He done?" But they shouted all the more, "Crucify Him!"

15 Wishing to satisfy the crowd, Pilate released Barabbas for them, and after having Jesus scourged, he handed Him over to be crucified.

16 The soldiers took Him away into the palace (that is, the Praetorium), and they *called together the whole *Roman* cohort.

17 They *dressed Him up in purple, and after twisting a crown of thorns, they put it on Him;

18 and they began to acclaim Him, "Hail, King of the Jews!"

> 19 They kept beating His head with a reed, and spitting on Him, and kneeling and bowing before Him.

20 After they had mocked Him, they took the purple robe off Him and put His *own* garments on Him. And they *led Him out to crucify Him.

21 They *pressed into service a passer-by coming from the country, Simon of

---

LIFE LESSONS

> **Mark 15:19 — *They kept beating His head with a reed, and spitting on Him, and kneeling and bowing before Him.***

*H*ow hard it would have been to take the brutality and cruel mocking, knowing that with a word Jesus could have summoned more than twelve legions of furious angels (Matt. 26:53)! Yet He bore it, for our sake.

Cyrene (the father of Alexander and Rufus), to bear His cross.

22 Then they *brought Him to the place Golgotha, which is translated, Place of a Skull.

23 They tried to give Him wine mixed with myrrh; but He did not take it.

24 And they *crucified Him, and *divided up His garments among themselves, casting lots for them *to decide* what each man should take.

Numbers 35:1—36:13

35 NOW the LORD spoke to Moses in the plains of Moab by the Jordan *opposite* Jericho, saying,

2 "Command the sons of Israel that they give to the Levites from the inheritance of their possession cities to live in; and you shall give to the Levites pasture lands around the cities.

3 "The cities shall be theirs to live in; and their pasture lands shall be for their cattle and for their herds and for all their beasts.

4 "The pasture lands of the cities which you shall give to the Levites shall *extend* from the wall of the city outward a thousand cubits around.

5 "You shall also measure outside the city on the east side two thousand cubits, and on the south side two thousand cubits, and on the west side two thousand cubits, and on the north side two thousand cubits, with the city in the center. This shall become theirs as pasture lands for the cities.

6 "The cities which you shall give to the Levites *shall be* the six cities of refuge, which you shall give for the manslayer to flee to; and in addition to them you shall give forty-two cities.

7 "All the cities which you shall give to the Levites *shall be* forty-eight cities, together with their pasture lands.

8 "As for the cities which you shall give from the possession of the sons of Israel, you shall take more from the larger and you shall take less from the smaller; each shall give some of his cities to the Levites in proportion to his possession which he inherits."

9 Then the LORD spoke to Moses, saying,

10 "Speak to the sons of Israel and say to them, 'When you cross the Jordan into the land of Canaan,

11 then you shall select for yourselves cities to be your cities of refuge, that the manslayer who has killed any person unintentionally may flee there.

12 'The cities shall be to you as a refuge from the avenger, so that the manslayer will not die until he stands before the congregation for trial.

13 'The cities which you are to give shall be your six cities of refuge.

14 'You shall give three cities across the Jordan and three cities in the land of Canaan; they are to be cities of refuge.

15 'These six cities shall be for refuge for the sons of Israel, and for the alien and for the sojourner among them; that anyone who kills a person unintentionally may flee there.

16 'But if he struck him down with an iron object, so that he died, he is a murderer; the murderer shall surely be put to death.

17 'If he struck him down with a stone in the hand, by which he will die, and *as a result* he died, he is a murderer; the murderer shall surely be put to death.

18 'Or if he struck him with a wooden object in the hand, by which he might die, and *as a result* he died, he is a murderer; the murderer shall surely be put to death.

19 'The blood avenger himself shall put the murderer to death; he shall put him to death when he meets him.

20 'If he pushed him of hatred, or threw something at him lying in wait and *as a result* he died,

21 or if he struck him down with his hand in enmity, and *as a result* he died, the one who struck him shall surely be put to death, he is a murderer; the blood avenger shall put the murderer to death when he meets him.

22 'But if he pushed him suddenly without enmity, or threw something at him without lying in wait,

23 or with any deadly object of stone, and without seeing it dropped on him so that he died, while he was not his enemy nor seeking his injury,

24 then the congregation shall judge between the slayer and the blood avenger according to these ordinances.

25 'The congregation shall deliver the manslayer from the hand of the blood avenger, and the congregation shall restore him to his city of refuge to which he fled; and he shall live in it until the death of the high priest who was anointed with the holy oil.

26 'But if the manslayer at any time goes beyond the border of his city of refuge to which he may flee,

27 and the blood avenger finds him outside the border of his city of refuge, and the blood avenger kills the manslayer, he will not be guilty of blood

28 because he should have remained in his city of refuge until the death of the high priest. But after the death of the high priest the manslayer shall return to the land of his possession.

29 'These things shall be for a statutory ordinance to you throughout your generations in all your dwellings.

30 'If anyone kills a person, the murderer shall be put to death at the evidence of witnesses, but no person shall be put to death on the testimony of one witness.

31 'Moreover, you shall not take ransom for the life of a murderer who is guilty of death, but he shall surely be put to death.

32 'You shall not take ransom for him who has fled to his city of refuge, that he may return to live in the land before the death of the priest.

33 'So you shall not pollute the land in which you are; for blood pollutes the land and no expiation can be made for the land for the blood that is shed on it, except by the blood of him who shed it.

34 'You shall not defile the land in which you live, in the midst of which I dwell; for I the LORD am dwelling in the midst of the sons of Israel.'"

36 AND the heads of the fathers' *households* of the family of the sons of Gilead, the son of Machir, the son of Manasseh, of the families of the sons of Joseph, came near and spoke before Moses and before the leaders, the heads of the fathers' *households* of the sons of Israel,

2 and they said, "The LORD commanded my lord to give the land by lot to the sons of Israel as an inheritance, and my lord was commanded by the LORD to give the

---

LIFE LESSONS

➢ Numbers 35:34 — *"You shall not defile the land in which you live . . . for I the LORD am dwelling in the midst of the sons of Israel."*

*W*e are never to forget that our holy God lives among us. That knowledge alone should shape the way we live. We are accountable to Him in every aspect of our lives.

inheritance of Zelophehad our brother to his daughters.

3 "But if they marry one of the sons of the *other* tribes of the sons of Israel, their inheritance will be withdrawn from the inheritance of our fathers and will be added to the inheritance of the tribe to which they belong; thus it will be withdrawn from our allotted inheritance.

4 "When the jubilee of the sons of Israel comes, then their inheritance will be added to the inheritance of the tribe to which they belong; so their inheritance will be withdrawn from the inheritance of the tribe of our fathers."

5 Then Moses commanded the sons of Israel according to the word of the LORD, saying, "The tribe of the sons of Joseph are right in *their* statements.

6 "This is what the LORD has commanded concerning the daughters of Zelophehad, saying, 'Let them marry whom they wish; only they must marry within the family of the tribe of their father.'

7 "Thus no inheritance of the sons of Israel shall be transferred from tribe to tribe, for the sons of Israel shall each hold to the inheritance of the tribe of his fathers.

8 "Every daughter who comes into possession of an inheritance of any tribe of the sons of Israel shall be wife to one of the family of the tribe of her father, so that the sons of Israel each may possess the inheritance of his fathers.

9 "Thus no inheritance shall be transferred from one tribe to another tribe, for the tribes of the sons of Israel shall each hold to his own inheritance."

10 Just as the LORD had commanded Moses, so the daughters of Zelophehad did:

11 Mahlah, Tirzah, Hoglah, Milcah and Noah, the daughters of Zelophehad married their uncles' sons.

12 They married *those* from the families of the sons of Manasseh the son of Joseph, and their inheritance remained with the tribe of the family of their father.

13 These are the commandments and the ordinances which the LORD commanded to the sons of Israel through Moses in the plains of Moab by the Jordan *opposite* Jericho.

✦ Psalm 35:17–28

17 Lord, how long will You look on?
Rescue my soul from their ravages,
My only *life* from the lions.

18 I will give You thanks in the great congregation;
I will praise You among a mighty throng.

19 Do not let those who are wrongfully my enemies rejoice over me;
Nor let those who hate me without cause wink maliciously.

20 For they do not speak peace,
But they devise deceitful words against those who are quiet in the land.

21 They opened their mouth wide against me;
They said, "Aha, aha, our eyes have seen it!"

22 You have seen it, O LORD, do not keep silent;
O Lord, do not be far from me.

23 Stir up Yourself, and awake to my right
And to my cause, my God and my Lord.

24 Judge me, O LORD my God, according to Your righteousness,
And do not let them rejoice over me.

25 Do not let them say in their heart, "Aha, our desire!"
Do not let them say, "We have swallowed him up!"

26 Let those be ashamed and humiliated altogether who rejoice at my distress;
Let those be clothed with shame and dishonor who magnify themselves over me.

LIFE LESSONS

➤ **Psalm 35:24 — *Judge me, O LORD my God, according to Your righteousness.***

*W*e pray powerfully when we pray in line with the righteousness of God—that is, when we pray for what is right, good, glorifying to Him, and beneficial for His people. The Lord delights in such prayers.

➤ **Psalm 35:27 — Let them shout for joy and rejoice, who favor my vindication; and let them say continually, "The Lord be magnified, who delights in the prosperity of His servant."**

W̲hen things don't go well, we may think the Lord has rejected us. But the truth is He takes great pleasure in our prosperity and rejoices in our happiness. However, God's first priority is our spiritual wellbeing. He loves us and He is always providing for us—even in hard times.

27 Let them shout for joy and rejoice,
     who favor my vindication;
   And let them say continually, "The
     Lord be magnified,
   Who delights in the prosperity of
     His servant."
28 And my tongue shall declare Your
     righteousness
   And Your praise all day long.

Proverbs 12:3

3 A man will not be established by
     wickedness,
   But the root of the righteous will
     not be moved.

Mark 15:25–47

25 It was the third hour when they crucified Him.
26 The inscription of the charge against Him read, "THE KING OF THE JEWS."
27 They *crucified two robbers with Him, one on His right and one on His left.
28 [And the Scripture was fulfilled which says, "And He was numbered with transgressors."]
29 Those passing by were hurling abuse at Him, wagging their heads, and saying, "Ha! You who *are going to* destroy the temple and rebuild it in three days,
30 save Yourself, and come down from the cross!"
31 In the same way the chief priests also, along with the scribes, were mocking *Him* among themselves and saying, "He saved others; He cannot save Himself.
32 "Let *this* Christ, the King of Israel, now come down from the cross, so that we may see and believe!" Those who were crucified with Him were also insulting Him.
33 When the sixth hour came, darkness fell over the whole land until the ninth hour.
34 At the ninth hour Jesus cried out with a loud voice, "Eloi, Eloi, lama sabachthani?" which is translated, "My God, My God, why have You forsaken Me?"
35 When some of the bystanders heard it, they *began* saying, "Behold, He is calling for Elijah."
36 Someone ran and filled a sponge with sour wine, put it on a reed, and gave Him a drink, saying, "Let us see whether Elijah will come to take Him down."
37 And Jesus uttered a loud cry, and breathed His last.
38 And the veil of the temple was torn in two from top to bottom.
39 When the centurion, who was standing right in front of Him, saw the way He breathed His last, he said, "Truly this man was the Son of God!"
40 There were also *some* women looking on from a distance, among whom *were* Mary Magdalene, and Mary the mother of James the Less and Joses, and Salome.

➤ **Mark 15:34 — Jesus cried out with a loud voice . . . "My God, My God, why have You forsaken Me?"**

I̲n His darkest hour, when He carried the sins of the entire world on His back, Jesus fixed His mind on the words of Scripture. Read Psalm 22 to see how God comforted Him, even on the Cross.

➤ **Mark 15:38 — And the veil of the temple was torn in two from top to bottom.**

B̲y tearing the thick, heavy veil of the temple from top to bottom, God signified that He, through the death of His Son, had made free access to heaven possible for all those who trust in Jesus Christ as their Lord and Savior.

Life Examples:

THE CENTURION:
A Bold Confession

MARK 15:39

*T*he breastplate that covered his heart bore the seal of his master, Caesar. He felt pride in commanding a hundred elite Roman soldiers.

The centurion looked at the crosses and stood vigil as death reduced them to a mass of lifeless flesh. Yet one victim seemed unlike any the veteran soldier had ever seen. This Man didn't fight as the others had. Nor did He beg or curse, condemn or plead for mercy. In fact, He did something that tore at the centurion's heart.

He forgave.

In all of his career, only Jesus had ever offered the centurion mercy. Even though he stood for everything that put Christ on that cross, Jesus forgave him. In that moment, he could utter only one confession: "Truly this man was the Son of God!" (Mark 15:39).

Two thousand years later, people still look upon Jesus, the resurrected Son of God. What is your confession about Him?

---

41 When He was in Galilee, they used to follow Him and minister to Him; and *there were* many other women who came up with Him to Jerusalem.

42 When evening had already come, because it was the preparation day, that is, the day before the Sabbath,

43 Joseph of Arimathea came, a prominent member of the Council, who himself was waiting for the kingdom of God; and he gathered up courage and went in before Pilate, and asked for the body of Jesus.

44 Pilate wondered if He was dead by this time, and summoning the centurion, he questioned him as to whether He was already dead.

45 And ascertaining this from the centurion, he granted the body to Joseph.

46 Joseph bought a linen cloth, took Him down, wrapped Him in the linen cloth and laid Him in a tomb which had been hewn out in the rock; and he rolled a stone against the entrance of the tomb.

47 Mary Magdalene and Mary the *mother* of Joses were looking on *to see* where He was laid.

LIFE LESSONS

➤ **Mark 15:43 —** *Joseph of Arimathea . . . went in before Pilate, and asked for the body of Jesus.*

*T*o this point, Joseph had been a "secret" disciple for fear he might jeopardize his position. But when all the Lord's disciples ran, he stepped forward and made public his allegiance to Christ.

Deuteronomy 1:1—2:37

1 THESE are the words which Moses spoke to all Israel across the Jordan in the wilderness, in the Arabah opposite Suph, between Paran and Tophel and Laban and Hazeroth and Dizahab.

2 It is eleven days' *journey* from Horeb by the way of Mount Seir to Kadesh-barnea.

3 In the fortieth year, on the first *day* of the eleventh month, Moses spoke to the children of Israel, according to all that the LORD had commanded him to *give* to them,

4 after he had defeated Sihon the king of the Amorites, who lived in Heshbon, and Og the king of Bashan, who lived in Ashtaroth and Edrei.

5 Across the Jordan in the land of Moab, Moses undertook to expound this law, saying,

6 "The LORD our God spoke to us at Horeb, saying, 'You have stayed long enough at this mountain.

7 'Turn and set your journey, and go to the hill country of the Amorites, and to all their neighbors in the Arabah, in the

hill country and in the lowland and in the Negev and by the seacoast, the land of the Canaanites, and Lebanon, as far as the great river, the river Euphrates.

8 'See, I have placed the land before you; go in and possess the land which the LORD swore to give to your fathers, to Abraham, to Isaac, and to Jacob, to them and their descendants after them.'

9 "I spoke to you at that time, saying, 'I am not able to bear *the burden* of you alone.

10 'The LORD your God has multiplied you, and behold, you are this day like the stars of heaven in number.

11 'May the LORD, the God of your fathers, increase you a thousand-fold more than you are and bless you, just as He has promised you!

12 'How can I alone bear the load and burden of you and your strife?

13 'Choose wise and discerning and experienced men from your tribes, and I will appoint them as your heads.'

14 "You answered me and said, 'The thing which you have said to do is good.'

15 "So I took the heads of your tribes, wise and experienced men, and appointed them heads over you, leaders of thousands and of hundreds, of fifties and of tens, and officers for your tribes.

16 "Then I charged your judges at that time, saying, 'Hear *the cases* between your fellow countrymen, and judge righteously between a man and his fellow countryman, or the alien who is with him.

17 'You shall not show partiality in judgment; you shall hear the small and the great alike. You shall not fear man, for the judgment is God's. The case that is too hard for you, you shall bring to me, and I will hear it.'

18 "I commanded you at that time all the things that you should do.

19 "Then we set out from Horeb, and went through all that great and terrible wilderness which you saw on the way to the hill country of the Amorites, just as the LORD our God had commanded us; and we came to Kadesh-barnea.

20 "I said to you, 'You have come to the hill country of the Amorites which the LORD our God is about to give us.

21 'See, the LORD your God has placed the land before you; go up, take possession, as the LORD, the God of your fathers, has spoken to you. Do not fear or be dismayed.'

22 "Then all of you approached me and said, 'Let us send men before us, that they may search out the land for us, and bring back to us word of the way by which we should go up and the cities which we shall enter.'

23 "The thing pleased me and I took twelve of your men, one man for each tribe.

24 "They turned and went up into the hill country, and came to the valley of Eshcol and spied it out.

25 "Then they took *some* of the fruit of the land in their hands and brought it down to us; and they brought us back a report and said, 'It is a good land which the LORD our God is about to give us.'

26 "Yet you were not willing to go up, but rebelled against the command of the LORD your God;

27 and you grumbled in your tents and said, 'Because the LORD hates us, He has brought us out of the land of Egypt to deliver us into the hand of the Amorites to destroy us.

28 'Where can we go up? Our brethren have made our hearts melt, saying, "The people are bigger and taller than we; the cities are large and fortified to heaven. And besides, we saw the sons of the Anakim there."'

29 "Then I said to you, 'Do not be shocked, nor fear them.

30 'The LORD your God who goes before you will Himself fight on your behalf, just as He did for you in Egypt before your eyes,

31 and in the wilderness where you saw how the LORD your God carried you, just as a man carries his son, in all the way which you have walked until you came to this place.'

LIFE LESSONS

Deuteronomy 1:13 — *"Choose wise and discerning and experienced men from your tribes, and I will appoint them as your heads."*

The kingdom of God cannot advance as it should without wise, understanding, and knowledgeable leaders who are filled with the Spirit of God. We do not move forward in godliness alone; we need each other.

LIFE LESSONS

➤ Deuteronomy 1:30 — *"The LORD your God who goes before you will Himself fight on your behalf."*

*E*ver since the garden of Eden, one of Satan's most successful tactics has been to get God's people to believe the Lord is not really loving and gracious. However, He is not only with us; He also goes ahead of us to prepare our way and give us success.

32 "But for all this, you did not trust the LORD your God,

33 who goes before you on *your* way, to seek out a place for you to encamp, in fire by night and cloud by day, to show you the way in which you should go.

34 "Then the LORD heard the sound of your words, and He was angry and took an oath, saying,

35 'Not one of these men, this evil generation, shall see the good land which I swore to give your fathers,

36 except Caleb the son of Jephunneh; he shall see it, and to him and to his sons I will give the land on which he has set foot, because he has followed the LORD fully.'

37 "The LORD was angry with me also on your account, saying, 'Not even you shall enter there.

38 'Joshua the son of Nun, who stands before you, he shall enter there; encourage him, for he will cause Israel to inherit it.

39 'Moreover, your little ones who you said would become a prey, and your sons, who this day have no knowledge of good or evil, shall enter there, and I will give it to them and they shall possess it.

40 'But as for you, turn around and set out for the wilderness by the way to the Red Sea.'

41 "Then you said to me, 'We have sinned against the LORD; we will indeed go up and fight, just as the LORD our God commanded us.' And every man of you girded on his weapons of war, and regarded it as easy to go up into the hill country.

42 "And the LORD said to me, 'Say to them, "Do not go up nor fight, for I am not among you; otherwise you will be defeated before your enemies."'

43 "So I spoke to you, but you would

not listen. Instead you rebelled against the command of the LORD, and acted presumptuously and went up into the hill country.

44 "The Amorites who lived in that hill country came out against you and chased you as bees do, and crushed you from Seir to Hormah.

45 "Then you returned and wept before the LORD; but the LORD did not listen to your voice nor give ear to you.

46 "So you remained in Kadesh many days, the days that you spent *there.*

2 "THEN we turned and set out for the wilderness by the way to the Red Sea, as the LORD spoke to me, and circled Mount Seir for many days.

2 "And the LORD spoke to me, saying,

3 'You have circled this mountain long enough. *Now* turn north,

4 and command the people, saying, "You will pass through the territory of your brothers the sons of Esau who live in Seir; and they will be afraid of you. So be very careful;

5 do not provoke them, for I will not give you any of their land, even *as little as* a footstep because I have given Mount Seir to Esau as a possession.

6 "You shall buy food from them with money so that you may eat, and you shall also purchase water from them with money so that you may drink.

7 "For the LORD your God has blessed ◄ you in all that you have done; He has known your wanderings through this great wilderness. These forty years the LORD your God has been with you; you have not lacked a thing."'

8 "So we passed beyond our brothers the sons of Esau, who live in Seir, away from the Arabah road, away from Elath and from Ezion-geber. And we turned and passed through by the way of the wilderness of Moab.

LIFE LESSONS

➤ Deuteronomy 2:7 — *"These forty years the LORD your God has been with you; you have not lacked a thing."*

*E*ven though Israel ended up in the wilderness because of disobedience, even there God blessed His people and gave them everything they needed. He tempers His justice with grace.

9 "Then the LORD said to me, 'Do not harass Moab, nor provoke them to war, for I will not give you any of their land as a possession, because I have given Ar to the sons of Lot as a possession.'

10 (The Emim lived there formerly, a people as great, numerous, and tall as the Anakim.

11 Like the Anakim, they are also regarded as Rephaim, but the Moabites call them Emim.

12 The Horites formerly lived in Seir, but the sons of Esau dispossessed them and destroyed them from before them and settled in their place, just as Israel did to the land of their possession which the LORD gave to them.)

13 'Now arise and cross over the brook Zered yourselves.' So we crossed over the brook Zered.

14 "Now the time that it took for us to come from Kadesh-barnea until we crossed over the brook Zered was thirty-eight years, until all the generation of the men of war perished from within the camp, as the LORD had sworn to them.

15 "Moreover the hand of the LORD was against them, to destroy them from within the camp until they all perished.

16 "So it came about when all the men of war had finally perished from among the people,

17 that the LORD spoke to me, saying,

18 'Today you shall cross over Ar, the border of Moab.

19 'When you come opposite the sons of Ammon, do not harass them nor provoke them, for I will not give you any of the land of the sons of Ammon as a possession, because I have given it to the sons of Lot as a possession.'

20 (It is also regarded as the land of the Rephaim, for Rephaim formerly lived in it, but the Ammonites call them Zamzummin,

21 a people as great, numerous, and tall as the Anakim, but the LORD destroyed them before them. And they dispossessed them and settled in their place,

22 just as He did for the sons of Esau, who live in Seir, when He destroyed the Horites from before them; they dispossessed them and settled in their place even to this day.

23 And the Avvim, who lived in villages as far as Gaza, the Caphtorim who came from Caphtor, destroyed them and lived in their place.)

24 'Arise, set out, and pass through the valley of Arnon. Look! I have given Sihon the Amorite, king of Heshbon, and his land into your hand; begin to take possession and contend with him in battle.

25 'This day I will begin to put the dread and fear of you upon the peoples everywhere under the heavens, who, when they hear the report of you, will tremble and be in anguish because of you.'

26 "So I sent messengers from the wilderness of Kedemoth to Sihon king of Heshbon with words of peace, saying,

27 'Let me pass through your land, I will travel only on the highway; I will not turn aside to the right or to the left.

28 'You will sell me food for money so that I may eat, and give me water for money so that I may drink, only let me pass through on foot,

29 just as the sons of Esau who live in Seir and the Moabites who live in Ar did for me, until I cross over the Jordan into the land which the LORD our God is giving to us.'

30 "But Sihon king of Heshbon was not willing for us to pass through his land; for the LORD your God hardened his spirit and made his heart obstinate, in order to deliver him into your hand, as he is today.

31 "The LORD said to me, 'See, I have begun to deliver Sihon and his land over to you. Begin to occupy, that you may possess his land.'

32 "Then Sihon with all his people came out to meet us in battle at Jahaz.

33 "The LORD our God delivered him over to us, and we defeated him with his sons and all his people.

34 "So we captured all his cities at that time and utterly destroyed the men, women and children of every city. We left no survivor.

35 "We took only the animals as our booty and the spoil of the cities which we had captured.

36 "From Aroer which is on the edge of the valley of Arnon and from the city which is in the valley, even to Gilead, there was no city that was too high for us; the LORD our God delivered all over to us.

37 "Only you did not go near to the land

of the sons of Ammon, all along the river Jabbok and the cities of the hill country, and wherever the LORD our God had commanded us.

Psalm 36:1–6

For the choir director. *A Psalm* of David the servant of the LORD.

36 TRANSGRESSION speaks to the ungodly within his heart;
There is no fear of God before his eyes.

2   For it flatters him in his *own* eyes
Concerning the discovery of his iniquity *and* the hatred *of it.*

3   The words of his mouth are wickedness and deceit;
He has ceased to be wise *and* to do good.

4   He plans wickedness upon his bed;
He sets himself on a path that is not good;
He does not despise evil.

5   Your lovingkindness, O LORD, extends to the heavens,
Your faithfulness *reaches* to the skies.

6   Your righteousness is like the mountains of God;
Your judgments are *like* a great deep.
O LORD, You preserve man and beast.

Proverbs 12:4–6

4   An excellent wife is the crown of her husband,
But she who shames *him* is like rottenness in his bones.

LIFE LESSONS

➤ **Psalm 36:5 —** *Your lovingkindness, O LORD, extends to the heavens, your faithfulness reaches to the skies.*

*G*od loves to show mercy and remains eternally trustworthy to do exactly what He has promised. If He seems to delay in working on your behalf, wait for Him. He will *never* be unfaithful to you.

5   The thoughts of the righteous are just,
But the counsels of the wicked are deceitful.

6   The words of the wicked lie in wait for blood,
But the mouth of the upright will deliver them.

Mark 16:1–20

16 WHEN the Sabbath was over, Mary Magdalene, and Mary the *mother* of James, and Salome, bought spices, so that they might come and anoint Him.

2   Very early on the first day of the week, they *came to the tomb when the sun had risen.

3   They were saying to one another, "Who will roll away the stone for us from the entrance of the tomb?"

4   Looking up, they *saw that the stone had been rolled away, although it was extremely large.

5   Entering the tomb, they saw a young man sitting at the right, wearing a white robe; and they were amazed.

6   And he *said to them, "Do not be amazed; you are looking for Jesus the Nazarene, who has been crucified. He has risen; He is not here; behold, *here is* the place where they laid Him.

7   "But go, tell His disciples and Peter, 'He is going ahead of you to Galilee; there you will see Him, just as He told you.'"

8   They went out and fled from the tomb, for trembling and astonishment had gripped them; and they said nothing to anyone, for they were afraid.

9   [Now after He had risen early on the first day of the week, He first appeared to Mary Magdalene, from whom He had cast out seven demons.

LIFE LESSONS

➤ **Mark 16:7 —** *"But go, tell His disciples and Peter, 'He is going ahead of you to Galilee.'"*

*O*nly Mark's Gospel tells us that the angel singled out Peter for the announcement that Christ had risen from the dead. Peter had denied the Lord three times—but Jesus showed him grace.

LIFE LESSONS

➤ **Mark 16:8** — *They went out and fled from the tomb, for trembling and astonishment had gripped them; and they said nothing to anyone, for they were afraid.*

The first hours after the resurrection were anything but a triumphant display of faith and courage. Though Jesus had told them repeatedly that He would rise from the dead, none of the Lord's disciples imagined that He really would. Fear reigned in them as long as they doubted. Our responsibility is always to remain faithful when things look their darkest because we know that God is going to redeem the situation in a manner "far more abundantly beyond all that we ask or think" (Eph. 3:20). God's work will always amaze us, so we must wait for it patiently and expectantly.

10 She went and reported to those who had been with Him, while they were mourning and weeping.
11 When they heard that He was alive and had been seen by her, they refused to believe it.
12 After that, He appeared in a different form to two of them while they were walking along on their way to the country.
13 They went away and reported it to the others, but they did not believe them either.
14 Afterward He appeared to the eleven themselves as they were reclining *at the table;* and He reproached them for their unbelief and hardness of heart, because they had not believed those who had seen Him after He had risen.
15 And He said to them, "Go into all the world and preach the gospel to all creation.
16 "He who has believed and has been

ANSWERS TO LIFE'S QUESTIONS

What tools has God provided to help me share my faith?

MARK 16:15, 16

The only way to reach spiritually blind, captive, and dead people is through the divine work of almighty God, who does not wish "for any to perish but for all to come to repentance" (2 Pet. 3:9). We are His tools; He is the power.

The apostle Paul explains, "For God has not given us a spirit of timidity, but of power and love and discipline" (2 Tim. 1:7). We do not have to be afraid to share our faith because He has given us three important tools to help us.

Power. The gospel of God opens blind eyes, rescues captives, and revives the dead. We share our faith by declaring that Christ died on the Cross for our sins, was buried, and rose from the dead. Lead the lost to consider who Jesus is because He is the One who provides salvation. Any rejection you experience thus centers on Him, not you. Always pray for His wisdom and strength when you tell others about His saving grace. It is the power of God through the Holy Spirit that changes lives (Acts 1:8).

Love. The greatest force on earth is the love of God. "By this all men will know that you are My disciples, if you have love for one another" (John 13:35). We can showcase His

love in countless ways (1 John 3:18). Listen to the words of a friend. Spend time with a parent or loved one. Keep a couple's child so they can enjoy a special night out. Invite a friend over. Deliver food to someone who is sick. We can love others through service, or we can love them with our words (Prov. 31:26). That means we encourage those who are lost by telling them about the Lord Jesus, who loves them unconditionally and wants to give them a new life.

Wisdom. The Christian faith is based on the unshakable Word of God and not fiction. Sharing our faith is never unreasonable or irrational—we are doing exactly what Jesus has commanded us to do: to proclaim the true message of the gospel to as many people as possible. We offer others the trustworthy testimony of Scripture and the reason for our faith (1 Pet. 3:15), which includes:

- The fact of the resurrection (1 Cor. 15:6). The resurrection is indeed a concrete, historical fact.
- The fact of fulfilled Scripture. Literally hundreds of Old Testament prophesies were fulfilled in the New Testament, including many intricate details of Jesus' birth, life, death, and resurrection.
- The fact of manuscript and archaeological evidence. Thousands of ancient manuscripts attest to the reliability of the Bible. Archaeological evidence has consistently verified the historical data of the Bible.

baptized shall be saved; but he who has disbelieved shall be condemned.

17 "These signs will accompany those who have believed: in My name they will cast out demons, they will speak with new tongues;

18 they will pick up serpents, and if they drink any deadly *poison,* it will not hurt them; they will lay hands on the sick, and they will recover."

19 So then, when the Lord Jesus had spoken to them, He was received up into heaven and sat down at the right hand of God.

20 And they went out and preached everywhere, while the Lord worked with them, and confirmed the word by the signs that followed.]

[*And they promptly reported all these instructions to Peter and his companions. And after that, Jesus Himself sent out through them from east to west the sacred and imperishable proclamation of eternal salvation.*]

MARCH 21

◈ Deuteronomy 3:1—4:49

3 "THEN" we turned and went up the road to Bashan, and Og, king of Bashan, with all his people came out to meet us in battle at Edrei.

2 "But the LORD said to me, 'Do not fear him, for I have delivered him and all his people and his land into your hand; and you shall do to him just as you did to Sihon king of the Amorites, who lived at Heshbon.'

3 "So the LORD our God delivered Og also, king of Bashan, with all his people into our hand, and we smote them until no survivor was left.

4 "We captured all his cities at that time; there was not a city which we did not take from them: sixty cities, all the region of Argob, the kingdom of Og in Bashan.

5 "All these were cities fortified with high walls, gates and bars, besides a great many unwalled towns.

6 "We utterly destroyed them, as we did to Sihon king of Heshbon, utterly destroying the men, women and children of every city.

7 "But all the animals and the spoil of the cities we took as our booty.

8 "Thus we took the land at that time from the hand of the two kings of the Amorites who were beyond the Jordan, from the valley of Arnon to Mount Hermon

9 (Sidonians call Hermon Sirion, and the Amorites call it Senir):

10 all the cities of the plateau and all Gilead and all Bashan, as far as Salecah and Edrei, cities of the kingdom of Og in Bashan.

11 (For only Og king of Bashan was left of the remnant of the Rephaim. Behold, his bedstead was an iron bedstead; it is in Rabbah of the sons of Ammon. Its length was nine cubits and its width four cubits by ordinary cubit.)

12 "So we took possession of this land at that time. From Aroer, which is by the valley of Arnon, and half the hill country of Gilead and its cities I gave to the Reubenites and to the Gadites.

13 "The rest of Gilead and all Bashan, the kingdom of Og, I gave to the half-tribe of Manasseh, all the region of Argob (concerning all Bashan, it is called the land of Rephaim.

14 Jair the son of Manasseh took all the region of Argob as far as the border of the Geshurites and the Maacathites, and called it, *that is,* Bashan, after his own name, Havvoth-jair, *as it is* to this day.)

15 "To Machir I gave Gilead.

16 "To the Reubenites and to the Gadites I gave from Gilead even as far as the valley of Arnon, the middle of the valley as a border and as far as the river Jabbok, the border of the sons of Ammon;

17 the Arabah also, with the Jordan as *a* border, from Chinnereth even as far as the sea of the Arabah, the Salt Sea, at the foot of the slopes of Pisgah on the east.

18 "Then I commanded you at that time, saying, 'The LORD your God has given you this land to possess it; all you valiant men shall cross over armed before your brothers, the sons of Israel.

19 'But your wives and your little ones and your livestock (I know that you have much livestock) shall remain in your cities which I have given you,

20 until the LORD gives rest to your fellow countrymen as to you, and they also possess the land which the LORD your God will give them beyond the Jordan. Then you may return every man to his possession which I have given you.'

21 "I commanded Joshua at that time, saying, 'Your eyes have seen all that the LORD your God has done to these two kings; so the LORD shall do to all the kingdoms into which you are about to cross.

➤ 22 'Do not fear them, for the LORD your God is the one fighting for you.'

23 "I also pleaded with the LORD at that time, saying,

24 'O Lord GOD, You have begun to show Your servant Your greatness and Your strong hand; for what god is there in heaven or on earth who can do such works and mighty acts as Yours?

25 'Let me, I pray, cross over and see the fair land that is beyond the Jordan, that good hill country and Lebanon.'

➤ 26 "But the LORD was angry with me on your account, and would not listen to me;

LIFE LESSONS

➤ **Deuteronomy 3:22 — "Do not fear them, for the LORD your God is the one fighting for you."**

God knew the tremendous obstacles that Joshua and the Israelites would face when conquering the Promised Land, and so He assured them that He would provide them with victory. They would not conquer in their own strength, but in His. Likewise, no matter what obstacles hinder you, the Lord can overcome it for you. Trust Him.

➤ **Deuteronomy 3:26 — "Enough! Speak to Me no more of this matter."**

The Bible teaches us to pray and keep on praying, and not to give up (Luke 18:1). We may call upon God for any reason, at any time, regarding any problem or difficulty or challenge. Yet there may come times when the Lord lets us know it is time to stop praying for a particular thing.

---

and the LORD said to me, 'Enough! Speak to Me no more of this matter.

27 'Go up to the top of Pisgah and lift up your eyes to the west and north and south and east, and see it with your eyes, for you shall not cross over this Jordan.

28 'But charge Joshua and encourage him and strengthen him, for he shall go across at the head of this people, and he will give them as an inheritance the land which you will see.'

29 "So we remained in the valley opposite Beth-peor.

4 "NOW, O Israel, listen to the statutes and the judgments which I am teaching you to perform, so that you may live and go in and take possession of the land which the LORD, the God of your fathers, is giving you.

2 "You shall not add to the word which I am commanding you, nor take away from it, that you may keep the commandments of the LORD your God which I command you.

3 "Your eyes have seen what the LORD has done in the case of Baal-peor, for all the men who followed Baal-peor, the LORD your God has destroyed them from among you.

4 "But you who held fast to the LORD your God are alive today, every one of you.

5 "See, I have taught you statutes and judgments just as the LORD my God commanded me, that you should do thus in the land where you are entering to possess it.

6 "So keep and do them, for that is your wisdom and your understanding in the sight of the peoples who will hear all these statutes and say, 'Surely this great nation is a wise and understanding people.'

7 "For what great nation is there that has a god so near to it as is the LORD our God whenever we call on Him?

8 "Or what great nation is there that has statutes and judgments as righteous as this whole law which I am setting before you today?

9 "Only give heed to yourself and keep your soul diligently, so that you do not forget the things which your eyes have seen and they do not depart from your heart all the days of your life; but make them known to your sons and your grandsons.

10 "*Remember* the day you stood before the LORD your God at Horeb, when the LORD said to me, 'Assemble the people to Me, that I may let them hear My words so they may learn to fear Me all the days they live on the earth, and that they may teach their children.'

11 "You came near and stood at the foot of the mountain, and the mountain burned with fire to the *very* heart of the heavens: darkness, cloud and thick gloom.

12 "Then the LORD spoke to you from the midst of the fire; you heard the sound of words, but you saw no form—only a voice.

13 "So He declared to you His covenant which He commanded you to perform, *that is,* the Ten Commandments; and He wrote them on two tablets of stone.

14 "The LORD commanded me at that time to teach you statutes and judgments, that you might perform them in the land where you are going over to possess it.

15 "So watch yourselves carefully, since you did not see any form on the day the LORD spoke to you at Horeb from the midst of the fire,

16 so that you do not act corruptly and make a graven image for yourselves in the form of any figure, the likeness of male or female,

17 the likeness of any animal that is on the earth, the likeness of any winged bird that flies in the sky,

18 the likeness of anything that creeps on the ground, the likeness of any fish that is in the water below the earth.

19 "And *beware* not to lift up your eyes to heaven and see the sun and the moon and the stars, all the host of heaven, and be drawn away and worship them and serve them, those which the LORD your God has allotted to all the peoples under the whole heaven.

20 "But the LORD has taken you and brought you out of the iron furnace, from Egypt, to be a people for His own possession, as today.

21 "Now the LORD was angry with me on your account, and swore that I would not cross the Jordan, and that I would not enter the good land which the LORD your God is giving you as an inheritance.

22 "For I will die in this land, I shall not cross the Jordan, but you shall cross and take possession of this good land.

23 "So watch yourselves, that you do not forget the covenant of the LORD your God which He made with you, and make for yourselves a graven image in the form of anything *against* which the LORD your God has commanded you.

24 "For the LORD your God is a consuming fire, a jealous God. ≺

25 "When you become the father of children and children's children and have remained long in the land, and act corruptly, and make an idol in the form of anything, and do that which is evil in the sight of the LORD your God *so as* to provoke Him to anger,

26 I call heaven and earth to witness against you today, that you will surely perish quickly from the land where you are going over the Jordan to possess it. You shall not live long on it, but will be utterly destroyed.

27 "The LORD will scatter you among the peoples, and you will be left few in number among the nations where the LORD drives you.

28 "There you will serve gods, the work of man's hands, wood and stone, which neither see nor hear nor eat nor smell.

29 "But from there you will seek the LORD your God, and you will find *Him* if you search for Him with all your heart and all your soul.

30 "When you are in distress and all these things have come upon you, in the latter days you will return to the LORD your God and listen to His voice.

31 "For the LORD your God is a compassionate God; He will not fail you nor ≺ destroy you nor forget the covenant with your fathers which He swore to them.

32 "Indeed, ask now concerning the former days which were before you, since the day that God created man on

---

LIFE LESSONS

➤ **Deuteronomy 4:24 —** *"For the LORD your God is a consuming fire, a jealous God."*

The Lord is jealous in the sense that He will not share the hearts of His people with anyone or anything else. We belong to Him alone. Intimacy with God is His highest priority for our lives.

➤ **Deuteronomy 4:31** — *"He will not fail you nor destroy you nor forget the covenant with your fathers."*

*W*e serve a God who is powerful, awesome, mighty, loving, compassionate, and fully worthy of our trust. The Lord never makes a promise He can't keep, and He never forgets the promises He has made.

the earth, and *inquire* from one end of the heavens to the other. Has *anything* been done like this great thing, or has *anything* been heard like it?

33 "Has *any* people heard the voice of God speaking from the midst of the fire, as you have heard *it*, and survived?

34 "Or has a god tried to go to take for himself a nation from within *another* nation by trials, by signs and wonders and by war and by a mighty hand and by an outstretched arm and by great terrors, as the LORD your God did for you in Egypt before your eyes?

35 "To you it was shown that you might know that the LORD, He is God; there is no other besides Him.

36 "Out of the heavens He let you hear His voice to discipline you; and on earth He let you see His great fire, and you heard His words from the midst of the fire.

37 "Because He loved your fathers, therefore He chose their descendants after them. And He personally brought you from Egypt by His great power,

38 driving out from before you nations greater and mightier than you, to bring you in *and* to give you their land for an inheritance, as it is today.

39 "Know therefore today, and take it to your heart, that the LORD, He is God in heaven above and on the earth below; there is no other.

40 "So you shall keep His statutes and His commandments which I am giving you today, that it may go well with you and with your children after you, and that you may live long on the land which the LORD your God is giving you for all time."

41 Then Moses set apart three cities across the Jordan to the east,

42 that a manslayer might flee there, who unintentionally slew his neighbor without having enmity toward him in time past; and by fleeing to one of these cities he might live:

43 Bezer in the wilderness on the

How does God get our attention?

DEUTERONOMY 4:32–40

A whistle can get our attention quickly. We use it to control unruly behavior, signal the start or finish of an event, or interrupt the action in a game. Regardless of who blows it, a whistle tells us to stop and listen.

What does God use to get our attention? Sometimes He uses the tool of a restless spirit or a vague dissatisfaction with life. He may use another person's words to help us recognize He is speaking to us, or He may allow our prayers to remain unanswered in order to prompt us to sharpen our focus on Him. He may also work through disappointments, difficulties, and failures to gain our attention. In each case, we are to stop and ask, "Lord, are You teaching me something?"

If we are wise, we will quickly seek Him out. In tragedies, financial reversals, and physical affliction, God wants to see if we will turn to Him and ask, "Lord, what would You have me learn from this?"

What does it take for the Lord to get our attention? Will a restless spirit cause us to seek godly counsel? Do we listen when God sends someone to point out His way? When blessings come, do we turn to Him and ask how He would like us to use them? Do we seek the Lord when our prayers go unanswered? How long does it take us to get past our emotions over disappointments, difficulties, and failures to listen to what our heavenly Father has to say? In times of great financial crisis, tragedy, or sickness, do our eyes and minds lift heavenward to seek God's love and wisdom?

Allow the events of your life—both the pleasant and the painful—to prompt you to turn to God and ask, "Lord, what are you teaching me?" Don't miss what the Lord wants to tell you. Begin *now* training yourself to give Him your full attention. Allow what happens in your day to draw you to Him. He is waiting for you.

plateau for the Reubenites, and Ramoth in Gilead for the Gadites, and Golan in Bashan for the Manassites.

44 Now this is the law which Moses set before the sons of Israel;

45 these are the testimonies and the statutes and the ordinances which Moses spoke to the sons of Israel, when they came out from Egypt,

46 across the Jordan, in the valley opposite Beth-peor, in the land of Sihon king of the Amorites who lived at Heshbon, whom Moses and the sons of Israel defeated when they came out from Egypt.

47 They took possession of his land and the land of Og king of Bashan, the two kings of the Amorites, *who were* across the Jordan to the east,

48 from Aroer, which is on the edge of the valley of Arnon, even as far as Mount Sion (that is, Hermon),

49 with all the Arabah across the Jordan to the east, even as far as the sea of the Arabah, at the foot of the slopes of Pisgah.

Psalm 36:7–12

7 How precious is Your
  lovingkindness, O God!
 And the children of men take refuge
  in the shadow of Your wings.

8 They drink their fill of the
  abundance of Your house;
 And You give them to drink of the
  river of Your delights.

9 For with You is the fountain of life;
 In Your light we see light.

10 O continue Your lovingkindness to
  those who know You,
 And Your righteousness to the
  upright in heart.

11 Let not the foot of pride come upon
  me,
 And let not the hand of the wicked
  drive me away.

12 There the doers of iniquity have
  fallen;
 They have been thrust down and
  cannot rise.

Proverbs 12:7

7 The wicked are overthrown and are
  no more,
 But the house of the righteous will
  stand.

Luke 1:1–20

1 INASMUCH as many have undertaken to compile an account of the things accomplished among us,

2 just as they were handed down to us by those who from the beginning were eyewitnesses and servants of the word,

3 it seemed fitting for me as well, having investigated everything carefully from the beginning, to write *it* out for you in consecutive order, most excellent Theophilus;

4 so that you may know the exact truth about the things you have been taught.

5 In the days of Herod, king of Judea, there was a priest named Zacharias, of the division of Abijah; and he had a wife from the daughters of Aaron, and her name was Elizabeth.

6 They were both righteous in the sight of God, walking blamelessly in all the commandments and requirements of the Lord.

LIFE LESSONS

➤ **Psalm 36:9 —** *For with You is the fountain of life; in Your light we see light.*

*G*od offers the only real life there is. When we give ourselves to Him and walk in the light He provides us—in His Word and by His Spirit—we begin to see more and more how we can enjoy life to the fullest.

➤ **Luke 1:4 —** *So that you may know the exact truth about the things you have been taught.*

*G*od wants us to know that the Bible teaches truth and can be trusted in all that it declares. The Gospels are not a collection of religious fairy tales. They are the source of eternal truth—God's Word.

7   But they had no child, because Elizabeth was barren, and they were both advanced in years.

8   Now it happened *that* while he was performing his priestly service before God in the *appointed* order of his division,

9   according to the custom of the priestly office, he was chosen by lot to enter the temple of the Lord and burn incense.

10   And the whole multitude of the people were in prayer outside at the hour of the incense offering.

11   And an angel of the Lord appeared to him, standing to the right of the altar of incense.

12   Zacharias was troubled when he saw *the angel*, and fear gripped him.

13   But the angel said to him, "Do not be afraid, Zacharias, for your petition has been heard, and your wife Elizabeth will bear you a son, and you will give him the name John.

14   "You will have joy and gladness, and many will rejoice at his birth.

15   "For he will be great in the sight of the Lord; and he will drink no wine or liquor, and he will be filled with the Holy Spirit while yet in his mother's womb.

16   "And he will turn many of the sons of Israel back to the Lord their God.

17   "It is he who will go *as a forerunner* before Him in the spirit and power of Elijah, TO TURN THE HEARTS OF THE FATHERS BACK TO THE CHILDREN, and the disobedient to the attitude of the righteous, so as to make ready a people prepared for the Lord."

18   Zacharias said to the angel, "How will I know this *for certain?* For I am an old man and my wife is advanced in years."

19   The angel answered and said to him, "I am Gabriel, who stands in the presence of God, and I have been sent to speak to you and to bring you this good news.

20   "And behold, you shall be silent and unable to speak until the day when these things take place, because you did not believe my words, which will be fulfilled in their proper time."

Deuteronomy 5:1—6:25

5 THEN Moses summoned all Israel and said to them:

"Hear, O Israel, the statutes and the ordinances which I am speaking today in your hearing, that you may learn them and observe them carefully.

2   "The LORD our God made a covenant with us at Horeb.

3   "The LORD did not make this covenant with our fathers, but with us, *with* all those of us alive here today.

4   "The LORD spoke to you face to face at the mountain from the midst of the fire,

5   *while* I was standing between the LORD and you at that time, to declare to you the word of the LORD; for you were afraid because of the fire and did not go up the mountain. He said,

6   'I am the LORD your God who brought you out of the land of Egypt, out of the house of slavery.

7   'You shall have no other gods before Me.

8   'You shall not make for yourself an idol, *or* any likeness *of* what is in heaven above or on the earth beneath or in the water under the earth.

9   'You shall not worship them or serve them; for I, the LORD your God, am a jealous God, visiting the iniquity of the fathers on the children, and on the third and the fourth *generations* of those who hate Me,

10   but showing lovingkindness to thousands, to those who love Me and keep My commandments.

11   'You shall not take the name of the LORD your God in vain, for the LORD will not leave him unpunished who takes His name in vain.

12   'Observe the sabbath day to keep it holy, as the LORD your God commanded you.

13   'Six days you shall labor and do all your work,

14   but the seventh day is a sabbath

of the LORD your God; *in it* you shall not do any work, you or your son or your daughter or your male servant or your female servant or your ox or your donkey or any of your cattle or your so-journer who stays with you, so that your male servant and your female servant may rest as well as you.

15 'You shall remember that you were a slave in the land of Egypt, and the LORD your God brought you out of there by a mighty hand and by an outstretched arm; therefore the LORD your God com-manded you to observe the sabbath day.

16 'Honor your father and your mother, as the LORD your God has commanded you, that your days may be prolonged and that it may go well with you on the land which the LORD your God gives you.

17 'You shall not murder.

18 'You shall not commit adultery.

19 'You shall not steal.

20 'You shall not bear false witness against your neighbor.

21 'You shall not covet your neigh-bor's wife, and you shall not desire your neighbor's house, his field or his male servant or his female servant, his ox or his donkey or anything that belongs to your neighbor.'

22 "These words the LORD spoke to all your assembly at the mountain from the midst of the fire, *of* the cloud and *of* the thick gloom, with a great voice, and He added no more. He wrote them on two tablets of stone and gave them to me.

23 "And when you heard the voice from the midst of the darkness, while the mountain was burning with fire, you came near to me, all the heads of your tribes and your elders.

24 "You said, 'Behold, the LORD our God has shown us His glory and His great-ness, and we have heard His voice from the midst of the fire; we have seen today that God speaks with man, yet He lives.

25 'Now then why should we die? For this great fire will consume us; if we hear the voice of the LORD our God any longer, then we will die.

26 'For who is there of all flesh who has heard the voice of the living God speak-ing from the midst of the fire, as we *have*, and lived?

27 'Go near and hear all that the LORD our God says; then speak to us all that the LORD our God speaks to you, and we will hear and do *it*.'

28 "The LORD heard the voice of your words when you spoke to me, and the LORD said to me, 'I have heard the voice of the words of this people which they have spoken to you. They have done well in all that they have spoken.

29 'Oh that they had such a heart in ◄ them, that they would fear Me and keep all My commandments always, that it may be well with them and with their sons forever!

30 'Go, say to them, "Return to your tents."

31 'But as for you, stand here by Me, that I may speak to you all the command-ments and the statutes and the judg-ments which you shall teach them, that they may observe *them* in the land which I give them to possess.'

32 "So you shall observe to do just as the LORD your God has commanded you; you shall not turn aside to the right or to the left.

33 "You shall walk in all the way which the LORD your God has commanded you, that you may live and that it may be well with you, and that you may prolong *your* days in the land which you will pos-sess.

6 "NOW this is the commandment, the statutes and the judgments which the LORD your God has commanded *me* to teach you, that you might do *them* in the land where you are going over to possess it,

2 so that you and your son and your grandson might fear the LORD your God,

---

LIFE LESSONS

➤ **Deuteronomy 5:29 —** *"Oh that they had such a heart in them, that they would fear Me and keep all My com-mandments always, that it may be well with them and with their sons forever!"*

*H*ere God states the desire of His own heart: He longs that a godly fear of Him would prompt us to eagerly keep His commandments, so that He could bless us and our descendants *forever*. God gives us His commandments for our good. By keeping them, His people gain not only life, but a *successful* life and a *long* life. That is a gracious God!

to keep all His statutes and His commandments which I command you, all the days of your life, and that your days may be prolonged.

3 "O Israel, you should listen and be careful to do *it*, that it may be well with you and that you may multiply greatly, just as the LORD, the God of your fathers, has promised you, *in* a land flowing with milk and honey.

4 "Hear, O Israel! The LORD is our God, the LORD is one!

5 "You shall love the LORD your God with all your heart and with all your soul and with all your might.

6 "These words, which I am commanding you today, shall be on your heart.

7 "You shall teach them diligently to your sons and shall talk of them when you sit in your house and when you walk by the way and when you lie down and when you rise up.

8 "You shall bind them as a sign on your hand and they shall be as frontals on your forehead.

9 "You shall write them on the doorposts of your house and on your gates.

10 "Then it shall come about when the LORD your God brings you into the land which He swore to your fathers,

---

LIFE LESSONS

➤ **Deuteronomy 6:4 — *"Hear, O Israel! The LORD is our God, the LORD is one!"***

This statement begins a section that is called the *Shema. Shema* is the Hebrew word for *hear*. The Jewish people would often pray Deuteronomy 6:4–9 as a confirmation of their belief in God. It's a wise practice to rehearse what you believe because when times of trouble come, the Holy Spirit will remind you of God's truth and comfort you.

➤ **Deuteronomy 6:5 — *"You shall love the LORD your God with all your heart and with all your soul and with all your might."***

Of all God's commandments, this is the central and most important one. When we love God first and foremost, obedience follows as a natural result and ceases to be a chore (John 14:15; 1 John 5:3).

Abraham, Isaac and Jacob, to give you, great and splendid cities which you did not build,

11 and houses full of all good things which you did not fill, and hewn cisterns which you did not dig, vineyards and olive trees which you did not plant, and you eat and are satisfied,

12 then watch yourself, that you do not forget the LORD who brought you from the land of Egypt, out of the house of slavery.

13 "You shall fear *only* the LORD your God; and you shall worship Him and swear by His name.

14 "You shall not follow other gods, any of the gods of the peoples who surround you,

15 for the LORD your God in the midst of you is a jealous God; otherwise the anger of the LORD your God will be kindled against you, and He will wipe you off the face of the earth.

16 "You shall not put the LORD your God to the test, as you tested *Him* at Massah.

17 "You should diligently keep the commandments of the LORD your God, and His testimonies and His statutes which He has commanded you.

18 "You shall do what is right and good in the sight of the LORD, that it may be well with you and that you may go in and possess the good land which the LORD swore to *give* your fathers,

19 by driving out all your enemies from before you, as the LORD has spoken.

20 "When your son asks you in time to come, saying, 'What *do* the testimonies and the statutes and the judgments *mean* which the LORD our God commanded you?'

21 then you shall say to your son, 'We were slaves to Pharaoh in Egypt, and the LORD brought us from Egypt with a mighty hand.

22 'Moreover, the LORD showed great and distressing signs and wonders before our eyes against Egypt, Pharaoh and all his household;

23 He brought us out from there in order to bring us in, to give us the land which He had sworn to our fathers.'

24 "So the LORD commanded us to observe all these statutes, to fear the LORD

our God for our good always and for our survival, as *it is* today.

25 "It will be righteousness for us if we are careful to observe all this commandment before the LORD our God, just as He commanded us.

Psalm 37:1–4

A Psalm of David.

37 DO not fret because of evildoers,
Be not envious toward wrongdoers.

2　For they will wither quickly like the grass
And fade like the green herb.

3　Trust in the LORD and do good;
Dwell in the land and cultivate faithfulness.

4　Delight yourself in the LORD;
And He will give you the desires of your heart.

Proverbs 12:8

8　A man will be praised according to his insight,
But one of perverse mind will be despised.

Luke 1:21–38

21　The people were waiting for Zacharias, and were wondering at his delay in the temple.

22　But when he came out, he was unable to speak to them; and they realized that he had seen a vision in the temple; and he kept making signs to them, and remained mute.

23　When the days of his priestly service were ended, he went back home.

24　After these days Elizabeth his wife became pregnant, and she kept herself in seclusion for five months, saying,

25　"This is the way the Lord has dealt with me in the days when He looked *with favor* upon *me*, to take away my disgrace among men."

26　Now in the sixth month the angel Gabriel was sent from God to a city in Galilee called Nazareth,

27　to a virgin engaged to a man whose name was Joseph, of the descendants of David; and the virgin's name was Mary.

28　And coming in, he said to her, "Greetings, favored one! The Lord *is* with you."

29　But she was very perplexed at *this* statement, and kept pondering what kind of salutation this was.

30　The angel said to her, "Do not be afraid, Mary; for you have found favor with God.

31　"And behold, you will conceive in your womb and bear a son, and you shall name Him Jesus.

32　"He will be great and will be called the Son of the Most High; and the Lord God will give Him the throne of His father David;

33　and He will reign over the house of Jacob forever, and His kingdom will have no end."

34　Mary said to the angel, "How can this be, since I am a virgin?"

35　The angel answered and said to her, "The Holy Spirit will come upon you, and the power of the Most High will overshadow you; and for that reason the holy Child shall be called the Son of God.

LIFE LESSONS

➢ **Psalm 37:3** — *Trust in the LORD and do good; dwell in the land and cultivate faithfulness.*

*G*od calls us to do good to others so that they might see His goodness in us. But unless we "cultivate faithfulness"—unless we stay in close fellowship with Him—we won't have much good to offer anyone.

➢ **Luke 1:30** — *"Do not be afraid, Mary; for you have found favor with God."*

*T*he favor of God is worth any discomfort it might entail. God chose Mary to give birth to the Savior of the world, but she also had to bear the public shame of people not understanding what God was doing through her and through Jesus.

Life Examples:

MARY: Woman of Faith

LUKE 1:31–38

*W*hen Mary was young, the customary age for betrothal was thirteen or fourteen. More than likely, she was a young girl when Joseph asked her to marry him. Can you imagine the excitement she felt? That quickly changed the moment the angel Gabriel stepped into her presence and announced she would have a son—and He would be the Savior of the world.

Jewish tradition demanded harsh treatment for unmarried pregnant women.

Religious leaders would have dealt with her severely. Yet Mary remained strong in her faith. She knew she had heard God's Word spoken to her, and she believed He would provide what she needed to do His will.

Mary was an ordinary girl with extraordinary, godly character that gave her an uncommon faith. Completely trusting in God, in every way she was a good and faithful servant. Mary provides a model of inspiration for each one of us. For the most part, she lived her life in relative obscurity—happy and even grateful to be used by God. Yet today the world continues to celebrate her obedience to the Lord.

36 "And behold, even your relative Elizabeth has also conceived a son in her old age; and she who was called barren is now in her sixth month.
➤ 37 "For nothing will be impossible with God."
38 And Mary said, "Behold, the bondslave of the Lord; may it be done to me according to your word." And the angel departed from her.

LIFE LESSONS

➤ **Luke 1:37 — *"For nothing will be impossible with God."***

*W*e can trust God even in the most difficult of circumstances because no problem is too tough for Him to handle and no challenge is beyond His power to overcome. He has the ability to do what He says He will do.

Deuteronomy 7:1—8:20

7"WHEN the LORD your God brings you into the land where you are entering to possess it, and clears away many nations before you, the Hittites and the Girgashites and the Amorites and the Canaanites and the Perizzites and the Hivites and the Jebusites, seven nations greater and stronger than you,
2 and when the LORD your God delivers them before you and you defeat them, then you shall utterly destroy them. You shall make no covenant with them and show no favor to them.
3 "Furthermore, you shall not intermarry with them; you shall not give your daughters to their sons, nor shall you take their daughters for your sons.
➤ 4 "For they will turn your sons away from following Me to serve other gods; then the anger of the LORD will be kindled against you and He will quickly destroy you.
5 "But thus you shall do to them: you shall tear down their altars, and smash their *sacred* pillars, and hew down their Asherim, and burn their graven images with fire.
6 "For you are a holy people to the LORD your God; the LORD your God has chosen you to be a people for His own possession out of all the peoples who are on the face of the earth.

LIFE LESSONS

➤ **Deuteronomy 7:4 — *"They will turn your sons away from following Me to serve other gods."***

*S*ince intimacy with God is His highest priority for our lives, no greater sin exists than to turn someone's heart away from the one true God.

➤ 7 "The LORD did not set His love on you nor choose you because you were more in number than any of the peoples, for you were the fewest of all peoples,

8 but because the LORD loved you and kept the oath which He swore to your forefathers, the LORD brought you out by a mighty hand and redeemed you from the house of slavery, from the hand of Pharaoh king of Egypt.

9 "Know therefore that the LORD your God, He is God, the faithful God, who keeps His covenant and His lovingkindness to a thousandth generation with those who love Him and keep His commandments;

10 but repays those who hate Him to their faces, to destroy them; He will not delay with him who hates Him, He will repay him to his face.

11 "Therefore, you shall keep the commandment and the statutes and the judgments which I am commanding you today, to do them.

12 "Then it shall come about, because you listen to these judgments and keep and do them, that the LORD your God will keep with you His covenant and His lovingkindness which He swore to your forefathers.

13 "He will love you and bless you and multiply you; He will also bless the fruit of your womb and the fruit of your ground, your grain and your new wine and your oil, the increase of your herd and the young of your flock, in the land which He swore to your forefathers to give you.

14 "You shall be blessed above all peoples; there will be no male or female barren among you or among your cattle.

15 "The LORD will remove from you all sickness; and He will not put on you any of the harmful diseases of Egypt which you have known, but He will lay them on all who hate you.

16 "You shall consume all the peoples whom the LORD your God will deliver to you; your eye shall not pity them, nor shall you serve their gods, for that *would be* a snare to you.

17 "If you should say in your heart, 'These nations are greater than I; how can I dispossess them?'

➤ 18 you shall not be afraid of them; you shall well remember what the LORD your God did to Pharaoh and to all Egypt:

LIFE LESSONS

➤ **Deuteronomy 7:7, 8 — *"You were the fewest of all peoples; but because the LORD loved you."***

*E*ven before God's chosen people entered the Promised Land, God assured them of His everlasting love. God does not love us because we're so loveable; He loves us because His nature is love and because of His promise to Abraham. We owe our salvation to the holy love of God, and nothing else.

➤ **Deuteronomy 7:18 — *"You shall not be afraid of them; you shall well remember what the LORD your God did to Pharaoh."***

*W*hen God calls us to some intimidating work, we are not to focus on our own abilities and strengths, but on His limitless power and grace. We succeed only when we align ourselves with Him. Our God really is both great and awesome—and He is with us! Today, not only is He with us, He is *in* us in the Person of the Holy Spirit. So what do we have to fear?

19 the great trials which your eyes saw and the signs and the wonders and the mighty hand and the outstretched arm by which the LORD your God brought you out. So shall the LORD your God do to all the peoples of whom you are afraid.

20 "Moreover, the LORD your God will send the hornet against them, until those who are left and hide themselves from you perish.

21 "You shall not dread them, for the LORD your God is in your midst, a great and awesome God.

22 "The LORD your God will clear away these nations before you little by little; you will not be able to put an end to them quickly, for the wild beasts would grow too numerous for you.

23 "But the LORD your God will deliver them before you, and will throw them into great confusion until they are destroyed.

24 "He will deliver their kings into your hand so that you will make their name perish from under heaven; no man will be able to stand before you until you have destroyed them.

25 "The graven images of their gods you

are to burn with fire; you shall not covet the silver or the gold that is on them, nor take it for yourselves, or you will be snared by it, for it is an abomination to the LORD your God.

26 "You shall not bring an abomination into your house, and like it come under the ban; you shall utterly detest it and you shall utterly abhor it, for it is something banned.

8 "ALL the commandments that I am commanding you today you shall be careful to do, that you may live and multiply, and go in and possess the land which the LORD swore to give to your forefathers.

2 "You shall remember all the way which the LORD your God has led you in the wilderness these forty years, that He might humble you, testing you, to know what was in your heart, whether you would keep His commandments or not.

3 "He humbled you and let you be hungry, and fed you with manna which you did not know, nor did your fathers know, that He might make you understand that man does not live by bread alone, but man lives by everything that proceeds out of the mouth of the LORD.

4 "Your clothing did not wear out on you, nor did your foot swell these forty years.

5 "Thus you are to know in your heart that the LORD your God was disciplining you just as a man disciplines his son.

6 "Therefore, you shall keep the commandments of the LORD your God, to walk in His ways and to fear Him.

7 "For the LORD your God is bringing you into a good land, a land of brooks of water, of fountains and springs, flowing forth in valleys and hills;

8 a land of wheat and barley, of vines and fig trees and pomegranates, a land of olive oil and honey;

9 a land where you will eat food without scarcity, in which you will not lack anything; a land whose stones are iron, and out of whose hills you can dig copper.

10 "When you have eaten and are satisfied, you shall bless the LORD your God for the good land which He has given you.

11 "Beware that you do not forget the LORD your God by not keeping His commandments and His ordinances and His statutes which I am commanding you today;

12 otherwise, when you have eaten and are satisfied, and have built good houses and lived in them,

13 and when your herds and your flocks multiply, and your silver and gold multiply, and all that you have multiplies,

14 then your heart will become proud and you will forget the LORD your God who brought you out from the land of Egypt, out of the house of slavery.

15 "He led you through the great and terrible wilderness, with its fiery serpents and scorpions and thirsty ground where there was no water; He brought water for you out of the rock of flint.

16 "In the wilderness He fed you manna which your fathers did not know, that He might humble you and that He might test you, to do good for you in the end.

17 "Otherwise, you may say in your heart, 'My power and the strength of my hand made me this wealth.'

18 "But you shall remember the LORD your God, for it is He who is giving you power to make wealth, that He may confirm His covenant which He swore to your fathers, as it is this day.

19 "It shall come about if you ever forget the LORD your God and go after other

---

LIFE LESSONS

➤ **Deuteronomy 8:16** — *"In the wilderness He fed you manna . . . that He might test you, to do good for you in the end."*

God promises to lead us, even when we walk through the wilderness. There He humbles us and tests us, to see whether we will obey Him, even when things get difficult. Even so, He does all this to do us "good in the end." We may not see that good right away, but if we will trust Him, He will bless us in His time.

➤ **Deuteronomy 8:18** — *"But you shall remember the LORD your God, for it is He who is giving you power to make wealth, that He may confirm His covenant which He swore to your fathers."*

Nothing in the Bible condemns hard work in the acquisition of material wealth. God wants us to remember, however, that our ability to earn wealth comes from Him and Him alone.

WHAT THE BIBLE SAYS ABOUT

How God Defines Wealth

Deuteronomy 8:17

*E*ach year various publications list the one hundred wealthiest people in America. The magazines categorize the individuals by total income, usually in the millions and billions. Such is the predominant viewpoint regarding the meaning of wealth.

But is that the way God defines wealth? Hardly. From God's standpoint, wealth includes much more than currency. The bank accounts of rich men and women may overflow, but misery often enshrouds their souls.

Biblical wealth, by contrast, may be defined as the ability to experience and enjoy God's presence. The poor individual who knows God as Savior has indescribable wealth compared to the rich one who rejects Him.

The Bible insists that God is the source of all gain: "Both riches and honor come from You, and You rule over all, and in Your hand is power and might; and it lies in Your hand to make great and to strengthen everyone" (1 Chr. 29:12).

Apart from the benevolence of God, we cannot amass wealth. While our labor, diligence, planning, and wisdom are vital, God remains the sole source of blessing. He is the fountainhead of health, food, sun, and all other elements necessary for life. As Creator, all of life is His gift. He is the Prime Giver. "Every good thing given and every perfect gift is from above, coming down from the Father of lights" (James 1:17).

As God prepared to take the Israelites into fertile and fruitful Canaan, He warned them not to forget the source of their newfound affluence, "Otherwise, you may say in your heart, 'My power and the strength of my hand made me this wealth.' But you shall remember the LORD your God, for it is He who is giving you power to make wealth" (Deut. 8:17, 18).

Since all wealth flows from the provision of God, our role is to act as sensible, faithful stewards. God gives it all and God owns it all. He designates us as caretakers of His assets. Our spending and investments then become extensions of His will. By following the careful guidelines of Scripture, we can wisely manage God's riches. ◈

---

gods and serve them and worship them, I testify against you today that you will surely perish.

20 "Like the nations that the LORD makes to perish before you, so you shall perish; because you would not listen to the voice of the LORD your God.

◈ Psalm 37:5–11

5 Commit your way to the LORD,
   Trust also in Him, and He will do it.
✳6 He will bring forth your
   righteousness as the light
   And your judgment as the noonday.
7 Rest in the LORD and wait patiently
   for Him;
   Do not fret because of him who
   prospers in his way,
   Because of the man who carries out
   wicked schemes.
8 Cease from anger and forsake
   wrath;

Do not fret; *it leads* only to
   evildoing.
9 For evildoers will be cut off,
   But those who wait for the LORD,
   they will inherit the land.
10 Yet a little while and the wicked
   man will be no more;
   And you will look carefully for his
   place and he will not be *there*.
11 But the humble will inherit the land
   And will delight themselves in
   abundant prosperity.

◈ Proverbs 12:9–10

9 Better is he who is lightly esteemed
   and has a servant
   Than he who honors himself and
   lacks bread.
10 A righteous man has regard for the
   life of his animal,
   But *even* the compassion of the
   wicked is cruel.

Luke 1:39–56

39 Now at this time Mary arose and went in a hurry to the hill country, to a city of Judah,
40 and entered the house of Zacharias and greeted Elizabeth.
41 When Elizabeth heard Mary's greeting, the baby leaped in her womb; and Elizabeth was filled with the Holy Spirit.
42 And she cried out with a loud voice and said, "Blessed *are* you among women, and blessed *is* the fruit of your womb!
43 "And how has it *happened* to me, that the mother of my Lord would come to me?
44 "For behold, when the sound of your greeting reached my ears, the baby leaped in my womb for joy.
45 "And blessed *is* she who believed that there would be a fulfillment of what had been spoken to her by the Lord."
46 And Mary said:
"My soul exalts the Lord,
47 And my spirit has rejoiced in God my Savior,
48 "For He has had regard for the humble state of His bondslave;
For behold, from this time on all generations will count me blessed.
49 "For the Mighty One has done great things for me;
And holy is His name.
50 "AND HIS MERCY IS UPON GENERATION AFTER GENERATION
TOWARD THOSE WHO FEAR HIM.

51 "He has done mighty deeds with His arm;
He has scattered *those who were* proud in the thoughts of their heart.
52 "He has brought down rulers from *their* thrones,
And has exalted those who were humble.
53 "HE HAS FILLED THE HUNGRY WITH GOOD THINGS;
And sent away the rich empty-handed.
54 "He has given help to Israel His servant,
In remembrance of His mercy,
55 As He spoke to our fathers,
To Abraham and his descendants forever."
56 And Mary stayed with her about three months, and *then* returned to her home.

LIFE LESSONS

> Luke 1:45 — *"Blessed is she who believed that there would be a fulfillment of what had been spoken to her by the Lord."*

What would have happened had Mary not believed Gabriel's words? Would she have disqualified herself from being the mother of Jesus? The fact is, she did believe and she obeyed God. Her obedience set the stage for the Lord's blessings. He not only fulfilled His word in her, He also used her to accomplish His prophecy to our lost and dying world.

Deuteronomy 9:1—10:22

9 "HEAR, O Israel! You are crossing over the Jordan today to go in to dispossess nations greater and mightier than you, great cities fortified to heaven,
2 a people great and tall, the sons of the Anakim, whom you know and of whom you have heard *it said,* 'Who can stand before the sons of Anak?'

3 "Know therefore today that it is the LORD your God who is crossing over before you as a consuming fire. He will destroy them and He will subdue them before you, so that you may drive them out and destroy them quickly, just as the LORD has spoken to you.
4 "Do not say in your heart when the LORD your God has driven them out before you, 'Because of my righteousness the LORD has brought me in to possess

this land,' but *it is* because of the wickedness of these nations *that* the LORD is dispossessing them before you.

5 "It is not for your righteousness or for the uprightness of your heart that you are going to possess their land, but *it is* because of the wickedness of these nations *that* the LORD your God is driving them out before you, in order to confirm the oath which the LORD swore to your fathers, to Abraham, Isaac and Jacob.

➤ 6 "Know, then, *it is* not because of your righteousness *that* the LORD your God is giving you this good land to possess, for you are a stubborn people.

7 "Remember, do not forget how you provoked the LORD your God to wrath in the wilderness; from the day that you left the land of Egypt until you arrived at this place, you have been rebellious against the LORD.

8 "Even at Horeb you provoked the LORD to wrath, and the LORD was so angry with you that He would have destroyed you.

9 "When I went up to the mountain to receive the tablets of stone, the tablets of the covenant which the LORD had made with you, then I remained on the mountain forty days and nights; I neither ate bread nor drank water.

10 "The LORD gave me the two tablets of stone written by the finger of God; and on them *were* all the words which the LORD had spoken with you at the mountain from the midst of the fire on the day of the assembly.

11 "It came about at the end of forty days and nights that the LORD gave me the two tablets of stone, the tablets of the covenant.

12 "Then the LORD said to me, 'Arise, go down from here quickly, for your people whom you brought out of Egypt have acted corruptly. They have quickly turned aside from the way which I commanded them; they have made a molten image for themselves.'

13 "The LORD spoke further to me, saying, 'I have seen this people, and indeed, it is a stubborn people.

14 'Let Me alone, that I may destroy them and blot out their name from under heaven; and I will make of you a nation mightier and greater than they.'

15 "So I turned and came down from the mountain while the mountain was burning with fire, and the two tablets of the covenant were in my two hands.

16 "And I saw that you had indeed sinned against the LORD your God. You had made for yourselves a molten calf; you had turned aside quickly from the way which the LORD had commanded you.

17 "I took hold of the two tablets and threw them from my hands and smashed them before your eyes.

18 "I fell down before the LORD, as at the first, forty days and nights; I neither ate bread nor drank water, because of all your sin which you had committed in doing what was evil in the sight of the LORD to provoke Him to anger.

19 "For I was afraid of the anger and hot displeasure with which the LORD was wrathful against you in order to destroy you, but the LORD listened to me that time also.

20 "The LORD was angry enough with Aaron to destroy him; so I also prayed for Aaron at the same time.

21 "I took your sinful *thing*, the calf which you had made, and burned it with fire and crushed it, grinding it very small until it was as fine as dust; and I threw its dust into the brook that came down from the mountain.

22 "Again at Taberah and at Massah and at Kibroth-hattaavah you provoked the LORD to wrath.

23 "When the LORD sent you from Kadesh-barnea, saying, 'Go up and possess the land which I have given you,' then you rebelled against the command of the LORD your God; you neither believed Him nor listened to His voice.

24 "You have been rebellious against the LORD from the day I knew you.

LIFE LESSONS

➤ **Deuteronomy 9:6 — *"Know, then, it is not because of your righteousness that the LORD your God is giving you this good land to possess, for you are a stubborn people."***

*T*he Lord does not shower us with His love because we deserve it, but because He is gracious and loving. "But God demonstrates His own love toward us, in that while we were yet sinners, Christ died for us" (Rom. 5:8).

25 "So I fell down before the LORD the forty days and nights, which I did because the LORD had said He would destroy you.

26 "I prayed to the LORD and said, 'O Lord GOD, do not destroy Your people, even Your inheritance, whom You have redeemed through Your greatness, whom You have brought out of Egypt with a mighty hand.

27 'Remember Your servants, Abraham, Isaac, and Jacob; do not look at the stubbornness of this people or at their wickedness or their sin.

28 'Otherwise the land from which You brought us may say, "Because the LORD was not able to bring them into the land which He had promised them and because He hated them He has brought them out to slay them in the wilderness."

29 'Yet they are Your people, even Your inheritance, whom You have brought out by Your great power and Your outstretched arm.'

10 "AT that time the LORD said to me, 'Cut out for yourself two tablets of stone like the former ones, and come up to Me on the mountain, and make an ark of wood for yourself.

2 'I will write on the tablets the words that were on the former tablets which you shattered, and you shall put them in the ark.'

3 "So I made an ark of acacia wood and cut out two tablets of stone like the former ones, and went up on the mountain with the two tablets in my hand.

4 "He wrote on the tablets, like the former writing, the Ten Commandments which the LORD had spoken to you on the mountain from the midst of the fire on the day of the assembly; and the LORD gave them to me.

5 "Then I turned and came down from the mountain and put the tablets in the ark which I had made; and there they are, as the LORD commanded me."

6 (Now the sons of Israel set out from Beeroth Bene-jaakan to Moserah. There Aaron died and there he was buried and Eleazar his son ministered as priest in his place.

7 From there they set out to Gudgodah, and from Gudgodah to Jotbathah, a land of brooks of water.

8 At that time the LORD set apart the tribe of Levi to carry the ark of the covenant of the LORD, to stand before the LORD to serve Him and to bless in His name until this day.

9 Therefore, Levi does not have a portion or inheritance with his brothers; the LORD is his inheritance, just as the LORD your God spoke to him.)

10 "I, moreover, stayed on the mountain forty days and forty nights like the first time, and the LORD listened to me that time also; the LORD was not willing to destroy you.

11 "Then the LORD said to me, 'Arise, proceed on your journey ahead of the people, that they may go in and possess the land which I swore to their fathers to give them.'

12 "Now, Israel, what does the LORD your God require from you, but to fear the LORD your God, to walk in all His ways and love Him, and to serve the LORD your God with all your heart and with all your soul,

13 and to keep the LORD'S commandments and His statutes which I am commanding you today for your good?

14 "Behold, to the LORD your God belong heaven and the highest heavens, the earth and all that is in it.

15 "Yet on your fathers did the LORD set His affection to love them, and He chose their descendants after them, even you above all peoples, as it is this day.

16 "So circumcise your heart, and stiffen your neck no longer.

17 "For the LORD your God is the God of gods and the Lord of lords, the great, the mighty, and the awesome God who does not show partiality nor take a bribe.

18 "He executes justice for the orphan

LIFE LESSONS

➤ **Deuteronomy 10:12 —** *"What does the LORD your God require from you, but to fear the LORD your God, to walk in all His ways and love Him, and to serve the LORD."*

*M*oses gives a condensed version of the law: (1) fear God; (2) walk in God's ways; (3) love God; (4) serve God wholeheartedly; (5) obey God. God promises to bless all those who live like this.

ANSWERS TO LIFE'S QUESTIONS

What does God require of us?

DEUTERONOMY 10:12, 13

Sometimes God's commands are as clear as the sun on a cloudless day. However, at times what He instructs you to do may seem as difficult as capturing the sun and putting it in your pocket—it's an impossible task.

The Israelites faced this dilemma when they stood on the verge of entering Canaan. God commanded that they take the land of promise by war; but after 40 years of wandering, no doubt they wondered if they had what it took to wage a successful campaign.

Yet, they were missing the point of the relationship they had with God. In Deuteronomy 10:12, 13 Moses admonished, "What does the LORD your God require from you, but to fear the LORD your God, to walk in all His ways and love Him, and to serve the LORD your God with all your heart and with all your soul, and to keep the LORD's commandments and His statutes which I am commanding you today for your good?"

God did not expect them to have a perfect battle plan—He simply wanted them to love Him. He did not ask them to win the war at any cost—He told them to simply trust His ways and obey His commands.

Moses understood that Israel could not be under God's protection without obedience and faith—without love for the One they were following. You must understand that as well.

God is not an impossible taskmaster; He won't set you up to fail. Rather, He is your loving God who is making a way for you through whatever challenges you face. Your responsibility is to walk in His ways.

Micah 6:8 explains, "He has told you, O man, what is good; and what does the LORD require of you but to do justice, to love kindness, and to walk humbly with your God?" What does that mean? It means that you are to exhibit the character of Christ—respectfully accepting God's instructions and serving Him out of love.

Understand that God wants to have a deep and abiding relationship with you, and He gladly prepares and empowers you for whatever He expects of you. The more you understand His ways, the more you're going to love Him and want to obey Him.

If you want to serve God and if you desire His protection, you must know Him, love Him, and obey Him. And no matter how difficult the challenges that arise, God will help you. In His will is the safest place for you to be. So, do not fear, for He is with you. He will give you the strength you need when you trust Him and do what He says.

and the widow, and shows His love for the alien by giving him food and clothing.

19 "So show your love for the alien, for you were aliens in the land of Egypt.

20 "You shall fear the LORD your God; you shall serve Him and cling to Him, and you shall swear by His name.

21 "He is your praise and He is your God, who has done these great and awesome things for you which your eyes have seen.

22 "Your fathers went down to Egypt seventy persons in all, and now the LORD your God has made you as numerous as the stars of heaven.

Psalm 37:12–17

12 The wicked plots against the righteous
  And gnashes at him with his teeth.

13 The Lord laughs at him,
  For He sees his day is coming.

14 The wicked have drawn the sword and bent their bow
  To cast down the afflicted and the needy,
  To slay those who are upright in conduct.

15 Their sword will enter their own heart,
  And their bows will be broken.

16 Better is the little of the righteous
  Than the abundance of many wicked.

17 For the arms of the wicked will be broken,
  But the LORD sustains the righteous.

Proverbs 12:11

11 He who tills his land will have plenty of bread,

But he who pursues worthless
things lacks sense.

Luke 1:57–80

57 Now the time had come for Elizabeth to give birth, and she gave birth to a son.
58 Her neighbors and her relatives heard that the Lord had displayed His great mercy toward her; and they were rejoicing with her.
59 And it happened that on the eighth day they came to circumcise the child, and they were going to call him Zacharias, after his father.
60 But his mother answered and said, "No indeed; but he shall be called John."
61 And they said to her, "There is no one among your relatives who is called by that name."
62 And they made signs to his father, as to what he wanted him called.
63 And he asked for a tablet and wrote as follows, "His name is John." And they were all astonished.
64 And at once his mouth was opened and his tongue *loosed*, and he *began* to speak in praise of God.
65 Fear came on all those living around them; and all these matters were being talked about in all the hill country of Judea.
66 All who heard them kept them in mind, saying, "What then will this child *turn out to* be?" For the hand of the Lord was certainly with him.
67 And his father Zacharias was filled with the Holy Spirit, and prophesied, saying:
68 "Blessed *be* the Lord God of Israel,
For He has visited us and
accomplished redemption for His people,
69 And has raised up a horn of salvation for us
In the house of David His servant—
70 As He spoke by the mouth of His holy prophets from of old—
71 Salvation FROM OUR ENEMIES,
And FROM THE HAND OF ALL WHO HATE US;
72 To show mercy toward our fathers,

And to remember His holy covenant,
73 The oath which He swore to Abraham our father,
74 To grant us that we, being rescued from the hand of our enemies, Might serve Him without fear,
75 In holiness and righteousness before Him all our days.
76 "And you, child, will be called the prophet of the Most High;
For you will go on BEFORE THE LORD TO PREPARE HIS WAYS;
77 To give to His people *the* knowledge of salvation
By the forgiveness of their sins,
78 Because of the tender mercy of our God,
With which the Sunrise from on high will visit us,
79 TO SHINE UPON THOSE WHO SIT IN DARKNESS AND THE SHADOW OF DEATH,
To guide our feet into the way of peace."

80 And the child continued to grow and to become strong in spirit, and he lived in the deserts until the day of his public appearance to Israel.

LIFE LESSONS

➤ **Luke 1:74–75 — "Serve Him without fear, in holiness and righteousness before Him all our days."**

Those who fear God do not have to fear anything else. When we commit ourselves wholeheartedly to serving God, we can enjoy the intense pleasures that come with holiness and righteousness.

➤ **Luke 1:78 — "The Sunrise from on high will visit us."**

Zacharias was referring to the prophecy of Malachi 4:2, "The sun of righteousness will rise." This of course, was speaking about the Messiah. By first listing God's covenants to David and Abraham (vv. 69, 73), and then referring to the last thing God said in Malachi, Zacharias was confirming that God had indeed kept every aspect of His promise to send the Messiah. The good news that Israel had been longing to hear had finally arrived.

Deuteronomy 11:1—12:32

11 "YOU shall therefore love the LORD your God, and always keep His charge, His statutes, His ordinances, and His commandments.

2 "Know this day that I *am* not *speaking* with your sons who have not known and who have not seen the discipline of the LORD your God—His greatness, His mighty hand and His outstretched arm,

3 and His signs and His works which He did in the midst of Egypt to Pharaoh the king of Egypt and to all his land;

4 and what He did to Egypt's army, to its horses and its chariots, when He made the water of the Red Sea to engulf them while they were pursuing you, and the LORD completely destroyed them;

5 and what He did to you in the wilderness until you came to this place;

6 and what He did to Dathan and Abiram, the sons of Eliab, the son of Reuben, when the earth opened its mouth and swallowed them, their households, their tents, and every living thing that followed them, among all Israel—

7 but your own eyes have seen all the great work of the LORD which He did.

8 "You shall therefore keep every commandment which I am commanding you today, so that you may be strong and go in and possess the land into which you are about to cross to possess it;

9 so that you may prolong *your* days on the land which the LORD swore to your fathers to give to them and to their descendants, a land flowing with milk and honey.

10 "For the land, into which you are entering to possess it, is not like the land of Egypt from which you came, where you used to sow your seed and water it with your foot like a vegetable garden.

11 "But the land into which you are about to cross to possess it, a land of hills and valleys, drinks water from the rain of heaven,

12 a land for which the LORD your God cares; the eyes of the LORD your God are always on it, from the beginning even to the end of the year.

➤ 13 "It shall come about, if you listen obediently to my commandments which I am commanding you today, to love the LORD your God and to serve Him with all your heart and all your soul,

14 that He will give the rain for your land in its season, the early and late rain, that you may gather in your grain and your new wine and your oil.

15 "He will give grass in your fields for your cattle, and you will eat and be satisfied.

16 "Beware that your hearts are not ◄ deceived, and that you do not turn away and serve other gods and worship them.

17 "Or the anger of the LORD will be kindled against you, and He will shut up the heavens so that there will be no rain and the ground will not yield its fruit; and you will perish quickly from the good land which the LORD is giving you.

18 "You shall therefore impress these words of mine on your heart and on your soul; and you shall bind them as a sign on your hand, and they shall be as frontals on your forehead.

19 "You shall teach them to your sons, talking of them when you sit in your house and when you walk along the road and when you lie down and when you rise up.

20 "You shall write them on the doorposts of your house and on your gates,

21 so that your days and the days of your sons may be multiplied on the land which the LORD swore to your fathers to

---

LIFE LESSONS

➤ **Deuteronomy 11:13–14** — *"If you listen obediently to my . . . that He will give the rain for your land in its season."*

*O*ur God provides for those who love Him and who obey His commandments. In today's uncertain world, it's good to be in the hands of a loving God who knows what we need before we even ask Him for it.

➤ **Deuteronomy 11:16** — *"Beware that your hearts are not deceived, and that you do not turn away and serve other gods."*

*M*ost people do not simply wake up one day and decide to abandon God. Deception usually plays a large role—just as it did in Eden, just as it will at the end of time (Gen. 3:13; Matt. 24:5).

give them, as long as the heavens *remain* above the earth.

22 "For if you are careful to keep all this commandment which I am commanding you to do, to love the LORD your God, to walk in all His ways and hold fast to Him,

23 then the LORD will drive out all these nations from before you, and you will dispossess nations greater and mightier than you.

24 "Every place on which the sole of your foot treads shall be yours; your border will be from the wilderness to Lebanon, *and* from the river, the river Euphrates, as far as the western sea.

25 "No man will be able to stand before you; the LORD your God will lay the dread of you and the fear of you on all the land on which you set foot, as He has spoken to you.

26 "See, I am setting before you today a blessing and a curse:

27 the blessing, if you listen to the commandments of the LORD your God, which I am commanding you today;

28 and the curse, if you do not listen to the commandments of the LORD your God, but turn aside from the way which I am commanding you today, by following other gods which you have not known.

29 "It shall come about, when the LORD your God brings you into the land where you are entering to possess it, that you shall place the blessing on Mount Gerizim and the curse on Mount Ebal.

30 "Are they not across the Jordan, west of the way toward the sunset, in the land of the Canaanites who live in the Arabah, opposite Gilgal, beside the oaks of Moreh?

31 "For you are about to cross the Jordan to go in to possess the land which the LORD your God is giving you, and you shall possess it and live in it,

32 and you shall be careful to do all the statutes and the judgments which I am setting before you today.

12 "THESE are the statutes and the judgments which you shall carefully observe in the land which the LORD, the God of your fathers, has given you to possess as long as you live on the earth.

2 "You shall utterly destroy all the places where the nations whom you shall dispossess serve their gods, on the high mountains and on the hills and under every green tree.

3 "You shall tear down their altars and smash their *sacred* pillars and burn their Asherim with fire, and you shall cut down the engraved images of their gods and obliterate their name from that place.

4 "You shall not act like this toward the ◄ LORD your God.

5 "But you shall seek *the* LORD at the place which the LORD your God will choose from all your tribes, to establish His name there for His dwelling, and there you shall come.

6 "There you shall bring your burnt offerings, your sacrifices, your tithes, the contribution of your hand, your votive offerings, your freewill offerings, and the firstborn of your herd and of your flock.

7 "There also you and your households shall eat before the LORD your God, and rejoice in all your undertakings in which the LORD your God has blessed you.

8 "You shall not do at all what we are doing here today, every man *doing* whatever is right in his own eyes;

9 for you have not as yet come to the resting place and the inheritance which the LORD your God is giving you.

10 "When you cross the Jordan and live in the land which the LORD your God is giving you to inherit, and He gives you rest from all your enemies around *you* so that you live in security,

11 then it shall come about that the place in which the LORD your God will choose for His name to dwell, there you shall bring all that I command you: your burnt offerings and your sacrifices, your tithes and the contribution of your hand, and all your choice votive offerings which you will vow to the LORD.

12 "And you shall rejoice before the LORD your God, you and your sons and daughters, your male and female servants, and the Levite who is within your

---

LIFE LESSONS

➤ **Deuteronomy 12:4 —** *"You shall not act like this toward the LORD your God."*

*A*ll worship is not godly worship. God calls us to worship Him in Spirit and in truth, and not all forms of worship fit this criteria.

gates, since he has no portion or inheritance with you.

13 "Be careful that you do not offer your burnt offerings in every *cultic* place you see,

14 but in the place which the LORD chooses in one of your tribes, there you shall offer your burnt offerings, and there you shall do all that I command you.

15 "However, you may slaughter and eat meat within any of your gates, whatever you desire, according to the blessing of the LORD your God which He has given you; the unclean and the clean may eat of it, as of the gazelle and the deer.

16 "Only you shall not eat the blood; you are to pour it out on the ground like water.

17 "You are not allowed to eat within your gates the tithe of your grain or new wine or oil, or the firstborn of your herd or flock, or any of your votive offerings which you vow, or your freewill offerings, or the contribution of your hand.

➤ **18** "But you shall eat them before the LORD your God in the place which the LORD your God will choose, you and your son and daughter, and your male and female servants, and the Levite who is within your gates; and you shall rejoice before the LORD your God in all your undertakings.

19 "Be careful that you do not forsake the Levite as long as you live in your land.

20 "When the LORD your God extends your border as He has promised you, and you say, 'I will eat meat,' because you desire to eat meat, *then* you may eat meat, whatever you desire.

21 "If the place which the LORD your God chooses to put His name is too far from you, then you may slaughter of your herd and flock which the LORD has given you, as I have commanded you; and you may eat within your gates whatever you desire.

22 "Just as a gazelle or a deer is eaten, so

you will eat it; the unclean and the clean alike may eat of it.

23 "Only be sure not to eat the blood, for the blood is the life, and you shall not eat the life with the flesh.

24 "You shall not eat it; you shall pour it out on the ground like water.

25 "You shall not eat it, so that it may be well with you and your sons after you, for you will be doing what is right in the sight of the LORD.

26 "Only your holy things which you may have and your votive offerings, you shall take and go to the place which the LORD chooses.

27 "And you shall offer your burnt offerings, the flesh and the blood, on the altar of the LORD your God; and the blood of your sacrifices shall be poured out on the altar of the LORD your God, and you shall eat the flesh.

28 "Be careful to listen to all these words which I command you, so that it may be well with you and your sons after you forever, for you will be doing what is good and right in the sight of the LORD your God. ✳

29 "When the LORD your God cuts off before you the nations which you are going in to dispossess, and you dispossess them and dwell in their land,

30 beware that you are not ensnared to follow them, after they are destroyed before you, and that you do not inquire after their gods, saying, 'How do these nations serve their gods, that I also may do likewise?'

31 "You shall not behave thus toward the LORD your God, for every abominable act which the LORD hates they have done for their gods; for they even burn their sons and daughters in the fire to their gods.

32 "Whatever I command you, you shall be careful to do; you shall not add to nor take away from it.

LIFE LESSONS

➤ **Deuteronomy 12:18** — *"You shall rejoice before the LORD your God in all your undertakings."*

*G*od wants a happy people who rejoice in all they do, not a dour company of saints who focus on all the evil in the world. Oneness with God produces peace and joy, not chaos and grumbling.

✦ Psalm 37:18–22

18 The LORD knows the days of the
    blameless,
    And their inheritance will be
    forever.
19 They will not be ashamed in the
    time of evil,
    And in the days of famine they will
    have abundance. ✳

20 But the wicked will perish;
And the enemies of the LORD will be
like the glory of the pastures,
They vanish—like smoke they
vanish away.
21 The wicked borrows and does not
pay back,
But the righteous is gracious and
gives.
22 For those blessed by Him will
inherit the land,
But those cursed by Him will be cut
off.

Proverbs 12:12–14

12 The wicked man desires the booty
of evil men,
But the root of the righteous yields
fruit.
13 An evil man is ensnared by the
transgression of his lips,

But the righteous will escape from
trouble.
14 A man will be satisfied with good
by the fruit of his words,
And the deeds of a man's hands will
return to him.

Luke 2:1–24

2 NOW in those days a decree went out
from Caesar Augustus, that a census
be taken of all the inhabited earth.
2   This was the first census taken while
Quirinius was governor of Syria.
3   And everyone was on his way to register for the census, each to his own city.
4   Joseph also went up from Galilee,
from the city of Nazareth, to Judea, to
the city of David which is called Bethlehem, because he was of the house and
family of David,
5   in order to register along with Mary,

ANSWERS TO LIFE'S QUESTIONS

What are the characteristics of a godly man?

LUKE 2:1–20

*U*ntil he became engaged to Mary, Joseph's life probably resembled that of most other men in his hometown. No doubt he had business concerns and goals for the future. But nothing seriously interrupted his daily routine until Mary informed him she was pregnant. This was when his life changed rapidly.

The news was shocking to him, and rather than disgrace Mary, Joseph planned to send her away (Matt. 1:19). But God saw the confusion building within Joseph's mind and sent His angel to guide him: "Joseph, son of David, do not be afraid to take Mary as your wife; for the Child who has been conceived in her is of the Holy Spirit. She will bear a Son; and you shall call His name Jesus, for He will save His people from their sins" (Matt. 1:20, 21). From this point on, Joseph never questioned the Lord's method or motive. He realized the God of the universe had chosen him to watch over Mary and the Son she would have. He remained faithful not only to his wife, but also to the Lord.

Joseph showed courage by ignoring the ugly rumors swirling around town about Mary's pregnancy; he valued God's plan above what others thought of him. He remained sensitive to the Holy Spirit, demonstrated by his acceptance of His guidance. After the birth of Jesus, an angel appeared to him, warning him of impending danger. Joseph immediately took Mary and Jesus to Egypt, where they found safety until the threat passed (Matt. 2:13–15). As we look at the life of Joseph, we find that he was a humble man who honored God by obeying His Word. He remained consistent and content, and he could be counted on to follow the Lord regardless, of the personal costs.

How can you grow in your faith to become a godly individual? Begin by committing yourself to a consistent, daily walk with Christ. Attend a church where the Word of God is proclaimed as the standard of life. Make a commitment to God and to your loved ones that you will not abandon your devotion to Christ or to them.

You will gain a sense of godly responsibility when you stand up for what is right. A committed Christian is not easily swayed, but is filled with conviction, faith, and a desire to know God intimately. When Joseph had no one else to guide and comfort him, he turned to God and found the strength and love he needed to get through the most difficult of circumstances.

You will too. Will you make Joseph's spiritual commitment your own today?

who was engaged to him, and was with child.

6   While they were there, the days were completed for her to give birth.

7   And she gave birth to her firstborn son; and she wrapped Him in cloths, and laid Him in a manger, because there was no room for them in the inn.

8   In the same region there were *some* shepherds staying out in the fields and keeping watch over their flock by night.

9   And an angel of the Lord suddenly stood before them, and the glory of the Lord shone around them; and they were terribly frightened.

10   But the angel said to them, "Do not be afraid; for behold, I bring you good news of great joy which will be for all the people;

11   for today in the city of David there has been born for you a Savior, who is Christ the Lord.

12   "This *will be* a sign for you: you will find a baby wrapped in cloths and lying in a manger."

13   And suddenly there appeared with the angel a multitude of the heavenly host praising God and saying,

---

LIFE LESSONS

> Luke 2:10 — *"Do not be afraid; for behold, I bring you good news of great joy which will be for all the people."*

The angel told the shepherds not to fear, but to open their eyes and look for the wonderfully good thing that God was doing for them and for the whole world—something that would bring great joy to everyone.

---

14   "Glory to God in the highest,
   And on earth peace among men
      with whom He is pleased."

15   When the angels had gone away from them into heaven, the shepherds *began* saying to one another, "Let us go straight to Bethlehem then, and see this thing that has happened which the Lord has made known to us."

16   So they came in a hurry and found their way to Mary and Joseph, and the baby as He lay in the manger.

17   When they had seen this, they made known the statement which had been told them about this Child.

18   And all who heard it wondered at the things which were told them by the shepherds.

19   But Mary treasured all these things, pondering them in her heart.

20   The shepherds went back, glorifying and praising God for all that they had heard and seen, just as had been told them.

21   And when eight days had passed, before His circumcision, His name was *then* called Jesus, the name given by the angel before He was conceived in the womb.

22   And when the days for their purification according to the law of Moses were completed, they brought Him up to Jerusalem to present Him to the Lord

23   (as it is written in the Law of the Lord, "EVERY *firstborn* MALE THAT OPENS THE WOMB SHALL BE CALLED HOLY TO THE LORD"),

24   and to offer a sacrifice according to what was said in the Law of the Lord, "A PAIR OF TURTLEDOVES OR TWO YOUNG PIGEONS."

MARCH 26

Deuteronomy 13:1—14:29

13 "IF a prophet or a dreamer of dreams arises among you and gives you a sign or a wonder,

2   and the sign or the wonder comes true, concerning which he spoke to you, saying, 'Let us go after other gods (whom you have not known) and let us serve them,'

3   you shall not listen to the words of that prophet or that dreamer of dreams; for the LORD your God is testing you to find out if you love the LORD your God with all your heart and with all your soul.

4   "You shall follow the LORD your God and fear Him; and you shall keep His commandments, listen to His voice, serve Him, and cling to Him.

5   "But that prophet or that dreamer of

dreams shall be put to death, because he has counseled rebellion against the LORD your God who brought you from the land of Egypt and redeemed you from the house of slavery, to seduce you from the way in which the LORD your God commanded you to walk. So you shall purge the evil from among you.

6 "If your brother, your mother's son, or your son or daughter, or the wife you cherish, or your friend who is as your own soul, entice you secretly, saying, 'Let us go and serve other gods' (whom neither you nor your fathers have known,

7 of the gods of the peoples who are around you, near you or far from you, from one end of the earth to the other end),

8 you shall not yield to him or listen to him; and your eye shall not pity him, nor shall you spare or conceal him.

9 "But you shall surely kill him; your hand shall be first against him to put him to death, and afterwards the hand of all the people.

10 "So you shall stone him to death because he has sought to seduce you from the LORD your God who brought you out from the land of Egypt, out of the house of slavery.

11 "Then all Israel will hear and be afraid, and will never again do such a wicked thing among you.

12 "If you hear in one of your cities, which the LORD your God is giving you to live in, *anyone* saying *that*

13 some worthless men have gone out from among you and have seduced the inhabitants of their city, saying, 'Let us go and serve other gods' (whom you have not known),

14 then you shall investigate and

search out and inquire thoroughly. If it is true *and* the matter established that this abomination has been done among you,

15 you shall surely strike the inhabitants of that city with the edge of the sword, utterly destroying it and all that is in it and its cattle with the edge of the sword.

16 "Then you shall gather all its booty into the middle of its open square and burn the city and all its booty with fire as a whole burnt offering to the LORD your God; and it shall be a ruin forever. It shall never be rebuilt.

17 "Nothing from that which is put under the ban shall cling to your hand, in order that the LORD may turn from His burning anger and show mercy to you, and have compassion on you and make you increase, just as He has sworn to your fathers,

18 if you will listen to the voice of the LORD your God, keeping all His commandments which I am commanding you today, and doing what is right in the sight of the LORD your God.

14 "YOU are the sons of the LORD your God; you shall not cut yourselves nor shave your forehead for the sake of the dead.

2 "For you are a holy people to the LORD your God, and the LORD has chosen you to be a people for His own possession out of all the peoples who are on the face of the earth. ✳

3 "You shall not eat any detestable thing.

4 "These are the animals which you may eat: the ox, the sheep, the goat,

5 the deer, the gazelle, the roebuck, the wild goat, the ibex, the antelope and the mountain sheep.

6 "Any animal that divides the hoof and has the hoof split in two *and* chews the cud, among the animals, that you may eat.

7 "Nevertheless, you are not to eat of these among those which chew the cud, or among those that divide the hoof in two: the camel and the rabbit and the shaphan, for though they chew the cud, they do not divide the hoof; they are unclean for you.

8 "The pig, because it divides the hoof but *does* not *chew* the cud, it is unclean for you. You shall not eat any of their flesh nor touch their carcasses.

9 "These you may eat of all that are in water: anything that has fins and scales you may eat,

10 but anything that does not have fins and scales you shall not eat; it is unclean for you.

11 "You may eat any clean bird.

12 "But these are the ones which you shall not eat: the eagle and the vulture and the buzzard,

13 and the red kite, the falcon, and the kite in their kinds,

14 and every raven in its kind,

15 and the ostrich, the owl, the sea gull, and the hawk in their kinds,

16 the little owl, the great owl, the white owl,

17 the pelican, the carrion vulture, the cormorant,

18 the stork, and the heron in their kinds, and the hoopoe and the bat.

19 "And all the teeming life with wings are unclean to you; they shall not be eaten.

20 "You may eat any clean bird.

21 "You shall not eat anything which dies *of itself*. You may give it to the alien who is in your town, so that he may eat it, or you may sell it to a foreigner, for you are a holy people to the LORD your God. You shall not boil a young goat in its mother's milk.

22 "You shall surely tithe all the produce from what you sow, which comes out of the field every year.

23 "You shall eat in the presence of the LORD your God, at the place where He chooses to establish His name, the tithe of your grain, your new wine, your oil, and the firstborn of your herd and your flock, so that you may learn to fear the LORD your God always.

24 "If the distance is so great for you that you are not able to bring *the tithe*, since the place where the LORD your God chooses to set His name is too far away from you when the LORD your God blesses you,

25 then you shall exchange *it* for money, and bind the money in your hand and go to the place which the LORD your God chooses.

26 "You may spend the money for whatever your heart desires: for oxen, or sheep, or wine, or strong drink, or whatever your heart desires; and there you shall eat in the presence of the LORD your God and rejoice, you and your household.

27 "Also you shall not neglect the Levite who is in your town, for he has no portion or inheritance among you.

28 "At the end of every third year you shall bring out all the tithe of your produce in that year, and shall deposit *it* in your town.

29 "The Levite, because he has no portion or inheritance among you, and the alien, the orphan and the widow who are in your town, shall come and eat and be satisfied, in order that the LORD your God may bless you in all the work of your hand which you do.

✷ Psalm 37:23–29

23 The steps of a man are established by the LORD,
   And He delights in his way.

24 When he falls, he will not be hurled headlong, ✳
   Because the LORD is the One who holds his hand.

25 I have been young and now I am old,
   Yet I have not seen the righteous forsaken
   Or his descendants begging bread.

26 All day long he is gracious and lends,
   And his descendants are a blessing.

27 Depart from evil and do good,
   So you will abide forever.

28 For the LORD loves justice
   And does not forsake His godly ones;
   They are preserved forever,
   But the descendants of the wicked will be cut off.

29 The righteous will inherit the land
   And dwell in it forever.

✷ Proverbs 12:15–16

15 The way of a fool is right in his own eyes, ◄
   But a wise man is he who listens to counsel. ✳

16 A fool's anger is known at once,
   But a prudent man conceals dishonor.

✦ Luke 2:25–52

25 And there was a man in Jerusalem whose name was Simeon; and this man was righteous and devout, looking for the consolation of Israel; and the Holy Spirit was upon him.
26 And it had been revealed to him by the Holy Spirit that he would not see death before he had seen the Lord's Christ.
27 And he came in the Spirit into the temple; and when the parents brought in the child Jesus, to carry out for Him the custom of the Law,
28 then he took Him into his arms, and blessed God, and said,
29 "Now Lord, You are releasing Your bond-servant to depart in peace, According to Your word;
30 For my eyes have seen Your salvation,
31 Which You have prepared in the presence of all peoples,
32 A LIGHT OF REVELATION TO THE GENTILES, And the glory of Your people Israel."

33 And His father and mother were amazed at the things which were being said about Him.
34 And Simeon blessed them and said to Mary His mother, "Behold, this *Child* is appointed for the fall and rise of many in Israel, and for a sign to be opposed—
35 and a sword will pierce even your own soul—to the end that thoughts from many hearts may be revealed."
36 And there was a prophetess, Anna the daughter of Phanuel, of the tribe of Asher. She was advanced in years and had lived with *her* husband seven years after her marriage,
37 and then as a widow to the age of eighty-four. She never left the temple, serving night and day with fastings and prayers.
38 At that very moment she came up and *began* giving thanks to God, and continued to speak of Him to all those who were looking for the redemption of Jerusalem.
39 When they had performed everything according to the Law of the Lord, they returned to Galilee, to their own city of Nazareth.
40 The Child continued to grow and become strong, increasing in wisdom; and the grace of God was upon Him.
41 Now His parents went to Jerusalem every year at the Feast of the Passover.
42 And when He became twelve, they went up *there* according to the custom of the Feast;
43 and as they were returning, after spending the full number of days, the boy Jesus stayed behind in Jerusalem. But His parents were unaware of it,
44 but supposed Him to be in the caravan,

SIMEON: Whole in the Arms of God

LUKE 2:25–35

*A*s he made his way to the temple, we may wonder if Simeon thought, *"The years must be catching up to me. How long will I have to wait for God to answer my prayer?"* How long had it been since he had received the special word of the Lord? Five years? Ten years? It didn't matter. Each day brought him closer to the fulfillment of God's promise that "he would not see death before he had seen the Lord's Christ" (Luke 2:26).

At that moment, a young couple emerged onto the temple porch with a newborn son. *The Child!* Simeon thought. He approached the young family, took the babe in his arms, and immediately knew *this* was the One for whom he had waited so long.

The Lord always keeps His promises. And this faithful servant of God had the opportunity to witness the Savior as promised. He took Jesus in his arms and blessed Him saying, "Now Lord, You are releasing Your bond-servant to depart in peace, according to Your word; for my eyes have seen Your salvation" (Luke 2:29, 30).

➤ **Luke 2:40 —** *The Child continued to grow and become strong, increasing in wisdom; and the grace of God was upon Him.*

*J*esus had to grow, just like every other human child. He became strong in spirit and filled with wisdom because He grew up in the grace of God. God's grace is what makes us both strong and wise.

and went a day's journey; and they *began* looking for Him among their relatives and acquaintances.

45 When they did not find Him, they returned to Jerusalem looking for Him.

46 Then, after three days they found Him in the temple, sitting in the midst of the teachers, both listening to them and asking them questions.

➤ 47 And all who heard Him were amazed at His understanding and His answers.

48 When they saw Him, they were astonished; and His mother said to Him, "Son, why have You treated us this way? Behold, Your father and I have been anxiously looking for You."

49 And He said to them, "Why is it that you were looking for Me? Did you not know that I had to be in My Father's *house?*"

➤ 50 But they did not understand the statement which He had made to them.

➤ 51 And He went down with them and came to Nazareth, and He continued in subjection to them; and His mother treasured all *these* things in her heart.

52 And Jesus kept increasing in wisdom and stature, and in favor with God and men.

➤ **Luke 2:47 —** *And all who heard Him were amazed at His understanding and His answers.*

*T*he wisdom of God is astounding. Even the teachers of the law and temple scholars were completely amazed at Christ's spiritual insight—especially at such a young age. Yet remember, "The fear of the Lord is the beginning of wisdom, and the knowledge of the Holy One is understanding" (Prov. 9:10). The Lord's remarkable knowledge and understanding are available to all who truly believe in Him (Jer. 33:3; 1 Cor. 1:18—2:16; James 1:5, 6). Do you need God's wisdom for your situation? Then trust and obey Him, because He will surely reveal Himself to you as you seek Him (Luke 11:9, 10).

➤ **Luke 2:50 —** *But they did not understand the statement which He had made to them.*

*E*ven as a boy, Jesus spoke of spiritual issues in ways that His hearers often did not understand. Serious Christ followers, however, strive to gain understanding, as did Mary (Luke 2:51) and His disciples (Luke 8:9).

➤ **Luke 2:51 —** *And He went down with them and came to Nazareth, and He continued in subjection to them.*

*J*esus is the only begotten Son of God, but He was placed in the care and under the authority of His earthly parents, Mary and Joseph. He submitted to them, not as an inferior, but as an example of obedience to us.

MARCH 27

Deuteronomy 15:1—16:22

15"AT the end of *every* seven years you shall grant a remission *of debts.*

2 "This is the manner of remission: every creditor shall release what he has loaned to his neighbor; he shall not

exact it of his neighbor and his brother, because the Lord's remission has been proclaimed.

3 "From a foreigner you may exact *it*, but your hand shall release whatever of yours is with your brother.

4 "However, there will be no poor among you, since the Lord will surely bless you in the land which the Lord

your God is giving you as an inheritance to possess,

5 if only you listen obediently to the voice of the LORD your God, to observe carefully all this commandment which I am commanding you today.

6 "For the LORD your God will bless you as He has promised you, and you will lend to many nations, but you will not borrow; and you will rule over many nations, but they will not rule over you.

7 "If there is a poor man with you, one of your brothers, in any of your towns in your land which the LORD your God is giving you, you shall not harden your heart, nor close your hand from your poor brother;

8 but you shall freely open your hand to him, and shall generously lend him sufficient for his need *in* whatever he lacks.

9 "Beware that there is no base thought in your heart, saying, 'The seventh year, the year of remission, is near,' and your eye is hostile toward your poor brother, and you give him nothing; then he may cry to the LORD against you, and it will be a sin in you.

10 "You shall generously give to him, and your heart shall not be grieved when you give to him, because for this thing the LORD your God will bless you in all your work and in all your undertakings.

11 "For the poor will never cease *to be* in the land; therefore I command you, saying, 'You shall freely open your hand to your brother, to your needy and poor in your land.'

12 "If your kinsman, a Hebrew man or woman, is sold to you, then he shall serve you six years, but in the seventh year you shall set him free.

13 "When you set him free, you shall not send him away empty-handed.

14 "You shall furnish him liberally from your flock and from your threshing floor and from your wine vat; you shall give to him as the LORD your God has blessed you.

15 "You shall remember that you were a slave in the land of Egypt, and the LORD your God redeemed you; therefore I command you this today.

16 "It shall come about if he says to you, 'I will not go out from you,' because he loves you and your household, since he fares well with you;

17 then you shall take an awl and pierce it through his ear into the door, and he shall be your servant forever. Also you shall do likewise to your maidservant.

18 "It shall not seem hard to you when you set him free, for he has given you six years *with* double the service of a hired man; so the LORD your God will bless you in whatever you do.

19 "You shall consecrate to the LORD your God all the firstborn males that are born of your herd and of your flock; you shall not work with the firstborn of your herd, nor shear the firstborn of your flock.

20 "You and your household shall eat it every year before the LORD your God in the place which the LORD chooses.

21 "But if it has any defect, *such as* lameness or blindness, *or* any serious defect, you shall not sacrifice it to the LORD your God.

22 "You shall eat it within your gates; the unclean and the clean alike *may eat it*, as a gazelle or a deer.

23 "Only you shall not eat its blood; you are to pour it out on the ground like water.

16 "OBSERVE the month of Abib and celebrate the Passover to the LORD your God, for in the month of Abib the LORD your God brought you out of Egypt by night.

2 "You shall sacrifice the Passover to the LORD your God from the flock and the herd, in the place where the LORD chooses to establish His name.

3 "You shall not eat leavened bread with it; seven days you shall eat with it unleavened bread, the bread of affliction (for you came out of the land of Egypt in haste), so that you may remember all the days of your life the day when you came out of the land of Egypt.

4 "For seven days no leaven shall be

LIFE LESSONS

➤ **Deuteronomy 15:11** — *"For the poor will never cease to be in the land; therefore I command you, saying, 'You shall freely open your hand to your brother.'"*

*B*oth Moses and Jesus told us the poor would always live among us (Matt. 26:11). Therefore we are always to remain generous.

seen with you in all your territory, and none of the flesh which you sacrifice on the evening of the first day shall remain overnight until morning.

5 "You are not allowed to sacrifice the Passover in any of your towns which the LORD your God is giving you;

6 but at the place where the LORD your God chooses to establish His name, you shall sacrifice the Passover in the evening at sunset, at the time that you came out of Egypt.

7 "You shall cook and eat it in the place which the LORD your God chooses. In the morning you are to return to your tents.

8 "Six days you shall eat unleavened bread, and on the seventh day there shall be a solemn assembly to the LORD your God; you shall do no work on it.

9 "You shall count seven weeks for yourself; you shall begin to count seven weeks from the time you begin to put the sickle to the standing grain.

10 "Then you shall celebrate the Feast of Weeks to the LORD your God with a tribute of a freewill offering of your hand, which you shall give just as the LORD your God blesses you;

11 and you shall rejoice before the LORD your God, you and your son and your daughter and your male and female servants and the Levite who is in your town, and the stranger and the orphan and the widow who are in your midst, in the place where the LORD your God chooses to establish His name.

12 "You shall remember that you were a slave in Egypt, and you shall be careful to observe these statutes.

13 "You shall celebrate the Feast of Booths seven days after you have gathered in from your threshing floor and your wine vat;

14 and you shall rejoice in your feast, you and your son and your daughter and your male and female servants and the Levite and the stranger and the orphan and the widow who are in your towns.

15 "Seven days you shall celebrate a feast to the LORD your God in the place which the LORD chooses, because the LORD your God will bless you in all your produce and in all the work of your hands, so that you will be altogether joyful.

16 "Three times in a year all your males shall appear before the LORD your God in the place which He chooses, at the Feast of Unleavened Bread and at the Feast of Weeks and at the Feast of Booths, and they shall not appear before the LORD empty-handed.

17 "Every man shall give as he is able, according to the blessing of the LORD your God which He has given you.

18 "You shall appoint for yourself judges and officers in all your towns which the LORD your God is giving you, according to your tribes, and they shall judge the people with righteous judgment.

19 "You shall not distort justice; you shall not be partial, and you shall not take a bribe, for a bribe blinds the eyes of the wise and perverts the words of the righteous.

20 "Justice, and only justice, you shall pursue, that you may live and possess the land which the LORD your God is giving you.

21 "You shall not plant for yourself an Asherah of any kind of tree beside the altar of the LORD your God, which you shall make for yourself.

22 "You shall not set up for yourself a sacred pillar which the LORD your God hates.

Psalm 37:30–36

30 The mouth of the righteous utters wisdom,
And his tongue speaks justice.

31 The law of his God is in his heart;
His steps do not slip.

LIFE LESSONS

➤ Deuteronomy 16:17 — *"Every man shall give as he is able, according to the blessing of the LORD."*

*I*n both the Old and New Testaments, God instructs His people to give back to the Lord a proportionate amount, as He had blessed them (2 Cor. 8:12). This is above the first ten percent—or tithe—which we owe to God (Lev. 27:30; Mal. 3:8, 10); rather, it is a gift of love in thankfulness for His generosity and grace. Always remember, no one ever out gives God!

WHAT THE BIBLE SAYS ABOUT ⊙

God's Schedule

Psalm 37:34

*D*o you feel as if things are not going the way you planned? As if God is on a completely different schedule than you are? Well, He probably is.

Remember that God's master plan is to develop a loving, personal relationship with you. Though life will often bring you pain, suffering, and developments you would not choose, you can always be confident that God finds a way to use everything for your good. God is developing you into a mature believer—and that includes showing you how to wait patiently for Him.

So why should you trust God's timing? Here are some excellent reasons:

1. *God's schedule is best for you because He is all-knowing.*

God is aware of every detail of your life—past, present, or future. He's also aware of what you will need for challenges ahead. God's knowledge is complete. Therefore, since God is aware of things that you have no way of knowing—and is providing for things you don't even realize you need—you should trust His timing.

2. *God's schedule is best for you because He is all-wise.*

It is foolish to think that anyone knows the absolute best thing to do in every situation because everyone makes mistakes. Of course, you probably already realize that you make your decisions based upon an imperfect per-

ception of the future. God's wisdom, on the other hand, is infinite and perfect. Though your heart can lie to you, He never will. The Father will take His time teaching you all that you need to know through His Holy Spirit who lives within you.

3. *God's schedule is best for you because He is all-loving.*

The most important reason to live by God's schedule is the simple fact that He loves you and wants what's best for you. His schedule is built around a wonderful future of godly maturity and fellowship with Him. Time is simply one of the tools He uses to teach you, train you, and mold you. His love reaches to the tiniest details of your life, uses every experience for your best, and is absolutely unconditional.

The rewards of learning to live by God's timing are infinite. You have a new peace and assurance, because you no longer try to make time serve your own end. You have renewed strength, so that you can run and not be weary, and walk without fainting (Is. 40:28–31). And you learn to trust Him more because you see God redeeming your time and working through you powerfully.

Therefore, realize that you're not sufficient within yourself—that you must live by God's timing because you know that yours won't work. Trust God completely knowing you're in His care, and be patient no matter what happens. And finally, have the courage and self-discipline to wait upon God.

Isaiah 64:4 tells us, "For from days of old they have not heard or perceived by ear, nor has the eye seen a God besides You, who acts in behalf of the one who waits for Him. ⊙

---

32   The wicked spies upon the righteous
      And seeks to kill him.
33   The LORD will not leave him in his hand
      Or let him be condemned when he is judged.
34   Wait for the LORD and keep His way,
      And He will exalt you to inherit the land;
      When the wicked are cut off, you will see it.
35   I have seen a wicked, violent man
      Spreading himself like a luxuriant tree in its native soil.

36   Then he passed away, and lo, he was no more;
      I sought for him, but he could not be found.

⊙ Proverbs 12:17–19

17   He who speaks truth tells what is right,
      But a false witness, deceit.
18   There is one who speaks rashly like the thrusts of a sword,
      But the tongue of the wise brings healing.

19 Truthful lips will be established
forever,
But a lying tongue is only for a
moment.

Luke 3:1–38

3 NOW in the fifteenth year of the reign of Tiberius Caesar, when Pontius Pilate was governor of Judea, and Herod was tetrarch of Galilee, and his brother Philip was tetrarch of the region of Ituraea and Trachonitis, and Lysanias was tetrarch of Abilene,
2   in the high priesthood of Annas and Caiaphas, the word of God came to John, the son of Zacharias, in the wilderness.
3   And he came into all the district around the Jordan, preaching a baptism of repentance for the forgiveness of sins;
4   as it is written in the book of the words of Isaiah the prophet,
"THE VOICE OF ONE CRYING IN THE
WILDERNESS,
'MAKE READY THE WAY OF THE LORD,
MAKE HIS PATHS STRAIGHT.
5   'EVERY RAVINE WILL BE FILLED,
AND EVERY MOUNTAIN AND HILL WILL
BE BROUGHT LOW;
THE CROOKED WILL BECOME STRAIGHT,
AND THE ROUGH ROADS SMOOTH;
6   AND ALL FLESH WILL SEE THE
SALVATION OF GOD.'"
7   So he *began* saying to the crowds who were going out to be baptized by him, "You brood of vipers, who warned you to flee from the wrath to come?
8   "Therefore bear fruits in keeping with repentance, and do not begin to say to yourselves, 'We have Abraham for our father,' for I say to you that from these stones God is able to raise up children to Abraham.
9   "Indeed the axe is already laid at the root of the trees; so every tree that does not bear good fruit is cut down and thrown into the fire."
10   And the crowds were questioning him, saying, "Then what shall we do?"
11   And he would answer and say to them, "The man who has two tunics is to share with him who has none; and he who has food is to do likewise."
12   And *some* tax collectors also came

to be baptized, and they said to him, "Teacher, what shall we do?"
13   And he said to them, "Collect no more than what you have been ordered to."
14   *Some* soldiers were questioning him, saying, "And *what about* us, what shall we do?" And he said to them, "Do not take money from anyone by force, or accuse *anyone* falsely, and be content with your wages."
15   Now while the people were in a state of expectation and all were wondering in their hearts about John, as to whether he was the Christ,
16   John answered and said to them all, "As for me, I baptize you with water; but One is coming who is mightier than I, and I am not fit to untie the thong of His sandals; He will baptize you with the Holy Spirit and fire.
17   "His winnowing fork is in His hand to thoroughly clear His threshing floor, and to gather the wheat into His barn; but He will burn up the chaff with unquenchable fire."
18   So with many other exhortations he preached the gospel to the people.
19   But when Herod the tetrarch was reprimanded by him because of Herodias, his brother's wife, and because of all the wicked things which Herod had done,

---

LIFE LESSONS

➤ Luke 3:11 — *And he would answer and say to them, "The man who has two tunics is to share with him who has none; and he who has food is to do likewise."*

*A*n intimate relationship with God is about far more than enjoying warm feelings toward the Creator of the universe. Any genuine love of God moves a person to real acts of love toward others (1 John 3:17).

➤ Luke 3:14 — *"Do not take money from anyone by force, or accuse anyone falsely, and be content with your wages."*

*J*ohn the Baptist did not advise soldiers to go into another profession. He did, however, instruct them to act justly and mercifully with those under their authority.

20 Herod also added this to them all: he locked John up in prison.

21 Now when all the people were baptized, Jesus was also baptized, and while He was praying, heaven was opened,

22 and the Holy Spirit descended upon Him in bodily form like a dove, and a voice came out of heaven, "You are My beloved Son, in You I am well-pleased."

➤ 23 When He began His ministry, Jesus Himself was about thirty years of age, being, as was supposed, the son of Joseph, the son of Eli,

24 the son of Matthat, the son of Levi, the son of Melchi, the son of Jannai, the son of Joseph,

25 the son of Mattathias, the son of Amos, the son of Nahum, the son of Hesli, the son of Naggai,

26 the son of Maath, the son of Mattathias, the son of Semein, the son of Josech, the son of Joda,

27 the son of Joanan, the son of Rhesa,

LIFE LESSONS

➤ **Luke 3:23 —** *When He began His ministry, Jesus Himself was about thirty years of age.*

*G*od spent three decades preparing Jesus for His ministry, most of it in almost total obscurity. Anyone whom God uses greatly He first puts through a period of preparation.

---

the son of Zerubbabel, the son of Shealtiel, the son of Neri,

28 the son of Melchi, the son of Addi, the son of Cosam, the son of Elmadam, the son of Er,

29 the son of Joshua, the son of Eliezer, the son of Jorim, the son of Matthat, the son of Levi,

30 the son of Simeon, the son of Judah, the son of Joseph, the son of Jonam, the son of Eliakim,

31 the son of Melea, the son of Menna, the son of Mattatha, the son of Nathan, the son of David,

32 the son of Jesse, the son of Obed, the son of Boaz, the son of Salmon, the son of Nahshon,

33 the son of Amminadab, the son of Admin, the son of Ram, the son of Hezron, the son of Perez, the son of Judah,

34 the son of Jacob, the son of Isaac, the son of Abraham, the son of Terah, the son of Nahor,

35 the son of Serug, the son of Reu, the son of Peleg, the son of Heber, the son of Shelah,

36 the son of Cainan, the son of Arphaxad, the son of Shem, the son of Noah, the son of Lamech,

37 the son of Methuselah, the son of Enoch, the son of Jared, the son of Mahalaleel, the son of Cainan,

38 the son of Enosh, the son of Seth, the son of Adam, the son of God.

Deuteronomy 17:1—18:22

17 "YOU shall not sacrifice to the LORD your God an ox or a sheep which has a blemish *or* any defect, for that is a detestable thing to the LORD your God.

2 "If there is found in your midst, in any of your towns, which the LORD your God is giving you, a man or a woman who does what is evil in the sight of the LORD your God, by transgressing His covenant,

3 and has gone and served other gods and worshiped them, or the sun or the

moon or any of the heavenly host, which I have not commanded,

4 and if it is told you and you have heard of it, then you shall inquire thoroughly. Behold, if it is true and the thing certain that this detestable thing has been done in Israel,

5 then you shall bring out that man or that woman who has done this evil deed to your gates, *that is*, the man or the woman, and you shall stone them to death.

6 "On the evidence of two witnesses or three witnesses, he who is to die shall be put to death; he shall not be put to death on the evidence of one witness.

7 "The hand of the witnesses shall be first against him to put him to death, and afterward the hand of all the people. So you shall purge the evil from your midst.

8 "If any case is too difficult for you to decide, between one kind of homicide or another, between one kind of lawsuit or another, and between one kind of assault or another, being cases of dispute in your courts, then you shall arise and go up to the place which the LORD your God chooses.

9 "So you shall come to the Levitical priest or the judge who is *in office* in those days, and you shall inquire *of them* and they will declare to you the verdict in the case.

10 "You shall do according to the terms of the verdict which they declare to you from that place which the LORD chooses; and you shall be careful to observe according to all that they teach you.

11 "According to the terms of the law which they teach you, and according to the verdict which they tell you, you shall do; you shall not turn aside from the word which they declare to you, to the right or the left.

12 "The man who acts presumptuously by not listening to the priest who stands there to serve the LORD your God, nor to the judge, that man shall die; thus you shall purge the evil from Israel.

13 "Then all the people will hear and be afraid, and will not act presumptuously again.

14 "When you enter the land which the LORD your God gives you, and you possess it and live in it, and you say, 'I will set a king over me like all the nations who are around me,'

15 you shall surely set a king over you whom the LORD your God chooses, *one* from among your countrymen you shall set as king over yourselves; you may not put a foreigner over yourselves who is not your countryman.

16 "Moreover, he shall not multiply horses for himself, nor shall he cause the people to return to Egypt to multiply horses, since the LORD has said to you, 'You shall never again return that way.'

17 "He shall not multiply wives for himself, or else his heart will turn away; nor shall he greatly increase silver and gold for himself.

18 "Now it shall come about when he sits on the throne of his kingdom, he shall write for himself a copy of this law on a scroll in the presence of the Levitical priests.

19 "It shall be with him and he shall read it all the days of his life, that he may learn to fear the LORD his God, by carefully observing all the words of this law and these statutes,

20 that his heart may not be lifted up above his countrymen and that he may not turn aside from the commandment, to the right or the left, so that he and his sons may continue long in his kingdom in the midst of Israel.

18 "THE Levitical priests, the whole tribe of Levi, shall have no portion or inheritance with Israel; they shall eat the LORD'S offerings by fire and His portion.

2 "They shall have no inheritance among their countrymen; the LORD is their inheritance, as He promised them.

3 "Now this shall be the priests' due from the people, from those who offer a sacrifice, either an ox or a sheep, of which they shall give to the priest the shoulder and the two cheeks and the stomach.

4 "You shall give him the first fruits of your grain, your new wine, and your oil, and the first shearing of your sheep.

5 "For the LORD your God has chosen him and his sons from all your tribes, to stand and serve in the name of the LORD forever.

6 "Now if a Levite comes from any of your towns throughout Israel where he resides, and comes whenever he desires to the place which the LORD chooses,

7 then he shall serve in the name of

LIFE LESSONS

➤ **Deuteronomy 17:19 — *"It shall be with him and he shall read it all the days of his life, that he may learn to fear the LORD his God."***

*D*aily Bible study helps us to fear God and obey His commands; it keeps us humble and lengthens our lives. God's Word is an anchor in times of storm—it sustains us and helps us maintain the course He has planned for us.

WHAT THE BIBLE SAYS ABOUT ⊕

The Forbidden Practice of the Occult

Deuteronomy 18:9–14

Most believers readily recognize the Bible forbids Satan worship and witchcraft. They might not, however, so quickly identify other practices as occult. Although some Christians may consider it harmless fun to consult their horoscopes in the daily newspaper; God says it is not. In fact, He forbids His people from engaging in astrology or any kind of fortune-telling (Lev. 20:27; Deut. 18:9–14; Is. 44:25; 47:12, 13; Jer. 27:9; Ezek. 13:8). The Bible also condemns other magical practices, such as casting enchantments and contacting the dead through mediums (Lev. 19:31; 2 Kin. 17:16–18; 21:6).

Have you ever sought out your horoscope, had your palm read, used a Ouija board, or researched your astrological sign? Did it ever cross your mind it could be extremely dangerous to do so? These are all gateways to serious spiritual bondage. We must remember the enemy of our souls is very cunning—preying on our seemingly harmless desire for knowledge of the future to trap us and lead us to destruction.

No one should *ever* experiment with the occult. There are spiritual forces far more powerful than we can imagine constantly trying to defeat us and keep us from what God created us to be. When we engage in occult activity, we open a door to Satan, giving him access to our lives.

Instead, you must learn to "put on the full armor of God, so that you will be able to stand firm against the schemes of the devil. . . . so that you will be able to resist in the evil day, and having done everything, to stand firm" (Eph. 6:11, 13). Listen to God, obey His Word, rely on His power against the dark forces, and don't ever wander into the devil's territory: "Your adversary, the devil, prowls around like a roaring lion, seeking someone to devour" (1 Pet. 5:8). You can resist him, standing firm in your faith that in Christ, he has already been defeated—you already have the victory. ⊕

---

the LORD his God, like all his fellow Levites who stand there before the LORD.
8 "They shall eat equal portions, except *what they receive* from the sale of their fathers' *estates.*
9 "When you enter the land which the LORD your God gives you, you shall not learn to imitate the detestable things of those nations.
10 "There shall not be found among you anyone who makes his son or his daughter pass through the fire, one who uses divination, one who practices witchcraft, or one who interprets omens, or a sorcerer,
11 or one who casts a spell, or a medium, or a spiritist, or one who calls up the dead.
12 "For whoever does these things is detestable to the LORD; and because of these detestable things the LORD your God will drive them out before you.
13 "You shall be blameless before the LORD your God.
14 "For those nations, which you shall dispossess, listen to those who practice witchcraft and to diviners, but as for you,

the LORD your God has not allowed you *to do so.*
15 "The LORD your God will raise up for you a prophet like me from among you, from your countrymen, you shall listen to him.
16 "This is according to all that you asked of the LORD your God in Horeb on the day of the assembly, saying, 'Let me not hear again the voice of the LORD my God, let me not see this great fire anymore, or I will die.'

LIFE LESSONS

➤ **Deuteronomy 18:18 —** *"I will raise up a prophet . . . and I will put My words in his mouth."*

A true prophet such as Moses, Isaiah, and Jeremiah faithfully declares the full counsel of God. Although much more than a mere prophet, Jesus Christ also fulfilled this prophecy during His earthly ministry—speaking only what the Father gave Him to declare (John 4:25, 26; 8:28; 12:49, 50; 17:8).

17 "The LORD said to me, 'They have spoken well.

➤ 18 'I will raise up a prophet from among their countrymen like you, and I will put My words in his mouth, and he shall speak to them all that I command him.

19 'It shall come about that whoever will not listen to My words which he shall speak in My name, I Myself will require it of him.

20 'But the prophet who speaks a word presumptuously in My name which I have not commanded him to speak, or which he speaks in the name of other gods, that prophet shall die.'

21 "You may say in your heart, 'How will we know the word which the LORD has not spoken?'

➤ 22 "When a prophet speaks in the name of the LORD, if the thing does not come about or come true, that is the thing which the LORD has not spoken. The prophet has spoken it presumptuously; you shall not be afraid of him.

Psalm 37:37–40

37 Mark the blameless man, and behold the upright;
For the man of peace will have a posterity.
38 But transgressors will be altogether destroyed;

LIFE LESSONS

➤ **Deuteronomy 18:22** — *"When a prophet speaks . . . if the thing does not come about or come true . . . the Lord has not spoken."*

*S*ince God always keeps His promises and always fulfills His Word, any prophecy or prediction that fails to come true has a source other than God.

➤ **Psalm 37:39** — *The salvation of the righteous is from the LORD; He is their strength in time of trouble.*

*W*hen hard times come, we often feel listless, powerless, weak, and worried. We must find our strength in God, for His might never wavers.

The posterity of the wicked will be cut off.
39 But the salvation of the righteous is from the LORD;
He is their strength in time of trouble.
40 The LORD helps them and delivers them;
He delivers them from the wicked and saves them,
Because they take refuge in Him.

Proverbs 12:20–22

20 Deceit is in the heart of those who devise evil,
But counselors of peace have joy.
21 No harm befalls the righteous,
But the wicked are filled with trouble.
22 Lying lips are an abomination to the LORD,
But those who deal faithfully are His delight.

Luke 4:1–30

4 JESUS, full of the Holy Spirit, returned from the Jordan and was led around by the Spirit in the wilderness
2 for forty days, being tempted by the devil. And He ate nothing during those days, and when they had ended, He became hungry.
3 And the devil said to Him, "If You are the Son of God, tell this stone to become bread."
4 And Jesus answered him, "It is written, 'MAN SHALL NOT LIVE ON BREAD ALONE.'"
5 And he led Him up and showed Him all the kingdoms of the world in a moment of time.
6 And the devil said to Him, "I will give You all this domain and its glory; for it has been handed over to me, and I give it to whomever I wish.
7 "Therefore if You worship before me, it shall all be Yours."
8 Jesus answered him, "It is written,

'YOU SHALL WORSHIP THE LORD YOUR GOD AND SERVE HIM ONLY.'"

9 And he led Him to Jerusalem and had Him stand on the pinnacle of the temple, and said to Him, "If You are the Son of God, throw Yourself down from here;

10 for it is written,

'HE WILL COMMAND HIS ANGELS
　　CONCERNING YOU TO GUARD YOU,'

11 and,

'ON *their* HANDS THEY WILL BEAR YOU
　　UP,
SO THAT YOU WILL NOT STRIKE YOUR
　　FOOT AGAINST A STONE.'"

12 And Jesus answered and said to him, "It is said, 'YOU SHALL NOT PUT THE LORD YOUR GOD TO THE TEST.'"

13 When the devil had finished every temptation, he left Him until an opportune time.

14 And Jesus returned to Galilee in the power of the Spirit, and news about Him spread through all the surrounding district.

15 And He *began* teaching in their synagogues and was praised by all.

16 And He came to Nazareth, where He had been brought up; and as was His custom, He entered the synagogue on the Sabbath, and stood up to read.

17 And the book of the prophet Isaiah was handed to Him. And He opened the book and found the place where it was written,

18 "THE SPIRIT OF THE LORD IS UPON
　　ME,
BECAUSE HE ANOINTED ME TO PREACH
　　THE GOSPEL TO THE POOR.
HE HAS SENT ME TO PROCLAIM
　　RELEASE TO THE CAPTIVES,
AND RECOVERY OF SIGHT TO THE
　　BLIND,
TO SET FREE THOSE WHO ARE
　　OPPRESSED,

19 TO PROCLAIM THE FAVORABLE YEAR OF
　　THE LORD."

20 And He closed the book, gave it back to the attendant and sat down; and the eyes of all in the synagogue were fixed on Him.

21 And He began to say to them, "Today this Scripture has been fulfilled in your hearing."

22 And all were speaking well of Him,

LIFE LESSONS

➤ **Luke 4:14** — *And Jesus returned to Galilee in the power of the Spirit.*

*L*uke shows us that Jesus fulfilled His entire ministry by relying on the power and direction of the Holy Spirit. When we rely on the Spirit as Jesus did, we can follow in His ministry footsteps.

➤ **Luke 4:21** — *"Today this Scripture has been fulfilled in your hearing."*

*T*hose in the synagogue understood that the text Jesus read (Isaiah 61) referred to the prophesied Messiah. Therefore, at the outset of His ministry, Jesus announced that He is the Savior and Redeemer whom Israel and the world had been awaiting.

---

and wondering at the gracious words which were falling from His lips; and they were saying, "Is this not Joseph's son?"

23 And He said to them, "No doubt you will quote this proverb to Me, 'Physician, heal yourself! Whatever we heard was done at Capernaum, do here in your hometown as well.'"

24 And He said, "Truly I say to you, no prophet is welcome in his hometown.

25 "But I say to you in truth, there were many widows in Israel in the days of Elijah, when the sky was shut up for three years and six months, when a great famine came over all the land;

26 and yet Elijah was sent to none of them, but only to Zarephath, *in the land* of Sidon, to a woman who was a widow.

27 "And there were many lepers in Israel in the time of Elisha the prophet; and none of them was cleansed, but only Naaman the Syrian."

28 And all *the people* in the synagogue were filled with rage as they heard these things;

29 and they got up and drove Him out of the city, and led Him to the brow of the hill on which their city had been built, in order to throw Him down the cliff.

30 But passing through their midst, He went His way.

Deuteronomy 19:1—20:20

19 "WHEN the LORD your God cuts off the nations, whose land the LORD your God gives you, and you dispossess them and settle in their cities and in their houses,

2   you shall set aside three cities for yourself in the midst of your land, which the LORD your God gives you to possess.

3   "You shall prepare the roads for yourself, and divide into three parts the territory of your land which the LORD your God will give you as a possession, so that any manslayer may flee there.

4   "Now this is the case of the manslayer who may flee there and live: when he kills his friend unintentionally, not hating him previously—

➤ 5   as when *a man* goes into the forest with his friend to cut wood, and his hand swings the axe to cut down the tree, and the iron *head* slips off the handle and strikes his friend so that he dies—he may flee to one of these cities and live;

6   otherwise the avenger of blood might pursue the manslayer in the heat of his anger, and overtake him, because the way is long, and take his life, though he was not deserving of death, since he had not hated him previously.

7   "Therefore, I command you, saying, 'You shall set aside three cities for yourself.'

8   "If the LORD your God enlarges your territory, just as He has sworn to your fathers, and gives you all the land which He promised to give your fathers—

9   if you carefully observe all this commandment which I command you today, to love the LORD your God, and to walk in His ways always—then you shall add three more cities for yourself, besides these three.

10   "So innocent blood will not be shed in the midst of your land which the LORD your God gives you as an inheritance, and bloodguiltiness be on you.

11   "But if there is a man who hates his neighbor and lies in wait for him and rises up against him and strikes him so that he dies, and he flees to one of these cities,

12   then the elders of his city shall send and take him from there and deliver him into the hand of the avenger of blood, that he may die.

13   "You shall not pity him, but you shall purge the blood of the innocent from Israel, that it may go well with you.

14   "You shall not move your neighbor's boundary mark, which the ancestors have set, in your inheritance which you will inherit in the land that the LORD your God gives you to possess.

15   "A single witness shall not rise up against a man on account of any iniquity or any sin which he has committed; on the evidence of two or three witnesses a matter shall be confirmed.

16   "If a malicious witness rises up against a man to accuse him of wrongdoing,

17   then both the men who have the dispute shall stand before the LORD, before the priests and the judges who will be *in office* in those days.

18   "The judges shall investigate thoroughly, and if the witness is a false witness *and* he has accused his brother falsely,

19   then you shall do to him just as he had intended to do to his brother. Thus you shall purge the evil from among you.

20   "The rest will hear and be afraid, and will never again do such an evil thing among you.

21   "Thus you shall not show pity: life for life, eye for eye, tooth for tooth, hand for hand, foot for foot.

20 "WHEN you go out to battle against ◄ your enemies and see horses and chariots *and* people more numerous than you, do not be afraid of them; for the LORD your God, who brought you up from the land of Egypt, is with you.

2   "When you are approaching the battle, the priest shall come near and speak to the people.

LIFE LESSONS

➤ **Deuteronomy 19:5 — *"He may flee to one of these cities and live."***

*A*ccidents and tragedies occur in a fallen world, and although God may not tell us why, He does instruct us how to respond. He also assumes full responsibility for our needs when we obey Him.

LIFE PRINCIPLE   4

THE AWARENESS OF GOD'S PRESENCE ENER-
GIZES US FOR OUR WORK.

DEUTERONOMY 20:1

*H*ow can you get the most out of your
work? Here are three suggestions.

1. View yourself as a servant.

Jesus came to earth not to be served, but to
serve—and He instructed us to adopt the same
attitude (Matt. 20:25–28). Paul wrote, "Slaves,
in all things obey those who are your masters
on earth, not with external service, as those
who merely please men, but with sincerity of
heart, fearing the Lord" (Col. 3:22).

If Paul told slaves to do their work heartily
(and they received no paycheck), then what
about the rest of us who *do* get paid? "Well,
they don't pay me nearly enough," you may
say. Okay, perhaps you are not paid adequately—but taking longer lunch hours, clock-
ing out early, or coming in late is not the way
to even things out. If you are compensated for
eight hours, you need to give eight full hours.
Why? Because you are a servant of God, and as
His representative, you have a responsibility to
do good work.

Besides, the best pathway to promotion is
servanthood. Whoever wants to be a leader
must adopt an attitude of humility (Mark
9:35). A prideful employee is seldom seen as
a candidate for promotion. Instead, it is the
humble, godly worker who diligently labors
that management sees as leadership material.
Never doubt the impact of your attitude on
everyone around you—the boss included!

But who's your real employer? That leads us
to our second suggestion.

*2. Realize that you work for the Lord
Himself.*

Your employer exercises supervisory authority over you, but Jesus Christ is your Lord.
You work for *Him*: "Whatever you do, do
your work heartily, as for the Lord rather than
for men" (Col. 3:23).

If you are a Christian, Jesus Christ is the
supervisor at your place of work—and He
not only watches you from afar, He's right
there with you. You and I need to give a full
day's labor, regardless of whether we think
management is fair. Jesus is ultimately the One
we serve, and He's always on site. You and

I should do our very best because the Holy
Spirit is present, equipping, and energizing us.

We make a terrible mistake by segment-
ing life. We may think that Monday through
Friday we go to work, Saturday we play, and
Sunday we worship. God has not designed life
that way. If Jesus Christ is our Savior, we can't
exclude Him from *any* part of life. It isn't right
to teach a Sunday school class with everything
we have, then meander into work the rest of
the week—we must honor and glorify Him in
everything we do. It eliminates the temptation
of doing our work merely to be seen by men
when we commit ourselves wholeheartedly
Jesus (Matt. 6:24).

Do I mean that your mundane job is also
the Lord's work? Yes! *Ministry is not just what
you do at church.* You worship God every day
of the week—on Sunday, you do so in church;
on Monday through Friday, you show your
devotion to Him by doing a good job at work.
Your exalted status as a child of God dignifies
your labor, and your office or place of employ-
ment should be better off because you are
there.

You serve the Lord Jesus Christ (Col. 3:24).
Do you have a good testimony in the marketplace for Him? Are you one of your company's
most faithful employees because you serve
God? Does your attitude reflect the joy you
have in considering Him the *real* CEO?

*3. Realize your pay comes both now and here-
after.*

Paul wrote, "From the Lord you will receive
the reward of the inheritance" (Col. 3:24). Of
course, you must get paid now to take care
of your household expenses. But if you have
done your very best and given all you have,
you will never really get paid all you are worth.
The wonderful thing to remember is this: you
may get insufficient wages here, but you will
get rewarded beyond measure in heaven. God
will much more than equalize everything in
the Judgment (1 Cor. 3:11–15; 2 Cor. 5:9,
10; Eph. 6:7, 8), and He will certainly reward
you justly.

Do you see yourself as a servant? Do you
consider Him your real Boss and work in a
manner honoring to the Lord, no matter how
menial or boring your job might seem? Have
you realized that you have a tremendous
reward coming later for faithful labor performed now? If so, you are getting the most
out of your work. ❂

3 "He shall say to them, 'Hear, O Israel, you are approaching the battle against your enemies today. Do not be faint-hearted. Do not be afraid, or panic, or tremble before them,
4 for the LORD your God is the one who goes with you, to fight for you against your enemies, to save you.'
5 "The officers also shall speak to the people, saying, 'Who is the man that has built a new house and has not dedicated it? Let him depart and return to his house, otherwise he might die in the battle and another man would dedicate it.
6 'Who is the man that has planted a vineyard and has not begun to use its fruit? Let him depart and return to his house, otherwise he might die in the battle and another man would begin to use its fruit.
7 'And who is the man that is engaged to a woman and has not married her? Let him depart and return to his house, otherwise he might die in the battle and another man would marry her.'
8 "Then the officers shall speak further to the people and say, 'Who is the man that is afraid and fainthearted? Let him depart and return to his house, so that he might not make his brothers' hearts melt like his heart.'
9 "When the officers have finished speaking to the people, they shall appoint commanders of armies at the head of the people.

10 "When you approach a city to fight against it, you shall offer it terms of peace.
11 "If it agrees to make peace with you and opens to you, then all the people who are found in it shall become your forced labor and shall serve you.
12 "However, if it does not make peace with you, but makes war against you, then you shall besiege it.
13 "When the LORD your God gives it into your hand, you shall strike all the men in it with the edge of the sword.
14 "Only the women and the children and the animals and all that is in the city, all its spoil, you shall take as booty for yourself; and you shall use the spoil of your enemies which the LORD your God has given you.
15 "Thus you shall do to all the cities that are very far from you, which are not of the cities of these nations nearby.
16 "Only in the cities of these peoples that the LORD your God is giving you as an inheritance, you shall not leave alive anything that breathes.
17 "But you shall utterly destroy them, the Hittite and the Amorite, the Canaanite and the Perizzite, the Hivite and the Jebusite, as the LORD your God has commanded you,
18 so that they may not teach you to do according to all their detestable things which they have done for their gods, so that you would sin against the LORD your God.
19 "When you besiege a city a long time, to make war against it in order to capture it, you shall not destroy its trees by swinging an axe against them; for you may eat from them, and you shall not cut them down. For is the tree of the field a man, that it should be besieged by you?
20 "Only the trees which you know are not fruit trees you shall destroy and cut down, that you may construct siege-works against the city that is making war with you until it falls.

LIFE LESSONS

➤ Deuteronomy 20:1 — *"When you go out to battle against your enemies . . . do not be afraid of them; for the LORD your God . . . is with you."*

The number, strength, and hostility of our enemies matter little when the Lord is with us. As He delivered Israel from Egypt, so He can deliver us from our enemies. His presence energizes us and empowers us to accomplish anything He calls us to do.

➤ Deuteronomy 20:7 — *"Let him depart and return to his house, otherwise he might die in the battle and another man would marry her."*

The Lord did not promise His people that they would suffer no casualties when they followed Him into battle, only that they would surely triumph.

✦ Psalm 38:1–8

A Psalm of David, for a memorial.

38 O LORD, rebuke me not in Your wrath,
And chasten me not in Your burning anger.

2   For Your arrows have sunk deep
      into me,
    And Your hand has pressed down
      on me.
3   There is no soundness in my flesh
      because of Your indignation;
    There is no health in my bones
      because of my sin.
➤ 4   For my iniquities are gone over my
      head;
    As a heavy burden they weigh too
      much for me.
5   My wounds grow foul *and* fester
    Because of my folly.
6   I am bent over and greatly bowed
      down;
    I go mourning all day long.
7   For my loins are filled with burning,
    And there is no soundness in my
      flesh.
8   I am benumbed and badly crushed;
    I groan because of the agitation of
      my heart.

Proverbs 12:23–25

23 A prudent man conceals knowledge,
    But the heart of fools proclaims
      folly.
24 The hand of the diligent will rule,
    But the slack *hand* will be put to
      forced labor.
➤ 25 Anxiety in a man's heart weighs it
      down,
    But a good word makes it glad.

Luke 4:31–44

31 And He came down to Capernaum,
a city of Galilee, and He was teaching
them on the Sabbath;
32 and they were amazed at His teaching, for His message was with authority.
33 In the synagogue there was a man
possessed by the spirit of an unclean
demon, and he cried out with a loud
voice,
34 "Let us alone! What business do we
have with each other, Jesus of Nazareth?
Have You come to destroy us? I know
who You are—the Holy One of God!"
35 But Jesus rebuked him, saying, "Be
quiet and come out of him!" And when

the demon had thrown him down in the
midst *of the people,* he came out of him
without doing him any harm.
36 And amazement came upon them
all, and they *began* talking with one
another saying, "What is this message?
For with authority and power He commands the unclean spirits and they come
out.'"
37 And the report about Him was
spreading into every locality in the surrounding district.
38 Then He got up and *left* the synagogue, and entered Simon's home. Now
Simon's mother-in-law was suffering
from a high fever, and they asked Him to
help her.
39 And standing over her, He rebuked
the fever, and it left her; and she immediately got up and waited on them.
40 While the sun was setting, all those
who had any *who were* sick with various
diseases brought them to Him; and laying His hands on each one of them, He
was healing them.
41 Demons also were coming out of
many, shouting, "You are the Son of
God!" But rebuking them, He would not
allow them to speak, because they knew
Him to be the Christ.

LIFE LESSONS

➤ **Psalm 38:4** — *For my iniquities are
gone over my head; as a heavy burden
they weigh too much for me.*

God knows that our sins weigh us
down and keep us from His best.
When we confess them, He takes them
off our shoulders and enables us to walk
with our heads upright once again.

➤ **Proverbs 12:25** — *Anxiety in a man's
heart weighs it down, but a good word
makes it glad.*

We should become experts at giving
encouragement (Heb. 3:13). The
world has more than enough naysayers,
critics, scoffers, ridiculers, and detractors.
A "good word" is hard to find, which
is why Colossians 3:16 admonishes, "Let
the word of Christ richly dwell within
you, with all wisdom teaching and
admonishing one another with psalms
and hymns and spiritual songs, singing with thankfulness in your hearts to
God."

42 When day came, Jesus left and went to a secluded place; and the crowds were searching for Him, and came to Him and tried to keep Him from going away from them.

43 But He said to them, "I must preach the kingdom of God to the other cities also, for I was sent for this purpose." *

44 So He kept on preaching in the synagogues of Judea.

MARCH 30

Deuteronomy 21:1—22:30

21 "IF a slain person is found lying in the open country in the land which the LORD your God gives you to possess, *and* it is not known who has struck him,

2 then your elders and your judges shall go out and measure *the distance* to the cities which are around the slain one.

3 "It shall be that the city which is nearest to the slain man, that is, the elders of that city, shall take a heifer of the herd, which has not been worked and which has not pulled in a yoke;

4 and the elders of that city shall bring the heifer down to a valley with running water, which has not been plowed or sown, and shall break the heifer's neck there in the valley.

5 "Then the priests, the sons of Levi, shall come near, for the LORD your God has chosen them to serve Him and to bless in the name of the LORD; and every dispute and every assault shall be settled by them.

6 "All the elders of that city which is nearest to the slain man shall wash their hands over the heifer whose neck was broken in the valley;

7 and they shall answer and say, 'Our hands did not shed this blood, nor did our eyes see *it.*

8 'Forgive Your people Israel whom You have redeemed, O LORD, and do not place the guilt of innocent blood in the midst of Your people Israel.' And the bloodguiltiness shall be forgiven them.

9 "So you shall remove the guilt of innocent blood from your midst, when you do what is right in the eyes of the LORD.

10 "When you go out to battle against your enemies, and the LORD your God delivers them into your hands and you take them away captive,

11 and see among the captives a beautiful woman, and have a desire for her and would take her as a wife for yourself,

12 then you shall bring her home to your house, and she shall shave her head and trim her nails.

13 "She shall also remove the clothes of her captivity and shall remain in your house, and mourn her father and mother a full month; and after that you may go in to her and be her husband and she shall be your wife.

14 "It shall be, if you are not pleased with her, then you shall let her go wherever she wishes; but you shall certainly not sell her for money, you shall not mistreat her, because you have humbled her.

15 "If a man has two wives, the one loved and the other unloved, and *both* the loved and the unloved have borne him sons, if the firstborn son belongs to the unloved,

16 then it shall be in the day he wills what he has to his sons, he cannot make the son of the loved the firstborn before the son of the unloved, who is the firstborn.

17 "But he shall acknowledge the firstborn, the son of the unloved, by giving him a double portion of all that he has, for he is the beginning of his strength; to him belongs the right of the firstborn.

18 "If any man has a stubborn and rebellious son who will not obey his father or his mother, and when they chastise him, he will not even listen to them,

19 then his father and mother shall seize him, and bring him out to the elders of his city at the gateway of his hometown.

20 "They shall say to the elders of his city, 'This son of ours is stubborn and rebellious, he will not obey us, he is a glutton and a drunkard.'

21 "Then all the men of his city shall

stone him to death; so you shall remove the evil from your midst, and all Israel will hear *of it* and fear.

22 "If a man has committed a sin worthy of death and he is put to death, and you hang him on a tree,

➤ 23 his corpse shall not hang all night on the tree, but you shall surely bury him on the same day (for he who is hanged is accursed of God), so that you do not defile your land which the LORD your God gives you as an inheritance.

22 "YOU shall not see your countryman's ox or his sheep straying away, and pay no attention to them; you shall certainly bring them back to your countryman.

2 "If your countryman is not near you, or if you do not know him, then you shall bring it home to your house, and it shall remain with you until your countryman looks for it; then you shall restore it to him.

3 "Thus you shall do with his donkey, and you shall do the same with his garment, and you shall do likewise with anything lost by your countryman, which he has lost and you have found. You are not allowed to neglect *them.*

4 "You shall not see your countryman's donkey or his ox fallen down on the way, and pay no attention to them; you shall certainly help him to raise *them* up.

5 "A woman shall not wear man's clothing, nor shall a man put on a woman's clothing; for whoever does these things is an abomination to the LORD your God.

6 "If you happen to come upon a bird's nest along the way, in any tree or on the ground, with young ones or eggs, and the mother sitting on the young or on the

eggs, you shall not take the mother with the young;

7 you shall certainly let the mother go, but the young you may take for yourself, in order that it may be well with you and that you may prolong your days.

8 "When you build a new house, you shall make a parapet for your roof, so that you will not bring bloodguilt on your house if anyone falls from it.

9 "You shall not sow your vineyard with two kinds of seed, or all the produce of the seed which you have sown and the increase of the vineyard will become defiled.

10 "You shall not plow with an ox and a donkey together.

11 "You shall not wear a material mixed of wool and linen together.

12 "You shall make yourself tassels on the four corners of your garment with which you cover yourself.

13 "If any man takes a wife and goes in to her and *then* turns against her,

14 and charges her with shameful deeds and publicly defames her, and says, 'I took this woman, *but* when I came near her, I did not find her a virgin,'

15 then the girl's father and her mother shall take and bring out the *evidence* of the girl's virginity to the elders of the city at the gate.

16 "The girl's father shall say to the elders, 'I gave my daughter to this man for a wife, but he turned against her;

17 and behold, he has charged her with shameful deeds, saying, "I did not find your daughter a virgin." But this is the evidence of my daughter's virginity.' And they shall spread the garment before the elders of the city.

18 "So the elders of that city shall take the man and chastise him,

19 and they shall fine him a hundred *shekels* of silver and give it to the girl's father, because he publicly defamed a virgin of Israel. And she shall remain his wife; he cannot divorce her all his days.

20 "But if this charge is true, that the girl was not found a virgin,

21 then they shall bring out the girl to the doorway of her father's house, and the men of her city shall stone her to death because she has committed an act of folly in Israel by playing the harlot in her father's house; thus you shall purge the evil from among you.

22 "If a man is found lying with a

---

married woman, then both of them shall die, the man who lay with the woman, and the woman; thus you shall purge the evil from Israel.

23 "If there is a girl who is a virgin engaged to a man, and *another* man finds her in the city and lies with her,

24 then you shall bring them both out to the gate of that city and you shall stone them to death; the girl, because she did not cry out in the city, and the man, because he has violated his neighbor's wife. Thus you shall purge the evil from among you.

25 "But if in the field the man finds the girl who is engaged, and the man forces her and lies with her, then only the man who lies with her shall die.

26 "But you shall do nothing to the girl; there is no sin in the girl worthy of death, for just as a man rises against his neighbor and murders him, so is this case.

27 "When he found her in the field, the engaged girl cried out, but there was no one to save her.

28 "If a man finds a girl who is a virgin, who is not engaged, and seizes her and lies with her and they are discovered,

29 then the man who lay with her shall give to the girl's father fifty *shekels* of silver, and she shall become his wife because he has violated her; he cannot divorce her all his days.

30 "A man shall not take his father's wife so that he will not uncover his father's skirt.

Psalm 38:9–22

9 Lord, all my desire is before You;
  And my sighing is not hidden from
    You.
10 My heart throbs, my strength fails
    me;
  And the light of my eyes, even that
    has gone from me.
11 My loved ones and my friends stand
    aloof from my plague;
  And my kinsmen stand afar off.
12 Those who seek my life lay snares
    for me;
  And those who seek to injure me
    have threatened destruction,
  And they devise treachery all day
    long.
13 But I, like a deaf man, do not hear;
  And *I am* like a mute man who does
    not open his mouth.
14 Yes, I am like a man who does not
    hear,
  And in whose mouth are no
    arguments.
15 For I hope in You, O LORD;
  You will answer, O Lord my God.

Life Examples:

Keep It Real

PSALM 38:9, 10

Sometimes it's difficult to be real with people. You don't know how they'll react to what you share with them. Will they be shocked by your admissions? Will they reject or mock you? Will they betray your secrets to others? If you've been hurt, it can become harder and harder to reveal your heart.

But you can always be open with God because He knows the un-sugarcoated truth—all of your hopes, dreams, fears, wounds, insecurities, transgressions, and faults—all of it. King David writes, "Lord, all my desire is before You; and my sighing is not hidden from You. My heart throbs, my strength fails me; and the light of my eyes, even that has gone from me" (Ps. 38:9, 10).

Friend, God knows you—and He knows

what is going on in you right now as you read this devotion. Whatever it is, perhaps you can't share it with others. Whether it's because you feel they just won't understand the stress of your situation, because you don't want to burden them with your troubles, or because you're simply too uncomfortable to share it—you're carrying it alone when you don't have to.

Realize God loves and accepts you, no matter what is going on with you. He wants an intimate relationship with you, and He is eager to show you His presence, power, wisdom, and unconditional love in the most difficult circumstances of your life.

Whatever it is burdening your heart—give it to God. He already understands your pain and knows how to heal it. Open your heart to Him, confide in Him, and trust Him with your most profound thoughts and feelings. You'll see that the Savior of your soul is also the dearest friend you'll ever know.

16 For I said, "May they not rejoice
      over me,
   Who, when my foot slips, would
      magnify themselves against me."
17 For I am ready to fall,
   And my sorrow is continually
      before me.
18 For I confess my iniquity;
   I am full of anxiety because of my
      sin.
19 But my enemies are vigorous *and*
      strong,
   And many are those who hate me
      wrongfully.
20 And those who repay evil for good,
   They oppose me, because I follow
      what is good.
21 Do not forsake me, O LORD;
   O my God, do not be far from me!
22 Make haste to help me,
   O Lord, my salvation!

✦ Proverbs 12:26–28

26 The righteous is a guide to his
      neighbor,
   But the way of the wicked leads
      them astray.
27 A lazy man does not roast his prey,
   But the precious possession of a
      man *is* diligence.
✴ 28 In the way of righteousness is life,
   And in *its* pathway there is no
      death.

✦ Luke 5:1–16

5 NOW it happened that while the
   crowd was pressing around Him and
listening to the word of God, He was
standing by the lake of Gennesaret;
2   and He saw two boats lying at the
edge of the lake; but the fishermen had
gotten out of them and were washing
their nets.
3   And He got into one of the boats,
which was Simon's, and asked him to put
out a little way from the land. And He
sat down and *began* teaching the people
from the boat.
4   When He had finished speaking, He
said to Simon, "Put out into the deep
water and let down your nets for a catch."

5   Simon answered and said, "Master,
we worked hard all night and caught
nothing, but I will do as You say *and* let
down the nets."
6   When they had done this, they enclosed a great quantity of fish, and their
nets *began* to break;
7   so they signaled to their partners in
the other boat for them to come and help
them. And they came and filled both of
the boats, so that they began to sink.
8   But when Simon Peter saw *that*, he
fell down at Jesus' feet, saying, "Go away
from me Lord, for I am a sinful man!"
9   For amazement had seized him and
all his companions because of the catch
of fish which they had taken;
10 and so also *were* James and John,
sons of Zebedee, who were partners with
Simon. And Jesus said to Simon, "Do not
fear, from now on you will be catching
men."
11 When they had brought their boats ≺
to land, they left everything and followed
Him.
12 While He was in one of the cities,
behold, *there was* a man covered with
leprosy; and when he saw Jesus, he fell
on his face and implored Him, saying,
"Lord, if You are willing, You can make
me clean."
13 And He stretched out His hand and ≺
touched him, saying, "I am willing; be

LIFE LESSONS

≻ **Luke 5:11 —** *When they had brought
their boats to land, they left everything
and followed Him.*

*T*he particulars of what Jesus requires
of His disciples vary tremendously,
but of all followers He demands total
allegiance. He must be Lord of all, not
merely one significant voice among
many others.

≻ **Luke 5:13 —** *He stretched out His
hand and touched him, saying, "I am
willing; be cleansed." And immediately
the leprosy left him.*

*J*esus did not have to touch people
to cure them (Luke 7:1–10), but He
made a point of compassionately touching the leper—a man no one dared to
touch. Jesus always gives us exactly what
we need.

cleansed." And immediately the leprosy left him.

14 And He ordered him to tell no one, "But go and show yourself to the priest and make an offering for your cleansing, just as Moses commanded, as a testimony to them."

15 But the news about Him was spreading even farther, and large crowds were gathering to hear *Him* and to be healed of their sicknesses.

16 But Jesus Himself would *often* slip away to the wilderness and pray.

LIFE LESSONS

> Luke 5:16 — *Jesus Himself would often slip away to the wilderness and pray.*

*J*esus cherished his times alone in prayer. As our example, He shows us none can afford to skip our devotional times alone with the Lord. We were made for an intimate relationship with Him, and that cannot happen if we never communicate with Him or listen to Him.

MARCH 31

◈ Deuteronomy 23:1—24:22

23 "NO one who is emasculated or has his male organ cut off shall enter the assembly of the LORD.

2 "No one of illegitimate birth shall enter the assembly of the LORD; none of his *descendants*, even to the tenth generation, shall enter the assembly of the LORD.

3 "No Ammonite or Moabite shall enter the assembly of the LORD; none of their *descendants*, even to the tenth generation, shall ever enter the assembly of the LORD,

4 because they did not meet you with food and water on the way when you came out of Egypt, and because they hired against you Balaam the son of Beor from Pethor of Mesopotamia, to curse you.

5 "Nevertheless, the LORD your God was not willing to listen to Balaam, but the LORD your God turned the curse into a blessing for you because the LORD your God loves you.

6 "You shall never seek their peace or their prosperity all your days.

7 "You shall not detest an Edomite, for he is your brother; you shall not detest an Egyptian, because you were an alien in his land.

8 "The sons of the third generation who are born to them may enter the assembly of the LORD.

9 "When you go out as an army against your enemies, you shall keep yourself from every evil thing.

10 "If there is among you any man who is unclean because of a nocturnal emission, then he must go outside the camp; he may not reenter the camp.

11 "But it shall be when evening approaches, he shall bathe himself with water, and at sundown he may reenter the camp.

12 "You shall also have a place outside the camp and go out there,

13 and you shall have a spade among your tools, and it shall be when you sit down outside, you shall dig with it and shall turn to cover up your excrement.

14 "Since the LORD your God walks in the midst of your camp to deliver you and to defeat your enemies before you, therefore your camp must be holy; and He must not see anything indecent among you or He will turn away from you.

15 "You shall not hand over to his master a slave who has escaped from his master to you.

LIFE LESSONS

> Deuteronomy 23:12 — *"You shall also have a place outside the camp."*

*L*ong before humankind knew anything about the connection between personal hygiene and good health, God gave His people commands to keep them physically healthy. Obedience always brings blessing!

16 "He shall live with you in your midst, in the place which he shall choose in one of your towns where it pleases him; you shall not mistreat him.

17 "None of the daughters of Israel shall be a cult prostitute, nor shall any of the sons of Israel be a cult prostitute.

18 "You shall not bring the hire of a harlot or the wages of a dog into the house of the LORD your God for any votive offering, for both of these are an abomination to the LORD your God.

19 "You shall not charge interest to your countrymen: interest on money, food, or anything that may be loaned at interest.

20 "You may charge interest to a foreigner, but to your countrymen you shall not charge interest, so that the LORD your God may bless you in all that you undertake in the land which you are about to enter to possess.

21 "When you make a vow to the LORD your God, you shall not delay to pay it, for it would be sin in you, and the LORD your God will surely require it of you.

22 "However, if you refrain from vowing, it would not be sin in you.

23 "You shall be careful to perform what goes out from your lips, just as you have voluntarily vowed to the LORD your God, what you have promised.

24 "When you enter your neighbor's vineyard, then you may eat grapes until you are fully satisfied, but you shall not put any in your basket.

25 "When you enter your neighbor's standing grain, then you may pluck the heads with your hand, but you shall not wield a sickle in your neighbor's standing grain.

24 "WHEN a man takes a wife and marries her, and it happens that she finds no favor in his eyes because he has found some indecency in her, and he writes her a certificate of divorce and puts it in her hand and sends her out from his house,

2 and she leaves his house and goes and becomes another man's wife,

3 and if the latter husband turns against her and writes her a certificate of divorce and puts it in her hand and sends her out of his house, or if the latter husband dies who took her to be his wife,

4 then her former husband who sent her away is not allowed to take her again to be his wife, since she has been defiled; for that is an abomination before the LORD, and you shall not bring sin on the land which the LORD your God gives you as an inheritance.

5 "When a man takes a new wife, he shall not go out with the army nor be charged with any duty; he shall be free at home one year and shall give happiness to his wife whom he has taken.

6 "No one shall take a handmill or an upper millstone in pledge, for he would be taking a life in pledge.

7 "If a man is caught kidnapping any of his countrymen of the sons of Israel, and he deals with him violently or sells him, then that thief shall die; so you shall purge the evil from among you.

8 "Be careful against an infection of leprosy, that you diligently observe and do according to all that the Levitical priests teach you; as I have commanded them, so you shall be careful to do.

9 "Remember what the LORD your God did to Miriam on the way as you came out of Egypt.

10 "When you make your neighbor a loan of any sort, you shall not enter his house to take his pledge.

11 "You shall remain outside, and the man to whom you make the loan shall bring the pledge out to you.

12 "If he is a poor man, you shall not sleep with his pledge.

13 "When the sun goes down you shall surely return the pledge to him, that he may sleep in his cloak and bless you; and it will be righteousness for you before the LORD your God.

14 "You shall not oppress a hired servant who is poor and needy, whether he is one of your countrymen or one of your aliens who is in your land in your towns.

LIFE LESSONS

➤ **Deuteronomy 24:5** — *"When a man takes a new wife, he shall not go out with the army nor be charged with any duty; he shall be free at home one year and shall give happiness to his wife whom he has taken."*

God is most concerned about our holiness, but He is not unconcerned about our happiness, as this verse demonstrates. God wants us to have strong families and to experience His joy.

15 "You shall give him his wages on his day before the sun sets, for he is poor and sets his heart on it; so that he will not cry against you to the LORD and it become sin in you.

➤ 16 "Fathers shall not be put to death for *their* sons, nor shall sons be put to death for *their* fathers; everyone shall be put to death for his own sin.

17 "You shall not pervert the justice due an alien *or* an orphan, nor take a widow's garment in pledge.

18 "But you shall remember that you were a slave in Egypt, and that the LORD your God redeemed you from there; therefore I am commanding you to do this thing.

19 "When you reap your harvest in your field and have forgotten a sheaf in the field, you shall not go back to get it; it shall be for the alien, for the orphan, and for the widow, in order that the LORD your God may bless you in all the work of your hands.

20 "When you beat your olive tree, you shall not go over the boughs again; it shall be for the alien, for the orphan, and for the widow.

21 "When you gather the grapes of your vineyard, you shall not go over it again; it shall be for the alien, for the orphan, and for the widow.

➤ 22 "You shall remember that you were a slave in the land of Egypt; therefore I am commanding you to do this thing.

✦ Psalm 39:1–6

For the choir director, for Jeduthun.
A Psalm of David.

➤ **39** I SAID, "I will guard my ways
That I may not sin with my tongue;
I will guard my mouth as with a muzzle
While the wicked are in my presence."
2 I was mute and silent,
I refrained *even* from good,
And my sorrow grew worse.
3 My heart was hot within me,
While I was musing the fire burned;
Then I spoke with my tongue:
✱ 4 "LORD, make me to know my end
And what is the extent of my days;
Let me know how transient I am.

5 "Behold, You have made my days *as* handbreadths,
And my lifetime as nothing in Your sight;
Surely every man at his best is a mere breath.   Selah.
6 "Surely every man walks about as a phantom;
Surely they make an uproar for nothing;
He amasses *riches* and does not know who will gather them.

✦ Proverbs 13:1–3

13 A WISE son *accepts his* father's discipline,
But a scoffer does not listen to rebuke.
2 From the fruit of a man's mouth he enjoys good,

LIFE LESSONS

➤ **Deuteronomy 24:16 — *"Everyone shall be put to death for his own sin."***

*W*e are all responsible to God for our own lives. We do not accrue the righteousness of our ancestors, nor must we pay for the sins of our forbearers. God judges each person individually.

➤ **Deuteronomy 24:22 — *"You shall remember that you were a slave in the land of Egypt."***

*G*od often reminded Israel they had been slaves in Egypt. Why? To foster compassion in them for the downtrodden. Likewise, He reminds us we once were estranged from Him so that we will be faithful to proclaim the Good News to those who are lost (Eph. 2:12, 13, 17). We are to be a compassionate people— both to the poor and to those who are perishing.

➤ **Psalm 39:1 — *"I will guard my ways that I may not sin with my tongue."***

*W*e should always be aware of our speech and take special caution when in the presence of unbelievers. We should never give anyone a reason to reject God because we've said something ungodly (Col. 4:5, 6).

LIFE LESSONS

➤ **Proverbs 13:3** — *The one who guards his mouth preserves his life; the one who opens wide his lips comes to ruin.*

"*L*oose lips sink ships," was a popular World War II motto. It reminded people to guard their words so nothing they said would endanger American troops. Preventing casualties in the spiritual wars we engage in every day as believers takes the same kind of caution. We should not allow gossip to imperil our testimonies as we seek to win the lost (James 3:5–10).

But the desire of the treacherous is violence.

➤ 3   The one who guards his mouth
        preserves his life;
✳   The one who opens wide his lips
        comes to ruin.

Luke 5:17–39

17   One day He was teaching; and there were *some* Pharisees and teachers of the law sitting *there*, who had come from every village of Galilee and Judea and *from* Jerusalem; and the power of the Lord was *present* for Him to perform healing.
18   And *some* men *were* carrying on a bed a man who was paralyzed; and they were trying to bring him in and to set him down in front of Him.
19   But not finding any *way* to bring him in because of the crowd, they went up on the roof and let him down through the tiles with his stretcher, into the middle *of the crowd,* in front of Jesus.
20   Seeing their faith, He said, "Friend, your sins are forgiven you."
21   The scribes and the Pharisees began to reason, saying, "Who is this *man* who speaks blasphemies? Who can forgive sins, but God alone?"
22   But Jesus, aware of their reasonings, answered and said to them, "Why are you reasoning in your hearts?
23   "Which is easier, to say, 'Your sins have been forgiven you,' or to say, 'Get up and walk'?
24   "But, so that you may know that the

Son of Man has authority on earth to forgive sins,"—He said to the paralytic—"I say to you, get up, and pick up your stretcher and go home."
25   Immediately he got up before them, and picked up what he had been lying on, and went home glorifying God.
26   They were all struck with astonishment and *began* glorifying God; and they were filled with fear, saying, "We have seen remarkable things today."
27   After that He went out and noticed a tax collector named Levi sitting in the tax booth, and He said to him, "Follow Me."
28   And he left everything behind, and got up and *began* to follow Him.
29   And Levi gave a big reception for Him in his house; and there was a great crowd of tax collectors and other *people* who were reclining *at the table* with them.
30   The Pharisees and their scribes *began* grumbling at His disciples, saying, "Why do you eat and drink with the tax collectors and sinners?"
31   And Jesus answered and said to them, "*It is* not those who are well who need a physician, but those who are sick.
32   "I have not come to call the righteous but sinners to repentance."
33   And they said to Him, "The disciples of John often fast and offer prayers, the *disciples* of the Pharisees also do the same, but Yours eat and drink."
34   And Jesus said to them, "You cannot make the attendants of the bridegroom fast while the bridegroom is with them, can you?
35   "But *the* days will come; and when the bridegroom is taken away from them, then they will fast in those days."
36   And He was also telling them a parable: "No one tears a piece of cloth from a new garment and puts it on an old garment; otherwise he will both tear the new, and the piece from the new will not match the old.
37   "And no one puts new wine into old wineskins; otherwise the new wine will burst the skins and it will be spilled out, and the skins will be ruined.
38   "But new wine must be put into fresh   ✳ wineskins.
39   "And no one, after drinking old *wine* wishes for new; for he says, 'The old is good *enough.*'"

Life Examples:

New Wineskins

LUKE 5:37–39

*T*echnology is an amazing thing. Before the invention of the printing press in 1440, every manuscript was written by hand—a long, painstaking process that would take an enormous amount of time. Still, even after mechanization was applied to the process, the first edition of the Gutenberg Bible took about three years to produce—from 1452 to circa 1455—and there were only 180 copies. Even so, it was a massive advancement.

Of course, improvements would continue over the years. Almost 260 years later, the first typewriter appeared on the scene. A century after that, in 1831, the first electric telegraph emerged. In 1876, Thomas Edison patented the mimeograph, which is the precursor to today's copy machines. That same year, Alexander Graham Bell invented the telephone.

Guglielmo Marconi sent the first radio signal in 1895, and by 1902 he discovered the way to transmit a radio signal across the Atlantic Ocean. Then in 1925, John Logie Baird sent the very first television signal.

By the late 1970s, home computers and cell phones were making their way into the marketplace. However, it was not until the mid-1990s that the World Wide Web was born—connecting the entire world through the Internet.

Why this lesson in technology? Along the way, there have been people who've spoken out against technology due to their fear of change. Yet in 1971, God gave me a vision for how technology could be used to spread the gospel. My heart's desire is to get the gospel to as many people as possible, as clearly as possible, as irresistibly as possible, and as quickly as possible—all to God's glory.

Still, I understand people's reticence to embrace new sources of communication. Jesus said in Luke 5:39, "And no one, after drinking old wine wishes for new; for he says, 'The old is good enough.'"

Those who were accustomed to only hearing preachers from pulpits probably didn't care much for gospel programming on the radio. Those who enjoyed listening to Bible teaching on the radio were probably skeptical about television. And those who have benefited from TV programs such as In Touch may not really know what to think about things such as "podcasts" and streaming the gospel message on the Internet.

Even so, we have to understand that as the world changes the way it communicates, we must take every opportunity to reach people with the good news of salvation—we must change, too.

Jesus said, "And no one puts new wine into old wineskins; otherwise the new wine will burst the skins and it will be spilled out, and the skins will be ruined" (Luke 5:37, 38). What this means is we can't just keep doing the same old thing. We must do our best as new methods arise to communicate the gospel to as many people as possible, as clearly as possible, as irresistibly as possible, as quickly as possible, all for God's glory—no matter what the technology.

The content, my friend, is always the same. The gospel doesn't change. Just as wine will always be made with grapes, so the gospel will always be centered on the blood of Christ. The Cross will always be our focus. That will never vary—even if the way we communicate its message does.

Deuteronomy 25:1—26:19

25 "IF there is a dispute between men and they go to court, and the judges decide their case, and they justify the righteous and condemn the wicked,

2 then it shall be if the wicked man deserves to be beaten, the judge shall then make him lie down and be beaten in his presence with the number of stripes according to his guilt.

3 "He may beat him forty times *but* no more, so that he does not beat him with many more stripes than these and your brother is not degraded in your eyes.

4 "You shall not muzzle the ox while he is threshing.

5 "When brothers live together and one of them dies and has no son, the wife of the deceased shall not be *married* outside *the family* to a strange man. Her husband's brother shall go in to her and take her to himself as wife and perform the duty of a husband's brother to her.

6 "It shall be that the firstborn whom she bears shall assume the name of his dead brother, so that his name will not be blotted out from Israel.

7 "But if the man does not desire to take his brother's wife, then his brother's wife shall go up to the gate to the elders and say, 'My husband's brother refuses to establish a name for his brother in Israel; he is not willing to perform the duty of a husband's brother to me.'

8 "Then the elders of his city shall summon him and speak to him. And *if* he persists and says, 'I do not desire to take her,'

9 then his brother's wife shall come to him in the sight of the elders, and pull his sandal off his foot and spit in his face; and she shall declare, 'Thus it is done to the man who does not build up his brother's house.'

10 "In Israel his name shall be called, 'The house of him whose sandal is removed.'

11 "If *two* men, a man and his countryman, are struggling together, and the wife of one comes near to deliver her husband from the hand of the one who is striking him, and puts out her hand and seizes his genitals,

12 then you shall cut off her hand; you shall not show pity.

13 "You shall not have in your bag differing weights, a large and a small.

14 "You shall not have in your house differing measures, a large and a small. ≺

15 "You shall have a full and just weight; you shall have a full and just measure, that your days may be prolonged in the land which the LORD your God gives you.

16 "For everyone who does these things, everyone who acts unjustly is an abomination to the LORD your God.

17 "Remember what Amalek did to you along the way when you came out from Egypt,

18 how he met you along the way and attacked among you all the stragglers at your rear when you were faint and weary; and he did not fear God.

19 "Therefore it shall come about when the LORD your God has given you rest from all your surrounding enemies, in the land which the LORD your God gives you as an inheritance to possess, you shall blot out the memory of Amalek from under heaven; you must not forget.

26 "THEN it shall be, when you enter the land which the LORD your God gives you as an inheritance, and you possess it and live in it,

2 that you shall take some of the first of all the produce of the ground which you bring in from your land that the LORD your God gives you, and you shall put *it* in a basket and go to the place where the LORD your God chooses to establish His name.

3 "You shall go to the priest who is in office at that time and say to him, 'I declare this day to the LORD my God that I have entered the land which the LORD swore to our fathers to give us.'

4 "Then the priest shall take the basket

LIFE LESSONS

≻ **Deuteronomy 25:14** — *"You shall not have in your house differing measures, a large and a small."*

*G*od is concerned about every aspect of our lives—not only our "religious" duties, but our civic ones as well. We are to live all of our lives for His glory (1 Cor. 10:31).

from your hand and set it down before the altar of the LORD your God.

5 "You shall answer and say before the LORD your God, 'My father was a wandering Aramean, and he went down to Egypt and sojourned there, few in number; but there he became a great, mighty and populous nation.

6 'And the Egyptians treated us harshly and afflicted us, and imposed hard labor on us.

➤ 7 'Then we cried to the LORD, the God of our fathers, and the LORD heard our voice and saw our affliction and our toil and our oppression;

8 and the LORD brought us out of Egypt with a mighty hand and an outstretched arm and with great terror and with signs and wonders;

9 and He has brought us to this place and has given us this land, a land flowing with milk and honey.

✳ 10 'Now behold, I have brought the first of the produce of the ground which You, O LORD have given me.' And you shall set it down before the LORD your God, and worship before the LORD your God;

➤ 11 and you and the Levite and the alien who is among you shall rejoice in all the good which the LORD your God has given you and your household.

12 "When you have finished paying all the tithe of your increase in the third year, the year of tithing, then you shall give it to the Levite, to the stranger, to the orphan and to the widow, that they may eat in your towns and be satisfied.

13 "You shall say before the LORD your God, 'I have removed the sacred *portion* from *my* house, and also have given it to the Levite and the alien, the orphan and the widow, according to all Your commandments which You have commanded me; I have not transgressed or forgotten any of Your commandments.

14 'I have not eaten of it while mourning, nor have I removed any of it while I was unclean, nor offered any of it to the dead. I have listened to the voice of the LORD my God; I have done according to all that You have commanded me.

15 'Look down from Your holy habitation, from heaven, and bless Your people Israel, and the ground which You have given us, a land flowing with milk and honey, as You swore to our fathers.'

16 "This day the LORD your God commands you to do these statutes and ordinances. You shall therefore be careful to do them with all your heart and with all your soul.

17 "You have today declared the LORD to be your God, and that you would walk in His ways and keep His statutes, His commandments and His ordinances, and listen to His voice.

18 "The LORD has today declared you to be His people, a treasured possession, as He promised you, and that you should keep all His commandments;

19 and that He will set you high above all nations which He has made, for praise, fame, and honor; and that you shall be a consecrated people to the LORD your God, as He has spoken."

LIFE LESSONS

➤ **Deuteronomy 26:7 —** *"Then we cried to the Lord . . . and the LORD heard our voice and saw our affliction."*

*I*t is good to remember and to declare to others how the Lord has rescued us in times past. These remembrances strengthen our faith and give us the courage to endure difficult times.

➤ **Deuteronomy 26:11 —** *"You shall rejoice in all the good which the LORD your God has given you and your household."*

*W*hy is it so important to "rejoice in all the good which the LORD your God has given you"? Rejoicing in God is a powerful way to draw close to Him, which is the very reason He created us.

◆ Psalm 39:7–11

7 "And now, Lord, for what do I wait?   ✳
    My hope is in You.
8 "Deliver me from all my
        transgressions;
    Make me not the reproach of the
        foolish.
9 "I have become mute, I do not open
        my mouth,
    Because it is You who have done *it*.

10 "Remove Your plague from me;
   Because of the opposition of Your
   hand I am perishing.
➤ 11 "With reproofs You chasten a man
      for iniquity;
   You consume as a moth what is
      precious to him;
   Surely every man is a mere breath.
                                    Selah.

Proverbs 13:4–6

4   The soul of the sluggard craves and
      gets nothing,
   But the soul of the diligent is made
      fat.
5   A righteous man hates falsehood,
   But a wicked man acts disgustingly
      and shamefully.
6   Righteousness guards the one
      whose way is blameless,
   But wickedness subverts the
      sinner.

Luke 6:1–26

6 NOW it happened that He was passing through *some* grainfields on a
Sabbath; and His disciples were picking
the heads of grain, rubbing them in their
hands, and eating *the grain.*
2   But some of the Pharisees said,
"Why do you do what is not lawful on
the Sabbath?"
3   And Jesus answering them said,
"Have you not even read what David did
when he was hungry, he and those who
were with him,
4   how he entered the house of God,
and took and ate the consecrated bread
which is not lawful for any to eat except
the priests alone, and gave it to his companions?"
5   And He was saying to them, "The
Son of Man is Lord of the Sabbath."
6   On another Sabbath He entered the
synagogue and was teaching; and there
was a man there whose right hand was
withered.
7   The scribes and the Pharisees were
watching Him closely *to see* if He healed
on the Sabbath, so that they might find
reason to accuse Him.
8   But He knew what they were thinking, and He said to the man with the
withered hand, "Get up and come
forward!" And he got up and came forward.
9   And Jesus said to them, "I ask you, is
it lawful to do good or to do harm on the
Sabbath, to save a life or to destroy it?"
10   After looking around at them all,
He said to him, "Stretch out your hand!"
And he did *so;* and his hand was restored.
11   But they themselves were filled with
rage, and discussed together what they
might do to Jesus.
12   It was at this time that He went off to
the mountain to pray, and He spent the
whole night in prayer to God.
13   And when day came, He called His
disciples to Him and chose twelve of
them, whom He also named as apostles:
14   Simon, whom He also named Peter,
and Andrew his brother; and James and
John; and Philip and Bartholomew;
15   and Matthew and Thomas; James
the son of Alphaeus, and Simon who was
called the Zealot;
16   Judas *the son* of James, and Judas
Iscariot, who became a traitor.

LIFE LESSONS

➤ **Psalm 39:11 —** *Surely every man is a
mere breath.*

L ife passes with lightning speed. We
   are on this earth for only a short
time, so we must be diligent to live
wisely and well. We may appear before
God tomorrow—so let us live for Him
today.

➤ **Luke 6:9 —** *"Is it lawful to do good or
to do harm on the Sabbath, to save a life
or to destroy it?"*

E very law or commandment God ever
   gave to His people He gave for his or
her good (Deut. 10:13). The Father takes
no pleasure in laws that destroy or injure,
so the answer to Jesus' question should
have been obvious.

ANSWERS TO LIFE'S QUESTIONS

Why do I sometimes fail to hear God when He speaks?

LUKE 6:12

*W*hy do so many of us fail to hear what God is saying? We want to know His will for us, but we cannot perceive Him speaking to us. Like David, we pray, "O my God, I cry by day, but You do not answer; and by night, but I have no rest" (Ps. 22:2). Why can't we hear His voice?

One significant obstacle is that we often consider the act of listening to be a passive experience—we assume we can simply sit and absorb what is being said. Good listening, however, is an active endeavor, involving both attitude and action.

We will have difficulty listening if we come to God with uncertainty, doubting that He is going to speak. Instead, we are to approach God confidently and expectantly, anticipating He will communicate with us. Such an attitude expresses our faith and demonstrates we believe His promises.

Another problem is disobedience. God instructs us, but we do not like His answer. Perhaps we want more information before we step out in faith (Judg. 6:36–40). Maybe the Lord is commanding us to release something that is important to us (2 Sam. 12:13–23) or directing us to act in a way that is terrifying, challenging, or unpleasant (Jon. 1:1–3). Either way, we want Him to change His mind and plan.

The prophet Jeremiah repeatedly reminded his people that although God had been speaking to them, they refused to hear Him. "I spoke to you in your prosperity," the Lord declared through the prophet, "but you said, 'I will not listen!' This has been your practice from your youth, that you have not obeyed My voice" (Jer. 22:21). We often have the same problem. The Lord may be speaking to us, but we've blocked Him out. However, we must repent of our faithlessness and disobedience and immediately do whatever He's commanded.

Sometimes God is silent simply to build our faith and relationship with Him. Sometimes He withholds information until we are prepared to pay attention and obey Him—trusting even when we cannot hear His voice. In such instances, we're told, "Cease striving, and know that I am God" (Ps. 46:10). We must approach the Lord with an attitude of patience and confidence (Ps. 40:1) and listen for Him actively. Colossians 3:16 says, "Let the word of Christ richly dwell within you, with all wisdom." In other words, as we read and meditate on Scripture, we are to humbly and submissively allow the truth of His Word to penetrate deep within our hearts and overflow to our actions. We must come quietly to Him and allow Him to do the talking. While there is nothing wrong with keeping a prayer list, a devotional time ought to include more than just a litany of requests. We should take time to hear what God says to us.

Keep on listening attentively and prepare to submit to whatever the Lord tells you. Your heavenly Father *will* speak, and when He does, He will bless you greatly.

---

17 Jesus came down with them and stood on a level place; and *there was* a large crowd of His disciples, and a great throng of people from all Judea and Jerusalem and the coastal region of Tyre and Sidon,

18 who had come to hear Him and to be healed of their diseases; and those who were troubled with unclean spirits were being cured.

19 And all the people were trying to touch Him, for power was coming from Him and healing *them* all.

20 And turning His gaze toward His disciples, He *began* to say, "Blessed *are* you *who are* poor, for yours is the kingdom of God.

21 "Blessed *are* you who hunger now, for you shall be satisfied. Blessed *are* you who weep now, for you shall laugh.

22 "Blessed are you when men hate you, and ostracize you, and insult you, and scorn your name as evil, for the sake of the Son of Man.

23 "Be glad in that day and leap *for joy*, for behold, your reward is great in heaven. For in the same way their fathers used to treat the prophets.

24 "But woe to you who are rich, for you are receiving your comfort in full.

25 "Woe to you who are well-fed now, for you shall be hungry. Woe *to you* who laugh now, for you shall mourn and weep.

26 "Woe *to you* when all men speak well of you, for their fathers used to treat the false prophets in the same way.

27 THEN Moses and the elders of Israel charged the people, saying, "Keep all the commandments which I command you today.

2 "So it shall be on the day when you cross the Jordan to the land which the LORD your God gives you, that you shall set up for yourself large stones and coat them with lime

3 and write on them all the words of this law, when you cross over, so that you may enter the land which the LORD your God gives you, a land flowing with milk and honey, as the LORD, the God of your fathers, promised you.

4 "So it shall be when you cross the Jordan, you shall set up on Mount Ebal, these stones, as I am commanding you today, and you shall coat them with lime.

5 "Moreover, you shall build there an altar to the LORD your God, an altar of stones; you shall not wield an iron *tool* on them.

6 "You shall build the altar of the LORD your God of uncut stones, and you shall offer on it burnt offerings to the LORD your God;

7 and you shall sacrifice peace offerings and eat there, and rejoice before the LORD your God.

8 "You shall write on the stones all the words of this law very distinctly."

9 Then Moses and the Levitical priests spoke to all Israel, saying, "Be silent and listen, O Israel! This day you have become a people for the LORD your God.

10 "You shall therefore obey the LORD your God, and do His commandments and His statutes which I command you today."

11 Moses also charged the people on that day, saying,

12 "When you cross the Jordan, these shall stand on Mount Gerizim to bless the people: Simeon, Levi, Judah, Issachar, Joseph, and Benjamin.

13 "For the curse, these shall stand on Mount Ebal: Reuben, Gad, Asher, Zebulun, Dan, and Naphtali.

14 "The Levites shall then answer and say to all the men of Israel with a loud voice,

15 'Cursed is the man who makes an idol or a molten image, an abomination to the LORD, the work of the hands of the craftsman, and sets *it* up in secret.' And all the people shall answer and say, 'Amen.'

16 'Cursed is he who dishonors his father or mother.' And all the people shall say, 'Amen.'

17 'Cursed is he who moves his neighbor's boundary mark.' And all the people shall say, 'Amen.'

18 'Cursed is he who misleads a blind *person* on the road.' And all the people shall say, 'Amen.'

19 'Cursed is he who distorts the justice due an alien, orphan, and widow.' And all the people shall say, 'Amen.'

20 'Cursed is he who lies with his father's wife, because he has uncovered his father's skirt.' And all the people shall say, 'Amen.'

21 'Cursed is he who lies with any animal.' And all the people shall say, 'Amen.'

22 'Cursed is he who lies with his sister, the daughter of his father or of his mother.' And all the people shall say, 'Amen.'

23 'Cursed is he who lies with his mother-in-law.' And all the people shall say, 'Amen.'

24 'Cursed is he who strikes his neighbor in secret.' And all the people shall say, 'Amen.'

25 'Cursed is he who accepts a bribe to strike down an innocent person.' And all the people shall say, 'Amen.'

LIFE LESSONS

➤ **Deuteronomy 27:2, 3 —** *"You shall set up for yourself large stones and . . . write on them all the words of this law."*

*G*od did not want His people to forget His Law once they crossed over the Jordan River and received the Land of Promise, so He commanded them to put it in full public view. How do you remind yourself to remember God's Word?

➤ **Deuteronomy 27:15 —** *"All the people shall answer and say, 'Amen.'"*

*O*ur faith is never a solitary business, but is meant to grow in community.

26 'Cursed is he who does not confirm the words of this law by doing them.' And all the people shall say, 'Amen.'

28 "NOW it shall be, if you diligently obey the LORD your God, being careful to do all His commandments which I command you today, the LORD your God will set you high above all the nations of the earth.

2 "All these blessings will come upon you and overtake you if you obey the LORD your God:

3 "Blessed *shall* you *be* in the city, and blessed *shall* you *be* in the country.

4 "Blessed *shall be* the offspring of your body and the produce of your ground and the offspring of your beasts, the increase of your herd and the young of your flock.

5 "Blessed *shall be* your basket and your kneading bowl.

6 "Blessed *shall* you *be* when you come in, and blessed *shall* you *be* when you go out.

7 "The LORD shall cause your enemies who rise up against you to be defeated before you; they will come out against you one way and will flee before you seven ways.

8 "The LORD will command the blessing

LIFE LESSONS

➤ **Deuteronomy 28:4** — *"Blessed shall be the offspring of your body and the produce of your ground and the offspring of your beasts, the increase of your herd and the young of your flock."*

God left no doubt about the kinds of blessings in store for those who obey Him. No matter where we live, what we do, or where we go, if we obey God's commandments, we can be assured of His blessing.

➤ **Deuteronomy 28:7** — *"The LORD shall cause your enemies who rise up against you to be defeated before you."*

God spoke these words to a people about to face great dangers from their enemies. Yet He assured them— and us today—that no enemy can stand against Him. He passionately defends those who belong to Him.

Life Examples:

Taking God Seriously

DEUTERONOMY 28

Throughout the Bible, there are two kinds of pronouncements God makes. The first kind is God's *absolute declaration*. He makes an absolute declaration when He tells us what He will do. As a rule, these acts of God are absolutely independent of any involvement on our part. They are promises God will see accomplished, regardless of our input.

For example, God promised our salvation through an absolute declaration. God said in Jeremiah 31:33, 34, "I will be their God, and they shall be My people . . . For I will forgive their iniquity, and their sin I will remember no more." God provided salvation for us when we had no power to ask for it (Rom. 5:8). Therefore, God's provision of salvation was made through an absolute declaration.

The second kind of proclamation God makes is a *conditional statement*. These declarations invite us into an active relationship with God. For example, in Deuteronomy 28:1, 2, God is speaking to the nation of Israel, getting them ready to enter the Promised Land. He says, "If you diligently obey the LORD your God, being careful to do all His commandments . . . the LORD your God will set you high above all the nations of the earth. All these blessings will come upon you and overtake you if you obey the LORD your God."

In other words, the people of Israel had some input in the outcome. They had a choice in the matter. They could either obey God and receive His blessing, or they could rebel against Him and endure His wrath.

Regardless of whether His promise is conditional or absolute, God will always do exactly what He says He will do. He will always keep His Word to us. Unfortunately, we are living in an age when people don't really believe that. Our society doesn't take God very seriously. However, we as believers must earnestly believe God will do as He says without exception.

Joshua 23:14 proclaims, "You know in all your hearts and in all your souls that not one word of all the good words which the LORD your God spoke concerning you has failed; all have been fulfilled for you, not one of them has failed." Be assured, His Word will never fail you.

Therefore, today and every day, take God seriously. Trust Him for whatever He has promised. He will certainly reward your obedience, and you will never be disappointed.

upon you in your barns and in all that you put your hand to, and He will bless you in the land which the LORD your God gives you.

9 "The LORD will establish you as a holy people to Himself, as He swore to you, if you keep the commandments of the LORD your God and walk in His ways.

10 "So all the peoples of the earth will see that you are called by the name of the LORD, and they will be afraid of you.

11 "The LORD will make you abound in prosperity, in the offspring of your body and in the offspring of your beast and in the produce of your ground, in the land which the LORD swore to your fathers to give you.

12 "The LORD will open for you His good storehouse, the heavens, to give rain to your land in its season and to bless all the work of your hand; and you shall lend to many nations, but you shall not borrow.

13 "The LORD will make you the head and not the tail, and you only will be above, and you will not be underneath, if you listen to the commandments of the LORD your God, which I charge you today, to observe *them* carefully,

14 and do not turn aside from any of the words which I command you today, to the right or to the left, to go after other gods to serve them.

15 "But it shall come about, if you do not obey the LORD your God, to observe to do all His commandments and His statutes with which I charge you today, that all these curses will come upon you and overtake you:

16 "Cursed *shall* you *be* in the city, and cursed *shall* you *be* in the country.

17 "Cursed *shall be* your basket and your kneading bowl.

18 "Cursed *shall be* the offspring of your body and the produce of your ground, the increase of your herd and the young of your flock.

19 "Cursed *shall* you *be* when you come in, and cursed *shall* you *be* when you go out.

20 "The LORD will send upon you curses, confusion, and rebuke, in all you undertake to do, until you are destroyed and until you perish quickly, on account of the evil of your deeds, because you have forsaken Me.

21 "The LORD will make the pestilence cling to you until He has consumed you from the land where you are entering to possess it.

22 "The LORD will smite you with consumption and with fever and with inflammation and with fiery heat and with the sword and with blight and with mildew, and they will pursue you until you perish.

23 "The heaven which is over your head shall be bronze, and the earth which is under you, iron.

24 "The LORD will make the rain of your land powder and dust; from heaven it shall come down on you until you are destroyed.

25 "The LORD shall cause you to be defeated before your enemies; you will go out one way against them, but you will flee seven ways before them, and you will be *an example of* terror to all the kingdoms of the earth.

26 "Your carcasses will be food to all birds of the sky and to the beasts of the earth, and there will be no one to frighten *them* away.

27 "The LORD will smite you with the boils of Egypt and with tumors and with the scab and with the itch, from which you cannot be healed.

28 "The LORD will smite you with madness and with blindness and with bewilderment of heart;

29 and you will grope at noon, as the blind man gropes in darkness, and you will not prosper in your ways; but you shall only be oppressed and robbed continually, with none to save you.

30 "You shall betroth a wife, but another man will violate her; you shall build a house, but you will not live in it; you shall plant a vineyard, but you will not use its fruit.

31 "Your ox shall be slaughtered before your eyes, but you will not eat of it; your donkey shall be torn away from you, and will not be restored to you; your sheep shall be given to your enemies, and you will have none to save you.

32 "Your sons and your daughters shall be given to another people, while your eyes look on and yearn for them continually; but there will be nothing you can do.

33 "A people whom you do not know shall eat up the produce of your ground and all your labors, and you will never

be anything but oppressed and crushed continually.

34 "You shall be driven mad by the sight of what you see.

35 "The LORD will strike you on the knees and legs with sore boils, from which you cannot be healed, from the sole of your foot to the crown of your head.

36 "The LORD will bring you and your king, whom you set over you, to a nation which neither you nor your fathers have known, and there you shall serve other gods, wood and stone.

37 "You shall become a horror, a proverb, and a taunt among all the people where the LORD drives you.

38 "You shall bring out much seed to the field but you will gather in little, for the locust will consume it.

39 "You shall plant and cultivate vineyards, but you will neither drink of the wine nor gather *the grapes*, for the worm will devour them.

40 "You shall have olive trees throughout your territory but you will not anoint yourself with the oil, for your olives will drop off.

41 "You shall have sons and daughters but they will not be yours, for they will go into captivity.

42 "The cricket shall possess all your trees and the produce of your ground.

43 "The alien who is among you shall rise above you higher and higher, but you will go down lower and lower.

44 "He shall lend to you, but you will not lend to him; he shall be the head, and you will be the tail.

45 "So all these curses shall come on you and pursue you and overtake you until you are destroyed, because you would not obey the LORD your God by keeping His commandments and His statutes which He commanded you.

46 "They shall become a sign and a wonder on you and your descendants forever.

47 "Because you did not serve the LORD your God with joy and a glad heart, for the abundance of all things;

48 therefore you shall serve your enemies whom the LORD will send against you, in hunger, in thirst, in nakedness, and in the lack of all things; and He will put an iron yoke on your neck until He has destroyed you.

49 "The LORD will bring a nation against you from afar, from the end of the earth, as the eagle swoops down, a nation whose language you shall not understand,

50 a nation of fierce countenance who will have no respect for the old, nor show favor to the young.

51 "Moreover, it shall eat the offspring of your herd and the produce of your ground until you are destroyed, who also leaves you no grain, new wine, or oil, nor the increase of your herd or the young of your flock until they have caused you to perish.

52 "It shall besiege you in all your towns until your high and fortified walls in which you trusted come down throughout your land, and it shall besiege you in all your towns throughout your land which the LORD your God has given you.

53 "Then you shall eat the offspring of your own body, the flesh of your sons and of your daughters whom the LORD your God has given you, during the siege and the distress by which your enemy will oppress you.

54 "The man who is refined and very delicate among you shall be hostile toward his brother and toward the wife he cherishes and toward the rest of his children who remain,

55 so that he will not give *even* one of them any of the flesh of his children which he will eat, since he has nothing *else* left, during the siege and the distress by which your enemy will oppress you in all your towns.

56 "The refined and delicate woman among you, who would not venture to set the sole of her foot on the ground for delicateness and refinement, shall be hostile toward the husband she cherishes and toward her son and daughter,

57 and toward her afterbirth which issues from between her legs and toward her children whom she bears; for she will eat them secretly for lack of anything *else*, during the siege and the distress by which your enemy will oppress you in your towns.

58 "If you are not careful to observe all the words of this law which are written in this book, to fear this honored and awesome name, the LORD your God,

59 then the LORD will bring extraordinary plagues on you and your descen-

dants, even severe and lasting plagues, and miserable and chronic sicknesses.
60 "He will bring back on you all the diseases of Egypt of which you were afraid, and they will cling to you.
61 "Also every sickness and every plague which, not written in the book of this law, the LORD will bring on you until you are destroyed.
62 "Then you shall be left few in number, whereas you were as numerous as the stars of heaven, because you did not obey the LORD your God.
63 "It shall come about that as the LORD delighted over you to prosper you, and multiply you, so the LORD will delight over you to make you perish and destroy you; and you will be torn from the land where you are entering to possess it.
64 "Moreover, the LORD will scatter you among all peoples, from one end of the earth to the other end of the earth; and there you shall serve other gods, wood and stone, which you or your fathers have not known.
65 "Among those nations you shall find no rest, and there will be no resting place for the sole of your foot; but there the LORD will give you a trembling heart, failing of eyes, and despair of soul.
66 "So your life shall hang in doubt before you; and you will be in dread night and day, and shall have no assurance of your life.
67 "In the morning you shall say, 'Would that it were evening!' And at evening you shall say, 'Would that it were morning!' because of the dread of your heart which you dread, and for the sight of your eyes which you will see.
68 "The LORD will bring you back to Egypt in ships, by the way about which I spoke to you, 'You will never see it again!' And there you will offer yourselves for sale to your enemies as male and female slaves, but there will be no buyer."

Psalm 39:12, 13

12 "Hear my prayer, O LORD, and give
    ear to my cry;
    Do not be silent at my tears;
    For I am a stranger with You,
    A sojourner like all my fathers.

13 "Turn Your gaze away from me, that
    I may smile *again*
    Before I depart and am no more."

Proverbs 13:7, 8

7   There is one who pretends to be
    rich, but has nothing;
    Another pretends to be poor, but
    has great wealth.
8   The ransom of a man's life is his
    wealth,
    But the poor hears no rebuke.

Luke 6:27–49

27 "But I say to you who hear, love your enemies, do good to those who hate you,
28 bless those who curse you, pray for those who mistreat you.
29 "Whoever hits you on the cheek, offer him the other also; and whoever takes away your coat, do not withhold your shirt from him either.
30 "Give to everyone who asks of you, and whoever takes away what is yours, do not demand it back.
31 "Treat others the same way you want them to treat you.
32 "If you love those who love you, what credit is *that* to you? For even sinners love those who love them.
33 "If you do good to those who do good to you, what credit is *that* to you? For even sinners do the same.
34 "If you lend to those from whom you expect to receive, what credit is *that* to you? Even sinners lend to sinners in order to receive back the same *amount*.
35 "But love your enemies, and do ◄

LIFE LESSONS

➤ Luke 6:35 — *"He Himself is kind to ungrateful and evil men."*

If God were not kind to the unappreciative and ungodly, where would any of us be (Rom. 5:8)? The Lord will always judge sin, but He desires for us to turn from our sin and receive His salvation so He can bless us, not judge us (1 Pet. 3:9).

good, and lend, expecting nothing in return; and your reward will be great, and you will be sons of the Most High; for He Himself is kind to ungrateful and evil *men.*

36 "Be merciful, just as your Father is merciful.

37 "Do not judge, and you will not be judged; and do not condemn, and you will not be condemned; pardon, and you will be pardoned.

38 "Give, and it will be given to you. They will pour into your lap a good measure—pressed down, shaken together, *and* running over. For by your standard of measure it will be measured to you in return."

39 And He also spoke a parable to them: "A blind man cannot guide a blind man, can he? Will they not both fall into a pit?

40 "A pupil is not above his teacher; but everyone, after he has been fully trained, will be like his teacher.

41 "Why do you look at the speck that is in your brother's eye, but do not notice the log that is in your own eye?

42 "Or how can you say to your brother, 'Brother, let me take out the speck that is in your eye,' when you yourself do not see the log that is in your own eye? You hypocrite, first take the log out of your own eye, and then you will see clearly to take out the speck that is in your brother's eye.

43 "For there is no good tree which produces bad fruit, nor, on the other hand, a bad tree which produces good fruit.

44 "For each tree is known by its own fruit. For men do not gather figs from

thorns, nor do they pick grapes from a briar bush.

45 "The good man out of the good treasure of his heart brings forth what is good; and the evil *man* out of the evil *treasure* brings forth what is evil; for his mouth speaks from that which fills his heart.

46 "Why do you call Me, 'Lord, Lord,' and do not do what I say?

47 "Everyone who comes to Me and hears My words and acts on them, I will show you whom he is like:

48 he is like a man building a house, who dug deep and laid a foundation on the rock; and when a flood occurred, the torrent burst against that house and could not shake it, because it had been well built.

49 "But the one who has heard and has not acted *accordingly,* is like a man who built a house on the ground without any foundation; and the torrent burst against it and immediately it collapsed, and the ruin of that house was great."

APRIL 3

Deuteronomy 29:1—30:20

29 THESE are the words of the covenant which the LORD commanded Moses to make with the sons of Israel in the land of Moab, besides the covenant which He had made with them at Horeb.

2 And Moses summoned all Israel and said to them, "You have seen all that the LORD did before your eyes in the land of

Egypt to Pharaoh and all his servants and all his land;

3 the great trials which your eyes have seen, those great signs and wonders.

4 "Yet to this day the LORD has not given you a heart to know, nor eyes to see, nor ears to hear.

5 "I have led you forty years in the wilderness; your clothes have not worn out on you, and your sandal has not worn out on your foot.

LIFE LESSONS

➤ Deuteronomy 29:4 — *"The Lord has not given you a heart to know, nor eyes to see, nor ears to hear."*

*W*hat the Lord had not given to His people Israel, He has given to believers. His Holy Spirit dwells within us and teaches us what is ours through Jesus Christ (Jer. 31:31-34; Ezek. 36:26; Eph. 1:18).

6 "You have not eaten bread, nor have you drunk wine or strong drink, in order that you might know that I am the LORD your God.

7 "When you reached this place, Sihon the king of Heshbon and Og the king of Bashan came out to meet us for battle, but we defeated them;

8 and we took their land and gave it as an inheritance to the Reubenites, the Gadites, and the half-tribe of the Manassites.

9 "So keep the words of this covenant to do them, that you may prosper in all that you do.

10 "You stand today, all of you, before the LORD your God: your chiefs, your tribes, your elders and your officers, *even* all the men of Israel,

11 your little ones, your wives, and the alien who is within your camps, from the one who chops your wood to the one who draws your water,

12 that you may enter into the covenant with the LORD your God, and into His oath which the LORD your God is making with you today,

13 in order that He may establish you today as His people and that He may be your God, just as He spoke to you and as He swore to your fathers, to Abraham, Isaac, and Jacob.

14 "Now not with you alone am I making this covenant and this oath,

15 but both with those who stand here with us today in the presence of the LORD our God and with those who are not with us here today

16 (for you know how we lived in the land of Egypt, and how we came through the midst of the nations through which you passed;

17 moreover, you have seen their abominations and their idols *of* wood,

stone, silver, and gold, which *they had* with them);

18 so that there will not be among you a man or woman, or family or tribe, whose heart turns away today from the LORD our God, to go and serve the gods of those nations; that there will not be among you a root bearing poisonous fruit and wormwood.

19 "It shall be when he hears the words of this curse, that he will boast, saying, 'I have peace though I walk in the stubbornness of my heart in order to destroy the watered *land* with the dry.'

20 "The LORD shall never be willing to forgive him, but rather the anger of the LORD and His jealousy will burn against that man, and every curse which is written in this book will rest on him, and the LORD will blot out his name from under heaven.

21 "Then the LORD will single him out for adversity from all the tribes of Israel, according to all the curses of the covenant which are written in this book of the law.

22 "Now the generation to come, your sons who rise up after you and the foreigner who comes from a distant land, when they see the plagues of the land and the diseases with which the LORD has afflicted it, will say,

23 'All its land is brimstone and salt, a burning waste, unsown and unproductive, and no grass grows in it, like the overthrow of Sodom and Gomorrah, Admah and Zeboiim, which the LORD overthrew in His anger and in His wrath.'

24 "All the nations will say, 'Why has the LORD done thus to this land? Why this great outburst of anger?'

25 "Then *men* will say, 'Because they forsook the covenant of the LORD, the God of their fathers, which He made with them when He brought them out of the land of Egypt.

26 'They went and served other gods and worshiped them, gods whom they have not known and whom He had not allotted to them.

27 'Therefore, the anger of the LORD burned against that land, to bring upon it every curse which is written in this book;

28 and the LORD uprooted them from their land in anger and in fury and in great wrath, and cast them into another land, as *it is* this day.'

➤ **29** "The secret things belong to the LORD our God, but the things revealed belong to us and to our sons forever, that we may observe all the words of this law.

30 "SO it shall be when all of these things have come upon you, the blessing and the curse which I have set before you, and you call *them* to mind in all nations where the LORD your God has banished you,

2 and you return to the LORD your God and obey Him with all your heart and soul according to all that I command you today, you and your sons,

3 then the LORD your God will restore you from captivity, and have compassion on you, and will gather you again from all the peoples where the LORD your God has scattered you.

4 "If your outcasts are at the ends of the earth, from there the LORD your God will gather you, and from there He will bring you back.

5 "The LORD your God will bring you into the land which your fathers possessed, and you shall possess it; and He will prosper you and multiply you more than your fathers.

6 "Moreover the LORD your God will circumcise your heart and the heart of your descendants, to love the LORD your God with all your heart and with all your soul, so that you may live.

7 "The LORD your God will inflict all these curses on your enemies and on those who hate you, who persecuted you.

8 "And you shall again obey the LORD, and observe all His commandments which I command you today.

➤ **9** "Then the LORD your God will prosper you abundantly in all the work of your hand, in the offspring of your body and in the offspring of your cattle and in the produce of your ground, for the LORD will again rejoice over you for good, just as He rejoiced over your fathers;

10 if you obey the LORD your God to keep His commandments and His statutes which are written in this book of the law, if you turn to the LORD your God with all your heart and soul.

11 "For this commandment which I command you today is not too difficult for you, nor is it out of reach.

12 "It is not in heaven, that you should say, 'Who will go up to heaven for us to get it for us and make us hear it, that we may observe it?'

13 "Nor is it beyond the sea, that you should say, 'Who will cross the sea for us to get it for us and make us hear it, that we may observe it?'

14 "But the word is very near you, in your mouth and in your heart, that you may observe it.

15 "See, I have set before you today life and prosperity, and death and adversity;

16 in that I command you today to love the LORD your God, to walk in His ways and to keep His commandments and His statutes and His judgments, that you may live and multiply, and that the LORD your God may bless you in the land where you are entering to possess it.

17 "But if your heart turns away and you will not obey, but are drawn away and worship other gods and serve them,

18 I declare to you today that you shall surely perish. You will not prolong *your* days in the land where you are crossing the Jordan to enter and possess it.

19 "I call heaven and earth to witness against you today, that I have set before you life and death, the blessing and the curse. So choose life in order that you ✳ may live, you and your descendants,

20 by loving the LORD your God, by

---

obeying His voice, and by holding fast to Him; for this is your life and the length of your days, that you may live in the land which the LORD swore to your fathers, to Abraham, Isaac, and Jacob, to give them."

Psalm 40:1–5

For the choir director. A Psalm of David.

40 I WAITED patiently for the LORD; And He inclined to me and heard my cry.
2 He brought me up out of the pit of destruction, out of the miry clay, And He set my feet upon a rock making my footsteps firm.
3 He put a new song in my mouth, a song of praise to our God; Many will see and fear And will trust in the LORD.
4 How blessed is the man who has made the LORD his trust, And has not turned to the proud, nor to those who lapse into falsehood.
5 Many, O LORD my God, are the wonders which You have done, And Your thoughts toward us; There is none to compare with You. If I would declare and speak of them,

They would be too numerous to count.

Proverbs 13:9, 10

9 The light of the righteous rejoices, But the lamp of the wicked goes out.
10 Through insolence comes nothing but strife, But wisdom is with those who receive counsel.

◈ Luke 7:1–30

7 WHEN He had completed all His discourse in the hearing of the people, He went to Capernaum.

ANSWERS TO LIFE'S QUESTIONS

Where can I look for good advice?

PROVERBS 13:10

*P*roverbs has a lot to say about the value of wise counsel. Proverbs 13:10 declares, "Through insolence comes nothing but strife, but wisdom is with those who receive counsel." Proverbs 15:22 proclaims, "Without consultation, plans are frustrated, but with many counselors they succeed." And Proverbs 20:5 instructs us, "A plan in the heart of a man is like deep water, but a man of understanding draws it out."

I remember my grandfather's words: "Charles, whatever you do in life, always obey God fully. If He tells you to run your head through a brick wall, go forward, expecting Him to make a hole." I have never forgotten his advice, and it has been a cornerstone of my

personal ministry over the years. It reminds me that the most important counsel we can ever get comes from the Lord Himself.

Regardless of the situation or circumstance, we should always go first to God for *His* counsel. We should remember what King Jehoshaphat told King Ahab of Israel: "Please inquire first for the word of the LORD" (1 Kings 22:5). When we do so, we go to the wellspring of all wisdom, for we go to "the LORD of hosts, who has made his counsel wonderful and His wisdom great" (Is. 28:29).

God sometimes leads us to seek advice from others. When He does so, He wants us to examine the lifestyle of the person from whom we hope to receive counsel. If "the fear of the LORD is the beginning of wisdom" (Prov. 9:10), then we had better know where the person stands with the Lord. Consider the spiritual and moral track record of anyone from whom you obtain important advice or counsel, especially if the decision you make affects your entire family and future.

2 And a centurion's slave, who was highly regarded by him, was sick and about to die.

3 When he heard about Jesus, he sent some Jewish elders asking Him to come and save the life of his slave.

4 When they came to Jesus, they earnestly implored Him, saying, "He is worthy for You to grant this to him;

5 for he loves our nation and it was he who built us our synagogue."

6 Now Jesus *started* on His way with them; and when He was not far from the house, the centurion sent friends, saying to Him, "Lord, do not trouble Yourself further, for I am not worthy for You to come under my roof;

7 for this reason I did not even consider myself worthy to come to You, but *just* say the word, and my servant will be healed.

8 "For I also am a man placed under authority, with soldiers under me; and I say to this one, 'Go!' and he goes, and to another, 'Come!' and he comes, and to my slave, 'Do this!' and he does it."

9 Now when Jesus heard this, He marveled at him, and turned and said to the crowd that was following Him, "I say to you, not even in Israel have I found such great faith."

10 When those who had been sent returned to the house, they found the slave in good health.

11 Soon afterwards He went to a city called Nain; and His disciples were going along with Him, accompanied by a large crowd.

12 Now as He approached the gate of the city, a dead man was being carried out, the only son of his mother, and she was a widow; and a sizeable crowd from the city was with her.

13 When the Lord saw her, He felt compassion for her, and said to her, "Do not weep."

14 And He came up and touched the coffin; and the bearers came to a halt. And He said, "Young man, I say to you, arise!"

15 The dead man sat up and began to speak. And *Jesus* gave him back to his mother.

16 Fear gripped them all, and they *began* glorifying God, saying, "A great prophet has arisen among us!" and, "God has visited His people!"

17 This report concerning Him went out all over Judea and in all the surrounding district.

18 The disciples of John reported to him about all these things.

19 Summoning two of his disciples, John sent them to the Lord, saying, "Are You the Expected One, or do we look for someone else?"

20 When the men came to Him, they said, "John the Baptist has sent us to You, to ask, 'Are You the Expected One, or do we look for someone else?'"

21 At that very time He cured many *people* of diseases and afflictions and evil spirits; and He gave sight to many *who were* blind.

22 And He answered and said to them, "Go and report to John what you have seen and heard: *the* BLIND RECEIVE SIGHT, *the* lame walk, *the* lepers are cleansed, and *the* deaf hear, *the* dead are raised up, *the* POOR HAVE THE GOSPEL PREACHED TO THEM.

23 "Blessed is he who does not take offense at Me."

24 When the messengers of John had left, He began to speak to the crowds about John, "What did you go out into the wilderness to see? A reed shaken by the wind?

25 "But what did you go out to see? A man dressed in soft clothing? Those who are splendidly clothed and live in luxury are *found* in royal palaces!

26 "But what did you go out to see? A prophet? Yes, I say to you, and one who is more than a prophet.

27 "This is the one about whom it is written,

'BEHOLD, I SEND MY MESSENGER AHEAD OF YOU,

LIFE LESSONS

➤ **Luke 7:21 —** *He cured many people of diseases and afflictions and evil spirits; and He gave sight to many who were blind.*

*I*n prison, John had begun to doubt whether Jesus was the promised Messiah. In His grace, the Lord showed the discouraged John the truth. In the number and variety of His miracles, Jesus was doing what no Old Testament prophet had ever done.

Who will prepare Your way before You.'

28 "I say to you, among those born of women there is no one greater than John; yet he who is least in the kingdom of God is greater than he."
29 When all the people and the tax collectors heard *this*, they acknowledged God's justice, having been baptized with the baptism of John.
➤ 30 But the Pharisees and the lawyers rejected God's purpose for themselves, not having been baptized by John.

◈ Deuteronomy 31:1—32:52

31 SO Moses went and spoke these words to all Israel.
2 And he said to them, "I am a hundred and twenty years old today; I am no longer able to come and go, and the LORD has said to me, 'You shall not cross this Jordan.'
3 "It is the LORD your God who will cross ahead of you; He will destroy these nations before you, and you shall dispossess them. Joshua is the one who will

---

ANSWERS TO LIFE'S QUESTIONS

How can I find courage in the face of stiff challenges?

DEUTERONOMY 31:1–6

*A*ny time God requires us to face trials and tribulations, He always provides the courage to meet the demand. David was a man of great courage—not merely human courage, but courage rooted in the sovereignty of God. In 1 Samuel 17, we see God's supernatural strength in action in the life of David.

Defeat is never a viable option for the person of courage. As David faced Goliath, he never considered defeat an option. People of courage refuse to look for ways of escape. They set their gaze on advancement and victory. Never go into battle entertaining thoughts of defeat; you will lose every time. Men and women of courage know their success lies with our unshakable God.

Courageous people recall past victories and God's faithfulness. At times, David had faced enemies just as vicious as Goliath. In the moments before the battle, he recalled how God had strengthened him in the past to kill both a lion and a bear. David expected the same help to strengthen him against Goliath.

Courage is a result of having the right attitude. David realized he could not win in his own strength. He knew God had to be with him, or he would suffer defeat.

Courageous people look to God and trust His guidance. David's brothers mocked him. Saul doubted him. Goliath made fun of him. But their negative talk did not affect David. Every time God calls you to follow Him, expect opposition, even from surprising sources.

Genuine courage is not chilled by inner fears or outward difficulties. The person of courage isn't interested in those who refuse to believe God. Take time to study God's Word and apply His principles to your life. You can always face your enemies head on when you stand on the promises of God's Word.

A courageous person applies resources at hand in creative ways. David chose five smooth stones and a slingshot as his weapons instead of the bulky armor of Saul. He faced Goliath clothed in the strong faith of the living God. Mere men cannot penetrate nor defeat God-centered faith!

A person with the attribute of courage confronts an opponent with confidence that God will ultimately give him success if he obeys Him. When we face life's trials as David did, by faith, we become men and women of courage—and the victory is always ours.

cross ahead of you, just as the LORD has spoken.

4 "The LORD will do to them just as He did to Sihon and Og, the kings of the Amorites, and to their land, when He destroyed them.

5 "The LORD will deliver them up before you, and you shall do to them according to all the commandments which I have commanded you.

6 "Be strong and courageous, do not be afraid or tremble at them, for the LORD your God is the one who goes with you. He will not fail you or forsake you."

7 Then Moses called to Joshua and said to him in the sight of all Israel, "Be strong and courageous, for you shall go with this people into the land which the LORD has sworn to their fathers to give them, and you shall give it to them as an inheritance.

8 "The LORD is the one who goes ahead of you; He will be with you. He will not fail you or forsake you. Do not fear or be dismayed."

9 So Moses wrote this law and gave it to the priests, the sons of Levi who carried the ark of the covenant of the LORD, and to all the elders of Israel.

10 Then Moses commanded them, saying, "At the end of *every* seven years, at the time of the year of remission of debts, at the Feast of Booths,

11 when all Israel comes to appear before the LORD your God at the place which He will choose, you shall read this law in front of all Israel in their hearing.

12 "Assemble the people, the men and the women and children and the alien who is in your town, so that they may hear and learn and fear the LORD your God, and be careful to observe all the words of this law.

13 "Their children, who have not known, will hear and learn to fear the LORD your God, as long as you live on the land which you are about to cross the Jordan to possess."

14 Then the LORD said to Moses, "Behold, the time for you to die is near; call Joshua, and present yourselves at the tent of meeting, that I may commission him." So Moses and Joshua went and presented themselves at the tent of meeting.

15 The LORD appeared in the tent in a pillar of cloud, and the pillar of cloud stood at the doorway of the tent.

16 The LORD said to Moses, "Behold, you are about to lie down with your fathers; and this people will arise and play the harlot with the strange gods of the land, into the midst of which they are going, and will forsake Me and break My covenant which I have made with them.

17 "Then My anger will be kindled against them in that day, and I will forsake them and hide My face from them, and they will be consumed, and many evils and troubles will come upon them; so that they will say in that day, 'Is it not because our God is not among us that these evils have come upon us?'

18 "But I will surely hide My face in that day because of all the evil which they will do, for they will turn to other gods.

19 "Now therefore, write this song for yourselves, and teach it to the sons of Israel; put it on their lips, so that this song may be a witness for Me against the sons of Israel.

20 "For when I bring them into the land flowing with milk and honey, which I swore to their fathers, and they have eaten and are satisfied and become prosperous, then they will turn to other gods and serve them, and spurn Me and break My covenant.

21 "Then it shall come about, when many evils and troubles have come upon them, that this song will testify before them as a witness (for it shall not be forgotten from the lips of their descendants); for I know their intent which they are developing today, before I have brought them into the land which I swore."

22 So Moses wrote this song the same day, and taught it to the sons of Israel.

23 Then He commissioned Joshua the son of Nun, and said, "Be strong and

---

LIFE LESSONS

➤ Deuteronomy 31:6 — *"Do not be afraid or tremble at them, for the LORD your God is the one who goes with you."*

*C*ould anything feel more disconcerting or frightening than having to face a terrible trial all by yourself? God tells us those who know Him never have to worry. He is always right there with us in the most joyous and most difficult of times.

courageous, for you shall bring the sons of Israel into the land which I swore to them, and I will be with you."

24 It came about, when Moses finished writing the words of this law in a book until they were complete,

25 that Moses commanded the Levites who carried the ark of the covenant of the LORD, saying,

26 "Take this book of the law and place it beside the ark of the covenant of the LORD your God, that it may remain there as a witness against you.

27 "For I know your rebellion and your stubbornness; behold, while I am still alive with you today, you have been rebellious against the LORD; how much more, then, after my death?

28 "Assemble to me all the elders of your tribes and your officers, that I may speak these words in their hearing and call the heavens and the earth to witness against them.

29 "For I know that after my death you will act corruptly and turn from the way which I have commanded you; and evil will befall you in the latter days, for you will do that which is evil in the sight of the LORD, provoking Him to anger with the work of your hands."

30 Then Moses spoke in the hearing of all the assembly of Israel the words of this song, until they were complete:

32 "GIVE ear, O heavens, and let me speak;
And let the earth hear the words of my mouth.

2 "Let my teaching drop as the rain,
My speech distill as the dew,
As the droplets on the fresh grass
And as the showers on the herb.

3 "For I proclaim the name of the LORD;
Ascribe greatness to our God!

➤ 4 "The Rock! His work is perfect,
For all His ways are just;
A God of faithfulness and without injustice,
Righteous and upright is He.

5 "They have acted corruptly toward Him,
They are not His children, because of their defect;
But are a perverse and crooked generation.

6 "Do you thus repay the LORD,
O foolish and unwise people?

Is not He your Father who has bought you?
He has made you and established you.

7 "Remember the days of old,
Consider the years of all generations.
Ask your father, and he will inform you,
Your elders, and they will tell you.

8 "When the Most High gave the nations their inheritance,
When He separated the sons of man,
He set the boundaries of the peoples
According to the number of the sons of Israel.

9 "For the LORD'S portion is His people;
Jacob is the allotment of His inheritance.

10 "He found him in a desert land,
And in the howling waste of a wilderness;
He encircled him, He cared for him,
He guarded him as the pupil of His eye.

11 "Like an eagle that stirs up its nest,
That hovers over its young,
He spread His wings and caught them,
He carried them on His pinions.

12 "The LORD alone guided him,
And there was no foreign god with him.

13 "He made him ride on the high places of the earth,
And he ate the produce of the field;
And He made him suck honey from the rock,
And oil from the flinty rock,

14 Curds of cows, and milk of the flock,
With fat of lambs,

And rams, the breed of Bashan, and
goats,
With the finest of the wheat—
And of the blood of grapes you
drank wine.

15 "But Jeshurun grew fat and kicked—
You are grown fat, thick, and
sleek—
Then he forsook God who made
him,
And scorned the Rock of his
salvation.

16 "They made Him jealous with
strange gods;
With abominations they provoked
Him to anger.

17 "They sacrificed to demons who
were not God,
To gods whom they have not
known,
New gods who came lately,
Whom your fathers did not dread.

18 "You neglected the Rock who begot
you,
And forgot the God who gave you
birth.

19 "The LORD saw this, and spurned
them
Because of the provocation of His
sons and daughters.

20 "Then He said, 'I will hide My face
from them,
I will see what their end shall be;
For they are a perverse generation,
Sons in whom is no faithfulness.

21 'They have made Me jealous with
what is not God;
They have provoked Me to anger
with their idols.
So I will make them jealous with
those who are not a people;
I will provoke them to anger with a
foolish nation,

22 For a fire is kindled in My anger,
And burns to the lowest part of
Sheol,
And consumes the earth with its
yield,
And sets on fire the foundations of
the mountains.

23 'I will heap misfortunes on them;
I will use My arrows on them.

24 'They will be wasted by famine, and
consumed by plague
And bitter destruction;
And the teeth of beasts I will send
upon them,

With the venom of crawling things
of the dust.

25 'Outside the sword will bereave,
And inside terror—
Both young man and virgin,
The nursling with the man of gray
hair.

26 'I would have said, "I will cut them
to pieces,
I will remove the memory of them
from men,"

27 Had I not feared the provocation by
the enemy,
That their adversaries would
misjudge,
That they would say, "Our hand is
triumphant,
And the LORD has not done all
this."'

28 "For they are a nation lacking in
counsel,
And there is no understanding in
them.

29 "Would that they were wise, that
they understood this,
That they would discern their
future!

30 "How could one chase a thousand,
And two put ten thousand to flight,
Unless their Rock had sold them,
And the LORD had given them up?

31 "Indeed their rock is not like our
Rock,
Even our enemies themselves judge
this.

32 "For their vine is from the vine of
Sodom,
And from the fields of Gomorrah;
Their grapes are grapes of poison,
Their clusters, bitter.

33 "Their wine is the venom of serpents,
And the deadly poison of cobras.

34 'Is it not laid up in store with Me,
Sealed up in My treasuries?

35 'Vengeance is Mine, and retribution,
In due time their foot will slip;
For the day of their calamity is near,
And the impending things are
hastening upon them.'

36 "For the LORD will vindicate His
people,
And will have compassion on His
servants,
When He sees that their strength is
gone,
And there is none remaining, bond
or free.

LIFE LESSONS

> **Deuteronomy 32:36** — *"For the LORD will vindicate His people, and will have compassion on His servants."*

God both judges and restores His people. He loves us too much to allow us to stay disconnected from His love. He will move to restore the intimacy He desires with us, no matter what it takes.

37 "And He will say, 'Where are their gods,
 The rock in which they sought refuge?
38 'Who ate the fat of their sacrifices,
 And drank the wine of their drink offering?
 Let them rise up and help you,
 Let them be your hiding place!
39 'See now that I, I am He,
 And there is no god besides Me;
 It is I who put to death and give life.
 I have wounded and it is I who heal,
 And there is no one who can deliver from My hand.
40 'Indeed, I lift up My hand to heaven,
 And say, as I live forever,
41 If I sharpen My flashing sword,
 And My hand takes hold on justice,
 I will render vengeance on My adversaries,
 And I will repay those who hate Me.
42 'I will make My arrows drunk with blood,
 And My sword will devour flesh,
 With the blood of the slain and the captives,
 From the long-haired leaders of the enemy.'
43 "Rejoice, O nations, *with* His people;
 For He will avenge the blood of His servants,
 And will render vengeance on His adversaries,
 And will atone for His land *and* His people."

44 Then Moses came and spoke all the words of this song in the hearing of the people, he, with Joshua the son of Nun.
45 When Moses had finished speaking all these words to all Israel,
46 he said to them, "Take to your heart all the words with which I am warning you today, which you shall command your sons to observe carefully, *even* all the words of this law.
47 "For it is not an idle word for you; indeed it is your life. And by this word you will prolong your days in the land, which you are about to cross the Jordan to possess."

48 The LORD spoke to Moses that very same day, saying,
49 "Go up to this mountain of the Abarim, Mount Nebo, which is in the land of Moab opposite Jericho, and look at the land of Canaan, which I am giving to the sons of Israel for a possession.
50 "Then die on the mountain where you ascend, and be gathered to your people, as Aaron your brother died on Mount Hor and was gathered to his people,
51 because you broke faith with Me in the midst of the sons of Israel at the waters of Meribah-kadesh, in the wilderness of Zin, because you did not treat Me as holy in the midst of the sons of Israel.
52 "For you shall see the land at a distance, but you shall not go there, into the land which I am giving the sons of Israel."

Psalm 40:6–12

6 Sacrifice and meal offering You have not desired;
 My ears You have opened;
 Burnt offering and sin offering You have not required.
7 Then I said, "Behold, I come;
 In the scroll of the book it is written of me.
8 I delight to do Your will, O my God;
 Your Law is within my heart."

LIFE LESSONS

> **Psalm 40:8** — *I delight to do Your will, O my God; your Law is within my heart.*

God isn't seeking men and women who will obey Him grudgingly, reluctantly, and resentfully. He desires children who will delight to obey Him, who find pleasure in living out the commands that reflect His heart.

9   I have proclaimed glad tidings
of righteousness in the great
congregation;
Behold, I will not restrain my lips,
O LORD, You know.

10 I have not hidden Your
righteousness within my heart;
I have spoken of Your faithfulness
and Your salvation;
I have not concealed Your
lovingkindness and Your truth
from the great congregation.

11 You, O LORD, will not withhold Your
compassion from me;
Your lovingkindness and Your truth
will continually preserve me.

12 For evils beyond number have
surrounded me;
My iniquities have overtaken me, so
that I am not able to see;
They are more numerous than the
hairs of my head,
And my heart has failed me.

Proverbs 13:11, 12

11 Wealth *obtained* by fraud dwindles,
But the one who gathers by labor
increases *it*.

✳ 12 Hope deferred makes the heart sick,
But desire fulfilled is a tree of life.

Luke 7:31–50

31 "To what then shall I compare the
men of this generation, and what are
they like?
32 "They are like children who sit in
the market place and call to one another,
and they say, 'We played the flute for
you, and you did not dance; we sang a
dirge, and you did not weep.'
33 "For John the Baptist has come eating no bread and drinking no wine, and
you say, 'He has a demon!'
34 "The Son of Man has come eating
and drinking, and you say, 'Behold, a
gluttonous man and a drunkard, a friend
of tax collectors and sinners!'
35 "Yet wisdom is vindicated by all her
children."
36 Now one of the Pharisees was requesting Him to dine with him, and He

entered the Pharisee's house and reclined *at the table.*
37 And there was a woman in the city
who was a sinner; and when she learned
that He was reclining *at the table* in the
Pharisee's house, she brought an alabaster vial of perfume,
38 and standing behind *Him* at His feet,
weeping, she began to wet His feet with
her tears, and kept wiping them with the
hair of her head, and kissing His feet and
anointing them with the perfume.
39 Now when the Pharisee who had invited Him saw this, he said to himself, "If
this man were a prophet He would know
who and what sort of person this woman
is who is touching Him, that she is a sinner."
40 And Jesus answered him, "Simon, I
have something to say to you." And he
replied, "Say it, Teacher."
41 "A moneylender had two debtors:
one owed five hundred denarii, and the
other fifty.
42 "When they were unable to repay, he
graciously forgave them both. So which
of them will love him more?"
43 Simon answered and said, "I suppose the one whom he forgave more."
And He said to him, "You have judged
correctly."
44 Turning toward the woman, He said
to Simon, "Do you see this woman? I entered your house; you gave Me no water
for My feet, but she has wet My feet with
her tears and wiped them with her hair.
45 "You gave Me no kiss; but she, since
the time I came in, has not ceased to kiss
My feet.
46 "You did not anoint My head with
oil, but she anointed My feet with perfume.

LIFE LESSONS

➤ **Luke 7:47 — "For this reason I say to
you, her sins, which are many, have been
forgiven, for she loved much; but he who
is forgiven little, loves little."**

*I*f we do not see the magnitude of
our sin, the Lord's sacrifice may not
seem significant to us. But when we
understand the true condition of our sinful hearts and the terrible penalty of our
transgressions, His immense sacrifice will
inspire our deep love and devotion.

47 "For this reason I say to you, her sins, which are many, have been forgiven, for she loved much; but he who is forgiven little, loves little."
48 Then He said to her, "Your sins have been forgiven."

49 Those who were reclining *at the table* with Him began to say to themselves, "Who is this *man* who even forgives sins?"
50 And He said to the woman, "Your faith has saved you; go in peace."

Deuteronomy 33:1—34:12

33 NOW this is the blessing with which Moses the man of God blessed the sons of Israel before his death.
2 He said,
"The LORD came from Sinai,
  And dawned on them from Seir;
  He shone forth from Mount Paran,
  And He came from the midst of ten
    thousand holy ones;
  At His right hand there was flashing
    lightning for them.
3 "Indeed, He loves the people;
  All Your holy ones are in Your
    hand,
  And they followed in Your steps;
  Everyone receives of Your words.
4 "Moses charged us with a law,
  A possession for the assembly of
    Jacob.
5 "And He was king in Jeshurun,
  When the heads of the people were
    gathered,
  The tribes of Israel together.
6 "May Reuben live and not die,
  Nor his men be few."
7 And this regarding Judah; so he said,
  "Hear, O LORD, the voice of Judah,
  And bring him to his people.
  With his hands he contended for
    them,
  And may You be a help against his
    adversaries."
8 Of Levi he said,
  "*Let* Your Thummim and Your Urim
    belong to Your godly man,
  Whom You proved at Massah,
  With whom You contended at the
    waters of Meribah;
9 Who said of his father and his
    mother,
  'I did not consider them';

And he did not acknowledge his
    brothers,
  Nor did he regard his own sons,
  For they observed Your word,
  And kept Your covenant.
10 "They shall teach Your ordinances to
    Jacob,
  And Your law to Israel.
  They shall put incense before You,
  And whole burnt offerings on Your
    altar.
11 "O LORD, bless his substance,
  And accept the work of his hands;
  Shatter the loins of those who rise
    up against him,
  And those who hate him, so that
    they will not rise *again*."
12 Of Benjamin he said,
  "May the beloved of the LORD dwell
    in security by Him,
  Who shields him all the day,
  And he dwells between His
    shoulders."
13 Of Joseph he said,
  "Blessed of the LORD *be* his land,
  With the choice things of heaven,
    with the dew,
  And from the deep lying beneath,
14 And with the choice yield of the sun,
  And with the choice produce of the
    months.
15 "And with the best things of the
    ancient mountains,
  And with the choice things of the
    everlasting hills,
16 And with the choice things of the
    earth and its fullness,
  And the favor of Him who dwelt in
    the bush.
  Let it come to the head of Joseph,
  And to the crown of the head of
    the one distinguished among his
    brothers.
17 "As the firstborn of his ox, majesty is
    his,

And his horns are the horns of the
wild ox;
With them he will push the peoples,
All at once, to the ends of the earth.
And those are the ten thousands of
Ephraim,
And those are the thousands of
Manasseh."

18 Of Zebulun he said,
"Rejoice, Zebulun, in your going
forth,
And, Issachar, in your tents.

19 "They will call peoples to the
mountain;
There they will offer righteous sacrifices;
For they will draw out the abundance of the seas,
And the hidden treasures of the
sand."

20 Of Gad he said,
"Blessed is the one who enlarges Gad;
He lies down as a lion,
And tears the arm, also the crown of
the head.

21 "Then he provided the first part for
himself,
For there the ruler's portion was
reserved;
And he came with the leaders of the
people;
He executed the justice of the LORD,
And His ordinances with Israel."

22 Of Dan he said,
"Dan is a lion's whelp,
That leaps forth from Bashan."

23 Of Naphtali he said,
"O Naphtali, satisfied with favor,
And full of the blessing of the LORD,
Take possession of the sea and the
south."

24 Of Asher he said,
"More blessed than sons is Asher;
May he be favored by his brothers,
And may he dip his foot in oil.

25 "Your locks will be iron and bronze,
And according to your days, so will
your leisurely walk be.

26 "There is none like the God of
Jeshurun,
Who rides the heavens to your help,
And through the skies in His
majesty.

➤ 27 "The eternal God is a dwelling place,
And underneath are the everlasting
arms;

And He drove out the enemy from
before you,
And said, 'Destroy!'

28 "So Israel dwells in security,
The fountain of Jacob secluded,
In a land of grain and new wine;
His heavens also drop down dew.

29 "Blessed are you, O Israel;
Who is like you, a people saved by
the LORD,
Who is the shield of your help
And the sword of your majesty!
So your enemies will cringe before
you,
And you will tread upon their high
places."

34 NOW Moses went up from the
plains of Moab to Mount Nebo, to
the top of Pisgah, which is opposite Jericho. And the LORD showed him all the
land, Gilead as far as Dan,
2 and all Naphtali and the land of
Ephraim and Manasseh, and all the land
of Judah as far as the western sea,
3 and the Negev and the plain in the
valley of Jericho, the city of palm trees,
as far as Zoar.
4 Then the LORD said to him, "This
is the land which I swore to Abraham,
Isaac, and Jacob, saying, 'I will give it to
your descendants'; I have let you see it
with your eyes, but you shall not go over
there."
5 So Moses the servant of the LORD
died there in the land of Moab, according
to the word of the LORD.
6 And He buried him in the valley in
the land of Moab, opposite Beth-peor;
but no man knows his burial place to this
day.
7 Although Moses was one hundred
and twenty years old when he died, his
eye was not dim, nor his vigor abated.

LIFE LESSONS

➤ **Deuteronomy 33:27** — *"The eternal
God is a dwelling place, and underneath
are the everlasting arms; and He drove
out the enemy from before you."*

C an we have a better friend than one
who is infinitely strong and mighty,
yet at the same time loving and gentle?
Our God tenderly loves us and protects
us, yet has defeated all our spiritual
enemies, including the devil.

➤ **Deuteronomy 34:6 — And He buried him in the valley in the land of Moab . . . but no man knows his burial place to this day.**

*G*od buried Moses in a grave He kept secret. As great as Moses was, he was only a man, and God did not want anyone to remember him as anything but a man.

8   So the sons of Israel wept for Moses in the plains of Moab thirty days; then the days of weeping *and* mourning for Moses came to an end.

9   Now Joshua the son of Nun was filled with the spirit of wisdom, for Moses had laid his hands on him; and the sons of Israel listened to him and did as the LORD had commanded Moses.

10   Since that time no prophet has risen in Israel like Moses, whom the LORD knew face to face,

11   for all the signs and wonders which the LORD sent him to perform in the land of Egypt against Pharaoh, all his servants, and all his land,

12   and for all the mighty power and for all the great terror which Moses performed in the sight of all Israel.

Psalm 40:13–17

13   Be pleased, O LORD, to deliver me;
     Make haste, O LORD, to help me.
14   Let those be ashamed and
          humiliated together
     Who seek my life to destroy it;
     Let those be turned back and
          dishonored
     Who delight in my hurt.
15   Let those be appalled because of
          their shame
     Who say to me, "Aha, aha!"
16   Let all who seek You rejoice and be
          glad in You;
     Let those who love Your salvation
          say continually,
     "The LORD be magnified!"
17   Since I am afflicted and needy,
     Let the Lord be mindful of me.
     You are my help and my deliverer;
     Do not delay, O my God.

Proverbs 13:13, 14

13   The one who despises the word will
          be in debt to it,
     But the one who fears the
          commandment will be rewarded.
14   The teaching of the wise is a
          fountain of life,
     To turn aside from the snares of
          death.

Luke 8:1–25

8 SOON afterwards, He *began* going around from one city and village to another, proclaiming and preaching the kingdom of God. The twelve were with Him,

2   and *also* some women who had been healed of evil spirits and sicknesses: Mary who was called Magdalene, from whom seven demons had gone out,

3   and Joanna the wife of Chuza, Herod's steward, and Susanna, and many others who were contributing to their support out of their private means.

4   When a large crowd was coming together, and those from the various cities were journeying to Him, He spoke by way of a parable:

5   "The sower went out to sow his seed; and as he sowed, some fell beside the road, and it was trampled under foot and the birds of the air ate it up.

6   "Other *seed* fell on rocky *soil*, and as soon as it grew up, it withered away, because it had no moisture.

➤ **Luke 8:2, 3 — Some women . . . were contributing to their support out of their private means.**

*L*uke came from a culture that largely dismissed or at least downplayed the importance of women, yet he often highlights the contributions of women in the ministry of Jesus. He thus anticipates the message of Galatians 3:28, "There is neither Jew nor Greek, there is neither slave nor free man, there is neither male nor female; for you are all one in Christ Jesus."

7 "Other *seed* fell among the thorns; and the thorns grew up with it and choked it out.

8 "Other *seed* fell into the good soil, and grew up, and produced a crop a hundred times as great." As He said these things, He would call out, "He who has ears to hear, let him hear."

9 His disciples *began* questioning Him as to what this parable meant.

10 And He said, "To you it has been granted to know the mysteries of the kingdom of God, but to the rest *it is* in parables, so that SEEING THEY MAY NOT SEE, AND HEARING THEY MAY NOT UNDERSTAND.

11 "Now the parable is this: the seed is the word of God.

12 "Those beside the road are those who have heard; then the devil comes and takes away the word from their heart, so that they will not believe and be saved.

13 "Those on the rocky *soil are* those who, when they hear, receive the word with joy; and these have no *firm* root; they believe for a while, and in time of temptation fall away.

14 "The *seed* which fell among the thorns, these are the ones who have heard, and as they go on their way they are choked with worries and riches and pleasures of *this* life, and bring no fruit to maturity.

15 "But the *seed* in the good soil, these are the ones who have heard the word in an honest and good heart, and hold it fast, and bear fruit with perseverance.

WHAT THE BIBLE SAYS ABOUT ⊕

That the World Would Know Him

Luke 8:16

*T*hese three questions are eternally significant: *Who is God? What is He like? Can we know Him?* The world is filled with religions that claim to give the answers to these questions. However, when you trust Jesus Christ as your Lord and Savior, you have the truth: God is our Father, He is loving, and He is most certainly knowable through a relationship with Jesus Christ.

Jesus said in John 8:12, "I am the Light of the world; he who follows Me will not walk in the darkness, but will have the Light of life."

That is why you are told in Luke 8:16, "Now no one after lighting a lamp covers it over with a container, or puts it under a bed; but he puts it on a lampstand, so that those who come in may see the light." You have come to know the Light of the World, Jesus Christ. You cannot hide that you know Him. Rather, you must allow His light to shine through you so others can also have His light—so that they can also accept the salvation He offers.

This is what God wants most for your life— for you to have a saving knowledge of Jesus Christ, to grow daily in your walk with Him, to live out the plan He has for your life, and to tell others about His great gift of salvation.

The desire of the Father's heart is for all people to know Him. As 1 Timothy 2:3, 4 tell us, "God our Savior, who desires all men to be saved and to come to the knowledge of the truth." Christ died for the sins of everyone in this world, and He desires everyone to be rescued from its grip.

God's provision of forgiveness of sins and of eternal life in heaven is offered to every person on earth. He did not create mankind to be lost for all eternity (2 Pet. 3:9)—though some people will choose to be lost through their own stubborn wills (John 3:17, 18). For this reason, He sends us to every corner of the earth to share the gospel.

Before Jesus left this earth to sit at the right hand of the Father, He left us with a powerful commandment. Matthew 28:19, 20 says, "Go therefore and make disciples of all the nations, baptizing them in the name of the Father and the Son and the Holy Spirit, teaching them to observe all that I commanded you; and lo, I am with you always, even to the end of the age." We call this the *Great Commission*, and it is His desire that we spread His gospel across the world until every living soul has heard it.

God will enable and empower each of us to witness for Him through His Holy Spirit. Then we have the incredible opportunity to tell others about the desire of God's heart—that they would know Him and grow in Him.

Don't hide the light of God within you— share it with this lost world that needs it so desperately. ⊕

16 "Now no one after lighting a lamp covers it over with a container, or puts it under a bed; but he puts it on a lampstand, so that those who come in may see the light.

17 "For nothing is hidden that will not become evident, nor *anything* secret that will not be known and come to light.

18 "So take care how you listen; for whoever has, to him *more* shall be given; and whoever does not have, even what he thinks he has shall be taken away from him."

19 And His mother and brothers came to Him, and they were unable to get to Him because of the crowd.

20 And it was reported to Him, "Your mother and Your brothers are standing outside, wishing to see You."

21 But He answered and said to them,

"My mother and My brothers are these who hear the word of God and do it."

22 Now on one of *those* days Jesus and His disciples got into a boat, and He said to them, "Let us go over to the other side of the lake." So they launched out.

23 But as they were sailing along He fell asleep; and a fierce gale of wind descended on the lake, and they *began* to be swamped and to be in danger.

24 They came to Jesus and woke Him up, saying, "Master, Master, we are perishing!" And He got up and rebuked the wind and the surging waves, and they stopped, and it became calm.

25 And He said to them, "Where is your faith?" They were fearful and amazed, saying to one another, "Who then is this, that He commands even the winds and the water, and they obey Him?"

Joshua 1:1—2:24

1 NOW it came about after the death of Moses the servant of the LORD, that the LORD spoke to Joshua the son of Nun, Moses' servant, saying,

2 "Moses My servant is dead; now therefore arise, cross this Jordan, you and all this people, to the land which I am giving to them, to the sons of Israel.

3 "Every place on which the sole of your foot treads, I have given it to you, just as I spoke to Moses.

4 "From the wilderness and this Lebanon, even as far as the great river, the river Euphrates, all the land of the Hittites, and as far as the Great Sea toward the setting of the sun will be your territory.

5 "No man will *be able to* stand before you all the days of your life. Just as I have been with Moses, I will be with you; I will not fail you or forsake you.

6 "Be strong and courageous, for you shall give this people possession of the land which I swore to their fathers to give them.

7 "Only be strong and very courageous; be careful to do according to all the law which Moses My servant commanded you; do not turn from it to the right or

to the left, so that you may have success wherever you go.

8 "This book of the law shall not depart from your mouth, but you shall meditate on it day and night, so that you may be careful to do according to all that is written in it; for then you will make your way prosperous, and then you will have success.

9 "Have I not commanded you? Be strong and courageous! Do not tremble or be dismayed, for the LORD your God is with you wherever you go."

10 Then Joshua commanded the officers of the people, saying,

LIFE LESSONS

➤ **Joshua 1:5 — "No man shall be able to stand before you . . . I will not fail you or forsake you."**

*B*efore Joshua gave his first order or made his first move as the new leader of Israel, he listened for the voice of God. Listening to the Father is essential to walking with Him and securing His blessings. When we do the His will in His way with His help, no one and nothing can stand in the way of our success. The key is seeking the presence of the Lord.

ANSWERS TO LIFE'S QUESTIONS

How can I find courage in times of adversity?

JOSHUA 1:6-9

*I*n many ways, adversity is like boot camp; it is rigorous, painful, and challenging. Difficulties cause us to adopt new routines and habits; to mature in the physical, mental, emotional, and spiritual aspects of our being; and to grow in our relationships with the Lord.

During times of trial, we need to remain courageous and faithful. We also need to remain steadfast in our devotion to the Lord as we battle feelings of doubt, fear, and limitation. He will provide strength and hope not only to endure the hardship, but also to make the changes required of us so we can claim the blessings of God.

Thankfully, we can trust the Holy Spirit to "transform the body of our humble state into conformity with the body of His glory" (Phil. 3:21). By His Spirit, God can and will change us so we live a life honoring our Savior, Jesus Christ, and facing every hurdle with valor.

As a close associate of Moses, Joshua had grown in his faith and leadership abilities. He also knew all about adversity. Without question, the forty years of wandering in the wilderness had subjected him to physical, relational, spiritual, emotional, and mental hardships that helped him understand the harsh realities of pain and suffering. Yet Joshua also knew the Lord was with him and the nation of Israel. This assurance gave him all he needed to persevere, no matter how difficult the situation became.

When the time came for the people of God to cross the Jordan River and inhabit the Land of Promise, the Lord named Joshua as the leader to succeed Moses and admonished him about being courageous:

- "Be strong and courageous, for you shall give this people possession of the land which I swore to their fathers to give them" (Josh. 1:6).
- "Only be strong and very courageous; be careful to do according to all the law which Moses My servant commanded you" (Josh. 1:7).
- "Have I not commanded you? Be strong and courageous! Do not tremble or be dismayed, for the LORD your God is with you wherever you go" (Josh. 1:9).

Note the three things that required Joshua to be brave: (1) making decisions that affected other people under his leadership; (2) keeping the laws and commandments, even as changes occurred; and (3) remembering continually that the Lord was with him, despite what circumstances might indicate to the contrary.

There will be times when each of us needs courage in exactly the same three areas. The storms of life will strike without warning, and we will find ourselves crying out to God. We need His wisdom, hope, and assurance. When we measure life's challenges and trials against His mighty power, we gain the courage we need to proceed to triumph because He has already won the eternal victory for us.

---

11 "Pass through the midst of the camp and command the people, saying, 'Prepare provisions for yourselves, for within three days you are to cross this Jordan, to go in to possess the land which the LORD your God is giving you, to possess it.'"

12 To the Reubenites and to the Gadites and to the half-tribe of Manasseh, Joshua said,

13 "Remember the word which Moses the servant of the LORD commanded you, saying, 'The LORD your God gives you rest and will give you this land.'

14 "Your wives, your little ones, and your cattle shall remain in the land

---

LIFE LESSONS

➤ **Joshua 1:8 — "You shall meditate on it day and night, so that you may be careful to do according to all that is written in it."**

*T*he Lord gave Joshua the same command he issued to future Israelite kings in Deuteronomy 17:19—he was to meditate on the Word of God every day. Knowledge of God's will is crucial to doing it.

➤ **Joshua 1:9 — "Be strong and courageous! Do not tremble or be dismayed, for the LORD your God is with you wherever you go."**

*I*t's easy to focus on our problems, which we can see, and not on God, whom we can't. As Joshua discovered, God is with us no matter where we are or how big our problems seem.

which Moses gave you beyond the Jordan, but you shall cross before your brothers in battle array, all your valiant warriors, and shall help them,

15 until the LORD gives your brothers rest, as *He gives* you, and they also possess the land which the LORD your God is giving them. Then you shall return to your own land, and possess that which Moses the servant of the LORD gave you beyond the Jordan toward the sunrise."

16 They answered Joshua, saying, "All that you have commanded us we will do, and wherever you send us we will go.

17 "Just as we obeyed Moses in all things, so we will obey you; only may the LORD your God be with you as He was with Moses.

18 "Anyone who rebels against your command and does not obey your words in all that you command him, shall be put to death; only be strong and courageous."

2 THEN Joshua the son of Nun sent two men as spies secretly from Shittim, saying, "Go, view the land, especially Jericho." So they went and came into the house of a harlot whose name was Rahab, and lodged there.

2 It was told the king of Jericho, saying, "Behold, men from the sons of Israel have come here tonight to search out the land."

3 And the king of Jericho sent *word* to Rahab, saying, "Bring out the men who have come to you, who have entered your house, for they have come to search out all the land."

4 But the woman had taken the two men and hidden them, and she said, "Yes, the men came to me, but I did not know where they were from.

5 "It came about when *it was time* to shut the gate at dark, that the men went out; I do not know where the men went. Pursue them quickly, for you will overtake them."

6 But she had brought them up to the roof and hidden them in the stalks of flax which she had laid in order on the roof.

7 So the men pursued them on the road to the Jordan to the fords; and as soon as those who were pursuing them had gone out, they shut the gate.

8 Now before they lay down, she came up to them on the roof,

9 and said to the men, "I know that the LORD has given you the land, and that the

terror of you has fallen on us, and that all the inhabitants of the land have melted away before you.

10 "For we have heard how the LORD dried up the water of the Red Sea before you when you came out of Egypt, and what you did to the two kings of the Amorites who were beyond the Jordan, to Sihon and Og, whom you utterly destroyed.

11 "When we heard *it*, our hearts melted ◄ and no courage remained in any man any longer because of you; for the LORD your God, He is God in heaven above and on earth beneath.

12 "Now therefore, please swear to me by the LORD, since I have dealt kindly with you, that you also will deal kindly with my father's household, and give me a pledge of truth,

13 and spare my father and my mother and my brothers and my sisters, with all who belong to them, and deliver our lives from death."

14 So the men said to her, "Our life for yours if you do not tell this business of ours; and it shall come about when the LORD gives us the land that we will deal kindly and faithfully with you."

15 Then she let them down by a rope through the window, for her house was on the city wall, so that she was living on the wall.

16 She said to them, "Go to the hill country, so that the pursuers will not happen upon you, and hide yourselves there for three days until the pursuers return. Then afterward you may go on your way."

17 The men said to her, "We *shall be* free from this oath to you which you have made us swear,

---

LIFE LESSONS

► Joshua 2:11 — *"The LORD your God, He is God in heaven above and on earth beneath."*

Genuine faith can take root in the unlikeliest of soils, as it did in the heart of the pagan prostitute Rahab. She had heard enough to believe—and the Lord saved her (Heb. 11:31). God always follows through on His promises—but it encourages us greatly when, in His grace, He gives us a foretaste of that fulfilled promise.

18 unless, when we come into the land, you tie this cord of scarlet thread in the window through which you let us down, and gather to yourself into the house your father and your mother and your brothers and all your father's household. 19 "It shall come about that anyone who goes out of the doors of your house into the street, his blood *shall be* on his own head, and we *shall be* free; but anyone who is with you in the house, his blood *shall be* on our head if a hand is *laid* on him. 20 "But if you tell this business of ours, then we shall be free from the oath which you have made us swear."

21 She said, "According to your words, so be it." So she sent them away, and they departed; and she tied the scarlet cord in the window.

22 They departed and came to the hill country, and remained there for three days until the pursuers returned. Now the pursuers had sought *them* all along the road, but had not found *them*.

23 Then the two men returned and came down from the hill country and crossed over and came to Joshua the son of Nun, and they related to him all that had happened to them.

24 They said to Joshua, "Surely the LORD has given all the land into our hands; moreover, all the inhabitants of the land have melted away before us."

Psalm 41:1–13

For the choir director. A Psalm of David.

41 HOW blessed is he who considers the helpless;
   The LORD will deliver him in a day of trouble.
2 The LORD will protect him and keep him alive,
   And he shall be called blessed upon the earth;
   And do not give him over to the desire of his enemies.
3 The LORD will sustain him upon his sickbed;
   In his illness, You restore him to health.
4 As for me, I said, "O LORD, be gracious to me;

   Heal my soul, for I have sinned against You."
5 My enemies speak evil against me, "When will he die, and his name perish?"
6 And when he comes to see *me*, he speaks falsehood;
   His heart gathers wickedness to itself;
   When he goes outside, he tells it.
7 All who hate me whisper together against me;
   Against me they devise my hurt, *saying,*
8 "A wicked thing is poured out upon him,
   That when he lies down, he will not rise up again."
9 Even my close friend in whom I trusted,
   Who ate my bread,
   Has lifted up his heel against me.
10 But You, O LORD, be gracious to me and raise me up,
   That I may repay them.
11 By this I know that You are pleased with me,
   Because my enemy does not shout in triumph over me.
12 As for me, You uphold me in my integrity,
   And You set me in Your presence forever.
13 Blessed be the LORD, the God of Israel,
   From everlasting to everlasting.
   Amen and Amen.

Proverbs 13:15, 16

15 Good understanding produces favor,

LIFE LESSONS

> **Psalm 41:9** — *Even my close friend in whom I trusted, who ate my bread, has lifted up his heel against me.*

*J*esus applied this verse to Judas Iscariot as a fulfillment of biblical prophecy (John 13:18). Just because someone says, "Lord, Lord," does not mean they have a genuine relationship with God (Matt. 7:21).

But the way of the treacherous is
   hard.
16 Every prudent man acts with
   knowledge,
   But a fool displays folly.

✦ Luke 8:26–56

26 Then they sailed to the country of
the Gerasenes, which is opposite Galilee.
27 And when He came out onto the
land, He was met by a man from the city
who was possessed with demons; and
who had not put on any clothing for a
long time, and was not living in a house,
but in the tombs.
28 Seeing Jesus, he cried out and fell
before Him, and said in a loud voice,
"What business do we have with each
other, Jesus, Son of the Most High God?
I beg You, do not torment me."
29 For He had commanded the unclean
spirit to come out of the man. For it had
seized him many times; and he was
bound with chains and shackles and kept
under guard, and yet he would break his
bonds and be driven by the demon into
the desert.
30 And Jesus asked him, "What is your
name?" And he said, "Legion"; for many
demons had entered him.
31 They were imploring Him not to
command them to go away into the
abyss.
32 Now there was a herd of many swine
feeding there on the mountain; and the
demons implored Him to permit them to
enter the swine. And He gave them permission.
33 And the demons came out of the
man and entered the swine; and the herd
rushed down the steep bank into the lake
and was drowned.
34 When the herdsmen saw what had
happened, they ran away and reported it
in the city and out in the country.
35 The people went out to see what had
happened; and they came to Jesus, and
found the man from whom the demons
had gone out, sitting down at the feet of
Jesus, clothed and in his right mind; and
they became frightened.
36 Those who had seen it reported to
them how the man who was demon-
possessed had been made well.

37 And all the people of the country of
the Gerasenes and the surrounding district asked Him to leave them, for they
were gripped with great fear; and He got
into a boat and returned.
38 But the man from whom the demons
had gone out was begging Him that he
might accompany Him; but He sent him
away, saying,
39 "Return to your house and describe
what great things God has done for you."
So he went away, proclaiming throughout the whole city what great things
Jesus had done for him.
40 And as Jesus returned, the people
welcomed Him, for they had all been
waiting for Him.
41 And there came a man named Jairus,
and he was an official of the synagogue;
and he fell at Jesus' feet, and began to
implore Him to come to his house;
42 for he had an only daughter, about
twelve years old, and she was dying. But
as He went, the crowds were pressing
against Him.
43 And a woman who had a hemorrhage for twelve years, and could not be
healed by anyone,
44 came up behind Him and touched
the fringe of His cloak, and immediately
her hemorrhage stopped.
45 And Jesus said, "Who is the one
who touched Me?" And while they were
all denying it, Peter said, "Master, the
people are crowding and pressing in on
You."
46 But Jesus said, "Someone did touch
Me, for I was aware that power had gone
out of Me."
47 When the woman saw that she had
not escaped notice, she came trembling
and fell down before Him, and declared
in the presence of all the people the reason why she had touched Him, and how
she had been immediately healed.
48 And He said to her, "Daughter, your
faith has made you well; go in peace."
49 While He was still speaking, someone *came from the house of the synagogue official, saying, "Your daughter
has died; do not trouble the Teacher
anymore."
50 But when Jesus heard this, He answered him, "Do not be afraid any longer; only believe, and she will be made
well."
51 When He came to the house, He did

not allow anyone to enter with Him, except Peter and John and James, and the girl's father and mother.

52 Now they were all weeping and lamenting for her; but He said, "Stop weeping, for she has not died, but is asleep."

➤ 53 And they *began* laughing at Him, knowing that she had died.

54 He, however, took her by the hand and called, saying, "Child, arise!"

55 And her spirit returned, and she got up immediately; and He gave orders for *something* to be given her to eat.

56 Her parents were amazed; but He instructed them to tell no one what had happened.

LIFE LESSONS

➤ **Luke 8:53 — *And they began laughing at Him, knowing that she had died.***

*A*s a physician, Luke wanted his audience to know the child Jesus healed was really and truly dead. One day, Jesus will destroy death altogether (1 Cor. 15:21); but even before then, He showed His mastery over it.

Joshua 3:1—4:24

3 THEN Joshua rose early in the morning; and he and all the sons of Israel set out from Shittim and came to the Jordan, and they lodged there before they crossed.

2 At the end of three days the officers went through the midst of the camp;

3 and they commanded the people, saying, "When you see the ark of the covenant of the LORD your God with the Levitical priests carrying it, then you shall set out from your place and go after it.

➤ 4 "However, there shall be between you and it a distance of about 2,000 cubits by measure. Do not come near it, that you may know the way by which you shall go, for you have not passed this way before."

5 Then Joshua said to the people, "Consecrate yourselves, for tomorrow the LORD will do wonders among you."

6 And Joshua spoke to the priests, saying, "Take up the ark of the covenant and cross over ahead of the people." So they took up the ark of the covenant and went ahead of the people.

7 Now the LORD said to Joshua, "This day I will begin to exalt you in the sight of all Israel, that they may know that just as I have been with Moses, I will be with you.

8 "You shall, moreover, command the priests who are carrying the ark of the covenant, saying, 'When you come to the edge of the waters of the Jordan, you shall stand *still* in the Jordan.'"

9 Then Joshua said to the sons of Israel, "Come here, and hear the words of the LORD your God."

10 Joshua said, "By this you shall know ➤ that the living God is among you, and that He will assuredly dispossess from before you the Canaanite, the Hittite, the Hivite, the Perizzite, the Girgashite, the Amorite, and the Jebusite.

11 "Behold, the ark of the covenant of the Lord of all the earth is crossing over ahead of you into the Jordan.

12 "Now then, take for yourselves twelve

LIFE LESSONS

➤ **Joshua 3:4 — *"Do not come near it, that you may know the way by which you shall go, for you have not passed this way before."***

*S*ince the Israelites had never traveled this path before, they wisely chose to follow the lead of God, in this case by trailing the ark of the covenant. The Lord leads, we are to follow.

➤ **Joshua 3:10 — *"Know that the living God is among you, and that He will assuredly dispossess from before you the Canaanites."***

*W*hen the living God is among us, no problem is insurmountable. The awareness of His presence energizes us for our work.

⊕ **LIFE PRINCIPLE** | **5**

GOD DOES NOT REQUIRE US TO UNDERSTAND HIS WILL, JUST OBEY IT, EVEN IF IT SEEMS UNREASONABLE.

JOSHUA 3:8

*D*o you often find yourself wondering why God doesn't answer your prayers, or why, despite all your best efforts, the circumstances of your life still don't work out? The answer could lie in your level of obedience to the Lord. Or waiting may be the result of God wanting you to be still, trust Him, and watch for His cue to move forward.

Any area of disobedience needs to be addressed. Sin prevents us from experiencing His best. Perhaps God has asked something of you, and in response, you have either ignored His words or done only part of what He asked. True obedience to God means doing what He says, when He says it, how He says it should be done, and as long as He says to do it—regardless of whether or not you understand the reasons for it—until what He says is accomplished.

Before you try to make a list of everything God has ever asked you to do or not do, consider this: Is there one particular area of your life in which you struggle to obey the Lord? As you read Scripture, does He continually bring a specific sin to mind? When you go to Him in prayer, does the same issue surface repeatedly? If the Lord is bringing something to your mind right now, consider this: It could be you have been living in the same uncomfortable situation for years because at some point, you chose to do things your way instead of God's way.

Following His will instead of your own can make a tremendous difference in your life, which is why you must make obedience to Him your top priority. But to do so, you need to understand why submission plays such an important role in your relationship with God.

An excellent biblical example to illustrate the point is Noah—a man who obeyed the Lord, even when what He asked him to do didn't seem to make much sense. The Lord God called him to build an enormous ark—something that seemed both impossible and illogical—and Noah complied without asking questions (Gen. 6–9).

Will it always be popular to obey God? No. Will people criticize you? Probably. Will they think you do some ridiculous things? No doubt. Will they laugh at you? Yes. But think about this: Noah chose to walk with God in the midst of a corrupt society. In fact, it had grown so wicked God determined to destroy every living human being on the face of this earth, with the exception of one family—Noah's. We can only imagine what the people must have said to Noah as they watched him day after day. But soon after the raindrops started falling, all mocking stopped.

Noah obeyed God despite what other people thought of him, and the Lord spared him from the great flood that covered the earth. If he had listened to his critics, Noah would not have built the ark, and he would have been swept away with everyone else. Instead, he chose to obey God, regardless of any misgivings he might have had.

When we choose the path of obedience, we must be prepared for the negative responses we will undoubtedly receive, knowing that God has an excellent reason for His command and will help us in extraordinary ways. We must never focus on the things or the people who try to distract us from doing God's will. The Holy Spirit enables us to obey every one of God's commandments and always directs us in the very best way possible. Therefore, whatever He requires of us—whether it be painful or joyful, profitable or costly, reasonable or peculiar—our heavenly Father will give us the ability and strength to be faithful, regardless of what others think or how our circumstances appear.

Obedience must be a priority in every believer's life. It is the only way you will ever become the person God wants you to be and the only way you will ever achieve the things in life He has so wonderfully prepared for you. It is the Holy Spirit who enables you to walk obediently before the Lord in His strength and His power.

So choose to obey Him, even if you don't understand why He asks you to do something. Have faith in the fact His instructions are for your good (Jer. 29:11). That way, you can become the person He wants you to be, do the work He desires of you, bear the fruit He enables you to bear, and receive all the blessings He has prepared for you. ◈

men from the tribes of Israel, one man for each tribe.

13 "It shall come about when the soles of the feet of the priests who carry the ark of the LORD, the Lord of all the earth, rest in the waters of the Jordan, the waters of the Jordan will be cut off, *and* the waters which are flowing down from above will stand in one heap."

14 So when the people set out from their tents to cross the Jordan with the priests carrying the ark of the covenant before the people,

15 and when those who carried the ark came into the Jordan, and the feet of the priests carrying the ark were dipped in the edge of the water (for the Jordan overflows all its banks all the days of harvest),

16 the waters which were flowing down from above stood *and* rose up in one heap, a great distance away at Adam, the city that is beside Zarethan; and those which were flowing down toward the sea of the Arabah, the Salt Sea, were completely cut off. So the people crossed opposite Jericho.

17 And the priests who carried the ark of the covenant of the LORD stood firm on dry ground in the middle of the Jordan while all Israel crossed on dry ground, until all the nation had finished crossing the Jordan.

4 NOW when all the nation had finished crossing the Jordan, the LORD spoke to Joshua, saying,

2 "Take for yourselves twelve men from the people, one man from each tribe,

3 and command them, saying, 'Take up for yourselves twelve stones from here out of the middle of the Jordan, from the place where the priests' feet are standing firm, and carry them over with you and lay them down in the lodging place where you will lodge tonight.'"

4 So Joshua called the twelve men whom he had appointed from the sons of Israel, one man from each tribe;

5 and Joshua said to them, "Cross again to the ark of the LORD your God into the middle of the Jordan, and each of you take up a stone on his shoulder, according to the number of the tribes of the sons of Israel.

6 "Let this be a sign among you, so that when your children ask later, saying, 'What do these stones mean to you?'

7 then you shall say to them, 'Because the waters of the Jordan were cut off before the ark of the covenant of the LORD; when it crossed the Jordan, the waters of the Jordan were cut off.' So these stones shall become a memorial to the sons of Israel forever."

8 Thus the sons of Israel did as Joshua commanded, and took up twelve stones from the middle of the Jordan, just as the LORD spoke to Joshua, according to the number of the tribes of the sons of Israel; and they carried them over with them to the lodging place and put them down there.

9 Then Joshua set up twelve stones in the middle of the Jordan at the place where the feet of the priests who carried the ark of the covenant were standing, and they are there to this day.

10 For the priests who carried the ark were standing in the middle of the Jordan until everything was completed that the LORD had commanded Joshua to speak to the people, according to all that Moses had commanded Joshua. And the people hurried and crossed;

11 and when all the people had finished crossing, the ark of the LORD and the priests crossed before the people.

12 The sons of Reuben and the sons of Gad and the half-tribe of Manasseh crossed over in battle array before the sons of Israel, just as Moses had spoken to them;

13 about 40,000 equipped for war, crossed for battle before the LORD to the desert plains of Jericho.

14 On that day the LORD exalted Joshua in the sight of all Israel; so that they revered him, just as they had revered Moses all the days of his life.

15 Now the LORD said to Joshua,

16 "Command the priests who carry the

LIFE LESSONS

➤ **Joshua 4:7 — "These stones shall become a memorial to the sons of Israel forever."**

*F*or years after Israel had defeated Jericho, the people could look at the stones taken from the Jordan's dry river-bed and remember God's work on their behalf. What "memorial stones" remind you of God's work in your own life?

ark of the testimony that they come up from the Jordan."
17 So Joshua commanded the priests, saying, "Come up from the Jordan."
18 It came about when the priests who carried the ark of the covenant of the LORD had come up from the middle of the Jordan, and the soles of the priests' feet were lifted up to the dry ground, that the waters of the Jordan returned to their place, and went over all its banks as before.
19 Now the people came up from the Jordan on the tenth of the first month and camped at Gilgal on the eastern edge of Jericho.
20 Those twelve stones which they had taken from the Jordan, Joshua set up at Gilgal.
21 He said to the sons of Israel, "When your children ask their fathers in time to come, saying, 'What are these stones?'
22 then you shall inform your children, saying, 'Israel crossed this Jordan on dry ground.'
23 "For the LORD your God dried up the waters of the Jordan before you until you had crossed, just as the LORD your God had done to the Red Sea, which He dried up before us until we had crossed;
24 that all the peoples of the earth may know that the hand of the LORD is mighty, so that you may fear the LORD your God forever."

Psalm 42:1–5

BOOK 2

For the choir director.
A Maskil of the sons of Korah.

42 AS the deer pants for the water brooks,
So my soul pants for You, O God.
2 My soul thirsts for God, for the living God;
When shall I come and appear before God?
3 My tears have been my food day and night,
While *they* say to me all day long, "Where is your God?"
4 These things I remember and I pour out my soul within me.
For I used to go along with

the throng *and* lead them in procession to the house of God,
With the voice of joy and thanksgiving, a multitude keeping festival.
5 Why are you in despair, O my soul? And *why* have you become disturbed within me?
Hope in God, for I shall again praise Him
For the help of His presence.

Proverbs 13:17, 18

17 A wicked messenger falls into adversity,
But a faithful envoy *brings* healing.
18 Poverty and shame *will come* to him who neglects discipline,
But he who regards reproof will be honored.

Luke 9:1–17

9 AND He called the twelve together, and gave them power and authority over all the demons and to heal diseases.
2 And He sent them out to proclaim the kingdom of God and to perform healing.

LIFE LESSONS

➢ Joshua 4:24 — *"That all the peoples of the earth may know that the hand of the LORD is mighty, so that you may fear the LORD your God forever."*

What happens to God's people has ramifications far beyond their own lives. The Lord wants the entire world to know Him, and He "advertises" His activity through us.

➢ Proverbs 13:18 — *Poverty and shame will come to him who neglects discipline, but he who regards reproof will be honored.*

We all need correction at many points along life's journey, but not all of us graciously and willingly accept the correction we need. We need correction to keep us off the wrong path that leads to the wrong destination.

3 And He said to them, "Take nothing for *your* journey, neither a staff, nor a bag, nor bread, nor money; and do not *even* have two tunics apiece.

4 "Whatever house you enter, stay there until you leave that city.

5 "And as for those who do not receive you, as you go out from that city, shake the dust off your feet as a testimony against them."

6 Departing, they *began* going throughout the villages, preaching the gospel and healing everywhere.

7 Now Herod the tetrarch heard of all that was happening; and he was greatly perplexed, because it was said by some that John had risen from the dead,

8 and by some that Elijah had appeared, and by others that one of the prophets of old had risen again.

9 Herod said, "I myself had John beheaded; but who is this man about whom I hear such things?" And he kept trying to see Him.

10 When the apostles returned, they gave an account to Him of all that they had done. Taking them with Him, He withdrew by Himself to a city called Bethsaida.

11 But the crowds were aware of this and followed Him; and welcoming them, He *began* speaking to them about the kingdom of God and curing those who had need of healing.

12 Now the day was ending, and the twelve came and said to Him, "Send the crowd away, that they may go into the surrounding villages and countryside and find lodging and get something to eat; for here we are in a desolate place."

13 But He said to them, "You give them something to eat!" And they said, "We have no more than five loaves and two fish, unless perhaps we go and buy food for all these people."

14 (For there were about five thousand men.) And He said to His disciples, "Have them sit down *to eat* in groups of about fifty each."

15 They did so, and had them all sit down.

16 Then He took the five loaves and the two fish, and looking up to heaven, He blessed them, and broke *them,* and kept giving *them* to the disciples to set before the people.

17 And they all ate and were satisfied; and the broken pieces which they had left over were picked up, twelve baskets *full.*

LIFE LESSONS

➤ **Luke 9:13 — *"Give them something to eat!"***

*T*he Lord will never command us to do something without also providing whatever we need to obey His command. In this case, His command seemed impossible; but He provided what He told them to give.

APRIL 8

Joshua 5:1—6:27

5 NOW it came about when all the kings of the Amorites who *were* beyond the Jordan to the west, and all the kings of the Canaanites who *were* by the sea, heard how the LORD had dried up the waters of the Jordan before the sons of Israel until they had crossed, that their hearts melted, and there was no spirit in them any longer because of the sons of Israel.

2 At that time the LORD said to Joshua, "Make for yourself flint knives and circumcise again the sons of Israel the second time."

3 So Joshua made himself flint knives and circumcised the sons of Israel at Gibeath-haaraloth.

4 This is the reason why Joshua circumcised them: all the people who came out of Egypt who were males, all the men of war, died in the wilderness along the way after they came out of Egypt.

5 For all the people who came out were circumcised, but all the people who were born in the wilderness along the way as they came out of Egypt had not been circumcised.

6 For the sons of Israel walked forty

years in the wilderness, until all the nation, *that is*, the men of war who came out of Egypt, perished because they did not listen to the voice of the LORD, to whom the LORD had sworn that He would not let them see the land which the LORD had sworn to their fathers to give us, a land flowing with milk and honey.

7 Their children whom He raised up in their place, Joshua circumcised; for they were uncircumcised, because they had not circumcised them along the way.

➤ 8 Now when they had finished circumcising all the nation, they remained in their places in the camp until they were healed.

9 Then the LORD said to Joshua, "Today I have rolled away the reproach of Egypt from you." So the name of that place is called Gilgal to this day.

10 While the sons of Israel camped at Gilgal they observed the Passover on the evening of the fourteenth day of the month on the desert plains of Jericho.

11 On the day after the Passover, on that very day, they ate some of the produce of the land, unleavened cakes and parched *grain*.

12 The manna ceased on the day after they had eaten some of the produce of the land, so that the sons of Israel no longer had manna, but they ate some of the yield of the land of Canaan during that year.

13 Now it came about when Joshua was by Jericho, that he lifted up his eyes and looked, and behold, a man was standing opposite him with his sword drawn in his hand, and Joshua went to him and said to him, "Are you for us or for our adversaries?"

➤ 14 He said, "No; rather I indeed come now *as* captain of the host of the LORD." And Joshua fell on his face to the earth, and bowed down, and said to him, "What has my lord to say to his servant?"

15 The captain of the LORD'S host said to Joshua, "Remove your sandals from your feet, for the place where you are standing is holy." And Joshua did so.

6 NOW Jericho was tightly shut because of the sons of Israel; no one went out and no one came in.

2 The LORD said to Joshua, "See, I have given Jericho into your hand, with its king *and* the valiant warriors.

3 "You shall march around the city, all

the men of war circling the city once. You shall do so for six days.

4 "Also seven priests shall carry seven trumpets of rams' horns before the ark; then on the seventh day you shall march around the city seven times, and the priests shall blow the trumpets.

5 "It shall be that when they make a ◄ long blast with the ram's horn, and when you hear the sound of the trumpet, all the people shall shout with a great shout; and the wall of the city will fall down flat, and the people will go up every man straight ahead."

6 So Joshua the son of Nun called the priests and said to them, "Take up the ark of the covenant, and let seven priests carry seven trumpets of rams' horns before the ark of the LORD."

7 Then he said to the people, "Go forward, and march around the city, and let the armed men go on before the ark of the LORD."

8 And it was *so*, that when Joshua had

LIFE LESSONS

➤ **Joshua 5:8 —** *When they had finished circumcising all the nation, they remained in their places in the camp until they were healed.*

*W*hile the men healed from their painful circumcisions, they remained vulnerable to attack from hostile forces (Gen. 34:1–29). Yet our sovereign God protected them, even then (Josh. 5:1). God provides exactly what we need, when we need it. In fact, He assumes full responsibility for our needs when we obey Him.

➤ **Joshua 5:14 —** *"I indeed come now as captain of the host of the LORD."*

*T*he question is never, "Is God on our side?" but rather "Are we on God's side?" God does not choose sides, but He invites us to choose His side.

➤ **Joshua 6:5 —** *"All the people shall shout with a great shout; and the wall of the city will fall down flat."*

*A*s a soldier, Joshua must have seen these instructions as very strange. Yet as a man of God, he immediately obeyed. God does not require us to understand His will, just obey it, whether it makes sense or not.

Life Examples:

Already Won

JOSHUA 6:1, 2

*I*t was huge and it stood in their way. As Joshua looked at the fortifications of Jericho, he realized taking the city was no small task, especially with the seemingly impenetrable wall that stood before him.

However, God promised Joshua Israel would triumph, and Joshua believed Him. Joshua 6:5 records God's command, "It shall be that when they make a long blast with the ram's horn, and when you hear the sound of the trumpet, all the people shall shout with a great shout; and the wall of the city will fall down flat, and the people will go up every man straight ahead."

To God, the conquest of Jericho was already accomplished. It wasn't about a trumpet sound or about the Israelites shouting—anymore than the parting of the Red Sea had

been accomplished by Moses' rod (Ex. 14:16). Rather, the marching and the yelling were about obedience. It was about whether the Israelites would submit to the One who had already delivered the city to them.

And they did.

Hebrews 11:30 records, "By faith the walls of Jericho fell down after they had been encircled for seven days." For generations to come, the children of Israel would ask about the onslaught at Jericho. Their parents would respond that it was by shouts and trumpet blasts that the walls were destroyed because the power of God was with them. No battering ram technology, no modern warfare strategy was necessary—only obedience.

The lesson for you remains that God has a way for you to overcome your obstacles by His power. The Lord's command to you may not be what you expect, but it is exactly what is needed. The victory is already won, and all you have to do to claim it is submit to Him. Are you willing to obey Him?

---

spoken to the people, the seven priests carrying the seven trumpets of rams' horns before the LORD went forward and blew the trumpets; and the ark of the covenant of the LORD followed them.

9 The armed men went before the priests who blew the trumpets, and the rear guard came after the ark, while they continued to blow the trumpets.

10 But Joshua commanded the people, saying, "You shall not shout nor let your voice be heard nor let a word proceed out of your mouth, until the day I tell you, 'Shout!' Then you shall shout!"

11 So he had the ark of the LORD taken around the city, circling *it* once; then they came into the camp and spent the night in the camp.

12 Now Joshua rose early in the morning, and the priests took up the ark of the LORD.

13 The seven priests carrying the seven trumpets of rams' horns before the ark of the LORD went on continually, and blew the trumpets; and the armed men went before them and the rear guard came after the ark of the LORD, while they continued to blow the trumpets.

14 Thus the second day they marched around the city once and returned to the camp; they did so for six days.

15 Then on the seventh day they rose early at the dawning of the day and marched around the city in the same manner seven times; only on that day they marched around the city seven times.

16 At the seventh time, when the priests blew the trumpets, Joshua said to the people, "Shout! For the LORD has given you the city.

17 "The city shall be under the ban, it and all that is in it belongs to the LORD; only Rahab the harlot and all who are with her in the house shall live, because she hid the messengers whom we sent.

18 "But as for you, only keep yourselves from the things under the ban, so that you do not covet *them* and take some of the things under the ban, and make the camp of Israel accursed and bring trouble on it.

19 "But all the silver and gold and articles of bronze and iron are holy to the LORD; they shall go into the treasury of the LORD."

20 So the people shouted, and *priests* blew the trumpets; and when the people heard the sound of the trumpet, the people shouted with a great shout and the wall fell down flat, so that the people went up into the city, every man straight ahead, and they took the city.

21 They utterly destroyed everything in the city, both man and woman, young and old, and ox and sheep and donkey, with the edge of the sword.

22 Joshua said to the two men who had spied out the land, "Go into the harlot's house and bring the woman and all she has out of there, as you have sworn to her."
23 So the young men who were spies went in and brought out Rahab and her father and her mother and her brothers and all she had; they also brought out all her relatives and placed them outside the camp of Israel.
24 They burned the city with fire, and all that was in it. Only the silver and gold, and articles of bronze and iron, they put into the treasury of the house of the LORD.
25 However, Rahab the harlot and her father's household and all she had, Joshua spared; and she has lived in the midst of Israel to this day, for she hid the messengers whom Joshua sent to spy out Jericho.
26 Then Joshua made them take an oath at that time, saying, "Cursed before the LORD is the man who rises up and builds this city Jericho; with *the loss of* his firstborn he shall lay its foundation, and with *the loss of* his youngest son he shall set up its gates."
27 So the LORD was with Joshua, and his fame was in all the land.

Psalm 42:6–11

6 O my God, my soul is in despair
within me;
Therefore I remember You from the
land of the Jordan
And the peaks of Hermon, from
Mount Mizar.
7 Deep calls to deep at the sound of
Your waterfalls;

All Your breakers and Your waves
have rolled over me.
8 The LORD will command His
lovingkindness in the daytime;
And His song will be with me in the
night,
A prayer to the God of my life.
9 I will say to God my rock, "Why
have You forgotten me?
Why do I go mourning because of
the oppression of the enemy?"
10 As a shattering of my bones, my
adversaries revile me,
While they say to me all day long,
"Where is your God?"
11 Why are you in despair, O my soul?
And why have you become
disturbed within me?
Hope in God, for I shall yet praise
Him,
The help of my countenance and my
God.

Proverbs 13:19–21

19 Desire realized is sweet to the soul,
But it is an abomination to fools to
turn away from evil.
20 He who walks with wise men will be
wise,
But the companion of fools will
suffer harm.
21 Adversity pursues sinners,
But the righteous will be rewarded
with prosperity.

Luke 9:18–36

18 And it happened that while He was
praying alone, the disciples were with

LIFE LESSONS

➤ **Joshua 6:26 — *"Cursed before the LORD is the man who rises up and builds this city Jericho."***

The curse of Joshua on Jericho came into force many centuries later in the time of King Ahab, when a man named Hiel rebuilt it—at the very cost prophesied by Joshua (1 Kin. 16:34).

➤ **Psalm 42:11 — *Why are you in despair, O my soul? . . . Hope in God, for I shall yet praise Him.***

Sometimes we do not know why we feel discouraged, down, or sad. It is good at those times to consciously put our hope in God, to draw on His strength, and to anticipate the grace He will show us.

LIFE LESSONS

> Luke 9:18 — *While He was praying alone, the disciples were with Him.*

The disciples often saw Jesus off by Himself, praying to His Father. Eventually, they asked Him to teach them to pray as He did (Luke 11:1). Do our prayer lives inspire others to want to pray as we do?

Him, and He questioned them, saying, "Who do the people say that I am?"

19 They answered and said, "John the Baptist, and others *say* Elijah; but others, that one of the prophets of old has risen again."

20 And He said to them, "But who do you say that I am?" And Peter answered and said, "The Christ of God."

21 But He warned them and instructed *them* not to tell this to anyone,

22 saying, "The Son of Man must suffer many things and be rejected by the elders and chief priests and scribes, and be killed and be raised up on the third day."

23 And He was saying to *them* all, "If anyone wishes to come after Me, he must deny himself, and take up his cross daily and follow Me.

24 "For whoever wishes to save his life will lose it, but whoever loses his life for My sake, he is the one who will save it.

25 "For what is a man profited if he gains the whole world, and loses or forfeits himself?

26 "For whoever is ashamed of Me and My words, the Son of Man will be ashamed of him when He comes in His glory, and *the glory* of the Father and of the holy angels.

27 "But I say to you truthfully, there are some of those standing here who will not taste death until they see the kingdom of God."

28 Some eight days after these sayings, He took along Peter and John and James, and went up on the mountain to pray.

29 And while He was praying, the appearance of His face became different, and His clothing *became* white *and* gleaming.

30 And behold, two men were talking with Him; and they were Moses and Elijah,

31 who, appearing in glory, were speaking of His departure which He was about to accomplish at Jerusalem.

32 Now Peter and his companions had been overcome with sleep; but when they were fully awake, they saw His glory and the two men standing with Him.

33 And as these were leaving Him, Peter said to Jesus, "Master, it is good for us to be here; let us make three tabernacles: one for You, and one for Moses, and one for Elijah"—not realizing what he was saying.

34 While he was saying this, a cloud formed and *began* to overshadow them; and they were afraid as they entered the cloud.

35 Then a voice came out of the cloud, saying, "This is My Son, *My* Chosen One; listen to Him!"

36 And when the voice had spoken, Jesus was found alone. And they kept silent, and reported to no one in those days any of the things which they had seen.

APRIL 9

 Joshua 7:1—8:35

7 BUT the sons of Israel acted unfaithfully in regard to the things under the ban, for Achan, the son of Carmi, the son of Zabdi, the son of Zerah, from the tribe of Judah, took some of the things under the ban, therefore the anger of the LORD burned against the sons of Israel.

2 Now Joshua sent men from Jericho to Ai, which is near Beth-aven, east of Bethel, and said to them, "Go up and spy out the land." So the men went up and spied out Ai.

3 They returned to Joshua and said to him, "Do not let all the people go up; *only* about two or three thousand men need go up to Ai; do not make all the people toil up there, for they are few."

Life Examples:

How Listening Spares Us Pain

JOSHUA 7:1–13

*L*istening does more than give us necessary information. Sometimes it spells the difference between success and failure, joy and sorrow, pleasure and pain. The failure to listen can cause us a great deal of heartache.

A good example of this is found in Joshua 7:1–13. Immediately after God gave the Israelites a great victory at Jericho, Joshua sent a group of soldiers to spy on the little town of Ai. He then commissioned a small force to overthrow it. Although Ai paled in size to Jericho, the Israelites were soundly defeated in a serious setback that caused grief and fear throughout the Israelite camp.

What differed in the two campaigns? First, God gave Joshua an order to defeat Jericho and promised He would give the city into Joshua's hand. Second, God gave Joshua the military strategy by which the victory could be won (Josh. 6). The victory was God's, and He received full glory for it.

The Lord no doubt had a battle plan for Ai, but Joshua didn't ask to hear it. Instead he sent out spies, and when they came back with

a report that Ai could easily be taken, he dispatched a few thousand men without consulting God. He relied solely on human opinion.

In addition, God had commanded the people not to touch the "accursed things" of Jericho—items considered unclean according to the Law, including various personal effects. They were to take only the silver, gold, bronze, and iron vessels for the house of the Lord and were to burn the rest (Josh. 6:18). But Achan chose not to obey the Lord. He brought accursed things into the camp, including a beautiful garment from Shinar (or Babylonia). He also took two hundred shekels of silver and a bar of gold for himself, burying them in the ground beneath his tent. It was only a matter of time before the Lord exposed Achan's sin.

Israel's defeat at Ai was humiliating. Had Joshua listened for the Lord's counsel before moving against the city, no doubt God would have revealed what Achan had done. The problem probably would have been solved, and the assault on Ai would have been successful. Sin robs us of the opportunity to live rightly before God. It entreats us to turn aside to selfish action while ignoring the ways of the Lord. But we do not have to fall for Satan's sinful folly. We have the power of Christ living within us, and we can learn how to walk in God's truth and power.

4 So about three thousand men from the people went up there, but they fled from the men of Ai.
➤ 5 The men of Ai struck down about thirty-six of their men, and pursued them from the gate as far as Shebarim and struck them down on the descent, so the hearts of the people melted and became as water.
6 Then Joshua tore his clothes and fell to the earth on his face before the ark of the LORD until the evening, *both* he and the elders of Israel; and they put dust on their heads.

LIFE LESSONS

➤ **Joshua 7:5 — *The men of Ai struck down about thirty-six of their men.***

*T*hirty-six soldiers of Israel died in a failed attack on the little town of Ai because the people had not inquired of the Lord before they acted. Prayer is life's greatest time saver—and often a life saver as well.

7 Joshua said, "Alas, O Lord GOD, why did You ever bring this people over the Jordan, *only* to deliver us into the hand of the Amorites, to destroy us? If only we had been willing to dwell beyond the Jordan!
8 "O Lord, what can I say since Israel has turned *their* back before their enemies?
9 "For the Canaanites and all the inhabitants of the land will hear of it, and they will surround us and cut off our name from the earth. And what will You do for Your great name?"
10 So the LORD said to Joshua, "Rise up! Why is it that you have fallen on your face?
11 "Israel has sinned, and they have also transgressed My covenant which I commanded them. And they have even taken some of the things under the ban and have both stolen and deceived. Moreover, they have also put *them* among their own things.
12 "Therefore the sons of Israel cannot

stand before their enemies; they turn *their* backs before their enemies, for they have become accursed. I will not be with you anymore unless you destroy the things under the ban from your midst.

➤ 13 "Rise up! Consecrate the people and say, 'Consecrate yourselves for tomorrow, for thus the LORD, the God of Israel, has said, "There are things under the ban in your midst, O Israel. You cannot stand before your enemies until you have removed the things under the ban from your midst."

14 'In the morning then you shall come near by your tribes. And it shall be that the tribe which the LORD takes *by lot* shall come near by families, and the family which the LORD takes shall come near by households, and the household which the LORD takes shall come near man by man.

15 'It shall be that the one who is taken with the things under the ban shall be burned with fire, he and all that belongs to him, because he has transgressed the covenant of the LORD, and because he has committed a disgraceful thing in Israel.'"

16 So Joshua arose early in the morning and brought Israel near by tribes, and the tribe of Judah was taken.

17 He brought the family of Judah near, and he took the family of the Zerahites; and he brought the family of the Zerahites near man by man, and Zabdi was taken.

18 He brought his household near man by man; and Achan, son of Carmi, son of Zabdi, son of Zerah, from the tribe of Judah, was taken.

19 Then Joshua said to Achan, "My son, I implore you, give glory to the LORD, the God of Israel, and give praise to Him; and tell me now what you have done. Do not hide it from me."

20 So Achan answered Joshua and said, "Truly, I have sinned against the LORD, the God of Israel, and this is what I did:

21 when I saw among the spoil a beautiful mantle from Shinar and two hundred shekels of silver and a bar of gold fifty shekels in weight, then I coveted them and took them; and behold, they are concealed in the earth inside my tent with the silver underneath it."

22 So Joshua sent messengers, and they ran to the tent; and behold, it was concealed in his tent with the silver underneath it.

23 They took them from inside the tent and brought them to Joshua and to all the sons of Israel, and they poured them out before the LORD.

24 Then Joshua and all Israel with him, took Achan the son of Zerah, the silver, the mantle, the bar of gold, his sons, his daughters, his oxen, his donkeys, his sheep, his tent and all that belonged to him; and they brought them up to the valley of Achor.

25 Joshua said, "Why have you troubled us? The LORD will trouble you this day." And all Israel stoned them with stones; and they burned them with fire after they had stoned them with stones.

26 They raised over him a great heap of stones that stands to this day, and the LORD turned from the fierceness of His anger. Therefore the name of that place has been called the valley of Achor to this day.

8 NOW the LORD said to Joshua, "Do not fear or be dismayed. Take all the people of war with you and arise, go up to Ai; see, I have given into your hand the king of Ai, his people, his city, and his land.

2 "You shall do to Ai and its king just

LIFE LESSONS

➤ **Joshua 7:13 — "Consecrate yourselves for tomorrow, for thus the LORD, the God of Israel, has said, 'There are things under the ban in your midst, O Israel.'"**

There is a time for prayer, and there is a time for action. Because Joshua missed his time of prayer, God required him to take swift, decisive, and sobering action to rid the camp of sin.

➤ **Joshua 7:21 — "I coveted them and took them."**

Sin begins in the heart. Achan's problems began when he broke the last commandment about coveting, the very sin the apostle Paul noted in himself (Rom. 7:7). It takes God's Spirit within us to create a new, obedient heart.

as you did to Jericho and its king; you shall take only its spoil and its cattle as plunder for yourselves. Set an ambush for the city behind it."

3 So Joshua rose with all the people of war to go up to Ai; and Joshua chose 30,000 men, valiant warriors, and sent them out at night.

4 He commanded them, saying, "See, you are going to ambush the city from behind it. Do not go very far from the city, but all of you be ready.

5 "Then I and all the people who are with me will approach the city. And when they come out to meet us as at the first, we will flee before them.

6 "They will come out after us until we have drawn them away from the city, for they will say, 'They are fleeing before us as at the first.' So we will flee before them.

7 "And you shall rise from your ambush and take possession of the city, for the LORD your God will deliver it into your hand.

8 "Then it will be when you have seized the city, that you shall set the city on fire. You shall do it according to the word of the LORD. See, I have commanded you."

9 So Joshua sent them away, and they went to the place of ambush and remained between Bethel and Ai, on the west side of Ai; but Joshua spent that night among the people.

10 Now Joshua rose early in the morning and mustered the people, and he went up with the elders of Israel before the people to Ai.

11 Then all the people of war who were with him went up and drew near, and arrived in front of the city, and camped on the north side of Ai. Now there was a valley between him and Ai.

12 And he took about 5,000 men and set them in ambush between Bethel and Ai, on the west side of the city.

13 So they stationed the people, all the army that was on the north side of the city, and its rear guard on the west side of the city, and Joshua spent that night in the midst of the valley.

14 It came about when the king of Ai saw it, that the men of the city hurried and rose up early and went out to meet Israel in battle, he and all his people at the appointed place before the desert plain. But he did not know that there was an ambush against him behind the city.

15 Joshua and all Israel pretended to be beaten before them, and fled by the way of the wilderness.

16 And all the people who were in the city were called together to pursue them, and they pursued Joshua and were drawn away from the city.

17 So not a man was left in Ai or Bethel who had not gone out after Israel, and they left the city unguarded and pursued Israel.

18 Then the LORD said to Joshua, "Stretch out the javelin that is in your hand toward Ai, for I will give it into your hand." So Joshua stretched out the javelin that was in his hand toward the city.

19 The men in ambush rose quickly from their place, and when he had stretched out his hand, they ran and entered the city and captured it, and they quickly set the city on fire.

20 When the men of Ai turned back and looked, behold, the smoke of the city ascended to the sky, and they had no place to flee this way or that, for the people who had been fleeing to the wilderness turned against the pursuers.

21 When Joshua and all Israel saw that the men in ambush had captured the city and that the smoke of the city ascended, they turned back and slew the men of Ai.

22 The others came out from the city to encounter them, so that they were trapped in the midst of Israel, some on this side and some on that side; and they slew them until no one was left of those who survived or escaped.

23 But they took alive the king of Ai and brought him to Joshua.

24 Now when Israel had finished killing all the inhabitants of Ai in the field in the wilderness where they pursued them, and all of them were fallen by the edge of the sword until they were destroyed, then all Israel returned to Ai and struck it with the edge of the sword.

25 All who fell that day, both men and women, were 12,000—all the people of Ai.

26 For Joshua did not withdraw his hand with which he stretched out the javelin until he had utterly destroyed all the inhabitants of Ai.

27 Israel took only the cattle and the spoil of that city as plunder for themselves, according to the word of the LORD which He had commanded Joshua.
28 So Joshua burned Ai and made it a heap forever, a desolation until this day.
29 He hanged the king of Ai on a tree until evening; and at sunset Joshua gave command and they took his body down from the tree and threw it at the entrance of the city gate, and raised over it a great heap of stones *that stands* to this day.
30 Then Joshua built an altar to the LORD, the God of Israel, in Mount Ebal,
31 just as Moses the servant of the LORD had commanded the sons of Israel, as it is written in the book of the law of Moses, an altar of uncut stones on which no man had wielded an iron *tool;* and they offered burnt offerings on it to the LORD, and sacrificed peace offerings.
32 He wrote there on the stones a copy of the law of Moses, which he had written, in the presence of the sons of Israel.
33 All Israel with their elders and officers and their judges were standing on both sides of the ark before the Levitical priests who carried the ark of the covenant of the LORD, the stranger as well as the native. Half of them *stood* in front of Mount Gerizim and half of them in front of Mount Ebal, just as Moses the servant of the LORD had given command at first to bless the people of Israel.
34 Then afterward he read all the words of the law, the blessing and the curse, according to all that is written in the book of the law.
35 There was not a word of all that Moses had commanded which Joshua did not read before all the assembly of Israel with the women and the little ones and the strangers who were living among them.

Psalm 43:1–5

43 VINDICATE me, O God, and plead my case against an ungodly nation;
O deliver me from the deceitful and unjust man!
2 For You are the God of my strength; why have You rejected me?

Why do I go mourning because of the oppression of the enemy?
3 O send out Your light and Your truth, let them lead me;
Let them bring me to Your holy hill
And to Your dwelling places.
4 Then I will go to the altar of God, To God my exceeding joy;
And upon the lyre I shall praise You, O God, my God.
5 Why are you in despair, O my soul?
And why are you disturbed within me?
Hope in God, for I shall again praise Him,
The help of my countenance and my God.

Proverbs 13:22, 23

22 A good man leaves an inheritance to his children's children,
And the wealth of the sinner is stored up for the righteous.
23 Abundant food *is in* the fallow ground of the poor,
But it is swept away by injustice.

Luke 9:37–62

37 On the next day, when they came down from the mountain, a large crowd met Him.
38 And a man from the crowd shouted, saying, "Teacher, I beg You to look at my son, for he is my only *boy,*
39 and a spirit seizes him, and he suddenly screams, and it throws him into a

LIFE LESSONS

➤ **Psalm 43:3 — *O send out Your light and Your truth, let them lead me.***

One of the ways God draws us to Himself is by leading us to worship Him with His people. His Word consistently encourages us to gather with other believers to hear His truth and to praise Him together.

convulsion with foaming *at the mouth;* and only with difficulty does it leave him, mauling him *as it leaves.*
40 "I begged Your disciples to cast it out, and they could not."
41 And Jesus answered and said, "You unbelieving and perverted generation, how long shall I be with you and put up with you? Bring your son here."
42 While he was still approaching, the demon slammed him *to the ground* and threw him into a convulsion. But Jesus rebuked the unclean spirit, and healed the boy and gave him back to his father.
43 And they were all amazed at the greatness of God.

But while everyone was marveling at all that He was doing, He said to His disciples,
44 "Let these words sink into your ears; for the Son of Man is going to be delivered into the hands of men."
45 But they did not understand this statement, and it was concealed from them so that they would not perceive it; and they were afraid to ask Him about this statement.
46 An argument started among them as to which of them might be the greatest.
47 But Jesus, knowing what they were thinking in their heart, took a child and stood him by His side,
48 and said to them, "Whoever receives this child in My name receives Me, and whoever receives Me receives Him who sent Me; for the one who is least among all of you, this is the one who is great."
49 John answered and said, "Master, we saw someone casting out demons in Your name; and we tried to prevent him because he does not follow along with us."

50 But Jesus said to him, "Do not hinder *him;* for he who is not against you is for you."
51 When the days were approaching for His ascension, He was determined to go to Jerusalem;
52 and He sent messengers on ahead of Him, and they went and entered a village of the Samaritans to make arrangements for Him.
53 But they did not receive Him, because He was traveling toward Jerusalem.
54 When His disciples James and John saw *this,* they said, "Lord, do You want us to command fire to come down from heaven and consume them?"
55 But He turned and rebuked them, [and said, "You do not know what kind of spirit you are of;
56 for the Son of Man did not come to destroy men's lives, but to save them."] And they went on to another village.
57 As they were going along the road, someone said to Him, "I will follow You wherever You go."
58 And Jesus said to him, "The foxes have holes and the birds of the air *have* nests, but the Son of Man has nowhere to lay His head."
59 And He said to another, "Follow Me." But he said, "Lord, permit me first to go and bury my father."
60 But He said to him, "Allow the dead to bury their own dead; but as for you, go and proclaim everywhere the kingdom of God."
61 Another also said, "I will follow You, Lord; but first permit me to say good-bye to those at home."
62 But Jesus said to him, "No one, after putting his hand to the plow and looking back, is fit for the kingdom of God."

LIFE LESSONS

➤ **Luke 9:43 — *They were all amazed at the greatness of God.***

*T*he majesty of God takes many forms. In this case, it amounted to His irresistible power over an unclean spirit. What do you think of when you consider the majesty of God? What amazes you about Him?

➤ **Luke 9:55 — *"You do not know what kind of spirit you are of."***

*T*he disciples had no idea yet of whom they really were in Christ. Sometimes we too do not act like the new men and women in Christ we really are. However, we are new creations all the same (2 Cor. 5:17).

Joshua 9:1—10:43

9 NOW it came about when all the kings who were beyond the Jordan, in the hill country and in the lowland and on all the coast of the Great Sea toward Lebanon, the Hittite and the Amorite, the Canaanite, the Perizzite, the Hivite and the Jebusite, heard of it,

2 that they gathered themselves together with one accord to fight with Joshua and with Israel.

3 When the inhabitants of Gibeon heard what Joshua had done to Jericho and to Ai,

4 they also acted craftily and set out as envoys, and took worn-out sacks on their donkeys, and wineskins worn-out and torn and mended,

5 and worn-out and patched sandals on their feet, and worn-out clothes on themselves; and all the bread of their provision was dry *and* had become crumbled.

6 They went to Joshua to the camp at Gilgal and said to him and to the men of Israel, "We have come from a far country; now therefore, make a covenant with us."

7 The men of Israel said to the Hivites, "Perhaps you are living within our land; how then shall we make a covenant with you?"

8 But they said to Joshua, "We are your servants." Then Joshua said to them, "Who are you and where do you come from?"

9 They said to him, "Your servants have come from a very far country because of the fame of the LORD your God; for we have heard the report of Him and all that He did in Egypt,

10 and all that He did to the two kings of the Amorites who were beyond the Jordan, to Sihon king of Heshbon and to Og king of Bashan who was at Ashtaroth.

11 "So our elders and all the inhabitants of our country spoke to us, saying, 'Take provisions in your hand for the journey, and go to meet them and say to them,

---

ANSWERS TO LIFE'S QUESTIONS

How should I respond to failure or setbacks?

JOSHUA 7-10

*W*hen the men of Israel returned in defeat from Ai, Joshua needed some answers and so turned immediately to prayer. He tore his garments, an act of grief, and fell on his face in humiliation before the ark of the covenant until nightfall. All of the elders joined him. Joshua cried out to God, "O Lord GOD, why did You ever bring this people over the Jordan, only to deliver us into the hand of the Amorites, to destroy us?" (Josh. 7:7).

Joshua asked the wrong question—a question many of us ask when unexpected trouble strikes. Often our first impulse is to ask why or to blame God for the tragedy or problem overwhelming us. We cry out, "Why me? What did I do to deserve this? Why did You allow me to get in this mess?" Though all of us have asked them, these are not the right questions. When difficulty comes, we need to ask the Lord one question: "What do You want me to learn in this situation?" We can express our hurt or frustration, but the bottom line must always be one of surrender and openness to His will for us.

Sometimes, we may need to change a habit or correct a bad attitude. Perhaps we need to deal with some area of sin or poor judgment. When Joshua stopped pouring out his frustration, God said, "Rise up! Why is it that you have fallen on your face? Israel has sinned, and they have also transgressed My covenant which I commanded them . . . Therefore the sons of Israel cannot stand before their enemies" (Josh. 7:10–12).

When we go to the Lord in prayer, we must be willing to hear what He says. Often, we don't stop to listen to Him. We must learn to wait to hear His response when we voice our petitions.

This is especially true when we pray in the aftermath of a setback or defeat. It is also vitally important when we are tempted to blame God or become angry over our troubles. We must be willing to accept His assessment of our situation, which often includes Him correcting an ungodly behavior or attitude in us.

Once the Lord reveals to us what we need to do, nothing more needs to be said. We must accept God's will and immediately move to obey Him. Our obedience may include asking Him to forgive us and to help us obey Him in the future. It may also require we make amends or take specific actions that will help right the wrong. Whatever the case, our submission to His direction must follow quickly.

"We are your servants; now then, make a covenant with us.'''

12 "This our bread *was* warm *when* we took it for our provisions out of our houses on the day that we left to come to you; but now behold, it is dry and has become crumbled.

13 "These wineskins which we filled were new, and behold, they are torn; and these our clothes and our sandals are worn out because of the very long journey."

14 So the men *of Israel* took some of their provisions, and did not ask for the counsel of the LORD.

15 Joshua made peace with them and made a covenant with them, to let them live; and the leaders of the congregation swore *an oath* to them.

16 It came about at the end of three days after they had made a covenant with them, that they heard that they were neighbors and that they were living within their land.

17 Then the sons of Israel set out and came to their cities on the third day. Now their cities *were* Gibeon and Chephirah and Beeroth and Kiriath-jearim.

18 The sons of Israel did not strike them because the leaders of the congregation had sworn to them by the LORD the God of Israel. And the whole congregation grumbled against the leaders.

➤ 19 But all the leaders said to the whole congregation, "We have sworn to them by the LORD, the God of Israel, and now we cannot touch them.

20 "This we will do to them, even let them live, so that wrath will not be upon us for the oath which we swore to them."

21 The leaders said to them, "Let them live." So they became hewers of wood and drawers of water for the whole congregation, just as the leaders had spoken to them.

22 Then Joshua called for them and spoke to them, saying, "Why have you deceived us, saying, 'We are very far from you,' when you are living within our land?

23 "Now therefore, you are cursed, and you shall never cease being slaves, both hewers of wood and drawers of water for the house of my God."

24 So they answered Joshua and said, "Because it was certainly told your servants that the LORD your God had commanded His servant Moses to give you all the land, and to destroy all the inhabitants of the land before you; therefore we feared greatly for our lives because of you, and have done this thing.

25 "Now behold, we are in your hands; do as it seems good and right in your sight to do to us."

26 Thus he did to them, and delivered them from the hands of the sons of Israel, and they did not kill them.

27 But Joshua made them that day hewers of wood and drawers of water for the congregation and for the altar of the LORD, to this day, in the place which He would choose.

10 NOW it came about when Adoni-zedek king of Jerusalem heard that Joshua had captured Ai, and had utterly destroyed it (just as he had done to Jericho and its king, so he had done to Ai and its king), and that the inhabitants of Gibeon had made peace with Israel and were within their land,

2 that he feared greatly, because Gibeon *was* a great city, like one of the royal cities, and because it was greater than Ai, and all its men *were* mighty.

3 Therefore Adoni-zedek king of Jerusalem sent *word* to Hoham king of Hebron and to Piram king of Jarmuth and to Japhia king of Lachish and to Debir king of Eglon, saying,

4 "Come up to me and help me, and let us attack Gibeon, for it has made peace with Joshua and with the sons of Israel."

5 So the five kings of the Amorites, the king of Jerusalem, the king of Hebron, the king of Jarmuth, the king of Lachish, *and* the king of Eglon, gathered together and went up, they with all their armies, and camped by Gibeon and fought against it.

6 Then the men of Gibeon sent *word* to Joshua to the camp at Gilgal, saying,

"Do not abandon your servants; come up to us quickly and save us and help us, for all the kings of the Amorites that live in the hill country have assembled against us."

7 So Joshua went up from Gilgal, he and all the people of war with him and all the valiant warriors.

8 The LORD said to Joshua, "Do not fear them, for I have given them into your hands; not one of them shall stand before you."

9 So Joshua came upon them suddenly by marching all night from Gilgal.

10 And the LORD confounded them before Israel, and He slew them with a great slaughter at Gibeon, and pursued them by the way of the ascent of Beth-horon and struck them as far as Azekah and Makkedah.

11 As they fled from before Israel, while they were at the descent of Beth-horon, the LORD threw large stones from heaven on them as far as Azekah, and they died; there were more who died from the hailstones than those whom the sons of Israel killed with the sword.

➤ 12 Then Joshua spoke to the LORD in the day when the LORD delivered up the Amorites before the sons of Israel, and he said in the sight of Israel,

"O sun, stand still at Gibeon,
And O moon in the valley of Aijalon."

13 So the sun stood still, and the moon stopped,
Until the nation avenged themselves of their enemies.
Is it not written in the book of Jashar? And the sun stopped in the middle of the sky and did not hasten to go down for about a whole day.

14 There was no day like that before it or after it, when the LORD listened to the voice of a man; for the LORD fought for Israel.

15 Then Joshua and all Israel with him returned to the camp to Gilgal.

16 Now these five kings had fled and hidden themselves in the cave at Makkedah.

17 It was told Joshua, saying, "The five kings have been found hidden in the cave at Makkedah."

18 Joshua said, "Roll large stones against the mouth of the cave, and assign men by it to guard them;

19 but do not stay there yourselves; pursue your enemies and attack them in the rear. Do not allow them to enter their cities, for the LORD your God has delivered them into your hand."

20 It came about when Joshua and the sons of Israel had finished slaying them with a very great slaughter, until they were destroyed, and the survivors who remained of them had entered the fortified cities,

21 that all the people returned to the camp to Joshua at Makkedah in peace. No one uttered a word against any of the sons of Israel.

22 Then Joshua said, "Open the mouth of the cave and bring these five kings out to me from the cave."

23 They did so, and brought these five kings out to him from the cave: the king of Jerusalem, the king of Hebron, the king of Jarmuth, the king of Lachish, and the king of Eglon.

24 When they brought these kings out to Joshua, Joshua called for all the men of Israel, and said to the chiefs of the men of war who had gone with him, "Come near, put your feet on the necks of these kings." So they came near and put their feet on their necks.

25 Joshua then said to them, "Do not ◄ fear or be dismayed! Be strong and courageous, for thus the LORD will do to all your enemies with whom you fight."

LIFE LESSONS

➤ **Joshua 10:12** — *"O sun, stand still at Gibeon, and O moon in the valley of Aijalon."*

*W*e do not know how God accomplished this great miracle; we know only that He did it in response to believing prayer. God invites us to partner with Him in the work of His kingdom, but we must never forget we are very much the junior partners.

➤ **Joshua 10:25** — *"Do not fear or be dismayed! Be strong and courageous, for thus the LORD will do to all your enemies."*

*A*t the beginning of his military career, Joshua needed to be encouraged by his people (Josh. 1:16-18). Here he encourages them. We need each other more than we know.

26 So afterward Joshua struck them and put them to death, and he hanged them on five trees; and they hung on the trees until evening.

27 It came about at sunset that Joshua gave a command, and they took them down from the trees and threw them into the cave where they had hidden themselves, and put large stones over the mouth of the cave, to this very day.

28 Now Joshua captured Makkedah on that day, and struck it and its king with the edge of the sword; he utterly destroyed it and every person who was in it. He left no survivor. Thus he did to the king of Makkedah just as he had done to the king of Jericho.

29 Then Joshua and all Israel with him passed on from Makkedah to Libnah, and fought against Libnah.

30 The LORD gave it also with its king into the hands of Israel, and he struck it and every person who was in it with the edge of the sword. He left no survivor in it. Thus he did to its king just as he had done to the king of Jericho.

31 And Joshua and all Israel with him passed on from Libnah to Lachish, and they camped by it and fought against it.

32 The LORD gave Lachish into the hands of Israel; and he captured it on the second day, and struck it and every person who was in it with the edge of the sword, according to all that he had done to Libnah.

33 Then Horam king of Gezer came up to help Lachish, and Joshua defeated him and his people until he had left him no survivor.

34 And Joshua and all Israel with him passed on from Lachish to Eglon, and they camped by it and fought against it.

35 They captured it on that day and struck it with the edge of the sword; and he utterly destroyed that day every person who was in it, according to all that he had done to Lachish.

36 Then Joshua and all Israel with him went up from Eglon to Hebron, and they fought against it.

37 They captured it and struck it and its king and all its cities and all the persons who were in it with the edge of the sword. He left no survivor, according to all that he had done to Eglon. And he utterly destroyed it and every person who was in it.

38 Then Joshua and all Israel with him returned to Debir, and they fought against it.

39 He captured it and its king and all its cities, and they struck them with the edge of the sword, and utterly destroyed every person who was in it. He left no survivor. Just as he had done to Hebron, so he did to Debir and its king, as he had also done to Libnah and its king.

40 Thus Joshua struck all the land, ⊰ the hill country and the Negev and the lowland and the slopes and all their kings. He left no survivor, but he utterly destroyed all who breathed, just as the LORD, the God of Israel, had commanded.

41 Joshua struck them from Kadesh-barnea even as far as Gaza, and all the country of Goshen even as far as Gibeon.

42 Joshua captured all these kings and their lands at one time, because the LORD, the God of Israel, fought for Israel.

43 So Joshua and all Israel with him returned to the camp at Gilgal.

✦ Psalm 44:1–3

For the choir director.
A Maskil of the sons of Korah.

44 O GOD, we have heard with our ears,
    Our fathers have told us
    The work that You did in their days,
    In the days of old.
2   You with Your own hand drove out the nations;
    Then You planted them;
    You afflicted the peoples,
    Then You spread them abroad.
3   For by their own sword they did not ✳ possess the land,

LIFE LESSONS

➤ **Joshua 10:40** — *Joshua . . . utterly destroyed all who breathed, just as the LORD, the God of Israel, had commanded.*

A story like the annihilation of the Canaanites often makes us wince, but it illustrates God's implacable hatred of sin. The Lord destroyed those nations due to sin (Gen. 15:16; Deut. 9:5). Sin always brings His wrath.

And their own arm did not save
them,
But Your right hand and Your arm
and the light of Your presence,
For You favored them.

Proverbs 13:24, 25

24 He who withholds his rod hates his
son,
But he who loves him disciplines
him diligently.
25 The righteous has enough to satisfy
his appetite,
But the stomach of the wicked is in
need.

Luke 10:1–24

10 NOW after this the Lord appointed
seventy others, and sent them in
pairs ahead of Him to every city and
place where He Himself was going to
come.
2 And He was saying to them, "The
harvest is plentiful, but the laborers are
few; therefore beseech the Lord of the
harvest to send out laborers into His harvest.
3 "Go; behold, I send you out as lambs
in the midst of wolves.
4 "Carry no money belt, no bag, no
shoes; and greet no one on the way.
5 "Whatever house you enter, first say,
'Peace be to this house.'
6 "If a man of peace is there, your
peace will rest on him; but if not, it will
return to you.
7 "Stay in that house, eating and
drinking what they give you; for the

laborer is worthy of his wages. Do not
keep moving from house to house.
8 "Whatever city you enter and they
receive you, eat what is set before you;
9 and heal those in it who are sick, and
say to them, 'The kingdom of God has
come near to you.'
10 "But whatever city you enter and
they do not receive you, go out into its
streets and say,
11 'Even the dust of your city which
clings to our feet we wipe off in protest
against you; yet be sure of this, that the
kingdom of God has come near.'
12 "I say to you, it will be more tolerable in that day for Sodom than for that
city.
13 "Woe to you, Chorazin! Woe to you,
Bethsaida! For if the miracles had been
performed in Tyre and Sidon which
occurred in you, they would have repented long ago, sitting in sackcloth and
ashes.
14 "But it will be more tolerable for
Tyre and Sidon in the judgment than for
you.
15 "And you, Capernaum, will not be
exalted to heaven, will you? You will be
brought down to Hades!
16 "The one who listens to you listens to
Me, and the one who rejects you rejects
Me; and he who rejects Me rejects the
One who sent Me."
17 The seventy returned with joy, saying, "Lord, even the demons are subject
to us in Your name."
18 And He said to them, "I was watching Satan fall from heaven like lightning.
19 "Behold, I have given you authority
to tread on serpents and scorpions, and
over all the power of the enemy, and
nothing will injure you.
20 "Nevertheless do not rejoice in this,
that the spirits are subject to you, but

LIFE LESSONS

➤ **Luke 10:2 — "Beseech the Lord of the
harvest to send out laborers into His harvest."**

The Lord invites us to partner with Him
in expanding His kingdom. The curious fact is, even when he uses an angel
in an evangelistic role, He still leaves
the proclamation of the message to us
(Acts 10).

➤ **Luke 10:20 — "Rejoice that your names
are recorded in heaven."**

We tend to get excited about miracles
like curing cancer and casting out
demons, but the Lord insists the greatest miracle is our salvation. Evangelism is
therefore a greater work than we imagine (John 14:12).

rejoice that your names are recorded in heaven."
21 At that very time He rejoiced greatly in the Holy Spirit, and said, "I praise You, O Father, Lord of heaven and earth, that You have hidden these things from *the* wise and intelligent and have revealed them to infants. Yes, Father, for this way was well-pleasing in Your sight.
22 "All things have been handed over to Me by My Father, and no one knows who the Son is except the Father, and who the Father is except the Son, and anyone to whom the Son wills to reveal *Him*."
23 Turning to the disciples, He said privately, "Blessed *are* the eyes which see the things you see;
24 for I say to you, that many prophets and kings wished to see the things which you see, and did not see *them*, and to hear the things which you hear, and did not hear *them*."

Joshua 11:1—12:24

11 THEN it came about, when Jabin king of Hazor heard *of it*, that he sent to Jobab king of Madon and to the king of Shimron and to the king of Achshaph,
2 and to the kings who were of the north in the hill country, and in the Arabah—south of Chinneroth and in the lowland and on the heights of Dor on the west—
3 to the Canaanite on the east and on the west, and the Amorite and the Hittite and the Perizzite and the Jebusite in the hill country, and the Hivite at the foot of Hermon in the land of Mizpeh.
4 They came out, they and all their armies with them, *as* many people as the sand that is on the seashore, with very many horses and chariots.
5 So all of these kings having agreed to meet, came and encamped together at the waters of Merom, to fight against Israel.
6 Then the LORD said to Joshua, "Do not be afraid because of them, for tomorrow at this time I will deliver all of them slain before Israel; you shall hamstring their horses and burn their chariots with fire."
7 So Joshua and all the people of war with him came upon them suddenly by the waters of Merom, and attacked them.
8 The LORD delivered them into the hand of Israel, so that they defeated them, and pursued them as far as Great Sidon and Misrephoth-maim and the valley of Mizpeh to the east; and they struck them until no survivor was left to them.
9 Joshua did to them as the LORD had told him; he hamstrung their horses and burned their chariots with fire.
10 Then Joshua turned back at that time, and captured Hazor and struck its king with the sword; for Hazor formerly was the head of all these kingdoms.
11 They struck every person who was in it with the edge of the sword, utterly destroying *them*; there was no one left who breathed. And he burned Hazor with fire.
12 Joshua captured all the cities of these kings, and all their kings, and he struck them with the edge of the sword, *and* utterly destroyed them; just as Moses the servant of the LORD had commanded.
13 However, Israel did not burn any cities that stood on their mounds, except Hazor alone, *which* Joshua burned.
14 All the spoil of these cities and the cattle, the sons of Israel took as their plunder; but they struck every man with the edge of the sword, until they had destroyed them. They left no one who breathed.
15 Just as the LORD had commanded Moses his servant, so Moses commanded Joshua, and so Joshua did; he left nothing undone of all that the LORD had commanded Moses.

LIFE LESSONS

➤ **Joshua 11:11** — *They struck every person who was in it with the edge of the sword, utterly destroying them.*

*U*nreserved and total obedience leads to unreserved and total blessing (Josh. 11: 23).

16 Thus Joshua took all that land: the hill country and all the Negev, all that land of Goshen, the lowland, the Arabah, the hill country of Israel and its lowland
17 from Mount Halak, that rises toward Seir, even as far as Baal-gad in the valley of Lebanon at the foot of Mount Hermon. And he captured all their kings and struck them down and put them to death.
18 Joshua waged war a long time with all these kings.
19 There was not a city which made peace with the sons of Israel except the Hivites living in Gibeon; they took them all in battle.
20 For it was of the LORD to harden their hearts, to meet Israel in battle in order that he might utterly destroy them, that they might receive no mercy, but that he might destroy them, just as the LORD had commanded Moses.
21 Then Joshua came at that time and cut off the Anakim from the hill country, from Hebron, from Debir, from Anab and from all the hill country of Judah and from all the hill country of Israel. Joshua utterly destroyed them with their cities.
22 There were no Anakim left in the land of the sons of Israel; only in Gaza, in Gath, and in Ashdod some remained.
23 So Joshua took the whole land, according to all that the LORD had spoken to Moses, and Joshua gave it for an inheritance to Israel according to their divisions by their tribes. Thus the land had rest from war.

12 NOW these are the kings of the land whom the sons of Israel defeated, and whose land they possessed beyond the Jordan toward the sunrise, from the valley of the Arnon as far as Mount Hermon, and all the Arabah to the east:
2 Sihon king of the Amorites, who lived in Heshbon, *and* ruled from Aroer, which is on the edge of the valley of the Arnon, both the middle of the valley and half of Gilead, even as far as the brook Jabbok, the border of the sons of Ammon;
3 and the Arabah as far as the Sea of Chinneroth toward the east, and as far as the sea of the Arabah, *even* the Salt Sea, eastward toward Beth-jeshimoth, and on the south, at the foot of the slopes of Pisgah;

4 and the territory of Og king of Bashan, one of the remnant of Rephaim, who lived at Ashtaroth and at Edrei,
5 and ruled over Mount Hermon and Salecah and all Bashan, as far as the border of the Geshurites and the Maacathites, and half of Gilead, *as far as* the border of Sihon king of Heshbon.
6 Moses the servant of the LORD and the sons of Israel defeated them; and Moses the servant of the LORD gave it to the Reubenites and the Gadites and the half-tribe of Manasseh as a possession.
7 Now these are the kings of the land whom Joshua and the sons of Israel defeated beyond the Jordan toward the west, from Baal-gad in the valley of Lebanon even as far as Mount Halak, which rises toward Seir; and Joshua gave it to the tribes of Israel as a possession according to their divisions,
8 in the hill country, in the lowland, in the Arabah, on the slopes, and in the wilderness, and in the Negev; the Hittite,

---

LIFE LESSONS

➤ **Joshua 11:20 —** *For it was of the LORD to harden their hearts, to meet Israel in battle in order that he might utterly destroy them.*

*O*ur sovereign God hardens the hearts of some so that He might execute His judgment on them. He can take even opposition and use it for His glory and our benefit.

➤ **Joshua 11:23 —** *Joshua took the whole land, according to all that the LORD had spoken to Moses.*

*S*ometimes God doesn't keep His promises when or how we thought He would. God told Moses Israel would take possession of the Promised Land, and that's just what happened—in God's way and in God's timing.

➤ **Joshua 12:6 —** *Moses the servant of the LORD gave it to the Reubenites and the Gadites and the half-tribe of Manasseh.*

*I*t is wise to rehearse the spiritual victories God gives us. We do well to periodically remind ourselves of the truth we already know, so we do not forget and act foolishly (2 Pet. 1:12).

the Amorite and the Canaanite, the Perizzite, the Hivite and the Jebusite:
9 the king of Jericho, one; the king of Ai, which is beside Bethel, one;
10 the king of Jerusalem, one; the king of Hebron, one;
11 the king of Jarmuth, one; the king of Lachish, one;
12 the king of Eglon, one; the king of Gezer, one;
13 the king of Debir, one; the king of Geder, one;
14 the king of Hormah, one; the king of Arad, one;
15 the king of Libnah, one; the king of Adullam, one;
16 the king of Makkedah, one; the king of Bethel, one;
17 the king of Tappuah, one; the king of Hepher, one;
18 the king of Aphek, one; the king of Lasharon, one;
19 the king of Madon, one; the king of Hazor, one;
20 the king of Shimron-meron, one; the king of Achshaph, one;
21 the king of Taanach, one; the king of Megiddo, one;
22 the king of Kedesh, one; the king of Jokneam in Carmel, one;
23 the king of Dor in the heights of Dor, one; the king of Goiim in Gilgal, one;
24 the king of Tirzah, one: in all, thirty-one kings.

◈ Psalm 44:4–19

4 You are my King, O God;
 Command victories for Jacob.
5 Through You we will push back our adversaries;
 Through Your name we will trample down those who rise up against us.
6 For I will not trust in my bow,
 Nor will my sword save me.
7 But You have saved us from our adversaries,
 And You have put to shame those who hate us.
8 In God we have boasted all day long,
 And we will give thanks to Your name forever. Selah.
9 Yet You have rejected *us* and brought us to dishonor,
 And do not go out with our armies.

10 You cause us to turn back from the adversary;
 And those who hate us have taken spoil for themselves.
11 You give us as sheep to be eaten And have scattered us among the nations.
12 You sell Your people cheaply,
 And have not profited by their sale.
13 You make us a reproach to our neighbors,
 A scoffing and a derision to those around us.
14 You make us a byword among the nations,
 A laughingstock among the peoples.
15 All day long my dishonor is before me
 And my humiliation has overwhelmed me,
16 Because of the voice of him who reproaches and reviles,
 Because of the presence of the enemy and the avenger.
17 All this has come upon us, but we have not forgotten You,
 And we have not dealt falsely with Your covenant.
18 Our heart has not turned back,
 And our steps have not deviated from Your way,
19 Yet You have crushed us in a place of jackals
 And covered us with the shadow of death.

◈ Proverbs 14:1, 2

14 THE wise woman builds her house,
 But the foolish tears it down with her own hands.

LIFE LESSONS

➢ **Psalm 44:7 — *You have saved us from our adversaries, and You have put to shame those who hate us.***

Regardless of the resources God gives us, we must not trust in them for success. We must put our hope in Him alone. We should ask Him how to use those resources, but never count on them for deliverance.

2   He who walks in his uprightness
     fears the LORD,
     But he who is devious in his ways
     despises Him.

Luke 10:25–42

25   And a lawyer stood up and put Him
to the test, saying, "Teacher, what shall I
do to inherit eternal life?"
26   And He said to him, "What is written
in the Law? How does it read to you?"
27   And he answered, "YOU SHALL LOVE
THE LORD YOUR GOD WITH ALL YOUR HEART,
AND WITH ALL YOUR SOUL, AND WITH ALL
YOUR STRENGTH, AND WITH ALL YOUR MIND;
AND YOUR NEIGHBOR AS YOURSELF."
28   And He said to him, "You have answered correctly; DO THIS AND YOU WILL
LIVE."
29   But wishing to justify himself, he
said to Jesus, "And who is my neighbor?"
30   Jesus replied and said, "A man was
going down from Jerusalem to Jericho,
and fell among robbers, and they stripped
him and beat him, and went away leaving
him half dead.
31   "And by chance a priest was going
down on that road, and when he saw him,
he passed by on the other side.
32   "Likewise a Levite also, when he
came to the place and saw him, passed by
on the other side.
33   "But a Samaritan, who was on a journey, came upon him; and when he saw
him, he felt compassion,
34   and came to him and bandaged up
his wounds, pouring oil and wine on
them; and he put him on his own beast,

and brought him to an inn and took care
of him.
35   "On the next day he took out two
denarii and gave them to the innkeeper
and said, 'Take care of him; and whatever more you spend, when I return I will
repay you.'
36   "Which of these three do you think
proved to be a neighbor to the man who
fell into the robbers' *hands?*"
37   And he said, "The one who showed
mercy toward him." Then Jesus said to
him, "Go and do the same."
38   Now as they were traveling along, He
entered a village; and a woman named
Martha welcomed Him into her home.
39   She had a sister called Mary, who
was seated at the Lord's feet, listening to
His word.
40   But Martha was distracted with all
her preparations; and she came up *to
Him* and said, "Lord, do You not care that
my sister has left me to do all the serving
alone? Then tell her to help me."
41   But the Lord answered and said to
her, "Martha, Martha, you are worried
and bothered about so many things;
42   but *only* one thing is necessary, for
Mary has chosen the good part, which
shall not be taken away from her."

LIFE LESSONS

➤ Luke 10:42 — *"Mary has chosen the
good part, which shall not be taken
away from her."*

God created us to enjoy a deep and
intimate relationship with Himself.
While works of service are important,
they must never eclipse the fellowship
He wants to experience with each of us.

Life Examples:

MARY of Bethany: A Life Devoted to God

LUKE 10:38–42

Each time we look at the life of Mary
of Bethany through the window
afforded us in the Gospels, we find her at the
feet of Jesus (John 11:32; 12:3). In Mary, Jesus
discerned a heart of devotion and true love
for the things of God (Luke 10:42).
Mary accepted Jesus' words when He

spoke of His death and resurrection, and she
applied them to her life by humbling herself
before God and desiring only to serve the
Lord. Her attitude marked her as a woman
mighty in spirit—and you, too, can have this
trait when you commit yourself to Christ.
Ask the Lord to make you aware of anything that keeps you from sitting at His feet
in wholehearted devotion. Pray for the Holy
Spirit to give you a deep love for God's Word.
This is what Mary cherished—the Word of
God spoken to her. It can be your greatest
source of comfort and hope as well.

Joshua 13:1—14:15

13 NOW Joshua was old *and* advanced in years when the LORD said to him, "You are old *and* advanced in years, and very much of the land remains to be possessed.

2 "This is the land that remains: all the regions *of* the Philistines and all *those of* the Geshurites;

3 from the Shihor which is east of Egypt, even as far as the border of Ekron to the north (it is counted as Canaanite); the five lords of the Philistines: the Gazite, the Ashdodite, the Ashkelonite, the Gittite, the Ekronite; and the Avvite

4 to the south, all the land of the Canaanite, and Mearah that belongs to the Sidonians, as far as Aphek, to the border of the Amorite;

5 and the land of the Gebalite, and all of Lebanon, toward the east, from Baal-gad below Mount Hermon as far as Lebo-hamath.

6 "All the inhabitants of the hill country from Lebanon as far as Misrephoth-maim, all the Sidonians, I will drive them out from before the sons of Israel; only allot it to Israel for an inheritance as I have commanded you.

7 "Now therefore, apportion this land for an inheritance to the nine tribes and the half-tribe of Manasseh."

8 With the other half-tribe, the Reubenites and the Gadites received their inheritance which Moses gave them beyond the Jordan to the east, just as Moses the servant of the LORD gave to them;

9 from Aroer, which is on the edge of the valley of the Arnon, with the city which is in the middle of the valley, and all the plain of Medeba, as far as Dibon;

10 and all the cities of Sihon king of the Amorites, who reigned in Heshbon, as far as the border of the sons of Ammon;

11 and Gilead, and the territory of the Geshurites and Maacathites, and all Mount Hermon, and all Bashan as far as Salecah;

12 all the kingdom of Og in Bashan, who reigned in Ashtaroth and in Edrei (he alone was left of the remnant of the Rephaim); for Moses struck them and dispossessed them.

13 But the sons of Israel did not dispossess the Geshurites or the Maacathites; for Geshur and Maacath live among Israel until this day.

14 Only to the tribe of Levi he did not give an inheritance; the offerings by fire to the LORD, the God of Israel, are their inheritance, as He spoke to him.

15 So Moses gave *an inheritance* to the tribe of the sons of Reuben according to their families.

16 Their territory was from Aroer, which is on the edge of the valley of the Arnon, with the city which is in the middle of the valley and all the plain by Medeba;

17 Heshbon, and all its cities which are on the plain: Dibon and Bamoth-baal and Beth-baal-meon,

18 and Jahaz and Kedemoth and Mephaath,

19 and Kiriathaim and Sibmah and Zereth-shahar on the hill of the valley,

20 and Beth-peor and the slopes of Pisgah and Beth-jeshimoth,

21 even all the cities of the plain and all the kingdom of Sihon king of the Amorites who reigned in Heshbon, whom Moses struck with the chiefs of Midian, Evi and Rekem and Zur and Hur and Reba, the princes of Sihon, who lived in the land.

22 The sons of Israel also killed Balaam the son of Beor, the diviner, with the sword among *the rest of* their slain.

23 The border of the sons of Reuben was the Jordan. This was the inheritance of the sons of Reuben according to their families, the cities and their villages.

24 Moses also gave *an inheritance* to the tribe of Gad, to the sons of Gad, according to their families.

25 Their territory was Jazer, and all the cities of Gilead, and half the land of the sons of Ammon, as far as Aroer which is before Rabbah;

26 and from Heshbon as far as Ramath-mizpeh and Betonim, and from Mahanaim as far as the border of Debir;

27 and in the valley, Beth-haram and Beth-nimrah and Succoth and Zaphon, the rest of the kingdom of Sihon king of Heshbon, with the Jordan as a border, as far as the *lower* end of the Sea of Chinnereth beyond the Jordan to the east.

28 This is the inheritance of the sons of Gad according to their families, the cities and their villages.

29 Moses also gave *an inheritance* to the half-tribe of Manasseh; and it was for the half-tribe of the sons of Manasseh according to their families.

30 Their territory was from Mahanaim, all Bashan, all the kingdom of Og king of Bashan, and all the towns of Jair, which are in Bashan, sixty cities;

31 also half of Gilead, with Ashtaroth and Edrei, the cities of the kingdom of Og in Bashan, *were* for the sons of Machir the son of Manasseh, for half of the sons of Machir according to their families.

32 These are *the territories* which Moses apportioned for an inheritance in the plains of Moab, beyond the Jordan at Jericho to the east.

33 But to the tribe of Levi, Moses did not give an inheritance; the LORD, the God of Israel, is their inheritance, as He had promised to them.

14 NOW these are *the territories* which the sons of Israel inherited in the land of Canaan, which Eleazar the priest, and Joshua the son of Nun, and the heads of the households of the tribes of the sons of Israel apportioned to them for an inheritance,

2 by the lot of their inheritance, as the LORD commanded through Moses, for the nine tribes and the half-tribe.

3 For Moses had given the inheritance of the two tribes and the half-tribe

beyond the Jordan; but he did not give an inheritance to the Levites among them.

4 For the sons of Joseph were two tribes, Manasseh and Ephraim, and they did not give a portion to the Levites in the land, except cities to live in, with their pasture lands for their livestock and for their property.

5 Thus the sons of Israel did just as the LORD had commanded Moses, and they divided the land.

6 Then the sons of Judah drew near to Joshua in Gilgal, and Caleb the son of Jephunneh the Kenizzite said to him, "You know the word which the LORD spoke to Moses the man of God concerning you and me in Kadesh-barnea.

7 "I was forty years old when Moses the servant of the LORD sent me from Kadesh-barnea to spy out the land, and I brought word back to him as *it was* in my heart.

8 "Nevertheless my brethren who went up with me made the heart of the people melt with fear; but I followed the LORD my God fully.

9 "So Moses swore on that day, saying, 'Surely the land on which your foot has trodden will be an inheritance to you and to your children forever, because you have followed the LORD my God fully.'

10 "Now behold, the LORD has let me live, just as He spoke, these forty-five years, from the time that the LORD spoke this word to Moses, when Israel walked in the wilderness; and now behold, I am eighty-five years old today.

11 "I am still as strong today as I was in the day Moses sent me; as my strength was then, so my strength is now, for war and for going out and coming in.

12 "Now then, give me this hill country about which the LORD spoke on that day,

LIFE LESSONS

➤ **Joshua 14:9 — "Surely the land on which your foot has trodden will be an inheritance to you and to your children forever, because you have followed the LORD my God fully."**

*W*hen we choose to wholly follow the Lord, He will move heaven and earth, if necessary, to fulfill His good promises to us.

for you heard on that day that Anakim *were* there, with great fortified cities; perhaps the LORD will be with me, and I will drive them out as the LORD has spoken."

13 So Joshua blessed him and gave Hebron to Caleb the son of Jephunneh for an inheritance.

14 Therefore, Hebron became the inheritance of Caleb the son of Jephunneh the Kenizzite until this day, because he followed the LORD God of Israel fully.

15 Now the name of Hebron was formerly Kiriath-arba; *for Arba* was the greatest man among the Anakim. Then the land had rest from war.

Psalm 44:20–26

20 If we had forgotten the name of our God
Or extended our hands to a strange god,
21 Would not God find this out?
For He knows the secrets of the heart.
22 But for Your sake we are killed all day long;
We are considered as sheep to be slaughtered.
23 Arouse Yourself, why do You sleep, O Lord?
Awake, do not reject us forever.
24 Why do You hide Your face
And forget our affliction and our oppression?
25 For our soul has sunk down into the dust;
Our body cleaves to the earth.
26 Rise up, be our help,
And redeem us for the sake of Your lovingkindness.

LIFE LESSONS

➤ **Psalm 44:22 — *But for Your sake we are killed all day long; we are considered as sheep to be slaughtered.***

*P*aul quotes this unsettling verse in the middle of a passage extolling God's love (Rom. 8:36). Why? Because he wanted us to know that even in the worst of circumstances, God's love for us remains unchanged.

Proverbs 14:3

3 In the mouth of the foolish is a rod for *his* back,
But the lips of the wise will protect them.

Luke 11:1–28

11 IT happened that while Jesus was praying in a certain place, after He had finished, one of His disciples said to Him, "Lord, teach us to pray just as John also taught his disciples."
2 And He said to them, "When you pray, say:
'Father, hallowed be Your name.
Your kingdom come.
3 'Give us each day our daily bread.
4 'And forgive us our sins,
For we ourselves also forgive everyone who is indebted to us.
And lead us not into temptation.'"
5 Then He said to them, "Suppose one of you has a friend, and goes to him at midnight and says to him, 'Friend, lend me three loaves;
6 for a friend of mine has come to me from a journey, and I have nothing to set before him';
7 and from inside he answers and says, 'Do not bother me; the door has already been shut and my children and I are in bed; I cannot get up and give you *anything*.'
8 "I tell you, even though he will not get up and give him *anything* because he is his friend, yet because of his persistence he will get up and give him as much as he needs.
9 "So I say to you, ask, and it will be given to you; seek, and you will find; knock, and it will be opened to you.
10 "For everyone who asks, receives; and he who seeks, finds; and to him who knocks, it will be opened.
11 "Now suppose one of you fathers is asked by his son for a fish; he will not give him a snake instead of a fish, will he?
12 "Or *if* he is asked for an egg, he will not give him a scorpion, will he?
13 "If you then, being evil, know how

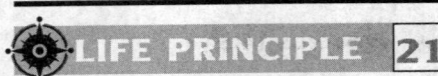

LIFE PRINCIPLE 21

OBEDIENCE ALWAYS BRINGS BLESSING.

LUKE 11:28

*The Lord's simple requests often serve as step-ping-stones to life's most wonderful blessings. Simon Peter illustrates what can happen when we say yes to God.

One day a large crowd pressed around Jesus while He preached (Luke 5:1–11). The Lord wanted to use Peter's boat as a floating platform from which to address the multitude, so He asked the future apostle to push the vessel out a little way from shore (v. 3). This was not in itself a particularly remarkable request, but Peter's compliance paved the way for a life-changing blessing. From his example, we also learn how essential it is to obey God, even in the smallest matters.

The noisy crowd received the first blessing of Peter's obedience; the people could now clearly hear Jesus' words. At the conclusion of the lesson, the Lord said to Peter, "Put out into the deep water and let down your nets for a catch" (v. 4)—a second opportunity to say yes or no. But this time, Peter may have felt tempted to decline. After all, he was a seasoned fisherman. He had worked the entire night for a catch but had returned empty-handed. Now this young teacher—a carpenter, by the way, not a fisher-man—was asking him to go fishing again?

Peter's reply demonstrates the beginning of a lifetime of faith in God. He said, "Master, we worked hard all night and caught nothing, but *I will* do as You say and let down the nets" (v. 50, emphasis added). The soon-to-be disciple chose to obey the Lord and to leave the consequences of his decision to Him.

Notice what happened as a result of Peter's obe-dience—Jesus demonstrated His power and sover-eignty. Peter and his partners may have started the day off thinking their efforts had yielded nothing. But they ended it in complete amazement because they pulled in not one but *two* overflowing boatloads of fish (v. 7). Saying yes to the Lord's request resulted in a miracle that transformed not only one fisherman's life, but also the lives of the entire group.

Consider three reasons why obedience is critical to the successful Christian life:

1. Obeying God in small matters is an essential step in receiving God's greatest blessings.

Suppose Peter had said, "Look, I'm busy clean-ing my nets right now. I can't help You because I'm going fishing again tonight." Or he could have said, "Why don't You ask to use that other boat over there?" Or, "I've already been fishing today; it would be a waste of time to go again." If Peter had said anything other than yes, he would have missed the greatest fishing experience of his life. But because of Peter's obedience, the Lord arranged a miracle he would never forget.

Often, God's greatest blessings come as a result of our willingness to do something that appears very insignificant. So ask yourself, "Has God been chal-lenging me to do something seemingly unimportant that I have not yet made an effort to accomplish? Is there anything I have rationalized by saying, 'It's too difficult,' 'I don't want to,' or 'I have to pray about it first'"?

2. Our obedience always benefits others.

Think of how many people were blessed by Peter's obedience. Not only could the crowd see the Lord and hear His lesson, but Jesus Himself also benefited—preaching from the boat enabled him to sit down in comfort while He spoke (v. 3). Then, of course, Peter's friends had a very profitable day—they took in two vessels so full of fish that both began to sink. More importantly, they had the opportunity to witness the Lord's supernatural provision.

God often rewards others—in particular, those closest to us—as a result of our obedience. For example, when a father obeys the Lord, his entire family reaps the reward of God's blessings. Likewise, a child's obedience will bless his or her parents. This does not mean those who choose to disobey the Lord will escape His discipline because of some-one else's godly walk. His call to obedience always demands our response. However, when we live obe-dient lives, those who know and love us will sense the peace and joy He has given us. Instead of conflict, there will be contentment—and that is just one part of experiencing God's goodness.

3. When we obey God, we will never be disappointed.

Peter no doubt assumed that Jesus' fishing instruc-tions would amount to a waste of time. But when he complied with the Lord's simple request, Christ brought about a miracle that gripped the disciple with amazement. Jesus turned an empty boat into a full one. We, like Peter, must recognize obeying God is *always* the wisest course of action. He can also take our emptiness—whether related to finances, rela-tionships, or careers—and change it into something splendid.

Perhaps you have hesitated to obey God because you fear the consequences of your decision. But the Lord's command is for you to fear Him above all else. The same sovereign, omnipotent God who keeps your heart beating and the planets orbiting is more than able to handle the results of your obedi-ence. When He tells you to do something and you know without a doubt it is His will, then you need to obey based solely on who is doing the talking.

When you choose to obey the Lord, He will bless you. This is because obedience *always* leads to bless-ing. I have always told people who say they do not understand why God is asking them to do a certain thing that if they will obey Him, He will reward them with a sense of peace and joy that compares to nothing this world has to offer. Therefore, set a goal to obey the Lord, and watch Him work in your life. ◀

23 and Kedesh and Hazor and Ithnan,
24 Ziph and Telem and Bealoth,
25 and Hazor-hadattah and Kerioth-hezron (that is, Hazor),
26 Amam and Shema and Moladah,
27 and Hazar-gaddah and Heshmon and Beth-pelet,
28 and Hazar-shual and Beersheba and Biziothiah,
29 Baalah and Iim and Ezem,
30 and Eltolad and Chesil and Hormah,
31 and Ziklag and Madmannah and Sansannah,
32 and Lebaoth and Shilhim and Ain and Rimmon; in all, twenty-nine cities with their villages.
33 In the lowland: Eshtaol and Zorah and Ashnah,
34 and Zanoah and En-gannim, Tappuah and Enam,
35 Jarmuth and Adullam, Socoh and Azekah,
36 and Shaaraim and Adithaim and Gederah and Gederothaim; fourteen cities with their villages.
37 Zenan and Hadashah and Migdal-gad,
38 and Dilean and Mizpeh and Joktheel,
39 Lachish and Bozkath and Eglon,
40 and Cabbon and Lahmas and Chitlish,
41 and Gederoth, Beth-dagon and Naamah and Makkedah; sixteen cities with their villages.
42 Libnah and Ether and Ashan,
43 and Iphtah and Ashnah and Nezib,
44 and Keilah and Achzib and Mareshah; nine cities with their villages.
45 Ekron, with its towns and its villages;
46 from Ekron even to the sea, all that were by the side of Ashdod, with their villages.
47 Ashdod, its towns and its villages; Gaza, its towns and its villages; as far as the brook of Egypt and the Great Sea, even its coastline.
48 In the hill country: Shamir and Jattir and Socoh,
49 and Dannah and Kiriath-sannah (that is, Debir),
50 and Anab and Eshtemoh and Anim,
51 and Goshen and Holon and Giloh; eleven cities with their villages.
52 Arab and Dumah and Eshan,

53 and Janum and Beth-tappuah and Aphekah,
54 and Humtah and Kiriath-arba (that is, Hebron), and Zior; nine cities with their villages.
55 Maon, Carmel and Ziph and Juttah,
56 and Jezreel and Jokdeam and Zanoah,
57 Kain, Gibeah and Timnah; ten cities with their villages.
58 Halhul, Beth-zur and Gedor,
59 and Maarath and Beth-anoth and Eltekon; six cities with their villages.
60 Kiriath-baal (that is, Kiriath-jearim), and Rabbah; two cities with their villages.
61 In the wilderness: Beth-arabah, Middin and Secacah,
62 and Nibshan and the City of Salt and Engedi; six cities with their villages.
63 Now as for the Jebusites, the inhabitants of Jerusalem, the sons of Judah could not drive them out; so the Jebusites live with the sons of Judah at Jerusalem until this day.

16 THEN the lot for the sons of Joseph went from the Jordan at Jericho to the waters of Jericho on the east into the wilderness, going up from Jericho through the hill country to Bethel.
2 It went from Bethel to Luz, and continued to the border of the Archites at Ataroth.
3 It went down westward to the territory of the Japhletites, as far as the territory of lower Beth-horon even to Gezer, and it ended at the sea.
4 The sons of Joseph, Manasseh and Ephraim, received their inheritance.
5 Now this was the territory of the sons of Ephraim according to their families: the border of their inheritance eastward was Ataroth-addar, as far as upper Beth-horon.
6 Then the border went westward at

LIFE LESSONS

➤ Joshua 15:63 — *Now as for the Jebusites, the inhabitants of Jerusalem, the sons of Judah could not drive them out.*

The Jebusite city of Jerusalem did not fall to the Israelites until the time of David (2 Sam. 5:6, 7). Sometimes God waits to fulfill His promises; but He always keeps His word in the end.

Michmethath on the north, and the border turned about eastward to Taanath-shiloh and continued *beyond* it to the east of Janoah.

7 It went down from Janoah to Ataroth and to Naarah, then reached Jericho and came out at the Jordan.

8 From Tappuah the border continued westward to the brook of Kanah, and it ended at the sea. This is the inheritance of the tribe of the sons of Ephraim according to their families,

9 *together* with the cities which were set apart for the sons of Ephraim in the midst of the inheritance of the sons of Manasseh, all the cities with their villages.

10 But they did not drive out the Canaanites who lived in Gezer, so the Canaanites live in the midst of Ephraim to this day, and they became forced laborers.

Psalm 45:1–5

For the choir director; according to the Shoshannim. A Maskil of the sons of Korah. A Song of Love.

45 MY heart overflows with a good theme;
I address my verses to the King;
My tongue is the pen of a ready writer.

2 You are fairer than the sons of men;
Grace is poured upon Your lips;
Therefore God has blessed You forever.

3 Gird Your sword on *Your* thigh,
O Mighty One,
In Your splendor and Your majesty!

4 And in Your majesty ride on victoriously,
For the cause of truth and meekness *and* righteousness;
Let Your right hand teach You awesome things.

5 Your arrows are sharp;
The peoples fall under You;
Your arrows are in the heart of the King's enemies.

Proverbs 14:4, 5

4 Where no oxen are, the manger is clean,

But much revenue *comes* by the strength of the ox.

5 A trustworthy witness will not lie,
But a false witness utters lies.

Luke 11:29–54

29 As the crowds were increasing, He began to say, "This generation is a wicked generation; it seeks for a sign, and *yet* no sign will be given to it but the sign of Jonah.

30 "For just as Jonah became a sign to the Ninevites, so will the Son of Man be to this generation.

31 "The Queen of the South will rise up with the men of this generation at the judgment and condemn them, because she came from the ends of the earth to hear the wisdom of Solomon; and behold, something greater than Solomon is here.

32 "The men of Nineveh will stand up with this generation at the judgment and condemn it, because they repented at the preaching of Jonah; and behold, something greater than Jonah is here.

33 "No one, after lighting a lamp, puts it away in a cellar nor under a basket, but on the lampstand, so that those who enter may see the light.

34 "The eye is the lamp of your body; when your eye is clear, your whole body also is full of light; but when it is bad, your body also is full of darkness.

35 "Then watch out that the light in you is not darkness.

36 "If therefore your whole body is full of light, with no dark part in it, it will be wholly illumined, as when the lamp illumines you with its rays."

37 Now when He had spoken, a Pharisee *asked Him to have lunch with him;

LIFE LESSONS

➤ **Luke 11:35 — *"Then watch out that the light in you is not darkness."***

*H*ow can the light within us actually be darkness? It happens when we mistake religious dogmatism and man-made tradition for genuine spirituality—"zeal for God, but not in accordance with knowledge" (Rom. 10:2).

and He went in, and reclined *at the table.*

38 When the Pharisee saw it, he was surprised that He had not first ceremonially washed before the meal.

39 But the Lord said to him, "Now you Pharisees clean the outside of the cup and of the platter; but inside of you, you are full of robbery and wickedness.

40 "You foolish ones, did not He who made the outside make the inside also?

41 "But give that which is within as charity, and then all things are clean for you.

42 "But woe to you Pharisees! For you pay tithe of mint and rue and every *kind of* garden herb, and *yet* disregard justice and the love of God; but these are the things you should have done without neglecting the others.

43 "Woe to you Pharisees! For you love the chief seats in the synagogues and the respectful greetings in the market places.

44 "Woe to you! For you are like concealed tombs, and the people who walk over *them* are unaware *of it.*"

➤ 45 One of the lawyers *said to Him in reply, "Teacher, when You say this, You insult us too."

46 But He said, "Woe to you lawyers as well! For you weigh men down with burdens hard to bear, while you yourselves will not even touch the burdens with one of your fingers.

47 "Woe to you! For you build the tombs of the prophets, and *it was* your fathers *who* killed them.

48 "So you are witnesses and approve the deeds of your fathers; because it was they who killed them, and you build *their* tombs.

49 "For this reason also the wisdom of God said, 'I will send to them prophets and apostles, and *some* of them they will kill and *some* they will persecute,

50 so that the blood of all the prophets, shed since the foundation of the world, may be charged against this generation,

51 from the blood of Abel to the blood of Zechariah, who was killed between the altar and the house *of God;* yes, I tell you, it shall be charged against this generation.'

52 "Woe to you lawyers! For you have taken away the key of knowledge; you yourselves did not enter, and you hindered those who were entering."

53 When He left there, the scribes and the Pharisees began to be very hostile and to question Him closely on many subjects,

54 plotting against Him to catch *Him* in something He might say.

Joshua 17:1—18:28

17 NOW *this* was the lot for the tribe of Manasseh, for he was the first-born of Joseph. To Machir the firstborn of Manasseh, the father of Gilead, were allotted Gilead and Bashan, because he was a man of war.

2 So *the lot* was *made* for the rest of the sons of Manasseh according to their families: for the sons of Abiezer and for the sons of Helek and for the sons of Asriel and for the sons of Shechem and for the sons of Hepher and for the sons of Shemida; these *were* the male descendants of Manasseh the son of Joseph according to their families.

3 However, Zelophehad, the son of Hepher, the son of Gilead, the son of Machir, the son of Manasseh, had no sons, only daughters; and these are the names of his daughters: Mahlah and Noah, Hoglah, Milcah and Tirzah.

4 They came near before Eleazar the ➤ priest and before Joshua the son of Nun

and before the leaders, saying, "The LORD commanded Moses to give us an inheritance among our brothers." So according to the command of the LORD he gave them an inheritance among their father's brothers.

5 Thus there fell ten portions to Manasseh, besides the land of Gilead and Bashan, which is beyond the Jordan, 6 because the daughters of Manasseh received an inheritance among his sons. And the land of Gilead belonged to the rest of the sons of Manasseh.

7 The border of Manasseh ran from Asher to Michmethath which was east of Shechem; then the border went southward to the inhabitants of En-tappuah. 8 The land of Tappuah belonged to Manasseh, but Tappuah on the border of Manasseh *belonged* to the sons of Ephraim.

9 The border went down to the brook of Kanah, southward of the brook (these cities *belonged* to Ephraim among the cities of Manasseh), and the border of Manasseh *was* on the north side of the brook and it ended at the sea.

10 The south side *belonged* to Ephraim and the north side to Manasseh, and the sea was their border; and they reached to Asher on the north and to Issachar on the east.

11 In Issachar and in Asher, Manasseh had Beth-shean and its towns and Ibleam and its towns, and the inhabitants of Dor and its towns, and the inhabitants of En-dor and its towns, and the inhabitants of Taanach and its towns, and the inhabitants of Megiddo and its towns, the third is Napheth.

12 But the sons of Manasseh could not take possession of these cities, because the Canaanites persisted in living in that land.

13 It came about when the sons of Israel became strong, they put the Canaanites to forced labor, but they did not drive them out completely.

14 Then the sons of Joseph spoke to Joshua, saying, "Why have you given me only one lot and one portion for an inheritance, since I am a numerous people whom the LORD has thus far blessed?"

15 Joshua said to them, "If you are a numerous people, go up to the forest and clear a place for yourself there in the land of the Perizzites and of the Rephaim, since the hill country of Ephraim is too narrow for you."

16 The sons of Joseph said, "The hill country is not enough for us, and all the Canaanites who live in the valley land have chariots of iron, both those who are in Beth-shean and its towns and those who are in the valley of Jezreel."

17 Joshua spoke to the house of Joseph, to Ephraim and Manasseh, saying, "You are a numerous people and have great power; you shall not have one lot *only*, 18 but the hill country shall be yours. ⊰ For though it is a forest, you shall clear it, and to its farthest borders it shall be yours; for you shall drive out the Canaanites, even though they have chariots of iron *and* though they are strong."

18 THEN the whole congregation of the sons of Israel assembled themselves at Shiloh, and set up the tent of meeting there; and the land was subdued before them.

2 There remained among the sons of Israel seven tribes who had not divided their inheritance.

3 So Joshua said to the sons of Israel, ⊰ "How long will you put off entering to take possession of the land which the LORD, the God of your fathers, has given you?

LIFE LESSONS

➢ **Joshua 17:4 — "The LORD commanded Moses to give us an inheritance among our brothers."**

*W*e should never hesitate to come before the Lord and ask Him to do what He has promised, even if it seems out of the ordinary. James tells us, "You do not have because you do not ask" (James 4:2).

➢ **Joshua 17:18 — "The hill country shall be yours . . . for you shall drive out the Canaanites."**

*I*f we are to fully benefit from the promises of God, we have our own work to do. God requires His people to put forth great effort in their lives of faith (1 Cor. 4:12).

LIFE LESSONS

➢ Joshua 18:3 — *"How long will you put off entering to take possession of the land which the LORD, the God of your fathers, has given you?"*

What keeps you from claiming the territory God wants to give you? What is holding you back from acting on His promises? How long will you neglect to possess the land God has given to you?

4 "Provide for yourselves three men from each tribe that I may send them, and that they may arise and walk through the land and write a description of it according to their inheritance; then they shall return to me.

5 "They shall divide it into seven portions; Judah shall stay in its territory on the south, and the house of Joseph shall stay in their territory on the north.

6 "You shall describe the land in seven divisions, and bring *the description* here to me. I will cast lots for you here before the LORD our God.

7 "For the Levites have no portion among you, because the priesthood of the LORD is their inheritance. Gad and Reuben and the half-tribe of Manasseh also have received their inheritance eastward beyond the Jordan, which Moses the servant of the LORD gave them."

8 Then the men arose and went, and Joshua commanded those who went to describe the land, saying, "Go and walk through the land and describe it, and return to me; then I will cast lots for you here before the LORD in Shiloh."

9 So the men went and passed through the land, and described it by cities in seven divisions in a book; and they came to Joshua to the camp at Shiloh.

10 And Joshua cast lots for them in Shiloh before the LORD, and there Joshua divided the land to the sons of Israel according to their divisions.

11 Now the lot of the tribe of the sons of Benjamin came up according to their families, and the territory of their lot lay between the sons of Judah and the sons of Joseph.

12 Their border on the north side was from the Jordan, then the border went up to the side of Jericho on the north, and went up through the hill country westward, and it ended at the wilderness of Beth-aven.

13 From there the border continued to Luz, to the side of Luz (that is, Bethel) southward; and the border went down to Ataroth-addar, near the hill which *lies* on the south of lower Beth-horon.

14 The border extended *from there* and turned round on the west side southward, from the hill which *lies* before Beth-horon southward; and it ended at Kiriath-baal (that is, Kiriath-jearim), a city of the sons of Judah. This *was* the west side.

15 Then the south side *was* from the edge of Kiriath-jearim, and the border went westward and went to the fountain of the waters of Nephtoah.

16 The border went down to the edge of the hill which is in the valley of Ben-hinnom, which is in the valley of Rephaim northward; and it went down to the valley of Hinnom, to the slope of the Jebusite southward, and went down to En-rogel.

17 It extended northward and went to En-shemesh and went to Geliloth, which is opposite the ascent of Adummim, and it went down to the stone of Bohan the son of Reuben.

18 It continued to the side in front of the Arabah northward and went down to the Arabah.

19 The border continued to the side of Beth-hoglah northward; and the border ended at the north bay of the Salt Sea, at the south end of the Jordan. This *was* the south border.

20 Moreover, the Jordan was its border on the east side. This *was* the inheritance of the sons of Benjamin, according to their families *and* according to its borders all around.

21 Now the cities of the tribe of the sons of Benjamin according to their families were Jericho and Beth-hoglah and Emek-keziz,

22 and Beth-arabah and Zemaraim and Bethel,

23 and Avvim and Parah and Ophrah,

24 and Chephar-ammoni and Ophni and Geba; twelve cities with their villages.

25 Gibeon and Ramah and Beeroth,

26 and Mizpeh and Chephirah and Mozah,

27   and Rekem and Irpeel and Taralah,
28   and Zelah, Haeleph and the Jebusite
(that is, Jerusalem), Gibeah, Kiriath;
fourteen cities with their villages. This is
the inheritance of the sons of Benjamin
according to their families.

Psalm 45:6–17

6   Your throne, O God, is forever and
     ever;
     A scepter of uprightness is the
     scepter of Your kingdom.
➤ 7 You have loved righteousness and
     hated wickedness;
     Therefore God, Your God, has
     anointed You
     With the oil of joy above Your
     fellows.
8   All Your garments are *fragrant
     with* myrrh and aloes *and*
     cassia;
     Out of ivory palaces stringed
     instruments have made You
     glad.
9   Kings' daughters are among Your
     noble ladies;
     At Your right hand stands the queen
     in gold from Ophir.
10   Listen, O daughter, give attention
     and incline your ear:
     Forget your people and your father's
     house;
11   Then the King will desire your
     beauty.
     Because He is your Lord, bow down
     to Him.
12   The daughter of Tyre *will come*
     with a gift;
     The rich among the people will seek
     your favor.

LIFE LESSONS

➤ **Psalm 45:7 —** *You have loved righteousness and hated wickedness; therefore God, Your God, has anointed You
with the oil of joy.*

*I*t really is *not* more fun to do evil
than to do good. When we willingly
obey God, He rewards our obedience
with "the oil of joy," a satisfaction and
joy that penetrates all the way to the
heart.

13   The King's daughter is all glorious
     within;
     Her clothing is interwoven with
     gold.
14   She will be led to the King in
     embroidered work;
     The virgins, her companions who
     follow her,
     Will be brought to You.
15   They will be led forth with gladness
     and rejoicing;
     They will enter into the King's
     palace.
16   In place of your fathers will be your
     sons;
     You shall make them princes in all
     the earth.
17   I will cause Your name to be
     remembered in all generations;
     Therefore the peoples will give You
     thanks forever and ever.

Proverbs 14:6

6   A scoffer seeks wisdom and *finds*
     none,
     But knowledge is easy to one who
     has understanding.

Luke 12:1–34

12 UNDER these circumstances, after
   so many thousands of people had
gathered together that they were stepping on one another, He began saying
to His disciples first *of all,* "Beware of
the leaven of the Pharisees, which is
hypocrisy.
2   "But there is nothing covered up that
will not be revealed, and hidden that will
not be known.
3   "Accordingly, whatever you have
said in the dark will be heard in the light,
and what you have whispered in the
inner rooms will be proclaimed upon the
housetops.
4   "I say to you, My friends, do not be
afraid of those who kill the body and
after that have no more that they can do.
5   "But I will warn you whom to fear:
fear the One who, after He has killed, has
authority to cast into hell; yes, I tell you,
fear Him!

➤ 6 "Are not five sparrows sold for two cents? *Yet* not one of them is forgotten before God.

7 "Indeed, the very hairs of your head are all numbered. Do not fear; you are more valuable than many sparrows.

8 "And I say to you, everyone who confesses Me before men, the Son of Man will confess him also before the angels of God;

9 but he who denies Me before men will be denied before the angels of God.

10 "And everyone who speaks a word against the Son of Man, it will be forgiven him; but he who blasphemes against the Holy Spirit, it will not be forgiven him.

11 "When they bring you before the synagogues and the rulers and the authorities, do not worry about how or what you are to speak in your defense, or what you are to say;

12 for the Holy Spirit will teach you in that very hour what you ought to say."

13 Someone in the crowd said to Him, "Teacher, tell my brother to divide the *family* inheritance with me."

14 But He said to him, "Man, who appointed Me a judge or arbitrator over you?"

➤ 15 Then He said to them, "Beware, and be on your guard against every form of greed; for not *even* when one has an abundance does his life consist of his possessions."

16 And He told them a parable, saying, "The land of a rich man was very productive.

17 "And he began reasoning to himself, saying, 'What shall I do, since I have no place to store my crops?'

18 "Then he said, 'This is what I will do: I will tear down my barns and build larger ones, and there I will store all my grain and my goods.

19 'And I will say to my soul, "Soul, you have many goods laid up for many years *to come*; take your ease, eat, drink *and* be merry."'

20 "But God said to him, 'You fool! This *very* night your soul is required of you; and *now* who will own what you have prepared?'

21 "So is the man who stores up treasure for himself, and is not rich toward God."

22 And He said to His disciples, "For this reason I say to you, do not worry about *your* life, *as to* what you will eat; nor for your body, *as to* what you will put on.

23 "For life is more than food, and the body more than clothing.

24 "Consider the ravens, for they neither sow nor reap; they have no storeroom nor barn, and *yet* God feeds them; how much more valuable you are than the birds!

25 "And which of you by worrying can add a *single* hour to his life's span?

26 "If then you cannot do even a very little thing, why do you worry about other matters?

27 "Consider the lilies, how they grow: they neither toil nor spin; but I tell you, not even Solomon in all his glory clothed himself like one of these.

28 "But if God so clothes the grass in the field, which is *alive* today and tomorrow is thrown into the furnace, how much more *will He clothe* you? You men of little faith!

29 "And do not seek what you will eat and what you will drink, and do not keep worrying.

30 "For all these things the nations of the world eagerly seek; but your Father knows that you need these things.

31 "But seek His kingdom, and these things will be added to you.

LIFE LESSONS

➤ **Luke 12:6** — *"Are not five sparrows sold for two cents? Yet not one of them is forgotten before God."*

The Lord remembers even the sparrows that end up for sale at the market and knows their plight. You can trust He knows your situation and how best to deliver you from your troubles. Trust Him.

➤ **Luke 12:15** — *"Beware, and be on your guard against every form of greed; for not even when one has an abundance does his life consist of his possessions."*

True satisfaction in life flows out of fulfilling the purpose for which we were created—to enjoy an intimate relationship with God. As a substitute for the Lord, acquiring material excess only makes the heart feel hollow (Eccl. 6:2).

WHAT THE BIBLE SAYS ABOUT

Money and Worries

Luke 12:13–34

*E*very day you face decisions that express what you really believe about God—you're constantly making choices that demonstrate who and what you truly depend upon for your security. Of course, for most people, nothing represents a breach in security or inspires fear as quickly as concerns over money. Of all Satan's schemes, his deception concerning wealth has become one of the most successful in turning people's hearts away from God. First Timothy 6:10 reminds us, "For the love of money is a root of all sorts of evil, and some by longing for it have wandered away from the faith and pierced themselves with many griefs."

Satan will frequently use the perceived need for material security against you—motivating you through fear of the future to choose against trusting God. This can happen in many different ways, but it generally involves clear-cut (albeit difficult) choices that will either honor God or temporarily calm your fears. On one side is God's way—the path He has directed you to through His Word and Spirit. On the other side is the "common sense" choice—the option that appeals to earthly wisdom.

For the man in the crowd, the issue was his inheritance. In Luke 12:13 he said, "Teacher, tell my brother to divide the family inheritance with me." Although the man may have had a right to the inheritance, Jesus saw right away it was a stumbling block to him—it was blind-ing him to the truly important issues. Not only was the man willing to divide his family over his claim, but his desire for his portion of the inheritance was impeding him from receiving the salvation Jesus was preaching. The Lord was there to offer him eternal life, and all he could think about was the money owed to him.

That is why Jesus responded, "Beware, and be on your guard against every form of greed; for not even when one has an abundance does his life consist of his possessions" (Luke 12:15). Though here on earth it may seem like money moves the world, it doesn't. God does. Your wealth—or lack thereof—has nothing to do with your security. It is only a mirage of a world that is fading away (James 1:11; 1 Pet. 1:24). Only God keeps you truly safe. He is the one who feeds you and clothes you (Luke 12:22–29). He is the One who protects your life and will one day require it of you (Luke 12:20).

Whenever you are confronted with a dilemma about monetary issues, do what honors God. Always remember Jesus' words of encouragement: "Do not be afraid, little flock, for your Father has chosen gladly to give you the kingdom. Sell your possessions and give to charity; make yourselves money belts which do not wear out, an unfailing treasure in heaven, where no thief comes near nor moth destroys. For where your treasure is, there your heart will be also" (Luke 12:32–34).

You are worth so much more than the assets in your portfolio, and your Father knows your needs even before you ask Him. Therefore, do not fear. Honor God and trust Him to be your security in every situation. When He is your treasure, you truly have everything you need.

---

32 "Do not be afraid, little flock, for your Father has chosen gladly to give you the kingdom.
33 "Sell your possessions and give to charity; make yourselves money belts which do not wear out, an unfailing treasure in heaven, where no thief comes near nor moth destroys.
34 "For where your treasure is, there your heart will be also.

Joshua 19:1—20:9

19 THEN the second lot fell to Simeon, to the tribe of the sons of Simeon according to their families, and their inheritance was in the midst of the inheritance of the sons of Judah.
2   So they had as their inheritance Beersheba or Sheba and Moladah,

3 and Hazar-shual and Balah and Ezem,

4 and Eltolad and Bethul and Hormah,

5 and Ziklag and Beth-marcaboth and Hazar-susah,

6 and Beth-lebaoth and Sharuhen; thirteen cities with their villages;

7 Ain, Rimmon and Ether and Ashan; four cities with their villages;

8 and all the villages which *were* around these cities as far as Baalath-beer, Ramah of the Negev. This *was* the inheritance of the tribe of the sons of Simeon according to their families.

9 The inheritance of the sons of Simeon *was taken* from the portion of the sons of Judah, for the share of the sons of Judah was too large for them; so the sons of Simeon received *an* inheritance in the midst of Judah's inheritance.

10 Now the third lot came up for the sons of Zebulun according to their families. And the territory of their inheritance was as far as Sarid.

11 Then their border went up to the west and to Maralah, it then touched Dabbesheth and reached to the brook that is before Jokneam.

12 Then it turned from Sarid to the east toward the sunrise as far as the border of Chisloth-tabor, and it proceeded to Daberath and up to Japhia.

13 From there it continued eastward toward the sunrise to Gath-hepher, to Eth-kazin, and it proceeded to Rimmon which stretches to Neah.

14 The border circled around it on the north to Hannathon, and it ended at the valley of Iphtahel.

15 *Included* also *were* Kattah and Nahalal and Shimron and Idalah and Bethlehem; twelve cities with their villages.

16 This *was* the inheritance of the sons of Zebulun according to their families, these cities with their villages.

17 The fourth lot fell to Issachar, to the sons of Issachar according to their families.

18 Their territory was to Jezreel and *included* Chesulloth and Shunem,

19 and Hapharaim and Shion and Anaharath,

20 and Rabbith and Kishion and Ebez,

21 and Remeth and En-gannim and En-haddah and Beth-pazzez.

22 The border reached to Tabor and Shahazumah and Beth-shemesh, and their border ended at the Jordan; sixteen cities with their villages.

23 This *was* the inheritance of the tribe of the sons of Issachar according to their families, the cities with their villages.

24 Now the fifth lot fell to the tribe of the sons of Asher according to their families.

25 Their territory was Helkath and Hali and Beten and Achshaph,

26 and Allammelech and Amad and Mishal; and it reached to Carmel on the west and to Shihor-libnath.

27 It turned toward the east to Beth-dagon and reached to Zebulun, and to the valley of Iphtahel northward to Beth-emek and Neiel; then it proceeded on north to Cabul,

28 and Ebron and Rehob and Hammon and Kanah, as far as Great Sidon.

29 The border turned to Ramah and to the fortified city of Tyre; then the border turned to Hosah, and it ended at the sea by the region of Achzib.

30 *Included* also *were* Ummah, and Aphek and Rehob; twenty-two cities with their villages.

31 This *was* the inheritance of the tribe of the sons of Asher according to their families, these cities with their villages.

32 The sixth lot fell to the sons of Naphtali; to the sons of Naphtali according to their families.

33 Their border was from Heleph, from the oak in Zaanannim and Adami-nekeb and Jabneel, as far as Lakkum, and it ended at the Jordan.

34 Then the border turned westward to Aznoth-tabor and proceeded from there to Hukkok; and it reached to Zebulun on the south and touched Asher on the west, and to Judah at the Jordan toward the east.

35 The fortified cities *were* Ziddim, Zer and Hammath, Rakkath and Chinnereth,

36 and Adamah and Ramah and Hazor,

37 and Kedesh and Edrei and En-hazor,

38 and Yiron and Migdal-el, Horem and Beth-anath and Beth-shemesh; nineteen cities with their villages.

39 This *was* the inheritance of the tribe of the sons of Naphtali according to their families, the cities with their villages.

40 The seventh lot fell to the tribe of the sons of Dan according to their families.

41 The territory of their inheritance was Zorah and Eshtaol and Ir-shemesh,

42 and Shaalabbin and Aijalon and Ithlah,

43 and Elon and Timnah and Ekron,
44 and Eltekeh and Gibbethon and Baalath,
45 and Jehud and Bene-berak and Gath-rimmon,
46 and Me-jarkon and Rakkon, with the territory over against Joppa.
47 The territory of the sons of Dan proceeded beyond them; for the sons of Dan went up and fought with Leshem and captured it. Then they struck it with the edge of the sword and possessed it and settled in it; and they called Leshem Dan after the name of Dan their father.
48 This *was* the inheritance of the tribe of the sons of Dan according to their families, these cities with their villages.
49 When they finished apportioning the land for inheritance by its borders, the sons of Israel gave an inheritance in their midst to Joshua the son of Nun.
50 In accordance with the command of the LORD they gave him the city for which he asked, Timnath-serah in the hill country of Ephraim. So he built the city and settled in it.
51 These are the inheritances which Eleazar the priest, and Joshua the son of Nun, and the heads of the households of the tribes of the sons of Israel distributed by lot in Shiloh before the LORD at the doorway of the tent of meeting. So they finished dividing the land.

20 THEN the LORD spoke to Joshua, saying,
2 "Speak to the sons of Israel, saying, 'Designate the cities of refuge, of which I spoke to you through Moses,
3 that the manslayer who kills any person unintentionally, without premeditation, may flee there, and they shall become your refuge from the avenger of blood.
4 'He shall flee to one of these cities, and shall stand at the entrance of the gate of the city and state his case in the hearing of the elders of that city; and they shall take him into the city to them and give him a place, so that he may dwell among them.
5 'Now if the avenger of blood pursues him, then they shall not deliver the manslayer into his hand, because he struck his neighbor without premeditation and did not hate him beforehand.
6 'He shall dwell in that city until he stands before the congregation for judgment, until the death of the one who is

high priest in those days. Then the manslayer shall return to his own city and to his own house, to the city from which he fled.'"
7 So they set apart Kedesh in Galilee in the hill country of Naphtali and Shechem in the hill country of Ephraim, and Kiriath-arba (that is, Hebron) in the hill country of Judah.
8 Beyond the Jordan east of Jericho, they designated Bezer in the wilderness on the plain from the tribe of Reuben, and Ramoth in Gilead from the tribe of Gad, and Golan in Bashan from the tribe of Manasseh.
9 These were the appointed cities for all the sons of Israel and for the stranger who sojourns among them, that whoever kills any person unintentionally may flee there, and not die by the hand of the avenger of blood until he stands before the congregation.

Psalm 46:1–6

For the choir director. *A Psalm* of the sons of Korah, set to Alamoth. A Song.

46 GOD is our refuge and strength,
A very present help in trouble.
2 Therefore we will not fear, though the earth should change

LIFE LESSONS

Joshua 19:51 — *These are the inheritances which Eleazar . . . and the heads of . . . Israel distributed by lot in Shiloh before the LORD.*

*E*verything we do should be done for the Lord. Where we live, who we marry, how we make a living—all these things are proper issues to bring before the Lord in prayer.

Psalm 46:1 — *God is our refuge and strength, a very present help in trouble.*

*O*n some days, we may feel as if our world has been shaken, and everything we depend upon has been cast into the sea. But if we put our hope in God, we have no need to fear, because He is truly the refuge who can never be moved. In fact, sometimes He will allow our earthly securities to fail us so we will learn to depend upon Him.

And though the mountains slip into the heart of the sea;

3 Though its waters roar *and* foam,
Though the mountains quake at its swelling pride. Selah.

4 There is a river whose streams make glad the city of God,
The holy dwelling places of the Most High.

5 God is in the midst of her, she will not be moved;
God will help her when morning dawns.

6 The nations made an uproar, the kingdoms tottered;
He raised His voice, the earth melted.

✦ Proverbs 14:7–11

7 Leave the presence of a fool,
Or you will not discern words of knowledge.

8 The wisdom of the sensible is to understand his way,
But the foolishness of fools is deceit.

9 Fools mock at sin,
But among the upright there is good will.

10 The heart knows its own bitterness,
And a stranger does not share its joy.

11 The house of the wicked will be destroyed,
But the tent of the upright will flourish.

✦ Luke 12:35–59

35 "Be dressed in readiness, and *keep* your lamps lit.
36 "Be like men who are waiting for their master when he returns from the wedding feast, so that they may immediately open *the door* to him when he comes and knocks.

ANSWERS TO LIFE'S QUESTIONS

How can I deal with the anger or bitterness of another?

PROVERBS 14:10

*T*he unfortunate fact is, sooner or later all of us will run into someone who feels angry or bitter toward us. What should you do when you find yourself the object of another's bitterness? How should you respond to someone's red-hot anger aimed straight at you? Responding to bitterness with more bitterness only leads to a combative and explosive situation. So what should you do?

First, tell yourself the truth about the situation. What happened? How did the situation unfold? Are you really at fault? It may be you can't entirely reconstruct the event in question, but try your best to honestly recall what led to the outburst.

Second, listen carefully to what the bitter person is saying. Bitterness and anger are usually the offshoots of deep hurt. Say something like, "It seems you are really upset. Can we talk about it?" Even such a simple question may help defuse the situation. Although you may not be able to uproot the bitterness in someone else's life, you can stop it from taking root in your own heart by asking God to help you understand why this person feels the way he or she does.

Third, any time you come under personal attack, it is important to recall God's personal love for you. You may have made mistakes, but that does not change the Lord's feelings about you. Ask Him to encourage you through His Word.

Fourth, ask God to help you respond with His love and grace, and to protect you from angry attacks. In Psalm 64, we read how David prayed for God's deliverance from the attacks of an embittered enemy. He wrote, "They aimed bitter speech as their arrow, to shoot from concealment at the blameless" (Ps. 64:3, 4). At times, the angry person will attack by turning others against you with their accusations. Yet you should not fear their venom because God protects and vindicates His people (Ps. 64:7–10).

Bitterness is a much deeper and more complex reaction than a simple expression of quick anger. It is a satanic stronghold that needs to be faced in an honest manner. God tells us to beware "that no root of bitterness springing up causes trouble, and by it many be defiled" (Heb. 12:15).

When you find yourself the target of a bitter accusation or a hateful personal attack, pray for God's protection. Ask Him to give you wisdom in dealing with the other person, as well as a healthy perspective on the entire matter. Your reaction to the assault is the most important issue with God. Therefore, be firm but loving in what you say and do.

➤ 37 "Blessed are those slaves whom the master will find on the alert when he comes; truly I say to you, that he will gird himself *to serve*, and have them recline *at the table*, and will come up and wait on them.

38 "Whether he comes in the second watch, or even in the third, and finds *them* so, blessed are those *slaves*.

39 "But be sure of this, that if the head of the house had known at what hour the thief was coming, he would not have allowed his house to be broken into.

40 "You too, be ready; for the Son of Man is coming at an hour that you do not expect."

41 Peter said, "Lord, are You addressing this parable to us, or to everyone *else* as well?"

42 And the Lord said, "Who then is the faithful and sensible steward, whom his master will put in charge of his servants, to give them their rations at the proper time?

43 "Blessed is that slave whom his master finds so doing when he comes.

44 "Truly I say to you that he will put him in charge of all his possessions.

45 "But if that slave says in his heart, 'My master will be a long time in coming,' and begins to beat the slaves, *both* men and women, and to eat and drink and get drunk;

46 the master of that slave will come on a day when he does not expect *him* and at an hour he does not know, and will cut him in pieces, and assign him a place with the unbelievers.

47 "And that slave who knew his master's will and did not get ready or act in accord with his will, will receive many lashes,

➤ 48 but the one who did not know *it*, and committed deeds worthy of a flogging,

will receive but few. From everyone who has been given much, much will be required; and to whom they entrusted much, of him they will ask all the more.

49 "I have come to cast fire upon the earth; and how I wish it were already kindled!

50 "But I have a baptism to undergo, and how distressed I am until it is accomplished!

51 "Do you suppose that I came to grant peace on earth? I tell you, no, but rather division;

52 for from now on five *members* in one household will be divided, three against two and two against three.

53 "They will be divided, father against son and son against father, mother against daughter and daughter against mother, mother-in-law against daughter-in-law and daughter-in-law against mother-in-law."

54 And He was also saying to the crowds, "When you see a cloud rising in the west, immediately you say, 'A shower is coming,' and so it turns out.

55 "And when *you see* a south wind blowing, you say, 'It will be a hot day,' and it turns out *that way*.

56 "You hypocrites! You know how to analyze the appearance of the earth and the sky, but why do you not analyze this present time?

57 "And why do you not even on your own initiative judge what is right?

58 "For while you are going with your opponent to appear before the magistrate, on *your* way *there* make an effort to settle with him, so that he may not drag you before the judge, and the judge turn you over to the officer, and the officer throw you into prison.

59 "I say to you, you will not get out of there until you have paid the very last cent."

LIFE LESSONS

➤ **Luke 12:37** — *"Blessed are those slaves whom the master will find on the alert when he comes . . . He will . . . come up and wait on them."*

Servants serve and masters get served—at least, that's the way it works in this world. But Jesus says that He, the Master, will serve His faithful, prepared servants when He returns to settle accounts.

➤ **Luke 12:48** — *"From everyone who has been given much, much will be required."*

Jesus does not give us gifts, talents, and resources merely to spend them on ourselves. He gives them to us so we will use them to expand His kingdom and meet the needs of others, especially fellow believers.

21 THEN the heads of households of the Levites approached Eleazar the priest, and Joshua the son of Nun, and the heads of households of the tribes of the sons of Israel.

2 They spoke to them at Shiloh in the land of Canaan, saying, "The LORD commanded through Moses to give us cities to live in, with their pasture lands for our cattle."

3 So the sons of Israel gave the Levites from their inheritance these cities with their pasture lands, according to the command of the LORD.

4 Then the lot came out for the families of the Kohathites. And the sons of Aaron the priest, who were of the Levites, received thirteen cities by lot from the tribe of Judah and from the tribe of the Simeonites and from the tribe of Benjamin.

5 The rest of the sons of Kohath received ten cities by lot from the families of the tribe of Ephraim and from the tribe of Dan and from the half-tribe of Manasseh.

6 The sons of Gershon received thirteen cities by lot from the families of the tribe of Issachar and from the tribe of Asher and from the tribe of Naphtali and from the half-tribe of Manasseh in Bashan.

7 The sons of Merari according to their families received twelve cities from the tribe of Reuben and from the tribe of Gad and from the tribe of Zebulun.

8 Now the sons of Israel gave by lot to the Levites these cities with their pasture lands, as the LORD had commanded through Moses.

9 They gave these cities which are *here* mentioned by name from the tribe of the sons of Judah and from the tribe of the sons of Simeon;

10 and they were for the sons of Aaron, one of the families of the Kohathites, of the sons of Levi, for the lot was theirs first.

11 Thus they gave them Kiriath-arba, *Arba being* the father of Anak (that is, Hebron), in the hill country of Judah, with its surrounding pasture lands.

12 But the fields of the city and its villages they gave to Caleb the son of Jephunneh as his possession.

13 So to the sons of Aaron the priest they gave Hebron, the city of refuge for the manslayer, with its pasture lands, and Libnah with its pasture lands,

14 and Jattir with its pasture lands and Eshtemoa with its pasture lands,

15 and Holon with its pasture lands and Debir with its pasture lands,

16 and Ain with its pasture lands and Juttah with its pasture lands *and* Beth-shemesh with its pasture lands; nine cities from these two tribes.

17 From the tribe of Benjamin, Gibeon with its pasture lands, Geba with its pasture lands,

18 Anathoth with its pasture lands and Almon with its pasture lands; four cities.

19 All the cities of the sons of Aaron, the priests, were thirteen cities with their pasture lands.

20 Then the cities from the tribe of Ephraim were allotted to the families of the sons of Kohath, the Levites, *even to* the rest of the sons of Kohath.

21 They gave them Shechem, the city of refuge for the manslayer, with its pasture lands, in the hill country of Ephraim, and Gezer with its pasture lands,

22 and Kibzaim with its pasture lands and Beth-horon with its pasture lands; four cities.

23 From the tribe of Dan, Elteke with its pasture lands, Gibbethon with its pasture lands,

24 Aijalon with its pasture lands, Gath-rimmon with its pasture lands; four cities.

25 From the half-tribe of Manasseh, *they allotted* Taanach with its pasture lands and Gath-rimmon with its pasture lands; two cities.

26 All the cities with their pasture lands for the families of the rest of the sons of Kohath were ten.

27 To the sons of Gershon, one of the families of the Levites, from the half-tribe of Manasseh, *they gave* Golan in Bashan, the city of refuge for the manslayer, with its pasture lands, and Be-eshterah with its pasture lands; two cities.

28 From the tribe of Issachar, *they gave* Kishion with its pasture lands, Daberath with its pasture lands,

29   Jarmuth with its pasture lands, Engannim with its pasture lands; four cities.
30   From the tribe of Asher, *they gave* Mishal with its pasture lands, Abdon with its pasture lands,
31   Helkath with its pasture lands and Rehob with its pasture lands; four cities.
32   From the tribe of Naphtali, *they gave* Kedesh in Galilee, the city of refuge for the manslayer, with its pasture lands and Hammoth-dor with its pasture lands and Kartan with its pasture lands; three cities.
33   All the cities of the Gershonites according to their families were thirteen cities with their pasture lands.
34   To the families of the sons of Merari, the rest of the Levites, *they gave* from the tribe of Zebulun, Jokneam with its pasture lands and Kartah with its pasture lands.
35   Dimnah with its pasture lands, Nahalal with its pasture lands; four cities.
36   From the tribe of Reuben, *they gave* Bezer with its pasture lands and Jahaz with its pasture lands,
37   Kedemoth with its pasture lands and Mephaath with its pasture lands; four cities.
38   From the tribe of Gad, *they gave* Ramoth in Gilead, the city of refuge for the manslayer, with its pasture lands and Mahanaim with its pasture lands,
39   Heshbon with its pasture lands, Jazer with its pasture lands; four cities in all.
40   All *these were* the cities of the sons of Merari according to their families, the rest of the families of the Levites; and their lot was twelve cities.
41   All the cities of the Levites in the midst of the possession of the sons of Israel were forty-eight cities with their pasture lands.
42   These cities each had its surrounding pasture lands; thus *it was* with all these cities.
43   So the LORD gave Israel all the land which He had sworn to give to their fathers, and they possessed it and lived in it.
44   And the LORD gave them rest on every side, according to all that He had sworn to their fathers, and no one of all their enemies stood before them; the LORD gave all their enemies into their hand.

45   Not one of the good promises which the LORD had made to the house of Israel failed; all came to pass.
22 THEN Joshua summoned the Reubenites and the Gadites and the half-tribe of Manasseh,
2   and said to them, "You have kept all that Moses the servant of the LORD commanded you, and have listened to my voice in all that I commanded you.
3   "You have not forsaken your brothers these many days to this day, but have kept the charge of the commandment of the LORD your God.
4   "And now the LORD your God has given rest to your brothers, as He spoke to them; therefore turn now and go to your tents, to the land of your possession, which Moses the servant of the LORD gave you beyond the Jordan.
5   "Only be very careful to observe the commandment and the law which Moses the servant of the LORD commanded you, to love the LORD your God and walk in all His ways and keep His commandments and hold fast to Him and serve Him with all your heart and with all your soul."
6   So Joshua blessed them and sent them away, and they went to their tents.
7   Now to the one half-tribe of Manasseh Moses had given *a possession* in Bashan, but to the other half Joshua gave *a possession* among their brothers westward beyond the Jordan. So when

---

LIFE LESSONS

➤ **Joshua 21:44 —** *The LORD gave them rest on every side.*

*G*od's good promises ultimately lead to peace and rest. He tells us that in "repentance and rest you will be saved, in quietness and trust is your strength" (Is. 30:15).

➤ **Joshua 22:5 —** *"Be very careful . . . to love the LORD your God and walk in all His ways and keep His commandments and hold fast to Him and serve Him with all your heart and with all your soul."*

*W*hat Joshua told the eastern tribes still holds true today. We will surely succeed if we: (1) love God; (2) walk in His ways; (3) keep His commandments; (4) hold fast to Him; (5) serve Him wholeheartedly.

Joshua sent them away to their tents, he blessed them,

8   and said to them, "Return to your tents with great riches and with very much livestock, with silver, gold, bronze, iron, and with very many clothes; divide the spoil of your enemies with your brothers."

9   The sons of Reuben and the sons of Gad and the half-tribe of Manasseh returned *home* and departed from the sons of Israel at Shiloh which is in the land of Canaan, to go to the land of Gilead, to the land of their possession which they had possessed, according to the command of the LORD through Moses.

10   When they came to the region of the Jordan which is in the land of Canaan, the sons of Reuben and the sons of Gad and the half-tribe of Manasseh built an altar there by the Jordan, a large altar in appearance.

11   And the sons of Israel heard *it* said, "Behold, the sons of Reuben and the sons of Gad and the half-tribe of Manasseh have built an altar at the frontier of the land of Canaan, in the region of the Jordan, on the side *belonging to* the sons of Israel."

12   When the sons of Israel heard *of it*, the whole congregation of the sons of Israel gathered themselves at Shiloh to go up against them in war.

13   Then the sons of Israel sent to the sons of Reuben and to the sons of Gad and to the half-tribe of Manasseh, into the land of Gilead, Phinehas the son of Eleazar the priest,

14   and with him ten chiefs, one chief for each father's household from each of the tribes of Israel; and each one of them *was* the head of his father's household among the thousands of Israel.

15   They came to the sons of Reuben and to the sons of Gad and to the half-tribe of Manasseh, to the land of Gilead, and they spoke with them saying,

16   "Thus says the whole congregation of the LORD, 'What is this unfaithful act which you have committed against the God of Israel, turning away from following the LORD this day, by building yourselves an altar, to rebel against the LORD this day?

17   'Is not the iniquity of Peor enough for us, from which we have not cleansed ourselves to this day, although a plague came on the congregation of the LORD,

18   that you must turn away this day from following the LORD? If you rebel against the LORD today, He will be angry with the whole congregation of Israel tomorrow.

19   'If, however, the land of your possession is unclean, then cross into the land of the possession of the LORD, where the LORD'S tabernacle stands, and take possession among us. Only do not rebel against the LORD, or rebel against us by building an altar for yourselves, besides the altar of the LORD our God.

20   'Did not Achan the son of Zerah act unfaithfully in the things under the ban, and wrath fall on all the congregation of Israel? And that man did not perish alone in his iniquity.'"

21   Then the sons of Reuben and the sons of Gad and the half-tribe of Manasseh answered and spoke to the heads of the families of Israel.

22   "The Mighty One, God, the LORD, the Mighty One, God, the LORD! He knows, and may Israel itself know. If *it was* in rebellion, or if in an unfaithful act against the LORD do not save us this day!

23   "If we have built us an altar to turn away from following the LORD, or if to offer a burnt offering or grain offering on it, or if to offer sacrifices of peace offerings on it, may the LORD Himself require it.

24   "But truly we have done this out of concern, for a reason, saying, 'In time to come your sons may say to our sons, "What have you to do with the LORD, the God of Israel?

25   "For the LORD has made the Jordan a border between us and you, *you* sons of Reuben and sons of Gad; you have no portion in the LORD." So your sons may make our sons stop fearing the LORD.'

26   "Therefore we said, 'Let us build an altar, not for burnt offering or for sacrifice;

27   rather it shall be a witness between us and you and between our generations after us, that we are to perform the service of the LORD before Him with our burnt offerings, and with our sacrifices and with our peace offerings, so that your sons will not say to our sons in time to come, "You have no portion in the LORD."'

28 "Therefore we said, 'It shall also come about if they say *this* to us or to our generations in time to come, then we shall say, "See the copy of the altar of the LORD which our fathers made, not for burnt offering or for sacrifice; rather it is a witness between us and you."'

29 "Far be it from us that we should rebel against the LORD and turn away from following the LORD this day, by building an altar for burnt offering, for grain offering or for sacrifice, besides the altar of the LORD our God which is before His tabernacle."

30 So when Phinehas the priest and the leaders of the congregation, even the heads of the families of Israel who *were* with him, heard the words which the sons of Reuben and the sons of Gad and the sons of Manasseh spoke, it pleased them.

31 And Phinehas the son of Eleazar the priest said to the sons of Reuben and to the sons of Gad and to the sons of Manasseh, "Today we know that the LORD is in our midst, because you have not committed this unfaithful act against the LORD; now you have delivered the sons of Israel from the hand of the LORD."

32 Then Phinehas the son of Eleazar the priest and the leaders returned from the sons of Reuben and from the sons of Gad, from the land of Gilead to the land of Canaan, to the sons of Israel, and brought back word to them.

➢ 33 The word pleased the sons of Israel, and the sons of Israel blessed God; and they did not speak of going up against them in war to destroy the land in which the sons of Reuben and the sons of Gad were living.

34 The sons of Reuben and the sons of Gad called the altar *Witness;* "For," *they said,* "it is a witness between us that the LORD is God."

Psalm 46:7–11

7 The LORD of hosts is with us;
 The God of Jacob is our stronghold.
                                    Selah.

8 Come, behold the works of the LORD,
 Who has wrought desolations in the earth.

9 He makes wars to cease to the end of the earth;
 He breaks the bow and cuts the spear in two;
 He burns the chariots with fire.

10 "Cease *striving* and know that I am God;
 I will be exalted among the nations,
 I will be exalted in the earth."

11 The LORD of hosts is with us;
 The God of Jacob is our stronghold.
                                    Selah.

Proverbs 14:12, 13

12 There is a way *which seems* right to a man,
 But its end is the way of death.

13 Even in laughter the heart may be in pain,
 And the end of joy may be grief.

Luke 13:1–22

13 NOW on the same occasion there were some present who reported to Him about the Galileans whose blood Pilate had mixed with their sacrifices.

2 And Jesus said to them, "Do you suppose that these Galileans were *greater* sinners than all *other* Galileans because they suffered this *fate?*

LIFE LESSONS

➢ **Joshua 22:33 —** *The word pleased the sons of Israel, and the sons of Israel blessed God.*

*G*od loves to bless His children, but it is also appropriate for His children to bless Him. How? With the only thing we have to give: a "sacrifice of praise" (Heb. 13:15).

➢ **Psalm 46:10 —** *Cease striving and know that I am God.*

*O*nly in the rarest of circumstances, and then usually in judgment, does God display His glory in blinding flashes impossible to ignore. Most of the time, we meet Him in the quietness of our hearts.

Life Examples:

Confidence in Times of Distress

PS. 46:10, 11

*M*ost of us feel distraught at some point in our lives. When stress in daily living becomes unbearable, we want to escape. We may want out of jobs, relationships, a church, a neighborhood, or some other difficult situation. We think we can't handle things the way they are because they cause us too much stress, so we decide to walk away ... move on ... head for anywhere but where we are.

What does the Bible tell us about handling stress? How are we to respond when our fallen human nature cries out for us to stop and run?

God has a powerful truth for us. We do not handle stressful situations by fighting against them; instead, He calls us to be at rest in Him. To the psalmist, this meant being still and knowing God (Ps. 46:10). To the apostle Peter, it meant refusing to carry burdens not meant for him: "casting all your anxiety on Him, because He cares for you" (1 Pet. 5:7). Jesus described it as a peacefulness that we both find and receive as we spend time learning from Him (Matt. 11:28–30). Our human instinct clamors for us to escape—but God calls us to draw near, and absorb the truths of Scripture.

Most of all, the Lord wants us to know Him. As we believe in His sovereignty (1 Chr. 29:11) and accept both the absolute goodness of His plans (Jer. 29:11) and His deep, abiding love for us (Eph. 3:17–19), we will grow in trust. Then we will find it easier to "be still" and not to respond like the world which says, "I'm out of here!"

Our stress need not become *distress*. When we feel stress, we do not have to feel defeated and give in to the temptation to give up and run. With an accurate understanding of our heavenly Father and a firm belief in His care, we will be able to walk through the worst of circumstances with inner quietness (Gal. 5:22) and genuine confidence (Heb. 13:6).

This is our privilege as God's children.

➤ 3 "I tell you, no, but unless you repent, you will all likewise perish.

4 "Or do you suppose that those eighteen on whom the tower in Siloam fell and killed them were *worse* culprits than all the men who live in Jerusalem?

5 "I tell you, no, but unless you repent, you will all likewise perish."

6 And He *began* telling this parable: "A man had a fig tree which had been planted in his vineyard; and he came looking for fruit on it and did not find any.

7 "And he said to the vineyard-keeper, 'Behold, for three years I have come looking for fruit on this fig tree without finding any. Cut it down! Why does it even use up the ground?'

LIFE LESSONS

➤ **Luke 13:3 —** *"Unless you repent, you will all likewise perish."*

*T*he victims of tragedies are not necessarily the recipients of divine judgment. Yet because we live in a dangerous world where tragedies occur without warning, we must always be ready to meet our God.

8 "And he answered and said to him, 'Let it alone, sir, for this year too, until I dig around it and put in fertilizer;

9 and if it bears fruit next year, *fine*; but if not, cut it down.'"

10 And He was teaching in one of the synagogues on the Sabbath.

11 And there was a woman who for eighteen years had had a sickness caused by a spirit; and she was bent double, and could not straighten up at all.

12 When Jesus saw her, He called her over and said to her, "Woman, you are freed from your sickness."

13 And He laid His hands on her; and immediately she was made erect again and *began* glorifying God.

14 But the synagogue official, indignant because Jesus had healed on the Sabbath, *began* saying to the crowd in response, "There are six days in which work should be done; so come during them and get healed, and not on the Sabbath day."

15 But the Lord answered him and said, "You hypocrites, does not each of you on the Sabbath untie his ox or his donkey from the stall and lead him away to water *him*?

16 "And this woman, a daughter of Abraham as she is, whom Satan has bound for eighteen long years, should she not have been released from this bond on the Sabbath day?"

LIFE LESSONS

➤ Luke 13:16 — *"And this woman . . . whom Satan has bound for eighteen long years, should she not have been released from this bond on the Sabbath day?"*

*W*hen we care more for keeping rules than we do for the welfare of people made in God's image, we miss the entire point of our existence. The Bible says, "Love is the fulfillment of the law" (Rom. 13:10).

APRIL 17

Joshua 23:1—24:33

23 NOW it came about after many days, when the LORD had given rest to Israel from all their enemies on every side, and Joshua was old, advanced in years,

2 that Joshua called for all Israel, for their elders and their heads and their judges and their officers, and said to them, "I am old, advanced in years.

3 "And you have seen all that the LORD your God has done to all these nations because of you, for the LORD your God is He who has been fighting for you.

4 "See, I have apportioned to you these nations which remain as an inheritance for your tribes, with all the nations which I have cut off, from the Jordan even to the Great Sea toward the setting of the sun.

5 "The LORD your God, He will thrust them out from before you and drive them from before you; and you will possess their land, just as the LORD your God promised you.

6 "Be very firm, then, to keep and do all that is written in the book of the law of Moses, so that you may not turn aside from it to the right hand or to the left,

7 so that you will not associate with these nations, these which remain among

17 As He said this, all His opponents were being humiliated; and the entire crowd was rejoicing over all the glorious things being done by Him.

18 So He was saying, "What is the kingdom of God like, and to what shall I compare it?

19 "It is like a mustard seed, which a man took and threw into his own garden; and it grew and became a tree, and THE BIRDS OF THE AIR NESTED IN ITS BRANCHES."

20 And again He said, "To what shall I compare the kingdom of God?

21 "It is like leaven, which a woman took and hid in three pecks of flour until it was all leavened."

22 And He was passing through from one city and village to another, teaching, and proceeding on His way to Jerusalem.

you, or mention the name of their gods, or make *anyone* swear *by them,* or serve them, or bow down to them.

8 "But you are to cling to the LORD your God, as you have done to this day.

9 "For the LORD has driven out great and strong nations from before you; and as for you, no man has stood before you to this day.

10 "One of your men puts to flight a thousand, for the LORD your God is He who fights for you, just as He promised you.

11 "So take diligent heed to yourselves to love the LORD your God.

12 "For if you ever go back and cling to the rest of these nations, these which remain among you, and intermarry with them, so that you associate with them and they with you,

13 know with certainty that the LORD your God will not continue to drive these nations out from before you; but they will be a snare and a trap to you, and a whip on your sides and thorns in your eyes, until you perish from off this good land which the LORD your God has given you.

14 "Now behold, today I am going the way of all the earth, and you know in all your hearts and in all your souls that not one word of all the good words which the LORD your God spoke concerning you has failed; all have been fulfilled for you, not one of them has failed.

15 "It shall come about that just as all the good words which the LORD your God spoke to you have come upon you, so the LORD will bring upon you all the threats, until He has destroyed you from off this good land which the LORD your God has given you.

16 "When you transgress the covenant of the LORD your God, which He commanded you, and go and serve other gods and bow down to them, then the anger of the LORD will burn against you, and you will perish quickly from off the good land which He has given you."

24 THEN Joshua gathered all the tribes of Israel to Shechem, and called for the elders of Israel and for their heads and their judges and their officers; and they presented themselves before God.

2 Joshua said to all the people, "Thus says the LORD, the God of Israel, 'From ancient times your fathers lived beyond the River, *namely*, Terah, the father of Abraham and the father of Nahor, and they served other gods.

3 'Then I took your father Abraham from beyond the River, and led him through all the land of Canaan, and multiplied his descendants and gave him Isaac.

4 'To Isaac I gave Jacob and Esau, and to Esau I gave Mount Seir to possess it; but Jacob and his sons went down to Egypt.

5 'Then I sent Moses and Aaron, and I plagued Egypt by what I did in its midst; and afterward I brought you out.

6 'I brought your fathers out of Egypt, and you came to the sea; and Egypt pursued your fathers with chariots and horsemen to the Red Sea.

7 'But when they cried out to the LORD, He put darkness between you and the Egyptians, and brought the sea upon them and covered them; and your own eyes saw what I did in Egypt. And you lived in the wilderness for a long time.

8 'Then I brought you into the land of the Amorites who lived beyond the Jordan, and they fought with you; and I gave them into your hand, and you took possession of their land when I destroyed them before you.

9 'Then Balak the son of Zippor, king of Moab, arose and fought against Israel, and he sent and summoned Balaam the son of Beor to curse you.

10 'But I was not willing to listen to Balaam. So he had to bless you, and I delivered you from his hand.

11 'You crossed the Jordan and came to Jericho; and the citizens of Jericho fought against you, *and* the Amorite and the Perizzite and the Canaanite and the Hittite and the Girgashite, the Hivite and the Jebusite. Thus I gave them into your hand.

12 'Then I sent the hornet before you and it drove out the two kings of the Amorites from before you, *but* not by your sword or your bow.

13 'I gave you a land on which you had not labored, and cities which you had not built, and you have lived in them; you are eating of vineyards and olive groves which you did not plant.'

14 "Now, therefore, fear the LORD and serve Him in sincerity and truth; and put away the gods which your fathers served beyond the River and in Egypt, and serve the LORD.

15 "If it is disagreeable in your sight to serve the LORD, choose for yourselves today whom you will serve: whether the gods which your fathers served which were beyond the River, or the gods of the Amorites in whose land you are living; but as for me and my house, we will serve the LORD."

16 The people answered and said, "Far be it from us that we should forsake the LORD to serve other gods;

17 for the LORD our God is He who

LIFE LESSONS

➤ **Joshua 23:13 —** *"They will be a snare and a trap to you."*

*W*hen God tells us we need to rid our lives of certain things, we are wise to obey. Bad things happen when we give the devil a foothold (Eph. 4:27). It takes courage to obey God, and as His people we need to encourage one another daily, "so that none of you will be hardened by the deceitfulness of sin" (Heb. 3:13).

➤ **Joshua 24:12 —** *"I sent the hornet before you and it drove out the two kings of the Amorites from before you."*

*O*ur sovereign God can use even wild creatures to bring about His will and bless His people. *Nothing* is beyond His control, and *everything* can be a mighty tool in His hand.

brought us and our fathers up out of the land of Egypt, from the house of bondage, and who did these great signs in our sight and preserved us through all the way in which we went and among all the peoples through whose midst we passed.

18 "The LORD drove out from before us all the peoples, even the Amorites who lived in the land. We also will serve the LORD, for He is our God."

19 Then Joshua said to the people, "You will not be able to serve the LORD, for He is a holy God. He is a jealous God; He will not forgive your transgression or your sins.

20 "If you forsake the LORD and serve foreign gods, then He will turn and do you harm and consume you after He has done good to you."

21 The people said to Joshua, "No, but we will serve the LORD."

22 Joshua said to the people, "You are witnesses against yourselves that you have chosen for yourselves the LORD, to serve Him." And they said, "We are witnesses."

23 "Now therefore, put away the foreign gods which are in your midst, and incline your hearts to the LORD, the God of Israel."

24 The people said to Joshua, "We will serve the LORD our God and we will obey His voice."

25 So Joshua made a covenant with the people that day, and made for them a statute and an ordinance in Shechem.

26 And Joshua wrote these words in the book of the law of God; and he took a large stone and set it up there under the oak that was by the sanctuary of the LORD.

27 Joshua said to all the people, "Behold, this stone shall be for a witness against us, for it has heard all the words of the LORD which He spoke to us; thus it shall be for a witness against you, so that you do not deny your God."

28 Then Joshua dismissed the people, each to his inheritance.

29 It came about after these things that Joshua the son of Nun, the servant of the LORD, died, being one hundred and ten years old.

30 And they buried him in the territory of his inheritance in Timnath-serah, which is in the hill country of Ephraim, on the north of Mount Gaash.

31 Israel served the LORD all the days of Joshua and all the days of the elders who survived Joshua, and had known all the deeds of the LORD which He had done for Israel.

32 Now they buried the bones of Joseph, which the sons of Israel brought up from Egypt, at Shechem, in the piece of ground which Jacob had bought from the sons of Hamor the father of Shechem for one hundred pieces of money; and they became the inheritance of Joseph's sons.

33 And Eleazar the son of Aaron died; and they buried him at Gibeah of Phinehas his son, which was given him in the hill country of Ephraim.

Psalm 47:1–9

For the choir director. A Psalm of the sons of Korah.

47 O CLAP your hands, all peoples;
Shout to God with the voice of joy.

2 For the LORD Most High is to be feared,
A great King over all the earth.

3 He subdues peoples under us
And nations under our feet.

4 He chooses our inheritance for us,
The glory of Jacob whom He loves.
Selah.

5 God has ascended with a shout,
The LORD, with the sound of a trumpet.

6 Sing praises to God, sing praises;
Sing praises to our King, sing praises.

7 For God is the King of all the earth;
Sing praises with a skillful psalm.

8 God reigns over the nations,
God sits on His holy throne.

9 The princes of the people have assembled themselves as the people of the God of Abraham,
For the shields of the earth belong to God;
He is highly exalted.

LIFE LESSONS

➤ Joshua 24:24 — "We will serve the LORD our God and we will obey His voice."

*W*hat a motto for success! When we make the Lord our own, choose to serve Him, open our ears to hear His Word, and obey Him, then our own Promised Land opens wide before us.

Proverbs 14:14

14 The backslider in heart will have
his fill of his own ways,
But a good man will *be satisfied*
with his.

Luke 13:23–35

23 And someone said to Him, "Lord, are
there *just* a few who are being saved?"
And He said to them,
24 "Strive to enter through the narrow
door; for many, I tell you, will seek to
enter and will not be able.
25 "Once the head of the house gets
up and shuts the door, and you begin

LIFE LESSONS

➤ **Psalm 47:7 — *God is the King of all
the earth; sing praises with a skillful
psalm.***

*A*re hymns better than praise songs?
Are choruses superior to cantatas?
We weary ourselves with foolish ques-
tions, when we should be asking, "Am
I growing in my understanding of God
through my worship?"

Life Examples:

The Narrow Way

LUKE 13:24

*M*artial artist Morihei Ueshiba once
philosophized, "There are many
paths leading to the top of Mount Fuji."
His statement reflected the idea that many
people believe, which is that there are many
ways to find God. Life is a journey, and people
are free to choose their own path to the deity
of their choice.

However, Jesus completely refuted that
idea. In Luke 13:24, He said, "Strive to enter
through the narrow door; for many, I tell you,
will seek to enter and will not be able." In
other words, there are people who will spend
their entire lives pursuing a deity that cannot
save them, and they will not realize it until it's
too late. It's a horrifying thought.

So why do so many people think there is
more than one way to find God?

Generally, the belief that there is more
than one path to God stems from the fact that
in every society in the world (it doesn't make
any difference how civilized or uncivilized),
there are always people who believe in some
kind of deity. Therefore, many anthropolo-
gists and sociologists reason there is no one
true religion—everyone simply worships the
deity which best reflects their environmental
influences.

Such scientists conclude everyone is entitled to his or her own idea of God—including
believing there is no such thing as a supreme
being. Unfortunately, that's human reasoning. It sounds logical, but the problem is it's
a complete contradiction to the way the one
true God has provided for us to know Him
(John 3:16–18).

Why are there so many cultures with so
many deities? Romans 1:20 explains, "Since
the creation of the world His invisible attributes, His eternal power and divine nature,
have been clearly seen, being understood
through what has been made, so that they are
without excuse." People are without excuse
in knowing God exists. Every culture has a
concept of God—He's clearly seen throughout
nature. However, it's not up to us to imagine
who He is or to create Him out of our own
reasoning or culture. Rather, we must look
to the way He's revealed Himself to us, which
is through the person of Jesus Christ (Matt.
11:27; John 14:7).

Unfortunately, people are sometimes
offended when Christians say Jesus Christ is
the only way to God because they say God
wouldn't exclude from heaven all the people
who don't believe in Christ. However, their
reasoning is completely wrong. It's not that
the one true God is exclusive. In fact, He is
completely *inclusive*. Jesus said in John 12:32,
"I, if I am lifted up from the earth, will draw
all peoples to Myself." Jesus offers salvation to
everyone. Jesus would never turn away someone who put his or her faith in Him (Rom.
10:9–13).

Though life may be a journey, and though
there may be a multitude of roads to the
earthly Mount Fuji, there's only one way to
God—by accepting Jesus Christ as your Lord
and Savior (John 14:6; Acts 4:12). Christ offers
the only road that leads to salvation. Though
the world may offer an abundance of choices,
they'll never lead to what you're really looking for (Prov. 14:12). The only right choice
is the road God offers through Jesus Christ.
Though that path is the narrow one, it's
always wide open to you. Trust Him.

to stand outside and knock on the door, saying, 'Lord, open up to us!' then He will answer and say to you, 'I do not know where you are from.'

26 "Then you will begin to say, 'We ate and drank in Your presence, and You taught in our streets';

27 and He will say, 'I tell you, I do not know where you are from; DEPART FROM ME, ALL YOU EVILDOERS.'

28 "In that place there will be weeping and gnashing of teeth when you see Abraham and Isaac and Jacob and all the prophets in the kingdom of God, but yourselves being thrown out.

29 "And they will come from east and west and from north and south, and will recline *at the table* in the kingdom of God.

30 "And behold, *some* are last who will be first and *some* are first who will be last."

31 Just at that time some Pharisees approached, saying to Him, "Go away, leave here, for Herod wants to kill You."

32 And He said to them, "Go and tell that fox, 'Behold, I cast out demons and perform cures today and tomorrow, and the third *day* I reach My goal.'

33 "Nevertheless I must journey on today and tomorrow and the next *day;* for it cannot be that a prophet would perish outside of Jerusalem.

34 "O Jerusalem, Jerusalem, *the city* that kills the prophets and stones those sent to her! How often I wanted to gather your children together, just as a hen *gathers* her brood under her wings, and you would not *have it!*

35 "Behold, your house is left to you *desolate;* and I say to you, you will not see Me until *the time* comes when you say, 'BLESSED IS HE WHO COMES IN THE NAME OF THE LORD!'"

Judges 1:1—2:23

1 NOW it came about after the death of Joshua that the sons of Israel inquired of the LORD, saying, "Who shall go up first for us against the Canaanites, to fight against them?"

2 The LORD said, "Judah shall go up; behold, I have given the land into his hand."

3 Then Judah said to Simeon his brother, "Come up with me into the territory allotted me, that we may fight against the Canaanites; and I in turn will go with you into the territory allotted you." So Simeon went with him.

4 Judah went up, and the LORD gave the Canaanites and the Perizzites into their hands, and they defeated ten thousand men at Bezek.

5 They found Adoni-bezek in Bezek and fought against him, and they defeated the Canaanites and the Perizzites.

6 But Adoni-bezek fled; and they pursued him and caught him and cut off his thumbs and big toes.

7 Adoni-bezek said, "Seventy kings with their thumbs and their big toes cut off used to gather up *scraps* under my

table; as I have done, so God has repaid me." So they brought him to Jerusalem and he died there.

8 Then the sons of Judah fought against Jerusalem and captured it and struck it with the edge of the sword and set the city on fire.

LIFE LESSONS

> Judges 1:1 — *After the death of Joshua . . . Israel inquired of the LORD, saying, "Who shall go up first for us against the Canaanites?"*

The book of Judges begins well, with the successors to Joshua asking the Lord for His guidance and direction. Joshua had taught them to listen to God, and as a result, they enjoyed a successful walk with Him.

> Judges 1:8 — *Judah fought against Jerusalem and captured it.*

The men of Judah did not capture all of Jerusalem (Judg. 1:21). Not until much later did David take the Jebusite inner citadel (2 Sam. 5:7). Sometimes we have to wait for God to give us final victory.

9 Afterward the sons of Judah went down to fight against the Canaanites living in the hill country and in the Negev and in the lowland.

10 So Judah went against the Canaanites who lived in Hebron (now the name of Hebron formerly *was* Kiriath-arba); and they struck Sheshai and Ahiman and Talmai.

11 Then from there he went against the inhabitants of Debir (now the name of Debir formerly *was* Kiriath-sepher).

12 And Caleb said, "The one who attacks Kiriath-sepher and captures it, I will even give him my daughter Achsah for a wife."

13 Othniel the son of Kenaz, Caleb's younger brother, captured it; so he gave him his daughter Achsah for a wife.

14 Then it came about when she came *to him,* that she persuaded him to ask her father for a field. Then she alighted from her donkey, and Caleb said to her, "What do you want?"

15 She said to him, "Give me a blessing, since you have given me the land of the Negev, give me also springs of water." So Caleb gave her the upper springs and the lower springs.

16 The descendants of the Kenite, Moses' father-in-law, went up from the city of palms with the sons of Judah, to the wilderness of Judah which is in the south of Arad; and they went and lived with the people.

17 Then Judah went with Simeon his brother, and they struck the Canaanites living in Zephath, and utterly destroyed it. So the name of the city was called Hormah.

18 And Judah took Gaza with its territory and Ashkelon with its territory and Ekron with its territory.

19 Now the LORD was with Judah, and they took possession of the hill country; but they could not drive out the inhabitants of the valley because they had iron chariots.

20 Then they gave Hebron to Caleb, as Moses had promised; and he drove out from there the three sons of Anak.

21 But the sons of Benjamin did not drive out the Jebusites who lived in Jerusalem; so the Jebusites have lived with the sons of Benjamin in Jerusalem to this day.

22 Likewise the house of Joseph went up against Bethel, and the LORD was with them.

23 The house of Joseph spied out Bethel (now the name of the city was formerly Luz).

24 The spies saw a man coming out of the city and they said to him, "Please show us the entrance to the city and we will treat you kindly."

25 So he showed them the entrance to the city, and they struck the city with the edge of the sword, but they let the man and all his family go free.

26 The man went into the land of the Hittites and built a city and named it Luz which is its name to this day.

27 But Manasseh did not take possession of Beth-shean and its villages, or Taanach and its villages, or the inhabitants of Dor and its villages, or the inhabitants of Ibleam and its villages, or the inhabitants of Megiddo and its villages; so the Canaanites persisted in living in that land.

28 It came about when Israel became strong, that they put the Canaanites to forced labor, but they did not drive them out completely.

29 Ephraim did not drive out the Canaanites who were living in Gezer; so the Canaanites lived in Gezer among them.

30 Zebulun did not drive out the inhabitants of Kitron, or the inhabitants of Nahalol; so the Canaanites lived among them and became subject to forced labor.

31 Asher did not drive out the inhabitants of Acco, or the inhabitants of Sidon, or of Ahlab, or of Achzib, or of Helbah, or of Aphik, or of Rehob.

32 So the Asherites lived among the Canaanites, the inhabitants of the land; for they did not drive them out.

33 Naphtali did not drive out the inhabitants of Beth-shemesh, or the inhabitants of Beth-anath, but lived among the Canaanites, the inhabitants of the land; and the inhabitants of Beth-shemesh and Beth-anath became forced labor for them.

34 Then the Amorites forced the sons of Dan into the hill country, for they did not allow them to come down to the valley;

35 yet the Amorites persisted in living in Mount Heres, in Aijalon and in Shaalbim; but when the power of the house of Joseph grew strong, they became forced labor.

36 The border of the Amorites ran from the ascent of Akrabbim, from Sela and upward.

2 NOW the angel of the LORD came up from Gilgal to Bochim. And he said, "I brought you up out of Egypt and led you into the land which I have sworn to your fathers; and I said, 'I will never break My covenant with you,

2 and as for you, you shall make no covenant with the inhabitants of this land; you shall tear down their altars.' But you have not obeyed Me; what is this you have done?

3 "Therefore I also said, 'I will not drive them out before you; but they will become as thorns in your sides and their gods will be a snare to you.'"

4 When the angel of the LORD spoke these words to all the sons of Israel, the people lifted up their voices and wept.

5 So they named that place Bochim; and there they sacrificed to the LORD.

6 When Joshua had dismissed the people, the sons of Israel went each to his inheritance to possess the land.

7 The people served the LORD all the days of Joshua, and all the days of the elders who survived Joshua, who had seen all the great work of the LORD which He had done for Israel.

8 Then Joshua the son of Nun, the servant of the LORD, died at the age of one hundred and ten.

9 And they buried him in the territory of his inheritance in Timnath-heres, in the hill country of Ephraim, north of Mount Gaash.

10 All that generation also were gathered to their fathers; and there arose another generation after them who did not know the LORD, nor yet the work which He had done for Israel.

11 Then the sons of Israel did evil in the sight of the LORD and served the Baals,

➤ 12 and they forsook the LORD, the God of their fathers, who had brought them out of the land of Egypt, and followed other gods from among the gods of the peoples who were around them, and bowed themselves down to them; thus they provoked the LORD to anger.

13 So they forsook the LORD and served Baal and the Ashtaroth.

14 The anger of the LORD burned against Israel, and He gave them into the hands of plunderers who plundered them; and He sold them into the hands of their enemies around them, so that they could no longer stand before their enemies.

15 Wherever they went, the hand of the LORD was against them for evil, as the LORD had spoken and as the LORD had sworn to them, so that they were severely distressed.

16 Then the LORD raised up judges who delivered them from the hands of those who plundered them.

17 Yet they did not listen to their judges, for they played the harlot after other gods and bowed themselves down to them. They turned aside quickly from the way in which their fathers had walked in obeying the commandments of the LORD; they did not do as their fathers.

18 When the LORD raised up judges for ◄ them, the LORD was with the judge and delivered them from the hand of their enemies all the days of the judge; for the LORD was moved to pity by their groaning because of those who oppressed and afflicted them.

19 But it came about when the judge died, that they would turn back and act more corruptly than their fathers, in following other gods to serve them and bow down to them; they did not abandon their practices or their stubborn ways.

LIFE LESSONS

➤ **Judges 2:12 — They forsook the LORD, the God of their fathers . . . thus they provoked the LORD to anger.**

The Lord predicted if the people did not completely remove the pagan influence from their land, they would eventually serve pagan gods (Judg. 2:3). Incomplete obedience has dire consequences. Will we continue to trust the Lord and obey His Word when the going gets tough? Our answers will determine whether we ultimately succeed or fail.

➤ **Judges 2:18 — The LORD was moved to pity by their groaning because of those who oppressed and afflicted them.**

Where would we be if the Lord did not temper His judgment with mercy? He is a holy God with a loving heart—and for that reason, we continue to live and breathe.

LIFE PRINCIPLE 6

YOU REAP WHAT YOU SOW, MORE THAN YOU
SOW, AND LATER THAN YOU SOW.

JUDGES 2:1–4

Today is the father of tomorrow.
What we are today is the result of what
we have been thinking and the way we have lived
in the past. Those who act wisely today will have
wisdom in the future to make wise decisions.
The same is true when we come to the subject of
finances. Those who save wisely today will have
plenty tomorrow. Those who spend everything
they have today will have little or nothing in the
future. It is a shortsighted person who thinks
only of the now, doing as little as possible, for
on payday he will have no way to avoid the poor
quality and small quantity of his rewards. The
nation of Israel had to learn this in a very personal
way. Their waywardness and failure to do what
God instructed them to do often placed them in a
position where they would not have His blessings.

The Lord gives principles in Scripture to serve
as warnings and as an encouragement. His Word
states, "Do not be deceived, God is not mocked;
for whatever a man sows, this he will also reap"
(Gal. 6:7). This is an unalterable law that affects
everyone in every area of life, family, work, and
pleasure.

Every farmer understands the meaning of this
principle: We reap what we sow, more than we
sow, and later than we sow. Let's look at each part
of the principle to make sure we understand its
full implications.

*1. The principle applies to everyone, both
Christians and non-Christians.*

This principle is irrevocable; there is no escape,
either the believer or for the unbeliever. It is a law
of life.

Did you notice how Galatians 6:7 begins? It
says, "Do not be deceived, God is not mocked."
Herein lies the root cause of the careless and
indulgent lifestyle of many people. They *are*
deceived. They either do not believe the truth, or
they think they will somehow be the exceptions to
God's laws.

To mock God is to turn up one's nose at Him,
to hope to outwit Him—a foolish thought, as
2 Corinthians 5:10 reveals: "We must all appear
before the judgment seat of Christ, so that each
one may be recompensed for his deeds in the
body, according to what he has done, whether
good or bad."

If you were required to appear before the
judgment seat of Christ in the next five minutes,
what kind of crops would you have to show?

2. We reap what we sow.

The fact that we reap what we sow is good
news for those who sow good habits, but a
frightening thought for those currently involved
in ungodly activities such as promiscuity, drug
and alcohol abuse, neglect of family, or mistreat-
ment of others in order to climb the ladder of
success. We cannot sow crabgrass and expect to
reap pineapples. We cannot sow disobedience to
God and expect to reap His blessing. What we
sow, we reap. Let us not deceive ourselves: we
will reap the harvest of our lives.

3. We reap more than we sow.

Why do farmers plant their seed? Because
they expect to harvest a great deal more than
they sow. A single seed that sprouts can yield
dozens, scores, even hundreds of seeds. It is the
same way with both sin and righteousness—a
small decision to do either good or bad reaps a
much bigger crop, for either joy or sorrow.

Jesus used the picture of a sprouting seed
to show that when we allow God's Word to
produce good things in us, the results multiply: "The one on whom seed was sown on the
good soil, this is the man who hears the word
and understands it; who indeed bears fruit and
brings forth, some a hundredfold, some sixty,
and some thirty" (Matt. 13:23). On the other
side of the ledger, the prophet Hosea describes
what awaits those who choose to sow seeds of
wickedness: "They sow the wind and they reap
the whirlwind" (Hos. 8:7).

4. We reap later than we sow.

Some are deceived because their present seed
does not appear to be producing an immediate
crop. So they continue down their course, mistakenly believing there will never be a harvest.
But unlike the crops of the field, which get
harvested at approximately the same time each
year, there is no regular timetable for the harvest
of life. Some crops we reap quickly; others take a
long time. But do not be deceived—their season
will come. And by going the second mile now
and giving more than is required, we will reap
rich dividends later.

"For whatever a man sows, this he will also
reap." What a comforting and assuring
thought to those who faithfully labor under
difficult circumstances! Faithfulness in such situations *will* produce a rich harvest in the
future, for our heavenly Father always keeps
His promises.

20 So the anger of the LORD burned against Israel, and He said, "Because this nation has transgressed My covenant which I commanded their fathers and has not listened to My voice,

21 I also will no longer drive out before them any of the nations which Joshua left when he died,

22 in order to test Israel by them, whether they will keep the way of the LORD to walk in it as their fathers did, or not."

23 So the LORD allowed those nations to remain, not driving them out quickly; and He did not give them into the hand of Joshua.

Psalm 48:1–8

A Song; a Psalm of the sons of Korah.

48 GREAT is the LORD, and greatly to be praised,
In the city of our God, His holy mountain.

2 Beautiful in elevation, the joy of the whole earth,
Is Mount Zion *in* the far north,
The city of the great King.

3 God, in her palaces,
Has made Himself known as a stronghold.

4 For, lo, the kings assembled themselves,
They passed by together.

5 They saw *it*, then they were amazed;
They were terrified, they fled in alarm.

6 Panic seized them there,
Anguish, as of a woman in childbirth.

7 With the east wind
You break the ships of Tarshish.

8 As we have heard, so have we seen
In the city of the LORD of hosts, in the city of our God;
God will establish her forever.
                                    Selah.

Proverbs 14:15–17

15 The naive believes everything,
But the sensible man considers his steps.

16 A wise man is cautious and turns away from evil,
But a fool is arrogant and careless.

17 A quick-tempered man acts foolishly,
And a man of evil devices is hated.

Luke 14:1–24

14 IT happened that when He went into the house of one of the leaders of the Pharisees on *the* Sabbath to eat bread, they were watching Him closely.

2 And there in front of Him was a man suffering from dropsy.

3 And Jesus answered and spoke to the lawyers and Pharisees, saying, "Is it lawful to heal on the Sabbath, or not?"

4 But they kept silent. And He took hold of him and healed him, and sent him away.

5 And He said to them, "Which one of you will have a son or an ox fall into a well, and will not immediately pull him out on a Sabbath day?"

6 And they could make no reply to this.

7 And He *began* speaking a parable to the invited guests when He noticed how they had been picking out the places of honor *at the table*, saying to them,

8 "When you are invited by someone to a wedding feast, do not take the place of honor, for someone more distinguished than you may have been invited by him,

9 and he who invited you both will come and say to you, 'Give *your* place to this man,' and then in disgrace you proceed to occupy the last place.

10 "But when you are invited, go and recline at the last place, so that when the one who has invited you comes, he may say to you, 'Friend, move up higher'; then you will have honor in the sight of all who are at the table with you.

11 "For everyone who exalts himself will be humbled, and he who humbles himself will be exalted."

12 And He also went on to say to the one who had invited Him, "When you give a luncheon or a dinner, do not invite your friends or your brothers or your relatives or rich neighbors, otherwise they may also invite you in return and *that* will be your repayment.

13 "But when you give a reception, invite *the* poor, *the* crippled, *the* lame, *the* blind,

➤ 14 and you will be blessed, since they do not have *the means* to repay you; for you will be repaid at the resurrection of the righteous."

15 When one of those who were reclining *at the table* with Him heard this, he said to Him, "Blessed is everyone who will eat bread in the kingdom of God!"

16 But He said to him, "A man was giving a big dinner, and he invited many;

17 and at the dinner hour he sent his slave to say to those who had been invited, 'Come; for everything is ready now.'

18 "But they all alike began to make excuses. The first one said to him, 'I have bought a piece of land and I need to go out and look at it; please consider me excused.'

19 "Another one said, 'I have bought five yoke of oxen, and I am going to try them out; please consider me excused.'

20 "Another one said, 'I have married a wife, and for that reason I cannot come.'

21 "And the slave came *back* and reported this to his master. Then the head of the household became angry and said to his slave, 'Go out at once into the streets and lanes of the city and bring in here the poor and crippled and blind and lame.'

22 "And the slave said, 'Master, what you commanded has been done, and still there is room.'

23 "And the master said to the slave, ◄ 'Go out into the highways and along the hedges, and compel *them* to come in, so that my house may be filled.

24 'For I tell you, none of those men who were invited shall taste of my dinner.'"

LIFE LESSONS

➤ **Luke 14:14 —** *"You will be repaid at the resurrection of the righteous."*

*N*o one ever outgives God. Any kind deed or blessing we bestow upon someone else, in Jesus' name and for His sake, will be repaid in abundance. God loves to reward His faithful people!

➤ **Luke 14:23 —** *"Go out into the highways and along the hedges, and compel them to come in, so that my house may be filled."*

*F*ar from wanting to exclude people from heaven, God desires "all men to be saved and to come to the knowledge of the truth" (1 Tim. 2:4).

Judges 3:1—4:24

3 NOW these are the nations which the LORD left, to test Israel by them (*that is*, all who had not experienced any of the wars of Canaan;

2 only in order that the generations of the sons of Israel might be taught war, those who had not experienced it formerly).

3 *These nations are:* the five lords of the Philistines and all the Canaanites and the Sidonians and the Hivites who lived in Mount Lebanon, from Mount Baal-hermon as far as Lebo-hamath.

4 They were for testing Israel, to find out if they would obey the commandments of the LORD, which He had commanded their fathers through Moses.

5 The sons of Israel lived among the Canaanites, the Hittites, the Amorites, the Perizzites, the Hivites, and the Jebusites;

6 and they took their daughters for ◄ themselves as wives, and gave their own daughters to their sons, and served their gods.

LIFE LESSONS

➤ **Judges 3:6 —** *They took their daughters for themselves as wives, and gave their own daughters to their sons, and served their gods.*

*M*arriage can make or break one's faith. Judges declares Israel fell into idolatry by marrying into it, just as King Solomon would many years later (1 Kin. 11:4). Christians are not to marry unbelievers—period (2 Cor. 6:14).

7   The sons of Israel did what was evil in the sight of the LORD, and forgot the LORD their God and served the Baals and the Asheroth.

8   Then the anger of the LORD was kindled against Israel, so that He sold them into the hands of Cushan-rishathaim king of Mesopotamia; and the sons of Israel served Cushan-rishathaim eight years.

9   When the sons of Israel cried to the LORD, the LORD raised up a deliverer for the sons of Israel to deliver them, Othniel the son of Kenaz, Caleb's younger brother.

10   The Spirit of the LORD came upon him, and he judged Israel. When he went out to war, the LORD gave Cushan-rishathaim king of Mesopotamia into his hand, so that he prevailed over Cushan-rishathaim.

11   Then the land had rest forty years. And Othniel the son of Kenaz died.

➤ 12   Now the sons of Israel again did evil in the sight of the LORD. So the LORD strengthened Eglon the king of Moab against Israel, because they had done evil in the sight of the LORD.

13   And he gathered to himself the sons of Ammon and Amalek; and he went and defeated Israel, and they possessed the city of the palm trees.

14   The sons of Israel served Eglon the king of Moab eighteen years.

15   But when the sons of Israel cried to the LORD, the LORD raised up a deliverer for them, Ehud the son of Gera, the Benjamite, a left-handed man. And the sons of Israel sent tribute by him to Eglon the king of Moab.

16   Ehud made himself a sword which had two edges, a cubit in length, and he bound it on his right thigh under his cloak.

17   He presented the tribute to Eglon king of Moab. Now Eglon was a very fat man.

18   It came about when he had finished presenting the tribute, that he sent away the people who had carried the tribute.

19   But he himself turned back from the idols which were at Gilgal, and said, "I have a secret message for you, O king." And he said, "Keep silence." And all who attended him left him.

20   Ehud came to him while he was sitting alone in his cool roof chamber. And Ehud said, "I have a message from God for you." And he arose from his seat.

21   Ehud stretched out his left hand, took the sword from his right thigh and thrust it into his belly.

22   The handle also went in after the blade, and the fat closed over the blade, for he did not draw the sword out of his belly; and the refuse came out.

23   Then Ehud went out into the vestibule and shut the doors of the roof chamber behind him, and locked *them.*

24   When he had gone out, his servants came and looked, and behold, the doors of the roof chamber were locked; and they said, "He is only relieving himself in the cool room."

25   They waited until they became anxious; but behold, he did not open the doors of the roof chamber. Therefore they took the key and opened them, and behold, their master had fallen to the floor dead.

26   Now Ehud escaped while they were delaying, and he passed by the idols and escaped to Seirah.

27   It came about when he had arrived, that he blew the trumpet in the hill country of Ephraim; and the sons of Israel went down with him from the hill country, and he *was* in front of them.

28   He said to them, "Pursue *them,* for the LORD has given your enemies the Moabites into your hands." So they went down after him and seized the fords of the Jordan opposite Moab, and did not allow anyone to cross.

29   They struck down at that time about ten thousand Moabites, all robust and valiant men; and no one escaped.

30   So Moab was subdued that day under the hand of Israel. And the land was undisturbed for eighty years.

31   After him came Shamgar the son of

LIFE LESSONS

➤ **Judges 3:12** — *The LORD strengthened Eglon the king of Moab against Israel, because they had done evil in the sight of the LORD.*

*W*hen we make a habit of disobeying God, He may take an active role in increasing the power of our enemies. He does this so we will repent and return to Him—not to destroy us.

Anath, who struck down six hundred Philistines with an oxgoad; and he also saved Israel.

4 THEN the sons of Israel again did evil in the sight of the LORD, after Ehud died.

2 And the LORD sold them into the hand of Jabin king of Canaan, who reigned in Hazor; and the commander of his army was Sisera, who lived in Harosheth-hagoyim.

3 The sons of Israel cried to the LORD; for he had nine hundred iron chariots, and he oppressed the sons of Israel severely for twenty years.

4 Now Deborah, a prophetess, the wife of Lappidoth, was judging Israel at that time.

5 She used to sit under the palm tree of Deborah between Ramah and Bethel in the hill country of Ephraim; and the sons of Israel came up to her for judgment.

6 Now she sent and summoned Barak the son of Abinoam from Kedesh-naphtali, and said to him, "Behold, the LORD, the God of Israel, has commanded, 'Go and march to Mount Tabor, and take with you ten thousand men from the sons of Naphtali and from the sons of Zebulun.

7 'I will draw out to you Sisera, the commander of Jabin's army, with his chariots and his many *troops* to the river Kishon, and I will give him into your hand.'"

8 Then Barak said to her, "If you will go with me, then I will go; but if you will not go with me, I will not go."

9 She said, "I will surely go with you; nevertheless, the honor shall not be yours on the journey that you are about to take, for the LORD will sell Sisera into the hands of a woman." Then Deborah arose and went with Barak to Kedesh.

10 Barak called Zebulun and Naphtali together to Kedesh, and ten thousand men went up with him; Deborah also went up with him.

11 Now Heber the Kenite had separated himself from the Kenites, from the sons of Hobab the father-in-law of Moses, and had pitched his tent as far away as the oak in Zaanannim, which is near Kedesh.

12 Then they told Sisera that Barak the son of Abinoam had gone up to Mount Tabor.

13 Sisera called together all his chariots, nine hundred iron chariots, and all the people who *were* with him, from Harosheth-hagoyim to the river Kishon.

14 Deborah said to Barak, "Arise! For this is the day in which the LORD has given Sisera into your hands; behold, the LORD has gone out before you." So Barak went down from Mount Tabor with ten thousand men following him.

15 The LORD routed Sisera and all *his* ◄

LIFE LESSONS

➤ **Judges 4:15 —** *The LORD routed Sisera.*

*T*he Bible declares *the Lord* routed Sisera; the sword of Barak and his men were only secondary. As David said years later, "The LORD does not deliver by sword or by spear; for the battle is the LORD's" (1 Sam. 17:47).

Life Examples:

DEBORAH: A Mother in Israel

JUDGES 4:4–10

*T*he Bible doesn't tell us much about Deborah other than to call her a prophetess, a highly esteemed judge of Israel, and the wife of Lappidoth. We don't know if Scripture's description of her as "a mother in Israel" (Judg. 5:7) means she had children or she cared for Israel as only a loving mother could. Also, Scripture does not indicate why God chose her to become a judge. Certainly, this action seems strange given the fact the culture was one generally ruled by men. However, God is not bound by tradition. He sees the hearts of the individuals who serve Him and is motivated to use them for His purposes.

Deborah loved the Lord and served Him faithfully. We do know the people trusted her; even the commander of the army, Barak, respected her leadership.

As we study the life of Deborah, we realize it doesn't take a certain set of credentials to become an effective servant of God. There is only one requirement—a heart willing to be used by Him. The Lord uses the person who listens to Him and obeys Him. Deborah made herself available to God, and He gave her the ability to be victorious.

chariots and all *his* army with the edge of the sword before Barak; and Sisera alighted from *his* chariot and fled away on foot.
16 But Barak pursued the chariots and the army as far as Harosheth-hagoyim, and all the army of Sisera fell by the edge of the sword; not even one was left.
17 Now Sisera fled away on foot to the tent of Jael the wife of Heber the Kenite, for *there was* peace between Jabin the king of Hazor and the house of Heber the Kenite.
18 Jael went out to meet Sisera, and said to him, "Turn aside, my master, turn aside to me! Do not be afraid." And he turned aside to her into the tent, and she covered him with a rug.
19 He said to her, "Please give me a little water to drink, for I am thirsty." So she opened a bottle of milk and gave him a drink; then she covered him.
20 He said to her, "Stand in the doorway of the tent, and it shall be if anyone comes and inquires of you, and says, 'Is there anyone here?' that you shall say, 'No.'"
21 But Jael, Heber's wife, took a tent peg and seized a hammer in her hand, and went secretly to him and drove the peg into his temple, and it went through into the ground; for he was sound asleep and exhausted. So he died.
22 And behold, as Barak pursued Sisera, Jael came out to meet him and said to him, "Come, and I will show you the man whom you are seeking." And he entered with her, and behold Sisera was lying dead with the tent peg in his temple.
23 So God subdued on that day Jabin the king of Canaan before the sons of Israel.
24 The hand of the sons of Israel pressed heavier and heavier upon Jabin the king of Canaan, until they had destroyed Jabin the king of Canaan.

Psalm 48:9–14

9 We have thought on Your
   lovingkindness, O God,
   In the midst of Your temple.
➤ 10 As is Your name, O God,
   So is Your praise to the ends of the
   earth;

LIFE LESSONS

➤ **Psalm 48:10 — *As is Your name, O God, so is Your praise to the ends of the earth.***

*G*od deserves our best praise and worship, for He has the best name in the entire universe. The style never matters so much as the heart. Regardless of what we sing, do we bring to Him our best?

Your right hand is full of
   righteousness.
11 Let Mount Zion be glad,
   Let the daughters of Judah rejoice
   Because of Your judgments.
12 Walk about Zion and go around
   her;
   Count her towers;
13 Consider her ramparts;
   Go through her palaces,
   That you may tell *it* to the next
   generation.
14 For such is God,
   Our God forever and ever;
   He will guide us until death.

Proverbs 14:18, 19

18 The naive inherit foolishness,
   But the sensible are crowned with
   knowledge.
19 The evil will bow down before the
   good,
   And the wicked at the gates of the
   righteous.

Luke 14:25–35

25 Now large crowds were going along with Him; and He turned and said to them,
26 "If anyone comes to Me, and does not hate his own father and mother and wife and children and brothers and sisters, yes, and even his own life, he cannot be My disciple.
27 "Whoever does not carry his own cross and come after Me cannot be My disciple.
28 "For which one of you, when he wants to build a tower, does not first sit

➤ Luke 14:26 — *"If anyone comes to Me, and does not hate . . . his own life, he cannot be My disciple."*

*J*esus calls for an exclusive commitment from His disciples. Everything else should pale in comparison to our love for Him because He alone must be enthroned in our hearts.

down and calculate the cost to see if he has enough to complete it?

29 "Otherwise, when he has laid a foundation and is not able to finish, all who observe it begin to ridicule him,

30 saying, 'This man began to build and was not able to finish.'

31 "Or what king, when he sets out to meet another king in battle, will not first sit down and consider whether he is strong enough with ten thousand *men* to encounter the one coming against him with twenty thousand?

32 "Or else, while the other is still far away, he sends a delegation and asks for terms of peace.

33 "So then, none of you can be My disciple who does not give up all his own possessions.

34 "Therefore, salt is good; but if even salt has become tasteless, with what will it be seasoned?

35 "It is useless either for the soil or for the manure pile; it is thrown out. He who has ears to hear, let him hear."

Judges 5:1—6:40

5 THEN Deborah and Barak the son of Abinoam sang on that day, saying,

2 "That the leaders led in Israel,
That the people volunteered,
Bless the LORD!

3 "Hear, O kings; give ear, O rulers!
I—to the LORD, I will sing,
I will sing praise to the LORD, the God of Israel.

4 "LORD, when You went out from Seir,
When You marched from the field of Edom,
The earth quaked, the heavens also dripped,
Even the clouds dripped water.

5 "The mountains quaked at the presence of the LORD,
This Sinai, at the presence of the LORD, the God of Israel.

6 "In the days of Shamgar the son of Anath,
In the days of Jael, the highways were deserted,
And travelers went by roundabout ways.

7 "The peasantry ceased, they ceased in Israel,
Until I, Deborah, arose,
Until I arose, a mother in Israel.

8 "New gods were chosen;

Then war *was* in the gates.
Not a shield or a spear was seen Among forty thousand in Israel.

9 "My heart *goes out* to the commanders of Israel,
The volunteers among the people;
Bless the LORD!

10 "You who ride on white donkeys,
You who sit on *rich* carpets,
And you who travel on the road—sing!

11 "At the sound of those who divide *flocks* among the watering places,
There they shall recount the righteous deeds of the LORD,
The righteous deeds for His peasantry in Israel.
Then the people of the LORD went down to the gates.

12 "Awake, awake, Deborah;
Awake, awake, sing a song!
Arise, Barak, and take away your captives, O son of Abinoam.

13 "Then survivors came down to the nobles;
The people of the LORD came down to me as warriors.

14 "From Ephraim those whose root is in Amalek *came down*,
Following you, Benjamin, with your peoples;
From Machir commanders came down,

LIFE LESSONS

➤ **Judges 5:13** — *"The people of the LORD came down to me as warriors."*

When we face off against the mighty, we need the Lord to help us. If we want to win, we will get on our knees in prayer. The secret to success remains the same throughout the Bible: the presence of God. When He is with us—or more accurately, when we are with Him—success naturally follows.

And from Zebulun those who wield the staff of office.

15 "And the princes of Issachar *were* with Deborah;
As *was* Issachar, so *was* Barak;
Into the valley they rushed at his heels;
Among the divisions of Reuben
There were great resolves of heart.

16 "Why did you sit among the sheepfolds,
To hear the piping for the flocks?
Among the divisions of Reuben
There were great searchings of heart.

17 "Gilead remained across the Jordan;
And why did Dan stay in ships?
Asher sat at the seashore,
And remained by its landings.

18 "Zebulun *was* a people who despised their lives *even* to death,
And Naphtali also, on the high places of the field.

19 "The kings came *and* fought;
Then fought the kings of Canaan
At Taanach near the waters of Megiddo;
They took no plunder in silver.

20 "The stars fought from heaven,
From their courses they fought against Sisera.

21 "The torrent of Kishon swept them away,
The ancient torrent, the torrent Kishon.
O my soul, march on with strength.

22 "Then the horses' hoofs beat
From the dashing, the dashing of his valiant steeds.

23 'Curse Meroz,' said the angel of the LORD,
'Utterly curse its inhabitants;
Because they did not come to the help of the LORD,

To the help of the LORD against the warriors.'

24 "Most blessed of women is Jael,
The wife of Heber the Kenite;
Most blessed is she of women in the tent.

25 "He asked for water *and* she gave him milk;
In a magnificent bowl she brought him curds.

26 "She reached out her hand for the tent peg,
And her right hand for the workmen's hammer.
Then she struck Sisera, she smashed his head;
And she shattered and pierced his temple.

27 "Between her feet he bowed, he fell, he lay;
Between her feet he bowed, he fell;
Where he bowed, there he fell dead.

28 "Out of the window she looked and lamented,
The mother of Sisera through the lattice,
'Why does his chariot delay in coming?
Why do the hoofbeats of his chariots tarry?'

29 "Her wise princesses would answer her,
Indeed she repeats her words to herself,

30 'Are they not finding, are they not dividing the spoil?
A maiden, two maidens for every warrior;
To Sisera a spoil of dyed work,
A spoil of dyed work embroidered,
Dyed work of double embroidery on the neck of the spoiler?'

31 "Thus let all Your enemies perish, O LORD;
But let those who love Him be like the rising of the sun in its might."
And the land was undisturbed for forty years.

6 THEN the sons of Israel did what was evil in the sight of the LORD; and the LORD gave them into the hands of Midian seven years. 2 The power of Midian prevailed against Israel. Because of Midian the sons of Israel made for themselves the dens which were in the mountains and the caves and the strongholds.

3 For it was when Israel had sown, that the Midianites would come up with the Amalekites and the sons of the east and go against them.

4 So they would camp against them and destroy the produce of the earth as far as Gaza, and leave no sustenance in Israel as well as no sheep, ox, or donkey.

5 For they would come up with their livestock and their tents, they would come in like locusts for number, both they and their camels were innumerable; and they came into the land to devastate it.

6 So Israel was brought very low because of Midian, and the sons of Israel cried to the LORD.

7 Now it came about when the sons of Israel cried to the LORD on account of Midian,

8 that the LORD sent a prophet to the sons of Israel, and he said to them, "Thus says the LORD, the God of Israel, 'It was I who brought you up from Egypt and brought you out from the house of slavery.

9 'I delivered you from the hands of the Egyptians and from the hands of all your oppressors, and dispossessed them before you and gave you their land,

➤ 10 and I said to you, "I am the LORD your God; you shall not fear the gods of the Amorites in whose land you live. But you have not obeyed Me."'"

11 Then the angel of the LORD came and sat under the oak that was in Ophrah, which belonged to Joash the Abiezrite as his son Gideon was beating out wheat in the wine press in order to save it from the Midianites.

➤ 12 The angel of the LORD appeared to him and said to him, "The LORD is with you, O valiant warrior."

13 Then Gideon said to him, "O my lord, if the LORD is with us, why then has all this happened to us? And where are all His miracles which our fathers told us about, saying, 'Did not the LORD bring us up from Egypt?' But now the LORD has abandoned us and given us into the hand of Midian."

14 The LORD looked at him and said, "Go in this your strength and deliver Israel from the hand of Midian. Have I not sent you?"

15 He said to Him, "O Lord, how shall I deliver Israel? Behold, my family is the

---

---

least in Manasseh, and I am the youngest in my father's house."

16 But the LORD said to him, "Surely I will be with you, and you shall defeat Midian as one man."

17 So Gideon said to Him, "If now I have found favor in Your sight, then show me a sign that it is You who speak with me.

18 "Please do not depart from here, until I come back to You, and bring out my offering and lay it before You." And He said, "I will remain until you return."

19 Then Gideon went in and prepared a young goat and unleavened bread from an ephah of flour; he put the meat in a basket and the broth in a pot, and brought them out to him under the oak and presented them.

20 The angel of God said to him, "Take the meat and the unleavened bread and lay them on this rock, and pour out the broth." And he did so.

21 Then the angel of the LORD put out the end of the staff that was in his hand and touched the meat and the unleavened bread; and fire sprang up from the rock and consumed the meat and the unleavened bread. Then the angel of the LORD vanished from his sight.

22 When Gideon saw that he was the angel of the LORD, he said, "Alas, O Lord GOD! For now I have seen the angel of the LORD face to face."

23 The LORD said to him, "Peace to you, do not fear; you shall not die."

24 Then Gideon built an altar there to the LORD and named it The LORD is Peace. To this day it is still in Ophrah of the Abiezrites.

25 Now on the same night the LORD said to him, "Take your father's bull and a second bull seven years old, and pull down the altar of Baal which belongs to your father, and cut down the Asherah that is beside it;

26 and build an altar to the LORD your God on the top of this stronghold in an orderly manner, and take a second bull and offer a burnt offering with the wood of the Asherah which you shall cut down."

27 Then Gideon took ten men of his servants and did as the LORD had spoken to him; and because he was too afraid of his father's household and the men of the city to do it by day, he did it by night.

28 When the men of the city arose early in the morning, behold, the altar of Baal was torn down, and the Asherah which was beside it was cut down, and the second bull was offered on the altar which had been built.

29 They said to one another, "Who did this thing?" And when they searched about and inquired, they said, "Gideon the son of Joash did this thing."

30 Then the men of the city said to Joash, "Bring out your son, that he may die, for he has torn down the altar of Baal, and indeed, he has cut down the Asherah which was beside it."

31 But Joash said to all who stood against him, "Will you contend for Baal, or will you deliver him? Whoever will plead for him shall be put to death by morning. If he is a god, let him contend for himself, because someone has torn down his altar."

32 Therefore on that day he named him Jerubbaal, that is to say, "Let Baal contend against him," because he had torn down his altar.

33 Then all the Midianites and the Amalekites and the sons of the east assembled themselves; and they crossed over and camped in the valley of Jezreel.

34 So the Spirit of the LORD came upon Gideon; and he blew a trumpet, and the Abiezrites were called together to follow him.

35 He sent messengers throughout Manasseh, and they also were called

LIFE LESSONS

> **Judges 6:34 — *The Spirit of the LORD came upon Gideon.***

*W*hen the Spirit of the living God fills us, "impossibilities" become possible. As Paul writes, "For God has not given us a spirit of timidity, but of power and love and discipline" (2 Tim. 1:7).

together to follow him; and he sent messengers to Asher, Zebulun, and Naphtali, and they came up to meet them.

36 Then Gideon said to God, "If You will deliver Israel through me, as You have spoken,

37 behold, I will put a fleece of wool on the threshing floor. If there is dew on the fleece only, and it is dry on all the ground, then I will know that You will deliver Israel through me, as You have spoken."

38 And it was so. When he arose early the next morning and squeezed the fleece, he drained the dew from the fleece, a bowl full of water.

39 Then Gideon said to God, "Do not let Your anger burn against me that I may speak once more; please let me make a test once more with the fleece, let it now be dry only on the fleece, and let there be dew on all the ground."

40 God did so that night; for it was dry only on the fleece, and dew was on all the ground.

Psalm 49:1–9

For the choir director. A Psalm of the sons of Korah.

49 HEAR this, all peoples;
Give ear, all inhabitants of the world,

2 Both low and high,
Rich and poor together.

3 My mouth will speak wisdom,
And the meditation of my heart *will be* understanding.

4 I will incline my ear to a proverb;
I will express my riddle on the harp.

5 Why should I fear in days of adversity,
When the iniquity of my foes surrounds me,

ANSWERS TO LIFE'S QUESTIONS

Is "fleece throwing" a good way to discover the will of God?

JUDGES 6:36–40

Some try to determine God's will by "throwing fleeces." We say, "If X happens, then I'll do one thing; but if Z happens, then I'll do another." But how does such a strategy differ from treating the will of God like a coin toss and basing our decisions on whether it falls on heads or tails? In most cases, putting out a fleece demonstrates not a robust faith in God, but an unhealthy suspicion He doesn't have our best interests at heart and He really can't be trusted to fulfill His promises.

We find the act of fleece throwing in the Book of Judges, when God calls Gideon to fight the Midianites (Judg. 6:36–40). It is obvious Gideon did not feel confident about the divine assignment the Lord had given him. Instead of going forward in faith, he put out his fleece, not to discover the will of God, but in an effort to gain reassurance he would have success. Notice three things about this questionable practice.

First, the fleece throwing was Gideon's idea, not God's. Nowhere in Scripture does the Lord authorize such a practice or call it a desirable method for knowing His purposes. When God makes His will clear, He expects us to trust Him.

Second, only here in Scripture is this method used. No one else employs it.

Third, Gideon laid out the fleece so he could know God's will. He knew what the Lord had instructed him to do, but he did it to gain confidence in the outcome God had already promised. Gideon understood the Lord wanted him to lead the people into battle against the Midianites. The armies had already gathered for war (Judg. 6:33), and he was the nation's leader. He simply wanted an extraordinary sign from God that he and the Israelites would succeed. At some point, each one of us has done the same thing. We go back to God in prayer, seeking His encouragement.

Repeatedly in Scripture, the Lord calls us to be faithful. Genuine trust in God means we follow Him wherever He leads and do whatever He directs, without any concern for the outcome. Job had the right idea: "Though He slay me, I will hope in Him" (Job 13:15).

Gideon's actions indicated he really did not believe God would do what He said He would do. Still, there was a great desire within his heart to trust the Lord, and this is what God saw in his life. The Lord calls us to a different path and walk. It is a walk of faith, not one of fear, doubt, or worry. The psalmist wrote: "God is our refuge and strength, a very present help in trouble. Therefore we will not fear, though the earth should change and though the mountains slip into the heart of the sea" (Ps. 46:1, 2).

6 Even those who trust in their wealth
And boast in the abundance of their riches?
7 No man can by any means redeem *his* brother
Or give to God a ransom for him—
8 For the redemption of his soul is costly,
And he should cease *trying* forever—
9 That he should live on eternally,
That he should not undergo decay.

Proverbs 14:20, 21

20 The poor is hated even by his neighbor,
But those who love the rich are many.
21 He who despises his neighbor sins,
But happy is he who is gracious to the poor.

Luke 15:1–10

15 NOW all the tax collectors and the sinners were coming near Him to listen to Him.
2 Both the Pharisees and the scribes *began* to grumble, saying, "This man receives sinners and eats with them."
3 So He told them this parable, saying,
4 "What man among you, if he has a hundred sheep and has lost one of them, does not leave the ninety-nine in the open pasture and go after the one which is lost until he finds it?
5 "When he has found it, he lays it on his shoulders, rejoicing.
6 "And when he comes home, he calls together his friends and his neighbors, saying to them, 'Rejoice with me, for I have found my sheep which was lost!'
7 "I tell you that in the same way, there will be *more* joy in heaven over

one sinner who repents than over ninety-nine righteous persons who need no repentance.

8 "Or what woman, if she has ten silver coins and loses one coin, does not light a lamp and sweep the house and search carefully until she finds it?

9 "When she has found it, she calls together her friends and neighbors, saying, 'Rejoice with me, for I have found the coin which I had lost!'

10 "In the same way, I tell you, there is joy in the presence of the angels of God over one sinner who repents."

LIFE LESSONS

➤ **Luke 15:6 — "Rejoice with me, for I have found my sheep which was lost!"**

*T*he Lord is neither cold-hearted nor matter-of-fact about finding His lost sheep and bringing them home. He takes great joy and feels great excitement in re-establishing a close bond with His wandering ones.

➤ **Luke 15:10 — "There is joy in the presence of the angels of God over one sinner who repents."**

*J*esus cannot talk about heaven and about the redeemed who populate it without talking about joy and gladness. Heaven is a very happy place because joy is an attribute of God (Gal. 5:22).

APRIL 21

🧭 Judges 7:1—8:35

7 THEN Jerubbaal (that is, Gideon) and all the people who were with him, rose early and camped beside the spring of Harod; and the camp of Midian was on the north side of them by the hill of Moreh in the valley.

➤ 2 The LORD said to Gideon, "The people who are with you are too many for Me to give Midian into their hands, for Israel would become boastful, saying, 'My own power has delivered me.'

3 "Now therefore come, proclaim in the hearing of the people, saying, 'Whoever is afraid and trembling, let him return and depart from Mount Gilead.'" So 22,000 people returned, but 10,000 remained.

4 Then the LORD said to Gideon, "The people are still too many; bring them down to the water and I will test them for you there. Therefore it shall be that he of whom I say to you, 'This one shall go with you,' he shall go with you; but everyone of whom I say to you, 'This one shall not go with you,' he shall not go."

5 So he brought the people down to the water. And the LORD said to Gideon, "You shall separate everyone who laps the water with his tongue as a dog laps, as well as everyone who kneels to drink."

6 Now the number of those who lapped, putting their hand to their mouth, was 300 men; but all the rest of the people kneeled to drink water.

7 The LORD said to Gideon, "I will deliver you with the 300 men who lapped and will give the Midianites into your hands; so let all the *other* people go, each man to his home."

8 So the 300 men took the people's provisions and their trumpets into their hands. And Gideon sent all the *other*

LIFE LESSONS

➤ **Judges 7:2 — "The people who are with you are too many."**

*W*hen God wants to act mightily in our lives, He may first reduce our physical resources in order to demonstrate that He accomplishes the feat and not we ourselves.

➤ **Judges 7:7 — "I will deliver you with the 300 men who lapped and will give the Midianites into your hands."**

*O*n hearing these odd instructions for battle, Gideon may have felt as Joshua did many years before at Jericho. But both men obeyed, and both men experienced God's great victory on their behalf.

men of Israel, each to his tent, but retained the 300 men; and the camp of Midian was below him in the valley.

9 Now the same night it came about that the LORD said to him, "Arise, go down against the camp, for I have given it into your hands.

10 "But if you are afraid to go down, go with Purah your servant down to the camp,

11 and you will hear what they say; and afterward your hands will be strengthened that you may go down against the camp." So he went with Purah his servant down to the outposts of the army that was in the camp.

12 Now the Midianites and the Amalekites and all the sons of the east were lying in the valley as numerous as locusts; and their camels were without number, as numerous as the sand on the seashore.

13 When Gideon came, behold, a man was relating a dream to his friend. And he said, "Behold, I had a dream; a loaf of barley bread was tumbling into the camp of Midian, and it came to the tent and struck it so that it fell, and turned it upside down so that the tent lay flat."

14 His friend replied, "This is nothing less than the sword of Gideon the son of Joash, a man of Israel; God has given Midian and all the camp into his hand."

15 When Gideon heard the account of the dream and its interpretation, he bowed in worship. He returned to the camp of Israel and said, "Arise, for the LORD has given the camp of Midian into your hands."

16 He divided the 300 men into three companies, and he put trumpets and empty pitchers into the hands of all of them, with torches inside the pitchers.

17 He said to them, "Look at me and do likewise. And behold, when I come to the outskirts of the camp, do as I do.

18 "When I and all who are with me blow the trumpet, then you also blow the trumpets all around the camp and say, 'For the LORD and for Gideon.'"

19 So Gideon and the hundred men who were with him came to the outskirts of the camp at the beginning of the middle watch, when they had just posted the watch; and they blew the trumpets and smashed the pitchers that were in their hands.

20 When the three companies blew the

Life Examples:

Adversity Reveals Our Strengths and Weaknesses

JUDGES 7:9–15

*W*hen adversity strikes, we discover the depth of our spiritual characters. Perhaps you've said in the aftermath of some hardship, "Before this happened, I never would have thought I could deal with something like this."

Gideon had that type of understanding. When the angel of the Lord said to him, "The LORD is with you, O valiant warrior," Gideon automatically responded, "O my lord, if the LORD is with us, why then has all this happened to us? . . . The LORD has abandoned us" (Judg. 6:12, 13). He saw himself and his people as weak and unworthy. The Lord replied almost as if He hadn't heard him: "Go in this your strength and deliver Israel from the hand of Midian. Have I not sent you?" (v. 14).

Again, Gideon replied with an extremely low view of himself: "O Lord, how shall I deliver Israel? Behold, my family is the least in Manasseh, and I am the youngest in my

father's house" (v. 15). Once more the Lord encouraged his servant, "Surely I will be with you, and you shall defeat Midian as one man" (v. 16).

Friend, when the Lord calls you strong, don't declare yourself weak!

When the Lord says you are forgiven, don't dwell on your sins!

When the Lord says you are righteous, don't see yourself as guilty!

Never try to cope with adversity on your own apart from God. You need His wisdom and strength. We can do very little to help ourselves. We need His ability every hour of every day of every year. He is our ever-present help (Ps. 46:1).

Our strength lies in the Lord and not in ourselves. There is no comparison between the might and ability of God and of humankind. He is infinite; we are finite. When we rely on the Lord, we have access to His unlimited power and wisdom; therefore, we will not end up as failures. When we attempt to rely on ourselves, however, usually we fail miserably—and often suffer even more adversity. Don't make that mistake!

trumpets and broke the pitchers, they held the torches in their left hands and the trumpets in their right hands for blowing, and cried, "A sword for the LORD and for Gideon!"

21 Each stood in his place around the camp; and all the army ran, crying out as they fled.

22 When they blew 300 trumpets, the LORD set the sword of one against another even throughout the whole army; and the army fled as far as Beth-shittah toward Zererah, as far as the edge of Abel-meholah, by Tabbath.

23 The men of Israel were summoned from Naphtali and Asher and all Manasseh, and they pursued Midian.

24 Gideon sent messengers throughout all the hill country of Ephraim, saying, "Come down against Midian and take the waters before them, as far as Beth-barah and the Jordan." So all the men of Ephraim were summoned and they took the waters as far as Beth-barah and the Jordan.

25 They captured the two leaders of Midian, Oreb and Zeeb, and they killed Oreb at the rock of Oreb, and they killed Zeeb at the wine press of Zeeb, while they pursued Midian; and they brought the heads of Oreb and Zeeb to Gideon from across the Jordan.

8 THEN the men of Ephraim said to him, "What is this thing you have done to us, not calling us when you went to fight against Midian?" And they contended with him vigorously.

2 But he said to them, "What have I done now in comparison with you? Is not the gleaning *of the grapes* of Ephraim better than the vintage of Abiezer?

3 "God has given the leaders of Midian, Oreb and Zeeb into your hands; and what was I able to do in comparison with you?" Then their anger toward him subsided when he said that.

4 Then Gideon and the 300 men who were with him came to the Jordan *and* crossed over, weary yet pursuing.

5 He said to the men of Succoth, "Please give loaves of bread to the people who are following me, for they are weary, and I am pursuing Zebah and Zalmunna, the kings of Midian."

6 The leaders of Succoth said, "Are the hands of Zebah and Zalmunna already

in your hands, that we should give bread to your army?"

7 Gideon said, "All right, when the LORD has given Zebah and Zalmunna into my hand, then I will thrash your bodies with the thorns of the wilderness and with briers."

8 He went up from there to Penuel and spoke similarly to them; and the men of Penuel answered him just as the men of Succoth had answered.

9 So he spoke also to the men of Penuel, saying, "When I return safely, I will tear down this tower."

10 Now Zebah and Zalmunna were in Karkor, and their armies with them, about 15,000 men, all who were left of the entire army of the sons of the east; for the fallen were 120,000 swordsmen.

11 Gideon went up by the way of those who lived in tents on the east of Nobah and Jogbehah, and attacked the camp when the camp was unsuspecting.

12 When Zebah and Zalmunna fled, he pursued them and captured the two kings of Midian, Zebah and Zalmunna, and routed the whole army.

13 Then Gideon the son of Joash returned from the battle by the ascent of Heres.

14 And he captured a youth from Succoth and questioned him. Then *the youth* wrote down for him the princes of Succoth and its elders, seventy-seven men.

15 He came to the men of Succoth and said, "Behold Zebah and Zalmunna, concerning whom you taunted me, saying, 'Are the hands of Zebah and Zalmunna already in your hand, that we should give bread to your men who are weary?'"

16 He took the elders of the city, and thorns of the wilderness and briers, and he disciplined the men of Succoth with them.

17 He tore down the tower of Penuel and killed the men of the city.

18 Then he said to Zebah and Zalmunna, "What kind of men *were* they whom you killed at Tabor?" And they said, "They were like you, each one resembling the son of a king."

19 He said, "They *were* my brothers, the sons of my mother. *As* the LORD lives, if only you had let them live, I would not kill you."

20 So he said to Jether his firstborn, "Rise, kill them." But the youth did not

30 but when this son of yours came, who has devoured your wealth with prostitutes, you killed the fattened calf for him.'

31 "And he said to him, 'Son, you have always been with me, and all that is mine is yours.

32 'But we had to celebrate and rejoice, for this brother of yours was dead and *has begun* to live, and *was* lost and has been found.'"

LIFE LESSONS

> Luke 15:32 — *"We had to celebrate and rejoice, for this brother of yours was dead and has begun to live."*

*A*part from a close relationship with God, we have nothing to look forward to but death. However, connecting with Him on a deep level brings merriment, gladness, and joy—both for us and for God.

Judges 9:1—10:18

9 AND Abimelech the son of Jerubbaal went to Shechem to his mother's relatives, and spoke to them and to the whole clan of the household of his mother's father, saying,

2 "Speak, now, in the hearing of all the leaders of Shechem, 'Which is better for you, that seventy men, all the sons of Jerubbaal, rule over you, or that one man rule over you?' Also, remember that I am your bone and your flesh."

3 And his mother's relatives spoke all these words on his behalf in the hearing of all the leaders of Shechem; and they were inclined to follow Abimelech, for they said, "He is our relative."

4 They gave him seventy *pieces* of silver from the house of Baal-berith with which Abimelech hired worthless and reckless fellows, and they followed him.

5 Then he went to his father's house at Ophrah and killed his brothers the sons of Jerubbaal, seventy men, on one stone. But Jotham the youngest son of Jerubbaal was left, for he hid himself.

LIFE LESSONS

> Judges 9:4 — *Abimelech hired worthless and reckless fellows; and they followed him.*

*G*od may allow worthless and reckless men to assume power for a time, but in the end, their evil deeds catch up with them. Just as God blesses obedience, so He judges disobedience.

6 All the men of Shechem and all Beth-millo assembled together, and they went and made Abimelech king, by the oak of the pillar which was in Shechem.

7 Now when they told Jotham, he went and stood on the top of Mount Gerizim, and lifted his voice and called out. Thus he said to them, "Listen to me, O men of Shechem, that God may listen to you.

8 "Once the trees went forth to anoint a king over them, and they said to the olive tree, 'Reign over us!'

9 "But the olive tree said to them, 'Shall I leave my fatness with which God and men are honored, and go to wave over the trees?'

10 "Then the trees said to the fig tree, 'You come, reign over us!'

11 "But the fig tree said to them, 'Shall I leave my sweetness and my good fruit, and go to wave over the trees?'

12 "Then the trees said to the vine, 'You come, reign over us!'

13 "But the vine said to them, 'Shall I leave my new wine, which cheers God and men, and go to wave over the trees?'

14 "Finally all the trees said to the bramble, 'You come, reign over us!'

15 "The bramble said to the trees, 'If in truth you are anointing me as king over you, come and take refuge in my shade; but if not, may fire come out from the bramble and consume the cedars of Lebanon.'

16 "Now therefore, if you have dealt in truth and integrity in making Abimelech king, and if you have dealt well with Jerubbaal and his house, and have dealt with him as he deserved—

17 for my father fought for you and risked his life and delivered you from the hand of Midian;

18 but you have risen against my father's house today and have killed his sons, seventy men, on one stone, and have made Abimelech, the son of his maidservant, king over the men of Shechem, because he is your relative—

19 if then you have dealt in truth and integrity with Jerubbaal and his house this day, rejoice in Abimelech, and let him also rejoice in you.

20 "But if not, let fire come out from Abimelech and consume the men of Shechem and Beth-millo; and let fire come out from the men of Shechem and from Beth-millo, and consume Abimelech."

21 Then Jotham escaped and fled, and went to Beer and remained there because of Abimelech his brother.

22 Now Abimelech ruled over Israel three years.

23 Then God sent an evil spirit between Abimelech and the men of Shechem; and the men of Shechem dealt treacherously with Abimelech,

24 so that the violence done to the seventy sons of Jerubbaal might come, and their blood might be laid on Abimelech their brother, who killed them, and on the men of Shechem, who strengthened his hands to kill his brothers.

25 The men of Shechem set men in ambush against him on the tops of the mountains, and they robbed all who might pass by them along the road; and it was told to Abimelech.

26 Now Gaal the son of Ebed came with his relatives, and crossed over into Shechem; and the men of Shechem put their trust in him.

27 They went out into the field and gathered the grapes of their vineyards and trod them, and held a festival; and they went into the house of their god, and ate and drank and cursed Abimelech.

28 Then Gaal the son of Ebed said, "Who is Abimelech, and who is Shechem, that we should serve him? Is he not the son of Jerubbaal, and is Zebul not his lieutenant? Serve the men of Hamor the father of Shechem; but why should we serve him?

29 "Would, therefore, that this people

were under my authority! Then I would remove Abimelech." And he said to Abimelech, "Increase your army and come out."

30 When Zebul the ruler of the city heard the words of Gaal the son of Ebed, his anger burned.

31 He sent messengers to Abimelech deceitfully, saying, "Behold, Gaal the son of Ebed and his relatives have come to Shechem; and behold, they are stirring up the city against you.

32 "Now therefore, arise by night, you and the people who are with you, and lie in wait in the field.

33 "In the morning, as soon as the sun is up, you shall rise early and rush upon the city; and behold, when he and the people who are with him come out against you, you shall do to them whatever you can."

34 So Abimelech and all the people who were with him arose by night and lay in wait against Shechem in four companies.

35 Now Gaal the son of Ebed went out and stood in the entrance of the city gate; and Abimelech and the people who were with him arose from the ambush.

36 When Gaal saw the people, he said to Zebul, "Look, people are coming down from the tops of the mountains." But Zebul said to him, "You are seeing the shadow of the mountains as if they were men."

37 Gaal spoke again and said, "Behold, people are coming down from the highest part of the land, and one company comes by the way of the diviners' oak."

38 Then Zebul said to him, "Where is your boasting now with which you said, 'Who is Abimelech that we should serve him?' Is this not the people whom you despised? Go out now and fight with them!"

39 So Gaal went out before the leaders of Shechem and fought with Abimelech.

40 Abimelech chased him, and he fled before him; and many fell wounded up to the entrance of the gate.

41 Then Abimelech remained at Arumah, but Zebul drove out Gaal and his relatives so that they could not remain in Shechem.

42 Now it came about the next day, that the people went out to the field, and it was told to Abimelech.

43 So he took his people and divided them into three companies, and lay in

wait in the field; when he looked and saw the people coming out from the city, he arose against them and slew them.

44 Then Abimelech and the company who was with him dashed forward and stood in the entrance of the city gate; the other two companies then dashed against all who *were* in the field and slew them.

45 Abimelech fought against the city all that day, and he captured the city and killed the people who *were* in it; then he razed the city and sowed it with salt.

46 When all the leaders of the tower of Shechem heard of *it*, they entered the inner chamber of the temple of El-berith.

47 It was told Abimelech that all the leaders of the tower of Shechem were gathered together.

48 So Abimelech went up to Mount Zalmon, he and all the people who *were* with him; and Abimelech took an axe in his hand and cut down a branch from the trees, and lifted it and laid *it* on his shoulder. Then he said to the people who *were* with him, "What you have seen me do, hurry *and* do likewise."

49 All the people also cut down each one his branch and followed Abimelech, and put *them* on the inner chamber and set the inner chamber on fire over those *inside,* so that all the men of the tower of Shechem also died, about a thousand men and women.

50 Then Abimelech went to Thebez, and he camped against Thebez and captured it.

51 But there was a strong tower in the center of the city, and all the men and women with all the leaders of the city fled there and shut themselves in; and they went up on the roof of the tower.

52 So Abimelech came to the tower and fought against it, and approached the entrance of the tower to burn it with fire.

53 But a certain woman threw an upper millstone on Abimelech's head, crushing his skull.

54 Then he called quickly to the young man, his armor bearer, and said to him, "Draw your sword and kill me, so that it will not be said of me, 'A woman slew him.'" So the young man pierced him through, and he died.

55 When the men of Israel saw that Abimelech was dead, each departed to his home.

56 Thus God repaid the wickedness of Abimelech, which he had done to his father in killing his seventy brothers.

57 Also God returned all the wickedness of the men of Shechem on their heads, and the curse of Jotham the son of Jerubbaal came upon them.

10 NOW after Abimelech died, Tola the son of Puah, the son of Dodo, a man of Issachar, arose to save Israel; and he lived in Shamir in the hill country of Ephraim.

2 He judged Israel twenty-three years. Then he died and was buried in Shamir.

3 After him, Jair the Gileadite arose and judged Israel twenty-two years.

4 He had thirty sons who rode on thirty donkeys, and they had thirty cities in the land of Gilead that are called Havvoth-jair to this day.

5 And Jair died and was buried in Kamon.

6 Then the sons of Israel again did evil in the sight of the LORD, served the Baals and the Ashtaroth, the gods of Aram, the gods of Sidon, the gods of Moab, the gods of the sons of Ammon, and the gods of the Philistines; thus they forsook the LORD and did not serve Him.

7 The anger of the LORD burned against Israel, and He sold them into the hands of the Philistines and into the hands of the sons of Ammon.

8 They afflicted and crushed the sons of Israel that year; for eighteen years they *afflicted* all the sons of Israel who were beyond the Jordan in Gilead in the land of the Amorites.

9 The sons of Ammon crossed the Jordan to fight also against Judah, Benjamin, and the house of Ephraim, so that Israel was greatly distressed.

10 Then the sons of Israel cried out to the LORD, saying, "We have sinned against You, for indeed, we have forsaken our God and served the Baals."

11 The LORD said to the sons of Israel, "*Did I* not *deliver you* from the Egyptians, the Amorites, the sons of Ammon, and the Philistines?

12 "Also when the Sidonians, the Amalekites and the Maonites oppressed you, you cried out to Me, and I delivered you from their hands.

13 "Yet you have forsaken Me and served other gods; therefore I will no longer deliver you.

14 "Go and cry out to the gods which you have chosen; let them deliver you in the time of your distress."

15 The sons of Israel said to the LORD, "We have sinned, do to us whatever seems good to You; only please deliver us this day."

➤ 16 So they put away the foreign gods from among them and served the LORD; and He could bear the misery of Israel no longer.

17 Then the sons of Ammon were summoned and they camped in Gilead. And the sons of Israel gathered together and camped in Mizpah.

18 The people, the leaders of Gilead, said to one another, "Who is the man who will begin to fight against the sons of Ammon? He shall become head over all the inhabitants of Gilead."

◈ Psalm 50:1–6

A Psalm of Asaph.

50 THE Mighty One, God, the LORD, has spoken,
And summoned the earth from the rising of the sun to its setting.

2 Out of Zion, the perfection of beauty,
God has shone forth.

3 May our God come and not keep silence;
Fire devours before Him,
And it is very tempestuous around Him.

4 He summons the heavens above,
And the earth, to judge His people;

✴ 5 "Gather My godly ones to Me,
Those who have made a covenant with Me by sacrifice."

6 And the heavens declare His righteousness,
For God Himself is judge.   Selah.

LIFE LESSONS

➤ **Judges 10:16** — *He could bear the misery of Israel no longer.*

*G*od will always judge sin, but He longs to show mercy. His first inclination, is always to redeem and rescue.

◈ Proverbs 14:25–27

25 A truthful witness saves lives,
But he who utters lies is treacherous.

26 In the fear of the LORD there is strong confidence,
And his children will have refuge.

27 The fear of the LORD is a fountain of life, ✴
That one may avoid the snares of death.

◈ Luke 16:1–31

16 NOW He was also saying to the disciples, "There was a rich man who had a manager, and this *manager* was reported to him as squandering his possessions.

2 "And he called him and said to him, 'What is this I hear about you? Give an accounting of your management, for you can no longer be manager.'

3 "The manager said to himself, 'What shall I do, since my master is taking the management away from me? I am not strong enough to dig; I am ashamed to beg.

4 'I know what I shall do, so that when I am removed from the management people will welcome me into their homes.'

5 "And he summoned each one of his master's debtors, and he *began* saying to the first, 'How much do you owe my master?'

6 "And he said, 'A hundred measures of oil.' And he said to him, 'Take your bill, and sit down quickly and write fifty.'

7 "Then he said to another, 'And how much do you owe?' And he said, 'A hundred measures of wheat.' He *said to him, 'Take your bill, and write eighty.'

8 "And his master praised the unrighteous manager because he had acted shrewdly; for the sons of this age are more shrewd in relation to their own kind than the sons of light.

9 "And I say to you, make friends for yourselves by means of the wealth of unrighteousness, so that when it fails, they will receive you into the eternal dwellings.

10 "He who is faithful in a very little

thing is faithful also in much; and he who is unrighteous in a very little thing is unrighteous also in much.

11 "Therefore if you have not been faithful in the *use of* unrighteous wealth, who will entrust the true *riches* to you?

12 "And if you have not been faithful in *the use of* that which is another's, who will give you that which is your own?

13 "No servant can serve two masters; for either he will hate the one and love the other, or else he will be devoted to one and despise the other. You cannot serve God and wealth."

14 Now the Pharisees, who were lovers of money, were listening to all these things and were scoffing at Him.

15 And He said to them, "You are those who justify yourselves in the sight of men, but God knows your hearts; for that which is highly esteemed among men is detestable in the sight of God.

16 "The Law and the Prophets *were proclaimed* until John; since that time the gospel of the kingdom of God has been preached, and everyone is forcing his way into it.

17 "But it is easier for heaven and earth to pass away than for one stroke of a letter of the Law to fail.

18 "Everyone who divorces his wife and marries another commits adultery, and he who marries one who is divorced from a husband commits adultery.

19 "Now there was a rich man, and he

LIFE LESSONS

➢ **Luke 16:10 — *"He who is faithful in a very little thing is faithful also in much."***

Faithfulness in the small assignments the Lord gives us qualifies us for the opportunity to serve in greater and more influential ways. Be faithful where God plants you, and watch the awesome things He will do through your life.

➢ **Luke 16:15 — *"For that which is highly esteemed among men is detestable in the sight of God."***

There is nothing wrong with being successful; the problem arises in how we try to go about it. God says that to be great in the kingdom of heaven we must humbly serve others and glorify Him—not flaunt how great we are.

---

habitually dressed in purple and fine linen, joyously living in splendor every day.

20 "And a poor man named Lazarus was laid at his gate, covered with sores,

21 and longing to be fed with the *crumbs* which were falling from the rich man's table; besides, even the dogs were coming and licking his sores.

22 "Now the poor man died and was carried away by the angels to Abraham's bosom; and the rich man also died and was buried.

23 "In Hades he lifted up his eyes, being

Life Examples:

The Consequences of Being Spiritually Shortsighted

LUKE 16:19–26

Nothing stopped the rich man from getting what he wanted. While he was on earth, he seemed to possess every creature comfort. On the other hand, there was a beggar named Lazarus who was poor and sickly. He lacked even the most basic of needs. Though it seemed the rich man was blessed and Lazarus cursed, everything changed drastically when they both died.

In Luke 16, Jesus tells the story of how Lazarus went to heaven, while the rich man was condemned to torment. As Lazarus stood with Abraham, they looked across the chasm

and heard the rich man's pleas for a drop of water to cool his burning tongue.

However, Abraham replied, "Between us and you there is a great chasm fixed, so that those who wish to come over from here to you will not be able, and that none may cross over from there to us" (Luke 16:26).

The rich man had been spiritually shortsighted in thinking whatever built bridges for him on earth would do so in heaven. H. Alford wrote, "The most dreadful torment of the lost, in fact that which constitutes their state of torment, will be this coming to themselves, when too late for repentance."

Do you struggle with unbelief, thinking your earthly resources will save you in heaven? Do not give in to spiritual shortsightedness. Rather, allow God to open your eyes to His wondrous truth. Then you can repent and receive the free gift of salvation.

in torment, and *saw Abraham far away and Lazarus in his bosom.
24 "And he cried out and said, 'Father Abraham, have mercy on me, and send Lazarus so that he may dip the tip of his finger in water and cool off my tongue, for I am in agony in this flame.'
25 "But Abraham said, 'Child, remember that during your life you received your good things, and likewise Lazarus bad things; but now he is being comforted here, and you are in agony.
26 'And besides all this, between us and you there is a great chasm fixed, so that those who wish to come over from here to you will not be able, and *that* none may cross over from there to us.'
27 "And he said, 'Then I beg you, father, that you send him to my father's house—
28 for I have five brothers—in order that he may warn them, so that they will not also come to this place of torment.'

29 "But Abraham *said, 'They have Moses and the Prophets; let them hear them.'
30 "But he said, 'No, father Abraham, but if someone goes to them from the dead, they will repent!'
31 "But he said to him, 'If they do not listen to Moses and the Prophets, they will not be persuaded even if someone rises from the dead.'"

LIFE LESSONS

➤ Luke 16:31 — *"If they do not listen to Moses and the Prophets, they will not be persuaded even if someone rises from the dead."*

*M*iracles never *make* anyone believe. Jesus performed all kinds of miracles—including raising people from the dead (Luke 7:12-15; 8:49-55; John 11:1-44)—and His enemies still crucified Him.

APRIL 23

◈ Judges 11:1—12:15

11 NOW Jephthah the Gileadite was a valiant warrior, but he was the son of a harlot. And Gilead was the father of Jephthah.
2 Gilead's wife bore him sons; and when his wife's sons grew up, they drove Jephthah out and said to him, "You shall not have an inheritance in our father's house, for you are the son of another woman."
3 So Jephthah fled from his brothers and lived in the land of Tob; and worthless fellows gathered themselves about Jephthah, and they went out with him.
4 It came about after a while that the sons of Ammon fought against Israel.
5 When the sons of Ammon fought against Israel, the elders of Gilead went to get Jephthah from the land of Tob;
6 and they said to Jephthah, "Come and be our chief that we may fight against the sons of Ammon."
7 Then Jephthah said to the elders of Gilead, "Did you not hate me and drive me from my father's house? So why have

you come to me now when you are in trouble?"
8 The elders of Gilead said to Jephthah, "For this reason we have now returned to you, that you may go with us and fight with the sons of Ammon and become head over all the inhabitants of Gilead."
9 So Jephthah said to the elders of Gilead, "If you take me back to fight against the sons of Ammon and the LORD gives them up to me, will I become your head?"
10 The elders of Gilead said to Jephthah, "The LORD is witness between us; surely we will do as you have said."
11 Then Jephthah went with the elders of Gilead, and the people made him head and chief over them; and Jephthah spoke all his words before the LORD at Mizpah.
12 Now Jephthah sent messengers to the king of the sons of Ammon, saying, "What is between you and me, that you have come to me to fight against my land?"
13 The king of the sons of Ammon said to the messengers of Jephthah, "Because Israel took away my land when they came up from Egypt, from the Arnon as

far as the Jabbok and the Jordan; therefore, return them peaceably now."

14 But Jephthah sent messengers again to the king of the sons of Ammon,

15 and they said to him, "Thus says Jephthah, 'Israel did not take away the land of Moab nor the land of the sons of Ammon.

16 'For when they came up from Egypt, and Israel went through the wilderness to the Red Sea and came to Kadesh,

17 then Israel sent messengers to the king of Edom, saying, "Please let us pass through your land," but the king of Edom would not listen. And they also sent to the king of Moab, but he would not consent. So Israel remained at Kadesh.

18 'Then they went through the wilderness and around the land of Edom and the land of Moab, and came to the east side of the land of Moab, and they camped beyond the Arnon; but they did not enter the territory of Moab, for the Arnon *was* the border of Moab.

19 'And Israel sent messengers to Sihon king of the Amorites, the king of Heshbon, and Israel said to him, "Please let us pass through your land to our place."

20 'But Sihon did not trust Israel to pass through his territory; so Sihon gathered all his people and camped in Jahaz and fought with Israel.

21 'The LORD, the God of Israel, gave Sihon and all his people into the hand of Israel, and they defeated them; so Israel possessed all the land of the Amorites, the inhabitants of that country.

22 'So they possessed all the territory of the Amorites, from the Arnon as far as the Jabbok, and from the wilderness as far as the Jordan.

23 'Since now the LORD, the God of Israel, drove out the Amorites from before His people Israel, are you then to possess it?

➤ 24 'Do you not possess what Chemosh your god gives you to possess? So whatever the LORD our God has driven out before us, we will possess it.

25 'Now are you any better than Balak the son of Zippor, king of Moab? Did he ever strive with Israel, or did he ever fight against them?

26 'While Israel lived in Heshbon and its villages, and in Aroer and its villages, and in all the cities that are on the banks of the Arnon, three hundred years, why

did you not recover them within that time?

27 'I therefore have not sinned against you, but you are doing me wrong by making war against me; may the LORD, the Judge, judge today between the sons of Israel and the sons of Ammon.' "

28 But the king of the sons of Ammon disregarded the message which Jephthah sent him.

29 Now the Spirit of the LORD came upon Jephthah, so that he passed through Gilead and Manasseh; then he passed through Mizpah of Gilead, and from Mizpah of Gilead he went on to the sons of Ammon.

30 Jephthah made a vow to the LORD and said, "If You will indeed give the sons of Ammon into my hand,

31 then it shall be that whatever comes out of the doors of my house to meet me when I return in peace from the sons of Ammon, it shall be the LORD's, and I will offer it up as a burnt offering."

32 So Jephthah crossed over to the sons of Ammon to fight against them; and the LORD gave them into his hand.

33 He struck them with a very great slaughter from Aroer to the entrance of Minnith, twenty cities, and as far as Abel-keramim. So the sons of Ammon were subdued before the sons of Israel.

34 When Jephthah came to his house at Mizpah, behold, his daughter was coming out to meet him with tambourines and with dancing. Now she was his one *and* only child; besides her he had no son or daughter.

35 When he saw her, he tore his clothes and said, "Alas, my daughter! You have brought me very low, and you are among those who trouble me; for I have given my word to the LORD, and I cannot take *it* back."

36 So she said to him, "My father, you

WHAT THE BIBLE SAYS ABOUT

Vows

Judges 11:29–40

*I*s there something you want that blazes in your heart like an ever-burning fire? You think about it all the time, and it takes all the faith you have to wait for it patiently. You'd do almost anything to have it; and though God has already promised to give you the desires of your heart (Ps. 37:4), you feel as if you need to go the extra mile to motivate God to give it to you—and you offer God a deal you believe He can't refuse.

This is the way Jephthah's tragedy began. As war with the Ammonites loomed ahead of him, a passion for victory burned in his heart. He pleaded with God in Judges 11:30, 31, "If You will indeed give the sons of Ammon into my hand, then it shall be that whatever comes out of the doors of my house to meet me when I return in peace from the sons of Ammon, it shall be the LORD's, and I will offer it up as a burnt offering."

Even though Jephthah knew the territory the Ammonites wanted rightfully belonged to Israel—and though he realized God would protect the inheritance He had given them (Judg. 11:15–24)—it seems Jephthah still doubted. Whether it was to show his devotion to the Lord or to move God to act in Israel's favor, Jephthah made a vow he would soon deeply regret—without consulting God whether he should make the vow or not.

Doubt makes us do many things that are not God's will for us. Jephthath learned this the hard way. When he returned home from successfully defeating the Ammonites, Judges 11:34 tells us, "Behold, his daughter was coming out to meet him with tambourines and with dancing. Now she was his one and only

child." What a sad and horrible day. Although Jephthath had won the victory, he would have to sacrifice his only child in order to fulfill his vow—and he knew he couldn't go back on his word to God (Num. 30:2).

The question remains: *Was it really necessary?*

In fact, the answer is most definitely *no!* Jephthah's sacrifice wasn't necessary. God desires obedience rather than sacrifice (1 Sam. 15:22). The Lord promised, "If you diligently obey the LORD your God . . . the LORD your God will set you high above all the nations of the earth. . . . The LORD shall cause your enemies who rise up against you to be defeated before you" (Deut. 28:1, 7). God was going to give Jephthah the triumph anyway, but because of his doubt in God, he paid a great price.

Understand that God does what He wants (Ps. 115:3; 135:6)—your vows do not move Him. Your epic acts of sacrifice will not cause Him to adjust His timetable. In fact, your pledges may be evidence to Him that your faith still isn't mature enough for what He wants to give you.

Jesus said, "Again, you have heard that the ancients were told, 'You shall not make false vows, but shall fulfill your vows to the LORD.' But I say to you, make no oath at all, either by heaven, for it is the throne of God . . . But let your statement be, 'Yes, yes' or 'No, no'; anything beyond these is of evil" (Matt. 5:33, 34, 37).

Friend, don't fall into the trap of the evil one, thinking you can convince God through vows to give you the desire of your heart—that road will only lead to heartache. Rather, obey God, count on His promises, and express your faith. He will do as He says. He will most certainly fulfill His promises to you above and beyond what you can imagine (Josh. 23:14; Eph. 3:20). As Jephthah learned, the consequences of living any other way are far too great. ◈

---

have given your word to the LORD; do to me as you have said, since the LORD has avenged you of your enemies, the sons of Ammon."
37 She said to her father, "Let this thing be done for me; let me alone two months, that I may go to the mountains and weep because of my virginity, I and my companions."
38 Then he said, "Go." So he sent her

away for two months; and she left with her companions, and wept on the mountains because of her virginity.
39 At the end of two months she returned to her father, who did to her according to the vow which he had made; and she had no relations with a man. Thus it became a custom in Israel,
40 that the daughters of Israel went yearly to commemorate the daughter of

Jephthah the Gileadite four days in the year.

12 THEN the men of Ephraim were summoned, and they crossed to Zaphon and said to Jephthah, "Why did you cross over to fight against the sons of Ammon without calling us to go with you? We will burn your house down on you."

2 Jephthah said to them, "I and my people were at great strife with the sons of Ammon; when I called you, you did not deliver me from their hand.

➤ 3 "When I saw that you would not deliver me, I took my life in my hands and crossed over against the sons of Ammon, and the LORD gave them into my hand. Why then have you come up to me this day to fight against me?"

4 Then Jephthah gathered all the men of Gilead and fought Ephraim; and the men of Gilead defeated Ephraim, because they said, "You are fugitives of Ephraim, O Gileadites, in the midst of Ephraim and in the midst of Manasseh."

5 The Gileadites captured the fords of the Jordan opposite Ephraim. And it happened when any of the fugitives of Ephraim said, "Let me cross over," the men of Gilead would say to him, "Are you an Ephraimite?" If he said, "No,"

6 then they would say to him, "Say now, 'Shibboleth.'" But he said, "Sibboleth," for he could not pronounce it correctly. Then they seized him and slew him at the fords of the Jordan. Thus there fell at that time 42,000 of Ephraim.

7 Jephthah judged Israel six years. Then Jephthah the Gileadite died and was buried in one of the cities of Gilead.

8 Now Ibzan of Bethlehem judged Israel after him.

9 He had thirty sons, and thirty daughters whom he gave in marriage outside the family, and he brought in thirty daughters from outside for his sons. And he judged Israel seven years.

10 Then Ibzan died and was buried in Bethlehem.

11 Now Elon the Zebulunite judged Israel after him; and he judged Israel ten years.

12 Then Elon the Zebulunite died and was buried at Aijalon in the land of Zebulun.

13 Now Abdon the son of Hillel the Pirathonite judged Israel after him.

14 He had forty sons and thirty grandsons who rode on seventy donkeys; and he judged Israel eight years.

15 Then Abdon the son of Hillel the Pirathonite died and was buried at Pirathon in the land of Ephraim, in the hill country of the Amalekites.

Psalm 50:7–15

7 "Hear, O My people, and I will speak;
   O Israel, I will testify against you;
   I am God, your God.

8 "I do not reprove you for your sacrifices,
   And your burnt offerings are continually before Me.

9 "I shall take no young bull out of your house
   Nor male goats out of your folds.

10 "For every beast of the forest is Mine,
   The cattle on a thousand hills.

11 "I know every bird of the mountains,
   And everything that moves in the field is Mine.

12 "If I were hungry I would not tell you,
   For the world is Mine, and all it contains.

13 "Shall I eat the flesh of bulls
   Or drink the blood of male goats?

14 "Offer to God a sacrifice of thanksgiving
   And pay your vows to the Most High;

15 Call upon Me in the day of trouble;
   I shall rescue you, and you will honor Me."

LIFE LESSONS

➤ **Judges 12:3 — "I took my life in my hands and crossed over against the sons of Ammon, and the LORD gave them into my hand."**

*W*hen in faith and obedience we do what God has called us to do—even though no one else supports us—He does for us what we cannot do for ourselves. God takes care of our needs when we obey Him.

Proverbs 14:28

28 In a multitude of people is a king's
    glory,
    But in the dearth of people is a
    prince's ruin.

Luke 17:1–19

17 HE said to His disciples, "It is inevitable that stumbling blocks come, but woe to him through whom they come!
2 "It would be better for him if a millstone were hung around his neck and he were thrown into the sea, than that he would cause one of these little ones to stumble.
3 "Be on your guard! If your brother sins, rebuke him; and if he repents, forgive him.
4 "And if he sins against you seven times a day, and returns to you seven times, saying, 'I repent,' forgive him."
5 The apostles said to the Lord, "Increase our faith!"
6 And the Lord said, "If you had faith like a mustard seed, you would say to this mulberry tree, 'Be uprooted and be planted in the sea'; and it would obey you.
7 "Which of you, having a slave plowing or tending sheep, will say to him when he has come in from the field, 'Come immediately and sit down to eat'?
8 "But will he not say to him, 'Prepare something for me to eat, and properly clothe yourself and serve me while I eat and drink; and afterward you may eat and drink'?
9 "He does not thank the slave because he did the things which were commanded, does he?
10 "So you too, when you do all the things which are commanded you, say, 'We are unworthy slaves; we have done only that which we ought to have done.'"
11 While He was on the way to Jerusalem, He was passing between Samaria and Galilee.
12 As He entered a village, ten leprous men who stood at a distance met Him;
13 and they raised their voices, saying, "Jesus, Master, have mercy on us!"
14 When He saw them, He said to them, "Go and show yourselves to the priests." And as they were going, they were cleansed.
15 Now one of them, when he saw that he had been healed, turned back, glorifying God with a loud voice,
16 and he fell on his face at His feet, giving thanks to Him. And he was a Samaritan.
17 Then Jesus answered and said, "Were there not ten cleansed? But the nine—where are they?
18 "Was no one found who returned to give glory to God, except this foreigner?"
19 And He said to him, "Stand up and go; your faith has made you well."

LIFE LESSONS

➤ **Luke 17:4 — "If he sins against you seven times a day, and returns to you seven times, saying, 'I repent,' forgive him."**

Jesus is not encouraging irresponsible behavior on the part of the offender, but merciful and gracious behavior on the part of the offended. For "just as the Lord forgave you, so also should you" (Col. 3:13).

➤ **Luke 17:5 — "Increase our faith!"**

We do not need more faith to comply with the Lord's instructions, but genuine faith. It's not the amount that matters—even a mustard seed of faith will do. The almighty power of God can work in an amazing way through a willing vessel (2 Cor. 4:7).

➤ **Luke 17:10 — "We are unworthy slaves; we have done only that which we ought to have done."**

Jesus does not want us to grow proud over the things He enables us to accomplish by His Spirit. So Paul writes, "If I preach the gospel, I have nothing to boast of, for I am under compulsion" (1 Cor. 9:16).

➤ **Luke 17:18 — "Was no one found who returned to give glory to God, except this foreigner?"**

Often, the most unlikely people are the ones who obey God and give Him glory. The Lord always accepts their praise and frequently uses them as the examples of a righteous heart.

Judges 13:1—14:20

13 NOW the sons of Israel again did evil in the sight of the LORD, so that the LORD gave them into the hands of the Philistines forty years.

2 There was a certain man of Zorah, of the family of the Danites, whose name was Manoah; and his wife was barren and had borne no *children.*

3 Then the angel of the LORD appeared to the woman and said to her, "Behold now, you are barren and have borne no *children,* but you shall conceive and give birth to a son.

4 "Now therefore, be careful not to drink wine or strong drink, nor eat any unclean thing.

5 "For behold, you shall conceive and give birth to a son, and no razor shall come upon his head, for the boy shall be a Nazirite to God from the womb; and he shall begin to deliver Israel from the hands of the Philistines."

6 Then the woman came and told her husband, saying, "A man of God came to me and his appearance was like the

Life Examples:

Barren?

JUDGES 13

*T*hough things have changed in modern times, to be childless in ancient Israel was a terrible hardship. The barren woman was considered cursed by God (Ex. 23:26; Deut. 7:4). The very meaning of the word *barren* betrayed its dire consequences. It signified the family would be *uprooted*—that there would be no descendants and no successors.

Children, after all, were considered God's blessing (Ps. 128:3, 4). Psalm 127:4, 5, explains, "Like arrows in the hand of a warrior, so are the children of one's youth. How blessed is the man whose quiver is full of them; they will not be ashamed." Of course, without children, there would be no one to care for the woman and her husband in their old age. There would be no grandchildren to delight them. The family line would end—to her disgrace.

It was in this condition that the Angel of the Lord found Manoah's wife—a failure by the standards of her culture. Yet his wonderful words changed her life: "Behold now, you are barren and have borne no children, but you shall conceive and give birth to a son" (Judg. 13:3). From one moment to the next, God changed her situation completely.

Perhaps you, like Manoah's wife, are wholeheartedly praying for a child. Or maybe there are other things God has promised you that are on your heart—a spouse, a better financial situation, or even good health. No doubt it's difficult to watch as other people are so abundantly blessed with the very thing you pray so hard for. You may even question why God made it so easy for them when they don't appreciate what they have.

Please understand, this isn't a competition—it isn't about who gets the blessing first. Rather, it's about who will honor God with what they've been given.

God honored Manoah's wife with the birth of Samson—a man who would be very important to Israel. In Judges 13:5, the Angel of the Lord declared, "He shall begin to deliver Israel from the hands of the Philistines." There were many other barren women throughout the Bible who were blessed to bear powerful men of God as well: Sarah, who gave birth to Isaac; Rebekah, who bore Jacob; Rachel, who was Joseph's mother; Hannah, the mother of the prophet Samuel; and Elizabeth, who delivered John the Baptist; among others. All of these men had a powerful part in God's plan—in the fulfillment of God's promises.

Although you've not yet received your request, God knows how deeply you long for it—and He's providing it for you in a manner that will show you His great and mighty power. God always works in the most adverse circumstances to build your faith and your relationship with Him.

So instead of despairing, ask God to show you His will and help you to be obedient to His plan. Make knowing Him the object of your pursuit (Matt. 6:33). Then, thank God that when He fulfills His promise to you, you won't take it for granted. You'll know the priceless nature of the gift God's given you, and you'll honor Him with it every day of your life.

appearance of the angel of God, very awesome. And I did not ask him where he *came* from, nor did he tell me his name.

7 "But he said to me, 'Behold, you shall conceive and give birth to a son, and now you shall not drink wine or strong drink nor eat any unclean thing, for the boy shall be a Nazirite to God from the womb to the day of his death.'"

➤ 8 Then Manoah entreated the LORD and said, "O Lord, please let the man of God whom You have sent come to us again that he may teach us what to do for the boy who is to be born."

9 God listened to the voice of Manoah; and the angel of God came again to the woman as she was sitting in the field, but Manoah her husband was not with her.

10 So the woman ran quickly and told her husband, "Behold, the man who came the *other* day has appeared to me."

11 Then Manoah arose and followed his wife, and when he came to the man he said to him, "Are you the man who spoke to the woman?" And he said, "I am."

12 Manoah said, "Now when your words come *to pass*, what shall be the boy's mode of life and his vocation?"

13 So the angel of the LORD said to Manoah, "Let the woman pay attention to all that I said.

14 "She should not eat anything that comes from the vine nor drink wine or strong drink, nor eat any unclean thing; let her observe all that I commanded."

15 Then Manoah said to the angel of the LORD, "Please let us detain you so that we may prepare a young goat for you."

➤ 16 The angel of the LORD said to Manoah, "Though you detain me, I will not eat your food, but if you prepare a burnt offering, *then* offer it to the LORD." For Manoah did not know that he was the angel of the LORD.

17 Manoah said to the angel of the LORD, "What is your name, so that when your words come *to pass*, we may honor you?"

18 But the angel of the LORD said to him, "Why do you ask my name, seeing it is wonderful?"

19 So Manoah took the young goat with the grain offering and offered it on the rock to the LORD, and He performed wonders while Manoah and his wife looked on.

20 For it came about when the flame went up from the altar toward heaven, that the angel of the LORD ascended in the flame of the altar. When Manoah and his wife saw *this*, they fell on their faces to the ground.

21 Now the angel of the LORD did not appear to Manoah or his wife again. Then Manoah knew that he was the angel of the LORD.

22 So Manoah said to his wife, "We will surely die, for we have seen God."

23 But his wife said to him, "If the LORD ◄ had desired to kill us, He would not have accepted a burnt offering and a grain offering from our hands, nor would He have shown us all these things, nor would He have let us hear *things* like this at this time."

24 Then the woman gave birth to a son and named him Samson; and the child grew up and the LORD blessed him.

25 And the Spirit of the LORD began to stir him in Mahaneh-dan, between Zorah and Eshtaol.

LIFE LESSONS

➤ **Judges 13:8 —** *"O Lord, please let the man of God whom You have sent come to us again that he may teach us what to do for the boy."*

*I*n the midst of a disobedient, idolatrous nation, Manoah and his wife stand out as faithful people of God. They sought His counsel on how to rear their child in difficult times, and the Lord answered their prayers.

➤ **Judges 13:16 —** *For Manoah did not know that he was the angel of the LORD.*

*H*ow many of our ordinary encounters are actually appointments with God's heavenly ambassadors? We will never know this side of heaven; that is one reason why we must treat every encounter as a divine appointment (Heb. 13:2).

➤ **Judges 13:23 —** *"If the LORD had desired to kill us, He would not have accepted a burnt offering."*

*T*he Lord does not desire to bring us harm but to bless us. He will bless us if we will take to heart His gracious promises and obey His word by the power of His Spirit.

14 THEN Samson went down to Timnah and saw a woman in Timnah, *one* of the daughters of the Philistines.
2 So he came back and told his father and mother, "I saw a woman in Timnah, *one* of the daughters of the Philistines; now therefore, get her for me as a wife."
3 Then his father and his mother said to him, "Is there no woman among the daughters of your relatives, or among all our people, that you go to take a wife from the uncircumcised Philistines?" But Samson said to his father, "Get her for me, for she looks good to me."
➤ 4 However, his father and mother did not know that it was of the LORD, for He was seeking an occasion against the Philistines. Now at that time the Philistines were ruling over Israel.
5 Then Samson went down to Timnah with his father and mother, and came as far as the vineyards of Timnah; and behold, a young lion *came* roaring toward him.
6 The Spirit of the LORD came upon him mightily, so that he tore him as one tears a young goat though he had nothing in his hand; but he did not tell his father or mother what he had done.
7 So he went down and talked to the woman; and she looked good to Samson.
8 When he returned later to take her, he turned aside to look at the carcass of the lion; and behold, a swarm of bees and honey were in the body of the lion.
9 So he scraped the honey into his hands and went on, eating as he went. When he came to his father and mother, he gave *some* to them and they ate *it;* but he did not tell them that he had scraped the honey out of the body of the lion.
10 Then his father went down to the woman; and Samson made a feast there, for the young men customarily did this.
11 When they saw him, they brought thirty companions to be with him.
12 Then Samson said to them, "Let me now propound a riddle to you; if you will indeed tell it to me within the seven days of the feast, and find it out, then I will give you thirty linen wraps and thirty changes of clothes.
13 "But if you are unable to tell me, then you shall give me thirty linen wraps and thirty changes of clothes." And they said to him, "Propound your riddle, that we may hear it."
14 So he said to them,

"Out of the eater came something to eat,
And out of the strong came something sweet."

But they could not tell the riddle in three days.
15 Then it came about on the fourth day that they said to Samson's wife, "Entice your husband, so that he will tell us the riddle, or we will burn you and your father's house with fire. Have you invited us to impoverish us? Is this not *so?*"
16 Samson's wife wept before him and said, "You only hate me, and you do not love me; you have propounded a riddle to the sons of my people, and have not told *it* to me." And he said to her, "Behold, I have not told *it* to my father or mother; so should I tell you?"
17 However she wept before him seven days while their feast lasted. And on the seventh day he told her because she pressed him so hard. She then told the riddle to the sons of her people.
18 So the men of the city said to him on the seventh day before the sun went down,

"What is sweeter than honey?
And what is stronger than a lion?"

And he said to them,

"If you had not plowed with my heifer,
You would not have found out my riddle."

19 Then the Spirit of the LORD came upon him mightily, and he went down to Ashkelon and killed thirty of them and took their spoil and gave the changes *of clothes* to those who told the riddle. And his anger burned, and he went up to his father's house.

LIFE LESSONS

➤ **Judges 14:4 — *His father and mother did not know that it was of the LORD, for He was seeking an occasion against the Philistines.***

Samson's desire for a Philistine wife clearly transgressed God's law (Deut. 7:3, 4). Yet God used even his disobedience for the good of His people. Note, however, that Samson himself never received a blessing for his rebellious choice.

20 But Samson's wife was *given* to his companion who had been his friend.

Psalm 50:16–23

16 But to the wicked God says,
  "What right have you to tell of My statutes
  And to take My covenant in your mouth?
17 "For you hate discipline,
  And you cast My words behind you.
18 "When you see a thief, you are pleased with him,
  And you associate with adulterers.
19 "You let your mouth loose in evil
  And your tongue frames deceit.
20 "You sit and speak against your brother;
  You slander your own mother's son.
21 "These things you have done and I kept silence;
  You thought that I was just like you;
  I will reprove you and state *the case* in order before your eyes.
22 "Now consider this, you who forget God,
  Or I will tear *you* in pieces, and there will be none to deliver.
23 "He who offers a sacrifice of thanksgiving honors Me;
  And to him who orders *his* way *aright*
  I shall show the salvation of God."

Proverbs 14:29, 30

➤ 29 He who is slow to anger has great understanding,
  But he who is quick-tempered exalts folly.

LIFE LESSONS

➤ **Proverbs 14:29 —** *He who is slow to anger has great understanding, but he who is quick-tempered exalts folly.*

*I*t may feel good (for a short while) to vent our fury at someone, but "the anger of man does not achieve the righteousness of God" (James 1:20). Failure to control a quick temper leads only to heartache (Eph. 4:26, 27).

30 A tranquil heart is life to the body,
  But passion is rottenness to the bones.

Luke 17:20–37

20 Now having been questioned by the Pharisees as to when the kingdom of God was coming, He answered them and said, "The kingdom of God is not coming with signs to be observed;
21 nor will they say, 'Look, here *it is!*' or, 'There *it is!*' For behold, the kingdom of God is in your midst."
22 And He said to the disciples, "The days will come when you will long to see one of the days of the Son of Man, and you will not see it.
23 "They will say to you, 'Look there! Look here!' Do not go away, and do not run after *them.*
24 "For just like the lightning, when it flashes out of one part of the sky, shines to the other part of the sky, so will the Son of Man be in His day.
25 "But first He must suffer many things and be rejected by this generation.
26 "And just as it happened in the days of Noah, so it will be also in the days of the Son of Man:
27 they were eating, they were drinking, they were marrying, they were being given in marriage, until the day that Noah entered the ark, and the flood came and destroyed them all.
28 "It was the same as happened in the days of Lot: they were eating, they were drinking, they were buying, they were selling, they were planting, they were building;
29 but on the day that Lot went out from Sodom it rained fire and brimstone from heaven and destroyed them all.
30 "It will be just the same on the day that the Son of Man is revealed.
31 "On that day, the one who is on the housetop and whose goods are in the house must not go down to take them out; and likewise the one who is in the field must not turn back.
32 "Remember Lot's wife.
33 "Whoever seeks to keep his life will lose it, and whoever loses *his life* will preserve it.

34 "I tell you, on that night there will be two in one bed; one will be taken and the other will be left.
35 "There will be two women grinding at the same place; one will be taken and the other will be left.

36 ["Two men will be in the field; one will be taken and the other will be left."]
37 And answering they *said to Him, "Where, Lord?" And He said to them, "Where the body is, there also the vultures will be gathered."

Judges 15:1—16:31

15 BUT after a while, in the time of wheat harvest, Samson visited his wife with a young goat, and said, "I will go in to my wife in her room." But her father did not let him enter.
2 Her father said, "I really thought that you hated her intensely; so I gave her to your companion. Is not her younger sister more beautiful than she? Please let her be yours instead."
3 Samson then said to them, "This time I shall be blameless in regard to the Philistines when I do them harm."
4 Samson went and caught three hundred foxes, and took torches, and turned the foxes tail to tail and put one torch in the middle between two tails.
5 When he had set fire to the torches, he released the foxes into the standing grain of the Philistines, thus burning up both the shocks and the standing grain, along with the vineyards and groves.
6 Then the Philistines said, "Who did this?" And they said, "Samson, the son-in-law of the Timnite, because he took his wife and gave her to his companion." So the Philistines came up and burned her and her father with fire.
7 Samson said to them, "Since you act like this, I will surely take revenge on you, but after that I will quit."
8 He struck them ruthlessly with a great slaughter; and he went down and lived in the cleft of the rock of Etam.
9 Then the Philistines went up and camped in Judah, and spread out in Lehi.
10 The men of Judah said, "Why have you come up against us?" And they said, "We have come up to bind Samson in order to do to him as he did to us."
11 Then 3,000 men of Judah went down to the cleft of the rock of Etam and said

to Samson, "Do you not know that the Philistines are rulers over us? What then is this that you have done to us?" And he said to them, "As they did to me, so I have done to them."
12 They said to him, "We have come down to bind you so that we may give you into the hands of the Philistines." And Samson said to them, "Swear to me that you will not kill me."
13 So they said to him, "No, but we will bind you fast and give you into their hands; yet surely we will not kill you." Then they bound him with two new ropes and brought him up from the rock.
14 When he came to Lehi, the Philistines shouted as they met him. And the Spirit of the LORD came upon him mightily so that the ropes that were on his arms were as flax that is burned with fire, and his bonds dropped from his hands.
15 He found a fresh jawbone of a donkey, so he reached out and took it and killed a thousand men with it.
16 Then Samson said,
"With the jawbone of a donkey,
    Heaps upon heaps,
With the jawbone of a donkey
    I have killed a thousand men."
17 When he had finished speaking, he threw the jawbone from his hand; and he named that place Ramath-lehi.
18 Then he became very thirsty, and he ◄

LIFE LESSONS

➤ **Judges 15:18 — He became very thirsty, and he called to the LORD.**

Although Samson had many serious character flaws, he is included in the "hall of faith" (Heb.13:32). God listened to his pleas for help. But imagine what the Lord could have done through a wholeheartedly obedient Samson!

called to the LORD and said, "You have given this great deliverance by the hand of Your servant, and now shall I die of thirst and fall into the hands of the uncircumcised?"

19 But God split the hollow place that is in Lehi so that water came out of it. When he drank, his strength returned and he revived. Therefore he named it En-hakkore, which is in Lehi to this day.

20 So he judged Israel twenty years in the days of the Philistines.

16 NOW Samson went to Gaza and saw a harlot there, and went in to her.

2 *When it was told* to the Gazites, saying, "Samson has come here," they surrounded *the place* and lay in wait for him all night at the gate of the city. And they kept silent all night, saying, "*Let us wait* until the morning light, then we will kill him."

3 Now Samson lay until midnight, and at midnight he arose and took hold of the doors of the city gate and the two posts and pulled them up along with the bars; then he put them on his shoulders and carried them up to the top of the mountain which is opposite Hebron.

4 After this it came about that he loved a woman in the valley of Sorek, whose name was Delilah.

5 The lords of the Philistines came up to her and said to her, "Entice him, and see where his great strength *lies* and how we may overpower him that we may bind him to afflict him. Then we will each give you eleven hundred *pieces* of silver."

6 So Delilah said to Samson, "Please tell me where your great strength is and how you may be bound to afflict you."

7 Samson said to her, "If they bind me with seven fresh cords that have not been dried, then I will become weak and be like any *other* man."

8 Then the lords of the Philistines brought up to her seven fresh cords that had not been dried, and she bound him with them.

9 Now she had *men* lying in wait in an inner room. And she said to him, "The Philistines are upon you, Samson!" But he snapped the cords as a string of tow snaps when it touches fire. So his strength was not discovered.

10 Then Delilah said to Samson, "Behold, you have deceived me and told me lies; now please tell me how you may be bound."

11 He said to her, "If they bind me tightly with new ropes which have not been used, then I will become weak and be like any *other* man."

12 So Delilah took new ropes and bound him with them and said to him, "The Philistines are upon you, Samson!" For the *men* were lying in wait in the inner room. But he snapped the ropes from his arms like a thread.

13 Then Delilah said to Samson, "Up to now you have deceived me and told me lies; tell me how you may be bound." And he said to her, "If you weave the seven locks of my hair with the web [and fasten it with a pin, then I will become weak and be like any other man."

14 So while he slept, Delilah took the seven locks of his hair and wove them into the web]. And she fastened *it* with the pin and said to him, "The Philistines are upon you, Samson!" But he awoke from his sleep and pulled out the pin of the loom and the web.

15 Then she said to him, "How can you say, 'I love you,' when your heart is not with me? You have deceived me these three times and have not told me where your great strength is."

16 It came about when she pressed him daily with her words and urged him, that his soul was annoyed to death.

17 So he told her all *that was* in his heart and said to her, "A razor has never come on my head, for I have been a Nazirite to God from my mother's womb. If I am shaved, then my strength will leave me and I will become weak and be like any *other* man."

LIFE LESSONS

➤ Judges 16:15 — *"How can you say, 'I love you,' when your heart is not with me?"*

*I*t is easy to say, "I love you," but real, godly love always wants the best for the other person. Samson did not want the best for Delilah, nor did she want the best for him. Lust is a very poor substitute for love.

18 When Delilah saw that he had told her all *that was* in his heart, she sent and called the lords of the Philistines, saying, "Come up once more, for he has told me all *that is* in his heart." Then the lords of the Philistines came up to her and brought the money in their hands.

➤ **19** She made him sleep on her knees, and called for a man and had him shave off the seven locks of his hair. Then she began to afflict him, and his strength left him.

➤ **20** She said, "The Philistines are upon you, Samson!" And he awoke from his sleep and said, "I will go out as at other times and shake myself free." But he did not know that the LORD had departed from him.

21 Then the Philistines seized him and gouged out his eyes; and they brought him down to Gaza and bound him with bronze chains, and he was a grinder in the prison.

22 However, the hair of his head began to grow again after it was shaved off.

23 Now the lords of the Philistines assembled to offer a great sacrifice to Dagon their god, and to rejoice, for they said,

"Our god has given Samson our
    enemy into our hands."

24 When the people saw him, they praised their god, for they said,

"Our god has given our enemy into
    our hands,
Even the destroyer of our country,
Who has slain many of us."

25 It so happened when they were in high spirits, that they said, "Call for Samson, that he may amuse us." So they called for Samson from the prison, and he entertained them. And they made him stand between the pillars.

26 Then Samson said to the boy who was holding his hand, "Let me feel the pillars on which the house rests, that I may lean against them."

27 Now the house was full of men and women, and all the lords of the Philistines were there. And about 3,000 men and women were on the roof looking on while Samson was amusing *them.*

28 Then Samson called to the LORD and said, "O Lord GOD, please remember me and please strengthen me just this time, O God, that I may at once be avenged of the Philistines for my two eyes."

29 Samson grasped the two middle pillars on which the house rested, and braced himself against them, the one with his right hand and the other with his left.

30 And Samson said, "Let me die with the Philistines!" And he bent with all his might so that the house fell on the lords and all the people who were in it. So the dead whom he killed at his death were more than those whom he killed in his life.

31 Then his brothers and all his father's household came down, took him, brought him up and buried him between Zorah and Eshtaol in the tomb of Manoah his father. Thus he had judged Israel twenty years.

LIFE LESSONS

➤ **Judges 16:19 — *She began to afflict him, and his strength left him.***

*H*ow quickly some love turns to torment! Spent lust often generates feelings of hatred more potent than the earlier feelings of love (2 Sam. 13:15).

➤ **Judges 16:20 — *He did not know that the LORD had departed from him.***

*S*amson had fallen so low spiritually he could not tell the difference between the Lord's presence and His absence. While God's Spirit will never leave believers in Christ, His blessings may. That hinges on our obedience.

✦ **Psalm 51:1–6**

For the choir director. A Psalm of David, when Nathan the prophet came to him, after he had gone in to Bathsheba.

51 BE gracious to me, O God,
    according to Your
    lovingkindness;
  According to the greatness of
    Your compassion blot out my
    transgressions.
2 Wash me thoroughly from my
    iniquity
  And cleanse me from my sin.
3 For I know my transgressions,
  And my sin is ever before me.

Life Examples:

DAVID: A Case Study in Repentance

PSALM 51:1–6

*W*hat happens when we sin and delay our repentance? Are there consequences?

When David committed adultery with Bathsheba, he didn't repent immediately. Only some time later did David admit to his sin. Even then, he didn't do it on his own accord; God had to send a prophet to confront him (2 Sam. 12:1–14). Only after Nathan's visit did David confess his sin and then repent of it. God's discipline followed, in a severe form—perhaps so severe because of David's failure to repent sooner.

If you and I deal with our sin genuinely, openly, and immediately, God can lessen the severity of our discipline. This makes sense in light of the nature of discipline. Discipline is designed to get us to change, to obey. If the Lord sees that we want to cooperate and we have purposed in our hearts to obey the next time, then stern discipline is not usually needed.

4   Against You, You only, I have sinned
     And done what is evil in Your sight,
     So that You are justified when You speak
     And blameless when You judge.
5   Behold, I was brought forth in iniquity,
     And in sin my mother conceived me.
6   Behold, You desire truth in the innermost being,
     And in the hidden part You will make me know wisdom.

Proverbs 14:31, 32

31   He who oppresses the poor taunts his Maker,
      But he who is gracious to the needy honors Him.
32   The wicked is thrust down by his wrongdoing,
      But the righteous has a refuge when he dies.

Luke 18:1–23

18 NOW He was telling them a parable to show that at all times they ought to pray and not to lose heart,
2   saying, "In a certain city there was a judge who did not fear God and did not respect man.
3   "There was a widow in that city, and she kept coming to him, saying, 'Give me legal protection from my opponent.'
4   "For a while he was unwilling; but afterward he said to himself, 'Even though I do not fear God nor respect man,
5   yet because this widow bothers me, I will give her legal protection, otherwise by continually coming she will wear me out.'"
6   And the Lord said, "Hear what the unrighteous judge *said;
7   now, will not God bring about justice for His elect who cry to Him day and night, and will He delay long over them?
8   "I tell you that He will bring about justice for them quickly. However, when the Son of Man comes, will He find faith on the earth?"

LIFE LESSONS

➤ **Psalm 51:4** — *Against You, You only, I have sinned.*

*D*avid sinned by committing adultery with Uriah's wife and plotting his murder (2 Sam. 11). He had made an adulteress of Bathsheba and had dishonored his people, Israel. Yet all sin is ultimately against God and requires His forgiveness—first and foremost.

➤ **Luke 18:1** — *Now He was telling them a parable to show that at all times they ought to pray and not to lose heart.*

*T*here may be many reasons why God does not always answer our prayers quickly, but until He lets us know that we should stop praying about something, He calls us to persevere in faith and keep asking.

9 And He also told this parable to some people who trusted in themselves that they were righteous, and viewed others with contempt:

10 "Two men went up into the temple to pray, one a Pharisee and the other a tax collector.

11 "The Pharisee stood and was praying this to himself: 'God, I thank You that I am not like other people: swindlers, unjust, adulterers, or even like this tax collector.

12 'I fast twice a week; I pay tithes of all that I get.'

13 "But the tax collector, standing some distance away, was even unwilling to lift up his eyes to heaven, but was beating his breast, saying, 'God, be merciful to me, the sinner!'

14 "I tell you, this man went to his house justified rather than the other; for everyone who exalts himself will be humbled, but he who humbles himself will be exalted."

15 And they were bringing even their babies to Him so that He would touch them, but when the disciples saw it, they *began* rebuking them.

16 But Jesus called for them, saying, "Permit the children to come to Me, and do not hinder them, for the kingdom of God belongs to such as these.

17 "Truly I say to you, whoever does not receive the kingdom of God like a child will not enter it *at all.*"

18 A ruler questioned Him, saying, "Good Teacher, what shall I do to inherit eternal life?"

19 And Jesus said to him, "Why do you call Me good? No one is good except God alone.

20 "You know the commandments, 'DO NOT COMMIT ADULTERY, DO NOT MURDER, DO NOT STEAL, DO NOT BEAR FALSE WITNESS, HONOR YOUR FATHER AND MOTHER.'"

21 And he said, "All these things I have kept from *my* youth."

22 When Jesus heard *this*, He said to him, "One thing you still lack; sell all that you possess and distribute it to the poor, and you shall have treasure in heaven; and come, follow Me."

23 But when he had heard these things, he became very sad, for he was extremely rich.

Judges 17:1—19:30

17 NOW there was a man of the hill country of Ephraim whose name was Micah.

2 He said to his mother, "The eleven hundred *pieces* of silver which were taken from you, about which you uttered a curse in my hearing, behold, the silver is with me; I took it." And his mother said, "Blessed be my son by the LORD."

3 He then returned the eleven hundred *pieces* of silver to his mother, and his mother said, "I wholly dedicate the silver from my hand to the LORD for my son to make a graven image and a molten image; now therefore, I will return them to you."

4 So when he returned the silver to his mother, his mother took two hundred *pieces* of silver and gave them to the silversmith who made them into a graven image and a molten image, and they were in the house of Micah.

5 And the man Micah had a shrine and he made an ephod and household idols and consecrated one of his sons, that he might become his priest.

6 In those days there was no king in Israel; every man did what was right in his own eyes.

7 Now there was a young man from Bethlehem in Judah, of the family of

LIFE LESSONS

➤ **Judges 17:3 —** *"I wholly dedicate the silver from my hand to the LORD for my son to make a graven image and a molten image."*

*T*his woman tried to wed idolatry with worship of the true God. But we can never worship God *and* something else. The Lord deserves our exclusive devotion.

Judah, who was a Levite; and he was staying there.

8 Then the man departed from the city, from Bethlehem in Judah, to stay wherever he might find *a place*; and as he made his journey, he came to the hill country of Ephraim to the house of Micah.

9 Micah said to him, "Where do you come from?" And he said to him, "I am a Levite from Bethlehem in Judah, and I am going to stay wherever I may find *a place*."

10 Micah then said to him, "Dwell with me and be a father and a priest to me, and I will give you ten *pieces* of silver a year, a suit of clothes, and your maintenance." So the Levite went *in*.

11 The Levite agreed to live with the man, and the young man became to him like one of his sons.

12 So Micah consecrated the Levite, and the young man became his priest and lived in the house of Micah.

➤ 13 Then Micah said, "Now I know that the LORD will prosper me, seeing I have a Levite as priest."

18 IN those days there was no king of Israel; and in those days the tribe of the Danites was seeking an inheritance for themselves to live in, for until that day an inheritance had not been allotted to them as a possession among the tribes of Israel.

LIFE LESSONS

➤ **Judges 17:6** — *In those days there was no king in Israel; every man did what was right in his own eyes.*

*M*oses had warned against "every man doing whatever is right in his own eyes" (Deut. 12:8). But when God's people refuse to obey Him, that's exactly what starts to happen. And the result is chaos, as Judges proves.

➤ **Judges 17:13** — *"Now I know that the LORD will prosper me, seeing I have a Levite as priest."*

*T*he Word of God makes clear the Lord's blessing does not come because of the observation of rituals or by special connections to religious people. His blessings are given to those who obey Him.

---

2 So the sons of Dan sent from their family five men out of their whole number, valiant men from Zorah and Eshtaol, to spy out the land and to search it; and they said to them, "Go, search the land." And they came to the hill country of Ephraim, to the house of Micah, and lodged there.

3 When they were near the house of Micah, they recognized the voice of the young man, the Levite; and they turned aside there and said to him, "Who brought you here? And what are you doing in this *place*? And what do you have here?"

4 He said to them, "Thus and so has Micah done to me, and he has hired me and I have become his priest."

5 They said to him, "Inquire of God, please, that we may know whether our way on which we are going will be prosperous."

6 The priest said to them, "Go in peace; your way in which you are going has the LORD's approval."

7 Then the five men departed and came to Laish and saw the people who were in it living in security, after the manner of the Sidonians, quiet and secure; for there was no ruler humiliating *them* for anything in the land, and they were far from the Sidonians and had no dealings with anyone.

8 When they came back to their brothers at Zorah and Eshtaol, their brothers said to them, "What *do* you *report*?"

9 They said, "Arise, and let us go up against them; for we have seen the land, and behold, it is very good. And will you sit still? Do not delay to go, to enter, to possess the land.

10 "When you enter, you will come to a secure people with a spacious land; for God has given it into your hand, a place where there is no lack of anything that is on the earth."

11 Then from the family of the Danites, from Zorah and from Eshtaol, six hundred men armed with weapons of war set out.

12 They went up and camped at Kiriath-jearim in Judah. Therefore they called that place Mahaneh-dan to this day; behold, it is west of Kiriath-jearim.

13 They passed from there to the hill country of Ephraim and came to the house of Micah.
14 Then the five men who went to spy out the country of Laish said to their kinsmen, "Do you know that there are in these houses an ephod and household idols and a graven image and a molten image? Now therefore, consider what you should do."
15 They turned aside there and came to the house of the young man, the Levite, to the house of Micah, and asked him of his welfare.
16 The six hundred men armed with their weapons of war, who were of the sons of Dan, stood by the entrance of the gate.
17 Now the five men who went to spy out the land went up *and* entered there, *and* took the graven image and the ephod and household idols and the molten image, while the priest stood by the entrance of the gate with the six hundred men armed with weapons of war.
18 When these went into Micah's house and took the graven image, the ephod and household idols and the molten image, the priest said to them, "What are you doing?"
19 They said to him, "Be silent, put your hand over your mouth and come with us, and be to us a father and a priest. Is it better for you to be a priest to the house of one man, or to be priest to a tribe and a family in Israel?"
20 The priest's heart was glad, and he took the ephod and household idols and the graven image and went among the people.
21 Then they turned and departed, and put the little ones and the livestock and the valuables in front of them.
22 When they had gone some distance from the house of Micah, the men who *were* in the houses near Micah's house assembled and overtook the sons of Dan.
23 They cried to the sons of Dan, who turned around and said to Micah, "What is *the matter* with you, that you have assembled together?"
24 He said, "You have taken away my gods which I made, and the priest, and have gone away, and what do I have be-

sides? So how can you say to me, 'What is *the matter* with you?'"
25 The sons of Dan said to him, "Do not let your voice be heard among us, or else fierce men will fall upon you and you will lose your life, with the lives of your household."
26 So the sons of Dan went on their way; and when Micah saw that they were too strong for him, he turned and went back to his house.
27 Then they took what Micah had made and the priest who had belonged to him, and came to Laish, to a people quiet and secure, and struck them with the edge of the sword; and they burned the city with fire.
28 And there was no one to deliver *them,* because it was far from Sidon and they had no dealings with anyone, and it was in the valley which is near Beth-rehob. And they rebuilt the city and lived in it.
29 They called the name of the city Dan, after the name of Dan their father who was born in Israel; however, the name of the city formerly was Laish.
30 The sons of Dan set up for them- ◄ selves the graven image; and Jonathan, the son of Gershom, the son of Manasseh, he and his sons were priests to the tribe of the Danites until the day of the captivity of the land.
31 So they set up for themselves Micah's graven image which he had made, all the time that the house of God was at Shiloh.

19 NOW it came about in those days, when there was no king in Israel, that there was a certain Levite staying in the remote part of the hill country of Ephraim, who took a concubine for himself from Bethlehem in Judah.
2 But his concubine played the harlot

against him, and she went away from him to her father's house in Bethlehem in Judah, and was there for a period of four months.

3   Then her husband arose and went after her to speak tenderly to her in order to bring her back, taking with him his servant and a pair of donkeys. So she brought him into her father's house, and when the girl's father saw him, he was glad to meet him.

4   His father-in-law, the girl's father, detained him; and he remained with him three days. So they ate and drank and lodged there.

5   Now on the fourth day they got up early in the morning, and he prepared to go; and the girl's father said to his son-in-law, "Sustain yourself with a piece of bread, and afterward you may go."

6   So both of them sat down and ate and drank together; and the girl's father said to the man, "Please be willing to spend the night, and let your heart be merry."

7   Then the man arose to go, but his father-in-law urged him so that he spent the night there again.

8   On the fifth day he arose to go early in the morning, and the girl's father said, "Please sustain yourself, and wait until afternoon"; so both of them ate.

9   When the man arose to go along with his concubine and servant, his father-in-law, the girl's father, said to him, "Behold now, the day has drawn to a close; please spend the night. Lo, the day is coming to an end; spend the night here that your heart may be merry. Then tomorrow you may arise early for your journey so that you may go home."

10   But the man was not willing to spend the night, so he arose and departed and came to a place opposite Jebus (that is, Jerusalem). And there were with him a pair of saddled donkeys; his concubine also was with him.

11   When they were near Jebus, the day was almost gone; and the servant said to his master, "Please come, and let us turn aside into this city of the Jebusites and spend the night in it."

12   However, his master said to him, "We will not turn aside into the city of foreigners who are not of the sons of Israel; but we will go on as far as Gibeah."

13   He said to his servant, "Come and let us approach one of these places; and we will spend the night in Gibeah or Ramah."

14   So they passed along and went their way, and the sun set on them near Gibeah which belongs to Benjamin.

15   They turned aside there in order to enter and lodge in Gibeah. When they entered, they sat down in the open square of the city, for no one took them into his house to spend the night.

16   Then behold, an old man was coming out of the field from his work at evening. Now the man was from the hill country of Ephraim, and he was staying in Gibeah, but the men of the place were Benjamites.

17   And he lifted up his eyes and saw the traveler in the open square of the city; and the old man said, "Where are you going, and where do you come from?"

18   He said to him, "We are passing from Bethlehem in Judah to the remote part of the hill country of Ephraim, for I am from there, and I went to Bethlehem in Judah. But I am now going to my house, and no man will take me into his house.

19   "Yet there is both straw and fodder for our donkeys, and also bread and wine for me, your maidservant, and the young man who is with your servants; there is no lack of anything."

20   The old man said, "Peace to you. Only let me take care of all your needs; however, do not spend the night in the open square."

21   So he took him into his house and gave the donkeys fodder, and they washed their feet and ate and drank.

22   While they were celebrating, behold, the men of the city, certain worthless fellows, surrounded the house, pounding the door; and they spoke to the owner of the house, the old man, saying, "Bring out the man who came into your house that we may have relations with him."

23   Then the man, the owner of the house, went out to them and said to them, "No, my fellows, please do not act so wickedly; since this man has come

into my house, do not commit this act of folly.

24 "Here is my virgin daughter and his concubine. Please let me bring them out that you may ravish them and do to them whatever you wish. But do not commit such an act of folly against this man."

➤ 25 But the men would not listen to him. So the man seized his concubine and brought *her* out to them; and they raped her and abused her all night until morning, then let her go at the approach of dawn.

26 As the day began to dawn, the woman came and fell down at the doorway of the man's house where her master was, until *full* daylight.

27 When her master arose in the morning and opened the doors of the house and went out to go on his way, then behold, his concubine was lying at the doorway of the house with her hands on the threshold.

28 He said to her, "Get up and let us go," but there was no answer. Then he placed her on the donkey; and the man arose and went to his home.

29 When he entered his house, he took a knife and laid hold of his concubine and cut her in twelve pieces, limb by limb, and sent her throughout the territory of Israel.

30 All who saw *it* said, "Nothing like this has *ever* happened or been seen from the day when the sons of Israel came up from the land of Egypt to this day. Consider it, take counsel and speak up!"

◈ Psalm 51:7–11

7 Purify me with hyssop, and I shall be clean;

Wash me, and I shall be whiter than snow.

8 Make me to hear joy and gladness, Let the bones which You have broken rejoice.

9 Hide Your face from my sins And blot out all my iniquities.

10 Create in me a clean heart, O God, And renew a steadfast spirit within me.

11 Do not cast me away from Your presence And do not take Your Holy Spirit from me.

◈ Proverbs 14:33–35

33 Wisdom rests in the heart of one who has understanding, But in the hearts of fools it is made known.

34 Righteousness exalts a nation, But sin is a disgrace to *any* people. ✳

35 The king's favor is toward a servant who acts wisely, But his anger is toward him who acts shamefully.

◈ Luke 18:24–43

24 And Jesus looked at him and said, "How hard it is for those who are wealthy to enter the kingdom of God!

25 "For it is easier for a camel to go through the eye of a needle than for a rich man to enter the kingdom of God."

26 They who heard it said, "Then who can be saved?"

27 But He said, "The things that are impossible with people are possible with God."

28 Peter said, "Behold, we have left our own *homes* and followed You."

29 And He said to them, "Truly I say to ✳ you, there is no one who has left house or wife or brothers or parents or children, for the sake of the kingdom of God,

30 who will not receive many times as much at this time and in the age to come, eternal life."

LIFE LESSONS

➤ **Judges 19:25 — *The man seized his concubine and brought her out to them.***

*W*hen everyone does what is right in his own eyes, before long moral conditions sink to the perverted level of Sodom (Gen. 19:1–8). We need the Word of God to show us the right way.

ANSWERS TO LIFE'S QUESTIONS

What should I do when I feel distant from God?

PSALM 51:11

It's safe to say no believer alive today has avoided those "desert" times when he or she just didn't feel the presence of God. It's a problem all of us have to confront at some point along the way.

Many factors can make us feel distant from our heavenly Father. Sometimes, it's a matter of our accuser, the devil, whispering in our ears and speaking his deception. At other times, these "distant" times turn out to be seasons when God is trying to bring us closer to Himself. But sometimes it's a matter of our need to do some inner "housecleaning."

Nothing can make us feel more distant from God than unconfessed sin. While our failures do not stop His unconditional love for us, they can drive an emotional and spiritual wedge between us and Him.

Throughout the Book of Judges, we read how the nation of Israel sinned and drifted in its devotion to the Lord. Many times when our hearts become entangled with disobedience and the things of this world, God will allow us to experience a feeling of distance between Him and us. This is exactly what Israel should have felt in those dark days.

The people should have recognized their spiritual poverty. Instead, they continued to worship Baal without regard for the holy nature of God and His intimate love for them. Therefore, He allowed them to go through a time of testing. In Judges 6:6 we read, "Israel was brought very low because of Midian, and the sons of Israel cried to the LORD." Here we see at work an important principle regarding repentance and regaining favor with the Lord.

When we realize our error and cry out to the Lord, He turns in our direction. He never comes, however, as if being summoned by a superior. He comes when our hearts have been broken and when at last we realize our need for Him. When we humbly confess our sins and our dependence on Him, He hears our prayers and brings deliverance from sin (Judg. 8:28; 1 John 1:9).

If you are experiencing a time of coolness in your relationship with God, don't hesitate to turn to Him in prayer. Confess any known sin, and ask Him to restore the sweetness of His fellowship to your heart.

---

31 Then He took the twelve aside and said to them, "Behold, we are going up to Jerusalem, and all things which are written through the prophets about the Son of Man will be accomplished.

32 "For He will be handed over to the Gentiles, and will be mocked and mistreated and spit upon,

33 and after they have scourged Him, they will kill Him; and the third day He will rise again."

➤ **34** But the disciples understood none of these things, and *the meaning of* this statement was hidden from them, and they did not comprehend the things that were said.

35 As Jesus was approaching Jericho, a blind man was sitting by the road begging.

36 Now hearing a crowd going by, he *began* to inquire what this was.

37 They told him that Jesus of Nazareth was passing by.

38 And he called out, saying, "Jesus, Son of David, have mercy on me!"

39 Those who led the way were sternly telling him to be quiet; but he kept crying out all the more, "Son of David, have mercy on me!"

40 And Jesus stopped and commanded that he be brought to Him; and when he came near, He questioned him,

41 "What do you want Me to do for you?" And he said, "Lord, *I want* to regain my sight!"

42 And Jesus said to him, "Receive your sight; your faith has made you well."

43 Immediately he regained his sight and *began* following Him, glorifying God; and when all the people saw it, they gave praise to God.

LIFE LESSONS

➤ **Luke 18:34 — *The disciples understood none of these things.***

Why did the disciples so frequently misunderstand Jesus' words? Can we blame faulty expectations, disobedience, or some other cause? Luke says the truth was hidden from them. Those who really want to know will persevere to reach understanding.

20 THEN all the sons of Israel from Dan to Beersheba, including the land of Gilead, came out, and the congregation assembled as one man to the LORD at Mizpah.

2 The chiefs of all the people, *even* of all the tribes of Israel, took their stand in the assembly of the people of God, 400,000 foot soldiers who drew the sword.

3 (Now the sons of Benjamin heard that the sons of Israel had gone up to Mizpah.) And the sons of Israel said, "Tell *us,* how did this wickedness take place?"

4 So the Levite, the husband of the woman who was murdered, answered and said, "I came with my concubine to spend the night at Gibeah which belongs to Benjamin.

5 "But the men of Gibeah rose up against me and surrounded the house at night because of me. They intended to kill me; instead, they ravished my concubine so that she died.

6 "And I took hold of my concubine and cut her in pieces and sent her throughout the land of Israel's inheritance; for they have committed a lewd and disgraceful act in Israel.

7 "Behold, all you sons of Israel, give your advice and counsel here."

8 Then all the people arose as one man, saying, "Not one of us will go to his tent, nor will any of us return to his house.

9 "But now this is the thing which we will do to Gibeah; *we will go up* against it by lot.

10 "And we will take 10 men out of 100 throughout the tribes of Israel, and 100 out of 1,000, and 1,000 out of 10,000 to supply food for the people, that when they come to Gibeah of Benjamin, they may punish *them* for all the disgraceful acts that they have committed in Israel."

11 Thus all the men of Israel were gathered against the city, united as one man.

12 Then the tribes of Israel sent men through the entire tribe of Benjamin, saying, "What is this wickedness that has taken place among you?

13 "Now then, deliver up the men, the worthless fellows in Gibeah, that we may put them to death and remove *this* wickedness from Israel." But the sons of Benjamin would not listen to the voice of their brothers, the sons of Israel.

14 The sons of Benjamin gathered from the cities to Gibeah, to go out to battle against the sons of Israel.

15 From the cities on that day the sons of Benjamin were numbered, 26,000 men who draw the sword, besides the inhabitants of Gibeah who were numbered, 700 choice men.

16 Out of all these people 700 choice men were left-handed; each one could sling a stone at a hair and not miss.

17 Then the men of Israel besides Benjamin were numbered, 400,000 men who draw the sword; all these were men of war.

18 Now the sons of Israel arose, went up to Bethel, and inquired of God and said, "Who shall go up first for us to battle against the sons of Benjamin?" Then the LORD said, "Judah *shall go up* first."

19 So the sons of Israel arose in the morning and camped against Gibeah.

20 The men of Israel went out to battle against Benjamin, and the men of Israel arrayed for battle against them at Gibeah.

21 Then the sons of Benjamin came out of Gibeah and felled to the ground on that day 22,000 men of Israel.

22 But the people, the men of Israel, encouraged themselves and arrayed for battle again in the place where they had arrayed themselves the first day.

23 The sons of Israel went up and wept before the LORD until evening, and inquired of the LORD, saying, "Shall we again draw near for battle against the sons of my brother Benjamin?" And the LORD said, "Go up against him."

24 Then the sons of Israel came against the sons of Benjamin the second day.

25 Benjamin went out against them from Gibeah the second day and felled to the ground again 18,000 men of the sons of Israel; all these drew the sword.

26 Then all the sons of Israel and all the people went up and came to Bethel and wept; thus they remained there before the LORD and fasted that day until evening. And they offered burnt offerings and peace offerings before the LORD.

27 The sons of Israel inquired of the

LORD (for the ark of the covenant of God *was* there in those days,

28 and Phinehas the son of Eleazar, Aaron's son, stood before it to *minister* in those days), saying, "Shall I yet again go out to battle against the sons of my brother Benjamin, or shall I cease?" And the LORD said, "Go up, for tomorrow I will deliver them into your hand."

29 So Israel set men in ambush around Gibeah.

30 The sons of Israel went up against the sons of Benjamin on the third day and arrayed themselves against Gibeah as at other times.

31 The sons of Benjamin went out against the people and were drawn away from the city, and they began to strike and kill some of the people as at other times, on the highways, one of which goes up to Bethel and the other to Gibeah, *and* in the field, about thirty men of Israel.

32 The sons of Benjamin said, "They are struck down before us, as at the first." But the sons of Israel said, "Let us flee that we may draw them away from the city to the highways."

33 Then all the men of Israel arose from their place and arrayed themselves at Baal-tamar; and the men of Israel in ambush broke out of their place, even out of Maareh-geba.

34 When ten thousand choice men from all Israel came against Gibeah, the battle became fierce; but Benjamin did not know that disaster was close to them.

35 And the LORD struck Benjamin before Israel, so that the sons of Israel destroyed 25,100 men of Benjamin that day, all who draw the sword.

36 So the sons of Benjamin saw that they were defeated. When the men of Israel gave ground to Benjamin because they relied on the men in ambush whom they had set against Gibeah,

37 the men in ambush hurried and rushed against Gibeah; the men in ambush also deployed and struck all the city with the edge of the sword.

38 Now the appointed sign between the men of Israel and the men in ambush was that they would make a great cloud of smoke rise from the city.

39 Then the men of Israel turned in the battle, and Benjamin began to strike and kill about thirty men of Israel, for they said, "Surely they are defeated before us, as in the first battle."

40 But when the cloud began to rise from the city in a column of smoke, Benjamin looked behind them; and behold, the whole city was going up *in smoke* to heaven.

41 Then the men of Israel turned, and the men of Benjamin were terrified; for they saw that disaster was close to them.

42 Therefore, they turned their backs before the men of Israel toward the direction of the wilderness, but the battle overtook them while those who came out of the cities destroyed them in the midst of them.

43 They surrounded Benjamin, pursued them without rest *and* trod them down opposite Gibeah toward the east.

44 Thus 18,000 men of Benjamin fell; all these were valiant warriors.

45 The rest turned and fled toward the wilderness to the rock of Rimmon, but they caught 5,000 of them on the highways and overtook them at Gidom and killed 2,000 of them.

46 So all of Benjamin who fell that day ◄ were 25,000 men who draw the sword; all these were valiant warriors.

47 But 600 men turned and fled toward the wilderness to the rock of Rimmon, and they remained at the rock of Rimmon four months.

48 The men of Israel then turned back against the sons of Benjamin and struck them with the edge of the sword, both the entire city with the cattle and all that they found; they also set on fire all the cities which they found.

21 NOW the men of Israel had sworn in Mizpah, saying, "None of us shall give his daughter to Benjamin in marriage."

LIFE LESSONS

➤ Judges 20:46 — *So all of Benjamin who fell that day were 25,000 men who draw the sword.*

*T*he tribe of Benjamin lost more than 25,000 men in battle, while Israel lost over 40,000 of its men—a bloody civil war that didn't need to happen. When we lose connection to God's Word, we lose our senses and make extremely bad decisions (Prov. 16:25).

Judges 20:1—21:25

20 THEN all the sons of Israel from Dan to Beersheba, including the land of Gilead, came out, and the congregation assembled as one man to the LORD at Mizpah.
2 The chiefs of all the people, *even* of all the tribes of Israel, took their stand in the assembly of the people of God, 400,000 foot soldiers who drew the sword.
3 (Now the sons of Benjamin heard that the sons of Israel had gone up to Mizpah.) And the sons of Israel said, "Tell *us*, how did this wickedness take place?"
4 So the Levite, the husband of the woman who was murdered, answered and said, "I came with my concubine to spend the night at Gibeah which belongs to Benjamin.
5 "But the men of Gibeah rose up against me and surrounded the house at night because of me. They intended to kill me; instead, they ravished my concubine so that she died.
6 "And I took hold of my concubine and cut her in pieces and sent her throughout the land of Israel's inheritance; for they have committed a lewd and disgraceful act in Israel.
7 "Behold, all you sons of Israel, give your advice and counsel here."
8 Then all the people arose as one man, saying, "Not one of us will go to his tent, nor will any of us return to his house.
9 "But now this is the thing which we will do to Gibeah; *we will go up* against it by lot.
10 "And we will take 10 men out of 100 throughout the tribes of Israel, and 100 out of 1,000, and 1,000 out of 10,000 to supply food for the people, that when they come to Gibeah of Benjamin, they may punish *them* for all the disgraceful acts that they have committed in Israel."
11 Thus all the men of Israel were gathered against the city, united as one man.
12 Then the tribes of Israel sent men through the entire tribe of Benjamin, saying, "What is this wickedness that has taken place among you?
13 "Now then, deliver up the men, the worthless fellows in Gibeah, that we may put them to death and remove *this* wickedness from Israel." But the sons of Benjamin would not listen to the voice of their brothers, the sons of Israel.
14 The sons of Benjamin gathered from the cities to Gibeah, to go out to battle against the sons of Israel.
15 From the cities on that day the sons of Benjamin were numbered, 26,000 men who draw the sword, besides the inhabitants of Gibeah who were numbered, 700 choice men.
16 Out of all these people 700 choice men were left-handed; each one could sling a stone at a hair and not miss.
17 Then the men of Israel besides Benjamin were numbered, 400,000 men who draw the sword; all these were men of war.
18 Now the sons of Israel arose, went up to Bethel, and inquired of God and said, "Who shall go up first for us to battle against the sons of Benjamin?" Then the LORD said, "Judah *shall go up* first."
19 So the sons of Israel arose in the morning and camped against Gibeah.
20 The men of Israel went out to battle against Benjamin, and the men of Israel arrayed for battle against them at Gibeah.
21 Then the sons of Benjamin came out of Gibeah and felled to the ground on that day 22,000 men of Israel.
22 But the people, the men of Israel, encouraged themselves and arrayed for battle again in the place where they had arrayed themselves the first day.
23 The sons of Israel went up and wept before the LORD until evening, and inquired of the LORD, saying, "Shall we again draw near for battle against the sons of my brother Benjamin?" And the LORD said, "Go up against him."
24 Then the sons of Israel came against the sons of Benjamin the second day.
25 Benjamin went out against them from Gibeah the second day and felled to the ground again 18,000 men of the sons of Israel; all these drew the sword.
26 Then all the sons of Israel and all the people went up and came to Bethel and wept; thus they remained there before the LORD and fasted that day until evening. And they offered burnt offerings and peace offerings before the LORD.
27 The sons of Israel inquired of the

LORD (for the ark of the covenant of God *was* there in those days,

28 and Phinehas the son of Eleazar, Aaron's son, stood before it to *minister* in those days), saying, "Shall I yet again go out to battle against the sons of my brother Benjamin, or shall I cease?" And the LORD said, "Go up, for tomorrow I will deliver them into your hand."

29 So Israel set men in ambush around Gibeah.

30 The sons of Israel went up against the sons of Benjamin on the third day and arrayed themselves against Gibeah as at other times.

31 The sons of Benjamin went out against the people and were drawn away from the city, and they began to strike and kill some of the people as at other times, on the highways, one of which goes up to Bethel and the other to Gibeah, *and* in the field, about thirty men of Israel.

32 The sons of Benjamin said, "They are struck down before us, as at the first." But the sons of Israel said, "Let us flee that we may draw them away from the city to the highways."

33 Then all the men of Israel arose from their place and arrayed themselves at Baal-tamar; and the men of Israel in ambush broke out of their place, even out of Maareh-geba.

34 When ten thousand choice men from all Israel came against Gibeah, the battle became fierce; but Benjamin did not know that disaster was close to them.

35 And the LORD struck Benjamin before Israel, so that the sons of Israel destroyed 25,100 men of Benjamin that day, all who draw the sword.

36 So the sons of Benjamin saw that they were defeated. When the men of Israel gave ground to Benjamin because they relied on the men in ambush whom they had set against Gibeah,

37 the men in ambush hurried and rushed against Gibeah; the men in ambush also deployed and struck all the city with the edge of the sword.

38 Now the appointed sign between the men of Israel and the men in ambush was that they would make a great cloud of smoke rise from the city.

39 Then the men of Israel turned in the battle, and Benjamin began to strike and kill about thirty men of Israel, for they said, "Surely they are defeated before us, as in the first battle."

40 But when the cloud began to rise from the city in a column of smoke, Benjamin looked behind them; and behold, the whole city was going up *in smoke* to heaven.

41 Then the men of Israel turned, and the men of Benjamin were terrified; for they saw that disaster was close to them.

42 Therefore, they turned their backs before the men of Israel toward the direction of the wilderness, but the battle overtook them while those who came out of the cities destroyed them in the midst of them.

43 They surrounded Benjamin, pursued them without rest *and* trod them down opposite Gibeah toward the east.

44 Thus 18,000 men of Benjamin fell; all these were valiant warriors.

45 The rest turned and fled toward the wilderness to the rock of Rimmon, but they caught 5,000 of them on the highways and overtook them at Gidom and killed 2,000 of them.

46 So all of Benjamin who fell that day ◁ were 25,000 men who draw the sword; all these were valiant warriors.

47 But 600 men turned and fled toward the wilderness to the rock of Rimmon, and they remained at the rock of Rimmon four months.

48 The men of Israel then turned back against the sons of Benjamin and struck them with the edge of the sword, both the entire city with the cattle and all that they found; they also set on fire all the cities which they found.

21 NOW the men of Israel had sworn in Mizpah, saying, "None of us shall give his daughter to Benjamin in marriage."

LIFE LESSONS

> ➤ Judges 20:46 — *So all of Benjamin who fell that day were 25,000 men who draw the sword.*

The tribe of Benjamin lost more than 25,000 men in battle, while Israel lost over 40,000 of its men—a bloody civil war that didn't need to happen. When we lose connection to God's Word, we lose our senses and make extremely bad decisions (Prov. 16:25).

2   So the people came to Bethel and sat there before God until evening, and lifted up their voices and wept bitterly.

3   They said, "Why, O LORD, God of Israel, has this come about in Israel, so that one tribe should be *missing* today in Israel?"

4   It came about the next day that the people arose early and built an altar there and offered burnt offerings and peace offerings.

5   Then the sons of Israel said, "Who is there among all the tribes of Israel who did not come up in the assembly to the LORD?" For they had taken a great oath concerning him who did not come up to the LORD at Mizpah, saying, "He shall surely be put to death."

6   And the sons of Israel were sorry for their brother Benjamin and said, "One tribe is cut off from Israel today.

7   "What shall we do for wives for those who are left, since we have sworn by the LORD not to give them any of our daughters in marriage?"

8   And they said, "What one is there of the tribes of Israel who did not come up to the LORD at Mizpah?" And behold, no one had come to the camp from Jabesh-gilead to the assembly.

9   For when the people were numbered, behold, not one of the inhabitants of Jabesh-gilead was there.

10 And the congregation sent 12,000 of the valiant warriors there, and commanded them, saying, "Go and strike the inhabitants of Jabesh-gilead with the edge of the sword, with the women and the little ones.

11 "This is the thing that you shall do: you shall utterly destroy every man and every woman who has lain with a man."

12 And they found among the inhabitants of Jabesh-gilead 400 young virgins who had not known a man by lying with him; and they brought them to the camp at Shiloh, which is in the land of Canaan.

13 Then the whole congregation sent *word* and spoke to the sons of Benjamin who were at the rock of Rimmon, and proclaimed peace to them.

14 Benjamin returned at that time, and they gave them the women whom they had kept alive from the women of Jabesh-gilead; yet they were not enough for them.

15 And the people were sorry for Ben-

jamin because the LORD had made a breach in the tribes of Israel.

16 Then the elders of the congregation said, "What shall we do for wives for those who are left, since the women are destroyed out of Benjamin?"

17 They said, "*There must be* an inheritance for the survivors of Benjamin, so that a tribe will not be blotted out from Israel.

18 "But we cannot give them wives of our daughters." For the sons of Israel had sworn, saying, "Cursed is he who gives a wife to Benjamin."

19 So they said, "Behold, there is a feast of the LORD from year to year in Shiloh, which is on the north side of Bethel, on the east side of the highway that goes up from Bethel to Shechem, and on the south side of Lebonah."

20 And they commanded the sons of Benjamin, saying, "Go and lie in wait in the vineyards,

21 and watch; and behold, if the daughters of Shiloh come out to take part in the dances, then you shall come out of the vineyards and each of you shall catch his wife from the daughters of Shiloh, and go to the land of Benjamin.

22 "It shall come about, when their fathers or their brothers come to complain to us, that we shall say to them, 'Give them to us voluntarily, because we did not take for each man *of Benjamin* a wife in battle, nor did you give *them* to them, *else* you would now be guilty.'"

23 The sons of Benjamin did so, and took wives according to their number from those who danced, whom they carried away. And they went and returned to their inheritance and rebuilt the cities and lived in them.

24 The sons of Israel departed from there at that time, every man to his tribe and family, and each one of them went out from there to his inheritance.

25 In those days there was no king in Israel; everyone did what was right in his own eyes.

✦ Psalm 51:12–19

12 Restore to me the joy of Your
         salvation
      And sustain me with a willing spirit.

13   *Then* I will teach transgressors
Your ways,
And sinners will be converted to
You.
14   Deliver me from bloodguiltiness,
O God, the God of my salvation;
Then my tongue will joyfully sing of
Your righteousness.
15   O Lord, open my lips,
That my mouth may declare Your
praise.
16   For You do not delight in sacrifice,
otherwise I would give it;
You are not pleased with burnt
offering.
17   The sacrifices of God are a broken
spirit;
A broken and a contrite heart,
O God, You will not despise.
18   By Your favor do good to Zion;
Build the walls of Jerusalem.
19   Then You will delight in righteous
sacrifices,
In burnt offering and whole burnt
offering;
Then young bulls will be offered on
Your altar.

Proverbs 15:1–3

15 A GENTLE answer turns away
wrath,
But a harsh word stirs up anger.
2   The tongue of the wise makes
knowledge acceptable,
But the mouth of fools spouts folly.
3   The eyes of the LORD are in every
place,
Watching the evil and the good.

Luke 19:1–27

19 HE entered Jericho and was passing through.
2   And there was a man called by the
name of Zaccheus; he was a chief tax
collector and he was rich.
3   Zaccheus was trying to see who
Jesus was, and was unable because of
the crowd, for he was small in stature.
4   So he ran on ahead and climbed up
into a sycamore tree in order to see Him,
for He was about to pass through that way.

5   When Jesus came to the place, He
looked up and said to him, "Zaccheus,
hurry and come down, for today I must
stay at your house."
6   And he hurried and came down and
received Him gladly.
7   When they saw it, they all *began* to
grumble, saying, "He has gone to be the
guest of a man who is a sinner."
8   Zaccheus stopped and said to the
Lord, "Behold, Lord, half of my possessions I will give to the poor, and if I have
defrauded anyone of anything, I will give
back four times as much."
9   And Jesus said to him, "Today salvation has come to this house, because he,
too, is a son of Abraham.
10   "For the Son of Man has come to
seek and to save that which was lost."
11   While they were listening to these
things, Jesus went on to tell a parable,
because He was near Jerusalem, and
they supposed that the kingdom of God
was going to appear immediately.
12   So He said, "A nobleman went to a
distant country to receive a kingdom for
himself, and *then* return.
13   "And he called ten of his slaves, and
gave them ten minas and said to them,
'Do business *with this* until I come *back*.'
14   "But his citizens hated him and sent
a delegation after him, saying, 'We do
not want this man to reign over us.'
15   "When he returned, after receiv-

LIFE LESSONS

➤ **Psalm 51:12 — *Restore to me the joy
of Your salvation and sustain me with a
willing spirit.***

*A*lthough we can never lose our
salvation once we genuinely come
to Christ by faith, we can lose the *joy*
of our salvation through our sin. Only
through confession and reliance on His
Spirit can we return to peace with the
Lord and contentment in our souls.

➤ **Proverbs 15:3 — *The eyes of the LORD
are in every place, watching the evil and
the good.***

*N*othing ever escapes the notice of
God, so nothing ever surprises Him.
He always has the right plans in place to
accomplish precisely what He desires—
for reward or for judgment.

ZACCHEUS: A Life That Counts

LUKE 19:1–10

*I*t wasn't easy being one of the most hated (and shortest) men in the city, but Zaccheus the tax collector had learned to handle it. His life was characterized by dishonesty and greed. He had not only collected taxes from the people of his hometown, but he had added an extra tariff for himself. He also had learned to overcome obstacles in unorthodox ways—which may be how he ended up in a tree trying to get a glimpse of the Messiah as He passed by.

Jesus knew who he was. He also knew that though Zaccheus had wealth, his life was void of peace, joy, and contentment. So when He saw him peering down from the tree, the Lord said, "Zaccheus, hurry and come down, for today I must stay at your house" (Luke 19:5). Within moments, the despised tax collector climbed down from his perch and walked with the Savior to his home.

Have you every considered how God is willing to meet you right where you are? All He wants you to do is to admit your need for Him. He wants you to do what this man did—turn your life over to Him.

After meeting Jesus, Zaccheus stopped cheating the people and promised to restore four times all he had taken. He eagerly surrendered everything he had to Christ. For all his shortcomings, Zaccheus realized following the Savior was the only way to true meaning and purpose. He had spent many lonely nights counting money. But from this point on, he wanted his life to count for the kingdom of God.

---

ing the kingdom, he ordered that these slaves, to whom he had given the money, be called to him so that he might know what business they had done.

16 "The first appeared, saying, 'Master, your mina has made ten minas more.'

17 "And he said to him, 'Well done, good slave, because you have been faithful in a very little thing, you are to be in authority over ten cities.'

18 "The second came, saying, 'Your mina, master, has made five minas.'

19 "And he said to him also, 'And you are to be over five cities.'

20 "Another came, saying, 'Master, here is your mina, which I kept put away in a handkerchief;

21 for I was afraid of you, because you are an exacting man; you take up what you did not lay down and reap what you did not sow.'

22 "He *said to him, 'By your own words I will judge you, you worthless slave. Did you know that I am an exacting man, taking up what I did not lay down and reaping what I did not sow?

23 'Then why did you not put my money in the bank, and having come, I would have collected it with interest?'

24 "Then he said to the bystanders, 'Take the mina away from him and give it to the one who has the ten minas.'

25 "And they said to him, 'Master, he has ten minas *already.*'

26 "I tell you that to everyone who has, more shall be given, but from the one who does not have, even what he does have shall be taken away.

27 "But these enemies of mine, who did not want me to reign over them, bring them here and slay them in my presence."

LIFE LESSONS

➤ Luke 19:10 — *"For the Son of Man has come to seek and to save that which was lost."*

*T*he Lord does not merely provide us with an example of godly living, but He makes it possible for us to enjoy an intimate relationship with Himself. All of us "have sinned and fall short of the glory of God" (Rom. 3:23), which means we are all lost. Yet Christ came to earth to save us (John 3:16-18). He did for us what we could never do on our own (Rom. 5:1, 2).

➤ Luke 19:12 — *"A nobleman went to a distant country to receive a kingdom for himself, and then return."*

*J*esus gave a few clues like this one to indicate He might not return to earth physically for a long time after His ascension. Until He comes again in His glory, we are to continue to faithfully do His work in the power of the Holy Spirit— who is always with us (John 9:4; 14:16, 17, 26; 16:13, 14).

Ruth 1:1—2:23

1 NOW it came about in the days when the judges governed, that there was a famine in the land. And a certain man of Bethlehem in Judah went to sojourn in the land of Moab with his wife and his two sons.

2 The name of the man *was* Elimelech, and the name of his wife, Naomi; and the names of his two sons *were* Mahlon and Chilion, Ephrathites of Bethlehem in Judah. Now they entered the land of Moab and remained there.

3 Then Elimelech, Naomi's husband, died; and she was left with her two sons.

4 They took for themselves Moabite women *as* wives; the name of the one was Orpah and the name of the other Ruth. And they lived there about ten years.

5 Then both Mahlon and Chilion also died, and the woman was bereft of her two children and her husband.

➤ 6 Then she arose with her daughters-in-law that she might return from the land of Moab, for she had heard in the land of Moab that the LORD had visited His people in giving them food.

7 So she departed from the place where she was, and her two daughters-in-law with her; and they went on the way to return to the land of Judah.

8 And Naomi said to her two daughters-in-law, "Go, return each of you to her mother's house. May the LORD deal kindly with you as you have dealt with the dead and with me.

9 "May the LORD grant that you may find rest, each in the house of her husband." Then she kissed them, and they lifted up their voices and wept.

10 And they said to her, "*No*, but we will surely return with you to your people."

11 But Naomi said, "Return, my daughters. Why should you go with me? Have I yet sons in my womb, that they may be your husbands?

12 "Return, my daughters! Go, for I am too old to have a husband. If I said I have hope, if I should even have a husband tonight and also bear sons,

13 would you therefore wait until they were grown? Would you therefore refrain from marrying? No, my daughters; for it is harder for me than for you, for the hand of the LORD has gone forth against me."

14 And they lifted up their voices and wept again; and Orpah kissed her mother-in-law, but Ruth clung to her.

15 Then she said, "Behold, your sister-in-law has gone back to her people and her gods; return after your sister-in-law."

16 But Ruth said, "Do not urge me to leave you *or* turn back from following you; for where you go, I will go, and where you lodge, I will lodge. Your people *shall be* my people, and your God, my God. ✳

17 "Where you die, I will die, and there I will be buried. Thus may the LORD do to me, and worse, if *anything but* death parts you and me."

18 When she saw that she was determined to go with her, she said no more to her.

19 So they both went until they came to Bethlehem. And when they had come to Bethlehem, all the city was stirred because of them, and the women said, "Is this Naomi?"

20 She said to them, "Do not call me Naomi; call me Mara, for the Almighty has dealt very bitterly with me.

21 "I went out full, but the LORD has ◄ brought me back empty. Why do you call me Naomi, since the LORD has witnessed against me and the Almighty has afflicted me?"

22 So Naomi returned, and with her Ruth the Moabitess, her daughter-in-law,

---

LIFE LESSONS

➤ **Ruth 1:6 — *She had heard in the land of Moab that the LORD had visited His people in giving them food.***

*W*ondrous indeed is the grace of our Lord, who does not forsake us when we wander, but draws and restores us with His cords of love.

➤ **Ruth 1:21 — *"The Almighty has afflicted me."***

*H*ardship has a way of prompting us to believe God has turned against us, even though we can see no reason for it. But the Lord is good, and He knows how to turn sad stories into joyful ones.

Life Examples:

NAOMI: Sowing in the Midst of Suffering

RUTH 1:11-22

*A*s Naomi looked at the shambles of her life, she could see only a barren field of sorrow—yet she clung to the roots of hope. *Even though my sons and husband are gone,* she may have thought, *perhaps I may yet see fruitfulness in my life.*

God had not abandoned her, and in time Naomi reaped a rich, unexpected yield of love. Her daughter-in-law, Ruth, looked tenderly into her face and declared her firm commitment to stay with her, even all the way to death (Ruth 1:16, 17). Naomi placed her faith in the Lord, and He provided for her.

Whatever situation you face, the Lord is with you and can sustain you. Though there may be no fruit now, the grains of love and faithfulness you have scattered will produce a rich harvest. Will you persevere as Naomi did, and sow in the midst of suffering?

---

who returned from the land of Moab. And they came to Bethlehem at the beginning of barley harvest.

➤ 2 NOW Naomi had a kinsman of her husband, a man of great wealth, of the family of Elimelech, whose name was Boaz.
2 And Ruth the Moabitess said to Naomi, "Please let me go to the field and glean among the ears of grain after one in whose sight I may find favor." And she said to her, "Go, my daughter."
3 So she departed and went and gleaned in the field after the reapers; and she happened to come to the portion of the field belonging to Boaz, who was of the family of Elimelech.
4 Now behold, Boaz came from Bethlehem and said to the reapers, "May the LORD be with you." And they said to him, "May the LORD bless you."
5 Then Boaz said to his servant who was in charge of the reapers, "Whose young woman is this?"
6 The servant in charge of the reapers replied, "She is the young Moabite woman who returned with Naomi from the land of Moab.

LIFE LESSONS

➤ **Ruth 2:1** — *Now Naomi had a kinsman of her husband, a man of great wealth, of the family of Elimelech, whose name was Boaz.*

*B*oaz had wealth but no wife; Ruth had poverty and no husband. Both demonstrated their commitment to God by their lives. And for such people, the Lord loves to take deficits and turn them into unbelievable assets.

7 "And she said, 'Please let me glean and gather after the reapers among the sheaves.' Thus she came and has remained from the morning until now; she has been sitting in the house for a little while."
8 Then Boaz said to Ruth, "Listen carefully, my daughter. Do not go to glean in another field; furthermore, do not go on from this one, but stay here with my maids.
9 "Let your eyes be on the field which they reap, and go after them. Indeed, I have commanded the servants not to touch you. When you are thirsty, go to the water jars and drink from what the servants draw."
10 Then she fell on her face, bowing to the ground and said to him, "Why have I found favor in your sight that you should take notice of me, since I am a foreigner?"
11 Boaz replied to her, "All that you have done for your mother-in-law after the death of your husband has been fully reported to me, and how you left your father and your mother and the land of your birth, and came to a people that you did not previously know.
12 "May the LORD reward your work, and your wages be full from the LORD, the God of Israel, under whose wings you have come to seek refuge."
13 Then she said, "I have found favor in your sight, my lord, for you have comforted me and indeed have spoken kindly to your maidservant, though I am not like one of your maidservants."
14 At mealtime Boaz said to her, "Come here, that you may eat of the bread and dip your piece of bread in the vinegar." So she sat beside the reapers; and he

served her roasted grain, and she ate and was satisfied and had some left.

➤ 15 When she rose to glean, Boaz commanded his servants, saying, "Let her glean even among the sheaves, and do not insult her.

16 "Also you shall purposely pull out for her *some grain* from the bundles and leave *it* that she may glean, and do not rebuke her."

17 So she gleaned in the field until evening. Then she beat out what she had gleaned, and it was about an ephah of barley.

18 She took *it* up and went into the city, and her mother-in-law saw what she had gleaned. She also took *it* out and gave Naomi what she had left after she was satisfied.

19 Her mother-in-law then said to her, "Where did you glean today and where did you work? May he who took notice of you be blessed." So she told her mother-in-law with whom she had worked and said, "The name of the man with whom I worked today is Boaz."

➤ 20 Naomi said to her daughter-in-law, "May he be blessed of the LORD who has not withdrawn his kindness to the living and to the dead." Again Naomi said to her, "The man is our relative, he is one of our closest relatives."

21 Then Ruth the Moabitess said, "Furthermore, he said to me, 'You should

---

LIFE LESSONS

➤ **Ruth 2:15 —** *"Let her glean even among the sheaves, and do not insult her."*

*B*oaz did not act so generously to Ruth because he knew what was coming. He acted generously because he had made generosity a habit. "He who is generous will be blessed" (Prov. 22:9).

➤ **Ruth 2:20 —** *"May he be blessed of the LORD who has not withdrawn his kindness to the living and to the dead."*

*A*lthough a discouraged believer may say foolish and rash things while in pain, God's grace within remains and erupts into praise when He once more shows His favor. Even this shows His goodness.

---

stay close to my servants until they have finished all my harvest.'"

22 Naomi said to Ruth her daughter-in-law, "It is good, my daughter, that you go out with his maids, so that *others* do not fall upon you in another field."

23 So she stayed close by the maids of Boaz in order to glean until the end of the barley harvest and the wheat harvest. And she lived with her mother-in-law.

◈ **Psalm 52:1–5**

For the choir director. A Maskil of David, when Doeg the Edomite came and told Saul and said to him, "David has come to the house of Ahimelech."

52 WHY do you boast in evil,
   O mighty man?
   The lovingkindness of God *endures*
      all day long.
2 Your tongue devises destruction,
   Like a sharp razor, O worker of
      deceit.
3 You love evil more than good,
   Falsehood more than speaking what
      is right.   Selah.
4 You love all words that devour,
   O deceitful tongue.
5 But God will break you down
      forever;
   He will snatch you up and tear you
      away from *your* tent,
   And uproot you from the land of the
      living.   Selah.

◈ **Proverbs 15:4, 5**

4 A soothing tongue is a tree of life,
   But perversion in it crushes the
      spirit.
5 A fool rejects his father's discipline,
   But he who regards reproof is
      sensible.

◈ **Luke 19:28–48**

28 After He had said these things, He was going on ahead, going up to Jerusalem.

29 When He approached Bethphage and Bethany, near the mount that is called Olivet, He sent two of the disciples,
30 saying, "Go into the village ahead of *you*; there, as you enter, you will find a colt tied on which no one yet has ever sat; untie it and bring it *here*.
31 "If anyone asks you, 'Why are you untying it?' you shall say, 'The Lord has need of it.'"
32 So those who were sent went away and found it just as He had told them.
33 As they were untying the colt, its owners said to them, "Why are you untying the colt?"
34 They said, "The Lord has need of it."
35 They brought it to Jesus, and they threw their coats on the colt and put Jesus *on it*.
36 As He was going, they were spreading their coats on the road.
37 As soon as He was approaching, near the descent of the Mount of Olives, the whole crowd of the disciples began to praise God joyfully with a loud voice for all the miracles which they had seen,
38 shouting:

"BLESSED IS THE KING WHO COMES IN
    THE NAME OF THE LORD;
Peace in heaven and glory in the
    highest!"

39 Some of the Pharisees in the crowd said to Him, "Teacher, rebuke Your disciples."
40 But Jesus answered, "I tell you, if these become silent, the stones will cry out!"
41 When He approached *Jerusalem*, He saw the city and wept over it,

42 saying, "If you had known in this day, even you, the things which make for peace! But now they have been hidden from your eyes.
43 "For the days will come upon you when your enemies will throw up a barricade against you, and surround you and hem you in on every side,
44 and they will level you to the ground and your children within you, and they will not leave in you one stone upon another, because you did not recognize the time of your visitation."
45 Jesus entered the temple and began to drive out those who were selling,
46 saying to them, "It is written, 'AND MY HOUSE SHALL BE A HOUSE OF PRAYER,' but you have made it a ROBBERS' DEN."
47 And He was teaching daily in the temple; but the chief priests and the scribes and the leading men among the people were trying to destroy Him,
48 and they could not find anything that they might do, for all the people were hanging on to every word He said.

Ruth 3:1—4:22

3 THEN Naomi her mother-in-law said to her, "My daughter, shall I not seek security for you, that it may be well with you?
2 "Now is not Boaz our kinsman, with whose maids you were? Behold, he winnows barley at the threshing floor tonight.

3 "Wash yourself therefore, and anoint yourself and put on your *best* clothes, and go down to the threshing floor; *but* do not make yourself known to the man until he has finished eating and drinking.
4 "It shall be when he lies down, that you shall notice the place where he lies, and you shall go and uncover his feet and lie down; then he will tell you what you shall do."
5 She said to her, "All that you say I will do."

6   So she went down to the threshing
floor and did according to all that her
mother-in-law had commanded her.
7   When Boaz had eaten and drunk
and his heart was merry, he went to lie
down at the end of the heap of grain; and
she came secretly, and uncovered his
feet and lay down.
8   It happened in the middle of the
night that the man was startled and bent
forward; and behold, a woman was lying
at his feet.
9   He said, "Who are you?" And she answered, "I am Ruth your maid. So spread
your covering over your maid, for you
are a close relative."
10   Then he said, "May you be blessed of
the LORD, my daughter. You have shown
your last kindness to be better than
the first by not going after young men,
whether poor or rich.
11 "Now, my daughter, do not fear. I will
do for you whatever you ask, for all my
people in the city know that you are a
woman of excellence.
12 "Now it is true I am a close relative;
however, there is a relative closer than I.
13 "Remain this night, and when morning comes, if he will redeem you, good;
let him redeem you. But if he does not
wish to redeem you, then I will redeem
you, as the LORD lives. Lie down until
morning."
14   So she lay at his feet until morning
and rose before one could recognize another; and he said, "Let it not be known
that the woman came to the threshing
floor."
15   Again he said, "Give me the cloak
that is on you and hold it." So she held it,
and he measured six *measures* of barley
and laid *it* on her. Then she went into the
city.
16   When she came to her mother-in-law,

she said, "How did it go, my daughter?"
And she told her all that the man had done
for her.
17   She said, "These six *measures* of
barley he gave to me, for he said, 'Do
not go to your mother-in-law empty-
handed.'"
18   Then she said, "Wait, my daughter,
until you know how the matter turns
out; for the man will not rest until he has
settled it today."

4 NOW Boaz went up to the gate and
sat down there, and behold, the close
relative of whom Boaz spoke was passing by, so he said, "Turn aside, friend,
sit down here." And he turned aside and
sat down.
2   He took ten men of the elders of the
city and said, "Sit down here." So they
sat down.
3   Then he said to the closest relative,
"Naomi, who has come back from the
land of Moab, has to sell the piece of land
which belonged to our brother Elimelech.
4   "So I thought to inform you, saying,
'Buy *it* before those who are sitting *here*,
and before the elders of my people. If
you will redeem *it*, redeem *it*; but if not,
tell me that I may know; for there is no
one but you to redeem *it*, and I am after
you.'" And he said, "I will redeem *it*."
5   Then Boaz said, "On the day you buy
the field from the hand of Naomi, you
must also acquire Ruth the Moabitess,
the widow of the deceased, in order to
raise up the name of the deceased on his
inheritance."
6   The closest relative said, "I cannot
redeem *it* for myself, because I would
jeopardize my own inheritance. Redeem
it for yourself; you *may have* my right of
redemption, for I cannot redeem *it*."
7   Now this was *the custom* in former

LIFE LESSONS

➤ Ruth 3:10 — *"You have shown your
last kindness to be better than the first by
not going after young men."*

*A*pparently, it had never occurred to
Boaz a beautiful and faithful young
woman such as Ruth could show a personal interest in him. God loves to shower
His obedient people with amazing blessings!

➤ Ruth 3:18 — *"Wait, my daughter, until
you know how the matter turns out; for
the man will not rest until he has settled
it today."*

*T*here is a time to act, and there is a
time to wait. When we have done
what we should do, we must wait to see
what God will do.

times in Israel concerning the redemption and the exchange *of land* to confirm any matter: a man removed his sandal and gave it to another; and this was the *manner of* attestation in Israel.

8   So the closest relative said to Boaz, "Buy *it* for yourself." And he removed his sandal.

9   Then Boaz said to the elders and all the people, "You are witnesses today that I have bought from the hand of Naomi all that belonged to Elimelech and all that belonged to Chilion and Mahlon.

10 "Moreover, I have acquired Ruth the Moabitess, the widow of Mahlon, to be my wife in order to raise up the name of the deceased on his inheritance, so that the name of the deceased will not be cut off from his brothers or from the court of his *birth* place; you are witnesses today."

11   All the people who were in the court, and the elders, said, "*We are* witnesses. May the LORD make the woman who is coming into your home like Rachel and Leah, both of whom built the house of Israel; and may you achieve wealth in Ephrathah and become famous in Bethlehem.

12 "Moreover, may your house be like the house of Perez whom Tamar bore to Judah, through the offspring which the LORD will give you by this young woman."

13   So Boaz took Ruth, and she became his wife, and he went in to her. And the LORD enabled her to conceive, and she gave birth to a son.

14   Then the women said to Naomi, "Blessed is the LORD who has not left you without a redeemer today, and may his name become famous in Israel.

15 "May he also be to you a restorer of life and a sustainer of your old age; for your daughter-in-law, who loves you and is better to you than seven sons, has given birth to him."

16   Then Naomi took the child and laid him in her lap, and became his nurse.

17   The neighbor women gave him a name, saying, "A son has been born to Naomi!" So they named him Obed. He is the father of Jesse, the father of David.

18   Now these are the generations of Perez: to Perez was born Hezron,

19   and to Hezron was born Ram, and to Ram, Amminadab,

20   and to Amminadab was born Nahshon, and to Nahshon, Salmon,

---

LIFE LESSONS

➤ Ruth 4:11 — *"May you achieve wealth in Ephrathah and become famous in Bethlehem."*

*T*he elders of Bethlehem had no way of knowing the blessing they pronounced upon Boaz would come abundantly true, for the child to come of this new couple would be an ancestor of Jesus Christ.

➤ Ruth 4:15 — *"Your daughter-in-law, who loves you and is better to you than seven sons, has given birth to him."*

*N*aomi had lost two sons, but in a devoted and virtuous daughter-in-law she found someone better than seven sons—and in the end, a grandson who gave her great joy in her old age. God loves to bless His faithful people!

Life Examples:

RUTH: Loyal to the End

RUTH 4:13–22

*A*fter the death of her Hebrew husband, Ruth could have remained in her own culture—the expected and easier route—but instead chose to travel with Naomi, her mother-in-law. She traveled with Naomi back to Bethlehem, a place totally foreign to her. Why did she do this? The reason seemed very logical from her point of view: she had a fierce loyalty to her bereaved mother-in-law.

Loyalty ties individuals together. True loyalty is seldom easy—it takes both patience and a willingness to be inconvenienced. Genuine, loyal people adjust their schedules to meet the needs of those they serve, and loyalty often comes at a price. Ruth, for example, made a tremendous sacrifice by leaving her family and friends behind in order to serve Naomi.

Ultimately, however, godly loyalty tends to yield a great reward. God saw Ruth's deep, abiding loyalty and rewarded her by giving her a loving husband and a beautiful son—but most of all, by placing her in the family line of Jesus Christ.

21 and to Salmon was born Boaz, and to Boaz, Obed,
22 and to Obed was born Jesse, and to Jesse, David.

✦ Psalm 52:6–9

6 The righteous will see and fear,
And will laugh at him, *saying,*
7 "Behold, the man who would not make God his refuge,
But trusted in the abundance of his riches
And was strong in his *evil* desire."
➤ 8 But as for me, I am like a green olive tree in the house of God;
I trust in the lovingkindness of God forever and ever.
✳ 9 I will give You thanks forever, because You have done *it,*
And I will wait on Your name, for *it is* good, in the presence of Your godly ones.

✦ Proverbs 15:6, 7

6 Great wealth is *in* the house of the righteous,
But trouble is in the income of the wicked.
7 The lips of the wise spread knowledge,
But the hearts of fools are not so.

✦ Luke 20:1–26

20 ON one of the days while He was teaching the people in the temple and preaching the gospel, the chief priests and the scribes with the elders confronted *Him,*

LIFE LESSONS

➤ **Psalm 52:8 —** *I trust in the lovingkindness of God forever and ever.*

*G*od will never run out of mercy, love, or grace. There will never come a day when He says, "I'm tired. Come back in a month." Because He never changes, we have an unchanging hope (Heb. 13:8).

---

2 and they spoke, saying to Him, "Tell us by what authority You are doing these things, or who is the one who gave You this authority?"
3 Jesus answered and said to them, "I will also ask you a question, and you tell Me:
4 "Was the baptism of John from heaven or from men?"
5 They reasoned among themselves, saying, "If we say, 'From heaven,' He will say, 'Why did you not believe him?'
6 "But if we say, 'From men,' all the people will stone us to death, for they are convinced that John was a prophet."
7 So they answered that they did not know where *it came* from.
8 And Jesus said to them, "Nor will I tell you by what authority I do these things."
9 And He began to tell the people this parable: "A man planted a vineyard and rented it out to vine-growers, and went on a journey for a long time.
10 "At the *harvest* time he sent a slave to the vine-growers, so that they would give him *some* of the produce of the vineyard; but the vine-growers beat him and sent him away empty-handed.
11 "And he proceeded to send another slave; and they beat him also and treated him shamefully and sent him away empty-handed.
12 "And he proceeded to send a third; and this one also they wounded and cast out.
13 "The owner of the vineyard said, 'What shall I do? I will send my beloved son; perhaps they will respect him.'
14 "But when the vine-growers saw him, they reasoned with one another, saying, 'This is the heir; let us kill him so that the inheritance will be ours.'
15 "So they threw him out of the vineyard and killed him. What, then, will the owner of the vineyard do to them?
16 "He will come and destroy these vine-growers and will give the vineyard to others." When they heard it, they said, "May it never be!"
17 But Jesus looked at them and said, "What then is this that is written:
'THE STONE WHICH THE BUILDERS REJECTED,
THIS BECAME THE CHIEF CORNER *stone*'? ✳
18 "Everyone who falls on that stone will be broken to pieces; but on whomever it falls, it will scatter him like dust."

19 The scribes and the chief priests tried to lay hands on Him that very hour, and they feared the people; for they understood that He spoke this parable against them.

➤ 20 So they watched Him, and sent spies who pretended to be righteous, in order

that they might catch Him in some statement, so that they *could* deliver Him to the rule and the authority of the governor.

21 They questioned Him, saying, "Teacher, we know that You speak and teach correctly, and You are not partial to any, but teach the way of God in truth.

22 "Is it lawful for us to pay taxes to Caesar, or not?"

23 But He detected their trickery and said to them,

24 "Show Me a denarius. Whose likeness and inscription does it have?" They said, "Caesar's."

25 And He said to them, "Then render to Caesar the things that are Caesar's, and to God the things that are God's."

26 And they were unable to catch Him in a saying in the presence of the people; and being amazed at His answer, they became silent.

1 Samuel 1:1—3:21

1 NOW there was a certain man from Ramathaim-zophim from the hill country of Ephraim, and his name was Elkanah the son of Jeroham, the son of Elihu, the son of Tohu, the son of Zuph, an Ephraimite.

2 He had two wives: the name of one was Hannah and the name of the other Peninnah; and Peninnah had children, but Hannah had no children.

3 Now this man would go up from his city yearly to worship and to sacrifice to the LORD of hosts in Shiloh. And the two sons of Eli, Hophni and Phinehas, were priests to the LORD there.

4 When the day came that Elkanah sacrificed, he would give portions to Peninnah his wife and to all her sons and her daughters;

➤ 5 but to Hannah he would give a double portion, for he loved Hannah, but the LORD had closed her womb.

6 Her rival, however, would provoke her bitterly to irritate her, because the LORD had closed her womb.

7 It happened year after year, as often as she went up to the house of the LORD, she would provoke her; so she wept and would not eat.

8 Then Elkanah her husband said to her, "Hannah, why do you weep and why do you not eat and why is your heart sad? Am I not better to you than ten sons?"

9 Then Hannah rose after eating and drinking in Shiloh. Now Eli the priest was sitting on the seat by the doorpost of the temple of the LORD.

10 She, greatly distressed, prayed to the LORD and wept bitterly.

11 She made a vow and said, "O LORD

Life Examples:

HANNAH: Asking in Faith

1 SAMUEL 1:10, 11

*H*annah is an excellent biblical example of asking in faith. She had married a man named Elkanah—and so had someone else. Through the years, Elkanah's second wife, Peninnah, bore several sons and daughters to him, while Hannah remained barren. Hannah longed for a baby of her own.

Finally, one year Hannah went to the doorway of the tabernacle and wept and prayed to the Lord in great anguish, asking for a son and vowing to give him to the Lord (1 Sam. 1:10, 11). The Lord heard Hannah's request and answered it. Nine months later she bore a son named Samuel, who grew up to become the prophet and judge of all Israel.

Would Samuel have been born if Hannah had not asked God to give her a son? The Bible seems to answer, "No." Samuel appeared on the scene in direct response to Hannah's heartfelt request.

of hosts, if You will indeed look on the affliction of Your maidservant and remember me, and not forget Your maidservant, but will give Your maidservant a son, then I will give him to the LORD all the days of his life, and a razor shall never come on his head."
12 Now it came about, as she continued praying before the LORD, that Eli was watching her mouth.
13 As for Hannah, she was speaking in her heart, only her lips were moving, but her voice was not heard. So Eli thought she was drunk.
14 Then Eli said to her, "How long will you make yourself drunk? Put away your wine from you."
15 But Hannah replied, "No, my lord, I am a woman oppressed in spirit; I have drunk neither wine nor strong drink, but I have poured out my soul before the LORD.
16 "Do not consider your maidservant as a worthless woman, for I have spoken until now out of my great concern and provocation."
17 Then Eli answered and said, "Go in peace; and may the God of Israel grant your petition that you have asked of Him."
➤ 18 She said, "Let your maidservant find favor in your sight." So the woman went her way and ate, and her face was no longer *sad.*
19 Then they arose early in the morning and worshiped before the LORD, and returned again to their house in Ramah. And Elkanah had relations with Hannah his wife, and the LORD remembered her.
20 It came about in due time, after Hannah had conceived, that she gave birth to a son; and she named him Samuel,

saying, "Because I have asked him of the LORD."
21 Then the man Elkanah went up with all his household to offer to the LORD the yearly sacrifice and *pay* his vow.
22 But Hannah did not go up, for she said to her husband, "I *will not go up* until the child is weaned; then I will bring him, that he may appear before the LORD and stay there forever."
23 Elkanah her husband said to her, "Do what seems best to you. Remain until you have weaned him; only may the LORD confirm His word." So the woman remained and nursed her son until she weaned him.
24 Now when she had weaned him, she took him up with her, with a three-year-old bull and one ephah of flour and a jug of wine, and brought him to the house of the LORD in Shiloh, although the child was young.
25 Then they slaughtered the bull, and brought the boy to Eli.
26 She said, "Oh, my lord! As your soul lives, my lord, I am the woman who stood here beside you, praying to the LORD.

LIFE LESSONS

➤ **1 Samuel 1:18 — *The woman went her way and ate, and her face was no longer sad.***

*H*annah left behind her grief, not when her circumstances changed— they hadn't—but after she poured out her soul to the Lord. Because of her sorrow, she connected with God on a deeper level than she had never known.

27 "For this boy I prayed, and the LORD has given me my petition which I asked of Him.

28 "So I have also dedicated him to the LORD; as long as he lives he is dedicated to the LORD." And he worshiped the LORD there.

➤ 2 THEN Hannah prayed and said,
"My heart exults in the LORD;
My horn is exalted in the LORD,
My mouth speaks boldly against my
  enemies,
Because I rejoice in Your salvation.

2 "There is no one holy like the LORD,
Indeed, there is no one besides You,
Nor is there any rock like our God.

3 "Boast no more so very proudly,
Do not let arrogance come out of
  your mouth;
For the LORD is a God of knowledge,
And with Him actions are weighed.

4 "The bows of the mighty are
  shattered,
But the feeble gird on strength.

5 "Those who were full hire
  themselves out for bread,
But those who were hungry cease
  to hunger.
Even the barren gives birth to
  seven,
But she who has many children
  languishes.

6 "The LORD kills and makes alive;
He brings down to Sheol and raises
  up.

7 "The LORD makes poor and rich;
He brings low, He also exalts.

8 "He raises the poor from the dust,
He lifts the needy from the ash heap
To make them sit with nobles,
And inherit a seat of honor;
For the pillars of the earth are the
  LORD'S,
And He set the world on them.

9 "He keeps the feet of His godly ones,
But the wicked ones are silenced in
  darkness;
For not by might shall a man
  prevail.

10 "Those who contend with the LORD
  will be shattered;
Against them He will thunder in the
  heavens,
The LORD will judge the ends of the
  earth;
And He will give strength to His
  king,

And will exalt the horn of His
  anointed."

11 Then Elkanah went to his home at Ramah. But the boy ministered to the LORD before Eli the priest.

12 Now the sons of Eli were worthless men; they did not know the LORD

13 and the custom of the priests with the people. When any man was offering a sacrifice, the priest's servant would come while the meat was boiling, with a three-pronged fork in his hand.

14 Then he would thrust it into the pan, or kettle, or caldron, or pot; all that the fork brought up the priest would take for himself. Thus they did in Shiloh to all the Israelites who came there.

15 Also, before they burned the fat, the priest's servant would come and say to the man who was sacrificing, "Give the priest meat for roasting, as he will not take boiled meat from you, only raw."

16 If the man said to him, "They must surely burn the fat first, and then take as much as you desire," then he would say, "No, but you shall give it to me now; and if not, I will take it by force."

17 Thus the sin of the young men was ◄ very great before the LORD, for the men despised the offering of the LORD.

18 Now Samuel was ministering before the LORD, as a boy wearing a linen ephod.

LIFE LESSONS

➤ **1 Samuel 2:1** — *"My mouth speaks boldly against my enemies, because I rejoice in Your salvation."*

*W*e can smile at our enemies when we remember we serve a God who takes great delight in redeeming us. When we rejoice in the Lord, and not merely in His blessings, we find a joy that cannot be found anywhere else.

➤ **1 Samuel 2:17** — *Thus the sin of the young men was very great before the LORD.*

*G*od takes it very seriously when leaders, by their evil conduct, make it difficult for or prevent people from worshiping Him in spirit and in truth. He wants a close relationship with us, and He will move against anything that stands in the way.

19 And his mother would make him a little robe and bring it to him from year to year when she would come up with her husband to offer the yearly sacrifice. 20 Then Eli would bless Elkanah and his wife and say, "May the LORD give you children from this woman in place of the one she dedicated to the LORD." And they went to their own home.

21 The LORD visited Hannah; and she conceived and gave birth to three sons and two daughters. And the boy Samuel grew before the LORD.

22 Now Eli was very old; and he heard all that his sons were doing to all Israel, and how they lay with the women who served at the doorway of the tent of meeting.

23 He said to them, "Why do you do such things, the evil things that I hear from all these people?

24 "No, my sons; for the report is not good which I hear the LORD's people circulating.

25 "If one man sins against another, God will mediate for him; but if a man sins against the LORD, who can intercede for him?" But they would not listen to the voice of their father, for the LORD desired to put them to death.

26 Now the boy Samuel was growing in stature and in favor both with the LORD and with men.

27 Then a man of God came to Eli and said to him, "Thus says the LORD, 'Did I not indeed reveal Myself to the house of your father when they were in Egypt in bondage to Pharaoh's house?

28 'Did I not choose them from all the tribes of Israel to be My priests, to go up to My altar, to burn incense, to carry an ephod before Me; and did I not give to the house of your father all the fire offerings of the sons of Israel?

29 'Why do you kick at My sacrifice and at My offering which I have commanded in My dwelling, and honor your sons above Me, by making yourselves fat with the choicest of every offering of My people Israel?'

30 "Therefore the LORD God of Israel declares, 'I did indeed say that your house and the house of your father should walk before Me forever'; but now the LORD declares, 'Far be it from Me—for those who honor Me I will honor, and those who despise Me will be lightly esteemed.

31 'Behold, the days are coming when I will break your strength and the strength of your father's house so that there will not be an old man in your house.

32 'You will see the distress of My dwelling, in spite of all the good that I do for Israel; and an old man will not be in your house forever.

33 'Yet I will not cut off every man of yours from My altar so that your eyes will fail from weeping and your soul grieve, and all the increase of your house will die in the prime of life.

34 'This will be the sign to you which will come concerning your two sons, Hophni and Phinehas: on the same day both of them will die.

35 'But I will raise up for Myself a faithful priest who will do according to what is in My heart and in My soul; and I will build him an enduring house, and he will walk before My anointed always.

36 'Everyone who is left in your house will come and bow down to him for a piece of silver or a loaf of bread and say, "Please assign me to one of the priest's offices so that I may eat a piece of bread."'"

3 NOW the boy Samuel was ministering to the LORD before Eli. And word from the LORD was rare in those days, visions were infrequent.

2 It happened at that time as Eli was lying down in his place (now his eyesight had begun to grow dim and he could not see well),

3 and the lamp of God had not yet gone out, and Samuel was lying down in the temple of the LORD where the ark of God was,

4 that the LORD called Samuel; and he said, "Here I am."

5 Then he ran to Eli and said, "Here I am, for you called me." But he said, "I did not call, lie down again." So he went and lay down.

6 The LORD called yet again, "Samuel!" So Samuel arose and went to Eli and said, "Here I am, for you called me." But he answered, "I did not call, my son, lie down again."

7 Now Samuel did not yet know the LORD, nor had the word of the LORD yet been revealed to him.

8 So the LORD called Samuel again for the third time. And he arose and went to Eli and said, "Here I am, for you called

LIFE LESSONS

➤ **1 Samuel 3:7 —** *Now Samuel did not yet know the LORD.*

*W*hen God first spoke to Samuel, the boy didn't yet know His voice—but he learned to hear it. The Lord desires that we enjoy a close relationship with Him, and He will do everything necessary to make it possible.

me." Then Eli discerned that the LORD was calling the boy.

9 And Eli said to Samuel, "Go lie down, and it shall be if He calls you, that you shall say, 'Speak, LORD, for Your servant is listening.'" So Samuel went and lay down in his place.

10 Then the LORD came and stood and called as at other times, "Samuel! Samuel!" And Samuel said, "Speak, for Your servant is listening."

11 The LORD said to Samuel, "Behold, I am about to do a thing in Israel at which both ears of everyone who hears it will tingle.

12 "In that day I will carry out against Eli all that I have spoken concerning his house, from beginning to end.

13 "For I have told him that I am about to judge his house forever for the iniquity which he knew, because his sons brought a curse on themselves and he did not rebuke them.

14 "Therefore I have sworn to the house of Eli that the iniquity of Eli's house shall not be atoned for by sacrifice or offering forever."

15 So Samuel lay down until morning. Then he opened the doors of the house of the LORD. But Samuel was afraid to tell the vision to Eli.

16 Then Eli called Samuel and said, "Samuel, my son." And he said, "Here I am."

17 He said, "What is the word that He spoke to you? Please do not hide it from me. May God do so to you, and more also, if you hide anything from me of all the words that He spoke to you."

18 So Samuel told him everything and hid nothing from him. And he said, "It is the LORD; let Him do what seems good to Him."

19 Thus Samuel grew and the LORD was with him and let none of his words fail.

20 All Israel from Dan even to Beersheba knew that Samuel was confirmed as a prophet of the LORD.

21 And the LORD appeared again at Shiloh, because the LORD revealed Himself to Samuel at Shiloh by the word of the LORD.

✦ Psalm 53:1–6

For the choir director; according to Mahalath. A Maskil of David.

53 THE fool has said in his heart,
    "There is no God,"
They are corrupt, and have
    committed abominable injustice;
There is no one who does good.

2 God has looked down from heaven
    upon the sons of men
To see if there is anyone who
    understands,
Who seeks after God.

3 Every one of them has turned
    aside; together they have become
    corrupt;
There is no one who does good, not
    even one.

4 Have the workers of wickedness no
    knowledge,
Who eat up My people *as though*
    they ate bread
And have not called upon God?

5 There they were in great fear *where*
    no fear had been;
For God scattered the bones of him
    who encamped against you;
You put *them* to shame, because
    God had rejected them.

6 Oh, that the salvation of Israel
    would come out of Zion!
When God restores His captive
    people,
Let Jacob rejoice, let Israel be glad.

✦ Proverbs 15:8–11

8 The sacrifice of the wicked is an
    abomination to the LORD,
But the prayer of the upright is His
    delight.

9 The way of the wicked is an
    abomination to the LORD,

But He loves one who pursues
righteousness.
10 Grievous punishment is for him
who forsakes the way;
He who hates reproof will die.
11 Sheol and Abaddon *lie open* before
the LORD,
How much more the hearts of men!

◈ Luke 20:27–47

27 Now there came to Him some of the Sadducees (who say that there is no resurrection),
28 and they questioned Him, saying, "Teacher, Moses wrote for us that IF A MAN'S BROTHER DIES, having a wife, AND HE IS CHILDLESS, HIS BROTHER SHOULD MARRY THE WIFE AND RAISE UP CHILDREN TO HIS BROTHER.
29 "Now there were seven brothers; and the first took a wife and died childless;
30 and the second
31 and the third married her; and in the same way all seven died, leaving no children.
32 "Finally the woman died also.
33 "In the resurrection therefore, which one's wife will she be? For all seven had married her."
34 Jesus said to them, "The sons of this age marry and are given in marriage,
35 but those who are considered worthy to attain to that age and the resurrection from the dead, neither marry nor are given in marriage;
36 for they cannot even die anymore, because they are like angels, and are sons of God, being sons of the resurrection.
37 "But that the dead are raised, even Moses showed, in the *passage about the burning* bush, where he calls the Lord

THE GOD OF ABRAHAM, AND THE GOD OF ISAAC, AND THE GOD OF JACOB.
38 "Now He is not the God of the dead but of the living; for all live to Him."
39 Some of the scribes answered and said, "Teacher, You have spoken well."
40 For they did not have courage to question Him any longer about anything.
41 Then He said to them, "How *is it that* they say the Christ is David's son?
42 "For David himself says in the book of Psalms,
'THE LORD SAID TO MY LORD,
"SIT AT MY RIGHT HAND,
43 UNTIL I MAKE YOUR ENEMIES A
FOOTSTOOL FOR YOUR FEET."'
44 "Therefore David calls Him 'Lord,' and how is He his son?"
45 And while all the people were listening, He said to the disciples,
46 "Beware of the scribes, who like to walk around in long robes, and love respectful greetings in the market places, and chief seats in the synagogues and places of honor at banquets,
47 who devour widows' houses, and for appearance's sake offer long prayers. These will receive greater condemnation."

LIFE LESSONS

➤ Luke 20:47 — *"These will receive greater condemnation."*

*G*od's judgment will fall more severely on those who pretend to serve Him for their own personal gains and who use their religious credentials to deceive others. Although there is no longer condemnation for believers (Rom. 8:1), those who faithfully obey the Lord will receive greater rewards than those who disregard their divine assignments or serve God for their own selfish motives.

1 Samuel 4:1—5:12

4 THUS the word of Samuel came to all Israel. Now Israel went out to meet the Philistines in battle and camped beside Ebenezer while the Philistines camped in Aphek.

2 The Philistines drew up in battle array to meet Israel. When the battle spread, Israel was defeated before the Philistines who killed about four thousand men on the battlefield.

➤ 3 When the people came into the camp, the elders of Israel said, "Why has the LORD defeated us today before the Philistines? Let us take to ourselves from Shiloh the ark of the covenant of the LORD, that it may come among us and deliver us from the power of our enemies."

4 So the people sent to Shiloh, and from there they carried the ark of the covenant of the LORD of hosts who sits *above* the cherubim; and the two sons of Eli, Hophni and Phinehas, *were* there with the ark of the covenant of God.

5 As the ark of the covenant of the LORD came into the camp, all Israel shouted with a great shout, so that the earth resounded.

6 When the Philistines heard the noise of the shout, they said, "What *does* the noise of this great shout in the camp of the Hebrews *mean?*" Then they understood that the ark of the LORD had come into the camp.

7 The Philistines were afraid, for they said, "God has come into the camp." And they said, "Woe to us! For nothing like this has happened before.

8 "Woe to us! Who shall deliver us from the hand of these mighty gods? These are the gods who smote the Egyptians with all *kinds of* plagues in the wilderness.

9 "Take courage and be men, O Philistines, or you will become slaves to the Hebrews, as they have been slaves to you; therefore, be men and fight."

10 So the Philistines fought and Israel was defeated, and every man fled to his tent; and the slaughter was very great, for there fell of Israel thirty thousand foot soldiers.

11 And the ark of God was taken; and the two sons of Eli, Hophni and Phinehas, died.

12 Now a man of Benjamin ran from the battle line and came to Shiloh the same day with his clothes torn and dust on his head.

13 When he came, behold, Eli was sitting on *his* seat by the road eagerly watching, because his heart was trembling for the ark of God. So the man came to tell *it* in the city, and all the city cried out.

14 When Eli heard the noise of the outcry, he said, "What *does* the noise of this commotion *mean?*" Then the man came hurriedly and told Eli.

LIFE LESSONS

➤ 1 Samuel 4:3 — *"Let us take to ourselves from Shiloh the ark of the covenant of the LORD, that it may come among us and deliver us from the power of our enemies."*

No religious artifact or ceremony, no matter how sacred, can rescue us. Israel's leaders thought the ark of the covenant could save them, but it had no power to do so. God alone rescues.

Life Examples:

SAMUEL: Learning to Hear God's Voice

1 SAMUEL 4:1

As one of the mightiest prophets of the Old Testament, it's no coincidence Samuel's first divine assignment was for him to learn how to hear God's voice—to recognize Him when He called.

As 1 Samuel 3:1–10 tells us, young Samuel, entrusted to the care of Eli the priest, was lying down one evening when the Lord spoke. At first, Samuel didn't know whom he was hearing; he thought Eli was calling him. But finally, after Eli told Samuel three times he had not called, Eli realized it was the Lord. Therefore, he instructed the boy to respond, "Speak, LORD, for Your servant is listening" (v. 9).

Isn't that a beautiful way to answer God? "Speak, LORD, for Your servant is listening." Eli taught Samuel how to listen to the Father—and if we are going to be men and women of God, we too must learn how to recognize His efforts to speak to us.

15 Now Eli was ninety-eight years old, and his eyes were set so that he could not see.

16 The man said to Eli, "I am the one who came from the battle line. Indeed, I escaped from the battle line today." And he said, "How did things go, my son?"

17 Then the one who brought the news replied, "Israel has fled before the Philistines and there has also been a great slaughter among the people, and your two sons also, Hophni and Phinehas, are dead, and the ark of God has been taken."

18 When he mentioned the ark of God, Eli fell off the seat backward beside the gate, and his neck was broken and he died, for he was old and heavy. Thus he judged Israel forty years.

19 Now his daughter-in-law, Phinehas's wife, was pregnant and about to give birth; and when she heard the news that the ark of God was taken and that her father-in-law and her husband had died, she kneeled down and gave birth, for her pains came upon her.

20 And about the time of her death the women who stood by her said to her, "Do not be afraid, for you have given birth to a son." But she did not answer or pay attention.

21 And she called the boy Ichabod, saying, "The glory has departed from Israel," because the ark of God was taken and because of her father-in-law and her husband.

22 She said, "The glory has departed from Israel, for the ark of God was taken."

5 NOW the Philistines took the ark of God and brought it from Ebenezer to Ashdod.

2 Then the Philistines took the ark of God and brought it to the house of Dagon and set it by Dagon.

3 When the Ashdodites arose early the next morning, behold, Dagon had fallen on his face to the ground before the ark of the LORD. So they took Dagon and set him in his place again.

4 But when they arose early the next morning, behold, Dagon had fallen on his face to the ground before the ark of the LORD. And the head of Dagon and both the palms of his hands were cut off on the threshold; only the trunk of Dagon was left to him.

5 Therefore neither the priests of Dagon nor all who enter Dagon's house tread on the threshold of Dagon in Ashdod to this day.

6 Now the hand of the LORD was heavy on the Ashdodites, and He ravaged them and smote them with tumors, both Ashdod and its territories.

7 When the men of Ashdod saw that it was so, they said, "The ark of the God of Israel must not remain with us, for His hand is severe on us and on Dagon our god."

8 So they sent and gathered all the lords of the Philistines to them and said, "What shall we do with the ark of the God of Israel?" And they said, "Let the ark of the God of Israel be brought around to Gath." And they brought the ark of the God of Israel *around*.

9 After they had brought it around, the hand of the LORD was against the city with very great confusion; and He smote the men of the city, both young and old, so that tumors broke out on them.

10 So they sent the ark of God to Ekron. And as the ark of God came to Ekron the Ekronites cried out, saying, "They have brought the ark of the God of Israel around to us, to kill us and our people."

LIFE LESSONS

> **1 Samuel 5:2 — *Then the Philistines took the ark of God and brought it to the house of Dagon and set it by Dagon.***

*T*he Philistines placed the ark of the covenant in the temple of Dagon to demonstrate their deity had triumphed over Israel's God. But even in what seemed like a moment of defeat, the Lord showed Himself strong and the Ruler of all (Ps. 103:19). He irrefutably established Himself as the only true God (1 Sam. 5:3-6).

> **1 Samuel 5:9 — *The LORD was against the city with a very great confusion.***

*T*he Lord wanted the Philistines to know what had happened did not occur by chance—He had been behind it all (1 Sam. 6:5). God desires for the entire world to acknowledge Him as Lord (Is. 45:23; Rom. 14:11), and He works through us to display His glory (Matt. 5:16).

11 They sent therefore and gathered all the lords of the Philistines and said, "Send away the ark of the God of Israel, and let it return to its own place, so that it will not kill us and our people." For there was a deadly confusion throughout the city; the hand of God was very heavy there.
12 And the men who did not die were smitten with tumors and the cry of the city went up to heaven.

 Psalm 54:1–7

For the choir director; on stringed instruments. A Maskil of David, when the Ziphites came and said to Saul, "Is not David hiding himself among us?"

54 SAVE me, O God, by Your name,
And vindicate me by Your power.
2 Hear my prayer, O God;
Give ear to the words of my mouth.
3 For strangers have risen against me
And violent men have sought my life;
They have not set God before them.   Selah.
4 Behold, God is my helper;
The Lord is the sustainer of my soul.
5 He will recompense the evil to my foes;
Destroy them in Your faithfulness.
6 Willingly I will sacrifice to You;
I will give thanks to Your name,
O Lord, for it is good.
7 For He has delivered me from all trouble,

LIFE LESSONS

➢ **Psalm 54:6 — *Willingly I will sacrifice to You; I will give thanks to Your name, O Lord, for it is good.***

*W*hat does it mean to willingly sacrifice to God? It means that we voluntarily and gladly put something precious of ours in His gracious hands, knowing we can never out give Him. No offering is ultimately a sacrifice because we give nothing to Him that He has not first given to us.

And my eye has looked *with satisfaction* upon my enemies.

 Proverbs 15:12, 13

12 A scoffer does not love one who reproves him,
He will not go to the wise.
13 A joyful heart makes a cheerful face,
But when the heart is sad, the spirit is broken.

Luke 21:1–19

21 AND He looked up and saw the rich putting their gifts into the treasury.
2 And He saw a poor widow putting in two small copper coins.
3 And He said, "Truly I say to you, this poor widow put in more than all *of them;*
4 for they all out of their surplus put into the offering; but she out of her poverty put in all that she had to live on."
5 And while some were talking about the temple, that it was adorned with beautiful stones and votive gifts, He said,
6 "*As for* these things which you are looking at, the days will come in which there will not be left one stone upon another which will not be torn down."
7 They questioned Him, saying, "Teacher, when therefore will these things happen? And what *will be* the sign when these things are about to take place?"
8 And He said, "See to it that you are not misled; for many will come in My name, saying, 'I am *He*,' and, 'The time is near.' Do not go after them.
9 "When you hear of wars and disturbances, do not be terrified; for these things must take place first, but the end *does* not *follow* immediately."
10 Then He continued by saying to them, "Nation will rise against nation and kingdom against kingdom,
11 and there will be great earthquakes, and in various places plagues and

famines; and there will be terrors and great signs from heaven.

12 "But before all these things, they will lay their hands on you and will persecute you, delivering you to the synagogues and prisons, bringing you before kings and governors for My name's sake.

➤ 13 "It will lead to an opportunity for your testimony.

14 "So make up your minds not to prepare beforehand to defend yourselves;

✳ 15 for I will give you utterance and wisdom which none of your opponents will be able to resist or refute.

16 "But you will be betrayed even by parents and brothers and relatives and friends, and they will put *some* of you to death,

17 and you will be hated by all because of My name.

➤ 18 "Yet not a hair of your head will perish.

19 "By your endurance you will gain your lives.

LIFE LESSONS

➤ **Luke 21:13 — "It will lead to an opportunity for your testimony."**

*J*ust as the imprisonments of the apostle Paul turned out to be divine opportunities to testify to the gospel of Christ (Acts 9:15; Phil. 1:12), so God will use persecutions to make His Word known.

➤ **Luke 21:18 — "Not a hair of your head will perish."**

*J*esus reminds believers that He will always remain in control and every detail of our lives will be safe in His loving hands. Although we will certainly face persecution, not a hair of our heads will be touched without His permission. And if we lose our lives for His sake, it will be according to His purpose and timing. Our eternal life is secure and our victory is guaranteed. So we should not worry, but should always stand firm in our faith in the Lord.

---

1 Samuel 6:1—7:17

6 NOW the ark of the LORD had been in the country of the Philistines seven months.

2 And the Philistines called for the priests and the diviners, saying, "What shall we do with the ark of the LORD? Tell us how we shall send it to its place."

3 They said, "If you send away the ark of the God of Israel, do not send it empty; but you shall surely return to Him a guilt offering. Then you will be healed and it will be known to you why His hand is not removed from you."

4 Then they said, "What shall be the guilt offering which we shall return to Him?" And they said, "Five golden tumors and five golden mice *according to* the number of the lords of the Philistines, for one plague was on all of you and on your lords.

5 "So you shall make likenesses of your tumors and likenesses of your mice that ravage the land, and you shall give glory to the God of Israel; perhaps He will ease His hand from you, your gods, and your land.

6 "Why then do you harden your hearts as the Egyptians and Pharaoh hardened their hearts? When He had severely dealt with them, did they not allow the people to go, and they departed?

7 "Now therefore, take and prepare a new cart and two milch cows on which there has never been a yoke; and hitch the cows to the cart and take their calves home, away from them.

8 "Take the ark of the LORD and place it on the cart; and put the articles of gold which you return to Him as a guilt offering in a box by its side. Then send it away that it may go.

9 "Watch, if it goes up by the way of its own territory to Beth-shemesh, then He has done us this great evil. But if not, then we will know that it was not His hand that struck us; it happened to us by chance."

10 Then the men did so, and took two

milch cows and hitched them to the cart, and shut up their calves at home.
11 They put the ark of the LORD on the cart, and the box with the golden mice and the likenesses of their tumors.
12 And the cows took the straight way in the direction of Beth-shemesh; they went along the highway, lowing as they went, and did not turn aside to the right or to the left. And the lords of the Philistines followed them to the border of Beth-shemesh.
13 Now *the people of* Beth-shemesh were reaping their wheat harvest in the valley, and they raised their eyes and saw the ark and were glad to see *it.*
14 The cart came into the field of Joshua the Beth-shemite and stood there where there *was* a large stone; and they split the wood of the cart and offered the cows as a burnt offering to the LORD.
15 The Levites took down the ark of the LORD and the box that was with it, in which were the articles of gold, and put them on the large stone; and the men of Beth-shemesh offered burnt offerings and sacrificed sacrifices that day to the LORD.
16 When the five lords of the Philistines saw it, they returned to Ekron that day.
17 These are the golden tumors which the Philistines returned for a guilt offering to the LORD: one for Ashdod, one for Gaza, one for Ashkelon, one for Gath, one for Ekron;
18 and the golden mice, *according to* the number of all the cities of the Philistines belonging to the five lords, both of fortified cities and of country villages. The large stone on which they set the ark of the LORD *is a witness* to this day in the field of Joshua the Beth-shemite.
➤ 19 He struck down some of the men of Beth-shemesh because they had looked into the ark of the LORD. He struck down of all the people, 50,070 men, and the people mourned because the LORD had struck the people with a great slaughter.
20 The men of Beth-shemesh said, "Who is able to stand before the LORD, this holy God? And to whom shall He go up from us?"
21 So they sent messengers to the inhabitants of Kiriath-jearim, saying, "The Philistines have brought back the ark of the LORD; come down and take it up to you."

7 AND the men of Kiriath-jearim came and took the ark of the LORD and brought it into the house of Abinadab on the hill, and consecrated Eleazar his son to keep the ark of the LORD.
2 From the day that the ark remained at Kiriath-jearim, the time was long, for it was twenty years; and all the house of Israel lamented after the LORD.
3 Then Samuel spoke to all the house ◄ of Israel, saying, "If you return to the LORD with all your heart, remove the foreign gods and the Ashtaroth from among you and direct your hearts to the LORD and serve Him alone; and He will deliver you from the hand of the Philistines."
4 So the sons of Israel removed the Baals and the Ashtaroth and served the LORD alone.
5 Then Samuel said, "Gather all Israel to Mizpah and I will pray to the LORD for you."
6 They gathered to Mizpah, and drew water and poured it out before the LORD, and fasted on that day and said there, "We have sinned against the LORD." And Samuel judged the sons of Israel at Mizpah.
7 Now when the Philistines heard that the sons of Israel had gathered to Mizpah, the lords of the Philistines went up against Israel. And when the sons of Israel heard it, they were afraid of the Philistines.
8 Then the sons of Israel said to Samuel, "Do not cease to cry to the LORD our

---

LIFE LESSONS

➤ **1 Samuel 6:19** — *He struck down some of the men of Beth-shemesh because they had looked into the ark of the LORD.*

*I*n His grace, God brought the ark back to Israel. But in His holiness, He struck down some Israelites who treated the ark as a curiosity and an idol rather than as a symbol of God's glory.

➤ **1 Samuel 7:3** — *"If you return to the LORD with all your heart, remove the foreign gods."*

*G*od demands and deserves our exclusive loyalty and love. He made us for Himself, and we have no higher calling than to draw near to Him.

ANSWERS TO LIFE'S QUESTIONS

How can I know it's God's voice I hear and not something else?

1 SAMUEL 7

*T*he book of 1 Samuel describes how the boy Samuel came to hear and understand the spoken word of God. The Bible records that the word of the Lord was rare in those days; Samuel, therefore, had to learn how to recognize the voice of God and not get it mixed up with ideas that conflicted with the Lord's true character.

Samuel not only learned to hear the words of God clearly, he also came to speak them with authority. So the Bible says of him, "The LORD was with him and let none of his words fail. All Israel from Dan to Beersheba knew that Samuel was confirmed as a prophet of the LORD" (1 Sam. 3:19, 20).

We sometimes let our preconceptions about God influence what we think we hear from Him. If, for instance, we think of God as a wise and caring counselor, we will be open to the love He has for us in the midst of calamities brought on by our own foolishness. If, however, we think of God as a vindictive judge, we will expect to hear words of condemnation and harsh punishment when we act foolishly.

Our relationships with God influence how we hear Him. If we approach the Lord as His saved children living under His grace, then we come with the assurance He will speak the words we really need—even if they are not what we want to hear. When we understand that He infinitely loves us, then we can believe everything He says.

This same problem occurs in any area where our idea of God's character conflicts with Scripture. We may think of Him as a generous provider or become deceived and view Him as being stingy. We may view Him as a faithful, trustworthy guide or be misled in thinking He is a fair-weather friend.

Too many Christians fall for twisted conceptions of God that misrepresent our gracious, consistent, patient, trustworthy Father. We have all heard too many unbiblical ideas offered as if they were gospel truth, and such error can lead us into horrible emotional and spiritual bondage.

Our view of God must remain correct and biblically informed. By knowing Him as the God of love (1 John 4:8) who wants us to approach the throne of grace boldly (Heb. 4:16), we will trust more completely whatever He tells us. Take the advice of 1 Thessalonians 5:21, and test whatever you hear against the truth of Scripture.

God for us, that He may save us from the hand of the Philistines."

9 Samuel took a suckling lamb and offered it for a whole burnt offering to the LORD; and Samuel cried to the LORD for Israel and the LORD answered him.

10 Now Samuel was offering up the burnt offering, and the Philistines drew near to battle against Israel. But the LORD thundered with a great thunder on that day against the Philistines and confused them, so that they were routed before Israel.

11 The men of Israel went out of Mizpah and pursued the Philistines, and struck them down as far as below Bethcar.

12 Then Samuel took a stone and set it between Mizpah and Shen, and named it Ebenezer, saying, "Thus far the LORD has helped us."

13 So the Philistines were subdued and they did not come anymore within the border of Israel. And the hand of the LORD was against the Philistines all the days of Samuel.

14 The cities which the Philistines had taken from Israel were restored to Israel, from Ekron even to Gath; and Israel delivered their territory from the hand of the Philistines. So there was peace between Israel and the Amorites.

15 Now Samuel judged Israel all the days of his life.

16 He used to go annually on circuit to Bethel and Gilgal and Mizpah, and he judged Israel in all these places.

17 Then his return *was* to Ramah, for his house *was* there, and there he judged Israel; and he built there an altar to the LORD.

Psalm 55:1–8

For the choir director; on stringed instruments. A Maskil of David.

55 GIVE ear to my prayer, O God; And do not hide Yourself from my supplication.

2 Give heed to me and answer me;

I am restless in my complaint and
am surely distracted,

3 Because of the voice of the enemy,
Because of the pressure of the
wicked;
For they bring down trouble upon
me
And in anger they bear a grudge
against me.

4 My heart is in anguish within me,
And the terrors of death have fallen
upon me.

5 Fear and trembling come upon me,
And horror has overwhelmed me.

➤ 6 I said, "Oh, that I had wings like a
dove!
I would fly away and be at rest.

7 "Behold, I would wander far away,
I would lodge in the wilderness.
                      Selah.

8 "I would hasten to my place of refuge
From the stormy wind *and* tempest."

✦ Proverbs 15:14

14 The mind of the intelligent seeks
knowledge,
But the mouth of fools feeds on
folly.

✦ Luke 21:20–38

20 "But when you see Jerusalem surrounded by armies, then recognize that
her desolation is near.
21 "Then those who are in Judea must
flee to the mountains, and those who are
in the midst of the city must leave, and
those who are in the country must not
enter the city;
22 because these are days of vengeance,
so that all things which are written will
be fulfilled.
23 "Woe to those who are pregnant and
to those who are nursing babies in those
days; for there will be great distress upon
the land and wrath to this people;
24 and they will fall by the edge of the
sword, and will be led captive into all the
nations; and Jerusalem will be trampled
under foot by the Gentiles until the times
of the Gentiles are fulfilled.
✳ 25 "There will be signs in sun and moon
and stars, and on the earth dismay among
nations, in perplexity at the roaring of the
sea and the waves,
26 men fainting from fear and the expectation of the things which are coming
upon the world; for the powers of the
heavens will be shaken.
27 "Then they will see THE SON OF MAN
COMING IN A CLOUD with power and great
glory.
28 "But when these things begin to
take place, straighten up and lift up your
heads, because your redemption is drawing near."
29 Then He told them a parable: "Behold the fig tree and all the trees;
30 as soon as they put forth *leaves*, you
see it and know for yourselves that summer is now near.
31 "So you also, when you see these
things happening, recognize that the
kingdom of God is near.
32 "Truly I say to you, this generation
will not pass away until all things take
place.
33 "Heaven and earth will pass away,
but My words will not pass away.
34 "Be on guard, so that your hearts ➤
will not be weighted down with dissipation and drunkenness and the worries of
life, and that day will not come on you
suddenly like a trap;

LIFE LESSONS

➤ **Psalm 55:6 — "Oh, that I had wings
like a dove! I would fly away and be at
rest."**

*W*hen the walls close in and the floor
gives way, we often wish we could
be anywhere but where God has put us.
Trusting the Lord, however, means looking beyond what we can see to what He
sees.

➤ **Luke 21:34 — "Be on guard, so . . .
that day will not come on you suddenly."**

*A*constant awareness that the Lord
could return at any time keeps us
spiritually alert and living productively
for the kingdom of God. When our focus
is on Christ's Second Coming, we will not
be as concerned with the trivial matters
of life but will be motivated to obey Him
and will diligently work to tell all people
of the salvation He offers.

35 for it will come upon all those who dwell on the face of all the earth.

➤ 36 "But keep on the alert at all times, praying that you may have strength to escape all these things that are about to take place, and to stand before the Son of Man."

37 Now during the day He was teaching in the temple, but at evening He would go out and spend the night on the mount that is called Olivet.

38 And all the people would get up early in the morning *to come* to Him in the temple to listen to Him.

LIFE LESSONS

➤ Luke 21:36 — *"But keep on the alert at all times, praying that you may have strength to escape all these things that are about to take place."*

*G*od Himself instructs us to pray so that we might escape certain kinds of trials and tribulations. We need faith to bear the suffering encountered at times in our lives, and we need faith to pray for God to spare us any unnecessary suffering.

MAY 3

◈ 1 Samuel 8:1—9:27

*8*AND it came about when Samuel was old that he appointed his sons judges over Israel.

2 Now the name of his firstborn was Joel, and the name of his second, Abijah; *they* were judging in Beersheba.

➤ 3 His sons, however, did not walk in his ways, but turned aside after dishonest gain and took bribes and perverted justice.

4 Then all the elders of Israel gathered together and came to Samuel at Ramah;

LIFE LESSONS

➤ 1 Samuel 8:3 — *His sons, however, did not walk in his ways, but turned aside after dishonest gain and took bribes and perverted justice.*

*A*s godly as Samuel was, his children did not walk in the ways of God. Regardless of how involved in ministry we are, we cannot afford to neglect the spiritual training of our children.

➤ 1 Samuel 8:6 — *"Give us a king to judge us." And Samuel prayed to the* LORD.

*E*ven in his old age, Samuel sought to hear the voice of God when confronted with a challenge. He didn't think he knew it all. Rather, he went to the Lord for guidance. So should we.

---

5 and they said to him, "Behold, you have grown old, and your sons do not walk in your ways. Now appoint a king for us to judge us like all the nations."

6 But the thing was displeasing in the ◄ sight of Samuel when they said, "Give us a king to judge us." And Samuel prayed to the LORD.

7 The LORD said to Samuel, "Listen to the voice of the people in regard to all that they say to you, for they have not rejected you, but they have rejected Me from being king over them.

8 "Like all the deeds which they have done since the day that I brought them up from Egypt even to this day—in that they have forsaken Me and served other gods—so they are doing to you also.

9 "Now then, listen to their voice; however, you shall solemnly warn them and tell them of the procedure of the king who will reign over them."

10 So Samuel spoke all the words of the LORD to the people who had asked of him a king.

11 He said, "This will be the procedure of the king who will reign over you: he will take your sons and place *them* for himself in his chariots and among his horsemen and they will run before his chariots.

12 "He will appoint for himself commanders of thousands and of fifties, and *some* to do his plowing and to reap his harvest and to make his weapons of war and equipment for his chariots.

13 "He will also take your daughters for perfumers and cooks and bakers.

14 "He will take the best of your fields and your vineyards and your olive groves and give *them* to his servants.
15 "He will take a tenth of your seed and of your vineyards and give to his officers and to his servants.
16 "He will also take your male servants and your female servants and your best young men and your donkeys and use *them* for his work.
17 "He will take a tenth of your flocks, and you yourselves will become his servants.
18 "Then you will cry out in that day because of your king whom you have chosen for yourselves, but the LORD will not answer you in that day."
➤ 19 Nevertheless, the people refused to listen to the voice of Samuel, and they said, "No, but there shall be a king over us,
20 that we also may be like all the nations, that our king may judge us and go out before us and fight our battles."
21 Now after Samuel had heard all the words of the people, he repeated them in the LORD'S hearing.
22 The LORD said to Samuel, "Listen to their voice and appoint them a king." So Samuel said to the men of Israel, "Go every man to his city."
9 NOW there was a man of Benjamin whose name was Kish the son of Abiel, the son of Zeror, the son of Becorath, the son of Aphiah, the son of a Benjamite, a mighty man of valor.
2 He had a son whose name was Saul, a choice and handsome *man*, and there was not a more handsome person than he among the sons of Israel; from his shoulders and up he was taller than any of the people.
3 Now the donkeys of Kish, Saul's

LIFE LESSONS

➤ **1 Samuel 8:19, 20 — *"There shall be a king over us, that we also may be like all the nations."***

*T*he Lord is the only King the people of Israel ever needed. Unfortunately, in every culture and time, God's people feel a tug to be like those around them—to conform to the customs of their unbelieving neighbors. But Jesus tells us, "Do not be like them" (Matt. 6:8). Only He has the right to rule your heart.

---

father, were lost. So Kish said to his son Saul, "Take now with you one of the servants, and arise, go search for the donkeys."
4 He passed through the hill country of Ephraim and passed through the land of Shalishah, but they did not find *them*. Then they passed through the land of Shaalim, but *they were* not *there*. Then he passed through the land of the Benjamites, but they did not find *them*.
5 When they came to the land of Zuph, Saul said to his servant who was with him, "Come, and let us return, or else my father will cease *to be concerned* about the donkeys and will become anxious for us."
6 He said to him, "Behold now, there is a man of God in this city, and the man is held in honor; all that he says surely comes true. Now let us go there, perhaps he can tell us about our journey on which we have set out."
7 Then Saul said to his servant, "But behold, if we go, what shall we bring the man? For the bread is gone from our sack and there is no present to bring to the man of God. What do we have?"
8 The servant answered Saul again and said, "Behold, I have in my hand a fourth of a shekel of silver; I will give *it* to the man of God and he will tell us our way."
9 (Formerly in Israel, when a man went to inquire of God, he used to say, "Come, and let us go to the seer"; for *he who is called* a prophet now was formerly called a seer.)
10 Then Saul said to his servant, "Well said; come, let us go." So they went to the city where the man of God was.
11 As they went up the slope to the city, they found young women going out to draw water and said to them, "Is the seer here?"
12 They answered them and said, "He is; see, *he is* ahead of you. Hurry now, for he has come into the city today, for the people have a sacrifice on the high place today.
13 "As soon as you enter the city you will find him before he goes up to the high place to eat, for the people will not eat until he comes, because he must bless the sacrifice; afterward those who are invited will eat. Now therefore, go up for you will find him at once."

14 So they went up to the city. As they came into the city, behold, Samuel was coming out toward them to go up to the high place.
15 Now a day before Saul's coming, the LORD had revealed *this* to Samuel saying,
➤ 16 "About this time tomorrow I will send you a man from the land of Benjamin, and you shall anoint him to be prince over My people Israel; and he will deliver My people from the hand of the Philistines. For I have regarded My people, because their cry has come to Me."
17 When Samuel saw Saul, the LORD said to him, "Behold, the man of whom I spoke to you! This one shall rule over My people."
18 Then Saul approached Samuel in the gate and said, "Please tell me where the seer's house is."
19 Samuel answered Saul and said, "I am the seer. Go up before me to the high place, for you shall eat with me today; and in the morning I will let you go, and will tell you all that is on your mind.
20 "As for your donkeys which were lost three days ago, do not set your mind on them, for they have been found. And for whom is all that is desirable in Israel? Is it not for you and for all your father's household?"
➤ 21 Saul replied, "Am I not a Benjamite, of the smallest of the tribes of Israel, and my family the least of all the families of the tribe of Benjamin? Why then do you speak to me in this way?"
22 Then Samuel took Saul and his servant and brought them into the hall and gave them a place at the head of those who were invited, who were about thirty men.
23 Samuel said to the cook, "Bring the portion that I gave you, concerning which I said to you, 'Set it aside.'"
24 Then the cook took up the leg with what was on it and set *it* before Saul. And *Samuel* said, "Here is what has been reserved! Set *it* before you *and* eat, because it has been kept for you until the appointed time, since I said I have invited the people." So Saul ate with Samuel that day.
25 When they came down from the high place into the city, *Samuel* spoke with Saul on the roof.

26 And they arose early; and at daybreak Samuel called to Saul on the roof, saying, "Get up, that I may send you away." So Saul arose, and both he and Samuel went out into the street.
27 As they were going down to the edge of the city, Samuel said to Saul, "Say to the servant that he might go ahead of us and pass on, but you remain standing now, that I may proclaim the word of God to you."

Psalm 55:9–15

9 Confuse, O Lord, divide their tongues,
   For I have seen violence and strife in the city.
10 Day and night they go around her upon her walls,
   And iniquity and mischief are in her midst.
11 Destruction is in her midst;
   Oppression and deceit do not depart from her streets.
12 For it is not an enemy who reproaches me,
   Then I could bear *it*;
   Nor is it one who hates me who has exalted himself against me,
   Then I could hide myself from him.
13 But it is you, a man my equal,

LIFE LESSONS

➤ **1 Samuel 9:16** — *"I will send you a man from the land of Benjamin, and you shall anoint him to be prince over My people Israel."*

God often uses misfortune to bring us to the very place where He will show us His will. The dark moments of life will last only so long as is necessary for God to accomplish His purpose in us.

➤ **1 Samuel 9:21** — *"Am I not a Benjamite, of . . . the least of all the families of the tribe of Benjamin?"*

Like Gideon before him, Saul thought of himself as small, unimportant, and powerless. But God loves to use "the weak things of the world to shame the things which are strong" (1 Cor. 1:27).

JUDAS: "Rabbi" Is Not Enough

LUKE 22:1–6

*J*udas Iscariot powerfully reminds us of the horrific possibilities within every human heart. While he called Jesus "Rabbi" (Matt. 26:25, 49), there is no record he ever used the term "Lord." Sadly, he shows us that we can claim allegiance to Christ without ever truly believing in Him as our Lord and Savior (Matt. 7:22, 23). This is the case with those who believe Jesus was a good teacher but deny Him as the only way to the Father (John 14:6). This is also the case for those who profess to know Him but do so only for their own gain.

Whatever his reason for handing over the Lord Jesus, we know that sin had so blinded Judas that he could not see the Way, the Truth, and the Life. He pridefully took matters into his own hands and later regretted all that he did (Matt. 27:3–5).

Judas' story of betrayal still resonates, not only because of his evil kiss (Luke 22:47, 48), but also because we realize the wickedness of our own flesh. How many of us attend church regularly and give Jesus intellectual assent but not our hearts? How many of us call Him King only as a way to achieve our own thrones?

What kind of kiss do *we* give the Lord?

My companion and my familiar friend;
14 We who had sweet fellowship together
Walked in the house of God in the throng.
15 Let death come deceitfully upon them;
Let them go down alive to Sheol,
For evil is in their dwelling, in their midst.

Proverbs 15:15–17

15 All the days of the afflicted are bad,
But a cheerful heart *has* a continual feast.
16 Better is a little with the fear of the LORD
Than great treasure and turmoil with it.
17 Better is a dish of vegetables where love is
Than a fattened ox *served* with hatred.

Luke 22:1–23

22 NOW the Feast of Unleavened Bread, which is called the Passover, was approaching.
2 The chief priests and the scribes were seeking how they might put Him to death; for they were afraid of the people.

3 And Satan entered into Judas who was called Iscariot, belonging to the number of the twelve.
4 And he went away and discussed with the chief priests and officers how he might betray Him to them.
5 They were glad and agreed to give him money.
6 So he consented, and *began* seeking a good opportunity to betray Him to them apart from the crowd.
7 Then came the *first* day of Unleavened Bread on which the Passover *lamb* had to be sacrificed.
8 And Jesus sent Peter and John, saying, "Go and prepare the Passover for us, so that we may eat it."
9 They said to Him, "Where do You want us to prepare it?"
10 And He said to them, "When you have

LIFE LESSONS

➤ Luke 22:3 — *And Satan entered into Judas who was called Iscariot, belonging to the number of the twelve.*

*A*lthough others such as Saul (1 Sam. 16:14) and the Gadarene demoniacs (Matt. 8:28-33) were tormented by evil spirits, Judas is the only person whom the Bible explicitly says was possessed by Satan. Many Bible scholars believe the Antichrist will be as well (Rev. 12–13). Both men are called "the son of perdition" (John 17:12; 2 Thess. 2:3). Whenever we refuse to submit to God's will, we are aiding the enemy's plan (John 8:42-47).

entered the city, a man will meet you carrying a pitcher of water; follow him into the house that he enters.

11 "And you shall say to the owner of the house, 'The Teacher says to you, "Where is the guest room in which I may eat the Passover with My disciples?"'

12 "And he will show you a large, furnished upper room; prepare it there."

13 And they left and found *everything* just as He had told them; and they prepared the Passover.

14 When the hour had come, He reclined *at the table*, and the apostles with Him.

15 And He said to them, "I have earnestly desired to eat this Passover with you before I suffer;

16 for I say to you, I shall never again eat it until it is fulfilled in the kingdom of God."

17 And when He had taken a cup *and* given thanks, He said, "Take this and share it among yourselves;

18 for I say to you, I will not drink of the fruit of the vine from now on until the kingdom of God comes."

19 And when He had taken *some* bread *and* given thanks, He broke it and gave it to them, saying, "This is My body which is given for you; do this in remembrance of Me."

20 And in the same way *He took* the cup after they had eaten, saying, "This cup which is poured out for you is the new covenant in My blood.

21 "But behold, the hand of the one betraying Me is with Mine on the table.

22 "For indeed, the Son of Man is going as it has been determined; but woe to that man by whom He is betrayed!"

23 And they began to discuss among themselves which one of them it might be who was going to do this thing.

MAY 4

1 Samuel 10:1—11:15

10 THEN Samuel took the flask of oil, poured it on his head, kissed him and said, "Has not the LORD anointed you a ruler over His inheritance?

2 "When you go from me today, then you will find two men close to Rachel's tomb in the territory of Benjamin at Zelzah; and they will say to you, 'The donkeys which you went to look for have been found. Now behold, your father has ceased to be concerned about the donkeys and is anxious for you, saying, "What shall I do about my son?"'

3 "Then you will go on further from there, and you will come as far as the oak of Tabor, and there three men going up to God at Bethel will meet you, one carrying three young goats, another carrying three loaves of bread, and another carrying a jug of wine;

4 and they will greet you and give you two *loaves* of bread, which you will accept from their hand.

5 "Afterward you will come to the hill of God where the Philistine garrison is; and it shall be as soon as you have come there to the city, that you will meet a group of prophets coming down from the high place with harp, tambourine, flute, and a lyre before them, and they will be prophesying.

6 "Then the Spirit of the LORD will come upon you mightily, and you shall prophesy with them and be changed into another man.

7 "It shall be when these signs come to you, do for yourself what the occasion requires, for God is with you.

8 "And you shall go down before me to Gilgal; and behold, I will come down to you to offer burnt offerings and sacrifice peace offerings. You shall wait seven days until I come to you and show you what you should do."

9 Then it happened when he turned his back to leave Samuel, God changed his heart; and all those signs came about on that day.

10 When they came to the hill there, behold, a group of prophets met him; and the Spirit of God came upon him mightily, so that he prophesied among them.

11 It came about, when all who knew him previously saw that he prophesied now with the prophets, that the people

➤ **1 Samuel 10:9 —** *When he turned his back to leave Samuel . . . God changed his heart.*

We should pray for God to give us hearts that love, serve, and obey Him. It's only with a heart that is completely submitted to Him that we will be able to live the life He calls us to (Ezek. 36:26, 27).

said to one another, "What has happened to the son of Kish? Is Saul also among the prophets?"
12 A man there said, "Now, who is their father?" Therefore it became a proverb: "Is Saul also among the prophets?"
13 When he had finished prophesying, he came to the high place.
14 Now Saul's uncle said to him and his servant, "Where did you go?" And he said, "To look for the donkeys. When we saw that they could not be found, we went to Samuel."
15 Saul's uncle said, "Please tell me what Samuel said to you."
16 So Saul said to his uncle, "He told us plainly that the donkeys had been found." But he did not tell him about the matter of the kingdom which Samuel had mentioned.

17 Thereafter Samuel called the people together to the LORD at Mizpah;
18 and he said to the sons of Israel, "Thus says the LORD, the God of Israel, 'I brought Israel up from Egypt, and I delivered you from the hand of the Egyptians and from the power of all the kingdoms that were oppressing you.'
19 "But you have today rejected your God, who delivers you from all your calamities and your distresses; yet you have said, 'No, but set a king over us!' Now therefore, present yourselves before the LORD by your tribes and by your clans."
20 Thus Samuel brought all the tribes of Israel near, and the tribe of Benjamin was taken by lot.
21 Then he brought the tribe of Benjamin near by its families, and the Matrite family was taken. And Saul the son of Kish was taken; but when they looked for him, he could not be found.
22 Therefore they inquired further of the LORD, "Has the man come here yet?" So the LORD said, "Behold, he is hiding himself by the baggage."
23 So they ran and took him from there, and when he stood among the people, he was taller than any of the people from his shoulders upward.
24 Samuel said to all the people, "Do

ANSWERS TO LIFE'S QUESTIONS

What should I do when I feel the need to act in haste?

1 SAMUEL 10:8

At times we may feel an overwhelming urge to act spontaneously—to throw caution to the wind and take control of a situation. In times like these, we must make sure our actions line up with God's will. If they do not, our rash behavior may lead to terrible heartache.

This is what happened to King Saul; he lost his throne because he acted hastily. The prophet Samuel told him to wait for him seven days at Gilgal, "Until I come to you and show you what you should do" (1 Sam. 10:8). By the seventh day, Samuel still hadn't arrived. With a hostile Philistine army pressing in on him, Saul decided to take matters in his own hands, preparing burnt offerings to gain the Lord's favor. As soon as he completed the offering, Samuel

appeared. Saul made excuses, but his rashness disqualified him for a long and peaceful reign (1 Sam. 13:13, 14). Getting ahead of God is a terrible mistake with destructive consequences.

On the other hand, Nehemiah, cupbearer to King Artaxerxes, patiently waited for God's timing—with glorious results. He fasted and prayed "for days" (Neh. 1:4), then waited for an opportunity to bring his concern before the king. Rather than dash into action, Nehemiah waited before God. In fact, he beseeched the Lord for a period of four months, until one day the king himself asked Nehemiah why he seemed so downcast. Nehemiah explained the situation, and within days, the king sent him off to Jerusalem with all the necessary authority and building materials (Neh. 2:1–11). Nehemiah waited until God put all the particulars in place, and then he moved swiftly—according to God's will.

We should do the same. As Psalm 27:14 exhorts, "Wait for the LORD; be strong and let your heart take courage; yes, wait for the LORD."

you see him whom the LORD has chosen? Surely there is no one like him among all the people." So all the people shouted and said, "*Long* live the king!"

25 Then Samuel told the people the ordinances of the kingdom, and wrote *them* in the book and placed *it* before the LORD. And Samuel sent all the people away, each one to his house.

26 Saul also went to his house at Gibeah; and the valiant *men* whose hearts God had touched went with him.

➢ 27 But certain worthless men said, "How can this one deliver us?" And they despised him and did not bring him any present. But he kept silent.

11 NOW Nahash the Ammonite came up and besieged Jabesh-gilead; and all the men of Jabesh said to Nahash, "Make a covenant with us and we will serve you."

2 But Nahash the Ammonite said to them, "I will make *it* with you on this condition, that I will gouge out the right eye of every one of you, thus I will make it a reproach on all Israel."

3 The elders of Jabesh said to him, "Let us alone for seven days, that we may send messengers throughout the territory of Israel. Then, if there is no one to deliver us, we will come out to you."

4 Then the messengers came to Gibeah of Saul and spoke these words in the hearing of the people, and all the people lifted up their voices and wept.

5 Now behold, Saul was coming from the field behind the oxen, and he said, "What is *the matter* with the people that they weep?" So they related to him the words of the men of Jabesh.

6 Then the Spirit of God came upon Saul mightily when he heard these words, and he became very angry.

7 He took a yoke of oxen and cut them in pieces, and sent *them* throughout the territory of Israel by the hand of messengers, saying, "Whoever does not come out after Saul and after Samuel, so shall it be done to his oxen." Then the dread of the LORD fell on the people, and they came out as one man.

8 He numbered them in Bezek; and the sons of Israel were 300,000, and the men of Judah 30,000.

9 They said to the messengers who had come, "Thus you shall say to the men of Jabesh-gilead, 'Tomorrow, by the time the sun is hot, you will have deliverance.'" So the messengers went and told the men of Jabesh; and they were glad.

10 Then the men of Jabesh said, "Tomorrow we will come out to you, and you may do to us whatever seems good to you."

11 The next morning Saul put the people in three companies; and they came into the midst of the camp at the morning watch and struck down the Ammonites until the heat of the day. Those who survived were scattered, so that no two of them were left together.

12 Then the people said to Samuel, "Who is he that said, 'Shall Saul reign over us?' Bring the men, that we may put them to death."

13 But Saul said, "Not a man shall be put to death this day, for today the LORD has accomplished deliverance in Israel."

14 Then Samuel said to the people, "Come and let us go to Gilgal and renew the kingdom there."
15 So all the people went to Gilgal, and there they made Saul king before the LORD in Gilgal. There they also offered sacrifices of peace offerings before the LORD; and there Saul and all the men of Israel rejoiced greatly.

Psalm 55:16–23

16 As for me, I shall call upon God,
　　And the LORD will save me.
17 Evening and morning and at noon,
　　I will complain and murmur,
　　And He will hear my voice.
18 He will redeem my soul in peace
　　from the battle *which is* against
　　me,
　　For they are many *who strive* with
　　me.
19 God will hear and answer them—
　　Even the one who sits enthroned
　　from of old—　　　　　Selah.
　　With whom there is no change,
　　And who do not fear God.
20 He has put forth his hands against
　　those who were at peace with
　　him;
　　He has violated his covenant.
21 His speech was smoother than
　　butter,
　　But his heart was war;
　　His words were softer than oil,
　　Yet they were drawn swords.
22 Cast your burden upon the LORD
　　and He will sustain you;
　　He will never allow the righteous to
　　be shaken.
23 But You, O God, will bring them
　　down to the pit of destruction;
　　Men of bloodshed and deceit will
　　not live out half their days.
　　But I will trust in You.

Proverbs 15:18–20

18 A hot-tempered man stirs up strife,
　　But the slow to anger calms a
　　dispute.
19 The way of the lazy is as a hedge of
　　thorns,

　　But the path of the upright is a
　　highway.
20 A wise son makes a father glad,
　　But a foolish man despises his
　　mother.

Luke 22:24–46

24 And there arose also a dispute among them *as to* which one of them was regarded to be greatest.
25 And He said to them, "The kings of the Gentiles lord it over them; and those who have authority over them are called 'Benefactors.'
26 "But *it is* not this way with you, but the one who is the greatest among you must become like the youngest, and the leader like the servant.
27 "For who is greater, the one who reclines *at the table* or the one who serves? Is it not the one who reclines *at the table*? But I am among you as the one who serves.
28 "You are those who have stood by Me in My trials;
29 and just as My Father has granted Me a kingdom, I grant you
30 that you may eat and drink at My table in My kingdom, and you will sit on thrones judging the twelve tribes of Israel.
31 "Simon, Simon, behold, Satan has ⟨ demanded *permission* to sift you like wheat;
32 but I have prayed for you, that your faith may not fail; and you, when once you have turned again, strengthen your brothers."
33 But he said to Him, "Lord, with You I am ready to go both to prison and to death!"

> ·　·　·　L I F E　L E S S O N S　·　·　·

➤ **Luke 22:31** — *"Simon, Simon, behold, Satan has demanded permission to sift you like wheat."*

*W*hen Peter denied Jesus three times, the enemy was invisibly working behind the scenes to encourage his spiritual failure. We must always remain on the alert to detect the activity of our adversary so we can resist him and stand firm in the faith (1 Pet. 5:8-11).

34 And He said, "I say to you, Peter, the rooster will not crow today until you have denied three times that you know Me."

35 And He said to them, "When I sent you out without money belt and bag and sandals, you did not lack anything, did you?" They said, "No, nothing."

36 And He said to them, "But now, whoever has a money belt is to take it along, likewise also a bag, and whoever has no sword is to sell his coat and buy one.

37 "For I tell you that this which is written must be fulfilled in Me, 'AND HE WAS NUMBERED WITH TRANSGRESSORS'; for that which refers to Me has *its* fulfillment."

38 They said, "Lord, look, here are two swords." And He said to them, "It is enough."

39 And He came out and proceeded as was His custom to the Mount of Olives; and the disciples also followed Him.

40 When He arrived at the place, He said to them, "Pray that you may not enter into temptation."

41 And He withdrew from them about a stone's throw, and He knelt down and *began* to pray,

42 saying, "Father, if You are willing, remove this cup from Me; yet not My will, but Yours be done."

43 Now an angel from heaven appeared to Him, strengthening Him.

44 And being in agony He was praying very fervently; and His sweat became like drops of blood, falling down upon the ground.

45 When He rose from prayer, He came to the disciples and found them sleeping from sorrow,

46 and said to them, "Why are you sleeping? Get up and pray that you may not enter into temptation."

LIFE LESSONS

➤ **Luke 22:43 —** *Now an angel from heaven appeared to Him, strengthening Him.*

*D*uring Jesus' most difficult hour, when He had to make the final decision to accept His Father's will and march to the Cross, God sent Him angelic help to encourage Him. The Father will always give us just what we need.

MAY 5

◈ 1 Samuel 12:1—13:23

12 THEN Samuel said to all Israel, "Behold, I have listened to your voice in all that you said to me and I have appointed a king over you.

2 "Now, here is the king walking before you, but I am old and gray, and behold my sons are with you. And I have walked before you from my youth even to this day.

3 "Here I am; bear witness against me before the LORD and His anointed. Whose ox have I taken, or whose donkey have I taken, or whom have I defrauded? Whom have I oppressed, or from whose hand have I taken a bribe to blind my eyes with it? I will restore *it* to you."

4 They said, "You have not defrauded us or oppressed us or taken anything from any man's hand."

5 He said to them, "The LORD is witness against you, and His anointed is witness this day that you have found nothing in my hand." And they said, "*He* is witness."

6 Then Samuel said to the people, "It is the LORD who appointed Moses and Aaron and who brought your fathers up from the land of Egypt.

7 "So now, take your stand, that I may

LIFE LESSONS

➤ **1 Samuel 12:3 —** *"Whom have I defrauded?"*

*I*ntegrity is the consuming desire to acknowledge, obey, and honor the Father in all we do, as well as being ready to confess and repent of sin as soon as it is found in us. It is expressed in both our private and public behavior—in how we treat others and how we act when no one is watching. When we have integrity, we leave no ground for accusation—our lives speak for us (Matt. 7:16-18).

plead with you before the LORD concerning all the righteous acts of the LORD which He did for you and your fathers.
8 "When Jacob went into Egypt and your fathers cried out to the LORD, then the LORD sent Moses and Aaron who brought your fathers out of Egypt and settled them in this place.
9 "But they forgot the LORD their God, so He sold them into the hand of Sisera, captain of the army of Hazor, and into the hand of the Philistines and into the hand of the king of Moab, and they fought against them.
10 "They cried out to the LORD and said, 'We have sinned because we have forsaken the LORD and have served the Baals and the Ashtaroth; but now deliver us from the hands of our enemies, and we will serve You.'
11 "Then the LORD sent Jerubbaal and Bedan and Jephthah and Samuel, and delivered you from the hands of your enemies all around, so that you lived in security.
12 "When you saw that Nahash the king of the sons of Ammon came against you, you said to me, 'No, but a king shall reign over us,' although the LORD your God was your king.
13 "Now therefore, here is the king whom you have chosen, whom you have asked for, and behold, the LORD has set a king over you.
14 "If you will fear the LORD and serve Him, and listen to His voice and not rebel against the command of the LORD, then both you and also the king who reigns over you will follow the LORD your God.
15 "If you will not listen to the voice of the LORD, but rebel against the command of the LORD, then the hand of the LORD will be against you, as it was against your fathers.
16 "Even now, take your stand and see this great thing which the LORD will do before your eyes.
17 "Is it not the wheat harvest today? I will call to the LORD, that He may send thunder and rain. Then you will know and see that your wickedness is great which you have done in the sight of the LORD by asking for yourselves a king."
18 So Samuel called to the LORD, and the LORD sent thunder and rain that day; and all the people greatly feared the LORD and Samuel.

19 Then all the people said to Samuel, "Pray for your servants to the LORD your God, so that we may not die, for we have added to all our sins this evil by asking for ourselves a king."
20 Samuel said to the people, "Do not fear. You have committed all this evil, yet do not turn aside from following the LORD, but serve the LORD with all your heart.
21 "You must not turn aside, for then you would go after futile things which can not profit or deliver, because they are futile.
22 "For the LORD will not abandon His people on account of His great name, because the LORD has been pleased to make you a people for Himself.
23 "Moreover, as for me, far be it from me that I should sin against the LORD by ceasing to pray for you; but I will instruct you in the good and right way.
24 "Only fear the LORD and serve Him in truth with all your heart; for consider what great things He has done for you.
25 "But if you still do wickedly, both you and your king will be swept away."
13 SAUL was thirty years old when he began to reign, and he reigned forty two years over Israel.
2 Now Saul chose for himself 3,000 men of Israel, of which 2,000 were with Saul in Michmash and in the hill country of Bethel, while 1,000 were with Jonathan at Gibeah of Benjamin. But he sent away the rest of the people, each to his tent.
3 Jonathan smote the garrison of the Philistines that was in Geba, and the

---

LIFE LESSONS

➤ 1 Samuel 12:21 — "You must not turn aside, for then you would go after futile things which can not profit or deliver, because they are futile."

How often do we go after futile things that can neither bless nor deliver us? Even if we get these things, we end up with precisely nothing—because anything we acquire outside God's will eventually turns to ashes. Remember, intimacy with the Lord is always His highest priority for our lives, and He will never disappoint us.

ANSWERS TO LIFE'S QUESTIONS

What does the Bible say to lonely people?

1 SAMUEL 12:22

*T*ime and again throughout the Old Testament, we find the Lord reaching out to His people, revealing Himself to them, desiring to be with them, and communicating with them. In 1 Samuel 12:22, we find this promise of God: "The LORD will not abandon His people on account of His great name, because the LORD has been pleased to make you a people for Himself." God desires companionship, fellowship, and communion with those who will reciprocate His expressions of friendship.

We can count on the close communion of the Lord, even if everyone else abandons us. We see this in the life of Jesus. On the very night He was arrested and put on trial—the trial that led to His crucifixion—He said to His disciples, "Behold, an hour is coming, and has already come, for you to be scattered, each to his own home, and to leave Me alone." Can you hear the pain in that statement? Jesus knew what it meant to be lonely! But then He said, "And yet I am not alone, because the Father is with Me" (John 16:32). Jesus knew what it was to be comforted, even in the face of abandonment.

When loneliness engulfs us, the first thing we must do is turn our focus away from what we don't have to what we do have. What do we have, you may ask?

God Himself!

You can never be alone once you have trusted Jesus Christ as your Savior. He promises that He dwells within you when you have received Him into your life and that He is connected to you, just as a vine and a branch are connected. In the same way that sap flows through a vine and its branches, so too the love of Christ flows in you and through you. He abides in you, and you abide in Him. You are one being with Christ. You share with Him the most intimate relationship possible—an eternal, spiritual intimacy (John 15:1–9).

The depth of that intimacy, to a great extent, is up to you. How much do you desire intimacy with the Lord? How much do you allow Him to fill you up with His presence? How willing are you for Him to reveal Himself to you? Even so, you can never totally isolate yourself from the Lord. He is always there, desiring to move ever closer to you.

Philistines heard of *it*. Then Saul blew the trumpet throughout the land, saying, "Let the Hebrews hear."

4 All Israel heard the news that Saul had smitten the garrison of the Philistines, and also that Israel had become odious to the Philistines. The people were then summoned to Saul at Gilgal.

5 Now the Philistines assembled to fight with Israel, 30,000 chariots and 6,000 horsemen, and people like the sand which is on the seashore in abundance; and they came up and camped in Michmash, east of Beth-aven.

6 When the men of Israel saw that they were in a strait (for the people were hard-pressed), then the people hid themselves in caves, in thickets, in cliffs, in cellars, and in pits.

7 Also *some of* the Hebrews crossed the Jordan into the land of Gad and Gilead. But as for Saul, he *was* still in Gilgal, and all the people followed him trembling.

8 Now he waited seven days, according to the appointed time set by Samuel, but Samuel did not come to Gilgal; and the people were scattering from him.

9 So Saul said, "Bring to me the burnt offering and the peace offerings." And he offered the burnt offering.

10 As soon as he finished offering the burnt offering, behold, Samuel came; and Saul went out to meet him *and* to greet him.

11 But Samuel said, "What have you done?" And Saul said, "Because I saw that the people were scattering from me, and that you did not come within the appointed days, and that the Philistines were assembling at Michmash,

12 therefore I said, 'Now the Philistines will come down against me at Gilgal, and I have not asked the favor of the LORD.' So I forced myself and offered the burnt offering."

13 Samuel said to Saul, "You have acted foolishly; you have not kept the commandment of the LORD your God, which He commanded you, for now the LORD would have established your kingdom over Israel forever.

14 "But now your kingdom shall not ◄ endure. The LORD has sought out for Himself a man after His own heart, and the LORD has appointed him as ruler over

> **1 Samuel 13:14 — "The LORD has appointed him as ruler over His people."**

Saul wanted to act on his terms, rather than in obedience to God. He did not yet realize our intimacy with and obedience to the Lord determines the impact of our lives. God has a plan for us, and we become all He has created us to be as we grow in our faith and our relationship with Him. If we refuse to trust Him (as Saul did), we forfeit the blessings He has for us. If we are faithful, He will surely reward us.

His people, because you have not kept what the LORD commanded you."
15 Then Samuel arose and went up from Gilgal to Gibeah of Benjamin. And Saul numbered the people who were present with him, about six hundred men.
16 Now Saul and his son Jonathan and the people who were present with them were staying in Geba of Benjamin while the Philistines camped at Michmash.
17 And the raiders came from the camp of the Philistines in three companies: one company turned toward Ophrah, to the land of Shual,
18 and another company turned toward Beth-horon, and another company turned toward the border which overlooks the valley of Zeboim toward the wilderness.
19 Now no blacksmith could be found in all the land of Israel, for the Philistines said, "Otherwise the Hebrews will make swords or spears."
20 So all Israel went down to the Philistines, each to sharpen his plowshare, his mattock, his axe, and his hoe.
21 The charge was two-thirds of a shekel for the plowshares, the mattocks, the forks, and the axes, and to fix the hoes.
22 So it came about on the day of battle that neither sword nor spear was found in the hands of any of the people who *were* with Saul and Jonathan, but they were found with Saul and his son Jonathan.
23 And the garrison of the Philistines went out to the pass of Michmash.

Psalm 56:1–13

For the choir director; according to Jonath elem rehokim. A Mikhtam of David, when the Philistines seized him in Gath.

56 BE gracious to me, O God, for man has trampled upon me; Fighting all day long he oppresses me.
2 My foes have trampled upon me all day long, For they are many who fight proudly against me.
3 When I am afraid, I will put my trust in You.
4 In God, whose word I praise, In God I have put my trust; I shall not be afraid. What can *mere* man do to me?
5 All day long they distort my words; All their thoughts are against me for evil.
6 They attack, they lurk, They watch my steps, As they have waited *to take* my life.
7 Because of wickedness, cast them forth, In anger put down the peoples, O God!
8 You have taken account of my wanderings; Put my tears in Your bottle. Are *they* not in Your book?
9 Then my enemies will turn back in the day when I call; This I know, that God is for me.
10 In God, *whose* word I praise, In the LORD, *whose* word I praise,
11 In God I have put my trust, I shall not be afraid. What can man do to me?
12 Your vows are *binding* upon me, O God; I will render thank offerings to You.

> **Psalm 56:3 — When I am afraid, I will put my trust in You.**

The psalmist does not say, "*If* something ever scares me," he says, "*When* I am afraid." Fear is a natural human reaction to danger. God does not tell us to ignore our fears but to bring them to Him.

13 For You have delivered my soul
      from death,
    Indeed my feet from stumbling,
    So that I may walk before God
    In the light of the living.

Proverbs 15:21–23

21 Folly is joy to him who lacks sense,
    But a man of understanding walks
      straight.
➤ 22 Without consultation, plans are
      frustrated,
    But with many counselors they
      succeed.
✳ 23 A man has joy in an apt answer,
    And how delightful is a timely
      word!

Luke 22:47–71

47 While He was still speaking, behold,
a crowd *came*, and the one called Judas,
one of the twelve, was preceding them;
and he approached Jesus to kiss Him.
48 But Jesus said to him, "Judas, are
you betraying the Son of Man with a
kiss?"
49 When those who were around Him
saw what was going to happen, they
said, "Lord, shall we strike with the
sword?"
50 And one of them struck the slave of
the high priest and cut off his right ear.
51 But Jesus answered and said, "Stop!
No more of this." And He touched his ear
and healed him.
52 Then Jesus said to the chief priests
and officers of the temple and elders who
had come against Him, "Have you come

out with swords and clubs as you would
against a robber?
53 "While I was with you daily in the
temple, you did not lay hands on Me; but
this hour and the power of darkness are
yours."
54 Having arrested Him, they led Him
away and brought Him to the house of
the high priest; but Peter was following
at a distance.
55 After they had kindled a fire in the
middle of the courtyard and had sat
down together, Peter was sitting among
them.
56 And a servant-girl, seeing him as he
sat in the firelight and looking intently at
him, said, "This man was with Him too."
57 But he denied *it*, saying, "Woman, I
do not know Him."
58 A little later, another saw him and
said, "You are *one* of them too!" But
Peter said, "Man, I am not!"
59 After about an hour had passed,
another man *began* to insist, saying,
"Certainly this man also was with Him,
for he is a Galilean too."
60 But Peter said, "Man, I do not know
what you are talking about." Immediately, while he was still speaking, a
rooster crowed.
61 The Lord turned and looked at Peter. ◄
And Peter remembered the word of the
Lord, how He had told him, "Before a
rooster crows today, you will deny Me
three times."
62 And he went out and wept bitterly.
63 Now the men who were holding
Jesus in custody were mocking Him and
beating Him,
64 and they blindfolded Him and were
asking Him, saying, "Prophesy, who is
the one who hit You?"
65 And they were saying many other
things against Him, blaspheming.

LIFE LESSONS

➤ **Proverbs 15:22** — *Without consultation, plans are frustrated, but with many counselors they succeed.*

Since none of us has an unlimited
perspective, we frequently need the
godly expertise and viewpoints of others
to inform our most important decisions
and plans. God often uses the counsel of
other believers to show us His will.

➤ **Luke 22:61** — *The Lord turned and looked at Peter.*

What kind of look was it? One that
expressed compassion? Disappointment? Resignation? Sorrow? We don't
know. We only know that Jesus used it to
remind Peter of His prophetic word, and
that look caused Peter to weep.

66 When it was day, the Council of elders of the people assembled, both chief priests and scribes, and they led Him away to their council *chamber*, saying,
67 "If You are the Christ, tell us." But He said to them, "If I tell you, you will not believe;
68 and if I ask a question, you will not answer.

69 "But from now on THE SON OF MAN WILL BE SEATED AT THE RIGHT HAND of the power OF GOD."
70 And they all said, "Are You the Son of God, then?" And He said to them, "Yes, I am."
71 Then they said, "What further need do we have of testimony? For we have heard it ourselves from His own mouth."

1 Samuel 14:1—15:35

14 NOW the day came that Jonathan, the son of Saul, said to the young man who was carrying his armor, "Come and let us cross over to the Philistines' garrison that is on the other side." But he did not tell his father.
2 Saul was staying in the outskirts of Gibeah under the pomegranate tree which is in Migron. And the people who *were* with him *were* about six hundred men,
3 and Ahijah, the son of Ahitub, Ichabod's brother, the son of Phinehas, the son of Eli, the priest of the LORD at Shiloh, was wearing an ephod. And the people did not know that Jonathan had gone.
4 Between the passes by which Jonathan sought to cross over to the Philistines' garrison, there was a sharp crag on the one side and a sharp crag on the other side, and the name of the one was Bozez, and the name of the other Seneh.
5 The one crag rose on the north opposite Michmash, and the other on the south opposite Geba.
6 Then Jonathan said to the young man who was carrying his armor, "Come and let us cross over to the garrison of these uncircumcised; perhaps the LORD will work for us, for the LORD is not restrained to save by many or by few."
7 His armor bearer said to him, "Do all that is in your heart; turn yourself, *and* here I am with you according to your desire."
8 Then Jonathan said, "Behold, we will cross over to the men and reveal ourselves to them.
9 "If they say to us, 'Wait until we come to you'; then we will stand in our place and not go up to them.
10 "But if they say, 'Come up to us,' then we will go up, for the LORD has given them into our hands; and this shall be the sign to us."
11 When both of them revealed themselves to the garrison of the Philistines, the Philistines said, "Behold, Hebrews are coming out of the holes where they have hidden themselves."
12 So the men of the garrison hailed Jonathan and his armor bearer and said, "Come up to us and we will tell you something." And Jonathan said to his armor bearer, "Come up after me, for the LORD has given them into the hands of Israel."
13 Then Jonathan climbed up on his hands and feet, with his armor bearer behind him; and they fell before Jonathan, and his armor bearer put some to death after him.
14 That first slaughter which Jonathan and his armor bearer made was about twenty men within about half a furrow in an acre of land.
15 And there was a trembling in the

LIFE LESSONS

➤ **1 Samuel 14:6 — *"For the LORD is not restrained to save by many or by few."***

*J*onathan had a spirit very different from that of his father. Saul feared men; Jonathan feared God. And so the Lord did mighty things through Jonathan.

camp, in the field, and among all the people. Even the garrison and the raiders trembled, and the earth quaked so that it became a great trembling.

16 Now Saul's watchmen in Gibeah of Benjamin looked, and behold, the multitude melted away; and they went here and *there*.

17 Saul said to the people who *were* with him, "Number now and see who has gone from us." And when they had numbered, behold, Jonathan and his armor bearer were not *there*.

18 Then Saul said to Ahijah, "Bring the ark of God here." For the ark of God was at that time with the sons of Israel.

19 While Saul talked to the priest, the commotion in the camp of the Philistines continued and increased; so Saul said to the priest, "Withdraw your hand."

20 Then Saul and all the people who *were* with him rallied and came to the battle; and behold, every man's sword was against his fellow, *and there was* very great confusion.

21 Now the Hebrews *who* were with the Philistines previously, who went up with them all around in the camp, even they also *turned* to be with the Israelites who *were* with Saul and Jonathan.

22 When all the men of Israel who had hidden themselves in the hill country of Ephraim heard that the Philistines had fled, even they also pursued them closely in the battle.

23 So the LORD delivered Israel that day, and the battle spread beyond Beth-aven.

24 Now the men of Israel were hard-pressed on that day, for Saul had put the people under oath, saying, "Cursed be the man who eats food before evening, and until I have avenged myself on my enemies." So none of the people tasted food.

25 All *the people of* the land entered the forest, and there was honey on the ground.

26 When the people entered the forest, behold, *there was* a flow of honey; but no man put his hand to his mouth, for the people feared the oath.

27 But Jonathan had not heard when his father put the people under oath; therefore, he put out the end of the staff that *was* in his hand and dipped it in the honeycomb, and put his hand to his mouth, and his eyes brightened.

28 Then one of the people said, "Your father strictly put the people under oath, saying, 'Cursed be the man who eats food today.'" And the people were weary.

29 Then Jonathan said, "My father has troubled the land. See now, how my eyes have brightened because I tasted a little of this honey.

30 "How much more, if only the people had eaten freely today of the spoil of their enemies which they found! For now the slaughter among the Philistines has not been great."

31 They struck among the Philistines that day from Michmash to Aijalon. And the people were very weary.

32 The people rushed greedily upon the spoil, and took sheep and oxen and calves, and slew *them* on the ground; and the people ate *them* with the blood.

33 Then they told Saul, saying, "Behold, the people are sinning against the LORD by eating with the blood." And he said, "You have acted treacherously; roll a great stone to me today."

34 Saul said, "Disperse yourselves among the people and say to them, 'Each one of you bring me his ox or his sheep, and slaughter *it* here and eat; and do not sin against the LORD by eating with the blood.'" So all the people that night brought each one his ox with him and slaughtered *it* there.

35 And Saul built an altar to the LORD; it was the first altar that he built to the LORD.

36 Then Saul said, "Let us go down after the Philistines by night and take spoil among them until the morning light, and let us not leave a man of them." And they said, "Do whatever seems good to you." So the priest said, "Let us draw near to God here."

37 Saul inquired of God, "Shall I go down after the Philistines? Will You give them into the hand of Israel?" But He did not answer him on that day.

38 Saul said, "Draw near here, all you chiefs of the people, and investigate and see how this sin has happened today.

39 "For as the LORD lives, who delivers Israel, though it is in Jonathan my son, he shall surely die." But not one of all the people answered him.

40 Then he said to all Israel, "You shall be on one side and I and Jonathan my son will be on the other side." And the people said to Saul, "Do what seems good to you."
41 Therefore, Saul said to the LORD, the God of Israel, "Give a perfect *lot*." And Jonathan and Saul were taken, but the people escaped.
42 Saul said, "Cast *lots* between me and Jonathan my son." And Jonathan was taken.
43 Then Saul said to Jonathan, "Tell me what you have done." So Jonathan told him and said, "I indeed tasted a little honey with the end of the staff that was in my hand. Here I am, I must die!"
44 Saul said, "May God do this *to me* and more also, for you shall surely die, Jonathan."
45 But the people said to Saul, "Must Jonathan die, who has brought about this great deliverance in Israel? Far from it! As the LORD lives, not one hair of his head shall fall to the ground, for he has worked with God this day." So the people rescued Jonathan and he did not die.
46 Then Saul went up from pursuing the Philistines, and the Philistines went to their own place.
47 Now when Saul had taken the kingdom over Israel, he fought against all his enemies on every side, against Moab, the sons of Ammon, Edom, the kings of Zobah, and the Philistines; and wherever he turned, he inflicted punishment.
48 He acted valiantly and defeated the Amalekites, and delivered Israel from the hands of those who plundered them.
49 Now the sons of Saul were Jonathan and Ishvi and Malchi-shua; and the names of his two daughters *were these:* the name of the firstborn Merab and the name of the younger Michal.
50 The name of Saul's wife was Ahinoam the daughter of Ahimaaz. And the name of the captain of his army was Abner the son of Ner, Saul's uncle.
51 Kish *was* the father of Saul, and Ner the father of Abner *was* the son of Abiel.
52 Now the war against the Philistines was severe all the days of Saul; and when Saul saw any mighty man or any valiant man, he attached him to his staff.

15 THEN Samuel said to Saul, "The LORD sent me to anoint you as king over His people, over Israel; now therefore, listen to the words of the LORD.
2 "Thus says the LORD of hosts, 'I will punish Amalek *for* what he did to Israel, how he set himself against him on the way while he was coming up from Egypt.
3 'Now go and strike Amalek and utterly destroy all that he has, and do not spare him; but put to death both man and woman, child and infant, ox and sheep, camel and donkey.' "
4 Then Saul summoned the people and numbered them in Telaim, 200,000 foot soldiers and 10,000 men of Judah.
5 Saul came to the city of Amalek and set an ambush in the valley.
6 Saul said to the Kenites, "Go, depart, go down from among the Amalekites, so that I do not destroy you with them; for you showed kindness to all the sons of Israel when they came up from Egypt." So the Kenites departed from among the Amalekites.
7 So Saul defeated the Amalekites, from Havilah as you go to Shur, which is east of Egypt.
8 He captured Agag the king of the Amalekites alive, and utterly destroyed all the people with the edge of the sword.
9 But Saul and the people spared Agag and the best of the sheep, the oxen, the fatlings, the lambs, and all that was good, and were not willing to destroy them utterly; but everything despised and worthless, that they utterly destroyed.
10 Then the word of the LORD came to Samuel, saying,
11 "I regret that I have made Saul king, for he has turned back from following Me and has not carried out My

---

LIFE LESSONS

➤ **1 Samuel 15:12 — *"Saul came to Carmel, and behold, he set up a monument for himself."***

*T*he young man who once thought of himself as small and unable to lead Israel (1 Sam. 9:21; 10:20-22; 15:17) arrogantly set up a monument to honor himself. When we cease to follow the Lord wholeheartedly, we follow our prideful hearts to our own destruction.

ANSWERS TO LIFE'S QUESTIONS

What role does obedience play in a mature Christian's life?

1 SAMUEL 15:22

Those who know the greatness and goodness of God—and those who seek to identify fully with Christ's life—have a great passion to obey God.

Obedience is active, not passive. It is joyfully living out what we know to be true, right, and good. It is to follow the Lord daily, saying and doing what Jesus would do if He were living in our place. Obedience is total submission to what God desires.

Our heavenly Father places a high value on obedience. He prefers it even to sacrifice, or the outward expression of worship (1 Sam. 15:22). In fact, our obedience is the ultimate expression of worship and service (Prov. 21:3).

Mature Christians express their desire to obey God in three general ways:
1. *A passion to know the Bible.*

To know what God requires of us, we must know what He has commanded. God's commandments have not changed through the ages, nor have they been altered according to culture, custom, or technological advances. God's Word is absolute and enduring (Josh. 24:24; Ps. 119:15, 16, 105, 106; 143:10).
2. *A passion to live in righteousness.*

Very simply, living in righteousness is doing what is right before the Lord. It means gladly keeping His commandments and statutes. It is turning away from sin and toward what is holy and acceptable to God (Ps. 97:10–12; Prov. 11:30; 12:12, 13; Rom. 2:7–10; Heb. 12:1, 2).
3. *A passion to receive daily direction from the Lord.*

To have a heart for obedience is to have a deep desire to receive daily direction from the Holy Spirit. To obey is to "walk in His ways," step by step—trusting that God is leading you and that He will correct you should you make an error. We must observe what God is doing around us and daily ask Him, "What is Your will, Lord?" (Ps. 25:4, 5; 141:3, 4, 8–10; Jer. 42:1–6).

Ultimately, these three desires work together. The more we explore God's Word, the greater our understanding of righteousness and how the Holy Spirit works in us to do God's will. The more we trust the Holy Spirit, the more He reminds us of God's Word and leads us into righteousness. The more we desire to be right before the Father, the more we will want to read His Word and listen for His voice.

---

commands." And Samuel was distressed and cried out to the LORD all night.

> 12 Samuel rose early in the morning to meet Saul; and it was told Samuel, saying, "Saul came to Carmel, and behold, he set up a monument for himself, then turned and proceeded on down to Gilgal."

13 Samuel came to Saul, and Saul said to him, "Blessed are you of the LORD! I have carried out the command of the LORD."

14 But Samuel said, "What then is this bleating of the sheep in my ears, and the lowing of the oxen which I hear?"

15 Saul said, "They have brought them from the Amalekites, for the people spared the best of the sheep and oxen, to sacrifice to the LORD your God; but the rest we have utterly destroyed."

16 Then Samuel said to Saul, "Wait, and let me tell you what the LORD said to me last night." And he said to him, "Speak!"

17 Samuel said, "Is it not true, though you were little in your own eyes, you were *made* the head of the tribes of Israel? And the LORD anointed you king over Israel,

18 and the LORD sent you on a mission, and said, 'Go and utterly destroy the sinners, the Amalekites, and fight against them until they are exterminated.'

19 "Why then did you not obey the voice of the LORD, but rushed upon the spoil and did what was evil in the sight of the LORD?"

20 Then Saul said to Samuel, "I did obey the voice of the LORD, and went on the mission on which the LORD sent me, and have brought back Agag the king of Amalek, and have utterly destroyed the Amalekites.

21 "But the people took *some* of the spoil, sheep and oxen, the choicest of the things devoted to destruction, to sacrifice to the LORD your God at Gilgal."

22 Samuel said,

"Has the LORD as much delight in
    burnt offerings and sacrifices
As in obeying the voice of the
    LORD?

> Behold, to obey is better than
>   sacrifice,
> *And* to heed than the fat of rams.
23 "For rebellion is as the sin of
>   divination,
> And insubordination is as iniquity
>   and idolatry.
> Because you have rejected the word
>   of the LORD,
> He has also rejected you from *being*
>   king."

➢ 24 Then Saul said to Samuel, "I have sinned; I have indeed transgressed the command of the LORD and your words, because I feared the people and listened to their voice.
25 "Now therefore, please pardon my sin and return with me, that I may worship the LORD."
26 But Samuel said to Saul, "I will not return with you; for you have rejected the word of the LORD, and the LORD has rejected you from being king over Israel."
27 As Samuel turned to go, *Saul* seized the edge of his robe, and it tore.
28 So Samuel said to him, "The LORD has torn the kingdom of Israel from you today and has given it to your neighbor, who is better than you.
29 "Also the Glory of Israel will not lie or change His mind; for He is not a man that He should change His mind."
30 Then he said, "I have sinned; *but* please honor me now before the elders of my people and before Israel, and go back with me, that I may worship the LORD your God."
31 So Samuel went back following Saul, and Saul worshiped the LORD.
32 Then Samuel said, "Bring me Agag, the king of the Amalekites." And Agag came to him cheerfully. And Agag said, "Surely the bitterness of death is past."
33 But Samuel said, "As your sword

has made women childless, so shall your mother be childless among women." And Samuel hewed Agag to pieces before the LORD at Gilgal.
34 Then Samuel went to Ramah, but Saul went up to his house at Gibeah of Saul.
35 Samuel did not see Saul again until the day of his death; for Samuel grieved over Saul. And the LORD regretted that He had made Saul king over Israel.

◈ Psalm 57:1–3

For the choir director; *set to* Al-tashheth.
A Mikhtam of David, when he fled from
Saul in the cave.

57 BE gracious to me, O God, be
>   gracious to me,
> For my soul takes refuge in You;
> And in the shadow of Your wings I
>   will take refuge
> Until destruction passes by.
2 I will cry to God Most High,
> To God who accomplishes *all things*
>   for me.
3 He will send from heaven and save
>   me;
> He reproaches him who tramples
>   upon me.   Selah.
> God will send forth His
>   lovingkindness and His truth.

Proverbs 15:24, 25

24 The path of life *leads* upward for the
 wise
 That he may keep away from Sheol
 below.
25 The LORD will tear down the house
 of the proud,
 But He will establish the boundary
 of the widow.

Luke 23:1–25

23 THEN the whole body of them
 got up and brought Him before
Pilate.
2 And they began to accuse Him, saying, "We found this man misleading our
nation and forbidding to pay taxes to
Caesar, and saying that He Himself is
Christ, a King."
3 So Pilate asked Him, saying, "Are
You the King of the Jews?" And He answered him and said, "*It is as* you say."
4 Then Pilate said to the chief priests
and the crowds, "I find no guilt in this
man."
5 But they kept on insisting, saying,
"He stirs up the people, teaching all over
Judea, starting from Galilee even as far
as this place."
6 When Pilate heard it, he asked
whether the man was a Galilean.
7 And when he learned that He belonged to Herod's jurisdiction, he sent
Him to Herod, who himself also was in
Jerusalem at that time.
8 Now Herod was very glad when he
saw Jesus; for he had wanted to see Him
for a long time, because he had been
hearing about Him and was hoping to
see some sign performed by Him.
9 And he questioned Him at some
length; but He answered him nothing.
10 And the chief priests and the scribes
were standing there, accusing Him vehe-
mently.
11 And Herod with his soldiers, after
treating Him with contempt and mocking Him, dressed Him in a gorgeous robe
and sent Him back to Pilate.
12 Now Herod and Pilate became
friends with one another that very day;

for before they had been enemies with
each other.
13 Pilate summoned the chief priests
and the rulers and the people,
14 and said to them, "You brought this
man to me as one who incites the people
to rebellion, and behold, having examined Him before you, I have found no
guilt in this man regarding the charges
which you make against Him.
15 "No, nor has Herod, for he sent Him
back to us; and behold, nothing deserving death has been done by Him.
16 "Therefore I will punish Him and release Him."
17 [Now he was obliged to release to
them at the feast one prisoner.]
18 But they cried out all together, saying, "Away with this man, and release
for us Barabbas!"
19 (He was one who had been thrown
into prison for an insurrection made in
the city, and for murder.)
20 Pilate, wanting to release Jesus, addressed them again,
21 but they kept on calling out, saying,
"Crucify, crucify Him!"
22 And he said to them the third time,
"Why, what evil has this man done? I
have found in Him no guilt *demanding*
death; therefore I will punish Him and
release Him."
23 But they were insistent, with loud
voices asking that He be crucified. And
their voices *began* to prevail.
24 And Pilate pronounced sentence that
their demand be granted.
25 And he released the man they were
asking for who had been thrown into
prison for insurrection and murder, but
he delivered Jesus to their will.

LIFE LESSONS

➤ **Luke 23:8 —** *Now Herod was very
glad when he saw Jesus; for he . . . was
hoping to see some sign performed by
Him.*

*H*erod had no interest in Jesus the
 Messiah or Jesus the Savior; he simply wanted to see wonders performed
for him. Yet Jesus refused to speak a
single word to the king. No one can ever
manipulate Him into doing his or her
bidding.

1 Samuel 16:1—17:58

16 NOW the LORD said to Samuel, "How long will you grieve over Saul, since I have rejected him from being king over Israel? Fill your horn with oil and go; I will send you to Jesse the Bethlehemite, for I have selected a king for Myself among his sons."

2 But Samuel said, "How can I go? When Saul hears *of it,* he will kill me." And the LORD said, "Take a heifer with you and say, 'I have come to sacrifice to the LORD.'

3 "You shall invite Jesse to the sacrifice, and I will show you what you shall do; and you shall anoint for Me the one whom I designate to you."

4 So Samuel did what the LORD said, and came to Bethlehem. And the elders of the city came trembling to meet him and said, "Do you come in peace?"

5 He said, "In peace; I have come to sacrifice to the LORD. Consecrate yourselves and come with me to the sacrifice." He also consecrated Jesse and his sons and invited them to the sacrifice.

6 When they entered, he looked at Eliab and thought, "Surely the LORD'S anointed is before Him."

7 But the LORD said to Samuel, "Do not look at his appearance or at the height of his stature, because I have rejected him; for God *sees* not as man sees, for man looks at the outward appearance, but the LORD looks at the heart."

8 Then Jesse called Abinadab and made

LIFE LESSONS

➤ 1 Samuel 16:7 — *"For man looks at the outward appearance, but the LORD looks at the heart."*

Before Samuel had even met David, the Lord had chosen him to lead Israel (1 Sam. 13:14). Yet even a godly man like Samuel couldn't help but judge a man by his appearance. This is why we must continually go to the Lord for His wisdom; only He sees the heart. At his young age, David already knew the importance of obeying God fully, which is why the Lord could work through him and develop him into the ruler Israel needed (1 Sam. 16:7; Acts 13:22).

---

him pass before Samuel. And he said, "The LORD has not chosen this one either."

9 Next Jesse made Shammah pass by. And he said, "The LORD has not chosen this one either."

10 Thus Jesse made seven of his sons pass before Samuel. But Samuel said to Jesse, "The LORD has not chosen these."

11 And Samuel said to Jesse, "Are these all the children?" And he said, "There remains yet the youngest, and behold, he is tending the sheep." Then Samuel said to Jesse, "Send and bring him; for we will not sit down until he comes here."

12 So he sent and brought him in. Now he was ruddy, with beautiful eyes and a handsome appearance. And the LORD said, "Arise, anoint him; for this is he."

13 Then Samuel took the horn of oil and anointed him in the midst of his brothers; and the Spirit of the LORD came mightily upon David from that day forward. And Samuel arose and went to Ramah.

14 Now the Spirit of the LORD departed from Saul, and an evil spirit from the LORD terrorized him.

15 Saul's servants then said to him, "Behold now, an evil spirit from God is terrorizing you.

16 "Let our lord now command your servants who are before you. Let them seek a man who is a skillful player on the harp; and it shall come about when the evil spirit from God is on you, that he shall play *the harp* with his hand, and you will be well."

17 So Saul said to his servants, "Provide for me now a man who can play well and bring *him* to me."

18 Then one of the young men said, "Behold, I have seen a son of Jesse the Bethlehemite who is a skillful musician, a mighty man of valor, a warrior, one prudent in speech, and a handsome man; and the LORD is with him."

19 So Saul sent messengers to Jesse and said, "Send me your son David who is with the flock."

20 Jesse took a donkey *loaded with* bread and a jug of wine and a young goat, and sent *them* to Saul by David his son.

21 Then David came to Saul and attended him; and Saul loved him greatly, and he became his armor bearer.

22 Saul sent to Jesse, saying, "Let David now stand before me, for he has found favor in my sight."

LIFE LESSONS

➤ **1 Samuel 16:19 — *"Send me your son David."***

*A*fter David was anointed by Samuel, he went back to the flocks—an act that revealed his character. He was willing to do whatever the Lord wanted, and it was because of his faith that God used him so powerfully. Just as He sent Moses into the household of Pharaoh to train him, at the right time, the Lord sent David into Saul's palace for preparation. God always equips us for the tasks He gives us.

23 So it came about whenever the *evil* spirit from God came to Saul, David would take the harp and play *it* with his hand; and Saul would be refreshed and be well, and the evil spirit would depart from him.

17 NOW the Philistines gathered their armies for battle; and they were gathered at Socoh which belongs to Judah, and they camped between Socoh and Azekah, in Ephes-dammim.

2 Saul and the men of Israel were gathered and camped in the valley of Elah, and drew up in battle array to encounter the Philistines.

3 The Philistines stood on the mountain on one side while Israel stood on the mountain on the other side, with the valley between them.

4 Then a champion came out from the armies of the Philistines named Goliath, from Gath, whose height was six cubits and a span.

5 *He had* a bronze helmet on his head, and he was clothed with scale-armor which weighed five thousand shekels of bronze.

6 *He* also *had* bronze greaves on his legs and a bronze javelin *slung* between his shoulders.

7 The shaft of his spear was like a weaver's beam, and the head of his spear *weighed* six hundred shekels of iron; his shield-carrier also walked before him.

8 He stood and shouted to the ranks of Israel and said to them, "Why do you come out to draw up in battle array? Am I not the Philistine and you servants of Saul? Choose a man for yourselves and let him come down to me.

9 "If he is able to fight with me and kill me, then we will become your servants; but if I prevail against him and kill him, then you shall become our servants and serve us."

10 Again the Philistine said, "I defy the ranks of Israel this day; give me a man that we may fight together."

11 When Saul and all Israel heard these words of the Philistine, they were dismayed and greatly afraid.

12 Now David was the son of the Ephrathite of Bethlehem in Judah, whose name was Jesse, and he had eight sons. And Jesse was old in the days of Saul, advanced *in years* among men.

13 The three older sons of Jesse had gone after Saul to the battle. And the names of his three sons who went to the battle were Eliab the firstborn, and the second to him Abinadab, and the third Shammah.

14 David was the youngest. Now the three oldest followed Saul,

15 but David went back and forth from Saul to tend his father's flock at Bethlehem.

16 The Philistine came forward morning and evening for forty days and took his stand.

17 Then Jesse said to David his son, "Take now for your brothers an ephah of this roasted grain and these ten loaves and run to the camp to your brothers.

18 "Bring also these ten cuts of cheese to the commander of *their* thousand, and look into the welfare of your brothers, and bring back news of them.

19 "For Saul and they and all the men of Israel are in the valley of Elah, fighting with the Philistines."

20 So David arose early in the morning and left the flock with a keeper and took *the supplies* and went as Jesse had commanded him. And he came to the circle of the camp while the army was going out in battle array shouting the war cry.

21 Israel and the Philistines drew up in battle array, army against army.

22 Then David left his baggage in the care of the baggage keeper, and ran to the battle line and entered in order to greet his brothers.

23 As he was talking with them, behold, the champion, the Philistine from Gath named Goliath, was coming up from the army of the Philistines, and he spoke

these same words; and David heard *them.*

24 When all the men of Israel saw the man, they fled from him and were greatly afraid.

25 The men of Israel said, "Have you seen this man who is coming up? Surely he is coming up to defy Israel. And it will be that the king will enrich the man who kills him with great riches and will give him his daughter and make his father's house free in Israel."

26 Then David spoke to the men who were standing by him, saying, "What will be done for the man who kills this Philistine and takes away the reproach from Israel? For who is this uncircumcised Philistine, that he should taunt the armies of the living God?"

27 The people answered him in accord with this word, saying, "Thus it will be done for the man who kills him."

28 Now Eliab his oldest brother heard when he spoke to the men; and Eliab's anger burned against David and he said, "Why have you come down? And with whom have you left those few sheep in the wilderness? I know your insolence and the wickedness of your heart; for you have come down in order to see the battle."

29 But David said, "What have I done now? Was it not just a question?"

30 Then he turned away from him to another and said the same thing; and the people answered the same thing as before.

31 When the words which David spoke were heard, they told *them* to Saul, and he sent for him.

32 David said to Saul, "Let no man's heart fail on account of him; your servant will go and fight with this Philistine."

➤ 33 Then Saul said to David, "You are not able to go against this Philistine to fight with him; for you are *but* a youth while he has been a warrior from his youth."

34 But David said to Saul, "Your servant was tending his father's sheep. When a lion or a bear came and took a lamb from the flock,

35 I went out after him and attacked him, and rescued *it* from his mouth; and when he rose up against me, I seized *him*

by his beard and struck him and killed him.

36 "Your servant has killed both the lion and the bear; and this uncircumcised Philistine will be like one of them, since he has taunted the armies of the living God."

37 And David said, "The LORD who delivered me from the paw of the lion and from the paw of the bear, He will deliver me from the hand of this Philistine." And Saul said to David, "Go, and may the LORD be with you."

38 Then Saul clothed David with his garments, and put a bronze helmet on his head, and he clothed him with armor.

39 David girded his sword over his armor and tried to walk, for he had not tested *them.* So David said to Saul, "I cannot go with these, for I have not tested *them.*" And David took them off.

40 He took his stick in his hand and chose for himself five smooth stones from the brook, and put them in the shepherd's bag which he had, even in *his* pouch, and his sling was in his hand; and he approached the Philistine.

41 Then the Philistine came on and approached David, with the shield-bearer in front of him.

42 When the Philistine looked and saw David, he disdained him; for he was *but* a youth, and ruddy, with a handsome appearance.

43 The Philistine said to David, "Am I a dog, that you come to me with sticks?" And the Philistine cursed David by his gods.

44 The Philistine also said to David, "Come to me, and I will give your flesh to the birds of the sky and the beasts of the field."

LIFE LESSONS

➤ **1 Samuel 17:33 — *"You are not able to go against this Philistine to fight with him."***

Saul had trained himself to look at things only through the eyes of the flesh; he had forgotten how to see with eyes of faith. But trusting God means looking beyond what we can see to what He sees. David knew the Lord would be victorious and, because of it, he proceeded with confidence.

ANSWERS TO LIFE'S QUESTIONS

What role does faith play in doing great things for God?

1 SAMUEL 17

Faith is *believing God will do as He has promised*. It is not a power. It's not something we have to drum up inside ourselves. Faith is trusting that God will honor His promises.

The famous story of David and Goliath illustrates this well. The armies of Israel had lined up on one side of the valley, while the Philistines had lined up on the other. Every day the giant warrior, Goliath, would walk down into the valley and taunt the armies of Israel.

One day young David arrived on the scene with a fresh outlook. Notice what he said when he heard Goliath's arrogant threats: "Who is this uncircumcised Philistine, that he should taunt the armies of the living God?" (1 Sam. 17:26).

David didn't see Goliath as merely the enemy of Israel. He saw him as *God's enemy*— and David knew that God could take Goliath out of the picture with no problem. So he acted on his faith.

Hundreds, maybe even thousands, of Israelite soldiers had greater training to do battle with Goliath than David. But they responded to the giant's threats with paralyzing fear, stress, and anxious frustration. David, on the other hand, didn't seem upset at all. Why? Because he knew it was God's battle, not his. Apart from the Lord, he knew he didn't stand a chance. But with the help of the Lord, he knew everything would turn out all right.

Neither David nor the soldiers of Israel had the natural ability to defeat the giant. But while one party focused on its inability—and therefore panicked—the other party focused on God's provision—and therefore remained confident. The only difference was focus.

David did *exactly what he knew how to do, while trusting God to do the rest.* That is what living by faith boils down to: living in the confidence that God is supremely faithful to keep His word. So David gathered a few stones, walked down into the valley, and carried on a short but direct exchange with Goliath. Then he loaded his sling and fired the one shot that changed his life and the course of Israel's future. Once that stone left David's sling, God stepped in to do what only He could do. And Goliath went down in defeat.

Friend, that is faith in action! And it is how great triumphs originate and conclude.

---

45 Then David said to the Philistine, "You come to me with a sword, a spear, and a javelin, but I come to you in the name of the LORD of hosts, the God of the armies of Israel, whom you have taunted.

46 "This day the LORD will deliver you up into my hands, and I will strike you down and remove your head from you. And I will give the dead bodies of the army of the Philistines this day to the birds of the sky and the wild beasts of the earth, that all the earth may know that there is a God in Israel,

47 and that all this assembly may know that the LORD does not deliver by sword or by spear; for the battle is the LORD's and He will give you into our hands."

48 Then it happened when the Philistine rose and came and drew near to meet David, that David ran quickly toward the battle line to meet the Philistine.

49 And David put his hand into his bag and took from it a stone and slung *it*, and struck the Philistine on his forehead.

And the stone sank into his forehead, so that he fell on his face to the ground.

50 Thus David prevailed over the Philistine with a sling and a stone, and he struck the Philistine and killed him; but there was no sword in David's hand.

51 Then David ran and stood over the Philistine and took his sword and drew it out of its sheath and killed him, and cut

LIFE LESSONS

➤ **1 Samuel 17:45 —** *"You come to me with a sword, a spear, and a javelin, ?but I come to you in the name of the LORD of hosts, the God of the armies of Israel, whom you have taunted."*

A sword, a spear, and a javelin are no match for an active faith in the living Lord. As Isaiah 54:17 affirms, "No weapon that is formed against you will prosper . . . this is the heritage of the servants of the LORD." David knew God was with him, and already he had seen what His presence could accomplish. So he voiced his confidence, to the glory of the Lord.

off his head with it. When the Philistines saw that their champion was dead, they fled.
52 The men of Israel and Judah arose and shouted and pursued the Philistines as far as the valley, and to the gates of Ekron. And the slain Philistines lay along the way to Shaaraim, even to Gath and Ekron.
53 The sons of Israel returned from chasing the Philistines and plundered their camps.
54 Then David took the Philistine's head and brought it to Jerusalem, but he put his weapons in his tent.
55 Now when Saul saw David going out against the Philistine, he said to Abner the commander of the army, "Abner, whose son is this young man?" And Abner said, "By your life, O king, I do not know."
56 The king said, "You inquire whose son the youth is."
57 So when David returned from killing the Philistine, Abner took him and brought him before Saul with the Philistine's head in his hand.
58 Saul said to him, "Whose son are you, young man?" And David answered, "I am the son of your servant Jesse the Bethlehemite."

Psalm 57:4–11

4   My soul is among lions;
    I must lie among those who breathe
       forth fire,
    Even the sons of men, whose teeth
       are spears and arrows
    And their tongue a sharp sword.
5   Be exalted above the heavens,
      O God;
    Let Your glory *be* above all the earth.
6   They have prepared a net for my
      steps;
    My soul is bowed down;
    They dug a pit before me;
    They *themselves* have fallen into
       the midst of it.   Selah.
7   My heart is steadfast, O God, my
      heart is steadfast;
    I will sing, yes, I will sing praises!
8   Awake, my glory!
    Awake, harp and lyre!
    I will awaken the dawn.

9   I will give thanks to You, O Lord,
      among the peoples;
    I will sing praises to You among the
      nations.
10 For Your lovingkindness is great to
      the heavens
    And Your truth to the clouds.
11 Be exalted above the heavens,
      O God;
    Let Your glory *be* above all the
      earth.

Proverbs 15:26

26 Evil plans are an abomination to the
    LORD,
    But pleasant words are pure.

Luke 23:26–56

26 When they led Him away, they seized a man, Simon of Cyrene, coming in from the country, and placed on him the cross to carry behind Jesus.
27 And following Him was a large crowd of the people, and of women who were mourning and lamenting Him.
28 But Jesus turning to them said, "Daughters of Jerusalem, stop weeping for Me, but weep for yourselves and for your children.
29 "For behold, the days are coming when they will say, 'Blessed are the barren, and the wombs that never bore, and the breasts that never nursed.'
30 "Then they will begin TO SAY TO THE MOUNTAINS, 'FALL ON US,' AND TO THE HILLS, 'COVER US.'
31 "For if they do these things when the tree is green, what will happen when it is dry?"
32 Two others also, who were criminals, were being led away to be put to death with Him.
33 When they came to the place called The Skull, there they crucified Him and the criminals, one on the right and the other on the left.
34 But Jesus was saying, "Father, forgive them; for they do not know what they are doing." And they cast lots, dividing up His garments among themselves.
35 And the people stood by, looking

on. And even the rulers were sneering at Him, saying, "He saved others; let Him save Himself if this is the Christ of God, His Chosen One."

36 The soldiers also mocked Him, coming up to Him, offering Him sour wine,

37 and saying, "If You are the King of the Jews, save Yourself!"

38 Now there was also an inscription above Him, "THIS IS THE KING OF THE JEWS."

39 One of the criminals who were hanged *there* was hurling abuse at Him, saying, "Are You not the Christ? Save Yourself and us!"

40 But the other answered, and rebuking him said, "Do you not even fear God, since you are under the same sentence of condemnation?

41 "And we indeed *are suffering* justly, for we are receiving what we deserve for our deeds; but this man has done nothing wrong."

42 And he was saying, "Jesus, remember me when You come in Your kingdom!"

43 And He said to him, "Truly I say to you, today you shall be with Me in Paradise."

44 It was now about the sixth hour, and darkness fell over the whole land until the ninth hour,

45 because the sun was obscured; and the veil of the temple was torn in two.

46 And Jesus, crying out with a loud voice, said, "Father, INTO YOUR HANDS I COMMIT MY SPIRIT." Having said this, He breathed His last.

47 Now when the centurion saw what had happened, he *began* praising God, saying, "Certainly this man was innocent."

48 And all the crowds who came together for this spectacle, when they observed what had happened, *began* to return, beating their breasts.

49 And all His acquaintances and the women who accompanied Him from Gal-

ilee were standing at a distance, seeing these things.

50 And a man named Joseph, who was a member of the Council, a good and righteous man

51 (he had not consented to their plan and action), *a man* from Arimathea, a city of the Jews, who was waiting for the kingdom of God;

52 this man went to Pilate and asked for the body of Jesus.

53 And he took it down and wrapped it in a linen cloth, and laid Him in a tomb cut into the rock, where no one had ever lain.

54 It was the preparation day, and the Sabbath was about to begin.

55 Now the women who had come with Him out of Galilee followed, and saw the tomb and how His body was laid.

56 Then they returned and prepared spices and perfumes.

And on the Sabbath they rested according to the commandment.

LIFE LESSONS

> Luke 23:43 — *"Today you shall be with Me in Paradise."*

One thief had a change of heart while on the Cross, and Jesus accepted his expression of faith as genuine. Did the thief deserve such mercy? No. None of us do. But the point is that God's grace saves us, not our merit.

> Luke 23:55 — *Now the women who had come with Him out of Galilee followed, and saw the tomb and how His body was laid.*

People who want to discredit the Resurrection have at times claimed the disciples went to the wrong grave. But this verse shows that the women carefully noted which tomb held Jesus' body.

---

1 Samuel 18:1—19:24

18 NOW it came about when he had finished speaking to Saul, that the soul of Jonathan was knit to the soul of David, and Jonathan loved him as himself.

2 Saul took him that day and did not let him return to his father's house.

3 Then Jonathan made a covenant with David because he loved him as himself.

4 Jonathan stripped himself of the robe that was on him and gave it to David, with his armor, including his sword and his bow and his belt.

5 So David went out wherever Saul sent him, *and* prospered; and Saul set him over the men of war. And it was pleasing in the sight of all the people and also in the sight of Saul's servants.

6 It happened as they were coming, when David returned from killing the Philistine, that the women came out of all the cities of Israel, singing and dancing, to meet King Saul, with tambourines, with joy and with musical instruments.

7 The women sang as they played, and said,

"Saul has slain his thousands,
And David his ten thousands."

➤ 8 Then Saul became very angry, for this saying displeased him; and he said, "They have ascribed to David ten thousands, but to me they have ascribed thousands. Now what more can he have but the kingdom?"

9 Saul looked at David with suspicion from that day on.

10 Now it came about on the next day that an evil spirit from God came mightily upon Saul, and he raved in the midst of the house, while David was playing *the harp* with his hand, as usual; and a spear *was* in Saul's hand.

11 Saul hurled the spear for he thought,

LIFE LESSONS

➤ **1 Samuel 18:1 —** *The soul of Jonathan was knit to the soul of David.*

*J*onathan recognized in David a kindred spirit, a man who loved the Lord wholeheartedly, as he did. Their close friendship blessed not only themselves but also eventually all of Israel. We need each other to move forward in faith.

➤ **1 Samuel 18:8 —** *"They have ascribed to David ten thousands, but to me they have ascribed thousands."*

*I*nstead of dwelling on the great deliverance God had just brought about through David, Saul focused on what he considered a slight to himself. This burning jealousy eventually consumed Saul, ultimately leading to the destruction of his life and family.

"I will pin David to the wall." But David escaped from his presence twice.

12 Now Saul was afraid of David, for the LORD was with him but had departed from Saul.

13 Therefore Saul removed him from his presence and appointed him as his commander of a thousand; and he went out and came in before the people.

14 David was prospering in all his ways for the LORD *was* with him.

15 When Saul saw that he was prospering greatly, he dreaded him.

16 But all Israel and Judah loved David, and he went out and came in before them.

✳

17 Then Saul said to David, "Here is my older daughter Merab; I will give her to you as a wife, only be a valiant man for me and fight the LORD'S battles." For Saul thought, "My hand shall not be against him, but let the hand of the Philistines be against him."

18 But David said to Saul, "Who am I, and what is my life *or* my father's family in Israel, that I should be the king's son-in-law?"

19 So it came about at the time when Merab, Saul's daughter, should have been given to David, that she was given to Adriel the Meholathite for a wife.

20 Now Michal, Saul's daughter, loved David. When they told Saul, the thing was agreeable to him.

21 Saul thought, "I will give her to him that she may become a snare to him, and that the hand of the Philistines may be against him." Therefore Saul said to David, "For a second time you may be my son-in-law today."

22 Then Saul commanded his servants, "Speak to David secretly, saying, 'Behold, the king delights in you, and all his servants love you; now therefore, become the king's son-in-law.'"

23 So Saul's servants spoke these words to David. But David said, "Is it trivial in your sight to become the king's son-in-law, since I am a poor man and lightly esteemed?"

24 The servants of Saul reported to him according to these words *which* David spoke.

25 Saul then said, "Thus you shall say to David, 'The king does not desire any dowry except a hundred foreskins of the Philistines, to take vengeance on the

Life Examples:

The Deadliness of Anger

1 SAMUEL 18

*F*ew people in Scripture exhibited as much anger as King Saul. His anger seemed to erupt when David returned from battle and the women greeted him with this song: "Saul has slain his thousands, and David his ten thousands." Scripture tells us, "Saul became very angry, for this saying displeased him" (1 Sam. 18:7, 8).

In his anger and jealousy, Saul:
- Twice threw his spear at David, trying to pin him to the wall (1 Sam. 18:10, 11; 19:9, 10).
- Put David in a position of authority, hoping that he would fail to lead wisely and thus be discredited (1 Sam. 18:12–15).
- Required that David kill one hundred Philistines before he would give him his daughter in marriage, hoping that David would die while fighting the Philistines (1 Sam. 18:25–29).
- Pursued David continually for more than a decade, forcing him to live in exile and move frequently from hiding place to hiding place (1 Sam. 24; 26).

Not only did Saul pursue David without mercy, he also ordered the murder of those who helped David. He even turned on his own son with murderous intent (1 Sam. 20:30). Saul's anger had no end.

It is easy to see anger at work in a person such as Saul. Boiling rage results in violent outbursts that manifest themselves repeatedly over time. The angry person often has visible changes in physical appearance, such as dilated eyes and tense muscles. Internally, blood pressure rises, and the stomach feels as if it is tied in knots.

It is far more difficult to recognize anger in ourselves. We tend to tolerate a great deal of anger in our personal lives. Some even see anger as a sign of strength or power.

God's Word, however, forbids such an ungodly tolerance for anger. Such anger damages emotional health and wellbeing, hampering spiritual growth and witness. God closely links "wrath" with the work of the evil one in our lives. So Scripture admonishes us clearly: "Do not let the sun go down on your anger, and do not give the devil an opportunity" (Eph. 4:26, 27).

---

king's enemies.'" Now Saul planned to make David fall by the hand of the Philistines.

26 When his servants told David these words, it pleased David to become the king's son-in-law. Before the days had expired

27 David rose up and went, he and his men, and struck down two hundred men among the Philistines. Then David brought their foreskins, and they gave them in full number to the king, that he might become the king's son-in-law. So Saul gave him Michal his daughter for a wife.

28 When Saul saw and knew that the LORD was with David, and *that* Michal, Saul's daughter, loved him,

29 then Saul was even more afraid of David. Thus Saul was David's enemy continually.

30 Then the commanders of the Philistines went out *to battle,* and it happened as often as they went out, that David behaved himself more wisely than all the servants of Saul. So his name was highly esteemed.

19 NOW Saul told Jonathan his son and all his servants to put David to death. But Jonathan, Saul's son, greatly delighted in David.

2 So Jonathan told David saying, "Saul my father is seeking to put you to death. Now therefore, please be on guard in the morning, and stay in a secret place and hide yourself.

3 "I will go out and stand beside my father in the field where you are, and I will speak with my father about you; if I find out anything, then I will tell you."

4 Then Jonathan spoke well of David to Saul his father and said to him, "Do not let the king sin against his servant David, since he has not sinned against you, and since his deeds *have been* very beneficial to you.

5 "For he took his life in his hand and struck the Philistine, and the LORD brought about a great deliverance for all Israel; you saw *it* and rejoiced. Why then will you sin against innocent blood by putting David to death without a cause?"

6 Saul listened to the voice of Jonathan, and Saul vowed, "As the LORD lives, he shall not be put to death."

7 Then Jonathan called David, and Jonathan told him all these words. And

Jonathan brought David to Saul, and he was in his presence as formerly.

8 When there was war again, David went out and fought with the Philistines and defeated them with great slaughter, so that they fled before him.

9 Now there was an evil spirit from the LORD on Saul as he was sitting in his house with his spear in his hand, and David was playing *the harp* with *his* hand.

10 Saul tried to pin David to the wall with the spear, but he slipped away out of Saul's presence, so that he stuck the spear into the wall. And David fled and escaped that night.

11 Then Saul sent messengers to David's house to watch him, in order to put him to death in the morning. But Michal, David's wife, told him, saying, "If you do not save your life tonight, tomorrow you will be put to death."

12 So Michal let David down through a window, and he went out and fled and escaped.

13 Michal took the household idol and laid *it* on the bed, and put a quilt of goats' *hair* at its head, and covered *it* with clothes.

14 When Saul sent messengers to take David, she said, "He is sick."

15 Then Saul sent messengers to see David, saying, "Bring him up to me on his bed, that I may put him to death."

16 When the messengers entered, behold, the household idol *was* on the bed with the quilt of goats' *hair* at its head.

17 So Saul said to Michal, "Why have you deceived me like this and let my enemy go, so that he has escaped?" And Michal said to Saul, "He said to me, 'Let me go! Why should I put you to death?'"

18 Now David fled and escaped and came to Samuel at Ramah, and told him all that Saul had done to him. And he and Samuel went and stayed in Naioth.

19 It was told Saul, saying, "Behold, David is at Naioth in Ramah."

➤ 20 Then Saul sent messengers to take David, but when they saw the company of the prophets prophesying, with Samuel standing *and* presiding over them, the Spirit of God came upon the messengers of Saul; and they also prophesied.

21 When it was told Saul, he sent other messengers, and they also prophesied. So Saul sent messengers again the third time, and they also prophesied.

LIFE LESSONS

➤ **1 Samuel 19:20 — *The Spirit of God came upon the messengers of Saul; and they also prophesied.***

*G*od protects His children in the most surprising ways. He does not need weapons of war or fast horses; He can cause even our mortal enemies to act in ways contrary to their nature because He is absolutely sovereign!

---

22 Then he himself went to Ramah and came as far as the large well that is in Secu; and he asked and said, "Where are Samuel and David?" And *someone* said, "Behold, they are at Naioth in Ramah."

23 He proceeded there to Naioth in Ramah; and the Spirit of God came upon him also, so that he went along prophesying continually until he came to Naioth in Ramah.

24 He also stripped off his clothes, and he too prophesied before Samuel and lay down naked all that day and all that night. Therefore they say, "Is Saul also among the prophets?"

 Psalm 58:1–11

For the choir director; *set to* Al-tashheth.
A Mikhtam of David.

58 DO you indeed speak
righteousness, O gods?
Do you judge uprightly, O sons of men?

2 No, in heart you work unrighteousness;
On earth you weigh out the violence of your hands.

3 The wicked are estranged from the womb;
These who speak lies go astray from birth.

4 They have venom like the venom of a serpent;
Like a deaf cobra that stops up its ear,

5 So that it does not hear the voice of charmers,
Or a skillful caster of spells.

6 O God, shatter their teeth in their mouth;
Break out the fangs of the young lions, O LORD.

7 Let them flow away like water that
   runs off;
   When he aims his arrows, let them
   be as headless shafts.
8 *Let them be* as a snail which melts
   away as it goes along,
   Like the miscarriages of a woman
   which never see the sun.
9 Before your pots can feel *the fire of*
   thorns
   He will sweep them away with a
   whirlwind, the green and the
   burning alike.
10 The righteous will rejoice when he
   sees the vengeance;
   He will wash his feet in the blood of
   the wicked.
11 And men will say, "Surely there is a
   reward for the righteous;
   Surely there is a God who judges on
   earth!"

Proverbs 15:27–30

27 He who profits illicitly troubles his
   own house,
   But he who hates bribes will live.
28 The heart of the righteous ponders
   how to answer,
   But the mouth of the wicked pours
   out evil things.
29 The LORD is far from the wicked,
   But He hears the prayer of the
   righteous.
30 Bright eyes gladden the heart;
   Good news puts fat on the bones.

Luke 24:1–35

24 BUT on the first day of the week,
   at early dawn, they came to the
tomb bringing the spices which they had
prepared.
2 And they found the stone rolled
away from the tomb,
3 but when they entered, they did not
find the body of the Lord Jesus.
4 While they were perplexed about
this, behold, two men suddenly stood
near them in dazzling clothing;
5 and as *the women* were terrified and
bowed their faces to the ground, *the men*

said to them, "Why do you seek the living One among the dead?
6 "He is not here, but He has risen. Remember how He spoke to you while He
was still in Galilee,
7 saying that the Son of Man must be
delivered into the hands of sinful men, and
be crucified, and the third day rise again."
8 And they remembered His words,
9 and returned from the tomb and reported all these things to the eleven and
to all the rest.
10 Now they were Mary Magdalene and
Joanna and Mary the *mother* of James;
also the other women with them were
telling these things to the apostles.
11 But these words appeared to them
as nonsense, and they would not believe
them.
12 But Peter got up and ran to the tomb;
stooping and looking in, he *saw the linen
wrappings only; and he went away to his
home, marveling at what had happened.
13 And behold, two of them were going
that very day to a village named Em-
maus, which was about seven miles from
Jerusalem.
14 And they were talking with each
other about all these things which had
taken place.
15 While they were talking and discussing, Jesus Himself approached and
began traveling with them.
16 But their eyes were prevented from
recognizing Him.
17 And He said to them, "What are
these words that you are exchanging
with one another as you are walking?"
And they stood still, looking sad.
18 One *of them,* named Cleopas, an-

LIFE LESSONS

➤ **Luke 24:16 — *But their eyes were prevented from recognizing Him.***

In many accounts of the post-
resurrection appearances of Jesus,
the disciples did not at first recognize
the Lord. It took some real convincing to
get the disciples to believe Jesus really
had risen from the dead. Usually it took
hearing His voice or seeing Him perform
some recognizable action to open their
eyes. Only after they became convinced
of its truth did they become powerhouse
witnesses for Christ.

swered and said to Him, "Are You the only one visiting Jerusalem and unaware of the things which have happened here in these days?"

19 And He said to them, "What things?" And they said to Him, "The things about Jesus the Nazarene, who was a prophet mighty in deed and word in the sight of God and all the people,

20 and how the chief priests and our rulers delivered Him to the sentence of death, and crucified Him.

21 "But we were hoping that it was He who was going to redeem Israel. Indeed, besides all this, it is the third day since these things happened.

22 "But also some women among us amazed us. When they were at the tomb early in the morning,

23 and did not find His body, they came, saying that they had also seen a vision of angels who said that He was alive.

24 "Some of those who were with us went to the tomb and found it just exactly as the women also had said; but Him they did not see."

25 And He said to them, "O foolish men and slow of heart to believe in all that the prophets have spoken!

26 "Was it not necessary for the Christ to suffer these things and to enter into His glory?"

27 Then beginning with Moses and with all the prophets, He explained to them the things concerning Himself in all the Scriptures.

28 And they approached the village where they were going, and He acted as though He were going farther.

29 But they urged Him, saying, "Stay with us, for it is *getting* toward evening, and the day is now nearly over." So He went in to stay with them.

30 When He had reclined *at the table* with them, He took the bread and blessed *it*, and breaking *it*, He *began* giving *it* to them.

31 Then their eyes were opened and they recognized Him; and He vanished from their sight.

32 They said to one another, "Were not our hearts burning within us while He was speaking to us on the road, and He was explaining the Scriptures to us?"

33 And they got up that very hour and returned to Jerusalem, and found gathered together the eleven and those who were with them,

34 saying, "The Lord has really risen and has appeared to Simon."

35 They *began* to relate their experiences on the road and how He was recognized by them in the breaking of the bread.

◈ 1 Samuel 20:1—21:15

20 THEN David fled from Naioth in Ramah, and came and said to Jonathan, "What have I done? What is my iniquity? And what is my sin before your father, that he is seeking my life?"

2 He said to him, "Far from it, you shall not die. Behold, my father does nothing either great or small without disclosing it to me. So why should my father hide this thing from me? It is not so!"

3 Yet David vowed again, saying, "Your father knows well that I have found favor in your sight, and he has said, 'Do not let Jonathan know this, or he will be grieved.' But truly as the

LORD lives and as your soul lives, there is hardly a step between me and death."

4 Then Jonathan said to David, "Whatever you say, I will do for you."

5 So David said to Jonathan, "Behold, tomorrow is the new moon, and I ought to sit down to eat with the king. But let me go, that I may hide myself in the field until the third evening.

6 "If your father misses me at all, then say, 'David earnestly asked *leave* of me to run to Bethlehem his city, because it is the yearly sacrifice there for the whole family.'

7 "If he says, 'It is good,' your servant *will be* safe; but if he is very angry, know that he has decided on evil.

8 "Therefore deal kindly with your servant, for you have brought your servant

into a covenant of the LORD with you. But if there is iniquity in me, put me to death yourself; for why then should you bring me to your father?"

9 Jonathan said, "Far be it from you! For if I should indeed learn that evil has been decided by my father to come upon you, then would I not tell you about it?"

10 Then David said to Jonathan, "Who will tell me if your father answers you harshly?"

11 Jonathan said to David, "Come, and let us go out into the field." So both of them went out to the field.

➤ 12 Then Jonathan said to David, "The LORD, the God of Israel, be witness! When I have sounded out my father about this time tomorrow, or the third day, behold, if there is good feeling toward David, shall I not then send to you and make it known to you?

13 "If it please my father to do you harm, may the LORD do so to Jonathan and more also, if I do not make it known to you and send you away, that you may go in safety. And may the LORD be with you as He has been with my father.

14 "If I am still alive, will you not show me the lovingkindness of the LORD, that I may not die?

15 "You shall not cut off your lovingkindness from my house forever, not even when the LORD cuts off every one of the enemies of David from the face of the earth."

16 So Jonathan made a covenant with the house of David, saying, "May the LORD require it at the hands of David's enemies."

17 Jonathan made David vow again because of his love for him, because he loved him as he loved his own life.

18 Then Jonathan said to him, "Tomorrow is the new moon, and you will be missed because your seat will be empty.

19 "When you have stayed for three days, you shall go down quickly and come to the place where you hid yourself on that eventful day, and you shall remain by the stone Ezel.

20 "I will shoot three arrows to the side, as though I shot at a target.

21 "And behold, I will send the lad, saying, 'Go, find the arrows.' If I specifically say to the lad, 'Behold, the arrows are on this side of you, get them,' then come; for there is safety for you and no harm, as the LORD lives.

22 "But if I say to the youth, 'Behold, the arrows are beyond you,' go, for the LORD has sent you away.

23 "As for the agreement of which you and I have spoken, behold, the LORD is between you and me forever."

24 So David hid in the field; and when the new moon came, the king sat down to eat food.

25 The king sat on his seat as usual, the seat by the wall; then Jonathan rose up and Abner sat down by Saul's side, but David's place was empty.

26 Nevertheless Saul did not speak anything that day, for he thought, "It is an accident, he is not clean, surely he is not clean."

27 It came about the next day, the second day of the new moon, that David's place was empty; so Saul said to Jonathan his son, "Why has the son of Jesse not come to the meal, either yesterday or today?"

28 Jonathan then answered Saul, "David earnestly asked leave of me to go to Bethlehem,

29 for he said, 'Please let me go, since our family has a sacrifice in the city, and my brother has commanded me to attend. And now, if I have found favor in your sight, please let me get away that I may see my brothers.' For this reason he has not come to the king's table."

30 Then Saul's anger burned against Jonathan and he said to him, "You son of a perverse, rebellious woman! Do I not know that you are choosing the son of Jesse to your own shame and to the shame of your mother's nakedness?

31 "For as long as the son of Jesse lives on the earth, neither you nor your kingdom will be established. Therefore now, send and bring him to me, for he must surely die."

32 But Jonathan answered Saul his fa-

LIFE LESSONS

➤ 1 Samuel 20:12, 13 — "The LORD, the God of Israel, be witness!"

Jonathan cast his entire friendship with David in spiritual terms, making the Lord the centerpiece of their relationship. That is always the way to the closest and best of friendships.

WHAT THE BIBLE SAYS ABOUT ◈

The Need for Christian Friendship

1 Samuel 20

*A*dversity often brings us face-to-face with our need to associate with a different group of people. Perhaps we need to sever ties with others. Perhaps we need new friends. Perhaps we need to align ourselves more closely with Christian believers.

God made us for fellowship, communication with other human beings, and communication with Himself. None of us were designed to go it alone. We need other people, and they need us.

At times, however, we make unwise associations. We choose the wrong friend, employer, partner, or employee. And inevitably, our bad choices bring us adversity.

David and Jonathan provide us with a good model for true friendship. Jonathan's love for his friend caused him to act in several specific ways:

- He warned David of possible danger (1 Sam. 19:1–3).
- He spoke well of David, even to a person who considered David an enemy and who was angry with Jonathan for having David as a friend (1 Sam. 19:4, 5).
- He sought to do what David needed him to do (1 Sam. 20:4).
- He risked his life in defending David (1 Sam. 20:30–33).
- He helped David escape death (1 Sam. 20:35–42).

Jonathan voiced one of the greatest statements of friendship in the Bible when he said to David, "Go in safety, inasmuch as we have sworn to each other in the name of the LORD, saying, 'The LORD will be between me and you, and between my descendants and your descendants forever'" (1 Sam. 20:42). Now *that's* friendship!

Paul describes Christian friendship in what we have come to call the love chapter of the Bible, 1 Corinthians 13. He describes Christian friendship as: patient, kind, and humble (v. 4); polite, selfless, unruffled, and positive (v. 5); magnanimous and rooted in truth (v. 6); and supportive, hopeful, and enduring (v. 7).

Such love, Paul said, "never fails" (v. 8). And such friendships are divine blessings in our lives, God's rich rewards to us on this earth. ◈

---

ther and said to him, "Why should he be put to death? What has he done?"

33 Then Saul hurled his spear at him to strike him down; so Jonathan knew that his father had decided to put David to death.

34 Then Jonathan arose from the table in fierce anger, and did not eat food on the second day of the new moon, for he was grieved over David because his father had dishonored him.

35 Now it came about in the morning that Jonathan went out into the field for the appointment with David, and a little lad *was* with him.

36 He said to his lad, "Run, find now the arrows which I am about to shoot." As the lad was running, he shot an arrow past him.

37 When the lad reached the place of the arrow which Jonathan had shot, Jonathan called after the lad and said, "Is not the arrow beyond you?"

38 And Jonathan called after the lad, "Hurry, be quick, do not stay!" And

Jonathan's lad picked up the arrow and came to his master.

39 But the lad was not aware of anything; only Jonathan and David knew about the matter.

40 Then Jonathan gave his weapons to his lad and said to him, "Go, bring *them* to the city."

41 When the lad was gone, David rose from the south side and fell on his face to the ground, and bowed three times. And they kissed each other and wept together, but David *wept* the more.

42 Jonathan said to David, "Go in safety, inasmuch as we have sworn to each other in the name of the LORD, saying, 'The LORD will be between me and you, and between my descendants and your descendants forever.'" Then he rose and departed, while Jonathan went into the city.

21 THEN David came to Nob to Ahimelech the priest; and Ahimelech came trembling to meet David and said to him, "Why are you alone and no one with you?"

2 David said to Ahimelech the priest, "The king has commissioned me with a matter and has said to me, 'Let no one know anything about the matter on which I am sending you and with which I have commissioned you; and I have directed the young men to a certain place.' 3 "Now therefore, what do you have on hand? Give me five loaves of bread, or whatever can be found." 4 The priest answered David and said, "There is no ordinary bread on hand, but there is consecrated bread; if only the young men have kept themselves from women." 5 David answered the priest and said to him, "Surely women have been kept from us as previously when I set out and the vessels of the young men were holy, though it was an ordinary journey; how much more then today will their vessels be holy?" 6 So the priest gave him consecrated *bread;* for there was no bread there but the bread of the Presence which was removed from before the LORD, in order to put hot bread *in its place* when it was taken away. 7 Now one of the servants of Saul was there that day, detained before the LORD; and his name was Doeg the Edomite, the chief of Saul's shepherds. 8 David said to Ahimelech, "Now is there not a spear or a sword on hand? For I brought neither my sword nor my weapons with me, because the king's matter was urgent." 9 Then the priest said, "The sword of Goliath the Philistine, whom you killed in the valley of Elah, behold, it is wrapped in a cloth behind the ephod; if you would take it for yourself, take *it.* For there is no other except it here." And David said, "There is none like it; give it to me." 10 Then David arose and fled that day from Saul, and went to Achish king of Gath. 11 But the servants of Achish said to him, "Is this not David the king of the land? Did they not sing of this one as they danced, saying,

'Saul has slain his thousands,
And David his ten thousands'?"

12 David took these words to heart and greatly feared Achish king of Gath. 13 So he disguised his sanity before them, and acted insanely in their hands, and scribbled on the doors of the gate, and let his saliva run down into his beard. 14 Then Achish said to his servants, "Behold, you see the man behaving as a madman. Why do you bring him to me? 15 "Do I lack madmen, that you have brought this one to act the madman in my presence? Shall this one come into my house?"

Psalm 59:1–5

For the choir director; *set to* Al-tashheth. A Mikhtam of David, when Saul sent *men* and they watched the house in order to kill him.

59 DELIVER me from my enemies,
     O my God;
     Set me *securely* on high away from
       those who rise up against me.
2   Deliver me from those who do
       iniquity
     And save me from men of
       bloodshed.
3   For behold, they have set an
       ambush for my life;
     Fierce men launch an attack against
       me,
     Not for my transgression nor for my
       sin, O LORD,
4   For no guilt of *mine,* they run and
       set themselves against me.
     Arouse Yourself to help me, and see!
5   You, O LORD God of hosts, the God
       of Israel,
     Awake to punish all the nations;
     Do not be gracious to any *who are*
       treacherous in iniquity.   Selah.

Proverbs 15:31–33

31   He whose ear listens to the
       life-giving reproof
     Will dwell among the wise.
32   He who neglects discipline despises
       himself,
     But he who listens to reproof
       acquires understanding.
33   The fear of the LORD is the
       instruction for wisdom,
     And before honor *comes* humility.

Luke 24:36–53

36 While they were telling these things, He Himself stood in their *said to them, "Peace be to Yere seeing 37 But they were * fright-ened and thought Why are you a spirit. *ubts arise in 38 And He say My feet, that it troubled, and see, for a spirit your hearts *bones as you see 39 "See N is I Myse *ad said this, He does n *ds and His feet. that *ould not believe *it* 40 and amazement, He *you anything here to *n a piece of a broiled

*k it and ate *it* before

*e said to them, "These are My *nich I spoke to you while I was *with you, that all things which are *ritten about Me in the Law of Moses and the Prophets and the Psalms must be fulfilled."
45 Then He opened their minds to understand the Scriptures,
46 and He said to them, "Thus it is written, that the Christ would suffer and rise again from the dead the third day,
47 and that repentance for forgiveness of sins would be proclaimed in His name to all the nations, beginning from Jerusalem.
48 "You are witnesses of these things.
49 "And behold, I am sending forth the promise of My Father upon you; but you are to stay in the city until you are clothed with power from on high."
50 And He led them out as far as Bethany, and He lifted up His hands and blessed them.
51 While He was blessing them, He parted from them and was carried up into heaven.
52 And they, after worshiping Him, returned to Jerusalem with great joy,
53 and were continually in the temple praising God,

LIFE LESSONS

➤ **Luke 24:41 — *"Have you anything here to eat?"***

*J*esus had to prove to His unbelieving disciples that He was not a ghost and was not a figment of their imaginations before they would accept the truth of His bodily resurrection.

➤ **Luke 24:45 — *He opened their minds to understand the Scriptures.***

*T*he things of the Spirit of God are foolishness to the unbelieving natural man (1 Cor. 2:14). It always takes the Lord's wisdom and influence to help us understand and accept the truth of His Word.

1 Samuel 22:1—23:29

22 SO David departed from there and escaped to the cave of Adullam; and when his brothers and all his father's household heard *of it*, they went down there to him.
2 Everyone who was in distress, and everyone who was in debt, and everyone who was discontented gathered to him; and he became captain over them. Now there were about four hundred men with him.
3 And David went from there to Mizpah of Moab; and he said to the king of Moab, "Please let my father and my mother come *and stay* with you until I know what God will do for me."
4 Then he left them with the king of Moab; and they stayed with him all the time that David was in the stronghold.
5 The prophet Gad said to David, "Do not stay in the stronghold; depart, and go into the land of Judah." So David

---

---

departed and went into the forest of Hereth.

6   Then Saul heard that David and the men who were with him had been discovered. Now Saul was sitting in Gibeah, under the tamarisk tree on the height with his spear in his hand, and all his servants were standing around him.

7   Saul said to his servants who stood around him, "Hear now, O Benjamites! Will the son of Jesse also give to all of you fields and vineyards? Will he make you all commanders of thousands and commanders of hundreds?

8   "For all of you have conspired against me so that there is no one who discloses to me when my son makes *a covenant* with the son of Jesse, and there is none of you who is sorry for me or discloses to me that my son has stirred up my servant against me to lie in ambush, as *it is* this day."

9   Then Doeg the Edomite, who was standing by the servants of Saul, said, "I saw the son of Jesse coming to Nob, to Ahimelech the son of Ahitub.

10 "He inquired of the LORD for him, gave him provisions, and gave him the sword of Goliath the Philistine."

11   Then the king sent someone to summon Ahimelech the priest, the son of Ahitub, and all his father's household, the priests who were in Nob; and all of them came to the king.

12   Saul said, "Listen now, son of Ahitub." And he answered, "Here I am, my lord."

13   Saul then said to him, "Why have you and the son of Jesse conspired against me, in that you have given him bread and a sword and have inquired of God for him, so that he would rise up against me by lying in ambush as *it is* this day?"

14   Then Ahimelech answered the king

and sa[...]
servants "And who among all your
the king [...] faithful as David, even
over your [...] in-law, who is captain
house? [...]nd is honored in your
15 "Did I jus[...]nquire of God for
him today? Fa[...]me! Do not let
the king imput[...] his servant
or to any of the [...]y father,
for your servant [...]at all of
this whole affair." [...]
16   But the king sa[...]
die, Ahimelech, you a[...]
household!"

17   And the king said to[...]
were attending him, "T[...]
put the priests of the LORD[...]
cause their hand also is wi[...]
because they knew that he[...]
and did not reveal it to me." B[...]
vants of the king were not will[...]
forth their hands to attack the p[...]
the LORD.

18   Then the king said to Doeg,[...]
turn around and attack the priests."[...]
Doeg the Edomite turned around a[...]
attacked the priests, and he killed th[...]
day eighty-five men who wore the line[...]
ephod.

19   And he struck Nob the city of the[...]
priests with the edge of the sword, both men and women, children and infants; also oxen, donkeys, and sheep *he struck* with the edge of the sword.

20   But one son of Ahimelech the son of Ahitub, named Abiathar, escaped and fled after David.

21   Abiathar told David that Saul had killed the priests of the LORD.

22   Then David said to Abiathar, "I knew on that day, when Doeg the Edomite was there, that he would surely tell Saul. I have brought about *the death* of every person in your father's household.

23 "Stay with me; do not be afraid, for he who seeks my life seeks your life, for you are safe with me."

23 THEN they told David, saying, "Behold, the Philistines are fighting against Keilah and are plundering the threshing floors."

2   So David inquired of the LORD, saying, "Shall I go and attack these Philistines?" And the LORD said to David, "Go and attack the Philistines and deliver Keilah."

3   But David's men said to him, "Be-

Luke 24:36–53

36 While they were telling these things, He Himself stood in their midst and *said to them, "Peace be to you."

37 But they were startled and frightened and thought that they were seeing a spirit.

38 And He said to them, "Why are you troubled, and why do doubts arise in your hearts?

39 "See My hands and My feet, that it is I Myself; touch Me and see, for a spirit does not have flesh and bones as you see that I have."

40 And when He had said this, He showed them His hands and His feet.

➤ **41** While they still could not believe *it* because of their joy and amazement, He said to them, "Have you anything here to eat?"

42 They gave Him a piece of a broiled fish;

43 and He took it and ate *it* before them.

44 Now He said to them, "These are My words which I spoke to you while I was still with you, that all things which are written about Me in the Law of Moses and the Prophets and the Psalms must be fulfilled."

➤ **45** Then He opened their minds to understand the Scriptures,

✳ **46** and He said to them, "Thus it is written, that the Christ would suffer and rise again from the dead the third day,

47 and that repentance for forgiveness of sins would be proclaimed in His name to all the nations, beginning from Jerusalem.

48 "You are witnesses of these things.

49 "And behold, I am sending forth the promise of My Father upon you; but you are to stay in the city until you are clothed with power from on high."

50 And He led them out as far as Bethany, and He lifted up His hands and blessed them.

51 While He was blessing them, He parted from them and was carried up into heaven.

52 And they, after worshiping Him, returned to Jerusalem with great joy,

53 and were continually in the temple praising God,

LIFE LESSONS

➤ **Luke 24:41 —** *"Have you anything here to eat?"*

*J*esus had to prove to His unbelieving disciples that He was not a ghost and was not a figment of their imaginations before they would accept the truth of His bodily resurrection.

➤ **Luke 24:45 —** *He opened their minds to understand the Scriptures.*

*T*he things of the Spirit of God are foolishness to the unbelieving natural man (1 Cor. 2:14). It always takes the Lord's wisdom and influence to help us understand and accept the truth of His Word.

1 Samuel 22:1—23:29

22 SO David departed from there and escaped to the cave of Adullam; and when his brothers and all his father's household heard of *it,* they went down there to him.

2 Everyone who was in distress, and everyone who was in debt, and everyone who was discontented gathered to him; and he became captain over them. Now

there were about four hundred men with him.

3 And David went from there to Mizpah of Moab; and he said to the king of Moab, "Please let my father and my mother come *and stay* with you until I know what God will do for me."

4 Then he left them with the king of Moab; and they stayed with him all the time that David was in the stronghold.

5 The prophet Gad said to David, "Do not stay in the stronghold; depart, and go into the land of Judah." So David

LIFE LESSONS

➤ 1 Samuel 22:3 — *"Please let my father and my mother come and stay with you until I know what God will do for me."*

*W*hile David had the anointing of God, he did not have a detailed map of his future. So he trusted the Lord to lead him wisely in both the things he could do and the things he could not do.

departed and went into the forest of Hereth.

6 Then Saul heard that David and the men who were with him had been discovered. Now Saul was sitting in Gibeah, under the tamarisk tree on the height with his spear in his hand, and all his servants were standing around him.

7 Saul said to his servants who stood around him, "Hear now, O Benjamites! Will the son of Jesse also give to all of you fields and vineyards? Will he make you all commanders of thousands and commanders of hundreds?

8 "For all of you have conspired against me so that there is no one who discloses to me when my son makes *a covenant* with the son of Jesse, and there is none of you who is sorry for me or discloses to me that my son has stirred up my servant against me to lie in ambush, as *it is* this day."

9 Then Doeg the Edomite, who was standing by the servants of Saul, said, "I saw the son of Jesse coming to Nob, to Ahimelech the son of Ahitub.

10 "He inquired of the LORD for him, gave him provisions, and gave him the sword of Goliath the Philistine."

11 Then the king sent someone to summon Ahimelech the priest, the son of Ahitub, and all his father's household, the priests who were in Nob; and all of them came to the king.

12 Saul said, "Listen now, son of Ahitub." And he answered, "Here I am, my lord."

13 Saul then said to him, "Why have you and the son of Jesse conspired against me, in that you have given him bread and a sword and have inquired of God for him, so that he would rise up against me by lying in ambush as *it is* this day?"

14 Then Ahimelech answered the king and said, "And who among all your servants is as faithful as David, even the king's son-in-law, who is captain over your guard, and is honored in your house?

15 "Did I *just* begin to inquire of God for him today? Far be it from me! Do not let the king impute anything to his servant *or* to any of the household of my father, for your servant knows nothing at all of this whole affair."

16 But the king said, "You shall surely die, Ahimelech, you and all your father's household!"

17 And the king said to the guards who were attending him, "Turn around and put the priests of the LORD to death, because their hand also is with David and because they knew that he was fleeing and did not reveal it to me." But the servants of the king were not willing to put forth their hands to attack the priests of the LORD.

18 Then the king said to Doeg, "You turn around and attack the priests." And Doeg the Edomite turned around and attacked the priests, and he killed that day eighty-five men who wore the linen ephod.

19 And he struck Nob the city of the priests with the edge of the sword, both men and women, children and infants; also oxen, donkeys, and sheep *he struck* with the edge of the sword.

20 But one son of Ahimelech the son of Ahitub, named Abiathar, escaped and fled after David.

21 Abiathar told David that Saul had killed the priests of the LORD.

22 Then David said to Abiathar, "I knew on that day, when Doeg the Edomite was there, that he would surely tell Saul. I have brought about *the death* of every person in your father's household.

23 "Stay with me; do not be afraid, for he who seeks my life seeks your life, for you are safe with me."

23 THEN they told David, saying, "Behold, the Philistines are fighting against Keilah and are plundering the threshing floors."

2 So David inquired of the LORD, saying, "Shall I go and attack these Philistines?" And the LORD said to David, "Go and attack the Philistines and deliver Keilah."

3 But David's men said to him, "Be-

➤ **John 1:1** — *In the beginning was the Word, and the Word was with God, and the Word was God.*

*A*t the beginning of his Gospel, John tells us Jesus was far more than just a great teacher or a mighty prophet; in fact, He was God. Jesus is "the exact representation" of God's person (Heb. 1:3).

WHAT THE BIBLE SAYS ABOUT

The Important Message

John 1:1–18

*F*our hundred years of silence. It had been so long since God had spoken through one of His prophets, the people of Israel wondered if He would ever speak again—or if He had forgotten the covenants He'd established with their forefathers Abraham and David (Gen. 12:1–3; 15; 2 Sam. 7:8–16).

As happens with any pregnant pause or prolonged time of quiet, their ears strained in anticipation. They were hungry for a word.

So God sent *the* Word.

But this time, the Word came as it had never come before. "And the Word became flesh, and dwelt among us, and we saw His glory, glory as of the only begotten from the Father, full of grace and truth" (John 1:14).

The Word that had been with God in the creation of the world and all the life in it (Gen. 1; John 1:2, 3), now came to the world to offer a new covenant and a new life (Jer. 31:33; John 1:4).

During the 400 years of silence, God had readied the world for the Word to travel through it. Under the influence of Alexander the Great (356–323 B.C.), Greek—the language of science, medicine, and philosophy—made communicating the Word much easier than it had ever been. Also, because of the roads and general peace (Pax Romana) of the Roman Empire, missionaries could travel everywhere with less difficulty.

Finally, there were many times more Jews scattered throughout the Roman Empire than there were in Israel proper—giving evangelists synagogues and Jewish communities from

Him, and apart from Him nothing came into being that has come into being.
4 In Him was life, and the life was the Light of men.
5 The Light shines in the darkness, and the darkness did not comprehend it.
6 There came a man sent from God, whose name was John.
7 He came as a witness, to testify about the Light, so that all might believe through him.

which to preach the good news throughout the known world.

It was in this global climate that God sent His Word.

What was His message?

"'THEY SHALL CALL HIS NAME IMMANUEL,' which translated means, 'GOD WITH US'" (Matt. 1:23).

"You shall call His name Jesus, for He will save His people from their sins" (Matt. 1:21).

"But as many as received Him, to them He gave the right to become children of God, even to those who believe in His name, who were born, not of blood nor of the will of the flesh nor of the will of man, but of God" (John 1:12, 13).

Through the Word, all the families of the world were blessed (Rev. 5:9), in fulfillment of God's promise to Abraham (Gen. 12:3). Through the Word, the throne of David was established forever (Rev. 22:16)—not merely in an earthly kingdom, but one that will reign forever (Luke 1:31–33). And through the Word, God saves us.

Friend, have you been waiting for a word from God? Have you been straining your ears because of the silence? Look to *the* Word. Look to Jesus. Just as the time of silence was preparation for Christ's coming, God is readying His message to you in a manner that you cannot imagine.

God is with you. He will save you from your sins. If Jesus Christ is your Savior, you are a child of God, and what He is providing for you will not be accomplished through flesh or the will of man—but by the power of God. He *always* keeps His promises.

Remember that God will move heaven and earth to show you His will. If He's silent now, it's because He wants you to realize His next message is extremely important.

So keep listening ... you don't want to miss it. ◈

8   He was not the Light, but *he came* to testify about the Light.
9   There was the true Light which, coming into the world, enlightens every man.
10   He was in the world, and the world was made through Him, and the world did not know Him.
11   He came to His own, and those who were His own did not receive Him.
12   But as many as received Him, to them He gave the right to become children of God, *even* to those who believe in His name,
✳ 13   who were born, not of blood nor of the will of the flesh nor of the will of man, but of God.
➤ 14   And the Word became flesh, and dwelt among us, and we saw His glory, glory as of the only begotten from the Father, full of grace and truth.
15   John *testified about Him and cried out, saying, "This was He of whom I said,

LIFE LESSONS

➤ **John 1:14 — *And the Word became flesh, and dwelt among us, and we saw His glory, glory as of the only begotten from the Father, full of grace and truth.***

*W*hatever Jesus does, He does with grace. Whatever He says, He says in truth. If you want to understand what God is like, look to Jesus (John 1:18; 14:9).

'He who comes after me has a higher rank than I, for He existed before me.'"
16   For of His fullness we have all received, and grace upon grace.
17   For the Law was given through Moses; grace and truth were realized through Jesus Christ.
18   No one has seen God at any time; the only begotten God who is in the bosom of the Father, He has explained *Him*.

MAY 11

1 Samuel 24:1—25:44

24 NOW when Saul returned from pursuing the Philistines, he was told, saying, "Behold, David is in the wilderness of Engedi."
2   Then Saul took three thousand chosen men from all Israel and went to seek David and his men in front of the Rocks of the Wild Goats.
3   He came to the sheepfolds on the way, where there *was* a cave; and Saul went in to relieve himself. Now David and his men were sitting in the inner recesses of the cave.
4   The men of David said to him, "Behold, *this is* the day of which the LORD said to you, 'Behold; I am about to give your enemy into your hand, and you shall do to him as it seems good to you.'" Then David arose and cut off the edge of Saul's robe secretly.
5   It came about afterward that David's conscience bothered him because he had cut off the edge of Saul's *robe.*
➤ 6   So he said to his men, "Far be it from
✳ me because of the LORD that I should

do this thing to my lord, the LORD's anointed, to stretch out my hand against him, since he is the LORD's anointed."
7   David persuaded his men with *these* words and did not allow them to rise up against Saul. And Saul arose, left the cave, and went on *his* way.
8   Now afterward David arose and went out of the cave and called after Saul, saying, "My lord the king!" And when Saul looked behind him, David bowed with his face to the ground and prostrated himself.

LIFE LESSONS

➤ **1 Samuel 24:6 — *"Far be it from me because of the LORD that I should do this thing to my lord, the LORD's anointed."***

*B*ecause God had anointed Saul, David refused to lay a hand on him. He honored the Lord by sparing Saul's life, and he continued to trust that God would put him on the throne—in His time. This is the essence of true faith: we refuse to run ahead of the Lord's plan. Rather, we exalt Him in everything we do, knowing He is faithful and just to keep His promises to us.

9   David said to Saul, "Why do you listen to the words of men, saying, 'Behold, David seeks to harm you'?
10 "Behold, this day your eyes have seen that the LORD had given you today into my hand in the cave, and some said to kill you, but *my eye* had pity on you; and I said, 'I will not stretch out my hand against my lord, for he is the LORD's anointed.'
11 "Now, my father, see! Indeed, see the edge of your robe in my hand! For in that I cut off the edge of your robe and did not kill you, know and perceive that there is no evil or rebellion in my hands, and I have not sinned against you, though you are lying in wait for my life to take it.
12 "May the LORD judge between you and me, and may the LORD avenge me on you; but my hand shall not be against you.
13 "As the proverb of the ancients says, 'Out of the wicked comes forth wickedness'; but my hand shall not be against you.
14 "After whom has the king of Israel come out? Whom are you pursuing? A dead dog, a single flea?
15 "The LORD therefore be judge and decide between you and me; and may He see and plead my cause and deliver me from your hand."
16 When David had finished speaking these words to Saul, Saul said, "Is this your voice, my son David?" Then Saul lifted up his voice and wept.
17 He said to David, "You are more righteous than I; for you have dealt well with me, while I have dealt wickedly with you.
18 "You have declared today that you have done good to me, that the LORD delivered me into your hand and *yet* you did not kill me.
19 "For if a man finds his enemy, will he let him go away safely? May the LORD

therefore reward you with good in return for what you have done to me this day.
20 "Now, behold, I know that you will surely be king, and that the kingdom of Israel will be established in your hand.
21 "So now swear to me by the LORD that you will not cut off my descendants after me and that you will not destroy my name from my father's household."
22 David swore to Saul. And Saul went to his home, but David and his men went up to the stronghold.

25 THEN Samuel died; and all Israel gathered together and mourned for him, and buried him at his house in Ramah. And David arose and went down to the wilderness of Paran.
2 Now *there was* a man in Maon whose business was in Carmel; and the man was very rich, and he had three thousand sheep and a thousand goats. And it came about while he was shearing his sheep in Carmel
3 (now the man's name was Nabal, and his wife's name was Abigail. And the woman was intelligent and beautiful in appearance, but the man was harsh and evil in *his* dealings, and he was a Calebite),
4 that David heard in the wilderness that Nabal was shearing his sheep.
5 So David sent ten young men; and David said to the young men, "Go up to Carmel, visit Nabal and greet him in my name;
6 and thus you shall say, 'Have a long life, peace be to you, and peace be to your house, and peace be to all that you have.
7 'Now I have heard that you have shearers; now your shepherds have been with us and we have not insulted them, nor have they missed anything all the days they were in Carmel.
8 'Ask your young men and they will tell you. Therefore let *my* young men find favor in your eyes, for we have come on a festive day. Please give whatever you find at hand to your servants and to your son David.'"
9   When David's young men came, they spoke to Nabal according to all these words in David's name; then they waited.
10 But Nabal answered David's servants and said, "Who is David? And who is the son of Jesse? There are many

---

LIFE LESSONS

➤ **1 Samuel 24:12 —** *"May the LORD avenge me on you; but my hand shall not be against you."*

*D*avid would not dishonor the Lord as Saul had done before him (1 Sam. 13:8-14; 15:10-23). If Saul needed to be removed as king to make way for David, then God would have to do it. Even when urged by his friends, David would not strike the Lord's anointed.

servants today who are each breaking away from his master.

11 "Shall I then take my bread and my water and my meat that I have slaughtered for my shearers, and give it to men whose origin I do not know?"

12 So David's young men retraced their way and went back; and they came and told him according to all these words.

13 David said to his men, "Each *of you* gird on his sword." So each man girded on his sword. And David also girded on his sword, and about four hundred men went up behind David while two hundred stayed with the baggage.

14 But one of the young men told Abigail, Nabal's wife, saying, "Behold, David sent messengers from the wilderness to greet our master, and he scorned them.

15 "Yet the men were very good to us, and we were not insulted, nor did we miss anything as long as we went about with them, while we were in the fields.

16 "They were a wall to us both by night and by day, all the time we were with them tending the sheep.

17 "Now therefore, know and consider what you should do, for evil is plotted against our master and against all his household; and he is such a worthless man that no one can speak to him."

18 Then Abigail hurried and took two hundred *loaves* of bread and two jugs of wine and five sheep already prepared and five measures of roasted grain and a hundred clusters of raisins and two hundred cakes of figs, and loaded *them* on donkeys.

19 She said to her young men, "Go on before me; behold, I am coming after you." But she did not tell her husband Nabal.

20 It came about as she was riding on her donkey and coming down by the hidden part of the mountain, that behold, David and his men were coming down toward her; so she met them.

➤ 21 Now David had said, "Surely in vain I have guarded all that this *man* has in the wilderness, so that nothing was missed of all that belonged to him; and he has returned me evil for good.

22 "May God do so to the enemies of David, and more also, if by morning I leave *as much as* one male of any who belong to him."

23 When Abigail saw David, she hurried and dismounted from her donkey, and

fell on her face before David and bowed herself to the ground.

24 She fell at his feet and said, "On me alone, my lord, be the blame. And please let your maidservant speak to you, and listen to the words of your maidservant.

25 "Please do not let my lord pay attention to this worthless man, Nabal, for as his name is, so is he. Nabal is his name and folly is with him; but I your maidservant did not see the young men of my lord whom you sent.

26 "Now therefore, my lord, as the LORD lives, and as your soul lives, since the LORD has restrained you from shedding blood, and from avenging yourself by your own hand, now then let your enemies and those who seek evil against my lord, be as Nabal.

27 "Now let this gift which your maidservant has brought to my lord be given to the young men who accompany my lord.

28 "Please forgive the transgression of your maidservant; for the LORD will certainly make for my lord an enduring house, because my lord is fighting the battles of the LORD, and evil will not be found in you all your days.

29 "Should anyone rise up to pursue you and to seek your life, then the life of my lord shall be bound in the bundle of the living with the LORD your God; but the lives of your enemies He will sling out as from the hollow of a sling.

30 "And when the LORD does for my lord according to all the good that He has spoken concerning you, and appoints you ruler over Israel,

31 this will not cause grief or a troubled heart to my lord, both by having shed blood without cause and by my lord having avenged himself. When the LORD deals well with my lord, then remember your maidservant."

LIFE LESSONS

➤ **1 Samuel 25:21 —** *"He has returned me evil for good."*

Sometimes we may doubt whether it benefits us to do good—especially when those we help treat us badly in return. But God's Word tells us, "Let us not lose heart in doing good, for in due time we will reap if we do not grow weary" (Gal. 6:9).

32 Then David said to Abigail, "Blessed be the LORD God of Israel, who sent you this day to meet me,
33 and blessed be your discernment, and blessed be you, who have kept me this day from bloodshed and from avenging myself by my own hand.
34 "Nevertheless, as the LORD God of Israel lives, who has restrained me from harming you, unless you had come quickly to meet me, surely there would not have been left to Nabal until the morning light *as much as* one male."
35 So David received from her hand what she had brought him and said to her, "Go up to your house in peace. See, I have listened to you and granted your request."
36 Then Abigail came to Nabal, and behold, he was holding a feast in his house, like the feast of a king. And Nabal's heart was merry within him, for he was very drunk; so she did not tell him anything at all until the morning light.
37 But in the morning, when the wine had gone out of Nabal, his wife told him these things, and his heart died within him so that he became *as* a stone.
38 About ten days later, the LORD struck Nabal and he died.
39 When David heard that Nabal was dead, he said, "Blessed be the LORD, who has pleaded the cause of my reproach from the hand of Nabal and has kept back His servant from evil. The LORD has also returned the evildoing of Nabal on his own head." Then David sent a proposal to Abigail, to take her as his wife.
40 When the servants of David came to Abigail at Carmel, they spoke to her, saying, "David has sent us to you to take you as his wife."
41 She arose and bowed with her face to the ground and said, "Behold, your maidservant is a maid to wash the feet of my lord's servants."
42 Then Abigail quickly arose, and rode on a donkey, with her five maidens who attended her; and she followed the messengers of David and became his wife.
43 David had also taken Ahinoam of Jezreel, and they both became his wives.
44 Now Saul had given Michal his daughter, David's wife, to Palti the son of Laish, who was from Gallim.

Psalm 60:1–5

For the choir director; according to Shushan Eduth. A Mikhtam of David, to teach; when he struggled with Aram-naharaim and with Aram-zobah, and Joab returned, and smote twelve thousand of Edom in the Valley of Salt.

60 O GOD, You have rejected us.
     You have broken us;
     You have been angry; O, restore us.
2 You have made the land quake, You have split it open;
     Heal its breaches, for it totters.
3 You have made Your people experience hardship;
     You have given us wine to drink that makes us stagger.
4 You have given a banner to those who fear You,
     That it may be displayed because of the truth.   Selah.
5 That Your beloved may be delivered, Save with Your right hand, and answer us!

Proverbs 16:3

3 Commit your works to the LORD
     And your plans will be established.

LIFE LESSONS

1 Samuel 25:34 — *"The LORD God of Israel . . . has restrained me from harming you."*

It was Abigail's quick thinking and wise actions that kept David from annihilating all the males in Nabal's family, but David rightly saw it as the Lord keeping him from bloodshed. Our sovereign Lord works in many ways!

Proverbs 16:3 — *Commit your works to the LORD and your plans will be established.*

How do we commit our works to the Lord? Not merely by asking Him to bless what we've already done, but by committing ourselves completely to *His* plans before, during, and after we have done our work.

John 1:19–51

19 This is the testimony of John, when the Jews sent to him priests and Levites from Jerusalem to ask him, "Who are you?"
20 And he confessed and did not deny, but confessed, "I am not the Christ."
21 They asked him, "What then? Are you Elijah?" And he *said, "I am not." "Are you the Prophet?" And he answered, "No."
22 Then they said to him, "Who are you, so that we may give an answer to those who sent us? What do you say about yourself?"
23 He said, "I am A VOICE OF ONE CRYING IN THE WILDERNESS, 'MAKE STRAIGHT THE WAY OF THE LORD,' as Isaiah the prophet said."
24 Now they had been sent from the Pharisees.
25 They asked him, and said to him, "Why then are you baptizing, if you are not the Christ, nor Elijah, nor the Prophet?"
26 John answered them saying, "I baptize in water, *but* among you stands One whom you do not know.
27 "*It is* He who comes after me, the thong of whose sandal I am not worthy to untie."
28 These things took place in Bethany beyond the Jordan, where John was baptizing.
29 The next day he *saw Jesus coming to him and *said, "Behold, the Lamb of God who takes away the sin of the world!
30 "This is He on behalf of whom I said, 'After me comes a Man who has a higher rank than I, for He existed before me.'
31 "I did not recognize Him, but so that

LIFE LESSONS

➤ John 1:29 — *"Behold, the Lamb of God who takes away the sin of the world!"*

Jesus is our Passover Lamb who willingly took the punishment we deserve (1 Cor. 5:7). God "made Him who knew no sin to be sin on our behalf, so that we might become the righteousness of God in Him" (2 Cor. 5:21).

He might be manifested to Israel, I came baptizing in water."
32 John testified saying, "I have seen the Spirit descending as a dove out of heaven, and He remained upon Him.
33 "I did not recognize Him, but He who sent me to baptize in water said to me, 'He upon whom you see the Spirit descending and remaining upon Him, this is the One who baptizes in the Holy Spirit.'
34 "I myself have seen, and have testified that this is the Son of God."
35 Again the next day John was standing with two of his disciples,
36 and he looked at Jesus as He walked, and *said, "Behold, the Lamb of God!"
37 The two disciples heard him speak, and they followed Jesus.
38 And Jesus turned and saw them following, and *said to them, "What do you seek?" They said to Him, "Rabbi (which translated means Teacher), where are You staying?"
39 He *said to them, "Come, and you will see." So they came and saw where He was staying; and they stayed with Him that day, for it was about the tenth hour.
40 One of the two who heard John *speak* and followed Him, was Andrew, Simon Peter's brother.
41 He *found first his own brother Simon and *said to him, "We have found the Messiah" (which translated means Christ).
42 He brought him to Jesus. Jesus looked at him and said, "You are Simon the son of John; you shall be called Cephas" (which is translated Peter).
43 The next day He purposed to go into Galilee, and He *found Philip. And Jesus *said to him, "Follow Me."
44 Now Philip was from Bethsaida, of the city of Andrew and Peter.
45 Philip *found Nathanael and *said to him, "We have found Him of whom Moses in the Law and *also* the Prophets wrote—Jesus of Nazareth, the son of Joseph."
46 Nathanael said to him, "Can any good thing come out of Nazareth?" Philip *said to him, "Come and see."
47 Jesus saw Nathanael coming to Him, and *said of him, "Behold, an Israelite indeed, in whom there is no deceit!"
48 Nathanael *said to Him, "How do

WHAT THE BIBLE SAYS ABOUT

Welcoming the King

John 1:19–34

*I*n ancient times, the arrival of a king was heralded so his subjects could prepare for his appearance. Certainly the king deserved to be celebrated as the ruler of the land, so cities would hold great festivals with much fanfare and pageantry. Everything would be cleaned and repaired so that the king would see his dominion at its best.

When the King of Kings came to earth, the same was true. Could any less be done for the Savior of the world? "As it is written in Isaiah the prophet: 'BEHOLD, I SEND MY MESSENGER AHEAD OF YOU, WHO WILL PREPARE YOUR WAY. THE VOICE OF ONE CRYING IN THE WILDERNESS, "MAKE READY THE WAY OF THE LORD; MAKE HIS PATHS STRAIGHT"'" (Mark 1:2, 3).

Who was that messenger, and how does one make straight the path of the Lord—preparing a people for His coming? Mark 1:4 tells us, "John the Baptist appeared in the wilderness preaching a baptism of repentance for the forgiveness of sins."

When Jesus began His ministry, He was heralded by John's baptism of repentance. John didn't ready a city to greet a mere earthly king; rather, he prepared people's hearts to receive a Savior. John said, "I did not recognize Him, but so that He might be manifested to Israel, I came baptizing in water" (John 1:31).

Why baptism by water? Why was this the way chosen by God to proclaim the coming of the King?

During that time, when Gentiles converted to Judaism, they were baptized to show a complete, all-encompassing change of attitude. They went from knowledge of false gods to recognition of the one true God. The baptism John brought was for Jews and Gentiles alike—also showing a change in attitude. Yet this baptism was not only about recognizing the one true God; it was about agreeing fully with the Lord about their sinful nature.

John's father, Zechariah, prophesied about him, saying, "And you, child, will be called the prophet of the Most High; for you will go on BEFORE THE LORD TO PREPARE HIS WAYS; To give to His people the knowledge of salvation by the forgiveness of their sins" (Luke 1:76, 77).

John helped people know they were sinful, but he also proclaimed the good news that the forgiveness of their sins was coming soon. In John 1:29, 34, he describes the moment when John's teaching was fulfilled. "The next day he saw Jesus coming to him and said, 'Behold, the Lamb of God who takes away the sin of the world! ... I myself have seen, and have testified that this is the Son of God.'"

John pointed toward Christ as the Son of God who had come for the forgiveness of sins. John's ministry was essential to the establishment of the new covenant because he instructed people on how to get ready for the King. He told the multitudes that the attitude for receiving Christ was repentance and that it was only through the lowly heart of one regretting his or her sin that the King could truly be welcomed (2 Cor. 7:10). ◈

You know me?" Jesus answered and said to him, "Before Philip called you, when you were under the fig tree, I saw you."
49 Nathanael answered Him, "Rabbi, You are the Son of God; You are the King of Israel."
50 Jesus answered and said to him, "Be-

cause I said to you that I saw you under the fig tree, do you believe? You will see greater things than these."
51 And He *said to him, "Truly, truly, I say to you, you will see the heavens opened and the angels of God ascending and descending on the Son of Man."

◈ 1 Samuel 26:1—27:12

26 THEN the Ziphites came to Saul at Gibeah, saying, "Is not David

hiding on the hill of Hachilah, *which is before Jeshimon?*"
2 So Saul arose and went down to the wilderness of Ziph, having with him three thousand chosen men of Israel, to

search for David in the wilderness of Ziph.

3   Saul camped in the hill of Hachilah, which is before Jeshimon, beside the road, and David was staying in the wilderness. When he saw that Saul came after him into the wilderness,

4   David sent out spies, and he knew that Saul was definitely coming.

5   David then arose and came to the place where Saul had camped. And David saw the place where Saul lay, and Abner the son of Ner, the commander of his army; and Saul was lying in the circle of the camp, and the people were camped around him.

6   Then David said to Ahimelech the Hittite and to Abishai the son of Zeruiah, Joab's brother, saying, "Who will go down with me to Saul in the camp?" And Abishai said, "I will go down with you."

7   So David and Abishai came to the people by night, and behold, Saul lay sleeping inside the circle of the camp with his spear stuck in the ground at his head; and Abner and the people were lying around him.

8   Then Abishai said to David, "Today God has delivered your enemy into your hand; now therefore, please let me strike him with the spear to the ground with one stroke, and I will not strike him the second time."

9   But David said to Abishai, "Do not destroy him, for who can stretch out his hand against the LORD's anointed and be without guilt?"

➤ 10   David also said, "As the LORD lives, surely the LORD will strike him, or his day will come that he dies, or he will go down into battle and perish.

11   "The LORD forbid that I should stretch out my hand against the LORD's anointed; but now please take the spear that is at

his head and the jug of water, and let us go."

12   So David took the spear and the jug of water from *beside* Saul's head, and they went away, but no one saw or knew *it,* nor did any awake, for they were all asleep, because a sound sleep from the LORD had fallen on them.

13   Then David crossed over to the other side and stood on top of the mountain at a distance *with* a large area between them.

14   David called to the people and to Abner the son of Ner, saying, "Will you not answer, Abner?" Then Abner replied, "Who are you who calls to the king?"

15   So David said to Abner, "Are you not a man? And who is like you in Israel? Why then have you not guarded your lord the king? For one of the people came to destroy the king your lord.

16   "This thing that you have done is not good. As the LORD lives, *all* of you must surely die, because you did not guard your lord, the LORD's anointed. And now, see where the king's spear is and the jug of water that was at his head."

17   Then Saul recognized David's voice and said, "Is this your voice, my son David?" And David said, "It is my voice, my lord the king."

18   He also said, "Why then is my lord pursuing his servant? For what have I done? Or what evil is in my hand?

19   "Now therefore, please let my lord the king listen to the words of his servant. If the LORD has stirred you up against me, let Him accept an offering; but if it is men, cursed are they before the LORD, for they have driven me out today so that I would have no attachment with the inheritance of the LORD, saying, 'Go, serve other gods.'

20   "Now then, do not let my blood fall to the ground away from the presence of the LORD; for the king of Israel has come out to search for a single flea, just as one hunts a partridge in the mountains."

21   Then Saul said, "I have sinned. Return, my son David, for I will not harm ◄ you again because my life was precious in your sight this day. Behold, I have played the fool and have committed a serious error."

22   David replied, "Behold the spear of

LIFE LESSONS

➤ **1 Samuel 26:10** — *"The LORD will strike him."*

*O*nce more David refused to kill Saul when he had the chance. David's aide saw the opportunity as a divine blessing, but David saw it as a test. He would wait for God to act in His own time.

the king! Now let one of the young men come over and take it.

23 "The LORD will repay each man *for* his righteousness and his faithfulness; for the LORD delivered you into *my* hand today, but I refused to stretch out my hand against the LORD'S anointed.

24 "Now behold, as your life was highly valued in my sight this day, so may my life be highly valued in the sight of the LORD, and may He deliver me from all distress."

25 Then Saul said to David, "Blessed are you, my son David; you will both accomplish much and surely prevail." So David went on his way, and Saul returned to his place.

27 THEN David said to himself, "Now I will perish one day by the hand of Saul. There is nothing better for me than to escape into the land of the Philistines. Saul then will despair of searching for me anymore in all the territory of Israel, and I will escape from his hand."

2 So David arose and crossed over, he and the six hundred men who were with him, to Achish the son of Maoch, king of Gath.

3 And David lived with Achish at Gath, he and his men, each with his household, *even* David with his two wives, Ahinoam the Jezreelitess, and Abigail the Carmelitess, Nabal's widow.

4 Now it was told Saul that David had fled to Gath, so he no longer searched for him.

5 Then David said to Achish, "If now I have found favor in your sight, let them give me a place in one of the cities in the country, that I may live there; for why should your servant live in the royal city with you?"

6 So Achish gave him Ziklag that day; therefore Ziklag has belonged to the kings of Judah to this day.

7 The number of days that David lived in the country of the Philistines was a year and four months.

8 Now David and his men went up and raided the Geshurites and the Girzites and the Amalekites; for they were the inhabitants of the land from ancient times, as you come to Shur even as far as the land of Egypt.

9 David attacked the land and did not leave a man or a woman alive, and he took away the sheep, the cattle, the donkeys, the camels, and the clothing. Then he returned and came to Achish.

10 Now Achish said, "Where have you made a raid today?" And David said, "Against the Negev of Judah and against the Negev of the Jerahmeelites and against the Negev of the Kenites."

11 David did not leave a man or a woman alive to bring to Gath, saying, "Otherwise they will tell about us, saying, 'So has David done and so *has been* his practice all the time he has lived in the country of the Philistines.'"

12 So Achish believed David, saying, "He has surely made himself odious among his people Israel; therefore he will become my servant forever."

Psalm 60:6–12

6 God has spoken in His holiness:
    "I will exult, I will portion out
        Shechem and measure out the
        valley of Succoth.
7 "Gilead is Mine, and Manasseh is
        Mine;
    Ephraim also is the helmet of My
        head;
    Judah is My scepter.
8 "Moab is My washbowl;
    Over Edom I shall throw My shoe;
    Shout loud, O Philistia, because of
        Me!"
9 Who will bring me into the besieged
        city?
    Who will lead me to Edom?
10 Have not You Yourself, O God,
        rejected us?
    And will You not go forth with our
        armies, O God?

11 O give us help against the
       adversary,
     For deliverance by man is in vain.
12 Through God we shall do valiantly,
     And it is He who will tread down
       our adversaries.

Proverbs 16:4, 5

4   The LORD has made everything for
       its own purpose,
     Even the wicked for the day of
       evil.
5   Everyone who is proud in heart is
       an abomination to the LORD;
     Assuredly, he will not be
       unpunished.

John 2:1–25

2 ON the third day there was a wedding in Cana of Galilee, and the mother of Jesus was there;
2   and both Jesus and His disciples were invited to the wedding.
3   When the wine ran out, the mother of Jesus *said to Him, "They have no wine."
4   And Jesus *said to her, "Woman, what does that have to do with us? My hour has not yet come."
5   His mother *said to the servants, "Whatever He says to you, do it."
6   Now there were six stone waterpots set there for the Jewish custom of purification, containing twenty or thirty gallons each.
7   Jesus *said to them, "Fill the waterpots with water." So they filled them up to the brim.

8   And He *said to them, "Draw *some* out now and take it to the headwaiter." So they took it *to him.*
9   When the headwaiter tasted the water which had become wine, and did not know where it came from (but the servants who had drawn the water knew), the headwaiter *called the bridegroom,
10 and *said to him, "Every man serves the good wine first, and when *the people* have drunk freely, *then he serves* the poorer *wine; but* you have kept the good wine until now."
11 This beginning of *His* signs Jesus did in Cana of Galilee, and manifested His glory, and His disciples believed in Him.
12 After this He went down to Capernaum, He and His mother and *His* brothers and His disciples; and they stayed there a few days.
13 The Passover of the Jews was near, and Jesus went up to Jerusalem.
14 And He found in the temple those who were selling oxen and sheep and doves, and the money changers seated *at their tables.*
15 And He made a scourge of cords, and drove *them* all out of the temple, with the sheep and the oxen; and He poured out the coins of the money changers and overturned their tables;
16 and to those who were selling the doves He said, "Take these things away; stop making My Father's house a place of business."
17 His disciples remembered that it was

WHAT THE BIBLE SAYS ABOUT

Between Passover and Pentecost

John 2:20–22

When Jesus spoke to the disciples about being raised from the dead in three days, it didn't make sense to them initially. Yet John 2:22 tells us, "When He was raised from the dead, His disciples remembered that He said this; and they believed the Scripture and the word which Jesus had spoken."

They still may not have understood the full significance of what had occurred and what it really meant that the temple of His body had been raised. However, the feasts of the Lord help us to understand what happened.

During the Passover Feast, Jesus became our sacrificial Lamb (1 Cor. 5:7). It's easy for us to see the spiritual significance of what occurred because we know His death and resurrection marked the beginning of the new covenant. Yet we often think the next feast the disciples celebrated was Pentecost—when the Holy Spirit empowered the church. Unfortunately, there's a feast we often miss.

Though Pentecost—also known as the Feast of Weeks—refers to the fiftieth day of the Hebrew harvest, the harvest actually started on the third day after Passover with the Feast of Firstfruits. Jesus rose from the dead on the Feast of Firstfruits—which makes sense because Jesus is "the firstborn over all creation" (Col. 1:15). In 1 Corinthians 15:20, Paul writes, "Christ is risen from the dead, and has become the first fruits of those who have fallen asleep."

During Firstfruits, people brought offerings of barley—the first crop of the year—to the temple. When God accepted it, it meant He was promising to provide them with the rest of the harvest (Lev. 23:9–14; Prov. 3:9, 10). Likewise, Jesus' resurrection is given as a guarantee we will live forever.

Now understand, when Jesus said, "Destroy this temple, and in three days I will raise it up" (John 2:19), He wasn't only talking about His crucifixion and His resurrection. He was saying that the way people worship and the way the church would function would completely change, too.

Remember, Jesus said, "God is spirit, and those who worship Him must worship in spirit and truth" (John 4:24). No longer would people go to the temple to make offerings because Christ became our offering—and we ourselves became an offering as well (Rom. 12:1). On the Feast of Firstfruits, Jesus raised a new temple in us. We became God's temple. Paul writes, "Your body is a temple of the Holy Spirit who is in you, whom you have from God" (1 Cor. 6:19).

We are the new temple. When they tore Christ down, God raised us up. We are an acceptable offering to the Lord because Christ made us acceptable.

The Romans destroyed the earthly temple—the one mentioned in John 2:20—in A.D. 70, and today what stands in its place is the Muslim Dome of the Rock and Al-Aqsa Mosque. However, we no longer look to a temple that can be destroyed. Rather, we are the temple that will last forever—and that grows in strength with each person who believes in Jesus Christ as his or her Savior (Eph. 2:20–22).

What can we learn from this? What should we take away from the Feast of Firstfruits? In all things we must imitate Christ—the first of the harvest—and have the eternal perspective He had. Jesus came to give us everlasting life and to change our focus from the temporary to the eternal.

Is there something you are struggling with today—some temple being torn down in your life? Jesus is raising it up again, but not necessarily in the way you think. Jesus has a better, eternal vision for your life than you can imagine, so trust Him. And be assured what He's building in you will last forever (2 Cor. 4:16–18). ◈

---

written, "ZEAL FOR YOUR HOUSE WILL CONSUME ME."
18 The Jews then said to Him, "What sign do You show us as your authority for doing these things?"
19 Jesus answered them, "Destroy this temple, and in three days I will raise it up."

20 The Jews then said, "It took forty-six years to build this temple, and will You raise it up in three days?"
21 But He was speaking of the temple of His body.
22 So when He was raised from the dead, His disciples remembered that He

LIFE LESSONS

➤ **John 2:22 — So when He was raised from the dead, His disciples remembered that He said this; and they believed the Scripture.**

Sometimes we hesitate to spend time in God's Word because we don't feel as though we're getting anything out of it. But often a text does not "click" in our minds until some time later.

said this; and they believed the Scripture and the word which Jesus had spoken.
23 Now when He was in Jerusalem at the Passover, during the feast, many believed in His name, observing His signs which He was doing.
24 But Jesus, on His part, was not entrusting Himself to them, for He knew all men,
25 and because He did not need anyone to testify concerning man, for He Himself knew what was in man.

MAY 13

1 Samuel 28:1–25

28 NOW it came about in those days that the Philistines gathered their armed camps for war, to fight against Israel. And Achish said to David, "Know assuredly that you will go out with me in the camp, you and your men."
2 David said to Achish, "Very well, you shall know what your servant can do." So Achish said to David, "Very well, I will make you my bodyguard for life."
3 Now Samuel was dead, and all Israel had lamented him and buried him in Ramah, his own city. And Saul had removed from the land those who were mediums and spiritists.
4 So the Philistines gathered together and came and camped in Shunem; and Saul gathered all Israel together and they camped in Gilboa.
5 When Saul saw the camp of the Philistines, he was afraid and his heart trembled greatly.
6 When Saul inquired of the LORD, the LORD did not answer him, either by dreams or by Urim or by prophets.
➤ 7 Then Saul said to his servants, "Seek for me a woman who is a medium, that I may go to her and inquire of her." And his servants said to him, "Behold, there is a woman who is a medium at En-dor."
8 Then Saul disguised himself by putting on other clothes, and went, he and two men with him, and they came to the woman by night; and he said, "Conjure up for me, please, and bring up for me whom I shall name to you."

9 But the woman said to him, "Behold, you know what Saul has done, how he has cut off those who are mediums and spiritists from the land. Why are you then laying a snare for my life to bring about my death?"
10 Saul vowed to her by the LORD, saying, "As the LORD lives, no punishment shall come upon you for this thing." ◄
11 Then the woman said, "Whom shall I bring up for you?" And he said, "Bring up Samuel for me."
12 When the woman saw Samuel, she cried out with a loud voice; and the woman spoke to Saul, saying, "Why have you deceived me? For you are Saul."
13 The king said to her, "Do not be afraid; but what do you see?" And the

LIFE LESSONS

➤ **1 Samuel 28:7 — "Seek for me a woman who is a medium."**

Once more Saul allowed his fear to spur him on to a foolish and wicked choice (Lev. 19:31; 20:6; Deut. 18:10-12). If we do not deal with our fear by bringing it to the Lord, it will eventually crush us.

➤ **1 Samuel 28:10 — "As the LORD lives, no punishment shall come upon you for this thing."**

Saul no longer knew right from wrong—godly from wicked. He even vowed not to do what the Lord had commanded (Lev. 20:27)! Outward professions of faith will never substitute for genuine, obedient faith.

woman said to Saul, "I see a divine being coming up out of the earth."

14   He said to her, "What is his form?" And she said, "An old man is coming up, and he is wrapped with a robe." And Saul knew that it was Samuel, and he bowed with his face to the ground and did homage.

15   Then Samuel said to Saul, "Why have you disturbed me by bringing me up?" And Saul answered, "I am greatly distressed; for the Philistines are waging war against me, and God has departed from me and no longer answers me, either through prophets or by dreams; therefore I have called you, that you may make known to me what I should do."

16   Samuel said, "Why then do you ask me, since the LORD has departed from you and has become your adversary?

17   "The LORD has done accordingly as He spoke through me; for the LORD has torn the kingdom out of your hand and given it to your neighbor, to David.

18   "As you did not obey the LORD and did not execute His fierce wrath on Amalek, so the LORD has done this thing to you this day.

19   "Moreover the LORD will also give over Israel along with you into the hands of the Philistines, therefore tomorrow you and your sons will be with me. Indeed the LORD will give over the army of Israel into the hands of the Philistines!"

20   Then Saul immediately fell full length upon the ground and was very afraid because of the words of Samuel; also there was no strength in him, for he had eaten no food all day and all night.

21   The woman came to Saul and saw that he was terrified, and said to him, "Behold, your maidservant has obeyed you, and I have taken my life in my hand and have listened to your words which you spoke to me.

22   "So now also, please listen to the voice of your maidservant, and let me set a piece of bread before you that you may eat and have strength when you go on your way."

23   But he refused and said, "I will not eat." However, his servants together with the woman urged him, and he listened to them. So he arose from the ground and sat on the bed.

24   The woman had a fattened calf in the house, and she quickly slaughtered it; and she took flour, kneaded it and baked unleavened bread from it.

25   She brought it before Saul and his servants, and they ate. Then they arose and went away that night.

Psalm 61:1–4

For the choir director; on a stringed instrument. A Psalm of David.

61 HEAR my cry, O God;
         Give heed to my prayer.
2   From the end of the earth I call to
         You when my heart is faint;
         Lead me to the rock that is higher
         than I.
3   For You have been a refuge for me,
         A tower of strength against the
         enemy.
4   Let me dwell in Your tent forever;
         Let me take refuge in the shelter of
         Your wings.   Selah.

Proverbs 16:6

6   By lovingkindness and truth
         iniquity is atoned for,
         And by the fear of the LORD one
         keeps away from evil.

LIFE LESSONS

➤ **1 Samuel 28:19 —** *"The LORD will also give over Israel along with you into the hands of the Philistines."*

Samuel still proclaimed the same uncompromising message he delivered while alive—and the Lord still fulfilled all that the prophet said (1 Sam. 3:19; 31:1-7). God's Word is a rock on which we can build our entire lives (Matt. 7:24, 25).

➤ **Psalm 61:2 —** *Lead me to the rock that is higher than I.*

The Lord is our Rock—our unshakable foundation that will never fail. No matter where in the world we travel, no matter what challenges we face, God goes before us, inviting us to entrust our troubles and emotions to Him. If we will just look up, He will be there, and He will lead us to triumph.

John 3:1–18

3 NOW there was a man of the Pharisees, named Nicodemus, a ruler of the Jews;
2 this man came to Jesus by night and said to Him, "Rabbi, we know that You have come from God *as* a teacher; for no one can do these signs that You do unless God is with him."
3 Jesus answered and said to him, "Truly, truly, I say to you, unless one is born again he cannot see the kingdom of God."
4 Nicodemus *said to Him, "How can a man be born when he is old? He cannot enter a second time into his mother's womb and be born, can he?"
5 Jesus answered, "Truly, truly, I say to you, unless one is born of water and the Spirit he cannot enter into the kingdom of God.
6 "That which is born of the flesh is flesh, and that which is born of the Spirit is spirit.
7 "Do not be amazed that I said to you, 'You must be born again.'

8 "The wind blows where it wishes and you hear the sound of it, but do not know where it comes from and where it is going; so is everyone who is born of the Spirit."
9 Nicodemus said to Him, "How can these things be?"
10 Jesus answered and said to him, "Are you the teacher of Israel and do not understand these things?
11 "Truly, truly, I say to you, we speak of what we know and testify of what we have seen, and you do not accept our testimony.
12 "If I told you earthly things and you do not believe, how will you believe if I tell you heavenly things?
13 "No one has ascended into heaven, but He who descended from heaven: the Son of Man.
14 "As Moses lifted up the serpent in the wilderness, even so must the Son of Man be lifted up;
15 so that whoever believes will in Him have eternal life.
16 "For God so loved the world, that He gave His only begotten Son, that whoever believes in Him shall not perish, but have eternal life.

Life Examples:

NICODEMUS: Unclean but Unblemished

JOHN 3:1–18

*I*t all started at night, when Nicodemus, a Pharisee and "a ruler of the Jews" (John 3:1) came to the Light (John 3:21). Nicodemus makes three appearances in the Bible (John 3:1–21; 7:50–52; 19:39–42), and by the third time, we see that the truth Jesus planted in his heart had powerfully taken root. Although Jesus had been condemned by Nicodemus' colleagues (Luke 23:13–24), it no longer made a difference to him. Nicodemus knew Jesus was the true Messiah—the hope of Israel and the world.

How do we know he arrived at this decision? Normally the bodies of those who had been crucified were thrown on the trash heap of the city. Yet after Christ was removed from the Cross, Joseph of Arimathea claimed His body, prepared it for burial, and then placed Him in a brand new tomb. Nicodemus was right beside Joseph. He brought myrrh and aloes and assisted in Christ's burial (John 19:38–41). It is believed the spices used

for the Lord's burial were those personally belonging to Nicodemus. Instead of saving them for his own burial, he gave them to Jesus as an offering of love and devotion. John 19:39 tells us these spices weighed "about a hundred pounds weight," which would have been the amount used to bury a great king—not merely a good man or a simple teacher. Nicodemus acknowledged that Jesus is the Son of God, and treated Him with great respect.

We also know that according to the Law of Moses, no priest was to "defile himself for a dead person" (Lev. 21:1)—touching the deceased body would make him unclean. Yet that also did not matter to Nicodemus because he realized that in his new eternal life, he was completely unblemished (John 3:16).

Today, Nicodemus' example still teaches us. We learn from him that Jesus is always there for us, night or day. We learn that in God's perfect timing, He will answer our most confounding questions. We learn that regardless of our status, nothing is more important than the life of Christ within us. And we learn that no matter how great our sacrifice, it can never compare to Christ's sacrifice for us.

➤ 17 "For God did not send the Son into the world to judge the world, but that the world might be saved through Him.
➤ 18 "He who believes in Him is not judged; he who does not believe has been judged already, because he has not believed in the name of the only begotten Son of God.

LIFE LESSONS

➤ **John 3:17 — "For God did not send the Son into the world to judge the world, but that the world might be saved through Him."**

*W*hile Jesus says that all judgment has been committed to Him (John 5:22), He assures us that He did not come to earth to judge us but to save us. As James says, "Mercy triumphs over judgment" (James 2:13).

➤ **John 3:18 — "He who believes in Him is not judged; he who does not believe has been judged already."**

*T*hose who place their faith in Jesus will never be condemned because Jesus has already taken their punishment upon Himself. But those who reject Jesus as Savior must bear the full penalty of their sins.

M A Y 14

1 Samuel 29:1—31:13

29 NOW the Philistines gathered together all their armies to Aphek, while the Israelites were camping by the spring which is in Jezreel.
2   And the lords of the Philistines were proceeding on by hundreds and by thousands, and David and his men were proceeding on in the rear with Achish.
3   Then the commanders of the Philistines said, "What *are* these Hebrews *doing here?*" And Achish said to the commanders of the Philistines, "Is this not David, the servant of Saul the king of Israel, who has been with me these days, or *rather* these years, and I have found no fault in him from the day he deserted *to me* to this day?"
4   But the commanders of the Philistines were angry with him, and the commanders of the Philistines said to him, "Make the man go back, that he may return to his place where you have assigned him, and do not let him go down to battle with us, or in the battle he may become an adversary to us. For with what could this *man* make himself acceptable to his lord? *Would it* not *be* with the heads of these men?
5   "Is this not David, of whom they sing in the dances, saying,

'Saul has slain his thousands,
And David his ten thousands'?"

6   Then Achish called David and said to him, "*As* the LORD lives, you *have been* upright, and your going out and your coming in with me in the army are pleasing in my sight; for I have not found evil in you from the day of your coming to me to this day. Nevertheless, you are not pleasing in the sight of the lords.
7   "Now therefore return and go in peace, that you may not displease the lords of the Philistines."
8   David said to Achish, "But what have I done? And what have you found in your servant from the day when I came before you to this day, that I may not go and fight against the enemies of my lord the king?"
9   But Achish replied to David, "I know that you are pleasing in my sight, like an angel of God; nevertheless the commanders of the Philistines have said, 'He must not go up with us to the battle.'
10 "Now then arise early in the morning with the servants of your lord who have come with you, and as soon as you have arisen early in the morning and have light, depart."
11 So David arose early, he and his men, to depart in the morning to return to the land of the Philistines. And the Philistines went up to Jezreel.

30 THEN it happened when David ◄ and his men came to Ziklag on the third day, that the Amalekites had made a raid on the Negev and on Ziklag, and had overthrown Ziklag and burned it with fire;

2   and they took captive the women *and all* who were in it, both small and great, without killing anyone, and carried *them* off and went their way.

3   When David and his men came to the city, behold, it was burned with fire, and their wives and their sons and their daughters had been taken captive.

4   Then David and the people who were with him lifted their voices and wept until there was no strength in them to weep.

5   Now David's two wives had been taken captive, Ahinoam the Jezreelitess and Abigail the widow of Nabal the Carmelite.

6   Moreover David was greatly distressed because the people spoke of stoning him, for all the people were embittered, each one because of his sons and his daughters. But David strengthened himself in the LORD his God.

7   Then David said to Abiathar the priest, the son of Ahimelech, "Please bring me the ephod." So Abiathar brought the ephod to David.

8   David inquired of the LORD, saying, "Shall I pursue this band? Shall I overtake them?" And He said to him, "Pursue, for you will surely overtake them, and you will surely rescue *all.*"

9   So David went, he and the six hundred men who were with him, and came to the brook Besor, *where* those left behind remained.

10 But David pursued, he and four hundred men, for two hundred who were too exhausted to cross the brook Besor remained *behind.*

LIFE LESSONS

➤ **1 Samuel 30:1 — *The Amalekites had made a raid on the Negev and on Ziklag.***

*I*t's no wonder the Philistines gave David Ziklag—it was constantly in danger of invading armies. Yet God was working through the adversity to train David to be a wise king who would trust Him, even in the most difficult situations. The dark moments of our lives will last only so long as is necessary for God to accomplish His purpose, molding us into godly people.

---

11 Now they found an Egyptian in the field and brought him to David, and gave him bread and he ate, and they provided him water to drink.

12 They gave him a piece of fig cake and two clusters of raisins, and he ate; then his spirit revived. For he had not eaten bread or drunk water for three days and three nights.

13 David said to him, "To whom do you belong? And where are you from?" And he said, "I am a young man of Egypt, a servant of an Amalekite; and my master left me behind when I fell sick three days ago.

14 "We made a raid on the Negev of the Cherethites, and on that which belongs to Judah, and on the Negev of Caleb, and we burned Ziklag with fire."

15 Then David said to him, "Will you bring me down to this band?" And he said, "Swear to me by God that you will not kill me or deliver me into the hands of my master, and I will bring you down to this band."

16 When he had brought him down, behold, they were spread over all the land, eating and drinking and dancing because of all the great spoil that they had taken from the land of the Philistines and from the land of Judah.

17 David slaughtered them from the twilight until the evening of the next day; and not a man of them escaped, except four hundred young men who rode on camels and fled.

18 So David recovered all that the Amalekites had taken, and rescued his two wives.

19 But nothing of theirs was missing, whether small or great, sons or daughters, spoil or anything that they had taken for themselves; David brought *it* all back.

20 So David had captured all the sheep and the cattle *which the people* drove ahead of the *other* livestock, and they said, "This is David's spoil."

21 When David came to the two hundred men who were too exhausted to follow David, who had also been left at the brook Besor, and they went out to meet David and to meet the people who were with him, then David approached the people and greeted them.

22 Then all the wicked and worthless men among those who went with David

THE DARK MOMENTS OF OUR LIFE WILL LAST
ONLY SO LONG AS IS NECESSARY FOR GOD TO
ACCOMPLISH HIS PURPOSE IN US.

---

1 SAMUEL 30:1–6

*I*f you want God's best for your life and desire to be used by Him, at some point you will have to travel the road of adversity. He can and will use adversity in your life for a good purpose. Yet many people view adversity as only negative and defeating. You don't have to be among them!

God has designed adversity, regardless of its source, to become a turning point from which you take your greatest leaps forward in spiritual growth. He allows adversity to remain in your life only until He accomplishes His purpose in you. He will not keep it in your life one second longer than is necessary.

Some people are almost wiped out by trials, while others learn to stand in the confidence of God's faithfulness. The latter have an overwhelming sense of stability and immovable strength. They weather the storms with heads held high, confident, bold, and not discouraged by any obstacle that comes along. They feel absolutely certain God is going to see them through the heartache and bring them out whole, joyful, and more mature on the other side.

Adversity also shows us where we stand in our faith. Do we doubt God? Or do we thank Him for His faithfulness during the stressful, heart-wrenching times? Do we trust that He will never leave or forsake us? Adversity is God's most accurate measure of our faith—it reveals our endurance level. None of us knows how much difficulty we can withstand until we are tried.

Right now, right where you are, remember this: *God has put a limit on all adversity.* Because you are a child of God, the Holy Spirit is living inside of you, and He knows how much you can bear. The psalmist said: "Many are the afflictions of the righteous, but the LORD delivers him out of them all" (Ps. 34:19). And, "Just as a father has compassion on his children, so the LORD has compassion on those who fear Him. For He Himself knows our frame; He is mindful that we are but dust" (Ps. 103:13, 14).

When we learn and mature in the midst of tremendous adversity, God is pleased because He sees His purpose being fulfilled in us. We are growing spiritually, becoming stronger in areas of weakness, and increasingly being conformed to the likeness of Christ. God is thrilled when we respond correctly to adversity!

There are three principles we can learn when we face adversity:

❶ **Adversity is God's choice tool for building godly, spiritual character into our lives. Until we experience heartache, disappointment, and pain, we are not properly equipped for service (2 Cor. 1:3–7). He uses adversity to mold and shape us; He does not bring it into our lives without purpose.**

❷ **Adversity usually comes in the areas where we feel the most confident. God wants to break us of the idea we are sufficient on our own. He made us for a loving, intimate relationship with Himself, and He uses adversity to remind us of the fact that we are dependent upon Him.**

❸ **God's ultimate design is to conform us to the likeness of Jesus. Through adversity, God develops the fruit of the Spirit—love, joy, peace, patience, kindness, goodness, faithfulness, gentleness, and self-control (Gal. 5:22, 23)—in us.**

God also accomplishes several goals in our lives by allowing suffering and heartache. Adversity:

- Gets our attention.
- Reveals our weaknesses and strengths.
- Increases our aversion to sin.
- Demonstrates His faithfulness.
- Strengthens our faith.
- Removes our pride and self-centeredness.
- Prepares us for future service.
- Enables us to comfort others facing adversity.

Through adversity, God is molding you into a mature and effective servant. When you know Christ as your Savior, God sees you as a saint—sometimes struggling, sometimes falling, but justified, redeemed, forgiven, and reconciled to Him. He sees a person full of His unconditional love, indwelt by His presence, sealed by the Holy Spirit of promise, whose name is written in the Lamb's Book of Life. He also sees all of your potential—all the good you could accomplish for His kingdom. So take comfort, adversity won't take up permanent residence in your life. But when it's present, it can develop good things if you're willing to trust Him. Therefore, no matter what dark moments you may walk through, be confident He's going to bring you into the light. And when He does, it will certainly be worth it. ◉

LIFE LESSONS

➤ **1 Samuel 30:20 —** *"This is David's spoil."*

*A*s He had done with Joseph centuries before, God took a personal tragedy for David and turned it into a personal blessing by increasing his flocks. Obedience always brings blessing, even in dark and puzzling times.

said, "Because they did not go with us, we will not give them any of the spoil that we have recovered, except to every man his wife and his children, that they may lead *them* away and depart."

23 Then David said, "You must not do so, my brothers, with what the LORD has given us, who has kept us and delivered into our hand the band that came against us.

24 "And who will listen to you in this matter? For as his share is who goes down to the battle, so shall his share be who stays by the baggage; they shall share alike."

25 So it has been from that day forward, that he made it a statute and an ordinance for Israel to this day.

26 Now when David came to Ziklag, he sent *some* of the spoil to the elders of Judah, to his friends, saying, "Behold, a gift for you from the spoil of the enemies of the LORD:

27 to those who were in Bethel, and to those who were in Ramoth of the Negev, and to those who were in Jattir,

28 and to those who were in Aroer, and to those who were in Siphmoth, and to those who were in Eshtemoa,

29 and to those who were in Racal, and to those who were in the cities of the Jerahmeelites, and to those who were in the cities of the Kenites,

30 and to those who were in Hormah, and to those who were in Bor-ashan, and to those who were in Athach,

31 and to those who were in Hebron, and to all the places where David himself and his men were accustomed to go."

31 NOW the Philistines were fighting against Israel, and the men of Israel fled from before the Philistines and fell slain on Mount Gilboa.

➤ 2 The Philistines overtook Saul and his sons; and the Philistines killed Jona-than and Abinadab and Malchi-shua the sons of Saul.

3 The battle went heavily against Saul, and the archers hit him; and he was badly wounded by the archers.

4 Then Saul said to his armor bearer, "Draw your sword and pierce me through with it, otherwise these uncircumcised will come and pierce me through and make sport of me." But his armor bearer would not, for he was greatly afraid. So Saul took his sword and fell on it.

5 When his armor bearer saw that Saul was dead, he also fell on his sword and died with him.

6 Thus Saul died with his three sons, his armor bearer, and all his men on that day together.

7 When the men of Israel who were on the other side of the valley, with those who were beyond the Jordan, saw that the men of Israel had fled and that Saul and his sons were dead, they abandoned the cities and fled; then the Philistines came and lived in them.

8 It came about on the next day when the Philistines came to strip the slain, that they found Saul and his three sons fallen on Mount Gilboa.

9 They cut off his head and stripped off his weapons, and sent *them* through-

LIFE LESSONS

➤ **1 Samuel 30:22 —** *All the wicked and worthless men ... said, "Because they did not go with us, we will not give them any of the spoil."*

*E*ven after times of victory, "the wicked and the worthless" can raise their complaints. God allows the wheat and the tares to grow together (Matt. 13:24–30), and we must be ready for this—and make sure we know how to handle their criticism with God's grace.

➤ **1 Samuel 31:2 —** *The Philistines overtook Saul and his sons; and the Philistines killed Jonathan and Abinadab and Malchi-shua the sons of Saul.*

*J*onathan loved God and delighted in his close friend, David—yet the Lord allowed the Philistines to kill him. Why? We could speculate, but God does not tell us why. Even in tragedy, our job is to trust.

out the land of the Philistines, to carry the good news to the house of their idols and to the people.

10 They put his weapons in the temple of Ashtaroth, and they fastened his body to the wall of Beth-shan.

11 Now when the inhabitants of Jabesh-gilead heard what the Philistines had done to Saul,

12 all the valiant men rose and walked all night, and took the body of Saul and the bodies of his sons from the wall of Beth-shan, and they came to Jabesh and burned them there.

13 They took their bones and buried them under the tamarisk tree at Jabesh, and fasted seven days.

Psalm 61:5–8

5 For You have heard my vows, O God;
  You have given *me* the inheritance
    of those who fear Your name.
6 You will prolong the king's life;
  His years will be as many
    generations.

7 He will abide before God forever;
  Appoint lovingkindness and truth
    that they may preserve him.
8 So I will sing praise to Your name
    forever,
  That I may pay my vows day by day.

Proverbs 16:7–9

7 When a man's ways are pleasing to
    the LORD,
  He makes even his enemies to be at
    peace with him.
8 Better is a little with righteousness
  Than great income with injustice.

LIFE LESSONS

➤ **1 Samuel 31:9 — *They cut off his head and stripped off his weapons.***

*G*od sometimes allows His enemies to triumph—even celebrate and believe that they have overcome Him—but only for a while. God takes the long view of history, and always triumphs in the end.

9 The mind of man plans his way,
  But the LORD directs his steps.

John 3:19–36

19 "This is the judgment, that the Light has come into the world, and men loved the darkness rather than the Light, for their deeds were evil.

20 "For everyone who does evil hates the Light, and does not come to the Light for fear that his deeds will be exposed.

21 "But he who practices the truth comes to the Light, so that his deeds may be manifested as having been wrought in God."

22 After these things Jesus and His disciples came into the land of Judea, and there He was spending time with them and baptizing.

23 John also was baptizing in Aenon near Salim, because there was much water there; and *people* were coming and were being baptized—

24 for John had not yet been thrown into prison.

25 Therefore there arose a discussion on the part of John's disciples with a Jew about purification.

26 And they came to John and said to him, "Rabbi, He who was with you beyond the Jordan, to whom you have testified, behold, He is baptizing and all are coming to Him."

27 John answered and said, "A man can receive nothing unless it has been given him from heaven.

28 "You yourselves are my witnesses that I said, 'I am not the Christ,' but, 'I have been sent ahead of Him.'

29 "He who has the bride is the bridegroom; but the friend of the bridegroom, who stands and hears him, rejoices greatly because of the bridegroom's voice. So this joy of mine has been made full.

30 "He must increase, but I must decrease.

31 "He who comes from above is above all, he who is of the earth is from the earth and speaks of the earth. He who comes from heaven is above all.

32 "What He has seen and heard, of that He testifies; and no one receives His testimony.

33 "He who has received His testimony has set his seal to *this*, that God is true.

34 "For He whom God has sent speaks the words of God; for He gives the Spirit without measure.

35 "The Father loves the Son and has given all things into His hand.

36 "He who believes in the Son has eternal life; but he who does not obey the Son will not see life, but the wrath of God abides on him."

MAY 15

⊙ 2 Samuel 1:1—2:32

1 NOW it came about after the death of Saul, when David had returned from the slaughter of the Amalekites, that David remained two days in Ziklag.

2 On the third day, behold, a man came out of the camp from Saul, with his clothes torn and dust on his head. And it came about when he came to David that he fell to the ground and prostrated himself.

3 Then David said to him, "From where do you come?" And he said to him, "I have escaped from the camp of Israel."

4 David said to him, "How did things go? Please tell me." And he said, "The people have fled from the battle, and also many of the people have fallen and are dead; and Saul and Jonathan his son are dead also."

5 So David said to the young man who told him, "How do you know that Saul and his son Jonathan are dead?"

6 The young man who told him said, "By chance I happened to be on Mount Gilboa, and behold, Saul was leaning on his spear. And behold, the chariots and the horsemen pursued him closely.

7 "When he looked behind him, he saw me and called to me. And I said, 'Here I am.'

8 "He said to me, 'Who are you?' And I answered, 'I am an Amalekite.'

9 "Then he said to me, 'Please stand beside me and kill me, for agony has seized me because my life still lingers in me.'

10 "So I stood beside him and killed him, because I knew that he could not live after he had fallen. And I took the crown which *was* on his head and the bracelet which *was* on his arm, and I have brought them here to my lord."

11 Then David took hold of his clothes and tore them, and so also *did* all the men who *were* with him.

12 They mourned and wept and fasted until evening for Saul and his son Jonathan and for the people of the LORD and the house of Israel, because they had fallen by the sword.

13 David said to the young man who told him, "Where are you from?" And he answered, "I am the son of an alien, an Amalekite."

14 Then David said to him, "How is it you were not afraid to stretch out your hand to destroy the LORD'S anointed?"

15 And David called one of the young men and said, "Go, cut him down." So he struck him and he died.

16 David said to him, "Your blood is on your head, for your mouth has testified

against you, saying, 'I have killed the LORD's anointed.'"

17 Then David chanted with this lament over Saul and Jonathan his son,

18 and he told *them* to teach the sons of Judah *the song of* the bow; behold, it is written in the book of Jashar.

19 "Your beauty, O Israel, is slain on
    your high places!
How have the mighty fallen!

20 "Tell *it* not in Gath,
    Proclaim it not in the streets of
        Ashkelon,
    Or the daughters of the Philistines
        will rejoice,
    The daughters of the uncircumcised
        will exult.

21 "O mountains of Gilboa,
    Let not dew or rain be on you, nor
        fields of offerings;
    For there the shield of the mighty
        was defiled,
    The shield of Saul, not anointed
        with oil.

22 "From the blood of the slain, from
        the fat of the mighty,
    The bow of Jonathan did not turn
        back,
    And the sword of Saul did not
        return empty.

23 "Saul and Jonathan, beloved and
        pleasant in their life,
    And in their death they were not
        parted;
    They were swifter than eagles,
    They were stronger than lions.

24 "O daughters of Israel, weep over
        Saul,
    Who clothed you luxuriously in
        scarlet,
    Who put ornaments of gold on your
        apparel.

25 "How have the mighty fallen in the
        midst of the battle!
    Jonathan is slain on your high
        places.

➤ **26** "I am distressed for you, my brother
        Jonathan;
    You have been very pleasant to me.
    Your love to me was more wonderful
    Than the love of women.

27 "How have the mighty fallen,
    And the weapons of war perished!"

➤ **2** THEN it came about afterwards that David inquired of the LORD, saying, "Shall I go up to one of the cities of Judah?" And the LORD said to him, "Go up." So David said, "Where shall I go up?" And He said, "To Hebron."

2 So David went up there, and his two wives also, Ahinoam the Jezreelitess and Abigail the widow of Nabal the Carmelite.

3 And David brought up his men who *were* with him, each with his household; and they lived in the cities of Hebron.

4 Then the men of Judah came and there anointed David king over the house of Judah.

And they told David, saying, "It was the men of Jabesh-gilead who buried Saul."

5 David sent messengers to the men of Jabesh-gilead, and said to them, "May you be blessed of the LORD because you have shown this kindness to Saul your lord, and have buried him.

6 "Now may the LORD show lovingkindness and truth to you; and I also will show this goodness to you, because you have done this thing.

7 "Now therefore, let your hands be strong and be valiant; for Saul your lord is dead, and also the house of Judah has anointed me king over them."

8 But Abner the son of Ner, commander of Saul's army, had taken Ishbosheth the son of Saul and brought him over to Mahanaim.

9 He made him king over Gilead, over the Ashurites, over Jezreel, over

---

LIFE LESSONS

➤ **2 Samuel 1:26 —** *"I am distressed for you, my brother Jonathan; you have been very pleasant to me."*

*D*avid honored Saul in his lament, but he celebrated Jonathan, his dear friend. David became what he was at least in part because of Jonathan. Friends play an important role in supporting us spiritually and helping us grow in our love for the Lord.

➤ **2 Samuel 2:1 —** *"Shall I go up to one of the cities of Judah?"*

*D*avid asked God for His leading in the matter of where he should live and was careful to obey the Lord's direction in every aspect of his life. Like David, if we want God's best for us, we must obey Him completely (Prov. 16:3).

Life Examples:

DAVID: Competent Over Time

2 SAMUEL 2

*W*hat happens when we sin and delay our repentance? Are there consequences?

When David committed adultery with Bathsheba, he didn't repent immediately. Only some time later did David admit to his sin. Even then, he didn't do it on his own accord; God had to send a prophet to confront him (2 Sam. 12:1–14).

It was only after Nathan's visit did David confess his sin and then repent of it. God's discipline followed, in a severe form—perhaps so severe because of his failure to repent sooner.

If you and I deal with our sins genuinely, openly, and immediately, God can lessen the severity of our discipline. This makes sense in the light of the nature of discipline. Discipline is designed to get us to change, to obey. If God sees that we want to cooperate and that we have purposed in our hearts to obey the next time, then stern discipline is not as necessary.

Ephraim, and over Benjamin, even over all Israel.

➤ 10 Ish-bosheth, Saul's son, was forty years old when he became king over Israel, and he was king for two years. The house of Judah, however, followed David.
11 The time that David was king in Hebron over the house of Judah was seven years and six months.
12 Now Abner the son of Ner, went out from Mahanaim to Gibeon with the servants of Ish-bosheth the son of Saul.
13 And Joab the son of Zeruiah and the servants of David went out and met them by the pool of Gibeon; and they sat down, one on the one side of the pool and the other on the other side of the pool.
14 Then Abner said to Joab, "Now let the young men arise and hold a contest before us." And Joab said, "Let them arise."
15 So they arose and went over by count, twelve for Benjamin and Ish-bosheth the son of Saul, and twelve of the servants of David.
16 Each one of them seized his opponent by the head and *thrust* his sword in his opponent's side; so they fell down

together. Therefore that place was called Helkath-hazzurim, which is in Gibeon.
17 That day the battle was very severe, and Abner and the men of Israel were beaten before the servants of David.
18 Now the three sons of Zeruiah were there, Joab and Abishai and Asahel; and Asahel *was as* swift-footed as one of the gazelles which is in the field.
19 Asahel pursued Abner and did not turn to the right or to the left from following Abner.
20 Then Abner looked behind him and said, "Is that you, Asahel?" And he answered, "It is I."
21 So Abner said to him, "Turn to your right or to your left, and take hold of one of the young men for yourself, and take for yourself his spoil." But Asahel was not willing to turn aside from following him.
22 Abner repeated again to Asahel, "Turn aside from following me. Why should I strike you to the ground? How then could I lift up my face to your brother Joab?"
23 However, he refused to turn aside; therefore Abner struck him in the belly with the butt end of the spear, so that the spear came out at his back. And he fell there and died on the spot. And it came about that all who came to the place where Asahel had fallen and died, stood still.
24 But Joab and Abishai pursued Abner, and when the sun was going down, they came to the hill of Ammah, which is in front of Giah by the way of the wilderness of Gibeon.
25 The sons of Benjamin gathered together behind Abner and became one

---

LIFE LESSONS

➤ **2 Samuel 2:10** — *Ish-bosheth, Saul's son, was forty years old when he became king over Israel.*

*A*bner, not the Lord, made Saul's son, Ish-bosheth, king over Israel. Abner's plan brought the nation nothing but heartache and civil war. Whatever we acquire outside of God's will eventually turns to ashes.

band, and they stood on the top of a certain hill.

26 Then Abner called to Joab and said, "Shall the sword devour forever? Do you not know that it will be bitter in the end? How long will you refrain from telling the people to turn back from following their brothers?"

27 Joab said, "As God lives, if you had not spoken, surely then the people would have gone away in the morning, each from following his brother."

28 So Joab blew the trumpet; and all the people halted and pursued Israel no longer, nor did they continue to fight anymore.

29 Abner and his men then went through the Arabah all that night; so they crossed the Jordan, walked all morning, and came to Mahanaim.

30 Then Joab returned from following Abner; when he had gathered all the people together, nineteen of David's servants besides Asahel were missing.

31 But the servants of David had struck down many of Benjamin and Abner's men, *so that* three hundred and sixty men died.

32 And they took up Asahel and buried him in his father's tomb which was in Bethlehem. Then Joab and his men went all night until the day dawned at Hebron.

◈ Psalm 62:1–4

For the choir director; according to Jeduthun. A Psalm of David.

62 MY soul *waits* in silence for God only;
    From Him is my salvation.
✳ 2 He only is my rock and my salvation,
    My stronghold; I shall not be greatly shaken.
3 How long will you assail a man,
    That you may murder *him*, all of you,
    Like a leaning wall, like a tottering fence?
4 They have counseled only to thrust
    him down from his high position;
    They delight in falsehood;
    They bless with their mouth,
    But inwardly they curse.   Selah.

◈ Proverbs 16:10–12

10 A divine decision is in the lips of the king;
    His mouth should not err in judgment.
11 A just balance and scales belong to the LORD;
    All the weights of the bag are His concern.

12 It is an abomination for kings to commit wicked acts,
    For a throne is established on righteousness.

◈ John 4:1–30

4 THEREFORE when the Lord knew that the Pharisees had heard that Jesus was making and baptizing more disciples than John

2 (although Jesus Himself was not baptizing, but His disciples were),

3 He left Judea and went away again into Galilee.

4 And He had to pass through Samaria.

5 So He *came to a city of Samaria called Sychar, near the parcel of ground that Jacob gave to his son Joseph;

6 and Jacob's well was there. So Jesus, being wearied from His journey, was sitting thus by the well. It was about the sixth hour.

7 There *came a woman of Samaria to draw water. Jesus *said to her, "Give Me a drink."

8 For His disciples had gone away into the city to buy food.

9 Therefore the Samaritan woman *said to Him, "How is it that You, being a Jew, ask me for a drink since I am a Samaritan woman?" (For Jews have no dealings with Samaritans.)

10 Jesus answered and said to her, "If ◄ you knew the gift of God, and who it is who says to you, 'Give Me a drink,' you would have asked Him, and He would have given you living water."

11 She *said to Him, "Sir, You have nothing to draw with and the well is deep; where then do You get that living water?

12 "You are not greater than our father Jacob, are You, who gave us the well, and drank of it himself and his sons and his cattle?"

13 Jesus answered and said to her, "Everyone who drinks of this water will thirst again;

14 but whoever drinks of the water that I will give him shall never thirst; but the water that I will give him will become in him a well of water springing up to eternal life."

15 The woman *said to Him, "Sir, give me this water, so I will not be thirsty nor come all the way here to draw."

16 He *said to her, "Go, call your husband and come here."

17 The woman answered and said, "I have no husband." Jesus *said to her, "You have correctly said, 'I have no husband';

18 for you have had five husbands, and the one whom you now have is not your husband; this you have said truly."

19 The woman *said to Him, "Sir, I perceive that You are a prophet.

20 "Our fathers worshiped in this mountain, and you *people* say that in Jerusalem is the place where men ought to worship."

21 Jesus *said to her, "Woman, believe Me, an hour is coming when neither in this mountain nor in Jerusalem will you worship the Father.

22 "You worship what you do not know; we worship what we know, for salvation is from the Jews.

23 "But an hour is coming, and now is, when the true worshipers will worship the Father in spirit and truth; for such people the Father seeks to be His worshipers.

24 "God is spirit, and those who worship Him must worship in spirit and truth."

25 The woman *said to Him, "I know that Messiah is coming (He who is called Christ); when that One comes, He will declare all things to us."

26 Jesus *said to her, "I who speak to you am *He*."

27 At this point His disciples came, and they were amazed that He had been speaking with a woman, yet no one said, "What do You seek?" or, "Why do You speak with her?"

28 So the woman left her waterpot, and went into the city and *said to the men,

29 "Come, see a man who told me all the things that I *have* done; this is not the Christ, is it?"

30 They went out of the city, and were coming to Him.

LIFE LESSONS

> John 4:10 — *"He would have given you living water."*

*E*ven when God asks us to do certain things, it's really an invitation to receive greater things from Him. Jesus asked the woman for a drink of water so He could offer her living waater.

> John 4:23 — *"True worshipers will worship the Father in spirit and truth."*

*T*he Lord actively seeks men and women who will eagerly worship Him according to the truth of the Word and by the power of the Holy Spirit.

MAY 16

◈ 2 Samuel 3:1—4:12

3 NOW there was a long war between the house of Saul and the house of David; and David grew steadily stronger, but the house of Saul grew weaker continually.

2 Sons were born to David at Hebron: his firstborn was Amnon, by Ahinoam the Jezreelitess;

3 and his second, Chileab, by Abigail the widow of Nabal the Carmelite; and the third, Absalom the son of Maacah, the daughter of Talmai, king of Geshur;

4 and the fourth, Adonijah the son of Haggith; and the fifth, Shephatiah the son of Abital;

5　and the sixth, Ithream, by David's wife Eglah. These were born to David at Hebron.

6　It came about while there was war between the house of Saul and the house of David that Abner was making himself strong in the house of Saul.

7　Now Saul had a concubine whose name was Rizpah, the daughter of Aiah; and Ish-bosheth said to Abner, "Why have you gone in to my father's concubine?"

8　Then Abner was very angry over the words of Ish-bosheth and said, "Am I a dog's head that belongs to Judah? Today I show kindness to the house of Saul your father, to his brothers and to his friends, and have not delivered you into the hands of David; and yet today you charge me with a guilt concerning the woman.

9　"May God do so to Abner, and more also, if as the LORD has sworn to David, I do not accomplish this for him,

10　to transfer the kingdom from the house of Saul and to establish the throne of David over Israel and over Judah, from Dan even to Beersheba."

11　And he could no longer answer Abner a word, because he was afraid of him.

12　Then Abner sent messengers to David in his place, saying, "Whose is the land? Make your covenant with me, and behold, my hand shall be with you to bring all Israel over to you."

13　He said, "Good! I will make a covenant with you, but I demand one thing of you, namely, you shall not see my face unless you first bring Michal, Saul's daughter, when you come to see me."

14　So David sent messengers to Ish-bosheth, Saul's son, saying, "Give me my wife Michal, to whom I was betrothed for a hundred foreskins of the Philistines."

15　Ish-bosheth sent and took her from *her* husband, from Paltiel the son of Laish.

16　But her husband went with her, weeping as he went, and followed her as far as Bahurim. Then Abner said to him, "Go, return." So he returned.

17　Now Abner had consultation with the elders of Israel, saying, "In times past you were seeking for David to be king over you.

18　"Now then, do *it!* For the LORD has spoken of David, saying, 'By the hand of My servant David I will save My people Israel from the hand of the Philistines and from the hand of all their enemies.'"

19　Abner also spoke in the hearing of Benjamin; and in addition Abner went to speak in the hearing of David in Hebron all that seemed good to Israel and to the whole house of Benjamin.

20　Then Abner and twenty men with him came to David at Hebron. And David made a feast for Abner and the men who were with him.

21　Abner said to David, "Let me arise and go and gather all Israel to my lord the king, that they may make a covenant with you, and that you may be king over all that your soul desires." So David sent Abner away, and he went in peace.

22　And behold, the servants of David and Joab came from a raid and brought much spoil with them; but Abner was not with David in Hebron, for he had sent him away, and he had gone in peace.

23　When Joab and all the army that was with him arrived, they told Joab, saying, "Abner the son of Ner came to the king, and he has sent him away, and he has gone in peace."

24　Then Joab came to the king and said, "What have you done? Behold, Abner came to you; why then have you sent him away and he is already gone?

25　"You know Abner the son of Ner, that he came to deceive you and to learn of your going out and coming in and to find out all that you are doing."

26　When Joab came out from David, he sent messengers after Abner, and they brought him back from the well of Sirah; but David did not know *it.*

27　So when Abner returned to Hebron, Joab took him aside into the middle of the gate to speak with him privately, and there he struck him in the belly so that he died on account of the blood of Asahel his brother.

28 Afterward when David heard it, he said, "I and my kingdom are innocent before the LORD forever of the blood of Abner the son of Ner.

29 "May it fall on the head of Joab and on all his father's house; and may there not fail from the house of Joab one who has a discharge, or who is a leper, or who takes hold of a distaff, or who falls by the sword, or who lacks bread."

30 So Joab and Abishai his brother killed Abner because he had put their brother Asahel to death in the battle at Gibeon.

31 Then David said to Joab and to all the people who were with him, "Tear your clothes and gird on sackcloth and lament before Abner." And King David walked behind the bier.

32 Thus they buried Abner in Hebron; and the king lifted up his voice and wept at the grave of Abner, and all the people wept.

33 The king chanted a *lament* for Abner and said,

"Should Abner die as a fool dies?
34 "Your hands were not bound, nor
        your feet put in fetters;
    As one falls before the wicked, you
        have fallen."

And all the people wept again over him.

35 Then all the people came to persuade David to eat bread while it was still day; but David vowed, saying, "May God do so to me, and more also, if I taste bread or anything else before the sun goes down."

36 Now all the people took note *of it,* and it pleased them, just as everything the king did pleased all the people.

37 So all the people and all Israel understood that day that it had not been *the will* of the king to put Abner the son of Ner to death.

38 Then the king said to his servants, "Do you not know that a prince and a great man has fallen this day in Israel?

39 "I am weak today, though anointed king; and these men the sons of Zeruiah are too difficult for me. May the LORD repay the evildoer according to his evil."

4 NOW when Ish-bosheth, Saul's son, heard that Abner had died in Hebron, he lost courage, and all Israel was disturbed.

2 Saul's son *had* two men who were commanders of bands: the name of the one was Baanah and the name of the other Rechab, sons of Rimmon the Beerothite, of the sons of Benjamin (for Beeroth is also considered *part* of Benjamin,

3 and the Beerothites fled to Gittaim and have been aliens there until this day).

4 Now Jonathan, Saul's son, had a son crippled in his feet. He was five years old when the report of Saul and Jonathan came from Jezreel, and his nurse took him up and fled. And it happened that in her hurry to flee, he fell and became lame. And his name was Mephibosheth.

5 So the sons of Rimmon the Beerothite, Rechab and Baanah, departed and came to the house of Ish-bosheth in the heat of the day while he was taking his midday rest.

6 They came to the middle of the house as if to get wheat, and they struck him in the belly; and Rechab and Baanah his brother escaped.

7 Now when they came into the house, as he was lying on his bed in his bedroom, they struck him and killed him and beheaded him. And they took his head and traveled by way of the Arabah all night.

8 Then they brought the head of Ish-bosheth to David at Hebron and said to the king, "Behold, the head of Ish-bosheth the son of Saul, your enemy, who sought your life; thus the LORD has given my lord the king vengeance this day on Saul and his descendants."

9 David answered Rechab and Baanah

LIFE LESSONS

➤ **2 Samuel 4:8 —** *Then they brought the head of Ish-bosheth to David at Hebron.*

*D*avid was not impressed by spiritual words when he saw evil deeds. As a man after God's own heart, he could not delight in wickedness, even if it appeared to benefit him.

➤ **2 Samuel 4:9 —** *"As the Lord lives, who has redeemed my life from all distress."*

*T*he Lord loves to redeem our lives from distress. David realized that only God could free him from adversity.

his brother, sons of Rimmon the Beer-othite, and said to them, "As the LORD lives, who has redeemed my life from all distress,
10 when one told me, saying, 'Behold, Saul is dead,' and thought he was bring-ing good news, I seized him and killed him in Ziklag, which was the reward I gave him for *his* news.
11 "How much more, when wicked men have killed a righteous man in his own house on his bed, shall I not now require his blood from your hand and destroy you from the earth?"
12 Then David commanded the young men, and they killed them and cut off their hands and feet and hung them up beside the pool in Hebron. But they took the head of Ish-bosheth and buried it in the grave of Abner in Hebron.

Psalm 62:5–12

5 My soul, wait in silence for God only,
    For my hope is from Him.

6 He only is my rock and my
      salvation,
    My stronghold; I shall not be
      shaken.
7 On God my salvation and my glory
      rest;
    The rock of my strength, my refuge
      is in God.
8 Trust in Him at all times, O people;
    Pour out your heart before Him;
    God is a refuge for us.   Selah.
9 Men of low degree are only vanity
      and men of rank are a lie;
    In the balances they go up;
    They are together lighter than
      breath.
10 Do not trust in oppression
    And do not vainly hope in robbery;
    If riches increase, do not set *your*
      heart *upon them.*
11 Once God has spoken;
    Twice I have heard this:
    That power belongs to God;
12 And lovingkindness is Yours,
      O Lord,
    For You recompense a man
      according to his work.

ANSWERS TO LIFE'S QUESTIONS

What does it mean to sit before the Lord?

PSALM 62:5–8

Perhaps the greatest key to spiritual growth is spending time alone with the Lord. This means taking the time to speak with God about whatever is on your heart—and, even more importantly, allowing Him to speak to you.

God called King David "a man after My own heart" (Acts 13:22). To win that kind of reputation, David first needed to know the mind and heart of God so that he might be and do what the Lord desired of him. David sought to know God. He frequently "inquired" of the Lord. He spent time in the Lord's presence, singing to Him from the depths of his heart. In 2 Samuel 7:18 we read, "Then David the king went in and sat before the LORD, and he said, 'Who am I, O Lord GOD, and what is my house, that You have brought me this far?'"

What did it mean for David to sit before the Lord? It means that he spent time alone in the presence of God, communicating with the Lord from the depths of his heart, asking Him questions, and listening quietly for the Lord's answers.

Jesus frequently sought time apart with His heavenly Father. Time with the Father provided Him with a source of comfort and strength. Jesus also sought time alone with His disciples so that He might teach them and they might find spiritual refreshment (Luke 9:17–24).

We are wise if we choose to spend time alone with God, in a place without distractions or interruptions, for a period sufficient for us to relax completely and focus our attention fully upon the Lord and His Word. We must be willing to wait in the Lord's presence until we receive God's directives or His words of comfort.

Why don't many of us desire to spend time alone with God? The foremost reason is we don't feel sure of our relationships with God and, therefore, we feel afraid of Him.

But those who are born again spiritually have a Father-child relationship with the Lord. Our heavenly Father loves us unconditionally and deals with us tenderly and patiently. The more we learn what He's really like—the more we see Him as He truly is—the more we will long to spend time alone with Him . . . and the more we will know the fullness of His grace.

✦ Proverbs 16:13–15

13 Righteous lips are the delight of
      kings,
      And he who speaks right is
      loved.
14 The fury of a king is *like*
      messengers of death,
      But a wise man will appease it.
15 In the light of a king's face is
      life,
      And his favor is like a cloud with
      the spring rain.

◎ John 4:31–54

31 Meanwhile the disciples were urging Him, saying, "Rabbi, eat."
32 But He said to them, "I have food to eat that you do not know about."
33 So the disciples were saying to one another, "No one brought Him *anything* to eat, did he?"
34 Jesus *said to them, "My food is to do the will of Him who sent Me and to accomplish His work.
35 "Do you not say, 'There are yet four months, and *then* comes the harvest'? Behold, I say to you, lift up your eyes and look on the fields, that they are white for harvest.
36 "Already he who reaps is receiving wages and is gathering fruit for life eternal; so that he who sows and he who reaps may rejoice together.
37 "For in this *case* the saying is true, 'One sows and another reaps.'

38 "I sent you to reap that for which you have not labored; others have labored and you have entered into their labor."
39 From that city many of the Samaritans believed in Him because of the word of the woman who testified, "He told me all the things that I *have* done."
40 So when the Samaritans came to Jesus, they were asking Him to stay with them; and He stayed there two days.
41 Many more believed because of His word;
42 and they were saying to the woman, "It is no longer because of what you said that we believe, for we have heard for ourselves and know that this One is indeed the Savior of the world."
43 After the two days He went forth from there into Galilee.
44 For Jesus Himself testified that a prophet has no honor in his own country.
45 So when He came to Galilee, the Galileans received Him, having seen all the things that He did in Jerusalem at the feast; for they themselves also went to the feast.
46 Therefore He came again to Cana of Galilee where He had made the water wine. And there was a royal official whose son was sick at Capernaum.
47 When he heard that Jesus had come out of Judea into Galilee, he went to Him and was imploring *Him* to come down and heal his son; for he was at the point of death.
48 So Jesus said to him, "Unless you

people see signs and wonders, you *simply* will not believe."
49 The royal official *said to Him, "Sir, come down before my child dies."
50 Jesus *said to him, "Go; your son lives." The man believed the word that Jesus spoke to him and started off.
51 As he was now going down, *his* slaves met him, saying that his son was living.
52 So he inquired of them the hour

when he began to get better. Then they said to him, "Yesterday at the seventh hour the fever left him."
53 So the father knew that *it was* at that hour in which Jesus said to him, "Your son lives"; and he himself believed and his whole household.
54 This is again a second sign that Jesus performed when He had come out of Judea into Galilee.

✦ 2 Samuel 5:1—6:23

5THEN all the tribes of Israel came to David at Hebron and said, "Behold, we are your bone and your flesh.
2 "Previously, when Saul was king over us, you were the one who led Israel out and in. And the LORD said to you, 'You will shepherd My people Israel, and you will be a ruler over Israel.'"
3 So all the elders of Israel came to the king at Hebron, and King David made a covenant with them before the LORD at Hebron; then they anointed David king over Israel.
4 David was thirty years old when he became king, *and* he reigned forty years.
5 At Hebron he reigned over Judah seven years and six months, and in Jerusalem he reigned thirty-three years over all Israel and Judah.
6 Now the king and his men went to Jerusalem against the Jebusites, the inhabitants of the land, and they said to David, "You shall not come in here, but the blind and lame will turn you away"; thinking, "David cannot enter here."
7 Nevertheless, David captured the stronghold of Zion, that is the city of David.
8 David said on that day, "Whoever would strike the Jebusites, let him reach the lame and the blind, who are hated by David's soul, through the water tunnel." Therefore they say, "The blind or the lame shall not come into the house."
9 So David lived in the stronghold and called it the city of David. And David built all around from the Millo and inward.

10 David became greater and greater, ◄ for the LORD God of hosts was with him.
11 Then Hiram king of Tyre sent messengers to David with cedar trees and carpenters and stonemasons; and they built a house for David.
12 And David realized that the LORD had established him as king over Israel, and that He had exalted his kingdom for the sake of His people Israel.
13 Meanwhile David took more concubines and wives from Jerusalem, after he came from Hebron; and more sons and daughters were born to David.
14 Now these are the names of those who were born to him in Jerusalem: Shammua, Shobab, Nathan, Solomon,
15 Ibhar, Elishua, Nepheg, Japhia,
16 Elishama, Eliada and Eliphelet.
17 When the Philistines heard that they had anointed David king over Israel, all the Philistines went up to seek out David; and when David heard *of it*, he went down to the stronghold.
18 Now the Philistines came and spread themselves out in the valley of Rephaim.
19 Then David inquired of the LORD,

L I F E   L E S S O N S

➤ **2 Samuel 5:10 —** *David became greater and greater, for the LORD God of hosts was with him.*

*W*hen we follow the Lord wholeheartedly as David did, we too will enjoy His wonderful presence. And just as He did with David, He can cause us to grow in godliness and even to become great for the sake of His kingdom (Matt. 18:1–5; 20:26–28; 23:11, 12).

saying, "Shall I go up against the Philistines? Will You give them into my hand?" And the LORD said to David, "Go up, for I will certainly give the Philistines into your hand."

20 So David came to Baal-perazim and defeated them there; and he said, "The LORD has broken through my enemies before me like the breakthrough of waters." Therefore he named that place Baal-perazim.

21 They abandoned their idols there, so David and his men carried them away.

22 Now the Philistines came up once again and spread themselves out in the valley of Rephaim.

23 When David inquired of the LORD, He said, "You shall not go *directly* up; circle around behind them and come at them in front of the balsam trees.

24 "It shall be, when you hear the sound of marching in the tops of the balsam trees, then you shall act promptly, for then the LORD will have gone out before you to strike the army of the Philistines."

25 Then David did so, just as the LORD had commanded him, and struck down the Philistines from Geba as far as Gezer.

6 NOW David again gathered all the chosen men of Israel, thirty thousand.

2 And David arose and went with all the people who were with him to Baale-judah, to bring up from there the ark of God which is called by the Name, the very name of the LORD of hosts who is enthroned *above* the cherubim.

3 They placed the ark of God on a new cart that they might bring it from the house of Abinadab which was on the hill; and Uzzah and Ahio, the sons of Abinadab, were leading the new cart.

4 So they brought it with the ark of God from the house of Abinadab, which was on the hill; and Ahio was walking ahead of the ark.

5 Meanwhile, David and all the house of Israel were celebrating before the LORD with all kinds of *instruments made of* fir wood, and with lyres, harps, tambourines, castanets and cymbals.

6 But when they came to the threshing floor of Nacon, Uzzah reached out toward the ark of God and took hold of it, for the oxen nearly upset *it*.

7 And the anger of the LORD burned against Uzzah, and God struck him down there for his irreverence; and he died there by the ark of God.

8 David became angry because of the LORD's outburst against Uzzah, and that place is called Perez-uzzah to this day.

9 So David was afraid of the LORD that day; and he said, "How can the ark of the LORD come to me?"

10 And David was unwilling to move the ark of the LORD into the city of David with him; but David took it aside to the house of Obed-edom the Gittite.

11 Thus the ark of the LORD remained in the house of Obed-edom the Gittite three months, and the LORD blessed Obed-edom and all his household.

12 Now it was told King David, saying, "The LORD has blessed the house of Obed-edom and all that belongs to him, on account of the ark of God." David went and brought up the ark of God from the house of Obed-edom into the city of David with gladness.

13 And so it was, that when the bearers of the ark of the LORD had gone six paces, he sacrificed an ox and a fatling.

14 And David was dancing before the LORD with all *his* might, and David was wearing a linen ephod.

15 So David and all the house of Israel were bringing up the ark of the LORD with shouting and the sound of the trumpet.

16 Then it happened *as* the ark of the LORD came into the city of David that Michal the daughter of Saul looked out of the window and saw King David leaping and dancing before the LORD; and she despised him in her heart.

17 So they brought in the ark of the

LIFE LESSONS

➤ **2 Samuel 6:9 — *So David was afraid of the LORD that day.***

*D*avid failed to consult the Word of God before he moved the ark. If he had, he would have learned the specific way God instructed His people to transport it (Ex. 25:12–14). God never blesses disobedience. And David, the man after God's own heart, learned a hard lesson about the infinite holiness of God and the necessity of obeying His words completely. God is our Friend, but He never ceases to be Lord.

LORD and set it in its place inside the tent which David had pitched for it; and David offered burnt offerings and peace offerings before the LORD.

18 When David had finished offering the burnt offering and the peace offering, he blessed the people in the name of the LORD of hosts.

19 Further, he distributed to all the people, to all the multitude of Israel, both to men and women, a cake of bread and one of dates and one of raisins to each one. Then all the people departed each to his house.

20 But when David returned to bless his household, Michal the daughter of Saul came out to meet David and said, "How the king of Israel distinguished himself today! He uncovered himself today in the eyes of his servants' maids as one of the foolish ones shamelessly uncovers himself!"

21 So David said to Michal, "*It was* before the LORD, who chose me above your father and above all his house, to appoint me ruler over the people of the LORD, over Israel; therefore I will celebrate before the LORD.

22 "I will be more lightly esteemed than this and will be humble in my own eyes, but with the maids of whom you have spoken, with them I will be distinguished."

23 Michal the daughter of Saul had no child to the day of her death.

✦ Psalm 63:1–11

A Psalm of David, when he was in the wilderness of Judah.

63 O GOD, You are my God; I shall
seek You earnestly;
My soul thirsts for You, my flesh
yearns for You,

In a dry and weary land where
there is no water.
2 Thus I have seen You in the
sanctuary,
To see Your power and Your glory.
3 Because Your lovingkindness is
better than life,
My lips will praise You.
4 So I will bless You as long as I live;
I will lift up my hands in Your name.
5 My soul is satisfied as with marrow
and fatness,
And my mouth offers praises with
joyful lips.
6 When I remember You on my bed,
I meditate on You in the night watches,
7 For You have been my help,
And in the shadow of Your wings
I sing for joy.
8 My soul clings to You;
Your right hand upholds me.
9 But those who seek my life to
destroy it,
Will go into the depths of the earth.
10 They will be delivered over to the
power of the sword;
They will be a prey for foxes.
11 But the king will rejoice in God;
Everyone who swears by Him will
glory,
For the mouths of those who speak
lies will be stopped.

✦ Proverbs 16:16, 17

16 How much better it is to get wisdom
than gold!
And to get understanding is to be
chosen above silver.
17 The highway of the upright is to
depart from evil;
He who watches his way preserves
his life.

LIFE LESSONS

➤ **Psalm 63:1 — *My soul thirsts for You.***

*D*o you long for God as the psalmist did? Do you seek Him earnestly and pursue Him throughout your day? Your intimacy with the Lord will determine the impact of your life. So go before His throne often with confidence because only He can fill the hunger of your soul.

➤ **Psalm 63:6 — *I meditate on You in the night watches.***

*W*hen God brings a matter to your attention at bedtime, don't ignore it. Pursue it. If he is causing you to feel restless, ask Him what He wants you to do. He always speaks when you make yourself available to Him.

WHAT THE BIBLE SAYS ABOUT

Seeking the Lord

Psalm 63:1–5

*H*ave you experienced times in your spiritual life when you don't feel the presence of God? You know God is there, but you just don't feel His presence. You know He's promised to answer your prayers, but when you pray, you don't see much evidence He is listening. You get to the point where you read the Bible, and it's just black print on white pages—nothing about it comforts or motivates you.

You're going through a dry and weary time in your spiritual life. Like David, you cry out, "O God . . . my soul thirsts for You, my flesh yearns for You, in a dry and weary land where there is no water" (Ps. 63:1).

If you keep a diary of your spiritual life with the Lord, more than likely, here is what you'll discover: Those times when you don't feel God's presence usually come when your mind is focused on other things—on something other than Jesus Christ. Although you have Jesus in your life, He's not your first priority.

So what did David do when he felt those dry times? He wrote, "I have seen You in the sanctuary, to see Your power and Your glory" (Ps. 63:2). David sought the Lord. We should, too. Here are eight excellent reasons we should seek the Lord.

1. *We seek the Lord because Jesus Christ desires to be the object of our affections.*

Christ wants to be our focus—the most important person in our lives, whom we adore. We were created to love and worship God—that's our primary purpose. Our service should be the overflow of a life of worship and love (Luke 10:27).

2. *We seek the Lord because He wants to have fellowship with us.*

God created us to have fellowship with Him and to express His love toward us. He desires to love us and be our Friend. He is not only our Savior, Lord, Judge, Master, and King—He is our Beloved. Jesus wants us to build a relationship with Him—loving each other and fellowshiping with each other (John 14:23).

3. *We seek the Lord so that we learn to depend upon Him.*

God is our Provider and the source of all things. He satisfies all of our needs. Therefore, God wants us to learn to depend upon Him for everything, not just come to Him in times of desperation. He is eager to meet all of our needs (Phil. 4:19).

4. *We seek the Lord because God knows the pressure the world puts on us.*

God knows the pressure of the world is powerful. It's very easy for us to lose our focus on the Lord because the devil is always attacking us with temptations. Unless you and I seek Jesus Christ constantly, we will be tempted away from serving the Lord. Though we'll never lose our salvation, we'll lose the focus of our attention and our desire for Him. Therefore, we must seek God constantly so we can live obediently before Him and experience His victory over the world (John 16:33).

5. *We seek the Lord because anything else we seek will disappoint us.*

If we seek anything else in life other than Christ, the deepest needs of our hearts won't be satisfied. Only Jesus Christ can fill our most profound needs (Ps. 145:16).

6. *We seek the Lord for our own protection.*

If we do not deliberately choose to seek the Lord, we will do evil. Why? Because if we don't seek God, we'll drift away from Him and the pressures of this world will succeed in tempting us. We cannot fight temptation on our own. Rather, we can only fight our sin nature by maintaining a close relationship with Christ (Rom. 7).

7. *We seek the Lord because Christ is everything to us.*

Jesus is everything we need. This doesn't mean we should quit our jobs. Performing our vocations is different from seeking the Lord and looking to Him to meet our needs. In fact, the careers God has called us to fulfill are part of His plan for our lives. However, a job should never be the main thing we seek because it can't satisfy our needs as Jesus can. Everything we have comes as a result of Him living within us (John 17:3).

8. *We seek the Lord because we become what we focus on most.*

If you focus on negative things, you will become negative. If you focus on sensual things, you will become sensual. If you focus on materialistic things, you will become materialistic. Whatever you and I focus on most, that is what we become (3 John 1:11).

Therefore, seek the Lord. Love Him, focus upon Him, and become like Him. Seek Him every day of your life, for as long as you live. He will be your oasis in the dry times of your life, and like David you'll say, "My soul is satisfied as with marrow and fatness, and my mouth offers praises with joyful lips" (Ps. 63:5). ◈

John 5:1–23

5 AFTER these things there was a feast of the Jews, and Jesus went up to Jerusalem.
2 Now there is in Jerusalem by the sheep *gate* a pool, which is called in Hebrew Bethesda, having five porticoes.
3 In these lay a multitude of those who were sick, blind, lame, and withered, [waiting for the moving of the waters;
4 for an angel of the Lord went down at certain seasons into the pool and stirred up the water; whoever then first, after the stirring up of the water, stepped in was made well from whatever disease with which he was afflicted.]
5 A man was there who had been ill for thirty-eight years.
6 When Jesus saw him lying *there,* and knew that he had already been a long time *in that condition,* He *said to him, "Do you wish to get well?"
7 The sick man answered Him, "Sir, I have no man to put me into the pool when the water is stirred up, but while I am coming, another steps down before me."
8 Jesus *said to him, "Get up, pick up your pallet and walk."
9 Immediately the man became well, and picked up his pallet and *began* to walk.
Now it was the Sabbath on that day.
10 So the Jews were saying to the man who was cured, "It is the Sabbath, and it is not permissible for you to carry your pallet."
11 But he answered them, "He who made me well was the one who said to me, 'Pick up your pallet and walk.' "
12 They asked him, "Who is the man who said to you, 'Pick up *your pallet* and walk'?"
13 But the man who was healed did not know who it was, for Jesus had slipped away while there was a crowd in *that* place.
14 Afterward Jesus *found him in the temple and said to him, "Behold, you have become well; do not sin anymore, so that nothing worse happens to you."
15 The man went away, and told the Jews that it was Jesus who had made him well.
16 For this reason the Jews were persecuting Jesus, because He was doing these things on the Sabbath.

17 But He answered them, "My Father is working until now, and I Myself am working."
18 For this reason therefore the Jews were seeking all the more to kill Him, because He not only was breaking the Sabbath, but also was calling God His own Father, making Himself equal with God.
19 Therefore Jesus answered and was saying to them, "Truly, truly, I say to you, the Son can do nothing of Himself, unless *it is* something He sees the Father doing; for whatever the Father does, these things the Son also does in like manner.
20 "For the Father loves the Son, and shows Him all things that He Himself is doing; and *the Father* will show Him greater works than these, so that you will marvel.
21 "For just as the Father raises the dead and gives them life, even so the Son also gives life to whom He wishes.
22 "For not even the Father judges anyone, but He has given all judgment to the Son,
23 so that all will honor the Son even as they honor the Father. He who does not honor the Son does not honor the Father who sent Him.

LIFE LESSONS

➤ **John 5:14 — *"You have become well; do not sin anymore, so that nothing worse happens to you."***

Not all sickness is a result of sin (John 9:3), but some may be. Paul told the Corinthians that because of their sin, "many among you are weak and sick, and a number sleep" (1 Cor. 11:30).

➤ **John 5:18 — *The Jews were seeking all the more to kill Him, because He . . . was calling God His own Father, making Himself equal with God.***

Instead of being joyful to have God in their presence, His opponents became angry and murderous because of their jealousy and desire for power. How do you react to God's presence? Do you rejoice that He is with you and obey His commands, or do you struggle with Him for control? You'll never lose by obeying God, but you may forfeit everything by standing against Him. Therefore, choose wisely.

7 NOW it came about when the king lived in his house, and the LORD had given him rest on every side from all his enemies,

2 that the king said to Nathan the prophet, "See now, I dwell in a house of cedar, but the ark of God dwells within tent curtains."

3 Nathan said to the king, "Go, do all that is in your mind, for the LORD is with you."

4 But in the same night the word of the LORD came to Nathan, saying,

5 "Go and say to My servant David, 'Thus says the LORD, "Are you the one who should build Me a house to dwell in?

6 "For I have not dwelt in a house since the day I brought up the sons of Israel from Egypt, even to this day; but I have been moving about in a tent, even in a tabernacle.

7 "Wherever I have gone with all the sons of Israel, did I speak a word with one of the tribes of Israel, which I commanded to shepherd My people Israel, saying, 'Why have you not built Me a house of cedar?'"'

➤ 8 "Now therefore, thus you shall say to My servant David, 'Thus says the LORD of hosts, "I took you from the pasture, from following the sheep, to be ruler over My people Israel.

9 "I have been with you wherever you have gone and have cut off all your enemies from before you; and I will make you a great name, like the names of the great men who are on the earth.

10 "I will also appoint a place for My people Israel and will plant them, that they may live in their own place and not be disturbed again, nor will the wicked afflict them any more as formerly,

11 even from the day that I commanded judges to be over My people Israel; and I will give you rest from all your enemies. The LORD also declares to you that the LORD will make a house for you.

12 "When your days are complete and you lie down with your fathers, I will raise up your descendant after you, who will come forth from you, and I will establish his kingdom.

13 "He shall build a house for My name, and I will establish the throne of his kingdom forever.

14 "I will be a father to him and he will be a son to Me; when he commits iniquity, I will correct him with the rod of men and the strokes of the sons of men,

15 but My lovingkindness shall not depart from him, as I took it away from Saul, whom I removed from before you.

16 "Your house and your kingdom shall endure before Me forever; your throne shall be established forever."'"

17 In accordance with all these words and in all this vision, so Nathan spoke to David.

18 Then David the king went in and sat before the LORD, and he said, "Who am I, O Lord GOD, and what is my house, that You have brought me this far?

19 "And yet this was insignificant in Your eyes, O Lord GOD, for You have spoken also of the house of Your servant concerning the distant future. And this is the custom of man, O Lord GOD.

20 "Again what more can David say to You? For You know Your servant, O Lord GOD!

21 "For the sake of Your word, and according to Your own heart, You have done all this greatness to let Your servant know.

22 "For this reason You are great, O Lord GOD; for there is none like You, and there is no God besides You, according to all that we have heard with our ears.

23 "And what one nation on the earth is like Your people Israel, whom God went to redeem for Himself as a people and to make a name for Himself, and to do a great thing for You and awesome things for Your land, before Your people whom You have redeemed for Yourself from Egypt, from nations and their gods?

LIFE LESSONS

➤ **2 Samuel 7:8 — "I took you from the pasture, from following the sheep, to be ruler over My people Israel."**

*W*hen we begin to enjoy some success, we would do well to remind ourselves of where we came from and how we arrived at our place of blessing. It is all God's doing—every good thing we have comes from His hand (James 1:17).

WHAT THE BIBLE SAYS ABOUT ◉

The Immense Value of Meditation

2 Samuel 7:29

The mere mention of the word "meditation" tends to conjure up images foreign to the Western mind. Perhaps that's why so many contemporary believers have removed the word from their vocabulary. But we do this at our great peril because scriptural meditation greatly helps us to listen accurately to God.

King David pursued this godly endeavor fervently and fruitfully. Many psalms resulted from his quiet waiting and reflecting upon God. As a "man after [God's] heart" (Acts 13:22), David first had to know the mind and heart of God. To a large extent, David accomplished this through the persistent practice of godly meditation.

In our over-scheduled lives, we often find it difficult to see a purpose in what we do. With so many things and people clamoring for our time, we must return to one of life's most important activities—meditation.

Godly meditation means lifting your heart heavenward and listening to God. It is focusing your attention on Christ and shutting out everything else. Without practicing daily meditation on the Lord, it is impossible to experience:

- *Holiness of heart*: Meditation allows you to concentrate on who God is and to grow into oneness with Him.
- *Contentment*: With meditation on God comes great contentment of soul.
- *Being a help to someone else*: If we don't draw our strength from God, we soon run out of strength.

In order to continue the habit of meditating on the Lord, we must guard against meditating simply out of habit. We must have a pure purpose for meditation: to get to know God more intimately. We must also have a plan for when we come to Him, including a portion of time when we meditate on His Word, and a prayer journal in which to offer up prayers and write what God tells us through the Holy Spirit and Scripture.

Meditate on the Lord—His majesty, glory, goodness, faithfulness, and promises. Meditate on who He is—and you will come to know His character and His presence in a deep, fresh way. ◉

24 "For You have established for Yourself Your people Israel as Your own people forever, and You, O LORD, have become their God.
25 "Now therefore, O LORD God, the word that You have spoken concerning Your servant and his house, confirm *it* forever, and do as You have spoken,
26 that Your name may be magnified forever, by saying, 'The LORD of hosts is God over Israel'; and may the house of Your servant David be established before You.
27 "For You, O LORD of hosts, the God of Israel, have made a revelation to Your servant, saying, 'I will build you a house'; therefore Your servant has found courage to pray this prayer to You.
28 "Now, O Lord GOD, You are God, and Your words are truth, and You have promised this good thing to Your servant.
29 "Now therefore, may it please You to bless the house of Your servant, that it may continue forever before You. For You, O Lord GOD, have spoken; and with Your blessing may the house of Your servant be blessed forever."

8 NOW after this it came about that David defeated the Philistines and subdued them; and David took control of the chief city from the hand of the Philistines.
2 He defeated Moab, and measured them with the line, making them lie down on the ground; and he measured

LIFE LESSONS

➤ **2 Samuel 7:29 — "Bless the house of Your servant, that it may continue forever before You."**

David responded to God's gracious promise by praising Him for fulfilling His pledge and giving Him all the glory. David understood that by praying according to the Lord's promise, he aligned himself with His will. We can and should do the same.

two lines to put to death and one full line to keep alive. And the Moabites became servants to David, bringing tribute.

3 Then David defeated Hadadezer, the son of Rehob king of Zobah, as he went to restore his rule at the River.

4 David captured from him 1,700 horsemen and 20,000 foot soldiers; and David hamstrung the chariot horses, but reserved *enough* of them for 100 chariots.

5 When the Arameans of Damascus came to help Hadadezer, king of Zobah, David killed 22,000 Arameans.

6 Then David put garrisons among the Arameans of Damascus, and the Arameans became servants to David, bringing tribute. And the LORD helped David wherever he went.

7 David took the shields of gold which were carried by the servants of Hadadezer and brought them to Jerusalem.

8 From Betah and from Berothai, cities of Hadadezer, King David took a very large amount of bronze.

9 Now when Toi king of Hamath heard that David had defeated all the army of Hadadezer,

10 Toi sent Joram his son to King David to greet him and bless him, because he had fought against Hadadezer and defeated him; for Hadadezer had been at war with Toi. And *Joram* brought with him articles of silver, of gold and of bronze.

11 King David also dedicated these to the LORD, with the silver and gold that he had dedicated from all the nations which he had subdued:

12 from Aram and Moab and the sons of Ammon and the Philistines and Amalek, and from the spoil of Hadadezer, son of Rehob, king of Zobah.

13 So David made a name *for himself* when he returned from killing 18,000 Arameans in the Valley of Salt.

14 He put garrisons in Edom. In all Edom he put garrisons, and all the Edomites became servants to David. And the LORD helped David wherever he went.

15 So David reigned over all Israel; and David administered justice and righteousness for all his people.

16 Joab the son of Zeruiah *was* over the army, and Jehoshaphat the son of Ahilud *was* recorder.

17 Zadok the son of Ahitub and Ahime-lech the son of Abiathar *were* priests, and Seraiah *was* secretary.

18 Benaiah the son of Jehoiada was over the Cherethites and the Pelethites; and David's sons were chief ministers.

Psalm 64:1–10

For the choir director. A Psalm of David.

64 HEAR my voice, O God, in my complaint;
Preserve my life from dread of the enemy.

2 Hide me from the secret counsel of evildoers,
From the tumult of those who do iniquity,

3 Who have sharpened their tongue like a sword.
They aimed bitter speech *as* their arrow,

4 To shoot from concealment at the blameless;
Suddenly they shoot at him, and do not fear.

5 They hold fast to themselves an evil purpose;
They talk of laying snares secretly;
They say, "Who can see them?"

6 They devise injustices, *saying,*
"We are ready with a well-conceived plot";

LIFE LESSONS

➤ **2 Samuel 8:6** — *The LORD helped David wherever he went.*

*A*s the Lord preserved David wherever he went, so He can protect us wherever we go. If we make the Lord our delight and obey Him as David did, then He will bless us and give us success, just as He did for David.

➤ **Psalm 64:2** — *Hide me from the secret counsel of evildoers.*

*B*elievers sometimes become targets because they stand for God (Matt. 5:10-12; Luke 10:16). Unseen enemies may seek to injure us and cause us trouble. Yet God doesn't want us to worry about these things but to bring them to Him and obey Him. He knows all about them and knows just how to respond.

For the inward thought and the
   heart of a man are deep.
7 But God will shoot at them with an
   arrow;
   Suddenly they will be wounded.
8 So they will make him stumble;
   Their own tongue is against them;
   All who see them will shake the
   head.
9 Then all men will fear,
   And they will declare the work of
   God,
   And will consider what He has done.
10 The righteous man will be glad in
   the LORD and will take refuge in
   Him;
   And all the upright in heart will
   glory.

Proverbs 16:18, 19

18 Pride *goes* before destruction,
   And a haughty spirit before
   stumbling.
19 It is better to be humble in spirit
   with the lowly
   Than to divide the spoil with the
   proud.

John 5:24–47

24 "Truly, truly, I say to you, he who
hears My word, and believes Him who
sent Me, has eternal life, and does not
come into judgment, but has passed out
of death into life.
25 "Truly, truly, I say to you, an hour is
coming and now is, when the dead will
hear the voice of the Son of God, and
those who hear will live.
26 "For just as the Father has life in
Himself, even so He gave to the Son also
to have life in Himself;
27 and He gave Him authority to execute judgment, because He is *the* Son of
Man.
28 "Do not marvel at this; for an hour
is coming, in which all who are in the
tombs will hear His voice,
29 and will come forth; those who did
the good *deeds* to a resurrection of life,
those who committed the evil *deeds* to a
resurrection of judgment.

30 "I can do nothing on My own initiative. As I hear, I judge; and My judgment
is just, because I do not seek My own
will, but the will of Him who sent Me.
31 "If I *alone* testify about Myself, My
testimony is not true.
32 "There is another who testifies of
Me, and I know that the testimony which
He gives about Me is true.
33 "You have sent to John, and he has
testified to the truth.
34 "But the testimony which I receive is
not from man, but I say these things so
that you may be saved.
35 "He was the lamp that was burning
and was shining and you were willing to
rejoice for a while in his light.
36 "But the testimony which I have is
greater than *the testimony of* John; for
the works which the Father has given
Me to accomplish—the very works that I
do—testify about Me, that the Father has
sent Me.
37 "And the Father who sent Me, He has
testified of Me. You have neither heard
His voice at any time nor seen His form.
38 "You do not have His word abiding in
you, for you do not believe Him whom He
sent.

LIFE LESSONS

➤ **John 5:29 — *"Come forth; those who
did the good deeds to a resurrection of
life, those who committed the evil deeds
to a resurrection of judgment."***

*E*very person who has ever lived will
one day stand before God at the
judgment, either to receive rewards for
Spirit-empowered activity and faith in
Christ, or to receive condemnation for
self-focused behavior. An eager anticipation of the Lord's return keeps us living
productively.

➤ **John 5:30 — *"I do not seek My own
will, but the will of Him who sent Me."***

*W*e have the wonderful opportunity
to glorify the Lord with our lives
(1 Cor. 6:20)—to walk in His footsteps
(Eph. 5:1, 2) and resemble Him in our
characters (Gal. 5:22, 23). This begins by
asking whether we seek after our own
goals or the will of God. As believers,
we've been called to allow Jesus to live
His life through us so that others can be
saved—and that's just what we must do.

39 "You search the Scriptures because you think that in them you have eternal life; it is these that testify about Me;
40 and you are unwilling to come to Me so that you may have life.
41 "I do not receive glory from men;
42 but I know you, that you do not have the love of God in yourselves.
43 "I have come in My Father's name, and you do not receive Me; if another comes in his own name, you will receive him.
44 "How can you believe, when you receive glory from one another and you do not seek the glory that is from the *one and* only God?
45 "Do not think that I will accuse you before the Father; the one who accuses you is Moses, in whom you have set your hope.
46 "For if you believed Moses, you would believe Me, for he wrote about Me.
47 "But if you do not believe his writings, how will you believe My words?"

MAY 19

2 Samuel 9:1—10:19

9 THEN David said, "Is there yet anyone left of the house of Saul, that I may show him kindness for Jonathan's sake?"
2 Now there was a servant of the house of Saul whose name was Ziba, and they called him to David; and the king said to him, "Are you Ziba?" And he said, "*I am* your servant."
3 The king said, "Is there not yet anyone of the house of Saul to whom I may show the kindness of God?" And Ziba said to the king, "There is still a son of Jonathan who is crippled in both feet."
4 So the king said to him, "Where is he?" And Ziba said to the king, "Behold, he is in the house of Machir the son of Ammiel in Lo-debar."
5 Then King David sent and brought him from the house of Machir the son of Ammiel, from Lo-debar.
6 Mephibosheth, the son of Jonathan the son of Saul, came to David and fell on his face and prostrated himself. And David said, "Mephibosheth." And he said, "Here is your servant!"
➤ 7 David said to him, "Do not fear, for I will surely show kindness to you for the sake of your father Jonathan, and will restore to you all the land of your grandfather Saul; and you shall eat at my table regularly."
8 Again he prostrated himself and said, "What is your servant, that you should regard a dead dog like me?"
9 Then the king called Saul's servant Ziba and said to him, "All that belonged to Saul and to all his house I have given to your master's grandson.
10 "You and your sons and your servants shall cultivate the land for him, and you shall bring in *the produce* so that your master's grandson may have food; nevertheless Mephibosheth your master's grandson shall eat at my table regularly." Now Ziba had fifteen sons and twenty servants.
11 Then Ziba said to the king, "According to all that my lord the king commands his servant so your servant will do." So Mephibosheth ate at David's table as one of the king's sons.
12 Mephibosheth had a young son whose name was Mica. And all who lived in the house of Ziba were servants to Mephibosheth.
13 So Mephibosheth lived in Jerusalem, for he ate at the king's table regularly. Now he was lame in both feet.
10 NOW it happened afterwards that the king of the Ammonites died, and Hanun his son became king in his place.

LIFE LESSONS

➤ **2 Samuel 9:7 — *"Do not fear, for I will surely show kindness to you for the sake of your father Jonathan."***

D avid remembered the promise he had made to Jonathan (1 Sam. 20:14–17) and worked hard to honor it. He remembered with gratitude his friend's help and responded with generosity toward Jonathan's child.

WHAT THE BIBLE SAYS ABOUT ◈
Loving the Unlovable

2 Samuel 9

*W*hat do you do when someone cuts you off in traffic or a friend has offended you? Do you become hurt by the thoughtless or deliberate actions done toward you? Do you immediately forgive those who hurt you, or do you sulk with feelings of unforgiveness? How do you typically react?

Jesus tells us our behavior must radically differ from that of the world: "I say to you, love your enemies and pray for those who persecute you" (Matt. 5:44). So what should you do when someone offends you? Follow these basic steps to ensure a Christ-centered response.

1. Forgive the offender.

Hurt, when not addressed properly, turns into bitterness and an unforgiving spirit. Through the grace of Jesus Christ, you have the spiritual resources to forgive others (Matt. 18:21–35; Eph. 4:32). When you release someone of a debt he or she owes, a spirit of unforgiveness or bitterness no longer binds you. You are free to see that individual as Christ does—anger no longer has the power to rule your life and decisions. Forgiveness does not mean that what the person did was right. It means that you have turned him or her over to God. You are no longer holding on to the unforgiveness, and you are free to live fully for Jesus Christ.

2. Seek to understand before you seek to be understood.

Practice the skill of listening, and try to imagine the perspective of the offender. What might have motivated his actions? What is going on in her life? Many times, a person who hurts you is also a victim of hurt. Understanding the offender's private pain could be a key step toward reconciliation or preventing further conflicts.

3. Speak with noncombative yet truthful words.

Speaking the truth in love does not mean that your words will lack impact. Sometimes the truth can be very unsettling, and the individual who has wounded you may need to grapple with some tough issues regarding his or her thoughtless actions toward you.

Only the Lord can work in a person's heart. You can pressure him or her for an apology, but God is the One who must convict the other person that what he or she has done is wrong. Your best course of action is to extend patience, love, and forgiveness because this is what the Lord extends to you. And one day even your "worst enemy" could become your best friend in Christ. Whatever the result, you can be sure of God's blessing as you seek His way of dealing with those who hurt you. ◈

---

2 Then David said, "I will show kindness to Hanun the son of Nahash, just as his father showed kindness to me." So David sent some of his servants to console him concerning his father. But when David's servants came to the land of the Ammonites,

3 the princes of the Ammonites said to Hanun their lord, "Do you think that David is honoring your father because he has sent consolers to you? Has David not sent his servants to you in order to search the city, to spy it out and overthrow it?"

4 So Hanun took David's servants and shaved off half of their beards, and cut off their garments in the middle as far as their hips, and sent them away.

5 When they told it to David, he sent to meet them, for the men were greatly humiliated. And the king said, "Stay at Jericho until your beards grow, and then return."

6 Now when the sons of Ammon saw that they had become odious to David, the sons of Ammon sent and hired the Arameans of Beth-rehob and the Arameans of Zobah, 20,000 foot soldiers, and the king of Maacah with 1,000 men, and the men of Tob with 12,000 men.

7 When David heard of it, he sent Joab and all the army, the mighty men.

8 The sons of Ammon came out and drew up in battle array at the entrance of the city, while the Arameans of Zobah and of Rehob and the men of Tob and Maacah were by themselves in the field.

9 Now when Joab saw that the battle was set against him in front and in the rear, he selected from all the choice men of Israel, and arrayed them against the Arameans.

10 But the remainder of the people he placed in the hand of Abishai his brother, and he arrayed *them* against the sons of Ammon.

11 He said, "If the Arameans are too strong for me, then you shall help me, but if the sons of Ammon are too strong for you, then I will come to help you.

➤ 12 "Be strong, and let us show ourselves courageous for the sake of our people and for the cities of our God; and may the LORD do what is good in His sight."

13 So Joab and the people who were with him drew near to the battle against the Arameans, and they fled before him.

14 When the sons of Ammon saw that the Arameans fled, they *also* fled before Abishai and entered the city. Then Joab returned from *fighting* against the sons of Ammon and came to Jerusalem.

15 When the Arameans saw that they had been defeated by Israel, they gathered themselves together.

16 And Hadadezer sent and brought out the Arameans who were beyond the River, and they came to Helam; and Shobach the commander of the army of Hadadezer led them.

17 Now when it was told David, he gathered all Israel together and crossed the Jordan, and came to Helam. And the Arameans arrayed themselves to meet David and fought against him.

18 But the Arameans fled before Israel, and David killed 700 charioteers of the Arameans and 40,000 horsemen and struck down Shobach the commander of their army, and he died there.

19 When all the kings, servants of Hadadezer, saw that they were defeated by Israel, they made peace with Israel and served them. So the Arameans feared to help the sons of Ammon anymore.

Psalm 65:1–8

For the choir director. A Psalm of David. A Song.

65 THERE will be silence before You, *and* praise in Zion, O God, And to You the vow will be performed.

2 O You who hear prayer, To You all men come.

3 Iniquities prevail against me; As for our transgressions, You forgive them.

4 How blessed is the one whom You choose and bring near *to You* To dwell in Your courts. We will be satisfied with the goodness of Your house, Your holy temple.

5 By awesome *deeds* You answer us in righteousness, O God of our salvation, You who are the trust of all the ends of the earth and of the farthest sea;

6 Who establishes the mountains by His strength, Being girded with might;

7 Who stills the roaring of the seas, The roaring of their waves, And the tumult of the peoples.

LIFE LESSONS

➤ **2 Samuel 10:12 — "May the LORD do what is good in His sight."**

*W*hen we face some major challenge, we can do no better than to find courage in God and to ask Him to "do what is good in His sight." The Lord loves to honor those who honor Him (1 Sam. 2:30).

➤ **Psalm 65:5 — *By awesome deeds You answer us in righteousness, O God of our salvation.***

*S*ome answers to prayer can be described with no better word than "awesome." Has God ever answered your prayers in a way that filled you with awe? Do you need His awe-inspiring intervention right now? Then pray and with faith expect Him to do amazing things on your behalf.

➤ **Psalm 65:7 — *Who stills the roaring of the seas, the roaring of their waves, and the tumult of the peoples.***

*D*uring His earthly ministry, Jesus both stilled the raging sea and stilled the angry mob (Mark 4:39; Luke 4:29, 30)— and demonstrated His divine sovereignty as Lord of all.

8   They who dwell in the ends *of the earth* stand in awe of Your signs;
You make the dawn and the sunset shout for joy.

Proverbs 16:20, 21

➤ 20   He who gives attention to the word will find good,
And blessed is he who trusts in the LORD.
✳ 21   The wise in heart will be called understanding,
And sweetness of speech increases persuasiveness.

John 6:1–21

6 AFTER these things Jesus went away to the other side of the Sea of Galilee (or Tiberias).
2   A large crowd followed Him, because they saw the signs which He was performing on those who were sick.
3   Then Jesus went up on the mountain, and there He sat down with His disciples.
4   Now the Passover, the feast of the Jews, was near.
5   Therefore Jesus, lifting up His eyes and seeing that a large crowd was coming to Him, *said to Philip, "Where are we to buy bread, so that these may eat?"
➤ 6   This He was saying to test him, for He Himself knew what He was intending to do.
7   Philip answered Him, "Two hundred denarii worth of bread is not sufficient for them, for everyone to receive a little."
8   One of His disciples, Andrew, Simon Peter's brother, *said to Him,
9   "There is a lad here who has five barley loaves and two fish, but what are these for so many people?"
10   Jesus said, "Have the people sit down." Now there was much grass in the place. So the men sat down, in number about five thousand.
11   Jesus then took the loaves, and having given thanks, He distributed to those who were seated; likewise also of the fish as much as they wanted.

12   When they were filled, He *said to His disciples, "Gather up the leftover fragments so that nothing will be lost."
13   So they gathered them up, and filled twelve baskets with fragments from the five barley loaves which were left over by those who had eaten.
14   Therefore when the people saw the sign which He had performed, they said, "This is truly the Prophet who is to come into the world."
15   So Jesus, perceiving that they were intending to come and take Him by force to make Him king, withdrew again to the mountain by Himself alone.
16   Now when evening came, His disciples went down to the sea,
17   and after getting into a boat, they *started to* cross the sea to Capernaum. It had already become dark, and Jesus had not yet come to them.
18   The sea *began* to be stirred up because a strong wind was blowing.
19   Then, when they had rowed about three or four miles, they *saw Jesus walking on the sea and drawing near to the boat; and they were frightened.
20   But He *said to them, "It is I; do not ✳ be afraid."
21   So they were willing to receive Him into the boat, and immediately the boat was at the land to which they were going.

LIFE LESSONS

➤ **Proverbs 16:20 — *And blessed is he who trusts in the LORD.***

*N*o one will ever find true happiness by disobeying a clear command of God. Our joy is found in trusting the Lord and becoming all He created us to be. Those who disobey show they do not truly trust that He has their best interests at heart.

➤ **John 6:6 — *This He was saying to test him, for He Himself knew what He was intending to do.***

*A*t times, the Lord will set a seemingly impossible task before us to test us and see whether we react in fear or faith. This is because he is training us to have faith in Him, and trusting Him means looking beyond what we can see and do to what He is able to accomplish.

2 Samuel 11:1—12:31

11 THEN it happened in the spring, at the time when kings go out *to battle*, that David sent Joab and his servants with him and all Israel, and they destroyed the sons of Ammon and besieged Rabbah. But David stayed at Jerusalem.

2 Now when evening came David arose from his bed and walked around on the roof of the king's house, and from the roof he saw a woman bathing; and the woman was very beautiful in appearance.

3 So David sent and inquired about the woman. And one said, "Is this not Bathsheba, the daughter of Eliam, the wife of Uriah the Hittite?"

4 David sent messengers and took her, and when she came to him, he lay with her; and when she had purified herself from her uncleanness, she returned to her house.

5 The woman conceived; and she sent and told David, and said, "I am pregnant."

6 Then David sent to Joab, *saying*, "Send me Uriah the Hittite." So Joab sent Uriah to David.

7 When Uriah came to him, David asked

LIFE LESSONS

➤ **2 Samuel 11:2** — *From the roof he saw a woman bathing; and the woman was very beautiful in appearance.*

*D*avid did not sin by catching a glimpse of a bathing beauty. He sinned when he failed to take his eyes off of her. Soon he discovered that lust gives birth to sin, and full-grown sin brings forth death (James 1:15).

ANSWERS TO LIFE'S QUESTIONS

How can we effectively guard against temptation?

2 SAMUEL 11:2–4

*A*ll temptation begins with a single thought. We have the ability to choose to ignore it or to allow it to remain in our minds. If it remains, more than likely it will gain a foothold within us. Temptation in and of itself is not sinful. It entices us to sin and to disobey God. If not checked, it leads to disappointment, failure, rejection, isolation, and a host of other consequences. The apostle Paul instructed the Corinthians to bring "every thought captive to the obedience of Christ" (2 Cor. 10:5).

Through the presence of the Holy Spirit, we have the ability to screen, select, admit, and cultivate what goes into our minds. By His power, we can prevent our minds from taking a wrong turn and wandering into evil, but we must choose to focus on what is godly and good (Phil. 4:8).

Through Christ, we also have the ability to choose *how* we will think about what we perceive with our senses. While we have no control over some things that come into our field of vision or within our range of hearing, we *do* control how we will think about what we perceive or sense and how we will act on that information.

For example, David *saw* Bathsheba. One night he was out walking on his balcony, and while surveying the city below, he saw a beautiful woman bathing. That could have been the end of the story. But it turned out quite differently for David. Without question, he could have turned and walked back into his palace and thought nothing more about what he had seen.

Instead, he began to *think* about Bathsheba. He allowed his heart to be tempted and he dismissed the Lord's command to avoid adultery. Instead, he rushed to sin and "inquired about the woman" (2 Sam. 11:3). More than likely, he imagined what it would be like to get closer to her and what it might be like to be with her physically. Eventually, he sent for her and sinned against God. David suffered serious consequences as a result of his decision. This one act of disobedience followed him the rest of his life. While he sought God's forgiveness and received it, the shadow of his sin never vanished from his life or the lives of his family members who followed him.

When things come into our range of sensation or perception, we must immediately evaluate them through the "filter" of God's Word. If we find ourselves dwelling on a thought, we must ask ourselves, "Why am I thinking this? What is at the root of my thought? What will happen if I continue to think this way? Is that really the direction I want my life to go?" Never act on ungodly impulses, desires, and lusts. You can *choose* to think godly thoughts, act according to His will, and "do all [things] to the glory of God" (1 Cor. 10:31).

concerning the welfare of Joab and the people and the state of the war.

8 Then David said to Uriah, "Go down to your house, and wash your feet." And Uriah went out of the king's house, and a present from the king was sent out after him.

9 But Uriah slept at the door of the king's house with all the servants of his lord, and did not go down to his house.

10 Now when they told David, saying, "Uriah did not go down to his house," David said to Uriah, "Have you not come from a journey? Why did you not go down to your house?"

11 Uriah said to David, "The ark and Israel and Judah are staying in temporary shelters, and my lord Joab and the servants of my lord are camping in the open field. Shall I then go to my house to eat and to drink and to lie with my wife? By your life and the life of your soul, I will not do this thing."

12 Then David said to Uriah, "Stay here today also, and tomorrow I will let you go." So Uriah remained in Jerusalem that day and the next.

13 Now David called him, and he ate and drank before him, and he made him drunk; and in the evening he went out to lie on his bed with his lord's servants, but he did not go down to his house.

14 Now in the morning David wrote a letter to Joab and sent it by the hand of Uriah.

15 He had written in the letter, saying, "Place Uriah in the front line of the fiercest battle and withdraw from him, so that he may be struck down and die."

16 So it was as Joab kept watch on the city, that he put Uriah at the place where he knew there were valiant men.

17 The men of the city went out and fought against Joab, and some of the people among David's servants fell; and Uriah the Hittite also died.

18 Then Joab sent and reported to David all the events of the war.

19 He charged the messenger, saying, "When you have finished telling all the events of the war to the king,

20 and if it happens that the king's wrath rises and he says to you, 'Why did you go so near to the city to fight? Did you not know that they would shoot from the wall?

21 'Who struck down Abimelech the son of Jerubbesheth? Did not a woman throw an upper millstone on him from the wall so that he died at Thebez? Why did you go so near the wall?'—then you shall say, 'Your servant Uriah the Hittite is dead also.'"

22 So the messenger departed and came and reported to David all that Joab had sent him to tell.

23 The messenger said to David, "The men prevailed against us and came out against us in the field, but we pressed them as far as the entrance of the gate.

24 "Moreover, the archers shot at your servants from the wall; so some of the king's servants are dead, and your servant Uriah the Hittite is also dead."

25 Then David said to the messenger, ◄ "Thus you shall say to Joab, 'Do not let this thing displease you, for the sword devours one as well as another; make your battle against the city stronger and overthrow it'; and so encourage him."

26 Now when the wife of Uriah heard that Uriah her husband was dead, she mourned for her husband.

27 When the time of mourning was over, David sent and brought her to his house and she became his wife; then she bore him a son. But the thing that David had done was evil in the sight of the LORD.

12 THEN the LORD sent Nathan to David. And he came to him and said,

"There were two men in one city, the
    one rich and the other poor.

2 "The rich man had a great many
    flocks and herds.

3 "But the poor man had nothing
    except one little ewe lamb
    Which he bought and nourished;

LIFE LESSONS

➤ **2 Samuel 11:25 — "Do not let this thing displease you, for the sword devours one as well as another."**

*U*nconfessed sin has a way of making us callous toward the value of human life. It deadens the spirit and distances us from God. Without confession and repentance, we descend even further into the prison of sin.

And it grew up together with him
and his children.
It would eat of his bread and drink
of his cup and lie in his bosom,
And was like a daughter to him.
4   "Now a traveler came to the rich
man,
And he was unwilling to take from
his own flock or his own herd,
To prepare for the wayfarer who
had come to him;
Rather he took the poor man's ewe
lamb and prepared it for the man
who had come to him."

5   Then David's anger burned greatly
against the man, and he said to Nathan,
"As the LORD lives, surely the man who
has done this deserves to die.
6   "He must make restitution for the
lamb fourfold, because he did this thing
and had no compassion."
7   Nathan then said to David, "You
are the man! Thus says the LORD God of
Israel, 'It is I who anointed you king over
Israel and it is I who delivered you from
the hand of Saul.
8   'I also gave you your master's house
and your master's wives into your care,
and I gave you the house of Israel and
Judah; and if *that had been* too little,
I would have added to you many more
things like these!
9   'Why have you despised the word of
the LORD by doing evil in His sight? You
have struck down Uriah the Hittite with
the sword, have taken his wife to be your
wife, and have killed him with the sword
of the sons of Ammon.
10   'Now therefore, the sword shall
never depart from your house, because
you have despised Me and have taken
the wife of Uriah the Hittite to be your
wife.'
11   "Thus says the LORD, 'Behold, I will
raise up evil against you from your own
household; I will even take your wives
before your eyes and give *them* to your
companion, and he will lie with your
wives in broad daylight.
12   'Indeed you did it secretly, but I will
do this thing before all Israel, and under
the sun.'"
13   Then David said to Nathan, "I have
sinned against the LORD." And Nathan
said to David, "The LORD also has taken
away your sin; you shall not die.
14   "However, because by this deed you
have given occasion to the enemies of
the LORD to blaspheme, the child also
that is born to you shall surely die."
15   So Nathan went to his house.
Then the LORD struck the child that
Uriah's widow bore to David, so that he
was *very* sick.
16   David therefore inquired of God for
the child; and David fasted and went and
lay all night on the ground.
17   The elders of his household stood
beside him in order to raise him up from
the ground, but he was unwilling and
would not eat food with them.
18   Then it happened on the seventh
day that the child died. And the servants
of David were afraid to tell him that the
child was dead, for they said, "Behold,
while the child was *still* alive, we spoke
to him and he did not listen to our voice.
How then can we tell him that the child is
dead, since he might do *himself* harm!"
19   But when David saw that his servants were whispering together, David
perceived that the child was dead; so
David said to his servants, "Is the child
dead?" And they said, "He is dead."
20   So David arose from the ground,
washed, anointed *himself*, and changed
his clothes; and he came into the house
of the LORD and worshiped. Then he
came to his own house, and when he requested, they set food before him and he
ate.
21   Then his servants said to him, "What
is this thing that you have done? While
the child was alive, you fasted and wept;
but when the child died, you arose and
ate food."
22   He said, "While the child was *still*
alive, I fasted and wept; for I said, 'Who

LIFE LESSONS

> **2 Samuel 12:4 — "He took the poor
> man's ewe lamb and prepared it for the
> man who had come to him."**

Nathan used a story that reminded
David of his youth to break through
the king's resistance and bring him to
a place of repentance. We must correct
others in love with the hope of restoring them; and a prayer-bathed, Spirit-led
approach will accomplish far more than
our self-righteous arguments ever can
(Matt. 18:15; 2 Cor. 7:9-10).

knows, the LORD may be gracious to me, that the child may live.'

23 "But now he has died; why should I fast? Can I bring him back again? I will go to him, but he will not return to me."

➤ 24 Then David comforted his wife Bathsheba, and went in to her and lay with her; and she gave birth to a son, and he named him Solomon. Now the LORD loved him

25 and sent word through Nathan the prophet, and he named him Jedidiah for the LORD's sake.

26 Now Joab fought against Rabbah of the sons of Ammon and captured the royal city.

27 Joab sent messengers to David and said, "I have fought against Rabbah, I have even captured the city of waters.

28 "Now therefore, gather the rest of the people together and camp against the city and capture it, or I will capture the city myself and it will be named after me."

29 So David gathered all the people and went to Rabbah, fought against it and captured it.

30 Then he took the crown of their king from his head; and its weight was a talent of gold, and in it was a precious stone; and it was placed on David's head. And he brought out the spoil of the city in great amounts.

31 He also brought out the people who were in it, and set them under saws, sharp iron instruments, and iron axes, and made them pass through the brick-kiln. And thus he did to all the cities of the sons of Ammon. Then David and all the people returned to Jerusalem.

◈ Psalm 65:9–13

9 You visit the earth and cause it to
     overflow;
  You greatly enrich it;
  The stream of God is full of water;
  You prepare their grain, for thus You
     prepare the earth.
10 You water its furrows abundantly,
  You settle its ridges,
  You soften it with showers,
  You bless its growth.
11 You have crowned the year with
     Your bounty,
  And Your paths drip with fatness.
12 The pastures of the wilderness drip,
  And the hills gird themselves with
     rejoicing.
13 The meadows are clothed with
     flocks
  And the valleys are covered with
     grain;
  They shout for joy, yes, they sing.

LIFE LESSONS

➤ **2 Samuel 12:22 —** *"While the child was still alive, I fasted and wept; for I said, 'Who knows, the LORD may be gracious to me, that the child may live.'"*

*T*he Lord expresses His grace to us when he gives us what we do not merit. In this case, David knew he had sinned and did not deserve for his baby to live, but he pleaded for God to reconsider taking his son. However, understanding that His grace is undeserved, David did not become bitter over the child's death. Though it was difficult, he humbly accepted the Lord's will.

➤ **2 Samuel 12:24 —** *And she gave birth to a son, and he named him Solomon. Now the LORD loved him.*

*W*hy did the Lord love Solomon? Look no further than His grace. David did not deserve it, and the newborn Solomon certainly had not earned it. God's love always originates in His own character, not ours.

◈ Proverbs 16:22–24

22 Understanding is a fountain of life
     to one who has it,
  But the discipline of fools is folly.
23 The heart of the wise instructs his
     mouth
  And adds persuasiveness to his lips. ✳
24 Pleasant words are a honeycomb,
  Sweet to the soul and healing to the
     bones.

◈ John 6:22–51

22 The next day the crowd that stood on the other side of the sea saw that there

was no other small boat there, except one, and that Jesus had not entered with His disciples into the boat, but *that* His disciples had gone away alone.

23 There came other small boats from Tiberias near to the place where they ate the bread after the Lord had given thanks.

24 So when the crowd saw that Jesus was not there, nor His disciples, they themselves got into the small boats, and came to Capernaum seeking Jesus.

25 When they found Him on the other side of the sea, they said to Him, "Rabbi, when did You get here?"

26 Jesus answered them and said, "Truly, truly, I say to you, you seek Me, not because you saw signs, but because you ate of the loaves and were filled.

27 "Do not work for the food which perishes, but for the food which endures to eternal life, which the Son of Man will give to you, for on Him the Father, God, has set His seal."

28 Therefore they said to Him, "What shall we do, so that we may work the works of God?"

29 Jesus answered and said to them, "This is the work of God, that you believe in Him whom He has sent."

30 So they said to Him, "What then do You do for a sign, so that we may see, and believe You? What work do You perform?

31 "Our fathers ate the manna in the wilderness; as it is written, 'HE GAVE THEM BREAD OUT OF HEAVEN TO EAT.'"

32 Jesus then said to them, "Truly, truly, I say to you, it is not Moses who has given you the bread out of heaven, but it is My Father who gives you the true bread out of heaven.

33 "For the bread of God is that which comes down out of heaven, and gives life to the world."

34 Then they said to Him, "Lord, always give us this bread."

35 Jesus said to them, "I am the bread of life; he who comes to Me will not hunger, and he who believes in Me will never thirst.

36 "But I said to you that you have seen Me, and yet do not believe.

37 "All that the Father gives Me will come to Me, and the one who comes to Me I will certainly not cast out.

38 "For I have come down from heaven, not to do My own will, but the will of Him who sent Me.

39 "This is the will of Him who sent Me, that of all that He has given Me I lose nothing, but raise it up on the last day.

40 "For this is the will of My Father, that everyone who beholds the Son and believes in Him will have eternal life, and I Myself will raise him up on the last day."

41 Therefore the Jews were grumbling about Him, because He said, "I am the bread that came down out of heaven."

42 They were saying, "Is not this Jesus, the son of Joseph, whose father and mother we know? How does He now say, 'I have come down out of heaven'?"

43 Jesus answered and said to them, "Do not grumble among yourselves.

44 "No one can come to Me unless the Father who sent Me draws him; and I will raise him up on the last day.

45 "It is written in the prophets, 'AND THEY SHALL ALL BE TAUGHT OF GOD.' Everyone who has heard and learned from the Father, comes to Me.

46 "Not that anyone has seen the Father, except the One who is from God; He has seen the Father.

47 "Truly, truly, I say to you, he who believes has eternal life.

48 "I am the bread of life.

49 "Your fathers ate the manna in the wilderness, and they died.

50 "This is the bread which comes down out of heaven, so that one may eat of it and not die.

51 "I am the living bread that came down out of heaven; if anyone eats of this bread, he will live forever; and the bread also which I will give for the life of the world is My flesh."

LIFE LESSONS

➤ **John 6:38 —** *"For I have come down from heaven, not to do My own will, but the will of Him who sent Me."*

*W*e never grow out of our need to obey God; obedience always remains a part of our relationships with Him. Jesus was the Son of God, yet He continually named obedience to His Father as His number one desire.

13 NOW it was after this that Absalom the son of David had a beautiful sister whose name was Tamar, and Amnon the son of David loved her.

2 Amnon was so frustrated because of his sister Tamar that he made himself ill, for she was a virgin, and it seemed hard to Amnon to do anything to her.

3 But Amnon had a friend whose name was Jonadab, the son of Shimeah, David's brother; and Jonadab was a very shrewd man.

4 He said to him, "O son of the king, why are you so depressed morning after morning? Will you not tell me?" Then Amnon said to him, "I am in love with Tamar, the sister of my brother Absalom."

5 Jonadab then said to him, "Lie down on your bed and pretend to be ill; when your father comes to see you, say to him, 'Please let my sister Tamar come and give me *some* food to eat, and let her prepare the food in my sight, that I may see *it* and eat from her hand.'"

6 So Amnon lay down and pretended to be ill; when the king came to see him, Amnon said to the king, "Please let my sister Tamar come and make me a couple of cakes in my sight, that I may eat from her hand."

7 Then David sent to the house for Tamar, saying, "Go now to your brother Amnon's house, and prepare food for him."

8 So Tamar went to her brother Amnon's house, and he was lying down. And she took dough, kneaded *it,* made cakes in his sight, and baked the cakes.

9 She took the pan and dished *them* out before him, but he refused to eat. And Amnon said, "Have everyone go out from me." So everyone went out from him.

10 Then Amnon said to Tamar, "Bring the food into the bedroom, that I may eat from your hand." So Tamar took the cakes which she had made and brought them into the bedroom to her brother Amnon.

11 When she brought *them* to him to eat, he took hold of her and said to her, "Come, lie with me, my sister."

12 But she answered him, "No, my brother, do not violate me, for such a thing is not done in Israel; do not do this disgraceful thing!

13 "As for me, where could I get rid of my reproach? And as for you, you will be like one of the fools in Israel. Now therefore, please speak to the king, for he will not withhold me from you."

14 However, he would not listen to her; since he was stronger than she, he violated her and lay with her.

15 Then Amnon hated her with a very ◄ great hatred; for the hatred with which he hated her was greater than the love with which he had loved her. And Amnon said to her, "Get up, go away!"

16 But she said to him, "No, because this wrong in sending me away is greater than the other that you have done to me!" Yet he would not listen to her.

17 Then he called his young man who attended him and said, "Now throw this woman out of my *presence,* and lock the door behind her."

18 Now she had on a long-sleeved garment; for in this manner the virgin daughters of the king dressed themselves in robes. Then his attendant took her out and locked the door behind her.

19 Tamar put ashes on her head and tore her long-sleeved garment which *was* on her; and she put her hand on her head and went away, crying aloud as she went.

20 Then Absalom her brother said to her, "Has Amnon your brother been with you? But now keep silent, my sister, he is your brother; do not take this matter to heart." So Tamar remained and was desolate in her brother Absalom's house.

21 Now when King David heard of all these matters, he was very angry.

22 But Absalom did not speak to ◄ Amnon either good or bad; for Absalom hated Amnon because he had violated his sister Tamar.

LIFE LESSONS

► **2 Samuel 13:15 — *Then Amnon hated her with a very great hatred.***

*L*ust relieved frequently gives way to hatred expressed. It often masquerades as love, but lust and love result in profoundly different outcomes.

23 Now it came about after two full
years that Absalom had sheepshearers
in Baal-hazor, which is near Ephraim,
and Absalom invited all the king's sons.
24 Absalom came to the king and said,
"Behold now, your servant has sheepshearers; please let the king and his
servants go with your servant."
25 But the king said to Absalom, "No,
my son, we should not all go, for we will
be burdensome to you." Although he
urged him, he would not go, but blessed
him.
26 Then Absalom said, "If not, please
let my brother Amnon go with us." And
the king said to him, "Why should he go
with you?"
27 But when Absalom urged him, he let
Amnon and all the king's sons go with
him.
28 Absalom commanded his servants,
saying, "See now, when Amnon's heart
is merry with wine, and when I say to
you, 'Strike Amnon,' then put him to
death. Do not fear; have not I myself
commanded you? Be courageous and be
valiant."
29 The servants of Absalom did
to Amnon just as Absalom had commanded. Then all the king's sons arose
and each mounted his mule and fled.
30 Now it was while they were on the
way that the report came to David, saying, "Absalom has struck down all the
king's sons, and not one of them is left."
31 Then the king arose, tore his clothes
and lay on the ground; and all his servants were standing by with clothes torn.
32 Jonadab, the son of Shimeah, David's brother, responded, "Do not let
my lord suppose they have put to death
all the young men, the king's sons, for
Amnon alone is dead; because by the

intent of Absalom this has been determined since the day that he violated his
sister Tamar.
33 "Now therefore, do not let my lord the
king take the report to heart, namely, 'all
the king's sons are dead,' for only Amnon
is dead."
34 Now Absalom had fled. And the
young man who was the watchman
raised his eyes and looked, and behold,
many people were coming from the road
behind him by the side of the mountain.
35 Jonadab said to the king, "Behold,
the king's sons have come; according to
your servant's word, so it happened."
36 As soon as he had finished speaking,
behold, the king's sons came and lifted
their voices and wept; and also the king
and all his servants wept very bitterly.
37 Now Absalom fled and went to Talmai the son of Ammihud, the king of
Geshur. And *David* mourned for his son
every day.
38 So Absalom had fled and gone to
Geshur, and was there three years.
39 *The heart of* King David longed to
go out to Absalom; for he was comforted
concerning Amnon, since he was dead.

14 NOW Joab the son of Zeruiah perceived that the king's heart *was
inclined* toward Absalom.
2 So Joab sent to Tekoa and brought a
wise woman from there and said to her,
"Please pretend to be a mourner, and
put on mourning garments now, and do
not anoint yourself with oil, but be like a
woman who has been mourning for the
dead many days;
3 then go to the king and speak to him
in this manner." So Joab put the words in
her mouth.
4 Now when the woman of Tekoa
spoke to the king, she fell on her face to
the ground and prostrated herself and
said, "Help, O king."
5 The king said to her, "What is your
trouble?" And she answered, "Truly I am
a widow, for my husband is dead.
6 "Your maidservant had two sons, but
the two of them struggled together in the
field, and there was no one to separate
them, so one struck the other and killed
him.
7 "Now behold, the whole family has
risen against your maidservant, and they
say, 'Hand over the one who struck his
brother, that we may put him to death

for the life of his brother whom he killed, and destroy the heir also.' Thus they will extinguish my coal which is left, so as to leave my husband neither name nor remnant on the face of the earth."

8 Then the king said to the woman, "Go to your house, and I will give orders concerning you."

9 The woman of Tekoa said to the king, "O my lord, the king, the iniquity is on me and my father's house, but the king and his throne are guiltless."

10 So the king said, "Whoever speaks to you, bring him to me, and he will not touch you anymore."

11 Then she said, "Please let the king remember the Lord your God, so that the avenger of blood will not continue to destroy, otherwise they will destroy my son." And he said, "As the Lord lives, not one hair of your son shall fall to the ground."

12 Then the woman said, "Please let your maidservant speak a word to my lord the king." And he said, "Speak."

13 The woman said, "Why then have you planned such a thing against the people of God? For in speaking this word the king is as one who is guilty, in that the king does not bring back his banished one.

14 "For we will surely die and are like water spilled on the ground which cannot be gathered up again. Yet God does not take away life, but plans ways so that the banished one will not be cast out from him.

15 "Now the reason I have come to speak this word to my lord the king is that the people have made me afraid; so your maidservant said, 'Let me now speak to the king, perhaps the king will perform the request of his maidservant.

16 'For the king will hear and deliver his maidservant from the hand of the man who would destroy both me and my son from the inheritance of God.'

17 "Then your maidservant said, 'Please let the word of my lord the king be comforting, for as the angel of God, so is my lord the king to discern good and evil. And may the Lord your God be with you.'"

18 Then the king answered and said to the woman, "Please do not hide anything from me that I am about to ask you." And

the woman said, "Let my lord the king please speak."

19 So the king said, "Is the hand of Joab with you in all this?" And the woman replied, "As your soul lives, my lord the king, no one can turn to the right or to the left from anything that my lord the king has spoken. Indeed, it was your servant Joab who commanded me, and it was he who put all these words in the mouth of your maidservant;

20 in order to change the appearance of things your servant Joab has done this thing. But my lord is wise, like the wisdom of the angel of God, to know all that is in the earth."

21 Then the king said to Joab, "Behold now, I will surely do this thing; go therefore, bring back the young man Absalom."

22 Joab fell on his face to the ground, prostrated himself and blessed the king; then Joab said, "Today your servant knows that I have found favor in your sight, O my lord, the king, in that the king has performed the request of his servant."

23 So Joab arose and went to Geshur and brought Absalom to Jerusalem.

24 However the king said, "Let him turn to his own house, and let him not see my face." So Absalom turned to his own house and did not see the king's face.

25 Now in all Israel was no one as handsome as Absalom, so highly praised; from the sole of his foot to the crown of his head there was no defect in him.

26 When he cut the hair of his head (and it was at the end of every year that he cut it, for it was heavy on him so he cut it), he weighed the hair of his head at 200 shekels by the king's weight.

27 To Absalom there were born three sons, and one daughter whose name was Tamar; she was a woman of beautiful appearance.

28 Now Absalom lived two full years in Jerusalem, and did not see the king's face.

29 Then Absalom sent for Joab, to send him to the king, but he would not come to him. So he sent again a second time, but he would not come.

30 Therefore he said to his servants, "See, Joab's field is next to mine, and he has barley there; go and set it on fire." So Absalom's servants set the field on fire.

31 Then Joab arose, came to Absalom at his house and said to him, "Why have your servants set my field on fire?"

➤ 32 Absalom answered Joab, "Behold, I sent for you, saying, 'Come here, that I may send you to the king, to say, "Why have I come from Geshur? It would be better for me still to be there."' Now therefore, let me see the king's face, and if there is iniquity in me, let him put me to death."

33 So when Joab came to the king and told him, he called for Absalom. Thus he came to the king and prostrated himself on his face to the ground before the king, and the king kissed Absalom.

Psalm 66:1–7

For the choir director. A Song. A Psalm.

66 SHOUT joyfully to God, all the earth;

2 Sing the glory of His name;
     Make His praise glorious.

3 Say to God, "How awesome are Your works!
     Because of the greatness of Your power Your enemies will give feigned obedience to You.

4 "All the earth will worship You,
     And will sing praises to You;
     They will sing praises to Your name."   Selah.

5 Come and see the works of God,
     Who is awesome in His deeds toward the sons of men.

6 He turned the sea into dry land;
     They passed through the river on foot;
     There let us rejoice in Him!

7 He rules by His might forever;

LIFE LESSONS

➤ **2 Samuel 14:32** — *"Let me see the king's face, and if there is iniquity in me, let him put me to death."*

*A*bsalom never repented of his sin. In fact, his words and actions show he felt justified in murdering Amnon and setting fire to Joab's field. He wanted the king's acceptance, not forgiveness. But such unremorseful pride always causes more trouble in the end.

His eyes keep watch on the nations;
     Let not the rebellious exalt themselves.   Selah.

Proverbs 16:25, 26

25 There is a way *which seems* right to a man,
     But its end is the way of death.

26 A worker's appetite works for him,
     For his hunger urges him *on*.

John 6:52–71

52 Then the Jews *began* to argue with one another, saying, "How can this man give us *His* flesh to eat?"

53 So Jesus said to them, "Truly, truly, I say to you, unless you eat the flesh of the Son of Man and drink His blood, you have no life in yourselves.

54 "He who eats My flesh and drinks My blood has eternal life, and I will raise him up on the last day.

55 "For My flesh is true food, and My blood is true drink.

56 "He who eats My flesh and drinks My blood abides in Me, and I in him.

57 "As the living Father sent Me, and I live because of the Father, so he who eats Me, he also will live because of Me.

58 "This is the bread which came down out of heaven; not as the fathers ate and died; he who eats this bread will live forever."

59 These things He said in the synagogue as He taught in Capernaum.

60 Therefore many of His disciples, when they heard *this* said, "This is a difficult statement; who can listen to it?"

61 But Jesus, conscious that His disciples grumbled at this, said to them, "Does this cause you to stumble?

62 "*What* then if you see the Son of Man ascending to where He was before?

63 "It is the Spirit who gives life; the flesh profits nothing; the words that I have spoken to you are spirit and are life.

64 "But there are some of you who do not believe." For Jesus knew from the beginning who they were who did not believe, and who it was that would betray Him.

WHAT THE BIBLE SAYS ABOUT

Difficulties and Victories

John 6:44–69

The Christian life is difficult, and no one knew that better than the disciples. As they listened to Jesus speak about His mission on earth, they were challenged. The things He spoke of were hard to accept.

Scripture teaches, "Many of His disciples, when they heard this said, 'This is a difficult statement; who can listen to it?' . . . As a result of this many of His disciples withdrew and were not walking with Him anymore" (John 6:60, 66).

Perhaps you have encountered difficulties that have made you want to turn away, but you didn't. The disciples faced the Crucifixion, which was the most disheartening and dreadful event they could ever experience. Their hopes and dreams of an earthly Savior were destroyed. But they also experienced the glory of the resurrection, which showed them God's greater mission of salvation.

The disciples who stayed with Christ were able to see Jesus raised from the grave. Peter testified, "Therefore let all the house of Israel know for certain that God has made Him both Lord and Christ—this Jesus whom you crucified" (Acts 2:36). Peter was able to see God's victory.

If any of your dreams seem to have died, don't walk away from the Savior. Jesus desires to show you His glory in the most difficult issues you face. No matter how trying the situation, if you stand by the Savior, you will see the victory.

---

65 And He was saying, "For this reason I have said to you, that no one can come to Me unless it has been granted him from the Father."
➤ 66 As a result of this many of His disciples withdrew and were not walking with Him anymore.
67 So Jesus said to the twelve, "You do not want to go away also, do you?"
➤ 68 Simon Peter answered Him, "Lord, to whom shall we go? You have words of eternal life.
69 "We have believed and have come to know that You are the Holy One of God."
70 Jesus answered them, "Did I Myself not choose you, the twelve, and *yet* one of you is a devil?"
71 Now He meant Judas *the son* of Simon Iscariot, for he, one of the twelve, was going to betray Him.

LIFE LESSONS

➤ **John 6:66 — *As a result of this many of His disciples withdrew and were not walking with Him anymore.***

Jesus did not try to talk unwilling disciples into staying with Him, nor did He make things easier for them so they would reconsider their relationship with Him. He wants eager followers, not fickle fans.

➤ **John 6:68 — *"Lord, to whom shall we go? You have words of eternal life."***

Times come for all of us when a life of faith in Christ seems more difficult than we expected. Yet here's the question each of us must answer: *Where can we find a better offer than the eternal life Jesus alone promises?*

---

2 Samuel 15:1—16:23

15 NOW it came about after this that Absalom provided for himself a chariot and horses and fifty men as runners before him.
2 Absalom used to rise early and stand beside the way to the gate; and when any man had a suit to come to the king for judgment, Absalom would call to him and say, "From what city are you?" And he would say, "Your servant is from one of the tribes of Israel."
3 Then Absalom would say to him, "See, your claims are good and right, but no man listens to you on the part of the king."
4 Moreover, Absalom would say, "Oh

that one would appoint me judge in the land, then every man who has any suit or cause could come to me and I would give him justice."

5 And when a man came near to prostrate himself before him, he would put out his hand and take hold of him and kiss him.

➤ 6 In this manner Absalom dealt with all Israel who came to the king for judgment; so Absalom stole away the hearts of the men of Israel.

7 Now it came about at the end of forty years that Absalom said to the king, "Please let me go and pay my vow which I have vowed to the LORD, in Hebron.

8 "For your servant vowed a vow while I was living at Geshur in Aram, saying, 'If the LORD shall indeed bring me back to Jerusalem, then I will serve the LORD.'"

9 The king said to him, "Go in peace." So he arose and went to Hebron.

10 But Absalom sent spies throughout all the tribes of Israel, saying, "As soon as you hear the sound of the trumpet, then you shall say, 'Absalom is king in Hebron.'"

11 Then two hundred men went with Absalom from Jerusalem, who were invited and went innocently, and they did not know anything.

12 And Absalom sent for Ahithophel the Gilonite, David's counselor, from his city Giloh, while he was offering the sacrifices. And the conspiracy was strong, for the people increased continually with Absalom.

13 Then a messenger came to David, saying, "The hearts of the men of Israel are with Absalom."

14 David said to all his servants who were with him at Jerusalem, "Arise and let us flee, for *otherwise* none of us will escape from Absalom. Go in haste, or he will overtake us quickly and bring down calamity on us and strike the city with the edge of the sword."

15 Then the king's servants said to the king, "Behold, your servants *are ready to do* whatever my lord the king chooses."

16 So the king went out and all his household with him. But the king left ten concubines to keep the house.

17 The king went out and all the people with him, and they stopped at the last house.

18 Now all his servants passed on beside him, all the Cherethites, all the Pelethites and all the Gittites, six hundred men who had come with him from Gath, passed on before the king.

19 Then the king said to Ittai the Gittite, "Why will you also go with us? Return and remain with the king, for you are a foreigner and also an exile; *return* to your own place.

20 "You came *only* yesterday, and shall I today make you wander with us, while I go where I will? Return and take back your brothers; mercy and truth be with you."

21 But Ittai answered the king and said, ◄ "As the LORD lives, and as my lord the king lives, surely wherever my lord the king may be, whether for death or for life, there also your servant will be."

22 Therefore David said to Ittai, "Go and pass over." So Ittai the Gittite passed over with all his men and all the little ones who *were* with him.

23 While all the country was weeping with a loud voice, all the people passed over. The king also passed over the brook Kidron, and all the people passed over toward the way of the wilderness.

24 Now behold, Zadok also *came*, and all the Levites with him carrying the ark of the covenant of God. And they set down the ark of God, and Abiathar came up until all the people had finished passing from the city.

25 The king said to Zadok, "Return the ◄ ark of God to the city. If I find favor in the sight of the LORD, then He will bring me back again and show me both it and His habitation.

---

26 "But if He should say thus, 'I have no delight in you,' behold, here I am, let Him do to me as seems good to Him."
27 The king said also to Zadok the priest, "Are you *not* a seer? Return to the city in peace and your two sons with you, your son Ahimaaz and Jonathan the son of Abiathar.
28 "See, I am going to wait at the fords of the wilderness until word comes from you to inform me."
29 Therefore Zadok and Abiathar returned the ark of God to Jerusalem and remained there.
30 And David went up the ascent of the *Mount of* Olives, and wept as he went, and his head was covered and he walked barefoot. Then all the people who were with him each covered his head and went up weeping as they went.
31 Now someone told David, saying, "Ahithophel is among the conspirators with Absalom." And David said, "O LORD, I pray, make the counsel of Ahithophel foolishness."
32 It happened as David was coming to the summit, where God was worshiped, that behold, Hushai the Archite met him with his coat torn and dust on his head.
33 David said to him, "If you pass over with me, then you will be a burden to me.
34 "But if you return to the city, and say to Absalom, 'I will be your servant, O king; as I have been your father's servant in time past, so I will now be your servant,' then you can thwart the counsel of Ahithophel for me.
35 "Are not Zadok and Abiathar the priests with you there? So it shall be that whatever you hear from the king's house, you shall report to Zadok and Abiathar the priests.
36 "Behold their two sons are with them

there, Ahimaaz, Zadok's son and Jonathan, Abiathar's son; and by them you shall send me everything that you hear."
37 So Hushai, David's friend, came into the city, and Absalom came into Jerusalem.

16 NOW when David had passed a little beyond the summit, behold, Ziba the servant of Mephibosheth met him with a couple of saddled donkeys, and on them *were* two hundred loaves of bread, a hundred clusters of raisins, a hundred summer fruits, and a jug of wine.
2 The king said to Ziba, "Why do you have these?" And Ziba said, "The donkeys are for the king's household to ride, and the bread and summer fruit for the young men to eat, and the wine, for whoever is faint in the wilderness to drink."
3 Then the king said, "And where is your master's son?" And Ziba said to the king, "Behold, he is staying in Jerusalem, for he said, 'Today the house of Israel will restore the kingdom of my father to me.'"
4 So the king said to Ziba, "Behold, all that belongs to Mephibosheth is yours." And Ziba said, "I prostrate myself; let me find favor in your sight, O my lord, the king!"
5 When King David came to Bahurim, behold, there came out from there a man of the family of the house of Saul whose name was Shimei, the son of Gera; he came out cursing continually as he came.
6 He threw stones at David and at all the servants of King David; and all the people and all the mighty men were at his right hand and at his left.
7 Thus Shimei said when he cursed, "Get out, get out, you man of bloodshed, and worthless fellow!
8 "The LORD has returned upon you all the bloodshed of the house of Saul, in whose place you have reigned; and the LORD has given the kingdom into the hand of your son Absalom. And behold, you are *taken* in your own evil, for you are a man of bloodshed!"
9 Then Abishai the son of Zeruiah said to the king, "Why should this dead dog curse my lord the king? Let me go over now and cut off his head."
10 But the king said, "What have I to do with you, O sons of Zeruiah? If he curses,

---

LIFE LESSONS

➤ **2 Samuel 15:25** — *"Return the ark of God to the city. If I find favor in the sight of the LORD, then He will bring me back again and show me both it and His habitation."*

*D*avid had learned to trust in the grace and mercy of the Lord, even though he did not know what lay ahead for him. God assumes full responsibility for our needs when we obey him.

LIFE PRINCIPLE 8

FIGHT ALL YOUR BATTLES ON YOUR KNEES
AND YOU WIN EVERY TIME.

2 SAMUEL 15:31

The term *resistance movement* describes situations in which oppressed people rise up against their oppressors. Resistance fighters take the stance, "I'm not going to stand idly by and allow this evil to continue. I choose to resist the wrongs. Whether I live or die in resisting my oppressor, I will no longer live as I have been."

Resistance in prayer is the biblical approach to confronting and overcoming the devil. Peter wrote, "But resist him, firm in your faith" (1 Pet. 5:9). James echoed this teaching: "Submit therefore to God. Resist the devil and he will flee from you. Draw near to God and He will draw near to you" (James 4:7, 8). Both Peter and James make it clear we are to actively resist evil through our persevering prayers.

On the surface, resistance may appear to be passive. In practice, it is anything but passive. It is an active stance, both intentional and powerful.

What would you do if a weight began to press against you, attempting to push you off a position that is rightfully yours? How would you resist? You would lean into the weight and press back. The pressure you exert would equal or exceed the pressure exerted against you. That's a posture of resistance.

Resistance is first and foremost a firm decision to join the struggle against evil in prayer, rather than turning away, backing off, or retreating. Such resistance takes strength and courage. It also takes patience and perseverance. That's why Luke includes a parable designed to teach us "at all times [we] ought to pray and not to lose heart" (Luke 18:1).

Peter and James point to two key words at the heart of our ability to resist the devil through our prayers: submission to God and faith.

Submission to God is saying, "I can't, but You can." In our battlefield prayers we might say, "Lord, I can't defeat the devil on my own. But with You I can." This is the position the apostle Paul took when he said, "I can do all things through Him who strengthens me" (Phil. 4:13).

James taught that submission occurs when we seek to develop a closer relationship to God. As we spend time with God, we get to know Him better and discover *how* He wants us to overcome evil and experience blessing.

We draw near to God through prayer and by spending time in His Word. We draw near to God when we set aside time solely to listen to God and to wait upon Him for direction and guidance. We draw near to God when we periodically shut ourselves away, closing off all other influences that might distract us from knowing Him better. The better we know Him, the more we see His awesome power, experience His vast love, learn from His wisdom, and grow in our faith. We come to an even greater realization: "Yes, God *can* defeat the devil on my behalf. Yes, God *will* win in any conflict with the devil. Yes, God *does* want me to be able to overcome my adversary and to live in victory in Christ Jesus."

Faith is saying to God, "I believe You will." In our battle to overcome the enemy, we might pray this way: "I believe You will defeat the enemy and cause him to flee from me as I resist him and put my trust in You." Again and again, David made this declaration of faith to the Lord: "O my God, in You I trust" (Ps. 25:2; also 31:6; 55:23; 56:3; 143:8). Perfect faith views the battle as being done and God gaining the victory. When David said, "In You I trust," he meant: "It is done. Lord, You are perfect in nature. You do all things well. And You have victory over all my enemies." He had absolute faith in God's ability. There was no hint of "I hope He will" because David knew it was as good as done.

We grow in faith by exercising it, by trusting God in situation after situation, circumstance after circumstance, relationship after relationship. We develop a personal history in which we obey God and He remains faithful in His loving care of us.

It is impossible for you to resist the devil for very long if you do not believe that Christ Jesus through you can and *will* defeat the devil. Furthermore, you can remain firm in your faith only when you completely submit to God—in all areas of your life. When you refuse to submit a problem or area to the Lord, you are saying, "I can handle this. I don't need Your help." That's precisely what Satan wants you to do: trust your ability and not in omnipotent God. It is also the place where he will level his greatest attack against you!

The good news is God has given each of us a measure of faith to develop. He also gives us the ability to trust Him and surrender our lives to Him. We can stand firm and resist the enemy, but only by the power of God. He is the One who hears our prayers and rushes to our defense. When we pray, Satan flees. ◈

and if the Lord has told him, 'Curse David,' then who shall say, 'Why have you done so?'"
11 Then David said to Abishai and to all his servants, "Behold, my son who came out from me seeks my life; how much more now this Benjamite? Let him alone and let him curse, for the Lord has told him.
12 "Perhaps the Lord will look on my affliction and return good to me instead of his cursing this day."
13 So David and his men went on the way; and Shimei went along on the hillside parallel with him and as he went he cursed and cast stones and threw dust at him.
14 The king and all the people who were with him arrived weary and he refreshed himself there.
15 Then Absalom and all the people, the men of Israel, entered Jerusalem, and Ahithophel with him.
16 Now it came about when Hushai the Archite, David's friend, came to Absalom, that Hushai said to Absalom, "Long live the king! Long live the king!"
17 Absalom said to Hushai, "Is this your loyalty to your friend? Why did you not go with your friend?"
18 Then Hushai said to Absalom, "No! For whom the Lord, this people, and all the men of Israel have chosen, his I will be, and with him I will remain.
19 "Besides, whom should I serve? Should I not serve in the presence of his son? As I have served in your father's presence, so I will be in your presence."
20 Then Absalom said to Ahithophel, "Give your advice. What shall we do?"
21 Ahithophel said to Absalom, "Go in to your father's concubines, whom he has left to keep the house; then all Israel will hear that you have made yourself odious to your father. The hands of all who are with you will also be strengthened."
22 So they pitched a tent for Absalom on the roof, and Absalom went in to his father's concubines in the sight of all Israel.
23 The advice of Ahithophel, which he gave in those days, was as if one inquired of the word of God; so was all the advice of Ahithophel regarded by both David and Absalom.

Psalm 66:8–15

8 Bless our God, O peoples,
And sound His praise abroad,
9 Who keeps us in life
And does not allow our feet to slip.
10 For You have tried us, O God;
You have refined us as silver is refined.
11 You brought us into the net;
You laid an oppressive burden upon our loins.
12 You made men ride over our heads;
We went through fire and through water,
Yet You brought us out into a place of abundance.
13 I shall come into Your house with burnt offerings;
I shall pay You my vows,
14 Which my lips uttered
And my mouth spoke when I was in distress.
15 I shall offer to You burnt offerings of fat beasts,
With the smoke of rams;
I shall make an offering of bulls with male goats.   Selah.

Proverbs 16:27–30

27 A worthless man digs up evil,
While his words are like scorching fire.
28 A perverse man spreads strife,
And a slanderer separates intimate friends.
29 A man of violence entices his neighbor
And leads him in a way that is not good.

LIFE LESSONS

➤ Psalm 66:10 — For You have tried us, O God; You have refined us as silver is refined.

God tests every believer, both to reveal the character of his or her heart and to lead him or her into a deeper relationship with Himself. We tend to learn more in the valley than on the mountaintop.

30 He who winks his eyes *does so* to
    devise perverse things;
    He who compresses his lips brings
    evil to pass.

John 7:1–27

7 AFTER these things Jesus was walking in Galilee, for He was unwilling
to walk in Judea because the Jews were
seeking to kill Him.
2 Now the feast of the Jews, the Feast
of Booths, was near.
3 Therefore His brothers said to Him,
"Leave here and go into Judea, so that
Your disciples also may see Your works
which You are doing.
4 "For no one does anything in secret
when he himself seeks to be *known*
publicly. If You do these things, show
Yourself to the world."
5 For not even His brothers were believing in Him.
6 So Jesus *said to them, "My time is
not yet here, but your time is always opportune.
7 "The world cannot hate you, but it
hates Me because I testify of it, that its
deeds are evil.
8 "Go up to the feast yourselves; I do
not go up to this feast because My time
has not yet fully come."
9 Having said these things to them, He
stayed in Galilee.
10 But when His brothers had gone up
to the feast, then He Himself also went
up, not publicly, but as if, in secret.
11 So the Jews were seeking Him at the
feast and were saying, "Where is He?"
12 There was much grumbling among
the crowds concerning Him; some were
saying, "He is a good man"; others were
saying, "No, on the contrary, He leads
the people astray."
13 Yet no one was speaking openly of
Him for fear of the Jews.
14 But when it was now the midst of the
feast Jesus went up into the temple, and
began to teach.
15 The Jews then were astonished, saying, "How has this man become learned,
having never been educated?"
16 So Jesus answered them and said,
"My teaching is not Mine, but His who
sent Me.

17 "If anyone is willing to do His will, he
will know of the teaching, whether it is of
God or *whether* I speak from Myself.
18 "He who speaks from himself seeks
his own glory; but He who is seeking the
glory of the One who sent Him, He is true,
and there is no unrighteousness in Him.
19 "Did not Moses give you the Law,
and *yet* none of you carries out the Law?
Why do you seek to kill Me?"
20 The crowd answered, "You have a
demon! Who seeks to kill You?"
21 Jesus answered them, "I did one
deed, and you all marvel.
22 "For this reason Moses has given
you circumcision (not because it is from
Moses, but from the fathers), and on *the*
Sabbath you circumcise a man.
23 "If a man receives circumcision on
the Sabbath so that the Law of Moses
will not be broken, are you angry with
Me because I made an entire man well
on *the* Sabbath?
24 "Do not judge according to appearance, but judge with righteous judgment."
25 So some of the people of Jerusalem
were saying, "Is this not the man whom
they are seeking to kill?
26 "Look, He is speaking publicly, and
they are saying nothing to Him. The rulers do not really know that this is the
Christ, do they?
27 "However, we know where this man
is from; but whenever the Christ may
come, no one knows where He is from."

LIFE LESSONS

**John 7:5 — *For not even His brothers
were believing in Him.***

Jesus' younger brothers had grown up
with Him in Nazareth, and while they
might have heard about His extraordinary birth, they did not believe in Him
until after the Resurrection. Only then
did they come to faith.

**John 7:17 — *"He will know of the
teaching, whether it is of God or whether
I speak from Myself."***

The best way to understand the Word
of God is to decide to obey it, whatever it says. We put ourselves in great
spiritual danger by trying to understand
the Bible without first committing to
obey God (Luke 12:47, 48).

17 FURTHERMORE, Ahithophel said to Absalom, "Please let me choose 12,000 men that I may arise and pursue David tonight.

2 "I will come upon him while he is weary and exhausted and terrify him, so that all the people who are with him will flee. Then I will strike down the king alone,

3 and I will bring back all the people to you. The return of everyone depends on the man you seek; then all the people will be at peace."

4 So the plan pleased Absalom and all the elders of Israel.

5 Then Absalom said, "Now call Hushai the Archite also, and let us hear what he has to say."

6 When Hushai had come to Absalom, Absalom said to him, "Ahithophel has spoken thus. Shall we carry out his plan? If not, you speak."

7 So Hushai said to Absalom, "This time the advice that Ahithophel has given is not good."

8 Moreover, Hushai said, "You know your father and his men, that they are mighty men and they are fierce, like a bear robbed of her cubs in the field. And your father is an expert in warfare, and will not spend the night with the people.

9 "Behold, he has now hidden himself in one of the caves or in another place; and it will be when he falls on them at the first attack, that whoever hears it will say, 'There has been a slaughter among the people who follow Absalom.'

10 "And even the one who is valiant, whose heart is like the heart of a lion, will completely lose heart; for all Israel knows that your father is a mighty man and those who are with him are valiant men.

11 "But I counsel that all Israel be surely gathered to you, from Dan even to Beersheba, as the sand that is by the sea in abundance, and that you personally go into battle.

12 "So we shall come to him in one of the places where he can be found, and we will fall on him as the dew falls on the ground; and of him and of all the men who are with him, not even one will be left.

13 "If he withdraws into a city, then all Israel shall bring ropes to that city, and we will drag it into the valley until not even a small stone is found there."

14 Then Absalom and all the men of Israel said, "The counsel of Hushai the Archite is better than the counsel of Ahithophel." For the LORD had ordained to thwart the good counsel of Ahithophel, so that the LORD might bring calamity on Absalom.

15 Then Hushai said to Zadok and to Abiathar the priests, "This is what Ahithophel counseled Absalom and the elders of Israel, and this is what I have counseled.

16 "Now therefore, send quickly and tell David, saying, 'Do not spend the night at the fords of the wilderness, but by all means cross over, or else the king and all the people who are with him will be destroyed.'"

17 Now Jonathan and Ahimaaz were staying at En-rogel, and a maidservant would go and tell them, and they would go and tell King David, for they could not be seen entering the city.

18 But a lad did see them and told Absalom; so the two of them departed quickly and came to the house of a man in Bahurim, who had a well in his courtyard, and they went down into it.

19 And the woman took a covering and spread it over the well's mouth and scattered grain on it, so that nothing was known.

20 Then Absalom's servants came to the woman at the house and said, "Where are Ahimaaz and Jonathan?" And the woman said to them, "They have crossed the brook of water." And when they searched and could not find them, they returned to Jerusalem.

21 It came about after they had departed that they came up out of the well and went and told King David; and they said to David, "Arise and cross over the water quickly for thus Ahithophel has counseled against you."

22 Then David and all the people who were with him arose and crossed the Jordan; and by dawn not even one remained who had not crossed the Jordan.

23 Now when Ahithophel saw that his counsel was not followed, he saddled his donkey and arose and went to his home,

to his city, and set his house in order, and strangled himself; thus he died and was buried in the grave of his father.

24 Then David came to Mahanaim. And Absalom crossed the Jordan, he and all the men of Israel with him.

25 Absalom set Amasa over the army in place of Joab. Now Amasa was the son of a man whose name was Ithra the Israelite, who went in to Abigail the daughter of Nahash, sister of Zeruiah, Joab's mother.

26 And Israel and Absalom camped in the land of Gilead.

27 Now when David had come to Mahanaim, Shobi the son of Nahash from Rabbah of the sons of Ammon, Machir the son of Ammiel from Lo-debar, and Barzillai the Gileadite from Rogelim,

28 brought beds, basins, pottery, wheat, barley, flour, parched *grain*, beans, lentils, parched *seeds*,

29 honey, curds, sheep, and cheese of the herd, for David and for the people who *were* with him, to eat; for they said, "The people are hungry and weary and thirsty in the wilderness."

18 THEN David numbered the people who were with him and set over them commanders of thousands and commanders of hundreds.

2 David sent the people out, one third under the command of Joab, one third under the command of Abishai the son of Zeruiah, Joab's brother, and one third under the command of Ittai the Gittite. And the king said to the people, "I myself will surely go out with you also."

3 But the people said, "You should not go out; for if we indeed flee, they will not care about us; even if half of us die, they will not care about us. But you are worth ten thousand of us; therefore now it is better that you *be ready* to help us from the city."

4 Then the king said to them, "Whatever seems best to you I will do." So the king stood beside the gate, and all the people went out by hundreds and thousands.

5 The king charged Joab and Abishai and Ittai, saying, "*Deal* gently for my sake with the young man Absalom." And all the people heard when the king charged all the commanders concerning Absalom.

6 Then the people went out into the field against Israel, and the battle took place in the forest of Ephraim.

7 The people of Israel were defeated there before the servants of David, and the slaughter there that day was great, 20,000 men.

8 For the battle there was spread over the whole countryside, and the forest devoured more people that day than the sword devoured.

9 Now Absalom happened to meet the servants of David. For Absalom was riding on *his* mule, and the mule went under the thick branches of a great oak. And his head caught fast in the oak, so he was left hanging between heaven and earth, while the mule that was under him kept going.

10 When a certain man saw *it,* he told Joab and said, "Behold, I saw Absalom hanging in an oak."

11 Then Joab said to the man who had told him, "Now behold, you saw *him!* Why then did you not strike him there to the ground? And I would have given you ten *pieces* of silver and a belt."

12 The man said to Joab, "Even if I should receive a thousand *pieces of* silver in my hand, I would not put out my hand against the king's son; for in our hearing the king charged you and Abishai and Ittai, saying, 'Protect for me the young man Absalom!'

13 "Otherwise, if I had dealt treacherously against his life (and there is nothing hidden from the king), then you yourself would have stood aloof."

14 Then Joab said, "I will not waste time here with you." So he took three spears in his hand and thrust them through the heart of Absalom while he was yet alive in the midst of the oak.

15 And ten young men who carried Joab's armor gathered around and struck Absalom and killed him.

16 Then Joab blew the trumpet, and the people returned from pursuing Israel, for Joab restrained the people.

17 They took Absalom and cast him into a deep pit in the forest and erected over him a very great heap of stones. And all Israel fled, each to his tent.

18 Now Absalom in his lifetime had taken and set up for himself a pillar which is in the King's Valley, for he said, "I have no son to preserve my name." So he named the pillar after his own name,

and it is called Absalom's Monument to this day.

19 Then Ahimaaz the son of Zadok said, "Please let me run and bring the king news that the LORD has freed him from the hand of his enemies."

20 But Joab said to him, "You are not the man to carry news this day, but you shall carry news another day; however, you shall carry no news today because the king's son is dead."

21 Then Joab said to the Cushite, "Go, tell the king what you have seen." So the Cushite bowed to Joab and ran.

22 Now Ahimaaz the son of Zadok said once more to Joab, "But whatever happens, please let me also run after the Cushite." And Joab said, "Why would you run, my son, since you will have no reward for going?"

23 "But whatever happens," *he said,* "I will run." So he said to him, "Run." Then Ahimaaz ran by way of the plain and passed up the Cushite.

24 Now David was sitting between the two gates; and the watchman went up to the roof of the gate by the wall, and raised his eyes and looked, and behold, a man running by himself.

25 The watchman called and told the king. And the king said, "If he is by himself there is good news in his mouth." And he came nearer and nearer.

26 Then the watchman saw another man running; and the watchman called to the gatekeeper and said, "Behold, *another* man running by himself." And the king said, "This one also is bringing good news."

27 The watchman said, "I think the running of the first one is like the running of Ahimaaz the son of Zadok." And the king said, "This is a good man and comes with good news."

28 Ahimaaz called and said to the king, "All is well." And he prostrated himself before the king with his face to the ground. And he said, "Blessed is the LORD your God, who has delivered up the men who lifted their hands against my lord the king."

29 The king said, "Is it well with the young man Absalom?" And Ahimaaz answered, "When Joab sent the king's servant, and your servant, I saw a great tumult, but I did not know what *it was.*"

30 Then the king said, "Turn aside and stand here." So he turned aside and stood still.

31 Behold, the Cushite arrived, and the Cushite said, "Let my lord the king receive good news, for the LORD has freed you this day from the hand of all those who rose up against you."

32 Then the king said to the Cushite, "Is it well with the young man Absalom?" And the Cushite answered, "Let the enemies of my lord the king, and all who rise up against you for evil, be as that young man!"

33 The king was deeply moved and went up to the chamber over the gate and wept. And thus he said as he walked, "O my son Absalom, my son, my son Absalom! Would I had died instead of you, O Absalom, my son, my son!"

Psalm 66:16–20

16 Come *and* hear, all who fear God,
And I will tell of what He has done
for my soul.
17 I cried to Him with my mouth,
And He was extolled with my
tongue.
18 If I regard wickedness in my heart, ◄
The Lord will not hear;
19 But certainly God has heard;
He has given heed to the voice of
my prayer.

LIFE LESSONS

➤ **2 Samuel 18:18** — *Absalom in his lifetime had taken and set up for himself a pillar which is in the King's Valley.*

*A*bsalom left behind a stone monument in his name, but nothing else. Whatever we acquire outside of God's will turns to ashes.

➤ **Psalm 66:18** — *If I regard wickedness in my heart, the Lord will not hear.*

*I*f we refuse to admit to some sin, despite the conviction of the Holy Spirit on our hearts, we hinder our own prayers. God blesses obedience, not stubbornness.

20 Blessed be God,
Who has not turned away my prayer
Nor His lovingkindness from me.

Proverbs 16:31, 32

31 A gray head is a crown of glory;
It is found in the way of righteousness.
32 He who is slow to anger is better
than the mighty,
And he who rules his spirit, than he
who captures a city.

John 7:28–53

28 Then Jesus cried out in the temple,
teaching and saying, "You both know Me
and know where I am from; and I have
not come of Myself, but He who sent Me
is true, whom you do not know.
29 "I know Him, because I am from
Him, and He sent Me."

WHAT THE BIBLE SAYS ABOUT

Signs

John 7:28–31

*H*ow many signs are enough? For those
in the crowd who believed in Jesus,
He had done enough. They said, "When the
Christ comes, He will not perform more signs
than those which this man has, will He?" (John
7:31). Others were doubtful—they needed
more wonders before they could believe.

Do you ever feel as if you need a big,
obvious sign from God? Do you ever want
proof God is going to do as He says? Would a
miraculous gesture convince you God is going
to be faithful?

In Luke 16, Jesus answered such a sign-
based faith with a parable. As the rich man
faced the torments of perdition, he felt certain
that if his brothers had a special messenger,
they would take heed of the judgment awaiting them. Therefore, the rich man asked
Abraham to send the poor man, Lazarus, back
to earth from heaven to give his brothers the
message of salvation.

30 So they were seeking to seize Him;
and no man laid his hand on Him, because His hour had not yet come.
31 But many of the crowd believed in
Him; and they were saying, "When the
Christ comes, He will not perform more
signs than those which this man has,
will He?"
32 The Pharisees heard the crowd mut-
tering these things about Him, and the
chief priests and the Pharisees sent officers to seize Him.
33 Therefore Jesus said, "For a little
while longer I am with you, then I go to
Him who sent Me.

LIFE LESSONS

➤ *John 7:30 — So they were seeking to
seize Him; and no man laid his hand on
Him, because His hour had not yet come.*

*S*everal times Jesus' opponents wanted
to take Him by force or eliminate
Him, but God did not permit any of their
plans to succeed until they fit His timing.
His sovereign will controls all of history.

However, Abraham did not honor his
request. Rather, he revealed a sobering truth,
"If they do not listen to Moses and the Prophets, they will not be persuaded even if someone rises from the dead" (Luke 16:31).

Jesus voiced a similar theme in John 7:28,
"You both know Me and know where I am
from; and I have not come of Myself, but He
who sent Me is true." You know Christ and
His character. You know He has the ability and
wisdom to help you. After all that, do you still
doubt?

Miraculous signs and wonders will hardly
convince people who do not believe God's
track record. A. W. Tozer has written, "The
unbelieving mind would not be convinced by
any proof, and the worshiping heart needs
none."

Do you keep asking for signs in order to
believe? Then you're asking for the wrong
thing. Instead, look to God. He has been faithful throughout history, and He will most certainly be faithful to you. If you need assurances of the trustworthiness of His character,
you have a huge treasure trove of examples in
Scripture. Make your faith sure—He will do as
He has said, you can be certain of it. ◉

34 "You will seek Me, and will not find Me; and where I am, you cannot come."
35 The Jews then said to one another, "Where does this man intend to go that we will not find Him? He is not intending to go to the Dispersion among the Greeks, and teach the Greeks, is He?
36 "What is this statement that He said, 'You will seek Me, and will not find Me; and where I am, you cannot come'?"
➤ 37 Now on the last day, the great *day* of the feast, Jesus stood and cried out, saying, "If anyone is thirsty, let him come to Me and drink.
38 "He who believes in Me, as the Scripture said, 'From his innermost being will flow rivers of living water.'"
39 But this He spoke of the Spirit, whom those who believed in Him were to receive; for the Spirit was not yet *given*, because Jesus was not yet glorified.
40 *Some* of the people therefore, when

LIFE LESSONS

➤ **John 7:37 — "If anyone is thirsty, let him come to Me and drink."**

*B*ecause God made us for an intimate relationship with Himself, our deepest needs cannot be met anywhere else but in Him. Jesus offers the only satisfaction for spiritual thirst.

---

they heard these words, were saying, "This certainly is the Prophet."
41 Others were saying, "This is the Christ." Still others were saying, "Surely the Christ is not going to come from Galilee, is He?
42 "Has not the Scripture said that the Christ comes from the descendants of David, and from Bethlehem, the village where David was?"
43 So a division occurred in the crowd because of Him.
44 Some of them wanted to seize Him, but no one laid hands on Him.
45 The officers then came to the chief priests and Pharisees, and they said to them, "Why did you not bring Him?"
46 The officers answered, "Never has a man spoken the way this man speaks."
47 The Pharisees then answered them, "You have not also been led astray, have you?
48 "No one of the rulers or Pharisees has believed in Him, has he?
49 "But this crowd which does not know the Law is accursed."
50 Nicodemus (he who came to Him before, being one of them) *said to them,
51 "Our Law does not judge a man unless it first hears from him and knows what he is doing, does it?"
52 They answered him, "You are not also from Galilee, are you? Search, and see that no prophet arises out of Galilee."
53 [Everyone went to his home.

---

2 Samuel 19:1—20:26

19 THEN it was told Joab, "Behold, the king is weeping and mourns for Absalom."
2 The victory that day was turned to mourning for all the people, for the people heard *it* said that day, "The king is grieved for his son."
3 So the people went by stealth into the city that day, as people who are humiliated steal away when they flee in battle.
4 The king covered his face and cried

out with a loud voice, "O my son Absalom, O Absalom, my son, my son!"
5 Then Joab came into the house to

LIFE LESSONS

➤ **2 Samuel 19:4 — "O my son Absalom, O Absalom, my son, my son!"**

*A*lthough David did everything he could to protect him, Absalom still lost his life. That is what always happens when a person harbors unforgiveness and revenge in his heart—he hurts the people around him unnecessarily and eventually destroys himself.

the king and said, "Today you have covered with shame the faces of all your servants, who today have saved your life and the lives of your sons and daughters, the lives of your wives, and the lives of your concubines,

6   by loving those who hate you, and by hating those who love you. For you have shown today that princes and servants are nothing to you; for I know this day that if Absalom were alive and all of us were dead today, then you would be pleased.

7   "Now therefore arise, go out and speak kindly to your servants, for I swear by the LORD, if you do not go out, surely not a man will pass the night with you, and this will be worse for you than all the evil that has come upon you from your youth until now."

8   So the king arose and sat in the gate. When they told all the people, saying, "Behold, the king is sitting in the gate," then all the people came before the king. Now Israel had fled, each to his tent.

9   All the people were quarreling throughout all the tribes of Israel, saying, "The king delivered us from the hand of our enemies and saved us from the hand of the Philistines, but now he has fled out of the land from Absalom.

10 "However, Absalom, whom we anointed over us, has died in battle. Now then, why are you silent about bringing the king back?"

11 Then King David sent to Zadok and Abiathar the priests, saying, "Speak to the elders of Judah, saying, 'Why are you the last to bring the king back to his house, since the word of all Israel has come to the king, even to his house?

12 'You are my brothers; you are my bone and my flesh. Why then should you be the last to bring back the king?'

13 "Say to Amasa, 'Are you not my bone and my flesh? May God do so to me, and more also, if you will not be commander of the army before me continually in place of Joab.'"

14 Thus he turned the hearts of all the men of Judah as one man, so that they sent word to the king, saying, "Return, you and all your servants."

15 The king then returned and came as far as the Jordan. And Judah came to Gilgal in order to go to meet the king, to bring the king across the Jordan.

16 Then Shimei the son of Gera, the Benjamite who was from Bahurim, hurried and came down with the men of Judah to meet King David.

17 There were a thousand men of Benjamin with him, with Ziba the servant of the house of Saul, and his fifteen sons and his twenty servants with him; and they rushed to the Jordan before the king.

18 Then they kept crossing the ford to bring over the king's household, and to do what was good in his sight. And Shimei the son of Gera fell down before the king as he was about to cross the Jordan.

19 So he said to the king, "Let not my lord consider me guilty, nor remember what your servant did wrong on the day when my lord the king came out from Jerusalem, so that the king would take it to heart.

20 "For your servant knows that I have sinned; therefore behold, I have come today, the first of all the house of Joseph to go down to meet my lord the king."

21 But Abishai the son of Zeruiah said, "Should not Shimei be put to death for this, because he cursed the LORD's anointed?"

22 David then said, "What have I to do with you, O sons of Zeruiah, that you should this day be an adversary to me? Should any man be put to death in Israel today? For do I not know that I am king over Israel today?"

23 The king said to Shimei, "You shall not die." Thus the king swore to him.

24 Then Mephibosheth the son of Saul came down to meet the king; and he had neither cared for his feet, nor trimmed his mustache, nor washed his clothes, from the day the king departed until the day he came home in peace.

25 It was when he came from Jerusalem to meet the king, that the king said to him, "Why did you not go with me, Mephibosheth?"

26 So he answered, "O my lord, the king, my servant deceived me; for your servant said, 'I will saddle a donkey for myself that I may ride on it and go with the king,' because your servant is lame.

27 "Moreover, he has slandered your servant to my lord the king; but my lord the king is like the angel of God, therefore do what is good in your sight.

28 "For all my father's household was

nothing but dead men before my lord the king; yet you set your servant among those who ate at your own table. What right do I have yet that I should complain anymore to the king?"

29 So the king said to him, "Why do you still speak of your affairs? I have decided, 'You and Ziba shall divide the land.'"

30 Mephibosheth said to the king, "Let him even take it all, since my lord the king has come safely to his own house."

31 Now Barzillai the Gileadite had come down from Rogelim; and he went on to the Jordan with the king to escort him over the Jordan.

32 Now Barzillai was very old, being eighty years old; and he had sustained the king while he stayed at Mahanaim, for he was a very great man.

33 The king said to Barzillai, "You cross over with me and I will sustain you in Jerusalem with me."

34 But Barzillai said to the king, "How long have I yet to live, that I should go up with the king to Jerusalem?

35 "I am now eighty years old. Can I distinguish between good and bad? Or can your servant taste what I eat or what I drink? Or can I hear anymore the voice of singing men and women? Why then should your servant be an added burden to my lord the king?

36 "Your servant would merely cross over the Jordan with the king. Why should the king compensate me *with* this reward?

37 "Please let your servant return, that I may die in my own city near the grave of my father and my mother. However, here is your servant Chimham, let him cross over with my lord the king, and do for him what is good in your sight."

38 The king answered, "Chimham shall cross over with me, and I will do for him what is good in your sight; and whatever you require of me, I will do for you."

39 All the people crossed over the Jordan and the king crossed too. The king then kissed Barzillai and blessed him, and he returned to his place.

40 Now the king went on to Gilgal, and Chimham went on with him; and all the people of Judah and also half the people of Israel accompanied the king.

41 And behold, all the men of Israel came to the king and said to the king, "Why had our brothers the men of Judah stolen you away, and brought the king and his household and all David's men with him over the Jordan?"

42 Then all the men of Judah answered the men of Israel, "Because the king is a close relative to us. Why then are you angry about this matter? Have we eaten at all at the king's *expense*, or has anything been taken for us?"

43 But the men of Israel answered the men of Judah and said, "We have ten parts in the king, therefore we also have more *claim* on David than you. Why then did you treat us with contempt? Was it not our advice first to bring back our king?" Yet the words of the men of Judah were harsher than the words of the men of Israel.

20 NOW a worthless fellow happened to be there whose name was Sheba, the son of Bichri, a Benjamite; and he blew the trumpet and said,

"We have no portion in David,
Nor do we have inheritance in the son of Jesse;
Every man to his tents, O Israel!"

2 So all the men of Israel withdrew from following David *and* followed Sheba the son of Bichri; but the men of Judah remained steadfast to their king, from the Jordan even to Jerusalem.

3 Then David came to his house at Jerusalem, and the king took the ten women, the concubines whom he had left to keep the house, and placed them under guard and provided them with sustenance, but did not go in to them. So they were shut up until the day of their death, living as widows.

4 Then the king said to Amasa, "Call out the men of Judah for me within three days, and be present here yourself."

5 So Amasa went to call out *the men of* Judah, but he delayed longer than the set time which he had appointed him.

6 And David said to Abishai, "Now Sheba the son of Bichri will do us more harm than Absalom; take your lord's servants and pursue him, so that he does not find for himself fortified cities and escape from our sight."

7 So Joab's men went out after him, along with the Cherethites and the Pelethites and all the mighty men; and they went out from Jerusalem to pursue Sheba the son of Bichri.

8. When they were at the large stone which is in Gibeon, Amasa came to meet them. Now Joab was dressed in his military attire, and over it was a belt with a sword in its sheath fastened at his waist; and as he went forward, it fell out.

9 Joab said to Amasa, "Is it well with you, my brother?" And Joab took Amasa by the beard with his right hand to kiss him.

10 But Amasa was not on guard against the sword which was in Joab's hand so he struck him in the belly with it and poured out his inward parts on the ground, and did not *strike* him again, and he died. Then Joab and Abishai his brother pursued Sheba the son of Bichri.

11 Now there stood by him one of Joab's young men, and said, "Whoever favors Joab and whoever is for David, *let him* follow Joab."

12 But Amasa lay wallowing in *his* blood in the middle of the highway. And when the man saw that all the people stood still, he removed Amasa from the highway into the field and threw a garment over him when he saw that everyone who came by him stood still.

13 As soon as he was removed from the highway, all the men passed on after Joab to pursue Sheba the son of Bichri.

14 Now he went through all the tribes of Israel to Abel, even Beth-maacah, and all the Berites; and they were gathered together and also went after him.

15 They came and besieged him in Abel Beth-maacah, and they cast up a siege ramp against the city, and it stood by the rampart; and all the people who were with Joab were wreaking destruction in order to topple the wall.

16 Then a wise woman called from the city, "Hear, hear! Please tell Joab, 'Come here that I may speak with you.'"

17 So he approached her, and the woman said, "Are you Joab?" And he answered, "I am." Then she said to him, "Listen to the words of your maidservant." And he answered, "I am listening."

18 Then she spoke, saying, "Formerly they used to say, 'They will surely ask *advice* at Abel,' and thus they ended *the* dispute.

19 "I am of those who are peaceable *and* faithful in Israel. You are seeking to destroy a city, even a mother in Israel. Why would you swallow up the inheritance of the LORD?"

20 Joab replied, "Far be it, far be it from me that I should swallow up or destroy!

21 "Such is not the case. But a man from the hill country of Ephraim, Sheba the son of Bichri by name, has lifted up his hand against King David. Only hand him over, and I will depart from the city." And the woman said to Joab, "Behold, his head will be thrown to you over the wall."

22 Then the woman wisely came to all the people. And they cut off the head of Sheba the son of Bichri and threw it to Joab. So he blew the trumpet, and they were dispersed from the city, each to his tent. Joab also returned to the king at Jerusalem.

23 Now Joab was over the whole army of Israel, and Benaiah the son of Jehoiada was over the Cherethites and the Pelethites;

24 and Adoram was over the forced labor, and Jehoshaphat the son of Ahilud was the recorder;

25 and Sheva was scribe, and Zadok and Abiathar were priests;

26 and Ira the Jairite was also a priest to David.

Psalm 67:1–7

For the choir director; with stringed instruments. A Psalm. A Song.

67 GOD be gracious to us and bless us,
    And cause His face to shine upon us—   Selah.
2   That Your way may be known on the earth,
    Your salvation among all nations.

LIFE LESSONS

➤ **Psalm 67:1** — *God be gracious to us and bless us, and cause His face to shine upon us.*

*A*s sinners saved by grace, we all need God's mercy. We all need His blessing. Life goes much better when His face shines upon us. Therefore, why not ask God for all three, as the psalmist did?

3   Let the peoples praise You, O God;
Let all the peoples praise You.

4   Let the nations be glad and sing for
joy;
For You will judge the peoples with
uprightness
And guide the nations on the
earth.   Selah.

5   Let the peoples praise You, O God;
Let all the peoples praise You.

6   The earth has yielded its produce;
God, our God, blesses us.

7   God blesses us,
That all the ends of the earth may
fear Him.

Proverbs 16:33—17:1

33   The lot is cast into the lap,
But its every decision is from the
LORD.

17 BETTER is a dry morsel and
quietness with it
Than a house full of feasting with
strife.

John 8:1–27

8 BUT Jesus went to the Mount of
Olives.

2   Early in the morning He came again
into the temple, and all the people were
coming to Him; and He sat down and
began to teach them.

3   The scribes and the Pharisees
*brought a woman caught in adultery,
and having set her in the center *of the
court,*

4   they *said to Him, "Teacher, this
woman has been caught in adultery, in
the very act.

5   "Now in the Law Moses commanded
us to stone such women; what then do
You say?"

6   They were saying this, testing Him,
so that they might have grounds for accusing Him. But Jesus stooped down and
with His finger wrote on the ground.

7   But when they persisted in asking
Him, He straightened up, and said to
them, "He who is without sin among you,
let him *be the* first to throw a stone at
her."

8   Again He stooped down and wrote
on the ground.

9   When they heard it, they *began* to
go out one by one, beginning with the
older ones, and He was left alone, and
the woman, where she was, in the center
of the court.

10   Straightening up, Jesus said to her,
"Woman, where are they? Did no one
condemn you?"

11   She said, "No one, Lord." And Jesus
said, "I do not condemn you, either. Go.
From now on sin no more."]

12   Then Jesus again spoke to them,
saying, "I am the Light of the world;
he who follows Me will not walk in the
darkness, but will have the Light of life."

13   So the Pharisees said to Him, "You
are testifying about Yourself; Your testimony is not true."

14   Jesus answered and said to them,
"Even if I testify about Myself, My testimony is true, for I know where I came
from and where I am going; but you do
not know where I come from or where I
am going.

15   "You judge according to the flesh; I
am not judging anyone.

16   "But even if I do judge, My judgment
is true; for I am not alone *in it,* but I and
the Father who sent Me.

17   "Even in your law it has been written
that the testimony of two men is true.

18   "I am He who testifies about Myself,
and the Father who sent Me testifies
about Me."

19   So they were saying to Him, "Where
is Your Father?" Jesus answered, "You
know neither Me nor My Father; if you
knew Me, you would know My Father
also."

20   These words He spoke in the treasury, as He taught in the temple; and no
one seized Him, because His hour had
not yet come.

LIFE LESSONS

➢ **John 8:11 —** *"I do not condemn you,
either. Go. From now on sin no more."*

*J*esus is gracious and merciful, but He
never ceases to be holy. He calls us
to a life of holiness and obedience to
His Father, and He gives us the spiritual
resources we need to walk in righteousness.

Why does God tell us to avoid evil and "sin no more"?

JOHN 8:11

*T*hose who hope that God will tolerate a little sinfulness generally do so because of iniquity in their own lives. They do nothing about their sin, even though they recognize it as wrong.

"But we are all sinful," you may protest. "None of us is perfect." True. Romans 3:23 says plainly, "All have sinned and fall short of the glory of God."

But recognizing our sin should compel us to do something about it. When we understand we have violated God's will, we need to come to the Father and say, "I need Your forgiveness. Please wash me and make me clean in Your sight." When we recognize we have acted wrongly toward our neighbors or have disobeyed God, we should not casually brush aside our offenses as if to say, "Well, that's just my human nature!" Rather, we need to come to God and say, "I have sinned. Have mercy upon me. Transform me, Lord, into the likeness of Christ so I won't desire to do this again!"

Deuteronomy 19:19, 20 give clear instructions in how to deal with our sin: "You shall purge the evil from among you. The rest will hear and be afraid, and will never again do such an evil thing among you." Centuries later, Jesus told a woman caught in the act of blatant sin, "Go. From now on sin no more" (John 8:11).

Facing the fact we are sinful creatures is not the same as tolerating sin in our lives. Scripture teaches us God desires for us to hate sin and its consequences and to completely avoid evil.

We are not to imitate evil.
We are not to embrace evil.
We are not to flirt with evil.
We are not to be curious about evil.
Rather, we are to turn our backs on it and run from it at full speed.

Why does God want you to flee from evil? Because He desires to protect you from sin's terrible consequences! The Lord knows what you will reap when you sow sinfulness—a harvest of terrible consequences, including anguish, trials, heartaches, and adversity.

Don't do it. Instead, flee from evil, and experience the blessings of the Lord.

---

21 Then He said again to them, "I go away, and you will seek Me, and will die in your sin; where I am going, you cannot come."
22 So the Jews were saying, "Surely He will not kill Himself, will He, since He says, 'Where I am going, you cannot come'?"
23 And He was saying to them, "You are from below, I am from above; you are of this world, I am not of this world.
24 "Therefore I said to you that you will die in your sins; for unless you believe that I am *He*, you will die in your sins."
25 So they were saying to Him, "Who are You?" Jesus said to them, "What have I been saying to you *from* the beginning?
26 "I have many things to speak and to judge concerning you, but He who sent Me is true; and the things which I heard from Him, these I speak to the world."
27 They did not realize that He had been speaking to them about the Father.

MAY 25

2 Samuel 21:1—22:51

➤ **21** NOW there was a famine in the days of David for three years, year after year; and David sought the presence of the LORD. And the LORD said, "It is for Saul and his bloody house, because he put the Gibeonites to death."
2 So the king called the Gibeonites and spoke to them (now the Gibeonites

LIFE LESSONS

➤ **2 Samuel 21:1** — *"It is for Saul and his bloody house, because he put the Gibeonites to death."*

*S*aul in his mistaken zeal had violated a covenant made in God's name (Josh. 9:16–21), and Israel paid for it. We reap what we sow, more than we sow, and later than we sow.

were not of the sons of Israel but of the remnant of the Amorites, and the sons of Israel made a covenant with them, but Saul had sought to kill them in his zeal for the sons of Israel and Judah).

3 Thus David said to the Gibeonites, "What should I do for you? And how can I make atonement that you may bless the inheritance of the LORD?"

4 Then the Gibeonites said to him, "We have no *concern* of silver or gold with Saul or his house, nor is it for us to put any man to death in Israel." And he said, "I will do for you whatever you say."

5 So they said to the king, "The man who consumed us and who planned to exterminate us from remaining within any border of Israel,

6 let seven men from his sons be given to us, and we will hang them before the LORD in Gibeah of Saul, the chosen of the LORD." And the king said, "I will give *them.*"

7 But the king spared Mephibosheth, the son of Jonathan the son of Saul, because of the oath of the LORD which was between them, between David and Saul's son Jonathan.

8 So the king took the two sons of Rizpah the daughter of Aiah, Armoni and Mephibosheth whom she had borne to Saul, and the five sons of Merab the daughter of Saul, whom she had borne to Adriel the son of Barzillai the Meholathite.

9 Then he gave them into the hands of the Gibeonites, and they hanged them in the mountain before the LORD, so that the seven of them fell together; and they were put to death in the first days of harvest at the beginning of barley harvest.

10 And Rizpah the daughter of Aiah took sackcloth and spread it for herself on the rock, from the beginning of harvest until it rained on them from the sky; and she allowed neither the birds of the sky to rest on them by day nor the beasts of the field by night.

11 When it was told David what Rizpah the daughter of Aiah, the concubine of Saul, had done,

12 then David went and took the bones of Saul and the bones of Jonathan his son from the men of Jabesh-gilead, who had stolen them from the open square of Beth-shan, where the Philistines had hanged them on the day the Philistines struck down Saul in Gilboa.

13 He brought up the bones of Saul and the bones of Jonathan his son from there, and they gathered the bones of those who had been hanged.

14 They buried the bones of Saul and Jonathan his son in the country of Benjamin in Zela, in the grave of Kish his father; thus they did all that the king commanded, and after that God was moved by prayer for the land.

15 Now when the Philistines were at war again with Israel, David went down and his servants with him; and as they fought against the Philistines, David became weary.

16 Then Ishbi-benob, who was among the descendants of the giant, the weight of whose spear was three hundred *shekels* of bronze in weight, was girded with a new *sword,* and he intended to kill David.

17 But Abishai the son of Zeruiah helped him, and struck the Philistine and killed him. Then the men of David swore to him, saying, "You shall not go out again with us to battle, so that you do not extinguish the lamp of Israel."

18 Now it came about after this that there was war again with the Philistines at Gob; then Sibbecai the Hushathite struck down Saph, who was among the descendants of the giant.

19 There was war with the Philistines again at Gob, and Elhanan the son of Jaare-oregim the Bethlehemite killed Goliath the Gittite, the shaft of whose spear was like a weaver's beam.

20 There was war at Gath again, where there was a man of *great* stature who had six fingers on each hand and six toes on each foot, twenty-four in number; and he also had been born to the giant.

21 When he defied Israel, Jonathan the son of Shimei, David's brother, struck him down.

22 These four were born to the giant in Gath, and they fell by the hand of David and by the hand of his servants.

22 AND David spoke the words of this song to the LORD in the day that the LORD delivered him from the hand of all his enemies and from the hand of Saul.

2 He said,

"The LORD is my rock and my
    fortress and my deliverer;

3   My God, my rock, in whom I take
refuge,
My shield and the horn of my
salvation, my stronghold and my
refuge;
My savior, You save me from
violence.

4   "I call upon the LORD, who is worthy
to be praised,
And I am saved from my enemies.

5   "For the waves of death
encompassed me;
The torrents of destruction
overwhelmed me;

6   The cords of Sheol surrounded me;
The snares of death confronted me.

7   "In my distress I called upon the
LORD,
Yes, I cried to my God;
And from His temple He heard my
voice,
And my cry for help *came* into His
ears.

8   "Then the earth shook and quaked,
The foundations of heaven were
trembling
And were shaken, because He was
angry.

9   "Smoke went up out of His nostrils,
Fire from His mouth devoured;
Coals were kindled by it.

10   "He bowed the heavens also, and
came down
With thick darkness under His feet.

11   "And He rode on a cherub and flew;
And He appeared on the wings of
the wind.

12   "And He made darkness canopies
around Him,
A mass of waters, thick clouds of the
sky.

13   "From the brightness before Him
Coals of fire were kindled.

14   "The LORD thundered from heaven,
And the Most High uttered His
voice.

15   "And He sent out arrows, and
scattered them,
Lightning, and routed them.

16   "Then the channels of the sea
appeared,
The foundations of the world were
laid bare
By the rebuke of the LORD,
At the blast of the breath of His
nostrils.

17   "He sent from on high, He took me;
He drew me out of many waters.

18   "He delivered me from my strong
enemy,
From those who hated me, for they
were too strong for me.

19   "They confronted me in the day of
my calamity,
But the LORD was my support.

20   "He also brought me forth into a
broad place;
He rescued me, because He
delighted in me.

21   "The LORD has rewarded me
according to my righteousness;
According to the cleanness of my
hands He has recompensed me.

22   "For I have kept the ways of the
LORD,
And have not acted wickedly
against my God.

23   "For all His ordinances *were* before
me,
And *as for* His statutes, I did not
depart from them.

24   "I was also blameless toward Him,
And I kept myself from my iniquity.

25   "Therefore the LORD has
recompensed me according to my
righteousness,
According to my cleanness before
His eyes.

26   "With the kind You show Yourself
kind,
With the blameless You show
Yourself blameless;

27   With the pure You show Yourself
pure,
And with the perverted You show
Yourself astute.

28   "And You save an afflicted people;
But Your eyes are on the haughty
whom You abase.

LIFE LESSONS

➤ **2 Samuel 22:18** — *He delivered me
from my strong enemy, from those who
hated me, for they were too strong for
me.*

*O*ur enemies are often too strong for
us, but they are never too strong for
the Lord. As Isaiah 45:17 promises, "No
weapon that is formed against you will
prosper . . . This is the heritage of the
servants of the LORD."

LIFE LESSONS

➤ **2 Samuel 22:28 —** *And You save an afflicted people; but Your eyes are on the haughty whom You abase.*

*T*hroughout Scripture, God tells us He will save the humble but oppose the proud (Prov. 3:34; James 4:6; 1 Pet. 5:5). The proud try to put themselves in God's place—and that He will never allow.

29 "For You are my lamp, O LORD;
　　And the LORD illumines my
　　darkness.
30 "For by You I can run upon a troop;
　　By my God I can leap over a wall.
31 "As for God, His way is blameless;
　　The word of the LORD is tested;
　　He is a shield to all who take refuge
　　in Him.
32 "For who is God, besides the LORD?
　　And who is a rock, besides our
　　God?
33 "God is my strong fortress;
　　And He sets the blameless in His
　　way.
34 "He makes my feet like hinds' *feet,*
　　And sets me on my high places.
35 "He trains my hands for battle,
　　So that my arms can bend a bow of
　　bronze.
36 "You have also given me the shield
　　of Your salvation,
　　And Your help makes me great.
37 "You enlarge my steps under me,
　　And my feet have not slipped.
38 "I pursued my enemies and
　　destroyed them,
　　And I did not turn back until they
　　were consumed.
39 "And I have devoured them and
　　shattered them, so that they did
　　not rise;
　　And they fell under my feet.
40 "For You have girded me with
　　strength for battle;
　　You have subdued under me those
　　who rose up against me.
41 "You have also made my enemies
　　turn *their* backs to me,
　　And I destroyed those who hated
　　me.
42 "They looked, but there was none to
　　save;
　　Even to the LORD, but He did not
　　answer them.

43 "Then I pulverized them as the dust
　　of the earth;
　　I crushed *and* stamped them as the
　　mire of the streets.
44 "You have also delivered me from
　　the contentions of my people;
　　You have kept me as head of the
　　nations;
　　A people whom I have not known
　　serve me.
45 "Foreigners pretend obedience to me;
　　As soon as they hear, they obey me.
46 "Foreigners lose heart,
　　And come trembling out of their
　　fortresses.
47 "The LORD lives, and blessed be my
　　rock;
　　And exalted be God, the rock of my
　　salvation,
48 The God who executes vengeance
　　for me,
　　And brings down peoples under me,
49 Who also brings me out from my
　　enemies;
　　You even lift me above those who
　　rise up against me;
　　You rescue me from the violent
　　man.
50 "Therefore I will give thanks to You,
　　O LORD, among the nations,
　　And I will sing praises to Your
　　name.
51 "*He* is a tower of deliverance to His
　　king,
　　And shows lovingkindness to His
　　anointed,
　　To David and his descendants
　　forever."

✦ Psalm 68:1–6

For the choir director. A Psalm of David.
A Song.

68 LET God arise, let His enemies be
　　　scattered,
　　And let those who hate Him flee
　　before Him.
2　As smoke is driven away, *so* drive
　　them away;
　　As wax melts before the fire,
　　So let the wicked perish before God.
3　But let the righteous be glad; let
　　them exult before God;
　　Yes, let them rejoice with gladness.

4   Sing to God, sing praises to His
    name;
    Lift up *a song* for Him who rides
        through the deserts,
    Whose name is the LORD, and exult
        before Him.
5   A father of the fatherless and a
        judge for the widows,
    Is God in His holy habitation.
6   God makes a home for the lonely;
    He leads out the prisoners into
        prosperity,
    Only the rebellious dwell in a
        parched land.

Proverbs 17:2–4

2   A servant who acts wisely will rule
        over a son who acts shamefully,
    And will share in the inheritance
        among brothers.
3   The refining pot is for silver and the
        furnace for gold,
    But the LORD tests hearts.
4   An evildoer listens to wicked lips;
    A liar pays attention to a destructive
        tongue.

John 8:28–59

28 So Jesus said, "When you lift up the
Son of Man, then you will know that
I am *He*, and I do nothing on My own
initiative, but I speak these things as the
Father taught Me.
29 "And He who sent Me is with Me; He
has not left Me alone, for I always do the
things that are pleasing to Him."
30 As He spoke these things, many
came to believe in Him.
31 So Jesus was saying to those Jews
who had believed Him, "If you continue
in My word, *then* you are truly disciples
of Mine;
32 and you will know the truth, and the
truth will make you free."
33 They answered Him, "We are Abraham's descendants and have never yet
been enslaved to anyone; how is it that
You say, 'You will become free'?"
34 Jesus answered them, "Truly, truly, I
say to you, everyone who commits sin is
the slave of sin.

35 "The slave does not remain in the
house forever; the son does remain forever.
36 "So if the Son makes you free, you
will be free indeed.
37 "I know that you are Abraham's
descendants; yet you seek to kill Me,
because My word has no place in you.
38 "I speak the things which I have seen
with *My* Father; therefore you also do
the things which you heard from *your*
father."
39 They answered and said to Him,
"Abraham is our father." Jesus *said to
them, "If you are Abraham's children, do
the deeds of Abraham.
40 "But as it is, you are seeking to kill
Me, a man who has told you the truth,
which I heard from God; this Abraham
did not do.
41 "You are doing the deeds of your
father." They said to Him, "We were not
born of fornication; we have one Father:
God."
42 Jesus said to them, "If God were
your Father, you would love Me, for I
proceeded forth and have come from
God, for I have not even come on My
own initiative, but He sent Me.
43 "Why do you not understand what I
am saying? *It is* because you cannot hear
My word.

ANSWERS TO LIFE'S QUESTIONS

What does it mean to be set free in Christ?

JOHN 8:31, 32

The scribes and Pharisees were intent on trapping Jesus, so they brought Him a woman who had been caught in the act of adultery and said, "Teacher, this woman has been caught in adultery, in the very act. Now in the Law Moses commanded us to stone such women; what then do You say?" (John 8:4, 5).

Instead of being ensnared by their words, Jesus turned the situation into an opportunity to teach the crowd about His liberating love in action. He said, "He who is without sin among you, let him be the first to throw a stone at her. . . . Woman, where are they? Did no one condemn you? . . . I do not condemn you, either. Go. From now on sin no more" (John 8:7, 10, 11). The woman walked away forgiven, free, and saved from certain doom.

A little later, Jesus proclaimed: "If you continue in My word, then you are truly disciples of Mine; and you will know the truth, and the truth will make you free" (John 8:31, 32). Consider these verses the believer's emancipation proclamation. In verses 34–36, Jesus explains: "Truly, truly, I say to you, everyone who commits sin is the slave of sin. The slave does not remain in the house forever; the son does remain forever. So if the Son makes you free, you will be free indeed." How are we liberated to live in Christ?

1. Through Jesus' death on the Cross and resurrection, we are freed from the *penalty* of sin. Like the woman caught in adultery, we are no longer condemned for what we've done. Christ pays our sin

debt in full so we can be reconciled to the Father (Rom. 5:10; 6:23; Col. 1:19–22).

2. We are released from the *power* of sin. Our sin nature no longer dominates us—leading us from one unsatisfying and destructive transgression to another. Rather, we are free to seek and know God through the power and presence of His Holy Spirit (Rom. 8:2–17). Jesus told the woman, "Go. From now on sin no more" (John 8:11), not as a terrible requirement for earning His forgiveness, but as a declaration of what is possible when we follow Him (1 Cor. 6:11–20).

3. We are liberated from the *purpose* of sin. James 1:15 tells us, "When sin is accomplished, it brings forth death." The goal of our iniquities is usually to exalt ourselves or fill our own needs, but the outcome is always ruination. Perhaps this woman was seeking love, acceptance, or security; yet, she was obviously going about getting it in the wrong way—destroying herself and her dignity. However, Christ sets us free to become everything God created us to be to His honor and glory (John 10:10; Eph. 2:10).

4. We are unshackled from the *personality* of sin. To the scribes and the Pharisees, this woman would always be known by the name "sinner," and perhaps that is how she thought of herself as well. However, when Jesus comes into our lives, we are no longer known for our iniquities. Rather, we are recognized as belonging to the One who has covered our iniquities with His blood. Our transgressions are no longer our identities because Christ makes us into new creations (Rom. 8:1; 2 Cor. 5:17).

What can you do to begin living in the freedom Jesus purchased for you on the Cross? There is no formula for discovering the richness of His truth. But by obeying and trusting in Him, you'll be on the road to the liberated life He designed for you.

---

44 "You are of *your* father the devil, and you want to do the desires of your father. He was a murderer from the beginning, and does not stand in the truth because there is no truth in him. Whenever he speaks a lie, he speaks from his own *nature*, for he is a liar and the father of lies. 45 "But because I speak the truth, you do not believe Me. 46 "Which one of you convicts Me of sin? If I speak truth, why do you not believe Me? 47 "He who is of God hears the words of God; for this reason you do not hear *them*, because you are not of God." 48 The Jews answered and said to Him,

"Do we not say rightly that You are a Samaritan and have a demon?" 49 Jesus answered, "I do not have a demon; but I honor My Father, and you dishonor Me. 50 "But I do not seek My glory; there is One who seeks and judges. 51 "Truly, truly, I say to you, if anyone keeps My word he will never see death." 52 The Jews said to Him, "Now we know that You have a demon. Abraham died, and the prophets *also*; and You say, 'If anyone keeps My word, he will never taste of death.' 53 "Surely You are not greater than our father Abraham, who died? The prophets died too; whom do You make Yourself out *to be*?"

54 Jesus answered, "If I glorify Myself, My glory is nothing; it is My Father who glorifies Me, of whom you say, 'He is our God';

55 and you have not come to know Him, but I know Him; and if I say that I do not know Him, I will be a liar like you, but I do know Him and keep His word.

56 "Your father Abraham rejoiced to see My day, and he saw *it* and was glad."

57 So the Jews said to Him, "You are not yet fifty years old, and have You seen Abraham?"

➤ 58 Jesus said to them, "Truly, truly, I say to you, before Abraham was born, I am."

59 Therefore they picked up stones to throw at Him, but Jesus hid Himself and went out of the temple.

LIFE LESSONS

➤ **John 8:58** — *"Truly, truly, I say to you, before Abraham was born, I am."*

*T*his may be the clearest claim Jesus ever made to be God in the flesh. He called Himself by the divine name, "I AM" (Ex. 3:14; Is. 42:8) and said that He existed long before Abraham lived.

MAY 26

2 Samuel 23:1—24:25

23 NOW these are the last words of David.

David the son of Jesse declares,
  The man who was raised on high declares,
  The anointed of the God of Jacob,
  And the sweet psalmist of Israel,

2 "The Spirit of the LORD spoke by me,
  And His word was on my tongue.

3 "The God of Israel said,
  The Rock of Israel spoke to me,
  'He who rules over men righteously,
  Who rules in the fear of God,

4 Is as the light of the morning *when* the sun rises,
  A morning without clouds,
  When the tender grass *springs* out of the earth,
  Through sunshine after rain.'

5 "Truly is not my house so with God?
  For He has made an everlasting covenant with me,
  Ordered in all things, and secured;
  For all my salvation and all *my* desire,
  Will He not indeed make *it* grow?

6 "But the worthless, every one of them will be thrust away like thorns,
  Because they cannot be taken in hand;

7 But the man who touches them

Must be armed with iron and the shaft of a spear,
  And they will be completely burned with fire in *their* place."

8 These are the names of the mighty men whom David had: Josheb-basshebeth a Tahchemonite, chief of the captains, he was *called* Adino the Eznite, because of eight hundred slain *by him* at one time;

9 and after him was Eleazar the son of Dodo the Ahohite, one of the three mighty men with David when they defied the Philistines who were gathered there to battle and the men of Israel had withdrawn.

10 He arose and struck the Philistines until his hand was weary and clung to the sword, and the LORD brought about a great victory that day; and the people returned after him only to strip *the slain*.

11 Now after him was Shammah the son of Agee a Hararite. And the Philistines were gathered into a troop where there was a plot of ground full of lentils, and the people fled from the Philistines.

12 But he took his stand in the midst of the plot, defended it and struck the Philistines; and the LORD brought about a great victory.

13 Then three of the thirty chief men went down and came to David in the harvest time to the cave of Adullam, while the troop of the Philistines was camping in the valley of Rephaim.

14 David was then in the stronghold, while the garrison of the Philistines was then in Bethlehem.
15 David had a craving and said, "Oh that someone would give me water to drink from the well of Bethlehem which is by the gate!"
16 So the three mighty men broke through the camp of the Philistines, and drew water from the well of Bethlehem which was by the gate, and took *it* and brought *it* to David. Nevertheless he would not drink it, but poured it out to the LORD;
17 and he said, "Be it far from me, O LORD, that I should do this. *Shall I drink* the blood of the men who went in *jeopardy* of their lives?" Therefore he would not drink it. These things the three mighty men did.
18 Abishai, the brother of Joab, the son of Zeruiah, was chief of the thirty. And he swung his spear against three hundred and killed *them*, and had a name as well as the three.
19 He was most honored of the thirty, therefore he became their commander; however, he did not attain to the three.
20 Then Benaiah the son of Jehoiada, the son of a valiant man of Kabzeel, who had done mighty deeds, killed the two *sons of* Ariel of Moab. He also went down and killed a lion in the middle of a pit on a snowy day.
21 He killed an Egyptian, an impressive man. Now the Egyptian *had* a spear in his hand, but he went down to him with a club and snatched the spear from the Egyptian's hand and killed him with his own spear.
22 These *things* Benaiah the son of Jehoiada did, and had a name as well as the three mighty men.
23 He was honored among the thirty, but he did not attain to the three. And David appointed him over his guard.
24 Asahel the brother of Joab was among the thirty; Elhanan the son of Dodo of Bethlehem,
25 Shammah the Harodite, Elika the Harodite,
26 Helez the Paltite, Ira the son of Ikkesh the Tekoite,
27 Abiezer the Anathothite, Mebunnai the Hushathite,
28 Zalmon the Ahohite, Maharai the Netophathite,

29 Heleb the son of Baanah the Netophathite, Ittai the son of Ribai of Gibeah of the sons of Benjamin,
30 Benaiah a Pirathonite, Hiddai of the brooks of Gaash,
31 Abi-albon the Arbathite, Azmaveth the Barhumite,
32 Eliahba the Shaalbonite, the sons of Jashen, Jonathan,
33 Shammah the Hararite, Ahiam the son of Sharar the Ararite,
34 Eliphelet the son of Ahasbai, the son of the Maacathite, Eliam the son of Ahithophel the Gilonite,
35 Hezro the Carmelite, Paarai the Arbite,
36 Igal the son of Nathan of Zobah, Bani the Gadite,
37 Zelek the Ammonite, Naharai the Beerothite, armor bearers of Joab the son of Zeruiah,
38 Ira the Ithrite, Gareb the Ithrite,
39 Uriah the Hittite; thirty-seven in all.

24 NOW again the anger of the LORD burned against Israel, and it incited David against them to say, "Go, number Israel and Judah."
2 The king said to Joab the commander of the army who was with him, "Go about now through all the tribes of Israel, from Dan to Beersheba, and register the people, that I may know the number of the people."
3 But Joab said to the king, "Now may the LORD your God add to the people a hundred times as many as they are, while the eyes of my lord the king *still* see; but why does my lord the king delight in this thing?"
4 Nevertheless, the king's word prevailed against Joab and against the commanders of the army. So Joab and the commanders of the army went out from the presence of the king to register the people of Israel.
5 They crossed the Jordan and camped in Aroer, on the right side of the city that is in the middle of the valley of Gad and toward Jazer.
6 Then they came to Gilead and to the land of Tahtim-hodshi, and they came to Dan-jaan and around to Sidon,
7 and came to the fortress of Tyre and to all the cities of the Hivites and of the Canaanites, and they went out to the south of Judah, *to* Beersheba.
8 So when they had gone about through

the whole land, they came to Jerusalem at the end of nine months and twenty days.
9 And Joab gave the number of the registration of the people to the king; and there were in Israel eight hundred thousand valiant men who drew the sword, and the men of Judah were five hundred thousand men.
10 Now David's heart troubled him after he had numbered the people. So David said to the LORD, "I have sinned greatly in what I have done. But now, O LORD, please take away the iniquity of Your servant, for I have acted very foolishly."
11 When David arose in the morning, the word of the LORD came to the prophet Gad, David's seer, saying,
12 "Go and speak to David, 'Thus the LORD says, "I am offering you three things; choose for yourself one of them, which I will do to you."'"
13 So Gad came to David and told him, and said to him, "Shall seven years of famine come to you in your land? Or will you flee three months before your foes while they pursue you? Or shall there be three days' pestilence in your land? Now consider and see what answer I shall return to Him who sent me."
➤ 14 Then David said to Gad, "I am in great distress. Let us now fall into the hand of the LORD for His mercies are great, but do not let me fall into the hand of man."
15 So the LORD sent a pestilence upon Israel from the morning until the appointed time, and seventy thousand men of the people from Dan to Beersheba died.
16 When the angel stretched out his hand toward Jerusalem to destroy it, the LORD relented from the calamity and said to the angel who destroyed the people, "It is enough! Now relax your hand!"

And the angel of the LORD was by the threshing floor of Araunah the Jebusite.
17 Then David spoke to the LORD when he saw the angel who was striking down the people, and said, "Behold, it is I who have sinned, and it is I who have done wrong; but these sheep, what have they done? Please let Your hand be against me and against my father's house."
18 So Gad came to David that day and said to him, "Go up, erect an altar to the LORD on the threshing floor of Araunah the Jebusite."
19 David went up according to the word of Gad, just as the LORD had commanded.
20 Araunah looked down and saw the king and his servants crossing over toward him; and Araunah went out and bowed his face to the ground before the king.
21 Then Araunah said, "Why has my lord the king come to his servant?" And David said, "To buy the threshing floor from you, in order to build an altar to the LORD, that the plague may be held back from the people."
22 Araunah said to David, "Let my lord the king take and offer up what is good in his sight. Look, the oxen for the burnt offering, the threshing sledges and the yokes of the oxen for the wood.
23 "Everything, O king, Araunah gives to the king." And Araunah said to the king, "May the LORD your God accept you."
24 However, the king said to Araunah, "No, but I will surely buy it from you for a price, for I will not offer burnt offerings to the LORD my God which cost me nothing." So David bought the threshing floor and the oxen for fifty shekels of silver.
25 David built there an altar to the LORD and offered burnt offerings and peace offerings. Thus the LORD was moved by prayer for the land, and the plague was held back from Israel.

LIFE LESSONS

➤ **2 Samuel 24:14 —** *"Let us now fall into the hand of the LORD for His mercies are great."*

*D*avid counted on the mercy of God, not to remove from him all consequences for his sin, but to spare his life and the life of his nation. Even in judgment, God shows mercy.

➤ **2 Samuel 24:24 —** *"For I will not offer burnt offerings to the LORD my God which cost me nothing."*

*D*avid felt he could not honor God by offering a gift that cost him nothing. The Lord wants our best, not because He needs it, but because by giving we demonstrate that our goods are not our God.

Psalm 68:7–10

7   O God, when You went forth before
    Your people,
    When You marched through the
    wilderness,   Selah.
8   The earth quaked;
    The heavens also dropped *rain* at
    the presence of God;
    Sinai itself *quaked* at the presence
    of God, the God of Israel.
9   You shed abroad a plentiful rain,
    O God;
    You confirmed Your inheritance
    when it was parched.
10 Your creatures settled in it;
    You provided in Your goodness for
    the poor, O God.

Proverbs 17:5, 6

5   He who mocks the poor taunts his
    Maker;
    He who rejoices at calamity will not
    go unpunished.
6   Grandchildren are the crown of old
    men,
    And the glory of sons is their
    fathers.

WHAT THE BIBLE SAYS ABOUT

Trading Our Weakness for God's Strength

John 9:1–15

*W*ere they purposefully adding insult
to injury? As the people gathered
around the blind man, they proclaimed that
his sin was the reason he could not see. This
is often the plight of someone going through
suffering. As much pain as the sufferer is in,
people are eager to point out that he or she
must have done something to deserve it.

Have you ever experienced this or are you
facing it now? When trials in your life are
overwhelming, and people offer no comfort—
only condemnation—it can almost be too
much for the heart to handle.

John 9:1–23

9 AS He passed by, He saw a man blind
  from birth.
2   And His disciples asked Him, "Rabbi,
who sinned, this man or his parents, that
he would be born blind?"
3   Jesus answered, "*It was* neither *that*
this man sinned, nor his parents; but *it
was* so that the works of God might be
displayed in him.
4   "We must work the works of Him
who sent Me as long as it is day; night is
coming when no one can work.
5   "While I am in the world, I am the
Light of the world."
6   When He had said this, He spat on
the ground, and made clay of the spittle,
and applied the clay to his eyes,

Yet even as struggles and criticism com-
pound in your life, the Lord offers hope. In
John 9:3 Jesus told the crowd, "It was neither
that this man sinned, nor his parents; but it
was so that the works of God might be displayed in him." Whatever your trial, you can
eagerly expect that God is going to display His
glory through you.

That is why Paul wrote in 2 Corinthians
12:10, "Therefore I am well content with
weaknesses, with insults, with distresses, with
persecutions, with difficulties, for Christ's sake;
for when I am weak, then I am strong."

Paul knew that whatever the situation,
God would prevail. This is true for you as
well. Life is hard, often unjustly so, and people are often critical. But God loves you and
He is your hope. Count on Him to be your
strength, and His glory will be shown
through you. ◈

LIFE LESSONS

➤ **John 9:3** — *"It was neither that this man sinned, nor his parents; but it was so that the works of God might be displayed in him."*

It is always dangerous to assume that some sin is to blame for a physical ailment. In this case, Jesus said that God designed the man's blindness to provide a platform for exalting His glory.

7 and said to him, "Go, wash in the pool of Siloam" (which is translated, Sent). So he went away and washed, and came *back* seeing.

8 Therefore the neighbors, and those who previously saw him as a beggar, were saying, "Is not this the one who used to sit and beg?"

9 Others were saying, "This is he," *still* others were saying, "No, but he is like him." He kept saying, "I am the one."

10 So they were saying to him, "How then were your eyes opened?"

11 He answered, "The man who is called Jesus made clay, and anointed my eyes, and said to me, 'Go to Siloam and wash'; so I went away and washed, and I received sight."

12 They said to him, "Where is He?" He *said, "I do not know."

13 They *brought to the Pharisees the man who was formerly blind.

14 Now it was a Sabbath on the day when Jesus made the clay and opened his eyes.

15 Then the Pharisees also were asking him again how he received his sight. And he said to them, "He applied clay to my eyes, and I washed, and I see."

16 Therefore some of the Pharisees were saying, "This man is not from God, because He does not keep the Sabbath." But others were saying, "How can a man who is a sinner perform such signs?" And there was a division among them.

17 So they *said to the blind man again, "What do you say about Him, since He opened your eyes?" And he said, "He is a prophet."

18 The Jews then did not believe *it* of him, that he had been blind and had received sight, until they called the parents of the very one who had received his sight,

19 and questioned them, saying, "Is this your son, who you say was born blind? Then how does he now see?"

20 His parents answered them and said, "We know that this is our son, and that he was born blind;

21 but how he now sees, we do not know; or who opened his eyes, we do not know. Ask him; he is of age, he will speak for himself."

22 His parents said this because they were afraid of the Jews; for the Jews had already agreed that if anyone confessed Him to be Christ, he was to be put out of the synagogue.

23 For this reason his parents said, "He is of age; ask him."

1 Kings 1:1—2:46

1 NOW King David was old, advanced in age; and they covered him with clothes, but he could not keep warm.

2 So his servants said to him, "Let them seek a young virgin for my lord the king, and let her attend the king and become his nurse; and let her lie in your bosom, that my lord the king may keep warm."

3 So they searched for a beautiful girl throughout all the territory of Israel, and found Abishag the Shunammite, and brought her to the king.

4 The girl was very beautiful; and she became the king's nurse and served him, but the king did not cohabit with her.

5 Now Adonijah the son of Haggith exalted himself, saying, "I will be king." So he prepared for himself chariots and horsemen with fifty men to run before him.

6 His father had never crossed him at any time by asking, "Why have you done so?" And he was also a very handsome man, and he was born after Absalom.

7 He had conferred with Joab the son of Zeruiah and with Abiathar the priest; and following Adonijah they helped him.
8 But Zadok the priest, Benaiah the son of Jehoiada, Nathan the prophet, Shimei, Rei, and the mighty men who belonged to David, were not with Adonijah.
9 Adonijah sacrificed sheep and oxen and fatlings by the stone of Zoheleth, which is beside En-rogel; and he invited all his brothers, the king's sons, and all the men of Judah, the king's servants.
10 But he did not invite Nathan the prophet, Benaiah, the mighty men, and Solomon his brother.
11 Then Nathan spoke to Bathsheba the mother of Solomon, saying, "Have you not heard that Adonijah the son of Haggith has become king, and David our lord does not know *it?*
12 "So now come, please let me give you counsel and save your life and the life of your son Solomon.
13 "Go at once to King David and say to him, 'Have you not, my lord, O king, sworn to your maidservant, saying, "Surely Solomon your son shall be king after me, and he shall sit on my throne"? Why then has Adonijah become king?'
14 "Behold, while you are still there speaking with the king, I will come in after you and confirm your words."
15 So Bathsheba went in to the king in the bedroom. Now the king was very old, and Abishag the Shunammite was ministering to the king.
16 Then Bathsheba bowed and prostrated herself before the king. And the king said, "What do you wish?"
17 She said to him, "My lord, you swore to your maidservant by the Lord your God, *saying,* 'Surely your son Solomon shall be king after me and he shall sit on my throne.'
18 "Now, behold, Adonijah is king; and now, my lord the king, you do not know *it.*
19 "He has sacrificed oxen and fatlings and sheep in abundance, and has invited all the sons of the king and Abiathar the priest and Joab the commander of the army, but he has not invited Solomon your servant.
20 "As for you now, my lord the king, the eyes of all Israel are on you, to tell them who shall sit on the throne of my lord the king after him.

21 "Otherwise it will come about, as soon as my lord the king sleeps with his fathers, that I and my son Solomon will be considered offenders."
22 Behold, while she was still speaking with the king, Nathan the prophet came in.
23 They told the king, saying, "Here is Nathan the prophet." And when he came in before the king, he prostrated himself before the king with his face to the ground.
24 Then Nathan said, "My lord the king, have you said, 'Adonijah shall be king after me, and he shall sit on my throne'?
25 "For he has gone down today and has sacrificed oxen and fatlings and sheep in abundance, and has invited all the king's sons and the commanders of the army and Abiathar the priest, and behold, they are eating and drinking before him; and they say, 'Long live King Adonijah!'
26 "But me, *even* me your servant, and Zadok the priest and Benaiah the son of Jehoiada and your servant Solomon, he has not invited.
27 "Has this thing been done by my lord the king, and you have not shown to your servants who should sit on the throne of my lord the king after him?"
28 Then King David said, "Call Bathsheba to me." And she came into the king's presence and stood before the king.
29 The king vowed and said, "As the Lord lives, who has redeemed my life from all distress,
30 surely as I vowed to you by the Lord the God of Israel, saying, 'Your son Solomon shall be king after me, and he shall sit on my throne in my place'; I will indeed do so this day."
31 Then Bathsheba bowed with her face to the ground, and prostrated herself before the king and said, "May my lord King David live forever."
32 Then King David said, "Call to me Zadok the priest, Nathan the prophet, and Benaiah the son of Jehoiada." And they came into the king's presence.
33 The king said to them, "Take with you the servants of your lord, and have my son Solomon ride on my own mule, and bring him down to Gihon.
34 "Let Zadok the priest and Nathan the prophet anoint him there as king over Israel, and blow the trumpet and say, 'Long live King Solomon!'

35 "Then you shall come up after him, and he shall come and sit on my throne and be king in my place; for I have appointed him to be ruler over Israel and Judah."

36 Benaiah the son of Jehoiada answered the king and said, "Amen! Thus may the LORD, the God of my lord the king, say.

37 "As the LORD has been with my lord the king, so may He be with Solomon, and make his throne greater than the throne of my lord King David!"

38 So Zadok the priest, Nathan the prophet, Benaiah the son of Jehoiada, the Cherethites, and the Pelethites went down and had Solomon ride on King David's mule, and brought him to Gihon.

39 Zadok the priest then took the horn of oil from the tent and anointed Solomon. Then they blew the trumpet, and all the people said, "Long live King Solomon!"

40 All the people went up after him, and the people were playing on flutes and rejoicing with great joy, so that the earth shook at their noise.

41 Now Adonijah and all the guests who were with him heard it as they finished eating. When Joab heard the sound of the trumpet, he said, "Why is the city making such an uproar?"

42 While he was still speaking, behold, Jonathan the son of Abiathar the priest came. Then Adonijah said, "Come in, for you are a valiant man and bring good news."

43 But Jonathan replied to Adonijah, "No! Our lord King David has made Solomon king.

44 "The king has also sent with him Zadok the priest, Nathan the prophet, Benaiah the son of Jehoiada, the Cherethites, and the Pelethites; and they have made him ride on the king's mule.

45 "Zadok the priest and Nathan the prophet have anointed him king in Gihon, and they have come up from there rejoicing, so that the city is in an uproar. This is the noise which you have heard.

46 "Besides, Solomon has even taken his seat on the throne of the kingdom.

47 "Moreover, the king's servants came to bless our lord King David, saying, 'May your God make the name of Solomon better than your name and his throne greater than your throne!' And the king bowed himself on the bed.

48 "The king has also said thus, 'Blessed be the LORD, the God of Israel, who has granted one to sit on my throne today while my own eyes see it.'"

49 Then all the guests of Adonijah were terrified; and they arose and each went on his way.

50 And Adonijah was afraid of Solomon, and he arose, went and took hold of the horns of the altar.

51 Now it was told Solomon, saying, "Behold, Adonijah is afraid of King Solomon, for behold, he has taken hold of the horns of the altar, saying, 'Let King Solomon swear to me today that he will not put his servant to death with the sword.'"

52 Solomon said, "If he is a worthy man, not one of his hairs will fall to the ground; but if wickedness is found in him, he will die."

53 So King Solomon sent, and they brought him down from the altar. And he came and prostrated himself before King Solomon, and Solomon said to him, "Go to your house."

2 AS David's time to die drew near, he charged Solomon his son, saying,

2 "I am going the way of all the earth. Be strong, therefore, and show yourself a man.

3 "Keep the charge of the LORD your God, to walk in His ways, to keep His statutes, His commandments, His ordinances, and His testimonies, according to what is written in the Law of Moses, that you may succeed in all that you do and wherever you turn,

4 so that the LORD may carry out His promise which He spoke concerning me, saying, 'If your sons are careful of their way, to walk before Me in truth with all their heart and with all their soul, you shall not lack a man on the throne of Israel.'

LIFE LESSONS

➤ 1 Kings 1:51 — "Behold, Adonijah is afraid of King Solomon, for behold, he has taken hold of the horns of the altar."

There is a big difference between regretting the consequences of sin and repenting of it. Adonijah feared the possible ramifications of his actions, but he never repudiated them. And eventually that would cost him everything.

5 "Now you also know what Joab the son of Zeruiah did to me, what he did to the two commanders of the armies of Israel, to Abner the son of Ner, and to Amasa the son of Jether, whom he killed; he also shed the blood of war in peace. And he put the blood of war on his belt about his waist, and on his sandals on his feet.

6 "So act according to your wisdom, and do not let his gray hair go down to Sheol in peace.

7 "But show kindness to the sons of Barzillai the Gileadite, and let them be among those who eat at your table; for they assisted me when I fled from Absalom your brother.

8 "Behold, there is with you Shimei the son of Gera the Benjamite, of Bahurim; now it was he who cursed me with a violent curse on the day I went to Mahanaim. But when he came down to me at the Jordan, I swore to him by the LORD, saying, 'I will not put you to death with the sword.'

➤ 9 "Now therefore, do not let him go unpunished, for you are a wise man; and you will know what you ought to do to him, and you will bring his gray hair down to Sheol with blood."

10 Then David slept with his fathers and was buried in the city of David.

11 The days that David reigned over Israel *were* forty years: seven years he reigned in Hebron and thirty-three years he reigned in Jerusalem.

12 And Solomon sat on the throne of David his father, and his kingdom was firmly established.

13 Now Adonijah the son of Haggith came to Bathsheba the mother of Solomon. And she said, "Do you come peacefully?" And he said, "Peacefully."

14 Then he said, "I have something *to say* to you." And she said, "Speak."

➤ 15 So he said, "You know that the kingdom was mine and that all Israel expected me to be king; however, the kingdom has turned about and become my brother's, for it was his from the LORD.

16 "Now I am making one request of you; do not refuse me." And she said to him, "Speak."

17 Then he said, "Please speak to Solomon the king, for he will not refuse you, that he may give me Abishag the Shunammite as a wife."

18 Bathsheba said, "Very well; I will speak to the king for you."

19 So Bathsheba went to King Solomon to speak to him for Adonijah. And the king arose to meet her, bowed before her, and sat on his throne; then he had a throne set for the king's mother, and she sat on his right.

20 Then she said, "I am making one small request of you; do not refuse me." And the king said to her, "Ask, my mother, for I will not refuse you."

21 So she said, "Let Abishag the Shunammite be given to Adonijah your brother as a wife."

22 King Solomon answered and said to his mother, "And why are you asking Abishag the Shunammite for Adonijah? Ask for him also the kingdom—for he is my older brother—even for him, for Abiathar the priest, and for Joab the son of Zeruiah!"

23 Then King Solomon swore by the LORD, saying, "May God do so to me and more also, if Adonijah has not spoken this word against his own life.

24 "Now therefore, as the LORD lives, who has established me and set me on the throne of David my father and who has made me a house as He promised, surely Adonijah shall be put to death today."

25 So King Solomon sent Benaiah the son of Jehoiada; and he fell upon him so that he died.

LIFE LESSONS

➤ **1 Kings 2:6, 9 — *"Act according to your wisdom . . . for you are a wise man; and you will know what you ought to do."***

*E*ven at the beginning of his reign, Solomon was considered a wise man. Yet God is able to multiply even what we have so that we can better serve Him and bless His people.

➤ **1 Kings 2:17 — *"Give me Abishag the Shunammite as a wife."***

*A*donijah revealed a heart still bent on evil when he requested to marry King David's concubine. By joining himself with a member of David's harem, he was strengthening his claim to the throne and trying to gain an advantage over Solomon (1 Kin. 2:21-25). However, God will never bless those who work against His will.

26 Then to Abiathar the priest the king said, "Go to Anathoth to your own field, for you deserve to die; but I will not put you to death at this time, because you carried the ark of the Lord GOD before my father David, and because you were afflicted in everything with which my father was afflicted."
27 So Solomon dismissed Abiathar from being priest to the LORD, in order to fulfill the word of the LORD, which He had spoken concerning the house of Eli in Shiloh.
28 Now the news came to Joab, for Joab had followed Adonijah, although he had not followed Absalom. And Joab fled to the tent of the LORD and took hold of the horns of the altar.
29 It was told King Solomon that Joab had fled to the tent of the LORD, and behold, he is beside the altar. Then Solomon sent Benaiah the son of Jehoiada, saying, "Go, fall upon him."
30 So Benaiah came to the tent of the LORD and said to him, "Thus the king has said, 'Come out.'" But he said, "No, for I will die here." And Benaiah brought the king word again, saying, "Thus spoke Joab, and thus he answered me."
31 The king said to him, "Do as he has spoken and fall upon him and bury him, that you may remove from me and from my father's house the blood which Joab shed without cause.
32 "The LORD will return his blood on his own head, because he fell upon two men more righteous and better than he and killed them with the sword, while my father David did not know it: Abner the son of Ner, commander of the army of Israel, and Amasa the son of Jether, commander of the army of Judah.
33 "So shall their blood return on the head of Joab and on the head of his descendants forever; but to David and his descendants and his house and his throne, may there be peace from the LORD forever."
34 Then Benaiah the son of Jehoiada went up and fell upon him and put him to death, and he was buried at his own house in the wilderness.
35 The king appointed Benaiah the son of Jehoiada over the army in his place, and the king appointed Zadok the priest in the place of Abiathar.
36 Now the king sent and called for Shimei and said to him, "Build for yourself a house in Jerusalem and live there, and do not go out from there to any place.
37 "For on the day you go out and cross over the brook Kidron, you will know for certain that you shall surely die; your blood shall be on your own head."
38 Shimei then said to the king, "The word is good. As my lord the king has said, so your servant will do." So Shimei lived in Jerusalem many days.
39 But it came about at the end of three years, that two of the servants of Shimei ran away to Achish son of Maacah, king of Gath. And they told Shimei, saying, "Behold, your servants are in Gath."
40 Then Shimei arose and saddled his donkey, and went to Gath to Achish to look for his servants. And Shimei went and brought his servants from Gath.
41 It was told Solomon that Shimei had gone from Jerusalem to Gath, and had returned.
42 So the king sent and called for Shimei and said to him, "Did I not make you swear by the LORD and solemnly warn you, saying, 'You will know for certain that on the day you depart and go anywhere, you shall surely die'? And you said to me, 'The word which I have heard is good.'
43 "Why then have you not kept the oath of the LORD, and the command which I have laid on you?"
44 The king also said to Shimei, "You know all the evil which you acknowledge in your heart, which you did to my father David; therefore the LORD shall return your evil on your own head.
45 "But King Solomon shall be blessed, and the throne of David shall be established before the LORD forever."
46 So the king commanded Benaiah the son of Jehoiada, and he went out and fell upon him so that he died.

Thus the kingdom was established in the hands of Solomon.

Psalm 68:11–14

11 The Lord gives the command;
   The women who proclaim the *good*
      tidings are a great host:
12 "Kings of armies flee, they flee,
   And she who remains at home will
      divide the spoil!"

13 When you lie down among the
      sheepfolds,
    You are like the wings of a dove
      covered with silver,
    And its pinions with glistening gold.
14 When the Almighty scattered the
      kings there,
    It was snowing in Zalmon.

Proverbs 17:7–9

7   Excellent speech is not fitting for a
      fool,
    Much less are lying lips to a prince.
8   A bribe is a charm in the sight of its
      owner;
    Wherever he turns, he prospers.
9   He who conceals a transgression
      seeks love,
    But he who repeats a matter
      separates intimate friends.

John 9:24–41

24 So a second time they called the man
    who had been blind, and said to him,
    "Give glory to God; we know that this
    man is a sinner."
25 He then answered, "Whether He is
    a sinner, I do not know; one thing I do
    know, that though I was blind, now I
    see."

LIFE LESSONS

➤ **John 9:24 — "Give glory to God; we
know that this man is a sinner."**

*R*eligious speech often cloaks the
darkest of hearts. These leaders
wanted the man to speak a vicious lie
about God's Son—something that, far
from honoring God, would anger and
offend Him.

26 So they said to him, "What did He do
to you? How did He open your eyes?"
27 He answered them, "I told you already and you did not listen; why do you
want to hear *it* again? You do not want
to become His disciples too, do you?"
28 They reviled him and said, "You
are His disciple, but we are disciples of
Moses.
29 "We know that God has spoken to
Moses, but as for this man, we do not
know where He is from."
30 The man answered and said to them,
"Well, here is an amazing thing, that you
do not know where He is from, and yet
He opened my eyes.
31 "We know that God does not hear
sinners; but if anyone is God-fearing and
does His will, He hears him.
32 "Since the beginning of time it has
never been heard that anyone opened
the eyes of a person born blind.
33 "If this man were not from God, He
could do nothing."
34 They answered him, "You were born

Life Examples:

Now I See

JOHN 9:24–33

*H*e was free! Unfettered by unseen
obstacles and emancipated from
blindness, the man rejoiced because Jesus had
healed him. Yet the Pharisees could not accept
it, and they certainly were not celebrating. As
they questioned him, the Pharisees became
increasingly argumentative.

So the man answered them, "I told you
already and you did not listen; why do you
want to hear it again? You do not want to
become His disciples too, do you?" (John 9:27)

Perhaps there have been areas of your
life greatly affected by your relationship
with Christ. Do not be surprised when people

have a hard time understanding the ways He
has worked because recognizing God's work
requires faith.

However, your reaction should be like
that of the blind man. He was thankful for
what Jesus had done, and he was willing to
tell people it was Jesus who had healed his
blindness. He was even so bold as to suggest
the Pharisees should want to become disciples
as well!

Charles de Foucauld wrote, "Crosses
release us from this world and by doing so
bind us to God." The man was bound to God
because he had been freed from his blindness.

Your crosses will bind you to God as well.
Give thanks for how He has healed you, and
rely on Him for your strength. Tell people
what He has done in your life, and He will
make you a great witness for Him.

entirely in sins, and are you teaching us?" So they put him out.

➤ 35 Jesus heard that they had put him out, and finding him, He said, "Do you believe in the Son of Man?"

LIFE LESSONS

➤ **John 9:35** — *Jesus heard that they had put him out, and finding him, He said, "Do you believe in the Son of Man?"*

*J*esus sought the man out after He heard what the religious leaders had done to him. He does the same thing with us. He seeks us out, offering us His help and encouragement to walk with God.

MAY 28

1 Kings 3:1—4:34

3 THEN Solomon formed a marriage alliance with Pharaoh king of Egypt, and took Pharaoh's daughter and brought her to the city of David until he had finished building his own house and the house of the LORD and the wall around Jerusalem.

2 The people were still sacrificing on the high places, because there was no house built for the name of the LORD until those days.

➤ 3 Now Solomon loved the LORD, walking in the statutes of his father David, except he sacrificed and burned incense on the high places.

4 The king went to Gibeon to sacrifice there, for that was the great high place; Solomon offered a thousand burnt offerings on that altar.

5 In Gibeon the LORD appeared to Solomon in a dream at night; and God said, "Ask what *you wish* Me to give you."

6 Then Solomon said, "You have shown great lovingkindness to Your servant David my father, according as he walked before You in truth and righteousness and uprightness of heart toward You; and You have reserved for him this great lovingkindness, that You have given him a son to sit on his throne, as *it is* this day.

36 He answered, "Who is He, Lord, that I may believe in Him?"

37 Jesus said to him, "You have both seen Him, and He is the one who is talking with you."

38 And he said, "Lord, I believe." And he worshiped Him.

39 And Jesus said, "For judgment I came into this world, so that those who do not see may see, and that those who see may become blind."

40 Those of the Pharisees who were with Him heard these things and said to Him, "We are not blind too, are we?"

41 Jesus said to them, "If you were blind, you would have no sin; but since you say, 'We see,' your sin remains.

7 "Now, O LORD my God, You have made Your servant king in place of my father David, yet I am but a little child; I do not know how to go out or come in.

8 "Your servant is in the midst of Your people which You have chosen, a great people who are too many to be numbered or counted.

9 "So give Your servant an understanding heart to judge Your people to discern between good and evil. For who is able to judge this great people of Yours?"

10 It was pleasing in the sight of the Lord that Solomon had asked this thing.

11 God said to him, "Because you have asked this thing and have not asked for yourself long life, nor have asked riches for yourself, nor have you asked for the life of your enemies, but have asked for yourself discernment to understand justice,

12 behold, I have done according to your

LIFE LESSONS

➤ **1 Kings 3:3** — *Now Solomon loved the LORD, walking in the statutes of his father David, except he sacrificed and burned incense on the high places.*

*A*t the beginning, Solomon loved the Lord and obeyed His commandments. But note the one word that led to his downfall: "except." The Lord wants wholehearted commitment to Him, not partial devotion.

WHAT THE BIBLE SAYS ABOUT ⊕

Asking God for Specific Things

1 Kings 3:5

Many Bible passages challenge believers to ask God for very specific things. Read the following familiar verses to remind yourself how important it is to ask God for the things you need. God expects you to *ask*!

- In Gibeon the LORD appeared to Solomon in a dream at night; and God said, "Ask what you wish me to give you." (1 Kin. 3:5)
- [Jesus said,] "And all things you ask in prayer, believing, you will receive." (Matt. 21:22)
- [Jesus said,] "Until now you have asked for nothing in My name; ask and you will receive, so that your joy may be made full." (John 16:24)
- But if any of you lacks wisdom, let him ask of God, who gives to all generously and without reproach, and it will be given to him. But he must ask in faith without any doubting, for the one who

doubts is like the surf of the sea, driven and tossed by the wind. (James 1:5, 6)

If we were to summarize these verses, we would find some very clear and concise principles related to our asking:

- God wants us to ask Him to meet all of our needs.
- God delights in revealing to us His desires and His ways of doing things.
- We can ask God for all things, including those that relate to the natural world.
- We are wise to ask in agreement with others.
- We must always ask in faith and in the name of Jesus.
- God will respond to our need not in a way that opposes His commandments, but in a way that pleases Him and brings Him glory.
- We can be assured that whenever we ask God for something, He hears and responds to us, giving us precisely what we need—which may not be what we think we need, but which always benefits us most.

The Bible tells us, "You do not have because you do not ask" (James 4:2). For what things in your life have you failed to ask God? ⊕

words. Behold, I have given you a wise and discerning heart, so that there has been no one like you before you, nor shall one like you arise after you.

13 "I have also given you what you have not asked, both riches and honor, so that there will not be any among the kings like you all your days.

14 "If you walk in My ways, keeping My

LIFE LESSONS

➤ **1 Kings 3:9 —** *"Give Your servant an understanding heart to judge Your people to discern between good and evil. For who is able to judge this great people of Yours?"*

Solomon wanted the ability to wisely lead his people, which was a good and honorable request that greatly pleased God. After all, "The fear of the LORD is the beginning of wisdom" (Prov. 9:10). Because Solomon made such an excellent request and sought he Lord, He gave him not only what He needed, but He gave him more than he ever could have dreamed (2 Chr. 1:10-12).

statutes and commandments, as your father David walked, then I will prolong your days."

15 Then Solomon awoke, and behold, it was a dream. And he came to Jerusalem and stood before the ark of the covenant of the Lord, and offered burnt offerings and made peace offerings, and made a feast for all his servants.

16 Then two women who were harlots came to the king and stood before him.

17 The one woman said, "Oh, my lord, this woman and I live in the same house; and I gave birth to a child while she *was* in the house.

18 "It happened on the third day after I gave birth, that this woman also gave birth to a child, and we were together. There was no stranger with us in the house, only the two of us in the house.

19 "This woman's son died in the night, because she lay on it.

20 "So she arose in the middle of the night and took my son from beside me while your maidservant slept, and laid him in her bosom, and laid her dead son in my bosom.

21 "When I rose in the morning to nurse my son, behold, he was dead; but when I looked at him carefully in the morning, behold, he was not my son, whom I had borne."

22 Then the other woman said, "No! For the living one is my son, and the dead one is your son." But the first woman said, "No! For the dead one is your son, and the living one is my son." Thus they spoke before the king.

23 Then the king said, "The one says, 'This is my son who is living, and your son is the dead one'; and the other says, 'No! For your son is the dead one, and my son is the living one.'"

24 The king said, "Get me a sword." So they brought a sword before the king.

25 The king said, "Divide the living child in two, and give half to the one and half to the other."

26 Then the woman whose child was the living one spoke to the king, for she was deeply stirred over her son and said, "Oh, my lord, give her the living child, and by no means kill him." But the other said, "He shall be neither mine nor yours; divide him!"

27 Then the king said, "Give the first woman the living child, and by no means kill him. She is his mother."

28 When all Israel heard of the judgment which the king had handed down, they feared the king, for they saw that the wisdom of God was in him to administer justice.

4 NOW King Solomon was king over all Israel.

2 These were his officials: Azariah the son of Zadok was the priest;

3 Elihoreph and Ahijah, the sons of Shisha were secretaries; Jehoshaphat the son of Ahilud was the recorder;

4 and Benaiah the son of Jehoiada was over the army; and Zadok and Abiathar were priests;

5 and Azariah the son of Nathan was over the deputies; and Zabud the son of Nathan, a priest, was the king's friend;

6 and Ahishar was over the household; and Adoniram the son of Abda was over the men subject to forced labor.

7 Solomon had twelve deputies over all Israel, who provided for the king and his household; each man had to provide for a month in the year.

8 These are their names: Ben-hur, in the hill country of Ephraim;

9 Ben-deker in Makaz and Shaalbim and Beth-shemesh and Elonbeth-hanan;

10 Ben-hesed, in Arubboth (Socoh was his and all the land of Hepher);

11 Ben-abinadab, in all the height of Dor (Taphath the daughter of Solomon was his wife);

12 Baana the son of Ahilud, in Taanach and Megiddo, and all Beth-shean which is beside Zarethan below Jezreel, from Beth-shean to Abel-meholah as far as the other side of Jokmeam;

13 Ben-geber, in Ramoth-gilead (the towns of Jair, the son of Manasseh, which are in Gilead were his: the region of Argob, which is in Bashan, sixty great cities with walls and bronze bars were his);

14 Ahinadab the son of Iddo, in Mahanaim;

15 Ahimaaz, in Naphtali (he also married Basemath the daughter of Solomon);

16 Baana the son of Hushai, in Asher and Bealoth;

17 Jehoshaphat the son of Paruah, in Issachar;

18 Shimei the son of Ela, in Benjamin;

19 Geber the son of Uri, in the land of Gilead, the country of Sihon king of the Amorites and of Og king of Bashan; and he was the only deputy who was in the land.

20 Judah and Israel were as numerous as the sand that is on the seashore in abundance; they were eating and drinking and rejoicing.

21 Now Solomon ruled over all the kingdoms from the River to the land of the Philistines and to the border of Egypt; they brought tribute and served Solomon all the days of his life.

22 Solomon's provision for one day was thirty kors of fine flour and sixty kors of meal,

23 ten fat oxen, twenty pasture-fed oxen, a hundred sheep besides deer, gazelles, roebucks, and fattened fowl.

24 For he had dominion over everything west of the River, from Tiphsah even to Gaza, over all the kings west of the River; and he had peace on all sides around about him.

25 So Judah and Israel lived in safety, every man under his vine and his fig tree,

from Dan even to Beersheba, all the days of Solomon.
26 Solomon had 40,000 stalls of horses for his chariots, and 12,000 horsemen.
27 Those deputies provided for King Solomon and all who came to King Solomon's table, each in his month; they left nothing lacking.
28 They also brought barley and straw for the horses and swift steeds to the place where it should be, each according to his charge.
29 Now God gave Solomon wisdom and very great discernment and breadth of mind, like the sand that is on the seashore.
30 Solomon's wisdom surpassed the wisdom of all the sons of the east and all the wisdom of Egypt.
31 For he was wiser than all men, than Ethan the Ezrahite, Heman, Calcol and Darda, the sons of Mahol; and his fame was *known* in all the surrounding nations.
32 He also spoke 3,000 proverbs, and his songs were 1,005.
33 He spoke of trees, from the cedar that is in Lebanon even to the hyssop that grows on the wall; he spoke also of animals and birds and creeping things and fish.
34 Men came from all peoples to hear the wisdom of Solomon, from all the kings of the earth who had heard of his wisdom.

Psalm 68:15–20

15 A mountain of God is the mountain of Bashan;
A mountain *of many* peaks is the mountain of Bashan.
16 Why do you look with envy, O mountains with *many* peaks, At the mountain which God has desired for His abode?
Surely the LORD will dwell *there* forever.
17 The chariots of God are myriads, thousands upon thousands;
The Lord is among them *as at* Sinai, in holiness.
18 You have ascended on high, You have led captive *Your* captives;
You have received gifts among men, Even *among* the rebellious also, that the LORD God may dwell *there*.

19 Blessed be the Lord, who daily bears our burden,
The God *who* is our salvation. Selah.
20 God is to us a God of deliverances;
And to GOD the Lord belong escapes from death.

Proverbs 17:10–12

10 A rebuke goes deeper into one who has understanding
Than a hundred blows into a fool.
11 A rebellious man seeks only evil, So a cruel messenger will be sent against him.
12 Let a man meet a bear robbed of her cubs,
Rather than a fool in his folly.

John 10:1–21

10 "TRULY, truly, I say to you, he who does not enter by the door into the fold of the sheep, but climbs up some other way, he is a thief and a robber.
2 "But he who enters by the door is a shepherd of the sheep.
3 "To him the doorkeeper opens, and the sheep hear his voice, and he calls his own sheep by name and leads them out.
4 "When he puts forth all his own, he goes ahead of them, and the sheep follow him because they know his voice.
5 "A stranger they simply will not follow, but will flee from him, because they do not know the voice of strangers."
6 This figure of speech Jesus spoke to them, but they did not understand what those things were which He had been saying to them.

LIFE LESSONS

➤ **Psalm 68:19 — *Blessed be the Lord, who daily bears our burden, the God who is our salvation.***

*W*e will never know how the Lord "bears our burden" every day of our lives. We take for granted many of His blessings: life, food, shelter, friends, family, and clothes. But we should always praise Him for who He is!

7   So Jesus said to them again, "Truly, truly, I say to you, I am the door of the sheep.

8   "All who came before Me are thieves and robbers, but the sheep did not hear them.

➤ 9   "I am the door; if anyone enters through Me, he will be saved, and will go in and out and find pasture.

✱ 10   "The thief comes only to steal and kill and destroy; I came that they may have life, and have *it* abundantly.

➤ 11   "I am the good shepherd; the good shepherd lays down His life for the sheep.

12   "He who is a hired hand, and not a shepherd, who is not the owner of the sheep, sees the wolf coming, and leaves the sheep and flees, and the wolf snatches them and scatters *them*.

13   "*He flees* because he is a hired hand and is not concerned about the sheep.

14   "I am the good shepherd, and I know My own and My own know Me,

15   even as the Father knows Me and I know the Father; and I lay down My life for the sheep.

16   "I have other sheep, which are not of this fold; I must bring them also, and they will hear My voice; and they will become one flock *with* one shepherd.

➤ 17   "For this reason the Father loves Me, because I lay down My life so that I may take it again.

18   "No one has taken it away from Me, but I lay it down on My own initiative. I have authority to lay it down, and I have authority to take it up again. This commandment I received from My Father."

LIFE LESSONS

➤ **John 10:9 — "I am the door; if anyone enters through Me, he will be saved, and will go in and out and find pasture."**

*J*esus is not one of many doors to the Father—He is the only door. He never claimed to be one route among several to an intimate relationship with God but insisted He was the only way.

➤ **John 10:11 — "I am the good shepherd; the good shepherd lays down His life for the sheep."**

*J*esus willingly gave His life to save ours, so how can we think He would ever keep back from us anything that would truly benefit us? He is the *Good* Shepherd.

➤ **John 10:17 — "The Father loves Me, because I lay down My life so that I may take it again."**

*G*od gave Jesus the authority both to offer His life as a sacrifice for our sins and to rise from the dead in power and great glory. Jesus' death and resurrection were equally planned from eternity (Rev. 13:8).

19   A division occurred again among the Jews because of these words.

20   Many of them were saying, "He has a demon and is insane. Why do you listen to Him?"

21   Others were saying, "These are not the sayings of one demon-possessed. A demon cannot open the eyes of the blind, can he?"

MAY 29

1 Kings 5:1—6:38

5 NOW Hiram king of Tyre sent his servants to Solomon, when he heard that they had anointed him king in place of his father, for Hiram had always been a friend of David.

2   Then Solomon sent *word* to Hiram, saying,

3   "You know that David my father was unable to build a house for the name of the Lord his God because of the wars which surrounded him, until the Lord put them under the soles of his feet.

4   "But now the Lord my God has given me rest on every side; there is neither adversary nor misfortune.

5   "Behold, I intend to build a house for the name of the Lord my God, as the ✱ Lord spoke to David my father, saying, 'Your son, whom I will set on your throne in your place, he will build the house for My name.'

6 "Now therefore, command that they cut for me cedars from Lebanon, and my servants will be with your servants; and I will give you wages for your servants according to all that you say, for you know that there is no one among us who knows how to cut timber like the Sidonians."

7 When Hiram heard the words of Solomon, he rejoiced greatly and said, "Blessed be the LORD today, who has given to David a wise son over this great people."

8 So Hiram sent *word* to Solomon, saying, "I have heard *the message* which you have sent me; I will do what you desire concerning the cedar and cypress timber.

9 "My servants will bring *them* down from Lebanon to the sea; and I will make them into rafts *to go* by sea to the place where you direct me, and I will have them broken up there, and you shall carry *them* away. Then you shall accomplish my desire by giving food to my household."

10 So Hiram gave Solomon as much as he desired of the cedar and cypress timber.

11 Solomon then gave Hiram 20,000 kors of wheat as food for his household, and twenty kors of beaten oil; thus Solomon would give Hiram year by year.

➤ 12 The LORD gave wisdom to Solomon, just as He promised him; and there was peace between Hiram and Solomon, and the two of them made a covenant.

13 Now King Solomon levied forced laborers from all Israel; and the forced laborers numbered 30,000 men.

14 He sent them to Lebanon, 10,000 a month in relays; they were in Lebanon a month *and* two months at home. And Adoniram *was* over the forced laborers.

15 Now Solomon had 70,000 transporters, and 80,000 hewers *of stone* in the mountains,

16 besides Solomon's 3,300 chief deputies who *were* over the project *and* who ruled over the people who were doing the work.

17 Then the king commanded, and they quarried great stones, costly stones, to lay the foundation of the house with cut stones.

18 So Solomon's builders and Hiram's builders and the Gebalites cut them, and prepared the timbers and the stones to build the house.

6 NOW it came about in the four hundred and eightieth year after the sons of Israel came out of the land of Egypt, in the fourth year of Solomon's reign over Israel, in the month of Ziv which is the second month, that he began to build the house of the LORD.

2 As for the house which King Solomon built for the LORD, its length *was* sixty cubits and its width twenty *cubits* and its height thirty cubits.

3 The porch in front of the nave of the house *was* twenty cubits in length, corresponding to the width of the house, *and* its depth along the front of the house *was* ten cubits.

4 Also for the house he made windows with *artistic* frames.

5 Against the wall of the house he built stories encompassing the walls of the house around both the nave and the inner sanctuary; thus he made side chambers all around.

6 The lowest story *was* five cubits wide, and the middle *was* six cubits wide, and the third *was* seven cubits wide; for on the outside he made offsets *in the wall* of the house all around in order that *the beams* would not be inserted in the walls of the house.

7 The house, while it was being built, was built of stone prepared at the quarry, and there was neither hammer nor axe nor any iron tool heard in the house while it was being built.

8 The doorway for the lowest side chamber *was* on the right side of the house; and they would go up by winding stairs to the middle *story,* and from the middle to the third.

9 So he built the house and finished it; and he covered the house with beams and planks of cedar.

10 He also built the stories against the whole house, each five cubits high; and

---

LIFE LESSONS

➤ **1 Kings 5:12 —** *The LORD gave wisdom to Solomon, just as He promised him.*

*T*he Lord always follows through on His promises. We may not see how He could fulfill a promise, but trusting God means looking beyond what we can see to what God can see.

they were fastened to the house with timbers of cedar.

11 Now the word of the LORD came to Solomon saying,

➤ 12 "Concerning this house which you are building, if you will walk in My statutes and execute My ordinances and keep all My commandments by walking in them, then I will carry out My word with you which I spoke to David your father.

13 "I will dwell among the sons of Israel, and will not forsake My people Israel."

14 So Solomon built the house and finished it.

15 Then he built the walls of the house on the inside with boards of cedar; from the floor of the house to the ceiling he overlaid the walls on the inside with wood, and he overlaid the floor of the house with boards of cypress.

16 He built twenty cubits on the rear part of the house with boards of cedar from the floor to the ceiling; he built them for it on the inside as an inner sanctuary, even as the most holy place.

17 The house, that is, the nave in front of the inner sanctuary, was forty cubits long.

18 There was cedar on the house within, carved in the shape of gourds and open flowers; all was cedar, there was no stone seen.

19 Then he prepared an inner sanctuary within the house in order to place there the ark of the covenant of the LORD.

20 The inner sanctuary was twenty cubits in length, twenty cubits in width, and twenty cubits in height, and he overlaid it with pure gold. He also overlaid the altar with cedar.

21 So Solomon overlaid the inside of the house with pure gold. And he drew chains of gold across the front of the inner sanctuary, and he overlaid it with gold.

22 He overlaid the whole house with gold, until all the house was finished. Also the whole altar which was by the inner sanctuary he overlaid with gold.

23 Also in the inner sanctuary he made two cherubim of olive wood, each ten cubits high.

24 Five cubits was the one wing of the cherub and five cubits the other wing of the cherub; from the end of one wing to the end of the other wing were ten cubits.

25 The other cherub was ten cubits; both the cherubim were of the same measure and the same form.

26 The height of the one cherub was ten cubits, and so was the other cherub.

27 He placed the cherubim in the midst of the inner house, and the wings of the cherubim were spread out, so that the wing of the one was touching the one wall, and the wing of the other cherub was touching the other wall. So their wings were touching each other in the center of the house.

28 He also overlaid the cherubim with gold.

29 Then he carved all the walls of the house round about with carved engravings of cherubim, palm trees, and open flowers, inner and outer sanctuaries.

30 He overlaid the floor of the house with gold, inner and outer sanctuaries.

31 For the entrance of the inner sanctuary he made doors of olive wood, the lintel and five-sided doorposts.

32 So he made two doors of olive wood, and he carved on them carvings of cherubim, palm trees, and open flowers, and overlaid them with gold; and he spread the gold on the cherubim and on the palm trees.

33 So also he made for the entrance of the nave four-sided doorposts of olive wood

34 and two doors of cypress wood; the two leaves of the one door turned on pivots, and the two leaves of the other door turned on pivots.

35 He carved on it cherubim, palm trees, and open flowers; and he overlaid them with gold evenly applied on the engraved work.

36 He built the inner court with three rows of cut stone and a row of cedar beams.

37 In the fourth year the foundation of

LIFE LESSONS

➤ **1 Kings 6:12** — *"If you will walk in My statutes . . . then I will carry out My word with you."*

$\mathcal{M}$any of God's promises to us are conditional in nature: *if* we will do this, *then* God will do that. He is under no obligation to fulfill a conditional promise if we neglect our part of the deal.

the house of the LORD was laid, in the month of Ziv.
38 In the eleventh year, in the month of Bul, which is the eighth month, the house was finished throughout all its parts and according to all its plans. So he was seven years in building it.

Psalm 68:21–27

21 Surely God will shatter the head of His enemies,
  The hairy crown of him who goes on in his guilty deeds.
22 The Lord said, "I will bring *them* back from Bashan.
  I will bring *them* back from the depths of the sea;
23 That your foot may shatter *them* in blood,
  The tongue of your dogs *may have* its portion from *your* enemies."
24 They have seen Your procession, O God,
  The procession of my God, my King, into the sanctuary.
25 The singers went on, the musicians after *them*,
  In the midst of the maidens beating tambourines.
26 Bless God in the congregations,
  Even the LORD, *you who are* of the fountain of Israel.
27 There is Benjamin, the youngest, ruling them,
  The princes of Judah *in their* throng,
  The princes of Zebulun, the princes of Naphtali.

Proverbs 17:13–15

13 He who returns evil for good,
  Evil will not depart from his house.
14 The beginning of strife is *like* letting out water,
  So abandon the quarrel before it breaks out.
15 He who justifies the wicked and he who condemns the righteous,
  Both of them alike are an abomination to the LORD.

John 10:22–42

22 At that time the Feast of the Dedication took place at Jerusalem;
23 it was winter, and Jesus was walking in the temple in the portico of Solomon.
24 The Jews then gathered around Him, and were saying to Him, "How long will You keep us in suspense? If You are the Christ, tell us plainly."
25 Jesus answered them, "I told you, and you do not believe; the works that I do in My Father's name, these testify of Me.
26 "But you do not believe because you are not of My sheep.
27 "My sheep hear My voice, and I know them, and they follow Me;
28 and I give eternal life to them, and they will never perish; and no one will snatch them out of My hand.
29 "My Father, who has given *them* to Me, is greater than all; and no one is able to snatch *them* out of the Father's hand.
30 "I and the Father are one."
31 The Jews picked up stones again to stone Him.
32 Jesus answered them, "I showed you many good works from the Father; for which of them are you stoning Me?"
33 The Jews answered Him, "For a good work we do not stone You, but for blasphemy; and because You, being a man, make Yourself out *to be* God."
34 Jesus answered them, "Has it not been written in your Law, 'I SAID, YOU ARE GODS'?
35 "If he called them gods, to whom the word of God came (and the Scripture cannot be broken),

---

LIFE LESSONS

➤ **John 10:30 — *"I and the Father are one."***

*W*hen Jesus used the words "I" and "the Father," He proclaimed a clear distinction in the two divine Persons. But in saying they "are one," He proclaimed their unity of nature and equality—and His hearers understood His claim. There is only one God, but we know Him in three persons: Father, Son, and Holy Spirit.

WHAT THE BIBLE SAYS ABOUT

About Hanukkah

John 10:22, 23

John 10:22, 23 tell us, "At that time the Feast of the Dedication took place at Jerusalem; it was winter, and Jesus was walking in the temple in the portico of Solomon." It's one of those details that seem to be as an afterthought. However, it's a great blessing for us when we truly look at it. That's because the Feast of Dedication is actually *Hanukkah*, and here we see that Jesus made the effort to go to the Temple to celebrate it. Because *Hanukkah* is part of His heritage, it's part of ours as Christians, too. In fact, *Hanukkah* holds great promise and encouragement for us as believers.

The story of *Hanukkah* actually begins in Daniel 8:8–12 and is continued in Daniel 11:29–32. Here, Daniel prophesied that after a great defeat against the south, a brutal ruler would retreat to Israel and take his fury out on the people there. "He will be disheartened and will return and become enraged at the holy covenant and take action; so he will come back and show regard for those who forsake the holy covenant. Forces from him will arise, desecrate the sanctuary fortress, and do away with the regular sacrifice. And they will set up the abomination of desolation. By smooth words he will turn to godlessness those who act wickedly toward the covenant, but the people who know their God will display strength and take action" (Dan. 11:30–32).

History shows Daniel's prophecy came true through the evil man named Antiochus Epiphanes. After an Egyptian and Roman coalition trounced him, he did indeed return to Israel. He knew that in order to subjugate the Israelites, he would have to separate them from their God because the Lord was their strength and sense of identity. So, as Daniel prophesied, Epiphanes's forces eliminated the offerings and forbade the Israelites to circumcise their sons, which struck at the heart of their covenant with God (Gen. 17:10–14).

It was a terrible time. From 40,000 to 80,000 Jews were slaughtered, and 40,000 more were sold into slavery. Worst of all, Epiphanes went into the holy temple of God and sacrificed a pig on the altar to Zeus. He also destroyed every copy of the Torah he could find—killing whoever was hiding in it.

The persecution began in Jerusalem and quickly spread throughout Israel. Yet in the town of Modin, an old priest named Matthias refused to sacrifice to Epiphanes' gods. Along with his son, Judas Maccabeus, Matthias was able to defeat all of Epiphanes' soldiers. They joined forces with the Hasidim—mighty orthodox warriors—and went throughout the land, driving out the sinners and tearing down altars to Epiphanes' gods. God won amazing victories through his little army. As Daniel 11:32 had promised, "The people who know their God will display strength and take action."

Finally, Epiphanes's got so sick of being defeated by them that he sent half of all his forces—over 65,000 soldiers—against Maccabeus's 10,000-man army. The Israelites prayed, fasted, and tithed. Then, they sounded the trumpets and gave a shout. And they beat the enemy handily!

After that, Maccabeus's men fought their way to Jerusalem to address what had been done at the temple. They were heartbroken by what they found there, but they set about cleansing it. They did everything as the Law commanded—they consecrated and dedicated the temple to God for eight days (Ex. 29:37).

Now, there was a great miracle that happened during the consecration. In order to have a proper dedication, it was necessary to keep the lamps burning before the Lord from morning to evening (Ex. 27:20, 21). However, they only found one unpolluted vessel of oil with the seal of the high priest, which was only enough for one day. Yet miraculously, that one vessel burned all eight days of the dedication—until they could consecrate more. They had been faithful to God, and now He was showing Himself faithful to them!

Imagine Jesus walking along the colonnade of the same temple that had been reclaimed almost two centuries beforehand, thinking about what happened during those eight days of consecration. Like Maccabeus, He was going to vanquish an enemy that had defiled God's people.

This time, however, the miraculous light would not last for only eight days. This time, Christ was bringing the true light—the light of eternity—to people (John 1:4, 9). Jesus said in John 8:12, "I am the Light of the world; he who follows Me will not walk in the darkness, but will have the Light of life." This time what was being consecrated was not a temple of stone and mortar, but of flesh and blood (1 Cor. 3:16, 17; 6:16, 19).

The world, like Epiphanes, will do everything in its power to separate us from our God because He is our strength, our identity, and our salvation. However, Jesus promises, "I give eternal life to them, and they will never perish; and no one will snatch them out of My hand" (John 10:28). No one can defile what Christ has made clean. And as His people, He has made us undefileable and inextinguishable.

Hanukkah is more than a festival of lights—it's the celebration of God helping His people when they had lost all hope. That's how we were when we were lost in sin. But now, we have the light and the temple that will last forever. ◈

36 do you say of Him, whom the Father sanctified and sent into the world, 'You are blaspheming,' because I said, 'I am the Son of God'?
37 "If I do not do the works of My Father, do not believe Me;
38 but if I do them, though you do not believe Me, believe the works, so that you may know and understand that the Father is in Me, and I in the Father."
39 Therefore they were seeking again to seize Him, and He eluded their grasp.
40 And He went away again beyond the Jordan to the place where John was first baptizing, and He was staying there.
41 Many came to Him and were say-

---

ing, "While John performed no sign, yet everything John said about this man was true."
42 Many believed in Him there.

---

1 Kings 7:1—8:66

7 NOW Solomon was building his own house thirteen years, and he finished all his house.
2 He built the house of the forest of Lebanon; its length was 100 cubits and its width 50 cubits and its height 30 cubits, on four rows of cedar pillars with cedar beams on the pillars.
3 It was paneled with cedar above the side chambers which were on the 45 pillars, 15 in each row.
4 There were artistic window frames in three rows, and window was opposite window in three ranks.
5 All the doorways and doorposts had squared artistic frames, and window was opposite window in three ranks.
6 Then he made the hall of pillars; its length was 50 cubits and its width 30 cubits, and a porch was in front of them and pillars and a threshold in front of them.
7 He made the hall of the throne where he was to judge, the hall of judgment, and it was paneled with cedar from floor to floor.
8 His house where he was to live, the other court inward from the hall, was of the same workmanship. He also made a house like this hall for Pharaoh's daughter, whom Solomon had married.
9 All these were of costly stones, of stone cut according to measure, sawed with saws, inside and outside; even from the foundation to the coping, and so on the outside to the great court.
10 The foundation was of costly stones, even large stones, stones of ten cubits and stones of eight cubits.
11 And above were costly stones, stone cut according to measure, and cedar.
12 So the great court all around had three rows of cut stone and a row of cedar beams even as the inner court of the house of the LORD, and the porch of the house.
13 Now King Solomon sent and brought Hiram from Tyre.
14 He was a widow's son from the tribe of Naphtali, and his father was a man of Tyre, a worker in bronze; and he was filled with wisdom and understanding and skill for doing any work in bronze. So he came to King Solomon and performed all his work.
15 He fashioned the two pillars of bronze; eighteen cubits was the height of one pillar, and a line of twelve cubits measured the circumference of both.
16 He also made two capitals of molten bronze to set on the tops of the pillars; the height of the one capital was five cubits and the height of the other capital was five cubits.
17 There were nets of network and twisted threads of chainwork for the capitals which were on the top of the pillars;

seven for the one capital and seven for the other capital.

18 So he made the pillars, and two rows around on the one network to cover the capitals which were on the top of the pomegranates; and so he did for the other capital.

19 The capitals which *were* on the top of the pillars in the porch were of lily design, four cubits.

20 *There were* capitals on the two pillars, even above *and* close to the rounded projection which was beside the network; and the pomegranates *numbered* two hundred in rows around both capitals.

21 Thus he set up the pillars at the porch of the nave; and he set up the right pillar and named it Jachin, and he set up the left pillar and named it Boaz.

22 On the top of the pillars was lily design. So the work of the pillars was finished.

23 Now he made the sea of cast *metal* ten cubits from brim to brim, circular in form, and its height was five cubits, and thirty cubits in circumference.

24 Under its brim gourds went around encircling it ten to a cubit, completely surrounding the sea; the gourds were in two rows, cast with the rest.

25 It stood on twelve oxen, three facing north, three facing west, three facing south, and three facing east; and the sea *was set* on top of them, and all their rear parts *turned* inward.

26 It was a handbreadth thick, and its brim was made like the brim of a cup, *as* a lily blossom; it could hold two thousand baths.

27 Then he made the ten stands of bronze; the length of each stand was four cubits and its width four cubits and its height three cubits.

28 This was the design of the stands: they had borders, even borders between the frames,

29 and on the borders which were between the frames *were* lions, oxen and cherubim; and on the frames there *was* a pedestal above, and beneath the lions and oxen *were* wreaths of hanging work.

30 Now each stand had four bronze wheels with bronze axles, and its four feet had supports; beneath the basin *were* cast supports with wreaths at each side.

31 Its opening inside the crown at the top *was* a cubit, and its opening *was* round like the design of a pedestal, a cubit and a half; and also on its opening *there were* engravings, and their borders were square, not round.

32 The four wheels *were* underneath the borders, and the axles of the wheels *were* on the stand. And the height of a wheel *was* a cubit and a half.

33 The workmanship of the wheels *was* like the workmanship of a chariot wheel. Their axles, their rims, their spokes, and their hubs *were* all cast.

34 Now *there were* four supports at the four corners of each stand; its supports *were* part of the stand itself.

35 On the top of the stand *there was* a circular form half a cubit high, and on the top of the stand its stays and its borders *were* part of it.

36 He engraved on the plates of its stays and on its borders, cherubim, lions and palm trees, according to the clear space on each, with wreaths *all* around.

37 He made the ten stands like this: all of them had one casting, one measure and one form.

38 He made ten basins of bronze, one basin held forty baths; each basin *was* four cubits, *and* on each of the ten stands *was* one basin.

39 Then he set the stands, five on the right side of the house and five on the left side of the house; and he set the sea *of cast metal* on the right side of the house eastward toward the south.

40 Now Hiram made the basins and the shovels and the bowls. So Hiram finished doing all the work which he performed for King Solomon *in* the house of the LORD:

41 the two pillars and the *two* bowls of the capitals which *were* on the top of the two pillars, and the two networks to cover the two bowls of the capitals which *were* on the top of the pillars;

42 and the four hundred pomegranates for the two networks, two rows of pomegranates for each network to cover the two bowls of the capitals which *were* on the tops of the pillars;

43 and the ten stands with the ten basins on the stands;

44 and the one sea and the twelve oxen under the sea;

45 and the pails and the shovels and

the bowls; even all these utensils which Hiram made for King Solomon *in* the house of the LORD *were* of polished bronze.

46　In the plain of the Jordan the king cast them, in the clay ground between Succoth and Zarethan.

47　Solomon left all the utensils *unweighed,* because *they were* too many; the weight of the bronze could not be ascertained.

48　Solomon made all the furniture which *was in* the house of the LORD: the golden altar and the golden table on which *was* the bread of the Presence;

49　and the lampstands, five on the right side and five on the left, in front of the inner sanctuary, of pure gold; and the flowers and the lamps and the tongs, of gold;

50　and the cups and the snuffers and the bowls and the spoons and the fire-pans, of pure gold; and the hinges both for the doors of the inner house, the most holy place, *and* for the doors of the house, *that is,* of the nave, of gold.

51　Thus all the work that King Solomon performed *in* the house of the LORD was finished. And Solomon brought in the things dedicated by his father David, the silver and the gold and the utensils, *and* he put them in the treasuries of the house of the LORD.

8 THEN Solomon assembled the elders of Israel and all the heads of the tribes, the leaders of the fathers' *households* of the sons of Israel, to King Solomon in Jerusalem, to bring up the ark of the covenant of the LORD from the city of David, which is Zion.

2　All the men of Israel assembled themselves to King Solomon at the feast, in the month Ethanim, which is the seventh month.

3　Then all the elders of Israel came, and the priests took up the ark.

4　They brought up the ark of the LORD and the tent of meeting and all the holy utensils, which were in the tent, and the priests and the Levites brought them up.

5　And King Solomon and all the congregation of Israel, who were assembled to him, were with him before the ark, sacrificing so many sheep and oxen they could not be counted or numbered.

6　Then the priests brought the ark of the covenant of the LORD to its place, into the inner sanctuary of the house, to the most holy place, under the wings of the cherubim.

7　For the cherubim spread *their* wings over the place of the ark, and the cherubim made a covering over the ark and its poles from above.

8　But the poles were so long that the ends of the poles could be seen from the holy place before the inner sanctuary, but they could not be seen outside; they are there to this day.

9　There was nothing in the ark except the two tablets of stone which Moses put there at Horeb, where the LORD made a covenant with the sons of Israel, when they came out of the land of Egypt.

10　It happened that when the priests came from the holy place, the cloud filled the house of the LORD,

11　so that the priests could not stand to minister because of the cloud, for the glory of the LORD filled the house of the LORD.

12　Then Solomon said,
　　"The LORD has said that He would
　　　　dwell in the thick cloud.
13　"I have surely built You a lofty
　　　　house,
　　A place for Your dwelling forever."

14　Then the king faced about and blessed all the assembly of Israel, while all the assembly of Israel was standing.

15　He said, "Blessed be the LORD, the God of Israel, who spoke with His mouth to my father David and has fulfilled *it* with His hand, saying,

16　'Since the day that I brought My people Israel from Egypt, I did not choose a city out of all the tribes of Israel *in which*

LIFE LESSONS

➤ **1 Kings 8:10 —** *It happened that when the priests came from the holy place, the cloud filled the house of the LORD.*

S ometimes the presence of the Lord becomes so obvious and mighty that we must cease our ministering and simply worship. Our God fills the universe, yet He chose to dwell in a special way in the Jerusalem temple. Today, He lives not in a manmade temple, but in the hearts of all those who believe in Christ (1 Cor. 6:19). In those moments of intimacy we fulfill our highest purpose.

to build a house that My name might be there, but I chose David to be over My people Israel.'

17 "Now it was in the heart of my father David to build a house for the name of the LORD, the God of Israel.

18 "But the LORD said to my father David, 'Because it was in your heart to build a house for My name, you did well that it was in your heart.

19 'Nevertheless you shall not build the house, but your son who will be born to you, he will build the house for My name.'

20 "Now the LORD has fulfilled His word which He spoke; for I have risen in place of my father David and sit on the throne of Israel, as the LORD promised, and have built the house for the name of the LORD, the God of Israel.

21 "There I have set a place for the ark, in which is the covenant of the LORD, which He made with our fathers when He brought them from the land of Egypt."

22 Then Solomon stood before the altar of the LORD in the presence of all the assembly of Israel and spread out his hands toward heaven.

23 He said, "O LORD, the God of Israel, there is no God like You in heaven above or on earth beneath, keeping covenant and *showing* lovingkindness to Your servants who walk before You with all their heart,

➤ 24 who have kept with Your servant, my father David, that which You have promised him; indeed, You have spoken with Your mouth and have fulfilled it with Your hand as it is this day.

LIFE LESSONS

➤ **1 Kings 8:24 — "Who have kept with Your servant, my father David, that which You have promised him."**

*I*t honors God and blesses us when we publicly acknowledge that our God keeps all of His promises. He is absolutely trustworthy, and we can build our lives on His Word. It is important to periodically gather as the people of God to celebrate with joyful and glad hearts all the good the Lord does for us. This not only honors Him; it encourages us to stay true to Him.

---

25 "Now therefore, O LORD, the God of Israel, keep with Your servant David my father that which You have promised him, saying, 'You shall not lack a man to sit on the throne of Israel, if only your sons take heed to their way to walk before Me as you have walked.'

26 "Now therefore, O God of Israel, let Your word, I pray, be confirmed which You have spoken to Your servant, my father David.

27 "But will God indeed dwell on the earth? Behold, heaven and the highest heaven cannot contain You, how much less this house which I have built!

28 "Yet have regard to the prayer of Your servant and to his supplication, O LORD my God, to listen to the cry and to the prayer which Your servant prays before You today;

29 that Your eyes may be open toward this house night and day, toward the place of which You have said, 'My name shall be there,' to listen to the prayer which Your servant shall pray toward this place.

30 "Listen to the supplication of Your servant and of Your people Israel, when they pray toward this place; hear in heaven Your dwelling place; hear and forgive.

31 "If a man sins against his neighbor and is made to take an oath, and he comes *and* takes an oath before Your altar in this house,

32 then hear in heaven and act and judge Your servants, condemning the wicked by bringing his way on his own head and justifying the righteous by giving him according to his righteousness.

33 "When Your people Israel are defeated before an enemy, because they have sinned against You, if they turn to You again and confess Your name and pray and make supplication to You in this house,

34 then hear in heaven, and forgive the sin of Your people Israel, and bring them back to the land which You gave to their fathers.

35 "When the heavens are shut up and there is no rain, because they have sinned against You, and they pray toward this place and confess Your name and turn from their sin when You afflict them,

36 then hear in heaven and forgive the

sin of Your servants and of Your people Israel, indeed, teach them the good way in which they should walk. And send rain on Your land, which You have given Your people for an inheritance.

37 "If there is famine in the land, if there is pestilence, if there is blight or mildew, locust or grasshopper, if their enemy besieges them in the land of their cities, whatever plague, whatever sickness there is,

➤ 38 whatever prayer or supplication is made by any man or by all Your people Israel, each knowing the affliction of his own heart, and spreading his hands toward this house;

39 then hear in heaven Your dwelling place, and forgive and act and render to each according to all his ways, whose heart You know, for You alone know the hearts of all the sons of men,

40 that they may fear You all the days that they live in the land which You have given to our fathers.

41 "Also concerning the foreigner who is not of Your people Israel, when he comes from a far country for Your name's sake

42 (for they will hear of Your great name and Your mighty hand, and of Your outstretched arm); when he comes and prays toward this house,

➤ 43 hear in heaven Your dwelling place, and do according to all for which the foreigner calls to You, in order that all the peoples of the earth may know Your name, to fear You, as do Your people Israel, and that they may know that this house which I have built is called by Your name.

44 "When Your people go out to battle against their enemy, by whatever way You shall send them, and they pray to the LORD toward the city which You have chosen and the house which I have built for Your name,

45 then hear in heaven their prayer and their supplication, and maintain their cause.

46 "When they sin against You (for there is no man who does not sin) and You are angry with them and deliver them to an enemy, so that they take them away captive to the land of the enemy, far off or near;

47 if they take thought in the land where they have been taken captive, and repent and make supplication to You in the land of those who have taken them captive, saying, 'We have sinned and have committed iniquity, we have acted wickedly';

48 if they return to You with all their heart and with all their soul in the land of their enemies who have taken them captive, and pray to You toward their land which You have given to their fathers, the city which You have chosen, and the house which I have built for Your name;

49 then hear their prayer and their supplication in heaven Your dwelling place, and maintain their cause,

50 and forgive Your people who have sinned against You and all their transgressions which they have transgressed against You, and make them objects of compassion before those who have taken them captive, that they may have compassion on them

51 (for they are Your people and Your inheritance which You have brought forth from Egypt, from the midst of the iron furnace),

52 that Your eyes may be open to the supplication of Your servant and to the supplication of Your people Israel, to listen to them whenever they call to You.

53 "For You have separated them from all the peoples of the earth as Your

---

LIFE LESSONS

➤ **1 Kings 8:38** — *"Each knowing the affliction of his own heart."*

*I*t is important that each of us knows "the affliction of his own heart." We are not to dwell morbidly over our own sinfulness, but we need to know our personal tendencies toward certain kinds of sin. Since we are all prone to wandering (1 Kin. 8:46), it is wise to pray regularly for God to give us a great love for Him and to grant us the desire to walk in His ways, joyfully obeying His Word.

➤ **1 Kings 8:43** — *"That all the peoples of the earth may know Your name, to fear You."*

*F*rom the very beginning, God desired that the entire world come to know, love, worship, and serve Him. Intimacy with God is His highest priority everywhere on earth.

inheritance, as You spoke through Moses Your servant, when You brought our fathers forth from Egypt, O Lord GOD."
54 When Solomon had finished praying this entire prayer and supplication to the LORD, he arose from before the altar of the LORD, from kneeling on his knees with his hands spread toward heaven.
55 And he stood and blessed all the assembly of Israel with a loud voice, saying:
56 "Blessed be the LORD, who has given rest to His people Israel, according to all that He promised; not one word has failed of all His good promise, which He promised through Moses His servant.
57 "May the LORD our God be with us, as He was with our fathers; may He not leave us or forsake us,
58 that He may incline our hearts to Himself, to walk in all His ways and to keep His commandments and His statutes and His ordinances, which He commanded our fathers.
59 "And may these words of mine, with which I have made supplication before the LORD, be near to the LORD our God day and night, that He may maintain the cause of His servant and the cause of His people Israel, as each day requires,
60 so that all the peoples of the earth may know that the LORD is God; there is no one else.
61 "Let your heart therefore be wholly devoted to the LORD our God, to walk in His statutes and to keep His commandments, as at this day."
62 Now the king and all Israel with him offered sacrifice before the LORD.
63 Solomon offered for the sacrifice of peace offerings, which he offered to the LORD, 22,000 oxen and 120,000 sheep. So the king and all the sons of Israel dedicated the house of the LORD.
64 On the same day the king consecrated the middle of the court that was before the house of the LORD, because there he offered the burnt offering and the grain offering and the fat of the peace offerings; for the bronze altar that was before the LORD was too small to hold the burnt offering and the grain offering and the fat of the peace offerings.
65 So Solomon observed the feast at that time, and all Israel with him, a great assembly from the entrance of Hamath

to the brook of Egypt, before the LORD our God, for seven days and seven more days, even fourteen days.
66 On the eighth day he sent the people away and they blessed the king. Then they went to their tents joyful and glad of heart for all the goodness that the LORD had shown to David His servant and to Israel His people.

Psalm 68:28–35

28 Your God has commanded your strength;
Show Yourself strong, O God, who have acted on our behalf.
29 Because of Your temple at Jerusalem
Kings will bring gifts to You.
30 Rebuke the beasts in the reeds,
The herd of bulls with the calves of the peoples,
Trampling under foot the pieces of silver;
He has scattered the peoples who delight in war.
31 Envoys will come out of Egypt;
Ethiopia will quickly stretch out her hands to God.
32 Sing to God, O kingdoms of the earth,
Sing praises to the Lord,   Selah.
33 To Him who rides upon the highest heavens, which are from ancient times;
Behold, He speaks forth with His voice, a mighty voice.
34 Ascribe strength to God;
His majesty is over Israel
And His strength is in the skies.
35 O God, You are awesome from Your sanctuary.
The God of Israel Himself gives strength and power to the people.
Blessed be God!

Proverbs 17:16, 17

16 Why is there a price in the hand of a fool to buy wisdom,
When he has no sense?

✳ 17 A friend loves at all times,
And a brother is born for adversity.

John 11:1–29

11 NOW a certain man was sick, Lazarus of Bethany, the village of Mary and her sister Martha.

2 It was the Mary who anointed the Lord with ointment, and wiped His feet with her hair, whose brother Lazarus was sick.

3 So the sisters sent *word* to Him, saying, "Lord, behold, he whom You love is sick."

➤ 4 But when Jesus heard *this*, He said, "This sickness is not to end in death, but for the glory of God, so that the Son of God may be glorified by it."

5 Now Jesus loved Martha and her sister and Lazarus.

6 So when He heard that he was sick, He then stayed two days *longer* in the place where He was.

7 Then after this He *said to the disciples, "Let us go to Judea again."

8 The disciples *said to Him, "Rabbi, the Jews were just now seeking to stone You, and are You going there again?"

9 Jesus answered, "Are there not twelve hours in the day? If anyone walks in the day, he does not stumble, because he sees the light of this world.

10 "But if anyone walks in the night, he stumbles, because the light is not in him."

11 This He said, and after that He *said to them, "Our friend Lazarus has fallen asleep; but I go, so that I may awaken him out of sleep."

12 The disciples then said to Him, "Lord, if he has fallen asleep, he will recover."

13 Now Jesus had spoken of his death, but they thought that He was speaking of literal sleep.

14 So Jesus then said to them plainly, "Lazarus is dead,

15 and I am glad for your sakes that I ◄ was not there, so that you may believe; but let us go to him."

16 Therefore Thomas, who is called Didymus, said to *his* fellow disciples, "Let us also go, so that we may die with Him."

17 So when Jesus came, He found that

LIFE LESSONS

➤ **John 11:4 — *"This sickness is not to end in death, but for the glory of God."***

*J*esus did not mean that Lazarus would not die—he did—but that the episode would not *end* in death. When Jesus is involved, death ends nothing; as the Lord of life, He triumphs even over death.

➤ **John 11:15 — *"I am glad for your sakes that I was not there, so that you may believe."***

*W*e have to understand God is far more concerned with growing our faith than with making us comfortable. Jesus said He was "glad" about the death of Lazarus because He valued his friends' faith over their tears.

Life Examples:

MARTHA: Worship as You Work

JOHN 11:19–44

*A*fter Jesus raised her brother Lazarus from the dead, Martha finally understood the awesome power of Christ. She knew that nothing she could do would ever honor Him sufficiently—yet she also realized He would gladly receive anything done for Him out of a heart of genuine devotion (John 11:19–44).

God invites you to use your gifts to express praise to Him, especially if you use them with a grateful, joyful heart. If, however, they become your avenue for seeking acceptance and prestige—as with Martha at the beginning (Luke 10:38–42)—then they can become a source of bitterness and resentment. Your actions can either proclaim Christ or they can seek your own advancement. You can use your talents with an attitude of praise or an attitude of self-promotion.

As you express your gifts today, consider your testimony. Will you serve out of praise to Him? Will you choose work or worship?

he had already been in the tomb four days.

18 Now Bethany was near Jerusalem, about two miles off;

19 and many of the Jews had come to Martha and Mary, to console them concerning *their* brother.

20 Martha therefore, when she heard that Jesus was coming, went to meet Him, but Mary stayed at the house.

21 Martha then said to Jesus, "Lord, if You had been here, my brother would not have died.

22 "Even now I know that whatever You ask of God, God will give You."

23 Jesus *said to her, "Your brother will rise again."

24 Martha *said to Him, "I know that he will rise again in the resurrection on the last day."

25 Jesus said to her, "I am the resurrection and the life; he who believes in Me will live even if he dies,

26 and everyone who lives and believes in Me will never die. Do you believe this?"

27 She *said to Him, "Yes, Lord; I have believed that You are the Christ, the Son of God, *even* He who comes into the world."

28 When she had said this, she went away and called Mary her sister, saying secretly, "The Teacher is here and is calling for you."

29 And when she heard it, she *got up quickly and was coming to Him.

---

1 Kings 9:1—10:29

9 NOW it came about when Solomon had finished building the house of the LORD, and the king's house, and all that Solomon desired to do,

2 that the LORD appeared to Solomon a second time, as He had appeared to him at Gibeon.

3 The LORD said to him, "I have heard your prayer and your supplication, which you have made before Me; I have consecrated this house which you have built by putting My name there forever, and My eyes and My heart will be there perpetually.

4 "As for you, if you will walk before Me as your father David walked, in integrity of heart and uprightness, doing according to all that I have commanded

you *and* will keep My statutes and My ordinances,

5 then I will establish the throne of your kingdom over Israel forever, just as I promised to your father David, saying, 'You shall not lack a man on the throne of Israel.'

6 "But if you or your sons indeed turn away from following Me, and do not keep My commandments and My statutes which I have set before you, and go and serve other gods and worship them,

7 then I will cut off Israel from the land which I have given them, and the house which I have consecrated for My name, I will cast out of My sight. So Israel will become a proverb and a byword among all peoples.

8 "And this house will become a heap of ruins; everyone who passes by will be astonished and hiss and say, 'Why has the LORD done thus to this land and to this house?'

9 "And they will say, 'Because they forsook the LORD their God, who brought their fathers out of the land of Egypt, and adopted other gods and worshiped them and served them, therefore the LORD has brought all this adversity on them.'"

10 It came about at the end of twenty years in which Solomon had built the two houses, the house of the LORD and the king's house

LIFE LESSONS

➤ **1 Kings 9:3 — *"I have heard your prayer."***

*W*hen we bring our requests to God, He hears. It may not always seem as though He hears. Sometimes it may feel as though we speak into the air. But He hears, and He acts for those who wait for Him.

11 (Hiram king of Tyre had supplied Solomon with cedar and cypress timber and gold according to all his desire), then King Solomon gave Hiram twenty cities in the land of Galilee.

12 So Hiram came out from Tyre to see the cities which Solomon had given him, and they did not please him.

13 He said, "What are these cities which you have given me, my brother?" So they were called the land of Cabul to this day.

14 And Hiram sent to the king 120 talents of gold.

15 Now this is the account of the forced labor which King Solomon levied to build the house of the LORD, his own house, the Millo, the wall of Jerusalem, Hazor, Megiddo, and Gezer.

16 For Pharaoh king of Egypt had gone up and captured Gezer and burned it with fire, and killed the Canaanites who lived in the city, and had given it as a dowry to his daughter, Solomon's wife.

17 So Solomon rebuilt Gezer and the lower Beth-horon

18 and Baalath and Tamar in the wilderness, in the land of Judah,

19 and all the storage cities which Solomon had, even the cities for his chariots and the cities for his horsemen, and all that it pleased Solomon to build in Jerusalem, in Lebanon, and in all the land under his rule.

20 As for all the people who were left of the Amorites, the Hittites, the Perizzites, the Hivites and the Jebusites, who were not of the sons of Israel,

21 their descendants who were left after them in the land whom the sons of Israel were unable to destroy utterly, from them Solomon levied forced laborers, even to this day.

22 But Solomon did not make slaves of the sons of Israel; for they were men of war, his servants, his princes, his captains, his chariot commanders, and his horsemen.

23 These were the chief officers who were over Solomon's work, five hundred and fifty, who ruled over the people doing the work.

24 As soon as Pharaoh's daughter came up from the city of David to her house which Solomon had built for her, then he built the Millo.

25 Now three times in a year Solomon offered burnt offerings and peace offerings on the altar which he built to the LORD, burning incense with them on the altar which was before the LORD. So he finished the house.

26 King Solomon also built a fleet of ships in Ezion-geber, which is near Eloth on the shore of the Red Sea, in the land of Edom.

27 And Hiram sent his servants with the fleet, sailors who knew the sea, along with the servants of Solomon.

28 They went to Ophir and took four hundred and twenty talents of gold from there, and brought it to King Solomon.

10 NOW when the queen of Sheba heard about the fame of Solomon concerning the name of the LORD, she came to test him with difficult questions.

2 So she came to Jerusalem with a very large retinue, with camels carrying spices and very much gold and precious stones. When she came to Solomon, she spoke with him about all that was in her heart.

3 Solomon answered all her questions; nothing was hidden from the king which he did not explain to her.

4 When the queen of Sheba perceived all the wisdom of Solomon, the house that he had built,

5 the food of his table, the seating of his servants, the attendance of his waiters and their attire, his cupbearers, and his stairway by which he went up to the house of the LORD, there was no more spirit in her.

6 Then she said to the king, "It was a true report which I heard in my own land about your words and your wisdom.

7 "Nevertheless I did not believe the reports, until I came and my eyes had seen it. And behold, the half was not told me. You exceed in wisdom and prosperity the report which I heard.

8 "How blessed are your men, how blessed are these your servants who stand before you continually and hear your wisdom.

9 "Blessed be the LORD your God who delighted in you to set you on the throne of Israel; because the LORD loved Israel forever, therefore He made you king, to do justice and righteousness."

10 She gave the king a hundred and twenty talents of gold, and a very great amount of spices and precious stones. Never again did such abundance of spices

come in as that which the queen of Sheba gave King Solomon.

11 Also the ships of Hiram, which brought gold from Ophir, brought in from Ophir a very great *number of* almug trees and precious stones.

12 The king made of the almug trees supports for the house of the LORD and for the king's house, also lyres and harps for the singers; such almug trees have not come in *again* nor have they been seen to this day.

13 King Solomon gave to the queen of Sheba all her desire which she requested, besides what he gave her according to his royal bounty. Then she turned and went to her own land together with her servants.

14 Now the weight of gold which came in to Solomon in one year was 666 talents of gold,

15 besides *that* from the traders and the wares of the merchants and all the kings of the Arabs and the governors of the country.

16 King Solomon made 200 large shields of beaten gold, using 600 *shekels of* gold on each large shield.

17 *He made* 300 shields of beaten gold, using three minas of gold on each shield, and the king put them in the house of the forest of Lebanon.

18 Moreover, the king made a great throne of ivory and overlaid it with refined gold.

19 *There were* six steps to the throne and a round top to the throne at its rear, and arms on each side of the seat, and two lions standing beside the arms.

20 Twelve lions were standing there on the six steps on the one side and on the other; nothing like *it* was made for any other kingdom.

21 All King Solomon's drinking vessels *were* of gold, and all the vessels of the house of the forest of Lebanon *were* of pure gold. None was of silver; it was not considered valuable in the days of Solomon.

22 For the king had at sea the ships of Tarshish with the ships of Hiram; once every three years the ships of Tarshish came bringing gold and silver, ivory and apes and peacocks.

➤ 23 So King Solomon became greater than all the kings of the earth in riches and in wisdom.

24 All the earth was seeking the presence of Solomon, to hear his wisdom which God had put in his heart.

25 They brought every man his gift, articles of silver and gold, garments, weapons, spices, horses, and mules, so much year by year.

26 Now Solomon gathered chariots and horsemen; and he had 1,400 chariots and 12,000 horsemen, and he stationed them in the chariot cities and with the king in Jerusalem.

27 The king made silver *as common* as stones in Jerusalem, and he made cedars as plentiful as sycamore trees that are in the lowland.

28 Also Solomon's import of horses was from Egypt and Kue, *and* the king's merchants procured *them* from Kue for a price.

29 A chariot was imported from Egypt for 600 *shekels* of silver, and a horse for 150; and by the same means they exported them to all the kings of the Hittites and to the kings of the Arameans.

⊕　**Psalm 69:1–4**

For the choir director; according to Shoshannim. *A Psalm* of David.

69 SAVE me, O God,
　　For the waters have threatened my
　　　life.

2　I have sunk in deep mire, and there
　　　is no foothold;
　　I have come into deep waters, and a
　　　flood overflows me.

3　I am weary with my crying; my
　　　throat is parched;
　　My eyes fail while I wait for my God.

4　Those who hate me without a cause
　　　are more than the hairs of my
　　　head;

Those who would destroy me are powerful, being wrongfully my enemies;
What I did not steal, I then have to restore.

 Proverbs 17:18, 19

18 A man lacking in sense pledges
And becomes guarantor in the presence of his neighbor.
19 He who loves transgression loves strife;
He who raises his door seeks destruction.

John 11:30–57

30 Now Jesus had not yet come into the village, but was still in the place where Martha met Him.
31 Then the Jews who were with her in the house, and consoling her, when they saw that Mary got up quickly and went

out, they followed her, supposing that she was going to the tomb to weep there.
32 Therefore, when Mary came where Jesus was, she saw Him, and fell at His feet, saying to Him, "Lord, if You had been here, my brother would not have died."
33 When Jesus therefore saw her weeping, and the Jews who came with her *also* weeping, He was deeply moved in spirit and was troubled,
34 and said, "Where have you laid him?" They *said to Him, "Lord, come and see."
35 Jesus wept.
36 So the Jews were saying, "See how He loved him!"
37 But some of them said, "Could not this man, who opened the eyes of the blind man, have kept this man also from dying?"
38 So Jesus, again being deeply moved within, *came to the tomb. Now it was a cave, and a stone was lying against it.
39 Jesus *said, "Remove the stone." Martha, the sister of the deceased, *said to Him, "Lord, by this time there will be a stench, for he has been *dead* four days."
40 Jesus *said to her, "Did I not say to you that if you believe, you will see the glory of God?"

WHAT THE BIBLE SAYS ABOUT

God's Forever Love

John 11:30–45

*F*irst Corinthians 13 is probably the most widely quoted passage in the world on the subject of love. Verse 13 says, "But now faith, hope, love, abide these three; but the greatest of these is love."

We recognize that Jesus demonstrated sacrificial love for us by dying for our sins, making possible our forgiveness and restoring us to fellowship with the Father. Yet we often fail to realize that Christ's love goes even beyond the Cross.

Everything we do, don't do, face, and don't face is touched by His continuing love. Everything about us hinges on love because God, who is love, created us in His image (1 John 4:8, 16). Because God loves us, He gives us blessings and lets us share them. When we pray and are told to wait, it is because He loves us and knows we need time to grow.

When the overwhelming choices before us make it hard to know which way is up, our Lord and Savior shows us our need to depend on His guiding love.

Jesus demonstrated this kind of amazing love to Mary and Martha upon Lazarus' death. John 11:6 says, "So when He heard that he was sick, He then stayed two days longer in the place where He was." Jesus knew Mary and Martha needed to grieve in order to grow. He allowed the sisters' pain *because* He loved them.

Until we come to understand and believe at our deepest, innermost level that God is love, we will struggle with trusting Him, yielding to Him, obeying Him, and serving Him wholeheartedly. One of the keys to our spiritual growth as Christians is believing in God's love—even when we cannot see it.

While we are to live in faith and hope, our most important dwelling place is God's love. Without making His love our ultimate dwelling, we cannot fully live in faith and hope. We should refuse to take a step or a breath without remaining keenly sensitive to "the greatest of these"—our Father's love.

➤ **John 11:37** — *"Could not this man, who opened the eyes of the blind man, have kept this man also from dying?"*

Yes, Jesus could have; but He chose to do something else. He did not spare His friends even great grief because it benefited them more in the end to witness His power over death (Rom. 8:18).

41 So they removed the stone. Then Jesus raised His eyes, and said, "Father, I thank You that You have heard Me.

42 "I knew that You always hear Me; but because of the people standing around I said it, so that they may believe that You sent Me."

43 When He had said these things, He cried out with a loud voice, "Lazarus, come forth."

44 The man who had died came forth, bound hand and foot with wrappings, and his face was wrapped around with a cloth. Jesus *said to them, "Unbind him, and let him go."

45 Therefore many of the Jews who came to Mary, and saw what He had done, believed in Him.

46 But some of them went to the Pharisees and told them the things which Jesus had done.

47 Therefore the chief priests and the Pharisees convened a council, and were saying, "What are we doing? For this man is performing many signs.

48 "If we let Him *go on* like this, all men will believe in Him, and the Romans will come and take away both our place and our nation."

49 But one of them, Caiaphas, who was high priest that year, said to them, "You know nothing at all,

50 nor do you take into account that it is expedient for you that one man die for the people, and that the whole nation not perish."

51 Now he did not say this on his own initiative, but being high priest that year, he prophesied that Jesus was going to die for the nation,

52 and not for the nation only, but in order that He might also gather together into one the children of God who are scattered abroad.

53 So from that day on they planned together to kill Him.

54 Therefore Jesus no longer continued to walk publicly among the Jews, but went away from there to the country near the wilderness, into a city called Ephraim; and there He stayed with the disciples.

55 Now the Passover of the Jews was near, and many went up to Jerusalem out of the country before the Passover to purify themselves.

56 So they were seeking for Jesus, and were saying to one another as they stood in the temple, "What do you think; that He will not come to the feast at all?"

57 Now the chief priests and the Pharisees had given orders that if anyone knew where He was, he was to report it, so that they might seize Him.

1 Kings 11:1—12:33

11 NOW King Solomon loved many foreign women along with the daughter of Pharaoh: Moabite, Ammonite, Edomite, Sidonian, and Hittite women,

2 from the nations concerning which the LORD had said to the sons of Israel, "You shall not associate with them, nor shall they associate with you, *for* they will surely turn your heart away after their gods." Solomon held fast to these in love.

3 He had seven hundred wives, princesses, and three hundred concubines, and his wives turned his heart away.

4 For when Solomon was old, his wives turned his heart away after other gods; and his heart was not wholly devoted to the LORD his God, as the heart of David his father *had been.*

5 For Solomon went after Ashtoreth the goddess of the Sidonians and after Milcom the detestable idol of the Ammonites.

6 Solomon did what was evil in the sight of the LORD, and did not follow the LORD fully, as David his father *had done.*

7 Then Solomon built a high place for Chemosh the detestable idol of Moab, on the mountain which is east of Jerusalem, and for Molech the detestable idol of the sons of Ammon.

8 Thus also he did for all his foreign wives, who burned incense and sacrificed to their gods.

9 Now the LORD was angry with Solomon because his heart was turned away from the LORD, the God of Israel, who had appeared to him twice,

10 and had commanded him concerning this thing, that he should not go after other gods; but he did not observe what the LORD had commanded.

11 So the LORD said to Solomon, "Because you have done this, and you have not kept My covenant and My statutes, which I have commanded you, I will surely tear the kingdom from you, and will give it to your servant.

12 "Nevertheless I will not do it in your days for the sake of your father David, *but* I will tear it out of the hand of your son.

13 "However, I will not tear away all the kingdom, *but* I will give one tribe to your son for the sake of My servant David and for the sake of Jerusalem which I have chosen."

14 Then the LORD raised up an adversary to Solomon, Hadad the Edomite; he was of the royal line in Edom.

15 For it came about, when David was in Edom, and Joab the commander of the army had gone up to bury the slain, and had struck down every male in Edom

16 (for Joab and all Israel stayed there six months, until he had cut off every male in Edom),

17 that Hadad fled to Egypt, he and certain Edomites of his father's servants with him, while Hadad *was* a young boy.

18 They arose from Midian and came to Paran; and they took men with them from Paran and came to Egypt, to Pharaoh king of Egypt, who gave him a house and assigned him food and gave him land.

19 Now Hadad found great favor before Pharaoh, so that he gave him in marriage the sister of his own wife, the sister of Tahpenes the queen.

20 The sister of Tahpenes bore his son Genubath, whom Tahpenes weaned in Pharaoh's house; and Genubath was in Pharaoh's house among the sons of Pharaoh.

21 But when Hadad heard in Egypt that David slept with his fathers and that Joab the commander of the army was

---

LIFE LESSONS

➤ **1 Kings 11:1 — *King Solomon loved many foreign women.***

*E*verything the Lord had forbidden kings to do in Deuteronomy 17:16, 17, Solomon did. He accumulated Egyptian horses, silver, gold, and foreign wives—and so lost the blessing of God.

➤ **1 Kings 11:14 — *Then the LORD raised up an adversary to Solomon.***

*W*hen the Lord raises up an adversary against us, He does so not only to discipline us, but also to bring us back to wholehearted devotion to Him. Even in judgment, He shows mercy.

ANSWERS TO LIFE'S QUESTIONS

Where do we draw the line between healthy and unhealthy compromise?

1 KINGS 11:1–13

*C*ompromise can be defined as making a concession in order to gain something. At times, compromise can be a good thing. If you've ever had to compromise on what restaurant to choose or how much to pay for a new car, you don't need an explanation of how compromise works.

We engage in *healthy* compromise when we can work with another without compromising our core values and beliefs. Every healthy human relationship experiences an element of give and take. *Unhealthy* compromise, on the other hand, involves abandoning sound and godly ideas and standards, leaving us morally and spiritually bankrupt.

The story of Solomon illustrates how unhealthy compromise ends in tragedy. Solomon surpassed every ruler of his time in wisdom and riches. People from all around the world sought out Solomon for his wisdom. Yet Solomon deliberately disobeyed God's warning against intermarriage with other religions (Deut. 7:3; 1 Kin. 11:1, 2). The result? Solomon's heart turned away from absolute devotion to God and began to cling to the false deities of his wives. Don't be deceived. Stepping away from God's truth always begins with what appears to be a harmless deed. But the end result is deep regret, sorrow, bondage, and emotional and spiritual separation from God.

We live in a world full of temptations that urge us to compromise our godly values. But when we choose to compromise, we pay a price, even though it may not seem immediately apparent to others (or even to ourselves). Satan wants us to believe the lie that no one gets hurt when we compromise our core values. But that lie has cost men their jobs and ministries, children their innocence, and at times, it has cost individuals their very lives.

God's righteousness is forever. He doesn't accept any compromise of His holy standards. Consider Solomon—after his compromise came collapse. God didn't waste any words. He said He would rip the kingdom out of Solomon's hands because of his compromise, and that is exactly what happened (1 Kin. 11:11).

Unhealthy compromise is costly. It corrupts. It brings collapse.

Has God revealed an area of compromise in your life? Perhaps you've crossed the line from flirting with compromise to jumping headlong into some ungodly activity. Satan is both cunning and powerful, and if he can get you to give up what is important to you, he can send you down a dark road that could cost you dearly. Don't fall for it. Don't give in. Don't compromise your faith. Obey God, trust Him, and allow Him to mold your life so that all you do reflects His love, goodness, holiness, and truth to others.

---

dead, Hadad said to Pharaoh, "Send me away, that I may go to my own country." 22 Then Pharaoh said to him, "But what have you lacked with me, that behold, you are seeking to go to your own country?" And he answered, "Nothing; nevertheless you must surely let me go."

23 God also raised up *another* adversary to him, Rezon the son of Eliada, who had fled from his lord Hadadezer king of Zobah.

24 He gathered men to himself and became leader of a marauding band, after David slew them of *Zobah*; and they went to Damascus and stayed there, and reigned in Damascus.

25 So he was an adversary to Israel all the days of Solomon, along with the evil that Hadad *did*; and he abhorred Israel and reigned over Aram.

26 Then Jeroboam the son of Nebat, an Ephraimite of Zeredah, Solomon's servant, whose mother's name was Zeruah, a widow, also rebelled against the king.

27 Now this was the reason why he rebelled against the king: Solomon built the Millo, *and* closed up the breach of the city of his father David.

28 Now the man Jeroboam was a valiant warrior, and when Solomon saw that the young man was industrious, he appointed him over all the forced labor of the house of Joseph.

29 It came about at that time, when Jeroboam went out of Jerusalem, that the prophet Ahijah the Shilonite found him on the road. Now Ahijah had clothed himself with a new cloak; and both of them were alone in the field.

30 Then Ahijah took hold of the new cloak which was on him and tore it into twelve pieces.

31 He said to Jeroboam, "Take for your-

self ten pieces; for thus says the LORD, the God of Israel, 'Behold, I will tear the kingdom out of the hand of Solomon and give you ten tribes

32 (but he will have one tribe, for the sake of My servant David and for the sake of Jerusalem, the city which I have chosen from all the tribes of Israel),

33 because they have forsaken Me, and have worshiped Ashtoreth the goddess of the Sidonians, Chemosh the god of Moab, and Milcom the god of the sons of Ammon; and they have not walked in My ways, doing what is right in My sight and *observing* My statutes and My ordinances, as his father David *did.*

34 'Nevertheless I will not take the whole kingdom out of his hand, but I will make him ruler all the days of his life, for the sake of My servant David whom I chose, who observed My commandments and My statutes;

35 but I will take the kingdom from his son's hand and give it to you, *even* ten tribes.

36 'But to his son I will give one tribe, that My servant David may have a lamp always before Me in Jerusalem, the city where I have chosen for Myself to put My name.

37 'I will take you, and you shall reign over whatever you desire, and you shall be king over Israel.

38 'Then it will be, that if you listen to all that I command you and walk in My ways, and do what is right in My sight by observing My statutes and My commandments, as My servant David did, then I will be with you and build you an enduring house as I built for David, and I will give Israel to you.

39 'Thus I will afflict the descendants of David for this, but not always.'"

➤ 40 Solomon sought therefore to put Jeroboam to death; but Jeroboam arose and fled to Egypt to Shishak king of Egypt, and he was in Egypt until the death of Solomon.

41 Now the rest of the acts of Solomon and whatever he did, and his wisdom, are they not written in the book of the acts of Solomon?

42 Thus the time that Solomon reigned in Jerusalem over all Israel was forty years.

43 And Solomon slept with his fathers and was buried in the city of his father

David, and his son Rehoboam reigned in his place.

12 THEN Rehoboam went to Shechem, for all Israel had come to Shechem to make him king.

2 Now when Jeroboam the son of Nebat heard *of it,* he was living in Egypt (for he was yet in Egypt, where he had fled from the presence of King Solomon).

3 Then they sent and called him, and Jeroboam and all the assembly of Israel came and spoke to Rehoboam, saying,

4 "Your father made our yoke hard; now therefore lighten the hard service of your father and his heavy yoke which he put on us, and we will serve you."

5 Then he said to them, "Depart for three days, then return to me." So the people departed.

6 King Rehoboam consulted with the elders who had served his father Solomon while he was still alive, saying, "How do you counsel *me* to answer this people?"

7 Then they spoke to him, saying, "If you will be a servant to this people today, and will serve them and grant them their petition, and speak good words to them, then they will be your servants forever."

8 But he forsook the counsel of the elders which they had given him, and consulted with the young men who grew up with him and served him.

9 So he said to them, "What counsel do you give that we may answer this people who have spoken to me, saying, 'Lighten the yoke which your father put on us'?"

10 The young men who grew up with him spoke to him, saying, "Thus you shall say to this people who spoke to you, saying, 'Your father made our yoke heavy, now you make it lighter for us!' But you

shall speak to them, 'My little finger is thicker than my father's loins!

11 'Whereas my father loaded you with a heavy yoke, I will add to your yoke; my father disciplined you with whips, but I will discipline you with scorpions.'"

12 Then Jeroboam and all the people came to Rehoboam on the third day as the king had directed, saying, "Return to me on the third day."

13 The king answered the people harshly, for he forsook the advice of the elders which they had given him,

14 and he spoke to them according to the advice of the young men, saying, "My father made your yoke heavy, but I will add to your yoke; my father disciplined you with whips, but I will discipline you with scorpions."

15 So the king did not listen to the people; for it was a turn *of events* from the LORD, that He might establish His word, which the LORD spoke through Ahijah the Shilonite to Jeroboam the son of Nebat.

16 When all Israel *saw* that the king did not listen to them, the people answered the king, saying,

"What portion do we have in David?
We have no inheritance in the son of Jesse;
To your tents, O Israel!
Now look after your own house, David!"

So Israel departed to their tents.

17 But as for the sons of Israel who lived in the cities of Judah, Rehoboam reigned over them.

18 Then King Rehoboam sent Adoram, who was over the forced labor, and all Israel stoned him to death. And King Rehoboam made haste to mount his chariot to flee to Jerusalem.

19 So Israel has been in rebellion against the house of David to this day.

20 It came about when all Israel heard that Jeroboam had returned, that they sent and called him to the assembly and made him king over all Israel. None but the tribe of Judah followed the house of David.

21 Now when Rehoboam had come to Jerusalem, he assembled all the house of Judah and the tribe of Benjamin, 180,000 chosen men who were warriors, to fight against the house of Israel to restore the kingdom to Rehoboam the son of Solomon.

22 But the word of God came to Shemaiah the man of God, saying,

23 "Speak to Rehoboam the son of Solomon, king of Judah, and to all the house of Judah and Benjamin and to the rest of the people, saying,

24 'Thus says the LORD, "You must not go up and fight against your relatives the sons of Israel; return every man to his house, for this thing has come from Me."'" So they listened to the word of the LORD, and returned and went *their way* according to the word of the LORD.

25 Then Jeroboam built Shechem in the hill country of Ephraim, and lived there. And he went out from there and built Penuel.

26 Jeroboam said in his heart, "Now the kingdom will return to the house of David.

27 "If this people go up to offer sacrifices in the house of the LORD at Jerusalem, then the heart of this people will return to their lord, *even* to Rehoboam king of Judah; and they will kill me and return to Rehoboam king of Judah."

28 So the king consulted, and made two ◄ golden calves, and he said to them, "It is too much for you to go up to Jerusalem; behold your gods, O Israel, that brought you up from the land of Egypt."

29 He set one in Bethel, and the other he put in Dan.

30 Now this thing became a sin, for the people went *to worship* before the one as far as Dan.

31 And he made houses on high places, and made priests from among all the people who were not of the sons of Levi.

32 Jeroboam instituted a feast in the eighth month on the fifteenth day of the month, like the feast which is in Judah, and he went up to the altar; thus he did

---

LIFE LESSONS

➤ **1 Kings 12:28** — *The king . . . made two golden calves.*

Centuries before, the Israelites had constructed a golden idol and proclaimed, "This is your god, O Israel, who brought you up from the land of Egypt" (Ex. 32:4). Satan seldom changes his tactics; unfortunately, he doesn't need to.

in Bethel, sacrificing to the calves which he had made. And he stationed in Bethel the priests of the high places which he had made.

33 Then he went up to the altar which he had made in Bethel on the fifteenth day in the eighth month, even in the month which he had devised in his own heart; and he instituted a feast for the sons of Israel and went up to the altar to burn incense.

◈ Psalm 69:5–15

5 O God, it is You who knows my folly,
    And my wrongs are not hidden
        from You.
➤ 6 May those who wait for You not
        be ashamed through me, O Lord
        GOD of hosts;
    May those who seek You not be
        dishonored through me, O God of
        Israel,
7 Because for Your sake I have borne
        reproach;
    Dishonor has covered my face.
8 I have become estranged from my
        brothers
    And an alien to my mother's sons.
9 For zeal for Your house has
        consumed me,
    And the reproaches of those who
        reproach You have fallen on me.
10 When I wept in my soul with
        fasting,
    It became my reproach.
11 When I made sackcloth my
        clothing,
    I became a byword to them.
12 Those who sit in the gate talk
        about me,
    And I *am* the song of the drunkards.

LIFE LESSONS

➤ **Psalm 69:6 —** *May those who wait for*
You not be ashamed through me.

*W*hat we do and how we live has a profound effect on those around us. People are watching us, even when we don't realize it. Pray that God will enable us to represent Him well, at all times.

---

13 But as for me, my prayer is to You,
        O LORD, at an acceptable time;
    O God, in the greatness of Your
        lovingkindness,
    Answer me with Your saving truth.
14 Deliver me from the mire and do
        not let me sink;
    May I be delivered from my foes
        and from the deep waters.
15 May the flood of water not overflow
        me
    Nor the deep swallow me up,
    Nor the pit shut its mouth on me.

◈ Proverbs 17:20—22

20 He who has a crooked mind finds
        no good,
    And he who is perverted in his
        language falls into evil.
21 He who sires a fool *does so* to his
        sorrow,
    And the father of a fool has no joy.
22 A joyful heart is good medicine,
    But a broken spirit dries up the
        bones.

◈ John 12:1–26

12 JESUS, therefore, six days before the Passover, came to Bethany where Lazarus was, whom Jesus had raised from the dead.

2 So they made Him a supper there, and Martha was serving; but Lazarus was one of those reclining *at the table* with Him.

3 Mary then took a pound of very costly perfume of pure nard, and anointed the feet of Jesus and wiped His feet with her hair; and the house was filled with the fragrance of the perfume.

4 But Judas Iscariot, one of His disciples, who was intending to betray Him, *said,

5 "Why was this perfume not sold for three hundred denarii and given to poor *people?*"

6 Now he said this, not because he was concerned about the poor, but because he was a thief, and as he had the money box, he used to pilfer what was put into it.

7 Therefore Jesus said, "Let her alone,

so that she may keep it for the day of My burial.

8 "For you always have the poor with you, but you do not always have Me."

9 The large crowd of the Jews then learned that He was there; and they came, not for Jesus' sake only, but that they might also see Lazarus, whom He raised from the dead.

10 But the chief priests planned to put Lazarus to death also;

11 because on account of him many of the Jews were going away and were believing in Jesus.

12 On the next day the large crowd who had come to the feast, when they heard that Jesus was coming to Jerusalem,

13 took the branches of the palm trees and went out to meet Him, and *began to shout, "Hosanna! BLESSED IS HE WHO COMES IN THE NAME OF THE LORD, even the King of Israel."

14 Jesus, finding a young donkey, sat on it; as it is written,

15 "FEAR NOT, DAUGHTER OF ZION; BEHOLD, YOUR KING IS COMING, SEATED ON A DONKEY'S COLT."

➤ 16 These things His disciples did not understand at the first; but when Jesus was glorified, then they remembered that these things were written of Him, and that they had done these things to Him.

17 So the people, who were with Him when He called Lazarus out of the tomb and raised him from the dead, continued to testify *about Him.

18 For this reason also the people went and met Him, because they heard that He had performed this sign.

19 So the Pharisees said to one another, "You see that you are not doing any good; look, the world has gone after Him."

20 Now there were some Greeks among those who were going up to worship at the feast;

21 these then came to Philip, who was from Bethsaida of Galilee, and *began to ask him, saying, "Sir, we wish to see Jesus."

22 Philip *came and *told Andrew; Andrew and Philip *came and *told Jesus.

23 And Jesus *answered them, saying, "The hour has come for the Son of Man to be glorified.

24 "Truly, truly, I say to you, unless a grain of wheat falls into the earth and dies, it remains alone; but if it dies, it bears much fruit.

25 "He who loves his life loses it, and he who hates his life in this world will keep it to life eternal.

26 "If anyone serves Me, he must follow Me; and where I am, there My servant will be also; if anyone serves Me, the Father will honor him.

JUNE 2

1 Kings 13:1—14:31

➤ **13** NOW behold, there came a man of God from Judah to Bethel by the word of the LORD, while Jeroboam was standing by the altar to burn incense.

2 He cried against the altar by the word of the LORD, and said, "O altar, altar, thus says the LORD, 'Behold, a son shall be born to the house of David,

Josiah by name; and on you he shall sacrifice the priests of the high places who burn incense on you, and human bones shall be burned on you.'"

3 Then he gave a sign the same day, saying, "This is the sign which the LORD has spoken, 'Behold, the altar shall be split apart and the ashes which are on it shall be poured out.'"

4 Now when the king heard the saying of the man of God, which he cried against the altar in Bethel, Jeroboam stretched out his hand from the altar, saying, "Seize him." But his hand which he stretched out against him dried up, so that he could not draw it back to himself.

5 The altar also was split apart and the ashes were poured out from the altar, according to the sign which the man of God had given by the word of the LORD.

6 The king said to the man of God, "Please entreat the LORD your God, and pray for me, that my hand may be restored to me." So the man of God entreated the LORD, and the king's hand was restored to him, and it became as it was before.

7 Then the king said to the man of God, "Come home with me and refresh yourself, and I will give you a reward."

8 But the man of God said to the king, "If you were to give me half your house I would not go with you, nor would I eat bread or drink water in this place.

9 "For so it was commanded me by the word of the LORD, saying, 'You shall eat no bread, nor drink water, nor return by the way which you came.'"

10 So he went another way and did not return by the way which he came to Bethel.

11 Now an old prophet was living in Bethel; and his sons came and told him all the deeds which the man of God had done that day in Bethel; the words which he had spoken to the king, these also they related to their father.

12 Their father said to them, "Which way did he go?" Now his sons had seen the way which the man of God who came from Judah had gone.

13 Then he said to his sons, "Saddle the donkey for me." So they saddled the donkey for him and he rode away on it.

14 So he went after the man of God and found him sitting under an oak; and he said to him, "Are you the man of God

who came from Judah?" And he said, "I am."

15 Then he said to him, "Come home with me and eat bread."

16 He said, "I cannot return with you, nor go with you, nor will I eat bread or drink water with you in this place.

17 "For a command came to me by the word of the LORD, 'You shall eat no bread, nor drink water there; do not return by going the way which you came.'"

18 He said to him, "I also am a prophet like you, and an angel spoke to me by the word of the LORD, saying, 'Bring him back with you to your house, that he may eat bread and drink water.'" But he lied to him.

19 So he went back with him, and ate bread in his house and drank water.

20 Now it came about, as they were sitting down at the table, that the word of the LORD came to the prophet who had brought him back;

21 and he cried to the man of God who came from Judah, saying, "Thus says the LORD, 'Because you have disobeyed the command of the LORD, and have not observed the commandment which the LORD your God commanded you,

22 but have returned and eaten bread and drunk water in the place of which He said to you, "Eat no bread and drink no water"; your body shall not come to the grave of your fathers.'"

23 It came about after he had eaten bread and after he had drunk, that he saddled the donkey for him, for the prophet whom he had brought back.

24 Now when he had gone, a lion met him on the way and killed him, and his body was thrown on the road, with the donkey standing beside it; the lion also was standing beside the body.

25 And behold, men passed by and saw the body thrown on the road, and the lion standing beside the body; so they came and told it in the city where the old prophet lived.

26 Now when the prophet who brought him back from the way heard it, he said, "It is the man of God, who disobeyed the command of the LORD; therefore the LORD has given him to the lion, which has torn him and killed him, according to the word of the LORD which He spoke to him."

27 Then he spoke to his sons, saying,

"Saddle the donkey for me." And they saddled *it.*

28 He went and found his body thrown on the road with the donkey and the lion standing beside the body; the lion had not eaten the body nor torn the donkey.

29 So the prophet took up the body of the man of God and laid it on the donkey and brought it back, and he came to the city of the old prophet to mourn and to bury him.

30 He laid his body in his own grave, and they mourned over him, *saying,* "Alas, my brother!"

31 After he had buried him, he spoke to his sons, saying, "When I die, bury me in the grave in which the man of God is buried; lay my bones beside his bones.

32 "For the thing shall surely come to pass which he cried by the word of the LORD against the altar in Bethel and against all the houses of the high places which are in the cities of Samaria."

➤ 33 After this event Jeroboam did not return from his evil way, but again he made priests of the high places from among all the people; any who would, he ordained, to be priests of the high places.

34 This event became sin to the house of Jeroboam, even to blot *it* out and destroy *it* from off the face of the earth.

14 AT that time Abijah the son of Jeroboam became sick.

➤ 2 Jeroboam said to his wife, "Arise now, and disguise yourself so that they will not know that you are the wife of Jeroboam, and go to Shiloh; behold, Ahijah the prophet is there, who spoke concerning me *that I would be* king over this people.

3 "Take ten loaves with you, *some* cakes and a jar of honey, and go to him. He will tell you what will happen to the boy."

4 Jeroboam's wife did so, and arose and went to Shiloh, and came to the house of Ahijah. Now Ahijah could not see, for his eyes were dim because of his age.

5 Now the LORD had said to Ahijah, "Behold, the wife of Jeroboam is coming to inquire of you concerning her son, for he is sick. You shall say thus and thus to her, for it will be when she arrives that she will pretend to be another woman."

6 When Ahijah heard the sound of her feet coming in the doorway, he said,

"Come in, wife of Jeroboam, why do you pretend to be another woman? For I am sent to you *with* a harsh *message.*

7 "Go, say to Jeroboam, 'Thus says the LORD God of Israel, "Because I exalted you from among the people and made you leader over My people Israel,

8 and tore the kingdom away from the house of David and gave it to you— yet you have not been like My servant David, who kept My commandments and who followed Me with all his heart, to do only that which was right in My sight;

9 you also have done more evil than all who were before you, and have gone and made for yourself other gods and molten images to provoke Me to anger, and have cast Me behind your back—

10 therefore behold, I am bringing calamity on the house of Jeroboam, and will cut off from Jeroboam every male person, both bond and free in Israel, and I will make a clean sweep of the house of Jeroboam, as one sweeps away dung until it is all gone.

11 "Anyone belonging to Jeroboam who dies in the city the dogs will eat. And he who dies in the field the birds of the heavens will eat; for the LORD has spoken *it.*"'

12 "Now you, arise, go to your house. When your feet enter the city the child will die.

13 "All Israel shall mourn for him and ◄

---

bury him, for he alone of Jeroboam's *family* will come to the grave, because in him something good was found toward the LORD God of Israel in the house of Jeroboam.

14 "Moreover, the LORD will raise up for Himself a king over Israel who will cut off the house of Jeroboam this day and from now on.

15 "For the LORD will strike Israel, as a reed is shaken in the water; and He will uproot Israel from this good land which He gave to their fathers, and will scatter them beyond the *Euphrates* River, because they have made their Asherim, provoking the LORD to anger.

16 "He will give up Israel on account of the sins of Jeroboam, which he committed and with which he made Israel to sin."

17 Then Jeroboam's wife arose and departed and came to Tirzah. As she was entering the threshold of the house, the child died.

18 All Israel buried him and mourned for him, according to the word of the LORD which He spoke through His servant Ahijah the prophet.

19 Now the rest of the acts of Jeroboam, how he made war and how he reigned, behold, they are written in the Book of the Chronicles of the Kings of Israel.

20 The time that Jeroboam reigned *was* twenty-two years; and he slept with his fathers, and Nadab his son reigned in his place.

21 Now Rehoboam the son of Solomon reigned in Judah. Rehoboam was forty-one years old when he became king, and he reigned seventeen years in Jerusalem, the city which the LORD had chosen from all the tribes of Israel to put His name there. And his mother's name was Naamah the Ammonitess.

22 Judah did evil in the sight of the LORD, and they provoked Him to jealousy more than all that their fathers had done, with the sins which they committed.

23 For they also built for themselves high places and *sacred* pillars and Asherim on every high hill and beneath every luxuriant tree.

24 There were also male cult prostitutes in the land. They did according to all the abominations of the nations which the LORD dispossessed before the sons of Israel.

25 Now it happened in the fifth year of King Rehoboam, that Shishak the king of Egypt came up against Jerusalem.

26 He took away the treasures of the house of the LORD and the treasures of the king's house, and he took everything, even taking all the shields of gold which Solomon had made.

27 So King Rehoboam made shields of bronze in their place, and committed them to the care of the commanders of the guard who guarded the doorway of the king's house.

28 Then it happened as often as the king entered the house of the LORD, that the guards would carry them and would bring them back into the guards' room.

29 Now the rest of the acts of Rehoboam and all that he did, are they not written in the Book of the Chronicles of the Kings of Judah?

30 There was war between Rehoboam and Jeroboam continually.

31 And Rehoboam slept with his fathers and was buried with his fathers in the city of David; and his mother's name was Naamah the Ammonitess. And Abijam his son became king in his place.

LIFE LESSONS

➤ 1 Kings 14:13 — *"He alone of Jeroboam's family will come to the grave, because in him something good was found toward the LORD God of Israel."*

*J*eroboam had so dishonored the Lord that God pronounced the terrible judgment, "Anyone belonging to Jeroboam who dies in the city the dogs will eat. And he who dies in the field the birds of the heavens will eat" (1 Kin. 14:11). Jeroboam's line would end and his family would be completely humiliated by being left dishonorably unburied. Yet God shows mercy, even in the midst of His judgment. The Lord said He would allow the only one in Jeroboam's family who had any good in him to be mourned properly.

◈ **Psalm 69:16–21**

16 Answer me, O LORD, for Your
       lovingkindness is good;
     According to the greatness of Your
       compassion, turn to me,

17 And do not hide Your face from
    Your servant,
    For I am in distress; answer me
    quickly.
18 Oh draw near to my soul *and*
    redeem it;
    Ransom me because of my enemies!
19 You know my reproach and my
    shame and my dishonor;
    All my adversaries are before You.
20 Reproach has broken my heart and
    I am so sick.
    And I looked for sympathy, but
    there was none,
    And for comforters, but I found
    none.
➤ 21 They also gave me gall for my food
    And for my thirst they gave me
    vinegar to drink.

✦ Proverbs 17:23, 24

23 A wicked man receives a bribe from
    the bosom
    To pervert the ways of justice.
24 Wisdom is in the presence of the
    one who has understanding,
    But the eyes of a fool are on the
    ends of the earth.

✦ John 12:27–50

27 "Now My soul has become troubled; and what shall I say, 'Father, save Me from this hour'? But for this purpose I came to this hour.
28 "Father, glorify Your name." Then a voice came out of heaven: "I have both glorified it, and will glorify it again."
29 So the crowd *of people* who stood by and heard it were saying that it had thundered; others were saying, "An angel has spoken to Him."
30 Jesus answered and said, "This voice has not come for My sake, but for your sakes.
31 "Now judgment is upon this world; now the ruler of this world will be cast out.
➤ 32 "And I, if I am lifted up from the earth, will draw all men to Myself."
33 But He was saying this to indicate the kind of death by which He was to die.

34 The crowd then answered Him, "We have heard out of the Law that the Christ is to remain forever; and how can You say, 'The Son of Man must be lifted up'? Who is this Son of Man?"
35 So Jesus said to them, "For a little while longer the Light is among you. Walk while you have the Light, so that darkness will not overtake you; he who walks in the darkness does not know where he goes.
36 "While you have the Light, believe in the Light, so that you may become sons of Light."
These things Jesus spoke, and He went away and hid Himself from them.
37 But though He had performed so many signs before them, *yet* they were not believing in Him.
38 *This was* to fulfill the word of Isaiah the prophet which he spoke: "LORD, WHO HAS BELIEVED OUR REPORT? AND TO WHOM HAS THE ARM OF THE LORD BEEN REVEALED?"
39 For this reason they could not believe, for Isaiah said again,
40 "HE HAS BLINDED THEIR EYES AND HE HARDENED THEIR HEART, SO THAT THEY WOULD NOT SEE WITH THEIR EYES AND PERCEIVE WITH THEIR HEART, AND BE CONVERTED AND I HEAL THEM."
41 These things Isaiah said because he saw His glory, and he spoke of Him.
42 Nevertheless many even of the rulers believed in Him, but because of the

---

LIFE LESSONS

➤ **Psalm 69:21** — *They also gave me gall for my food and for my thirst they gave me vinegar to drink.*

*I*n fulfillment of this passage, the Roman soldiers crucifying Jesus gave Him wine mixed with gall to make it bitter. Later, others gave Him wine vinegar to drink (Matt. 27:34, 48; John 19:28-30).

➤ **John 12:32** — *"And I, if I am lifted up from the earth, will draw all men to Myself."*

*J*esus says that He draws all peoples to Himself. We are to represent Him as well as we can and allow Him to live through us, but we can never convert anyone. It is Christ's responsibility to cause faith to take root in human hearts, not ours.

WHAT THE BIBLE SAYS ABOUT

Lifted Up?

John 12:27–36

*B*eing "lifted up" sounded good, until the disciples realized Jesus was "saying this to indicate the kind of death by which He was to die" (John 12:33). They had hoped He—as the Messiah—would inaugurate a powerful earthly kingdom. However, all His talk of death quickly dashed their hopes.

What was even more confusing was that when Jesus had spoken about being lifted up earlier, He had explained it would be "as Moses lifted up the serpent in the wilderness" (John 3:14). That called to mind the well-known and terrible episode in Israel's history (Num. 21:1–9).

The incident Jesus spoke of occurred after God gave the Israelites victory over the Canaanites at Hormah. Though they had triumphed over their enemies, the Israelites were depressed and complaining. They were disheartened because instead of heading forward to the Promised Land, it looked like they were headed backwards—back to the Red Sea where they had narrowly escaped the Egyptian army.

God was leading them around the enemy territory of Edom, but they didn't care. They were tired, and it felt as if this journey in the wilderness would never end. Why was God doing this? In their discouragement, they "spoke against God and Moses, 'Why have you brought us up out of Egypt to die in the wilderness? For there is no food and no water, and we loathe this miserable food'" (Num. 21:5).

It was unthinkable that the people who had been saved out of Egypt by God's mighty hand would address Him and His servant Moses in such an ungrateful manner—and God's anger burned against them. He sent fiery serpents to bite the people, and many of them did not survive. This frightful plague of snakes lasted until they were willing to repent (Num. 21:7).

Then, in His mercy, "The LORD said to Moses, 'Make a fiery serpent, and set it on a standard; and it shall come about, that everyone who is bitten, when he looks at it, he will live.' "

Understand this: As long as the fiery snakes were under the people's feet, they were deadly. However, as soon as Moses lifted one up and the people looked upon it, God made it the catalyst for their healing.

The same is true for your relationship with Jesus. As long as you hold Him under your feet—in the sense that you don't believe in Him because of your pride or limited vision—your own actions will condemn you (1 Pet. 2:6–8). However, when you lift Christ up—honoring what He did for you on the Cross—then you will be healed.

In John 12, Jesus taught this to the disciples. He knew they would be tempted by discouragement after the crucifixion, and He wanted them to understand His death on the Cross was the beginning of the true victory—that being lifted up was the way all peoples would be saved (v. 32). Even though the disciple's goals of participating in an earthly kingdom were destroyed, Christ was showing them they would inherit a better kingdom in heaven.

It can be difficult to remain faithful when your circumstances seem to be taking you away from your goals instead of towards them. However, don't make the mistake the Israelites did by speaking against God. Such faithless actions dishonor the Lord and hurt your spirit. They reveal the condition of your heart is not right.

Instead, when you feel weary and disheartened, look to Christ—lift Him up in your life and praise Him. He knows your journey is long and difficult. He understands your heart can only handle so much (Ps. 103:14). Yet surely, the "backwards" steps you're taking are leading you to an even better goal. As long as you're looking to Jesus, He'll give you the strength and encouragement you need to carry on (Matt. 11:28–30). And the best thing about His plan is that along the way, as He's exalted in you, others will be saved. ◈

Pharisees they were not confessing *Him*, for fear that they would be put out of the synagogue;
43 for they loved the approval of men rather than the approval of God.

44 And Jesus cried out and said, "He who believes in Me, does not believe in Me but in Him who sent Me.
45 "He who sees Me sees the One who sent Me.

46 "I have come *as* Light into the world, so that everyone who believes in Me will not remain in darkness.
47 "If anyone hears My sayings and does not keep them, I do not judge him; for I did not come to judge the world, but to save the world.
48 "He who rejects Me and does not receive My sayings, has one who judges him; the word I spoke is what will judge him at the last day.
49 "For I did not speak on My own initiative, but the Father Himself who sent Me has given Me a commandment *as to* what to say and what to speak.
50 "I know that His commandment is eternal life; therefore the things I speak, I speak just as the Father has told Me."

JUNE 3

1 Kings 15:1—16:34

15 NOW in the eighteenth year of King Jeroboam, the son of Nebat, Abijam became king over Judah.
2 He reigned three years in Jerusalem; and his mother's name was Maacah the daughter of Abishalom.
3 He walked in all the sins of his father which he had committed before him; and his heart was not wholly devoted to the LORD his God, like the heart of his father David.
4 But for David's sake the LORD his God gave him a lamp in Jerusalem, to raise up his son after him and to establish Jerusalem;
5 because David did what was right in the sight of the LORD, and had not turned aside from anything that He commanded him all the days of his life, except in the case of Uriah the Hittite.
6 There was war between Rehoboam and Jeroboam all the days of his life.
7 Now the rest of the acts of Abijam and all that he did, are they not written in the Book of the Chronicles of the Kings of Judah? And there was war between Abijam and Jeroboam.
8 And Abijam slept with his fathers and they buried him in the city of David; and Asa his son became king in his place.
9 So in the twentieth year of Jeroboam the king of Israel, Asa began to reign as king of Judah.
10 He reigned forty-one years in Jerusalem; and his mother's name was Maacah the daughter of Abishalom.
11 Asa did what was right in the sight of the LORD, like David his father.
12 He also put away the male cult prostitutes from the land and removed all the idols which his fathers had made.
13 He also removed Maacah his mother from *being* queen mother, because she had made a horrid image as an Asherah; and Asa cut down her horrid image and burned *it* at the brook Kidron.
14 But the high places were not taken away; nevertheless the heart of Asa was wholly devoted to the LORD all his days.
15 He brought into the house of the LORD the dedicated things of his father and his own dedicated things: silver and gold and utensils.
16 Now there was war between Asa and Baasha king of Israel all their days.
17 Baasha king of Israel went up against Judah and fortified Ramah in order to prevent *anyone* from going out or coming in to Asa king of Judah.
18 Then Asa took all the silver and the gold which were left in the treasuries of the house of the LORD and the treasuries of the king's house, and delivered them into the hand of his servants. And King Asa sent them to Ben-hadad the

LIFE LESSONS

➤ **1 Kings 15:18 —** *Asa took all the silver and the gold which were left in the treasuries of the house of the LORD and . . . sent them to Ben-hadad.*

We must always avoid the temptation of relying on our own reasoning and resources rather than on trusting God to help us and protect us.

son of Tabrimmon, the son of Hezion, king of Aram, who lived in Damascus, saying,
19 "Let there be a treaty between you and me, as between my father and your father. Behold, I have sent you a present of silver and gold; go, break your treaty with Baasha king of Israel so that he will withdraw from me."
20 So Ben-hadad listened to King Asa and sent the commanders of his armies against the cities of Israel, and conquered Ijon, Dan, Abel-beth-maacah and all Chinneroth, besides all the land of Naphtali.
21 When Baasha heard of it, he ceased fortifying Ramah and remained in Tirzah.
22 Then King Asa made a proclamation to all Judah—none was exempt—and they carried away the stones of Ramah and its timber with which Baasha had built. And King Asa built with them Geba of Benjamin and Mizpah.
23 Now the rest of all the acts of Asa and all his might and all that he did and the cities which he built, are they not written in the Book of the Chronicles of the Kings of Judah? But in the time of his old age he was diseased in his feet.
24 And Asa slept with his fathers and was buried with his fathers in the city of David his father; and Jehoshaphat his son reigned in his place.
25 Now Nadab the son of Jeroboam became king over Israel in the second year of Asa king of Judah, and he reigned over Israel two years.
26 He did evil in the sight of the LORD, and walked in the way of his father and in his sin which he made Israel sin.
27 Then Baasha the son of Ahijah of the house of Issachar conspired against him, and Baasha struck him down at Gibbethon, which belonged to the Philistines, while Nadab and all Israel were laying siege to Gibbethon.
➤ 28 So Baasha killed him in the third year of Asa king of Judah and reigned in his place.
29 It came about as soon as he was king, he struck down all the household of Jeroboam. He did not leave to Jeroboam any persons alive, until he had destroyed them, according to the word of the LORD,

which He spoke by His servant Ahijah the Shilonite,
30 and because of the sins of Jeroboam which he sinned, and which he made Israel sin, because of his provocation with which he provoked the LORD God of Israel to anger.
31 Now the rest of the acts of Nadab and all that he did, are they not written in the Book of the Chronicles of the Kings of Israel?
32 There was war between Asa and Baasha king of Israel all their days.
33 In the third year of Asa king of Judah, Baasha the son of Ahijah became king over all Israel at Tirzah, and reigned twenty-four years.
34 He did evil in the sight of the LORD, and walked in the way of Jeroboam and in his sin which he made Israel sin.

16 NOW the word of the LORD came to Jehu the son of Hanani against Baasha, saying,
2 "Inasmuch as I exalted you from the dust and made you leader over My people Israel, and you have walked in the way of Jeroboam and have made My people Israel sin, provoking Me to anger with their sins,
3 behold, I will consume Baasha and his house, and I will make your house like the house of Jeroboam the son of Nebat.
4 "Anyone of Baasha who dies in the city the dogs will eat, and anyone of his who dies in the field the birds of the heavens will eat."
5 Now the rest of the acts of Baasha and what he did and his might, are they not written in the Book of the Chronicles of the Kings of Israel?

LIFE LESSONS

➤ 1 Kings 15:28 — *Baasha killed him in the third year of Asa king of Judah and reigned in his place.*

*J*eroboam could have established an enduring royal line if he had chosen to obey the Lord (1 Kin. 11:31-38). Instead, he rebelled and so brought on his family a deadly curse (1 Kin. 14:9-14). God wants us to obey Him and enjoy life at its very best, which only He can offer us.

6 And Baasha slept with his fathers and was buried in Tirzah, and Elah his son became king in his place.

7 Moreover, the word of the LORD through the prophet Jehu the son of Hanani also came against Baasha and his household, both because of all the evil which he did in the sight of the LORD, provoking Him to anger with the work of his hands, in being like the house of Jeroboam, and because he struck it.

8 In the twenty-sixth year of Asa king of Judah, Elah the son of Baasha became king over Israel at Tirzah, *and reigned* two years.

9 His servant Zimri, commander of half his chariots, conspired against him. Now he *was* at Tirzah drinking himself drunk in the house of Arza, who *was* over the household at Tirzah.

10 Then Zimri went in and struck him and put him to death in the twenty-seventh year of Asa king of Judah, and became king in his place.

11 It came about when he became king, as soon as he sat on his throne, that he killed all the household of Baasha; he did not leave a single male, neither of his relatives nor of his friends.

12 Thus Zimri destroyed all the household of Baasha, according to the word of the LORD, which He spoke against Baasha through Jehu the prophet,

13 for all the sins of Baasha and the sins of Elah his son, which they sinned and which they made Israel sin, provoking the LORD God of Israel to anger with their idols.

14 Now the rest of the acts of Elah and all that he did, are they not written in the Book of the Chronicles of the Kings of Israel?

15 In the twenty-seventh year of Asa king of Judah, Zimri reigned seven days at Tirzah. Now the people were camped against Gibbethon, which belonged to the Philistines.

16 The people who were camped heard it said, "Zimri has conspired and has also struck down the king." Therefore all Israel made Omri, the commander of the army, king over Israel that day in the camp.

17 Then Omri and all Israel with him went up from Gibbethon and besieged Tirzah.

18 When Zimri saw that the city was taken, he went into the citadel of the king's house and burned the king's house over him with fire, and died,

19 because of his sins which he sinned, doing evil in the sight of the LORD, walking in the way of Jeroboam, and in his sin which he did, making Israel sin.

20 Now the rest of the acts of Zimri and his conspiracy which he carried out, are they not written in the Book of the Chronicles of the Kings of Israel?

21 Then the people of Israel were divided into two parts: half of the people followed Tibni the son of Ginath, to make him king; the *other* half followed Omri.

22 But the people who followed Omri prevailed over the people who followed Tibni the son of Ginath. And Tibni died and Omri became king.

23 In the thirty-first year of Asa king of Judah, Omri became king over Israel *and reigned* twelve years; he reigned six years at Tirzah.

24 He bought the hill Samaria from Shemer for two talents of silver; and he built on the hill, and named the city which he built Samaria, after the name of Shemer, the owner of the hill.

25 Omri did evil in the sight of the LORD, and acted more wickedly than all who *were* before him.

26 For he walked in all the way of Jeroboam the son of Nebat and in his sins which he made Israel sin, provoking the LORD God of Israel with their idols.

27 Now the rest of the acts of Omri which he did and his might which he showed, are they not written in the Book of the Chronicles of the Kings of Israel?

28 So Omri slept with his fathers and

LIFE LESSONS

➤ **1 Kings 16:18 —** *He went into the citadel of the king's house and burned the king's house over him with fire, and died.*

Sometimes God allows wicked men to flourish for years; sometimes he judges them very quickly. The evil King Zimri lasted just seven days. God is sovereign, and "removes kings and establishes kings" (Dan. 2:21).

➤ **1 Kings 16:30 — Ahab the son of Omri did evil in the sight of the LORD more than all who were before him.**

*A*lthough King Ahab did more evil than all his predecessors, the Lord allowed him to reign for twenty-two years. However, we should never mistake God's patience for either indulgence or indifference (Jer. 5:12-17; Zeph. 1:12). "It is appointed for men to die once and after this comes judgment" (Heb. 9:27).

was buried in Samaria; and Ahab his son became king in his place.
29 Now Ahab the son of Omri became king over Israel in the thirty-eighth year of Asa king of Judah, and Ahab the son of Omri reigned over Israel in Samaria twenty-two years.
➤ **30** Ahab the son of Omri did evil in the sight of the LORD more than all who were before him.
31 It came about, as though it had been a trivial thing for him to walk in the sins of Jeroboam the son of Nebat, that he married Jezebel the daughter of Ethbaal king of the Sidonians, and went to serve Baal and worshiped him.
32 So he erected an altar for Baal in the house of Baal which he built in Samaria.
33 Ahab also made the Asherah. Thus Ahab did more to provoke the LORD God of Israel than all the kings of Israel who were before him.
34 In his days Hiel the Bethelite built Jericho; he laid its foundations with the *loss of* Abiram his firstborn, and set up its gates with the *loss of* his youngest son Segub, according to the word of the LORD, which He spoke by Joshua the son of Nun.

Psalm 69:22–28

22 May their table before them become a snare;
And when they are in peace, *may it* become a trap.
23 May their eyes grow dim so that they cannot see,

And make their loins shake continually.
24 Pour out Your indignation on them,
And may Your burning anger overtake them.
25 May their camp be desolate;
May none dwell in their tents.
26 For they have persecuted him whom You Yourself have smitten,
And they tell of the pain of those whom You have wounded.
27 Add iniquity to their iniquity,
And may they not come into Your righteousness.
28 May they be blotted out of the book of life
And may they not be recorded with the righteous.

Proverbs 17:25, 26

25 A foolish son is a grief to his father
And bitterness to her who bore him.
26 It is also not good to fine the righteous,
Nor to strike the noble for *their* uprightness.

John 13:1–20

13 NOW before the Feast of the Passover, Jesus knowing that His hour had come that He would depart out of this world to the Father, having loved His own who were in the world, He loved them to the end.
2 During supper, the devil having already put into the heart of Judas Iscariot, *the son* of Simon, to betray Him,
3 *Jesus*, knowing that the Father had

➤ **John 13:1 — He loved them to the end.**

*J*esus always finishes what He starts. He never drops someone in midstream or gives up on a person halfway to the finish line. "He who began a good work in you will perfect it" (Phil. 1:6).

Life Examples:

Dirty No More

JOHN 13:3-10

*A*s Peter approached Jesus, he looked at the menial stance of the Rabboni. He was kneeling, towel wrapped around His waist, and basin filled with water on the floor next to Him. Then, Jesus reached out for the foot of His disciple.

His action made Peter recoil. The Teacher he most respected was in the position of the lowest servant. How could he allow so great a man to do so humble a service? Peter would not allow Him to do it. Jesus responded, "If I do not wash you, you have no part with Me" (John 13:8).

How often has this happened to the believer who is so discouraged or ashamed of his sin that he cannot face God? The Lord desires to cleanse His child from all sin, yet the believer is tempted to walk away from God because the process is humbling.

Like Peter, you may feel unworthy of Jesus washing your feet and cry out, "Never shall You wash my feet!" (John 13:8). But the Lord must purify you so that you can fully enjoy all the blessings of God's presence.

Whatever shame you are struggling with, the Lord understands, and He wants to gently scrub it from your life. His desire is for you to cast off all the "dirt" which makes you unrighteous and feel the cleanliness of being one of His children. He is the only one who can do it. Will you let Him?

---

given all things into His hands, and that He had come forth from God and was going back to God,

4 *got up from supper, and *laid aside His garments; and taking a towel, He girded Himself.

5 Then He *poured water into the basin, and began to wash the disciples' feet and to wipe them with the towel with which He was girded.

6 So He *came to Simon Peter. He *said to Him, "Lord, do You wash my feet?"

7 Jesus answered and said to him, "What I do you do not realize now, but you will understand hereafter."

8 Peter *said to Him, "Never shall You wash my feet!" Jesus answered him, "If I do not wash you, you have no part with Me."

9 Simon Peter *said to Him, "Lord, *then wash* not only my feet, but also my hands and my head."

10 Jesus *said to him, "He who has bathed needs only to wash his feet, but is completely clean; and you are clean, but not all *of you.*"

11 For He knew the one who was betraying Him; for this reason He said, "Not all of you are clean."

12 So when He had washed their feet, and taken His garments and reclined *at the table* again, He said to them, "Do you know what I have done to you?

13 "You call Me Teacher and Lord; and you are right, for *so* I am.

14 "If I then, the Lord and the Teacher, washed your feet, you also ought to wash one another's feet.

15 "For I gave you an example that you also should do as I did to you.

16 "Truly, truly, I say to you, a slave is not greater than his master, nor *is* one who is sent greater than the one who sent him.

17 "If you know these things, you are ◄ blessed if you do them.

18 "I do not speak of all of you. I know the ones I have chosen; but *it is* that the Scripture may be fulfilled, 'HE WHO EATS MY BREAD HAS LIFTED UP HIS HEEL AGAINST ME.'

19 "From now on I am telling you before *it* comes to pass, so that when it does occur, you may believe that I am He.

20 "Truly, truly, I say to you, he who receives whomever I send receives Me; and he who receives Me receives Him who sent Me."

LIFE LESSONS

➤ John 13:17 — *"If you know these things, you are blessed if you do them."*

*K*nowing and doing are two separate things. Jesus reserves His blessing not merely for those who know His will, but for those who know it *and* do it as well. Genuine faith always leads to godly action, and we know that whatever He leads us to do for His name's sake, He will use powerfully for His glory, even if we can't yet see how (Phil. 1:6).

1 Kings 17:1—18:46

17 NOW Elijah the Tishbite, who was of the settlers of Gilead, said to Ahab, "As the LORD, the God of Israel lives, before whom I stand, surely there shall be neither dew nor rain these years, except by my word."

2 The word of the LORD came to him, saying,

3 "Go away from here and turn eastward, and hide yourself by the brook Cherith, which is east of the Jordan.

4 "It shall be that you will drink of the brook, and I have commanded the ravens to provide for you there."

5 So he went and did according to the word of the LORD, for he went and lived by the brook Cherith, which is east of the Jordan.

6 The ravens brought him bread and meat in the morning and bread and meat in the evening, and he would drink from the brook.

7 It happened after a while that the brook dried up, because there was no rain in the land.

8 Then the word of the LORD came to him, saying,

9 "Arise, go to Zarephath, which belongs to Sidon, and stay there; behold, I have commanded a widow there to provide for you."

10 So he arose and went to Zarephath, and when he came to the gate of the city, behold, a widow was there gathering sticks; and he called to her and said, "Please get me a little water in a jar, that I may drink."

11 As she was going to get *it*, he called to her and said, "Please bring me a piece of bread in your hand."

12 But she said, "As the LORD your God lives, I have no bread, only a handful of flour in the bowl and a little oil in the jar; and behold, I am gathering a few sticks that I may go in and prepare for me and my son, that we may eat it and die."

13 Then Elijah said to her, "Do not fear; go, do as you have said, but make me a little bread cake from it first and bring *it* out to me, and afterward you may make *one* for yourself and for your son.

14 "For thus says the LORD God of Israel, 'The bowl of flour shall not be exhausted, nor shall the jar of oil be empty, until the day that the LORD sends rain on the face of the earth.'"

15 So she went and did according to the word of Elijah, and she and he and her household ate for *many* days.

16 The bowl of flour was not exhausted nor did the jar of oil become empty, according to the word of the LORD which He spoke through Elijah.

17 Now it came about after these things that the son of the woman, the mistress of the house, became sick; and his sickness was so severe that there was no breath left in him.

18 So she said to Elijah, "What do I have to do with you, O man of God? You have come to me to bring my iniquity to remembrance and to put my son to death!"

19 He said to her, "Give me your son." Then he took him from her bosom and carried him up to the upper room where he was living, and laid him on his own bed.

20 He called to the LORD and said, "O LORD my God, have You also brought calamity to the widow with whom I am staying, by causing her son to die?"

21 Then he stretched himself upon the

LIFE LESSONS

➤ 1 Kings 17:6 — *The ravens brought him bread and meat . . . and he would drink from the brook.*

*W*e should never question how God will provide for us. The Creator and Owner of all that exists can command the wind and waves to be still (Luke 8:24) and ravens to bring us food. Surely, there is nothing we'll ever need that He cannot provide.

➤ 1 Kings 17:17 — *His sickness was so severe that there was no breath left in him.*

*T*ragedy comes into the life of the faithful, just as it does to the lives of the ungodly. But for obedient believers, God takes everything—even heartbreaking situations—and uses them for His glory (Rom. 8:28).

child three times, and called to the LORD and said, "O LORD my God, I pray You, let this child's life return to him."

22 The LORD heard the voice of Elijah, and the life of the child returned to him and he revived.

23 Elijah took the child and brought him down from the upper room into the house and gave him to his mother; and Elijah said, "See, your son is alive."

24 Then the woman said to Elijah, "Now I know that you are a man of God and that the word of the LORD in your mouth is truth."

18 NOW it happened *after* many days that the word of the LORD came to Elijah in the third year, saying, "Go, show yourself to Ahab, and I will send rain on the face of the earth."

2 So Elijah went to show himself to Ahab. Now the famine *was* severe in Samaria.

3 Ahab called Obadiah who *was* over the household. (Now Obadiah feared the LORD greatly;

4 for when Jezebel destroyed the prophets of the LORD, Obadiah took a hundred prophets and hid them by fifties in a cave, and provided them with bread and water.)

5 Then Ahab said to Obadiah, "Go through the land to all the springs of water and to all the valleys; perhaps we will find grass and keep the horses and mules alive, and not have to kill some of the cattle."

6 So they divided the land between them to survey it; Ahab went one way by himself and Obadiah went another way by himself.

7 Now as Obadiah was on the way, behold, Elijah met him, and he recognized him and fell on his face and said, "Is this you, Elijah my master?"

8 He said to him, "It is I. Go, say to your master, 'Behold, Elijah *is here.*'"

9 He said, "What sin have I committed, that you are giving your servant into the hand of Ahab to put me to death?

10 "As the LORD your God lives, there is no nation or kingdom where my master has not sent to search for you; and when they said, 'He is not *here,*' he made the kingdom or nation swear that they could not find you.

11 "And now you are saying, 'Go, say to your master, "Behold, Elijah *is here.*"'

12 "It will come about when I leave you that the Spirit of the LORD will carry you where I do not know; so when I come and tell Ahab and he cannot find you, he will kill me, although I your servant have feared the LORD from my youth.

13 "Has it not been told to my master what I did when Jezebel killed the prophets of the LORD, that I hid a hundred prophets of the LORD by fifties in a cave, and provided them with bread and water?

14 "And now you are saying, 'Go, say to your master, "Behold, Elijah *is here*"'; he will then kill me."

15 Elijah said, "As the LORD of hosts lives, before whom I stand, I will surely show myself to him today."

16 So Obadiah went to meet Ahab and told him; and Ahab went to meet Elijah.

17 When Ahab saw Elijah, Ahab said to him, "Is this you, you troubler of Israel?"

18 He said, "I have not troubled Israel, but you and your father's house *have,* because you have forsaken the commandments of the LORD and you have followed the Baals.

19 "Now then send *and* gather to me all Israel at Mount Carmel, *together* with 450 prophets of Baal and 400 prophets of the Asherah, who eat at Jezebel's table."

20 So Ahab sent *a message* among all the sons of Israel and brought the prophets together at Mount Carmel.

21 Elijah came near to all the people

LIFE LESSONS

1 Kings 18:3 — *Ahab called Obadiah who was over the household. (Now Obadiah feared the LORD greatly.)*

*G*od often puts a godly man in the service of a wicked man, not to frustrate or aggravate him, but to provide a unique platform from which to rescue and bless His people (1 Kin. 18:4, 13).

---

1 Kings 18:21 — *"How long will you hesitate between two opinions? If the LORD is God, follow Him."*

*A*t some point, we have to make up our minds: Will we serve God or not? Do we believe He is who He claims to be or not? We have to take a stand and move on from there. No one can "hesitate between two opinions" forever.

How to Pray with Authority

1 KINGS 18:20–40

*T*he prophet Elijah is an amazing example of what can happen when believers pray with authority. When we come confidently to God, asking Him to work in ways that will bring glory to Himself, He is moved to action. When the people of Israel and the prophets of Baal gathered at Mt. Carmel for a "showdown," Elijah confidently prayed: "O LORD, the God of Abraham, Isaac and Israel, today let it be known that You are God in Israel and that I am Your servant and I have done all these things at Your word. Answer me, O LORD, answer me, that this people may know that You, O LORD, are God, and that You have turned their heart back again" (1 Kin. 18:36, 37).

When Elijah finished his prayer, God sent fire from heaven. This fire consumed the sacrifice, as well as the wood, stones, dust, and all the water in the trench. When the people saw it, they fell on their faces and said, "The LORD, He is God; the LORD, He is God" (v. 39).

Notice how Elijah addressed the situation: he didn't pray in secret, off in some corner where no one could see or hear him. He prayed openly and publicly. There was nothing tricky or shady about what he did; there was no doubt about what he said.

God tells us to come boldly into His presence. He grants us the privilege to come before Him with authority because of our position in Christ Jesus. We are to be bold in our faith that God will do what He desires to do and what He says He will do.

The New Testament tells us, "We do not have a high priest who cannot sympathize with our weaknesses, but One who has been tempted in all things as *we are, yet* without sin. Therefore let us draw near with confidence to the throne of grace, so that we may receive mercy and find grace to help in time of need" (Heb. 4:15, 16), and, "Let us draw near with a sincere heart in full assurance of faith" (Heb. 10:22). We have God's invitation. Will we accept?

---

and said, "How long *will* you hesitate between two opinions? If the LORD is God, follow Him; but if Baal, follow him." But the people did not answer him a word.
22 Then Elijah said to the people, "I alone am left a prophet of the LORD, but Baal's prophets are 450 men.
23 "Now let them give us two oxen; and let them choose one ox for themselves and cut it up, and place it on the wood, but put no fire *under it;* and I will prepare the other ox and lay it on the wood, and I will not put a fire *under it.*
24 "Then you call on the name of your god, and I will call on the name of the LORD, and the God who answers by fire, He is God." And all the people said, "That is a good idea."
25 So Elijah said to the prophets of Baal, "Choose one ox for yourselves and prepare it first for you are many, and call on the name of your god, but put no fire *under it.*"
26 Then they took the ox which was given them and they prepared it and called on the name of Baal from morning until noon saying, "O Baal, answer us." But there was no voice and no one answered. And they leaped about the altar which they made.

27 It came about at noon, that Elijah mocked them and said, "Call out with a loud voice, for he is a god; either he is occupied or gone aside, or is on a journey, or perhaps he is asleep and needs to be awakened."
28 So they cried with a loud voice and cut themselves according to their custom with swords and lances until the blood gushed out on them.
29 When midday was past, they raved until the time of the offering of the *evening* sacrifice; but there was no voice, no one answered, and no one paid attention.
30 Then Elijah said to all the people, "Come near to me." So all the people came near to him. And he repaired the altar of the LORD which had been torn down.
31 Elijah took twelve stones according to the number of the tribes of the sons of Jacob, to whom the word of the LORD had come, saying, "Israel shall be your name."
32 So with the stones he built an altar in the name of the LORD, and he made a trench around the altar, large enough to hold two measures of seed.
33 Then he arranged the wood and cut the ox in pieces and laid *it* on the wood.

34 And he said, "Fill four pitchers with water and pour *it* on the burnt offering and on the wood." And he said, "Do it a second time," and they did it a second time. And he said, "Do it a third time," and they did it a third time.

35 The water flowed around the altar and he also filled the trench with water.

36 At the time of the offering of the *evening* sacrifice, Elijah the prophet came near and said, "O LORD, the God of Abraham, Isaac and Israel, today let it be known that You are God in Israel and that I am Your servant and I have done all these things at Your word.

37 "Answer me, O LORD, answer me, that this people may know that You, O LORD, are God, and *that* You have turned their heart back again."

38 Then the fire of the LORD fell and consumed the burnt offering and the wood and the stones and the dust, and licked up the water that was in the trench.

39 When all the people saw it, they fell on their faces; and they said, "The LORD, He is God; the LORD, He is God."

40 Then Elijah said to them, "Seize the prophets of Baal; do not let one of them escape." So they seized them; and Elijah brought them down to the brook Kishon, and slew them there.

41 Now Elijah said to Ahab, "Go up, eat and drink; for there is the sound of the roar of a *heavy* shower."

42 So Ahab went up to eat and drink. But Elijah went up to the top of Carmel; and he crouched down on the earth and put his face between his knees.

43 He said to his servant, "Go up now, look toward the sea." So he went up and looked and said, "There is nothing." And he said, "Go back" seven times.

44 It came about at the seventh *time*, that he said, "Behold, a cloud as small as a man's hand is coming up from the sea." And he said, "Go up, say to Ahab, 'Prepare *your chariot* and go down, so that the *heavy* shower does not stop you.'"

45 In a little while the sky grew black with clouds and wind, and there was a heavy shower. And Ahab rode and went to Jezreel.

46 Then the hand of the LORD was on Elijah, and he girded up his loins and outran Ahab to Jezreel.

Psalm 69:29–36

29 But I am afflicted and in pain;
May Your salvation, O God, set me *securely* on high.

30 I will praise the name of God with song
And magnify Him with thanksgiving.

31 And it will please the LORD better than an ox
Or a young bull with horns and hoofs.

32 The humble have seen *it and* are glad;
You who seek God, let your heart revive.

33 For the LORD hears the needy
And does not despise His *who are* prisoners.

34 Let heaven and earth praise Him,
The seas and everything that moves in them.

35 For God will save Zion and build the cities of Judah,
That they may dwell there and possess it.

36 The descendants of His servants will inherit it,
And those who love His name will dwell in it.

Proverbs 17:27, 28

27 He who restrains his words has knowledge,
And he who has a cool spirit is a man of understanding.

28 Even a fool, when he keeps silent, is considered wise;
When he closes his lips, he is *considered* prudent.

LIFE LESSONS

➤ Proverbs 17:28 — *Even a fool, when he keeps silent, is considered wise.*

There are times when we must speak up (Esth. 4:14; Acts 18:9), but there are vastly more times when we should keep silent. We must listen to the Lord's instruction and engage our minds before we attempt to open our mouths.

John 13:21–38

21 When Jesus had said this, He became troubled in spirit, and testified and said, "Truly, truly, I say to you, that one of you will betray Me."
22 The disciples *began* looking at one another, at a loss *to know* of which one He was speaking.
23 There was reclining on Jesus' bosom one of His disciples, whom Jesus loved.
24 So Simon Peter *gestured to him, and *said to him, "Tell *us* who it is of whom He is speaking."
25 He, leaning back thus on Jesus' bosom, *said to Him, "Lord, who is it?"
26 Jesus then *answered, "That is the one for whom I shall dip the morsel and give it to him." So when He had dipped the morsel, He *took and *gave it to Judas, *the son* of Simon Iscariot.
27 After the morsel, Satan then entered into him. Therefore Jesus *said to him, "What you do, do quickly."
28 Now no one of those reclining *at the table* knew for what purpose He had said this to him.
29 For some were supposing, because Judas had the money box, that Jesus was saying to him, "Buy the things we have need of for the feast"; or else, that he should give something to the poor.
30 So after receiving the morsel he went out immediately; and it was night.
31 Therefore when he had gone out, Jesus *said, "Now is the Son of Man glorified, and God is glorified in Him;

32 if God is glorified in Him, God will also glorify Him in Himself, and will glorify Him immediately.
33 "Little children, I am with you a little while longer. You will seek Me; and as I said to the Jews, now I also say to you, 'Where I am going, you cannot come.'
34 "A new commandment I give to you, that you love one another, even as I have loved you, that you also love one another.
35 "By this all men will know that you are My disciples, if you have love for one another."
36 Simon Peter *said to Him, "Lord, where are You going?" Jesus answered, "Where I go, you cannot follow Me now; but you will follow later."
37 Peter *said to Him, "Lord, why can I not follow You right now? I will lay down my life for You."
38 Jesus *answered, "Will you lay down your life for Me? Truly, truly, I say to you, a rooster will not crow until you deny Me three times.

1 Kings 19:1—20:43

19 NOW Ahab told Jezebel all that Elijah had done, and how he had killed all the prophets with the sword.
2 Then Jezebel sent a messenger to Elijah, saying, "So may the gods do to me and even more, if I do not make your life as the life of one of them by tomorrow about this time."
3 And he was afraid and arose and ran

for his life and came to Beersheba, which belongs to Judah, and left his servant there.

4   But he himself went a day's journey into the wilderness, and came and sat down under a juniper tree; and he requested for himself that he might die, and said, "It is enough; now, O LORD, take my life, for I am not better than my fathers."

5   He lay down and slept under a juniper tree; and behold, there was an angel touching him, and he said to him, "Arise, eat."

6   Then he looked and behold, there was at his head a bread cake *baked on* hot stones, and a jar of water. So he ate and drank and lay down again.

7   The angel of the LORD came again a second time and touched him and said, "Arise, eat, because the journey is too great for you."

8   So he arose and ate and drank, and went in the strength of that food forty days and forty nights to Horeb, the mountain of God.

9   Then he came there to a cave and lodged there; and behold, the word of the LORD *came* to him, and He said to him, "What are you doing here, Elijah?"

10   He said, "I have been very zealous for the LORD, the God of hosts; for the sons of Israel have forsaken Your covenant, torn down Your altars and killed Your prophets with the sword. And I alone am left; and they seek my life, to take it away."

11   So He said, "Go forth and stand on the mountain before the LORD." And behold, the LORD was passing by! And a great and strong wind was rending the mountains and breaking in pieces the rocks before the LORD; *but* the LORD *was* not in the wind. And after the wind an earthquake, *but* the LORD *was* not in the earthquake.

12   After the earthquake a fire, *but* the LORD *was* not in the fire; and after the fire a sound of a gentle blowing.

13   When Elijah heard *it*, he wrapped his face in his mantle and went out and stood in the entrance of the cave. And behold, a voice *came* to him and said, "What are you doing here, Elijah?"

14   Then he said, "I have been very zealous for the LORD, the God of hosts; for

---

ANSWERS TO LIFE'S QUESTIONS

How can I develop and maintain an attitude of active listening before the Lord?

1 KINGS 19:11–13

*M*any people seem uncomfortable with silence, especially if they are alone. In silence, however, we are able to hear the "sound of gentle blowing" (1 Kin. 19:12)—the voice of the Lord. Certainly the prophet Elijah knew this. After receiving a death threat from Queen Jezebel, Elijah escaped to an isolated desert area. There in a cave, he heard the Lord say to him:

" 'Go forth and stand on the mountain before the LORD.' And behold, the LORD was passing by! And a great and strong wind was rending the mountains and breaking in pieces the rocks before the LORD; but the LORD was not in the wind. And after the wind an earthquake, but the LORD was not in the earthquake. After the earthquake a fire, but the LORD was not in the fire; and after the fire a sound of a gentle blowing. When Elijah heard it, he wrapped his face in his mantle and went out and stood in the entrance of the cave. And behold, a voice came to him and said, 'What are you doing here, Elijah?' " (1 Kin. 19:11–13).

Quietness is essential to listening. If we are too busy to sit in silence in God's presence; if we are preoccupied with thoughts or concerns about the day; if we have filled our minds for hour upon hour with carnal interference and aimless chatter—then we are going to have difficulty listening for His still, small voice.

At some point during the day, be still before the Lord in prayer. You may find that late night or early morning is a good time of solitude and quiet for you. A noonday walk in the park may be a time when you can quiet your soul before the Lord. Ask the Lord to reveal to you a time and a place where you might turn off the cares and worries of the world for a few moments and listen to Him.

So often we spend our prayer time talking to the Lord without spending any time simply waiting in silence to see what He has to say to us. Take time to intentionally sit or kneel in silence before the Lord. Empty your mind of all other thoughts. Concentrate on His Word and His presence with you. Ask Him to speak to you.

the sons of Israel have forsaken Your covenant, torn down Your altars and killed Your prophets with the sword. And I alone am left; and they seek my life, to take it away."

15 The LORD said to him, "Go, return on your way to the wilderness of Damascus, and when you have arrived, you shall anoint Hazael king over Aram;

16 and Jehu the son of Nimshi you shall anoint king over Israel; and Elisha the son of Shaphat of Abel-meholah you shall anoint as prophet in your place.

17 "It shall come about, the one who escapes from the sword of Hazael, Jehu shall put to death, and the one who escapes from the sword of Jehu, Elisha shall put to death.

18 "Yet I will leave 7,000 in Israel, all the knees that have not bowed to Baal and every mouth that has not kissed him."

19 So he departed from there and found Elisha the son of Shaphat, while he was plowing with twelve pairs of oxen before him, and he with the twelfth. And Elijah passed over to him and threw his mantle on him.

20 He left the oxen and ran after Elijah and said, "Please let me kiss my father and my mother, then I will follow you." And he said to him, "Go back again, for what have I done to you?"

21 So he returned from following him, and took the pair of oxen and sacrificed them and boiled their flesh with the implements of the oxen, and gave it to the people and they ate. Then he arose and followed Elijah and ministered to him.

20 NOW Ben-hadad king of Aram gathered all his army, and there *were* thirty-two kings with him, and

---

LIFE LESSONS

➤ **1 Kings 19:18 — "Yet I will leave 7,000 in Israel, all the knees that have not bowed to Baal."**

*E*ven in the worst of times, God will not leave Himself without a remnant as a witness. When we feel isolated and all alone, we aren't; the Lord is at work in hearts that we may not even know about. Therefore, we should eagerly watch for His activity in other people's lives.

---

horses and chariots. And he went up and besieged Samaria and fought against it.

2 Then he sent messengers to the city to Ahab king of Israel and said to him, "Thus says Ben-hadad,

3 'Your silver and your gold are mine; your most beautiful wives and children are also mine.'"

4 The king of Israel replied, "It is according to your word, my lord, O king; I am yours, and all that I have."

5 Then the messengers returned and said, "Thus says Ben-hadad, 'Surely, I sent to you saying, "You shall give me your silver and your gold and your wives and your children,"

6 but about this time tomorrow I will send my servants to you, and they will search your house and the houses of your servants; and whatever is desirable in your eyes, they will take in their hand and carry away.'"

7 Then the king of Israel called all the elders of the land and said, "Please observe and see how this man is looking for trouble; for he sent to me for my wives and my children and my silver and my gold, and I did not refuse him."

8 All the elders and all the people said to him, "Do not listen or consent."

9 So he said to the messengers of Ben-hadad, "Tell my lord the king, 'All that you sent for to your servant at the first I will do, but this thing I cannot do.'" And the messengers departed and brought him word again.

10 Ben-hadad sent to him and said, "May the gods do so to me and more also, if the dust of Samaria will suffice for handfuls for all the people who follow me."

11 Then the king of Israel replied, "Tell *him,* 'Let not him who girds on *his armor* boast like him who takes *it* off.'"

12 When *Ben-hadad* heard this message, as he was drinking with the kings in the temporary shelters, he said to his servants, "Station *yourselves.*" So they stationed *themselves* against the city.

13 Now behold, a prophet approached Ahab king of Israel and said, "Thus says the LORD, 'Have you seen all this great multitude? Behold, I will deliver them into your hand today, and you shall know that I am the LORD.'"

14 Ahab said, "By whom?" So he said, "Thus says the LORD, 'By the young men of the rulers of the provinces.'" Then he said, "Who shall begin the battle?" And he answered, "You."

15 Then he mustered the young men of the rulers of the provinces, and there were 232; and after them he mustered all the people, *even* all the sons of Israel, 7,000.

16 They went out at noon, while Benhadad was drinking himself drunk in the temporary shelters with the thirty-two kings who helped him.

17 The young men of the rulers of the provinces went out first; and Ben-hadad sent out and they told him, saying, "Men have come out from Samaria."

18 Then he said, "If they have come out for peace, take them alive; or if they have come out for war, take them alive."

19 So these went out from the city, the young men of the rulers of the provinces, and the army which followed them.

20 They killed each his man; and the Arameans fled and Israel pursued them, and Ben-hadad king of Aram escaped on a horse with horsemen.

21 The king of Israel went out and struck the horses and chariots, and killed the Arameans with a great slaughter.

22 Then the prophet came near to the king of Israel and said to him, "Go, strengthen yourself and observe and see what you have to do; for at the turn of the year the king of Aram will come up against you."

23 Now the servants of the king of Aram said to him, "Their gods are gods of the mountains, therefore they were stronger than we; but rather let us fight against them in the plain, *and* surely we will be stronger than they.

24 "Do this thing: remove the kings, each from his place, and put captains in their place,

25 and muster an army like the army that you have lost, horse for horse, and chariot for chariot. Then we will fight against them in the plain, and surely we will be stronger than they." And he listened to their voice and did so.

26 At the turn of the year, Ben-hadad mustered the Arameans and went up to Aphek to fight against Israel.

27 The sons of Israel were mustered and were provisioned and went to meet them; and the sons of Israel camped before them like two little flocks of goats, but the Arameans filled the country.

28 Then a man of God came near and spoke to the king of Israel and said, "Thus says the LORD, 'Because the Arameans have said, "The LORD is a god of *the* mountains, but He is not a god of *the* valleys," therefore I will give all this great multitude into your hand, and you shall know that I am the LORD.'"

29 So they camped one over against the other seven days. And on the seventh day the battle was joined, and the sons of Israel killed *of* the Arameans 100,000 foot soldiers in one day.

30 But the rest fled to Aphek into the city, and the wall fell on 27,000 men who were left. And Ben-hadad fled and came into the city into an inner chamber.

31 His servants said to him, "Behold now, we have heard that the kings of the house of Israel are merciful kings, please let us put sackcloth on our loins and ropes on our heads, and go out to the king of Israel; perhaps he will save your life."

32 So they girded sackcloth on their loins and *put* ropes on their heads, and came to the king of Israel and said, "Your servant Ben-hadad says, 'Please let me live.'" And he said, "Is he still alive? He is my brother."

33 Now the men took this as an omen, and quickly catching his word said, "Your brother Ben-hadad." Then he said, "Go, bring him." Then Ben-hadad came out to him, and he took him up into the chariot.

34 *Ben-hadad* said to him, "The cities which my father took from your father I will restore, and you shall make streets for yourself in Damascus, as my father made in Samaria." *Ahab said,* "And I will let you go with this covenant." So he made a covenant with him and let him go.

35 Now a certain man of the sons of the prophets said to another by the word of the LORD, "Please strike me." But the man refused to strike him.

36 Then he said to him, "Because you have not listened to the voice of the LORD, behold, as soon as you have departed from me, a lion will kill you." And as soon as he had departed from him a lion found him and killed him.

37 Then he found another man and

said, "Please strike me." And the man struck him, wounding him.

38 So the prophet departed and waited for the king by the way, and disguised himself with a bandage over his eyes.

39 As the king passed by, he cried to the king and said, "Your servant went out into the midst of the battle; and behold, a man turned aside and brought a man to me and said, 'Guard this man; if for any reason he is missing, then your life shall be for his life, or else you shall pay a talent of silver.'

40 "While your servant was busy here and there, he was gone." And the king of Israel said to him, "So shall your judgment be; you yourself have decided it."

41 Then he hastily took the bandage away from his eyes, and the king of Israel recognized him that he was of the prophets.

42 He said to him, "Thus says the LORD, 'Because you have let go out of your hand the man whom I had devoted to destruction, therefore your life shall go for his life, and your people for his people.'"

43 So the king of Israel went to his house sullen and vexed, and came to Samaria.

Psalm 70:1–5

For the choir director. A Psalm of David; for a memorial.

70 O GOD, hasten to deliver me;
O LORD, hasten to my help!

2 Let those be ashamed and humiliated
Who seek my life;
Let those be turned back and dishonored
Who delight in my hurt.

3 Let those be turned back because of their shame
Who say, "Aha, aha!"

4 Let all who seek You rejoice and be glad in You;
And let those who love Your salvation say continually,
"Let God be magnified."

5 But I am afflicted and needy;
Hasten to me, O God!
You are my help and my deliverer;
O LORD, do not delay.

Proverbs 18:1, 2

18 HE who separates himself seeks his own desire,
He quarrels against all sound wisdom.

2 A fool does not delight in understanding,
But only in revealing his own mind.

John 14:1–31

14 "DO not let your heart be troubled; believe in God, believe also in Me.

2 "In My Father's house are many dwelling places; if it were not so, I would have told you; for I go to prepare a place for you.

3 "If I go and prepare a place for you, I will come again and receive you to Myself, that where I am, there you may be also.

4 "And you know the way where I am going."

5 Thomas *said to Him, "Lord, we do not know where You are going, how do we know the way?"

6 Jesus *said to him, "I am the way, and the truth, and the life; no one comes to the Father but through Me.

7 "If you had known Me, you would have known My Father also; from now on you know Him, and have seen Him."

8 Philip *said to Him, "Lord, show us the Father, and it is enough for us."

9 Jesus *said to him, "Have I been so long with you, and yet you have not come to know Me, Philip? He who has seen Me has seen the Father; how can you say, 'Show us the Father'?

10 "Do you not believe that I am in the Father, and the Father is in Me? The words that I say to you I do not speak on

LIFE LESSONS

➤ **John 14:6 — "I am the way, and the truth, and the life; no one comes to the Father but through Me."**

The truth is very narrow—the only way someone can come to the Father is through Jesus, who lived a completely sinless life in thought, word, and deed.

LIFE LESSONS

➤ John 14:9 — *"He who has seen Me has seen the Father."*

*I*n Jesus, we have more than just a representation of theological attributes. He is God in the flesh, and when we gaze upon Him, we behold our Lord.

My own initiative, but the Father abiding in Me does His works.

11 "Believe Me that I am in the Father and the Father is in Me; otherwise believe because of the works themselves.

12 "Truly, truly, I say to you, he who believes in Me, the works that I do, he will do also; and greater *works* than these he will do; because I go to the Father.

13 "Whatever you ask in My name, that will I do, so that the Father may be glorified in the Son.

14 "If you ask Me anything in My name, I will do *it*.

15 "If you love Me, you will keep My commandments.

16 "I will ask the Father, and He will give you another Helper, that He may be with you forever;

17 *that is* the Spirit of truth, whom the world cannot receive, because it does not see Him or know Him, *but* you know Him because He abides with you and will be in you.

18 "I will not leave you as orphans; I will come to you.

19 "After a little while the world will no longer see Me, but you *will* see Me; because I live, you will live also.

20 "In that day you will know that I am in My Father, and you in Me, and I in you.

21 "He who has My commandments and keeps them is the one who loves Me; and he who loves Me will be loved by My Father, and I will love him and will disclose Myself to him."

22 Judas (not Iscariot) *said to Him, "Lord, what then has happened that You are going to disclose Yourself to us and not to the world?"

➤ 23 Jesus answered and said to him, "If anyone loves Me, he will keep My word; and My Father will love him, and We will come to him and make Our abode with him.

24 "He who does not love Me does not keep My words; and the word which you hear is not Mine, but the Father's who sent Me.

25 "These things I have spoken to you while abiding with you.

26 "But the Helper, the Holy Spirit, whom the Father will send in My name, He will teach you all things, and bring to your remembrance all that I said to you.

27 "Peace I leave with you; My peace I give to you; not as the world gives do I give to you. Do not let your heart be troubled, nor let it be fearful.

28 "You heard that I said to you, 'I go away, and I will come to you.' If you loved Me, you would have rejoiced because I go to the Father, for the Father is greater than I.

29 "Now I have told you before it happens, so that when it happens, you may believe.

30 "I will not speak much more with you, for the ruler of the world is coming, and he has nothing in Me;

31 but so that the world may know that I love the Father, I do exactly as the Father commanded Me. Get up, let us go from here.

LIFE LESSONS

➤ John 14:23 — *"If anyone loves Me, he will keep My word; and . . . We will . . . make Our abode with him."*

*W*e love and obey Jesus by depending on His power to enable us to do what He compels us to do. An intimate relationship with Him leads to willing, devoted, joyful obedience, and the deeper our intimacy with Him, the greater the impact our lives will have for His kingdom.

➤ John 14:27 — *"Peace I leave with you; My peace I give to you; not as the world gives do I give to you. Do not let your heart be troubled, nor let it be fearful."*

*T*he peace of Jesus "surpasses all comprehension" (Phil. 4:7) because its source is Christ Himself. His peace keeps us from fear and worry because it brings us straight to Him and teaches us to depend on Him in everything we face. We know that no matter what our circumstances, the Lord Jesus will sustain us, strengthen us, and enable us to walk through it victoriously.

21 NOW it came about after these things that Naboth the Jezreelite had a vineyard which *was* in Jezreel beside the palace of Ahab king of Samaria.
2 Ahab spoke to Naboth, saying, "Give me your vineyard, that I may have it for a vegetable garden because it is close beside my house, and I will give you a better vineyard than it in its place; if you like, I will give you the price of it in money."
3 But Naboth said to Ahab, "The LORD forbid me that I should give you the inheritance of my fathers."
4 So Ahab came into his house sullen and vexed because of the word which Naboth the Jezreelite had spoken to him; for he said, "I will not give you the inheritance of my fathers." And he lay down on his bed and turned away his face and ate no food.
5 But Jezebel his wife came to him and said to him, "How is it that your spirit is so sullen that you are not eating food?"
6 So he said to her, "Because I spoke to Naboth the Jezreelite and said to him, 'Give me your vineyard for money; or else, if it pleases you, I will give you a vineyard in its place.' But he said, 'I will not give you my vineyard.'"
7 Jezebel his wife said to him, "Do you now reign over Israel? Arise, eat bread, and let your heart be joyful; I will give you the vineyard of Naboth the Jezreelite."
8 So she wrote letters in Ahab's name and sealed them with his seal, and sent letters to the elders and to the nobles who were living with Naboth in his city.
9 Now she wrote in the letters, saying, "Proclaim a fast and seat Naboth at the head of the people;
10 and seat two worthless men before him, and let them testify against him, saying, 'You cursed God and the king.' Then take him out and stone him to death."
11 So the men of his city, the elders and the nobles who lived in his city, did as Jezebel had sent *word* to them, just as it was written in the letters which she had sent them.
12 They proclaimed a fast and seated Naboth at the head of the people.

13 Then the two worthless men came in and sat before him; and the worthless men testified against him, even against Naboth, before the people, saying, "Naboth cursed God and the king." So they took him outside the city and stoned him to death with stones.
14 Then they sent *word* to Jezebel, saying, "Naboth has been stoned and is dead."
15 When Jezebel heard that Naboth had been stoned and was dead, Jezebel said to Ahab, "Arise, take possession of the vineyard of Naboth, the Jezreelite, which he refused to give you for money; for Naboth is not alive, but dead."
16 When Ahab heard that Naboth was dead, Ahab arose to go down to the vineyard of Naboth the Jezreelite, to take possession of it.
17 Then the word of the LORD came to Elijah the Tishbite, saying,
18 "Arise, go down to meet Ahab king of Israel, who is in Samaria; behold, he is in the vineyard of Naboth where he has gone down to take possession of it.
19 "You shall speak to him, saying, 'Thus says the LORD, "Have you murdered and also taken possession?"' And you shall speak to him, saying, 'Thus says the LORD, "In the place where the dogs licked up the blood of Naboth the dogs will lick up your blood, even yours."'"
20 Ahab said to Elijah, "Have you found me, O my enemy?" And he answered, "I have found *you*, because you have sold yourself to do evil in the sight of the LORD.
21 "Behold, I will bring evil upon you, and will utterly sweep you away, and will cut off from Ahab every male, both bond and free in Israel;
22 and I will make your house like the house of Jeroboam the son of Nebat, and like the house of Baasha the son of Ahijah, because of the provocation with

---

LIFE LESSONS

➤ 1 Kings 21:14 — *"Naboth . . . is dead."*

*N*aboth lost his life for obeying God, while Jezebel got her way by disobeying Him (Ex. 23:7). Yet this life is not all there is, and the Lord promises to set all accounts right (Rom. 2:6–8).

which you have provoked *Me* to anger, and *because* you have made Israel sin.

23 "Of Jezebel also has the LORD spoken, saying, 'The dogs will eat Jezebel in the district of Jezreel.'

24 "The one belonging to Ahab, who dies in the city, the dogs will eat, and the one who dies in the field the birds of heaven will eat."

➤ 25 Surely there was no one like Ahab who sold himself to do evil in the sight of the LORD, because Jezebel his wife incited him.

26 He acted very abominably in following idols, according to all that the Amorites had done, whom the LORD cast out before the sons of Israel.

27 It came about when Ahab heard these words, that he tore his clothes and put on sackcloth and fasted, and he lay in sackcloth and went about despondently.

28 Then the word of the LORD came to Elijah the Tishbite, saying,

29 "Do you see how Ahab has humbled himself before Me? Because he has humbled himself before Me, I will not bring the evil in his days, *but* I will bring the evil upon his house in his son's days."

22 THREE years passed without war between Aram and Israel.

2 In the third year Jehoshaphat the king of Judah came down to the king of Israel.

3 Now the king of Israel said to his servants, "Do you know that Ramoth-gilead belongs to us, and we are still doing nothing to take it out of the hand of the king of Aram?"

4 And he said to Jehoshaphat, "Will you go with me to battle at Ramoth-gilead?" And Jehoshaphat said to the king of Israel, "I am as you are, my people as your people, my horses as your horses."

5 Moreover, Jehoshaphat said to the king of Israel, "Please inquire first for the word of the LORD."

6 Then the king of Israel gathered the prophets together, about four hundred men, and said to them, "Shall I go against Ramoth-gilead to battle or shall I refrain?" And they said, "Go up, for the Lord will give *it* into the hand of the king."

7 But Jehoshaphat said, "Is there not yet a prophet of the LORD here that we may inquire of him?"

8 The king of Israel said to Jehoshaphat, "There is yet one man by whom we may inquire of the LORD, but I hate him, because he does not prophesy good concerning me, but evil. *He is* Micaiah son of Imlah." But Jehoshaphat said, "Let not the king say so."

9 Then the king of Israel called an officer and said, "Bring quickly Micaiah son of Imlah."

10 Now the king of Israel and Jehoshaphat king of Judah were sitting each on his throne, arrayed in *their* robes, at the threshing floor at the entrance of the gate of Samaria; and all the prophets were prophesying before them.

11 Then Zedekiah the son of Chenaanah made horns of iron for himself and said, "Thus says the LORD, 'With these you will gore the Arameans until they are consumed.'"

12 All the prophets were prophesying thus, saying, "Go up to Ramoth-gilead and prosper, for the LORD will give *it* into the hand of the king."

13 Then the messenger who went to summon Micaiah spoke to him saying, "Behold now, the words of the prophets are uniformly favorable to the king. Please let your word be like the word of one of them, and speak favorably."

14 But Micaiah said, "As the LORD lives, what the LORD says to me, that I shall speak."

15 When he came to the king, the king said to him, "Micaiah, shall we go to Ramoth-gilead to battle, or shall we refrain?" And he answered him, "Go up and succeed, and the LORD will give *it* into the hand of the king."

16 Then the king said to him, "How many times must I adjure you to speak to me nothing but the truth in the name of the LORD?"

17 So he said,

LIFE LESSONS

➤ **1 Kings 21:25 — *Jezebel his wife incited him.***

*T*ime after time in the Bible we see how a poor choice of mate leads to physical, spiritual, and moral ruin. What kind of king might Ahab have become had he married a godly woman? We'll never know.

"I saw all Israel
Scattered on the mountains,
Like sheep which have no shepherd.
And the LORD said, 'These have no
    master.
Let each of them return to his house
    in peace.'"
18 Then the king of Israel said to Jehoshaphat, "Did I not tell you that he
would not prophesy good concerning
me, but evil?"
19 Micaiah said, "Therefore, hear the
word of the LORD. I saw the LORD sitting
on His throne, and all the host of heaven
standing by Him on His right and on His
left.
20 "The LORD said, 'Who will entice
Ahab to go up and fall at Ramoth-
gilead?' And one said this while another
said that.
21 "Then a spirit came forward and
stood before the LORD and said, 'I will
entice him.'
22 "The LORD said to him, 'How?' And
he said, 'I will go out and be a deceiving
spirit in the mouth of all his prophets.'
Then He said, 'You are to entice *him* and
also prevail. Go and do so.'
23 "Now therefore, behold, the LORD has
put a deceiving spirit in the mouth of all
these your prophets; and the LORD has
proclaimed disaster against you."
24 Then Zedekiah the son of Chenaanah came near and struck Micaiah on
the cheek and said, "How did the Spirit of
the LORD pass from me to speak to you?"
25 Micaiah said, "Behold, you shall see
on that day when you enter an inner
room to hide yourself."
26 Then the king of Israel said, "Take
Micaiah and return him to Amon the
governor of the city and to Joash the
king's son;
27 and say, 'Thus says the king, "Put this
man in prison and feed him sparingly with
bread and water until I return safely."'"
28 Micaiah said, "If you indeed return
safely the LORD has not spoken by me."
And he said, "Listen, all you people."
29 So the king of Israel and Jehoshaphat
king of Judah went up against Ramoth-
gilead.
30 The king of Israel said to Jehoshaphat, "I will disguise myself and
go into the battle, but you put on your
robes." So the king of Israel disguised
himself and went into the battle.

31 Now the king of Aram had commanded the thirty-two captains of his
chariots, saying, "Do not fight with small
or great, but with the king of Israel
alone."
32 So when the captains of the chariots
saw Jehoshaphat, they said, "Surely it is
the king of Israel," and they turned aside
to fight against him, and Jehoshaphat
cried out.
33 When the captains of the chariots
saw that it was not the king of Israel,
they turned back from pursuing him.
34 Now a certain man drew his bow at ◄
random and struck the king of Israel in
a joint of the armor. So he said to the
driver of his chariot, "Turn around and
take me out of the fight; for I am severely
wounded."
35 The battle raged that day, and the
king was propped up in his chariot in
front of the Arameans, and died at evening, and the blood from the wound ran
into the bottom of the chariot.
36 Then a cry passed throughout the
army close to sunset, saying, "Every man
to his city and every man to his country."
37 So the king died and was brought
to Samaria, and they buried the king in
Samaria.
38 They washed the chariot by the pool
of Samaria, and the dogs licked up his
blood (now the harlots bathed themselves *there*), according to the word of
the LORD which He spoke.
39 Now the rest of the acts of Ahab and
all that he did and the ivory house which
he built and all the cities which he built,
are they not written in the Book of the
Chronicles of the Kings of Israel?
40 So Ahab slept with his fathers, and
Ahaziah his son became king in his place.
41 Now Jehoshaphat the son of Asa became king over Judah in the fourth year
of Ahab king of Israel.
42 Jehoshaphat was thirty-five years old

LIFE LESSONS

➤ **1 Kings 22:34** — *A certain man drew
his bow at random and struck the king of
Israel in a joint of the armor.*

*G*od takes seemingly random acts and
uses them to fulfill His will and His
Word (2 Chr. 18:28-34). Only our sovereign Lord can do that!

when he became king, and he reigned twenty-five years in Jerusalem. And his mother's name was Azubah the daughter of Shilhi.

43 He walked in all the way of Asa his father; he did not turn aside from it, doing right in the sight of the LORD. However, the high places were not taken away; the people still sacrificed and burnt incense on the high places.

44 Jehoshaphat also made peace with the king of Israel.

45 Now the rest of the acts of Jehoshaphat, and his might which he showed and how he warred, are they not written in the Book of the Chronicles of the Kings of Judah?

46 The remnant of the sodomites who remained in the days of his father Asa, he expelled from the land.

47 Now there was no king in Edom; a deputy was king.

48 Jehoshaphat made ships of Tarshish to go to Ophir for gold, but they did not go for the ships were broken at Ezion-geber.

49 Then Ahaziah the son of Ahab said to Jehoshaphat, "Let my servants go with your servants in the ships." But Jehoshaphat was not willing.

50 And Jehoshaphat slept with his fathers and was buried with his fathers in the city of his father David, and Jehoram his son became king in his place.

51 Ahaziah the son of Ahab became king over Israel in Samaria in the seventeenth year of Jehoshaphat king of Judah, and he reigned two years over Israel.

52 He did evil in the sight of the LORD and walked in the way of his father and in the way of his mother and in the way of Jeroboam the son of Nebat, who caused Israel to sin.

53 So he served Baal and worshiped him and provoked the LORD God of Israel to anger, according to all that his father had done.

Psalm 71:1–8

71 IN You, O LORD, I have taken refuge;
Let me never be ashamed.

2 In Your righteousness deliver me and rescue me;
Incline Your ear to me and save me.

3 Be to me a rock of habitation to which I may continually come;
You have given commandment to save me,
For You are my rock and my fortress.

4 Rescue me, O my God, out of the hand of the wicked,
Out of the grasp of the wrongdoer and ruthless man,

5 For You are my hope;
O Lord GOD, *You are* my confidence from my youth.

6 By You I have been sustained from *my* birth;
You are He who took me from my mother's womb;
My praise is continually of You.

7 I have become a marvel to many,
For You are my strong refuge.

8 My mouth is filled with Your praise
And with Your glory all day long.

Proverbs 18:3–5

3 When a wicked man comes, contempt also comes,
And with dishonor *comes* scorn.

4 The words of a man's mouth are deep waters;
The fountain of wisdom is a bubbling brook.

5 To show partiality to the wicked is not good,
Nor to thrust aside the righteous in judgment.

John 15:1–27

15 "I AM the true vine, and My Father is the vinedresser.

LIFE LESSONS

➤ Psalm 71:5 — *For You are my hope; O Lord GOD.*

Some caution against leading children to Christ too early, but this is a mistake. If you don't teach your children to have faith in Jesus, others will convince them to trust in something else (Prov. 22:6; Matt. 19:13, 14; 2 Tim. 3:14-16).

2 "Every branch in Me that does not bear fruit, He takes away; and every *branch* that bears fruit, He prunes it so that it may bear more fruit.

3 "You are already clean because of the word which I have spoken to you.

➤ 4 "Abide in Me, and I in you. As the branch cannot bear fruit of itself unless it abides in the vine, so neither *can* you unless you abide in Me.

5 "I am the vine, you are the branches; he who abides in Me and I in him, he bears much fruit, for apart from Me you can do nothing.

6 "If anyone does not abide in Me, he is thrown away as a branch and dries up; and they gather them, and cast them into the fire and they are burned.

7 "If you abide in Me, and My words abide in you, ask whatever you wish, and it will be done for you.

✳ 8 "My Father is glorified by this, that you bear much fruit, and *so* prove to be My disciples.

9 "Just as the Father has loved Me, I have also loved you; abide in My love.

10 "If you keep My commandments, you will abide in My love; just as I have kept My Father's commandments and abide in His love.

➤ 11 "These things I have spoken to you so that My joy may be in you, and *that* your joy may be made full.

LIFE LESSONS

➤ **John 15:4 —** *"As the branch cannot bear fruit of itself unless it abides in the vine, so neither can you unless you abide in Me."*

*T*he only way we can play a significant role in the kingdom of God is to allow Jesus to live His life in and through us. While apart from Him we can do nothing, in Him we can do anything He calls us to do.

➤ **John 15:11 —** *"These things I have spoken to you so that My joy may be in you, and that your joy may be made full."*

*T*he Word of God, living and growing within us, produces lasting and increasing joy. A lack of joy in a Christian's life often can be traced to a lack of concentrated devotional time in God's Word or disobedience.

---

12 "This is My commandment, that you love one another, just as I have loved you.

13 "Greater love has no one than this, that one lay down his life for his friends.

14 "You are My friends if you do what I command you.

15 "No longer do I call you slaves, for the slave does not know what his master is doing; but I have called you friends, for all things that I have heard from My Father I have made known to you.

16 "You did not choose Me but I chose you, and appointed you that you would go and bear fruit, and *that* your fruit would remain, so that whatever you ask of the Father in My name He may give to you.

17 "This I command you, that you love one another.

18 "If the world hates you, you know that it has hated Me before *it hated* you.

19 "If you were of the world, the world would love its own; but because you are not of the world, but I chose you out of the world, because of this the world hates you.

20 "Remember the word that I said to you, 'A slave is not greater than his master.' If they persecuted Me, they will also persecute you; if they kept My word, they will keep yours also.

21 "But all these things they will do to you for My name's sake, because they do not know the One who sent Me.

22 "If I had not come and spoken to them, they would not have sin, but now they have no excuse for their sin.

23 "He who hates Me hates My Father also.

24 "If I had not done among them the works which no one else did, they would not have sin; but now they have both seen and hated Me and My Father as well.

25 "But *they have done this* to fulfill the word that is written in their Law, 'THEY HATED ME WITHOUT A CAUSE.'

26 "When the Helper comes, whom I will send to you from the Father, *that is* the Spirit of truth who proceeds from the Father, He will testify about Me,

27 and you *will* testify also, because you have been with Me from the beginning.

WHAT THE BIBLE SAYS ABOUT

The Best Friend You Will Ever Have

John 15:13

*M*any of us know the familiar hymn, "What a Friend We Have in Jesus." We all consider our Savior a great friend—but none of us have an exhaustive knowledge of the heights, depths, and breadth of His amazing friendship. Consider just a few of the elements of Jesus' loving relationship with you:
1. He has committed Himself to you as a friend for life. In fact, this commitment lasts more than an earthly lifetime; it's eternal. He will never leave you, no matter what you do. You may suffer some dashed expectations in your lifetime, but the Lord Himself will never disappoint you.
2. He remains open to you at all times. Jesus will show you as much about Himself as you desire to learn and are able to appreciate. He will never keep from you anything about Himself that you need to know.

3. He renews His loving overtures to you every day. He knows how to meet your deepest longings, and He remains sensitive to your wants as well as your needs.
Jesus is an inspiring, comforting listener who hears exactly what you say and always provides the very best for you.
What kind of friend is Jesus? John 15:13 answers the question: "Greater love has no one than this, that one lay down his life for his friends." Jesus is the kind of friend who willingly laid down His life as payment for your sins—past, present, and future. Without complaint, He bore all your sorrows and suffering while pledging never to leave you or forsake you (John 14:18). Jesus is the friend who sticks closer than a brother (Prov. 18:24), the friend who walks by your side through everything.
And because Jesus gave Himself for all people, we His followers should give ourselves completely to Him (2 Cor. 5:14, 15). "Therefore, we are ambassadors for Christ, as though God were making an appeal through us; we beg you on behalf of Christ, be reconciled to God" (2 Cor. 5:20). Who in your circle of influence needs to be reconciled to God? Who do you know that needs to find a friend in Jesus? ◈

JUNE 7

◈ 2 Kings 1:1—2:25

1 NOW Moab rebelled against Israel after the death of Ahab.
2 And Ahaziah fell through the lattice in his upper chamber which *was* in Samaria, and became ill. So he sent messengers and said to them, "Go, inquire of Baal-zebub, the god of Ekron, whether I will recover from this sickness."
3 But the angel of the LORD said to Elijah the Tishbite, "Arise, go up to meet the messengers of the king of Samaria and say to them, 'Is it because there is no God in Israel *that* you are going to inquire of Baal-zebub, the god of Ekron?'
4 "Now therefore thus says the LORD, 'You shall not come down from the bed where you have gone up, but you shall surely die.'" Then Elijah departed.
5 When the messengers returned to him he said to them, "Why have you returned?"

6 They said to him, "A man came up to meet us and said to us, 'Go, return to the king who sent you and say to him, "Thus says the LORD, 'Is it because there is no God in Israel *that* you are sending to inquire of Baal-zebub, the god of Ekron? Therefore you shall not come down from the bed where you have gone up, but shall surely die.'""
7 He said to them, "What kind of man was he who came up to meet you and spoke these words to you?"
8 They answered him, "*He was* a hairy man with a leather girdle bound about his loins." And he said, "It is Elijah the Tishbite."
9 Then *the king* sent to him a captain of fifty with his fifty. And he went up to him, and behold, he was sitting on the top of the hill. And he said to him, "O man of God, the king says, 'Come down.'"
10 Elijah replied to the captain of fifty, "If I am a man of God, let fire come down ◄

from heaven and consume you and your fifty." Then fire came down from heaven and consumed him and his fifty.

11 So he again sent to him another captain of fifty with his fifty. And he said to him, "O man of God, thus says the king, 'Come down quickly.'"

12 Elijah replied to them, "If I am a man of God, let fire come down from heaven and consume you and your fifty." Then the fire of God came down from heaven and consumed him and his fifty.

13 So he again sent the captain of a third fifty with his fifty. When the third captain of fifty went up, he came and bowed down on his knees before Elijah, and begged him and said to him, "O man of God, please let my life and the lives of these fifty servants of yours be precious in your sight.

14 "Behold fire came down from heaven and consumed the first two captains of fifty with their fifties; but now let my life be precious in your sight."

15 The angel of the LORD said to Elijah, "Go down with him; do not be afraid of him." So he arose and went down with him to the king.

16 Then he said to him, "Thus says the LORD, 'Because you have sent messengers to inquire of Baal-zebub, the god of Ekron—is it because there is no God in Israel to inquire of His word?—therefore you shall not come down from the bed where you have gone up, but shall surely die.'"

17 So Ahaziah died according to the word of the LORD which Elijah had spoken. And because he had no son, Jehoram became king in his place in the second year of Jehoram the son of Jehoshaphat, king of Judah.

18 Now the rest of the acts of Ahaziah which he did, are they not written in the Book of the Chronicles of the Kings of Israel?

2 AND it came about when the LORD was about to take up Elijah by a whirlwind to heaven, that Elijah went with Elisha from Gilgal.

2 Elijah said to Elisha, "Stay here please, for the LORD has sent me as far as Bethel." But Elisha said, "As the LORD lives and as you yourself live, I will not leave you." So they went down to Bethel.

3 Then the sons of the prophets who *were at* Bethel came out to Elisha and said to him, "Do you know that the LORD will take away your master from over you today?" And he said, "Yes, I know; be still."

4 Elijah said to him, "Elisha, please stay here, for the LORD has sent me to Jericho." But he said, "As the LORD lives, and as you yourself live, I will not leave you." So they came to Jericho.

5 The sons of the prophets who *were* at Jericho approached Elisha and said to him, "Do you know that the LORD will take away your master from over you today?" And he answered, "Yes, I know; be still."

6 Then Elijah said to him, "Please stay here, for the LORD has sent me to the Jordan." And he said, "As the LORD lives, and as you yourself live, I will not leave you." So the two of them went on.

7 Now fifty men of the sons of the prophets went and stood opposite *them* at a distance, while the two of them stood by the Jordan.

8 Elijah took his mantle and folded it together and struck the waters, and they were divided here and there, so that the two of them crossed over on dry ground.

9 When they had crossed over, Elijah ◄ said to Elisha, "Ask what I shall do for you before I am taken from you." And

Elisha said, "Please, let a double portion of your spirit be upon me."

10 He said, "You have asked a hard thing. *Nevertheless,* if you see me when I am taken from you, it shall be so for you; but if not, it shall not be *so.*"

11 As they were going along and talking, behold, *there appeared* a chariot of fire and horses of fire which separated the two of them. And Elijah went up by a whirlwind to heaven.

12 Elisha saw *it* and cried out, "My father, my father, the chariots of Israel and its horsemen!" And he saw Elijah no more. Then he took hold of his own clothes and tore them in two pieces.

13 He also took up the mantle of Elijah that fell from him and returned and stood by the bank of the Jordan.

14 He took the mantle of Elijah that fell from him and struck the waters and said, "Where is the LORD, the God of Elijah?" And when he also had struck the waters, they were divided here and there; and Elisha crossed over.

15 Now when the sons of the prophets who *were* at Jericho opposite *him* saw him, they said, "The spirit of Elijah rests on Elisha." And they came to meet him and bowed themselves to the ground before him.

16 They said to him, "Behold now, there are with your servants fifty strong men, please let them go and search for your master; perhaps the Spirit of the LORD has taken him up and cast him on some mountain or into some valley." And he said, "You shall not send."

17 But when they urged him until he was ashamed, he said, "Send." They sent therefore fifty men; and they searched three days but did not find him.

18 They returned to him while he was staying at Jericho; and he said to them, "Did I not say to you, 'Do not go'?"

19 Then the men of the city said to Elisha, "Behold now, the situation of this city is pleasant, as my lord sees; but the water is bad and the land is unfruitful."

20 He said, "Bring me a new jar, and put salt in it." So they brought *it* to him.

➤ 21 He went out to the spring of water and threw salt in it and said, "Thus says the LORD, 'I have purified these waters; there shall not be from there death or unfruitfulness any longer.'"

22 So the waters have been purified to this day, according to the word of Elisha which he spoke.

23 Then he went up from there to Bethel; and as he was going up by the way, young lads came out from the city and mocked him and said to him, "Go up, you baldhead; go up, you baldhead!"

24 When he looked behind him and saw them, he cursed them in the name of the LORD. Then two female bears came out of the woods and tore up forty-two lads of their number.

25 He went from there to Mount Carmel, and from there he returned to Samaria.

Psalm 71:9–16

9 Do not cast me off in the time of old age;
   Do not forsake me when my strength fails.

10 For my enemies have spoken against me;
   And those who watch for my life have consulted together,

11 Saying, "God has forsaken him;
   Pursue and seize him, for there is no one to deliver."

12 O God, do not be far from me;
   O my God, hasten to my help!

13 Let those who are adversaries of my soul be ashamed *and* consumed;
   Let them be covered with reproach and dishonor, who seek to injure me.

14 But as for me, I will hope continually,
   And will praise You yet more and more.

15 My mouth shall tell of Your righteousness
   And of Your salvation all day long;
   For I do not know the sum *of them.*

LIFE LESSONS

➤ **2 Kings 2:21 — *"Thus says the LORD, 'I have purified these waters.'"***

*T*he salt did not purify the water, nor did Elisha's words; it was God Himself at work. While God chooses to work through people to accomplish His purposes, He is always the One in control.

16 I will come with the mighty deeds of
the Lord GOD;
I will make mention of Your
righteousness, Yours alone.

Proverbs 18:6–8

6 A fool's lips bring strife,
And his mouth calls for blows.
7 A fool's mouth is his ruin,
And his lips are the snare of his soul.
8 The words of a whisperer are like
dainty morsels,
And they go down into the
innermost parts of the body.

John 16:1–33

16 "THESE things I have spoken to
you so that you may be kept from
stumbling.
2 "They will make you outcasts from
the synagogue, but an hour is coming for
everyone who kills you to think that he
is offering service to God.
3 "These things they will do because
they have not known the Father or Me.
4 "But these things I have spoken to
you, so that when their hour comes, you
may remember that I told you of them.
These things I did not say to you at the
beginning, because I was with you.
5 "But now I am going to Him who
sent Me; and none of you asks Me,
'Where are You going?'
6 "But because I have said these things
to you, sorrow has filled your heart.
7 "But I tell you the truth, it is to your
advantage that I go away; for if I do not
go away, the Helper will not come to you;
but if I go, I will send Him to you.
8 "And He, when He comes, will convict the world concerning sin and righteousness and judgment;
9 concerning sin, because they do not
believe in Me;
10 and concerning righteousness, because I go to the Father and you no longer see Me;
11 and concerning judgment, because
the ruler of this world has been judged.
12 "I have many more things to say to
you, but you cannot bear them now.

13 "But when He, the Spirit of truth,
comes, He will guide you into all the
truth; for He will not speak on His own
initiative, but whatever He hears, He will
speak; and He will disclose to you what
is to come.
14 "He will glorify Me, for He will take
of Mine and will disclose it to you.
15 "All things that the Father has are
Mine; therefore I said that He takes of
Mine and will disclose it to you.
16 "A little while, and you will no longer see Me; and again a little while, and
you will see Me."
17 Some of His disciples then said to
one another, "What is this thing He is
telling us, 'A little while, and you will
not see Me; and again a little while, and
you will see Me'; and, 'because I go to the
Father'?"
18 So they were saying, "What is this
that He says, 'A little while'? We do not
know what He is talking about."
19 Jesus knew that they wished to question Him, and He said to them, "Are you
deliberating together about this, that I
said, 'A little while, and you will not see
Me, and again a little while, and you will
see Me'?
20 "Truly, truly, I say to you, that you
will weep and lament, but the world will
rejoice; you will grieve, but your grief
will be turned into joy.
21 "Whenever a woman is in labor she
has pain, because her hour has come; but
when she gives birth to the child, she no
longer remembers the anguish because
of the joy that a child has been born into
the world.
22 "Therefore you too have grief now;
but I will see you again, and your heart
will rejoice, and no one will take your joy
away from you.

LIFE LESSONS

➤ **John 16:22 — "You too have grief
now; but I will see you again, and your
heart will rejoice, and no one will take
your joy away from you."**

Sorrow and happiness are both a part
of the human experience, and both
depend largely on circumstances. When
we unite ourselves to the risen Christ,
however, He gives us a joy that no obstacle, problem, or situation can take away.

WHAT THE BIBLE SAYS ABOUT ◉

How the Holy Spirit Guides Us

John 16:13

If you've ever wished you could immediately understand God's will when going through a difficult situation, you're in good company. We've all faced challenging circumstances that have confounded us—we've had no idea how to proceed, and we've longed for the Lord's guidance, help, and provision. However, as believers, we must understand the Holy Spirit indwells us the moment we accept Jesus Christ as our Savior, and He has been given to us as an everlasting promise God will never leave us nor forsake us, no matter what happens (John 14:16–18; 1 Cor. 3:16; 6:17; 2 Cor. 1:21, 22; 5:5; Eph. 1:13; 4:30; 1 John 4:2, 13).

Although you may be facing a situation that makes you feel isolated, helpless, or directionless, understand you're never alone. The Holy Spirit is with you to live the life of Christ through you—helping you face every challenge in a godly, victorious manner. John 16:13, 14 promises, "He will guide you into all the truth; for He will not speak on His own initiative, but whatever He hears, He will speak; and He will disclose to you what is to come. He will glorify Me, for He will take of Mine and will disclose it to you."

How does the Holy Spirit help and direct you? He does so in a manner that is:

Practical. The Holy Spirit warns you of perils ahead and equips you to succeed in the tasks He has assigned to you. He knows exactly how much strength, wisdom, resources, and encouragement you need for whatever is ahead.

Personal. He lives inside of you and knows you even better than you know yourself. He understands exactly what you require to grow in the likeness of Christ, and He enables you to become the person the Lord created you to be.

Available. Twenty-four hours a day, 365 days a year, the Holy Spirit is there for you. He never sleeps but is constantly working in and through you for your good.

Dependable. There's no problem you face that God can't handle. In fact, not only will the Holy Spirit help you get through your heartaches, but He will also use your burdens to teach you about the love, wisdom, and power of God.

Even when you don't know what to ask for in prayer, the Holy Spirit will intervene for you (Rom. 8:26–29). Though God's Word may not make sense to you, He will show you what it means (1 Cor. 2:12–14). If there is something within you that is hindering God's work, He will reveal it to you (John 16:8). When you feel inadequate, He bestows you with the giftedness you need to live the Christian life (1 Cor. 12:4–11). And in your greatest moments of weakness and distress, the Holy Spirit can energize, encourage, and empower you to overcome whatever afflicts you (Rom. 5:3–5).

Therefore, don't hinder the Holy Spirit—He is your Helper, and His guidance is yours for the asking. Whenever you need Him, pray, listen, follow His direction, and confidently obey His promptings because you can be sure He will never lead you astray. ◉

---

23 "In that day you will not question Me about anything. Truly, truly, I say to you, if you ask the Father for anything in My name, He will give it to you.
➤ 24 "Until now you have asked for nothing in My name; ask and you will receive, so that your joy may be made full.
25 "These things I have spoken to you in figurative language; an hour is coming when I will no longer speak to you in figurative language, but will tell you plainly of the Father.
26 "In that day you will ask in My name, and I do not say to you that I will request of the Father on your behalf;
27 for the Father Himself loves you, because you have loved Me and have believed that I came forth from the Father.
28 "I came forth from the Father and have come into the world; I am leaving the world again and going to the Father."
29 His disciples *said, "Lo, now You

LIFE LESSONS

➤ **John 16:24** — *"Until now you have asked for nothing in My name; ask and you will receive."*

To ask in Jesus' name means to connect your request with the will, plans, purpose, and sovereignty.

are speaking plainly and are not using a figure of speech.

30 "Now we know that You know all things, and have no need for anyone to question You; by this we believe that You came from God."

31 Jesus answered them, "Do you now believe?

32 "Behold, an hour is coming, and has *already* come, for you to be scattered, each to his own *home,* and to leave Me alone; and *yet* I am not alone, because the Father is with Me.

➤ 33 "These things I have spoken to you, so that in Me you may have peace. In the world you have tribulation, but take courage; I have overcome the world."

2 Kings 3:1—4:44

3 NOW Jehoram the son of Ahab became king over Israel at Samaria in the eighteenth year of Jehoshaphat king of Judah, and reigned twelve years.

2 He did evil in the sight of the LORD, though not like his father and his mother; for he put away the *sacred* pillar of Baal which his father had made.

3 Nevertheless, he clung to the sins of Jeroboam the son of Nebat, which he made Israel sin; he did not depart from them.

4 Now Mesha king of Moab was a sheep breeder, and used to pay the king of Israel 100,000 lambs and the wool of 100,000 rams.

5 But when Ahab died, the king of Moab rebelled against the king of Israel.

6 And King Jehoram went out of Samaria at that time and mustered all Israel.

7 Then he went and sent *word* to Jehoshaphat the king of Judah, saying, "The king of Moab has rebelled against me. Will you go with me to fight against Moab?" And he said, "I will go up; I am as you are, my people as your people, my horses as your horses."

8 He said, "Which way shall we go up?" And he answered, "The way of the wilderness of Edom."

9 So the king of Israel went with the king of Judah and the king of Edom; and they made a circuit of seven days' journey, and there was no water for the army or for the cattle that followed them.

10 Then the king of Israel said, "Alas! For the LORD has called these three kings to give them into the hand of Moab."

11 But Jehoshaphat said, "Is there not a prophet of the LORD here, that we may inquire of the LORD by him?" And one of the king of Israel's servants answered and said, "Elisha the son of Shaphat is here, who used to pour water on the hands of Elijah."

12 Jehoshaphat said, "The word of the LORD is with him." So the king of Israel and Jehoshaphat and the king of Edom went down to him.

13 Now Elisha said to the king of Israel, "What do I have to do with you? Go to the prophets of your father and to the prophets of your mother." And the king of Israel said to him, "No, for the LORD has called these three kings *together* to give them into the hand of Moab."

14 Elisha said, "As the LORD of hosts lives, before whom I stand, were it not that I regard the presence of Jehoshaphat the king of Judah, I would not look at you nor see you.

15 "But now bring me a minstrel." And it came about, when the minstrel played, that the hand of the LORD came upon him.

16 He said, "Thus says the LORD, 'Make this valley full of trenches.'
17 "For thus says the LORD, 'You shall not see wind nor shall you see rain; yet that valley shall be filled with water, so that you shall drink, both you and your cattle and your beasts.
18 'This is but a slight thing in the sight of the LORD; He will also give the Moabites into your hand.
19 'Then you shall strike every fortified city and every choice city, and fell every good tree and stop all springs of water, and mar every good piece of land with stones.'"
20 It happened in the morning about the time of offering the sacrifice, that behold, water came by the way of Edom, and the country was filled with water.
21 Now all the Moabites heard that the kings had come up to fight against them. And all who were able to put on armor and older were summoned and stood on the border.
22 They rose early in the morning, and the sun shone on the water, and the Moabites saw the water opposite *them* as red as blood.
23 Then they said, "This is blood; the kings have surely fought together, and they have slain one another. Now therefore, Moab, to the spoil!"
24 But when they came to the camp of Israel, the Israelites arose and struck the Moabites, so that they fled before them; and they went forward into the land, slaughtering the Moabites.
25 Thus they destroyed the cities; and each one threw a stone on every piece of good land and filled it. So they stopped all the springs of water and felled all the good trees, until in Kir-haraseth *only* they left its stones; however, the slingers went about *it* and struck it.
26 When the king of Moab saw that the battle was too fierce for him, he took with him 700 men who drew swords, to break through to the king of Edom; but they could not.
27 Then he took his oldest son who was to reign in his place, and offered him as a burnt offering on the wall. And there came great wrath against Israel, and they departed from him and returned to their own land.

4 NOW a certain woman of the wives of the sons of the prophets cried out to Elisha, "Your servant my husband is dead, and you know that your servant feared the LORD; and the creditor has come to take my two children to be his slaves."
2 Elisha said to her, "What shall I do for you? Tell me, what do you have in the house?" And she said, "Your maidservant has nothing in the house except a jar of oil."
3 Then he said, "Go, borrow vessels at large for yourself from all your neighbors, *even* empty vessels; do not get a few.
4 "And you shall go in and shut the door behind you and your sons, and pour out into all these vessels, and you shall set aside what is full."
5 So she went from him and shut the door behind her and her sons; they were bringing *the vessels* to her and she poured.
6 When the vessels were full, she said to her son, "Bring me another vessel." And he said to her, "There is not one vessel more." And the oil stopped.
7 Then she came and told the man of God. And he said, "Go, sell the oil and pay your debt, and you *and* your sons can live on the rest."
8 Now there came a day when Elisha passed over to Shunem, where there was a prominent woman, and she persuaded him to eat food. And so it was, as often as he passed by, he turned in there to eat food.
9 She said to her husband, "Behold now, I perceive that this is a holy man of God passing by us continually.
10 "Please, let us make a little walled upper chamber and let us set a bed for him there, and a table and a chair and a lampstand; and it shall be, when he comes to us, *that* he can turn in there."
11 One day he came there and turned in to the upper chamber and rested.
12 Then he said to Gehazi his servant,

WHAT THE BIBLE SAYS ABOUT

Living Beyond Financial Indebtedness

2 Kings 4:1

*T*he Bible leaves no doubt about God's opinion regarding debt. The following two verses speak clearly on this subject, a painful one for millions:

"Owe nothing to anyone except to love one another; for he who loves his neighbor has fulfilled the law." (Rom. 13:8)

"The rich rules over the poor, and the borrower becomes the lender's slave." (Prov. 22:7)

As a nation, the United States has ignored these truths. It is not unusual to hear of people who are standing on the brink of bankruptcy. Many individuals feel as though they are no more than sixty days away from becoming homeless or in dire financial need. Sadly, our society has bought into a buy-now and pay-later philosophy.

We have believed a lie, and now we are choking on it. But God does not want His people to be in unnecessary financial debt. The only thing we are to owe others is our love, which we are to give freely and in tangible forms. Why is the Lord concerned about our debt? The price of indebtedness is steep. He knows when we are in financial bondage we are not completely free. We are bound to those who hold the deed to our debts.

Listen to the heart's cry of a widow who said to the prophet Elisha, "Your servant my husband is dead, and you know that your servant feared the LORD; and the creditor has come to take my two children to be his slaves" (2 Kin. 4:1). Because of the death of her husband, a prophet associated with Elisha, this woman and her family were deeply in debt. The woman appeared to have only one asset left—her children. And the creditor was coming to sell them into slavery so they could work off what they owed.

We may protest, "How horrible! How could a parent allow her children to work off a debt?" Yet that is exactly what we do when we teach our children debt is okay. Our children will be forced to pay for our foolishness.

God wants us to learn how to live free and not be enslaved to debt. You can do this when you apply His principles to your life. Begin by setting a goal to spend less, manage a budget—no matter how meager your income seems—and obey God by tithing your income. When you obey Him in these matters, you are saying, "Lord, I trust You. I want Your best, and I believe You will show me how to live correctly." ❖

"Call this Shunammite." And when he had called her, she stood before him.
13 He said to him, "Say now to her, 'Behold, you have been careful for us with all this care; what can I do for you? Would you be spoken for to the king or to the captain of the army?'" And she answered, "I live among my own people."
14 So he said, "What then is to be done for her?" And Gehazi answered, "Truly she has no son and her husband is old."
15 He said, "Call her." When he had called her, she stood in the doorway.
16 Then he said, "At this season next year you will embrace a son." And she said, "No, my lord, O man of God, do not lie to your maidservant."
17 The woman conceived and bore a son at that season the next year, as Elisha had said to her.
18 When the child was grown, the day came that he went out to his father to the reapers.

19 He said to his father, "My head, my head." And he said to his servant, "Carry him to his mother."
20 When he had taken him and brought ◄ him to his mother, he sat on her lap until noon, and *then* died.
21 She went up and laid him on the bed of the man of God, and shut *the door* behind him and went out.
22 Then she called to her husband and said, "Please send me one of the servants

LIFE LESSONS

➤ **2 Kings 4:20 — *When he had taken him and brought him to his mother, he sat on her lap until noon, and then died.***

*L*ife is never an unbroken string of joyful blessings and extraordinary miracles. We live in a fallen world where bad things happen. Yet God calls us to trust Him with the end of the story as well as its beginning.

and one of the donkeys, that I may run to the man of God and return."

23 He said, "Why will you go to him today? It is neither new moon nor sabbath." And she said, "*It will be* well."

24 Then she saddled a donkey and said to her servant, "Drive and go forward; do not slow down the pace for me unless I tell you."

25 So she went and came to the man of God to Mount Carmel.

When the man of God saw her at a distance, he said to Gehazi his servant, "Behold, there is the Shunammite.

26 "Please run now to meet her and say to her, 'Is it well with you? Is it well with your husband? Is it well with the child?'" And she answered, "It is well."

27 When she came to the man of God to the hill, she caught hold of his feet. And Gehazi came near to push her away; but the man of God said, "Let her alone, for her soul is troubled within her; and the LORD has hidden it from me and has not told me."

28 Then she said, "Did I ask for a son from my lord? Did I not say, 'Do not deceive me'?"

29 Then he said to Gehazi, "Gird up your loins and take my staff in your hand, and go your way; if you meet any man, do not salute him, and if anyone salutes you, do not answer him; and lay my staff on the lad's face."

30 The mother of the lad said, "As the LORD lives and as you yourself live, I will not leave you." And he arose and followed her.

31 Then Gehazi passed on before them and laid the staff on the lad's face, but there was no sound or response. So he returned to meet him and told him, "The lad has not awakened."

32 When Elisha came into the house, behold the lad was dead and laid on his bed.

33 So he entered and shut the door behind them both and prayed to the LORD.

34 And he went up and lay on the child, and put his mouth on his mouth and his eyes on his eyes and his hands on his hands, and he stretched himself on him; and the flesh of the child became warm.

35 Then he returned and walked in the house once back and forth, and went up and stretched himself on him; and the lad sneezed seven times and the lad opened his eyes.

36 He called Gehazi and said, "Call this Shunammite." So he called her. And when she came in to him, he said, "Take up your son."

37 Then she went in and fell at his feet and bowed herself to the ground, and she took up her son and went out.

38 When Elisha returned to Gilgal, *there was* a famine in the land. As the sons of the prophets were sitting before him, he said to his servant, "Put on the large pot and boil stew for the sons of the prophets."

39 Then one went out into the field to gather herbs, and found a wild vine and gathered from it his lap full of wild gourds, and came and sliced them into the pot of stew, for they did not know *what they were.*

40 So they poured *it* out for the men to eat. And as they were eating of the stew, they cried out and said, "O man of God, there is death in the pot." And they were unable to eat.

41 But he said, "Now bring meal." He threw it into the pot and said, "Pour *it* out for the people that they may eat." Then there was no harm in the pot.

42 Now a man came from Baal-shalishah, and brought the man of God bread of the first fruits, twenty loaves of barley and fresh ears of grain in his sack. And he said, "Give *them* to the people that they may eat."

43 His attendant said, "What, will I set this before a hundred men?" But he said, "Give *them* to the people that they may eat, for thus says the LORD, 'They shall eat and have *some* left over.'"

44 So he set *it* before them, and they ate and had *some* left over, according to the word of the LORD.

Psalm 71:17–24

17 O God, You have taught me from my youth,
   And I still declare Your wondrous deeds.

18 And even when *I am* old and gray,
   O God, do not forsake me,
   Until I declare Your strength to *this* generation,
   Your power to all who are to come.

19 For Your righteousness, O God,
   reaches to the heavens,
   You who have done great things;
   O God, who is like You?
20 You who have shown me many
      troubles and distresses
   Will revive me again,
   And will bring me up again from
      the depths of the earth.
21 May You increase my greatness
   And turn *to* comfort me.
22 I will also praise You with a harp,
   Even Your truth, O my God;
   To You I will sing praises with the
      lyre,
   O Holy One of Israel.
23 My lips will shout for joy when I
      sing praises to You;
   And my soul, which You have
      redeemed.
➤ 24 My tongue also will utter Your
      righteousness all day long;
   For they are ashamed, for they are
      humiliated who seek my hurt.

✦ Proverbs 18:9

9 He also who is slack in his work
   Is brother to him who destroys.

✦ John 17:1–26

17 JESUS spoke these things; and lift-
      ing up His eyes to heaven, He said,
"Father, the hour has come; glorify Your
Son, that the Son may glorify You,
2 even as You gave Him authority
over all flesh, that to all whom You have
given Him, He may give eternal life.
➤ 3 "This is eternal life, that they may
know You, the only true God, and Jesus
✳ Christ whom You have sent.
4 "I glorified You on the earth, having
accomplished the work which You have
given Me to do.
5 "Now, Father, glorify Me together
with Yourself, with the glory which I had
with You before the world was.
6 "I have manifested Your name to
the men whom You gave Me out of the
world; they were Yours and You gave
them to Me, and they have kept Your
word.

7 "Now they have come to know that
everything You have given Me is from
You;
8 for the words which You gave Me
I have given to them; and they received
them and truly understood that I came
forth from You, and they believed that
You sent Me.
9 "I ask on their behalf; I do not ask on
behalf of the world, but of those whom
You have given Me; for they are Yours;
10 and all things that are Mine are
Yours, and Yours are Mine; and I have
been glorified in them.
11 "I am no longer in the world; and *yet*
they themselves are in the world, and I
come to You. Holy Father, keep them in
Your name, *the name* which You have
given Me, that they may be one even as
We *are*.
12 "While I was with them, I was keeping them in Your name which You have
given Me; and I guarded them and not
one of them perished but the son of
perdition, so that the Scripture would be
fulfilled.
13 "But now I come to You; and these
things I speak in the world so that they
may have My joy made full in themselves.
14 "I have given them Your word; and
the world has hated them, because they

LIFE LESSONS

➤ **Psalm 71:24 — *My tongue also will
utter Your righteousness all day long.***

*W*hile faith is a deeply personal
   affair, God never meant for it to be
a solitary affair. We usually love speaking about what gives us joy. If the Lord is
our joy, then His Name should also be on
our tongues.

➤ **John 17:3 — *"This is eternal life, that
they may know You, the only true God,
and Jesus Christ whom You have sent."***

*S*ome believe eternal life can only
   be enjoyed after death. However,
Scripture is clear that you receive it the
moment you have faith in the risen Jesus
Christ and begin a relationship with Him.
You don't just receive the gift of living
forever—you are given the awesome
privilege of having a vibrant, growing
relationship with the Creator of all that
exists.

are not of the world, even as I am not of the world.

15 "I do not ask You to take them out of the world, but to keep them from the evil one.

16 "They are not of the world, even as I am not of the world.

17 "Sanctify them in the truth; Your word is truth.

18 "As You sent Me into the world, I also have sent them into the world.

19 "For their sakes I sanctify Myself, that they themselves also may be sanctified in truth.

➤ 20 "I do not ask on behalf of these alone, but for those also who believe in Me through their word;

21 that they may all be one; even as You, Father, *are* in Me and I in You, that they also may be in Us, so that the world may believe that You sent Me.

22 "The glory which You have given Me I have given to them, that they may be one, just as We are one;

23 I in them and You in Me, that they may be perfected in unity, so that the world may know that You sent Me, and loved them, even as You have loved Me.

➤ 24 "Father, I desire that they also, whom You have given Me, be with Me where I am, so that they may see My glory which You have given Me, for You loved Me before the foundation of the world.

25 "O righteous Father, although the world has not known You, yet I have known You; and these have known that You sent Me;

26 and I have made Your name known to them, and will make it known, so that the love with which You loved Me may be in them, and I in them."

LIFE LESSONS

➤ **John 17:20 — "I do not ask on behalf of these alone, but for those also who believe in Me through their word."**

*J*esus began His prayers for us way back in the Garden of Gethsemane before His arrest. We have trusted in Jesus through the word of the apostles, and this prayer of His is therefore for us.

➤ **John 17:24 — "Father, I desire that they also, whom You have given Me, be with Me where I am, so that they may see My glory."**

*H*ebrews 12:2 tells us, "Jesus ... for the joy set before Him endured the cross." What was His joy? Fulfilling the purpose for which He came—to restore our relationship with Him and show His glory. In the moments before He faced arrest, Jesus prayed for us in the Garden of Gethsemane. And because He triumphed on the Cross, not only has He achieved His mission, we can share in His joy as well.

JUNE 9

2 Kings 5:1—6:33

5 NOW Naaman, captain of the army of the king of Aram, was a great man with his master, and highly respected, because by him the LORD had given victory to Aram. The man was also a valiant warrior, *but he was* a leper.

2 Now the Arameans had gone out in bands and had taken captive a little girl from the land of Israel; and she waited on Naaman's wife.

3 She said to her mistress, "I wish that my master were with the prophet who is in Samaria! Then he would cure him of his leprosy."

4 Naaman went in and told his master, saying, "Thus and thus spoke the girl who is from the land of Israel."

5 Then the king of Aram said, "Go now, and I will send a letter to the king of Israel." He departed and took with him ten talents of silver and six thousand *shekels* of gold and ten changes of clothes.

6 He brought the letter to the king of Israel, saying, "And now as this letter comes to you, behold, I have sent Naaman my servant to you, that you may cure him of his leprosy."

7 When the king of Israel read the letter, he tore his clothes and said, "Am I God, to kill and to make alive, that this man is sending *word* to me to cure a man

of his leprosy? But consider now, and see how he is seeking a quarrel against me."

8   It happened when Elisha the man of God heard that the king of Israel had torn his clothes, that he sent *word* to the king, saying, "Why have you torn your clothes? Now let him come to me, and he shall know that there is a prophet in Israel."

9   So Naaman came with his horses and his chariots and stood at the doorway of the house of Elisha.

10   Elisha sent a messenger to him, saying, "Go and wash in the Jordan seven times, and your flesh will be restored to you and *you will* be clean."

11   But Naaman was furious and went away and said, "Behold, I thought, 'He will surely come out to me and stand and call on the name of the LORD his God, and wave his hand over the place and cure the leper.'

➤ 12   "Are not Abanah and Pharpar, the rivers of Damascus, better than all the waters of Israel? Could I not wash in them and be clean?" So he turned and went away in a rage.

13   Then his servants came near and spoke to him and said, "My father, had the prophet told you *to do some* great thing, would you not have done *it*? How much more *then*, when he says to you, 'Wash, and be clean'?"

14   So he went down and dipped *himself* seven times in the Jordan, according to

the word of the man of God; and his flesh was restored like the flesh of a little child and he was clean.

15   When he returned to the man of God with all his company, and came and stood before him, he said, "Behold now, I know that there is no God in all the earth, but in Israel; so please take a present from your servant now."

16   But he said, "As the LORD lives, before whom I stand, I will take nothing." And he urged him to take *it*, but he refused.

17   Naaman said, "If not, please let your servant at least be given two mules' load of earth; for your servant will no longer offer burnt offering nor will he sacrifice to other gods, but to the LORD.

18   "In this matter may the LORD pardon your servant: when my master goes into the house of Rimmon to worship there, and he leans on my hand and I bow myself in the house of Rimmon, when I bow myself in the house of Rimmon, the LORD pardon your servant in this matter."

19   He said to him, "Go in peace." So he departed from him some distance.

20   But Gehazi, the servant of Elisha the man of God, thought, "Behold, my master has spared this Naaman the Aramean, by not receiving from his hands what he brought. As the LORD lives, I will run after him and take something from him."

21   So Gehazi pursued Naaman. When Naaman saw one running after him, he came down from the chariot to meet him and said, "Is all well?"

22   He said, "All is well. My master has sent me, saying, 'Behold, just now two young men of the sons of the prophets have come to me from the hill country of Ephraim. Please give them a talent of silver and two changes of clothes.'"

23   Naaman said, "Be pleased to take two talents." And he urged him, and bound two talents of silver in two bags with two changes of clothes and gave them to two of his servants; and they carried *them* before him.

24   When he came to the hill, he took them from their hand and deposited them in the house, and he sent the men away, and they departed.

25   But he went in and stood before his master. And Elisha said to him, "Where

---

LIFE LESSONS

➤ **2 Kings 5:12 — Are not . . . the rivers of Damascus, better than all the waters of Israel? Could I not wash in them and be clean?**

Could God have healed Naaman immediately without him dipping in the Jordan's waters? Absolutely. However, in order for Naaman to recognize God as Lord (v. 15), he first had to submit to His authority. As we pray to God about our concerns, He may give us assignments that we consider somewhat demeaning from the world's point of view. However, as 1 Peter 5:6 instructs, "Therefore humble yourselves under the mighty hand of God, that He may exalt you at the proper time." As Naaman learned, saying yes to God is a step toward reward and spiritual victory.

have you been, Gehazi?" And he said, "Your servant went nowhere."

26 Then he said to him, "Did not my heart go *with you*, when the man turned from his chariot to meet you? Is it a time to receive money and to receive clothes and olive groves and vineyards and sheep and oxen and male and female servants?

27 "Therefore, the leprosy of Naaman shall cling to you and to your descendants forever." So he went out from his presence a leper *as white* as snow.

6 NOW the sons of the prophets said to Elisha, "Behold now, the place before you where we are living is too limited for us.

2 "Please let us go to the Jordan and each of us take from there a beam, and let us make a place there for ourselves where we may live." So he said, "Go."

3 Then one said, "Please be willing to go with your servants." And he answered, "I shall go."

4 So he went with them; and when they came to the Jordan, they cut down trees.

5 But as one was felling a beam, the axe head fell into the water; and he cried out and said, "Alas, my master! For it was borrowed."

6 Then the man of God said, "Where did it fall?" And when he showed him the place, he cut off a stick and threw *it* in there, and made the iron float.

7 He said, "Take it up for yourself." So he put out his hand and took it.

8 Now the king of Aram was warring against Israel; and he counseled with his servants saying, "In such and such a place shall be my camp."

9 The man of God sent *word* to the king of Israel saying, "Beware that you do not pass this place, for the Arameans are coming down there."

10 The king of Israel sent to the place about which the man of God had told him; thus he warned him, so that he guarded himself there, more than once or twice.

11 Now the heart of the king of Aram was enraged over this thing; and he called his servants and said to them, "Will you tell me which of us is for the king of Israel?"

12 One of his servants said, "No, my lord, O king; but Elisha, the prophet who is in Israel, tells the king of Israel the words that you speak in your bedroom."

13 So he said, "Go and see where he is, that I may send and take him." And it was told him, saying, "Behold, he is in Dothan."

14 He sent horses and chariots and a great army there, and they came by night and surrounded the city.

15 Now when the attendant of the man of God had risen early and gone out, behold, an army with horses and chariots was circling the city. And his servant said to him, "Alas, my master! What shall we do?"

16 So he answered, "Do not fear, for those who are with us are more than those who are with them."

17 Then Elisha prayed and said, "O Lord, I pray, open his eyes that he may see." And the Lord opened the servant's eyes and he saw; and behold, the mountain was full of horses and chariots of fire all around Elisha.

18 When they came down to him, Elisha prayed to the Lord and said, "Strike this people with blindness, I pray." So He struck them with blindness according to the word of Elisha.

19 Then Elisha said to them, "This is not the way, nor is this the city; follow me and I will bring you to the man whom you seek." And he brought them to Samaria.

20 When they had come into Samaria, Elisha said, "O Lord, open the eyes of these *men*, that they may see." So the Lord opened their eyes and they saw; and behold, they were in the midst of Samaria.

LIFE LESSONS

➤ **2 Kings 6:17** — *Behold, the mountain was full of horses and chariots of fire all around Elisha.*

Elisha did not pray his servant would stop seeing the enemy; he prayed he would start seeing the goodness and provision of the Lord. Trusting God means looking beyond what we can see to what He sees. Elisha understood this and learned to look beyond his own limited perspective to the Lord's reality. Because of his faith, God showed Elisha amazing things and did miracles through him.

LIFE PRINCIPLE 9

TRUSTING GOD MEANS LOOKING BEYOND
WHAT WE CAN SEE TO WHAT GOD SEES.

2 KINGS 6:17

Staring across the Elah Valley into the eyes of Goliath, David recalled the times God had delivered him from the brink of disaster. The Lord had always given him the ability he needed to triumph. Now he faced one of the greatest challenges of his life—a trained and well-armed warrior named Goliath.

At some point, each of us will face what seem to be mammoth trials and difficulties. This is why we must know how to respond to every threat by laying hold of the kind of victorious faith that looks beyond what we can see to what God sees.

The secret of David's success was his ability to trust and obey God. Had he looked merely at the giant challenge facing him, he would have turned around and run away, as did the rest of the Israelites. But through faith, David saw what his countrymen did not.

In times of extreme pressure, God stretches our faith and deepens our dependence on Him. Without a strong, abiding faith, we can quickly yield to temptation and fear, especially when the trial or difficulty is intense or prolonged. The Lord developed David's trust until it became unshakable.

Whatever Goliath you face, you need to bury one truth deep within your heart: God loves you, and when you place your trust in Him, He will help you to triumph. You may go through times of failure. Life may not always turn out the way you planned. But ultimately, God will be glorified and you will be blessed.

Every challenge presents an opportunity for the Lord to display His faithfulness and love. Instead of yielding to thoughts of fear and failure, make a commitment to trust God, even when you do not know what the next day will bring. Train yourself to look beyond what you can see to what He sees.

David founded his faith in the sovereignty of God, and that is why he knew he would not fail in his quest to defeat the Philistine giant. How can you gain the same faith?

Recall past victories. David recalled how God had delivered him from the paw of the lion and the grasp of the bear (1 Sam. 17:32–37). You first win spiritual victories in your mind. If you cave into feelings of fear and doubt, you will lose. When you focus on the truth of God's Word, you win every time.

Reject discouraging words. No one in the Israelite camp encouraged David in his quest to defeat Goliath. The soldiers laughed at him. His brothers felt embarrassed by his presence and urged him to go home. Even King Saul doubted David. If he had listened to their disparaging comments, he would have given up—but he turned his heart toward the Lord and there found the encouragement he needed.

Recognize the true nature of the battle. David entered the battle shouting to his arrogant opponent the memorable words, "The battle is the LORD's, and He will give you into our hands" (1 Sam. 17:47). What a victorious way to say, "God wins!"

Respond to the challenge with a positive confession. David asked the fearful Israelites, "For who is this uncircumcised Philistine, that he should taunt the armies of the living God?" (1 Sam. 17:26). To Saul he said, "The LORD . . . will deliver me from the hand of the Philistine." To Goliath he said, "I come to you in the name of the LORD of hosts, the God of the armies of Israel" (1 Sam. 17:37, 45). David firmly declared his belief that he could not lose because God was with him.

Rely on the power of God. David did not need a spear or a javelin to defeat Goliath. He needed only his faith and a homemade slingshot. "That all this assembly may know that the LORD does not deliver by sword or by spear" (1 Sam. 17:47). God provided the victory, and He received the glory.

Reckon the victory. Even before he stepped onto the battlefield, David knew he would not lose. He knew it wasn't his reputation on the line, but God's. He knew it wasn't his strength or cunning that would win the battle, but God's strength and wisdom.

You can face any circumstance with confidence and hope, because it is not your strength, wisdom, energy, or power that brings victory. Triumph comes because of Christ's ability. When you place your trust in Him, you tap into an irresistible force no one and nothing can successfully oppose. ◆

21 Then the king of Israel when he saw them, said to Elisha, "My father, shall I kill them? Shall I kill them?"

22 He answered, "You shall not kill *them*. Would you kill those you have taken captive with your sword and with your bow? Set bread and water before them, that they may eat and drink and go to their master."

23 So he prepared a great feast for them; and when they had eaten and drunk he sent them away, and they went to their master. And the marauding bands of Arameans did not come again into the land of Israel.

24 Now it came about after this, that Ben-hadad king of Aram gathered all his army and went up and besieged Samaria.

25 There was a great famine in Samaria; and behold, they besieged it, until a donkey's head was sold for eighty *shekels* of silver, and a fourth of a kab of dove's dung for five *shekels* of silver.

26 As the king of Israel was passing by on the wall a woman cried out to him, saying, "Help, my lord, O king!"

27 He said, "If the LORD does not help you, from where shall I help you? From the threshing floor, or from the wine press?"

28 And the king said to her, "What is the matter with you?" And she answered, "This woman said to me, 'Give your son that we may eat him today, and we will eat my son tomorrow.'

29 "So we boiled my son and ate him; and I said to her on the next day, 'Give your son, that we may eat him'; but she has hidden her son."

30 When the king heard the words of the woman, he tore his clothes—now he was passing by on the wall—and the people looked, and behold, he had sackcloth beneath on his body.

➤ 31 Then he said, "May God do so to me and more also, if the head of Elisha the son of Shaphat remains on him today."

32 Now Elisha was sitting in his house, and the elders were sitting with him. And *the king* sent a man from his presence; but before the messenger came to him, he said to the elders, "Do you see how this son of a murderer has sent to take away my head? Look, when the messenger comes, shut the door and hold the door shut against him. Is not the sound of his master's feet behind him?"

33 While he was still talking with them, ➤ behold, the messenger came down to him and he said, "Behold, this evil is from the LORD; why should I wait for the LORD any longer?"

Psalm 72:1–7

A Psalm of Solomon.

72 GIVE the king Your judgments, O God,
And Your righteousness to the king's son.

2 May he judge Your people with righteousness
And Your afflicted with justice.

3 Let the mountains bring peace to the people,
And the hills, in righteousness.

4 May he vindicate the afflicted of the people,
Save the children of the needy
And crush the oppressor.

5 Let them fear You while the sun *endures*,
And as long as the moon, throughout all generations.

6 May he come down like rain upon the mown grass,
Like showers that water the earth.

LIFE LESSONS

➤ **2 Kings 6:31** — *"May God do so to me and more also, if the head of Elisha the son of Shaphat remains on him today."*

*T*he king blamed Elisha for the disaster, rather than his own sin. As long as we blame others for the trouble our sin causes, we descend even further into destruction. Yet God wants us to confess and repent so He can restore our relationship with Him.

➤ **2 Kings 6:33** — *"This evil is from the LORD; why should I wait for the LORD any longer?"*

*T*he king correctly saw the calamity as from the Lord. But he was wrong about not waiting for God. The Lord acts on behalf of those who wait for Him, even when we do not understand His timing.

7 In his days may the righteous
   flourish,
   And abundance of peace till the
   moon is no more.

Proverbs 18:10, 11

10 The name of the LORD is a strong
    tower;
    The righteous runs into it and is
    safe.
11 A rich man's wealth is his strong
    city,
    And like a high wall in his own
    imagination.

John 18:1–18

18 WHEN Jesus had spoken these
words, He went forth with His disciples over the ravine of the Kidron,
where there was a garden, in which He
entered with His disciples.
2   Now Judas also, who was betraying
Him, knew the place, for Jesus had often
met there with His disciples.
3   Judas then, having received the
Roman cohort and officers from the chief
priests and the Pharisees, *came there
with lanterns and torches and weapons.
4   So Jesus, knowing all the things that
were coming upon Him, went forth and
*said to them, "Whom do you seek?"
5   They answered Him, "Jesus the Nazarene." He *said to them, "I am *He.*" And
Judas also, who was betraying Him, was
standing with them.
6   So when He said to them, "I am *He,*"
they drew back and fell to the ground.
7   Therefore He again asked them,
"Whom do you seek?" And they said,
"Jesus the Nazarene."
8   Jesus answered, "I told you that I am
He; so if you seek Me, let these go their
way,"
9   to fulfill the word which He spoke,
"Of those whom You have given Me I lost
not one."
10 Simon Peter then, having a sword,
drew it and struck the high priest's slave,
and cut off his right ear; and the slave's
name was Malchus.

11 So Jesus said to Peter, "Put the
sword into the sheath; the cup which the
Father has given Me, shall I not drink it?"
12 So the *Roman* cohort and the commander and the officers of the Jews, arrested Jesus and bound Him,
13 and led Him to Annas first; for he
was father-in-law of Caiaphas, who was
high priest that year.
14 Now Caiaphas was the one who
had advised the Jews that it was expedient for one man to die on behalf of the
people.
15 Simon Peter was following Jesus,
and *so was* another disciple. Now that
disciple was known to the high priest,
and entered with Jesus into the court of
the high priest,
16 but Peter was standing at the door
outside. So the other disciple, who was
known to the high priest, went out and
spoke to the doorkeeper, and brought
Peter in.
17 Then the slave-girl who kept the
door *said to Peter, "You are not also
one of this man's disciples, are you?" He
*said, "I am not."
18 Now the slaves and the officers were
standing *there,* having made a charcoal fire, for it was cold and they were
warming themselves; and Peter was also
with them, standing and warming himself.

LIFE LESSONS

➤ Proverbs 18:10 — *The name of the
LORD is a strong tower; the righteous runs
into it and is safe.*

*W*here do you run when trouble
comes? How do you react at
the first sign of hardship? Do you run
directly to God? Or do you flee to
earthly resources that are sure to fail
you?

➤ John 18:11 — *"The cup which the
Father has given Me, shall I not drink it?"*

*T*hree times in the Garden of Gethsemane Jesus had prayed that, if it
were possible, God would remove the
"cup" of the Cross from Him (Matt.
26:36–46). He didn't, and so now Jesus
would let nothing come between Him
and that cup.

2 Kings 7:1—8:29

7 THEN Elisha said, "Listen to the word of the LORD; thus says the LORD, 'Tomorrow about this time a measure of fine flour will be *sold* for a shekel, and two measures of barley for a shekel, in the gate of Samaria.'"

2 The royal officer on whose hand the king was leaning answered the man of God and said, "Behold, if the LORD should make windows in heaven, could this thing be?" Then he said, "Behold, you will see it with your own eyes, but you will not eat of it."

3 Now there were four leprous men at the entrance of the gate; and they said to one another, "Why do we sit here until we die?

4 "If we say, 'We will enter the city,' then the famine is in the city and we will die there; and if we sit here, we die also. Now therefore come, and let us go over to the camp of the Arameans. If they spare us, we will live; and if they kill us, we will but die."

5 They arose at twilight to go to the camp of the Arameans; when they came to the outskirts of the camp of the Arameans, behold, there was no one there.

6 For the Lord had caused the army of the Arameans to hear a sound of chariots and a sound of horses, *even* the sound of a great army, so that they said to one another, "Behold, the king of Israel has hired against us the kings of the Hittites and the kings of the Egyptians, to come upon us."

7 Therefore they arose and fled in the twilight, and left their tents and their horses and their donkeys, *even* the camp just as it was, and fled for their life.

8 When these lepers came to the outskirts of the camp, they entered one tent and ate and drank, and carried from there silver and gold and clothes, and went and hid *them*; and they returned and entered another tent and carried from there *also*, and went and hid *them*.

9 Then they said to one another, "We are not doing right. This day is a day of good news, but we are keeping silent; if we wait until morning light, punishment will overtake us. Now therefore come, let us go and tell the king's household."

10 So they came and called to the gatekeepers of the city, and they told them, saying, "We came to the camp of the Arameans, and behold, there was no one there, nor the voice of man, only the horses tied and the donkeys tied, and the tents just as they were."

11 The gatekeepers called and told *it* within the king's household.

12 Then the king arose in the night and said to his servants, "I will now tell you what the Arameans have done to us. They know that we are hungry; therefore they have gone from the camp to hide themselves in the field, saying, 'When they come out of the city, we will capture them alive and get into the city.'"

13 One of his servants said, "Please, let some *men* take five of the horses which remain, which are left in the city. Behold, they *will be in any case* like all the multitude of Israel who are left in it; behold, they *will be in any case* like all the multitude of Israel who have already perished, so let us send and see."

14 They took therefore two chariots with horses, and the king sent after the army of the Arameans, saying, "Go and see."

15 They went after them to the Jordan, and behold, all the way was full of clothes and equipment which the Arameans had thrown away in their haste. Then the messengers returned and told the king.

16 So the people went out and plundered

What steps can I take to hear from God?

2 KINGS 7:1

*T*hroughout the Bible, we read of prophets and other men and women of God who implored their people to hear the word of the Lord. Obviously, God earnestly wanted His people to hear His voice.

He still does.

So how do we hear God when He speaks to us today? What steps can we take to make ourselves ready to hear what He has to say?

There are times when we complicate the process. God may ask us to wait, or He may send an answer quickly. Some people act as if they want to receive a phone call from heaven in which the Lord details His plan for the next five years. He rarely, if ever, does something this emphatic. He wants us to learn to listen for His Spirit's voice, leading us into all truth.

Developing daily spiritual disciplines helps us to hear Him clearly and learn how to discern what is right. Ponder the following basic steps you can take to enable you to hear the Lord when He speaks to you:

• *Read God's Word*: By studying God's Word, we begin to see His established order for our lives. We learn about His truth, mercy, love, and forgiveness.

• *Seek Him in Prayer*: Many times, bowing our heads is the best way to see God's face and hear His voice. In opening ourselves up to Him in prayer, we can tell Him all we are feeling and all we are experiencing. Prayer is more than just a wish list for God—it's a conversation in which we interact with Him.

• *Meditate on His Truth*: Dwelling on what the Lord speaks to our hearts is a great way to let His truths take root in our souls. Not only will what we read and hear from Him impact our lives, but by meditating on it, He has the building materials to lay an unshakable foundation in our hearts. The psalmist said to the Lord, "I have more insight than all my teachers, for Your testimonies are my meditation" (Ps. 119:99).

• *Listen to Him*: You hear with your ears. If you have normal hearing, you can't help hearing sounds within a certain audio range. Listening, however, goes further, involving the mind. Genuine listening is active, meaning that it puts the mind in gear and pays attention to everything said, looking intently for the meaning. That's how God wants us to listen to Him—actively!

the camp of the Arameans. Then a measure of fine flour *was sold* for a shekel and two measures of barley for a shekel, according to the word of the LORD.

17 Now the king appointed the royal officer on whose hand he leaned to have charge of the gate; but the people trampled on him at the gate, and he died just as the man of God had said, who spoke when the king came down to him.

18 It happened just as the man of God had spoken to the king, saying, "Two measures of barley for a shekel and a measure of fine flour for a shekel, will be *sold* tomorrow about this time at the gate of Samaria."

19 Then the royal officer answered the man of God and said, "Now behold, if the LORD should make windows in heaven, could such a thing be?" And he said, "Behold, you will see it with your own eyes, but you will not eat of it."

20 And so it happened to him, for the people trampled on him at the gate and he died.

8 NOW Elisha spoke to the woman whose son he had restored to life, saying, "Arise and go with your household, and sojourn wherever you can sojourn; for the LORD has called for a famine, and it will even come on the land for seven years."

2 So the woman arose and did according to the word of the man of God, and she went with her household and sojourned in the land of the Philistines seven years.

3 At the end of seven years, the woman returned from the land of the Philistines; and she went out to appeal to the king for her house and for her field.

4 Now the king was talking with Gehazi, the servant of the man of God, saying, "Please relate to me all the great things that Elisha has done."

5 As he was relating to the king how he had restored to life the one who was dead, behold, the woman whose son he had restored to life appealed to the king for her house and for her field. And

Gehazi said, "My lord, O king, this is the woman and this is her son, whom Elisha restored to life."

6   When the king asked the woman, she related it to him. So the king appointed for her a certain officer, saying, "Restore all that was hers and all the produce of the field from the day that she left the land even until now."

7   Then Elisha came to Damascus. Now Ben-hadad king of Aram was sick, and it was told him, saying, "The man of God has come here."

8   The king said to Hazael, "Take a gift in your hand and go to meet the man of God, and inquire of the LORD by him, saying, 'Will I recover from this sickness?'"

9   So Hazael went to meet him and took a gift in his hand, even every kind of good thing of Damascus, forty camels' loads; and he came and stood before him and said, "Your son Ben-hadad king of Aram has sent me to you, saying, 'Will I recover from this sickness?'"

10   Then Elisha said to him, "Go, say to him, 'You will surely recover,' but the LORD has shown me that he will certainly die."

11   He fixed his gaze steadily on him until he was ashamed, and the man of God wept.

12   Hazael said, "Why does my lord weep?" Then he answered, "Because I know the evil that you will do to the sons of Israel: their strongholds you will set on fire, and their young men you will kill with the sword, and their little ones you will dash in pieces, and their women with child you will rip up."

13   Then Hazael said, "But what is your servant, who is but a dog, that he should do this great thing?" And Elisha answered, "The LORD has shown me that you will be king over Aram."

14   So he departed from Elisha and returned to his master, who said to him, "What did Elisha say to you?" And he answered, "He told me that you would surely recover."

15   On the following day, he took the cover and dipped it in water and spread it on his face, so that he died. And Hazael became king in his place.

16   Now in the fifth year of Joram the son of Ahab king of Israel, Jehoshaphat being then the king of Judah, Jehoram the son of Jehoshaphat king of Judah became king.

17   He was thirty-two years old when he became king, and he reigned eight years in Jerusalem.

18   He walked in the way of the kings of Israel, just as the house of Ahab had done, for the daughter of Ahab became his wife; and he did evil in the sight of the LORD.

19   However, the LORD was not willing to destroy Judah, for the sake of David His servant, since He had promised him to give a lamp to him through his sons always.

20   In his days Edom revolted from under the hand of Judah, and made a king over themselves.

21   Then Joram crossed over to Zair, and all his chariots with him. And he arose by night and struck the Edomites who had surrounded him and the captains of the chariots; but his army fled to their tents.

22   So Edom revolted against Judah to this day. Then Libnah revolted at the same time.

23   The rest of the acts of Joram and all that he did, are they not written in the Book of the Chronicles of the Kings of Judah?

24   So Joram slept with his fathers and was buried with his fathers in the city of David; and Ahaziah his son became king in his place.

25   In the twelfth year of Joram the son of Ahab king of Israel, Ahaziah the son of Jehoram king of Judah began to reign.

26   Ahaziah was twenty-two years old when he became king, and he reigned one year in Jerusalem. And his mother's name was Athaliah the granddaughter of Omri king of Israel.

LIFE LESSONS

> **2 Kings 8:18 — He walked in the way of the kings of Israel . . . for the daughter of Ahab became his wife.**

*J*ehoshaphat, the righteous king of Judah, foolishly allowed the crown prince, Jehoram, to marry the daughter of one of the most wicked kings in Israel's history (2 Chr. 18:1). And so all the good Jehoshaphat had accomplished quickly came unraveled.

27 He walked in the way of the house of Ahab and did evil in the sight of the LORD, like the house of Ahab *had done*, because he was a son-in-law of the house of Ahab.
28 Then he went with Joram the son of Ahab to war against Hazael king of Aram at Ramoth-gilead, and the Arameans wounded Joram.
29 So King Joram returned to be healed in Jezreel of the wounds which the Arameans had inflicted on him at Ramah when he fought against Hazael king of Aram. Then Ahaziah the son of Jehoram king of Judah went down to see Joram the son of Ahab in Jezreel because he was sick.

Psalm 72:8–16

8 May he also rule from sea to sea
  And from the River to the ends of the earth.
9 Let the nomads of the desert bow before him,
  And his enemies lick the dust.
10 Let the kings of Tarshish and of the islands bring presents;
  The kings of Sheba and Seba offer gifts.
11 And let all kings bow down before him,
  All nations serve him.
12 For he will deliver the needy when he cries for help,
  The afflicted also, and him who has no helper.
13 He will have compassion on the poor and needy,
  And the lives of the needy he will save.
14 He will rescue their life from oppression and violence,
  And their blood will be precious in his sight;
15 So may he live, and may the gold of Sheba be given to him;
  And let them pray for him continually;
  Let them bless him all day long.
16 May there be abundance of grain in the earth on top of the mountains;
  Its fruit will wave like *the cedars of* Lebanon;
  And may those from the city flourish like vegetation of the earth.

Proverbs 18:12, 13

12 Before destruction the heart of man is haughty,
  But humility *goes* before honor.
13 He who gives an answer before he hears,
  It is folly and shame to him.

John 18:19–40

19 The high priest then questioned Jesus about His disciples, and about His teaching.
20 Jesus answered him, "I have spoken openly to the world; I always taught in synagogues and in the temple, where all the Jews come together; and I spoke nothing in secret.
21 "Why do you question Me? Question those who have heard what I spoke to them; they know what I said."
22 When He had said this, one of the officers standing nearby struck Jesus, saying, "Is that the way You answer the high priest?"
23 Jesus answered him, "If I have spoken wrongly, testify of the wrong; but if rightly, why do you strike Me?"

LIFE LESSONS

➢ **Psalm 72:11 — *Let all kings bow down before him, all nations serve him.***

*O*ne day, perhaps soon, "every knee will bow" and "every tongue will confess that Jesus Christ is Lord, to the glory of God the Father" (Phil. 2:10, 11).

➢ **Proverbs 18:12 — *Before destruction the heart of man is haughty, but humility goes before honor.***

*B*eware of the temptation of pride, which is an exaggerated attentiveness to yourself and what you want. God hates pride, and whatever the Lord hates must be eliminated from your life. Pay attention to your thoughts and words. If your speech is characterized by lots of "I," "me," and "my," you're focusing on yourself far too much. Make sure your attention is centered on God.

24 So Annas sent Him bound to Caiaphas the high priest.

25 Now Simon Peter was standing and warming himself. So they said to him, "You are not also *one* of His disciples, are you?" He denied *it*, and said, "I am not."

26 One of the slaves of the high priest, being a relative of the one whose ear Peter cut off, *said, "Did I not see you in the garden with Him?"

27 Peter then denied *it* again, and immediately a rooster crowed.

28 Then they *led Jesus from Caiaphas into the Praetorium, and it was early; and they themselves did not enter into the Praetorium so that they would not be defiled, but might eat the Passover.

29 Therefore Pilate went out to them and *said, "What accusation do you bring against this Man?"

30 They answered and said to him, "If this Man were not an evildoer, we would not have delivered Him to you."

31 So Pilate said to them, "Take Him yourselves, and judge Him according to your law." The Jews said to him, "We are not permitted to put anyone to death,"

32 to fulfill the word of Jesus which He spoke, signifying by what kind of death He was about to die.

33 Therefore Pilate entered again into the Praetorium, and summoned Jesus and said to Him, "Are You the King of the Jews?"

34 Jesus answered, "Are you saying this on your own initiative, or did others tell you about Me?"

35 Pilate answered, "I am not a Jew, am I? Your own nation and the chief priests delivered You to me; what have You done?"

36 Jesus answered, "My kingdom is not of this world. If My kingdom were of this world, then My servants would be fighting so that I would not be handed over to the Jews; but as it is, My kingdom is not of this realm."

37 Therefore Pilate said to Him, "So You are a king?" Jesus answered, "You say *correctly* that I am a king. For this I have been born, and for this I have come into the world, to testify to the truth. Everyone who is of the truth hears My voice."

38 Pilate *said to Him, "What is truth?"

And when he had said this, he went out again to the Jews and *said to them, "I find no guilt in Him.

39 "But you have a custom that I release someone for you at the Passover; do you wish then that I release for you the King of the Jews?"

40 So they cried out again, saying, "Not this Man, but Barabbas." Now Barabbas was a robber.

LIFE LESSONS

➤ **John 18:36 —** *"My kingdom is not of this world."*

One day Jesus will return to earth "to rule all the nations with a rod of iron" (Rev. 12:5; see also Ps. 2:9; Rev. 2:27; 19:15). Until then, His kingdom focuses on redeeming the hearts of the lost.

JUNE 11

2 Kings 9:1—10:36

9 NOW Elisha the prophet called one of the sons of the prophets and said to him, "Gird up your loins, and take this flask of oil in your hand and go to Ramoth-gilead.

2 "When you arrive there, search out Jehu the son of Jehoshaphat the son of Nimshi, and go in and bid him arise from among his brothers, and bring him to an inner room.

3 "Then take the flask of oil and pour it on his head and say, 'Thus says the LORD, "I have anointed you king over Israel."' Then open the door and flee and do not wait."

4 So the young man, the servant of the prophet, went to Ramoth-gilead.

5 When he came, behold, the captains of the army were sitting, and he said, "I have a word for you, O captain." And Jehu said, "For which *one* of us?" And he said, "For you, O captain."

6 He arose and went into the house,

and he poured the oil on his head and said to him, "Thus says the LORD, the God of Israel, 'I have anointed you king over the people of the LORD, *even* over Israel.

7 'You shall strike the house of Ahab your master, that I may avenge the blood of My servants the prophets, and the blood of all the servants of the LORD, at the hand of Jezebel.

8 'For the whole house of Ahab shall perish, and I will cut off from Ahab every male person both bond and free in Israel.

9 'I will make the house of Ahab like the house of Jeroboam the son of Nebat, and like the house of Baasha the son of Ahijah.

10 'The dogs shall eat Jezebel in the territory of Jezreel, and none shall bury her.'" Then he opened the door and fled.

11 Now Jehu came out to the servants of his master, and one said to him, "Is all well? Why did this mad fellow come to you?" And he said to them, "You know *very well* the man and his talk."

12 They said, "It is a lie, tell us now." And he said, "Thus and thus he said to me, 'Thus says the LORD, "I have anointed you king over Israel."'"

13 Then they hurried and each man took his garment and placed it under him on the bare steps, and blew the trumpet, saying, "Jehu is king!"

14 So Jehu the son of Jehoshaphat the son of Nimshi conspired against Joram. Now Joram with all Israel was defending Ramoth-gilead against Hazael king of Aram,

15 but King Joram had returned to Jezreel to be healed of the wounds which the Arameans had inflicted on him when he fought with Hazael king of Aram. So Jehu said, "If this is your mind, *then* let no one escape *or* leave the city to go tell *it* in Jezreel."

16 Then Jehu rode in a chariot and went to Jezreel, for Joram was lying there. Ahaziah king of Judah had come down to see Joram.

17 Now the watchman was standing on the tower in Jezreel and he saw the company of Jehu as he came, and said, "I see a company." And Joram said, "Take a horseman and send him to meet them and let him say, 'Is it peace?'"

18 So a horseman went to meet him and said, "Thus says the king, 'Is it peace?'" And Jehu said, "What have you

to do with peace? Turn behind me." And the watchman reported, "The messenger came to them, but he did not return."

19 Then he sent out a second horseman, who came to them and said, "Thus says the king, 'Is it peace?'" And Jehu answered, "What have you to do with peace? Turn behind me."

20 The watchman reported, "He came even to them, and he did not return; and the driving is like the driving of Jehu the son of Nimshi, for he drives furiously."

21 Then Joram said, "Get ready." And they made his chariot ready. Joram king of Israel and Ahaziah king of Judah went out, each in his chariot, and they went out to meet Jehu and found him in the property of Naboth the Jezreelite.

22 When Joram saw Jehu, he said, "Is it peace, Jehu?" And he answered, "What peace, so long as the harlotries of your mother Jezebel and her witchcrafts are so many?"

23 So Joram reined about and fled and said to Ahaziah, "*There is* treachery, O Ahaziah!"

24 And Jehu drew his bow with his full strength and shot Joram between his arms; and the arrow went through his heart and he sank in his chariot.

25 Then *Jehu* said to Bidkar his officer, "Take *him* up and cast him into the property of the field of Naboth the Jezreelite, for I remember when you and I were riding together after Ahab his father, that the LORD laid this oracle against him:

26 'Surely I have seen yesterday the blood of Naboth and the blood of his sons,' says the LORD, 'and I will repay you in this property,' says the LORD. Now then, take and cast him into the property, according to the word of the LORD."

27 When Ahaziah the king of Judah saw *this,* he fled by the way of the garden house. And Jehu pursued him and said, "Shoot him too, in the chariot." *So they shot him* at the ascent of Gur, which is at Ibleam. But he fled to Megiddo and died there.

28 Then his servants carried him in a chariot to Jerusalem and buried him in his grave with his fathers in the city of David.

29 Now in the eleventh year of Joram, the son of Ahab, Ahaziah became king over Judah.

30 When Jehu came to Jezreel, Jezebel

heard *of it,* and she painted her eyes and adorned her head and looked out the window.

31 As Jehu entered the gate, she said, "Is it well, Zimri, your master's murderer?"

32 Then he lifted up his face to the window and said, "Who is on my side? Who?" And two or three officials looked down at him.

33 He said, "Throw her down." So they threw her down, and some of her blood was sprinkled on the wall and on the horses, and he trampled her under foot.

34 When he came in, he ate and drank; and he said, "See now to this cursed woman and bury her, for she is a king's daughter."

35 They went to bury her, but they found nothing more of her than the skull and the feet and the palms of her hands.

36 Therefore they returned and told him. And he said, "This is the word of the LORD, which He spoke by His servant Elijah the Tishbite, saying, 'In the property of Jezreel the dogs shall eat the flesh of Jezebel;

37 and the corpse of Jezebel will be as dung on the face of the field in the property of Jezreel, so they cannot say, "This is Jezebel."'"

10 NOW Ahab had seventy sons in Samaria. And Jehu wrote letters and sent *them* to Samaria, to the rulers of Jezreel, the elders, and to the guardians of *the children* of Ahab, saying,

2 "Now, when this letter comes to you, since your master's sons are with you,

as well as the chariots and horses and a fortified city and the weapons,

3 select the best and fittest of your master's sons, and set *him* on his father's throne, and fight for your master's house."

4 But they feared greatly and said, "Behold, the two kings did not stand before him; how then can we stand?"

5 And the one who *was* over the household, and he who *was* over the city, the elders, and the guardians of *the children,* sent *word* to Jehu, saying, "We are your servants, all that you say to us we will do, we will not make any man king; do what is good in your sight."

6 Then he wrote a letter to them a second time saying, "If you are on my side, and you will listen to my voice, take the heads of the men, your master's sons, and come to me at Jezreel tomorrow about this time." Now the king's sons, seventy persons, *were* with the great men of the city, *who* were rearing them.

7 When the letter came to them, they took the king's sons and slaughtered *them,* seventy persons, and put their heads in baskets, and sent *them* to him at Jezreel.

Life Examples:

ELIJAH: Responding to Stress

2 KINGS 9:36, 37

*S*tressful situations can drive us to inappropriate responses. The prophet Elijah illustrates the importance of viewing circumstances from the Lord's perspective.

God sent the prophet to rescue Israel from its moral and spiritual decline. Elijah confronted and defeated the prophets of Baal (1 Kin. 18:17–40), but the wicked Queen Jezebel immediately threatened to kill him for executing her false prophets.

Instead of holding fast to the Lord's faithfulness, Elijah panicked, ran, and hid (1 Kin. 19:3). Yet He reminded His prophet that His provision and protection was sufficient for his circumstances. Elijah was not alone, nor would God leave him to face the wrath of Jezebel by himself. In fact, there were seven thousand people in Israel who were also faithfully dedicated to God and who would never worship Jezebel's false deities. This encouraged Elijah, so the prophet returned to his mission for God.

Like Elijah, we need to rest in the Lord, recall His faithfulness, and trust Him for the future. He remains active in our lives, even when it feels as though we're alone and He has fallen silent. He's still with you, so be confident He will help you in whatever you are facing.

8 When the messenger came and told him, saying, "They have brought the heads of the king's sons," he said, "Put them in two heaps at the entrance of the gate until morning."

9 Now in the morning he went out and stood and said to all the people, "You are innocent; behold, I conspired against my master and killed him, but who killed all these?

10 "Know then that there shall fall to the earth nothing of the word of the LORD, which the LORD spoke concerning the house of Ahab, for the LORD has done what He spoke through His servant Elijah."

11 So Jehu killed all who remained of the house of Ahab in Jezreel, and all his great men and his acquaintances and his priests, until he left him without a survivor.

12 Then he arose and departed and went to Samaria. On the way while he was at Beth-eked of the shepherds,

13 Jehu met the relatives of Ahaziah king of Judah and said, "Who are you?" And they answered, "We are the relatives of Ahaziah; and we have come down to greet the sons of the king and the sons of the queen mother."

14 He said, "Take them alive." So they took them alive and killed them at the pit of Beth-eked, forty-two men; and he left none of them.

15 Now when he had departed from there, he met Jehonadab the son of Rechab *coming* to meet him; and he greeted him and said to him, "Is your heart right, as my heart is with your heart?" And Jehonadab answered, "It is." *Jehu said,* "If it is, give *me* your hand." And he gave him his hand, and he took him up to him into the chariot.

16 He said, "Come with me and see my zeal for the LORD." So he made him ride in his chariot.

17 When he came to Samaria, he killed all who remained to Ahab in Samaria, until he had destroyed him, according to the word of the LORD which He spoke to Elijah.

18 Then Jehu gathered all the people and said to them, "Ahab served Baal a little; Jehu will serve him much.

19 "Now, summon all the prophets of Baal, all his worshipers and all his priests; let no one be missing, for I have a great sacrifice for Baal; whoever is missing shall not live." But Jehu did it in cunning, so that he might destroy the worshipers of Baal.

20 And Jehu said, "Sanctify a solemn assembly for Baal." And they proclaimed *it.*

21 Then Jehu sent throughout Israel and all the worshipers of Baal came, so that there was not a man left who did not come. And when they went into the house of Baal, the house of Baal was filled from one end to the other.

22 He said to the one who *was* in charge of the wardrobe, "Bring out garments for all the worshipers of Baal." So he brought out garments for them.

23 Jehu went into the house of Baal with Jehonadab the son of Rechab; and he said to the worshipers of Baal, "Search and see that there is here with you none of the servants of the LORD, but only the worshipers of Baal."

24 Then they went in to offer sacrifices and burnt offerings.

Now Jehu had stationed for himself eighty men outside, and he had said, "The one who permits any of the men whom I bring into your hands to escape shall give up his life in exchange."

25 Then it came about, as soon as he had finished offering the burnt offering, that Jehu said to the guard and to the royal officers, "Go in, kill them; let none come out." And they killed them with the edge of the sword; and the guard and the royal officers threw *them* out, and went to the inner room of the house of Baal.

26 They brought out the *sacred* pillars of the house of Baal and burned them.

27 They also broke down the *sacred* pillar of Baal and broke down the house of Baal, and made it a latrine to this day.

28 Thus Jehu eradicated Baal out of Israel.

29 However, *as for* the sins of Jeroboam ◄ the son of Nebat, which he made Israel

---

LIFE LESSONS

➤ *2 Kings 10:29 — However, as for the sins of Jeroboam . . . which he made Israel sin, from these Jehu did not depart.*

*J*ehu obeyed the Word of the Lord as long as it advanced his goals. But to maintain control over his people, he followed the pattern set by the evil Jeroboam (1 Kin. 12:25-33). Incomplete obedience is blatant rebellion.

sin, from these Jehu did not depart, *even* the golden calves that *were* at Bethel and that *were* at Dan.

30 The LORD said to Jehu, "Because you have done well in executing what is right in My eyes, *and* have done to the house of Ahab according to all that *was* in My heart, your sons of the fourth generation shall sit on the throne of Israel."

31 But Jehu was not careful to walk in the law of the LORD, the God of Israel, with all his heart; he did not depart from the sins of Jeroboam, which he made Israel sin.

32 In those days the LORD began to cut off *portions* from Israel; and Hazael defeated them throughout the territory of Israel:

33 from the Jordan eastward, all the land of Gilead, the Gadites and the Reubenites and the Manassites, from Aroer, which is by the valley of the Arnon, even Gilead and Bashan.

34 Now the rest of the acts of Jehu and all that he did and all his might, are they not written in the Book of the Chronicles of the Kings of Israel?

35 And Jehu slept with his fathers, and they buried him in Samaria. And Jehoahaz his son became king in his place.

36 Now the time which Jehu reigned over Israel in Samaria *was* twenty-eight years.

Psalm 72:17–20

17 May his name endure forever;
  May his name increase as long as the sun *shines;*
  And let *men* bless themselves by him;
  Let all nations call him blessed.
18 Blessed be the LORD God, the God of Israel,
  Who alone works wonders.

LIFE LESSONS

➤ **Psalm 72:17 — *May his name endure forever . . . all nations call Him blessed.***

*J*esus will receive a kingdom that will never end, and He will rule over all nations in righteousness and truth. Then we will see the true blessing of our obedience.

19 And blessed be His glorious name forever;
  And may the whole earth be filled with His glory.
  Amen, and Amen.
20 The prayers of David the son of Jesse are ended.

Proverbs 18:14, 15

14 The spirit of a man can endure his sickness,
  But *as for* a broken spirit who can bear it?
15 The mind of the prudent acquires knowledge,
  And the ear of the wise seeks knowledge.

John 19:1–22

19 PILATE then took Jesus and scourged Him.
2 And the soldiers twisted together a crown of thorns and put it on His head, and put a purple robe on Him;
3 and they *began* to come up to Him and say, "Hail, King of the Jews!" and to give Him slaps *in the face.*
4 Pilate came out again and *said to them, "Behold, I am bringing Him out to you so that you may know that I find no guilt in Him."
5 Jesus then came out, wearing the crown of thorns and the purple robe. *Pilate* *said to them, "Behold, the Man!"
6 So when the chief priests and the officers saw Him, they cried out saying, "Crucify, crucify!" Pilate *said to them, "Take Him yourselves and crucify Him, for I find no guilt in Him."
7 The Jews answered him, "We have a law, and by that law He ought to die because He made Himself out *to be* the Son of God."
8 Therefore when Pilate heard this statement, he was *even* more afraid;
9 and he entered into the Praetorium again and *said to Jesus, "Where are You from?" But Jesus gave him no answer.
10 So Pilate *said to Him, "You do not speak to me? Do You not know that I

have authority to release You, and I have authority to crucify You?"
11 Jesus answered, "You would have no authority over Me, unless it had been given you from above; for this reason he who delivered Me to you has *the* greater sin."
12 As a result of this Pilate made efforts to release Him, but the Jews cried out saying, "If you release this Man, you are no friend of Caesar; everyone who makes himself out *to be* a king opposes Caesar."
13 Therefore when Pilate heard these words, he brought Jesus out, and sat down on the judgment seat at a place called The Pavement, but in Hebrew, Gabbatha.
14 Now it was the day of preparation for the Passover; it was about the sixth hour. And he *said to the Jews, "Behold, your King!"
15 So they cried out, "Away with *Him*, away with *Him*, crucify Him!" Pilate *said to them, "Shall I crucify your King?" The chief priests answered, "We have no king but Caesar."
16 So he then handed Him over to them to be crucified.
17 They took Jesus, therefore, and He went out, bearing His own cross, to the place called the Place of a Skull, which is called in Hebrew, Golgotha.
18 There they crucified Him, and with Him two other men, one on either side, and Jesus in between.

LIFE LESSONS

➤ **John 19:11 — *"You would have no authority over Me, unless it had been given you from above."***

*N*o one exercises any authority at all in this world unless the Lord first gives it to him or her (Prov. 21:1; Dan. 4:17; Rom. 13:1). As children of a sovereign God, we are *never* victims of our circumstances.

➤ **John 19:15 — *The chief priests answered, "We have no king but Caesar."***

*T*he opponents of Jesus wanted Him dead so badly they confessed Caesar as their only king, thus rejecting God as their King. No one speaking by the Spirit of the Lord could ever give total allegiance to a human ruler.

---

19 Pilate also wrote an inscription and put it on the cross. It was written, "JESUS THE NAZARENE, THE KING OF THE JEWS."
20 Therefore many of the Jews read this inscription, for the place where Jesus was crucified was near the city; and it was written in Hebrew, Latin *and* in Greek.
21 So the chief priests of the Jews were saying to Pilate, "Do not write, 'The King of the Jews'; but that He said, 'I am King of the Jews.'"
22 Pilate answered, "What I have written I have written."

---

2 Kings 11:1—13:25

11 WHEN Athaliah the mother of Ahaziah saw that her son was dead, she rose and destroyed all the royal offspring.
2 But Jehosheba, the daughter of King Joram, sister of Ahaziah, took Joash the son of Ahaziah and stole him from among the king's sons who were being put to death, and placed him and his nurse in the bedroom. So they hid him from Athaliah, and he was not put to death.
3 So he was hidden with her in the house of the LORD six years, while Athaliah was reigning over the land.
4 Now in the seventh year Jehoiada

LIFE LESSONS

➤ **2 Kings 11:2 — *Jehosheba . . . stole him from among the king's sons who were being put to death.***

*T*hrough Athaliah, Satan tried to wipe out the Davidic line and so frustrate the promise of God leading to the Messiah (2 Sam. 7:8-16). But no one, not even the devil, can derail any of the Lord's promises.

sent and brought the captains of hundreds of the Carites and of the guard, and brought them to him in the house of the LORD. Then he made a covenant with them and put them under oath in the house of the LORD, and showed them the king's son.

5 He commanded them, saying, "This is the thing that you shall do: one third of you, who come in on the sabbath and keep watch over the king's house

6 (one third also *shall be* at the gate Sur, and one third at the gate behind the guards), shall keep watch over the house for defense.

7 "Two parts of you, *even* all who go out on the sabbath, shall also keep watch over the house of the LORD for the king.

8 "Then you shall surround the king, each with his weapons in his hand; and whoever comes within the ranks shall be put to death. And be with the king when he goes out and when he comes in."

9 So the captains of hundreds did according to all that Jehoiada the priest commanded. And each one of them took his men who were to come in on the sabbath, with those who were to go out on the sabbath, and came to Jehoiada the priest.

10 The priest gave to the captains of hundreds the spears and shields that *had been* King David's, which *were* in the house of the LORD.

11 The guards stood each with his weapons in his hand, from the right side of the house to the left side of the house, by the altar and by the house, around the king.

12 Then he brought the king's son out and put the crown on him and *gave him* the testimony; and they made him king and anointed him, and they clapped their hands and said, "*Long* live the king!"

13 When Athaliah heard the noise of the guard *and of* the people, she came to the people in the house of the LORD.

14 She looked and behold, the king was standing by the pillar, according to the custom, with the captains and the trumpeters beside the king; and all the people of the land rejoiced and blew trumpets. Then Athaliah tore her clothes and cried, "Treason! Treason!"

15 And Jehoiada the priest commanded the captains of hundreds who were appointed over the army and said to them,

"Bring her out between the ranks, and whoever follows her put to death with the sword." For the priest said, "Let her not be put to death in the house of the LORD."

16 So they seized her, and when she arrived at the horses' entrance of the king's house, she was put to death there.

17 Then Jehoiada made a covenant be- ◄ tween the LORD and the king and the people, that they would be the LORD's people, also between the king and the people.

18 All the people of the land went to the house of Baal, and tore it down; his altars and his images they broke in pieces thoroughly, and killed Mattan the priest of Baal before the altars. And the priest appointed officers over the house of the LORD.

19 He took the captains of hundreds and the Carites and the guards and all the people of the land; and they brought the king down from the house of the LORD, and came by the way of the gate of the guards to the king's house. And he sat on the throne of the kings.

20 So all the people of the land rejoiced and the city was quiet. For they had put Athaliah to death with the sword at the king's house.

21 Jehoash was seven years old when he became king.

12 IN the seventh year of Jehu, Jehoash became king, and he reigned forty years in Jerusalem; and his mother's name was Zibiah of Beersheba.

2 Jehoash did right in the sight of the LORD all his days in which Jehoiada the priest instructed him.

3 Only the high places were not taken away; the people still sacrificed and burned incense on the high places.

4 Then Jehoash said to the priests, "All the money of the sacred things which is

---

LIFE LESSONS

➤ **2 Kings 11:17 — *Then Jehoiada made a covenant between the LORD and the king and the people, that they would be the LORD's people.***

*J*ehoiada is a bright light in a dark time. He demonstrates how we can remain faithful to God and His Word, even when the culture around us decays.

brought into the house of the LORD, in current money, *both* the money of each man's assessment *and* all the money which any man's heart prompts him to bring into the house of the LORD,
5　let the priests take it for themselves, each from his acquaintance; and they shall repair the damages of the house wherever any damage may be found."
6　But it came about that in the twenty-third year of King Jehoash the priests had not repaired the damages of the house.
7　Then King Jehoash called for Jehoiada the priest, and for the *other* priests and said to them, "Why do you not repair the damages of the house? Now therefore take no *more* money from your acquaintances, but pay it for the damages of the house."
8　So the priests agreed that they would take no *more* money from the people, nor repair the damages of the house.
9　But Jehoiada the priest took a chest and bored a hole in its lid and put it beside the altar, on the right side as one comes into the house of the LORD; and the priests who guarded the threshold put in it all the money which was brought into the house of the LORD.
10　When they saw that there was much money in the chest, the king's scribe and the high priest came up and tied *it* in bags and counted the money which was found in the house of the LORD.
11　They gave the money which was weighed out into the hands of those who did the work, who had the oversight of the house of the LORD; and they paid it out to the carpenters and the builders who worked on the house of the LORD;
12　and to the masons and the stonecutters, and for buying timber and hewn stone to repair the damages to the house of the LORD, and for all that was laid out for the house to repair it.
13　But there were not made for the house of the LORD silver cups, snuffers, bowls, trumpets, any vessels of gold, or vessels of silver from the money which was brought into the house of the LORD;
14　for they gave that to those who did the work, and with it they repaired the house of the LORD.
15　Moreover, they did not require an accounting from the men into whose hand they gave the money to pay to

those who did the work, for they dealt faithfully.
16　The money from the guilt offerings and the money from the sin offerings was not brought into the house of the LORD; it was for the priests.
17　Then Hazael king of Aram went up and fought against Gath and captured it, and Hazael set his face to go up to Jerusalem.
18　Jehoash king of Judah took all the sacred things that Jehoshaphat and Jehoram and Ahaziah, his fathers, kings of Judah, had dedicated, and his own sacred things and all the gold that was found among the treasuries of the house of the LORD and of the king's house, and sent *them* to Hazael king of Aram. Then he went away from Jerusalem.
19　Now the rest of the acts of Joash and all that he did, are they not written in the Book of the Chronicles of the Kings of Judah?
20　His servants arose and made a conspiracy and struck down Joash at the house of Millo *as he was* going down to Silla.
21　For Jozacar the son of Shimeath and Jehozabad the son of Shomer, his servants, struck *him* and he died; and they buried him with his fathers in the city of David, and Amaziah his son became king in his place.

13 IN the twenty-third year of Joash the son of Ahaziah, king of Judah, Jehoahaz the son of Jehu became king over Israel at Samaria, *and he reigned* seventeen years.
2　He did evil in the sight of the LORD, and followed the sins of Jeroboam the son of Nebat, with which he made Israel sin; he did not turn from them.
3　So the anger of the LORD was kindled against Israel, and He gave them continually into the hand of Hazael king of Aram, and into the hand of Ben-hadad the son of Hazael.
4　Then Jehoahaz entreated the favor of the LORD, and the LORD listened to him; for He saw the oppression of Israel, how the king of Aram oppressed them.
5　The LORD gave Israel a deliverer, so that they escaped from under the hand of the Arameans; and the sons of Israel lived in their tents as formerly.
6　Nevertheless they did not turn away from the sins of the house of Jeroboam,

with which he made Israel sin, but walked in them; and the Asherah also remained standing in Samaria.

7 For he left to Jehoahaz of the army not more than fifty horsemen and ten chariots and 10,000 footmen, for the king of Aram had destroyed them and made them like the dust at threshing.

8 Now the rest of the acts of Jehoahaz, and all that he did and his might, are they not written in the Book of the Chronicles of the Kings of Israel?

9 And Jehoahaz slept with his fathers, and they buried him in Samaria; and Joash his son became king in his place.

10 In the thirty-seventh year of Joash king of Judah, Jehoash the son of Jehoahaz became king over Israel in Samaria, *and reigned* sixteen years.

11 He did evil in the sight of the LORD; he did not turn away from all the sins of Jeroboam the son of Nebat, with which he made Israel sin, but he walked in them.

12 Now the rest of the acts of Joash and all that he did and his might with which he fought against Amaziah king of Judah, are they not written in the Book of the Chronicles of the Kings of Israel?

13 So Joash slept with his fathers, and Jeroboam sat on his throne; and Joash was buried in Samaria with the kings of Israel.

➤ 14 When Elisha became sick with the illness of which he was to die, Joash the king of Israel came down to him and wept over him and said, "My father, my father, the chariots of Israel and its horsemen!"

15 Elisha said to him, "Take a bow and arrows." So he took a bow and arrows.

16 Then he said to the king of Israel, "Put your hand on the bow." And he put his hand *on it,* then Elisha laid his hands on the king's hands.

17 He said, "Open the window toward the east," and he opened *it.* Then Elisha said, "Shoot!" And he shot. And he said, "The LORD'S arrow of victory, even the arrow of victory over Aram; for you will defeat the Arameans at Aphek until you have destroyed *them.*"

18 Then he said, "Take the arrows," and he took them. And he said to the king of Israel, "Strike the ground," and he struck *it* three times and stopped.

➤ 19 So the man of God was angry with him and said, "You should have struck

five or six times, then you would have struck Aram until you would have destroyed *it.* But now you shall strike Aram *only* three times."

20 Elisha died, and they buried him. Now the bands of the Moabites would invade the land in the spring of the year.

21 As they were burying a man, behold, they saw a marauding band; and they cast the man into the grave of Elisha. And when the man touched the bones of Elisha he revived and stood up on his feet.

22 Now Hazael king of Aram had oppressed Israel all the days of Jehoahaz.

23 But the LORD was gracious to them and had compassion on them and turned to them because of His covenant with Abraham, Isaac, and Jacob, and would not destroy them or cast them from His presence until now.

24 When Hazael king of Aram died, Ben-hadad his son became king in his place.

25 Then Jehoash the son of Jehoahaz took again from the hand of Ben-hadad

---

LIFE LESSONS

➤ **2 Kings 13:14 —** *When Elisha became sick with the illness of which he was to die.*

*E*lisha performed twice as many miracles as Elijah, yet he died of an illness while Elijah "went up by a whirlwind to heaven" (2 Kin. 2:11). Lack of faith? Hardly. God endorsed his ministry by performing one final miracle through him after his death (2 Kin. 13:21).

➤ **2 Kings 13:19 —** *"You should have struck five or six times, then you would have struck Aram until you would have destroyed it."*

*W*hen King Joash of Israel was instructed to strike the ground, it meant he was to shoot the arrows into the ground. He should have shot all the arrows he had taken up—signifying a complete trust in God for a total victory. Unfortunately, when Joash held the arrows back, it showed he didn't have a wholehearted trust in the Lord. The same is true for us. We must use all of our resources in God's service, not holding any back (2 Tim. 4:6). Everything we are and have belongs to Him.

the son of Hazael the cities which he had taken in war from the hand of Jehoahaz his father. Three times Joash defeated him and recovered the cities of Israel.

Psalm 73:1–9

BOOK 3
A Psalm of Asaph.

73
SURELY God is good to Israel,
To those who are pure in heart!
2 But as for me, my feet came close to stumbling,
My steps had almost slipped.
3 For I was envious of the arrogant
As I saw the prosperity of the wicked.
4 For there are no pains in their death,
And their body is fat.
5 They are not in trouble *as other* men,
Nor are they plagued like mankind.
6 Therefore pride is their necklace;
The garment of violence covers them.
7 Their eye bulges from fatness;
The imaginations of *their* heart run riot.
8 They mock and wickedly speak of oppression;
They speak from on high.
9 They have set their mouth against the heavens,
And their tongue parades through the earth.

Proverbs 18:16, 17

16 A man's gift makes room for him
And brings him before great men.
17 The first to plead his case *seems* right,
Until another comes and examines him.

John 19:23–42

23 Then the soldiers, when they had crucified Jesus, took His outer garments and made four parts, a part to every soldier and *also* the tunic; now the tunic was seamless, woven in one piece.
24 So they said to one another, "Let us not tear it, but cast lots for it, *to decide* whose it shall be"; *this was* to fulfill the Scripture: "THEY DIVIDED MY OUTER GARMENTS AMONG THEM, AND FOR MY CLOTHING THEY CAST LOTS."
25 Therefore the soldiers did these things.
But standing by the cross of Jesus were His mother, and His mother's sister, Mary the *wife* of Clopas, and Mary Magdalene.
26 When Jesus then saw His mother, and the disciple whom He loved standing nearby, He *said to His mother, "Woman, behold, your son!"
27 Then He *said to the disciple, "Behold, your mother!" From that hour the disciple took her into his own *household.*
28 After this, Jesus, knowing that all things had already been accomplished, to fulfill the Scripture, *said, "I am thirsty."
29 A jar full of sour wine was standing there; so they put a sponge full of the sour wine upon *a branch of* hyssop and brought it up to His mouth.
30 Therefore when Jesus had received the sour wine, He said, "It is finished!" And He bowed His head and gave up His spirit.

LIFE LESSONS

➤ **Proverbs 18:17 — *The first to plead his case seems right, until another comes and examines him.***

*W*e must guard against making snap judgments. Scripture insists that we listen to the testimony of two or three witnesses before making a decision, precisely so we don't make hasty mistakes (Deut. 19:15; Matt. 18:16; 2 Cor. 13:1; 1 Tim. 5:19).

➤ **John 19:26 — *"Woman, behold, your son!"***

*E*ven as He died, Jesus showed His deep and genuine concern for others. He called upon John the Beloved to care for his mother. "For even the Son of Man did not come to be served, but to serve, and to give His life a ransom for many" (Mark 10:45).

31 Then the Jews, because it was the day of preparation, so that the bodies would not remain on the cross on the Sabbath (for that Sabbath was a high day), asked Pilate that their legs might be broken, and *that* they might be taken away.
32 So the soldiers came, and broke the legs of the first man and of the other who was crucified with Him;
33 but coming to Jesus, when they saw that He was already dead, they did not break His legs.
34 But one of the soldiers pierced His side with a spear, and immediately blood and water came out.
35 And he who has seen has testified, and his testimony is true; and he knows that he is telling the truth, so that you also may believe.
36 For these things came to pass to fulfill

WHAT THE BIBLE SAYS ABOUT

As the King He Is

John 19:38–42

*B*odies that had been crucified were not given the honor and dignity of burial. Rather, they were flung on the city dung heap. It was the most humiliating and horrifying thing that could happen to a Jew … or anyone, for that matter. To be treated as refuse at death was the ultimate disgrace.

Had Jesus been the common criminal the religious leaders said He was His pierced and broken body would have been defiled with the rest of the thieves and scoundrels. However, as the Messiah and the Son of the living God, Jesus was buried in the manner befitting His person.

John 19:38–42 shows us the loving care with which Joseph of Arimathea and Nicodemus treated Jesus' body. "Joseph of Arimathea, being a disciple of Jesus, but a secret one for fear of the Jews, asked Pilate that he might take away the body of Jesus; and Pilate granted permission. So he came and took away His body. Nicodemus, who had first come to Him by night, also came, bringing a mixture of myrrh and aloes, about a hundred pounds weight. So they took the body of Jesus and bound it in linen wrappings with the spices, as is the burial custom of the Jews. Now in the place where He was crucified there was a garden, and in the garden a new tomb in which no one had yet been laid. Therefore because of the Jewish day of preparation, since the tomb was nearby, they laid Jesus there."

Understand that when Joseph of Arimathea and Nicodemus treated Jesus with tenderness and respect in His burial, it was to fulfill prophecy. Psalm 16:10 promises, "For You will not abandon my soul to Sheol; nor will You allow Your Holy One to undergo decay." God had promised the Messiah would not suffer decay in the grave. In faithfulness to His promise, God did not allow Jesus to be dishonored in His burial.

That's why Christ was buried in a tomb— and not just any tomb. Most burial chambers in Israel at the time had space for eight to 13 people, but the tomb they put Jesus in was brand new. It had just been cut out—there had never been a dead body there, which means it had never been defiled by death. So the body of the Messiah never inhabited a place with decay.

Also, during a burial, the body was usually watched, washed, anointed with preparatory spices, and either wrapped with cloth or bound in burial shrouds that were made of strips of linen. The face was bound separately with a face cloth or just covered. The 100 pounds of myrrh and aloes that Nicodemus brought were sufficient to treat 100 to 200 bodies—though it was customary to give monarchs and other highly respected officials that vast amount of spices. Jesus was treated like a king in every way.

God didn't just keep His Son from being treated like a criminal and put on the city trash heap. He didn't merely prevent Christ from seeing decay (Acts 2:31, 32; 13:34, 35, 37). Rather, even in death—however brief it was—the Father showed our Savior the honor and dignity reserved for kings (Phil. 2:9–11)!

Everything surrounding the crucifixion and resurrection of Jesus Christ shows us how God keeps every one of His promises. As Christians, this is extremely important because even when we don't realize it, God is keeping His promises to us in ways that go above and beyond what we could ever imagine (Eph. 3:20).

Therefore, trust Him! And honor Christ as King in your heart. ◈

the Scripture, "NOT A BONE OF HIM SHALL
BE BROKEN."
37 And again another Scripture says,
"THEY SHALL LOOK ON HIM WHOM THEY
PIERCED."
38 After these things Joseph of Arimathea, being a disciple of Jesus, but
a secret one for fear of the Jews, asked
Pilate that he might take away the body
of Jesus; and Pilate granted permission.
So he came and took away His body.
39 Nicodemus, who had first come to
Him by night, also came, bringing a mixture of myrrh and aloes, about a hundred
pounds weight.
40 So they took the body of Jesus and
bound it in linen wrappings with the
spices, as is the burial custom of the
Jews.
41 Now in the place where He was
crucified there was a garden, and in the
garden a new tomb in which no one had
yet been laid.
42 Therefore because of the Jewish
day of preparation, since the tomb was
nearby, they laid Jesus there.

2 Kings 14:1–29

14 IN the second year of Joash son of
Joahaz king of Israel, Amaziah the
son of Joash king of Judah became king.
2 He was twenty-five years old when
he became king, and he reigned twenty-
nine years in Jerusalem. And his mother's name was Jehoaddin of Jerusalem.
3 He did right in the sight of the LORD,
yet not like David his father; he did according to all that Joash his father had
done.
4 Only the high places were not taken
away; the people still sacrificed and
burned incense on the high places.
5 Now it came about, as soon as the
kingdom was firmly in his hand, that
he killed his servants who had slain the
king his father.
6 But the sons of the slayers he did not
put to death, according to what is written
in the book of the Law of Moses, as the
LORD commanded, saying, "The fathers
shall not be put to death for the sons, nor
the sons be put to death for the fathers;
but each shall be put to death for his own
sin."
7 He killed of Edom in the Valley of
Salt 10,000 and took Sela by war, and
named it Joktheel to this day.
8 Then Amaziah sent messengers to
Jehoash, the son of Jehoahaz son of Jehu,
king of Israel, saying, "Come, let us face
each other."
9 Jehoash king of Israel sent to Amaziah king of Judah, saying, "The thorn
bush which was in Lebanon sent to the
cedar which was in Lebanon, saying,
'Give your daughter to my son in marriage.' But there passed by a wild beast
that was in Lebanon, and trampled the
thorn bush.
10 "You have indeed defeated Edom,
and your heart has become proud. Enjoy
your glory and stay at home; for why
should you provoke trouble so that you,
even you, would fall, and Judah with
you?"
11 But Amaziah would not listen. So
Jehoash king of Israel went up; and he
and Amaziah king of Judah faced each
other at Beth-shemesh, which belongs to
Judah.
12 Judah was defeated by Israel, and
they fled each to his tent.
13 Then Jehoash king of Israel captured Amaziah king of Judah, the son
of Jehoash the son of Ahaziah, at Beth-
shemesh, and came to Jerusalem and
tore down the wall of Jerusalem from the
Gate of Ephraim to the Corner Gate, 400
cubits.

LIFE LESSONS

➤ **2 Kings 14:10 — "Your heart has
become proud."**

Pride can cause us to do foolish
things. God tells us, "Pride goes
before destruction, and a haughty spirit
before stumbling" (Prov. 16:18). The Lord
used a wicked king to admonish Amaziah, but he refused to listen.

14 He took all the gold and silver and all the utensils which were found in the house of the LORD, and in the treasuries of the king's house, the hostages also, and returned to Samaria.

15 Now the rest of the acts of Jehoash which he did, and his might and how he fought with Amaziah king of Judah, are they not written in the Book of the Chronicles of the Kings of Israel?

16 So Jehoash slept with his fathers and was buried in Samaria with the kings of Israel; and Jeroboam his son became king in his place.

17 Amaziah the son of Joash king of Judah lived fifteen years after the death of Jehoash son of Jehoahaz king of Israel.

18 Now the rest of the acts of Amaziah, are they not written in the Book of the Chronicles of the Kings of Judah?

19 They conspired against him in Jerusalem, and he fled to Lachish; but they sent after him to Lachish and killed him there.

20 Then they brought him on horses and he was buried at Jerusalem with his fathers in the city of David.

21 All the people of Judah took Azariah, who *was* sixteen years old, and made him king in the place of his father Amaziah.

22 He built Elath and restored it to Judah after the king slept with his fathers.

23 In the fifteenth year of Amaziah the son of Joash king of Judah, Jeroboam the son of Joash king of Israel became king in Samaria, *and reigned* forty-one years.

24 He did evil in the sight of the LORD; he did not depart from all the sins of Jeroboam the son of Nebat, which he made Israel sin.

25 He restored the border of Israel from the entrance of Hamath as far as the Sea of the Arabah, according to the word of the LORD, the God of Israel, which He spoke through His servant Jonah the son of Amittai, the prophet, who was of Gath-hepher.

26 For the LORD saw the affliction of Israel, *which was* very bitter; for there was neither bond nor free, nor was there any helper for Israel.

27 The LORD did not say that He would blot out the name of Israel from under heaven, but He saved them by the hand of Jeroboam the son of Joash.

28 Now the rest of the acts of Jeroboam and all that he did and his might, how he fought and how he recovered for Israel, Damascus and Hamath, *which had belonged* to Judah, are they not written in the Book of the Chronicles of the Kings of Israel?

29 And Jeroboam slept with his fathers, even with the kings of Israel, and Zechariah his son became king in his place.

⊕ Psalm 73:10–20

10 Therefore his people return to this place,
    And waters of abundance are drunk by them.

11 They say, "How does God know?
    And is there knowledge with the Most High?"

12 Behold, these are the wicked;
    And always at ease, they have increased *in* wealth.

13 Surely in vain I have kept my heart pure

LIFE LESSONS

➤ **2 Kings 14:27 — *He saved them by the hand of Jeroboam.***

*T*he sovereign Lord uses both good and evil men to fulfill His holy purposes. What He has said, He will do; but we must take care not to misrepresent or misconstrue His words.

➤ **Psalm 73:13 — *Surely in vain I have kept my heart pure.***

*E*veryone goes through times when they wonder if obeying the Lord is really worth it—especially when they see people who don't serve God having the success and prosperity they want. However, our obedience to Him is never in vain. Asaph the psalmist reminds us we are reaping a harvest in eternity (Ps. 73:17–19). Always remember, we reap what we sow, more than we sow, and later than we sow.

And washed my hands in
    innocence;
14 For I have been stricken all day
    long
And chastened every morning.
15 If I had said, "I will speak thus,"
Behold, I would have betrayed the
    generation of Your children.
16 When I pondered to understand
    this,
It was troublesome in my sight
17 Until I came into the sanctuary of
    God;
Then I perceived their end.
18 Surely You set them in slippery
    places;
You cast them down to destruction.
19 How they are destroyed in a
    moment!
They are utterly swept away by
    sudden terrors!
20 Like a dream when one awakes,
O Lord, when aroused, You will
    despise their form.

Proverbs 18:18, 19

18 The cast lot puts an end to strife
And decides between the mighty
    ones.
19 A brother offended is harder to be
    won than a strong city,
And contentions are like the bars of
    a citadel.

John 20:1–31

20 NOW on the first day of the week
Mary Magdalene *came early to
the tomb, while it *was still dark, and
*saw the stone already taken away from
the tomb.
2   So she *ran and *came to Simon
Peter and to the other disciple whom
Jesus loved, and *said to them, "They
have taken away the Lord out of the
tomb, and we do not know where they
have laid Him."
3   So Peter and the other disciple went
forth, and they were going to the tomb.
4   The two were running together; and

the other disciple ran ahead faster than
Peter and came to the tomb first;
5   and stooping and looking in, he *saw
the linen wrappings lying there; but he
did not go in.
6   And so Simon Peter also *came, following him, and entered the tomb; and
he *saw the linen wrappings lying there,
7   and the face-cloth which had been
on His head, not lying with the linen
wrappings, but rolled up in a place by
itself.
8   So the other disciple who had first
come to the tomb then also entered, and
he saw and believed.
9   For as yet they did not understand
the Scripture, that He must rise again
from the dead.
10 So the disciples went away again to
their own homes.
11 But Mary was standing outside the
tomb weeping; and so, as she wept, she
stooped and looked into the tomb;
12 and she *saw two angels in white sitting, one at the head and one at the feet,
where the body of Jesus had been lying.
13 And they *said to her, "Woman,
why are you weeping?" She *said to
them, "Because they have taken away
my Lord, and I do not know where they
have laid Him."
14 When she had said this, she turned
around and *saw Jesus standing there,
and did not know that it was Jesus.
15 Jesus *said to her, "Woman, why are
you weeping? Whom are you seeking?"
Supposing Him to be the gardener, she
*said to Him, "Sir, if you have carried
Him away, tell me where you have laid
Him, and I will take Him away."
16 Jesus *said to her, "Mary!" She
turned and *said to Him in Hebrew,
"Rabboni!" (which means, Teacher).
17 Jesus *said to her, "Stop clinging to
Me, for I have not yet ascended to the
Father; but go to My brethren and say to
them, 'I ascend to My Father and your
Father, and My God and your God.'"
18 Mary Magdalene *came, announcing
to the disciples, "I have seen the Lord,"
and that He had said these things to her.
19 So when it was evening on that day,
the first day of the week, and when the
doors were shut where the disciples
were, for fear of the Jews, Jesus came

and stood in their midst and *said to them, "Peace *be* with you."

20 And when He had said this, He showed them both His hands and His side. The disciples then rejoiced when they saw the Lord.

➤ 21 So Jesus said to them again, "Peace *be* with you; as the Father has sent Me, I also send you."

22 And when He had said this, He breathed on them and *said to them, "Receive the Holy Spirit.

23 "If you forgive the sins of any, *their* sins have been forgiven them; if you retain the *sins* of any, they have been retained."

24 But Thomas, one of the twelve, called Didymus, was not with them when Jesus came.

25 So the other disciples were saying to him, "We have seen the Lord!" But he said to them, "Unless I see in His hands the imprint of the nails, and put my finger into the place of the nails, and put my hand into His side, I will not believe."

26 After eight days His disciples were again inside, and Thomas with them. Jesus *came, the doors having been shut, and stood in their midst and said, "Peace *be* with you."

27 Then He *said to Thomas, "Reach here with your finger, and see My hands; and reach here your hand and put it into ✳ My side; and do not be unbelieving, but believing."

28 Thomas answered and said to Him, "My Lord and my God!"

29 Jesus *said to him, "Because you have seen Me, have you believed? Blessed *are* they who did not see, and yet believed."

30 Therefore many other signs Jesus also performed in the presence of the disciples, which are not written in this book;

31 but these have been written so that ◄ you may believe that Jesus is the Christ, the Son of God; and that believing you may have life in His name.

LIFE LESSONS

➤ **John 20:21 — *"As the Father has sent Me, I also send you."***

𝒯he Father sent His Son into the world to make it possible for sinful men and women to become holy, and the Son now sends His followers into the world to make it possible for others to hear about His provision.

➤ **John 20:31 — *These have been written so that you may believe that Jesus is the Christ, the Son of God; and that believing you may have life in His name.***

𝒥f the Word of God did not have the Lord's stamp of approval, it would have fallen into obscurity long ago. But as Isaiah 40:8 assures, "The word of our God stands forever." The Bible is His revelation to us, and through the work of the Holy Spirit, it will continue to accomplish His purpose—to lead people to eternal life in Christ (Is. 55:11; Matt. 5:18; Phil. 1:6).

Life Examples:

THOMAS: From Doubt to Faith

JOHN 20:24–29

𝒯he name Thomas is the Hebrew equivalent of the Greek name *Didymus,* which means "twin." Thomas reminds us of the similarities between doubt and faith—both originate from the same place: a confrontation with the unknown. Doubt concedes defeat, while faith claims the victory.

When Jesus appeared to Thomas, hope became reality. The resurrection renewed his confidence in God (John 20:24–29) and motivated him to spend the rest of his life proclaiming the certainty of the risen Christ. Tradition holds that Thomas spread the gospel to India and helped dispel others' disbelief about the resurrection.

If uncertainties have smothered your confidence in the Lord, remember His power so evident in the empty tomb. The crucifixion was not the end of the story—and neither is the trial you face. Choose the path of faith and declare that triumph lies just ahead. Allow His resurrection to strengthen your hope, renew your certainty, and be your greatest victory.

2 Kings 15:1—16:20

15 IN the twenty-seventh year of Jeroboam king of Israel, Azariah son of Amaziah king of Judah became king.
2 He was sixteen years old when he became king, and he reigned fifty-two years in Jerusalem; and his mother's name was Jecoliah of Jerusalem.
3 He did right in the sight of the LORD, according to all that his father Amaziah had done.
4 Only the high places were not taken away; the people still sacrificed and burned incense on the high places.
5 The LORD struck the king, so that he was a leper to the day of his death. And he lived in a separate house, while Jotham the king's son was over the household, judging the people of the land.
6 Now the rest of the acts of Azariah and all that he did, are they not written in the Book of the Chronicles of the Kings of Judah?
7 And Azariah slept with his fathers, and they buried him with his fathers in the city of David, and Jotham his son became king in his place.
8 In the thirty-eighth year of Azariah king of Judah, Zechariah the son of Jeroboam became king over Israel in Samaria for six months.
9 He did evil in the sight of the LORD, as his fathers had done; he did not depart from the sins of Jeroboam the son of Nebat, which he made Israel sin.
10 Then Shallum the son of Jabesh conspired against him and struck him before the people and killed him, and reigned in his place.
11 Now the rest of the acts of Zechariah, behold they are written in the Book of the Chronicles of the Kings of Israel.
12 This is the word of the LORD which He spoke to Jehu, saying, "Your sons to the fourth generation shall sit on the throne of Israel." And so it was.
13 Shallum son of Jabesh became king in the thirty-ninth year of Uzziah king of Judah, and he reigned one month in Samaria.
14 Then Menahem son of Gadi went up from Tirzah and came to Samaria, and struck Shallum son of Jabesh in Samaria, and killed him and became king in his place.
15 Now the rest of the acts of Shallum and his conspiracy which he made, behold they are written in the Book of the Chronicles of the Kings of Israel.
16 Then Menahem struck Tiphsah and all who were in it and its borders from Tirzah, because they did not open to him; therefore he struck it and ripped up all its women who were with child.
17 In the thirty-ninth year of Azariah king of Judah, Menahem son of Gadi became king over Israel and reigned ten years in Samaria.
18 He did evil in the sight of the LORD; he did not depart all his days from the sins of Jeroboam the son of Nebat, which he made Israel sin.
19 Pul, king of Assyria, came against the land, and Menahem gave Pul a thousand talents of silver so that his hand might be with him to strengthen the kingdom under his rule.
20 Then Menahem exacted the money from Israel, even from all the mighty men of wealth, from each man fifty shekels of silver to pay the king of Assyria. So the king of Assyria returned and did not remain there in the land.
21 Now the rest of the acts of Menahem and all that he did, are they not written in

---

LIFE LESSONS

➤ **2 Kings 15:5** — *The LORD struck the king, so that he was a leper to the day of his death.*

Why did God strike King Azariah (also called Uzziah) with leprosy? Second Chronicles 26:16–21 tells us that when the king had many military victories, he became proud and attempted to usurp the duties of a priest. God immediately made him a leper. Pride has terrible consequences.

➤ **2 Kings 15:16** — *They did not open to him; therefore he struck it and ripped up all its women who were with child.*

As God prepares to judge His rebellious people, He usually first gives them a taste of the judgment to come, giving them a further opportunity to repent. But Israel ignored His warnings.

the Book of the Chronicles of the Kings of Israel?

22 And Menahem slept with his fathers, and Pekahiah his son became king in his place.

23 In the fiftieth year of Azariah king of Judah, Pekahiah son of Menahem became king over Israel in Samaria, *and* *reigned* two years.

24 He did evil in the sight of the LORD; he did not depart from the sins of Jeroboam son of Nebat, which he made Israel sin.

25 Then Pekah son of Remaliah, his officer, conspired against him and struck him in Samaria, in the castle of the king's house with Argob and Arieh; and with him were fifty men of the Gileadites, and he killed him and became king in his place.

26 Now the rest of the acts of Pekahiah and all that he did, behold they are written in the Book of the Chronicles of the Kings of Israel.

27 In the fifty-second year of Azariah king of Judah, Pekah son of Remaliah became king over Israel in Samaria, *and* *reigned* twenty years.

28 He did evil in the sight of the LORD; he did not depart from the sins of Jeroboam son of Nebat, which he made Israel sin.

29 In the days of Pekah king of Israel, Tiglath-pileser king of Assyria came and captured Ijon and Abel-beth-maacah and Janoah and Kedesh and Hazor and Gilead and Galilee, all the land of Naphtali; and he carried them captive to Assyria.

30 And Hoshea the son of Elah made a conspiracy against Pekah the son of Remaliah, and struck him and put him to death and became king in his place, in the twentieth year of Jotham the son of Uzziah.

31 Now the rest of the acts of Pekah and all that he did, behold, they are written in the Book of the Chronicles of the Kings of Israel.

32 In the second year of Pekah the son of Remaliah king of Israel, Jotham the son of Uzziah king of Judah became king.

33 He was twenty-five years old when he became king, and he reigned sixteen years in Jerusalem; and his mother's name *was* Jerusha the daughter of Zadok.

34 He did what was right in the sight of the LORD; he did according to all that his father Uzziah had done.

35 Only the high places were not taken away; the people still sacrificed and burned incense on the high places. He built the upper gate of the house of the LORD.

36 Now the rest of the acts of Jotham and all that he did, are they not written in the Book of the Chronicles of the Kings of Judah?

37 In those days the LORD began to send Rezin king of Aram and Pekah the son of Remaliah against Judah.

38 And Jotham slept with his fathers, and he was buried with his fathers in the city of David his father; and Ahaz his son became king in his place.

16 IN the seventeenth year of Pekah the son of Remaliah, Ahaz the son of Jotham, king of Judah, became king.

2 Ahaz *was* twenty years old when he became king, and he reigned sixteen years in Jerusalem; and he did not do what was right in the sight of the LORD his God, as his father David *had done.*

3 But he walked in the way of the kings of Israel, and even made his son pass through the fire, according to the abominations of the nations whom the LORD had driven out from before the sons of Israel.

4 He sacrificed and burned incense on the high places and on the hills and under every green tree.

5 Then Rezin king of Aram and Pekah son of Remaliah, king of Israel, came up to Jerusalem to *wage* war; and they besieged Ahaz, but could not overcome him.

6 At that time Rezin king of Aram recovered Elath for Aram, and cleared the Judeans out of Elath entirely; and the Arameans came to Elath and have lived there to this day.

7 So Ahaz sent messengers to Tiglath-pileser king of Assyria, saying, "I am your servant and your son; come up and deliver me from the hand of the king of Aram and from the hand of the king of Israel, who are rising up against me."

8 Ahaz took the silver and gold that was found in the house of the LORD and in the treasuries of the king's house, and sent a present to the king of Assyria.

9 So the king of Assyria listened to him; and the king of Assyria went up

against Damascus and captured it, and carried *the people of* it away into exile to Kir, and put Rezin to death.

10 Now King Ahaz went to Damascus to meet Tiglath-pileser king of Assyria, and saw the altar which *was* at Damascus; and King Ahaz sent to Urijah the priest the pattern of the altar and its model, according to all its workmanship.

11 So Urijah the priest built an altar; according to all that King Ahaz had sent from Damascus, thus Urijah the priest made *it*, before the coming of King Ahaz from Damascus.

12 When the king came from Damascus, the king saw the altar; then the king approached the altar and went up to it,

13 and burned his burnt offering and his meal offering, and poured his drink offering and sprinkled the blood of his peace offerings on the altar.

14 The bronze altar, which *was* before the LORD, he brought from the front of the house, from between *his* altar and the house of the LORD, and he put it on the north side of *his* altar.

15 Then King Ahaz commanded Urijah the priest, saying, "Upon the great altar burn the morning burnt offering and the evening meal offering and the king's burnt offering and his meal offering, with the burnt offering of all the people of the land and their meal offering and their drink offerings; and sprinkle on it all the blood of the burnt offering and all the blood of the sacrifice. But the bronze altar shall be for me to inquire *by.*"

16 So Urijah the priest did according to all that King Ahaz commanded.

17 Then King Ahaz cut off the borders of the stands, and removed the laver from them; he also took down the sea from the bronze oxen which were under it and put it on a pavement of stone.

18 The covered way for the sabbath which they had built in the house, and the outer entry of the king, he removed from the house of the LORD because of the king of Assyria.

19 Now the rest of the acts of Ahaz which he did, are they not written in the Book of the Chronicles of the Kings of Judah?

20 So Ahaz slept with his fathers, and was buried with his fathers in the city of David; and his son Hezekiah reigned in his place.

Psalm 73:21–28

21 When my heart was embittered
    And I was pierced within,
22 Then I was senseless and
        ignorant;
    I was *like* a beast before You.
23 Nevertheless I am continually
        with You;
    You have taken hold of my right
        hand.
24 With Your counsel You will guide
        me,
    And afterward receive me to glory.
25 Whom have I in heaven *but You?*
    And besides You, I desire nothing
        on earth.
26 My flesh and my heart may fail,
    But God is the strength of my heart
        and my portion forever.
27 For, behold, those who are far from
        You will perish;
    You have destroyed all those who
        are unfaithful to You.
28 But as for me, the nearness of God
        is my good;
    I have made the Lord GOD my
        refuge,
    That I may tell of all Your works.

LIFE LESSONS

➤ **Psalm 73:22 — *Then I was senseless and ignorant; I was like a beast before You.***

*W*hen we leave the path God lays out for us and walk our own way, we may think (for a while) that we are pursuing a better or more enjoyable course of action. But sin is always the wrong choice. Always. When we realize the destruction our sin causes, we also recognize how senseless and ignorant we've been.

➤ **Psalm 73:26 — *My flesh and my heart may fail, but God is the strength of my heart and my portion forever.***

*S*ome people falsely believe only the weak need God, but the truth is that *all* of us are weary, inadequate, vulnerable, and helpless at one point or another. When we find our strength in the Lord, His power is perfected in our weakness (2 Cor. 12:9, 10).

ANSWERS TO LIFE'S QUESTIONS

How do I deal with burnout?

PSALM 73:26

*B*urnout. The very expression seems to make us sigh, doesn't it? In this fast-paced, overworked world, most of us have felt the tiring numbness of burnout. How should a believer in Christ respond to these feelings?

1. *Surrender.* You may think this means to throw up your hands and cry, "I give up!" But that is not what we must do. Rather, we should surrender everything we have to the Lord. His hands are large enough to hold anything we need Him to handle. Remember what God says: "It is I who made the earth, and created man upon it. I stretched out the heavens with My hands and I ordained all their host" (Is. 45:12). When we try to keep everything in our puny hands, we will eventually start dropping it all.

2. *Depend on Him.* Have you ever relinquished a concern to the Lord, only to find yourself trying to pull it back out of His hand? We tend to want to fix things ourselves. The truth is, however, only God has both the power and perspective to bring all matters to their proper conclusion (Rom.

11:33–36). When we try to take things back from Him, we only interfere with the solution He wants to bring about.

3. *Trust Him.* Do not overlook this vital point: God loves you! Because of His great love, God wants to take care of you—and that means He wants to handle all of your worries (Matt. 6:25–34).

God does not want you to run yourself into exhaustion, even by doing "good deeds" or "church work." Instead, He desires for you to rest in Him (Matt. 11:29, 30). You may have reached the end of your rope, but God never will: "Do you not know? Have you not heard? The Everlasting God, the LORD, the Creator of the ends of the earth does not become weary or tired. His understanding is inscrutable. He gives strength to the weary, and to him who lacks might He increases power. Though youths grow weary and tired, and vigorous young men stumble badly, yet those who wait for the LORD will gain new strength; they will mount up with wings like eagles, they will run and not get tired, they will walk and not become weary" (Is. 40:28–31).

Are you burning out? If so, return to the Flame and be rekindled today.

Proverbs 18:20, 21

20 With the fruit of a man's mouth his
  stomach will be satisfied;
  He will be satisfied *with* the product
  of his lips.

✳ 21 Death and life are in the power of
  the tongue,
  And those who love it will eat its fruit.

John 21:1–25

21 AFTER these things Jesus manifested Himself again to the disciples at the Sea of Tiberias, and He manifested *Himself* in this way.
2 Simon Peter, and Thomas called Didymus, and Nathanael of Cana in Galilee, and the *sons* of Zebedee, and two others of His disciples were together.
3 Simon Peter *said to them, "I am going fishing." They *said to him, "We will also come with you." They went out and got into the boat; and that night they caught nothing.

4 But when the day was now breaking, Jesus stood on the beach; yet the disciples did not know that it was Jesus.
5 So Jesus *said to them, "Children, you do not have any fish, do you?" They answered Him, "No."
6 And He said to them, "Cast the net on the right-hand side of the boat and you will find *a catch.*" So they cast, and then they were not able to haul it in because of the great number of fish.
7 Therefore that disciple whom Jesus loved *said to Peter, "It is the Lord." So when Simon Peter heard that it was the Lord, he put his outer garment on (for he was stripped *for work*), and threw himself into the sea.
8 But the other disciples came in the little boat, for they were not far from the land, but about one hundred yards away, dragging the net *full* of fish.
9 So when they got out on the land, they *saw a charcoal fire *already* laid and fish placed on it, and bread.
10 Jesus *said to them, "Bring some of the fish which you have now caught."
11 Simon Peter went up and drew the net to land, full of large fish, a hundred

and fifty-three; and although there were so many, the net was not torn.

➤ 12 Jesus *said to them, "Come *and* have breakfast." None of the disciples ventured to question Him, "Who are You?" knowing that it was the Lord.

13 Jesus *came and *took the bread and *gave *it* to them, and the fish likewise.

14 This is now the third time that Jesus was manifested to the disciples, after He was raised from the dead.

15 So when they had finished breakfast, Jesus *said to Simon Peter, "Simon, *son* of John, do you love Me more than these?" He *said to Him, "Yes, Lord; You know that I love You." He *said to him, "Tend My lambs."

16 He *said to him again a second time, "Simon, *son* of John, do you love Me?"

✱ He *said to Him, "Yes, Lord; You know that I love You." He *said to him, "Shepherd My sheep."

17 He *said to him the third time, "Simon, *son* of John, do you love Me?" Peter was grieved because He said to him the third time, "Do you love Me?" And he said to Him, "Lord, You know all things; You know that I love You." Jesus *said to him, "Tend My sheep.

18 "Truly, truly, I say to you, when you were younger, you used to gird yourself and walk wherever you wished; but when you grow old, you will stretch out your hands and someone else will gird you, and bring you where you do not wish to go."

➤ 19 Now this He said, signifying by what kind of death he would glorify God. And when He had spoken this, He *said to him, "Follow Me!"

20 Peter, turning around, *saw the disciple whom Jesus loved following *them;* the one who also had leaned back on His bosom at the supper and said, "Lord, who is the one who betrays You?"

21 So Peter seeing him *said to Jesus, "Lord, and what about this man?"

➤ 22 Jesus *said to him, "If I want him to remain until I come, what *is that* to you? You follow Me!"

23 Therefore this saying went out among the brethren that that disciple would not die; yet Jesus did not say to him that he would not die, but *only,* "If I want him to remain until I come, what *is that* to you?"

24 This is the disciple who is testifying to these things and wrote these things, and we know that his testimony is true.

25 And there are also many other things which Jesus did, which if they *were written in detail, I suppose that even the world itself *would not contain the books that *would be written.

LIFE LESSONS

➤ **John 21:12 —** *Jesus said to them, "Come and have breakfast."*

*I*f someone were making up the story, it would seem very odd to have the resurrected Savior making breakfast for His awestruck disciples. Yet God is interested in every detail of our lives, even the mundane ones.

➤ **John 21:19 —** *Signifying by what kind of death he would glorify God.*

*F*rom this moment on, Peter knew what kind of death—crucifixion—awaited him. Yet he loved the Savior who forgave him with such a passion that he never shrank from fulfilling his purpose, even to the very end.

➤ **John 21:22 —** *Jesus said to him, "If I want him to remain until I come, what is that to you? You follow Me!"*

*W*e are to concern ourselves with what God wants to do in our lives, not fret about what He might do in the life of another. We are not to compare or compete—we are to obey. What the Lord does with His other servants is His business, not ours.

---

2 Kings 17:1—18:37

17 IN the twelfth year of Ahaz king of Judah, Hoshea the son of Elah

became king over Israel in Samaria, *and reigned* nine years.

2 He did evil in the sight of the LORD, only not as the kings of Israel who were before him.

3   Shalmaneser king of Assyria came up against him, and Hoshea became his servant and paid him tribute.

4   But the king of Assyria found conspiracy in Hoshea, who had sent messengers to So king of Egypt and had offered no tribute to the king of Assyria, as *he had done* year by year; so the king of Assyria shut him up and bound him in prison.

5   Then the king of Assyria invaded the whole land and went up to Samaria and besieged it three years.

6   In the ninth year of Hoshea, the king of Assyria captured Samaria and carried Israel away into exile to Assyria, and settled them in Halah and Habor, *on* the river of Gozan, and in the cities of the Medes.

7   Now *this* came about because the sons of Israel had sinned against the LORD their God, who had brought them up from the land of Egypt from under the hand of Pharaoh, king of Egypt, and they had feared other gods

8   and walked in the customs of the nations whom the LORD had driven out before the sons of Israel, and *in the customs* of the kings of Israel which they had introduced.

9   The sons of Israel did things secretly which were not right against the LORD their God. Moreover, they built for themselves high places in all their towns, from watchtower to fortified city.

10   They set for themselves *sacred* pillars and Asherim on every high hill and under every green tree,

11   and there they burned incense on all the high places as the nations *did* which the LORD had carried away to exile before them; and they did evil things provoking the LORD.

12   They served idols, concerning which the LORD had said to them, "You shall not do this thing."

13   Yet the LORD warned Israel and Judah through all His prophets *and* every seer, saying, "Turn from your evil ways and keep My commandments, My statutes according to all the law which I commanded your fathers, and which I sent to you through My servants the prophets."

14   However, they did not listen, but stiffened their neck like their fathers, who did not believe in the LORD their God.

15   They rejected His statutes and His covenant which He made with their fathers and His warnings with which He warned them. And they followed vanity and became vain, and *went* after the nations which surrounded them, concerning which the LORD had commanded them not to do like them.

16   They forsook all the commandments of the LORD their God and made for themselves molten images, *even* two calves, and made an Asherah and worshiped all the host of heaven and served Baal.

17   Then they made their sons and their daughters pass through the fire, and practiced divination and enchantments, and sold themselves to do evil in the sight of the LORD, provoking Him.

18   So the LORD was very angry with Israel and removed them from His sight; none was left except the tribe of Judah.

19   Also Judah did not keep the commandments of the LORD their God, but walked in the customs which Israel had introduced.

20   The LORD rejected all the descendants of Israel and afflicted them and gave them into the hand of plunderers, until He had cast them out of His sight.

21   When He had torn Israel from the house of David, they made Jeroboam the son of Nebat king. Then Jeroboam drove Israel away from following the LORD and made them commit a great sin.

22   The sons of Israel walked in all the sins of Jeroboam which he did; they did not depart from them

23   until the LORD removed Israel from His sight, as He spoke through all His servants the prophets. So Israel was carried away into exile from their own land to Assyria until this day.

24   The king of Assyria brought *men* from Babylon and from Cuthah and from Avva and from Hamath and Sepharvaim, and settled *them* in the cities of Samaria in place of the sons of Israel. So they possessed Samaria and lived in its cities.

25   At the beginning of their living there, they did not fear the LORD; therefore the LORD sent lions among them which killed some of them.

26   So they spoke to the king of Assyria, saying, "The nations whom you have carried away into exile in the cities of Samaria do not know the custom of the god of the land; so he has sent lions among

them, and behold, they kill them because they do not know the custom of the god of the land."

27 Then the king of Assyria commanded, saying, "Take there one of the priests whom you carried away into exile and let him go and live there; and let him teach them the custom of the god of the land."

28 So one of the priests whom they had carried away into exile from Samaria came and lived at Bethel, and taught them how they should fear the LORD.

29 But every nation still made gods of its own and put them in the houses of the high places which the people of Samaria had made, every nation in their cities in which they lived.

30 The men of Babylon made Succoth-benoth, the men of Cuth made Nergal, the men of Hamath made Ashima,

31 and the Avvites made Nibhaz and Tartak; and the Sepharvites burned their children in the fire to Adrammelech and Anammelech the gods of Sepharvaim.

32 They also feared the LORD and appointed from among themselves priests of the high places, who acted for them in the houses of the high places.

➤ 33 They feared the LORD and served their own gods according to the custom of the nations from among whom they had been carried away into exile.

34 To this day they do according to the earlier customs: they do not fear the LORD, nor do they follow their statutes or their ordinances or the law, or the commandments which the LORD commanded the sons of Jacob, whom He named Israel;

35 with whom the LORD made a covenant and commanded them, saying, "You shall not fear other gods, nor bow down yourselves to them nor serve them nor sacrifice to them.

36 "But the LORD, who brought you up from the land of Egypt with great power and with an outstretched arm, Him you shall fear, and to Him you shall bow yourselves down, and to Him you shall sacrifice.

37 "The statutes and the ordinances and the law and the commandment which He wrote for you, you shall observe to do forever; and you shall not fear other gods.

38 "The covenant that I have made with you, you shall not forget, nor shall you fear other gods.

39 "But the LORD your God you shall fear; and He will deliver you from the hand of all your enemies."

40 However, they did not listen, but they did according to their earlier custom.

41 So while these nations feared the LORD, they also served their idols; their children likewise and their grandchildren, as their fathers did, so they do to this day.

18 NOW it came about in the third year of Hoshea, the son of Elah king of Israel, that Hezekiah the son of Ahaz king of Judah became king.

2 He was twenty-five years old when he became king, and he reigned twenty-nine years in Jerusalem; and his mother's name was Abi the daughter of Zechariah.

3 He did right in the sight of the LORD, according to all that his father David had done.

4 He removed the high places and broke down the *sacred* pillars and cut down the Asherah. He also broke in pieces the bronze serpent that Moses had made, for until those days the sons of Israel burned incense to it; and it was called Nehushtan.

5 He trusted in the LORD, the God of Israel; so that after him there was none like him among all the kings of Judah, nor *among those* who were before him.

6 For he clung to the LORD; he did not depart from following Him, but kept His commandments, which the LORD had commanded Moses.

7 And the LORD was with him; wherever he went he prospered. And he rebelled against the king of Assyria and did not serve him.

8 He defeated the Philistines as far as

Gaza and its territory, from watchtower to fortified city.

9 Now in the fourth year of King Hezekiah, which was the seventh year of Hoshea son of Elah king of Israel, Shalmaneser king of Assyria came up against Samaria and besieged it.

10 At the end of three years they captured it; in the sixth year of Hezekiah, which was the ninth year of Hoshea king of Israel, Samaria was captured.

11 Then the king of Assyria carried Israel away into exile to Assyria, and put them in Halah and on the Habor, the river of Gozan, and in the cities of the Medes,

12 because they did not obey the voice of the LORD their God, but transgressed His covenant, even all that Moses the servant of the LORD commanded; they would neither listen nor do it.

13 Now in the fourteenth year of King Hezekiah, Sennacherib king of Assyria came up against all the fortified cities of Judah and seized them.

14 Then Hezekiah king of Judah sent to the king of Assyria at Lachish, saying, "I have done wrong. Withdraw from me; whatever you impose on me I will bear." So the king of Assyria required of Hezekiah king of Judah three hundred talents of silver and thirty talents of gold.

15 Hezekiah gave him all the silver which was found in the house of the LORD, and in the treasuries of the king's house.

16 At that time Hezekiah cut off the gold from the doors of the temple of the LORD, and from the doorposts which Hezekiah king of Judah had overlaid, and gave it to the king of Assyria.

17 Then the king of Assyria sent Tartan and Rab-saris and Rabshakeh from Lachish to King Hezekiah with a large army to Jerusalem. So they went up and came to Jerusalem. And when they went up, they came and stood by the conduit of the upper pool, which is on the highway of the fuller's field.

18 When they called to the king, Eliakim the son of Hilkiah, who was over the household, and Shebnah the scribe and Joah the son of Asaph the recorder, came out to them.

19 Then Rabshakeh said to them, "Say now to Hezekiah, 'Thus says the great king, the king of Assyria, "What is this confidence that you have?

20 "You say (but they are only empty words), 'I have counsel and strength for the war.' Now on whom do you rely, that you have rebelled against me?

21 "Now behold, you rely on the staff of this crushed reed, even on Egypt; on which if a man leans, it will go into his hand and pierce it. So is Pharaoh king of Egypt to all who rely on him.

22 "But if you say to me, 'We trust in the LORD our God,' is it not He whose high places and whose altars Hezekiah has taken away, and has said to Judah and to Jerusalem, 'You shall worship before this altar in Jerusalem'?

23 "Now therefore, come, make a bargain with my master the king of Assyria, and I will give you two thousand horses, if you are able on your part to set riders on them.

24 "How then can you repulse one official of the least of my master's servants, and rely on Egypt for chariots and for horsemen?

25 "Have I now come up without the ◁ LORD'S approval against this place to destroy it? The LORD said to me, 'Go up against this land and destroy it.'"'"

26 Then Eliakim the son of Hilkiah, and Shebnah and Joah, said to Rabshakeh, "Speak now to your servants in Aramaic, for we understand it; and do not speak with us in Judean in the hearing of the people who are on the wall."

27 But Rabshakeh said to them, "Has my master sent me only to your master and to you to speak these words, and not to the men who sit on the wall, doomed to eat their own dung and drink their own urine with you?"

28 Then Rabshakeh stood and cried with a loud voice in Judean, saying, "Hear the word of the great king, the king of Assyria.

29 "Thus says the king, 'Do not let Hezekiah deceive you, for he will not be able to deliver you from my hand;

LIFE LESSONS

➤ 2 Kings 18:25 — *"The LORD said to me, 'Go up against this land and destroy it.'"*

The Assyrians had no command from the Lord to destroy Jerusalem, but they used religious language to dishearten God's people. We must always be discerning and not believe someone just because he uses the right words.

30 nor let Hezekiah make you trust in the LORD, saying, "The LORD will surely deliver us, and this city will not be given into the hand of the king of Assyria."

31 'Do not listen to Hezekiah, for thus says the king of Assyria, "Make your peace with me and come out to me, and eat each of his vine and each of his fig tree and drink each of the waters of his own cistern,

32 until I come and take you away to a land like your own land, a land of grain and new wine, a land of bread and vineyards, a land of olive trees and honey, that you may live and not die." But do not listen to Hezekiah when he misleads you, saying, "The LORD will deliver us."

33 'Has any one of the gods of the nations delivered his land from the hand of the king of Assyria?

34 'Where are the gods of Hamath and Arpad? Where are the gods of Sepharvaim, Hena and Ivvah? Have they delivered Samaria from my hand?

35 'Who among all the gods of the lands have delivered their land from my hand, that the LORD should deliver Jerusalem from my hand?'"

36 But the people were silent and answered him not a word, for the king's commandment was, "Do not answer him."

37 Then Eliakim the son of Hilkiah, who was over the household, and Shebna the scribe and Joah the son of Asaph, the recorder, came to Hezekiah with their clothes torn and told him the words of Rabshakeh.

✦ Psalm 74:1–8

A Maskil of Asaph.

➤ **74** O GOD, why have You rejected us forever?
Why does Your anger smoke against the sheep of Your pasture?

2 Remember Your congregation,
which You have purchased of old,
Which You have redeemed to be the tribe of Your inheritance;
And this Mount Zion, where You have dwelt.

3 Turn Your footsteps toward the perpetual ruins;

The enemy has damaged everything within the sanctuary.

4 Your adversaries have roared in the midst of Your meeting place;
They have set up their own standards for signs.

5 It seems as if one had lifted up *His* axe in a forest of trees.

6 And now all its carved work They smash with hatchet and hammers.

7 They have burned Your sanctuary to the ground;
They have defiled the dwelling place of Your name.

8 They said in their heart, "Let us completely subdue them."
They have burned all the meeting places of God in the land.

✦ Proverbs 18:22–24

22 He who finds a wife finds a good thing
And obtains favor from the LORD.

23 The poor man utters supplications,
But the rich man answers roughly.

24 A man of *too many* friends *comes* to ruin,
But there is a friend who sticks closer than a brother.

✦ Acts 1:1–26

1 THE first account I composed, Theophilus, about all that Jesus began to do and teach,

2 until the day when He was taken up *to heaven*, after He had by the Holy Spirit given orders to the apostles whom He had chosen.

3 To these He also presented Himself alive after His suffering, by many convincing proofs, appearing to them over *a period of* forty days and speaking of the things concerning the kingdom of God.

4 Gathering them together, He commanded them not to leave Jerusalem, but to wait for what the Father had promised, "Which," *He said,* "you heard of from Me;

5 for John baptized with water, but you will be baptized with the Holy Spirit not many days from now."

6 So when they had come together, they were asking Him, saying, "Lord, is it at this time You are restoring the kingdom to Israel?"

7 He said to them, "It is not for you to know times or epochs which the Father has fixed by His own authority;

8 but you will receive power when the Holy Spirit has come upon you; and you shall be My witnesses both in Jerusalem, and in all Judea and Samaria, and even to the remotest part of the earth."

9 And after He had said these things, He was lifted up while they were looking on, and a cloud received Him out of their sight.

10 And as they were gazing intently into the sky while He was going, behold,

two men in white clothing stood beside them.

11 They also said, "Men of Galilee, why do you stand looking into the sky? This Jesus, who has been taken up from you into heaven, will come in just the same way as you have watched Him go into heaven."

12 Then they returned to Jerusalem from the mount called Olivet, which is near Jerusalem, a Sabbath day's journey away.

13 When they had entered *the city,* they went up to the upper room where they were staying; that is, Peter and John and James and Andrew, Philip and Thomas,

LIFE LESSONS

➤ **Acts 1:11 — *"Men of Galilee, why do you stand looking into the sky?"***

*W*hy were they standing there and looking up at the sky? Because the risen Lord Jesus Christ was gloriously ascending to heaven at the Father's right hand. It is easy to get so mesmerized by the amazing power and miracles of God that we become mere observers rather than active participants in what He wants to do in this world. Yet God calls us to Spirit-empowered action, and we must tell others of the wonderful salvation He has provided for us.

Bartholomew and Matthew, James *the son* of Alphaeus, and Simon the Zealot, and Judas *the son* of James.
14　These all with one mind were continually devoting themselves to prayer, along with *the* women, and Mary the mother of Jesus, and with His brothers.
15　At this time Peter stood up in the midst of the brethren (a gathering of about one hundred and twenty persons was there together), and said,
16 "Brethren, the Scripture had to be fulfilled, which the Holy Spirit foretold by the mouth of David concerning Judas, who became a guide to those who arrested Jesus.
17 "For he was counted among us and received his share in this ministry."

18　(Now this man acquired a field with the price of his wickedness, and falling headlong, he burst open in the middle and all his intestines gushed out.
19　And it became known to all who were living in Jerusalem; so that in their own language that field was called Hakeldama, that is, Field of Blood.)
20 "For it is written in the book of Psalms,
　'LET HIS HOMESTEAD BE MADE
　　DESOLATE,
　AND LET NO ONE DWELL IN IT';
and,
　'LET ANOTHER MAN TAKE HIS OFFICE.'
21 "Therefore it is necessary that of the men who have accompanied us all the time that the Lord Jesus went in and out among us—
22　beginning with the baptism of John until the day that He was taken up from us—one of these *must* become a witness with us of His resurrection."
23　So they put forward two men, Joseph called Barsabbas (who was also called Justus), and Matthias.
24　And they prayed and said, "You, Lord, who know the hearts of all men, show which one of these two You have chosen
25　to occupy this ministry and apostleship from which Judas turned aside to go to his own place."
26　And they drew lots for them, and the lot fell to Matthias; and he was added to the eleven apostles.

2 Kings 19:1—21:26

19 AND when King Hezekiah heard *it*, he tore his clothes, covered himself with sackcloth and entered the house of the LORD.
2　Then he sent Eliakim who was over the household with Shebna the scribe and the elders of the priests, covered with sackcloth, to Isaiah the prophet the son of Amoz.
3　They said to him, "Thus says Hezekiah, 'This day is a day of distress, rebuke, and rejection; for children have

come to birth and there is no strength to *deliver.*
4　'Perhaps the LORD your God will hear all the words of Rabshakeh, whom his master the king of Assyria has sent to reproach the living God, and will rebuke the words which the LORD your God has heard. Therefore, offer a prayer for the remnant that is left.'"
5　So the servants of King Hezekiah came to Isaiah.
6　Isaiah said to them, "Thus you shall say to your master, 'Thus says the LORD, "Do not be afraid because of the words that you have heard, with which the

servants of the king of Assyria have blasphemed Me.

➤ 7 "Behold, I will put a spirit in him so that he will hear a rumor and return to his own land. And I will make him fall by the sword in his own land."'"

8 Then Rabshakeh returned and found the king of Assyria fighting against Libnah, for he had heard that the king had left Lachish.

9 When he heard *them* say concerning Tirhakah king of Cush, "Behold, he has come out to fight against you," he sent messengers again to Hezekiah saying,

10 'Thus you shall say to Hezekiah king of Judah, 'Do not let your God in whom you trust deceive you saying, "Jerusalem will not be given into the hand of the king of Assyria."

11 'Behold, you have heard what the kings of Assyria have done to all the lands, destroying them completely. So will you be spared?

12 'Did the gods of those nations which my fathers destroyed deliver them, *even* Gozan and Haran and Rezeph and the sons of Eden who *were* in Telassar?

13 'Where is the king of Hamath, the king of Arpad, the king of the city of Sepharvaim, and *of* Hena and Ivvah?'"

14 Then Hezekiah took the letter from the hand of the messengers and read it, and he went up to the house of the LORD and spread it out before the LORD.

15 Hezekiah prayed before the LORD and said, "O LORD, the God of Israel, who are enthroned *above* the cherubim, You are the God, You alone, of all the kingdoms of the earth. You have made heaven and earth.

16 "Incline Your ear, O LORD, and hear; open Your eyes, O LORD, and see; and listen to the words of Sennacherib, which he has sent to reproach the living God.

17 "Truly, O LORD, the kings of Assyria have devastated the nations and their lands

18 and have cast their gods into the fire, for they were not gods but the work of men's hands, wood and stone. So they have destroyed them.

19 "Now, O LORD our God, I pray, deliver
✻ us from his hand that all the kingdoms of the earth may know that You alone, O LORD, are God."

➤ 20 Then Isaiah the son of Amoz sent to Hezekiah saying, "Thus says the LORD,

the God of Israel, 'Because you have prayed to Me about Sennacherib king of Assyria, I have heard you.'

21 "This is the word that the LORD has spoken against him:

'She has despised you and mocked you,
The virgin daughter of Zion;
She has shaken *her* head behind you,
The daughter of Jerusalem!

22 'Whom have you reproached and blasphemed?
And against whom have you raised *your* voice,
And haughtily lifted up your eyes?
Against the Holy One of Israel!

23 'Through your messengers you have reproached the Lord,
And you have said, "With my many chariots
I came up to the heights of the mountains,
To the remotest parts of Lebanon;
And I cut down its tall cedars *and* its choice cypresses.
And I entered its farthest lodging place, its thickest forest.

24 "I dug *wells* and drank foreign waters,

LIFE LESSONS

➤ **2 Kings 19:7** — *"I will put a spirit in him so that he will hear a rumor and return to his own land. And I will make him fall by the sword in his own land."*

*E*veryone falls under God's sovereign power—even powerful enemy rulers. Though King Hezekiah was unable to stave off Sennacherib's onslaught or change the situation in any way—the Lord certainly could. And He did. Second Kings 19:35–37 testifies and history confirms that God kept His promise to Hezekiah. Sennacherib fell by the sword in Ninevah (2 Chr. 32:21). Everything concerning your circumstances—including the people in authority over you—is under God's sovereign hand (Prov. 21:1).

➤ **2 Kings 19:20** — *"Because you have prayed to Me about Sennacherib king of Assyria, I have heard you."*

*G*od acted in a mighty way against the king of Assyria because Hezekiah had prayed for Him to intervene. When we fight our battles on our knees, we win every time.

And with the sole of my feet I
   dried up
All the rivers of Egypt."
25 'Have you not heard?
   Long ago I did it;
From ancient times I planned it.
Now I have brought it to pass,
That you should turn fortified cities
   into ruinous heaps.
26 'Therefore their inhabitants were
   short of strength,
They were dismayed and put to
   shame;
They were as the vegetation of the
   field and as the green herb,
As grass on the housetops is
   scorched before it is grown up.
27 'But I know your sitting down,
And your going out and your
   coming in,
And your raging against Me.
28 'Because of your raging against Me,
And because your arrogance has
   come up to My ears,
Therefore I will put My hook in your
   nose,
And My bridle in your lips,
And I will turn you back by the way
   which you came.
29 'Then this shall be the sign for you:
you will eat this year what grows of
itself, in the second year what springs
from the same, and in the third year sow,
reap, plant vineyards, and eat their fruit.
30 'The surviving remnant of the house
of Judah will again take root downward
and bear fruit upward.
31 'For out of Jerusalem will go forth a
remnant, and out of Mount Zion survivors.
The zeal of the LORD will perform this.
32 'Therefore thus says the LORD concerning the king of Assyria, "He will not
come to this city or shoot an arrow there;
and he will not come before it with a
shield or throw up a siege ramp against it.
33 "By the way that he came, by the
same he will return, and he shall not
come to this city,"' declares the LORD.
34 'For I will defend this city to save it for
My own sake and for My servant David's
sake.'"
35 Then it happened that night that the
angel of the LORD went out and struck
185,000 in the camp of the Assyrians;
and when men rose early in the morning,
behold, all of them were dead.
36 So Sennacherib king of Assyria de-

LIFE LESSONS

➤ **2 Kings 19:35 — *The angel of the LORD
went out and struck 185,000 in the camp
of the Assyrians.***

A solitary angel killed 185,000 trained
Assyrian troops—the best in the
world at that time—in a single night.
"The angel of the LORD encamps around
those who fear Him, and rescues them"
(Ps. 34:7).

parted and returned *home*, and lived at
Nineveh.
37 It came about as he was worshiping in the house of Nisroch his god, that
Adrammelech and Sharezer killed him
with the sword; and they escaped into
the land of Ararat. And Esarhaddon his
son became king in his place.

20 IN those days Hezekiah became
mortally ill. And Isaiah the prophet
the son of Amoz came to him and said
to him, "Thus says the LORD, 'Set your
house in order, for you shall die and not
live.'"
2 Then he turned his face to the wall
and prayed to the LORD, saying,
3 "Remember now, O LORD, I beseech
You, how I have walked before You in
truth and with a whole heart and have
done what is good in Your sight." And
Hezekiah wept bitterly.
4 Before Isaiah had gone out of the
middle court, the word of the LORD came
to him, saying,
5 "Return and say to Hezekiah the
leader of My people, 'Thus says the LORD,
the God of your father David, "I have
heard your prayer, I have seen your tears;
behold, I will heal you. On the third day
you shall go up to the house of the LORD.
6 "I will add fifteen years to your life,
and I will deliver you and this city from
the hand of the king of Assyria; and I will
defend this city for My own sake and for
My servant David's sake."'"
7 Then Isaiah said, "Take a cake of
figs." And they took and laid *it* on the
boil, and he recovered.
8 Now Hezekiah said to Isaiah, "What
will be the sign that the LORD will heal
me, and that I shall go up to the house of
the LORD the third day?"
9 Isaiah said, "This shall be the sign to
you from the LORD, that the LORD will do

the thing that He has spoken: shall the shadow go forward ten steps or go back ten steps?"

10 So Hezekiah answered, "It is easy for the shadow to decline ten steps; no, but let the shadow turn backward ten steps."

11 Isaiah the prophet cried to the LORD, and He brought the shadow on the stairway back ten steps by which it had gone down on the stairway of Ahaz.

12 At that time Berodach-baladan a son of Baladan, king of Babylon, sent letters and a present to Hezekiah, for he heard that Hezekiah had been sick.

13 Hezekiah listened to them, and showed them all his treasure house, the silver and the gold and the spices and the precious oil and the house of his armor and all that was found in his treasuries. There was nothing in his house nor in all his dominion that Hezekiah did not show them.

14 Then Isaiah the prophet came to King Hezekiah and said to him, "What did these men say, and from where have they come to you?" And Hezekiah said, "They have come from a far country, from Babylon."

15 He said, "What have they seen in your house?" So Hezekiah answered, "They have seen all that is in my house; there is nothing among my treasuries that I have not shown them."

16 Then Isaiah said to Hezekiah, "Hear the word of the LORD.

➤ 17 'Behold, the days are coming when all that is in your house, and all that your fathers have laid up in store to this day will be carried to Babylon; nothing shall be left,' says the LORD.

18 'Some of your sons who shall issue from you, whom you will beget, will be taken away; and they will become officials in the palace of the king of Babylon.'"

19 Then Hezekiah said to Isaiah, "The word of the LORD which you have spoken is good." For he thought, "Is it not so, if there will be peace and truth in my days?"

20 Now the rest of the acts of Hezekiah and all his might, and how he made the pool and the conduit and brought water into the city, are they not written in the Book of the Chronicles of the Kings of Judah?

21 So Hezekiah slept with his fathers, and Manasseh his son became king in his place.

21 MANASSEH was twelve years old when he became king, and he reigned fifty-five years in Jerusalem; and his mother's name was Hephzibah.

2 He did evil in the sight of the LORD, according to the abominations of the nations whom the LORD dispossessed before the sons of Israel.

3 For he rebuilt the high places which Hezekiah his father had destroyed; and he erected altars for Baal and made an Asherah, as Ahab king of Israel had done, and worshiped all the host of heaven and served them.

4 He built altars in the house of the LORD, of which the LORD had said, "In Jerusalem I will put My name."

5 For he built altars for all the host of heaven in the two courts of the house of the LORD.

6 He made his son pass through the fire, practiced witchcraft and used divination, and dealt with mediums and spiritists. He did much evil in the sight of the LORD provoking *Him to anger.*

7 Then he set the carved image of Asherah that he had made, in the house of which the LORD said to David and to his son Solomon, "In this house and in Jerusalem, which I have chosen from all the tribes of Israel, I will put My name forever.

8 "And I will not make the feet of Israel wander anymore from the land which I gave their fathers, if only they will observe to do according to all that I have commanded them, and according to all the law that My servant Moses commanded them."

9 But they did not listen, and Manasseh seduced them to do evil more than the nations whom the LORD destroyed before the sons of Israel.

10 Now the LORD spoke through His servants the prophets, saying,
11 "Because Manasseh king of Judah has done these abominations, having done wickedly more than all the Amorites did who *were* before him, and has also made Judah sin with his idols;
12 therefore thus says the LORD, the God of Israel, 'Behold, I am bringing *such* calamity on Jerusalem and Judah, that whoever hears of it, both his ears will tingle.
13 'I will stretch over Jerusalem the line of Samaria and the plummet of the house of Ahab, and I will wipe Jerusalem as one wipes a dish, wiping it and turning it upside down.
14 'I will abandon the remnant of My inheritance and deliver them into the hand of their enemies, and they will become as plunder and spoil to all their enemies;
15 because they have done evil in My sight, and have been provoking Me to anger since the day their fathers came from Egypt, even to this day.'"
16 Moreover, Manasseh shed very much innocent blood until he had filled Jerusalem from one end to another; besides his sin with which he made Judah sin, in doing evil in the sight of the LORD.
17 Now the rest of the acts of Manasseh and all that he did and his sin which he committed, are they not written in the Book of the Chronicles of the Kings of Judah?
18 And Manasseh slept with his fathers and was buried in the garden of his own house, in the garden of Uzza, and Amon his son became king in his place.
19 Amon was twenty-two years old when he became king, and he reigned two years in Jerusalem; and his mother's name *was* Meshullemeth the daughter of Haruz of Jotbah.
20 He did evil in the sight of the LORD, as Manasseh his father had done.
21 For he walked in all the way that his father had walked, and served the idols that his father had served and worshiped them.
22 So he forsook the LORD, the God of his fathers, and did not walk in the way of the LORD.
23 The servants of Amon conspired against him and killed the king in his own house.
24 Then the people of the land killed all those who had conspired against King Amon, and the people of the land made Josiah his son king in his place.
25 Now the rest of the acts of Amon which he did, are they not written in the Book of the Chronicles of the Kings of Judah?
26 He was buried in his grave in the garden of Uzza, and Josiah his son became king in his place.

Psalm 74:9–17

9   We do not see our signs;
There is no longer any prophet,
Nor is there any among us who knows how long.
10   How long, O God, will the adversary revile,
And the enemy spurn Your name forever?
11   Why do You withdraw Your hand, even Your right hand?
From within Your bosom, destroy *them!*
12   Yet God is my king from of old,
Who works deeds of deliverance in the midst of the earth;
13   You divided the sea by Your strength;
You broke the heads of the sea monsters in the waters.
14   You crushed the heads of Leviathan;
You gave him as food for the creatures of the wilderness.
15   You broke open springs and torrents;
You dried up ever-flowing streams.
16   Yours is the day, Yours also is the night;
You have prepared the light and the sun.
17   You have established all the boundaries of the earth;
You have made summer and winter.

Proverbs 19:1, 2

19 BETTER is a poor man who walks in his integrity
Than he who is perverse in speech and is a fool.

2   Also it is not good for a person to be without knowledge,
And he who hurries his footsteps errs.

Acts 2:1–21

2 WHEN the day of Pentecost had come, they were all together in one place.
2   And suddenly there came from heaven a noise like a violent rushing wind, and it filled the whole house where they were sitting.
3   And there appeared to them tongues as of fire distributing themselves, and they rested on each one of them.
4   And they were all filled with the Holy Spirit and began to speak with other tongues, as the Spirit was giving them utterance.
5   Now there were Jews living in Jerusalem, devout men from every nation under heaven.
6   And when this sound occurred, the crowd came together, and were bewildered because each one of them was hearing them speak in his own language.
7   They were amazed and astonished, saying, "Why, are not all these who are speaking Galileans?

ANSWERS TO LIFE'S QUESTIONS

When and how am I filled with the Holy Spirit?

ACTS 2:4

*W*hat does the New Testament have to say about the believer's relationship with the Holy Spirit? It seems there is sometimes a debate concerning the activity of the Spirit in a person's life and how a believer experiences the Spirit-filled Christian life. But when we look at Scripture, we see there is no real cause for confusion.

The Holy Spirit arrived to establish the church on the day of Pentecost, and He was accompanied by extraordinary manifestations of His presence. These demonstrations were sign oriented, not character based. In other words, the Bible doesn't say that after being filled with the Holy Spirit, those in the Upper Room went out with great patience, kindness, gentleness, and so on (Gal. 5:22, 23). Rather, it says they immediately began speaking in other tongues. That is how the unbelievers who heard them knew that something supernatural had taken place (Acts 2:1–12).

Initially, it appeared the Spirit specifically came to indwell those gathered in the Upper Room to spread the gospel (Acts 2:3, 4). Soon, however, other believers also were filled with the Holy Spirit as they surrendered their lives to Jesus Christ (Acts 4:31; 9:17). It then became obvious that Christian believers everywhere were being blessed with the outpouring of the Spirit, and He was transforming their lives (Acts 10:45).

What then was the relationship between salvation and receiving the Spirit? Paul explained, "After listening to the message of truth, the gospel of your salvation—having also believed, you were sealed in Him with the Holy Spirit of promise, who is given as a pledge of our inheritance, with a view to the redemption of God's own possession, to the praise of His glory" (Eph. 1:13, 14).

Within a few years following the day of Pentecost, the gospel of Jesus Christ was being taught throughout the known world, and lives were being changed as a result of His Spirit. In fact, after the Book of Acts, the phrase "filled with the Spirit" was not used again, except for being mentioned in Ephesians 5:18. In that passage, Paul talks about surrendering to the influence of the Spirit—not to the indwelling ministry of the Holy Spirit, which every believer receives.

Today, God dwells in the hearts and lives of all who place their faith in His Son, the Lord Jesus Christ. Paul wrote, "By one Spirit we were all baptized into one body, whether Jews or Greeks, whether slaves or free, and we were all made to drink of one Spirit" (1 Cor. 12:13). The apostle John wrote, "By this we know that we abide in Him and He in us, because He has given us of His Spirit" (1 John 4:13). In fact, "If anyone does not have the Spirit of Christ, he does not belong to Him" (Rom. 8:9). We know we belong to Christ because His Spirit dwells in us.

We are filled with God's Spirit the moment we accept Christ as our personal Savior. We are not repeatedly refilled—we have all we are going to receive of the Spirit at salvation. However, as we grow in our Christian walk, we learn more about God's ways, character, and presence within us through His Spirit. The more about Him we know, love, and obey, the more we learn how to live life to the fullest. Some may say we receive more of the Holy Spirit, but just the opposite is true—the Spirit actually gains more of us.

LIFE LESSONS

➤ **Acts 2:4 — *They were all filled with the Holy Spirit and began to speak with other tongues, as the Spirit was giving them utterance.***

*T*o demonstrate to the disciples and to the unbelieving world that the Spirit had come in power on the church in a new way, the believers began to speak in languages they had never learned. However, understand that what they spoke were the dialects of the people from "his own language" (Acts 2:6). They did not speak meaningless babble or some unknown tongue; rather, they spoke the established languages of "devout men from every nation under heaven" that were present (Acts 2:5; see also Acts 2:9–11; 1 Cor. 14).

➤ **Acts 2:5 — *There were Jews living in Jerusalem, devout men from every nation under heaven.***

*W*hy were there people from every nation in Jerusalem? Because it was the Feast of Pentecost—also called the Feast of Weeks—which was the fiftieth day of the Hebrew harvest (Lev. 23:15-22; Deut. 16:9–12). It was a celebration of God's provision, and Jews from around the world would bring their offerings of thanksgiving to the temple. Little did they know God would change their lives in such a radical way, and they would become the harvest (Acts 2:41)!

8 "And how is it that we each hear *them* in our own language to which we were born?

9 "Parthians and Medes and Elamites, and residents of Mesopotamia, Judea and Cappadocia, Pontus and Asia,

10 Phrygia and Pamphylia, Egypt and the districts of Libya around Cyrene, and visitors from Rome, both Jews and proselytes,

11 Cretans and Arabs—we hear them in our *own* tongues speaking of the mighty deeds of God."

12 And they all continued in amazement and great perplexity, saying to one another, "What does this mean?"

13 But others were mocking and saying, "They are full of sweet wine."

14 But Peter, taking his stand with the eleven, raised his voice and declared to them: "Men of Judea and all you who live in Jerusalem, let this be known to you and give heed to my words.

15 "For these men are not drunk, as you suppose, for it is *only* the third hour of the day;

16 but this is what was spoken of through the prophet Joel:

17 'AND IT SHALL BE IN THE LAST DAYS,'
God says,
'THAT I WILL POUR FORTH OF MY SPIRIT
ON ALL MANKIND;
AND YOUR SONS AND YOUR DAUGHTERS
SHALL PROPHESY,
AND YOUR YOUNG MEN SHALL SEE
VISIONS,
AND YOUR OLD MEN SHALL DREAM
DREAMS;

18 EVEN ON MY BONDSLAVES, BOTH MEN
AND WOMEN,
I WILL IN THOSE DAYS POUR FORTH OF
MY SPIRIT
And they shall prophesy.

19 'AND I WILL GRANT WONDERS IN THE
SKY ABOVE
AND SIGNS ON THE EARTH BELOW,
BLOOD, AND FIRE, AND VAPOR OF
SMOKE.

20 'THE SUN WILL BE TURNED INTO
DARKNESS
AND THE MOON INTO BLOOD,
BEFORE THE GREAT AND GLORIOUS DAY
OF THE LORD SHALL COME.

21 'AND IT SHALL BE THAT EVERYONE WHO
CALLS ON THE NAME OF THE LORD
WILL BE SAVED.'

2 Kings 22:1—24:20

22 JOSIAH was eight years old when he became king, and he reigned

thirty-one years in Jerusalem; and his mother's name *was* Jedidah the daughter of Adaiah of Bozkath.

2 He did right in the sight of the LORD and walked in all the way of his father

David, nor did he turn aside to the right or to the left.

3 Now in the eighteenth year of King Josiah, the king sent Shaphan, the son of Azaliah the son of Meshullam the scribe, to the house of the LORD saying,

4 "Go up to Hilkiah the high priest that he may count the money brought in to the house of the LORD which the door-keepers have gathered from the people.

5 "Let them deliver it into the hand of the workmen who have the oversight of the house of the LORD, and let them give it to the workmen who are in the house of the LORD to repair the damages of the house,

6 to the carpenters and the builders and the masons and for buying timber and hewn stone to repair the house.

7 "Only no accounting shall be made with them for the money delivered into their hands, for they deal faithfully."

8 Then Hilkiah the high priest said to Shaphan the scribe, "I have found the book of the law in the house of the LORD." And Hilkiah gave the book to Shaphan who read it.

9 Shaphan the scribe came to the king and brought back word to the king and said, "Your servants have emptied out the money that was found in the house, and have delivered it into the hand of the workmen who have the oversight of the house of the LORD."

➤ 10 Moreover, Shaphan the scribe told the king saying, "Hilkiah the priest has given me a book." And Shaphan read it in the presence of the king.

11 When the king heard the words of the book of the law, he tore his clothes.

12 Then the king commanded Hilkiah the priest, Ahikam the son of Shaphan, Achbor the son of Micaiah, Shaphan the scribe, and Asaiah the king's servant saying,

13 "Go, inquire of the LORD for me and the people and all Judah concerning the words of this book that has been found, for great is the wrath of the LORD that burns against us, because our fathers have not listened to the words of this book, to do according to all that is written concerning us."

14 So Hilkiah the priest, Ahikam, Achbor, Shaphan, and Asaiah went to Huldah the prophetess, the wife of Shallum the son of Tikvah, the son of Harhas, keeper of the wardrobe (now she lived in Jerusalem in the Second Quarter); and they spoke to her.

15 She said to them, "Thus says the LORD God of Israel, 'Tell the man who sent you to me,

16 thus says the LORD, "Behold, I bring evil on this place and on its inhabitants, *even* all the words of the book which the king of Judah has read.

17 "Because they have forsaken Me and have burned incense to other gods that they might provoke Me to anger with all the work of their hands, therefore My wrath burns against this place, and it shall not be quenched."'

18 "But to the king of Judah who sent you to inquire of the LORD thus shall you say to him, 'Thus says the LORD God of Israel, "*Regarding* the words which you have heard,

19 because your heart was tender and you humbled yourself before the LORD when you heard what I spoke against this place and against its inhabitants that they should become a desolation and a curse, and you have torn your clothes and wept before Me, I truly have heard ✳ you," declares the LORD.

20 "Therefore, behold, I will gather you to your fathers, and you will be gathered to your grave in peace, and your eyes will not see all the evil which I will bring on this place."'" So they brought back word to the king.

23 THEN the king sent, and they gathered to him all the elders of Judah and of Jerusalem.

2 The king went up to the house of the LORD and all the men of Judah and all the inhabitants of Jerusalem with him, and the priests and the prophets and all the people, both small and great; and he read in their hearing all the words of the

WHAT THE BIBLE SAYS ABOUT

Founded in Faithfulness

2 Kings 22:1—23:3

*T*he heavy ancient scroll crinkled beneath his fingertips as Josiah began to unroll the book of the covenant. The people of Judah were still gathering before the temple. From the least to the greatest, they assembled to hear their king read from the sacred pages, which had been lost for many generations.

Josiah stood by the northern pillar of the temple, the appropriate place for a king. He glanced at the scroll and then looked south to the other pillar. The once bronze-covered column bore the name *Jachin*, which means, "He establishes."

He considered the strength of this monument, a poignant reminder of the power of the Lord God. It was not by man's strength that this nation had been brought into existence. Yahweh had established this nation and had placed David, his ancestor, on the throne.

The bronze had been stripped from the pillar, and Josiah was saddened by the desecration. Evil kings and foreign rulers had ransacked the treasures of the temple, dishonoring the sanctuary of Yahweh. The pine paneling, which had been covered with gold, was exposed like the sins of the people. He glanced down at the words of the covenant and sighed. Was Judah beyond the favor of the Lord? Had they sinned so profoundly and welcomed the foreign gods so willingly that God would reject them forever?

Josiah became king after the murder of his idolatrous father, Amon. Because he was only eight, he lacked instruction in the ways of the Lord. Having no living example to go by, he walked in the ways of his forefather, the great King David. Now, the words of the prophetess, Huldah, were the encouragement that Josiah needed. Through Huldah's words, Josiah was reassured that God had not rejected him. "Because your heart was tender and you humbled yourself before the LORD when you heard what I spoke against this place and against its inhabitants that they should become a desolation and a curse, and you have torn your

clothes and wept before Me, I truly have heard you," declares the LORD" (2 Kin. 22:19).

This northern pillar under which Josiah stood was called *Boaz*, or "by Him is he mighty." It was right that Josiah stood here, under the canopy of God's protection, to proclaim the covenant of the Lord. Like King David, Josiah's heart was set to rule Judah in a manner that would honor the Lord. He would carry out the commands of the Law with the strength Yahweh would give him.

Though he stood amidst the desolation of the temple, there was a foundation within him that could neither be shaken nor destroyed. Therefore, Josiah read from the ancient manuscript with confidence. He committed himself to follow the Lord, keeping all His mandates and decrees, renewing the covenant of his forefathers. As a result, all the people before him—from the least to the greatest—pledged themselves to the Lord.

Josiah's reforms throughout Judah and Samaria were extensive. In fact, his obedience was so great he stands out in Scripture as one of the most faithful kings. "Before him there was no king like him who turned to the LORD with all his heart and with all his soul and with all his might, according to all the law of Moses; nor did any like him arise after him" (2 Kin. 23:25).

Though there may be destruction and despair surrounding you, you have a sure foundation that will never fall. God's strength and your reliance upon His trustworthy character will sustain you when everything else begins to crumble.

The Lord did not accept Josiah because he had attained the most wealth or military victories. Rather, God accepted Josiah because he was obedient to His instruction. Josiah put all of his trust and hope in the covenant Yahweh had established, knowing the Lord would honor His Word. When you trust in the faultless character of God and allow His Word to dwell in you, you will have a foundation established that cannot be shaken.

No matter what trial or opposition you face, the foundation of the Lord's love and Word in your heart will endure. Like Josiah, God will help you. Make your heart tender, and humble yourself before the Lord. He will establish you, and by Him you will be mighty. ◉

book of the covenant which was found in the house of the LORD.

3   The king stood by the pillar and made a covenant before the LORD, to walk after the LORD, and to keep His

commandments and His testimonies and His statutes with all *his* heart and all *his* soul, to carry out the words of this covenant that were written in this book. And all the people entered into the covenant.

4   Then the king commanded Hilkiah the high priest and the priests of the second order and the doorkeepers, to bring out of the temple of the LORD all the vessels that were made for Baal, for Asherah, and for all the host of heaven; and he burned them outside Jerusalem in the fields of the Kidron, and carried their ashes to Bethel.

5   He did away with the idolatrous priests whom the kings of Judah had appointed to burn incense in the high places in the cities of Judah and in the surrounding area of Jerusalem, also those who burned incense to Baal, to the sun and to the moon and to the constellations and to all the host of heaven.

6   He brought out the Asherah from the house of the LORD outside Jerusalem to the brook Kidron, and burned it at the brook Kidron, and ground it to dust, and threw its dust on the graves of the common people.

7   He also broke down the houses of the *male* cult prostitutes which *were* in the house of the LORD, where the women were weaving hangings for the Asherah.

8   Then he brought all the priests from the cities of Judah, and defiled the high places where the priests had burned incense, from Geba to Beersheba; and he broke down the high places of the gates which *were* at the entrance of the gate of Joshua the governor of the city, which *were* on one's left at the city gate.

9   Nevertheless the priests of the high places did not go up to the altar of the LORD in Jerusalem, but they ate unleavened bread among their brothers.

10   He also defiled Topheth, which is in the valley of the son of Hinnom, that no man might make his son or his daughter pass through the fire for Molech.

11   He did away with the horses which the kings of Judah had given to the sun, at the entrance of the house of the LORD, by the chamber of Nathan-melech the official, which *was* in the precincts; and he burned the chariots of the sun with fire.

12   The altars which *were* on the roof, the upper chamber of Ahaz, which the kings of Judah had made, and the altars which Manasseh had made in the two courts of the house of the LORD, the king broke down; and he smashed them there and threw their dust into the brook Kidron.

13   The high places which *were* before Jerusalem, which *were* on the right of the mount of destruction which Solomon the king of Israel had built for Ashtoreth the abomination of the Sidonians, and for Chemosh the abomination of Moab, and for Milcom the abomination of the sons of Ammon, the king defiled.

14   He broke in pieces the *sacred* pillars and cut down the Asherim and filled their places with human bones.

15   Furthermore, the altar that *was* at Bethel *and* the high place which Jeroboam the son of Nebat, who made Israel sin, had made, even that altar and the high place he broke down. Then he demolished its stones, ground them to dust, and burned the Asherah.

16   Now when Josiah turned, he saw the graves that *were* there on the mountain, and he sent and took the bones from the graves and burned *them* on the altar and defiled it according to the word of the LORD which the man of God proclaimed, who proclaimed these things.

17   Then he said, "What is this monument that I see?" And the men of the city told him, "It is the grave of the man of God who came from Judah and proclaimed these things which you have done against the altar of Bethel."

18   He said, "Let him alone; let no one disturb his bones." So they left his bones undisturbed with the bones of the prophet who came from Samaria.

19   Josiah also removed all the houses of the high places which *were* in the cities of Samaria, which the kings of Israel had made provoking the LORD; and he did to them just as he had done in Bethel.

20   All the priests of the high places who *were* there he slaughtered on the altars and burned human bones on them; then he returned to Jerusalem.

21   Then the king commanded all the people saying, "Celebrate the Passover to the LORD your God as it is written in this book of the covenant."

22   Surely such a Passover had not been celebrated from the days of the judges who judged Israel, nor in all the days of the kings of Israel and of the kings of Judah.

23   But in the eighteenth year of King Josiah, this Passover was observed to the LORD in Jerusalem.

24   Moreover, Josiah removed the mediums and the spiritists and the teraphim

and the idols and all the abominations that were seen in the land of Judah and in Jerusalem, that he might confirm the words of the law which were written in the book that Hilkiah the priest found in the house of the LORD.

➤ 25 Before him there was no king like him who turned to the LORD with all his heart and with all his soul and with all his might, according to all the law of Moses; nor did any like him arise after him.

26 However, the LORD did not turn from the fierceness of His great wrath with which His anger burned against Judah, because of all the provocations with which Manasseh had provoked Him.

27 The LORD said, "I will remove Judah also from My sight, as I have removed Israel. And I will cast off Jerusalem, this city which I have chosen, and the temple of which I said, 'My name shall be there.'"

28 Now the rest of the acts of Josiah and all that he did, are they not written in the Book of the Chronicles of the Kings of Judah?

29 In his days Pharaoh Neco king of Egypt went up to the king of Assyria to the river Euphrates. And King Josiah went to meet him, and when *Pharaoh Neco* saw him he killed him at Megiddo.

30 His servants drove his body in a chariot from Megiddo, and brought him to Jerusalem and buried him in his own tomb. Then the people of the land took Jehoahaz the son of Josiah and anointed him and made him king in place of his father.

31 Jehoahaz was twenty-three years old when he became king, and he reigned three months in Jerusalem; and his mother's name was Hamutal the daughter of Jeremiah of Libnah.

32 He did evil in the sight of the LORD, according to all that his fathers had done.

33 Pharaoh Neco imprisoned him at Riblah in the land of Hamath, that he might not reign in Jerusalem; and he imposed on the land a fine of one hundred talents of silver and a talent of gold.

34 Pharaoh Neco made Eliakim the son of Josiah king in the place of Josiah his father, and changed his name to Jehoiakim. But he took Jehoahaz away and brought *him* to Egypt, and he died there.

35 So Jehoiakim gave the silver and gold to Pharaoh, but he taxed the land in order to give the money at the command of Pharaoh. He exacted the silver and gold from the people of the land, each according to his valuation, to give it to Pharaoh Neco.

36 Jehoiakim was twenty-five years old when he became king, and he reigned eleven years in Jerusalem; and his mother's name *was* Zebidah the daughter of Pedaiah of Rumah.

37 He did evil in the sight of the LORD, according to all that his fathers had done.

24 IN his days Nebuchadnezzar king of Babylon came up, and Jehoiakim became his servant *for* three years; then he turned and rebelled against him.

2 The LORD sent against him bands of Chaldeans, bands of Arameans, bands of Moabites, and bands of Ammonites. So He sent them against Judah to destroy it, according to the word of the LORD which He had spoken through His servants the prophets.

3 Surely at the command of the LORD it came upon Judah, to remove *them* from His sight because of the sins of Manasseh, according to all that he had done,

4 and also for the innocent blood which he shed, for he filled Jerusalem with innocent blood; and the LORD would not forgive.

5 Now the rest of the acts of Jehoiakim and all that he did, are they not written in the Book of the Chronicles of the Kings of Judah?

6 So Jehoiakim slept with his fathers, and Jehoiachin his son became king in his place.

7 The king of Egypt did not come out of his land again, for the king of Babylon

---

LIFE LESSONS

➤ **2 Kings 23:25 — *Before him there was no king like him who turned to the LORD with all his heart and with all his soul and with all his might.***

*G*enuine devotion to God involves much more than intense feeling or heightened emotion. Those who follow the Lord with all their hearts, souls, and might, also eagerly obey His commands.

had taken all that belonged to the king of Egypt from the brook of Egypt to the river Euphrates.

8 Jehoiachin was eighteen years old when he became king, and he reigned three months in Jerusalem; and his mother's name *was* Nehushta the daughter of Elnathan of Jerusalem.

9 He did evil in the sight of the LORD, according to all that his father had done.

10 At that time the servants of Nebuchadnezzar king of Babylon went up to Jerusalem, and the city came under siege.

11 And Nebuchadnezzar the king of Babylon came to the city, while his servants were besieging it.

12 Jehoiachin the king of Judah went out to the king of Babylon, he and his mother and his servants and his captains and his officials. So the king of Babylon took him captive in the eighth year of his reign.

13 He carried out from there all the treasures of the house of the LORD, and the treasures of the king's house, and cut in pieces all the vessels of gold which Solomon king of Israel had made in the temple of the LORD, just as the LORD had said.

14 Then he led away into exile all Jerusalem and all the captains and all the mighty men of valor, ten thousand captives, and all the craftsmen and the smiths. None remained except the poorest people of the land.

15 So he led Jehoiachin away into exile to Babylon; also the king's mother and the king's wives and his officials and the leading men of the land, he led away into exile from Jerusalem to Babylon.

16 All the men of valor, seven thousand, and the craftsmen and the smiths, one thousand, all strong and fit for war, and these the king of Babylon brought into exile to Babylon.

17 Then the king of Babylon made his uncle Mattaniah king in his place, and changed his name to Zedekiah.

18 Zedekiah was twenty-one years old when he became king, and he reigned eleven years in Jerusalem; and his mother's name was Hamutal the daughter of Jeremiah of Libnah.

19 He did evil in the sight of the LORD, according to all that Jehoiakim had done.

20 For through the anger of the LORD *this* came about in Jerusalem and Judah until He cast them out from His presence. And Zedekiah rebelled against the king of Babylon.

Psalm 74:18–23

18 Remember this, O LORD, that the enemy has reviled,
And a foolish people has spurned Your name.

19 Do not deliver the soul of Your turtledove to the wild beast;
Do not forget the life of Your afflicted forever.

20 Consider the covenant;
For the dark places of the land are full of the habitations of violence.

21 Let not the oppressed return dishonored;
Let the afflicted and needy praise Your name.

22 Arise, O God, *and* plead Your own cause;
Remember how the foolish man reproaches You all day long.

23 Do not forget the voice of Your adversaries,
The uproar of those who rise against You which ascends continually.

LIFE LESSONS

> **2 Kings 24:20 — *He cast them out from His presence.***

*M*ore than a hundred years after Isaiah made his prophecy about the fall of Jerusalem to the Babylonians, it happened. Though God seems to delay the fulfillment of His Word, "Wait for it; for it will certainly come, it will not delay" (Hab. 2:3).

> **Psalm 74:22 — *Arise, O God, and plead Your own cause; remember how the foolish man reproaches You all day long.***

*M*any Bible prayers are based on genuine concern for God's reputation and glory. When we are obediently focused on the Lord—asking Him to defend His name and to be exalted through us—we are praying according to His will.

Proverbs 19:3

3   The foolishness of man ruins his
       way,
     And his heart rages against the LORD.

Acts 2:22–47

22 "Men of Israel, listen to these words:
Jesus the Nazarene, a man attested to
you by God with miracles and wonders
and signs which God performed through
Him in your midst, just as you yourselves
know—
23 this *Man*, delivered over by the predetermined plan and foreknowledge of
God, you nailed to a cross by the hands
of godless men and put *Him* to death.
24 "But God raised Him up again, putting an end to the agony of death, since
it was impossible for Him to be held in its
power.
25 "For David says of Him,
     'I SAW THE LORD ALWAYS IN MY
          PRESENCE;
     FOR HE IS AT MY RIGHT HAND, SO THAT
          I WILL NOT BE SHAKEN.
26 'THEREFORE MY HEART WAS GLAD AND
          MY TONGUE EXULTED;
     MOREOVER MY FLESH ALSO WILL LIVE
          IN HOPE;
27 BECAUSE YOU WILL NOT ABANDON MY
          SOUL TO HADES,
     NOR ALLOW YOUR HOLY ONE TO
          UNDERGO DECAY.
28 'YOU HAVE MADE KNOWN TO ME THE
          WAYS OF LIFE;
     YOU WILL MAKE ME FULL OF GLADNESS
          WITH YOUR PRESENCE.'

LIFE LESSONS

> Acts 2:23 — *"This Man, delivered over
by the predetermined plan and foreknowledge of God, you nailed to a cross
by the hands of godless men and put
Him to death."*

In a way none of us can fully understand, God orchestrated all the
events of Jesus' arrest and death, yet
every individual who played a part in His
execution remained personally responsible for his choices and actions.

29 "Brethren, I may confidently say to
you regarding the patriarch David that
he both died and was buried, and his
tomb is with us to this day.
30 "And so, because he was a prophet
and knew that GOD HAD SWORN TO HIM
WITH AN OATH TO SEAT *one* OF HIS DESCEN-
DANTS ON HIS THRONE,
31 he looked ahead and spoke of the
resurrection of the Christ, that HE WAS
NEITHER ABANDONED TO HADES, NOR DID
His flesh SUFFER DECAY.
32 "This Jesus God raised up again, to
which we are all witnesses.
33 "Therefore having been exalted to the
right hand of God, and having received
from the Father the promise of the Holy
Spirit, He has poured forth this which
you both see and hear.
34 "For it was not David who ascended
into heaven, but he himself says:
     'THE LORD SAID TO MY LORD,
     "SIT AT MY RIGHT HAND,
35   UNTIL I MAKE YOUR ENEMIES A
          FOOTSTOOL FOR YOUR FEET."'
36 "Therefore let all the house of Israel
know for certain that God has made Him
both Lord and Christ—this Jesus whom
you crucified."
37 Now when they heard *this*, they
were pierced to the heart, and said to
Peter and the rest of the apostles, "Brethren, what shall we do?"
38 Peter *said* to them, "Repent, and
each of you be baptized in the name of
Jesus Christ for the forgiveness of your
sins; and you will receive the gift of the
Holy Spirit.
39 "For the promise is for you and your
children and for all who are far off, as
many as the Lord our God will call to
Himself."
40 And with many other words he solemnly testified and kept on exhorting
them, saying, "Be saved from this perverse generation!"
41 So then, those who had received his
word were baptized; and that day there
were added about three thousand souls.
42 They were continually devoting
themselves to the apostles' teaching and
to fellowship, to the breaking of bread
and to prayer.
43 Everyone kept feeling a sense of
awe; and many wonders and signs were
taking place through the apostles.

44   And all those who had believed were together and had all things in common;
45   and they *began* selling their property and possessions and were sharing them with all, as anyone might have need.
46   Day by day continuing with one mind in the temple, and breaking bread from house to house, they were taking their meals together with gladness and sincerity of heart,
47   praising God and having favor with all the people. And the Lord was adding to their number day by day those who were being saved.

JUNE 18

2 Kings 25:1–30

25 NOW in the ninth year of his reign, on the tenth day of the tenth month, Nebuchadnezzar king of Babylon came, he and all his army, against Jerusalem, camped against it and built a siege wall all around it.
2   So the city was under siege until the eleventh year of King Zedekiah.
3   On the ninth day of the *fourth* month the famine was so severe in the city that there was no food for the people of the land.
4   Then the city was broken into, and all the men of war *fled* by night by way of the gate between the two walls beside the king's garden, though the Chaldeans were all around the city. And they went by way of the Arabah.
5   But the army of the Chaldeans pursued the king and overtook him in the plains of Jericho and all his army was scattered from him.
6   Then they captured the king and brought him to the king of Babylon at Riblah, and he passed sentence on him.
7   They slaughtered the sons of Zedekiah before his eyes, then put out the eyes of Zedekiah and bound him with bronze fetters and brought him to Babylon.
8   Now on the seventh day of the fifth month, which was the nineteenth year of King Nebuchadnezzar, king of Babylon, Nebuzaradan the captain of the guard, a servant of the king of Babylon, came to Jerusalem.

9   He burned the house of the LORD, the king's house, and all the houses of Jerusalem; even every great house he burned with fire.
10   So all the army of the Chaldeans who *were with* the captain of the guard broke down the walls around Jerusalem.
11   Then the rest of the people who were left in the city and the deserters who had deserted to the king of Babylon and the rest of the people, Nebuzaradan the captain of the guard carried away into exile.
12   But the captain of the guard left some of the poorest of the land to be vinedressers and plowmen.
13   Now the bronze pillars which were in the house of the LORD, and the stands and the bronze sea which were in the house of the LORD, the Chaldeans broke in pieces and carried the bronze to Babylon.
14   They took away the pots, the shovels, the snuffers, the spoons, and all the bronze vessels which were used in *temple* service.
15   The captain of the guard also took away the firepans and the basins, what was fine gold and what was fine silver.
16   The two pillars, the one sea, and the stands which Solomon had made for the house of the LORD—the bronze of all these vessels was beyond weight.
17   The height of the one pillar was eighteen cubits, and a bronze capital was on it; the height of the capital was three cubits, with a network and pomegranates on the capital all around, all of

bronze. And the second pillar was like these with network.

18 Then the captain of the guard took Seraiah the chief priest and Zephaniah the second priest, with the three officers of the temple.

19 From the city he took one official who was overseer of the men of war, and five of the king's advisers who were found in the city; and the scribe of the captain of the army who mustered the people of the land; and sixty men of the people of the land who were found in the city.

20 Nebuzaradan the captain of the guard took them and brought them to the king of Babylon at Riblah.

21 Then the king of Babylon struck them down and put them to death at Riblah in the land of Hamath. So Judah was led away into exile from its land.

22 Now *as for* the people who were left in the land of Judah, whom Nebuchadnezzar king of Babylon had left, he appointed Gedaliah the son of Ahikam, the son of Shaphan over them.

23 When all the captains of the forces, they and *their* men, heard that the king of Babylon had appointed Gedaliah *governor*, they came to Gedaliah to Mizpah, namely, Ishmael the son of Nethaniah, and Johanan the son of Kareah, and Seraiah the son of Tanhumeth the Netophathite, and Jaazaniah the son of the Maacathite, they and their men.

24 Gedaliah swore to them and their men and said to them, "Do not be afraid of the servants of the Chaldeans; live in the land and serve the king of Babylon, and it will be well with you."

25 But it came about in the seventh month, that Ishmael the son of Nethaniah, the son of Elishama, of the royal family, came with ten men and struck Gedaliah down so that he died along with the Jews and the Chaldeans who were with him at Mizpah.

26 Then all the people, both small and great, and the captains of the forces arose and went to Egypt; for they were afraid of the Chaldeans.

27 Now it came about in the thirty-seventh year of the exile of Jehoiachin king of Judah, in the twelfth month, on the twenty-seventh *day* of the month, that Evil-merodach king of Babylon, in the year that he became king, released Jehoiachin king of Judah from prison;

28 and he spoke kindly to him and set his throne above the throne of the kings who *were* with him in Babylon.

29 Jehoiachin changed his prison clothes and had his meals in the king's presence regularly all the days of his life;

30 and for his allowance, a regular allowance was given him by the king, a portion for each day, all the days of his life.

Psalm 75:1–10

For the choir director; *set to* Al-tashheth. A Psalm of Asaph, a Song.

75 WE give thanks to You, O God, we give thanks,
For Your name is near;
Men declare Your wondrous works.

2 "When I select an appointed time,
It is I who judge with equity.

3 "The earth and all who dwell in it melt;
It is I who have firmly set its pillars. Selah.

4 "I said to the boastful, 'Do not boast,'
And to the wicked, 'Do not lift up the horn;

5 Do not lift up your horn on high,
Do not speak with insolent pride.'"

6 For not from the east, nor from the west,
Nor from the desert *comes* exaltation;

7 But God is the Judge;
He puts down one and exalts another.

8 For a cup is in the hand of the LORD, and the wine foams;
It is well mixed, and He pours out of this;
Surely all the wicked of the earth must drain *and* drink down its dregs.

LIFE LESSONS

➤ **Psalm 75:6 — *Not from the east, nor from the west, nor from the desert comes exaltation.***

*G*od's people are not to seek the favor of powerful figures in an attempt to selfishly advance their own careers or positions. We are to work "for the Lord rather than for men" and leave the outcome of our lives in His hands (Col. 3:23).

9   But as for me, I will declare *it* forever;
    I will sing praises to the God of Jacob.
10 And all the horns of the wicked He
      will cut off,
    But the horns of the righteous will
      be lifted up.

Proverbs 19:4, 5

4   Wealth adds many friends,
    But a poor man is separated from
      his friend.
5   A false witness will not go
      unpunished,
    And he who tells lies will not escape.

Acts 3:1–26

3 NOW Peter and John were going up to
  the temple at the ninth *hour*, the hour
of prayer.
2   And a man who had been lame from
his mother's womb was being carried
along, whom they used to set down every
day at the gate of the temple which is
called Beautiful, in order to beg alms of
those who were entering the temple.
3   When he saw Peter and John about
to go into the temple, he *began* asking to
receive alms.
4   But Peter, along with John, fixed his
gaze on him and said, "Look at us!"
5   And he *began* to give them his attention, expecting to receive something
from them.
6   But Peter said, "I do not possess silver and gold, but what I do have I give
to you: In the name of Jesus Christ the
Nazarene—walk!"
7   And seizing him by the right hand,
he raised him up; and immediately his
feet and his ankles were strengthened.
8   With a leap he stood upright and
began to walk; and he entered the temple
with them, walking and leaping and
praising God.
9   And all the people saw him walking
and praising God;

ANSWERS TO LIFE'S QUESTIONS

How do I deal with the temptation of pride?

PSALM 75:4–7

*B*efore his death, David told his son
and successor, Solomon, "As for you,
my son Solomon, know the God of your father,
and serve Him with a whole heart and a willing mind; for the LORD searches all hearts and
understands every intent of the thoughts. If
you seek Him, He will let you find him" (1 Chr.
28:9).

Our ability to know and seek God and
serve Him with our entire heart begins with
one word: humility. As the apostle James
wrote, "GOD IS OPPOSED TO THE PROUD, BUT GIVES
GRACE TO THE HUMBLE" (James 4:6).

Sadly, Solomon did not cling to his father's
words of advice. Instead, he abandoned his
instruction and married women who worshiped
other gods. But sin has consequences; and
while God did not forsake His promise, He did
remove His blessing from Solomon's life.

If you desire the Lord's wisdom, be sure
you are willing to humble yourself and follow
wisdom's pathway. God told Solomon he could
ask for anything and it would be his. Instead
of asking for great wealth or power, Solomon
chose to ask for wisdom, which God provided
abundantly. However, as Solomon grew older,
he relied on his own wisdom instead of leaning
on God. In his early years, he had trusted the
Lord and wanted to do His will. But eventually, Solomon stopped relying on the Lord and
began to rely entirely on his own ability. That
was his downfall.

When we fail to humbly listen to God . . .
• we begin to listen to the wrong voices:
  our own, the enemy's, and those who
  don't have God's very best for us in mind.
• we are easily deceived—and decisions
  outside the will of God quickly turn
  disastrous.
• we become prideful and express our
  independence from God in various
  haughty ways.
• we begin to make decisions that appeal
  to our own desires and not the Lord's.
• we hurt those around us.
• we miss out on God's very best.

How can you avoid these perils? Ask God to
open your heart to His truth. Be willing to obey
His Word, even if it means giving up something
you hold precious. Obedience is always better
than the richest sacrifice. Our God is the God
of restoration, and He will never refuse your
sincere desire to obey and please Him.

10 and they were taking note of him as being the one who used to sit at the Beautiful Gate of the temple to *beg* alms, and they were filled with wonder and amazement at what had happened to him.

11 While he was clinging to Peter and John, all the people ran together to them at the so-called portico of Solomon, full of amazement.

➤ 12 But when Peter saw *this,* he replied to the people, "Men of Israel, why are you amazed at this, or why do you gaze at us, as if by our own power or piety we had made him walk?

13 "The God of Abraham, Isaac and Jacob, the God of our fathers, has glorified His servant Jesus, *the one* whom you delivered and disowned in the presence of Pilate, when he had decided to release Him.

14 "But you disowned the Holy and Righteous One and asked for a murderer to be granted to you,

15 but put to death the Prince of life, *the one* whom God raised from the dead, *a fact* to which we are witnesses.

16 "And on the basis of faith in His name, *it is* the name of Jesus which has strengthened this man whom you see and know; and the faith which *comes* through Him has given him this perfect health in the presence of you all.

17 "And now, brethren, I know that you acted in ignorance, just as your rulers did also.

18 "But the things which God announced beforehand by the mouth of all the prophets, that His Christ would suffer, He has thus fulfilled.

19 "Therefore repent and return, so that your sins may be wiped away, in order that times of refreshing may come from the presence of the Lord;

20 and that He may send Jesus, the Christ appointed for you,

21 whom heaven must receive until *the* period of restoration of all things about which God spoke by the mouth of His holy prophets from ancient time.

22 "Moses said, 'THE LORD GOD WILL RAISE UP FOR YOU A PROPHET LIKE ME FROM YOUR BRETHREN; TO HIM YOU SHALL GIVE HEED to everything He says to you.

23 'And it will be that every soul that does not heed that prophet shall be utterly destroyed from among the people.'

24 "And likewise, all the prophets who have spoken, from Samuel and *his* successors onward, also announced these days.

25 "It is you who are the sons of the prophets and of the covenant which God made with your fathers, saying to Abraham, 'AND IN YOUR SEED ALL THE FAMILIES OF THE EARTH SHALL BE BLESSED.'

26 "For you first, God raised up His Servant and sent Him to bless you by turning every one *of you* from your wicked ways."

1 ADAM, Seth, Enosh,
2 Kenan, Mahalalel, Jared,
3 Enoch, Methuselah, Lamech,
4 Noah, Shem, Ham and Japheth.
5 The sons of Japheth *were* Gomer, Magog, Madai, Javan, Tubal, Meshech and Tiras.
6 The sons of Gomer *were* Ashkenaz, Diphath, and Togarmah.
7 The sons of Javan *were* Elishah, Tarshish, Kittim and Rodanim.
8 The sons of Ham *were* Cush, Mizraim, Put, and Canaan.
9 The sons of Cush *were* Seba, Havilah, Sabta, Raama and Sabteca; and the sons of Raamah *were* Sheba and Dedan.
10 Cush became the father of Nimrod; he began to be a mighty one in the earth.
11 Mizraim became the father of the people of Lud, Anam, Lehab, Naphtuh,
12 Pathrus, Casluh, from which the Philistines came, and Caphtor.
13 Canaan became the father of Sidon, his firstborn, Heth,
14 and the Jebusites, the Amorites, the Girgashites,
15 the Hivites, the Arkites, the Sinites,
16 the Arvadites, the Zemarites and the Hamathites.
17 The sons of Shem *were* Elam, Asshur, Arpachshad, Lud, Aram, Uz, Hul, Gether and Meshech.
18 Arpachshad became the father of Shelah and Shelah became the father of Eber.
19 Two sons were born to Eber, the name of the one was Peleg, for in his days the earth was divided, and his brother's name was Joktan.
20 Joktan became the father of Almodad, Sheleph, Hazarmaveth, Jerah,
21 Hadoram, Uzal, Diklah,
22 Ebal, Abimael, Sheba,
23 Ophir, Havilah and Jobab; all these *were* the sons of Joktan.
24 Shem, Arpachshad, Shelah,
25 Eber, Peleg, Reu,
26 Serug, Nahor, Terah,
27 Abram, that is Abraham.
28 The sons of Abraham *were* Isaac and Ishmael.
29 These are their genealogies: the firstborn of Ishmael *was* Nebaioth, then Kedar, Adbeel, Mibsam,
30 Mishma, Dumah, Massa, Hadad, Tema,
31 Jetur, Naphish and Kedemah; these *were* the sons of Ishmael.
32 The sons of Keturah, Abraham's concubine, *whom* she bore, *were* Zimran, Jokshan, Medan, Midian, Ishbak and Shuah. And the sons of Jokshan *were* Sheba and Dedan.
33 The sons of Midian were Ephah, Epher, Hanoch, Abida and Eldaah. All these were the sons of Keturah.
34 Abraham became the father of Isaac. The sons of Isaac *were* Esau and Israel.
35 The sons of Esau *were* Eliphaz, Reuel, Jeush, Jalam and Korah.
36 The sons of Eliphaz *were* Teman, Omar, Zephi, Gatam, Kenaz, Timna and Amalek.
37 The sons of Reuel *were* Nahath, Zerah, Shammah and Mizzah.
38 The sons of Seir *were* Lotan, Shobal, Zibeon, Anah, Dishon, Ezer and Dishan.
39 The sons of Lotan *were* Hori and Homam; and Lotan's sister *was* Timna.
40 The sons of Shobal *were* Alian, Manahath, Ebal, Shephi and Onam. And the sons of Zibeon *were* Aiah and Anah.
41 The son of Anah *was* Dishon. And the sons of Dishon *were* Hamran, Eshban, Ithran and Cheran.
42 The sons of Ezer *were* Bilhan, Zaavan and Jaakan. The sons of Dishan *were* Uz and Aran.
43 Now these are the kings who reigned in the land of Edom before any king of the sons of Israel reigned. Bela was the son of Beor, and the name of his city was Dinhabah.
44 When Bela died, Jobab the son of Zerah of Bozrah became king in his place.
45 When Jobab died, Husham of the land of the Temanites became king in his place.
46 When Husham died, Hadad the son of Bedad, who defeated Midian in the

---

LIFE LESSONS

➤ **1 Chronicles 1:1 — *Adam, Seth, Enosh.***

*W*hy spend such effort recording genealogies? For one thing, God wants us to remember the Bible recounts the lives of *real* people with *real* problems and *real* challenges we can relate to.

field of Moab, became king in his place; and the name of his city *was* Avith.
47 When Hadad died, Samlah of Masrekah became king in his place.
48 When Samlah died, Shaul of Rehoboth by the River became king in his place.
49 When Shaul died, Baal-hanan the son of Achbor became king in his place.
50 When Baal-hanan died, Hadad became king in his place; and the name of his city was Pai, and his wife's name was Mehetabel, the daughter of Matred, the daughter of Mezahab.
51 Then Hadad died.
Now the chiefs of Edom were: chief Timna, chief Aliah, chief Jetheth,
52 chief Oholibamah, chief Elah, chief Pinon,
53 chief Kenaz, chief Teman, chief Mibzar,
54 chief Magdiel, chief Iram. These *were* the chiefs of Edom.

2 THESE are the sons of Israel: Reuben, Simeon, Levi, Judah, Issachar, Zebulun,
2 Dan, Joseph, Benjamin, Naphtali, Gad and Asher.
3 The sons of Judah *were* Er, Onan and Shelah; *these* three were born to him by Bath-shua the Canaanitess. And Er, Judah's firstborn, was wicked in the sight of the LORD, so He put him to death.
4 Tamar his daughter-in-law bore him Perez and Zerah. Judah had five sons in all.
5 The sons of Perez *were* Hezron and Hamul.
6 The sons of Zerah *were* Zimri, Ethan, Heman, Calcol and Dara; five of them in all.
7 The son of Carmi *was* Achar, the troubler of Israel, who violated the ban.
8 The son of Ethan *was* Azariah.
9 Now the sons of Hezron, who were born to him *were* Jerahmeel, Ram and Chelubai.
10 Ram became the father of Amminadab, and Amminadab became the father of Nahshon, leader of the sons of Judah;
11 Nahshon became the father of Salma, Salma became the father of Boaz,
12 Boaz became the father of Obed, and Obed became the father of Jesse;
13 and Jesse became the father of Eliab his firstborn, then Abinadab the second, Shimea the third,

14 Nethanel the fourth, Raddai the fifth,
15 Ozem the sixth, David the seventh;
16 and their sisters *were* Zeruiah and Abigail. And the three sons of Zeruiah *were* Abshai, Joab and Asahel.
17 Abigail bore Amasa, and the father of Amasa was Jether the Ishmaelite.
18 Now Caleb the son of Hezron had sons by Azubah *his* wife, and by Jerioth; and these were her sons: Jesher, Shobab, and Ardon.
19 When Azubah died, Caleb married Ephrath, who bore him Hur.
20 Hur became the father of Uri, and Uri became the father of Bezalel.
21 Afterward Hezron went in to the daughter of Machir the father of Gilead, whom he married when he was sixty years old; and she bore him Segub.
22 Segub became the father of Jair, who had twenty-three cities in the land of Gilead.
23 But Geshur and Aram took the towns of Jair from them, with Kenath and its villages, *even* sixty cities. All these were the sons of Machir, the father of Gilead.
24 After the death of Hezron in Calebephrathah, Abijah, Hezron's wife, bore him Ashhur the father of Tekoa.
25 Now the sons of Jerahmeel the firstborn of Hezron *were* Ram the firstborn, then Bunah, Oren, Ozem *and* Ahijah.
26 Jerahmeel had another wife, whose name was Atarah; she was the mother of Onam.
27 The sons of Ram, the firstborn of Jerahmeel, were Maaz, Jamin and Eker.
28 The sons of Onam were Shammai and Jada. And the sons of Shammai *were* Nadab and Abishur.
29 The name of Abishur's wife *was* Abihail, and she bore him Ahban and Molid.
30 The sons of Nadab *were* Seled and Appaim, and Seled died without sons.
31 The son of Appaim *was* Ishi. And the son of Ishi *was* Sheshan. And the son of Sheshan *was* Ahlai.
32 The sons of Jada the brother of Shammai *were* Jether and Jonathan, and Jether died without sons.
33 The sons of Jonathan *were* Peleth and Zaza. These were the sons of Jerahmeel.
34 Now Sheshan had no sons, only daughters. And Sheshan had an Egyptian servant whose name was Jarha.
35 Sheshan gave his daughter to Jarha

his servant in marriage, and she bore him Attai.

36 Attai became the father of Nathan, and Nathan became the father of Zabad,
37 and Zabad became the father of Ephlal, and Ephlal became the father of Obed,
38 and Obed became the father of Jehu, and Jehu became the father of Azariah,
39 and Azariah became the father of Helez, and Helez became the father of Eleasah,
40 and Eleasah became the father of Sismai, and Sismai became the father of Shallum,
41 and Shallum became the father of Jekamiah, and Jekamiah became the father of Elishama.
42 Now the sons of Caleb, the brother of Jerahmeel, *were* Mesha his firstborn, who was the father of Ziph; and his son was Mareshah, the father of Hebron.
43 The sons of Hebron *were* Korah and Tappuah and Rekem and Shema.
44 Shema became the father of Raham, the father of Jorkeam; and Rekem became the father of Shammai.
45 The son of Shammai was Maon, and Maon *was* the father of Bethzur.
46 Ephah, Caleb's concubine, bore Haran, Moza and Gazez; and Haran became the father of Gazez.
47 The sons of Jahdai *were* Regem, Jotham, Geshan, Pelet, Ephah and Shaaph.
48 Maacah, Caleb's concubine, bore Sheber and Tirhanah.
49 She also bore Shaaph the father of Madmannah, Sheva the father of Machbena and the father of Gibea; and the daughter of Caleb *was* Achsah.
50 These were the sons of Caleb.

The sons of Hur, the firstborn of Ephrathah, *were* Shobal the father of Kiriath-jearim,
51 Salma the father of Bethlehem *and* Hareph the father of Beth-gader.
52 Shobal the father of Kiriath-jearim had sons: Haroeh, half of the Manahathites,
53 and the families of Kiriath-jearim: the Ithrites, the Puthites, the Shumathites and the Mishraites; from these came the Zorathites and the Eshtaolites.
54 The sons of Salma *were* Bethlehem and the Netophathites, Atroth-beth-joab and half of the Manahathites, the Zorites.
55 The families of scribes who lived at Jabez *were* the Tirathites, the Shime-

athites *and* the Sucathites. Those are the Kenites who came from Hammath, the father of the house of Rechab.

◈ Psalm 76:1–6

For the choir director; on stringed instruments.
A Psalm of Asaph, a Song.

76 GOD is known in Judah;
His name is great in Israel.
2 His tabernacle is in Salem;
His dwelling place also is in Zion.
3 There He broke the flaming arrows,
The shield and the sword and the
weapons of war.   Selah.
4 You are resplendent,
More majestic than the mountains of
prey.
5 The stouthearted were plundered,
They sank into sleep;
And none of the warriors could use
his hands.
6 At Your rebuke, O God of Jacob,
Both rider and horse were cast into
a dead sleep.

◈ Proverbs 19:6, 7

6 Many will seek the favor of a
generous man,
And every man is a friend to him
who gives gifts.
7 All the brothers of a poor man hate
him;
How much more do his friends
abandon him!
He pursues *them with* words, *but*
they are gone.

◈ Acts 4:1–22

4 AS they were speaking to the people, the priests and the captain of the temple *guard* and the Sadducees came up to them,
2 being greatly disturbed because they were teaching the people and proclaiming in Jesus the resurrection from the dead.
3 And they laid hands on them and put

them in jail until the next day, for it was already evening.

4 But many of those who had heard the message believed; and the number of the men came to be about five thousand.

5 On the next day, their rulers and elders and scribes were gathered together in Jerusalem;

6 and Annas the high priest *was there*, and Caiaphas and John and Alexander, and all who were of high-priestly descent.

7 When they had placed them in the center, they *began to* inquire, "By what power, or in what name, have you done this?"

8 Then Peter, filled with the Holy Spirit, said to them, "Rulers and elders of the people,

9 if we are on trial today for a benefit done to a sick man, as to how this man has been made well,

10 let it be known to all of you and to all the people of Israel, that by the name of Jesus Christ the Nazarene, whom you crucified, whom God raised from the dead—by this *name* this man stands here before you in good health.

11 "He is the STONE WHICH WAS REJECTED by you, THE BUILDERS, *but* WHICH BECAME THE CHIEF CORNER *stone.*

12 "And there is salvation in no one else; for there is no other name under heaven that has been given among men by which we must be saved."

13 Now as they observed the confidence of Peter and John and understood that they were uneducated and untrained men, they were amazed, and *began to* recognize them as having been with Jesus.

14 And seeing the man who had been healed standing with them, they had nothing to say in reply.

15 But when they had ordered them to leave the Council, they *began to* confer with one another,

16 saying, "What shall we do with these men? For the fact that a noteworthy miracle has taken place through them is apparent to all who live in Jerusalem, and we cannot deny it.

17 "But so that it will not spread any further among the people, let us warn them to speak no longer to any man in this name."

18 And when they had summoned them, they commanded them not to speak or teach at all in the name of Jesus.

19 But Peter and John answered and said to them, "Whether it is right in the sight of God to give heed to you rather than to God, you be the judge;

20 for we cannot stop speaking about what we have seen and heard."

21 When they had threatened them further, they let them go (finding no basis on which to punish them) on account of the people, because they were all glorifying God for what had happened;

22 for the man was more than forty years old on whom this miracle of healing had been performed.

LIFE LESSONS

➤ **Acts 4:12** — *"There is no other name under heaven that has been given among men by which we must be saved."*

*I*f Jesus did not really have to die to save us, then why would God send Him to the Cross? The Father doesn't make mistakes, and His wisdom is always sound. Jesus died so we might have eternal life. He says we can only come to Him through faith and acceptance of His life, death, and resurrection.

➤ **Acts 4:13** — *As they . . . understood that they were uneducated and untrained men, they were amazed, and began to recognize them as having been with Jesus.*

*R*eal success is never about your own intelligence, education, beauty, or talent. Rather, it is about the Lord Jesus Christ shining through you. Spend time with Him—in prayer and in God's Word—and obey Him wholeheartedly. That is when He is able to do the most amazing things through you (1 Cor. 1:26–31; 2 Cor. 4:7; 12:10).

➤ **Acts 4:19** — *"Whether it is right in the sight of God to give heed to you rather than to God, you be the judge."*

*W*e are always to *respect* authority, even when it appears to be wrong. But if some authority tells us to defy God and His commands, we are to disobey that authority. For Jesus' sake, we accept the consequences of our allegiance to Him, knowing He will reward us in the life to come (Matt. 5:10-12).

WHAT THE BIBLE SAYS ABOUT

The Positive Power of Confidence

Acts 4:5–21

When other people see confidence and assurance in a believer, they are influenced in a positive way. This was certainly true of Peter and John. In Acts 4, they went and courageously preached the gospel to the very people who had crucified Christ. Why? They knew Christ was the only way by which people could be saved (v. 12). Acts 4:13 tells us that when the religious leaders "observed the confidence of Peter and John and understood that they were uneducated and untrained men, they were amazed, and began to recognize them as having been with Jesus."

As believers, we have the power within us to be bold and confident. Our adequacy is not within ourselves. Rather, our adequacy comes from the indwelling presence of God.

Perhaps you doubt you can be as courageous as the disciples were. How can you develop confidence in your life?

1. *You develop confidence by knowing God is your heavenly Father, and He loves you unconditionally.*

Confidence begins to grow by knowing God. He is gracious, kind, tender, and forgiving. He is also faithful to keep every promise He's made to you. Realize the Father is committed to acting on your behalf in every situation, and He will only do what is good for you. Knowing Him helps you have the assurance to face every situation.

2. *You develop confidence by meditating upon the Word of God.*

An excellent way to build your confidence is to look at the ways God has worked in the lives of others throughout Scripture. You know that if He has worked powerfully in others' lives, then He can do so in your life, too. The Lord can build great confidence in you through His Word. Therefore, when you read the Bible, ask Him to speak to your heart.

3. *You develop confidence by drawing near to God in your prayers.*

You can't develop confidence by praying on the run; rather, you must spend time listening to Him. Often, you'll encounter difficulties that make you think, "God, humanly speaking, there is no way this could ever come out alright." These are the times when it's imperative to get on your face before God and tell Him how hopeless you feel about your situation. Confess that if He doesn't intervene, you won't be able to survive it. Then, having laid your genuine, heartfelt feelings before Him, refocus on the truth that God has promised to never forsake you. Recall what you know about Him, and confess your faith in Him. The Lord has never failed you, and He will never change. By the time you rise from your knees, you will have an awesome sense of confidence, and you will be able to see your situation from His perspective.

4. *You develop confidence by keeping your focus fixed upon God.*

After being criticized, beaten, shipwrecked, imprisoned, and left for dead, the apostle Paul confessed, "I can do all things through Him who strengthens me" (Phil. 4:13). Paul knew Christ personally, and he knew that if Jesus Christ could defeat sin and death, there was nothing he could face that Christ could not overcome. The good news is you can know Christ as deeply and as personally as Paul did.

Each of us has the privilege of waking every morning and saying, "Thank You Father for dwelling in me, for Your unconditional love, and for faithfully keeping Your promises. Thank You for providing what is good for me. I know with You, I can overcome any obstacle! I can face this day victoriously—no matter what—because You are with me." You have to believe God is who He says He is and He will do what He says He will do. If you are willing to make that choice, you can walk confidently, no matter what.

JUNE 20

🧭 1 Chronicles 3:1—4:43

3 NOW these were the sons of David who were born to him in Hebron: the firstborn *was* Amnon, by Ahinoam the Jezreelitess; the second *was* Daniel, by Abigail the Carmelitess;

2   the third *was* Absalom the son of Maachah, the daughter of Talmai king of Geshur; the fourth *was* Adonijah the son of Haggith;

3   the fifth *was* Shephatiah, by Abital; the sixth *was* Ithream, by his wife Eglah.
4   Six were born to him in Hebron, and there he reigned seven years and six months. And in Jerusalem he reigned thirty-three years.
5   These were born to him in Jerusalem: Shimea, Shobab, Nathan and Solomon, four, by Bath-shua the daughter of Ammiel;
6   and Ibhar, Elishama, Eliphelet,
7   Nogah, Nepheg and Japhia,
8   Elishama, Eliada and Eliphelet, nine.
9   All *these were* the sons of David, besides the sons of the concubines; and Tamar *was* their sister.
10   Now Solomon's son *was* Rehoboam, Abijah *was* his son, Asa his son, Jehoshaphat his son,
11   Joram his son, Ahaziah his son, Joash his son,
12   Amaziah his son, Azariah his son, Jotham his son,
13   Ahaz his son, Hezekiah his son, Manasseh his son,
14   Amon his son, Josiah his son.
15   The sons of Josiah *were* Johanan the firstborn, and the second *was* Jehoiakim, the third Zedekiah, the fourth Shallum.
16   The sons of Jehoiakim *were* Jeconiah his son, Zedekiah his son.
17   The sons of Jeconiah, the prisoner, *were* Shealtiel his son,
18   and Malchiram, Pedaiah, Shenazzar, Jekamiah, Hoshama and Nedabiah.
19   The sons of Pedaiah *were* Zerubbabel and Shimei. And the sons of Zerubbabel *were* Meshullam and Hananiah, and Shelomith *was* their sister;
20   and Hashubah, Ohel, Berechiah, Hasadiah and Jushab-hesed, five.
21   The sons of Hananiah *were* Pelatiah and Jeshaiah, the sons of Rephaiah, the sons of Arnan, the sons of Obadiah, the sons of Shecaniah.
22   The descendants of Shecaniah *were* Shemaiah, and the sons of Shemaiah: Hattush, Igal, Bariah, Neariah and Shaphat, six.
23   The sons of Neariah *were* Elioenai, Hizkiah and Azrikam, three.
24   The sons of Elioenai *were* Hodaviah, Eliashib, Pelaiah, Akkub, Johanan, Delaiah and Anani, seven.

4 THE sons of Judah *were* Perez, Hezron, Carmi, Hur and Shobal.

2   Reaiah the son of Shobal became the father of Jahath, and Jahath became the father of Ahumai and Lahad. These *were* the families of the Zorathites.
3   These *were* the sons of Etam: Jezreel, Ishma and Idbash; and the name of their sister *was* Hazzelelponi.
4   Penuel *was* the father of Gedor, and Ezer the father of Hushah. These *were* the sons of Hur, the firstborn of Ephrathah, the father of Bethlehem.
5   Ashhur, the father of Tekoa, had two wives, Helah and Naarah.
6   Naarah bore him Ahuzzam, Hepher, Temeni and Haahashtari. These were the sons of Naarah.
7   The sons of Helah *were* Zereth, Izhar and Ethnan.
8   Koz became the father of Anub and Zobebah, and the families of Aharhel the son of Harum.
9   Jabez was more honorable than his brothers, and his mother named him Jabez saying, "Because I bore *him* with pain."
10   Now Jabez called on the God of Israel, saying, "Oh that You would bless me indeed and enlarge my border, and that Your hand might be with me, and that You would keep *me* from harm that *it* may not pain me!" And God granted him what he requested.
11   Chelub the brother of Shuhah became the father of Mehir, who was the father of Eshton.
12   Eshton became the father of Bethrapha and Paseah, and Tehinnah the father of Ir-nahash. These are the men of Recah.
13   Now the sons of Kenaz *were* Othniel and Seraiah. And the sons of Othniel *were* Hathath and Meonothai.
14   Meonothai became the father of Ophrah, and Seraiah became the father of Joab the father of Ge-harashim, for they were craftsmen.

LIFE LESSONS

➤ **1 Chronicles 4:10** — *Jabez called on the God of Israel . . . God granted him what he requested.*

*J*abez lived an "honorable" life (1 Chr. 4:9) and made specific prayer requests to God—and the Lord heard him and answered his prayers.

15 The sons of Caleb the son of Jephunneh *were* Iru, Elah and Naam; and the son of Elah *was* Kenaz.

16 The sons of Jehallelel *were* Ziph and Ziphah, Tiria and Asarel.

17 The sons of Ezrah *were* Jether, Mered, Epher and Jalon. (And these are the sons of Bithia the daughter of Pharaoh, whom Mered took) and she conceived *and bore* Miriam, Shammai and Ishbah the father of Eshtemoa.

18 His Jewish wife bore Jered the father of Gedor, and Heber the father of Soco, and Jekuthiel the father of Zanoah.

19 The sons of the wife of Hodiah, the sister of Naham, *were* the fathers of Keilah the Garmite and Eshtemoa the Maacathite.

20 The sons of Shimon *were* Amnon and Rinnah, Benhanan and Tilon. And the sons of Ishi *were* Zoheth and Benzoheth.

21 The sons of Shelah the son of Judah *were* Er the father of Lecah and Laadah the father of Mareshah, and the families of the house of the linen workers at Beth-ashbea;

22 and Jokim, the men of Cozeba, Joash, Saraph, who ruled in Moab, and Jashubi-lehem. And the records are ancient.

23 These were the potters and the inhabitants of Netaim and Gederah; they lived there with the king for his work.

24 The sons of Simeon *were* Nemuel and Jamin, Jarib, Zerah, Shaul;

25 Shallum his son, Mibsam his son, Mishma his son.

26 The sons of Mishma *were* Hammuel his son, Zaccur his son, Shimei his son.

27 Now Shimei had sixteen sons and six daughters; but his brothers did not have many sons, nor did all their family multiply like the sons of Judah.

28 They lived at Beersheba, Moladah and Hazar-shual,

29 at Bilhah, Ezem, Tolad,

30 Bethuel, Hormah, Ziklag,

31 Beth-marcaboth, Hazar-susim, Beth-biri and Shaaraim. These *were* their cities until the reign of David.

32 Their villages *were* Etam, Ain, Rimmon, Tochen and Ashan, five cities;

33 and all their villages that *were* around the same cities as far as Baal. These *were* their settlements, and they have their genealogy.

34 Meshobab and Jamlech and Joshah the son of Amaziah,

35 and Joel and Jehu the son of Joshibiah, the son of Seraiah, the son of Asiel,

36 and Elioenai, Jaakobah, Jeshohaiah, Asaiah, Adiel, Jesimiel, Benaiah,

37 Ziza the son of Shiphi, the son of Allon, the son of Jedaiah, the son of Shimri, the son of Shemaiah;

38 these mentioned by name *were* leaders in their families; and their fathers' houses increased greatly.

39 They went to the entrance of Gedor, even to the east side of the valley, to seek pasture for their flocks.

40 They found rich and good pasture, and the land was broad and quiet and peaceful; for those who lived there formerly *were* Hamites.

41 These, recorded by name, came in the days of Hezekiah king of Judah, and attacked their tents and the Meunites who were found there, and destroyed them utterly to this day, and lived in their place, because there was pasture there for their flocks.

42 From them, from the sons of Simeon, five hundred men went to Mount Seir, with Pelatiah, Neariah, Rephaiah and Uzziel, the sons of Ishi, as their leaders.

43 They destroyed the remnant of the Amalekites who escaped, and have lived there to this day.

Psalm 76:7–12

7 You, even You, are to be feared;
  And who may stand in Your
    presence when once You are
    angry?

LIFE LESSONS

➤ **Psalm 76:7 — *You, even You, are to be feared.***

As believers, we must never lose our reverence for God, because when we do, we become weak, compromising, and complacent. He is our Judge and King, and He deserves nothing less than our wholehearted commitment and obedience.

8 You caused judgment to be heard
   from heaven;
   The earth feared and was still
9 When God arose to judgment,
   To save all the humble of the earth.
                       Selah.
10 For the wrath of man shall praise
    You;
    With a remnant of wrath You will
    gird Yourself.
11 Make vows to the LORD your God
    and fulfill *them;*
    Let all who are around Him bring
    gifts to Him who is to be
    feared.
12 He will cut off the spirit of
    princes;
    He is feared by the kings of the
    earth.

◈ Proverbs 19:8, 9

8 He who gets wisdom loves his own
    soul;
    He who keeps understanding will
    find good.
9 A false witness will not go
    unpunished,
    And he who tells lies will perish.

◈ Acts 4:23–37

23 When they had been released, they
went to their own *companions* and reported all that the chief priests and the
elders had said to them.
24 And when they heard *this,* they
lifted their voices to God with one accord
and said, "O Lord, it is You who MADE
THE HEAVEN AND THE EARTH AND THE SEA,
AND ALL THAT IS IN THEM,
25 who by the Holy Spirit, *through* the
mouth of our father David Your servant,
said,
  'WHY DID THE GENTILES RAGE,
  AND THE PEOPLES DEVISE FUTILE
    THINGS?
26 'THE KINGS OF THE EARTH TOOK THEIR
    STAND,
  AND THE RULERS WERE GATHERED
    TOGETHER
  AGAINST THE LORD AND AGAINST HIS
    CHRIST.'

27 "For truly in this city there were gathered together against Your holy servant
Jesus, whom You anointed, both Herod
and Pontius Pilate, along with the Gentiles and the peoples of Israel,
28 to do whatever Your hand and Your
purpose predestined to occur.
29 "And now, Lord, take note of their
threats, and grant that Your bond-
servants may speak Your word with all
confidence,
30 while You extend Your hand to
heal, and signs and wonders take place
through the name of Your holy servant
Jesus."
31 And when they had prayed, the
place where they had gathered together was shaken, and they were all
filled with the Holy Spirit and *began*
to speak the word of God with boldness.
32 And the congregation of those who
believed were of one heart and soul; and
not one *of them* claimed that anything
belonging to him was his own, but all
things were common property to them.
33 And with great power the apostles
were giving testimony to the resurrection
of the Lord Jesus, and abundant grace
was upon them all.
34 For there was not a needy person
among them, for all who were owners of
land or houses would sell them and bring
the proceeds of the sales

LIFE LESSONS

➤ **Acts 4:29 — *"Grant that Your bond-
servants may speak Your word with all
confidence."***

*I*n a world that does not seem to
respect God, we must pray for boldness and strength to represent Him well,
and by our words and actions be His vessels by which He draws others into saving relationships with Jesus Christ.

➤ **Acts 4:31 — *When they had prayed
. . . they were all filled with the Holy
Spirit and began to speak the word of
God with boldness.***

*T*here is no substitute for believers
regularly coming together for earnest prayer. God does amazing things in
response to the faith-filled prayers of His
people.

Life Examples:

BARNABAS: Always an Encouraging Word

ACTS 4:36

*W*herever Barnabas went, people's faces lit up. They knew his presence brought a kind word, a helpful suggestion, and a great deal of encouragement.

In fact, that's how he got his name. He was born Joseph, a Levite from Cyprus, but his reassuring and cheerful ways soon prompted the apostles to give him the nickname *Bar-*

nabas, which means "Son of Encouragement" (Acts 4:36).

Without Barnabas, there might never have been an apostle Paul. It was Barnabas who introduced Saul to the church when everyone else was afraid of him (Acts 9:26–30). And when the apostles sent Barnabas to check up on a young church, he "began to encourage them all with resolute heart to remain true to the Lord; for he was a good man, and full of the Holy Spirit and of faith" (Acts 11:23, 24).

Don't you agree we could use a few more believers like Barnabas?

---

35 and lay them at the apostles' feet, and they would be distributed to each as any had need.

36 Now Joseph, a Levite of Cyprian birth, who was also called Barnabas by

the apostles (which translated means Son of Encouragement),

37 and who owned a tract of land, sold it and brought the money and laid it at the apostles' feet.

---

1 Chronicles 5:1—6:81

5 NOW the sons of Reuben the firstborn of Israel (for he was the firstborn, but because he defiled his father's bed, his birthright was given to the sons of Joseph the son of Israel; so that he is not enrolled in the genealogy according to the birthright.

2 Though Judah prevailed over his brothers, and from him *came* the leader, yet the birthright belonged to Joseph),

3 the sons of Reuben the firstborn of Israel *were* Hanoch and Pallu, Hezron and Carmi.

4 The sons of Joel *were* Shemaiah his son, Gog his son, Shimei his son,

5 Micah his son, Reaiah his son, Baal his son,

6 Beerah his son, whom Tilgath-pilneser king of Assyria carried away into exile; he was leader of the Reubenites.

7 His kinsmen by their families, in the genealogy of their generations, *were* Jeiel the chief, then Zechariah

8 and Bela the son of Azaz, the son of Shema, the son of Joel, who lived in Aroer, even to Nebo and Baal-meon.

9 To the east he settled as far as the

entrance of the wilderness from the river Euphrates, because their cattle had increased in the land of Gilead.

10 In the days of Saul they made war with the Hagrites, who fell by their hand, so that they occupied their tents throughout all the land east of Gilead.

11 Now the sons of Gad lived opposite them in the land of Bashan as far as Salecah.

12 Joel *was* the chief and Shapham the second, then Janai and Shaphat in Bashan.

13 Their kinsmen of their fathers' households *were* Michael, Meshullam, Sheba, Jorai, Jacan, Zia and Eber, seven.

14 These *were* the sons of Abihail, the son of Huri, the son of Jaroah, the son of Gilead, the son of Michael, the son of Jeshishai, the son of Jahdo, the son of Buz;

15 Ahi the son of Abdiel, the son of Guni, *was* head of their fathers' households.

16 They lived in Gilead, in Bashan and in its towns, and in all the pasture lands of Sharon, as far as their borders.

17 All of these were enrolled in the genealogies in the days of Jotham king of Judah and in the days of Jeroboam king of Israel.

18 The sons of Reuben and the Gadites and the half-tribe of Manasseh, *consisting* of valiant men, men who bore shield and sword and shot with bow and *were* skillful in battle, *were* 44,760, who went to war.

19 They made war against the Hagrites, Jetur, Naphish and Nodab.

20 They were helped against them, and the Hagrites and all who *were* with them were given into their hand; for they cried out to God in the battle, and He answered their prayers because they trusted in Him.

21 They took away their cattle: their 50,000 camels, 250,000 sheep, 2,000 donkeys; and 100,000 men.

22 For many fell slain, because the war *was* of God. And they settled in their place until the exile.

23 Now the sons of the half-tribe of Manasseh lived in the land; from Bashan to Baal-hermon and Senir and Mount Hermon they were numerous.

24 These were the heads of their fathers' households, even Epher, Ishi, Eliel, Azriel, Jeremiah, Hodaviah and Jahdiel, mighty men of valor, famous men, heads of their fathers' households.

25 But they acted treacherously against the God of their fathers and played the harlot after the gods of the peoples of the land, whom God had destroyed before them.

26 So the God of Israel stirred up the spirit of Pul, king of Assyria, even the spirit of Tilgath-pilneser king of Assyria, and he carried them away into exile, namely the Reubenites, the Gadites and the half-tribe of Manasseh, and brought them to Halah, Habor, Hara and to the river of Gozan, to this day.

6 THE sons of Levi *were* Gershon, Kohath and Merari.

2 The sons of Kohath *were* Amram, Izhar, Hebron and Uzziel.

3 The children of Amram *were* Aaron, Moses and Miriam. And the sons of Aaron *were* Nadab, Abihu, Eleazar and Ithamar.

4 Eleazar became the father of Phinehas, *and* Phinehas became the father of Abishua,

5 and Abishua became the father of Bukki, and Bukki became the father of Uzzi,

6 and Uzzi became the father of Zera-

hiah, and Zerahiah became the father of Meraioth,

7 Meraioth became the father of Amariah, and Amariah became the father of Ahitub,

8 and Ahitub became the father of Zadok, and Zadok became the father of Ahimaaz,

9 and Ahimaaz became the father of Azariah, and Azariah became the father of Johanan,

10 and Johanan became the father of Azariah (it was he who served as the priest in the house which Solomon built in Jerusalem),

11 and Azariah became the father of Amariah, and Amariah became the father of Ahitub,

12 and Ahitub became the father of Zadok, and Zadok became the father of Shallum,

13 and Shallum became the father of Hilkiah, and Hilkiah became the father of Azariah,

14 and Azariah became the father of Seraiah, and Seraiah became the father of Jehozadak;

15 and Jehozadak went *along* when the LORD carried Judah and Jerusalem away into exile by Nebuchadnezzar.

16 The sons of Levi *were* Gershom, Kohath and Merari.

17 These are the names of the sons of Gershom: Libni and Shimei.

18 The sons of Kohath *were* Amram, Izhar, Hebron and Uzziel.

19 The sons of Merari *were* Mahli and Mushi. And these are the families of the Levites according to their fathers' *households.*

20 Of Gershom: Libni his son, Jahath his son, Zimmah his son,

21 Joah his son, Iddo his son, Zerah his son, Jeatherai his son.

22 The sons of Kohath *were* Amminadab his son, Korah his son, Assir his son,

23 Elkanah his son, Ebiasaph his son and Assir his son,

24 Tahath his son, Uriel his son, Uzziah his son and Shaul his son.

25 The sons of Elkanah *were* Amasai and Ahimoth.

26 *As for* Elkanah, the sons of Elkanah *were* Zophai his son and Nahath his son,

27 Eliab his son, Jeroham his son, Elkanah his son.

28 The sons of Samuel *were* Joel the firstborn, and Abijah the second.
29 The sons of Merari *were* Mahli, Libni his son, Shimei his son, Uzzah his son,
30 Shimea his son, Haggiah his son, Asaiah his son.
31 Now these are those whom David appointed over the service of song in the house of the LORD, after the ark rested *there*.
32 They ministered with song before the tabernacle of the tent of meeting, until Solomon had built the house of the LORD in Jerusalem; and they served in their office according to their order.
33 These are those who served with their sons: From the sons of the Kohathites *were* Heman the singer, the son of Joel, the son of Samuel,
34 the son of Elkanah, the son of Jeroham, the son of Eliel, the son of Toah,
35 the son of Zuph, the son of Elkanah, the son of Mahath, the son of Amasai,
36 the son of Elkanah, the son of Joel, the son of Azariah, the son of Zephaniah,
37 the son of Tahath, the son of Assir, the son of Ebiasaph, the son of Korah,
38 the son of Izhar, the son of Kohath, the son of Levi, the son of Israel.
39 *Heman's* brother Asaph stood at his right hand, even Asaph the son of Berechiah, the son of Shimea,
40 the son of Michael, the son of Baaseiah, the son of Malchijah,
41 the son of Ethni, the son of Zerah, the son of Adaiah,
42 the son of Ethan, the son of Zimmah, the son of Shimei,
43 the son of Jahath, the son of Gershom, the son of Levi.
44 On the left hand *were* their kinsmen the sons of Merari: Ethan the son of Kishi, the son of Abdi, the son of Malluch,
45 the son of Hashabiah, the son of Amaziah, the son of Hilkiah,
46 the son of Amzi, the son of Bani, the son of Shemer,
47 the son of Mahli, the son of Mushi, the son of Merari, the son of Levi.
48 Their kinsmen the Levites were appointed for all the service of the tabernacle of the house of God.
49 But Aaron and his sons offered on the altar of burnt offering and on the altar of incense, for all the work of the most holy place, and to make atonement for Israel, according to all that Moses the servant of God had commanded.

50 These are the sons of Aaron: Eleazar his son, Phinehas his son, Abishua his son,
51 Bukki his son, Uzzi his son, Zerahiah his son,
52 Meraioth his son, Amariah his son, Ahitub his son,
53 Zadok his son, Ahimaaz his son.
54 Now these are their settlements according to their camps within their borders. To the sons of Aaron of the families of the Kohathites (for theirs was the *first* lot),
55 to them they gave Hebron in the land of Judah and its pasture lands around it;
56 but the fields of the city and its villages, they gave to Caleb the son of Jephunneh.
57 To the sons of Aaron they gave the *following* cities of refuge: Hebron, Libnah also with its pasture lands, Jattir, Eshtemoa with its pasture lands,
58 Hilen with its pasture lands, Debir with its pasture lands,
59 Ashan with its pasture lands and Beth-shemesh with its pasture lands;
60 and from the tribe of Benjamin: Geba with its pasture lands, Allemeth with its pasture lands, and Anathoth with its pasture lands. All their cities throughout their families were thirteen cities.
61 Then to the rest of the sons of Kohath *were given* by lot, from the family of the tribe, from the half-tribe, the half of Manasseh, ten cities.
62 To the sons of Gershom, according to their families, *were given* from the tribe of Issachar and from the tribe of Asher, the tribe of Naphtali, and the tribe of Manasseh, thirteen cities in Bashan.
63 To the sons of Merari *were given* by lot, according to their families, from the tribe of Reuben, the tribe of Gad and the tribe of Zebulun, twelve cities.
64 So the sons of Israel gave to the Levites the cities with their pasture lands.
65 They gave by lot from the tribe of the sons of Judah, the tribe of the sons of Simeon and the tribe of the sons of Benjamin, these cities which are mentioned by name.
66 Now some of the families of the sons of Kohath had cities of their territory from the tribe of Ephraim.
67 They gave to them the *following* cities of refuge: Shechem in the hill country of Ephraim with its pasture lands, Gezer also with its pasture lands,

68 Jokmeam with its pasture lands, Beth-horon with its pasture lands,

69 Aijalon with its pasture lands and Gath-rimmon with its pasture lands;

70 and from the half-tribe of Manasseh: Aner with its pasture lands and Bileam with its pasture lands, for the rest of the family of the sons of Kohath.

71 To the sons of Gershom *were given,* from the family of the half-tribe of Manasseh: Golan in Bashan with its pasture lands and Ashtaroth with its pasture lands;

72 and from the tribe of Issachar: Kedesh with its pasture lands, Daberath with its pasture lands

73 and Ramoth with its pasture lands, Anem with its pasture lands;

74 and from the tribe of Asher: Mashal with its pasture lands, Abdon with its pasture lands,

75 Hukok with its pasture lands and Rehob with its pasture lands;

76 and from the tribe of Naphtali: Kedesh in Galilee with its pasture lands, Hammon with its pasture lands and Kiriathaim with its pasture lands.

77 To the rest of *the Levites,* the sons of Merari, *were given,* from the tribe of Zebulun: Rimmono with its pasture lands, Tabor with its pasture lands;

78 and beyond the Jordan at Jericho, on the east side of the Jordan, *were given them,* from the tribe of Reuben: Bezer in the wilderness with its pasture lands, Jahzah with its pasture lands,

79 Kedemoth with its pasture lands and Mephaath with its pasture lands;

80 and from the tribe of Gad: Ramoth in Gilead with its pasture lands, Mahanaim with its pasture lands,

81 Heshbon with its pasture lands and Jazer with its pasture lands.

◈ Psalm 77:1–3

For the choir director; according to Jeduthun. A Psalm of Asaph.

77 MY voice *rises* to God, and I will cry aloud;
My voice *rises* to God, and He will hear me.

2 In the day of my trouble I sought the Lord;

In the night my hand was stretched out without weariness;
My soul refused to be comforted.

3 *When* I remember God, then I am disturbed;
When I sigh, then my spirit grows faint. Selah.

◈ Proverbs 19:10–12

10 Luxury is not fitting for a fool;
Much less for a slave to rule over princes.

11 A man's discretion makes him slow to anger,
And it is his glory to overlook a transgression.

12 The king's wrath is like the roaring of a lion,
But his favor is like dew on the grass.

◈ Acts 5:1–21

5 BUT a man named Ananias, with his wife Sapphira, sold a piece of property,

2 and kept back *some* of the price for himself, with his wife's full knowledge, and bringing a portion of it, he laid it at the apostles' feet.

3 But Peter said, "Ananias, why has Satan filled your heart to lie to the Holy Spirit and to keep back *some* of the price of the land?

4 "While it remained *unsold,* did it not remain your own? And after it was sold, was it not under your control? Why is it that you have conceived this deed in

---

LIFE LESSONS

➤ **Proverbs 19:11 —** *A man's discretion makes him slow to anger, and it is his glory to overlook a transgression.*

*M*any of us get into trouble in our relationships because we insist on being "right." We demand that everyone see things our way; and because we refuse to overlook a transgression at times, we end up alienating our friends and family.

ANSWERS TO LIFE'S QUESTIONS

What place should money take in my life?

ACTS 5:1–11

For some people, money is central. They worship wealth, which means they devote most of their time, energy, and attention to its gain and use because they regard it as the key to power and prestige.

"Oh, I'd never worship the idol of affluence," you may say. But ask yourself these questions:

- How much time do I spend every day thinking about my financial life—my income, bills, past and upcoming purchases, and investments? In comparison, how much time do I spend meditating upon God's Word?
- How much time do I spend each week working, shopping, or dealing with money? (Be sure to include trips to automatic teller machines and the bank, discussions with your spouse about budgets or spending plans and habits, and the time you spend paying bills and balancing your checking account.) In comparison, how much time do I spend seeking God in prayer and Bible reading, or serving the Lord in church-related activities and outreach?

- Am I more likely to discuss with my family and friends a hot stock tip, the cost of an item, and a new business opportunity—or an insight I have into God's Word, the truths I gleaned from last Sunday's sermon, and the way in which the Holy Spirit has helped me during the day? Which topic is more likely to attract a greater amount of my energy, enthusiasm, or concern—more wealth or a deeper understanding of the Savior?

You may say you trust God in every area of your life—but do you conduct business transactions, make purchases and investments, or enter into moneymaking opportunities without asking His opinion or seeking His wisdom? When you leave the Lord out of your financial life, you are in grave danger of making money your idol.

So how can you make sure you don't fall into such a deadly trap? Begin by focusing on Philippians 4:19, where God promises to supply all your needs. All of us have very specific needs: emotional, physical, material, mental, and spiritual. God knows our needs must be met if we are to carry out the complete life plan He has ordained for us (Matt. 6:32). By making intimacy with God your number one priority in life, you can be assured He will meet all those needs: "Seek first His kingdom and His righteousness, and all these things will be added to you" (Matt. 6:33).

your heart? You have not lied to men but to God."

5 And as he heard these words, Ananias fell down and breathed his last; and great fear came over all who heard of it.

6 The young men got up and covered him up, and after carrying him out, they buried him.

7 Now there elapsed an interval of about three hours, and his wife came in, not knowing what had happened.

8 And Peter responded to her, "Tell me whether you sold the land for such and such a price?" And she said, "Yes, that was the price."

9 Then Peter *said* to her, "Why is it that you have agreed together to put the Spirit of the Lord to the test? Behold, the feet of those who have buried your husband are at the door, and they will carry you out *as well.*"

10 And immediately she fell at his feet and breathed her last, and the young

men came in and found her dead, and they carried her out and buried her beside her husband.

11 And great fear came over the whole ⟨

LIFE LESSONS

➤ Acts 5:11 — *Great fear came over the whole church, and over all who heard of these things.*

After Ananias and Sapphira were struck dead because they had lied to the Holy Spirit (Acts 5:3, 9), the people were reminded of God's perfect holiness. This filled them with fear that they would face the same end. We should learn a similar lesson. Although we live under His grace, God is righteous, and we are to be holy as He is because we are His ambassadors (Lev. 11:44; 19:2; 10:7; Eph. 1:4; Col. 1:22; 1 Pet. 1:13–16). True reverence of the Lord's holiness and power purifies the church and helps us to live in submission to Him.

church, and over all who heard of these things.

12 At the hands of the apostles many signs and wonders were taking place among the people; and they were all with one accord in Solomon's portico.

13 But none of the rest dared to associate with them; however, the people held them in high esteem.

14 And all the more believers in the Lord, multitudes of men and women, were constantly added to *their number,*

15 to such an extent that they even carried the sick out into the streets and laid them on cots and pallets, so that when Peter came by at least his shadow might fall on any one of them.

16 Also the people from the cities in the vicinity of Jerusalem were coming together, bringing people who were sick or afflicted with unclean spirits, and they were all being healed.

17 But the high priest rose up, along with all his associates (that is the sect of the Sadducees), and they were filled with jealousy.

18 They laid hands on the apostles and put them in a public jail.

19 But during the night an angel of the Lord opened the gates of the prison, and ✳ taking them out he said, ✦

20 "Go, stand and speak to the people ‹ in the temple the whole message of this Life."

21 Upon hearing *this,* they entered into the temple about daybreak and *began* to teach.

Now when the high priest and his associates came, they called the Council together, even all the Senate of the sons of Israel, and sent *orders* to the prison house for them to be brought.

LIFE LESSONS

➤ **Acts 5:20 — "Go, stand and speak to the people in the temple the whole message of this Life."**

*G*od did not break the disciples out of prison so they could escape to safety; He freed them so they could go right back to what they had been doing— preaching about His salvation to the people of Israel. God wants His words of life to go forth!

⟐ 1 Chronicles 7:1—8:40

7NOW the sons of Issachar *were* four: Tola, Puah, Jashub and Shimron.

2 The sons of Tola *were* Uzzi, Rephaiah, Jeriel, Jahmai, Ibsam and Samuel, heads of their fathers' households. *The sons* of Tola *were* mighty men of valor in their generations; their number in the days of David was 22,600.

3 The son of Uzzi *was* Izrahiah. And the sons of Izrahiah *were* Michael, Obadiah, Joel, Isshiah; all five of them *were* chief men.

4 With them by their generations according to their fathers' households were 36,000 troops of the army for war, for they had many wives and sons.

5 Their relatives among all the families of Issachar *were* mighty men of valor, enrolled by genealogy, in all 87,000.

6 *The sons of* Benjamin *were* three: Bela and Becher and Jediael.

7 The sons of Bela were five: Ezbon, Uzzi, Uzziel, Jerimoth and Iri. They *were* heads of fathers' households, mighty men of valor, and were 22,034 enrolled by genealogy.

8 The sons of Becher *were* Zemirah, Joash, Eliezer, Elioenai, Omri, Jeremoth, Abijah, Anathoth and Alemeth. All these *were* the sons of Becher.

9 They were enrolled by genealogy, according to their generations, heads of their fathers' households, 20,200 mighty men of valor.

10 The son of Jediael *was* Bilhan. And the sons of Bilhan *were* Jeush, Benjamin, Ehud, Chenaanah, Zethan, Tarshish and Ahishahar.

11 All these *were* sons of Jediael, according to the heads of their fathers' households, 17,200 mighty men of valor, who were ready to go out with the army to war.

12 Shuppim and Huppim *were* the sons of Ir; Hushim *was* the son of Aher.

13 The sons of Naphtali *were* Jahziel, Guni, Jezer, and Shallum, the sons of Bilhah.

14 The sons of Manasseh *were* Asriel, whom his Aramean concubine bore; she bore Machir the father of Gilead.

15 Machir took a wife for Huppim and Shuppim, whose sister's name was Maacah. And the name of the second was Zelophehad, and Zelophehad had daughters.

16 Maacah the wife of Machir bore a son, and she named him Peresh; and the name of his brother *was* Sheresh, and his sons *were* Ulam and Rakem.

17 The son of Ulam *was* Bedan. These *were* the sons of Gilead the son of Machir, the son of Manasseh.

18 His sister Hammolecheth bore Ishhod and Abiezer and Mahlah.

19 The sons of Shemida were Ahian and Shechem and Likhi and Aniam.

20 The sons of Ephraim *were* Shuthelah and Bered his son, Tahath his son, Eleadah his son, Tahath his son,

21 Zabad his son, Shuthelah his son, and Ezer and Elead whom the men of Gath who were born in the land killed, because they came down to take their livestock.

22 Their father Ephraim mourned many days, and his relatives came to comfort him.

23 Then he went in to his wife, and she conceived and bore a son, and he named him Beriah, because misfortune had come upon his house.

24 His daughter was Sheerah, who built lower and upper Beth-horon, also Uzzensheerah.

25 Rephah was his son *along* with Resheph, Telah his son, Tahan his son,

26 Ladan his son, Ammihud his son, Elishama his son,

27 Non his son and Joshua his son.

28 Their possessions and settlements *were* Bethel with its towns, and to the east Naaran, and to the west Gezer with its towns, and Shechem with its towns as far as Ayyah with its towns,

29 and along the borders of the sons of Manasseh, Beth-shean with its towns, Taanach with its towns, Megiddo with its towns, Dor with its towns. In these lived the sons of Joseph the son of Israel.

30 The sons of Asher *were* Imnah, Ishvah, Ishvi and Beriah, and Serah their sister.

31 The sons of Beriah *were* Heber and Malchiel, who was the father of Birzaith.

32 Heber became the father of Japhlet, Shomer and Hotham, and Shua their sister.

33 The sons of Japhlet *were* Pasach, Bimhal and Ashvath. These were the sons of Japhlet.

34 The sons of Shemer *were* Ahi and Rohgah, Jehubbah and Aram.

35 The sons of his brother Helem *were* Zophah, Imna, Shelesh and Amal.

36 The sons of Zophah *were* Suah, Harnepher, Shual, Beri and Imrah,

37 Bezer, Hod, Shamma, Shilshah, Ithran and Beera.

38 The sons of Jether *were* Jephunneh, Pispa and Ara.

39 The sons of Ulla *were* Arah, Hanniel and Rizia.

40 All these *were* the sons of Asher, heads of the fathers' houses, choice and mighty men of valor, heads of the princes. And the number of them enrolled by genealogy for service in war was 26,000 men.

8 AND Benjamin became the father of Bela his firstborn, Ashbel the second, Aharah the third,

2 Nohah the fourth and Rapha the fifth.

3 Bela had sons: Addar, Gera, Abihud,

4 Abishua, Naaman, Ahoah,

5 Gera, Shephuphan and Huram.

6 These are the sons of Ehud: these are the heads of fathers' *households* of the inhabitants of Geba, and they carried them into exile to Manahath,

7 namely, Naaman, Ahijah and Gera— he carried them into exile; and he became the father of Uzza and Ahihud.

8 Shaharaim became the father of children in the country of Moab after he had sent away Hushim and Baara his wives.

9 By Hodesh his wife he became the father of Jobab, Zibia, Mesha, Malcam,

10 Jeuz, Sachia, Mirmah. These were his sons, heads of fathers' *households*.

11 By Hushim he became the father of Abitub and Elpaal.

12 The sons of Elpaal *were* Eber, Misham, and Shemed, who built Ono and Lod, with its towns;

13 and Beriah and Shema, who were heads of fathers' *households* of the inhabitants of Aijalon, who put to flight the inhabitants of Gath;
14 and Ahio, Shashak and Jeremoth.
15 Zebadiah, Arad, Eder,
16 Michael, Ishpah and Joha *were* the sons of Beriah.
17 Zebadiah, Meshullam, Hizki, Heber,
18 Ishmerai, Izliah and Jobab *were* the sons of Elpaal.
19 Jakim, Zichri, Zabdi,
20 Elienai, Zillethai, Eliel,
21 Adaiah, Beraiah and Shimrath *were* the sons of Shimei.
22 Ishpan, Eber, Eliel,
23 Abdon, Zichri, Hanan,
24 Hananiah, Elam, Anthothijah,
25 Iphdeiah and Penuel *were* the sons of Shashak.
26 Shamsherai, Shehariah, Athaliah,
27 Jaareshiah, Elijah and Zichri *were* the sons of Jeroham.
28 These were heads of the fathers' *households* according to their generations, chief men who lived in Jerusalem.
29 Now in Gibeon, *Jeiel*, the father of Gibeon lived, and his wife's name was Maacah;
30 and his firstborn son *was* Abdon, then Zur, Kish, Baal, Nadab,
31 Gedor, Ahio and Zecher.
32 Mikloth became the father of Shimeah. And they also lived with their relatives in Jerusalem opposite their *other* relatives.
33 Ner became the father of Kish, and Kish became the father of Saul, and Saul became the father of Jonathan, Malchishua, Abinadab and Eshbaal.
34 The son of Jonathan *was* Meribbaal, and Merib-baal became the father of Micah.
35 The sons of Micah *were* Pithon, Melech, Tarea and Ahaz.
36 Ahaz became the father of Jehoaddah, and Jehoaddah became the father of Alemeth, Azmaveth and Zimri; and Zimri became the father of Moza.
37 Moza became the father of Binea; Raphah *was* his son, Eleasah his son, Azel his son.
38 Azel had six sons, and these *were* their names: Azrikam, Bocheru, Ishmael, Sheariah, Obadiah and Hanan. All these *were* the sons of Azel.
39 The sons of Eshek his brother *were* Ulam his firstborn, Jeush the second and Eliphelet the third.
40 The sons of Ulam were mighty men of valor, archers, and had many sons and grandsons, 150 *of them*. All these *were* of the sons of Benjamin.

Psalm 77:4–9

4 You have held my eyelids *open;*
   I am so troubled that I cannot speak.
5 I have considered the days of old,
   The years of long ago.
6 I will remember my song in the night;
   I will meditate with my heart,
   And my spirit ponders:
7 Will the Lord reject forever?
   And will He never be favorable again?
8 Has His lovingkindness ceased forever?
   Has *His* promise come to an end forever?
9 Has God forgotten to be gracious,
   Or has He in anger withdrawn His compassion?   Selah.

Proverbs 19:13, 14

13 A foolish son is destruction to his father,
   And the contentions of a wife are a constant dripping.
14 House and wealth are an inheritance from fathers,
   But a prudent wife is from the LORD.

LIFE LESSONS

➤ *Psalm 77:8 — Has His lovingkindness ceased forever? Has His promise come to an end forever?*

When we're in the middle of adversity the answers to these questions often seem to be "yes." In fact, however, God's mercy never ceases, and His promises never fail. The Lord is always compassionate and faithful to His promises. Always.

WHAT THE BIBLE SAYS ABOUT ◉

Fixing Your Thoughts

Psalm 77:4–10

*N*o doubt, you can understand where Asaph the psalmist was coming from when he wrote, "You have held my eyelids open; I am so troubled that I cannot speak." You've spent sleepless nights, tossing and turning in your bed, considering solution after solution for your dilemmas. Though your body is completely weary, you just can't shut your eyes. Because of the heaviness of exhaustion and helplessness, your lips are silent, but your tormented spirit is quietly crying, "Oh my Lord God, I don't know what to do!"

Please understand: just as a greasy, fast-food burger couldn't possibly help a bad case of indigestion, analyzing your plight over and over again will never help your troubled soul. Rather, you must redirect your focus.

Asaph wrote, "I will remember my song in the night; I will meditate with my heart, and my spirit ponders . . . It is my grief, that the right hand of the Most High has changed" (Ps. 77:6, 10). The only thing that will heal you and help you rest is to turn your thoughts to the faithfulness of God. That is why Paul wrote,

"Be anxious for nothing, but in everything by prayer and supplication with thanksgiving let your requests be made known to God. And the peace of God, which surpasses all comprehension, will guard your hearts and your minds in Christ Jesus. Finally, brethren, whatever is true, whatever is honorable, whatever is right, whatever is pure, whatever is lovely, whatever is of good repute, if there is any excellence and if anything worthy of praise, dwell on these things" (Phil. 4:6–8).

Here, Paul offers the blueprint for ending sleepless nights. First, pray out your anxieties—discuss your troubles with God, and give them to Him. Second, recall God's goodness to you with praise and gratefulness. When you remember God's amazing ability to create new solutions, His peace will begin to fill your soul. Third, fix your thoughts on the Lord's glorious character and nature: His omnipotence, omniscience, omnipresence, and unconditional love. Whenever your thoughts begin to stray back to your troubles, counter the attack with more of God's wonderful, never-changing attributes.

It will be difficult, and it will take all of your self-will, but you must change the focus of your mind to the God who will surely help you overcome every dilemma. Then, you will find, "He gives to His beloved even in his sleep" (Ps. 127:2). ◉

◉ Acts 5:22–42

22 But the officers who came did not find them in the prison; and they returned and reported back,
23 saying, "We found the prison house locked quite securely and the guards standing at the doors; but when we had opened up, we found no one inside."
24 Now when the captain of the temple *guard* and the chief priests heard these words, they were greatly perplexed about them as to what would come of this.
25 But someone came and reported to them, "The men whom you put in prison are standing in the temple and teaching the people!"
26 Then the captain went along with the officers and *proceeded* to bring them *back* without violence (for they were afraid of the people, that they might be stoned).

27 When they had brought them, they stood them before the Council. The high priest questioned them,
28 saying, "We gave you strict orders not to continue teaching in this name, and yet, you have filled Jerusalem with your teaching and intend to bring this man's blood upon us."
29 But Peter and the apostles answered, "We must obey God rather than men.
30 "The God of our fathers raised up Jesus, whom you had put to death by hanging Him on a cross.
31 "He is the one whom God exalted to His right hand as a Prince and a Savior, to grant repentance to Israel, and for-giveness of sins.
32 "And we are witnesses of these things; and *so is* the Holy Spirit, whom God has given to those who obey Him."
33 But when they heard this, they were cut to the quick and intended to kill them.

34 But a Pharisee named Gamaliel, a teacher of the Law, respected by all the people, stood up in the Council and gave orders to put the men outside for a short time.
35 And he said to them, "Men of Israel, take care what you propose to do with these men.
36 "For some time ago Theudas rose up, claiming to be somebody, and a group of about four hundred men joined up with him. But he was killed, and all who followed him were dispersed and came to nothing.
37 "After this man, Judas of Galilee rose up in the days of the census and drew away *some* people after him; he too perished, and all those who followed him were scattered.
➤ 38 "So in the present case, I say to you, stay away from these men and let them alone, for if this plan or action is of men, it will be overthrown;
39 but if it is of God, you will not be able to overthrow them; or else you may even be found fighting against God."
40 They took his advice; and after calling the apostles in, they flogged them and ordered them not to speak in the name of Jesus, and *then* released them.
➤ 41 So they went on their way from the presence of the Council, rejoicing that

they had been considered worthy to suffer shame for *His* name.
42 And every day, in the temple and from house to house, they kept right on teaching and preaching Jesus *as* the Christ.

LIFE LESSONS

➤ **Acts 5:38, 39 — *If this . . . is of men, it will be overthrown; but if it is of God, you will not be able to overthrow them; or else you . . . fighting against God.***

*G*amaliel's great wisdom was founded in the principle that whatever is done outside of God's will cannot last. However, whatever God does is eternal. God's great plans will never fail, so obey whatever He tells you to do.

➤ **Acts 5:41 — *They went on their way . . . rejoicing that they had been considered worthy to suffer shame for His name.***

*T*he Bible consistently recognizes that when people try to disgrace us because we confess Christ, we are receiving one of the greatest possible blessings—we have been given the privilege of identifying with out Savior (Matt. 5:10-12; Phil. 3:7-12).

---

1 Chronicles 9:1—10:14

➤ **9**SO all Israel was enrolled by genealogies; and behold, they are written

in the Book of the Kings of Israel. And Judah was carried away into exile to Babylon for their unfaithfulness.
2 Now the first who lived in their possessions in their cities *were* Israel, the priests, the Levites and the temple servants.
3 Some of the sons of Judah, of the sons of Benjamin and of the sons of Ephraim and Manasseh lived in Jerusalem:
4 Uthai the son of Ammihud, the son of Omri, the son of Imri, the son of Bani, from the sons of Perez the son of Judah.
5 From the Shilonites *were* Asaiah the firstborn and his sons.
6 From the sons of Zerah *were* Jeuel and their relatives, 690 *of them.*
7 From the sons of Benjamin *were*

LIFE LESSONS

➤ **1 Chronicles 9:1 — *Judah was carried away into exile to Babylon for their unfaithfulness.***

*J*udah was not taken captive to Babylon because it lacked political power, military strength, diplomatic connections, or financial resources. Unfaithfulness to God caused the exile. We reap what we sow, more than we sow, and later than we sow.

Sallu the son of Meshullam, the son of Hodaviah, the son of Hassenuah,
8 and Ibneiah the son of Jeroham, and Elah the son of Uzzi, the son of Michri, and Meshullam the son of Shephatiah, the son of Reuel, the son of Ibnijah;
9 and their relatives according to their generations, 956. All these *were* heads of fathers' *households* according to their fathers' houses.
10 From the priests *were* Jedaiah, Jehoiarib, Jachin,
11 and Azariah the son of Hilkiah, the son of Meshullam, the son of Zadok, the son of Meraioth, the son of Ahitub, the chief officer of the house of God;
12 and Adaiah the son of Jeroham, the son of Pashhur, the son of Malchijah, and Maasai the son of Adiel, the son of Jahzerah, the son of Meshullam, the son of Meshillemith, the son of Immer;
13 and their relatives, heads of their fathers' households, 1,760 very able men for the work of the service of the house of God.
14 Of the Levites *were* Shemaiah the son of Hasshub, the son of Azrikam, the son of Hashabiah, of the sons of Merari;
15 and Bakbakkar, Heresh and Galal and Mattaniah the son of Mica, the son of Zichri, the son of Asaph,
16 and Obadiah the son of Shemaiah, the son of Galal, the son of Jeduthun, and Berechiah the son of Asa, the son of Elkanah, who lived in the villages of the Netophathites.
17 Now the gatekeepers *were* Shallum and Akkub and Talmon and Ahiman and their relatives (Shallum the chief
18 *being stationed* until now at the king's gate to the east). These *were* the gatekeepers for the camp of the sons of Levi.
19 Shallum the son of Kore, the son of Ebiasaph, the son of Korah, and his relatives of his father's house, the Korahites, *were* over the work of the service, keepers of the thresholds of the tent; and their fathers had been over the camp of the LORD, keepers of the entrance.
20 Phinehas the son of Eleazar was ruler over them previously, *and* the LORD was with him.
21 Zechariah the son of Meshelemiah was gatekeeper of the entrance of the tent of meeting.
22 All these who were chosen to be

gatekeepers at the thresholds were 212. These were enrolled by genealogy in their villages, whom David and Samuel the seer appointed in their office of trust.
23 So they and their sons had charge of the gates of the house of the LORD, *even* the house of the tent, as guards.
24 The gatekeepers were on the four sides, to the east, west, north and south.
25 Their relatives in their villages *were* to come in every seven days from time to time *to be* with them;
26 for the four chief gatekeepers who *were* Levites, were in an office of trust, and were over the chambers and over the treasuries in the house of God.
27 They spent the night around the house of God, because the watch was committed to them; and they *were* in charge of opening *it* morning by morning.
28 Now some of them had charge of the utensils of service, for they counted them when they brought them in and when they took them out.
29 Some of them also were appointed over the furniture and over all the utensils of the sanctuary and over the fine flour and the wine and the oil and the frankincense and the spices.
30 Some of the sons of the priests prepared the mixing of the spices.
31 Mattithiah, one of the Levites, who was the firstborn of Shallum the Korahite, had the responsibility over the things which were baked in pans.
32 Some of their relatives of the sons of the Kohathites *were* over the showbread to prepare it every sabbath.
33 Now these are the singers, heads of fathers' *households* of the Levites, *who* lived in the chambers *of the temple* free *from other service*; for they were engaged in their work day and night.
34 These were heads of fathers' *households* of the Levites according to their generations, chief men, who lived in Jerusalem.
35 In Gibeon Jeiel the father of Gibeon lived, and his wife's name was Maacah,
36 and his firstborn son *was* Abdon, then Zur, Kish, Baal, Ner, Nadab,
37 Gedor, Ahio, Zechariah and Mikloth.
38 Mikloth became the father of Shimeam. And they also lived with their relatives in Jerusalem opposite their *other* relatives.
39 Ner became the father of Kish, and

Kish became the father of Saul, and Saul became the father of Jonathan, Malchishua, Abinadab and Eshbaal.
40 The son of Jonathan *was* Merib-baal; and Merib-baal became the father of Micah.
41 The sons of Micah *were* Pithon, Melech, Tahrea *and Ahaz*.
42 Ahaz became the father of Jarah, and Jarah became the father of Alemeth, Azmaveth and Zimri; and Zimri became the father of Moza,
43 and Moza became the father of Binea and Rephaiah his son, Eleasah his son, Azel his son.
44 Azel had six sons whose names are these: Azrikam, Bocheru and Ishmael and Sheariah and Obadiah and Hanan. These were the sons of Azel.

10 NOW the Philistines fought against Israel; and the men of Israel fled before the Philistines and fell slain on Mount Gilboa.
2 The Philistines closely pursued Saul and his sons, and the Philistines struck down Jonathan, Abinadab and Malchishua, the sons of Saul.
3 The battle became heavy against Saul, and the archers overtook him; and he was wounded by the archers.
4 Then Saul said to his armor bearer, "Draw your sword and thrust me through with it, otherwise these uncircumcised will come and abuse me." But his armor bearer would not, for he was greatly afraid. Therefore Saul took his sword and fell on it.
5 When his armor bearer saw that Saul was dead, he likewise fell on his sword and died.
6 Thus Saul died with his three sons, and all *those* of his house died together.
7 When all the men of Israel who were in the valley saw that they had fled, and that Saul and his sons were dead, they forsook their cities and fled; and the Philistines came and lived in them.
8 It came about the next day, when the Philistines came to strip the slain, that they found Saul and his sons fallen on Mount Gilboa.
9 So they stripped him and took his head and his armor and sent *messengers* around the land of the Philistines to carry the good news to their idols and to the people.
10 They put his armor in the house of their gods and fastened his head in the house of Dagon.

11 When all Jabesh-gilead heard all that the Philistines had done to Saul,
12 all the valiant men arose and took away the body of Saul and the bodies of his sons and brought them to Jabesh, and they buried their bones under the oak in Jabesh, and fasted seven days.
13 So Saul died for his trespass which ◁ he committed against the LORD, because of the word of the LORD which he did not keep; and also because he asked counsel of a medium, making inquiry *of it,*
14 and did not inquire of the LORD. Therefore He killed him and turned the kingdom to David the son of Jesse.

Psalm 77:10–15

10 Then I said, "It is my grief,   ◁
    That the right hand of the Most
    High has changed."
11 I shall remember the deeds of the
    LORD;   ✳
    Surely I will remember Your
    wonders of old.
12 I will meditate on all Your work
    And muse on Your deeds.
13 Your way, O God, is holy;
    What god is great like our God?
14 You are the God who works wonders;

LIFE LESSONS

➤ **1 Chronicles 10:13, 14 —** *Saul did not inquire of the LORD. Therefore He killed him and turned the kingdom to David the son of Jesse.*

*S*aul lost God's blessing, the kingdom, and his life because he refused to honor the Lord (1 Sam. 9—31). In all matters that require guidance, whether large or small, God wants us to come to Him first. If necessary, He will move heaven and earth to show us His will.

➤ **Psalm 77:10 —** *Then I said, "It is my grief, that the right hand of the Most High has changed."*

*W*hen hardship strikes and we feel at our lowest point, it will always bring us great comfort to dwell on the fact God never changes and He will always act on behalf of those who wait for Him (Is. 64:4).

ANSWERS TO LIFE'S QUESTIONS

How can I praise God when life doesn't go well?

PSALM 77:11, 12

*W*hen life's twists and turns take you down unexpected and difficult roads, it can sometimes be challenging to praise the Lord. Yet He seeks our praise in *all* things—whether they appear good to us or not (Heb. 13:15).

So how can you praise the Lord when adversity comes into your life?

First, remember that our God is good and *always* gives us ample reason to praise Him. When you find yourself not knowing how to praise the Lord because of your circumstances, try some of the following ideas:

- Make a list of blessings God has bestowed on you—from giving you friends and family to your salvation in His Son.
- Tell someone about your salvation experience. Re-telling the moment when God lovingly adopted you into His family helps you recall the beauty of His matchless grace.
- Read a psalm each day. David praised God through hardship and great trial. We can learn from his example.

- Try to imagine how God could use negative circumstances to glorify Himself. Could He use the loss of a job to help you focus on Him and find out how you can experience His best? Could He use an illness to give you the opportunity to minister to the souls of your doctors and nurses as they tend to your sick body?

Second, remember God's overriding purpose in your life is to mold you into the likeness of Christ (Rom. 8:29) so that you can have an intimate relationship with and glorify Him. Therefore, ask Him to change your perspective so you will see your circumstances as He does. For example, God has a decidedly different viewpoint on the death of believers than we often do: "Precious in the sight of the LORD is the death of His godly ones" (Ps. 116:15). When we begin to see things as He does, we begin to see the truth—and praise once more can find a home on our lips.

Third, by exercising your will, you can make a conscious choice to praise Him. David did this: "I will praise the LORD while I live; I will sing praises to my God while I have my being" (Ps. 146:2).

Despite how you may feel, praise really can flow from you like a fountain—beginning right now.

You have made known Your strength among the peoples.
15 You have by Your power redeemed Your people,
The sons of Jacob and Joseph. Selah.

Proverbs 19:15, 16

15 Laziness casts into a deep sleep,
And an idle man will suffer hunger.
16 He who keeps the commandment keeps his soul,
But he who is careless of conduct will die.

Acts 6:1–15

6 NOW at this time while the disciples were increasing *in number*, a complaint arose on the part of the Hellenistic *Jews* against the *native* Hebrews,

because their widows were being overlooked in the daily serving *of food*.
2 So the twelve summoned the congregation of the disciples and said, "It is not desirable for us to neglect the word of God in order to serve tables.
3 "Therefore, brethren, select from among you seven men of good reputation, full of the Spirit and of wisdom, whom we may put in charge of this task.
4 "But we will devote ourselves to prayer and to the ministry of the word."

LIFE LESSONS

➤ Acts 6:4 — *"We will devote ourselves to prayer and to the ministry of the word."*

*C*hurch leaders and teachers, in particular, must never skimp on their time spent in prayer and in God's Word. Since they will "incur a stricter judgment" (James 3:1), they need to make sure they stay close to God.

5   The statement found approval with the whole congregation; and they chose Stephen, a man full of faith and of the Holy Spirit, and Philip, Prochorus, Nicanor, Timon, Parmenas and Nicolas, a proselyte from Antioch.

6   And these they brought before the apostles; and after praying, they laid their hands on them.

7   The word of God kept on spreading; and the number of the disciples continued to increase greatly in Jerusalem, and a great many of the priests were becoming obedient to the faith.

8   And Stephen, full of grace and power, was performing great wonders and signs among the people.

9   But some men from what was called the Synagogue of the Freedmen, *including* both Cyrenians and Alexandrians, and some from Cilicia and Asia, rose up and argued with Stephen.

10   But they were unable to cope with the wisdom and the Spirit with which he was speaking.

➤ 11   Then they secretly induced men to say, "We have heard him speak blasphemous words against Moses and *against* God."

LIFE LESSONS

➤ Acts 6:11 — *"We have heard him speak blasphemous words against Moses and against God."*

*J*ust as the opponents of Jesus instructed witnesses to testify falsely against the Lord, so the opponents of Stephen followed the same strategy. Interestingly, neither man tried to refute the false charges because they knew that ultimately God would bring the truth to light.

---

12   And they stirred up the people, the elders and the scribes, and they came up to him and dragged him away and brought him before the Council.

13   They put forward false witnesses who said, "This man incessantly speaks against this holy place and the Law;

14   for we have heard him say that this Nazarene, Jesus, will destroy this place and alter the customs which Moses handed down to us."

15   And fixing their gaze on him, all who were sitting in the Council saw his face like the face of an angel.

---

1 Chronicles 11:1—12:40

11 THEN all Israel gathered to David at Hebron and said, "Behold, we are your bone and your flesh.

➤ 2   "In times past, even when Saul was king, you *were* the one who led out and brought in Israel; and the LORD your God said to you, 'You shall shepherd My people Israel, and you shall be prince over My people Israel.'"

3   So all the elders of Israel came to the king at Hebron, and David made a covenant with them in Hebron before the LORD; and they anointed David king over Israel, according to the word of the LORD through Samuel.

4   Then David and all Israel went to Jerusalem (that is, Jebus); and the Jebusites, the inhabitants of the land, *were* there.

5   The inhabitants of Jebus said to David, "You shall not enter here." Nevertheless David captured the stronghold of Zion (that is, the city of David).

6   Now David had said, "Whoever strikes down a Jebusite first shall be chief and commander." Joab the son of Zeruiah went up first, so he became chief.

LIFE LESSONS

➤ 1 Chronicles 11:2 — *"You shall shepherd My people Israel, and you shall be prince over My people Israel."*

*D*avid was to rule Israel much as he had shepherded his father's flocks: up close, tenderly, wisely, for their benefit, and not for his own gain. He was to be a living "example of God's care of us as the Great Shepherd" (Ps. 23; Heb. 13:20). David became great because the Lord was with him (1 Chr. 11:9). Only when David acted without the Lord did he fail.

7   Then David dwelt in the stronghold; therefore it was called the city of David.
8   He built the city all around, from the Millo even to the surrounding area; and Joab repaired the rest of the city.
9   David became greater and greater, for the LORD of hosts *was* with him.
10   Now these are the heads of the mighty men whom David had, who gave him strong support in his kingdom, together with all Israel, to make him king, according to the word of the LORD concerning Israel.
11   These *constitute* the list of the mighty men whom David had: Jashobeam, the son of a Hachmonite, the chief of the thirty; he lifted up his spear against three hundred whom he killed at one time.
12   After him was Eleazar the son of Dodo, the Ahohite, who *was* one of the three mighty men.
13   He was with David at Pasdammim when the Philistines were gathered together there to battle, and there was a plot of ground full of barley; and the people fled before the Philistines.
14   They took their stand in the midst of the plot and defended it, and struck down the Philistines; and the LORD saved them by a great victory.
15   Now three of the thirty chief men went down to the rock to David, into the cave of Adullam, while the army of the Philistines was camping in the valley of Rephaim.
16   David was then in the stronghold, while the garrison of the Philistines *was* then in Bethlehem.
17   David had a craving and said, "Oh that someone would give me water to drink from the well of Bethlehem, which is by the gate!"
18   So the three broke through the camp of the Philistines and drew water from the well of Bethlehem which *was* by the gate, and took *it* and brought *it* to David; nevertheless David would not drink it, but poured it out to the LORD;
19   and he said, "Be it far from me before my God that I should do this. Shall I drink the blood of these men *who went* at the risk of their lives? For at the risk of their lives they brought it." Therefore he would not drink it. These things the three mighty men did.
20   As for Abshai the brother of Joab, he was chief of the thirty, and he swung his spear against three hundred and killed them; and he had a name as well as the thirty.
21   Of the three in the second *rank* he was the most honored and became their commander; however, he did not attain to the *first* three.
22   Benaiah the son of Jehoiada, the son of a valiant man of Kabzeel, mighty in deeds, struck down the two *sons of* Ariel of Moab. He also went down and killed a lion inside a pit on a snowy day.
23   He killed an Egyptian, a man of *great* stature five cubits tall. Now in the Egyptian's hand *was* a spear like a weaver's beam, but he went down to him with a club and snatched the spear from the Egyptian's hand and killed him with his own spear.
24   These *things* Benaiah the son of Jehoiada did, and had a name as well as the three mighty men.
25   Behold, he was honored among the thirty, but he did not attain to the three; and David appointed him over his guard.
26   Now the mighty men of the armies *were* Asahel the brother of Joab, Elhanan the son of Dodo of Bethlehem,
27   Shammoth the Harorite, Helez the Pelonite,
28   Ira the son of Ikkesh the Tekoite, Abiezer the Anathothite,
29   Sibbecai the Hushathite, Ilai the Ahohite,
30   Maharai the Netophathite, Heled the son of Baanah the Netophathite,
31   Ithai the son of Ribai of Gibeah of the sons of Benjamin, Benaiah the Pirathonite,
32   Hurai of the brooks of Gaash, Abiel the Arbathite,
33   Azmaveth the Baharumite, Eliahba the Shaalbonite,
34   the sons of Hashem the Gizonite, Jonathan the son of Shagee the Hararite,
35   Ahiam the son of Sacar the Hararite, Eliphal the son of Ur,
36   Hepher the Mecherathite, Ahijah the Pelonite,
37   Hezro the Carmelite, Naarai the son of Ezbai,
38   Joel the brother of Nathan, Mibhar the son of Hagri,
39   Zelek the Ammonite, Naharai the Berothite, the armor bearer of Joab the son of Zeruiah,

40 Ira the Ithrite, Gareb the Ithrite,
41 Uriah the Hittite, Zabad the son of Ahlai,
42 Adina the son of Shiza the Reubenite, a chief of the Reubenites, and thirty with him,
43 Hanan the son of Maacah and Joshaphat the Mithnite,
44 Uzzia the Ashterathite, Shama and Jeiel the sons of Hotham the Aroerite,
45 Jediael the son of Shimri and Joha his brother, the Tizite,
46 Eliel the Mahavite and Jeribai and Joshaviah, the sons of Elnaam, and Ithmah the Moabite,
47 Eliel and Obed and Jaasiel the Mezobaite.

12 NOW these are the ones who came to David at Ziklag, while he was still restricted because of Saul the son of Kish; and they were among the mighty men who helped *him* in war.
2 They were equipped with bows, using both the right hand and the left *to sling* stones and *to shoot* arrows from the bow; *they were* Saul's kinsmen from Benjamin.
3 The chief was Ahiezer, then Joash, the sons of Shemaah the Gibeathite; and Jeziel and Pelet, the sons of Azmaveth, and Beracah and Jehu the Anathothite,
4 and Ishmaiah the Gibeonite, a mighty man among the thirty, and over the thirty. Then Jeremiah, Jahaziel, Johanan, Jozabad the Gederathite,
5 Eluzai, Jerimoth, Bealiah, Shemariah, Shephatiah the Haruphite,
6 Elkanah, Isshiah, Azarel, Joezer, Jashobeam, the Korahites,
7 and Joelah and Zebadiah, the sons of Jeroham of Gedor.
8 From the Gadites there came over to David in the stronghold in the wilderness, mighty men of valor, men trained for war, who could handle shield and spear, and whose faces were like the faces of lions, and *they were* as swift as the gazelles on the mountains.
9 Ezer *was* the first, Obadiah the second, Eliab the third,
10 Mishmannah the fourth, Jeremiah the fifth,
11 Attai the sixth, Eliel the seventh,
12 Johanan the eighth, Elzabad the ninth,
13 Jeremiah the tenth, Machbannai the eleventh.

14 These of the sons of Gad were captains of the army; he who was least was equal to a hundred and the greatest to a thousand.
15 These are the ones who crossed the Jordan in the first month when it was overflowing all its banks and they put to flight all those in the valleys, both to the east and to the west.
16 Then some of the sons of Benjamin and Judah came to the stronghold to David.
17 David went out to meet them, and said to them, "If you come peacefully to me to help me, my heart shall be united with you; but if to betray me to my adversaries, since there is no wrong in my hands, may the God of our fathers look on *it* and decide."
18 Then the Spirit came upon Amasai, ◄ who was the chief of the thirty, *and he said,*

"*We* are yours, O David,
And with you, O son of Jesse!
Peace, peace to you,
And peace to him who helps you;
Indeed, your God helps you!"

Then David received them and made them captains of the band.
19 From Manasseh also some defected to David when he was about to go to battle with the Philistines against Saul. But they did not help them, for the lords of the Philistines after consultation sent him away, saying, "At *the cost of* our heads he may defect to his master Saul."
20 As he went to Ziklag there defected to him from Manasseh: Adnah, Jozabad, Jediael, Michael, Jozabad, Elihu and Zillethai, captains of thousands who belonged to Manasseh.
21 They helped David against the band of raiders, for they were all mighty men of valor, and were captains in the army.
22 For day by day *men* came to David

LIFE LESSONS

➤ **1 Chronicles 12:18 — *"Peace, peace to you, and peace to him who helps you."***

W hen the Spirit leads us to join God's people in doing His work, we must listen and obey, regardless of how difficult the work appears. To walk in the Spirit is to obey the initial promptings of the Spirit.

to help him, until there was a great army like the army of God.

23 Now these are the numbers of the divisions equipped for war, who came to David at Hebron, to turn the kingdom of Saul to him, according to the word of the LORD.

24 The sons of Judah who bore shield and spear *were* 6,800, equipped for war.

25 Of the sons of Simeon, mighty men of valor for war, 7,100.

26 Of the sons of Levi 4,600.

27 Now Jehoiada was the leader of *the house of* Aaron, and with him were 3,700,

28 also Zadok, a young man mighty of valor, and of his father's house twenty-two captains.

29 Of the sons of Benjamin, Saul's kinsmen, 3,000; for until now the greatest part of them had kept their allegiance to the house of Saul.

30 Of the sons of Ephraim 20,800, mighty men of valor, famous men in their fathers' households.

31 Of the half-tribe of Manasseh 18,000, who were designated by name to come and make David king.

32 Of the sons of Issachar, men who understood the times, with knowledge of what Israel should do, their chiefs *were* two hundred; and all their kinsmen *were* at their command.

33 Of Zebulun, there were 50,000 who went out in the army, who could draw up in battle formation with all kinds of weapons of war and helped *David* with an undivided heart.

34 Of Naphtali *there were* 1,000 captains, and with them 37,000 with shield and spear.

35 Of the Danites who could draw up in battle formation, *there were* 28,600.

36 Of Asher *there were* 40,000 who went out in the army to draw up in battle formation.

37 From the other side of the Jordan, of the Reubenites and the Gadites and of the half-tribe of Manasseh, *there were* 120,000 with all *kinds* of weapons of war for the battle.

38 All these, being men of war who could draw up in battle formation, came to Hebron with a perfect heart to make David king over all Israel; and all the rest also of Israel were of one mind to make David king.

39 They were there with David three days, eating and drinking, for their kinsmen had prepared for them.

40 Moreover those who were near to them, *even* as far as Issachar and Zebulun and Naphtali, brought food on donkeys, camels, mules and on oxen, great quantities of flour cakes, fig cakes and bunches of raisins, wine, oil, oxen and sheep. There was joy indeed in Israel.

Psalm 77:16–20

16 The waters saw You, O God;
The waters saw You, they were in anguish;
The deeps also trembled.

17 The clouds poured out water;
The skies gave forth a sound;
Your arrows flashed here and there.

18 The sound of Your thunder was in the whirlwind;
The lightnings lit up the world;
The earth trembled and shook.

19 Your way was in the sea
And Your paths in the mighty waters,
And Your footprints may not be known.

20 You led Your people like a flock
By the hand of Moses and Aaron.

Proverbs 19:17–19

17 One who is gracious to a poor man lends to the LORD,
And He will repay him for his good deed.

18 Discipline your son while there is hope,
And do not desire his death.

LIFE LESSONS

➢ **Proverbs 19:17 — *One who is gracious to a poor man lends to the LORD, and He will repay him for his good deed.***

*N*othing you do for those in need is ever wasted. Even if your actions are unappreciated or unacknowledged here on earth, God knows what you've done and faithfully rewards you (Matt. 25:34–40).

WHAT THE BIBLE SAYS ABOUT ◉

The Key to Surviving the Tough Times in Life

Psalm 77:19, 20

*W*e can probably agree tough times in life are inescapable. Difficult circumstances take place in everyone's life. Some of the troubles we experience are those we bring upon ourselves, while others are the result of what God is doing in our lives. What is important is the way we respond to those tough times. We must decide whether we are going to let our burdens develop us or destroy us. Our success hinges upon our attitudes and responses to our circumstances.

Think about how the Israelites responded to their trials as they fled Egypt for the Promised Land. Some—like Moses and Joshua—engaged the long, arduous journey with confidence in God, and their characters became stronger because of it. Yet there were also those Israelites who were faithless, and they crumbled beneath their loads because they refused to trust in God. The difference was the way they responded to their problems.

Some of the most godly men and women I know are those who have walked through the most difficult times of heartbreak, loss, and persecution. Through it all, they committed themselves to being godly, strong, and courageous—and to continue trusting God, no matter what happened. Though they are just ordinary people, they have learned the key to surviving the tough times in life.

In Hebrews 11:27, Moses tells us, "He endured, as seeing Him who is unseen." He understood no circumstance was too difficult for God, and he knew that any problem or obstacle he encountered was surmountable through the wisdom and power of the Lord. This is the means by which we can have the indomitable faith that can conquer any dilemma. We can be strong and withstand any crushing pressure with the knowledge God will deliver us out of it.

For example, when the children of Israel were caught between the Egyptian army and the Red Sea, Moses was able to remain faithful—even though Psalm 77:19 reports, "Your way was in the sea and Your paths in the mighty waters, and Your footprints may not be known." Moses didn't know *how* God would deliver them, but he still knew that God *would* deliver them. So he said to Israel, "Do not fear! Stand by and see the salvation of the LORD which He will accomplish for you today" (Ex. 14:13).

Moses saw the One who is unseen—he saw God. If we forget everything else, we must remember this: The key to surviving tough times is learning to live with the continuing awareness of the presence of God.

Have you discovered that yet? Are you aware that every moment of your life, you are in the presence of almighty God? He is sovereign, loving, all knowing, and faithful. He is always with you—helping you, providing for you, and protecting you. There is no trouble, heartache, loss, or suffering that His loving hand cannot guide you through. Count on Him. You will not only survive the tough times, you will triumph in them. ◉

---

19   *A man of* great anger will bear the penalty,
     For if you rescue *him*, you will only have to do it again.

◉   Acts 7:1–21

7 THE high priest said, "Are these things so?"
2   And he said, "Hear me, brethren and fathers! The God of glory appeared to our father Abraham when he was in Mesopotamia, before he lived in Haran,

3   and said to him, 'LEAVE YOUR COUNTRY AND YOUR RELATIVES, AND COME INTO THE LAND THAT I WILL SHOW YOU.'
4 "Then he left the land of the Chaldeans and settled in Haran. From there, after his father died, *God* had him move to this country in which you are now living.
5 "But He gave him no inheritance in it, ◄ not even a foot of ground, and *yet*, even when he had no child, He promised that HE WOULD GIVE IT TO HIM AS A POSSESSION, AND TO HIS DESCENDANTS AFTER HIM.
6 "But God spoke to this effect, that his DESCENDANTS WOULD BE ALIENS IN A

LIFE LESSONS

➤ Acts 7:5 — *Even when [Abraham] had no child, He promised that He wouLd give it to him as a possession.*

*G*od's promises often come at times when all hope seems lost. Being so old, how could Abraham ever expect to have a son? Yet it is in the midst of the impossible that God best shows us His wondrous power and teaches us faith.

FOREIGN LAND, AND THAT THEY WOULD BE ENSLAVED AND MISTREATED FOR FOUR HUNDRED YEARS.

7 "'AND WHATEVER NATION TO WHICH THEY WILL BE IN BONDAGE I MYSELF WILL JUDGE,' said God, 'AND AFTER THAT THEY WILL COME OUT AND SERVE ME IN THIS PLACE.'

8 "And He gave him the covenant of circumcision; and so *Abraham* became the father of Isaac, and circumcised him on the eighth day; and Isaac *became the father of* Jacob, and Jacob *of* the twelve patriarchs.

➤ 9 "The patriarchs became jealous of Joseph and sold him into Egypt. *Yet* God was with him,

10 and rescued him from all his afflictions, and granted him favor and wisdom in the sight of Pharaoh, king of Egypt, and he made him governor over Egypt and all his household.

11 "Now a famine came over all Egypt and Canaan, and great affliction *with it,* and our fathers could find no food.

12 "But when Jacob heard that there was grain in Egypt, he sent our fathers *there* the first time.

13 "On the second *visit* Joseph made himself known to his brothers, and Joseph's family was disclosed to Pharaoh.

14 "Then Joseph sent *word* and invited Jacob his father and all his relatives to come to him, seventy-five persons *in all.*

15 "And Jacob went down to Egypt and *there* he and our fathers died.

16 "*From there* they were removed to Shechem and laid in the tomb which Abraham had purchased for a sum of money from the sons of Hamor in Shechem.

17 "But as the time of the promise was approaching which God had assured to Abraham, the people increased and multiplied in Egypt,

18 until THERE AROSE ANOTHER KING OVER EGYPT WHO KNEW NOTHING ABOUT JOSEPH.

19 "It was he who took shrewd advantage of our race and mistreated our fathers so that they would expose their infants and they would not survive.

20 "It was at this time that Moses was born; and he was lovely in the sight of God, and he was nurtured three months in his father's home.

21 "And after he had been set outside, Pharaoh's daughter took him away and nurtured him as her own son.

LIFE LESSONS

➤ Acts 7:9, 10 — *"God was with him, and rescued him from all his afflictions, and granted him favor and wisdom in the sight of Pharaoh."*

*S*tephen reminded his audience Joseph had been persecuted by his own brothers and that God used even their evil deeds for blessing (Gen. 37—47). The Lord always blesses obedience, in His own timing and in His own way.

JUNE 25

1 Chronicles 13:1—14:17

13 THEN David consulted with the captains of the thousands and the hundreds, even with every leader.

2 David said to all the assembly of Israel, "If it seems good to you, and if it is from the LORD our God, let us send everywhere to our kinsmen who remain in all the land of Israel, also to the priests and Levites who are with them in their cities with pasture lands, that they may meet with us;

3 and let us bring back the ark of our ≺ God to us, for we did not seek it in the days of Saul."

4 Then all the assembly said that they would do so, for the thing was right in the eyes of all the people.

LIFE LESSONS

➤ **1 Chronicles 13:3 — *And let us bring back the ark of our God to us, for we did not seek it in the days of Saul.*"**

*D*avid saw the ark as an invaluable aspect of Israel's worship because it was the centerpiece of the Day of Atonement (Lev. 16:29–34). He honored God's commands and used every means to draw even closer to Him. We are made for an intimate relationship with the Lord, and we should employ every godly means possible to draw close to Him.

5 So David assembled all Israel together, from the Shihor of Egypt even to the entrance of Hamath, to bring the ark of God from Kiriath-jearim.
6 David and all Israel went up to Baalah, *that is*, to Kiriath-jearim, which belongs to Judah, to bring up from there the ark of God, the LORD who is enthroned *above* the cherubim, where His name is called.
7 They carried the ark of God on a new cart from the house of Abinadab, and Uzza and Ahio drove the cart.
8 David and all Israel were celebrating before God with all *their* might, even with songs and with lyres, harps, tambourines, cymbals and with trumpets.
9 When they came to the threshing floor of Chidon, Uzza put out his hand to hold the ark, because the oxen nearly upset *it*.
10 The anger of the LORD burned against Uzza, so He struck him down because he put out his hand to the ark; and he died there before God.
11 Then David became angry because of the LORD'S outburst against Uzza; and he called that place Perez-uzza to this day.
12 David was afraid of God that day, saying, "How can I bring the ark of God *home* to me?"
13 So David did not take the ark with him to the city of David, but took it aside to the house of Obed-edom the Gittite.
➤ 14 Thus the ark of God remained with the family of Obed-edom in his house three months; and the LORD blessed the family of Obed-edom with all that he had.

14 NOW Hiram king of Tyre sent messengers to David with cedar trees, masons and carpenters, to build a house for him.

2 And David realized that the LORD had established him as king over Israel, *and* that his kingdom was highly exalted, for the sake of His people Israel.
3 Then David took more wives at Jerusalem, and David became the father of more sons and daughters.
4 These are the names of the children born *to him* in Jerusalem: Shammua, Shobab, Nathan, Solomon,
5 Ibhar, Elishua, Elpelet,
6 Nogah, Nepheg, Japhia,
7 Elishama, Beeliada and Eliphelet.
8 When the Philistines heard that David had been anointed king over all Israel, all the Philistines went up in search of David; and David heard of it and went out against them.
9 Now the Philistines had come and made a raid in the valley of Rephaim.
10 David inquired of God, saying, "Shall I go up against the Philistines? And will You give them into my hand?" Then the LORD said to him, "Go up, for I will give them into your hand."
11 So they came up to Baal-perazim, and David defeated them there; and David said, "God has broken through my enemies by my hand, like the breakthrough of waters." Therefore they named that place Baal-perazim.
12 They abandoned their gods there; so David gave the order and they were burned with fire.

LIFE LESSONS

➤ **1 Chronicles 13:14 — *Thus the ark of God remained with the family of Obed-edom . . . and the LORD blessed the family of Obed-edom.***

*G*od used His blessing on Obed-Edom's house to show David that although He would always judge sin, He desires to draw close to His people and bless them (2 Sam. 6:10–12).

➤ **1 Chronicles 14:12 — *David gave the order and they were burned with fire.***

*U*nlike some of his predecessors and many of his successors, David did not collect the idols of his defeated enemies, but burned them, as God commanded (Deut. 7:5). Obedience always brings blessing.

13 The Philistines made yet another raid in the valley.
14 David inquired again of God, and God said to him, "You shall not go up after them; circle around behind them and come at them in front of the balsam trees.
15 "It shall be when you hear the sound of marching in the tops of the balsam trees, then you shall go out to battle, for God will have gone out before you to strike the army of the Philistines."
16 David did just as God had commanded him, and they struck down the army of the Philistines from Gibeon even as far as Gezer.
17 Then the fame of David went out into all the lands; and the LORD brought the fear of him on all the nations.

✦ Psalm 78:1–11

A Maskil of Asaph.

78 LISTEN, O my people, to my instruction;
Incline your ears to the words of my mouth.
2 I will open my mouth in a parable;
I will utter dark sayings of old,
3 Which we have heard and known,
And our fathers have told us.
➤ **4** We will not conceal them from their children,
✳ But tell to the generation to come the praises of the LORD,
And His strength and His wondrous works that He has done.
5 For He established a testimony in Jacob
And appointed a law in Israel,
Which He commanded our fathers
That they should teach them to their children,
6 That the generation to come might know, *even* the children *yet* to be born,
That they may arise and tell *them* to their children,
7 That they should put their confidence in God
And not forget the works of God,
But keep His commandments,

8 And not be like their fathers,
A stubborn and rebellious generation,
A generation that did not prepare its heart
And whose spirit was not faithful to God.
9 The sons of Ephraim were archers equipped with bows,
Yet they turned back in the day of battle.
10 They did not keep the covenant of God
And refused to walk in His law;
11 They forgot His deeds
And His miracles that He had shown them.

✦ Proverbs 19:20, 21

20 Listen to counsel and accept discipline,
That you may be wise the rest of your days.
21 Many plans are in a man's heart,
But the counsel of the LORD will stand.

LIFE LESSONS

➤ **Psalm 78:4** — *We will not conceal them from their children, but tell to the generation to come the praises of the LORD.*

*I*t is our job to tell our children and the generations that follow us not only the great things God did in biblical times, but also the wonderful works He has performed in our own lives. They need to see the Lord at work in us.

➤ **Proverbs 19:21** — *Many plans are in a man's heart, but the counsel of the LORD will stand.*

*I*t is unfortunate when we make our own plans and forget to seek God's counsel because only His plan can stand—not our own. Therefore, seek the Lord in everything and obey Him. He will move heaven and earth to show you what to do, and your obedience to Him will bring greater blessings than your plans could ever hope to achieve.

WHAT THE BIBLE SAYS ABOUT ◈

The Value of Godly Counsel

Proverbs 19:20

God often uses other believers to strengthen, encourage, and enrich our lives. Despite countless negative influences around us, we can still find wisdom through the counsel of godly men and women.

A wonderful example of this is the prophet Nathan in his confrontation with King David

(2 Sam. 12:1–14). God used Nathan to bring His servant, David, to repentance. Although the intense conviction greatly pained David, it was absolutely necessary in order for him to regain a right relationship with God.

The Book of Proverbs teaches us repeatedly to seek out godly counsel (Prov. 12:15; 13:10; 15:31; 19:20). We must be careful to make sure the person giving us counsel is in step with the Lord. While we are all fellow travelers on the path toward godly wisdom, we would be wise to lean on each other for support along the way. ◈

◈ Acts 7:22–43

22 "Moses was educated in all the learning of the Egyptians, and he was a man of power in words and deeds.
23 "But when he was approaching the age of forty, it entered his mind to visit his brethren, the sons of Israel.
24 "And when he saw one of *them* being treated unjustly, he defended him and took vengeance for the oppressed by striking down the Egyptian.
25 "And he supposed that his brethren understood that God was granting them deliverance through him, but they did not understand.
26 "On the following day he appeared to them as they were fighting together, and he tried to reconcile them in peace, saying, 'Men, you are brethren, why do you injure one another?'
27 "But the one who was injuring his neighbor pushed him away, saying, 'WHO MADE YOU A RULER AND JUDGE OVER US?
28 'YOU DO NOT MEAN TO KILL ME AS YOU KILLED THE EGYPTIAN YESTERDAY, DO YOU?'
29 "At this remark, MOSES FLED AND BECAME AN ALIEN IN THE LAND OF MIDIAN, where he became the father of two sons.
30 "After forty years had passed, AN ANGEL APPEARED TO HIM IN THE WILDERNESS OF MOUNT Sinai, IN THE FLAME OF A BURNING THORN BUSH.
31 "When Moses saw it, he marveled at the sight; and as he approached to look *more* closely, there came the voice of the Lord:
32 'I AM THE GOD OF YOUR FATHERS, THE GOD OF ABRAHAM AND ISAAC AND JACOB.'

Moses shook with fear and would not venture to look.
33 "BUT THE LORD SAID TO HIM, 'TAKE OFF THE SANDALS FROM YOUR FEET, FOR THE PLACE ON WHICH YOU ARE STANDING IS HOLY GROUND.
34 'I HAVE CERTAINLY SEEN THE OPPRESSION OF MY PEOPLE IN EGYPT AND HAVE HEARD THEIR GROANS, AND I HAVE COME DOWN TO RESCUE THEM; COME NOW, AND I WILL SEND YOU TO EGYPT.'
35 "This Moses whom they disowned, ◄ saying, 'WHO MADE YOU A RULER AND A JUDGE?' is the one whom God sent *to be* both a ruler and a deliverer with the help of the angel who appeared to him in the thorn bush. ✳
36 "This man led them out, performing wonders and signs in the land of Egypt and in the Red Sea and in the wilderness for forty years.
37 "This is the Moses who said to sons of Israel, 'GOD WILL RAISE UP FOR YOU A PROPHET LIKE ME FROM YOUR BRETHREN.'
38 "This is the one who was in the congregation in the wilderness together

LIFE LESSONS

➤ **Acts 7:35 — *Moses whom they disowned . . . is the one whom God sent to be both a ruler and a deliverer.***

Just as the Hebrews initially rejected Moses, and the religious leaders renounced Jesus, people who truly love and serve God may experience opposition—even from the very people they are trying to help. Therefore, don't be discouraged when you face resistance. Obey God and He will show everyone He is the One working through you.

with the angel who was speaking to him on Mount Sinai, and *who was* with our fathers; and he received living oracles to pass on to you.

39 "Our fathers were unwilling to be obedient to him, but repudiated him and in their hearts turned back to Egypt,

40 SAYING TO AARON, 'MAKE FOR US GODS WHO WILL GO BEFORE US; FOR THIS MOSES WHO LED US OUT OF THE LAND OF EGYPT—WE DO NOT KNOW WHAT HAPPENED TO HIM.'

41 "At that time they made a calf and brought a sacrifice to the idol, and were rejoicing in the works of their hands.

42 "But God turned away and delivered them up to serve the host of heaven; as it is written in the book of the prophets, 'IT WAS NOT TO ME THAT YOU OFFERED VICTIMS AND SACRIFICES FORTY YEARS IN THE WILDERNESS, WAS IT, O HOUSE OF ISRAEL?

43 'YOU ALSO TOOK ALONG THE TABERNACLE OF MOLOCH AND THE STAR OF THE GOD ROMPHA, THE IMAGES WHICH YOU MADE TO WORSHIP. I ALSO WILL REMOVE YOU BEYOND BABYLON.'

JUNE 26

◈ 1 Chronicles 15:1—16:43

15 NOW *David* built houses for himself in the city of David; and he prepared a place for the ark of God and pitched a tent for it.

2 Then David said, "No one is to carry the ark of God but the Levites; for the LORD chose them to carry the ark of God and to minister to Him forever."

3 And David assembled all Israel at Jerusalem to bring up the ark of the LORD to its place which he had prepared for it.

4 David gathered together the sons of Aaron and the Levites:

5 of the sons of Kohath, Uriel the chief, and 120 of his relatives;

6 of the sons of Merari, Asaiah the chief, and 220 of his relatives;

7 of the sons of Gershom, Joel the chief, and 130 of his relatives;

8 of the sons of Elizaphan, Shemaiah the chief, and 200 of his relatives;

9 of the sons of Hebron, Eliel the chief, and 80 of his relatives;

10 of the sons of Uzziel, Amminadab the chief, and 112 of his relatives.

11 Then David called for Zadok and Abiathar the priests, and for the Levites, for Uriel, Asaiah, Joel, Shemaiah, Eliel and Amminadab,

12 and said to them, "You are the heads of the fathers' *households* of the Levites; consecrate yourselves both you and your relatives, that you may bring up the ark of the LORD God of Israel to *the place* that I have prepared for it.

13 "Because you did not *carry it* at the first, the LORD our God made an outburst on us, for we did not seek Him according to the ordinance."

14 So the priests and the Levites consecrated themselves to bring up the ark of the LORD God of Israel.

15 The sons of the Levites carried the ark of God on their shoulders with the poles thereon, as Moses had commanded according to the word of the LORD.

16 Then David spoke to the chiefs of the Levites to appoint their relatives the singers, with instruments of music, harps, lyres, loud-sounding cymbals, to raise sounds of joy.

17 So the Levites appointed Heman the son of Joel, and from his relatives, Asaph the son of Berechiah; and from the sons of Merari their relatives, Ethan the son of Kushaiah,

18 and with them their relatives of the second rank, Zechariah, Ben, Jaaziel, Shemiramoth, Jehiel, Unni, Eliab, Benaiah, Maaseiah, Mattithiah, Eliphelehu, Mikneiah, Obed-edom and Jeiel, the gatekeepers.

19 So the singers, Heman, Asaph and Ethan *were appointed* to sound aloud cymbals of bronze;

20 and Zechariah, Aziel, Shemiramoth, Jehiel, Unni, Eliab, Maaseiah and Benaiah, with harps *tuned* to alamoth;

21 and Mattithiah, Eliphelehu, Mikneiah, Obed-edom, Jeiel and Azaziah, to lead with lyres tuned to the sheminith.

22 Chenaniah, chief of the Levites, was *in charge of* the singing; he gave instruction in singing because he was skillful.
23 Berechiah and Elkanah were gatekeepers for the ark.
24 Shebaniah, Joshaphat, Nethanel, Amasai, Zechariah, Benaiah and Eliezer, the priests, blew the trumpets before the ark of God. Obed-edom and Jehiah also *were* gatekeepers for the ark.
25 So *it was* David, with the elders of Israel and the captains over thousands, who went to bring up the ark of the covenant of the LORD from the house of Obed-edom with joy.
➤ 26 Because God was helping the Levites who were carrying the ark of the covenant of the LORD, they sacrificed seven bulls and seven rams.
27 Now David was clothed with a robe of fine linen with all the Levites who were carrying the ark, and the singers and Chenaniah the leader of the singing *with* the singers. David also wore an ephod of linen.
➤ 28 Thus all Israel brought up the ark of the covenant of the LORD with shouting, and with sound of the horn, with trumpets, with loud-sounding cymbals, with harps and lyres.
➤ 29 It happened when the ark of the covenant of the LORD came to the city of David, that Michal the daughter of Saul looked out of the window and saw King David leaping and celebrating; and she despised him in her heart.

16 AND they brought in the ark of God and placed it inside the tent which David had pitched for it, and they offered burnt offerings and peace offerings before God.
2 When David had finished offering the burnt offering and the peace offerings, he blessed the people in the name of the LORD.
3 He distributed to everyone of Israel, both man and woman, to everyone a loaf of bread and a portion *of meat* and a raisin cake.
4 He appointed some of the Levites *as* ministers before the ark of the LORD, even to celebrate and to thank and praise the LORD God of Israel:
5 Asaph the chief, and second to him Zechariah, *then* Jeiel, Shemiramoth, Jehiel, Mattithiah, Eliab, Benaiah,

Obed-edom and Jeiel, with musical instruments, harps, lyres; also Asaph *played* loud-sounding cymbals,
6 and Benaiah and Jahaziel the priests *blew* trumpets continually before the ark of the covenant of God.
7 Then on that day David first as- ◄ signed Asaph and his relatives to give thanks to the LORD.
8 Oh give thanks to the LORD, call
　　upon His name;
　　Make known His deeds among the
　　peoples.

LIFE LESSONS

➤ **1 Chronicles 15:26 — *Because God was helping the Levites who were carrying the ark of the covenant of the LORD.***

*G*od helps us in the work He commissions us to do. He does not merely give us a task and leave us alone to do it; He gives us His strength, wisdom, and presence to make our work successful.

➤ **1 Chronicles 15:28 — *All Israel brought up the ark of the covenant of the LORD . . . with harps and lyres.***

*I*srael rejoiced that the ark of the covenant was in Jerusalem again because God's presence would appear above it (Ex. 25:22). Now that we have the Lord's presence with us always through the Holy Spirit, we may be tempted to take Him for granted. However, God's presence should always make us rejoice and worship.

➤ **1 Chronicles 15:29 — *She despised him in her heart.***

*D*avid's wife despised him when she saw him celebrating the return of the ark in a manner she thought undignified for a king. But God is after the heart, and David delighted to give his entire heart to the Lord, regardless of appearances.

➤ **1 Chronicles 16:7 — *David first assigned Asaph and his relatives to give thanks to the LORD.***

*D*avid, the great warrior-king, took great pleasure in crafting worship songs for praising the Lord. If we want to grow close to God, we must also make time for personal worship.

9 Sing to Him, sing praises to Him;
   Speak of all His wonders.
10 Glory in His holy name;
   Let the heart of those who seek the
      LORD be glad.
11 Seek the LORD and His strength;
   Seek His face continually.
12 Remember His wonderful deeds
      which He has done,
   His marvels and the judgments from
      His mouth,
13 O seed of Israel His servant,
   Sons of Jacob, His chosen ones!
14 He is the LORD our God;
   His judgments are in all the earth.
15 Remember His covenant forever,
   The word which He commanded to
      a thousand generations,
16 *The covenant* which He made with
      Abraham,
   And His oath to Isaac.
17 He also confirmed it to Jacob for a
      statute,
   To Israel as an everlasting covenant,
18 Saying, "To you I will give the land
      of Canaan,
   As the portion of your inheritance."
19 When they were only a few in number,
   Very few, and strangers in it,
20 And they wandered about from
      nation to nation,
   And from *one* kingdom to another
      people,
21 He permitted no man to oppress
      them,
   And He reproved kings for their
      sakes, *saying,*
22 "Do not touch My anointed ones,
   And do My prophets no harm."
23 Sing to the LORD, all the earth;
   Proclaim good tidings of His
      salvation from day to day.
24 Tell of His glory among the nations,
   His wonderful deeds among all the
      peoples.
25 For great is the LORD, and greatly to
      be praised;
   He also is to be feared above all gods.
26 For all the gods of the peoples are
      idols,
   But the LORD made the heavens.
27 Splendor and majesty are before Him,
   Strength and joy are in His place.
28 Ascribe to the LORD, O families of
      the peoples,
   Ascribe to the LORD glory and
      strength.

29 Ascribe to the LORD the glory due
      His name;
   Bring an offering, and come before
      Him;
   Worship the LORD in holy array.
30 Tremble before Him, all the earth;
   Indeed, the world is firmly
      established, it will not be moved.
31 Let the heavens be glad, and let the
      earth rejoice;
   And let them say among the
      nations, "The LORD reigns."
32 Let the sea roar, and all it contains;
   Let the field exult, and all that is in it.
33 Then the trees of the forest will sing
      for joy before the LORD;
   For He is coming to judge the earth.
34 O give thanks to the LORD, for *He is*
      good;
   For His lovingkindness is everlasting.
35 Then say, "Save us, O God of our
      salvation,
   And gather us and deliver us from
      the nations,
   To give thanks to Your holy name,
   And glory in Your praise."
36 Blessed be the LORD, the God of
      Israel,
   From everlasting even to
      everlasting.
Then all the people said, "Amen," and
praised the LORD.
37 So he left Asaph and his relatives
there before the ark of the covenant of
the LORD to minister before the ark continually, as every day's work required;
38 and Obed-edom with his 68 relatives;
Obed-edom, also the son of Jeduthun,
and Hosah as gatekeepers.
39 *He left* Zadok the priest and his relatives the priests before the tabernacle of
the LORD in the high place which *was* at
Gibeon,
40 to offer burnt offerings to the LORD
on the altar of burnt offering continually
morning and evening, even according to
all that is written in the law of the LORD,
which He commanded Israel.
41 With them *were* Heman and Jeduthun, and the rest who were chosen, who
were designated by name, to give thanks
to the LORD, because His lovingkindness
is everlasting.
42 And with them *were* Heman and
Jeduthun *with* trumpets and cymbals for
those who should sound aloud, and *with*

instruments *for* the songs of God, and the sons of Jeduthun for the gate.

43 Then all the people departed each to his house, and David returned to bless his household.

Psalm 78:12–16

12 He wrought wonders before their fathers
In the land of Egypt, in the field of Zoan.
13 He divided the sea and caused them to pass through,
And He made the waters stand up like a heap.
14 Then He led them with the cloud by day
And all the night with a light of fire.
15 He split the rocks in the wilderness
And gave *them* abundant drink like the ocean depths.
16 He brought forth streams also from the rock
And caused waters to run down like rivers.

Proverbs 19:22–24

22 What is desirable in a man is his kindness,
And *it is* better to be a poor man than a liar.
23 The fear of the LORD *leads* to life,
So that one may sleep satisfied, untouched by evil.
24 The sluggard buries his hand in the dish,
But will not even bring it back to his mouth.

Acts 7:44–60

44 "Our fathers had the tabernacle of testimony in the wilderness, just as He who spoke to Moses directed *him* to make it according to the pattern which he had seen.
45 "And having received it in their turn, our fathers brought it in with Joshua upon dispossessing the nations whom God drove out before our fathers, until the time of David.
46 "*David* found favor in God's sight, and asked that he might find a dwelling place for the God of Jacob.
47 "But it was Solomon who built a house for Him.
48 "However, the Most High does not dwell in *houses* made by *human* hands; as the prophet says:
49 'HEAVEN IS MY THRONE,
AND EARTH IS THE FOOTSTOOL OF MY FEET;
WHAT KIND OF HOUSE WILL YOU BUILD FOR ME?' says the Lord,
'OR WHAT PLACE IS THERE FOR MY REPOSE?
50 'WAS IT NOT MY HAND WHICH MADE ALL THESE THINGS?'
51 "You men who are stiff-necked and uncircumcised in heart and ears are always resisting the Holy Spirit; you are doing just as your fathers did.
52 "Which one of the prophets did your fathers not persecute? They killed those who had previously announced the coming of the Righteous One, whose betrayers and murderers you have now become;
53 you who received the law as ordained by angels, and *yet* did not keep it."
54 Now when they heard this, they were cut to the quick, and they *began* gnashing their teeth at him.
55 But being full of the Holy Spirit, he gazed intently into heaven and saw the glory of God, and Jesus standing at the right hand of God;
56 and he said, "Behold, I see the heavens opened up and the Son of Man standing at the right hand of God."
57 But they cried out with a loud voice, and covered their ears and rushed at him with one impulse.

LIFE LESSONS

➤ **Acts 7:56 — *"I see the heavens opened up and the Son of Man standing at the right hand of God."***

*W*e learn from several Bible passages when Jesus ascended to heaven, He "sat down at the right hand of God" (Mark 16:19; also Col. 3:1; Heb. 1:3; 10:12; 12:2). Yet to greet this first Christian martyr, the Lord stood.

58 When they had driven him out of the city, they *began* stoning *him*; and the witnesses laid aside their robes at the feet of a young man named Saul.
59 They went on stoning Stephen as he called on *the Lord* and said, "Lord Jesus, receive my spirit!"
60 Then falling on his knees, he cried out with a loud voice, "Lord, do not hold this sin against them!" Having said this, he fell asleep.

LIFE LESSONS

➤ **Acts 7:60 — "Lord, do not hold this sin against them!"**

*J*ust as Jesus asked His Father to forgive those who crucified Him (Luke 23:34), so Stephen asked God to give his murderers a chance to repent. The Father's grace enables us to do what we could never do on our own.

Life Examples:

STEPHEN: Echoing His Savior

ACTS 7:59, 60

*S*tephen slumped to the ground as blood and forgiveness poured from his lips. Nearby a young man watched, unaware this death would bring life to worldwide evangelism. Later, the young man who had supported the execution of Stephen because of his allegiance to Christ became the apostle Paul.

Stephen most revealed his Christlike qualities when under duress. As the stones assailed him, he cried, "Lord Jesus, receive my spirit!" (Acts 7:59). Then, as death inched closer with every blow, he echoed his Savior by praying aloud, "Lord, do not hold this sin against them!" (Acts 7:60).

The beauty of Stephen's final words can never be overstated. They most eloquently summarize the heart of the true Christian. They testified that the Lord of grace was living inside him. They spoke of ultimate love, and they were words that grabbed the attention of someone who was nearby—watching.

JUNE 27

◈ 1 Chronicles 17:1—18:17

17AND it came about, when David dwelt in his house, that David said to Nathan the prophet, "Behold, I am dwelling in a house of cedar, but the ark of the covenant of the LORD is under curtains."
2 Then Nathan said to David, "Do all that is in your heart, for God is with you."
3 It came about the same night that the word of God came to Nathan, saying,
4 "Go and tell David My servant, 'Thus says the LORD, "You shall not build a house for Me to dwell in;
5 for I have not dwelt in a house since the day that I brought up Israel to this day, but I have gone from tent to tent and from *one* dwelling place *to another.*
6 "In all places where I have walked with all Israel, have I spoken a word with any of the judges of Israel, whom I commanded to shepherd My people, saying, 'Why have you not built for Me a house of cedar?'"'
7 "Now, therefore, thus shall you say to My servant David, 'Thus says the LORD of hosts, "I took you from the pasture, from following the sheep, to be leader over My people Israel.
8 "I have been with you wherever you have gone, and have cut off all your enemies from before you; and I will make you a name like the name of the great ones who are in the earth.
9 "I will appoint a place for My people Israel, and will plant them, so that they may dwell in their own place and not be moved again; and the wicked will not waste them anymore as formerly,
10 even from the day that I commanded judges *to be* over My people Israel. And I will subdue all your enemies.
Moreover, I tell you that the LORD will build a house for you.
11 "When your days are fulfilled that

you must go *to be* with your fathers, that I will set up *one of* your descendants after you, who will be of your sons; and I will establish his kingdom.

12 "He shall build for Me a house, and I will establish his throne forever.

13 "I will be his father and he shall be My son; and I will not take My loving-kindness away from him, as I took it from him who was before you.

14 "But I will settle him in My house and in My kingdom forever, and his throne shall be established forever."'"

15 According to all these words and according to all this vision, so Nathan spoke to David.

➤ 16 Then David the king went in and sat before the LORD and said, "Who am I, O LORD God, and what is my house that You have brought me this far?

17 "This was a small thing in Your eyes, O God; but You have spoken of Your servant's house for a great while to come, and have regarded me according to the standard of a man of high degree, O LORD God.

18 "What more can David still *say* to You concerning the honor *bestowed* on

---

Your servant? For You know Your servant.

19 "O LORD, for Your servant's sake, and according to Your own heart, You have wrought all this greatness, to make known all these great things.

20 "O LORD, there is none like You, nor is there any God besides You, according to all that we have heard with our ears.

21 "And what one nation in the earth is like Your people Israel, whom God went to redeem for Himself *as* a people, to make You a name by great and terrible things, in driving out nations from before Your people, whom You redeemed out of Egypt?

Life Examples:

Better Plans

1 CHRONICLES 17:1–14

*H*e had come a long way from the sheep pen. As King David scanned the beautiful carvings, cedar paneling, and gold embellishments of his palace, he thought of how different his life was and how far God had brought him. Yes, it was the Lord who had done all of it—all of the victories, the successes, the wealth, the peace. Yet David felt the picture was still incomplete.

"Behold, I am dwelling in a house of cedar, but the ark of the covenant of the LORD is under curtains" (1 Chr. 17:1), he said to Nathan the prophet. The holy ark of the covenant—the place where the presence of God would appear—deserved better. The Lord was worthy to be honored after all He had done for Israel. How could David dwell in such opulence and not build a house for the One who had given him everything?

The Lord's response surprised him. "You shall not build a house for Me to dwell in" (1 Chr. 17:4). David's son Solomon would build the temple, but God had different plans for David.

Was David wrong for wanting to build a house for the Lord? Of course not! He wanted to honor God. However, as David no doubt learned from Samuel the prophet, "To obey is better than sacrifice" (1 Sam. 15:22).

God loves when our desire is to exalt Him. But there are times He will say no to our plans in order to accomplish more important things through us. We know this was true with David. First Chronicles 18:3 tells us, "He went to establish his rule to the Euphrates River," which fulfilled God's promise to Abraham, "To your descendants I have given this land, from the river of Egypt as far as the great river, the River Euphrates" (Gen. 15:18). David strengthened Israel by defeating the Philistines, Moabites, and Arameans. He also collected many of the materials that would ultimately be used in the temple (1 Chr. 18).

Sometimes God will stop us from doing something we believe is good to accomplish something better for His kingdom. Just remember, you don't have to think up pious acts to please God. Your obedience pleases Him immeasurably. Therefore, listen to the Lord and make sure whatever you do "for Him" comes first *from* Him.

22 "For Your people Israel You made Your own people forever, and You, O LORD, became their God.

23 "Now, O LORD, let the word that You have spoken concerning Your servant and concerning his house be established forever, and do as You have spoken.

24 "Let Your name be established and magnified forever, saying, 'The LORD of hosts is the God of Israel, *even* a God to Israel; and the house of David Your servant is established before You.'

25 "For You, O my God, have revealed to Your servant that You will build for him a house; therefore Your servant has found *courage* to pray before You.

26 "Now, O LORD, You are God, and have promised this good thing to Your servant.

27 "And now it has pleased You to bless the house of Your servant, that it may continue forever before You; for You, O LORD, have blessed, and it is blessed forever."

18 NOW after this it came about that David defeated the Philistines and subdued them and took Gath and its towns from the hand of the Philistines.

2 He defeated Moab, and the Moabites became servants to David, bringing tribute.

3 David also defeated Hadadezer king of Zobah *as far as* Hamath, as he went to establish his rule to the Euphrates River.

4 David took from him 1,000 chariots and 7,000 horsemen and 20,000 foot soldiers, and David hamstrung all the chariot horses, but reserved *enough* of them for 100 chariots.

5 When the Arameans of Damascus came to help Hadadezer king of Zobah, David killed 22,000 men of the Arameans.

6 Then David put *garrisons* among the Arameans of Damascus; and the Arameans became servants to David, bringing tribute. And the LORD helped David wherever he went.

7 David took the shields of gold which were carried by the servants of Hadadezer and brought them to Jerusalem.

➤ 8 Also from Tibhath and from Cun, cities of Hadadezer, David took a very large amount of bronze, with which Solomon made the bronze sea and the pillars and the bronze utensils.

9 Now when Tou king of Hamath heard

---

that David had defeated all the army of Hadadezer king of Zobah,

10 he sent Hadoram his son to King David to greet him and to bless him, because he had fought against Hadadezer and had defeated him; for Hadadezer had been at war with Tou. And *Hadoram brought* all kinds of articles of gold and silver and bronze.

11 King David also dedicated these to the LORD with the silver and the gold which he had carried away from all the nations: from Edom, Moab, the sons of Ammon, the Philistines, and from Amalek.

12 Moreover Abishai the son of Zeruiah defeated 18,000 Edomites in the Valley of Salt.

13 Then he put garrisons in Edom, and all the Edomites became servants to David. And the LORD helped David wherever he went.

14 So David reigned over all Israel; and he administered justice and righteousness for all his people.

15 Joab the son of Zeruiah *was* over the army, and Jehoshaphat the son of Ahilud *was* recorder;

16 and Zadok the son of Ahitub and Abimelech the son of Abiathar *were* priests, and Shavsha *was* secretary;

17 and Benaiah the son of Jehoiada *was* over the Cherethites and the Pelethites, and the sons of David *were* chiefs at the king's side.

Psalm 78:17–25

17 Yet they still continued to sin against Him,
To rebel against the Most High in the desert.

18 And in their heart they put God to
the test
By asking food according to their
desire.
19 Then they spoke against God;
They said, "Can God prepare a table
in the wilderness?
20 "Behold, He struck the rock so that
waters gushed out,
And streams were overflowing;
Can He give bread also?
Will He provide meat for His
people?"
21 Therefore the LORD heard and was
full of wrath;
And a fire was kindled against
Jacob
And anger also mounted against
Israel,
22 Because they did not believe in God
And did not trust in His salvation.
23 Yet He commanded the clouds
above
And opened the doors of heaven;
24 He rained down manna upon them
to eat
And gave them food from heaven.
25 Man did eat the bread of angels;
He sent them food in abundance.

Proverbs 19:25, 26

25 Strike a scoffer and the naive may
become shrewd,
But reprove one who has
understanding and he will gain
knowledge.
26 He who assaults *his* father *and*
drives *his* mother away
Is a shameful and disgraceful son.

Acts 8:1–25

8 SAUL was in hearty agreement with
putting him to death.
And on that day a great persecution
began against the church in Jerusalem,
and they were all scattered throughout
the regions of Judea and Samaria, except
the apostles.
2 *Some* devout men buried Stephen,
and made loud lamentation over him.
3 But Saul *began* ravaging the church,
entering house after house, and dragging
off men and women, he would put them
in prison.
4 Therefore, those who had been scattered went about preaching the word.
5 Philip went down to the city of Samaria and *began* proclaiming Christ to
them.
6 The crowds with one accord were
giving attention to what was said by
Philip, as they heard and saw the signs
which he was performing.
7 For *in the case of* many who had
unclean spirits, they were coming out
of them shouting with a loud voice; and
many who had been paralyzed and lame
were healed.
8 So there was much rejoicing in that
city.
9 Now there was a man named Simon,
who formerly was practicing magic in
the city and astonishing the people of
Samaria, claiming to be someone great;

LIFE LESSONS

➤ **Acts 8:3 — *But Saul began ravaging
the church, entering house after house,
and dragging off men and women, he
would put them in prison.***

Saul persecuted the church because
he saw Christians as a terrible threat
to the Jewish religion—he honestly
thought he was doing right. Yet this
goes to show that just because our
actions are in earnest does not mean
they honor God. Saul, who became the
apostle Paul, could never forget he tried
to destroy the church" (Gal. 1:13), and
called himself the "foremost of all" sinners (1 Tim. 1:15). Jesus often requires a
radical change in our attitudes, actions,
and understanding. Will you cling to
your erroneous ideas or immediately do
as He says? If you really love God and do
everything for Him, the choice will be
clear.

➤ **Acts 8:4 — *Therefore, those who had
been scattered went about preaching the
word.***

God is an expert at using even hardship and suffering for His glory and
our benefit. The opponents of Christ
intended their persecution to wipe out
the church. Instead, it spread more rapidly as believers fled into other regions.

10 and they all, from smallest to greatest, were giving attention to him, saying, "This man is what is called the Great Power of God."

11 And they were giving him attention because he had for a long time astonished them with his magic arts.

12 But when they believed Philip preaching the good news about the kingdom of God and the name of Jesus Christ, they were being baptized, men and women alike.

13 Even Simon himself believed; and after being baptized, he continued on with Philip, and as he observed signs and great miracles taking place, he was constantly amazed.

14 Now when the apostles in Jerusalem heard that Samaria had received the word of God, they sent them Peter and John,

15 who came down and prayed for them that they might receive the Holy Spirit.

16 For He had not yet fallen upon any of them; they had simply been baptized in the name of the Lord Jesus.

17 Then they *began* laying their hands on them, and they were receiving the Holy Spirit.

18 Now when Simon saw that the Spirit was bestowed through the laying on of the apostles' hands, he offered them money,

19 saying, "Give this authority to me as well, so that everyone on whom I lay my hands may receive the Holy Spirit."

20 But Peter said to him, "May your silver perish with you, because you thought you could obtain the gift of God with money!

21 "You have no part or portion in this matter, for your heart is not right before God.

22 "Therefore repent of this wickedness of yours, and pray the Lord that, if possible, the intention of your heart may be forgiven you.

23 "For I see that you are in the gall of ◄ bitterness and in the bondage of iniquity."

24 But Simon answered and said, "Pray to the Lord for me yourselves, so that nothing of what you have said may come upon me."

25 So, when they had solemnly testified and spoken the word of the Lord, they started back to Jerusalem, and were preaching the gospel to many villages of the Samaritans.

LIFE LESSONS

➤ Acts 8:23 — *"For I see that you are in the gall of bitterness and in the bondage of iniquity."*

*W*e do not know if Simon the sorcerer made a big error as a young Christian or whether he had never truly come to faith. But in either case, Peter rebuked him sharply—not to condemn him, but to rescue him.

JUNE 28

✦ 1 Chronicles 19:1—20:8

19 NOW it came about after this, that Nahash the king of the sons of Ammon died, and his son became king in his place.

2 Then David said, "I will show kindness to Hanun the son of Nahash, because his father showed kindness to me." So David sent messengers to console him concerning his father. And David's servants came into the land of the sons of Ammon to Hanun to console him.

3 But the princes of the sons of Ammon said to Hanun, "Do you think that David is honoring your father, in that he has sent comforters to you? Have not his servants come to you to search and to overthrow and to spy out the land?"

4 So Hanun took David's servants and shaved them and cut off their garments in the middle as far as their hips, and sent them away.

5 Then *certain persons* went and told David about the men. And he sent to meet them, for the men were greatly humiliated. And the king said, "Stay at Jericho until your beards grow, and *then* return."

6 When the sons of Ammon saw that they had made themselves odious to David, Hanun and the sons of Ammon sent 1,000 talents of silver to hire for themselves chariots and horsemen from Mesopotamia, from Aram-maacah and from Zobah.

7 So they hired for themselves 32,000 chariots, and the king of Maacah and his people, who came and camped before Medeba. And the sons of Ammon gathered together from their cities and came to battle.

8 When David heard *of it*, he sent Joab and all the army, the mighty men.

9 The sons of Ammon came out and drew up in battle array at the entrance of the city, and the kings who had come were by themselves in the field.

10 Now when Joab saw that the battle was set against him in front and in the rear, he selected from all the choice men of Israel and they arrayed themselves against the Arameans.

11 But the remainder of the people he placed in the hand of Abshai his brother; and they arrayed themselves against the sons of Ammon.

12 He said, "If the Arameans are too strong for me, then you shall help me; but if the sons of Ammon are too strong for you, then I will help you.

13 "Be strong, and let us show ourselves courageous for the sake of our people and for the cities of our God; and may the LORD do what is good in His sight."

14 So Joab and the people who were with him drew near to the battle against the Arameans, and they fled before him.

15 When the sons of Ammon saw that the Arameans fled, they also fled before Abshai his brother and entered the city. Then Joab came to Jerusalem.

16 When the Arameans saw that they had been defeated by Israel, they sent messengers and brought out the Arameans who were beyond the River, with Shophach the commander of the army of Hadadezer leading them.

17 When it was told David, he gathered all Israel together and crossed the Jordan, and came upon them and drew up in formation against them. And when David drew up in battle array against the Arameans, they fought against him.

18 The Arameans fled before Israel, and David killed of the Arameans 7,000 charioteers and 40,000 foot soldiers, and put to death Shophach the commander of the army.

19 So when the servants of Hadadezer saw that they were defeated by Israel, they made peace with David and served him. Thus the Arameans were not willing to help the sons of Ammon anymore.

20 THEN it happened in the spring, at the time when kings go out *to battle,* that Joab led out the army and ravaged the land of the sons of Ammon, and came and besieged Rabbah. But David stayed at Jerusalem. And Joab struck Rabbah and overthrew it.

2 David took the crown of their king from his head, and he found it to weigh a talent of gold, and there was a precious stone in it; and it was placed on David's head. And he brought out the spoil of the city, a very great amount.

3 He brought out the people who *were* in it, and cut *them* with saws and with sharp instruments and with axes. And thus David did to all the cities of the sons of Ammon. Then David and all the people returned *to* Jerusalem.

4 Now it came about after this, that war broke out at Gezer with the Philistines; then Sibbecai the Hushathite killed Sippai, one of the descendants of the giants, and they were subdued.

5 And there was war with the Philistines again, and Elhanan the son of Jair killed Lahmi the brother of Goliath the Gittite, the shaft of whose spear *was* like a weaver's beam.

6 Again there was war at Gath, where there was a man of *great* stature who had twenty-four fingers and toes, six *fingers on each hand* and six *toes on each foot;* and he also was descended from the giants.

7 When he taunted Israel, Jonathan the son of Shimea, David's brother, killed him.

8 These were descended from the giants in Gath, and they fell by the hand of David and by the hand of his servants.

Psalm 78:26–33

26 He caused the east wind to blow in the heavens

And by His power He directed the
south wind.

27 When He rained meat upon them
like the dust,
Even winged fowl like the sand of
the seas,

28 Then He let *them* fall in the midst of
their camp,
Round about their dwellings.

29 So they ate and were well filled,
And their desire He gave to them.

30 Before they had satisfied their
desire,
While their food was in their
mouths,

31 The anger of God rose against
them
And killed some of their stoutest
ones,
And subdued the choice men of
Israel.

32 In spite of all this they still sinned
And did not believe in His
wonderful works.

33 So He brought their days to an end
in futility
And their years in sudden terror.

Proverbs 19:27–29

27 Cease listening, my son, to
discipline,
And you will stray from the words
of knowledge.

28 A rascally witness makes a
mockery of justice,
And the mouth of the wicked
spreads iniquity.

29 Judgments are prepared for
scoffers,
And blows for the back of fools.

Acts 8:26–40

26 But an angel of the Lord spoke to
Philip saying, "Get up and go south to
the road that descends from Jerusalem
to Gaza." (This is a desert *road*.)

27 So he got up and went; and there was
an Ethiopian eunuch, a court official of
Candace, queen of the Ethiopians, who
was in charge of all her treasure; and he
had come to Jerusalem to worship,

28 and he was returning and sitting in
his chariot, and was reading the prophet
Isaiah.

29 Then the Spirit said to Philip, "Go up
and join this chariot."

30 Philip ran up and heard him reading
Isaiah the prophet, and said, "Do you
understand what you are reading?"

31 And he said, "Well, how could I, unless someone guides me?" And he invited
Philip to come up and sit with him.

32 Now the passage of Scripture which
he was reading was this:
"HE WAS LED AS A SHEEP TO
SLAUGHTER;
AND AS A LAMB BEFORE ITS SHEARER IS
SILENT,
SO HE DOES NOT OPEN HIS MOUTH.

33 "IN HUMILIATION HIS JUDGMENT WAS
TAKEN AWAY;
WHO WILL RELATE HIS GENERATION?
FOR HIS LIFE IS REMOVED FROM THE
EARTH."

34 The eunuch answered Philip and
said, "Please *tell me*, of whom does the
prophet say this? Of himself or of someone else?"

35 Then Philip opened his mouth,
and beginning from this Scripture he
preached Jesus to him.

LIFE LESSONS

➤ **Proverbs 19:27 — *Cease listening, my
son, to discipline, and you will stray from
the words of knowledge.***

*W*e must never stop learning. Not
only do we need reminders of
the principles we've already embraced
(2 Pet. 1:12), but new lessons always lie
ahead of us to continue our transformation into the image and character of
Christ (Rom. 8:29).

➤ **Acts 8:27 — *So he got up and went.***

*P*hilip didn't waste time arguing with
the angel of the Lord about why
he should go—he simply obeyed. Had
Philip demanded more details and spent
time debating the wisdom of the command, he would have missed the opportunity to influence a high official of the
Ethiopian court. Immediate obedience is
always necessary. This is why it's important to spend time alone with the Lord.
When He calls, you know His voice and
can act directly.

WHAT THE BIBLE SAYS ABOUT ◉

Baptism, Some Answers

Acts 8:26–39

After the time of Pentecost, a Christian named Philip had a conversation with a man from Ethiopia. Philip told his new friend the good news about Jesus Christ. Eventually the Ethiopian said, "Look! Water! What prevents me from being baptized?" (Acts 8:36).

Philip replied, "If you believe with all your heart, you may" (Acts 8:37). This passage raises several important questions about the practice of baptism.

1. *Who should be baptized?*

Some might assume anyone who wants to be a church member should be baptized. In reality, only those who believe in Jesus Christ as their Lord and Savior should be baptized. A mere mental affirmation of Christ's existence is not enough. Rather, if we truly believe in Jesus, we must do something about it—we must confess, repent, and live in a new way.

2. *What is the proper method of baptism?*

Christians throughout the world recognize three methods of baptism. The first of these involves pouring the water over the head of the new believer. The second involves sprinkling the water. The final method of baptism is the full immersion of the person into the water. The Greek words for "pour" and "sprinkle" are never used in the New Testament in reference to baptism. Rather, the word for *baptism* comes from the Greek word used to describe things such as sinking ships. Romans 6:4 tells us, "We have been buried with Him through baptism into death, so that as Christ was raised from the dead through the glory of the Father, so we too might walk in newness of life." This is why we baptize by immersion—it represents the meaning of baptism, and most vividly symbolizes the death and resurrection of Christ.

3. *What is the meaning of baptism?*

As stated before, the procedure of momentarily being immersed and being lifted presents a simple picture of the actions of Jesus Himself. He was killed, buried, and resurrected from death. When we trust Him as our Savior, we die to our old lives and are raised to walk in newness of life in Him. It also suggests that one day we will rise from death itself to live eternally in heaven.

4. *What is the proper time for baptism?*

When the Holy Spirit empowered the church at Pentecost, we know Peter preached the gospel and "those who had received his word were baptized; and that day there were added about three thousand souls" (Acts 2:41). In other words, as soon as the people believed in Christ, they were candidates for baptism. Philip's Ethiopian friend was baptized without delay. As a general rule, the time for baptism is immediately after conversion. When we procrastinate in following this command, we break the commitment we made to follow Christ, surrendering our lives to Him. Obedience should never be delayed.

5. *What is the relationship of baptism to salvation?*

The Word of God does not teach that baptism is a requirement for salvation nor that the act itself saves us. In fact, the thief on the cross beside Jesus was saved without baptism (Luke 23:43). The clear and consistent teaching of Scripture is that we are saved through the grace of God when we believe in Christ as our Savior (Eph. 2:8, 9). Baptism is our obedient response to Christ in thankfulness for our salvation.

6. *Why should we be baptized?*

The first reason we should be baptized is Jesus commanded it (Matt. 28:19). Second, He was baptized, and we should follow His example (Rom. 8:29). Third, baptism is a picture of the life, death, and resurrection of our Lord and Savior (Rom. 6:4). It serves as an encouragement to believers and a testimony to nonbelievers. Fourth, it is also a picture of our experience in salvation—that of dying to the old, sinful self, and rising to walk in the new life of the Holy Spirit. Fifth, baptism identifies us with the body of Christ. Finally, baptism declares our faith in a future bodily resurrection. For all these reasons, Christian baptism is a joy, privilege, and pleasure for the children of God. ◉

---

36 As they went along the road they came to some water; and the eunuch *said, "Look! Water! What prevents me from being baptized?"

37 [And Philip said, "If you believe with all your heart, you may." And he answered and said, "I believe that Jesus Christ is the Son of God."]

38 And he ordered the chariot to stop; and they both went down into the water,

Philip as well as the eunuch, and he baptized him.

39 When they came up out of the water, the Spirit of the Lord snatched Philip away; and the eunuch no longer saw him, but went on his way rejoicing.

40 But Philip found himself at Azotus, and as he passed through he kept preaching the gospel to all the cities until he came to Caesarea.

JUNE 29

1 Chronicles 21:1—22:19

21 THEN Satan stood up against Israel and moved David to number Israel.

2 So David said to Joab and to the princes of the people, "Go, number Israel from Beersheba even to Dan, and bring me *word* that I may know their number."

3 Joab said, "May the LORD add to His people a hundred times as many as they are! But, my lord the king, are they not all my lord's servants? Why does my lord seek this thing? Why should he be a cause of guilt to Israel?"

4 Nevertheless, the king's word prevailed against Joab. Therefore, Joab departed and went throughout all Israel, and came to Jerusalem.

5 Joab gave the number of the census of *all* the people to David. And all Israel were 1,100,000 men who drew the sword; and Judah *was* 470,000 men who drew the sword.

6 But he did not number Levi and Benjamin among them, for the king's command was abhorrent to Joab.

7 God was displeased with this thing, so He struck Israel.

8 David said to God, "I have sinned greatly, in that I have done this thing. But now, please take away the iniquity of Your servant, for I have done very foolishly."

9 The LORD spoke to Gad, David's seer, saying,

10 "Go and speak to David, saying, 'Thus says the LORD, "I offer you three things;

choose for yourself one of them, which I will do to you."'"

11 So Gad came to David and said to him, "Thus says the LORD, 'Take for yourself

12 either three years of famine, or three months to be swept away before your foes, while the sword of your enemies overtakes *you*, or else three days of the sword of the LORD, even pestilence in the land, and the angel of the LORD destroying throughout all the territory of Israel.' Now, therefore, consider what answer I shall return to Him who sent me."

13 David said to Gad, "I am in great distress; please let me fall into the hand of the LORD, for His mercies are very great. But do not let me fall into the hand of man."

14 So the LORD sent a pestilence on Israel; 70,000 men of Israel fell.

15 And God sent an angel to Jerusalem to destroy it; but as he was about to destroy *it*, the LORD saw and was sorry over

the calamity, and said to the destroying angel, "It is enough; now relax your hand." And the angel of the LORD was standing by the threshing floor of Ornan the Jebusite.

16 Then David lifted up his eyes and saw the angel of the LORD standing between earth and heaven, with his drawn sword in his hand stretched out over Jerusalem. Then David and the elders, covered with sackcloth, fell on their faces.

17 David said to God, "Is it not I who commanded to count the people? Indeed, I am the one who has sinned and done very wickedly, but these sheep, what have they done? O LORD my God, please let Your hand be against me and my father's household, but not against Your people that they should be plagued."

18 Then the angel of the LORD commanded Gad to say to David, that David should go up and build an altar to the LORD on the threshing floor of Ornan the Jebusite.

19 So David went up at the word of Gad, which he spoke in the name of the LORD.

20 Now Ornan turned back and saw the angel, and his four sons *who were* with him hid themselves. And Ornan was threshing wheat.

21 As David came to Ornan, Ornan looked and saw David, and went out from the threshing floor and prostrated himself before David with his face to the ground.

22 Then David said to Ornan, "Give me the site of *this* threshing floor, that I may build on it an altar to the LORD; for the full price you shall give it to me, that the plague may be restrained from the people."

23 Ornan said to David, "Take *it* for yourself; and let my lord the king do what is good in his sight. See, I will give the oxen for burnt offerings and the threshing sledges for wood and the wheat for the grain offering; I will give *it* all."

24 But King David said to Ornan, "No, but I will surely buy *it* for the full price; for I will not take what is yours for the LORD, or offer a burnt offering which costs me nothing."

25 So David gave Ornan 600 shekels of gold by weight for the site.

26 Then David built an altar to the LORD there and offered burnt offerings and peace offerings. And he called to the LORD and He answered him with fire from heaven on the altar of burnt offering.

27 The LORD commanded the angel, and he put his sword back in its sheath.

28 At that time, when David saw that the LORD had answered him on the threshing floor of Ornan the Jebusite, he offered sacrifice there.

29 For the tabernacle of the LORD, which Moses had made in the wilderness, and the altar of burnt offering *were* in the high place at Gibeon at that time.

30 But David could not go before it to inquire of God, for he was terrified by the sword of the angel of the LORD.

22 THEN David said, "This is the house of the LORD God, and this is the altar of burnt offering for Israel."

2 So David gave orders to gather the foreigners who were in the land of Israel, and he set stonecutters to hew out stones to build the house of God.

3 David prepared large quantities of iron to make the nails for the doors of the gates and for the clamps, and more bronze than could be weighed;

4 and timbers of cedar logs beyond number, for the Sidonians and Tyrians brought large quantities of cedar timber to David.

5 David said, "My son Solomon is young and inexperienced, and the house that is to be built for the LORD shall be exceedingly magnificent, famous and glorious throughout all lands. *Therefore* now I will make preparation for it." So David made ample preparations before his death.

6 Then he called for his son Solomon, and charged him to build a house for the LORD God of Israel.

LIFE LESSONS

> **1 Chronicles 21:16 —** *David lifted up his eyes and saw the angel of the LORD standing between earth and heaven.*

*A*t select times and places, God lifts the curtain obscuring our vision of spiritual realities, and we see clearly what He is doing—but He remains active even when we do not see (1 Cor. 2:9; 2 Cor. 4:17, 18).

7 David said to Solomon, "My son, I had intended to build a house to the name of the LORD my God.

8 "But the word of the LORD came to me, saying, 'You have shed much blood and have waged great wars; you shall not build a house to My name, because you have shed so much blood on the earth before Me.

9 'Behold, a son will be born to you, who shall be a man of rest; and I will give him rest from all his enemies on every side; for his name shall be Solomon, and I will give peace and quiet to Israel in his days.

10 'He shall build a house for My name, and he shall be My son and I will be his father; and I will establish the throne of his kingdom over Israel forever.'

11 "Now, my son, the LORD be with you that you may be successful, and build the house of the LORD your God just as He has spoken concerning you.

12 "Only the LORD give you discretion and understanding, and give you charge over Israel, so that you may keep the law of the LORD your God.

13 "Then you will prosper, if you are careful to observe the statutes and the ordinances which the LORD commanded Moses concerning Israel. Be strong and courageous, do not fear nor be dismayed.

14 "Now behold, with great pains I have prepared for the house of the LORD 100,000 talents of gold and 1,000,000 talents of silver, and bronze and iron beyond weight, for they are in great quantity; also timber and stone I have prepared, and you may add to them.

15 "Moreover, there are many workmen with you, stonecutters and masons of stone and carpenters, and all men who are skillful in every kind of work.

16 "Of the gold, the silver and the bronze and the iron there is no limit. Arise and work, and may the LORD be with you."

17 David also commanded all the leaders of Israel to help his son Solomon, saying,

18 "Is not the LORD your God with you? And has He not given you rest on every side? For He has given the inhabitants of the land into my hand, and the land is subdued before the LORD and before His people.

19 "Now set your heart and your soul to seek the LORD your God; arise, therefore, and build the sanctuary of the LORD God,

so that you may bring the ark of the covenant of the LORD and the holy vessels of God into the house that is to be built for the name of the LORD."

Psalm 78:34–39

34 When He killed them, then they sought Him,
    And returned and searched diligently for God;

35 And they remembered that God was their rock,
    And the Most High God their Redeemer.

36 But they deceived Him with their mouth
    And lied to Him with their tongue.

37 For their heart was not steadfast toward Him,
    Nor were they faithful in His covenant.

38 But He, being compassionate, forgave their iniquity and did not destroy them;
    And often He restrained His anger
    And did not arouse all His wrath.

39 Thus He remembered that they were but flesh,
    A wind that passes and does not return.

LIFE LESSONS

➤ 1 Chronicles 22:19 — *"Set your heart and your soul to seek the LORD your God."*

*W*e are to encourage one another to seek the Lord with all our hearts and souls; Hebrews 3:13 instructs us to do this daily. We need each other, for no Christian has ever been called to "go it alone" in his or her walk of faith.

➤ Psalm 78:38 — *But He, being compassionate, forgave their iniquity and did not destroy them.*

*I*t is a blessed truth that God "has not dealt with us according to our sins" (Ps. 103:10). For the sake of His name, He restrains His anger and pours out mercy—rather than wrath—for those who put their faith in His Son, Jesus Christ (Rom. 5:8–11).

Proverbs 20:1, 2

20 WINE is a mocker, strong drink a
brawler,
And whoever is intoxicated by it is
not wise.
2   The terror of a king is like the
growling of a lion;
He who provokes him to anger
forfeits his own life.

Acts 9:1–21

9 NOW Saul, still breathing threats and
murder against the disciples of the
Lord, went to the high priest,
2   and asked for letters from him to the
synagogues at Damascus, so that if he
found any belonging to the Way, both
men and women, he might bring them
bound to Jerusalem.
3   As he was traveling, it happened
that he was approaching Damascus, and
suddenly a light from heaven flashed
around him;
4   and he fell to the ground and heard a
voice saying to him, "Saul, Saul, why are
you persecuting Me?"
5   And he said, "Who are You, Lord?"
And He *said*, "I am Jesus whom you are
persecuting,
6   but get up and enter the city, and it
will be told you what you must do."
7   The men who traveled with him stood
speechless, hearing the voice but seeing
no one.
8   Saul got up from the ground, and
though his eyes were open, he could see
nothing; and leading him by the hand,
they brought him into Damascus.
9   And he was three days without sight,
and neither ate nor drank.
10   Now there was a disciple at Damascus named Ananias; and the Lord said to
him in a vision, "Ananias." And he said,
"Here I am, Lord."
11   And the Lord *said* to him, "Get up
and go to the street called Straight, and
inquire at the house of Judas for a man
from Tarsus named Saul, for he is praying,
12   and he has seen in a vision a man
named Ananias come in and lay his

hands on him, so that he might regain
his sight."
13   But Ananias answered, "Lord, I have
heard from many about this man, how
much harm he did to Your saints at Jerusalem;
14   and here he has authority from the
chief priests to bind all who call on Your
name."
15   But the Lord said to him, "Go, for he
is a chosen instrument of Mine, to bear
My name before the Gentiles and kings
and the sons of Israel;
16   for I will show him how much he
must suffer for My name's sake."
17   So Ananias departed and entered
the house, and after laying his hands on
him said, "Brother Saul, the Lord Jesus,
who appeared to you on the road by
which you were coming, has sent me so
that you may regain your sight and be
filled with the Holy Spirit."
18   And immediately there fell from his
eyes something like scales, and he regained his sight, and he got up and was
baptized;

LIFE LESSONS

**➤ Acts 9:4 — "Saul, Saul, why are you
persecuting Me?"**

Before the Apostle Paul knew Jesus
as his Savior, he was a prominent
Pharisee named Saul who persecuted
the church. He sent people who believed
in Jesus Christ to be tortured and put
to death. Saul honestly thought he was
serving God by arresting and imprison-
ing dangerous heretics. Yet Jesus told
him that by putting Christians to death,
he was persecuting God Himself. When
we bless other believers, we bless Christ;
and when we wound other believers, we
harm Him (Matt. 25:40, 45).

**➤ Acts 9:11 — "Get up and go to the
street called Straight, and inquire at the
house of Judas for a man from Tarsus
named Saul."**

The Lord gave Ananias an assignment he did not particularly like. He
objected that Saul was a dangerous man,
but the Lord repeated His command to
go. Unlike Jonah long before, Ananias
obeyed, and the church gained a new
apostle.

WHAT THE BIBLE SAYS ABOUT

How God Uses Adversity to Get Our Attention

Acts 9:1–21

*A*ny instructor will tell you, the first goal of a teacher is to raise a student's interest. You can't teach someone who isn't paying attention. The Lord sometimes uses adversity in our lives to cause us to focus on Him in a new way.

This is exactly what happened to Saul of Tarsus as he traveled to Damascus where he intended to bring great persecution upon the Christians in that city. Scripture tells us Saul was "breathing threats and murder against the disciples of the Lord" (Acts 9:1). It seemed his cruel mission nearly consumed him.

But God got Saul's attention in a way he never expected. He sent him crashing to the ground with a blazing light and instructed him to enter the city and there wait for instructions. When he opened his eyes, he found himself blind and having to ask others to lead him by the hand into the city.

Saul definitely received a wake-up call from the Lord that day. In one stunning moment, God gained Saul's undivided attention, striking him with the adversity of blindness and humbling him in front of his traveling companions. The Lord had Saul exactly where He wanted him.

Saul felt more than ready to listen when the Lord asked, "Why are you persecuting Me?" (Acts 9:14). Up to that point, he had no idea he was dishonoring God. In fact, he thought he was serving the Lord by ridding the world of Christians. A period of intense adversity resulted in a complete turnaround for Saul. Within a matter of days, he was proclaiming Jesus in the synagogues (Acts 9:20).

The Lord got Saul's full attention on the Damascus Road, and He used the temporary blindness and humiliation to transform the zealous Pharisee named Saul into the powerful apostle and missionary named Paul, who spread the gospel and planted churches across the Roman world.

God knew exactly what He was doing when He saved Paul. And He knows what He is doing in your life through the affliction you are facing. Never delay in responding to His call. When He allows difficulties in your life, seek Him, give Him your full attention, respond to His commands quickly and humbly, and listen for what He has to say to you. You will never regret giving your heart and life to the Savior. ◉

---

19 and he took food and was strengthened.

Now for several days he was with the disciples who were at Damascus,
20 and immediately he *began* to proclaim Jesus in the synagogues, saying, "He is the Son of God."

21 All those hearing him continued to be amazed, and were saying, "Is this not he who in Jerusalem destroyed those who called on this name, and *who* had come here for the purpose of bringing them bound before the chief priests?"

JUNE 30

◈ 1 Chronicles 23:1—25:31

23 NOW when David reached old age, he made his son Solomon king over Israel.
2 And he gathered together all the leaders of Israel with the priests and the Levites.
3 The Levites were numbered from thirty years old and upward, and their number by census of men was 38,000.

4 Of these, 24,000 were to oversee the work of the house of the LORD; and 6,000 *were* officers and judges,
5 and 4,000 *were* gatekeepers, and 4,000 *were* praising the LORD with the instruments which David made for giving praise.
6 David divided them into divisions according to the sons of Levi: Gershon, Kohath, and Merari.
7 Of the Gershonites *were* Ladan and Shimei.

8   The sons of Ladan *were* Jehiel the first and Zetham and Joel, three.

9   The sons of Shimei *were* Shelomoth and Haziel and Haran, three. These were the heads of the fathers' *households* of Ladan.

10   The sons of Shimei *were* Jahath, Zina, Jeush and Beriah. These four *were* the sons of Shimei.

11   Jahath was the first and Zizah the second; but Jeush and Beriah did not have many sons, so they became a father's household, one class.

12   The sons of Kohath *were* four: Amram, Izhar, Hebron and Uzziel.

13   The sons of Amram *were* Aaron and Moses. And Aaron was set apart to sanctify him as most holy, he and his sons forever, to burn incense before the LORD, to minister to Him and to bless in His name forever.

14   But *as for* Moses the man of God, his sons were named among the tribe of Levi.

15   The sons of Moses *were* Gershom and Eliezer.

16   The son of Gershom *was* Shebuel the chief.

17   The son of Eliezer was Rehabiah the chief; and Eliezer had no other sons, but the sons of Rehabiah were very many.

18   The son of Izhar was Shelomith the chief.

19   The sons of Hebron *were* Jeriah the first, Amariah the second, Jahaziel the third and Jekameam the fourth.

20   The sons of Uzziel *were* Micah the first and Isshiah the second.

21   The sons of Merari *were* Mahli and Mushi. The sons of Mahli *were* Eleazar and Kish.

22   Eleazar died and had no sons, but daughters only, so their brothers, the sons of Kish, took them *as wives*.

23   The sons of Mushi *were* three: Mahli, Eder and Jeremoth.

24   These were the sons of Levi according to their fathers' households, *even* the heads of the fathers' *households* of those of them who were counted, in the number of names by their census, doing the work for the service of the house of the LORD, from twenty years old and upward.

25   For David said, "The LORD God of Israel has given rest to His people, and He dwells in Jerusalem forever.

26   "Also, the Levites will no longer need to carry the tabernacle and all its utensils for its service."

27   For by the last words of David the sons of Levi *were* numbered from twenty years old and upward.

28   For their office is to assist the sons of Aaron with the service of the house of the LORD, in the courts and in the chambers and in the purifying of all holy things, even the work of the service of the house of God,

29   and with the showbread, and the fine flour for a grain offering, and unleavened wafers, or *what is baked in* the pan or what is well-mixed, and all measures of volume and size.

30   They are to stand every morning to thank and to praise the LORD, and likewise at evening,

31   and to offer all burnt offerings to the LORD, on the sabbaths, the new moons and the fixed festivals in the number *set* by the ordinance concerning them, continually before the LORD.

32   Thus they are to keep charge of the tent of meeting, and charge of the holy place, and charge of the sons of Aaron their relatives, for the service of the house of the LORD.

24 NOW the divisions of the descendants of Aaron *were these:* the sons of Aaron *were* Nadab, Abihu, Eleazar and Ithamar.

2   But Nadab and Abihu died before their father and had no sons. So Eleazar and Ithamar served as priests.

3   David, with Zadok of the sons of Eleazar and Ahimelech of the sons of Ithamar, divided them according to their offices for their ministry.

4   Since more chief men were found from the descendants of Eleazar than the descendants of Ithamar, they divided them thus: *there were* sixteen heads of fathers' households of the descendants of Eleazar and eight of the descendants of Ithamar, according to their fathers' households.

5   Thus they were divided by lot, the one as the other; for they were officers of the sanctuary and officers of God, both from the descendants of Eleazar and the descendants of Ithamar.

6   Shemaiah, the son of Nethanel the scribe, from the Levites, recorded them in the presence of the king, the princes,

Zadok the priest, Ahimelech the son of Abiathar, and the heads of the fathers' *households* of the priests and of the Levites; one father's household taken for Eleazar and one taken for Ithamar.

7 Now the first lot came out for Jehoiarib, the second for Jedaiah,

8 the third for Harim, the fourth for Seorim,

9 the fifth for Malchijah, the sixth for Mijamin,

10 the seventh for Hakkoz, the eighth for Abijah,

11 the ninth for Jeshua, the tenth for Shecaniah,

12 the eleventh for Eliashib, the twelfth for Jakim,

13 the thirteenth for Huppah, the fourteenth for Jeshebeab,

14 the fifteenth for Bilgah, the sixteenth for Immer,

15 the seventeenth for Hezir, the eighteenth for Happizzez,

16 the nineteenth for Pethahiah, the twentieth for Jehezkel,

17 the twenty-first for Jachin, the twenty-second for Gamul,

18 the twenty-third for Delaiah, the twenty-fourth for Maaziah.

19 These were their offices for their ministry when *they* came in to the house of the LORD according to the ordinance *given* to them through Aaron their father, just as the LORD God of Israel had commanded him.

20 Now for the rest of the sons of Levi: of the sons of Amram, Shubael; of the sons of Shubael, Jehdeiah.

21 Of Rehabiah: of the sons of Rehabiah, Isshiah the first.

22 Of the Izharites, Shelomoth; of the sons of Shelomoth, Jahath.

23 The sons of *Hebron:* Jeriah *the first,* Amariah the second, Jahaziel the third, Jekameam the fourth.

24 *Of* the sons of Uzziel, Micah; of the sons of Micah, Shamir.

25 The brother of Micah, Isshiah; of the sons of Isshiah, Zechariah.

26 The sons of Merari, Mahli and Mushi; the sons of Jaaziah, Beno.

27 The sons of Merari: by Jaaziah *were* Beno, Shoham, Zaccur and Ibri.

28 By Mahli: Eleazar, who had no sons.

29 By Kish: the sons of Kish, Jerahmeel.

30 The sons of Mushi: Mahli, Eder and Jerimoth. These *were* the sons of the Levites according to their fathers' households.

31 These also cast lots just as their relatives the sons of Aaron in the presence of David the king, Zadok, Ahimelech, and the heads of the fathers' *households* of the priests and of the Levites—the head of fathers' *households* as well as those of his younger brother.

25 MOREOVER, David and the commanders of the army set apart for the service *some* of the sons of Asaph and of Heman and of Jeduthun, who *were* to prophesy with lyres, harps and cymbals; and the number of those who performed their service was:

2 Of the sons of Asaph: Zaccur, Joseph, Nethaniah and Asharelah; the sons of Asaph *were* under the direction of Asaph, who prophesied under the direction of the king.

3 Of Jeduthun, the sons of Jeduthun: Gedaliah, Zeri, Jeshaiah, Shimei, Hashabiah and Mattithiah, six, under the direction of their father Jeduthun with the harp, who prophesied in giving thanks and praising the LORD.

4 Of Heman, the sons of Heman: Bukkiah, Mattaniah, Uzziel, Shebuel and Jerimoth, Hananiah, Hanani, Eliathah, Giddalti and Romamti-ezer, Joshbekashah, Mallothi, Hothir, Mahazioth.

5 All these *were* the sons of Heman the king's seer to exalt him according to the words of God, for God gave fourteen sons and three daughters to Heman.

6 All these were under the direction of their father to sing in the house of the LORD, with cymbals, harps and lyres, for the service of the house of God. Asaph, Jeduthun and Heman *were* under the direction of the king.

7 Their number who were trained in singing to the LORD, with their relatives, all who were skillful, *was* 288.

8 They cast lots for their duties, all alike, the small as well as the great, the teacher *as well* as the pupil.

9 Now the first lot came out for Asaph to Joseph, the second for Gedaliah, he with his relatives and sons *were* twelve;

10 the third to Zaccur, his sons and his relatives, twelve;

11 the fourth to Izri, his sons and his relatives, twelve;

12 the fifth to Nethaniah, his sons and his relatives, twelve;

13 the sixth to Bukkiah, his sons and his relatives, twelve;
14 the seventh to Jesharelah, his sons and his relatives, twelve;
15 the eighth to Jeshaiah, his sons and his relatives, twelve;
16 the ninth to Mattaniah, his sons and his relatives, twelve;
17 the tenth to Shimei, his sons and his relatives, twelve;
18 the eleventh to Azarel, his sons and his relatives, twelve;
19 the twelfth to Hashabiah, his sons and his relatives, twelve;
20 for the thirteenth, Shubael, his sons and his relatives, twelve;
21 for the fourteenth, Mattithiah, his sons and his relatives, twelve;
22 for the fifteenth to Jeremoth, his sons and his relatives, twelve;
23 for the sixteenth to Hananiah, his sons and his relatives, twelve;
24 for the seventeenth to Joshbekashah, his sons and his relatives, twelve;
25 for the eighteenth to Hanani, his sons and his relatives, twelve;
26 for the nineteenth to Mallothi, his sons and his relatives, twelve;

27 for the twentieth to Eliathah, his sons and his relatives, twelve;
28 for the twenty-first to Hothir, his sons and his relatives, twelve;
29 for the twenty-second to Giddalti, his sons and his relatives, twelve;
30 for the twenty-third to Mahazioth, his sons and his relatives, twelve;
31 for the twenty-fourth to Romamti-ezer, his sons and his relatives, twelve.

Psalm 78:40–55

40 How often they rebelled against
    Him in the wilderness
    And grieved Him in the desert!
41 Again and again they tempted God,
    And pained the Holy One of Israel.
42 They did not remember His power,
    The day when He redeemed them
    from the adversary,
43 When He performed His signs in
    Egypt
    And His marvels in the field of Zoan,
44 And turned their rivers to blood,
    And their streams, they could not
    drink.

WHAT THE BIBLE SAYS ABOUT

No Fear Because God Is Here

Psalm 78:52, 53

*I*t is a beautiful statement of God's leadership, "He led forth His own people like sheep and guided them in the wilderness like a flock; he led them safely, so that they did not fear" (Ps. 78:52, 53). The demoralized, slavery-worn Israelites needed the strong, gentle leadership of the Good Shepherd. He not only cared for their needs and protected them from their enemies, but He gave them a visible reminder of His powerful presence with them. Exodus 13:21 tells us, "The LORD was going before them in a pillar of cloud by day to lead them on the way, and in a pillar of fire by night to give them light, that they might travel by day and by night."

Though God may not be leading you in the same way He did the Israelites, there's an important principle here that can keep you from becoming discouraged. God is guiding you—showing you the way you should go—and as long as you maintain your focus on Him, you'll have no reason to fear. Unfortunately, our human tendency is to take our eyes off God and become overwhelmed by the perils that encircle us. It is then that we forget the magnificent power of our almighty God.

Are you afraid of something today? Is some situation gnawing away at you and causing you anxiety? Are you completely lost as to how to proceed? Then, put your focus back on the Lord.

His message to you is clear, "The LORD is the one who goes ahead of you; He will be with you. He will not fail you or forsake you. Do not fear or be dismayed" (Deut. 31:8). Your Good Shepherd has your every need in mind, and He is eminently capable of protecting you from every danger. Therefore, don't take your eyes off of Him. Obey Him in every step of faith He commands you to take, and do not be afraid. He will guide you through the wilderness, lead you in safety, and be your confidence in every situation. ◈

45 He sent among them swarms of flies
    which devoured them,
    And frogs which destroyed them.
46 He gave also their crops to the
    grasshopper
    And the product of their labor to the
    locust.
47 He destroyed their vines with
    hailstones
    And their sycamore trees with frost.
48 He gave over their cattle also to the
    hailstones
    And their herds to bolts of lightning.
49 He sent upon them His burning
    anger,
    Fury and indignation and trouble,
    A band of destroying angels.
50 He leveled a path for His anger;
    He did not spare their soul from
    death,
    But gave over their life to the plague;
51 And smote all the firstborn in Egypt,
    The first *issue* of their virility in the
    tents of Ham.
52 But He led forth His own people
    like sheep
    And guided them in the wilderness
    like a flock;
53 He led them safely, so that they did
    not fear;
    But the sea engulfed their enemies.
54 So He brought them to His holy land,
    To this hill country which His right
    hand had gained.
55 He also drove out the nations before
    them
    And apportioned them for an
    inheritance by measurement,
    And made the tribes of Israel dwell
    in their tents.

Proverbs 20:3

3 Keeping away from strife is an
    honor for a man,
    But any fool will quarrel.

Acts 9:22–43

22 But Saul kept increasing in strength
and confounding the Jews who lived at
Damascus by proving that this *Jesus* is
the Christ.

23 When many days had elapsed, the
Jews plotted together to do away with him,
24 but their plot became known to Saul.
They were also watching the gates day
and night so that they might put him to
death;
25 but his disciples took him by night
and let him down through *an opening in*
the wall, lowering him in a large basket.
26 When he came to Jerusalem, he was
trying to associate with the disciples; but
they were all afraid of him, not believing
that he was a disciple.
27 But Barnabas took hold of him and
brought him to the apostles and described to them how he had seen the
Lord on the road, and that He had talked
to him, and how at Damascus he had
spoken out boldly in the name of Jesus.
28 And he was with them, moving
about freely in Jerusalem, speaking out
boldly in the name of the Lord.
29 And he was talking and arguing with
the Hellenistic *Jews;* but they were attempting to put him to death.
30 But when the brethren learned *of it,*
they brought him down to Caesarea and
sent him away to Tarsus.
31 So the church throughout all Judea
and Galilee and Samaria enjoyed peace,
being built up; and going on in the fear of
the Lord and in the comfort of the Holy
Spirit, it continued to increase.

LIFE LESSONS

➤ Acts 9:22 — *Saul . . . confounding the
Jews who lived at Damascus by proving
that this Jesus is the Christ.*

Though Saul had worldly knowledge
    through his education as a Pharisee,
it didn't compare to the spiritual wisdom
he acquired when Jesus Christ became
his Savior. God can use your temporal
gifts and aptitudes in an amazing way
when they are under the control of His
Spirit.

➤ Acts 9:27 — *Barnabas took hold of
him and brought him to the apostles.*

The name *Barnabas* means "Son of
    Encouragement" (Acts 4:36), and
wherever we see him in the Book of
Acts, he is usually encouraging someone.
In this case he vouched for Saul when
everyone else was afraid of him.

32 Now as Peter was traveling through all *those regions,* he came down also to the saints who lived at Lydda.

33 There he found a man named Aeneas, who had been bedridden eight years, for he was paralyzed.

34 Peter said to him, "Aeneas, Jesus Christ heals you; get up and make your bed." Immediately he got up.

35 And all who lived at Lydda and Sharon saw him, and they turned to the Lord.

36 Now in Joppa there was a disciple named Tabitha (which translated *in Greek* is called Dorcas); this woman was abounding with deeds of kindness and charity which she continually did.

37 And it happened at that time that she fell sick and died; and when they had washed her body, they laid it in an upper room.

38 Since Lydda was near Joppa, the disciples, having heard that Peter was there, sent two men to him, imploring him, "Do not delay in coming to us."

39 So Peter arose and went with them. When he arrived, they brought him into the upper room; and all the widows stood beside him, weeping and showing all the tunics and garments that Dorcas used to make while she was with them.

40 But Peter sent them all out and knelt down and prayed, and turning to the body, he said, "Tabitha, arise." And she opened her eyes, and when she saw Peter, she sat up.

41 And he gave her his hand and raised her up; and calling the saints and widows, he presented her alive.

42 It became known all over Joppa, and many believed in the Lord.

43 And Peter stayed many days in Joppa with a tanner *named* Simon.

26 FOR the divisions of the gatekeepers *there were* of the Korahites, Meshelemiah the son of Kore, of the sons of Asaph.

2 Meshelemiah had sons: Zechariah the firstborn, Jediael the second, Zebadiah the third, Jathniel the fourth,

3 Elam the fifth, Johanan the sixth, Eliehoenai the seventh.

4 Obed-edom had sons: Shemaiah the firstborn, Jehozabad the second, Joah the third, Sacar the fourth, Nethanel the fifth,

5 Ammiel the sixth, Issachar the seventh *and* Peullethai the eighth; God had indeed blessed him.

6 Also to his son Shemaiah sons were born who ruled over the house of their father, for they were mighty men of valor.

7 The sons of Shemaiah *were* Othni, Rephael, Obed and Elzabad, whose brothers, Elihu and Semachiah, were valiant men.

8 All these *were* of the sons of Obed-edom; they and their sons and their relatives *were* able men with strength for the service, 62 from Obed-edom.

9 Meshelemiah had sons and relatives, 18 valiant men.

10 Also Hosah, *one* of the sons of Merari had sons: Shimri the first (although he was not the firstborn, his father made him first),

11 Hilkiah the second, Tebaliah the third, Zechariah the fourth; all the sons and relatives of Hosah *were* 13.

12 To these divisions of the gatekeepers, the chief men, *were given* duties like their relatives to minister in the house of the LORD.

13 They cast lots, the small and the great alike, according to their fathers' households, for every gate.

14 The lot to the east fell to Shelemiah. Then they cast lots *for* his son Zechariah, a counselor with insight, and his lot came out to the north.

15 For Obed-edom *it fell* to the south, and to his sons went the storehouse.

16 For Shuppim and Hosah *it was* to the west, by the gate of Shallecheth, on the ascending highway. Guard corresponded to guard.

17 On the east there were six Levites, on the north four daily, on the south four daily, and at the storehouse two by two.

18 At the Parbar on the west *there were* four at the highway and two at the Parbar.

19 These were the divisions of the gatekeepers of the sons of Korah and of the sons of Merari.

20 The Levites, their relatives, had charge of the treasures of the house of God and of the treasures of the dedicated gifts.

21 The sons of Ladan, the sons of the Gershonites belonging to Ladan, *namely*, the Jehielites, *were* the heads of the fathers' *households*, belonging to Ladan the Gershonite.

22 The sons of Jehieli, Zetham and Joel his brother, had charge of the treasures of the house of the LORD.

23 As for the Amramites, the Izharites, the Hebronites and the Uzzielites,

24 Shebuel the son of Gershom, the son of Moses, was officer over the treasures.

25 His relatives by Eliezer *were* Rehabiah his son, Jeshaiah his son, Joram his son, Zichri his son and Shelomoth his son.

26 This Shelomoth and his relatives had charge of all the treasures of the dedicated gifts which King David and the heads of the fathers' *households*, the commanders of thousands and hundreds, and the commanders of the army, had dedicated.

27 They dedicated part of the spoil won in battles to repair the house of the LORD.

28 And all that Samuel the seer had dedicated and Saul the son of Kish, Abner the son of Ner and Joab the son of Zeruiah, everyone who had dedicated *anything, all of this* was in the care of Shelomoth and his relatives.

29 As for the Izharites, Chenaniah and his sons were *assigned* to outside duties for Israel, as officers and judges.

30 As for the Hebronites, Hashabiah and his relatives, 1,700 capable men, had charge of the affairs of Israel west of the Jordan, for all the work of the LORD and the service of the king.

31 As for the Hebronites, Jerijah the chief (these Hebronites were investi-

gated according to their genealogies and fathers' *households,* in the fortieth year of David's reign, and men of outstanding capability were found among them at Jazer of Gilead)

32 and his relatives, capable men, *were* 2,700 in number, heads of fathers' *households.* And King David made them overseers of the Reubenites, the Gadites and the half-tribe of the Manassites concerning all the affairs of God and of the king.

27 NOW *this is* the enumeration of the sons of Israel, the heads of fathers' *households,* the commanders of thousands and of hundreds, and their officers who served the king in all the affairs of the divisions which came in and went out month by month throughout all the months of the year, each division *numbering* 24,000:

2 Jashobeam the son of Zabdiel had charge of the first division for the first month; and in his division *were* 24,000.

3 *He was* from the sons of Perez, *and was* chief of all the commanders of the army for the first month.

4 Dodai the Ahohite and his division had charge of the division for the second month, Mikloth *being* the chief officer; and in his division *were* 24,000.

5 The third commander of the army for the third month *was* Benaiah, the son of Jehoiada the priest, *as* chief; and in his division *were* 24,000.

6 This Benaiah *was* the mighty man of the thirty, and had charge of thirty; and over his division was Ammizabad his son.

7 The fourth for the fourth month *was* Asahel the brother of Joab, and Zebadiah his son after him; and in his division *were* 24,000.

8 The fifth for the fifth month *was* the commander Shamhuth the Izrahite; and in his division *were* 24,000.

9 The sixth for the sixth month *was* Ira the son of Ikkesh the Tekoite; and in his division *were* 24,000.

10 The seventh for the seventh month *was* Helez the Pelonite of the sons of Ephraim; and in his division *were* 24,000.

11 The eighth for the eighth month *was* Sibbecai the Hushathite of the Zerahites; and in his division *were* 24,000.

12 The ninth for the ninth month *was* Abiezer the Anathothite of the Benjamites; and in his division *were* 24,000.

13 The tenth for the tenth month *was* Maharai the Netophathite of the Zerahites; and in his division *were* 24,000.

14 The eleventh for the eleventh month *was* Benaiah the Pirathonite of the sons of Ephraim; and in his division *were* 24,000.

15 The twelfth for the twelfth month *was* Heldai the Netophathite of Othniel; and in his division *were* 24,000.

16 Now in charge of the tribes of Israel: chief officer for the Reubenites was Eliezer the son of Zichri; for the Simeonites, Shephatiah the son of Maacah;

17 for Levi, Hashabiah the son of Kemuel; for Aaron, Zadok;

18 for Judah, Elihu, *one* of David's brothers; for Issachar, Omri the son of Michael;

19 for Zebulun, Ishmaiah the son of Obadiah; for Naphtali, Jeremoth the son of Azriel;

20 for the sons of Ephraim, Hoshea the son of Azaziah; for the half-tribe of Manasseh, Joel the son of Pedaiah;

21 for the half-tribe of Manasseh in Gilead, Iddo the son of Zechariah; for Benjamin, Jaasiel the son of Abner;

22 for Dan, Azarel the son of Jeroham. These *were* the princes of the tribes of Israel.

23 But David did not count those twenty years of age and under, because the LORD had said He would multiply Israel as the stars of heaven.

24 Joab the son of Zeruiah had begun to count *them,* but did not finish; and because of this, wrath came upon Israel, and the number was not included in the account of the chronicles of King David.

25 Now Azmaveth the son of Adiel had charge of the king's storehouses. And Jonathan the son of Uzziah had charge of the storehouses in the country, in the cities, in the villages and in the towers.

26 Ezri the son of Chelub had charge of the agricultural workers who tilled the soil.

27 Shimei the Ramathite had charge of the vineyards; and Zabdi the Shiphmite had charge of the produce of the vineyards *stored* in the wine cellars.

28 Baal-hanan the Gederite had charge of the olive and sycamore trees in the Shephelah; and Joash had charge of the stores of oil.

29 Shitrai the Sharonite had charge of

the cattle which were grazing in Sharon; and Shaphat the son of Adlai had charge of the cattle in the valleys.
30　Obil the Ishmaelite had charge of the camels; and Jehdeiah the Meronothite had charge of the donkeys.
31　Jaziz the Hagrite had charge of the flocks. All these were overseers of the property which belonged to King David.
32　Also Jonathan, David's uncle, *was* a counselor, a man of understanding, and a scribe; and Jehiel the son of Hachmoni tutored the king's sons.
33　Ahithophel *was* counselor to the king; and Hushai the Archite *was* the king's friend.
34　Jehoiada the son of Benaiah, and Abiathar succeeded Ahithophel; and Joab was the commander of the king's army.

Psalm 78:56–66

56　Yet they tempted and rebelled
　　against the Most High God
　　And did not keep His testimonies,
57　But turned back and acted
　　treacherously like their fathers;
　　They turned aside like a treacherous
　　bow.
58　For they provoked Him with their
　　high places
　　And aroused His jealousy with their
　　graven images.
59　When God heard, He was filled with
　　wrath
　　And greatly abhorred Israel;
60　So that He abandoned the dwelling
　　place at Shiloh,
　　The tent which He had pitched
　　among men,
61　And gave up His strength to
　　captivity
　　And His glory into the hand of the
　　adversary.
62　He also delivered His people to the
　　sword,
　　And was filled with wrath at His
　　inheritance.
63　Fire devoured His young men,
　　And His virgins had no wedding
　　songs.
64　His priests fell by the sword,
　　And His widows could not weep.

65　Then the Lord awoke as *if from*
　　sleep,
　　Like a warrior overcome by wine.
66　He drove His adversaries backward;
　　He put on them an everlasting
　　reproach.

Proverbs 20:4, 5

4　The sluggard does not plow after
　　the autumn,
　　So he begs during the harvest and
　　has nothing.
5　A plan in the heart of a man is *like*
　　deep water,
　　But a man of understanding draws
　　it out.

Acts 10:1–23

10 NOW *there was* a man at Caesarea named Cornelius, a centurion of what was called the Italian cohort,
2　a devout man and one who feared God with all his household, and gave many alms to the *Jewish* people and prayed to God continually.
3　About the ninth hour of the day he clearly saw in a vision an angel of God who had *just* come in and said to him, "Cornelius!"
4　And fixing his gaze on him and being much alarmed, he said, "What is it, Lord?" And he said to him, "Your prayers and alms have ascended as a memorial before God.

LIFE LESSONS

➤ **Proverbs 20:4** — *The sluggard does not plow after the autumn, so he begs during the harvest and has nothing.*

God has not called us to be lazy. Slothfulness has consequences. The person who doesn't bother to work or prepare for the future will be very disappointed. God worked six days and then He rested. His example is one we should apply to our own lives so that we might be successful in all we do. This also is true in our spiritual lives. Spending time with Him reaps a bountiful reward.

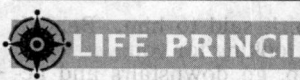

LIFE PRINCIPLE 22

TO WALK IN THE SPIRIT IS TO OBEY THE INITIAL PROMPTINGS OF THE SPIRIT.

ACTS 10:19

To whom do you turn for daily guidance on how to live or what decisions to make?

Scripture tells us the only Guide worth trusting is the Holy Spirit. He is the One who knows our pasts completely, from the moment we were conceived to the present, and who knows our futures. He knows God's plan and purpose for each of us, and He also knows what is good and right for us.

Jesus repeatedly referred to the Spirit as the "Spirit of truth." Note what He said about the Holy Spirit's activity in your life: "He will guide you into all the truth; for He will not speak on His own initiative, but whatever He hears, He will speak; and He will disclose to you what is to come" (John 16:13). The Spirit of truth is like an inner compass in our lives—always pointing us toward what Jesus would be, say, or do in any given moment.

God desires to make His will known to you. He wants you to know what to do and when to do it. Therefore, you can trust the Holy Spirit to be your daily Guide! After the Lord poured out the Holy Spirit on the disciples, they found themselves led in profound ways by the Spirit. The verses below give just a few examples of how the Holy Spirit dealt with God's people in ways that provided personal and specific guidance. What He did for them then, He desires to do for you today.

- "The Spirit told me to go with them without misgivings" (Acts 11:12).
- "While they were ministering to the Lord and fasting, the Holy Spirit said, 'Set apart for Me Barnabas and Saul for the work to which I have called them'" (Acts 13:2).
- "They passed through the Phrygian and Galatian region, having been forbidden by the Holy Spirit to speak the word in Asia" (Acts 16:6).

The leaders of the early church relied on the Holy Spirit to give them this kind of specific, personal guidance, and we are wise to do likewise. Both Romans 8:14 and Galatians 5:18 refer to our being "led by the Spirit"—the norm of the Christian life.

You may ask, "Are there any conditions placed upon the guidance of the Holy Spirit in our lives?"

Yes.

First, we must stay yielded to the Spirit. We must say yes to the Spirit when He prompts us to take a certain action or say a certain word. We must give mental assent to the Spirit's direction, and then we must actually obey His prompting and follow through by doing or saying what He has called us to do or say.

The Spirit often speaks to us in the stillness of our hearts with a word of conviction or assurance. When the Holy Spirit is directing us away from something harmful, we very often have a heaviness, feeling of trouble, foreboding, or uneasiness in our spirits. When the Holy Spirit is directing us toward helpful things, we tend to feel a deep inner peace, an eagerness to see what God will do, and a feeling of joy.

How can you know if you are yielded to the Holy Spirit? You are yielded to Him when you can say, "Here is what I desire. But if Your answer to this is 'no,' it's all right. I'll do what You say."

Second, we must believe and obey His guidance. We are more likely to hear what the Holy Spirit has to say if we are actively listening for Him to speak. We are more likely to see the Holy Spirit's direction if we are looking for Him. Hebrews 11:6 tells us that God is a "rewarder of those who seek Him." We are to be diligent in seeking His guidance, asking for it, watching for it, anticipating it, and receiving it.

The Holy Spirit has come to reveal the truth to us. He has come in His all-knowing ability to impart to us what we need to know in order to live obedient and faithful lives. Trust Him to guide you, now and always! ✦

5 "Now dispatch *some* men to Joppa and send for a man *named* Simon, who is also called Peter;

6 he is staying with a tanner *named* Simon, whose house is by the sea."

7 When the angel who was speaking to him had left, he summoned two of his servants and a devout soldier of those who were his personal attendants,

8 and after he had explained everything to them, he sent them to Joppa.

9 On the next day, as they were on their way and approaching the city, Peter went up on the housetop about the sixth hour to pray.

10 But he became hungry and was desiring to eat; but while they were making preparations, he fell into a trance;

11 and he *saw the sky opened up, and an object like a great sheet coming down, lowered by four corners to the ground,

12 and there were in it all *kinds of* four-footed animals and crawling creatures of the earth and birds of the air.

13 A voice came to him, "Get up, Peter, kill and eat!"

14 But Peter said, "By no means, Lord, for I have never eaten anything unholy and unclean."

15 Again a voice *came* to him a second time, "What God has cleansed, no *longer* consider unholy."

16 This happened three times, and immediately the object was taken up into the sky.

17 Now while Peter was greatly perplexed in mind as to what the vision which he had seen might be, behold, the men who had been sent by Cornelius, having asked directions for Simon's house, appeared at the gate;

18 and calling out, they were asking whether Simon, who was also called Peter, was staying there.

19 While Peter was reflecting on the vision, the Spirit said to him, "Behold, three men are looking for you.

20 "But get up, go downstairs and accompany them without misgivings, for I have sent them Myself."

21 Peter went down to the men and said, "Behold, I am the one you are looking for; what is the reason for which you have come?"

22 They said, "Cornelius, a centurion, a righteous and God-fearing man well spoken of by the entire nation of the Jews, was *divinely* directed by a holy angel to send for you *to come* to his house and hear a message from you."

23 So he invited them in and gave them lodging.

And on the next day he got up and went away with them, and some of the brethren from Joppa accompanied him.

LIFE LESSONS

➤ Acts 10:15 — *"What God has cleansed, no longer consider unholy."*

*G*od was addressing Peter's prejudice against Gentile believers. However, it's a message to us as well. We should never look down upon anyone the Father has saved—not because of race, economic status, or any other factor. As Philippians 2:3 instructs, "Do nothing from selfishness or empty conceit, but with humility of mind regard one another as more important than yourselves."

➤ Acts 10:20 — *"But get up, go downstairs and accompany them without misgivings, for I have sent them Myself."*

*H*ave you ever noticed God tends to guide us in stages? He rarely, if ever, gives us a roadmap to follow. Instead, He asks us to take His hand and go where He goes, without doubting our final destination.

JULY 2

1 Chronicles 28:1—29:30

28 NOW David assembled at Jerusalem all the officials of Israel, the princes of the tribes, and the commanders of the divisions that served the king, and the commanders of thousands, and the commanders of hundreds, and the overseers of all the property and livestock belonging to the king and his sons, with the officials and the mighty men, even all the valiant men.

2   Then King David rose to his feet and said, "Listen to me, my brethren and my people; I *had* intended to build a permanent home for the ark of the covenant of the LORD and for the footstool of our God. So I had made preparations to build *it.*

3   "But God said to me, 'You shall not build a house for My name because you are a man of war and have shed blood.'

4   "Yet, the LORD, the God of Israel, chose me from all the house of my father to be king over Israel forever. For He has chosen Judah to be a leader; and in the house of Judah, my father's house, and among the sons of my father He took pleasure in me to make *me* king over all Israel.

5   "Of all my sons (for the LORD has given me many sons), He has chosen my son Solomon to sit on the throne of the kingdom of the LORD over Israel.

6   "He said to me, 'Your son Solomon is the one who shall build My house and My courts; for I have chosen him to be a son to Me, and I will be a father to him.

7   'I will establish his kingdom forever if he resolutely performs My commandments and My ordinances, as is done now.'

8   "So now, in the sight of all Israel, the assembly of the LORD, and in the hearing of our God, observe and seek after all the commandments of the LORD your God so that you may possess the good land and bequeath *it* to your sons after you forever.

9   "As for you, my son Solomon, know the God of your father, and serve Him with a whole heart and a willing mind; for the LORD searches all hearts, and understands every intent of the thoughts. If you seek Him, He will let you find Him; but if you forsake Him, He will reject you forever.

10 "Consider now, for the LORD has chosen you to build a house for the sanctuary; be courageous and act."

11 Then David gave to his son Solomon the plan of the porch of *the temple,* its buildings, its storehouses, its upper rooms, its inner rooms and the room for the mercy seat;

12 and the plan of all that he had in mind, for the courts of the house of the LORD, and for all the surrounding rooms, for the storehouses of the house of God and for the storehouses of the dedicated things;

13 also for the divisions of the priests and the Levites and for all the work of the service of the house of the LORD and for all the utensils of service in the house of the LORD;

14 for the golden *utensils,* the weight of gold for all utensils for every kind of service; for the silver utensils, the weight *of silver* for all utensils for every kind of service;

15 and the weight *of gold* for the golden lampstands and their golden lamps, with the weight of each lampstand and its lamps; and *the weight of silver* for the silver lampstands, with the weight of each lampstand and its lamps according to the use of each lampstand;

16 and the gold by weight for the tables of showbread, for each table; and silver for the silver tables;

17 and the forks, the basins, and the pitchers of pure gold; and for the golden bowls with the weight for each bowl; and for the silver bowls with the weight for each bowl;

18 and for the altar of incense refined gold by weight; and gold for the model of the chariot, *even* the cherubim that spread out *their wings* and covered the ark of the covenant of the LORD.

19 "All *this,*" *said David,* "the LORD made me understand in writing by His hand upon me, all the details of this pattern."

20 Then David said to his son Solomon, "Be strong and courageous, and act; do not fear nor be dismayed, for the LORD God, my God, is with you. He will not fail you nor forsake you until all the work for the service of the house of the LORD is finished.

LIFE LESSONS

➤ **1 Chronicles 28:19** — *"The LORD made me understand in writing by His hand upon me, all the details of this pattern."*

*I*nspired by the Spirit of God, David drew up plans for the temple. If we will allow the Spirit to work unhindered in our lives, we can draw upon His guidance and wisdom in all areas of life.

21 "Now behold, *there are* the divisions of the priests and the Levites for all the service of the house of God, and every willing man of any skill will be with you in all the work for all kinds of service. The officials also and all the people will be entirely at your command."

29 THEN King David said to the entire assembly, "My son Solomon, whom alone God has chosen, is still young and inexperienced and the work is great; for the temple is not for man, but for the LORD God.

2 "Now with all my ability I have provided for the house of my God the gold for the *things of* gold, and the silver for the *things of* silver, and the bronze for the *things of* bronze, the iron for the *things of* iron, and wood for the *things of* wood, onyx stones and inlaid *stones,* stones of antimony and stones of various colors, and all kinds of precious stones and alabaster in abundance.

3 "Moreover, in my delight in the house of my God, the treasure I have of gold and silver, I give to the house of my God, over and above all that I have already provided for the holy temple,

4 *namely,* 3,000 talents of gold, of the gold of Ophir, and 7,000 talents of refined silver, to overlay the walls of the buildings;

5 of gold for the *things of* gold and of silver for the *things of* silver, that is, for all the work done by the craftsmen. Who then is willing to consecrate himself this day to the LORD?"

6 Then the rulers of the fathers' *households,* and the princes of the tribes of Israel, and the commanders of thousands and of hundreds, with the overseers over the king's work, offered willingly;

7 and for the service for the house of God they gave 5,000 talents and 10,000 darics of gold, and 10,000 talents of silver, and 18,000 talents of brass, and 100,000 talents of iron.

8 Whoever possessed *precious* stones gave them to the treasury of the house of the LORD, in care of Jehiel the Gershonite.

➤ 9 Then the people rejoiced because they had offered so willingly, for they made their offering to the LORD with a whole heart, and King David also rejoiced greatly.

10 So David blessed the LORD in the sight of all the assembly; and David said, "Blessed are You, O LORD God of Israel our father, forever and ever.

11 "Yours, O LORD, is the greatness and the power and the glory and the victory and the majesty, indeed everything that is in the heavens and the earth; Yours is the dominion, O LORD, and You exalt Yourself as head over all.

12 "Both riches and honor *come* from You, and You rule over all, and in Your hand is power and might; and it lies in Your hand to make great and to strengthen everyone.

13 "Now therefore, our God, we thank You, and praise Your glorious name.

14 "But who am I and who are my people that we should be able to offer as generously as this? For all things come from You, and from Your hand we have given You.

15 "For we are sojourners before You, and tenants, as all our fathers were; our days on the earth are like a shadow, and there is no hope.

16 "O LORD our God, all this abundance that we have provided to build You a house for Your holy name, it is from Your hand, and all is Yours.

17 "Since I know, O my God, that You try the heart and delight in uprightness, I, in the integrity of my heart, have willingly offered all these *things;* so now with joy I have seen Your people, who are present here, make *their* offerings willingly to You.

18 "O LORD, the God of Abraham, Isaac and Israel, our fathers, preserve this forever in the intentions of the heart of Your people, and direct their heart to You;

19 and give to my son Solomon a perfect heart to keep Your commandments, Your testimonies and Your statutes, and to do *them* all, and to build the temple, for which I have made provision."

20 Then David said to all the assembly, "Now bless the LORD your God." And all

ANSWERS TO LIFE'S QUESTIONS

Does God consider loyalty an important trait in His people?

1 CHRONICLES 29:19

*O*ur relationship with God is usually reflected in our relationships with other people. The more loyal we are to Him, the more loyal we tend to be with friends and family members. That's no accident.

The Father considers loyalty an important trait. David thought it so important that he prayed, "Give to my son Solomon a perfect heart to keep Your commandments, Your testimonies and Your statutes" (1 Chr. 29:19). God wants us to remain loyal to Him, and He wants us to remain loyal to the people He puts in our lives.

Perhaps this helps explain why we find so many beautiful pictures of loyalty in the Bible. For example, Jonathan remained loyal to David, even at the risk of his own health and safety (1 Sam. 18:4; 19:2). In the New Testament, we see a bond of loyalty between the apostle Paul and Barnabas, two men who helped change the course of the world for Christ, even though they couldn't always agree.

But perhaps one of the most beautiful pictures of loyalty in Scripture is that of Ruth for her mother-in-law, Naomi. Many people have inscribed her words on bracelets and pendants that they carry with them everywhere: "Where you go, I will go, and where you lodge, I will lodge. Your people shall be my people, and your God, my God. Where you die, I will die, and there I will be buried. Thus may the LORD do to me, and worse, if anything but death parts you and me" (Ruth 1:16, 17).

Loyalty comes from the heart. It is motivated by love and wants the best for the other person. A loyal person remains steadfast. You never have to beg the support of a loyal friend or coworker.

Loyalty also demands trust. It leaves no room for deception or mistrust. As a result, individuals loyal to one another relate at much deeper levels than others.

A loyal person makes for a reliable messenger. Disloyalty causes division, especially among Christians. Loyal friends defend the other person and refuse to listen to gossip. Loyalty speaks the truth. A loyal person has a strong sense of responsibility.

Genuine loyalty is not built around circumstances, environment, popularity, or convenience. True loyalty is built on devotion to God and love of others.

Finally, God always rewards those who remain loyal to Him and to the people He places in our lives. You can never out give God, even in loyalty.

---

the assembly blessed the LORD, the God of their fathers, and bowed low and did homage to the LORD and to the king.

21 On the next day they made sacrifices to the LORD and offered burnt offerings to the LORD, 1,000 bulls, 1,000 rams *and* 1,000 lambs, with their drink offerings and sacrifices in abundance for all Israel.

22 So they ate and drank that day before the LORD with great gladness.

And they made Solomon the son of David king a second time, and they anointed *him* as ruler for the LORD and Zadok as priest.

23 Then Solomon sat on the throne of the LORD as king instead of David his father; and he prospered, and all Israel obeyed him.

24 All the officials, the mighty men, and also all the sons of King David pledged allegiance to King Solomon.

25 The LORD highly exalted Solomon in the sight of all Israel, and bestowed on him royal majesty which had not been on any king before him in Israel.

26 Now David the son of Jesse reigned over all Israel.

27 The period which he reigned over Israel *was* forty years; he reigned in Hebron seven years and in Jerusalem thirty-three *years.*

28 Then he died in a ripe old age, full of days, riches and honor; and his son Solomon reigned in his place.

29 Now the acts of King David, from first to last, are written in the chronicles of Samuel the seer, in the chronicles of Nathan the prophet and in the chronicles of Gad the seer,

30 with all his reign, his power, and the circumstances which came on him, on Israel, and on all the kingdoms of the lands.

✦ Psalm 78:67–72

67 He also rejected the tent of Joseph,
    And did not choose the tribe of
        Ephraim,

68 But chose the tribe of Judah,
Mount Zion which He loved.
69 And He built His sanctuary like the
heights,
Like the earth which He has
founded forever.
70 He also chose David His servant
And took him from the sheepfolds;
71 From the care of the ewes with
suckling lambs He brought him
To shepherd Jacob His people,
And Israel His inheritance.
72 So he shepherded them according
to the integrity of his heart,
And guided them with his skillful
hands.

Proverbs 20:6, 7

6 Many a man proclaims his own
loyalty,
But who can find a trustworthy man?
7 A righteous man who walks in his
integrity—
How blessed are his sons after him.

Acts 10:24–48

24 On the following day he entered
Caesarea. Now Cornelius was waiting
for them and had called together his relatives and close friends.
25 When Peter entered, Cornelius met
him, and fell at his feet and worshiped
him.
26 But Peter raised him up, saying,
"Stand up; I too am *just* a man."
27 As he talked with him, he entered
and *found many people assembled.
28 And he said to them, "You yourselves know how unlawful it is for a
man who is a Jew to associate with a
foreigner or to visit him; and *yet* God has
shown me that I should not call any man
unholy or unclean.
29 "That is why I came without even
raising any objection when I was sent
for. So I ask for what reason you have
sent for me."
30 Cornelius said, "Four days ago to
this hour, I was praying in my house
during the ninth hour; and behold, a man
stood before me in shining garments,

31 and he *said, 'Cornelius, your prayer
has been heard and your alms have been
remembered before God.
32 'Therefore send to Joppa and invite
Simon, who is also called Peter, to come
to you; he is staying at the house of
Simon *the* tanner by the sea.'
33 "So I sent for you immediately, and
you have been kind enough to come.
Now then, we are all here present before
God to hear all that you have been commanded by the Lord."
34 Opening his mouth, Peter said:
"I most certainly understand *now*
that God is not one to show partiality,
35 but in every nation the man who
fears Him and does what is right is welcome to Him.
36 "The word which He sent to the sons
of Israel, preaching peace through Jesus
Christ (He is Lord of all)—
37 you yourselves know the thing
which took place throughout all Judea,
starting from Galilee, after the baptism
which John proclaimed.

LIFE LESSONS

Proverbs 20:7 — *A righteous man who
walks in his integrity—how blessed are
his sons after him.*

*I*t would be hard to think of a greater
legacy to leave behind than a personal record of godly integrity and
obedience. Those who faithfully demonstrate a deep, abiding love for the Lord
and exhibit a sound moral character in
obedience to Him bless their children
with a gift that lasts for generations.

Acts 10:28 — *"God has shown me
that I should not call any man unholy or
unclean."*

*A*s a *God-fearer*, Cornelius would have
believed in the God of Israel, but he
probably wasn't a Jewish convert in the
formal sense. This presented a unique
challenge to Peter because Jews were not
to associate with Gentiles (Acts 11:2, 3),
and there was a question about whether
Gentiles could become Christians without
first converting to Judaism (Acts 15:1–29).
Yet the Lord made it clear that no person
was to be called unclean. Jesus Christ
alone saves us, and the invitation is open
to whomever will believe in Him (Rom.
1:16; 10:9–12).

38 "You know of Jesus of Nazareth, how God anointed Him with the Holy Spirit and with power, and how He went about doing good and healing all who were oppressed by the devil, for God was with Him.

39 "We are witnesses of all the things He did both in the land of the Jews and in Jerusalem. They also put Him to death by hanging Him on a cross.

40 "God raised Him up on the third day and granted that He become visible,

41 not to all the people, but to witnesses who were chosen beforehand by God, that is, to us who ate and drank with Him after He arose from the dead.

42 "And He ordered us to preach to the people, and solemnly to testify that this is the One who has been appointed by God as Judge of the living and the dead.

43 "Of Him all the prophets bear witness that through His name everyone who believes in Him receives forgiveness of sins."

44 While Peter was still speaking these words, the Holy Spirit fell upon all those who were listening to the message.

45 All the circumcised believers who came with Peter were amazed, because the gift of the Holy Spirit had been poured out on the Gentiles also.

46 For they were hearing them speaking with tongues and exalting God. Then Peter answered,

47 "Surely no one can refuse the water for these to be baptized who have received the Holy Spirit just as we did, can he?"

48 And he ordered them to be baptized in the name of Jesus Christ. Then they asked him to stay on for a few days.

2 Chronicles 1:1—2:18

1 NOW Solomon the son of David established himself securely over his kingdom, and the LORD his God was with him and exalted him greatly.

2 Solomon spoke to all Israel, to the commanders of thousands and of hundreds and to the judges and to every leader in all Israel, the heads of the fathers' households.

3 Then Solomon and all the assembly with him went to the high place which was at Gibeon, for God's tent of meeting was there, which Moses the servant of the LORD had made in the wilderness.

4 However, David had brought up the ark of God from Kiriath-jearim to the place he had prepared for it, for he had pitched a tent for it in Jerusalem.

5 Now the bronze altar, which Bezalel the son of Uri, the son of Hur, had made, was there before the tabernacle of the LORD, and Solomon and the assembly sought it out.

6 Solomon went up there before the LORD to the bronze altar which *was* at the tent of meeting, and offered a thousand burnt offerings on it.

7 In that night God appeared to Solomon and said to him, "Ask what I shall give you."

8 Solomon said to God, "You have dealt with my father David with great lovingkindness, and have made me king in his place.

9 "Now, O LORD God, Your promise to my father David is fulfilled, for You have made me king over a people as numerous as the dust of the earth.

10 "Give me now wisdom and knowledge, that I may go out and come in before this people, for who can rule this great people of Yours?"

11 God said to Solomon, "Because you had this in mind, and did not ask for riches, wealth or honor, or the life of those who hate you, nor have you even asked for long life, but you have asked for yourself wisdom and knowledge that you may rule My people over whom I have made you king,

12 wisdom and knowledge have been granted to you. And I will give you riches and wealth and honor, such as none of the kings who were before you has possessed nor those who will come after you."

13 So Solomon went from the high place which was at Gibeon, from the tent of meeting, to Jerusalem, and he reigned over Israel.

14 Solomon amassed chariots and horsemen. He had 1,400 chariots and 12,000 horsemen, and he stationed them in the chariot cities and with the king at Jerusalem.

15 The king made silver and gold as

ANSWERS TO LIFE'S QUESTIONS

How can I gain wisdom from God?

2 CHRONICLES 1:8–13

A growing number of people in our world fail to seek God for His wisdom. Instead, they strive to satisfy their passions and desires without regard for their futures or the consequences of their decisions.

This is a dangerous way to live spiritually. When we try to live apart from the counsel of God's wisdom, we suffer disillusionment, fear, doubt, worry, and frustration. Our lives fall apart when we do not involve the Savior in our decisions.

The wisest approach to life's challenges is to seek God for His plan, direction, and spiritual insight. But how can we do that? The next time you face a challenge or an important decision, seek God's wisdom by doing the following:

- *Seek Him*—If you want to know the Father's heart on a given issue, or when you have to make a difficult decision, ask Him. Take time to pray. In your times of prayer, don't do all the talking. Listen for God's still, small voice whispering His words of guidance and encouragement to you.
- *Meditate on God's Word*—You will gain insight into the Father's mind and heart by studying Scripture and meditating on its truth. Difficult decisions become easier to make when He is the One guiding you.
- *Obey the principles of Scripture*—When you set your heart on obeying God, He will teach you how to apply His truth to your life. Then you will know the way of wisdom.
- *Observe the faithfulness of God*—The Lord has never failed to keep a single promise He has made. The Bible is full of testimonies that celebrate His goodness and love. Learn to claim His promises as you read His Word.
- *Heed godly counsel*—God can use a pastor or trusted Christian friend to help you see beyond your weaknesses. Don't hesitate to share your needs and fears with those who love the Lord.
- *Associate with wise people*—Choose your friends wisely. Include the Lord in every relationship, and you will establish a strong, godly base of counselors to support you in making wise decisions.

Because God loves us, we have no need to worry about the future. He has a plan, not only for our lives, but also for every problem we face. Oswald Chambers said, "All our fret and worry is caused by calculating without God." Take time today to renew your trust in God and His ability to provide the wisdom you need.

plentiful in Jerusalem as stones, and he made cedars as plentiful as sycamores in the lowland.
16 Solomon's horses were imported from Egypt and from Kue; the king's traders procured them from Kue for a price.
17 They imported chariots from Egypt for 600 *shekels* of silver apiece and horses for 150 apiece, and by the same means they exported them to all the kings of the Hittites and the kings of Aram.

2 NOW Solomon decided to build a house for the name of the LORD and a royal palace for himself.
2 So Solomon assigned 70,000 men to carry loads and 80,000 men to quarry *stone* in the mountains and 3,600 to supervise them.
3 Then Solomon sent *word* to Huram the king of Tyre, saying, "As you dealt with David my father and sent him cedars to build him a house to dwell in, so do for me.
4 "Behold, I am about to build a house for the name of the LORD my God, dedicating it to Him, to burn fragrant incense before Him and *to set out* the showbread continually, and to offer burnt offerings morning and evening, on sabbaths and on new moons and on the appointed feasts of the LORD our God, this *being required* forever in Israel.
5 "The house which I am about to build *will be* great, for greater is our God than all the gods.
6 "But who is able to build a house for Him, for the heavens and the highest heavens cannot contain Him? So who am I, that I should build a house for Him, except to burn *incense* before Him?
7 "Now send me a skilled man to work in gold, silver, brass and iron, and in

purple, crimson and violet *fabrics,* and who knows how to make engravings, to *work* with the skilled men whom I have in Judah and Jerusalem, whom David my father provided.
8 "Send me also cedar, cypress and algum timber from Lebanon, for I know that your servants know how to cut timber of Lebanon; and indeed my servants *will work* with your servants,
9 to prepare timber in abundance for me, for the house which I am about to build *will be* great and wonderful.
10 "Now behold, I will give to your servants, the woodsmen who cut the timber, 20,000 kors of crushed wheat and 20,000 kors of barley, and 20,000 baths of wine and 20,000 baths of oil."
11 Then Huram, king of Tyre, answered in a letter sent to Solomon: "Because the LORD loves His people, He has made you king over them."
12 Then Huram continued, "Blessed be the LORD, the God of Israel, who has made heaven and earth, who has given King David a wise son, endowed with discretion and understanding, who will build a house for the LORD and a royal palace for himself.
13 "Now I am sending Huram-abi, a skilled man, endowed with understanding,
14 the son of a Danite woman and a Tyrian father, who knows how to work in gold, silver, bronze, iron, stone and wood, *and* in purple, violet, linen and crimson fabrics, and *who knows how* to make all kinds of engravings and to execute any design which may be assigned to him, *to work* with your skilled men and with those of my lord David your father.
15 "Now then, let my lord send to his servants wheat and barley, oil and wine, of which he has spoken.
16 "We will cut whatever timber you need from Lebanon and bring it to you on rafts by sea to Joppa, so that you may carry it up to Jerusalem."
17 Solomon numbered all the aliens who *were* in the land of Israel, following the census which his father David had taken; and 153,600 were found.
18 He appointed 70,000 of them to carry loads and 80,000 to quarry *stones* in the mountains and 3,600 supervisors to make the people work.

LIFE LESSONS

➤ **2 Chronicles 2:5** — *"The house which I am about to build will be great, for greater is our God than all the gods."*

Solomon set about to build a glorious temple that would honor the Lord and show He was above all other deities. However, Jesus builds a more wonderful temple because He has established His dwelling place within us, the Church (1 Cor. 3:16, 17; 6:19, 20; Eph. 2:19–22).

Psalm 79:1–4

A Psalm of Asaph.

79 O GOD, the nations have invaded
Your inheritance;
They have defiled Your holy temple;
They have laid Jerusalem in ruins.

2 They have given the dead bodies
of Your servants for food to the
birds of the heavens,
The flesh of Your godly ones to the
beasts of the earth.

3 They have poured out their blood
like water round about Jerusalem;
And there was no one to bury them.

4 We have become a reproach to our
neighbors,
A scoffing and derision to those
around us.

Proverbs 20:8, 9

8 A king who sits on the throne of
justice
Disperses all evil with his eyes.

9 Who can say, "I have cleansed my
heart,
I am pure from my sin"?

Acts 11:1–30

11 NOW the apostles and the brethren
who were throughout Judea heard
that the Gentiles also had received the
word of God.

2 And when Peter came up to Jerusalem, those who were circumcised took
issue with him,

3 saying, "You went to uncircumcised
men and ate with them."

4 But Peter began *speaking* and *proceeded* to explain to them in orderly
sequence, saying,

5 "I was in the city of Joppa praying;
and in a trance I saw a vision, an object
coming down like a great sheet lowered
by four corners from the sky; and it came
right down to me,

6 and when I had fixed my gaze on
it and was observing it I saw the four-
footed animals of the earth and the wild

beasts and the crawling creatures and
the birds of the air.

7 "I also heard a voice saying to me,
'Get up, Peter; kill and eat.'

8 "But I said, 'By no means, Lord, for
nothing unholy or unclean has ever entered my mouth.'

9 "But a voice from heaven answered a
second time, 'What God has cleansed, no
longer consider unholy.'

10 "This happened three times, and everything was drawn back up into the sky.

11 "And behold, at that moment three
men appeared at the house in which we
were *staying*, having been sent to me
from Caesarea.

12 "The Spirit told me to go with them
without misgivings. These six brethren
also went with me and we entered the
man's house.

13 "And he reported to us how he had
seen the angel standing in his house, and
saying, 'Send to Joppa and have Simon,
who is also called Peter, brought here;

14 and he will speak words to you by
which you will be saved, you and all your
household.'

15 "And as I began to speak, the Holy
Spirit fell upon them just as *He did* upon
us at the beginning.

16 "And I remembered the word of the
Lord, how He used to say, 'John baptized
with water, but you will be baptized with
the Holy Spirit.'

17 "Therefore if God gave to them the
same gift as *He gave* to us also after believing in the Lord Jesus Christ, who was
I that I could stand in God's way?"

18 When they heard this, they quieted
down and glorified God, saying, "Well
then, God has granted to the Gentiles
also the repentance *that leads* to life."

LIFE LESSONS

➤ **Acts 11:18 —** *"God has granted to the
Gentiles also the repentance that leads
to life."*

*I*t had never occurred to the early Jewish believers that God might actually
give the Holy Spirit to believing Gentiles
as He had to believing Jews. But once
they saw the truth, they responded correctly by praising Him. Once we recognize
a clear move of God, we are wise to join
Him. It may not be what we expected or
hoped for, but He is in command, not us.

19 So then those who were scattered because of the persecution that occurred in connection with Stephen made their way to Phoenicia and Cyprus and Antioch, speaking the word to no one except to Jews alone.
20 But there were some of them, men of Cyprus and Cyrene, who came to Antioch and *began* speaking to the Greeks also, preaching the Lord Jesus.
21 And the hand of the Lord was with them, and a large number who believed turned to the Lord.
22 The news about them reached the ears of the church at Jerusalem, and they sent Barnabas off to Antioch.
➤ 23 Then when he arrived and witnessed the grace of God, he rejoiced and *began* to encourage them all with resolute heart to remain *true* to the Lord;
24 for he was a good man, and full of the Holy Spirit and of faith. And considerable numbers were brought to the Lord.
25 And he left for Tarsus to look for Saul;
26 and when he had found him, he brought him to Antioch. And for an entire year they met with the church and taught considerable numbers; and the disciples were first called Christians in Antioch.
27 Now at this time some prophets came down from Jerusalem to Antioch.
28 One of them named Agabus stood up and *began* to indicate by the Spirit that there would certainly be a great famine

all over the world. And this took place in the *reign* of Claudius.
29 And in the proportion that any of ◄ the disciples had means, each of them determined to send *a contribution* for the relief of the brethren living in Judea.
30 And this they did, sending it in charge of Barnabas and Saul to the elders.

LIFE LESSONS

➤ **Acts 11:23 — He . . . began to encourage them all with resolute heart to remain true to the Lord.**

*H*ow does one witness the grace of God? By observing its fruit: people being saved, dynamic worship, forgiving spirits, peace, joy, and so forth. We encourage such grace to flourish by exhorting each other to eagerly and tenaciously serve the living God.

➤ **Acts 11:29 — And in the proportion that any of the disciples had means, each of them determined to send a contribution for the relief of the brethren living in Judea.**

*A*long with the persecution and high taxation, the residents of Judea were about to face a great famine as well. So the disciples immediately decided to help. A heart genuinely touched by the love of God desires to meet the needs of fellow believers in distress (James 2:15–17). The Lord blesses us so that we might bless others.

JULY 4

2 Chronicles 3:1—4:22

3 THEN Solomon began to build the house of the LORD in Jerusalem on Mount Moriah, where *the* LORD had appeared to his father David, at the place that David had prepared on the threshing floor of Ornan the Jebusite.
2 He began to build on the second *day* in the second month of the fourth year of his reign.
3 Now these are the foundations which Solomon laid for building the house of

God. The length in cubits, according to the old standard *was* sixty cubits, and the width twenty cubits.
4 The porch which was in front of the house was as long as the width of the house, twenty cubits, and the height 120; and inside he overlaid it with pure gold.
5 He overlaid the main room with cypress wood and overlaid it with fine gold, and ornamented it with palm trees and chains.
6 Further, he adorned the house with precious stones; and the gold was gold from Parvaim.

7   He also overlaid the house with gold—the beams, the thresholds and its walls and its doors; and he carved cherubim on the walls.

8   Now he made the room of the holy of holies: its length across the width of the house *was* twenty cubits, and its width *was* twenty cubits; and he overlaid it with fine gold, *amounting* to 600 talents.

9   The weight of the nails was fifty shekels of gold. He also overlaid the upper rooms with gold.

10 Then he made two sculptured cherubim in the room of the holy of holies and overlaid them with gold.

11 The wingspan of the cherubim *was* twenty cubits; the wing of one, of five cubits, touched the wall of the house, and *its* other wing, of five cubits, touched the wing of the other cherub.

12 The wing of the other cherub, of five cubits, touched the wall of the house; and *its* other wing of five cubits was attached to the wing of the first cherub.

13 The wings of these cherubim extended twenty cubits, and they stood on their feet facing the *main* room.

14 He made the veil of violet, purple, crimson and fine linen, and he worked cherubim on it.

15 He also made two pillars for the front of the house, thirty-five cubits high, and the capital on the top of each *was* five cubits.

16 He made chains in the inner sanctuary and placed *them* on the tops of the pillars; and he made one hundred pomegranates and placed *them* on the chains.

17 He erected the pillars in front of the temple, one on the right and the other on the left, and named the one on the right Jachin and the one on the left Boaz.

4 THEN he made a bronze altar, twenty cubits in length and twenty cubits in width and ten cubits in height.

2   Also he made the cast *metal* sea, ten cubits from brim to brim, circular in form, and its height *was* five cubits and its circumference thirty cubits.

3   Now figures like oxen *were* under it *and* all around it, ten cubits, entirely encircling the sea. The oxen *were* in two rows, cast in one piece.

4   It stood on twelve oxen, three facing the north, three facing west, three facing south and three facing east; and the sea *was set* on top of them and all their hindquarters turned inwards.

5   It was a handbreadth thick, and its brim was made like the brim of a cup, *like* a lily blossom; it could hold 3,000 baths.

6   He also made ten basins in which to wash, and he set five on the right side and five on the left to rinse things for the burnt offering; but the sea *was* for the priests to wash in.

7   Then he made the ten golden lampstands in the way prescribed for them and he set them in the temple, five on the right side and five on the left.

8   He also made ten tables and placed them in the temple, five on the right side and five on the left. And he made one hundred golden bowls.

9   Then he made the court of the priests and the great court and doors for the court, and overlaid their doors with bronze.

10 He set the sea on the right side *of the house* toward the southeast.

11 Huram also made the pails, the shovels and the bowls. So Huram finished doing the work which he performed for King Solomon in the house of God:

12 the two pillars, the bowls and the two capitals on top of the pillars, and the two networks to cover the two bowls of the capitals which were on top of the pillars,

13 and the four hundred pomegranates for the two networks, two rows of pomegranates for each network to cover the two bowls of the capitals which were on the pillars.

14 He also made the stands and he made the basins on the stands,

15 *and* the one sea with the twelve oxen under it.

16 The pails, the shovels, the forks and all its utensils, Huram-abi made of polished bronze for King Solomon for the house of the Lord.

17 On the plain of the Jordan the king cast them in the clay ground between Succoth and Zeredah.

18 Thus Solomon made all these utensils in great quantities, for the weight of the bronze could not be found out.

19 Solomon also made all the things that *were* in the house of God: even the golden altar, the tables with the bread of the Presence on them,

20 the lampstands with their lamps of pure gold, to burn in front of the inner sanctuary in the way prescribed;

21 the flowers, the lamps, and the tongs of gold, of purest gold;
22 and the snuffers, the bowls, the spoons and the firepans of pure gold; and the entrance of the house, its inner doors for the holy of holies and the doors of the house, *that is,* of the nave, of gold.

◈ Psalm 79:5–10

5 How long, O LORD? Will You be
     angry forever?
     Will Your jealousy burn like fire?
6 Pour out Your wrath upon the
     nations which do not know You,
     And upon the kingdoms which do
     not call upon Your name.
7 For they have devoured Jacob
     And laid waste his habitation.
8 Do not remember the iniquities of
     our forefathers against us;
     Let Your compassion come quickly
       to meet us,
     For we are brought very low.
9 Help us, O God of our salvation, for
     the glory of Your name;
     And deliver us and forgive our sins
       for Your name's sake.
10 Why should the nations say,
     "Where is their God?"
     Let there be known among the
     nations in our sight,
     Vengeance for the blood of Your
     servants which has been shed.

◈ Proverbs 20:10–12

10 Differing weights and differing
     measures,
     Both of them are abominable to the
     LORD.
11 It is by his deeds that a lad
     distinguishes himself
     If his conduct is pure and right.
12 The hearing ear and the seeing eye,
     The LORD has made both of them.

◈ Acts 12:1–25

12 NOW about that time Herod the king laid hands on some who be-

longed to the church in order to mistreat them.
2 And he had James the brother of John put to death with a sword.
3 When he saw that it pleased the Jews, he proceeded to arrest Peter also. Now it was during the days of Unleavened Bread.
4 When he had seized him, he put him in prison, delivering him to four squads of soldiers to guard him, intending after the Passover to bring him out before the people.
5 So Peter was kept in the prison, but prayer for him was being made fervently by the church to God.
6 On the very night when Herod was about to bring him forward, Peter was sleeping between two soldiers, bound with two chains, and guards in front of the door were watching over the prison.
7 And behold, an angel of the Lord suddenly appeared and a light shone in the cell; and he struck Peter's side and woke him up, saying, "Get up quickly." And his chains fell off his hands.
8 And the angel said to him, "Gird yourself and put on your sandals." And he did so. And he *said to him, "Wrap your cloak around you and follow me."
9 And he went out and continued to follow, and he did not know that what was being done by the angel was real, but thought he was seeing a vision.
10 When they had passed the first and

LIFE LESSONS

➢ **Psalm 79:9** — *Help us, O God of our salvation, for the glory of Your name.*

*W*hen we pray about something for the sake of God's name, we urge Him to act in order to defend His reputation, to make His glory known, to honor Him and to let others see His majesty and greatness.

➢ **Acts 12:5** — *So Peter was kept in the prison, but prayer for him was being made fervently by the church to God.*

*T*he church had already lost one leader, James the brother of John, to the executioner (Acts 12:2). Now it appeared as though it would lose Peter, too. But God loves to perform miracles in response to corporate prayer!

LIFE LESSONS

➤ **Acts 12:9** — *He went out and continued to follow . . . but thought he was seeing a vision.*

*P*eter had seen visions from God before, and this scene looked so unusual he thought it had to be another one. But it wasn't; it was actually happening, just as he saw it. Nothing is impossible for God!

second guard, they came to the iron gate that leads into the city, which opened for them by itself; and they went out and went along one street, and immediately the angel departed from him.

11 When Peter came to himself, he said, "Now I know for sure that the Lord has sent forth His angel and rescued me from the hand of Herod and from all that the Jewish people were expecting."

12 And when he realized *this*, he went to the house of Mary, the mother of John who was also called Mark, where many were gathered together and were praying.

13 When he knocked at the door of the gate, a servant-girl named Rhoda came to answer.

14 When she recognized Peter's voice, because of her joy she did not open the gate, but ran in and announced that Peter was standing in front of the gate.

15 They said to her, "You are out of your mind!" But she kept insisting that it was so. They kept saying, "It is his angel."

16 But Peter continued knocking; and when they had opened *the door,* they saw him and were amazed.

17 But motioning to them with his hand to be silent, he described to them how the Lord had led him out of the prison. And he said, "Report these things to James and the brethren." Then he left and went to another place.

18 Now when day came, there was no small disturbance among the soldiers *as* to what could have become of Peter.

19 When Herod had searched for him and had not found him, he examined the guards and ordered that they be led away *to execution.* Then he went down from Judea to Caesarea and was spending time there.

20 Now he was very angry with the people of Tyre and Sidon; and with one accord they came to him, and having won over Blastus the king's chamberlain, they were asking for peace, because their country was fed by the king's country.

21 On an appointed day Herod, having put on his royal apparel, took his seat on the rostrum and *began* delivering an address to them.

22 The people kept crying out, "The voice of a god and not of a man!"

23 And immediately an angel of the Lord struck him because he did not give God the glory, and he was eaten by worms and died.

24 But the word of the Lord continued to grow and to be multiplied.

25 And Barnabas and Saul returned from Jerusalem when they had fulfilled their mission, taking along with *them* John, who was also called Mark.

Life Examples:

RHODA: Joy in Prayer

ACTS 12:12–17

*L*ate into the night, the church pled for God's mercy on behalf of their imprisoned leader, Peter.

Rhoda, a household servant, knew very well the believers who met in Mary's large house. But though they prayed earnestly for Peter, it seemed inevitable he would face a morning execution.

Suddenly a sharp rap at the door interrupted their prayers. Rhoda approached the entrance, listened—and heard a familiar voice. At the gate stood Peter! In her excitement, she forgot to let him in and instead ran to inform the praying church. "Peter is at the door!" she exclaimed. It wasn't until he stood among them, recounting his deliverance, that they jubilantly acknowledge the Lord's provision.

Just as Rhoda's gladness sustained her heart when life became painful, so the joy of Christ sustains you when the future appears impossible. The delight of your salvation helps you endure when disappointments and difficult issues assail you.

2 Chronicles 5:1—6:42

5 THUS all the work that Solomon performed for the house of the LORD was finished. And Solomon brought in the things that David his father had dedicated, even the silver and the gold and all the utensils, *and* put *them* in the treasuries of the house of God.

2 Then Solomon assembled to Jerusalem the elders of Israel and all the heads of the tribes, the leaders of the fathers' *households* of the sons of Israel, to bring up the ark of the covenant of the LORD out of the city of David, which is Zion.

3 All the men of Israel assembled themselves to the king at the feast, that is *in* the seventh month.

4 Then all the elders of Israel came, and the Levites took up the ark.

5 They brought up the ark and the tent of meeting and all the holy utensils which *were* in the tent; the Levitical priests brought them up.

6 And King Solomon and all the congregation of Israel who were assembled with him before the ark, were sacrificing so many sheep and oxen that they could not be counted or numbered.

7 Then the priests brought the ark of the covenant of the LORD to its place, into the inner sanctuary of the house, to the holy of holies, under the wings of the cherubim.

8 For the cherubim spread their wings over the place of the ark, so that the cherubim made a covering over the ark and its poles.

9 The poles were so long that the ends of the poles of the ark could be seen in front of the inner sanctuary, but they could not be seen outside; and they are there to this day.

10 There was nothing in the ark except the two tablets which Moses put *there* at Horeb, where the LORD made a covenant with the sons of Israel, when they came out of Egypt.

11 When the priests came forth from the holy place (for all the priests who were present had sanctified themselves, without regard to divisions),

12 and all the Levitical singers, Asaph, Heman, Jeduthun, and their sons and kinsmen, clothed in fine linen, with cymbals, harps and lyres, standing east of the altar, and with them one hundred and twenty priests blowing trumpets

13 in unison when the trumpeters and the singers were to make themselves heard with one voice to praise and to glorify the LORD, and when they lifted up their voice accompanied by trumpets and cymbals and instruments of music, and when they praised the LORD *saying,* "He indeed is good for His lovingkindness is everlasting," then the house, the house of the LORD, was filled with a cloud,

14 so that the priests could not stand ◄ to minister because of the cloud, for the glory of the LORD filled the house of God.

6 THEN Solomon said,
"The LORD has said that He would
dwell in the thick cloud.

2 "I have built You a lofty house,
And a place for Your dwelling
forever."

3 Then the king faced about and blessed all the assembly of Israel, while all the assembly of Israel was standing.

4 He said, "Blessed be the LORD, the God of Israel, who spoke with His mouth to my father David and has fulfilled *it* with His hands, saying,

5 'Since the day that I brought My people from the land of Egypt, I did not choose a city out of all the tribes of Israel *in which* to build a house that My name might be there, nor did I choose any man for a leader over My people Israel;

6 but I have chosen Jerusalem that My name might be there, and I have chosen David to be over My people Israel.'

LIFE LESSONS

➤ **2 Chronicles 5:14 — *The priests could not stand to minister of. . . the glory of the LORD filled the house of God.***

God's presence can be overpowering. When we see His work in action, we may find we are awestruck by His power and might. We may reason that we must do something in order to please Him. But what He wants is our full attention and obedience. True worship includes humble praise—not what we can do for Him, but our heartfelt expression of love and thankfulness. He is worthy of all our devotion, adoration, appreciation, and praise.

7 "Now it was in the heart of my father David to build a house for the name of the LORD, the God of Israel.
8 "But the LORD said to my father David, 'Because it was in your heart to build a house for My name, you did well that it was in your heart.
9 'Nevertheless you shall not build the house, but your son who will be born to you, he shall build the house for My name.'
10 "Now the LORD has fulfilled His word which He spoke; for I have risen in the place of my father David and sit on the throne of Israel, as the LORD promised, and have built the house for the name of the LORD, the God of Israel.
11 "There I have set the ark in which is the covenant of the LORD, which He made with the sons of Israel."
12 Then he stood before the altar of the LORD in the presence of all the assembly of Israel and spread out his hands.
13 Now Solomon had made a bronze platform, five cubits long, five cubits wide and three cubits high, and had set it in the midst of the court; and he stood on it, knelt on his knees in the presence of all the assembly of Israel and spread out his hands toward heaven.
14 He said, "O LORD, the God of Israel, there is no god like You in heaven or on earth, keeping covenant and *showing* lovingkindness to Your servants who walk before You with all their heart;
➤ 15 who has kept with Your servant David, my father, that which You have promised him; indeed You have spoken with Your mouth and have fulfilled it with Your hand, as it is this day.
16 "Now therefore, O LORD, the God of Israel, keep with Your servant David, my father, that which You have promised him, saying, 'You shall not lack a man to sit on the throne of Israel, if only your sons take heed to their way, to walk in My law as you have walked before Me.'

LIFE LESSONS

➤ **2 Chronicles 6:15** — *"You have spoken with Your mouth and have fulfilled it with Your hand, as it is this day."*

*T*he Lord doesn't leave it up to us to fulfill His promises. What God speaks with His mouth, He fulfills with His own hand.

---

17 "Now therefore, O LORD, the God of Israel, let Your word be confirmed which You have spoken to Your servant David.
18 "But will God indeed dwell with mankind on the earth? Behold, heaven and the highest heaven cannot contain You; how much less this house which I have built.
19 "Yet have regard to the prayer of Your servant and to his supplication, O LORD my God, to listen to the cry and to the prayer which Your servant prays before You;
20 that Your eye may be open toward this house day and night, toward the place of which You have said that *You would* put Your name there, to listen to the prayer which Your servant shall pray toward this place.
21 "Listen to the supplications of Your servant and of Your people Israel when they pray toward this place; hear from Your dwelling place, from heaven; hear and forgive.
22 "If a man sins against his neighbor and is made to take an oath, and he comes *and* takes an oath before Your altar in this house,
23 then hear from heaven and act and judge Your servants, punishing the wicked by bringing his way on his own head and justifying the righteous by giving him according to his righteousness.
24 "If Your people Israel are defeated before an enemy because they have sinned against You, and they return *to You* and confess Your name, and pray and make supplication before You in this house,
25 then hear from heaven and forgive the sin of Your people Israel, and bring them back to the land which You have given to them and to their fathers.
26 "When the heavens are shut up and there is no rain because they have sinned against You, and they pray toward this place and confess Your name, and turn from their sin when You afflict them;
27 then hear in heaven and forgive the sin of Your servants and Your people Israel, indeed, teach them the good way in which they should walk. And send rain on Your land which You have given to Your people for an inheritance.
28 "If there is famine in the land, if there is pestilence, if there is blight or mildew, if there is locust or grasshopper, if their enemies besiege them in the land

of their cities, whatever plague or whatever sickness *there is,*

➤ 29 whatever prayer or supplication is made by any man or by all Your people Israel, each knowing his own affliction and his own pain, and spreading his hands toward this house,

30 then hear from heaven Your dwelling place, and forgive, and render to each according to all his ways, whose heart You know for You alone know the hearts of the sons of men,

31 that they may fear You, to walk in Your ways as long as they live in the land which You have given to our fathers.

32 "Also concerning the foreigner who is not from Your people Israel, when he comes from a far country for Your great name's sake and Your mighty hand and Your outstretched arm, when they come and pray toward this house,

33 then hear from heaven, from Your dwelling place, and do according to all for which the foreigner calls to You, in order that all the peoples of the earth may know Your name, and fear You as *do* Your people Israel, and that they may know that this house which I have built is called by Your name.

34 "When Your people go out to battle against their enemies, by whatever way You shall send them, and they pray to You toward this city which You have chosen and the house which I have built for Your name,

35 then hear from heaven their prayer and their supplication, and maintain their cause.

36 "When they sin against You (for there is no man who does not sin) and You are angry with them and deliver them to an enemy, so that they take them away captive to a land far off or near,

37 if they take thought in the land where they are taken captive, and repent and make supplication to You in the land of their captivity, saying, 'We have sinned, we have committed iniquity and have acted wickedly';

38 if they return to You with all their heart and with all their soul in the land of their captivity, where they have been taken captive, and pray toward their land which You have given to their fathers and the city which You have chosen, and toward the house which I have built for Your name,

39 then hear from heaven, from Your dwelling place, their prayer and supplications, and maintain their cause and forgive Your people who have sinned against You.

40 "Now, O my God, I pray, let Your eyes be open and Your ears attentive to the prayer *offered* in this place.

41 "Now therefore arise, O LORD God, to Your resting place, You and the ark of Your might; let Your priests, O LORD God, be clothed with salvation and let Your godly ones rejoice in what is good.

42 "O LORD God, do not turn away the face of Your anointed; remember *Your* lovingkindness to Your servant David."

Psalm 79:11–13

11 Let the groaning of the prisoner
    come before You;
    According to the greatness of Your
    power preserve those who are
    doomed to die.

12 And return to our neighbors
    sevenfold into their bosom
    The reproach with which they have
    reproached You, O Lord.

13 So we Your people and the sheep of
    Your pasture
    Will give thanks to You forever;
    To all generations we will tell of
    Your praise.

Proverbs 20:13, 14

13 Do not love sleep, or you will
    become poor;

LIFE LESSONS

➤ **2 Chronicles 6:29, 30 — *"Hear from heaven Your dwelling place, and forgive, and render to each according to all his ways."***

*W*e might consider this verse an Old Testament version of Philippians 4:6: "In everything by prayer and supplication with thanksgiving let your requests be made known to God." The Lord invites our prayers!

ANSWERS TO LIFE'S QUESTIONS

How does my relationship with the Lord affect what and how I hear from Him?

PSALM 79:13

*O*ur relationships with God—the most important aspect of our lives—affect greatly what we hear when we pray and listen. The only message an unbeliever will ever hear from God is he is a sinner who needs Jesus as his Savior. Until that person knows Christ as his personal Messiah, he will not hear God speak on any subject other than salvation.

In the life of a believer, that speaker/hearer relationship has two main features.

First, we are saved. When by faith we receive Jesus Christ as our personal Savior, the Bible says we are born again. God takes us from the kingdom of darkness and places us into the kingdom of light. We become His children. Our salvation experience begins our relationship with Him.

Second, we are identified with Him. Our salvation takes care of our eternal security, while our identification takes care of our daily walk of victory. By identification, I mean Christ's life is now mine and mine is His. "It is no longer I who live, but Christ lives in me" (Gal. 2:20). What happened to Christ at Calvary also happened to me. Christ was crucified; I was crucified. Christ was buried; I was buried. Christ was raised; I was raised.

One who is safe and secure in the love of God and sustained by His grace now feels as if He is not distant. He now listens to Someone who loves him enough to bring him into a close, personal relationship—and that makes all the difference. We no longer come to Him, groping and pleading, wondering whether He accepts us.

Through my identification with Him, I come gladly and boldly, knowing I am accepted, not by my behavior, but because of my belief in Him and in what He has already accomplished. Therefore, I can approach Him with confidence and great assurance.

Jesus is now my personal, faithful, and merciful High Priest. He is my Father with whom I enjoy intimate communication. I no longer have to stand on the perimeter, squinting into the distance for a glimpse of His presence. Jesus has paid the price of my relationship with God through His shed blood so that now I am a full member of His own family, sitting daily before Him, totally secure in my sonship.

Open your eyes, *and* you will be
satisfied with food.
14 "Bad, bad," says the buyer,
But when he goes his way, then he
boasts.

Acts 13:1–25

13 NOW there were at Antioch, in the church that was *there*, prophets and teachers: Barnabas, and Simeon who was called Niger, and Lucius of Cyrene, and Manaen who had been brought up with Herod the tetrarch, and Saul.

2 While they were ministering to the Lord and fasting, the Holy Spirit said, "Set apart for Me Barnabas and Saul for the work to which I have called them."

3 Then, when they had fasted and prayed and laid their hands on them, they sent them away.

4 So, being sent out by the Holy Spirit, they went down to Seleucia and from there they sailed to Cyprus.

5 When they reached Salamis, they began to proclaim the word of God in the synagogues of the Jews; and they also had John as their helper.

6 When they had gone through the whole island as far as Paphos, they found a magician, a Jewish false prophet whose name was Bar-Jesus,

7 who was with the proconsul, Sergius Paulus, a man of intelligence. This man summoned Barnabas and Saul and sought to hear the word of God.

8 But Elymas the magician (for so his name is translated) was opposing them,

LIFE LESSONS

➤ **Acts 13:2 — *"Set apart for Me Barnabas and Saul for the work to which I have called them."***

*P*aul and Barnabas found the callings of their lives in the midst of praying and worshiping among their fellow believers—not on their own. God calls us to serve Him together, to show the world how relationships are supposed to work.

seeking to turn the proconsul away from the faith.

9 But Saul, who was also *known as* Paul, filled with the Holy Spirit, fixed his gaze on him,

10 and said, "You who are full of all deceit and fraud, you son of the devil, you enemy of all righteousness, will you not cease to make crooked the straight ways of the Lord?

11 "Now, behold, the hand of the Lord is upon you, and you will be blind and not see the sun for a time." And immediately a mist and a darkness fell upon him, and he went about seeking those who would lead him by the hand.

12 Then the proconsul believed when he saw what had happened, being amazed at the teaching of the Lord.

13 Now Paul and his companions put out to sea from Paphos and came to Perga in Pamphylia; but John left them and returned to Jerusalem.

14 But going on from Perga, they arrived at Pisidian Antioch, and on the Sabbath day they went into the synagogue and sat down.

15 After the reading of the Law and the Prophets the synagogue officials sent to them, saying, "Brethren, if you have any word of exhortation for the people, say it."

16 Paul stood up, and motioning with his hand said,

"Men of Israel, and you who fear God, listen:

17 "The God of this people Israel chose our fathers and made the people great during their stay in the land of Egypt, and with an uplifted arm He led them out from it.

18 "For a period of about forty years He put up with them in the wilderness.

19 "When He had destroyed seven nations in the land of Canaan, He distrib-

uted their land as an inheritance—*all of which took* about four hundred and fifty years.

20 "After these things He gave *them* judges until Samuel the prophet.

21 "Then they asked for a king, and God gave them Saul the son of Kish, a man of the tribe of Benjamin, for forty years.

22 "After He had removed him, He raised up David to be their king, concerning whom He also testified and said, 'I HAVE FOUND DAVID the son of Jesse, A MAN AFTER MY HEART, who will do all My will.'

23 "From the descendants of this man, according to promise, God has brought to Israel a Savior, Jesus,

24 after John had proclaimed before His coming a baptism of repentance to all the people of Israel.

25 "And while John was completing his course, he kept saying, 'What do you suppose that I am? I am not *He*. But behold, one is coming after me the sandals of whose feet I am not worthy to untie.'

LIFE LESSONS

➤ **Acts 13:23 — *From the descendants of this man, according to promise, God has brought to Israel a Savior, Jesus.***

*P*aul was always reminding the Jewish people that Christ was the fulfillment of God's covenants with David and Abraham. This is because from childhood, they would have looked forward to the Messiah; however, they were looking for an earthly deliverer, rather than the eternal salvation the Lord was offering. Their perception needed to change. Yet even when God is changing our understanding, we can always remember that Jesus not only saves us, He is the ultimate reminder God always keeps His promises!

---

2 Chronicles 7:1—8:18

7 NOW when Solomon had finished praying, fire came down from heaven and consumed the burnt offering and

the sacrifices, and the glory of the LORD filled the house.

2 The priests could not enter into the house of the LORD because the glory of the LORD filled the LORD's house.

3 All the sons of Israel, seeing the fire

come down and the glory of the LORD upon the house, bowed down on the pavement with their faces to the ground, and they worshiped and gave praise to the LORD, *saying*, "Truly He is good, truly His lovingkindness is everlasting."

4 Then the king and all the people offered sacrifice before the LORD.

5 King Solomon offered a sacrifice of 22,000 oxen and 120,000 sheep. Thus the king and all the people dedicated the house of God.

6 The priests stood at their posts, and the Levites also, with the instruments of music to the LORD, which King David had made for giving praise to the LORD— "for His lovingkindness is everlasting"— whenever he gave praise by their means, while the priests on the other side blew trumpets; and all Israel was standing.

7 Then Solomon consecrated the middle of the court that *was* before the house of the LORD, for there he offered the burnt offerings and the fat of the peace offerings because the bronze altar which Solomon had made was not able to contain the burnt offering, the grain offering and the fat.

8 So Solomon observed the feast at that time for seven days, and all Israel with him, a very great assembly *who came* from the entrance of Hamath to the brook of Egypt.

9 On the eighth day they held a solemn assembly, for the dedication of the altar they observed seven days and the feast seven days.

10 Then on the twenty-third day of the seventh month he sent the people to their tents, rejoicing and happy of heart because of the goodness that the LORD had shown to David and to Solomon and to His people Israel.

11 Thus Solomon finished the house of the LORD and the king's palace, and successfully completed all that he had planned on doing in the house of the LORD and in his palace.

12 Then the LORD appeared to Solomon at night and said to him, "I have heard your prayer and have chosen this place for Myself as a house of sacrifice.

13 "If I shut up the heavens so that there is no rain, or if I command the locust to devour the land, or if I send pestilence among My people,

14 and My people who are called by My name humble themselves and pray and seek My face and turn from their wicked ways, then I will hear from heaven, will forgive their sin and will heal their land.

15 "Now My eyes will be open and My ears attentive to the prayer *offered* in this place.

16 "For now I have chosen and consecrated this house that My name may be there forever, and My eyes and My heart will be there perpetually.

17 "As for you, if you walk before Me as your father David walked, even to do

---

according to all that I have commanded you, and will keep My statutes and My ordinances,

18 then I will establish your royal throne as I covenanted with your father David, saying, 'You shall not lack a man *to be* ruler in Israel.'

19 "But if you turn away and forsake My statutes and My commandments which I have set before you, and go and serve other gods and worship them,

20 then I will uproot you from My land which I have given you, and this house which I have consecrated for My name I will cast out of My sight and I will make it a proverb and a byword among all peoples.

21 "As for this house, which was exalted, everyone who passes by it will be astonished and say, 'Why has the LORD done thus to this land and to this house?'

22 "And they will say, 'Because they forsook the LORD, the God of their fathers who brought them from the land of Egypt, and they adopted other gods and worshiped them and served them; therefore He has brought all this adversity on them.'"

8 NOW it came about at the end of the twenty years in which Solomon had built the house of the LORD and his own house

2 that he built the cities which Huram had given to him, and settled the sons of Israel there.

3 Then Solomon went to Hamath-zobah and captured it.

4 He built Tadmor in the wilderness and all the storage cities which he had built in Hamath.

5 He also built upper Beth-horon and lower Beth-horon, fortified cities *with* walls, gates and bars;

6 and Baalath and all the storage cities that Solomon had, and all the cities for his chariots and cities for his horsemen, and all that it pleased Solomon to build in Jerusalem, in Lebanon, and in all the land under his rule.

7 All of the people who were left of the Hittites, the Amorites, the Perizzites, the Hivites and the Jebusites, who were not of Israel,

8 *namely,* from their descendants who were left after them in the land whom the sons of Israel had not destroyed, them Solomon raised as forced laborers to this day.

9 But Solomon did not make slaves for his work from the sons of Israel; they were men of war, his chief captains and commanders of his chariots and his horsemen.

10 These were the chief officers of King Solomon, two hundred and fifty who ruled over the people.

11 Then Solomon brought Pharaoh's ◄ daughter up from the city of David to the house which he had built for her, for he said, "My wife shall not dwell in the house of David king of Israel, because the places are holy where the ark of the LORD has entered."

12 Then Solomon offered burnt offerings to the LORD on the altar of the LORD which he had built before the porch;

13 and *did so* according to the daily rule, offering *them* up according to the commandment of Moses, for the sabbaths, the new moons and the three annual feasts—the Feast of Unleavened Bread, the Feast of Weeks and the Feast of Booths.

14 Now according to the ordinance of his father David, he appointed the divisions of the priests for their service, and the Levites for their duties of praise and ministering before the priests according to the daily rule, and the gatekeepers by their divisions at every gate; for David the man of God had so commanded.

15 And they did not depart from the commandment of the king to the priests and Levites in any manner or concerning the storehouses.

16 Thus all the work of Solomon was carried out from the day of the foundation of the house of the LORD, and until it was finished. So the house of the LORD was completed.

17 Then Solomon went to Ezion-geber and to Eloth on the seashore in the land of Edom.

LIFE LESSONS

➤ **2 Chronicles 8:11** — *"My wife shall not dwell in the house of David king of Israel, because the places are holy where the ark of the LORD has entered."*

Solomon understood he had married a woman who had no place in the worship of Israel and no connection to God. He knowingly sinned. But he did not realize how his sin would ruin him.

18 And Huram by his servants sent him ships and servants who knew the sea; and they went with Solomon's servants to Ophir, and took from there four hundred and fifty talents of gold and brought them to King Solomon.

Psalm 80:1–6

For the choir director; set to El Shoshannim; Eduth. A Psalm of Asaph.

80 OH, give ear, Shepherd of Israel, You who lead Joseph like a flock;
You who are enthroned *above* the cherubim, shine forth!

2 Before Ephraim and Benjamin and Manasseh, stir up Your power And come to save us!

3 O God, restore us
And cause Your face to shine *upon us*, and we will be saved.

4 O LORD God *of* hosts,
How long will You be angry with the prayer of Your people?

5 You have fed them with the bread of tears,
And You have made them to drink tears in large measure.

6 You make us an object of contention to our neighbors,
And our enemies laugh among themselves.

Proverbs 20:15

15 There is gold, and an abundance of jewels;
But the lips of knowledge are a more precious thing.

LIFE LESSONS

➤ **Psalm 80:3 — *O God, restore us and cause Your face to shine upon us, and we will be saved.***

*I*t would be great if we all marched from spiritual childhood to maturity without a hitch. But the truth is we all need to be restored from time to time. Prayer, confession, and repentance are all necessary steps to restoration.

Acts 13:26–52

26 "Brethren, sons of Abraham's family, and those among you who fear God, to us the message of this salvation has been sent.

27 "For those who live in Jerusalem, and their rulers, recognizing neither Him nor the utterances of the prophets which are read every Sabbath, fulfilled *these* by condemning *Him*.

28 "And though they found no ground for *putting Him to* death, they asked Pilate that He be executed.

29 "When they had carried out all that was written concerning Him, they took Him down from the cross and laid Him in a tomb.

30 "But God raised Him from the dead;

31 and for many days He appeared to those who came up with Him from Galilee to Jerusalem, the very ones who are now His witnesses to the people.

32 "And we preach to you the good news of the promise made to the fathers,

33 that God has fulfilled this *promise* to our children in that He raised up Jesus, as it is also written in the second Psalm, 'YOU ARE MY SON; TODAY I HAVE BEGOTTEN YOU.'

34 "*As for the fact* that He raised Him up from the dead, no longer to return to decay, He has spoken in this way: 'I WILL GIVE YOU THE HOLY *and* SURE *blessings* OF DAVID.'

35 "Therefore He also says in another *Psalm,* 'YOU WILL NOT ALLOW YOUR HOLY ONE TO UNDERGO DECAY.'

36 "For David, after he had served the purpose of God in his own generation, fell asleep, and was laid among his fathers and underwent decay;

37 but He whom God raised did not undergo decay.

38 "Therefore let it be known to you, brethren, that through Him forgiveness of sins is proclaimed to you,

39 and through Him everyone who believes is freed from all things, from which you could not be freed through the Law of Moses.

40 "Therefore take heed, so that the thing spoken of in the Prophets may not come upon *you:*

41 'BEHOLD, YOU SCOFFERS, AND MARVEL, AND PERISH;

F<small>OR</small> I <small>AM ACCOMPLISHING A WORK IN YOUR DAYS,</small>
A <small>WORK WHICH YOU WILL NEVER BELIEVE, THOUGH SOMEONE SHOULD DESCRIBE IT TO YOU.</small>'"

42 As Paul and Barnabas were going out, the people kept begging that these things might be spoken to them the next Sabbath.

43 Now when *the meeting of* the synagogue had broken up, many of the Jews and of the God-fearing proselytes followed Paul and Barnabas, who, speaking to them, were urging them to continue in the grace of God.

44 The next Sabbath nearly the whole city assembled to hear the word of the Lord.

45 But when the Jews saw the crowds, they were filled with jealousy and *began* contradicting the things spoken by Paul, and were blaspheming.

46 Paul and Barnabas spoke out boldly and said, "It was necessary that the word of God be spoken to you first; since you repudiate it and judge yourselves unworthy of eternal life, behold, we are turning to the Gentiles.

47 "For so the Lord has commanded us,
'I <small>HAVE PLACED</small> Y<small>OU AS A LIGHT FOR THE</small> G<small>ENTILES,</small>
T<small>HAT</small> Y<small>OU MAY BRING SALVATION TO THE END OF THE EARTH.</small>'"

48 When the Gentiles heard this, they *began* rejoicing and glorifying the word of the Lord; and as many as had been appointed to eternal life believed.

49 And the word of the Lord was being spread through the whole region.

50 But the Jews incited the devout women of prominence and the leading men of the city, and instigated a persecution against Paul and Barnabas, and drove them out of their district.

51 But they shook off the dust of their feet *in protest* against them and went to Iconium.

52 And the disciples were continually filled with joy and with the Holy Spirit.

LIFE LESSONS

➤ **Acts 13:47 — "I have placed you as a light for the Gentiles, that you may bring salvation to the end of the earth."**

Paul and Barnabas confronted the Jews with this verse from Isaiah 49:6 to remind them they were to encourage the Gentiles to know the Lord, not turn them away from His salvation and blessings. The same goes for us as believers—we were never meant to shut ourselves off completely from unbelievers; we are to be a light to them (Matt. 5:14–16). We must always lead others to Him, and with our conducts and testimonies, glorify Him.

➤ **Acts 13:52 — The disciples were continually filled with joy and with the Holy Spirit.**

God intends a life in step with His Spirit to be a life of joy. This doesn't mean there will never be sorrow. As we have seen, Paul and Barnabas experienced a great deal of heartache. It means that even in the midst of sorrow, the joy of the Spirit sustains us because we know God will always work powerfully through our obedience.

---

2 Chronicles 9:1—10:19

9 NOW when the queen of Sheba heard of the fame of Solomon, she came to Jerusalem to test Solomon with difficult questions. She had a very large retinue, with camels carrying spices and a large amount of gold and precious stones; and when she came to Solomon, she spoke with him about all that was on her heart.

2 Solomon answered all her questions; nothing was hidden from Solomon which he did not explain to her.

3 When the queen of Sheba had seen the wisdom of Solomon, the house which he had built,

4 the food at his table, the seating of his servants, the attendance of his ministers and their attire, his cupbearers and their attire, and his stairway by which he went up to the house of the L<small>ORD</small>, she was breathless.

5   Then she said to the king, "It was a true report which I heard in my own land about your words and your wisdom.
6   "Nevertheless I did not believe their reports until I came and my eyes had seen it. And behold, the half of the greatness of your wisdom was not told me. You surpass the report that I heard.
7   "How blessed are your men, how blessed are these your servants who stand before you continually and hear your wisdom.
8   "Blessed be the LORD your God who delighted in you, setting you on His throne as king for the LORD your God; because your God loved Israel establishing them forever, therefore He made you king over them, to do justice and righteousness."
9   Then she gave the king one hundred and twenty talents of gold and a very great *amount* of spices and precious stones; there had never been spice like that which the queen of Sheba gave to King Solomon.
10   The servants of Huram and the servants of Solomon who brought gold from Ophir, also brought algum trees and precious stones.
11   From the algum trees the king made steps for the house of the LORD and for the king's palace, and lyres and harps for the singers; and none like that was seen before in the land of Judah.
12   King Solomon gave to the queen of Sheba all her desire which she requested besides *a return for* what she had brought to the king. Then she turned and went to her own land with her servants.
13   Now the weight of gold which came to Solomon in one year was 666 talents of gold,

---

LIFE LESSONS

> **2 Chronicles 9:7** — *"How blessed are these your servants who stand before you continually and hear your wisdom."*

*P*erhaps Solomon listened too eagerly to glowing declarations of his great wisdom, and it eventually led to a prideful downfall (1 Kin. 11:4–10). He knew he had received this gift from God, yet maybe because of all the praise and success he received, he ultimately learned to trust the gift more than the Giver.

---

14   besides that which the traders and merchants brought; and all the kings of Arabia and the governors of the country brought gold and silver to Solomon.
15   King Solomon made 200 large shields of beaten gold, using 600 *shekels* of beaten gold on each large shield.
16   *He* made 300 shields of beaten gold, using three hundred shekels of gold on each shield, and the king put them in the house of the forest of Lebanon.
17   Moreover, the king made a great throne of ivory and overlaid it with pure gold.
18   *There were* six steps to the throne and a footstool in gold attached to the throne, and arms on each side of the seat, and two lions standing beside the arms.
19   Twelve lions were standing there on the six steps on the one side and on the other; nothing like *it* was made for any *other* kingdom.
20   All King Solomon's drinking vessels *were* of gold, and all the vessels of the house of the forest of Lebanon *were* of pure gold; silver was not considered valuable in the days of Solomon.
21   For the king had ships which went to Tarshish with the servants of Huram; once every three years the ships of Tarshish came bringing gold and silver, ivory and apes and peacocks.
22   So King Solomon became greater than all the kings of the earth in riches and wisdom.
23   And all the kings of the earth were seeking the presence of Solomon, to hear his wisdom which God had put in his heart.
24   They brought every man his gift, articles of silver and gold, garments, weapons, spices, horses and mules, so much year by year.
25   Now Solomon had 4,000 stalls for horses and chariots and 12,000 horsemen, and he stationed them in the chariot cities and with the king in Jerusalem.
26   He was the ruler over all the kings from the Euphrates River even to the land of the Philistines, and as far as the border of Egypt.
27   The king made silver *as common* as stones in Jerusalem, and he made cedars as plentiful as sycamore trees that are in the lowland.
28   And they were bringing horses for

Life Examples:

KING SOLOMON: We All Need God's Wisdom

2 CHRONICLES 9:5–8, 22, 23

*W*hen God invited Solomon to ask for whatever he wanted, the king requested wisdom (1 Kin. 3:9). That God-given wisdom taught Solomon only a fool tries to solve life's problems without the Lord's help.

Any time we spend wondering about how to get out of a touchy situation is time wasted. God's guidance is more than sufficient for all the tests or trials we might have to face—but in order to benefit from it, we have to seek it out, just as Solomon did so long ago.

In this life, tests come in all shapes and sizes. Some we anticipate; others blindside us. Some tests require us to endure; others involve making the right decision immediately. Regardless of the difficulty, God instructs us to come to Him for the wisdom we so desperately need.

Solomon from Egypt and from all countries.

29 Now the rest of the acts of Solomon, from first to last, are they not written in the records of Nathan the prophet, and in the prophecy of Ahijah the Shilonite, and in the visions of Iddo the seer concerning Jeroboam the son of Nebat?

30 Solomon reigned forty years in Jerusalem over all Israel.

31 And Solomon slept with his fathers and was buried in the city of his father David; and his son Rehoboam reigned in his place.

10 THEN Rehoboam went to Shechem, for all Israel had come to Shechem to make him king.

2 When Jeroboam the son of Nebat heard *of it* (for he was in Egypt where he had fled from the presence of King Solomon), Jeroboam returned from Egypt.

3 So they sent and summoned him. When Jeroboam and all Israel came, they spoke to Rehoboam, saying,

4 "Your father made our yoke hard; now therefore lighten the hard service of your father and his heavy yoke which he put on us, and we will serve you."

5 He said to them, "Return to me again in three days." So the people departed.

6 Then King Rehoboam consulted with the elders who had served his father Solomon while he was still alive, saying, "How do you counsel *me* to answer this people?"

7 They spoke to him, saying, "If you will be kind to this people and please them and speak good words to them, then they will be your servants forever."

8 But he forsook the counsel of the elders which they had given him, and consulted with the young men who grew up with him and served him.

9 So he said to them, "What counsel do you give that we may answer this people, who have spoken to me, saying, 'Lighten the yoke which your father put on us'?"

10 The young men who grew up with him spoke to him, saying, "Thus you shall say to the people who spoke to you, saying, 'Your father made our yoke heavy, but you make it lighter for us.' Thus you shall say to them, 'My little finger is thicker than my father's loins!

11 'Whereas my father loaded you with a heavy yoke, I will add to your yoke; my father disciplined you with whips, but I *will discipline you* with scorpions.'"

12 So Jeroboam and all the people came to Rehoboam on the third day as the king had directed, saying, "Return to me on the third day."

13 The king answered them harshly, and King Rehoboam forsook the counsel of the elders.

14 He spoke to them according to the advice of the young men, saying, "My father made your yoke heavy, but I will add to it; my father disciplined you with whips, but I *will discipline you* with scorpions."

15 So the king did not listen to the people, for it was a turn *of events* from God that the LORD might establish His word, which He spoke through Ahijah the Shilonite to Jeroboam the son of Nebat.

16 When all Israel *saw* that the king did not listen to them the people answered the king, saying,

"What portion do we have in David?

We have no inheritance in the son of Jesse.

Every man to your tents, O Israel;
  Now look after your own house,
      David."
So all Israel departed to their tents.
17 But as for the sons of Israel who
lived in the cities of Judah, Rehoboam
reigned over them.
18 Then King Rehoboam sent Hadoram,
who was over the forced labor, and the
sons of Israel stoned him to death. And
King Rehoboam made haste to mount his
chariot to flee to Jerusalem.
19 So Israel has been in rebellion
against the house of David to this day.

Psalm 80:7–13

7 O God of hosts, restore us
    And cause Your face to shine upon
      us, and we will be saved.
8 You removed a vine from Egypt;
    You drove out the nations and
      planted it.
9 You cleared the ground before it,
    And it took deep root and filled the
      land.
10 The mountains were covered with
      its shadow,
    And the cedars of God with its
      boughs.
11 It was sending out its branches to
      the sea
    And its shoots to the River.
12 Why have You broken down its
      hedges,
    So that all who pass that way pick
      its fruit?
13 A boar from the forest eats it away
    And whatever moves in the field
      feeds on it.

Proverbs 20:16–18

16 Take his garment when he becomes
      surety for a stranger;
    And for foreigners, hold him in
      pledge.
17 Bread obtained by falsehood is
      sweet to a man,
    But afterward his mouth will be
      filled with gravel.
18 Prepare plans by consultation,
    And make war by wise guidance.

Acts 14:1–28

14 IN Iconium they entered the syna-
    gogue of the Jews together, and
spoke in such a manner that a large
number of people believed, both of Jews
and of Greeks.
2 But the Jews who disbelieved stirred
up the minds of the Gentiles and embittered them against the brethren.
3 Therefore they spent a long time
there speaking boldly with reliance upon
the Lord, who was testifying to the word
of His grace, granting that signs and
wonders be done by their hands.
4 But the people of the city were divided; and some sided with the Jews, and
some with the apostles.
5 And when an attempt was made by
both the Gentiles and the Jews with their
rulers, to mistreat and to stone them,
6 they became aware of it and fled to
the cities of Lycaonia, Lystra and Derbe,
and the surrounding region;
7 and there they continued to preach
the gospel.
8 At Lystra a man was sitting who had
no strength in his feet, lame from his
mother's womb, who had never walked.
9 This man was listening to Paul as he
spoke, who, when he had fixed his gaze
on him and had seen that he had faith to
be made well,
10 said with a loud voice, "Stand upright
on your feet." And he leaped up and began
to walk.
11 When the crowds saw what Paul had
done, they raised their voice, saying in
the Lycaonian language, "The gods have
become like men and have come down to
us."
12 And they began calling Barnabas,
Zeus, and Paul, Hermes, because he was
the chief speaker.
13 The priest of Zeus, whose temple
was just outside the city, brought oxen
and garlands to the gates, and wanted to
offer sacrifice with the crowds.
14 But when the apostles Barnabas and
Paul heard of it, they tore their robes and
rushed out into the crowd, crying out
15 and saying, "Men, why are you
doing these things? We are also men of
the same nature as you, and preach the
gospel to you that you should turn from

these vain things to a living God, WHO MADE THE HEAVEN AND THE EARTH AND THE SEA AND ALL THAT IS IN THEM.

16 "In the generations gone by He permitted all the nations to go their own ways;

17 and yet He did not leave Himself without witness, in that He did good and gave you rains from heaven and fruitful seasons, satisfying your hearts with food and gladness."

18 *Even* saying these things, with difficulty they restrained the crowds from offering sacrifice to them.

➤ 19 But Jews came from Antioch and Iconium, and having won over the crowds, they stoned Paul and dragged him out of the city, supposing him to be dead.

20 But while the disciples stood around him, he got up and entered the city. The next day he went away with Barnabas to Derbe.

21 After they had preached the gospel to that city and had made many disciples, they returned to Lystra and to Iconium and to Antioch,

➤ 22 strengthening the souls of the disciples, encouraging them to continue in ✳ the faith, and *saying*, "Through many tribulations we must enter the kingdom of God."

23 When they had appointed elders for them in every church, having prayed with fasting, they commended them to the Lord in whom they had believed.

24 They passed through Pisidia and came into Pamphylia.

25 When they had spoken the word in Perga, they went down to Attalia.

26 From there they sailed to Antioch, from which they had been commended to the grace of God for the work that they had accomplished.

27 When they had arrived and gathered the church together, they *began* to report

all things that God had done with them and how He had opened a door of faith to the Gentiles.

28 And they spent a long time with the disciples.

2 Chronicles 11:1—12:16

11 NOW when Rehoboam had come to Jerusalem, he assembled the house of Judah and Benjamin, 180,000 chosen men who were warriors, to fight

against Israel to restore the kingdom to Rehoboam.

2 But the word of the LORD came to Shemaiah the man of God, saying,

3 "Speak to Rehoboam the son of Solomon, king of Judah, and to all Israel in Judah and Benjamin, saying,

➤ 4 'Thus says the LORD, "You shall not go up or fight against your relatives; return every man to his house, for this thing is from Me."'" So they listened to the words of the LORD and returned from going against Jeroboam.

5 Rehoboam lived in Jerusalem and built cities for defense in Judah.

6 Thus he built Bethlehem, Etam, Tekoa,

7 Beth-zur, Soco, Adullam,

8 Gath, Mareshah, Ziph,

9 Adoraim, Lachish, Azekah,

10 Zorah, Aijalon and Hebron, which are fortified cities in Judah and in Benjamin.

11 He also strengthened the fortresses and put officers in them and stores of food, oil and wine.

12 *He put* shields and spears in every city and strengthened them greatly. So he held Judah and Benjamin.

13 Moreover, the priests and the Levites who were in all Israel stood with him from all their districts.

14 For the Levites left their pasture lands and their property and came to Judah and Jerusalem, for Jeroboam and his sons had excluded them from serving as priests to the LORD.

➤ 15 He set up priests of his own for the high places, for the satyrs and for the calves which he had made.

16 Those from all the tribes of Israel who set their hearts on seeking the LORD God of Israel followed them to Jerusalem, to sacrifice to the LORD God of their fathers.

17 They strengthened the kingdom of Judah and supported Rehoboam the son of Solomon for three years, for they walked in the way of David and Solomon for three years.

18 Then Rehoboam took as a wife Mahalath the daughter of Jerimoth the son of David *and of* Abihail the daughter of Eliab the son of Jesse,

19 and she bore him sons: Jeush, Shemariah and Zaham.

20 After her he took Maacah the daughter of Absalom, and she bore him Abijah, Attai, Ziza and Shelomith.

21 Rehoboam loved Maacah the daughter of Absalom more than all his *other* wives and concubines. For he had taken eighteen wives and sixty concubines and

fathered twenty-eight sons and sixty daughters.

22 Rehoboam appointed Abijah the son of Maacah as head and leader among his brothers, for he *intended* to make him king.

23 He acted wisely and distributed some of his sons through all the territories of Judah and Benjamin to all the fortified cities, and he gave them food in abundance. And he sought many wives *for them.*

12 WHEN the kingdom of Rehoboam ◄ was established and strong, he and all Israel with him forsook the law of the LORD.

2 And it came about in King Rehoboam's fifth year, because they had been unfaithful to the LORD, that Shishak king of Egypt came up against Jerusalem

3 with 1,200 chariots and 60,000 horsemen. And the people who came with him from Egypt were without number: the Lubim, the Sukkiim and the Ethiopians.

4 He captured the fortified cities of Judah and came as far as Jerusalem.

5   Then Shemaiah the prophet came to Rehoboam and the princes of Judah who had gathered at Jerusalem because of Shishak, and he said to them, "Thus says the LORD, 'You have forsaken Me, so I also have forsaken you to Shishak.'"

6   So the princes of Israel and the king humbled themselves and said, "The LORD is righteous."

7   When the LORD saw that they humbled themselves, the word of the LORD came to Shemaiah, saying, "They have humbled themselves *so* I will not destroy them, but I will grant them some *measure* of deliverance, and My wrath shall not be poured out on Jerusalem by means of Shishak.

8   "But they will become his slaves so that they may learn *the difference between* My service and the service of the kingdoms of the countries."

9   So Shishak king of Egypt came up against Jerusalem, and took the treasures of the house of the LORD and the treasures of the king's palace. He took everything; he even took the golden shields which Solomon had made.

10   Then King Rehoboam made shields of bronze in their place and committed them to the care of the commanders of the guard who guarded the door of the king's house.

11   As often as the king entered the house of the LORD, the guards came and carried them and *then* brought them back into the guards' room.

12   And when he humbled himself, the anger of the LORD turned away from him, so as not to destroy *him* completely; and also conditions were good in Judah.

13   So King Rehoboam strengthened himself in Jerusalem and reigned. Now Rehoboam was forty-one years old when he began to reign, and he reigned seventeen years in Jerusalem, the city which the LORD had chosen from all the tribes of Israel, to put His name there. And his mother's name was Naamah the Ammonitess.

14   He did evil because he did not set his heart to seek the LORD.

15   Now the acts of Rehoboam, from first to last, are they not written in the records of Shemaiah the prophet and of Iddo the seer, according to genealogical enrollment? And *there were* wars between Rehoboam and Jeroboam continually.

16   And Rehoboam slept with his fathers and was buried in the city of David; and his son Abijah became king in his place.

✦ Psalm 80:14–19

14   O God *of* hosts, turn again now, we
          beseech You;
       Look down from heaven and see,
          and take care of this vine,
15   Even the shoot which Your right
          hand has planted,
       And on the son whom You have
          strengthened for Yourself.
16   It is burned with fire, it is cut
          down;
       They perish at the rebuke of Your
          countenance.
17   Let Your hand be upon the man of
          Your right hand,
       Upon the son of man whom You
          made strong for Yourself.
18   Then we shall not turn back from
          You;
       Revive us, and we will call upon
          Your name.
19   O LORD God of hosts, restore us;
       Cause Your face to shine *upon us,*
          and we will be saved.

LIFE LESSONS

➤ 2 Chronicles 12:1 — *When the kingdom of Rehoboam was established . . . he and all Israel with him forsook the law of the LORD.*

*I*f we should grow strong and prosperous, we must be aware of the temptation to attribute our prosperity to our own ingenuity (Deut. 8:17, 18). God alone supplies all we have, and we never outgrow our need for Him.

➤ 2 Chronicles 12:7 — *"I will not destroy them, but I will grant them some measure of deliverance."*

*I*n His grace, the Lord granted some deliverance to the disobedient leaders of Israel who humbled themselves— but He still let them experience the serious consequences of their rebellion.

Proverbs 20:19–21

19 He who goes about as a slanderer
reveals secrets,
Therefore do not associate with a
gossip.
20 He who curses his father or his
mother,
His lamp will go out in time of
darkness.
21 An inheritance gained hurriedly at
the beginning
Will not be blessed in the end.

Acts 15:1–21

15 SOME men came down from Judea
and *began* teaching the brethren,
"Unless you are circumcised according
to the custom of Moses, you cannot be
saved."
2 And when Paul and Barnabas had
great dissension and debate with them,
the brethren determined that Paul and
Barnabas and some others of them
should go up to Jerusalem to the apostles
and elders concerning this issue.
3 Therefore, being sent on their way
by the church, they were passing through
both Phoenicia and Samaria, describing
in detail the conversion of the Gentiles,
and were bringing great joy to all the
brethren.
4 When they arrived at Jerusalem,
they were received by the church and
the apostles and the elders, and they
reported all that God had done with
them.
5 But some of the sect of the Pharisees
who had believed stood up, saying, "It is
necessary to circumcise them and to direct them to observe the Law of Moses."
6 The apostles and the elders came
together to look into this matter.
7 After there had been much debate,
Peter stood up and said to them, "Brethren, you know that in the early days God
made a choice among you, that by my
mouth the Gentiles would hear the word
of the gospel and believe.
8 "And God, who knows the heart,
testified to them giving them the Holy
Spirit, just as He also did to us;

9 and He made no distinction between
us and them, cleansing their hearts by
faith.
10 "Now therefore why do you put God
to the test by placing upon the neck
of the disciples a yoke which neither
our fathers nor we have been able to
bear?
11 "But we believe that we are saved
through the grace of the Lord Jesus, in
the same way as they also are."
12 All the people kept silent, and they
were listening to Barnabas and Paul as
they were relating what signs and wonders God had done through them among
the Gentiles.
13 After they had stopped speaking,
James answered, saying, "Brethren, listen to me.
14 "Simeon has related how God first
concerned Himself about taking from
among the Gentiles a people for His
name.
15 "With this the words of the Prophets
agree, just as it is written,

LIFE LESSONS

➤ **Proverbs 20:19** — *Therefore do not
associate with a gossip.*

A person who enjoys speaking negatively about others may attempt to
draw you in with the secrets they know.
However, God's Word is clear that you
should "not associate with a gossip."
James 3:6 explains, "The tongue is a fire,
the very world of iniquity; the tongue is
set among our members as that which
defiles the entire body, and sets on fire
the course of our life." Gossip destroys
lives and dishonors God.

➤ **Acts 15:11** — *"Through the grace of
the Lord Jesus, in the same way as they
also are."*

M any of the Jewish Christians—those
called *Judaizers*—thought Gentile
believers should be required to keep
the law in order to attain salvation
(Acts 15:1, 5). To answer their claims, the
elders called the first conference of the
early church called the Jerusalem Council. In that meeting, the elders affirmed
the truth: we don't have to earn our
salvation through works or keeping
the law—Christ has given it to us freely
(Eph. 2:4–9).

WHAT THE BIBLE SAYS ABOUT

A Tradition of Works

Acts 15:1–21

Though we know salvation is by grace through faith (Eph. 2:8), we're all tempted to do something to earn our salvation. This was especially true of some of the Christian Jews in the early church. After centuries of observing the covenant of circumcision (Gen. 17:10–14), many of them did not believe they should give it up. These people were called Judaizers, and they said, "Unless you are circumcised according to the custom of Moses, you cannot be saved" (Acts 15:1). Though they agreed that salvation was through Jesus Christ, they said that a person was also required to keep the law in order to attain salvation. It was their tradition, handed down from their forefathers throughout the ages, and they couldn't let it go.

Of course, it was also a violation of everything that the apostles had been teaching—especially to the new Gentile believers. They recognized that keeping the law would be terribly difficult for the Gentile Christians who were unaccustomed to Jewish practices. Therefore, the elders decided to call a meeting to discuss the dispute (Acts 15:2). This was the beginning of what was called the Jerusalem Council, which was the first conference held by the early church.

Peter explained the gospel of grace by saying, "in the early days God made a choice among you, that by my mouth the Gentiles would hear the word of the gospel and believe. And God, who knows the heart, testified to them giving them the Holy Spirit, just as He also did to us; and He made no distinction between us and them, cleansing their hearts by faith. Now therefore why do you put God to the test by placing upon the neck of the disciples a yoke which neither our fathers nor we have been able to bear? But we believe that we are saved through the grace of the Lord Jesus, in the same way as they also are" (Acts 15:7–11).

Peter was not setting aside the law. Rather, he was saying the law was a yoke that revealed their need for a Savior (Rom. 3:19, 20; Gal. 3:19–25). Although circumcision had been an outward sign of devotion to God, it was never enough for salvation (Matt. 23:13–28; Luke 11:39–52; Gal. 2:16). Only faith in Jesus Christ could truly purify their hearts.

Are you used to working your way through life? Did you have to earn your parent's love or others' acceptance? Are you accustomed to being judged by how you perform? Like the Judaizers, those past experiences and "traditions" may be clouding your understanding of how to relate to Christ.

Instead of circumcising your flesh with outward signs, Christ circumcises your heart and spirit, making you holy from the inside (Deut 30:6; Jer. 4:4; Rom. 2:25–29; 1 Cor. 7:19; Gal. 5:1–6). If you've trusted Jesus Christ as your Savior, you have been set free from sin. Your sin-debt has been paid completely. Salvation is no longer an issue—you can't increase it or lose it by what you do.

You don't have to work your way to salvation—Christ has given it to you freely. You don't have to earn God's love—He loves you unconditionally. And you won't be judged by your performance; rather, what God cares about is your obedience and faith.

Sometimes this is a difficult truth to get used to, but it is immensely important that you embrace it because it will set you free to serve God out of love and trust.

Therefore, understand once and for all, "God, being rich in mercy, because of His great love with which He loved us, even when we were dead in our transgressions, made us alive together with Christ . . . it is the gift of God; not as a result of works" (Eph. 2:4, 5, 8, 9). Therefore, let go of those old, powerless traditions and hold on to Christ. Stop working, and start enjoying the freedom God's love gives you. ◉

---

16 'AFTER THESE THINGS I will return,
   AND I WILL REBUILD THE TABERNACLE
      OF DAVID WHICH HAS FALLEN,
   AND I WILL REBUILD ITS RUINS,
   AND I WILL RESTORE IT,

✴ 17 SO THAT THE REST OF MANKIND MAY
      SEEK THE LORD,

AND ALL THE GENTILES WHO ARE
      CALLED BY MY NAME,'
18 SAYS THE LORD, WHO MAKES THESE
      THINGS KNOWN FROM LONG AGO.
19 "Therefore it is my judgment that we do not trouble those who are turning to God from among the Gentiles,

20 but that we write to them that they abstain from things contaminated by idols and from fornication and from what is strangled and from blood.

21 "For Moses from ancient generations has in every city those who preach him, since he is read in the synagogues every Sabbath."

2 Chronicles 13:1—14:15

13 IN the eighteenth year of King Jeroboam, Abijah became king over Judah.
2 He reigned three years in Jerusalem; and his mother's name was Micaiah the daughter of Uriel of Gibeah.

Now there was war between Abijah and Jeroboam.
3 Abijah began the battle with an army of valiant warriors, 400,000 chosen men, while Jeroboam drew up in battle formation against him with 800,000 chosen men *who were* valiant warriors.
4 Then Abijah stood on Mount Zemaraim, which is in the hill country of Ephraim, and said, "Listen to me, Jeroboam and all Israel:
5 "Do you not know that the LORD God of Israel gave the rule over Israel forever to David and his sons by a covenant of salt?
6 "Yet Jeroboam the son of Nebat, the servant of Solomon the son of David, rose up and rebelled against his master,
7 and worthless men gathered about him, scoundrels, who proved too strong for Rehoboam, the son of Solomon, when he was young and timid and could not hold his own against them.
8 "So now you intend to resist the kingdom of the LORD through the sons of David, being a great multitude and *having* with you the golden calves which Jeroboam made for gods for you.
9 "Have you not driven out the priests of the LORD, the sons of Aaron and the Levites, and made for yourselves priests like the peoples of *other* lands? Whoever comes to consecrate himself with a young bull and seven rams, even he may become a priest of *what are* no gods.
10 "But as for us, the LORD is our God, and we have not forsaken Him; and the sons of Aaron are ministering to the LORD as priests, and the Levites attend to their work.
11 "Every morning and evening they burn to the LORD burnt offerings and fragrant incense, and the showbread is *set* on the clean table, and the golden lampstand with its lamps is *ready* to light every evening; for we keep the charge of the LORD our God, but you have forsaken Him.
12 "Now behold, God is with us at *our* head and His priests with the signal trumpets to sound the alarm against you. O sons of Israel, do not fight against the LORD God of your fathers, for you will not succeed."
13 But Jeroboam had set an ambush to come from the rear, so that *Israel* was in front of Judah and the ambush was behind them.
14 When Judah turned around, behold, they were attacked both front and rear; so they cried to the LORD, and the priests blew the trumpets.
15 Then the men of Judah raised a war cry, and when the men of Judah raised the war cry, then it was that God routed Jeroboam and all Israel before Abijah and Judah.
16 When the sons of Israel fled before Judah, God gave them into their hand.
17 Abijah and his people defeated them with a great slaughter, so that 500,000 chosen men of Israel fell slain.
18 Thus the sons of Israel were subdued ◄ at that time, and the sons of Judah conquered because they trusted in the LORD, the God of their fathers.
19 Abijah pursued Jeroboam and captured from him *several* cities, Bethel with its villages, Jeshanah with its villages and Ephron with its villages.

LIFE LESSONS

➤ **2 Chronicles 13:18 — *The sons of Judah conquered because they trusted in the Lord, the God of their fathers.***

*T*he people of Judah prevailed despite clever military tactics by the enemy. Why? Only one reason: they relied on the Lord, and He delivered them.

20 Jeroboam did not again recover strength in the days of Abijah; and the LORD struck him and he died.
21 But Abijah became powerful; and took fourteen wives to himself, and became the father of twenty-two sons and sixteen daughters.
22 Now the rest of the acts of Abijah, and his ways and his words are written in the treatise of the prophet Iddo.

14 SO Abijah slept with his fathers, and they buried him in the city of David, and his son Asa became king in his place. The land was undisturbed for ten years during his days.
2 Asa did good and right in the sight of the LORD his God,
3 for he removed the foreign altars and high places, tore down the *sacred* pillars, cut down the Asherim,
4 and commanded Judah to seek the LORD God of their fathers and to observe the law and the commandment.
5 He also removed the high places and the incense altars from all the cities of Judah. And the kingdom was undisturbed under him.
6 He built fortified cities in Judah, since the land was undisturbed, and there was no one at war with him during those years, because the LORD had given him rest.
7 For he said to Judah, "Let us build these cities and surround *them* with walls and towers, gates and bars. The land is still ours because we have sought the LORD our God; we have sought Him, and He has given us rest on every side." So they built and prospered.
8 Now Asa had an army of 300,000 from Judah, bearing large shields and spears, and 280,000 from Benjamin, bearing shields and wielding bows; all of them were valiant warriors.
9 Now Zerah the Ethiopian came out against them with an army of a million men and 300 chariots, and he came to Mareshah.
10 So Asa went out to meet him, and they drew up in battle formation in the valley of Zephathah at Mareshah.
11 Then Asa called to the LORD his God and said, "LORD, there is no one besides You to help *in the battle* between the powerful and those who have no strength; so help us, O LORD our God, for we trust in You, and in Your name have we come against this multitude. O LORD, You are our God; let not man prevail against You."

LIFE LESSONS

➤ **2 Chronicles 14:2, 4 — Asa . . . commanded Judah to seek the LORD God of their fathers and to observe the law and the commandment.**

*I*t is impossible to obey the Lord without first seeking Him, because listening to God is essential to walking with Him. If we want to stay in the center of His will, we must draw near to Him, appropriate His strength, and obey His commands by the power of His Spirit.

➤ **2 Chronicles 14:11 — "LORD, there is no one besides You to help."**

*W*ith such a large Ethiopian army attacking Judah (2 Chr. 14:8, 9), Asa realized there was nowhere to turn for help but to the Lord. However, God easily delivered the victory (2 Chr. 14:12–15). When we fight our battles on our knees, we win every time.

---

12 So the LORD routed the Ethiopians before Asa and before Judah, and the Ethiopians fled.
13 Asa and the people who *were* with him pursued them as far as Gerar; and so many Ethiopians fell that they could not recover, for they were shattered before the LORD and before His army. And they carried away very much plunder.
14 They destroyed all the cities around Gerar, for the dread of the LORD had fallen on them; and they despoiled all the cities, for there was much plunder in them.
15 They also struck down those who owned livestock, and they carried away large numbers of sheep and camels. Then they returned to Jerusalem.

Psalm 81:1–5

For the choir director; on the Gittith.
A Psalm of Asaph.

81 SING for joy to God our strength;
Shout joyfully to the God of Jacob.
2 Raise a song, strike the timbrel,
The sweet sounding lyre with the harp.
3 Blow the trumpet at the new moon,
At the full moon, on our feast day.
4 For it is a statute for Israel,
An ordinance of the God of Jacob.

5 He established it for a testimony in
Joseph
When he went throughout the land
of Egypt.
I heard a language that I did not
know:

Proverbs 20:22, 23

22 Do not say, "I will repay evil";
Wait for the LORD, and He will save
you.
23 Differing weights are an
abomination to the LORD,
And a false scale is not good.

Acts 15:22–41

22 Then it seemed good to the apostles
and the elders, with the whole church, to
choose men from among them to send to
Antioch with Paul and Barnabas—Judas
called Barsabbas, and Silas, leading men
among the brethren,
23 and they sent this letter by them,
"The apostles and the brethren who
are elders, to the brethren in Antioch
and Syria and Cilicia who are from
the Gentiles, greetings.
24 "Since we have heard that some of
our number to whom we gave no
instruction have disturbed you with
their words, unsettling your souls,
25 it seemed good to us, having become of
one mind, to select men to send to you
with our beloved Barnabas and Paul,
26 men who have risked their lives for
the name of our Lord Jesus Christ.
27 "Therefore we have sent Judas and
Silas, who themselves will also report
the same things by word *of mouth.*
28 "For it seemed good to the Holy
Spirit and to us to lay upon you no
greater burden than these essentials:
29 that you abstain from things sacrificed to idols and from blood and from
things strangled and from fornication;
if you keep yourselves free from such
things, you will do well. Farewell."
30 So when they were sent away, they
went down to Antioch; and having gathered the congregation together, they delivered the letter.

31 When they had read it, they rejoiced
because of its encouragement.
32 Judas and Silas, also being prophets
themselves, encouraged and strengthened
the brethren with a lengthy message.
33 After they had spent time *there*, they
were sent away from the brethren in
peace to those who had sent them out.
34 [But it seemed good to Silas to remain there.]
35 But Paul and Barnabas stayed in Antioch, teaching and preaching with many
others also, the word of the Lord.
36 After some days Paul said to Barnabas, "Let us return and visit the brethren
in every city in which we proclaimed the
word of the Lord, *and see* how they are."
37 Barnabas wanted to take John,
called Mark, along with them also.
38 But Paul kept insisting that they
should not take him along who had deserted them in Pamphylia and had not
gone with them to the work.
39 And there occurred such a sharp dis-

LIFE LESSONS

> **Proverbs 20:22** — *Do not say, "I will
repay evil"; wait for the LORD, and He will
save you.*

*R*evenge isn't your responsibility;
it's God's (Luke 18:7; Rom. 12:19).
Though it's only human to want to
mete out your own justice, it is not the
Lord's will for you to take matters into
your own hands. Rather, allow Him to
avenge you. Even if you never see justice
done on earth, you can be sure God will
accomplish what He's promised you.

> **Acts 15:28** — *"It seemed good to the
Holy Spirit and to us."*

*T*he early church reached consensus on this and other crucial issues
through respectful discussion, earnest
prayer, careful listening, and study of
Scripture. The same must hold true for
churches and believers today.

> **Acts 15:39** — *There occurred such a
sharp disagreement that they separated
from one another.*

*E*ven mature, godly believers can have
disagreements that lead to a parting
of ways. Yet God used the split between
Paul and Barnabas to send out two missionary teams instead of one.

WHAT THE BIBLE SAYS ABOUT

Checking Up

Acts 15:36

*Y*esterday, you read about the Jerusalem Council, where the apostles defended new believers against those who would enslave them again to works. The council authored letters to the churches, asserting they should not listen to the Judaizers who insisted that believers should live by all of the Jewish laws.

The council wrote, "Since we have heard that some who went out from us have troubled you with words, unsettling your souls, saying, 'You must be circumcised and keep the law'—to whom we gave no such commandment— it seemed good to us, being assembled with one accord, to send chosen men to you" (Acts 15:24, 25). Those men went and taught the affected churches the truth.

Now, Paul was among those men, and he did something very wise. He said, "Let us return and visit the brethren in every city in which we proclaimed the word of the Lord, and see how they are" (Acts 15:36). He realized that the Judaizers and other groups would not stop trying to spread their destructive views,

and he wanted to make sure the churches they'd planted were still honoring Christ.

Understand that we also have a responsibility towards those we lead to the Lord. We must make sure they have what they need to follow the Lord in obedience. Though we can't always be the ones who daily teach them to walk with Christ, we should be concerned for their welfare, as Paul was.

Paul wrote, "My children, with whom I am again in labor until Christ is formed in you—but I could wish to be present with you now" (Gal. 4:19, 20). Paul was involved in their spiritual growth even though he couldn't be present with them in person. He made sure they had everything they needed through his letters—which now comprise half of the New Testament—and through the capable, godly representatives he sent to check on them (1 Cor. 4:7; 2 Cor. 8:16–18; Eph. 6:21, 22; Phil. 2:19–30; Col. 4:7–9).

What about those you've led to the Lord? When was the last time you checked to make sure they weren't being led away by false doctrines but were serving the Lord in love and obedience? It may not always be possible to be with them, but as much as you're able, keep track of those you've introduced to the Savior. No doubt, you'll be blessed by the way they grow in the Lord. ❖

---

agreement that they separated from one another, and Barnabas took Mark with him and sailed away to Cyprus.
40 But Paul chose Silas and left, being

committed by the brethren to the grace of the Lord.
41 And he was traveling through Syria and Cilicia, strengthening the churches.

❖ 2 Chronicles 15:1—16:14

15 NOW the Spirit of God came on Azariah the son of Oded,
2 and he went out to meet Asa and said to him, "Listen to me, Asa, and all Judah and Benjamin: the LORD is with you when you are with Him. And if you seek Him, He will let you find Him; but if you forsake Him, He will forsake you.
3 "For many days Israel was without the true God and without a teaching priest and without law.
➤ 4 "But in their distress they turned to

the LORD God of Israel, and they sought Him, and He let them find Him.

LIFE LESSONS

➤ **2 Chronicles 15:4 — *"In their distress they turned to the LORD God of Israel, and they sought Him, and He let them find Him."***

*N*o matter our backgrounds, regardless of our personal histories, and/or despite the terrible things we may have done, God urges us to repent and turn to Him. When we seek Him, we will find Him.

5 "In those times there was no peace to him who went out or to him who came in, for many disturbances afflicted all the inhabitants of the lands.

6 "Nation was crushed by nation, and city by city, for God troubled them with every kind of distress.

7 "But you, be strong and do not lose courage, for there is reward for your work."

8 Now when Asa heard these words and the prophecy which Azariah the son of Oded the prophet spoke, he took courage and removed the abominable idols from all the land of Judah and Benjamin and from the cities which he had captured in the hill country of Ephraim. He then restored the altar of the LORD which was in front of the porch of the LORD.

9 He gathered all Judah and Benjamin and those from Ephraim, Manasseh and Simeon who resided with them, for many defected to him from Israel when they saw that the LORD his God was with him.

10 So they assembled at Jerusalem in the third month of the fifteenth year of Asa's reign.

11 They sacrificed to the LORD that day 700 oxen and 7,000 sheep from the spoil they had brought.

12 They entered into the covenant to seek the LORD God of their fathers with all their heart and soul;

13 and whoever would not seek the LORD God of Israel should be put to death, whether small or great, man or woman.

14 Moreover, they made an oath to the LORD with a loud voice, with shouting, with trumpets and with horns.

15 All Judah rejoiced concerning the oath, for they had sworn with their whole heart and had sought Him earnestly, and He let them find Him. So the LORD gave them rest on every side.

16 He also removed Maacah, the mother of King Asa, from the *position of* queen mother, because she had made a horrid image as an Asherah, and Asa cut down her horrid image, crushed *it* and burned *it* at the brook Kidron.

17 But the high places were not removed from Israel; nevertheless Asa's heart was blameless all his days.

18 He brought into the house of God the dedicated things of his father and his own dedicated things: silver and gold and utensils.

19 And there was no more war until the thirty-fifth year of Asa's reign.

16 IN the thirty-sixth year of Asa's reign Baasha king of Israel came up against Judah and fortified Ramah in order to prevent *anyone* from going out or coming in to Asa king of Judah.

2 Then Asa brought out silver and gold from the treasuries of the house of the LORD and the king's house, and sent them to Ben-hadad king of Aram, who lived in Damascus, saying,

3 "*Let there be* a treaty between you and me, *as* between my father and your father. Behold, I have sent you silver and gold; go, break your treaty with Baasha king of Israel so that he will withdraw from me."

4 So Ben-hadad listened to King Asa and sent the commanders of his armies against the cities of Israel, and they conquered Ijon, Dan, Abel-maim and all the store cities of Naphtali.

5 When Baasha heard *of it*, he ceased fortifying Ramah and stopped his work.

6 Then King Asa brought all Judah, and they carried away the stones of Ramah and its timber with which Baasha had been building, and with them he fortified Geba and Mizpah.

7 At that time Hanani the seer came to Asa king of Judah and said to him, "Because you have relied on the king of Aram and have not relied on the LORD your God, therefore the army of the king of Aram has escaped out of your hand.

8 "Were not the Ethiopians and the Lubim an immense army with very many chariots and horsemen? Yet because you relied on the LORD, He delivered them into your hand.

9 "For the eyes of the LORD move to and fro throughout the earth that He may strongly support those whose heart is completely His. You have acted foolishly in this. Indeed, from now on you will surely have wars."

10 Then Asa was angry with the seer

LIFE LESSONS

> **2 Chronicles 16:7** — *"You have relied on the king of Aram and have not relied on the LORD your God."*

*A*sa's political solution worked in the short term to remove a threat, but it backfired in the long run. Trusting God can be a day-by-day, moment-by-moment pursuit. We must trust the Lord today and every day.

LIFE PRINCIPLE 13

LISTENING TO GOD IS ESSENTIAL TO WALKING WITH GOD.

PSALM 81:8

*O*ne of the most important lessons we can learn is how to listen to God. In our complex and hectic lives, nothing is more urgent, nothing more necessary, and nothing more rewarding than hearing what God has to say to us and obeying Him.

A true conversation, of course, involves both talking and listening. Most of us do better with the talking part.

At one point, I became so occupied doing the Lord's work I had very little time for anything else. I preached six times a week, taped two television programs, and was the senior pastor of a large church. We also were developing an international broadcast ministry. I spent a great deal of time talking to God, but one day I realized I was not spending as much time *listening* to what He was saying to me. I knew something had to change. If we fail to learn how to listen to the Lord, we will make some very unwise and costly mistakes.

You may ask, "Does the Lord really speak to us today?" The Bible assures us He does. The book of Hebrews opens this way: "God, after He spoke long ago to the fathers in the prophets in many portions and in many ways, in these last days has spoken to us in His Son" (Heb. 1:1, 2). Our God is not silent. Our heavenly Father is alive and active. He speaks to us individually and in a way that we can hear

Him, receive His message, and obey Him. He is infinite, fully capable of communicating with each of us, right where we are—in the midst of our circumstances—in a very personal way.

This may be one of the most important concepts you will grasp in learning how to listen to God. When the Lord speaks, He is speaking to *you*. The Word of God contains His truth; therefore, take it personally. Allow His Holy Spirit to open your heart so you will have a deeper understanding of Scripture. When you do, you can begin to claim His promises for your life. You also will gain a deeper understanding of His provision, care, and love.

God is serious about His relationship with you. He speaks for your benefit, and it is important for you to listen to Him and respond in obedience. Sometimes He will challenge you to change your thinking or to release certain unhealthy feelings and opinions. Sometimes He will command you to change aspects of your behavior. Yet with every instruction He gives, you can be certain it is for your good. He desires to encourage and mature you so that you might live with greater joy and strength. He also wants to transform you into the likeness of His Son, Jesus Christ—helping you to become the very best you can be.

Learning to listen to God through the reading of His Word is the most important thing you can do because there is no other way to enjoy the amazingly wonderful abundant life He offers. Therefore, pay close attention to what He has to say, and He will certainly "tell you great and mighty things, which you do not know" (Jer. 33:3).

---

and put him in prison, for he was enraged at him for this. And Asa oppressed some of the people at the same time.
11 Now, the acts of Asa from first to last, behold, they are written in the Book of the Kings of Judah and Israel.
12 In the thirty-ninth year of his reign Asa became diseased in his feet. His disease was severe, yet even in his disease he did not seek the LORD, but the physicians.
13 So Asa slept with his fathers, having died in the forty-first year of his reign.
14 They buried him in his own tomb which he had cut out for himself in the city of David, and they laid him in the resting place which he had filled with

spices of various kinds blended by the perfumers' art; and they made a very great fire for him.

◈ **Psalm 81:6–10**

6 "I relieved his shoulder of the burden,
    His hands were freed from the basket.
7 "You called in trouble and I rescued you;
    I answered you in the hiding place of thunder;
    I proved you at the waters of Meribah.   Selah.

8   "Hear, O My people, and I will
       admonish you;
       O Israel, if you would listen to Me!
9   "Let there be no strange god among
       you;
       Nor shall you worship any foreign
       god.
10   "I, the LORD, am your God,
       Who brought you up from the land
       of Egypt;
       Open your mouth wide and I will
       fill it.

Proverbs 20:24, 25

24   Man's steps are *ordained* by the LORD,
       How then can man understand his
       way?
25   It is a trap for a man to say rashly,
       "It is holy!"
       And after the vows to make inquiry.

Acts 16:1–21

16 PAUL came also to Derbe and to
Lystra. And a disciple was there,
named Timothy, the son of a Jewish
woman who was a believer, but his father was a Greek,
2   and he was well spoken of by the
brethren who were in Lystra and Iconium.
3   Paul wanted this man to go with
him; and he took him and circumcised
him because of the Jews who were in
those parts, for they all knew that his
father was a Greek.
4   Now while they were passing
through the cities, they were delivering
the decrees which had been decided
upon by the apostles and elders who
were in Jerusalem, for them to observe.
5   So the churches were being strengthened in the faith, and were increasing in
number daily.
6   They passed through the Phrygian
and Galatian region, having been forbidden by the Holy Spirit to speak the word
in Asia;
7   and after they came to Mysia, they
were trying to go into Bithynia, and the
Spirit of Jesus did not permit them;
8   and passing by Mysia, they came
down to Troas.
9   A vision appeared to Paul in the

LIFE LESSONS

➢ **Psalm 81:10 —** *"Open your mouth
wide and I will fill it."*

*H*ere we see the heart of God: He
desires to bless His people beyond
their imaginations. But we also see our
part in the process: to willingly receive
what He has to offer by submitting ourselves to Him. We are filled only when
we obey His instructions.

➢ **Acts 16:6, 7 —** *Having been forbidden by the Holy Spirit to speak the word
in Asia . . . . they were trying to go into
Bithynia, and the Spirit of Jesus did not
permit them.*

*P*aul and his companions had developed a plan for evangelism they
tried to follow, but they never let their
plans get in the way of the Spirit's leading. Because they obeyed the Lord's
direction, they crossed the Aegean Sea
and went into new territory—Europe—
with the gospel. Paul planted churches
at Philippi, Thessalonica, and Berea,
which would prove to be very strategic
in the spread of Christianity.

night: a man of Macedonia was standing
and appealing to him, and saying, "Come
over to Macedonia and help us."
10   When he had seen the vision, immediately we sought to go into Macedonia,
concluding that God had called us to
preach the gospel to them.
11   So putting out to sea from Troas, we
ran a straight course to Samothrace, and
on the day following to Neapolis;
12   and from there to Philippi, which is a
leading city of the district of Macedonia,
a *Roman* colony; and we were staying in
this city for some days.
13   And on the Sabbath day we went
outside the gate to a riverside, where
we were supposing that there would be
a place of prayer; and we sat down and
began speaking to the women who had
assembled.
14   A woman named Lydia, from the
city of Thyatira, a seller of purple fabrics, a worshiper of God, was listening;
and the Lord opened her heart to respond to the things spoken by Paul.
15   And when she and her household
had been baptized, she urged us, saying,
"If you have judged me to be faithful to

LIFE LESSONS

➤ Acts 16:14 — *The Lord opened her heart to respond to the things spoken by Paul.*

*N*o one will respond to the gospel message unless God goes before us and sends His Spirit to do a work in human hearts. Jesus said, "No one can come to Me unless it has been granted him from the Father" (John 6:65).

the Lord, come into my house and stay." And she prevailed upon us.
16 It happened that as we were going to the place of prayer, a slave-girl having a spirit of divination met us, who was bringing her masters much profit by fortune-telling.
17 Following after Paul and us, she kept crying out, saying, "These men are bond-servants of the Most High God, who are proclaiming to you the way of salvation."
18 She continued doing this for many days. But Paul was greatly annoyed, and turned and said to the spirit, "I command you in the name of Jesus Christ to come out of her!" And it came out at that very moment.
19 But when her masters saw that their hope of profit was gone, they seized Paul and Silas and dragged them into the market place before the authorities,
20 and when they had brought them to the chief magistrates, they said, "These men are throwing our city into confusion, being Jews,
21 and are proclaiming customs which it is not lawful for us to accept or to observe, being Romans."

2 Chronicles 17:1—18:34

17 JEHOSHAPHAT his son then became king in his place, and made his position over Israel firm.
2 He placed troops in all the fortified cities of Judah, and set garrisons in the land of Judah and in the cities of Ephraim which Asa his father had captured.
3 The LORD was with Jehoshaphat because he followed the example of his father David's earlier days and did not seek the Baals,
4 but sought the God of his father, followed His commandments, and did not act as Israel did.
5 So the LORD established the kingdom in his control, and all Judah brought tribute to Jehoshaphat, and he had great riches and honor.
6 He took great pride in the ways of the LORD and again removed the high places and the Asherim from Judah.
7 Then in the third year of his reign he sent his officials, Ben-hail, Obadiah, Zechariah, Nethanel and Micaiah, to teach in the cities of Judah;
8 and with them the Levites, Shemaiah, Nethaniah, Zebadiah, Asahel, Shemiramoth, Jehonathan, Adonijah, Tobijah and Tobadonijah, the Levites; and with them Elishama and Jehoram, the priests.
9 They taught in Judah, *having* the book of the law of the LORD with them; and they went throughout all the cities of Judah and taught among the people.
10 Now the dread of the LORD was on all the kingdoms of the lands which *were* around Judah, so that they did not make war against Jehoshaphat.
11 Some of the Philistines brought gifts and silver as tribute to Jehoshaphat; the Arabians also brought him flocks, 7,700 rams and 7,700 male goats.
12 So Jehoshaphat grew greater and greater, and he built fortresses and store cities in Judah.

LIFE LESSONS

➤ 2 Chronicles 17:10 — *The dread of the LORD was on all the kingdoms of the lands which were around Judah, so that they did not make war against Jehoshaphat.*

*T*he Lord has untold weapons in His heavenly arsenal to protect His obedient people. Here He used a general sense of fear to keep Judah's enemies at bay. Who knows how the Lord is protecting you right now?

13 He had large supplies in the cities of Judah, and warriors, valiant men, in Jerusalem.

14 This was their muster according to their fathers' households: of Judah, commanders of thousands, Adnah *was* the commander, and with him 300,000 valiant warriors;

15 and next to him *was* Johanan the commander, and with him 280,000;

16 and next to him Amasiah the son of Zichri, who volunteered for the LORD, and with him 200,000 valiant warriors;

17 and of Benjamin, Eliada a valiant warrior, and with him 200,000 armed with bow and shield;

18 and next to him Jehozabad, and with him 180,000 equipped for war.

19 These are they who served the king, apart from those whom the king put in the fortified cities through all Judah.

18 NOW Jehoshaphat had great riches and honor; and he allied himself by marriage with Ahab.

2 Some years later he went down to *visit* Ahab at Samaria. And Ahab slaughtered many sheep and oxen for him and the people who were with him, and induced him to go up against Ramoth-gilead.

3 Ahab king of Israel said to Jehoshaphat king of Judah, "Will you go with me *against* Ramoth-gilead?" And he said to him, "I am as you are, and my people as your people, and we *will be* with you in the battle."

4 Moreover, Jehoshaphat said to the king of Israel, "Please inquire first for the word of the LORD."

5 Then the king of Israel assembled the prophets, four hundred men, and said to them, "Shall we go against Ramoth-gilead to battle, or shall I refrain?" And they said, "Go up, for God will give *it* into the hand of the king."

6 But Jehoshaphat said, "Is there not yet a prophet of the LORD here that we may inquire of him?"

7 The king of Israel said to Jehoshaphat, "There is yet one man by whom we may inquire of the LORD, but I hate him, for he never prophesies good concerning me but always evil. He is Micaiah, son of Imla." But Jehoshaphat said, "Let not the king say so."

8 Then the king of Israel called an officer and said, "Bring quickly Micaiah, Imla's son."

9 Now the king of Israel and Jehoshaphat the king of Judah were sitting each on his throne, arrayed in *their* robes, and *they* were sitting at the threshing floor at the entrance of the gate of Samaria; and all the prophets were prophesying before them.

10 Zedekiah the son of Chenaanah made horns of iron for himself and said, "Thus says the LORD, 'With these you shall gore the Arameans until they are consumed.'"

11 All the prophets were prophesying thus, saying, "Go up to Ramoth-gilead and succeed, for the LORD will give *it* into the hand of the king."

12 Then the messenger who went to summon Micaiah spoke to him saying, "Behold, the words of the prophets are uniformly favorable to the king. So please let your word be like one of them and speak favorably."

13 But Micaiah said, "As the LORD lives, what my God says, that I will speak."

14 When he came to the king, the king said to him, "Micaiah, shall we go to Ramoth-gilead to battle, or shall I refrain?" He said, "Go up and succeed, for they will be given into your hand."

15 Then the king said to him, "How many times must I adjure you to speak to me nothing but the truth in the name of the LORD?"

16 So he said,
"I saw all Israel
Scattered on the mountains,
Like sheep which have no shepherd;
And the LORD said,
'These have no master.
Let each of them return to his house in peace.'"

17 Then the king of Israel said to Jehoshaphat, "Did I not tell you that he would not prophesy good concerning me, but evil?"

18 Micaiah said, "Therefore, hear the word of the LORD. I saw the LORD sitting on His throne, and all the host of heaven standing on His right and on His left.

19 "The LORD said, 'Who will entice Ahab king of Israel to go up and fall at Ramoth-gilead?' And one said this while another said that.

20 "Then a spirit came forward and stood before the LORD and said, 'I will entice him.' And the LORD said to him, 'How?'

21 "He said, 'I will go and be a deceiving

spirit in the mouth of all his prophets.' Then He said, 'You are to entice *him* and prevail also. Go and do so.'

22 "Now therefore, behold, the LORD has put a deceiving spirit in the mouth of these your prophets, for the LORD has proclaimed disaster against you."

23 Then Zedekiah the son of Chenaanah came near and struck Micaiah on the cheek and said, "How did the Spirit of the LORD pass from me to speak to you?"

24 Micaiah said, "Behold, you will see on that day when you enter an inner room to hide yourself."

25 Then the king of Israel said, "Take Micaiah and return him to Amon the governor of the city and to Joash the king's son;

26 and say, 'Thus says the king, "Put this *man* in prison and feed him sparingly with bread and water until I return safely."'"

27 Micaiah said, "If you indeed return safely, the LORD has not spoken by me." And he said, "Listen, all you people."

28 So the king of Israel and Jehoshaphat king of Judah went up against Ramothgilead.

29 The king of Israel said to Jehoshaphat, "I will disguise myself and go into battle, but you put on your robes." So the king of Israel disguised himself, and they went into battle.

30 Now the king of Aram had commanded the captains of his chariots, saying, "Do not fight with small or great, but with the king of Israel alone."

31 So when the captains of the chariots saw Jehoshaphat, they said, "It is the king of Israel," and they turned aside to fight against him. But Jehoshaphat cried out, and the LORD helped him, and God diverted them from him.

32 When the captains of the chariots saw that it was not the king of Israel, they turned back from pursuing him.

33 A certain man drew his bow at random and struck the king of Israel in a joint of the armor. So he said to the driver of the chariot, "Turn around and take me out of the fight, for I am severely wounded."

34 The battle raged that day, and the king of Israel propped himself up in his chariot in front of the Arameans until the evening; and at sunset he died.

Psalm 81:11–16

11 "But My people did not listen to My voice,
And Israel did not obey Me.
12 "So I gave them over to the stubbornness of their heart,
To walk in their own devices.
13 "Oh that My people would listen to Me,
That Israel would walk in My ways!
14 "I would quickly subdue their enemies
And turn My hand against their adversaries.
15 "Those who hate the LORD would pretend obedience to Him,
And their time *of punishment* would be forever.
16 "But I would feed you with the finest of the wheat,
And with honey from the rock I would satisfy you."

LIFE LESSONS

2 Chronicles 18:31 — *Jehoshaphat cried out, and the LORD helped him.*

The Lord helped Jehoshaphat out of a tight spot he never should have been in. God is loving and merciful toward us, but we should never presume upon His grace. He warns us in Deuteronomy 6:16, 18, "You shall not put the LORD your God to the test. . . . You shall do what is right and good in the sight of the LORD, that it may be well with you."

2 Chronicles 18:33 — *A certain man drew his bow at random and struck the king of Israel in a joint of the armor.*

Though the Bible says this was a random action by some unknown man, this particular arrow had a divine appointment with the joints of Ahab's armor (1 Kin. 22:34). God can do whatever He pleases in order to fulfill His plans, even using seemingly haphazard events to further His will (Rom. 8:28).

Psalm 81:16 — *"With honey from the rock I would satisfy you."*

God loves to bless His people when we obey His commands. He wants us to always remember true satisfaction, peace, and joy come to us only through Him and not through any other means.

◈ Proverbs 20:26–28

26 A wise king winnows the wicked,
And drives the *threshing* wheel over
them.
27 The spirit of man is the lamp of the
LORD,
Searching all the innermost parts of
his being.
28 Loyalty and truth preserve the king,
And he upholds his throne by
righteousness.

◈ Acts 16:22–40

22 The crowd rose up together against
them, and the chief magistrates tore their
robes off them and proceeded to order
them to be beaten with rods.
23 When they had struck them with
many blows, they threw them into
prison, commanding the jailer to guard
them securely;
24 and he, having received such a command, threw them into the inner prison
and fastened their feet in the stocks.
25 But about midnight Paul and Silas
were praying and singing hymns of
praise to God, and the prisoners were
listening to them;
26 and suddenly there came a great
earthquake, so that the foundations of
the prison house were shaken; and immediately all the doors were opened and
everyone's chains were unfastened.
27 When the jailer awoke and saw the
prison doors opened, he drew his sword
and was about to kill himself, supposing
that the prisoners had escaped.

LIFE LESSONS

➤ Acts 16:25 — *But about midnight
Paul and Silas were praying and singing
hymns of praise to God.*

*P*aul and Silas had been attacked by a
mob, beaten by soldiers, thrown in
stocks and shoved into a cistern, which
served as a high-security prison cell. How
did they react? With prayer and singing!
Only the Spirit can produce such complete submission to the Father's will.

28 But Paul cried out with a loud voice,
saying, "Do not harm yourself, for we are
all here!"
29 And he called for lights and rushed
in, and trembling with fear he fell down
before Paul and Silas,
30 and after he brought them out, he
said, "Sirs, what must I do to be saved?"
31 They said, "Believe in the Lord
Jesus, and you will be saved, you and
your household."
32 And they spoke the word of the Lord
to him together with all who were in his
house.
33 And he took them that *very* hour of
the night and washed their wounds, and
immediately he was baptized, he and all
his *household*.
34 And he brought them into his house
and set food before them, and rejoiced
greatly, having believed in God with his
whole household.
35 Now when day came, the chief magistrates sent their policemen, saying,
"Release those men."
36 And the jailer reported these words
to Paul, *saying*, "The chief magistrates
have sent to release you. Therefore come
out now and go in peace."

Life Examples:

SILAS: Singing for Victory

ACTS 16:24–34

*A*s exhausted as he felt, Silas could
not sleep. The stale air in the inner
cell made breathing difficult, and the torment
of his wounds kept him from getting much-
needed sleep. Would he or Paul live to see
another day? Silas did not know.
Yet Silas neither meditated on injustice
nor despaired of his situation. Instead, faith
filled his heart. When Silas and Paul lifted
their voices in song, a violent earthquake
shook the prison. Soon they led the jailer and
his entire family to the Lord.
You have a song to sing as well. Though
your situation may feel overwhelming, are you
willing to trust God in your circumstances? Do
you believe no problem is beyond His power?
As you allow God to conduct the symphony of
your life, you will see Him shaking your own
prisons. Will you, like Silas, lift up your voice
to herald the coming victory?

37 But Paul said to them, "They have beaten us in public without trial, men who are Romans, and have thrown us into prison; and now are they sending us away secretly? No indeed! But let them come themselves and bring us out."
38 The policemen reported these words to the chief magistrates. They were afraid when they heard that they were Romans,
39 and they came and appealed to them, and when they had brought them out, they kept begging them to leave the city.
40 They went out of the prison and entered *the house of* Lydia, and when they saw the brethren, they encouraged them and departed.

✦ 2 Chronicles 19:1—20:17

19 THEN Jehoshaphat the king of Judah returned in safety to his house in Jerusalem.
2 Jehu the son of Hanani the seer went out to meet him and said to King Jehoshaphat, "Should you help the wicked and love those who hate the LORD and so *bring* wrath on yourself from the LORD?
3 "But there is *some* good in you, for you have removed the Asheroth from the land and you have set your heart to seek God."
4 So Jehoshaphat lived in Jerusalem and went out again among the people from Beersheba to the hill country of Ephraim and brought them back to the LORD, the God of their fathers.
5 He appointed judges in the land in all the fortified cities of Judah, city by city.
6 He said to the judges, "Consider what you are doing, for you do not judge for man but for the LORD who is with you when you render judgment.
7 "Now then let the fear of the LORD be upon you; be very careful what you do, for the LORD our God will have no part in unrighteousness or partiality or the taking of a bribe."
8 In Jerusalem also Jehoshaphat appointed some of the Levites and priests, and some of the heads of the fathers' *households* of Israel, for the judgment of the LORD and to judge disputes among the inhabitants of Jerusalem.
9 Then he charged them saying, "Thus you shall do in the fear of the LORD, faithfully and wholeheartedly.

10 "Whenever any dispute comes to you from your brethren who live in their cities, between blood and blood, between law and commandment, statutes and ordinances, you shall warn them so that they may not be guilty before the LORD, and wrath may *not* come on you and your brethren. Thus you shall do and you will not be guilty.
11 "Behold, Amariah the chief priest will be over you in all that pertains to the LORD, and Zebadiah the son of Ishmael, the ruler of the house of Judah, in all that pertains to the king. Also the Levites shall be officers before you. Act resolutely, and the LORD be with the upright."

20 NOW it came about after this that the sons of Moab and the sons of Ammon, together with some of the Meunites, came to make war against Jehoshaphat.
2 Then some came and reported to Jehoshaphat, saying, "A great multitude is coming against you from beyond the sea, out of Aram and behold, they are in Hazazon-tamar (that is Engedi)."
3 Jehoshaphat was afraid and turned his attention to seek the LORD, and proclaimed a fast throughout all Judah.
4 So Judah gathered together to seek help from the LORD; they even came from all the cities of Judah to seek the LORD.
5 Then Jehoshaphat stood in the assembly of Judah and Jerusalem, in the house of the LORD before the new court,
6 and he said, "O LORD, the God of our fathers, are You not God in the heavens? And are You not ruler over all the kingdoms of the nations? Power and might

LIFE PRINCIPLE 10

IF NECESSARY, GOD WILL MOVE HEAVEN AND
EARTH TO SHOW US HIS WILL.

2 CHRONICLES 20:12

God always wants the best for us, and
He is committed to showing us how to
follow the specific plan He has designed for
each of our lives. He wants us to listen for His
voice, to hear what He wants us to do, and
how He wants us to do it (Is. 30:19–21).

When we begin to wander from the course
God has set for us, He will take all kinds of
measures to capture our attention and protect
us from harm. He has a wide variety of ways to
help us to take notice, among them:

❶ A restless spirit
Sometimes God gets our attention by making us restless (Esth. 6). If you experience
restlessness deep within—something you cannot quite identify—then stop and pray, "Lord,
are You trying to say something to me?" Each
time God was about to move me from one
pastorate to another, I became very restless.

❷ A spoken word
God also gets our attenztion by using the
words of others. The Lord gave a message
both to young Samuel and to the old priest Eli
through this method (1 Sam. 3:4–18). If several people in a short span of time begin telling
you the same thing, then ask the Lord if He is
trying to speak to you through them.

❸ An unusual blessing
God may bless us in an unusual way to gain
our attention. Of course, if you are an overly
self-sufficient person, the Lord may more likely
use some other method to get your focus on
Him. But remember, no matter which method
He uses, it expresses His love.

❹ Unanswered prayer
Sometimes God will answer a prayer with
"no." Despite David's prayers for God to save
his infant son's life (the child born through the
king's adultery), the boy died (2 Sam. 12:15–
18). The Lord may remain silent to our prayers
as a way of prompting us to examine ourselves.

❺ Disappointment
When the nation of Israel refused God's
instruction to take possession of the Promised
Land, God judged the people for their unbelief. They quickly changed their minds and
announced they now desired to enter the land;

but the Lord said no, it was too late (Num.
14). God got their attention through a tremendous sense of disappointment. In a similar
way, the Lord may allow setbacks to keep us
from charting our own course.

❻ Extraordinary circumstances
Sometimes God will use unusual circumstances to get us to stop and listen. Moses saw
a flaming bush that did not burn up. As he
approached to investigate, the Lord spoke
to him from the fire (Ex. 3). You and I must
learn to look for the presence of God in every
circumstance of life. He leaves His footprints
and handiwork all around us.

❼ Defeat
God may use defeat to show us the truth.
Following their stunning victory over Jericho,
the Israelites approached a small town with
overconfidence and neglected to do what the
Lord had commanded (Josh. 7). God got
Joshua's attention by allowing the nation to
suffer an embarrassing defeat. But even this can
prove to be a great stepping-stone to success
when we pray, "Lord, what are You saying?
Help me to see where I have taken a wrong
turn."

❽ Financial troubles
In the time of the judges, when "every man
did what was right in his own eyes" (Judg.
17:6), the nation fell into idolatry and disobedience. God brought judgment through
the Midianites, who devastated the land. Only
when He took away every material belonging
did they cry out to Him (Judg. 6:3–6). The
Lord knew exactly what it would take to get
their attention. When they did return to Him,
He delivered them from their oppressors and
blessed them.

❾ Tragedy, sickness, and affliction
We should regard our tragedies and afflictions as reasons to inquire of the Lord, "What
are You trying to say?" When King Hezekiah
became prideful, God used illness to alert him
to the problem (2 Chr. 32:24). Similarly, when
Saul of Tarsus persecuted Christians, God
struck him with blindness—a tactic that certainly got his attention (Acts 9:1–19)!

The Father always knows exactly where you
are in your journey of faith and precisely what
it will take to get your attention. Stay alert;
notice if any of these divine methods are occur-
ring—or recurring—in your life. If they are, ask
Him what He wants to tell you. Be willing to
hear and obey what He says. ◆

are in Your hand so that no one can stand against You.

7 "Did You not, O our God, drive out the inhabitants of this land before Your people Israel and give it to the descendants of Abraham Your friend forever?

8 "They have lived in it, and have built You a sanctuary there for Your name, saying,

9 'Should evil come upon us, the sword, or judgment, or pestilence, or famine, we will stand before this house and before You (for Your name is in this house) and cry to You in our distress, and You will hear and deliver us.'

10 "Now behold, the sons of Ammon and Moab and Mount Seir, whom You did not let Israel invade when they came out of the land of Egypt (they turned aside from them and did not destroy them),

11 see how they are rewarding us by coming to drive us out from Your possession which You have given us as an inheritance.

12 "O our God, will You not judge them? For we are powerless before this great multitude who are coming against us; nor do we know what to do, but our eyes are on You."

13 All Judah was standing before the LORD, with their infants, their wives and their children.

14 Then in the midst of the assembly the Spirit of the LORD came upon Jahaziel the son of Zechariah, the son of Benaiah, the son of Jeiel, the son of Mattaniah, the Levite of the sons of Asaph;

15 and he said, "Listen, all Judah and the inhabitants of Jerusalem and King Jehoshaphat: thus says the LORD to you, 'Do not fear or be dismayed because of this great multitude, for the battle is not yours but God's.

16 'Tomorrow go down against them. Behold, they will come up by the ascent of Ziz, and you will find them at the end of the valley in front of the wilderness of Jeruel.

17 'You need not fight in this battle; station yourselves, stand and see the salvation of the LORD on your behalf, O Judah and Jerusalem.' Do not fear or be dismayed; tomorrow go out to face them, for the LORD is with you."

Psalm 82:1–8

A Psalm of Asaph.

82 GOD takes His stand in His own congregation;
He judges in the midst of the rulers.

2 How long will you judge unjustly
And show partiality to the wicked?
　　　　　　　　　　　　　　Selah.

3 Vindicate the weak and fatherless;
Do justice to the afflicted and destitute.

4 Rescue the weak and needy;
Deliver them out of the hand of the wicked.

5 They do not know nor do they understand;
They walk about in darkness;
All the foundations of the earth are shaken.

6 I said, "You are gods,
And all of you are sons of the Most High.

7 "Nevertheless you will die like men
And fall like any one of the princes."

8 Arise, O God, judge the earth!
For it is You who possesses all the nations.

LIFE LESSONS

2 Chronicles 20:15 — The battle is not yours but God's.

As believers, we never have to worry about how to engage our conflicts because they all belong to God. And being His, they are already won. Our responsibility is to obey whatever He instructs us to do and trust Him to show us His triumph. Always remember every blessing and success comes from the Lord, and no enemy will stand as long as He is leading the charge against them.

Psalm 82:6 — I said, "You are gods, and all of you are sons of the Most High."

Jesus quoted this verse to show He is the true Son of God and to highlight the staggering privilege of receiving the Word of God (John 10:34–36). Let us treat the Bible as the great gift it is, and daily feed upon it to honor the One who gave it to us.

Proverbs 20:29, 30

29 The glory of young men is their
        strength,
     And the honor of old men is their
        gray hair.
30 Stripes that wound scour away evil,
     And strokes *reach* the innermost
        parts.

Acts 17:1–15

17NOW when they had traveled
     through Amphipolis and Apollonia,
they came to Thessalonica, where there
was a synagogue of the Jews.
2   And according to Paul's custom, he
went to them, and for three Sabbaths
reasoned with them from the Scriptures,
3   explaining and giving evidence that
the Christ had to suffer and rise again
from the dead, and *saying*, "This Jesus
whom I am proclaiming to you is the
Christ."
4   And some of them were persuaded
and joined Paul and Silas, along with a
large number of the God-fearing Greeks
and a number of the leading women.
5   But the Jews, becoming jealous and
taking along some wicked men from
the market place, formed a mob and set
the city in an uproar; and attacking the
house of Jason, they were seeking to
bring them out to the people.
6   When they did not find them, they
began dragging Jason and some brethren before the city authorities, shouting,
"These men who have upset the world
have come here also;
7   and Jason has welcomed them, and
they all act contrary to the decrees of

Caesar, saying that there is another king,
Jesus."
8   They stirred up the crowd and the
city authorities who heard these things.
9   And when they had received a
pledge from Jason and the others, they
released them.
10 The brethren immediately sent Paul
and Silas away by night to Berea, and
when they arrived, they went into the
synagogue of the Jews.
11 Now these were more noble-minded
than those in Thessalonica, for they received the word with great eagerness,
examining the Scriptures daily *to see*
whether these things were so.
12 Therefore many of them believed,
along with a number of prominent Greek
women and men.
13 But when the Jews of Thessalonica
found out that the word of God had been
proclaimed by Paul in Berea also, they
came there as well, agitating and stirring
up the crowds.
14 Then immediately the brethren sent
Paul out to go as far as the sea; and Silas
and Timothy remained there.
15 Now those who escorted Paul brought
him as far as Athens; and receiving a
command for Silas and Timothy to come
to him as soon as possible, they left.

LIFE LESSONS

➢ **Acts 17:11 — *They received the word
with great eagerness, examining the
Scriptures daily to see whether these
things were so.***

*T*he Bereans didn't rely on Paul's word
     that the Old Testament prophesied
the ministry, sufferings, and resurrection of Christ. They studied Scripture for
themselves—and God commended them
for their diligence.

 JULY 13

2 Chronicles 20:18—22:12

18 Jehoshaphat bowed his head with
his face to the ground, and all Judah and
the inhabitants of Jerusalem fell down
before the LORD, worshiping the LORD.

19 The Levites, from the sons of the Kohathites and of the sons of the Korahites,
stood up to praise the LORD God of Israel,
with a very loud voice.
20 They rose early in the morning and
went out to the wilderness of Tekoa; and
when they went out, Jehoshaphat stood

and said, "Listen to me, O Judah and inhabitants of Jerusalem, put your trust in the LORD your God and you will be established. Put your trust in His prophets and succeed."

21 When he had consulted with the people, he appointed those who sang to the LORD and those who praised *Him* in holy attire, as they went out before the army and said, "Give thanks to the LORD, for His lovingkindness is everlasting."

➤ 22 When they began singing and praising, the LORD set ambushes against the sons of Ammon, Moab and Mount Seir, who had come against Judah; so they were routed.

23 For the sons of Ammon and Moab rose up against the inhabitants of Mount Seir destroying *them* completely; and when they had finished with the inhabitants of Seir, they helped to destroy one another.

24 When Judah came to the lookout of the wilderness, they looked toward the multitude, and behold, they *were* corpses lying on the ground, and no one had escaped.

➤ 25 When Jehoshaphat and his people came to take their spoil, they found much among them, *including* goods, garments and valuable things which they took for themselves, more than they could carry. And they were three days taking the spoil because there was so much.

26 Then on the fourth day they assembled in the valley of Beracah, for there they blessed the LORD. Therefore they have named that place "The Valley of Beracah" until today.

27 Every man of Judah and Jerusalem returned with Jehoshaphat at their head, returning to Jerusalem with joy, for the LORD had made them to rejoice over their enemies.

28 They came to Jerusalem with harps, lyres and trumpets to the house of the LORD.

29 And the dread of God was on all the kingdoms of the lands when they heard that the LORD had fought against the enemies of Israel.

30 So the kingdom of Jehoshaphat was at peace, for his God gave him rest on all sides.

31 Now Jehoshaphat reigned over Judah. He *was* thirty-five years old when he became king, and he reigned

in Jerusalem twenty-five years. And his mother's name *was* Azubah the daughter of Shilhi.

32 He walked in the way of his father Asa and did not depart from it, doing right in the sight of the LORD.

33 The high places, however, were not removed; the people had not yet directed their hearts to the God of their fathers.

34 Now the rest of the acts of Jehoshaphat, first to last, behold, they are written in the annals of Jehu the son of Hanani, which is recorded in the Book of the Kings of Israel.

35 After this Jehoshaphat king of Judah allied himself with Ahaziah king of Israel. He acted wickedly in so doing.

36 So he allied himself with him to

LIFE LESSONS

➤ **2 Chronicles 20:20 — *"Put your trust in the LORD your God and you will be established."***

*P*raise paves the way for a deep relationship with God and victory in our circumstances. When we begin to exalt Him, we become aware of how absolutely dependent upon Him we truly are and how completely able He is to help us. If you want to have a successful, fulfilling life, you can do no better than to worship the Lord and obey His Word.

➤ **2 Chronicles 20:22 — *When they began singing and praising, the LORD set ambushes against the sons of Ammon, Moab and Mount Seir.***

*I*t doesn't matter if God's commands don't make sense—like forming a choir to stand up to an army—obey them anyway. The Lord has already won our battles for us, and His interest in involving us is to build our faith. This is why He will often command us to do things that seem unreasonable—to see if we'll trust Him. We must always put all of our hope in His almighty hand.

➤ **2 Chronicles 20:25 — *They were three days taking the spoil because there was so much.***

*T*he very thing Satan had intended to use against God's people, the Lord used to bless and enrich them. The Father loves to answer the prayers of His obedient people in surprising ways!

ANSWERS TO LIFE'S QUESTIONS

What is our authority in prayer?

2 CHRONICLES 20:18–22

One day King Jehoshaphat and the people of Judah saw that a great multitude had risen up against them. Three groups of aggressors—the Moabites, the Ammonites, and the Meunites—launched a major assault against Jerusalem.

Jehoshaphat felt deeply afraid, but rather than cower in fear, he "turned his attention to seek the LORD" (2 Chr. 20:3). He proclaimed a fast throughout all Judah and called the people together to join him in seeking the Lord. He stood before the people in the house of the Lord and prayed, "O LORD, the God of our fathers, are You not God in the heavens? And are you not ruler over all the kingdoms of the nations? Power and might are in Your hand so that no one can stand against You" (2 Chr. 20:6).

Jehoshaphat did not express doubt in the power of God, but rather publicly proclaimed his trust in almighty God. He declared he was putting all of his hope in the Lord of unlimited power. In addition, Jehoshaphat stated very plainly that he, even as king of Judah, stood in total humility and weakness before the Lord. He claimed no authority in or for himself. He said to God:

- You are the One who gave us this land.
- You are the One who has allowed Your people to dwell in it and build a sanctuary in it.
- You are the One who said we should cry out to You in our affliction and You would hear and save us.
- You are the One who told us to spare these enemy people when we first came to occupy this land.
- You are the only One capable of judging these enemies who are rising against us—we have no power and no plan.

He concluded his prayer by admitting, "Our eyes are on You" (2 Chr. 20:12). In effect, Jehoshaphat was saying, "If You don't exercise Your authority in this matter, we are doomed. We are putting our entire trust and confidence in You and You alone."

We see no trace of egotism in Jehoshaphat. He made no demand of God to do something He did not desire to do. Jehoshaphat claimed no authority in or power for himself. However, he wisely recognized all power and authority rest in the Lord alone—and from that understanding he petitioned the God of heaven and was blessed with the victory (1 Chr. 20:22–24).

---

make ships to go to Tarshish, and they made the ships in Ezion-geber.

➤ 37 Then Eliezer the son of Dodavahu of Mareshah prophesied against Jehoshaphat saying, "Because you have allied yourself with Ahaziah, the LORD has destroyed your works." So the ships were broken and could not go to Tarshish.

LIFE LESSONS

➤ **2 Chronicles 20:37 — "Because you have allied yourself with Ahaziah, the LORD has destroyed your works."**

Most of us have at least one "blind spot" that gives us trouble. Jehoshaphat's was his tendency to make foolish alliances outside of God's will. He discovered whatever we acquire outside of the will of God turns to ashes. The Bible tells us, "Do not be deceived: 'Bad company corrupts good morals'" (1 Cor. 15:33). Through his unholy alliance with the wicked Ahab and Ahaziah, Jehoshaphat ended up ruining his own family.

21 THEN Jehoshaphat slept with his fathers and was buried with his fathers in the city of David, and Jehoram his son became king in his place.
2 He had brothers, the sons of Jehoshaphat: Azariah, Jehiel, Zechariah, Azaryahu, Michael and Shephatiah. All these *were* the sons of Jehoshaphat king of Israel.
3 Their father gave them many gifts of silver, gold and precious things, with fortified cities in Judah, but he gave the kingdom to Jehoram because he was the firstborn.
4 Now when Jehoram had taken over the kingdom of his father and made himself secure, he killed all his brothers with the sword, and some of the rulers of Israel also.
5 Jehoram *was* thirty-two years old when he became king, and he reigned eight years in Jerusalem.
6 He walked in the way of the kings of Israel, just as the house of Ahab did (for Ahab's daughter was his wife), and he did evil in the sight of the LORD.
7 Yet the LORD was not willing to

destroy the house of David because of the covenant which He had made with David, and since He had promised to give a lamp to him and his sons forever.

8 In his days Edom revolted against the rule of Judah and set up a king over themselves.

9 Then Jehoram crossed over with his commanders and all his chariots with him. And he arose by night and struck down the Edomites who were surrounding him and the commanders of the chariots.

10 So Edom revolted against Judah to this day. Then Libnah revolted at the same time against his rule, because he had forsaken the LORD God of his fathers.

11 Moreover, he made high places in the mountains of Judah, and caused the inhabitants of Jerusalem to play the harlot and led Judah astray.

12 Then a letter came to him from Elijah the prophet saying, "Thus says the LORD God of your father David, 'Because you have not walked in the ways of Jehoshaphat your father and the ways of Asa king of Judah,

13 but have walked in the way of the kings of Israel, and have caused Judah and the inhabitants of Jerusalem to play the harlot as the house of Ahab played the harlot, and you have also killed your brothers, your own family, who were better than you,

14 behold, the LORD is going to strike your people, your sons, your wives and all your possessions with a great calamity;

15 and you will suffer severe sickness, a disease of your bowels, until your bowels come out because of the sickness, day by day.'"

16 Then the LORD stirred up against Jehoram the spirit of the Philistines and the Arabs who bordered the Ethiopians;

17 and they came against Judah and invaded it, and carried away all the possessions found in the king's house together with his sons and his wives, so that no son was left to him except Jehoahaz, the youngest of his sons.

18 So after all this the LORD smote him in his bowels with an incurable sickness.

19 Now it came about in the course of time, at the end of two years, that his bowels came out because of his sickness and he died in great pain. And his people made no fire for him like the fire for his fathers.

20 He was thirty-two years old when he became king, and he reigned in Jerusalem eight years; and he departed with no one's regret, and they buried him in the city of David, but not in the tombs of the kings.

22 THEN the inhabitants of Jerusalem made Ahaziah, his youngest son, king in his place, for the band of men who came with the Arabs to the camp had slain all the older *sons.* So Ahaziah the son of Jehoram king of Judah began to reign.

2 Ahaziah *was* twenty-two years old when he became king, and he reigned one year in Jerusalem. And his mother's name was Athaliah, the granddaughter of Omri.

3 He also walked in the ways of the house of Ahab, for his mother was his counselor to do wickedly.

4 He did evil in the sight of the LORD like the house of Ahab, for they were his counselors after the death of his father, to his destruction.

5 He also walked according to their counsel, and went with Jehoram the son of Ahab king of Israel to wage war against Hazael king of Aram at Ramoth-gilead. But the Arameans wounded Joram.

6 So he returned to be healed in Jezreel of the wounds which they had inflicted on him at Ramah, when he fought against Hazael king of Aram. And Ahaziah, the son of Jehoram king of Judah, went down to see Jehoram the son of Ahab in Jezreel, because he was sick.

7 Now the destruction of Ahaziah was from God, in that he went to Joram. For when he came, he went out with Jehoram against Jehu the son of Nimshi, whom the LORD had anointed to cut off the house of Ahab.

8 It came about when Jehu was executing judgment on the house of Ahab, he found the princes of Judah and the sons of Ahaziah's brothers ministering to Ahaziah, and slew them.

9 He also sought Ahaziah, and they caught him while he was hiding in Samaria; they brought him to Jehu, put him to death and buried him. For they said, "He is the son of Jehoshaphat, who

sought the LORD with all his heart." So there was no one of the house of Ahaziah to retain the power of the kingdom.

10 Now when Athaliah the mother of Ahaziah saw that her son was dead, she rose and destroyed all the royal offspring of the house of Judah.

11 But Jehoshabeath the king's daughter took Joash the son of Ahaziah, and stole him from among the king's sons who were being put to death, and placed him and his nurse in the bedroom. So Jehoshabeath, the daughter of King Jehoram, the wife of Jehoiada the priest (for she was the sister of Ahaziah), hid him from Athaliah so that she would not put him to death.

12 He was hidden with them in the house of God six years while Athaliah reigned over the land.

Psalm 83:1–8

A Song, a Psalm of Asaph.

83 O GOD, do not remain quiet; Do not be silent and, O God, do not be still.

2 For behold, Your enemies make an uproar,
And those who hate You have exalted themselves.

3 They make shrewd plans against Your people,
And conspire together against Your treasured ones.

4 They have said, "Come, and let us wipe them out as a nation,
That the name of Israel be remembered no more."

5 For they have conspired together with one mind;

6 The tents of Edom and the Ishmaelites,
Moab and the Hagrites;

7 Gebal and Ammon and Amalek,
Philistia with the inhabitants of Tyre;

8 Assyria also has joined with them;
They have become a help to the children of Lot.   Selah.

Proverbs 21:1

21 THE king's heart is *like* channels of water in the hand of the LORD;
He turns it wherever He wishes.

Acts 17:16–34

16 Now while Paul was waiting for them at Athens, his spirit was being provoked within him as he was observing the city full of idols.

17 So he was reasoning in the synagogue with the Jews and the God-fearing *Gentiles*, and in the market place every day with those who happened to be present.

18 And also some of the Epicurean and Stoic philosophers were conversing with him. Some were saying, "What would this idle babbler wish to say?" Others, "He seems to be a proclaimer of strange deities,"—because he was preaching Jesus and the resurrection.

19 And they took him and brought him to the Areopagus, saying, "May we know what this new teaching is which you are proclaiming?

20 "For you are bringing some strange things to our ears; so we want to know what these things mean."

21 (Now all the Athenians and the strangers visiting there used to spend their time in nothing other than telling or hearing something new.)

22 So Paul stood in the midst of the Areopagus and said, "Men of Athens, I observe that you are very religious in all respects.

23 "For while I was passing through and examining the objects of your worship, I also found an altar with this inscription,

---

LIFE LESSONS

➤ **Psalm 83:1 —** *O God, do not remain quiet; do not be silent and, O God, do not be still.*

The Book of Psalms is full of pleas for God to act in power and to rescue His beleaguered people. Often the Lord does not act until we acknowledge we're helpless on our own to resolve our troubles. That way, when He acts, He receives all the glory.

'TO AN UNKNOWN GOD.' Therefore what you worship in ignorance, this I proclaim to you.

24 "The God who made the world and all things in it, since He is Lord of heaven and earth, does not dwell in temples made with hands;

25 nor is He served by human hands, as though He needed anything, since He Himself gives to all *people* life and breath and all things;

26 and He made from one *man* every nation of mankind to live on all the face of the earth, having determined *their* appointed times and the boundaries of their habitation,

27 that they would seek God, if perhaps they might grope for Him and find Him, though He is not far from each one of us;

28 for in Him we live and move and exist, as even some of your own poets have said, 'For we also are His children.'

29 "Being then the children of God, we ought not to think that the Divine Nature is like gold or silver or stone, an image formed by the art and thought of man.

30 "Therefore having overlooked the times of ignorance, God is now declaring to men that all *people* everywhere should repent,

31 because He has fixed a day in which He will judge the world in righteousness through a Man whom He has appointed, having furnished proof to all men by raising Him from the dead."

32 Now when they heard of the resurrection of the dead, some *began* to sneer, but others said, "We shall hear you again concerning this."

33 So Paul went out of their midst.

34 But some men joined him and believed, among whom also were Dionysius the Areopagite and a woman named Damaris and others with them.

2 Chronicles 23:1—24:27

23 NOW in the seventh year Jehoiada strengthened himself, and took captains of hundreds: Azariah the son of Jeroham, Ishmael the son of Johanan, Azariah the son of Obed, Maaseiah the son of Adaiah, and Elishaphat the son of Zichri, *and they entered* into a covenant with him.

2 They went throughout Judah and gathered the Levites from all the cities of Judah, and the heads of the fathers' *households* of Israel, and they came to Jerusalem.

3 Then all the assembly made a covenant with the king in the house of God. And Jehoiada said to them, "Behold, the king's son shall reign, as the LORD has spoken concerning the sons of David.

4 "This is the thing which you shall do: one third of you, of the priests and Levites who come in on the sabbath, *shall be* gatekeepers,

5 and one third *shall be* at the king's house, and a third at the Gate of the Foundation; and all the people *shall be* in the courts of the house of the LORD.

6 "But let no one enter the house of the LORD except the priests and the ministering Levites; they may enter, for they are holy. And let all the people keep the charge of the LORD.

7 "The Levites will surround the king, each man with his weapons in his hand; and whoever enters the house, let him be killed. Thus be with the king when he comes in and when he goes out."

8 So the Levites and all Judah did according to all that Jehoiada the priest commanded. And each one of them took

his men who were to come in on the sabbath, with those who were to go out on the sabbath, for Jehoiada the priest did not dismiss *any of* the divisions.

9 Then Jehoiada the priest gave to the captains of hundreds the spears and the large and small shields which had been King David's, which were in the house of God.

10 He stationed all the people, each man with his weapon in his hand, from the right side of the house to the left side of the house, by the altar and by the house, around the king.

11 Then they brought out the king's son and put the crown on him, and *gave him* the testimony and made him king. And Jehoiada and his sons anointed him and said, "*Long* live the king!"

12 When Athaliah heard the noise of the people running and praising the king, she came into the house of the LORD to the people.

13 She looked, and behold, the king was standing by his pillar at the entrance, and the captains and the trumpeters *were* beside the king. And all the people of the land rejoiced and blew trumpets, the singers with *their* musical instruments leading the praise. Then Athaliah tore her clothes and said, "Treason! Treason!"

14 Jehoiada the priest brought out the captains of hundreds who were appointed over the army and said to them, "Bring her out between the ranks; and whoever follows her, put to death with the sword." For the priest said, "Let her not be put to death in the house of the LORD."

15 So they seized her, and when she arrived at the entrance of the Horse Gate of the king's house, they put her to death there.

16 Then Jehoiada made a covenant between himself and all the people and the king, that they would be the LORD's people.

17 And all the people went to the house of Baal and tore it down, and they broke in pieces his altars and his images, and killed Mattan the priest of Baal before the altars.

18 Moreover, Jehoiada placed the offices of the house of the LORD under the authority of the Levitical priests, whom David had assigned over the house of the LORD, to offer the burnt offerings of the LORD, as it is written in the law of Moses—with rejoicing and singing according to the order of David.

19 He stationed the gatekeepers of the house of the LORD, so that no one would enter *who was* in any way unclean.

20 He took the captains of hundreds, the nobles, the rulers of the people and all the people of the land, and brought the king down from the house of the LORD, and came through the upper gate to the king's house. And they placed the king upon the royal throne.

21 So all of the people of the land rejoiced and the city was quiet. For they had put Athaliah to death with the sword.

24 JOASH *was* seven years old when he became king, and he reigned forty years in Jerusalem; and his mother's name *was* Zibiah from Beersheba.

2 Joash did what was right in the sight of the LORD all the days of Jehoiada the priest.

3 Jehoiada took two wives for him, and he became the father of sons and daughters.

4 Now it came about after this that Joash decided to restore the house of the LORD.

5 He gathered the priests and Levites and said to them, "Go out to the cities of Judah and collect money from all Israel to repair the house of your God annually, and you shall do the matter quickly." But the Levites did not act quickly.

6 So the king summoned Jehoiada the chief *priest* and said to him, "Why have you not required the Levites to bring in from Judah and from Jerusalem the levy *fixed by* Moses the servant of the LORD on the congregation of Israel for the tent of the testimony?"

7 For the sons of the wicked Athaliah had broken into the house of God and even used the holy things of the house of the LORD for the Baals.

8 So the king commanded, and they made a chest and set it outside by the gate of the house of the LORD.

9 They made a proclamation in Judah and Jerusalem to bring to the LORD the levy *fixed by* Moses the servant of God on Israel in the wilderness.

10 All the officers and all the people rejoiced and brought in their levies and dropped *them* into the chest until they had finished.

WHAT THE BIBLE SAYS ABOUT
Avoiding the Disaster of Drifting

2 Chronicles 24

King Joash drifted. Though he started out as a godly man who loved and obeyed the Lord, once the positive influence in his life—Jehoida the priest—died, it was all downhill. Second Chronicles 24:17, 18 explains, "The officials of Judah came and bowed down to the king, and the king listened to them. They abandoned the house of the LORD, the God of their fathers, and served the Asherim and the idols; so wrath came."

Joash rejected God and died a hated, apostate, evil king, who wasn't even good enough to be buried in the tomb with the other kings of Judah (see 2 Chr. 24:24, 25). He drifted away from the Lord because he wasn't anchored in God's truth. Rather, he became caught up in the current of other people's opinions, and that led him to destruction.

Have you found yourself drifting in your spiritual life? You're not reading the Bible as often or getting on your knees in prayer before God like you once did. Maybe you've taken up with the wrong crowd and haven't attended worship services in a long time. The most disturbing part of it is you just don't feel God's presence anymore. Something is happening to your spiritual life—and it isn't good. You're drifting, which means you're headed for trouble.

It's very easy to drift because you get caught up in the ways of the world. On the other hand, it takes a great deal of effort to stay on track with God because you're constantly fighting the world's current. This is why any one of us can drift. When we get tired or lazy—or we lose the person who helps us stay on track—we're all in danger of neglecting our relationships with Him.

Understand God wants to give you purpose and direction for your life—direction that will lead you to abundant life, rather than the ruin of drifting. This is why God disciplines disobedience. Hebrews 12:10 tells us, "He disciplines us for our good, so that we may share His holiness." God won't allow us to drift away from His Word, His will, or His purpose for our lives without divine discipline because He loves us and wants what's best for us. However, God also wants us to have a positive, godly role in His kingdom work, and we can't as long as we're participating in a life of sin.

So, how do we stop ourselves from drifting?
1. *We prevent ourselves from drifting by anchoring to the Word of God.*

First, we must be anchored to the Word of God. Everything we need to know—everything that will keep us safely on course—is in the Bible, and God wants to teach us through it. He lifts verses off its pages and applies them to our minds and hearts, giving us clear direction. Whenever we need counsel about what to do, we can always look to God's Word.
2. *We prevent ourselves from drifting by obeying the Word of God.*

We shouldn't only read the Bible; rather, we should think about it, absorb it, and do as it tells us to do. In order to stop ourselves from drifting, we must obey God's Word and make it an integral part of our lives. We've got to be willing to submit to whatever He commands us to do.
3. *We prevent ourselves from drifting by surrendering our lives to God.*

The third way we stop ourselves from drifting is very simple, but also extremely difficult: We must surrender our lives completely to God and submit ourselves to Him before we get out of bed each morning. Begin the day with this simple prayer: "Lord Jesus, I surrender my entire life to You today. I am completely Yours." Then, when some conflict, challenge, or temptation comes along, the Spirit of God will remind us we have committed ourselves to obedience.
4. *We prevent ourselves from drifting by staying on guard.*

Understand Satan is an enemy who will do whatever it takes to get us to drift away from God. Therefore, we must stay on guard against the schemes of the enemy.

Have you been drifting? Do you lack the power and joy of the Christian life? How do you get back on track when you've been drifting? First, acknowledge you've been drifting away from God by confessing your sin. Second, repent. This means you admit what you should be doing, which is being wholeheartedly devoted to your Lord and Savior.

If you don't change your course, you're ultimately going to destroy your life like King Joash did. But if you get right with God, you'll be back on track to experience His very best for your life. ◉

11 It came about whenever the chest was brought in to the king's officer by the Levites, and when they saw that there was much money, then the king's scribe and the chief priest's officer would come, empty the chest, take it, and return it to its place. Thus they did daily and collected much money.
12 The king and Jehoiada gave it to those who did the work of the service of the house of the LORD; and they hired masons and carpenters to restore the house of the LORD, and also workers in iron and bronze to repair the house of the LORD.
13 So the workmen labored, and the repair work progressed in their hands, and they restored the house of God according to its specifications and strengthened it.
14 When they had finished, they brought the rest of the money before the king and Jehoiada; and it was made into utensils for the house of the LORD, utensils for the service and the burnt offering, and pans and utensils of gold and silver. And they offered burnt offerings in the house of the LORD continually all the days of Jehoiada.
15 Now when Jehoiada reached a ripe old age he died; he was one hundred and thirty years old at his death.
16 They buried him in the city of David among the kings, because he had done well in Israel and to God and His house.
17 But after the death of Jehoiada the officials of Judah came and bowed down to the king, and the king listened to them.
18 They abandoned the house of the LORD, the God of their fathers, and served the Asherim and the idols; so wrath came upon Judah and Jerusalem for this their guilt.
19 Yet He sent prophets to them to bring them back to the LORD; though they testified against them, they would not listen.
20 Then the Spirit of God came on Zechariah the son of Jehoiada the priest; and he stood above the people and said to them, "Thus God has said, 'Why do you transgress the commandments of the LORD and do not prosper? Because you have forsaken the LORD, He has also forsaken you.'"
21 So they conspired against him and at the command of the king they stoned him to death in the court of the house of the LORD.
22 Thus Joash the king did not remember the kindness which his father Je-

hoiada had shown him, but he murdered his son. And as he died he said, "May the LORD see and avenge!"
23 Now it happened at the turn of the year that the army of the Arameans came up against him; and they came to Judah and Jerusalem, destroyed all the officials of the people from among the people, and sent all their spoil to the king of Damascus.
24 Indeed the army of the Arameans came with a small number of men; yet the LORD delivered a very great army into their hands, because they had forsaken the LORD, the God of their fathers. Thus they executed judgment on Joash.
25 When they had departed from him (for they left him very sick), his own servants conspired against him because of the blood of the son of Jehoiada the priest, and murdered him on his bed. So he died, and they buried him in the city of David, but they did not bury him in the tombs of the kings.
26 Now these are those who conspired against him: Zabad the son of Shimeath the Ammonitess, and Jehozabad the son of Shimrith the Moabitess.
27 As to his sons and the many oracles against him and the rebuilding of the house of God, behold, they are written in the treatise of the Book of the Kings. Then Amaziah his son became king in his place.

Psalm 83:9–18

9 Deal with them as with Midian,
As with Sisera and Jabin at the torrent of Kishon,

LIFE LESSONS

➤ 2 Chronicles 24:24 — The LORD delivered a very great army into their hands, because they had forsaken the LORD, the God of their fathers.

Just as God handed over huge enemy armies to the small but faithful forces of Judah (2 Chr. 14:12; 20:22), so He handed Joash's huge but unfaithful army over to a small pagan force. The presence of God and our obedience to Him—not the size of the army—are what really matter in every battle.

10 Who were destroyed at En-dor,
    Who became as dung for the
        ground.
11 Make their nobles like Oreb and
        Zeeb
    And all their princes like Zebah and
        Zalmunna,
12 Who said, "Let us possess for
        ourselves
    The pastures of God."
13 O my God, make them like the
        whirling dust,
    Like chaff before the wind.
14 Like fire that burns the forest
    And like a flame that sets the
        mountains on fire,
15 So pursue them with Your tempest
    And terrify them with Your storm.
16 Fill their faces with dishonor,
    That they may seek Your name,
        O LORD.
17 Let them be ashamed and dismayed
        forever,
    And let them be humiliated and
        perish,
18 That they may know that You
        alone, whose name is the LORD,
    Are the Most High over all the
        earth.

✦ Proverbs 21:2, 3

2   Every man's way is right in his own
        eyes,
    But the LORD weighs the hearts.
3   To do righteousness and justice
    Is desired by the LORD more than
        sacrifice.

✦ Acts 18:1–28

18 AFTER these things he left Athens
    and went to Corinth.
2   And he found a Jew named Aquila,
a native of Pontus, having recently come
from Italy with his wife Priscilla, because
Claudius had commanded all the Jews to
leave Rome. He came to them,
3   and because he was of the same
trade, he stayed with them and they were
working, for by trade they were tent-
makers.
4   And he was reasoning in the synagogue every Sabbath and trying to persuade Jews and Greeks.
5   But when Silas and Timothy came
down from Macedonia, Paul *began* devoting himself completely to the word,
solemnly testifying to the Jews that
Jesus was the Christ.
6   But when they resisted and blasphemed, he shook out his garments and
said to them, "Your blood *be* on your
own heads! I am clean. From now on I
will go to the Gentiles."
7   Then he left there and went to the
house of a man named Titius Justus, a
worshiper of God, whose house was next
to the synagogue.
8   Crispus, the leader of the synagogue,
believed in the Lord with all his household, and many of the Corinthians when
they heard were believing and being
baptized.
9   And the Lord said to Paul in the
night by a vision, "Do not be afraid *any
longer,* but go on speaking and do not be
silent;
10 for I am with you, and no man will
attack you in order to harm you, for I
have many people in this city."
11 And he settled *there* a year and six
months, teaching the word of God among
them.

LIFE LESSONS

➤ **Proverbs 21:3** — *To do righteousness
and justice is desired by the LORD more
than sacrifice.*

God wants your heart. He is not interested in outward compliance without
an inward desire to willingly and joyfully
obey Him. In fact, He hates religious
pretense because it shows contempt for
His chief desire—which is for a deep,
intimate relationship with us (Amos
5:21–24).

➤ **Acts 18:4** — *He was reasoning in the
synagogue every Sabbath and trying to
persuade Jews and Greeks.*

Paul had a Bible-centered, thoughtful
approach to evangelism. He persuaded people of the truth of the gospel
and was able to respond to others' questions because of His knowledge of God's
Word and submission to the Spirit. We
must be ready to do the same (2 Tim.
2:15; 2 Pet. 3:15).

12 But while Gallio was proconsul of Achaia, the Jews with one accord rose up against Paul and brought him before the judgment seat,
13 saying, "This man persuades men to worship God contrary to the law."
14 But when Paul was about to open his mouth, Gallio said to the Jews, "If it were a matter of wrong or of vicious crime, O Jews, it would be reasonable for me to put up with you;
15 but if there are questions about words and names and your own law, look after it yourselves; I am unwilling to be a judge of these matters."
16 And he drove them away from the judgment seat.
17 And they all took hold of Sosthenes, the leader of the synagogue, and *began* beating him in front of the judgment seat. But Gallio was not concerned about any of these things.
18 Paul, having remained many days longer, took leave of the brethren and put out to sea for Syria, and with him were Priscilla and Aquila. In Cenchrea he had his hair cut, for he was keeping a vow.
19 They came to Ephesus, and he left them there. Now he himself entered the synagogue and reasoned with the Jews.
20 When they asked him to stay for a longer time, he did not consent,
21 but taking leave of them and saying, "I will return to you again if God wills," he set sail from Ephesus.
22 When he had landed at Caesarea, he went up and greeted the church, and went down to Antioch.
23 And having spent some time *there*, he left and passed successively through the Galatian region and Phrygia, strengthening all the disciples.
24 Now a Jew named Apollos, an Alexandrian by birth, an eloquent man, came to Ephesus; and he was mighty in the Scriptures.

LIFE LESSONS

➤ **Acts 18:9, 10 — *"Go on speaking and do not be silent; for I am with you, and no man will attack you in order to harm you, for I have many people in this city."***

$\mathcal{P}$aul took courage in his evangelistic efforts because: (1) Jesus told him to keep speaking; (2) He promised to be with him; (3) He promised to protect him; and (4) He promised him success. We can take courage for identical reasons. Every time God calls us to do anything, He assures us He will be with us.

➤ **Acts 18:27, 28 — *He greatly helped those who had believed through grace . . . demonstrating by the Scriptures that Jesus was the Christ.***

$\mathcal{T}$hrough grace people believe in Christ, and through grace they come to understand His will by grasping the instruction of the Bible. And through grace God gives us gifted teachers to help us understand.

25 This man had been instructed in the way of the Lord; and being fervent in spirit, he was speaking and teaching accurately the things concerning Jesus, being acquainted only with the baptism of John;
26 and he began to speak out boldly in the synagogue. But when Priscilla and Aquila heard him, they took him aside and explained to him the way of God more accurately.
27 And when he wanted to go across ◄ to Achaia, the brethren encouraged him and wrote to the disciples to welcome him; and when he had arrived, he greatly helped those who had believed through grace,
28 for he powerfully refuted the Jews in public, demonstrating by the Scriptures that Jesus was the Christ.

JULY 15

◈ 2 Chronicles 25:1—27:9

25 AMAZIAH was twenty-five years old when he became king, and he reigned twenty-nine years in Jerusalem. And his mother's name was Jehoaddan of Jerusalem.
2 He did right in the sight of the LORD, yet not with a whole heart.

3 Now it came about as soon as the kingdom was firmly in his grasp, that he killed his servants who had slain his father the king.

4 However, he did not put their children to death, but *did* as it is written in the law in the book of Moses, which the LORD commanded, saying, "Fathers shall not be put to death for sons, nor sons be put to death for fathers, but each shall be put to death for his own sin."

5 Moreover, Amaziah assembled Judah and appointed them according to *their* fathers' households under commanders of thousands and commanders of hundreds throughout Judah and Benjamin; and he took a census of those from twenty years old and upward and found them to be 300,000 choice men, *able* to go to war *and* handle spear and shield.

6 He hired also 100,000 valiant warriors out of Israel for one hundred talents of silver.

7 But a man of God came to him saying, "O king, do not let the army of Israel go with you, for the LORD is not with Israel *nor with* any of the sons of Ephraim.

8 "But if you do go, do *it*, be strong for the battle; *yet* God will bring you down before the enemy, for God has power to help and to bring down."

➤ 9 Amaziah said to the man of God, "But what *shall we* do for the hundred talents which I have given to the troops of Israel?" And the man of God answered, "The LORD has much more to give you than this."

10 Then Amaziah dismissed them, the troops which came to him from Ephraim, to go home; so their anger burned against Judah and they returned home in fierce anger.

11 Now Amaziah strengthened himself and led his people forth, and went to the Valley of Salt and struck down 10,000 of the sons of Seir.

---

12 The sons of Judah also captured 10,000 alive and brought them to the top of the cliff and threw them down from the top of the cliff, so that they were all dashed to pieces.

13 But the troops whom Amaziah sent back from going with him to battle, raided the cities of Judah, from Samaria to Beth-horon, and struck down 3,000 of them and plundered much spoil.

14 Now after Amaziah came from slaughtering the Edomites, he brought the gods of the sons of Seir, set them up as his gods, bowed down before them and burned incense to them.

15 Then the anger of the LORD burned against Amaziah, and He sent him a prophet who said to him, "Why have you sought the gods of the people who have not delivered their own people from your hand?"

16 As he was talking with him, the king said to him, "Have we appointed you a royal counselor? Stop! Why should you be struck down?" Then the prophet stopped and said, "I know that God has planned to destroy you, because you have done this and have not listened to my counsel."

17 Then Amaziah king of Judah took counsel and sent to Joash the son of Jehoahaz the son of Jehu, the king of Israel, saying, "Come, let us face each other."

18 Joash the king of Israel sent to Amaziah king of Judah, saying, "The thorn bush which was in Lebanon sent to the cedar which was in Lebanon, saying, 'Give your daughter to my son in marriage.' But there passed by a wild beast that was in Lebanon and trampled the thorn bush.

19 "You said, 'Behold, you have defeated Edom.' And your heart has become proud in boasting. Now stay at home; for why should you provoke trouble so that you, even you, would fall and Judah with you?"

20 But Amaziah would not listen, for it was from God, that He might deliver them into the hand *of Joash* because they had sought the gods of Edom.

21 So Joash king of Israel went up, and he and Amaziah king of Judah faced each other at Beth-shemesh, which belonged to Judah.

22 Judah was defeated by Israel, and they fled each to his tent.

23 Then Joash king of Israel captured Amaziah king of Judah, the son of Joash the son of Jehoahaz, at Beth-shemesh, and brought him to Jerusalem and tore down the wall of Jerusalem from the Gate of Ephraim to the Corner Gate, 400 cubits.

24 *He took* all the gold and silver and all the utensils which were found in the house of God with Obed-edom, and the treasures of the king's house, the hostages also, and returned to Samaria.

25 And Amaziah, the son of Joash king of Judah, lived fifteen years after the death of Joash, son of Jehoahaz, king of Israel.

26 Now the rest of the acts of Amaziah, from first to last, behold, are they not written in the Book of the Kings of Judah and Israel?

27 From the time that Amaziah turned away from following the LORD they conspired against him in Jerusalem, and he fled to Lachish; but they sent after him to Lachish and killed him there.

28 Then they brought him on horses and buried him with his fathers in the city of Judah.

26 AND all the people of Judah took Uzziah, who *was* sixteen years old, and made him king in the place of his father Amaziah.

2 He built Eloth and restored it to Judah after the king slept with his fathers.

3 Uzziah was sixteen years old when he became king, and he reigned fifty-two years in Jerusalem; and his mother's name was Jechiliah of Jerusalem.

4 He did right in the sight of the LORD according to all that his father Amaziah had done.

5 He continued to seek God in the days of Zechariah, who had understanding through the vision of God; and as long as he sought the LORD, God prospered him.

6 Now he went out and warred against the Philistines, and broke down the wall of Gath and the wall of Jabneh and the wall of Ashdod; and he built cities in *the area of* Ashdod and among the Philistines.

7 God helped him against the Philistines, and against the Arabians who lived in Gur-baal, and the Meunites.

8 The Ammonites also gave tribute to Uzziah, and his fame extended to the border of Egypt, for he became very strong.

9 Moreover, Uzziah built towers in Jerusalem at the Corner Gate and at the Valley Gate and at the corner buttress and fortified them.

10 He built towers in the wilderness and hewed many cisterns, for he had much livestock, both in the lowland and in the plain. *He also had* plowmen and vinedressers in the hill country and the fertile fields, for he loved the soil.

11 Moreover, Uzziah had an army ready for battle, which entered combat by divisions according to the number of their muster, prepared by Jeiel the scribe and Maaseiah the official, under the direction of Hananiah, one of the king's officers.

12 The total number of the heads of the households, of valiant warriors, was 2,600.

13 Under their direction was an elite army of 307,500, who could wage war with great power, to help the king against the enemy.

14 Moreover, Uzziah prepared for all the army shields, spears, helmets, body armor, bows and sling stones.

15 In Jerusalem he made engines *of war* invented by skillful men to be on the towers and on the corners for the purpose of shooting arrows and great stones. Hence his fame spread afar, for he was marvelously helped until he *was* strong.

16 But when he became strong, his ◄ heart was so proud that he acted corruptly, and he was unfaithful to the LORD his God, for he entered the temple of the LORD to burn incense on the altar of incense.

17 Then Azariah the priest entered after

LIFE LESSONS

➤ **2 Chronicles 26:16 — *When he became strong, his heart was so proud that he acted corruptly.***

*O*ur greatest tests often come, not during times of weakness or tragedy, but in times of prosperity and success. Pride brings down more men and women than any weapon of war ever invented.

UZZIAH: The Downfall of Pride

2 CHRONICLES 26:16–23

*W*hen we rely on our own strength to combat sin or achieve our goals, we ensure our defeat. After all, whatever we acquire outside of God's will eventually turns to ashes. A good example of this was King Uzziah of Judah.

Uzziah was a great reformer and ferocious warrior who enjoyed great success "as long as he sought the LORD" (2 Chr. 26:5). He could have enjoyed a lifetime of victory if he had kept his focus on God.

Unfortunately, Uzziah turned his attention to all he had accomplished and gave in to pride. Predictably, corrupt behavior and unfaithfulness to the Lord followed.

Eventually, so altered by his pride, he believed he was above the law and entered the temple to do what was strictly forbidden by God's Word (Ex. 30). The Lord consequently struck Uzziah with leprosy for usurping the work of the priests and defiling the temple, and he died tragically because of his sin (2 Cor. 26:16–23).

Pride will take us places we have no business being; and before long, it will destroy us. If we want to walk with God, we must listen when He tells us to humble ourselves and obey Him.

---

him and with him eighty priests of the LORD, valiant men.
18 They opposed Uzziah the king and said to him, "It is not for you, Uzziah, to burn incense to the LORD, but for the priests, the sons of Aaron who are consecrated to burn incense. Get out of the sanctuary, for you have been unfaithful and will have no honor from the LORD God."
19 But Uzziah, with a censer in his hand for burning incense, was enraged; and while he was enraged with the priests, the leprosy broke out on his forehead before the priests in the house of the LORD, beside the altar of incense.
20 Azariah the chief priest and all the priests looked at him, and behold, he *was* leprous on his forehead; and they hurried him out of there, and he himself also hastened to get out because the LORD had smitten him.
21 King Uzziah was a leper to the day of his death; and he lived in a separate house, being a leper, for he was cut off from the house of the LORD. And Jotham his son *was* over the king's house judging the people of the land.
22 Now the rest of the acts of Uzziah, first to last, the prophet Isaiah, the son of Amoz, has written.
23 So Uzziah slept with his fathers, and they buried him with his fathers in the field of the grave which belonged to the kings, for they said, "He is a leper." And Jotham his son became king in his place.

27 JOTHAM was twenty-five years old when he became king, and he reigned sixteen years in Jerusalem. And his mother's name was Jerushah the daughter of Zadok.
2 He did right in the sight of the LORD, according to all that his father Uzziah had done; however he did not enter the temple of the LORD. But the people continued acting corruptly.
3 He built the upper gate of the house of the LORD, and he built extensively the wall of Ophel.
4 Moreover, he built cities in the hill country of Judah, and he built fortresses and towers on the wooded *hills.*
5 He fought also with the king of the Ammonites and prevailed over them so that the Ammonites gave him during that year one hundred talents of silver, ten thousand kors of wheat and ten thousand of barley. The Ammonites also paid him this *amount* in the second and in the third year.
6 So Jotham became mighty because he ordered his ways before the LORD his God.
7 Now the rest of the acts of Jotham, even all his wars and his acts, behold, they are written in the Book of the Kings of Israel and Judah.
8 He was twenty-five years old when he became king, and he reigned sixteen years in Jerusalem.
9 And Jotham slept with his fathers, and they buried him in the city of David; and Ahaz his son became king in his place.

Psalm 84:1–7

For the choir director; on the Gittith.
A Psalm of the sons of Korah.

84 HOW lovely are Your dwelling
places, O LORD of hosts!
2   My soul longed and even yearned
for the courts of the LORD;
My heart and my flesh sing for joy
to the living God.
3   The bird also has found a house,
And the swallow a nest for herself,
where she may lay her young,
Even Your altars, O LORD of hosts,
My King and my God.
4   How blessed are those who dwell in
Your house!
They are ever praising You.   Selah.
5   How blessed is the man whose
strength is in You,
In whose heart are the highways *to*
Zion!
6   Passing through the valley of Baca
they make it a spring;
The early rain also covers it with
blessings.
7   They go from strength to strength,
Every one of them appears before
God in Zion.

Proverbs 21:4, 5

4   Haughty eyes and a proud heart,
The lamp of the wicked, is sin.
5   The plans of the diligent *lead* surely
to advantage,
But everyone who is hasty *comes*
surely to poverty.

Acts 19:1–20

19 IT happened that while Apollos was
at Corinth, Paul passed through the
upper country and came to Ephesus, and
found some disciples.
2   He said to them, "Did you receive
the Holy Spirit when you believed?" And
they *said* to him, "No, we have not even
heard whether there is a Holy Spirit."
3   And he said, "Into what then were

you baptized?" And they said, "Into
John's baptism."
4   Paul said, "John baptized with the
baptism of repentance, telling the people
to believe in Him who was coming after
him, that is, in Jesus."
5   When they heard this, they were
baptized in the name of the Lord Jesus.
6   And when Paul had laid his hands
upon them, the Holy Spirit came on
them, and they *began* speaking with
tongues and prophesying.
7   There were in all about twelve men.
8   And he entered the synagogue and
continued speaking out boldly for three
months, reasoning and persuading *them*
about the kingdom of God.
9   But when some were becoming hardened and disobedient, speaking evil of the
Way before the people, he withdrew from
them and took away the disciples, reasoning daily in the school of Tyrannus.
10 This took place for two years, so that
all who lived in Asia heard the word of
the Lord, both Jews and Greeks.
11 God was performing extraordinary
miracles by the hands of Paul,
12 so that handkerchiefs or aprons
were even carried from his body to the
sick, and the diseases left them and the
evil spirits went out.
13 But also some of the Jewish exor-
cists, who went from place to place, attempted to name over those who had the

---

LIFE LESSONS

➢ **Proverbs 21:5 —** *The plans of the dili-*
gent lead surely to advantage, but every-
one who is hasty comes surely to poverty.

"*G*et rich quick" schemes have been
around for millennia, and they've
never worked. For every man who gets
rich quick, ten thousand get poor even
quicker.

➢ **Acts 19:11 —** *God was performing*
extraordinary miracles by the hands of
Paul.

*T*he same Spirit who worked miracles
through Old Testament prophets
such as Elijah and Elisha, and who performed great signs through Jesus and
Peter, now worked similar miracles
through Paul. Where faith meets God,
extraordinary things happen.

evil spirits the name of the Lord Jesus, saying, "I adjure you by Jesus whom Paul preaches."

14 Seven sons of one Sceva, a Jewish chief priest, were doing this.

15 And the evil spirit answered and said to them, "I recognize Jesus, and I know about Paul, but who are you?"

16 And the man, in whom was the evil spirit, leaped on them and subdued all of them and overpowered them, so that they fled out of that house naked and wounded.

17 This became known to all, both Jews and Greeks, who lived in Ephesus; and fear fell upon them all and the name of the Lord Jesus was being magnified.

18 Many also of those who had believed kept coming, confessing and disclosing their practices.

19 And many of those who practiced magic brought their books together and *began* burning them in the sight of everyone; and they counted up the price of them and found it fifty thousand pieces of silver.

20 So the word of the Lord was growing mightily and prevailing.

LIFE LESSONS

➤ **Acts 19:20 — *The word of the Lord was growing mightily and prevailing.***

*G*od loves to honor His Word so that it grows mightily and prevails. If we want to be connected with such a mighty move of God, we must faithfully proclaim His Word through the power of His Spirit.

✦ 2 Chronicles 28:1—29:36

28AHAZ *was* twenty years old when he became king, and he reigned sixteen years in Jerusalem; and he did not do right in the sight of the LORD as David his father *had done.*

2 But he walked in the ways of the kings of Israel; he also made molten images for the Baals.

3 Moreover, he burned incense in the valley of Ben-hinnom and burned his sons in fire, according to the abominations of the nations whom the LORD had driven out before the sons of Israel.

4 He sacrificed and burned incense on the high places, on the hills and under every green tree.

5 Wherefore, the LORD his God delivered him into the hand of the king of Aram; and they defeated him and carried away from him a great number of captives and brought *them* to Damascus. And he was also delivered into the hand of the king of Israel, who inflicted him with heavy casualties.

➤ 6 For Pekah the son of Remaliah slew in Judah 120,000 in one day, all valiant men, because they had forsaken the LORD God of their fathers.

7 And Zichri, a mighty man of Ephraim, slew Maaseiah the king's son and Azrikam the ruler of the house and Elkanah the second to the king.

8 The sons of Israel carried away captive of their brethren 200,000 women, sons and daughters; and they took also a great deal of spoil from them, and brought the spoil to Samaria.

9 But a prophet of the LORD was there, whose name *was* Oded; and he went out to meet the army which came to Samaria and said to them, "Behold, because the LORD, the God of your fathers, was angry with Judah, He has delivered them into your hand, and you have slain them in a rage *which* has even reached heaven.

10 "Now you are proposing to subjugate

LIFE LESSONS

➤ **2 Chronicles 28:6 — *Pekah . . . slew in Judah 120,000 in one day, all valiant men, because they had forsaken the LORD God.***

*E*ven multitudes of valiant men cannot prosper when they forsake the living God. The Lord promised that if His people abandoned Him, "I will forsake them and . . . they will be consumed" (Deut. 31:17).

for yourselves the people of Judah and Jerusalem for male and female slaves. Surely, *do* you not *have* transgressions of your own against the LORD your God?

11 "Now therefore, listen to me and return the captives whom you captured from your brothers, for the burning anger of the LORD is against you."

12 Then some of the heads of the sons of Ephraim—Azariah the son of Johanan, Berechiah the son of Meshillemoth, Jehizkiah the son of Shallum, and Amasa the son of Hadlai—arose against those who were coming from the battle,

13 and said to them, "You must not bring the captives in here, for you are proposing *to bring* upon us guilt against the LORD adding to our sins and our guilt; for our guilt is great so that *His* burning anger is against Israel."

14 So the armed men left the captives and the spoil before the officers and all the assembly.

15 Then the men who were designated by name arose, took the captives, and they clothed all their naked ones from the spoil; and they gave them clothes and sandals, fed them and gave them drink, anointed them *with oil,* led all their feeble ones on donkeys, and brought them to Jericho, the city of palm trees, to their brothers; then they returned to Samaria.

16 At that time King Ahaz sent to the kings of Assyria for help.

17 For again the Edomites had come and attacked Judah and carried away captives.

18 The Philistines also had invaded the cities of the lowland and of the Negev of Judah, and had taken Beth-shemesh, Aijalon, Gederoth, and Soco with its villages, Timnah with its villages, and Gimzo with its villages, and they settled there.

19 For the LORD humbled Judah because of Ahaz king of Israel, for he had brought about a lack of restraint in Judah and was very unfaithful to the LORD.

20 So Tilgath-pilneser king of Assyria came against him and afflicted him instead of strengthening him.

21 Although Ahaz took a portion out of the house of the LORD and out of the palace of the king and of the princes, and gave *it* to the king of Assyria, it did not help him.

22 Now in the time of his distress this same King Ahaz became yet more unfaithful to the LORD.

23 For he sacrificed to the gods of Damascus which had defeated him, and said, "Because the gods of the kings of Aram helped them, I will sacrifice to them that they may help me." But they became the downfall of him and all Israel.

24 Moreover, when Ahaz gathered together the utensils of the house of God, he cut the utensils of the house of God in pieces; and he closed the doors of the house of the LORD and made altars for himself in every corner of Jerusalem.

25 In every city of Judah he made high places to burn incense to other gods, and provoked the LORD, the God of his fathers, to anger.

26 Now the rest of his acts and all his ways, from first to last, behold, they are written in the Book of the Kings of Judah and Israel.

27 So Ahaz slept with his fathers, and they buried him in the city, in Jerusalem, for they did not bring him into the tombs of the kings of Israel; and Hezekiah his son reigned in his place.

29 HEZEKIAH became king *when he was* twenty-five years old; and he reigned twenty-nine years in Jerusalem. And his mother's name *was* Abijah, the daughter of Zechariah.

2 He did right in the sight of the LORD, according to all that his father David had done.

3 In the first year of his reign, in the first month, he opened the doors of the house of the LORD and repaired them.

4 He brought in the priests and the Levites and gathered them into the square on the east.

5 Then he said to them, "Listen to me, O Levites. Consecrate yourselves now, and consecrate the house of the LORD,

---

LIFE LESSONS

➤ **2 Chronicles 28:22 —** *King Ahaz became yet more unfaithful to the LORD.*

*G*od wants to use our times of adversity to bring us closer to Him, not to drive us further away. We usually learn more in our valley experiences than on our mountaintops.

the God of your fathers, and carry the uncleanness out from the holy place.

6 "For our fathers have been unfaithful and have done evil in the sight of the LORD our God, and have forsaken Him and turned their faces away from the dwelling place of the LORD, and have turned *their* backs.

7 "They have also shut the doors of the porch and put out the lamps, and have not burned incense or offered burnt offerings in the holy place to the God of Israel.

8 "Therefore the wrath of the LORD was against Judah and Jerusalem, and He has made them an object of terror, of horror, and of hissing, as you see with your own eyes.

9 "For behold, our fathers have fallen by the sword, and our sons and our daughters and our wives are in captivity for this.

10 "Now it is in my heart to make a covenant with the LORD God of Israel, that His burning anger may turn away from us.

11 "My sons, do not be negligent now, for the LORD has chosen you to stand before Him, to minister to Him, and to be His ministers and burn incense."

12 Then the Levites arose: Mahath, the son of Amasai and Joel the son of Azariah, from the sons of the Kohathites; and from the sons of Merari, Kish the son of Abdi and Azariah the son of Jehallelel; and from the Gershonites, Joah the son of Zimmah and Eden the son of Joah;

13 and from the sons of Elizaphan, Shimri and Jeiel; and from the sons of Asaph, Zechariah and Mattaniah;

14 and from the sons of Heman, Jehiel and Shimei; and from the sons of Jeduthun, Shemaiah and Uzziel.

15 They assembled their brothers, consecrated themselves, and went in to cleanse the house of the LORD, according

to the commandment of the king by the words of the LORD.

16 So the priests went in to the inner part of the house of the LORD to cleanse *it*, and every unclean thing which they found in the temple of the LORD they brought out to the court of the house of the LORD. Then the Levites received *it* to carry out to the Kidron valley.

17 Now they began the consecration on the first *day* of the first month, and on the eighth day of the month they entered the porch of the LORD. Then they consecrated the house of the LORD in eight days, and finished on the sixteenth day of the first month.

18 Then they went in to King Hezekiah and said, "We have cleansed the whole house of the LORD, the altar of burnt offering with all of its utensils, and the table of showbread with all of its utensils.

19 "Moreover, all the utensils which King Ahaz had discarded during his reign in his unfaithfulness, we have prepared and consecrated; and behold, they are before the altar of the LORD."

20 Then King Hezekiah arose early and assembled the princes of the city and went up to the house of the LORD.

21 They brought seven bulls, seven rams, seven lambs and seven male goats for a sin offering for the kingdom, the sanctuary, and Judah. And he ordered the priests, the sons of Aaron, to offer *them* on the altar of the LORD.

22 So they slaughtered the bulls, and the priests took the blood and sprinkled it on the altar. They also slaughtered the rams and sprinkled the blood on the altar; they slaughtered the lambs also and sprinkled the blood on the altar.

23 Then they brought the male goats of the sin offering before the king and the assembly, and they laid their hands on them.

24 The priests slaughtered them and purged the altar with their blood to atone for all Israel, for the king ordered the burnt offering and the sin offering for all Israel.

25 He then stationed the Levites in the house of the LORD with cymbals, with harps and with lyres, according to the command of David and of Gad the king's seer, and of Nathan the prophet; for the command was from the LORD through His prophets.

26 The Levites stood with the *musical* instruments of David, and the priests with the trumpets.

27 Then Hezekiah gave the order to offer the burnt offering on the altar. When the burnt offering began, the song to the LORD also began with the trumpets, *accompanied* by the instruments of David, king of Israel.

28 While the whole assembly worshiped, the singers also sang and the trumpets sounded; all this *continued* until the burnt offering was finished.

29 Now at the completion of the burnt offerings, the king and all who were present with him bowed down and worshiped.

30 Moreover, King Hezekiah and the officials ordered the Levites to sing praises to the LORD with the words of David and Asaph the seer. So they sang praises with joy, and bowed down and worshiped.

31 Then Hezekiah said, "Now *that* you have consecrated yourselves to the LORD, come near and bring sacrifices and thank offerings to the house of the LORD." And the assembly brought sacrifices and thank offerings, and all those who were willing *brought* burnt offerings.

32 The number of the burnt offerings which the assembly brought was 70 bulls, 100 rams, and 200 lambs; all these were for a burnt offering to the LORD.

33 The consecrated things were 600 bulls and 3,000 sheep.

34 But the priests were too few, so that they were unable to skin all the burnt offerings; therefore their brothers the Levites helped them until the work was completed and until the *other* priests had consecrated themselves. For the Levites were more conscientious to consecrate themselves than the priests.

35 There *were* also many burnt offerings with the fat of the peace offerings and with the libations for the burnt offerings. Thus the service of the house of the LORD was established *again*.

36 Then Hezekiah and all the people rejoiced over what God had prepared for the people, because the thing came about suddenly.

Psalm 84:8–12

8 O Lᴏʀᴅ God of hosts, hear my prayer;
   Give ear, O God of Jacob!   Selah.
9 Behold our shield, O God,
   And look upon the face of Your
      anointed.
➤ 10 For a day in Your courts is better
      than a thousand *outside.*
   I would rather stand at the
      threshold of the house of my God
   Than dwell in the tents of
      wickedness.
✳ 11 For the Lᴏʀᴅ God is a sun and shield;
   The Lᴏʀᴅ gives grace and glory;
   No good thing does He withhold
      from those who walk uprightly.
12 O Lᴏʀᴅ of hosts,
   How blessed is the man who trusts
      in You!

Proverbs 21:6–8

6 The acquisition of treasures by a
      lying tongue
   Is a fleeting vapor, the pursuit of
      death.

LIFE LESSONS

➤ **2 Chronicles 29:36** — *Then Hezekiah and all the people rejoiced over
what God had prepared for the people,
because the thing came about suddenly.*

*G*ood things can happen suddenly
   when God goes ahead of us to prepare hearts. We can rejoice that He
makes it a habit to go ahead of His obedient people (Ex. 23:20; Deut. 31:3; Matt.
26:32).

➤ **Psalm 84:10** — *A day in Your courts is
better than a thousand outside. I would
rather stand at the threshold of the
house of my God than dwell in the tents
of wickedness.*

*S*ince we were made for an intimate
   relationship with God, a humble
place of service with Him is better than
an exalted position of power or fame in
the world without Him. We find deep
and ultimate satisfaction in Christ alone.

7 The violence of the wicked will drag
      them away,
   Because they refuse to act with
      justice.
8 The way of a guilty man is crooked,
   But as for the pure, his conduct is
      upright.

Acts 19:21–41

21 Now after these things were finished, Paul purposed in the Spirit to go to
Jerusalem after he had passed through
Macedonia and Achaia, saying, "After I
have been there, I must also see Rome."
22 And having sent into Macedonia two
of those who ministered to him, Timothy
and Erastus, he himself stayed in Asia
for a while.
23 About that time there occurred no
small disturbance concerning the Way.
24 For a man named Demetrius, a silversmith, who made silver shrines of
Artemis, was bringing no little business
to the craftsmen;
25 these he gathered together with the
workmen of similar *trades,* and said,
"Men, you know that our prosperity depends upon this business.
26 "You see and hear that not only in
Ephesus, but in almost all of Asia, this
Paul has persuaded and turned away a
considerable number of people, saying
that gods made with hands are no gods
at all.
27 "Not only is there danger that this
trade of ours fall into disrepute, but also
that the temple of the great goddess
Artemis be regarded as worthless and
that she whom all of Asia and the world
worship will even be dethroned from her
magnificence."
28 When they heard *this* and were filled
with rage, they *began* crying out, saying,
"Great is Artemis of the Ephesians!"
29 The city was filled with the confusion, and they rushed with one accord
into the theater, dragging along Gaius
and Aristarchus, Paul's traveling companions from Macedonia.
30 And when Paul wanted to go into
the assembly, the disciples would not let
him.
31 Also some of the Asiarchs who were

friends of his sent to him and repeatedly urged him not to venture into the theater. 32 So then, some were shouting one thing and some another, for the assembly was in confusion and the majority did not know for what reason they had come together. 33 Some of the crowd concluded *it was* Alexander, since the Jews had put him forward; and having motioned with his hand, Alexander was intending to make a defense to the assembly. 34 But when they recognized that he was a Jew, a *single* outcry arose from them all as they shouted for about two hours, "Great is Artemis of the Ephesians!" 35 After quieting the crowd, the town clerk *said, "Men of Ephesus, what man is there after all who does not know that the city of the Ephesians is guardian of the temple of the great Artemis and of the *image* which fell down from heaven? 36 "So, since these are undeniable facts, you ought to keep calm and to do nothing rash. 37 "For you have brought these men *here* who are neither robbers of temples nor blasphemers of our goddess.

38 "So then, if Demetrius and the craftsmen who are with him have a complaint against any man, the courts are in session and proconsuls are *available;* let them bring charges against one another. 39 "But if you want anything beyond this, it shall be settled in the lawful assembly. 40 "For indeed we are in danger of being accused of a riot in connection with today's events, since there is no *real* cause *for it,* and in this connection we will be unable to account for this disorderly gathering." 41 After saying this he dismissed the assembly.

LIFE LESSONS

➤ **Acts 19:32 — *The assembly was in confusion and the majority did not know for what reason they had come together.***

*A*ngry mobs are generally not good places to reason out disputes. When Paul wanted to speak to the volatile crowd—to reason and persuade, as was his custom—the disciples did not let him (Acts 19:30).

JULY 17

2 Chronicles 30:1—31:21

30 NOW Hezekiah sent to all Israel and Judah and wrote letters also to Ephraim and Manasseh, that they should come to the house of the LORD at Jerusalem to celebrate the Passover to the LORD God of Israel. 2 For the king and his princes and all the assembly in Jerusalem had decided to celebrate the Passover in the second month, 3 since they could not celebrate it at that time, because the priests had not consecrated themselves in sufficient numbers, nor had the people been gathered to Jerusalem. 4 Thus the thing was right in the sight of the king and all the assembly. 5 So they established a decree to circulate a proclamation throughout all Israel from Beersheba even to Dan, that they should come to celebrate the Passover to the LORD God of Israel at Jerusalem. For they had not celebrated *it* in great numbers as it was prescribed. 6 The couriers went throughout all Israel and Judah with the letters from the hand of the king and his princes, even according to the command of the king, saying, "O sons of Israel, return to the LORD God of Abraham, Isaac and Israel, that He may return to those of you who escaped *and* are left from the hand of the kings of Assyria. 7 "Do not be like your fathers and your brothers, who were unfaithful to the LORD God of their fathers, so that He made them a horror, as you see. 8 "Now do not stiffen your neck like your fathers, but yield to the LORD and enter His sanctuary which He has consecrated forever, and serve the LORD your God, that His burning anger may turn away from you.

➤ 9 "For if you return to the LORD, your brothers and your sons *will find* compassion before those who led them captive and will return to this land. For the LORD your God is gracious and compassionate, and will not turn *His* face away from you if you return to Him."

10 So the couriers passed from city to city through the country of Ephraim and Manasseh, and as far as Zebulun, but they laughed them to scorn and mocked them.

11 Nevertheless some men of Asher, Manasseh and Zebulun humbled themselves and came to Jerusalem.

➤ 12 The hand of God was also on Judah to give them one heart to do what the king and the princes commanded by the word of the LORD.

13 Now many people were gathered at Jerusalem to celebrate the Feast of Unleavened Bread in the second month, a very large assembly.

14 They arose and removed the altars which *were* in Jerusalem; they also removed all the incense altars and cast *them* into the brook Kidron.

15 Then they slaughtered the Passover *lambs* on the fourteenth of the second month. And the priests and Levites were ashamed of themselves, and consecrated themselves and brought burnt offerings to the house of the LORD.

16 They stood at their stations after their custom, according to the law of Moses the man of God; the priests sprinkled the blood *which they received* from the hand of the Levites.

17 For *there were* many in the assembly who had not consecrated themselves; therefore, the Levites *were* over the slaughter of the Passover *lambs* for everyone who *was* unclean, in order to consecrate *them* to the LORD.

18 For a multitude of the people, *even* many from Ephraim and Manasseh, Issachar and Zebulun, had not purified themselves, yet they ate the Passover otherwise than prescribed. For Hezekiah prayed for them, saying, "May the good LORD pardon

19 everyone who prepares his heart to seek God, the LORD God of his fathers, though not according to the purification *rules* of the sanctuary."

20 So the LORD heard Hezekiah and healed the people.

21 The sons of Israel present in Jerusalem celebrated the Feast of Unleavened Bread *for* seven days with great joy, and the Levites and the priests praised the LORD day after day with loud instruments to the LORD.

22 Then Hezekiah spoke encouragingly to all the Levites who showed good insight *in the things* of the LORD. So they ate for the appointed seven days, sacrificing peace offerings and giving thanks to the LORD God of their fathers.

23 Then the whole assembly decided to celebrate *the feast* another seven days, so they celebrated the seven days with joy.

24 For Hezekiah king of Judah had contributed to the assembly 1,000 bulls and 7,000 sheep, and the princes had contributed to the assembly 1,000 bulls and 10,000 sheep; and a large number of priests consecrated themselves.

25 All the assembly of Judah rejoiced, with the priests and the Levites and all the assembly that came from Israel, both the sojourners who came from the land of Israel and those living in Judah.

26 So there was great joy in Jerusalem, because there was nothing like this in Jerusalem since the days of Solomon the son of David, king of Israel.

27 Then the Levitical priests arose and blessed the people; and their voice was heard and their prayer came to His holy dwelling place, to heaven.

LIFE LESSONS

➤ **2 Chronicles 30:9** — *The LORD your God is gracious and compassionate, and will not turn His face away from you if you return to Him.*

*S*ome people worry that they have committed "the unpardonable sin" (Matt. 12:31), but God will never turn away anyone who genuinely repents of his sin and places his faith in Christ.

➤ **2 Chronicles 30:12** — *The hand of God was also on Judah to give them one heart to do what the king and the princes commanded.*

*W*hen everyone's focus is on the Lord and everyone's heart is committed to obeying Him, there will be unity and harmony among the people. Only God can give a people "one heart."

31 NOW when all this was finished, all Israel who were present went out to the cities of Judah, broke the pillars in pieces, cut down the Asherim and pulled down the high places and the altars throughout all Judah and Benjamin, as well as in Ephraim and Manasseh, until they had destroyed them all. Then all the sons of Israel returned to their cities, each to his possession.

2 And Hezekiah appointed the divisions of the priests and the Levites by their divisions, each according to his service, *both* the priests and the Levites, for burnt offerings and for peace offerings, to minister and to give thanks and to praise in the gates of the camp of the LORD.

3 *He* also *appointed* the king's portion of his goods for the burnt offerings, *namely,* for the morning and evening burnt offerings, and the burnt offerings for the sabbaths and for the new moons and for the fixed festivals, as it is written in the law of the LORD.

4 Also he commanded the people who lived in Jerusalem to give the portion due to the priests and the Levites, that they might devote themselves to the law of the LORD.

5 As soon as the order spread, the sons of Israel provided in abundance the first fruits of grain, new wine, oil, honey and of all the produce of the field; and they brought in abundantly the tithe of all.

6 The sons of Israel and Judah who lived in the cities of Judah also brought in the tithe of oxen and sheep, and the tithe of sacred gifts which were consecrated to the LORD their God, and placed *them* in heaps.

7 In the third month they began to make the heaps, and finished *them* by the seventh month.

8 When Hezekiah and the rulers came and saw the heaps, they blessed the LORD and His people Israel.

9 Then Hezekiah questioned the priests and the Levites concerning the heaps.

10 Azariah the chief priest of the house of Zadok said to him, "Since the contributions began to be brought into the house of the LORD, we have had enough to eat with plenty left over, for the LORD has blessed His people, and this great quantity is left over."

11 Then Hezekiah commanded *them* to prepare rooms in the house of the LORD, and they prepared *them*.

12 They faithfully brought in the contributions and the tithes and the consecrated things; and Conaniah the Levite *was* the officer in charge of them and his brother Shimei *was* second.

13 Jehiel, Azaziah, Nahath, Asahel, Jerimoth, Jozabad, Eliel, Ismachiah, Mahath and Benaiah *were* overseers under the authority of Conaniah and Shimei his brother by the appointment of King Hezekiah, and Azariah *was* the *chief* officer of the house of God.

14 Kore the son of Imnah the Levite, the keeper of the eastern *gate, was* over the freewill offerings of God, to apportion the contributions for the LORD and the most holy things.

15 Under his authority *were* Eden, Miniamin, Jeshua, Shemaiah, Amariah and Shecaniah in the cities of the priests, to distribute faithfully *their portions* to their brothers by divisions, whether great or small,

16 without regard to their genealogical enrollment, to the males from thirty years old and upward—everyone who entered the house of the LORD for his daily obligations—for their work in their duties according to their divisions;

17 as well as the priests who were enrolled genealogically according to their fathers' households, and the Levites from twenty years old and upwards, by their duties *and* their divisions.

18 The genealogical enrollment *included* all their little children, their wives, their sons and their daughters, for the whole assembly, for they consecrated themselves faithfully in holiness.

19 Also for the sons of Aaron the priests *who were* in the pasture lands of their cities, or in each and every city, *there were* men who were designated by name to distribute portions to every male among the priests and to everyone genealogically enrolled among the Levites.

20 Thus Hezekiah did throughout all Judah; and he did what *was* good, right and true before the LORD his God.

21 Every work which he began in the service of the house of God in law and in commandment, seeking his God, he did with all his heart and prospered.

Psalm 85:1–7

For the choir director.
A Psalm of the sons of Korah.

85 O LORD, You showed favor to
Your land;
You restored the captivity of Jacob.
2 You forgave the iniquity of Your
people;
You covered all their sin.   Selah.
3 You withdrew all Your fury;
You turned away from Your burning
anger.
4 Restore us, O God of our salvation,
And cause Your indignation toward
us to cease.
5 Will You be angry with us forever?
Will You prolong Your anger to all
generations?

LIFE LESSONS

➤ 2 Chronicles 31:21 — *Seeking his God,
he did with all his heart and prospered.*

*W*hen we seek the Lord with all our
hearts, the natural result is joyful
and earnest obedience—and obedience
always brings blessing.

➤ Psalm 85:6 — *Will You not Yourself
revive us again, that Your people may
rejoice in You?*

*S*piritual revival is not only about
restoring a right relationship with
God; it is also about returning to a place
where we can delight in Him and joyfully celebrate His goodness, love, and
mercy.

---

6 Will You not Yourself revive us
again,
That Your people may rejoice in
You?
7 Show us Your lovingkindness,
O LORD,
And grant us Your salvation.

Proverbs 21:9–11

9 It is better to live in a corner of a roof
Than in a house shared with a
contentious woman.
10 The soul of the wicked desires evil;
His neighbor finds no favor in his
eyes.
11 When the scoffer is punished, the
naive becomes wise;
But when the wise is instructed, he
receives knowledge.

Acts 20:1–16

20 AFTER the uproar had ceased, Paul
sent for the disciples, and when he
had exhorted them and taken his leave of
them, he left to go to Macedonia.
2 When he had gone through those
districts and had given them much exhortation, he came to Greece.
3 And *there* he spent three months,
and when a plot was formed against him
by the Jews as he was about to set sail
for Syria, he decided to return through
Macedonia.
4 And he was accompanied by Sop-
ater of Berea, *the son* of Pyrrhus, and

Life Examples:

TYCHICUS: Beloved
Messenger

ACTS 20:4

*E*ach time Tychicus is mentioned in
Scripture (Acts 20:4; Eph. 6:21; 2 Tim.
4:12; Titus 3:12), he is running errands for the
apostle Paul, then a prisoner in Rome. In a
sense, he is Paul's "messenger boy."
Paul himself wrote, "Tychicus, our beloved
brother and faithful servant and fellow bond-
servant in the Lord, will bring you informa-

tion. For I have sent him to you for this very
purpose, that you may know about our circumstances and that he may encourage your
hearts" (Col. 4:7, 8).
We might feel tempted to evaluate
Tychicus' ministry as minor, especially when
compared to Paul's. But do you realize that
Tychicus delivered Paul's messages to several
churches, and thus played a major part in distributing the Word of God? Is that unimportant? Absolutely not! Tychicus had a crucial
ministry, and he fulfilled it.
Will you allow him to inspire you to fulfill
your own crucial ministry, whatever it is?

by Aristarchus and Secundus of the Thessalonians, and Gaius of Derbe, and Timothy, and Tychicus and Trophimus of Asia.

5   But these had gone on ahead and were waiting for us at Troas.

6   We sailed from Philippi after the days of Unleavened Bread, and came to them at Troas within five days; and there we stayed seven days.

7   On the first day of the week, when we were gathered together to break bread, Paul *began* talking to them, intending to leave the next day, and he prolonged his message until midnight.

8   There were many lamps in the upper room where we were gathered together.

9   And there was a young man named Eutychus sitting on the window sill, sinking into a deep sleep; and as Paul kept on talking, he was overcome by sleep and fell down from the third floor and was picked up dead.

10   But Paul went down and fell upon him, and after embracing him, he said, "Do not be troubled, for his life is in him."

11   When he had gone *back* up and had broken the bread and eaten, he talked with them a long while until daybreak, and then left.

12   They took away the boy alive, and were greatly comforted.

13   But we, going ahead to the ship, set sail for Assos, intending from there to take Paul on board; for so he had arranged it, intending himself to go by land.

14   And when he met us at Assos, we took him on board and came to Mitylene.

15   Sailing from there, we arrived the following day opposite Chios; and the next day we crossed over to Samos; and the day following we came to Miletus.

16   For Paul had decided to sail past Ephesus so that he would not have to spend time in Asia; for he was hurrying to be in Jerusalem, if possible, on the day of Pentecost.

JULY 18

2 Chronicles 32:1—33:25

32 AFTER these acts of faithfulness Sennacherib king of Assyria came and invaded Judah and besieged the fortified cities, and thought to break into them for himself.

2   Now when Hezekiah saw that Sennacherib had come and that he intended to make war on Jerusalem,

3   he decided with his officers and his warriors to cut off the *supply of* water from the springs which *were* outside the city, and they helped him.

4   So many people assembled and stopped up all the springs and the stream which flowed through the region, saying, "Why should the kings of Assyria come and find abundant water?"

5   And he took courage and rebuilt all the wall that had been broken down and erected towers on it, and *built* another outside wall and strengthened the Millo *in* the city of David, and made weapons and shields in great number.

6   He appointed military officers over the people and gathered them to him in the square at the city gate, and spoke encouragingly to them, saying,

7   "Be strong and courageous, do not fear or be dismayed because of the king of Assyria nor because of all the horde that is with him; for the one with us is greater than the one with him.

8   "With him is *only* an arm of flesh, but with us is the LORD our God to help us and to fight our battles." And the people relied on the words of Hezekiah king of Judah.

LIFE LESSONS

➤ **2 Chronicles 32:3 —** *He decided with his officers and his warriors to cut off the supply of water from the springs which were outside the city.*

*H*ezekiah not only prayed to God for deliverance when the Assyrians advanced against him; he also took wise action. Faithful, believing prayer does not mean passivity or inaction; rather, it means active listening for the Lord and immediate obedience to the initial promptings of the Holy Spirit.

WHAT THE BIBLE SAYS ABOUT ◈

The Feeble Arm of Flesh

2 Chronicles 32:7, 8

To the Assyrian invader Sennacherib, Jerusalem was no problem. After all, Sennacherib's mighty forces had already conquered the majority of fortified cities in Judah and had no reason to think Jerusalem would be any different. The odds were definitely in Assyria's favor.

Yet Sennacherib failed to factor in the one thing that had always saved Judah in the past—the aid of the Lord God.

However, King Hezekiah of Judah had not forgotten the faithfulness of God, and he encouraged the people by saying, "Be strong and courageous, do not fear or be dismayed because of the king of Assyria nor because of all the horde that is with him; for the one with us is greater than the one with him. With him is only an arm of flesh, but with us is the LORD our God to help us and to fight our battles" (2 Chr. 32:7, 8).

Remember Hezekiah's wise words whenever you face obstacles and troubles that are far bigger than you could possibly handle: Your God is with you, and He will fight your battles. The arm of flesh is always weak and inadequate against the limitless power of the living God. In fact, the arm of flesh eventually returns to dust, but God is eternal and will never fail you.

History shows that God defeated Sennacherib, and sent him "in shame to his own land" (2 Chr. 32:21). God will defeat your troubles as well. However, you must remain strong and courageous—trusting God in every circumstance and obeying whatever He says.

His resources never fall short and His wisdom cannot be outmatched. God's help is real and available to you today. Will you trust Him? ◈

---

9 After this Sennacherib king of Assyria sent his servants to Jerusalem while he *was* besieging Lachish with all his forces with him, against Hezekiah king of Judah and against all Judah who *were* at Jerusalem, saying,
10 "Thus says Sennacherib king of Assyria, 'On what are you trusting that you are remaining in Jerusalem under siege?
11 'Is not Hezekiah misleading you to give yourselves over to die by hunger and by thirst, saying, "The LORD our God will deliver us from the hand of the king of Assyria"?
12 'Has not the same Hezekiah taken away His high places and His altars, and said to Judah and Jerusalem, "You shall worship before one altar, and on it you shall burn incense"?
13 'Do you not know what I and my fathers have done to all the peoples of the lands? Were the gods of the nations of the lands able at all to deliver their land from my hand?
14 'Who *was there* among all the gods of those nations which my fathers utterly destroyed who could deliver his people out of my hand, that your God should be able to deliver you from my hand?
15 'Now therefore, do not let Hezekiah deceive you or mislead you like this, and do not believe him, for no god of any nation or kingdom was able to deliver his people from my hand or from the hand of my fathers. How much less will your God deliver you from my hand?'"
16 His servants spoke further against the LORD God and against His servant Hezekiah.
17 He also wrote letters to insult the LORD God of Israel, and to speak against Him, saying, "As the gods of the nations of the lands have not delivered their people from my hand, so the God of Hezekiah will not deliver His people from my hand."
18 They called this out with a loud voice in the language of Judah to the people of Jerusalem who were on the wall, to frighten and terrify them, so that they might take the city.
19 They spoke of the God of Jerusalem as of the gods of the peoples of the earth, the work of men's hands.
20 But King Hezekiah and Isaiah the prophet, the son of Amoz, prayed about this and cried out to heaven.
21 And the LORD sent an angel who destroyed every mighty warrior, commander and officer in the camp of the

king of Assyria. So he returned in shame to his own land. And when he had entered the temple of his god, some of his own children killed him there with the sword.

22   So the LORD saved Hezekiah and the inhabitants of Jerusalem from the hand of Sennacherib the king of Assyria and from the hand of all *others,* and guided them on every side.

23   And many were bringing gifts to the LORD at Jerusalem and choice presents to Hezekiah king of Judah, so that he was exalted in the sight of all nations thereafter.

24   In those days Hezekiah became mortally ill; and he prayed to the LORD, and the LORD spoke to him and gave him a sign.

25   But Hezekiah gave no return for the benefit he received, because his heart was proud; therefore wrath came on him and on Judah and Jerusalem.

26   However, Hezekiah humbled the pride of his heart, both he and the inhabitants of Jerusalem, so that the wrath of the LORD did not come on them in the days of Hezekiah.

27   Now Hezekiah had immense riches and honor; and he made for himself treasuries for silver, gold, precious stones, spices, shields and all kinds of valuable articles,

28   storehouses also for the produce of grain, wine and oil, pens for all kinds of cattle and sheepfolds for the flocks.

29   He made cities for himself and acquired flocks and herds in abundance, for God had given him very great wealth.

30   It was Hezekiah who stopped the upper outlet of the waters of Gihon and directed them to the west side of the city of David. And Hezekiah prospered in all that he did.

➤ 31   Even *in the matter of* the envoys of the rulers of Babylon, who sent to him to inquire the wonder that had happened in the land, God left him *alone only* to test him, that He might know all that was in his heart.

32   Now the rest of the acts of Hezekiah and his deeds of devotion, behold, they are written in the vision of Isaiah the prophet, the son of Amoz, in the Book of the Kings of Judah and Israel.

33   So Hezekiah slept with his fathers, and they buried him in the upper section

---

of the tombs of the sons of David; and all Judah and the inhabitants of Jerusalem honored him at his death. And his son Manasseh became king in his place.

33 MANASSEH was twelve years old when he became king, and he reigned fifty-five years in Jerusalem.

2   He did evil in the sight of the LORD according to the abominations of the nations whom the LORD dispossessed before the sons of Israel.

3   For he rebuilt the high places which Hezekiah his father had broken down; he also erected altars for the Baals and made Asherim, and worshiped all the host of heaven and served them.

4   He built altars in the house of the LORD of which the LORD had said, "My name shall be in Jerusalem forever."

5   For he built altars for all the host of heaven in the two courts of the house of the LORD.

6   He made his sons pass through the fire in the valley of Ben-hinnom; and he practiced witchcraft, used divination, practiced sorcery and dealt with mediums and spiritists. He did much evil in the sight of the LORD, provoking Him *to anger.*

7   Then he put the carved image of the idol which he had made in the house of God, of which God had said to David and to Solomon his son, "In this house and in Jerusalem, which I have chosen from all the tribes of Israel, I will put My name forever;

8   and I will not again remove the foot of Israel from the land which I have appointed for your fathers, if only they will observe to do all that I have commanded them according to all the law, the statutes and the ordinances *given* through Moses."

9 Thus Manasseh misled Judah and the inhabitants of Jerusalem to do more evil than the nations whom the LORD destroyed before the sons of Israel.
10 The LORD spoke to Manasseh and his people, but they paid no attention.
11 Therefore the LORD brought the commanders of the army of the king of Assyria against them, and they captured Manasseh with hooks, bound him with bronze *chains* and took him to Babylon.
12 When he was in distress, he entreated the LORD his God and humbled himself greatly before the God of his fathers.
13 When he prayed to Him, He was moved by his entreaty and heard his supplication, and brought him again to Jerusalem to his kingdom. Then Manasseh knew that the LORD *was* God.
14 Now after this he built the outer wall of the city of David on the west side of Gihon, in the valley, even to the entrance of the Fish Gate; and he encircled the Ophel *with it* and made it very high. Then he put army commanders in all the fortified cities of Judah.
15 He also removed the foreign gods and the idol from the house of the LORD, as well as all the altars which he had built on the mountain of the house of the LORD and in Jerusalem, and he threw *them* outside the city.
16 He set up the altar of the LORD and sacrificed peace offerings and thank offerings on it; and he ordered Judah to serve the LORD God of Israel.
17 Nevertheless the people still sacrificed in the high places, *although* only to the LORD their God.
18 Now the rest of the acts of Manasseh even his prayer to his God, and the words of the seers who spoke to him in the name of the LORD God of Israel, behold, they are among the records of the kings of Israel.
19 His prayer also and *how God* was entreated by him, and all his sin, his unfaithfulness, and the sites on which he built high places and erected the Asherim and the carved images, before he humbled himself, behold, they are written in the records of the Hozai.
20 So Manasseh slept with his fathers, and they buried him in his own house. And Amon his son became king in his place.

21 Amon *was* twenty-two years old when he became king, and he reigned two years in Jerusalem.
22 He did evil in the sight of the LORD as Manasseh his father had done, and Amon sacrificed to all the carved images which his father Manasseh had made, and he served them.
23 Moreover, he did not humble himself before the LORD as his father Manasseh had done, but Amon multiplied guilt.
24 Finally his servants conspired against him and put him to death in his own house.
25 But the people of the land killed all the conspirators against King Amon, and the people of the land made Josiah his son king in his place.

◈ Psalm 85:8–13

8   I will hear what God the LORD will
      say;
    For He will speak peace to His
      people, to His godly ones;
    But let them not turn back to folly.
9   Surely His salvation is near to those
      who fear Him,
    That glory may dwell in our land.
10 Lovingkindness and truth have met
      together;
    Righteousness and peace have
      kissed each other.
11 Truth springs from the earth,
    And righteousness looks down
      from heaven.
12 Indeed, the LORD will give what is
      good,
    And our land will yield its
      produce.

LIFE LESSONS

➤ **Psalm 85:8 —** *He will speak peace to His people, to His godly ones; but let them not turn back to folly.*

Salvation not only rescues us from the penalty of our sins; it delivers us from bondage to our transgressions and the impulse to practice them (Rom. 6:17–19). Paul wrote, "It was for freedom that Christ set us free; therefore keep standing firm and do not be subject again to a yoke of slavery" (Gal. 5:1).

13 Righteousness will go before
    Him
    And will make His footsteps into a
    way.

Proverbs 21:12

12 The righteous one considers the
    house of the wicked,
    Turning the wicked to ruin.

Acts 20:17–38

17 From Miletus he sent to Ephesus and
called to him the elders of the church.
18 And when they had come to him, he
said to them,
    "You yourselves know, from the first
day that I set foot in Asia, how I was with
you the whole time,
19 serving the Lord with all humility
and with tears and with trials which
came upon me through the plots of the
Jews;
20 how I did not shrink from declaring
to you anything that was profitable, and
teaching you publicly and from house to
house,
21 solemnly testifying to both Jews and
Greeks of repentance toward God and
faith in our Lord Jesus Christ.
22 "And now, behold, bound by the
Spirit, I am on my way to Jerusalem,
not knowing what will happen to me
there,
23 except that the Holy Spirit solemnly
testifies to me in every city, saying that
bonds and afflictions await me.
24 "But I do not consider my life of any
account as dear to myself, so that I may
finish my course and the ministry which
I received from the Lord Jesus, to testify
solemnly of the gospel of the grace of
God.
25 "And now, behold, I know that all of
you, among whom I went about preaching the kingdom, will no longer see my
face.
26 "Therefore, I testify to you this day
that I am innocent of the blood of all
men.
27 "For I did not shrink from declaring to
you the whole purpose of God.

28 "Be on guard for yourselves and for
all the flock, among which the Holy
Spirit has made you overseers, to shepherd the church of God which He purchased with His own blood.
29 "I know that after my departure savage wolves will come in among you, not
sparing the flock;
30 and from among your own selves
men will arise, speaking perverse things,
to draw away the disciples after them.
31 "Therefore be on the alert, remembering that night and day for a period of
three years I did not cease to admonish
each one with tears.
32 "And now I commend you to God and
to the word of His grace, which is able to
build *you* up and to give *you* the inheritance among all those who are sanctified.
33 "I have coveted no one's silver or gold
or clothes.
34 "You yourselves know that these
hands ministered to my *own* needs and
to the men who were with me.

➤ 35 "In everything I showed you that by working hard in this manner you must help the weak and remember the words of the Lord Jesus, that He Himself said, 'It is more blessed to give than to receive.'"

36 When he had said these things, he knelt down and prayed with them all.

37 And they *began* to weep aloud and embraced Paul, and repeatedly kissed him,

38 grieving especially over the word which he had spoken, that they would not see his face again. And they were accompanying him to the ship.

LIFE LESSONS

➤ **Acts 20:35 — "The Lord Jesus ... said, 'It is more blessed to give than to receive.'"**

*N*one of the four canonical Gospels record this saying of Jesus; however, it reflects Christ's attitude throughout His ministry. "The Son of Man did not come to be served, but to serve, and to give His life a ransom for many" (Mark 10:45). It is more blessed to give because that is when we best resemble Christ (Matt. 10:8; 25:34–40; Mark 9:35; James 2:15–17).

---

2 Chronicles 34:1—36:23

34 JOSIAH *was* eight years old when he became king, and he reigned thirty-one years in Jerusalem.

2 He did right in the sight of the LORD, and walked in the ways of his father David and did not turn aside to the right or to the left.

3 For in the eighth year of his reign while he was still a youth, he began to seek the God of his father David; and in the twelfth year he began to purge Judah and Jerusalem of the high places, the Asherim, the carved images and the molten images.

4 They tore down the altars of the Baals in his presence, and the incense altars that were high above them he chopped down; also the Asherim, the carved images and the molten images he broke in pieces and ground to powder and scattered *it* on the graves of those who had sacrificed to them.

5 Then he burned the bones of the priests on their altars and purged Judah and Jerusalem.

6 In the cities of Manasseh, Ephraim, Simeon, even as far as Naphtali, in their surrounding ruins,

7 he also tore down the altars and beat the Asherim and the carved images into powder, and chopped down all the incense altars throughout the land of Israel. Then he returned to Jerusalem.

8 Now in the eighteenth year of his reign, when he had purged the land and the house, he sent Shaphan the son of Azaliah, and Maaseiah an official of the city, and Joah the son of Joahaz the recorder, to repair the house of the LORD his God.

9 They came to Hilkiah the high priest and delivered the money that was brought into the house of God, which the Levites, the doorkeepers, had collected from Manasseh and Ephraim, and from all the remnant of Israel, and from all Judah and Benjamin and the inhabitants of Jerusalem.

10 Then they gave *it* into the hands of the workmen who had the oversight of the house of the LORD, and the workmen who were working in the house of the LORD used it to restore and repair the house.

11 They in turn gave *it* to the carpenters and to the builders to buy quarried stone and timber for couplings and to make beams for the houses which the kings of Judah had let go to ruin.

12 The men did the work faithfully with foremen over them to supervise: Jahath and Obadiah, the Levites of the sons of Merari, Zechariah and Meshullam of the sons of the Kohathites, and the Levites, all who were skillful with musical instruments.

13 *They were* also over the burden bearers, and supervised all the workmen from job to job; and *some* of the Levites *were* scribes and officials and gatekeepers.

Life Examples:

JOSIAH: Committed to Following the Lord

2 CHRONICLES 34

*J*osiah became king of Judah when he was just eight years old after the murder of his idolatrous father, Amon. Having no living example and no parental instruction in the ways of God, he walked in the ways of his forefather, King David.

He committed himself to follow the Lord, keeping all His mandates and decrees. When he renewed the covenant of his forefathers, all the people with him pledged themselves to the Lord as well. Josiah's extensive reforms throughout Judah and Samaria make him stand out as one of Judah's most faithful kings (2 Kin. 23:25).

When you make the Lord and His Word the focus of your life, He will help you, just as He did Josiah. Make your heart tender, and humble yourself before the Lord. He will establish you, and by Him you will become mighty for God.

14 When they were bringing out the money which had been brought into the house of the LORD, Hilkiah the priest found the book of the law of the LORD *given* by Moses.

15 Hilkiah responded and said to Shaphan the scribe, "I have found the book of the law in the house of the LORD." And Hilkiah gave the book to Shaphan.

16 Then Shaphan brought the book to the king and reported further word to the king, saying, "Everything that was entrusted to your servants they are doing.

17 "They have also emptied out the money which was found in the house of the LORD, and have delivered it into the hands of the supervisors and the workmen."

18 Moreover, Shaphan the scribe told the king saying, "Hilkiah the priest gave me a book." And Shaphan read from it in the presence of the king.

19 When the king heard the words of the law, he tore his clothes.

20 Then the king commanded Hilkiah, Ahikam the son of Shaphan, Abdon the son of Micah, Shaphan the scribe, and Asaiah the king's servant, saying,

21 "Go, inquire of the LORD for me and for those who are left in Israel and in Judah, concerning the words of the book which has been found; for great is the wrath of the LORD which is poured out on us because our fathers have not observed the word of the LORD, to do according to all that is written in this book."

22 So Hilkiah and *those* whom the king had told went to Huldah the prophetess, the wife of Shallum the son of Tokhath, the son of Hasrah, the keeper of the wardrobe (now she lived in Jerusalem in the Second Quarter); and they spoke to her regarding this.

23 She said to them, "Thus says the LORD, the God of Israel, 'Tell the man who sent you to Me,

24 thus says the LORD, "Behold, I am bringing evil on this place and on its inhabitants, *even* all the curses written in the book which they have read in the presence of the king of Judah.

25 "Because they have forsaken Me and have burned incense to other gods, that they might provoke Me to anger with all the works of their hands; therefore My wrath will be poured out on this place and it shall not be quenched."'

26 "But to the king of Judah who sent you to inquire of the LORD, thus you will say to him, 'Thus says the LORD God of Israel *regarding* the words which you have heard,

27 "Because your heart was tender and you humbled yourself before God when you heard His words against this place and against its inhabitants, and *because* ✳ you humbled yourself before Me, tore your clothes and wept before Me, I truly have heard you," declares the LORD.

28 "Behold, I will gather you to your fathers and you shall be gathered to your grave in peace, so your eyes will not see all the evil which I will bring on this place and on its inhabitants."'" And they brought back word to the king.

29 Then the king sent and gathered all the elders of Judah and Jerusalem.

30 The king went up to the house of the LORD and all the men of Judah, the inhabitants of Jerusalem, the priests, the Levites and all the people, from the greatest to the least; and he read in their

hearing all the words of the book of the covenant which was found in the house of the LORD.
31 Then the king stood in his place and made a covenant before the LORD to walk after the LORD, and to keep His commandments and His testimonies and His statutes with all his heart and with all his soul, to perform the words of the covenant written in this book.
32 Moreover, he made all who were present in Jerusalem and Benjamin to stand with him. So the inhabitants of Jerusalem did according to the covenant of God, the God of their fathers.
33 Josiah removed all the abominations from all the lands belonging to the sons of Israel, and made all who were present in Israel to serve the LORD their God. Throughout his lifetime they did not turn from following the LORD God of their fathers.

35 THEN Josiah celebrated the Passover to the LORD in Jerusalem, and they slaughtered the Passover animals on the fourteenth day of the first month.
2 He set the priests in their offices and encouraged them in the service of the house of the LORD.
➤ 3 He also said to the Levites who taught all Israel and who were holy to the LORD, "Put the holy ark in the house which Solomon the son of David king of Israel built; it will be a burden on your shoulders no longer. Now serve the LORD your God and His people Israel.
4 "Prepare yourselves by your fathers' households in your divisions, according to the writing of David king of Israel and according to the writing of his son Solomon.
5 "Moreover, stand in the holy place according to the sections of the fathers'

households of your brethren the lay people, and according to the Levites, by division of a father's household.
6 "Now slaughter the Passover animals, sanctify yourselves and prepare for your brethren to do according to the word of the LORD by Moses."
7 Josiah contributed to the lay people, to all who were present, flocks of lambs and young goats, all for the Passover offerings, numbering 30,000 plus 3,000 bulls; these were from the king's possessions.
8 His officers also contributed a freewill offering to the people, the priests and the Levites. Hilkiah and Zechariah and Jehiel, the officials of the house of God, gave to the priests for the Passover offerings 2,600 from the flocks and 300 bulls.
9 Conaniah also, and Shemaiah and Nethanel, his brothers, and Hashabiah and Jeiel and Jozabad, the officers of the Levites, contributed to the Levites for the Passover offerings 5,000 from the flocks and 500 bulls.
10 So the service was prepared, and the priests stood at their stations and the Levites by their divisions according to the king's command.
11 They slaughtered the Passover animals, and while the priests sprinkled the blood received from their hand, the Levites skinned them.
12 Then they removed the burnt offerings that they might give them to the sections of the fathers' households of the lay people to present to the LORD, as it is written in the book of Moses. They did this also with the bulls.
13 So they roasted the Passover animals on the fire according to the ordinance, and they boiled the holy things in pots, in kettles, in pans, and carried them speedily to all the lay people.
14 Afterwards they prepared for themselves and for the priests, because the priests, the sons of Aaron, were offering the burnt offerings and the fat until night; therefore the Levites prepared for themselves and for the priests, the sons of Aaron.
15 The singers, the sons of Asaph, were also at their stations according to the command of David, Asaph, Heman, and Jeduthun the king's seer; and the gatekeepers at each gate did not have to

depart from their service, because the Levites their brethren prepared for them.

16 So all the service of the LORD was prepared on that day to celebrate the Passover, and to offer burnt offerings on the altar of the LORD according to the command of King Josiah.

17 Thus the sons of Israel who were present celebrated the Passover at that time, and the Feast of Unleavened Bread seven days.

18 There had not been celebrated a Passover like it in Israel since the days of Samuel the prophet; nor had any of the kings of Israel celebrated such a Passover as Josiah did with the priests, the Levites, all Judah and Israel who were present, and the inhabitants of Jerusalem.

19 In the eighteenth year of Josiah's reign this Passover was celebrated.

20 After all this, when Josiah had set the temple in order, Neco king of Egypt came up to make war at Carchemish on the Euphrates, and Josiah went out to engage him.

21 But Neco sent messengers to him, saying, "What have we to do with each other, O King of Judah? *I am* not *coming* against you today but against the house with which I am at war, and God has ordered me to hurry. Stop for your own sake from *interfering with* God who is with me, so that He will not destroy you."

> 22 However, Josiah would not turn away from him, but disguised himself in order to make war with him; nor did he listen to the words of Neco from the mouth of God, but came to make war on the plain of Megiddo.

23 The archers shot King Josiah, and the king said to his servants, "Take me away, for I am badly wounded."

24 So his servants took him out of the chariot and carried him in the second chariot which he had, and brought him to Jerusalem where he died and was buried in the tombs of his fathers. All Judah and Jerusalem mourned for Josiah.

25 Then Jeremiah chanted a lament for Josiah. And all the male and female singers speak about Josiah in their lamentations to this day. And they made them an ordinance in Israel; behold, they are also written in the Lamentations.

26 Now the rest of the acts of Josiah and his deeds of devotion as written in the law of the LORD,

27 and his acts, first to last, behold, they are written in the Book of the Kings of Israel and Judah.

36 THEN the people of the land took Joahaz the son of Josiah, and made him king in place of his father in Jerusalem.

2 Joahaz was twenty-three years old when he became king, and he reigned three months in Jerusalem.

3 Then the king of Egypt deposed him at Jerusalem, and imposed on the land a fine of one hundred talents of silver and one talent of gold.

4 The king of Egypt made Eliakim his brother king over Judah and Jerusalem, and changed his name to Jehoiakim. But Neco took Joahaz his brother and brought him to Egypt.

5 Jehoiakim was twenty-five years old when he became king, and he reigned eleven years in Jerusalem; and he did evil in the sight of the LORD his God.

6 Nebuchadnezzar king of Babylon came up against him and bound him with bronze *chains* to take him to Babylon.

7 Nebuchadnezzar also brought *some* of the articles of the house of the LORD to Babylon and put them in his temple at Babylon.

8 Now the rest of the acts of Jehoiakim and the abominations which he did, and what was found against him, behold, they are written in the Book of the Kings of Israel and Judah. And Jehoiachin his son became king in his place.

9 Jehoiachin was eight years old when he became king, and he reigned three months and ten days in Jerusalem, and he did evil in the sight of the LORD.

10 At the turn of the year King Nebuchadnezzar sent and brought him to

Babylon with the valuable articles of the house of the LORD, and he made his kinsman Zedekiah king over Judah and Jerusalem.

11 Zedekiah was twenty-one years old when he became king, and he reigned eleven years in Jerusalem.

12 He did evil in the sight of the LORD his God; he did not humble himself before Jeremiah the prophet who spoke for the LORD.

13 He also rebelled against King Nebuchadnezzar who had made him swear *allegiance* by God. But he stiffened his neck and hardened his heart against turning to the LORD God of Israel.

14 Furthermore, all the officials of the priests and the people were very unfaithful *following* all the abominations of the nations; and they defiled the house of the LORD which He had sanctified in Jerusalem.

15 The LORD, the God of their fathers, sent *word* to them again and again by His messengers, because He had compassion on His people and on His dwelling place;

16 but they *continually* mocked the messengers of God, despised His words and scoffed at His prophets, until the wrath of the LORD arose against His people, until there was no remedy.

17 Therefore He brought up against them the king of the Chaldeans who slew their young men with the sword in the house of their sanctuary, and had no compassion on young man or virgin, old man or infirm; He gave *them* all into his hand.

18 All the articles of the house of God, great and small, and the treasures of the house of the LORD, and the treasures of the king and of his officers, he brought *them* all to Babylon.

19 Then they burned the house of God and broke down the wall of Jerusalem, and burned all its fortified buildings with fire and destroyed all its valuable articles.

20 Those who had escaped from the sword he carried away to Babylon; and they were servants to him and to his sons until the rule of the kingdom of Persia,

21 to fulfill the word of the LORD by the mouth of Jeremiah, until the land had enjoyed its sabbaths. All the days of its desolation it kept sabbath until seventy years were complete.

22 Now in the first year of Cyrus king of Persia—in order to fulfill the word of the LORD by the mouth of Jeremiah—the LORD stirred up the spirit of Cyrus king of Persia, so that he sent a proclamation throughout his kingdom, and also *put it* in writing, saying,

23 "Thus says Cyrus king of Persia, 'The LORD, the God of heaven, has given me all the kingdoms of the earth, and He has appointed me to build Him a house in Jerusalem, which is in Judah. Whoever there is among you of all His people, may the LORD his God be with him, and let him go up!'"

✦ Psalm 86:1–5

A Prayer of David.

86 INCLINE Your ear, O LORD, *and* answer me;
For I am afflicted and needy.

2 Preserve my soul, for I am a godly man;
O You my God, save Your servant who trusts in You.

3 Be gracious to me, O Lord,
For to You I cry all day long.

LIFE LESSONS

➤ **2 Chronicles 36:16 —** *They continually mocked the messengers of God, despised His words and scoffed at His prophets, until the wrath of the LORD arose against His people.*

*W*hen a culture or a person comes to despise God's Word and habitually mocks and scoffs at His messengers, judgment cannot be far away. Judah's judgment came in 586 B.C. with the fall of Jerusalem, the destruction of the temple, and the exile of her people to Babylon.

➤ **2 Chronicles 36:23 —** *"He has appointed me to build Him a house in Jerusalem."*

*P*agan king Nebuchadnezzar of Babylon carried Judah into exile (2 Kin. 24:10—25:21; 2 Chr. 36:20), and another pagan king, Cyrus of Persia, sent them back to the Promised Land (2 Chr. 36:22, 23; Ezra 1:1–4). Our sovereign God allows the dark moments of our lives to last only so long as it takes for Him to accomplish His purposes in us.

4   Make glad the soul of Your
        servant,
    For to You, O Lord, I lift up my
        soul.
5   For You, Lord, are good, and
        ready to forgive,
    And abundant in lovingkindness
        to all who call upon You.

Proverbs 21:13, 14

13 He who shuts his ear to the cry of
        the poor
    Will also cry himself and not be
        answered.
14 A gift in secret subdues anger,
    And a bribe in the bosom, strong
        wrath.

Acts 21:1–17

21 WHEN we had parted from them
    and had set sail, we ran a straight
course to Cos and the next day to Rhodes
and from there to Patara;
2   and having found a ship crossing
over to Phoenicia, we went aboard and
set sail.
3   When we came in sight of Cyprus,
leaving it on the left, we kept sailing to
Syria and landed at Tyre; for there the
ship was to unload its cargo.
4   After looking up the disciples, we
stayed there seven days; and they kept
telling Paul through the Spirit not to set
foot in Jerusalem.
5   When our days there were ended,
we left and started on our journey, while
they all, with wives and children, escorted us until we were out of the city.
After kneeling down on the beach and
praying, we said farewell to one another.
6   Then we went on board the ship, and
they returned home again.
7   When we had finished the voyage
from Tyre, we arrived at Ptolemais, and
after greeting the brethren, we stayed
with them for a day.
8   On the next day we left and came
to Caesarea, and entering the house of
Philip the evangelist, who was one of the
seven, we stayed with him.

9   Now this man had four virgin daughters who were prophetesses.
10 As we were staying there for some
days, a prophet named Agabus came
down from Judea.
11 And coming to us, he took Paul's belt
and bound his own feet and hands, and
said, "This is what the Holy Spirit says:
'In this way the Jews at Jerusalem will
bind the man who owns this belt and deliver him into the hands of the Gentiles.'"
12 When we had heard this, we as well
as the local residents began begging him
not to go up to Jerusalem.
13 Then Paul answered, "What are you
doing, weeping and breaking my heart?
For I am ready not only to be bound, but
even to die at Jerusalem for the name of
the Lord Jesus."
14 And since he would not be persuaded, we fell silent, remarking, "The
will of the Lord be done!"
15 After these days we got ready and
started on our way up to Jerusalem.
16 Some of the disciples from Caesarea
also came with us, taking us to Mnason
of Cyprus, a disciple of long standing
with whom we were to lodge.
17 After we had arrived in Jerusalem, the
brethren received us gladly.

LIFE LESSONS

➤ **Acts 21:13 — "I am ready not only to
be bound, but even to die at Jerusalem
for the name of the Lord Jesus."**

The potential loss of his life did not
dissuade Paul from doing what he
believed God had called him to do. He
fit the mold of those described in Revelation 12:11 who "did not love their life
even when faced with death."

➤ **Acts 21:14 — "The will of the Lord be
done!"**

Paul could not be talked out of his
dangerous plan because he was
committed to God's will for his life.
Paul's friends had to submit themselves
to the Lord and release Paul to God's
care. Sometimes, the Lord calls us to do
difficult things. Whether He leads you
or another to follow Him, respond as
Jesus did in the garden of Gethsemane:
"Not My will, but Yours be done" (Luke
22:42).

Ezra 1:1—2:70

➤ 1 NOW in the first year of Cyrus king of Persia, in order to fulfill the word of the LORD by the mouth of Jeremiah, the LORD stirred up the spirit of Cyrus king of Persia, so that he sent a proclamation throughout all his kingdom, and also *put it* in writing, saying:

2 "Thus says Cyrus king of Persia, 'The LORD, the God of heaven, has given me all the kingdoms of the earth and He has appointed me to build Him a house in Jerusalem, which is in Judah.

3 'Whoever there is among you of all His people, may his God be with him! Let him go up to Jerusalem which is in
✳ Judah and rebuild the house of the LORD, the God of Israel; He is the God who is in Jerusalem.

4 'Every survivor, at whatever place he may live, let the men of that place support him with silver and gold, with goods and cattle, together with a freewill offering for the house of God which is in Jerusalem.'"

➤ 5 Then the heads of fathers' *households* of Judah and Benjamin and the priests and the Levites arose, even everyone whose spirit God had stirred to go up and rebuild the house of the LORD which is in Jerusalem.

6 All those about them encouraged them with articles of silver, with gold, with goods, with cattle and with valuables, aside from all that was given as a freewill offering.

7 Also King Cyrus brought out the articles of the house of the LORD, which Nebuchadnezzar had carried away from Jerusalem and put in the house of his gods;

8 and Cyrus, king of Persia, had them brought out by the hand of Mithredath the treasurer, and he counted them out to Sheshbazzar, the prince of Judah.

9 Now this *was* their number: 30 gold dishes, 1,000 silver dishes, 29 duplicates;

10 30 gold bowls, 410 silver bowls of a second *kind and* 1,000 other articles.

11 All the articles of gold and silver *numbered* 5,400. Sheshbazzar brought them all up with the exiles who went up from Babylon to Jerusalem.

LIFE LESSONS

➤ **Ezra 1:1 — *The LORD stirred up the spirit of Cyrus king of Persia.***

*J*ust as the Lord stirred up the spirit of Cyrus to act on behalf of His people, so can He act in the hearts of those in authority over you for your benefit. He is sovereign, and He acts in response to your faithful prayers and obedience.

➤ **Ezra 1:5 — *Then . . . arose . . . everyone whose spirit God had stirred to go up and rebuild the house of the LORD which is in Jerusalem.***

*G*od not only moves unbelievers such as Cyrus to act in certain ways, but He also moves the spirits of His people to particular actions. To walk in the Spirit is to obey the initial promptings of the Spirit.

Life Examples:

CYRUS: An Instrument of God

EZRA 1:1

*M*ighty men and ruthless conquerors may come and go, imposing their will on those in their path—but the Bible reminds us that the will of only one Ruler ultimately matters.

While the decree of the Persian king Cyrus sent Ezra back to Jerusalem, Scripture makes it clear he did only what God prompted him to do. The Bible says, "In order to fulfill the word of the LORD by the mouth of Jeremiah, the LORD stirred up the spirit of Cyrus king of Persia, so that he sent a proclamation throughout all his kingdom" (Ezra 1:1; also 2 Chr. 36:22).

This had been prophesied more than a century before by the prophet Isaiah who called Cyrus God's "anointed" (Is. 45:1) and "shepherd" (Is. 44:28). Isaiah said the king would do everything the Lord had called him to do—even though God had said of Cyrus, "you have not known Me" (Is. 45:4). God rules all—even the actions of pagan kings (Prov. 21:1). And He uses whomever He chooses. The Lord has the authority to engineer whatever circumstances necessary in order to fulfill His promises to His people. Therefore, always trust His mighty hand.

2 NOW these are the people of the province who came up out of the captivity of the exiles whom Nebuchadnezzar the king of Babylon had carried away to Babylon, and returned to Jerusalem and Judah, each to his city.

2 These came with Zerubbabel, Jeshua, Nehemiah, Seraiah, Reelaiah, Mordecai, Bilshan, Mispar, Bigvai, Rehum *and* Baanah.

The number of the men of the people of Israel:

3 the sons of Parosh, 2,172;
4 the sons of Shephatiah, 372;
5 the sons of Arah, 775;
6 the sons of Pahath-moab of the sons of Jeshua *and* Joab, 2,812;
7 the sons of Elam, 1,254;
8 the sons of Zattu, 945;
9 the sons of Zaccai, 760;
10 the sons of Bani, 642;
11 the sons of Bebai, 623;
12 the sons of Azgad, 1,222;
13 the sons of Adonikam, 666;
14 the sons of Bigvai, 2,056;
15 the sons of Adin, 454;
16 the sons of Ater of Hezekiah, 98;
17 the sons of Bezai, 323;
18 the sons of Jorah, 112;
19 the sons of Hashum, 223;
20 the sons of Gibbar, 95;
21 the men of Bethlehem, 123;
22 the men of Netophah, 56;
23 the men of Anathoth, 128;
24 the sons of Azmaveth, 42;
25 the sons of Kiriath-arim, Chephirah and Beeroth, 743;
26 the sons of Ramah and Geba, 621;
27 the men of Michmas, 122;
28 the men of Bethel and Ai, 223;
29 the sons of Nebo, 52;
30 the sons of Magbish, 156;
31 the sons of the other Elam, 1,254;
32 the sons of Harim, 320;
33 the sons of Lod, Hadid and Ono, 725;
34 the men of Jericho, 345;
35 the sons of Senaah, 3,630.
36 The priests: the sons of Jedaiah of the house of Jeshua, 973;
37 the sons of Immer, 1,052;
38 the sons of Pashhur, 1,247;
39 the sons of Harim, 1,017.
40 The Levites: the sons of Jeshua and Kadmiel, of the sons of Hodaviah, 74.
41 The singers: the sons of Asaph, 128.
42 The sons of the gatekeepers: the sons of Shallum, the sons of Ater, the sons of Talmon, the sons of Akkub, the sons of Hatita, the sons of Shobai, in all 139.
43 The temple servants: the sons of Ziha, the sons of Hasupha, the sons of Tabbaoth,
44 the sons of Keros, the sons of Siaha, the sons of Padon,
45 the sons of Lebanah, the sons of Hagabah, the sons of Akkub,
46 the sons of Hagab, the sons of Shalmai, the sons of Hanan,
47 the sons of Giddel, the sons of Gahar, the sons of Reaiah,
48 the sons of Rezin, the sons of Nekoda, the sons of Gazzam,
49 the sons of Uzza, the sons of Paseah, the sons of Besai,
50 the sons of Asnah, the sons of Meunim, the sons of Nephisim,
51 the sons of Bakbuk, the sons of Hakupha, the sons of Harhur,
52 the sons of Bazluth, the sons of Mehida, the sons of Harsha,
53 the sons of Barkos, the sons of Sisera, the sons of Temah,
54 the sons of Neziah, the sons of Hatipha.
55 The sons of Solomon's servants: the sons of Sotai, the sons of Hassophereth, the sons of Peruda,
56 the sons of Jaalah, the sons of Darkon, the sons of Giddel,
57 the sons of Shephatiah, the sons of Hattil, the sons of Pochereth-hazzebaim, the sons of Ami.
58 All the temple servants and the sons of Solomon's servants were 392.
59 Now these are those who came up from Tel-melah, Tel-harsha, Cherub, Addan *and* Immer, but they were not able to give evidence of their fathers' households and their descendants, whether they were of Israel:
60 the sons of Delaiah, the sons of Tobiah, the sons of Nekoda, 652.
61 Of the sons of the priests: the sons of Habaiah, the sons of Hakkoz, the sons of Barzillai, who took a wife from the daughters of Barzillai the Gileadite, and he was called by their name.
62 These searched *among* their ancestral registration, but they could not be located; therefore they were considered unclean *and excluded* from the priesthood.
63 The governor said to them that they

should not eat from the most holy things until a priest stood up with Urim and Thummim.

64 The whole assembly numbered 42,360,

65 besides their male and female servants who numbered 7,337; and they had 200 singing men and women.

66 Their horses were 736; their mules, 245;

67 their camels, 435; *their* donkeys, 6,720.

68 Some of the heads of fathers' *households*, when they arrived at the house of the LORD which is in Jerusalem, offered willingly for the house of God to restore it on its foundation.

➤ **69** According to their ability they gave to the treasury for the work 61,000 gold drachmas and 5,000 silver minas and 100 priestly garments.

70 Now the priests and the Levites, some of the people, the singers, the gate-keepers and the temple servants lived in their cities, and all Israel in their cities.

Psalm 86:6–10

➤ 6 Give ear, O LORD, to my prayer;
✳   And give heed to the voice of my
      supplications!
➤ 7 In the day of my trouble I shall call
      upon You,
    For You will answer me.
8 There is no one like You among the
      gods, O Lord,
    Nor are there any works like
      Yours.
9 All nations whom You have made
      shall come and worship before
      You, O Lord,
    And they shall glorify Your name.
10 For You are great and do wondrous
      deeds;
    You alone are God.

Proverbs 21:15, 16

15 The exercise of justice is joy for the
      righteous,
    But is terror to the workers of
      iniquity.

16 A man who wanders from the way
      of understanding
    Will rest in the assembly of the
      dead.

Acts 21:18–40

18 And the following day Paul went in with us to James, and all the elders were present.

19 After he had greeted them, he *began* to relate one by one the things which God had done among the Gentiles through his ministry.

LIFE LESSONS

➤ **Ezra 2:69 — *According to their ability they gave to the treasury for the work.***

*A*fter the tithe, which we give in faith, God asks us to give according to our ability, not according to what we do not have (Acts 11:29; 2 Cor. 8:12). He wants us to be faithful and generous in giving so that we can reflect His character. He also wants to teach us, "It is more blessed to give than to receive" (Acts 20:35). The truth is we can never out give Him. We give because He has first given to us.

➤ **Psalm 86:6 — *Give ear, O LORD, to my prayer.***

*I*f God already knows all our desires and needs, then why should we pray? One word: *relationship.* The Lord wants us to express ourselves to Him. If He were always to fill our needs without our seeking Him, we would never be vulnerable with Him. However, when we pray, we open ourselves to receive His love, power, wisdom, and provision.

➤ **Psalm 86:7 — *I shall call upon You, for You will answer me.***

*I*t takes faith to pray. That's probably why it's sometimes so hard to get on our knees before God—we wonder, *What good will it do?* However, we are assured the Lord hears us and provides for our needs when we seek Him. Therefore, don't look for other ways to solve your problems. Rather, call upon Him with full assurance that He will help you.

20 And when they heard it they *began* glorifying God; and they said to him, "You see, brother, how many thousands there are among the Jews of those who have believed, and they are all zealous for the Law;
21 and they have been told about you, that you are teaching all the Jews who are among the Gentiles to forsake Moses, telling them not to circumcise their children nor to walk according to the customs.
22 "What, then, is *to be done?* They will certainly hear that you have come.
23 "Therefore do this that we tell you. We have four men who are under a vow;
24 take them and purify yourself along with them, and pay their expenses so that they may shave their heads; and all will know that there is nothing to the things which they have been told about you, but that you yourself also walk orderly, keeping the Law.
25 "But concerning the Gentiles who have believed, we wrote, having decided that they should abstain from meat sacrificed to idols and from blood and from what is strangled and from fornication."
26 Then Paul took the men, and the next day, purifying himself along with them, went into the temple giving notice of the completion of the days of purification, until the sacrifice was offered for each one of them.
27 When the seven days were almost over, the Jews from Asia, upon seeing him in the temple, *began* to stir up all the crowd and laid hands on him,
28 crying out, "Men of Israel, come to our aid! This is the man who preaches to all men everywhere against our people and the Law and this place; and besides he has even brought Greeks into the temple and has defiled this holy place."
29 For they had previously seen Trophimus the Ephesian in the city with him, and they supposed that Paul had brought him into the temple.
30 Then all the city was provoked, and the people rushed together, and taking hold of Paul they dragged him out of the temple, and immediately the doors were shut.
31 While they were seeking to kill him, a report came up to the commander of the *Roman* cohort that all Jerusalem was in confusion.
32 At once he took along *some* soldiers ◄ and centurions and ran down to them; and when they saw the commander and the soldiers, they stopped beating Paul.
33 Then the commander came up and took hold of him, and ordered him to be bound with two chains; and he *began* asking who he was and what he had done.
34 But among the crowd some were shouting one thing *and* some another, and when he could not find out the facts because of the uproar, he ordered him to be brought into the barracks.
35 When he got to the stairs, he was carried by the soldiers because of the violence of the mob;
36 for the multitude of the people kept following them, shouting, "Away with him!"
37 As Paul was about to be brought into the barracks, he said to the commander, "May I say something to you?" And he *said, "Do you know Greek?
38 "Then you are not the Egyptian who some time ago stirred up a revolt and led the four thousand men of the Assassins out into the wilderness?"
39 But Paul said, "I am a Jew of Tarsus in Cilicia, a citizen of no insignificant city; and I beg you, allow me to speak to the people."
40 When he had given him permission, Paul, standing on the stairs, motioned to the people with his hand; and when there was a great hush, he spoke to them in the Hebrew dialect, saying,

---

LIFE LESSONS

➤ **Acts 21:32 — *And when they saw the commander and the soldiers, they stopped beating Paul.***

*E*ven before Paul's conversion, Jesus told Ananias, "I will show him how much he must suffer for My name's sake" (Acts 9:16). Paul was repeatedly beaten and in peril of his life, but he did not lose faith because of the adversity (2 Cor. 11:23–33). Instead, he rejoiced in his identification with Christ and believed that God would preserve him until His purpose for him was fulfilled (2 Cor. 12:7–10; Phil. 3:10–12).

Ezra 3:1—4:24

3 NOW when the seventh month came, and the sons of Israel *were* in the cities, the people gathered together as one man to Jerusalem.

2 Then Jeshua the son of Jozadak and his brothers the priests, and Zerubbabel the son of Shealtiel and his brothers arose and built the altar of the God of Israel to offer burnt offerings on it, as it is written in the law of Moses, the man of God.

3 So they set up the altar on its foundation, for they were terrified because of the peoples of the lands; and they offered burnt offerings on it to the LORD, burnt offerings morning and evening.

4 They celebrated the Feast of Booths, as it is written, and *offered* the fixed number of burnt offerings daily, according to the ordinance, as each day required;

5 and afterward *there was* a continual burnt offering, also for the new moons and for all the fixed festivals of the LORD that were consecrated, and from everyone who offered a freewill offering to the LORD.

6 From the first day of the seventh month they began to offer burnt offerings to the LORD, but the foundation of the temple of the LORD had not been laid.

7 Then they gave money to the masons and carpenters, and food, drink and oil to the Sidonians and to the Tyrians, to bring cedar wood from Lebanon to the sea at Joppa, according to the permission they had from Cyrus king of Persia.

8 Now in the second year of their coming to the house of God at Jerusalem in the second month, Zerubbabel the son of Shealtiel and Jeshua the son of Jozadak and the rest of their brothers the priests and the Levites, and all who came from the captivity to Jerusalem, began *the work* and appointed the Levites from twenty years and older to oversee the work of the house of the LORD.

9 Then Jeshua *with* his sons and brothers stood united *with* Kadmiel and his sons, the sons of Judah *and* the sons of Henadad *with* their sons and brothers the Levites, to oversee the workmen in the temple of God.

10 Now when the builders had laid the foundation of the temple of the LORD, the priests stood in their apparel with trumpets, and the Levites, the sons of Asaph, with cymbals, to praise the LORD according to the directions of King David of Israel.

11 They sang, praising and giving thanks to the LORD, *saying,* "For He is good, for His lovingkindness is upon Israel forever." And all the people shouted with a great shout when they praised the LORD because the foundation of the house of the LORD was laid.

12 Yet many of the priests and Levites and heads of fathers' *households,* the old men who had seen the first temple, wept with a loud voice when the foundation of this house was laid before their eyes, while many shouted aloud for joy,

13 so that the people could not distinguish the sound of the shout of joy from the sound of the weeping of the people, for the people shouted with a loud shout, and the sound was heard far away.

4 NOW when the enemies of Judah and Benjamin heard that the people of the exile were building a temple to the LORD God of Israel,

2 they approached Zerubbabel and the heads of fathers' *households,* and said to them, "Let us build with you, for we, like you, seek your God; and we have been sacrificing to Him since the days of Esarhaddon king of Assyria, who brought us up here."

3 But Zerubbabel and Jeshua and the rest of the heads of fathers' *households* of Israel said to them, "You have nothing in common with us in building a house to our God; but we ourselves will together build to the LORD God of Israel, as King Cyrus, the king of Persia has commanded us."

LIFE LESSONS

➤ **Ezra 4:2 —** *"Let us build with you, for we, like you, seek your God."*

*T*he adversaries of God and of His people do not always attack with a frontal assault; sometimes they try to seem friendly and sympathetic. A life of faith requires us to remain alert at all times (1 Pet. 5:8).

ANSWERS TO LIFE'S QUESTIONS

How can I find the strength to endure when I face spiritual opposition?

EZRA 4:1–24

*I*n the Book of Ezra we read of a beleaguered people who faced opposition in doing what God had commissioned them to do. They sought to rebuild the holy temple that was destroyed by Nebuchadnezzar's forces decades earlier, and they faced stiff opposition from the locals, deceitful offers of "help," and open attacks from the outside.

Still, God's people successfully completed the temple restoration. How? By developing a spiritual quality we all need in the Christian life: endurance.

God knows the Christian life is not easy. And it never will become easy, no matter how long we live. In this world, we will face opposition, both from the world and from the enemy of our souls, the devil. Jesus told us, "In the world you will have tribulation" (John 16:33).

Surrounded by such opposition, if we're going to live in a way that pleases God, then we must develop endurance. The Bible is full of examples of those who endured opposition to their work and who received their reward as a result. Hebrews 11, often called the "Hall of Faith", lists some of those heroes.

But what exactly is involved in developing endurance? At least four things play a big role:

1. *Receiving encouragement from others.*

The writer of Hebrews encourages us to ponder the lives of those he lists in chapter 11. He refers to them as "a cloud of witnesses" (Heb. 12:1). We cannot see this great cloud of witnesses, but we can read about them in God's Word and glean from their inspiring stories of endurance.

2. *Getting rid of hindrances.*

Hebrews tells us, "Let us also lay aside every encumbrance and the sin which so entangles us" (12:1). This means we need to identify those things that could slow us down including any sin God brings to our attention.

3. *Running the race.*

Hebrews 12:1 ends by telling us, "Let us run with endurance the race that is set before us." When the going gets rough, we don't run away. We can't be quitters. Rather, we continue on in confident trust, and the longer we persevere, the stronger our faith in Him becomes.

4. *Fixing our eyes on Christ.*

Hebrews 12:2 advises us to keep "fixing our eyes on Jesus, the author and perfecter of our faith." Nothing helps us endure like seeing the final prize before us—and that prize is Christ Himself. Do you want the prize? Then you must endure. And Jesus promises to help you.

---

4 Then the people of the land discouraged the people of Judah, and frightened them from building,

5 and hired counselors against them to frustrate their counsel all the days of Cyrus king of Persia, even until the reign of Darius king of Persia.

6 Now in the reign of Ahasuerus, in the beginning of his reign, they wrote an accusation against the inhabitants of Judah and Jerusalem.

7 And in the days of Artaxerxes, Bishlam, Mithredath, Tabeel and the rest of his colleagues wrote to Artaxerxes king of Persia; and the text of the letter was written in Aramaic and translated *from* Aramaic.

8 Rehum the commander and Shimshai the scribe wrote a letter against Jerusalem to King Artaxerxes, as follows—

9 then *wrote* Rehum the commander and Shimshai the scribe and the rest of their colleagues, the judges and the lesser governors, the officials, the secretaries, the men of Erech, the Babylonians, the men of Susa, that is, the Elamites,

10 and the rest of the nations which the great and honorable Osnappar deported and settled in the city of Samaria, and in the rest of the region beyond the River. Now

11 this is the copy of the letter which they sent to him:

"To King Artaxerxes: Your servants, the men in the region beyond the River, and now

12 let it be known to the king that the Jews who came up from you have come to us at Jerusalem; they are rebuilding the rebellious and evil city and are finishing the walls and repairing the foundations.

13 "Now let it be known to the king, that if that city is rebuilt and the walls are finished, they will not pay tribute, custom or toll, and it will damage the revenue of the kings.

14 "Now because we are in the service of the palace, and it is not fitting for us to see the king's dishonor, therefore we have sent and informed the king,
15 so that a search may be made in the record books of your fathers. And you will discover in the record books and learn that that city is a rebellious city and damaging to kings and provinces, and that they have incited revolt within it in past days; therefore that city was laid waste.
16 "We inform the king that if that city is rebuilt and the walls finished, as a result you will have no possession in *the province* beyond the River."
17 *Then* the king sent an answer to Rehum the commander, to Shimshai the scribe, and to the rest of their colleagues who live in Samaria and in the rest of *the provinces* beyond the River: "Peace. And now
18 the document which you sent to us has been translated and read before me.
19 "A decree has been issued by me, and a search has been made and it has been discovered that that city has risen up against the kings in past days, that rebellion and revolt have been perpetrated in it,
20 that mighty kings have ruled over Jerusalem, governing all *the provinces* beyond the River, and that tribute, custom and toll were paid to them.
21 "So, now issue a decree to make these men stop *work*, that this city may not be rebuilt until a decree is issued by me.
22 "Beware of being negligent in carrying out this *matter*; why should damage increase to the detriment of the kings?"
➤ 23 Then as soon as the copy of King Artaxerxes' document was read before Rehum and Shimshai the scribe and their colleagues, they went in haste to Jerusalem to the Jews and stopped them by force of arms.
24 Then work on the house of God in Jerusalem ceased, and it was stopped until the second year of the reign of Darius king of Persia.

🔶 Psalm 86:11–17

➤ 11 Teach me Your way, O LORD;
✳   I will walk in Your truth;
         Unite my heart to fear Your name.

12 I will give thanks to You, O Lord my God, with all my heart,
         And will glorify Your name forever.
13 For Your lovingkindness toward me is great,
         And You have delivered my soul from the depths of Sheol.
14 O God, arrogant men have risen up against me,
         And a band of violent men have sought my life,
         And they have not set You before them.
15 But You, O Lord, are a God merciful and gracious,
         Slow to anger and abundant in lovingkindness and truth.
16 Turn to me, and be gracious to me; Oh grant Your strength to Your servant,
         And save the son of Your handmaid.
17 Show me a sign for good,
         That those who hate me may see *it* and be ashamed,
         Because You, O LORD, have helped me and comforted me.

🔶 Proverbs 21:17, 18

17 He who loves pleasure *will become* a poor man;

LIFE LESSONS

➤ **Ezra 4:23 — *They went in haste to Jerusalem to the Jews and stopped them by force of arms.***

Sometimes God allows opposition to His will to succeed for a time. We may not know why, and unexpected developments may dishearten us. But we can learn through adversity and take our greatest leaps forward spiritually through our troubles if we will trust and obey God.

➤ **Psalm 86:11 — *Unite my heart to fear Your name.***

Our hearts can be a jumble of conflicting emotions and competing interests—we can feel torn in several directions. So God instructs us to pray for a united heart, at one in Him.

He who loves wine and oil will not
become rich.
18 The wicked is a ransom for the
righteous,
And the treacherous is in the place
of the upright.

Acts 22:1–30

22 "BRETHREN and fathers, hear my
defense which I now *offer* to you."
2   And when they heard that he was
addressing them in the Hebrew dialect,
they became even more quiet; and he
*said,
3   "I am a Jew, born in Tarsus of Cilicia, but brought up in this city, educated
under Gamaliel, strictly according to the
law of our fathers, being zealous for God
just as you all are today.
4   "I persecuted this Way to the death,
binding and putting both men and
women into prisons,
5   as also the high priest and all the
Council of the elders can testify. From
them I also received letters to the brethren, and started off for Damascus in
order to bring even those who were there
to Jerusalem as prisoners to be punished.
6   "But it happened that as I was on
my way, approaching Damascus about
noontime, a very bright light suddenly
flashed from heaven all around me,
7   and I fell to the ground and heard a
voice saying to me, 'Saul, Saul, why are
you persecuting Me?'
8   "And I answered, 'Who are You,
Lord?' And He said to me, 'I am Jesus the
Nazarene, whom you are persecuting.'
9   "And those who were with me saw
the light, to be sure, but did not understand the voice of the One who was
speaking to me.
10 "And I said, 'What shall I do, Lord?'
And the Lord said to me, 'Get up and go
on into Damascus, and there you will be
told of all that has been appointed for
you to do.'
11 "But since I could not see because of
the brightness of that light, I was led by
the hand by those who were with me and
came into Damascus.
12 "A certain Ananias, a man who was
devout by the standard of the Law, *and*

well spoken of by all the Jews who lived
there,
13 came to me, and standing near said
to me, 'Brother Saul, receive your sight!'
And at that very time I looked up at him.
14 "And he said, 'The God of our fathers
has appointed you to know His will and
to see the Righteous One and to hear an
utterance from His mouth.
15 'For you will be a witness for Him
to all men of what you have seen and
heard.
16 'Now why do you delay? Get up and
be baptized, and wash away your sins,
calling on His name.'
17 "It happened when I returned to Jerusalem and was praying in the temple,
that I fell into a trance,
18 and I saw Him saying to me, 'Make
haste, and get out of Jerusalem quickly,
because they will not accept your testimony about Me.'
19 "And I said, 'Lord, they themselves
understand that in one synagogue after
another I used to imprison and beat
those who believed in You.
20 'And when the blood of Your witness Stephen was being shed, I also was
standing by approving, and watching out

LIFE LESSONS

➤ **Acts 22:9 — *"Those who were with
me saw the light, to be sure, but did not
understand the voice of the One who
was speaking to me."***

*A*cts 9:7 reports that the men, "stood
speechless, hearing the voice." So is
this a contradiction? No. The Greek term
translated "hear" can mean both "to
perceive sound" and "to understand."
The men heard, but they did not understand.

➤ **Acts 22:14 — *"The God of our fathers
has appointed you to know His will and
to see the Righteous One and to hear an
utterance from His mouth."***

*P*aul never forgot the words of Ananias—that God had chosen him to
both see and hear Jesus and to know His
will. He never allowed affliction to shake
him. Instead, he embraced God's call
wholeheartedly and understood that the
adversity he experienced was a bridge
to a deeper relationship with the Lord
(2 Cor. 1:3–10; 4:7–18).

for the coats of those who were slaying him.'

21 "And He said to me, 'Go! For I will send you far away to the Gentiles.'"

22 They listened to him up to this statement, and *then* they raised their voices and said, "Away with such a fellow from the earth, for he should not be allowed to live!"

23 And as they were crying out and throwing off their cloaks and tossing dust into the air,

24 the commander ordered him to be brought into the barracks, stating that he should be examined by scourging so that he might find out the reason why they were shouting against him that way.

25 But when they stretched him out with thongs, Paul said to the centurion who was standing by, "Is it lawful for you to scourge a man who is a Roman and uncondemned?"

26 When the centurion heard *this*, he went to the commander and told him, saying, "What are you about to do? For this man is a Roman."

27 The commander came and said to him, "Tell me, are you a Roman?" And he said, "Yes."

28 The commander answered, "I acquired this citizenship with a large sum of money." And Paul said, "But I was actually born *a citizen*."

29 Therefore those who were about ◄ to examine him immediately let go of him; and the commander also was afraid when he found out that he was a Roman, and because he had put him in chains.

30 But on the next day, wishing to know for certain why he had been accused by the Jews, he released him and ordered the chief priests and all the Council to assemble, and brought Paul down and set him before them.

LIFE LESSONS

➤ **Acts 22:29** — *The commander also was afraid when he found out that he was a Roman, and because he had put him in chains.*

*I*t was a serious offense to injure or harm a Roman citizen who had not been convicted of an offense in a Roman court of law. Paul did not hesitate to use the law when it helped his cause.

Ezra 5:1—6:22

5 WHEN the prophets, Haggai the prophet and Zechariah the son of Iddo, prophesied to the Jews who were in Judah and Jerusalem in the name of the God of Israel, who was over them,

2 then Zerubbabel the son of Shealtiel and Jeshua the son of Jozadak arose and began to rebuild the house of God which is in Jerusalem; and the prophets of God were with them supporting them.

3 At that time Tattenai, the governor of *the province* beyond the River, and Shethar-bozenai and their colleagues came to them and spoke to them thus, "Who issued you a decree to rebuild this temple and to finish this structure?"

4 Then we told them accordingly what the names of the men were who were reconstructing this building.

5 But the eye of their God was on the elders of the Jews, and they did not stop them until a report could come to Darius, and then a written reply be returned concerning it.

6 *This is* the copy of the letter which Tattenai, the governor of *the province* beyond the River, and Shethar-bozenai and his colleagues the officials, who were beyond the River, sent to Darius the king.

7 They sent a report to him in which it was written thus: "To Darius the king, all peace.

8 "Let it be known to the king that we have gone to the province of Judah, to the house of the great God, which is being built with huge stones, and beams are being laid in the walls; and this work is going on with great care and is succeeding in their hands.

9 "Then we asked those elders and said to them thus, 'Who issued you a

decree to rebuild this temple and to finish this structure?'

10 "We also asked them their names so as to inform you, and that we might write down the names of the men who were at their head.

11 "Thus they answered us, saying, 'We are the servants of the God of heaven and earth and are rebuilding the temple that was built many years ago, which a great king of Israel built and finished.

12 'But because our fathers had provoked the God of heaven to wrath, He gave them into the hand of Nebuchadnezzar king of Babylon, the Chaldean, who destroyed this temple and deported the people to Babylon.

13 'However, in the first year of Cyrus king of Babylon, King Cyrus issued a decree to rebuild this house of God.

14 'Also the gold and silver utensils of the house of God which Nebuchadnezzar had taken from the temple in Jerusalem, and brought them to the temple of Babylon, these King Cyrus took from the temple of Babylon and they were given to one whose name was Sheshbazzar, whom he had appointed governor.

15 'He said to him, "Take these utensils, go and deposit them in the temple in Jerusalem and let the house of God be rebuilt in its place."

16 'Then that Sheshbazzar came and laid the foundations of the house of God in Jerusalem; and from then until now it has been under construction and it is not yet completed.'

17 "Now if it pleases the king, let a search be conducted in the king's treasure house, which is there in Babylon, if it be that a decree was issued by King Cyrus to rebuild this house of God at Jerusalem; and let the king send to us his decision concerning this matter."

6 THEN King Darius issued a decree, and search was made in the archives, where the treasures were stored in Babylon.

2 In Ecbatana in the fortress, which is in the province of Media, a scroll was found and there was written in it as follows: "Memorandum—

3 "In the first year of King Cyrus, Cyrus the king issued a decree: 'Concerning the house of God at Jerusalem, let the temple, the place where sacrifices are offered, be rebuilt and let its foundations

be retained, its height being 60 cubits and its width 60 cubits;

4 with three layers of huge stones and one layer of timbers. And let the cost be paid from the royal treasury.

5 'Also let the gold and silver utensils of the house of God, which Nebuchadnezzar took from the temple in Jerusalem and brought to Babylon, be returned and brought to their places in the temple in Jerusalem; and you shall put them in the house of God.'

6 "Now therefore, Tattenai, governor of the province beyond the River, Shethar-bozenai and your colleagues, the officials of the provinces beyond the River, keep away from there.

7 "Leave this work on the house of God alone; let the governor of the Jews and the elders of the Jews rebuild this house of God on its site.

8 "Moreover, I issue a decree concerning what you are to do for these elders of Judah in the rebuilding of this house of God: the full cost is to be paid to these people from the royal treasury out of the taxes of the provinces beyond the River, and that without delay.

9 "Whatever is needed, both young bulls, rams, and lambs for a burnt offering to the God of heaven, and wheat, salt, wine and anointing oil, as the priests in Jerusalem request, it is to be given to them daily without fail,

10 that they may offer acceptable sacrifices to the God of heaven and pray for the life of the king and his sons.

11 "And I issued a decree that any man who violates this edict, a timber shall be drawn from his house and he shall be impaled on it and his house shall be made a refuse heap on account of this.

12 "May the God who has caused His ◄

name to dwell there overthrow any king or people who attempts to change *it*, so as to destroy this house of God in Jerusalem. I, Darius, have issued *this* decree, let *it* be carried out with all diligence!"

13 Then Tattenai, the governor of *the province* beyond the River, Shethar-bozenai and their colleagues carried out *the decree* with all diligence, just as King Darius had sent.

14 And the elders of the Jews were successful in building through the prophesying of Haggai the prophet and Zechariah the son of Iddo. And they finished building according to the command of the God of Israel and the decree of Cyrus, Darius, and Artaxerxes king of Persia.

15 This temple was completed on the third day of the month Adar; it was the sixth year of the reign of King Darius.

➤ 16 And the sons of Israel, the priests, the Levites and the rest of the exiles, celebrated the dedication of this house of God with joy.

17 They offered for the dedication of this temple of God 100 bulls, 200 rams, 400 lambs, and as a sin offering for all Israel 12 male goats, corresponding to the number of the tribes of Israel.

18 Then they appointed the priests to their divisions and the Levites in their orders for the service of God in Jerusalem, as it is written in the book of Moses.

19 The exiles observed the Passover on the fourteenth of the first month.

20 For the priests and the Levites had purified themselves together; all of them were pure. Then they slaughtered the Passover *lamb* for all the exiles, both for their brothers the priests and for themselves.

➤ 21 The sons of Israel who returned from exile and all those who had separated themselves from the impurity of the nations of the land to *join* them, to seek the LORD God of Israel, ate *the Passover*.

➤ 22 And they observed the Feast of Unleavened Bread seven days with joy, for the LORD had caused them to rejoice, and

✳ had turned the heart of the king of Assyria toward them to encourage them in the work of the house of God, the God of Israel.

LIFE LESSONS

➤ **Ezra 6:16 — *The sons of Israel, the priests, the Levites and the rest of the exiles, celebrated the dedication of this house of God with joy.***

*N*o life of faith is complete without regular celebrations of joy. In fact, joy is a natural product of the faithful, Spirit-filled life (Gal 5:22). Jesus said, "These things I have spoken to you so that My joy may be in you, and that your joy may be made full" (John 15:11).

➤ **Ezra 6:21 — *The sons of Israel who returned from exile and all those who had separated themselves from the impurity of the nations of the land to join them, to seek the LORD God of Israel, ate the Passover.***

*I*f we truly want to seek the Lord, we have to separate ourselves from the evil practices of an unbelieving world. James reminds us, "Friendship with the world is hostility toward God" (James 4:4).

➤ **Ezra 6:22 — *The LORD had caused them to rejoice, and had turned the heart of the king of Assyria toward them.***

*A*s God had done with King Cyrus, He turned King Darius' heart towards the Israelites. Though sometimes it may seem as if people in authority are acting without accountability, they are all ultimately responsible to God. No one can stop His good purposes, and if the Lord chooses a pagan king to do His will, then He will turn the king's heart "wherever He wishes" and do as He pleases (Prov. 21:1).

Psalm 87:1–7

A Psalm of the sons of Korah. A Song.

87 HIS foundation is in the holy mountains.

2 The LORD loves the gates of Zion
More than all the *other* dwelling
places of Jacob.

3 Glorious things are spoken of you,
O city of God.   Selah.

4 "I shall mention Rahab and Babylon
among those who know Me;
Behold, Philistia and Tyre with
Ethiopia:

'This one was born there.'"

5 But of Zion it shall be said, "This
one and that one were born in
her";
And the Most High Himself will
establish her.
6 The LORD will count when He
registers the peoples,
"This one was born there."   Selah.
7 Then those who sing as well as
those who play the flutes *shall
say,*
"All my springs *of joy* are in you."

Proverbs 21:19, 20

19 It is better to live in a desert land
Than with a contentious and vexing
woman.
20 There is precious treasure and oil in
the dwelling of the wise,
But a foolish man swallows it up.

Acts 23:1–15

23 PAUL, looking intently at the
Council, said, "Brethren, I have
lived my life with a perfectly good conscience before God up to this day."
2 The high priest Ananias commanded
those standing beside him to strike him
on the mouth.
3 Then Paul said to him, "God is going
to strike you, you whitewashed wall! Do
you sit to try me according to the Law,
and in violation of the Law order me to
be struck?"
4 But the bystanders said, "Do you
revile God's high priest?"
5 And Paul said, "I was not aware,
brethren, that he was high priest; for it is
written, 'YOU SHALL NOT SPEAK EVIL OF A
RULER OF YOUR PEOPLE.'"
6 But perceiving that one group were
Sadducees and the other Pharisees, Paul
began crying out in the Council, "Brethren, I am a Pharisee, a son of Pharisees; I
am on trial for the hope and resurrection
of the dead!"
7 As he said this, there occurred a dissension between the Pharisees and Sadducees, and the assembly was divided.
8 For the Sadducees say that there

is no resurrection, nor an angel, nor a
spirit, but the Pharisees acknowledge
them all.
9 And there occurred a great uproar;
and some of the scribes of the Pharisaic
party stood up and *began* to argue heat-
edly, saying, "We find nothing wrong
with this man; suppose a spirit or an
angel has spoken to him?"
10 And as a great dissension was developing, the commander was afraid Paul
would be torn to pieces by them and
ordered the troops to go down and take
him away from them by force, and bring
him into the barracks.
11 But on the night *immediately* following, the Lord stood at his side and said,
"Take courage; for as you have solemnly
witnessed to My cause at Jerusalem, so
you must witness at Rome also."

LIFE LESSONS

**➤ Acts 23:6 — *"I am on trial for the hope
and resurrection of the dead!"***

*P*aul had broken no regulation, but
there was no one present to defend
him. So he heeded the Lord's counsel to
be "shrewd as serpents and innocent as
doves" (Matt. 10:16). He clearly stated
the reason for his trial—highlighting
the theological differences between the
Pharisees and the Sadducees, dividing
the Sanhedrin, and eventually ending
the trial (Acts 23:10). As believers, we
are not without defense; rather, we obey
God completely and leave the consequences to Him.

**➤ Acts 23:11 — *"Take courage; for as
you have solemnly witnessed to My
cause at Jerusalem, so you must witness
at Rome also."***

*I*t was a dark time for Paul. Certainly
his hopes of continuing to testify for
the Lord in Jerusalem were quashed by
the proceedings before the Sanhedrin
(Acts 23:1–10). Yet in this disheartening
moment, Jesus encourages him. The Lord
had told Ananias that Paul would bear His
name "before the Gentiles and kings and
the sons of Israel" (Acts 9:15). Here, Christ
reminds Paul of the promise He had given:
he would preach the gospel in Rome.
Likewise, no matter how discouraging
your circumstances appear, you can trust
God to fulfill His promises to you.

WHAT THE BIBLE SAYS ABOUT ◉

The Warnings of Our Conscience

Acts 23:1

*W*hat do the following situations have in common: You go off your diet—because the chocolate is just too tempting. You find yourself looking at someone lustfully. You gossip about your friend, or you lie to someone. What do all those situations have in common? Your conscience is going to bother you when you do them—and you must deal with what your conscience is telling you.

So the question is: How do you deal with your conscience? Do you realize it's a gift from God, given to protect you from doing things that will ultimately destroy you? Your conscience must be cared for because it is the moral capacity that enables you to distinguish between what's right and what's wrong—between what's good and what's best in your life.

However, what happens to the conscience when it's ignored or when we respond wrongly to its warnings? The Bible gives us seven words that relate to the condition of our conscience in each of its possible stages.

1. A *good* conscience.

In Acts 23:1, Paul says, "I have lived my life with a perfectly good conscience before God up to this day." That may be difficult to believe considering that Paul persecuted the church before he was saved. However, because Paul acted in ignorance (1 Tim. 1:13), and because he changed his ways the moment he understood the truth, he could say that his conscience was good. When Jesus Christ changed his life, he realized that all of his programming was wrong. People sometimes believe they're doing the right thing—when they are actually violating God's Word—because that's the way they've been programmed.

2. A *blameless* conscience.

Then, in Acts 24:16, Paul says, "I also do my best to maintain always a blameless conscience both before God and before men." A blameless conscience means that he is working at being godly and disciplined. Paul was willing to do whatever was necessary to make sure he was right with God—to keep his conscience from convicting him. A blameless conscience can only occur through obedience to the Holy Spirit.

3. A *clear* conscience.

Paul also said, "I serve with a clear conscience" (2 Tim. 1:3). A clear conscience is one that's quiet—clean and without regret. Paul didn't waste time; rather, he was always prepared for whatever God called him to do—and he always gave God his very best. Paul remained true to the Word of God, and never compromised his convictions.

4. A *weak* conscience.

Paul also dealt with people with a weak conscience—people who were not as mature in the

faith. We are responsible for living a life that won't hinder young, immature believers. Other Christians are looking to us as examples of how they can live the Christian life. Therefore, we must ask ourselves, "If I participate in that, will it hurt my testimony?" If we engage in activities that cause others to fall, we're accountable to God for our actions.

5. A *defiled* conscience.

Of course, when a person begins to sin against God and doesn't acknowledge that he's accountable to Him, he's defiling his conscience. And the longer he defiles it, the dirtier it gets. His testimony is destroyed. Our conscience is like a window—when it's clean, more light can come in. However, if we allow it to be soiled, the light becomes dimmer, until we don't even realize we're walking in the dark. This happens when we watch what other people are doing instead of looking to God's Word.

6. An *evil* conscience.

Then there is the evil conscience, which is one that is continually in sin. An evil conscience is one that does things a child of God could never do—it is a way of life. An evil conscience doesn't care that there's a God at all, and it will suffer the consequences that God warns us about in His Word.

7. A *seared* conscience.

If we took a branding iron and put it on our arm, the flesh would become so damaged that it would have no feeling at all. That's what sin does—it hardens the heart and conscience until the person doesn't feel anything. The conscience is seared, and the person can no longer hear the truth.

So how do we keep a blameless conscience?

- We must trust Jesus Christ as our personal Savior and Lord.
- We must set the Word of God as our standard for living.
- We must not allow anything in our lives that contradicts the Word of God.
- We must surrender to the Holy Spirit.
- We must have daily cleansing by confessing our sin and repenting of it.

We must keep a clear, blameless conscience before God because it's such a blessing to us. When our conscience is pure and clean, we'll have courage that most people don't have—because no matter what we're accused of, we'll know that we're in God's will and have done the right thing.

We'll also have God's all-surpassing peace in our hearts. We'll be able to remain calm and silent when everything is in turmoil because our heavenly Father is with us. We'll be fearless because God is on our side, and He faithfully takes care of His own.

And finally, we'll know that we have a mighty testimony because there's power and boldness in a clean, blameless conscience. We'll be standing on the truth, righteousness, and wisdom of God—and there's no better platform on which to stand! ◉

12 When it was day, the Jews formed a conspiracy and bound themselves under an oath, saying that they would neither eat nor drink until they had killed Paul.
13 There were more than forty who formed this plot.
14 They came to the chief priests and the elders and said, "We have bound ourselves under a solemn oath to taste nothing until we have killed Paul.
15 "Now therefore, you and the Council notify the commander to bring him down to you, as though you were going to determine his case by a more thorough investigation; and we for our part are ready to slay him before he comes near *the place.*"

Ezra 7:1—8:36

7 NOW after these things, in the reign of Artaxerxes king of Persia, *there went up* Ezra son of Seraiah, son of Azariah, son of Hilkiah,
2 son of Shallum, son of Zadok, son of Ahitub,
3 son of Amariah, son of Azariah, son of Meraioth,
4 son of Zerahiah, son of Uzzi, son of Bukki,
5 son of Abishua, son of Phinehas, son of Eleazar, son of Aaron the chief priest.
6 This Ezra went up from Babylon, and he was a scribe skilled in the law of Moses, which the LORD God of Israel had given; and the king granted him all he requested because the hand of the LORD his God *was* upon him.
7 Some of the sons of Israel and some of the priests, the Levites, the singers, the gatekeepers and the temple servants went up to Jerusalem in the seventh year of King Artaxerxes.
8 He came to Jerusalem in the fifth month, which was in the seventh year of the king.
9 For on the first of the first month he began to go up from Babylon; and on the first of the fifth month he came to Jerusalem, because the good hand of his God *was* upon him.
10 For Ezra had set his heart to study the law of the LORD and to practice *it,* and to teach *His* statutes and ordinances in Israel.
11 Now this is the copy of the decree which King Artaxerxes gave to Ezra the priest, the scribe, learned in the words of the commandments of the LORD and His statutes to Israel:

12 "Artaxerxes, king of kings, to Ezra the priest, the scribe of the law of the God of heaven, perfect *peace.* And now
13 I have issued a decree that any of the people of Israel and their priests and the Levites in my kingdom who are willing to go to Jerusalem, may go with you.
14 "Forasmuch as you are sent by the king and his seven counselors to inquire concerning Judah and Jerusalem according to the law of your God which is in your hand,
15 and to bring the silver and gold, which the king and his counselors have freely offered to the God of Israel, whose dwelling is in Jerusalem,
16 with all the silver and gold which you find in the whole province of Babylon, along with the freewill offering of the people and of the priests, who offered willingly for the house of their God which is in Jerusalem;
17 with this money, therefore, you shall diligently buy bulls, rams and lambs, with their grain offerings and their drink offerings and offer them on the altar of the house of your God which is in Jerusalem.
18 "Whatever seems good to you and to your brothers to do with the rest of the silver and gold, you may do according to the will of your God.
19 "Also the utensils which are given to you for the service of the house of your God, deliver in full before the God of Jerusalem.
20 "The rest of the needs for the house of your God, for which you may have occasion to provide, provide *for it* from the royal treasury.
21 "I, even I, King Artaxerxes, issue a decree to all the treasurers who are *in the provinces* beyond the River, that whatever Ezra the priest, the scribe of

Life Examples:

EZRA: Applying God's Word

EZRA 7:10

*E*zra is a great example of what commitment to applying God's Word can do for both an individual and a nation.

The Persian king Artaxerxes gave Ezra permission to travel from Babylon to his ancestral homeland in Jerusalem. As a godly priest, Ezra felt compelled to improve the spiritual condition of the remnant of his people, so he worked diligently to bring about several religious and cultural reforms among his discouraged countrymen.

Ezra's life demonstrates the importance not merely of learning and knowing the Word of God, but also of regularly applying it in daily life. Because God had put him in a position of spiritual authority, Ezra also did everything he could think of to pass on to others what he had learned in his Bible study. Ezra wasn't just a hearer of God's Word; he was also an effective and deeply committed doer of it (James 1:22).

---

the law of the God of heaven, may require of you, it shall be done diligently, 22 *even* up to 100 talents of silver, 100 kors of wheat, 100 baths of wine, 100 baths of oil, and salt as needed.

23 "Whatever is commanded by the God of heaven, let it be done with zeal for the house of the God of heaven, so that there will not be wrath against the kingdom of the king and his sons.

24 "We also inform you that it is not allowed to impose tax, tribute or toll *on* any of the priests, Levites, singers, doorkeepers, Nethinim or servants of this house of God.

25 "You, Ezra, according to the wisdom of your God which is in your hand, appoint magistrates and judges that they may judge all the people who are in *the province* beyond the River, *even* all those who know the laws of your God; and you may teach anyone who is ignorant *of them.*

26 "Whoever will not observe the law of your God and the law of the king, let judgment be executed upon him strictly, whether for death or for banishment or for confiscation of goods or for imprisonment."

27 Blessed be the LORD, the God of our fathers, who has put *such a thing* as this in the king's heart, to adorn the house of the LORD which is in Jerusalem,

28 and has extended lovingkindness to me before the king and his counselors and before all the king's mighty princes. Thus I was strengthened according to the hand of the LORD my God upon me, and I gathered leading men from Israel to go up with me.

8 NOW these are the heads of their fathers' *households* and the genealogical enrollment of those who went up with me from Babylon in the reign of King Artaxerxes:

2 of the sons of Phinehas, Gershom; of the sons of Ithamar, Daniel; of the sons of David, Hattush;

3 of the sons of Shecaniah *who was* of the sons of Parosh, Zechariah and with him 150 males *who were in* the genealogical list;

4 of the sons of Pahath-moab, Eliehoenai

LIFE LESSONS

➤ **Ezra 7:25 — *You, Ezra, according to the wisdom of your God which is in your hand, appoint magistrates and judges that they may judge all the people.***

*T*he king did not grant Ezra all of his requests simply because something odd came over him. He had been watching Ezra, and he recognized him as a man with God-given wisdom. Our behavior does *matter* (Prov. 14:35).

➤ **Ezra 7:28 — *I was strengthened according to the hand of the LORD my God upon me.***

*G*od shows us He is with us in a million different, meaningful ways. For Ezra, the letter from King Artaxerxes was confirmation that he was doing the Lord's will. The Father will show us we are on the correct course through His Word, the counsel of others, songs, and other means that are significant to us. How does God show you that you are on the right track?

the son of Zerahiah and 200 males with him;

5   of the sons of Zattu, Shecaniah, the son of Jahaziel and 300 males with him;

6   and of the sons of Adin, Ebed the son of Jonathan and 50 males with him;

7   and of the sons of Elam, Jeshaiah the son of Athaliah and 70 males with him;

8   and of the sons of Shephatiah, Zebadiah the son of Michael and 80 males with him;

9   of the sons of Joab, Obadiah the son of Jehiel and 218 males with him;

10   and of the sons of Bani, Shelomith, the son of Josiphiah and 160 males with him;

11   and of the sons of Bebai, Zechariah the son of Bebai and 28 males with him;

12   and of the sons of Azgad, Johanan the son of Hakkatan and 110 males with him;

13   and of the sons of Adonikam, the last ones, these being their names, Eliphelet, Jeuel and Shemaiah, and 60 males with them;

14   and of the sons of Bigvai, Uthai and Zabbud, and 70 males with them.

15   Now I assembled them at the river that runs to Ahava, where we camped for three days; and when I observed the people and the priests, I did not find any Levites there.

16   So I sent for Eliezer, Ariel, Shemaiah, Elnathan, Jarib, Elnathan, Nathan, Zechariah and Meshullam, leading men, and for Joiarib and Elnathan, teachers.

17   I sent them to Iddo the leading man at the place Casiphia; and I told them what to say to Iddo and his brothers, the temple servants at the place Casiphia, that is, to bring ministers to us for the house of our God.

18   According to the good hand of our God upon us they brought us a man of insight of the sons of Mahli, the son of Levi, the son of Israel, namely Sherebiah, and his sons and brothers, 18 men;

19   and Hashabiah and Jeshaiah of the sons of Merari, with his brothers and their sons, 20 men;

20   and 220 of the temple servants, whom David and the princes had given for the service of the Levites, all of them designated by name.

21   Then I proclaimed a fast there at the river of Ahava, that we might humble ourselves before our God to seek from Him a safe journey for us, our little ones, and all our possessions.

22   For I was ashamed to request from the king troops and horsemen to protect us from the enemy on the way, because we had said to the king, "The hand of our God is favorably disposed to all those who seek Him, but His power and His anger are against all those who forsake Him."

23   So we fasted and sought our God concerning this matter, and He listened to our entreaty.

24   Then I set apart twelve of the leading priests, Sherebiah, Hashabiah, and with them ten of their brothers;

25   and I weighed out to them the silver, the gold and the utensils, the offering for the house of our God which the king and his counselors and his princes and all Israel present there had offered.

26   Thus I weighed into their hands 650 talents of silver, and silver utensils worth 100 talents, and 100 gold talents,

27   and 20 gold bowls worth 1,000 darics, and two utensils of fine shiny bronze, precious as gold.

28   Then I said to them, "You are holy to the LORD, and the utensils are holy; and the silver and the gold are a freewill offering to the LORD God of your fathers.

29   "Watch and keep them until you weigh them before the leading priests, the Levites and the heads of the fathers' households of Israel at Jerusalem, in the chambers of the house of the LORD."

30   So the priests and the Levites accepted the weighed out silver and gold and the utensils, to bring them to Jerusalem to the house of our God.

31   Then we journeyed from the river ◄ Ahava on the twelfth of the first month to

---

LIFE LESSONS

➤ **Ezra 8:31 — The hand of our God was over us, and He delivered us from the hand of the enemy and the ambushes by the way.**

*W*ould Ezra have arrived safely at Jerusalem without prayer? Would bandits have ambushed him or enemies attacked him had he not knelt before the Lord? Because he did not want to find out, he fought and won those battles ahead of time through prayer.

go to Jerusalem; and the hand of our God was over us, and He delivered us from the hand of the enemy and the ambushes by the way.
32 Thus we came to Jerusalem and remained there three days.
33 On the fourth day the silver and the gold and the utensils were weighed out in the house of our God into the hand of Meremoth the son of Uriah the priest, and with him *was* Eleazar the son of Phinehas; and with them *were* the Levites, Jozabad the son of Jeshua and Noadiah the son of Binnui.
34 Everything *was* numbered and weighed, and all the weight was recorded at that time.
35 The exiles who had come from the captivity offered burnt offerings to the God of Israel: 12 bulls for all Israel, 96 rams, 77 lambs, 12 male goats for a sin offering, all as a burnt offering to the LORD.
36 Then they delivered the king's edicts to the king's satraps and to the governors *in the provinces* beyond the River, and they supported the people and the house of God.

Psalm 88:1–5

A Song. A Psalm of the sons of Korah. For the choir director; according to Mahalath Leannoth. A Maskil of Heman the Ezrahite.

88 O LORD, the God of my salvation, I have cried out by day and in the night before You.
2 Let my prayer come before You; Incline Your ear to my cry!
➤ 3 For my soul has had enough troubles, And my life has drawn near to Sheol.

4 I am reckoned among those who go down to the pit; I have become like a man without strength,
5 Forsaken among the dead, Like the slain who lie in the grave, Whom You remember no more, And they are cut off from Your hand.

Proverbs 21:21, 22

21 He who pursues righteousness and loyalty Finds life, righteousness and honor. ✳
22 A wise man scales the city of the mighty And brings down the stronghold in which they trust.

Acts 23:16–35

16 But the son of Paul's sister heard of ◄ their ambush, and he came and entered the barracks and told Paul.
17 Paul called one of the centurions to him and said, "Lead this young man to the commander, for he has something to report to him."
18 So he took him and led him to the commander and *said, "Paul the prisoner called me to him and asked me to lead this young man to you since he has something to tell you."
19 The commander took him by the hand and stepping aside, *began* to inquire of him privately, "What is it that you have to report to me?"
20 And he said, "The Jews have agreed to ask you to bring Paul down tomorrow

---

LIFE LESSONS

➤ **Psalm 88:3** — *My soul has had enough troubles, and my life has drawn near to Sheol.*

*O*bedience leads to blessing, but that doesn't mean you will have a trouble-free life. Paul and Barnabas said, "Through many tribulations we must enter the kingdom of God" (Acts 14:22).

➤ **Acts 23:16** — *The son of Paul's sister heard of their ambush, and he came and entered the barracks and told Paul.*

*W*e must never imagine that God *must* work in a certain way. Here He rescued Paul, not through a miracle, but through the sharp ears of his nephew. The Lord works in ways we cannot anticipate.

to the Council, as though they were going to inquire somewhat more thoroughly about him.

21 "So do not listen to them, for more than forty of them are lying in wait for him who have bound themselves under a curse not to eat or drink until they slay him; and now they are ready and waiting for the promise from you."

22 So the commander let the young man go, instructing him, "Tell no one that you have notified me of these things."

23 And he called to him two of the centurions and said, "Get two hundred soldiers ready by the third hour of the night to proceed to Caesarea, with seventy horsemen and two hundred spearmen."

24 *They were* also to provide mounts to put Paul on and bring him safely to Felix the governor.

25 And he wrote a letter having this form:

26 "Claudius Lysias, to the most excellent governor Felix, greetings.

27 "When this man was arrested by the Jews and was about to be slain by them, I came up to them with the troops and rescued him, having learned that he was a Roman.

28 "And wanting to ascertain the charge for which they were accusing him, I brought him down to their Council;

29 and I found him to be accused over questions about their Law, but under no accusation deserving death or imprisonment.

30 "When I was informed that there would be a plot against the man, I sent him to you at once, also instructing his accusers to bring charges against him before you."

31 So the soldiers, in accordance with their orders, took Paul and brought him by night to Antipatris.

32 But the next day, leaving the horsemen to go on with him, they returned to the barracks.

33 When these had come to Caesarea and delivered the letter to the governor, they also presented Paul to him.

34 When he had read it, he asked from what province he was, and when he learned that he was from Cilicia,

35 he said, "I will give you a hearing after your accusers arrive also," giving orders for him to be kept in Herod's Praetorium.

JULY 24

✦ Ezra 9:1—10:44

9 NOW when these things had been completed, the princes approached me, saying, "The people of Israel and the priests and the Levites have not separated themselves from the peoples of the lands, according to their abominations, *those* of the Canaanites, the Hittites, the Perizzites, the Jebusites, the Ammonites, the Moabites, the Egyptians and the Amorites.

2 "For they have taken some of their daughters *as wives* for themselves and for their sons, so that the holy race has intermingled with the peoples of the lands; indeed, the hands of the princes and the rulers have been foremost in this unfaithfulness."

➤ 3 When I heard about this matter, I tore my garment and my robe, and pulled some of the hair from my head and my beard, and sat down appalled.

4 Then everyone who trembled at the words of the God of Israel on account of the unfaithfulness of the exiles gathered to me, and I sat appalled until the evening offering.

5 But at the evening offering I arose

from my humiliation, even with my garment and my robe torn, and I fell on my knees and stretched out my hands to the LORD my God;

6 and I said, "O my God, I am ashamed and embarrassed to lift up my face to You, my God, for our iniquities have risen above our heads and our guilt has grown even to the heavens.

7 "Since the days of our fathers to this day we *have been* in great guilt, and on account of our iniquities we, our kings *and* our priests have been given into the hand of the kings of the lands, to the sword, to captivity and to plunder and to open shame, as *it is* this day.

8 "But now for a brief moment grace has been *shown* from the LORD our God, to leave us an escaped remnant and to give us a peg in His holy place, that our God may enlighten our eyes and grant us a little reviving in our bondage.

9 "For we are slaves; yet in our bondage our God has not forsaken us, but has extended lovingkindness to us in the sight of the kings of Persia, to give us reviving to raise up the house of our God, to restore its ruins and to give us a wall in Judah and Jerusalem.

10 "Now, our God, what shall we say after this? For we have forsaken Your commandments,

11 which You have commanded by Your servants the prophets, saying, 'The land which you are entering to possess is an unclean land with the uncleanness of the peoples of the lands, with their abominations which have filled it from end to end *and* with their impurity.

12 'So now do not give your daughters to their sons nor take their daughters to your sons, and never seek their peace or their prosperity, that you may be strong and eat the good *things* of the land and leave *it* as an inheritance to your sons forever.'

13 "After all that has come upon us for our evil deeds and our great guilt, since You our God have requited *us* less than our iniquities *deserve*, and have given us an escaped remnant as this,

14 shall we again break Your commandments and intermarry with the peoples who commit these abominations? Would You not be angry with us to the point of destruction, until there is no remnant nor any who escape?

15 "O LORD God of Israel, You are righteous, for we have been left an escaped remnant, as *it is* this day; behold, we are before You in our guilt, for no one can stand before You because of this."

10 NOW while Ezra was praying and making confession, weeping and prostrating himself before the house of God, a very large assembly, men, women and children, gathered to him from Israel; for the people wept bitterly.

2 Shecaniah the son of Jehiel, one of the sons of Elam, said to Ezra, "We have been unfaithful to our God and have married foreign women from the peoples of the land; yet now there is hope for Israel in spite of this.

3 "So now let us make a covenant with our God to put away all the wives and their children, according to the counsel of my lord and of those who tremble at the commandment of our God; and let it be done according to the law.

4 "Arise! For *this* matter is your responsibility, but we will be with you; be courageous and act."

5 Then Ezra rose and made the leading priests, the Levites and all Israel, take oath that they would do according to this proposal; so they took the oath.

6 Then Ezra rose from before the house of God and went into the chamber of Jehohanan the son of Eliashib. Although he went there, he did not eat bread nor drink water, for he was mourning over the unfaithfulness of the exiles.

LIFE LESSONS

> **Ezra 9:9 —** *"We are slaves; yet in our bondage our God has not forsaken us, but has extended lovingkindness to us in the sight of the kings of Persia."*

*E*ven in judgment, God loves to show mercy. We must be careful not to presume upon His grace, but rather must thank Him for it and obey His Word out of a grateful heart of love and devotion.

> **Ezra 10:3 —** *"Tremble at the commandment of our God."*

*W*hy should we "tremble at the commandment of our God"? Because He always means what He says, in regard to both blessing and judgment. We need more love and reverence for His Word!

7   They made a proclamation throughout Judah and Jerusalem to all the exiles, that they should assemble at Jerusalem,
8   and that whoever would not come within three days, according to the counsel of the leaders and the elders, all his possessions should be forfeited and he himself excluded from the assembly of the exiles.
9   So all the men of Judah and Benjamin assembled at Jerusalem within the three days. It was the ninth month on the twentieth of the month, and all the people sat in the open square *before* the house of God, trembling because of this matter and the heavy rain.
10 Then Ezra the priest stood up and said to them, "You have been unfaithful and have married foreign wives adding to the guilt of Israel.
11 "Now therefore, make confession to the LORD God of your fathers and do His will; and separate yourselves from the peoples of the land and from the foreign wives."
12 Then all the assembly replied with a loud voice, "That's right! As you have said, so it is our duty to do.
13 "But there are many people; it is the rainy season and we are not able to stand in the open. Nor *can* the task *be done* in one or two days, for we have transgressed greatly in this matter.
14 "Let our leaders represent the whole assembly and let all those in our cities who have married foreign wives come at appointed times, together with the elders and judges of each city, until the fierce anger of our God on account of this matter is turned away from us."
15 Only Jonathan the son of Asahel and Jahzeiah the son of Tikvah opposed this, with Meshullam and Shabbethai the Levite supporting them.
16 But the exiles did so. And Ezra the priest selected men *who were* heads of fathers' *households* for *each of* their father's households, all of them by name. So they convened on the first day of the tenth month to investigate the matter.
17 They finished *investigating* all the men who had married foreign wives by the first day of the first month.
18 Among the sons of the priests who had married foreign wives were found of the sons of Jeshua the son of Jozadak, and his brothers: Maaseiah, Eliezer, Jarib and Gedaliah.

19 They pledged to put away their wives, and being guilty, *they offered* a ram of the flock for their offense.
20 Of the sons of Immer *there were* Hanani and Zebadiah;
21 and of the sons of Harim: Maaseiah, Elijah, Shemaiah, Jehiel and Uzziah;
22 and of the sons of Pashhur: Elioenai, Maaseiah, Ishmael, Nethanel, Jozabad and Elasah.
23 Of Levites *there were* Jozabad, Shimei, Kelaiah (that is, Kelita), Pethahiah, Judah and Eliezer.
24 Of the singers *there was* Eliashib; and of the gatekeepers: Shallum, Telem and Uri.
25 Of Israel, of the sons of Parosh *there were* Ramiah, Izziah, Malchijah, Mijamin, Eleazar, Malchijah and Benaiah;
26 and of the sons of Elam: Mattaniah, Zechariah, Jehiel, Abdi, Jeremoth and Elijah;
27 and of the sons of Zattu: Elioenai, Eliashib, Mattaniah, Jeremoth, Zabad and Aziza;
28 and of the sons of Bebai: Jehohanan, Hananiah, Zabbai *and* Athlai;
29 and of the sons of Bani: Meshullam, Malluch and Adaiah, Jashub, Sheal *and* Jeremoth;
30 and of the sons of Pahath-moab: Adna, Chelal, Benaiah, Maaseiah, Mattaniah, Bezalel, Binnui and Manasseh;
31 and *of* the sons of Harim: Eliezer, Isshijah, Malchijah, Shemaiah, Shimeon,
32 Benjamin, Malluch *and* Shemariah;
33 of the sons of Hashum: Mattenai, Mattattah, Zabad, Eliphelet, Jeremai, Manasseh *and* Shimei;
34 of the sons of Bani: Maadai, Amram, Uel,
35 Benaiah, Bedeiah, Cheluhi,
36 Vaniah, Meremoth, Eliashib,
37 Mattaniah, Mattenai, Jaasu,
38 Bani, Binnui, Shimei,
39 Shelemiah, Nathan, Adaiah,
40 Machnadebai, Shashai, Sharai,
41 Azarel, Shelemiah, Shemariah,
42 Shallum, Amariah *and* Joseph.
43 Of the sons of Nebo *there were* Jeiel, Mattithiah, Zabad, Zebina, Jaddai, Joel *and* Benaiah.
44 All these had married foreign wives, and some of them had wives *by whom* they had children.

Psalm 88:6–10

6 You have put me in the lowest pit,
   In dark places, in the depths.
7 Your wrath has rested upon me,
   And You have afflicted me with all
      Your waves.   Selah.
8 You have removed my
      acquaintances far from me;
   You have made me an object of
      loathing to them;
   I am shut up and cannot go out.
9 My eye has wasted away because of
      affliction;
   I have called upon You every day,
      O LORD;
   I have spread out my hands to You.
10 Will You perform wonders for the
      dead?
   Will the departed spirits rise and
      praise You?   Selah.

Proverbs 21:23, 24

23 He who guards his mouth and his
      tongue,
   Guards his soul from troubles.
24 "Proud," "Haughty," "Scoffer," are
      his names,
   Who acts with insolent pride.

Acts 24:1–27

24 AFTER five days the high priest
   Ananias came down with some elders, with an attorney named Tertullus,
and they brought charges to the governor against Paul.
2 After Paul had been summoned, Tertullus began to accuse him, saying to the
governor,
   "Since we have through you attained
much peace, and since by your provi-
dence reforms are being carried out for
this nation,
3 we acknowledge this in every way
and everywhere, most excellent Felix,
with all thankfulness.
4 "But, that I may not weary you any
further, I beg you to grant us, by your
kindness, a brief hearing.

5 "For we have found this man a real
pest and a fellow who stirs up dissension among all the Jews throughout the
world, and a ringleader of the sect of the
Nazarenes.
6 "And he even tried to desecrate the
temple; and then we arrested him. [We
wanted to judge him according to our
own Law.
7 "But Lysias the commander came
along, and with much violence took him
out of our hands,
8 ordering his accusers to come before you.] By examining him yourself
concerning all these matters you will be
able to ascertain the things of which we
accuse him."
9 The Jews also joined in the attack,
asserting that these things were so.
10 When the governor had nodded for
him to speak, Paul responded:
   "Knowing that for many years you
have been a judge to this nation, I cheerfully make my defense,
11 since you can take note of the fact
that no more than twelve days ago I went
up to Jerusalem to worship.
12 "Neither in the temple, nor in the
synagogues, nor in the city itself did they
find me carrying on a discussion with
anyone or causing a riot.
13 "Nor can they prove to you the
charges of which they now accuse me.
14 "But this I admit to you, that according to the Way which they call a sect I do
serve the God of our fathers, believing
everything that is in accordance with the
Law and that is written in the Prophets;
15 having a hope in God, which these
men cherish themselves, that there shall
certainly be a resurrection of both the
righteous and the wicked.

LIFE LESSONS

➤ Acts 24:14 — "I do serve the God of
our fathers, believing everything that is
in accordance with the Law and that is
written in the Prophets."

Paul did not see the Christian faith
as an alternative to his Jewish
upbringing, but as the fulfillment of it.
He worshiped the same God he always
had, and had complete faith in the same
Scripture.

WHAT THE BIBLE SAYS ABOUT

A Clear Conscience

Acts 24:16

*W*hen you are tempted to do the wrong thing, do you listen to your conscience or do you just ignore it and keep going? Although sometimes it will seem as if people are acting without a conscience, we all have one. It is a gift from God that we should care for and give great attention to because it is given to us for our own protection.

Every day we face decisions that involve our conscience, and it sends up red flags when we are about to do something wrong. When our conscience speaks and we ignore it, it is like taking a knife and dulling the edges. It becomes ineffective. If we disregard our conscience long enough, we'll make a mess of our lives (1 Tim. 1:18–20).

This is when we are most vulnerable to false doctrines and sin, and it's why people throughout the centuries have worshiped all types of things. Their belief systems have disappeared. In order to quiet their conscience, they've changed the way they think. They've deliberately chosen to exchange the truth of God for a lie (Rom. 1:21–25). However, no one is going to get away with that. God will allow their hearts to be given over to darkness. Whoever violates the laws of God will suffer the consequences.

Is it safe, then, to let our conscience be our guide? Not really. It all depends upon how our conscience has been programmed. Has it been programmed with the Word of God? When the Word of God becomes the grid of truth that protects our conscience, then we know we can respond in the right way. This is because the Holy Spirit enables us to understand the truth and will guide us to do the right thing.

However, understand that the Holy Spirit isn't your conscience. Every person has a conscience—that's why there are people who know right from wrong, even though they aren't Christians. However, only those who've received Jesus as their Savior have the Holy Spirit. The Holy Spirit works in conjunction with our conscience and works to strengthen us, teaching us the truth.

We know we can dull our conscience, but the good news is that we can also make it stronger. Paul said, "I also do my best to maintain always a blameless conscience both before God and before men" (Acts 24:16). How do we do so? We program ourselves with the absolute truth of God's Word. His way is the best way, and it's the only way to find happiness, peace, joy, and eternal security. We must have His Word and His Spirit as our defense.

Are you going to take heed of your conscience? Are you going to listen to what God is saying to you? Or are you going to do everything your way?

Remember, your conscience is a gift of God to protect you. Take good care of it. Get in the Word of God, and obey the leading of the Spirit. Make sure that you program your grid system based on God's truth. And strengthen your conscience by seeking the Lord. Then you, too, will have a conscience without offense toward God and men. ❖

---

16 "In view of this, I also do my best to maintain always a blameless conscience *both* before God and before men.
17 "Now after several years I came to bring alms to my nation and to present offerings;
18 in which they found me *occupied* in the temple, having been purified, without *any* crowd or uproar. But *there were* some Jews from Asia—
19 who ought to have been present before you and to make accusation, if they should have anything against me.
20 "Or else let these men themselves tell what misdeed they found when I stood before the Council,

---

LIFE LESSONS

➤ **Acts 24:16** — *"I also do my best to maintain always a blameless conscience both before God and before men."*

*W*hen Paul talks about a blameless conscience, he is referring to one that is devoid of any guilt toward another person or toward the Lord. The apostle never tried to earn right standing before God, but he did strive to live out the righteousness that had been given to him through faith in Jesus. Paul wanted his conduct to reflect well on his Savior, and his conscience affirmed that he was honoring Christ.

21 other than for this one statement which I shouted out while standing among them, 'For the resurrection of the dead I am on trial before you today.'"
22 But Felix, having a more exact knowledge about the Way, put them off, saying, "When Lysias the commander comes down, I will decide your case."
23 Then he gave orders to the centurion for him to be kept in custody and *yet* have *some* freedom, and not to prevent any of his friends from ministering to him.
24 But some days later Felix arrived with Drusilla, his wife who was a Jewess, and sent for Paul and heard him *speak* about faith in Christ Jesus.
25 But as he was discussing righteousness, self-control and the judgment to come, Felix became frightened and said, "Go away for the present, and when I find time I will summon you."

26 At the same time too, he was hoping that money would be given him by Paul; therefore he also used to send for him quite often and converse with him.
27 But after two years had passed, Felix was succeeded by Porcius Festus, and wishing to do the Jews a favor, Felix left Paul imprisoned.

Nehemiah 1:1—2:20

1 THE words of Nehemiah the son of Hacaliah.

Now it happened in the month Chislev, *in* the twentieth year, while I was in Susa the capitol,
2 that Hanani, one of my brothers, and some men from Judah came; and I asked them concerning the Jews who had escaped *and* had survived the captivity, and about Jerusalem.
3 They said to me, "The remnant there in the province who survived the captivity are in great distress and reproach, and the wall of Jerusalem is broken down and its gates are burned with fire."
4 When I heard these words, I sat down and wept and mourned for days; and I was fasting and praying before the God of heaven.
5 I said, "I beseech You, O LORD God of heaven, the great and awesome God, who preserves the covenant and lovingkindness for those who love Him and keep His commandments,
6 let Your ear now be attentive and Your eyes open to hear the prayer of Your servant which I am praying before

You now, day and night, on behalf of the sons of Israel Your servants, confessing the sins of the sons of Israel which we have sinned against You; I and my father's house have sinned.
7 "We have acted very corruptly against You and have not kept the commandments, nor the statutes, nor the ordinances which You commanded Your servant Moses.
8 "Remember the word which You commanded Your servant Moses, saying, 'If you are unfaithful I will scatter you among the peoples;
9 but *if* you return to Me and keep My commandments and do them, though

WHAT THE BIBLE SAYS ABOUT

Effectively Tackling a Prayer Burden

Nehemiah 1:4–6

*W*hen Nehemiah heard that his people lived in great distress and reproach, that the walls of Jerusalem lay in ruins, and that the gates of the city remained burned and broken, he responded with prayer:

"I sat down and wept and mourned for days and I was fasting and praying before the God of heaven. I said, 'I beseech You, O LORD God of heaven, the great and awesome God, who preserves the covenant and lovingkindness for those who love Him and keep His commandments, let Your ear now be attentive and Your eyes open to hear the prayer of Your servant which I am praying before You now, day and night'" (Neh. 1:4–6).

Nehemiah was experiencing a prayer burden.

A prayer burden can be defined as a strong motivation to pray for others and to carry the needs of others before God in prayer until He responds.

The Bible has a great deal to say about burdens. We are to bear one another's burdens (Gal. 6:2). We are to go the second mile in helping another person (Matt. 5:41). Much of our ability to bear natural burdens is derived from developing our ability to carry spiritual burdens in prayer.

A sense of spiritual weight usually accompanies a prayer burden—a heaviness of heart and emotion, a spirit of mourning, or a feeling of restlessness. We can't seem to shift ourselves away from a problem or need that has come to our attention.

This is what happened with Nehemiah, so he prayed in faith that God would restore Jerusalem. And God answered his prayer by sending him to Jerusalem to lead the effort of rebuilding the wall.

James 5:16 promises, "The effective prayer of a righteous man can accomplish much." If you feel burdened to pray for another person, then commit yourself to wholehearted intercession with thanksgiving and praise that God will act on that person's behalf (Phil. 4:6, 7). Then, listen to Him and obey. He may very well work through you as part of His answer.

And like Nehemiah, you will be greatly blessed when you see God doing mighty things in response to your prayers. ◈

---

those of you who have been scattered were in the most remote part of the heavens, I will gather them from there and will bring them to the place where I have chosen to cause My name to dwell.' 10 "They are Your servants and Your people whom You redeemed by Your great power and by Your strong hand. 11 "O Lord, I beseech You, may Your ear be attentive to the prayer of Your servant and the prayer of Your servants who delight to revere Your name, and make Your servant successful today and grant him compassion before this man."

Now I was the cupbearer to the king.

2 AND it came about in the month Nisan, in the twentieth year of King Artaxerxes, that wine *was* before him, and I took up the wine and gave it to the king. Now I had not been sad in his presence.
2 So the king said to me, "Why is your face sad though you are not sick? This is nothing but sadness of heart." Then I was very much afraid.

3 I said to the king, "Let the king live forever. Why should my face not be sad when the city, the place of my fathers' tombs, lies desolate and its gates have been consumed by fire?"
4 Then the king said to me, "What would you request?" So I prayed to the God of heaven.
5 I said to the king, "If it please the

LIFE LESSONS

> Nehemiah 2:4 — *Then the king said to me, "What would you request?" So I prayed to the God of heaven.*

*T*his must be one of the shortest prayers on record, uttered wordlessly in the seconds after the king's question. Nehemiah needed wisdom to know what to ask for, so in this brief moment, he silently submitted himself to the Lord's direction. He knew that with God leading him, mighty things had already happened and would continue to come to pass.

king, and if your servant has found favor before you, send me to Judah, to the city of my fathers' tombs, that I may rebuild it."

6 Then the king said to me, the queen sitting beside him, "How long will your journey be, and when will you return?" So it pleased the king to send me, and I gave him a definite time.

7 And I said to the king, "If it please the king, let letters be given me for the governors *of the provinces* beyond the River, that they may allow me to pass through until I come to Judah,

8 and a letter to Asaph the keeper of the king's forest, that he may give me timber to make beams for the gates of the fortress which is by the temple, for the wall of the city and for the house to which I will go." And the king granted *them* to me because the good hand of my God *was* on me.

9 Then I came to the governors *of the provinces* beyond the River and gave them the king's letters. Now the king had sent with me officers of the army and horsemen.

10 When Sanballat the Horonite and Tobiah the Ammonite official heard *about it*, it was very displeasing to them that someone had come to seek the welfare of the sons of Israel.

11 So I came to Jerusalem and was there three days.

➤ 12 And I arose in the night, I and a few men with me. I did not tell anyone what my God was putting into my mind to do for Jerusalem and there was no animal with me except the animal on which I was riding.

13 So I went out at night by the Valley Gate in the direction of the Dragon's Well and *on* to the Refuse Gate, inspecting the walls of Jerusalem which were broken down and its gates which were consumed by fire.

14 Then I passed on to the Fountain Gate and the King's Pool, but there was no place for my mount to pass.

15 So I went up at night by the ravine and inspected the wall. Then I entered the Valley Gate again and returned.

16 The officials did not know where I had gone or what I had done; nor had I as yet told the Jews, the priests, the nobles, the officials or the rest who did the work.

17 Then I said to them, "You see the bad situation we are in, that Jerusalem is desolate and its gates burned by fire. Come, let us rebuild the wall of Jerusalem so that we will no longer be a reproach."

18 I told them how the hand of my God had been favorable to me and also about the king's words which he had spoken to me. Then they said, "Let us arise and build." So they put their hands to the good *work.*

19 But when Sanballat the Horonite and Tobiah the Ammonite official, and Geshem the Arab heard *it*, they mocked us and despised us and said, "What is this thing you are doing? Are you rebelling against the king?"

20 So I answered them and said to ➤ them, "The God of heaven will give us success; therefore we His servants will arise and build, but you have no portion, right or memorial in Jerusalem."

LIFE LESSONS

➤ **Nehemiah 2:12 —** *I arose in the night, I and a few men with me. I did not tell anyone what my God was putting into my mind to do for Jerusalem.*

*N*ehemiah showed himself to be a man of God when he obeyed the initial promptings of His Spirit. Though Nehemiah had been given the authority to repair Jerusalem's walls, he wisely chose not to tell anyone his purpose or plan until he had seen all of the destruction. That way, he could make an unbiased assessment of the situation. Though we may want to shout from the mountaintops what the Lord is calling us to do, the wisest thing is to be discreet until He releases us to announce our intentions.

➤ **Nehemiah 2:20 —** *"The God of heaven will give us success; therefore we His servants will arise and build."*

*N*ehemiah was a man of great confidence because he understood the trustworthy and loving nature of the Lord. He understood his task to be not primarily political or civic, but spiritual, even though it concerned the building of a physical wall. When God puts something on our hearts, the core issue is always spiritual—whether or not we will trust Him.

Psalm 88:11–18

11 Will Your lovingkindness be
   declared in the grave,
   Your faithfulness in Abaddon?
12 Will Your wonders be made known
   in the darkness?
   And Your righteousness in the land
   of forgetfulness?
13 But I, O LORD, have cried out to You
   for help,
   And in the morning my prayer
   comes before You.
14 O LORD, why do You reject my soul?
   Why do You hide Your face from
   me?
15 I was afflicted and about to die from
   my youth on;
   I suffer Your terrors; I am overcome.
16 Your burning anger has passed over
   me;
   Your terrors have destroyed me.
17 They have surrounded me like
   water all day long;
   They have encompassed me
   altogether.
18 You have removed lover and friend
   far from me;
   My acquaintances are in darkness.

Proverbs 21:25, 26

25 The desire of the sluggard puts him
   to death,
   For his hands refuse to work;
26 All day long he is craving,
   While the righteous gives and does
   not hold back.

Acts 25:1–27

25 FESTUS then, having arrived in the
province, three days later went up
to Jerusalem from Caesarea.
2 And the chief priests and the leading
men of the Jews brought charges against
Paul, and they were urging him,
3 requesting a concession against
Paul, that he might have him brought to
Jerusalem (at the same time, setting an
ambush to kill him on the way).

4 Festus then answered that Paul
was being kept in custody at Caesarea
and that he himself was about to leave
shortly.
5 "Therefore," he *said, "let the influential men among you go there with me,
and if there is anything wrong about the
man, let them prosecute him."
6 After he had spent not more than
eight or ten days among them, he went
down to Caesarea, and on the next day
he took his seat on the tribunal and ordered Paul to be brought.
7 After Paul arrived, the Jews who
had come down from Jerusalem stood
around him, bringing many and serious
charges against him which they could
not prove,
8 while Paul said in his own defense, "I
have committed no offense either against
the Law of the Jews or against the temple or against Caesar."
9 But Festus, wishing to do the Jews a
favor, answered Paul and said, "Are you
willing to go up to Jerusalem and stand
trial before me on these charges?"
10 But Paul said, "I am standing before
Caesar's tribunal, where I ought to be
tried. I have done no wrong to the Jews,
as you also very well know.
11 "If, then, I am a wrongdoer and have
committed anything worthy of death, I
do not refuse to die; but if none of those
things is true of which these men accuse
me, no one can hand me over to them. I
appeal to Caesar."
12 Then when Festus had conferred with
his council, he answered, "You have appealed to Caesar, to Caesar you shall go."
13 Now when several days had elapsed,
King Agrippa and Bernice arrived at
Caesarea and paid their respects to Festus.
14 While they were spending many
days there, Festus laid Paul's case before
the king, saying, "There is a man who
was left as a prisoner by Felix;
15 and when I was at Jerusalem, the
chief priests and the elders of the Jews
brought charges against him, asking for
a sentence of condemnation against him.
16 "I answered them that it is not the
custom of the Romans to hand over any
man before the accused meets his accusers face to face and has an opportunity to
make his defense against the charges.
17 "So after they had assembled here, I

did not delay, but on the next day took my seat on the tribunal and ordered the man to be brought before me.

18 "When the accusers stood up, they *began* bringing charges against him not of such crimes as I was expecting,

➤ 19 but they *simply* had some points of disagreement with him about their own religion and about a dead man, Jesus, whom Paul asserted to be alive.

20 "Being at a loss how to investigate such matters, I asked whether he was willing to go to Jerusalem and there stand trial on these matters.

21 "But when Paul appealed to be held in custody for the Emperor's decision, I ordered him to be kept in custody until I send him to Caesar."

22 Then Agrippa *said* to Festus, "I also would like to hear the man myself." "Tomorrow," he *said, "you shall hear him."

23 So, on the next day when Agrippa came together with Bernice amid great pomp, and entered the auditorium accompanied by the commanders and the prominent men of the city, at the command of Festus, Paul was brought in.

24 Festus *said, "King Agrippa, and all you gentlemen here present with us, you see this man about whom all the people of the Jews appealed to me, both at Jerusalem and here, loudly declaring that he ought not to live any longer.

25 "But I found that he had committed nothing worthy of death; and since he himself appealed to the Emperor, I decided to send him.

26 "Yet I have nothing definite about him to write to my lord. Therefore I have brought him before you *all* and especially before you, King Agrippa, so that after the investigation has taken place, I may have something to write.

27 "For it seems absurd to me in sending a prisoner, not to indicate also the charges against him." ◄

LIFE LESSONS

➤ **Acts 25:19** — *"They . . . had some points of disagreement with him about their own religion and about a dead man, Jesus, whom Paul asserted to be alive."*

To the Roman governor Festus, the gospel was nothing but the religious fantasy of a superstitious and contentious people. We should not be surprised when non-believers treat it as myth. However, we should live our lives in a manner that testifies to the truth of the gospel so that those who are lost can believe and be saved (2 Tim. 2:24–26).

➤ **Acts 25:27** — *"For it seems absurd to me in sending a prisoner, not to indicate also the charges against him."*

Festus could not see how Paul had violated the Jewish law and hoped that Agrippa—who knew the Jews well—could help him formulate some kind of legal charge against him that would make sense to the Romans. As we learn through Paul, Joseph (Gen. 39), and Stephen (Acts 7:54–60), sometimes people will charge us unfairly because we stand for the Lord. However, He will vindicate us, so we should trust Him and continue to obey Him faithfully (Ps. 7:8–10; 10:17, 18; 26:1–3; 43; 54; 109:26–31).

JULY 26

⊕ **Nehemiah 3:1—5:19**

3 THEN Eliashib the high priest arose with his brothers the priests and built the Sheep Gate; they consecrated it and hung its doors. They consecrated the wall to the Tower of the Hundred *and* the Tower of Hananel.

2 Next to him the men of Jericho built, and next to them Zaccur the son of Imri built.

3 Now the sons of Hassenaah built the Fish Gate; they laid its beams and hung its doors with its bolts and bars.

4 Next to them Meremoth the son of Uriah the son of Hakkoz made repairs. And next to him Meshullam the son of Berechiah the son of Meshezabel made repairs. And next to him Zadok the son of Baana *also* made repairs.

5 Moreover, next to him the Tekoites made repairs, but their nobles did not support the work of their masters.

6 Joiada the son of Paseah and Meshullam the son of Besodeiah repaired the Old Gate; they laid its beams and hung its doors with its bolts and its bars.
7 Next to them Melatiah the Gibeonite and Jadon the Meronothite, the men of Gibeon and of Mizpah, also made repairs for the official seat of the governor *of the province* beyond the River.
8 Next to him Uzziel the son of Harhaiah of the goldsmiths made repairs. And next to him Hananiah, one of the perfumers, made repairs, and they restored Jerusalem as far as the Broad Wall.
9 Next to them Rephaiah the son of Hur, the official of half the district of Jerusalem, made repairs.
10 Next to them Jedaiah the son of Harumaph made repairs opposite his house. And next to him Hattush the son of Hashabneiah made repairs.
11 Malchijah the son of Harim and Hasshub the son of Pahath-moab repaired another section and the Tower of Furnaces.
12 Next to him Shallum the son of Hallohesh, the official of half the district of Jerusalem, made repairs, he and his daughters.
13 Hanun and the inhabitants of Zanoah repaired the Valley Gate. They built it and hung its doors with its bolts and its bars, and a thousand cubits of the wall to the Refuse Gate.
14 Malchijah the son of Rechab, the official of the district of Beth-haccherem repaired the Refuse Gate. He built it and hung its doors with its bolts and its bars.
15 Shallum the son of Col-hozeh, the official of the district of Mizpah, repaired the Fountain Gate. He built it, covered it and hung its doors with its bolts and its bars, and the wall of the Pool of Shelah at the king's garden as far as the steps that descend from the city of David.
16 After him Nehemiah the son of Azbuk, official of half the district of Beth-zur, made repairs as far as *a point* opposite the tombs of David, and as far as the artificial pool and the house of the mighty men.
17 After him the Levites carried out repairs *under* Rehum the son of Bani. Next to him Hashabiah, the official of half the district of Keilah, carried out repairs for his district.

18 After him their brothers carried out repairs *under* Bavvai the son of Henadad, official of *the other* half of the district of Keilah.
19 Next to him Ezer the son of Jeshua, the official of Mizpah, repaired another section in front of the ascent of the armory at the Angle.
20 After him Baruch the son of Zabbai zealously repaired another section, from the Angle to the doorway of the house of Eliashib the high priest.
21 After him Meremoth the son of Uriah the son of Hakkoz repaired another section, from the doorway of Eliashib's house even as far as the end of his house.
22 After him the priests, the men of the valley, carried out repairs.
23 After them Benjamin and Hasshub carried out repairs in front of their house. After them Azariah the son of Maaseiah, son of Ananiah, carried out repairs beside his house.
24 After him Binnui the son of Henadad repaired another section, from the house of Azariah as far as the Angle and as far as the corner.
25 Palal the son of Uzai *made repairs* in front of the Angle and the tower projecting from the upper house of the king, which is by the court of the guard. After him Pedaiah the son of Parosh *made repairs*.
26 The temple servants living in Ophel *made repairs* as far as the front of the Water Gate toward the east and the projecting tower.
27 After them the Tekoites repaired another section in front of the great projecting tower and as far as the wall of Ophel.
28 Above the Horse Gate the priests carried out repairs, each in front of his house.
29 After them Zadok the son of Immer carried out repairs in front of his house. And after him Shemaiah the son of Shecaniah, the keeper of the East Gate, carried out repairs.
30 After him Hananiah the son of Shelemiah, and Hanun the sixth son of Zalaph, repaired another section. After him Meshullam the son of Berechiah carried out repairs in front of his own quarters.
31 After him Malchijah, one of the goldsmiths, carried out repairs as far as the house of the temple servants and of the merchants, in front of the Inspection

Gate and as far as the upper room of the corner.

32 Between the upper room of the corner and the Sheep Gate the goldsmiths and the merchants carried out repairs.

4 NOW it came about that when Sanballat heard that we were rebuilding the wall, he became furious and very angry and mocked the Jews.

2 He spoke in the presence of his brothers and the wealthy *men* of Samaria and said, "What are these feeble Jews doing? Are they going to restore *it* for themselves? Can they offer sacrifices? Can they finish in a day? Can they revive the stones from the dusty rubble even the burned ones?"

3 Now Tobiah the Ammonite *was* near him and he said, "Even what they are building—if a fox should jump on *it*, he would break their stone wall down!"

4 Hear, O our God, how we are despised! Return their reproach on their own heads and give them up for plunder in a land of captivity.

5 Do not forgive their iniquity and let not their sin be blotted out before You, for they have demoralized the builders.

6 So we built the wall and the whole wall was joined together to half its *height*, for the people had a mind to work.

7 Now when Sanballat, Tobiah, the Arabs, the Ammonites and the Ashdodites heard that the repair of the walls of Jerusalem went on, *and* that the breaches began to be closed, they were very angry.

8 All of them conspired together to come *and* fight against Jerusalem and to cause a disturbance in it.

9 But we prayed to our God, and because of them we set up a guard against them day and night.

10 Thus in Judah it was said,
"The strength of the burden bearers
    is failing,
Yet there is much rubbish;
And we ourselves are unable
To rebuild the wall."

11 Our enemies said, "They will not know or see until we come among them, kill them and put a stop to the work."

12 When the Jews who lived near them came and told us ten times, "They will come up against us from every place where you may turn,"

13 then I stationed *men* in the lowest parts of the space behind the wall, the exposed places, and I stationed the people in families with their swords, spears and bows.

14 When I saw *their fear*, I rose and spoke to the nobles, the officials and the rest of the people: "Do not be afraid of them; remember the Lord who is great and awesome, and fight for your brothers, your sons, your daughters, your wives and your houses."

Life Examples:

NEHEMIAH: Daring to Believe

NEHEMIAH 4:14

*D*espite moments of doubt and unease, Nehemiah demonstrated great faith in God. Driven by a vision he believed came from God, he dared to trust in the sovereign Lord who always keeps His promises.

Nehemiah told the people, "The God of heaven will give us success; therefore we His servants will arise and build" (Neh. 2:20). Nehemiah understood that if he didn't depend on God to get the job done, it would never get done. But he also understood that genuine belief requires practical action, so he told his colleagues, "Remember the Lord, who is great and awesome, and fight for your brothers" (Neh. 4:14).

Because Nehemiah trusted God and moved forward, he successfully completed the vision God had given him. Whatever challenge confronts you, God has promised to grant you success when you put your trust in Him.

15 When our enemies heard that it was known to us, and that God had frustrated their plan, then all of us returned to the wall, each one to his work.

16 From that day on, half of my servants carried on the work while half of them held the spears, the shields, the bows and the breastplates; and the captains *were* behind the whole house of Judah.

17 Those who were rebuilding the wall and those who carried burdens took *their* load with one hand doing the work and the other holding a weapon.

18 As for the builders, each *wore* his sword girded at his side as he built, while the trumpeter *stood* near me.

19 I said to the nobles, the officials and the rest of the people, "The work is great and extensive, and we are separated on the wall far from one another.

20 "At whatever place you hear the sound of the trumpet, rally to us there. Our God will fight for us."

21 So we carried on the work with half of them holding spears from dawn until the stars appeared.

22 At that time I also said to the people, "Let each man with his servant spend the night within Jerusalem so that they may be a guard for us by night and a laborer by day."

23 So neither I, my brothers, my servants, nor the men of the guard who followed me, none of us removed our clothes, each *took* his weapon *even to* the water.

5 NOW there was a great outcry of the people and of their wives against their Jewish brothers.

2 For there were those who said, "We, our sons and our daughters are many; therefore let us get grain that we may eat and live."

3 There were others who said, "We are mortgaging our fields, our vineyards and our houses that we might get grain because of the famine."

4 Also there were those who said, "We have borrowed money for the king's tax *on* our fields and our vineyards.

5 "Now our flesh is like the flesh of our brothers, our children like their children. Yet behold, we are forcing our sons and our daughters to be slaves, and some of our daughters are forced into bondage

already, and we are helpless because our fields and vineyards belong to others."

6 Then I was very angry when I had heard their outcry and these words.

7 I consulted with myself and contended with the nobles and the rulers and said to them, "You are exacting usury, each from his brother!" Therefore, I held a great assembly against them.

8 I said to them, "We according to our ability have redeemed our Jewish brothers who were sold to the nations; now would you even sell your brothers that they may be sold to us?" Then they were silent and could not find a word *to say*.

9 Again I said, "The thing which you are doing is not good; should you not walk in the fear of our God because of the reproach of the nations, our enemies?

10 "And likewise I, my brothers and my servants are lending them money and grain. Please, let us leave off this usury.

11 "Please, give back to them this very day their fields, their vineyards, their olive groves and their houses, also the hundredth *part* of the money and of the grain, the new wine and the oil that you are exacting from them."

12 Then they said, "We will give *it* back and will require nothing from them; we

---

LIFE LESSONS

➤ **Nehemiah 5:7 —** *I consulted with myself and contended with the nobles and the rulers.*

A solid prayer life and a close relationship with God do not minimize the need for clear and profound thinking. Rather, our communion with the Lord empowers and sharpens our thoughts and increases our wisdom.

➤ **Nehemiah 5:9 —** *"Should you not walk in the fear of our God because of the reproach of the nations?"*

P art of walking in the fear of God means that we watch carefully how we behave in front of those who do not yet know Him. As Paul wrote, "Conduct yourselves with wisdom toward outsiders, making the most of the opportunity" (Col. 4:5). Our interactions with them may be what the Lord works through to draw them to Himself.

will do exactly as you say." So I called the priests and took an oath from them that they would do according to this promise.

13 I also shook out the front of my garment and said, "Thus may God shake out every man from his house and from his possessions who does not fulfill this promise; even thus may he be shaken out and emptied." And all the assembly said, "Amen!" And they praised the LORD. Then the people did according to this promise.

14 Moreover, from the day that I was appointed to be their governor in the land of Judah, from the twentieth year to the thirty-second year of King Artaxerxes, *for* twelve years, neither I nor my kinsmen have eaten the governor's food *allowance.*

15 But the former governors who were before me laid burdens on the people and took from them bread and wine besides forty shekels of silver; even their servants domineered the people. But I did not do so because of the fear of God.

16 I also applied myself to the work on this wall; we did not buy any land, and all my servants were gathered there for the work.

17 Moreover, *there were* at my table one hundred and fifty Jews and officials, besides those who came to us from the nations that were around us.

18 Now that which was prepared for each day was one ox *and* six choice sheep, also birds were prepared for me; and once in ten days all sorts of wine *were furnished* in abundance. Yet for all this I did not demand the governor's food *allowance,* because the servitude was heavy on this people.

19 Remember me, O my God, for good, *according to* all that I have done for this people.

Psalm 89:1–4

A Maskil of Ethan ^the Ezrahite.

89 I WILL sing of the lovingkindness of the LORD forever;
To all generations I will make known Your faithfulness with my mouth.

2 For I have said, "Lovingkindness will be built up forever;
In the heavens You will establish Your faithfulness."
3 "I have made a covenant with My chosen;
I have sworn to David My servant,
4 I will establish your seed forever
And build up your throne to all generations."   Selah.

Proverbs 21:27

27 The sacrifice of the wicked is an abomination,
How much more when he brings it with evil intent!

Acts 26:1–32

26 AGRIPPA said to Paul, "You are permitted to speak for yourself." Then Paul stretched out his hand and *proceeded* to make his defense:

2 "In regard to all the things of which I am accused by the Jews, I consider myself fortunate, King Agrippa, that I am about to make my defense before you today;

3 especially because you are an expert in all customs and questions among *the* Jews; therefore I beg you to listen to me patiently.

4 "So then, all Jews know my manner of life from my youth up, which from the beginning was spent among my *own* nation and at Jerusalem;

5 since they have known about me for a long time, if they are willing to testify, that I lived *as* a Pharisee according to the strictest sect of our religion.

6 "And now I am standing trial for the hope of the promise made by God to our fathers;

7 *the promise* to which our twelve tribes hope to attain, as they earnestly serve *God* night and day. And for this hope, O King, I am being accused by Jews.

8 "Why is it considered incredible among you *people* if God does raise the dead?

9 "So then, I thought to myself that I ◄

LIFE LESSONS

➢ **Acts 26:9 —** *"I thought to myself that I had to do many things hostile to the name of Jesus of Nazareth."*

*P*aul could understand the animosity of the Jewish leaders against him because only a few years before he had shared their fierce hatred of Christianity (Acts 8:1–3). He knew one could feel as if they were doing right and serving God while being deeply wrong and persecuting Him (Acts 9:1–5). This is why it's so important to have a vibrant, growing relationship with the Lord instead of merely doing pious acts.

had to do many things hostile to the name of Jesus of Nazareth.

10 "And this is just what I did in Jerusalem; not only did I lock up many of the saints in prisons, having received authority from the chief priests, but also when they were being put to death I cast my vote against them.

11 "And as I punished them often in all the synagogues, I tried to force them to blaspheme; and being furiously enraged at them, I kept pursuing them even to foreign cities.

12 "While so engaged as I was journeying to Damascus with the authority and commission of the chief priests,

13 at midday, O King, I saw on the way a light from heaven, brighter than the sun, shining all around me and those who were journeying with me.

14 "And when we had all fallen to the ground, I heard a voice saying to me in the Hebrew dialect, 'Saul, Saul, why are you persecuting Me? It is hard for you to kick against the goads.'

15 "And I said, 'Who are You, Lord?' And the Lord said, 'I am Jesus whom you are persecuting.

16 'But get up and stand on your feet; for this purpose I have appeared to you, to appoint you a minister and a witness not only to the things which you have seen, but also to the things in which I will appear to you;

17 rescuing you from the *Jewish* people and from the Gentiles, to whom I am sending you,

18 to open their eyes so that they may turn from darkness to light and from the dominion of Satan to God, that they

may receive forgiveness of sins and an inheritance among those who have been sanctified by faith in Me.'

19 "So, King Agrippa, I did not prove disobedient to the heavenly vision,

20 but *kept* declaring both to those of Damascus first, and *also* at Jerusalem and *then* throughout all the region of Judea, and *even* to the Gentiles, that they should repent and turn to God, performing deeds appropriate to repentance.

21 "For this reason *some* Jews seized me in the temple and tried to put me to death.

22 "So, having obtained help from God, I stand to this day testifying both to small and great, stating nothing but what the Prophets and Moses said was going to take place;

23 that the Christ was to suffer, *and* that by reason of *His* resurrection from the dead He would be the first to proclaim light both to the *Jewish* people and to the Gentiles."

24 While *Paul* was saying this in his defense, Festus *said in a loud voice, "Paul, you are out of your mind! *Your* great learning is driving you mad."

25 But Paul *said, "I am not out of my mind, most excellent Festus, but I utter words of sober truth.

26 "For the king knows about these matters, and I speak to him also with confidence, since I am persuaded that none of these things escape his notice; for this has not been done in a corner.

27 "King Agrippa, do you believe the Prophets? I know that you do."

28 Agrippa *replied* to Paul, "In a short time you will persuade me to become a Christian."

LIFE LESSONS

➢ **Acts 26:20 —** *"Repent and turn to God, performing deeds appropriate to repentance."*

*T*he gospel teaches that we receive divine grace through faith in Jesus Christ. Although our salvation is not contingent upon our works, our Christian testimonies are—we need to repent of our sin and behave in a godly manner so that the Lord will be glorified through us. God's grace gives us the ability and the desire to obey, not the right to disobey.

29 And Paul *said,* "I would wish to God, that whether in a short or long time, not only you, but also all who hear me this day, might become such as I am, except for these chains."

30 The king stood up and the governor and Bernice, and those who were sitting with them,

31 and when they had gone aside, they *began* talking to one another, saying, "This man is not doing anything worthy of death or imprisonment."

➤ 32 And Agrippa said to Festus, "This man might have been set free if he had not appealed to Caesar."

LIFE LESSONS

➤ Acts 26:32 — *"This man might have been set free if he had not appealed to Caesar."*

*W*as this an immense mistake on Paul's part? No. Rather, Paul's appeal to Caesar helped to fulfill God's command to Paul, "As you have solemnly witnessed to My cause at Jerusalem, so you must witness at Rome also" (Acts 23:11). Paul's goal was to get to Rome, and his appeal to Caesar meant he was going courtesy of the Roman government—with an armed escort, no less!

JULY 27

◈ Nehemiah 6:1—7:73

6 NOW when it was reported to Sanballat, Tobiah, to Geshem the Arab and to the rest of our enemies that I had rebuilt the wall, and *that* no breach remained in it, although at that time I had not set up the doors in the gates,

➤ 2 then Sanballat and Geshem sent *a message* to me, saying, "Come, let us meet together at Chephirim in the plain of Ono." But they were planning to harm me.

3 So I sent messengers to them, saying, "I am doing a great work and I cannot come down. Why should the work stop while I leave it and come down to you?"

4 They sent *messages* to me four times in this manner, and I answered them in the same way.

5 Then Sanballat sent his servant to me in the same manner a fifth time with an open letter in his hand.

LIFE LESSONS

➤ Nehemiah 6:2 — *They were planning to harm me.*

*W*hat the devil cannot accomplish by scorn and intimidation, he will try to accomplish by deception and hateful schemes. Only by immersing ourselves in the Word of God and through prayer will we avoid his traps.

6 In it was written, "It is reported among the nations, and Gashmu says, that you and the Jews are planning to rebel; therefore you are rebuilding the wall. And you are to be their king, according to these reports.

7 "You have also appointed prophets to proclaim in Jerusalem concerning you, 'A king is in Judah!' And now it will be reported to the king according to these reports. So come now, let us take counsel together."

8 Then I sent *a message* to him saying, "Such things as you are saying have not been done, but you are inventing them in your own mind."

9 For all of them were *trying* to frighten us, thinking, "They will become discouraged with the work and it will not be done." But now, O God, strengthen my hands.

10 When I entered the house of Shemaiah the son of Delaiah, son of Mehetabel, who was confined at home, he said, "Let us meet together in the house of God, within the temple, and let us close the doors of the temple, for they are coming to kill you, and they are coming to kill you at night."

11 But I said, "Should a man like me flee? And could one such as I go into the temple to save his life? I will not go in."

12 Then I perceived that surely God had not sent him, but he uttered *his* prophecy against me because Tobiah and Sanballat had hired him.

➤ 13 He was hired for this reason, that I might become frightened and act accordingly and sin, so that they might have an evil report in order that they could reproach me.

14 Remember, O my God, Tobiah and Sanballat according to these works of theirs, and also Noadiah the prophetess and the rest of the prophets who were *trying* to frighten me.

15 So the wall was completed on the twenty-fifth of *the month* Elul, in fifty-two days.

16 When all our enemies heard of *it*, and all the nations surrounding us saw
✳ *it*, they lost their confidence; for they recognized that this work had been accomplished with the help of our God.

17 Also in those days many letters went from the nobles of Judah to Tobiah, and Tobiah's *letters* came to them.

18 For many in Judah were bound by oath to him because he was the son-in-law of Shecaniah the son of Arah, and his son Jehohanan had married the daughter of Meshullam the son of Berechiah.

19 Moreover, they were speaking about his good deeds in my presence and reported my words to him. Then Tobiah sent letters to frighten me.

7 NOW when the wall was rebuilt and I had set up the doors, and the gatekeepers and the singers and the Levites were appointed,

2 then I put Hanani my brother, and Hananiah the commander of the fortress, in charge of Jerusalem, for he was a faithful man and feared God more than many.

3 Then I said to them, "Do not let the gates of Jerusalem be opened until the sun is hot, and while they are standing *guard*, let them shut and bolt the doors. Also appoint guards from the inhabitants of Jerusalem, each at his post, and each in front of his own house."

4 Now the city was large and spacious, but the people in it were few and the houses were not built.

➤ 5 Then my God put it into my heart to assemble the nobles, the officials and the people to be enrolled by genealogies. Then I found the book of the genealogy of those who came up first in which I found the following record:

6 These are the people of the province

➤ **Nehemiah 6:13 — *He was hired for this reason, that I might become frightened.***

*W*e hurt our own cause when we give in to fear and intimidation and act as though the Lord God almighty does not reign on high. Though we should proceed cautiously in precarious situations like Nehemiah was experiencing, we never have a reason to be cowardly (Josh. 1:9).

➤ **Nehemiah 7:5 — *God put it into my heart to assemble the nobles, the officials and the people to be enrolled by genealogies.***

*T*hroughout the centuries, the Jewish people kept very accurate genealogical records. Mainly, because of the land division the Lord had given each tribe as an inheritance (Josh. 11:23), but also to keep track of the family line through which the Messiah would come (Gen. 49:10; 1 Kin. 2:45; Matt. 1:1–17; Luke 3:23–38). So the Lord prompted Nehemiah to continue this important work.

who came up from the captivity of the exiles whom Nebuchadnezzar the king of Babylon had carried away, and who returned to Jerusalem and Judah, each to his city,

7 who came with Zerubbabel, Jeshua, Nehemiah, Azariah, Raamiah, Nahamani, Mordecai, Bilshan, Mispereth, Bigvai, Nehum, Baanah.

The number of men of the people of Israel:

8 the sons of Parosh, 2,172;

9 the sons of Shephatiah, 372;

10 the sons of Arah, 652;

11 the sons of Pahath-moab of the sons of Jeshua and Joab, 2,818;

12 the sons of Elam, 1,254;

13 the sons of Zattu, 845;

14 the sons of Zaccai, 760;

15 the sons of Binnui, 648;

16 the sons of Bebai, 628;

17 the sons of Azgad, 2,322;

18 the sons of Adonikam, 667;

19 the sons of Bigvai, 2,067;

20 the sons of Adin, 655;

21 the sons of Ater, of Hezekiah, 98;

22 the sons of Hashum, 328;

23 the sons of Bezai, 324;

24 the sons of Hariph, 112;
25 the sons of Gibeon, 95;
26 the men of Bethlehem and Netophah, 188;
27 the men of Anathoth, 128;
28 the men of Beth-azmaveth, 42;
29 the men of Kiriath-jearim, Chephirah and Beeroth, 743;
30 the men of Ramah and Geba, 621;
31 the men of Michmas, 122;
32 the men of Bethel and Ai, 123;
33 the men of the other Nebo, 52;
34 the sons of the other Elam, 1,254;
35 the sons of Harim, 320;
36 the men of Jericho, 345;
37 the sons of Lod, Hadid and Ono, 721;
38 the sons of Senaah, 3,930.
39 The priests: the sons of Jedaiah of the house of Jeshua, 973;
40 the sons of Immer, 1,052;
41 the sons of Pashhur, 1,247;
42 the sons of Harim, 1,017.
43 The Levites: the sons of Jeshua, of Kadmiel, of the sons of Hodevah, 74.
44 The singers: the sons of Asaph, 148.
45 The gatekeepers: the sons of Shallum, the sons of Ater, the sons of Talmon, the sons of Akkub, the sons of Hatita, the sons of Shobai, 138.
46 The temple servants: the sons of Ziha, the sons of Hasupha, the sons of Tabbaoth,
47 the sons of Keros, the sons of Sia, the sons of Padon,
48 the sons of Lebana, the sons of Hagaba, the sons of Shalmai,
49 the sons of Hanan, the sons of Giddel, the sons of Gahar,
50 the sons of Reaiah, the sons of Rezin, the sons of Nekoda,
51 the sons of Gazzam, the sons of Uzza, the sons of Paseah,
52 the sons of Besai, the sons of Meunim, the sons of Nephushesim,
53 the sons of Bakbuk, the sons of Hakupha, the sons of Harhur,
54 the sons of Bazlith, the sons of Mehida, the sons of Harsha,
55 the sons of Barkos, the sons of Sisera, the sons of Temah,
56 the sons of Neziah, the sons of Hatipha.
57 The sons of Solomon's servants: the sons of Sotai, the sons of Sophereth, the sons of Perida,

58 the sons of Jaala, the sons of Darkon, the sons of Giddel,
59 the sons of Shephatiah, the sons of Hattil, the sons of Pochereth-hazzebaim, the sons of Amon.
60 All the temple servants and the sons of Solomon's servants *were* 392.
61 These *were* they who came up from Tel-melah, Tel-harsha, Cherub, Addon and Immer; but they could not show their fathers' houses or their descendants, whether they were of Israel:
62 the sons of Delaiah, the sons of Tobiah, the sons of Nekoda, 642.
63 Of the priests: the sons of Hobaiah, the sons of Hakkoz, the sons of Barzillai, who took a wife of the daughters of Barzillai, the Gileadite, and was named after them.
64 These searched *among* their ancestral registration, but it could not be located; therefore they were considered unclean *and excluded* from the priesthood.
65 The governor said to them that they should not eat from the most holy things until a priest arose with Urim and Thummim.
66 The whole assembly together *was* 42,360,
67 besides their male and their female servants, of whom *there were* 7,337; and they had 245 male and female singers.
68 Their horses were 736; their mules, 245;
69 *their* camels, 435; *their* donkeys, 6,720.
70 Some from among the heads of fathers' *households* gave to the work. The governor gave to the treasury 1,000 gold drachmas, 50 basins, 530 priests' garments.
71 Some of the heads of fathers' *households* gave into the treasury of the work 20,000 gold drachmas and 2,200 silver minas.
72 That which the rest of the people gave was 20,000 gold drachmas and 2,000 silver minas and 67 priests' garments.
73 Now the priests, the Levites, the gatekeepers, the singers, some of the people, the temple servants and all Israel, lived in their cities.

And when the seventh month came, the sons of Israel *were* in their cities.

Psalm 89:5–10

5   The heavens will praise Your
      wonders, O LORD;
      Your faithfulness also in the
      assembly of the holy ones.
6   For who in the skies is comparable
      to the LORD?
      Who among the sons of the mighty
      is like the LORD,
7   A God greatly feared in the council
      of the holy ones,
      And awesome above all those who
      are around Him?
8   O LORD God of hosts, who is like
      You, O mighty LORD?
      Your faithfulness also surrounds
      You.
9   You rule the swelling of the sea;
      When its waves rise, You still
      them.
10 You Yourself crushed Rahab like
      one who is slain;
      You scattered Your enemies with
      Your mighty arm.

Proverbs 21:28

28 A false witness will perish,
      But the man who listens to the
      truth will speak forever.

Acts 27:1–26

27 WHEN it was decided that we
      would sail for Italy, they proceeded

LIFE LESSONS

> Psalm 89:6 — Who among the sons of
the mighty is like the LORD?

*T*hough other people will fail us—
either for intentional or unintentional reasons—God never will. So why
do we still rely on others more than on
Him? Perhaps we do so because we can
see, hear, and touch other people, and
the Lord is not tangible with our physical senses. Still, He is real, and He will
always be a better help to us than any
person could hope to be.

to deliver Paul and some other prisoners
to a centurion of the Augustan cohort
named Julius.
2   And embarking in an Adramyttian
ship, which was about to sail to the regions along the coast of Asia, we put out
to sea accompanied by Aristarchus, a
Macedonian of Thessalonica.
3   The next day we put in at Sidon; and
Julius treated Paul with consideration
and allowed him to go to his friends and
receive care.
4   From there we put out to sea and
sailed under the shelter of Cyprus because the winds were contrary.
5   When we had sailed through the sea
along the coast of Cilicia and Pamphylia,
we landed at Myra in Lycia.
6   There the centurion found an Alexandrian ship sailing for Italy, and he put
us aboard it.
7   When we had sailed slowly for a
good many days, and with difficulty had
arrived off Cnidus, since the wind did not
permit us to go farther, we sailed under
the shelter of Crete, off Salmone;
8   and with difficulty sailing past it we
came to a place called Fair Havens, near
which was the city of Lasea.
9   When considerable time had passed
and the voyage was now dangerous,
since even the fast was already over,
Paul began to admonish them,
10 and said to them, "Men, I perceive
that the voyage will certainly be with
damage and great loss, not only of the
cargo and the ship, but also of our lives."
11 But the centurion was more persuaded by the pilot and the captain of
the ship than by what was being said by
Paul.
12 Because the harbor was not suitable
for wintering, the majority reached a
decision to put out to sea from there, if
somehow they could reach Phoenix, a
harbor of Crete, facing southwest and
northwest, and spend the winter there.
13 When a moderate south wind came
up, supposing that they had attained
their purpose, they weighed anchor and
began sailing along Crete, close inshore.
14 But before very long there rushed
down from the land a violent wind,
called Euraquilo;
15 and when the ship was caught in it
and could not face the wind, we gave way
to it and let ourselves be driven along.

WHAT THE BIBLE SAYS ABOUT

A Surprise and a Welcome Visit

Acts 27:13–26

*D*o you like surprise visits? For most of us, it depends upon who appears at the door. When God makes a surprise visit, He brings a message and purpose we could never anticipate.

In Acts 27:13–26, we see God make a surprise visit to Paul during his final, disastrous, maelstrom-tossed voyage to Rome. Acts 27:20 tells us, "Since neither sun nor stars appeared for many days, and no small storm was assailing us, from then on all hope of our being saved was gradually abandoned." Without tackle or food, the 276 passengers knew there was no way they could survive the terrible storm.

In the moment most bereft of hope, God sent word to Paul through an angel. Paul, in return, announced His message to his shipmates. He said, "For this very night an angel of the God to whom I belong and whom I serve stood before me, saying, 'Do not be afraid, Paul; you must stand before Caesar; and behold, God has granted you all those who are sailing with you' " (vv. 23, 24).

There are some important things we can learn about God's surprise visits through this account of Paul's life.

1. *When God visits, He comes in His own timing.*

Though we may wonder why God chose to wait so long to address the passengers on that ship, we know one thing for sure: The hope He offered was very welcome to them. God works on the basis of His perfect knowledge and purposes, rather than our understanding or impatience.

2. *When God visits, we feel an awesome sense of His presence.*

It is when we're most helpless that we best appreciate God's strength and provision. We can almost imagine the amazing emotion that swept through these people, knowing that holy God was coming to their aid.

3. *When God visits, He has a specific purpose for us.*

The Lord's specific message to Paul was that He would indeed fulfill His purpose in Paul's life. God had previously commanded, "As you have solemnly witnessed to My cause at Jerusalem, so you must witness at Rome also" (Acts 23:11). Then He confirmed, "Do not be afraid, Paul; you must stand before Caesar" (Acts 27:24). God encouraged Paul by letting him know he was still on the right track—even if his circumstances seemed to suggest otherwise.

4. *The greater your task or His purpose, the more likely His visit will be.*

Understand that Paul was on his way to his final place of ministry: Rome. This was a critical time in his life, and he needed God's encouragement to remain strong and courageous for his final assignment.

God still makes surprise visits today because He has a wonderful and significant purpose for every one of us. He is interested in the details of our lives—whether we're peacefully sailing or tempest-tossed. He wants to give us confidence and involve us in His plan. He also wants others to be encouraged and saved through us.

So welcome Him and embrace Him. His surprise visits will always be right on time. ◈

---

16 Running under the shelter of a small island called Clauda, we were scarcely able to get the *ship's* boat under control. 17 After they had hoisted it up, they used supporting cables in undergirding the ship; and fearing that they might run aground on *the shallows* of Syrtis, they let down the sea anchor and in this way let themselves be driven along. 18 The next day as we were being violently storm-tossed, they began to jettison the cargo; 19 and on the third day they threw the ship's tackle overboard with their own hands.

20 Since neither sun nor stars appeared ◁ for many days, and no small storm was assailing *us*, from then on all hope of our being saved was gradually abandoned. 21 When they had gone a long time without food, then Paul stood up in their midst and said, "Men, you ought to have followed my advice and not to have set sail from Crete and incurred this damage and loss. 22 "*Yet* now I urge you to keep up your

courage, for there will be no loss of life among you, but *only* of the ship.

23 "For this very night an angel of the God to whom I belong and whom I serve stood before me,

24 saying, 'Do not be afraid, Paul; you must stand before Caesar; and behold, God has granted you all those who are sailing with you.'

25 "Therefore, keep up your courage, men, for I believe God that it will turn out exactly as I have been told.

26 "But we must run aground on a certain island."

LIFE LESSONS

➢ **Acts 27:20 — *All hope of our being saved was gradually abandoned.***

*H*ardships and trials can last for so long that we begin to despair that God will ever rescue us from our troubles. Yet He remains faithful, and difficult circumstances never indicate that He has lost interest in us. Rather, our adversity will be a bridge to a deeper relationship with Him if we'll trust Him.

➢ **Acts 27:25 — *""Keep up your courage, men, for I believe God that it will turn out exactly as I have been told."***

*W*hen times become difficult, those who do not have a relationship with God can take courage from those who do if believers maintain and display their trust in the Lord. Paul's faith encouraged many unbelievers, and many came to know Jesus Christ as their Savior through his consistent testimony.

JULY 28

Nehemiah 8:1—9:38

8 AND all the people gathered as one man at the square which was in front of the Water Gate, and they asked Ezra the scribe to bring the book of the law of Moses which the LORD had given to Israel.

2 Then Ezra the priest brought the law before the assembly of men, women and all who *could* listen with understanding, on the first day of the seventh month.

3 He read from it before the square which was in front of the Water Gate from early morning until midday, in the presence of men and women, those who could understand; and all the people were attentive to the book of the law.

4 Ezra the scribe stood at a wooden podium which they had made for the purpose. And beside him stood Mattithiah, Shema, Anaiah, Uriah, Hilkiah, and Maaseiah on his right hand; and Pedaiah, Mishael, Malchijah, Hashum, Hashbaddanah, Zechariah *and* Meshullam on his left hand.

5 Ezra opened the book in the sight of all the people for he was standing above all the people; and when he opened it, all the people stood up.

6 Then Ezra blessed the LORD the great God. And all the people answered, "Amen, Amen!" while lifting up their hands; then they bowed low and worshiped the LORD with *their* faces to the ground.

7 Also Jeshua, Bani, Sherebiah, Jamin, Akkub, Shabbethai, Hodiah, Maaseiah, Kelita, Azariah, Jozabad, Hanan, Pelaiah, the Levites, explained the law to the people while the people *remained* in their place.

8 They read from the book, from the law of God, translating to give the sense so that they understood the reading.

LIFE LESSONS

➢ **Nehemiah 8:6 — *They bowed low and worshiped the LORD with their faces to the ground.***

*D*o you ever worship with your face to the ground? If not, you should. Such a posture reminds us that God is the King and we are His subjects. He is sovereign; we are not.

9   Then Nehemiah, who was the governor, and Ezra the priest *and* scribe, and the Levites who taught the people said to all the people, "This day is holy to the LORD your God; do not mourn or weep." For all the people were weeping when they heard the words of the law.

10   Then he said to them, "Go, eat of the fat, drink of the sweet, and send portions to him who has nothing prepared; for this day is holy to our Lord. Do not be grieved, for the joy of the LORD is your strength."

11   So the Levites calmed all the people, saying, "Be still, for the day is holy; do not be grieved."

12   All the people went away to eat, to drink, to send portions and to celebrate a great festival, because they understood the words which had been made known to them.

13   Then on the second day the heads of fathers' *households* of all the people, the priests and the Levites were gathered to Ezra the scribe that they might gain insight into the words of the law.

14   They found written in the law how the LORD had commanded through Moses that the sons of Israel should live in booths during the feast of the seventh month.

15   So they proclaimed and circulated a proclamation in all their cities and in Jerusalem, saying, "Go out to the hills, and bring olive branches and wild olive branches, myrtle branches, palm branches and branches of *other* leafy trees, to make booths, as it is written."

16   So the people went out and brought *them* and made booths for themselves, each on his roof, and in their courts and in the courts of the house of God, and in the square at the Water Gate and in the square at the Gate of Ephraim.

17   The entire assembly of those who had returned from the captivity made booths and lived in them. The sons of Israel had indeed not done so from the days of Joshua the son of Nun to that day. And there was great rejoicing.

18   He read from the book of the law of God daily, from the first day to the last day. And they celebrated the feast seven days, and on the eighth day *there was* a solemn assembly according to the ordinance.

9   NOW on the twenty-fourth day of this month the sons of Israel assembled with fasting, in sackcloth and with dirt upon them.

2   The descendants of Israel separated themselves from all foreigners, and stood and confessed their sins and the iniquities of their fathers.

3   While they stood in their place, they read from the book of the law of the LORD their God for a fourth of the day; and for *another* fourth they confessed and worshiped the LORD their God.

4   Now on the Levites' platform stood Jeshua, Bani, Kadmiel, Shebaniah, Bunni, Sherebiah, Bani *and* Chenani, and they cried with a loud voice to the LORD their God.

5   Then the Levites, Jeshua, Kadmiel, Bani, Hashabneiah, Sherebiah, Hodiah,

---

LIFE LESSONS

➤ **Nehemiah 8:8** — *They read from the book, from the law of God, translating to give the sense so that they understood the reading.*

*W*hile all of us need to immerse ourselves in the Word of God on our own, there is no substitute for regularly gathering as His people to hear the Bible clearly explained and applied.

➤ **Nehemiah 8:10** — *"The joy of the LORD is your strength."*

*H*ow is God's joy our strength? Hebrews 12:2 tells us, "Jesus . . . for the joy set before Him endured the cross." The Lord's delight is in forgiving us and saving us. His happiness is in showing love to all who believe in Him. Therefore, whenever we feel weak and helpless, we need to remember that He loves to step in and deliver us. Then His joy really will be our strength.

➤ **Nehemiah 9:2** — *The descendants of Israel . . . stood and confessed their sins.*

*W*hy confess our sins? First, because God tells us to (James 5:16). Second, because confessing a sin breaks its power over us, since the power of sin grows more readily when it is hidden. If God speaks to your heart about something in His Word, be honest with Him. He will faithfully forgive and restore you.

ANSWERS TO LIFE'S QUESTIONS

What good does fasting do us?

NEHEMIAH 9:1

*U*pon hearing the sad news of Jerusalem's pitiful state, Nehemiah agonized over the city's plight. His response can teach us something useful: "When I heard these words, I sat down and wept and mourned for days; and I was fasting and praying before the God of heaven" (Neh. 1:4).

When we reach points of despondency, despair, confusion, or desperation, going before the Lord in prayer and fasting can bring peace, clarity, and direction to our situations. Jerusalem's devastation led Nehemiah to his knees in prayer and fasting.

Fasting in the biblical context means to abstain from food for a given period of time. Fasting doesn't just mean "going hungry" for a few days. It means abstaining for the purpose of focusing your attention on God and what He has to say to you.

Consider many excellent reasons for fasting:

To receive divine intervention when we are helpless. Nehemiah needed God's guidance, so he fasted and prayed—and he received what he needed.

To know God's will for our lives. When

Daniel felt unsure about the Lord's next step for his life, he sought Him through fasting (Dan. 9:3). Fasting clears the mind and allows us to hear more clearly what God is saying to us.

To respond to times of crisis. During times of crisis, we need more than ever to focus on what God wants us to do. When King Jehoshaphat and Judah faced the terrible armies of the Moabites, Ammonites, and Meunites, fasting was the recommended course of action (2 Chr. 20:3).

To prepare for ministry. We need to clearly hear the Lord's voice before we embark on His work (Acts 13:1–3). As we prepare for what God calls us to, fasting puts us in a proper attitude of dependence on Him and shows we are willing to conform to His purpose and image.

For personal cleansing. Fasting is often practiced as a means of personal cleansing for the physical body, as a way to remove impurities. But it works the same way in our spiritual lives. When we realize that we are steeped in sin, fasting helps bring healing and cleansing (Joel 2:12).

For victory over temptation, habits, and bondage. Fasting equips us for the battle we wage against Satan and against our own flesh. When we fail repeatedly to defeat some sin, we should seek the Lord's help—and fasting is one of the spiritual disciplines that can help us secure victory (Is. 58:6).

Shebaniah *and* Pethahiah, said, "Arise, bless the LORD your God forever and ever!

O may Your glorious name be blessed
And exalted above all blessing and
　　praise!
6 "You alone are the LORD.
You have made the heavens,
The heaven of heavens with all their
　　host,
The earth and all that is on it,
The seas and all that is in them,
You give life to all of them
And the heavenly host bows down
　　before You.
7 "You are the LORD God,
Who chose Abram
And brought him out from Ur of the
　　Chaldees,
And gave him the name Abraham.
8 "You found his heart faithful before
　　You,
And made a covenant with him
To give *him* the land of the
　　Canaanite,

Of the Hittite and the Amorite,
Of the Perizzite, the Jebusite and
　　the Girgashite—
To give *it* to his descendants.
And You have fulfilled Your promise,
For You are righteous.
9 "You saw the affliction of our fathers
　　in Egypt,
And heard their cry by the Red Sea.
10 "Then You performed signs and
　　wonders against Pharaoh,
Against all his servants and all the
　　people of his land;
For You knew that they acted
　　arrogantly toward them,
And made a name for Yourself as *it*
　　is this day.
11 "You divided the sea before them,
So they passed through the midst of
　　the sea on dry ground;
And their pursuers You hurled into
　　the depths,
Like a stone into raging waters.
12 "And with a pillar of cloud You led
　　them by day,

And with a pillar of fire by night
To light for them the way
In which they were to go.
13 "Then You came down on Mount
Sinai,
And spoke with them from heaven;
You gave them just ordinances and
true laws,
Good statutes and commandments.
14 "So You made known to them Your
holy sabbath,
And laid down for them
commandments, statutes and law,
Through Your servant Moses.
15 "You provided bread from heaven
for them for their hunger,
You brought forth water from a rock
for them for their thirst,
And You told them to enter in order
to possess
The land which You swore to give
them.
16 "But they, our fathers, acted
arrogantly;
They became stubborn and would
not listen to Your commandments.
17 "They refused to listen,
And did not remember Your
wondrous deeds which You had
performed among them;
So they became stubborn and
appointed a leader to return to
their slavery in Egypt.
But You are a God of forgiveness,
Gracious and compassionate,
Slow to anger and abounding in
lovingkindness;
And You did not forsake them.
18 "Even when they made for
themselves
A calf of molten metal
And said, 'This is your God
Who brought you up from Egypt,'
And committed great blasphemies,
19 You, in Your great compassion,
Did not forsake them in the
wilderness;
The pillar of cloud did not leave
them by day,
To guide them on their way,
Nor the pillar of fire by night, to
light for them the way in which
they were to go.
20 "You gave Your good Spirit to
instruct them,
Your manna You did not withhold
from their mouth,

And You gave them water for their
thirst.
21 "Indeed, forty years You provided
for them in the wilderness *and*
they were not in want;
Their clothes did not wear out, nor
did their feet swell.
22 "You also gave them kingdoms and
peoples,
And allotted *them* to them as a
boundary.
They took possession of the land of
Sihon the king of Heshbon
And the land of Og the king of
Bashan.
23 "You made their sons numerous as
the stars of heaven,
And You brought them into the
land
Which You had told their fathers to
enter and possess.
24 "So their sons entered and possessed
the land.
And You subdued before them
the inhabitants of the land, the
Canaanites,
And You gave them into their hand,
with their kings and the peoples
of the land,
To do with them as they desired.
25 "They captured fortified cities and a
fertile land.
They took possession of houses full
of every good thing,
Hewn cisterns, vineyards, olive
groves,
Fruit trees in abundance.
So they ate, were filled and grew
fat,
And reveled in Your great goodness.
26 "But they became disobedient and
rebelled against You,
And cast Your law behind their
backs
And killed Your prophets who had
admonished them
So that they might return to You,
And they committed great
blasphemies.
27 "Therefore You delivered them into
the hand of their oppressors who
oppressed them,
But when they cried to You in the
time of their distress,
You heard from heaven, and
according to Your great
compassion

You gave them deliverers who delivered them from the hand of their oppressors.

28 "But as soon as they had rest, they did evil again before You;
Therefore You abandoned them to the hand of their enemies, so that they ruled over them.
When they cried again to You, You heard from heaven,
And many times You rescued them according to Your compassion,

29 And admonished them in order to turn them back to Your law.
Yet they acted arrogantly and did not listen to Your commandments but sinned against Your ordinances,
By which if a man observes them he shall live.
And they turned a stubborn shoulder and stiffened their neck, and would not listen.

30 "However, You bore with them for many years,
And admonished them by Your Spirit through Your prophets,
Yet they would not give ear.
Therefore You gave them into the hand of the peoples of the lands.

31 "Nevertheless, in Your great compassion You did not make an end of them or forsake them,
For You are a gracious and compassionate God.

32 "Now therefore, our God, the great, the mighty, and the awesome God, who keeps covenant and lovingkindness,
Do not let all the hardship seem insignificant before You,
Which has come upon us, our kings, our princes, our priests, our prophets, our fathers and on all Your people,
From the days of the kings of Assyria to this day.

33 "However, You are just in all that has come upon us;
For You have dealt faithfully, but we have acted wickedly.

34 "For our kings, our leaders, our priests and our fathers have not kept Your law
Or paid attention to Your commandments and Your admonitions with which You have admonished them.

35 "But they, in their own kingdom, With Your great goodness which You gave them,
With the broad and rich land which You set before them,
Did not serve You or turn from their evil deeds.

36 "Behold, we are slaves today,
And as to the land which You gave to our fathers to eat of its fruit and its bounty,
Behold, we are slaves in it.

37 "Its abundant produce is for the kings
Whom You have set over us because of our sins;
They also rule over our bodies And over our cattle as they please,
So we are in great distress.

38 "Now because of all this
We are making an agreement in writing;
And on the sealed document *are the names of* our leaders, our Levites *and* our priests."

Psalm 89:11–18

11 The heavens are Yours, the earth also is Yours;
The world and all it contains, You have founded them.

12 The north and the south, You have created them;
Tabor and Hermon shout for joy at Your name.

13 You have a strong arm;
Your hand is mighty, Your right hand is exalted.

14 Righteousness and justice are the foundation of Your throne;
Lovingkindness and truth go before You.

15 How blessed are the people who know the joyful sound!
O Lord, they walk in the light of Your countenance.

16 In Your name they rejoice all the day,
And by Your righteousness they are exalted.

17 For You are the glory of their strength,
And by Your favor our horn is exalted.

18 For our shield belongs to the Lord,
And our king to the Holy One of
Israel.

◈ Proverbs 21:29–31

29 A wicked man displays a bold face,
But as for the upright, he makes his
way sure.
30 There is no wisdom and no
understanding
And no counsel against the Lord.
31 The horse is prepared for the day of
battle,
But victory belongs to the Lord.

◈ Acts 27:27–44

27 But when the fourteenth night came,
as we were being driven about in the
Adriatic Sea, about midnight the sailors
began to surmise that they were approaching some land.
28 They took soundings and found *it to
be* twenty fathoms; and a little farther on
they took another sounding and found *it
to be* fifteen fathoms.
29 Fearing that we might run aground
somewhere on the rocks, they cast four
anchors from the stern and wished for
daybreak.
30 But as the sailors were trying to escape from the ship and had let down the
ship's boat into the sea, on the pretense of
intending to lay out anchors from the bow,
31 Paul said to the centurion and to the
soldiers, "Unless these men remain in the
ship, you yourselves cannot be saved."
32 Then the soldiers cut away the ropes
of the *ship's* boat and let it fall away.
33 Until the day was about to dawn,
Paul was encouraging them all to take
some food, saying, "Today is the fourteenth day that you have been constantly
watching and going without eating, having taken nothing.
34 "Therefore I encourage you to take
some food, for this is for your preservation, for not a hair from the head of any
of you will perish."
35 Having said this, he took bread and
gave thanks to God in the presence of all,
and he broke it and began to eat.

36 All of them were encouraged and
they themselves also took food.
37 All of us in the ship were two hundred and seventy-six persons.
38 When they had eaten enough, they
began to lighten the ship by throwing out
the wheat into the sea.
39 When day came, they could not recognize the land; but they did observe a
bay with a beach, and they resolved to
drive the ship onto it if they could.
40 And casting off the anchors, they
left them in the sea while at the same
time they were loosening the ropes of the
rudders; and hoisting the foresail to the
wind, they were heading for the beach.
41 But striking a reef where two seas
met, they ran the vessel aground; and the
prow stuck fast and remained immovable, but the stern *began* to be broken up
by the force *of the waves.*
42 The soldiers' plan was to kill the
prisoners, so that none *of them* would
swim away and escape;
43 but the centurion, wanting to bring
Paul safely through, kept them from
their intention, and commanded that
those who could swim should jump overboard first and get to land,
44 and the rest *should follow,* some on
planks, and others on various things
from the ship. And so it happened that
they all were brought safely to land.

LIFE LESSONS

➤ **Proverbs 21:31** — *The horse is prepared for the day of battle, but victory
belongs to the Lord.*

*T*here's nothing wrong with preparation. In fact, it is essential that we
always be ready for whatever the Lord
calls us to do (Matt. 25:1–13). However,
the power and wisdom behind any victory is from God. Our resources will never
be enough, but God's will never fail.

➤ **Acts 27:44** — *All were brought safely
to land.*

*G*od had promised that everyone on
board would be saved, and so it happened. Some swam, some floated on
boards or pieces of the ship, but everyone made it to shore safely. We never go
wrong by trusting God's Word!

Nehemiah 10:1—11:36

10 NOW on the sealed document *were the names of:* Nehemiah the governor, the son of Hacaliah, and Zedekiah,

2 Seraiah, Azariah, Jeremiah,

3 Pashhur, Amariah, Malchijah,

4 Hattush, Shebaniah, Malluch,

5 Harim, Meremoth, Obadiah,

6 Daniel, Ginnethon, Baruch,

7 Meshullam, Abijah, Mijamin,

8 Maaziah, Bilgai, Shemaiah. These *were* the priests.

9 And the Levites: Jeshua the son of Azaniah, Binnui of the sons of Henadad, Kadmiel;

10 also their brothers Shebaniah, Hodiah, Kelita, Pelaiah, Hanan,

11 Mica, Rehob, Hashabiah,

12 Zaccur, Sherebiah, Shebaniah,

13 Hodiah, Bani, Beninu.

14 The leaders of the people: Parosh, Pahath-moab, Elam, Zattu, Bani,

15 Bunni, Azgad, Bebai,

16 Adonijah, Bigvai, Adin,

17 Ater, Hezekiah, Azzur,

18 Hodiah, Hashum, Bezai,

19 Hariph, Anathoth, Nebai,

20 Magpiash, Meshullam, Hezir,

21 Meshezabel, Zadok, Jaddua,

22 Pelatiah, Hanan, Anaiah,

23 Hoshea, Hananiah, Hasshub,

24 Hallohesh, Pilha, Shobek,

25 Rehum, Hashabnah, Maaseiah,

26 Ahiah, Hanan, Anan,

27 Malluch, Harim, Baanah.

28 Now the rest of the people, the priests, the Levites, the gatekeepers, the singers, the temple servants and all those who had separated themselves from the peoples of the lands to the law of God, their wives, their sons and their daughters, all those who had knowledge and understanding,

29 are joining with their kinsmen, their nobles, and are taking on themselves a curse and an oath to walk in God's law, which was given through Moses, God's servant, and to keep and to observe all the commandments of GOD our Lord, and His ordinances and His statutes;

30 and that we will not give our daughters to the peoples of the land or take their daughters for our sons.

31 As for the peoples of the land who bring wares or any grain on the sabbath day to sell, we will not buy from them on the sabbath or a holy day; and we will forego *the crops* the seventh year and the exaction of every debt.

32 We also placed ourselves under obligation to contribute yearly one third of a shekel for the service of the house of our God:

33 for the showbread, for the continual grain offering, for the continual burnt offering, the sabbaths, the new moon, for the appointed times, for the holy things and for the sin offerings to make atonement for Israel, and all the work of the house of our God.

34 Likewise we cast lots for the supply of wood *among* the priests, the Levites and the people so that they might bring it to the house of our God, according to our fathers' households, at fixed times annually, to burn on the altar of the LORD our God, as it is written in the law;

35 and that they might bring the first fruits of our ground and the first fruits of all the fruit of every tree to the house of the LORD annually,

36 and bring to the house of our God the firstborn of our sons and of our cattle, and the firstborn of our herds and our flocks as it is written in the law, for the priests who are ministering in the house of our God.

37 We will also bring the first of our dough, our contributions, the fruit of every tree, the new wine and the oil to the priests at the chambers of the house of our God, and the tithe of our ground to the Levites, for the Levites are they who receive the tithes in all the rural towns.

38 The priest, the son of Aaron, shall be with the Levites when the Levites receive

---

LIFE LESSONS

➤ **Nehemiah 10:38 — *The priest . . . and the Levites shall bring up the tenth of the tithes to the house of our God.***

*G*iving back to God has always been an important part of a walk of faith. By giving, we acknowledge that everything we have comes from His hand and that only He—not earthly wealth—has a claim to our hearts. No one ever out gives God!

WHAT THE BIBLE SAYS ABOUT

The Danger of Drifting

Nehemiah 10:28–39

As the people settled back into Jerusalem after Nehemiah had rebuilt the wall, they were intent on being right with the Lord. Nehemiah 10:29 tells us that they "are taking on themselves a curse and an oath to walk in God's law, which was given through Moses, God's servant, and to keep and to observe all the commandments of GOD our Lord, and His ordinances and His statutes." Why were they so motivated? Because they knew their ancestors had drifted away from God and sinned against Him—and the result was decades of captivity in foreign lands. They didn't want to make the same mistake.

Drifting is extremely dangerous, and like the penitent Israelites, we cannot afford to do it. We must decide whether we're going to float or start paddling. Are we going to have direction and purpose in life, or are we going to let this world take us down its destructive path?

Understand that when we go with the current, we'll be disappointed and ultimately destroyed. We need a rudder and a sense of direction. We must keep God as the focus of our lives.

What are the indications that we're beginning to drift?

1. *We know we're drifting when we lose interest in God's Word.*

The first sign that we're drifting is that our interest in God's Word decreases. However, the Bible is our instruction book—if we want to know how to live, we must look to the Bible (Psalm 119:9–11). We must meditate upon it, or every area of our lives will be affected.

2. *We know we're drifting when we neglect to pray.*

The second indication that we're drifting is that we lose our passion for prayer and stop crying out to God. The problem comes when things are going so well that we don't feel the need to pray. However, that's when we should pray the most because when we drop our guard, Satan attacks. Prayer is the way we communicate with God—the navigator of our lives. Without Him, we can't fight the current or steer our way through the narrow moral, financial, relational, and spiritual channels of our lives—and calamity is the result.

3. *We know we're drifting when we lose interest in church.*

The third indication that we're drifting is that we stop meeting together with other Christians at church and other fellowship or ministry opportunities. We're to worship, sing, preach the gospel, fellowship, pray together, and encourage one another—and there's no excuse for missing out

on that (Heb. 10:24, 25). If you're not involved in a church, ask God where you should go. Anytime we're under the preaching and teaching of God's Word, He is directing us and will stop us from drifting.

4. *We know we're drifting when we don't give our time or money.*

The fourth indication that we're drifting is that we stop giving our money and time. Some people will say, "I can't afford to give my tithe or spend time serving God." However, you can't afford not to do it. When we are faithful to do as God says, He makes the remainder much more valuable to us—He multiplies what we give to Him (Luke 6:38). However, when we drift in the stewardship of our time and money, it affects everything in our lives negatively.

5. *We know we're drifting when we don't share Jesus with anyone.*

The fifth indication that we're drifting is that we never talk to anyone about Jesus. We say we're so busy that we just don't have time to talk to others about the Lord. What we're really saying is that we don't want to paddle against the current of the culture, which we know is anti-Christian. In today's world, it's just not politically correct to talk to people about Jesus. But we have no obligation before God to be politically correct. Rather, we have a divine obligation to be biblically correct—because if we're biblically correct, people's lives will change, and we'll positively impact society.

6. *We know we're drifting when we no longer feel close to God.*

The sixth indication that we're drifting is that we don't feel as close to the Lord as we once did. Of course, it's because we're not reading His Word, praying, going to church, giving, or witnessing anymore. What we're losing is the most intimate relationship that we could ever have. Our relationships with God are deeper than any other relationship, and only He knows how to satisfy us. Why do we forsake that relationship? We do so because of the influence of other people and the lure of the world's ways. When we do that, we miss the Father's best for our lives. If we want His best, we must be willing to fight against the current.

When the Israelites returned to Jerusalem, they wanted God's best, so they established their commitment to Him and devoted themselves to serving Him and following His leadership.

Do you want God's best for your life, too? More than likely, you'd say, "Yes!" Then you must understand there's a price to pay. What are you willing to do to engage in the Father's divine, loving plan? It starts by analyzing why you're drifting. Ultimately, you drift because you've chosen to.

Don't destroy your life—don't drift so far that God must discipline you to bring you back. The Israelites learned their lesson. Will you follow their example? ◈

tithes, and the Levites shall bring up the tenth of the tithes to the house of our God, to the chambers of the storehouse. 39 For the sons of Israel and the sons of Levi shall bring the contribution of the grain, the new wine and the oil to the chambers; there are the utensils of the sanctuary, the priests who are ministering, the gatekeepers and the singers. Thus we will not neglect the house of our God.

11 NOW the leaders of the people lived in Jerusalem, but the rest of the people cast lots to bring one out of ten to live in Jerusalem, the holy city, while nine-tenths *remained* in the *other* cities.
2 And the people blessed all the men who volunteered to live in Jerusalem.
3 Now these are the heads of the provinces who lived in Jerusalem, but in the cities of Judah each lived on his own property in their cities—the Israelites, the priests, the Levites, the temple servants and the descendants of Solomon's servants.
4 Some of the sons of Judah and some of the sons of Benjamin lived in Jerusalem. From the sons of Judah: Athaiah the son of Uzziah, the son of Zechariah, the son of Amariah, the son of Shephatiah, the son of Mahalalel, of the sons of Perez;
5 and Maaseiah the son of Baruch, the son of Col-hozeh, the son of Hazaiah, the son of Adaiah, the son of Joiarib, the son of Zechariah, the son of the Shilonite.
6 All the sons of Perez who lived in Jerusalem were 468 able men.
7 Now these are the sons of Benjamin: Sallu the son of Meshullam, the son of Joed, the son of Pedaiah, the son of Kolaiah, the son of Maaseiah, the son of Ithiel, the son of Jeshaiah;

LIFE LESSONS

➤ **Nehemiah 11:2 —** *The people blessed all the men who volunteered to live in Jerusalem.*

It could not have been easy to leave a comfortable home in order to live in the ruined city, but many did this for the good of God's people. How often do we sacrifice for the benefit of other believers?

---

8 and after him Gabbai *and* Sallai, 928.
9 Joel the son of Zichri was their overseer, and Judah the son of Hassenuah was second in command of the city.
10 From the priests: Jedaiah the son of Joiarib, Jachin,
11 Seraiah the son of Hilkiah, the son of Meshullam, the son of Zadok, the son of Meraioth, the son of Ahitub, the leader of the house of God,
12 and their kinsmen who performed the work of the temple, 822; and Adaiah the son of Jeroham, the son of Pelaliah, the son of Amzi, the son of Zechariah, the son of Pashhur, the son of Malchijah,
13 and his kinsmen, heads of fathers' *households*, 242; and Amashsai the son of Azarel, the son of Ahzai, the son of Meshillemoth, the son of Immer,
14 and their brothers, valiant warriors, 128. And their overseer was Zabdiel, the son of Haggedolim.
15 Now from the Levites: Shemaiah the son of Hasshub, the son of Azrikam, the son of Hashabiah, the son of Bunni;
16 and Shabbethai and Jozabad, from the leaders of the Levites, who were in charge of the outside work of the house of God;
17 and Mattaniah the son of Mica, the son of Zabdi, the son of Asaph, who was the leader in beginning the thanksgiving at prayer, and Bakbukiah, the second among his brethren; and Abda the son of Shammua, the son of Galal, the son of Jeduthun.
18 All the Levites in the holy city *were* 284.
19 Also the gatekeepers, Akkub, Talmon and their brethren who kept watch at the gates, *were* 172.
20 The rest of Israel, of the priests *and* of the Levites, *were* in all the cities of Judah, each on his own inheritance.
21 But the temple servants were living in Ophel, and Ziha and Gishpa were in charge of the temple servants.
22 Now the overseer of the Levites in Jerusalem was Uzzi the son of Bani, the son of Hashabiah, the son of Mattaniah, the son of Mica, from the sons of Asaph, who were the singers for the service of the house of God.
23 For *there was* a commandment from the king concerning them and a firm regulation for the song leaders day by day.

24 Pethahiah the son of Meshezabel, of the sons of Zerah the son of Judah, was the king's representative in all matters concerning the people.

25 Now as for the villages with their fields, some of the sons of Judah lived in Kiriath-arba and its towns, in Dibon and its towns, and in Jekabzeel and its villages,

26 and in Jeshua, in Moladah and Beth-pelet,

27 and in Hazar-shual, in Beersheba and its towns,

28 and in Ziklag, in Meconah and in its towns,

29 and in En-rimmon, in Zorah and in Jarmuth,

30 Zanoah, Adullam, and their villages, Lachish and its fields, Azekah and its towns. So they encamped from Beer-sheba as far as the valley of Hinnom.

31 The sons of Benjamin also *lived* from Geba *onward*, at Michmash and Aija, at Bethel and its towns,

32 at Anathoth, Nob, Ananiah,

33 Hazor, Ramah, Gittaim,

34 Hadid, Zeboim, Neballat,

35 Lod and Ono, the valley of crafts-men.

36 From the Levites, *some* divisions in Judah belonged to Benjamin.

Psalm 89:19–29

19 Once You spoke in vision to Your godly ones,
And said, "I have given help to one who is mighty;
I have exalted one chosen from the people.

20 "I have found David My servant;
With My holy oil I have anointed him,

21 With whom My hand will be established;
My arm also will strengthen him.

22 "The enemy will not deceive him,
Nor the son of wickedness afflict him.

23 "But I shall crush his adversaries before him,
And strike those who hate him.

24 "My faithfulness and My lovingkindness will be with him,

And in My name his horn will be exalted.

25 "I shall also set his hand on the sea
And his right hand on the rivers.

26 "He will cry to Me, 'You are my Father,
My God, and the rock of my salvation.'

27 "I also shall make him *My* firstborn,
The highest of the kings of the earth.

28 "My lovingkindness I will keep for him forever,
And My covenant shall be confirmed to him.

29 "So I will establish his descendants forever
And his throne as the days of heaven.

Proverbs 22:1, 2

22 A GOOD name is to be more desired than great wealth,
Favor is better than silver and gold.
2 The rich and the poor have a common bond,
The LORD is the maker of them all.

Acts 28:1–31

28 WHEN they had been brought safely through, then we found out that the island was called Malta.

2 The natives showed us extraordinary kindness; for because of the rain that had set in and because of the cold, they kindled a fire and received us all.

3 But when Paul had gathered a bundle of sticks and laid them on the fire, a

---

LIFE LESSONS

> **Acts 28:3 —** *A viper came out because of the heat and fastened itself on his hand.*

*G*od had just rescued Paul from drowning at sea, and immediately he suffered another kind of trouble. Yet the Lord used both difficult incidents to showcase His power and love to those who did not yet believe in Him.

viper came out because of the heat and fastened itself on his hand.

4   When the natives saw the creature hanging from his hand, they *began* saying to one another, "Undoubtedly this man is a murderer, and though he has been saved from the sea, justice has not allowed him to live."

5   However he shook the creature off into the fire and suffered no harm.

6   But they were expecting that he was about to swell up or suddenly fall down dead. But after they had waited a long time and had seen nothing unusual happen to him, they changed their minds and *began* to say that he was a god.

7   Now in the neighborhood of that place were lands belonging to the leading man of the island, named Publius, who welcomed us and entertained us courteously three days.

8   And it happened that the father of Publius was lying *in bed* afflicted with *recurrent* fever and dysentery; and Paul went in *to see* him and after he had prayed, he laid his hands on him and healed him.

9   After this had happened, the rest of the people on the island who had diseases were coming to him and getting cured.

10   They also honored us with many marks of respect; and when we were setting sail, they supplied *us* with all we needed.

11   At the end of three months we set sail on an Alexandrian ship which had wintered at the island, and which had the Twin Brothers for its figurehead.

12   After we put in at Syracuse, we stayed there for three days.

13   From there we sailed around and arrived at Rhegium, and a day later a south wind sprang up, and on the second day we came to Puteoli.

14   There we found *some* brethren, and were invited to stay with them for seven days; and thus we came to Rome.

➤ 15   And the brethren, when they heard about us, came from there as far as the Market of Appius and Three Inns to meet us; and when Paul saw them, he thanked God and took courage.

16   When we entered Rome, Paul was allowed to stay by himself, with the soldier who was guarding him.

17   After three days Paul called together those who were the leading men of the

LIFE LESSONS

➤ **Acts 28:15 — *When Paul saw them, he thanked God and took courage.***

Paul usually traveled in ministry teams and sought out brothers and sisters in Christ wherever he went. He always drew on the strength, faith, wisdom, and prayers of fellow believers for encouragement. He knew that no Christian can grow in faith apart from connecting deeply with others in the body of Christ.

Jews, and when they came together, he *began* saying to them, "Brethren, though I had done nothing against our people or the customs of our fathers, yet I was delivered as a prisoner from Jerusalem into the hands of the Romans.

18   "And when they had examined me, they were willing to release me because there was no ground for putting me to death.

19   "But when the Jews objected, I was forced to appeal to Caesar, not that I had any accusation against my nation.

20   "For this reason, therefore, I requested to see you and to speak with you, for I am wearing this chain for the sake of the hope of Israel."

21   They said to him, "We have neither received letters from Judea concerning you, nor have any of the brethren come here and reported or spoken anything bad about you.

22   "But we desire to hear from you what your views are; for concerning this sect, it is known to us that it is spoken against everywhere."

23   When they had set a day for Paul, they came to him at his lodging in large numbers; and he was explaining to them by solemnly testifying about the kingdom of God and trying to persuade them concerning Jesus, from both the Law of Moses and from the Prophets, from morning until evening.

24   Some were being persuaded by the ◄ things spoken, but others would not believe.

25   And when they did not agree with one another, they *began* leaving after Paul had spoken one *parting* word, "The Holy Spirit rightly spoke through Isaiah the prophet to your fathers,

26 saying,
'GO TO THIS PEOPLE AND SAY,
"YOU WILL KEEP ON HEARING, BUT WILL NOT UNDERSTAND;
AND YOU WILL KEEP ON SEEING, BUT WILL NOT PERCEIVE;
27 FOR THE HEART OF THIS PEOPLE HAS BECOME DULL,

AND WITH THEIR EARS THEY SCARCELY HEAR,
AND THEY HAVE CLOSED THEIR EYES;
OTHERWISE THEY MIGHT SEE WITH THEIR EYES,
AND HEAR WITH THEIR EARS,
AND UNDERSTAND WITH THEIR HEART AND RETURN,
AND I WOULD HEAL THEM."'
28 "Therefore let it be known to you that this salvation of God has been sent to the Gentiles; they will also listen."
29 [When he had spoken these words, the Jews departed, having a great dispute among themselves.]
30 And he stayed two full years in his own rented quarters and was welcoming all who came to him,
31 preaching the kingdom of God and teaching concerning the Lord Jesus Christ with all openness, unhindered.

Nehemiah 12:1—13:31

12 NOW these are the priests and the Levites who came up with Zerubbabel the son of Shealtiel, and Jeshua: Seraiah, Jeremiah, Ezra,
2 Amariah, Malluch, Hattush,
3 Shecaniah, Rehum, Meremoth,
4 Iddo, Ginnethoi, Abijah,
5 Mijamin, Maadiah, Bilgah,
6 Shemaiah and Joiarib, Jedaiah,
7 Sallu, Amok, Hilkiah and Jedaiah. These were the heads of the priests and their kinsmen in the days of Jeshua.
8 The Levites *were* Jeshua, Binnui, Kadmiel, Sherebiah, Judah, *and* Mattaniah *who was* in charge of the songs of thanksgiving, he and his brothers.
9 Also Bakbukiah and Unni, their brothers, stood opposite them in *their* service divisions.
10 Jeshua became the father of Joiakim, and Joiakim became the father of Eliashib, and Eliashib became the father of Joiada,
11 and Joiada became the father of Jonathan, and Jonathan became the father of Jaddua.

12 Now in the days of Joiakim, the priests, the heads of fathers' *households* were: of Seraiah, Meraiah; of Jeremiah, Hananiah;
13 of Ezra, Meshullam; of Amariah, Jehohanan;
14 of Malluchi, Jonathan; of Shebaniah, Joseph;
15 of Harim, Adna; of Meraioth, Helkai;
16 of Iddo, Zechariah; of Ginnethon, Meshullam;
17 of Abijah, Zichri; of Miniamin, of Moadiah, Piltai;
18 of Bilgah, Shammua; of Shemaiah, Jehonathan;
19 of Joiarib, Mattenai; of Jedaiah, Uzzi;
20 of Sallai, Kallai; of Amok, Eber;
21 of Hilkiah, Hashabiah; of Jedaiah, Nethanel.
22 As for the Levites, the heads of fathers' *households* were registered in the days of Eliashib, Joiada, and Johanan and Jaddua; so *were* the priests in the reign of Darius the Persian.
23 The sons of Levi, the heads of fathers' *households*, were registered in the Book of the Chronicles up to the days of Johanan the son of Eliashib.

24 The heads of the Levites *were* Hashabiah, Sherebiah and Jeshua the son of Kadmiel, with their brothers opposite them, to praise *and* give thanks, as prescribed by David the man of God, division corresponding to division.

25 Mattaniah, Bakbukiah, Obadiah, Meshullam, Talmon *and* Akkub *were* gatekeepers keeping watch at the storehouses of the gates.

26 These *served* in the days of Joiakim the son of Jeshua, the son of Jozadak, and in the days of Nehemiah the governor and of Ezra the priest *and* scribe.

➤ 27 Now at the dedication of the wall of Jerusalem they sought out the Levites from all their places, to bring them to Jerusalem so that they might celebrate the dedication with gladness, with hymns of thanksgiving and with songs *to the accompaniment* of cymbals, harps and lyres.

28 So the sons of the singers were assembled from the district around Jerusalem, and from the villages of the Netophathites,

29 from Beth-gilgal and from *their* fields in Geba and Azmaveth, for the singers had built themselves villages around Jerusalem.

30 The priests and the Levites purified themselves; they also purified the people, the gates and the wall.

31 Then I had the leaders of Judah come up on top of the wall, and I appointed two great choirs, the first proceeding to the right on top of the wall toward the Refuse Gate.

32 Hoshaiah and half of the leaders of Judah followed them,

33 with Azariah, Ezra, Meshullam,

34 Judah, Benjamin, Shemaiah, Jeremiah,

35 and some of the sons of the priests with trumpets; *and* Zechariah the son of Jonathan, the son of Shemaiah, the son of Mattaniah, the son of Micaiah, the son of Zaccur, the son of Asaph,

36 and his kinsmen, Shemaiah, Azarel, Milalai, Gilalai, Maai, Nethanel, Judah *and* Hanani, with the musical instruments of David the man of God. And Ezra the scribe went before them.

37 At the Fountain Gate they went directly up the steps of the city of David by the stairway of the wall above the house of David to the Water Gate on the east.

38 The second choir proceeded to the left, while I followed them with half of the people on the wall, above the Tower of Furnaces, to the Broad Wall,

39 and above the Gate of Ephraim, by the Old Gate, by the Fish Gate, the Tower of Hananel and the Tower of the Hundred, as far as the Sheep Gate; and they stopped at the Gate of the Guard.

40 Then the two choirs took their stand in the house of God. So did I and half of the officials with me;

41 and the priests, Eliakim, Maaseiah, Miniamin, Micaiah, Elioenai, Zechariah and Hananiah, with the trumpets;

42 and Maaseiah, Shemaiah, Eleazar, Uzzi, Jehohanan, Malchijah, Elam and Ezer. And the singers sang, with Jezrahiah *their* leader,

43 and on that day they offered great sacrifices and rejoiced because God had given them great joy, even the women and children rejoiced, so that the joy of Jerusalem was heard from afar.

44 On that day men were also appointed over the chambers for the stores, the contributions, the first fruits and the tithes, to gather into them from the fields of the cities the portions required by the law for the priests and Levites; for Judah rejoiced over the priests and Levites who served.

45 For they performed the worship of their God and the service of purification, together with the singers and the gatekeepers in accordance with the command of David *and* of his son Solomon.

46 For in the days of David and Asaph, in ancient times, *there were* leaders of the singers, songs of praise and hymns of thanksgiving to God.

47 So all Israel in the days of Zerubbabel and Nehemiah gave the portions

---

LIFE LESSONS

➤ **Nehemiah 12:27 — *At the dedication of the wall of Jerusalem they sought out the Levites . . . that they might celebrate the dedication with gladness, with hymns of thanksgiving.***

*I*t is good to celebrate what God has accomplished through His willing servants. This not only honors and praises the Lord, who made it possible, but encourages us to acknowledge His gracious work through us.

due the singers and the gatekeepers as each day required, and set apart the consecrated *portion* for the Levites, and the Levites set apart the consecrated *portion* for the sons of Aaron.

13 ON that day they read aloud from the book of Moses in the hearing of the people; and there was found written in it that no Ammonite or Moabite should ever enter the assembly of God, 2 because they did not meet the sons of Israel with bread and water, but hired Balaam against them to curse them. However, our God turned the curse into a blessing.
3 So when they heard the law, they excluded all foreigners from Israel.
4 Now prior to this, Eliashib the priest, who was appointed over the chambers of the house of our God, being related to Tobiah,
5 had prepared a large room for him, where formerly they put the grain offerings, the frankincense, the utensils and the tithes of grain, wine and oil prescribed for the Levites, the singers and the gatekeepers, and the contributions for the priests.
6 But during all this *time* I was not in Jerusalem, for in the thirty-second year of Artaxerxes king of Babylon I had gone to the king. After some time, however, I asked leave from the king,
7 and I came to Jerusalem and learned about the evil that Eliashib had done for Tobiah, by preparing a room for him in the courts of the house of God.
8 It was very displeasing to me, so I threw all of Tobiah's household goods out of the room.
9 Then I gave an order and they cleansed the rooms; and I returned there the utensils of the house of God with the grain offerings and the frankincense.
10 I also discovered that the portions of the Levites had not been given *them*, so that the Levites and the singers who performed the service had gone away, each to his own field.
11 So I reprimanded the officials and said, "Why is the house of God forsaken?" Then I gathered them together and restored them to their posts.
12 All Judah then brought the tithe of the grain, wine and oil into the storehouses.
13 In charge of the storehouses I appointed Shelemiah the priest, Zadok the

scribe, and Pedaiah of the Levites, and in addition to them was Hanan the son of Zaccur, the son of Mattaniah; for they were considered reliable, and it was their task to distribute to their kinsmen.
14 Remember me for this, O my God, and do not blot out my loyal deeds which I have performed for the house of my God and its services.
15 In those days I saw in Judah some who were treading wine presses on the sabbath, and bringing in sacks of grain and loading *them* on donkeys, as well as wine, grapes, figs and all kinds of loads, and they brought *them* into Jerusalem on the sabbath day. So I admonished *them* on the day they sold food.
16 Also men of Tyre were living there *who* imported fish and all kinds of merchandise, and sold *them* to the sons of Judah on the sabbath, even in Jerusalem.
17 Then I reprimanded the nobles of Judah and said to them, "What is this evil thing you are doing, by profaning the sabbath day?
18 "Did not your fathers do the same, so that our God brought on us and on this city all this trouble? Yet you are adding to the wrath on Israel by profaning the sabbath."
19 It came about that just as it grew dark at the gates of Jerusalem before the sabbath, I commanded that the doors should be shut and that they should not open them until after the sabbath. Then I stationed some of my servants at the gates *so that* no load would enter on the sabbath day.
20 Once or twice the traders and merchants of every kind of merchandise spent the night outside Jerusalem.
21 Then I warned them and said to them, "Why do you spend the night in

---

LIFE LESSONS

➢ **Nehemiah 13:21 —** *"Why do you spend the night in front of the wall? If you do so again, I will use force against you."*

Too many of us confuse the words "nice" and "godly." They are not the same thing. A godly man may at times have to speak forcefully and with great zeal, whereas a nice man might avoid the situation.

front of the wall? If you do so again, I will use force against you." From that time on they did not come on the sabbath.

22 And I commanded the Levites that they should purify themselves and come as gatekeepers to sanctify the sabbath day. *For* this also remember me, O my God, and have compassion on me according to the greatness of Your lovingkindness.

23 In those days I also saw that the Jews had married women from Ashdod, Ammon *and* Moab.

24 As for their children, half spoke in the language of Ashdod, and none of them was able to speak the language of Judah, but the language of his own people.

25 So I contended with them and cursed them and struck some of them and pulled out their hair, and made them swear by God, "You shall not give your daughters to their sons, nor take of their daughters for your sons or for yourselves.

26 "Did not Solomon king of Israel sin regarding these things? Yet among the many nations there was no king like him, and he was loved by his God, and God made him king over all Israel; nevertheless the foreign women caused even him to sin.

27 "Do we then hear about you that you have committed all this great evil by acting unfaithfully against our God by marrying foreign women?"

28 Even one of the sons of Joiada, the son of Eliashib the high priest, was a son-in-law of Sanballat the Horonite, so I drove him away from me.

29 Remember them, O my God, because they have defiled the priesthood and the covenant of the priesthood and the Levites.

30 Thus I purified them from everything foreign and appointed duties for the priests and the Levites, each in his task,

31 and *I arranged* for the supply of wood at appointed times and for the first fruits. Remember me, O my God, for good.

Psalm 89:30-37

30 "If his sons forsake My law
   And do not walk in My judgments,

31 If they violate My statutes
   And do not keep My
      commandments,

32 Then I will punish their
      transgression with the rod
   And their iniquity with stripes.

33 "But I will not break off My
      lovingkindness from him,
   Nor deal falsely in My faithfulness.

34 "My covenant I will not violate,
   Nor will I alter the utterance of My
      lips.

35 "Once I have sworn by My holiness;
   I will not lie to David.

36 "His descendants shall endure
      forever
   And his throne as the sun before Me.

37 "It shall be established forever like
      the moon,
   And the witness in the sky is
      faithful."   Selah.

Proverbs 22:3, 4

3 The prudent sees the evil and hides
      himself,
   But the naive go on, and are
      punished for it.

4 The reward of humility *and* the fear
      of the LORD
   Are riches, honor and life.

Romans 1:1-32

1 PAUL, a bond-servant of Christ Jesus, called *as* an apostle, set apart for the gospel of God,

LIFE LESSONS

➤ **Psalm 89:35, 36** — *Once I have sworn by My holiness; I will not lie to David. His descendants shall endure forever and his throne as the sun before Me.*

The fulfillment of God's promise to David came through Jesus Christ. Jesus was not only the accomplishment of the Lord's guarantee to David (2 Sam. 7:12–16) but also of over 300 prophesies and pledges throughout history to everyone from Adam to Zacharias. God always fulfills His promises to the letter.

2   which He promised beforehand through His prophets in the holy Scriptures,

3   concerning His Son, who was born of a descendant of David according to the flesh,

4   who was declared the Son of God with power by the resurrection from the dead, according to the Spirit of holiness, Jesus Christ our Lord,

5   through whom we have received grace and apostleship to bring about *the* obedience of faith among all the Gentiles for His name's sake,

6   among whom you also are the called of Jesus Christ;

7   to all who are beloved of God in Rome, called *as* saints: Grace to you and peace from God our Father and the Lord Jesus Christ.

8   First, I thank my God through Jesus Christ for you all, because your faith is being proclaimed throughout the whole world.

9   For God, whom I serve in my spirit in the *preaching of the* gospel of His Son, is my witness *as to* how unceasingly I make mention of you,

10   always in my prayers making request, if perhaps now at last by the will of God I may succeed in coming to you.

11   For I long to see you so that I may impart some spiritual gift to you, that you may be established;

12   that is, that I may be encouraged together with you *while* among you, each of us by the other's faith, both yours and mine.

13   I do not want you to be unaware, brethren, that often I have planned to come to you (and have been prevented so far) so that I may obtain some fruit among you also, even as among the rest of the Gentiles.

14   I am under obligation both to Greeks and to barbarians, both to the wise and to the foolish.

15   So, for my part, I am eager to preach the gospel to you also who are in Rome.

16   For I am not ashamed of the gospel, for it is the power of God for salvation to everyone who believes, to the Jew first and also to the Greek.

17   For in it *the* righteousness of God is revealed from faith to faith; as it is written, "BUT THE RIGHTEOUS *man* SHALL LIVE BY FAITH."

18   For the wrath of God is revealed from heaven against all ungodliness and unrighteousness of men who suppress the truth in unrighteousness,

19   because that which is known about God is evident within them; for God made it evident to them.

20   For since the creation of the world His invisible attributes, His eternal power and divine nature, have been clearly seen, being understood through what has been made, so that they are without excuse.

21   For even though they knew God, they did not honor Him as God or give thanks, but they became futile in their speculations, and their foolish heart was darkened.

22   Professing to be wise, they became fools,

23   and exchanged the glory of the incorruptible God for an image in the form of corruptible man and of birds and four-footed animals and crawling creatures.

24   Therefore God gave them over in the lusts of their hearts to impurity, so that their bodies would be dishonored among them.

25   For they exchanged the truth of God for a lie, and worshiped and served the creature rather than the Creator, who is blessed forever. Amen.

LIFE LESSONS

➤ **Romans 1:16 —** *I am not ashamed of the gospel, for it is the power of God for salvation to everyone who believes.*

*W*e must never feel ashamed of our connection to Christ or to the salvation that He freely offers to all. It is a high privilege to represent Him, and we must do so with boldness and enthusiasm.

➤ **Romans 1:17 —** *"The righteous man shall live by faith."*

*W*e live the entire Christian life by faith in the Lord who teaches, empowers, and equips us to please Him (Heb. 11:1, 6). We take hold of grace for salvation and for growing in godliness by trusting Him. God loves to honor faith because faith honors Him. It is when we submit ourselves in full obedience to Him that He is glorified in and through us.

WHAT THE BIBLE SAYS ABOUT

Knowing God: The Role of Creation

Romans 1:20–23

The Father has given us His creation to demonstrate His power and to give us knowledge about Himself. In fact, God has revealed Himself enough through creation that it's inexcusable for people to deny the fact that He exists. Romans 1:20 testifies, "Since the creation of the world His invisible attributes, His eternal power and divine nature, have been clearly seen, being understood through what has been made, so that they are without excuse."

What is the purpose of creation? The Father formed this universe to bring glory to Himself. Therefore, even without a Bible, you can see evidence of Him. Since God has made His existence obvious through nature we know that the people who reject Him—claiming that there is no God—do so because they want to continue doing things their own way. They refuse to acknowledge that He exists because they don't want to be accountable to Him. Unfortunately, we also know "There is a way which seems right to a man, but its end is the way of death" (Prov. 14:12). Those who seek their own way are ultimately headed for destruction.

Of course, that's not to say that creation is a complete revelation of God or that it's adequate for salvation, which is only through Jesus Christ. However, it shows us that we don't have any excuses—God does exist. It explains why in every culture there is a belief in some kind of god. It's natural for people to believe in a higher being, which is why people ultimately feel accountable to standards of right and wrong.

So of what use is the knowledge that is seen in creation? We can use it to draw other people to the one true God. We see a great example of this when Paul preached to the people of Athens at Mars Hill. He said, "Men of Athens, I observe that you are very religious in all respects. For while I was passing through and examining the objects of your worship, I also found an altar with this inscription, 'TO AN UNKNOWN GOD' Therefore what you worship in ignorance, this I proclaim to you. The God who made the world and all things in it, since He is Lord of heaven and earth" (Acts 17:22–24).

People want to know the true God, so proclaim Him openly and with boldness. He wants to make Himself known to them, and between your testimony and the witness of creation, He will. ◈

---

26 For this reason God gave them over to degrading passions; for their women exchanged the natural function for that which is unnatural,
27 and in the same way also the men abandoned the natural function of the woman and burned in their desire toward one another, men with men committing indecent acts and receiving in their own persons the due penalty of their error.
28 And just as they did not see fit to acknowledge God any longer, God gave them over to a depraved mind, to do those things which are not proper,
29 being filled with all unrighteousness, wickedness, greed, evil; full of envy, murder, strife, deceit, malice; *they are* gossips,
30 slanderers, haters of God, insolent, arrogant, boastful, inventors of evil, disobedient to parents,
31 without understanding, untrustworthy, unloving, unmerciful;
32 and although they know the ordinance of God, that those who practice such things are worthy of death, they not only do the same, but also give hearty approval to those who practice them.

LIFE LESSONS

➢ Romans 1:24 — *God gave them over in the lusts of their hearts to impurity, so that their bodies would be dishonored among them.*

Too many people reject the truth because it interferes with their lifestyles. They participate in every form of sin in an attempt to satisfy their needs, but all they are doing is moving further away from filling the empty void within them—what only the Lord can do. Even deeper emptiness, dissatisfaction, and hopelessness always result. Eventually, those transgressions take over their lives and destroy them (Rom. 1:26, 28).

Esther 1:1—2:23

1 NOW it took place in the days of Ahasuerus, the Ahasuerus who reigned from India to Ethiopia over 127 provinces,
2   in those days as King Ahasuerus sat on his royal throne which *was* at the citadel in Susa,
3   in the third year of his reign he gave a banquet for all his princes and attendants, the army *officers* of Persia and Media, the nobles and the princes of his provinces being in his presence.
4   And he displayed the riches of his royal glory and the splendor of his great majesty for many days, 180 days.
5   When these days were completed, the king gave a banquet lasting seven days for all the people who were present at the citadel in Susa, from the greatest to the least, in the court of the garden of the king's palace.
6   *There were hangings of* fine white and violet linen held by cords of fine purple linen on silver rings and marble columns, *and* couches of gold and silver on a mosaic pavement of porphyry, marble, mother-of-pearl and precious stones.
7   Drinks were served in golden vessels of various kinds, and the royal wine was plentiful according to the king's bounty.
8   The drinking was *done* according to the law, there was no compulsion, for so the king had given orders to each official of his household that he should do according to the desires of each person.
9   Queen Vashti also gave a banquet for the women in the palace which belonged to King Ahasuerus.
10   On the seventh day, when the heart of the king was merry with wine, he commanded Mehuman, Biztha, Harbona, Bigtha, Abagtha, Zethar and Carkas, the seven eunuchs who served in the presence of King Ahasuerus,
11   to bring Queen Vashti before the king with *her* royal crown in order to display her beauty to the people and the princes, for she was beautiful.
12   But Queen Vashti refused to come at the king's command delivered by the eunuchs. Then the king became very angry and his wrath burned within him.
13   Then the king said to the wise men who understood the times—for it was the custom of the king so *to speak* before all who knew law and justice
14   and were close to him: Carshena, Shethar, Admatha, Tarshish, Meres, Marsena and Memucan, the seven princes of Persia and Media who had access to the king's presence and sat in the first place in the kingdom—
15   "According to law, what is to be done with Queen Vashti, because she did not obey the command of King Ahasuerus *delivered* by the eunuchs?"
16   In the presence of the king and the princes, Memucan said, "Queen Vashti has wronged not only the king but *also* all the princes and all the peoples who are in all the provinces of King Ahasuerus.
17   "For the queen's conduct will become known to all the women causing them to look with contempt on their husbands by saying, 'King Ahasuerus commanded Queen Vashti to be brought in to his presence, but she did not come.'
18   "This day the ladies of Persia and Media who have heard of the queen's conduct will speak in *the same way* to all the king's princes, and there will be plenty of contempt and anger.
19   "If it pleases the king, let a royal edict be issued by him and let it be written in the laws of Persia and Media so that it cannot be repealed, that Vashti may no longer come into the presence of King Ahasuerus, and let the king give her royal position to another who is more worthy than she.
20   "When the king's edict which he will make is heard throughout all his kingdom, great as it is, then all women will give honor to their husbands, great and small."
21   *This* word pleased the king and the

---

princes, and the king did as Memucan proposed.

22 So he sent letters to all the king's provinces, to each province according to its script and to every people according to their language, that every man should be the master in his own house and the one who speaks in the language of his own people.

2 AFTER these things when the anger of King Ahasuerus had subsided, he remembered Vashti and what she had done and what had been decreed against her.

2 Then the king's attendants, who served him, said, "Let beautiful young virgins be sought for the king.

3 "Let the king appoint overseers in all the provinces of his kingdom that they may gather every beautiful young virgin to the citadel of Susa, to the harem, into the custody of Hegai, the king's eunuch, who is in charge of the women; and let their cosmetics be given *them*.

4 "Then let the young lady who pleases the king be queen in place of Vashti." And the matter pleased the king, and he did accordingly.

5 *Now* there was at the citadel in Susa a Jew whose name was Mordecai, the son of Jair, the son of Shimei, the son of Kish, a Benjamite,

6 who had been taken into exile from Jerusalem with the captives who had been exiled with Jeconiah king of Judah, whom Nebuchadnezzar the king of Babylon had exiled.

7 He was bringing up Hadassah, that is Esther, his uncle's daughter, for she had no father or mother. Now the young lady was beautiful of form and face, and when her father and her mother died, Mordecai took her as his own daughter.

8 So it came about when the command and decree of the king were heard and many young ladies were gathered to the citadel of Susa into the custody of Hegai, that Esther was taken to the king's palace into the custody of Hegai, who was in charge of the women.

9 Now the young lady pleased him and found favor with him. So he quickly provided her with her cosmetics and food, gave her seven choice maids from the king's palace and transferred her and her maids to the best place in the harem.

10 Esther did not make known her people or her kindred, for Mordecai had instructed her that she should not make *them* known.

11 Every day Mordecai walked back and forth in front of the court of the harem to learn how Esther was and how she fared.

12 Now when the turn of each young lady came to go in to King Ahasuerus, after the end of her twelve months under the regulations for the women—for the days of their beautification were completed as follows: six months with oil of myrrh and six months with spices and the cosmetics for women—

13 the young lady would go in to the king in this way: anything that she desired was given her to take with her from the harem to the king's palace.

14 In the evening she would go in and in the morning she would return to the second harem, to the custody of Shaashgaz, the king's eunuch who was in charge of the concubines. She would not again go in to the king unless the king delighted in her and she was summoned by name.

15 Now when the turn of Esther, the ◄ daughter of Abihail the uncle of Mordecai who had taken her as his daughter, came to go in to the king, she did not request anything except what Hegai, the king's eunuch who was in charge of the women, advised. And Esther found favor in the eyes of all who saw her.

16 So Esther was taken to King Ahasuerus to his royal palace in the tenth month which is the month Tebeth, in the seventh year of his reign.

17 The king loved Esther more than ✳ all the women, and she found favor and

---

LIFE LESSONS

➢ **Esther 2:15 —** *She did not request anything except what Hegai, the king's eunuch who was in charge of the women, advised.*

*E*sther not only had an obedient spirit, but she also possessed a humble heart. She realized that she did not know best in this unfamiliar situation and so wisely acted on the advice of a more experienced person.

kindness with him more than all the virgins, so that he set the royal crown on her head and made her queen instead of Vashti.

18 Then the king gave a great banquet, Esther's banquet, for all his princes and his servants; he also made a holiday for the provinces and gave gifts according to the king's bounty.

19 When the virgins were gathered together the second time, then Mordecai was sitting at the king's gate.

20 Esther had not yet made known her kindred or her people, even as Mordecai had commanded her; for Esther did what Mordecai told her as she had done when under his care.

21 In those days, while Mordecai was sitting at the king's gate, Bigthan and Teresh, two of the king's officials from those who guarded the door, became angry and sought to lay hands on King Ahasuerus.

22 But the plot became known to Mordecai and he told Queen Esther, and Esther informed the king in Mordecai's name.

23 Now when the plot was investigated and found *to be so*, they were both hanged on a gallows; and it was written in the Book of the Chronicles in the king's presence.

◈ Psalm 89:38–45

38 But You have cast off and rejected,
    You have been full of wrath against
    Your anointed.
39 You have spurned the covenant of
    Your servant;
    You have profaned his crown in the
    dust.
40 You have broken down all his
    walls;
    You have brought his strongholds to
    ruin.
41 All who pass along the way plunder
    him;
    He has become a reproach to his
    neighbors.
42 You have exalted the right hand of
    his adversaries;
    You have made all his enemies
    rejoice.

43 You also turn back the edge of his
    sword
    And have not made him stand in
    battle.
44 You have made his splendor to
    cease
    And cast his throne to the ground.
45 You have shortened the days of his
    youth;
    You have covered him with shame.
                                    Selah.

◈ Proverbs 22:5, 6

5   Thorns *and* snares are in the way of
    the perverse;
    He who guards himself will be far
    from them.
6   Train up a child in the way he
    should go,
    Even when he is old he will not
    depart from it.

◈ Romans 2:1–29

2 THEREFORE you have no excuse, everyone of you who passes judgment, for in that which you judge another, you condemn yourself; for you who judge practice the same things.

2   And we know that the judgment of God rightly falls upon those who practice such things.

3   But do you suppose this, O man, when you pass judgment on those who practice such things and do the same

yourself, that you will escape the judgment of God?

➤ 4　Or do you think lightly of the riches of His kindness and tolerance and patience, not knowing that the kindness of God leads you to repentance?

➤ 5　But because of your stubbornness and unrepentant heart you are storing up wrath for yourself in the day of wrath and revelation of the righteous judgment of God,

6　who WILL RENDER TO EACH PERSON ACCORDING TO HIS DEEDS:

7　to those who by perseverance in doing good seek for glory and honor and immortality, eternal life;

8　but to those who are selfishly ambitious and do not obey the truth, but obey unrighteousness, wrath and indignation.

9　*There will be* tribulation and distress for every soul of man who does evil, of the Jew first and also of the Greek,

10　but glory and honor and peace to everyone who does good, to the Jew first and also to the Greek.

11　For there is no partiality with God.

12　For all who have sinned without the Law will also perish without the Law, and all who have sinned under the Law will be judged by the Law;

13　for *it is* not the hearers of the Law *who* are just before God, but the doers of the Law will be justified.

14　For when Gentiles who do not have the Law do instinctively the things of the Law, these, not having the Law, are a law to themselves,

15　in that they show the work of the Law written in their hearts, their conscience bearing witness and their thoughts alternately accusing or else defending them,

➤ 16　on the day when, according to my gospel, God will judge the secrets of men through Christ Jesus.

17　But if you bear the name "Jew" and rely upon the Law and boast in God,

18　and know *His* will and approve the things that are essential, being instructed out of the Law,

19　and are confident that you yourself are a guide to the blind, a light to those who are in darkness,

20　a corrector of the foolish, a teacher of the immature, having in the Law the embodiment of knowledge and of the truth,

21　you, therefore, who teach another, do you not teach yourself? You who preach that one shall not steal, do you steal?

22　You who say that one should not commit adultery, do you commit adultery? You who abhor idols, do you rob temples?

23　You who boast in the Law, through your breaking the Law, do you dishonor God?

24　For "THE NAME OF GOD IS BLASPHEMED ◄ AMONG THE GENTILES BECAUSE OF YOU," just as it is written.

25　For indeed circumcision is of value if you practice the Law; but if you are a transgressor of the Law, your circumcision has become uncircumcision.

26　So if the uncircumcised man keeps the requirements of the Law, will not his

---

LIFE LESSONS

➤ **Romans 2:5, 6 — God . . . "will render to each person according to his deeds."**

*W*hen asked, many people explain they are going to heaven, "Because I am a good person." They measure their worthiness by their own standards and disregard God's (Rom. 2:1–4). Throughout the Bible we learn that God will reward believers for their Spirit-empowered good works and will punish the lost for their unbelief and flesh-driven evil deeds (Ps. 28:4; 62:12; Prov. 24:12; Jer. 17:10; Matt. 16:27; Rev. 2:23; 20:12, 13). In the end, only God's judgment will matter, and without faith in Jesus Christ, no one will find a home in heaven.

➤ **Romans 2:16 — God will judge the secrets of men through Christ Jesus.**

*W*hether we like it or not, we are accountable for *everything* we do and say because at the judgment, every secret motivation, desire, and act will come out into the open. Jesus said, "Nothing is hidden that will not become evident, nor anything secret that will not be known and come to light" (Luke 8:17). Are there undisclosed sins in your life? If Jesus is your Savior, you are forgiven for *all* of your transgressions. He has removed the penalty of your sin and has left you spotless in return.

How does my conscience differ from the guidance of the Holy Spirit?

ROMANS 2:14, 15

*T*he conscience functions similar to a computer. A computer is programmed to respond in specific ways to specific information. It also responds to information based on the commands it has been programmed to follow.

When you click your word processing application, your computer knows which program to open. For the most part, computers are simply responders.

The conscience is a responder as well. It responds to certain input, just as it has been programmed. Paul described it like this: "For when Gentiles who do not have the Law do instinctively the things of the Law, these, not having the Law, are a law to themselves, in that they show the work of the Law written in their hearts, their conscience bearing witness and their thoughts alternately accusing or else defending them" (Rom. 2:14, 15).

God has programmed His moral code into the heart of every man and woman. We are born with it. When a person's actions or thoughts violate that code, the conscience

responds by sending a "no" message to the brain. On the other hand, when the act or thought goes along with the preprogrammed moral code, the conscience says "go."

Notice that Paul says our thoughts sometimes point out the legitimacy of certain actions. When that happens, if the actions line up with the law of God written in our hearts, the conscience gives us the go-ahead.

When you became a Christian, a change began to occur in your conscience. The basic moral code that everyone has at birth started to be overhauled. The Spirit of truth took up residency in your heart. Then, whether you were aware of it or not, He immediately set about to reprogram your conscience. Whereas before you had a general sense of right and wrong, the Holy Spirit began renewing your mind to more specific and complete truths (1 Cor. 2:10–13).

You participate in this renewal process every time you read your Bible, attend worship, memorize a verse, or pray. The Holy Spirit uses all this input to reprogram the database through which your conscience evaluates every opportunity, thought, invitation, word, and deed.

As this process continues, your conscience tunes in with the moral code of the Holy Spirit—a code reflecting the moral and ethical standards of God. This process sensitizes you not only to God's moral standards but also to the will of God.

uncircumcision be regarded as circumcision?
27 And he who is physically uncircumcised, if he keeps the Law, will he not judge you who though having the letter *of the Law* and circumcision are a transgressor of the Law?
28 For he is not a Jew who is one outwardly, nor is circumcision that which is outward in the flesh.
✳ 29 But he is a Jew who is one inwardly; and circumcision is that which is of the heart, by the Spirit, not by the letter; and his praise is not from men, but from God.

➤ **Romans 2:24 — *"The name of God is blasphemed among the Gentiles because of you."***

*W*hether we realize it or not, unbelievers are watching us—how we conduct ourselves and how we treat others. God intends for what they see in us to attract them to Himself (Matt. 5:16). Unfortunately, when we foolishly disobey the Lord, the opposite often happens. How do others respond to God because of your example?

Esther 3:1—4:17

3 AFTER these events King Ahasuerus promoted Haman, the son of Hammedatha the Agagite, and advanced him and established his authority over all the princes who *were* with him.

2 All the king's servants who were at the king's gate bowed down and paid homage to Haman; for so the king had commanded concerning him. But Mordecai neither bowed down nor paid homage.

3 Then the king's servants who were at the king's gate said to Mordecai, "Why are you transgressing the king's command?"

4 Now it was when they had spoken daily to him and he would not listen to them, that they told Haman to see whether Mordecai's reason would stand; for he had told them that he was a Jew.

5 When Haman saw that Mordecai neither bowed down nor paid homage to him, Haman was filled with rage.

6 But he disdained to lay hands on Mordecai alone, for they had told him *who* the people of Mordecai *were;* therefore Haman sought to destroy all the Jews, the people of Mordecai, who *were* throughout the whole kingdom of Ahasuerus.

7 In the first month, which is the month Nisan, in the twelfth year of King Ahasuerus, Pur, that is the lot, was cast before Haman from day to day and from month *to month,* until the twelfth month, that is the month Adar.

8 Then Haman said to King Ahasuerus, "There is a certain people scattered and dispersed among the peoples in all the provinces of your kingdom; their laws are different from *those* of all *other* people and they do not observe the king's laws, so it is not in the king's interest to let them remain.

9 "If it is pleasing to the king, let it be decreed that they be destroyed, and I will pay ten thousand talents of silver into the hands of those who carry on the *king's* business, to put into the king's treasuries."

10 Then the king took his signet ring from his hand and gave it to Haman, the son of Hammedatha the Agagite, the enemy of the Jews.

11 The king said to Haman, "The silver is yours, and the people *also,* to do with them as you please."

12 Then the king's scribes were summoned on the thirteenth day of the first month, and it was written just as Haman commanded to the king's satraps, to the governors who were over each province and to the princes of each people, each province according to its script, each people according to its language, being written in the name of King Ahasuerus and sealed with the king's signet ring.

13 Letters were sent by couriers to all the king's provinces to destroy, to kill and to annihilate all the Jews, both young and old, women and children, in one day, the thirteenth *day* of the twelfth month, which is the month Adar, and to seize their possessions as plunder.

14 A copy of the edict to be issued as law in every province was published to all the peoples so that they should be ready for this day.

15 The couriers went out impelled by the king's command while the decree was issued at the citadel in Susa; and while the king and Haman sat down to drink, the city of Susa was in confusion.

4 WHEN Mordecai learned all that had been done, he tore his clothes, put on sackcloth and ashes, and went out into the midst of the city and wailed loudly and bitterly.

2 He went as far as the king's gate, for no one was to enter the king's gate clothed in sackcloth.

3 In each and every province where

LIFE LESSONS

> **Esther 3:2 — *Mordecai neither bowed down nor paid homage.***

*M*ordecai owed his allegiance to God alone and refused to bow in worship to any man, regardless of how powerful he might be. If we fear the Lord, we will not be afraid of anyone. People who do not know God will often try to convince us, urge us, and even coerce us into violating our convictions. But if we wish to honor Him, we will obey His voice above all others.

the command and decree of the king came, there was great mourning among the Jews, with fasting, weeping and wailing; and many lay on sackcloth and ashes.

4 Then Esther's maidens and her eunuchs came and told her, and the queen writhed in great anguish. And she sent garments to clothe Mordecai that he might remove his sackcloth from him, but he did not accept *them*.

5 Then Esther summoned Hathach from the king's eunuchs, whom the king had appointed to attend her, and ordered him *to go* to Mordecai to learn what this *was* and why it *was*.

6 So Hathach went out to Mordecai to the city square in front of the king's gate.

7 Mordecai told him all that had happened to him, and the exact amount of money that Haman had promised to pay to the king's treasuries for the destruction of the Jews.

8 He also gave him a copy of the text of the edict which had been issued in Susa for their destruction, that he might show Esther and inform her, and to order her to go in to the king to implore his favor and to plead with him for her people.

9 Hathach came back and related Mordecai's words to Esther.

10 Then Esther spoke to Hathach and ordered him *to reply* to Mordecai:

11 "All the king's servants and the people of the king's provinces know that for any man or woman who comes to the king to the inner court who is not summoned, he has but one law, that he be put to death, unless the king holds out to him the golden scepter so that he may live. And I have not been summoned to come to the king for these thirty days."

12 They related Esther's words to Mordecai.

13 Then Mordecai told *them* to reply to Esther, "Do not imagine that you in the king's palace can escape any more than all the Jews.

➤ 14 "For if you remain silent at this time, ✳ relief and deliverance will arise for the Jews from another place and you and your father's house will perish. And who knows whether you have not attained royalty for such a time as this?"

15 Then Esther told *them* to reply to Mordecai,

16 "Go, assemble all the Jews who are found in Susa, and fast for me; do not eat or drink for three days, night or day. I and my maidens also will fast in the same way. And thus I will go in to the king, which is not according to the law; and if I perish, I perish."

17 So Mordecai went away and did just as Esther had commanded him.

✦ Psalm 89:46–52

46 How long, O LORD?
Will You hide Yourself forever?
Will Your wrath burn like fire?

47 Remember what my span of life is;
For what vanity You have created all
the sons of men!

48 What man can live and not see
death?
Can he deliver his soul from the
power of Sheol
                              Selah.

49 Where are Your former
lovingkindnesses, O Lord,
Which You swore to David in Your
faithfulness?

50 Remember, O Lord, the reproach of
Your servants;
How I bear in my bosom *the
reproach of* all the many peoples,

51 With which Your enemies have
reproached, O LORD,
With which they have reproached
the footsteps of Your anointed.

WHAT THE BIBLE SAYS ABOUT

The Benefits of Prayer and Fasting

Esther 4:16

*W*hen God calls us to prayer and fasting, He always does so for our benefit. Scripture points out at least seven benefits to prayer and fasting:

1. *Our attitudes, feelings, and thoughts are sifted, pruned, purified, and readied for greater ministry with God.* By fasting and praying, we become more disciplined toward the things of the Father. We show our willingness for Him to cut away from us those things that will slow us down, make us stumble, or keep us from His plans and purposes.

2. *We are able to discern more clearly the will of God for our lives.* Fasting clears our spiritual eyes and ears so we can accurately discern what God desires to reveal to us.

3. *We are confronted with our sins and shortcomings so we might confess them to God, receive forgiveness for them, and walk in His righteousness.* Through fasting and prayer we demonstrate our desire for God to break stubborn, sinful habits within us. As we pray, He cleanses and purifies us from the very things that keep us entangled in sin.

4. *We experience a release of supernatural power.* Genuine fasting and prayer can result in spiritual growth, including a renewed outpouring of supernatural power. Certain problems and situations cannot be resolved apart from fasting and prayer (Matt. 17:21).

5. *We can influence national issues and concerns through our prayers.* In 2 Chronicles 7:14, God promises, "[If] My people who are called by My name humble themselves and pray and seek My face and turn from their wicked ways, then I will hear from heaven, will forgive their sin and will heal their land."

6. *We can help build up God's people.* Prayer keeps the church body connected to its Head—Jesus Christ. Through prayer the church can understand His will for ministry—filling us with His love for the lost and His power to further His kingdom.

7. *Our minds are sharpened.* When we fast and pray, we begin to understand the Word of God as never before. We become sensitive to God's timing and direction, with an increased awareness and ability to discern His will. We become keenly aware of what God desires to do and accomplish not only in our lives, but also in the lives of those around us. ◈

---

52   Blessed be the LORD forever!
     Amen and Amen.

◈   Proverbs 22:7, 8

7   The rich rules over the poor,
    And the borrower *becomes* the
      lender's slave.
8   He who sows iniquity will reap
    vanity,
    And the rod of his fury will perish.

◈   Romans 3:1–31

3 THEN what advantage has the Jew? Or what is the benefit of circumcision?
2   Great in every respect. First of all, that they were entrusted with the oracles of God.

3   What then? If some did not believe, their unbelief will not nullify the faithfulness of God, will it?
4   May it never be! Rather, let God be found true, though every man *be found* a liar, as it is written,

    "THAT YOU MAY BE JUSTIFIED IN YOUR
      WORDS,
    AND PREVAIL WHEN YOU ARE JUDGED."

5   But if our unrighteousness demonstrates the righteousness of God, what shall we say? The God who inflicts wrath is not unrighteous, is He? (I am speaking in human terms.)
6   May it never be! For otherwise, how will God judge the world?
7   But if through my lie the truth of God abounded to His glory, why am I also still being judged as a sinner?
8   And why not *say* (as we are slanderously reported and as some claim that we say), "Let us do evil that good may come"? Their condemnation is just.

9 What then? Are we better than they? Not at all; for we have already charged that both Jews and Greeks are all under sin;

10 as it is written,

"THERE IS NONE RIGHTEOUS, NOT EVEN ONE;

11 THERE IS NONE WHO UNDERSTANDS,

THERE IS NONE WHO SEEKS FOR GOD;

12 ALL HAVE TURNED ASIDE, TOGETHER THEY HAVE BECOME USELESS;

THERE IS NONE WHO DOES GOOD,

THERE IS NOT EVEN ONE."

13 "THEIR THROAT IS AN OPEN GRAVE,

WITH THEIR TONGUES THEY KEEP DECEIVING,"

"THE POISON OF ASPS IS UNDER THEIR LIPS";

14 "WHOSE MOUTH IS FULL OF CURSING AND BITTERNESS";

15 "THEIR FEET ARE SWIFT TO SHED BLOOD,

16 DESTRUCTION AND MISERY ARE IN THEIR PATHS,

17 AND THE PATH OF PEACE THEY HAVE NOT KNOWN."

18 "THERE IS NO FEAR OF GOD BEFORE THEIR EYES."

19 Now we know that whatever the Law says, it speaks to those who are under the Law, so that every mouth may be closed and all the world may become accountable to God;

20 because by the works of the Law no flesh will be justified in His sight; for through the Law *comes* the knowledge of sin.

21 But now apart from the Law *the* righteousness of God has been manifested, being witnessed by the Law and the Prophets,

22 even *the* righteousness of God through faith in Jesus Christ for all those who believe; for there is no distinction;

23 for all have sinned and fall short of the glory of God,

24 being justified as a gift by His grace through the redemption which is in Christ Jesus;

25 whom God displayed publicly as a propitiation in His blood through faith. *This was* to demonstrate His righteousness, because in the forbearance of God He passed over the sins previously committed;

26 for the demonstration, *I say,* of His righteousness at the present time, so that He would be just and the justifier of the one who has faith in Jesus.

27 Where then is boasting? It is excluded. By what kind of law? Of works? No, but by a law of faith.

28 For we maintain that a man is justified by faith apart from works of the Law.

29 Or is God *the God* of Jews only? Is He not *the God* of Gentiles also? Yes, of Gentiles also,

30 since indeed God who will justify the circumcised by faith and the uncircumcised through faith is one.

31 Do we then nullify the Law through faith? May it never be! On the contrary, we establish the Law.

LIFE LESSONS

➤ **Romans 3:8 — *Why not say . . . "Let us do evil that good may come"?***

Some opponents of Paul claimed the apostle's teaching on grace amounted to saying "I'm saved anyway, so I might as well sin. God's grace will take care of it." Paul condemned this distortion of grace.

➤ **Romans 3:18 — *"There is no fear of God before their eyes."***

All sin eventually comes down to the refusal to fear the Lord. All of the sins that Paul lists have their source in a rebellious attitude that will not honor God as God.

➤ **Romans 3:20 — *Through the Law comes the knowledge of sin.***

The Father gave His people the law so they could understand their need for grace, not so that they could try to "earn" their way into His favor. The law shows us our sin; it doesn't empower us to follow it.

➤ **Romans 3:23 — *All have sinned and fall short of the glory of God.***

Jesus alone, among all of the billions of human beings ever born on this planet, lived His entire life by the power of the Spirit, always doing His Father's will and never committing a single sin (John 8:46; Heb. 4:15).

Esther 5:1—6:14

5 NOW it came about on the third day that Esther put on her royal robes and stood in the inner court of the king's palace in front of the king's rooms, and the king was sitting on his royal throne in the throne room, opposite the entrance to the palace.

2   When the king saw Esther the queen standing in the court, she obtained favor in his sight; and the king extended to Esther the golden scepter which *was* in his hand. So Esther came near and touched the top of the scepter.

3   Then the king said to her, "What is *troubling* you, Queen Esther? And what is your request? Even to half of the kingdom it shall be given to you."

4   Esther said, "If it pleases the king, may the king and Haman come this day to the banquet that I have prepared for him."

5   Then the king said, "Bring Haman quickly that we may do as Esther desires." So the king and Haman came to the banquet which Esther had prepared.

6   As they drank their wine at the banquet, the king said to Esther, "What is your petition, for it shall be granted to you. And what is your request? Even to half of the kingdom it shall be done."

7   So Esther replied, "My petition and my request is:

8   if I have found favor in the sight of the king, and if it pleases the king to grant my petition and do what I request, may the king and Haman come to the banquet which I will prepare for them, and tomorrow I will do as the king says."

9   Then Haman went out that day glad and pleased of heart; but when Haman saw Mordecai in the king's gate and that he did not stand up or tremble before him, Haman was filled with anger against Mordecai.

10   Haman controlled himself, however, went to his house and sent for his friends and his wife Zeresh.

11   Then Haman recounted to them the glory of his riches, and the number of his sons, and every *instance* where the king had magnified him and how he had promoted him above the princes and servants of the king.

12   Haman also said, "Even Esther the queen let no one but me come with the king to the banquet which she had prepared; and tomorrow also I am invited by her with the king.

13   "Yet all of this does not satisfy me every time I see Mordecai the Jew sitting at the king's gate."

14   Then Zeresh his wife and all his friends said to him, "Have a gallows fifty cubits high made and in the morning ask the king to have Mordecai hanged on it; then go joyfully with the king to the banquet." And the advice pleased Haman, so he had the gallows made.

6 DURING that night the king could not sleep so he gave an order to bring the book of records, the chronicles, and they were read before the king.

2   It was found written what Mordecai had reported concerning Bigthana and Teresh, two of the king's eunuchs who were doorkeepers, that they had sought to lay hands on King Ahasuerus.

3   The king said, "What honor or dignity has been bestowed on Mordecai for this?" Then the king's servants who attended him said, "Nothing has been done for him."

4   So the king said, "Who is in the court?" Now Haman had just entered the outer court of the king's palace in order to speak to the king about hanging Mordecai on the gallows which he had prepared for him.

5   The king's servants said to him, "Behold, Haman is standing in the court." And the king said, "Let him come in."

6   So Haman came in and the king said to him, "What is to be done for the man whom the king desires to honor?" And Haman said to himself, "Whom would the king desire to honor more than me?"

LIFE LESSONS

➤ Esther 5:4 — *"If it pleases the king, may the king and Haman come this day to the banquet that I have prepared for him."*

*E*sther demonstrates as well as anyone in Scripture the wisdom of God's Word when it tells us to honor those who deserve honor, such as the king (Rom. 13:1–7; 1 Pet. 2:17). God honors us when we honor His Word!

KING AHASUERUS: A Restless Spirit

ESTHER 6:1

God often uses a restless spirit to get a person's attention.

After Haman tricked King Ahasuerus into signing an edict for the annihilation of the Jews, the king could not sleep. Because of his restless spirit, he "gave an order to bring the book of records, the chronicles, and they were read before the king" (Esth. 6:1). That night, Ahasuerus discovered that Mordecai had earlier saved the king's life. In the end, Mordecai was honored—and Haman died on the gallows.

God frequently uses a persistent restlessness to direct us. This type of restlessness originates in the deepest aspect of a person's being and persists over time.

When you have that feeling, stop and ask the Father what He is trying to say. Spend extended time in the Word and in prayer. Set aside a block of time to quiet yourself before the Lord so you can hear from Him clearly.

7 Then Haman said to the king, "For the man whom the king desires to honor, 8 let them bring a royal robe which the king has worn, and the horse on which the king has ridden, and on whose head a royal crown has been placed; 9 and let the robe and the horse be handed over to one of the king's most noble princes and let them array the man whom the king desires to honor and lead him on horseback through the city square, and proclaim before him, 'Thus it shall be done to the man whom the king desires to honor.'"

10 Then the king said to Haman, "Take quickly the robes and the horse as you have said, and do so for Mordecai the Jew, who is sitting at the king's gate; do not fall short in anything of all that you have said."

11 So Haman took the robe and the horse, and arrayed Mordecai, and led him *on horseback* through the city square, and proclaimed before him, "Thus it shall be done to the man whom the king desires to honor."

12 Then Mordecai returned to the king's gate. But Haman hurried home, mourning, with *his* head covered.

13 Haman recounted to Zeresh his wife and all his friends everything that had happened to him. Then his wise men and Zeresh his wife said to him, "If Mordecai, before whom you have begun to fall, is of Jewish origin, you will not overcome him, but will surely fall before him."

14 While they were still talking with him, the king's eunuchs arrived and hastily brought Haman to the banquet which Esther had prepared.

Psalm 90:1–6

BOOK 4

A Prayer of Moses, the man of God.

90 LORD, You have been our dwelling place in all generations.
2 Before the mountains were born
Or You gave birth to the earth and the world,
Even from everlasting to everlasting, You are God.
3 You turn man back into dust
And say, "Return, O children of men."
4 For a thousand years in Your sight
Are like yesterday when it passes by,
Or *as* a watch in the night.
5 You have swept them away like a flood, they fall asleep;

LIFE LESSONS

➤ **Esther 6:10** — *"Take quickly the robes and the horse as you have said, and do so for Mordecai the Jew."*

God loves to use for good what men intend for evil. In doing so, He shows that He alone is sovereign.

➤ **Psalm 90:4** — *For a thousand years in Your sight are like yesterday when it passes by, or as a watch in the night.*

Because God is infinite and "lives forever" (Is. 57:15), He is not bound by the same constraints of time that limit and frustrate us. What seems like a delay to us is right on time to Him.

In the morning they are like grass
which sprouts anew.

6   In the morning it flourishes and
sprouts anew;
Toward evening it fades and withers
away.

Proverbs 22:9

9   He who is generous will be blessed,
For he gives some of his food to the
poor.

Romans 4:1–25

4 WHAT then shall we say that Abraham, our forefather according to the
flesh, has found?
2   For if Abraham was justified by
works, he has something to boast about,
but not before God.
3   For what does the Scripture say?
"ABRAHAM BELIEVED GOD, AND IT WAS
CREDITED TO HIM AS RIGHTEOUSNESS."
4   Now to the one who works, his wage
is not credited as a favor, but as what is
due.
5   But to the one who does not work,
but believes in Him who justifies the ungodly, his faith is credited as righteousness,
6   just as David also speaks of the
blessing on the man to whom God credits
righteousness apart from works:
7   "BLESSED ARE THOSE WHOSE LAWLESS
       DEEDS HAVE BEEN FORGIVEN,
    AND WHOSE SINS HAVE BEEN COVERED.
8   "BLESSED IS THE MAN WHOSE SIN
       THE LORD WILL NOT TAKE INTO
       ACCOUNT."
9   Is this blessing then on the circumcised, or on the uncircumcised also? For
we say, "FAITH WAS CREDITED TO ABRAHAM
AS RIGHTEOUSNESS."
10   How then was it credited? While he
was circumcised, or uncircumcised? Not
while circumcised, but while uncircumcised;
11   and he received the sign of circumcision, a seal of the righteousness of the
faith which he had while uncircumcised,
so that he might be the father of all who

believe without being circumcised, that
righteousness might be credited to them,
12   and the father of circumcision to
those who not only are of the circumcision, but who also follow in the steps of
the faith of our father Abraham which he
had while uncircumcised.
13   For the promise to Abraham or to
his descendants that he would be heir of
the world was not through the Law, but
through the righteousness of faith.
14   For if those who are of the Law are
heirs, faith is made void and the promise
is nullified;
15   for the Law brings about wrath, but
where there is no law, there also is no
violation.
16   For this reason *it is* by faith, in order
that *it may be* in accordance with grace,
so that the promise will be guaranteed
to all the descendants, not only to those
who are of the Law, but also to those
who are of the faith of Abraham, who is
the father of us all,
17   (as it is written, "A FATHER OF MANY
NATIONS HAVE I MADE YOU") in the presence of Him whom he believed, *even*
God, who gives life to the dead and calls
into being that which does not exist.
18   In hope against hope he believed, so
that he might become a father of many
nations according to that which had been
spoken, "SO SHALL YOUR DESCENDANTS BE."
19   Without becoming weak in faith he
contemplated his own body, now as good
as dead since he was about a hundred
years old, and the deadness of Sarah's
womb;
20   yet, with respect to the promise of
God, he did not waver in unbelief but
grew strong in faith, giving glory to God,
21   and being fully assured that what
God had promised, He was able also to
perform.

LIFE LESSONS

➤ **Romans 4:3 — *"Abraham believed
God, and it was credited to him as righteousness."***

*P*aul used the example of Abraham,
who lived long before the Mosaic
law, to show that the only way for
any sinful person to come into a right
relationship with God is by grace
through faith.

22 Therefore IT WAS ALSO CREDITED TO HIM AS RIGHTEOUSNESS.
23 Now not for his sake only was it written that it was credited to him,
24 but for our sake also, to whom it will be credited, as those who believe in Him who raised Jesus our Lord from the dead,
25 *He* who was delivered over because of our transgressions, and was raised because of our justification.

Esther 7:1—8:17

7 NOW the king and Haman came to drink *wine* with Esther the queen.
2 And the king said to Esther on the second day also as they drank their wine at the banquet, "What is your petition, Queen Esther? It shall be granted you. And what is your request? Even to half of the kingdom it shall be done."
➤ 3 Then Queen Esther replied, "If I have found favor in your sight, O king, and if it pleases the king, let my life be given me as my petition, and my people as my request;
4 for we have been sold, I and my people, to be destroyed, to be killed and to be annihilated. Now if we had only been sold as slaves, men and women, I would have remained silent, for the trouble would not be commensurate with the annoyance to the king."
5 Then King Ahasuerus asked Queen Esther, "Who is he, and where is he, who would presume to do thus?"
6 Esther said, "A foe and an enemy is this wicked Haman!" Then Haman became terrified before the king and queen.
7 The king arose in his anger from drinking wine *and went* into the palace garden; but Haman stayed to beg for his life from Queen Esther, for he saw that harm had been determined against him by the king.
8 Now when the king returned from the palace garden into the place where they were drinking wine, Haman was falling on the couch where Esther was. Then the king said, "Will he even assault the queen with me in the house?" As the word went out of the king's mouth, they covered Haman's face.
9 Then Harbonah, one of the eunuchs who *were* before the king said, "Behold indeed, the gallows standing at Haman's house fifty cubits high, which Haman made for Mordecai who spoke good on behalf of the king!" And the king said, "Hang him on it."
10 So they hanged Haman on the gallows which he had prepared for Mordecai, and the king's anger subsided.
8 ON that day King Ahasuerus gave the house of Haman, the enemy of the

Jews, to Queen Esther; and Mordecai came before the king, for Esther had disclosed what he was to her.

➤ 2 The king took off his signet ring which he had taken away from Haman, and gave it to Mordecai. And Esther set Mordecai over the house of Haman.

3 Then Esther spoke again to the king, fell at his feet, wept and implored him to avert the evil *scheme* of Haman the Agagite and his plot which he had devised against the Jews.

4 The king extended the golden scepter to Esther. So Esther arose and stood before the king.

5 Then she said, "If it pleases the king and if I have found favor before him and the matter *seems* proper to the king and I am pleasing in his sight, let it be written to revoke the letters devised by Haman, the son of Hammedatha the Agagite, which he wrote to destroy the Jews who are in all the king's provinces.

6 "For how can I endure to see the calamity which will befall my people, and how can I endure to see the destruction of my kindred?"

7 So King Ahasuerus said to Queen Esther and to Mordecai the Jew, "Behold, I have given the house of Haman to Esther, and him they have hanged on the gallows because he had stretched out his hands against the Jews.

8 "Now you write to the Jews as you see fit, in the king's name, and seal *it* with the king's signet ring; for a decree which is written in the name of the king and sealed with the king's signet ring may not be revoked."

9 So the king's scribes were called at that time in the third month (that is, the month Sivan), on the twenty-third day; and it was written according to all that Mordecai commanded to the Jews, the satraps, the governors and the princes of the provinces which *extended* from India to Ethiopia, 127 provinces, to every province according to its script, and to every people according to their language as well as to the Jews according to their script and their language.

10 He wrote in the name of King Ahasuerus, and sealed it with the king's signet ring, and sent letters by couriers on horses, riding on steeds sired by the royal stud.

11 In them the king granted the Jews who were in each and every city *the right* to assemble and to defend their lives, to destroy, to kill and to annihilate the entire army of any people or province which might attack them, including children and women, and to plunder their spoil,

12 on one day in all the provinces of King Ahasuerus, the thirteenth *day* of the twelfth month (that is, the month Adar).

13 A copy of the edict to be issued as law in each and every province was published to all the peoples, so that the Jews would be ready for this day to avenge themselves on their enemies.

14 The couriers, hastened and impelled by the king's command, went out, riding on the royal steeds; and the decree was given out at the citadel in Susa.

15 Then Mordecai went out from the presence of the king in royal robes of blue and white, with a large crown of gold and a garment of fine linen and purple; and the city of Susa shouted and rejoiced.

16 For the Jews there was light and gladness and joy and honor.

17 In each and every province and in each and every city, wherever the king's commandment and his decree arrived, ✳ there was gladness and joy for the Jews, a feast and a holiday. And many among the peoples of the land became Jews, for the dread of the Jews had fallen on them.

LIFE LESSONS

➤ **Esther 8:2 —** *Esther set Mordecai over the house of Haman.*

*T*he story of Mordecai and Haman well illustrates Proverbs 13:22: "A good man leaves an inheritance to his children's children, and the wealth of the sinner is stored up for the righteous."

Psalm 90:7–17

7 For we have been consumed by Your anger
And by Your wrath we have been dismayed.

8 You have placed our iniquities before You,

Our secret *sins* in the light of Your presence.
9 For all our days have declined in Your fury;
We have finished our years like a sigh.
10 As for the days of our life, they contain seventy years,
Or if due to strength, eighty years,
Yet their pride is *but* labor and sorrow;
For soon it is gone and we fly away.
11 Who understands the power of Your anger
And Your fury, according to the fear that is due You?
12 So teach us to number our days,
That we may present to You a heart of wisdom.
13 Do return, O LORD; how long *will it be?*
And be sorry for Your servants.
➤ 14 O satisfy us in the morning with Your lovingkindness,
That we may sing for joy and be glad all our days.
15 Make us glad according to the days You have afflicted us,
And the years we have seen evil.
16 Let Your work appear to Your servants
And Your majesty to their children.
✳ 17 Let the favor of the Lord our God be upon us;
And confirm for us the work of our hands;
Yes, confirm the work of our hands.

Proverbs 22:10, 11

10 Drive out the scoffer, and contention will go out,
Even strife and dishonor will cease.
11 He who loves purity of heart
✳ *And* whose speech is gracious, the king is his friend.

Romans 5:1–21

➤ **5** THEREFORE, having been justified by faith, we have peace with God through our Lord Jesus Christ,
2 through whom also we have ob-tained our introduction by faith into this grace in which we stand; and we exult in hope of the glory of God.
3 And not only this, but we also exult ◄ in our tribulations, knowing that tribula-tion brings about perseverance;
4 and perseverance, proven character; and proven character, hope;
5 and hope does not disappoint, be-cause the love of God has been poured out within our hearts through the Holy Spirit who was given to us.
6 For while we were still helpless, at the right time Christ died for the un-godly.
7 For one will hardly die for a righ-teous man; though perhaps for the good man someone would dare even to die.
8 But God demonstrates His own love ◄ toward us, in that while we were yet sin-ners, Christ died for us.
9 Much more then, having now been justified by His blood, we shall be saved from the wrath *of God* through Him.

LIFE LESSONS

➤ **Psalm 90:14 — *O satisfy us in the morning with Your lovingkindness.***

God wants our relationships with Him to fill us with joy and gladness as an example to the world of His goodness and mercy. "In Your presence is fullness of joy" (Ps. 16:11).

➤ **Romans 5:1 — *Therefore, having been justified by faith, we have peace with God through our Lord Jesus Christ.***

For those who place their faith in the risen Christ, the war with heaven is over. We move from darkness to light, from enemies to beloved children, from death to life. God showers His peace on those who trust Him.

➤ **Romans 5:3, 4 — *We also exult in our tribulations, knowing that tribulation brings about perseverance; and perse-verance, proven character; and proven character, hope.***

Trials, difficulties, and adversities are often God's way of maturing us into people who look more like His Son. Trials are never easy, but by faith we can begin to understand how the Father uses them for our good.

WHAT THE BIBLE SAYS ABOUT ◉

The Grace in Which We Stand

Romans 5:1–5

When we think of grace, we think of God's unmerited favor, and rightly so. He forgives us out of His unconditional love. Therefore, we cannot earn our salvation, nor can we do anything to lose it.

Unfortunately, there are some who fall for the lie that God's grace stops doing its work in us after we receive Jesus as our Savior. They forfeit the peace that He has provided them without need because they don't realize that His grace is founded in a love that is secure—not unpredictable or temporary. The selfless mercy that the Father continually shows us is the very love Jesus displayed at Calvary.

In Romans 5:1-2, the apostle Paul explains, "We have peace with God through our Lord Jesus Christ, through whom also we have obtained our introduction by faith into this grace in which we stand; and we exult in hope of the glory of God."

We stand securely in God's love because of Christ—not by our own merit. However, many people become confused because of the troubles they endure. They believe that they have somehow fallen from the Father's favor because of the pain they face. Yet Paul dem-onstrates that God uses even our heartaches for our good.

Paul wrote, "We also exult in our tribulations, knowing that tribulation brings about perseverance; and perseverance, proven character; and proven character, hope; and hope does not disappoint, because the love of God has been poured out within our hearts through the Holy Spirit who was given to us" (Rom. 5:3–5).

Problems will come into your life; however, they're no reason to believe that God has stopped loving you or that you've somehow lost His grace. Just the opposite is true—He has allowed this suffering so that you will learn to persevere so that you will develop His character and so you will have hope. Because of His great love for you, the Lord wants you to experience His eternal, abundant life more deeply. But the only way to prepare you for it is through hardship. Even your trials are the outpouring of His grace.

Therefore, instead of doubting God's love because of your troubles, rejoice in them. As 1 Peter 4:12, 13 admonishes, "Do not be surprised at the fiery ordeal among you, which comes upon you for your testing, as though some strange thing were happening to you; but to the degree that you share the sufferings of Christ, keep on rejoicing, so that also at the revelation of His glory you may rejoice with exultation." ◉

LIFE LESSONS

➤ **Romans 5:8 — God demonstrates His own love toward us, in that while we were yet sinners, Christ died for us.**

Jesus did not die only for nice or good people. He gave His sinless life for everyone. And He did this because of God's amazing love.

---

10 For if while we were enemies we were reconciled to God through the death of His Son, much more, having been reconciled, we shall be saved by His life.
11 And not only this, but we also exult in God through our Lord Jesus Christ, through whom we have now received the reconciliation.

12 Therefore, just as through one man sin entered into the world, and death through sin, and so death spread to all men, because all sinned—
13 for until the Law sin was in the world, but sin is not imputed when there is no law.
14 Nevertheless death reigned from Adam until Moses, even over those who had not sinned in the likeness of the offense of Adam, who is a type of Him who was to come.
15 But the free gift is not like the transgression. For if by the transgression of the one the many died, much more did the grace of God and the gift by the grace of the one Man, Jesus Christ, abound to the many.
16 The gift is not like *that which came* through the one who sinned; for on the one hand the judgment *arose* from one

transgression resulting in condemnation, but on the other hand the free gift *arose* from many transgressions resulting in justification.

17 For if by the transgression of the one, death reigned through the one, much more those who receive the abundance of grace and of the gift of righteousness will reign in life through the One, Jesus Christ.

18 So then as through one transgression there resulted condemnation to all men, even so through one act of righteousness there resulted justification of life to all men.

19 For as through the one man's disobedience the many were made sinners, even so through the obedience of the One the many will be made righteous.

20 The Law came in so that the transgression would increase; but where sin increased, grace abounded all the more,

21 so that, as sin reigned in death, even so grace would reign through righteousness to eternal life through Jesus Christ our Lord.

✦ Esther 9:1—10:3

9 NOW in the twelfth month (that is, the month Adar), on the thirteenth day when the king's command and edict were about to be executed, on the day when the enemies of the Jews hoped to gain the mastery over them, it was turned to the contrary so that the Jews themselves gained the mastery over those who hated them.

2 The Jews assembled in their cities throughout all the provinces of King Ahasuerus to lay hands on those who sought their harm; and no one could stand before them, for the dread of them had fallen on all the peoples.

3 Even all the princes of the provinces, the satraps, the governors and those who were doing the king's business assisted the Jews, because the dread of Mordecai had fallen on them.

LIFE LESSONS

➤ **Esther 9:1 —** *The Jews themselves gained the mastery over those who hated them.*

*H*aman did not live to see the total reversal of his diabolical plan, yet Esther and Mordecai did—they saw the amazing ways God answered their prayers and delivered them. Therefore, never lose heart when things seem bleak. Instead, remember that God loves to act on behalf of those who wait for Him!

---

4 Indeed, Mordecai was great in the king's house, and his fame spread throughout all the provinces; for the man Mordecai became greater and greater.

5 Thus the Jews struck all their enemies with the sword, killing and destroying; and they did what they pleased to those who hated them.

6 At the citadel in Susa the Jews killed and destroyed five hundred men,

7 and Parshandatha, Dalphon, Aspatha,

8 Poratha, Adalia, Aridatha,

9 Parmashta, Arisai, Aridai and Vaizatha,

10 the ten sons of Haman the son of Hammedatha, the Jews' enemy; but they did not lay their hands on the plunder.

11 On that day the number of those who were killed at the citadel in Susa was reported to the king.

12 The king said to Queen Esther, "The Jews have killed and destroyed five hundred men and the ten sons of Haman at the citadel in Susa. What then have they done in the rest of the king's provinces! Now what is your petition? It shall even be granted you. And what is your further request? It shall also be done."

13 Then said Esther, "If it pleases the king, let tomorrow also be granted to the Jews who are in Susa to do according to the edict of today; and let Haman's ten sons be hanged on the gallows."

14 So the king commanded that it should be done so; and an edict was issued in Susa, and Haman's ten sons were hanged.

15 The Jews who were in Susa assembled also on the fourteenth day of the month Adar and killed three hundred men in Susa, but they did not lay their hands on the plunder.

16 Now the rest of the Jews who *were* in the king's provinces assembled, to defend their lives and rid themselves of their enemies, and kill 75,000 of those who hated them; but they did not lay their hands on the plunder.

17 *This was done* on the thirteenth day of the month Adar, and on the fourteenth day they rested and made it a day of feasting and rejoicing.

18 But the Jews who were in Susa assembled on the thirteenth and the fourteenth of the same month, and they rested on the fifteenth day and made it a day of feasting and rejoicing.

19 Therefore the Jews of the rural areas, who live in the rural towns, make the fourteenth day of the month Adar *a* holiday for rejoicing and feasting and sending portions *of food* to one another.

20 Then Mordecai recorded these events, and he sent letters to all the Jews who were in all the provinces of King Ahasuerus, both near and far,

21 obliging them to celebrate the fourteenth day of the month Adar, and the fifteenth day of the same month, annually,

22 because on those days the Jews rid themselves of their enemies, and *it was* a month which was turned for them from sorrow into gladness and from mourning into a holiday; that they should make them days of feasting and rejoicing and sending portions *of food* to one another and gifts to the poor.

23 Thus the Jews undertook what they had started to do, and what Mordecai had written to them.

24 For Haman the son of Hammedatha, the Agagite, the adversary of all the Jews, had schemed against the Jews to destroy them and had cast Pur, that is the lot, to disturb them and destroy them.

25 But when it came to the king's attention, he commanded by letter that his wicked scheme which he had devised against the Jews, should return on his own head and that he and his sons should be hanged on the gallows.

26 Therefore they called these days Purim after the name of Pur. And because of the instructions in this letter, both what they had seen in this regard and what had happened to them,

27 the Jews established and made a custom for themselves and for their descendants and for all those who allied themselves with them, so that they would not fail to celebrate these two days according to their regulation and according to their appointed time annually.

28 So these days were to be remembered and celebrated throughout every generation, every family, every province and every city; and these days of Purim were not to fail from among the Jews, or their memory fade from their descendants.

29 Then Queen Esther, daughter of Abihail, with Mordecai the Jew, wrote with full authority to confirm this second letter about Purim.

30 He sent letters to all the Jews, to the 127 provinces of the kingdom of Ahasuerus, *namely,* words of peace and truth,

31 to establish these days of Purim at their appointed times, just as Mordecai the Jew and Queen Esther had established for them, and just as they had established for themselves and for their descendants with instructions for their times of fasting and their lamentations.

32 The command of Esther established these customs for Purim, and it was written in the book.

10 NOW King Ahasuerus laid a tribute on the land and on the coastlands of the sea.

2 And all the accomplishments of his authority and strength, and the full account of the greatness of Mordecai to which the king advanced him, are they not written in the Book of the Chronicles of the Kings of Media and Persia?

3 For Mordecai the Jew was second

LIFE LESSONS

➤ **Esther 10:3 —** *For Mordecai the Jew was second only to King Ahasuerus, and great among the Jews.*

*M*ordecai took his place, along with Joseph and Daniel before him, as a godly man living in exile who God raised to a position of authority second only to the king. The Lord is sovereign, and He is always good!

Life Examples:

MORDECAI: Bowing Before No Man

ESTHER 10:3

If anyone ever had reason to compromise on what he knew was right, it was Mordecai. He had a choice: either bow before a powerful official, Haman, or lose his life. Mordecai stood strong, however, and refused to disobey God's commandment against bowing in worship to anyone but Him (Ex. 20:3; Lev. 26:1; Josh. 23:16).

Day after day, the other officials tried to reason with Mordecai, but he still refused to bow. Perhaps he remembered God's words: "Who are you that you are afraid of man who dies and of the son of man who is made like grass, that you have forgotten the LORD your Maker" (Is. 51:12, 13).

In the end, God not only spared Mordecai's life, but He made him a powerful and honored public official (Esth. 10:3). God means it when He says, "Those who honor Me I will honor" (1 Sam. 2:30)!

only to King Ahasuerus, and great among the Jews and in favor with his many kinsmen, one who sought the good of his people and one who spoke for the welfare of his whole nation.

Psalm 91:1–6

91 HE who dwells in the shelter of the Most High
Will abide in the shadow of the Almighty.
2 I will say to the LORD, "My refuge and my fortress,
My God, in whom I trust!"
3 For it is He who delivers you from the snare of the trapper
And from the deadly pestilence.
4 He will cover you with His pinions,
And under His wings you may seek refuge;
His faithfulness is a shield and bulwark.
5 You will not be afraid of the terror by night,
Or of the arrow that flies by day;
6 Of the pestilence that stalks in darkness,
Or of the destruction that lays waste at noon.

Proverbs 22:12

12 The eyes of the LORD preserve knowledge,
But He overthrows the words of the treacherous man.

Romans 6:1–23

6 WHAT shall we say then? Are we to continue in sin so that grace may increase?
2 May it never be! How shall we who died to sin still live in it?
3 Or do you not know that all of us who have been baptized into Christ Jesus have been baptized into His death?
4 Therefore we have been buried with Him through baptism into death, so that as Christ was raised from the dead through the glory of the Father, so we too might walk in newness of life.
5 For if we have become united with *Him* in the likeness of His death, certainly

LIFE LESSONS

➤ **Psalm 91:5 — *You will not be afraid of the terror by night, or of the arrow that flies by day.***

Sometimes it may feel as if our nights are filled with terror and that we do have figurative arrows flying at us by day. Yet when we find our security in the Lord, they do not have to terrify or intimidate us; He is our safety, and in Him we find rest.

➤ **Romans 6:2 — *How shall we who died to sin still live in it?***

Paul could not imagine why anyone who genuinely loves Christ would want to continue committing the very sins that cost Jesus His life. How could any real believer glory in what God abhors?

we shall also be *in the likeness* of His resurrection,

➤ 6   knowing this, that our old self was crucified with *Him*, in order that our body of sin might be done away with, so that we would no longer be slaves to sin;

7   for he who has died is freed from sin.

8   Now if we have died with Christ, we believe that we shall also live with Him,

9   knowing that Christ, having been raised from the dead, is never to die again; death no longer is master over Him.

10   For the death that He died, He died to sin once for all; but the life that He lives, He lives to God.

➤ 11   Even so consider yourselves to be dead to sin, but alive to God in Christ Jesus.

12   Therefore do not let sin reign in your mortal body so that you obey its lusts,

13   and do not go on presenting the members of your body to sin *as* instruments of unrighteousness; but present yourselves to God as those alive from the dead, and your members *as* instruments of righteousness to God.

14   For sin shall not be master over you, for you are not under law but under grace.

15   What then? Shall we sin because we are not under law but under grace? May it never be!

16   Do you not know that when you present yourselves to someone *as* slaves for obedience, you are slaves of the one whom you obey, either of sin resulting in death, or of obedience resulting in righteousness?

17   But thanks be to God that though you were slaves of sin, you became obedient from the heart to that form of teaching to which you were committed,

18   and having been freed from sin, you became slaves of righteousness.

19   I am speaking in human terms because of the weakness of your flesh. For

just as you presented your members as slaves to impurity and to lawlessness, resulting in *further* lawlessness, so now present your members as slaves to righteousness, resulting in sanctification.

20   For when you were slaves of sin, you were free in regard to righteousness.

21   Therefore what benefit were you then deriving from the things of which you are now ashamed? For the outcome of those things is death.

22   But now having been freed from sin and enslaved to God, you derive your benefit, resulting in sanctification, and the outcome, eternal life.

23   For the wages of sin is death, but the free gift of God is eternal life in Christ Jesus our Lord.

LIFE LESSONS

➤ **Romans 6:6** — *Our old self was crucified with Him, in order that . . . we would no longer be slaves to sin.*

*B*efore we came to Christ, sin had a choke hold on our lives, and we could do nothing but serve it as its obedient slaves. Through the death and resurrection of Christ, however, we received a new nature and the power to live for God.

➤ **Romans 6:11** — *Even so consider yourselves to be dead to sin, but alive to God in Christ Jesus.*

*I*f we have died to sin by accepting Jesus as our Lord and Savior, we will have the resurrected life of Christ within us. Neither sin nor death will ever be our master again. Death has been defeated because He gives us life without end with Him in heaven. Until we reach our new heavenly home, we are to draw on the power of the Spirit to put to death the sin that still wants to express itself and obey God for His glory.

AUGUST 5

 Job 1:1—2:13

1 THERE was a man in the land of Uz whose name was Job; and that man

was blameless, upright, fearing God and turning away from evil.

2   Seven sons and three daughters were born to him.

3   His possessions also were 7,000 sheep, 3,000 camels, 500 yoke of oxen,

500 female donkeys, and very many servants; and that man was the greatest of all the men of the east.

4 His sons used to go and hold a feast in the house of each one on his day, and they would send and invite their three sisters to eat and drink with them.

5 When the days of feasting had completed their cycle, Job would send and consecrate them, rising up early in the morning and offering burnt offerings *according to* the number of them all; for Job said, "Perhaps my sons have sinned and cursed God in their hearts." Thus Job did continually.

6 Now there was a day when the sons of God came to present themselves before the LORD, and Satan also came among them.

7 The LORD said to Satan, "From where do you come?" Then Satan answered the LORD and said, "From roaming about on the earth and walking around on it."

8 The LORD said to Satan, "Have you considered My servant Job? For there is no one like him on the earth, a blameless and upright man, fearing God and turning away from evil."

9 Then Satan answered the LORD, "Does Job fear God for nothing?

10 "Have You not made a hedge about him and his house and all that he has, on every side? You have blessed the work of his hands, and his possessions have increased in the land.

11 "But put forth Your hand now and touch all that he has; he will surely curse You to Your face."

12 Then the LORD said to Satan, "Behold, all that he has is in your power, only do not put forth your hand on him." So Satan departed from the presence of the LORD.

13 Now on the day when his sons and his daughters were eating and drinking wine in their oldest brother's house,

14 a messenger came to Job and said, "The oxen were plowing and the donkeys feeding beside them,

15 and the Sabeans attacked and took them. They also slew the servants with the edge of the sword, and I alone have escaped to tell you."

16 While he was still speaking, another also came and said, "The fire of God fell from heaven and burned up the sheep and the servants and consumed them, and I alone have escaped to tell you."

17 While he was still speaking, another also came and said, "The Chaldeans formed three bands and made a raid on the camels and took them and slew the servants with the edge of the sword, and I alone have escaped to tell you."

18 While he was still speaking, another also came and said, "Your sons and your daughters were eating and drinking wine in their oldest brother's house,

19 and behold, a great wind came from across the wilderness and struck the four corners of the house, and it fell on the young people and they died, and I alone have escaped to tell you."

20 Then Job arose and tore his robe and shaved his head, and he fell to the ground and worshiped.

21 He said,

"Naked I came from my mother's womb,
And naked I shall return there.
The LORD gave and the LORD has taken away.
Blessed be the name of the LORD."

22 Through all this Job did not sin nor did he blame God.

2 AGAIN there was a day when the sons of God came to present themselves

---

LIFE LESSONS

➤ **Job 1:10 —** *"Have You not made a hedge about him and his house and all that he has, on every side?"*

*J*ob had no idea of the extent of God's protection that surrounded him and his family. We probably do not, either. Yet when we joyfully obey God by His Spirit, as Job did, the Lord helps us, protects us, and provides for our needs (Ps. 34).

➤ **Job 1:20 —** *Then Job arose and tore his robe and shaved his head, and he fell to the ground and worshiped.*

*W*hen tragedy strikes, believers hurt just as much as anyone else. They grieve, but not "as do the rest who have no hope" (1 Thess. 4:13). We can worship, even in tragedy, because nothing can separate us from God and His love.

WHAT THE BIBLE SAYS ABOUT ◉

How God Limits Our Adversity

Job 1:1—2:6

Although God may allow Satan to persecute and accuse us, He places limitations on the enemy's actions. Satan does not have free access to our lives. Only God, who created us, has the right to deal with us at every turn in life.

In the case of Job, the Lord stopped the enemy and commanded him: "Do not put forth your hand on him" (Job 1:12). The Lord allowed His servant Job to be tested, but notice He limited what Satan could do. The Lord is omniscient, omnipotent, and omnipresent. Nothing is greater—no sin or disease— than Him. He gave Satan strict instructions: "Spare his life" (Job 2:6), and the enemy had to comply—just as he complies today with God's limitations on the amount of adversity, suffering, and sorrow we experience.

There is a limit to adversity. It may seem that your sorrow will never pass, but it will. Remember that today's troubles are God's opportunities for Him to prove His faithfulness. He will only allow the trial to continue until He accomplishes His purpose in your life. Crises will pass. Circumstances do change. Situations evolve. Yet in everything, God works in and through our adversity and brings it to an end according to His timetable.

The enemy may attempt to wear you down, but you have an eternal source of strength living within you that cannot be defeated. Satan knows that as believers we belong to God. We are saved through His grace and by faith in His Son. Therefore, the enemy shifts his attention and seeks to fill our hearts with fear, doubt, and discouragement in an effort to tempt us into giving up.

Under extreme pressure, Job's faith remained firmly set on God. The same can be true for us. When adversity comes, we do not have to bend or yield to defeat. In 2 Corinthians 4:8, 9 the apostle Paul writes, "We are afflicted in every way, but not crushed; perplexed, but not despairing; persecuted, but not forsaken; struck down, but not destroyed." The Lord will not allow the enemy to destroy us; therefore, we must continue to trust God and resist the devil even when we're weary (Gal. 6:9).

Furthermore, the Lord works through adversity, allowing it in our lives for a season to accomplish an important purpose in us. Isaiah 30:20, 21 teaches, "Although the Lord has given you bread of privation and water of oppression, He, your Teacher will no longer hide Himself, but your eyes will behold your Teacher." In other words, the dark moments of our lives will last only so long as is necessary for God to accomplish His purpose in us.

What good news this is! The Father will not only limit our trials and tribulations, but He will draw us deeper into relationship with Himself, working everything out for our good (Rom. 8:28). Certainly, this is a good reason to praise Him! ◈

---

before the LORD, and Satan also came among them to present himself before the LORD.
2   The LORD said to Satan, "Where have you come from?" Then Satan answered the LORD and said, "From roaming about on the earth and walking around on it."
3   The LORD said to Satan, "Have you considered My servant Job? For there is no one like him on the earth, a blameless and upright man fearing God and turning away from evil. And he still holds fast his integrity, although you incited Me against him to ruin him without cause."
4   Satan answered the LORD and said, "Skin for skin! Yes, all that a man has he will give for his life.
5   "However, put forth Your hand now, and touch his bone and his flesh; he will curse You to Your face."
6   So the LORD said to Satan, "Behold, he is in your power, only spare his life."
7   Then Satan went out from the presence of the LORD and smote Job with sore boils from the sole of his foot to the crown of his head.
8   And he took a potsherd to scrape himself while he was sitting among the ashes.
9   Then his wife said to him, "Do you still hold fast your integrity? Curse God and die!"
10 But he said to her, "You speak as one of the foolish women speaks. Shall we indeed accept good from God and not

accept adversity?" In all this Job did not sin with his lips.

11 Now when Job's three friends heard of all this adversity that had come upon him, they came each one from his own place, Eliphaz the Temanite, Bildad the Shuhite and Zophar the Naamathite; and they made an appointment together to come to sympathize with him and comfort him.

12 When they lifted up their eyes at a distance and did not recognize him, they raised their voices and wept. And each of them tore his robe and they threw dust over their heads toward the sky.

13 Then they sat down on the ground with him for seven days and seven nights with no one speaking a word to him, for they saw that *his* pain was very great.

Psalm 91:7–13

7 A thousand may fall at your side
     And ten thousand at your right
          hand,
     But it shall not approach you.
8 You will only look on with your eyes
     And see the recompense of the
          wicked.
9 For you have made the LORD, my
          refuge,
     Even the Most High, your dwelling
          place.
10 No evil will befall you,
     Nor will any plague come near your
          tent.
11 For He will give His angels charge
          concerning you,
     To guard you in all your ways.
12 They will bear you up in their
          hands,
     That you do not strike your foot
          against a stone.
13 You will tread upon the lion and
          cobra,
     The young lion and the serpent you
          will trample down.

Proverbs 22:13, 14

13 The sluggard says, "There is a lion
          outside;
     I will be killed in the streets!"

14 The mouth of an adulteress is a
          deep pit;
     He who is cursed of the LORD will
          fall into it.

Romans 7:1–25

7 OR do you not know, brethren (for I am speaking to those who know the law), that the law has jurisdiction over a person as long as he lives?

2 For the married woman is bound by law to her husband while he is living; but if her husband dies, she is released from the law concerning the husband.

3 So then, if while her husband is living she is joined to another man, she shall be called an adulteress; but if her husband dies, she is free from the law, so that she is not an adulteress though she is joined to another man.

4 Therefore, my brethren, you also were made to die to the Law through the body of Christ, so that you might be joined to another, to Him who was raised from the dead, in order that we might bear fruit for God.

5 For while we were in the flesh, the sinful passions, which were *aroused* by the Law, were at work in the members of our body to bear fruit for death.

6 But now we have been released from the Law, having died to that by which we were bound, so that we serve in newness of the Spirit and not in oldness of the letter.

7 What shall we say then? Is the Law sin? May it never be! On the contrary, I would not have come to know sin except through the Law; for I would not have known about coveting if the Law had not said, "YOU SHALL NOT COVET."

8 But sin, taking opportunity through the commandment, produced in me coveting of every kind; for apart from the Law sin *is* dead.

9 I was once alive apart from the Law; but when the commandment came, sin became alive and I died;

10 and this commandment, which was to result in life, proved to result in death for me;

11 for sin, taking an opportunity through the commandment, deceived me and through it killed me.

➤ 12 So then, the Law is holy, and the commandment is holy and righteous and good.

13 Therefore did that which is good become *a cause of* death for me? May it never be! Rather it was sin, in order that it might be shown to be sin by effecting my death through that which is good, so that through the commandment sin would become utterly sinful.

14 For we know that the Law is spiritual, but I am of flesh, sold into bondage to sin.

➤ 15 For what I am doing, I do not understand; for I am not practicing what I *would* like to do, but I am doing the very thing I hate.

16 But if I do the very thing I do not want *to do*, I agree with the Law, *confessing* that the Law is good.

17 So now, no longer am I the one doing it, but sin which dwells in me.

➤ 18 For I know that nothing good dwells in me, that is, in my flesh; for the willing is present in me, but the doing of the good *is* not.

19 For the good that I want, I do not do, but I practice the very evil that I do not want.

20 But if I am doing the very thing I do not want, I am no longer the one doing it, but sin which dwells in me.

21 I find then the principle that evil is present in me, the one who wants to do good.

22 For I joyfully concur with the law of God in the inner man,

✳ 23 but I see a different law in the members of my body, waging war against the law of my mind and making me a

LIFE LESSONS

➤ **Romans 7:12 — *So then, the Law is holy, and the commandment is holy and righteous and good.***

The Bible reveals to us the character of God—His holiness, righteousness, justice, goodness, kindness, and more. As a reflection of Him, His Holy Word both celebrates His perfect nature and reveals to us our own fallen nature.

➤ **Romans 7:15 — *For what I am doing, I do not understand; for I am not practicing what I would like to do.***

We all can relate to the fierce internal struggle that Paul describes. Until we stand in Jesus' presence, we will all experience this battle. The only way to win it is by joyfully tapping into the Spirit's overcoming power.

➤ **Romans 7:18 — *For the willing is present in me, but the doing of the good is not.***

We simply do not have the power by ourselves to do what pleases God. Even the "good things" we do in our own strength make us prideful and dishonoring to God (Is. 64:6).

prisoner of the law of sin which is in my members.

24 Wretched man that I am! Who will set me free from the body of this death?

25 Thanks be to God through Jesus Christ our Lord! So then, on the one hand I myself with my mind am serving the law of God, but on the other, with my flesh the law of sin.

  Job 3:1—4:21

3 AFTERWARD Job opened his mouth and cursed the day of his *birth*.

2 And Job said,

3 "Let the day perish on which I was to be born,
    And the night *which* said, 'A boy is conceived.'

4 "May that day be darkness;

Let not God above care for it,
    Nor light shine on it.

5 "Let darkness and black gloom claim it;
    Let a cloud settle on it;
    Let the blackness of the day terrify it.

6 "*As for* that night, let darkness seize it;
    Let it not rejoice among the days of the year;

Let it not come into the number of
the months.

7 "Behold, let that night be barren;
Let no joyful shout enter it.

8 "Let those curse it who curse the day,
Who are prepared to rouse
Leviathan.

9 "Let the stars of its twilight be
darkened;
Let it wait for light but have none,
And let it not see the breaking
dawn;

10 Because it did not shut the opening
of my *mother's* womb,
Or hide trouble from my eyes.

11 "Why did I not die at birth,
Come forth from the womb and
expire?

12 "Why did the knees receive me,
And why the breasts, that I should
suck?

13 "For now I would have lain down
and been quiet;
I would have slept then, I would
have been at rest,

14 With kings and *with* counselors of
the earth,
Who rebuilt ruins for themselves;

15 Or with princes who had gold,
Who were filling their houses *with*
silver.

16 "Or like a miscarriage which is
discarded, I would not be,
As infants that never saw light.

17 "There the wicked cease from raging,
And there the weary are at rest.

18 "The prisoners are at ease together;
They do not hear the voice of the
taskmaster.

19 "The small and the great are there,
And the slave is free from his
master.

20 "Why is light given to him who
suffers,
And life to the bitter of soul,

21 Who long for death, but there is
none,
And dig for it more than for hidden
treasures,

22 Who rejoice greatly,
And exult when they find the grave?

23 "*Why is light given* to a man whose
way is hidden,
And whom God has hedged in?

24 "For my groaning comes at the sight
of my food,
And my cries pour out like water.

25 "For what I fear comes upon me,
And what I dread befalls me.

26 "I am not at ease, nor am I quiet,
And I am not at rest, but turmoil
comes."

4 THEN Eliphaz the Temanite answered

2 "If one ventures a word with you,
will you become impatient?
But who can refrain from speaking?

3 "Behold you have admonished
many,
And you have strengthened weak
hands.

4 "Your words have helped the
tottering to stand,
And you have strengthened feeble
knees.

5 "But now it has come to you, and
you are impatient;
It touches you, and you are
dismayed.

6 "Is not your fear *of God* your
confidence,
And the integrity of your ways your
hope?

7 "Remember now, who *ever* perished
being innocent?
Or where were the upright
destroyed?

8 "According to what I have seen,
those who plow iniquity
And those who sow trouble harvest
it.

9 "By the breath of God they perish,
And by the blast of His anger they
come to an end.

10 "The roaring of the lion and the
voice of the *fierce* lion,
And the teeth of the young lions are
broken.

LIFE LESSONS

> **Job 3:25 — *"For what I fear comes
upon me, and what I dread befalls me."***

*I*ntense suffering often prompts us to
say things we don't really mean. Fortunately, we serve a God who "is mindful that we are but dust" (Ps. 103:14)
and who promises not to break the
bruised reed of our souls (Is. 42:3). We all
have secret fears and worries, things that
make us say, "If *this* happened, I don't
know what I'd do." The Lord wants us to
take even these fears to Him and say, "I
put my trust in You."

11 "The lion perishes for lack of prey,
　And the whelps of the lioness are
　　scattered.
12 "Now a word was brought to me
　　stealthily,
　And my ear received a whisper of it.
13 "Amid disquieting thoughts from the
　　visions of the night,
　When deep sleep falls on men,
14 Dread came upon me, and
　　trembling,
　And made all my bones shake.
15 "Then a spirit passed by my face;
　The hair of my flesh bristled up.
16 "It stood still, but I could not discern
　　its appearance;
　A form *was* before my eyes;
　There was silence, then I heard a
　　voice:
➤ 17 'Can mankind be just before God?
　Can a man be pure before his
　　Maker?
18 'He puts no trust even in His servants;
　And against His angels He charges
　　error.
19 'How much more those who dwell in
　　houses of clay,
　Whose foundation is in the dust,
　Who are crushed before the moth!
20 'Between morning and evening they
　　are broken in pieces;
　Unobserved, they perish forever.
21 'Is not their tent-cord plucked up
　　within them?
　They die, yet without wisdom.'

Psalm 91:14-16

14 "Because he has loved Me, therefore
　　I will deliver him;
　I will set him *securely* on high,
　　because he has known My name.
➤ 15 "He will call upon Me, and I will
　　answer him;
　I will be with him in trouble;
　I will rescue him and honor him.
16 "With a long life I will satisfy him
　And let him see My salvation."

Proverbs 22:15

15 Foolishness is bound up in the heart
　of a child;

The rod of discipline will remove it
　far from him.

Romans 8:1-21

8 THEREFORE there is now no condemnation for those who are in Christ Jesus.
2 For the law of the Spirit of life in Christ Jesus has set you free from the law of sin and of death.
3 For what the Law could not do, weak as it was through the flesh, God *did*: sending His own Son in the likeness of sinful flesh and *as an offering* for sin, He condemned sin in the flesh,
4 so that the requirement of the Law might be fulfilled in us, who do not walk according to the flesh but according to the Spirit.
5 For those who are according to the flesh set their minds on the things of the flesh, but those who are according to the Spirit, the things of the Spirit.
6 For the mind set on the flesh is death, but the mind set on the Spirit is life and peace,
7 because the mind set on the flesh is hostile toward God; for it does not subject itself to the law of God, for it is not even able *to do so*,

LIFE LESSONS

➤ **Job 4:17 — "Can mankind be just before God?"**

*W*henever we fault God's handling of the universe or angrily blame Him for a personal hardship, we are in fact calling ourselves more gracious and righteous than He is—and that's always a dangerous and foolish place to be.

➤ **Psalm 91:15 — *He will call upon Me, and I will answer him; I will be with him in trouble; I will rescue him and honor him.***

*I*n prayer, we connect our need to God's supply. We bring our emptiness to His fullness and ask Him to satisfy us. Our deficits are no match for the Lord's abundance, and our cries find a home in His ears.

ANSWERS TO LIFE'S QUESTIONS

Why do I still have the impulse to sin?

ROMANS 8:1–11

*W*hen you placed your faith in Jesus Christ to forgive you of all of your sins, were you filled with joy because of your new life in Him? Did the ungodly things you once did lose their attraction? Did you feel like you never wanted to sin again?

Sometimes at the beginning of our relationships with Christ, we begin to feel as if we could conquer every evil impulse. Unfortunately, that feeling of invincibility does not last long. We stumble badly. New temptations and trials bring to light areas of weakness in our lives that we thought we had conquered. We feel confused, ashamed, and even alarmed. We wonder, *How could this happen? I thought I was supposed to be free from sin!*

The truth is, Jesus *has* liberated us from our sins—but we must cooperate with what He has done for us. Paul wrote, "It was for freedom that Christ set us free; therefore keep standing firm and do not be subject again to a yoke of slavery" (Gal. 5:1). In other words, God has broken sin's hold over us and has given us His Spirit who directs us in living a life of freedom that is pleasing to Him. However, we can forfeit our liberty by selfishly choosing our way instead of God's.

This is the basis of sin—we disobey the Lord in order to satisfy our own fleshly desires. Paul explains, "The flesh sets its desire against the Spirit, and the Spirit against the flesh; for these are in opposition to one another, so that you may not do the things that you please" (Gal. 5:17). The impulse to sin—also called the *sin nature*—remains within us and must be surrendered to God. This does not happen overnight but is the continuing work of the Spirit within us. Paul affirms, "Walk by the Spirit, and you will not carry out the desire of the flesh" (Gal. 5:16).

If you have accepted Christ as your Savior, you have been united with Him. His likeness and holiness are present within your life, and He empowers you to resist temptation. Therefore, you must have faith that He can remove ungodly strongholds within your heart and that He will continuously work to set you free from *all* sin and bondage. Your responsibility is to say "no" to sin and "yes" to Him as He provides the all-encompassing liberty that your soul craves.

➤ 8 and those who are in the flesh cannot please God.

9 However, you are not in the flesh but in the Spirit, if indeed the Spirit of God dwells in you. But if anyone does not have the Spirit of Christ, he does not belong to Him.

10 If Christ is in you, though the body is dead because of sin, yet the spirit is alive because of righteousness.

11 But if the Spirit of Him who raised Jesus from the dead dwells in you, He who raised Christ Jesus from the dead will also give life to your mortal bodies through His Spirit who dwells in you.

12 So then, brethren, we are under obligation, not to the flesh, to live according to the flesh—

➤ 13 for if you are living according to the flesh, you must die; but if by the Spirit you are putting to death the deeds of the body, you will live.

14 For all who are being led by the Spirit of God, these are sons of God.

15 For you have not received a spirit of slavery leading to fear again, but you have received a spirit of adoption as sons by which we cry out, "Abba! Father!"

16 The Spirit Himself testifies with our spirit that we are children of God,

LIFE LESSONS

➤ **Romans 8:8 —** *Those who are in the flesh cannot please God.*

*S*ince the flesh naturally puts itself first and does everything it can to honor itself, nothing done "in the flesh" can honor or please God. We please the Lord only when we depend on Him to do through us what we cannot.

➤ **Romans 8:13 —** *If you are living according to the flesh, you must die; but if by the Spirit you are putting to death the deeds of the body, you will live.*

*G*race does not change the nature of sin; sin leads to death—always. Grace never makes sin less deadly. Instead, grace enables us to rely on the power of the Spirit to put to death our sinful urges and desires.

17 and if children, heirs also, heirs of God and fellow heirs with Christ, if indeed we suffer with *Him* so that we may also be glorified with *Him*.

18 For I consider that the sufferings of this present time are not worthy to be compared with the glory that is to be revealed to us.

19 For the anxious longing of the creation waits eagerly for the revealing of the sons of God.

20 For the creation was subjected to futility, not willingly, but because of Him who subjected it, in hope

21 that the creation itself also will be set free from its slavery to corruption into the freedom of the glory of the children of God.

AUGUST 7

Job 5:1—6:30

5 "CALL now, is there anyone who
   will answer you?
   And to which of the holy ones will
   you turn?

2 "For anger slays the foolish man,
   And jealousy kills the simple.

3 "I have seen the foolish taking root,
   And I cursed his abode immediately.

4 "His sons are far from safety,
   They are even oppressed in the gate,
   And there is no deliverer.

5 "His harvest the hungry devour
   And take it to a *place of* thorns,
   And the schemer is eager for their
   wealth.

6 "For affliction does not come from
   the dust,
   Nor does trouble sprout from the
   ground,

7 For man is born for trouble,
   As sparks fly upward.

➤ 8 "But as for me, I would seek God,
   And I would place my cause before
   God;

9 Who does great and unsearchable
   things,
   Wonders without number.

10 "He gives rain on the earth
   And sends water on the fields,

11 So that He sets on high those who
   are lowly,

And those who mourn are lifted to
   safety.

12 "He frustrates the plotting of the
   shrewd,
   So that their hands cannot attain
   success.

13 "He captures the wise by their own
   shrewdness,
   And the advice of the cunning is
   quickly thwarted.

14 "By day they meet with darkness,
   And grope at noon as in the night.

15 "But He saves from the sword of
   their mouth,
   And the poor from the hand of the
   mighty.

16 "So the helpless has hope,
   And unrighteousness must shut its
   mouth.

17 "Behold, how happy is the man
   whom God reproves,

So do not despise the discipline of the Almighty.

18 "For He inflicts pain, and gives relief;
He wounds, and His hands *also* heal.

19 "From six troubles He will deliver you,
Even in seven evil will not touch you.

20 "In famine He will redeem you from death,
And in war from the power of the sword.

21 "You will be hidden from the scourge of the tongue,
And you will not be afraid of violence when it comes.

22 "You will laugh at violence and famine,
And you will not be afraid of wild beasts.

23 "For you will be in league with the stones of the field,
And the beasts of the field will be at peace with you.

24 "You will know that your tent is secure,
For you will visit your abode and fear no loss.

25 "You will know also that your descendants will be many,
And your offspring as the grass of the earth.

26 "You will come to the grave in full vigor,
Like the stacking of grain in its season.

27 "Behold this; we have investigated it, *and* so it is.
Hear it, and know for yourself."

6 THEN Job answered,
2 "Oh that my grief were actually weighed
And laid in the balances together with my calamity!

3 "For then it would be heavier than the sand of the seas;
Therefore my words have been rash.

4 "For the arrows of the Almighty are within me,
Their poison my spirit drinks;
The terrors of God are arrayed against me.

5 "Does the wild donkey bray over *his* grass,
Or does the ox low over his fodder?

6 "Can something tasteless be eaten without salt,
Or is there any taste in the white of an egg?

7 "My soul refuses to touch *them;*
They are like loathsome food to me.

8 "Oh that my request might come to pass,
And that God would grant my longing!

9 "Would that God were willing to crush me,
That He would loose His hand and cut me off!

10 "But it is still my consolation,
And I rejoice in unsparing pain,
That I have not denied the words of the Holy One.

11 "What is my strength, that I should wait?
And what is my end, that I should endure?

12 "Is my strength the strength of stones,
Or is my flesh bronze?

13 "Is it that my help is not within me,
And that deliverance is driven from me?

14 "For the despairing man *there should be* kindness from his friend;
So that he does not forsake the fear of the Almighty.

15 "My brothers have acted deceitfully like a wadi,
Like the torrents of wadis which vanish,

16 Which are turbid because of ice
And into which the snow melts.

17 "When they become waterless, they are silent,
When it is hot, they vanish from their place.

18 "The paths of their course wind along,
They go up into nothing and perish.

19 "The caravans of Tema looked,
The travelers of Sheba hoped for them.

20 "They were disappointed for they had trusted,
They came there and were confounded.

21 "Indeed, you have now become such,
You see a terror and are afraid.

22 "Have I said, 'Give me *something,*'
Or, 'Offer a bribe for me from your wealth,'

23 Or, 'Deliver me from the hand of the adversary,'

Or, 'Redeem me from the hand of
the tyrants'?

24 "Teach me, and I will be silent;
And show me how I have erred.

25 "How painful are honest words!
But what does your argument prove?

➤ 26 "Do you intend to reprove *my* words,
When the words of one in despair
belong to the wind?

27 "You would even cast *lots* for the
orphans
And barter over your friend.

28 "Now please look at me,
And *see* if I lie to your face.

29 "Desist now, let there be no injustice;
Even desist, my righteousness is yet
in it.

30 "Is there injustice on my tongue?
Cannot my palate discern
calamities?

🔹 Psalm 92:1–7

A Psalm, a Song for the Sabbath day.

92 IT is good to give thanks to the
LORD

✳ And to sing praises to Your name,
O Most High;

➤ 2 To declare Your lovingkindness in
the morning
And Your faithfulness by night,

3 With the ten-stringed lute and with
the harp,
With resounding music upon the lyre.

4 For You, O LORD, have made me
glad by what You have done,
I will sing for joy at the works of
Your hands.

5 How great are Your works, O LORD!
Your thoughts are very deep.

6 A senseless man has no knowledge,
Nor does a stupid man understand
this:

7 That when the wicked sprouted up
like grass
And all who did iniquity flourished,
It *was only* that they might be
destroyed forevermore.

🔹 Proverbs 22:16

16 He who oppresses the poor to make
more for himself

Or who gives to the rich, *will* only
come to poverty.

🔹 Romans 8:22–39

22 For we know that the whole creation
groans and suffers the pains of childbirth
together until now.

23 And not only this, but also we ourselves, having the first fruits of the Spirit,
even we ourselves groan within ourselves, waiting eagerly for *our* adoption
as sons, the redemption of our body.

24 For in hope we have been saved, but
hope that is seen is not hope; for who
hopes for what he *already* sees?

25 But if we hope for what we do not
see, with perseverance we wait eagerly
for it.

26 In the same way the Spirit also helps
our weakness; for we do not know how
to pray as we should, but the Spirit Himself intercedes for *us* with groanings too
deep for words;

27 and He who searches the hearts
knows what the mind of the Spirit is,

LIFE LESSONS

➤ **Job 6:26 — *"Do you intend to reprove
my words, when the words of one in
despair belong to the wind?"***

*G*odly people in pain usually know
when they speak rashly and unwisely,
but they just can't seem to help themselves; their desperation drives them to
it. Because people in great pain often
say things they don't really mean, we
must not judge too harshly their words,
even when they offend us. In these
times, we must remain "quick to hear,
slow to speak" (James 1:19). As Peter
says, "love for one another, because love
covers a multitude of sins" (1 Pet. 4:8).

➤ **Psalm 92:2 — *Declare Your lovingkindness in the morning and Your faithfulness by night.***

*T*his verse points to the moment-by-
moment relationship that God wants
with us. He has little interest in a law
("do this in the morning and this in the
evening"); rather, He wants to enjoy our
company all day long.

because He intercedes for the saints according to *the will of* God.

➤ 28 And we know that God causes all things to work together for good to those who love God, to those who are called according to *His* purpose.

29 For those whom He foreknew, He also predestined *to become* conformed to the image of His Son, so that He would be the firstborn among many brethren;

30 and these whom He predestined, He also called; and these whom He called, He also justified; and these whom He justified, He also glorified.

➤ 31 What then shall we say to these things? If God *is* for us, who *is* against us?

32 He who did not spare His own Son, but delivered Him over for us all, how will He not also with Him freely give us all things?

33 Who will bring a charge against God's elect? God is the one who justifies;

34 who is the one who condemns? Christ Jesus is He who died, yes, rather who was raised, who is at the right hand of God, who also intercedes for us.

LIFE LESSONS

➤ **Romans 8:28 —** *All things to work together for good to those who love God, to those who are called according to His purpose.*

*O*n this side of heaven we may never understand how all things can work together for good for God's children. Though not all things we experience are in themselves pleasant or helpful—some of them are very painful—we are promised that God uses *everything* for our benefit. Therefore, we must have faith that He will turn our failures and hardships into opportunities for spiritual growth.

➤ **Romans 8:31 —** *If God is for us, who is against us?*

*A*lthough people may be against us—causing us trouble, pain, and sorrow—nothing can ultimately triumph over us when we are believers. God wins and we are guaranteed to share in His victory.

ANSWERS TO LIFE'S QUESTIONS

What does God really think of me?

ROMANS 8:38, 39

I never thought much about whether God liked me or approved of me when I was a young man. I knew He *loved* me, but I never thought about whether He *liked* me. If someone had pressed me on the point, I probably would have concluded that the Lord "somewhat" liked me. I don't think I would have said that He liked me through and through.

Only after I truly experienced God's love—His total, unconditional, overwhelming, abundant love—could I say with all honesty, "Yes, God likes me. He approves of me. He likes spending time with me. He likes being with me. He likes hearing me when I pray to Him, and He also enjoys talking with me through His Word. I believe He loves me. He knows I make mistakes, but He sees my heart and my desire to know Him better each day."

I didn't come to that position on the basis of things I had accomplished or actions I had taken. Rather, I came to that position solely because I had a new appreciation for God's grace at work in my life. The Lord certainly does expect obedience, but the fact is, I had done nothing and could do nothing to win His approval. He likes me just the way I am because He created me to be just the way I am. His approval of me isn't based on anything I have accomplished or might accomplish in the future. He approves of me because I stand forgiven before Him, and I'm forgiven because I have accepted Jesus Christ as my Savior and have received His forgiveness. That makes me *totally* acceptable to Him.

The first four chapters of Romans make it very clear that we can't save ourselves. We are all sinners and have fallen short of the glory of God (Rom. 3:23). But because of what Jesus Christ did for us on the Cross, by faith we are "justified as a gift by His grace" (Rom. 3:24).

Jesus has done for you what you cannot do. He purchased full approval and forgiveness for you. You cannot have grace without the Cross. But because of the Cross, you have full access to His grace.

Grace is God's kindness and goodness toward you without regard to worth or merit. As a believer, you have a duty to obey the Lord. But you can't earn grace, buy it, or barter with God to receive it. Grace is His free gift to you. There is only one thing you can do in regard to grace: Receive it gladly!

35 Who will separate us from the love of Christ? Will tribulation, or distress, or persecution, or famine, or nakedness, or peril, or sword?
36 Just as it is written,

"FOR YOUR SAKE WE ARE BEING PUT TO
DEATH ALL DAY LONG;
WE WERE CONSIDERED AS SHEEP TO BE
SLAUGHTERED."

37 But in all these things we overwhelmingly conquer through Him who loved us.
38 For I am convinced that neither death, nor life, nor angels, nor principalities, nor things present, nor things to come, nor powers,
39 nor height, nor depth, nor any other

created thing, will be able to separate us from the love of God, which is in Christ Jesus our Lord.

AUGUST 8

Job 7:1—8:22

7 "IS not man forced to labor on earth,
And *are not* his days like the days of a hired man?
2 "As a slave who pants for the shade,
And as a hired man who eagerly waits for his wages,
3 So am I allotted months of vanity,
And nights of trouble are appointed me.
4 "When I lie down I say,
'When shall I arise?'
But the night continues,
And I am continually tossing until dawn.
5 "My flesh is clothed with worms and a crust of dirt,
My skin hardens and runs.
6 "My days are swifter than a weaver's shuttle,
And come to an end without hope.
7 "Remember that my life is *but* breath;
My eye will not again see good.
8 "The eye of him who sees me will behold me no longer;
Your eyes *will be* on me, but I will not be.
9 "When a cloud vanishes, it is gone,
So he who goes down to Sheol does not come up.
10 "He will not return again to his house,

Nor will his place know him anymore.
11 "Therefore I will not restrain my mouth;
I will speak in the anguish of my spirit,
I will complain in the bitterness of my soul.
12 "Am I the sea, or the sea monster,
That You set a guard over me?
13 "If I say, 'My bed will comfort me,
My couch will ease my complaint,'
14 Then You frighten me with dreams
And terrify me by visions;
15 So that my soul would choose suffocation,
Death rather than my pains.
16 "I waste away; I will not live forever.
Leave me alone, for my days are *but* a breath.
17 "What is man that You magnify him,
And that You are concerned about him,

18 That You examine him every
    morning
    And try him every moment?
19 "Will You never turn Your gaze
    away from me,
    Nor let me alone until I swallow my
    spittle?
20 "Have I sinned? What have I done to
    You,
    O watcher of men?
    Why have You set me as Your target,
    So that I am a burden to myself?
21 "Why then do You not pardon my
    transgression
    And take away my iniquity?
    For now I will lie down in the dust;
    And You will seek me, but I will not
    be."

8 THEN Bildad the Shuhite answered,
2   "How long will you say these
    things,
    And the words of your mouth be a
    mighty wind?
3   "Does God pervert justice?
    Or does the Almighty pervert what
    is right?
➤ 4   "If your sons sinned against Him,
    Then He delivered them into the
    power of their transgression.
5   "If you would seek God
    And implore the compassion of the
    Almighty,
6   If you are pure and upright,
    Surely now He would rouse Himself
    for you
    And restore your righteous estate.
7   "Though your beginning was
    insignificant,
    Yet your end will increase greatly.
8   "Please inquire of past generations,
    And consider the things searched
    out by their fathers.
9   "For we are only of yesterday and
    know nothing,

LIFE LESSONS

➤ **Job 8:4 — "If your sons sinned against Him, then He delivered them into the power of their transgression."**

*J*ob lost his sons tragically, and now his friend worsens his pain by suggesting that they deserved it. The truth is, we don't usually know the reason behind someone's misfortune — and to speculate like this is a sin.

    Because our days on earth are as a
    shadow.
10 "Will they not teach you and tell you,
    And bring forth words from their
    minds?
11 "Can the papyrus grow up without a
    marsh?
    Can the rushes grow without water?
12 "While it is still green and not cut
    down,
    Yet it withers before any other
    plant.
13 "So are the paths of all who forget
    God;
    And the hope of the godless will
    perish,
14 Whose confidence is fragile,
    And whose trust a spider's web.
15 "He trusts in his house, but it does
    not stand;
    He holds fast to it, but it does not
    endure.
16 "He thrives before the sun,
    And his shoots spread out over his
    garden.
17 "His roots wrap around a rock pile,
    He grasps a house of stones.
18 "If he is removed from his place,
    Then it will deny him, saying, 'I
    never saw you.'
19 "Behold, this is the joy of His way;
    And out of the dust others will spring.
20 "Lo, God will not reject a man of
    integrity,
    Nor will He support the evildoers.
21 "He will yet fill your mouth with
    laughter
    And your lips with shouting.
22 "Those who hate you will be clothed
    with shame,
    And the tent of the wicked will be
    no longer."

Psalm 92:8–15

8   But You, O LORD, are on high
    forever.
9   For, behold, Your enemies, O LORD,
    For, behold, Your enemies will
    perish;
    All who do iniquity will be
    scattered.
10 But You have exalted my horn like
    that of the wild ox;
    I have been anointed with fresh oil.

WHAT THE BIBLE SAYS ABOUT

Staying Young All Your Life

Psalm 92:12–15

Some people are old before their fortieth birthday; others reach ninety and still seem young. What is the difference? Attitude. The body will age, but we get old only if we choose to do so. However, God desires that believers live each day fully so that He can use us. As Psalm 92:13, 14 promises: "Planted in the house of the LORD, they will flourish in the courts of our God. They will still yield fruit in old age."

What does this mean for us as believers?

First, we need to keep learning. Some people are satisfied with their present level of knowledge because learning something new would tax their brain. But discovering fresh concepts guarantees we can continue being productive in this world.

Of course, Scripture should be our first source of knowledge. When we gain God's perspective, anxiety and fear diminish so that our bodies and minds can function at optimum levels. In addition, we should read up on whatever interests us, become involved in new projects, and learn to use technology.

Keeping up with new technology seems harder the more birthdays we have, but it helps to keep us young. That's why I offer another suggestion—keep laboring. I'm not against retirement, but leaving a vocation is no reason to stop working.

Just as certain fruit improves as trees age, years of a faithful walk with God should yield greater fruit in the believer's life. Look for service opportunities through the church and other ministries.

If the Father blesses you with many years, bless Him with useful service. The longer you stay young, the more valuable you are as a servant in His kingdom. ◈

---

11 And my eye has looked *exultantly*
    upon my foes,
    My ears hear of the evildoers who
      rise up against me.
12 The righteous man will flourish like
    the palm tree,
    He will grow like a cedar in
      Lebanon.
13 Planted in the house of the LORD,
    They will flourish in the courts of
      our God.
➤ 14 They will still yield fruit in old age;
✳   They shall be full of sap and very
      green,
15 To declare that the LORD is
    upright;
    He is my rock, and there is no
      unrighteousness in Him.

LIFE LESSONS

➤ **Psalm 92:14 — *They will still yield fruit in old age; they shall be full of sap and very green.***

Bodies grow old and frail, but God wants us to bear fruit as long as we live on this earth. The kind of fruit may vary depending on our season of life, but He calls us to fruitfulness in all seasons.

◈ Proverbs 22:17–21

17 Incline your ear and hear the words
    of the wise,
    And apply your mind to my
      knowledge;
18 For it will be pleasant if you keep
    them within you,
    That they may be ready on your
      lips.
19 So that your trust may be in the
    LORD,
    I have taught you today, even you.
20 Have I not written to you excellent
    things
    Of counsels and knowledge,
21 To make you know the certainty of
    the words of truth
    That you may correctly answer him
      who sent you?

◈ Romans 9:1–15

9 I AM telling the truth in Christ, I am not lying, my conscience testifies with me in the Holy Spirit,
2 that I have great sorrow and unceasing grief in my heart.

➤ 3 For I could wish that I myself were accursed, *separated* from Christ for the sake of my brethren, my kinsmen according to the flesh,

✳ 4 who are Israelites, to whom belongs the adoption as sons, and the glory and the covenants and the giving of the Law and the *temple* service and the promises,

5 whose are the fathers, and from whom is the Christ according to the flesh, who is over all, God blessed forever. Amen.

6 But *it is* not as though the word of God has failed. For they are not all Israel who are *descended* from Israel;

7 nor are they all children because they are Abraham's descendants, but: "THROUGH ISAAC YOUR DESCENDANTS WILL BE NAMED."

8 That is, it is not the children of the flesh who are children of God, but the children of the promise are regarded as descendants.

9 For this is the word of promise: "AT THIS TIME I WILL COME, AND SARAH SHALL HAVE A SON."

10 And not only this, but there was Rebekah also, when she had conceived *twins* by one man, our father Isaac;

11 for though *the twins* were not yet born and had not done anything good or bad, so that God's purpose according to *His* choice would stand, not because of works but because of Him who calls,

12 it was said to her, "THE OLDER WILL SERVE THE YOUNGER."

13 Just as it is written, "JACOB I LOVED, BUT ESAU I HATED."

14 What shall we say then? There is no injustice with God, is there? May it never be!

15 For He says to Moses, "I WILL HAVE ◄ MERCY ON WHOM I HAVE MERCY, AND I WILL HAVE COMPASSION ON WHOM I HAVE COMPASSION."

LIFE LESSONS

➤ **Romans 9:3 — *I could wish that I myself were accursed, separated from Christ for the sake of my brethren.***

*D*espite his frequent ill treatment at the hands of his Jewish countrymen, Paul had an intense desire for them to come to faith in Christ and so experience the new life available in Him. How badly do *we* want people to know Jesus?

➤ **Romans 9:15 — *"I will have mercy on whom I have mercy."***

*G*od blesses people with His grace and mercy, not because they deserve it but because it is His nature to grant grace and mercy. Grace nor mercy can be demanded—they can only be gratefully accepted.

AUGUST 9

Job 9:1—10:22

9 THEN Job answered,
2   "In truth I know that this is so;
But how can a man be in the right before God?

3 "If one wished to dispute with Him,
He could not answer Him once in a thousand *times*.

4 "Wise in heart and mighty in strength,
Who has defied Him without harm?

5 "*It is God* who removes the mountains, they know not *how*,
When He overturns them in His anger;

6 Who shakes the earth out of its place,
And its pillars tremble;

7 Who commands the sun not to shine,
And sets a seal upon the stars;

8 Who alone stretches out the heavens
And tramples down the waves of the sea;

9 Who makes the Bear, Orion and the Pleiades,
And the chambers of the south;

10 Who does great things, unfathomable,
And wondrous works without number.

11 "Were He to pass by me, I would not
  see Him;
    Were He to move past *me,* I would
    not perceive Him.
12 "Were He to snatch away, who could
  restrain Him?
    Who could say to Him, 'What are
    You doing?'
13 "God will not turn back His anger;
    Beneath Him crouch the helpers of
    Rahab.
14 "How then can I answer Him,
    And choose my words before Him?
15 "For though I were right, I could not
  answer;
    I would have to implore the mercy
    of my judge.
16 "If I called and He answered me,
    I could not believe that He was
    listening to my voice.
17 "For He bruises me with a tempest
    And multiplies my wounds without
    cause.
18 "He will not allow me to get my
  breath,
    But saturates me with bitterness.
19 "If *it is a matter* of power, behold,
    He is the strong one!
    And if *it is a matter* of justice, who
    can summon Him?
20 "Though I am righteous, my mouth
    will condemn me;
    Though I am guiltless, He will
    declare me guilty.
21 "I am guiltless;
    I do not take notice of myself;
    I despise my life.
22 "It is *all* one; therefore I say,
    'He destroys the guiltless and the
    wicked.'
23 "If the scourge kills suddenly,
    He mocks the despair of the
    innocent.
24 "The earth is given into the hand of
    the wicked;
    He covers the faces of its judges.
    If *it is* not He, then who is it?
25 "Now my days are swifter than a
  runner;
    They flee away, they see no good.
26 "They slip by like reed boats,
    Like an eagle that swoops on its
    prey.
27 "Though I say, 'I will forget my
  complaint,
    I will leave off my *sad* countenance
    and be cheerful,'

28 I am afraid of all my pains,
    I know that You will not acquit me.
29 "I am accounted wicked,
    Why then should I toil in vain?
30 "If I should wash myself with snow
    And cleanse my hands with lye,
31 Yet You would plunge me into the
  pit,
    And my own clothes would abhor
    me.
32 "For *He is* not a man as I am that I
    may answer Him,
    That we may go to court together.
33 "There is no umpire between us,
    Who may lay his hand upon us
    both.
34 "Let Him remove His rod from me,
    And let not dread of Him terrify me.
35 "*Then* I would speak and not fear
    Him;
    But I am not like that in myself.

10 "I LOATHE my own life;
    I will give full vent to my
      complaint;
    I will speak in the bitterness of my
      soul.
2 "I will say to God, 'Do not condemn
  me;
    Let me know why You contend with
    me.
3 'Is it right for You indeed to
  oppress,
    To reject the labor of Your hands,
    And to look favorably on the
    schemes of the wicked?
4 'Have You eyes of flesh?
    Or do You see as a man sees?
5 'Are Your days as the days of a
  mortal,
    Or Your years as man's years,
6 That You should seek for my guilt
    And search after my sin?
7 'According to Your knowledge I am
    indeed not guilty,

· · · · LIFE LESSONS · · · ·

➤ **Job 9:33 — *"There is no umpire
between us, who may lay his hand upon
us both."***

*J*ob needed what we have: a sympathetic mediator between holy God
and sinful people. Here's the good news:
"For there is one God, and one mediator also between God and men, the man
Christ Jesus" (1 Tim. 2:5).

Yet there is no deliverance from
Your hand.
8 'Your hands fashioned and made me
altogether,
And would You destroy me?
9 'Remember now, that You have
made me as clay;
And would You turn me into dust
again?
10 'Did You not pour me out like milk
And curdle me like cheese;
11 Clothe me with skin and flesh,
And knit me together with bones
and sinews?
➤ 12 'You have granted me life and
lovingkindness;
And Your care has preserved my
spirit.
13 'Yet these things You have
concealed in Your heart;
I know that this is within You:
14 If I sin, then You would take note of
me,
And would not acquit me of my
guilt.
15 'If I am wicked, woe to me!
And if I am righteous, I dare not lift
up my head.
I am sated with disgrace and
conscious of my misery.
16 'Should my head be lifted up, You
would hunt me like a lion;
And again You would show Your
power against me.
17 'You renew Your witnesses against
me
And increase Your anger toward me;
Hardship after hardship is with me.
18 'Why then have You brought me out
of the womb?
Would that I had died and no eye
had seen me!
19 'I should have been as though I had
not been,
Carried from womb to tomb.'
➤ 20 "Would He not let my few days
alone?
Withdraw from me that I may have
a little cheer
21 Before I go—and I shall not
return—
To the land of darkness and deep
shadow,
22 The land of utter gloom as darkness
itself,
Of deep shadow without order,
And which shines as the darkness."

Psalm 93:1–5

93 THE LORD reigns, He is clothed
with majesty; ◄
The LORD has clothed and girded
Himself with strength;
Indeed, the world is firmly
established, it will not be moved. ✳
2 Your throne is established from of
old;
You are from everlasting.
3 The floods have lifted up, O LORD,
The floods have lifted up their voice,
The floods lift up their pounding
waves.
4 More than the sounds of many
waters,
Than the mighty breakers of the
sea,
The LORD on high is mighty.
5 Your testimonies are fully
confirmed;

LIFE LESSONS

➤ **Job 10:12** — *"You have granted me
life and lovingkindness; and Your care
has preserved my spirit."*

Even in the middle of their bitter complaints, those with a genuine heart
for God continue to hope in His grace
and remember His many blessings. God
sustains us, even when we cannot see His
hand in our situations.

➤ **Job 10:20** — *"Would He not let my
few days alone? Withdraw from me that
I may have a little cheer."*

When we feel most discouraged
and worn out, we may wish that
the Lord would just leave us alone—but
thankfully He never does. He promises
us, "I WILL NEVER DESERT YOU, NOR WILL I EVER
FORSAKE YOU" (Heb. 13:5).

➤ **Psalm 93:1** — *The LORD reigns, He
is clothed with majesty . . . The LORD
has clothed and girded Himself with
strength.*

We are children of a sovereign God
who has the power and wisdom to
make happen everything He desires to
do. Nothing can frustrate His plans, and
no one can derail His promises. That's
why we can trust Him!

Holiness befits Your house,
O LORD, forevermore.

Proverbs 22:22, 23

22 Do not rob the poor because he is
poor,
Or crush the afflicted at the gate;
23 For the LORD will plead their case
And take the life of those who rob
them.

Romans 9:16–33

16 So then it *does* not *depend* on the
man who wills or the man who runs, but
on God who has mercy.
17 For the Scripture says to Pharaoh,
"FOR THIS VERY PURPOSE I RAISED YOU
UP, TO DEMONSTRATE MY POWER IN YOU,
AND THAT MY NAME MIGHT BE PROCLAIMED
THROUGHOUT THE WHOLE EARTH."
18 So then He has mercy on whom He
desires, and He hardens whom He desires.
19 You will say to me then, "Why does
He still find fault? For who resists His
will?"
20 On the contrary, who are you, O
man, who answers back to God? The
thing molded will not say to the molder,
"Why did you make me like this," will it?
21 Or does not the potter have a right
over the clay, to make from the same
lump one vessel for honorable use and
another for common use?
22 What if God, although willing to
demonstrate His wrath and to make
His power known, endured with much
patience vessels of wrath prepared for
destruction?
23 And *He did so* to make known the
riches of His glory upon vessels of mercy,
which He prepared beforehand for glory,
24 *even* us, whom He also called, not
from among Jews only, but also from
among Gentiles.
25 As He says also in Hosea,
"I WILL CALL THOSE WHO WERE NOT MY
PEOPLE, 'MY PEOPLE,'
AND HER WHO WAS NOT BELOVED,
'BELOVED.'"
26 "AND IT SHALL BE THAT IN THE PLACE

WHERE IT WAS SAID TO THEM, 'YOU
ARE NOT MY PEOPLE,'
THERE THEY SHALL BE CALLED SONS OF
THE LIVING GOD."
27 Isaiah cries out concerning Israel,
"THOUGH THE NUMBER OF THE SONS OF IS-
RAEL BE LIKE THE SAND OF THE SEA, IT IS THE
REMNANT THAT WILL BE SAVED;
28 FOR THE LORD WILL EXECUTE HIS WORD
ON THE EARTH, THOROUGHLY AND QUICKLY."
29 And just as Isaiah foretold,
"UNLESS THE LORD OF SABAOTH HAD
LEFT TO US A POSTERITY,
WE WOULD HAVE BECOME LIKE SODOM,
AND WOULD HAVE RESEMBLED
GOMORRAH."
30 What shall we say then? That Gen-
tiles, who did not pursue righteousness,
attained righteousness, even the righ-
teousness which is by faith;
31 but Israel, pursuing a law of righ-
teousness, did not arrive at *that* law.
32 Why? Because *they did* not *pursue it*
by faith, but as though *it were* by works.
They stumbled over the stumbling stone,
33 just as it is written,
"BEHOLD, I LAY IN ZION A STONE OF
STUMBLING AND A ROCK OF OFFENSE,
AND HE WHO BELIEVES IN HIM WILL
NOT BE DISAPPOINTED."

LIFE LESSONS

➤ **Romans 9:18 —** *Whom He desires, and
He hardens.*

*W*e know God wants all to come to
repentance (2 Pet. 3:9). So how is
it, then, that He also hardens people's
hearts? Understand that Pharaoh had
five opportunities to repent during the first five
plagues to repent. Yet we see repeatedly
that "Pharaoh hardened his heart" (Ex.
8:32; Ex. 7:13, 23; 8:15, 19; 9:7). It was
not until the sixth plague that God gave
Pharaoh over to His sinfulness: "The LORD
hardened Pharaoh's heart" (Ex. 9:12).
The Lord is God, and He reserves the
right to decide when enough is truly
enough.

➤ **Romans 9:27 —** *"The remnant that
will be saved."*

*T*he idea of the remnant appears
throughout Scripture (2 Kin. 19:30,
31; Ezra 9:8; Is. 10:20). In His grace, God
preserves a small portion of His people
Israel until the day He rescues them all.

WHAT THE BIBLE SAYS ABOUT

Molded by the Master

Romans 9:20, 21

When the potter takes the lump of clay, he knows what he wants to do with it—whether he wants to create a beautiful vase, bowl, or pitcher. He already knows what it is going to become. He takes the lump of clay, places it on the pottery wheel, and begins to shape it. However, the only way the potter can form this piece of clay into something beautiful is by getting it to the center of the wheel.

I learned this when I went to a pottery house. As I watched people molding their clay creations, one of the artisans told me, "I have to get this right in the center of the wheel because if I don't, I can't mold it correctly."

One of the reasons God is not able to make us into the people He wants us to be is because we rebel against Him—we insist on doing things our way and get out of the center of His will. If we insist on questioning and contradicting Him, we'll never experience God's best.

Romans 9:20, 21 warns, "Who are you, O man, who answers back to God? The thing molded will not say to the molder, 'Why did you make me like this,' will it? Or does not the potter have a right over the clay, to make from the same lump one vessel for honorable use and another for common use?"

God is daily molding us through our circumstances, and we need to trust Him—our faith in Him is absolutely crucial. To follow are six words to describe our Master Potter that will help us when our faith falters:

1. *Power.*

God has power in our lives because He is omnipotent—He is all-powerful. He can do anything He chooses to do. However, the Father gave us a will of our own because He wants us to love Him freely. Now, there is no such thing as an absolutely free will because God is in ultimate control over all things. He allows our free will up to a certain point; however, the Master Potter has the ultimate power over the clay.

2. *Purpose.*

God has a specific purpose in mind for each of us—and He created us with qualities that will fulfill that purpose.

3. *Plan.*

God has a plan. His plan is to mold us and work daily to conform us to the likeness of His Son Jesus Christ throughout our lives.

4. *Patience.*

God never hurries. Spiritual maturity is not something that can be rushed. It continues on, even when we are older. We cannot rush Him because becoming like Jesus Christ involves a lifetime process of learning the ways of God.

5. *Perseverance.*

When the potter finds imperfections in the clay, he puts it back on the wheel and reshapes it. He never throws it away. Likewise, God never discards us. He will never throw us away. The all-powerful, loving hand of our Father has the power to overcome any obstacle in our lives. He alone can make us into something extraordinary.

6. *Personal.*

God forms each one of us individually. He can do so because He is infinite in power, wisdom, and love. He knows exactly what He has planned for each of us.

Therefore, trust the Master Potter! Trust the One who is powerful, who has a purpose and a plan for you, who is patient with you, who perseveres with you, and who loves you deeply and personally. As He molds you, learn from Him—cling to Him. He is molding you into an amazing vessel for His work, and He is creating a future for you that is better than you could ever imagine. You're a masterpiece waiting to happen, so submit to His touch. ❖

❖ **Job 11:1—12:25**

11 THEN Zophar the Naamathite answered,

2 "Shall a multitude of words go unanswered,
   And a talkative man be acquitted?
3 "Shall your boasts silence men?
   And shall you scoff and none rebuke?

4 "For you have said, 'My teaching is
    pure,
    And I am innocent in your eyes.'
5 "But would that God might speak,
    And open His lips against you,
6   And show you the secrets of
    wisdom!
    For sound wisdom has two sides.
    Know then that God forgets a part
    of your iniquity.
➤ 7 "Can you discover the depths of God?
    Can you discover the limits of the
    Almighty?
8 "*They are* high as the heavens, what
    can you do?
    Deeper than Sheol, what can you
    know?
9 "Its measure is longer than the earth
    And broader than the sea.
10 "If He passes by or shuts up,
    Or calls an assembly, who can
    restrain Him?
11 "For He knows false men,
    And He sees iniquity without
    investigating.
12 "An idiot will become intelligent
    When the foal of a wild donkey is
    born a man.
13 "If you would direct your heart right
    And spread out your hand to Him,
14 If iniquity is in your hand, put it far
    away,
    And do not let wickedness dwell in
    your tents;
15 "Then, indeed, you could lift up your
    face without *moral* defect,
    And you would be steadfast and not
    fear.
16 "For you would forget *your* trouble,
    As waters that have passed by, you
    would remember *it.*
17 "Your life would be brighter than
    noonday;
    Darkness would be like the
    morning.

18 "Then you would trust, because there
    is hope;
    And you would look around and
    rest securely.
19 "You would lie down and none
    would disturb *you,*
    And many would entreat your favor.
20 "But the eyes of the wicked will fail,
    And there will be no escape for
    them;
    And their hope is to breathe their
    last."

12 THEN Job responded,
2   "Truly then you are the people,
    And with you wisdom will die!
3 "But I have intelligence as well as
    you;
    I am not inferior to you.
    And who does not know such things
    as these?
4 "I am a joke to my friends,   ◄
    The one who called on God and He
    answered him;
    The just *and* blameless *man* is a
    joke.
5 "He who is at ease holds calamity in
    contempt,
    As prepared for those whose feet
    slip.
6 "The tents of the destroyers prosper,
    And those who provoke God are
    secure,
    Whom God brings into their power.
7 "But now ask the beasts, and let
    them teach you;
    And the birds of the heavens, and
    let them tell you.
8 "Or speak to the earth, and let it
    teach you;
    And let the fish of the sea declare to
    you.
9 "Who among all these does not
    know
    That the hand of the LORD has done
    this,

LIFE LESSONS

➤ **Job 11:7 — "Can you discover the
depths of God?"**

*Z*ophar asked good questions, but
he should have directed them at
himself, not merely at Job. "God is in
heaven," the Bible tells us, "and you are
on earth; therefore let your words be
few" (Eccl. 5:2).

➤ **Job 12:4 — "I am a joke to my friends
. . . the just and blameless man is a joke."**

*G*od had called Job a "blameless and
upright man, fearing God and turning away from evil" (Job 1:8). Yet Job's
friends mocked and ridiculed him in his
distress. When will we learn the truth of
Matthew 12:7—that God desires mercy?

10 In whose hand is the life of every
living thing,
And the breath of all mankind?
11 "Does not the ear test words,
As the palate tastes its food?
12 "Wisdom is with aged men,
With long life is understanding.
➤ 13 "With Him are wisdom and might;
To Him belong counsel and
understanding.
14 "Behold, He tears down, and it
cannot be rebuilt;
He imprisons a man, and there can
be no release.
15 "Behold, He restrains the waters, and
they dry up;
And He sends them out, and they
inundate the earth.
16 "With Him are strength and sound
wisdom,
The misled and the misleader
belong to Him.
17 "He makes counselors walk barefoot
And makes fools of judges.
18 "He loosens the bond of kings
And binds their loins with a girdle.
19 "He makes priests walk barefoot
And overthrows the secure ones.
20 "He deprives the trusted ones of
speech
And takes away the discernment of
the elders.
21 "He pours contempt on nobles
And loosens the belt of the strong.
22 "He reveals mysteries from the
darkness
And brings the deep darkness into
light.
23 "He makes the nations great, then
destroys them;
He enlarges the nations, then leads
them away.
24 "He deprives of intelligence the
chiefs of the earth's people

LIFE LESSONS

➤ **Job 12:13** — *"With Him are wisdom
and might; to Him belong counsel and
understanding."*

When we find ourselves in painful
and distressing circumstances, we
must turn to the Lord for His wisdom,
strength, guidance, and knowledge.
Where else can we go to find the help
we need?

And makes them wander in a
pathless waste.
25 "They grope in darkness with no
light,
And He makes them stagger like a
drunken man."

Psalm 94:1–11

94 O LORD, God of vengeance,
God of vengeance, shine forth!
2   Rise up, O Judge of the earth,
Render recompense to the proud.
3   How long shall the wicked,
O LORD,
How long shall the wicked exult?
4   They pour forth *words*, they speak
arrogantly;
All who do wickedness vaunt
themselves.
5   They crush Your people, O LORD,
And afflict Your heritage.
6   They slay the widow and the
stranger
And murder the orphans.
7   They have said, "The LORD does not
see,
Nor does the God of Jacob pay
heed."
8   Pay heed, you senseless among the
people;
And when will you understand,
stupid ones?
9   He who planted the ear, does He
not hear?
He who formed the eye, does He not
see?
10 He who chastens the nations, will
He not rebuke,
Even He who teaches man
knowledge?
11 The LORD knows the thoughts of
man,
That they are a *mere* breath.

Proverbs 22:24, 25

24 Do not associate with a man *given*
to anger;
Or go with a hot-tempered man,
25 Or you will learn his ways
And find a snare for yourself.

Romans 10:1–21

10 BRETHREN, my heart's desire and my prayer to God for them is for *their* salvation.

2 For I testify about them that they have a zeal for God, but not in accordance with knowledge.

3 For not knowing about God's righteousness and seeking to establish their own, they did not subject themselves to the righteousness of God.

4 For Christ is the end of the law for righteousness to everyone who believes.

5 For Moses writes that the man who practices the righteousness which is based on law shall live by that righteousness.

6 But the righteousness based on faith speaks as follows: "DO NOT SAY IN YOUR HEART, 'WHO WILL ASCEND INTO HEAVEN?' (that is, to bring Christ down),

7 or 'WHO WILL DESCEND INTO THE ABYSS?' (that is, to bring Christ up from the dead)."

8 But what does it say? "THE WORD IS NEAR YOU, IN YOUR MOUTH AND IN YOUR HEART"—that is, the word of faith which we are preaching,

9 that if you confess with your mouth Jesus *as* Lord, and believe in your heart that God raised Him from the dead, you will be saved;

10 for with the heart a person believes, resulting in righteousness, and with the mouth he confesses, resulting in salvation.

11 For the Scripture says, "WHOEVER BELIEVES IN HIM WILL NOT BE DISAPPOINTED."

12 For there is no distinction between Jew and Greek; for the same *Lord* is Lord of all, abounding in riches for all who call on Him;

13 for "WHOEVER WILL CALL ON THE NAME OF THE LORD WILL BE SAVED."

14 How then will they call on Him in whom they have not believed? How will they believe in Him whom they have not heard? And how will they hear without a preacher?

15 How will they preach unless they are sent? Just as it is written, "HOW BEAUTIFUL ARE THE FEET OF THOSE WHO BRING GOOD NEWS OF GOOD THINGS!"

16 However, they did not all heed the good news; for Isaiah says, "LORD, WHO HAS BELIEVED OUR REPORT?"

17 So faith *comes* from hearing, and hearing by the word of Christ.

18 But I say, surely they have never heard, have they? Indeed they have;
"THEIR VOICE HAS GONE OUT INTO ALL THE EARTH,
AND THEIR WORDS TO THE ENDS OF THE WORLD."

19 But I say, surely Israel did not know, did they? First Moses says,
"I WILL MAKE YOU JEALOUS BY THAT WHICH IS NOT A NATION,
BY A NATION WITHOUT UNDERSTANDING WILL I ANGER YOU."

20 And Isaiah is very bold and says,
"I WAS FOUND BY THOSE WHO DID NOT SEEK ME,
I BECAME MANIFEST TO THOSE WHO DID NOT ASK FOR ME."

21 But as for Israel He says, "ALL THE DAY LONG I HAVE STRETCHED OUT MY HANDS TO A DISOBEDIENT AND OBSTINATE PEOPLE."

LIFE LESSONS

➤ Romans 10:4 — *For Christ is the end of the law for righteousness to everyone who believes.*

*W*hen we place our faith in Christ, God looks at us just as He looks at Jesus—who completely obeyed the whole law without exception and without fault. The perfect record of Christ becomes ours through faith.

➤ Romans 10:13 — *"Whoever will call on the name of the Lord will be saved."*

*J*esus is our ultimate, final, and complete sacrifice, and salvation is open to every person, regardless of who they are or what they have done. This is why the promise is: *whoever* puts his faith in Christ *will* be saved and *will* receive eternal life. It is absolutely guaranteed to any person who receives His grace—He will never reject them.

➤ Romans 10:17 — *So faith comes from hearing, and hearing by the word of Christ.*

*L*istening to God is essential to walking with Him. The Lord blesses us when we hear His promises and respond in faith to them.

WHAT THE BIBLE SAYS ABOUT

Why We Confess the Resurrection

Romans 10:8–13

*I*n Romans 10:8, 9, Paul declares, "'THE WORD IS NEAR YOU, IN YOUR MOUTH AND IN YOUR HEART'—that is, the word of faith which we are preaching, that if you confess with your mouth Jesus as Lord, and believe in your heart that God raised Him from the dead, you will be saved."

Many of the world's religions claim to have the truth of salvation. But of all the prophets who have lived in this world, all of them are dead—except for one. Those dead prophets can do nothing for us—and neither can their religions.

However, Jesus Christ—not only the one living prophet, but also the Savior of the world—has conquered death. His tomb is empty, He sits at the right hand of the Father in heaven, and He is interceding on our behalf..

Jesus came to earth, not only to teach, preach, heal, and forgive us, but to give us resurrection life! Paul writes, "The Father of glory . . . give to you a spirit of wisdom and of revelation in the knowledge of Him . . . that you will know what is the hope of His calling, what are the riches of the glory of His inheritance in the saints, and what is the surpassing greatness of His power toward us who believe. These are in accordance with the working of the strength of His might which He brought about in Christ, when He raised Him from the dead" (Eph. 1:17–20). We have the power of God in our lives—the power that defeats death! Can anything we face require more power than that?

Christ also gives us the hope of heaven and the encouragement of knowing that we need never fear death. Similarly, our loved ones are not doomed to the cold caskets of this world. If they die in Christ as believers, they will be in the presence of almighty God. And one day, when Christ returns, we will all be raised in bodily resurrection. We will be transformed to the redeemed heavenly bodies that we will have for all eternity.

Why, then, do we confess the resurrection? Because Christ is risen! And we know that since Christ has risen from the grave, we will too—not only from the death that awaits every individual, but also from all the miseries that this world contains (Rom. 6:4–11; 1 Cor. 15:20–22; 2 Cor. 4:14; Phil 3:10, 11). ◈

AUGUST 11

◈ Job 13:1—14:22

13 "BEHOLD, my eye has seen all this,
My ear has heard and understood it.
2 "What you know I also know;
I am not inferior to you.
3 "But I would speak to the Almighty,
And I desire to argue with God.
4 "But you smear with lies;
You are all worthless physicians.
➤ 5 "O that you would be completely silent,
And that it would become your wisdom!
6 "Please hear my argument
And listen to the contentions of my lips.

7 "Will you speak what is unjust for God,
And speak what is deceitful for Him?
8 "Will you show partiality for Him?

LIFE LESSONS

➤ **Job 13:5 — "O that you would be completely silent, and that it would become your wisdom!"**

*V*ery often—more frequently than we know—our best counsel and most helpful advice is to say precisely nothing. "Even a fool, when he keeps silent, is considered wise; when he closes his lips, he is considered prudent" (Prov. 17:28).

Will you contend for God?
9 "Will it be well when He examines
you?
Or will you deceive Him as one
deceives a man?
10 "He will surely reprove you
If you secretly show partiality.
11 "Will not His majesty terrify you,
And the dread of Him fall on you?
12 "Your memorable sayings are
proverbs of ashes,
Your defenses are defenses of clay.
13 "Be silent before me so that I may
speak;
Then let come on me what may.
14 "Why should I take my flesh in my
teeth
And put my life in my hands?
➤ 15 "Though He slay me,
✳ I will hope in Him.
Nevertheless I will argue my ways
before Him.
16 "This also will be my salvation,
For a godless man may not come
before His presence.
17 "Listen carefully to my speech,
And let my declaration *fill* your ears.
18 "Behold now, I have prepared my
case;
I know that I will be vindicated.
19 "Who will contend with me?
For then I would be silent and die.
20 "Only two things do not do to me,
Then I will not hide from Your face:
21 Remove Your hand from me,
And let not the dread of You terrify
me.
22 "Then call, and I will answer;
Or let me speak, then reply to me.
23 "How many are my iniquities and
sins?

Make known to me my rebellion
and my sin.
24 "Why do You hide Your face
And consider me Your enemy?
25 "Will You cause a driven leaf to
tremble?
Or will You pursue the dry chaff?
26 "For You write bitter things against
me
And make me to inherit the
iniquities of my youth.
27 "You put my feet in the stocks
And watch all my paths;
You set a limit for the soles of my
feet,
28 While I am decaying like a rotten
thing,
Like a garment that is moth-eaten.

14 "MAN, who is born of woman,
Is short-lived and full of turmoil.
2 "Like a flower he comes forth and
withers.
He also flees like a shadow and
does not remain.
3 "You also open Your eyes on him
And bring him into judgment with
Yourself.
4 "Who can make the clean out of the ◄
unclean?
No one!

LIFE LESSONS

➤ **Job 13:15** — *"Though He slay me,
I will hope in Him."*

*G*od is either worth trusting all the
way to the end, or He's not worth
trusting at all. As Peter proclaimed,
"Lord, to whom shall we go? You have
words of eternal life" (John 6:68).

Life Examples:

JOB: Choosing to Trust

JOB 13:15

*J*ob was a good and righteous man
who walked in the ways of the Lord.
In fact, his righteousness prompted God to
say of him, "For there is no one like him on
the earth" (Job 1:8). The Lord blessed Job for
his righteousness, and so Job earned the title,
"the greatest of all the men of the east" (Job
1:3).
Yet Job endured unspeakable suffering.

Though he had done nothing wrong, he lost
everything—his family, his wealth, his reputation, even his health. If that weren't enough,
his wife and his friends offered him no real
comfort. Job's friends told him that he had
suffered because of some hidden sin in his life.
Job is a stark biblical example of a fact we
need to understand: even those who are right
before God suffer. Will we allow the suffering
to tear down our faith or build it up? These
are our only choices.
Job chose to place his trust in God, his
Redeemer, and was rewarded for his faith (see
Job 19:25, 26; 42:1-6, 10-17).

LIFE LESSONS

➤ **Job 14:4 — *"Who can make the clean out of the unclean? No one!"***

*W*e have no more power to turn our sins into righteousness than a leopard can change its spots (see Jer. 13:23). Yet Christ has the power to remove our sins and replace them with His holiness— if we will trust Him.

5 "Since his days are determined,
  The number of his months is with You;
  And his limits You have set so that he cannot pass.
6 "Turn Your gaze from him that he may rest,
  Until he fulfills his day like a hired man.
7 "For there is hope for a tree,
  When it is cut down, that it will sprout again,
  And its shoots will not fail.
8 "Though its roots grow old in the ground
  And its stump dies in the dry soil,
9 At the scent of water it will flourish
  And put forth sprigs like a plant.
10 "But man dies and lies prostrate.
  Man expires, and where is he?
11 "As water evaporates from the sea,
  And a river becomes parched and dried up,
12 So man lies down and does not rise.
  Until the heavens are no longer,
  He will not awake nor be aroused out of his sleep.
13 "Oh that You would hide me in Sheol,
  That You would conceal me until Your wrath returns *to You,*
  That You would set a limit for me and remember me!
➤ 14 "If a man dies, will he live *again?*
  All the days of my struggle I will wait
  Until my change comes.
15 "You will call, and I will answer You;
  You will long for the work of Your hands.
16 "For now You number my steps,
  You do not observe my sin.
17 "My transgression is sealed up in a bag,
  And You wrap up my iniquity.

18 "But the falling mountain crumbles away,
  And the rock moves from its place;
19 Water wears away stones,
  Its torrents wash away the dust of the earth;
  So You destroy man's hope.
20 "You forever overpower him and he departs;
  You change his appearance and send him away.
21 "His sons achieve honor, but he does not know *it;*
  Or they become insignificant, but he does not perceive it.
22 "But his body pains him,
  And he mourns only for himself."

◈ **Psalm 94:12–19**

12 Blessed is the man whom You chasten, O LORD,
  And whom You teach out of Your law;
13 That You may grant him relief from the days of adversity,
  Until a pit is dug for the wicked.
14 For the LORD will not abandon His people,
  Nor will He forsake His inheritance.
15 For judgment will again be righteous,

LIFE LESSONS

➤ **Job 14:14 — *"If a man dies, will he live again?"***

*T*here is life after death, but only the saved will enjoy it in God's presence. "He who believes in the Son has eternal life; but he who does not obey the Son will not see life, but the wrath of God abides on him" (John 3:36).

➤ **Psalm 94:12, 13 — *Blessed is the man whom You . . . teach out of Your law; that You may grant him relief from the days of adversity.***

*I*n this verse, God gives us yet another reason to study His Word. Through Scripture, He shows us how we have contributed to our afflictions and teaches us to repent. He also instructs us in how to avoid stumbling in the future.

And all the upright in heart will
   follow it.
16 Who will stand up for me against
   evildoers?
   Who will take his stand for
     me against those who do
     wickedness?
17 If the LORD had not been my help,
   My soul would soon have dwelt in
     the abode of silence.
18 If I should say, "My foot has
     slipped,"
   Your lovingkindness, O LORD, will
     hold me up.
19 When my anxious thoughts multiply
     within me,
   Your consolations delight my soul.

⊕ Proverbs 22:26, 27

26 Do not be among those who give
     pledges,
   Among those who become
     guarantors for debts.
27 If you have nothing with which to
     pay,
   Why should he take your bed from
     under you?

⊕ Romans 11:1–18

11 I SAY then, God has not rejected
His people, has He? May it never
be! For I too am an Israelite, a descendant of Abraham, of the tribe of Benjamin.
2 God has not rejected His people
whom He foreknew. Or do you not know
what the Scripture says in *the passage
about* Elijah, how he pleads with God
against Israel?
3 "Lord, THEY HAVE KILLED YOUR PROPH-
ETS, THEY HAVE TORN DOWN YOUR ALTARS,
AND I ALONE AM LEFT, AND THEY ARE SEEK-
ING MY LIFE."
4 But what is the divine response to
him? "I HAVE KEPT for Myself SEVEN THOU-
SAND MEN WHO HAVE NOT BOWED THE KNEE
TO BAAL."
5 In the same way then, there has also
come to be at the present time a remnant
according to God's gracious choice.
6 But if it is by grace, it is no longer on

the basis of works, otherwise grace is no
longer grace.
7 What then? What Israel is seeking,
it has not obtained, but those who were
chosen obtained it, and the rest were
hardened;
8 just as it is written,
   "GOD GAVE THEM A SPIRIT OF STUPOR,
   EYES TO SEE NOT AND EARS TO HEAR
     NOT,
   DOWN TO THIS VERY DAY."
9 And David says,
   "LET THEIR TABLE BECOME A SNARE AND
     A TRAP,
   AND A STUMBLING BLOCK AND A
     RETRIBUTION TO THEM.
10 "LET THEIR EYES BE DARKENED TO SEE
     NOT,
   AND BEND THEIR BACKS FOREVER."
11 I say then, they did not stumble so as
to fall, did they? May it never be! But by
their transgression salvation *has come* to
the Gentiles, to make them jealous.
12 Now if their transgression is riches
for the world and their failure is riches
for the Gentiles, how much more will
their fulfillment be!
13 But I am speaking to you who are
Gentiles. Inasmuch then as I am an apostle of Gentiles, I magnify my ministry,
14 if somehow I might move to jealousy
my fellow countrymen and save some of
them.
15 For if their rejection is the reconciliation of the world, what will *their* acceptance be but life from the dead?
16 If the first piece *of dough* is holy, the
lump is also; and if the root is holy, the
branches are too.
17 But if some of the branches were

LIFE LESSONS

➤ **Romans 11:18** — *If you are arrogant,
remember that it is not you who supports the root, but the root supports you.*

*H*ere, Paul was exhorting the Gentiles to remember they were being
grafted in to the covenants that the Lord
had given to Abraham, David, and the
nation of Israel by God's mercy. Likewise,
we must always remember that our faith
has a context and a history. We cannot
be true students of the New Testament
without also embracing the Old Testament.

broken off, and you, being a wild olive, were grafted in among them and became partaker with them of the rich root of the olive tree,

18 do not be arrogant toward the branches; but if you are arrogant, *remember that* it is not you who supports the root, but the root *supports* you.

Job 15:1—16:22

15 THEN Eliphaz the Temanite responded,

2 "Should a wise man answer with windy knowledge
And fill himself with the east wind?

3 "Should he argue with useless talk,
Or with words which are not profitable?

4 "Indeed, you do away with reverence
And hinder meditation before God.

5 "For your guilt teaches your mouth,
And you choose the language of the crafty.

6 "Your own mouth condemns you, and not I;
And your own lips testify against you.

7 "Were you the first man to be born,
Or were you brought forth before the hills?

8 "Do you hear the secret counsel of God,
And limit wisdom to yourself?

9 "What do you know that we do not know?
What do you understand that we do not?

10 "Both the gray-haired and the aged are among us,
Older than your father.

11 "Are the consolations of God too small for you,

Even the word *spoken* gently with you?

12 "Why does your heart carry you away?
And why do your eyes flash,

13 That you should turn your spirit against God
And allow *such* words to go out of your mouth?

14 "What is man, that he should be pure,
Or he who is born of a woman, that he should be righteous?

15 "Behold, He puts no trust in His holy ones,
And the heavens are not pure in His sight;

16 How much less one who is detestable and corrupt,
Man, who drinks iniquity like water!

17 "I will tell you, listen to me;
And what I have seen I will also declare;

18 What wise men have told,
And have not concealed from their fathers,

19 To whom alone the land was given,
And no alien passed among them.

20 "The wicked man writhes in pain all *his* days,
And numbered are the years stored up for the ruthless.

21 "Sounds of terror are in his ears;
While at peace the destroyer comes upon him.

22 "He does not believe that he will return from darkness,
And he is destined for the sword.

23 "He wanders about for food, saying, 'Where is it?'
He knows that a day of darkness is at hand.

24 "Distress and anguish terrify him,
They overpower him like a king ready for the attack,

25 Because he has stretched out his hand against God

LIFE LESSONS

➤ Job 15:9 — *"What do you know that we do not know?"*

*W*hen people start to "measure themselves by themselves and compare themselves," they "are without understanding" (2 Cor. 10:12). Why? We are all ignorant in ways unknown to us—especially when compared to God.

And conducts himself arrogantly
    against the Almighty.
26 "He rushes headlong at Him
    With his massive shield.
27 "For he has covered his face with his
    fat
    And made his thighs heavy with
    flesh.
28 "He has lived in desolate cities,
    In houses no one would inhabit,
    Which are destined to become ruins.
29 "He will not become rich, nor will his
    wealth endure;
    And his grain will not bend down to
    the ground.
30 "He will not escape from darkness;
    The flame will wither his shoots,
    And by the breath of His mouth he
    will go away.
31 "Let him not trust in emptiness,
    deceiving himself;
    For emptiness will be his reward.
32 "It will be accomplished before his
    time,
    And his palm branch will not be
    green.
33 "He will drop off his unripe grape
    like the vine,
    And will cast off his flower like the
    olive tree.
34 "For the company of the godless is
    barren,
    And fire consumes the tents of the
    corrupt.
35 "They conceive mischief and bring
    forth iniquity,
    And their mind prepares deception."

16 THEN Job answered,
2   "I have heard many such things;
    Sorry comforters are you all.
3 "Is there *no* limit to windy words?
    Or what plagues you that you
    answer?
4 "I too could speak like you,
    If I were in your place.
    I could compose words against you
    And shake my head at you.
➤ 5 "I could strengthen you with my
    mouth,
    And the solace of my lips could
    lessen *your* pain.
6 "If I speak, my pain is not lessened,
    And if I hold back, what has left me?
7 "But now He has exhausted me;
    You have laid waste all my
    company.
8 "You have shriveled me up,

It has become a witness;
    And my leanness rises up against me,
    It testifies to my face.
9 "His anger has torn me and hunted   ➤
    me down,
    He has gnashed at me with His
    teeth;
    My adversary glares at me.
10 "They have gaped at me with their
    mouth,
    They have slapped me on the cheek
    with contempt;
    They have massed themselves
    against me.
11 "God hands me over to ruffians
    And tosses me into the hands of the
    wicked.
12 "I was at ease, but He shattered me,
    And He has grasped me by the neck
    and shaken me to pieces;
    He has also set me up as His target.
13 "His arrows surround me.
    Without mercy He splits my kidneys
    open;
    He pours out my gall on the ground.
14 "He breaks through me with breach
    after breach;
    He runs at me like a warrior.
15 "I have sewed sackcloth over my
    skin
    And thrust my horn in the dust.
16 "My face is flushed from weeping,
    And deep darkness is on my eyelids,

LIFE LESSONS

➤ **Job 16:5 —** *"I could strengthen you
with my mouth, and the solace of my lips
could lessen your pain."*

Our words have the power to tear
down and bring grief or the power
to give strength and comfort. Every
day we choose what kind of power we
will wield—and God is watching (Matt.
12:36).

➤ **Job 16:9 —** *"His anger has torn me
and hunted me down, he has gnashed at
me with His teeth; my adversary glares
at me."*

When we pray in our anguish and
nothing seems to change, and we
cry out in our pain and it only increases,
we wonder if God has become our
enemy. Never! He loves us and always
will (Rom. 8:39).

What role does Satan play in our adversity?

JOB 16:11

Several biblical accounts illustrate Satan's role in adversity. We find the clearest example in the story of Job. Those who attribute all adversity to sin or to a lack of faith sometimes have a difficult time with this narrative. Though some may speculate that Job's problems are due to pride or the sin of his children, there is no real evidence for this. The Book of Job is the story of one man's faith under trial. Job faced the fires of hopelessness, rejection, intense physical pain, and deep emotional sorrow, and he passed the test. He was a man who "was blameless, upright, fearing God and turning away from evil." Later in the same chapter, the Lord Himself says of Job, "There is no one like him on the earth, a blameless and upright man, fearing God and turning away from evil" (Job 1:8).

Job was a righteous man whose adversity did *not* come as a result of sin. In fact, an ensuing discussion between God and Satan spells out why Job suffered the way he did. Satan accused Job of following God only because the Lord had blessed him and protected him. Take away that protection, Satan challenged, and Job would curse God to His face.

So Satan set out to destroy all Job had. Yet Job continued to serve God and walk in His ways. Satan then made another request of God, asking Him permission to afflict Job's body (Job 2:4–7).

Clearly, Job's adversity was initiated by Satan who asked God for permission to send trouble into Job's life. God, in turn, allowed the enemy to afflict Job in a limited way. Permission for the trial came from God; but adversity came from the devil.

Peter reminded his readers that Satan "prowls" around like a lion, seeking those he can destroy (1 Pet. 5:8). We may think Peter's words refer only to Satan's involvement in our temptations. However, the enemy is crafty and he wants to use suffering of any kind to destroy us. He roams the earth, looking for opportunities to bring adversity into our lives in an all out attempt to harm the body of Christ. However, he is a defeated foe. Jesus Christ won the ultimate victory on the Cross and because He lives within us, we can have this same victory. We may have to face serious threats at times, but like Job, we can respond to the trial by holding firm in our faith.

Not only does adversity train us to trust God, it also can be a bridge to a deeper relationship with Him. At the end of his season of suffering, Job praised the Lord, saying, "I have heard of You by the hearing of the ear; but now my eye sees You" (Job 42:5).

---

17 Although there is no violence in my hands,
    And my prayer is pure.
18 "O earth, do not cover my blood,
    And let there be no *resting* place for my cry.
19 "Even now, behold, my witness is in heaven,
    And my advocate is on high.
20 "My friends are my scoffers;
    My eye weeps to God.
21 "O that a man might plead with God
    As a man with his neighbor!
22 "For when a few years are past,
    I shall go the way of no return.

 Psalm 94:20–23

20 Can a throne of destruction be allied with You,
    One which devises mischief by decree?

21 They band themselves together against the life of the righteous
    And condemn the innocent to death.
22 But the LORD has been my stronghold,
    And my God the rock of my refuge.
23 He has brought back their wickedness upon them
    And will destroy them in their evil;
    The LORD our God will destroy them.

Proverbs 22:28, 29

28 Do not move the ancient boundary
    Which your fathers have set.
29 Do you see a man skilled in his work?
    He will stand before kings;
    He will not stand before obscure men.

Romans 11:19–36

19 You will say then, "Branches were broken off so that I might be grafted in."
20 Quite right, they were broken off for their unbelief, but you stand by your faith. Do not be conceited, but fear;
21 for if God did not spare the natural branches, He will not spare you, either.
22 Behold then the kindness and severity of God; to those who fell, severity, but to you, God's kindness, if you continue in His kindness; otherwise you also will be cut off.
23 And they also, if they do not continue in their unbelief, will be grafted in, for God is able to graft them in again.
24 For if you were cut off from what is by nature a wild olive tree, and were grafted contrary to nature into a cultivated olive tree, how much more will these who are the natural *branches* be grafted into their own olive tree?
25 For I do not want you, brethren, to be uninformed of this mystery—so that you will not be wise in your own estimation—that a partial hardening has happened to Israel until the fullness of the Gentiles has come in;
26 and so all Israel will be saved; just as it is written,
"THE DELIVERER WILL COME FROM ZION,
HE WILL REMOVE UNGODLINESS FROM
JACOB."
27 "THIS IS MY COVENANT WITH THEM,
WHEN I TAKE AWAY THEIR SINS."
28 From the standpoint of the gospel they are enemies for your sake, but from the standpoint of God's choice they are beloved for the sake of the fathers;
29 for the gifts and the calling of God are irrevocable.
30 For just as you once were disobedient to God, but now have been shown mercy because of their disobedience,
31 so these also now have been disobedient, that because of the mercy shown to you they also may now be shown mercy.
32 For God has shut up all in disobedience so that He may show mercy to all.
33 Oh, the depth of the riches both of the wisdom and knowledge of God! How unsearchable are His judgments and unfathomable His ways!
34 For WHO HAS KNOWN THE MIND OF THE LORD, OR WHO BECAME HIS COUNSELOR?
35 Or WHO HAS FIRST GIVEN TO HIM THAT IT MIGHT BE PAID BACK TO HIM AGAIN?
36 For from Him and through Him and to Him are all things. To Him *be* the glory forever. Amen.

LIFE LESSONS

> **Romans 11:22 — *Behold then the kindness and severity of God.***

*P*aul urges us to remember that God is loving and holy, gracious and just, patient and faithful to *all* of His Word. "Knowing the fear of the Lord, we persuade men" (2 Cor. 5:11).

> **Romans 11:29 — *For the gifts and the calling of God are irrevocable.***

*O*nce you have placed your faith in God, He will never cast you away. The Lord will never abandon you, reject you, or turn you away. As a loving Father He will discipline you, but He will never leave you.

> **Romans 11:33 — *How unsearchable are His judgments and unfathomable His ways!***

*W*e will never completely understand God's ways or grasp why He does what He does, but we *can* worship Him for the goodness, love, and mercy that He has already shown us!

Job 17:1—18:21

17 "MY spirit is broken, my days are extinguished,
The grave is *ready* for me.

2 "Surely mockers are with me,
     And my eye gazes on their provocation.
3 "Lay down, now, a pledge for me
     with Yourself;
     Who is there that will be my
     guarantor?

4 "For You have kept their heart from
  understanding,
  Therefore You will not exalt *them*.
5 "He who informs against friends for
  a share *of the spoil*,
  The eyes of his children also will
  languish.
6 "But He has made me a byword of
  the people,
  And I am one at whom men spit.
7 "My eye has also grown dim because
  of grief,
  And all my members are as a
  shadow.
8 "The upright will be appalled at this,
  And the innocent will stir up
  himself against the godless.
9 "Nevertheless the righteous will hold
  to his way,
  And he who has clean hands will
  grow stronger and stronger.
10 "But come again all of you now,
  For I do not find a wise man among
  you.
11 "My days are past, my plans are torn
  apart,
  Even the wishes of my heart.
12 "They make night into day, *saying*,
  'The light is near,' in the presence of
  darkness.
13 "If I look for Sheol as my home,
  I make my bed in the darkness;
14 If I call to the pit, 'You are my
  father';
  To the worm, 'my mother and my
  sister';
➤ 15 Where now is my hope?
  And who regards my hope?
16 "Will it go down with me to Sheol?
  Shall we together go down into the
  dust?"

18 THEN Bildad the Shuhite responded,
2 "How long will you hunt for words?

Show understanding and then we
  can talk.
3 "Why are we regarded as beasts,
  As stupid in your eyes?
4 "O you who tear yourself in your
  anger—
  For your sake is the earth to be
  abandoned,
  Or the rock to be moved from its
  place?
5 "Indeed, the light of the wicked goes
  out,
  And the flame of his fire gives no
  light.
6 "The light in his tent is darkened,
  And his lamp goes out above him.
7 "His vigorous stride is shortened,
  And his own scheme brings him
  down.
8 "For he is thrown into the net by his
  own feet,
  And he steps on the webbing.
9 "A snare seizes *him* by the heel,
  And a trap snaps shut on him.
10 "A noose for him is hidden in the
  ground,
  And a trap for him on the path.
11 "All around terrors frighten him,
  And harry him at every step.
12 "His strength is famished,
  And calamity is ready at his side.
13 "His skin is devoured by disease,
  The firstborn of death devours his
  limbs.
14 "He is torn from the security of his
  tent,
  And they march him before the king
  of terrors.
15 "There dwells in his tent nothing of
  his;
  Brimstone is scattered on his
  habitation.
16 "His roots are dried below,
  And his branch is cut off above.
17 "Memory of him perishes from the
  earth,
  And he has no name abroad.
18 "He is driven from light into
  darkness,
  And chased from the inhabited
  world.
19 "He has no offspring or posterity
  among his people,
  Nor any survivor where he
  sojourned.
20 "Those in the west are appalled at
  his fate,

And those in the east are seized
   with horror.
21 "Surely such are the dwellings of the
   wicked,
   And this is the place of him who
    does not know God."

Psalm 95:1–5

95 O COME, let us sing for joy to the
   LORD,
   Let us shout joyfully to the rock of
    our salvation.
2 Let us come before His presence
   with thanksgiving,
   Let us shout joyfully to Him with
    psalms.
3 For the LORD is a great God
   And a great King above all gods,
4 In whose hand are the depths of the
   earth,
   The peaks of the mountains are His
    also.
5 The sea is His, for it was He who
   made it,
   And His hands formed the dry
    land.

Proverbs 23:1–3

23 WHEN you sit down to dine with
   a ruler,
   Consider carefully what is before
    you,
2 And put a knife to your throat
   If you are a man of *great* appetite.
3 Do not desire his delicacies,
   For it is deceptive food.

Romans 12:1–21

12 THEREFORE I urge you, brethren,
   by the mercies of God, to present
your bodies a living and holy sacrifice,
acceptable to God, *which is* your spiritual service of worship.
2 And do not be conformed to this
world, but be transformed by the renewing of your mind, so that you may prove
what the will of God is, that which is
good and acceptable and perfect.

3 For through the grace given to me I
say to everyone among you not to think
more highly of himself than he ought to
think; but to think so as to have sound
judgment, as God has allotted to each a
measure of faith.
4 For just as we have many members
in one body and all the members do not
have the same function,
5 so we, who are many, are one body
in Christ, and individually members one
of another.
6 Since we have gifts that differ according to the grace given to us, *each
of us is to exercise them accordingly*: if
prophecy, according to the proportion of
his faith;

LIFE LESSONS

➤ **Romans 12:1** — *Present your bodies
a living and holy sacrifice, acceptable to
God.*

*P*aul encourages us to turn ourselves
over to God each day, lay our wills
on the altar before Him, and ask Him to
use us for His glory and the good of His
people.

➤ **Romans 12:2** — *Do not be conformed
to this world, but be transformed by the
renewing of your mind.*

*T*ransformation begins with our thinking and with our commitment to
listening to and obeying God. Our minds
are renewed as we study His Word, and
our hearts are changed as we submit to
Him. We do not merely try hard to sin less.
We learn to depend upon Him, observe
His commands, and trust Him to mold us
into people who please Him. It is then
we discover how awesome it is to live in
the center of His will because it is life at
its very best—and there is nothing in this
world that compares to it.

➤ **Romans 12:5** — *We, who are many,
are one body in Christ, and individually
members one of another.*

*G*od is never pleased when someone
says, "I love Jesus, but I don't need
the church." No Christian has ever been
called to "go it alone" in his or her walk
of faith. We need one another, and we
should serve and support each other
with love and gladness.

ANSWERS TO LIFE'S QUESTIONS

What does it mean to be conformed to the truth?

ROMANS 12:2

*P*aul wrote that the Lord has predestined us "to become conformed to the image of His Son" (Rom. 8:29)—but just *how* is God going to accomplish such a job?

Answer: by revealing the truth of His likeness.

As the truth confronts us, we can do one of two things: Either we can refuse to be pushed into God's mold, or we can yield to Him and be fashioned into His likeness.

I once preached a series of sermons entitled, "How the Truth Can Set You Free." Week after week, people would say to me, "I want to tell you how the Lord has set me free. Last week's message changed my life." After they walked away, I would often think, *God, what about me? I'm the one who told them.* I knew I was not living as free as the Father wanted me to. After months of seeing other lives changed, God finally changed my own life in a remarkable way.

I learned that I had to *listen in order to comprehend* and to *comprehend in order to*

be conformed to His truth. God never speaks in order to entertain us; He speaks that we may be made like Jesus. James says, "If anyone is a hearer of the word and not a doer, he is like a man who looks at his natural face in a mirror; for once he has looked at himself and gone away, he has immediately forgotten what kind of person he was" (1:23, 24). Obedience must accompany understanding. We are either in the process of resisting God's truth or in the process of being shaped by His truth.

After spending several years with Paul, Timothy, the apostle's protégé, began shepherding the work of the gospel in Ephesus and Asia Minor. As he labored there, Paul wrote to him saying, "Let no one look down on your youthfulness, but rather in speech, conduct, love, faith and purity, show yourself an example of those who believe" (1 Tim. 4:12).

In the Second Epistle to Timothy, Paul penned these words: "For I am mindful of the sincere faith within you, which first dwelt in your grandmother Lois and your mother Eunice, and I am sure that it is in you as well" (2 Tim. 1:5).

Timothy didn't just *know* the truth; he allowed its power to transform him in such a way that his life became a constant example of godliness. How? Through the unfolding ministry of God's Word.

---

7 if service, in his serving; or he who teaches, in his teaching;

8 or he who exhorts, in his exhortation; he who gives, with liberality; he who leads, with diligence; he who shows mercy, with cheerfulness.

9 *Let* love *be* without hypocrisy. Abhor what is evil; cling to what is good.

10 *Be* devoted to one another in brotherly love; give preference to one another in honor;

11 not lagging behind in diligence, fervent in spirit, serving the Lord;

12 rejoicing in hope, persevering in tribulation, devoted to prayer,

13 contributing to the needs of the saints, practicing hospitality.

14 Bless those who persecute you; bless and do not curse.

> 15 Rejoice with those who rejoice, and weep with those who weep.

16 Be of the same mind toward one another; do not be haughty in mind, but associate with the lowly. Do not be wise in your own estimation.

17 Never pay back evil for evil to any-

one. Respect what is right in the sight of all men.

18 If possible, so far as it depends on you, be at peace with all men.

19 Never take your own revenge, beloved, but leave room for the wrath *of God*, for it is written, "VENGEANCE IS MINE, I WILL REPAY," says the Lord.

20 "BUT IF YOUR ENEMY IS HUNGRY, FEED HIM, AND IF HE IS THIRSTY, GIVE HIM A DRINK; FOR IN SO DOING YOU WILL HEAP BURNING COALS ON HIS HEAD."

21 Do not be overcome by evil, but overcome evil with good.

LIFE LESSONS

> **Romans 12:15 — *Rejoice with those who rejoice, and weep with those who weep.***

*B*oth rejoicing and weeping imply genuine, heartfelt emotion. This kind of keenly felt connection happens only when we choose to invest ourselves deeply in the lives of other believers.

Job 19:1—20:29

19 THEN Job responded,
2 "How long will you torment me
And crush me with words?

3 "These ten times you have insulted
me;
You are not ashamed to wrong me.

4 "Even if I have truly erred,
My error lodges with me.

5 "If indeed you vaunt yourselves
against me
And prove my disgrace to me,

6 Know then that God has wronged
me
And has closed His net around me.

7 "Behold, I cry, 'Violence!' but I get
no answer;
I shout for help, but there is no
justice.

8 "He has walled up my way so that I
cannot pass,
And He has put darkness on my
paths.

9 "He has stripped my honor from me
And removed the crown from my
head.

10 "He breaks me down on every side,
and I am gone;
And He has uprooted my hope like
a tree.

11 "He has also kindled His anger
against me
And considered me as His enemy.

12 "His troops come together,
And build up their way against me
And camp around my tent.

13 "He has removed my brothers far
from me,
And my acquaintances are
completely estranged from me.

14 "My relatives have failed,
And my intimate friends have
forgotten me.

15 "Those who live in my house and my
maids consider me a stranger.
I am a foreigner in their sight.

16 "I call to my servant, but he does not
answer;
I have to implore him with my mouth.

17 "My breath is offensive to my wife,
And I am loathsome to my own
brothers.

18 "Even young children despise me;
I rise up and they speak against me.

ANSWERS TO LIFE'S QUESTIONS

How can I handle criticism during times of adversity?

JOB 19:17–26

*I*n times of adversity, life can sometimes seem so bleak and dark that we feel on the verge of giving up hope. Others around us may foretell doom and encourage us to face what they see as inevitable. Job's wife was one such person. After painful boils covered Job from the soles of his feet to the crown of his head, she said to him, "Do you still hold fast your integrity? Curse God and die!" (Job 2:9).

Job wisely responded to her, "You speak as one of the foolish women speaks. Shall we indeed accept good from God, and not accept adversity?" Scripture adds this important line: "In all this Job did not sin with his lips" (Job 2:10).

When you face difficult circumstances and then have to endure negative opinions and comments from others, you need the courage to stay positive—to continue to believe that the Lord is with you. Many times, hope and

faith are not automatic responses to hardship and trial. They require an exercise of the will, bolstered with courage. So the psalmist said, "Why are you in despair, O my soul? And why have you become disturbed within me? Hope in God, for I shall again praise Him for the help of His presence" (Ps. 42:5).

At times, you must say aloud to yourself, "I know that God has a purpose in this. I know that He will bring me through this. I know that He is my good and loving Father and that He is doing a good and eternal work in my life." If no one else speaks hope to you, then you need to speak it to yourself.

You may also need courage to withstand the enemies moving against your life—in other words, those who are causing your adversity. Moses realized that Joshua and the Israelites would face such trials, so he said to God's people, "Be strong and courageous, do not be afraid or tremble at them, for the LORD your God is the one who goes with you. He will not fail you or forsake you" (Deut. 31:6).

Ask the Lord to give you the courage to continue to believe in Him and in His presence with you as you go through adversity. Ask Him to renew your hope and faith. And know that He loves to honor such faithful requests.

19 "All my associates abhor me,
   And those I love have turned
      against me.
20 "My bone clings to my skin and my
      flesh,
   And I have escaped *only* by the skin
      of my teeth.
21 "Pity me, pity me, O you my friends,
   For the hand of God has struck me.
22 "Why do you persecute me as God
      does,
   And are not satisfied with my flesh?
➤ 23 "Oh that my words were written!
   Oh that they were inscribed in a book!
24 "That with an iron stylus and lead
   They were engraved in the rock
      forever!
25 "As for me, I know that my
      Redeemer lives,
   And at the last He will take His
      stand on the earth.
26 "Even after my skin is destroyed,
   Yet from my flesh I shall see God;
27 Whom I myself shall behold,
   And whom my eyes will see and not
      another.
   My heart faints within me!
28 "If you say, 'How shall we persecute
      him?'
   And 'What pretext for a case
      against him can we find?'
29 "*Then* be afraid of the sword for
      yourselves,
   For wrath *brings* the punishment of
      the sword,
   So that you may know there is
      judgment."

20 THEN Zophar the Naamathite an-
      swered,
2 "Therefore my disquieting thoughts
      make me respond,
   Even because of my inward agitation.
3 "I listened to the reproof which
      insults me,
   And the spirit of my understanding
      makes me answer.
➤ 4 "Do you know this from of old,
   From the establishment of man on
      earth,
5 That the triumphing of the wicked
      is short,
   And the joy of the godless
      momentary?
6 "Though his loftiness reaches the
      heavens,
   And his head touches the clouds,
7 He perishes forever like his refuse;

Those who have seen him will say,
   'Where is he?'
8 "He flies away like a dream, and
      they cannot find him;
   Even like a vision of the night he is
      chased away.
9 "The eye which saw him sees him no
      longer,
   And his place no longer beholds
      him.
10 "His sons favor the poor,
   And his hands give back his wealth.
11 "His bones are full of his youthful
      vigor,
   But it lies down with him in the dust.
12 "Though evil is sweet in his mouth
   And he hides it under his tongue,
13 *Though* he desires it and will not let
      it go,
   But holds it in his mouth,
14 *Yet* his food in his stomach is
      changed
   To the venom of cobras within him.
15 "He swallows riches,
   But will vomit them up;
   God will expel them from his belly.
16 "He sucks the poison of cobras;
   The viper's tongue slays him.

LIFE LESSONS

➤ **Job 19:23 — "Oh that my words were
written! Oh that they were inscribed in
a book!"**

*E*ven as Job spoke these words, God's
plan was to put them in the Book of
books—the Bible—for all time and for
the benefit of His hurting people. He is
at work, even when we do not know it.

➤ **Job 20:4, 5 — "Do you know . . . that
the triumphing of the wicked is short?"**

*A*gain, Zophar mistakenly blames sin
for Job's great losses and troubles.
Although it is true "the joy of the godless is momentary," Zophar fails to see
that the suffering of the righteous is
also short, and that the agony of the
godly is but for a moment as well (Rom.
8:18). Our present pain does not necessarily mean God is disciplining us (Heb.
12:5–11). However, as with Job, we can
be sure that if we trust and obey the
Lord, our "momentary, light affliction is
producing for us an eternal weight of
glory far beyond all comparison" (2 Cor.
4:17).

17 "He does not look at the streams,
　The rivers flowing with honey and
　　curds.
18 "He returns what he has attained
　And cannot swallow *it*;
　As to the riches of his trading,
　He cannot even enjoy *them*.
19 "For he has oppressed *and* forsaken
　　the poor;
　He has seized a house which he has
　　not built.
20 "Because he knew no quiet within
　　him,
　He does not retain anything he
　　desires.
21 "Nothing remains for him to devour,
　Therefore his prosperity does not
　　endure.
22 "In the fullness of his plenty he will
　　be cramped;
　The hand of everyone who suffers
　　will come *against* him.
23 "When he fills his belly,
　God will send His fierce anger on him
　And will rain *it* on him while he is
　　eating.
24 "He may flee from the iron weapon,
　But the bronze bow will pierce him.
25 "It is drawn forth and comes out of
　　his back,
　Even the glittering point from his gall.
　Terrors come upon him,
26 Complete darkness is held in
　　reserve for his treasures,
　And unfanned fire will devour him;
　It will consume the survivor in his
　　tent.
27 "The heavens will reveal his iniquity,
　And the earth will rise up against
　　him.
28 "The increase of his house will
　　depart;
　His possessions will flow away in
　　the day of His anger.
29 "This is the wicked man's portion
　　from God,
　Even the heritage decreed to him by
　　God."

🔹 Psalm 95:6–11

6　Come, let us worship and bow
　　down,
　Let us kneel before the LORD our
　　Maker.

7　For He is our God,
　And we are the people of His
　　pasture and the sheep of His
　　hand.
　Today, if you would hear His voice,
8　Do not harden your hearts, as at
　　Meribah,
　As in the day of Massah in the
　　wilderness,
9　"When your fathers tested Me,
　They tried Me, though they had
　　seen My work.
10 "For forty years I loathed *that*
　　generation,
　And said they are a people who err
　　in their heart,
　And they do not know My ways.
11 "Therefore I swore in My anger,
　Truly they shall not enter into My
　　rest."

🔹 Proverbs 23:4, 5

4　Do not weary yourself to gain
　　wealth,
　Cease from your consideration
　　of it.
5　When you set your eyes on it, it is
　　gone.
　For *wealth* certainly makes itself
　　wings
　Like an eagle that flies *toward* the
　　heavens.

🔹 Romans 13:1–14

13 EVERY person is to be in subjec-
　　tion to the governing authorities.
For there is no authority except from

God, and those which exist are established by God.

2　Therefore whoever resists authority has opposed the ordinance of God; and they who have opposed will receive condemnation upon themselves.

3　For rulers are not a cause of fear for good behavior, but for evil. Do you want to have no fear of authority? Do what is good and you will have praise from the same;

4　for it is a minister of God to you for good. But if you do what is evil, be afraid; for it does not bear the sword for nothing; for it is a minister of God, an avenger who brings wrath on the one who practices evil.

5　Therefore it is necessary to be in subjection, not only because of wrath, but also for conscience' sake.

6　For because of this you also pay taxes, for *rulers* are servants of God, devoting themselves to this very thing.

7　Render to all what is due them: tax to whom tax *is due;* custom to whom custom; fear to whom fear; honor to whom honor.

8　Owe nothing to anyone except to love one another; for he who loves his neighbor has fulfilled *the* law.

9　For this, "YOU SHALL NOT COMMIT ADULTERY, YOU SHALL NOT MURDER, YOU SHALL NOT STEAL, YOU SHALL NOT COVET," and if there is any other commandment, it is summed up in this saying, "YOU SHALL LOVE YOUR NEIGHBOR AS YOURSELF."

10　Love does no wrong to a neighbor; therefore love is the fulfillment of *the* law.

11　*Do* this, knowing the time, that it is already the hour for you to awaken from sleep; for now salvation is nearer to us than when we believed.

12　The night is almost gone, and the day is near. Therefore let us lay aside the deeds of darkness and put on the armor of light.

13　Let us behave properly as in the day, not in carousing and drunkenness, not in sexual promiscuity and sensuality, not in strife and jealousy.

14　But put on the Lord Jesus Christ, and make no provision for the flesh in regard to *its* lusts.

LIFE LESSONS

➤ **Romans 13:1 —** *For there is no authority except from God, and those which exist are established by God.*

*J*oseph submitted to the Egyptian authorities; Daniel submitted to the Babylonian authorities; Mordecai submitted to the Persian authorities; Jesus submitted to the Roman authorities. While none of these regimes were godly, God had authorized them all.

➤ **Romans 13:10 —** *Love is the fulfillment of the law.*

*G*od is love, and the law reflects His character. Therefore, love is the fulfillment of the law. Obedience is never about slavishly following rules, but always about eagerly pleasing our loving Lord.

➤ **Romans 13:14 —** *Put on the Lord Jesus Christ, and make no provision for the flesh in regard to its lusts.*

*W*hen we know we should avoid a certain place but we go there anyway, it is sin. When we recognize that a particular activity is a temptation but still participate in it, we are dishonoring the Lord.

Job 21:1—22:30

21 THEN Job answered,
2　"Listen carefully to my speech,
And let this be your *way of* consolation.

3　"Bear with me that I may speak;
Then after I have spoken, you may mock.

4　"As for me, is my complaint to man?
And why should I not be impatient?

5　"Look at me, and be astonished,
And put *your* hand over *your* mouth.

6 "Even when I remember, I am
    disturbed,
    And horror takes hold of my flesh.
7 "Why do the wicked *still* live,
    Continue on, also become very
    powerful?
8 "Their descendants are established
    with them in their sight,
    And their offspring before their
    eyes,
9 Their houses are safe from fear,
    And the rod of God is not on them.
10 "His ox mates without fail;
    His cow calves and does not abort.
11 "They send forth their little ones like
    the flock,
    And their children skip about.
12 "They sing to the timbrel and harp
    And rejoice at the sound of the flute.
13 "They spend their days in prosperity,
    And suddenly they go down to
    Sheol.
14 "They say to God, 'Depart from us!
    We do not even desire the
    knowledge of Your ways.
15 'Who is the Almighty, that we
    should serve Him,
    And what would we gain if we
    entreat Him?'
16 "Behold, their prosperity is not in
    their hand;
    The counsel of the wicked is far
    from me.
17 "How often is the lamp of the wicked
    put out,
    Or does their calamity fall on them?
    Does God apportion destruction in
    His anger?
18 "Are they as straw before the wind,
    And like chaff which the storm
    carries away?
19 "*You say,* 'God stores away a man's
    iniquity for his sons.'
    Let God repay him so that he may
    know *it.*
20 "Let his own eyes see his decay,
    And let him drink of the wrath of
    the Almighty.
21 "For what does he care for his
    household after him,
    When the number of his months is
    cut off?
22 "Can anyone teach God knowledge,
    In that He judges those on high?
23 "One dies in his full strength,
    Being wholly at ease and satisfied;
24 His sides are filled out with fat,

And the marrow of his bones is
    moist,
25 While another dies with a bitter
    soul,
    Never even tasting *anything* good.
26 "Together they lie down in the dust,
    And worms cover them.
27 "Behold, I know your thoughts,
    And the plans by which you would
    wrong me.
28 "For you say, 'Where is the house of
    the nobleman,
    And where is the tent, the dwelling
    places of the wicked?'
29 "Have you not asked wayfaring
    men,
    And do you not recognize their
    witness?
30 "For the wicked is reserved for the
    day of calamity;
    They will be led forth at the day of
    fury.
31 "Who will confront him with his
    actions,
    And who will repay him for what he
    has done?
32 "While he is carried to the grave,
    Men will keep watch over *his* tomb.
33 "The clods of the valley will gently
    cover him;
    Moreover, all men will follow after
    him,
    While countless ones *go* before him.
34 "How then will you vainly comfort
    me,
    For your answers remain *full of*
    falsehood?"

22 THEN Eliphaz the Temanite re-
        sponded,
2 "Can a vigorous man be of use to
    God,
    Or a wise man be useful to himself?
3 "Is there any pleasure to the
    Almighty if you are righteous,   ◄

LIFE LESSONS

➤ **Job 22:3 — *"Is there any pleasure to
the Almighty if you are righteous?"***

*E*liphaz may seem to imply "no" to
both of these questions, but actually
the answers are "yes" and "yes." In fact,
God delights in the obedience of His
people (1 Sam. 15:22) and "favors those
who fear Him, those who wait for His
lovingkindness" (Ps. 147:11).

Or profit if you make your ways
perfect?
4 "Is it because of your reverence that
He reproves you,
That He enters into judgment against
you?
5 "Is not your wickedness great,
And your iniquities without end?
6 "For you have taken pledges of your
brothers without cause,
And stripped men naked.
7 "To the weary you have given no
water to drink,
And from the hungry you have
withheld bread.
8 "But the earth belongs to the mighty
man,
And the honorable man dwells in it.
9 "You have sent widows away empty,
And the strength of the orphans has
been crushed.
10 "Therefore snares surround you,
And sudden dread terrifies you,
11 Or darkness, so that you cannot see,
And an abundance of water covers
you.
12 "Is not God *in* the height of heaven?
Look also at the distant stars, how
high they are!
13 "You say, 'What does God know?
Can He judge through the thick
darkness?
14 'Clouds are a hiding place for Him,
so that He cannot see;
And He walks on the vault of
heaven.'
15 "Will you keep to the ancient path
Which wicked men have trod,
16 Who were snatched away before
their time,
Whose foundations were washed
away by a river?
17 "They said to God, 'Depart from us!'
And 'What can the Almighty do to
them?'
18 "Yet He filled their houses with good
things;
But the counsel of the wicked is far
from me.
19 "The righteous see and are glad,
And the innocent mock them,
20 *Saying,* 'Truly our adversaries are
cut off,
And their abundance the fire has
consumed.'
21 "Yield now and be at peace with
Him;

Thereby good will come to you.
22 "Please receive instruction from His
mouth
And establish His words in your
heart.
23 "If you return to the Almighty, you
will be restored;
If you remove unrighteousness far
from your tent,
24 And place *your* gold in the dust,
And *the gold of* Ophir among the
stones of the brooks,
25 Then the Almighty will be your gold
And choice silver to you.
26 "For then you will delight in the
Almighty
And lift up your face to God.
27 "You will pray to Him, and He will
hear you;
And you will pay your vows.
28 "You will also decree a thing, and it
will be established for you;
And light will shine on your ways.
29 "When you are cast down, you will
speak with confidence,
And the humble person He will
save.
30 "He will deliver one who is not
innocent,
And he will be delivered through
the cleanness of your hands."

✦ Psalm 96:1–6

96 SING to the LORD a new song;
Sing to the LORD, all the earth.
2 Sing to the LORD, bless His name;
Proclaim good tidings of His
salvation from day to day.
3 Tell of His glory among the nations,
His wonderful deeds among all the
peoples.
4 For great is the LORD and greatly to
be praised;
He is to be feared above all gods.

LIFE LESSONS

➤ **Psalm 96:1** — *Sing to the LORD a new
song.*

Why does Scripture encourage us to
sing a new song to the Lord? New
songs help us to see God in a fresh light
and to appreciate Him in a new way.

5　For all the gods of the peoples are
　　idols,
　　But the LORD made the heavens.
6　Splendor and majesty are before
　　Him,
　　Strength and beauty are in His
　　sanctuary.

Proverbs 23:6–8

6　Do not eat the bread of a selfish
　　man,
　　Or desire his delicacies;
7　For as he thinks within himself, so
　　he is.
　　He says to you, "Eat and drink!"
　　But his heart is not with you.
8　You will vomit up the morsel you
　　have eaten,
　　And waste your compliments.

Romans 14:1–23

14NOW accept the one who is weak
in faith, *but* not for *the purpose of*
passing judgment on his opinions.
2　One person has faith that he may
eat all things, but he who is weak eats
vegetables *only*.
3　The one who eats is not to regard
with contempt the one who does not eat,
and the one who does not eat is not to
judge the one who eats, for God has accepted him.
4　Who are you to judge the servant of
another? To his own master he stands or
falls; and he will stand, for the Lord is
able to make him stand.
➤ 5　One person regards one day above
another, another regards every day *alike*.
Each person must be fully convinced in
his own mind.
6　He who observes the day, observes it
for the Lord, and he who eats, does so for
the Lord, for he gives thanks to God; and
he who eats not, for the Lord he does not
eat, and gives thanks to God.
7　For not one of us lives for himself,
and not one dies for himself;
➤ 8　for if we live, we live for the Lord, or
if we die, we die for the Lord; therefore
whether we live or die, we are the Lord's.
9　For to this end Christ died and lived

again, that He might be Lord both of the
dead and of the living.
10　But you, why do you judge your
brother? Or you again, why do you regard your brother with contempt? For we
will all stand before the judgment seat of
God.
11　For it is written,
　　"AS I LIVE, SAYS THE LORD, EVERY KNEE
　　　　SHALL BOW TO ME,
　　　AND EVERY TONGUE SHALL GIVE PRAISE
　　　　TO GOD."
12　So then each one of us will give an ◄
account of himself to God.
13　Therefore let us not judge one another anymore, but rather determine
this—not to put an obstacle or a stumbling block in a brother's way.
14　I know and am convinced in the
Lord Jesus that nothing is unclean in
itself; but to him who thinks anything to
be unclean, to him it is unclean.
15　For if because of food your brother
is hurt, you are no longer walking according to love. Do not destroy with your
food him for whom Christ died.

LIFE LESSONS

➤ **Romans 14:5 —** *Each person must be
fully convinced in his own mind.*

God wants us to learn how to live by
faith, which means He wants us to
develop personal convictions based on
our ongoing relationships with Him.

➤ **Romans 14:8 —** *For if we live, we live
for the Lord, or if we die, we die for the
Lord; therefore whether we live or die,
we are the Lord's.*

Everything we do should reflect well
on and be in submission to the Savior
who bought us with His own blood. Even
the way we die should witness to the
goodness of Jesus Christ. Every moment
of every day we belong to Him.

➤ **Romans 14:12 —** *Each one of us will
give an account of himself to God.*

What sort of account would you have
to give to Jesus of the way you
lived this past week? What would you
tell Him about the way you lived today?
Would He be happy about your plans for
tomorrow?

WHAT THE BIBLE SAYS ABOUT

Jesus Christ Is Lord

Romans 14:7–12

Is Jesus Christ the Lord of my life? I've asked myself that question many times. On one occasion, I was in the hospital because I had worn myself out. I was so busy with religious activities I had exhausted myself and had to be taken to the hospital for rest.

If you had asked me, I would have told you I was doing it all for Jesus' sake. However, was I truly pleasing God with my grueling busyness? No! I had thought my motivation was good, but deep down I knew it wasn't right. I was doing everything *for* Jesus, but I was not obeying Him—which is what He really wanted.

As I lay in that hospital bed, I thought about my relationship with Jesus Christ. I realized how foolish I had been. I prayed, "Lord, how will I know when You are the Lord of my life? What do I need to do?" I took out some paper and a pencil and began writing. I couldn't write fast enough. The Lord gave me some very important statements to measure my life by, and these helped me immeasurably:

1. *Jesus Christ is the Lord of my life when I obey the initial promptings of the Holy Spirit without arguing with Him.*

There are many times when God gives us a command that we should obey immediately. However, we begin to argue with Him because we want to do things our own way.

But in every situation, we must recognize the Lord's authority, wisdom, and power—whether it appears to be good for us or not. Our perception of God's command is never the issue. Our only right response is to step out in faith and obey Him. We must answer "yes" to His leading and guidance in every situation.

2. *I know that Jesus Christ is Lord of my life when I am committed to following His will, even though I may not know what His will is.*

The Father does not show us every detail of His will for us, and we must simply trust Him. However, if we insist on knowing every detail of His plan, we are actually rebelling against Him. We must leave all the consequences of our obedience to Him. If He is the King of all

creation and omniscient (knowing all things), omnipotent, (all powerful), and omnipresent (He is always with us), then what do we have to worry about? Since He is able to do anything, loves us unconditionally, and is always with us, we truly have nothing to fear.

3. *I know that Jesus Christ is Lord of my life when I am available to serve Him no matter what He requires of me.*

We cannot say that Jesus is Lord if we've decided we don't want to serve Him. To follow Jesus means that we are giving our lives to Him.

4. *Jesus Christ is Lord of my life when pleasing Him takes precedence over pleasing any other person.*

Jesus Christ is Lord of my life when pleasing Him is more important to us than pleasing anyone else in the world—including ourselves.

5. *Jesus Christ is Lord of my life when I recognize that He is the source of all I need and I go to Him as that source.*

The lordship of Jesus Christ should eliminate our worries because He will give us everything we need. The Lord can meet every need we have. If He cannot, then He is not God!

6. *Jesus Christ is Lord of my life when I recognize His ownership of all that I am and all that I have.*

Jesus Christ is the owner of everything that exists. He has it all in His keeping. When we recognize that He is the owner—the One who possesses all that we are and all that we have—then we will begin to understand what it means to have Christ as the Lord of our lives.

7. *Jesus Christ is Lord of my life when I learn to turn difficulties and failures into opportunities for growth.*

He is Lord when we see everything as an opportunity to grow in Christ's likeness. God uses everything for our good—even our difficulties. This is why we must view everything that comes into our lives as something that He alone is going to work through.

8. *Jesus Christ is Lord of my life when knowing Him becomes the obsession of my life.*

Therefore, trust God and make Him your focus—your obsession! Allow Him to be the Lord of your life. Then you will know you are reaching the potential you were created for and living the very best life possible. ◈

16 Therefore do not let what is for you a good thing be spoken of as evil;

17 for the kingdom of God is not eating and drinking, but righteousness and peace and joy in the Holy Spirit.

18 For he who in this *way* serves Christ is acceptable to God and approved by men.

19 So then we pursue the things which make for peace and the building up of one another.

20 Do not tear down the work of God for the sake of food. All things indeed are clean, but they are evil for the man who eats and gives offense.

21 It is good not to eat meat or to drink wine, or *to do anything* by which your brother stumbles.

22 The faith which you have, have as your own conviction before God. Happy is he who does not condemn himself in what he approves.

23 But he who doubts is condemned if he eats, because *his eating is* not from faith; and whatever is not from faith is sin.

LIFE LESSONS

➤ **Romans 14:23 —** *Whatever is not from faith is sin.*

*W*e are to live our entire lives relying on the power of grace as it comes to us through faith. If we are not sure that something we would like to do honors God—if we cannot do it in faith—then we should refrain.

AUGUST 16

Job 23:1—25:6

23 THEN Job replied,
2 "Even today my complaint is rebellion;
His hand is heavy despite my groaning.

3 "Oh that I knew where I might find Him,
That I might come to His seat!

4 "I would present *my* case before Him
And fill my mouth with arguments.

5 "I would learn the words *which* He would answer,
And perceive what He would say to me.

6 "Would He contend with me by the greatness of *His* power?
No, surely He would pay attention to me.

7 "There the upright would reason with Him;
And I would be delivered forever from my Judge.

8 "Behold, I go forward but He is not *there*,
And backward, but I cannot perceive Him;

9 When He acts on the left, I cannot behold *Him*;

He turns on the right, I cannot see Him.

10 "But He knows the way I take;
When He has tried me, I shall come forth as gold.

11 "My foot has held fast to His path;
I have kept His way and not turned aside.

12 "I have not departed from the command of His lips;
I have treasured the words of His mouth more than my necessary food.

13 "But He is unique and who can turn Him?
And *what* His soul desires, that He does.

14 "For He performs what is appointed for me,

LIFE LESSONS

➤ **Job 23:12 —** *"I have treasured the words of His mouth more than my necessary food."*

*I*f we turn away from the Lord when hard times hit, where will we find hope, peace, or truth? God's Word is an immovable anchor in times of storm and living bread for those who hunger for righteousness (Matt. 5:6).

And many such *decrees* are with Him.

15 "Therefore, I would be dismayed at His presence;
　　When I consider, I am terrified of Him.

16 "*It is* God *who* has made my heart faint,
　　And the Almighty *who* has dismayed me,

17 But I am not silenced by the darkness,
　　Nor deep gloom *which* covers me.

24 "WHY are times not stored up by the Almighty,
　　And why do those who know Him not see His days?

2 "Some remove the landmarks;
　　They seize and devour flocks.

3 "They drive away the donkeys of the orphans;
　　They take the widow's ox for a pledge.

4 "They push the needy aside from the road;
　　The poor of the land are made to hide themselves altogether.

5 "Behold, as wild donkeys in the wilderness
　　They go forth seeking food in their activity,
　　As bread for *their* children in the desert.

6 "They harvest their fodder in the field
　　And glean the vineyard of the wicked.

7 "They spend the night naked, without clothing,
　　And have no covering against the cold.

8 "They are wet with the mountain rains
　　And hug the rock for want of a shelter.

9 "Others snatch the orphan from the breast,
　　And against the poor they take a pledge.

10 "They cause *the poor* to go about naked without clothing,
　　And they take away the sheaves from the hungry.

11 "Within the walls they produce oil;
　　They tread wine presses but thirst.

12 "From the city men groan,
　　And the souls of the wounded cry out;
　　Yet God does not pay attention to folly.

13 "Others have been with those who rebel against the light;
　　They do not want to know its ways
　　Nor abide in its paths.

14 "The murderer arises at dawn;
　　He kills the poor and the needy,
　　And at night he is as a thief.

15 "The eye of the adulterer waits for the twilight,
　　Saying, 'No eye will see me.'
　　And he disguises his face.

Life Examples:

JOB'S FRIENDS: Adamant, but Wrong

JOB 23:10–13

*E*liphaz, Bildad, and Zophar heard of Job's plight and felt deeply burdened to comfort their old friend. But what they saw staggered them. They gasped, cried out, and tore their clothes—a demonstration of deep grief. Finally, they sat with Job and remained silent. They stayed that way for seven days (Job 2:11-13).

Once they opened their mouths, however, Job's visitors didn't offer much help. They judged his pitiful situation to be the consequence of sin and kept insisting that adversity comes only to the wicked, not to the righteous. Job suffered, but not because he had failed the Lord or done something wrong. Therefore, he rejected their diagnosis and held fast to his faith in God.

In the end, the Lord had the final word, and He rebuked Eliphaz, Bildad, and Zophar (Job 42:7–9). When God restored Job twofold, He proved Himself—and His promises—ever faithful. And He showed that blessings for obedience do not guarantee a life free of adversity.

16 "In the dark they dig into houses,
     They shut themselves up by day;
     They do not know the light.
17 "For the morning is the same to him
         as thick darkness,
     For he is familiar with the terrors of
         thick darkness.
18 "They are insignificant on the
         surface of the water;
     Their portion is cursed on the
         earth.
     They do not turn toward the
         vineyards.
19 "Drought and heat consume the
         snow waters,
     So does Sheol those who have
         sinned.
20 "A mother will forget him;
     The worm feeds sweetly till he is no
         longer remembered.
     And wickedness will be broken like
         a tree.
21 "He wrongs the barren woman
     And does no good for the widow.
22 "But He drags off the valiant by His
         power;
     He rises, but no one has assurance
         of life.
23 "He provides them with security, and
         they are supported;
     And His eyes are on their ways.
24 "They are exalted a little while, then
         they are gone;
     Moreover, they are brought low and
         like everything gathered up;
     Even like the heads of grain they
         are cut off.
25 "Now if it is not so, who can prove
         me a liar,
     And make my speech worthless?"

25 THEN Bildad the Shuhite an-
     swered,
2 "Dominion and awe belong to Him
     Who establishes peace in His
         heights.
3 "Is there any number to His troops?
     And upon whom does His light not
         rise?
4 "How then can a man be just with
         God?
     Or how can he be clean who is born
         of woman?
5 "If even the moon has no
         brightness
     And the stars are not pure in His
         sight,

6 How much less man, that
         maggot,
     And the son of man, that worm!"

◈ Psalm 96:7–10

7 Ascribe to the LORD, O families of
         the peoples,
     Ascribe to the LORD glory and
         strength.
8 Ascribe to the LORD the glory of His
         name;
     Bring an offering and come into His
         courts.
9 Worship the LORD in holy attire;
     Tremble before Him, all the earth.
10 Say among the nations, "The LORD
         reigns;
     Indeed, the world is firmly
         established, it will not be moved;
     He will judge the peoples with
         equity."

◈ Proverbs 23:9

9 Do not speak in the hearing of a
         fool,
     For he will despise the wisdom of
         your words.

LIFE LESSONS

➤ **Psalm 96:9 —** *Worship the LORD in holy
attire!*

*W*e are to worship the Lord for His
     beautiful holiness—His purity, His
righteousness, His spotlessness—as we
worship Him beautifully through pure,
blameless, and upright lives.

➤ **Romans 15:2 —** *Each of us is to please
his neighbor for his good, to his edification.*

*I*f we are serious about our Christian
     faith, we *must* take into consider-
ation how our actions affect others. We
cannot mature in our relationships with
the Lord in isolation from others, and
whenever we interact with others, we
should have edifying them and glorifying God as our goal.

Romans 15:1–24

15 NOW we who are strong ought to bear the weaknesses of those without strength and not *just* please ourselves.

2 Each of us is to please his neighbor for his good, to his edification.

3 For even Christ did not please Himself; but as it is written, "THE REPROACHES OF THOSE WHO REPROACHED YOU FELL ON ME."

4 For whatever was written in earlier times was written for our instruction, so that through perseverance and the encouragement of the Scriptures we might have hope.

5 Now may the God who gives perseverance and encouragement grant you to be of the same mind with one another according to Christ Jesus,

6 so that with one accord you may with one voice glorify the God and Father of our Lord Jesus Christ.

7 Therefore, accept one another, just as Christ also accepted us to the glory of God.

8 For I say that Christ has become a servant to the circumcision on behalf of the truth of God to confirm the promises *given* to the fathers,

9 and for the Gentiles to glorify God for His mercy; as it is written,

"THEREFORE I WILL GIVE PRAISE TO YOU AMONG THE GENTILES,
AND I WILL SING TO YOUR NAME."

10 Again he says,

"REJOICE, O GENTILES, WITH HIS PEOPLE."

11 And again,

"PRAISE THE LORD ALL YOU GENTILES,
AND LET ALL THE PEOPLES PRAISE HIM."

12 Again Isaiah says,

"THERE SHALL COME THE ROOT OF JESSE,
AND HE WHO ARISES TO RULE OVER THE GENTILES,
IN HIM SHALL THE GENTILES HOPE."

13 Now may the God of hope fill you with all joy and peace in believing, so that you will abound in hope by the power of the Holy Spirit.

14 And concerning you, my brethren, I myself also am convinced that you yourselves are full of goodness, filled with all knowledge and able also to admonish one another.

15 But I have written very boldly to you on some points so as to remind you again, because of the grace that was given me from God,

16 to be a minister of Christ Jesus to the Gentiles, ministering as a priest the gospel of God, so that *my* offering of the Gentiles may become acceptable, sanctified by the Holy Spirit.

17 Therefore in Christ Jesus I have found reason for boasting in things pertaining to God.

18 For I will not presume to speak of anything except what Christ has accomplished through me, resulting in the obedience of the Gentiles by word and deed,

19 in the power of signs and wonders, in the power of the Spirit; so that from Jerusalem and round about as far as Illyricum I have fully preached the gospel of Christ.

20 And thus I aspired to preach the gospel, not where Christ was *already* named, so that I would not build on another man's foundation;

21 but as it is written,

"THEY WHO HAD NO NEWS OF HIM SHALL SEE,
AND THEY WHO HAVE NOT HEARD SHALL UNDERSTAND."

22 For this reason I have often been prevented from coming to you;

23 but now, with no further place for me in these regions, and since I have had for many years a longing to come to you

24 whenever I go to Spain—for I hope to see you in passing, and to be helped on my way there by you, when I have first enjoyed your company for a while—

LIFE LESSONS

➤ **Romans 15:13 —** *Now may the God of hope fill you with all joy and peace in believing.*

The Christian life is to be characterized by hope, joy, and peace. As we grow in His grace, God wants us to experience each of them in increasing measure. If they're lacking, we know something has gone wrong.

Job 26:1–14

26THEN Job responded,
2 "What a help you are to the weak!
How you have saved the arm without strength!
3 "What counsel you have given to *one* without wisdom!
What helpful insight you have abundantly provided!
4 "To whom have you uttered words?
And whose spirit was expressed through you?
5 "The departed spirits tremble
Under the waters and their inhabitants.
6 "Naked is Sheol before Him,
And Abaddon has no covering.
➤ 7 "He stretches out the north over empty space
And hangs the earth on nothing.
8 "He wraps up the waters in His clouds,
And the cloud does not burst under them.
9 "He obscures the face of the full moon
And spreads His cloud over it.
10 "He has inscribed a circle on the surface of the waters
At the boundary of light and darkness.
11 "The pillars of heaven tremble
And are amazed at His rebuke.
12 "He quieted the sea with His power,
And by His understanding He shattered Rahab.
13 "By His breath the heavens are cleared;
His hand has pierced the fleeing serpent.
➤ 14 "Behold, these are the fringes of His ways;
And how faint a word we hear of Him!
But His mighty thunder, who can understand?"

Psalm 96:11–13

11 Let the heavens be glad, and let the earth rejoice;
Let the sea roar, and all it contains;
12 Let the field exult, and all that is in it.
Then all the trees of the forest will sing for joy
13 Before the Lord, for He is coming,
For He is coming to judge the earth.
He will judge the world in righteousness
And the peoples in His faithfulness.

Proverbs 23:10–12

10 Do not move the ancient boundary
Or go into the fields of the fatherless,
11 For their Redeemer is strong;
He will plead their case against you.
12 Apply your heart to discipline
And your ears to words of knowledge.

Romans 15:25–33

25 but now, I am going to Jerusalem serving the saints.
26 For Macedonia and Achaia have been

LIFE LESSONS

➤ **Job 26:7 — "He . . . hangs the earth on nothing."**

*W*ho but God could take nothing and hang the world on it? Isn't this just how the Lord helps us—in a way that is beyond our understanding and imagination? Although we see no solution to our problems and have no way to handle them on our own, God has a way. He can make a solution where there was none before. We cannot possibly know the extraordinary manner by which the Father is going to work on our behalf; however, we should always trust and obey Him being sure that He will.

➤ **Job 26:14 — *These are the fringes of His ways.***

*T*he greatest forces in nature give nothing but the tiniest hint of God's immeasurable power. Yet He makes all that power available to us through prayer!

WHAT THE BIBLE SAYS ABOUT

The Power of His Ways

Job 26:7–14

The greatest forces in nature give nothing but the tiniest hint of God's immeasurable power. That was Job's message to his friends when he said, "He . . . hangs the earth on nothing . . . The pillars of heaven tremble and are amazed at His rebuke. He quieted the sea with His power . . . By His breath the heavens are cleared . . . Behold, these are the fringes of His ways; and how faint a word we hear of Him!" (Job 26:7, 11–14).

God makes all that abundant power available to us through prayer. How amazing! The mighty hand that created the heavens is available to you as you kneel before Him and put your trust in Him.

What is it that burdens your heart today? Is it some desperate need or long unfulfilled desire? Is your intercession filled with concern over the welfare of another? Is there some obstacle that blocks your path or some challenge for which you do not have strength? Do not despair! The One who is able to shake the heavens and stir the seas is able to help you.

Ephesians 1:19, 20 admonishes you to embrace the "surpassing greatness of His power toward us who believe . . . the working of the strength of His might which He brought about in Christ, when He raised Him from the dead and seated Him at His right hand in the heavenly places." In other words, what God offers you is the same amazing strength, wisdom, and love that accomplished the resurrection of Christ from the dead and that raised Him to His throne in heaven! Really, is there anything that you could face that needs more power than that?

No matter what worries you, one thing is for sure: You cannot possibly know the extraordinary manner by which God is going to work it all out. So pray to Him, and express your trust in His magnificent ways. There may be much you don't understand about *how* He's going to help you, but you can be sure He *will*. And when He does, it will shake your world—for good! ◈

---

pleased to make a contribution for the poor among the saints in Jerusalem.
27 Yes, they were pleased *to do so*, and they are indebted to them. For if the Gentiles have shared in their spiritual things, they are indebted to minister to them also in material things.
28 Therefore, when I have finished this, and have put my seal on this fruit of theirs, I will go on by way of you to Spain.
29 I know that when I come to you, I will come in the fullness of the blessing of Christ.
➤ 30 Now I urge you, brethren, by our Lord Jesus Christ and by the love of the Spirit, to strive together with me in your prayers to God for me,
31 that I may be rescued from those who are disobedient in Judea, and *that* my service for Jerusalem may prove acceptable to the saints;
32 so that I may come to you in joy by the will of God and find *refreshing* rest in your company.
33 Now the God of peace be with you all. Amen.

LIFE LESSONS

➤ **Proverbs 23:11 — *For their Redeemer is strong; He will plead their case against you.***

In ancient times, there were none more helpless than the orphans and widows. However, because they were often powerless and vulnerable, God pledged Himself to be their Redeemer and Defender. Those who took advantage of them because they seemed to be easy targets soon discovered that the Lord God Himself was their protector.

➤ **Romans 15:30 — *Strive together with me in your prayers to God for me.***

Paul, the great apostle, frequently asked others to pray for him. God loves to answer our prayers for our brothers and sisters in Christ. The Lord wants us to regularly lift each other up to the throne of grace so we can grow as the body of Christ, and so we can experience His powerful presence and provision together (Matt. 18:19, 20).

Job 27:1—28:28

27 THEN Job continued his discourse and said,

2 "As God lives, who has taken away my right,
And the Almighty, who has embittered my soul,

➤ 3 For as long as life is in me,
And the breath of God is in my nostrils,

4 My lips certainly will not speak unjustly,
Nor will my tongue mutter deceit.

5 "Far be it from me that I should declare you right;
Till I die I will not put away my integrity from me.

6 "I hold fast my righteousness and will not let it go.
My heart does not reproach any of my days.

7 "May my enemy be as the wicked
And my opponent as the unjust.

8 "For what is the hope of the godless when he is cut off,
When God requires his life?

9 "Will God hear his cry
When distress comes upon him?

10 "Will he take delight in the Almighty?
Will he call on God at all times?

11 "I will instruct you in the power of God;
What is with the Almighty I will not conceal.

12 "Behold, all of you have seen *it*;
Why then do you act foolishly?

13 "This is the portion of a wicked man from God,
And the inheritance *which* tyrants receive from the Almighty.

14 "Though his sons are many, they are destined for the sword;

And his descendants will not be satisfied with bread.

15 "His survivors will be buried because of the plague,
And their widows will not be able to weep.

16 "Though he piles up silver like dust
And prepares garments as *plentiful as* the clay,

17 He may prepare *it,* but the just will wear *it*
And the innocent will divide the silver.

18 "He has built his house like the spider's web,
Or as a hut *which* the watchman has made.

19 "He lies down rich, but never again;
He opens his eyes, and it is no longer.

20 "Terrors overtake him like a flood;
A tempest steals him away in the night.

21 "The east wind carries him away, and he is gone,
For it whirls him away from his place.

22 "For it will hurl at him without sparing;
He will surely try to flee from its power.

23 "*Men* will clap their hands at him
And will hiss him from his place.

28 "SURELY there is a mine for silver
And a place where they refine gold.

2 "Iron is taken from the dust,
And copper is smelted from rock.

3 "*Man* puts an end to darkness,
And to the farthest limit he searches out
The rock in gloom and deep shadow.

4 "He sinks a shaft far from habitation,
Forgotten by the foot;
They hang and swing to and fro far from men.

5 "The earth, from it comes food,
And underneath it is turned up as fire.

6 "Its rocks are the source of sapphires,
And its dust *contains* gold.

7 "The path no bird of prey knows,
Nor has the falcon's eye caught sight of it.

LIFE LESSONS

➤ **Job 27:3, 4 — "The breath of God is in my nostrils."**

*E*very breath we take is really the breath of God. It belongs to Him, and He can take it back at any time. So let us use our breath to glorify and praise Him, so long as we have it.

8　"The proud beasts have not trodden
　　it,
　　Nor has the *fierce* lion passed over
　　it.
9　"He puts his hand on the flint;
　　He overturns the mountains at the
　　base.
10　"He hews out channels through the
　　rocks,
　　And his eye sees anything precious.
11　"He dams up the streams from
　　flowing,
　　And what is hidden he brings out to
　　the light.
12　"But where can wisdom be found?
　　And where is the place of
　　understanding?
13　"Man does not know its value,
　　Nor is it found in the land of the
　　living.
14　"The deep says, 'It is not in me';
　　And the sea says, 'It is not with me.'
15　"Pure gold cannot be given in
　　exchange for it,
　　Nor can silver be weighed as its
　　price.
16　"It cannot be valued in the gold of
　　Ophir,
　　In precious onyx, or sapphire.
17　"Gold or glass cannot equal it,
　　Nor can it be exchanged for articles
　　of fine gold.
18　"Coral and crystal are not to be
　　mentioned;
　　And the acquisition of wisdom is
　　above *that of* pearls.
19　"The topaz of Ethiopia cannot equal
　　it,
　　Nor can it be valued in pure gold.
20　"Where then does wisdom come
　　from?
　　And where is the place of
　　understanding?
21　"Thus it is hidden from the eyes of
　　all living
　　And concealed from the birds of the
　　sky.
22　"Abaddon and Death say,
　　'With our ears we have heard a
　　report of it.'
23　"God understands its way,
　　And He knows its place.
24　"For He looks to the ends of the
　　earth
　　And sees everything under the
　　heavens.
25　"When He imparted weight to the wind

And meted out the waters by
　　measure,
26　When He set a limit for the rain
　　And a course for the thunderbolt,
27　Then He saw it and declared it;
　　He established it and also searched
　　it out.
28　"And to man He said, 'Behold, the
　　fear of the Lord, that is
　　wisdom;
　　And to depart from evil is
　　understanding.'"

Psalm 97:1–6

97　THE LORD reigns, let the earth
　　rejoice;
　　Let the many islands be glad.
2　Clouds and thick darkness surround
　　Him;
　　Righteousness and justice are the
　　foundation of His throne.
3　Fire goes before Him
　　And burns up His adversaries round
　　about.
4　His lightnings lit up the world;
　　The earth saw and trembled.
5　The mountains melted like wax at
　　the presence of the LORD,
　　At the presence of the Lord of the
　　whole earth.
6　The heavens declare His
　　righteousness,
　　And all the peoples have seen His
　　glory.

Proverbs 23:13, 14

13　Do not hold back discipline from
　　the child,

LIFE LESSONS

➤ **Job 28:28** — *"Behold, the fear of the Lord, that is wisdom; and to depart from evil is understanding."*

*W*hy is it wise to fear the Lord? How do we show insight when we obey Him? One day we will stand before Him, "that each one may be recompensed for his deeds in the body . . . whether good or bad" (2 Cor. 5:10).

Although you strike him with the rod, he will not die.

14 You shall strike him with the rod
And rescue his soul from Sheol.

Romans 16:1–27

16 I COMMEND to you our sister Phoebe, who is a servant of the church which is at Cenchrea;
2 that you receive her in the Lord in a manner worthy of the saints, and that you help her in whatever matter she may have need of you; for she herself has also been a helper of many, and of myself as well.
3 Greet Prisca and Aquila, my fellow workers in Christ Jesus,
4 who for my life risked their own necks, to whom not only do I give thanks, but also all the churches of the Gentiles;
5 also greet the church that is in their house. Greet Epaenetus, my beloved, who is the first convert to Christ from Asia.
6 Greet Mary, who has worked hard for you.
7 Greet Andronicus and Junias, my kinsmen and my fellow prisoners, who are outstanding among the apostles, who also were in Christ before me.
8 Greet Ampliatus, my beloved in the Lord.
9 Greet Urbanus, our fellow worker in Christ, and Stachys my beloved.
10 Greet Apelles, the approved in Christ. Greet those who are of the *household* of Aristobulus.
11 Greet Herodion, my kinsman. Greet those of the *household* of Narcissus, who are in the Lord.
12 Greet Tryphaena and Tryphosa, workers in the Lord. Greet Persis the beloved, who has worked hard in the Lord.
13 Greet Rufus, a choice man in the Lord, also his mother and mine.
14 Greet Asyncritus, Phlegon, Hermes, Patrobas, Hermas and the brethren with them.
15 Greet Philologus and Julia, Nereus and his sister, and Olympas, and all the saints who are with them.
16 Greet one another with a holy kiss. All the churches of Christ greet you.

17 Now I urge you, brethren, keep your eye on those who cause dissensions and hindrances contrary to the teaching which you learned, and turn away from them.
18 For such men are slaves, not of our Lord Christ but of their own appetites; and by their smooth and flattering speech they deceive the hearts of the unsuspecting.
19 For the report of your obedience has reached to all; therefore I am rejoicing over you, but I want you to be wise in what is good and innocent in what is evil.
20 The God of peace will soon crush Satan under your feet.
The grace of our Lord Jesus be with you.
21 Timothy my fellow worker greets

LIFE LESSONS

➤ **Romans 16:17 —** *Those who cause dissensions and hindrances contrary to the teaching which you learned, and turn away from them.*

*D*ivision is a sure mark of the enemy's work. God calls His people to unity in order to demonstrate His love to the world (John 13:35; 15:8–17). When it is missing, we become ineffective (1 Cor. 13:1–3). That is why the enemy will attempt to set believers against each other, because while we are busy arguing within the church, we are failing to show the lost Christ's love (2 Tim. 2:14–26).

➤ **Romans 16:19 —** *Be wise in what is good and innocent in what is evil.*

*W*e are on the wrong track if we are constantly asking, "What's wrong with doing that?" This is a question for immature believers, not growing ones. God wants us to focus on His will for us and growing in the likeness of Christ—not on why He has instructed us to avoid certain activities and attitudes.

➤ **Romans 16:25 —** *Now to Him who is able to establish you according to my gospel.*

*A*ll Christian growth ultimately comes down to our willing submission to the Lord—the only One who can conform us to His image and mature our faith.

WHAT THE BIBLE SAYS ABOUT

Avoiding Counterfeits

Romans 16:17–20

*T*he news is filled with the resourceful (but reprehensible) ways that people invent to do evil. The wicked are always finding novel ways to take advantage of others and to evade capture by clever disguises. It is very difficult to see the danger approaching, and even more complicated to see justice done after they've escaped.

Unfortunately, the same is true within the church, which is why Paul admonished Roman believers: "I urge you, brethren, keep your eye on those who cause dissensions and hindrances contrary to the teaching which you learned, and turn away from them. For such men are slaves, not of our Lord Christ but of their own appetites; and by their smooth flattering speech they deceive the hearts of the unsuspecting."

False teachers are everywhere—especially targeting the believers and congregations that are being most effective for Christ. Satan is our enemy, and he doesn't want the church to be successful. Therefore, he sends his servants disguised as believers to destroy it from the inside.

However, because of Paul's warning, we know what to look for. We can identify false teachers by their messages because they are not promoting the unity of the Spirit. Rather, they are inciting dissension among the brethren and contradicting the gospel message and/or adding to it in some way. They invite people to doubt that we can know Christ personally through the Bible and indwelling Holy Spirit, saying that something extra is needed—and, of course, only they know what that additional information is.

We can also recognize false teachers by what motivates them. Is Christ always at the forefront of their words and actions? Or are they motivated by power, wealth, and publicity? Do they imitate Christ's holy character and His attitude of loving servanthood? Or do they display an air of superiority and demand that people obey them? Are they pouring themselves out to build God's heavenly kingdom? Or are they using improper means to promote their own earthly realms?

Finally, we will know false teachers by the outcome of their efforts. Though it may appear that their ministries are growing, we must ask ourselves if people in their ministries are actually accepting Christ, or are they merely being drawn away from other Christian organizations and congregations? When looking closely at what is really going on, we may find they have alienated more people from Christ than they've "reached." However, the outcome of a healthy, God-honoring ministry is always mature believers in Christ.

In Romans 16:19 Paul wrote, "I want you to be wise in what is good and innocent in what is evil." Because it is impossible to keep up with all the ways that wicked people will try to attack the church, this cannot be our focus. Rather, as Paul admonished, we must be wise in what is good. We must focus on the Word of God. We must have deep, intimate relationships with the Lord Jesus Christ. Then we will be aware of what the false teachers are doing and we won't be enticed by their "smooth and flattering speech" (Rom. 16:18). Instead, we will be victorious over them because "the God of peace will soon crush Satan under [our] feet" (Rom. 16:20). ◉

---

you, and *so do* Lucius and Jason and Sosipater, my kinsmen.
22 I, Tertius, who write this letter, greet you in the Lord.
23 Gaius, host to me and to the whole church, greets you. Erastus, the city treasurer greets you, and Quartus, the brother.
24 [The grace of our Lord Jesus Christ be with you all. Amen.]
➤ **25** Now to Him who is able to establish you according to my gospel and the preaching of Jesus Christ, according to the revelation of the mystery which has been kept secret for long ages past,
26 but now is manifested, and by the Scriptures of the prophets, according to the commandment of the eternal God, has been made known to all the nations, *leading* to obedience of faith;
27 to the only wise God, through Jesus Christ, be the glory forever. Amen.

Job 29:1—30:31

29 AND Job again took up his discourse and said,

2 "Oh that I were as in months gone by,
As in the days when God watched over me;

3 When His lamp shone over my head,
And by His light I walked through darkness;

4 As I was in the prime of my days,
When the friendship of God *was* over my tent;

5 When the Almighty was yet with me,
And my children were around me;

6 When my steps were bathed in butter,
And the rock poured out for me streams of oil!

7 "When I went out to the gate of the city,
When I took my seat in the square,

8 The young men saw me and hid themselves,
And the old men arose *and* stood.

9 "The princes stopped talking
And put *their* hands on their mouths;

10 The voice of the nobles was hushed,
And their tongue stuck to their palate.

11 "For when the ear heard, it called me blessed,
And when the eye saw, it gave witness of me,

12 Because I delivered the poor who cried for help,
And the orphan who had no helper.

13 "The blessing of the one ready to perish came upon me,

And I made the widow's heart sing for joy.

14 "I put on righteousness, and it clothed me;
My justice was like a robe and a turban.

15 "I was eyes to the blind
And feet to the lame.

16 "I was a father to the needy,
And I investigated the case which I did not know.

17 "I broke the jaws of the wicked
And snatched the prey from his teeth.

18 "Then I thought, 'I shall die in my nest,
And I shall multiply *my* days as the sand.

19 'My root is spread out to the waters,
And dew lies all night on my branch.

20 'My glory is *ever* new with me,
And my bow is renewed in my hand.'

21 "To me they listened and waited,
And kept silent for my counsel.

22 "After my words they did not speak again,
And my speech dropped on them.

23 "They waited for me as for the rain,
And opened their mouth as for the spring rain.

24 "I smiled on them when they did not believe,
And the light of my face they did not cast down.

25 "I chose a way for them and sat as chief,
And dwelt as a king among the troops,
As one who comforted the mourners.

30 "BUT now those younger than I mock me,
Whose fathers I disdained to put with the dogs of my flock.

2 "Indeed, what *good was* the strength of their hands to me?
Vigor had perished from them.

3 "From want and famine they are gaunt
Who gnaw the dry ground by night in waste and desolation.

4 Who pluck mallow by the bushes,
And whose food is the root of the broom shrub.

LIFE LESSONS

➤ **Job 29:2 —** *"Oh that I were as in months gone by, as in the days when God watched over me."*

*J*ob did not realize that, even as he uttered this wish, God was *still* closely and lovingly watching over him. His hardships did not mean that the Lord had abandoned him. The same is true for you.

5 "They are driven from the
community;
They shout against them as *against*
a thief,

6 So that they dwell in dreadful
valleys,
In holes of the earth and of the
rocks.

7 "Among the bushes they cry out;
Under the nettles they are gathered
together.

8 "Fools, even those without a name,
They were scourged from the land.

9 "And now I have become their taunt,
I have even become a byword to
them.

10 "They abhor me *and* stand aloof
from me,
And they do not refrain from
spitting at my face.

11 "Because He has loosed His
bowstring and afflicted me,
They have cast off the bridle before
me.

12 "On the right hand their brood
arises;
They thrust aside my feet and build
up against me their ways of
destruction.

13 "They break up my path,
They profit from my destruction;
No one restrains them.

14 "As *through* a wide breach they
come,
Amid the tempest they roll on.

15 "Terrors are turned against me;
They pursue my honor as the wind,
And my prosperity has passed away
like a cloud.

16 "And now my soul is poured out
within me;
Days of affliction have seized me.

17 "At night it pierces my bones within
me,
And my gnawing *pains* take no rest.

18 "By a great force my garment is
distorted;
It binds me about as the collar of
my coat.

19 "He has cast me into the mire,
And I have become like dust and
ashes.

➤ 20 "I cry out to You for help, but You do
not answer me;
I stand up, and You turn Your
attention against me.

21 "You have become cruel to me;

With the might of Your hand You
persecute me.

22 "You lift me up to the wind *and*
cause me to ride;
And You dissolve me in a storm.

23 "For I know that You will bring me
to death
And to the house of meeting for all
living.

24 "Yet does not one in a heap of ruins
stretch out *his* hand,
Or in his disaster therefore cry out
for help?

25 "Have I not wept for the one whose
life is hard?
Was not my soul grieved for the
needy?

26 "When I expected good, then evil
came;
When I waited for light, then
darkness came.

27 "I am seething within and cannot
relax;
Days of affliction confront me.

28 "I go about mourning without
comfort;
I stand up in the assembly *and* cry
out for help.

29 "I have become a brother to jackals
And a companion of ostriches.

30 "My skin turns black on me,
And my bones burn with fever.

31 "Therefore my harp is turned to
mourning,
And my flute to the sound of those
who weep.

Psalm 97:7–12

7 Let all those be ashamed who serve
graven images,
Who boast themselves of idols;
Worship Him, all you gods.

8 Zion heard *this* and was glad,
   And the daughters of Judah have
      rejoiced
   Because of Your judgments, O LORD.
9 For You are the LORD Most High
      over all the earth;
   You are exalted far above all gods.
10 Hate evil, you who love the LORD,
   Who preserves the souls of His
      godly ones;
   He delivers them from the hand of
      the wicked.
11 Light is sown *like seed* for the
      righteous
   And gladness for the upright in
      heart.
12 Be glad in the LORD, you righteous
      ones,
   And give thanks to His holy name.

◈ Proverbs 23:15, 16

15 My son, if your heart is wise,
   My own heart also will be glad;
16 And my inmost being will rejoice
   When your lips speak what is right.

◈ 1 Corinthians 1:1–31

1 PAUL, called *as* an apostle of Jesus
  Christ by the will of God, and Sosthenes our brother,
2 To the church of God which is at
Corinth, to those who have been sanctified in Christ Jesus, saints by calling,
with all who in every place call on the
name of our Lord Jesus Christ, their *Lord*
and ours:
3 Grace to you and peace from God
our Father and the Lord Jesus Christ.
4 I thank my God always concerning you for the grace of God which was
given you in Christ Jesus,
5 that in everything you were enriched in Him, in all speech and all knowledge,
6 even as the testimony concerning
Christ was confirmed in you,
7 so that you are not lacking in any
gift, awaiting eagerly the revelation of
our Lord Jesus Christ,
8 who will also confirm you to the end,
blameless in the day of our Lord Jesus
Christ.

9 God is faithful, through whom you
were called into fellowship with His Son,
Jesus Christ our Lord.
10 Now I exhort you, brethren, by the
name of our Lord Jesus Christ, that you
all agree and that there be no divisions
among you, but that you be made complete in the same mind and in the same
judgment.
11 For I have been informed concerning
you, my brethren, by Chloe's *people*, that
there are quarrels among you.
12 Now I mean this, that each one of
you is saying, "I am of Paul," and "I
of Apollos," and "I of Cephas," and "I of
Christ."
13 Has Christ been divided? Paul was
not crucified for you, was he? Or were
you baptized in the name of Paul?
14 I thank God that I baptized none of
you except Crispus and Gaius,

LIFE LESSONS

➤ **Psalm 97:10 — *Hate evil, you who
love the Lord.***

*A*s our taste for the Lord and His
loving, holy nature grows, our
distaste for anything that dishonors and
displeases Him should also increase. Our
love for God should prompt us to help
others draw near to Him as well.

➤ **1 Corinthians 1:2 — *To those who
have been sanctified in Christ Jesus,
saints by calling.***

*E*very believer in Jesus is *sanctified*—
set apart to God, released from the
power of sin, and actively transformed
into His image. Therefore, Christians are
called saints—holy members of His family—and should be "zealous for good
deeds" (Titus 2:14).

➤ **1 Corinthians 1:10 — *That you be
made complete in the same mind and in
the same judgment.***

*J*esus prayed for the unity of His
followers before His arrest and crucifixion, and Paul also made frequent
appeals so that believers "may be one"
(John 17:11, 22). The joyful unity of
Christians is a powerful testimony to the
world that the gospel of love we preach
is real, unique, powerful, and welcoming
to whomever will believe in the Lord.

WHAT THE BIBLE SAYS ABOUT

About God's Wrath

1 Corinthians 1:17–24

Most people enjoy hearing of the Father's incredible love—but what about His wrath? The wrath of God is described many times in His Word because His character is holy. Habakkuk 1:13 says, "Your eyes are too pure to approve evil, and You can not look on wickedness with favor."

The natural consequence of our sin is a sentence of death (Rom. 6:23). Many people fail to understand the lethal nature of sin, but God takes it very seriously. He knows sin destroys anything it touches. When we reject God's forgiveness of sin through Christ, we reject the only thing that can divert His wrath from us.

Romans 1:18 tells us that "the wrath of God is revealed from heaven against all ungodliness and unrighteousness of men who suppress the truth in unrighteousness." Anyone who denies, ignores, or rebels against God has rejected the only defense that's been provided against His awesome anger. Romans 2:5 confirms, "But because of your stubbornness and unrepentant heart you are storing up wrath for yourself in the day of wrath and revelation of the righteous judgment of God."

Yet on the Cross, we see that the wrath that was due to all humanity was laid upon God's perfect Son—the only person who never sinned at all. The atoning death of Jesus Christ is where the holy wrath and the abounding love of God intersect. It's where our sin is judged according to His holiness and where we are reconciled to God so that we may live eternally in His holy presence.

Apart from Jesus Christ, we will experience the wrath of God. However, when we accept Christ as our Lord and Savior, we need never fear God's wrath again. The glorious truth is that through Christ we are forgiven and our names are written in the Lamb's Book of Life. Therefore, rejoice and proclaim to others how they can avoid God's wrath as well. ◉

---

15 so that no one would say you were baptized in my name.

16 Now I did baptize also the household of Stephanas; beyond that, I do not know whether I baptized any other.

17 For Christ did not send me to baptize, but to preach the gospel, not in cleverness of speech, so that the cross of Christ would not be made void.

18 For the word of the cross is foolishness to those who are perishing, but to us who are being saved it is the power of God.

19 For it is written,
"I WILL DESTROY THE WISDOM OF THE WISE,
AND THE CLEVERNESS OF THE CLEVER I WILL SET ASIDE."

20 Where is the wise man? Where is the scribe? Where is the debater of this age? Has not God made foolish the wisdom of the world?

21 For since in the wisdom of God the world through its wisdom did not *come to* know God, God was well-pleased through the foolishness of the message preached to save those who believe.

22 For indeed Jews ask for signs and Greeks search for wisdom;

23 but we preach Christ crucified, to Jews a stumbling block and to Gentiles foolishness,

24 but to those who are the called, both Jews and Greeks, Christ the power of God and the wisdom of God.

25 Because the foolishness of God is wiser than men, and the weakness of God is stronger than men.

26 For consider your calling, brethren, that there were not many wise according to the flesh, not many mighty, not many noble;

27 but God has chosen the foolish things of the world to shame the wise, and God has chosen the weak things of the world to shame the things which are strong,

LIFE LESSONS

➤ **1 Corinthians 1:27 — *God has chosen the weak things of the world to shame the things which are strong.***

The Lord loves to use weak, despised, and seemingly inconsequential things, people, and events to demonstrate His majesty so "that the surpassing greatness of the power will be of God and not from ourselves" (2 Cor. 4:7).

28 and the base things of the world and the despised God has chosen, the things that are not, so that He may nullify the things that are,
29 so that no man may boast before God.

30 But by His doing you are in Christ Jesus, who became to us wisdom from God, and righteousness and sanctification, and redemption,
31 so that, just as it is written, "LET HIM WHO BOASTS, BOAST IN THE LORD."

AUGUST 20

Job 31:1—32:22

> **31** "I HAVE made a covenant with my eyes;
How then could I gaze at a virgin?
2 "And what is the portion of God from above
Or the heritage of the Almighty from on high?
3 "Is it not calamity to the unjust
And disaster to those who work iniquity?
> 4 "Does He not see my ways
And number all my steps?
5 "If I have walked with falsehood,
And my foot has hastened after deceit,
6 Let Him weigh me with accurate scales,
And let God know my integrity.
7 "If my step has turned from the way,
Or my heart followed my eyes,
Or if any spot has stuck to my hands,

8 Let me sow and another eat,
And let my crops be uprooted.
9 "If my heart has been enticed by a woman,
Or I have lurked at my neighbor's doorway,
10 May my wife grind for another,
And let others kneel down over her.
11 "For that would be a lustful crime;
Moreover, it would be an iniquity *punishable by* judges.
12 "For it would be fire that consumes to Abaddon,
And would uproot all my increase.
13 "If I have despised the claim of my male or female slaves
When they filed a complaint against me,
14 What then could I do when God arises?
And when He calls me to account, what will I answer Him?
15 "Did not He who made me in the womb make him,
And the same one fashion us in the womb?
16 "If I have kept the poor from *their* desire,
Or have caused the eyes of the widow to fail,
17 Or have eaten my morsel alone,
And the orphan has not shared it
18 (But from my youth he grew up with me as with a father,
And from infancy I guided her),
19 If I have seen anyone perish for lack of clothing,
Or that the needy had no covering,
20 If his loins have not thanked me,
And if he has not been warmed with the fleece of my sheep,
21 If I have lifted up my hand against the orphan,
Because I saw I had support in the gate,

LIFE LESSONS

> **Job 31:1 — *"I have made a covenant with my eyes."***

*J*ob was committed to honoring God completely. He refused to take any step toward sin—which included not looking at anyone or anything that could cause him to stumble (James 1:14, 15).

> **Job 31:4 — *"Does He not see my ways and number all my steps?"***

*G*od does indeed see everything we do, hear everything we say, and record everywhere we go. He desires an intimate relationship with us, and His intimate knowledge of us makes that possible.

22 Let my shoulder fall from the
      socket,
    And my arm be broken off at the
      elbow.
23 "For calamity from God is a terror to
      me,
    And because of His majesty I can
      do nothing.
24 "If I have put my confidence *in* gold,
    And called fine gold my trust,
25 If I have gloated because my wealth
      was great,
    And because my hand had secured
      so much;
26 If I have looked at the sun when it
      shone
    Or the moon going in splendor,
27 And my heart became secretly
      enticed,
    And my hand threw a kiss from my
      mouth,
28 That too would have been an
      iniquity *calling for* judgment,
    For I would have denied God above.
29 "Have I rejoiced at the extinction of
      my enemy,
    Or exulted when evil befell him?
30 "No, I have not allowed my mouth to
      sin
    By asking for his life in a curse.
31 "Have the men of my tent not said,
    'Who can find one who has not been
      satisfied with his meat'?
32 "The alien has not lodged outside,
    For I have opened my doors to the
      traveler.
33 "Have I covered my transgressions
      like Adam,
    By hiding my iniquity in my bosom,
34 Because I feared the great
      multitude,
    And the contempt of families
      terrified me,
    And kept silent and did not go out
      of doors?
35 "Oh that I had one to hear me!
    Behold, here is my signature;
    Let the Almighty answer me!
    And the indictment which my
      adversary has written,
36 Surely I would carry it on my
      shoulder,
    I would bind it to myself like a
      crown.
37 "I would declare to Him the number
      of my steps;

    Like a prince I would approach
      Him.
38 "If my land cries out against me,
    And its furrows weep together;
39 If I have eaten its fruit without
      money,
    Or have caused its owners to lose
      their lives,
40 Let briars grow instead of wheat,
    And stinkweed instead of barley."
The words of Job are ended.

32 THEN these three men ceased answering Job, because he was righteous in his own eyes.
2   But the anger of Elihu the son of
Barachel the Buzite, of the family of Ram
burned; against Job his anger burned
because he justified himself before God.
3   And his anger burned against his
three friends because they had found no
answer, and yet had condemned Job.
4   Now Elihu had waited to speak to
Job because they were years older than
he.
5   And when Elihu saw that there was
no answer in the mouth of the three men
his anger burned.
6   So Elihu the son of Barachel the
Buzite spoke out and said,
    "I am young in years and you are
      old;
    Therefore I was shy and afraid to
      tell you what I think.
7   "I thought age should speak,
    And increased years should teach
      wisdom.
8   "But it is a spirit in man,
    And the breath of the Almighty
      gives them understanding.
9   "The abundant *in years* may not be
      wise,
    Nor may elders understand justice.
10 "So I say, 'Listen to me,
    I too will tell what I think.'
11 "Behold, I waited for your words,
    I listened to your reasonings,
    While you pondered what to say.
12 "I even paid close attention to you;
    Indeed, there was no one who
      refuted Job,
    Not one of you who answered his
      words.
13 "Do not say,
    'We have found wisdom;
    God will rout him, not man.'
14 "For he has not arranged *his* words
      against me,

Nor will I reply to him with your
    arguments.
15 "They are dismayed, they no longer
    answer;
    Words have failed them.
16 "Shall I wait, because they do not
    speak,
    Because they stop *and* no longer
    answer?
17 "I too will answer my share,
    I also will tell my opinion.
➤ 18 "For I am full of words;
    The spirit within me constrains
    me.
19 "Behold, my belly is like unvented
    wine,
    Like new wineskins it is about to
    burst.
20 "Let me speak that I may get relief;
    Let me open my lips and answer.
21 "Let me now be partial to no one,
    Nor flatter *any* man.
22 "For I do not know how to flatter,
    Else my Maker would soon take me
    away.

✦ Psalm 98:1–3

A Psalm.

98 O SING to the LORD a new song,
    For He has done wonderful
        things,
    His right hand and His holy arm
        have gained the victory for Him.
2   The LORD has made known His
        salvation;
    He has revealed His righteousness
        in the sight of the nations.
3   He has remembered His
        lovingkindness and His
        faithfulness to the house of
        Israel;
    All the ends of the earth have seen
        the salvation of our God.

✦ Proverbs 23:17, 18

17 Do not let your heart envy sinners,
    But *live* in the fear of the LORD
        always.
18 Surely there is a future,
    And your hope will not be cut off.

✦ 1 Corinthians 2:1–16

2 AND when I came to you, brethren,
    I did not come with superiority of
speech or of wisdom, proclaiming to you
the testimony of God.
2   For I determined to know nothing ◄
among you except Jesus Christ, and Him
crucified.
3   I was with you in weakness and in
fear and in much trembling,
4   and my message and my preaching
were not in persuasive words of wisdom,
but in demonstration of the Spirit and of
power,
5   so that your faith would not rest on ◄
the wisdom of men, but on the power of
God.

LIFE LESSONS

➤ **Job 32:18 —** *"I am full of words; the
spirit within me constrains me."*

*E*lihu had a difficult time holding his
    tongue. He thought he had much
to add, but in fact he merely restated
the foolish things already said. "When
there are many words, transgression is
unavoidable" (Prov. 10:19).

➤ **1 Corinthians 2:2 —** *I determined to
know nothing among you except Jesus
Christ, and Him crucified.*

*P*aul could have preached about a
    thousand different topics, but he
knew the Corinthians needed most to
hear about how the death of Christ
could free anyone from the power of
sin. So the apostle preached the simple,
life-changing truth of the gospel, knowing that Jesus had promised, "I, if I am
lifted up from the earth, will draw all
men to Myself" (John 12:32).

➤ **1 Corinthians 2:5 —** *Your faith would
not rest on the wisdom of men, but on
the power of God.*

*A*lthough we should organize our
    thoughts about our faith and be
able to explain it effectively to anyone
who might ask (1 Pet. 3:15), we must
remember that the power of the gospel
comes not in our careful explanations
but in the mighty resurrection of Christ
and His power to draw people to Himself (John 6:44; 12:32).

6 Yet we do speak wisdom among those who are mature; a wisdom, however, not of this age nor of the rulers of this age, who are passing away;

7 but we speak God's wisdom in a mystery, the hidden *wisdom* which God predestined before the ages to our glory;

8 *the wisdom* which none of the rulers of this age has understood; for if they had understood it they would not have crucified the Lord of glory;

9 but just as it is written,

"Things which eye has not seen and ear has not heard,
And *which* have not entered the heart of man,
All that God has prepared for those who love Him."

10 For to us God revealed *them* through the Spirit; for the Spirit searches all things, even the depths of God.

11 For who among men knows the *thoughts* of a man except the spirit of the man which is in him? Even so the *thoughts* of God no one knows except the Spirit of God.

12 Now we have received, not the spirit of the world, but the Spirit who is from God, so that we may know the things freely given to us by God,

13 which things we also speak, not in words taught by human wisdom, but in those taught by the Spirit, combining spiritual *thoughts* with spiritual *words*.

14 But a natural man does not accept

LIFE LESSONS

> **1 Corinthians 2:12 — *We have received . . . the Spirit who is from God.***

*G*od never wants us to guess about what lies ahead for us nor what we should do. In fact, if necessary, He will move heaven and earth to show us His will. He has given us His Word and Spirit to empower us and help us understand what He has planned. This is why it is absolutely essential that we remain faithful in prayer and in the study of His Word—so we can walk with Him in a daily relationship and discover the plan and the principles He wants us to live by.

ANSWERS TO LIFE'S QUESTIONS

How can I rightly comprehend God's truth?

1 CORINTHIANS 2:9, 10

*W*henever God speaks to us, *His first goal is that we may comprehend the truth.* He desires that we fully understand His meaning.

God has given His Holy Spirit to each one of us. As believers, we can have a personal relationship with the Father because the Spirit lives within us. He knows the mind of God perfectly (1 Cor. 2:10), and He communicates to our spirits the truth God wants us to hear. He wants us to grow in three primary areas:

1. *The truth about Himself.*

God wants us to fully grasp His majesty, holiness, power, love, grace, and joy. When we begin to comprehend these mighty truths about the person of God, we find our lives enriched, enabled, and energized. Paul wrote that his ultimate aim in life was to know Christ (Phil. 3:10).

2. *The truth about ourselves.*

God wants us to realize our part in His eternal plan. But most of all, He wants us to know

our position in Christ. Since we are one with Him, all of His divine privileges become ours. His righteousness is ours because He abides in us. We can appropriate His wisdom and sanctification because we belong to Him. Our names are written in the Lamb's Book of Life, and this ensures our eternal status as God's children.

3. *The truth about other people.*

God wants us to view people as His chosen instruments and His creations. Some years ago, the Father began sifting me, sanding me, and pruning me—until I thought nothing would be left. A friend walked with me through this deep valley. Sometimes, my words may have seemed harsh, but he never reacted. He would just say, "I understand. What can I do to help?" He never rejected me or showed disappointment; he never angrily admonished me. When I poured out my feelings to him, he just loved me. He wept with me, prayed with me, laughed with me, and patiently listened to me. Through his unwavering love, we developed an unbreakable bond of deep friendship that strengthened my own intimacy with God.

When we begin to understand the truth of who God is and gain a better understanding of ourselves as well as others, we become thoroughly equipped to be fruitful, productive servants on earth.

the things of the Spirit of God, for they are foolishness to him; and he cannot understand them, because they are spiritually appraised.

15 But he who is spiritual appraises all things, yet he himself is appraised by no one.

16 For WHO HAS KNOWN THE MIND OF THE LORD, THAT HE WILL INSTRUCT HIM? But we have the mind of Christ.

AUGUST 21

Job 33:1—34:37

33 "HOWEVER now, Job, please hear my speech,
And listen to all my words.

2 "Behold now, I open my mouth,
My tongue in my mouth speaks.

3 "My words are *from* the uprightness of my heart,
And my lips speak knowledge sincerely.

4 "The Spirit of God has made me,
And the breath of the Almighty gives me life.

5 "Refute me if you can;
Array yourselves before me, take your stand.

6 "Behold, I belong to God like you;
I too have been formed out of the clay.

7 "Behold, no fear of me should terrify you,
Nor should my pressure weigh heavily on you.

8 "Surely you have spoken in my hearing,
And I have heard the sound of *your* words:

9 'I am pure, without transgression;
I am innocent and there is no guilt in me.

10 'Behold, He invents pretexts against me;
He counts me as His enemy.

11 'He puts my feet in the stocks;
He watches all my paths.'

12 "Behold, let me tell you, you are not right in this,
For God is greater than man.

13 "Why do you complain against Him That He does not give an account of all His doings?

14 "Indeed God speaks once,
Or twice, *yet* no one notices it.

15 "In a dream, a vision of the night,
When sound sleep falls on men,
While they slumber in their beds,

16 Then He opens the ears of men,
And seals their instruction,

17 That He may turn man aside *from his* conduct,
And keep man from pride;

18 He keeps back his soul from the pit,
And his life from passing over into Sheol.

19 "Man is also chastened with pain on his bed,
And with unceasing complaint in his bones;

20 So that his life loathes bread,
And his soul favorite food.

21 "His flesh wastes away from sight,
And his bones which were not seen stick out.

22 "Then his soul draws near to the pit,
And his life to those who bring death.

23 "If there is an angel *as* mediator for him,
One out of a thousand,
To remind a man what is right for him,

24 Then let him be gracious to him, and say,
'Deliver him from going down to the pit,
I have found a ransom';

25 Let his flesh become fresher than in youth,

LIFE LESSONS

➤ **Job 33:14 —** *"Indeed God speaks once, or twice, yet no one notices it."*

*G*od desires to speak to us in any number of ways—some of them quite surprising—so we must always keep our ears open and our spirits ready to listen for His voice.

Let him return to the days of his
youthful vigor;

26 Then he will pray to God, and He
will accept him,
That he may see His face with joy,
And He may restore His
righteousness to man.

27 "He will sing to men and say,
'I have sinned and perverted what is
right,
And it is not proper for me.

28 'He has redeemed my soul from
going to the pit,
And my life shall see the light.'

29 "Behold, God does all these
oftentimes with men,

30 To bring back his soul from the pit,
That he may be enlightened with
the light of life.

31 "Pay attention, O Job, listen to me;
Keep silent, and let me speak.

32 "*Then* if you have anything to say,
answer me;
Speak, for I desire to justify you.

33 "If not, listen to me;
Keep silent, and I will teach you
wisdom."

34

THEN Elihu continued and said,
2 "Hear my words, you wise men,
And listen to me, you who know.

3 "For the ear tests words
As the palate tastes food.

4 "Let us choose for ourselves what is
right;
Let us know among ourselves what
is good.

5 "For Job has said, 'I am righteous,
But God has taken away my right;

6 Should I lie concerning my right?
My wound is incurable, *though I am*
without transgression.'

7 "What man is like Job,
Who drinks up derision like water,

8 Who goes in company with the
workers of iniquity,
And walks with wicked men?

9 "For he has said, 'It profits a man
nothing
When he is pleased with God.'

10 "Therefore, listen to me, you men of
understanding.
Far be it from God to do
wickedness,
And from the Almighty to do wrong.

11 "For He pays a man according to his
work,

And makes him find it according to
his way.

12 "Surely, God will not act wickedly,   ◄
And the Almighty will not pervert
justice.

13 "Who gave Him authority over the
earth?
And who has laid *on Him* the whole
world?

14 "If He should determine to do so,
If He should gather to Himself His
spirit and His breath,

15 All flesh would perish together,
And man would return to dust.

16 "But if *you have* understanding, hear
this;
Listen to the sound of my words.

17 "Shall one who hates justice rule?
And will you condemn the righteous
mighty One,

18 Who says to a king, 'Worthless
one,'
To nobles, 'Wicked ones';

19 Who shows no partiality to princes
Nor regards the rich above the
poor,
For they all are the work of His
hands?

20 "In a moment they die, and at
midnight
People are shaken and pass away,
And the mighty are taken away
without a hand.

21 "For His eyes are upon the ways of a
man,
And He sees all his steps.

22 "There is no darkness or deep
shadow
Where the workers of iniquity may
hide themselves.

23 "For He does not *need to* consider a
man further,
That he should go before God in
judgment.

LIFE LESSONS

➤ **Job 34:12** — *"Surely, God will not act
wickedly, and the Almighty will not pervert justice."*

*W*e may not understand why God
allows bad things to happen to
godly people, but we never have to
wonder about His character. He will
always do what is right. This truth will
never change.

24 "He breaks in pieces mighty men
     without inquiry,
    And sets others in their place.
25 "Therefore He knows their works,
    And He overthrows *them* in the
    night,
    And they are crushed.
26 "He strikes them like the wicked
    In a public place,
27 Because they turned aside from
    following Him,
    And had no regard for any of His
    ways;
28 So that they caused the cry of the
    poor to come to Him,
    And that He might hear the cry of
    the afflicted—
29 When He keeps quiet, who then can
    condemn?
    And when He hides His face, who
    then can behold Him,
    That is, in regard to both nation and
    man?—
30 So that godless men would not rule
    Nor be snares of the people.
31 "For has anyone said to God,
    'I have borne *chastisement*;
    I will not offend *anymore*;
32 Teach me what I do not see;
    If I have done iniquity,
    I will not do it again'?
33 "Shall He recompense on your terms,
    because you have rejected *it*?
    For you must choose, and not I;
    Therefore declare what you know.
34 "Men of understanding will say to
    me,
    And a wise man who hears me,
35 'Job speaks without knowledge,
    And his words are without wisdom.
36 'Job ought to be tried to the limit,
    Because he answers like wicked men.
37 'For he adds rebellion to his sin;
    He claps his hands among us,
    And multiplies his words against
    God.'"

Psalm 98:4–9

4 Shout joyfully to the LORD, all the
    earth;
    Break forth and sing for joy and
    sing praises.
5 Sing praises to the LORD with the
    lyre,
    With the lyre and the sound of
    melody.
6 With trumpets and the sound of the
    horn
    Shout joyfully before the King, the
    LORD.
7 Let the sea roar and all it contains,
    The world and those who dwell
    in it.
8 Let the rivers clap their hands,
    Let the mountains sing together for
    joy
9 Before the LORD, for He is coming
    to judge the earth;
    He will judge the world with
    righteousness
    And the peoples with equity.

Proverbs 23:19–21

19 Listen, my son, and be wise,
    And direct your heart in the way.
20 Do not be with heavy drinkers of
    wine,
    Or with gluttonous eaters of meat;
21 For the heavy drinker and the
    glutton will come to poverty,
    And drowsiness will clothe *one* with
    rags.

1 Corinthians 3:1–23

3 AND I, brethren, could not speak to
you as to spiritual men, but as to men
of flesh, as to infants in Christ.
2 I gave you milk to drink, not solid
food; for you were not yet able *to receive*
it. Indeed, even now you are not yet able,

LIFE LESSONS

➤ **Psalm 98:9 —** *He will judge the world*
with righteousness.

W hen He returns, Jesus will fulfill this
verse and bring justice to our troubled world. Peter affirmed, "He ordered
us to preach to the people, and solemnly
to testify that this is the One who has
been appointed by God as Judge of the
living and the dead. . . . Everyone who
believes in Him receives forgiveness of
sins" (Acts 10:42, 43).

WHAT THE BIBLE SAYS ABOUT ◈

How God Judges and Rewards Our Work

1 Corinthians 3:6–15

Though we consider the apostle Paul to be the greatest missionary in history, he received more lashes and stones than honorary banquets, and he spent more time in jail than in mansions. How did he continue under such duress? He looked ahead to God's reward: "In the future there is laid up for me the crown of righteousness, which the Lord, the righteous Judge, will award to me on that day" (2 Tim. 4:8).

Why would Moses leave the luxury of Pharaoh's palace for the harshness of the desert? It was because he considered the "reproach of Christ greater riches than the treasures of Egypt; for he was looking to the reward" (Heb. 11:26). Serving God yielded Moses a vast storehouse of heavenly reward, even though it meant a lifetime of struggle.

Every act, word, and thought will be credited by Christ: "Each will receive his own reward according to his own labor" (1 Cor. 3:8). If we seek to glorify God with a diligent and humble spirit, our laurels will multiply. If we seek merely to please others and reap their praise, then our rewards will shrink.

Rewards are not limited to the hereafter. Whenever we follow the principles of Scripture, we enjoy the blessings of obedience: "The one who fears the commandment will be rewarded" (Prov. 13:13).

When Peter reminded Jesus that he had left everything behind to follow the Messiah, Christ responded, "There is no one who has left house or wife or brothers or parents or children, for the sake of the kingdom of God, who will not receive many times as much at this time and in the age to come, eternal life" (Luke 18:29, 30).

When one knows and serves God, every product of his or her life will be rewarded, either in this life or in heaven. The Father watches over all our ways, and He has promised to perfectly reward us. All those who serve "the Lord Christ" (Col. 3:24) will be rewarded on the day of judgment of believers. The Christian who seeks to please God lays up treasures that can never be devalued or depleted. ◈

➤ 3 for you are still fleshly. For since there is jealousy and strife among you, are you not fleshly, and are you not walking like mere men? 4 For when one says, "I am of Paul," and another, "I am of Apollos," are you not *mere* men? 5 What then is Apollos? And what is Paul? Servants through whom you believed, even as the Lord gave *opportunity* to each one. 6 I planted, Apollos watered, but God was causing the growth.

LIFE LESSONS

➤ **1 Corinthians 3:3 — *Are you not fleshly, and are you not walking like mere men?***

No Christian should ever give the excuse, "I'm only human," when he or she succumbs to some temptation. Only carnal Christians could give such an excuse, for the Spirit gives us the ability to do what "mere men" cannot.

7 So then neither the one who plants nor the one who waters is anything, but God who causes the growth. 8 Now he who plants and he who waters are one; but each will receive his own reward according to his own labor. 9 For we are God's fellow workers; you are God's field, God's building. 10 According to the grace of God which was given to me, like a wise master builder I laid a foundation, and another ✳ is building on it. But each man must be careful how he builds on it. 11 For no man can lay a foundation other than the one which is laid, which is Jesus Christ. 12 Now if any man builds on the foundation with gold, silver, precious stones, wood, hay, straw, 13 each man's work will become evident; ◄ for the day will show it because it is *to be* revealed with fire, and the fire itself will test the quality of each man's work. 14 If any man's work which he has built on it remains, he will receive a reward.

LIFE LESSONS

> ➤ **1 Corinthians 3:13 — *It is to be revealed with fire.***

*H*ere, Paul speaks about the judgment believers will face—not concerning salvation, but of the quality of our service to Christ. This was a warning to those whose only purpose was to achieve power and prominence in the church. When we stand before the Lord, it will become absolutely clear what we accomplished for Him through the Spirit and what we did in our own power. God knows our motives, and no one will be able to oppose or resist His judgment.

> ➤ **1 Corinthians 3:15 — *If any man's work is burned up, he will suffer loss; but he himself will be saved, yet so as through fire.***

*E*very believer in Christ already has eternal life; that question was settled forever at the Cross. But rewards for service are another matter entirely. Some will receive many; others will get none—all according to the truth we understood, the opportunities we used to share the truth, and how we responded in obedience to Him.

15 If any man's work is burned up, he will suffer loss; but he himself will be saved, yet so as through fire. ⎠

16 Do you not know that you are a temple of God and *that* the Spirit of God dwells in you?

17 If any man destroys the temple of God, God will destroy him, for the temple of God is holy, and that is what you are.

18 Let no man deceive himself. If any man among you thinks that he is wise in this age, he must become foolish, so that he may become wise.

19 For the wisdom of this world is foolishness before God. For it is written, "*He is* THE ONE WHO CATCHES THE WISE IN THEIR CRAFTINESS";

20 and again, "THE LORD KNOWS THE REASONINGS of the wise, THAT THEY ARE USELESS."

21 So then let no one boast in men. For all things belong to you,

22 whether Paul or Apollos or Cephas or the world or life or death or things present or things to come; all things belong to you,

23 and you belong to Christ; and Christ belongs to God.

  Job 35:1—36:33

35 THEN Elihu continued and said,
2 "Do you think this is according to justice?
Do you say, 'My righteousness is more than God's'?

3 "For you say, 'What advantage will it be to You?
What profit will I have, more than if I had sinned?'

4 "I will answer you,
And your friends with you.

5 "Look at the heavens and see;
And behold the clouds—they are higher than you.

6 "If you have sinned, what do you accomplish against Him?
And if your transgressions are many, what do you do to Him?

7 "If you are righteous, what do you give to Him,
Or what does He receive from your hand?

8 "Your wickedness is for a man like yourself,
And your righteousness is for a son of man.

9 "Because of the multitude of oppressions they cry out;
They cry for help because of the arm of the mighty.

10 "But no one says, 'Where is God my Maker,
Who gives songs in the night,

11 Who teaches us more than the beasts of the earth
And makes us wiser than the birds of the heavens?'

12 "There they cry out, but He does not answer
Because of the pride of evil men.

13 "Surely God will not listen to an
empty *cry*,
Nor will the Almighty regard it.

14 "How much less when you say you
do not behold Him,
The case is before Him, and you
must wait for Him!

15 "And now, because He has not
visited *in* His anger,
Nor has He acknowledged
transgression well,

16 So Job opens his mouth emptily;
He multiplies words without
knowledge."

36 THEN Elihu continued and said,
2 "Wait for me a little, and I will
show you
That there is yet more to be said in
God's behalf.

3 "I will fetch my knowledge from
afar,
And I will ascribe righteousness to
my Maker.

4 "For truly my words are not false;
One who is perfect in knowledge is
with you.

5 "Behold, God is mighty but does not
despise *any*;
He is mighty in strength of
understanding.

6 "He does not keep the wicked alive,
But gives justice to the afflicted.

7 "He does not withdraw His eyes from
the righteous;
But with kings on the throne
He has seated them forever, and
they are exalted.

8 "And if they are bound in fetters,
And are caught in the cords of
affliction,

9 Then He declares to them their
work
And their transgressions, that they
have magnified themselves.

10 "He opens their ear to instruction,
And commands that they return
from evil.

11 "If they hear and serve *Him*,
They will end their days in
prosperity
And their years in pleasures.

12 "But if they do not hear, they shall
perish by the sword
And they will die without
knowledge.

13 "But the godless in heart lay up
anger;

They do not cry for help when He
binds them.

14 "They die in youth,
And their life *perishes* among the
cult prostitutes.

15 "He delivers the afflicted in their   ≺
affliction,
And opens their ear in *time of*
oppression.

16 "Then indeed, He enticed you from
the mouth of distress,
Instead of it, a broad place with no
constraint;
And that which was set on your
table was full of fatness.

17 "But you were full of judgment on
the wicked;
Judgment and justice take hold *of
you*.

18 "*Beware* that wrath does not entice
you to scoffing;
And do not let the greatness of the
ransom turn you aside.

19 "Will your riches keep you from
distress,
Or all the forces of *your* strength?

20 "Do not long for the night,
When people vanish in their place.

21 "Be careful, do not turn to evil,
For you have preferred this to
affliction.

22 "Behold, God is exalted in His power;
Who is a teacher like Him?

23 "Who has appointed Him His way,
And who has said, 'You have done
wrong'?

24 "Remember that you should exalt
His work,
Of which men have sung.

25 "All men have seen it;
Man beholds from afar.

26 "Behold, God is exalted, and we do
not know *Him*;
The number of His years is
unsearchable.

LIFE LESSONS

≻ **Job 36:15** — *"He delivers the afflicted
in their affliction, and opens their ear in
time of oppression."*

*G*od wants to use our afflictions, and
the way He delivers us from them, to
lead us into a deeper and richer relationship with Him. We should treat adversity
as a bridge to a closer walk with God.

27 "For He draws up the drops of water,
    They distill rain from the mist,
28 Which the clouds pour down,
    They drip upon man abundantly.
29 "Can anyone understand the
    spreading of the clouds,
    The thundering of His pavilion?
30 "Behold, He spreads His lightning
    about Him,
    And He covers the depths of the
    sea.
31 "For by these He judges peoples;
    He gives food in abundance.
32 "He covers *His* hands with the
    lightning,
    And commands it to strike the
    mark.
33 "Its noise declares His presence;
    The cattle also, concerning what is
    coming up.

◈ Psalm 99:1–9

99 THE LORD reigns, let the peoples
    tremble;
    He is enthroned *above* the
    cherubim, let the earth shake!
2 The LORD is great in Zion,
    And He is exalted above all the
    peoples.
3 Let them praise Your great and
    awesome name;
    Holy is He.
4 The strength of the King loves
    justice;
    You have established equity;
    You have executed justice and
    righteousness in Jacob.
5 Exalt the LORD our God
    And worship at His footstool;
    Holy is He.
6 Moses and Aaron were among His
    priests,
    And Samuel was among those who
    called on His name;
    They called upon the LORD and He
    answered them.
7 He spoke to them in the pillar of
    cloud;
    They kept His testimonies
    And the statute that He gave
    them.
8 O LORD our God, You answered
    them;
    You were a forgiving God to them,

And *yet* an avenger of their *evil*
    deeds.
9 Exalt the LORD our God
    And worship at His holy hill,
    For holy is the LORD our God.

◈ Proverbs 23:22–25

22 Listen to your father who begot
    you,
    And do not despise your mother
    when she is old.
23 Buy truth, and do not sell *it*,
    Get wisdom and instruction and
    understanding.
24 The father of the righteous will
    greatly rejoice,
    And he who sires a wise son will be
    glad in him.
25 Let your father and your mother be
    glad,
    And let her rejoice who gave birth
    to you.

◈ 1 Corinthians 4:1–21

4 LET a man regard us in this manner,
    as servants of Christ and stewards of
the mysteries of God.
2   In this case, moreover, it is required

LIFE LESSONS

➤ **Psalm 99:1 —** *The Lord reigns, let the*
peoples tremble.

*W*hy should we tremble when we
    ponder God's sovereignty? Why
should our hearts be moved when we
consider His presence? Because He is
"the King of kings and Lord of lords,
who alone possesses immortality "
(1 Tim. 6:15, 16).

➤ **Psalm 99:8 —** *You were a forgiving*
God to them, and yet an avenger of their
evil deeds.

*G*od's forgiveness is not incompatible
    with or opposed to His discipline.
When we place our faith in Christ, He
forgives our sins—past, present, and
future—but He still promises to discipline us when necessary (Heb. 12:4–11).

of stewards that one be found trustworthy.

3   But to me it is a very small thing that I may be examined by you, or by *any* human court; in fact, I do not even examine myself.

4   For I am conscious of nothing against myself, yet I am not by this acquitted; but the one who examines me is the Lord.

5   Therefore do not go on passing judgment before the time, *but wait* until the Lord comes who will both bring to light the things hidden in the darkness and disclose the motives of *men's* hearts; and then each man's praise will come to him from God.

6   Now these things, brethren, I have figuratively applied to myself and Apollos for your sakes, so that in us you may learn not to exceed what is written, so that no one of you will become arrogant in behalf of one against the other.

7   For who regards you as superior? What do you have that you did not receive? And if you did receive it, why do you boast as if you had not received it?

8   You are already filled, you have already become rich, you have become kings without us; and indeed, *I* wish that you had become kings so that we also might reign with you.

9   For, I think, God has exhibited us apostles last of all, as men condemned to death; because we have become a spectacle to the world, both to angels and to men.

10   We are fools for Christ's sake, but you are prudent in Christ; we are weak, but you are strong; you are distinguished, but we are without honor.

11   To this present hour we are both hungry and thirsty, and are poorly clothed, and are roughly treated, and are homeless;

12   and we toil, working with our own hands; when we are reviled, we bless; when we are persecuted, we endure;

13   when we are slandered, we try to conciliate; we have become as the scum of the world, the dregs of all things, *even* until now.

14   I do not write these things to shame you, but to admonish you as my beloved children.

15   For if you were to have countless

➤ **1 Corinthians 4:5 —** *Therefore do not go on passing judgment before the time, but wait until the Lord comes.*

*N*one of us are in a position to assess the motivations of the human heart—especially when it comes to another's service to the Lord. While the Bible does instruct us to react in a certain way to sinful behavior (1 Cor. 5:2), we are not to judge another's intentions. Often our opinion of their actions has more to do with our own failings than theirs (Luke 6:36-49).

➤ **1 Corinthians 4:7 —** *What do you have that you did not receive?*

*I*n an ultimate sense, human arrogance makes very little sense because we never accomplish *anything* except by using the gifts, talents, energies, inspirations—and even breaths—that God gives to us.

➤ **1 Corinthians 4:14 —** *I do not write these things to shame you, but to admonish you as my beloved children.*

*P*aul learned such a loving attitude from Christ Himself. The Lord does not correct us in order to humiliate us but because He loves us and wants to spare us the pain that our sinful actions always bring.

---

tutors in Christ, yet *you would* not *have* many fathers, for in Christ Jesus I became your father through the gospel.

16   Therefore I exhort you, be imitators of me.

17   For this reason I have sent to you Timothy, who is my beloved and faithful child in the Lord, and he will remind you of my ways which are in Christ, just as I teach everywhere in every church.

18   Now some have become arrogant, as though I were not coming to you.

19   But I will come to you soon, if the Lord wills, and I shall find out, not the words of those who are arrogant but their power.

20   For the kingdom of God does not consist in words but in power.

21   What do you desire? Shall I come to you with a rod, or with love and a spirit of gentleness?

Life Examples:

TIMOTHY: A Man Who Honored God

1 CORINTHIANS 4:17

Timothy, born half Greek and half Jew, probably accepted Christ in his hometown of Lystra during Paul's first missionary journey. The apostle learned of Timothy's growth in his walk with Christ and made the young man his aide during his second missionary journey.

The name Timothy means "one who honors God," and Paul entrusted him with the toughest of assignments in Ephesus, Corinth, Macedonia, and Thessalonica. As an adult, Timothy, in an ultimate display of his commitment to Christ, submitted to the painful procedure of circumcision to accommodate Paul's preaching to Jews (Acts 16:3). The writer of Hebrews reports that at some point Timothy also was imprisoned (Heb. 13:23).

Scripture reveals that at times, Timothy was timid, probably earlier in life. But he devoted himself to the Lord, and spent his young adult years traversing the world so that he could preach the gospel. He continues to inspire us toward courage and boldness, even when we feel we naturally lack these qualities.

Job 37:1—38:41

37 "AT this also my heart trembles,
And leaps from its place.

2 "Listen closely to the thunder of His
voice,
And the rumbling that goes out
from His mouth.

3 "Under the whole heaven He lets it
loose,
And His lightning to the ends of the
earth.

4 "After it, a voice roars;
He thunders with His majestic
voice,
And He does not restrain the
lightnings when His voice is
heard.

5 "God thunders with His voice
wondrously,
Doing great things which we cannot
comprehend.

6 "For to the snow He says, 'Fall on the
earth,'
And to the downpour and the rain,
'Be strong.'

7 "He seals the hand of every man,
That all men may know His work.

8 "Then the beast goes into its lair
And remains in its den.

9 "Out of the south comes the storm,
And out of the north the cold.

10 "From the breath of God ice is
made,

And the expanse of the waters is
frozen.

11 "Also with moisture He loads the
thick cloud;
He disperses the cloud of His
lightning.

12 "It changes direction, turning around
by His guidance,
That it may do whatever He
commands it
On the face of the inhabited
earth.

13 "Whether for correction, or for His
world,
Or for lovingkindness, He causes it
to happen.

14 "Listen to this, O Job,
Stand and consider the wonders of
God.

15 "Do you know how God establishes
them,
And makes the lightning of His
cloud to shine?

16 "Do you know about the layers of the
thick clouds,
The wonders of one perfect in
knowledge,

17 You whose garments are hot,
When the land is still because of the
south wind?

18 "Can you, with Him, spread out the
skies,
Strong as a molten mirror?

19 "Teach us what we shall say to Him;
We cannot arrange *our case*
because of darkness.

20 "Shall it be told Him that I would
speak?
Or should a man say that he would
be swallowed up?

21 "Now men do not see the light which
is bright in the skies;
But the wind has passed and cleared
them.

22 "Out of the north comes golden
splendor;
Around God is awesome majesty.

23 "The Almighty—we cannot find Him;
He is exalted in power
And He will not do violence
to justice and abundant
righteousness.

24 "Therefore men fear Him;
He does not regard any who are
wise of heart."

38 THEN the LORD answered Job out
of the whirlwind and said,

2 "Who is this that darkens counsel
By words without knowledge?

3 "Now gird up your loins like a man,
And I will ask you, and you instruct
Me!

4 "Where were you when I laid the
foundation of the earth?
Tell *Me*, if you have understanding,

5 Who set its measurements? Since
you know.
Or who stretched the line on it?

6 "On what were its bases sunk?
Or who laid its cornerstone,

7 When the morning stars sang
together
And all the sons of God shouted for
joy?

LIFE LESSONS

> **Job 38:1** — *Then the LORD answered
Job out of the whirlwind.*

*G*od speaks to His people through
His Word, through other believers,
in circumstances, in dreams, in visions,
by angels, out of whirlwinds, and even
through donkeys. Are we listening?

> **Job 38:4** — *"Where were you when I
laid the foundations of the earth?"*

*I*t is good to remind ourselves that
the Lord is God and we are not. He
is the Creator; we are the created. He is
the Original; we are the image. He is our
Friend, but not our peer.

---

8 "Or *who* enclosed the sea with
doors
When, bursting forth, it went out
from the womb;

9 When I made a cloud its garment
And thick darkness its swaddling
band,

10 And I placed boundaries on it
And set a bolt and doors,

11 And I said, 'Thus far you shall
come, but no farther;
And here shall your proud waves
stop'?

12 "Have you ever in your life
commanded the morning,
And caused the dawn to know its
place,

13 That it might take hold of the ends
of the earth,
And the wicked be shaken out of it?

14 "It is changed like clay *under* the
seal;
And they stand forth like a garment.

15 "From the wicked their light is
withheld,
And the uplifted arm is broken.

16 "Have you entered into the springs of
the sea
Or walked in the recesses of the
deep?

17 "Have the gates of death been
revealed to you,
Or have you seen the gates of deep
darkness?

18 "Have you understood the expanse
of the earth?
Tell *Me*, if you know all this.

19 "Where is the way to the dwelling of
light?
And darkness, where is its place,

20 That you may take it to its territory
And that you may discern the paths
to its home?

21 "You know, for you were born then,
And the number of your days is
great!

22 "Have you entered the storehouses of
the snow,
Or have you seen the storehouses of
the hail,

23 Which I have reserved for the time
of distress,
For the day of war and battle?

24 "Where is the way that the light is
divided,
Or the east wind scattered on the
earth?

25 "Who has cleft a channel for the
     flood,
    Or a way for the thunderbolt,
26 To bring rain on a land without
     people,
    On a desert without a man in it,
27 To satisfy the waste and desolate
     land
    And to make the seeds of grass to
     sprout?
28 "Has the rain a father?
    Or who has begotten the drops of
     dew?
29 "From whose womb has come the
     ice?
    And the frost of heaven, who has
     given it birth?
30 "Water becomes hard like stone,
    And the surface of the deep is
     imprisoned.
31 "Can you bind the chains of the
     Pleiades,
    Or loose the cords of Orion?
32 "Can you lead forth a constellation in
     its season,
    And guide the Bear with her
     satellites?
33 "Do you know the ordinances of the
     heavens,
    Or fix their rule over the earth?
34 "Can you lift up your voice to the
     clouds,
    So that an abundance of water will
     cover you?
35 "Can you send forth lightnings that
     they may go
    And say to you, 'Here we are'?
36 "Who has put wisdom in the
     innermost being
    Or given understanding to the
     mind?
37 "Who can count the clouds by
     wisdom,
    Or tip the water jars of the
     heavens,
38 When the dust hardens into a mass
    And the clods stick together?
39 "Can you hunt the prey for the
     lion,
    Or satisfy the appetite of the young
     lions,
40 When they crouch in *their* dens
    And lie in wait in *their* lair?
41 "Who prepares for the raven its
     nourishment
    When its young cry to God
    And wander about without food?

Psalm 100:1–5

A Psalm for Thanksgiving.

100 SHOUT joyfully to the LORD, all
     the earth.
2   Serve the LORD with gladness;
    Come before Him with joyful
     singing.
3   Know that the LORD Himself is God;
    It is He who has made us, and not
     we ourselves;
    We are His people and the sheep of
     His pasture.
4   Enter His gates with thanksgiving
    And His courts with praise.
    Give thanks to Him, bless His
     name.
5   For the LORD is good;
    His lovingkindness is everlasting
    And His faithfulness to all
     generations.

Proverbs 23:26–28

26   Give me your heart, my son,
    And let your eyes delight in my
     ways.
27   For a harlot is a deep pit
    And an adulterous woman is a
     narrow well.
28   Surely she lurks as a robber,
    And increases the faithless among
     men.

1 Corinthians 5:1–13

5 IT is actually reported that there is
immorality among you, and immorality of such a kind as does not exist even

LIFE LESSONS

➤ **Psalm 100:3 — *We are His people.***

*G*od is the Shepherd; we are His flock.
He is our Father; we are His children.
He is the Creator; we were formed by His
hand. When we remember these basic
truths, we will honor Him and will have
more motivation and confidence for
whatever situation comes along.

ANSWERS TO LIFE'S QUESTIONS

What happens when we praise God?

PSALM 100:1–5

*P*erhaps no book exemplifies the spirit of praise and worship more than the Book of Psalms. It records more verses of praise than any other book of the Bible. Obviously, God wants the praises of His people.

The Father tells us to give Him thanks in everything (1 Thess. 5:18), even when things press against our souls. We may not understand what is happening; we may never understand. But His will in each circumstance is that we praise and thank Him.

But why? It is because praise is the clearest and most direct means by which you declare your dependence on God. It repeats your trust in Him in the midst of darkness. It confesses your allegiance and devotion to the One who was crucified for you and to whom you are eternally joined.

Consider a few of the specific benefits we derive from praising the Lord:

Praise magnifies God: Praise puts our focus on God, not on our problems. His power, presence, and ability transform our thinking.

Praise humbles us: When we worship God, we gain a right view of ourselves. Praise deflates excess pride and ego. We gain a healthy self-image, based on His view of us. By removing pride, praise strengthens us against temptation.

Praise reveals our devotion to God: If I love Christ, I will praise Him. If He has first place in my life, I will honor Him with worship and thanksgiving.

Praise motivates us to holy living: Praise opens our hearts to want to live the way God desires—holy and separated unto Him, to do His will above our own, to want to be like Him more than like anyone else. The more we worship Him, the more like Him we will become.

Praise increases our joy: Joy is the constant companion of praise. If we feel depressed or discouraged, praising God will soon bring us joy.

Praise establishes our faith: The greater we see our God, the smaller we see our problems.

Praise elevates our emotions: Worry, fear, and doubt cannot survive for long in an atmosphere of praise.

If you want to see a difference in your relationship with Christ and in your walk with Him, start to praise Him today. Continue, even when you feel like giving up. Commit yourself to a life of praise and fellowship with Jesus—and experience the fullness of what God means by "joy."

---

among the Gentiles, that someone has his father's wife.

➤ 2 You have become arrogant and have not mourned instead, so that the one who had done this deed would be removed from your midst.

3 For I, on my part, though absent in body but present in spirit, have already judged him who has so committed this, as though I were present.

4 In the name of our Lord Jesus, when you are assembled, and I with you in spirit, with the power of our Lord Jesus,

➤ 5 *I have decided* to deliver such a one to Satan for the destruction of his flesh, so that his spirit may be saved in the day of the Lord Jesus.

6 Your boasting is not good. Do you not know that a little leaven leavens the whole lump *of dough*?

✳ 7 Clean out the old leaven so that you may be a new lump, just as you are *in fact* unleavened. For Christ our Passover also has been sacrificed.

8 Therefore let us celebrate the feast, not with old leaven, nor with the leaven

---

LIFE LESSONS

➤ **1 Corinthians 5:2 — *You have become arrogant and have not mourned instead.***

*A*pparently, the Corinthians felt proud that they could tolerate such a shocking sin. Perhaps they congratulated themselves that their love could overlook the kind of behavior that ordinarily brought condemnation. However, their tolerance was allowing the church to remain defiled.

➤ **1 Corinthians 5:5 — *Deliver such a one to Satan for the destruction of his flesh, so that his spirit may be saved in the day of the Lord Jesus.***

*B*latant and persistent sin on the part of believers can have serious consequences, not only for those in the church, but also for those who do not believe in Christ. If His followers are no different from the world, why should they believe in Him? Many times, we must allow people to bear the full ramifications of their actions without interfering in the hope that they will repent of their sin and turn to God.

of malice and wickedness, but with the unleavened bread of sincerity and truth.

9 I wrote you in my letter not to associate with immoral people;

10 I *did* not at all *mean* with the immoral people of this world, or with the covetous and swindlers, or with idolaters, for then you would have to go out of the world.

➤ 11 But actually, I wrote to you not to associate with any so-called brother if he is an immoral person, or covetous, or an idolater, or a reviler, or a drunkard, or a swindler—not even to eat with such a one.

12 For what have I to do with judging

LIFE LESSONS

➤ **1 Corinthians 5:11 — *Not even to eat with such a one.***

This kind of church discipline does not sound either loving or kind to many today, but it is much less loving and kind to tolerate a sin that can lead to serious personal and corporate injury.

outsiders? Do you not judge those who are within *the church*?

13 But those who are outside, God judges. REMOVE THE WICKED MAN FROM AMONG YOURSELVES.

AUGUST 24

✦ Job 39:1—40:24

39 "DO you know the time the mountain goats give birth?
Do you observe the calving of the deer?

2 "Can you count the months they fulfill,
Or do you know the time they give birth?

3 "They kneel down, they bring forth their young,
They get rid of their labor pains.

4 "Their offspring become strong, they grow up in the open field;
They leave and do not return to them.

5 "Who sent out the wild donkey free?
And who loosed the bonds of the swift donkey,

6 To whom I gave the wilderness for a home
And the salt land for his dwelling place?

7 "He scorns the tumult of the city,
The shoutings of the driver he does not hear.

8 "He explores the mountains for his pasture
And searches after every green thing.

9 "Will the wild ox consent to serve you,

Or will he spend the night at your manger?

10 "Can you bind the wild ox in a furrow with ropes,
Or will he harrow the valleys after you?

11 "Will you trust him because his strength is great
And leave your labor to him?

12 "Will you have faith in him that he will return your grain
And gather *it from* your threshing floor?

13 "The ostriches' wings flap joyously
With the pinion and plumage of love,

14 For she abandons her eggs to the earth
And warms them in the dust,

15 And she forgets that a foot may crush them,
Or that a wild beast may trample them.

16 "She treats her young cruelly, as if *they* were not hers;
Though her labor be in vain, *she* is unconcerned;

17 Because God has made her forget wisdom,
And has not given her a share of understanding.

18 "When she lifts herself on high,
She laughs at the horse and his rider.

19 "Do you give the horse *his* might?

Do you clothe his neck with a mane?

20 "Do you make him leap like the locust?
His majestic snorting is terrible.

21 "He paws in the valley, and rejoices in *his* strength;
He goes out to meet the weapons.

22 "He laughs at fear and is not dismayed;
And he does not turn back from the sword.

23 "The quiver rattles against him,
The flashing spear and javelin.

24 "With shaking and rage he races over the ground,
And he does not stand still at the voice of the trumpet.

25 "As often as the trumpet *sounds* he says, 'Aha!'
And he scents the battle from afar,
And the thunder of the captains and the war cry.

26 "Is it by your understanding that the hawk soars,
Stretching his wings toward the south?

27 "Is it at your command that the eagle mounts up
And makes his nest on high?

28 "On the cliff he dwells and lodges,
Upon the rocky crag, an inaccessible place.

29 "From there he spies out food;
His eyes see *it* from afar.

30 "His young ones also suck up blood;
And where the slain are, there is he."

40 THEN the LORD said to Job,
2 "Will the faultfinder contend with the Almighty?
Let him who reproves God answer it."

3 Then Job answered the LORD and said,

4 "Behold, I am insignificant; what can I reply to You?
I lay my hand on my mouth.

5 "Once I have spoken, and I will not answer;
Even twice, and I will add nothing more."

6 Then the LORD answered Job out of the storm and said,

7 "Now gird up your loins like a man;
I will ask you, and you instruct Me.

8 "Will you really annul My judgment?
Will you condemn Me that you may be justified?

9 "Or do you have an arm like God,
And can you thunder with a voice like His?

10 "Adorn yourself with eminence and dignity,
And clothe yourself with honor and majesty.

11 "Pour out the overflowings of your anger,
And look on everyone who is proud, and make him low.

12 "Look on everyone who is proud, *and* humble him,
And tread down the wicked where they stand.

13 "Hide them in the dust together;
Bind them in the hidden *place*.

14 "Then I will also confess to you,
That your own right hand can save you.

15 "Behold now, Behemoth, which I made as well as you;
He eats grass like an ox.

16 "Behold now, his strength in his loins
And his power in the muscles of his belly.

17 "He bends his tail like a cedar;
The sinews of his thighs are knit together.

18 "His bones are tubes of bronze;
His limbs are like bars of iron.

LIFE LESSONS

➤ **Job 40:4 — "Behold, I am insignificant; what can I reply to You?"**

*E*ven a blameless and upright man sees himself as insignificant when confronted by the majestic holiness of almighty God. Yet we can come boldly into the Lord's presence when we come in faith, wrapped in Christ's righteousness (Heb. 4:16).

➤ **Job 40:8 — "Will you condemn Me that you may be justified?"**

*W*e may not always understand God's ways, but we must never presume to judge His ways. He is "a God of faithfulness and without injustice, righteous and upright is He" (Deut. 32:4).

19 "He is the first of the ways of God;
   Let his maker bring near his
      sword.
20 "Surely the mountains bring him
      food,
   And all the beasts of the field play
      there.
21 "Under the lotus plants he lies
      down,
   In the covert of the reeds and the
      marsh.
22 "The lotus plants cover him with
      shade;
   The willows of the brook surround
      him.
23 "If a river rages, he is not alarmed;
   He is confident, though the Jordan
      rushes to his mouth.
24 "Can anyone capture him when he is
      on watch,
   With barbs can anyone pierce *his*
      nose?

Psalm 101:1–4

A Psalm of David.

101 I WILL sing of lovingkindness
      and justice,
   To You, O LORD, I will sing praises.

➤ 2 I will give heed to the blameless
      way.
   When will You come to me?
   I will walk within my house in the
      integrity of my heart.

➤ 3 I will set no worthless thing before
      my eyes;
   I hate the work of those who fall
      away;
   It shall not fasten its grip on me.

4 A perverse heart shall depart from
      me;
   I will know no evil.

Proverbs 23:29–30

29 Who has woe? Who has sorrow?
   Who has contentions? Who has
      complaining?
   Who has wounds without cause?
   Who has redness of eyes?
30 Those who linger long over
      wine,

Those who go to taste mixed
   wine.

1 Corinthians 6:1–20

6 DOES any one of you, when he has a
   case against his neighbor, dare to go
to law before the unrighteous and not
before the saints?
2   Or do you not know that the saints
will judge the world? If the world is
judged by you, are you not competent *to
constitute* the smallest law courts?
3   Do you not know that we will judge
angels? How much more matters of this
life?
4   So if you have law courts dealing
with matters of this life, do you appoint
them as judges who are of no account in
the church?
5   I say *this* to your shame. *Is it so, that*
there is not among you one wise man
who will be able to decide between his
brethren,
6   but brother goes to law with brother,
and that before unbelievers?
7   Actually, then, it is already a defeat
for you, that you have lawsuits with one
another. Why not rather be wronged?
Why not rather be defrauded?
8   On the contrary, you yourselves wrong

LIFE LESSONS

➤ **Psalm 101:2 —** *I will walk within my
house in the integrity of my heart.*

*I*t's one thing to behave in a godly
way in public when you know many
eyes are watching. It's another to reflect
His goodness and righteousness at home,
where only family members see. God
calls us to both.

➤ **Psalm 101:3 —** *I will set no worthless
thing before my eyes.*

*H*ow many wrong relationships begin
with just a harmless glance? How
many thefts start with an envious gaze?
How many addictive habits take hold
from prolonged exposure to the wrong
thing? If we wish to avoid doing evil, we
must stay far away from any situation,
attitude, or habit that could cause us to
stumble.

ANSWERS TO LIFE'S QUESTIONS

Is there a limit to God's forgiveness?

1 CORINTHIANS 6:9–11

*D*o you ever ask yourself:
- Can I ever be free of the weight of my sin and guilt?
- Will God forgive my *every* sin?

I have good news for you! Your loving, heavenly Father will forgive you of *all* your sins. You can be released today from your sins if you will do what God says.

The apostle Paul dealt with an instance of gross sexual immorality in the Corinthian church: a man was sexually involved with his stepmother. Against that backdrop, Paul wrote, "Do not be deceived; neither fornicators, nor idolaters, nor adulterers, nor effeminate, nor homosexuals, nor thieves, nor the covetous, nor drunkards, nor revilers, nor swindlers, will inherit the kingdom of God. Such were some of you; but you were washed, but you were sanctified, but you were justified in the name of the Lord Jesus Christ and in the Spirit of our God" (1 Cor. 6:9–11).

This passage holds three great messages for us.

First, it tells us that sin is sin. God doesn't differentiate between one type of sin and another. Most of us wouldn't consider slan-derers in the same "sin boat" as thieves, but sin is sin. There are, however, some sins that I believe are tremendously ensnaring. The effect of sexual sin reaches deep into the soul. It is so ensnaring that many find it difficult to shake free, but God's love and ability to rescue, forgive, and restore is greater still. There is mercy at the Cross, and it is available to all who draw near to Christ.

Second, it tells us that sin is a lifestyle, a state of being. Paul declared that sin had been the identity of the Corinthians. Sin had been their all-consuming character. Paul called them former *thieves*—people who had stolen as a way of life. He didn't say, "Some of you had one too many drinks on occasion." He said some in the Corinthian church were *drunkards*. Sin isn't just something you *do*. Rather, sinful is what you *are*.

Third, it tells us that all types of sin can be forgiven. Paul declared, "Such *were* some of you." And then Paul reminded them that they were no longer whom they had been, but they had been washed, sanctified, and justified in the name of the Lord Jesus and by the Spirit of God. The Corinthians found a new life and a new identity in Christ Jesus. You can as well.

Nothing is beyond God's forgiveness. No sin is too great or too awful for God to forgive. No person is so deep in sin, so ingrained in a wicked lifestyle, or so steeped in evil that he or she cannot be saved. The only requirement is that you accept His forgiveness. Will you?

---

and defraud. *You do* this even to *your* brethren.

9 Or do you not know that the unrighteous will not inherit the kingdom of God? Do not be deceived; neither fornicators, nor idolaters, nor adulterers, nor effeminate, nor homosexuals,

10 nor thieves, nor *the* covetous, nor drunkards, nor revilers, nor swindlers, will inherit the kingdom of God.

LIFE LESSONS

➤ **1 Corinthians 6:12 —** *All things are lawful for me, but I will not be mastered by anything.*

*P*aul had no interest in allowing the sinful patterns from which he had escaped through God's grace to enslave him again. He didn't ask, "What's wrong with it?" as much as, "Is this the Lord's will for me? Will it honor and glorify Him?"

11 Such were some of you; but you were washed, but you were sanctified, but you were justified in the name of the Lord Jesus Christ and in the Spirit of our God.

12 All things are lawful for me, but not ◄ all things are profitable. All things are lawful for me, but I will not be mastered by anything.

13 Food is for the stomach and the stomach is for food, but God will do away with both of them. Yet the body is not for immorality, but for the Lord, and the Lord is for the body.

14 Now God has not only raised the Lord, but will also raise us up through His power.

15 Do you not know that your bodies are members of Christ? Shall I then take away the members of Christ and make them members of a prostitute? May it never be!

16 Or do you not know that the one who

joins himself to a prostitute is one body *with her?* For He says, "THE TWO SHALL BECOME ONE FLESH."

17 But the one who joins himself to the Lord is one spirit *with Him.*

18 Flee immorality. Every *other* sin that a man commits is outside the body, but the immoral man sins against his own body.

19 Or do you not know that your body is a temple of the Holy Spirit who is in you, whom you have from God, and that you are not your own?

20 For you have been bought with a price: therefore glorify God in your body.

AUGUST 25

Job 41:1—42:17

41 "CAN you draw out Leviathan with a fishhook?
Or press down his tongue with a cord?

2 "Can you put a rope in his nose
Or pierce his jaw with a hook?

3 "Will he make many supplications to you,
Or will he speak to you soft words?

4 "Will he make a covenant with you?
Will you take him for a servant forever?

5 "Will you play with him as with a bird,
Or will you bind him for your maidens?

6 "Will the traders bargain over him?
Will they divide him among the merchants?

7 "Can you fill his skin with harpoons,
Or his head with fishing spears?

8 "Lay your hand on him;
Remember the battle; you will not do it again!

9 "Behold, your expectation is false;
Will you be laid low even at the sight of him?

10 "No one is so fierce that he dares to arouse him;
Who then is he that can stand before Me?

11 "Who has given to Me that I should repay *him?*

Whatever is under the whole heaven is Mine.

12 "I will not keep silence concerning his limbs,
Or his mighty strength, or his orderly frame.

13 "Who can strip off his outer armor?
Who can come within his double mail?

14 "Who can open the doors of his face?
Around his teeth there is terror.

15 "*His* strong scales are *his* pride,
Shut up *as with* a tight seal.

16 "One is so near to another
That no air can come between them.

17 "They are joined one to another;
They clasp each other and cannot be separated.

18 "His sneezes flash forth light,
And his eyes are like the eyelids of the morning.

19 "Out of his mouth go burning torches;
Sparks of fire leap forth.

20 "Out of his nostrils smoke goes forth
As *from* a boiling pot and *burning* rushes.

21 "His breath kindles coals,
And a flame goes forth from his mouth.

22 "In his neck lodges strength,
And dismay leaps before him.

23 "The folds of his flesh are joined together,
Firm on him and immovable.

24 "His heart is as hard as a stone,
Even as hard as a lower millstone.

25 "When he raises himself up, the
    mighty fear;
    Because of the crashing they are
    bewildered.
26 "The sword that reaches him cannot
    avail,
    Nor the spear, the dart or the
    javelin.
27 "He regards iron as straw,
    Bronze as rotten wood.
28 "The arrow cannot make him flee;
    Slingstones are turned into stubble
    for him.
29 "Clubs are regarded as stubble;
    He laughs at the rattling of the
    javelin.
30 "His underparts are *like* sharp
    potsherds;
    He spreads out *like* a threshing
    sledge on the mire.
31 "He makes the depths boil like a pot;
    He makes the sea like a jar of
    ointment.
32 "Behind him he makes a wake to
    shine;
    One would think the deep to be
    gray-haired.
33 "Nothing on earth is like him,
    One made without fear.
34 "He looks on everything that is high;
    He is king over all the sons of
    pride."

42 THEN Job answered the LORD and
    said,
2   "I know that You can do all things,
    And that no purpose of Yours can be
    thwarted.
3   'Who is this that hides counsel
    without knowledge?'
    "Therefore I have declared that
    which I did not understand,
    Things too wonderful for me, which
    I did not know."
4   'Hear, now, and I will speak;
    I will ask You, and You instruct me.'
5   "I have heard of You by the hearing
    of the ear;
    But now my eye sees You;
6   Therefore I retract,
    And I repent in dust and ashes."

7   It came about after the LORD had
spoken these words to Job, that the LORD
said to Eliphaz the Temanite, "My wrath
is kindled against you and against your
two friends, because you have not spoken of Me what is right as My servant
Job has.

8   "Now therefore, take for yourselves
seven bulls and seven rams, and go to
My servant Job, and offer up a burnt
offering for yourselves, and My servant
Job will pray for you. For I will accept
him so that I may not do with you *according to your* folly, because you have
not spoken of Me what is right, as My
servant Job has."
9   So Eliphaz the Temanite and Bildad
the Shuhite *and* Zophar the Naamathite
went and did as the LORD told them; and
the LORD accepted Job.
10 The LORD restored the fortunes of
Job when he prayed for his friends, and
the LORD increased all that Job had twofold.
11 Then all his brothers and all his sisters and all who had known him before
came to him, and they ate bread with
him in his house; and they consoled him
and comforted him for all the adversities
that the LORD had brought on him. And
each one gave him one piece of money,
and each a ring of gold.
12 The LORD blessed the latter *days* of
Job more than his beginning; and he had

LIFE LESSONS

**➤ Job 42:5, 6 — "I have heard of You by
the hearing of the ear; but now my eye
sees You."**

*I*t is one thing to learn facts about
God from a safe distance. It is quite
another to know Him personally, intimately, up close, and face-to-face. "Who
would not fear You, O King of the
nations?" (Jer. 10:7).

**➤ Job 42:8 — "My servant Job will pray
for you. For I will accept him."**

*I*n his time of trouble, Job wondered
whether God even heard his pain-
filled prayers—but not only had the Lord
heard him, He accepted both him and
his prayers. God acts on behalf of those
who wait for Him!

**➤ Job 42:12 — The LORD blessed the lat-
ter days of Job more than his beginning.**

*J*ob found that life has its highs and
lows, its delights and its tragedies.
But through it all, God is there—and so
is His blessing for faithful obedience.

LIFE PRINCIPLE **11**

GOD ASSUMES FULL RESPONSIBILITY FOR OUR
NEEDS WHEN WE OBEY HIM.

JOB 42:7–17

*D*o you really believe God is able and eager
to meet all of your needs? Most people
would say yes. But when difficulty comes, problems
arise, and sorrow strikes, we often wonder where
God is and how we can trust Him. But the Lord is
not only capable of meeting all of our needs, He also
is able to satisfy the deepest desires of our hearts.

Some question this reasoning. They say, "I know
God is capable of meeting my needs, but will He?
Doesn't He know that I'm struggling?" The Lord
knows the battle that is ensuing around your life.

And while questions like these are asked by each
one of us at some point, we need to learn a deeper
principle: how to focus on our faith when we are
under trial. God is committed to meeting our needs,
but first He wants to know that we are committed
to living our lives for Him.

Jesus told His disciples not to worry. He admonished them to "Seek first His kingdom and His righteousness and all these things will be added to you"
(Matt. 6:33). This is a promise, a commitment, and
a pledge of action that we can claim. God knows we
have emotional and material needs—food, shelter, a
sense of belonging, and clothing. But Jesus was telling His followers that the focus of their lives should
not be set on material products or "feel good" experiences. Instead, they were to set their hearts—like
flint—on God and His kingdom, then every need
and desire they had would be met.

The value of any commitment is based upon two
things:

1. The ability of the promise maker to fulfill the
promise.

2. The integrity of the promise maker, whether he
has the character to follow through on the promise.

God certainly qualifies on both accounts. He
has all the wisdom, power, and ability necessary to
fulfill His promises to us. He also has proven integrity—He always keeps His promises. He is utterly
faithful to His Word. He is holy and immutable;
He is unchanging. His commandments, statutes,
and promises have not changed; they reflect our
unchanging God. He is "the same yesterday and
today and forever" (Heb. 13:8).

When you have an unmet need, you first need to
pray and tell the Lord what you are facing. Prayer is
an act of faith. It declares your trust in God and His
ability. Many times, He allows a need to come so
that He can teach you to trust Him in a greater way.
No problem is too complicated or too difficult for
Him to handle.

The real questions that we must answer are:

"How are you responding in the midst of your
circumstance or situation?" And, "Are you trusting
Him or are you frantically looking for a way out of
the difficulty without discovering what He wants
you to learn?"

Jesus pledged that God would meet your needs
when you "seek first His kingdom and His righteousness." This means that He is obligated to
meet your needs when you faithfully obey and trust
Him. When you are walking in step with Him, He
assumes full responsibility for the answer to your
needs, problems, challenges, and circumstances of
life. But there is a catch: He does this according
to His will, purpose, plan, and timing. And meeting needs does not necessarily mean meeting every
desire that we have. He may choose to answer
our prayers quickly, or He may wait for a season.
Regardless, when the answer comes, it will be perfect and it will encourage us.

One of God's greatest desires is for us to learn to
trust His wisdom and timing. Do you have a pre-
conceived idea about how He must act to meet your
needs or whom He may use to meet them? Many
people have said, "Well, if this man would just do
such and such or that woman would agree to do so
and so, then my need would be met." Or they have
said, "Well, I did such and such and therefore God
must do this and that."

People who make statements such as these
are not really trusting the Lord. Rather, they are
demanding that He exert His power on behalf of
their wishes and commands. Anytime we "expect"
God to move a certain way, we have missed the
deeper lesson that He wants us to learn.

Faith requires complete trust in Him, even when
we do not understand why He has allowed circumstances to unfold a certain way. Think of all the
people in the Bible who trusted the Lord and gained
a wondrous victory: Moses, David, Esther, Jeremiah,
Elijah, the disciples, Mary, and many more. We
should never obey Him merely to manipulate our
situations. God knows our hearts. When we are surrendered to Him, He sees our devotion and goes to
work on our behalf.

The Father calls us to trust Him, and Him alone,
to meet our needs and to be our total source of supply. Furthermore, He requires that we obey Him as
part of our trusting Him. Therefore, tell Him,
"Lord, I trust You completely to meet my needs, in
Your timing and according to Your methods. I want
to lay down my selfish hopes, dreams, and desires.
Mold these so that they represent Your will for my
life. And I will continue to obey You, by the power
of Your Spirit, believing that as I do, You will take
care of me." You can count on the Father's love,
wisdom, power, and grace. He has never failed you.
He is the God who cares, and He will provide what
you need at just the right time. When He does, it
will be abundantly beyond all you imagined. ◈

14,000 sheep and 6,000 camels and 1,000 yoke of oxen and 1,000 female donkeys.
13 He had seven sons and three daughters.
14 He named the first Jemimah, and the second Keziah, and the third Keren-happuch.
15 In all the land no women were found so fair as Job's daughters; and their father gave them inheritance among their brothers.
16 After this, Job lived 140 years, and saw his sons and his grandsons, four generations.
17 And Job died, an old man and full of days.

Psalm 101:5–8

5 Whoever secretly slanders his
    neighbor, him I will destroy;
    No one who has a haughty look and
    an arrogant heart will I endure.
6 My eyes shall be upon the faithful
    of the land, that they may dwell
    with me;
    He who walks in a blameless way is
    the one who will minister to me.
7 He who practices deceit shall not
    dwell within my house;
    He who speaks falsehood shall not
    maintain his position before me.
8 Every morning I will destroy all the
    wicked of the land,
    So as to cut off from the city of the
    LORD all those who do iniquity.

Proverbs 23:31–35

31 Do not look on the wine when it is
    red,
    When it sparkles in the cup,
    When it goes down smoothly;
32 At the last it bites like a serpent
    And stings like a viper.
33 Your eyes will see strange things
    And your mind will utter perverse
    things.
34 And you will be like one who lies
    down in the middle of the sea,
    Or like one who lies down on the
    top of a mast.

35 "They struck me, *but* I did not
    become ill;
    They beat me, *but* I did not know *it.*
    When shall I awake?
    I will seek another drink."

1 Corinthians 7:1–19

7 NOW concerning the things about which you wrote, it is good for a man not to touch a woman.
2 But because of immoralities, each man is to have his own wife, and each woman is to have her own husband.
3 The husband must fulfill his duty to his wife, and likewise also the wife to her husband.
4 The wife does not have authority over her own body, but the husband *does;* and likewise also the husband does not have authority over his own body, but the wife *does.*
5 Stop depriving one another, except by agreement for a time, so that you may devote yourselves to prayer, and come together again so that Satan will not tempt you because of your lack of self-control.
6 But this I say by way of concession, not of command.
7 Yet I wish that all men were even as I myself am. However, each man has his own gift from God, one in this manner, and another in that.
8 But I say to the unmarried and to widows that it is good for them if they remain even as I.
9 But if they do not have self-control, let them marry; for it is better to marry than to burn *with passion.*
10 But to the married I give instructions,

LIFE LESSONS

➤ **1 Corinthians 7:5** — *Stop depriving one another, except by agreement for a time, so that you may devote yourselves to prayer, and come together again.*

S exual expression is a key and vital part of every Christian marriage. Believing couples should abstain from it only (1) by mutual consent, (2) for a limited time, and (3) for a specific prayer need.

not I, but the Lord, that the wife should not leave her husband

> 11 (but if she does leave, she must remain unmarried, or else be reconciled to her husband), and that the husband should not divorce his wife.

12 But to the rest I say, not the Lord, that if any brother has a wife who is an unbeliever, and she consents to live with him, he must not divorce her.

13 And a woman who has an unbelieving husband, and he consents to live with her, she must not send her husband away.

14 For the unbelieving husband is sanctified through his wife, and the unbelieving wife is sanctified through her believing husband; for otherwise your children are unclean, but now they are holy.

15 Yet if the unbelieving one leaves, let him leave; the brother or the sister is not under bondage in such *cases*, but God has called us to peace.

16 For how do you know, O wife, whether you will save your husband? Or how do you know, O husband, whether you will save your wife?

17 Only, as the Lord has assigned to each one, as God has called each, in this manner let him walk. And so I direct in all the churches. ✳

18 Was any man called *when he was already* circumcised? He is not to become uncircumcised. Has anyone been called in uncircumcision? He is not to be circumcised.

19 Circumcision is nothing, and uncircumcision is nothing, but *what matters is* the keeping of the commandments of God. ◄

LIFE LESSONS

> **1 Corinthians 7:11 —** *If she does leave, she must remain unmarried, or else be reconciled to her husband.*

*P*aul follows the lead of the Old Testament and of Jesus on the topic of divorce. His teaching on grace does not mean that spouses can divorce at will; it means that God can give them the strength to persevere.

> **1 Corinthians 7:19 —** *What matters is the keeping of the commandments of God.*

*R*ituals help us only insofar as they move us toward God; in and of themselves, they have no intrinsic value. God values devoted obedience far more than adherence to religious regulations (1 Sam. 15:22).

AUGUST 26

◈ Ecclesiastes 1:1—2:26

1 THE words of the Preacher, the son of David, king in Jerusalem.

2 "Vanity of vanities," says the Preacher, "Vanity of vanities! All is vanity."

3 What advantage does man have in all his work
   Which he does under the sun?

4 A generation goes and a generation comes,
   But the earth remains forever.

5 Also, the sun rises and the sun sets;
   And hastening to its place it rises there *again*.

6 Blowing toward the south,
   Then turning toward the north,

The wind continues swirling along;
   And on its circular courses the wind returns.

7 All the rivers flow into the sea,
   Yet the sea is not full.
   To the place where the rivers flow,
   There they flow again.

8 All things are wearisome;
   Man is not able to tell *it*.
   The eye is not satisfied with seeing,
   Nor is the ear filled with hearing.

9 That which has been is that which will be,
   And that which has been done is that which will be done.
   So there is nothing new under the sun.

10 Is there anything of which one might say,

"See this, it is new"?
Already it has existed for ages
Which were before us.

11 There is no remembrance of earlier
things;
And also of the later things which
will occur,
There will be for them no
remembrance
Among those who will come later *still.*

12 I, the Preacher, have been king over
Israel in Jerusalem.

13 And I set my mind to seek and explore
by wisdom concerning all that has been
done under heaven. *It* is a grievous task
which God has given to the sons of men to
be afflicted with.

14 I have seen all the works which have
been done under the sun, and behold, all
is vanity and striving after wind.

15 What is crooked cannot be straightened and what is lacking cannot be
counted.

16 I said to myself, "Behold, I have
magnified and increased wisdom more
than all who were over Jerusalem before
me; and my mind has observed a wealth
of wisdom and knowledge."

17 And I set my mind to know wisdom
and to know madness and folly; for I realized that this also is striving after wind.

➤ 18 Because in much wisdom there is
much grief, and increasing knowledge
results in increasing pain.

2 I SAID to myself, "Come now, I will
test you with pleasure. So enjoy yourself." And behold, it too was futility.

2 I said of laughter, "It is madness,"
and of pleasure, "What does it accomplish?"

3 I explored with my mind *how* to
stimulate my body with wine while my
mind was guiding *me* wisely, and how to
take hold of folly, until I could see what
good there is for the sons of men to do
under heaven the few years of their lives.

4 I enlarged my works: I built houses
for myself, I planted vineyards for myself;

5 I made gardens and parks for myself
and I planted in them all kinds of fruit
trees;

6 I made ponds of water for myself
from which to irrigate a forest of growing trees.

7 I bought male and female slaves and
I had homeborn slaves. Also I possessed

flocks and herds larger than all who preceded me in Jerusalem.

8 Also, I collected for myself silver
and gold and the treasure of kings and
provinces. I provided for myself male
and female singers and the pleasures of
men—many concubines.

9 Then I became great and increased
more than all who preceded me in Jerusalem. My wisdom also stood by me.

10 All that my eyes desired I did not
refuse them. I did not withhold my heart
from any pleasure, for my heart was
pleased because of all my labor and this
was my reward for all my labor.

11 Thus I considered all my activities ◄
which my hands had done and the labor
which I had exerted, and behold all was
vanity and striving after wind and there
was no profit under the sun.

12 So I turned to consider wisdom,
madness and folly; for what *will* the man
do who will come after the king *except*
what has already been done?

13 And I saw that wisdom excels folly
as light excels darkness.

14 The wise man's eyes are in his head,
but the fool walks in darkness. And yet I
know that one fate befalls them both.

15 Then I said to myself, "As is the fate
of the fool, it will also befall me. Why
then have I been extremely wise?" So I
said to myself, "This too is vanity."

16 For there is no lasting remembrance of the wise man *as* with the fool,

---

LIFE LESSONS

➤ **Ecclesiastes 1:18** — *Because in much
wisdom there is much grief, and increasing knowledge results in increasing pain.*

Solomon's big mistake was that he
depended on his great wisdom,
rather than on his relationship with
God. We were made for an intimate
relationship with the Lord, and pursuing
anything apart from Him will lead to discouragement.

➤ **Ecclesiastes 2:11** — *I considered all my
activities which my hands had done . . .
all was vanity.*

Solomon climbed the world's ladder of
success, only to find it leaning against
the wrong wall. When we walk through
life with God, we find ultimate meaning.

inasmuch as in the coming days all will be forgotten. And how the wise man and the fool alike die!

➤ 17 So I hated life, for the work which had been done under the sun was grievous to me; because everything is futility and striving after wind.

18 Thus I hated all the fruit of my labor for which I had labored under the sun, for I must leave it to the man who will come after me.

19 And who knows whether he will be a wise man or a fool? Yet he will have control over all the fruit of my labor for which I have labored by acting wisely under the sun. This too is vanity.

20 Therefore I completely despaired of all the fruit of my labor for which I had labored under the sun.

WHAT THE BIBLE SAYS ABOUT

Enjoying God's Presence

Ecclesiastes 2:26

*R*epeatedly in Scripture, we find there is great joy and awe for believers in the presence of the Lord (Ps. 16:11; 21:6; 95:2; Is. 64:3–5; Jude 1:24, 25). Ecclesiastes 2:26 tells us, "To a person who is good in His sight He has given wisdom and knowledge and joy." Why, then, do so many people fail to enjoy God's presence?

First, some may not really know Him. Sometimes people mistakenly see God as an untouchable, invisible force caring very little about His creation. But nothing is further from the truth. He desires a close, abiding relationship with you. When you fail to realize the depth of His love, you miss a great blessing. He says to you today, "I have loved you with an everlasting love; therefore I have drawn you with lovingkindness" (Jer. 31:3). The Father cares for you deeply, and when you spend time with Him, He expresses that love to you.

Second, some have an erroneous view of God's attitude. Our heavenly Father is not legalistic, expecting you to live by rituals and regulations. Rather, He cares about your heart—about your love for Him and your sincere desire to obey Him. Remember, "God did not send the Son into the world to judge the world, but that the world might be saved through Him" (John 3:17). You do not have to earn His acceptance. You do not have to work for His care. When you spend time in His pres-

ence, He teaches you His ways and how to live each day.

Third, as hard as it is to imagine, some people are simply afraid of God. They see Him as unpredictable and full of wrath. Although He calls you to have reverence for Him—to respect His holiness—He does not want you to be afraid of Him with a human fear. He tells us to fear Him, but we do this with a reverent fear—one worships the Lord, acknowledging our love for Him.

1 John 4:18 tells us, "There is no fear in love; but perfect love casts out fear, because fear involves punishment." This is why He so often tells His people, "Do not fear" (Gen. 15:1; Josh. 8:1; Luke 1:30). Our lives are in His hands, and He will lead, protect, and provide for us when we seek Him—not punish us.

Fourth, sin breaks the fellowship God wants us to enjoy with Him. Sin not only blocks His best for us, it stops us from experiencing His wonderful presence. Yet not only does God extend forgiveness, He also promises restoration to us. When we forsake our sin—repenting of it—He brings us back into fellowship and the blessing of His love.

Fifth, some people refuse to believe that the Father accepts them. There is absolutely nothing you can do to save yourself or to become more acceptable to Him. The Lord loves you the way you are! He never approves of sin, but He also is committed to loving you and teaching you how to know Him better.

How can you begin to enjoy God? Realize that He enjoys being with you, and then learn to spend time with Him—trusting Him to meet all your needs. ◉

21 When there is a man who has labored with wisdom, knowledge and skill, then he gives his legacy to one who has not labored with them. This too is vanity and a great evil.

22 For what does a man get in all his labor and in his striving with which he labors under the sun?

23 Because all his days his task is painful and grievous; even at night his mind does not rest. This too is vanity.

24 There is nothing better for a man *than* to eat and drink and tell himself that his labor is good. This also I have seen that it is from the hand of God.

25 For who can eat and who can have enjoyment without Him?

26 For to a person who is good in His sight He has given wisdom and knowledge and joy, while to the sinner He has given the task of gathering and collecting so that he may give to one who is good in God's sight. This too is vanity and striving after wind.

◈ Psalm 102:1–11

A Prayer of the Afflicted when he is faint and pours out his complaint before the LORD.

102 HEAR my prayer, O LORD!
And let my cry for help come to
You.
2 Do not hide Your face from me in
the day of my distress;
Incline Your ear to me;
In the day when I call answer me
quickly.
3 For my days have been consumed
in smoke,
And my bones have been scorched
like a hearth.
4 My heart has been smitten like
grass and has withered away,
Indeed, I forget to eat my bread.
5 Because of the loudness of my
groaning
My bones cling to my flesh.
6 I resemble a pelican of the
wilderness;
I have become like an owl of the
waste places.
7 I lie awake,
I have become like a lonely bird on
a housetop.

8 My enemies have reproached me all
day long;
Those who deride me have used my
name as a curse.
9 For I have eaten ashes like bread
And mingled my drink with
weeping
10 Because of Your indignation and
Your wrath,
For You have lifted me up and cast
me away.
11 My days are like a lengthened
shadow,
And I wither away like grass.

◈ Proverbs 24:1, 2

24 DO not be envious of evil men,
Nor desire to be with them;
2 For their minds devise violence,
And their lips talk of trouble.

◈ 1 Corinthians 7:20–40

20 Each man must remain in that condition in which he was called.
21 Were you called while a slave? Do not worry about it; but if you are able also to become free, rather do that.

LIFE LESSONS

➤ **Proverbs 24:2 —** *For their minds devise violence, and their lips talk of trouble.*

*I*t may seem like the wicked have better lives than we do, but it's a big mistake to envy them. In the end, they have nothing, but the believer can say, "God is the strength of my heart and my portion forever" (Ps. 73:26).

➤ **1 Corinthians 7:20 —** *Each man must remain in that condition in which he was called.*

"*I*'d serve God if only I had a better job, a better home, a better spouse, and a better position." Ever hear anything like this? The truth is, your ministry does not start some time in the future when your circumstances change. It begins the moment you believe in Christ. Serve Him obediently with this is view.

22 For he who was called in the Lord while a slave, is the Lord's freedman; likewise he who was called while free, is Christ's slave.
23 You were bought with a price; do not become slaves of men.
※ 24 Brethren, each one is to remain with God in that *condition* in which he was called.
25 Now concerning virgins I have no command of the Lord, but I give an opinion as one who by the mercy of the Lord is trustworthy.
26 I think then that this is good in view of the present distress, that it is good for a man to remain as he is.
27 Are you bound to a wife? Do not seek to be released. Are you released from a wife? Do not seek a wife.
28 But if you marry, you have not sinned; and if a virgin marries, she has not sinned. Yet such will have trouble in this life, and I am trying to spare you.
29 But this I say, brethren, the time has been shortened, so that from now on those who have wives should be as though they had none;
30 and those who weep, as though they did not weep; and those who rejoice, as though they did not rejoice; and those who buy, as though they did not possess;
31 and those who use the world, as though they did not make full use of it; for the form of this world is passing away.
32 But I want you to be free from concern. One who is unmarried is concerned about the things of the Lord, how he may please the Lord;
33 but one who is married is concerned about the things of the world, how he may please his wife,
34 and *his interests* are divided. The woman who is unmarried, and the virgin, is concerned about the things of the Lord, that she may be holy both in body and spirit; but one who is married is concerned about the things of the world, how she may please her husband.
35 This I say for your own benefit; not to put a restraint upon you, but to promote what is appropriate and *to secure* undistracted devotion to the Lord.
36 But if any man thinks that he is acting unbecomingly toward his virgin *daughter*, if she is past her youth, and if it must be so, let him do what he wishes, he does not sin; let her marry.
37 But he who stands firm in his heart, being under no constraint, but has authority over his own will, and has decided this in his own heart, to keep his own virgin *daughter*, he will do well.
38 So then both he who gives his own virgin *daughter* in marriage does well, and he who does not give her in marriage will do better.
39 A wife is bound as long as her husband lives; but if her husband is dead, she is free to be married to whom she wishes, only in the Lord.
40 But in my opinion she is happier if she remains as she is; and I think that I also have the Spirit of God.

AUGUST 27

Ecclesiastes 3:1–22

➤ **3** THERE is an appointed time for everything. And there is a time for every event under heaven—
2   A time to give birth and a time to die;
     A time to plant and a time to uproot what is planted.
3   A time to kill and a time to heal;
     A time to tear down and a time to build up.
4   A time to weep and a time to laugh;
     A time to mourn and a time to dance.
5   A time to throw stones and a time to gather stones;

LIFE LESSONS

➤ **Ecclesiastes 3:1 — *There is an appointed time for everything. And there is a time for every event under heaven.***

*I*n His wisdom and sovereignty, God sets an appropriate time for everything. At the right time, Christ was born (Gal. 4:4); at the right time, He lifts us up (1 Pet. 5:6). Don't run ahead of God's timing! His blessings are always worth the wait.

WHAT THE BIBLE SAYS ABOUT ◈

Beautiful Eventually

Ecclesiastes 3:1–14

Think about the promise of Ecclesiastes 3:11, "He has made everything appropriate in its time." This signifies that there will be unavoidable things in your life that appear to be ugly, unwanted, and uncomfortable. I'm sure there are things that immediately spring to your mind—and there's nothing good about them as far as you can see.

Perhaps that's because there are just too many overwhelming unknowns about your situation that blind you to the good God is doing. Or perhaps you're simply too bogged down and disheartened by your load to imagine it ever getting any better. Don't be surprised when I tell you there will be seasons like this in your life (1 Pet. 4:12, 13).

Why does God burden us with such times? The second part of Ecclesiastes 3:11 teaches, "He has also set eternity in their heart, yet so that man will not find out the work which God has done from the beginning even to the end."

Though you may never know everything the Father is doing in your life, you can always count on the fact that He is preparing your heart for eternity. Second Corinthians 4:17 says, "For momentary, light affliction is producing for us an eternal weight of glory far beyond all comparison." Your seasons of trial—however long and heavy they may seem—are brief and light compared to the great things God is doing in you (Rom. 8:18–21, 28).

As you've been promised in Ecclesiastes 3:11, your difficult situations will eventually be beautiful in your sight. Is that hard for you to envision? God's wonderful plans for you are by definition beyond imagination (Eph. 3:20, 21). Until you see His lovely workmanship taking shape in your circumstances, simply hold on to His promise. Eventually, your season of trial and difficulty will be over, and you will find that it was all worthwhile. ◈

A time to embrace and a time to shun embracing.
6　A time to search and a time to give up as lost;
A time to keep and a time to throw away.
7　A time to tear apart and a time to sew together;
A time to be silent and a time to speak.
8　A time to love and a time to hate;
A time for war and a time for peace.
9　What profit is there to the worker from that in which he toils?
10　I have seen the task which God has given the sons of men with which to occupy themselves.
11　He has made everything appropriate in its time. He has also set eternity in their heart, yet so that man will not find out the work which God has done from the beginning even to the end.
12　I know that there is nothing better for them than to rejoice and to do good in one's lifetime;
13　moreover, that every man who eats and drinks sees good in all his labor—it is the gift of God.
14　I know that everything God does will remain forever; there is nothing to add to it and there is nothing to take from it, for God has so worked that men should fear Him.
15　That which is has been already and that which will be has already been, for God seeks what has passed by.
16　Furthermore, I have seen under the sun *that* in the place of justice there is wickedness and in the place of righteousness there is wickedness.

LIFE LESSONS

➤ **Ecclesiastes 3:12 —** *I know that there is nothing better for them than to rejoice and to do good in one's lifetime.*

God "richly supplies us with all things to enjoy," but He warns us not "to fix [our] hope on the uncertainty of riches" and urges us to "be rich in good works, to be generous and ready to share" (1 Tim. 6:17, 18). There is nothing more satisfying and joyous in life than to do the Father's will and fulfill the purpose for which we were created (Eph. 2:10). Therefore, we must always remain focused on Him, rather than being distracted by the things of this world (1 Tim. 6:10–19).

17 I said to myself, "God will judge both the righteous man and the wicked man," for a time for every matter and for every deed is there.
18 I said to myself concerning the sons of men, "God has surely tested them in order for them to see that they are but beasts."
19 For the fate of the sons of men and the fate of beasts is the same. As one dies so dies the other; indeed, they all have the same breath and there is no advantage for man over beast, for all is vanity.
20 All go to the same place. All came from the dust and all return to the dust.
21 Who knows that the breath of man ascends upward and the breath of the beast descends downward to the earth?
22 I have seen that nothing is better than that man should be happy in his activities, for that is his lot. For who will bring him to see what will occur after him?

Psalm 102:12–17

12 But You, O LORD, abide forever,
And Your name to all generations.
13 You will arise and have compassion on Zion;
For it is time to be gracious to her,
For the appointed time has come.
14 Surely Your servants find pleasure in her stones
And feel pity for her dust.
15 So the nations will fear the name of the LORD
And all the kings of the earth Your glory.
16 For the LORD has built up Zion;
He has appeared in His glory.
17 He has regarded the prayer of the destitute
And has not despised their prayer.

Proverbs 24:3, 4

3 By wisdom a house is built,
And by understanding it is established;
4 And by knowledge the rooms are filled
With all precious and pleasant riches.

1 Corinthians 8:1–13

8 NOW concerning things sacrificed to idols, we know that we all have knowledge. Knowledge makes arrogant, but love edifies.
2 If anyone supposes that he knows anything, he has not yet known as he ought to know;
3 but if anyone loves God, he is known by Him.
4 Therefore concerning the eating of things sacrificed to idols, we know that there is no such thing as an idol in the world, and that there is no God but one.
5 For even if there are so-called gods whether in heaven or on earth, as indeed there are many gods and many lords,
6 yet for us there is but one God, the Father, from whom are all things and we exist for Him; and one Lord, Jesus Christ, by whom are all things, and we exist through Him.
7 However not all men have this knowledge; but some, being accustomed to the idol until now, eat food as if it were sacrificed to an idol; and their conscience being weak is defiled.
8 But food will not commend us to God; we are neither the worse if we do not eat, nor the better if we do eat.
9 But take care that this liberty of yours

LIFE LESSONS

➤ **1 Corinthians 8:1 — Knowledge makes arrogant, but love edifies.**

God wants us to keep learning about Him and His ways, not merely to add to our storehouse of knowledge and to promote ourselves, but to better serve Him and His people. Knowledge that is led by the Spirit and expressed with godly love can be a powerful tool He uses to transform a person's life.

➤ **1 Corinthians 8:6 — There is but one God, the Father . . . and one Lord Jesus Christ, by whom are all things.**

Paul often speaks of the Father and the Son in equal but complementary ways. We serve one God through one Lord by one Spirit.

does not somehow become a stumbling block to the weak.

10 For if someone sees you, who have knowledge, dining in an idol's temple, will not his conscience, if he is weak, be strengthened to eat things sacrificed to idols?

11 For through your knowledge he who is weak is ruined, the brother for whose sake Christ died.

12 And so, by sinning against the brethren and wounding their conscience when it is weak, you sin against Christ.

LIFE LESSONS

➤ **1 Corinthians 8:11** — *For through your knowledge he who is weak is ruined, the brother for whose sake Christ died?*

*P*aul teaches us that love always desires the best for those it loves, even if that means self-denial.

13 Therefore, if food causes my brother to stumble, I will never eat meat again, so that I will not cause my brother to stumble.

◈ Ecclesiastes 4:1—6:12

4 THEN I looked again at all the acts of oppression which were being done under the sun. And behold I *saw* the tears of the oppressed and *that* they had no one to comfort *them*; and on the side of their oppressors was power, but they had no one to comfort *them*.

2 So I congratulated the dead who are already dead more than the living who are still living.

3 But better *off* than both of them is the one who has never existed, who has never seen the evil activity that is done under the sun.

4 I have seen that every labor and every skill which is done is *the result of* rivalry between a man and his neighbor. This too is vanity and striving after wind.

5 The fool folds his hands and consumes his own flesh.

6 One hand full of rest is better than two fists full of labor and striving after wind.

7 Then I looked again at vanity under the sun.

8 There was a certain man without a dependent, having neither a son nor a brother, yet there was no end to all his labor. Indeed, his eyes were not satisfied with riches *and he never asked,* "And for whom am I laboring and depriving myself of pleasure?" This too is vanity and it is a grievous task.

9 Two are better than one because they have a good return for their labor.

10 For if either of them falls, the one will lift up his companion. But woe to the one who falls when there is not another to lift him up.

11 Furthermore, if two lie down together they keep warm, but how can one be warm *alone*?

12 And if one can overpower him who is alone, two can resist him. A cord of three *strands* is not quickly torn apart.

LIFE LESSONS

➤ **Ecclesiastes 4:6** — *One hand full of rest is better than two fists full of labor and striving after wind.*

*P*aul wrote, "godliness actually is a means of great gain when accompanied by contentment" (1 Tim. 6:6). In other words, when we submit to God—resting in Him and trusting Him to take care of the consequences of our obedience—He supplies everything we need. Therefore, we should find all of our joy and fulfillment in Him. Those who walk closely with God can learn "to be content in whatever circumstances . . . the secret of being filled and going hungry, both of having abundance and suffering need" (Phil. 4:11, 12).

➤ **Ecclesiastes 4:10** — *Woe the one who falls when there is not another to lift him up.*

*G*od never calls on any of His children to "go it alone" in their walks with Him. We need each other, not only to receive help and encouragement, but to give it as well.

13 A poor yet wise lad is better than an old and foolish king who no longer knows *how* to receive instruction.

14 For he has come out of prison to become king, even though he was born poor in his kingdom.

15 I have seen all the living under the sun throng to the side of the second lad who replaces him.

16 There is no end to all the people, to all who were before them, and even the ones who will come later will not be happy with him, for this too is vanity and striving after wind.

5 GUARD your steps as you go to the house of God and draw near to listen rather than to offer the sacrifice of fools; for they do not know they are doing evil.

2 Do not be hasty in word or impulsive in thought to bring up a matter in the presence of God. For God is in heaven and you are on the earth; therefore let your words be few.

3 For the dream comes through much effort and the voice of a fool through many words.

4 When you make a vow to God, do not be late in paying it; for *He takes* no delight in fools. Pay what you vow!

5 It is better that you should not vow than that you should vow and not pay.

6 Do not let your speech cause you to sin and do not say in the presence of the messenger *of God* that it was a mistake. Why should God be angry on account of your voice and destroy the work of your hands?

7 For in many dreams and in many words there is emptiness. Rather, fear God.

8 If you see oppression of the poor and denial of justice and righteousness in the province, do not be shocked at the sight; for one official watches over another official, and there are higher officials over them.

9 After all, a king who cultivates the field is an advantage to the land.

10 He who loves money will not be satisfied with money, nor he who loves abundance *with its* income. This too is vanity.

11 When good things increase, those who consume them increase. So what is the advantage to their owners except to look on?

12 The sleep of the working man is pleasant, whether he eats little or much; but the full stomach of the rich man does not allow him to sleep.

13 There is a grievous evil *which* I have seen under the sun: riches being hoarded by their owner to his hurt.

14 When those riches were lost through a bad investment and he had fathered a son, then there was nothing to support him.

15 As he had come naked from his mother's womb, so will he return as he came. He will take nothing from the fruit of his labor that he can carry in his hand.

16 This also is a grievous evil—exactly as a man is born, thus will he die. So what is the advantage to him who toils for the wind?

17 Throughout his life *he* also eats in darkness with great vexation, sickness and anger.

18 Here is what I have seen to be good and fitting: to eat, to drink and enjoy oneself in all one's labor in which he toils under the sun *during* the few years of his life which God has given him; for this is his reward.

Life Examples:

THE PREACHER: Rich Doesn't Mean Expensive

ECCLESIASTES 5:10–20

*T*he Preacher is a great example of how "the good life" lacks the power to make anyone truly happy. He wrote that he built houses, planted vineyards, made gardens and orchards, possessed flocks and herds, and collected silver and gold and the treasures of kings. He did not refuse himself any desire.

And what was the result? "All was vanity and striving after wind" (Eccl. 2:11).

The richest moments in life are generally *not* the most expensive—the laughter of a child, a hug from a grandparent, a cup of coffee with a friend, a fishing trip with Dad, an "I love you" from Mom. The next time you find yourself wishing you had more earthly wealth, ask God to show you how rich you really are in Him. Realize that when you believe in Him, you are blessed with the immeasurable treasures of heaven that will surely never fade (Matt. 6:19–21; Eph. 1:3, 4; 1 Tim. 6:10–19).

LIFE LESSONS

➤ **Ecclesiastes 5:19 —** *As for every man to whom God has given riches and wealth . . . this is the gift of God.*

*G*od allows certain amounts of wealth and possessions to come into our hands so that we might use them to bless others. We are to be a funnel for God's blessings, not a container in which to hoard them.

➤ 19 Furthermore, as for every man to whom God has given riches and wealth, He has also empowered him to eat from them and to receive his reward and rejoice in his labor; this is the gift of God. 20 For he will not often consider the years of his life, because God keeps him occupied with the gladness of his heart.

6 THERE is an evil which I have seen under the sun and it is prevalent among men— 2 a man to whom God has given riches and wealth and honor so that his soul lacks nothing of all that he desires; yet God has not empowered him to eat from them, for a foreigner enjoys them. This is vanity and a severe affliction. 3 If a man fathers a hundred *children* and lives many years, however many they be, but his soul is not satisfied with good things and he does not even have a *proper* burial, *then* I say, "Better the miscarriage than he, 4 for it comes in futility and goes into obscurity; and its name is covered in obscurity. 5 "It never sees the sun and it never knows *anything*; it is better off than he. 6 "Even if the *other* man lives a thousand years twice and does not enjoy good things—do not all go to one place?" 7 All a man's labor is for his mouth and yet the appetite is not satisfied. 8 For what advantage does the wise man have over the fool? What *advantage* does the poor man have, knowing *how* to walk before the living? 9 What the eyes see is better than what the soul desires. This too is futility and a striving after wind. 10 Whatever exists has already been named, and it is known what man is; for he cannot dispute with him who is stronger than he is.

11 For there are many words which increase futility. What *then* is the advantage to a man? 12 For who knows what is good for a man during *his* lifetime, *during* the few years of his futile life? He will spend them like a shadow. For who can tell a man what will be after him under the sun?

Psalm 102:18–28

18 This will be written for the generation to come,　　　　◄
That a people yet to be created may praise the LORD.
19 For He looked down from His holy height;
From heaven the LORD gazed upon the earth,
20 To hear the groaning of the prisoner,
To set free those who were doomed to death,
21 That *men* may tell of the name of the LORD in Zion
And His praise in Jerusalem,
22 When the peoples are gathered together,
And the kingdoms, to serve the LORD.
23 He has weakened my strength in the way;
He has shortened my days.
24 I say, "O my God, do not take me away in the midst of my days,
Your years are throughout all generations.
25 "Of old You founded the earth,
And the heavens are the work of Your hands.
26 "Even they will perish, but You endure;
And all of them will wear out like a garment;
Like clothing You will change them and they will be changed.

✳

LIFE LESSONS

➤ **Psalm 102:18 —** *A people yet to be created may praise the Lord.*

*W*e are the "people yet to be created" spoken of in this verse. *You* are a fulfillment of prophecy! But to fulfill it completely, you must be in the habit of praising the Lord. Are you?

27 "But You are the same,
   And Your years will not come to an
   end.
28 "The children of Your servants will
   continue,
   And their descendants will be
   established before You."

⊕ Proverbs 24:5, 6

5 A wise man is strong,
   And a man of knowledge increases
   power.
6 For by wise guidance you will wage
   war,
   And in abundance of counselors
   there is victory.

⊕ 1 Corinthians 9:1–27

9 AM I not free? Am I not an apostle?
  Have I not seen Jesus our Lord? Are
you not my work in the Lord?
2   If to others I am not an apostle, at
least I am to you; for you are the seal of
my apostleship in the Lord.
3   My defense to those who examine
me is this:
4   Do we not have a right to eat and
drink?
5   Do we not have a right to take along
a believing wife, even as the rest of the
apostles and the brothers of the Lord and
Cephas?
6   Or do only Barnabas and I not have
a right to refrain from working?
7   Who at any time serves as a soldier
at his own expense? Who plants a vineyard and does not eat the fruit of it? Or
who tends a flock and does not use the
milk of the flock?
8   I am not speaking these things according to human judgment, am I? Or
does not the Law also say these things?
9   For it is written in the Law of Moses,
"YOU SHALL NOT MUZZLE THE OX WHILE
HE IS THRESHING." God is not concerned
about oxen, is He?
10 Or is He speaking altogether for our
sake? Yes, for our sake it was written,
because the plowman ought to plow in
hope, and the thresher to thresh in hope
of sharing the crops.

11 If we sowed spiritual things in you,
is it too much if we reap material things
from you?
12 If others share the right over you, do
we not more? Nevertheless, we did not
use this right, but we endure all things
so that we will cause no hindrance to the
gospel of Christ.
13 Do you not know that those who perform sacred services eat the food of the
temple, and those who attend regularly to
the altar have their share from the altar?
14 So also the Lord directed those who
proclaim the gospel to get their living
from the gospel.
15 But I have used none of these things.
And I am not writing these things so that
it will be done so in my case; for it would
be better for me to die than have any
man make my boast an empty one.
16 For if I preach the gospel, I have
nothing to boast of, for I am under compulsion; for woe is me if I do not preach
the gospel.
17 For if I do this voluntarily, I have a
reward; but if against my will, I have a
stewardship entrusted to me.
18 What then is my reward? That, when
I preach the gospel, I may offer the gospel without charge, so as not to make full
use of my right in the gospel.
19 For though I am free from all men, I
have made myself a slave to all, so that I
may win more.
20 To the Jews I became as a Jew, so
that I might win Jews; to those who are
under the Law, as under the Law though
not being myself under the Law, so that I
might win those who are under the Law;
21 to those who are without law, as without law, though not being without the law
of God but under the law of Christ, so that
I might win those who are without law.
22 To the weak I became weak, that I ◄

LIFE LESSONS

➤ **1 Corinthians 9:22** — *I have become
all things to all men, so that I may by all
means save some.*

*P*aul never compromised his convictions or his calling, but he was more
than willing to find common ground and
meet his audience wherever it happened
to be. More than anything, he wanted
to lead people to life in Christ.

might win the weak; I have become all things to all men, so that I may by all means save some.

23 I do all things for the sake of the gospel, so that I may become a fellow partaker of it.

24 Do you not know that those who run in a race all run, but *only* one receives the prize? Run in such a way that you may win.

25 Everyone who competes in the games exercises self-control in all things. They then *do it* to receive a perishable wreath, but we an imperishable.

26 Therefore I run in such a way, as not without aim; I box in such a way, as not beating the air;

27 but I discipline my body and make it

LIFE LESSONS

➤ **1 Corinthians 9:24 —** *Run in such a way that you may win.*

*W*e will not accomplish much in life if we do not have a clear purpose and mission in mind. The only way to consistently hit the mark is to take careful aim. What is your own life mission? It is a great privilege to serve the Lord, but it is also our duty. The amazing thing is that God has promised to reward us richly for what we do for Him and what we allow Him to do through us.

my slave, so that, after I have preached to others, I myself will not be disqualified.

Ecclesiastes 7:1–29

7 A GOOD name is better than a good ointment,
And the day of *one's* death is better than the day of one's birth.

2 It is better to go to a house of mourning
Than to go to a house of feasting,
Because that is the end of every man,
And the living takes *it* to heart.

3 Sorrow is better than laughter,
For when a face is sad a heart may be happy.

4 The mind of the wise is in the house of mourning,
While the mind of fools is in the house of pleasure.

5 It is better to listen to the rebuke of a wise man
Than for one to listen to the song of fools.

6 For as the crackling of thorn bushes under a pot,
So is the laughter of the fool;
And this too is futility.

7 For oppression makes a wise man mad,
And a bribe corrupts the heart.

8 The end of a matter is better than its beginning;

Patience of spirit is better than haughtiness of spirit.

9 Do not be eager in your heart to be angry,
For anger resides in the bosom of fools.

10 Do not say, "Why is it that the former days were better than these?"
For it is not from wisdom that you ask about this.

11 Wisdom along with an inheritance is good
And an advantage to those who see the sun.

LIFE LESSONS

➤ **Ecclesiastes 7:5 —** *It is better to listen to the rebuke of a wise man than for one to listen to the song of fools.*

*W*e live in an entertainment age in which people increasingly value mindless diversions over substantive pursuits that might require some thinking. However, everything we listen to affects how we think and make decisions—for godliness or wickedness. That's why as Christians we are to be "destroying speculations and every lofty thing raised up against the knowledge of God, and we are taking every thought captive to the obedience of Christ" (2 Cor. 10:5).

WHAT THE BIBLE SAYS ABOUT

How to Control Our Anger

Ecclesiastes 7:9

*I*n Isaiah 64:9, the prophet implores God with these words: "Do not be angry beyond measure, O LORD, nor remember iniquity forever." From this passage we learn that the Father measures His anger in a way appropriate to each occasion. We, too, can learn how to control our anger and focus it so that we do no harm. How do we go about doing that?

Ephesians 4:26 exhorts us to control our anger so we do not sin. While anger itself is not sinful, it can quickly lead to this. A line exists that we must not cross. How do we know when we have crossed it? Clearly we must avoid verbal abuse and physical violence, but anger can lead to other sins just as deadly. Whenever you see the following in your life, you know you have crossed the line:

1. *Strife*—Proverbs 29:22 tells us "an angry man stirs up strife." Strife can take many forms, but it always pits one person against another, even if things don't become loud or violent. Isaiah warned against employers who took unfair advantage of their workers, yet tried to cover their tracks with religious observance: "Behold, on the day of your fast you find your desire, and drive hard all your workers. Behold, you fast for contention and strife and to strike with a wicked fist" (Is. 58:3, 4). But it wouldn't work. For all of their rituals, their voices would not be "heard on high" (Is. 58:4).

2. *Bitterness*—Psalm 30:5 says that God's "anger is but for a moment," and Ephesians 4:26 warns us against staying angry overnight. Extended anger usually leads to bitterness. So God instructs us, "Let all bitterness and wrath and anger and clamor and slander be put away from you, along with all malice" (Eph. 4:31).

3. *Isolation*—Nursing anger leads people to avoid each other and eventually to cut off their relationships altogether. Proverbs 18:1 warns, "He who separates himself seeks his own desire, he quarrels against all sound wisdom." Eventually, being right about an issue becomes more important to us than showing the love of God to others, which contradicts the Lord's command: "The Lord's bond-servant must not be quarrelsome, but be kind to all, able to teach, patient when wronged, with gentleness correcting those who are in opposition, if perhaps God may grant them repentance leading to the knowledge of the truth" (2 Tim. 2:24, 25).

4. *Retaliation*—Romans 12:19 addresses this directly: "Never take your own revenge, beloved, but leave room for the wrath of God, for it is written, 'Vengeance is Mine, I will repay,' says the Lord."

Remember, "The anger of man does not achieve the righteousness of God" (James 1:20). Therefore, when you find yourself crossing the line and becoming angry beyond measure, submit yourself to God and "do not give the devil an opportunity" (Eph. 4:27). Confess your feelings, pray for the person who has infuriated you, and ask for the Lord's guidance in the situation. Surely, the Lord will give you "such a word as is good for edification according to the need of the moment, so that it will give grace to those who hear" (Eph. 4:29).

---

12 For wisdom is protection *just as*
        money is protection,
    But the advantage of knowledge is
        that wisdom preserves the lives of
        its possessors.
13 Consider the work of God,
    For who is able to straighten what
        He has bent?
➤ 14 In the day of prosperity be happy,
    But in the day of adversity
        consider—
    God has made the one as well as
        the other
    So that man will not discover
        anything *that will be* after him.

15 I have seen everything during my lifetime of futility; there is a righteous man

LIFE LESSONS

➤ **Ecclesiastes 7:14 —** *God has made the one as well as the other.*

*W*e tend to see good times as the blessing of God and bad times as the work of the devil, but such a view is shortsighted. Nothing reaches us without first passing through the hands of our sovereign God—and He uses adversity to deepen our relationships with Him.

who perishes in his righteousness and there is a wicked man who prolongs *his life* in his wickedness.

16 Do not be excessively righteous and do not be overly wise. Why should you ruin yourself?

17 Do not be excessively wicked and do not be a fool. Why should you die before your time?

18 It is good that you grasp one thing and also not let go of the other; for the one who fears God comes forth with both of them.

19 Wisdom strengthens a wise man more than ten rulers who are in a city.

20 Indeed, there is not a righteous man on earth who *continually* does good and who never sins.

21 Also, do not take seriously all words which are spoken, so that you will not hear your servant cursing you.

22 For you also have realized that you likewise have many times cursed others.

23 I tested all this with wisdom, *and* I said, "I will be wise," but it was far from me.

24 What has been is remote and exceedingly mysterious. Who can discover it?

25 I directed my mind to know, to investigate and to seek wisdom and an explanation, and to know the evil of folly and the foolishness of madness.

26 And I discovered more bitter than death the woman whose heart is snares and nets, whose hands are chains. One who is pleasing to God will escape from her, but the sinner will be captured by her.

27 "Behold, I have discovered this," says the Preacher, "*adding* one thing to another to find an explanation,

28 which I am still seeking but have not found. I have found one man among a thousand, but I have not found a woman among all these.

29 "Behold, I have found only this, that God made men upright, but they have sought out many devices."

✛ Psalm 103:1–5

A Psalm of David.

103 BLESS the LORD, O my soul,
And all that is within me, *bless*
His holy name.

2 Bless the LORD, O my soul,
And forget none of His benefits;

3 Who pardons all your iniquities,
Who heals all your diseases;

4 Who redeems your life from the pit,
Who crowns you with lovingkindness and compassion;

5 Who satisfies your years with good things,
So that your youth is renewed like the eagle.

✛ Proverbs 24:7–9

7 Wisdom is *too* exalted for a fool,
He does not open his mouth in the gate.

8 One who plans to do evil,
Men will call a schemer.

9 The devising of folly is sin,
And the scoffer is an abomination to men.

✛ 1 Corinthians 10:1–18

10 FOR I do not want you to be unaware, brethren, that our fathers were all under the cloud and all passed through the sea;

2 and all were baptized into Moses in the cloud and in the sea;

3 and all ate the same spiritual food;

4 and all drank the same spiritual drink, for they were drinking from a spiritual rock which followed them; and the rock was Christ.

5 Nevertheless, with most of them God was not well-pleased; for they were laid low in the wilderness.

6 Now these things happened as

LIFE LESSONS

➤ **Psalm 103:1 — *Bless the Lord, O my soul, and all that is within me, bless His holy name.***

*G*od wants every part of us—body, soul and spirit—to grow close to Him and enter into a joyful relationship with Him. He seeks worshipers who will gladly give everything they are to Him.

examples for us, so that we would not crave evil things as they also craved.

7 Do not be idolaters, as some of them were; as it is written, "THE PEOPLE SAT DOWN TO EAT AND DRINK, AND STOOD UP TO PLAY."

8 Nor let us act immorally, as some of them did, and twenty-three thousand fell in one day.

9 Nor let us try the Lord, as some of them did, and were destroyed by the serpents.

10 Nor grumble, as some of them did, and were destroyed by the destroyer.

➤ 11 Now these things happened to them as an example, and they were written for our instruction, upon whom the ends of the ages have come.

12 Therefore let him who thinks he stands take heed that he does not fall.

13 No temptation has overtaken you but such as is common to man; and God is faithful, who will not allow you to be tempted beyond what you are able, but with the temptation will provide the way of escape also, so that you will be able to endure it.

14 Therefore, my beloved, flee from idolatry.

15 I speak as to wise men; you judge what I say.

16 Is not the cup of blessing which we bless a sharing in the blood of Christ? Is not the bread which we break a sharing in the body of Christ?

17 Since there is one bread, we who are many are one body; for we all partake of the one bread.

18 Look at the nation Israel; are not those who eat the sacrifices sharers in the altar?

Ecclesiastes 8:1—10:20

8 WHO is like the wise man and who knows the interpretation of a matter? A man's wisdom illumines him and causes his stern face to beam.

2 I say, "Keep the command of the king because of the oath before God.

3 "Do not be in a hurry to leave him. Do not join in an evil matter, for he will do whatever he pleases."

4 Since the word of the king is authoritative, who will say to him, "What are you doing?"

➤ 5 He who keeps a *royal* command experiences no trouble, for a wise heart knows the proper time and procedure.

6 For there is a proper time and procedure for every delight, though a man's trouble is heavy upon him.

7 If no one knows what will happen, who can tell him when it will happen?

8 No man has authority to restrain the wind with the wind, or authority over the day of death; and there is no discharge in the time of war, and evil will not deliver those who practice it.

9 All this I have seen and applied my mind to every deed that has been done under the sun wherein a man has exercised authority over *another* man to his hurt.

10 So then, I have seen the wicked buried, those who used to go in and out from the holy place, and they are *soon*

forgotten in the city where they did thus. This too is futility.

11 Because the sentence against an evil deed is not executed quickly, therefore the hearts of the sons of men among them are given fully to do evil.

12 Although a sinner does evil a hundred *times* and may lengthen his *life*, still I know that it will be well for those who fear God, who fear Him openly.

13 But it will not be well for the evil man and he will not lengthen his days like a shadow, because he does not fear God.

14 There is futility which is done on the earth, that is, there are righteous men to whom it happens according to the deeds of the wicked. On the other hand, there are evil men to whom it happens according to the deeds of the righteous. I say that this too is futility.

15 So I commended pleasure, for there is nothing good for a man under the sun except to eat and to drink and to be merry, and this will stand by him in his toils *throughout* the days of his life which God has given him under the sun.

16 When I gave my heart to know wisdom and to see the task which has been done on the earth (even though one should never sleep day or night),

17 and I saw every work of God, *I concluded* that man cannot discover the work which has been done under the sun. Even though man should seek laboriously, he will not discover; and though the wise man should say, "I know," he cannot discover.

9 FOR I have taken all this to my heart and explain it that righteous men, wise men, and their deeds are in the hand of God. Man does not know whether *it will be* love or hatred; anything awaits him.

2 It is the same for all. There is one fate for the righteous and for the wicked; for the good, for the clean and for the unclean; for the man who offers a sacrifice and for the one who does not sacrifice. As the good man is, so is the sinner; as the swearer is, so is the one who is afraid to swear.

3 This is an evil in all that is done under the sun, that there is one fate for all men. Furthermore, the hearts of the sons of men are full of evil and insanity is in their hearts throughout their lives. Afterwards they *go* to the dead.

4 For whoever is joined with all the living, there is hope; surely a live dog is better than a dead lion.

5 For the living know they will die; but the dead do not know anything, nor have they any longer a reward, for their memory is forgotten.

6 Indeed their love, their hate and their zeal have already perished, and they will no longer have a share in all that is done under the sun.

7 Go *then*, eat your bread in happiness and drink your wine with a cheerful heart; for God has already approved your works.

8 Let your clothes be white all the time, and let not oil be lacking on your head.

9 Enjoy life with the woman whom you love all the days of your fleeting life which He has given to you under the sun; for this is your reward in life and in your toil in which you have labored under the sun.

10 Whatever your hand finds to do, do *it* with *all* your might; for there is no activity or planning or knowledge or wisdom in Sheol where you are going.

11 I again saw under the sun that the race is not to the swift and the battle is not to the warriors, and neither is bread to the wise nor wealth to the discerning nor favor to men of ability; for time and chance overtake them all.

LIFE LESSONS

➤ **Ecclesiastes 9:2** — *One fate for the righteous and for the wicked.*

*G*ood things can happen to bad people, and bad things can happen to good people. That's the world we live in. But this world is coming to an end, and when it does, God will reveal a very different story.

➤ **Ecclesiastes 9:10** — *Whatever your hand finds to do, do it with all your might.*

*G*od doesn't appreciate partial obedience—He sees it as disobedience and denounces halfhearted devotion to Him (Rev. 3:15, 16). God urges us to work at whatever He gives us to do with all our hearts (Col. 3:23). Enthusiasm for Him should translate into enthusiasm for life.

ANSWERS TO LIFE'S QUESTIONS

How can I find fulfillment in my work?

ECCLESIASTES 9:10

*W*e all enjoy weekends. Recreation with our families and friends is important for a well-balanced life. But if we live for the weekends only, we thwart God's desire to bless us in the task that occupies most of our adult life—work—whether you are a stay at home mom or someone who heads out each morning to an office or a job.

Work is not the result of the curse placed on humanity when Adam and Eve sinned. God had instructed them to reap the fruit of the earth *before* the fall (Gen. 1:27–30). Work is a gift from God—given for our enjoyment and blessing. That is why the Preacher wrote, "I know that there is nothing better for them than to rejoice and to do good in one's lifetime; moreover, that every man who eats and drinks sees good in all his labor—it is the gift of God" (Eccl. 3:12, 13).

"Wait a minute," you might be saying. "If you knew who my boss is, you would understand! How can I possibly enjoy my work with such an unpleasant supervisor?"

True enough, some work may not fit our ideal job descriptions—but consider the alternative. Have you ever known anyone to feel happy and satisfied while standing in an unemployment line? If you have a job, thank God for it.

Wherever you find yourself working today—on the factory line, under a sink, at a desk, in a truck, or on the phone—thank the Lord for your work. It may be less than perfect, but that is where God has placed you, at least for now.

We must come to see every detail of our jobs as an opportunity to serve God. The apostle Paul tells us, "Whether, then, you eat or drink or whatever you do, do all to the glory of God" (1 Cor. 10:31). And he reminds us, "Whatever you do, do your work heartily, as for the Lord rather than for men, knowing that from the Lord you will receive the reward of the inheritance. It is the Lord Christ whom you serve" (Col. 3:23, 24). Such an attitude can transform the workplace from a mere workstation to a practical pulpit that says more about your relationship with Christ than words ever could.

See work as God's gift! Give Him thanks for the opportunity and the privilege of working—not just for a living but also for Him. Then you can start anticipating the weekday as much as the weekend.

---

12 Moreover, man does not know his time: like fish caught in a treacherous net and birds trapped in a snare, so the sons of men are ensnared at an evil time when it suddenly falls on them.
13 Also this I came to see as wisdom under the sun, and it impressed me.
14 There was a small city with few men in it and a great king came to it, surrounded it and constructed large siegeworks against it.
15 But there was found in it a poor wise man and he delivered the city by his wisdom. Yet no one remembered that poor man.
16 So I said, "Wisdom is better than strength." But the wisdom of the poor man is despised and his words are not heeded.
17 The words of the wise heard in quietness are *better* than the shouting of a ruler among fools.
18 Wisdom is better than weapons of war, but one sinner destroys much good.

10 DEAD flies make a perfumer's oil stink, so a little foolishness is weightier than wisdom *and* honor.

2 A wise man's heart *directs him* toward the right, but the foolish man's heart *directs him* toward the left.
3 Even when the fool walks along the road, his sense is lacking and he demonstrates to everyone *that* he is a fool.
4 If the ruler's temper rises against you, do not abandon your position, because composure allays great offenses.
5 There is an evil I have seen under the sun, like an error which goes forth from the ruler—
6 folly is set in many exalted places while rich men sit in humble places.
7 I have seen slaves *riding* on horses and princes walking like slaves on the land.
8 He who digs a pit may fall into it, and a serpent may bite him who breaks through a wall.
9 He who quarries stones may be hurt by them, and he who splits logs may be endangered by them.
10 If the axe is dull and he does not sharpen *its* edge, then he must exert more strength. Wisdom has the advantage of giving success.

11 If the serpent bites before being charmed, there is no profit for the charmer.

12 Words from the mouth of a wise man are gracious, while the lips of a fool consume him;

13 the beginning of his talking is folly and the end of it is wicked madness.

14 Yet the fool multiplies words. No man knows what will happen, and who can tell him what will come after him?

15 The toil of a fool so wearies him that he does not even know how to go to a city.

16 Woe to you, O land, whose king is a lad and whose princes feast in the morning.

17 Blessed are you, O land, whose king is of nobility and whose princes eat at the appropriate time—for strength and not for drunkenness.

18 Through indolence the rafters sag, and through slackness the house leaks.

19 Men prepare a meal for enjoyment, and wine makes life merry, and money is the answer to everything.

20 Furthermore, in your bedchamber do not curse a king, and in your sleeping rooms do not curse a rich man, for a bird of the heavens will carry the sound and the winged creature will make the matter known.

Psalm 103:6–14

6 The LORD performs righteous deeds
   And judgments for all who are
      oppressed.

7 He made known His ways to Moses,
   His acts to the sons of Israel.

8 The LORD is compassionate and
      gracious,
   Slow to anger and abounding in
      lovingkindness.

9 He will not always strive with us,
   Nor will He keep His anger forever.

10 He has not dealt with us according
      to our sins,
   Nor rewarded us according to our
      iniquities.

11 For as high as the heavens are
      above the earth,
   So great is His lovingkindness
      toward those who fear Him.

12 As far as the east is from the west,

So far has He removed our
   transgressions from us.

13 Just as a father has compassion on
      his children,
   So the LORD has compassion on
      those who fear Him.

14 For He Himself knows our frame;
   He is mindful that we are but dust.

Proverbs 24:10–12

10 If you are slack in the day of distress,
   Your strength is limited.

11 Deliver those who are being taken
      away to death,
   And those who are staggering to
      slaughter, Oh hold them back.

12 If you say, "See, we did not know this,"
   Does He not consider it who weighs
      the hearts?
   And does He not know it who keeps
      your soul?
   And will He not render to man
      according to his work?

1 Corinthians 10:19–33

19 What do I mean then? That a thing sacrificed to idols is anything, or that an idol is anything?

20 No, but I say that the things which the Gentiles sacrifice, they sacrifice to demons and not to God; and I do not want you to become sharers in demons.

21 You cannot drink the cup of the Lord and the cup of demons; you cannot partake of the table of the Lord and the table of demons.

22 Or do we provoke the Lord to jealousy? We are not stronger than He, are we?

LIFE LESSONS

➤ Psalm 103:13 — Just as a father has compassion on his children, so the Lord has compassion on those who fear Him.

How does a father have compassion on His children? He considers their weaknesses, immaturities, and ignorances, and He does not require of them more than they can handle. Our Father does the same with us (1 Cor. 10:13).

➤ **23** All things are lawful, but not all things are profitable. All things are lawful, but not all things edify.

24 Let no one seek his own *good,* but that of his neighbor.

25 Eat anything that is sold in the meat market without asking questions for conscience' sake;

26 FOR THE EARTH IS THE LORD'S, AND ALL IT CONTAINS.

27 If one of the unbelievers invites you and you want to go, eat anything that is set before you without asking questions for conscience' sake.

28 But if anyone says to you, "This is meat sacrificed to idols," do not eat *it,* for the sake of the one who informed *you,* and for conscience' sake;

29 I mean not your own conscience, but the other *man's;* for why is my freedom judged by another's conscience?

30 If I partake with thankfulness, why am I slandered concerning that for which I give thanks?

➤ ✱ **31** Whether, then, you eat or drink or whatever you do, do all to the glory of God.

LIFE LESSONS

➤ **1 Corinthians 10:23 — *All things are lawful, but not all things are profitable. All things are lawful, but not all things edify.***

*G*od wants us to move beyond merely debating whether something is wrong or right, and instead choose actions that build up the faith of others.

➤ **1 Corinthians 10:31 — *Do all to the glory of God.***

*T*here could hardly be a better standard of behavior than this. Before you commit to any action, ask yourself, "Can I do this to the glory of God? Would this action put God's reputation in a good light?"

---

32 Give no offense either to Jews or to Greeks or to the church of God;

33 just as I also please all men in all things, not seeking my own profit but the *profit* of the many, so that they may be saved.

AUGUST 31

◈ Ecclesiastes 11:1—12:14

11 CAST your bread on the surface of the waters, for you will find it after many days.

2 Divide your portion to seven, or even to eight, for you do not know what misfortune may occur on the earth.

3 If the clouds are full, they pour out rain upon the earth; and whether a tree falls toward the south or toward the north, wherever the tree falls, there it lies.

➤ **4** He who watches the wind will not sow and he who looks at the clouds will not reap.

➤ **5** Just as you do not know the path of the wind and how bones *are formed* in the womb of the pregnant woman, so you do not know the activity of God who makes all things.

6 Sow your seed in the morning and do not be idle in the evening, for you do not know whether morning or evening sowing will succeed, or whether both of them alike will be good.

LIFE LESSONS

➤ **Ecclesiastes 11:4 — *He who watches the wind will not sow and he who looks at the clouds will not reap.***

*T*he procrastinator can easily miss out on God's best for his life. Instead, our callings are always to obey the initial promptings of His Holy Spirit. Therefore, let your motto be, "I'll obey immediately, as the Lord directs and enables me."

➤ **Ecclesiastes 11:5 — *You do not know the activity of God who makes all things.***

*G*od's ways are higher than ours, and His thoughts far loftier and greater (Is. 55:8, 9). Yet He reveals exactly what we need so that we can follow Him joyfully and successfully (Deut. 29:29). Let us treasure God's Word!

WHAT THE BIBLE SAYS ABOUT ◉

The Value of Diligence

Ecclesiastes 11:6

You've probably heard the old sayings, "The early bird gets the worm" and "sharp as a tack." But have you ever considered that both describe a character trait that the Bible says is vital to any successful venture?

This character trait is diligence, frequently contrasted in the Bible with laziness and procrastination. The Hebrew language uses two word pictures to illustrate diligence: "dawn" and "knife," thus portraying an individual who is fully awake and alert (the early bird) and whose skills are sharpened and honed (sharp as a tack).

"He who watches the wind will not sow and he who looks at the clouds will not reap," the Preacher tells us (Eccl. 11:4). We can't spend our time daydreaming, nor can we wait to get started until all conditions look absolutely optimal. "Sow your seed in the morning and do not be idle in the evening, for you do not know whether morning or evening sowing will succeed, or whether both of them alike will be good" (Eccl. 11:6).

The lazy man is always dreaming and wanting but never willing to pay the price of perseverance. Thus he comes to frustration and emptiness. Yet a diligent man is a satisfied man.

Before the apostle Peter listed the character-building blocks of faith, virtue, knowledge, and self-control, he exhorted his readers to apply "all diligence" in acquiring them (2 Pet. 1:5). Such qualities are not found in a superficial Christian. They take root in one's character only through steadfast application and pursuit.

The overriding motivation for the cultivation and attainment of diligence is not material gain, but the urgency of our Christian witness. "We must work the works of Him who sent Me as long as it is day," Jesus said. "Night is coming when no one can work" (John 9:4).

Our pilgrimage on earth is brief. A diligent believer alert to every opportunity to share Christ and make Him known will have the greatest influence on the kingdom of God. Time is precious. We redeem it for His purposes as we remain diligent in our work, our study, our witness, and our prayers. ◉

---

7 The light is pleasant, and *it is* good for the eyes to see the sun.

8 Indeed, if a man should live many years, let him rejoice in them all, and let him remember the days of darkness, for they will be many. Everything that is to come *will be* futility.

9 Rejoice, young man, during your childhood, and let your heart be pleasant during the days of young manhood. And follow the impulses of your heart and the desires of your eyes. Yet know that God will bring you to judgment for all these things.

10 So, remove grief and anger from your heart and put away pain from your body, because childhood and the prime of life are fleeting.

➤ 12 REMEMBER also your Creator in the days of your youth, before the evil days come and the years draw near when you will say, "I have no delight in them";

2 before the sun and the light, the moon and the stars are darkened, and clouds return after the rain;

3 in the day that the watchmen of the house tremble, and mighty men stoop, the grinding ones stand idle because they are few, and those who look through windows grow dim;

4 and the doors on the street are shut as the sound of the grinding mill is low, and one will arise at the sound of the bird, and all the daughters of song will sing softly.

5 Furthermore, men are afraid of a high place and of terrors on the road; the almond tree blossoms, the grasshopper drags himself along, and the caperberry is ineffective. For man goes to his eternal home while mourners go about in the street.

LIFE LESSONS

➤ **Ecclesiastes 12:1 —** *Remember also your Creator in the days of your youth.*

Toward the end of his life, Solomon did not walk with God, and so he dreaded growing old. Let us strive to be more like Moses, who at the end still had bright eyes and a zest for life (Deut. 34:7).

6　*Remember Him* before the silver cord is broken and the golden bowl is crushed, the pitcher by the well is shattered and the wheel at the cistern is crushed;

7　then the dust will return to the earth as it was, and the spirit will return to God who gave it.

8　"Vanity of vanities," says the Preacher, "all is vanity!"

9　In addition to being a wise man, the Preacher also taught the people knowledge; and he pondered, searched out and arranged many proverbs.

10　The Preacher sought to find delightful words and to write words of truth correctly.

11　The words of wise men are like goads, and masters of *these* collections are like well-driven nails; they are given by one Shepherd.

12　But beyond this, my son, be warned: the writing of many books is endless, and excessive devotion *to books* is wearying to the body.

➤ 13　The conclusion, when all has been heard, *is*: fear God and keep His commandments, because this *applies to* every person.

✳ 14　For God will bring every act to judgment, everything which is hidden, whether it is good or evil.

✦ Psalm 103:15–22

15　As for man, his days are like grass;
　　As a flower of the field, so he
　　　flourishes.

16　When the wind has passed over it, it
　　is no more,
　　And its place acknowledges it no
　　　longer.

LIFE LESSONS

➤ **Ecclesiastes 12:13 —** *Fear God and keep His commandments, because this applies to every person.*

*F*rom Genesis to Revelation, God instructs and urges His people to obey His commands and to fear His great name. Yet we are to do so with joy in our souls and love in our hearts (Deut. 6:5, 6; Matt. 22:37; John 15: 9-11; Eph. 6:24).

17　But the lovingkindness of the LORD
　　is from everlasting to everlasting
　　on those who fear Him,
　　And His righteousness to children's　✳
　　　children,

18　To those who keep His covenant
　　And remember His precepts to do
　　　them.

19　The LORD has established His
　　throne in the heavens,
　　And His sovereignty rules over all.

20　Bless the LORD, you His angels,
　　Mighty in strength, who perform His
　　　word,
　　Obeying the voice of His word!

21　Bless the LORD, all you His hosts,
　　You who serve Him, doing His will.

22　Bless the LORD, all you works of
　　His,
　　In all places of His dominion;
　　Bless the LORD, O my soul!

✦ Proverbs 24:13, 14

13　My son, eat honey, for it is good,
　　Yes, the honey from the comb is
　　　sweet to your taste;

14　Know *that* wisdom is thus for your　✳
　　soul;
　　If you find *it*, then there will be a
　　　future,
　　And your hope will not be cut off.

✦ 1 Corinthians 11:1–16

11 BE imitators of me, just as I also am　✳ of Christ.

2　Now I praise you because you remember me in everything and hold firmly to the traditions, just as I delivered them to you.

3　But I want you to understand that Christ is the head of every man, and the man is the head of a woman, and God is the head of Christ.

4　Every man who has *something* on his head while praying or prophesying disgraces his head.

5　But every woman who has her head uncovered while praying or prophesying disgraces her head, for she is one and the same as the woman whose head is shaved.

6 For if a woman does not cover her head, let her also have her hair cut off; but if it is disgraceful for a woman to have her hair cut off or her head shaved, let her cover her head.

7 For a man ought not to have his head covered, since he is the image and glory of God; but the woman is the glory of man.

8 For man does not originate from woman, but woman from man;

9 for indeed man was not created for the woman's sake, but woman for the man's sake.

10 Therefore the woman ought to have *a symbol of* authority on her head, because of the angels.

11 However, in the Lord, neither is woman independent of man, nor is man independent of woman.

12 For as the woman originates from the man, so also the man *has his birth* through the woman; and all things originate from God.

13 Judge for yourselves: is it proper for a woman to pray to God *with her head* uncovered?

14 Does not even nature itself teach you that if a man has long hair, it is a dishonor to him,

15 but if a woman has long hair, it is a glory to her? For her hair is given to her for a covering.

16 But if one is inclined to be contentious, we have no other practice, nor have the churches of God.

Song of Solomon 1:1—2:17

1 THE Song of Songs, which is Solomon's.
2 "May he kiss me with the kisses of his mouth!
For your love is better than wine.
3 "Your oils have a pleasing fragrance,
Your name is *like* purified oil;
Therefore the maidens love you.
➤ 4 "Draw me after you *and* let us run *together!*
The king has brought me into his chambers."
"We will rejoice in you and be glad;
We will extol your love more than wine.
Rightly do they love you."
5 "I am black but lovely,
O daughters of Jerusalem,
Like the tents of Kedar,
Like the curtains of Solomon.
6 "Do not stare at me because I am swarthy,
For the sun has burned me.
My mother's sons were angry with me;
They made me caretaker of the vineyards,
But I have not taken care of my own vineyard.
7 "Tell me, O you whom my soul loves,
Where do you pasture *your flock,*
Where do you make *it* lie down at noon?
For why should I be like one who veils herself
Beside the flocks of your companions?"
8 "If you yourself do not know,
Most beautiful among women,
Go forth on the trail of the flock
And pasture your young goats
By the tents of the shepherds.
9 "To me, my darling, you are like
My mare among the chariots of Pharaoh.
10 "Your cheeks are lovely with ornaments,
Your neck with strings of beads."
11 "We will make for you ornaments of gold
With beads of silver."
12 "While the king was at his table,
My perfume gave forth its fragrance.
13 "My beloved is to me a pouch of myrrh
Which lies all night between my breasts.
14 "My beloved is to me a cluster of henna blossoms
In the vineyards of Engedi."
15 "How beautiful you are, my darling,
How beautiful you are!
Your eyes are *like* doves."
16 "How handsome you are, my beloved,
And so pleasant!
Indeed, our couch is luxuriant!
17 "The beams of our houses are cedars,
Our rafters, cypresses.

2 "I AM the rose of Sharon,
The lily of the valleys."
2 "Like a lily among the thorns,
So is my darling among the maidens."
3 "Like an apple tree among the trees of the forest,
So is my beloved among the young men.
In his shade I took great delight and sat down,
And his fruit was sweet to my taste.
4 "He has brought me to *his* banquet hall,
And his banner over me is love.
5 "Sustain me with raisin cakes,
Refresh me with apples,
Because I am lovesick.
6 "Let his left hand be under my head
And his right hand embrace me."

LIFE LESSONS

➤ **Song of Solomon 1:4 —** *We will rejoice in you and be glad; we will extol your love.*

No Christian has ever been called to "go it alone" in his or her walk of faith. To make both our marriages and our churches work as God wants them to, we must get involved with trustworthy, mature believers who help us grow in our relationships with Christ and in our giftedness. No one grows in perpetual solitude. Therefore, we must consciously devote time to developing our friendships with other godly believers.

WHAT THE BIBLE SAYS ABOUT

God as Our Lover

Song of Solomon 2:4

Love is the greatest gift God offers us. And yet, it is the one we have the most difficulty receiving. Why?

First, sometimes we do not think we deserve His love—which is true. "God demonstrates His own love toward us," the apostle Paul writes, "in that while we were yet sinners, Christ died for us" (Rom. 5:8).

Second, we often do not understand God's unconditional love, because its quality differs so much from our own. We somehow believe that He loves us the way we love others. Such a viewpoint, however, leaves us doubtful that He will always love us as the Bible promises He will (Jer. 31:1).

Love is a sacrificial commitment to the peace, security, joy, and development of another person (1 Cor. 13:4–8). The Father's love is not based on emotion but flows out of His changeless character. The Bible tells us that God is love (1 John 4:8). Since it is impossible for Him to do anything contrary to His nature, His love will forever remain certain and dependable.

In addition, He gives us His love as a gift. James 1:17 teaches, "Every perfect gift is from above, coming down from the Father of lights, with whom there is no variation or shifting shadow." Because God does not change, His love for us exists independently from our actions. We cannot earn it or give anything in return for it—the Lord offers His love to us freely, as a gift.

The love of our heavenly Father is perfect—it is wonderful, faultless, unfailing, forgiving, and unconditional. You cannot increase His love for you in any way, and you certainly cannot stop Him from caring about you. Since His love for you is perfect, you can be sure He is with you forever—leading you in the way that is best and providing everything you need. Therefore, forget any misconceptions you have about whether or not the Lord accepts you. Release all those feelings of unworthiness and fears of being forsaken. God has always loved you and always will. Rejoice that His banner over you is love (Song 2:4).

---

7 "I adjure you, O daughters of
        Jerusalem,
    By the gazelles or by the hinds of
        the field,
    That you do not arouse or awaken
        my love
    Until she pleases."
8 "Listen! My beloved!
    Behold, he is coming,
    Climbing on the mountains,
    Leaping on the hills!
9 "My beloved is like a gazelle or a
        young stag.
    Behold, he is standing behind our
        wall,
    He is looking through the windows,
    He is peering through the lattice.
10 "My beloved responded and said to
        me,
    'Arise, my darling, my beautiful one,
    And come along.
11 'For behold, the winter is past,
    The rain is over *and* gone.
12 'The flowers have *already* appeared
        in the land;
    The time has arrived for pruning
        the vines,

And the voice of the turtledove has
        been heard in our land.
13 'The fig tree has ripened its figs,
    And the vines in blossom have
        given forth *their* fragrance.
    Arise, my darling, my beautiful
        one,
    And come along!'"
14 "O my dove, in the clefts of the
        rock,
    In the secret place of the steep
        pathway,
    Let me see your form,
    Let me hear your voice;
    For your voice is sweet,
    And your form is lovely."

LIFE LESSONS

➤ **Song of Solomon 2:13** — *"Arise my darling, my beautiful one, and come along!"*

Marital love will not flourish without some "alone time" between lovers. In a similar way, our relationships with God will not blossom without spending some private time with Him.

15 "Catch the foxes for us,
     The little foxes that are ruining the
       vineyards,
     While our vineyards are in
       blossom."
16 "My beloved is mine, and I am
       his;
     He pastures *his flock* among the
       lilies.
17 "Until the cool of the day when the
       shadows flee away,
     Turn, my beloved, and be like a
       gazelle
     Or a young stag on the mountains
       of Bether."

Psalm 104:1–9

104 BLESS the LORD, O my soul!
       O LORD my God, You are very
         great;
     You are clothed with splendor and
       majesty,
2   Covering Yourself with light as with
       a cloak,
     Stretching out heaven like a *tent*
       curtain.
3   He lays the beams of His upper
       chambers in the waters;
     He makes the clouds His chariot;
     He walks upon the wings of the
       wind;
4   He makes the winds His
       messengers,
     Flaming fire His ministers.
5   He established the earth upon its
       foundations,
     So that it will not totter forever and
       ever.
6   You covered it with the deep as
       with a garment;
     The waters were standing above the
       mountains.
7   At Your rebuke they fled,
     At the sound of Your thunder they
       hurried away.
8   The mountains rose; the valleys
       sank down
     To the place which You established
       for them.
9   You set a boundary that they may
       not pass over,
     So that they will not return to cover
       the earth.

Proverbs 24:15, 16

15 Do not lie in wait, O wicked man,
     against the dwelling of the
       righteous;
   Do not destroy his resting place;
16 For a righteous man falls seven
     times, and rises again,
   But the wicked stumble in *time of
     calamity.*

1 Corinthians 11:17–34

17 But in giving this instruction, I do
not praise you, because you come together not for the better but for the
worse.
18 For, in the first place, when you
come together as a church, I hear that
divisions exist among you; and in part I
believe it.
19 For there must also be factions
among you, so that those who are approved may become evident among you.
20 Therefore when you meet together,
it is not to eat the Lord's Supper,
21 for in your eating each one takes his
own supper first; and one is hungry and
another is drunk.
22 What! Do you not have houses in
which to eat and drink? Or do you de-

LIFE LESSONS

**Psalm 104:4 — *He makes the winds His
messengers, flaming fire His ministers.***

The angels of God are not the cute,
harmless little cherubs often pictured
in popular culture. They are spirits of
enormous power who are sent to do
God's will. In His mercy, the Lord often
sends them to help us.

**1 Corinthians 11:22 — *Do you despise
the church of God and shame those who
have nothing?***

While we all come to faith as individuals, God calls us to express our
faith in community. When we act without consideration for other members of
Christ's body, we despise the church He
died for.

spise the church of God and shame those who have nothing? What shall I say to you? Shall I praise you? In this I will not praise you.

23 For I received from the Lord that which I also delivered to you, that the Lord Jesus in the night in which He was betrayed took bread;

24 and when He had given thanks, He broke it and said, "This is My body, which is for you; do this in remembrance of Me."

25 In the same way *He took* the cup also after supper, saying, "This cup is the new covenant in My blood; do this, as often as you drink *it,* in remembrance of Me."

26 For as often as you eat this bread and drink the cup, you proclaim the Lord's death until He comes.

27 Therefore whoever eats the bread or drinks the cup of the Lord in an unworthy manner, shall be guilty of the body and the blood of the Lord.

28 But a man must examine himself, and in so doing he is to eat of the bread and drink of the cup.

29 For he who eats and drinks, eats and drinks judgment to himself if he does not judge the body rightly.

30 For this reason many among you are weak and sick, and a number sleep.

31 But if we judged ourselves rightly, we would not be judged.

32 But when we are judged, we are disciplined by the Lord so that we will not be condemned along with the world.

33 So then, my brethren, when you come together to eat, wait for one another.

34 If anyone is hungry, let him eat at home, so that you will not come together for judgment. The remaining matters I will arrange when I come.

LIFE LESSONS

➤ **1 Corinthians 11:26 — *As often as you eat this bread and drink the cup, you proclaim the Lord's death until He comes.***

The Lord's Supper not only looks back at Christ's sacrifice and gives Him praise for His great gift of salvation to us, but it also looks ahead to the day when we will see Him again and enjoy our heavenly home with Him forever.

➤ **1 Corinthians 11:32 — *When we are judged, we are disciplined by the Lord so that we will not be condemned along with the world.***

God disciplines His erring children because He wants to spare us the greater pain that comes with persistent disobedience (Heb. 12:5-13). His mercy prompts His discipline.

SEPTEMBER 2

Song of Solomon 3:1—4:16

3 "ON my bed night after night I
　　　sought him
　　Whom my soul loves;
　　I sought him but did not find him.

2 'I must arise now and go about the
　　　city;
　　In the streets and in the squares
　　I must seek him whom my soul loves.'
　　I sought him but did not find him.

3 "The watchmen who make the
　　　rounds in the city found me,
　　And I said, 'Have you seen him
　　　whom my soul loves?'

4 "Scarcely had I left them

When I found him whom my soul
　　　loves;
　　I held on to him and would not let
　　　him go
　　Until I had brought him to my
　　　mother's house,
　　And into the room of her who
　　　conceived me."

5 "I adjure you, O daughters of
　　　Jerusalem,
　　By the gazelles or by the hinds of
　　　the field,
　　That you will not arouse or awaken
　　my love
　　Until she pleases."

6 "What is this coming up from the
　　　wilderness

Like columns of smoke,
Perfumed with myrrh and
  frankincense,
With all scented powders of the
  merchant?
7 "Behold, it is the *traveling* couch of
     Solomon;
   Sixty mighty men around it,
   Of the mighty men of Israel.
8 "All of them are wielders of the
     sword,
   Expert in war;
   Each man has his sword at his side,
   Guarding against the terrors of the
     night.
9 "King Solomon has made for himself
     a sedan chair
   From the timber of Lebanon.
10 "He made its posts of silver,
   Its back of gold
   And its seat of purple fabric,
   With its interior lovingly fitted out
   By the daughters of Jerusalem.
11 "Go forth, O daughters of Zion,
   And gaze on King Solomon with the
     crown
   With which his mother has crowned
     him
   On the day of his wedding,
   And on the day of his gladness of
     heart."

4 "HOW beautiful you are, my darling,
   How beautiful you are!
   Your eyes are *like* doves behind
     your veil;
   Your hair is like a flock of goats
   That have descended from Mount
     Gilead.
2 "Your teeth are like a flock of *newly*
     shorn ewes
   Which have come up from *their*
     washing,
   All of which bear twins,
   And not one among them has lost
     her young.
3 "Your lips are like a scarlet thread,
   And your mouth is lovely.
   Your temples are like a slice of a
     pomegranate
   Behind your veil.
4 "Your neck is like the tower of
     David,
   Built with rows of stones
   On which are hung a thousand
     shields,
   All the round shields of the mighty
     men.

5 "Your two breasts are like two
     fawns,
   Twins of a gazelle
   Which feed among the lilies.
6 "Until the cool of the day
   When the shadows flee away,
   I will go my way to the mountain of
     myrrh
   And to the hill of frankincense.
7 "You are altogether beautiful, my
     darling,
   And there is no blemish in you.
8 "*Come* with me from Lebanon, *my*
     bride,
   May you come with me from
     Lebanon.
   Journey down from the summit of
     Amana,
   From the summit of Senir and
     Hermon,
   From the dens of lions,
   From the mountains of leopards.
9 "You have made my heart beat
     faster, my sister, *my* bride;
   You have made my heart beat faster
     with a single *glance* of your eyes,
   With a single strand of your
     necklace.
10 "How beautiful is your love, my
     sister, *my* bride!
   How much better is your love than
     wine,
   And the fragrance of your oils
   Than all *kinds* of spices!
11 "Your lips, *my* bride, drip honey;
   Honey and milk are under your
     tongue,
   And the fragrance of your garments
     is like the fragrance of Lebanon.
12 "A garden locked is my sister, *my*
     bride,
   A rock garden locked, a spring
     sealed up.
13 "Your shoots are an orchard of
     pomegranates

LIFE LESSONS

➤ **Song of Solomon 4:9 —** *"You have
made my heart beat faster . . . with a
single glance of your eyes."*

*N*ot only do husbands and wives need
to praise each other's good qualities, but in the best marriages, they also
love to describe the wonderful ways they
make each other feel.

With choice fruits, henna with nard
plants,

14 Nard and saffron, calamus and
cinnamon,
With all the trees of frankincense,
Myrrh and aloes, along with all the
finest spices.

15 "*You are* a garden spring,
A well of fresh water,
And streams *flowing* from Lebanon."

➤ 16 "Awake, O north *wind*,
And come, *wind* of the south;
Make my garden breathe out
fragrance,
Let its spices be wafted abroad.
May my beloved come into his
garden
And eat its choice fruits!"

LIFE LESSONS

➤ **Song of Solomon 4:16 — "*May my beloved come into his garden and eat its choice fruits!*"**

*W*hile sex is not the all-important prize our culture claims, it is a delightful and important part of any growing marriage. So Paul instructs, "Stop depriving one another, except by agreement for a time" (1 Cor. 7:5).

Psalm 104:10–23

10 He sends forth springs in the
valleys;
They flow between the mountains;

11 They give drink to every beast of
the field;
The wild donkeys quench their thirst.

12 Beside them the birds of the
heavens dwell;
They lift up *their* voices among the
branches.

13 He waters the mountains from His
upper chambers;
The earth is satisfied with the fruit
of His works.

14 He causes the grass to grow for the
cattle,
And vegetation for the labor of man,
So that he may bring forth food
from the earth,

15 And wine which makes man's heart
glad,
So that he may make *his* face
glisten with oil,
And food which sustains man's
heart.

16 The trees of the LORD drink their
fill,
The cedars of Lebanon which He
planted,

17 Where the birds build their nests,
And the stork, whose home is the fir
trees.

18 The high mountains are for the wild
goats;

The cliffs are a refuge for the
shephanim.

19 He made the moon for the seasons;
The sun knows the place of its
setting.

20 You appoint darkness and it
becomes night,
In which all the beasts of the forest
prowl about.

21 The young lions roar after their
prey
And seek their food from God.

22 *When* the sun rises they withdraw
And lie down in their dens.

23 Man goes forth to his work
And to his labor until evening.

Proverbs 24:17, 18

17 Do not rejoice when your enemy
falls,
And do not let your heart be glad
when he stumbles;

18 Or the LORD will see *it* and be
displeased,
And turn His anger away from him.

1 Corinthians 12:1–31

12 NOW concerning spiritual *gifts*,
brethren, I do not want you to be
unaware.

2 You know that when you were pa-
gans, *you were* led astray to the mute
idols, however you were led.

3 Therefore I make known to you that
no one speaking by the Spirit of God
says, "Jesus is accursed"; and no one can
say, "Jesus is Lord," except by the Holy
Spirit.

4   Now there are varieties of gifts, but the same Spirit.

5   And there are varieties of ministries, and the same Lord.

6   There are varieties of effects, but the same God who works all things in all *persons.*

➤ 7   But to each one is given the manifestation of the Spirit for the common good.

8   For to one is given the word of wisdom through the Spirit, and to another the word of knowledge according to the same Spirit;

9   to another faith by the same Spirit, and to another gifts of healing by the one Spirit,

10   and to another the effecting of miracles, and to another prophecy, and to another the distinguishing of spirits, to another *various* kinds of tongues, and to another the interpretation of tongues.

➤ 11   But one and the same Spirit works all these things, distributing to each one individually just as He wills.

✳ 12   For even as the body is one and *yet* has many members, and all the members of the body, though they are many, are one body, so also is Christ.

13   For by one Spirit we were all baptized into one body, whether Jews or Greeks, whether slaves or free, and we were all made to drink of one Spirit.

14   For the body is not one member, but many.

15   If the foot says, "Because I am not a hand, I am not *a part* of the body," it is not for this reason any the less *a part* of the body.

16   And if the ear says, "Because I am not an eye, I am not *a part* of the body," it is not for this reason any the less *a part* of the body.

17   If the whole body were an eye, where would the hearing be? If the whole were hearing, where would the sense of smell be?

18   But now God has placed the members, each one of them, in the body, just as He desired.

19   If they were all one member, where would the body be?

20   But now there are many members, but one body.

21   And the eye cannot say to the hand, "I have no need of you"; or again the head to the feet, "I have no need of you."

22   On the contrary, it is much truer that the members of the body which seem to be weaker are necessary;

23   and those *members* of the body which we deem less honorable, on these we bestow more abundant honor, and our less presentable members become much more presentable,

24   whereas our more presentable members have no need *of it.* But God has *so* composed the body, giving more abundant honor to that *member* which lacked,

25   so that there may be no division in the body, but *that* the members may have the same care for one another.

26   And if one member suffers, all the ◄ members suffer with it; if *one* member is honored, all the members rejoice with it.

27   Now you are Christ's body, and individually members of it.

28   And God has appointed in the church, first apostles, second prophets, third teachers, then miracles, then gifts

---

LIFE LESSONS

➤ **1 Corinthians 12:7 —** *To each one is given the manifestation of the Spirit for the common good*

*A*t the time we come to faith in Christ, every believer receives at least one spiritual gift—not merely to encourage and build up our own relationship with the Lord, but to edify the entire church.

➤ **1 Corinthians 12:11 —** *One and the same Spirit works all these things, distributing to each one individually just as He wills.*

*G*od distributes spiritual gifts as He sees fit. While a church can and should "desire earnestly spiritual gifts" (1 Cor. 41:1), individual believers are never encouraged to request specific gifts. The Spirit gives us the talents that are necessary for the tasks He wants us to accomplish.

➤ **1 Corinthians 12:26 —** *If one member suffers, all the members suffer with it.*

*T*his verse gives the reason for Paul's instruction: "Rejoice with those who rejoice, and weep with those who weep" (Rom. 12:15). Since we all belong to each other, we should desire and work for each other's benefit as if doing so for ourselves (Matt. 22:39).

WHAT THE BIBLE SAYS ABOUT

Holy Diversity

1 Corinthians 12:1–31

There is great diversity in the body of Christ. There are many parts and roles, but they all come together in the name of the Lord. In John 17:23, Jesus prays for believers, "that they may be perfected in unity, so that the world may know that You sent Me, and loved them, even as You have loved Me." Along with the unique work of others, you have a part in building the kingdom of God. Christ works in the entire process to bring success to the effort.

First Corinthians 12:7 tells you why God gave you such unique gifts and attributes: "To each one is given the manifestation of the Spirit for the common good." God gives you distinct abilities because the church needs *you*. The Lord could do His work in the world without You, but because of your need for relationship with Him and His desire for fellowship with you, He includes you in His work.

Ralph Waldo Emerson once wrote, "The only gift is a portion of thyself." This is especially true when considering the work of the church. There is no greater gift you can give to the Lord or to the church than yourself. Others in your community of believers will learn about Jesus through you as you gain knowledge of Him through them. Are you willing to take up the work God has for you and give a portion of yourself to be Christ's body in the world?

Is there any area in which you could use your gifts and talents to serve other believers? Write down any areas you can think of and pray for God to reveal what place He has for you in the body of Christ. ◈

---

of healings, helps, administrations, *various* kinds of tongues.
29 All are not apostles, are they? All are not prophets, are they? All are not teachers, are they? All are not *workers of miracles*, are they?

30 All do not have gifts of healings, do they? All do not speak with tongues, do they? All do not interpret, do they?
31 But earnestly desire the greater gifts.
And I show you a still more excellent way.

◈ Song of Solomon 5:1—6:13

5 "I HAVE come into my garden, my sister, *my* bride;
   I have gathered my myrrh along with my balsam.
   I have eaten my honeycomb and my honey;
   I have drunk my wine and my milk.
   Eat, friends;
   Drink and imbibe deeply, O lovers."
2 "I was asleep but my heart was awake.
   A voice! My beloved was knocking:
   'Open to me, my sister, my darling,
   My dove, my perfect one!
   For my head is drenched with dew,
   My locks with the damp of the night.'
3 "I have taken off my dress,
   How can I put it on *again*?

   I have washed my feet,
   How can I dirty them *again*?
4 "My beloved extended his hand through the opening,
   And my feelings were aroused for him.
5 "I arose to open to my beloved;
   And my hands dripped with myrrh,
   And my fingers with liquid myrrh,
   On the handles of the bolt.
6 "I opened to my beloved,
   But my beloved had turned away *and* had gone!
   My heart went out *to him* as he spoke.
   I searched for him but I did not find him;
   I called him but he did not answer me.
7 "The watchmen who make the rounds in the city found me,
   They struck me *and* wounded me;

The guardsmen of the walls took
away my shawl from me.
8 "I adjure you, O daughters of
Jerusalem,
If you find my beloved,
As to what you will tell him:
For I am lovesick."
9 "What kind of beloved is your beloved,
O most beautiful among women?
What kind of beloved is your
beloved,
That thus you adjure us?"
10 "My beloved is dazzling and ruddy,
Outstanding among ten thousand.
11 "His head is *like* gold, pure gold;
His locks are *like* clusters of dates
And black as a raven.
12 "His eyes are like doves
Beside streams of water,
Bathed in milk,
And reposed in *their* setting.
13 "His cheeks are like a bed of balsam,
Banks of sweet-scented herbs;
His lips are lilies
Dripping with liquid myrrh.
14 "His hands are rods of gold
Set with beryl;
His abdomen is carved ivory
Inlaid with sapphires.
15 "His legs are pillars of alabaster
Set on pedestals of pure gold;
His appearance is like Lebanon
Choice as the cedars.
➤ 16 "His mouth is *full of* sweetness.
And he is wholly desirable.
This is my beloved and this is my
friend,
O daughters of Jerusalem."

6 "WHERE has your beloved gone,
O most beautiful among women?
Where has your beloved turned,
That we may seek him with you?"
2 "My beloved has gone down to his
garden,
To the beds of balsam,
To pasture *his flock* in the gardens
And gather lilies.
➤ 3 "I am my beloved's and my beloved
is mine,
He who pastures *his flock* among
the lilies."
4 "You are as beautiful as Tirzah, my
darling,
As lovely as Jerusalem,
As awesome as an army with
banners.
5 "Turn your eyes away from me,
For they have confused me;

Your hair is like a flock of goats
That have descended from Gilead.
6 "Your teeth are like a flock of ewes
Which have come up from *their*
washing,
All of which bear twins,
And not one among them has lost
her young.
7 "Your temples are like a slice of a
pomegranate
Behind your veil.
8 "There are sixty queens and eighty
concubines,
And maidens without number;
9 *But* my dove, my perfect one, is
unique:
She is her mother's only *daughter*;
She is the pure *child* of the one who
bore her.
The maidens saw her and called her
blessed,
The queens and the concubines
also, and they praised her, *saying*,
10 'Who is this that grows like the dawn,
As beautiful as the full moon,
As pure as the sun,
As awesome as an army with
banners?'
11 "I went down to the orchard of nut
trees
To see the blossoms of the valley,
To see whether the vine had budded
Or the pomegranates had bloomed.
12 "Before I was aware, my soul set me
Over the chariots of my noble people."
13 "Come back, come back,
O Shulammite;

LIFE LESSONS

➤ **Song of Solomon 5:16 —** *"This is my beloved and this is my friend."*

*H*ow many marriages fall apart
because spouses forget to nurture their friendship along with their
romance? All-important relationships are
first good friendships—and that includes
the ones we have with God (James 2:23).

➤ **Song of Solomon 6:3 —** *"I am my beloved's and my beloved is mine."*

*H*usbands and wives do not "own"
each other, but they do belong to
each other in an exclusive way that no
one else can share. They become "one
flesh" (Gen. 2:24; Matt. 19:5, 6).

ANSWERS TO LIFE'S QUESTIONS

What does God's love look like?

SONG OF SOLOMON 6:4

*T*he notion of "true love" dominates much of popular culture. We purchase cards, shop for gifts, and plan romantic outings with our cherished one in mind.

God Himself places a high value on love (1 Cor. 13:13) and delights in expressing His wonderful love to us. Much of the time, however, we don't feel loved, do we? Sin has spoiled our capacity to understand God's love, to receive His love, and to love Him in return.

Our Savior, Jesus Christ, has remedied this problem. By liberating us from the power of sin and providing us with a new nature, we can now understand—at least, a little—our heavenly Father's wonderful love for us.

Divine love is *unconditional*—He showers us with it, regardless of who we are, where we have been, or what mistakes we have made. What matters to the Lord is that we belong to Him.

His love for us is also *absolute*—it never wavers or varies and knows no limitations. It always seeks our best, helping us to grow into the likeness of Jesus. Even when God disciplines us, He does so as a loving Father.

Understanding how much we are loved and accepting God's love for us frees us to live and love God's way. By loving Him with all our heart, soul, mind, and strength, we find the wisdom and power to love our neighbors in return.

What does loving God look like? Loving God means spending time deepening our relationships with Jesus Christ. We love Him when we give ourselves wholeheartedly to knowing Him and learning what pleases Him. We express our love when we give ourselves to Him and when we make a commitment to obey Him.

The Word of God also tells us that when we love others we are loving Jesus (Matt. 25:40). Loving others God's way means we will pursue His best for them. We will ask the Father to show us what we can say and do on behalf of others. We will seek to answer the question, "How can I build them up and help them grow into Christ's likeness?" When we love people in obedience to the Lord, we will find ourselves looking for ways to express His love to them. Love demonstrates that we belong to Jesus (John 13:35).

We are created to be lovers of God and others. Won't you receive His outpouring of love today?

Come back, come back, that we may
    gaze at you!"
"Why should you gaze at the
    Shulammite,
    As at the dance of the two companies?

◈ Psalm 104:24–30

➤ 24   O Lord, how many are Your works!
        In wisdom You have made them all;
        The earth is full of Your possessions.
25   There is the sea, great and broad,

LIFE LESSONS

➤ **Psalm 104:24 — *O Lord, how many are Your works! In wisdom You have made them all.***

*C*reation reveals that God has a vast intellect that we cannot completely comprehend. Our knowledge is finite while His is infinite. But as believers, we have the mind of Jesus Christ, and He provides the wisdom we need for every situation (1 Cor. 2:16).

    In which are swarms without number,
    Animals both small and great.
26   There the ships move along,
    And Leviathan, which You have
      formed to sport in it.
27   They all wait for You
    To give them their food in due season.
28   You give to them, they gather *it* up;   ✳
    You open Your hand, they are
      satisfied with good.
29   You hide Your face, they are
      dismayed;
    You take away their spirit, they expire
    And return to their dust.
30   You send forth Your Spirit, they are
      created;
    And You renew the face of the
      ground.

◈ Proverbs 24:19, 20

19   Do not fret because of evildoers
    Or be envious of the wicked;
20   For there will be no future for the evil
      man;

The lamp of the wicked will be put out.

1 Corinthians 13:1–13

13 IF I speak with the tongues of men and of angels, but do not have love, I have become a noisy gong or a clanging cymbal.
2 If I have *the gift of* prophecy, and know all mysteries and all knowledge; and if I have all faith, so as to remove mountains, but do not have love, I am nothing.
3   And if I give all my possessions to feed *the poor,* and if I surrender my body to be burned, but do not have love, it profits me nothing.
4   Love is patient, love is kind *and* is not jealous; love does not brag *and* is not arrogant,
5   does not act unbecomingly; it does not seek its own, is not provoked, does not take into account a wrong *suffered,*
6   does not rejoice in unrighteousness, but rejoices with the truth;
7   bears all things, believes all things, hopes all things, endures all things.
8   Love never fails; but if *there are gifts* of prophecy, they will be done away; if *there are* tongues, they will cease; if *there is* knowledge, it will be done away.
9   For we know in part and we prophesy in part;
10   but when the perfect comes, the partial will be done away.
11   When I was a child, I used to speak like a child, think like a child, reason like a child; when I became a man, I did away with childish things.

LIFE LESSONS

➤ **1 Corinthians 13:3 —** *If I give all my possessions to feed the poor . . . but do not have love, it profits me nothing.*

*L*ove means action, but it also means more than that. A person can literally give up his life for others—the supreme self-sacrifice—and yet do it without love. Love has a caring element that prompts its action.

➤ **1 Corinthians 13:9 —** *We know in part and we prophesy in part.*

*G*od does not give any of His children a complete picture of what He is doing or what He has planned to do in the world, but He reveals it to us as we work together in unity. We need to depend upon one another not only to experience His love and know His will, but also to fulfill His mission in the world.

➤ **1 Corinthians 13:13 —** *Faith, hope, love, abide these three; but the greatest of these is love.*

*O*ur hope will be fulfilled in heaven because we will have everything we've ever hoped for. Our faith will be complete because we will see the King in His glory. And His love will remain forever because the fruit of His love—our salvation—will endure always, to His honor, praise, and glory.

12   For now we see in a mirror dimly, but then face to face; now I know in part, but then I will know fully just as I also have been fully known.
13   But now faith, hope, love, abide these three; but the greatest of these is love.

SEPTEMBER 4

Song of Solomon 7:1—8:14

7 "HOW beautiful are your feet in sandals,
O prince's daughter!
The curves of your hips are like jewels,
The work of the hands of an artist.
2 "Your navel is *like* a round goblet
Which never lacks mixed wine;

Your belly is like a heap of wheat
Fenced about with lilies.
3 "Your two breasts are like two fawns,
Twins of a gazelle.
4 "Your neck is like a tower of ivory,
Your eyes *like* the pools in Heshbon
By the gate of Bath-rabbim;
Your nose is like the tower of
Lebanon,
Which faces toward Damascus.
5 "Your head crowns you like Carmel,

And the flowing locks of your head
     are like purple threads;
     The king is captivated by *your*
     tresses.
6 "How beautiful and how delightful
     you are,
     My love, with *all* your charms!
7 "Your stature is like a palm tree,
     And your breasts are *like its*
     clusters.
8 "I said, 'I will climb the palm tree,
     I will take hold of its fruit stalks.'
     Oh, may your breasts be like
     clusters of the vine,
     And the fragrance of your breath
     like apples,
9 And your mouth like the best
     wine!"
     "It goes *down* smoothly for my
     beloved,
     Flowing gently *through* the lips of
     those who fall asleep.
10 "I am my beloved's,
     And his desire is for me.
11 "Come, my beloved, let us go out into
     the country,
     Let us spend the night in the
     villages.
12 "Let us rise early *and* go to the
     vineyards;
     Let us see whether the vine has
     budded
     And its blossoms have opened,
     And whether the pomegranates
     have bloomed.
     There I will give you my love.
13 "The mandrakes have given forth
     fragrance;
     And over our doors are all choice
     fruits,
     Both new and old,
     Which I have saved up for you, my
     beloved.

8 "OH that you were like a brother to
     me
     Who nursed at my mother's breasts.
     If I found you outdoors, I would kiss
     you;
     No one would despise me, either.
2 "I would lead you *and* bring you
     Into the house of my mother, who
     used to instruct me;
     I would give you spiced wine
     to drink from the juice of my
     pomegranates.
3 "Let his left hand be under my head
     And his right hand embrace me."

4 "I want you to swear, O daughters of
     Jerusalem,
     Do not arouse or awaken *my* love
     Until she pleases."
5 "Who is this coming up from the
     wilderness
     Leaning on her beloved?"
     "Beneath the apple tree I awakened
     you;
     There your mother was in labor
     with you,
     There she was in labor *and* gave
     you birth.
6 "Put me like a seal over your heart,   ◄
     Like a seal on your arm.
     For love is as strong as death,
     Jealousy is as severe as Sheol;
     Its flashes are flashes of fire,
     The *very* flame of the Lord.
7 "Many waters cannot quench love,
     Nor will rivers overflow it;
     If a man were to give all the riches
     of his house for love,
     It would be utterly despised."
8 "We have a little sister,
     And she has no breasts;
     What shall we do for our sister
     On the day when she is spoken
     for?
9 "If she is a wall,
     We will build on her a battlement of
     silver;
     But if she is a door,
     We will barricade her with planks
     of cedar."
10 "I was a wall, and my breasts were
     like towers;
     Then I became in his eyes as one
     who finds peace.
11 "Solomon had a vineyard at
     Baal-hamon;
     He entrusted the vineyard to
     caretakers.

LIFE LESSONS

➤ **Song of Solomon 8:6 —** *"Put me like a seal over your heart."*

True devotion begins in the heart and works its way out in loving expressions involving the rest of the body. Spouses want and need all of each other—and God wants the same thing from us. He wants our devotion and, in return, gives to us His heart—which is totally committed to us at every turn.

WHAT THE BIBLE SAYS ABOUT

Sweet Meditation

Psalm 104:34

*D*o you ever feel like you're on a one-way call with God, and you're not sure whether He is being silent or if He's just completely disconnected? We all have seasons when we feel this way. We want to please Him, so we voice all the religious things we know to say. Yet somehow we know deep within that our prayer lives are not as they're supposed to be.

Although God gladly welcomes us into His presence and hears all of our requests, it's always important to be respectful when praying to Him. Ecclesiastes 5:1, 2 says, "Guard your steps as you go to the house of God and draw near to listen . . . Do not be hasty in word or impulsive in thought to bring up a matter in the presence of God[.] For God is in heaven and you on earth; therefore let your words be few."

Instead of going to God with our long lists of requests, we should approach His throne with the desire to simply listen.

Is that difficult for you to do? Then picture God on His majestic, heavenly throne. Imagine the cherubim praising Him and the saints worshiping at His feet. Envision the stars rushing to do His will and the earth as His footstool. His wisdom, power, and love are laid out before you—not in a philosophical sense; but rather, the reality of them can be seen in a million different ways.

We tend to forget who God really is. If we had a medical or mechanical issue, we would seek out the advice of an expert in that field. We would listen carefully to their wisdom about what to do to rectify our situations. Yet God is the Creator and Sustainer of the universe, and when we pray, we spend very little time listening. It's no wonder that we often miss the life-giving counsel that we most need.

Therefore, when you pray today, don't be full of words. Rather, as Habakkuk 2:20 instructs, "The Lord is in His holy temple. Let all the earth be silent before Him." Quietly seek God's wisdom. He delights in teaching you how to have a deeper relationship with Him and how to serve Him with honor and strength. Trust Him to show you His ways and to answer everything that concerns you. When you listen, you will hear the words that almighty God is sharing with you and the secrets He's revealing to you (Ps. 25:12, 14; Jer. 33:3). ◈

Each one was to bring a thousand
  shekels of silver for its fruit.
12 "My very own vineyard is at my
  disposal;
The thousand *shekels* are for you,
  Solomon,
And two hundred are for those who
  take care of its fruit."
13 "O you who sit in the gardens,
My companions are listening for
  your voice—
Let me hear it!"
14 "Hurry, my beloved,
And be like a gazelle or a young
  stag
On the mountains of spices."

◈ Psalm 104:31–35

31 Let the glory of the Lord endure
  forever;
Let the Lord be glad in His works;

32 He looks at the earth, and it
  trembles;
He touches the mountains, and they
  smoke.
33 I will sing to the Lord as long as I
  live;
I will sing praise to my God while I
  have my being.
34 Let my meditation be pleasing to
  Him;
As for me, I shall be glad in the
  Lord.
35 Let sinners be consumed from the
  earth
And let the wicked be no more.
Bless the Lord, O my soul.
Praise the Lord!

◈ Proverbs 24:21, 22

21 My son, fear the Lord and the
  king;

Do not associate with those who are given to change,

22 For their calamity will rise suddenly,
And who knows the ruin *that comes* from both of them?

1 Corinthians 14:1–20

14 PURSUE love, yet desire earnestly spiritual *gifts*, but especially that you may prophesy.
2 For one who speaks in a tongue does not speak to men but to God; for no one understands, but in *his* spirit he speaks mysteries.
3 But one who prophesies speaks to men for edification and exhortation and consolation.
4 One who speaks in a tongue edifies himself; but one who prophesies edifies the church.
5 Now I wish that you all spoke in tongues, but *even* more that you would prophesy; and greater is one who prophesies than one who speaks in tongues, unless he interprets, so that the church may receive edifying.
6 But now, brethren, if I come to you speaking in tongues, what will I profit you unless I speak to you either by way of revelation or of knowledge or of prophecy or of teaching?
7 Yet *even* lifeless things, either flute or harp, in producing a sound, if they do not produce a distinction in the tones, how will it be known what is played on the flute or on the harp?
8 For if the bugle produces an indistinct sound, who will prepare himself for battle?
9 So also you, unless you utter by the tongue speech that is clear, how will be known what is spoken? For you will be speaking into the air.
10 There are, perhaps, a great many kinds of languages in the world, and no *kind* is without meaning.
11 If then I do not know the meaning of the language, I will be to the one who speaks a barbarian, and the one who speaks will be a barbarian to me.
12 So also you, since you are zealous of spiritual *gifts*, seek to abound for the edification of the church.

13 Therefore let one who speaks in a tongue pray that he may interpret.
14 For if I pray in a tongue, my spirit prays, but my mind is unfruitful.
15 What is *the outcome* then? I will pray with the spirit and I will pray with the mind also; I will sing with the spirit and I will sing with the mind also.
16 Otherwise if you bless in the spirit *only*, how will the one who fills the place of the ungifted say the "Amen" at your giving of thanks, since he does not know what you are saying?
17 For you are giving thanks well enough, but the other person is not edified.
18 I thank God, I speak in tongues more than you all;
19 however, in the church I desire to speak five words with my mind so that I may instruct others also, rather than ten thousand words in a tongue.
20 Brethren, do not be children in your thinking; yet in evil be infants, but in your thinking be mature.

LIFE LESSONS

➤ **1 Corinthians 14:12 —** *Since you are zealous of spiritual gifts, seek to abound for the edification of the church.*

God wants us to grow in grace, learn about Him, and serve others *together.* Why together? Because our unity of heart and action best shows the power of the Father's love.

➤ **1 Corinthians 14:19 —** *In the church I desire to speak five words with my mind so that I may instruct others also, rather than ten thousand words in a tongue.*

Originally seen at the empowering of the church at Pentecost, the ability to speak diverse languages was given so the early church could spread the gospel all around the world (Acts 2:4). Yet what Paul is speaking of here is that many of the believers in Corinth were imitating other religions by babbling meaninglessly. What they were doing was neither of the Spirit nor edifying to other believers; rather, they were trying to show off their "super-spirituality." So Paul reiterated to them the real power of the Spirit is seen in the teaching and maturing of the church.

Isaiah 1:1—2:22

1 THE vision of Isaiah the son of Amoz concerning Judah and Jerusalem, which he saw during the reigns of Uzziah, Jotham, Ahaz *and* Hezekiah, kings of Judah.

2 Listen, O heavens, and hear,
O earth;
For the LORD speaks,
"Sons I have reared and brought up,
But they have revolted against Me.

3 "An ox knows its owner,
And a donkey its master's manger,
But Israel does not know,
My people do not understand."

4 Alas, sinful nation,
People weighed down with iniquity,
Offspring of evildoers,
Sons who act corruptly!
They have abandoned the LORD,
They have despised the Holy One of Israel,
They have turned away from Him.

5 Where will you be stricken again,
As you continue in *your* rebellion?
The whole head is sick
And the whole heart is faint.

6 From the sole of the foot even to the head
There is nothing sound in it,
Only bruises, welts and raw wounds,
Not pressed out or bandaged,
Nor softened with oil.

7 Your land is desolate,
Your cities are burned with fire,
Your fields—strangers are devouring them in your presence;
It is desolation, as overthrown by strangers.

8 The daughter of Zion is left like a shelter in a vineyard,
Like a watchman's hut in a cucumber field, like a besieged city.

9 Unless the LORD of hosts
Had left us a few survivors,
We would be like Sodom,
We would be like Gomorrah.

10 Hear the word of the LORD,
You rulers of Sodom;
Give ear to the instruction of our God,
You people of Gomorrah.

11 "What are your multiplied sacrifices to Me?"
Says the LORD.
"I have had enough of burnt offerings of rams
And the fat of fed cattle;
And I take no pleasure in the blood of bulls, lambs or goats.

12 "When you come to appear before Me,
Who requires of you this trampling of My courts?

13 "Bring your worthless offerings no longer,
Incense is an abomination to Me.
New moon and sabbath, the calling of assemblies—
I cannot endure iniquity and the solemn assembly.

14 "I hate your new moon *festivals* and your appointed feasts,
They have become a burden to Me;
I am weary of bearing *them*.

15 "So when you spread out your hands *in prayer*,
I will hide My eyes from you;
Yes, even though you multiply prayers,
I will not listen.
Your hands are covered with blood.

16 "Wash yourselves, make yourselves clean;
Remove the evil of your deeds from My sight.
Cease to do evil,

17 Learn to do good;
Seek justice,
Reprove the ruthless,
Defend the orphan,
Plead for the widow.

18 "Come now, and let us reason together,"
Says the LORD,
"Though your sins are as scarlet,
They will be as white as snow;

LIFE LESSONS

➤ **Isaiah 1:18 — *"Come now, and let us reason together."***

*D*ialogue builds relationships. Genuine prayer has all of the qualities and characteristics of a deeply meaningful conversation between two people. This image of God and man sitting down together for a good talk is our best image of prayer.

Though they are red like crimson,
They will be like wool.

19 "If you consent and obey,
You will eat the best of the land;

20 "But if you refuse and rebel,
You will be devoured by the sword."
Truly, the mouth of the LORD has
spoken.

21 How the faithful city has become a
harlot,
She *who* was full of justice!
Righteousness once lodged in her,
But now murderers.

22 Your silver has become dross,
Your drink diluted with water.

23 Your rulers are rebels
And companions of thieves;
Everyone loves a bribe
And chases after rewards.
They do not defend the orphan,
Nor does the widow's plea come
before them.

24 Therefore the Lord GOD of hosts,
The Mighty One of Israel, declares,
"Ah, I will be relieved of My
adversaries
And avenge Myself on My foes.

25 "I will also turn My hand against
you,
And will smelt away your dross as
with lye
And will remove all your alloy.

26 "Then I will restore your judges as at
the first,
And your counselors as at the
beginning;
After that you will be called the city
of righteousness,
A faithful city."

27 Zion will be redeemed with justice
And her repentant ones with
righteousness.

28 But transgressors and sinners will
be crushed together,
And those who forsake the LORD
will come to an end.

29 Surely you will be ashamed of the
oaks which you have desired,
And you will be embarrassed at the
gardens which you have chosen.

30 For you will be like an oak whose
leaf fades away
Or as a garden that has no water.

31 The strong man will become
tinder,
His work also a spark.
Thus they shall both burn together

And there will be none to quench
them.

2 THE word which Isaiah the son of
Amoz saw concerning Judah and Jerusalem.

2 Now it will come about that
In the last days
The mountain of the house of the
LORD
Will be established as the chief of
the mountains,
And will be raised above the hills;
And all the nations will stream to it.

3 And many peoples will come and
say,
"Come, let us go up to the mountain
of the LORD,
To the house of the God of Jacob;
That He may teach us concerning
His ways
And that we may walk in His paths."
For the law will go forth from Zion
And the word of the LORD from
Jerusalem.

4 And He will judge between the
nations,
And will render decisions for many
peoples;
And they will hammer their swords
into plowshares and their spears
into pruning hooks.
Nation will not lift up sword against
nation,
And never again will they learn
war.

5 Come, house of Jacob, and let us
walk in the light of the LORD.

6 For You have abandoned Your
people, the house of Jacob,
Because they are filled *with
influences* from the east,

LIFE LESSONS

➤ **Isaiah 2:3** — *"Come, let us go up to
the . . . house of the God of Jacob; that
He may teach us concerning His ways
and that we may walk in His paths."*

God designed the life of faith to be
lived and expressed in a community
of like-minded believers (1 Cor. 12:7-14;
Eph. 4:4-13; Heb. 10:24, 25). He teaches
us His ways, so that *we* can walk in His
paths. If you're trying to go it alone in
your faith, you'll never grow like the
Father wants you to.

And *they are* soothsayers like the Philistines,
And they strike *bargains* with the children of foreigners.

7 Their land has also been filled with silver and gold
And there is no end to their treasures;
Their land has also been filled with horses
And there is no end to their chariots.

8 Their land has also been filled with idols;
They worship the work of their hands,
That which their fingers have made.

9 So the *common* man has been humbled
And the man *of importance* has been abased,
But do not forgive them.

10 Enter the rock and hide in the dust
From the terror of the LORD and from the splendor of His majesty.

11 The proud look of man will be abased
And the loftiness of man will be humbled,
And the LORD alone will be exalted in that day.

12 For the LORD of hosts will have a day *of reckoning*
Against everyone who is proud and lofty
And against everyone who is lifted up,
That he may be abased.

13 And *it will be* against all the cedars of Lebanon that are lofty and lifted up,
Against all the oaks of Bashan,

14 Against all the lofty mountains,
Against all the hills that are lifted up,

15 Against every high tower,
Against every fortified wall,

16 Against all the ships of Tarshish
And against all the beautiful craft.

➤ 17 The pride of man will be humbled
And the loftiness of men will be abased;
And the LORD alone will be exalted in that day,

18 But the idols will completely vanish.

19 *Men* will go into caves of the rocks
And into holes of the ground

Before the terror of the LORD
And the splendor of His majesty,
When He arises to make the earth tremble.

20 In that day men will cast away to the moles and the bats
Their idols of silver and their idols of gold,
Which they made for themselves to worship,

21 In order to go into the caverns of the rocks and the clefts of the cliffs
Before the terror of the LORD and the splendor of His majesty,
When He arises to make the earth tremble.

22 Stop regarding man, whose breath *of life* is in his nostrils;
For why should he be esteemed?

✦ Psalm 105:1–6

105 OH give thanks to the LORD,
call upon His name;
Make known His deeds among the peoples.

2 Sing to Him, sing praises to Him;
Speak of all His wonders.

3 Glory in His holy name;
Let the heart of those who seek the LORD be glad.   ✳

LIFE LESSONS

➤ **Isaiah 2:17 —** *The pride of man will be humbled and the loftiness of men will be abased; and the LORD alone will be exalted in that day.*

A day is coming when human pride and arrogance will be smashed forever, and the entire world will acknowledge that God alone rules. As followers of Christ, we can anticipate that day by willingly humbling ourselves.

➤ **Psalm 105:4 —** *Seek the LORD and His strength; seek His face continually.*

*S*ince God is infinite, we will never run out of new and surprising territory to explore regarding His holy, unchanging character and nature. The great adventure of seeking God and His ways will continue our entire lives.

➤ 4   Seek the LORD and His strength;
      Seek His face continually.
5   Remember His wonders which He
      has done,
      His marvels and the judgments
      uttered by His mouth,
6   O seed of Abraham, His servant,
      O sons of Jacob, His chosen ones!

Proverbs 24:23–25

23   These also are sayings of the wise.
     To show partiality in judgment is
     not good.
24   He who says to the wicked, "You
     are righteous,"
     Peoples will curse him, nations will
     abhor him;
25   But to those who rebuke the *wicked*
     will be delight,
     And a good blessing will come upon
     them.

1 Corinthians 14:21–40

21   In the Law it is written, "BY MEN
OF STRANGE TONGUES AND BY THE LIPS OF
STRANGERS I WILL SPEAK TO THIS PEOPLE,
AND EVEN SO THEY WILL NOT LISTEN TO ME,"
says the Lord.
22   So then tongues are for a sign, not to
those who believe but to unbelievers; but
prophecy *is for a sign*, not to unbelievers
but to those who believe.
23   Therefore if the whole church assem-
bles together and all speak in tongues,
and ungifted men or unbelievers enter,
will they not say that you are mad?
24   But if all prophesy, and an unbeliever or an ungifted man enters, he is
convicted by all, he is called to account
by all;
25   the secrets of his heart are disclosed;
and so he will fall on his face and worship God, declaring that God is certainly
among you.
26   What is *the outcome* then, brethren?
When you assemble, each one has a
psalm, has a teaching, has a revelation,
has a tongue, has an interpretation. Let
all things be done for edification.
27   If anyone speaks in a tongue, *it*

should be by two or at the most three,
and *each* in turn, and one must interpret;
28   but if there is no interpreter, he must
keep silent in the church; and let him
speak to himself and to God.
29   Let two or three prophets speak, and
let the others pass judgment.
30   But if a revelation is made to another
who is seated, the first one must keep
silent.
31   For you can all prophesy one by one,
so that all may learn and all may be exhorted;
32   and the spirits of prophets are subject to prophets;
33   for God is not *a God* of confusion ◄
but of peace, as in all the churches of the ✴
saints.
34   The women are to keep silent in the
churches; for they are not permitted to
speak, but are to subject themselves, just
as the Law also says.
35   If they desire to learn anything, let
them ask their own husbands at home;
for it is improper for a woman to speak
in church.
36   Was it from you that the word of
God *first* went forth? Or has it come to
you only?
37   If anyone thinks he is a prophet

LIFE LESSONS

➤ **1 Corinthians 14:33 —** *God is not a
God of confusion but of peace.*

*G*od does not tell one person to do
something that completely contradicts and invalidates what He told
someone else to do. Nor does He ever
command anything that is in opposition
to His eternal Word. He is the Lord of
order, so when He brings us into fellowship with the rest of His church, He has
special plans to use our gifts and talents
within that group, and He keeps us unified with the rest of the body through
His Holy Spirit.

➤ **1 Corinthians 14:40 —** *All things must
be done properly and in an orderly manner.*

*C*onfusion is never a sign of God's leading. When something spirals out of
control, you can be sure that He did not
design it. He may lead in unusual ways,
but He will never guide us in a manner
inconsistent with His holiness and Word.

WHAT THE BIBLE SAYS ABOUT

A Well-Ordered Body

1 Corinthians 14:33

The human body is a complicated structure. It's known to house 60 to 75 trillion cells, and each cell is composed of 90 trillion atoms.

Every minute, 70,000 miles of blood vessels travel through the entire distance of the body and back; and every second, a minimum of 100,000 chemical reactions occur in the brain. In an inch of skin there are 19 million cells, 60 hairs, 90 oil glands, 19 feet of blood vessels, 625 sweat glands, and 19,000 sensory cells. DNA has more than 80,000 pieces of information.

Yes, the human body is an intricate, wonderful system. The workings of it are beyond our comprehension. Even doctors and scientists cannot possibly describe all the intricacies and mysteries of it—how the muscles, tendons, nerves, bones, cells, and systems all coordinate in an orderly manner to keep you going.

Interestingly, Scripture refers to the church as the body of Christ. Romans 12:4–6 teaches, "For just as we have many members in one body and all the members do not have the same function, so we, who are many, are one body in Christ, and individually members one of another. Since we have gifts that differ according to the grace given to us, each of us is to exercise them accordingly."

God did not create us to be exactly alike. Just as all of the parts of the body are different, He created us with specific purposes to fulfill. However, everything works together for His glory. As 1 Corinthians 14:33 teaches, "God is not a God of confusion but of peace, as in all the churches of the saints."

Like the human body, the church is a living organism that is constantly growing and changing. But understand that it does so in an organized, obedient, godly fashion—not in chaos. When Christ brings you into fellowship with the rest of His church, He has special plans to use your gifts and talents within that group, and He keeps you unified with the rest of the body through the Holy Spirit.

Is there dissension in the church? Has something gone wrong within the body? Is there someone calling for conformity instead of unanimity? Ephesians 4:1–3 has the prescription for restoring harmony, "Walk in a manner worthy of the calling with which you have been called, with all humility and gentleness, with patience, showing tolerance for one another in love, being diligent to preserve the unity of the Spirit in the bond of peace." In humility, respect the members of the body for their unique area of service, and seek the Spirit to restore unity within the fellowship.

or spiritual, let him recognize that the things which I write to you are the Lord's commandment.
38 But if anyone does not recognize *this*, he is not recognized.

39 Therefore, my brethren, desire earnestly to prophesy, and do not forbid to speak in tongues.
40 But all things must be done properly and in an orderly manner.

SEPTEMBER 6

Isaiah 3:1—4:6

3 FOR behold, the Lord GOD of hosts is going to remove from Jerusalem and Judah
Both supply and support, the whole supply of bread
And the whole supply of water;
2 The mighty man and the warrior,
The judge and the prophet,
The diviner and the elder,
3 The captain of fifty and the honorable man,
The counselor and the expert artisan,
And the skillful enchanter.
4 And I will make mere lads their princes,
And capricious children will rule over them,
5 And the people will be oppressed,
Each one by another, and each one by his neighbor;

The youth will storm against the
 elder
And the inferior against the
 honorable.
6 When a man lays hold of his
 brother in his father's house,
 saying,
 "You have a cloak, you shall be our
 ruler,
And these ruins will be under your
 charge,"
7 He will protest on that day, saying,
 "I will not be *your* healer,
For in my house there is neither
 bread nor cloak;
You should not appoint me ruler of
 the people."
➤ 8 For Jerusalem has stumbled and
 Judah has fallen,
Because their speech and their
 actions are against the LORD,
To rebel against His glorious
 presence.
9 The expression of their faces bears
 witness against them,
And they display their sin like
 Sodom;
They do not *even* conceal *it.*
Woe to them!
For they have brought evil on
 themselves.
➤ 10 Say to the righteous that *it will go*
 well *with them,*

For they will eat the fruit of their
 actions.
11 Woe to the wicked! *It will go* badly
 with him,
For what he deserves will be done
 to him.
12 O My people! Their oppressors are
 children,
And women rule over them.
O My people! Those who guide you
 lead *you* astray
And confuse the direction of your
 paths.
13 The LORD arises to contend,
And stands to judge the people.
14 The LORD enters into judgment with
 the elders and princes of His
 people,
"It is you who have devoured the
 vineyard;
The plunder of the poor is in your
 houses.
15 "What do you mean by crushing My
 people
And grinding the face of the poor?"
Declares the Lord GOD of hosts.
16 Moreover, the LORD said, "Because
 the daughters of Zion are proud
And walk with heads held high and
 seductive eyes,
And go along with mincing steps
And tinkle the bangles on their feet,
17 Therefore the Lord will afflict the
 scalp of the daughters of Zion
 with scabs,
And the LORD will make their
 foreheads bare."
18 In that day the Lord will take away
the beauty of *their* anklets, headbands,
crescent ornaments,
19 dangling earrings, bracelets, veils,
20 headdresses, ankle chains, sashes,
perfume boxes, amulets,
21 finger rings, nose rings,
22 festal robes, outer tunics, cloaks,
money purses,
23 hand mirrors, undergarments, turbans and veils.
24 Now it will come about that instead
 of sweet perfume there will be
 putrefaction;
Instead of a belt, a rope;
Instead of well-set hair, a plucked-out
 scalp;
Instead of fine clothes, a donning of
 sackcloth;
And branding instead of beauty.

25 Your men will fall by the sword
    And your mighty ones in battle.
26 And her gates will lament and mourn,
    And deserted she will sit on the
    ground.

4 FOR seven women will take hold of one man in that day, saying, "We will eat our own bread and wear our own clothes, only let us be called by your name; take away our reproach!"

2 In that day the Branch of the LORD will be beautiful and glorious, and the fruit of the earth *will be* the pride and the adornment of the survivors of Israel.

3 It will come about that he who is left in Zion and remains in Jerusalem will be called holy—everyone who is recorded for life in Jerusalem.

4 When the Lord has washed away the filth of the daughters of Zion and purged the bloodshed of Jerusalem from her midst, by the spirit of judgment and the spirit of burning,

5 then the LORD will create over the whole area of Mount Zion and over her assemblies a cloud by day, even smoke, and the brightness of a flaming fire by night; for over all the glory will be a canopy.

6 There will be a shelter to *give* shade from the heat by day, and refuge and protection from the storm and the rain.

Psalm 105:7–22

7 He is the LORD our God;
    His judgments are in all the earth.
8 He has remembered His covenant
    forever,
    The word which He commanded to
    a thousand generations,
9 *The covenant* which He made with
    Abraham,
    And His oath to Isaac.
10 Then He confirmed it to Jacob for a
    statute,
    To Israel as an everlasting covenant,
11 Saying, "To you I will give the land
    of Canaan
    As the portion of your inheritance,"
12 When they were only a few men in
    number,
    Very few, and strangers in it.
13 And they wandered about from
    nation to nation,

From *one* kingdom to another people.
14 He permitted no man to oppress them,
    And He reproved kings for their sakes:
15 "Do not touch My anointed ones,
    And do My prophets no harm."
16 And He called for a famine upon the land;
    He broke the whole staff of bread.
17 He sent a man before them,
    Joseph, *who* was sold as a slave.
18 They afflicted his feet with fetters,
    He himself was laid in irons;
19 Until the time that his word came to pass,
    The word of the LORD tested him.
20 The king sent and released him,
    The ruler of peoples, and set him free.
21 He made him lord of his house
    And ruler over all his possessions,
22 To imprison his princes at will,
    That he might teach his elders wisdom.

Proverbs 24:26, 27

26 He kisses the lips
    Who gives a right answer.

LIFE LESSONS

➤ Isaiah 4:2 — *In that day the Branch of the LORD will be beautiful and glorious.*

Isaiah is the first prophet to call the coming Messiah by the name "Branch"—depicting Him as bearing the fruit of salvation for the kingdom of God (45:8). Isaiah sees a time when Jesus will reign in glory and bring justice and righteousness to the entire world (Is. 11:1; Jer. 23:5; 33:15; Zech. 3:8, 9).

➤ Psalm 105:19 — *The word of the LORD tested him.*

Whomever God uses greatly, He first tests thoroughly. As a teenager, Joseph had dreams that his brothers and father would one day bow down before him (Gen. 37:5-10). But before that happened, he had to endure much hardship (50:20).

27 Prepare your work outside
And make it ready for yourself in
the field;
Afterwards, then, build your house.

◈ 1 Corinthians 15:1–28

15 NOW I make known to you, brethren, the gospel which I preached to you, which also you received, in which also you stand,
2 by which also you are saved, if you hold fast the word which I preached to you, unless you believed in vain.
3 For I delivered to you as of first importance what I also received, that Christ died for our sins according to the Scriptures,
4 and that He was buried, and that He was raised on the third day according to the Scriptures,
5 and that He appeared to Cephas, then to the twelve.
6 After that He appeared to more than five hundred brethren at one time, most of whom remain until now, but some have fallen asleep;
7 then He appeared to James, then to all the apostles;
8 and last of all, as to one untimely born, He appeared to me also.
9 For I am the least of the apostles, and not fit to be called an apostle, because I persecuted the church of God.
10 But by the grace of God I am what I am, and His grace toward me did not prove vain; but I labored even more than all of them, yet not I, but the grace of God with me.

LIFE LESSONS

➤ **1 Corinthians 15:10 —** *I labored even more than all of them, yet not I, but the grace of God with me.*

*A*nything worthwhile that we accomplish for God is done in obedience to Him through the guidance and empowering of His Holy Spirit. His grace prompts us to get busy, not to become lazy.

---

11 Whether then *it was* I or they, so we preach and so you believed.
12 Now if Christ is preached, that He has been raised from the dead, how do some among you say that there is no resurrection of the dead?
13 But if there is no resurrection of the dead, not even Christ has been raised;
14 and if Christ has not been raised, then our preaching is vain, your faith also is vain.
15 Moreover we are even found *to be* false witnesses of God, because we testified against God that He raised Christ, whom He did not raise, if in fact the dead are not raised.
16 For if the dead are not raised, not even Christ has been raised;
17 and if Christ has not been raised, your faith is worthless; you are still in your sins.
18 Then those also who have fallen asleep in Christ have perished.
19 If we have hoped in Christ in this life only, we are of all men most to be pitied.
20 But now Christ has been raised from the dead, the first fruits of those who are asleep.

Life Examples:

JAMES: A Changed Man

1 CORINTHIANS 15:5–8

*A*t the beginning, James refused to believe in either the ministry or the deity of Jesus, his brother (John 7:5). James' disbelief remained steadfast throughout Jesus' earthly life. Only after the resurrection did he finally realize the truth.

In 1 Corinthians 15:5–8, Paul lists those to whom the risen Christ appeared. There, along with the disciples, James is singled out. Soon after the resurrection, James and his brothers joined the disciples in devoting themselves to prayer as they awaited the Holy Spirit (Acts 1:14).

James—not Peter or one of the other disciples—led the Jerusalem church through its early days. The missionaries who informed this church of their activities reported to James, its leader (Acts 15:12–21; 21:18).

James proves that even when you feel the most comfortable with the Lord—even when you believe you have Him figured out—He can still surprise you and change your world.

21 For since by a man *came* death, by a man also *came* the resurrection of the dead.

22 For as in Adam all die, so also in Christ all will be made alive.

23 But each in his own order: Christ the first fruits, after that those who are Christ's at His coming,

24 then *comes* the end, when He hands over the kingdom to the God and Father, when He has abolished all rule and all authority and power.

25 For He must reign until He has put all His enemies under His feet.

26 The last enemy that will be abolished is death.

27 For HE HAS PUT ALL THINGS IN SUBJECTION UNDER HIS FEET. But when He says, "All things are put in subjection," it is evident that He is excepted who put all things in subjection to Him.

28 When all things are subjected to Him, then the Son Himself also will be subjected to the One who subjected all things to Him, so that God may be all in all.

SEPTEMBER 7

 Isaiah 5:1—6:13

5 LET me sing now for my well-beloved
  A song of my beloved concerning His vineyard.
  My well-beloved had a vineyard on a fertile hill.

2 He dug it all around, removed its stones,
  And planted it with the choicest vine.
  And He built a tower in the middle of it
  And also hewed out a wine vat in it;
  Then He expected *it* to produce good grapes,
  But it produced *only* worthless ones.

3 "And now, O inhabitants of Jerusalem and men of Judah,
  Judge between Me and My vineyard.

4 "What more was there to do for My vineyard that I have not done in it?
  Why, when I expected *it* to produce good grapes did it produce worthless ones?

5 "So now let Me tell you what I am going to do to My vineyard:

I will remove its hedge and it will be consumed;
  I will break down its wall and it will become trampled ground.

6 "I will lay it waste;
  It will not be pruned or hoed,
  But briars and thorns will come up.
  I will also charge the clouds to rain no rain on it."

7 For the vineyard of the LORD of hosts is the house of Israel
  And the men of Judah His delightful plant.
  Thus He looked for justice, but behold, bloodshed;
  For righteousness, but behold, a cry of distress.

8 Woe to those who add house to house *and* join field to field,
  Until there is no more room,
  So that you have to live alone in the midst of the land!

9 In my ears the LORD of hosts *has* sworn, "Surely, many houses shall become desolate,
  Even great and fine ones, without occupants.

10 "For ten acres of vineyard will yield only one bath *of wine,*
  And a homer of seed will yield *but* an ephah of grain."

11 Woe to those who rise early in the
       morning that they may pursue
       strong drink,
    Who stay up late in the evening that
       wine may inflame them!

12 Their banquets are *accompanied* by
       lyre and harp, by tambourine and
       flute, and by wine;
    But they do not pay attention to the
       deeds of the LORD,
    Nor do they consider the work of
       His hands.

13 Therefore My people go into exile
       for their lack of knowledge;
    And their honorable men are
       famished,
    And their multitude is parched with
       thirst.

14 Therefore Sheol has enlarged its
       throat and opened its mouth
       without measure;
    And Jerusalem's splendor, her
       multitude, her din *of revelry* and
       the jubilant within her, descend
       into it.

15 So the *common* man will be humbled
       and the man of *importance* abased,
    The eyes of the proud also will be
       abased.

16 But the LORD of hosts will be
       exalted in judgment,
    And the holy God will show Himself
       holy in righteousness.

17 Then the lambs will graze as in
       their pasture,
    And strangers will eat in the waste
       places of the wealthy.

18 Woe to those who drag iniquity
       with the cords of falsehood,
    And sin as if with cart ropes;

19 Who say, "Let Him make speed, let
       Him hasten His work, that we
       may see *it*;
    And let the purpose of the Holy One
       of Israel draw near

    And come to pass, that we may
       know *it!*"

20 Woe to those who call evil good,
       and good evil;
    Who substitute darkness for light
       and light for darkness;
    Who substitute bitter for sweet and
       sweet for bitter!

21 Woe to those who are wise in their
       own eyes
    And clever in their own sight!

22 Woe to those who are heroes in
       drinking wine
    And valiant men in mixing strong
       drink,

23 Who justify the wicked for a bribe,
    And take away the rights of the
       ones who are in the right!

24 Therefore, as a tongue of fire
       consumes stubble
    And dry grass collapses into the
       flame,
    So their root will become like rot and
       their blossom blow away as dust;
    For they have rejected the law of the
       LORD of hosts
    And despised the word of the Holy
       One of Israel.

25 On this account the anger of the LORD
       has burned against His people,
    And He has stretched out His hand
       against them and struck them
       down.
    And the mountains quaked, and
       their corpses lay like refuse in the
       middle of the streets.
    For all this His anger is not spent,
    But His hand is still stretched out.

26 He will also lift up a standard to the
       distant nation,
    And will whistle for it from the ends
       of the earth;
    And behold, it will come with speed
       swiftly.

27 No one in it is weary or stumbles,

LIFE LESSONS

➤ **Isaiah 5:12 — *They do not pay attention to the deeds of the LORD.***

God gives us music, food, and celebrations to enjoy but never to enjoy
apart from Him, instead of Him, or in
neglect of Him. He is to be at the center
of all we do, all the time.

➤ **Isaiah 5:20 — *Woe to those who call
evil good, and good evil.***

When God in His Word calls something
evil, it is evil. When He labels a thing
bitter, no multitude of religious authorities can make it sweet through their
solemn declarations. God is our absolute
authority.

None slumbers or sleeps;
Nor is the belt at its waist undone,
Nor its sandal strap broken.

28   Its arrows are sharp and all its
         bows are bent;
      The hoofs of its horses seem like
         flint and its *chariot* wheels like a
         whirlwind.

29   Its roaring is like a lioness, and it
         roars like young lions;
      It growls as it seizes the prey
      And carries *it* off with no one to
         deliver *it*.

30   And it will growl over it in that day
         like the roaring of the sea.
      If one looks to the land, behold,
         there is darkness *and* distress;
      Even the light is darkened by its
         clouds.

6 IN the year of King Uzziah's death I
    saw the Lord sitting on a throne, lofty
and exalted, with the train of His robe
filling the temple.
2   Seraphim stood above Him, each
having six wings: with two he covered
his face, and with two he covered his
feet, and with two he flew.
3   And one called out to another and
said,
      "Holy, Holy, Holy, is the LORD of hosts,
      The whole earth is full of His glory."
4   And the foundations of the thresholds trembled at the voice of him who
called out, while the temple was filling
with smoke.
5   Then I said,
      "Woe is me, for I am ruined!
      Because I am a man of unclean lips,
      And I live among a people of
         unclean lips;

For my eyes have seen the King, the
LORD of hosts."
6   Then one of the seraphim flew to me
with a burning coal in his hand, which he
had taken from the altar with tongs.
7   He touched my mouth *with it* and
said, "Behold, this has touched your lips;
and your iniquity is taken away and your
sin is forgiven."
8   Then I heard the voice of the Lord,
saying, "Whom shall I send, and who will
go for Us?" Then I said, "Here am I. Send
me!"
9   He said, "Go, and tell this people:
      'Keep on listening, but do not perceive;
      Keep on looking, but do not
         understand.'
10 "Render the hearts of this people
         insensitive,

LIFE LESSONS

➤ **Isaiah 6:3 — "Holy, holy, holy, is the LORD of hosts."**

*W*hen the seraphim announced God's holiness, they were stating an unshakable truth. The Lord is utterly perfect in His holiness. The repetition emphasizes that He is absolutely pure, completely separated from sin, wholly righteous, just, and spotless.

➤ **Isaiah 6:8 — "Here am I. Send me!"**

*G*od first *prepared* Isaiah for service and then Isaiah *offered* himself to the Lord. God will never call us to do something for which He hasn't equipped us. He wants ready, willing servants who will obey Him wholeheartedly.

Life Examples:

ISAIAH: A Life-Changing Encounter

ISAIAH 6:1–8

*I*saiah's entire life changed when he saw the majestic Lord seated on His heavenly throne. His awesome vision of God pierced him to the very core and prompted him to cry out, "I am a man of unclean lips . . . for my eyes have seen the King, the LORD of hosts" (Is. 6:5).
      You will never deal effectively with your sin without first realizing who God is. When

you study His Word and begin to grasp His holiness, a deep reverence for Him begins to grow in your heart. Like Isaiah, you are humbled before Him and realize that you fall far short of His holiness. Yet before discouragement creeps in, remember God loves you with an everlasting love.
      Through Jesus' death on the Cross, God takes away your sins and shows you His amazing love. The crucifixion and resurrection are the beautiful visions God gives *you* of His awesome holiness and majesty.
      Have you had a life-altering encounter with the Lord? Isaiah did—and it transformed his life forever.

Their ears dull,
And their eyes dim,
Otherwise they might see with their
eyes,
Hear with their ears,
Understand with their hearts,
And return and be healed."
11 Then I said, "Lord, how long?" And
He answered,
"Until cities are devastated *and*
without inhabitant,
Houses are without people
And the land is utterly desolate,
12 "The LORD has removed men far
away,
And the forsaken places are many
in the midst of the land.
13 "Yet there will be a tenth portion in
it,
And it will again be *subject* to
burning,
Like a terebinth or an oak
Whose stump remains when it is
felled.
The holy seed is its stump."

◈ Psalm 105:23–36

23 Israel also came into Egypt;
Thus Jacob sojourned in the land of
Ham.
24 And He caused His people to be
very fruitful,
And made them stronger than their
adversaries.
25 He turned their heart to hate His
people,
To deal craftily with His servants.
26 He sent Moses His servant,
And Aaron, whom He had chosen.
27 They performed His wondrous acts
among them,
And miracles in the land of Ham.
28 He sent darkness and made *it* dark;
And they did not rebel against His
words.
29 He turned their waters into blood
And caused their fish to die.
30 Their land swarmed with frogs
Even in the chambers of their kings.
31 He spoke, and there came a swarm
of flies
And gnats in all their territory.
32 He gave them hail for rain,
And flaming fire in their land.

33 He struck down their vines also and
their fig trees,
And shattered the trees of their
territory.
34 He spoke, and locusts came,
And young locusts, even without
number,
35 And ate up all vegetation in their
land,
And ate up the fruit of their ground.
36 He also struck down all the
firstborn in their land,
The first fruits of all their vigor.

◈ Proverbs 24:28, 29

28 Do not be a witness against your
neighbor without cause,
And do not deceive with your lips.
29 Do not say, "Thus I shall do to him
as he has done to me;
I will render to the man according
to his work."

◈ 1 Corinthians 15:29–58

29 Otherwise, what will those do who
are baptized for the dead? If the dead
are not raised at all, why then are they
baptized for them?
30 Why are we also in danger every
hour?
31 I affirm, brethren, by the boasting
in you which I have in Christ Jesus our
Lord, I die daily.
32 If from human motives I fought
with wild beasts at Ephesus, what does
it profit me? If the dead are not raised,
LET US EAT AND DRINK, FOR TOMORROW WE
DIE.

LIFE LESSONS

➤ **Proverbs 24:29** — *Do not say, "Thus I
shall do to him as he has done to me."*

*I*t is not up to us to settle accounts
and to avenge what we see as injustices. Often, we do not have all the facts,
and we may not understand everything
going on. Since God knows everything,
He says, "Vengeance is Mine, I will
repay" (Rom. 12:19).

33 Do not be deceived: "Bad company corrupts good morals."

34 Become sober-minded as you ought, and stop sinning; for some have no knowledge of God. I speak *this* to your shame.

35 But someone will say, "How are the dead raised? And with what kind of body do they come?"

36 You fool! That which you sow does not come to life unless it dies;

37 and that which you sow, you do not sow the body which is to be, but a bare grain, perhaps of wheat or of something else.

38 But God gives it a body just as He wished, and to each of the seeds a body of its own.

39 All flesh is not the same flesh, but there is one *flesh* of men, and another flesh of beasts, and another flesh of birds, and another of fish.

40 There are also heavenly bodies and earthly bodies, but the glory of the heavenly is one, and the *glory* of the earthly is another.

41 There is one glory of the sun, and another glory of the moon, and another glory of the stars; for star differs from star in glory.

42 So also is the resurrection of the dead. It is sown a perishable *body*, it is raised an imperishable *body*;

43 it is sown in dishonor, it is raised in glory; it is sown in weakness, it is raised in power;

44 it is sown a natural body, it is raised a spiritual body. If there is a natural body, there is also a spiritual *body*.

45 So also it is written, "The first MAN, Adam, BECAME A LIVING SOUL." The last Adam *became* a life-giving spirit.

46 However, the spiritual is not first, but the natural; then the spiritual.

47 The first man is from the earth, earthy; the second man is from heaven.

48 As is the earthy, so also are those who are earthy; and as is the heavenly, so also are those who are heavenly.

49 Just as we have borne the image of the earthy, we will also bear the image of the heavenly.

50 Now I say this, brethren, that flesh and blood cannot inherit the kingdom of God; nor does the perishable inherit the imperishable.

51 Behold, I tell you a mystery; we will not all sleep, but we will all be changed,

52 in a moment, in the twinkling of an eye, at the last trumpet; for the trumpet will sound, and the dead will be raised imperishable, and we will be changed.

53 For this perishable must put on the imperishable, and this mortal must put on immortality.

54 But when this perishable will have put on the imperishable, and this mortal will have put on immortality, then will come about the saying that is written, "DEATH IS SWALLOWED UP in victory. ✳

55 "O DEATH, WHERE IS YOUR VICTORY? O DEATH, WHERE IS YOUR STING?"

56 The sting of death is sin, and the power of sin is the law;

57 but thanks be to God, who gives us the victory through our Lord Jesus Christ.

58 Therefore, my beloved brethren, be ◄ steadfast, immovable, always abounding in the work of the Lord, knowing that your toil is not *in* vain in the Lord.

LIFE LESSONS

➤ **1 Corinthians 15:58 — *Be steadfast, immovable, always abounding in the work of the Lord, knowing that your toil is not in vain in the Lord.***

Our work for God has value and meaning because He is the one behind it, empowering us through His Spirit and He has promised to give us success and reward us well for our faithful service.

Isaiah 7:1—8:22

7 NOW it came about in the days of Ahaz, the son of Jotham, the son of Uzziah, king of Judah, that Rezin the king of Aram and Pekah the son of Remaliah, king of Israel, went up to Jerusalem to *wage* war against it, but could not conquer it.

WHAT THE BIBLE SAYS ABOUT ◈

The Coming of Christ

Isaiah 7:14

Since creation, God had been orchestrating world affairs to set the stage for the arrival of His Son. During that time, He used prophecy to keep alive people's hope for a fresh beginning and a new relationship with Him.

So many Messianic predictions are recorded in the Old Testament that the likelihood of one man fulfilling them all was slim. However, Jesus Christ's birth, life, and death happened exactly as the prophets foretold. Isaiah proclaimed, "Behold, a virgin will be with child and bear a son, and she will call His name Immanuel" (7:14). "Immanuel" means "God with us" and functions more as a title than a proper name. The angel told Mary to call her Son "Jesus," which means "God saves." So Jesus is the God among us who saves (Matt. 1:21, 23).

Micah told the Jewish people their leader would come from the tiny town of Bethlehem (Micah 5:2). The timing of the Messiah's arrival was revealed to Daniel, who recorded the timeline in his writings. (Note: The word "weeks" in Daniel 9:25, 26 actually has the meaning of "seven years"—just as in Genesis 29:27.)

God Himself gave a direct prophecy in Genesis 3:15 when He told Satan, "I will put enmity between . . . your seed and her seed; He shall bruise you on the head, and you shall bruise Him on the heel." It was an indication that Christ would defeat him. A careful comparison of Jesus' life with the prophecies of Scripture leads to only one conclusion: Jesus is the promised Messiah, who brings every willing person into a new covenant relationship with the Father.

The hope of a coming Messiah sustained the Israelites through centuries of chaos, confusion, and captivity. That messianic hope is still available in our day through the One who came, died, and rose again for us. Those of us who have received Jesus Christ as our Savior have an unbreakable covenant relationship with God and the promise of eternity with Him. ◈

---

2 When it was reported to the house of David, saying, "The Arameans have camped in Ephraim," his heart and the hearts of his people shook as the trees of the forest shake with the wind.
3 Then the LORD said to Isaiah, "Go out now to meet Ahaz, you and your son Shear-jashub, at the end of the conduit of the upper pool, on the highway to the fuller's field,
4 and say to him, 'Take care and be calm, have no fear and do not be fainthearted because of these two stubs of smoldering firebrands, on account of the fierce anger of Rezin and Aram and the son of Remaliah.
5 'Because Aram, *with* Ephraim and the son of Remaliah, has planned evil against you, saying,
6 "Let us go up against Judah and terrorize it, and make for ourselves a breach in its walls and set up the son of Tabeel as king in the midst of it,"
7 thus says the Lord GOD: "It shall not stand nor shall it come to pass.
8 "For the head of Aram is Damascus and the head of Damascus is Rezin (now within another 65 years Ephraim will be shattered, *so that it is* no longer a people),
9 and the head of Ephraim is Samaria and the head of Samaria is the son of Remaliah. If you will not believe, you surely shall not last." '"
10 Then the LORD spoke again to Ahaz, saying,
11 "Ask a sign for yourself from the LORD your God; make *it* deep as Sheol or high as heaven."
12 But Ahaz said, "I will not ask, nor will I test the LORD!"
13 Then he said, "Listen now, O house of David! Is it too slight a thing for you to try the patience of men, that you will try the patience of my God as well?
14 "Therefore the Lord Himself will give you a sign: Behold, a virgin will be with child and bear a son, and she will call His name Immanuel.
15 "He will eat curds and honey at the time He knows *enough* to refuse evil and choose good.
16 "For before the boy will know *enough* to refuse evil and choose good, the land whose two kings you dread will be forsaken.

17 "The LORD will bring on you, on your people, and on your father's house such days as have never come since the day that Ephraim separated from Judah, the king of Assyria."

18 In that day the LORD will whistle for the fly that is in the remotest part of the rivers of Egypt and for the bee that is in the land of Assyria.

19 They will all come and settle on the steep ravines, on the ledges of the cliffs, on all the thorn bushes and on all the watering places.

20 In that day the Lord will shave with a razor, hired from regions beyond the Euphrates (*that is*, with the king of Assyria), the head and the hair of the legs; and it will also remove the beard.

21 Now in that day a man may keep alive a heifer and a pair of sheep;

22 and because of the abundance of the milk produced he will eat curds, for everyone that is left within the land will eat curds and honey.

23 And it will come about in that day, that every place where there used to be a thousand vines, *valued* at a thousand *shekels* of silver, will become briars and thorns.

24 *People* will come there with bows and arrows because all the land will be briars and thorns.

25 As for all the hills which used to be cultivated with the hoe, you will not go there for fear of briars and thorns; but they will become a place for pasturing oxen and for sheep to trample.

8 THEN the LORD said to me, "Take for yourself a large tablet and write on it in ordinary letters: Swift is the booty, speedy is the prey.

2 "And I will take to Myself faithful witnesses for testimony, Uriah the priest and Zechariah the son of Jeberechiah."

3 So I approached the prophetess, and she conceived and gave birth to a son. Then the LORD said to me, "Name him Maher-shalal-hash-baz;

4 for before the boy knows how to cry out 'My father' or 'My mother,' the wealth of Damascus and the spoil of Samaria will be carried away before the king of Assyria."

5 Again the LORD spoke to me further, saying,

6 "Inasmuch as these people have rejected the gently flowing waters of Shiloah

And rejoice in Rezin and the son of Remaliah;

7 "Now therefore, behold, the Lord is about to bring on them the strong and abundant waters of the Euphrates,
Even the king of Assyria and all his glory;
And it will rise up over all its channels and go over all its banks.

8 "Then it will sweep on into Judah, it will overflow and pass through,
It will reach even to the neck;
And the spread of its wings will fill the breadth of your land,
O Immanuel.

9 "Be broken, O peoples, and be shattered;
And give ear, all remote places of the earth.
Gird yourselves, yet be shattered;
Gird yourselves, yet be shattered.

10 "Devise a plan, but it will be thwarted;
State a proposal, but it will not stand,
For God is with us."

11 For thus the LORD spoke to me with mighty power and instructed me not to walk in the way of this people, saying,

12 "You are not to say, '*It is* a conspiracy!' In regard to all that this people call a conspiracy,
And you are not to fear what they fear or be in dread of *it*.

13 "It is the LORD of hosts whom you should regard as holy.
And He shall be your fear,
And He shall be your dread.

14 "Then He shall become a sanctuary;
But to both the houses of Israel,
a stone to strike and a rock to stumble over,
And a snare and a trap for the inhabitants of Jerusalem.

15 "Many will stumble over them,

Then they will fall and be broken;
They will even be snared and caught."

16 Bind up the testimony, seal the law among my disciples.

17 And I will wait for the LORD who is hiding His face from the house of Jacob; I will even look eagerly for Him.

18 Behold, I and the children whom the LORD has given me are for signs and wonders in Israel from the LORD of hosts, who dwells on Mount Zion.

19 When they say to you, "Consult the mediums and the spiritists who whisper and mutter," should not a people consult their God? *Should they consult* the dead on behalf of the living?

20 To the law and to the testimony! If they do not speak according to this word, it is because they have no dawn.

21 They will pass through the land hard-pressed and famished, and it will turn out that when they are hungry, they will be enraged and curse their king and their God as they face upward.

22 Then they will look to the earth, and behold, distress and darkness, the gloom of anguish; and *they will be* driven away into darkness.

◉ Psalm 105:37–45

37 Then He brought them out with
    silver and gold,
And among His tribes there was not
    one who stumbled.

38 Egypt was glad when they departed,
For the dread of them had fallen
    upon them.

39 He spread a cloud for a covering,
And fire to illumine by night.

LIFE LESSONS

➤ **Isaiah 8:20 —** *If they do not speak according to this word, it is because they have no dawn.*

*W*e live in a time when men demean the Bible and value their wisdom and insight above all else. But they are foolish to disregard the Word of God! Regardless of current opinion, Scripture proclaims the truth and will be completely vindicated. And those who defy the Lord "will be driven away into darkness" (Is. 8:22).

---

40 They asked, and He brought quail,
And satisfied them with the bread
    of heaven.

41 He opened the rock and water flowed
    out;
It ran in the dry places *like* a river.

42 For He remembered His holy word
With Abraham His servant;

43 And He brought forth His people
    with joy,
His chosen ones with a joyful shout.

44 He gave them also the lands of the
    nations,
That they might take possession of
    the fruit of the peoples' labor,

45 So that they might keep His statutes
And observe His laws,
Praise the LORD!

◉ Proverbs 24:30–34

30 I passed by the field of the sluggard
And by the vineyard of the man
    lacking sense,

31 And behold, it was completely
    overgrown with thistles;
Its surface was covered with nettles,
And its stone wall was broken down.

32 When I saw, I reflected upon it;
I looked, *and* received instruction.

33 "A little sleep, a little slumber,
A little folding of the hands to rest,"

34 Then your poverty will come *as* a
    robber
And your want like an armed man.

◉ 1 Corinthians 16:1–24

16 NOW concerning the collection for the saints, as I directed the churches of Galatia, so do you also.

2 On the first day of every week each one of you is to put aside and save, as he may prosper, so that no collections be made when I come.

3 When I arrive, whomever you may approve, I will send them with letters to carry your gift to Jerusalem;

4 and if it is fitting for me to go also, they will go with me.

5 But I will come to you after I go through Macedonia, for I am going through Macedonia;

LIFE LESSONS

> **1 Corinthians 16:2 —** *On the first day of the week each one of you is to put aside and save.*

*P*aul instructs believers to give to present their offerings to the Lord on a regular, proportional basis. Giving should be a consistent discipline in our lives, rather than a sporadic practice. We should honor the Lord with what He asks of us—which is a *tithe,* or ten percent, of our income (Mal. 3:10)—with a heart thankful for all He has already provided for us.

6   and perhaps I will stay with you, or even spend the winter, so that you may send me on my way wherever I may go.

7   For I do not wish to see you now *just* in passing; for I hope to remain with you for some time, if the Lord permits.

8   But I will remain in Ephesus until Pentecost;

9   for a wide door for effective *service* has opened to me, and there are many adversaries.

10   Now if Timothy comes, see that he is with you without cause to be afraid, for he is doing the Lord's work, as I also am.

11   So let no one despise him. But send him on his way in peace, so that he may come to me; for I expect him with the brethren.

12   But concerning Apollos our brother, I encouraged him greatly to come to you with the brethren; and it was not at all *his* desire to come now, but he will come when he has opportunity.

13   Be on the alert, stand firm in the faith, act like men, be strong.

14   Let all that you do be done in love.

15   Now I urge you, brethren (you know the household of Stephanas, that they were the first fruits of Achaia, and that they have devoted themselves for ministry to the saints),

16   that you also be in subjection to such men and to everyone who helps in the work and labors.

17   I rejoice over the coming of Stephanas and Fortunatus and Achaicus, because they have supplied what was lacking on your part.

18   For they have refreshed my spirit and yours. Therefore acknowledge such men.

19   The churches of Asia greet you. Aquila and Prisca greet you heartily in the Lord, with the church that is in their house.

20   All the brethren greet you. Greet one another with a holy kiss.

21   The greeting is in my own hand—Paul.

22   If anyone does not love the Lord, he is to be accursed. Maranatha.

23   The grace of the Lord Jesus be with you.

24   My love be with you all in Christ Jesus. Amen.

LIFE LESSONS

> **1 Corinthians 16:7 —** *I hope to remain with you for some time, if the Lord permits.*

*P*aul always sought the Lord for direction in his life. Though he may have had personal desires to stay at a particular church, travel to a certain region to evangelize the people, or visit a beloved congregation, he wisely left those plans in God's hands to fulfill or alter as He deemed best.

> **1 Corinthians 16:9 —** *A wide door for effective service has opened to me, and there are many adversaries.*

*T*he blessing of God—in this case, the opening of a wide door of ministry—often comes with difficulties—such as adversaries or other challenges. We should not grow discouraged by the obstacles or become presumptuous because of the blessings. Rather, we must remain obedient to the Lord and seek His will for every situation.

> **1 Corinthians 16:22 —** *If anyone does not love the Lord, he is to be accursed. Maranatha.*

*M*aranatha means, "Come, Lord Jesus" or, "The Lord is coming soon." There will come a time when Jesus Christ will sit on the Great White Throne and pass judgment on all who refused to believe in Him (Rev. 20:11–15). When that happens, it will be too late for unbelievers to turn to Him in faith and embrace His gift of salvation. That is why the right time to be reconciled to God is always *right now* (2 Cor. 5:10) because we do not know when He will return (Heb. 9:27).

Isaiah 9:1—10:34

9 BUT there will be no *more* gloom for her who was in anguish; in earlier times He treated the land of Zebulun and the land of Naphtali with contempt, but later on He shall make *it* glorious, by the way of the sea, on the other side of Jordan, Galilee of the Gentiles.

2 The people who walk in darkness
   Will see a great light;
   Those who live in a dark land,
   The light will shine on them.
3 You shall multiply the nation,
   You shall increase their gladness;
   They will be glad in Your presence
   As with the gladness of harvest,
   As men rejoice when they divide the spoil.
4 For You shall break the yoke of
   their burden and the staff on their shoulders,
   The rod of their oppressor, as at the battle of Midian.
5 For every boot of the booted
   warrior in the *battle* tumult,
   And cloak rolled in blood, will be
   for burning, fuel for the fire.
6 For a child will be born to us, a son
   will be given to us;
   And the government will rest on His shoulders;
   And His name will be called
      Wonderful Counselor, Mighty God,
   Eternal Father, Prince of Peace.
7 There will be no end to the
   increase of *His* government or of peace,
   On the throne of David and over his kingdom,
   To establish it and to uphold it with
      justice and righteousness
   From then on and forevermore.
   The zeal of the LORD of hosts will accomplish this.
8 The Lord sends a message against Jacob,
   And it falls on Israel.
9 And all the people know *it*,
   That is, Ephraim and the
      inhabitants of Samaria,
   Asserting in pride and in arrogance of heart:
10 "The bricks have fallen down,

   But we will rebuild with smooth stones;
   The sycamores have been cut down,
   But we will replace *them* with cedars."
11 Therefore the LORD raises against
   them adversaries from Rezin
   And spurs their enemies on,
12 The Arameans on the east and the
   Philistines on the west;
   And they devour Israel with gaping jaws.
   In *spite of* all this, His anger does not turn away
   And His hand is still stretched out.
13 Yet the people do not turn back to
   Him who struck them,
   Nor do they seek the LORD of hosts.
14 So the LORD cuts off head and tail
   from Israel,
   Both palm branch and bulrush in a single day.
15 The head is the elder and honorable man,
   And the prophet who teaches falsehood is the tail.
16 For those who guide this people are
   leading *them* astray;

LIFE LESSONS

Isaiah 9:2 — *The people who walk in darkness will see a great light.*

Jesus grew up in Nazareth of Galilee. His parents learned that He would be "A Light of revelation to the gentiles" (Luke 2:32), and He called Himself "the Light of the world" (John 8:12).

Isaiah 9:13 — *The people do not turn back to Him who struck them, nor do they seek the LORD of hosts.*

God spent many years warning Israel to turn from her wicked ways before He finally sent the Assyrians to destroy the nation and carry her people into captivity. He uses adversity to turn us to Him, not to destroy us. The dark moments of our lives will last only so long as is necessary for God to accomplish His purpose in us. "His anger is but for a moment, His favor is for a lifetime" (Ps. 30:5).

And those who are guided by them
are brought to confusion.

17 Therefore the Lord does not take
pleasure in their young men,
Nor does He have pity on their
orphans or their widows;
For every one of them is godless
and an evildoer,
And every mouth is speaking
foolishness.
In *spite of* all this, His anger does
not turn away
And His hand is still stretched out.

18 For wickedness burns like a fire;
It consumes briars and thorns;
It even sets the thickets of the forest
aflame
And they roll upward in a column of
smoke.

19 By the fury of the LORD of hosts the
land is burned up,
And the people are like fuel for the
fire;
No man spares his brother.

20 They slice off *what is* on the right
hand but *still* are hungry,
And they eat *what is* on the left
hand but they are not satisfied;
Each of them eats the flesh of his
own arm.

21 Manasseh *devours* Ephraim, and
Ephraim Manasseh,
And together they are against
Judah.
In *spite of* all this, His anger does
not turn away
And His hand is still stretched out.

10 WOE to those who enact evil
statutes
And to those who constantly record
unjust decisions,

2 So as to deprive the needy of
justice
And rob the poor of My people of
their rights,
So that widows may be their spoil
And that they may plunder the
orphans.

3 Now what will you do in the day of
punishment,
And in the devastation which will
come from afar?
To whom will you flee for help?
And where will you leave your
wealth?

4 Nothing *remains* but to crouch
among the captives

Or fall among the slain.
In *spite of* all this, His anger does
not turn away
And His hand is still stretched out.

5 Woe to Assyria, the rod of My
anger
And the staff in whose hands is My
indignation,

6 I send it against a godless nation
And commission it against the
people of My fury
To capture booty and to seize
plunder,
And to trample them down like mud
in the streets.

7 Yet it does not so intend,
Nor does it plan so in its heart,
But rather it is its purpose to
destroy
And to cut off many nations.

8 For it says, "Are not my princes all
kings?

9 "Is not Calno like Carchemish,
Or Hamath like Arpad,
Or Samaria like Damascus?

10 "As my hand has reached to the
kingdoms of the idols,
Whose graven images *were* greater
than those of Jerusalem and
Samaria,

11 Shall I not do to Jerusalem and her
images
Just as I have done to Samaria and
her idols?"

12 So it will be that when the Lord has
completed all His work on Mount Zion
and on Jerusalem, *He will say,* "I will
punish the fruit of the arrogant heart of
the king of Assyria and the pomp of his
haughtiness."

13 For he has said,
"By the power of my hand and by
my wisdom I did *this,*
For I have understanding;
And I removed the boundaries of
the peoples
And plundered their treasures,
And like a mighty man I brought
down *their* inhabitants,

14 And my hand reached to the riches
of the peoples like a nest,
And as one gathers abandoned
eggs, I gathered all the earth;
And there was not one that flapped
its wing or opened *its* beak or
chirped."

➤ 15 Is the axe to boast itself over the
   one who chops with it?
   Is the saw to exalt itself over the
   one who wields it?
   That would be like a club wielding
   those who lift it,
   Or like a rod lifting *him who* is not
   wood.
16 Therefore the Lord, the GOD of
   hosts, will send a wasting disease
   among his stout warriors;
   And under his glory a fire will be
   kindled like a burning flame.
17 And the light of Israel will become a
   fire and his Holy One a flame,
   And it will burn and devour his
   thorns and his briars in a single
   day.
18 And He will destroy the glory of his
   forest and of his fruitful garden,
   both soul and body,
   And it will be as when a sick man
   wastes away.
19 And the rest of the trees of his
   forest will be so small in number
   That a child could write them down.
20 Now in that day the remnant of Israel, and those of the house of Jacob who
   have escaped, will never again rely on
   the one who struck them, but will truly
   rely on the LORD, the Holy One of Israel.
21 A remnant will return, the remnant
   of Jacob, to the mighty God.
22 For though your people, O Israel,
   may be like the sand of the sea,
   Only a remnant within them will
   return;
   A destruction is determined,
   overflowing with righteousness.
23 For a complete destruction, one that
is decreed, the Lord GOD of hosts will
execute in the midst of the whole land.
24 Therefore thus says the Lord GOD of
hosts, "O My people who dwell in Zion,
do not fear the Assyrian who strikes you

with the rod and lifts up his staff against
you, the way Egypt *did*.
25 "For in a very little while My indignation *against you* will be spent and My
anger *will be directed* to their destruction."
26 The LORD of hosts will arouse a
scourge against him like the slaughter of
Midian at the rock of Oreb; and His staff
will be over the sea and He will lift it up
the way *He did* in Egypt.
27 So it will be in that day, that his burden will be removed from your shoulders
and his yoke from your neck, and the
yoke will be broken because of fatness.
28 He has come against Aiath,
   He has passed through Migron;
   At Michmash he deposited his
   baggage.
29 They have gone through the pass,
   saying,
   "Geba will be our lodging place."
   Ramah is terrified, and Gibeah of
   Saul has fled away.
30 Cry aloud with your voice,
   O daughter of Gallim!
   Pay attention, Laishah *and* wretched
   Anathoth!
31 Madmenah has fled.
   The inhabitants of Gebim have
   sought refuge.
32 Yet today he will halt at Nob;
   He shakes his fist at the mountain
   of the daughter of Zion, the hill of
   Jerusalem.
33 Behold, the Lord, the GOD of hosts,
   will lop off the boughs with a
   terrible crash;
   Those also who are tall in stature
   will be cut down
   And those who are lofty will be
   abased.
34 He will cut down the thickets of the
   forest with an iron *axe*,
   And Lebanon will fall by the Mighty
   One.

LIFE LESSONS

➤ Isaiah 10:15 — *Is the axe to boast
itself over the one who chops with it?*

*A*ny success we achieve and any
accomplishments we make we owe
to the will and favor of God. As Paul
asks, "For who regards you as superior?
What do you have that you did not
receive?" (1 Cor. 4:7).

◈ **Psalm 106:1–5**

106 PRAISE the LORD!
Oh give thanks to the LORD, for
   He is good;
For His lovingkindness is
   everlasting.

2   Who can speak of the mighty deeds
of the LORD,
Or can show forth all His praise?
3   How blessed are those who keep
justice,
Who practice righteousness at all
times!
4   Remember me, O LORD, in *Your*
favor toward Your people;
Visit me with Your salvation,
5   That I may see the prosperity of
Your chosen ones,
That I may rejoice in the gladness of
Your nation,
That I may glory with Your
inheritance.

Proverbs 25:1, 2

25 THESE also are proverbs of Solomon which the men of Hezekiah,
king of Judah, transcribed.
2   It is the glory of God to conceal a
matter,
But the glory of kings is to search
out a matter.

2 Corinthians 1:1–24

1 PAUL, an apostle of Christ Jesus
by the will of God, and Timothy *our*
brother,
To the church of God which is at
Corinth with all the saints who are
throughout Achaia:
2   Grace to you and peace from God
our Father and the Lord Jesus Christ.
3   Blessed *be* the God and Father of our
Lord Jesus Christ, the Father of mercies
and God of all comfort,
4   who comforts us in all our affliction so that we will be able to comfort
those who are in any affliction with the
comfort with which we ourselves are
comforted by God.
5   For just as the sufferings of Christ
are ours in abundance, so also our comfort is abundant through Christ.
6   But if we are afflicted, it is for your
comfort and salvation; or if we are comforted, it is for your comfort, which is
effective in the patient enduring of the
same sufferings which we also suffer;

7   and our hope for you is firmly
grounded, knowing that as you are sharers of our sufferings, so also you are
sharers of our comfort.
8   For we do not want you to be unaware, brethren, of our affliction which
came *to us* in Asia, that we were burdened excessively, beyond our strength,
so that we despaired even of life;
9   indeed, we had the sentence of death
within ourselves so that we would not
trust in ourselves, but in God who raises
the dead;
10   who delivered us from so great a
peril of death, and will deliver *us*, He on
whom we have set our hope. And He will
yet deliver us,
11   you also joining in helping us
through your prayers, so that thanks
may be given by many persons on our
behalf for the favor bestowed on us
through *the prayers of* many.
12   For our proud confidence is this: the
testimony of our conscience, that in holiness and godly sincerity, not in fleshly
wisdom but in the grace of God, we have
conducted ourselves in the world, and
especially toward you.
13   For we write nothing else to you
than what you read and understand, and
I hope you will understand until the end;

LIFE LESSONS

> **Proverbs 25:2 —** *It is the glory of God
to conceal a matter.*

*G*od not only reveals things we do not
know, but He also hides things that
we *cannot* know them. Elisha found this
out (see 2 Kin. 4:27), as did Moses (see
Deut. 29:29). And Isaiah says, "You are a
God who hides Himself" (Is. 45:15).

> **2 Corinthians 1:4 —** *That we will be
able to comfort those who are in any
affliction.*

*S*ometimes God allows us to fall into
deep valleys in order to show us we
are never really in control. He alone is
always in control, and He knows how
to rescue us from impossible situations
(v. 9). When trials come, we can be sure
God will come to our aid. Why? It is His
nature—He is "the Father of mercies"
and the "God of all comfort". And He is
training us to comfort others.

WHAT THE BIBLE SAYS ABOUT

Encouragement for a Troubled Heart

2 Corinthians 1:3–11

*R*ead a book on leadership, and it will direct you to pore over the biographies of great leaders and imitate their techniques. As a Christian, you are directed to emulate Christ. However, you can never forget that Jesus' role was that of the Suffering Servant.

Second Corinthians 1:3, 4 teaches, "Blessed be the God and Father of our Lord Jesus Christ, the Father of mercies and God of all comfort, who comforts us in all our affliction so that we will be able to comfort those who are in any affliction with the comfort with which we ourselves are comforted by God."

If you are wondering about your sufferings, understand that you are being trained to be a servant as Jesus was. You are learning how to comfort others in the midst of their great afflictions.

It is truly an amazing and blessed thing to lift someone up in the midst of his or her trials and heartaches. However, this cannot be done simply by exuberance or flattery. On the contrary, true, priceless encouragement can only come from a heart that has likewise suffered.

That is why in 2 Corinthians 1:6 Paul teaches, "If we are afflicted, it is for your comfort and salvation; or if we are comforted, it is for your comfort, which is effective in the patient enduring of the same sufferings which we also suffer. Or if we are comforted, it is for your consolation and salvation."

Are you suffering? Are there trials and hardships which overcome your soul and bring salty, bitter tears to your eyes? God is making you into one of those precious servants who gladden the heart and bring sunshine to the lives of many. He is making you into an encourager.

Wouldn't this be a wondrous gift to give another—support and strength, with no fear? This is the servanthood that Jesus is developing in you. You will learn by His example as His power is shown through your troubles. And you will teach others so that they may walk in His ways as well.

You have been chosen to be a blessing. Take heart in the fact that you, like our Suffering Servant Jesus and the apostle Paul, have been afflicted for the comfort and salvation of others. ◈

---

14 just as you also partially did understand us, that we are your reason to be proud as you also are ours, in the day of our Lord Jesus.
15 In this confidence I intended at first to come to you, so that you might twice receive a blessing;
16 that is, to pass your way into Macedonia, and again from Macedonia to come to you, and by you to be helped on my journey to Judea.
17 Therefore, I was not vacillating when I intended to do this, was I? Or what I purpose, do I purpose according to the flesh, so that with me there will be yes, yes and no, no *at the same time?*
18 But as God is faithful, our word to you is not yes and no.
19 For the Son of God, Christ Jesus, who was preached among you by us—by me and Silvanus and Timothy—was not yes and no, but is yes in Him.
20 For as many as are the promises of God, in Him they are yes; therefore also through Him is our Amen to the glory of God through us.
21 Now He who establishes us with you in Christ and anointed us is God, ◄
22 who also sealed us and gave *us* the Spirit in our hearts as a pledge.
23 But I call God as witness to my soul, that to spare you I did not come again to Corinth.
24 Not that we lord it over your faith, but are workers with you for your joy; for in your faith you are standing firm.

Isaiah 11:1—12:6

11 THEN a shoot will spring from the stem of Jesse,
And a branch from his roots will bear fruit.

2 The Spirit of the LORD will rest on Him,
The spirit of wisdom and understanding,
The spirit of counsel and strength,
The spirit of knowledge and the fear of the LORD.

3 And He will delight in the fear of the LORD,
And He will not judge by what His eyes see,
Nor make a decision by what His ears hear;

4 But with righteousness He will judge the poor,
And decide with fairness for the afflicted of the earth;
And He will strike the earth with the rod of His mouth,
And with the breath of His lips He will slay the wicked.

5 Also righteousness will be the belt about His loins,
And faithfulness the belt about His waist.

6 And the wolf will dwell with the lamb,
And the leopard will lie down with the young goat,
And the calf and the young lion and the fatling together;
And a little boy will lead them.

7 Also the cow and the bear will graze,
Their young will lie down together,
And the lion will eat straw like the ox.

8 The nursing child will play by the hole of the cobra,
And the weaned child will put his hand on the viper's den.

9 They will not hurt or destroy in all My holy mountain,
For the earth will be full of the knowledge of the LORD
As the waters cover the sea.

10 Then in that day
The nations will resort to the root of Jesse,
Who will stand as a signal for the peoples;
And His resting place will be glorious.

11 Then it will happen on that day that the Lord
Will again recover the second time with His hand
The remnant of His people, who will remain,
From Assyria, Egypt, Pathros, Cush, Elam, Shinar, Hamath,
And from the islands of the sea.

12 And He will lift up a standard for the nations
And assemble the banished ones of Israel,
And will gather the dispersed of Judah
From the four corners of the earth.

13 Then the jealousy of Ephraim will depart,
And those who harass Judah will be cut off;
Ephraim will not be jealous of Judah,
And Judah will not harass Ephraim.

14 They will swoop down on the slopes of the Philistines on the west;
Together they will plunder the sons of the east;
They will possess Edom and Moab,
And the sons of Ammon will be subject to them.

LIFE LESSONS

➤ Isaiah 11:3 — *He will delight in the fear of the LORD.*

Isaiah foresaw that Jesus would "delight" in the fear of God. He didn't mean that Jesus would delight in the emotion so much as in the awesome, majestic, all-powerful God who inspires godly fear.

➤ Isaiah 11:9 — *For the earth will be full of the knowledge of the LORD as the waters cover the sea.*

We look forward to the day when God will rule on earth as He does in heaven, a day when righteousness will reign and evil will not be allowed to oppress anyone.

15 And the LORD will utterly destroy
The tongue of the Sea of Egypt;
And He will wave His hand over the River
With His scorching wind;
And He will strike it into seven streams
And make *men* walk over dry-shod.
16 And there will be a highway from Assyria
For the remnant of His people who will be left,
Just as there was for Israel
In the day that they came up out of the land of Egypt.

12 THEN you will say on that day,
"I will give thanks to You, O LORD;
For although You were angry with me,
Your anger is turned away,
And You comfort me.
2 "Behold, God is my salvation,
I will trust and not be afraid;
For the LORD GOD is my strength and song,
And He has become my salvation."

3 Therefore you will joyously draw water
From the springs of salvation.

LIFE LESSONS

➤ *Isaiah 12:2 — Behold, God is my salvation, I will trust and not be afraid.*

*W*hen hard times come, we always have the choice of whether to trust God or become fearful. No matter how overwhelming your circumstances become, trusting Him is the right choice. Faith gives us the ability to see what God sees. Therefore, do not fear. Rather, be confident that the Lord will be your defense.

➤ *Isaiah 12:3 — Therefore you will joyously draw water from the springs of salvation.*

*O*ur salvation should give us joy every day, not merely in the period immediately following our conversion. God's salvation is not about eternal life only but also about abundant life right now.

ANSWERS TO LIFE'S QUESTIONS

When is the appropriate time to praise the Lord?

ISAIAH 12

*P*raise the Lord often, regardless of your circumstances. Many people exalt Him only when something good happens to them or when they receive an unexpected blessing—but the Lord is worthy of our adoration at all times, in all circumstances.

However, we never should praise Him on the basis of our circumstances. We should exalt Him because He is worthy of our devotion and because we love Him. Therefore, praise Him on the basis of who He is in the midst of your circumstances.

Don't limit your worship to the songs you sing at Sunday church services. Praise the Lord often, in both words and songs that you create spontaneously. All around you, at all times, you can find countless things for which to praise God. Look for those things, and throughout the day, voice your heartfelt praise and thanksgiving to Him.

When you ride alone in your car, get into an empty elevator, sit alone in your office or work space, or find yourself alone in your home, take every opportunity to voice praise to the Lord for who He is. Honor Him for what He has done through the ages, for what He has done in your life and in the lives of your loved ones, and for what you know without a doubt the Lord is doing for you and will do for you both now and throughout all eternity.

You can never run out of things for which to praise the Lord!

When you voice your gratefulness to God, you open yourself up to experiencing His presence with you. The Bible tells us that the Lord is "enthroned" in the praises of His people (Ps. 22:3).

The greater your praise, the smaller your problems will appear.

The more frequent your praise, the less you will find yourself with time to worry or feel anxious.

The more you praise Him, the more you are going to see things worthy of His praise.

As you exalt Him, your entire attitude will shift from an unhealthy "I focus" and "problem focus," to a healthy and joyful "God focus" and "answer focus." So take a cue from the prophet Isaiah and proclaim: "O LORD, You are my God; I will exalt You, I will give thanks to Your name; for you have worked wonders, plans formed long ago, with perfect faithfulness" (Is. 25:1).

4   And in that day you will say,
    "Give thanks to the LORD, call on His
        name.
    Make known His deeds among the
        peoples;
    Make *them* remember that His
        name is exalted."
5   Praise the LORD in song, for He has
        done excellent things;
    Let this be known throughout the
        earth.
6   Cry aloud and shout for joy,
    O inhabitant of Zion,
    For great in your midst is the Holy
        One of Israel.

◈ Psalm 106:6–18

6 We have sinned like our fathers,
    We have committed iniquity, we
        have behaved wickedly.
7   Our fathers in Egypt did not
        understand Your wonders;
    They did not remember Your
        abundant kindnesses,
    But rebelled by the sea, at the Red
        Sea.
8   Nevertheless He saved them for the
        sake of His name,
    That He might make His power
        known.
9   Thus He rebuked the Red Sea and it
        dried up,
    And He led them through the deeps,
        as through the wilderness.
10 So He saved them from the hand of
        the one who hated *them*,
    And redeemed them from the hand
        of the enemy.
11 The waters covered their
        adversaries;
    Not one of them was left.
12 Then they believed His words;
    They sang His praise.
13 They quickly forgot His works;
    They did not wait for His counsel,
14 But craved intensely in the
        wilderness,
    And tempted God in the desert.
15 So He gave them their request,
    But sent a wasting disease among
        them.
16 When they became envious of
        Moses in the camp,

And of Aaron, the holy one of the
    LORD,
17 The earth opened and swallowed up
        Dathan,
    And engulfed the company of
        Abiram.
18 And a fire blazed up in their
        company;
    The flame consumed the wicked.

◈ Proverbs 25:3–5

3   *As* the heavens for height and the
        earth for depth,
    So the heart of kings is
        unsearchable.
4   Take away the dross from the
        silver,
    And there comes out a vessel for the
        smith;
5   Take away the wicked before the
        king,
    And his throne will be established
        in righteousness.

◈ 2 Corinthians 2:1–17

2 BUT I determined this for my own
    sake, that I would not come to you in
sorrow again.
2   For if I cause you sorrow, who then
makes me glad but the one whom I made
sorrowful?
3   This is the very thing I wrote you, so
that when I came, I would not have sorrow from those who ought to make me
rejoice; having confidence in you all that
my joy would be *the joy* of you all.
4   For out of much affliction and anguish of heart I wrote to you with many
tears; not so that you would be made sorrowful, but that you might know the love
which I have especially for you.
5   But if any has caused sorrow, he has
caused sorrow not to me, but in some
degree—in order not to say too much—to
all of you.
6   Sufficient for such a one is this ◄
punishment which *was inflicted* by the
majority,
7   so that on the contrary you should
rather forgive and comfort *him*, other-

wise such a one might be overwhelmed by excessive sorrow.

8 Wherefore I urge you to reaffirm *your* love for him.

9 For to this end also I wrote, so that I might put you to the test, whether you are obedient in all things.

10 But one whom you forgive anything, I *forgive* also; for indeed what I have forgiven, if I have forgiven anything, *I did it* for your sakes in the presence of Christ,

11 so that no advantage would be taken of us by Satan, for we are not ignorant of his schemes.

12 Now when I came to Troas for the gospel of Christ and when a door was opened for me in the Lord,

13 I had no rest for my spirit, not finding Titus my brother; but taking my leave of them, I went on to Macedonia.

14 But thanks be to God, who always leads us in triumph in Christ, and manifests through us the sweet aroma of the knowledge of Him in every place.

15 For we are a fragrance of Christ to God among those who are being saved and among those who are perishing;

16 to the one an aroma from death to death, to the other an aroma from life to life. And who is adequate for these things?

LIFE LESSONS

➤ **2 Corinthians 2:6, 7 — *Otherwise such a one might be overwhelmed by excessive sorrow.***

*G*od's desire in discipline is always restoration and renewal—not retribution and rejection. Sorrow has value only insofar as it moves someone to repentance and back into full fellowship. We should never take God's discipline as a sign of His hostility toward us or disinterest in us but rather as a sure token of His love. His goal is never to grieve us, but to get us back on a road to life.

➤ **2 Corinthians 2:14 — *Thanks be to God, who always leads us in triumph in Christ.***

*P*aul does not mean that things always turn out the way we want; but in Christ we are always on the road to victory. Setbacks happen, but they are never final or fatal because the Lord will assuredly triumph in the end (Rom. 8:28).

---

17 For we are not like many, peddling the word of God, but as from sincerity, but as from God, we speak in Christ in the sight of God.

Isaiah 13:1—14:32

13 THE oracle concerning Babylon which Isaiah the son of Amoz saw.

2 Lift up a standard on the bare hill,
   Raise your voice to them,
   Wave the hand that they may enter
      the doors of the nobles.

3 I have commanded My consecrated
      ones,
   I have even called My mighty
      warriors,
   My proudly exulting ones,
   To *execute* My anger.

4 A sound of tumult on the
      mountains,
   Like that of many people!
   A sound of the uproar of kingdoms,
   Of nations gathered together!
   The LORD of hosts is mustering the
      army for battle.

5 They are coming from a far country,
   From the farthest horizons,
   The LORD and His instruments of
      indignation,
   To destroy the whole land.

6 Wail, for the day of the LORD is
      near!
   It will come as destruction from the
      Almighty.

7 Therefore all hands will fall limp,
   And every man's heart will melt.

8 They will be terrified,
   Pains and anguish will take hold of
      them;
   They will writhe like a woman in
      labor,
   They will look at one another in
      astonishment,
   Their faces aflame.

9 Behold, the day of the LORD is
      coming,
   Cruel, with fury and burning anger,

To make the land a desolation;
And He will exterminate its sinners
    from it.
10 For the stars of heaven and their
        constellations
    Will not flash forth their light;
    The sun will be dark when it rises
    And the moon will not shed its light.
11 Thus I will punish the world for its
        evil
    And the wicked for their iniquity;
    I will also put an end to the
        arrogance of the proud
    And abase the haughtiness of the
        ruthless.
12 I will make mortal man scarcer than
        pure gold
    And mankind than the gold of
        Ophir.
13 Therefore I will make the heavens
        tremble,
    And the earth will be shaken from
        its place
    At the fury of the LORD of hosts
    In the day of His burning anger.
14 And it will be that like a hunted
        gazelle,
    Or like sheep with none to gather
        them,
    They will each turn to his own
        people,
    And each one flee to his own land.
15 Anyone who is found will be thrust
        through,
    And anyone who is captured will
        fall by the sword.
16 Their little ones also will be dashed
        to pieces
    Before their eyes;
    Their houses will be plundered
    And their wives ravished.
➤ 17 Behold, I am going to stir up the
        Medes against them,

LIFE LESSONS

➤ **Isaiah 13:17 — "Behold, I am going to stir up the Medes against them."**

*W*hen Isaiah made this prophecy, the Babylonians were far from the world's mightiest superpower and more than 150 years away from conquering Judah. Yet God foresaw their rise *and* their fall. Eventually, it was the Medes and Persians who toppled Babylon, just as God declared.

Who will not value silver or take
    pleasure in gold.
18 And *their* bows will mow down the
        young men,
    They will not even have compassion
        on the fruit of the womb,
    Nor will their eye pity children.
19 And Babylon, the beauty of
        kingdoms, the glory of the
        Chaldeans' pride,
    Will be as when God overthrew
        Sodom and Gomorrah.
20 It will never be inhabited or lived in
        from generation to generation;
    Nor will the Arab pitch *his* tent
        there,
    Nor will shepherds make *their*
        flocks lie down there.
21 But desert creatures will lie down
        there,
    And their houses will be full of
        owls;
    Ostriches also will live there, and
        shaggy goats will frolic there.
22 Hyenas will howl in their fortified
        towers
    And jackals in their luxurious
        palaces.
    Her *fateful* time also will soon come
    And her days will not be prolonged.

14 WHEN the LORD will have compassion on Jacob and again choose Israel, and settle them in their own land, then strangers will join them and attach themselves to the house of Jacob.
2   The peoples will take them along and bring them to their place, and the house of Israel will possess them as an inheritance in the land of the LORD as male servants and female servants; and they will take their captors captive and will rule over their oppressors.
3   And it will be in the day when the LORD gives you rest from your pain and turmoil and harsh service in which you have been enslaved,
4   that you will take up this taunt against the king of Babylon, and say,
    "How the oppressor has ceased,
    And how fury has ceased!
5   "The LORD has broken the staff of
        the wicked,
    The scepter of rulers
6   Which used to strike the peoples in
        fury with unceasing strokes,
    Which subdued the nations in anger
        with unrestrained persecution.

7 "The whole earth is at rest *and* is
    quiet;
    They break forth into shouts of joy.
8 "Even the cypress trees rejoice over
    you, *and* the cedars of Lebanon,
    saying,
    'Since you were laid low, no *tree*
    cutter comes up against us.'
9 "Sheol from beneath is excited over
    you to meet you when you come;
    It arouses for you the spirits of the
    dead, all the leaders of the earth;
    It raises all the kings of the nations
    from their thrones.
10 "They will all respond and say to you,
    'Even you have been made weak as
    we,
    You have become like us.
11 'Your pomp *and* the music of your
    harps
    Have been brought down to Sheol;
    Maggots are spread out *as your bed*
    beneath you
    And worms are your covering.'
12 "How you have fallen from heaven,
    O star of the morning, son of the
    dawn!
    You have been cut down to the
    earth,
    You who have weakened the nations!
➤ 13 "But you said in your heart,
    'I will ascend to heaven;
    I will raise my throne above the
    stars of God,
    And I will sit on the mount of
    assembly
    In the recesses of the north.
14 'I will ascend above the heights of
    the clouds;
    I will make myself like the Most
    High.'
15 "Nevertheless you will be thrust
    down to Sheol,
    To the recesses of the pit.
16 "Those who see you will gaze at you,
    They will ponder over you, *saying,*
    'Is this the man who made the earth
    tremble,
    Who shook kingdoms,
17 Who made the world like a
    wilderness
    And overthrew its cities,
    Who did not allow his prisoners to
    go home?'
18 "All the kings of the nations lie in
    glory,
    Each in his own tomb.

19 "But you have been cast out of your
    tomb
    Like a rejected branch,
    Clothed with the slain who are
    pierced with a sword,
    Who go down to the stones of the
    pit
    Like a trampled corpse.
20 "You will not be united with them in
    burial,
    Because you have ruined your
    country,
    You have slain your people.
    May the offspring of evildoers not
    be mentioned forever.
21 "Prepare for his sons a place of
    slaughter
    Because of the iniquity of their
    fathers.
    They must not arise and take
    possession of the earth
    And fill the face of the world with
    cities."
22 "I will rise up against them," declares
the LORD of hosts, "and will cut off from
Babylon name and survivors, offspring
and posterity," declares the LORD.
23 "I will also make it a possession for
the hedgehog and swamps of water, and
I will sweep it with the broom of destruction," declares the LORD of hosts.
24 The LORD of hosts has sworn saying, ◄
"Surely, just as I have intended so it has ✳
happened, and just as I have planned so
it will stand,
25 to break Assyria in My land, and I

LIFE LESSONS

➤ **Isaiah 14:13 — *"I will ascend to heaven; I will raise my throne above the stars of God."***

*I*saiah uses the arrogant king of Babylon to picture the insolent pride of
Satan. The devil fell from his lofty position because he wanted to usurp God's
place. He even tried to get Jesus to worship him (Matt. 4:9).

➤ **Isaiah 14:24 — *"Just as I have planned so it will stand."***

*G*od will always follow through on
both His promises and His warnings.
He tells us, "Whatever a man sows, this
he will also reap" (Gal. 6:7), and we are
foolish if we fail to heed His warning.

will trample him on My mountains. Then his yoke will be removed from them and his burden removed from their shoulder.
26 "This is the plan devised against the whole earth; and this is the hand that is stretched out against all the nations.
27 "For the LORD of hosts has planned, and who can frustrate *it*? And as for His stretched-out hand, who can turn it back?"
28 In the year that King Ahaz died this oracle came:
29 "Do not rejoice, O Philistia, all of you,
Because the rod that struck you is broken;
For from the serpent's root a viper will come out,
And its fruit will be a flying serpent.
30 "Those who are most helpless will eat,
And the needy will lie down in security;
I will destroy your root with famine,
And it will kill off your survivors.

31 "Wail, O gate; cry, O city;
Melt away, O Philistia, all of you;
For smoke comes from the north,
And there is no straggler in his ranks.
32 "How then will one answer the messengers of the nation?
That the LORD has founded Zion,
And the afflicted of His people will seek refuge in it."

◈ Psalm 106:19–23

19 They made a calf in Horeb
And worshiped a molten image.
20 Thus they exchanged their glory
For the image of an ox that eats grass.
21 They forgot God their Savior,
Who had done great things in Egypt,
22 Wonders in the land of Ham
And awesome things by the Red Sea.

How can I become a godly influence on others?

PSALM 106:23

*T*he United States Marine Corps is always on the lookout for what it calls "a few good men." The eyes of the Lord are likewise scanning the earth in order to find godly men and women who will step forward and use their influence to exalt Him (2 Chr. 16:9). We see this in Ezekiel, where God says, "I searched for a man among them who would build up the wall and stand in the gap before Me for the land, so that I would not destroy it" (Ezek. 22:30).

A gap is a place where error or falsehood has crept in, allowing satanic confusion and inviting the judgment of God. Sometimes these gaps are so serious they imperil entire nations. Such a time faced Israel following the exodus. But the Word of God records this remarkable statement: "Therefore He said that He would destroy them, had not Moses His chosen one stood in the breach before Him, to turn away His wrath from destroying them" (Ps. 106:23).

Few of us will ever be called upon to save a nation. But we can build up walls of protection around our families and churches by insisting on speaking the entire counsel of God (Acts

20:26–31). We can resist the devil daily and refuse the sensuality and perversions of this age. In Moses' day, one man made all the difference. Why not be the one who makes a difference today?

A prostitute named Rahab made the right choice and became the ancestor of the Messiah (Josh. 6:17, 25; Matt. 1:5; Heb. 11:31; James 2:25). A widow named Ruth chose the God of Israel, became the great-grandmother of King David, and was also the forbearer of Christ (Ruth 1:16, 17; 4:13–22; Matt. 1:5). An infertile wife named Hannah poured out her soul to God and became the mother of Samuel (1 Sam. 1:9–20). A man called Abram responded to God, left his relatives behind, and became the father of all who believe (Gen. 12:1–5; Rom. 4; Gal. 3). A woman named Mary poured expensive perfume on Jesus' head and gained for herself an eternal monument in history (Mark 14:3–9).

Who are the influential people of this earth? They are the ones who leave all to follow the Lord—men and women who prove themselves to be "blameless and innocent, children of God above reproach in the midst of a crooked and perverse generation, among whom [they] appear as lights in the world" (Phil. 2:15). You may doubt that your light shines brightly by this world's standards—but since God calls you a luminary, keep on shining!

23   Therefore He said that He would
         destroy them,
     Had not Moses His chosen one
         stood in the breach before Him,
     To turn away His wrath from
         destroying *them*.

Proverbs 25:6, 7

6   Do not claim honor in the presence
         of the king,
     And do not stand in the place of
         great men;
7   For it is better that it be said to you,
         "Come up here,"
     Than for you to be placed lower in
         the presence of the prince,
     Whom your eyes have seen.

2 Corinthians 3:1–18

3ARE we beginning to commend ourselves again? Or do we need, as some,
letters of commendation to you or from
you?
2   You are our letter, written in our
hearts, known and read by all men;
3   being manifested that you are a letter of Christ, cared for by us, written not
with ink but with the Spirit of the living
God, not on tablets of stone but on tablets of human hearts.
4   Such confidence we have through
Christ toward God.
5   Not that we are adequate in ourselves to consider anything as *coming*
from ourselves, but our adequacy is from
God,
6   who also made us adequate *as* servants of a new covenant, not of the letter
but of the Spirit; for the letter kills, but
the Spirit gives life.
7   But if the ministry of death, in letters
engraved on stones, came with glory,
so that the sons of Israel could not look
intently at the face of Moses because of
the glory of his face, fading *as* it was,
8   how will the ministry of the Spirit
fail to be even more with glory?
9   For if the ministry of condemnation
has glory, much more does the ministry
of righteousness abound in glory.
10   For indeed what had glory, in this

case has no glory because of the glory
that surpasses *it*.
11   For if that which fades away *was*
with glory, much more that which remains *is* in glory.
12   Therefore having such a hope, we
use great boldness in *our* speech,
13   and *are* not like Moses, *who* used to
put a veil over his face so that the sons of
Israel would not look intently at the end
of what was fading away.
14   But their minds were hardened; for
until this very day at the reading of the
old covenant the same veil remains un-
lifted, because it is removed in Christ.
15   But to this day whenever Moses is
read, a veil lies over their heart;
16   but whenever a person turns to the
Lord, the veil is taken away.
17   Now the Lord is the Spirit, and
where the Spirit of the Lord is, *there* is
liberty.
18   But we all, with unveiled face, be-
holding as in a mirror the glory of the
Lord, are being transformed into the
same image from glory to glory, just as
from the Lord, the Spirit.

LIFE LESSONS

➤ **2 Corinthians 3:5 —** *Our adequacy is*
from God.

*N*o one is so talented or capable that
he or she can succeed in life or ministry without depending on God every
step of the way. Jesus said, "Apart from
Me you can do nothing" (John 15:5).

➤ **2 Corinthians 3:17 —** *Where the Spirit*
of the Lord is, there is liberty.

*W*hen Jesus comes into a human
heart by faith, through the Spirit
He sets that person free from the bondage of sin, the chains of death, and the
futile attempt of trying to become righteous through self-effort.

➤ **2 Corinthians 3:18 —** *We all . . . are*
being transformed into the same image
from glory to glory.

*T*he Lord is after transformed lives,
not merely reformed ones. Part of
that transformation happens as we train
our minds to focus on the person of
Jesus. As we meditate on Him, the Spirit
begins molding us into His image.

Isaiah 15:1—16:14

15 THE oracle concerning Moab.
Surely in a night Ar of Moab is
devastated *and* ruined;
Surely in a night Kir of Moab is
devastated *and* ruined.

2 They have gone up to the temple
and *to* Dibon, *even* to the high
places to weep.
Moab wails over Nebo and
Medeba;
Everyone's head is bald *and* every
beard is cut off.

3 In their streets they have girded
themselves with sackcloth;
On their housetops and in their
squares
Everyone is wailing, dissolved in
tears.

4 Heshbon and Elealeh also cry out,
Their voice is heard all the way to
Jahaz;
Therefore the armed men of Moab
cry aloud;
His soul trembles within him.

5 My heart cries out for Moab;
His fugitives are as far as Zoar *and*
Eglath-shelishiyah,
For they go up the ascent of Luhith
weeping;
Surely on the road to Horonaim
they raise a cry of distress over
their ruin.

6 For the waters of Nimrim are
desolate.
Surely the grass is withered, the
tender grass died out,
There is no green thing.

7 Therefore the abundance *which*
they have acquired and stored up
They carry off over the brook of
Arabim.

8 For the cry of distress has gone
around the territory of Moab,
Its wail *goes* as far as Eglaim and
its wailing even to Beer-elim.

9 For the waters of Dimon are full of
blood;
Surely I will bring added *woes* upon
Dimon,
A lion upon the fugitives of Moab
and upon the remnant of the
land.

16 SEND the *tribute* lamb to the ruler
of the land,
From Sela by way of the wilderness
to the mountain of the daughter
of Zion.

2 Then, like fleeing birds *or* scattered
nestlings,
The daughters of Moab will be at
the fords of the Arnon.

3 "Give *us* advice, make a decision;
Cast your shadow like night at high
noon;
Hide the outcasts, do not betray the
fugitive.

4 "Let the outcasts of Moab stay with
you;
Be a hiding place to them from the
destroyer."
For the extortioner has come to an
end, destruction has ceased,
Oppressors have completely
disappeared from the land.

5 A throne will even be established in
lovingkindness,
And a judge will sit on it in
faithfulness in the tent of
David;
Moreover, he will seek justice
And be prompt in righteousness.

6 We have heard of the pride of
Moab, an excessive pride;
Even of his arrogance, pride, and
fury;
His idle boasts are false.

7 Therefore Moab will wail; everyone
of Moab will wail.
You will moan for the raisin cakes
of Kir-hareseth
As those who are utterly stricken.

8 For the fields of Heshbon have
withered, the vines of Sibmah *as
well*;
The lords of the nations have
trampled down its choice
clusters
Which reached as far as Jazer *and*
wandered to the deserts;
Its tendrils spread themselves out
and passed over the sea.

9 Therefore I will weep bitterly for
Jazer, for the vine of Sibmah;
I will drench you with my tears,
O Heshbon and Elealeh;
For the shouting over your summer
fruits and your harvest has fallen
away.

10　Gladness and joy are taken away
　　　from the fruitful field;
　　In the vineyards also there will
　　　be no cries of joy or jubilant
　　　shouting,
　　No treader treads out wine in the
　　　presses,
　　For I have made the shouting to
　　　cease.
11　Therefore my heart intones like a
　　　harp for Moab
　　And my inward feelings for
　　　Kir-hareseth.
12　So it will come about when Moab
　　　presents himself,
　　When he wearies himself upon *his*
　　　high place
　　And comes to his sanctuary to
　　　pray,
　　That he will not prevail.
13　This is the word which the LORD
spoke earlier concerning Moab.
14　But now the LORD speaks, saying,
"Within three years, as a hired man
would count them, the glory of Moab
will be degraded along with all *his* great
population, and *his* remnant will be very
small *and* impotent."

Psalm 106:24–31

24　Then they despised the pleasant
　　　land;
　　They did not believe in His word,
25　But grumbled in their tents;
　　They did not listen to the voice of
　　　the LORD.
26　Therefore He swore to them
　　That He would cast them down in
　　　the wilderness,
27　And that He would cast their seed
　　　among the nations
　　And scatter them in the lands.
28　They joined themselves also to
　　　Baal-peor,
　　And ate sacrifices offered to the
　　　dead.
29　Thus they provoked *Him* to anger
　　　with their deeds,
　　And the plague broke out among
　　　them.
30　Then Phinehas stood up and
　　　interposed,
　　And so the plague was stayed.

31　And it was reckoned to him for
　　　righteousness,
　　To all generations forever.

Proverbs 25:8–10

8　Do not go out hastily to argue *your*
　　　case;
　　Otherwise, what will you do in the
　　　end,
　　When your neighbor humiliates
　　　you?
9　Argue your case with your
　　　neighbor,
　　And do not reveal the secret of
　　　another,
10　Or he who hears *it* will reproach
　　　you,
　　And the evil report about you will
　　　not pass away.

2 Corinthians 4:1–18

4 THEREFORE, since we have this ministry, as we received mercy, we do not
lose heart,
2　but we have renounced the things
hidden because of shame, not walking
in craftiness or adulterating the word of
God, but by the manifestation of truth
commending ourselves to every man's
conscience in the sight of God.
3　And even if our gospel is veiled, it is
veiled to those who are perishing,
4　in whose case the god of this world
has blinded the minds of the unbelieving
so that they might not see the light of the
gospel of the glory of Christ, who is the
image of God.

LIFE LESSONS

➤ **2 Corinthians 4:4** — *The god of this
world has blinded the minds of the
unbelieving.*

*W*e would spare ourselves a lot of
anxiety in our efforts at evangelism
if we would remember that witnessing
to others about Christ means serious
spiritual warfare. Satan actively opposes
our efforts (Matt. 13:19).

5 For we do not preach ourselves but Christ Jesus as Lord, and ourselves as your bond-servants for Jesus' sake.

6 For God, who said, "Light shall shine out of darkness," is the One who has shone in our hearts to give the Light of the knowledge of the glory of God in the face of Christ.

➤ 7 But we have this treasure in earthen vessels, so that the surpassing greatness of the power will be of God and not from ourselves;

8 *we are* afflicted in every way, but not crushed; perplexed, but not despairing;

9 persecuted, but not forsaken; struck down, but not destroyed;

10 always carrying about in the body the dying of Jesus, so that the life of Jesus also may be manifested in our body.

11 For we who live are constantly being delivered over to death for Jesus' sake, so that the life of Jesus also may be manifested in our mortal flesh.

12 So death works in us, but life in you.

13 But having the same spirit of faith, according to what is written, "I BELIEVED, THEREFORE I SPOKE," we also believe, therefore we also speak,

14 knowing that He who raised the Lord Jesus will raise us also with Jesus and will present us with you.

15 For all things *are* for your sakes, so that the grace which is spreading to more and more people may cause the giving of thanks to abound to the glory of God.

✳ 16 Therefore we do not lose heart, but though our outer man is decaying, yet our inner man is being renewed day by day.

17 For momentary, light affliction is ◄ producing for us an eternal weight of glory far beyond all comparison,

18 while we look not at the things which are seen, but at the things which are not seen; for the things which are seen are temporal, but the things which are not seen are eternal.

LIFE LESSONS

➤ **2 Corinthians 4:7 —** *We have this treasure in earthen vessels, so that the surpassing greatness of the power will be of God and not from ourselves.*

*W*hen we think we must be strong and capable in order to serve God, we miss the point of how He works entirely. We are like jars of clay—common, weak, and valued by what we contain. It is Christ in us who gives us worth, power, wisdom, and joy. He accomplishes His will through us in a manner that is far above and beyond our human abilities so that others will see what He has done and want to know Him, too.

➤ **2 Corinthians 4:17 —** *Momentary, light affliction is producing for us an eternal weight of glory far beyond all comparison.*

*A*ny sacrifice we make or hardship we endure for the Lord's sake and in obedience to His commands never goes unnoticed. We are assured that He will amply reward what we suffered and bless us for our faithfulness to Him (Mark 10:28–30).

Life Examples:

PAUL: Strength in Weakness

2 CORINTHIANS 4:7–18

*A*s a young man, Paul trained under one of the greatest Jewish scholars of his time. He understood the elements of the law and practiced them with great zeal. Yet when he came face-to-face with Jesus Christ, his life changed forever. He no longer viewed the world through human eyes. God gave him spiritual insight that far surpassed anything he had known.

Still, he had to be broken further so that he could be used in an even greater way. God allowed Paul to be buffeted by many severe trials in order to humble him and remove the potential for pride (2 Cor. 12:7). Through his times of weakness, the apostle Paul learned a new and unexpected principle: *Weakness is strength.*

When God humbles us before Him, He sees the meekness of our hearts and sends His strength and blessings into our lives. Frailty in a certain area should never bring embarrassment.

⊕ **Isaiah 17:1—18:7**

17 THE oracle concerning Damascus.
"Behold, Damascus is about to be
removed from being a city
And will become a fallen ruin.

2 "The cities of Aroer are forsaken;
They will be for flocks to lie down in,
And there will be no one to frighten
them.

3 "The fortified city will disappear
from Ephraim,
And sovereignty from Damascus
And the remnant of Aram;
They will be like the glory of the
sons of Israel,"
Declares the LORD of hosts.

4 Now in that day the glory of Jacob
will fade,
And the fatness of his flesh will
become lean.

5 It will be even like the reaper
gathering the standing grain,
As his arm harvests the ears,
Or it will be like one gleaning ears
of grain
In the valley of Rephaim.

6 Yet gleanings will be left in it like
the shaking of an olive tree,
Two *or* three olives on the topmost
bough,
Four *or* five on the branches of a
fruitful tree,
Declares the LORD, the God of
Israel.

➤ 7 In that day man will have regard for
✳ his Maker
And his eyes will look to the Holy
One of Israel.

8 He will not have regard for the
altars, the work of his hands,

Nor will he look to that which his
fingers have made,
Even the Asherim and incense
stands.

9 In that day their strong cities will be
like forsaken places in the forest,
Or like branches which they
abandoned before the sons of
Israel;
And the land will be a desolation.

10 For you have forgotten the God of
your salvation
And have not remembered the rock
of your refuge.
Therefore you plant delightful plants
And set them with vine slips of a
strange *god.*

11 In the day that you plant *it* you
carefully fence *it* in,
And in the morning you bring your
seed to blossom;
But the harvest will *be* a heap
In a day of sickliness and incurable
pain.

12 Alas, the uproar of many peoples
Who roar like the roaring of the seas,
And the rumbling of nations
Who rush on like the rumbling of
mighty waters!

13 The nations rumble on like the
rumbling of many waters,
But He will rebuke them and they
will flee far away,
And be chased like chaff in the
mountains before the wind,
Or like whirling dust before a gale.

14 At evening time, behold, *there is*
terror!
Before morning they are no more.
Such *will be* the portion of those
who plunder us
And the lot of those who pillage us.

18 ALAS, oh land of whirring wings
Which lies beyond the rivers of
Cush,

2 Which sends envoys by the sea,
Even in papyrus vessels on the
surface of the waters.
Go, swift messengers, to a nation
tall and smooth,
To a people feared far and wide,
A powerful and oppressive nation
Whose land the rivers divide.

3 All you inhabitants of the world and
dwellers on earth,
As soon as a standard is raised on
the mountains, you will see *it,*

LIFE LESSONS

➤ **Isaiah 17:7 — *In that day man will
have regard for his Maker and his eyes
will look to the Holy One of Israel.***

*I*n this verse, Isaiah foresees how the
people will return to the Lord. We
should not wait until disaster drives us
to our knees. Rather, we can look to our
Maker and have respect for the Holy
One of Israel right now. At this very
moment, we can enjoy the blessings of
intimate relationship with God.

And as soon as the trumpet is
blown, you will hear *it*.
4   For thus the LORD has told me,
"I will look from My dwelling place
quietly
Like dazzling heat in the sunshine,
Like a cloud of dew in the heat of
harvest."
5   For before the harvest, as soon as
the bud blossoms
And the flower becomes a ripening
grape,
Then He will cut off the sprigs with
pruning knives
And remove *and* cut away the
spreading branches.
6   They will be left together for
mountain birds of prey,
And for the beasts of the earth;
And the birds of prey will spend the
summer *feeding* on them,
And all the beasts of the earth will
spend harvest time on them.
7   At that time a gift of homage will be
brought to the LORD of hosts
From a people tall and smooth,
Even from a people feared far and
wide,
A powerful and oppressive nation,
Whose land the rivers divide—
To the place of the name of the
LORD of hosts, *even* Mount Zion.

Psalm 106:32–39

32   They also provoked *Him* to wrath at
the waters of Meribah,
So that it went hard with Moses on
their account;
33   Because they were rebellious
against His Spirit,
He spoke rashly with his lips.
34   They did not destroy the peoples,
As the LORD commanded them,
35   But they mingled with the nations
And learned their practices,
36   And served their idols,
Which became a snare to them.
37   They even sacrificed their sons and
their daughters to the demons,
38   And shed innocent blood,
The blood of their sons and their
daughters,
Whom they sacrificed to the idols of
Canaan;

And the land was polluted with the
blood.
39   Thus they became unclean in their
practices,
And played the harlot in their
deeds.

Proverbs 25:11, 12

11   *Like* apples of gold in settings of
silver
Is a word spoken in right
circumstances.
12   *Like* an earring of gold and an
ornament of fine gold
Is a wise reprover to a listening ear.

2 Corinthians 5:1–21

5 FOR we know that if the earthly tent
which is our house is torn down, we
have a building from God, a house not
made with hands, eternal in the heavens.
2   For indeed in this *house* we groan,
longing to be clothed with our dwelling
from heaven,
3   inasmuch as we, having put it on,
will not be found naked.
4   For indeed while we are in this tent,
we groan, being burdened, because we
do not want to be unclothed but to be
clothed, so that what is mortal will be
swallowed up by life.
5   Now He who prepared us for this
very purpose is God, who gave to us the
Spirit as a pledge.
6   Therefore, being always of good
courage, and knowing that while we are
at home in the body we are absent from
the Lord—
7   for we walk by faith, not by sight—

LIFE LESSONS

➤ **2 Corinthians 5:7** — *We walk by faith,
not by sight.*

Paul writes this verse in the context
of the resurrection of the body.
We remain confident that we will live
again in a new and glorified body—not
because we see it but because we trust
the One who gave the promise.

8 we are of good courage, I say, and prefer rather to be absent from the body and to be at home with the Lord.

➤ 9 Therefore we also have as our ambition, whether at home or absent, to be pleasing to Him.

10 For we must all appear before the judgment seat of Christ, so that each one may be recompensed for his deeds in the body, according to what he has done, whether good or bad.

11 Therefore, knowing the fear of the Lord, we persuade men, but we are made manifest to God; and I hope that we are made manifest also in your consciences.

12 We are not again commending ourselves to you but *are* giving you an occasion to be proud of us, so that you will have *an answer* for those who take pride in appearance and not in heart.

13 For if we are beside ourselves, it is

WHAT THE BIBLE SAYS ABOUT

Accountability Relationships

2 Corinthians 5:10

*I*n an age of individual rights, the principle of accountability often runs strongly against the popular grain. Our pride, egotism, and self-sufficiency rebel against the concept of being accountable to one another for our conduct.

Yet accountability is a strong biblical teaching and concept that is crucial to our spiritual growth and fellowship with God. Scripture tells us that we are accountable to the Lord and also to others. We don't get to do whatever we please.

Godly accountability provides a wise set of checks and balances. Whether it is a supervisor at work or a personal friend, we need someone who is willing to admonish, encourage, and walk with us through trial and blessing. The Lord allows others to observe and confront us over our areas of weakness. In fact, a godly friend will not shrink back and tell us only what we want to hear.

Let's face it: No one likes to admit his or her shortcomings. But by submitting to God or one in authority over us, we become spiritual winners. We stimulate our performance and help keep ourselves from turning freedom into a license to sin against the Lord.

LIFE LESSONS

➤ **2 Corinthians 5:9 — We . . . have as our ambition, whether at home or absent, to be pleasing to Him.**

*I*f we love the Lord, we will make it our aim and our delight to please Him by the way we live. Why? Because it does not make sense for us to rely on God for our eternal future while doubting His instruction and provision for today. If we desire to make our faith in Him sure and mature in our relationships with Him, we must trust and obey Him, no matter what circumstances we face.

---

for God; if we are of sound mind, it is for you.

14 For the love of Christ controls us, having concluded this, that one died for all, therefore all died;

Even though he was the preeminent apostle of his day, Paul remained accountable to his home church at Antioch, returning there on occasion to report on his journeys. He also was accountable to the leaders in Jerusalem. As a temperamental young preacher, Timothy was accountable to Paul. Jesus had sent out His disciples, not just for mutual support, but also for accountability.

Our ultimate accountability, of course, is to the Lord. "So then each one of us will give an account of himself to God" (Rom. 14:12). Knowing that we must one day answer to God should be a powerful incentive for holiness and obedience. "For we must all appear before the judgment seat of Christ, so that each one may be recompensed for his deeds in the body, according to what he has done, whether good or bad" (2 Cor. 5:10).

Becoming a Christian does not relieve us of personal responsibility. Although our sins have been forgiven through Christ's sacrifice, we still are responsible for our behavior. What we do on earth *matters*. We are free in Christ, but we are also bondservants of Christ.

God has so designed us that we need to remain continually aware of our accountability to our all-knowing Creator, as well as our accountability in personal relationships. "Iron sharpens iron, so one man sharpens another" (Prov. 27:17).

15 and He died for all, so that they who live might no longer live for themselves, but for Him who died and rose again on their behalf. 16 Therefore from now on we recognize no one according to the flesh; even though we have known Christ according to the flesh, yet now we know *Him in this way* no longer. 17 Therefore if anyone is in Christ, *he is* a new creature; the old things passed away; behold, new things have come. 18 Now all *these* things are from God, who reconciled us to Himself through Christ and gave us the ministry of reconciliation, 19 namely, that God was in Christ reconciling the world to Himself, not counting their trespasses against them, and He has committed to us the word of reconciliation. 20 Therefore, we are ambassadors for Christ, as though God were making an appeal through us; we beg you on behalf of Christ, be reconciled to God. 21 He made Him who knew no sin *to be* sin on our behalf, so that we might become the righteousness of God in Him.

LIFE LESSONS

> 2 Corinthians 5:19 — *God was in Christ reconciling the world to Himself.*

*G*od created us to be united with Him in an intimate love relationship, and He has entrusted us with the task of telling the world what He has done to make it possible for everyone who has faith in Him to enjoy eternal life and an intimate relationship with Him. Through the Cross, we have the privilege of embracing and enjoying His loving presence forever.

> 2 Corinthians 5:21 — *He made Him who knew no sin to be sin on our behalf, so that we might become the righteousness of God in Him.*

*G*od took the sins of the entire world and, on the Cross, placed them on Jesus Christ, the One who had never committed a single sin. Jesus took our punishment so that we might receive His righteousness.

SEPTEMBER 14

Isaiah 19:1—20:6

19 THE oracle concerning Egypt.
Behold, the LORD is riding on a
swift cloud and is about to come
to Egypt;
The idols of Egypt will tremble at
His presence,
And the heart of the Egyptians will
melt within them.
2 "So I will incite Egyptians against
Egyptians;
And they will each fight against
his brother and each against his
neighbor,
City against city *and* kingdom
against kingdom.
3 "Then the spirit of the Egyptians will
be demoralized within them;
And I will confound their strategy,
So that they will resort to idols and
ghosts of the dead

And to mediums and spiritists.
4 "Moreover, I will deliver the
Egyptians into the hand of a cruel
master,
And a mighty king will rule over
them," declares the Lord GOD of
hosts.
5 The waters from the sea will dry up,
And the river will be parched and dry.
6 The canals will emit a stench,
The streams of Egypt will thin out
and dry up;
The reeds and rushes will rot away.
7 The bulrushes by the Nile, by the
edge of the Nile
And all the sown fields by the Nile
Will become dry, be driven away,
and be no more.
8 And the fishermen will lament,
And all those who cast a line into
the Nile will mourn,
And those who spread nets on the
waters will pine away.

9   Moreover, the manufacturers of
      linen made from combed flax
    And the weavers of white cloth will
      be utterly dejected.
10 And the pillars *of Egypt* will be
      crushed;
    All the hired laborers will be
      grieved in soul.
11 The princes of Zoan are mere
      fools;
    The advice of Pharaoh's wisest
      advisers has become stupid.
    How can you *men* say to Pharaoh,
    "I am a son of the wise, a son of
      ancient kings"?
12 Well then, where are your wise
      men?
    Please let them tell you,
    And let them understand what the
      LORD of hosts
    Has purposed against Egypt.
13 The princes of Zoan have acted
      foolishly,
    The princes of Memphis are
      deluded;
    Those who are the cornerstone of
      her tribes
    Have led Egypt astray.
14 The LORD has mixed within her a
      spirit of distortion;
    They have led Egypt astray in all
      that it does,
    As a drunken man staggers in his
      vomit.
15 There will be no work for Egypt
    Which *its* head or tail, *its* palm
      branch or bulrush, may do.
16 In that day the Egyptians will become like women, and they will tremble
and be in dread because of the waving of
the hand of the LORD of hosts, which He
is going to wave over them.
17 The land of Judah will become a
terror to Egypt; everyone to whom it is
mentioned will be in dread of it, because
of the purpose of the LORD of hosts which
He is purposing against them.
18 In that day five cities in the land of
Egypt will be speaking the language of
Canaan and swearing *allegiance* to the
LORD of hosts; one will be called the City
of Destruction.
19 In that day there will be an altar
to the LORD in the midst of the land of
Egypt, and a pillar to the LORD near its
border.

20 It will become a sign and a witness
to the LORD of hosts in the land of Egypt;
for they will cry to the LORD because of
oppressors, and He will send them a Savior and a Champion, and He will deliver
them.
21 Thus the LORD will make Himself
known to Egypt, and the Egyptians will
know the LORD in that day. They will
even worship with sacrifice and offering,
and will make a vow to the LORD and
perform it.
22 The LORD will strike Egypt, striking
but healing; so they will return to the
LORD, and He will respond to them and
will heal them.
23 In that day there will be a highway
from Egypt to Assyria, and the Assyrians
will come into Egypt and the Egyptians
into Assyria, and the Egyptians will worship with the Assyrians.
24 In that day Israel will be the third
party with Egypt and Assyria, a blessing
in the midst of the earth,
25 whom the LORD of hosts has blessed,
saying, "Blessed is Egypt My people, and
Assyria the work of My hands, and Israel
My inheritance."

20 IN the year that the commander
came to Ashdod, when Sargon the
king of Assyria sent him and he fought
against Ashdod and captured it,

LIFE LESSONS

> Isaiah 19:20 — *He will send them
a Savior and a Champion, and He will
deliver them.*

*W*e expect the Bible to tell us of a
Savior coming to deliver Israel—but
this text speaks of a Savior coming to
rescue Egypt, Israel's longtime nemesis!
Our God wants to bless all peoples.

> Isaiah 19:25 — *"Blessed is Egypt My
people, and Assyria the work of My
hands, and Israel My inheritance."*

*I*n the Exodus, God severely judged
Egypt; He destroyed Assyria after the
deportation of the northern kingdom;
and many times He judged rebellious
Israel. Yet God loves to show mercy, not
exercise judgment. He strikes with the
hope of healing and turning rebellious
hearts back to Him (Is. 19:22).

> 2 at that time the LORD spoke through Isaiah the son of Amoz, saying, "Go and loosen the sackcloth from your hips and take your shoes off your feet." And he did so, going naked and barefoot.

3 And the LORD said, "Even as My servant Isaiah has gone naked and barefoot three years as a sign and token against Egypt and Cush,

4 so the king of Assyria will lead away the captives of Egypt and the exiles of Cush, young and old, naked and barefoot with buttocks uncovered, to the shame of Egypt.

5 "Then they will be dismayed and ashamed because of Cush their hope and Egypt their boast.

6 "So the inhabitants of this coastland will say in that day, 'Behold, such is our hope, where we fled for help to be delivered from the king of Assyria; and we, how shall we escape?'"

⊕ Psalm 106:40–48

40 Therefore the anger of the LORD
    was kindled against His people
    And He abhorred His inheritance.

41 Then He gave them into the hand of
    the nations,
    And those who hated them ruled
    over them.

42 Their enemies also oppressed
    them,
    And they were subdued under their
    power.

43 Many times He would deliver
    them;
    They, however, were rebellious in
    their counsel,
    And *so* sank down in their
    iniquity.

44 Nevertheless He looked upon their
    distress
    When He heard their cry;

45 And He remembered His covenant
    for their sake,
    And relented according to the
    greatness of His lovingkindness.

46 He also made them *objects* of
    compassion
    In the presence of all their captors.

47 Save us, O LORD our God,
    And gather us from among the
    nations,
    To give thanks to Your holy name
    And glory in Your praise.

48 Blessed be the LORD, the God of
    Israel,
    From everlasting even to
    everlasting.
    And let all the people say, "Amen."
    Praise the LORD!

◈ Proverbs 25:13

13 Like the cold of snow in the time of
    harvest
    Is a faithful messenger to those who
    send him,
    For he refreshes the soul of his
    masters.

2 Corinthians 6:1–18

6 AND working together *with Him*, we also urge you not to receive the grace of God in vain—

2　for He says,

"AT THE ACCEPTABLE TIME I LISTENED TO YOU,

AND ON THE DAY OF SALVATION I HELPED YOU."

Behold, now is "THE ACCEPTABLE TIME," behold, now is "THE DAY OF SALVATION"—

3　giving no cause for offense in anything, so that the ministry will not be discredited,

4　but in everything commending ourselves as servants of God, in much endurance, in afflictions, in hardships, in distresses,

5　in beatings, in imprisonments, in tumults, in labors, in sleeplessness, in hunger,

6　in purity, in knowledge, in patience, in kindness, in the Holy Spirit, in genuine love,

7　in the word of truth, in the power of God; by the weapons of righteousness for the right hand and the left,

8　by glory and dishonor, by evil report and good report; *regarded* as deceivers and yet true;

9　as unknown yet well-known, as dying yet behold, we live; as punished yet not put to death,

10　as sorrowful yet always rejoicing, as poor yet making many rich, as having nothing yet possessing all things.

11　Our mouth has spoken freely to you, O Corinthians, our heart is opened wide.

12　You are not restrained by us, but you are restrained in your own affections.

13　Now in a like exchange—I speak as to children—open wide *to us* also.

14　Do not be bound together with unbelievers; for what partnership have righteousness and lawlessness, or what fellowship has light with darkness?

15　Or what harmony has Christ with Belial, or what has a believer in common with an unbeliever?

16　Or what agreement has the temple of

WHAT THE BIBLE SAYS ABOUT

A Warning Against Compromise

2 Corinthians 6:14–17

*G*od tells us not to be bound to people who don't believe in Jesus Christ—just like He told Israel to be separated from the pagan nations around them. Paul writes in 2 Corinthians 6:14, "Do not be bound together with unbelievers; for what partnership have righteousness and lawlessness, or what fellowship has light with darkness?"

We must be careful in how we live because compromise can be destructive. It can lead us to take a step in the wrong direction—a direction that could eventually lead us to ungodly, harmful actions. This is because compromise is like a slide: We begin with godly convictions and good morals, but the moment we negotiate with the world and validate the ways of evil, our values begin to slip. Each conciliation leads to a more serious cooperation with sin.

That's especially true when we try to nuance our convictions concerning the Word of God. In fact, we take our first step in the wrong direction when we make judgments about what is significant and insignificant in the Word of God. We start the slide by choosing what we want to believe. From there, each compromise weakens our conscience and desensitizes our spirit to the Father's commands. When that happens, we are in more trouble than we are capable of realizing. When living in sin no longer bothers us, we've stopped listening to the Holy Spirit—who alerts us to sin in the first place.

The unfortunate truth is: When we compromise with evil, we always lose. We will miss the abundant lives God has for us. We will fail to recognize His wonderful purpose for our lives and therefore miss the fulfillment and blessings that are available to us. The more we compromise, the more we will suffer the consequences.

Are you heading in the right direction? Are you doing as God instructed you to do? Are you waiting for His timing? If not, get off that sure path to destruction and get right with God. Surrender your life to Christ, and obey God in everything you do. The world can only offer you heartache, and that is never worth giving up the wonderful plan God has for you.

LIFE LESSONS

➢ **2 Corinthians 6:14 — *Do not be bound together with unbelievers.***

*G*od tells us not to be bound to unbelievers because of their influence in our lives. Did He say we should not love the lost? No. Did He tell us to treat them unkindly? No. Rather, He says we must be careful how we live. If the enemy gains a foothold in our lives by tempting us to compromise our faith and demonstration of God's love and forgiveness, he will make significant strides toward undermining our relationships with the Lord and our testimonies for Him.

God with idols? For we are the temple of the living God; just as God said,

"I WILL DWELL IN THEM AND WALK
   AMONG THEM;
AND I WILL BE THEIR GOD, AND THEY
   SHALL BE MY PEOPLE.

17 "Therefore, COME OUT FROM THEIR
MIDST AND BE SEPARATE," says the
Lord.
"AND DO NOT TOUCH WHAT IS
   UNCLEAN;
And I will welcome you.

18 "And I will be a father to you,
And you shall be sons and
   daughters to Me,"
Says the Lord Almighty.

SEPTEMBER 15

Isaiah 21:1—22:25

21 THE oracle concerning the wilderness of the sea.
As windstorms in the Negev sweep
   on,
It comes from the wilderness, from
   a terrifying land.

2 A harsh vision has been shown to
   me;
The treacherous one *still* deals
   treacherously, and the destroyer
   still destroys.
Go up, Elam, lay siege, Media;
I have made an end of all the
   groaning she has caused.

3 For this reason my loins are full of
   anguish;
Pains have seized me like the pains
   of a woman in labor.
I am so bewildered I cannot hear, so
   terrified I cannot see.

4 My mind reels, horror overwhelms
   me;
The twilight I longed for has been
   turned for me into trembling.

5 They set the table, they spread out
   the cloth, they eat, they drink;
"Rise up, captains, oil the shields,"

6 For thus the Lord says to me,
"Go, station the lookout, let him
   report what he sees.

7 "When he sees riders, horsemen in
   pairs,

A train of donkeys, a train of
   camels,
Let him pay close attention, very
   close attention."

8 Then the lookout called,
"O Lord, I stand continually by day
   on the watchtower,
And I am stationed every night at
   my guard post.

9 "Now behold, here comes a troop of
   riders, horsemen in pairs."
And one said, "Fallen, fallen is
   Babylon;
And all the images of her gods are
   shattered on the ground."

10 O my threshed *people*, and my
   afflicted of the threshing floor!
What I have heard from the LORD of
   hosts,
The God of Israel, I make known to
   you.

11 The oracle concerning Edom.
One keeps calling to me from Seir,
"Watchman, how far gone is the
   night?
Watchman, how far gone is the
   night?"

12 The watchman says,
"Morning comes but also night.
If you would inquire, inquire;
Come back again."

13 The oracle about Arabia.
In the thickets of Arabia you must
   spend the night,
O caravans of Dedanites.

14 Bring water for the thirsty,
O inhabitants of the land of Tema,
Meet the fugitive with bread.

15 For they have fled from the swords,
From the drawn sword, and from
the bent bow
And from the press of battle.

16 For thus the Lord said to me, "In a year, as a hired man would count it, all the splendor of Kedar will terminate;

17 and the remainder of the number of bowmen, the mighty men of the sons of Kedar, will be few; for the LORD God of Israel has spoken."

22 THE oracle concerning the valley of vision.

What is the matter with you now,
that you have all gone up to the
housetops?

2 You who were full of noise,
You boisterous town, you exultant
city;
Your slain were not slain with the
sword,
Nor did they die in battle.

3 All your rulers have fled together,
And have been captured without the
bow;
All of you who were found were
taken captive together,
Though they had fled far away.

4 Therefore I say, "Turn your eyes
away from me,
Let me weep bitterly,
Do not try to comfort me
concerning the destruction of the
daughter of my people."

5 For the Lord GOD of hosts has a
day of panic, subjugation and
confusion
In the valley of vision,
A breaking down of walls
And a crying to the mountain.

6 Elam took up the quiver
With the chariots, infantry *and*
horsemen;
And Kir uncovered the shield.

7 Then your choicest valleys were full
of chariots,
And the horsemen took up fixed
positions at the gate.

8 And He removed the defense of
Judah.
In that day you depended on the
weapons of the house of the
forest,

9 And you saw that the breaches

In the *wall* of the city of David were
many;
And you collected the waters of the
lower pool.

10 Then you counted the houses of
Jerusalem
And tore down houses to fortify the
wall.

11 And you made a reservoir between
the two walls
For the waters of the old pool.
But you did not depend on Him who
made it,
Nor did you take into consideration
Him who planned it long ago.

12 Therefore in that day the Lord GOD
of hosts called *you* to weeping, to
wailing,
To shaving the head and to wearing
sackcloth.

13 Instead, there is gaiety and
gladness,
Killing of cattle and slaughtering of
sheep,
Eating of meat and drinking of
wine:
"Let us eat and drink, for tomorrow
we may die."

14 But the LORD of hosts revealed
Himself to me,
"Surely this iniquity shall not be
forgiven you
Until you die," says the Lord GOD of
hosts.

15 Thus says the Lord GOD of hosts,
"Come, go to this steward,
To Shebna, who is in charge of the
royal household,

16 'What right do you have here,
And whom do you have here,
That you have hewn a tomb for
yourself here,
You who hew a tomb on the height,
You who carve a resting place for
yourself in the rock?

17 'Behold, the LORD is about to hurl
you headlong, O man.
And He is about to grasp you firmly

18 *And* roll you tightly like a ball,
To be cast into a vast country;
There you will die
And there your splendid chariots
will be,
You shame of your master's house.'

19 "I will depose you from your office,
And I will pull you down from your
station.

20 "Then it will come about in that day,
    That I will summon My servant
    Eliakim the son of Hilkiah,
21 And I will clothe him with your
    tunic
    And tie your sash securely about
    him.
    I will entrust him with your
    authority,
    And he will become a father to the
    inhabitants of Jerusalem and to
    the house of Judah.
22 "Then I will set the key of the house
    of David on his shoulder,
    When he opens no one will shut,
    When he shuts no one will open.
23 "I will drive him *like* a peg in a firm
    place,
    And he will become a throne of
    glory to his father's house.
24 "So they will hang on him all the
glory of his father's house, offspring and
issue, all the least of vessels, from bowls
to all the jars.
25 "In that day," declares the LORD of
hosts, "the peg driven in a firm place will
give way; it will even break off and fall,
and the load hanging on it will be cut off,
for the LORD has spoken."

Psalm 107:1–8

BOOK 5

107 OH give thanks to the LORD, for
    He is good,
    For His lovingkindness is
    everlasting.
2 Let the redeemed of the LORD say
    so,
    Whom He has redeemed from the
    hand of the adversary
3 And gathered from the lands,
    From the east and from the west,
    From the north and from the south.
4 They wandered in the wilderness in
    a desert region;
    They did not find a way to an
    inhabited city.
5 *They were* hungry and thirsty;
    Their soul fainted within them.
6 Then they cried out to the LORD in
    their trouble;
    He delivered them out of their
    distresses.

7 He led them also by a straight way,
    To go to an inhabited city.
8 Let them give thanks to the LORD
    for His lovingkindness,
    And for His wonders to the sons of
    men!

Proverbs 25:14–16

14 *Like* clouds and wind without rain
    Is a man who boasts of his gifts
    falsely.
15 By forbearance a ruler may be
    persuaded,
    And a soft tongue breaks the bone.
16 Have you found honey? Eat *only*
    what you need,
    That you not have it in excess and
    vomit it.

2 Corinthians 7:1–16

7 THEREFORE, having these promises,
    beloved, let us cleanse ourselves from
all defilement of flesh and spirit, perfecting holiness in the fear of God.
2   Make room for us *in your hearts;* we
wronged no one, we corrupted no one,
we took advantage of no one.
3   I do not speak to condemn you, for

LIFE LESSONS

> Isaiah 22:22 — *"When He opens no one will shut, when He shuts no one will open."*

The writer of Revelation 3:7 applied these similar words to Jesus. When He gives us an open door and beckons us to walk through it, He expects us to step through it by faith.

> 2 Corinthians 7:1 — *Let us cleanse ourselves from all defilement of flesh and spirit, perfecting holiness in the fear of God.*

The promises of God are meant to lead us to purity of life, but they do not do so automatically. As we wait in faith for them to be fulfilled, we learn to flee from sin, rely on Him, take comfort in His Word, and listen for His voice.

WHAT THE BIBLE SAYS ABOUT ◉

A Call to Repentance

2 Corinthians 7:8–12

*P*aul wanted the best for the people in Corinth. He greatly loved the church and actively worked for the good of its members. During a trip to Macedonia, Paul realized that the ethical and doctrinal problems in Corinth were so great that, without correction, they would result in the ruination of the church.

Therefore, Paul wrote a stinging disciplinary letter to the church. Preferring the people of Corinth to be wounded in correction and healed rather than continue on the pathway of sin and death, he rebuked them.

It is similar in concept to what one finds in cancer treatments. The manner by which cancer is treated is by radiation or chemotherapy, which destroys harmful cells. Though the remedy is often harsh and draining, it stops the cancer's consumption of the body.

In 2 Corinthians 7:10 Paul wrote, "For the sorrow that is according to the will of God produces a repentance without regret, leading to salvation."

The Lord does not desire to see you face pain and suffering. But at times there are such destructive things at work in your life that He must root them out. His desire is for you to repent. The Father kills the cancerous cells of sin so that you might be able to enjoy the abundant life He has for you.

God invites you to confess your sins to Him. Acknowledge the sins which plague you so that He can help you live the bountiful life you were intended to live. ◉

I have said before that you are in our hearts to die together and to live together.

4 Great is my confidence in you; great is my boasting on your behalf. I am filled with comfort; I am overflowing with joy in all our affliction.

5 For even when we came into Macedonia our flesh had no rest, but we were afflicted on every side: conflicts without, fears within.

➤ 6 But God, who comforts the depressed, comforted us by the coming of Titus;

7 and not only by his coming, but also by the comfort with which he was comforted in you, as he reported to us your longing, your mourning, your zeal for me; so that I rejoiced even more.

8 For though I caused you sorrow by my letter, I do not regret it; though I did regret it—*for* I see that that letter caused you sorrow, though only for a while—

➤ 9 I now rejoice, not that you were made sorrowful, but that you were made sorrowful to *the point of* repentance; for you were made sorrowful according to *the will of* God, so that you might not suffer loss in anything through us.

➤ 10 For the sorrow that is according to *the will of* God produces a repentance *without regret, leading* to salvation, but the sorrow of the world produces death.

11 For behold what earnestness this very thing, this godly sorrow, has produced in you: what vindication of yourselves, what indignation, what fear, what longing, what zeal, what avenging of wrong! In everything you demonstrated yourselves to be innocent in the matter.

12 So although I wrote to you, *it was* not for the sake of the offender nor for the sake of the one offended, but that your earnestness on our behalf might be made known to you in the sight of God.

LIFE LESSONS

➤ **2 Corinthians 7:6** — *God, who comforts the depressed, comforted us by the coming of Titus.*

*H*ow often do we miss God's answers to prayer because we don't recognize them when they come? We look for something miraculous, unusual, spectacular—and God sends us Titus.

➤ **2 Corinthians 7:9** — *I rejoice, not that you were made sorrowful, but that you were made sorrowful to the point of repentance.*

*T*he Father chastens us, not so that we will feel shamed, but so that our sorrow will lead us to repentance and restored fellowship with God. The *result* makes Him happy, not the means He uses to achieve the result.

13 For this reason we have been comforted.

And besides our comfort, we rejoiced even much more for the joy of Titus, because his spirit has been refreshed by you all.

14 For if in anything I have boasted to him about you, I was not put to shame; but as we spoke all things to you in truth, so also our boasting before Titus proved to be *the* truth.

15 His affection abounds all the more toward you, as he remembers the obedience of you all, how you received him with fear and trembling.

16 I rejoice that in everything I have confidence in you.

SEPTEMBER 16

Isaiah 23:1—24:23

23 THE oracle concerning Tyre.
Wail, O ships of Tarshish,
For *Tyre* is destroyed, without house
or harbor;
It is reported to them from the land
of Cyprus.

2 Be silent, you inhabitants of the
coastland,
You merchants of Sidon;
Your messengers crossed the sea

3 And *were* on many waters.
The grain of the Nile, the harvest of
the River was her revenue;
And she was the market of nations.

4 Be ashamed, O Sidon;
For the sea speaks, the stronghold
of the sea, saying,
"I have neither travailed nor given
birth,
I have neither brought up young
men *nor* reared virgins."

5 When the report *reaches* Egypt,
They will be in anguish at the report
of Tyre.

6 Pass over to Tarshish;
Wail, O inhabitants of the coastland.

7 Is this your jubilant *city*,
Whose origin is from antiquity,
Whose feet used to carry her to
colonize distant places?

8 Who has planned this against Tyre,
the bestower of crowns,

Whose merchants were princes,
whose traders were the honored
of the earth?

9 The LORD of hosts has planned it, to
defile the pride of all beauty,
To despise all the honored of the
earth.

10 Overflow your land like the Nile,
O daughter of Tarshish,
There is no more restraint.

11 He has stretched His hand out over
the sea,
He has made the kingdoms tremble;
The LORD has given a command
concerning Canaan to demolish
its strongholds.

12 He has said, "You shall exult no
more, O crushed virgin daughter
of Sidon.
Arise, pass over to Cyprus; even
there you will find no rest."

13 Behold, the land of the Chaldeans—
this is the people *which* was not; Assyria
appointed it for desert creatures—they
erected their siege towers, they stripped
its palaces, they made it a ruin.

14 Wail, O ships of Tarshish,
For your stronghold is destroyed.

15 Now in that day Tyre will be forgotten for seventy years like the days of one king. At the end of seventy years it will happen to Tyre as *in* the song of the harlot:

16 Take *your* harp, walk about the city,
O forgotten harlot;

Pluck the strings skillfully, sing
  many songs,
That you may be remembered.

17 It will come about at the end of seventy years that the LORD will visit Tyre. Then she will go back to her harlot's wages and will play the harlot with all the kingdoms on the face of the earth.
18 Her gain and her harlot's wages will be set apart to the LORD; it will not be stored up or hoarded, but her gain will become sufficient food and choice attire for those who dwell in the presence of the LORD.

24 BEHOLD, the LORD lays the earth waste, devastates it, distorts its surface and scatters its inhabitants.
2 And the people will be like the priest, the servant like his master, the maid like her mistress, the buyer like the seller, the lender like the borrower, the creditor like the debtor.
3 The earth will be completely laid waste and completely despoiled, for the LORD has spoken this word.
4 The earth mourns *and* withers, the world fades *and* withers, the exalted of the people of the earth fade away.
5 The earth is also polluted by its inhabitants, for they transgressed laws, violated statutes, broke the everlasting covenant.
6 Therefore, a curse devours the earth, and those who live in it are held guilty. Therefore, the inhabitants of the earth are burned, and few men are left.
7 The new wine mourns,
  The vine decays,
  All the merry-hearted sigh.
8 The gaiety of tambourines ceases,
  The noise of revelers stops,
  The gaiety of the harp ceases.
9 They do not drink wine with song;
  Strong drink is bitter to those who
    drink it.
10 The city of chaos is broken down;
  Every house is shut up so that none
    may enter.
11 There is an outcry in the streets
    concerning the wine;
  All joy turns to gloom.
  The gaiety of the earth is banished.
12 Desolation is left in the city
  And the gate is battered to ruins.
13 For thus it will be in the midst of the
    earth among the peoples,
  As the shaking of an olive tree,

As the gleanings when the grape
  harvest is over.
14 They raise their voices, they shout
    for joy;
  They cry out from the west
    concerning the majesty of the LORD.
15 Therefore glorify the LORD in the
    east,
  The name of the LORD, the God of
    Israel,
  In the coastlands of the sea.
16 From the ends of the earth we hear
    songs, "Glory to the Righteous
    One,"
  But I say, "Woe to me! Woe to me!
    Alas for me!
  The treacherous deal treacherously,
  And the treacherous deal very
    treacherously."
17 Terror and pit and snare
  Confront you, O inhabitant of the
    earth.
18 Then it will be that he who flees the
    report of disaster will fall into the
    pit,
  And he who climbs out of the pit
    will be caught in the snare;
  For the windows above are opened,
    and the foundations of the earth
    shake.
19 The earth is broken asunder,
  The earth is split through,
  The earth is shaken violently.
20 The earth reels to and fro like a
    drunkard

LIFE LESSONS

Isaiah 24:6 — *A curse devours the earth, and those who live in it are held guilty.*

Sin not only destroys us spiritually, it also plays havoc with the earth. Paul says, "The whole creation groans and suffers the pains of childbirth" (Rom. 8:22) and looks forward to its day of redemption.

Isaiah 24:20 — *Its transgression is heavy upon it.*

The prophets speak often about "the Day of the LORD," describing it as a time of horrific destruction, planet-wide judgments, and fierce divine wrath. Jesus said, "Unless those days had been cut short, no life would have been saved" (Matt. 24:22).

WHAT THE BIBLE SAYS ABOUT

Our Basic Needs

Psalm 107:9

*E*very individual is a beautiful and unique creation, complete with needs and desires specific to his or her own life. Some needs, however, are universal. That is, all people experience them in their lives.

The first is a sense of *belonging*. Everyone feels the need to fit in somewhere. The joy you feel when surrounded by intimate friends and family is powerful evidence of this truth. The discomfort associated with moving to a job or home where no one knows you also reveals how powerful this need is in our lives.

Another universal need is a sense of *worth*. It is important for all of us to be able to say, "I matter." Yet many people are not convinced

this is true. They're overcome by a disfigured self-image that's stealing the joy of the Lord from their lives.

A third universal need is a sense of *competence*. We need to know for certain that we can accomplish what the Lord puts before us. A lack of confidence in His power and provision in our lives can be devastating.

God responded to every one of these universal needs at the Cross. We belong because our heavenly Father called us into His holy family. We have worth because Jesus paid such a great price for our salvation. And we are competent because God has sent His Holy Spirit to indwell and empower us. A breakdown in any one of these areas will have a tremendous impact on our spiritual growth.

Are you struggling with any of these universal needs? If so, lay them before the Lord today. Then trust Him to make you the complete person He created you to be. ◈

And it totters like a shack,
For its transgression is heavy upon it,
And it will fall, never to rise again.
21 So it will happen in that day,
That the LORD will punish the host of heaven on high,
And the kings of the earth on earth.
22 They will be gathered together
Like prisoners in the dungeon,
And will be confined in prison;
And after many days they *will be* punished.
23 Then the moon will be abashed and the sun ashamed,
For the LORD of hosts will reign on Mount Zion and in Jerusalem,
And *His* glory will be before His elders.

◈ Psalm 107:9–22

9 For He has satisfied the thirsty soul,
And the hungry soul He has filled with what is good.
10 There were those who dwelt in darkness and in the shadow of death,
Prisoners in misery and chains,
11 Because they had rebelled against the words of God

And spurned the counsel of the Most High.
12 Therefore He humbled their heart with labor;
They stumbled and there was none to help.
13 Then they cried out to the LORD in their trouble;
He saved them out of their distresses.
14 He brought them out of darkness and the shadow of death
And broke their bands apart.
15 Let them give thanks to the LORD for His lovingkindness,
And for His wonders to the sons of men!
16 For He has shattered gates of bronze
And cut bars of iron asunder.
17 Fools, because of their rebellious way,
And because of their iniquities, were afflicted.
18 Their soul abhorred all kinds of food,
And they drew near to the gates of death.
19 Then they cried out to the LORD in their trouble;
He saved them out of their distresses.
20 He sent His word and healed them,
And delivered *them* from their destructions.

LIFE LESSONS

➤ **Psalm 107:19 — *They cried out to the LORD in their trouble; He saved them out of their distresses.***

Sometimes, the trouble that comes upon us is really a blessing in disguise, for it prompts us to seek God as never before. Are you in some trouble today? Then call upon the Lord for He delights in rescuing you.

21 Let them give thanks to the LORD
   for His lovingkindness,
   And for His wonders to the sons of
   men!
22 Let them also offer sacrifices of
   thanksgiving,
   And tell of His works with joyful
   singing.

Proverbs 25:17

17 Let your foot rarely be in your
   neighbor's house,
   Or he will become weary of you and
   hate you.

2 Corinthians 8:1–24

8 NOW, brethren, we *wish to* make known to you the grace of God which has been given in the churches of Macedonia,
2 that in a great ordeal of affliction their abundance of joy and their deep poverty overflowed in the wealth of their liberality.
3 For I testify that according to their ability, and beyond their ability, *they gave* of their own accord,
4 begging us with much urging for the favor of participation in the support of the saints,
➤ 5 and *this*, not as we had expected, but they first gave themselves to the Lord and to us by the will of God.
6 So we urged Titus that as he had previously made a beginning, so he would also complete in you this gracious work as well.

7 But just as you abound in everything, in faith and utterance and knowledge and in all earnestness and in the love we inspired in you, *see* that you abound in this gracious work also.
8 I am not speaking *this* as a command, but as proving through the earnestness of others the sincerity of your love also. ✳
9 For you know the grace of our Lord ≺ Jesus Christ, that though He was rich, yet for your sake He became poor, so that you through His poverty might become rich.
10 I give *my* opinion in this matter, for this is to your advantage, who were the first to begin a year ago not only to do *this*, but also to desire *to do it*.
11 But now finish doing it also, so that just as *there was* the readiness to desire it, so *there may be* also the completion of it by your ability.
12 For if the readiness is present, it is

LIFE LESSONS

➤ **2 Corinthians 8:5 — *They first gave themselves to the Lord and to us by the will of God.***

Believers in Jerusalem were suffering badly. Along with a famine in the region (Acts 11:27–30), many had been disowned by their families and had lost the ability to support themselves. To make matters worse, they were being double taxed by the Jewish and Roman authorities. Why were the Macedonian Christians so eager to help them? They were wholeheartedly committed to the Lord, and His priorities had become theirs.

➤ **2 Corinthians 8:9 — *For your sake He became poor, so that you through His poverty might become rich.***

The Lord Jesus left the magnificence and splendor of His kingdom in heaven, where He is adored and abounding in every way. He chose the limitation, suffering, and lowliness of a human body so He could personally demonstrate His great love to us. God is not after our time, talents, or bank account. He already owns the world and everything in it (Ex. 19:5). His greatest desire is to have a personal and intimate relationship with you for all eternity.

acceptable according to what *a person* has, not according to what he does not have.

13 For *this* is not for the ease of others *and* for your affliction, but by way of equality—

14 at this present time your abundance *being a supply* for their need, so that their abundance also may become *a supply* for your need, that there may be equality;

15 as it is written, "HE WHO *gathered* MUCH DID NOT HAVE TOO MUCH, AND HE WHO *gathered* LITTLE HAD NO LACK."

16 But thanks be to God who puts the same earnestness on your behalf in the heart of Titus.

➤ 17 For he not only accepted our appeal, but being himself very earnest, he has gone to you of his own accord.

18 We have sent along with him the brother whose fame in *the things of* the gospel *has spread* through all the churches;

19 and not only *this*, but he has also been appointed by the churches to travel with us in this gracious work, which is being administered by us for the glory of the Lord Himself, and *to show* our readiness,

20 taking precaution so that no one will discredit us in our administration of this generous gift;

21 for we have regard for what is honorable, not only in the sight of the Lord, but also in the sight of men.

22 We have sent with them our brother, whom we have often tested and found diligent in many things, but now even more diligent because of *his* great confidence in you.

23 As for Titus, *he is* my partner and fellow worker among you; as for our brethren, *they are* messengers of the churches, a glory to Christ.

24 Therefore openly before the churches, show them the proof of your love and of our reason for boasting about you.

LIFE LESSONS

➤ **2 Corinthians 8:17 —** *He has gone to you of his own accord.*

*H*ere we see the sovereignty of God and the free will of man working hand-in-hand. The Lord put a concern into Titus' heart, and Titus responded to Him in obedience, gladly acting on that concern of his own accord.

SEPTEMBER 17

✦ Isaiah 25:1—26:21

25 O LORD, You are my God;
I will exalt You, I will give
thanks to Your name;
For You have worked wonders,
Plans *formed* long ago, with perfect
faithfulness.

2 For You have made a city into a heap,
A fortified city into a ruin;
A palace of strangers is a city no
more,
It will never be rebuilt.

3 Therefore a strong people will
glorify You;
Cities of ruthless nations will revere
You.

➤ 4 For You have been a defense for the
helpless,
A defense for the needy in his
distress,

A refuge from the storm, a shade
from the heat;
For the breath of the ruthless
Is like a *rain* storm *against* a wall.

5 Like heat in drought, You subdue
the uproar of aliens;
Like heat by the shadow of a cloud,
the song of the ruthless is silenced.

6 The LORD of hosts will prepare a lavish
banquet for all peoples on this mountain;

LIFE LESSONS

➤ **Isaiah 25:4 —** *You have been a . . . refuge from the storm.*

*G*od gives strength to the weak, shelter to the homeless, and shade to those fainting in the scorching sun. Our Redeemer is all this to us and so much more. He assumes full responsibility for our needs when we obey Him.

A banquet of aged wine, choice
pieces with marrow,
And refined, aged wine.
7 And on this mountain He will
swallow up the covering which is
over all peoples,
Even the veil which is stretched
over all nations.
8 He will swallow up death for all
time,
And the Lord GOD will wipe tears
away from all faces,
And He will remove the reproach of
His people from all the earth;
For the LORD has spoken.
9 And it will be said in that day,
"Behold, this is our God for whom
we have waited that He might
save us.
This is the LORD for whom we have
waited;
Let us rejoice and be glad in His
salvation."
10 For the hand of the LORD will rest
on this mountain,
And Moab will be trodden down in
his place
As straw is trodden down in the
water of a manure pile.
11 And he will spread out his hands in
the middle of it
As a swimmer spreads out *his
hands* to swim,
But *the Lord* will lay low his pride
together with the trickery of his
hands.
12 The unassailable fortifications of
your walls He will bring down,
Lay low *and* cast to the ground,
even to the dust.

26 IN that day this song will be sung
in the land of Judah:
"We have a strong city;
He sets up walls and ramparts for
security.
2 "Open the gates, that the righteous
nation may enter,
The one that remains faithful.
3 "The steadfast of mind You will keep
in perfect peace,
Because he trusts in You.
4 "Trust in the LORD forever,
For in GOD the LORD, *we have* an
everlasting Rock.
5 "For He has brought low those who
dwell on high, the unassailable
city;

He lays it low, He lays it low to the
ground, He casts it to the dust.
6 "The foot will trample it,
The feet of the afflicted, the steps of
the helpless."
7 The way of the righteous is smooth;
O Upright One, make the path of
the righteous level.
8 Indeed, *while following* the way of
Your judgments, O LORD,
We have waited for You eagerly;
Your name, even Your memory, is
the desire of *our* souls.
9 At night my soul longs for You,
Indeed, my spirit within me seeks
You diligently;
For when the earth experiences Your
judgments
The inhabitants of the world learn
righteousness.
10 *Though* the wicked is shown favor,
He does not learn righteousness;
He deals unjustly in the land of
uprightness,
And does not perceive the majesty
of the LORD.
11 O LORD, Your hand is lifted up *yet*
they do not see it.
They see *Your* zeal for the people
and are put to shame;
Indeed, fire will devour Your
enemies.
12 LORD, You will establish peace for us,
Since You have also performed for
us all our works.
13 O LORD our God, other masters
besides You have ruled us;

LIFE LESSONS

➤ **Isaiah 26:8** — *Your name, even Your
memory, is the desire of our souls.*

*G*od designed us to enjoy a heart-to-
heart closeness with Him, and we
find our lives' highest calling and priority
in knowing Him intimately, obeying Him
faithfully, and loving Him deeply.

➤ **Isaiah 26:12** — *LORD, You will establish
peace for us.*

*T*o live the Christian life is to allow
Jesus to live His life in us and through
us. That means that all we accomplish,
we accomplish through His Spirit. And
that kind of wonderful partnership
results in peace.

But through You alone we confess
   Your name.

14 The dead will not live, the departed
   spirits will not rise;
   Therefore You have punished and
   destroyed them,
   And You have wiped out all
   remembrance of them.

15 You have increased the nation,
   O LORD,
   You have increased the nation, You
   are glorified;
   You have extended all the borders
   of the land.

16 O LORD, they sought You in distress;
   They could only whisper a prayer,
   Your chastening was upon them.

17 As the pregnant woman approaches
   the time to give birth,
   She writhes *and* cries out in her
   labor pains,
   Thus were we before You, O LORD.

18 We were pregnant, we writhed *in
   labor,*
   We gave birth, as it seems, *only* to
   wind.
   We could not accomplish
   deliverance for the earth,
   Nor were inhabitants of the world
   born.

19 Your dead will live;
   Their corpses will rise.
   You who lie in the dust, awake and
   shout for joy,
   For your dew *is as* the dew of the
   dawn,
   And the earth will give birth to the
   departed spirits.

20 Come, my people, enter into your
   rooms
   And close your doors behind you;
   Hide for a little while
   Until indignation runs *its* course.

21 For behold, the LORD is about to
   come out from His place
   To punish the inhabitants of the
   earth for their iniquity;
   And the earth will reveal her
   bloodshed
   And will no longer cover her slain.

Psalm 107:23-32

23 Those who go down to the sea in
   ships,

Who do business on great waters;

24 They have seen the works of the
   LORD,
   And His wonders in the deep.

25 For He spoke and raised up a
   stormy wind,
   Which lifted up the waves of the
   sea.

26 They rose up to the heavens, they
   went down to the depths;
   Their soul melted away in *their*
   misery.

27 They reeled and staggered like a
   drunken man,
   And were at their wits' end.

28 Then they cried to the LORD in their
   trouble,
   And He brought them out of their
   distresses.

29 He caused the storm to be still,
   So that the waves of the sea were
   hushed.

30 Then they were glad because they
   were quiet,
   So He guided them to their desired
   haven.

31 Let them give thanks to the LORD
   for His lovingkindness,
   And for His wonders to the sons of
   men!

32 Let them extol Him also in the
   congregation of the people,
   And praise Him at the seat of the
   elders.

Proverbs 25:18, 19

18 *Like* a club and a sword and a sharp
   arrow
   Is a man who bears false witness
   against his neighbor.

19 *Like* a bad tooth and an unsteady
   foot
   Is confidence in a faithless man in
   time of trouble.

2 Corinthians 9:1-15

9 FOR it is superfluous for me to write to
   you about this ministry to the saints;
2 for I know your readiness, of which
   I boast about you to the Macedonians,
   namely, that Achaia has been prepared

⊙ LIFE PRINCIPLE   23

YOU CAN NEVER OUTGIVE GOD.

2 CORINTHIANS 9:8

King David knew God had prospered him and given him rest from all his enemies. One day he looked around at his comfortable home and said to Nathan the prophet, "See now, I dwell in a house of cedar, but the ark of God dwells within tent curtains" (2 Sam. 7:2). He wanted to build a temple for God—no small undertaking.

But God had a much bigger gift in mind for David. He said, "The LORD also declares to you that the LORD will make a house for you . . . Your house and your kingdom shall endure before Me forever" (2 Sam. 7:11, 16).

This story powerfully reminds us that we can *never* outgive God. While He invites our gifts and offerings, He will always give us far more than we could possibly give Him. He will never be a debtor to anyone.

Jesus declared that any who gave one of His followers even a cup of water in His name would be lavishly rewarded (Mark 9:41). He once illustrated God's generosity by describing how a wealthy "Lord" rewarded servants with multiple cities in return for their doubling the little bit of money he had given them. Peter once boasted to the Lord, "Behold, we have left our own homes and followed you" (Luke 18:28). He probably expected a pat on the back. Instead Jesus told him, "Truly I say to you, there is no one who has left house or wife or brothers or parents or children, for the sake of the kingdom of God, who will not receive many times as much at this time and in the age to come, eternal life" (18:29, 30).

In one of the clearest examples of this principle in Scripture, Jesus tells us, "Give, and it will be given to you. They will pour into your lap a good measure—pressed down, shaken together, and running over. For by your standard of measure it will be measured to you in return" (Luke 6:38).

It's just a fact: you can never outgive God.

The Old Testament prophet Malachi certainly believed this principle. Through him, God instructed the people to bring Him the full tithe and said, "'Test Me now in this,' says the LORD of hosts, 'if I will not open for you the windows of heaven and pour out for you a blessing until it overflows' " (Mal. 3:10).

To tithe is to give ten percent of our incomes to God for His work. All that we have is a gift from God; therefore, a tithe is a mere portion of what

He has already given to us. If we obey God's Word and cheerfully give the portion He has requested of us, He will bless us and the work of His kingdom.

Years ago, God led us to purchase property for the expansion of First Baptist Atlanta. We began to pray He would provide the funds we needed.

I also prayed specifically He would show me what He wanted me to give. I had given financially, but I sensed there was something more that He was requiring.

It wasn't long before He began to impress upon me to give my camera equipment to the building fund. I love photography. It is my favorite hobby. However, God's conviction was strong and to the point. There was no way I wanted to avoid making the right decision. I knew that my obedience would lead to blessing. If He wanted my cameras, I wanted to give them to Him. After all, He owned them anyway.

A few days later, I sold my equipment and gave the money to the building fund. Many of the other members of our congregation also gave personal possessions and treasures. It was a great time in our fellowship for seeking God's will with our finances and also allowing Him to prove His faithfulness to each one of us. When it came time to sign the paperwork for our new property, we had the money we needed and did not have to borrow a single copper penny.

Several months later, a woman rang my doorbell. When I opened it, I noticed she had two very large shopping bags. She asked, "Are you Charles Stanley?" I didn't know what to think but I replied, "Yes, I am."

Then she said, "This is for you." She set the bags down and turned and walked away. I looked inside of one of them and immediately recognized my camera equipment. God had returned every lens and every camera body to me. Is this the way He works? I believe it is. Many times, He tests us to see where our true devotion is located. Is it in things, or is it in Him?

He challenges us to give Him the privilege to prove Himself and has promised to bless us in return (Prov. 3:9, 10). When we obey, He will protect our finances, just as He protected His obedient people in the Old Testament from the insects that otherwise would have devoured their crops.

The psalmist asked, "What shall I render to the LORD for all His benefits toward me?" (Ps. 116:12). The question could be translated, "How can I repay the Lord for all His goodness toward me?"

The answer is, we can't. No one can because no man or woman can outgive the Lord. ⊛

since last year, and your zeal has stirred up most of them.

3   But I have sent the brethren, in order that our boasting about you may not be made empty in this case, so that, as I was saying, you may be prepared;

4   otherwise if any Macedonians come with me and find you unprepared, we—not to speak of you—will be put to shame by this confidence.

5   So I thought it necessary to urge the brethren that they would go on ahead to you and arrange beforehand your previously promised bountiful gift, so that the same would be ready as a bountiful gift and not affected by covetousness.

6   Now this I say, he who sows sparingly will also reap sparingly, and he who sows bountifully will also reap bountifully.

7   Each one must do just as he has purposed in his heart, not grudgingly or under compulsion, for God loves a cheerful giver.

8   And God is able to make all grace abound to you, so that always having all sufficiency in everything, you may have an abundance for every good deed;

9   as it is written,
"HE SCATTERED ABROAD, HE GAVE TO THE POOR,
HIS RIGHTEOUSNESS ENDURES FOREVER."

10   Now He who supplies seed to the sower and bread for food will supply and multiply your seed for sowing and increase the harvest of your righteousness;

11   you will be enriched in everything for all liberality, which through us is producing thanksgiving to God.

12   For the ministry of this service is not only fully supplying the needs of the saints, but is also overflowing through many thanksgivings to God.

13   Because of the proof given by this ministry, they will glorify God for your obedience to your confession of the gospel of Christ and for the liberality of your contribution to them and to all,

14   while they also, by prayer on your behalf, yearn for you because of the surpassing grace of God in you.

15   Thanks be to God for His indescribable gift!

LIFE LESSONS

➤ **2 Corinthians 9:7 — God loves a cheerful giver.**

In giving, as in all other areas of Christian living, God wants our hearts to respond to Him in obedience. He wants willing, joyful, eager participation in His work, not grumbling or halfhearted compliance.

➤ **2 Corinthians 9:8 — God is able to make all grace abound to you.**

God's grace sustains us throughout our lives. His grace gives us our daily bread, supplies us with lungs full of air, and grants us the ability to make a living. The Father wants an abundant life for us; His grace makes it possible.

➤ **2 Corinthians 9:15 — Thanks be to God for His indescribable gift!**

The greatest gift we could ever receive is the marvelous grace of God, which hit its apex in the gift of His Son, Jesus Christ. The only reason we have the privilege of giving is that the Father has already given far more than we ever could.

◈ **Isaiah 27:1—28:15**

27 IN that day the LORD will punish Leviathan the fleeing serpent,
With His fierce and great and mighty sword,
Even Leviathan the twisted serpent;

And He will kill the dragon who lives in the sea.

2   In that day,
"A vineyard of wine, sing of it!

3   "I, the LORD, am its keeper;
I water it every moment.
So that no one will damage it,
I guard it night and day.

4 "I have no wrath.
   Should someone give Me briars *and*
     thorns in battle,
   Then I would step on them, I would
     burn them completely.
5 "Or let him rely on My protection,
   Let him make peace with Me,
   Let him make peace with Me."
6 In the days to come Jacob will take
     root,
   Israel will blossom and sprout,
   And they will fill the whole world
     with fruit.
7 Like the striking of Him who has
     struck them, has He struck them?
   Or like the slaughter of His slain,
     have they been slain?
8 You contended with them by
     banishing them, by driving them
     away.
   With His fierce wind He has expelled
     them on the day of the east wind.
9 Therefore through this Jacob's
     iniquity will be forgiven;
   And this will be the full price of the
     pardoning of his sin:
   When he makes all the altar stones
     like pulverized chalk stones;
   When Asherim and incense altars
     will not stand.
10 For the fortified city is isolated,
   A homestead forlorn and forsaken
     like the desert;
   There the calf will graze,
   And there it will lie down and feed
     on its branches.
11 When its limbs are dry, they are
     broken off;
   Women come *and* make a fire with
     them,
   For they are not a people of
     discernment,
   Therefore their Maker will not have
     compassion on them.
   And their Creator will not be
     gracious to them.
12 In that day the LORD will start *His*
threshing from the flowing stream of the
Euphrates to the brook of Egypt, and you
will be gathered up one by one, O sons of
Israel.
13 It will come about also in that day
that a great trumpet will be blown, and
those who were perishing in the land of
Assyria and who were scattered in the
land of Egypt will come and worship the
LORD in the holy mountain at Jerusalem.

28

WOE to the proud crown of the
   drunkards of Ephraim,
And to the fading flower of its
   glorious beauty,
Which is at the head of the fertile
   valley
Of those who are overcome with
   wine!
2 Behold, the Lord has a strong and
     mighty *agent;*
   As a storm of hail, a tempest of
     destruction,
   Like a storm of mighty overflowing
     waters,
   He has cast *it* down to the earth
     with *His* hand.
3 The proud crown of the drunkards
     of Ephraim is trodden under
     foot.
4 And the fading flower of its glorious
     beauty,
   Which is at the head of the fertile
     valley,
   Will be like the first-ripe fig prior to
     summer,
   Which one sees,
   And as soon as it is in his hand,
   He swallows it.
5 In that day the LORD of hosts will   ≺
     become a beautiful crown
   And a glorious diadem to the
     remnant of His people;
6 A spirit of justice for him who sits
     in judgment,
   A strength to those who repel the
     onslaught at the gate.
7 And these also reel with wine and
     stagger from strong drink:
   The priest and the prophet reel with
     strong drink,
   They are confused by wine, they
     stagger from strong drink;

LIFE LESSONS

≻ **Isaiah 28:5** — *In that day the LORD of
hosts will become a beautiful crown and
a glorious diadem to the remnant of His
people.*

*D*o you consider your relationship
   with the Lord your greatest treasure
and the deepest joy of your heart? He
longs to be nearer and dearer to us than
our parents, spouses, friends, or children.
We are His treasure, and He wants to be
ours.

They reel while having visions,
They totter *when rendering*
  judgment.
8   For all the tables are full of filthy
   vomit, without a *single clean*
   place.
9   "To whom would He teach
   knowledge,
   And to whom would He interpret
   the message?
   Those *just* weaned from milk?
   Those *just* taken from the breast?
10   "For *He says,*
   'Order on order, order on order,
   Line on line, line on line,
   A little here, a little there.'"
11   Indeed, He will speak to this
   people
   Through stammering lips and a
   foreign tongue,
12   He who said to them, "Here is rest,
   give rest to the weary,"
   And, "Here is repose," but they
   would not listen.
13   So the word of the LORD to them
   will be,
   "Order on order, order on order,
   Line on line, line on line,
   A little here, a little there,"
   That they may go and stumble
   backward, be broken, snared and
   taken captive.
14   Therefore, hear the word of the
   LORD, O scoffers,
   Who rule this people who are in
   Jerusalem,
15   Because you have said, "We have
   made a covenant with death,
   And with Sheol we have made a
   pact.
   The overwhelming scourge will not
   reach us when it passes by,
   For we have made falsehood our
   refuge and we have concealed
   ourselves with deception."

Psalm 107:33–43

33   He changes rivers into a wilderness
   And springs of water into a thirsty
   ground;
34   A fruitful land into a salt waste,
   Because of the wickedness of those
   who dwell in it.

35   He changes a wilderness into a pool
   of water
   And a dry land into springs of
   water;
36   And there He makes the hungry to
   dwell,
   So that they may establish an
   inhabited city,
37   And sow fields and plant vineyards,
   And gather a fruitful harvest.
38   Also He blesses them and they
   multiply greatly,
   And He does not let their cattle
   decrease.
39   When they are diminished and
   bowed down
   Through oppression, misery and
   sorrow,
40   He pours contempt upon princes
   And makes them wander in a
   pathless waste.
41   But He sets the needy securely on
   high away from affliction,
   And makes *his* families like a flock.
42   The upright see it and are glad;
   But all unrighteousness shuts its
   mouth.
43   Who is wise? Let him give heed to
   these things,
   And consider the lovingkindnesses
   of the LORD.

Proverbs 25:20

20   *Like* one who takes off a garment
   on a cold day, *or like* vinegar on
   soda,
   Is he who sings songs to a troubled
   heart.

2 Corinthians 10:1–18

10 NOW I, Paul, myself urge you by
the meekness and gentleness of
Christ—I who am meek when face to
face with you, but bold toward you when
absent!
2   I ask that when I am present I
need not be bold with the confidence
with which I propose to be courageous
against some, who regard us as if we
walked according to the flesh.

➤ 3　For though we walk in the flesh, we do not war according to the flesh,

4　for the weapons of our warfare are not of the flesh, but divinely powerful for the destruction of fortresses.

➤ 5　*We are* destroying speculations and every lofty thing raised up against the ✱ knowledge of God, and *we are* taking every thought captive to the obedience of Christ,

6　and we are ready to punish all disobedience, whenever your obedience is complete.

7　You are looking at things as they are outwardly. If anyone is confident in himself that he is Christ's, let him consider this again within himself, that just as he is Christ's, so also are we.

8　For even if I boast somewhat further about our authority, which the Lord gave for building you up and not for destroying you, I will not be put to shame,

9　for I do not wish to seem as if I would terrify you by my letters.

10　For they say, "His letters are weighty and strong, but his personal presence is unimpressive and his speech contemptible."

LIFE LESSONS

➤ **2 Corinthians 10:3 — *Though we walk in the flesh, we do not war according to the flesh.***

*W*e do not yet have our glorified bodies; we still live in tents of unredeemed flesh. Yet because the Spirit of the living God dwells within us, we serve Him not in the flesh but through faith in His Spirit.

➤ **2 Corinthians 10:5 — *We are taking every thought captive to the obedience of Christ.***

*P*aul speaks a great deal about training the mind to think in a way that honors God because the mind is the primary battlefield for spiritual warfare. Remember, what you focus your mind on has lasting ramifications. This is because a thought reaps an action; an action reaps a habit; a habit reaps your character; and your character reaps your destiny. Therefore, reject anything that does not honor Christ in your thinking (Phil. 4:8, 9; Col. 3:2).

ANSWERS TO LIFE'S QUESTIONS

What does it mean to do spiritual battle?

2 CORINTHIANS 10:3–7

*T*he conflict within you between the flesh and the Spirit is a form of spiritual warfare, and you win much of the battle just by realizing that the struggle exists.

Sin is still a powerful force, but it can no longer control you unless you allow it to do so. You are not doomed to failure, and to believe otherwise is to remain in needless, painful bondage. That breaks the heart of the Lord and grieves the Spirit (Eph. 4:30).

The truth is, you cannot wander too far, fail too many times, or exceed Christ's forgiveness. When you repent and turn to Him, He restores you to fellowship as though nothing had ever happened.

Peter denied Jesus three times, despite his boasts to remain faithful; yet the Lord forgave him and made him a powerful leader in the early church. Peter had learned his lesson well. Though he surely experienced other failures and setbacks, he knew that his Savior remained forever at his side, ready to forgive.

Notice what an older and wiser Peter had to say about God's grace: "His divine power has granted to us everything pertaining to life and godliness, through the true knowledge of Him who called us by His own glory and excellence. For by these He has granted to us His precious and magnificent promises, so that by them you may become partakers of the divine nature, having escaped the corruption that is in the world by lust" (2 Pet. 1:3, 4).

You are on an ever-upward climb to holiness, set apart for God's purposes. As you learn to say no to the power of sin and to rest in His grace, you are made free to obey with renewed vigor and understanding. It is imperative to grasp that obedience is always a choice; you decide whether you will yield to God and so become more like Christ.

You have a great potential to live free and holy through Jesus Christ, but God will never force you to do what He desires. Yet He longs for you to turn to Him in every spiritual conflict, acknowledge your weakness, and ask for His power to say no.

Are you tired of fighting a losing battle? Do you secretly feel like a failure? It's not true! And the sooner you learn to rejoice and grow in the reality of your identity in Him, the sooner you will experience the thrill of victory.

11 Let such a person consider this, that what we are in word by letters when absent, such persons *we are* also in deed when present.

12 For we are not bold to class or compare ourselves with some of those who commend themselves; but when they measure themselves by themselves and compare themselves with themselves, they are without understanding.

13 But we will not boast beyond *our* measure, but within the measure of the sphere which God apportioned to us as a measure, to reach even as far as you.

14 For we are not overextending ourselves, as if we did not reach to you, for we were the first to come even as far as you in the gospel of Christ;

15 not boasting beyond *our* measure, *that is,* in other men's labors, but with the hope that as your faith grows, we will be, within our sphere, enlarged even more by you,

16 so as to preach the gospel even to the regions beyond you, *and* not to boast in what has been accomplished in the sphere of another.

17 But HE WHO BOASTS IS TO BOAST IN THE LORD.

18 For it is not he who commends himself that is approved, but he whom the Lord commends.

SEPTEMBER 19

Isaiah 28:16—29:24

16 Therefore thus says the Lord GOD,
　　"Behold, I am laying in Zion a stone,
　　　a tested stone,
　　A costly cornerstone *for* the
　　　foundation, firmly placed.
　　He who believes *in it* will not be
　　　disturbed.

17 "I will make justice the measuring
　　　line
　　And righteousness the level;
　　Then hail will sweep away the
　　　refuge of lies
　　And the waters will overflow the
　　　secret place.

18 "Your covenant with death will be
　　　canceled,
　　And your pact with Sheol will not
　　　stand;
　　When the overwhelming scourge
　　　passes through,
　　Then you become its trampling
　　　place.

19 "As often as it passes through, it will
　　　seize you;

　　For morning after morning it will
　　　pass through, *anytime* during the
　　　day or night,
　　And it will be sheer terror to
　　　understand what it means."

20 The bed is too short on which to
　　　stretch out,
　　And the blanket is too small to wrap
　　　oneself in.

21 For the LORD will rise up as *at*
　　　Mount Perazim,
　　He will be stirred up as in the valley
　　　of Gibeon,
　　To do His task, His unusual task,
　　And to work His work, His
　　　extraordinary work.

22 And now do not carry on as
　　　scoffers,
　　Or your fetters will be made
　　　stronger;
　　For I have heard from the Lord GOD
　　　of hosts
　　Of decisive destruction on all the
　　　earth.

23 Give ear and hear my voice,
　　Listen and hear my words.

24 Does the farmer plow continually to
　　　plant seed?

WHAT THE BIBLE SAYS ABOUT

When the Milling Ends

Isaiah 28:28

Sometimes it will feel as if God's hand is heavy upon you—as if He is refining and sifting you for some reason known only to Him. During those times, trials will grind at you from inside and out in a seemingly unending process.

When such seasons linger for you, look to Isaiah 28:28 for comfort. The prophet writes,

"Grain for bread is crushed, indeed, he does not continue to thresh it forever."

God will not discipline you too much—He won't allow the process to destroy you. Rather, He knows just the amount of threshing and milling that's required to make you especially effective for ministry. And the best news is: it won't last forever.

Just as the farmer who is an expert in the possibilities of each grain of wheat, barley, or oat, God knows exactly how to develop you into the person He created you to be.

Trust Him. Soon the refining will be over and the result will be worth it. ◈

Does he *continually* turn and harrow the ground?
25 Does he not level its surface
And sow dill and scatter cummin
And plant wheat in rows,
Barley in its place and rye within its area?
26 For his God instructs and teaches him properly.
27 For dill is not threshed with a threshing sledge,
Nor is the cartwheel driven over cummin;
But dill is beaten out with a rod, and cummin with a club.
28 *Grain for* bread is crushed,
Indeed, he does not continue to thresh it forever.
Because the wheel of *his* cart and his horses *eventually* damage *it*,
He does not thresh it longer.
29 This also comes from the LORD of hosts,
Who has made *His* counsel wonderful and *His* wisdom great.

29 WOE, O Ariel, Ariel the city *where* David *once* camped!

LIFE LESSONS

➤ **Isaiah 28:29 — *This also comes from the LORD of hosts, who has made His counsel wonderful and His wisdom great.***

Have you experienced the wonderful counsel of God? Have you asked Him to guide you so you will accomplish His will? He wants to lead you into a great future—but you must listen to His voice and obey His directions.

Add year to year, observe *your* feasts on schedule.
2 I will bring distress to Ariel,
And she will be *a city of* lamenting and mourning;
And she will be like an Ariel to me.
3 I will camp against you encircling *you,*
And I will set siegeworks against you,
And I will raise up battle towers against you.
4 Then you will be brought low;
From the earth you will speak,
And from the dust *where* you are prostrate
Your words *will* come.
Your voice will also be like that of a spirit from the ground,
And your speech will whisper from the dust.
5 But the multitude of your enemies will become like fine dust,
And the multitude of the ruthless ones like the chaff which blows away;
And it will happen instantly, suddenly.
6 From the LORD of hosts you will be punished with thunder and earthquake and loud noise,
With whirlwind and tempest and the flame of a consuming fire.
7 And the multitude of all the nations who wage war against Ariel,
Even all who wage war against her and her stronghold, and who distress her,
Will be like a dream, a vision of the night.

8   It will be as when a hungry man
        dreams—
    And behold, he is eating;
    But when he awakens, his hunger is
        not satisfied,
    Or as when a thirsty man dreams—
    And behold, he is drinking,
    But when he awakens, behold, he is
        faint
    And his thirst is not quenched.
    Thus the multitude of all the nations
        will be
    Who wage war against Mount
        Zion.
9   Be delayed and wait,
    Blind yourselves and be blind;
    They become drunk, but not with
        wine,
    They stagger, but not with strong
        drink.
10 For the LORD has poured over you a
        spirit of deep sleep,
    He has shut your eyes, the
        prophets;
    And He has covered your heads, the
        seers.
11 The entire vision will be to you like
    the words of a sealed book, which when
    they give it to the one who is literate,
    saying, "Please read this," he will say, "I
    cannot, for it is sealed."
12 Then the book will be given to the
    one who is illiterate, saying, "Please read
    this." And he will say, "I cannot read."
➤ 13 Then the Lord said,
    "Because this people draw near with
        their words
    And honor Me with their lip
        service,
    But they remove their hearts far
        from Me,
    And their reverence for Me consists
        of tradition learned by rote,

LIFE LESSONS

➤ **Isaiah 29:13 — "This people draw near
with their word and honor Me with their
lip service, but they remove their hearts
far from Me."**

*G*od isn't just unimpressed with pas-
sionless prayers and dead devotion,
He detests them. He has no interest in
outward compliance devoid of inward
desire to please Him. He wants *us,* not
our words, deeds, or possessions.

---

14 Therefore behold, I will once
        again deal marvelously with this
        people, wondrously marvelous;
    And the wisdom of their wise men
        will perish,
    And the discernment of their
        discerning men will be
        concealed."
15 Woe to those who deeply hide their
        plans from the LORD,
    And whose deeds are done in a dark
        place,
    And they say, "Who sees us?" or
        "Who knows us?"
16 You turn things around!
    Shall the potter be considered as
        equal with the clay,
    That what is made would say to its
        maker, "He did not make me";
    Or what is formed say to him
        who formed it, "He has no
        understanding"?
17 Is it not yet just a little while
    Before Lebanon will be turned into
        a fertile field,
    And the fertile field will be
        considered as a forest?
18 On that day the deaf will hear
        words of a book,
    And out of their gloom and
        darkness the eyes of the blind will
        see.
19 The afflicted also will increase their
        gladness in the LORD,
    And the needy of mankind will
        rejoice in the Holy One of Israel.
20 For the ruthless will come to an end
        and the scorner will be finished,
    Indeed all who are intent on doing
        evil will be cut off;
21 Who cause a person to be indicted
        by a word,
    And ensnare him who adjudicates
        at the gate,
    And defraud the one in the right
        with meaningless arguments.
22 Therefore thus says the LORD, who
    redeemed Abraham, concerning the
    house of Jacob:
    "Jacob shall not now be ashamed,
        nor shall his face now turn pale;
23 But when he sees his children, the
        work of My hands, in his midst,
    They will sanctify My name;
    Indeed, they will sanctify the Holy
        One of Jacob

And will stand in awe of the God of Israel.

➤ 24 "Those who err in mind will know the truth,
And those who criticize will accept instruction.

◈ **Psalm 108:1–6**

A Song, a Psalm of David.

108 MY heart is steadfast, O God;
I will sing, I will sing praises,
even with my soul.
2 Awake, harp and lyre;
I will awaken the dawn!
3 I will give thanks to You, O LORD,
among the peoples,
And I will sing praises to You among
the nations.
4 For Your lovingkindness is great
above the heavens,
And Your truth *reaches* to the
skies.
5 Be exalted, O God, above the
heavens,
And Your glory above all the earth.
✳ 6 That Your beloved may be
delivered,
Save with Your right hand, and
answer me!

◈ **Proverbs 25:21, 22**

21 If your enemy is hungry, give him
food to eat;
And if he is thirsty, give him water
to drink;
✳ 22 For you will heap burning coals on
his head,
And the LORD will reward you.

◈ **2 Corinthians 11:1–15**

11 I WISH that you would bear with
me in a little foolishness; but indeed you are bearing with me.
2 For I am jealous for you with a godly
jealousy; for I betrothed you to one husband, so that to Christ I might present
you *as* a pure virgin.

3 But I am afraid that, as the serpent ⋖
deceived Eve by his craftiness, your
minds will be led astray from the sim-
plicity and purity *of devotion* to Christ.
4 For if one comes and preaches another Jesus whom we have not preached,
or you receive a different spirit which
you have not received, or a different
gospel which you have not accepted, you
bear *this* beautifully.
5 For I consider myself not in the least
inferior to the most eminent apostles.
6 But even if I am unskilled in speech,
yet I am not *so* in knowledge; in fact, in
every way we have made *this* evident to
you in all things.
7 Or did I commit a sin in humbling
myself so that you might be exalted,
because I preached the gospel of God to
you without charge?
8 I robbed other churches by taking
wages *from them* to serve you;
9 and when I was present with you
and was in need, I was not a burden to

LIFE LESSONS

➤ *Isaiah 29:24 — "Those who err in mind
will know the truth, and those who criticize will accept instruction."*

God disciplines us to sanctify us—to
conform us to His will and to the
image of Christ (Heb. 12:1-14). He uses
adversity to strengthen and teach us
about Himself and His unfailing love.
Many times, we learn more in our valley
experiences than on the mountaintops.

➤ *2 Corinthians 11:3 — As the serpent
deceived Eve by his craftiness, your
minds will be led astray from the simplic-
ity and purity of devotion to Christ.*

God wants us to enjoy an intimate
relationship with Him—that is His
primary goal for our existence. He
redeemed us by His grace so that we
could spend eternity with Him. So the
enemy does whatever he can to discourage us and prevent us from growing
closer to the Lord. This is a mission that
began in the Garden of Eden (Gen. 3)
and that continues with false teachers
today. However, we do not have to fall
for his tactics. We can resist the evil one
by staying faithful and obedient to the
Lord and not falling for lies that contradict His Word.

anyone; for when the brethren came from Macedonia they fully supplied my need, and in everything I kept myself from being a burden to you, and will continue to do so.

10 As the truth of Christ is in me, this boasting of mine will not be stopped in the regions of Achaia.

11 Why? Because I do not love you? God knows I do!

12 But what I am doing I will continue to do, so that I may cut off opportunity from those who desire an opportunity to be regarded just as we are in the matter about which they are boasting.

13 For such men are false apostles, deceitful workers, disguising themselves as apostles of Christ.

LIFE LESSONS

> **2 Corinthians 11:14 — *Satan disguises himself as an angel of light.***

*C*ults and false religions through the ages have often begun out of interactions with beings who presented themselves as angels. Demonic double agents can do a great deal of harm, and we must beware of them.

---

14 No wonder, for even Satan disguises himself as an angel of light. ◄

15 Therefore it is not surprising if his servants also disguise themselves as servants of righteousness, whose end will be according to their deeds.

SEPTEMBER 20

Isaiah 30:1—32:20

► **30** "WOE to the rebellious children," declares the LORD,
"Who execute a plan, but not Mine,
And make an alliance, but not of My Spirit,
In order to add sin to sin;

2 Who proceed down to Egypt
Without consulting Me,
To take refuge in the safety of Pharaoh
And to seek shelter in the shadow of Egypt!

3 "Therefore the safety of Pharaoh will be your shame

LIFE LESSONS

> **Isaiah 30:1 — *"Woe to the rebellious children . . . who execute a plan, but not Mine."***

*W*e find it terribly easy to jump ahead of the Lord, to get our plans in order and our projects in motion before we ask Him for His counsel. But He wants to be first in our deliberations, not an afterthought. Remember, to live the Christian life is to allow Jesus to live His life in and through us. We are to obey His plans, not demand that He bless ours.

And the shelter in the shadow of Egypt, your humiliation.

4 "For their princes are at Zoan
And their ambassadors arrive at Hanes.

5 "Everyone will be ashamed because of a people who cannot profit them,
Who are not for help or profit, but for shame and also for reproach."

6 The oracle concerning the beasts of the Negev.

Through a land of distress and anguish,
From where *come* lioness and lion, viper and flying serpent,
They carry their riches on the backs of young donkeys
And their treasures on camels' humps,
To a people who cannot profit *them*;

7 Even Egypt, whose help is vain and empty.
Therefore, I have called her
"Rahab who has been exterminated."

8 Now go, write it on a tablet before them
And inscribe it on a scroll,
That it may serve in the time to come
As a witness forever.

9 For this is a rebellious people, false sons,

Sons who refuse to listen
To the instruction of the LORD;

10 Who say to the seers, "You must not
see *visions*";
And to the prophets, "You must not
prophesy to us what is right,
Speak to us pleasant words,
Prophesy illusions.

11 "Get out of the way, turn aside from
the path,
Let us hear no more about the Holy
One of Israel."

12 Therefore thus says the Holy One of
Israel,
"Since you have rejected this word
And have put your trust in
oppression and guile, and have
relied on them,

13 Therefore this iniquity will be to
you
Like a breach about to fall,
A bulge in a high wall,
Whose collapse comes suddenly in
an instant,

14 Whose collapse is like the smashing
of a potter's jar,
So ruthlessly shattered
That a sherd will not be found
among its pieces
To take fire from a hearth
Or to scoop water from a cistern."

15 For thus the Lord GOD, the Holy One
of Israel, has said,
"In repentance and rest you will be
saved,
In quietness and trust is your
strength."
But you were not willing,

16 And you said, "No, for we will flee
on horses,"
Therefore you shall flee!
"And we will ride on swift *horses*,"
Therefore those who pursue you
shall be swift.

17 One thousand *will flee* at the threat
of one *man;*
You will flee at the threat of five,
Until you are left as a flag on a
mountain top
And as a signal on a hill.

18 Therefore the LORD longs to be
gracious to you,
And therefore He waits on high to
have compassion on you.
For the LORD is a God of justice;
How blessed are all those who long
for Him.

19 O people in Zion, inhabitant in Jerusalem, you will weep no longer. He will
surely be gracious to you at the sound
of your cry; when He hears it, He will
answer you.

20 Although the Lord has given you
bread of privation and water of oppression, *He,* your Teacher will no longer
hide Himself, but your eyes will behold
your Teacher.

21 Your ears will hear a word behind
you, "This is the way, walk in it," whenever you turn to the right or to the
left.

22 And you will defile your graven
images overlaid with silver, and your
molten images plated with gold. You will
scatter them as an impure thing, *and* say
to them, "Be gone!"

23 Then He will give *you* rain for the
seed which you will sow in the ground,
and bread *from* the yield of the ground,
and it will be rich and plenteous; on that
day your livestock will graze in a roomy
pasture.

24 Also the oxen and the donkeys
which work the ground will eat salted
fodder, which has been winnowed with
shovel and fork.

25 On every lofty mountain and on
every high hill there will be streams

LIFE LESSONS

➤ **Isaiah 30:15 —** *"In quietness and trust
is your strength."*

*P*aul tells us, "Give yourselves fully to
the work of the Lord, because you
know that your labor in the Lord is not in
vain" (1 Cor. 15:58). Never strive for *anything* apart from the empowering of His
Spirit. Dependence upon the Lord leads
to a quiet, confident spirit.

➤ **Isaiah 30:21 —** *"This is the way, walk
in it."*

*T*he Lord promises to lead and to guide
His people. He doesn't make it difficult for us to find Him and His will. On
the contrary, God will move heaven and
earth to show us His will, if necessary. If
we really want to do His will, He promises
to make it clear to us.

WHAT THE BIBLE SAYS ABOUT

The Adventure of Obedience

Isaiah 30:21

Christians sometimes approach obedience as a way of avoiding the negative consequences of disobedience. They see obedience as a burden, not as the road to blessing.

But God intended our walks of faith to be great adventures, motivated by our love for Jesus Christ. Obedience is about expressing our love for and trust in God, not about avoiding unpleasant consequences. That is why John can say, "This is the love of God, that we keep His commandments; and His commandments are not burdensome" (1 John 5:3).

When we place our trust in the omnipotence of the Lord and act on His prompting, life becomes worthwhile and purposeful. We need not be afraid of the future because God already knows the outcome of our obedience—and we can trust in His promise that He works everything out for our good (Rom. 8:28). Although we may not understand how, we are confident that the Lord is continuously moving us through a variety of circumstances toward His overriding purpose for our lives. However, if we fail to obey Him because of a mistaken desire for safety, we reject the opportunity for God to demonstrate His awesome power in us.

Small choices to submit to God's will may seem insignificant, but they lead toward a lifetime of walking with Him. And as His children, we should ask Him to lead us each day. "What would You have me say here, Lord?" or "What is the best decision now?" We must learn to listen to our heavenly Father and remain sensitive to the quiet voice that prompts us throughout the day. Isaiah says, "Your ears will hear a word behind you, 'This is the way, walk in it,' whenever you turn to the right or to the left" (Is. 30:21).

When we keep our minds focused on Him, we begin to understand the significance of our decisions and how He is guiding us along the adventurous path of His will. Ultimately, this awareness will lead to a fulfilling, meaningful life of walking with the Lord and receiving His best for us.

As you look at the day ahead of you—what is *your* next step of obedience? No matter how He directs you, trust Him and do exactly as He says. You'll be glad you did. ◈

---

running with water on the day of the great slaughter, when the towers fall.
26 The light of the moon will be as the light of the sun, and the light of the sun will be seven times *brighter*, like the light of seven days, on the day the LORD binds up the fracture of His people and heals the bruise He has inflicted.
27 Behold, the name of the LORD
   comes from a remote place;
   Burning is His anger and dense is
      His smoke;
   His lips are filled with indignation
   And His tongue is like a consuming
      fire;
28 His breath is like an overflowing
      torrent,
   Which reaches to the neck,
   To shake the nations back and forth
      in a sieve,
   And to *put* in the jaws of the peoples
      the bridle which leads to ruin.
29 You will have songs as in the night
      when you keep the festival,
   And gladness of heart as when one
      marches to *the sound of* the flute,

To go to the mountain of the LORD,
   to the Rock of Israel.
30 And the LORD will cause His voice
      of authority to be heard,
   And the descending of His arm to
      be seen in fierce anger,
   And *in* the flame of a consuming fire
   In cloudburst, downpour and
      hailstones.
31 For at the voice of the LORD Assyria
      will be terrified,
   When He strikes with the rod.
32 And every blow of the rod of
      punishment,
   Which the LORD will lay on him,
   Will be with *the music of*
      tambourines and lyres;
   And in battles, brandishing
      weapons, He will fight them.
33 For Topheth has long been ready,
   Indeed, it has been prepared for the
      king.
   He has made it deep and large,
   A pyre of fire with plenty of wood;
   The breath of the LORD, like a
      torrent of brimstone, sets it afire.

➤ **31** WOE to those who go down to
Egypt for help
And rely on horses,
And trust in chariots because they
are many
And in horsemen because they are
very strong,
But they do not look to the Holy
One of Israel, nor seek the LORD!

2 Yet He also is wise and will bring
disaster
And does not retract His words,
But will arise against the house of
evildoers
And against the help of the workers
of iniquity.

3 Now the Egyptians are men and not
God,
And their horses are flesh and not
spirit;
So the LORD will stretch out His hand,
And he who helps will stumble
And he who is helped will fall,
And all of them will come to an end
together.

4 For thus says the LORD to me,
"As the lion or the young lion growls
over his prey,
Against which a band of shepherds
is called out,
And he will not be terrified at their
voice nor disturbed at their noise,
So will the LORD of hosts come
down to wage war on Mount Zion
and on its hill."

5 Like flying birds so the LORD of
hosts will protect Jerusalem.
He will protect and deliver *it*;
He will pass over and rescue *it*.

6 Return to Him from whom you have
deeply defected, O sons of Israel.

7 For in that day every man will cast
away his silver idols and his gold idols,
which your sinful hands have made for
you as a sin.

LIFE LESSONS

➤ **Isaiah 31:1 — *Woe to those who go
down to Egypt for help and rely on
horses.***

*T*o what do you instinctively turn for
help, other than God? Those other
things may seem more practical to eyes
of flesh, but only God provides aid that
will endure and that leads to victory.

---

8 And the Assyrian will fall by a
sword not of man,
And a sword not of man will devour
him.
So he will not escape the sword,
And his young men will become
forced laborers.

9 "His rock will pass away because of
panic,
And his princes will be terrified at
the standard,"
Declares the LORD, whose fire is
in Zion and whose furnace is in
Jerusalem.

32 BEHOLD, a king will reign
righteously
And princes will rule justly.

2 Each will be like a refuge from the
wind
And a shelter from the storm,
Like streams of water in a dry
country,
Like the shade of a huge rock in a
parched land.

3 Then the eyes of those who see will
not be blinded,
And the ears of those who hear will
listen.

4 The mind of the hasty will discern
the truth,
And the tongue of the stammerers
will hasten to speak clearly.

5 No longer will the fool be called
noble,
Or the rogue be spoken of *as*
generous.

6 For a fool speaks nonsense,
And his heart inclines toward
wickedness:
To practice ungodliness and to
speak error against the LORD,
To keep the hungry person
unsatisfied
And to withhold drink from the
thirsty.

7 As for a rogue, his weapons are evil;
He devises wicked schemes
To destroy *the* afflicted with slander,
Even though *the* needy one speaks
what is right.

8 But the noble man devises noble
plans;
And by noble plans he stands.

9 Rise up, you women who are at ease,
And hear my voice;
Give ear to my word,
You complacent daughters.

10 Within a year and *a few* days
    You will be troubled, O complacent
    daughters;
    For the vintage is ended,
    And the *fruit* gathering will not come.
11 Tremble, you *women* who are at
    ease;
    Be troubled, you complacent
    daughters;
    Strip, undress and put *sackcloth* on
    your waist,
12 Beat your breasts for the pleasant
    fields, for the fruitful vine,
13 For the land of my people *in which*
    thorns *and* briars shall come up;
    Yea, for all the joyful houses *and for*
    the jubilant city.
14 Because the palace has been
    abandoned, the populated city
    forsaken.
    Hill and watch-tower have become
    caves forever,
    A delight for wild donkeys, a
    pasture for flocks;
15 Until the Spirit is poured out upon
    us from on high,
    And the wilderness becomes a
    fertile field,
    And the fertile field is considered as
    a forest.
16 Then justice will dwell in the
    wilderness
    And righteousness will abide in the
    fertile field.
17 And the work of righteousness will
    be peace,
    And the service of righteousness,
    quietness and confidence forever.
18 Then my people will live in a
    peaceful habitation,
    And in secure dwellings and in
    undisturbed resting places;
19 And it will hail when the forest
    comes down,
    And the city will be utterly laid low.
20 How blessed will you be, you who
    sow beside all waters,
    Who let out freely the ox and the
    donkey.

Psalm 108:7–13

7   God has spoken in His holiness:
    "I will exult, I will portion out
    Shechem

And measure out the valley of
Succoth.
8   "Gilead is Mine, Manasseh is Mine;
    Ephraim also is the helmet of My
    head;
    Judah is My scepter.
9   "Moab is My washbowl;
    Over Edom I shall throw My shoe;
    Over Philistia I will shout aloud."
10 Who will bring me into the besieged
    city?
    Who will lead me to Edom?
11 Have not You Yourself, O God,
    rejected us?
    And will You not go forth with our
    armies, O God?
12 Oh give us help against the adversary,
    For deliverance by man is in vain.
13 Through God we will do valiantly,
    And it is He who shall tread down
    our adversaries.

Proverbs 25:23, 24

23 The north wind brings forth rain,
    And a backbiting tongue, an angry
    countenance.
24 It is better to live in a corner of the
    roof
    Than in a house shared with a
    contentious woman.

2 Corinthians 11:16–33

16 Again I say, let no one think me
foolish; but if *you do,* receive me even as
foolish, so that I also may boast a little.
17 What I am saying, I am not saying as
the Lord would, but as in foolishness, in
this confidence of boasting.

LIFE LESSONS

➤ **Psalm 108:12** — *Oh give us help
against the adversary, for deliverance by
man is in vain.*

The real question is, "Where do we
go *first* when trouble hits?" Do we
rush to secure the aid of a friend or
relative? Or do we take our problems
directly to the Lord, and ask Him to send
us the help we need?

18 Since many boast according to the flesh, I will boast also.

19 For you, being *so* wise, tolerate the foolish gladly.

20 For you tolerate it if anyone enslaves you, anyone devours you, anyone takes advantage of you, anyone exalts himself, anyone hits you in the face.

21 To *my* shame I *must* say that we have been weak *by comparison*.

But in whatever respect anyone *else* is bold—I speak in foolishness—I am just as bold myself.

22 Are they Hebrews? So am I. Are they Israelites? So am I. Are they descendants of Abraham? So am I.

23 Are they servants of Christ?—I speak as if insane—I more so; in far more labors, in far more imprisonments, beaten times without number, often in danger of death.

24 Five times I received from the Jews thirty-nine *lashes*.

25 Three times I was beaten with rods, once I was stoned, three times I was shipwrecked, a night and a day I have spent in the deep.

26 *I have been* on frequent journeys, in dangers from rivers, dangers from robbers, dangers from *my* countrymen, dangers from the Gentiles, dangers in the city, dangers in the wilderness, dangers on the sea, dangers among false brethren;

27 *I have been* in labor and hardship, through many sleepless nights, in hunger and thirst, often without food, in cold and exposure.

28 Apart from *such* external things, there is the daily pressure on me *of* concern for all the churches.

29 Who is weak without my being ◄ weak? Who is led into sin without my intense concern?

30 If I have to boast, I will boast of what pertains to my weakness.

31 The God and Father of the Lord Jesus, He who is blessed forever, knows that I am not lying.

32 In Damascus the ethnarch under Aretas the king was guarding the city of the Damascenes in order to seize me,

33 and I was let down in a basket through a window in the wall, and *so* escaped his hands.

LIFE LESSONS

➤ **2 Corinthians 11:29 —** *Who is led into sin without my intense concern?*

The apostle Paul had been through so much in his obedience to the Lord, yet God worked through those trials to transform him into an effective minister of the gospel. He understood weakness and temptation, and he had experienced physical pain, sorrow, frustration, persecution, and fear. He could speak to people's deepest concerns and needs. Likewise, the Lord will use adversity in our lives to bring us into a deeper relationship with Himself and also so we will be able to reach those who need Him.

Isaiah 33:1—34:17

33 WOE to you, O destroyer,
While you were not destroyed;
And he who is treacherous, while
others did not deal treacherously
with him.
As soon as you finish destroying,
you will be destroyed;
As soon as you cease to deal
treacherously, *others* will deal
treacherously with you.

➤ 2 O LORD, be gracious to us; we have
waited for You.

Be their strength every morning,
Our salvation also in the time of
distress.

3 At the sound of the tumult peoples
flee;
At the lifting up of Yourself nations
disperse.

4 Your spoil is gathered *as* the
caterpillar gathers;
As locusts rushing about men rush
about on it.

5 The LORD is exalted, for He dwells
on high;
He has filled Zion with justice and
righteousness.

> **Isaiah 33:2 — *Be their strength every morning.***

*W*hen you first get out of bed in the morning, do you go to the Lord in prayer? Each one of us should begin his or her day by dedicating it to Him and gratefully acknowledging His love, power, wisdom, and guidance. The awareness of His presence will surely energize us for whatever is ahead.

6   And He will be the stability of your times,
     A wealth of salvation, wisdom and knowledge;
     The fear of the LORD is his treasure.

7   Behold, their brave men cry in the streets,
     The ambassadors of peace weep bitterly.

8   The highways are desolate, the traveler has ceased,
     He has broken the covenant, he has despised the cities,
     He has no regard for man.

9   The land mourns *and* pines away,
     Lebanon is shamed *and* withers;
     Sharon is like a desert plain,
     And Bashan and Carmel lose *their* foliage.

10 "Now I will arise," says the LORD,
     "Now I will be exalted, now I will be lifted up.

11 "You have conceived chaff, you will give birth to stubble;
     My breath will consume you like a fire.

12 "The peoples will be burned to lime,
     Like cut thorns which are burned in the fire.

13 "You who are far away, hear what I have done;
     And you who are near, acknowledge My might."

14 Sinners in Zion are terrified;
     Trembling has seized the godless.
     "Who among us can live with the consuming fire?
     Who among us can live with continual burning?"

15 He who walks righteously and speaks with sincerity,
     He who rejects unjust gain
     And shakes his hands so that they hold no bribe;

He who stops his ears from hearing about bloodshed
And shuts his eyes from looking upon evil;

16 He will dwell on the heights,
     His refuge will be the impregnable rock;
     His bread will be given *him*,
     His water will be sure.

17 Your eyes will see the King in His beauty;
     They will behold a far-distant land.

18 Your heart will meditate on terror:
     "Where is he who counts?
     Where is he who weighs?
     Where is he who counts the towers?"

19 You will no longer see a fierce people,
     A people of unintelligible speech which no one comprehends,
     Of a stammering tongue which no one understands.

20 Look upon Zion, the city of our appointed feasts;
     Your eyes will see Jerusalem, an undisturbed habitation,
     A tent which will not be folded;
     Its stakes will never be pulled up,
     Nor any of its cords be torn apart.

21 But there the majestic *One*, the LORD, will be for us
     A place of rivers *and* wide canals
     On which no boat with oars will go,
     And on which no mighty ship will pass—

22 For the LORD is our judge,
     The LORD is our lawgiver,
     The LORD is our king;
     He will save us—

23 Your tackle hangs slack;
     It cannot hold the base of its mast firmly,
     Nor spread out the sail.
     Then the prey of an abundant spoil will be divided;
     The lame will take the plunder.

> **Isaiah 33:22 — *The LORD is our king; He will save us.***

*G*od is our Judge—He decides whether our deeds are good or evil (2 Cor. 5:10). He is our Lawgiver—He instructs us how to live. And He is our King—He rules over all. How amazing that He is also our Savior!

24 And no resident will say, "I am sick";
The people who dwell there will be
forgiven *their* iniquity.

34

DRAW near, O nations, to hear;
and listen, O peoples!
Let the earth and all it contains
hear, and the world and all that
springs from it.

2 For the LORD's indignation is
against all the nations,
And *His* wrath against all their
armies;
He has utterly destroyed them,
He has given them over to slaughter.

3 So their slain will be thrown out,
And their corpses will give off their
stench,
And the mountains will be drenched
with their blood.

➤ 4 And all the host of heaven will wear
away,
And the sky will be rolled up like a
scroll;
All their hosts will also wither
away
As a leaf withers from the vine,
Or as *one* withers from the fig tree.

5 For My sword is satiated in heaven,
Behold it shall descend for
judgment upon Edom
And upon the people whom I have
devoted to destruction.

6 The sword of the LORD is filled with
blood,
It is sated with fat, with the blood of
lambs and goats,
With the fat of the kidneys of rams.
For the LORD has a sacrifice in
Bozrah
And a great slaughter in the land of
Edom.

7 Wild oxen will also fall with them
And young bulls with strong ones;
Thus their land will be soaked with
blood,

And their dust become greasy with
fat.

8 For the LORD has a day of
vengeance,
A year of recompense for the cause
of Zion.

9 Its streams will be turned into pitch,
And its loose earth into brimstone,
And its land will become burning
pitch.

10 It will not be quenched night or day;
Its smoke will go up forever.
From generation to generation it
will be desolate;
None will pass through it forever
and ever.

11 But pelican and hedgehog will
possess it,
And owl and raven will dwell in it;
And He will stretch over it the line
of desolation
And the plumb line of emptiness.

12 Its nobles—there is no one there
Whom they may proclaim king—
And all its princes will be nothing.

13 Thorns will come up in its fortified
towers,
Nettles and thistles in its fortified
cities;
It will also be a haunt of jackals
And an abode of ostriches.

14 The desert creatures will meet with
the wolves,
The hairy goat also will cry to its
kind;
Yes, the night monster will settle
there
And will find herself a resting place.

15 The tree snake will make its nest
and lay *eggs* there,
And it will hatch and gather *them*
under its protection.
Yes, the hawks will be gathered
there,
Every one with its kind.

16 Seek from the book of the LORD,
and read:
Not one of these will be missing;
None will lack its mate.
For His mouth has commanded,
And His Spirit has gathered them.

17 He has cast the lot for them,
And His hand has divided it to them
by line.
They shall possess it forever;
From generation to generation they
will dwell in it.

LIFE LESSONS

➤ **Isaiah 34:4 —** *All the host of heaven
will wear away, and the sky will be rolled
up like a scroll.*

*P*eter saw this same staggering event,
and asked, "Since all these things
are to be destroyed in this way, what
sort of people ought you to be in holy
conduct and godliness?" (2 Pet. 3:11).

Psalm 109:1–5

For the choir director. A Psalm of David.

109 O GOD of my praise,
Do not be silent!

2   For they have opened the wicked
and deceitful mouth against me;
They have spoken against me with a
lying tongue.

3   They have also surrounded me with
words of hatred,
And fought against me without cause.

➤ 4   In return for my love they act as my
accusers;
But I am *in* prayer.

5   Thus they have repaid me evil for
good
And hatred for my love.

Proverbs 25:25, 26

25   *Like* cold water to a weary soul,
So is good news from a distant land.

26   *Like* a trampled spring and a
polluted well
Is a righteous man who gives way
before the wicked.

2 Corinthians 12:1–21

12 BOASTING is necessary, though it
is not profitable; but I will go on to
visions and revelations of the Lord.

2   I know a man in Christ who fourteen
years ago—whether in the body I do not
know, or out of the body I do not know,
God knows—such a man was caught up
to the third heaven.

3   And I know how such a man—
whether in the body or apart from the
body I do not know, God knows—

4   was caught up into Paradise and
heard inexpressible words, which a man
is not permitted to speak.

5   On behalf of such a man I will boast;
but on my own behalf I will not boast,
except in regard to *my* weaknesses.

6   For if I do wish to boast I will not be
foolish, for I will be speaking the truth;
but I refrain *from this,* so that no one will
credit me with more than he sees *in* me or
hears from me.

7   Because of the surpassing greatness
of the revelations, for this reason, to keep
me from exalting myself, there was given
me a thorn in the flesh, a messenger of
Satan to torment me—to keep me from
exalting myself!

8   Concerning this I implored the Lord
three times that it might leave me.

9   And He has said to me, "My grace is
sufficient for you, for power is perfected
in weakness." Most gladly, therefore, I
will rather boast about my weaknesses,
so that the power of Christ may dwell in
me.

10   Therefore I am well content with
weaknesses, with insults, with distresses,
with persecutions, with difficulties, for
Christ's sake; for when I am weak, then I
am strong.

11   I have become foolish; you yourselves compelled me. Actually I should
have been commended by you, for in no
respect was I inferior to the most eminent
apostles, even though I am a nobody.

12   The signs of a true apostle were performed among you with all perseverance,
by signs and wonders and miracles.

13   For in what respect were you treated
as inferior to the rest of the churches,
except that I myself did not become a
burden to you? Forgive me this wrong!

14   Here for this third time I am ready to
come to you, and I will not be a burden to
you; for I do not seek what is yours, but
you; for children are not responsible to
save up for *their* parents, but parents for
their children.

15   I will most gladly spend and be ex-
pended for your souls. If I love you more,
am I to be loved less?

16   But be that as it may, I did not burden you myself; nevertheless, crafty fellow that I am, I took you in by deceit.

17   *Certainly* I have not taken advan-

LIFE LESSONS

 **Psalm 109:4 — *In return for my love
they act as my accusers; but I am in
prayer.***

*W*hen someone betrays us or turns
against us, God instructs us not
to seek revenge but to seek His face in
prayer. He knows how to best deal with
the situation, and we need to hear from
Him.

What value could there possibly be in weakness?

2 CORINTHIANS 12:9

*N*one of us can escape the pressures of life. Most of us know what it feels like to be disappointed. We know the painfulness of embarrassment, the sting of rejection, and the sorrow of failure. There will always be times when our circumstances seem to be overwhelming.

What is out of control in your life? Is there a financial need? Maybe you face a relationship crisis and are urgently praying for God's wisdom.

Regardless of your situation, you can trust this principle: *Whatever brings you to your knees in weakness carries the greatest potential for your personal success and spiritual victory.*

Even though Paul could have listed many personal accomplishments, he chose to tell his audience what he saw as the key to experiencing a victorious life: accepting his weakness so that the strength of Christ might live fully in him. "I will rather boast about my weaknesses, so that the power of Christ may dwell in me" (2 Cor. 12:9).

We do not know the trial that Paul faced;

he called it a "thorn in the flesh" (v. 7). In the Greek, the word thorn means a stake used for torturing or impaling someone—no gentle affliction! He writes that it buffeted him, indicating that the trial was either ongoing or recurring. When the apostle felt he could no longer withstand the blows, God reassured him that His grace was sufficient for anything he faced.

Strength that withstands the stresses and blows of this life comes from only one Source—the eternal, indwelling presence of God. What the world views as strong is really nothing more than weakness under wraps.

When we accept our weaknesses and the fact that we cannot handle life on our own, God goes to work. He sends encouragement and a sense of creativity, helping us to try new avenues that lead to hope and fresh beginnings.

Are you weary from trying? Has exhaustion left its mark? Are you afraid others will see your weaknesses and laugh? Could a thorn in your life expose your deepest fear? Let it go. Release your fears to Jesus who loves you. Let Him strengthen you. Nothing compares to the freedom that waits for you within His loving arms. Nothing will ever bring more completion to your heart and soul than knowing the unconditional love of God. It is yours today—if you choose it.

---

tage of you through any of those whom I have sent to you, have I?
18 I urged Titus *to go*, and I sent the brother with him. Titus did not take any advantage of you, did he? Did we not conduct ourselves in the same spirit *and walk* in the same steps?
19 All this time you have been thinking that we are defending ourselves to you. *Actually*, it is in the sight of God that we have been speaking in Christ; and all for your upbuilding, beloved.
20 For I am afraid that perhaps when

I come I may find you to be not what I wish and may be found by you to be not what you wish; that perhaps *there will be* strife, jealousy, angry tempers, disputes, slanders, gossip, arrogance, disturbances;
21 I am afraid that when I come again ◄ my God may humiliate me before you, and I may mourn over many of those who have sinned in the past and not repented of the impurity, immorality and sensuality which they have practiced.

LIFE LESSONS

➤ **2 Corinthians 12:14** — *I will not be a burden to you; for I do not seek what is yours, but you.*

*P*aul lived the way he did as a reflection of how God worked in his own life. He didn't want the material resources of his friends; he wanted *them*. Just so, God doesn't need or want our possessions—He wants *us*.

➤ **2 Corinthians 12:21** — *I may mourn over many of those who have sinned in the past and not repented.*

*I*f God's Word condemns some practice, it's wrong, regardless of how we may feel about it. It is a serious thing to sin against the Lord, know it, and not repent of it. Unrepentant sin always brings the discipline of God.

Isaiah 35:1—36:22

35 THE wilderness and the desert will be glad,
And the Arabah will rejoice and blossom;
Like the crocus
2 It will blossom profusely
And rejoice with rejoicing and shout of joy.
The glory of Lebanon will be given to it,
The majesty of Carmel and Sharon.
They will see the glory of the LORD,
The majesty of our God.
3 Encourage the exhausted, and strengthen the feeble.
4 Say to those with anxious heart,
"Take courage, fear not.
Behold, your God will come *with* vengeance;
The recompense of God will come,
But He will save you,"
5 Then the eyes of the blind will be opened
And the ears of the deaf will be unstopped.
6 Then the lame will leap like a deer,
And the tongue of the mute will shout for joy.
For waters will break forth in the wilderness
And streams in the Arabah.
7 The scorched land will become a pool
And the thirsty ground springs of water;
In the haunt of jackals, its resting place,
Grass *becomes* reeds and rushes.
8 A highway will be there, a roadway,
And it will be called the Highway of Holiness.
The unclean will not travel on it,

But it *will* be for him who walks *that* way,
And fools will not wander *on it.*
9 No lion will be there,
Nor will any vicious beast go up on it;
These will not be found there.
But the redeemed will walk *there,*
10 And the ransomed of the LORD will return
And come with joyful shouting to Zion,
With everlasting joy upon their heads.
They will find gladness and joy,
And sorrow and sighing will flee away.

36 NOW in the fourteenth year of King Hezekiah, Sennacherib king of Assyria came up against all the fortified cities of Judah and seized them.
2 And the king of Assyria sent Rabshakeh from Lachish to Jerusalem to King Hezekiah with a large army. And he stood by the conduit of the upper pool on the highway of the fuller's field.
3 Then Eliakim the son of Hilkiah, who was over the household, and Shebna the scribe, and Joah the son of Asaph, the recorder, came out to him.
4 Then Rabshakeh said to them, "Say now to Hezekiah, 'Thus says the great king, the king of Assyria, "What is this confidence that you have?
5 "I say, 'Your counsel and strength for the war are only empty words.' Now on whom do you rely, that you have rebelled against me?
6 "Behold, you rely on the staff of this crushed reed, *even* on Egypt, on which if a man leans, it will go into his hand and pierce it. So is Pharaoh king of Egypt to all who rely on him.
7 "But if you say to me, 'We trust in the LORD our God,' is it not He whose high places and whose altars Hezekiah has taken away and has said to Judah and to Jerusalem, 'You shall worship before this altar'?
8 "Now therefore, come make a bargain with my master the king of Assyria, and I will give you two thousand horses, if you are able on your part to set riders on them.
9 "How then can you repulse one official of the least of my master's servants and rely on Egypt for chariots and for horsemen?
10 "Have I now come up without the

LIFE LESSONS

➤ **Isaiah 35:2 — *They will see the glory of the LORD, the majesty of our God.***

*A*lthough we can experience some of the glory and excellence of God right now, "We see in a mirror dimly" (1 Cor. 13:12). One day, however, we will not only see His glory; we will share in it (Rom. 8:17).

WHAT THE BIBLE SAYS ABOUT ⊕

The Making of an Encourager

Isaiah 35:3, 4

Sometimes it takes only one word, a smile, or a grasp of the hand. Sometimes it means standing by someone during a particularly hard time and helping him or her not give in to despair.

What does encouragement mean to you? Can you recall a time when someone came alongside you for the sole purpose of lifting your spirits or making you smile?

Have you ever done that for a hurting person? It feels good to know you're loved. It feels especially good in those low moments when you can't see ahead clearly, when you don't grasp God's perspective and vision for your life. Isaiah 35:3, 4 admonishes, "Encourage the exhausted, and strengthen the feeble. Say to those with anxious heart, 'Take courage, fear not. Behold, your God will come with vengeance; the recompense of God will come, but He will save you.' "

The Father has given each of us special tasks within the body of Christ, and those with the gift of exhortation or encouragement (Rom. 12:8) can rejoice in their unique and tender ministries. But encouragement isn't strictly the domain of those to whom the Lord has given a special gift; it's not an activity exclusively for those with naturally bubbly or warm personalities. Encouragement is the wonderful, God-given function of everyone who belongs to Jesus Christ.

In the early days of the church, new believers badly needed encouragement. Societal pressures mounted, persecution multiplied, and few had access to the apostle's teaching (1 Thess. 3:1–10).

Very often, encouragement for the early church came in the form of a person, as it does today. Sometimes just the sight of a certain loved one can reinvigorate your spirits and remove your focus from yourself. Sometimes Paul sent Timothy. More than once, he sent his associate, Tychicus, as a special envoy of joy.

The ministry of encouragement is indispensible, both to you and to the body of Christ. There is no such thing as a person who doesn't need encouragement.

By seeking ways to daily encourage those with whom you interact, you further the potential for meaningful, Christ-centered relationships. As Paul told the persecuted Thessalonians, "Encourage one another and build up one another, just as you also are doing . . . Admonish the unruly, encourage the fainthearted, help the weak, be patient with everyone" (1 Thess. 5:11, 14). ⊕

LORD'S approval against this land to destroy it? The LORD said to me, 'Go up against this land and destroy it.'"'"
11 Then Eliakim and Shebna and Joah said to Rabshakeh, "Speak now to your

LIFE LESSONS

➤ **Isaiah 36:7 — "Is it not He whose high places and whose altars Hezekiah has taken away?"**

Hezekiah removed those altars out of obedience to God, and he trusted Him to protect Judah despite the Assyrian threat. Those who do not know the Lord simply cannot understand what true faith is (1 Cor. 1:18–31; 2:14, 15). Even though a place or a ritual may be considered religious, it does not necessarily honor the Lord. People may try to lump all faiths and spiritual practices together, but there is only one true God and one way to be saved (Acts 4:10–12).

servants in Aramaic, for we understand *it*; and do not speak with us in Judean in the hearing of the people who are on the wall."
12 But Rabshakeh said, "Has my master sent me only to your master and to you to speak these words, *and* not to the men who sit on the wall, *doomed* to eat their own dung and drink their own urine with you?"
13 Then Rabshakeh stood and cried with a loud voice in Judean and said, "Hear the words of the great king, the king of Assyria.
14 "Thus says the king, 'Do not let Hezekiah deceive you, for he will not be able to deliver you;
15 nor let Hezekiah make you trust in ◄ the LORD, saying, "The LORD will surely deliver us, this city will not be given into the hand of the king of Assyria."
16 'Do not listen to Hezekiah,' for thus says the king of Assyria, 'Make your peace

with me and come out to me, and eat each of his vine and each of his fig tree and drink each of the waters of his own cistern,
17 until I come and take you away to a land like your own land, a land of grain and new wine, a land of bread and vineyards.
18 'Beware that Hezekiah does not mislead you, saying, "The LORD will deliver us." Has any one of the gods of the nations delivered his land from the hand of the king of Assyria?
19 'Where are the gods of Hamath and Arpad? Where are the gods of Sepharvaim? And when have they delivered Samaria from my hand?
20 'Who among all the gods of these lands have delivered their land from my hand, that the LORD would deliver Jerusalem from my hand?'"
21 But they were silent and answered him not a word; for the king's commandment was, "Do not answer him."
22 Then Eliakim the son of Hilkiah, who was over the household, and Shebna the scribe and Joah the son of Asaph, the recorder, came to Hezekiah with their clothes torn and told him the words of Rabshakeh.

✦ Psalm 109:6–13

6 Appoint a wicked man over him,
 And let an accuser stand at his right hand.
7 When he is judged, let him come forth guilty,
 And let his prayer become sin.
8 Let his days be few;
 Let another take his office.
9 Let his children be fatherless
 And his wife a widow.

10 Let his children wander about and beg;
 And let them seek *sustenance* far from their ruined homes.
11 Let the creditor seize all that he has,
 And let strangers plunder the product of his labor.
12 Let there be none to extend lovingkindness to him,
 Nor any to be gracious to his fatherless children.
13 Let his posterity be cut off;
 In a following generation let their name be blotted out.

✦ Proverbs 25:27, 28

27 It is not good to eat much honey,
 Nor is it glory to search out one's own glory.
28 *Like* a city that is broken into *and* without walls
 Is a man who has no control over his spirit.

✦ 2 Corinthians 13:1–14

13 THIS is the third time I am coming to you. EVERY FACT IS TO BE CONFIRMED BY THE TESTIMONY OF TWO OR THREE WITNESSES.
2 I have previously said when present the second time, and though now absent I say in advance to those who have sinned in the past and to all the rest *as well*, that if I come again I will not spare *anyone*,
3 since you are seeking for proof of the Christ who speaks in me, and who is not weak toward you, but mighty in you.

4 For indeed He was crucified because of weakness, yet He lives because of the power of God. For we also are weak in Him, yet we will live with Him because of the power of God *directed* toward you.

➤ 5 Test yourselves *to see* if you are in the faith; examine yourselves! Or do you not recognize this about yourselves, that Jesus Christ is in you—unless indeed you fail the test?

6 But I trust that you will realize that we ourselves do not fail the test.

7 Now we pray to God that you do no wrong; not that we ourselves may appear approved, but that you may do what is right, even though we may appear unapproved.

8 For we can do nothing against the truth, but *only* for the truth.

9 For we rejoice when we ourselves are weak but you are strong; this we also pray for, that you be made complete.

10 For this reason I am writing these things while absent, so that when present I *need* not use severity, in accordance with the authority which the Lord gave me for building up and not for tearing down.

11 Finally, brethren, rejoice, be made complete, be comforted, be like-minded, live in peace; and the God of love and peace will be with you.

12 Greet one another with a holy kiss.

13 All the saints greet you.

14 The grace of the Lord Jesus Christ, ◄ and the love of God, and the fellowship of the Holy Spirit, be with you all.

LIFE LESSONS

➤ **2 Corinthians 13:5 — *Test yourselves to see if you are in the faith.***

*D*espite the Corinthians' problems, Paul could see their genuine spiritual gifts, their repentance, and their love for God, and he wanted these things to encourage them to further growth. Likewise, we must always make sure we are maturing in our walks with Him by examining whether or not we are expressing His likeness and character in increasing measure (2 Pet. 1:3–8).

➤ **2 Corinthians 13:14 — *The grace of the Lord Jesus Christ, and the love of God, and the fellowship of the Holy Spirit, be with you all.***

*I*n this simple but beautiful benediction, Paul calls attention to all three Persons of the Trinity. As the Godhead, He works together for our spiritual growth and for joy in the Christian life.

SEPTEMBER 23

 Isaiah 37:1—38:22

37 AND when King Hezekiah heard *it*, he tore his clothes, covered himself with sackcloth and entered the house of the LORD.

2 Then he sent Eliakim who was over the household with Shebna the scribe and the elders of the priests, covered with sackcloth, to Isaiah the prophet, the son of Amoz.

3 They said to him, "Thus says Hezekiah, 'This day is a day of distress, rebuke and rejection; for children have come to birth, and there is no strength to deliver.

➤ 4 'Perhaps the LORD your God will hear the words of Rabshakeh, whom his master the king of Assyria has sent to reproach the living God, and will rebuke the words which the LORD your God has heard. Therefore, offer a prayer for the remnant that is left.'"

5 So the servants of King Hezekiah came to Isaiah.

6 Isaiah said to them, "Thus you shall say to your master, 'Thus says the LORD, "Do not be afraid because of the words

---

LIFE LESSONS

➤ **Isaiah 37:4 — *"Offer a prayer for the remnant."***

*I*ndividual prayer is crucial, but corporate prayer is also important. Throughout the Bible we see godly leaders organizing their people to pray as a group. But how can we pray corporately if we never gather with God's people?

that you have heard, with which the servants of the king of Assyria have blasphemed Me.

7 "Behold, I will put a spirit in him so that he will hear a rumor and return to his own land. And I will make him fall by the sword in his own land."'"

8 Then Rabshakeh returned and found the king of Assyria fighting against Libnah, for he had heard that the king had left Lachish.

9 When he heard *them* say concerning Tirhakah king of Cush, "He has come out to fight against you," and when he heard *it* he sent messengers to Hezekiah, saying,

10 "Thus you shall say to Hezekiah king of Judah, 'Do not let your God in whom you trust deceive you, saying, "Jerusalem will not be given into the hand of the king of Assyria."

11 'Behold, you have heard what the kings of Assyria have done to all the lands, destroying them completely. So will you be spared?

12 'Did the gods of those nations which my fathers have destroyed deliver them, *even* Gozan and Haran and Rezeph and the sons of Eden who *were* in Telassar?

13 'Where is the king of Hamath, the king of Arpad, the king of the city of Sepharvaim, *and of* Hena and Ivvah?'"

14 Then Hezekiah took the letter from the hand of the messengers and read it, and he went up to the house of the LORD and spread it out before the LORD.

15 Hezekiah prayed to the LORD saying,

16 "O LORD of hosts, the God of Israel, who is enthroned *above* the cherubim, You are the God, You alone, of all the kingdoms of the earth. You have made heaven and earth.

17 "Incline Your ear, O LORD, and hear; open Your eyes, O LORD, and see; and listen to all the words of Sennacherib, who sent *them* to reproach the living God.

18 "Truly, O LORD, the kings of Assyria have devastated all the countries and their lands,

19 and have cast their gods into the fire, for they were not gods but the work of men's hands, wood and stone. So they have destroyed them.

20 "Now, O LORD our God, deliver us from his hand that all the kingdoms of the earth may know that You alone, LORD, are God."

21 Then Isaiah the son of Amoz sent word to Hezekiah, saying, "Thus says the LORD, the God of Israel, 'Because you have prayed to Me about Sennacherib king of Assyria,

22 this is the word that the LORD has spoken against him:

"She has despised you and mocked you,
The virgin daughter of Zion;
She has shaken *her* head behind you,
The daughter of Jerusalem!

23 "Whom have you reproached and blasphemed?
And against whom have you raised *your* voice
And haughtily lifted up your eyes?
Against the Holy One of Israel!

24 "Through your servants you have reproached the Lord,
And you have said, 'With my many chariots I came up to the heights of the mountains,
To the remotest parts of Lebanon;
And I cut down its tall cedars *and* its choice cypresses.
And I will go to its highest peak, its thickest forest.

25 'I dug *wells* and drank waters,
And with the sole of my feet I dried up All the rivers of Egypt.'

26 "Have you not heard?
Long ago I did it,
From ancient times I planned it.
Now I have brought it to pass,
That you should turn fortified cities into ruinous heaps.

27 "Therefore their inhabitants were short of strength,
They were dismayed and put to shame;
They were *as* the vegetation of the field and *as* the green herb,
As grass on the housetops is scorched before it is grown up.

LIFE LESSONS

➤ Isaiah 37:20 — *"God, deliver us from his hand that all the kingdoms of the earth may know that You alone, LORD, are God."*

*H*ezekiah prayed that God would act on Judah's behalf so that the world might know that He is Lord. "He is a rewarder of those who seek Him" (Heb. 11:6).

28 "But I know your sitting down
    And your going out and your
        coming in
    And your raging against Me.
29 "Because of your raging against Me
    And because your arrogance has
        come up to My ears,
    Therefore I will put My hook in
        your nose
    And My bridle in your lips,
    And I will turn you back by the way
        which you came.
30 "Then this shall be the sign for you:
you will eat this year what grows of
itself, in the second year what springs
from the same, and in the third year sow,
reap, plant vineyards and eat their fruit.
31 "The surviving remnant of the house
of Judah will again take root downward
and bear fruit upward.
32 "For out of Jerusalem will go forth a
remnant and out of Mount Zion survivors. The zeal of the LORD of hosts will
perform this."'
33 "Therefore, thus says the LORD concerning the king of Assyria, 'He will not
come to this city or shoot an arrow there;
and he will not come before it with a
shield, or throw up a siege ramp against it.
34 'By the way that he came, by the same
he will return, and he will not come to
this city,' declares the LORD.
35 'For I will defend this city to save it
for My own sake and for My servant
David's sake.'"
36 Then the angel of the LORD went out
and struck 185,000 in the camp of the Assyrians; and when men arose early in the
morning, behold, all of these were dead.
37 So Sennacherib king of Assyria departed and returned *home* and lived at
Nineveh.
38 It came about as he was worshiping in the house of Nisroch his god, that
Adrammelech and Sharezer his sons
killed him with the sword; and they escaped into the land of Ararat. And Esarhaddon his son became king in his place.

38 IN those days Hezekiah became
mortally ill. And Isaiah the prophet
the son of Amoz came to him and said to
him, "Thus says the LORD, 'Set your house
in order, for you shall die and not live.'"
2 Then Hezekiah turned his face to the
wall and prayed to the LORD,
3 and said, "Remember now, O LORD, I
beseech You, how I have walked before

You in truth and with a whole heart, and
have done what is good in Your sight."
And Hezekiah wept bitterly.
4 Then the word of the LORD came to
Isaiah, saying,
5 "Go and say to Hezekiah, 'Thus says
the LORD, the God of your father David,
"I have heard your prayer, I have seen
your tears; behold, I will add fifteen
years to your life.
6 "I will deliver you and this city from
the hand of the king of Assyria; and I will
defend this city."'
7 "This shall be the sign to you from
the LORD, that the LORD will do this thing
that He has spoken:
8 "Behold, I will cause the shadow on
the stairway, which has gone down with
the sun on the stairway of Ahaz, to go
back ten steps." So the sun's *shadow*
went back ten steps on the stairway on
which it had gone down.
9 A writing of Hezekiah king of Judah
after his illness and recovery:
10 I said, "In the middle of my life
    I am to enter the gates of Sheol;
    I am to be deprived of the rest of my
        years."
11 I said, "I will not see the LORD,
    The LORD in the land of the living;
    I will look on man no more among
        the inhabitants of the world.
12 "Like a shepherd's tent my dwelling is
        pulled up and removed from me;
    As a weaver I rolled up my life.
    He cuts me off from the loom;
    From day until night You make an
        end of me.
13 "I composed *my soul* until morning.
    Like a lion—so He breaks all my
        bones,
    From day until night You make an
        end of me.
14 "Like a swallow, *like* a crane, so I ◁
    twitter;

LIFE LESSONS

➤ **Isaiah 38:14 —** *My eyes look wistfully
to the heights.*

*W*e should not feel surprised if God
seems to delay in delivering us from
some trouble. Sometimes He makes us
wait longer than we think we can hold
on. But genuine trust perseveres, no
matter what.

I moan like a dove;
My eyes look wistfully to the heights;
O Lord, I am oppressed, be my
security.
15 "What shall I say?
For He has spoken to me, and He
Himself has done it;
I will wander about all my years
because of the bitterness of my
soul.
16 "O Lord, by *these* things *men* live,
And in all these is the life of my spirit;
O restore me to health and let me live!
17 "Lo, for *my own* welfare I had great
bitterness;
It is You who has kept my soul from
the pit of nothingness,
For You have cast all my sins behind
Your back.
18 "For Sheol cannot thank You,
Death cannot praise You;
Those who go down to the pit
cannot hope for Your faithfulness.
19 "It is the living who give thanks to
You, as I do today;
A father tells his sons about Your
faithfulness.
20 "The LORD will surely save me;
So we will play my songs on
stringed instruments
All *the* days of our life at the house
of the LORD."
21 Now Isaiah had said, "Let them take
a cake of figs and apply it to the boil, that
he may recover."
22 Then Hezekiah had said, "What is
the sign that I shall go up to the house of
the LORD?"

Psalm 109:14–20

14 Let the iniquity of his fathers be
remembered before the LORD,
And do not let the sin of his mother
be blotted out.
15 Let them be before the LORD
continually,
That He may cut off their memory
from the earth;
16 Because he did not remember to
show lovingkindness,
But persecuted the afflicted and
needy man,
And the despondent in heart, to put
them to death.

17 He also loved cursing, so it came to
him;
And he did not delight in blessing,
so it was far from him.
18 But he clothed himself with cursing
as with his garment,
And it entered into his body like
water
And like oil into his bones.
19 Let it be to him as a garment with
which he covers himself,
And for a belt with which he
constantly girds himself.
20 Let this be the reward of my
accusers from the LORD,
And of those who speak evil against
my soul.

Proverbs 26:1

26 LIKE snow in summer and like
rain in harvest,
So honor is not fitting for a fool.

Galatians 1:1–24

1 PAUL, an apostle (not *sent* from men
nor through the agency of man, but
through Jesus Christ and God the Father,
who raised Him from the dead),
2 and all the brethren who are with
me,
To the churches of Galatia:
3 Grace to you and peace from God
our Father and the Lord Jesus Christ,
4 who gave Himself for our sins so
that He might rescue us from this present

LIFE LESSONS

➤ **Galatians 1:3, 4** — *. . . so that He
might rescue us from this present evil
age.*

*J*esus saved us out of this evil age—
a time when people do and worship whatever they please but find no
fulfillment, love, or comfort. He does
this so that we might become "blameless and innocent, children of God above
reproach in the midst of a crooked and
perverse generation, among whom you
appear as lights in the world" (Phil.
2:15).

ANSWERS TO LIFE'S QUESTIONS

How can I have God's peace?

GALATIANS 1:3

The key element in true, lasting peace is the presence of God. Isaiah says to God, "The steadfast of mind You will keep in perfect peace, because he trusts in You" (Is. 26:3). Christ is our peace—His presence is the presence of peace within us (Eph. 2:14). And so Jesus declares, "In Me you may have peace" (John 16:33).

What is this peace? It is an inner sense of contentment and quietness, regardless of life's circumstances. It is steadfast confidence in our ever-faithful, immutable heavenly Father. It is the presence of joy in the midst of unhappiness.

True peace does not merely dull our pain. A person who has genuine, godly peace can endure an avalanche of hardship and difficulty and still enjoy an inner peace that surpasses all human understanding. Why? Because it does not come from pleasant circumstances, nice events, or good things others may do for us. Instead, it is based on the fact that the Spirit of our holy, omnipotent, and never-changing God lives within us.

Does enjoying God's perfect peace mean that you'll never feel the effects of the storms raging around you? Hardly. But His peace is complete, adequate, and sufficient for anything you face. Keep in mind three keys to experiencing sustained peace.

1. *Focus on God.* Perfect peace comes when you fix your mind on God. You must discipline yourself to meditate on the Lord's presence and work. When you spend time concentrating on a problem, does it not seem to grow bigger? In the same way, you will have a greater sense of God's presence and provision as you fix your mind on Him.

2. *Trust Him.* You never have to worry about God acting too late or providing insufficient help. His timing and purposes are perfect. In fact, He uses your tribulations to reveal more of Himself to you. His Word is full of rock-solid promises, many of which involve granting you peace. Know that He will always honor them!

3. *Meditate on His Word.* Psalm 119:165 emphasizes that those who love God's Word have great peace. Your most precious material possession is your Bible. Every believer should love God's Word and feast on it daily. If you love it, you're going to believe what it says—and then it will guide and anchor your life.

---

evil age, according to the will of our God and Father,
5   to whom *be* the glory forevermore. Amen.
6   I am amazed that you are so quickly deserting Him who called you by the grace of Christ, for a different gospel;
7   which is *really* not another; only there are some who are disturbing you and want to distort the gospel of Christ.
➤ 8   But even if we, or an angel from heaven, should preach to you a gospel contrary to what we have preached to you, he is to be accursed!
9   As we have said before, so I say again now, if any man is preaching to you a gospel contrary to what you received, he is to be accursed!
10   For am I now seeking the favor of men, or of God? Or am I striving to please men? If I were still trying to please
✳ men, I would not be a bond-servant of Christ.
➤ 11   For I would have you know, brethren, that the gospel which was preached by me is not according to man.
12   For I neither received it from man,

nor was I taught it, but I *received it* through a revelation of Jesus Christ.
13   For you have heard of my former manner of life in Judaism, how I used

LIFE LESSONS

➤ **Galatians 1:8** — *Even if we, or an angel from heaven, should preach to you a gospel contrary to what we have preached to you, he is to be accursed.*

Whenever someone promotes a restored gospel, secret gospel, fresh gospel, or any other gospel that deviates from what the Bible clearly teaches, you must flee! That person promotes death, not life.

➤ **Galatians 1:11** — *The gospel which was preached by me is not according to man.*

The gospel of salvation by grace through faith—by which we receive new life through the risen Savior, Jesus Christ—is no human invention. Paul did not conceive it, nor did the other disciples. It comes directly from God.

to persecute the church of God beyond measure and tried to destroy it;

14 and I was advancing in Judaism beyond many of my contemporaries among my countrymen, being more extremely zealous for my ancestral traditions.

15 But when God, who had set me apart *even* from my mother's womb and called me through His grace, was pleased

16 to reveal His Son in me so that I might preach Him among the Gentiles, I did not immediately consult with flesh and blood,

17 nor did I go up to Jerusalem to those who were apostles before me; but I went away to Arabia, and returned once more to Damascus.

18 Then three years later I went up to Jerusalem to become acquainted with Cephas, and stayed with him fifteen days.

19 But I did not see any other of the apostles except James, the Lord's brother.

20 (Now in what I am writing to you, I assure you before God that I am not lying.)

21 Then I went into the regions of Syria and Cilicia.

22 I was *still* unknown by sight to the churches of Judea which were in Christ;

23 but only, they kept hearing, "He who once persecuted us is now preaching the faith which he once tried to destroy."

24 And they were glorifying God because of me.

SEPTEMBER 24

Isaiah 39:1—40:31

39 AT that time Merodach-baladan son of Baladan, king of Babylon, sent letters and a present to Hezekiah, for he heard that he had been sick and had recovered.

2 Hezekiah was pleased, and showed them *all* his treasure house, the silver and the gold and the spices and the precious oil and his whole armory and all that was found in his treasuries. There was nothing in his house nor in all his dominion that Hezekiah did not show them.

3 Then Isaiah the prophet came to King Hezekiah and said to him, "What did these men say, and from where have they come to you?" And Hezekiah said, "They have come to me from a far country, from Babylon."

4 He said, "What have they seen in your house?" So Hezekiah answered, "They have seen all that is in my house; there is nothing among my treasuries that I have not shown them."

5 Then Isaiah said to Hezekiah, "Hear the word of the LORD of hosts,

6 'Behold, the days are coming when all that is in your house and all that your fathers have laid up in store to this day will be carried to Babylon; nothing will be left,' says the LORD.

7 'And *some* of your sons who will issue from you, whom you will beget, will be taken away, and they will become officials in the palace of the king of Babylon.'"

8 Then Hezekiah said to Isaiah, "The word of the LORD which you have spoken is good." For he thought, "For there will be peace and truth in my days."

40 "COMFORT, O comfort My people," says your God.

2 "Speak kindly to Jerusalem;
And call out to her, that her warfare has ended,
That her iniquity has been removed,
That she has received of the LORD'S hand
Double for all her sins."

3 A voice is calling,
"Clear the way for the LORD in the wilderness;

LIFE LESSONS

> **Isaiah 40:1 — *"Comfort, O comfort My people," says your God.***

*G*od revealed Israel's destruction and her eventual re-gathering and redemption to Isaiah. Even before His judgment fell, He had a plan in place to show His people grace. That is the Father's way—bringing hope in the midst of suffering.

Make smooth in the desert a
highway for our God.
4 "Let every valley be lifted up,
And every mountain and hill be
made low;
And let the rough ground become a
plain,
And the rugged terrain a broad
valley;
5 Then the glory of the LORD will be
revealed,
And all flesh will see *it* together;
For the mouth of the LORD has
spoken."
6 A voice says, "Call out."
Then he answered, "What shall I call
out?"
All flesh is grass, and all its
loveliness is like the flower of the
field.
7 The grass withers, the flower fades,
When the breath of the LORD blows
upon it;
Surely the people are grass.
➤ 8 The grass withers, the flower fades,
But the word of our God stands
forever.
9 Get yourself up on a high mountain,
O Zion, bearer of good news,
Lift up your voice mightily,
O Jerusalem, bearer of good news;
Lift *it* up, do not fear.
Say to the cities of Judah,
"Here is your God!"
10 Behold, the Lord GOD will come
with might,
With His arm ruling for Him.
Behold, His reward is with Him
And His recompense before Him.
11 Like a shepherd He will tend His
flock,
In His arm He will gather the
lambs
And carry *them* in His bosom;

He will gently lead the nursing
ewes.
12 Who has measured the waters in
the hollow of His hand,
And marked off the heavens by the
span,
And calculated the dust of the earth
by the measure,
And weighed the mountains in a
balance
And the hills in a pair of scales?
13 Who has directed the Spirit of the
LORD,
Or as His counselor has informed
Him?
14 With whom did He consult and *who*
gave Him understanding?
And *who* taught Him in the path
of justice and taught Him
knowledge
And informed Him of the way of
understanding?
15 Behold, the nations are like a drop
from a bucket,
And are regarded as a speck of dust
on the scales;
Behold, He lifts up the islands like
fine dust.
16 Even Lebanon is not enough to burn,
Nor its beasts enough for a burnt
offering.
17 All the nations are as nothing before
Him,
They are regarded by Him as less
than nothing and meaningless.
18 To whom then will you liken God?
Or what likeness will you compare
with Him?
19 *As for* the idol, a craftsman casts it,
A goldsmith plates it with gold,
And a silversmith *fashions* chains of
silver.
20 He who is too impoverished for
such an offering
Selects a tree that does not rot;
He seeks out for himself a skillful
craftsman
To prepare an idol that will not
totter.
21 Do you not know? Have you not
heard?
Has it not been declared to you
from the beginning?
Have you not understood from the
foundations of the earth?
22 It is He who sits above the circle of
the earth,

LIFE LESSONS

➤ **Isaiah 40:8 —** *"The grass withers, the flower fades, but the word of our God stands forever."*

*C*ritics have attacked the Bible for
centuries, but it still stands. They die;
it remains. Their works are forgotten; it
still changes lives through the power of
the Holy Spirit. We can depend on the
trustworthy Word of God.

And its inhabitants are like
grasshoppers,
Who stretches out the heavens like
a curtain
And spreads them out like a tent to
dwell in.

23 He *it is* who reduces rulers to
nothing,
Who makes the judges of the earth
meaningless.

24 Scarcely have they been planted,
Scarcely have they been sown,
Scarcely has their stock taken root
in the earth,
But He merely blows on them, and
they wither,
And the storm carries them away
like stubble.

➤ 25 "To whom then will you liken Me
That I would be *his* equal?" says the
Holy One.

26 Lift up your eyes on high
And see who has created these
stars,
The One who leads forth their host
by number,
He calls them all by name;
Because of the greatness of His
might and the strength of *His*
power,
Not one *of them* is missing.

27 Why do you say, O Jacob, and
assert, O Israel,
"My way is hidden from the LORD,
And the justice due me escapes the
notice of my God"?

28 Do you not know? Have you not
heard?
The Everlasting God, the LORD, the
Creator of the ends of the earth
Does not become weary or tired.
His understanding is inscrutable.

29 He gives strength to the weary,
And to *him who* lacks might He
increases power.

30 Though youths grow weary and
tired,
And vigorous young men stumble
badly,

31 Yet those who wait for the LORD
Will gain new strength;
They will mount up *with* wings like
eagles,
They will run and not get tired,
They will walk and not become
weary.

◈ Psalm 109:21–25

21 But You, O GOD, the Lord, deal
kindly with me for Your name's
sake;
Because Your lovingkindness is
good, deliver me;

22 For I am afflicted and needy,
And my heart is wounded within
me.

23 I am passing like a shadow when it
lengthens;
I am shaken off like the locust.

24 My knees are weak from fasting,
And my flesh has grown lean,
without fatness.

25 I also have become a reproach to
them;
When they see me, they wag their
head.

◈ Proverbs 26:2

2 Like a sparrow in *its* flitting, like a
swallow in *its* flying,
So a curse without cause does not
alight.

◈ Galatians 2:1–21

2 THEN after an interval of fourteen
years I went up again to Jerusalem
with Barnabas, taking Titus along also.
2 It was because of a revelation that I
went up; and I submitted to them the gospel which I preach among the Gentiles,
but *I did so* in private to those who were
of reputation, for fear that I might be running, or had run, in vain.

LIFE LESSONS

➤ Isaiah 40:25 — *"To whom then will
you liken Me that I would be his equal?"
says the Holy One.*

*G*od has no rivals, no peers, and no
equals. Satan is merely a fallen angel.
God therefore deserves all our trust, and
promises to reward that trust in ways
beyond our comprehension.

3 But not even Titus, who was with me, though he was a Greek, was compelled to be circumcised.

➤ 4 But *it was* because of the false brethren secretly brought in, who had sneaked in to spy out our liberty which we have in Christ Jesus, in order to bring us into bondage.

5 But we did not yield in subjection to them for even an hour, so that the truth of the gospel would remain with you.

6 But from those who were of high reputation (what they were makes no difference to me; God shows no partiality)—well, those who were of reputation contributed nothing to me.

7 But on the contrary, seeing that I had been entrusted with the gospel to the uncircumcised, just as Peter *had been* to the circumcised

8 (for He who effectually worked for Peter in *his* apostleship to the circumcised effectually worked for me also to the Gentiles),

9 and recognizing the grace that had been given to me, James and Cephas and John, who were reputed to be pillars, gave to me and Barnabas the right hand of fellowship, so that we *might go* to the Gentiles and they to the circumcised.

10 *They* only *asked* us to remember the poor—the very thing I also was eager to do.

11 But when Cephas came to Antioch, I opposed him to his face, because he stood condemned.

12 For prior to the coming of certain men from James, he used to eat with the Gentiles; but when they came, he *began* to withdraw and hold himself aloof, fearing the party of the circumcision.

➤ 13 The rest of the Jews joined him in hypocrisy, with the result that even Barnabas was carried away by their hypocrisy.

14 But when I saw that they were not straightforward about the truth of the gospel, I said to Cephas in the presence of all, "If you, being a Jew, live like the Gentiles and not like the Jews, how *is it that* you compel the Gentiles to live like Jews?

15 "We *are* Jews by nature and not sinners from among the Gentiles;

16 nevertheless knowing that a man is not justified by the works of the Law but through faith in Christ Jesus, even we have believed in Christ Jesus, so that we may be justified by faith in Christ and not by the works of the Law; since by the works of the Law no flesh will be justified.

17 "But if, while seeking to be justified in Christ, we ourselves have also been found sinners, is Christ then a minister of sin? May it never be!

18 "For if I rebuild what I have *once* destroyed, I prove myself to be a transgressor.

19 "For through the Law I died to the Law, so that I might live to God.

20 "I have been crucified with Christ; ◄ and it is no longer I who live, but Christ lives in me; and the *life* which I now live ✳ in the flesh I live by faith in the Son of God, who loved me and gave Himself up for me.

21 "I do not nullify the grace of God, for if righteousness *comes* through the Law, then Christ died needlessly."

LIFE LESSONS

➤ **Galatians 2:4** — *False brethren secretly . . . sneaked in to spy out our liberty.*

𝒯here is something about freedom that many people, even within the church, simply cannot tolerate. They will try all sorts of tactics, both obvious and veiled, to bring you under their control. Don't let them. Trust in God.

➤ **Galatians 2:13** — *Even Barnabas was carried away by their hypocrisy.*

𝒲e should never imagine that our sin affects only ourselves and no one else. Peter didn't mean for his sin to infect others, but it did. That's why we have to rely on God's Spirit to help us avoid spreading spiritual disease.

➤ **Galatians 2:20** — *I have been crucified with Christ; and it is no longer I who live, but Christ lives in me.*

𝓛iving the Christian life does not mean that we just try to do our best. Rather, it means we allow Jesus Christ to live in and through us by faith. When we invite Christ to work in our lives and obey His commands, we become His representatives, and He works through us so others will be saved.

LIFE PRINCIPLE 24

To live the Christian life is to allow
Jesus to live His life in and through us.

GALATIANS 2:20

*M*any Christians today seem content to
live what they think is an *adequate*
Christian life. They believe that if they go to
church, read their Bible occasionally, and say
their prayers once in a while, they will be all
right with God. Occasionally, they may be
inspired to go above and beyond their normal
routines and volunteer to serve others as an
usher, a member of a church committee, or
even go on a short-term mission trip. Though
they go through the motions of being a "good
Christian," they do not enjoy the power, peace,
and joy that should come with the abundant life
Jesus promised (John 10:10). Eventually, the
counterfeit Christian life they are living becomes
a burden and does not comfort them when the
storms of adversity assail.

This was not what you were created for. God
does not call you or any believer to a marginal
Christian life characterized by chores and rituals.
He desires to have a daily relationship with you
where you experience His presence and trust Him
for wisdom, courage, and strength in all situations.
With every step you take, decision you make,
conversation you have, and thought you entertain,
the Lord wants to glorify Himself through you.
He desires to shine in your life—with His love,
joy, peace, patience, kindness, goodness, faithfulness, gentleness, and self-control illuminating your
unique talents, traits, and personality as you walk
in obedience to Him.

In other words, to live the Christian life is
to allow Jesus to live in and through you. That
is why Paul wrote, "I have been crucified with
Christ; and it is no longer I who live, but Christ
lives in me; and the life which I now live in
the flesh I live by faith in the Son of God, who
loved me and gave Himself up for me" (Gal.
2:20).

How do you allow Jesus to do so? In what
way does He live in and through you? If these
two questions seem difficult or confusing to
you, you aren't alone. Many people never realize
how powerfully Christ could demonstrate His
life through them. This is because many believe
that the key to living the Christian life starts

with pious acts, when it really begins with a
deep, intimate relationship with Him.

Therefore, to answer the first question: *How
do you allow Jesus to do this?*—you must realize
the answer comes by working on your relationship with Christ. You do this through Bible
study, prayer, worship, and fellowship with other
believers. You not only learn *about* Him, but
you must listen *to* Him, because He will teach
you how *to* love Him, live for Him, and walk in
His ways.

The answer to the second question: *In what
way does He live in and through you?*—is as
unique as each believer who follows Him. This
is because He has a special purpose for your life,
and the most important thing you can ever do is
simply obey Him—no matter what He tells you
to do. God will allow situations and troubles in
your life that only He can solve. This is so He
can demonstrate His glory, power, love, and
wisdom through you.

Is there anything distracting you from having an intimate relationship with the Lord?
Have you failed to trust God's sovereignty? Are
you worried that you're not doing enough to
deserve a relationship with Him or that you
could lose the eternal life He has given you?
Then you need to return to the basic truth that
your salvation is through faith in Christ and not
by works. There is absolutely nothing you can
do to earn it or be worthy of it. Therefore, there
is nothing you can do or fail to do that would
cause you to forfeit it.

The issue is not your salvation but the impact
of your life for Christ and the joy and fulfillment
you receive from Him. God does not call you
to an *adequate* life—He wants it to be *extraordinary*. However, for you to experience the
life He planned for you, you must stop being
distracted by peripheral issues and focus your
attention completely on Him. Can you do it?
Can you trust Jesus to live His life through you
and take care of all that troubles you?

Of course you can! The God who redeems
you can teach you how to live for Him. The
Savior you trusted for your eternity is more than
capable of taking care of all the matters that burden you daily. He can shine through you
brightly so that others can know Him and be
saved. Therefore, die to your notions of what
the Christian life should be so you can experience true life in Him. ❖

Isaiah 41:1—42:25

41 "COASTLANDS, listen to Me in silence,
And let the peoples gain new strength;
Let them come forward, then let them speak;
Let us come together for judgment.

2 "Who has aroused one from the east
Whom He calls in righteousness to His feet?
He delivers up nations before him
And subdues kings.
He makes them like dust with his sword,
As the wind-driven chaff with his bow.

3 "He pursues them, passing on in safety,
By a way he had not been traversing with his feet.

➤ 4 "Who has performed and accomplished *it*,
Calling forth the generations from the beginning?
'I, the LORD, am the first, and with the last. I am He.'"

5 The coastlands have seen and are afraid;
The ends of the earth tremble;
They have drawn near and have come.

6 Each one helps his neighbor
And says to his brother, "Be strong!"

7 So the craftsman encourages the smelter,
And he who smooths *metal* with the hammer *encourages* him who beats the anvil,
Saying of the soldering, "It is good";
And he fastens it with nails,
So that it will not totter.

8 "But you, Israel, My servant,
Jacob whom I have chosen,
Descendant of Abraham My friend,

9 You whom I have taken from the ends of the earth,
And called from its remotest parts
And said to you, 'You are My servant,
I have chosen you and not rejected you.

10 'Do not fear, for I am with you;
Do not anxiously look about you, for I am your God.
I will strengthen you, surely I will help you,
Surely I will uphold you with My righteous right hand.'

11 "Behold, all those who are angered at you will be shamed and dishonored;
Those who contend with you will be as nothing and will perish.

12 "You will seek those who quarrel with you, but will not find them,
Those who war with you will be as nothing and non-existent.

13 "For I am the LORD your God, who upholds your right hand,
Who says to you, 'Do not fear, I will help you.'

14 "Do not fear, you worm Jacob, you men of Israel;
I will help you," declares the LORD,
"and your Redeemer is the Holy One of Israel.

15 "Behold, I have made you a new, sharp threshing sledge with double edges;
You will thresh the mountains and pulverize *them*,
And will make the hills like chaff.

16 "You will winnow them, and the wind will carry them away,
And the storm will scatter them;

LIFE LESSONS

➤ **Isaiah 41:4 — *"I, the LORD, am the first, and with the last I am He."***

*I*n the Book of Revelation, we find that Jesus is called "the first and the last" (Rev. 1:17; 2:8; 22:13). He who has always existed from before the beginning of all things—and who will always reign throughout eternity—knows how to rescue us from all our troubles.

➤ **Isaiah 41:10 — *"Do not fear, for I am with you."***

*A*t some point, each of us will face circumstances that cause anxiety. When we do, we must remember we are God's children. We have the power to overcome fear when we apply His Word to our lives—remembering that He is always with us and will never fail or forsake us.

WHAT THE BIBLE SAYS ABOUT

God's Empowering Presence

Isaiah 41:8–14

*W*hen did you last feel the presence of God in your life? I don't mean a merely intellectual recognition that He is with you, for He is everywhere. Rather, when did you last recognize in your heart that the Lord is personally, intimately abiding in you?

If you are like many believers, it may have been a while since you really felt His presence. Too many people go about their lives without a genuine sense of God's closeness. What a tragedy!

Repeatedly in Scripture, we see that whenever God calls someone into His service, He first reminds the person of His enduring presence. We see this in the stories of Moses (Ex. 3:11, 12), Joshua (Josh. 1:1–9), Gideon (Judg. 6:12), and Jeremiah (Jer. 1:6–8), to name just a few. These men discovered, as we can, that the awareness of God's presence energizes us for our work.

Why does God repeatedly assure His followers of His presence? He does so because we need to be reminded of the reason for our confidence. Each time God calls a servant into action, He essentially says, "You can be strong and courageous because I am with you. Victory isn't about *your* abilities, *your* strength, *your* skill, *your* armor, *your* gifts, or *your* dedication; it has to do with *My* presence. You can be strong because I will be strong in you."

When Jeremiah trembled at the thought of the difficult ministry ahead of him, the Lord strengthened him with these words: "'They will fight against you, but they will not overcome you, for I am with you to deliver you'" (Jer. 1:19).

God knows how difficult life can be, and He knows every detail of each struggle you will ever face. As a believer in Christ Jesus, you can trust that your heavenly Father will keep His Word. He is with you right now, and He always will be, as He promises in His Word: "'I will never desert, nor will I ever forsake you,' so that we may confidently say, 'The LORD is my helper, I will not be afraid. What will man do to me?'" (Heb. 13:5, 6). ◈

But you will rejoice in the LORD,
   You will glory in the Holy One of
     Israel.
17 "The afflicted and needy are seeking
     water, but there is none,
   And their tongue is parched with
     thirst;
   I, the LORD, will answer them
     Myself,
   As the God of Israel I will not
     forsake them.
18 "I will open rivers on the bare
     heights
   And springs in the midst of the
     valleys;
   I will make the wilderness a pool of
     water
   And the dry land fountains of water.
19 "I will put the cedar in the
     wilderness,
   The acacia and the myrtle and the
     olive tree;
   I will place the juniper in the desert
   Together with the box tree and the
     cypress,
20 That they may see and recognize,
   And consider and gain insight as
     well,

That the hand of the LORD has done
     this,
   And the Holy One of Israel has
     created it.
21 "Present your case," the LORD says.
   "Bring forward your strong
     arguments,"
   The King of Jacob says.
22 Let them bring forth and declare to
     us what is going to take place;
   As for the former *events*, declare
     what they *were*,
   That we may consider them and
     know their outcome.
   Or announce to us what is coming;
23 Declare the things that are going to
     come afterward,
   That we may know that you are
     gods;
   Indeed, do good or evil, that we may
     anxiously look about us and fear
     together.
24 Behold, you are of no account,
   And your work amounts to nothing;
   He who chooses you is an
     abomination.
25 "I have aroused one from the north,
     and he has come;

From the rising of the sun he will
call on My name;
And he will come upon rulers as
upon mortar,
Even as the potter treads clay."

26 Who has declared *this* from the
beginning, that we might know?
Or from former times, that we may
say, "*He is* right!"?
Surely there was no one who
declared,
Surely there was no one who
proclaimed,
Surely there was no one who heard
your words.

27 "Formerly *I said* to Zion, 'Behold,
here they are.'
And to Jerusalem, 'I will give a
messenger of good news.'

28 "But when I look, there is no one,
And there is no counselor among
them
Who, if I ask, can give an answer.

29 "Behold, all of them are false;
Their works are worthless,
Their molten images are wind and
emptiness.

42 "BEHOLD, My Servant, whom I
uphold;
My chosen one *in whom* My soul
delights.
I have put My Spirit upon Him;
He will bring forth justice to the
nations.

2 "He will not cry out or raise *His voice*,
Nor make His voice heard in the
street.

3 "A bruised reed He will not break
And a dimly burning wick He will
not extinguish;
He will faithfully bring forth justice.

4 "He will not be disheartened or
crushed

LIFE LESSONS

➤ **Isaiah 42:3 —** *A bruised reed He will
not break and a dimly burning wick He
will not extinguish.*

*G*od lifts up those who are broken in
spirit. When our hearts are turned
toward Him, He will not crush us. We
may experience trials, but we will not
experience spiritual defeat. He treats the
person who is bruised and weakened
with great tenderness.

Until He has established justice in
the earth;
And the coastlands will wait
expectantly for His law."

5 Thus says God the LORD,
Who created the heavens and
stretched them out,
Who spread out the earth and its
offspring,
Who gives breath to the people on it
And spirit to those who walk in it,

6 "I am the LORD, I have called You in
righteousness,
I will also hold You by the hand and
watch over You,
And I will appoint You as a covenant
to the people,
As a light to the nations,

7 To open blind eyes,
To bring out prisoners from the
dungeon
And those who dwell in darkness
from the prison.

8 "I am the LORD, that is My name;
I will not give My glory to another,
Nor My praise to graven images.

9 "Behold, the former things have
come to pass,
Now I declare new things;
Before they spring forth I proclaim
them to you."

10 Sing to the LORD a new song,
Sing His praise from the end of the
earth!
You who go down to the sea, and all
that is in it.
You islands, and those who dwell on
them.

11 Let the wilderness and its cities lift
up *their voices*,
The settlements where Kedar
inhabits.
Let the inhabitants of Sela sing
aloud,
Let them shout for joy from the tops
of the mountains.

12 Let them give glory to the LORD
And declare His praise in the
coastlands.

13 The LORD will go forth like a
warrior,
He will arouse *His* zeal like a man
of war.
He will utter a shout, yes, He will
raise a war cry.
He will prevail against His enemies.

14 "I have kept silent for a long time,

I have kept still and restrained
Myself.
Now like a woman in labor I will
groan,
I will both gasp and pant.
15 "I will lay waste the mountains and
hills
And wither all their vegetation;
I will make the rivers into
coastlands
And dry up the ponds.
16 "I will lead the blind by a way they
do not know,
In paths they do not know I will
guide them.
I will make darkness into light
before them
And rugged places into plains.
These are the things I will do,
And I will not leave them undone."
17 They will be turned back *and* be
utterly put to shame,
Who trust in idols,
Who say to molten images,
"You are our gods."
18 Hear, you deaf!
And look, you blind, that you may
see.
19 Who is blind but My servant,
Or so deaf as My messenger whom I
send?
Who is so blind as he that is at
peace *with Me*,
Or so blind as the servant of the
LORD?
20 You have seen many things, but you
do not observe *them;*
Your ears are open, but none hears.
21 The LORD was pleased for His
righteousness' sake
To make the law great and glorious.
22 But this is a people plundered and
despoiled;
All of them are trapped in caves,
Or are hidden away in prisons;
They have become a prey with none
to deliver *them,*
And a spoil, with none to say, "Give
them back!"
23 Who among you will give ear to
this?
Who will give heed and listen
hereafter?
24 Who gave Jacob up for spoil, and
Israel to plunderers?
Was it not the LORD, against whom
we have sinned,

And in whose ways they were not
willing to walk,
And whose law they did not obey?
25 So He poured out on him the heat of
His anger
And the fierceness of battle;
And it set him aflame all around,
Yet he did not recognize *it;*
And it burned him, but he paid no
attention.

Psalm 109:26–31

26 Help me, O LORD my God;
Save me according to Your
lovingkindness.
27 And let them know that this is Your
hand;
You, LORD, have done it.
28 Let them curse, but You bless;
When they arise, they shall be
ashamed,
But Your servant shall be glad.
29 Let my accusers be clothed with
dishonor,
And let them cover themselves with
their own shame as with a robe.
30 With my mouth I will give thanks
abundantly to the LORD;
And in the midst of many I will
praise Him.
31 For He stands at the right hand of
the needy,
To save him from those who judge
his soul.

Proverbs 26:3–6

3 A whip is for the horse, a bridle for
the donkey,
And a rod for the back of fools.

LIFE LESSONS

➤ **Psalm 109:27** — *Let them know that
this is Your hand; You,* LORD, *have done it.*

*W*hen we pray for someone's deliverance or for God to intervene in
some situation, it is entirely appropriate
to ask Him to make it plain that what
happens is no coincidence, but a direct
answer to our prayers.

➤ 4   Do not answer a fool according to his folly,
Or you will also be like him.
5   Answer a fool as his folly *deserves*,
That he not be wise in his own eyes.
6   He cuts off *his own* feet *and* drinks violence
Who sends a message by the hand of a fool.

⊕ **Galatians 3:1–29**

3 YOU foolish Galatians, who has bewitched you, before whose eyes Jesus Christ was publicly portrayed *as* crucified?
2   This is the only thing I want to find out from you: did you receive the Spirit by the works of the Law, or by hearing with faith?
3   Are you so foolish? Having begun by the Spirit, are you now being perfected by the flesh?
4   Did you suffer so many things in vain—if indeed it was in vain?
5   So then, does He who provides you with the Spirit and works miracles among you, do it by the works of the Law, or by hearing with faith?
6   Even so Abraham BELIEVED GOD, AND IT WAS RECKONED TO HIM AS RIGHTEOUSNESS.
7   Therefore, be sure that it is those who are of faith who are sons of Abraham.
8   The Scripture, foreseeing that God would justify the Gentiles by faith, preached the gospel beforehand to Abra-ham, *saying*, "ALL THE NATIONS WILL BE BLESSED IN YOU."
9   So then those who are of faith are blessed with Abraham, the believer.
10   For as many as are of the works of the Law are under a curse; for it is written, "CURSED IS EVERYONE WHO DOES NOT ABIDE BY ALL THINGS WRITTEN IN THE BOOK OF THE LAW, TO PERFORM THEM."
11   Now that no one is justified by the Law before God is evident; for, "THE RIGHTEOUS MAN SHALL LIVE BY FAITH."
12   However, the Law is not of faith; on the contrary, "HE WHO PRACTICES THEM SHALL LIVE BY THEM."
13   Christ redeemed us from the curse of the Law, having become a curse for us—for it is written, "CURSED IS EVERYONE WHO HANGS ON A TREE"—
14   in order that in Christ Jesus the blessing of Abraham might come to the Gentiles, so that we would receive the promise of the Spirit through faith.
15   Brethren, I speak in terms of human relations: even though it is *only* a man's covenant, yet when it has been ratified, no one sets it aside or adds conditions to it.
16   Now the promises were spoken to Abraham and to his seed. He does not say, "And to seeds," as *referring* to many, but *rather* to one, "And to your seed," that is, Christ.
17   What I am saying is this: the Law, which came four hundred and thirty years later, does not invalidate a covenant previously ratified by God, so as to nullify the promise.
18   For if the inheritance is based on law, it is no longer based on a promise; but God has granted it to Abraham by means of a promise.
19   Why the Law then? It was added because of transgressions, having been ordained through angels by the agency of a mediator, until the seed would come to whom the promise had been made.
20   Now a mediator is not for one *party only*; whereas God is *only* one.
21   Is the Law then contrary to the promises of God? May it never be! For if a law had been given which was able to impart life, then righteousness would indeed have been based on law.
22   But the Scripture has shut up everyone under sin, so that the promise by

---

LIFE LESSONS

➤ **Proverbs 26:4, 5 — *Do not answer a fool according to his folly, or you will also be like him. Answer a fool as his folly deserves, that he be not wise in his own eyes.***

Some may say, "There you have it: a direct contradiction in the Bible!" Well, not quite. Both statements can be true, although in different situations and at different times. It takes a wise person to know which one applies.

faith in Jesus Christ might be given to those who believe.

23 But before faith came, we were kept in custody under the law, being shut up to the faith which was later to be revealed.

➤ 24 Therefore the Law has become our tutor *to lead us* to Christ, so that we may be justified by faith.

25 But now that faith has come, we are no longer under a tutor.

26 For you are all sons of God through faith in Christ Jesus.

27 For all of you who were baptized into Christ have clothed yourselves with ✳ Christ.

➤ 28 There is neither Jew nor Greek, there is neither slave nor free man, there is neither male nor female; for you are all one in Christ Jesus.

29 And if you belong to Christ, then you are Abraham's descendants, heirs according to promise.

LIFE LESSONS

➤ **Galatians 3:24 —** *The Law has become our tutor to lead us to Christ, so that we may be justified by faith.*

*T*he purpose of the Law was to lead us to a complete realization of our inadequacy—to show us that we can never make ourselves acceptable to God by our own efforts. We are absolutely dependent upon Him to provide it for us, which He did through Jesus Christ our Savior.

➤ **Galatians 3:28 —** *You are all one in Christ Jesus.*

*G*od does not play favorites (Acts 10:34; Rom. 2:11); He has no favorite sons or daughters. We all come to Him with exactly the same level of need, and He makes us into a single unit, the body of Christ.

SEPTEMBER 26

❋ Isaiah 43:1—44:28

43 BUT now, thus says the LORD, your Creator, O Jacob,
And He who formed you, O Israel,
"Do not fear, for I have redeemed you;
I have called you by name; you are Mine!

✳ 2 "When you pass through the waters, I will be with you;
And through the rivers, they will not overflow you.
When you walk through the fire, you will not be scorched,
Nor will the flame burn you.

3 "For I am the LORD your God, The Holy One of Israel, your Savior;
I have given Egypt as your ransom, Cush and Seba in your place.

4 "Since you are precious in My sight, *Since* you are honored and I love you,
I will give *other* men in your place and *other* peoples in exchange for your life.

5 "Do not fear, for I am with you;
I will bring your offspring from the east,

And gather you from the west.

6 "I will say to the north, 'Give *them* up!'
And to the south, 'Do not hold *them* back.'
Bring My sons from afar
And My daughters from the ends of the earth,

7 Everyone who is called by My name,
And whom I have created for My glory,
Whom I have formed, even whom I have made."

8 Bring out the people who are blind, even though they have eyes,
And the deaf, even though they have ears.

LIFE LESSONS

➤ **Isaiah 43:7 —** *"Everyone who is called by My name, and whom I have created for My glory."*

*D*o you realize that God has created *you* for His glory? He wants the world to see His majesty and goodness through you, and He wants to crown you with His own splendor.

9 All the nations have gathered
together
So that the peoples may be
assembled.
Who among them can declare this
And proclaim to us the former
things?
Let them present their witnesses
that they may be justified,
Or let them hear and say, "It is true."
10 "You are My witnesses," declares the
LORD,
"And My servant whom I have
chosen,
So that you may know and believe
Me
And understand that I am He.
Before Me there was no God
formed,
And there will be none after Me.
11 "I, even I, am the LORD,
And there is no savior besides Me.
12 "It is I who have declared and saved
and proclaimed,
And there was no strange *god*
among you;
So you are My witnesses," declares
the LORD,
"And I am God.
13 "Even from eternity I am He,
And there is none who can deliver
out of My hand;
I act and who can reverse it?"
14 Thus says the LORD your Redeemer,
the Holy One of Israel,
"For your sake I have sent to
Babylon,
And will bring them all down as
fugitives,
Even the Chaldeans, into the ships
in which they rejoice.
15 "I am the LORD, your Holy One,
The Creator of Israel, your King."
16 Thus says the LORD,
Who makes a way through the sea
And a path through the mighty
waters,
17 Who brings forth the chariot and
the horse,
The army and the mighty man
(They will lie down together *and* not
rise again;
They have been quenched *and*
extinguished like a wick):
18 "Do not call to mind the former
things,
Or ponder things of the past.

19 "Behold, I will do something new,
Now it will spring forth;
Will you not be aware of it?
I will even make a roadway in the
wilderness,
Rivers in the desert.
20 "The beasts of the field will glorify
Me,
The jackals and the ostriches,
Because I have given waters in the
wilderness
And rivers in the desert,
To give drink to My chosen people.
21 "The people whom I formed for
Myself
Will declare My praise.
22 "Yet you have not called on Me,
O Jacob;
But you have become weary of Me,
O Israel.
23 "You have not brought to Me the
sheep of your burnt offerings,
Nor have you honored Me with your
sacrifices.
I have not burdened you with
offerings,
Nor wearied you with incense.
24 "You have bought Me not sweet cane
with money,
Nor have you filled Me with the fat
of your sacrifices;
Rather you have burdened Me with
your sins,
You have wearied Me with your
iniquities.
25 "I, even I, am the one who wipes out
your transgressions for My own
sake,
And I will not remember your sins.
26 "Put Me in remembrance, let us
argue our case together;
State your *cause*, that you may be
proved right.
27 "Your first forefather sinned,

LIFE LESSONS

➤ **Isaiah 43:20 —** *"I have given waters in
the wilderness and rivers in the desert, to
give drink to My chosen people."*

*G*od does not promise to keep us out
of the wilderness or away from the
desert. But when we belong to Him, He
does promise to sustain us there and
renew our lives, even in the tough times.

And your spokesmen have
  transgressed against Me.
28 "So I will pollute the princes of the
    sanctuary,
    And I will consign Jacob to the ban
    and Israel to revilement.

44 "BUT now listen, O Jacob, My
    servant,
    And Israel, whom I have chosen:
2   Thus says the LORD who made you
     And formed you from the womb,
       who will help you,
     'Do not fear, O Jacob My servant;
     And you Jeshurun whom I have
       chosen.
3   'For I will pour out water on the
       thirsty *land*
     And streams on the dry ground;
     I will pour out My Spirit on your
       offspring
     And My blessing on your
       descendants;
4   And they will spring up among the
       grass
     Like poplars by streams of water.'
5   "This one will say, 'I am the LORD's';
     And that one will call on the name
       of Jacob;
     And another will write *on* his hand,
       'Belonging to the LORD,'
     And will name Israel's name with
       honor.
6   "Thus says the LORD, the King of
Israel and his Redeemer, the LORD of
hosts:
     'I am the first and I am the last,
     And there is no God besides Me.
7   'Who is like Me? Let him proclaim
       and declare it;
     Yes, let him recount it to Me in
       order,
     From the time that I established the
       ancient nation.
     And let them declare to them the
       things that are coming
     And the events that are going to
       take place.
➤ 8 'Do not tremble and do not be
       afraid;
     Have I not long since announced *it*
       to you and declared *it*?
     And you are My witnesses.
     Is there any God besides Me,
     Or is there any *other* Rock?
     I know of none.'"
9   Those who fashion a graven image
are all of them futile, and their precious

things are of no profit; even their own
witnesses fail to see or know, so that
they will be put to shame.
10   Who has fashioned a god or cast an
idol to no profit?
11   Behold, all his companions will be
put to shame, for the craftsmen themselves are mere men. Let them all assemble themselves, let them stand up, let
them tremble, let them together be put
to shame.
12   The man shapes iron into a cutting
tool and does his work over the coals,
fashioning it with hammers and working it with his strong arm. He also gets
hungry and his strength fails; he drinks
no water and becomes weary.
13   *Another* shapes wood, he extends
a measuring line; he outlines it with
red chalk. He works it with planes and
outlines it with a compass, and makes it
like the form of a man, like the beauty of
man, so that it may sit in a house.
14   Surely he cuts cedars for himself,
and takes a cypress or an oak and raises
it for himself among the trees of the forest. He plants a fir, and the rain makes it
grow.
15   Then it becomes *something* for a
man to burn, so he takes one of them
and warms himself; he also makes a fire
to bake bread. He also makes a god and
worships it; he makes it a graven image
and falls down before it.
16   Half of it he burns in the fire; over
this half he eats meat as he roasts a roast
and is satisfied. He also warms himself
and says, "Aha! I am warm, I have seen
the fire."
17   But the rest of it he makes into a god,
his graven image. He falls down before
it and worships; he also prays to it and
says, "Deliver me, for you are my god."
18   They do not know, nor do they

LIFE LESSONS

➤ **Isaiah 44:8 — *"Is there any God
besides Me? Or is there any other Rock? I
know of none."***

Scripture consistently teaches that
only one true God exists. All other
"so-called gods" (1 Cor. 8:5) are actually nothing but demons trying to usurp
the worship that belongs to God alone
(1 Cor. 10:20).

WHAT THE BIBLE SAYS ABOUT ◉

How to Handle Feelings of Guilt

Isaiah 44:9–11

*M*any teachers find true-or-false tests a useful tool to determine what their students know. Some people are able to discern truth. Others ponder the question at length and realize they can't with confidence identify what is right and what is an error.

How would *you* answer the following questions?

True or False? *It is the responsibility of the Holy Spirit to convict us of sin.*

The answer is TRUE (John 16:8). When we have sinned, the Holy Spirit will reveal our guilt to us. Why? So we will ask God's forgiveness and allow Him to restore us to a proper fellowship with Him.

It is possible, of course, to engage in sin for so long feelings of shame and guilt evaporate. Isaiah marveled that his countrymen could create lifeless idols to worship and yet feel no shame (Is. 44:9–11). And the apostle Paul said that people can wallow in their transgressions for so long that their consciences become seared as with a hot iron (1 Tim. 4:2). Nevertheless, it is the Holy Spirit's job—*not* ours—to convict people of their sin.

True or False? *All guilty feelings are the result of sin.*

The answer is FALSE. We may feel guilty for various reasons. A wrong view of God may cause us to feel shame—especially if we mistakenly imagine Him gleefully noticing our mistakes, pointing His finger at us, or eagerly pronouncing judgment. At other times, we may have a sense of false guilt and not know why. The New Testament proclaims, "There is now no condemnation for those who are in Christ Jesus" (Rom. 8:1). Jesus came to take away our guilt (Is. 53:10)—and the Spirit-filled life is designed to overflow with joy and peace.

Therefore, when you feel guilty, ask God whether it is His Spirit convicting you or is it false guilt. If there is sin, He will reveal this to you so you can repent and turn away from it. Remember, when you ask for forgiveness, He is faithful and cleanses you from all sin (1 John 1:9).

Some of the guilt we experience comes from having a wrong view of God. The enemy tempts us into believing that the Lord is a hard taskmaster who could not possibly love us. The complete opposite is true. God is loving, compassionate, and intimately involved in our lives. He is eternally committed to our best and wants us to know how much He cares for us. When Satan raises an accusation against you, point him to the Cross and remind him that you are a forgiven, unconditionally, eternally-loved child of God. Accept the truth that the Lord loves you, and allow any "false" guilt feelings to melt away. ◉

---

understand, for He has smeared over their eyes so that they cannot see and their hearts so that they cannot comprehend.

19 No one recalls, nor is there knowledge or understanding to say, "I have burned half of it in the fire and also have baked bread over its coals. I roast meat and eat *it*. Then I make the rest of it into an abomination, I fall down before a block of wood!"

20 He feeds on ashes; a deceived heart has turned him aside. And he cannot deliver himself, nor say, "Is there not a lie in my right hand?"

21 "Remember these things, O Jacob,
And Israel, for you are My servant;
I have formed you, you are My servant,
O Israel, you will not be forgotten by Me.

22 "I have wiped out your
transgressions like a thick cloud
And your sins like a heavy mist.
Return to Me, for I have redeemed you."

23 Shout for joy, O heavens, for the LORD has done *it*!
Shout joyfully, you lower parts of the earth;
Break forth into a shout of joy, you mountains,
O forest, and every tree in it;
For the LORD has redeemed Jacob
And in Israel He shows forth His glory.

24 Thus says the LORD, your Redeemer, and the one who formed you from the womb,
"I, the LORD, am the maker of all things,

Stretching out the heavens by
Myself
And spreading out the earth all
alone,

25 Causing the omens of boasters to
fail,
Making fools out of diviners,
Causing wise men to draw back
And turning their knowledge into
foolishness,

26 Confirming the word of His
servant
And performing the purpose of His
messengers.
It is I who says of Jerusalem, 'She
shall be inhabited!'
And of the cities of Judah, 'They
shall be built,'
And I will raise up her ruins *again.*

27 "*It is I* who says to the depth of the
sea, 'Be dried up!'
And I will make your rivers dry.

28 "*It is I* who says of Cyrus, '*He is* My
shepherd!
And he will perform all My desire.'
And he declares of Jerusalem, 'She
will be built,'
And of the temple, 'Your foundation
will be laid.'"

Psalm 110:1–7

A Psalm of David.

110 THE LORD says to my Lord:
"Sit at My right hand
Until I make Your enemies a
footstool for Your feet."

2 The LORD will stretch forth Your
strong scepter from Zion,
saying,
"Rule in the midst of Your enemies."

3 Your people will volunteer freely in
the day of Your power;

LIFE LESSONS

➤ **Psalm 110:1 — *The LORD says to my
Lord: "Sit at My right hand."***

The New Testament quotes this psalm,
written by David, more than any
other. Jesus used this verse to prove that
He, the Messiah, was both David's "son"
and David's Lord (Matt. 22:41–46).

In holy array, from the womb of the
dawn,
Your youth are to You *as* the dew.

4 The LORD has sworn and will not
change His mind,
"You are a priest forever
According to the order of
Melchizedek."

5 The Lord is at Your right hand;
He will shatter kings in the day of
His wrath.

6 He will judge among the nations,
He will fill *them* with corpses,
He will shatter the chief men over a
broad country.

7 He will drink from the brook by the
wayside;
Therefore He will lift up *His* head.

Proverbs 26:7–9

7 *Like* the legs *which* are useless to
the lame,
So is a proverb in the mouth of
fools.

8 *Like* one who binds a stone in a
sling,
So is he who gives honor to a
fool.

9 *Like* a thorn *which* falls into the
hand of a drunkard,
So is a proverb in the mouth of
fools.

Galatians 4:1–31

4 NOW I say, as long as the heir is a
child, he does not differ at all from a
slave although he is owner of everything,

2 but he is under guardians and managers until the date set by the father.

3 So also we, while we were children,
were held in bondage under the elemental things of the world.

4 But when the fullness of the time
came, God sent forth His Son, born of a
woman, born under the Law,

5 so that He might redeem those who
were under the Law, that we might receive the adoption as sons.

6 Because you are sons, God has sent
forth the Spirit of His Son into our
hearts, crying, "Abba! Father!"

7   Therefore you are no longer a slave, but a son; and if a son, then an heir through God.

8   However at that time, when you did not know God, you were slaves to those which by nature are no gods.

9   But now that you have come to know God, or rather to be known by God, how is it that you turn back again to the weak and worthless elemental things, to which you desire to be enslaved all over again?

10   You observe days and months and seasons and years.

11   I fear for you, that perhaps I have labored over you in vain.

12   I beg of you, brethren, become as I *am*, for I also *have become* as you *are*. You have done me no wrong;

13   but you know that it was because of a bodily illness that I preached the gospel to you the first time;

14   and that which was a trial to you in my bodily condition you did not despise or loathe, but you received me as an angel of God, as Christ Jesus *Himself*.

15   Where then is that sense of blessing you had? For I bear you witness that, if possible, you would have plucked out your eyes and given them to me.

16   So have I become your enemy by telling you the truth?

17   They eagerly seek you, not commendably, but they wish to shut you out so that you will seek them.

18   But it is good always to be eagerly sought in a commendable manner, and not only when I am present with you.

19   My children, with whom I am again ◄ in labor until Christ is formed in you—

20   but I could wish to be present with you now and to change my tone, for I am perplexed about you.

21   Tell me, you who want to be under law, do you not listen to the law?

22   For it is written that Abraham had two sons, one by the bondwoman and one by the free woman.

23   But the son by the bondwoman was born according to the flesh, and the son by the free woman through the promise.

24   This is allegorically speaking, for these *women* are two covenants: one *proceeding* from Mount Sinai bearing children who are to be slaves; she is Hagar.

25   Now this Hagar is Mount Sinai in Arabia and corresponds to the present Jerusalem, for she is in slavery with her children.

26   But the Jerusalem above is free; she is our mother.

27   For it is written,

> "REJOICE, BARREN WOMAN WHO DOES
>   NOT BEAR;
> BREAK FORTH AND SHOUT, YOU WHO
>   ARE NOT IN LABOR;
> FOR MORE NUMEROUS ARE THE
>   CHILDREN OF THE DESOLATE
> THAN OF THE ONE WHO HAS A
>   HUSBAND."

28   And you brethren, like Isaac, are children of promise.

29   But as at that time he who was born according to the flesh persecuted him *who was born* according to the Spirit, so it is now also.

30   But what does the Scripture say?

> "CAST OUT THE BONDWOMAN AND HER
>   SON,
> FOR THE SON OF THE BONDWOMAN
>   SHALL NOT BE AN HEIR WITH THE SON
>   OF THE FREE WOMAN."

31   So then, brethren, we are not children of a bondwoman, but of the free woman.

LIFE LESSONS

➤ **Galatians 4:6 — "Abba! Father!"**

Abba is an Aramaic term for "father" suggesting warmth, closeness, confidence, and mutual delight. God wants to be our Abba, and His highest priority for our lives is an intimate relationship with Himself. So He sends His Spirit to indwell us—to show us what it means to be His children, to bless us with His great love, to reveal His purpose for creating us, and to empower us for all the great plans He has for our lives. He is loving and approachable, so call out in prayer to your beloved heavenly Father often.

➤ **Galatians 4:19 — I am again in labor until Christ is formed in you.**

The goal of Christian living is not to sin less, reform our manners, or do better than we used to. The goal is total transformation, to see Jesus formed in us. God wants us to increasingly resemble His Son.

Isaiah 45:1—46:13

45 THUS says the LORD to Cyrus His anointed,
Whom I have taken by the right hand,
To subdue nations before him
And to loose the loins of kings;
To open doors before him so that gates will not be shut:

2 "I will go before you and make the rough places smooth;
I will shatter the doors of bronze and cut through their iron bars.

3 "I will give you the treasures of darkness
And hidden wealth of secret places,
So that you may know that it is I,
The LORD, the God of Israel, who calls you by your name.

4 "For the sake of Jacob My servant,
And Israel My chosen one,
I have also called you by your name;
I have given you a title of honor
Though you have not known Me.

5 "I am the LORD, and there is no other;
Besides Me there is no God.
I will gird you, though you have not known Me;

6 That men may know from the rising to the setting of the sun
That there is no one besides Me.
I am the LORD, and there is no other,

7 The One forming light and creating darkness,
Causing well-being and creating calamity;
I am the LORD who does all these.

8 "Drip down, O heavens, from above,
And let the clouds pour down righteousness;
Let the earth open up and salvation bear fruit,
And righteousness spring up with it.
I, the LORD, have created it.

9 "Woe to *the one* who quarrels with his Maker—
An earthenware vessel among the vessels of earth!
Will the clay say to the potter, 'What are you doing?'
Or the thing you are making *say*, 'He has no hands'?

10 "Woe to him who says to a father,
'What are you begetting?'
Or to a woman, 'To what are you giving birth?'"

11 Thus says the LORD, the Holy One of Israel, and his Maker:
"Ask Me about the things to come concerning My sons,
And you shall commit to Me the work of My hands.

12 "It is I who made the earth, and created man upon it.
I stretched out the heavens with My hands
And I ordained all their host.

13 "I have aroused him in righteousness
And I will make all his ways smooth;
He will build My city and will let My exiles go free,
Without any payment or reward,"
says the LORD of hosts.

14 Thus says the LORD,
"The products of Egypt and the merchandise of Cush
And the Sabeans, men of stature,
Will come over to you and will be yours;
They will walk behind you, they will come over in chains
And will bow down to you;
They will make supplication to you:
'Surely, God is with you, and there is none else,
No other God.'"

15 Truly, You are a God who hides Himself,
O God of Israel, Savior!

16 They will be put to shame and even humiliated, all of them;
The manufacturers of idols will go away together in humiliation.

17 Israel has been saved by the LORD
With an everlasting salvation;
You will not be put to shame or humiliated
To all eternity.

18 For thus says the LORD, who created the heavens (He is the God who formed the earth and made it, He established it *and* did not create it a waste place, *but* formed it to be inhabited),
"I am the LORD, and there is none else.

19 "I have not spoken in secret,
In some dark land;

I did not say to the offspring of
Jacob,
'Seek Me in a waste place';
I, the LORD, speak righteousness,
Declaring things that are upright.
20 "Gather yourselves and come;
Draw near together, you fugitives of
the nations;
They have no knowledge,
Who carry about their wooden idol
And pray to a god who cannot
save.
21 "Declare and set forth *your case*;
Indeed, let them consult together.
Who has announced this from of
old?
Who has long since declared it?
Is it not I, the LORD?
And there is no other God besides
Me,
A righteous God and a Savior;
There is none except Me.
22 "Turn to Me and be saved, all the
ends of the earth;
For I am God, and there is no other.
23 "I have sworn by Myself,
The word has gone forth from My
mouth in righteousness
And will not turn back,
That to Me every knee will
bow, every tongue will swear
allegiance.
24 "They will say of Me, 'Only in the
LORD are righteousness and
strength.'
Men will come to Him,
And all who were angry at Him will
be put to shame.
25 "In the LORD all the offspring of
Israel
Will be justified and will glory."

46 BEL has bowed down, Nebo
stoops over;
Their images are *consigned* to the
beasts and the cattle.

The things that you carry are
burdensome,
A load for the weary *beast*.
2 They stooped over, they have
bowed down together;
They could not rescue the burden,
But have themselves gone into
captivity.
3 "Listen to Me, O house of Jacob,
And all the remnant of the house of
Israel,
You who have been borne by Me
from birth
And have been carried from the
womb;
4 Even to *your* old age I will be the
same,
And even to *your* graying years I
will bear *you*!
I have done *it*, and I will carry *you*;
And I will bear *you* and I will
deliver *you*.
5 "To whom would you liken Me
And make Me equal and compare
Me,
That we would be alike?
6 "Those who lavish gold from the
purse
And weigh silver on the scale
Hire a goldsmith, and he makes it
into a god;
They bow down, indeed they
worship it.
7 "They lift it upon the shoulder *and*
carry it;
They set it in its place and it stands
there.
It does not move from its place.
Though one may cry to it, it cannot
answer;
It cannot deliver him from his
distress.
8 "Remember this, and be assured;
Recall it to mind, you
transgressors.

LIFE LESSONS

➤ **Isaiah 45:19 — *"I have not spoken in
secret."***

*I*f we truly desire to know God's will
so that we may do it, the Father will
move heaven and earth, if necessary,
to show us what it is. We never have to
worry that we might inadvertently
miss it.

➤ **Isaiah 46:4 — *"Even to your graying
hairs I will bear you!"***

*A*s we grow older, we grow weaker
and frailer, but God never does. He
is the "Ancient of Days" (Dan. 7:9, 13, 22).
He remains infinitely strong and sustains
you today as He did Paul, Moses, Abraham, Noah, and Adam.

➤ 9 "Remember the former things long
      past,
    For I am God, and there is no
      other;
    I am God, and there is no one like
      Me,
10 Declaring the end from the
      beginning,
    And from ancient times things
      which have not been done,
    Saying, 'My purpose will be
      established,
    And I will accomplish all My good
      pleasure';
11 Calling a bird of prey from the
      east,
    The man of My purpose from a far
      country.
    Truly I have spoken; truly I will
      bring it to pass.
    I have planned *it, surely* I will
      do it.
12 "Listen to Me, you stubborn-minded,
    Who are far from righteousness.
13 "I bring near My righteousness, it is
      not far off;
    And My salvation will not delay.
    And I will grant salvation in Zion,
    And My glory for Israel.

✦ Psalm 111:1–6

111 PRAISE the LORD!
        I will give thanks to the LORD
          with all *my* heart,
    In the company of the upright and
      in the assembly.
➤ 2 Great are the works of the LORD;
    They are studied by all who delight
✱   in them.
3 Splendid and majestic is His work,
    And His righteousness endures
      forever.
4 He has made His wonders to be
      remembered;
    The LORD is gracious and
      compassionate.
5 He has given food to those who fear
      Him;
    He will remember His covenant
      forever.
6 He has made known to His people
      the power of His works,
    In giving them the heritage of the
      nations.

✦ Proverbs 26:10

10 *Like* an archer who wounds
      everyone,
    So is he who hires a fool or who
      hires those who pass by.

✦ Galatians 5:1–26

5 IT was for freedom that Christ set
    us free; therefore keep standing firm
and do not be subject again to a yoke of
slavery.
2   Behold I, Paul, say to you that if you
receive circumcision, Christ will be of no
benefit to you.
3   And I testify again to every man who
receives circumcision, that he is under
obligation to keep the whole Law.
4   You have been severed from Christ,
you who are seeking to be justified by
law; you have fallen from grace.
5   For we through the Spirit, by faith,
are waiting for the hope of righteousness.
6   For in Christ Jesus neither circumcision nor uncircumcision means anything, but faith working through love.
7   You were running well; who hindered you from obeying the truth?
8   This persuasion *did* not *come* from
Him who calls you.

LIFE LESSONS

➤ **Isaiah 46:9, 10** — *"I am God, and there
is no one like Me, declaring the end from
the beginning, and from ancient times
things which have not been done."*

*A*ccording to some estimates, almost
    thirty percent of the Bible con-
cerned future events at the time it was
written. God declares to us "the end
from the beginning" so that we might
trust both Him and His Word.

➤ **Psalm 111:2** — *Great are the works
of the LORD; they are studied by all who
delight in them.*

*W*e always take a keen interest in
    the activities and projects of those
we deeply love. So it is natural that we
should love to study the works of God,
beginning with the Bible.

9   A little leaven leavens the whole lump *of dough.*

10   I have confidence in you in the Lord that you will adopt no other view; but the one who is disturbing you will bear his judgment, whoever he is.

11   But I, brethren, if I still preach circumcision, why am I still persecuted? Then the stumbling block of the cross has been abolished.

12   I wish that those who are troubling you would even mutilate themselves.

➤ 13   For you were called to freedom, brethren; only *do* not *turn* your freedom into an opportunity for the flesh, but through love serve one another.

14   For the whole Law is fulfilled in one word, in the *statement,* "YOU SHALL LOVE YOUR NEIGHBOR AS YOURSELF."

15   But if you bite and devour one another, take care that you are not consumed by one another.

16   But I say, walk by the Spirit, and you will not carry out the desire of the flesh.

17   For the flesh sets its desire against the Spirit, and the Spirit against the flesh; for these are in opposition to one another, so that you may not do the things that you please.

18   But if you are led by the Spirit, you are not under the Law.

19   Now the deeds of the flesh are evident, which are: immorality, impurity, sensuality,

---

LIFE LESSONS

➤ **Galatians 5:13 — *Do not turn your freedom into an opportunity for the flesh, but through love serve one another.***

*W*e are free in Christ, but we do not have license to sin because it no longer fits who we are as the children of God. Rather, we have been set free from every encumbrance to become who He created us to be—those who build up and encourage others through creative, Spirit-led ministries. Why would anyone who truly loves Jesus want to use his or her cross-bought freedom to do anything that disgraces His name?

ANSWERS TO LIFE'S QUESTIONS

What is the fruit of the Spirit and how does it grow in me?

GALATIANS 5:22, 23

*B*elievers who truly walk in the Spirit radiate integrity. They do not hide their true feelings, harbor self-serving intentions, nor would they ever try to take advantage of you. In fact, you may feel as if you can trust them with your most intimate secrets. You may even find yourself opening up to them in a way that is quite uncharacteristic for you.

Spirit-filled believers do not pretend to be perfect. In fact, they often offer humble apologies before they are confronted with wrongdoing because the Spirit alerts them when they have offended or hurt someone. Secure in their relationships with the Lord and their worth in Him, they are able to respond quickly once they realize and admit their sin or error in judgment. They remember that the Holy Spirit is continually sanctifying them—transforming them into the image of Christ. Therefore, they are not discouraged, but are thankful that His grace is always available to them when they stumble and that He is teaching them to rise above their fleshly appetites and desires.

Specifically, their lives exude nine virtues: love, joy, peace, patience, kindness, goodness, faithfulness, gentleness, and self-control. This fruit is not simply a mark of the Spirit-filled life; it is the preeminent evidence of a life that is fully submitted to Jesus Christ.

When reading about God's gift of grace, ask Him to show you how you can be more grace-filled with others. He may help you recall the unkind things you've done in the past, but when you surrender your will to Him, He will make you a kinder person who reflects His love to many.

Do you see the problem?
"*I* want to be more kind."
"*I* need to act more loving."
"*I* need to exercise more self-control."
"*I*. . .I. . . .I. . . .I. . . .I. . ."

The fruit of the Spirit isn't produced when we focus on ourselves—it is a result of being singularly centered on Christ (John 15:5). These virtues aren't goals we can pursue, and they were never intended to demonstrate our dedication and resolve because *you and I cannot yield fruit.* Rather, the Holy Spirit is the producer and we are merely the bearers. And the harvest that results from our walk with Him merely reveals our dependency on and sensitivity to His promptings.

20 idolatry, sorcery, enmities, strife, jealousy, outbursts of anger, disputes, dissensions, factions,
21 envying, drunkenness, carousing, and things like these, of which I forewarn you, just as I have forewarned you, that those who practice such things will not inherit the kingdom of God.
22 But the fruit of the Spirit is love, joy, peace, patience, kindness, goodness, faithfulness,
23 gentleness, self-control; against such things there is no law.
24 Now those who belong to Christ Jesus have crucified the flesh with its passions and desires.
25 If we live by the Spirit, let us also walk by the Spirit.

LIFE LESSONS

➤ **Galatians 5:24 — *Those who belong to Christ have crucified the flesh with its passions and desires.***

*E*veryone who belongs to Christ has died with the Savior on the Cross. This means that we have given up our right to dictate the course of our lives because we realize that our fleshly inclinations only lead to disappointment and ruin (Prov. 14:12). We turn our lives over to the Lord because only He can lead us in the very best path possible.

26 Let us not become boastful, challenging one another, envying one another.

Isaiah 47:1—48:22

47 "COME down and sit in the dust,
　O virgin daughter of Babylon;
　Sit on the ground without a throne,
　O daughter of the Chaldeans!
　For you shall no longer be called
　　tender and delicate.
2　"Take the millstones and grind meal.
　Remove your veil, strip off the skirt,
　Uncover the leg, cross the rivers.
3　"Your nakedness will be uncovered,
　Your shame also will be exposed;
　I will take vengeance and will not
　　spare a man."
4　Our Redeemer, the LORD of hosts is
　　His name,
　The Holy One of Israel.
5　"Sit silently, and go into darkness,
　O daughter of the Chaldeans,
　For you will no longer be called
　The queen of kingdoms.
6　"I was angry with My people,
　I profaned My heritage
　And gave them into your hand.
　You did not show mercy to them,
　On the aged you made your yoke
　　very heavy.
7　"Yet you said, 'I will be a queen
　　forever.'
　These things you did not consider
　Nor remember the outcome of them.

8　"Now, then, hear this, you sensual
　　one,
　Who dwells securely,
　Who says in your heart,
　'I am, and there is no one besides
　　me.
　I will not sit as a widow,
　Nor know loss of children.'
9　"But these two things will come on
　　you suddenly in one day:
　Loss of children and widowhood.
　They will come on you in full
　　measure
　In spite of your many sorceries,
　In spite of the great power of your
　　spells.
10 "You felt secure in your wickedness
　　and said,
　'No one sees me,'
　Your wisdom and your knowledge,
　　they have deluded you;
　For you have said in your heart,
　'I am, and there is no one besides
　　me.'
11 "But evil will come on you
　Which you will not know how to
　　charm away;
　And disaster will fall on you
　For which you cannot atone;
　And destruction about which you do
　　not know
　Will come on you suddenly.
12 "Stand *fast* now in your spells

And in your many sorceries
With which you have labored from
your youth;
Perhaps you will be able to profit,
Perhaps you may cause trembling.
13 "You are wearied with your many
counsels;
Let now the astrologers,
Those who prophesy by the stars,
Those who predict by the new
moons,
Stand up and save you from what
will come upon you.
14 "Behold, they have become like
stubble,
Fire burns them;
They cannot deliver themselves
from the power of the flame;
There will be no coal to warm by
Nor a fire to sit before!
15 "So have those become to you with
whom you have labored,
Who have trafficked with you from
your youth;
Each has wandered in his own way;
There is none to save you.

48 "HEAR this, O house of Jacob,
who are named Israel
And who came forth from the loins
of Judah,
Who swear by the name of the LORD
And invoke the God of Israel,
But not in truth nor in
righteousness.
2 "For they call themselves after the
holy city
And lean on the God of Israel;
The LORD of hosts is His name.
3 "I declared the former things long ago
And they went forth from My
mouth, and I proclaimed them.
Suddenly I acted, and they came to
pass.
4 "Because I know that you are
obstinate,
And your neck is an iron sinew
And your forehead bronze,
5 Therefore I declared *them* to you
long ago,
Before they took place I proclaimed
them to you,
So that you would not say, 'My idol
has done them,
And my graven image and my molten
image have commanded them.'
6 "You have heard; look at all this.
And you, will you not declare it?

I proclaim to you new things from
this time,
Even hidden things which you have
not known.
7 "They are created now and not long
ago;
And before today you have not
heard them,
So that you will not say, 'Behold, I
knew them.'
8 "You have not heard, you have not
known.
Even from long ago your ear has
not been open,
Because I knew that you would deal
very treacherously;
And you have been called a rebel
from birth.
9 "For the sake of My name I delay My
wrath,
And *for* My praise I restrain *it* for you,
In order not to cut you off.
10 "Behold, I have refined you, but not
as silver;
I have tested you in the furnace of
affliction.
11 "For My own sake, for My own sake,
I will act;
For how can *My name* be profaned?
And My glory I will not give to
another.
12 "Listen to Me, O Jacob, even Israel
whom I called;
I am He, I am the first, I am also the
last.
13 "Surely My hand founded the earth,
And My right hand spread out the
heavens;
When I call to them, they stand
together.
14 "Assemble, all of you, and listen!

LIFE LESSONS

➤ **Isaiah 48:9** — *"For the sake of My name I delay My wrath, and for My praise I restrain it for you, in order not to cut you off."*

We owe our salvation to the love and grace of God that was expressed through the death and resurrection of the Lord Jesus Christ (Rom. 5:8), and not to anything else. He saved us for His name's sake, not because we deserved it or were somehow worthy (Eph. 2:8, 9; 2 Tim. 1:9).

Who among them has declared
these things?
The LORD loves him; he will carry
out His good pleasure on Babylon,
And His arm *will be against* the
Chaldeans.
15 "I, even I, have spoken; indeed I have
called him,
I have brought him, and He will
make his ways successful.
16 "Come near to Me, listen to this:
From the first I have not spoken in
secret,
From the time it took place, I was
there.
And now the Lord GOD has sent Me,
and His Spirit."
➤ 17 Thus says the LORD, your Redeemer,
the Holy One of Israel,
"I am the LORD your God, who
teaches you to profit,
Who leads you in the way you
should go.
18 "If only you had paid attention to My
commandments!
Then your well-being would have
been like a river,
And your righteousness like the
waves of the sea.
19 "Your descendants would have been
like the sand,
And your offspring like its grains;
Their name would never be cut off
or destroyed from My presence."
20 Go forth from Babylon! Flee from
the Chaldeans!
Declare with the sound of joyful
shouting, proclaim this,
Send it out to the end of the earth;
Say, "The LORD has redeemed His
servant Jacob."
21 They did not thirst when He led
them through the deserts.
He made the water flow out of the
rock for them;
He split the rock and the water
gushed forth.
22 "There is no peace for the wicked,"
says the LORD.

Psalm 111:7–10

7 The works of His hands are truth
and justice;
All His precepts are sure.

8 They are upheld forever and ever;
They are performed in truth and
uprightness.
9 He has sent redemption to His
people;
He has ordained His covenant
forever;
Holy and awesome is His name.
10 The fear of the LORD is the
beginning of wisdom;
A good understanding have
all those who do *His
commandments;*
His praise endures forever.

Proverbs 26:11, 12

11 Like a dog that returns to its vomit
Is a fool who repeats his folly.
12 Do you see a man wise in his own
eyes?
There is more hope for a fool than
for him.

Galatians 6:1–18

6 BRETHREN, even if anyone is caught
in any trespass, you who are spiritual,
restore such a one in a spirit of gentleness; *each one* looking to yourself, so
that you too will not be tempted.

LIFE LESSONS

➤ **Isaiah 48:17** — *"I am the LORD your
God, who teaches you to profit, who
leads you in the way you should go."*

*G*od may lead you into difficult circumstances (Mark 6:45–51), but wherever
He guides you, He does it "to do good
for you in the end" (Deut. 8:16).

➤ **Psalm 111:10** — *A good understanding have all those who do His commandments.*

*T*he more we strive by God's Spirit to
obey His commandments, the more
understanding He gives us of His Word.
Jesus said, "If anyone is willing to do
His will, he will know of the teaching,
whether it is of God" (John 7:17).

WHAT THE BIBLE SAYS ABOUT ◈

Bearing One Another's Burdens

Galatians 6:1–3

*M*any people object to the idea of accountability because they don't see how other people's actions are any of their business. But the Bible insists that we in the body of Christ all have a responsibility to one another.

Paul taught that if a believer is caught in sin, the strong members of the church are to help shoulder the responsibility of that person's sin. They are to work with the sinner to help him get back on track (Gal. 6:1–3). This implies that our sin is other people's business; and conversely, their sin becomes part of our responsibility. Nowhere in Scripture are we told that our sin is something just between God and us.

A woman in our church in Miami was married for only a short time when her husband revealed his homosexuality. Soon afterwards, he left her to be with his lover. She told me

something I will never forget. "After I was divorced," she said, "several of my friends came to me and said they knew he was gay before we married. When I asked them why they didn't say anything, they replied, 'We didn't think it was any of our business.'"

After hearing her story, I made up my mind never to stand by quietly and watch a friend make what I felt sure was a mistake. This resolution occasionally makes me very unpopular. People have left the church over things I have confronted them about. But when I start thinking that maybe I should keep my mouth shut, I always remember Solomon's words: "He who rebukes a man will afterward find more favor than he who flatters with the tongue" (Prov. 28:23).

It amazes me how often people come back to me or write letters to apologize for their reaction to my warnings. More often than not, they admit they should have listened.

Remember this, in an accountability relationship you are not responsible for how the other person responds to you. But you are responsible to tell the truth and then continue to love that person through the process. ◈

➢ 2　Bear one another's burdens, and thereby fulfill the law of Christ.
3　For if anyone thinks he is something when he is nothing, he deceives himself.
4　But each one must examine his own work, and then he will have *reason for* boasting in regard to himself alone, and not in regard to another.
5　For each one will bear his own load.
6　The one who is taught the word is to share all good things with the one who teaches *him.*
➢ 7　Do not be deceived, God is not

mocked; for whatever a man sows, this he will also reap.
8　For the one who sows to his own flesh will from the flesh reap corruption, but the one who sows to the Spirit will from the Spirit reap eternal life.
9　Let us not lose heart in doing good, ✳
for in due time we will reap if we do not grow weary.
10　So then, while we have opportunity, let us do good to all people, and especially to those who are of the household of the faith.

LIFE LESSONS

➢ **Galatians 6:2 — *Bear one another's burdens, and thereby fulfill the law of Christ.***

*N*o maturing Christian can ever say, "I don't need the church," because Jesus tells us that we all have work to do in the church—we must fulfill our role as part of the body. We cannot carry the burdens of those we never interact with. Therefore, we must continue to participate in the work, fellowship, and worship of the church—freely giving of ourselves just as Christ has given Himself to us.

➢ **Galatians 6:7 — *Do not be deceived.***

*D*o not be deceived by those who say that God does not care about how we live our lives. In fact, He cares immensely about our conduct and motives. The fact is we reap what we sow, more than we sow, and later than we sow. This means we bear the consequences of our choices for a long time—either for good or for bad. Be very careful to live in loving obedience to the Father.

11 See with what large letters I am writing to you with my own hand.

12 Those who desire to make a good showing in the flesh try to compel you to be circumcised, simply so that they will not be persecuted for the cross of Christ.

13 For those who are circumcised do not even keep the Law themselves, but they desire to have you circumcised so that they may boast in your flesh.

14 But may it never be that I would boast, except in the cross of our Lord Jesus Christ, through which the world has been crucified to me, and I to the world.

➤ 15 For neither is circumcision anything, nor uncircumcision, but a new creation.

16 And those who will walk by this rule, peace and mercy be upon them, and upon the Israel of God.

17 From now on let no one cause trouble for me, for I bear on my body the brand-marks of Jesus.

18 The grace of our Lord Jesus Christ be with your spirit, brethren. Amen.

LIFE LESSONS

➤ **Galatians 6:15** — *For neither is circumcision anything, nor uncircumcision, but a new creation.*

*G*od makes us into totally new people—not by assigning us religious rituals to observe or by reforming our behavior, but by making us into completely new creations (2 Cor. 5:17). He then gives us His nature by sending His Holy Spirit to indwell us and transform us into His likeness (1 Cor. 6:19, 20).

SEPTEMBER 29

Isaiah 49:1—50:11

49 LISTEN to Me, O islands,
And pay attention, you peoples
from afar.
The LORD called Me from the womb;
From the body of My mother He
named Me.

2 He has made My mouth like a sharp
sword,
In the shadow of His hand He has
concealed Me;
And He has also made Me a select
arrow,
He has hidden Me in His quiver.

3 He said to Me, "You are My
Servant, Israel,
In Whom I will show My glory."

4 But I said, "I have toiled in vain,
I have spent My strength for
nothing and vanity;
Yet surely the justice *due* to Me is
with the LORD,
And My reward with My God."

5 And now says the LORD, who
formed Me from the womb to be
His Servant,
To bring Jacob back to Him, so that
Israel might be gathered to Him

(For I am honored in the sight of the
LORD,
And My God is My strength),

6 He says, "It is too small a thing that
You should be My Servant
To raise up the tribes of Jacob and
to restore the preserved ones of
Israel;
I will also make You a light of the
nations
So that My salvation may reach to
the end of the earth."

7 Thus says the LORD, the Redeemer
of Israel *and* its Holy One,
To the despised One,
To the One abhorred by the nation,
To the Servant of rulers,
"Kings will see and arise,
Princes will also bow down,
Because of the LORD who is faithful,
the Holy One of Israel who has
chosen You."

8 Thus says the LORD,
"In a favorable time I have answered
You,
And in a day of salvation I have
helped You;
And I will keep You and give You for
a covenant of the people,
To restore the land, to make *them*
inherit the desolate heritages;

9 Saying to those who are bound, 'Go
     forth,'
   To those who are in darkness,
     'Show yourselves.'
   Along the roads they will feed,
   And their pasture *will be* on all bare
     heights.
10 "They will not hunger or thirst,
   Nor will the scorching heat or sun
     strike them down;
   For He who has compassion on
     them will lead them
   And will guide them to springs of
     water.
11 "I will make all My mountains a
     road,
   And My highways will be
     raised up.
12 "Behold, these will come from
     afar;
   And lo, these *will come* from the
     north and from the west,
   And these from the land of Sinim."
13 Shout for joy, O heavens! And
     rejoice, O earth!
   Break forth into joyful shouting,
     O mountains!
   For the LORD has comforted His
     people
   And will have compassion on His
     afflicted.
14 But Zion said, "The LORD has forsaken
     me,
   And the Lord has forgotten me."
➤ 15 "Can a woman forget her nursing
     child
   And have no compassion on the son
     of her womb?
✳   Even these may forget, but I will not
     forget you.
16 "Behold, I have inscribed you on the
     palms *of My hands*;
   Your walls are continually before
     Me.
17 "Your builders hurry;
   Your destroyers and devastators
   Will depart from you.

LIFE LESSONS

➤ **Isaiah 49:15 — *"I will not forget you."***

*G*od loves you more than any mother
has ever loved her own son or
daughter. Everything He does in your
life, He does out of love. He allows even
the hard times for your benefit.

---

18 "Lift up your eyes and look
     around;
   All of them gather together, they
     come to you.
   As I live," declares the LORD,
   "You will surely put on all of them
     as jewels and bind them on as a
     bride.
19 "For your waste and desolate places
     and your destroyed land—
   Surely now you will be too cramped
     for the inhabitants,
   And those who swallowed you will
     be far away.
20 "The children of whom you were
     bereaved will yet say in your
     ears,
   'The place is too cramped for me;
   Make room for me that I may live
     here.'
21 "Then you will say in your heart,
   'Who has begotten these for me,
   Since I have been bereaved of my
     children
   And am barren, an exile and a
     wanderer?
   And who has reared these?
   Behold, I was left alone;
   From where did these come?'"
22 Thus says the Lord GOD,
   "Behold, I will lift up My hand to the
     nations
   And set up My standard to the
     peoples;
   And they will bring your sons in
     their bosom,
   And your daughters will be carried
     on *their* shoulders.
23 "Kings will be your guardians,
   And their princesses your nurses.
   They will bow down to you with
     their faces to the earth
   And lick the dust of your feet;
   And *you* will know that I am the
     LORD;
   Those who hopefully wait for Me
     will not be put to shame.
24 "Can the prey be taken from the
     mighty man,
   Or the captives of a tyrant be
     rescued?"
25 Surely, thus says the LORD,
   "Even the captives of the mighty
     man will be taken away,
   And the prey of the tyrant will be
     rescued;

For I will contend with the one who
    contends with you,
And I will save your sons.

26 "I will feed your oppressors with
    their own flesh,
And they will become drunk with
    their own blood as with sweet
    wine;
And all flesh will know that I, the
    LORD, am your Savior
And your Redeemer, the Mighty
    One of Jacob."

50 THUS says the LORD,
"Where is the certificate of
    divorce
By which I have sent your mother
    away?
Or to whom of My creditors did I
    sell you?
Behold, you were sold for your
    iniquities,
And for your transgressions your
    mother was sent away.

2 "Why was there no man when I
    came?
When I called, *why* was there none
    to answer?
Is My hand so short that it cannot
    ransom?
Or have I no power to deliver?
Behold, I dry up the sea with My
    rebuke,
I make the rivers a wilderness;
Their fish stink for lack of water
And die of thirst.

3 "I clothe the heavens with
    blackness
And make sackcloth their
    covering."

4 The Lord GOD has given Me the
    tongue of disciples,
That I may know how to sustain the
    weary one with a word.
He awakens *Me* morning by
    morning,
He awakens My ear to listen as a
    disciple.

5 The Lord GOD has opened My
    ear;
And I was not disobedient
Nor did I turn back.

6 I gave My back to those who strike
    Me,
And My cheeks to those who pluck
    out the beard;
I did not cover My face from
    humiliation and spitting.

7 For the Lord GOD helps Me,
Therefore, I am not disgraced;
Therefore, I have set My face like
    flint,
And I know that I will not be
    ashamed.

8 He who vindicates Me is near;
Who will contend with Me?
Let us stand up to each other;
Who has a case against Me?
Let him draw near to Me.

9 Behold, the Lord GOD helps Me;
Who is he who condemns Me?
Behold, they will all wear out like a
    garment;
The moth will eat them.

10 Who is among you that fears the
    LORD,
That obeys the voice of His
    servant,
That walks in darkness and has no
    light?
Let him trust in the name of the
    LORD and rely on his God.

11 Behold, all you who kindle a
    fire,
Who encircle yourselves with
    firebrands,
Walk in the light of your fire
And among the brands you have
    set ablaze.
This you will have from My
    hand:
You will lie down in torment.

LIFE LESSONS

➤ **Isaiah 50:7 — *"I have set My face
like flint, and I know that I will not be
ashamed."***

*I*f you know that God is for you, then
you too can set your face like a flint,
and "be steadfast, immovable, always
abounding in the work of the Lord,
knowing that your toil is not in vain"
(1 Cor. 15:58).

➤ **Isaiah 50:10 — *"Who . . . walks in
darkness and has no light? Let him trust
in the name of the Lord and rely on his
God."***

*D*ark times come upon all of us; that's
part of life in a fallen world. But we
do not have to grope blindly, as those
without hope. We trust God in the dark,
take His hand, and go where He leads.

Psalm 112:1–4

112 PRAISE the LORD!
How blessed is the man who
fears the LORD,
Who greatly delights in His
commandments.
2 His descendants will be mighty on
earth;
The generation of the upright will
be blessed.
3 Wealth and riches are in his
house,
And his righteousness endures
forever.
4 Light arises in the darkness for the
upright;
He is gracious and compassionate
and righteous.

Proverbs 26:13–15

13 The sluggard says, "There is a lion
in the road!
A lion is in the open square!"
14 *As* the door turns on its hinges,
So *does* the sluggard on his bed.
15 The sluggard buries his hand in the
dish;
He is weary of bringing it to his
mouth again.

Ephesians 1:1–23

1 PAUL, an apostle of Christ Jesus by
the will of God,
To the saints who are at Ephesus
and *who are* faithful in Christ Jesus:
2 Grace to you and peace from God
our Father and the Lord Jesus Christ.
3 Blessed *be* the God and Father of
our Lord Jesus Christ, who has blessed
us with every spiritual blessing in the
heavenly *places* in Christ,
4 just as He chose us in Him before the
foundation of the world, that we would
be holy and blameless before Him. In
love
5 He predestined us to adoption as
sons through Jesus Christ to Himself, according to the kind intention of His will,

6 to the praise of the glory of His grace,
which He freely bestowed on us in the
Beloved.
7 In Him we have redemption through
His blood, the forgiveness of our trespasses, according to the riches of His
grace
8 which He lavished on us. In all wisdom and insight
9 He made known to us the mystery of
His will, according to His kind intention
which He purposed in Him
10 with a view to an administration
suitable to the fullness of the times, *that
is,* the summing up of all things in Christ,
things in the heavens and things on the
earth. In Him
11 also we have obtained an inheritance, having been predestined according to His purpose who works all things
after the counsel of His will,
12 to the end that we who were the first
to hope in Christ would be to the praise
of His glory.
13 In Him, you also, after listening to
the message of truth, the gospel of your
salvation—having also believed, you
were sealed in Him with the Holy Spirit
of promise,
14 who is given as a pledge of our inheritance, with a view to the redemption
of *God's own* possession, to the praise of
His glory.
15 For this reason I too, having heard
of the faith in the Lord Jesus which *exists* among you and your love for all the
saints,
16 do not cease giving thanks for you,
while making mention *of you* in my
prayers;
17 that the God of our Lord Jesus
Christ, the Father of glory, may give to

LIFE LESSONS

➢ **Ephesians 1:3 — *Blessed be the God
and Father of our Lord Jesus Christ, who
has blessed us with every spiritual blessing.***

God is generous when it comes to
bestowing His blessings to us, His
much-loved children. In fact, He has
already given us every spiritual blessing,
securing them for us in heaven, where
none can be stolen, damaged, or kept
back.

WHAT THE BIBLE SAYS ABOUT

The Holy Spirit in Us

Ephesians 1:13, 14

*D*id you know that we can short-circuit the effective work of the Holy Spirit in our lives by grieving Him? Paul wrote, "Do not grieve the Holy Spirit of God" (Eph. 4:30).

How do we grieve the Holy Spirit? We grieve Him when we disobey God's commandments and when we choose to act in unrighteous ways. In other words, we displease the Lord when we know what to do and then choose to do the opposite.

The Ephesians knew very well that it was not godly to lie, steal, remain angry with one another, or speak cutting, hurting words to each another. They knew that such evil things "give the devil an opportunity" (Eph. 4:27). Yet they became entangled in these very things, and they suffered in their relationships.

Paul lived and ministered among them for two years, and his ministry had a powerful impact on the entire city of Ephesus. He admonished them not to compromise their faith by doing the things common among the non-believers! He began with the basics of the Christian faith and taught them how to live godly lives.

When the Ephesians broke one of the most obvious of God's commandments, they caused sorrow to the Holy Spirit. Paul said, in effect, "Your ungodly behavior breaks the heart of God."

The Holy Spirit is grieved not only because our conduct tarnishes God's good name, but also because He loves us and deeply desires to reward us for our obedience. He longs to see the fruit of the Spirit alive and growing in our lives. He knows sin damages our relationships with God and with those we love. It saddles us with burdens that God never meant for us to bear. And He is grieved by our compromise and failure to live according to His standards.

So how can we avoid grieving the Spirit of God?

We can choose to keep His commandments and to lead a disciplined life by depending on the power of the Spirit. When we sin, we confess the sin immediately and repent of it, changing our minds and our behavior to conform to God's Word.

As we ask the Holy Spirit to lead us and help us every day, we gain His help to enjoy a successful Christian walk. He keeps our footing sure. ◉

---

you a spirit of wisdom and of revelation in the knowledge of Him.

➤ 18 *I pray that* the eyes of your heart may be enlightened, so that you will know what is the hope of His calling, what are the riches of the glory of His inheritance in the saints,

➤ 19 and what is the surpassing greatness of His power toward us who believe. *These are* in accordance with the working of the strength of His might

20 which He brought about in Christ, when He raised Him from the dead and seated Him at His right hand in the heavenly *places*,

21 far above all rule and authority and power and dominion, and every name that is named, not only in this age but also in the one to come.

22 And He put all things in subjection under His feet, and gave Him as head over all things to the church,

23 which is His body, the fullness of Him who fills all in all.

LIFE LESSONS

➤ **Ephesians 1:18 —** *Know what is the hope of His calling, what are the riches of the glory of His inheritance in the saints.*

*T*here is a big difference between having the blessings of God and actually enjoying them. We experience the riches of the Lord's grace by learning what blessings He has provided for us and then laying hold of them by faith.

➤ **Ephesians 1:19 —** *The surpassing greatness of His power toward us who believe.*

*T*he disciples continually marveled at the astounding miracles that the Lord performed (Matt. 9:33; 21:20; Mark 4:41). That same power is available to us by faith through the Spirit.

51 "LISTEN to me, you who pursue righteousness,
Who seek the LORD:
Look to the rock from which you were hewn
And to the quarry from which you were dug.

2 "Look to Abraham your father
And to Sarah who gave birth to you in pain;
When *he was but* one I called him,
Then I blessed him and multiplied him."

3 Indeed, the LORD will comfort Zion;
He will comfort all her waste places.
And her wilderness He will make like Eden,
And her desert like the garden of the LORD;
Joy and gladness will be found in her,
Thanksgiving and sound of a melody.

4 "Pay attention to Me, O My people,
And give ear to Me, O My nation;
For a law will go forth from Me,
And I will set My justice for a light of the peoples.

5 "My righteousness is near, My salvation has gone forth,
And My arms will judge the peoples;
The coastlands will wait for Me,
And for My arm they will wait expectantly.

6 "Lift up your eyes to the sky,
Then look to the earth beneath;
For the sky will vanish like smoke,
And the earth will wear out like a garment
And its inhabitants will die in like manner;
But My salvation will be forever,
And My righteousness will not wane.

7 "Listen to Me, you who know righteousness,
A people in whose heart is My law;
Do not fear the reproach of man,
Nor be dismayed at their revilings.

8 "For the moth will eat them like a garment,
And the grub will eat them like wool.
But My righteousness will be forever,
And My salvation to all generations."

9 Awake, awake, put on strength,
O arm of the LORD;
Awake as in the days of old, the generations of long ago.
Was it not You who cut Rahab in pieces,
Who pierced the dragon?

10 Was it not You who dried up the sea,
The waters of the great deep;
Who made the depths of the sea a pathway
For the redeemed to cross over?

11 So the ransomed of the LORD will return
And come with joyful shouting to Zion,
And everlasting joy *will be* on their heads.
They will obtain gladness and joy,
And sorrow and sighing will flee away.

12 "I, even I, am He who comforts you. ◄
Who are you that you are afraid of man who dies
And of the son of man who is made like grass,

13 That you have forgotten the LORD your Maker,
Who stretched out the heavens
And laid the foundations of the earth,
That you fear continually all day long because of the fury of the oppressor,
As he makes ready to destroy?
But where is the fury of the oppressor?

14 "The exile will soon be set free, and

LIFE LESSONS

➤ **Isaiah 51:12 — "I . . . am He who comforts you."**

*G*od does not leave us comfortless. He always comes with words of hope and mercy. His goal in allowing hurt is not to break us, but to teach us to draw close to Him in times of heartache and extreme pressure.

will not die in the dungeon, nor will his
bread be lacking.

15 "For I am the LORD your God, who
stirs up the sea and its waves roar (the
LORD of hosts is His name).

16 "I have put My words in your mouth
and have covered you with the shadow
of My hand, to establish the heavens, to
found the earth, and to say to Zion, 'You
are My people.'"

17 Rouse yourself! Rouse yourself!
    Arise, O Jerusalem,
    You who have drunk from the
        LORD's hand the cup of His anger;
    The chalice of reeling you have
        drained to the dregs.

18 There is none to guide her among
        all the sons she has borne,
    Nor is there one to take her by the
        hand among all the sons she has
        reared.

19 These two things have befallen you;
    Who will mourn for you?
    The devastation and destruction,
        famine and sword;
    How shall I comfort you?

20 Your sons have fainted,
    They lie *helpless* at the head of
        every street,
    Like an antelope in a net,
    Full of the wrath of the LORD,
    The rebuke of your God.

21 Therefore, please hear this, you
        afflicted,
    Who are drunk, but not with wine:

22 Thus says your Lord, the LORD,
        even your God
    Who contends for His people,
    "Behold, I have taken out of your
        hand the cup of reeling,
    The chalice of My anger;
    You will never drink it again.

23 "I will put it into the hand of your
        tormentors,
    Who have said to you, 'Lie down
        that we may walk over *you.*'
    You have even made your back like
        the ground
    And like the street for those who
        walk over *it.*"

52 AWAKE, awake,
    Clothe yourself in your strength,
        O Zion;
    Clothe yourself in your beautiful
        garments,
    O Jerusalem, the holy city;

For the uncircumcised and the
    unclean
Will no longer come into you.

2   Shake yourself from the dust, rise
        up,
    O captive Jerusalem;
    Loose yourself from the chains
        around your neck,
    O captive daughter of Zion.

3   For thus says the LORD, "You were ◄
sold for nothing and you will be redeemed without money."

4   For thus says the Lord GOD, "My
people went down at the first into Egypt
to reside there; then the Assyrian oppressed them without cause.

5   "Now therefore, what do I have here,"
declares the LORD, "seeing that My
people have been taken away without
cause?" *Again* the LORD declares, "Those
who rule over them howl, and My name
is continually blasphemed all day long.

6   "Therefore My people shall know My
name; therefore in that day I am the one
who is speaking, 'Here I am.'"

7   How lovely on the mountains
    Are the feet of him who brings good
        news,
    Who announces peace
    And brings good news of happiness,
    Who announces salvation,
    And says to Zion, "Your God
        reigns!"

8   Listen! Your watchmen lift up *their*
        voices,
    They shout joyfully together;
    For they will see with their own
        eyes
    When the LORD restores Zion.

9   Break forth, shout joyfully together,

LIFE LESSONS

➤ **Isaiah 52:3** — *"You were sold for
nothing and you will be redeemed without money."*

*W*hy do we sin? Although there
are many reasons—such as fear,
jealousy, insecurity, lust, unforgiveness,
compromise, and so forth—at the core
of all of them is pride. We sin because
we think we know better about what
we need than God does. But we always
get burned when we follow our plans
instead of His (Prov. 14:12). We sell ourselves into destruction for nothing. But
God buys us back with Himself.

You waste places of Jerusalem;
For the LORD has comforted His
   people,
He has redeemed Jerusalem.
10 The LORD has bared His holy arm
In the sight of all the nations,
That all the ends of the earth may
   see
The salvation of our God.
11 Depart, depart, go out from there,
Touch nothing unclean;
Go out of the midst of her, purify
   yourselves,
You who carry the vessels of the
   LORD.
12 But you will not go out in haste,
Nor will you go as fugitives;
For the LORD will go before you,
And the God of Israel *will be* your
   rear guard.
13 Behold, My servant will prosper,
He will be high and lifted up and
   greatly exalted.
14 Just as many were astonished at
   you, *My people,*
So His appearance was marred
   more than any man
And His form more than the sons of
   men.
15 Thus He will sprinkle many nations,
Kings will shut their mouths on
   account of Him;
For what had not been told them
   they will see,
And what they had not heard they
   will understand.

Psalm 112:5–10

5 It is well with the man who is
   gracious and lends;
He will maintain his cause in
   judgment.
6 For he will never be shaken;
The righteous will be remembered
   forever.
7 He will not fear evil tidings;
His heart is steadfast, trusting in the
   LORD.
8 His heart is upheld, he will not fear,
Until he looks *with satisfaction* on
   his adversaries.
9 He has given freely to the poor,
His righteousness endures forever;
His horn will be exalted in honor.

10 The wicked will see it and be
   vexed,
He will gnash his teeth and melt
   away;
The desire of the wicked will perish.

Proverbs 26:16

16 The sluggard is wiser in his own
   eyes
Than seven men who can give a
   discreet answer.

Ephesians 2:1–22

2 AND you were dead in your trespasses and sins,
2   in which you formerly walked according to the course of this world, according to the prince of the power of the
air, of the spirit that is now working in
the sons of disobedience.
3   Among them we too all formerly
lived in the lusts of our flesh, indulging
the desires of the flesh and of the mind,
and were by nature children of wrath,
even as the rest.
4   But God, being rich in mercy, because of His great love with which He
loved us,

LIFE LESSONS

Isaiah 52:14 — *His appearance was
marred more than any man and His form
more than the sons of men.*

*J*esus went through agony for our
sakes. He suffered, not through any
personal fault, but because of our sins.
He willingly died for us, that we might
live. What does He ask in return? "If you
love Me," He says, "you will keep my
commandments" (John 14:15).

Ephesians 2:2 — *The spirit that is now
working in the sons of disobedience.*

*A*s the "prince of the power of the
air," Satan is not limited to the
surface of the earth and so can move
quickly to try to prevent unbelievers
from coming to faith. Yet he is no match
for the Holy Spirit.

ANSWERS TO LIFE'S QUESTIONS

How can I develop a better self-image?

EPHESIANS 2:10

*O*n April 12, 1945, U.S. president Franklin Delano Roosevelt was sitting for a portrait, when he died suddenly of a cerebral hemorrhage. The "Unfinished Portrait," as it is called, remains on its easel, looking out on the world much as it did when artist Elizabeth Shoumatoff laid her brush down at the sight of the president's collapse.

The watercolor likeness of the president shows a man of inner strength and calm. Photographs taken days before and placed alongside the artist's canvas for reference, however, reveal a much different view. In them we see a national leader worn emotionally and physically from the political load he bore.

Later, Madam Shoumatoff returned to her work on the president's portrait. She did not choose to complete the watercolor, however. She saw it as complete in its own right. Instead, she began and finished a new portrait, painted in oil. It is a handsome rendering of a strong and confident President Roosevelt, with no visible flaws.

Have you ever wondered how God views your life? Do you worry that He sees your flaws and mistakes and loves you less? Do not worry! God knows you perfectly and loves you completely just the way you are. You are His masterpiece—His workmanship of grace and love—His work of art. He continues to paint the colors of your life in such a way that you will glorify Him.

The apostle Paul tells us: "We are His workmanship, created in Christ Jesus for good works, which God prepared beforehand so that we would walk in them" (Eph. 2:10).

By God's loving grace we are created in the image of Christ. Though our lives remain on the canvas, God has seen the finished portrait. His eternal eyes know exactly where we need His greatest attention. Every frustration, every disappointment, and every joy has a purpose (Rom. 8:28).

Many find this a hard concept to grasp. They see their lives as incomplete, much like the unfinished portrait of President Roosevelt. But God views you from a totally different perspective. When He sees your life, He sees a person of worth and great promise.

God rejoices over you, though He knows you are not yet what you will be when you step into His eternal presence (1 Cor. 13:12). Until that time, the Father is patiently molding and shaping your life into the image of His Son.

---

5   even when we were dead in our transgressions, made us alive together with Christ (by grace you have been saved),
6   and raised us up with Him, and seated us with Him in the heavenly *places* in Christ Jesus,
7   so that in the ages to come He might show the surpassing riches of His grace in kindness toward us in Christ Jesus.
8   For by grace you have been saved through faith; and that not of yourselves, *it is* the gift of God;
9   not as a result of works, so that no one may boast.

LIFE LESSONS

➤ **Ephesians 2:8 —** *By grace you have been saved through faith.*

*S*alvation is a gift of God, presented free and not in exchange for anything when we place our faith in Christ. It therefore magnifies God alone, since He blesses us not because of our merit but because of His goodness.

10 For we are His workmanship, created in Christ Jesus for good works, which God prepared beforehand so that we would walk in them.
11 Therefore remember that formerly you, the Gentiles in the flesh, who are called "Uncircumcision" by the so-called "Circumcision," *which is* performed in the flesh by human hands—
12 *remember* that you were at that time separate from Christ, excluded from the commonwealth of Israel, and strangers to the covenants of promise, having no hope and without God in the world.
13 But now in Christ Jesus you who formerly were far off have been brought near by the blood of Christ.
14 For He Himself is our peace, who made both *groups into* one and broke down the barrier of the dividing wall,
15 by abolishing in His flesh the enmity, *which is* the Law of commandments *contained* in ordinances, so that in Himself He might make the two into one new man, *thus* establishing peace,
16 and might reconcile them both in

LIFE LESSONS

➤ **Ephesians 2:13** — *You who formerly
were far off have been brought near by
the blood of Christ.*

*I*n Paul's day, there was a temptation
to view Jewish Christians as better
and more righteous than Gentile (or
non-Jewish) believers because of the
Lord's promises to Israel and their adherence to the laws and rituals of Judaism.
However, Paul reminds believers that
everyone is unclean before the Lord
and is saved by His grace alone. Now, in
Christ, both Jews and Gentiles have been
brought near and can enjoy fellowship
with God.

one body to God through the cross, by it
having put to death the enmity.

17 And He came and preached peace to
you who were far away, and peace to
those who were near;
18 for through Him we both have our
access in one Spirit to the Father.
19 So then you are no longer strangers
and aliens, but you are fellow citizens
with the saints, and are of God's household,
20 having been built on the foundation of the apostles and prophets,
Christ Jesus Himself being the corner
stone,
21 in whom the whole building, being
fitted together, is growing into a holy
temple in the Lord,
22 in whom you also are being built
together into a dwelling of God in the
Spirit.

Isaiah 53:1—54:17

53 WHO has believed our message?
And to whom has the arm of the
LORD been revealed?
2 For He grew up before Him like a
tender shoot,
And like a root out of parched
ground;
He has no *stately* form or majesty
That we should look upon Him,
Nor appearance that we should be
attracted to Him.
3 He was despised and forsaken of
men,
A man of sorrows and acquainted
with grief;
And like one from whom men hide
their face
He was despised, and we did not
esteem Him.
4 Surely our griefs He Himself bore,
And our sorrows He carried;
Yet we ourselves esteemed Him
stricken,
Smitten of God, and afflicted.
5 But He was pierced through for our
transgressions,
He was crushed for our iniquities;
The chastening for our well-being
fell upon Him,
And by His scourging we are healed.
6 All of us like sheep have gone astray,
Each of us has turned to his own
way;
But the LORD has caused the
iniquity of us all
To fall on Him.
7 He was oppressed and He was
afflicted,
Yet He did not open His mouth;
Like a lamb that is led to slaughter,
And like a sheep that is silent
before its shearers,
So He did not open His mouth.
8 By oppression and judgment He
was taken away;
And as for His generation, who
considered
That He was cut off out of the land
of the living
For the transgression of my people,
to whom the stroke *was due?*
9 His grave was assigned with wicked
men,

Yet He was with a rich man in His
death,
Because He had done no violence,
Nor was there any deceit in His
mouth.
10 But the LORD was pleased
To crush Him, putting *Him* to grief;
If He would render Himself *as a*
guilt offering,
He will see *His* offspring,
He will prolong *His* days,
And the good pleasure of the LORD
will prosper in His hand.
11 As a result of the anguish of His
soul,
He will see *it and* be satisfied;
By His knowledge the Righteous
One,
My Servant, will justify the many,
As He will bear their iniquities.
12 Therefore, I will allot Him a portion
with the great,
And He will divide the booty with
the strong;
Because He poured out Himself to
death,
And was numbered with the
transgressors;
Yet He Himself bore the sin of
many,
And interceded for the
transgressors.

54 "SHOUT for joy, O barren one,
you who have borne no *child;*
Break forth into joyful shouting
and cry aloud, you who have not
travailed;
For the sons of the desolate one *will
be* more numerous

LIFE LESSONS

➢ **Isaiah 53:11 — *The righteous One, My
Servant, will justify the many, as He will
bear their iniquities.***

*J*esus willingly became our substitute
on the Cross. God made Jesus "who
knew no sin to be sin on our behalf, so
that we might become the righteousness of God in Him" (2 Cor. 5:21). Christ
nailed your sins to the Cross and made
you "alive together with Him, having
forgiven us all our transgressions, having canceled out the certificate of debt
consisting of decrees against us" (Col.
2:13, 14).

ANSWERS TO LIFE'S QUESTIONS

Where is God when I'm in pain?

ISAIAH 53

Children periodically need painful immunizations. Often they do not understand that while inoculations hurt, they also protect from serious diseases. From their point of view, the doctor is assaulting them—and someone who loves them is allowing it!

Such an experience gives us a little insight into God's dealings with His own children. It helps to answer one of the questions we often ask when painful things happen to us: *Where is God?*

The Bible tells us that when the ancient Israelites suffered hardships, God usually made His presence known. He was right there with them. The prophet Isaiah points to the coming of Jesus Christ and His ability to identify with our needs: "In all their affliction He was afflicted" (Is. 63:9).

Do you remember your earthly father restraining you so that the doctor could administer the painful injection? Perhaps you recall him commenting that the experience hurt him more than it did you. That is exactly what God is describing in this passage. To a young mind, such an action seems utterly incomprehensible; but when we have children of our own, we grasp it clearly. Then we begin to understand what kind of Father we really have. He Himself enters into all our agony, and He has tasted our cup of suffering (Heb. 2:17, 18; 4:14–16).

Where is God when we suffer? He is where the pain is. "He was crushed for our iniquities; the chastening for our well-being fell upon Him" (Is. 53:5). God does not pick up and leave us when the hard times come. Instead, He is right there with us, ever mindful of the pain we endure.

But not only does God "feel" for us, He also acts on our behalf—even when we don't know it. So Isaiah says, "The angel of His presence saved them; in His love and in His mercy He redeemed them, and He lifted them and carried them all the days of old" (Is. 63:9). Did ancient Israel realize that God was carrying them through all their trials? No. But He did, nonetheless.

As you face adversity, look into the Savior's tear-stained face—you won't see anything but love. As we follow Jesus, we must bear the fellowship of His suffering. Paul reminds us, "For to you it has been granted for Christ's sake, not only to believe in Him, but also to suffer for His sake" (Phil. 1:29). We must go where He is—and just as He went to the cross, so must we bear our own cross daily (Luke 9:23). Yet in our affliction is one of the sweetest places to find Him, because not only do we experience His freedom, but also His resurrection life in us (Rom. 8:20, 21; 2 Cor. 4:10, 11; Phil. 3:7–11).

Than the sons of the married
    woman," says the LORD.
2 "Enlarge the place of your tent;
    Stretch out the curtains of your
      dwellings, spare not;
    Lengthen your cords
    And strengthen your pegs.
3 "For you will spread abroad to the
      right and to the left,
    And your descendants will possess
      nations
    And will resettle the desolate cities.
4 "Fear not, for you will not be put to
      shame;
    And do not feel humiliated, for you
      will not be disgraced;
    But you will forget the shame of
      your youth,
    And the reproach of your widowhood
      you will remember no more.
5 "For your husband is your Maker,
    Whose name is the LORD of hosts;
    And your Redeemer is the Holy One
      of Israel,

Who is called the God of all the
    earth.
6 "For the LORD has called you,
    Like a wife forsaken and grieved in
      spirit,
    Even like a wife of *one's* youth
      when she is rejected,"
    Says your God.
7 "For a brief moment I forsook you,
    But with great compassion I will
      gather you.
8 "In an outburst of anger
    I hid My face from you for a moment,

LIFE LESSONS

➤ **Isaiah 54:8** — *"With everlasting lovingkindness I will have compassion on you."*

God calls you to obey Him so "that the LORD may turn from His burning anger and show mercy to you, and have compassion on you and make you increase" (Deut. 13:17). He wants to do us good, not harm.

But with everlasting lovingkindness
I will have compassion on you,"
Says the LORD your Redeemer.

9 "For this is like the days of Noah to
Me,
When I swore that the waters of Noah
Would not flood the earth again;
So I have sworn that I will not be
angry with you
Nor will I rebuke you.

10 "For the mountains may be removed
and the hills may shake,
But My lovingkindness will not be
removed from you,
And My covenant of peace will not
be shaken,"
Says the LORD who has compassion
on you.

11 "O afflicted one, storm-tossed, *and*
not comforted,
Behold, I will set your stones in
antimony,
And your foundations I will lay in
sapphires.

12 "Moreover, I will make your
battlements of rubies,
And your gates of crystal,
And your entire wall of precious
stones.

13 "All your sons will be taught of the
LORD;
And the well-being of your sons will
be great.

14 "In righteousness you will be
established;
You will be far from oppression, for
you will not fear;
And from terror, for it will not come
near you.

15 "If anyone fiercely assails *you* it will
not be from Me.
Whoever assails you will fall
because of you.

16 "Behold, I Myself have created the
smith who blows the fire of coals
And brings out a weapon for its
work;
And I have created the destroyer to
ruin.

17 "No weapon that is formed against
you will prosper;
And every tongue that accuses you
in judgment you will condemn.
This is the heritage of the servants
of the LORD,
And their vindication is from Me,"
declares the LORD.

Psalm 113:1–4

11 3 PRAISE the LORD!
Praise, O servants of the LORD,
Praise the name of the LORD.

2 Blessed be the name of the LORD
From this time forth and forever.

3 From the rising of the sun to its
setting
The name of the LORD is to be
praised.

4 The LORD is high above all nations;
His glory is above the heavens.

Proverbs 26:17–19

17 *Like* one who takes a dog by the ears
Is he who passes by *and* meddles
with strife not belonging to him.

18 Like a madman who throws
Firebrands, arrows and death,

19 So is the man who deceives his
neighbor,
And says, "Was I not joking?"

Ephesians 3:1–21

3 FOR this reason I, Paul, the prisoner
of Christ Jesus for the sake of you
Gentiles—

2 if indeed you have heard of the stewardship of God's grace which was given
to me for you;

3 that by revelation there was made
known to me the mystery, as I wrote
before in brief.

4 By referring to this, when you read
you can understand my insight into the
mystery of Christ,

5 which in other generations was not
made known to the sons of men, as it has
now been revealed to His holy apostles
and prophets in the Spirit;

6 *to be specific,* that the Gentiles are
fellow heirs and fellow members of the
body, and fellow partakers of the promise in Christ Jesus through the gospel,

7 of which I was made a minister, according to the gift of God's grace which
was given to me according to the working of His power.

8   To me, the very least of all saints, this grace was given, to preach to the Gentiles the unfathomable riches of Christ,
9   and to bring to light what is the administration of the mystery which for ages has been hidden in God who created all things;
10   so that the manifold wisdom of God might now be made known through the church to the rulers and the authorities in the heavenly *places*.
11   *This was* in accordance with the eternal purpose which He carried out in Christ Jesus our Lord,
12   in whom we have boldness and confident access through faith in Him.
13   Therefore I ask you not to lose heart at my tribulations on your behalf, for they are your glory.
14   For this reason I bow my knees before the Father,
15   from whom every family in heaven and on earth derives its name,
16   that He would grant you, according to the riches of His glory, to be strengthened with power through His Spirit in the inner man,
17   so that Christ may dwell in your hearts through faith; *and* that you, being rooted and grounded in love,
18   may be able to comprehend with all the saints what is the breadth and length and height and depth,
19   and to know the love of Christ which surpasses knowledge, that you may be filled up to all the fullness of God.
20   Now to Him who is able to do far more abundantly beyond all that we ask or think, according to the power that works within us,
21   to Him *be* the glory in the church and in Christ Jesus to all generations forever and ever. Amen.

Isaiah 55:1—56:12

55 "HO! Every one who thirsts, come to the waters;
And you who have no money come, buy and eat.
Come, buy wine and milk
Without money and without cost.
2   "Why do you spend money for what is not bread,
And your wages for what does not satisfy?

Listen carefully to Me, and eat what
is good,
And delight yourself in abundance.

3   "Incline your ear and come to Me.
Listen, that you may live;
And I will make an everlasting
covenant with you,
According to the faithful mercies
shown to David.

4   "Behold, I have made him a witness
to the peoples,
A leader and commander for the
peoples.

5   "Behold, you will call a nation you
do not know,
And a nation which knows you not
will run to you,
Because of the LORD your God, even
the Holy One of Israel;
For He has glorified you."

➤ 6   Seek the LORD while He may be
found;
Call upon Him while He is near.

7   Let the wicked forsake his way
And the unrighteous man his
thoughts;
And let him return to the LORD,
And He will have compassion on
him,
And to our God,
For He will abundantly pardon.

8   "For My thoughts are not your
thoughts,
Nor are your ways My ways,"
declares the LORD.

➤ 9   "For *as* the heavens are higher than
the earth,
So are My ways higher than your
ways
And My thoughts than your
thoughts.

✳ 10   "For as the rain and the snow come
down from heaven,
And do not return there without
watering the earth
And making it bear and sprout,
And furnishing seed to the sower
and bread to the eater;

➤ 11   So will My word be which goes
forth from My mouth;
It will not return to Me empty,
Without accomplishing what I
desire,
And without succeeding *in the
matter* for which I sent it.

12   "For you will go out with joy
And be led forth with peace;

The mountains and the hills will
break forth into shouts of joy
before you,
And all the trees of the field will
clap *their* hands.

13   "Instead of the thorn bush the
cypress will come up,
And instead of the nettle the myrtle
will come up,
And it will be a memorial to the
LORD,
For an everlasting sign which will
not be cut off."

56 THUS says the LORD,
"Preserve justice and do
righteousness,
For My salvation is about to come
And My righteousness to be
revealed.

2   "How blessed is the man who does
this,
And the son of man who takes hold
of it;

LIFE LESSONS

➤ **Isaiah 55:6 —** *Seek the LORD while He
may be found.*

*T*he Lord invites us to come boldly
into His presence—any time of the
day or night—to receive His counsel,
confess our sins, make requests, and simply enjoy His company (Heb. 4:16).

➤ **Isaiah 55:9 —** *"As the heavens are
higher than the earth, so are My ways
higher than your ways."*

*E*ven when we do not understand
what God is up to in our lives—which
may happen frequently—He asks us to
trust Him. He knows what He is doing,
even if we cannot comprehend His methods or timing. To obey God is to bless
ourselves; to disobey Him is to curse ourselves. "I came," Jesus said, "that they
may have life, and have it abundantly"
(John 10:10).

➤ **Isaiah 55:11 —** *"My word . . . will not
return to Me empty."*

*T*he Lord promises to bless His Word,
and we are wise if we honor Him by
representing Scripture as accurately and
effectively as we can whenever we get
the opportunity to speak to others on
His behalf.

Who keeps from profaning the
sabbath,
And keeps his hand from doing any
evil."
3 Let not the foreigner who has joined
himself to the LORD say,
"The LORD will surely separate me
from His people."
Nor let the eunuch say, "Behold, I
am a dry tree."
4 For thus says the LORD,
"To the eunuchs who keep My
sabbaths,
And choose what pleases Me,
And hold fast My covenant,
5 To them I will give in My house and
within My walls a memorial,
And a name better than that of sons
and daughters;
I will give them an everlasting name
which will not be cut off.
6 "Also the foreigners who join
themselves to the LORD,
To minister to Him, and to love the
name of the LORD,
To be His servants, every one who
keeps from profaning the sabbath
And holds fast My covenant;
7 Even those I will bring to My holy
mountain
And make them joyful in My house
of prayer.
Their burnt offerings and their
sacrifices will be acceptable on
My altar;
For My house will be called a house
of prayer for all the peoples."
8 The Lord GOD, who gathers the
dispersed of Israel, declares,
"Yet others I will gather to them, to
those already gathered."
9 All you beasts of the field,
All you beasts in the forest,
Come to eat.
10 His watchmen are blind,
All of them know nothing.

LIFE LESSONS

➤ Isaiah 56:7 — *"My house will be called
a house of prayer."*

Jesus quoted this verse when He drove
the merchants and money changers
out of the temple (Mark 11:15–17). God
is serious about prayer and about His
people gathering to pray together.

All of them are mute dogs unable to
bark,
Dreamers lying down, who love to
slumber;
11 And the dogs are greedy, they are
not satisfied.
And they are shepherds who have
no understanding;
They have all turned to their own
way,
Each one to his unjust gain, to the
last one.
12 "Come," they say, "let us get wine,
and let us drink heavily of strong
drink;
And tomorrow will be like today,
only more so."

Psalm 113:5–9

5 Who is like the LORD our God,
Who is enthroned on high,
6 Who humbles Himself to behold
The things that are in heaven and
in the earth?
7 He raises the poor from the dust
And lifts the needy from the ash
heap,
8 To make *them* sit with princes,
With the princes of His people.
9 He makes the barren woman abide
in the house
As a joyful mother of children.
Praise the LORD!

Proverbs 26:20, 21

20 For lack of wood the fire goes out,
And where there is no whisperer,
contention quiets down.
21 *Like* charcoal to hot embers and
wood to fire,
So is a contentious man to kindle
strife.

Ephesians 4:1–32

4 THEREFORE I, the prisoner of the
Lord, implore you to walk in a manner worthy of the calling with which you
have been called,

2   with all humility and gentleness, with patience, showing tolerance for one another in love,

3   being diligent to preserve the unity of the Spirit in the bond of peace.

4   *There is* one body and one Spirit, just as also you were called in one hope of your calling;

5   one Lord, one faith, one baptism,

6   one God and Father of all who is over all and through all and in all.

7   But to each one of us grace was given according to the measure of Christ's gift.

8   Therefore it says,

"WHEN HE ASCENDED ON HIGH,
HE LED CAPTIVE A HOST OF CAPTIVES,
AND HE GAVE GIFTS TO MEN."

9   (Now this *expression*, "He ascended," what does it mean except that He also had descended into the lower parts of the earth?

10   He who descended is Himself also He who ascended far above all the heavens, so that He might fill all things.)

11   And He gave some *as* apostles, and some *as* prophets, and some *as* evangelists, and some *as* pastors and teachers,

12   for the equipping of the saints for the work of service, to the building up of the body of Christ;

13   until we all attain to the unity of the faith, and of the knowledge of the Son of God, to a mature man, to the measure of the stature which belongs to the fullness of Christ.

14   As a result, we are no longer to be children, tossed here and there by waves and carried about by every wind of doctrine, by the trickery of men, by craftiness in deceitful scheming;

15   but speaking the truth in love, we are to grow up in all *aspects* into Him who is the head, *even* Christ,

16   from whom the whole body, being fitted and held together by what every joint supplies, according to the proper working of each individual part, causes the growth of the body for the building up of itself in love.

17   So this I say, and affirm together with the Lord, that you walk no longer just as the Gentiles also walk, in the futility of their mind,

18   being darkened in their understanding, excluded from the life of God because of the ignorance that is in them, because of the hardness of their heart;

19   and they, having become callous, have given themselves over to sensuality for the practice of every kind of impurity with greediness.

20   But you did not learn Christ in this way,

21   if indeed you have heard Him and have been taught in Him, just as truth is in Jesus,

22   that, in reference to your former manner of life, you lay aside the old self, which is being corrupted in accordance with the lusts of deceit,

23   and that you be renewed in the spirit of your mind,

24   and put on the new self, which in ◄ *the likeness of* God has been created in righteousness and holiness of the truth.

25   Therefore, laying aside falsehood, SPEAK TRUTH EACH ONE *of you* WITH HIS NEIGHBOR, for we are members of one another.

26   BE ANGRY, AND *yet* DO NOT SIN; do not let the sun go down on your anger,

27   and do not give the devil an opportunity.

28   He who steals must steal no longer; but rather he must labor, performing with his own hands what is good, so that he will have *something* to share with one who has need.

29   Let no unwholesome word proceed from your mouth, but only such *a word*

LIFE LESSONS

➤ **Ephesians 4:1 —** *Walk in a manner worthy of the calling with which you have been called.*

*T*o walk worthy of Christ means that we are living in a manner that honors and pleases Him. We were "created in Christ Jesus for good works" (Eph. 2:10), and we should accomplish every assignment He gives us with love and devotion so that others will see our example and glorify Him.

➤ **Ephesians 4:24 —** *Put on the new self.*

*W*hen Paul tells us to "put on the new self," he means that we have to make a conscious, moment-by-moment choice to depend upon the Spirit's power to transform us into the likeness of Christ.

LIFE PRINCIPLE 25

GOD BLESSES US SO THAT WE MIGHT BLESS OTHERS.

EPHESIANS 4:28

*H*ow would you complete the following three statements?
1. God saved me because _____.
2. God's purpose for me is _____.
3. I am most like Jesus when I _____.

This little quiz is not to put you on the spot, but it is to set the proper framework for this life principle:

❶ God saved me because He loves me.

The sole reason God sent His Son to this world to die for our sins was because He loved us. When we acknowledge our sin and need for a Savior, He forgives us, grants us eternal life, and gives us the gift of His Holy Spirit out of His immeasurable love and grace. There is no other reason.

Many people seem to believe that God saves a man or woman because of the person's good works or service. Nothing could be further from the truth. No amount or type of service can earn salvation. The apostle Paul made this very clear when he wrote: "For by grace you have been saved through faith; and that not of yourselves, it is the gift of God; not as a result of works, so that no one may boast" (Eph. 2:8, 9). Even the faith by which we believe that God forgives us and saves us is a divine gift that flows from His love!

This point is critical to understand. Any good we do is in *response* to God's gifts of salvation, eternal life, and the Holy Spirit—never in order to earn, win, or warrant salvation.

❷ God's purpose for me is to bring Him glory.

God saved you and me so that we would serve as examples to others of His love and mercy at work in and through a human life.

Many people seem to think the only reason for salvation is so that a person will go to heaven when he dies. Eternal life is part of God's plan of forgiveness, but that is not the sole reason for our salvation. The Father saved us so that we each might reflect His nature—that we might be His people on this earth, doing the kinds of works that Jesus Himself

would do if He were walking in our shoes, through our world, during our lifetime. He desires to manifest His character through our personalities and giftedness.

When we allow His Holy Spirit to work in us and through us to others, we become vessels of His love in action. We begin to reflect His compassion, love, and mercy to others. And in so doing, we become His witnesses. We bring credit, honor, and glory to *Him*.

❸ I am most like Jesus when I serve others.

The foremost characteristic of the life of Jesus Christ was and is *service*. We are most like Him when we serve as He served.

Many seem to think that a person is most like Jesus when he preaches like Jesus preached, teaches like Jesus taught, heals like Jesus healed, or performs miracles like Jesus performed miracles. They look only at the outward manifestation of a person's witness and ministry.

They need to look beyond the outer manifestation to the motivation for Jesus' life. That motivation was always love. Jesus preached, taught, healed, and performed miracles in order to help others, never to call attention to Himself. He poured out His very life so that others might be saved. Paul wrote, "You know the grace of our Lord Jesus Christ, that though He was rich, yet for your sake He became poor, so that you through His poverty might become rich" (2 Cor. 8:9).

God calls us to serve one another just as Jesus did. He didn't save you or call you to service so that you might be exalted, praised, glorified, or put on a pedestal. He saved you so you could serve Him and others. When we do this, we honor Him with our lives. The most important thing you can do outside of accepting Christ as your Savior is to give your life to Him and allow Him to lead you each day.

Some mistakenly think that what we do is unimportant to God, but this is far from true. He has a plan for each one of us. When we make a decision to walk by faith, He will reveal it to us—and that plan always includes service and dedication to Him and to those He brings into our lives.

God loved us so that we might love others. He blesses us so that we might bless others. That's what the Christian life is all about. ❖

as is good for edification according to the need *of the moment,* so that it will give grace to those who hear.

30   Do not grieve the Holy Spirit of God, by whom you were sealed for the day of redemption.

31   Let all bitterness and wrath and anger and clamor and slander be put away from you, along with all malice.

32   Be kind to one another, tender-hearted, forgiving each other, just as God in Christ also has forgiven you.

OCTOBER 3

◈ Isaiah 57:1—58:14

57 THE righteous man perishes, and no man takes it to heart;
And devout men are taken away, while no one understands.
For the righteous man is taken away from evil,

2   He enters into peace;
They rest in their beds,
Each one who walked in his upright way.

3   "But come here, you sons of a sorceress,
Offspring of an adulterer and a prostitute.

4   "Against whom do you jest?
Against whom do you open wide your mouth
And stick out your tongue?
Are you not children of rebellion,
Offspring of deceit,

5   *Who* inflame yourselves among the oaks,
Under every luxuriant tree,
Who slaughter the children in the ravines,
Under the clefts of the crags?

6   "Among the smooth *stones* of the ravine
Is your portion, they are your lot;
Even to them you have poured out a drink offering,
You have made a grain offering.
Shall I relent concerning these things?

7   "Upon a high and lofty mountain
You have made your bed.
You also went up there to offer sacrifice.

8   "Behind the door and the doorpost
You have set up your sign;
Indeed, far removed from Me, you have uncovered yourself,
And have gone up and made your bed wide.

And you have made an agreement for yourself with them,
You have loved their bed,
You have looked on *their* manhood.

9   "You have journeyed to the king with oil
And increased your perfumes;
You have sent your envoys a great distance
And made *them* go down to Sheol.

10   "You were tired out by the length of your road,
Yet you did not say, 'It is hopeless.'
You found renewed strength,
Therefore you did not faint.

11   "Of whom were you worried and fearful
When you lied, and did not remember Me
Nor give *Me* a thought?
Was I not silent even for a long time
So you do not fear Me?

12   "I will declare your righteousness and your deeds,
But they will not profit you.

13   "When you cry out, let your collection *of idols* deliver you.
But the wind will carry all of them up,
And a breath will take *them away.*
But he who takes refuge in Me will inherit the land
And will possess My holy mountain."

LIFE LESSONS

➤ **Isaiah 57:11 — *"Was I not silent even for a long time so you do not fear Me?"***

The silence of God leads many to believe either that He doesn't exist or that He doesn't care enough to make Himself obvious. Both are mistakes. The Lord can roar, but He prefers to speak in a Shepherd's voice (Jer. 25:30; John 10:16).

14 And it will be said,
"Build up, build up, prepare the way,
Remove *every* obstacle out of the
way of My people."

➤ 15 For thus says the high and exalted
One
Who lives forever, whose name is
Holy,
"I dwell *on* a high and holy place,
And *also* with the contrite and lowly
of spirit
In order to revive the spirit of the
lowly
And to revive the heart of the contrite.

16 "For I will not contend forever,
Nor will I always be angry;
For the spirit would grow faint
before Me,
And the breath *of those whom* I
have made.

17 "Because of the iniquity of his unjust
gain I was angry and struck him;
I hid *My face* and was angry,
And he went on turning away, in the
way of his heart.

18 "I have seen his ways, but I will heal
him;
I will lead him and restore comfort
to him and to his mourners,

19 Creating the praise of the lips.
Peace, peace to him who is far and
to him who is near,"
Says the LORD, "and I will heal him."

20 But the wicked are like the tossing
sea,
For it cannot be quiet,
And its waters toss up refuse and
mud.

21 "There is no peace," says my God,
"for the wicked."

58 "CRY loudly, do not hold back;
Raise your voice like a trumpet,
And declare to My people their
transgression

And to the house of Jacob their
sins.

2 "Yet they seek Me day by day and
delight to know My ways,
As a nation that has done
righteousness
And has not forsaken the ordinance
of their God.
They ask Me *for* just decisions,
They delight in the nearness of God.

3 'Why have we fasted and You do not
see?
Why have we humbled ourselves
and You do not notice?'
Behold, on the day of your fast you
find *your* desire,
And drive hard all your workers.

4 "Behold, you fast for contention and
strife and to strike with a wicked
fist.
You do not fast like *you do* today to
make your voice heard on high.

5 "Is it a fast like this which I choose, a
day for a man to humble himself?
Is it for bowing one's head like a reed
And for spreading out sackcloth
and ashes as a bed?
Will you call this a fast, even an
acceptable day to the LORD?

6 "Is this not the fast which I choose,   ◄
To loosen the bonds of wickedness,
To undo the bands of the yoke,
And to let the oppressed go free
And break every yoke?

7 "Is it not to divide your bread with
the hungry
And bring the homeless poor into
the house;
When you see the naked, to cover
him;
And not to hide yourself from your
own flesh?

8 "Then your light will break out like
the dawn,

And your recovery will speedily
   spring forth;
And your righteousness will go
   before you;
The glory of the LORD will be your
   rear guard.
9 "Then you will call, and the LORD
   will answer;
You will cry, and He will say, 'Here I
   am.'
If you remove the yoke from your
   midst,
The pointing of the finger and
   speaking wickedness,
10 And if you give yourself to the
   hungry
And satisfy the desire of the
   afflicted,
Then your light will rise in
   darkness
And your gloom *will become* like
   midday.
11 "And the LORD will continually guide
   you,
And satisfy your desire in scorched
   places,
And give strength to your bones;
And you will be like a watered
   garden,
And like a spring of water whose
   waters do not fail.
12 "Those from among you will rebuild
   the ancient ruins;
You will raise up the age-old
   foundations;
And you will be called the repairer
   of the breach,
The restorer of the streets in which
   to dwell.
13 "If because of the sabbath, you turn
   your foot
From doing your *own* pleasure on
   My holy day,
And call the sabbath a delight, the
   holy *day* of the LORD honorable,
And honor it, desisting from your
   own ways,
From seeking your *own* pleasure
And speaking *your own* word,
14 Then you will take delight in the
   LORD,
And I will make you ride on the
   heights of the earth;
And I will feed you *with* the
   heritage of Jacob your father,
For the mouth of the LORD has
   spoken."

Psalm 114:1–8

114 WHEN Israel went forth from
      Egypt,
   The house of Jacob from a people of
      strange language,
2 Judah became His sanctuary,
   Israel, His dominion.
3 The sea looked and fled;
   The Jordan turned back.
4 The mountains skipped like rams,
   The hills, like lambs.
5 What ails you, O sea, that you flee?
   O Jordan, that you turn back?
6 O mountains, that you skip like
      rams?
   O hills, like lambs?
7 Tremble, O earth, before the Lord,
   Before the God of Jacob,
8 Who turned the rock into a pool of
      water,
   The flint into a fountain of water.

Proverbs 26:22

22 The words of a whisperer are like
      dainty morsels,
   And they go down into the
      innermost parts of the body.

Ephesians 5:1–14

5 THEREFORE be imitators of God, as
  beloved children;
2 and walk in love, just as Christ also
loved you and gave Himself up for us,
an offering and a sacrifice to God as a
fragrant aroma.
3 But immorality or any impurity or

LIFE LESSONS

➤ **Psalm 114:7 —** *Tremble, O earth,*
before the LORD, before the God of Jacob.

*T*here are at least two kinds of "trembling" in Scripture. Both describe
genuine fear in the presence of overwhelming power, but one takes quaking
pleasure in that power, while the other
sees in it only destruction.

WHAT THE BIBLE SAYS ABOUT

A Child's First Image of God

Ephesians 5:1, 2

A child's first image of God is his or her earthly father. We Christians spend a lot of time discussing ways to protect or improve our witness. We need to live our faith in front of coworkers and friends, but in the privacy of our homes, we also want our families to see Jesus in us. If we show forgiveness, patience, and acceptance, then our children will expect to find those traits in the Lord.

In a similar way, negative behaviors—for example, consistent harshness, busyness, or emotional neglect—also shape a child's view of God. I remember a young man who came

to me worried about his salvation. He had received Christ as his personal Savior but wasn't convinced that he was truly forgiven. When I opened the Word of God to share some assurances with him, he responded, "I believe them, but I'm just not sure God's promises apply to me." He seemed surprised when I then asked about his relationship with his father. During our conversation, it came out that his dad had often made promises he failed to keep. Now, years later, the son lacked certainty that God would keep His word.

Being a reflection of the heavenly Father requires no special skills; the only training guide we need is the Bible. By approaching fatherhood as an area of service and ministry, all men are able to be successful dads. As with any service rendered for God, the Holy Spirit offers fathers wisdom and guidance in the raising of children. ◈

greed must not even be named among you, as is proper among saints;
4 and *there must be no* filthiness and silly talk, or coarse jesting, which are not fitting, but rather giving of thanks.
5 For this you know with certainty, that no immoral or impure person or covetous man, who is an idolater, has an inheritance in the kingdom of Christ and God.
6 Let no one deceive you with empty words, for because of these things the

wrath of God comes upon the sons of disobedience.
7 Therefore do not be partakers with them;
8 for you were formerly darkness, but now you are Light in the Lord; walk as children of Light
9 (for the fruit of the Light *consists* in all goodness and righteousness and truth),
10 trying to learn what is pleasing to the Lord.
11 Do not participate in the unfruitful deeds of darkness, but instead even expose them;
12 for it is disgraceful even to speak of the things which are done by them in secret.
13 But all things become visible when they are exposed by the light, for everything that becomes visible is light.
14 For this reason it says,
"Awake, sleeper,
And arise from the dead,
And Christ will shine on you."

LIFE LESSONS

➤ Ephesians 5:1 — *Be imitators of God, as beloved children.*

If we are children of God, it only makes sense that we are to imitate our Father. And if we refuse to walk in the ways of our heavenly Father, there is biblical reason to wonder who our father really is (1 John 3:10).

Isaiah 59:1—60:22

59 BEHOLD, the LORD's hand is not so short
That it cannot save;

Nor is His ear so dull
That it cannot hear.
2 But your iniquities have made a separation between you and your God,
And your sins have hidden *His* face

from you so that He does not hear.

3 For your hands are defiled with blood
And your fingers with iniquity;
Your lips have spoken falsehood,
Your tongue mutters wickedness.

4 No one sues righteously and no one pleads honestly.
They trust in confusion and speak lies;
They conceive mischief and bring forth iniquity.

5 They hatch adders' eggs and weave the spider's web;
He who eats of their eggs dies,
And *from* that which is crushed a snake breaks forth.

6 Their webs will not become clothing,
Nor will they cover themselves with their works;
Their works are works of iniquity,
And an act of violence is in their hands.

7 Their feet run to evil,
And they hasten to shed innocent blood;
Their thoughts are thoughts of iniquity,
Devastation and destruction are in their highways.

8 They do not know the way of peace,
And there is no justice in their tracks;
They have made their paths crooked,
Whoever treads on them does not know peace.

9 Therefore justice is far from us,
And righteousness does not overtake us;
We hope for light, but behold, darkness,
For brightness, but we walk in gloom.

10 We grope along the wall like blind men,
We grope like those who have no eyes;
We stumble at midday as in the twilight,
Among those who are vigorous *we are* like dead men.

11 All of us growl like bears,
And moan sadly like doves;
We hope for justice, but there is none,
For salvation, *but* it is far from us.

12 For our transgressions are multiplied before You,
And our sins testify against us;
For our transgressions are with us,
And we know our iniquities:

13 Transgressing and denying the LORD,
And turning away from our God,
Speaking oppression and revolt,
Conceiving *in* and uttering from the heart lying words.

14 Justice is turned back,
And righteousness stands far away;
For truth has stumbled in the street,
And uprightness cannot enter.

15 Yes, truth is lacking;
And he who turns aside from evil makes himself a prey.
Now the LORD saw,
And it was displeasing in His sight that there was no justice.

16 And He saw that there was no man,
And was astonished that there was no one to intercede;
Then His own arm brought salvation to Him,
And His righteousness upheld Him.

17 He put on righteousness like a breastplate,
And a helmet of salvation on His head;
And He put on garments of vengeance for clothing
And wrapped Himself with zeal as a mantle.

18 According to *their* deeds, so He will repay,
Wrath to His adversaries, recompense to His enemies;
To the coastlands He will make recompense.

19 So they will fear the name of the LORD from the west
And His glory from the rising of the sun,
For He will come like a rushing stream

Which the wind of the LORD
drives.
20 "A Redeemer will come to Zion,
And to those who turn from
transgression in Jacob," declares
the LORD.
21 "As for Me, this is My covenant with
them," says the LORD: "My Spirit which
is upon you, and My words which I have
put in your mouth shall not depart from
your mouth, nor from the mouth of your
offspring, nor from the mouth of your
offspring's offspring," says the LORD,
"from now and forever."

60 "ARISE, shine; for your light has
come,
And the glory of the LORD has risen
upon you.
2 "For behold, darkness will cover the
earth
And deep darkness the peoples;
But the LORD will rise upon you
And His glory will appear upon you.
3 "Nations will come to your light,
And kings to the brightness of your
rising.
4 "Lift up your eyes round about and
see;
They all gather together, they come
to you.
Your sons will come from afar,
And your daughters will be carried
in the arms.
5 "Then you will see and be radiant,
And your heart will thrill and
rejoice;
Because the abundance of the sea
will be turned to you,
The wealth of the nations will come
to you.
6 "A multitude of camels will cover
you,
The young camels of Midian and
Ephah;
All those from Sheba will come;
They will bring gold and
frankincense,
And will bear good news of the
praises of the LORD.
7 "All the flocks of Kedar will be
gathered together to you,
The rams of Nebaioth will minister
to you;
They will go up with acceptance on
My altar,
And I shall glorify My glorious
house.

8 "Who are these who fly like a cloud
And like the doves to their lattices?
9 "Surely the coastlands will wait for
Me;
And the ships of Tarshish *will come*
first,
To bring your sons from afar,
Their silver and their gold with
them,
For the name of the LORD your God,
And for the Holy One of Israel
because He has glorified you.
10 "Foreigners will build up your walls,
And their kings will minister to you;
For in My wrath I struck you,
And in My favor I have had
compassion on you.
11 "Your gates will be open continually;
They will not be closed day or night,
So that *men* may bring to you the
wealth of the nations,
With their kings led in procession.
12 "For the nation and the kingdom
which will not serve you will
perish,
And the nations will be utterly
ruined.
13 "The glory of Lebanon will come to
you,
The juniper, the box tree and the
cypress together,
To beautify the place of My
sanctuary;
And I shall make the place of My
feet glorious.
14 "The sons of those who afflicted you
will come bowing to you,
And all those who despised you will
bow themselves at the soles of
your feet;
And they will call you the city of the
LORD,
The Zion of the Holy One of Israel.
15 "Whereas you have been forsaken
and hated
With no one passing through,
I will make you an everlasting pride,
A joy from generation to generation.
16 "You will also suck the milk of
nations
And suck the breast of kings;
Then you will know that I, the LORD,
am your Savior
And your Redeemer, the Mighty
One of Jacob.
17 "Instead of bronze I will bring gold,
And instead of iron I will bring silver,

And instead of wood, bronze,
And instead of stones, iron.
And I will make peace your
administrators
And righteousness your overseers.

18 "Violence will not be heard again in
your land,
Nor devastation or destruction
within your borders;
But you will call your walls
salvation, and your gates praise.

➤ 19 "No longer will you have the sun for
light by day,
Nor for brightness will the moon
give you light;
But you will have the LORD for an
everlasting light,
And your God for your glory.

✳ 20 "Your sun will no longer set,
Nor will your moon wane;
For you will have the LORD for an
everlasting light,
And the days of your mourning will
be over.

21 "Then all your people *will be*
righteous;
They will possess the land forever,
The branch of My planting,
The work of My hands,
That I may be glorified.

22 "The smallest one will become a clan,
And the least one a mighty nation.
I, the LORD, will hasten it in its time."

Psalm 115:1–8

➤ **115** NOT to us, O LORD, not to us,
But to Your name give glory
Because of Your lovingkindness,
because of Your truth.

✳ 2 Why should the nations say,
"Where, now, is their God?"

➤ 3 But our God is in the heavens;
He does whatever He pleases.

4 Their idols are silver and gold,
The work of man's hands.

5 They have mouths, but they cannot
speak;
They have eyes, but they cannot see;

6 They have ears, but they cannot
hear;
They have noses, but they cannot
smell;

7 They have hands, but they cannot
feel;

They have feet, but they cannot
walk;
They cannot make a sound with
their throat.

8 Those who make them will become
like them,
Everyone who trusts in them.

Proverbs 26:23

23 *Like* an earthen vessel overlaid with
silver dross
Are burning lips and a wicked
heart.

Ephesians 5:15–33

15 Therefore be careful how you walk,
not as unwise men but as wise,
16 making the most of your time, because the days are evil.

LIFE LESSONS

➤ **Isaiah 60:19 — *"You will have the LORD
for an everlasting light, and your God for
your glory."***

*J*ohn tells us that in the future New
Jerusalem there will be "no need of
the sun or of the moon to shine on it,
for the glory of God has illumined it, and
its lamp is the Lamb" (Rev. 21:23).

➤ **Psalm 115:1 — *To Your name give
glory because of Your lovingkindness,
because of Your truth.***

*G*od's mercy and truth make up a large
part of His glory, and when we pray
that He might gain glory for Himself by
answering our requests, we pray with
the kind of power that can move mountains.

➤ **Psalm 115:3 — *Our God is in the heavens; He does whatever He pleases.***

*T*o say that God is sovereign is to
say that He has the power and the
wisdom to accomplish everything and
anything He desires. He is the absolute
Monarch of the universe, and His will
rules all.

WHAT THE BIBLE SAYS ABOUT ◈

Giving Thanks in Everything

Ephesians 5:15–21

*W*hy would God command us to thank Him, regardless of the circumstances? The idea defies human logic. But then, the Lord rarely binds Himself to man-made rules. Scriptural principles serve specific purposes in the Christian's life. Gratitude keeps us aware of God's presence, which builds our trust and ultimately strengthens our witness.

We must realize that thankfulness is not based on emotions or a situation's outcome. We can be grateful, even during trials, because the Lord has promised to work everything for our good (Rom. 8:28). That means He has a purpose for every experience, pleasant or difficult. A big problem stacked against our small resources sends us running to Him, thankful He has committed to work it to our benefit.

The believer's part is to trust that God will bring good from trials and to discover His plan, which gives further reason for thanking Him. Understanding His intentions renews our strength for facing difficult trials. Expressing gratefulness changes our attitudes about God, ourselves, and our situations. Most people allow hurt and stress to form a pessimistic mindset, which negatively impacts every facet of their lives. But believers have God's Spirit working within to provide courage and a flow of thanksgiving.

When we demonstrate thankfulness in harsh circumstances, other people pay attention. Our coworkers, family, and friends will want for themselves the peace and energy we derive from a grateful relationship with the Lord. So whatever you experience today, go ahead and defy logic—praise God. ◈

---

17 So then do not be foolish, but understand what the will of the Lord is.
18 And do not get drunk with wine, for that is dissipation, but be filled with the Spirit,
19 speaking to one another in psalms and hymns and spiritual songs, singing and making melody with your heart to the Lord;
20 always giving thanks for all things in the name of our Lord Jesus Christ to God, even the Father;
21 and be subject to one another in the fear of Christ.
22 Wives, *be subject* to your own husbands, as to the Lord.
23 For the husband is the head of the wife, as Christ also is the head of the church, He Himself *being* the Savior of the body.
24 But as the church is subject to Christ, so also the wives *ought to be* to their husbands in everything.
25 Husbands, love your wives, just as Christ also loved the church and gave Himself up for her,
26 so that He might sanctify her, having cleansed her by the washing of water with the word,
27 that He might present to Himself the church in all her glory, having no spot or wrinkle or any such thing; but that she would be holy and blameless.

28 So husbands ought also to love their own wives as their own bodies. He who loves his own wife loves himself;
29 for no one ever hated his own flesh, but nourishes and cherishes it, just as Christ also *does* the church,
30 because we are members of His body.
31 FOR THIS REASON A MAN SHALL LEAVE HIS FATHER AND MOTHER AND SHALL BE JOINED TO HIS WIFE, AND THE TWO SHALL BECOME ONE FLESH.
32 This mystery is great; but I am speaking with reference to Christ and the church.
33 Nevertheless, each individual among you also is to love his own wife even as himself, and the wife must *see to it* that she respects her husband.

LIFE LESSONS

➤ **Ephesians 5:18 — *Be filled with the Spirit.***

*W*hen we talk about being filled with the Spirit of God, it does not mean that we receive something more from God. We are indwelt by the Spirit in full measure at the time of our salvation. Rather, being filled with the Spirit means that we live in submission to Him—or under His control. As he prompts and directs us, we immediately respond in obedience to His commands.

61

THE Spirit of the Lord GOD is upon me,
Because the LORD has anointed me
To bring good news to the afflicted;
He has sent me to bind up the brokenhearted,
To proclaim liberty to captives
And freedom to prisoners;

2 To proclaim the favorable year of the LORD
And the day of vengeance of our God;
To comfort all who mourn,

3 To grant those who mourn *in* Zion,
Giving them a garland instead of ashes,
The oil of gladness instead of mourning,
The mantle of praise instead of a spirit of fainting.
So they will be called oaks of righteousness,
The planting of the LORD, that He may be glorified.

4 Then they will rebuild the ancient ruins,
They will raise up the former devastations;
And they will repair the ruined cities,
The desolations of many generations.

5 Strangers will stand and pasture your flocks,
And foreigners will be your farmers and your vinedressers.

6 But you will be called the priests of the LORD;
You will be spoken of *as* ministers of our God.

LIFE LESSONS

➤ **Isaiah 61:1 —** *"The Lord has anointed Me to bring good news to the afflicted."*

Shortly after Jesus began His public ministry, He returned to his boyhood synagogue in Nazareth and delivered a short sermon based on this passage (Luke 4:16–21). He explained to the astonished crowd that He is the fulfillment of this Scripture.

You will eat the wealth of nations,
And in their riches you will boast.

7 Instead of your shame *you will have a* double *portion,*
And *instead of* humiliation they will shout for joy over their portion.
Therefore they will possess a double *portion* in their land,
Everlasting joy will be theirs.

8 For I, the LORD, love justice,
I hate robbery in the burnt offering;
And I will faithfully give them their recompense
And make an everlasting covenant with them.

9 Then their offspring will be known among the nations,
And their descendants in the midst of the peoples.
All who see them will recognize them
Because they are the offspring *whom* the LORD has blessed.

10 I will rejoice greatly in the LORD,
My soul will exult in my God;
For He has clothed me with garments of salvation,
He has wrapped me with a robe of righteousness,
As a bridegroom decks himself with a garland,
And as a bride adorns herself with her jewels.

11 For as the earth brings forth its sprouts,
And as a garden causes the things sown in it to spring up,
So the Lord GOD will cause righteousness and praise
To spring up before all the nations.

62

FOR Zion's sake I will not keep silent,
And for Jerusalem's sake I will not keep quiet,
Until her righteousness goes forth like brightness,
And her salvation like a torch that is burning.

2 The nations will see your righteousness,
And all kings your glory;
And you will be called by a new name
Which the mouth of the LORD will designate.

3 You will also be a crown of beauty in the hand of the LORD,

And a royal diadem in the hand of
your God.
4 It will no longer be said to you,
"Forsaken,"
Nor to your land will it any longer
be said, "Desolate";
But you will be called, "My delight
is in her,"
And your land, "Married";
For the LORD delights in you,
And *to Him* your land will be
married.
5 For *as* a young man marries a
virgin,
So your sons will marry you;
And *as* the bridegroom rejoices over
the bride,
So your God will rejoice over you.
6 On your walls, O Jerusalem, I have
appointed watchmen;
All day and all night they will never
keep silent.
You who remind the LORD, take no
rest for yourselves;
7 And give Him no rest until He
establishes
And makes Jerusalem a praise in
the earth.
8 The LORD has sworn by His right
hand and by His strong arm,
"I will never again give your grain *as*
food for your enemies;
Nor will foreigners drink your new
wine for which you have labored."
9 But those who garner it will eat it
and praise the LORD;
And those who gather it will drink
it in the courts of My sanctuary.
10 Go through, go through the gates,
Clear the way for the people;
Build up, build up the highway,
Remove the stones, lift up a
standard over the peoples.
11 Behold, the LORD has proclaimed to
the end of the earth,

Say to the daughter of Zion, "Lo,
your salvation comes;
Behold His reward is with Him, and
His recompense before Him."
12 And they will call them, "The holy
people,
The redeemed of the LORD";
And you will be called, "Sought out,
a city not forsaken."

◈ Psalm 115:9–13

9 O Israel, trust in the LORD;
He is their help and their shield.
10 O house of Aaron, trust in the
LORD;
He is their help and their shield.
11 You who fear the LORD, trust in the
LORD;
He is their help and their shield.
12 The LORD has been mindful of us;
He will bless *us;*
He will bless the house of Israel;
He will bless the house of Aaron.
13 He will bless those who fear the
LORD,
The small together with the great.

◈ Proverbs 26:24–26

24 He who hates disguises *it* with his
lips,
But he lays up deceit in his heart.
25 When he speaks graciously, do not
believe him,
For there are seven abominations in
his heart.
26 *Though his* hatred covers itself with
guile,
His wickedness will be revealed
before the assembly.

LIFE LESSONS

➢ **Isaiah 62:11** — *"Your salvation comes;
behold His reward is with Him."*

*J*esus is our salvation, and He is coming again to judge the world and
reward His followers. "Behold, I am coming quickly, and My reward is with Me, to
render to every man according to what
he has done" (Rev. 22:12).

➢ **Psalm 115:13** — *He will bless those
who fear the LORD, the small together
with the great.*

*G*od does not play favorites when it
comes to handing out His blessings. He
does not favor pastors more than policemen, or missionaries more than moms. If
you fear the Lord, He will bless you.

Ephesians 6:1–24

6 CHILDREN, obey your parents in the Lord, for this is right.

2 HONOR YOUR FATHER AND MOTHER (which is the first commandment with a promise),

3 SO THAT IT MAY BE WELL WITH YOU, AND THAT YOU MAY LIVE LONG ON THE EARTH.

4 Fathers, do not provoke your children to anger, but bring them up in the discipline and instruction of the Lord.

5 Slaves, be obedient to those who are your masters according to the flesh, with fear and trembling, in the sincerity of your heart, as to Christ;

6 not by way of eyeservice, as menpleasers, but as slaves of Christ, doing the will of God from the heart.

7 With good will render service, as to the Lord, and not to men,

8 knowing that whatever good thing each one does, this he will receive back from the Lord, whether slave or free.

9 And masters, do the same things to them, and give up threatening, knowing that both their Master and yours is in heaven, and there is no partiality with Him.

10 Finally, be strong in the Lord and in the strength of His might.

11 Put on the full armor of God, so that you will be able to stand firm against the schemes of the devil.

12 For our struggle is not against flesh and blood, but against the rulers, against the powers, against the world forces of this darkness, against the spiritual *forces* of wickedness in the heavenly *places*.

13 Therefore, take up the full armor of God, so that you will be able to resist in the evil day, and having done everything, to stand firm.

14 Stand firm therefore, HAVING GIRDED YOUR LOINS WITH TRUTH, and HAVING PUT ON THE BREASTPLATE OF RIGHTEOUSNESS,

15 and having shod YOUR FEET WITH THE PREPARATION OF THE GOSPEL OF PEACE;

16 in addition to all, taking up the shield of faith with which you will be able to extinguish all the flaming arrows of the evil *one*.

17 And take THE HELMET OF SALVATION, and the sword of the Spirit, which is the word of God.

18 With all prayer and petition pray at all times in the Spirit, and with this in view, be on the alert with all perseverance and petition for all the saints,

19 and *pray* on my behalf, that utterance may be given to me in the opening of my mouth, to make known with boldness the mystery of the gospel,

20 for which I am an ambassador in chains; that in *proclaiming* it I may speak boldly, as I ought to speak.

21 But that you also may know about my circumstances, how I am doing, Tychicus, the beloved brother and faithful minister in the Lord, will make everything known to you.

22 I have sent him to you for this very purpose, so that you may know about us, and that he may comfort your hearts.

23 Peace be to the brethren, and love with faith, from God the Father and the Lord Jesus Christ.

24 Grace be with all those who love our Lord Jesus Christ with incorruptible *love*.

LIFE LESSONS

Ephesians 6:8 — *Whatever good thing each one does, this he will receive back from the Lord.*

Throughout the Bible the Lord promises that He will generously reward His children for the good things they do in obedience to Him, no matter how small or insignificant it may seem. Faithful service yields wonderful blessings.

Ephesians 6:10 — *Be strong in the Lord and in the strength of His might.*

The only way to really be strong is to depend upon the unlimited power of God. We draw on His strength by faith, asking Him to supply us with the resources we lack so that we may be strong for Him.

Ephesians 6:18 — *With all prayer and petition pray at all times in the Spirit.*

None of us can long survive, let alone prosper, without the sincere prayers, love, support, and encouragement of other believers offered on our behalf. God has designed the Christian life as a community event, not as a solo endeavor.

WHAT THE BIBLE SAYS ABOUT

Dressed for the Battle

Ephesians 6:13–18

*W*e start our day by dressing appropriately for the weather or an activity. But many believers leave the house unprepared—they fail to arm themselves for spiritual warfare. Our first prayer before rising should include step-by-step application of God's armor.

First, we strap on the belt of truth. A leather apron protected the Roman soldier's abdomen; our protective girdle is the truth of who we are in Christ—saints with supernatural power from God's indwelling Spirit. Next, the breastplate deflects arrows. As difficult situations arise, we can repel the temptation to live by emotion—whether anger, fear, or dissatisfaction—and respond with a right spirit instead.

The sandals of peace help us to stand firm. Roman battle sandals usually had thick, spiked soles so that the soldier could anchor himself in the dirt. Regardless of the fierce enemy buffeting us, we can remain firmly planted in God's peaceful will. The shield of faith is no tiny, round piece of armor; it is door-sized equipment representing Christ's protection against anything Satan throws.

Faith brought us salvation—the point at which we exchanged our old thought patterns for new ways of thinking. Consequently, with salvation's helmet, we put on the mind of Christ, which gives us discernment and wisdom. Finally, we take up the sword of the Spirit so that we can combat Satan's lies with Scripture's truth.

Knowing precisely what we will face each day, the Lord has graciously provided the perfect equipment needed for our challenges. Always be sure to dress for battle. ◈

◈ Isaiah 63:1—64:12

63 WHO is this who comes from Edom,
    With garments of glowing colors from Bozrah,
    This One who is majestic in His apparel,
    Marching in the greatness of His strength?
    "It is I who speak in righteousness, mighty to save."

2   Why is Your apparel red,
    And Your garments like the one who treads in the wine press?
3   "I have trodden the wine trough alone,
    And from the peoples there was no man with Me.
    I also trod them in My anger
    And trampled them in My wrath;
    And their lifeblood is sprinkled on My garments,
    And I stained all My raiment.
4   "For the day of vengeance was in My heart,

    And My year of redemption has come.
5   "I looked, and there was no one to help,
    And I was astonished and there was no one to uphold;
    So My own arm brought salvation to Me,
    And My wrath upheld Me.
6   "I trod down the peoples in My anger
    And made them drunk in My wrath,
    And I poured out their lifeblood on the earth."

7   I shall make mention of the lovingkindnesses of the LORD, the praises of the LORD,
    According to all that the LORD has granted us,
    And the great goodness toward the house of Israel,
    Which He has granted them according to His compassion
    And according to the abundance of His lovingkindnesses.
8   For He said, "Surely, they are My people,

Sons who will not deal falsely."
So He became their Savior.
➤ 9 In all their affliction He was afflicted,
And the angel of His presence saved
them;
In His love and in His mercy He
redeemed them,
And He lifted them and carried
them all the days of old.
10 But they rebelled
And grieved His Holy Spirit;
Therefore He turned Himself to
become their enemy,
He fought against them.
11 Then His people remembered the
days of old, of Moses.
Where is He who brought them up
out of the sea with the shepherds
of His flock?
Where is He who put His Holy
Spirit in the midst of them,
12 Who caused His glorious arm to go
at the right hand of Moses,
Who divided the waters before
them to make for Himself an
everlasting name,
13 Who led them through the depths?
Like the horse in the wilderness,
they did not stumble;
14 As the cattle which go down into
the valley,
The Spirit of the LORD gave them rest.
So You led Your people,
To make for Yourself a glorious name.
15 Look down from heaven and see
from Your holy and glorious
habitation;
Where are Your zeal and Your
mighty deeds?
The stirrings of Your heart and Your
compassion are restrained toward
me.
16 For You are our Father, though
Abraham does not know us

And Israel does not recognize us.
You, O LORD, are our Father,
Our Redeemer from of old is Your
name.
17 Why, O LORD, do You cause us to
stray from Your ways
And harden our heart from fearing
You?
Return for the sake of Your servants,
the tribes of Your heritage.
18 Your holy people possessed Your
sanctuary for a little while,
Our adversaries have trodden it down.
19 We have become like those over
whom You have never ruled,
Like those who were not called by
Your name.

64 OH, that You would rend the
heavens and come down,
That the mountains might quake at
Your presence—
2 As fire kindles the brushwood, as
fire causes water to boil—
To make Your name known to Your
adversaries,
That the nations may tremble at
Your presence!
3 When You did awesome things
which we did not expect,
You came down, the mountains
quaked at Your presence.
4 For from days of old they have not ➤
heard or perceived by ear,
Nor has the eye seen a God besides
You,
Who acts in behalf of the one who
waits for Him.
5 You meet him who rejoices in doing
righteousness,
Who remembers You in Your ways.
Behold, You were angry, for we
sinned,
We continued in them a long time;
And shall we be saved?

LIFE LESSONS

➤ **Isaiah 63:9** — *In all their affliction He
was afflicted, and the angel of His presence saved them.*

*G*od understands what we are going
through. He feels what we feel,
and none of our anguish escapes His
attention. He also acts to save us and
rescue us.

➤ **Isaiah 64:4** — *Nor has the eye seen a
God besides You, who acts in behalf of
the one who waits for Him.*

*W*e cannot imagine how God will
move on our behalf—He does "far
more abundantly beyond all that we ask
or think" (Eph. 3:20)—but we confidently
expect that He *will* act when we wait for
Him in faith.

LIFE PRINCIPLE 14

GOD ACTS ON BEHALF OF THOSE WHO WAIT FOR HIM.

ISAIAH 64:4

*I*n this hurry-up world, waiting for anything can cause us to lose our temper and our good sense—more frequently than we care to admit! No one enjoys waiting in line. We don't like waiting at stoplights. We don't like waiting for dinner. We don't even like waiting for good things, like for fish to bite. We want what we want *right now*.

Yet the Word of God insists that we learn some of life's greatest lessons while we wait. Waiting rooms can be hard classrooms, but God promises vast rewards to those who wait for Him. God plans to use the long pauses in our lives for our blessing . . . if we let Him.

Why does the Father so often ask us to wait? Let's consider five major rewards of waiting.

❶ We discover God's will.

"The LORD is good to those who wait for Him, to the person who seeks Him" (Lam. 3:25). God does not allow delays in giving us the desire of our hearts to lead us along. Rather, we know that even as we wait, He is working all things together for our good and His glory (Rom. 8:28). Yet as we eagerly anticipate His provision, we must keep our eyes on Him—listening for His voice and direction. In that way, we learn to do His will and our relationships with Him grow deeper.

❷ We receive supernatural energy and strength.

God invites us to claim His promise in Isaiah 40:29–31: "He gives strength to the weary, and to him who lacks might He increases power. Though youths grow weary and tired, and vigorous young men stumble badly, yet those who wait for the LORD will gain new strength; they will mount up with wings like eagles, they will run and not get tired, they will walk and not become weary."

Just as God deepens our relationships with Him through times of waiting, He also increases our energy, faith, endurance, and strength. We grow in the likeness of Christ and all of His attributes—including in love, joy, peace, patience, kindness, goodness, faithfulness, gentleness, and self-control (Gal. 5:22, 23). Surely, waiting on Him is never wasted time!

❸ We win battles.

"Wait for the LORD, and He will save you" (Prov. 20:22). How wonderful to see the Lord rescue us and bless us with His favor! When we do things our way, in our own hurried time, we end up defeated. But when we wait on God and obey His commands, He ensures our victory and keeps us from foolish and precipitous acts.

❹ We see the fulfillment of our faith.

"Those who hopefully wait for Me will not be put to shame" (Is. 49:23). In the end, we'll never feel embarrassed for waiting on God; it's always the smart thing to do. Although others may encourage us to forge ahead instead of waiting on the Lord, we must remember that He is the only One who can truly help us, and that He will never let us down. And when we trust Him and obey, surely we will see the fulfillment of every hope we've entrusted to Him.

❺ We see God working on our behalf.

Isaiah spoke of the God "Who acts in behalf of the one who waits for Him" (Is. 64:4). What a wonderful promise! While *we* actively wait, *He* actively works. Think of this: every single day, we have the greatest Mediator working on our behalf. Even when things seem to go wrong, He is making sure that everything works according to His purpose.

Although waiting can be one of the more difficult things in the Christian life, it is *not* wasted time. God gives us instructions through periods of actively waiting. He may change our circumstances while we wait. He keeps us in step with Himself and prepares us for His answers. He uses the time to sift our motives and strengthen our faith. And when we choose to wait, God rewards us with blessings both large and unexpected.

Think of waiting on God as something like planting a garden. You put a seed under the soil and water it. And then you wait.

And wait.

And wait.

After the sun and rain nourish the earth, the seeds begin to grow; and one day, finally, you begin to see evidence of what you've planted. Now, suppose you had grown impatient and dug up your seeds because nothing seemed to be happening? You would have ruined your garden.

Remember, some fruit takes a long time to mature—and the One who wants to bring it forth in our lives knows exactly how long we need to wait. Therefore, trust Him and be patient, because He is producing the most wonderful and precious fruit that you could ever hope for or imagine. ❖

6   For all of us have become like one
    who is unclean,
    And all our righteous deeds are like
    a filthy garment;
    And all of us wither like a leaf,
    And our iniquities, like the wind,
    take us away.
7   There is no one who calls on Your
    name,
    Who arouses himself to take hold of
    You;
    For You have hidden Your face from
    us
    And have delivered us into the
    power of our iniquities.
➤ 8   But now, O LORD, You are our Father,
    We are the clay, and You our potter;
    And all of us are the work of Your
    hand.
9   Do not be angry beyond measure,
    O LORD,
    Nor remember iniquity forever;
    Behold, look now, all of us are Your
    people.
10 Your holy cities have become a
    wilderness,
    Zion has become a wilderness,
    Jerusalem a desolation.
11 Our holy and beautiful house,
    Where our fathers praised You,
    Has been burned by fire;
    And all our precious things have
    become a ruin.
12 Will You restrain Yourself at these
    things, O LORD?
    Will You keep silent and afflict us
    beyond measure?

Psalm 115:14–18

✳ 14 May the LORD give you increase,
    You and your children.

15 May you be blessed of the LORD,
    Maker of heaven and earth.
16 The heavens are the heavens of the
    LORD,
    But the earth He has given to the
    sons of men.
17 The dead do not praise the LORD,
    Nor do any who go down into
    silence;
18 But as for us, we will bless the LORD
    From this time forth and forever.
    Praise the LORD!

Proverbs 26:27

27 He who digs a pit will fall into it,
    And he who rolls a stone, it will
    come back on him.

Philippians 1:1–30

1 PAUL and Timothy, bond-servants of
    Christ Jesus,
    To all the saints in Christ Jesus who
are in Philippi, including the overseers
and deacons:
2   Grace to you and peace from God
our Father and the Lord Jesus Christ.
3   I thank my God in all my remembrance of you,
4   always offering prayer with joy in
my every prayer for you all,
5   in view of your participation in the
gospel from the first day until now.
6   For I am confident of this very thing, ◄
that He who began a good work in you
will perfect it until the day of Christ
Jesus.
7   For it is only right for me to feel this
way about you all, because I have you in

LIFE LESSONS

➤ **Isaiah 64:8** — *You [are] our potter; and
all of us are the work of Your hand.*

*A*s our Father, God acts for our benefit in ways that our minds cannot
always understand. As our Potter, He
molds us and shapes us in ways that
sometimes hurt. But always He deals with
us in love.

➤ **Philippians 1:6** — *He who began a
good work in you will perfect it.*

*G*od is always faithful to finish what
He begins—and He does so in a way
that is above and beyond all we can ask
or imagine. Never underestimate what He
will continue to do through your faithfulness long after you have completed your
obedient service to Him.

my heart, since both in my imprisonment and in the defense and confirmation of the gospel, you all are partakers of grace with me.

8 For God is my witness, how I long for you all with the affection of Christ Jesus.

9 And this I pray, that your love may abound still more and more in real knowledge and all discernment,

10 so that you may approve the things that are excellent, in order to be sincere and blameless until the day of Christ;

11 having been filled with the fruit of righteousness which *comes* through Jesus Christ, to the glory and praise of God.

12 Now I want you to know, brethren, that my circumstances have turned out for the greater progress of the gospel,

13 so that my imprisonment in *the cause of* Christ has become well known throughout the whole praetorian guard and to everyone else,

14 and that most of the brethren, trusting in the Lord because of my imprisonment, have far more courage to speak the word of God without fear.

15 Some, to be sure, are preaching Christ even from envy and strife, but some also from good will;

16 the latter *do it* out of love, knowing that I am appointed for the defense of the gospel;

17 the former proclaim Christ out of selfish ambition rather than from pure motives, thinking to cause me distress in my imprisonment.

18 What then? Only that in every way, whether in pretense or in truth, Christ is proclaimed; and in this I rejoice.

Yes, and I will rejoice,

19 for I know that this will turn out for my deliverance through your prayers and the provision of the Spirit of Jesus Christ,

20 according to my earnest expectation and hope, that I will not be put to shame in anything, but *that* with all boldness, Christ will even now, as always, be exalted in my body, whether by life or by death.

21 For to me, to live is Christ and to die is gain.

22 But if *I am* to live *on* in the flesh, this *will mean* fruitful labor for me; and I do not know which to choose.

23 But I am hard-pressed from both *directions,* having the desire to depart and be with Christ, for *that* is very much better;

24 yet to remain on in the flesh is more necessary for your sake.

25 Convinced of this, I know that I will remain and continue with you all for your progress and joy in the faith,

26 so that your proud confidence in me may abound in Christ Jesus through my coming to you again.

27 Only conduct yourselves in a manner worthy of the gospel of Christ, so that whether I come and see you or remain absent, I will hear of you that you are standing firm in one spirit, with one mind striving together for the faith of the gospel;

28 in no way alarmed by *your* opponents—which is a sign of destruction for them, but of salvation for you, and that *too,* from God.

29 For to you it has been granted for Christ's sake, not only to believe in Him, but also to suffer for His sake,

30 experiencing the same conflict which you saw in me, and now hear *to be* in me.

LIFE LESSONS

> **Philippians 1:21 — *For to me, to live is Christ.***

*P*aul did not want to do great things for God; He wanted God to do great things in and through him. His goal was to serve as the hands, feet, and mouth of Christ, doing in Christ's power what Christ would do.

> **Philippians 1:29 — *To you it has been granted for Christ's sake, not only to believe in Him, but also to suffer for His sake.***

*T*he word "granted" comes from the Greek term *charis,* often translated "gift." Believing in Christ is a gift of God, but so is suffering for Christ. If we would not refuse the first, neither should we the second (Rom. 8:17). God has a delightful way of turning negatives into positives. He loves to take things that Satan means for our harm and use them instead for His glory and our benefit.

65 "I PERMITTED Myself to be sought by those who did not ask *for Me*;
I permitted Myself to be found by those who did not seek Me.
I said, 'Here am I, here am I,'
To a nation which did not call on My name.

2 "I have spread out My hands all day long to a rebellious people,
Who walk *in* the way which is not good, following their own thoughts,

3 A people who continually provoke Me to My face,
Offering sacrifices in gardens and burning incense on bricks;

4 Who sit among graves and spend the night in secret places;
Who eat swine's flesh,
And the broth of unclean meat is *in* their pots.

5 "Who say, 'Keep to yourself, do not come near me,
For I am holier than you!'
These are smoke in My nostrils,
A fire that burns all the day.

6 "Behold, it is written before Me,
I will not keep silent, but I will repay;
I will even repay into their bosom,

7 Both their own iniquities and the iniquities of their fathers together," says the LORD.
"Because they have burned incense on the mountains
And scorned Me on the hills,
Therefore I will measure their former work into their bosom."

8 Thus says the LORD,
"As the new wine is found in the cluster,
And one says, 'Do not destroy it, for there is benefit in it,'
So I will act on behalf of My servants
In order not to destroy all of them.

9 "I will bring forth offspring from Jacob,
And an heir of My mountains from Judah;
Even My chosen ones shall inherit it,
And My servants will dwell there.

10 "Sharon will be a pasture land for flocks,
And the valley of Achor a resting place for herds,
For My people who seek Me.

11 "But you who forsake the LORD,
Who forget My holy mountain,
Who set a table for Fortune,
And who fill *cups* with mixed wine for Destiny,

12 I will destine you for the sword,
And all of you will bow down to the slaughter.
Because I called, but you did not answer;
I spoke, but you did not hear.
And you did evil in My sight
And chose that in which I did not delight."

13 Therefore, thus says the Lord GOD,
"Behold, My servants will eat, but you will be hungry.
Behold, My servants will drink, but you will be thirsty.
Behold, My servants will rejoice, but you will be put to shame.

14 "Behold, My servants will shout joyfully with a glad heart,
But you will cry out with a heavy heart,
And you will wail with a broken spirit.

15 "You will leave your name for a curse to My chosen ones,
And the Lord GOD will slay you.
But My servants will be called by another name.

16 "Because he who is blessed in the earth
Will be blessed by the God of truth;
And he who swears in the earth
Will swear by the God of truth;
Because the former troubles are forgotten,
And because they are hidden from My sight!

17 "For behold, I create new heavens and a new earth;
And the former things will not be remembered or come to mind.

18 "But be glad and rejoice forever in what I create;
For behold, I create Jerusalem *for* rejoicing
And her people *for* gladness.

19 "I will also rejoice in Jerusalem and be glad in My people;
And there will no longer be heard in her

The voice of weeping and the sound of crying.

20 "No longer will there be in it an infant *who lives but a few* days,
Or an old man who does not live out his days;
For the youth will die at the age of one hundred
And the one who does not reach the age of one hundred
Will be *thought* accursed.

21 "They will build houses and inhabit *them;*
They will also plant vineyards and eat their fruit.

22 "They will not build and another inhabit,
They will not plant and another eat;
For as the lifetime of a tree, *so will be* the days of My people,
And My chosen ones will wear out the work of their hands.

23 "They will not labor in vain,
Or bear *children* for calamity;
For they are the offspring of those blessed by the LORD,
And their descendants with them.

24 "It will also come to pass that before they call, I will answer; and while they are still speaking, I will hear.

25 "The wolf and the lamb will graze together, and the lion will eat straw like the ox; and dust will be the serpent's food. They will do no evil or harm in all My holy mountain," says the LORD.

66 THUS says the LORD,
"Heaven is My throne and the earth is My footstool.
Where then is a house you could build for Me?
And where is a place that I may rest?

2 "For My hand made all these things,
Thus all these things came into being," declares the LORD.

"But to this one I will look,
To him who is humble and contrite of spirit, and who trembles at My word.

3 "*But* he who kills an ox is *like* one who slays a man;
He who sacrifices a lamb is *like* the one who breaks a dog's neck;
He who offers a grain offering *is like one who offers* swine's blood;
He who burns incense is *like* the one who blesses an idol.
As they have chosen their *own* ways,
And their soul delights in their abominations,

4 So I will choose their punishments
And will bring on them what they dread.
Because I called, but no one answered;
I spoke, but they did not listen.
And they did evil in My sight
And chose that in which I did not delight."

5 Hear the word of the LORD, you who tremble at His word:
"Your brothers who hate you, who exclude you for My name's sake,
Have said, 'Let the LORD be glorified, that we may see your joy.'
But they will be put to shame.

6 "A voice of uproar from the city, a voice from the temple,
The voice of the LORD who is rendering recompense to His enemies.

7 "Before she travailed, she brought forth;
Before her pain came, she gave birth to a boy.

8 "Who has heard such a thing? Who has seen such things?
Can a land be born in one day?
Can a nation be brought forth all at once?
As soon as Zion travailed, she also brought forth her sons.

9 "Shall I bring to the point of birth and not give delivery?" says the LORD.
"Or shall I who gives delivery shut *the womb?*" says your God.

10 "Be joyful with Jerusalem and rejoice for her, all you who love her;

Be exceedingly glad with her, all
you who mourn over her,

11 That you may nurse and be satisfied
with her comforting breasts,
That you may suck and be delighted
with her bountiful bosom."

12 For thus says the LORD, "Behold, I
extend peace to her like a river,
And the glory of the nations like an
overflowing stream;
And you will be nursed, you will be
carried on the hip and fondled on
the knees.

13 "As one whom his mother comforts,
so I will comfort you;
And you will be comforted in
Jerusalem."

14 Then you will see *this*, and your
heart will be glad,
And your bones will flourish like
the new grass;
And the hand of the LORD will be
made known to His servants,
But He will be indignant toward His
enemies.

15 For behold, the LORD will come in
fire
And His chariots like the whirlwind,
To render His anger with fury,
And His rebuke with flames of fire.

16 For the LORD will execute judgment
by fire
And by His sword on all flesh,
And those slain by the LORD will be
many.

17 "Those who sanctify and purify
themselves *to* go to the gardens,
Following one in the center,
Who eat swine's flesh, detestable
things and mice,
Will come to an end altogether,"
declares the LORD.

18 "For I know their works and their
thoughts; the time is coming to gather
all nations and tongues. And they shall
come and see My glory.

19 "I will set a sign among them and will
send survivors from them to the nations:
Tarshish, Put, Lud, Meshech, Tubal and
Javan, to the distant coastlands that
have neither heard My fame nor seen
My glory. And they will declare My glory
among the nations.

20 "Then they shall bring all your brethren from all the nations as a grain offering to the LORD, on horses, in chariots,
in litters, on mules and on camels, to

My holy mountain Jerusalem," says the
LORD, "just as the sons of Israel bring
their grain offering in a clean vessel to
the house of the LORD.

21 "I will also take some of them for
priests *and* for Levites," says the LORD.

22 "For just as the new heavens and the
new earth
Which I make will endure before
Me," declares the LORD,
"So your offspring and your name
will endure.

23 "And it shall be from new moon to
new moon
And from sabbath to sabbath,
All mankind will come to bow down
before Me," says the LORD.

24 "Then they will go forth and look
On the corpses of the men
Who have transgressed against Me.
For their worm will not die
And their fire will not be quenched;
And they will be an abhorrence to
all mankind."

Psalm 116:1–4

116 I LOVE the LORD, because He
hears
My voice *and* my supplications.

2 Because He has inclined His ear to
me,
Therefore I shall call *upon Him* as
long as I live.

3 The cords of death encompassed me
And the terrors of Sheol came upon
me;
I found distress and sorrow.

4 Then I called upon the name of the
LORD:
"O LORD, I beseech You, save my
life!"

LIFE LESSONS

➤ **Isaiah 66:22 — *"The new heavens and
the new earth which I make will endure
before Me."***

*G*od loves us so much that He wants
our relationships with Him to continue to grow for all eternity. He will
never grow weary of us or abandon us,
and there will always be more of Him for
us to explore.

Proverbs 26:28

28 A lying tongue hates those it crushes,
And a flattering mouth works ruin.

Philippians 2:1–30

2 THEREFORE if there is any encouragement in Christ, if there is any consolation of love, if there is any fellowship of the Spirit, if any affection and compassion,
2 make my joy complete by being of the same mind, maintaining the same love, united in spirit, intent on one purpose.
3 Do nothing from selfishness or empty conceit, but with humility of mind regard one another as more important than yourselves;
4 do not *merely* look out for your own personal interests, but also for the interests of others.
5 Have this attitude in yourselves which was also in Christ Jesus,
6 who, although He existed in the form of God, did not regard equality with God a thing to be grasped,
7 but emptied Himself, taking the form of a bond-servant, *and* being made in the likeness of men.
8 Being found in appearance as a man, He humbled Himself by becoming obedient to the point of death, even death on a cross.
9 For this reason also, God highly exalted Him, and bestowed on Him the name which is above every name,
10 so that at the name of Jesus EVERY KNEE WILL BOW, of those who are in heaven and on earth and under the earth,
11 and that every tongue will confess that Jesus Christ is Lord, to the glory of God the Father.
12 So then, my beloved, just as you have always obeyed, not as in my presence only, but now much more in my absence, work out your salvation with fear and trembling;
13 for it is God who is at work in you, both to will and to work for *His* good pleasure.
14 Do all things without grumbling or disputing;

15 so that you will prove yourselves to be blameless and innocent, children of God above reproach in the midst of a crooked and perverse generation, among whom you appear as lights in the world,
16 holding fast the word of life, so that in the day of Christ I will have reason to glory because I did not run in vain nor toil in vain.
17 But even if I am being poured out as a drink offering upon the sacrifice and service of your faith, I rejoice and share my joy with you all.
18 You too, *I urge you*, rejoice in the same way and share your joy with me.
19 But I hope in the Lord Jesus to send Timothy to you shortly, so that I also may be encouraged when I learn of your condition.
20 For I have no one *else* of kindred spirit who will genuinely be concerned for your welfare.
21 For they all seek after their own interests, not those of Christ Jesus.

LIFE LESSONS

➤ **Philippians 2:2 — *Make my joy complete by being of the same mind.***

The joyful unity of believers in Christ offers a powerful testimony to the world that the God of love they preach is real, active, and eager to bring others into His loving family.

➤ **Philippians 2:12 — *Work out your salvation with fear and trembling.***

When Paul tells us to "work out" our own salvation "with fear and trembling," he means that we are to give careful attention to our actions and behavior, making sure that they well represent the One who saved us.

➤ **Philippians 2:15 — *You appear as lights in the world.***

God intends that His children act as beacons of light in this dark world—showing the way to spiritual safety for those who are lost (Matt. 5:14-16). But if our behavior as God's children is characterized by corruption, complaining, and self-centeredness, we will not differ from unbelievers—there will be nothing to recommend us or Christ in whom we believe for salvation.

WHAT THE BIBLE SAYS ABOUT

A Savior Freely Given

Philippians 2:5–18

*I*t's awe-inspiring to think that the One who has become our Savior has been watching the progress of the world since before the beginning. As He looked down from heaven, He realized that the only way to relieve our sin-saturated suffering was to come to earth to die for us. Jesus "emptied Himself, taking the form of a bond-servant, and being made in the likeness of men. Being found in appearance as a man, He humbled Himself by becoming obedient to the point of death, even death on a cross" (Phil. 2:7, 8). He had all of eternity stretched before Him and the throne of heaven beneath Him, yet He chose to submit His everlasting nature to the curse of mortal man: death. And we are able to enjoy everlasting life because of Jesus' victory over it.

God made provision for your sins through Jesus because He didn't want to be separated from you for eternity. He wanted you to see heaven—not just picture it in your mind. He wanted you to have a deep and wonder-ful relationship with Him, so He sanctified you—made you holy—through the blood of Christ. God could make all this provision for you because He is the King of kings. It is in His power to do as He pleases, and it pleased Him to have a relationship with you. The Holy One who was able to create the world and rule the universe is the One who wants you to know Him. He wants you to see His majesty in heaven and share it with Him.

Of course, that brings us to the question posed by Paul in Romans 8:32, "He who did not spare His own Son, but delivered Him over for us all, how will He not also with Him freely give us all things?" If Jesus would make the astounding sacrifice of leaving His magnificent throne in heaven to meet our most profound need of salvation—then how could we ever be so deceived as to imagine that He would abandon us in some lesser necessity?

Just as Christ has been watching the world's progress from before the beginning, He's been observing your growth as well—and He knows exactly what you're going through today. The Cross proves that there's nothing that can keep Him from helping you and showing you His love—not even death. Won't you trust Him with what concerns you? ◈

---

22 But you know of his proven worth, that he served with me in the furtherance of the gospel like a child *serving* his father.
23 Therefore I hope to send him immediately, as soon as I see how things go with me;
24 and I trust in the Lord that I myself also will be coming shortly.
25 But I thought it necessary to send to you Epaphroditus, my brother and fellow worker and fellow soldier, who is also your messenger and minister to my need;
26 because he was longing for you all and was distressed because you had heard that he was sick.

27 For indeed he was sick to the point of death, but God had mercy on him, and not on him only but also on me, so that I would not have sorrow upon sorrow.
28 Therefore I have sent him all the more eagerly so that when you see him again you may rejoice and I may be less concerned *about you.*
29 Receive him then in the Lord with all joy, and hold men like him in high regard;
30 because he came close to death for the work of Christ, risking his life to complete what was deficient in your service to me.

◈ **Jeremiah 1:1—2:37**

1 THE words of Jeremiah the son of Hilkiah, of the priests who were in Anathoth in the land of Benjamin,

2 to whom the word of the LORD came in the days of Josiah the son of Amon, king of Judah, in the thirteenth year of his reign.
3 It came also in the days of Jehoiakim the son of Josiah, king of Judah, until the

end of the eleventh year of Zedekiah the son of Josiah, king of Judah, until the exile of Jerusalem in the fifth month.

4 Now the word of the LORD came to me saying,

5 "Before I formed you in the womb I
    knew you,
And before you were born I
    consecrated you;
I have appointed you a prophet to
    the nations."

6 Then I said, "Alas, Lord GOD!
Behold, I do not know how to speak,
Because I am a youth."

7 But the LORD said to me,
"Do not say, 'I am a youth,'
Because everywhere I send you, you
    shall go,
And all that I command you, you
    shall speak.

8 "Do not be afraid of them,
For I am with you to deliver you,"
    declares the LORD.

9 Then the LORD stretched out His hand and touched my mouth, and the LORD said to me,

"Behold, I have put My words in
    your mouth.

10 "See, I have appointed you this day
    over the nations and over the
    kingdoms,
To pluck up and to break down,
To destroy and to overthrow,
To build and to plant."

11 The word of the LORD came to me saying, "What do you see, Jeremiah?" And I said, "I see a rod of an almond tree." 12 Then the LORD said to me, "You have seen well, for I am watching over My word to perform it."

13 The word of the LORD came to me a second time saying, "What do you see?" And I said, "I see a boiling pot, facing away from the north."

14 Then the LORD said to me, "Out of the north the evil will break forth on all the inhabitants of the land.

15 "For, behold, I am calling all the families of the kingdoms of the north," declares the LORD; "and they will come and they will set each one his throne at the entrance of the gates of Jerusalem, and against all its walls round about and against all the cities of Judah.

16 "I will pronounce My judgments on them concerning all their wickedness, whereby they have forsaken Me and have offered sacrifices to other gods, and worshiped the works of their own hands.

17 "Now, gird up your loins and arise, and speak to them all which I command you. Do not be dismayed before them, or I will dismay you before them.

18 "Now behold, I have made you today as a fortified city and as a pillar of iron and as walls of bronze against the whole land, to the kings of Judah, to its princes, to its priests and to the people of the land.

19 "They will fight against you, but they will not overcome you, for I am with you to deliver you," declares the LORD.

2 NOW the word of the LORD came to me saying,

2 "Go and proclaim in the ears of Jerusalem, saying, 'Thus says the LORD,

"I remember concerning you the
    devotion of your youth,
The love of your betrothals,
Your following after Me in the
    wilderness,
Through a land not sown.

3 "Israel was holy to the LORD,
The first of His harvest.
All who ate of it became guilty;
Evil came upon them," declares the
    LORD.'"

4 Hear the word of the LORD, O house of Jacob, and all the families of the house of Israel.

5 Thus says the LORD,

"What injustice did your fathers find
    in Me,
That they went far from Me
And walked after emptiness and
    became empty?

6 "They did not say, 'Where is the
    LORD
Who brought us up out of the land
    of Egypt,
Who led us through the wilderness,

Through a land of deserts and of pits,
Through a land of drought and of deep darkness,
Through a land that no one crossed
And where no man dwelt?'
7 "I brought you into the fruitful land
To eat its fruit and its good things.
But you came and defiled My land,
And My inheritance you made an abomination.
8 "The priests did not say, 'Where is the LORD?'
And those who handle the law did not know Me;
The rulers also transgressed against Me,
And the prophets prophesied by Baal
And walked after things that did not profit.
9 "Therefore I will yet contend with you," declares the LORD,
"And with your sons' sons I will contend.
10 "For cross to the coastlands of Kittim and see,
And send to Kedar and observe closely
And see if there has been such *a thing* as this!
11 "Has a nation changed gods
When they were not gods?
But My people have changed their glory
For that which does not profit.
12 "Be appalled, O heavens, at this,
And shudder, be very desolate," declares the LORD.
13 "For My people have committed two evils:
They have forsaken Me,
The fountain of living waters,
To hew for themselves cisterns,
Broken cisterns
That can hold no water.
14 "Is Israel a slave? Or is he a homeborn servant?
Why has he become a prey?
15 "The young lions have roared at him,
They have roared loudly.
And they have made his land a waste;
His cities have been destroyed, without inhabitant.
16 "Also the men of Memphis and Tahpanhes

Have shaved the crown of your head.
17 "Have you not done this to yourself
By your forsaking the LORD your God
When He led you in the way?
18 "But now what are you doing on the road to Egypt,
To drink the waters of the Nile?
Or what are you doing on the road to Assyria,
To drink the waters of the Euphrates?
19 "Your own wickedness will correct you,
And your apostasies will reprove you;
Know therefore and see that it is evil and bitter
For you to forsake the LORD your God,
And the dread of Me is not in you," declares the Lord GOD of hosts.
20 "For long ago I broke your yoke
And tore off your bonds;
But you said, 'I will not serve!'
For on every high hill
And under every green tree
You have lain down as a harlot.
21 "Yet I planted you a choice vine,
A completely faithful seed.
How then have you turned yourself before Me
Into the degenerate shoots of a foreign vine?
22 "Although you wash yourself with lye
And use much soap,
The stain of your iniquity is before Me," declares the Lord GOD.
23 "How can you say, 'I am not defiled,
I have not gone after the Baals'?
Look at your way in the valley!
Know what you have done!
You are a swift young camel entangling her ways,

LIFE LESSONS

➤ Jeremiah 2:19 — *"Your own wicked-ness will correct you."*

Some of the consequences for choosing sin are bound up in the sin itself—they include the punishment in their results (Rom. 1:18-32).

24 A wild donkey accustomed to the
   wilderness,
   That sniffs the wind in her passion.
   In *the time of* her heat who can turn
   her away?
   All who seek her will not become
   weary;
   In her month they will find her.
25 "Keep your feet from being unshod
   And your throat from thirst;
   But you said, 'It is hopeless!
   No! For I have loved strangers,
   And after them I will walk.'
26 "As the thief is shamed when he is
   discovered,
   So the house of Israel is shamed;
   They, their kings, their princes
   And their priests and their prophets,
27 Who say to a tree, 'You are my
   father,'
   And to a stone, 'You gave me birth.'
   For they have turned *their* back to
   Me,
   And not *their* face;
   But in the time of their trouble they
   will say,
   'Arise and save us.'
28 "But where are your gods
   Which you made for yourself?
   Let them arise, if they can save you
   In the time of your trouble;
   For *according to* the number of your
   cities
   Are your gods, O Judah.
29 "Why do you contend with Me?
   You have all transgressed against
   Me," declares the LORD.
30 "In vain I have struck your sons;
   They accepted no chastening.
   Your sword has devoured your
   prophets
   Like a destroying lion.
31 "O generation, heed the word of the
   LORD.
   Have I been a wilderness to Israel,
   Or a land of thick darkness?
   Why do My people say, 'We *are free
   to* roam;
   We will no longer come to You'?
> 32 "Can a virgin forget her ornaments,
   Or a bride her attire?
   Yet My people have forgotten Me
   Days without number.
33 "How well you prepare your way
   To seek love!
   Therefore even the wicked women
   You have taught your ways.

34 "Also on your skirts is found
   The lifeblood of the innocent poor;
   You did not find them breaking in.
   But in spite of all these things,
35 Yet you said, 'I am innocent;
   Surely His anger is turned away
   from me.'
   Behold, I will enter into judgment
   with you
   Because you say, 'I have not sinned.'
36 "Why do you go around so much
   Changing your way?
   Also, you will be put to shame by
   Egypt
   As you were put to shame by
   Assyria.
37 "From this *place* also you will go out
   With your hands on your head;
   For the LORD has rejected those in
   whom you trust,
   And you will not prosper with
   them."

Psalm 116:5–14

5 Gracious is the LORD, and righteous;
   Yes, our God is compassionate.
6 The LORD preserves the simple;
   I was brought low, and He saved
   me.
7 Return to your rest, O my soul,
   For the LORD has dealt bountifully
   with you.
8 For You have rescued my soul from
   death,
   My eyes from tears,
   My feet from stumbling.
9 I shall walk before the LORD
   In the land of the living.
10 I believed when I said,
   "I am greatly afflicted."
11 I said in my alarm,
   "All men are liars."

12 What shall I render to the LORD
For all His benefits toward me?
13 I shall lift up the cup of salvation
And call upon the name of the
LORD.
14 I shall pay my vows to the LORD,
Oh *may it be* in the presence of all
His people.

Proverbs 27:1

27 DO not boast about tomorrow,
For you do not know what a day
may bring forth.

Philippians 3:1–21

3 FINALLY, my brethren, rejoice in the
Lord. To write the same things *again*
is no trouble to me, and it is a safeguard
for you.
2 Beware of the dogs, beware of the
evil workers, beware of the false circumcision;
3 for we are the *true* circumcision, who
worship in the Spirit of God and glory in
Christ Jesus and put no confidence in the
flesh,
4 although I myself might have confidence even in the flesh. If anyone else
has a mind to put confidence in the flesh,
I far more:
5 circumcised the eighth day, of the
nation of Israel, of the tribe of Benjamin,
a Hebrew of Hebrews; as to the Law, a
Pharisee;
6 as to zeal, a persecutor of the church;
as to the righteousness which is in the
Law, found blameless.
7 But whatever things were gain to
me, those things I have counted as loss
for the sake of Christ.
8 More than that, I count all things to
be loss in view of the surpassing value
of knowing Christ Jesus my Lord, for
whom I have suffered the loss of all
things, and count them but rubbish so
that I may gain Christ,
9 and may be found in Him, not having a righteousness of my own derived
from *the* Law, but that which is through
faith in Christ, the righteousness which
comes from God on the basis of faith,

10 that I may know Him and the power
of His resurrection and the fellowship of
His sufferings, being conformed to His
death;
11 in order that I may attain to the resurrection from the dead.
12 Not that I have already obtained *it*
or have already become perfect, but I
press on so that I may lay hold of that for
which also I was laid hold of by Christ
Jesus.
13 Brethren, I do not regard myself as
having laid hold of *it* yet; but one thing
I do: forgetting what *lies* behind and
reaching forward to what *lies* ahead,
14 I press on toward the goal for the
prize of the upward call of God in Christ
Jesus.
15 Let us therefore, as many as are perfect, have this attitude; and if in anything
you have a different attitude, God will
reveal that also to you;
16 however, let us keep living by that
same *standard* to which we have attained.

LIFE LESSONS

> **Philippians 3:3 —** *We are the true cir-
cumcision, who worship in the Spirit of
God and glory in Christ Jesus and put no
confidence in the flesh.*

*T*rue religion is not a matter of carrying out traditions, rites, and rituals, but is always based in a genuine
and intimate relationship with God the
Father made possible by faith in Christ
and empowered by the Holy Spirit.

> **Philippians 3:8 —** *I count all things to
be loss in view of the surpassing value of
knowing Christ Jesus my Lord.*

*W*e never have to worry that we will
miss out on the good things in life
because of our Christian faith. *Nothing*
we give up because of our connection to
Christ has any lasting value.

> **Philippians 3:13 —** *Forgetting what
lies behind and reaching forward to what
lies ahead.*

*N*o matter what his circumstances, the
apostle Paul never settled for the
past. We, too, must press on with the
mindset that there is always something
more to be found in Christ.

LIFE PRINCIPLE 26

ADVERSITY IS A BRIDGE TO A DEEPER
RELATIONSHIP WITH GOD.

PHILIPPIANS 3:10, 11

*W*hat is God's goal in adversity? His basic objective is to draw us closer to Himself. He does not glory in pain or sorrow, but He uses these things to teach us about His love and faithfulness.

The moment adversity comes our vulnerability increases, and we may find ourselves wondering why God has allowed us to face such difficulty. Pain, disappointment, and trial are effective tools that He uses to drive us to Himself and to the Cross where we discover our personal need for a Savior. We are struck with a defining thought: *I need God.* We need His strength, wisdom, and forgiveness.

Whenever you are confronted by adversity, always remember that God has a purpose for allowing it to touch your life. He is never out of control. He has a plan and a goal, not just for this situation alone, but also for your entire life. In times of difficulty, He is your immovable strength (Prov. 18:10), and He has promised never to abandon you.

What are you to do when adversity strikes? The Book of Hebrews encourages us by saying, "Do not throw away your confidence, which has a great reward. For you have need of endurance, so that when you have done the will of God, you may receive what was promised" (Heb. 10:35, 36).

When adversity strikes, one of the first things we should do is turn to the Lord and ask Him to show us what we need to learn in the situation. We may initially battle feelings of disbelief or denial, but the overriding thought needs to be one of trust and faith in God's ability. The second step is to affirm our commitment to Him and set our focus on Him—not our circumstances. We see both of these portrayed in the lives of the men and women of the Bible.

Joseph's life especially was a study of faith, trust, and victory amid adversity. As a young man, he trusted and watched God take the cruelest act and turn it into a blessing. Sold into Egyptian bondage by his brothers, Joseph spent years bound and confined to a life of slavery. Even when it appeared that he would gain a reprieve from danger and heartache,

adversity struck a second time as he was falsely accused of a crime. Back to the dungeon he went, only this time with a stiffer sentence.

We may be tempted to think, "Poor Joseph!" But actually, he was right in the center of God's perfect plan. He may not have understood why he was in captivity, but he believed that he could trust God for his life and future.

Adversity was a keen tool in Joseph's life. The Lord used it to shape His servant for service. Joseph landed in a key leadership role that ultimately led to the preservation of the nation of Israel. Had he escaped from prison and gone into hiding, the entire nation of Israel would have missed God's blessing. And without the training that came as a result of severe disappointment, Joseph may have become proud and self-reliant. Instead, God used this young man's life to change the course of history.

People often ask, "What is the quickest way through seasons of adversity?" Many times there just is no quick solution to the trials we face. There is one sure way through the difficulties of life, however, and that is through obedience and surrender of selfish feelings and desires.

Adversity has a way of pushing us beyond ourselves where we find God waiting to gather us in His arms. It stirs us to pray like nothing else can. And it is in prayer that we find shelter from the storms of life. Held under the canopy of God's presence, we discover a sense of security and hope that we thought had evaded us.

Even when life seems emotionally and spiritually dark, He will be your light. You can be sure that God will use the trials you face to shape your life so that you reflect His love and care to others.

Never forget that God knows the future! He understands the advantage of adversity and how it can be used to strengthen your faith, refine your hope, and settle your heart into a place of contentment and trust. Without times of adversity, you would miss the powerful experience of God walking with you through the valley times of life.

Therefore, determine to keep the focus of your heart on Jesus. Don't let the negative talk of others tempt you to get off course. Stay close to the Lord in devotion and prayer. Read His Word. He will guide you through the greatest difficulty, and then you will know what it means to live in a broad place of blessing. ◈

17 Brethren, join in following my example, and observe those who walk according to the pattern you have in us.

18 For many walk, of whom I often told you, and now tell you even weeping, *that they are* enemies of the cross of Christ,

19 whose end is destruction, whose god is *their* appetite, and *whose* glory is in their shame, who set their minds on earthly things.

20 For our citizenship is in heaven, from which also we eagerly wait for a Savior, the Lord Jesus Christ;

21 who will transform the body of our humble state into conformity with the body of His glory, by the exertion of the power that He has even to subject all things to Himself.

OCTOBER 9

Jeremiah 3:1—4:31

3 GOD says, "If a husband divorces his wife
And she goes from him
And belongs to another man,
Will he still return to her?
Will not that land be completely polluted?
But you are a harlot *with* many lovers;
Yet you turn to Me," declares the LORD.

2 "Lift up your eyes to the bare heights and see;
Where have you not been violated?
By the roads you have sat for them
Like an Arab in the desert,
And you have polluted a land
With your harlotry and with your wickedness.

3 "Therefore the showers have been withheld,
And there has been no spring rain.
Yet you had a harlot's forehead;
You refused to be ashamed.

4 "Have you not just now called to Me,
'My Father, You are the friend of my youth?

5 'Will He be angry forever?
Will He be indignant to the end?'
Behold, you have spoken
And have done evil things,
And you have had your way."

6 Then the LORD said to me in the days of Josiah the king, "Have you seen what faithless Israel did? She went up on every high hill and under every green tree, and she was a harlot there.

7 "I thought, 'After she has done all these things she will return to Me'; but she did not return, and her treacherous sister Judah saw it.

8 "And I saw that for all the adulteries of faithless Israel, I had sent her away and given her a writ of divorce, yet her treacherous sister Judah did not fear; but she went and was a harlot also.

9 "Because of the lightness of her harlotry, she polluted the land and committed adultery with stones and trees.

10 "Yet in spite of all this her treacherous sister Judah did not return to Me with all her heart, but rather in deception," declares the LORD.

11 And the LORD said to me, "Faithless Israel has proved herself more righteous than treacherous Judah.

12 "Go and proclaim these words toward the north and say, ◀
'Return, faithless Israel,' declares the LORD;
'I will not look upon you in anger.
For I am gracious,' declares the LORD;
'I will not be angry forever.

13 'Only acknowledge your iniquity,
That you have transgressed against the LORD your God

LIFE LESSONS

➤ **Jeremiah 3:12 —** *"I will not look upon you in anger for I am gracious,"* declares the LORD.

God does not want to inflict His wrath upon us, but instead wants to show us mercy (Ezek. 18:21–23, 32; Rom. 2:4; 2 Pet. 3:9). He makes it possible for us to return to Him and know Him as our loving Savior.

And have scattered your favors to the
strangers under every green tree,
And you have not obeyed My voice,'
declares the LORD.
14 'Return, O faithless sons,' declares
the LORD;
'For I am a master to you,
And I will take you one from a city
and two from a family,
And I will bring you to Zion.'
15 "Then I will give you shepherds after
My own heart, who will feed you on
knowledge and understanding.
16 "It shall be in those days when you
are multiplied and increased in the land,"
declares the LORD, "they will no longer
say, 'The ark of the covenant of the
LORD.' And it will not come to mind, nor
will they remember it, nor will they miss
it, nor will it be made again.
17 "At that time they will call Jerusalem
'The Throne of the LORD,' and all the nations will be gathered to it, to Jerusalem,
for the name of the LORD; nor will they
walk anymore after the stubbornness of
their evil heart.
18 "In those days the house of Judah will
walk with the house of Israel, and they
will come together from the land of the
north to the land that I gave your fathers
as an inheritance.
19 "Then I said,
'How I would set you among My
sons
And give you a pleasant land,
The most beautiful inheritance of
the nations!'
And I said, 'You shall call Me, My
Father,
And not turn away from following
Me.'
20 "Surely, as a woman treacherously
departs from her lover,
So you have dealt treacherously
with Me,
O house of Israel," declares the
LORD.
21 A voice is heard on the bare
heights,
The weeping and the supplications
of the sons of Israel;
Because they have perverted their
way,
They have forgotten the LORD their
God.
22 "Return, O faithless sons,
I will heal your faithlessness."

"Behold, we come to You;
For You are the LORD our God.
23 "Surely, the hills are a deception,
A tumult on the mountains.
Surely in the LORD our God
Is the salvation of Israel.
24 "But the shameful thing has consumed the labor of our fathers since our
youth, their flocks and their herds, their
sons and their daughters.
25 "Let us lie down in our shame, and
let our humiliation cover us; for we have
sinned against the LORD our God, we and
our fathers, from our youth even to this
day. And we have not obeyed the voice
of the LORD our God."

4 "IF you will return, O Israel,"
declares the LORD,
"Then you should return to Me.
And if you will put away your
detested things from My
presence,
And will not waver,
2 And you will swear, 'As the LORD
lives,'
In truth, in justice and in
righteousness;
Then the nations will bless
themselves in Him,
And in Him they will glory."
3 For thus says the LORD to the men of
Judah and to Jerusalem,
"Break up your fallow ground,
And do not sow among thorns.
4 "Circumcise yourselves to the LORD
And remove the foreskins of your
heart,
Men of Judah and inhabitants of
Jerusalem,
Or else My wrath will go forth like
fire
And burn with none to quench it,
Because of the evil of your deeds."
5 Declare in Judah and proclaim in
Jerusalem, and say,
"Blow the trumpet in the land;
Cry aloud and say,
'Assemble yourselves, and let us go
Into the fortified cities.'
6 "Lift up a standard toward Zion!
Seek refuge, do not stand still,
For I am bringing evil from the
north,
And great destruction.
7 "A lion has gone up from his thicket,
And a destroyer of nations has set
out;

He has gone out from his place
To make your land a waste.
Your cities will be ruins
Without inhabitant.

8 "For this, put on sackcloth,
Lament and wail;
For the fierce anger of the LORD
Has not turned back from us."

9 "It shall come about in that day," declares the LORD, "that the heart of the king and the heart of the princes will fail; and the priests will be appalled and the prophets will be astounded."

10 Then I said, "Ah, Lord GOD! Surely You have utterly deceived this people and Jerusalem, saying, 'You will have peace'; whereas a sword touches the throat."

11 In that time it will be said to this people and to Jerusalem, "A scorching wind from the bare heights in the wilderness in the direction of the daughter of My people—not to winnow and not to cleanse,

12 a wind too strong for this—will come at My command; now I will also pronounce judgments against them.

13 "Behold, he goes up like clouds,
And his chariots like the whirlwind;
His horses are swifter than eagles.
Woe to us, for we are ruined!"

➤ 14 Wash your heart from evil,
O Jerusalem,
That you may be saved.
How long will your wicked thoughts
Lodge within you?

15 For a voice declares from Dan,
And proclaims wickedness from
Mount Ephraim.

16 "Report it to the nations, now!
Proclaim over Jerusalem,
'Besiegers come from a far country,
And lift their voices against the
cities of Judah.

17 'Like watchmen of a field they are
against her round about,

Because she has rebelled against Me,' declares the LORD.

18 "Your ways and your deeds
Have brought these things to you.
This is your evil. How bitter!
How it has touched your heart!"

19 My soul, my soul! I am in anguish!
Oh, my heart!
My heart is pounding in me;
I cannot be silent,
Because you have heard, O my soul,
The sound of the trumpet,
The alarm of war.

20 Disaster on disaster is proclaimed,
For the whole land is devastated;
Suddenly my tents are devastated,
My curtains in an instant.

21 How long must I see the standard
And hear the sound of the
trumpet?

22 "For My people are foolish,
They know Me not;
They are stupid children
And have no understanding.
They are shrewd to do evil,
But to do good they do not know."

23 I looked on the earth, and behold, it
was formless and void;
And to the heavens, and they had
no light.

24 I looked on the mountains, and
behold, they were quaking,
And all the hills moved to and fro.

25 I looked, and behold, there was no
man,
And all the birds of the heavens had
fled.

26 I looked, and behold, the fruitful
land was a wilderness,
And all its cities were pulled down
Before the LORD, before His fierce
anger.

27 For thus says the LORD,
"The whole land shall be a
desolation,
Yet I will not execute a complete
destruction.

28 "For this the earth shall mourn
And the heavens above be dark,
Because I have spoken, I have
purposed,
And I will not change My mind, nor
will I turn from it."

29 At the sound of the horseman and
bowman every city flees;
They go into the thickets and climb
among the rocks;

Every city is forsaken,
And no man dwells in them.
30 And you, O desolate one, what will
you do?
Although you dress in scarlet,
Although you decorate *yourself with*
ornaments of gold,
Although you enlarge your eyes
with paint,
In vain you make yourself beautiful.
Your lovers despise you;
They seek your life.
31 For I heard a cry as of a woman in
labor,
The anguish as of one giving birth
to her first child,
The cry of the daughter of Zion
gasping for breath,
Stretching out her hands, *saying,*
"Ah, woe is me, for I faint before
murderers."

Psalm 116:15–19

15 Precious in the sight of the LORD
Is the death of His godly ones.
16 O LORD, surely I am Your servant,
I am Your servant, the son of Your
handmaid,
You have loosed my bonds.
17 To You I shall offer a sacrifice of
thanksgiving,
And call upon the name of the
LORD.
18 I shall pay my vows to the LORD,
Oh *may it be* in the presence of all
His people,
19 In the courts of the LORD'S house,
In the midst of you, O Jerusalem.
Praise the LORD!

Proverbs 27:2

2 Let another praise you, and not
your own mouth;
A stranger, and not your own lips.

Philippians 4:1–23

4 THEREFORE, my beloved brethren
whom I long *to see,* my joy and
crown, in this way stand firm in the Lord,
my beloved.
2 I urge Euodia and I urge Syntyche to
live in harmony in the Lord.
3 Indeed, true companion, I ask you
also to help these women who have
shared my struggle in *the cause of* the
gospel, together with Clement also and
the rest of my fellow workers, whose
names are in the book of life.
4 Rejoice in the Lord always; again I
will say, rejoice!
5 Let your gentle *spirit* be known to all
men. The Lord is near.
6 Be anxious for nothing, but in everything by prayer and supplication with
thanksgiving let your requests be made
known to God.
7 And the peace of God, which surpasses all comprehension, will guard
your hearts and your minds in Christ
Jesus.

LIFE LESSONS

➤ **Psalm 116:15 —** *Precious in the sight
of the LORD is the death of His godly
ones.*

*W*e rightly grieve when a loved one
dies, but God has a very different
reaction: He rejoices that another one of
His children has entered His eternal presence. Death is not the end but a new
beginning.

➤ **Proverbs 27:2 —** *Let another praise
you, and not your own mouth.*

*O*ur God loathes human self-promotion.
Our society seems to take it for
granted, especially in athletics and entertainment, but "God is the Judge; He puts
down one and exalts another" (Ps. 75:7).

➤ **Philippians 4:6 —** *Be anxious for nothing, but in everything by prayer and
supplication with thanksgiving let your
requests be made known to God.*

*A*nxiety disappears when we learn
to take our concerns to God. He is
the only One who has the power and
the wisdom to deal with every issue perfectly. This is why we stand tallest and
strongest on our knees. When we are
submitted to the One who always works
in our best interest, we know we have
absolutely nothing to fear.

8   Finally, brethren, whatever is true, whatever is honorable, whatever is right, whatever is pure, whatever is lovely, whatever is of good repute, if there is any excellence and if anything worthy of praise, dwell on these things.

9   The things you have learned and received and heard and seen in me, practice these things, and the God of peace will be with you.

10   But I rejoiced in the Lord greatly, that now at last you have revived your concern for me; indeed, you were concerned *before*, but you lacked opportunity.

11   Not that I speak from want, for I have learned to be content in whatever circumstances I am.

12   I know how to get along with humble means, and I also know how to live in prosperity; in any and every circumstance I have learned the secret of being filled and going hungry, both of having abundance and suffering need.

13   I can do all things through Him who strengthens me.

14   Nevertheless, you have done well to share *with me* in my affliction.

15   You yourselves also know, Philippians, that at the first preaching of the gospel, after I left Macedonia, no church shared with me in the matter of giving and receiving but you alone;

16   for even in Thessalonica you sent *a gift* more than once for my needs.

17   Not that I seek the gift itself, but I seek for the profit which increases to your account.

18   But I have received everything in

ANSWERS TO LIFE'S QUESTIONS

Will God really meet all my needs?

PHILIPPIANS 4:19

*H*ave you ever pondered the real meaning of Philippians 4:19? If so, then you may also have encountered some frustration.

"What about this need I have had for years?" you wonder. "Doesn't God care about that aching hole in my heart? Why doesn't He just fill it by meeting my needs automatically?" The truth is: God wants us to trust Him and not look only for the blessing. In other words, keep our focus on the right thing, which is a personal relationship with the Savior. Circumstances have little to do with lasting joy. Peace, joy, and contentment come from knowing God and having a personal relationship with Him. The only way to be fully happy is to have a heart that is set on Jesus Christ. Then when difficulty comes, we won't feel lost, confused, or disillusioned.

Many people attempt to meet their own needs apart from God. But this never works. It only leads to frustration and deep disappointment. There will be times when we wonder if He hears our prayers. He always does. And He also is the only One who can answer correctly and satisfy the desires of our hearts. So why do we struggle? Usually, it is because we think we know better than God. We fail to realize we cannot meet our own needs *or* compel Him to comply with our personal desires, schedule, or concept of how we think something should be done.

The first step to having our needs met is to trust Him completely with the entirety of our lives. He knows what is best for us, and His purpose in allowing any delay is for our good. Waiting prepares us for a greater blessing. It strengthens our faith and reliance on Him and consequently rids us of a desire to be self-sufficient.

The second step is to obey Him and allow Him to work fully in our lives. Many times, He stretches our faith by allowing us to have a need. He knows how we will respond, but He wants us to learn how to say yes to His design—even when we do not have all the information and facts.

The third step is to trust and wait for Him. In a very real sense, your unmet need is a form of trial and temptation. It's a trial because its lack of fulfillment can feel truly painful, and it's a temptation because it urges you to turn away from God to meet your own needs. But James says, "Blessed is a man who perseveres under trial; for once he has been approved, he will receive the crown of life which the Lord has promised to those who love him" (James 1:12).

So what are you to do when the delay goes on, the pressure to give up increases, and you feel weary of beating yourself up with false guilt? It may sound like a platitude, but keep your eyes on the Lord and follow Him—no matter what. James tells us that the testing of our faith leads to perseverance, which works to make us "perfect and complete, lacking in nothing" (James 1:4).

Worked out on the journey of faith, such unwavering trust has profound results.

full and have an abundance; I am amply supplied, having received from Epaphroditus what you have sent, a fragrant aroma, an acceptable sacrifice, well-pleasing to God.

19 And my God will supply all your needs according to His riches in glory in Christ Jesus.

20 Now to our God and Father *be* the glory forever and ever. Amen.

21 Greet every saint in Christ Jesus. The brethren who are with me greet you.

22 All the saints greet you, especially those of Caesar's household.

23 The grace of the Lord Jesus Christ be with your spirit.

Jeremiah 5:1—6:30

5 "ROAM to and fro through the streets of Jerusalem,
And look now and take note.
And seek in her open squares,
If you can find a man,
If there is one who does justice, who seeks truth,
Then I will pardon her.

2 "And although they say, 'As the LORD lives,'
Surely they swear falsely."

3 O LORD, do not Your eyes *look* for truth?
You have smitten them,
But they did not weaken;
You have consumed them,
But they refused to take correction.
They have made their faces harder than rock;
They have refused to repent.

4 Then I said, "They are only the poor,
They are foolish;
For they do not know the way of the LORD
Or the ordinance of their God.

5 "I will go to the great
And will speak to them,
For they know the way of the LORD
And the ordinance of their God."
But they too, with one accord, have broken the yoke
And burst the bonds.

6 Therefore a lion from the forest will slay them,
A wolf of the deserts will destroy them,
A leopard is watching their cities.
Everyone who goes out of them will be torn in pieces,
Because their transgressions are many,
Their apostasies are numerous.

7 "Why should I pardon you?
Your sons have forsaken Me
And sworn by those who are not gods.
When I had fed them to the full,
They committed adultery
And trooped to the harlot's house.

8 "They were well-fed lusty horses,
Each one neighing after his neighbor's wife.

9 "Shall I not punish these *people*," declares the LORD,
"And on a nation such as this
Shall I not avenge Myself?

10 "Go up through her vine rows and destroy,
But do not execute a complete destruction;
Strip away her branches,
For they are not the LORD'S.

11 "For the house of Israel and the house of Judah
Have dealt very treacherously with Me," declares the LORD.

12 They have lied about the LORD
And said, "Not He;

➤ **Jeremiah 5:12 —** *They have lied about the LORD.*

*W*e lie about the Lord when we say that He takes pleasure in what the Bible calls evil, or when we say that He will bless what He has sworn to judge. God allows that to continue for a time— but not forever. God *always* judges sin and blesses obedience.

Misfortune will not come on us,
And we will not see sword or famine.
13 "The prophets are *as* wind,
And the word is not in them.
Thus it will be done to them!"
14 Therefore, thus says the LORD, the God of hosts,
"Because you have spoken this word,
Behold, I am making My words in your mouth fire
And this people wood, and it will consume them.
15 "Behold, I am bringing a nation against you from afar, O house of Israel," declares the LORD.
"It is an enduring nation,
It is an ancient nation,
A nation whose language you do not know,
Nor can you understand what they say.
16 "Their quiver is like an open grave,
All of them are mighty men.
17 "They will devour your harvest and your food;
They will devour your sons and your daughters;
They will devour your flocks and your herds;
They will devour your vines and your fig trees;
They will demolish with the sword your fortified cities in which you trust.
18 "Yet even in those days," declares the LORD, "I will not make you a complete destruction.
19 "It shall come about when they say, 'Why has the LORD our God done all these things to us?' then you shall say to them, 'As you have forsaken Me and

served foreign gods in your land, so you will serve strangers in a land that is not yours.'
20 "Declare this in the house of Jacob
And proclaim it in Judah, saying,
21 'Now hear this, O foolish and senseless people,
Who have eyes but do not see;
Who have ears but do not hear.
22 'Do you not fear Me?' declares the LORD.
'Do you not tremble in My presence?
For I have placed the sand as a boundary for the sea,
An eternal decree, so it cannot cross over it.
Though the waves toss, yet they cannot prevail;
Though they roar, yet they cannot cross over it.
23 'But this people has a stubborn and rebellious heart;
They have turned aside and departed.
24 'They do not say in their heart,
"Let us now fear the LORD our God,
Who gives rain in its season,
Both the autumn rain and the spring rain,
Who keeps for us
The appointed weeks of the harvest."
25 'Your iniquities have turned these away,
And your sins have withheld good from you.
26 'For wicked men are found among My people,
They watch like fowlers lying in wait;
They set a trap,
They catch men.
27 'Like a cage full of birds,
So their houses are full of deceit;
Therefore they have become great and rich.
28 'They are fat, they are sleek,
They also excel in deeds of wickedness;
They do not plead the cause,
The cause of the orphan, that they may prosper;
And they do not defend the rights of the poor.
29 'Shall I not punish these *people*?' declares the LORD,

'On a nation such as this
Shall I not avenge Myself?'

30 "An appalling and horrible thing
Has happened in the land:

31 The prophets prophesy falsely,
And the priests rule on their *own*
authority;
And My people love it so!
But what will you do at the end of
it?

6 "FLEE for safety, O sons of
Benjamin,
From the midst of Jerusalem!
Now blow a trumpet in Tekoa
And raise a signal over Beth-
haccerem;
For evil looks down from the north,
And a great destruction.

2 "The comely and dainty one, the
daughter of Zion, I will cut off.

3 "Shepherds and their flocks will
come to her,
They will pitch *their* tents around
her,
They will pasture each in his place.

4 "Prepare war against her;
Arise, and let us attack at noon.
Woe to us, for the day declines,
For the shadows of the evening
lengthen!

5 "Arise, and let us attack by night
And destroy her palaces!"

6 For thus says the LORD of hosts,
"Cut down her trees
And cast up a siege against
Jerusalem.
This is the city to be punished,
In whose midst there is only
oppression.

7 "As a well keeps its waters fresh,
So she keeps fresh her wickedness.
Violence and destruction are heard
in her;
Sickness and wounds are ever
before Me.

8 "Be warned, O Jerusalem,
Or I shall be alienated from you,
And make you a desolation,
A land not inhabited."

9 Thus says the LORD of hosts,
"They will thoroughly glean as the
vine the remnant of Israel;
Pass your hand again like a grape
gatherer
Over the branches."

10 To whom shall I speak and give
warning
That they may hear?
Behold, their ears are closed
And they cannot listen.
Behold, the word of the LORD has
become a reproach to them;
They have no delight in it.

11 But I am full of the wrath of the
LORD;
I am weary with holding *it* in.
"Pour *it* out on the children in the
street
And on the gathering of young men
together;
For both husband and wife shall be
taken,
The aged and the very old.

12 "Their houses shall be turned over to
others,
Their fields and their wives
together;
For I will stretch out My hand
Against the inhabitants of the land,"
declares the LORD.

13 "For from the least of them even to
the greatest of them,
Everyone is greedy for gain,
And from the prophet even to the
priest
Everyone deals falsely.

14 "They have healed the brokenness of ⊰
My people superficially,
Saying, 'Peace, peace,'
But there is no peace.

15 "Were they ashamed because of the
abomination they have done?
They were not even ashamed
at all;
They did not even know how to
blush.

LIFE LESSONS

⊰ **Jeremiah 6:14 —** *"They have healed
the brokenness of My people superficially, saying, 'Peace, peace,' but there is
no peace."*

*I*t was because of the love of God
that Jeremiah warned his erring
people to repent and turn back to God.
There is no genuine peace or safety
when we disobey God—no matter who
tells us there is. If we want to be safe
in God's arms, we must repent of our
sinfulness, stop seeking earthly forms of
comfort and security, and commit ourselves completely to Him.

Therefore they shall fall among
those who fall;
At the time that I punish them,
They shall be cast down," says the
LORD.

16 Thus says the LORD,
"Stand by the ways and see and ask
for the ancient paths,
Where the good way is, and walk
in it;
And you will find rest for your
souls.
But they said, 'We will not walk *in
it.*'

17 "And I set watchmen over you,
saying,
'Listen to the sound of the
trumpet!'
But they said, 'We will not listen.'

18 "Therefore hear, O nations,
And know, O congregation, what is
among them.

19 "Hear, O earth: behold, I am bringing
disaster on this people,
The fruit of their plans,
Because they have not listened to
My words,
And as for My law, they have
rejected it also.

20 "For what purpose does frankincense
come to Me from Sheba
And the sweet cane from a distant
land?
Your burnt offerings are not
acceptable
And your sacrifices are not pleasing
to Me."

21 Therefore, thus says the LORD,
"Behold, I am laying stumbling
blocks before this people.
And they will stumble against
them,
Fathers and sons together;
Neighbor and friend will perish."

22 Thus says the LORD,
"Behold, a people is coming from the
north land,
And a great nation will be aroused
from the remote parts of the
earth.

23 "They seize bow and spear;
They are cruel and have no mercy;
Their voice roars like the sea,
And they ride on horses,
Arrayed as a man for the battle
Against you, O daughter of
Zion!"

24 We have heard the report of it;
Our hands are limp.
Anguish has seized us,
Pain as of a woman in childbirth.

25 Do not go out into the field
And do not walk on the road,
For the enemy has a sword,
Terror is on every side.

26 O daughter of my people, put on
sackcloth
And roll in ashes;
Mourn as for an only son,
A lamentation most bitter.
For suddenly the destroyer
Will come upon us.

27 "I have made you an assayer *and* a
tester among My people,
That you may know and assay their
way."

28 All of them are stubbornly
rebellious,
Going about as a talebearer.
They are bronze and iron;
They, all of them, are corrupt.

29 The bellows blow fiercely,
The lead is consumed by the fire;
In vain the refining goes on,
But the wicked are not separated.

30 They call them rejected silver,
Because the LORD has rejected
them.

Psalm 117:1, 2

117 PRAISE the LORD, all
nations;
Laud Him, all peoples!
2 For His lovingkindness is great
toward us,
And the truth of the LORD is
everlasting.
Praise the LORD!

LIFE LESSONS

➤ **Psalm 117:2 — *The truth of the LORD is
everlasting.***

The Lord's truth does not change
from year to year, decade to decade,
or century to century. It does not vary
depending on current style or alter
based on popular opinion. In a world of
change, God's truth remains constant.

Proverbs 27:3, 4

3   A stone is heavy and the sand
        weighty,
     But the provocation of a fool is
        heavier than both of them.
4   Wrath is fierce and anger is a
        flood,
     But who can stand before jealousy?

Colossians 1:1–29

1 PAUL, an apostle of Jesus Christ
   by the will of God, and Timothy our
brother,
2   To the saints and faithful brethren in
Christ *who are* at Colossae: Grace to you
and peace from God our Father.
3   We give thanks to God, the Father
of our Lord Jesus Christ, praying always
for you,
4   since we heard of your faith in Christ
Jesus and the love which you have for all
the saints;
5   because of the hope laid up for you
in heaven, of which you previously heard
in the word of truth, the gospel
6   which has come to you, just as in all
the world also it is constantly bearing
fruit and increasing, even as *it has been
doing* in you also since the day you heard
of it and understood the grace of God in
truth;
7   just as you learned *it* from Epaphras,
our beloved fellow bond-servant, who is
a faithful servant of Christ on our behalf,
8   and he also informed us of your love
in the Spirit.
9   For this reason also, since the day
we heard *of it*, we have not ceased to
pray for you and to ask that you may be
filled with the knowledge of His will in
all spiritual wisdom and understanding,
➤ 10   so that you will walk in a manner
worthy of the Lord, to please *Him* in
all respects, bearing fruit in every good
work and increasing in the knowledge of
God;
11   strengthened with all power, according to His glorious might, for the attaining of all steadfastness and patience;
joyously
12   giving thanks to the Father, who has

qualified us to share in the inheritance of
the saints in Light.
13   For He rescued us from the domain ◄
of darkness, and transferred us to the
kingdom of His beloved Son,
14   in whom we have redemption, the
forgiveness of sins.
15   He is the image of the invisible God,
the firstborn of all creation.
16   For by Him all things were created,
both in the heavens and on earth, visible
and invisible, whether thrones or dominions or rulers or authorities—all things
have been created through Him and for
Him.
17   He is before all things, and in Him all
things hold together.
18   He is also head of the body, the
church; and He is the beginning, the
firstborn from the dead, so that He Himself will come to have first place in everything.
19   For it was the *Father's* good pleasure
for all the fullness to dwell in Him,

LIFE LESSONS

➤ **Colossians 1:10 —** *Walk in a manner
worthy of the Lord.*

*W*hat does it mean to walk worthy
of Christ's name? It means that our
conversations, conducts, and characters
are consistent with the person of Jesus
Christ—we live in a manner that represents Him with honor. When people
meet you, they see His likeness and are
drawn to Him. This can only be accomplished if you allow Jesus to live in and
through you.

➤ **Colossians 1:13 —** *He rescued us from
the domain of darkness, and transferred
us to the kingdom of His beloved Son.*

*P*agans in Colossae believed in
appeasing the chaotic and dangerous powers of darkness, and filled the
Christians there with fear. Though they
were right in believing that we are helpless to escape our bondage to the enemy
on our own, what they did not understand is that the Lord Jesus has defeated
Satan through His death on the Cross
and resurrection (Matt. 4:16; John 8:12;
12:46). Christ brings us into the light and
the life of freedom when we believe in
Him, so we have absolutely no reason to
fear the dominion of darkness.

WHAT THE BIBLE SAYS ABOUT

The Many Faces of Prayer

Colossians 1:9–12

Charles Finney, a nineteenth-century American evangelist, sometimes wrestled with what to say in prayer. One day a woman acquaintance fell deathly ill. She did not know Christ, but her husband asked Finney to pray for her.

Finney immediately became burdened for the woman, but he didn't know how to pray. Finally, after grasping for the right words, Finney received a breakthrough. He said he "was enabled to roll the burden upon" God and that he immediately felt sure the woman would not die.

Not long afterwards, the woman made a full recovery and committed her life to Christ.

There's much more to prayer, however, than a passionate plea for God to intervene. Paul often sprinkled his letters with intriguing prayers. We find one of them in Colossians 1:9–12. In seven requests, Paul covers every area of our lives that needs the daily touch of God:

1. *May we be filled with the knowledge of His will in all spiritual wisdom and understanding* (v. 9). Ask God to fill you with the spiritual wisdom and understanding you need as you walk in His will and study His Word.

2. *May we walk in a manner worthy of the Lord Jesus Christ* (v. 10). Jesus lived a blameless life, exactly what we should pursue.

3. *May we please God in all respects* (v. 10). Paul encourages believers to live a life pleasing to God and to excel in their Christian walk.

4. *May we bear fruit in every good work* (v. 10). We prove we are Jesus' disciples when we bear fruit.

5. *May we increase in the knowledge of God* (v. 10). We should ask for more and more knowledge from His tremendous resources.

6. *May we be strengthened with all power, according to His glorious might* (v. 11). Ask God to strengthen you to do His will for His glory—and He will do it.

7. *May our lives express joyous thanks to the Father for His grace to us* (v. 12). Our love for Him should run so deep that we can't help but give glory and honor to Him. ◈

---

20 and through Him to reconcile all things to Himself, having made peace through the blood of His cross; through Him, *I say*, whether things on earth or things in heaven.

21 And although you were formerly alienated and hostile in mind, *engaged* in evil deeds,

22 yet He has now reconciled you in His fleshly body through death, in order to present you before Him holy and blameless and beyond reproach—

23 if indeed you continue in the faith firmly established and steadfast, and not moved away from the hope of the gospel that you have heard, which was proclaimed in all creation under heaven, and of which I, Paul, was made a minister.

24 Now I rejoice in my sufferings for your sake, and in my flesh I do my share on behalf of His body, which is the church, in filling up what is lacking in Christ's afflictions.

25 Of *this church* I was made a minister according to the stewardship from God bestowed on me for your benefit, so that I might fully carry out the *preaching of* the word of God,

26 *that is*, the mystery which has been hidden from the *past* ages and generations, but has now been manifested to His saints,

27 to whom God willed to make known ◄ what is the riches of the glory of this mystery among the Gentiles, which is Christ in you, the hope of glory.

28 We proclaim Him, admonishing every man and teaching every man with all wisdom, so that we may present every man complete in Christ.

29 For this purpose also I labor, striving according to His power, which mightily works within me.

LIFE LESSONS

➤ **Colossians 1:27 —** *Christ in you, the hope of glory.*

In Old Testament times, the Holy Spirit came upon chosen men and women of God to enable them to accomplish His will. But no one ever imagined that He would actually take up residence in believers, as He does today.

Jeremiah 7:1—8:22

7THE word that came to Jeremiah from the LORD, saying,

2 "Stand in the gate of the LORD's house and proclaim there this word and say, 'Hear the word of the LORD, all you of Judah, who enter by these gates to worship the LORD!'"

3 Thus says the LORD of hosts, the God of Israel, "Amend your ways and your deeds, and I will let you dwell in this place.

4 "Do not trust in deceptive words, saying, 'This is the temple of the LORD, the temple of the LORD, the temple of the LORD.'

5 "For if you truly amend your ways and your deeds, if you truly practice justice between a man and his neighbor,

6 if you do not oppress the alien, the orphan, or the widow, and do not shed innocent blood in this place, nor walk after other gods to your own ruin,

7 then I will let you dwell in this place, in the land that I gave to your fathers forever and ever.

8 "Behold, you are trusting in deceptive words to no avail.

9 "Will you steal, murder, and commit adultery and swear falsely, and offer sacrifices to Baal and walk after other gods that you have not known,

10 then come and stand before Me in this house, which is called by My name, and say, 'We are delivered!'—that you may do all these abominations?

11 "Has this house, which is called by My name, become a den of robbers in your sight? Behold, I, even I, have seen it," declares the LORD.

12 "But go now to My place which was in Shiloh, where I made My name dwell at the first, and see what I did to it because of the wickedness of My people Israel.

13 "And now, because you have done all these things," declares the LORD, "and I spoke to you, rising up early and speaking, but you did not hear, and I called you but you did not answer,

14 therefore, I will do to the house which is called by My name, in which you trust, and to the place which I gave you and your fathers, as I did to Shiloh.

15 "I will cast you out of My sight, as I have cast out all your brothers, all the offspring of Ephraim.

16 "As for you, do not pray for this people, and do not lift up cry or prayer for them, and do not intercede with Me; for I do not hear you.

17 "Do you not see what they are doing in the cities of Judah and in the streets of Jerusalem?

18 "The children gather wood, and the fathers kindle the fire, and the women knead dough to make cakes for the queen of heaven; and they pour out drink offerings to other gods in order to spite Me.

19 "Do they spite Me?" declares the LORD. "Is it not themselves they spite, to their own shame?"

20 Therefore thus says the Lord GOD, "Behold, My anger and My wrath will be poured out on this place, on man and on beast and on the trees of the field and on the fruit of the ground; and it will burn and not be quenched."

21 Thus says the LORD of hosts, the God of Israel, "Add your burnt offerings to your sacrifices and eat flesh.

22 "For I did not speak to your fathers, or command them in the day that I brought them out of the land of Egypt, concerning burnt offerings and sacrifices.

23 "But this is what I commanded them, ◄ saying, 'Obey My voice, and I will be your God, and you will be My people; and you will walk in all the way which I command you, that it may be well with you.'

24 "Yet they did not obey or incline their ear, but walked in their own counsels and in the stubbornness of their evil heart, and went backward and not forward.

25 "Since the day that your fathers came out of the land of Egypt until this day, I

LIFE LESSONS

➤ **Jeremiah 7:23** — *"Obey My voice, and I will be your God, and you will be My people."*

God desires for you to be a whole person—growing in the likeness of Jesus Christ, fruitful, and fulfilling His purpose for your life. He also assumes full responsibility for our needs when we obey Him.

have sent you all My servants the prophets, daily rising early and sending *them*.
26 "Yet they did not listen to Me or incline their ear, but stiffened their neck; they did more evil than their fathers.
27 "You shall speak all these words to them, but they will not listen to you; and you shall call to them, but they will not answer you.
28 "You shall say to them, 'This is the nation that did not obey the voice of the LORD their God or accept correction; truth has perished and has been cut off from their mouth.
29 'Cut off your hair and cast *it* away,
　　And take up a lamentation on the
　　　　bare heights;
　　For the LORD has rejected and
　　　　forsaken
　　The generation of His wrath.'
30 "For the sons of Judah have done that which is evil in My sight," declares the LORD, "they have set their detestable things in the house which is called by My name, to defile it.
31 "They have built the high places of Topheth, which is in the valley of the son of Hinnom, to burn their sons and their daughters in the fire, which I did not command, and it did not come into My mind.
32 "Therefore, behold, days are coming," declares the LORD, "when it will no longer be called Topheth, or the valley of the son of Hinnom, but the valley of the Slaughter; for they will bury in Topheth because there is no *other* place.
33 "The dead bodies of this people will be food for the birds of the sky and for the beasts of the earth; and no one will frighten *them away.*
34 "Then I will make to cease from the cities of Judah and from the streets of Jerusalem the voice of joy and the voice of gladness, the voice of the bridegroom and the voice of the bride; for the land will become a ruin.

8 "AT that time," declares the LORD, "they will bring out the bones of the kings of Judah and the bones of its princes, and the bones of the priests and the bones of the prophets, and the bones of the inhabitants of Jerusalem from their graves.
2 "They will spread them out to the sun, the moon and to all the host of heaven, which they have loved and which they have served, and which they have gone after and which they have sought, and

which they have worshiped. They will not be gathered or buried; they will be as dung on the face of the ground.
3 "And death will be chosen rather than life by all the remnant that remains of this evil family, that remains in all the places to which I have driven them," declares the LORD of hosts.
4 "You shall say to them, 'Thus says the LORD,
　　"Do *men* fall and not get up again?
　　Does one turn away and not repent?
5 "Why then has this people, Jerusalem,
　　Turned away in continual apostasy?
　　They hold fast to deceit,
　　They refuse to return.
6 "I have listened and heard,
　　They have spoken what is not right;
　　No man repented of his wickedness,
　　Saying, 'What have I done?'
　　Everyone turned to his course,
　　Like a horse charging into the battle.
7 "Even the stork in the sky
　　Knows her seasons;
　　And the turtledove and the swift
　　　　and the thrush
　　Observe the time of their migration;
　　But My people do not know
　　The ordinance of the LORD.
8 "How can you say, 'We are wise,
　　And the law of the LORD is with us'?
　　But behold, the lying pen of the
　　　　scribes
　　Has made *it* into a lie.
9 "The wise men are put to shame,
　　They are dismayed and caught;
　　Behold, they have rejected the word
　　　　of the LORD,
　　And what kind of wisdom do they
　　　　have?
10 "Therefore I will give their wives to
　　　　others,
　　Their fields to new owners;

LIFE LESSONS

> **Jeremiah 8:9 — *"They have rejected the word of the LORD, and what kind of wisdom do they have?"***

Whenever we disobey the Word of God, we reject God's wisdom for our own. But it never turns out well. "There is a way which seems right to a man, but its end is the way of death" (Prov. 14:12). Any path apart from God's path leads to destruction.

WHAT THE BIBLE SAYS ABOUT

God as Our Comforter

Jeremiah 8:18

The recognition of God's power to heal your hurts is a key component to experiencing His tender love. In the midst of great pain, Jeremiah acknowledged his sadness and the ability of God to comfort him. So he cried out, "My sorrow is beyond healing, my heart is faint within me" (Jer. 8:18).

Centuries earlier, King David moaned, "Reproach has broken my heart and I am so sick. And I looked for sympathy, but there was none, and for comforters, but I found none" (Ps. 69:20). In the people around him, he could find no solace; but near the end of his song, his tune had changed: "You who seek God, let your heart revive. For the LORD hears the needy and does not despise His who are prisoners", (Ps. 69:32, 33).

Where do *you* look for comfort? If you have relied on human remedies, you know how their effectiveness diminishes over time. Some try food, alcohol, drugs, or escape into fantasy—anything to attempt to outrun the pain. But when the artificial glow wears off and the dream ends, the ache remains.

There is no such thing as a life without pain and trial, and therefore no such thing as a person without need of comfort. Don't let anyone deceive you into thinking that the key to leading a joy-filled Christian life is avoiding pain. That simply is not possible in this sinful world and neither is it profitable for us. God could choose to insulate you from hurt, but instead He allows you to experience the tough times that draw you closer to Him.

Out of your pain comes a need for God. As He ministers to you and you accept it with thanksgiving and a desire to learn, you become equipped to minister to those He places within your reach (2 Cor. 1:3, 4). Hurting individuals know there is no substitute for experience.

You can reach for God's comfort right now. Ask Him to give you solace—and find yourself wrapped in the love that will not let you go. ◈

Because from the least even to the greatest
Everyone is greedy for gain;
From the prophet even to the priest
Everyone practices deceit.
11 "They heal the brokenness of
the daughter of My people
superficially,
Saying, 'Peace, peace,'
But there is no peace.
12 "Were they ashamed because of the
abomination they had done?
They certainly were not ashamed,
And they did not know how to
blush;
Therefore they shall fall among
those who fall;
At the time of their punishment they
shall be brought down,"
Says the LORD.
13 "I will surely snatch them away,"
declares the LORD;
"There will be no grapes on the vine
And no figs on the fig tree,
And the leaf will wither;
And what I have given them will
pass away."'"
14 Why are we sitting still?

Assemble yourselves, and let us go
into the fortified cities
And let us perish there;
Because the LORD our God has
doomed us
And given us poisoned water to
drink,
For we have sinned against the
LORD.
15 *We* waited for peace, but no good
came;
For a time of healing, but behold,
terror!
16 From Dan is heard the snorting of
his horses;
At the sound of the neighing of his
stallions
The whole land quakes;
For they come and devour the land
and its fullness,
The city and its inhabitants.
17 "For behold, I am sending serpents
against you,
Adders, for which there is no charm,
And they will bite you," declares the
LORD.
18 My sorrow is beyond healing,
My heart is faint *within me!*

19 Behold, listen! The cry of the
daughter of my people from a
distant land:
"Is the LORD not in Zion? Is her King
not within her?"
"Why have they provoked Me with
their graven images, with foreign
idols?"
20 "Harvest is past, summer is ended,
And we are not saved."
21 For the brokenness of the daughter
of my people I am broken;
I mourn, dismay has taken hold of
me.
➤ 22 Is there no balm in Gilead?
Is there no physician there?
Why then has not the health of
the daughter of my people been
restored?

◈ Psalm 118:1–4

✳ **118** GIVE thanks to the LORD, for
He is good;
For His lovingkindness is everlasting.
2 Oh let Israel say,
"His lovingkindness is everlasting."
3 Oh let the house of Aaron say,
"His lovingkindness is everlasting."
4 Oh let those who fear the LORD say,
"His lovingkindness is everlasting."

◈ Proverbs 27:5, 6

5 Better is open rebuke
Than love that is concealed.
6 Faithful are the wounds of a friend,
But deceitful are the kisses of an
enemy.

◈ Colossians 2:1–23

2 FOR I want you to know how great
a struggle I have on your behalf and
for those who are at Laodicea, and for
all those who have not personally seen
my face,
2 that their hearts may be encouraged,
having been knit together in love, and
attaining to all the wealth that comes
from the full assurance of understand-

ing, *resulting* in a true knowledge of
God's mystery, *that is*, Christ *Himself*,
3 in whom are hidden all the treasures
of wisdom and knowledge.
4 I say this so that no one will delude
you with persuasive argument.
5 For even though I am absent in body,
nevertheless I am with you in spirit, rejoicing to see your good discipline and
the stability of your faith in Christ.
6 Therefore as you have received ◄
Christ Jesus the Lord, *so* walk in Him,
7 having been firmly rooted *and now*
being built up in Him and established in
your faith, just as you were instructed,
and overflowing with gratitude.
8 See to it that no one takes you
captive through philosophy and empty
deception, according to the tradition of ✳
men, according to the elementary principles of the world, rather than according
to Christ.
9 For in Him all the fullness of Deity ◄
dwells in bodily form,
10 and in Him you have been made
complete, and He is the head over all rule
and authority;
11 and in Him you were also circumcised with a circumcision made without
hands, in the removal of the body of the
flesh by the circumcision of Christ;
12 having been buried with Him in baptism, in which you were also raised up
with Him through faith in the working of
God, who raised Him from the dead.

LIFE LESSONS

➤ **Jeremiah 8:22 — *Why then has not
the health of the daughter of my people
been restored?***

*E*ven in Jeremiah's day, God offered
hope and healing to His spiritually
diseased people—but they had to come
to Him and accept His prescription to
find life. We will never find life anywhere else.

➤ **Colossians 2:6 — *As you have received
Christ Jesus the Lord, so walk in Him.***

*H*ow did you receive Jesus as your
Lord and Savior? By faith. And that
is exactly how you grow into maturity—
by faith. Through faith you depend upon
God's Spirit to mold you into the image
of Christ.

13 When you were dead in your transgressions and the uncircumcision of your flesh, He made you alive together with Him, having forgiven us all our transgressions,

14 having canceled out the certificate of debt consisting of decrees against us, which was hostile to us; and He has taken it out of the way, having nailed it to the cross.

15 When He had disarmed the rulers and authorities, He made a public display of them, having triumphed over them through Him.

16 Therefore no one is to act as your judge in regard to food or drink or in respect to a festival or a new moon or a Sabbath day—

17 things which are a *mere* shadow of what is to come; but the substance belongs to Christ.

18 Let no one keep defrauding you of your prize by delighting in self-abasement and the worship of the angels, taking his stand on *visions* he has seen, inflated without cause by his fleshly mind,

19 and not holding fast to the head, from whom the entire body, being supplied and held together by the joints and ligaments, grows with a growth which is from God.

20 If you have died with Christ to the elementary principles of the world, why, as if you were living in the world, do you submit yourself to decrees, such as,

21 "Do not handle, do not taste, do not touch!"

22 (which all *refer to* things destined to perish with use)—in accordance with the commandments and teachings of men?

23 These are matters which have, to be sure, the appearance of wisdom in self-made religion and self-abasement and severe treatment of the body, *but* are of no value against fleshly indulgence.

LIFE LESSONS

> **Colossians 2:9 — *For in Him all the fullness of Deity dwells in bodily form.***

*P*aul warned the Colossians to guard themselves against empty, deceptive philosophies that were based on limited human reasoning. It may be impossible for us to comprehend how Jesus could be totally human and totally divine at the same time (John 1:1, 14; Phil. 2:6–8). But that is the clear teaching of Scripture, and we must accept it—even if we do not understand it. Jesus said, "He who has seen Me has seen the Father" (John 14:9).

> **Colossians 2:23 — *These are matters which have, to be sure, the appearance of wisdom . . . but are of no value against fleshly indulgence.***

*I*n some ways, it may seem easier to live by a set of rules than to obey the Lord. But the truth is that pious regulations cannot change our nature—they can only temporarily suppress our true impulses. We must fight against anything that tempts us to conform to a legalistic mindset because that only leads to bondage. Spiritual problems can only be solved by the transformative power of His Holy Spirit.

Jeremiah 9:1—10:25

9 OH that my head were waters
And my eyes a fountain of tears,
  That I might weep day and night
  For the slain of the daughter of my
    people!
2 Oh that I had in the desert
  A wayfarers' lodging place;
  That I might leave my people
And go from them!
  For all of them are adulterers,
  An assembly of treacherous men.
3 "They bend their tongue *like* their
    bow;
  Lies and not truth prevail in the land;
  For they proceed from evil to evil,
  And they do not know Me," declares
    the LORD.
4 "Let everyone be on guard against
    his neighbor,

JEREMIAH: Sorrowful Compassion

JEREMIAH 9:1

*J*eremiah is often called the "weeping prophet," for little in his writings evokes ease or comfort. He wept because the people of his time had turned from God and had begun to reap the dreadful consequences of their sin.

He also wept because, with the vision of a true prophet of God, Jeremiah saw the devastation to come. And even though he occasionally urged the Lord to give His wandering people the full measure of what they deserved (Jer. 11:20), most of the time he pled for mercy and the divine grace needed to lead them back to repentance (Jer. 8:20–22).

Do we weep when we see people wandering away from God and heading straight toward judgment? Do we strive to show godly compassion to those in great spiritual danger? Or do we keep silent, hoping to see God's wrath poured out on our enemies?

And do not trust any brother;
Because every brother deals
  craftily,
And every neighbor goes about as a
  slanderer.
5 "Everyone deceives his neighbor
  And does not speak the truth,
  They have taught their tongue to
    speak lies;
  They weary themselves committing
    iniquity.
6 "Your dwelling is in the midst of
    deceit;
  Through deceit they refuse to know
    Me," declares the LORD.
7 Therefore thus says the LORD of hosts,
  "Behold, I will refine them and assay
    them;
  For what *else* can I do, because of
    the daughter of My people?
8 "Their tongue is a deadly arrow;
  It speaks deceit;
  With his mouth one speaks peace to
    his neighbor,
  But inwardly he sets an ambush for
    him.
9 "Shall I not punish them for these
    things?" declares the LORD.
  "On a nation such as this
  Shall I not avenge Myself?
10 "For the mountains I will take up a
    weeping and wailing,
  And for the pastures of the
    wilderness a dirge,
  Because they are laid waste so that
    no one passes through,
  And the lowing of the cattle is not
    heard;
  Both the birds of the sky and the
    beasts have fled; they are gone.
11 "I will make Jerusalem a heap of
    ruins,

A haunt of jackals;
  And I will make the cities of Judah
    a desolation, without inhabitant."
12 Who is the wise man that may understand this? And *who is* he to whom the mouth of the LORD has spoken, that he may declare it? Why is the land ruined, laid waste like a desert, so that no one passes through?
13 The LORD said, "Because they have forsaken My law which I set before them, and have not obeyed My voice nor walked according to it,
14 but have walked after the stubbornness of their heart and after the Baals, as their fathers taught them,"
15 therefore thus says the LORD of hosts, the God of Israel, "behold, I will feed them, this people, with wormwood and give them poisoned water to drink.
16 "I will scatter them among the nations, whom neither they nor their fathers have known; and I will send the sword after them until I have annihilated them."
17 Thus says the LORD of hosts,
  "Consider and call for the mourning
    women, that they may come;
  And send for the wailing women,
    that they may come!
18 "Let them make haste and take up a
    wailing for us,
  That our eyes may shed tears
  And our eyelids flow with water.
19 "For a voice of wailing is heard from
    Zion,
  'How are we ruined!
  We are put to great shame,
  For we have left the land,
  Because they have cast down our
    dwellings.'"
20 Now hear the word of the LORD,
  O you women,

And let your ear receive the word of
His mouth;
Teach your daughters wailing,
And everyone her neighbor a dirge.
21 For death has come up through our
windows;
It has entered our palaces
To cut off the children from the
streets,
The young men from the town
squares.
22 Speak, "Thus says the LORD,
'The corpses of men will fall like
dung on the open field,
And like the sheaf after the reaper,
But no one will gather *them.*'"

23 Thus says the LORD, "Let not a wise
man boast of his wisdom, and let not the
mighty man boast of his might, let not a
rich man boast of his riches;
24 but let him who boasts boast of this,
that he understands and knows Me, that
I am the LORD who exercises lovingkindness, justice and righteousness on earth;
for I delight in these things," declares the
LORD.
25 "Behold, the days are coming," declares the LORD, "that I will punish all
who are circumcised and yet uncircumcised—
26 Egypt and Judah, and Edom and the
sons of Ammon, and Moab and all those
inhabiting the desert who clip the hair
on their temples; for all the nations are
uncircumcised, and all the house of Israel
are uncircumcised of heart."

10 HEAR the word which the LORD
speaks to you, O house of Israel.
2 Thus says the LORD,
"Do not learn the way of the nations,
And do not be terrified by the signs
of the heavens
Although the nations are terrified
by them;
3 For the customs of the peoples are
delusion;
Because it is wood cut from the
forest,
The work of the hands of a
craftsman with a cutting tool.
4 "They decorate *it* with silver and
with gold;
They fasten it with nails and with
hammers
So that it will not totter.
5 "Like a scarecrow in a cucumber
field are they,

And they cannot speak;
They must be carried,
Because they cannot walk!
Do not fear them,
For they can do no harm,
Nor can they do any good."
6 There is none like You, O LORD;
You are great, and great is Your
name in might.
7 Who would not fear You, O King of
the nations?
Indeed it is Your due!
For among all the wise men of the
nations
And in all their kingdoms,
There is none like You.
8 But they are altogether stupid and
foolish
In their discipline of delusion—their
idol is wood!
9 Beaten silver is brought from
Tarshish,
And gold from Uphaz,
The work of a craftsman and of the
hands of a goldsmith;
Violet and purple are their clothing;
They are all the work of skilled
men.
10 But the LORD is the true God;
He is the living God and the
everlasting King.
At His wrath the earth quakes,

LIFE LESSONS

> Jeremiah 9:23, 24 — *"Let him who
boasts boast of this, that he understands
and knows Me."*

Intelligence, power, and riches all give
human beings the illusion of being in
control—but the illusion always comes to
an end. When we put our confidence in
God alone, however, we find that He is
truly worthy of our praise.

> Jeremiah 10:7 — *Who would not fear
You, O King of the nations? Indeed it is
Your due.*

The deities of the nations are merely
"the work of skilled men. But the
LORD is the true God; He is the living God
and the everlasting King" (Jer. 10:9, 10).
It is absurd that people would honor
the powerless idols of this world and yet
deny the One who really deserves our
respect, love, and obedience.

And the nations cannot endure His
indignation.

11 Thus you shall say to them, "The
gods that did not make the heavens and
the earth will perish from the earth and
from under the heavens."

12 *It is* He who made the earth by His
power,

Who established the world by His
wisdom;
And by His understanding He has
stretched out the heavens.

13 When He utters His voice, *there is* a
tumult of waters in the heavens,
And He causes the clouds to ascend
from the end of the earth;
He makes lightning for the rain,
And brings out the wind from His
storehouses.

14 Every man is stupid, devoid of
knowledge;
Every goldsmith is put to shame by
his idols;
For his molten images are
deceitful,
And there is no breath in them.

15 They are worthless, a work of
mockery;
In the time of their punishment they
will perish.

16 The portion of Jacob is not like
these;
For the Maker of all is He,
And Israel is the tribe of His
inheritance;
The LORD of hosts is His name.

17 Pick up your bundle from the
ground,
You who dwell under siege!

18 For thus says the LORD,
"Behold, I am slinging out the
inhabitants of the land
At this time,
And will cause them distress,
That they may be found."

19 Woe is me, because of my injury!
My wound is incurable.
But I said, "Truly this is a sickness,
And I must bear it."

20 My tent is destroyed,
And all my ropes are broken;
My sons have gone from me and are
no more.
There is no one to stretch out my
tent again
Or to set up my curtains.

21 For the shepherds have become
stupid
And have not sought the LORD;
Therefore they have not
prospered,
And all their flock is scattered.

22 The sound of a report! Behold, it
comes—
A great commotion out of the land
of the north—
To make the cities of Judah
A desolation, a haunt of jackals.

23 I know, O LORD, that a man's way is
not in himself,
Nor is it in a man who walks to
direct his steps.

24 Correct me, O LORD, but with
justice;
Not with Your anger, or You will
bring me to nothing.

25 Pour out Your wrath on the nations
that do not know You
And on the families that do not call
Your name;
For they have devoured Jacob;
They have devoured him and
consumed him
And have laid waste his
habitation.

Psalm 118:5–9

5 From *my* distress I called upon the
LORD;
The LORD answered me *and set me*
in a large place.

6 The LORD is for me; I will not fear;
What can man do to me?

7 The LORD is for me among those
who help me;

LIFE LESSONS

➤ **Psalm 118:8, 9 —** *It is better to take
refuge in the* LORD *than to trust in man.*

Even the best of friends can say one
thing and do another. Even the most
trusted public officials break their promises. God made us to depend on Him,
to look for His guidance, direction, and
counsel. We commit our lives to Him, not
merely for salvation, but for what we
need and where we go every moment of
our lives.

Therefore I will look *with satisfaction* on those who hate me.

➤ 8 It is better to take refuge in the LORD
Than to trust in man.

9 It is better to take refuge in the LORD
Than to trust in princes.

Proverbs 27:7

7 A sated man loathes honey,
But to a famished man any bitter thing is sweet.

Colossians 3:1–25

3 THEREFORE if you have been raised up with Christ, keep seeking the things above, where Christ is, seated at the right hand of God.

➤ 2 Set your mind on the things above, not on the things that are on earth.

3 For you have died and your life is hidden with Christ in God.

4 When Christ, who is our life, is revealed, then you also will be revealed with Him in glory.

5 Therefore consider the members of your earthly body as dead to immorality, impurity, passion, evil desire, and greed, which amounts to idolatry.

6 For it is because of these things that the wrath of God will come upon the sons of disobedience,

7 and in them you also once walked, when you were living in them.

8 But now you also, put them all aside: anger, wrath, malice, slander, *and* abusive speech from your mouth.

9 Do not lie to one another, since you laid aside the old self with its *evil* practices,

10 and have put on the new self who is being renewed to a true knowledge according to the image of the One who created him—

11 *a renewal* in which there is no *distinction between* Greek and Jew, circumcised and uncircumcised, barbarian, Scythian, slave and freeman, but Christ is all, and in all.

12 So, as those who have been chosen of God, holy and beloved, put on a heart of compassion, kindness, humility, gentleness and patience;

13 bearing with one another, and forgiving each other, whoever has a complaint against anyone; just as the Lord forgave you, so also should you.

14 Beyond all these things *put on* love, which is the perfect bond of unity.

15 Let the peace of Christ rule in your hearts, to which indeed you were called ✳ in one body; and be thankful.

16 Let the word of Christ richly dwell ◄ within you, with all wisdom teaching and admonishing one another with psalms *and* hymns *and* spiritual songs, singing with thankfulness in your hearts to God.

17 Whatever you do in word or deed, *do* all in the name of the Lord Jesus, giving thanks through Him to God the Father.

18 Wives, be subject to your husbands, as is fitting in the Lord.

19 Husbands, love your wives and do not be embittered against them.

20 Children, be obedient to your parents in all things, for this is well-pleasing to the Lord.

21 Fathers, do not exasperate your children, so that they will not lose heart.

22 Slaves, in all things obey those who

LIFE LESSONS

➤ **Colossians 3:2 —** *Set your mind on the things above, not on the things that are on earth.*

Transformation is God's goal for us, and we cooperate with His plan of spiritual metamorphosis when we train our minds to dwell on the things of God rather than on the things of the flesh.

➤ **Colossians 3:16 —** *Let the word of Christ richly dwell within you.*

Whatever we say to one another— whether we do so through sermons, lessons, testimonies, songs, or just casual conversations—should be with the purpose of spurring each other to love God more. We cannot grow in our relationships with Jesus or mature in our walks without the encouragement, help, and instruction of others.

are your masters on earth, not with external service, as those who *merely* please men, but with sincerity of heart, fearing the Lord.

23 Whatever you do, do your work heartily, as for the Lord rather than for men,

24 knowing that from the Lord you will receive the reward of the inheritance. It is the Lord Christ whom you serve.

25 For he who does wrong will receive the consequences of the wrong which he has done, and that without partiality.

OCTOBER 13

✦ Jeremiah 11:1—12:17

11 THE word which came to Jeremiah from the LORD, saying,

2 "Hear the words of this covenant, and speak to the men of Judah and to the inhabitants of Jerusalem;

3 and say to them, 'Thus says the LORD, the God of Israel, "Cursed is the man who does not heed the words of this covenant

4 which I commanded your forefathers in the day that I brought them out of the land of Egypt, from the iron furnace, saying, 'Listen to My voice, and do according to all which I command you; so you shall be My people, and I will be your God,'

5 in order to confirm the oath which I swore to your forefathers, to give them a land flowing with milk and honey, as *it is* this day."'" Then I said, "Amen, O LORD."

6 And the LORD said to me, "Proclaim all these words in the cities of Judah and in the streets of Jerusalem, saying, 'Hear the words of this covenant and do them.

7 'For I solemnly warned your fathers in the day that I brought them up from the land of Egypt, even to this day, warning persistently, saying, "Listen to My voice."

8 'Yet they did not obey or incline their ear, but walked, each one, in the stubbornness of his evil heart; therefore I brought on them all the words of this covenant, which I commanded *them* to do, but they did not.'"

9 Then the LORD said to me, "A con-

spiracy has been found among the men of Judah and among the inhabitants of Jerusalem.

10 "They have turned back to the iniquities of their ancestors who refused to hear My words, and they have gone after other gods to serve them; the house of Israel and the house of Judah have broken My covenant which I made with their fathers."

11 Therefore thus says the LORD, "Behold I am bringing disaster on them which they will not be able to escape; though they will cry to Me, yet I will not listen to them.

12 "Then the cities of Judah and the inhabitants of Jerusalem will go and cry to the gods to whom they burn incense, but they surely will not save them in the time of their disaster.

13 "For your gods are as many as your cities, O Judah; and as many as the streets of Jerusalem are the altars you have set up to the shameful thing, altars to burn incense to Baal.

14 "Therefore do not pray for this ◄

people, nor lift up a cry or prayer for them; for I will not listen when they call to Me because of their disaster.

15 "What right has My beloved in My house
When she has done many vile deeds?
Can the sacrificial flesh take away from you your disaster,
So *that* you can rejoice?"

16 The LORD called your name,
"A green olive tree, beautiful in fruit and form";
With the noise of a great tumult He has kindled fire on it,
And its branches are worthless.

17 The LORD of hosts, who planted you, has pronounced evil against you because of the evil of the house of Israel and of the house of Judah, which they have done to provoke Me by offering up sacrifices to Baal.

18 Moreover, the LORD made it known to me and I knew it;
Then You showed me their deeds.

19 But I was like a gentle lamb led to the slaughter;
And I did not know that they had devised plots against me, *saying*,
"Let us destroy the tree with its fruit,
And let us cut him off from the land of the living,
That his name be remembered no more."

20 But, O LORD of hosts, who judges righteously,
Who tries the feelings and the heart,
Let me see Your vengeance on them,
For to You have I committed my cause.

21 Therefore thus says the LORD concerning the men of Anathoth, who seek your life, saying, "Do not prophesy in the name of the LORD, so that you will not die at our hand";

22 therefore, thus says the LORD of hosts, "Behold, I am about to punish them! The young men will die by the sword, their sons and daughters will die by famine;

23 and a remnant will not be left to them, for I will bring disaster on the men of Anathoth—the year of their punishment."

12 RIGHTEOUS are You, O LORD,
that I would plead *my* case with You;

Indeed I would discuss matters of justice with You:
Why has the way of the wicked prospered?
Why are all those who deal in treachery at ease?

2 You have planted them, they have also taken root;
They grow, they have even produced fruit.
You are near to their lips
But far from their mind.

3 But You know me, O LORD;
You see me;
And You examine my heart's *attitude* toward You.
Drag them off like sheep for the slaughter
And set them apart for a day of carnage!

4 How long is the land to mourn
And the vegetation of the countryside to wither?
For the wickedness of those who dwell in it,
Animals and birds have been snatched away,
Because *men* have said, "He will not see our latter ending."

5 "If you have run with footmen and they have tired you out,
Then how can you compete with horses?
If you fall down in a land of peace,
How will you do in the thicket of the Jordan?

6 "For even your brothers and the household of your father,
Even they have dealt treacherously with you,
Even they have cried aloud after you.
Do not believe them, although they may say nice things to you."

7 "I have forsaken My house,

LIFE LESSONS

> Jeremiah 12:5 — *"If you have run with footmen and they have tired you out, then how can you compete with horses?"*

God encourages us, but He also challenges us. He speaks soft words to us when we need them, but He speaks harder words to us when we need them. He always gives us exactly what we need.

I have abandoned My inheritance;
I have given the beloved of My soul
Into the hand of her enemies.

8 "My inheritance has become to Me
Like a lion in the forest;
She has roared against Me;
Therefore I have come to hate her.

9 "Is My inheritance like a speckled
bird of prey to Me?
Are the birds of prey against her on
every side?
Go, gather all the beasts of the field,
Bring them to devour!

10 "Many shepherds have ruined My
vineyard,
They have trampled down My field;
They have made My pleasant field
A desolate wilderness.

11 "It has been made a desolation,
Desolate, it mourns before Me;
The whole land has been made
desolate,
Because no man lays it to heart.

12 "On all the bare heights in the
wilderness
Destroyers have come,
For a sword of the LORD is devouring
From one end of the land even to
the other;
There is no peace for anyone.

13 "They have sown wheat and have
reaped thorns,
They have strained themselves to no
profit.
But be ashamed of your harvest
Because of the fierce anger of the
LORD."

14 Thus says the LORD concerning all
My wicked neighbors who strike at the
inheritance with which I have endowed
My people Israel, "Behold I am about
to uproot them from their land and will
uproot the house of Judah from among
them.
15 "And it will come about that after I
have uprooted them, I will again have
compassion on them; and I will bring
them back, each one to his inheritance
and each one to his land.
16 "Then if they will really learn the
ways of My people, to swear by My
name, 'As the LORD lives,' even as they
taught My people to swear by Baal, they
will be built up in the midst of My people.
17 "But if they will not listen, then I will
uproot that nation, uproot and destroy
it," declares the LORD.

◈ Psalm 118:10–14

10 All nations surrounded me;
In the name of the LORD I will
surely cut them off.

11 They surrounded me, yes, they
surrounded me;
In the name of the LORD I will
surely cut them off.

12 They surrounded me like bees;
They were extinguished as a fire of
thorns;
In the name of the LORD I will
surely cut them off.

13 You pushed me violently so that I
was falling,
But the LORD helped me.

14 The LORD is my strength and song,
And He has become my salvation.   ✳

◈ Proverbs 27:8

8 Like a bird that wanders from her
nest,
So is a man who wanders from his
home.

◈ Colossians 4:1–18

4 MASTERS, grant to your slaves justice and fairness, knowing that you
too have a Master in heaven.
2 Devote yourselves to prayer, keeping alert in it with *an attitude of* thanksgiving;
3 praying at the same time for us as
well, that God will open up to us a door
for the word, so that we may speak forth
the mystery of Christ, for which I have
also been imprisoned;
4 that I may make it clear in the way I   ✳
ought to speak.
5 Conduct yourselves with wisdom to-   ◁
ward outsiders, making the most of the
opportunity.
6 Let your speech always be with
grace, *as though* seasoned with salt, so
that you will know how you should respond to each person.
7 As to all my affairs, Tychicus, *our*
beloved brother and faithful servant and

fellow bond-servant in the Lord, will bring you information.

8 For I have sent him to you for this very purpose, that you may know about our circumstances and that he may encourage your hearts;

9 and with him Onesimus, *our* faithful and beloved brother, who is one of your *number.* They will inform you about the whole situation here.

10 Aristarchus, my fellow prisoner, sends you his greetings; and *also* Barnabas's cousin Mark (about whom you received instructions; if he comes to you, welcome him);

11 and *also* Jesus who is called Justus; these are the only fellow workers for the kingdom of God who are from the circumcision, and they have proved to be an encouragement to me.

12 Epaphras, who is one of your number, a bondslave of Jesus Christ, sends you his greetings, always laboring earnestly for you in his prayers, that you may stand perfect and fully assured in all the will of God.

13 For I testify for him that he has a deep concern for you and for those who are in Laodicea and Hierapolis.

➤ 14 Luke, the beloved physician, sends you his greetings, and *also* Demas.

15 Greet the brethren who are in Laodicea and also Nympha and the church that is in her house.

16 When this letter is read among you, have it also read in the church of the Laodiceans; and you, for your part read my letter *that is coming* from Laodicea.

➤ 17 Say to Archippus, "Take heed to the ministry which you have received in the Lord, that you may fulfill it."

18 I, Paul, write this greeting with my own hand. Remember my imprisonment. Grace be with you.

---

13 THUS the LORD said to me, "Go and buy yourself a linen waistband and put it around your waist, but do not put it in water."

2 So I bought the waistband in accordance with the word of the LORD and put it around my waist.

3 Then the word of the LORD came to me a second time, saying,

4 "Take the waistband that you have bought, which is around your waist, and arise, go to the Euphrates and hide it there in a crevice of the rock."

5 So I went and hid it by the Euphrates, as the LORD had commanded me.

6 After many days the LORD said to me, "Arise, go to the Euphrates and take from there the waistband which I commanded you to hide there."

7 Then I went to the Euphrates and dug, and I took the waistband from the place where I had hidden it; and lo, the waistband was ruined, it was totally worthless.

8 Then the word of the LORD came to me, saying,

9 "Thus says the LORD, 'Just so will I destroy the pride of Judah and the great pride of Jerusalem.

10 'This wicked people, who refuse to listen to My words, who walk in the stubbornness of their hearts and have gone after other gods to serve them and to bow down to them, let them be just like this waistband which is totally worthless.

11 'For as the waistband clings to the waist of a man, so I made the whole household of Israel and the whole household of Judah cling to Me,' declares the LORD, 'that they might be for Me a people, for renown, for praise and for glory; but they did not listen.'

12 "Therefore you are to speak this word to them, 'Thus says the LORD, the God of Israel, "Every jug is to be filled with wine."' And when they say to you, 'Do we not very well know that every jug is to be filled with wine?'

13 then say to them, 'Thus says the LORD, "Behold I am about to fill all the inhabitants of this land—the kings that sit for David on his throne, the priests, the prophets—and all the inhabitants of Jerusalem—with drunkenness!

14 "I will dash them against each other, both the fathers and the sons together," declares the LORD. "I will not show pity nor be sorry nor have compassion so as not to destroy them."'"

15 Listen and give heed, do not be haughty,
For the LORD has spoken.

16 Give glory to the LORD your God,
Before He brings darkness
And before your feet stumble
On the dusky mountains,
And while you are hoping for light
He makes it into deep darkness,
And turns *it* into gloom.

17 But if you will not listen to it,
My soul will sob in secret for *such* pride;
And my eyes will bitterly weep
And flow down with tears,
Because the flock of the LORD has been taken captive.

18 Say to the king and the queen mother,
"Take a lowly seat,
For your beautiful crown
Has come down from your head."

LIFE LESSONS

Jeremiah 13:1 — *"Go and buy yourself a linen waistband and put it around your waist, but do not put it in water."*

*G*od often had His prophets participate in object lessons to illustrate His message to His people (Is. 20; Jer. 19; 32; Ezek. 4–5). Why did Jeremiah need to buy a linen sash and then ruin it (Jer. 13:1–7)? The Lord did not tell Jeremiah His full purpose until after the prophet had obeyed His commands (Jer. 13:8–11), but it turned out to be a powerful condemnation against Judah. We are to obey—even when God's instructions don't make sense to us.

Jeremiah 13:11 — *"That they might be for Me a people, for renown, for praise and for glory."*

*H*ere we see the heart of God: a passionate longing to become one with His people. He wants us to identify them with Him in such an intimate way that we are joyful whenever He receives glory. And whenever we succeed, everyone around us knows that it was His power and wisdom that truly achieved the victory (Matt. 5:16).

19 The cities of the Negev have been
   locked up,
   And there is no one to open *them*;
   All Judah has been carried into
   exile,
   Wholly carried into exile.
20 "Lift up your eyes and see
   Those coming from the north.
   Where is the flock that was given
   you,
   Your beautiful sheep?
21 "What will you say when He
   appoints over you—
   And you yourself had taught them—
   Former companions to be head over
   you?
   Will not pangs take hold of you
   Like a woman in childbirth?
22 "If you say in your heart,
   'Why have these things happened to
   me?'
   Because of the magnitude of your
   iniquity
   Your skirts have been removed
   And your heels have been exposed.
23 "Can the Ethiopian change his skin
   Or the leopard his spots?
   Then you also can do good
   Who are accustomed to doing evil.
24 "Therefore I will scatter them like
   drifting straw
   To the desert wind.
25 "This is your lot, the portion
   measured to you
   From Me," declares the LORD,
   "Because you have forgotten Me
   And trusted in falsehood.
26 "So I Myself have also stripped your
   skirts off over your face,
   That your shame may be seen.
27 "As for your adulteries and your
   lustful neighings,
   The lewdness of your prostitution
   On the hills in the field,
   I have seen your abominations.
   Woe to you, O Jerusalem!
   How long will you remain unclean?"

14 THAT which came as the word of
   the LORD to Jeremiah in regard to
the drought:
2 "Judah mourns
   And her gates languish;
   They sit on the ground in mourning,
   And the cry of Jerusalem has
   ascended.
3 "Their nobles have sent their
   servants for water;

They have come to the cisterns and
   found no water.
   They have returned with their
   vessels empty;
   They have been put to shame and
   humiliated,
   And they cover their heads.
4 "Because the ground is cracked,
   For there has been no rain on the
   land;
   The farmers have been put to
   shame,
   They have covered their heads.
5 "For even the doe in the field has
   given birth only to abandon *her
   young*,
   Because there is no grass.
6 "The wild donkeys stand on the bare
   heights;
   They pant for air like jackals,
   Their eyes fail
   For there is no vegetation.
7 "Although our iniquities testify
   against us,
   O LORD, act for Your name's sake!
   Truly our apostasies have been
   many,
   We have sinned against You.
8 "O Hope of Israel,
   Its Savior in time of distress,
   Why are You like a stranger in the
   land
   Or like a traveler who has pitched
   his *tent* for the night?
9 "Why are You like a man dismayed,
   Like a mighty man who cannot
   save?
   Yet You are in our midst, O LORD,
   And we are called by Your name;
   Do not forsake us!"

10 Thus says the LORD to this people,
"Even so they have loved to wander; they
have not kept their feet in check. Therefore the LORD does not accept them; now
He will remember their iniquity and call
their sins to account."
11 So the LORD said to me, "Do not pray
for the welfare of this people.
12 "When they fast, I am not going to
listen to their cry; and when they offer
burnt offering and grain offering, I am
not going to accept them. Rather I am
going to make an end of them by the
sword, famine and pestilence."
13 But, "Ah, Lord GOD!" I said, "Look,
the prophets are telling them, 'You will
not see the sword nor will you have

ANSWERS TO LIFE'S QUESTIONS

How does God define sin?

JEREMIAH 14:3–9

Sin is defined as "missing the mark"—just as an arrow misses a bull's-eye on a target. God's holiness is the standard we are to meet, and we miss it whenever we sin.

Another way to look at sin is that we "fall short" of God's perfect will. The Father desires that we live in wholeness and obey all His commands. When we fail to do so, we neither fulfill the purpose for which we were created nor glorify Him.

Still another aspect of sin is that we "trespass" or violate God's law and incur a penalty because of our guilt. The Lord specifically instructs that certain behaviors are destructive and off-limits, and when we defy Him, we reap the consequences of our disobedience. Jeremiah 2:13 tells us, "My people have committed two evils: They have forsaken Me, the fountain of living waters, to hew for themselves cisterns, broken cisterns that can hold no water." Cisterns are reservoirs dug into the earth, usually out of solid rock, designed to collect rainwater. A fountain, on the other hand, is a spring that bubbles up from the earth with an unending supply of fresh water.

Any time we attempt to meet our own needs or accomplish anything without God, we sin and set ourselves up for failure. We build broken cisterns that cannot hold water. As

Jesus once told a Samaritan woman by the well of Sychar, "If you knew the gift of God, and who it is who says to you, 'Give Me a drink,' you would have asked Him, and He would have given you living water" (John 4:10).

Too often, instead of choosing God's living water that could completely satisfy our thirst (Ps. 107:9; John 4:14; 6:35; Rev. 7:16, 17), we build our own cisterns—our own paths of fulfillment and even salvation, which are inherently unable to fill our needs (John 4:13). This is the nature of sin. We miss the mark—choosing our way instead of God's holy provision. We fall short of God's perfect plan—becoming completely dry of the hope and peace He wants to give us. And we trespass God's commands—suffering the consequences of our choices.

Proverbs 16:25 tells us, "There is a way which seems right to a man, but its end is the way of death." The Lord notes with sadness and certainty, "Have you not done this to yourself by your forsaking the LORD your God when He led you in the way?" (Jer. 2:17).

We have a choice to make. We can make our own broken cisterns and struggle because of our pride; or we can choose God's way, knowing that only He can bring us fulfillment.

Jesus has life to give, eternal and freely offered. His forgiveness—and the eternal life associated with it—is the fountain that will never fail us. So why not go to Him and quench our thirst with His living water? Surely He will satisfy even the deepest thirst of our soul.

---

famine, but I will give you lasting peace in this place.'"

14 Then the LORD said to me, "The prophets are prophesying falsehood in My name. I have neither sent them nor commanded them nor spoken to them; they are prophesying to you a false vision, divination, futility and the deception of their own minds.

15 "Therefore thus says the LORD concerning the prophets who are prophesying in My name, although it was not I who sent them—yet they keep saying, 'There will be no sword or famine in this land'—by sword and famine those prophets shall meet their end!

16 "The people also to whom they are prophesying will be thrown out into the streets of Jerusalem because of the famine and the sword; and there will be no one to bury them—neither them, nor their wives, nor their sons, nor their

daughters—for I will pour out their own wickedness on them.

17 "You will say this word to them,
  'Let my eyes flow down with tears
    night and day,
  And let them not cease;
  For the virgin daughter of my
    people has been crushed with a
    mighty blow,
  With a sorely infected wound.

18 'If I go out to the country,
  Behold, those slain with the sword!
  Or if I enter the city,
  Behold, diseases of famine!
  For both prophet and priest
  Have gone roving about in the land
    that they do not know.'"

19 Have You completely rejected
    Judah?
  Or have You loathed Zion?
  Why have You stricken us so that we
    are beyond healing?

We waited for peace, but nothing
 good *came;*
And for a time of healing, but
 behold, terror!

➢ 20 We know our wickedness,
 O LORD,
The iniquity of our fathers, for we
 have sinned against You.

21 Do not despise *us*, for Your own
 name's sake;
Do not disgrace the throne of Your
 glory;
Remember *and* do not annul Your
 covenant with us.

➢ 22 Are there any among the idols of
 the nations who give rain?
Or can the heavens grant
 showers?
Is it not You, O LORD our God?
Therefore we hope in You,
For You are the one who has done
 all these things.

Psalm 118:15–20

15 The sound of joyful shouting and
 salvation is in the tents of the
 righteous;
The right hand of the LORD does
 valiantly.

16 The right hand of the LORD is
 exalted;
The right hand of the LORD does
 valiantly.

17 I will not die, but live,
And tell of the works of the LORD.

18 The LORD has disciplined me
 severely,
But He has not given me over to
 death.

19 Open to me the gates of
 righteousness;
I shall enter through them, I shall
 give thanks to the LORD.

20 This is the gate of the LORD;
The righteous will enter through it.

Proverbs 27:9

9 Oil and perfume make the heart
 glad,
So a man's counsel is sweet to his
 friend.

1 Thessalonians 1:1–10

1 PAUL and Silvanus and Timothy,
 To the church of the Thessalonians
in God the Father and the Lord Jesus
Christ: Grace to you and peace.
2 We give thanks to God always for
all of you, making mention *of you* in our
prayers;
3 constantly bearing in mind your
work of faith and labor of love and steadfastness of hope in our Lord Jesus Christ
in the presence of our God and Father,
4 knowing, brethren beloved by God,
His choice of you;
5 for our gospel did not come to you
in word only, but also in power and in
the Holy Spirit and with full conviction;
just as you know what kind of men we
proved to be among you for your sake.
6 You also became imitators of us and ◁
of the Lord, having received the word in
much tribulation with the joy of the Holy
Spirit,

LIFE LESSONS

➢ **Jeremiah 14:20 — "We have sinned
against You."**

*W*hen we confess our sins, God
 removes the darkness of shame
and guilt that we feel and allows His
light to penetrate our souls and fill us
with life and joy.

➢ **Jeremiah 14:22 — *We hope in You, for
You are the one who has done all these
things.***

*W*e pray to God because He alone
 is the Creator. He created rain; He
made the clouds to nourish the land
with life-giving water. Since He alone
created the world, He alone has the
power to answer our prayers.

➢ **1 Thessalonians 1:6 — *You also
became imitators of us and of the Lord,
having received the word in much tribulation with the joy of the Holy Spirit.***

*T*he world does not see how joy and
 tribulation can possibly go together,
but throughout the Bible we see the
two of them paired. A life of faith may
entail adversity, but through it, we gain
a deeper relationship with the Lord.

➤ 7   so that you became an example to all the believers in Macedonia and in Achaia.
8   For the word of the Lord has sounded forth from you, not only in Macedonia and Achaia, but also in every place your faith toward God has gone forth, so that we have no need to say anything.
✳ 9   For they themselves report about us what kind of a reception we had with you, and how you turned to God from idols to serve a living and true God,
10   and to wait for His Son from heaven, whom He raised from the dead, *that is* Jesus, who rescues us from the wrath to come.

LIFE LESSONS

➤ **1 Thessalonians 1:7 —** *You became an example to all the believers in Macedonia and in Achaia.*

*T*he believers in Thessalonica were very young in the faith, but Paul saw their potential. If they remained firm in their faith, they could become a powerful witness to others in the region. He commended them for greatly inspiring others who heard their testimonies. Obedient submission to the Lord, not age, is what makes someone a good example.

OCTOBER 15

Jeremiah 15:1—16:21

15 THEN the LORD said to me, "Even though Moses and Samuel were to stand before Me, My heart would not be with this people; send them away from My presence and let them go!
2   "And it shall be that when they say to you, 'Where should we go?' then you are to tell them, 'Thus says the LORD:

"Those *destined* for death, to death;
And those *destined* for the sword, to the sword;
And those *destined* for famine, to famine;
And those *destined* for captivity, to captivity."'

3   "I will appoint over them four kinds *of* doom," declares the LORD: "the sword to slay, the dogs to drag off, and the birds of the sky and the beasts of the earth to devour and destroy.
4   "I will make them an object of horror among all the kingdoms of the earth because of Manasseh, the son of Hezekiah, the king of Judah, for what he did in Jerusalem.

5   "Indeed, who will have pity on you, O Jerusalem,
Or who will mourn for you,
Or who will turn aside to ask about your welfare?
6   "You who have forsaken Me," declares the LORD,
"You keep going backward.

So I will stretch out My hand against you and destroy you;
I am tired of relenting!
7   "I will winnow them with a winnowing fork
At the gates of the land;
I will bereave *them* of children, I will destroy My people;
They did not repent of their ways.
8   "Their widows will be more numerous before Me
Than the sand of the seas;
I will bring against them, against the mother of a young man,
A destroyer at noonday;
I will suddenly bring down on her Anguish and dismay.
9   "She who bore seven *sons* pines away;
Her breathing is labored.
Her sun has set while it was yet day;
She has been shamed and humiliated.
So I will give over their survivors to the sword
Before their enemies," declares the LORD.
10   Woe to me, my mother, that you have borne me
As a man of strife and a man of contention to all the land!
I have not lent, nor have men lent money to me,
Yet everyone curses me.
11   The LORD said, "Surely I will set you free for *purposes of* good;

LIFE PRINCIPLE **15**

BROKENNESS IS GOD'S REQUIREMENT FOR
MAXIMUM USEFULNESS.

JEREMIAH 15:19

So often, Christians struggle to get to
what they perceive as the top. They
forge their long list of accomplishments,
perhaps with the hope that they will one day
be able to hand it to God and say, "See what
I've done for You?"

However, God never accepts us on the
basis of what we've done; rather, He receives
us because of what Christ has done on the
cross (Eph 2:8, 9). This is why He instructs
us to stop depending on what we can accomplish and instead rely upon Him (Prov. 3:5,
6). However, that's not just for salvation but
for *every* aspect of life. He calls us to repent
of our sinful habits, self-reliance, and prideful
desires until we can truly say, "All that I am
and all that I have is God's. He is in me and
I am in Him, and that's all that matters."

What is God stripping away from your life?
What do you trust in more than the Lord?
God will break your dependence upon anything other than Himself no matter how long
it takes or how difficult the process may be.
He is committed to bringing you to a place of
wholeness and spiritual maturity—conforming
you to the likeness of His Son (Rom. 8:29)—
so that He can work through you and bring
others to wholeness and spiritual maturity
through your testimony (2 Cor. 1:3–7).

Maybe you are facing a time of brokenness
and it feels as though the emotional pain is
more than you can bear. Or perhaps you are
dealing with a series of disappointments that
have completely undermined your sense of
security. Instead of becoming fearful, ask the
Lord to reveal what He is teaching you.

The apostle Paul faced such a time of suffering, and he wrote, "I implored the Lord
three times that it might leave me" (2 Cor.
12:8). Although God did not remove the

"thorn" from him, He did help Paul to
understand that it was given to keep him from
exalting himself and from relying on anything
other than Christ (2 Cor. 12:7–11). The Lord
also taught the apostle that His grace would
always be sufficient for all of Paul's weaknesses.

The same is true for you. Whenever you
experience brokenness, God's grace can sustain and mature you. He will show you how
to relinquish your reliance on earthly forms
of security and teach you how to rest in His
wonderful provision and love. In that way,
you grow in the likeness of Christ and are
prepared for future service.

Peter wrote: "Beloved, do not be surprised
at the fiery ordeal among you, which comes
upon you for your testing, as though some
strange thing were happening to you; but to
the degree that you share the sufferings of
Christ, keep on rejoicing, so that also at the
revelation of His glory you may rejoice with
exultation" (1 Pet. 4:12, 13).

Keep in mind that God uses brokenness to
deepen your understanding in at least three
ways:

- You gain a new perspective of His mercy
  and provision and learn to depend on
  Him more.
- You develop a more complete comprehension of yourself.
- Your compassion and understanding for
  others' suffering grows.

Are you facing a season of trials and
brokenness? Then embrace the promise of
Jeremiah 15:19: "If you extract the precious
from the worthless, you will become My
spokesman." That is, if you trust in God and
learn from Him through your trial, He will
reveal Himself to you and work through you
in wonderful ways.

The Lord has one goal in mind for your
brokenness: spiritual victory. Therefore, be
confident that Jesus Christ can take your
weakness and turn it into strength, hope, and
honor. ◈

Surely I will cause the enemy to
   make supplication to you
In a time of disaster and a time of
   distress.
12 "Can anyone smash iron,
   Iron from the north, or bronze?
13 "Your wealth and your treasures
   I will give for booty without cost,
   Even for all your sins
   And within all your borders.
14 "Then I will cause your enemies to
   bring *it*
   Into a land you do not know;
   For a fire has been kindled in My
   anger,
   It will burn upon you."
15 You who know, O LORD,
   Remember me, take notice of me,
   And take vengeance for me on my
   persecutors.
   Do not, in view of Your patience,
   take me away;
   Know that for Your sake I endure
   reproach.
➤ 16 Your words were found and I ate
   them,
   And Your words became for me a
   joy and the delight of my heart;
   For I have been called by Your
   name,
   O LORD God of hosts.
17 I did not sit in the circle of
   merrymakers,
   Nor did I exult.
   Because of Your hand *upon me* I sat
   alone,
   For You filled me with indignation.
18 Why has my pain been perpetual
   And my wound incurable, refusing
   to be healed?

LIFE LESSONS

➤ **Jeremiah 15:16 — *Your words became
for me a joy and the delight of my heart;
for I have been called by Your name,
O LORD God of hosts.***

*G*od invites us to spend daily time with
Him in His Word and to remember
the great power, wisdom, and love He's
shown to His people throughout history,
which are also available to us. Through
Scripture and the work of His Holy Spirit,
He provides us with the spiritual guidance, joy, and strength we need to face
all of our challenges (Matt. 4:4).

Will You indeed be to me like a
   deceptive *stream*
With water that is unreliable?
19 Therefore, thus says the LORD,
   "If you return, then I will restore
   you—
   Before Me you will stand;
   And if you extract the precious from
   the worthless,
   You will become My spokesman.
   They for their part may turn to
   you,
   But as for you, you must not turn to
   them.
20 "Then I will make you to this
   people
   A fortified wall of bronze;
   And though they fight against you,
   They will not prevail over you;
   For I am with you to save you
   And deliver you," declares the LORD.
21 "So I will deliver you from the hand
   of the wicked,
   And I will redeem you from the
   grasp of the violent."

16 THE word of the LORD also came to
   me saying,
2   "You shall not take a wife for yourself
nor have sons or daughters in this place."
3   For thus says the LORD concerning the sons and daughters born in this
place, and concerning their mothers who
bear them, and their fathers who beget
them in this land:
4   "They will die of deadly diseases, they
will not be lamented or buried; they will
be as dung on the surface of the ground
and come to an end by sword and famine, and their carcasses will become food
for the birds of the sky and for the beasts
of the earth."
5   For thus says the LORD, "Do not enter
a house of mourning, or go to lament or
to console them; for I have withdrawn
My peace from this people," declares the
LORD, "My lovingkindness and compassion.
6   "Both great men and small will die in
this land; they will not be buried, they
will not be lamented, nor will anyone
gash himself or shave his head for them.
7   "Men will not break *bread* in mourning for them, to comfort anyone for the
dead, nor give them a cup of consolation
to drink for anyone's father or mother.
8   "Moreover you shall not go into a

house of feasting to sit with them to eat and drink."

9   For thus says the LORD of hosts, the God of Israel: "Behold, I am going to eliminate from this place, before your eyes and in your time, the voice of rejoicing and the voice of gladness, the voice of the groom and the voice of the bride.

10   "Now when you tell this people all these words, they will say to you, 'For what reason has the LORD declared all this great calamity against us? And what is our iniquity, or what is our sin which we have committed against the LORD our God?'

11   "Then you are to say to them, 'It is because your forefathers have forsaken Me,' declares the LORD, 'and have followed other gods and served them and bowed down to them; but Me they have forsaken and have not kept My law.

12   'You too have done evil, even more than your forefathers; for behold, you are each one walking according to the stubbornness of his own evil heart, without listening to Me.

13   'So I will hurl you out of this land into the land which you have not known, neither you nor your fathers; and there you will serve other gods day and night, for I will grant you no favor.'

14   "Therefore behold, days are coming," declares the LORD, "when it will no longer be said, 'As the LORD lives, who brought up the sons of Israel out of the land of Egypt,'

15   but, 'As the LORD lives, who brought up the sons of Israel from the land of the north and from all the countries where He had banished them.' For I will restore them to their own land which I gave to their fathers.

16   "Behold, I am going to send for many fishermen," declares the LORD, "and they will fish for them; and afterwards I will send for many hunters, and they will hunt them from every mountain and every hill and from the clefts of the rocks.

17   "For My eyes are on all their ways; they are not hidden from My face, nor is their iniquity concealed from My eyes.

18   "I will first doubly repay their iniquity and their sin, because they have polluted My land; they have filled My inheritance with the carcasses of their detestable idols and with their abominations."

19   O LORD, my strength and my stronghold,
    And my refuge in the day of distress,
    To You the nations will come
    From the ends of the earth and say,
    "Our fathers have inherited nothing but falsehood,
    Futility and things of no profit."

20   Can man make gods for himself?
    Yet they are not gods!

21   "Therefore behold, I am going to make them know—
    This time I will make them know
    My power and My might;
    And they shall know that My name is the LORD."

Psalm 118:21–24

21   I shall give thanks to You, for You have answered me,
    And You have become my salvation.

22   The stone which the builders rejected
    Has become the chief corner stone.

23   This is the LORD's doing;
    It is marvelous in our eyes.

24   This is the day which the LORD has made;
    Let us rejoice and be glad in it.

LIFE LESSONS

➤ **Jeremiah 16:16** — *"They will hunt them from every mountain and every hill and from the clefts of the rocks."*

*G*od will spare no effort to bless us, just as He promised. If we feel forgotten at the bottom of the sea or marooned on the far side of the moon, even from there He will retrieve us to bless us.

➤ **Psalm 118:22** — *The stone which the builders rejected has become the chief corner stone.*

*T*he religious leaders of Jesus' day rejected Him as the Messiah (Matt. 21:42), but as Peter declared, "God has made Him both Lord and Christ—this Jesus whom you crucified" (Acts 2:36).

✦ Proverbs 27:10

10 Do not forsake your own friend or
     your father's friend,
    And do not go to your brother's
     house in the day of your
     calamity;
    Better is a neighbor who is near
     than a brother far away.

✦ 1 Thessalonians 2:1–20

2 FOR you yourselves know, brethren,
that our coming to you was not in
vain,
2 but after we had already suffered
and been mistreated in Philippi, as you
know, we had the boldness in our God
to speak to you the gospel of God amid
much opposition.
3 For our exhortation does not *come*
from error or impurity or by way of deceit;
4 but just as we have been approved
by God to be entrusted with the gospel,
so we speak, not as pleasing men, but
God who examines our hearts.
5 For we never came with flattering
speech, as you know, nor with a pretext
for greed—God is witness—
6 nor did we seek glory from men,
either from you or from others, even
though as apostles of Christ we might
have asserted our authority.
7 But we proved to be gentle among
you, as a nursing *mother* tenderly cares
for her own children.
8 Having so fond an affection for you,
we were well-pleased to impart to you
not only the gospel of God but also our
own lives, because you had become very
dear to us.
9 For you recall, brethren, our labor
and hardship, *how* working night and
day so as not to be a burden to any of
you, we proclaimed to you the gospel of
God.
10 You are witnesses, and *so is* God,
how devoutly and uprightly and blamelessly we behaved toward you believers;
11 just as you know how we *were* exhorting and encouraging and imploring

each one of you as a father *would* his
own children,
12 so that you would walk in a manner
worthy of the God who calls you into His
own kingdom and glory.
13 For this reason we also constantly
thank God that when you received the
word of God which you heard from us,
you accepted *it* not *as* the word of men,
but *for* what it really is, the word of God,
which also performs its work in you who
believe.
14 For you, brethren, became imitators
of the churches of God in Christ Jesus
that are in Judea, for you also endured
the same sufferings at the hands of your
own countrymen, even as they *did* from
the Jews,
15 who both killed the Lord Jesus and
the prophets, and drove us out. They are
not pleasing to God, but hostile to all
men,
16 hindering us from speaking to the
Gentiles so that they may be saved; with
the result that they always fill up the
measure of their sins. But wrath has come
upon them to the utmost.
17 But we, brethren, having been taken

LIFE LESSONS

➤ **1 Thessalonians 2:2** — *We had the
boldness in our God to speak to you the
gospel of God amid much opposition.*

𝒯he best place to find courage to
express what we believe despite
adversity—really, the only reliable
place—is *in God.* Boldness inspired by
the Spirit cannot be quenched by suffering or conflict.

➤ **1 Thessalonians 2:11** — *We were
exhorting and encouraging and imploring each one of you as a father would his
own children.*

𝒫aul not only acted with tender care
toward these young Christian believers, but he also disciplined and admonished them as a loving father would.
God acts in both ways toward us as well
(Heb. 12:5–13). He loves us, but He also
instructs us in how to live the life He
created for us. Likewise, when we lead
others to the Lord, we must keep them
accountable and teach them to follow
Him in obedience.

away from you for a short while—in person, not in spirit—were all the more eager with great desire to see your face.

18 For we wanted to come to you—I, Paul, more than once—and *yet* Satan hindered us.

19 For who is our hope or joy or crown of exultation? Is it not even you, in the presence of our Lord Jesus at His coming?

20 For you are our glory and joy.

LIFE LESSONS

➤ **1 Thessalonians 2:18** — *We wanted to come to you—I, Paul, more than once—and yet Satan hindered us.*

Satan's opposition to the Lord's work is real and can definitely impede our progress, so we need to be aware of it. We must also understand as Paul did, that the enemy's might is no match for the awesome power of the living God.

OCTOBER 16

Jeremiah 17:1—18:23

17 THE sin of Judah is written down with an iron stylus; With a diamond point it is engraved upon the tablet of their heart And on the horns of their altars,

2 As they remember their children, So they *remember* their altars and their Asherim By green trees on the high hills.

3 O mountain of Mine in the countryside, I will give over your wealth and all your treasures for booty, Your high places for sin throughout your borders.

4 And you will, even of yourself, let go of your inheritance That I gave you; And I will make you serve your enemies In the land which you do not know; For you have kindled a fire in My anger Which will burn forever.

5 Thus says the LORD, "Cursed is the man who trusts in mankind And makes flesh his strength, And whose heart turns away from the LORD.

6 "For he will be like a bush in the desert And will not see when prosperity comes, But will live in stony wastes in the wilderness, A land of salt without inhabitant.

7 "Blessed is the man who trusts in the LORD And whose trust is the LORD.

8 "For he will be like a tree planted by the water, That extends its roots by a stream And will not fear when the heat comes; But its leaves will be green, And it will not be anxious in a year of drought Nor cease to yield fruit.

9 "The heart is more deceitful than all else

LIFE LESSONS

➤ **Jeremiah 17:5** — *"Cursed is the man who trusts in mankind and makes flesh his strength, and whose heart turns away from the LORD."*

God made us for a dynamic and deep relationship with Himself, and trying to replace Him with *anything* else will always result in a curse. We are to find our strength in Him, not in ourselves.

➤ **Jeremiah 17:9** — *"The heart is more deceitful than all else and is desperately sick; who can understand it?"*

Our hearts will lie to us, and our feelings are unreliable. Although they are a powerful part of who we are, we must realize that our emotions can lead us in devastating ways (Prov. 16:25; Eccl. 9:3). Only God knows the human heart and how to redeem it. So when it is hurting or moving us in a destructive manner, we must turn to our Maker to help us (1 John 3:20).

And is desperately sick;
Who can understand it?
10 "I, the LORD, search the heart,
I test the mind,
Even to give to each man according
to his ways,
According to the results of his
deeds.
11 "As a partridge that hatches eggs
which it has not laid,
So is he who makes a fortune, but
unjustly;
In the midst of his days it will
forsake him,
And in the end he will be a fool."
12 A glorious throne on high from the
beginning
Is the place of our sanctuary.
13 O LORD, the hope of Israel,
All who forsake You will be put to
shame.
Those who turn away on earth will
be written down,
Because they have forsaken the
fountain of living water, even the
LORD.
14 Heal me, O LORD, and I will be
healed;
Save me and I will be saved,
For You are my praise.
15 Look, they keep saying to me,
"Where is the word of the LORD?
Let it come now!"
16 But as for me, I have not hurried
away from *being* a shepherd after
You,
Nor have I longed for the woeful
day;
You Yourself know that the
utterance of my lips
Was in Your presence.
17 Do not be a terror to me;
You are my refuge in the day of
disaster.
18 Let those who persecute me be put
to shame, but as for me, let me
not be put to shame;
Let them be dismayed, but let me
not be dismayed.
Bring on them a day of disaster,
And crush them with twofold
destruction!
19 Thus the LORD said to me, "Go and
stand in the public gate, through which
the kings of Judah come in and go out,
as well as in all the gates of Jerusalem;
20 and say to them, 'Listen to the word
of the LORD, kings of Judah, and all
Judah and all inhabitants of Jerusalem
who come in through these gates:
21 'Thus says the LORD, "Take heed for
yourselves, and do not carry any load
on the sabbath day or bring anything in
through the gates of Jerusalem.
22 "You shall not bring a load out of
your houses on the sabbath day nor do
any work, but keep the sabbath day holy,
as I commanded your forefathers.
23 "Yet they did not listen or incline
their ears, but stiffened their necks in
order not to listen or take correction.
24 "But it will come about, if you listen
attentively to Me," declares the LORD, "to
bring no load in through the gates of this
city on the sabbath day, but to keep the
sabbath day holy by doing no work on it,
25 then there will come in through the
gates of this city kings and princes sitting on the throne of David, riding in
chariots and on horses, they and their
princes, the men of Judah and the inhabitants of Jerusalem, and this city will be
inhabited forever.
26 "They will come in from the cities of
Judah and from the environs of Jerusalem, from the land of Benjamin, from the
lowland, from the hill country and from
the Negev, bringing burnt offerings, sacrifices, grain offerings and incense, and
bringing sacrifices of thanksgiving to the
house of the LORD.
27 "But if you do not listen to Me to keep
the sabbath day holy by not carrying a
load and coming in through the gates
of Jerusalem on the sabbath day, then I
will kindle a fire in its gates and it will
devour the palaces of Jerusalem and not
be quenched."''

18 THE word which came to Jeremiah
from the LORD saying,
2 "Arise and go down to the potter's
house, and there I will announce My
words to you."
3 Then I went down to the potter's
house, and there he was, making something on the wheel.
4 But the vessel that he was making of
clay was spoiled in the hand of the potter; so he remade it into another vessel,
as it pleased the potter to make.
5 Then the word of the LORD came to
me saying,
6 "Can I not, O house of Israel, deal
with you as this potter *does*?" declares

WHAT THE BIBLE SAYS ABOUT

The Process of Spiritual Growth

Jeremiah 18:1–6

*Y*oung Christians sometimes complain that the Christian growth process feels slow and tedious. They can become discouraged and stop seeking God through prayer, Bible study, service, or fellowship with other believers because they want instant knowledge and maturity without expending the time and effort it takes to develop their faith.

Seasoned Christians may have some of the same difficulties, only in a different way. At times they may mistakenly perceive themselves as having all the knowledge necessary to live the Christian life. So, like the young believers, they may stop seeking God through prayer, Bible study, service, and fellowship with other believers, and risk becoming resistant to His commands and desensitized to sin.

Yet all believers are to be molded into the likeness of Christ, which is a lifelong process.

We are to grow as God's children and love Christ so deeply that we leave no opportunity for boredom or pride to mar our devotion to Him. As we allow the Lord to shape and mold us, we "will also bear the image of the heavenly," that is, Jesus Christ (1 Cor. 15:49).

Being molded and shaped into Christ's image, however, can take longer than we think and involve lessons we never imagined. We might not be able to discern how the Lord wants to shape us, which may cause us to resist His work to our own detriment. Yet the Lord says to us, "Behold, like the clay in the potter's hand, so are you in My hand" (Jer. 18:6). In order to become all we were created to be, we must submit ourselves to the shaping and molding of God's loving hands. Even when we cannot understand His plan, we must continue to trust Him to bring out our full potential.

The Potter longs to mold and shape your life—to mold you into something more beautiful and wonderful than you could ever imagine. Therefore, allow Him to take whatever time He needs to create in you a joy and devotion of immeasurable worth. ◈

---

the LORD. "Behold, like the clay in the potter's hand, so are you in My hand, O house of Israel.
7 "At one moment I might speak concerning a nation or concerning a kingdom to uproot, to pull down, or to destroy *it;*
8 if that nation against which I have spoken turns from its evil, I will relent concerning the calamity I planned to bring on it.
9 "Or at another moment I might speak concerning a nation or concerning a kingdom to build up or to plant *it;*
10 if it does evil in My sight by not

obeying My voice, then I will think better of the good with which I had promised to bless it.
11 "So now then, speak to the men of Judah and against the inhabitants of Jerusalem saying, 'Thus says the LORD, "Behold, I am fashioning calamity against you and devising a plan against you. Oh turn back, each of you from his evil way, and reform your ways and your deeds."'
12 "But they will say, 'It's hopeless! For we are going to follow our own plans, and each of us will act according to the stubbornness of his evil heart.'
13 "Therefore thus says the LORD,
'Ask now among the nations,
Who ever heard the like of this?
The virgin of Israel
Has done a most appalling thing.
14 'Does the snow of Lebanon forsake
the rock of the open country?
Or is the cold flowing water *from* a
foreign *land* ever snatched
away?
15 'For My people have forgotten Me,
They burn incense to worthless
gods

LIFE LESSONS

➤ **Jeremiah 18:6 — "Behold, like the clay in the potter's hand, so are you in My hand, O house of Israel!"**

*G*od wants to mold us and shape us into something of indescribable beauty. The process is not quick, nor does it always feel pleasant, but we can trust the hand of the Potter to finish what He has started.

And they have stumbled from their
ways,
From the ancient paths,
To walk in bypaths,
Not on a highway,
16 To make their land a desolation,
An object of perpetual hissing;
Everyone who passes by it will be
astonished
And shake his head.
17 'Like an east wind I will scatter
them
Before the enemy;
I will show them My back and not
My face
In the day of their calamity.'"
18 Then they said, "Come and let us devise plans against Jeremiah. Surely the
law is not going to be lost to the priest,
nor counsel to the sage, nor the *divine*
word to the prophet! Come on and let us
strike at him with *our* tongue, and let us
give no heed to any of his words."
19 Do give heed to me, O LORD,
And listen to what my opponents
are saying!
20 Should good be repaid with evil?
For they have dug a pit for me.
Remember how I stood before You
To speak good on their behalf,
So as to turn away Your wrath from
them.
21 Therefore, give their children over
to famine
And deliver them up to the power of
the sword;
And let their wives become childless
and widowed.
Let their men also be smitten to
death,
Their young men struck down by
the sword in battle.
22 May an outcry be heard from their
houses,
When You suddenly bring raiders
upon them;
For they have dug a pit to capture
me
And hidden snares for my feet.
23 Yet You, O LORD, know
All their deadly designs against me;
Do not forgive their iniquity
Or blot out their sin from Your sight.
But may they be overthrown before
You;
Deal with them in the time of Your
anger!

Psalm 118:25–29

25 O LORD, do save, we beseech You;
O LORD, we beseech You, do send
prosperity!
26 Blessed is the one who comes in the
name of the LORD;
We have blessed you from the house
of the LORD.
27 The LORD is God, and He has given
us light;
Bind the festival sacrifice with cords
to the horns of the altar.
28 You are my God, and I give thanks
to You;
You are my God, I extol You.
29 Give thanks to the LORD, for He is
good;
For His lovingkindness is
everlasting.

Proverbs 27:11, 12

11 Be wise, my son, and make my
heart glad,
That I may reply to him who
reproaches me.
12 A prudent man sees evil *and* hides
himself,
The naive proceed *and* pay the
penalty.

1 Thessalonians 3:1–13

3 THEREFORE when we could endure
it no longer, we thought it best to be
left behind at Athens alone,
2 and we sent Timothy, our brother
and God's fellow worker in the gospel of

LIFE LESSONS

➤ **Proverbs 27:12 —** *A prudent man sees evil and hides himself, the naive proceed and pay the penalty.*

Trust in God does not mean that we turn off our minds or skip through life without any thought about our surroundings or the challenges we face. Fools remain oblivious; the wise stay alert and take appropriate action.

Christ, to strengthen and encourage you as to your faith,

3   so that no one would be disturbed by these afflictions; for you yourselves know that we have been destined for this.

4   For indeed when we were with you, we *kept* telling you in advance that we were going to suffer affliction; and so it came to pass, as you know.

5   For this reason, when I could endure *it* no longer, I also sent to find out about your faith, for fear that the tempter might have tempted you, and our labor would be in vain.

6   But now that Timothy has come to us from you, and has brought us good news of your faith and love, and that you always think kindly of us, longing to see us just as we also long to see you,

7   for this reason, brethren, in all our distress and affliction we were comforted about you through your faith;

8   for now we *really* live, if you stand firm in the Lord.

9   For what thanks can we render to God for you in return for all the joy with which we rejoice before our God on your account,

10   as we night and day keep praying most earnestly that we may see your face, and may complete what is lacking in your faith?

11   Now may our God and Father Himself and Jesus our Lord direct our way to you;

12   and may the Lord cause you to increase and abound in love for one another, and for all people, just as we also do for you;

13   so that He may establish your hearts without blame in holiness before our God and Father at the coming of our Lord Jesus with all His saints.

LIFE LESSONS

> **1 Thessalonians 3:7 — *In all our distress and affliction we were comforted about you through your faith.***

*T*here is little so comforting as seeing your believing friends and loved ones growing closer to the Lord. Who might you encourage right now through your own maturing faith? Your example and testimony can help people to endure and stay faithful to the Lord during very difficult times (2 Cor. 1:3–11). Therefore when it is appropriate, share your experience with others.

> **1 Thessalonians 3:13 — *That He may establish your hearts without blame in holiness before our God and Father at the coming of our Lord Jesus.***

*T*he Bible very often connects holy living with the return of Christ. We do not know when we will see the Lord—either by our own death or because of His Second Coming. However, an eager anticipation of seeing Him face to face should keep us living productively and should inspire us to devote ourselves wholeheartedly to Him.

Jeremiah 19:1—20:18

19 THUS says the LORD, "Go and buy a potter's earthenware jar, and *take* some of the elders of the people and some of the senior priests.

2   "Then go out to the valley of Ben-hinnom, which is by the entrance of the potsherd gate, and proclaim there the words that I tell you,

3   and say, 'Hear the word of the LORD, O kings of Judah and inhabitants of Jerusalem: thus says the LORD of hosts, the God of Israel, "Behold I am about to bring a calamity upon this place, at which the ears of everyone that hears of it will tingle.

4   "Because they have forsaken Me and have made this an alien place and have burned sacrifices in it to other gods, that neither they nor their forefathers nor the kings of Judah had *ever* known, and *because* they have filled this place with the blood of the innocent

5   and have built the high places of

Baal to burn their sons in the fire as burnt offerings to Baal, a thing which I never commanded or spoke of, nor did it *ever* enter My mind;

6   therefore, behold, days are coming," declares the LORD, "when this place will no longer be called Topheth or the valley of Ben-hinnom, but rather the valley of Slaughter.

7   "I will make void the counsel of Judah and Jerusalem in this place, and I will cause them to fall by the sword before their enemies and by the hand of those who seek their life; and I will give over their carcasses as food for the birds of the sky and the beasts of the earth.

8   "I will also make this city a desolation and an *object of* hissing; everyone who passes by it will be astonished and hiss because of all its disasters.

9   "I will make them eat the flesh of their sons and the flesh of their daughters, and they will eat one another's flesh in the siege and in the distress with which their enemies and those who seek their life will distress them."'

10   "Then you are to break the jar in the sight of the men who accompany you

11   and say to them, 'Thus says the LORD of hosts, "Just so will I break this people and this city, even as one breaks a potter's vessel, which cannot again be repaired; and they will bury in Topheth because there is no *other* place for burial.

12   "This is how I will treat this place and its inhabitants," declares the LORD, "so as to make this city like Topheth.

13   "The houses of Jerusalem and the houses of the kings of Judah will be defiled like the place Topheth, because of all the houses on whose rooftops they burned sacrifices to all the heavenly host and poured out drink offerings to other gods."'"

14   Then Jeremiah came from Topheth, where the LORD had sent him to prophesy; and he stood in the court of the LORD's house and said to all the people:

15   "Thus says the LORD of hosts, the God of Israel, 'Behold, I am about to bring on this city and all its towns the entire calamity that I have declared against it, because they have stiffened their necks so as not to heed My words.'"

20 WHEN Pashhur the priest, the son of Immer, who was chief officer in the house of the LORD, heard Jeremiah prophesying these things,

2   Pashhur had Jeremiah the prophet ◄ beaten and put him in the stocks that were at the upper Benjamin Gate, which was by the house of the LORD.

3   On the next day, when Pashhur released Jeremiah from the stocks, Jeremiah said to him, "Pashhur is not the name the LORD has called you, but rather Magor-missabib.

4   "For thus says the LORD, 'Behold, I am going to make you a terror to yourself and to all your friends; and while your eyes look on, they will fall by the sword of their enemies. So I will give over all Judah to the hand of the king of Babylon, and he will carry them away as exiles to Babylon and will slay them with the sword.

5   'I will also give over all the wealth of this city, all its produce and all its costly things; even all the treasures of the kings of Judah I will give over to the hand of their enemies, and they will plunder them, take them away and bring them to Babylon.

6   'And you, Pashhur, and all who live in your house will go into captivity; and you will enter Babylon, and there you will die and there you will be buried, you and all your friends to whom you have falsely prophesied.'"

7   O LORD, You have deceived me and
        I was deceived;
    You have overcome me and
        prevailed.
    I have become a laughingstock all
        day long;
    Everyone mocks me.

LIFE LESSONS

➤ **Jeremiah 20:2** — *Pashhur had Jeremiah the prophet beaten and put him in the stocks.*

*J*eremiah suffered greatly for faithfully proclaiming the word that God told him to speak. To an observer, it might not have looked as though the Lord was rewarding Jeremiah's obedience. But this time of suffering did not define Jeremiah's life. We know that He avenged Jeremiah (Jer. 20:4–6), fulfilled His Word through him (2 Chr. 36:21; Ezra 1:1; Dan. 9:2; Matt. 2:17; 27:9), and was always faithful to deliver him (Jer. 1:8).

8　For each time I speak, I cry aloud;
　　I proclaim violence and destruction,
　　Because for me the word of the
　　　LORD has resulted
　　In reproach and derision all day
　　　long.
➤ 9　But if I say, "I will not remember
　　　Him
　　Or speak anymore in His name,"
　　Then in my heart it becomes like a
　　　burning fire
　　Shut up in my bones;
　　And I am weary of holding *it* in,
　　And I cannot endure *it.*
10　For I have heard the whispering of
　　　many,
　　"Terror on every side!
　　Denounce *him*; yes, let us denounce
　　　him!"
　　All my trusted friends,
　　Watching for my fall, say:
　　"Perhaps he will be deceived, so that
　　　we may prevail against him
　　And take our revenge on him."
11　But the LORD is with me like a dread
　　　champion;
　　Therefore my persecutors will
　　　stumble and not prevail.
　　They will be utterly ashamed,
　　　because they have failed,
　　With an everlasting disgrace that
　　　will not be forgotten.
12　Yet, O LORD of hosts, You who test
　　　the righteous,
　　Who see the mind and the heart;
　　Let me see Your vengeance on
　　　them;
　　For to You I have set forth my cause.
13　Sing to the LORD, praise the LORD!
　　For He has delivered the soul of the
　　　needy one
　　From the hand of evildoers.
14　Cursed be the day when I was born;
　　Let the day not be blessed when my
　　　mother bore me!

LIFE LESSONS

➤ **Jeremiah 20:9** — *"In my heart [His word] becomes like a burning fire shut up in my bones; and I am weary of holding it in, and I cannot endure it."*

*I*f your goals are truly from the Lord, your spirit will testify that you *must* accomplish them. You won't be able to do otherwise.

15　Cursed be the man who brought the
　　　news
　　To my father, saying,
　　"A baby boy has been born to you!"
　　And made him very happy.
16　But let that man be like the cities
　　Which the LORD overthrew without
　　　relenting,
　　And let him hear an outcry in the
　　　morning
　　And a shout of alarm at noon;
17　Because he did not kill me before
　　　birth,
　　So that my mother would have been
　　　my grave,
　　And her womb ever pregnant.
18　Why did I ever come forth from the
　　　womb
　　To look on trouble and sorrow,
　　So that my days have been spent in
　　　shame?

Psalm 119:1–8

× Aleph.

119 HOW blessed are those whose
　　　way is blameless,
　　Who walk in the law of the LORD.
2　How blessed are those who observe
　　　His testimonies,
　　Who seek Him with all *their* heart.
3　They also do no unrighteousness;
　　They walk in His ways.
4　You have ordained Your precepts,
　　That we should keep *them*
　　　diligently.
5　Oh that my ways may be established
　　To keep Your statutes!
6　Then I shall not be ashamed
　　When I look upon all Your
　　　commandments.
7　I shall give thanks to You with
　　　uprightness of heart,
　　When I learn Your righteous
　　　judgments.
8　I shall keep Your statutes;
　　Do not forsake me utterly!

Proverbs 27:13

13　Take his garment when he becomes
　　　surety for a stranger;

And for an adulterous woman hold
  him in pledge.

1 Thessalonians 4:1–18

4 FINALLY then, brethren, we request
  and exhort you in the Lord Jesus, that
as you received from us *instruction* as to
how you ought to walk and please God
(just as you actually do walk), that you
excel still more.
2   For you know what commandments
we gave you by *the authority of* the Lord
Jesus.
➤ 3   For this is the will of God, your sanctification; *that is,* that you abstain from
sexual immorality;
4   that each of you know how to possess his own vessel in sanctification and
honor,
5   not in lustful passion, like the Gentiles who do not know God;
6   *and* that no man transgress and defraud his brother in the matter because
the Lord is *the* avenger in all these
things, just as we also told you before
and solemnly warned *you.*
7   For God has not called us for the
purpose of impurity, but in sanctification.
8   So, he who rejects *this* is not rejecting man but the God who gives His Holy
Spirit to you.
9   Now as to the love of the brethren,
you have no need for *anyone* to write
to you, for you yourselves are taught by
God to love one another;
10   for indeed you do practice it toward
all the brethren who are in all Macedonia. But we urge you, brethren, to excel
still more,
➤ 11   and to make it your ambition to lead
a quiet life and attend to your own business and work with your hands, just as
we commanded you,
12   so that you will behave properly toward outsiders and not be in any need.
13   But we do not want you to be uninformed, brethren, about those who are
asleep, so that you will not grieve as do
the rest who have no hope.
14   For if we believe that Jesus died and
rose again, even so God will bring with
Him those who have fallen asleep in
Jesus.

15   For this we say to you by the word
of the Lord, that we who are alive and
remain until the coming of the Lord,
will not precede those who have fallen
asleep.

LIFE LESSONS

➤ **1 Thessalonians 4:3 — *This is the will
of God, your sanctification, that is, that
you abstain from sexual immorality.***

God calls you to a holy life because
  He wants you to enjoy all the blessings He has for you. That means He
puts boundaries on sex for your benefit—commanding that it be between a
man and a woman who are married to
each other because He cares about what
happens to you physically. However, no
matter what sin you've committed or
what sexual addiction has trapped you,
the Lord is *never* your enemy. He is your
biggest advocate, and He wants you to
experience His forgiveness, restoration,
and sanctification.

➤ **1 Thessalonians 4:11 — *Make it your
ambition to lead a quiet life and attend
to your own business and work with
your hands.***

The spirit-filled Christian life should
  not be characterized by drama and
disorder but by the unfettered peace of
God, steadfast self-control, and faithfulness to commitments (Gal. 5:22, 23).
Though the storms of adversity rage
in outward circumstances, the believer
continues to experience the quiet inward
confidence, which can only come from
the Lord.

➤ **1 Thessalonians 4:16 — *The Lord
Himself will descend from heaven with
a shout.***

This amazing passage describes the
  moment when the Lord returns for
His church—the dead in Christ will rise
and receive their glorified bodies, and
those who are alive will be gathered
directly into His presence. This should
not be confused with the Second Coming of the Lord, when Jesus stands upon
the Mount of Olives and establishes His
kingdom on earth (Matt. 25:31–46). The
rapture begins the wedding supper of
the Lamb (Matt. 25:1–13), and the Second Coming takes place after the banquet has concluded (Rev. 19:7—20:15).

WHAT THE BIBLE SAYS ABOUT

A Warning Against Sexual Sins

1 Thessalonians 4:1–8

Sexual sin promises immediate pleasure without penalty. Think about the movies that you see or the books you read. The people in them are committing all kinds of transgressions; and, of course, they always make it look like their lives are completely wonderful and fulfilling. However, the truth is that God did not create us to behave that way. The pleasure without penalty that the world promises is a big lie.

Sexual sin begins where all iniquity begins—with temptation, which is an enticement to do evil. Like any other transgression, sexual sin begins with a thought. From that thought, the imagination takes over because the person ponders what the experience would be like. Then, there is identification—the person takes on the character of his or her imagination. After that, the person's desire becomes stronger and more insistent—which can only be followed by the will to sin.

Be careful of what you think about. If you have ungodly thoughts in your mind, you must deal with them. Your imagination is an amazing gift from God; however, that gift can be perverted if you don't deal with your ungodly thoughts. Eventually, you'll live out those immoral fantasies.

Now, sex in itself is not a sin; in fact, it's a privilege given to us by God. However, there are certain boundaries that accompany that privilege. The sexual experience is reserved for a man and woman who are married to each other. When sex is enjoyed within the boundaries that God has given, it's good. Unfortunately, sex often isn't practiced out of genuine love for the other person; instead, people often engage in sex because of their own needs.

Again, the power of sexual sin is in its deceptive offer that you can have immediate pleasure without penalty. Let us think about that for a moment. What are the underlying causes of sexual sins?

1. The need for intimacy.

The need for intimacy is a legitimate need. However, there are many people who believe that they will eventually find someone who will fulfill their need for intimacy. Yet God created us to feel fulfillment in our relationships with Him above any other relationship.

2. The need for acceptance.

People believe that if they could just feel that somebody cares for them for a few moments then they will be all right. They are willing to give themselves over to someone else sexually just so that they will feel accepted for a little while. However, that's a terrible trap.

3. The need for fulfillment.

You will never have a sense of fulfillment as a result of sex because God did not make sex for that reason. Our fulfillment can only result from a relationship that is godly, wholesome, and divine.

4. The need to conquer.

Often, people are angry at the opposite sex, and they express their rage by conquering the opposite sex. Through sex, they believe the other people are surrendering themselves—at least for a time.

5. The desire for revenge.

Imagine a husband or a wife who thinks his or her spouse has been unfaithful to them. To get revenge, they go and have some kind of experience with someone else. Unfortunately, all that does is destroy whatever is left of the relationship. It's no way to have any kind of joy or fulfillment.

6. The need to build one's self-esteem.

People feel that they aren't attractive enough, wealthy enough, interesting enough, or smart enough. However, if they believe that sex can build up their self-esteem, they have been deceived. Instead, it's going to make the person feel less appealing, less attractive.

If you want love, acceptance, intimacy, victory, and fulfillment, there is only one place to find it—and that is through Jesus Christ. Therefore, accept Jesus Christ as your Lord and Savior. Seek Him every day of your life because it's in Him that all of your deepest needs are met. ◈

➤ 16 For the Lord Himself will descend from heaven with a shout, with the voice of *the* archangel and with the trumpet of God, and the dead in Christ will rise first. 17 Then we who are alive and remain will be caught up together with them in the clouds to meet the Lord in the air, and so we shall always be with the Lord. 18 Therefore comfort one another with these words.

21 THE word which came to Jeremiah from the LORD when King Zedekiah sent to him Pashhur the son of Malchijah, and Zephaniah the priest, the son of Maaseiah, saying,
2 "Please inquire of the LORD on our behalf, for Nebuchadnezzar king of Babylon is warring against us; perhaps the LORD will deal with us according to all His wonderful acts, so that the enemy will withdraw from us."
3 Then Jeremiah said to them, "You shall say to Zedekiah as follows:
4 'Thus says the LORD God of Israel, "Behold, I am about to turn back the weapons of war which are in your hands, with which you are warring against the king of Babylon and the Chaldeans who are besieging you outside the wall; and I will gather them into the center of this city.
5 "I Myself will war against you with an outstretched hand and a mighty arm, even in anger and wrath and great indignation.
6 "I will also strike down the inhabitants of this city, both man and beast; they will die of a great pestilence.
7 "Then afterwards," declares the LORD, "I will give over Zedekiah king of Judah and his servants and the people, even those who survive in this city from the pestilence, the sword and the famine, into the hand of Nebuchadnezzar king of Babylon, and into the hand of their foes and into the hand of those who seek their lives; and he will strike them down with the edge of the sword. He will not spare them nor have pity nor compassion."'
8 "You shall also say to this people, 'Thus says the LORD, "Behold, I set before you the way of life and the way of death.
9 "He who dwells in this city will die by the sword and by famine and by pestilence; but he who goes out and falls away to the Chaldeans who are besieging you will live, and he will have his own life as booty.
10 "For I have set My face against this city for harm and not for good," declares the LORD. "It will be given into the hand of the king of Babylon and he will burn it with fire."'
11 "Then *say* to the household of the king of Judah, 'Hear the word of the LORD,
12 O house of David, thus says the LORD:

"Administer justice every morning;
And deliver the *person* who has been robbed from the power of *his* oppressor,
That My wrath may not go forth like fire
And burn with none to extinguish *it*,
Because of the evil of their deeds.
13 "Behold, I am against you, O valley dweller,
O rocky plain," declares the LORD,
"You men who say, 'Who will come down against us?
Or who will enter into our habitations?'
14 "But I will punish you according to the results of your deeds," declares the LORD,
"And I will kindle a fire in its forest
That it may devour all its environs."'"

22 THUS says the LORD, "Go down to the house of the king of Judah, and there speak this word
2 and say, 'Hear the word of the LORD, O king of Judah, who sits on David's throne, you and your servants and your people who enter these gates.
3 'Thus says the LORD, "Do justice and righteousness, and deliver the one who has been robbed from the power of *his* oppressor. Also do not mistreat *or* do violence to the stranger, the orphan, or the widow; and do not shed innocent blood in this place.
4 "For if you men will indeed perform this thing, then kings will enter the gates of this house, sitting in David's place on his throne, riding in chariots and on horses, *even the king* himself and his servants and his people.
5 "But if you will not obey these words, I swear by Myself," declares the LORD, "that this house will become a desolation."'"
6 For thus says the LORD concerning the house of the king of Judah:

"You are *like* Gilead to Me,

Like the summit of Lebanon;
Yet most assuredly I will make you
like a wilderness,
Like cities which are not inhabited.
7 "For I will set apart destroyers
against you,
Each with his weapons;
And they will cut down your
choicest cedars
And throw *them* on the fire.
8 "Many nations will pass by this city;
and they will say to one another, 'Why
has the LORD done thus to this great
city?'
9 "Then they will answer, 'Because
they forsook the covenant of the LORD
their God and bowed down to other gods
and served them.'"
10 Do not weep for the dead or mourn
for him,
But weep continually for the one
who goes away;
For he will never return
Or see his native land.
11 For thus says the LORD in regard to
Shallum the son of Josiah, king of Judah,
who became king in the place of Josiah
his father, who went forth from this
place, "He will never return there;
12 but in the place where they led him
captive, there he will die and not see this
land again.
13 "Woe to him who builds his house
without righteousness
And his upper rooms without
justice,
Who uses his neighbor's services
without pay
And does not give him his wages,
14 Who says, 'I will build myself a
roomy house
With spacious upper rooms,
And cut out its windows,
Paneling *it* with cedar and painting
it bright red.'
15 "Do you become a king because you
are competing in cedar?
Did not your father eat and drink
And do justice and righteousness?
Then it was well with him.
16 "He pled the cause of the afflicted
and needy;
Then it was well.
Is not that what it means to know
Me?"
Declares the LORD.
17 "But your eyes and your heart

Are *intent* only upon your own
dishonest gain,
And on shedding innocent blood
And on practicing oppression and
extortion."
18 Therefore thus says the LORD in regard to Jehoiakim the son of Josiah, king
of Judah,
"They will not lament for him:
'Alas, my brother!' or, 'Alas, sister!'
They will not lament for him:
'Alas for the master!' or, 'Alas for
his splendor!'
19 "He will be buried with a donkey's
burial,
Dragged off and thrown out beyond
the gates of Jerusalem.
20 "Go up to Lebanon and cry out,
And lift up your voice in Bashan;
Cry out also from Abarim,
For all your lovers have been
crushed.
21 "I spoke to you in your prosperity;   ←
But you said, 'I will not listen!'
This has been your practice from
your youth,
That you have not obeyed My
voice.
22 "The wind will sweep away all your
shepherds,
And your lovers will go into
captivity;

LIFE LESSONS

➤ **Jeremiah 22:16 —** *"He pled the cause of the afflicted and needy; then it was well. Is not that what it means to know Me?"*

*T*o know God is not merely to have a peaceful feeling in the heart; to know God is to obey Him in acting for the benefit of others—especially for those who cannot pay you back (Matt. 28:19-20; John 15:10–14; 2 Cor. 9:6–9; James 2:15–17). Those who know God love to serve Him.

➤ **Jeremiah 22:21 —** *"This has been your practice from your youth, that you have not obeyed My voice."*

*G*od speaks to us in both our prosperity and our hardship; our job in both cases is to listen carefully for His voice, and to hear and obey what He says. What has God been saying to you lately?

Then you will surely be ashamed
and humiliated
Because of all your wickedness.
23 "You who dwell in Lebanon,
Nested in the cedars,
How you will groan when pangs
come upon you,
Pain like a woman in childbirth!
24 "As I live," declares the LORD, "even
though Coniah the son of Jehoiakim king
of Judah were a signet *ring* on My right
hand, yet I would pull you off;
25 and I will give you over into the hand
of those who are seeking your life, yes,
into the hand of those whom you dread,
even into the hand of Nebuchadnezzar
king of Babylon and into the hand of the
Chaldeans.
26 "I will hurl you and your mother who
bore you into another country where you
were not born, and there you will die.
27 "But as for the land to which they
desire to return, they will not return to it.
28 "Is this man Coniah a despised,
shattered jar?
Or is he an undesirable vessel?
Why have he and his descendants
been hurled out
And cast into a land that they had
not known?
29 "O land, land, land,
Hear the word of the LORD!
30 "Thus says the LORD,
'Write this man down childless,
A man who will not prosper in his
days;
For no man of his descendants will
prosper
Sitting on the throne of David
Or ruling again in Judah.'"

Psalm 119:9–16

ב Beth.

➤ 9 How can a young man keep his way
pure?
By keeping *it* according to Your
word.
✳ 10 With all my heart I have sought You;
Do not let me wander from Your
commandments.
11 Your word I have treasured in my
heart,
That I may not sin against You.

12 Blessed are You, O LORD;
Teach me Your statutes.
13 With my lips I have told of
All the ordinances of Your mouth.
14 I have rejoiced in the way of Your
testimonies,
As much as in all riches.
15 I will meditate on Your precepts
And regard Your ways.
16 I shall delight in Your statutes;
I shall not forget Your word.

Proverbs 27:14

14 He who blesses his friend with a
loud voice early in the morning,
It will be reckoned a curse to him.

1 Thessalonians 5:1–28

5 NOW as to the times and the epochs,
brethren, you have no need of anything to be written to you.
2 For you yourselves know full well ◄
that the day of the Lord will come just
like a thief in the night.
3 While they are saying, "Peace and
safety!" then destruction will come upon
them suddenly like labor pains upon a

LIFE LESSONS

➤ **Psalm 119:9** — *How can a young man
keep his way pure? By keeping it according to Your word.*

*I*f we want to please God and honor
Him with our lives, we must get to
know His Word. The Bible warns us of
dangers ahead, steers us toward the
heart of God, and gives us wisdom to
flourish in a dark age.

➤ **1 Thessalonians 5:2** — *You yourselves
know full well that the day of the Lord
will come just like a thief in the night.*

*W*hen will a thief strike? No one
knows. So it is with the return of
Christ. No one knows when He is coming
to gather us to Himself. But an eager
anticipation of His return should keep us
living hopefully and productively.

woman with child, and they will not escape.

4   But you, brethren, are not in darkness, that the day would overtake you like a thief;

5   for you are all sons of light and sons of day. We are not of night nor of darkness;

➤ 6   so then let us not sleep as others do, but let us be alert and sober.

7   For those who sleep do their sleeping at night, and those who get drunk get drunk at night.

8   But since we are of the day, let us be sober, having put on the breastplate of faith and love, and as a helmet, the hope of salvation.

9   For God has not destined us for wrath, but for obtaining salvation through our Lord Jesus Christ,

10   who died for us, so that whether we are awake or asleep, we will live together with Him.

11   Therefore encourage one another and build up one another, just as you also are doing.

12   But we request of you, brethren, that you appreciate those who diligently labor among you, and have charge over you in the Lord and give you instruction,

---

LIFE LESSONS

➤ **1 Thessalonians 5:6 —** *Let us not sleep as others do, but let us be alert and sober.*

*J*esus told us to watch for Him and keep at His business until He comes, and Paul merely elaborated on the same message. The prospect of Jesus' return should inspire us to keep working, not to get lazy.

➤ **1 Thessalonians 5:14 —** *Admonish the unruly, encourage the fainthearted, help the weak, be patient with everyone.*

*G*race ministers to different people in different ways, depending upon what they most need at the time. Some need stern warnings; others need comfort; some need help. But everyone needs patience, for we all fall short in many ways.

---

13   and that you esteem them very highly in love because of their work. Live in peace with one another.

14   We urge you, brethren, admonish the unruly, encourage the fainthearted, help the weak, be patient with everyone.

ANSWERS TO LIFE'S QUESTIONS

What does it mean to "pray without ceasing"?

1 THESSALONIANS 5:17

*W*hat did the apostle Paul mean by "pray without ceasing" (1 Thess. 5:17)? How is it possible to carry on with normal life if we do so?

First, the apostle did not mean that we should walk around all day mumbling to God. Rather, he taught that we can live in a constant attitude of intercession, even as we go about our daily routines. Of course, some days we'll pray much more than others. But regardless of the particular items on our "to do" list, we can maintain a natural, ongoing conversation with the Lord that encompasses our whole lives.

Should you pray about insignificant or mundane matters? Yes! God listens to *every* prayer. Since He is interested in every aspect of your life, He invites you to talk to Him about whatever concerns, interests, confuses, frightens, challenges, or in any way touches your life.

You should ask Him to help you with the small things like finding lost glasses or retrieving forgotten information. Because it is through such requests you learn that God is your gracious heavenly Father and you are His much-loved child.

Outsiders may consider such complete trust in the Lord foolhardy, but so what? Only through prayer can we tap into His limitless resources. Only by seeking Him can we test His promise: "If you ask Me anything in My name, I will do it" (John 14:14). Too often we limit our praying precisely because we do not cast ourselves wholeheartedly on His grace and mercy.

God has called us to be people of prayer, and regular communication creates intimate fellowship with our Savior. Through our time with Him, we discover His goodness, faithfulness, and wonderful direction for our lives. We also find the strength and wisdom for every turn on our path so we can experience all He has created us for. When we develop a prayerful outlook, eventually our communication with the Lord becomes our first instinct in *every* situation—not only when we face a challenge or encounter a difficulty. And in time, it will never occur to us to *not* pray.

15   See that no one repays another with evil for evil, but always seek after that which is good for one another and for all people.

16   Rejoice always;

17   pray without ceasing;

18   in everything give thanks; for this is God's will for you in Christ Jesus.

19   Do not quench the Spirit;

20   do not despise prophetic utterances.

21   But examine everything *carefully*; hold fast to that which is good;

22   abstain from every form of evil.

23   Now may the God of peace Himself sanctify you entirely; and may your spirit and soul and body be preserved complete, without blame at the coming of our Lord Jesus Christ.

24   Faithful is He who calls you, and He also will bring it to pass.

25   Brethren, pray for us.

26   Greet all the brethren with a holy kiss.

27   I adjure you by the Lord to have this letter read to all the brethren.

28   The grace of our Lord Jesus Christ be with you.

OCTOBER 19

◈ Jeremiah 23:1—24:10

23 "WOE to the shepherds who are destroying and scattering the sheep of My pasture!" declares the LORD.

2   Therefore thus says the LORD God of Israel concerning the shepherds who are tending My people: "You have scattered My flock and driven them away, and have not attended to them; behold, I am about to attend to you for the evil of your deeds," declares the LORD.

➤ 3   "Then I Myself will gather the remnant of My flock out of all the countries where I have driven them and bring them back to their pasture, and they will be fruitful and multiply.

4   "I will also raise up shepherds over them and they will tend them; and they will not be afraid any longer, nor be terrified, nor will any be missing," declares the LORD.

✳ 5   "Behold, *the* days are coming," declares the LORD,
"When I will raise up for David a
    righteous Branch;
And He will reign as king and act
    wisely
And do justice and righteousness in
    the land.

➤ 6   "In His days Judah will be saved,
And Israel will dwell securely;
And this is His name by which He
    will be called,
'The LORD our righteousness.'

7   "Therefore behold, *the* days are coming," declares the LORD, "when they will no longer say, 'As the LORD lives, who brought up the sons of Israel from the land of Egypt,'

8   but, 'As the LORD lives, who brought up and led back the descendants of the household of Israel from *the* north land and from all the countries where I had driven them.' Then they will live on their own soil."

9   As for the prophets:
My heart is broken within me,

LIFE LESSONS

➤ **Jeremiah 23:3** — *"I Myself will gather the remnant of My flock out of all the countries where I have driven them and bring them back to their pasture, and they will be fruitful and multiply."*

God desires to bless His people and to make them fruitful. This passage looked forward to a day when the Lord would gather His people to inhabit the Promised Land again, which happened during the reign of Persian king Cyrus (2 Chr. 36:22, 23; Ezra 1:1–3). Just as He fulfilled His promise to one day gather and bless Judah and Israel, so He longs to bless you when you obey Him.

➤ **Jeremiah 23:6** — *He will be called, "The LORD our righteousness."*

When we come to Jesus Christ in faith, *He* becomes our righteousness. We stand before God, not on the basis of our efforts or record, but because of what He has done for us on the cross and what He continues to do for us in our lives and throughout history.

All my bones tremble;
I have become like a drunken man,
Even like a man overcome with
　wine,
Because of the LORD
And because of His holy words.
10　For the land is full of adulterers;
For the land mourns because of the
　curse.
The pastures of the wilderness have
　dried up.
Their course also is evil
And their might is not right.
11　"For both prophet and priest are
　polluted;
Even in My house I have found their
　wickedness," declares the LORD.
12　"Therefore their way will be like
　slippery paths to them,
They will be driven away into the
　gloom and fall down in it;
For I will bring calamity upon them,
The year of their punishment,"
　declares the LORD.
13　"Moreover, among the prophets of
　Samaria I saw an offensive thing:
They prophesied by Baal and led
　My people Israel astray.
14　"Also among the prophets of
　Jerusalem I have seen a horrible
　thing:
The committing of adultery and
　walking in falsehood;
And they strengthen the hands of
　evildoers,
So that no one has turned back
　from his wickedness.
All of them have become to Me like
　Sodom,
And her inhabitants like Gomorrah.
15　"Therefore thus says the LORD of
hosts concerning the prophets,
'Behold, I am going to feed them
　wormwood
And make them drink poisonous
　water,
For from the prophets of Jerusalem
Pollution has gone forth into all the
　land.'"
16　Thus says the LORD of hosts,
"Do not listen to the words of the
　prophets who are prophesying to
　you.
They are leading you into futility;
They speak a vision of their own
　imagination,
Not from the mouth of the LORD.

17　"They keep saying to those who
　despise Me,
'The LORD has said, "You will have
　peace"';
And as for everyone who walks
　in the stubbornness of his own
　heart,
They say, 'Calamity will not come
　upon you.'
18　"But who has stood in the council of
　the LORD,
That he should see and hear His
　word?
Who has given heed to His word
　and listened?
19　"Behold, the storm of the LORD has
　gone forth in wrath,
Even a whirling tempest;
It will swirl down on the head of the
　wicked.
20　"The anger of the LORD will not turn
　back
Until He has performed and carried
　out the purposes of His heart;
In the last days you will clearly
　understand it.
21　"I did not send *these* prophets,
But they ran.
I did not speak to them,
But they prophesied.
22　"But if they had stood in My council,
Then they would have announced
　My words to My people,
And would have turned them back
　from their evil way
And from the evil of their deeds.
23　"Am I a God who is near," declares
　the LORD,
"And not a God far off?
24　"Can a man hide himself in hiding
　places
So I do not see him?" declares the
　LORD.
"Do I not fill the heavens and the
　earth?" declares the LORD.
25　"I have heard what the prophets

L I F E   L E S S O N S

➤ **Jeremiah 23:24 — *"Can a man hide
himself in hiding places so I do not see
him?"***

*G*od is never so busy managing the
universe that He has no time for you.
He can listen to your prayers even as He
cares for everything else.

have said who prophesy falsely in My name, saying, 'I had a dream, I had a dream!'

26 "How long? Is there *anything* in the hearts of the prophets who prophesy falsehood, even *these* prophets of the deception of their own heart,

27 who intend to make My people forget My name by their dreams which they relate to one another, just as their fathers forgot My name because of Baal?

28 "The prophet who has a dream may relate *his* dream, but let him who has My word speak My word in truth. What does straw have *in common* with grain?" declares the LORD.

29 "Is not My word like fire?" declares the LORD, "and like a hammer which shatters a rock?

30 "Therefore behold, I am against the prophets," declares the LORD, "who steal My words from each other.

31 "Behold, I am against the prophets," declares the LORD, "who use their tongues and declare, '*The Lord* declares.'

32 "Behold, I am against those who have prophesied false dreams," declares the LORD, "and related them and led My people astray by their falsehoods and reckless boasting; yet I did not send them or command them, nor do they furnish this people the slightest benefit," declares the LORD.

33 "Now when this people or the prophet or a priest asks you saying, 'What is the oracle of the LORD?' then you shall say to them, 'What oracle?' The LORD declares, 'I will abandon you.'

34 "Then as for the prophet or the priest or the people who say, 'The oracle of the LORD,' I will bring punishment upon that man and his household.

35 "Thus will each of you say to his neighbor and to his brother, 'What has the LORD answered?' or, 'What has the LORD spoken?'

36 "For you will no longer remember the oracle of the LORD, because every man's own word will become the oracle, and you have perverted the words of the living God, the LORD of hosts, our God.

37 "Thus you will say to *that* prophet, 'What has the LORD answered you?' and, 'What has the LORD spoken?'

38 "For if you say, 'The oracle of the LORD!' surely thus says the LORD, 'Because you said this word, "The oracle of the LORD!"

I have also sent to you, saying, "You shall not say, 'The oracle of the LORD!'"'

39 "Therefore behold, I will surely forget you and cast you away from My presence, along with the city which I gave you and your fathers.

40 "I will put an everlasting reproach on you and an everlasting humiliation which will not be forgotten."

24 AFTER Nebuchadnezzar king of Babylon had carried away captive Jeconiah the son of Jehoiakim, king of Judah, and the officials of Judah with the craftsmen and smiths from Jerusalem and had brought them to Babylon, the LORD showed me: behold, two baskets of figs set before the temple of the LORD!

2 One basket had very good figs, like first-ripe figs, and the other basket had very bad figs which could not be eaten due to rottenness.

3 Then the LORD said to me, "What do you see, Jeremiah?" And I said, "Figs, the good figs, very good; and the bad *figs*, very bad, which cannot be eaten due to rottenness."

4 Then the word of the LORD came to me, saying,

5 "Thus says the LORD God of Israel, 'Like these good figs, so I will regard as good the captives of Judah, whom I have sent out of this place *into* the land of the Chaldeans.

6 'For I will set My eyes on them for good, and I will bring them again to this land; and I will build them up and not overthrow them, and I will plant them and not pluck them up.

7 'I will give them a heart to know Me, for I am the LORD; and they will be My people, and I will be their God, for they will return to Me with their whole heart.

8 'But like the bad figs which cannot be eaten due to rottenness—indeed, thus says the LORD—so I will abandon Zedekiah king of Judah and his officials, and the remnant of Jerusalem who remain in this land and the ones who dwell in the land of Egypt.

9 'I will make them a terror *and an* evil for all the kingdoms of the earth, as a reproach and a proverb, a taunt and a curse in all places where I will scatter them.

10 'I will send the sword, the famine and the pestilence upon them until they are destroyed from the land which I gave to them and their forefathers.'"

WHAT THE BIBLE SAYS ABOUT

How to Increase Your Faith

2 Thessalonians 1:3, 4

What are some practical steps you can take to increase your level of faith today?

1. Read the Bible.

Romans 10:17 explains, "Faith comes from hearing, and hearing by the word of Christ." That is, you must feed your faith a steady diet of God's Word.

2. Exercise your faith.

An aspiring body-builder doesn't begin by lifting 500 pounds the first day. Rather, he exercises daily, gradually increasing his strength. Regularly exercising faith can bring about similar growth spiritually.

3. Embrace trials.

First Peter 1:3–9 reveals a shocking truth that adversity, addressed in God's power, creates greater faith. Just as a fire purifies

precious metals, hardship strips away all but the pure core of faith.

4. Examine the testimonies of others.

An individual's testimony is his own account of God's activity in his life. No one can ever deny, refute, or downplay another's testimony. When you hear of God's mighty deeds in someone else's life, your own faith in Him grows.

5. Pray.

You get to know someone by talking to him. That's just what prayer is: your personal communication with God. And don't just talk; be sure to spend time listening. the Lord wants to speak to you.

6. Practice obedience.

You will never grow in your faith if you consistently disobey what God tells you to do. Perfect faith is a by-product of obedience. Put yourself in a position to see God's best for your life, and your faith will soar.

Faith does not increase by accident. Growth takes time, dedication, and intentionality. Ask the Lord to help you exercise your faith today. ❂

❂ Psalm 119:17–24

▷ Gimel.

17 Deal bountifully with Your
    servant,
    That I may live and keep Your word.
18 Open my eyes, that I may behold
    Wonderful things from Your law.
19 I am a stranger in the earth;
    Do not hide Your commandments
    from me.
20 My soul is crushed with longing
    After Your ordinances at all times.
21 You rebuke the arrogant, the
    cursed,
    Who wander from Your
    commandments.
22 Take away reproach and contempt
    from me,
    For I observe Your testimonies.
23 Even though princes sit *and* talk
    against me,
    Your servant meditates on Your
    statutes.
24 Your testimonies also are my
    delight;
    They are my counselors.

❂ Proverbs 27:15, 16

15 A constant dripping on a day of
    steady rain
    And a contentious woman are
    alike;
16 He who would restrain her
    restrains the wind,
    And grasps oil with his right
    hand.

❂ 2 Thessalonians 1:1–12

1 PAUL and Silvanus and Timothy,
    To the church of the Thessalonians in God our Father and the Lord Jesus Christ:
2   Grace to you and peace from God the Father and the Lord Jesus Christ.
3   We ought always to give thanks to God for you, brethren, as is *only* fitting, because your faith is greatly enlarged, and the love of each one of you toward one another grows *ever* greater;
4   therefore, we ourselves speak proudly

LIFE LESSONS

> **2 Thessalonians 1:3 —** *We ought always to give thanks to God for you.*

A good way to tell if you are growing in your faith is to examine how you react toward your brothers and sisters in Christ. Does your love abound toward them? Do you feel a greater urgency to pray for them? Your love for God should inspire unity within the church.

of you among the churches of God for your perseverance and faith in the midst of all your persecutions and afflictions which you endure.

5   *This is* a plain indication of God's righteous judgment so that you will be considered worthy of the kingdom of God, for which indeed you are suffering.

6   For after all it is *only* just for God to repay with affliction those who afflict you,

7   and *to give* relief to you who are afflicted and to us as well when the Lord Jesus will be revealed from heaven with His mighty angels in flaming fire,

8   dealing out retribution to those who do not know God and to those who do not obey the gospel of our Lord Jesus.

➤ 9   These will pay the penalty of eternal destruction, away from the presence of the Lord and from the glory of His power,

10   when He comes to be glorified in His saints on that day, and to be marveled at among all who have believed—for our testimony to you was believed.

11   To this end also we pray for you always, that our God will count you worthy of your calling, and fulfill every desire for goodness and the work of faith with power,

12   so that the name of our Lord Jesus will be glorified in you, and you in Him, according to the grace of our God and *the* Lord Jesus Christ.

LIFE LESSONS

> **2 Thessalonians 1:9 —** *These will pay the penalty of eternal destruction, away from the presence of the Lord.*

F alse teachers were telling the people that when a person dies without Christ, they merely cease to live or are destroyed in some way. But this is not true. Every person will exist eternally—believers in heaven with the Lord and unbelievers in the eternal lake of fire that is never extinguished (Rev. 20:15; 21:8). Even though hell is described as a place of "weeping and gnashing of teeth" (Luke 13:28), the worst thing about it is not the physical suffering that will be involved but the intense loneliness of absolute separation from God.

> **2 Thessalonians 1:12 —** *The name of our Lord Jesus will be glorified in you.*

J esus is glorified in us when we eagerly do His will by submitting to the promptings of His Spirit. We must honor Jesus as Lord and acknowledge that He is infinitely worthy of our service because when we do He receives the honor, glory, power, and praise for the great things He does in and through us.

Jeremiah 25:1—26:24

25 THE word that came to Jeremiah concerning all the people of Judah, in the fourth year of Jehoiakim the son of Josiah, king of Judah (that was the first year of Nebuchadnezzar king of Babylon),

2   which Jeremiah the prophet spoke to all the people of Judah and to all the inhabitants of Jerusalem, saying,

3   "From the thirteenth year of Josiah the son of Amon, king of Judah, even to this day, these twenty-three years the word of the LORD has come to me, and I have spoken to you again and again, but you have not listened.

4   "And the LORD has sent to you all His servants the prophets again and again, but you have not listened nor inclined your ear to hear,

5   saying, 'Turn now everyone from his evil way and from the evil of your deeds,

and dwell on the land which the LORD has given to you and your forefathers forever and ever;

6 and do not go after other gods to serve them and to worship them, and do not provoke Me to anger with the work of your hands, and I will do you no harm.'

7 "Yet you have not listened to Me," declares the LORD, "in order that you might provoke Me to anger with the work of your hands to your own harm.

8 "Therefore thus says the LORD of hosts, 'Because you have not obeyed My words,

9 behold, I will send and take all the families of the north,' declares the LORD, 'and I will send to Nebuchadnezzar king of Babylon, My servant, and will bring them against this land and against its inhabitants and against all these nations round about; and I will utterly destroy them and make them a horror and a hissing, and an everlasting desolation.

10 'Moreover, I will take from them the voice of joy and the voice of gladness, the voice of the bridegroom and the voice of the bride, the sound of the millstones and the light of the lamp.

➤ 11 'This whole land will be a desolation and a horror, and these nations will serve the king of Babylon seventy years.

12 'Then it will be when seventy years are completed I will punish the king of Babylon and that nation,' declares the LORD, 'for their iniquity, and the land of the Chaldeans; and I will make it an everlasting desolation.

13 'I will bring upon that land all My words which I have pronounced against it, all that is written in this book which Jeremiah has prophesied against all the nations.

14 '(For many nations and great kings

LIFE LESSONS

➤ **Jeremiah 25:11 — *"This whole land will be a desolation and a horror, and these nations will serve the king of Babylon seventy years."***

*B*efore enemy troops ever set foot in Jerusalem, Jeremiah predicted that the Babylonian captivity would last seventy years. And that is exactly how long it lasted, no less, no more. You can always trust God's Word!

---

will make slaves of them, even them; and I will recompense them according to their deeds and according to the work of their hands.)'"

15 For thus the LORD, the God of Israel, says to me, "Take this cup of the wine of wrath from My hand and cause all the nations to whom I send you to drink it.

16 "They will drink and stagger and go mad because of the sword that I will send among them."

17 Then I took the cup from the LORD's hand and made all the nations to whom the LORD sent me drink it:

18 Jerusalem and the cities of Judah and its kings *and* its princes, to make them a ruin, a horror, a hissing and a curse, as it is this day;

19 Pharaoh king of Egypt, his servants, his princes and all his people;

20 and all the foreign people, all the kings of the land of Uz, all the kings of the land of the Philistines (even Ashkelon, Gaza, Ekron and the remnant of Ashdod);

21 Edom, Moab and the sons of Ammon;

22 and all the kings of Tyre, all the kings of Sidon and the kings of the coastlands which are beyond the sea;

23 and Dedan, Tema, Buz and all who cut the corners *of their hair*;

24 and all the kings of Arabia and all the kings of the foreign people who dwell in the desert;

25 and all the kings of Zimri, all the kings of Elam and all the kings of Media;

26 and all the kings of the north, near and far, one with another; and all the kingdoms of the earth which are upon the face of the ground, and the king of Sheshach shall drink after them.

27 "You shall say to them, 'Thus says the LORD of hosts, the God of Israel, "Drink, be drunk, vomit, fall and rise no more because of the sword which I will send among you."'

28 "And it will be, if they refuse to take the cup from your hand to drink, then you will say to them, 'Thus says the LORD of hosts: "You shall surely drink!

29 "For behold, I am beginning to work calamity in *this* city which is called by My name, and shall you be completely free from punishment? You will not be free from punishment; for I am summoning a sword against all the inhabitants of the earth," declares the LORD of hosts.'

30 "Therefore you shall prophesy against them all these words, and you shall say to them,

'The LORD will roar from on high
And utter His voice from His holy habitation;
He will roar mightily against His fold.
He will shout like those who tread *the grapes*,
Against all the inhabitants of the earth.

31 'A clamor has come to the end of the earth,
Because the LORD has a controversy with the nations.
He is entering into judgment with all flesh;
As for the wicked, He has given them to the sword,' declares the LORD."

32 Thus says the LORD of hosts,
"Behold, evil is going forth
From nation to nation,
And a great storm is being stirred up
From the remotest parts of the earth.

33 "Those slain by the LORD on that day will be from one end of the earth to the other. They will not be lamented, gathered or buried; they will be like dung on the face of the ground.

34 "Wail, you shepherds, and cry;
And wallow *in ashes*, you masters of the flock;
For the days of your slaughter and your dispersions have come,
And you will fall like a choice vessel.

35 "Flight will perish from the shepherds,
And escape from the masters of the flock.

36 "*Hear* the sound of the cry of the shepherds,
And the wailing of the masters of the flock!
For the LORD is destroying their pasture,

37 "And the peaceful folds are made silent
Because of the fierce anger of the LORD.

38 "He has left His hiding place like the lion;
For their land has become a horror

Because of the fierceness of the oppressing *sword*
And because of His fierce anger."

26 IN the beginning of the reign of Jehoiakim the son of Josiah, king of Judah, this word came from the LORD, saying,

2 "Thus says the LORD, 'Stand in the court of the LORD'S house, and speak to all the cities of Judah who have come to worship *in* the LORD'S house all the words that I have commanded you to speak to them. Do not omit a word!

3 'Perhaps they will listen and everyone will turn from his evil way, that I may repent of the calamity which I am planning to do to them because of the evil of their deeds.'

4 "And you will say to them, 'Thus says the LORD, "If you will not listen to Me, to walk in My law which I have set before you,

5 to listen to the words of My servants the prophets, whom I have been sending to you again and again, but you have not listened;

6 then I will make this house like Shiloh, and this city I will make a curse to all the nations of the earth."'"

7 The priests and the prophets and all the people heard Jeremiah speaking these words in the house of the LORD.

8 When Jeremiah finished speaking all that the LORD had commanded *him* to speak to all the people, the priests and the prophets and all the people seized him, saying, "You must die!

9 "Why have you prophesied in the name of the LORD saying, 'This house will be like Shiloh and this city will be desolate, without inhabitant'?" And all the people gathered about Jeremiah in the house of the LORD.

10 When the officials of Judah heard

LIFE LESSONS

➤ **Jeremiah 26:2 — "Stand in the court of the LORD's house, and speak . . . all the words that I have commanded you to speak."**

Jeremiah knew that partial obedience is blatant rebellion. He may have feared to speak every word that God told him to proclaim, but he did it. Only through the Spirit can we obey like this.

these things, they came up from the king's house to the house of the LORD and sat in the entrance of the New Gate of the LORD's *house.*

11 Then the priests and the prophets spoke to the officials and to all the people, saying, "A death sentence for this man! For he has prophesied against this city as you have heard in your hearing."

12 Then Jeremiah spoke to all the officials and to all the people, saying, "The LORD sent me to prophesy against this house and against this city all the words that you have heard.

13 "Now therefore amend your ways and your deeds and obey the voice of the LORD your God; and the LORD will change His mind about the misfortune which He has pronounced against you.

14 "But as for me, behold, I am in your hands; do with me as is good and right in your sight.

15 "Only know for certain that if you put me to death, you will bring innocent blood on yourselves, and on this city and on its inhabitants; for truly the LORD has sent me to you to speak all these words in your hearing."

16 Then the officials and all the people said to the priests and to the prophets, "No death sentence for this man! For he has spoken to us in the name of the LORD our God."

17 Then some of the elders of the land rose up and spoke to all the assembly of the people, saying,

18 "Micah of Moresheth prophesied in the days of Hezekiah king of Judah; and he spoke to all the people of Judah, saying, 'Thus the LORD of hosts has said,

"Zion will be plowed *as* a field,
And Jerusalem will become ruins,
And the mountain of the house as
the high places of a forest."'

19 "Did Hezekiah king of Judah and all Judah put him to death? Did he not fear the LORD and entreat the favor of the LORD, and the LORD changed His mind about the misfortune which He had pronounced against them? But we are committing a great evil against ourselves."

20 Indeed, there was also a man who prophesied in the name of the LORD, Uriah the son of Shemaiah from Kiriath-jearim; and he prophesied against this city and against this land words similar to all those of Jeremiah.

21 When King Jehoiakim and all his mighty men and all the officials heard his words, then the king sought to put him to death; but Uriah heard *it,* and he was afraid and fled and went to Egypt.

22 Then King Jehoiakim sent men to Egypt: Elnathan the son of Achbor and *certain* men with him *went* into Egypt.

23 And they brought Uriah from Egypt and led him to King Jehoiakim, who slew him with a sword and cast his dead body into the burial place of the common people.

24 But the hand of Ahikam the son of Shaphan was with Jeremiah, so that he was not given into the hands of the people to put him to death.

◈ **Psalm 119:25–32**

ד Daleth.

25 My soul cleaves to the dust;
   Revive me according to Your word.
26 I have told of my ways, and You
      have answered me;
   Teach me Your statutes.
27 Make me understand the way of
      Your precepts,
   So I will meditate on Your wonders.
28 My soul weeps because of grief;
   Strengthen me according to Your
      word.
29 Remove the false way from me,
   And graciously grant me Your law.
30 I have chosen the faithful way;
   I have placed Your ordinances
      before me.
31 I cling to Your testimonies;
   O LORD, do not put me to shame!
32 I shall run the way of Your
      commandments,
   For You will enlarge my heart.

LIFE LESSONS

➢ **Jeremiah 26:24 —** *The hand of Ahikam the son of Shaphan was with Jeremiah.*

*A*t strategic points along his difficult ministry, God provided Jeremiah with both encouragement and friends to help him complete his mission. He does the same for us, to help us succeed in our own divinely appointed tasks.

WHAT THE BIBLE SAYS ABOUT

God's Purpose in the Storm

Psalm 119:25–32

"My soul cleaves to the dust . . . My soul weeps because of grief" (Ps. 119:25, 28). Have you ever felt like that? Are you feeling desolation of a raging storm in your life today?

Believers have a choice about how they will respond to life's tempests. Either they can cast blame while becoming resentful and bitter, or they can turn to the Lord and ask, "What is Your purpose?"

Since recognizing God's purpose and plan is the way that faith grows, Christians may be tempted to ask, "Why?" However, like a child grasping new concepts, we learn step-by-step that God is faithful and will always do just as He promised.

For instance, in the Old Testament, King David made destructively wrong choices for which God allowed cleansing storms into his life. The leader of the nation had wandered off the right path, but painful experiences drove him back to the center of the Lord's will. We might consider the divine method cruel, but David would disagree. He wrote, "Before I was afflicted I went astray, but now I keep Your word. . . . It is good for me that I was afflicted, that I may learn Your statutes" (Psalm 119:67, 71).

Returning believers to right fellowship is only one of God's purposes for a life storm. Some difficulties are meant to blow away all distractions so we can focus our attention on the Lord. Other tempests break our worldly mold so that we can be conformed to the image of Jesus Christ. Our personal pleasure is not the top priority. God's primary concern is to shape a wise and obedient servant who loves Him.

When a storm rages in your life, understand that the Lord is already planning how to turn destruction into good. Seek His objective, then work with Him to achieve it. As we are promised in Romans 8:28, "We know that God causes all things to work together for good to those who love God, to those who are called according to His purpose."

 ### Proverbs 27:17

17 Iron sharpens iron,
   So one man sharpens another.

 ### 2 Thessalonians 2:1–17

2 NOW we request you, brethren, with regard to the coming of our Lord Jesus Christ and our gathering together to Him,
2 that you not be quickly shaken from your composure or be disturbed either by a spirit or a message or a letter as if from us, to the effect that the day of the Lord has come.
3 Let no one in any way deceive you, for *it will not come* unless the apostasy comes first, and the man of lawlessness is revealed, the son of destruction,
4 who opposes and exalts himself above every so-called god or object of worship, so that he takes his seat in the temple of God, displaying himself as being God.

5 Do you not remember that while I was still with you, I was telling you these things?
6 And you know what restrains him now, so that in his time he will be revealed.
7 For the mystery of lawlessness is already at work; only he who now restrains *will do so* until he is taken out of the way.
8 Then that lawless one will be revealed whom the Lord will slay with the breath of His mouth and bring to an end by the appearance of His coming;

LIFE LESSONS

> **2 Thessalonians 2:3** — *It will not come unless the apostasy comes first.*

The time is coming when many in the church will abandon sound doctrine and will instead endorse whatever heresy seems popular at the moment. At that time, the Antichrist will be revealed and will completely rebel against God's authority. Many will be led astray by his lies. The way to combat this apostasy is always to stay close to Jesus and teach others the truth of His Word.

➤ 9 *that is,* the one whose coming is in accord with the activity of Satan, with all power and signs and false wonders,

10 and with all the deception of wickedness for those who perish, because they did not receive the love of the truth so as to be saved.

11 For this reason God will send upon them a deluding influence so that they will believe what is false,

12 in order that they all may be judged who did not believe the truth, but took pleasure in wickedness.

13 But we should always give thanks to God for you, brethren beloved by the Lord, because God has chosen you from the beginning for salvation through sanctification by the Spirit and faith in the truth.

14 It was for this He called you through our gospel, that you may gain the glory of our Lord Jesus Christ.

15 So then, brethren, stand firm and hold to the traditions which you were taught, whether by word *of mouth* or by letter from us.

16 Now may our Lord Jesus Christ Himself and God our Father, who has loved us and given us eternal comfort and good hope by grace,

17 comfort and strengthen your hearts ◄ in every good work and word.

LIFE LESSONS

➤ **2 Thessalonians 2:9** — *The one whose coming is in accord with the activity of Satan, with all power and signs and false wonders.*

We must anchor our faith in the Word of God, not in miraculous signs and wonders, which can be fabricated. Satan will often counterfeit astounding works to deceive the weak into forsaking Christ. Therefore we must know God's Word so that we can oppose his lies and not be caught off guard.

➤ **2 Thessalonians 2:17** — *Comfort and strengthen your hearts in every good work and word.*

God comforts us in our distress, not merely to soothe our feelings, but so that we will find the strength and wisdom to minister to others (2 Cor. 1:3–7).

Jeremiah 27:1—28:17

27 IN the beginning of the reign of Zedekiah the son of Josiah, king of Judah, this word came to Jeremiah from the LORD, saying—

2 thus says the LORD to me—"Make for yourself bonds and yokes and put them on your neck,

3 and send word to the king of Edom, to the king of Moab, to the king of the sons of Ammon, to the king of Tyre and to the king of Sidon by the messengers who come to Jerusalem to Zedekiah king of Judah.

4 "Command them *to go* to their masters, saying, 'Thus says the LORD of hosts, the God of Israel, thus you shall say to your masters,

5 "I have made the earth, the men and the beasts which are on the face of the earth by My great power and by My out-stretched arm, and I will give it to the one who is pleasing in My sight.

6 "Now I have given all these lands into the hand of Nebuchadnezzar king of Babylon, My servant, and I have given him also the wild animals of the field to serve him.

7 "All the nations shall serve him and his son and his grandson until the time of his own land comes; then many nations and great kings will make him their servant.

8 "It will be, *that* the nation or the kingdom which will not serve him, Nebuchadnezzar king of Babylon, and which will not put its neck under the yoke of the king of Babylon, I will punish that nation with the sword, with famine and with pestilence," declares the LORD, "until I have destroyed it by his hand.

9 "But as for you, do not listen to your prophets, your diviners, your dreamers, your soothsayers or your sorcerers who

speak to you, saying, 'You will not serve the king of Babylon.'

10 "For they prophesy a lie to you in order to remove you far from your land; and I will drive you out and you will perish.

11 "But the nation which will bring its neck under the yoke of the king of Babylon and serve him, I will let remain on its land," declares the LORD, "and they will till it and dwell in it."'"

12 I spoke words like all these to Zedekiah king of Judah, saying, "Bring your necks under the yoke of the king of Babylon and serve him and his people, and live!

13 "Why will you die, you and your people, by the sword, famine and pestilence, as the LORD has spoken to that nation which will not serve the king of Babylon?

14 "So do not listen to the words of the prophets who speak to you, saying, 'You will not serve the king of Babylon,' for they prophesy a lie to you;

15 for I have not sent them," declares the LORD, "but they prophesy falsely in My name, in order that I may drive you out and that you may perish, you and the prophets who prophesy to you."

16 *Then* I spoke to the priests and to all this people, saying, "Thus says the LORD: Do not listen to the words of your prophets who prophesy to you, saying, 'Behold, the vessels of the LORD's house will now shortly be brought again from Babylon'; for they are prophesying a lie to you.

17 "Do not listen to them; serve the king of Babylon, and live! Why should this city become a ruin?

18 "But if they are prophets, and if the word of the LORD is with them, let them now entreat the LORD of hosts that the vessels which are left in the house of the LORD, in the house of the king of Judah and in Jerusalem may not go to Babylon.

19 "For thus says the LORD of hosts concerning the pillars, concerning the sea, concerning the stands and concerning the rest of the vessels that are left in this city,

20 which Nebuchadnezzar king of Babylon did not take when he carried into exile Jeconiah the son of Jehoiakim, king of Judah, from Jerusalem to Babylon, and all the nobles of Judah and Jerusalem.

21 "Yes, thus says the LORD of hosts, the God of Israel, concerning the vessels that are left in the house of the LORD and in the house of the king of Judah and in Jerusalem,

22 'They will be carried to Babylon and ◄ they will be there until the day I visit them,' declares the LORD. 'Then I will bring them back and restore them to this place.'"

28 NOW in the same year, in the beginning of the reign of Zedekiah king of Judah, in the fourth year, in the fifth month, Hananiah the son of Azzur, the prophet, who was from Gibeon, spoke to me in the house of the LORD in the presence of the priests and all the people, saying,

2 "Thus says the LORD of hosts, the God of Israel, 'I have broken the yoke of the king of Babylon.

3 'Within two years I am going to bring back to this place all the vessels of the LORD's house, which Nebuchadnezzar king of Babylon took away from this place and carried to Babylon.

4 'I am also going to bring back to this place Jeconiah the son of Jehoiakim, king of Judah, and all the exiles of Judah who went to Babylon,' declares the LORD, 'for I will break the yoke of the king of Babylon.'"

5 Then the prophet Jeremiah spoke to the prophet Hananiah in the presence of the priests and in the presence of all the people who were standing in the house of the LORD,

6 and the prophet Jeremiah said, "Amen! May the LORD do so; may the LORD confirm your words which you have prophesied to bring back the vessels of the LORD's house and all the exiles, from Babylon to this place.

7 "Yet hear now this word which I am about to speak in your hearing and in the hearing of all the people!

LIFE LESSONS

➤ **Jeremiah 27:22 — *"They will be carried to Babylon."***

*T*he Lord never abandoned His people, nor did He leave them alone—even though they spent years in captivity and longed for their homeland. Although we may likewise feel far from the blessings and promises He's made to us, God is still with us. And He will fulfill His word to us, but we must wait until He moves in His power and wisdom.

8 "The prophets who were before me and before you from ancient times prophesied against many lands and against great kingdoms, of war and of calamity and of pestilence.

9 "The prophet who prophesies of peace, when the word of the prophet comes to pass, then that prophet will be known *as* one whom the LORD has truly sent."

10 Then Hananiah the prophet took the yoke from the neck of Jeremiah the prophet and broke it.

11 Hananiah spoke in the presence of all the people, saying, "Thus says the LORD, 'Even so will I break within two full years the yoke of Nebuchadnezzar king of Babylon from the neck of all the nations.'" Then the prophet Jeremiah went his way.

12 The word of the LORD came to Jeremiah after Hananiah the prophet had broken the yoke from off the neck of the prophet Jeremiah, saying,

13 "Go and speak to Hananiah, saying, 'Thus says the LORD, "You have broken the yokes of wood, but you have made instead of them yokes of iron."

14 'For thus says the LORD of hosts, the God of Israel, "I have put a yoke of iron on the neck of all these nations, that they may serve Nebuchadnezzar king of Babylon; and they will serve him. And I have also given him the beasts of the field."'"

15 Then Jeremiah the prophet said to Hananiah the prophet, "Listen now, Hananiah, the LORD has not sent you, and you have made this people trust in a lie.

16 "Therefore thus says the LORD, 'Behold, I am about to remove you from the face of the earth. This year you are going to die, because you have counseled rebellion against the LORD.'"

17 So Hananiah the prophet died in the same year in the seventh month.

Psalm 119:33–40

ה He.

33 Teach me, O LORD, the way of Your statutes,
And I shall observe it to the end.

34 Give me understanding, that I may observe Your law
And keep it with all *my* heart.

35 Make me walk in the path of Your commandments,
For I delight in it.

36 Incline my heart to Your testimonies
And not to *dishonest* gain.

37 Turn away my eyes from looking at vanity,
And revive me in Your ways.

38 Establish Your word to Your servant,
As that which produces reverence for You.

39 Turn away my reproach which I dread,
For Your ordinances are good.

40 Behold, I long for Your precepts;
Revive me through Your righteousness.

Proverbs 27:18

18 He who tends the fig tree will eat its fruit,
And he who cares for his master will be honored.

2 Thessalonians 3:1–18

3 FINALLY, brethren, pray for us that the word of the Lord will spread rapidly and be glorified, just as *it did* also with you;

2 and that we will be rescued from perverse and evil men; for not all have faith.

LIFE LESSONS

➤ **Jeremiah 28:16, 17 — "This year you are going to die, because you have counseled rebellion against the LORD."**

How did Hananiah teach rebellion against the Lord? He did it through a message of false peace (Jer. 28:1–4). We never earn God's favor by convincing anyone that sin is anything other than sin. On the contrary, there is terrible judgment for the one who manipulates God's Word for his own gain.

LIFE PRINCIPLE **27**

PRAYER IS LIFE'S GREATEST TIME SAVER.

2 THESSALONIANS 3:1

*C*hange is never easy, especially when our choices affect other people. Change means important decisions will be made—which introduces the possibility of terrible mistakes and ongoing consequences. When we make those choices without seeking the Lord's leadership, we are headed for disaster. But when we pray to God, requesting His guidance and committing ourselves to His will, He moves in astounding ways to help us.

I remember the time when we needed to find a new property to house our "In Touch" television and radio ministry. Four months before we had to move, we found a building that we thought would be perfect. The only problem was that it cost $2.7 million. Several of our board members and executive staff felt good about the location and price, so they suggested we borrow the money for the property. Several others, however, rejected both the price and the idea of going into debt.

One Wednesday afternoon after that, a group of us met for a long time to discuss the move but were unable to come to any consensus. It was as if we were in a fog. We needed divine direction, and I knew we were not going to receive any sitting around that conference table. I asked my secretary to call Unicoi State Park and book some cabins for the following week. I understood that to stay there, we should have called four to six months in advance—it was unlikely they would have space for us. Ten minutes later, however, she returned and reported that we were all set.

On the morning we left for Unicoi, I asked a friend to negotiate with the owner to see if we could purchase the property for $2 million. I also asked our church administrator to see if we could possibly extend our stay at our current offices for six more months. Both told me they would do their best.

During the two hours I drove from Atlanta to the cabins, I thought and prayed. And God brought Zechariah 4:6 to my mind: "'Not by might nor by power, but by My Spirit,' says the LORD of hosts." I took it as a sign that He wanted to do something that we knew nothing about. So I prayed, "Lord, whatever You have in mind, please don't let us miss it!"

For two days, we did very little talking and a whole lot of praying. We cried out to God in desperation, realizing that a deadline was looming while our peace and unity were missing. During

one break, I called our administrator and discovered that we had been given an extension at our current location—we had six more months before we had to move. That was great news. Later, my friend called to tell me that the owner of the property had agreed to sell it to us for $2 million. There was only one problem. The building had a tenant who still had another six months on their lease. Moving them out early would cost us extra. We just kept praying.

When we left Unicoi two days later, we still didn't have any clear direction about how to purchase the building, but we were committed to waiting on God. We were confident that He had something different in mind other than borrowing the money and that it had already been worked out.

When I arrived home, I had a message to call a man I had never met. He was an "In Touch" viewer who was interested in helping the ministry. I called him back and he said, "Dr. Stanley, I have had you and your ministry on my mind the past several days. I notice that you never ask for money on the broadcast, and I was wondering if you had any needs."

I didn't know whether to laugh or cry. I explained our situation and then told him about our prayer meeting. He asked how much the building cost. I told him I thought we could get it for $2 million. He said, "I think I can handle that." And he did. We closed about 90 days later.

Can you imagine the mistake we would have made if we had not stopped to seek the Lord's guidance and had failed to trust in His provision? Can you imagine the time, energy, and resources we would have wasted if we had tried to acquire that property in our own strength instead of God's?

Prayer is always life's greatest time saver. You may be facing a great change or decision that seems overwhelming to you. The Lord knows exactly what you need, and He will *always* answer your prayers as is absolutely best for you. Therefore, spend time listening to Him, receiving His wisdom and direction, and drinking in His presence and power. Be quiet before Him, rest in Him, and allow Him to order your steps. He will keep you from moving in the wrong direction or from wasting your time doing useless things.

Are you willing to stop and listen to Him? Are you ready for Him to make you the most fruitful you can possibly be? Then no matter what you face, commit yourself to His schedule, wisdom, provision, and guidance through prayer. You'll find that your time with Him is the best investment you make every day. ◈

LIFE LESSONS

➤ **2 Thessalonians 3:2** — *That we will be rescued from perverse and evil men; for not all have faith.*

*W*hen the Word of God is preached, some will accept its life-giving message, and some will oppose it. It was that way in Paul's time, it continues to be true today, and opposition to the gospel will exist until the Lord returns. It is perfectly legitimate to pray for protection against those who reject God's Word.

3   But the Lord is faithful, and He will strengthen and protect you from the evil one.
4   We have confidence in the Lord concerning you, that you are doing and will continue to do what we command.
➤ 5   May the Lord direct your hearts into the love of God and into the steadfastness of Christ.
6   Now we command you, brethren, in the name of our Lord Jesus Christ, that you keep away from every brother who leads an unruly life and not according to the tradition which you received from us.
7   For you yourselves know how you ought to follow our example, because we did not act in an undisciplined manner among you,
8   nor did we eat anyone's bread without paying for it, but with labor and hardship we *kept* working night and day so that we would not be a burden to any of you;
9   not because we do not have the right to this, but in order to offer ourselves as a model for you, so that you would follow our example.
➤ 10   For even when we were with you, we used to give you this order: if anyone is not willing to work, then he is not to eat, either.
11   For we hear that some among you are leading an undisciplined life, doing no work at all, but acting like busybodies.
12   Now such persons we command and exhort in the Lord Jesus Christ to work in quiet fashion and eat their own bread.
13   But as for you, brethren, do not grow weary of doing good.
14   If anyone does not obey our instruction in this letter, take special note of that person and do not associate with him, so that he will be put to shame.
15   Yet do not regard him as an enemy, ◄ but admonish him as a brother.
16   Now may the Lord of peace Himself continually grant you peace in every circumstance. The Lord be with you all!
17   I, Paul, write this greeting with my own hand, and this is a distinguishing mark in every letter; this is the way I write.
18   The grace of our Lord Jesus Christ be with you all.

LIFE LESSONS

➤ **2 Thessalonians 3:5** — *May the Lord direct your hearts into the love of God and into the steadfastness of Christ.*

*T*his verse notes two crucial items necessary for spiritual growth. First, we must meditate on God's love for us and become increasingly convinced of it. Second, we must focus on Christ's return and wait patiently for it.

➤ **2 Thessalonians 3:10** — *If anyone is not willing to work, then he is not to eat, either.*

*S*ome of the Thessalonians were so convinced that Christ would return immediately, that they did not feel that it was necessary to work any longer. Others took advantage of the church's practice of charity and interdependence (Acts 2:42–47), living off the wealth of other believers. However, our belief in the Lord's return does not give us an excuse to be lazy. Instead, it should inspire us to do our very best in every situation—including our occupations—and keep us living productively for the sake of His kingdom.

➤ **2 Thessalonians 3:15** — *Do not regard him as an enemy, but admonish him as a brother.*

*W*e are not to associate with those who disobey God so that we do not likewise sin, but we must always remember that they are not the enemy (1 John 4:20). We should not be contentious or hateful towards them because they still need Christ. The Lord wants all to know Him and grow in an intimate relationship with Him. This should be our objective as well, so we must discipline and admonish others with this goal in view.

Jeremiah 29:1—30:24

29 NOW these are the words of the letter which Jeremiah the prophet sent from Jerusalem to the rest of the elders of the exile, the priests, the prophets and all the people whom Nebuchadnezzar had taken into exile from Jerusalem to Babylon.

2 (This was after King Jeconiah and the queen mother, the court officials, the princes of Judah and Jerusalem, the craftsmen and the smiths had departed from Jerusalem.)

3 *The letter was sent* by the hand of Elasah the son of Shaphan, and Gemariah the son of Hilkiah, whom Zedekiah king of Judah sent to Babylon to Nebuchadnezzar king of Babylon, saying,

4 "Thus says the LORD of hosts, the God of Israel, to all the exiles whom I have sent into exile from Jerusalem to Babylon,

5 'Build houses and live *in them*; and plant gardens and eat their produce.

6 'Take wives and become the fathers of sons and daughters, and take wives for your sons and give your daughters to husbands, that they may bear sons and daughters; and multiply there and do not decrease.

7 'Seek the welfare of the city where I have sent you into exile, and pray to the LORD on its behalf; for in its welfare you will have welfare.'

8 "For thus says the LORD of hosts, the God of Israel, 'Do not let your prophets who are in your midst and your diviners deceive you, and do not listen to the dreams which they dream.

9 'For they prophesy falsely to you in My name; I have not sent them,' declares the LORD.

10 "For thus says the LORD, 'When seventy years have been completed for Babylon, I will visit you and fulfill My good word to you, to bring you back to this place.

11 'For I know the plans that I have for you,' declares the LORD, 'plans for welfare and not for calamity to give you a future and a hope.

12 'Then you will call upon Me and come and pray to Me, and I will listen to you.

13 'You will seek Me and find *Me* when you search for Me with all your heart.

14 'I will be found by you,' declares the LORD, 'and I will restore your fortunes and will gather you from all the nations and from all the places where I have driven you,' declares the LORD, 'and I will bring you back to the place from where I sent you into exile.'

15 "Because you have said, 'The LORD has raised up prophets for us in Babylon'—

16 for thus says the LORD concerning the king who sits on the throne of David, and concerning all the people who dwell in this city, your brothers who did not go with you into exile—

17 thus says the LORD of hosts, 'Behold, I am sending upon them the sword, famine and pestilence, and I will make them like split-open figs that cannot be eaten due to rottenness.

18 'I will pursue them with the sword, with famine and with pestilence; and I will make them a terror to all the kingdoms of the earth, to be a curse and a horror and a hissing, and a reproach among all the nations where I have driven them,

19 because they have not listened to My words,' declares the LORD, 'which I sent to them again and again by My servants the prophets; but you did not listen,' declares the LORD.

LIFE LESSONS

> **Jeremiah 29:7 — *"Seek the welfare of the city where I have sent you into exile."***

*G*od caused His rebellious people to be carried away by force to wicked Babylon, and yet He instructed them to pray for the peace of the pagan city and to be obedient to Him. Even in Babylon, He wanted to have an intimate relationship with them and bless His people greatly.

> **Jeremiah 29:13 — *"You will seek Me and find Me when you search for Me with all your heart."***

*D*o you *really* want to know God's will for your life? Do you *really* want to learn His plans for you? The Father promises to reveal His will to everyone who will obey whatever He tells them to do.

ANSWERS TO LIFE'S QUESTIONS

How can I deal with discouragement?

JEREMIAH 29:10-14

*D*o you ever feel tempted to give up? Perhaps right now you feel over-looked, forgotten, mistreated, and you want to quit. Satan's goal is to get you to do just that—throw in the towel and call it quits. Discouragement is one of his most effective weapons.

But remember this: while disappointments are inevitable, discouragement is a choice. You do not have to yield to the devil's debilitating whispers of doubt and fear or be trapped in self-pity.

During a very troubling time in Israel's history, God directed Jeremiah to speak words of hope and encouragement to the disheartened exiles in Babylon: "I know the plans that I have for you,' declares the Lord, 'plans for welfare and not for calamity to give you a future and a hope." The people of Israel could avoid dis-couragement by remembering that God had wonderful plans for their future.

In Babylon, Israel sorted out her faith and rediscovered her deep need for the Lord. We must do the same. If we are ever going to reach our full potential, we must understand a very important truth: *God is for us.* He is not against us. He often uses trials to position us for greater blessing; and even in times of great disappointment, we can trust that He has our best in mind and will work all things out for our good. He knows how He wants to use the disappointment or hardship for our benefit, and He desires that we see Him as our only source of salvation and blessing.

When you feel tempted to yield to dis-couragement, go to God in prayer. Tell Him all you are feeling. God has an objective view of the situation. He sees the future and knows the direction your life will take. He also wants you to totally depend on Him and not rely on the compliments of others, earthly success, or worldly resources to make you happy. While disappointments will come—you live in a fallen world, after all—you can live above it by focus-ing your heart on Jesus Christ.

If you are in an emotionally or physically difficult spot right now, refuse to become dis-couraged. Ask the Lord to reveal His will and plan for your life. Commit yourself fully to Him and obey Him no matter what it costs you. If you take this approach, then God will provide for you in ways that far exceed human under-standing.

---

20 "You, therefore, hear the word of the LORD, all you exiles, whom I have sent away from Jerusalem to Babylon.
21 "Thus says the LORD of hosts, the God of Israel, concerning Ahab the son of Kolaiah and concerning Zedekiah the son of Maaseiah, who are prophesying to you falsely in My name, 'Behold, I will deliver them into the hand of Nebuchad-nezzar king of Babylon, and he will slay them before your eyes.
22 'Because of them a curse will be used by all the exiles from Judah who are in Babylon, saying, "May the LORD make you like Zedekiah and like Ahab, whom the king of Babylon roasted in the fire,
23 because they have acted foolishly in Israel, and have committed adultery with their neighbors' wives and have spoken words in My name falsely, which I did not command them; and I am He who knows and am a witness," declares the LORD.'"
24 To Shemaiah the Nehelamite you shall speak, saying,
25 "Thus says the LORD of hosts, the God of Israel, 'Because you have sent letters in your own name to all the people who are in Jerusalem, and to Zephaniah the son of Maaseiah, the priest, and to all the priests, saying,
26 "The LORD has made you priest instead of Jehoiada the priest, to be the overseer in the house of the LORD over every madman who prophesies, to put him in the stocks and in the iron collar,
27 now then, why have you not rebuked Jeremiah of Anathoth who prophesies to you?
28 "For he has sent to us in Babylon, say-ing, 'The exile will be long; build houses and live in them and plant gardens and eat their produce.'"'"
29 Zephaniah the priest read this letter to Jeremiah the prophet.
30 Then came the word of the LORD to Jeremiah, saying,
31 "Send to all the exiles, saying, 'Thus says the LORD concerning Shemaiah the Nehelamite, "Because Shemaiah has prophesied to you, although I did not

send him, and he has made you trust in a lie,"

32 therefore thus says the LORD, "Behold, I am about to punish Shemaiah the Nehelamite and his descendants; he will not have anyone living among this people, and he will not see the good that I am about to do to My people," declares the LORD, "because he has preached rebellion against the LORD."'"

30 THE word which came to Jeremiah from the LORD, saying,

2 "Thus says the LORD, the God of Israel, 'Write all the words which I have spoken to you in a book.

3 'For behold, days are coming,' declares the LORD, 'when I will restore the fortunes of My people Israel and Judah.' The LORD says, 'I will also bring them back to the land that I gave to their forefathers and they shall possess it.'"

4 Now these are the words which the LORD spoke concerning Israel and concerning Judah:

5 "For thus says the LORD,
'I have heard a sound of terror,
Of dread, and there is no peace.

6 'Ask now, and see
If a male can give birth.
Why do I see every man
With his hands on his loins, as a
woman in childbirth?
And why have all faces turned pale?

7 'Alas! for that day is great,
There is none like it;
And it is the time of Jacob's
distress,
But he will be saved from it.

8 'It shall come about on that day,' declares the LORD of hosts, 'that I will break his yoke from off their neck and will tear off their bonds; and strangers will no longer make them their slaves.

9 'But they shall serve the LORD their God and David their king, whom I will raise up for them.

10 'Fear not, O Jacob My servant,'
declares the LORD,
'And do not be dismayed, O Israel;
For behold, I will save you from afar
And your offspring from the land of
their captivity.
And Jacob will return and will be
quiet and at ease,
And no one will make him afraid.

➤ 11 'For I am with you,' declares the
LORD, 'to save you;

For I will destroy completely all the
nations where I have scattered
you,
Only I will not destroy you
completely.
But I will chasten you justly
And will by no means leave you
unpunished.'

12 "For thus says the LORD,
'Your wound is incurable
And your injury is serious.

13 'There is no one to plead your cause;
No healing for your sore,
No recovery for you.

14 'All your lovers have forgotten you,
They do not seek you;
For I have wounded you with the
wound of an enemy,
With the punishment of a cruel one,
Because your iniquity is great
And your sins are numerous.

15 'Why do you cry out over your
injury?
Your pain is incurable.
Because your iniquity is great
And your sins are numerous,
I have done these things to you.

16 'Therefore all who devour you will
be devoured;
And all your adversaries, every one
of them, will go into captivity;
And those who plunder you will be
for plunder,
And all who prey upon you I will
give for prey.

17 'For I will restore you to health
And I will heal you of your wounds,'
declares the LORD,
'Because they have called you an
outcast, saying:
"It is Zion; no one cares for her."'

18 "Thus says the LORD,
'Behold, I will restore the fortunes of
the tents of Jacob

And have compassion on his
dwelling places;
And the city will be rebuilt on its
ruin,
And the palace will stand on its
rightful place.

19 'From them will proceed
thanksgiving
And the voice of those who
celebrate;
And I will multiply them and they
will not be diminished;
I will also honor them and they will
not be insignificant.

20 'Their children also will be as
formerly,
And their congregation shall be
established before Me;
And I will punish all their
oppressors.

21 'Their leader shall be one of
them,
And their ruler shall come forth
from their midst;
And I will bring him near and he
shall approach Me;
For who would dare to risk his life
to approach Me?' declares the
LORD.

22 'You shall be My people,
And I will be your God.'"

23 Behold, the tempest of the LORD!
Wrath has gone forth,
A sweeping tempest;
It will burst on the head of the
wicked.

24 The fierce anger of the LORD will
not turn back
Until He has performed and until
He has accomplished
The intent of His heart;
In the latter days you will
understand this.

Psalm 119:41–48

ℶ Vav.

41 May Your lovingkindnesses also
come to me, O LORD,
Your salvation according to Your
word;

42 So I will have an answer for him
who reproaches me,
For I trust in Your word.

43 And do not take the word of truth
utterly out of my mouth,
For I wait for Your ordinances.

44 So I will keep Your law
continually,
Forever and ever.

45 And I will walk at liberty,
For I seek Your precepts.

46 I will also speak of Your testimonies
before kings
And shall not be ashamed.

47 I shall delight in Your
commandments,
Which I love.

48 And I shall lift up my hands to Your
commandments,
Which I love;
And I will meditate on Your statutes.

Proverbs 27:19

19 As in water face *reflects* face,
So the heart of man *reflects* man.

1 Timothy 1:1–20

1 PAUL, an apostle of Christ Jesus according to the commandment of God
our Savior, and of Christ Jesus, *who is*
our hope,
2 To Timothy, *my* true child in *the*
faith: Grace, mercy *and* peace from God
the Father and Christ Jesus our Lord.
3 As I urged you upon my departure
for Macedonia, remain on at Ephesus so
that you may instruct certain men not to
teach strange doctrines,
4 nor to pay attention to myths and ≺

LIFE LESSONS

➤ **1 Timothy 1:4 — *Nor to pay attention
to myths and endless genealogies, which
give rise to mere speculation rather than
furthering the administration of God
which is by faith.***

The goal of all Christian instruction
ought to be godly edification, which
does not merely fuel speculation or
cause useless arguments, but which helps
people in practical ways to grow closer
to God and each other.

endless genealogies, which give rise to mere speculation rather than *furthering* the administration of God which is by faith.

5 But the goal of our instruction is love from a pure heart and a good conscience and a sincere faith.

6 For some men, straying from these things, have turned aside to fruitless discussion,

7 wanting to be teachers of the Law, even though they do not understand either what they are saying or the matters about which they make confident assertions.

8 But we know that the Law is good, if one uses it lawfully,

9 realizing the fact that law is not made for a righteous person, but for those who are lawless and rebellious, for the ungodly and sinners, for the unholy and profane, for those who kill their fathers or mothers, for murderers

10 and immoral men and homosexuals and kidnappers and liars and perjurers, and whatever else is contrary to sound teaching,

11 according to the glorious gospel of the blessed God, with which I have been entrusted.

12 I thank Christ Jesus our Lord, who has strengthened me, because He considered me faithful, putting me into service,

13 even though I was formerly a blasphemer and a persecutor and a violent aggressor. Yet I was shown mercy because I acted ignorantly in unbelief;

14 and the grace of our Lord was more than abundant, with the faith and love which are *found* in Christ Jesus.

15 It is a trustworthy statement, deserving full acceptance, that Christ Jesus came into the world to save sinners, among whom I am foremost *of all.*

16 Yet for this reason I found mercy, so that in me as the foremost, Jesus Christ might demonstrate His perfect patience as an example for those who would believe in Him for eternal life.

17 Now to the King eternal, immortal, invisible, the only God, *be* honor and glory forever and ever. Amen.

18 This command I entrust to you, Timothy, *my* son, in accordance with the prophecies previously made concerning you, that by them you fight the good fight,

19 keeping faith and a good conscience, which some have rejected and suffered shipwreck in regard to their faith.

20 Among these are Hymenaeus and Alexander, whom I have handed over to Satan, so that they will be taught not to blaspheme.

LIFE LESSONS

➤ **1 Timothy 1:15** — *Christ Jesus came into the world to save sinners, among whom I am foremost of all.*

*N*o one persecuted the early Christian church more zealously than did Paul (previously called Saul) before he met Jesus Christ, and no one preached forgiveness as passionately and faithfully as Paul after he accepted the Lord's salvation (Acts 9:1–31; 22:1–21). The apostle received God's complete forgiveness— and so can you.

OCTOBER 23

◈ Jeremiah 31:1—32:44

31 "AT that time," declares the LORD, "I will be the God of all the families of Israel, and they shall be My people."

2 Thus says the LORD,
"The people who survived the sword
Found grace in the wilderness—
Israel, when it went to find its rest."

➤ 3 The LORD appeared to him from afar, *saying,*

LIFE LESSONS

➤ **Jeremiah 31:3** — *"I have loved you with an everlasting love."*

*G*od has pledged His love to you forever. He walks with you through disappointments and hardships, and nothing can separate you from His love (Rom. 8:31–39). Therefore, accept Him, cling to Him, and trust that His will for you is always the very best.

"I have loved you with an everlasting
love;
Therefore I have drawn you with
lovingkindness.

4 "Again I will build you and you will
be rebuilt,
O virgin of Israel!
Again you will take up your
tambourines,
And go forth to the dances of the
merrymakers.

5 "Again you will plant vineyards
On the hills of Samaria;
The planters will plant
And will enjoy *them*.

6 "For there will be a day when
watchmen
On the hills of Ephraim call out,
'Arise, and let us go up *to* Zion,
To the LORD our God.'"

7 For thus says the LORD,
"Sing aloud with gladness for Jacob,
And shout among the chief of the
nations;
Proclaim, give praise and say,
'O LORD, save Your people,
The remnant of Israel.'

8 "Behold, I am bringing them from
the north country,
And I will gather them from the
remote parts of the earth,
Among them the blind and the
lame,
The woman with child and she who
is in labor with child, together;
A great company, they will return
here.

9 "With weeping they will come,
And by supplication I will lead
them;
I will make them walk by streams of
waters,
On a straight path in which they
will not stumble;
For I am a father to Israel,
And Ephraim is My firstborn."

10 Hear the word of the LORD,
O nations,
And declare in the coastlands afar
off,
And say, "He who scattered Israel
will gather him
And keep him as a shepherd keeps
his flock."

11 For the LORD has ransomed Jacob
And redeemed him from the hand
of him who was stronger than he.

12 "They will come and shout for joy on
the height of Zion,
And they will be radiant over the
bounty of the LORD—
Over the grain and the new wine
and the oil,
And over the young of the flock and
the herd;
And their life will be like a watered
garden,
And they will never languish again.

13 "Then the virgin will rejoice in the
dance,
And the young men and the old,
together;
For I will turn their mourning into
joy
And will comfort them and give
them joy for their sorrow.

14 "I will fill the soul of the priests with
abundance,
And My people will be satisfied
with My goodness," declares the
LORD.

15 Thus says the LORD,
"A voice is heard in Ramah,
Lamentation *and* bitter weeping.
Rachel is weeping for her children;
She refuses to be comforted for her
children,
Because they are no more."

16 Thus says the LORD,
"Restrain your voice from weeping
And your eyes from tears;
For your work will be rewarded,"
declares the LORD,
"And they will return from the land
of the enemy.

17 "There is hope for your future,"
declares the LORD,
"And *your* children will return to
their own territory.

18 "I have surely heard Ephraim
grieving,
'You have chastised me, and I was
chastised,
Like an untrained calf;
Bring me back that I may be
restored,
For You are the LORD my God.

19 'For after I turned back, I repented;
And after I was instructed, I smote
on *my* thigh;
I was ashamed and also humiliated
Because I bore the reproach of my
youth.'

20 "Is Ephraim My dear son?

Is he a delightful child?
Indeed, as often as I have spoken
   against him,
I certainly *still* remember him;
Therefore My heart yearns for him;
I will surely have mercy on him,"
   declares the LORD.

21 "Set up for yourself roadmarks,
Place for yourself guideposts;
Direct your mind to the highway,
The way by which you went.
Return, O virgin of Israel,
Return to these your cities.

22 "How long will you go here and
   there,
O faithless daughter?
For the LORD has created a new
   thing in the earth—
A woman will encompass a man."

23 Thus says the LORD of hosts, the God
of Israel, "Once again they will speak
this word in the land of Judah and in its
cities when I restore their fortunes,
   'The LORD bless you, O abode of
      righteousness,
   O holy hill!'

24 "Judah and all its cities will dwell together in it, the farmer and they who go
about with flocks.

25 "For I satisfy the weary ones and refresh everyone who languishes."

26 At this I awoke and looked, and my
sleep was pleasant to me.

27 "Behold, days are coming," declares
the LORD, "when I will sow the house of
Israel and the house of Judah with the
seed of man and with the seed of beast.

28 "As I have watched over them to
pluck up, to break down, to overthrow,
to destroy and to bring disaster, so I will
watch over them to build and to plant,"
declares the LORD.

29 "In those days they will not say
   again,
   'The fathers have eaten sour grapes,
   And the children's teeth are set on
      edge.'

30 "But everyone will die for his own
iniquity; each man who eats the sour
grapes, his teeth will be set on edge.

31 "Behold, days are coming," declares
the LORD, "when I will make a new covenant with the house of Israel and with
the house of Judah,

32 not like the covenant which I made
with their fathers in the day I took them
by the hand to bring them out of the
land of Egypt, My covenant which they
broke, although I was a husband to
them," declares the LORD.

33 "But this is the covenant which I will
make with the house of Israel after those
days," declares the LORD, "I will put My
law within them and on their heart I will
write it; and I will be their God, and they
shall be My people.

34 "They will not teach again, each man
his neighbor and each man his brother,
saying, 'Know the LORD,' for they will all
know Me, from the least of them to the
greatest of them," declares the LORD, "for
I will forgive their iniquity, and their sin I
will remember no more."

35 Thus says the LORD,
Who gives the sun for light by day
And the fixed order of the moon
   and the stars for light by night,
Who stirs up the sea so that its
   waves roar;
The LORD of hosts is His name:

36 "If this fixed order departs
From before Me," declares the LORD,
"Then the offspring of Israel also will
   cease
From being a nation before Me
   forever."

37 Thus says the LORD,
"If the heavens above can be
   measured
And the foundations of the earth
   searched out below,
Then I will also cast off all the
   offspring of Israel
For all that they have done,"
   declares the LORD.

38 "Behold, days are coming," declares
the LORD, "when the city will be rebuilt
for the LORD from the Tower of Hananel
to the Corner Gate.

39 "The measuring line will go out farther straight ahead to the hill Gareb;
then it will turn to Goah.

LIFE LESSONS

➢ **Jeremiah 31:31 —** *"I will make a new
covenant."*

*W*e are a "new covenant" people, a
blessed group of men and women
who can come boldly into God's presence by His Spirit and through faith in
His Son, Jesus Christ (Heb. 8:7–13; 9:15;
12:24).

40 "And the whole valley of the dead bodies and of the ashes, and all the fields as far as the brook Kidron, to the corner of the Horse Gate toward the east, shall be holy to the LORD; it will not be plucked up or overthrown anymore forever."

32 THE word that came to Jeremiah from the LORD in the tenth year of Zedekiah king of Judah, which was the eighteenth year of Nebuchadnezzar.
2 Now at that time the army of the king of Babylon was besieging Jerusalem, and Jeremiah the prophet was shut up in the court of the guard, which *was in* the house of the king of Judah,
3 because Zedekiah king of Judah had shut him up, saying, "Why do you prophesy, saying, 'Thus says the LORD, "Behold, I am about to give this city into the hand of the king of Babylon, and he will take it;
4 and Zedekiah king of Judah will not escape out of the hand of the Chaldeans, but he will surely be given into the hand of the king of Babylon, and he will speak with him face to face and see him eye to eye;
5 and he will take Zedekiah to Babylon, and he will be there until I visit him," declares the LORD. "If you fight against the Chaldeans, you will not succeed"'?"
6 And Jeremiah said, "The word of the LORD came to me, saying,
7 'Behold, Hanamel the son of Shallum your uncle is coming to you, saying, "Buy for yourself my field which is at Anathoth, for you have the right of redemption to buy *it*."'
8 "Then Hanamel my uncle's son came to me in the court of the guard according to the word of the LORD and said to me, 'Buy my field, please, that is at Anathoth, which is in the land of Benjamin; for you have the right of possession and the redemption is yours; buy *it* for yourself.' Then I knew that this was the word of the LORD.
9 "I bought the field which was at Anathoth from Hanamel my uncle's son, and I weighed out the silver for him, seventeen shekels of silver.
10 "I signed and sealed the deed, and called in witnesses, and weighed out the silver on the scales.
11 "Then I took the deeds of purchase, both the sealed *copy containing* the terms and conditions and the open *copy;*

12 and I gave the deed of purchase to Baruch the son of Neriah, the son of Mahseiah, in the sight of Hanamel my uncle's *son* and in the sight of the witnesses who signed the deed of purchase, before all the Jews who were sitting in the court of the guard.
13 "And I commanded Baruch in their presence, saying,
14 'Thus says the LORD of hosts, the God of Israel, "Take these deeds, this sealed deed of purchase and this open deed, and put them in an earthenware jar, that they may last a long time."
15 'For thus says the LORD of hosts, the God of Israel, "Houses and fields and vineyards will again be bought in this land."'
16 "After I had given the deed of purchase to Baruch the son of Neriah, then I prayed to the LORD, saying,
17 'Ah Lord GOD! Behold, You have made the heavens and the earth by Your great power and by Your outstretched arm! Nothing is too difficult for You,
18 who shows lovingkindness to thousands, but repays the iniquity of fathers into the bosom of their children after them, O great and mighty God. The LORD of hosts is His name;
19 great in counsel and mighty in deed, whose eyes are open to all the ways of the sons of men, giving to everyone according to his ways and according to the fruit of his deeds;
20 who has set signs and wonders in the land of Egypt, *and* even to this day both in Israel and among mankind; and You have made a name for Yourself, as at this day.
21 'You brought Your people Israel out of the land of Egypt with signs and with wonders, and with a strong hand and with an outstretched arm and with great terror;
22 and gave them this land, which You swore to their forefathers to give them, a land flowing with milk and honey.
23 'They came in and took possession of it, but they did not obey Your voice or walk in Your law; they have done nothing of all that You commanded them to do; therefore You have made all this calamity come upon them.
24 'Behold, the siege ramps have reached the city to take it; and the city is given into the hand of the Chaldeans who

fight against it, because of the sword, the famine and the pestilence; and what You have spoken has come to pass; and behold, You see *it.*

25 'You have said to me, O Lord GOD, "Buy for yourself the field with money and call in witnesses"—although the city is given into the hand of the Chaldeans.'"

26 Then the word of the LORD came to Jeremiah, saying,

➤ 27 "Behold, I am the LORD, the God of all flesh; is anything too difficult for Me?"

28 Therefore thus says the LORD, "Behold, I am about to give this city into the hand of the Chaldeans and into the hand of Nebuchadnezzar king of Babylon, and he will take it.

29 "The Chaldeans who are fighting against this city will enter and set this city on fire and burn it, with the houses where *people* have offered incense to Baal on their roofs and poured out drink offerings to other gods to provoke Me to anger.

30 "Indeed the sons of Israel and the sons of Judah have been doing only evil in My sight from their youth; for the sons of Israel have been only provoking Me to anger by the work of their hands," declares the LORD.

31 "Indeed this city has been to Me *a provocation of* My anger and My wrath from the day that they built it, even to this day, so that it should be removed from before My face,

32 because of all the evil of the sons of Israel and the sons of Judah which they have done to provoke Me to anger—they, their kings, their leaders, their priests, their prophets, the men of Judah and the inhabitants of Jerusalem.

33 "They have turned *their* back to Me and not *their* face; though *I* taught them, teaching again and again, they would not listen and receive instruction.

34 "But they put their detestable things in the house which is called by My name, to defile it.

35 "They built the high places of Baal that are in the valley of Ben-hinnom to cause their sons and their daughters to pass through *the fire* to Molech, which I had not commanded them nor had it entered My mind that they should do this abomination, to cause Judah to sin.

36 "Now therefore thus says the LORD God of Israel concerning this city of which you say, 'It is given into the hand of the king of Babylon by sword, by famine and by pestilence.'

37 "Behold, I will gather them out of all the lands to which I have driven them in My anger, in My wrath and in great indignation; and I will bring them back to this place and make them dwell in safety.

38 "They shall be My people, and I will be their God;

➤ 39 and I will give them one heart and one way, that they may fear Me always, for their own good and for *the good of* their children after them.

40 "I will make an everlasting covenant with them that I will not turn away from them, to do them good; and I will put the fear of Me in their hearts so that they will not turn away from Me.

41 "I will rejoice over them to do them good and will faithfully plant them in this land with all My heart and with all My soul.

42 "For thus says the LORD, 'Just as I

LIFE LESSONS

➤ **Jeremiah 32:27** — *"Behold, I am the LORD, the God of all flesh; is anything too difficult for Me?"*

*A*braham had to learn this lesson (Gen. 18:14). Mary, the mother of Jesus, had to learn this lesson (Luke 1:37). Peter and the other disciples had to learn this lesson (Luke 18:27). And so do we.

➤ **Jeremiah 32:39** — *"I will give them one heart and one way, that they may fear Me always."*

*E*verything God does for us, He does for our good. He gives us a heart to love Him, a will to obey Him, and a spirit to fear Him for our good and the good of our children.

➤ **Jeremiah 32:42** — *"Just as I brought all this great disaster on this people, so I am going to bring on them all the good that I am promising them."*

*G*od keeps all of His promises, for both judgment and blessing—but He loves to bless His people, not judge them. He will not shrink from judging us (1 Pet. 4:17), but He would much prefer to bless us.

WHAT THE BIBLE SAYS ABOUT

Walking Through the Difficult Times

Psalm 119:49, 50

*J*ourneys through the valley are both inevitable and painful. However, they're also meant to be profitable. For example, trials can be times of discovery about God. When feelings of helplessness overtake us, He provides His strength to sustain us. When despair tries to close in, He invites us to experience His peace and promised rest (Matt. 11:28). In the midst of the clamoring pain, He offers Himself as our comforter and protector.

Other discoveries we make in severe crises have to do with ourselves. Terrible times test our faith and reveal our true character. When a crisis first hits, most of us will respond with alarm. Then, if our relationships with the Lord are weak, fear will increase. As the pressure continues, some of us will panic, some will seek ungodly counsel, and others will blame people or God for the problem. Instead of standing firm and looking to the Lord, we also try to find a way out on our own. These are signs of spiritual immaturity.

By contrast, those whose faith is strong will move from alarm to trust over time. We see this in the faith of David as he writes, "Remember the word to Your servant, in which You have made me hope. This is my comfort in my affliction, that Your word has revived me" (Ps. 119:49, 50). David centered his faith in God's Word and was rewarded for it.

We, too, must seek out the Lord through prayer and the Word, remembering His help to us in the past (Ps. 77:11–14). In this way, our endurance and confidence in Him will build and we will also believe His promises and trust Him to keep them, despite any evidence to the contrary. ◈

---

brought all this great disaster on this people, so I am going to bring on them all the good that I am promising them. 43 'Fields will be bought in this land of which you say, "It is a desolation, without man or beast; it is given into the hand of the Chaldeans." 44 'Men will buy fields for money, sign and seal deeds, and call in witnesses in the land of Benjamin, in the environs of Jerusalem, in the cities of Judah, in the cities of the hill country, in the cities of the lowland and in the cities of the Negev; for I will restore their fortunes,' declares the LORD."

◈ Psalm 119:49–56

ד Zayin.

49 Remember the word to Your servant,
In which You have made me hope.
50 This is my comfort in my affliction,
That Your word has revived me.
51 The arrogant utterly deride me,
Yet I do not turn aside from Your law.
52 I have remembered Your ordinances from of old, O LORD,
And comfort myself.

53 Burning indignation has seized me because of the wicked,
Who forsake Your law.
54 Your statutes are my songs
In the house of my pilgrimage.
55 O LORD, I remember Your name in the night,
And keep Your law.
56 This has become mine,
That I observe Your precepts.

◈ Proverbs 27:20

20 Sheol and Abaddon are never satisfied,
Nor are the eyes of man ever satisfied.

◈ 1 Timothy 2:1–15

2 FIRST of all, then, I urge that entreaties *and* prayers, petitions *and* thanksgivings, be made on behalf of all men, 2 for kings and all who are in authority, so that we may lead a tranquil and quiet life in all godliness and dignity.

3   This is good and acceptable in the sight of God our Savior,
4   who desires all men to be saved and to come to the knowledge of the truth.
5   For there is one God, *and* one mediator also between God and men, *the* man Christ Jesus,
6   who gave Himself as a ransom for all, the testimony *given* at the proper time.
7   For this I was appointed a preacher and an apostle (I am telling the truth, I am not lying) as a teacher of the Gentiles in faith and truth.
8   Therefore I want the men in every place to pray, lifting up holy hands, without wrath and dissension.
9   Likewise, *I want* women to adorn themselves with proper clothing, modestly and discreetly, not with braided hair and gold or pearls or costly garments,
10 but rather by means of good works, as is proper for women making a claim to godliness.
11 A woman must quietly receive instruction with entire submissiveness.
12 But I do not allow a woman to teach or exercise authority over a man, but to remain quiet.
13 For it was Adam who was first created, *and* then Eve.
14 And it *was* not Adam *who* was deceived, but the woman being deceived, fell into transgression.
15 But *women* will be preserved through the bearing of children if they continue in faith and love and sanctity with self-restraint.

LIFE LESSONS

➤ **1 Timothy 2:3, 4 — *God our Savior . . . desires all men to be saved and to come to the knowledge of the truth.***

*T*he Lord does not celebrate the need to judge wicked people, but is eager for the opportunity to redeem those who believe in His Son as Savior (2 Pet. 3:9). Jesus Christ has paid the penalty of our sin through His sacrificial, substitutionary, all-sufficient death (Rom. 6:23). This is the only way we are saved.

OCTOBER 24

Jeremiah 33:1—34:22

33 THEN the word of the LORD came to Jeremiah the second time, while he was still confined in the court of the guard, saying,
2   "Thus says the LORD who made *the earth*, the LORD who formed it to establish it, the LORD is His name,
3   'Call to Me and I will answer you, and I will tell you great and mighty things, which you do not know.'
4   "For thus says the LORD God of Israel concerning the houses of this city, and concerning the houses of the kings of Judah which are broken down *to make a defense* against the siege ramps and against the sword,
5   'While *they* are coming to fight with the Chaldeans and to fill them with the corpses of men whom I have slain in My anger and in My wrath, and I have hidden My face from this city because of all their wickedness:
6   'Behold, I will bring to it health and healing, and I will heal them; and I will reveal to them an abundance of peace and truth.
7   'I will restore the fortunes of Judah and the fortunes of Israel and will rebuild them as they were at first.
8   'I will cleanse them from all their iniquity by which they have sinned against Me, and I will pardon all their iniquities

---

LIFE LESSONS

➤ **Jeremiah 33:6 — *"I will bring to [this city] health and healing, and I will heal [My people]; and I will reveal to them an abundance of peace and truth."***

*F*or such a dark book, Jeremiah has some very beautiful promises for redemption and blessing. God desires to bring us health and healing, not sickness and injury. He wants to shower us with peace and truth, not keep either from us.

ANSWERS TO LIFE'S QUESTIONS

How can I make my prayer life fresh and new?

JEREMIAH 33:1–3

*T*he prophet Jeremiah was not a popular man. When he declared the truth God had given him—that Judah would soon start seventy long years in captivity—the people threw him into prison.

Yet in such dire circumstances, Jeremiah learned something profound about prayer. Jeremiah 33:1–3 says: "Then the word of the LORD came to Jeremiah the second time, while he was still confined in the court of the guard, saying, 'Thus says the LORD who made the earth, the LORD who formed it to establish it, the LORD is His name, "Call to Me and I will answer you, and I will tell you great and mighty things, which you do not know."'"

Prayer is a very real part of a vital relationship with God. It is not for some special spiritual elite; it is for *you*. Three principles within these verses can transform your old notions about prayer into something fresh and new.

First, God says, "Call to Me." He wants to hear from you. His loving, omnipotent heart desires to hear your innermost thoughts and feelings. He wants to hear from you in the hard times and when life is going smoothly. In fact, your sweetest times of prayer happen when you come before Him simply to praise, worship, and give thanks for what He has done.

Second, God says, "I will answer you." Do you believe that? Perhaps you once asked God for something He did not give you, and since then, you have harbored secret worries that He did not hear or did not care to answer. But God Himself says to you, "I will answer you." That answer may not take the form you anticipate or come when you desire, but He *will* respond. He might say "yes," "no," or "wait." You may not understand the reasons behind His answer—but you can trust that they are best for you (Rom. 8:28).

Third, God says, "I will show you great and mighty things, which you do not know." You have finite wisdom and understanding; God knows all. He knows the big picture; you see merely a tiny piece. When you ask Him to guide you, He works to direct you as a part of His higher vision and calling.

If you take that first step of calling out to Him, prayer can become an important part of a dynamic relationship with almighty God. Do it today—He waits to hear your voice.

---

by which they have sinned against Me and by which they have transgressed against Me.

➤ 9 'It will be to Me a name of joy, praise and glory before all the nations of the earth which will hear of all the good that I do for them, and they will fear and tremble because of all the good and all the peace that I make for it.'

10 "Thus says the LORD, 'Yet again there will be heard in this place, of which you say, "It is a waste, without man and without beast," *that is,* in the cities of Judah and in the streets of Jerusalem that are desolate, without man and without inhabitant and without beast,

11 the voice of joy and the voice of gladness, the voice of the bridegroom and the voice of the bride, the voice of those who say,

"Give thanks to the LORD of hosts,

For the LORD is good,

For His lovingkindness is everlasting";

and of those who bring a thank offering into the house of the LORD. For I will restore the fortunes of the land as they were at first,' says the LORD.

12 "Thus says the LORD of hosts, 'There will again be in this place which is waste, without man or beast, and in all its cities, a habitation of shepherds who rest their flocks.

13 'In the cities of the hill country, in the cities of the lowland, in the cities of the Negev, in the land of Benjamin, in the environs of Jerusalem and in the cities of Judah, the flocks will again pass under the hands of the one who numbers them,' says the LORD.

LIFE LESSONS

➤ **Jeremiah 33:9 —** *"They will fear and tremble because of all the good and all the peace that I make for it."*

*W*hen will we learn that the heart of God yearns to lavish joy, praise, honor, goodness, and peace on His obedient people? He does not wait in heaven for us to fail; rather, He looks "down from heaven upon the sons of men to see if there are any who understand, who seek after God" (Ps. 14:2) because He longs to bless us.

14 'Behold, days are coming,' declares the LORD, 'when I will fulfill the good word which I have spoken concerning the house of Israel and the house of Judah.

15 'In those days and at that time I will cause a righteous Branch of David to spring forth; and He shall execute justice and righteousness on the earth.

16 'In those days Judah will be saved and Jerusalem will dwell in safety; and this is *the name* by which she will be called: the LORD is our righteousness.'

17 "For thus says the LORD, 'David shall never lack a man to sit on the throne of the house of Israel;

18 and the Levitical priests shall never lack a man before Me to offer burnt offerings, to burn grain offerings and to prepare sacrifices continually.'"

19 The word of the LORD came to Jeremiah, saying,

20 "Thus says the LORD, 'If you can break My covenant for the day and My covenant for the night, so that day and night will not be at their appointed time,

21 then My covenant may also be broken with David My servant so that he will not have a son to reign on his throne, and with the Levitical priests, My ministers.

22 'As the host of heaven cannot be counted and the sand of the sea cannot be measured, so I will multiply the descendants of David My servant and the Levites who minister to Me.'"

23 And the word of the LORD came to Jeremiah, saying,

24 "Have you not observed what this people have spoken, saying, 'The two families which the LORD chose, He has rejected them'? Thus they despise My people, no longer are they as a nation in their sight.

25 "Thus says the LORD, 'If My covenant *for* day and night *stand* not, *and* the fixed patterns of heaven and earth I have not established,

26 then I would reject the descendants of Jacob and David My servant, not taking from his descendants rulers over the descendants of Abraham, Isaac and Jacob. But I will restore their fortunes and will have mercy on them.'"

34 THE word which came to Jeremiah from the LORD, when Nebuchadnezzar king of Babylon and all his army, with all the kingdoms of the earth that were under his dominion and all the peoples, were fighting against Jerusalem and against all its cities, saying,

2 "Thus says the LORD God of Israel, 'Go and speak to Zedekiah king of Judah and say to him: "Thus says the LORD, 'Behold, I am giving this city into the hand of the king of Babylon, and he will burn it with fire.

3 'You will not escape from his hand, for you will surely be captured and delivered into his hand; and you will see the king of Babylon eye to eye, and he will speak with you face to face, and you will go to Babylon.'"'

4 "Yet hear the word of the LORD, O Zedekiah king of Judah! Thus says the LORD concerning you, 'You will not die by the sword.

5 'You will die in peace; and as *spices* were burned for your fathers, the former kings who were before you, so they will burn *spices* for you; and they will lament for you, "Alas, lord!"' For I have spoken the word," declares the LORD.

6 Then Jeremiah the prophet spoke all these words to Zedekiah king of Judah in Jerusalem

7 when the army of the king of Babylon was fighting against Jerusalem and against all the remaining cities of Judah, *that is,* Lachish and Azekah, for they *alone* remained as fortified cities among the cities of Judah.

8 The word which came to Jeremiah from the LORD after King Zedekiah had made a covenant with all the people who were in Jerusalem to proclaim release to them:

9 that each man should set free his male servant and each man his female servant, a Hebrew man or a Hebrew woman; so that no one should keep them, a Jew his brother, in bondage.

10 And all the officials and all the people obeyed who had entered into the covenant that each man should set free his male servant and each man his female servant, so that no one should keep them any longer in bondage; they obeyed, and set *them free.*

11 But afterward they turned around and took back the male servants and the female servants whom they had set free, and brought them into subjection for male servants and for female servants.

12 Then the word of the LORD came to Jeremiah from the LORD, saying, **13** "Thus says the LORD God of Israel, 'I made a covenant with your forefathers in the day that I brought them out of the land of Egypt, from the house of bondage, saying, **14** "At the end of seven years each of you shall set free his Hebrew brother who has been sold to you and has served you six years, you shall send him out free from you; but your forefathers did not obey Me or incline their ear to Me. **15** "Although recently you *had* turned and done what is right in My sight, each man proclaiming release to his neighbor, and you had made a covenant before Me in the house which is called by My name. **16** "Yet you turned and profaned My name, and each man took back his male servant and each man his female servant whom you had set free according to their desire, and you brought them into subjection to be your male servants and female servants."' **17** "Therefore thus says the LORD, 'You have not obeyed Me in proclaiming release each man to his brother and each man to his neighbor. Behold, I am proclaiming a release to you,' declares the LORD, 'to the sword, to the pestilence and to the famine; and I will make you a terror to all the kingdoms of the earth. **18** 'I will give the men who have transgressed My covenant, who have not fulfilled the words of the covenant which they made before Me, *when* they cut the calf in two and passed between its parts— **19** the officials of Judah and the officials of Jerusalem, the court officers and the priests and all the people of the land who passed between the parts of the calf— **20** I will give them into the hand of their enemies and into the hand of those who seek their life. And their dead bodies will be food for the birds of the sky and the beasts of the earth. **21** 'Zedekiah king of Judah and his officials I will give into the hand of their enemies and into the hand of those who seek their life, and into the hand of the army of the king of Babylon which has gone away from you. **22** 'Behold, I am going to command,' declares the LORD, 'and I will bring them back to this city; and they will fight against it and take it and burn it with fire; and I will make the cities of Judah a desolation without inhabitant.'"

✦ Psalm 119:57–64

ה Heth.

57 The LORD is my portion;
    I have promised to keep Your words.
58 I sought Your favor with all *my* heart;
    Be gracious to me according to Your word.
59 I considered my ways
    And turned my feet to Your testimonies.
60 I hastened and did not delay
    To keep Your commandments.
61 The cords of the wicked have encircled me,
    But I have not forgotten Your law.
62 At midnight I shall rise to give thanks to You
    Because of Your righteous ordinances.
63 I am a companion of all those who fear You,
    And of those who keep Your precepts.
64 The earth is full of Your lovingkindness, O LORD;
    Teach me Your statutes.

✦ Proverbs 27:21

21 The crucible is for silver and the furnace for gold,
    And each *is tested* by the praise accorded him.

✦ 1 Timothy 3:1–16

3 IT is a trustworthy statement: if any man aspires to the office of overseer, it is a fine work he desires *to do.* **2** An overseer, then, must be above reproach, the husband of one wife, temperate, prudent, respectable, hospitable, able to teach, **3** not addicted to wine or pugnacious, but gentle, peaceable, free from the love of money.

4　*He must be* one who manages his own household well, keeping his children under control with all dignity

➤ 5　(but if a man does not know how to manage his own household, how will he take care of the church of God?),

➤ 6　*and* not a new convert, so that he will not become conceited and fall into the condemnation incurred by the devil.

7　And he must have a good reputation with those outside *the church*, so that he will not fall into reproach and the snare of the devil.

8　Deacons likewise *must be* men of dignity, not double-tongued, or addicted to much wine or fond of sordid gain,

✱ 9　*but* holding to the mystery of the faith with a clear conscience.

➤ 10　These men must also first be tested; then let them serve as deacons if they are beyond reproach.

11　Women *must* likewise *be* dignified, not malicious gossips, but temperate, faithful in all things.

12　Deacons must be husbands of *only* one wife, *and* good managers of *their* children and their own households.

13　For those who have served well as deacons obtain for themselves a high standing and great confidence in the faith that is in Christ Jesus.

14　I am writing these things to you, hoping to come to you before long;

➤ 15　but in case I am delayed, *I write* so that you will know how one ought to conduct himself in the household of God, which is the church of the living God, the pillar and support of the truth.

16　By common confession, great is the mystery of godliness:

He who was revealed in the flesh,
Was vindicated in the Spirit,
Seen by angels,
Proclaimed among the nations,
Believed on in the world,
Taken up in glory.

LIFE LESSONS

➤ **1 Timothy 3:5 — *If a man does not know how to manage his own household, how will he take care of the church of God?***

*B*efore God gives us greater responsibilities in a larger sphere of influence, He requires us to demonstrate our faithfulness to Him right where we are with those closest to us.

➤ **1 Timothy 3:6 — *So that he will not become conceited and fall into the condemnation incurred by the devil.***

*S*ometimes, when success comes too quickly, a person may be totally unprepared for it. He may not know how to deal with the admiration he's receiving. He becomes more focused on his own strengths, desires, and needs rather than on what is right in God sight, which means he's headed for trouble.

➤ **1 Timothy 3:10 — *These men must also first be tested; then let them serve as deacons.***

*A*t times, we see the passion, energy, talent, and desire of young believers and think they may be able to handle great responsibilities. However, it is not a person's enthusiasm that enables them to do ministry but their commitment to Christ and their steadfast obedience to Him. They must prove themselves faithful and godly in smaller tasks before they are ready to engage in more challenging ones (Matt. 25:14–30).

➤ **1 Timothy 3:15 — *Know how one ought to conduct himself in the household of God.***

*E*very believer is to bring honor to God, but it is especially important for church leaders to provide an authentic example of faith in action.

OCTOBER 25

 Jeremiah 35:1—36:32

35 THE word which came to Jeremiah from the LORD in the days of Je-

hoiakim the son of Josiah, king of Judah, saying,

2　"Go to the house of the Rechabites and speak to them, and bring them into the house of the LORD, into one of

12 Then the word of the LORD came to Jeremiah from the LORD, saying,
13 "Thus says the LORD God of Israel, 'I made a covenant with your forefathers in the day that I brought them out of the land of Egypt, from the house of bondage, saying,
14 "At the end of seven years each of you shall set free his Hebrew brother who has been sold to you and has served you six years, you shall send him out free from you; but your forefathers did not obey Me or incline their ear to Me.
15 "Although recently you *had* turned and done what is right in My sight, each man proclaiming release to his neighbor, and you had made a covenant before Me in the house which is called by My name.
16 "Yet you turned and profaned My name, and each man took back his male servant and each man his female servant whom you had set free according to their desire, and you brought them into subjection to be your male servants and female servants."'
17 "Therefore thus says the LORD, 'You have not obeyed Me in proclaiming release each man to his brother and each man to his neighbor. Behold, I am proclaiming a release to you,' declares the LORD, 'to the sword, to the pestilence and to the famine; and I will make you a terror to all the kingdoms of the earth.
18 'I will give the men who have transgressed My covenant, who have not fulfilled the words of the covenant which they made before Me, *when* they cut the calf in two and passed between its parts—
19 the officials of Judah and the officials of Jerusalem, the court officers and the priests and all the people of the land who passed between the parts of the calf—
20 I will give them into the hand of their enemies and into the hand of those who seek their life. And their dead bodies will be food for the birds of the sky and the beasts of the earth.
21 'Zedekiah king of Judah and his officials I will give into the hand of their enemies and into the hand of those who seek their life, and into the hand of the army of the king of Babylon which has gone away from you.
22 'Behold, I am going to command,' declares the LORD, 'and I will bring them back to this city; and they will fight against it and take it and burn it with fire; and I will make the cities of Judah a desolation without inhabitant.'"

Psalm 119:57–64

ח Heth.

57 The LORD is my portion;
    I have promised to keep Your words.
58 I sought Your favor with all *my*
      heart;
    Be gracious to me according to Your
      word.
59 I considered my ways
    And turned my feet to Your
      testimonies.
60 I hastened and did not delay
    To keep Your commandments.
61 The cords of the wicked have
      encircled me,
    But I have not forgotten Your law.
62 At midnight I shall rise to give
      thanks to You
    Because of Your righteous ordinances.
63 I am a companion of all those who
      fear You,
    And of those who keep Your precepts.
64 The earth is full of Your
      lovingkindness, O LORD;
    Teach me Your statutes.

Proverbs 27:21

21 The crucible is for silver and the
      furnace for gold,
    And each *is tested* by the praise
      accorded him.

1 Timothy 3:1–16

3 IT is a trustworthy statement: if any man aspires to the office of overseer, it is a fine work he desires *to do.*
2 An overseer, then, must be above reproach, the husband of one wife, temperate, prudent, respectable, hospitable, able to teach,
3 not addicted to wine or pugnacious, but gentle, peaceable, free from the love of money.

4   *He must be* one who manages his own household well, keeping his children under control with all dignity

➤ 5   (but if a man does not know how to manage his own household, how will he take care of the church of God?),

➤ 6   *and* not a new convert, so that he will not become conceited and fall into the condemnation incurred by the devil.

7   And he must have a good reputation with those outside *the church*, so that he will not fall into reproach and the snare of the devil.

8   Deacons likewise *must be* men of dignity, not double-tongued, or addicted to much wine or fond of sordid gain,

✳ 9   *but* holding to the mystery of the faith with a clear conscience.

➤ 10   These men must also first be tested; then let them serve as deacons if they are beyond reproach.

11   Women *must* likewise *be* dignified, not malicious gossips, but temperate, faithful in all things.

12   Deacons must be husbands of *only* one wife, *and* good managers of *their* children and their own households.

13   For those who have served well as deacons obtain for themselves a high standing and great confidence in the faith that is in Christ Jesus.

14   I am writing these things to you, hoping to come to you before long;

➤ 15   but in case I am delayed, *I write* so that you will know how one ought to conduct himself in the household of God, which is the church of the living God, the pillar and support of the truth.

16   By common confession, great is the mystery of godliness:

He who was revealed in the flesh,
Was vindicated in the Spirit,
Seen by angels,
Proclaimed among the nations,
Believed on in the world,
Taken up in glory.

OCTOBER 25

Jeremiah 35:1—36:32

35 THE word which came to Jeremiah from the LORD in the days of Jehoiakim the son of Josiah, king of Judah, saying,

2   "Go to the house of the Rechabites and speak to them, and bring them into the house of the LORD, into one of

the chambers, and give them wine to drink."

3 Then I took Jaazaniah the son of Jeremiah, son of Habazziniah, and his brothers and all his sons and the whole house of the Rechabites,

4 and I brought them into the house of the LORD, into the chamber of the sons of Hanan the son of Igdaliah, the man of God, which was near the chamber of the officials, which was above the chamber of Maaseiah the son of Shallum, the doorkeeper.

5 Then I set before the men of the house of the Rechabites pitchers full of wine and cups; and I said to them, "Drink wine!"

6 But they said, "We will not drink wine, for Jonadab the son of Rechab, our father, commanded us, saying, 'You shall not drink wine, you or your sons, forever.

7 'You shall not build a house, and you shall not sow seed and you shall not plant a vineyard or own one; but in tents you shall dwell all your days, that you may live many days in the land where you sojourn.'

8 "We have obeyed the voice of Jonadab the son of Rechab, our father, in all that he commanded us, not to drink wine all our days, we, our wives, our sons or our daughters,

9 nor to build ourselves houses to dwell in; and we do not have vineyard or field or seed.

10 "We have only dwelt in tents, and have obeyed and have done according to all that Jonadab our father commanded us.

11 "But when Nebuchadnezzar king of Babylon came up against the land, we said, 'Come and let us go to Jerusalem before the army of the Chaldeans and before the army of the Arameans.' So we have dwelt in Jerusalem."

12 Then the word of the LORD came to Jeremiah, saying,

13 "Thus says the LORD of hosts, the God of Israel, 'Go and say to the men of Judah and the inhabitants of Jerusalem, "Will you not receive instruction by listening to My words?" declares the LORD.

14 "The words of Jonadab the son of Rechab, which he commanded his sons not to drink wine, are observed. So they do not drink *wine* to this day, for they have obeyed their father's command. But I have spoken to you again and again; yet you have not listened to Me.

15 "Also I have sent to you all My servants the prophets, sending *them* again and again, saying: 'Turn now every man from his evil way and amend your deeds, and do not go after other gods to worship them. Then you will dwell in the land which I have given to you and to your forefathers; but you have not inclined your ear or listened to Me.

16 'Indeed, the sons of Jonadab the son of Rechab have observed the command of their father which he commanded them, but this people has not listened to Me.'"

17 "Therefore thus says the LORD, the God of hosts, the God of Israel, 'Behold, I am bringing on Judah and on all the inhabitants of Jerusalem all the disaster that I have pronounced against them; because I spoke to them but they did not listen, and I have called them but they did not answer.'"

18 Then Jeremiah said to the house of the Rechabites, "Thus says the LORD of hosts, the God of Israel, 'Because you have obeyed the command of Jonadab your father, kept all his commands and done according to all that he commanded you;

19 therefore thus says the LORD of hosts, the God of Israel, "Jonadab the son of Rechab shall not lack a man to stand before Me always."'"

36 IN the fourth year of Jehoiakim the son of Josiah, king of Judah, this word came to Jeremiah from the LORD, saying,

2 "Take a scroll and write on it all the words which I have spoken to you concerning Israel and concerning Judah, and concerning all the nations, from the day I *first* spoke to you, from the days of Josiah, even to this day.

3 "Perhaps the house of Judah will hear all the calamity which I plan to bring on them, in order that every man will turn from his evil way; then I will forgive their iniquity and their sin."

4 Then Jeremiah called Baruch the son of Neriah, and Baruch wrote on a scroll at the dictation of Jeremiah all the

words of the LORD which He had spoken to him.

5   Jeremiah commanded Baruch, saying, "I am restricted; I cannot go into the house of the LORD.

6   "So you go and read from the scroll which you have written at my dictation the words of the LORD to the people in the LORD's house on a fast day. And also you shall read them to all *the people of* Judah who come from their cities.

➤ 7   "Perhaps their supplication will come before the LORD, and everyone will turn from his evil way, for great is the anger and the wrath that the LORD has pronounced against this people."

8   Baruch the son of Neriah did according to all that Jeremiah the prophet commanded him, reading from the book the words of the LORD in the LORD's house.

9   Now in the fifth year of Jehoiakim the son of Josiah, king of Judah, in the ninth month, all the people in Jerusalem and all the people who came from the cities of Judah to Jerusalem proclaimed a fast before the LORD.

10   Then Baruch read from the book the words of Jeremiah in the house of the LORD in the chamber of Gemariah the son of Shaphan the scribe, in the upper court, at the entry of the New Gate of the LORD's house, to all the people.

11   Now when Micaiah the son of Gemariah, the son of Shaphan, had heard all the words of the LORD from the book,

12   he went down to the king's house, into the scribe's chamber. And behold, all the officials were sitting there—Elishama the scribe, and Delaiah the son of Shemaiah, and Elnathan the son of Achbor, and Gemariah the son of Shaphan, and Zedekiah the son of Hananiah, and all the *other* officials.

13   Micaiah declared to them all the words that he had heard when Baruch read from the book to the people.

14   Then all the officials sent Jehudi the son of Nethaniah, the son of Shelemiah, the son of Cushi, to Baruch, saying, "Take in your hand the scroll from which you have read to the people and come." So Baruch the son of Neriah took the scroll in his hand and went to them.

15   They said to him, "Sit down, please, and read it to us." So Baruch read it to them.

16   When they had heard all the words, they turned in fear one to another and said to Baruch, "We will surely report all these words to the king."

17   And they asked Baruch, saying, "Tell us, please, how did you write all these words? *Was it* at his dictation?"

18   Then Baruch said to them, "He dictated all these words to me, and I wrote them with ink on the book."

19   Then the officials said to Baruch, "Go, hide yourself, you and Jeremiah, and do not let anyone know where you are."

20   So they went to the king in the court, but they had deposited the scroll in the chamber of Elishama the scribe, and they reported all the words to the king.

21   Then the king sent Jehudi to get the scroll, and he took it out of the chamber of Elishama the scribe. And Jehudi read it to the king as well as to all the officials who stood beside the king.

22   Now the king was sitting in the winter house in the ninth month, with *a* fire burning in the brazier before him.

23   When Jehudi had read three or four columns, *the king* cut it with a scribe's knife and threw *it* into the fire that was in the brazier, until all the scroll was consumed in the fire that was in the brazier.

24   Yet the king and all his servants who ➤

LIFE LESSONS

➤ **Jeremiah 36:7** — *"Perhaps their supplication will come before the LORD, and everyone will turn from his evil way."*

*W*e should always urge men and women to repent and return to the Lord so that He might heal them (2 Cor. 5:20).

➤ **Jeremiah 36:24** — *Yet the king and all his servants who heard all these words were not afraid.*

*U*ntil God comes in judgment (Rev. 20:11–15), some may mock His Word and ridicule His servants. Yet a day is coming when, "At the name of Jesus every knee will bow, of those who are in heaven and on earth and under the earth, and that every tongue will confess that Jesus Christ is Lord, to the glory of God the Father" (Phil. 2:10, 11).

Life Examples:

KING JEHOIAKIM: God's Word Stands

JEREMIAH 36:30, 31

*T*he evil king Jehoiakim of Judah proves that while someone may physically destroy the pages of the Bible, no one may prevent the fulfillment of even a single word spoken by the mouth of God. His Word stands, regardless of what men may do.

When Jehoiakim heard words of divine judgment pronounced on him and his wicked kingdom, the king took the offending scroll and "cut it with a scribe's knife and threw it into the fire that was in the brazier, until all the scroll was consumed" (Jer. 36:23). He did so probably to show his contempt for the messenger and to demonstrate his lack of fear regarding the message.

God let the king's insolence stand for seven years. But when he refused to repent, the Lord fulfilled every threat that He had made regarding the king (Jer. 36:30, 31). God always keeps His promises, whether for blessing or judgment.

---

heard all these words were not afraid, nor did they rend their garments.
25 Even though Elnathan and Delaiah and Gemariah pleaded with the king not to burn the scroll, he would not listen to them.
26 And the king commanded Jerahmeel the king's son, Seraiah the son of Azriel, and Shelemiah the son of Abdeel to seize Baruch the scribe and Jeremiah the prophet, but the LORD hid them.
27 Then the word of the LORD came to Jeremiah after the king had burned the scroll and the words which Baruch had written at the dictation of Jeremiah, saying,
28 "Take again another scroll and write on it all the former words that were on the first scroll which Jehoiakim the king of Judah burned.
29 "And concerning Jehoiakim king of Judah you shall say, 'Thus says the LORD, "You have burned this scroll, saying, 'Why have you written on it that the king of Babylon will certainly come and destroy this land, and will make man and beast to cease from it?'"
30 'Therefore thus says the LORD concerning Jehoiakim king of Judah, "He shall have no one to sit on the throne of David, and his dead body shall be cast out to the heat of the day and the frost of the night.
31 "I will also punish him and his descendants and his servants for their iniquity, and I will bring on them and the inhabitants of Jerusalem and the men of Judah all the calamity that I have declared to them—but they did not listen."'"
32 Then Jeremiah took another scroll and gave it to Baruch the son of Neriah, the scribe, and he wrote on it at the dictation of Jeremiah all the words of the book which Jehoiakim king of Judah had burned in the fire; and many similar words were added to them.

✦ Psalm 119:65–70

ﬡ Teth.

65 You have dealt well with Your servant,
   O LORD, according to Your word.
66 Teach me good discernment and knowledge,
   For I believe in Your commandments.
67 Before I was afflicted I went astray,
   But now I keep Your word.
68 You are good and do good;
   Teach me Your statutes.
69 The arrogant have forged a lie against me;
   With all *my* heart I will observe Your precepts.
70 Their heart is covered with fat,
   But I delight in Your law.

LIFE LESSONS

➤ **Psalm 119:67 — *Before I was afflicted I went astray, but now I keep Your word.***

*G*od uses affliction, not as a whip to force us in line, but as a messenger to urge us back into a safe place. Affliction is a bridge to a deeper relationship with God.

Proverbs 27:22

22 Though you pound a fool in a
     mortar with a pestle along with
     crushed grain,
     Yet his foolishness will not depart
     from him.

1 Timothy 4:1–16

4 BUT the Spirit explicitly says that in
later times some will fall away from
the faith, paying attention to deceitful
spirits and doctrines of demons,
2   by means of the hypocrisy of liars
seared in their own conscience as with a
branding iron,
3   *men* who forbid marriage *and advocate* abstaining from foods which God
has created to be gratefully shared in by
those who believe and know the truth.
4   For everything created by God is
good, and nothing is to be rejected if it is
received with gratitude;
5   for it is sanctified by means of the
word of God and prayer.
6   In pointing out these things to the
brethren, you will be a good servant of
Christ Jesus, *constantly* nourished on
the words of the faith and of the sound
doctrine which you have been following.
7   But have nothing to do with worldly
fables fit only for old women. On the
other hand, discipline yourself for the
purpose of godliness;
8   for bodily discipline is only of little
profit, but godliness is profitable for all
things, since it holds promise for the
present life and *also* for the *life* to come.
9   It is a trustworthy statement deserving full acceptance.
10   For it is for this we labor and strive,
because we have fixed our hope on the
living God, who is the Savior of all men,
especially of believers.
11   Prescribe and teach these things.
12   Let no one look down on your youthfulness, but *rather* in speech, conduct,
love, faith *and* purity, show yourself an
example of those who believe.
13   Until I come, give attention to the
public reading *of Scripture*, to exhortation and teaching.

14   Do not neglect the spiritual gift
within you, which was bestowed on you
through prophetic utterance with the laying on of hands by the presbytery.
15   Take pains with these things; be
absorbed in them, so that your progress
will be evident to all.
16   Pay close attention to yourself and to
your teaching; persevere in these things,
for as you do this you will ensure salvation both for yourself and for those who
hear you.

LIFE LESSONS

**1 Timothy 4:1, 2 — *In later times some
will fall away from the faith, paying
attention to deceitful spirits and doctrines of demons . . . seared in their own
conscience as with a branding iron.***

A seared or burnt conscience can be
one that is beyond repair. It reflects
a rejection of God's truth. Ungodly and
deceptive doctrines have always plagued
the church, but the closer we draw to
the return of Christ, the more insidious,
prevalent, and aggressive false teachers
will become. That is why we must remain
vigilant and make sure we always lead
others to faith and obedience—especially as the Day of the Lord approaches.

**1 Timothy 4:12 — *In speech, conduct,
love, faith, and purity, show yourself as
an example to those who believe.***

Regardless of how old you are or
how long you have followed Christ,
you can become an excellent example
to others by submitting your life to
Christ and learning how to rely upon the
power and leading of the Spirit.

**1 Timothy 4:15 — *Take pains with
these things; be absorbed in them, so
that your progress will be evident to all.***

Why should we be diligent in reading
Scripture, teaching, encouraging
others, and practicing the spiritual gifts
the Lord has given us? Because this is the
way we learn more about God and how
to walk in His ways. As we live in active,
engaged obedience to the Lord—obeying the initial promptings of His Spirit
and clinging to His Word—we grow
and mature in His likeness (Gal. 5:22,
23; 2 Pet. 1:3–8).

Jeremiah 37:1—38:28

37 NOW Zedekiah the son of Josiah whom Nebuchadnezzar king of Babylon had made king in the land of Judah, reigned as king in place of Coniah the son of Jehoiakim.

2 But neither he nor his servants nor the people of the land listened to the words of the LORD which He spoke through Jeremiah the prophet.

3 Yet King Zedekiah sent Jehucal the son of Shelemiah, and Zephaniah the son of Maaseiah, the priest, to Jeremiah the prophet, saying, "Please pray to the LORD our God on our behalf."

4 Now Jeremiah was *still* coming in and going out among the people, for they had not *yet* put him in the prison.

5 Meanwhile, Pharaoh's army had set out from Egypt; and when the Chaldeans who had been besieging Jerusalem heard the report about them, they lifted the *siege* from Jerusalem.

6 Then the word of the LORD came to Jeremiah the prophet, saying,

7 "Thus says the LORD God of Israel, 'Thus you are to say to the king of Judah, who sent you to Me to inquire of Me: "Behold, Pharaoh's army which has come out for your assistance is going to return to its own land of Egypt.

8 "The Chaldeans will also return and fight against this city, and they will capture it and burn it with fire."'

9 "Thus says the LORD, 'Do not deceive yourselves, saying, "The Chaldeans will surely go away from us," for they will not go.

10 'For even if you had defeated the entire army of Chaldeans who were fighting against you, and there were *only* wounded men left among them, each man in his tent, they would rise up and burn this city with fire.'"

11 Now it happened when the army of the Chaldeans had lifted *the siege* from Jerusalem because of Pharaoh's army,

12 that Jeremiah went out from Jerusalem to go to the land of Benjamin in order to take possession of *some* property there among the people.

13 While he was at the Gate of Benjamin, a captain of the guard whose name was Irijah, the son of Shelemiah the son of Hananiah was there; and he arrested Jeremiah the prophet, saying, "You are going over to the Chaldeans!"

14 But Jeremiah said, "A lie! I am not going over to the Chaldeans"; yet he would not listen to him. So Irijah arrested Jeremiah and brought him to the officials.

15 Then the officials were angry at Jeremiah and beat him, and they put him in jail in the house of Jonathan the scribe, which they had made into the prison.

16 For Jeremiah had come into the dungeon, that is, the vaulted cell; and Jeremiah stayed there many days.

17 Now King Zedekiah sent and took him *out*; and in his palace the king secretly asked him and said, "Is there a word from the LORD?" And Jeremiah said, "There is!" Then he said, "You will be given into the hand of the king of Babylon!"

18 Moreover Jeremiah said to King Zedekiah, "In what *way* have I sinned against you, or against your servants, or against this people, that you have put me in prison?

19 "Where then are your prophets who prophesied to you, saying, 'The king of Babylon will not come against you or against this land'?

20 "But now, please listen, O my lord the king; please let my petition come before you and do not make me return to the house of Jonathan the scribe, that I may not die there."

21 Then King Zedekiah gave commandment, and they committed Jeremiah to the court of the guardhouse and gave him a loaf of bread daily from the bakers' street, until all the bread in the city was gone. So Jeremiah remained in the court of the guardhouse.

38 NOW Shephatiah the son of Mattan, and Gedaliah the son of

LIFE LESSONS

> Jeremiah 37:16 — *Jeremiah had come into the dungeon . . . and . . . stayed there many days.*

God never left Jeremiah, yet the prophet spent many lonely and discouraging days in His service. Jeremiah's obedience did not translate into instant and obvious blessing. It took faith for him to believe that God would remain faithful to the end.

Pashhur, and Jucal the son of Shelemiah, and Pashhur the son of Malchijah heard the words that Jeremiah was speaking to all the people, saying,

2 "Thus says the LORD, 'He who stays in this city will die by the sword and by famine and by pestilence, but he who goes out to the Chaldeans will live and have his *own* life as booty and stay alive.'

3 "Thus says the LORD, 'This city will certainly be given into the hand of the army of the king of Babylon and he will capture it.'"

4 Then the officials said to the king, "Now let this man be put to death, inasmuch as he is discouraging the men of war who are left in this city and all the people, by speaking such words to them; for this man is not seeking the well-being of this people but rather their harm."

5 So King Zedekiah said, "Behold, he is in your hands; for the king can *do* nothing against you."

6 Then they took Jeremiah and cast him into the cistern *of* Malchijah the king's son, which was in the court of the guardhouse; and they let Jeremiah down with ropes. Now in the cistern there was no water but only mud, and Jeremiah sank into the mud.

7 But Ebed-melech the Ethiopian, a eunuch, while he was in the king's palace, heard that they had put Jeremiah into the cistern. Now the king was sitting in the Gate of Benjamin;

8 and Ebed-melech went out from the king's palace and spoke to the king, saying,

➤ 9 "My lord the king, these men have acted wickedly in all that they have done to Jeremiah the prophet whom they have cast into the cistern; and he will die right where he is because of the famine, for there is no more bread in the city."

LIFE LESSONS

➤ **Jeremiah 38: 9 —** *"These men have acted wickedly in all that they have done to Jeremiah the prophet."*

*W*ith all Jeremiah's fellow Israelites around him, it took a foreigner, Ebed-melech the Ethiopian, to give him the help he needed. God often provides help from unexpected sources to show that He has accomplished the victory and deserves the glory.

10 Then the king commanded Ebed-melech the Ethiopian, saying, "Take thirty men from here under your authority and bring up Jeremiah the prophet from the cistern before he dies."

11 So Ebed-melech took the men under his authority and went into the king's palace to *a place* beneath the storeroom and took from there worn-out clothes and worn-out rags and let them down by ropes into the cistern to Jeremiah.

12 Then Ebed-melech the Ethiopian said to Jeremiah, "Now put these worn-out clothes and rags under your armpits under the ropes"; and Jeremiah did so.

13 So they pulled Jeremiah up with the ropes and lifted him out of the cistern, and Jeremiah stayed in the court of the guardhouse.

14 Then King Zedekiah sent and had Jeremiah the prophet brought to him at the third entrance that is in the house of the LORD; and the king said to Jeremiah, "I am going to ask you something; do not hide anything from me."

15 Then Jeremiah said to Zedekiah, "If I tell you, will you not certainly put me to death? Besides, if I give you advice, you will not listen to me."

16 But King Zedekiah swore to Jeremiah in secret saying, "As the LORD lives, who made this life for us, surely I will not put you to death nor will I give you over to the hand of these men who are seeking your life."

17 Then Jeremiah said to Zedekiah, "Thus says the LORD God of hosts, the God of Israel, 'If you will indeed go out to the officers of the king of Babylon, then you will live, this city will not be burned with fire, and you and your household will survive.

18 'But if you will not go out to the officers of the king of Babylon, then this city will be given over to the hand of the Chaldeans; and they will burn it with fire, and you yourself will not escape from their hand.'"

19 Then King Zedekiah said to Jeremiah, "I dread the Jews who have gone over to the Chaldeans, for they may give me over into their hand and they will abuse me."

20 But Jeremiah said, "They will not ◄ give you over. Please obey the LORD in what I am saying to you, that it may go well with you and you may live.

21 "But if you keep refusing to go out, this is the word which the LORD has shown me:

22 'Then behold, all of the women who have been left in the palace of the king of Judah are going to be brought out to the officers of the king of Babylon; and those women will say,

"Your close friends
Have misled and overpowered you;
While your feet were sunk in the mire,
They turned back."

23 'They will also bring out all your wives and your sons to the Chaldeans, and you yourself will not escape from their hand, but will be seized by the hand of the king of Babylon, and this city will be burned with fire.'"

24 Then Zedekiah said to Jeremiah, "Let no man know about these words and you will not die.

25 "But if the officials hear that I have talked with you and come to you and say to you, 'Tell us now what you said to the king and what the king said to you; do not hide it from us and we will not put you to death,'

26 then you are to say to them, 'I was presenting my petition before the king, not to make me return to the house of Jonathan to die there.'"

27 Then all the officials came to Jeremiah and questioned him. So he reported to them in accordance with all these words which the king had commanded; and they ceased speaking with him, since the conversation had not been overheard.

28 So Jeremiah stayed in the court of the guardhouse until the day that Jerusalem was captured.

✦ Psalm 119:71–80

71 It is good for me that I was afflicted,
That I may learn Your statutes.

72 The law of Your mouth is better to
     me
     Than thousands of gold and silver
     pieces.

> Yodh.

73 Your hands made me and fashioned
     me;
     Give me understanding, that I may
     learn Your commandments.
74 May those who fear You see me and
     be glad,
     Because I wait for Your word.
✳ 75 I know, O LORD, that Your
     judgments are righteous,
     And that in faithfulness You have
     afflicted me.
76 O may Your lovingkindness comfort
     me,
     According to Your word to Your
     servant.
77 May Your compassion come to me
     that I may live,
     For Your law is my delight.
78 May the arrogant be ashamed, for
     they subvert me with a lie;
     But I shall meditate on Your
     precepts.
79 May those who fear You turn to me,
     Even those who know Your
     testimonies.
80 May my heart be blameless in Your
     statutes,
     So that I will not be ashamed.

◈ Proverbs 27:23–27

23 Know well the condition of your
     flocks,
     And pay attention to your herds;
24 For riches are not forever,
     Nor does a crown *endure* to all
     generations.
25 *When* the grass disappears, the new
     growth is seen,
     And the herbs of the mountains are
     gathered in,
26 The lambs *will be* for your clothing,
     And the goats *will bring* the price of
     a field,
27 And *there will be* goats' milk
     enough for your food,
     For the food of your household,
     And sustenance for your maidens.

◈ 1 Timothy 5:1–25

5 DO not sharply rebuke an older man,
   but *rather* appeal to *him* as a father, *to*
the younger men as brothers,
2   the older women as mothers, *and* the
younger women as sisters, in all purity.
3   Honor widows who are widows indeed;
4   but if any widow has children or ◄
grandchildren, they must first learn to
practice piety in regard to their own
family and to make some return to their
parents; for this is acceptable in the sight
of God.
5   Now she who is a widow indeed and
who has been left alone, has fixed her
hope on God and continues in entreaties
and prayers night and day.
6   But she who gives herself to wanton
pleasure is dead even while she lives.
7   Prescribe these things as well, so
that they may be above reproach.
8   But if anyone does not provide for
his own, and especially for those of his
household, he has denied the faith and is
worse than an unbeliever.
9   A widow is to be put on the list only
if she is not less than sixty years old,
having been the wife of one man,
10 having a reputation for good works;
and if she has brought up children, if
she has shown hospitality to strangers,
if she has washed the saints' feet, if she
has assisted those in distress, *and* if
she has devoted herself to every good
work.

LIFE LESSONS

➤ **1 Timothy 5:4 — *If any widow has
children or grandchildren, they must first
learn to practice piety in regard to their
own family and to make some return to
their parents.***

This goes along with Paul's theme
that Christians should take care of
their families (1 Tim. 3:5). We should
honor our widows by caring for them
when they cannot take care of themselves. This may sound extremely difficult—and sometimes it will be. However,
whatever God calls us to do will be
worthwhile and will carry with it unfore-
seen—albeit priceless—blessings.

11 But refuse to put younger widows on the list, for when they feel sensual desires in disregard of Christ, they want to get married,

12 thus incurring condemnation, because they have set aside their previous pledge.

13 At the same time they also learn to be idle, as they go around from house to house; and not merely idle, but also gossips and busybodies, talking about things not proper to mention.

14 Therefore, I want younger widows to get married, bear children, keep house, and give the enemy no occasion for reproach;

15 for some have already turned aside to follow Satan.

16 If any woman who is a believer has dependent widows, she must assist them and the church must not be burdened, so that it may assist those who are widows indeed.

17 The elders who rule well are to be considered worthy of double honor, especially those who work hard at preaching and teaching.

18 For the Scripture says, "YOU SHALL NOT MUZZLE THE OX WHILE HE IS THRESHING," and "The laborer is worthy of his wages."

19 Do not receive an accusation against an elder except on the basis of two or three witnesses.

20 Those who continue in sin, rebuke in the presence of all, so that the rest also will be fearful of sinning.

21 I solemnly charge you in the presence of God and of Christ Jesus and of His chosen angels, to maintain these principles without bias, doing nothing in a spirit of partiality.

22 Do not lay hands upon anyone too hastily and thereby share responsibility

for the sins of others; keep yourself free from sin.

23 No longer drink water exclusively, but use a little wine for the sake of your stomach and your frequent ailments.

24 The sins of some men are quite evident, going before them to judgment; for others, their sins follow after.

25 Likewise also, deeds that are good are quite evident, and those which are otherwise cannot be concealed.

LIFE LESSONS

➣ **1 Timothy 5:20** — *Those who continue in sin, rebuke in the presence of all, so that the rest also will be fearful of sinning.*

*P*aul is speaking here of church leaders. If they abuse their positions and continue in their sin, they must be rebuked publicly—not to shame them, but to let everyone know that God does not approve of their behavior or condone their disobedience. "Teachers . . . will incur a stricter judgment" (James 3:1) because of their influence on the lives of others.

➣ **1 Timothy 5:24** — *The sins of some men are quite evident, going before them to judgment; for others, their sins follow after.*

*C*ertain transgressions are not as obvious as others. For example, some people do pious deeds within the church in order to promote themselves or subvert God's people. To us, it may look as if they are doing good, but they are really undermining the ministry and planting seeds of dissension. God knows the true intentions of our hearts and actions. Eventually, we reap what we sow, more than we sow, and later than we sow. No one gets away with sin.

 Jeremiah 39:1—40:16

39 NOW when Jerusalem was captured in the ninth year of Zedekiah king of Judah, in the tenth month, Nebuchadnezzar king of Babylon and all his

army came to Jerusalem and laid siege to it;

2 in the eleventh year of Zedekiah, in the fourth month, in the ninth day of the month, the city wall was breached.

3 Then all the officials of the king of Babylon came in and sat down at the

Middle Gate: Nergal-sar-ezer, Samgar-nebu, Sar-sekim the Rab-saris, Nergal-sar-ezer *the* Rab-mag, and all the rest of the officials of the king of Babylon.
4 When Zedekiah the king of Judah and all the men of war saw them, they fled and went out of the city at night by way of the king's garden through the gate between the two walls; and he went out toward the Arabah.
5 But the army of the Chaldeans pursued them and overtook Zedekiah in the plains of Jericho; and they seized him and brought him up to Nebuchadnezzar king of Babylon at Riblah in the land of Hamath, and he passed sentence on him.
6 Then the king of Babylon slew the sons of Zedekiah before his eyes at Riblah; the king of Babylon also slew all the nobles of Judah.
7 He then blinded Zedekiah's eyes and bound him in fetters of bronze to bring him to Babylon.
8 The Chaldeans also burned with fire the king's palace and the houses of the people, and they broke down the walls of Jerusalem.
9 As for the rest of the people who were left in the city, the deserters who had gone over to him and the rest of the people who remained, Nebuzaradan the captain of the bodyguard carried *them* into exile in Babylon.
10 But some of the poorest people who had nothing, Nebuzaradan the captain of the bodyguard left behind in the land of Judah, and gave them vineyards and fields at that time.
11 Now Nebuchadnezzar king of Babylon gave orders about Jeremiah through Nebuzaradan the captain of the bodyguard, saying,
12 "Take him and look after him, and do nothing harmful to him, but rather deal with him just as he tells you."
13 So Nebuzaradan the captain of the bodyguard sent *word*, along with Nebushazban the Rab-saris, and Nergal-sar-ezer the Rab-mag, and all the leading officers of the king of Babylon;
14 they even sent and took Jeremiah out of the court of the guardhouse and entrusted him to Gedaliah, the son of Ahikam, the son of Shaphan, to take him home. So he stayed among the people.
15 Now the word of the LORD had come

to Jeremiah while he was confined in the court of the guardhouse, saying,
16 "Go and speak to Ebed-melech the Ethiopian, saying, 'Thus says the LORD of hosts, the God of Israel, "Behold, I am about to bring My words on this city for disaster and not for prosperity; and they will take place before you on that day.
17 "But I will deliver you on that day," declares the LORD, "and you will not be given into the hand of the men whom you dread.
18 "For I will certainly rescue you, and you will not fall by the sword; but you will have your *own* life as booty, because you have trusted in Me," declares the LORD.'"

40 THE word which came to Jeremiah from the LORD after Nebuzaradan captain of the bodyguard had released him from Ramah, when he had taken him bound in chains among all the exiles of Jerusalem and Judah who were being exiled to Babylon.
2 Now the captain of the bodyguard had taken Jeremiah and said to him, "The LORD your God promised this calamity against this place;
3 and the LORD has brought *it* on and done just as He promised. Because you *people* sinned against the LORD and did not listen to His voice, therefore this thing has happened to you.
4 "But now, behold, I am freeing you today from the chains which are on your hands. If you would prefer to come with me to Babylon, come *along*, and I will look after you; but if you would prefer not to come with me to Babylon, never mind. Look, the whole land is before you; go wherever it seems good and right for you to go."
5 As Jeremiah was still not going back, *he said*, "Go on back then to Gedaliah the son of Ahikam, the son of Shaphan,

---

> • • • • • • • **LIFE LESSONS** • • • • • • •

> ➤ **Jeremiah 39:18 — "'You will have your own life as booty, because you have trusted in Me,' declares the LORD."**

*E*bed-melech the Ethiopian had no way of knowing that when he helped Jeremiah he was actually helping himself. He displayed his genuine faith by risking his life for the prophet, and God gave him his life as a reward.

whom the king of Babylon has appointed over the cities of Judah, and stay with him among the people; or else go anywhere it seems right for you to go." So the captain of the bodyguard gave him a ration and a gift and let him go.

6 Then Jeremiah went to Mizpah to Gedaliah the son of Ahikam and stayed with him among the people who were left in the land.

7 Now all the commanders of the forces that were in the field, they and their men, heard that the king of Babylon had appointed Gedaliah the son of Ahikam over the land and that he had put him in charge of the men, women and children, those of the poorest of the land who had not been exiled to Babylon.

8 So they came to Gedaliah at Mizpah, along with Ishmael the son of Nethaniah, and Johanan and Jonathan the sons of Kareah, and Seraiah the son of Tanhumeth, and the sons of Ephai the Netophathite, and Jezaniah the son of the Maacathite, *both* they and their men.

9 Then Gedaliah the son of Ahikam, the son of Shaphan, swore to them and to their men, saying, "Do not be afraid of serving the Chaldeans; stay in the land and serve the king of Babylon, that it may go well with you.

10 "Now as for me, behold, I am going to stay at Mizpah to stand *for you* before the Chaldeans who come to us; but as for you, gather in wine and summer fruit and oil and put *them* in your *storage* vessels, and live in your cities that you have taken over."

11 Likewise, also all the Jews who were in Moab and among the sons of Ammon and in Edom and who were in all the *other* countries, heard that the king of Babylon had left a remnant for Judah, and that he had appointed over them Gedaliah the son of Ahikam, the son of Shaphan.

12 Then all the Jews returned from all the places to which they had been driven away and came to the land of Judah, to Gedaliah at Mizpah, and gathered in wine and summer fruit in great abundance.

13 Now Johanan the son of Kareah and all the commanders of the forces that were in the field came to Gedaliah at Mizpah

14 and said to him, "Are you well aware that Baalis the king of the sons of Ammon

has sent Ishmael the son of Nethaniah to take your life?" But Gedaliah the son of Ahikam did not believe them.

15 Then Johanan the son of Kareah spoke secretly to Gedaliah in Mizpah, saying, "Let me go and kill Ishmael the son of Nethaniah, and not a man will know! Why should he take your life, so that all the Jews who are gathered to you would be scattered and the remnant of Judah would perish?"

16 But Gedaliah the son of Ahikam said to Johanan the son of Kareah, "Do not do this thing, for you are telling a lie about Ishmael."

 Psalm 119:81–88

ב **Kaph.**

81 My soul languishes for Your
     salvation;
   I wait for Your word.

82 My eyes fail *with longing* for Your
     word,
   While I say, "When will You comfort
     me?"

83 Though I have become like a
     wineskin in the smoke,
   I do not forget Your statutes.

84 How many are the days of Your
     servant?
   When will You execute judgment on
     those who persecute me?

85 The arrogant have dug pits for me,
   Men who are not in accord with
     Your law.

86 All Your commandments are faithful;
   They have persecuted me with a lie;
     help me!

87 They almost destroyed me on earth,
   But as for me, I did not forsake Your
     precepts.

88 Revive me according to Your
     lovingkindness,
   So that I may keep the testimony of
     Your mouth.

Proverbs 28:1

28 THE wicked flee when no one is
     pursuing,
   But the righteous are bold as a lion.

1 Timothy 6:1–21

6 ALL who are under the yoke as slaves are to regard their own masters as worthy of all honor so that the name of God and *our* doctrine will not be spoken against.

2   Those who have believers as their masters must not be disrespectful to them because they are brethren, but must serve them all the more, because those who partake of the benefit are believers and beloved. Teach and preach these *principles*.

3   If anyone advocates a different doctrine and does not agree with sound words, those of our Lord Jesus Christ, and with the doctrine conforming to godliness,

4   he is conceited *and* understands nothing; but he has a morbid interest in controversial questions and disputes about words, out of which arise envy, strife, abusive language, evil suspicions,

5   and constant friction between men of depraved mind and deprived of the truth, who suppose that godliness is a means of gain.

6   But godliness *actually* is a means of great gain when accompanied by contentment.

7   For we have brought nothing into the world, so we cannot take anything out of it either.

8   If we have food and covering, with these we shall be content.

9   But those who want to get rich fall into temptation and a snare and many foolish and harmful desires which plunge men into ruin and destruction.

10   For the love of money is a root of all sorts of evil, and some by longing for it have wandered away from the faith and pierced themselves with many griefs.

11   But flee from these things, you man of God, and pursue righteousness, godliness, faith, love, perseverance *and* gentleness.

12   Fight the good fight of faith; take hold of the eternal life to which you were called, and you made the good confession in the presence of many witnesses.

13   I charge you in the presence of God, who gives life to all things, and of Christ Jesus, who testified the good confession before Pontius Pilate,

14   that you keep the commandment without stain or reproach until the appearing of our Lord Jesus Christ,

15   which He will bring about at the proper time—He who is the blessed and only Sovereign, the King of kings and Lord of lords,

16   who alone possesses immortality and dwells in unapproachable light, whom no man has seen or can see. To Him *be* honor and eternal dominion! Amen.

17   Instruct those who are rich in this present world not to be conceited or to fix their hope on the uncertainty of riches, but on God, who richly supplies us with all things to enjoy.

18   *Instruct them* to do good, to be rich in good works, to be generous and ready to share,

19   storing up for themselves the treasure of a good foundation for the future,

LIFE LESSONS

➤ **1 Timothy 6:9 — *Those who want to get rich fall into temptation.***

The Bible condemns the desire to get rich, not because having money is a sin, but because money makes a terrible master. People who make it their goal to get rich do serve money—and therefore can't serve God (Matt. 6:24).

➤ **1 Timothy 6:12 — *Fight the good fight of faith.***

We must be unreservedly committed to Christ—regardless of our circumstances, challenges, or obstacles—realizing this leads to spiritual victory and eternal hope. We must believe in Him and obey with all our hearts, souls, minds, and strengths—standing firm for Him and representing Him well in the world so that others will believe in Him and be saved.

➤ **1 Timothy 6:18 — *Instruct them to do good, to be rich in good works.***

God blesses us financially and with our talents, not simply so that we can spend the resources He has given us on ourselves, but so that we can use them to help others and to expand His kingdom.

ANSWERS TO LIFE'S QUESTIONS

How can I learn to feel content?

1 TIMOTHY 6:7, 8

*M*any in today's workforce feel deeply discontented. "If only I had a better boss ... If only I could make more money ... If I could just work for *that* company ..." And so it goes.

Two thousand years ago, John the Baptist exhorted disgruntled Roman soldiers to be content with their wages (Luke 3:14). This is still good advice.

We can grow content when we see God as our sole Provider: "Give me neither poverty nor riches; feed me with the food that is my portion, that I not be full and deny You and say, 'Who is the Lord?' or that I not be in want and steal, and profane the name of my God" (Prov. 30:8, 9).

We can also grow discontent as we focus on the necessities of life. Paul reminds us: "For we have brought nothing into the world, so we cannot take anything out of it either. If we have food and covering, with these we shall be content" (1 Tim. 6:7, 8).

Much of our restlessness comes from desiring the many perks our affluent culture offers. But do we really need them? Can we get along without designer clothes? The answer is yes. While God often supplies many of our wants out of His goodness and grace, He really wants us to enjoy what He has given and have hearts of gratitude. He promises to supply our needs but when He gives us more than just the basics, we need to be very humble and grateful.

How do we become content? We do this by asking Him to teach us how to have gratitude for what we have, rather than complain about what we're missing: "Make sure that your character is free from the love of money, being content with what you have" (Heb. 13:5). Solomon said, "What the eyes see is better than what the soul desires" (Eccl. 6:9).

God already has blessed us with so much. And Satan is the one who seeks to redirect our focus to what eludes us, thus fostering a malignant virus of discontent. Instead of falling for his lies, why not take inventory of all that God has blessed you with and thank Him for each and every blessing?

We find our greatest source of contentment, of course, in a delightful relationship with Jesus Christ: "Not that I speak from want, for I have learned to be content in whatever circumstances I am ... I can do all things through Him who strengthens me" (Phil. 4:11, 13). Paul faced many trials and difficulties. Some were very hard to bear, but he was satisfied and content because he had an intimate relationship with the Savior and nothing had more value than this. Can you say that this is true of your life?

"Delight yourself in the Lord; and He will give you the desires of your heart" (Ps. 37:4).

---

so that they may take hold of that which is life indeed.
20 O Timothy, guard what has been entrusted to you, avoiding worldly *and* empty chatter *and* the opposing arguments of what is falsely called "knowledge"—
21 which some have professed and thus gone astray from the faith.

Grace be with you.

Jeremiah 41:1—42:22

41 IN the seventh month Ishmael the son of Nethaniah, the son of Elishama, of the royal family and *one* of the chief officers of the king, along with ten men, came to Mizpah to Gedaliah the son of Ahikam. While they were eating bread together there in Mizpah,
2 Ishmael the son of Nethaniah and the ten men who were with him arose and struck down Gedaliah the son of Ahikam, the son of Shaphan, with the sword and put to death the one whom the king of Babylon had appointed over the land.
3 Ishmael also struck down all the Jews who were with him, *that is* with Gedaliah at Mizpah, and the Chaldeans who were found there, the men of war.
4 Now it happened on the next day after the killing of Gedaliah, when no one knew about *it*,
5 that eighty men came from Shechem, from Shiloh, and from Samaria with their

beards shaved off and their clothes torn and their bodies gashed, having grain offerings and incense in their hands to bring to the house of the LORD.

6 Then Ishmael the son of Nethaniah went out from Mizpah to meet them, weeping as he went; and as he met them, he said to them, "Come to Gedaliah the son of Ahikam!"

7 Yet it turned out that as soon as they came inside the city, Ishmael the son of Nethaniah and the men that were with him slaughtered them *and cast them* into the cistern.

8 But ten men who were found among them said to Ishmael, "Do not put us to death; for we have stores of wheat, barley, oil and honey hidden in the field." So he refrained and did not put them to death along with their companions.

9 Now as for the cistern where Ishmael had cast all the corpses of the men whom he had struck down because of Gedaliah, it was the one that King Asa had made on account of Baasha, king of Israel; Ishmael the son of Nethaniah filled it with the slain.

10 Then Ishmael took captive all the remnant of the people who were in Mizpah, the king's daughters and all the people who were left in Mizpah, whom Nebuzaradan the captain of the bodyguard had put under the charge of Gedaliah the son of Ahikam; thus Ishmael the son of Nethaniah took them captive and proceeded to cross over to the sons of Ammon.

11 But Johanan the son of Kareah and all the commanders of the forces that were with him heard of all the evil that Ishmael the son of Nethaniah had done.

12 So they took all the men and went to fight with Ishmael the son of Nethaniah and they found him by the great pool that is in Gibeon.

13 Now as soon as all the people who were with Ishmael saw Johanan the son of Kareah and the commanders of the forces that were with him, they were glad.

14 So all the people whom Ishmael had taken captive from Mizpah turned around and came back, and went to Johanan the son of Kareah.

➤ 15 But Ishmael the son of Nethaniah escaped from Johanan with eight men and went to the sons of Ammon.

16 Then Johanan the son of Kareah and all the commanders of the forces that were with him took from Mizpah all the remnant of the people whom he had recovered from Ishmael the son of Nethaniah, after he had struck down Gedaliah the son of Ahikam, *that is,* the men who were soldiers, *the* women, *the* children, and *the* eunuchs, whom he had brought back from Gibeon.

17 And they went and stayed in Geruth Chimham, which is beside Bethlehem, in order to proceed into Egypt

18 because of the Chaldeans; for they were afraid of them, since Ishmael the son of Nethaniah had struck down Gedaliah the son of Ahikam, whom the king of Babylon had appointed over the land.

42 THEN all the commanders of the forces, Johanan the son of Kareah, Jezaniah the son of Hoshaiah, and all the people both small and great approached

2 and said to Jeremiah the prophet, "Please let our petition come before you, and pray for us to the LORD your God, *that is* for all this remnant; because we are left *but* a few out of many, as your own eyes *now* see us,

3 that the LORD your God may tell us

LIFE LESSONS

➤ **Jeremiah 41:15** — *Ishmael the son of Nethaniah escaped from Johanan with eight men and went to the sons of Ammon.*

In Hollywood, the bad guy is usually apprehended or defeated at the end of the movie. But the Bible is realistic; it admits that life doesn't always happen that way—at least, not on this side of heaven. But no one escapes the final judgment (Rev. 20:11–15).

➤ **Jeremiah 42:2, 3** — *"Pray for us . . . that the LORD your God may tell us the way in which we should walk and the thing that we should do."*

It is not hard to play the part of regular churchgoer and hymn-singer, but God is after genuine faith, not well-rehearsed lines spoken convincingly. The men said all the right words, but they had no intention of obeying the Lord. They already had a plan; they merely wanted Jeremiah to bless it. Such prayers and plans God will never honor.

the way in which we should walk and the thing that we should do."

4   Then Jeremiah the prophet said to them, "I have heard you. Behold, I am going to pray to the LORD your God in accordance with your words; and I will tell you the whole message which the LORD will answer you. I will not keep back a word from you."

5   Then they said to Jeremiah, "May the LORD be a true and faithful witness against us if we do not act in accordance with the whole message with which the LORD your God will send you to us.

6   "Whether it is pleasant or unpleasant, we will listen to the voice of the LORD our God to whom we are sending you, so that it may go well with us when we listen to the voice of the LORD our God."

7   Now at the end of ten days the word of the LORD came to Jeremiah.

8   Then he called for Johanan the son of Kareah and all the commanders of the forces that were with him, and for all the people both small and great,

9   and said to them, "Thus says the LORD the God of Israel, to whom you sent me to present your petition before Him:

10   'If you will indeed stay in this land, then I will build you up and not tear you down, and I will plant you and not uproot you; for I will relent concerning the calamity that I have inflicted on you.

11   'Do not be afraid of the king of Babylon, whom you are now fearing; do not be afraid of him,' declares the LORD, 'for I am with you to save you and deliver you from his hand.

12   'I will also show you compassion, so that he will have compassion on you and restore you to your own soil.

13   'But if you are going to say, "We will not stay in this land," so as not to listen to the voice of the LORD your God,

14   saying, "No, but we will go to the land of Egypt, where we will not see war or hear the sound of a trumpet or hunger for bread, and we will stay there";

15   then in that case listen to the word of the LORD, O remnant of Judah. Thus says the LORD of hosts, the God of Israel, "If you really set your mind to enter Egypt and go in to reside there,

16   then the sword, which you are afraid of, will overtake you there in the land of Egypt; and the famine, about which you

are anxious, will follow closely after you there in Egypt, and you will die there.

17   "So all the men who set their mind to go to Egypt to reside there will die by the sword, by famine and by pestilence; and they will have no survivors or refugees from the calamity that I am going to bring on them."'"

18   For thus says the LORD of hosts, the God of Israel, "As My anger and wrath have been poured out on the inhabitants of Jerusalem, so My wrath will be poured out on you when you enter Egypt. And you will become a curse, an object of horror, an imprecation and a reproach; and you will see this place no more."

19   The LORD has spoken to you, O remnant of Judah, "Do not go into Egypt!" You should clearly understand that today I have testified against you.

20   For you have only deceived your- ⤺ selves; for it is you who sent me to the LORD your God, saying, "Pray for us to the LORD our God; and whatever the LORD our God says, tell us so, and we will do it."

21   So I have told you today, but you have not obeyed the LORD your God, even in whatever He has sent me to tell you.

22   Therefore you should now clearly understand that you will die by the sword, by famine and by pestilence, in the place where you wish to go to reside.

✦ Psalm 119:89–96

ל Lamedh.

89   Forever, O LORD,
    Your word is settled in heaven.
90   Your faithfulness continues
        throughout all generations;
    You established the earth, and it
        stands.

LIFE LESSONS

➤ **Jeremiah 42:20 — "You have only deceived yourselves."**

*B*efore these men ever acted on their deception, Jeremiah openly revealed their hearts. We may fool others, but we do not fool God. We can never manipulate Him into giving us what we want.

91 They stand this day according to
Your ordinances,
For all things are Your servants.
92 If Your law had not been my
delight,
Then I would have perished in my
affliction.
93 I will never forget Your precepts,
For by them You have revived me.
94 I am Yours, save me;
For I have sought Your precepts.
95 The wicked wait for me to destroy
me;
I shall diligently consider Your
testimonies.
96 I have seen a limit to all perfection;
Your commandment is exceedingly
broad.

Proverbs 28:2

2 By the transgression of a land many
are its princes,
But by a man of understanding and
knowledge, so it endures.

2 Timothy 1:1–18

1 PAUL, an apostle of Christ Jesus
by the will of God, according to the
promise of life in Christ Jesus,
2 To Timothy, my beloved son: Grace,
mercy and peace from God the Father
and Christ Jesus our Lord.
3 I thank God, whom I serve with a
clear conscience the way my forefathers
did, as I constantly remember you in my
prayers night and day,
4 longing to see you, even as I recall
your tears, so that I may be filled with
joy.
5 For I am mindful of the sincere faith
within you, which first dwelt in your
grandmother Lois and your mother Eunice, and I am sure that it is in you as well.
6 For this reason I remind you to
kindle afresh the gift of God which is in
you through the laying on of my hands.
7 For God has not given us a spirit of
timidity, but of power and love and discipline.
8 Therefore do not be ashamed of
the testimony of our Lord or of me His

prisoner, but join with me in suffering
for the gospel according to the power
of God,
9 who has saved us and called us
with a holy calling, not according to our
works, but according to His own purpose and grace which was granted us in
Christ Jesus from all eternity,
10 but now has been revealed by the appearing of our Savior Christ Jesus, who
abolished death and brought life and immortality to light through the gospel,
11 for which I was appointed a preacher
and an apostle and a teacher.

LIFE LESSONS

> 2 Timothy 1:3 — *I constantly remem-
ber you in my prayers night and day.*

This was Paul's last letter. He knew
he would soon be facing death
and that he would no longer be able
to encourage Timothy and the many
who made up the churches that he had
helped to establish throughout the
known world. But he also knew that
the Holy Spirit would continue to guide
and lift up the body of Christ. Yet up to
the end, the apostle remained faithful
to pray for Timothy. Why? Because Paul
knew that every spiritual battle was won
on his knees in prayer. He testified, "I
know whom I have believed and I am
convinced that He is able to guard what
I have entrusted to Him"
(2 Tim. 1:12).

> 2 Timothy 1:6 — *Kindle afresh the gift
of God which is in you.*

God never takes away the spiritual
gifts He bestows upon us (Rom.
11:29), but they can lose their sharp
edge of effectiveness through our
neglect. God instructs us to use our gifts
for the benefit of His people (1 Pet. 4:10).

> 2 Timothy 1:8 — *Do not be ashamed
of the testimony of our Lord.*

Sometimes we may be tempted to
keep quiet about our faith in Christ
because of our fear of what others will
think of us. Yet it is a great privilege to
represent Him, and we must do so with
boldness and enthusiasm, remembering
that it may mean eternal life for those
who hear our testimonies and respond
to the Lord Jesus in faith.

ANSWERS TO LIFE'S QUESTIONS

How can I combat my fears?

2 TIMOTHY 1:7

*P*aul's words to Timothy are equally God's words to you. He has given each one of us "a spirit ... of power and love and discipline" (2 Tim. 1:7). Therefore, we never should respond to circumstances or people in fear because we have the power of God living within us—the very power that dispels all fear and anxiety.

1. Ask for God's help.

When fear strikes, immediately ask for God's help. Tap into His power and allow Him to encourage your heart. Remember when Peter tried to walk on the water to Jesus, but his fear overcame him (Matt. 14:30)? When he found himself in trouble and fear—sinking in the sea—he had the right response. He asked for God's help. "Lord, save me!" This is your best first response any time you feel fearful.

2. Ask the Lord to fill your heart with a sense of His abiding love.

Love is a powerful antidote to fear. God's love has the ability to eliminate it. I remember the first time I preached in my home church. I was young and had a "fear attack." I felt

the people would expect more from me than a group of strangers might expect. So what helped me? I read the words of the Lord to Joshua in Joshua 1:5–9, and then I turned my focus to the people of my home church. I felt overwhelmed by how much I loved them and how they had loved me through the years. By the time I stood in the pulpit, the fear had completely drained out of me. John tells us, "There is no fear in love; but perfect love casts out fear" (1 John 4:18). Ask your heavenly Father to impart to you more of Christ's love and to take away any torment you feel. As you do, fear will lose its grip on you.

3. Ask God to give you a sound mind, filled with and operating according to God's Word.

The basis for a sound mind is the Word of God. The more you know of God's promises and the more you live according to His commandments, the greater your strength to withstand fear. Use Scripture to speak directly to the source of your fear, just as Jesus quoted Scripture to Satan during His time of temptation in the wilderness (Luke 4:1–13).

When you feel gripped by fear, turn your gaze to Jesus, redirect your heart to His love, speak to your fear from the Word of God, and then respond boldly to the situation. The Lord's desire is for you to "Be strong and courageous" today (Josh. 1:9).

---

12 For this reason I also suffer these things, but I am not ashamed; for I know whom I have believed and I am convinced that He is able to guard what I have entrusted to Him until that day.
13 Retain the standard of sound words which you have heard from me, in the faith and love which are in Christ Jesus.
14 Guard, through the Holy Spirit who dwells in us, the treasure which has been entrusted to *you*.
15 You are aware of the fact that all

who are in Asia turned away from me, among whom are Phygelus and Hermogenes.
16 The Lord grant mercy to the house of Onesiphorus, for he often refreshed me and was not ashamed of my chains;
17 but when he was in Rome, he eagerly searched for me and found me—
18 the Lord grant to him to find mercy from the Lord on that day—and you know very well what services he rendered at Ephesus.

◈ Jeremiah 43:1—44:30

43 BUT as soon as Jeremiah, whom the LORD their God had sent, had finished telling all the people all the words of the LORD their God—that is, all these words—
2 Azariah the son of Hoshaiah, and Johanan the son of Kareah, and all the

arrogant men said to Jeremiah, "You are telling a lie! The LORD our God has not sent you to say, 'You are not to enter Egypt to reside there';
3 but Baruch the son of Neriah is inciting you against us to give us over into the hand of the Chaldeans, so they will put us to death or exile us to Babylon."
4 So Johanan the son of Kareah and all the commanders of the forces, and all

the people, did not obey the voice of the LORD to stay in the land of Judah.

➤ 5   But Johanan the son of Kareah and all the commanders of the forces took the entire remnant of Judah who had returned from all the nations to which they had been driven away, in order to reside in the land of Judah—

6   the men, the women, the children, the king's daughters and every person that Nebuzaradan the captain of the bodyguard had left with Gedaliah the son of Ahikam and grandson of Shaphan, together with Jeremiah the prophet and Baruch the son of Neriah—

7   and they entered the land of Egypt (for they did not obey the voice of the LORD) and went in as far as Tahpanhes.

8   Then the word of the LORD came to Jeremiah in Tahpanhes, saying,

9   "Take *some* large stones in your hands and hide them in the mortar in the brick *terrace* which is at the entrance of Pharaoh's palace in Tahpanhes, in the sight of some *of the* Jews;

10   and say to them, 'Thus says the LORD of hosts, the God of Israel, "Behold, I am going to send and get Nebuchadnezzar the king of Babylon, My servant, and I am going to set his throne *right* over these stones that I have hidden; and he will spread his canopy over them.

11   "He will also come and strike the land of Egypt; those who are *meant* for death *will be given over* to death, and those for captivity to captivity, and those for the sword to the sword.

12   "And I shall set fire to the temples of the gods of Egypt, and he will burn them and take them captive. So he will wrap himself with the land of Egypt as a shepherd wraps himself with his garment, and he will depart from there safely.

13   "He will also shatter the obelisks of Heliopolis, which is in the land of Egypt; and the temples of the gods of Egypt he will burn with fire." '"

44   THE word that came to Jeremiah for all the Jews living in the land of Egypt, those who were living in Migdol, Tahpanhes, Memphis, and the land of Pathros, saying,

2   "Thus says the LORD of hosts, the God of Israel, 'You yourselves have seen all the calamity that I have brought on Jerusalem and all the cities of Judah; and

behold, this day they are in ruins and no one lives in them,

3   because of their wickedness which they committed so as to provoke Me to anger by continuing to burn sacrifices *and* to serve other gods whom they had not known, *neither* they, you, nor your fathers.

4   'Yet I sent you all My servants the ◄ prophets, again and again, saying, "Oh, do not do this abominable thing which I hate."

5   'But they did not listen or incline their ears to turn from their wickedness, so as not to burn sacrifices to other gods.

6   'Therefore My wrath and My anger were poured out and burned in the cities of Judah and in the streets of Jerusalem, so they have become a ruin and a desolation as it is this day.

7   'Now then thus says the LORD God of hosts, the God of Israel, "Why are you doing great harm to yourselves, so as to cut off from you man and woman, child and infant, from among Judah, leaving yourselves without remnant,

8   provoking Me to anger with the works of your hands, burning sacrifices to other gods in the land of Egypt, where you are entering to reside, so that you might be cut off and become a curse and a reproach among all the nations of the earth?

LIFE LESSONS

➤ **Jeremiah 43:5, 6 —** *The commanders of the forces took the entire remnant of Judah . . . together with Jeremiah the prophet and Baruch the son of Neriah.*

*J*eremiah told the remnant not to move to Egypt, but they disobeyed and moved there anyway—and took him along as a captive. He suffered for their disobedience. By faith—he had nothing else—Jeremiah expected God to vindicate him.

➤ **Jeremiah 44:4 —** *"Do not do this abominable thing which I hate."*

*I*f necessary, God will move heaven and earth to show us His will and convict us of our sin. Will we listen carefully for what He says and obey Him? Or will we continue sinning without repentance?

9 "Have you forgotten the wickedness of your fathers, the wickedness of the kings of Judah, and the wickedness of their wives, your own wickedness, and the wickedness of your wives, which they committed in the land of Judah and in the streets of Jerusalem?

10 "But they have not become contrite even to this day, nor have they feared nor walked in My law or My statutes, which I have set before you and before your fathers."'

11 "Therefore thus says the LORD of hosts, the God of Israel, 'Behold, I am going to set My face against you for woe, even to cut off all Judah.

12 'And I will take away the remnant of Judah who have set their mind on entering the land of Egypt to reside there, and they will all meet their end in the land of Egypt; they will fall by the sword *and* meet their end by famine. Both small and great will die by the sword and famine; and they will become a curse, an object of horror, an imprecation and a reproach.

13 'And I will punish those who live in the land of Egypt, as I have punished Jerusalem, with the sword, with famine and with pestilence.

14 'So there will be no refugees or survivors for the remnant of Judah who have entered the land of Egypt to reside there and then to return to the land of Judah, to which they are longing to return and live; for none will return except *a few* refugees.'"

15 Then all the men who were aware that their wives were burning sacrifices to other gods, along with all the women who were standing by, *as* a large assembly, including all the people who were living in Pathros in the land of Egypt, responded to Jeremiah, saying,

16 "As for the message that you have spoken to us in the name of the LORD, we are not going to listen to you!

17 "But rather we will certainly carry out every word that has proceeded from our mouths, by burning sacrifices to the queen of heaven and pouring out drink offerings to her, just as we ourselves, our forefathers, our kings and our princes did in the cities of Judah and in the streets of Jerusalem; for *then* we had plenty of food and were well off and saw no misfortune.

18 "But since we stopped burning sacrifices to the queen of heaven and pouring out drink offerings to her, we have lacked everything and have met our end by the sword and by famine."

19 "And," *said the women,* "when we were burning sacrifices to the queen of heaven and were pouring out drink offerings to her, was it without our husbands that we made for her *sacrificial* cakes in her image and poured out drink offerings to her?"

20 Then Jeremiah said to all the people, to the men and women—even to all the people who were giving him *such* an answer—saying,

21 "As for the smoking sacrifices that you burned in the cities of Judah and in the streets of Jerusalem, you and your forefathers, your kings and your princes, and the people of the land, did not the LORD remember them and did not *all this* come into His mind?

22 "So the LORD was no longer able to endure *it,* because of the evil of your deeds, because of the abominations which you have committed; thus your land has become a ruin, an object of horror and a curse, without an inhabitant, as *it is* this day.

23 "Because you have burned sacrifices and have sinned against the LORD and not obeyed the voice of the LORD or walked in His law, His statutes or His testimonies, therefore this calamity has befallen you, as *it has* this day."

24 Then Jeremiah said to all the people, including all the women, "Hear the word of the LORD, all Judah who are in the land of Egypt,

25 thus says the LORD of hosts, the God of Israel, as follows: 'As for you and your wives, you have spoken with your mouths and fulfilled *it* with your hands, saying, "We will certainly perform our vows that we have vowed, to burn sacrifices to the queen of heaven and pour out drink offerings to her." Go ahead and confirm your vows, and certainly perform your vows!'

26 "Nevertheless hear the word of the LORD, all Judah who are living in the land of Egypt, 'Behold, I have sworn by My great name,' says the LORD, 'never shall My name be invoked again by the mouth of any man of Judah in all the land of Egypt, saying, "As the Lord GOD lives."

27 'Behold, I am watching over them for harm and not for good, and all the men of Judah who are in the land of Egypt will meet their end by the sword and by famine until they are completely gone.
28 'Those who escape the sword will return out of the land of Egypt to the land of Judah few in number. Then all the remnant of Judah who have gone to the land of Egypt to reside there will know whose word will stand, Mine or theirs.
29 'This will be the sign to you,' declares the LORD, 'that I am going to punish you in this place, so that you may know that My words will surely stand against you for harm.'
30 "Thus says the LORD, 'Behold, I am going to give over Pharaoh Hophra king of Egypt to the hand of his enemies, to the hand of those who seek his life, just as I gave over Zedekiah king of Judah to the hand of Nebuchadnezzar king of Babylon, who was his enemy and was seeking his life.'"

✦ Psalm 119:97–104

 מ Mem.

97 O how I love Your law!
   It is my meditation all the day.
98 Your commandments make me
      wiser than my enemies,
   For they are ever mine.
99 I have more insight than all my
      teachers,
   For Your testimonies are my
      meditation.
✳ 100 I understand more than the aged,
   Because I have observed Your
      precepts.
101 I have restrained my feet from
      every evil way,
   That I may keep Your word.
102 I have not turned aside from Your
      ordinances,
   For You Yourself have taught me.
103 How sweet are Your words to my
      taste!
   Yes, sweeter than honey to my
      mouth!
104 From Your precepts I get
      understanding;
   Therefore I hate every false way.

✦ Proverbs 28:3

3   A poor man who oppresses the
      lowly
   Is like a driving rain which leaves
      no food.

✦ 2 Timothy 2:1–26

2 YOU therefore, my son, be strong in ◄ the grace that is in Christ Jesus.
2   The things which you have heard from me in the presence of many witnesses, entrust these to faithful men who will be able to teach others also.
3   Suffer hardship with me, as a good ◄ soldier of Christ Jesus.
4   No soldier in active service entangles himself in the affairs of everyday life, so that he may please the one who enlisted him as a soldier.
5   Also if anyone competes as an athlete, he does not win the prize unless he competes according to the rules.
6   The hard-working farmer ought to be the first to receive his share of the crops.
7   Consider what I say, for the Lord ◄ will give you understanding in everything.
8   Remember Jesus Christ, risen from the dead, descendant of David, according to my gospel,

---

LIFE LESSONS

➤ 2 Timothy 2:1 — Be strong in the grace that is in Christ Jesus.

Paul doesn't encourage Timothy merely to "be strong"—any one can do that (1 Sam. 4:9). He encourages him to be strong in the grace of Jesus. Only in God's strength can we become strong.

➤ 2 Timothy 2:3 — Suffer hardship with me, as a good soldier of Christ Jesus.

If we are in a spiritual war, then we must be soldiers in God's army—and that's exactly what Paul tells Timothy. Soldiers are called on to endure hardship in order to win their wars ... and so are we.

WHAT THE BIBLE SAYS ABOUT ◉

Words That Build Eternally

2 Timothy 2:14–26

*Y*our words can build someone up or tear someone down. They can be a blessing or a curse. They can build bridges to the kingdom of God or put up roadblocks. Words reflect who you are.

George Crane said, "Language is the apparel in which your thoughts parade before the public."

What do your words show you to be clothed with? Do they witness to your love of God and dependence upon his grace? Or do your words testify to a sinful war in your heart? Do you encourage people toward Christ or dishearten them from ever entering the kingdom?

In 2 Timothy 2:24–26 Paul admonishes, "The Lord's bond-servant must not be quarrelsome, but be kind to all, able to teach, patient when wronged, with gentleness correcting those who are in opposition, if perhaps God may grant them repentance leading to the knowledge of the truth, and they may come to their senses and escape from the snare of the devil, having been held captive by him to do his will."

A servant of God should watch his or her words because words have eternal value to those who are listening to them. The more your words are clothed with grace, the more you can be sure you are building bridges to the kingdom. ◉

---

9 for which I suffer hardship even to imprisonment as a criminal; but the word of God is not imprisoned.
10 For this reason I endure all things for the sake of those who are chosen, so that they also may obtain the salvation which is in Christ Jesus *and* with *it* eternal glory.
11 It is a trustworthy statement:
For if we died with Him, we will also live with Him;
12 If we endure, we will also reign with Him;
If we deny Him, He also will deny us;
13 If we are faithless, He remains faithful, for He cannot deny Himself.
14 Remind *them* of these things, and solemnly charge *them* in the presence of God not to wrangle about words, which is useless *and leads* to the ruin of the hearers.
15 Be diligent to present yourself approved to God as a workman who does not need to be ashamed, accurately handling the word of truth.
16 But avoid worldly *and* empty chatter, for it will lead to further ungodliness,
17 and their talk will spread like gangrene. Among them are Hymenaeus and Philetus,
18 *men* who have gone astray from the truth saying that the resurrection has already taken place, and they upset the faith of some.
19 Nevertheless, the firm foundation of ◄ God stands, having this seal, "The Lord knows those who are His," and, "Everyone who names the name of the Lord is to abstain from wickedness."
20 Now in a large house there are not only gold and silver vessels, but also vessels of wood and of earthenware, and some to honor and some to dishonor.
21 Therefore, if anyone cleanses himself from these *things*, he will be a vessel

---

LIFE LESSONS

➤ **2 Timothy 2:7 — *The Lord will give you understanding in everything.***

*H*ow do we gain spiritual understanding? First, we have to meditate on what God says in His Word—pondering it and turning it over in our minds. Then we have to ask Him to apply His truth to our hearts in a practical way so we can live it out in obedience. Both work together.

➤ **2 Timothy 2:19 — *"Everyone who names the name of the Lord is to abstain from wickedness."***

*I*f we claim to be Christians, then we must live according to His calling and standards. His grace does not free us to sin; it gives us the strength and the desire to gladly submit to His will.

for honor, sanctified, useful to the Master, prepared for every good work.

22 Now flee from youthful lusts and pursue righteousness, faith, love *and* peace, with those who call on the Lord from a pure heart.

23 But refuse foolish and ignorant speculations, knowing that they produce quarrels.

24 The Lord's bond-servant must not be quarrelsome, but be kind to all, able to teach, patient when wronged,

25 with gentleness correcting those who are in opposition, if perhaps God may grant them repentance leading to the knowledge of the truth,

26 and they may come to their senses *and escape* from the snare of the devil, having been held captive by him to do his will.

Jeremiah 45:1—46:28

45 THIS is the message which Jeremiah the prophet spoke to Baruch the son of Neriah, when he had written down these words in a book at Jeremiah's dictation, in the fourth year of Jehoiakim the son of Josiah, king of Judah, saying:

2 "Thus says the LORD the God of Israel to you, O Baruch:

3 'You said, "Ah, woe is me! For the LORD has added sorrow to my pain; I am weary with my groaning and have found no rest."'

4 "Thus you are to say to him, 'Thus says the LORD, "Behold, what I have built I am about to tear down, and what I have planted I am about to uproot, that is, the whole land."

➤ 5 'But you, are you seeking great things for yourself? Do not seek *them*; for behold, I am going to bring disaster on all flesh,' declares the LORD, 'but I will give your life to you as booty in all the places where you may go.'"

LIFE LESSONS

➤ **Jeremiah 45:5 — "I will give your life to you as booty in all the places where you may go."**

*A*s He did with Ebed-melech, God promised to spare the life of Jeremiah's servant, Baruch, although His judgment would destroy Jerusalem. We must remember that God has a distinct plan for each of us, and it is always His very best for us.

---

46 THAT which came as the word of the LORD to Jeremiah the prophet concerning the nations.

2 To Egypt, concerning the army of Pharaoh Neco king of Egypt, which was by the Euphrates River at Carchemish, which Nebuchadnezzar king of Babylon defeated in the fourth year of Jehoiakim the son of Josiah, king of Judah:

3 "Line up the shield and buckler,
    And draw near for the battle!

4 "Harness the horses,
    And mount the steeds,
    And take your stand with helmets *on!*
    Polish the spears,
    Put on the scale-armor!

5 "Why have I seen *it?*
    They are terrified,
    They are drawing back,
    And their mighty men are defeated
    And have taken refuge in flight,
    Without facing back;
    Terror is on every side!"
    Declares the LORD.

6 Let not the swift man flee,
    Nor the mighty man escape;
    In the north beside the river Euphrates
    They have stumbled and fallen.

7 Who is this that rises like the Nile,
    Like the rivers whose waters surge about?

8 Egypt rises like the Nile,
    Even like the rivers whose waters surge about;
    And He has said, "I will rise and cover *that* land;
    I will surely destroy the city and its inhabitants."

9 Go up, you horses, and drive madly,
    you chariots,
    That the mighty men may march
    forward:
    Ethiopia and Put, that handle the
    shield,
    And the Lydians, that handle *and*
    bend the bow.
10 For that day belongs to the Lord
    GOD of hosts,
    A day of vengeance, so as to avenge
    Himself on His foes;
    And the sword will devour and be
    satiated
    And drink its fill of their blood;
    For there will be a slaughter for the
    Lord GOD of hosts,
    In the land of the north by the river
    Euphrates.
11 Go up to Gilead and obtain balm,
    O virgin daughter of Egypt!
    In vain have you multiplied
    remedies;
    There is no healing for you.
12 The nations have heard of your
    shame,
    And the earth is full of your cry *of*
    distress;
    For one warrior has stumbled over
    another,
    And both of them have fallen down
    together.

13 *This is* the message which the LORD spoke to Jeremiah the prophet about the coming of Nebuchadnezzar king of Babylon to smite the land of Egypt:

14 "Declare in Egypt and proclaim in
    Migdol,
    Proclaim also in Memphis and
    Tahpanhes;
    Say, 'Take your stand and get
    yourself ready,
    For the sword has devoured those
    around you.'
15 "Why have your mighty ones become
    prostrate?
    They do not stand because the LORD
    has thrust them down.
16 "They have repeatedly stumbled;
    Indeed, they have fallen one against
    another.
    Then they said, 'Get up! And let us
    go back
    To our own people and our native
    land
    Away from the sword of the
    oppressor.'

17 "They cried there, 'Pharaoh king of
    Egypt *is but* a big noise;
    He has let the appointed time pass
    by!'
18 "As I live," declares the King
    Whose name is the LORD of hosts,
    "Surely one shall come *who looms*
    up like Tabor among the
    mountains,
    Or like Carmel by the sea.
19 "Make your baggage ready for exile,
    O daughter dwelling in Egypt,
    For Memphis will become a
    desolation;
    It will even be burned down *and*
    bereft of inhabitants.
20 "Egypt is a pretty heifer,
    But a horsefly is coming from the
    north—it is coming!
21 "Also her mercenaries in her midst
    Are like fattened calves,
    For even they too have turned back
    and have fled away together;
    They did not stand *their ground.*
    For the day of their calamity has
    come upon them,
    The time of their punishment.
22 "Its sound moves along like a
    serpent;
    For they move on like an army
    And come to her as woodcutters
    with axes.
23 "They have cut down her forest,"
    declares the LORD;
    "Surely it will no *more* be found,
    Even though they are *now* more
    numerous than locusts
    And are without number.
24 "The daughter of Egypt has been put
    to shame,
    Given over to the power of the
    people of the north."

25 The LORD of hosts, the God of Israel, says, "Behold, I am going to punish Amon of Thebes, and Pharaoh, and Egypt along with her gods and her kings, even Pharaoh and those who trust in him.

26 "I shall give them over to the power of those who are seeking their lives, even into the hand of Nebuchadnezzar king of Babylon and into the hand of his officers. Afterwards, however, it will be inhabited as in the days of old," declares the LORD.

27 "But as for you, O Jacob My servant, do not fear,
    Nor be dismayed, O Israel!

For, see, I am going to save you
from afar,
And your descendants from the
land of their captivity;
And Jacob will return and be
undisturbed
And secure, with no one making
him tremble.

➤ 28 "O Jacob My servant, do not fear,"
declares the LORD,
"For I am with you.
For I will make a full end of all the
nations
Where I have driven you,
Yet I will not make a full end of you;
But I will correct you properly
And by no means leave you
unpunished."

Psalm 119:105–112

ב Nun.

➤ 105 Your word is a lamp to my feet
✳ And a light to my path.
106 I have sworn and I will confirm it,
That I will keep Your righteous
ordinances.
107 I am exceedingly afflicted;
Revive me, O LORD, according to
Your word.
108 O accept the freewill offerings of
my mouth, O LORD,
And teach me Your ordinances.
109 My life is continually in my hand,
Yet I do not forget Your law.
110 The wicked have laid a snare for
me,
Yet I have not gone astray from Your
precepts.
111 I have inherited Your testimonies
forever,
For they are the joy of my heart.
112 I have inclined my heart to perform
Your statutes
Forever, *even* to the end.

Proverbs 28:4

4   Those who forsake the law praise
the wicked,
But those who keep the law strive
with them.

2 Timothy 3:1–17

3 BUT realize this, that in the last days
difficult times will come.
2   For men will be lovers of self, lovers
of money, boastful, arrogant, revilers,
disobedient to parents, ungrateful, unholy,
3   unloving, irreconcilable, malicious
gossips, without self-control, brutal, haters of good,
4   treacherous, reckless, conceited, lovers of pleasure rather than lovers of God,
5   holding to a form of godliness, al- ◄
though they have denied its power;
Avoid such men as these.
6   For among them are those who enter

LIFE LESSONS

➤ **Jeremiah 46:28 — *"Do not fear . . . for
I am with you."***

*I*f God fills our hearts, then fear has
no place to make a home there. The
storms of life may assail us, but when
He is with us, we have no reason to be
afraid because His "perfect love casts
out fear" (1 John 4:18). We know we are
safe in His care, no matter what circumstances arise.

➤ **Psalm 119:105 — *Your word is a lamp
to my feet and a light to my path.***

*L*eft to ourselves, we often don't
know which way leads to life and
which way will end in death; we remain
in the dark. But God's Word provides us
with a searchlight to cut through the
darkness and lead us to safety.

➤ **2 Timothy 3:5 — *Holding to a form of
godliness, although they have denied its
power.***

*T*here are those who go through the
motions of religion but never genuinely trust the Lord as Savior. Because
of their unbelief, the subtle but deadly
sins of pride, greed, lust, unforgiveness,
gossip, and so forth flow from their lives.
To these, Jesus will say, "I never knew
you; depart from Me, you who practice
lawlessness" (Matt. 7:23). They are false
prophets who lead people astray, and
we should have nothing to do with
them.

WHAT THE BIBLE SAYS ABOUT ⊕

The Importance of Scripture

2 Timothy 3:16, 17

The truth of God's Word applies to all men and women in every culture, in every age, in every walk of life. It is His supernatural manual that alone reveals His mind and ways so that humankind may know and experience His presence and eternal love.

The Bible is God's written record of His works through the ages. It provides substantial evidence of His nature, plan, and purposes so that we can confidently place our faith in Him. Because we have His Word, we are not left to archaeological, historical, or theological guesswork. We can know how to live, make decisions, and worship the Lord, for "it is written" in His Word.

Scripture is divinely inspired. This means that He was involved in every detail that was recorded and written. It is God-breathed, and it is life's final and ultimate authority. The Bible is the "last word" on issues pertaining to God and His will. No individual, institution, or organization can supersede the authority of Scripture. Likewise, the Bible is God's guide to salvation and wise living. The psalmist wrote, "Your word is a lamp to my feet and a light to my path" (Ps. 119:105).

That is exactly why we are admonished not to add to or take away from Scripture (Rev. 22:18, 19). It perfectly expresses the decrees and judgments of almighty God. The Bible is authoritative because it is the truth: "The sum of Your word is truth" (Ps. 119:160).

Through the ministry of the Holy Spirit, the Bible enlightens each individual to recognize personal sin, the need for salvation, and the best possible life course. Without the Bible informing and illumining us, we would be hopelessly unable to know and follow the true and living God. When we say, "Oh, I just wish I could hear God speak to me!" we overlook the fact that He *has* spoken and is *still* speaking to us through His Word. He is never silent but is actively involved in every aspect of our lives (Rom. 3:2; Heb. 5:12).

The Bible is also profitable and nourishing. It provides us with an advantage in every department of life—family, business, and personal relationships. It is profitable because it reflects the wisdom of God; and when we abide by its teachings, we learn to live in His peace. As we meditate and consider its truth, our spirits and souls find nourishment. We become established and enriched in every experience of life by living according to God's perspective.

The Bible is the Book for everyone. It is revelation, inspiration, and communication of the Person and plan of the eternal, living, and powerful God. ⊕

---

into households and captivate weak women weighed down with sins, led on by various impulses,
7   always learning and never able to come to the knowledge of the truth.
8   Just as Jannes and Jambres opposed Moses, so these *men* also oppose the truth, men of depraved mind, rejected in regard to the faith.
9   But they will not make further progress; for their folly will be obvious to all, just as Jannes's and Jambres's folly was also.
10   Now you followed my teaching, conduct, purpose, faith, patience, love, perseverance,
11   persecutions, *and* sufferings, such as happened to me at Antioch, at Iconium *and* at Lystra; what persecutions I endured, and out of them all the Lord rescued me!

12   Indeed, all who desire to live godly in Christ Jesus will be persecuted.
13   But evil men and impostors will proceed *from bad* to worse, deceiving and being deceived.
14   You, however, continue in the things you have learned and become convinced

LIFE LESSONS

➤ **2 Timothy 3:12** — *All who desire to live godly in Christ Jesus will be persecuted.*

In our earthly reasoning, we sometimes believe that because God is all-powerful and loves us perfectly, He should protect us from all persecution and suffering. We fail to remember that He uses adversity to deepen our relationship with Him.

of, knowing from whom you have learned *them*,

15 and that from childhood you have known the sacred writings which are able to give you the wisdom that leads to salvation through faith which is in Christ Jesus.

➤ 16 All Scripture is inspired by God and profitable for teaching, for reproof, for correction, for training in righteousness;

17 so that the man of God may be adequate, equipped for every good work.

LIFE LESSONS

➤ **2 Timothy 3:16, 17 — *All Scripture is inspired by God . . . so that the man of God may be adequate, equipped for every good work.***

*G*od gave us Scripture for a particular reason: our growth in grace. It teaches us the truth about God, corrects us when we are wrong, and explains how to grow so that we can become effective ambassadors for Jesus Christ.

OCTOBER 31

Jeremiah 47:1—48:47

47 THAT which came as the word of the LORD to Jeremiah the prophet concerning the Philistines, before Pharaoh conquered Gaza.

2 Thus says the LORD:
"Behold, waters are going to rise
   from the north
And become an overflowing torrent,
And overflow the land and all its
   fullness,
The city and those who live in it;
And the men will cry out,
And every inhabitant of the land
   will wail.

3 "Because of the noise of the
   galloping hoofs of his stallions,
The tumult of his chariots, *and* the
   rumbling of his wheels,
The fathers have not turned back
   for *their* children,
Because of the limpness of *their*
   hands,

4 On account of the day that is
   coming
To destroy all the Philistines,
To cut off from Tyre and Sidon
Every ally that is left;
For the LORD is going to destroy the
   Philistines,
The remnant of the coastland of
   Caphtor.

5 "Baldness has come upon Gaza;
Ashkelon has been ruined.
O remnant of their valley,
How long will you gash yourself?

6 "Ah, sword of the LORD,
How long will you not be quiet?
Withdraw into your sheath;
Be at rest and stay still.

7 "How can it be quiet,
When the LORD has given it an
   order?
Against Ashkelon and against the
   seacoast—
There He has assigned it."

48 CONCERNING Moab. Thus says the LORD of hosts, the God of Israel,
"Woe to Nebo, for it has been
   destroyed;
Kiriathaim has been put to shame, it
   has been captured;
The lofty stronghold has been put to
   shame and shattered.

2 "There is praise for Moab no longer;
In Heshbon they have devised
   calamity against her:
'Come and let us cut her off from
   being a nation!'
You too, Madmen, will be silenced;
The sword will follow after you.

3 "The sound of an outcry from
   Horonaim,
'Devastation and great destruction!'

4 "Moab is broken,
Her little ones have sounded out a
   cry *of distress.*

5 "For by the ascent of Luhith
They will ascend with continual
   weeping;
For at the descent of Horonaim
They have heard the anguished cry
   of destruction.

6 "Flee, save your lives,

That you may be like a juniper in
  the wilderness.

7 "For because of your trust in your
    own achievements and treasures,
  Even you yourself will be captured;
  And Chemosh will go off into exile
  Together with his priests and his
    princes.

8 "A destroyer will come to every city,
  So that no city will escape;
  The valley also will be ruined
  And the plateau will be destroyed,
  As the LORD has said.

9 "Give wings to Moab,
  For she will flee away;
  And her cities will become a
    desolation,
  Without inhabitants in them.

10 "Cursed be the one who does the
     LORD'S work negligently,
   And cursed be the one who
     restrains his sword from blood.

11 "Moab has been at ease since his
     youth;
   He has also been undisturbed, *like
     wine* on its dregs,
   And he has not been emptied from
     vessel to vessel,
   Nor has he gone into exile.
   Therefore he retains his flavor,
   And his aroma has not changed.

12 "Therefore behold, the days are coming," declares the LORD, "when I will
send to him those who tip *vessels*, and
they will tip him over, and they will
empty his vessels and shatter his jars.

13 "And Moab will be ashamed of
Chemosh, as the house of Israel was
ashamed of Bethel, their confidence.

14 "How can you say, 'We are mighty
     warriors,
   And men valiant for battle'?

15 "Moab has been destroyed and men
     have gone up to his cities;
   His choicest young men have also
     gone down to the slaughter,"
   Declares the King, whose name is
     the LORD of hosts.

16 "The disaster of Moab will soon come,
   And his calamity has swiftly
     hastened.

17 "Mourn for him, all you who *live*
     around him,
   Even all of you who know his name;
   Say, 'How has the mighty scepter
     been broken,
   A staff of splendor!'

18 "Come down from your glory
   And sit on the parched ground,
   O daughter dwelling in Dibon,
   For the destroyer of Moab has come
     up against you,
   He has ruined your strongholds.

19 "Stand by the road and keep watch,
   O inhabitant of Aroer;
   Ask him who flees and her who
     escapes
   And say, 'What has happened?'

20 "Moab has been put to shame, for it
     has been shattered.
   Wail and cry out;
   Declare by the Arnon
   That Moab has been destroyed.

21 "Judgment has also come upon the
plain, upon Holon, Jahzah and against
Mephaath,

22 against Dibon, Nebo and Beth-
diblathaim,

23 against Kiriathaim, Beth-gamul and
Beth-meon,

24 against Kerioth, Bozrah and all the
cities of the land of Moab, far and near.

25 "The horn of Moab has been cut off
and his arm broken," declares the LORD.

26 "Make him drunk, for he has become
arrogant toward the LORD; so Moab will
wallow in his vomit, and he also will become a laughingstock.

27 "Now was not Israel a laughingstock
to you? Or was he caught among thieves?
For each time you speak about him you
shake *your head in scorn*.

28 "Leave the cities and dwell among
     the crags,
   O inhabitants of Moab,
   And be like a dove that nests
   Beyond the mouth of the chasm.

29 "We have heard of the pride of
     Moab—he *is* very proud—
   Of his haughtiness, his pride, his
     arrogance and his self-exaltation.

30 "I know his fury," declares the LORD,
   "But it is futile;
   His idle boasts have accomplished
     nothing.

31 "Therefore I will wail for Moab,
   Even for all Moab will I cry out;
   I will moan for the men of Kir-heres.

32 "More than the weeping for Jazer
   I will weep for you, O vine of
     Sibmah!
   Your tendrils stretched across the
     sea,
   They reached to the sea of Jazer;

Upon your summer fruits and your
grape harvest
The destroyer has fallen.
33 "So gladness and joy are taken away
From the fruitful field, even from
the land of Moab.
And I have made the wine to cease
from the wine presses;
No one will tread *them* with
shouting,
The shouting will not be shouts *of
joy.*
34 "From the outcry at Heshbon even to
Elealeh, even to Jahaz they have raised
their voice, from Zoar even to Horonaim
and to Eglath-shelishiyah; for even the
waters of Nimrim will become desolate.
35 "I will make an end of Moab," declares the LORD, "the one who offers *sacrifice* on the high place and the one who
burns incense to his gods.
36 "Therefore My heart wails for Moab
like flutes; My heart also wails like flutes
for the men of Kir-heres. Therefore they
have lost the abundance it produced.
37 "For every head is bald and every
beard cut short; there are gashes on all
the hands and sackcloth on the loins.
38 "On all the housetops of Moab and
in its streets there is lamentation everywhere; for I have broken Moab like an
undesirable vessel," declares the LORD.
39 "How shattered it is! *How* they have
wailed! How Moab has turned his back—
he is ashamed! So Moab will become a
laughingstock and an object of terror to
all around him."
40 For thus says the LORD:
"Behold, one will fly swiftly like an
eagle
And spread out his wings against
Moab.
41 "Kerioth has been captured
And the strongholds have been
seized,
So the hearts of the mighty men of
Moab in that day
Will be like the heart of a woman in
labor.
➤ 42 "Moab will be destroyed from *being*
a people
Because he has become arrogant
toward the LORD.
43 "Terror, pit and snare are *coming*
upon you,
O inhabitant of Moab," declares the
LORD.

44 "The one who flees from the terror
Will fall into the pit,
And the one who climbs up out of
the pit
Will be caught in the snare;
For I shall bring upon her, *even*
upon Moab,
The year of their punishment,"
declares the LORD.
45 "In the shadow of Heshbon
The fugitives stand without
strength;
For a fire has gone forth from
Heshbon
And a flame from the midst of
Sihon,
And it has devoured the forehead of
Moab
And the scalps of the riotous
revelers.
46 "Woe to you, Moab!
The people of Chemosh have
perished;
For your sons have been taken away
captive
And your daughters into captivity.
47 "Yet I will restore the fortunes of
Moab
In the latter days," declares the
LORD.
Thus far the judgment on Moab.

Psalm 119:113–120

ס   Samekh.

113 I hate those who are double-minded,
But I love Your law.
114 You are my hiding place and my
shield;
I wait for Your word.
115 Depart from me, evildoers,

LIFE LESSONS

➤ Jeremiah 48:42 — *"Moab will be
destroyed from being a people because
he has become arrogant toward the
LORD."*

*G*od *always* judges pride. Always.
Whether He finds the arrogance and
pride in the heart of an angel (Satan), a
man (Nebuchadnezzar), or a nation
(Moab), He will always judge it. He has
no rivals.

That I may observe the
commandments of my God.
116 Sustain me according to Your word,
that I may live;
And do not let me be ashamed of my
hope.
117 Uphold me that I may be safe,
That I may have regard for Your
statutes continually.
118 You have rejected all those who
wander from Your statutes,
For their deceitfulness is useless.
119 You have removed all the wicked of
the earth *like* dross;
Therefore I love Your testimonies.
120 My flesh trembles for fear of You,
And I am afraid of Your judgments.

Proverbs 28:5

5 Evil men do not understand justice,
But those who seek the LORD
understand all things.

2 Timothy 4:1–22

4 I SOLEMNLY charge *you* in the presence of God and of Christ Jesus, who
is to judge the living and the dead, and
by His appearing and His kingdom:
2 preach the word; be ready in season
and out of season; reprove, rebuke, exhort, with great patience and instruction.
3 For the time will come when they
will not endure sound doctrine; but
wanting to have their ears tickled, they
will accumulate for themselves teachers
in accordance to their own desires,
4 and will turn away their ears from
the truth and will turn aside to myths.
5 But you, be sober in all things, endure hardship, do the work of an evangelist, fulfill your ministry.
6 For I am already being poured out
as a drink offering, and the time of my
departure has come.
7 I have fought the good fight, I have
finished the course, I have kept the faith;
8 in the future there is laid up for me
the crown of righteousness, which the
Lord, the righteous Judge, will award to
me on that day; and not only to me, but
also to all who have loved His appearing.

9 Make every effort to come to me soon;
10 for Demas, having loved this present world, has deserted me and gone
to Thessalonica; Crescens *has gone* to
Galatia, Titus to Dalmatia.
11 Only Luke is with me. Pick up Mark
and bring him with you, for he is useful
to me for service.
12 But Tychicus I have sent to Ephesus.
13 When you come bring the cloak
which I left at Troas with Carpus, and
the books, especially the parchments.
14 Alexander the coppersmith did me
much harm; the Lord will repay him according to his deeds.
15 Be on guard against him yourself,
for he vigorously opposed our teaching.
16 At my first defense no one supported
me, but all deserted me; may it not be
counted against them.
17 But the Lord stood with me and
strengthened me, so that through me the
proclamation might be fully accomplished,
and that all the Gentiles might hear; and I
was rescued out of the lion's mouth.
18 The Lord will rescue me from every
evil deed, and will bring me safely to His

LIFE LESSONS

➤ **2 Timothy 4:3** — *They will not endure
sound doctrine; but . . . will accumulate
for themselves teachers.*

A time is coming when people will
outright reject the truth of God's
Word, picking and choosing what to
believe based on their desires and pref-
erences. They will follow the false doctrine of ungodly teachers who preach
what they want to hear. As they did in
Paul's time, they will persecute believers. However, we must remain steadfast
in our faith, knowing that we don't
answer to them. We are accountable to
Jesus, who will "judge the living and the
dead" (2 Tim. 4:1).

➤ **2 Timothy 4:7** — *I have fought the
good fight, I have finished the course, I
have kept the faith.*

A lthough Paul had been beaten,
imprisoned, shipwrecked, stoned,
and even left for dead, he never lost his
faith but followed the Lord Jesus based
on the truth of His Word and in anticipation of the rewards He had stored up for
him.

ANSWERS TO LIFE'S QUESTIONS

How can I cope with feelings of loneliness?

2 TIMOTHY 4:16–18

*P*aul endured prison alone, where he felt deeply isolated. In the last months of his life, he gave us the wonderful secret of what to do in times of intense loneliness.

First, he recognized the presence of God. He wrote that the Lord stood with him (2 Tim. 4:17). Paul couldn't change his situation, but in that lonely, damp prison cell, he remembered that God was with him.

Second, Paul dealt with loneliness by recalling how God faithfully strengthened him (2 Tim. 4:17). The Lord supported Paul, infusing him with strength. The apostle knew that no one could take his life without God's permission. We often quote Philippians 4:13: "I can do all things through Him who strengthens me." It is significant that Paul was confined to prison as he wrote these words. Even though he faced discouraging circumstances, he had an unwavering sense of hope within because he understood the truth that his life was totally under the omnipotent, watchful care of the Lord Jesus Christ.

Third, Paul combated his feelings of loneliness by reminding himself that he had the awesome privilege of fulfilling God's purpose for his life. What incredible encouragement that is—to know we are part of God's providential plan! David also found encouragement in the Lord's presence. Many of the psalms he penned were written as a result of the utmost dire situations. Yet he wrote these words: "This poor man cried and the Lord heard him and saved him out of all his trouble" (Psalm 34:6).

In his loneliness, Paul treasured the company of his friends. He wrote that Luke remained with him and urged Timothy and Mark to join him. He mentioned four people by name who comforted him: Eubulus, Pudens, Linus, and Claudia (2 Tim. 4:21). We know nothing about these four people, other than they stuck with the apostle Paul. That has to be one of the greatest compliments they could have been paid.

Finally, Paul asked Timothy to bring some books with him, "especially the parchments" (2 Tim. 4:13). These priceless documents were no doubt the Word of God. Knowing the apostle Paul, we may assume that he hungered for copies of Scripture. In an hour of great loneliness, the Word of God brings great comfort.

The Lord Jesus Christ felt totally alone as He faced His own death. The Bible says, "All the disciples left Him and fled" (Matt. 26:56). And on the Cross He cried out, "My God, My God, why have You forsaken Me?" (Matt. 27:46). Jesus knows all about loneliness. Yet He also knows the joy of being carried through the loneliest times on the wings of faith, confident that the Father will never abandon us. He stands as the ultimate example of One who faced the perils of loneliness without losing heart.

LIFE LESSONS

➤ **2 Timothy 4:17 — *The Lord stood with me and strengthened me.***

*W*hen everyone else abandons us, the Lord stands solidly by our side. When we feel absolutely spent, He gives us strength. When failure appears inevitable, He steps in and helps us to finish what He has called us to do.

heavenly kingdom; to Him *be* the glory forever and ever. Amen.
19 Greet Prisca and Aquila, and the household of Onesiphorus.
20 Erastus remained at Corinth, but Trophimus I left sick at Miletus.
21 Make every effort to come before winter. Eubulus greets you, also Pudens and Linus and Claudia and all the brethren.
22 The Lord be with your spirit. Grace be with you.

49 CONCERNING the sons of Ammon. Thus says the LORD:
"Does Israel have no sons?
Or has he no heirs?
Why then has Malcam taken possession of Gad
And his people settled in its cities?
2 "Therefore behold, the days are coming," declares the LORD,
"That I will cause a trumpet blast of war to be heard
Against Rabbah of the sons of Ammon;
And it will become a desolate heap,
And her towns will be set on fire.
Then Israel will take possession of his possessors,"
Says the LORD.
3 "Wail, O Heshbon, for Ai has been destroyed!
Cry out, O daughters of Rabbah,
Gird yourselves with sackcloth and lament,
And rush back and forth inside the walls;
For Malcam will go into exile
Together with his priests and his princes.
4 "How boastful you are about the valleys!
Your valley is flowing *away*,
O backsliding daughter
Who trusts in her treasures, *saying*,
'Who will come against me?'
5 "Behold, I am going to bring terror upon you,"
Declares the Lord GOD of hosts,
"From all *directions* around you;
And each of you will be driven out headlong,
With no one to gather the fugitives together.
6 "But afterward I will restore
The fortunes of the sons of Ammon,"
Declares the LORD.
7 Concerning Edom.
Thus says the LORD of hosts,
"Is there no longer any wisdom in Teman?
Has good counsel been lost to the prudent?
Has their wisdom decayed?

8 "Flee away, turn back, dwell in the depths,
O inhabitants of Dedan,
For I will bring the disaster of Esau upon him
At the time I punish him.
9 "If grape gatherers came to you,
Would they not leave gleanings?
If thieves *came* by night,
They would destroy *only* until they had enough.
10 "But I have stripped Esau bare,
I have uncovered his hiding places
So that he will not be able to conceal himself;
His offspring has been destroyed along with his relatives
And his neighbors, and he is no more.
11 "Leave your orphans behind, I will keep *them* alive;
And let your widows trust in Me."
12 For thus says the LORD, "Behold, those who were not sentenced to drink the cup will certainly drink *it*, and are you the one who will be completely acquitted? You will not be acquitted, but you will certainly drink *it*.
13 "For I have sworn by Myself," declares the LORD, "that Bozrah will become an object of horror, a reproach, a ruin and a curse; and all its cities will become perpetual ruins."
14 I have heard a message from the LORD,
And an envoy is sent among the nations, *saying*,
"Gather yourselves together and come against her,
And rise up for battle!"
15 "For behold, I have made you small among the nations,
Despised among men.
16 "As for the terror of you,
The arrogance of your heart has deceived you,
O you who live in the clefts of the rock,
Who occupy the height of the hill.
Though you make your nest as high as an eagle's,
I will bring you down from there," declares the LORD.
17 "Edom will become an object of horror; everyone who passes by it will be horrified and will hiss at all its wounds.

18 "Like the overthrow of Sodom and Gomorrah with its neighbors," says the LORD, "no one will live there, nor will a son of man reside in it.

➤ 19 "Behold, one will come up like a lion from the thickets of the Jordan against a perennially watered pasture; for in an instant I will make him run away from it, and whoever is chosen I shall appoint over it. For who is like Me, and who will summon Me *into court?* And who then is the shepherd who can stand against Me?"

20 Therefore hear the plan of the LORD which He has planned against Edom, and His purposes which He has purposed against the inhabitants of Teman: surely they will drag them off, *even* the little ones of the flock; surely He will make their pasture desolate because of them.

21 The earth has quaked at the noise of their downfall. There is an outcry! The noise of it has been heard at the Red Sea.

22 Behold, He will mount up and swoop like an eagle and spread out His wings against Bozrah; and the hearts of the mighty men of Edom in that day will be like the heart of a woman in labor.

23 Concerning Damascus.

"Hamath and Arpad are put to shame,
For they have heard bad news;
They are disheartened.
There is anxiety by the sea,
It cannot be calmed.

24 "Damascus has become helpless;
She has turned away to flee,
And panic has gripped her;
Distress and pangs have taken hold of her
Like a woman in childbirth.

25 "How the city of praise has not been deserted,
The town of My joy!

26 "Therefore, her young men will fall in her streets,

And all the men of war will be silenced in that day," declares the LORD of hosts.

27 "I will set fire to the wall of Damascus,
And it will devour the fortified towers of Ben-hadad."

28 Concerning Kedar and the kingdoms of Hazor, which Nebuchadnezzar king of Babylon defeated. Thus says the LORD,

"Arise, go up to Kedar
And devastate the men of the east.

29 "They will take away their tents and their flocks;
They will carry off for themselves
Their tent curtains, all their goods and their camels,
And they will call out to one another, 'Terror on every side!'

30 "Run away, flee! Dwell in the depths,
O inhabitants of Hazor," declares the LORD;
"For Nebuchadnezzar king of Babylon has formed a plan against you
And devised a scheme against you.

31 "Arise, go up against a nation which is at ease,
Which lives securely," declares the LORD.
"It has no gates or bars;
They dwell alone.

32 "Their camels will become plunder,
And their many cattle for booty,
And I will scatter to all the winds those who cut the corners *of their hair;*
And I will bring their disaster from every side," declares the LORD.

33 "Hazor will become a haunt of jackals,
A desolation forever;
No one will live there,
Nor will a son of man reside in it."

34 That which came as the word of the LORD to Jeremiah the prophet concerning Elam, at the beginning of the reign of Zedekiah king of Judah, saying:

35 "Thus says the LORD of hosts,
'Behold, I am going to break the bow of Elam,
The finest of their might.

36 'I will bring upon Elam the four winds
From the four ends of heaven,
And will scatter them to all these winds;
And there will be no nation

LIFE LESSONS

➤ Jeremiah 49:19 — *"Who is like Me?"*

*N*o one is like God (Is. 40:10–31). He has no peers, no equals, no judges, and no accusers. No one will prevent Him from accomplishing exactly as He plans.

To which the outcasts of Elam will
    not go.
37 'So I will shatter Elam before their
    enemies
    And before those who seek their
    lives;
    And I will bring calamity upon them,
    Even My fierce anger,' declares the
    LORD.
    'And I will send out the sword after
    them
    Until I have consumed them.
38 'Then I will set My throne in Elam
    And destroy out of it king and
    princes,'
    Declares the LORD.
39 'But it will come about in the last
    days
    That I will restore the fortunes of
    Elam,'"
    Declares the LORD.

50 THE word which the LORD spoke
concerning Babylon, the land of
the Chaldeans, through Jeremiah the
prophet:
2 "Declare and proclaim among the
    nations.
    Proclaim it and lift up a standard.
    Do not conceal *it but* say,
    'Babylon has been captured,
    Bel has been put to shame, Marduk
    has been shattered;
    Her images have been put to shame,
    her idols have been shattered.'
3 "For a nation has come up against her
out of the north; it will make her land
an object of horror, and there will be no
inhabitant in it. Both man and beast have
wandered off, they have gone away!
4 "In those days and at that time," declares the LORD, "the sons of Israel will
come, *both* they and the sons of Judah as
well; they will go along weeping as they
go, and it will be the LORD their God they
will seek.
5 "They will ask for the way to Zion,
turning their faces in its direction; they
will come that they may join themselves
to the LORD *in* an everlasting covenant
that will not be forgotten.
6 "My people have become lost sheep;
    Their shepherds have led them
    astray.
    They have made them turn aside *on*
    the mountains;
    They have gone along from
    mountain to hill

And have forgotten their resting
    place.
7 "All who came upon them have
    devoured them;
    And their adversaries have said, 'We
    are not guilty,
    Inasmuch as they have sinned
    against the LORD *who is* the
    habitation of righteousness,
    Even the LORD, the hope of their
    fathers.'
8 "Wander away from the midst of
    Babylon
    And go forth from the land of the
    Chaldeans;
    Be also like male goats at the head
    of the flock.
9 "For behold, I am going to arouse
    and bring up against Babylon
    A horde of great nations from the
    land of the north,
    And they will draw up *their* battle
    lines against her;
    From there she will be taken
    captive.
    Their arrows will be like an expert
    warrior
    Who does not return empty-handed.
10 "Chaldea will become plunder;
    All who plunder her will have
    enough," declares the LORD.
11 "Because you are glad, because you
    are jubilant,
    O you who pillage My heritage,
    Because you skip about like a
    threshing heifer
    And neigh like stallions,
12 Your mother will be greatly
    ashamed,
    She who gave you birth will be
    humiliated.
    Behold, *she will be* the least of the
    nations,
    A wilderness, a parched land and a
    desert.
13 "Because of the indignation of the
    LORD she will not be inhabited,
    But she will be completely desolate;
    Everyone who passes by Babylon
    will be horrified
    And will hiss because of all her
    wounds.
14 "Draw up your battle lines against
    Babylon on every side,
    All you who bend the bow;
    Shoot at her, do not be sparing with
    your arrows,

For she has sinned against the
Lord.
15 "Raise your battle cry against her on
every side!
She has given herself up, her pillars
have fallen,
Her walls have been torn down.
For this is the vengeance of the
Lord:
Take vengeance on her;
As she has done *to others, so* do to
her.
16 "Cut off the sower from Babylon
And the one who wields the sickle
at the time of harvest;
From before the sword of the
oppressor
They will each turn back to his own
people
And they will each flee to his own
land.
17 "Israel is a scattered flock, the lions
have driven *them* away. The first one
who devoured him was the king of Assyria, and this last one *who* has broken
his bones is Nebuchadnezzar king of
Babylon.
18 "Therefore thus says the Lord of
hosts, the God of Israel: 'Behold, I am
going to punish the king of Babylon and
his land, just as I punished the king of
Assyria.
19 'And I will bring Israel back to his
pasture and he will graze on Carmel and
Bashan, and his desire will be satisfied in
the hill country of Ephraim and Gilead.
20 'In those days and at that time,' declares the Lord, 'search will be made for
the iniquity of Israel, but there will be
none; and for the sins of Judah, but they
will not be found; for I will pardon those
whom I leave as a remnant.'
21 "Against the land of Merathaim, go
up against it,
And against the inhabitants of
Pekod.
Slay and utterly destroy them,"
declares the Lord,
"And do according to all that I have
commanded you.
22 "The noise of battle is in the land,
And great destruction.
23 "How the hammer of the whole earth
Has been cut off and broken!
How Babylon has become
An object of horror among the
nations!

24 "I set a snare for you and you were
also caught, O Babylon,
While you yourself were not aware;
You have been found and also
seized
Because you have engaged in
conflict with the Lord."
25 The Lord has opened His armory
And has brought forth the weapons
of His indignation,
For it is a work of the Lord God of
hosts
In the land of the Chaldeans.
26 Come to her from the farthest
border;
Open up her barns,
Pile her up like heaps
And utterly destroy her,
Let nothing be left to her.
27 Put all her young bulls to the sword;
Let them go down to the slaughter!
Woe be upon them, for their day has
come,
The time of their punishment.
28 There is a sound of fugitives
and refugees from the land of
Babylon,
To declare in Zion the vengeance of
the Lord our God,
Vengeance for His temple.
29 "Summon many against Babylon,
All those who bend the bow:
Encamp against her on every side,
Let there be no escape.
Repay her according to her work;
According to all that she has done,
so do to her;
For she has become arrogant
against the Lord,
Against the Holy One of Israel.
30 "Therefore her young men will fall in
her streets,
And all her men of war will be
silenced in that day," declares the
Lord.
31 "Behold, I am against you,
O arrogant one,"
Declares the Lord God of hosts,
"For your day has come,
The time when I will punish you.
32 "The arrogant one will stumble and
fall
With no one to raise him up;
And I will set fire to his cities
And it will devour all his environs."
33 Thus says the Lord of hosts,
"The sons of Israel are oppressed,

And the sons of Judah as well;
And all who took them captive have
held them fast,
They have refused to let them go.
34 "Their Redeemer is strong, the LORD
of hosts is His name;
He will vigorously plead their case
So that He may bring rest to the
earth,
But turmoil to the inhabitants of
Babylon.
35 "A sword against the Chaldeans,"
declares the LORD,
"And against the inhabitants of
Babylon
And against her officials and her
wise men!
36 "A sword against the oracle priests,
and they will become fools!
A sword against her mighty men,
and they will be shattered!
37 "A sword against their horses and
against their chariots
And against all the foreigners who
are in the midst of her,
And they will become women!
A sword against her treasures, and
they will be plundered!
38 "A drought on her waters, and they
will be dried up!
For it is a land of idols,
And they are mad over fearsome
idols.
39 "Therefore the desert creatures will
live there along with the jackals;
The ostriches also will live in it,
And it will never again be inhabited
Or dwelt in from generation to
generation.
40 "As when God overthrew Sodom
And Gomorrah with its neighbors,"
declares the LORD,
"No man will live there,
Nor will any son of man reside in it.
41 "Behold, a people is coming from the
north,
And a great nation and many kings
Will be aroused from the remote
parts of the earth.
42 "They seize their bow and javelin;
They are cruel and have no mercy.
Their voice roars like the sea;
And they ride on horses,
Marshalled like a man for the battle
Against you, O daughter of Babylon.
43 "The king of Babylon has heard the
report about them,

And his hands hang limp;
Distress has gripped him,
Agony like a woman in childbirth.
44 "Behold, one will come up like a lion
from the thicket of the Jordan to a perennially watered pasture; for in an instant
I will make them run away from it, and
whoever is chosen I will appoint over it.
For who is like Me, and who will summon
Me into court? And who then is the shepherd who can stand before Me?"
45 Therefore hear the plan of the LORD
which He has planned against Babylon,
and His purposes which He has purposed against the land of the Chaldeans:
surely they will drag them off, even the
little ones of the flock; surely He will
make their pasture desolate because of
them.
46 At the shout, "Babylon has been
seized!" the earth is shaken, and an outcry is heard among the nations.

◆ Psalm 119:121–128

ע Ayin.

121 I have done justice and righteousness;
Do not leave me to my oppressors.
122 Be surety for Your servant for
good;
Do not let the arrogant oppress me.
123 My eyes fail with longing for Your
salvation
And for Your righteous word.
124 Deal with Your servant according
to Your lovingkindness
And teach me Your statutes.
125 I am Your servant; give me
understanding,
That I may know Your testimonies.
126 It is time for the LORD to act,
For they have broken Your law.

LIFE LESSONS

➤ **Psalm 119:125 —** *I am Your servant;*
give me understanding, that I may know
Your testimonies.

God doesn't want ignorant servants,
but well-informed ones. Jesus tells us,
"I have called you friends, for all things
that I have heard from My Father I have
made known to you" (John 15:15). God's
Word tells us how to succeed.

Life Examples:

TITUS: Serving God with Abandon

TITUS 1

In the days following Titus' conversion, a deep love and mutual respect grew between him and the apostle Paul, a bond that lasted throughout their days. So strong was their connection that Paul referred to Titus as "my true child in a common faith" (Titus 1:4).

Paul saw in this new believer a rare and refreshing quality. Trustworthy and dependable as he was, it was no surprise that Paul would write of Titus, "He is my partner and fellow worker" (2 Cor. 8:23). Consequently, Titus traveled with Paul to places such as Corinth, Antioch, and Jerusalem.

Titus is a picture of God's grace. As a redeemed Gentile, he experienced intimate fellowship with the Lord. And because he willingly served unselfishly in places of obscurity, he became a treasured instrument for God's glory.

What could the Father do with us if we served Him with the same abandon as Titus?

127 Therefore I love Your commandments
     Above gold, yes, above fine gold.
128 Therefore I esteem right all *Your* precepts concerning everything,
     I hate every false way.

Proverbs 28:6

6   Better is the poor who walks in his integrity
     Than he who is crooked though he be rich.

Titus 1:1–16

1 PAUL, a bond-servant of God and an apostle of Jesus Christ, for the faith of those chosen of God and the knowledge of the truth which is according to godliness,
2   in the hope of eternal life, which God, who cannot lie, promised long ages ago,
3   but at the proper time manifested, *even* His word, in the proclamation with which I was entrusted according to the commandment of God our Savior,
4   To Titus, my true child in a common faith: Grace and peace from God the Father and Christ Jesus our Savior.
5   For this reason I left you in Crete, that you would set in order what remains and appoint elders in every city as I directed you,
6   *namely,* if any man is above reproach, the husband of one wife, having children who believe, not accused of dissipation or rebellion.
7   For the overseer must be above reproach as God's steward, not self-willed, not quick-tempered, not addicted to wine, not pugnacious, not fond of sordid gain,
8   but hospitable, loving what is good, sensible, just, devout, self-controlled,
9   holding fast the faithful word which is in accordance with the teaching, so that he will be able both to exhort in

LIFE LESSONS

Proverbs 28:6 — *Better is the poor who walks in his integrity than he who is crooked though he be rich.*

*N*o amount of money can make a vile person honorable, and no level of poverty can take the honor away from a person of integrity.

Titus 1:9 — *Holding fast the faithful word which is in accordance with the teaching, so that he will be able both to exhort in sound doctrine and to refute those who contradict.*

*T*o *hold fast* means to *grip tightly* and *apply* God's Word—this is absolutely essential for living a godly life because the Bible is an unshakable anchor in every situation. It has often been noted that the dirtier, the more used, and worn the pages in your Bible, the cleaner your heart. Why? Because "the word of God is living and active" (Heb. 4:12). Through the power of His Holy Spirit, Scripture transforms you—equipping you in sound doctrine to teach others and protecting you from those who oppose the Lord.

sound doctrine and to refute those who contradict.

10 For there are many rebellious men, empty talkers and deceivers, especially those of the circumcision,

11 who must be silenced because they are upsetting whole families, teaching things they should not *teach* for the sake of sordid gain.

12 One of themselves, a prophet of their own, said, "Cretans are always liars, evil beasts, lazy gluttons."

➤ 13 This testimony is true. For this reason reprove them severely so that they may be sound in the faith,

14 not paying attention to Jewish myths and commandments of men who turn away from the truth.

15 To the pure, all things are pure; but to those who are defiled and unbelieving, nothing is pure, but both their mind and their conscience are defiled.

➤ 16 They profess to know God, but by *their* deeds they deny *Him*, being detestable and disobedient and worthless for any good deed.

LIFE LESSONS

➤ **Titus 1:13 — *Reprove them severely so that they may be sound in the faith.***

*I*t's no fun to reprove someone severely. In fact, the apostle Paul often did it with weeping (Phil. 3:18). Unfortunately, it's sometimes unavoidable—as was the case with the believers in Crete who were being influenced by the ungodly culture surrounding them. When discipline becomes necessary, it's the most loving thing you can do.

➤ **Titus 1:16 — *They profess to know God, but in works they deny Him.***

*A*s believers, we are called to be set apart and reflect the godly character of Christ so others can know Him as Savior. Unfortunately, the world in which we live is opposed to this. So instead of challenging ungodly cultural norms or repenting from sinful behavior, we are sometimes tempted to compromise and avoid conflict. However, it is completely incompatible to confess Christ and ignore His commands.

◎ Jeremiah 51:1—52:34

51 THUS says the LORD:
"Behold, I am going to arouse against Babylon
And against the inhabitants of Leb-kamai
The spirit of a destroyer.

2 "I will dispatch foreigners to Babylon that they may winnow her
And may devastate her land;
For on every side they will be opposed to her
In the day of *her* calamity.

3 "Let not him who bends his bow bend *it*,
Nor let him rise up in his scale-armor;
So do not spare her young men;
Devote all her army to destruction.

4 "They will fall down slain in the land of the Chaldeans,
And pierced through in their streets."

5 For neither Israel nor Judah has been forsaken
By his God, the LORD of hosts,
Although their land is full of guilt
Before the Holy One of Israel.

6 Flee from the midst of Babylon,
And each of you save his life!
Do not be destroyed in her punishment,
For this is the LORD's time of vengeance;

LIFE LESSONS

➤ **Jeremiah 51:5 — *"For neither Israel nor Judah has been forsaken . . . although their land is full of guilt before the Holy One of Israel."***

*J*eremiah knew that while God would certainly judge His people for their sin, He would never completely abandon them. He had promised Abraham that He would be with them forever, and He always keeps His promises.

He is going to render recompense to
her.
7 Babylon has been a golden cup in
the hand of the Lord,
Intoxicating all the earth.
The nations have drunk of her wine;
Therefore the nations are going mad.
8 Suddenly Babylon has fallen and
been broken;
Wail over her!
Bring balm for her pain;
Perhaps she may be healed.
9 We applied healing to Babylon, but
she was not healed;
Forsake her and let us each go to
his own country,
For her judgment has reached to
heaven
And towers up to the very skies.
10 The Lord has brought about our
vindication;
Come and let us recount in Zion
The work of the Lord our God!
11 Sharpen the arrows, fill the quivers!
The Lord has aroused the spirit of
the kings of the Medes,
Because His purpose is against
Babylon to destroy it;
For it is the vengeance of the Lord,
vengeance for His temple.
12 Lift up a signal against the walls of
Babylon;
Post a strong guard,
Station sentries,
Place men in ambush!
For the Lord has both purposed
and performed
What He spoke concerning the
inhabitants of Babylon.
13 O you who dwell by many waters,
Abundant in treasures,
Your end has come,
The measure of your end.
14 The Lord of hosts has sworn by
Himself:
"Surely I will fill you with a
population like locusts,
And they will cry out with shouts of
victory over you."
15 It is He who made the earth by His
power,
Who established the world by His
wisdom,
And by His understanding He
stretched out the heavens.
16 When He utters His voice, there is a
tumult of waters in the heavens,

And He causes the clouds to ascend
from the end of the earth;
He makes lightning for the rain
And brings forth the wind from His
storehouses.
17 All mankind is stupid, devoid of
knowledge;
Every goldsmith is put to shame by
his idols,
For his molten images are deceitful,
And there is no breath in them.
18 They are worthless, a work of
mockery;
In the time of their punishment they
will perish.
19 The portion of Jacob is not like these;
For the Maker of all is He,
And of the tribe of His inheritance;
The Lord of hosts is His name.
20 He says, "You are My war-club, My
weapon of war;
And with you I shatter nations,
And with you I destroy kingdoms.
21 "With you I shatter the horse and his
rider,
And with you I shatter the chariot
and its rider,
22 And with you I shatter man and
woman,
And with you I shatter old man and
youth,
And with you I shatter young man
and virgin,
23 And with you I shatter the shepherd
and his flock,
And with you I shatter the farmer
and his team,
And with you I shatter governors
and prefects.
24 "But I will repay Babylon and all the
inhabitants of Chaldea for all their evil
that they have done in Zion before your
eyes," declares the Lord.
25 "Behold, I am against you,
O destroying mountain,
Who destroys the whole earth,"
declares the Lord,
"And I will stretch out My hand
against you,
And roll you down from the crags,
And I will make you a burnt out
mountain.
26 "They will not take from you even a
stone for a corner
Nor a stone for foundations,
But you will be desolate forever,"
declares the Lord.

27 Lift up a signal in the land,
Blow a trumpet among the nations!
Consecrate the nations against her,
Summon against her the kingdoms
of Ararat, Minni and Ashkenaz;
Appoint a marshal against her,
Bring up the horses like bristly
locusts.
28 Consecrate the nations against her,
The kings of the Medes,
Their governors and all their prefects,
And every land of their dominion.
29 So the land quakes and writhes,
For the purposes of the LORD
against Babylon stand,
To make the land of Babylon
A desolation without inhabitants.
30 The mighty men of Babylon have
ceased fighting,
They stay in the strongholds;
Their strength is exhausted,
They are becoming *like* women;
Their dwelling places are set on fire,
The bars of her *gates* are broken.
31 One courier runs to meet another,
And one messenger to meet another,
To tell the king of Babylon
That his city has been captured
from end *to end*;
32 The fords also have been seized,
And they have burned the marshes
with fire,
And the men of war are terrified.
33 For thus says the LORD of hosts, the
God of Israel:
"The daughter of Babylon is like a
threshing floor
At the time it is stamped firm;
Yet in a little while the time of
harvest will come for her."
34 "Nebuchadnezzar king of Babylon
has devoured me *and* crushed me,
He has set me down *like* an empty
vessel;
He has swallowed me like a monster,
He has filled his stomach with my
delicacies;
He has washed me away.
35 "May the violence *done* to me and to
my flesh be upon Babylon,"
The inhabitant of Zion will say;
And, "May my blood be upon the
inhabitants of Chaldea,"
Jerusalem will say.
36 Therefore thus says the LORD,
"Behold, I am going to plead your
case

And exact full vengeance for you;
And I will dry up her sea
And make her fountain dry.
37 "Babylon will become a heap *of
ruins*, a haunt of jackals,
An object of horror and hissing,
without inhabitants.
38 "They will roar together like young
lions,
They will growl like lions' cubs.
39 "When they become heated up, I will
serve *them* their banquet
And make them drunk, that they
may become jubilant
And may sleep a perpetual sleep
And not wake up," declares the
LORD.
40 "I will bring them down like lambs to
the slaughter,
Like rams together with male goats.
41 "How Sheshak has been captured,
And the praise of the whole earth
been seized!
How Babylon has become an object
of horror among the nations!
42 "The sea has come up over Babylon;
She has been engulfed with its
tumultuous waves.
43 "Her cities have become an object of
horror,
A parched land and a desert,
A land in which no man lives
And through which no son of man
passes.
44 "I will punish Bel in Babylon,
And I will make what he has
swallowed come out of his mouth;
And the nations will no longer
stream to him.
Even the wall of Babylon has fallen
down!
45 "Come forth from her midst, My
people,
And each of you save yourselves
From the fierce anger of the LORD.
46 "Now so that your heart does not
grow faint,
And you are not afraid at the report
that *will be* heard in the land—
For the report will come one year,
And after that another report in
another year,
And violence *will be* in the land
With ruler against ruler—
47 Therefore behold, days are coming
When I will punish the idols of
Babylon;

And her whole land will be put to
shame
And all her slain will fall in her midst.
48 "Then heaven and earth and all that
is in them
Will shout for joy over Babylon,
For the destroyers will come to her
from the north,"
Declares the LORD.
49 Indeed Babylon is to fall *for* the
slain of Israel,
As also for Babylon the slain of all
the earth have fallen.
50 You who have escaped the sword,
Depart! Do not stay!
Remember the LORD from afar,
And let Jerusalem come to your
mind.
51 We are ashamed because we have
heard reproach;
Disgrace has covered our faces,
For aliens have entered
The holy places of the LORD's house.
52 "Therefore behold, the days are
coming," declares the LORD,
"When I will punish her idols,
And the mortally wounded will
groan throughout her land.
53 "Though Babylon should ascend to
the heavens,
And though she should fortify her
lofty stronghold,
From Me destroyers will come to
her," declares the LORD.
54 The sound of an outcry from
Babylon,
And of great destruction from the
land of the Chaldeans!
55 For the LORD is going to destroy
Babylon,
And He will make *her* loud noise
vanish from her.
And their waves will roar like many
waters;
The tumult of their voices sounds
forth.
56 For the destroyer is coming against
her, against Babylon,
And her mighty men will be
captured,
Their bows are shattered;
For the LORD is a God of recompense,
He will fully repay.
57 "I will make her princes and her wise
men drunk,
Her governors, her prefects and her
mighty men,

That they may sleep a perpetual
sleep and not wake up,"
Declares the King, whose name is
the LORD of hosts.
58 Thus says the LORD of hosts,
"The broad wall of Babylon will be
completely razed
And her high gates will be set on fire;
So the peoples will toil for nothing,
And the nations become exhausted
only for fire."
59 The message which Jeremiah the
prophet commanded Seraiah the son of
Neriah, the grandson of Mahseiah, when
he went with Zedekiah the king of Judah
to Babylon in the fourth year of his reign.
(Now Seraiah was quartermaster.)
60 So Jeremiah wrote in a single scroll
all the calamity which would come upon
Babylon, *that is,* all these words which
have been written concerning Babylon.
61 Then Jeremiah said to Seraiah, "As
soon as you come to Babylon, then see
that you read all these words aloud,
62 and say, 'You, O LORD, have promised concerning this place to cut it off,
so that there will be nothing dwelling in
it, whether man or beast, but it will be a
perpetual desolation.'
63 "And as soon as you finish reading
this scroll, you will tie a stone to it and
throw it into the middle of the Euphrates,
64 and say, 'Just so shall Babylon sink
down and not rise again because of the
calamity that I am going to bring upon
her; and they will become exhausted.'"
Thus far are the words of Jeremiah.

52 ZEDEKIAH was twenty-one years
old when he became king, and he
reigned eleven years in Jerusalem; and
his mother's name was Hamutal the
daughter of Jeremiah of Libnah.
2 He did evil in the sight of the LORD
like all that Jehoiakim had done.
3 For through the anger of the LORD
this came about in Jerusalem and Judah
until He cast them out from His presence.
And Zedekiah rebelled against the king
of Babylon.
4 Now it came about in the ninth
year of his reign, on the tenth *day* of the
tenth month, that Nebuchadnezzar king
of Babylon came, he and all his army,
against Jerusalem, camped against it and
built a siege wall all around it.
5 So the city was under siege until the
eleventh year of King Zedekiah.

6 On the ninth *day* of the fourth month the famine was so severe in the city that there was no food for the people of the land.

7 Then the city was broken into, and all the men of war fled and went forth from the city at night by way of the gate between the two walls which *was* by the king's garden, though the Chaldeans were all around the city. And they went by way of the Arabah.

8 But the army of the Chaldeans pursued the king and overtook Zedekiah in the plains of Jericho, and all his army was scattered from him.

9 Then they captured the king and brought him up to the king of Babylon at Riblah in the land of Hamath, and he passed sentence on him.

10 The king of Babylon slaughtered the sons of Zedekiah before his eyes, and he also slaughtered all the princes of Judah in Riblah.

11 Then he blinded the eyes of Zedekiah; and the king of Babylon bound him with bronze fetters and brought him to Babylon and put him in prison until the day of his death.

12 Now on the tenth *day* of the fifth month, which was the nineteenth year of King Nebuchadnezzar, king of Babylon, Nebuzaradan the captain of the bodyguard, who was in the service of the king of Babylon, came to Jerusalem.

13 He burned the house of the LORD, the king's house and all the houses of Jerusalem; even every large house he burned with fire.

14 So all the army of the Chaldeans who *were* with the captain of the guard broke down all the walls around Jerusalem.

15 Then Nebuzaradan the captain of the guard carried away into exile some of the poorest of the people, the rest of the people who were left in the city, the deserters who had deserted to the king of Babylon and the rest of the artisans.

16 But Nebuzaradan the captain of the guard left some of the poorest of the land to be vinedressers and plowmen.

17 Now the bronze pillars which belonged to the house of the LORD and the stands and the bronze sea, which were in the house of the LORD, the Chaldeans broke in pieces and carried all their bronze to Babylon.

18 They also took away the pots, the shovels, the snuffers, the basins, the pans and all the bronze vessels which were used in *temple* service.

19 The captain of the guard also took away the bowls, the firepans, the basins, the pots, the lampstands, the pans and the drink offering bowls, what was fine gold and what was fine silver.

20 The two pillars, the one sea, and the twelve bronze bulls that were under the sea, *and* the stands, which King Solomon had made for the house of the LORD—the bronze of all these vessels was beyond weight.

21 As for the pillars, the height of each pillar *was* eighteen cubits, and it *was* twelve cubits in circumference and four fingers in thickness, *and* hollow.

22 Now a capital of bronze was on it; and the height of each capital was five cubits, with network and pomegranates upon the capital all around, all of bronze. And the second pillar was like these, including pomegranates.

23 There were ninety-six exposed pomegranates; all the pomegranates *numbered* a hundred on the network all around.

24 Then the captain of the guard took Seraiah the chief priest and Zephaniah the second priest, with the three officers of the temple.

25 He also took from the city one official who was overseer of the men of war, and seven of the king's advisers who were found in the city, and the scribe of the commander of the army who mustered the people of the land, and sixty men of the people of the land who were found in the midst of the city.

26 Nebuzaradan the captain of the guard took them and brought them to the king of Babylon at Riblah.

27 Then the king of Babylon struck them down and put them to death at Riblah in the land of Hamath. So Judah was led away into exile from its land.

28 These are the people whom Nebuchadnezzar carried away into exile: in the seventh year 3,023 Jews;

29 in the eighteenth year of Nebuchadnezzar 832 persons from Jerusalem;

30 in the twenty-third year of Nebuchadnezzar, Nebuzaradan the captain of the guard carried into exile 745 Jewish people; there were 4,600 persons in all.

31 Now it came about in the thirty-seventh year of the exile of Jehoiachin king of Judah, in the twelfth month, on the twenty-fifth of the month, that Evil-merodach king of Babylon, in the *first* year of his reign, showed favor to Jehoiachin king of Judah and brought him out of prison.

32 Then he spoke kindly to him and set his throne above the thrones of the kings who *were* with him in Babylon.

33 So Jehoiachin changed his prison clothes, and had his meals in the king's presence regularly all the days of his life.

➤ 34 For his allowance, a regular allowance was given him by the king of Babylon, a daily portion all the days of his life until the day of his death.

Psalm 119:129–136

ד Pe.

129 Your testimonies are wonderful;
    Therefore my soul observes them.
✳ 130 The unfolding of Your words gives light;
    It gives understanding to the simple.
131 I opened my mouth wide and panted,
    For I longed for Your commandments.
132 Turn to me and be gracious to me,
    After Your manner with those who love Your name.
133 Establish my footsteps in Your word,
    And do not let any iniquity have dominion over me.
134 Redeem me from the oppression of man,
    That I may keep Your precepts.
135 Make Your face shine upon Your servant,
    And teach me Your statutes.
136 My eyes shed streams of water,
    Because they do not keep Your law.

Proverbs 28:7, 8

7 He who keeps the law is a discerning son,
    But he who is a companion of gluttons humiliates his father.
8 He who increases his wealth by interest and usury

LIFE LESSONS

➤ **Jeremiah 52:34 — *A regular allowance was given him by the king of Babylon.***

*W*hile Jeremiah had predicted that King Jehoiachin (also called Coniah) would die in Babylon (Jer. 22:24-26), the false prophet Hananiah predicted that the king would return in triumph to Jerusalem (Jer. 28:4). This passage shows that Jeremiah's prophecies were ultimately proven true, and He was vindicated by God.

Gathers it for him who is gracious to the poor.

Titus 2:1–15

2 BUT as for you, speak the things which are fitting for sound doctrine.

2 Older men are to be temperate, dignified, sensible, sound in faith, in love, in perseverance.

3 Older women likewise are to be reverent in their behavior, not malicious gossips nor enslaved to much wine, teaching what is good,

4 so that they may encourage the young women to love their husbands, to love their children,

5 *to be* sensible, pure, workers at home, kind, being subject to their own husbands, so that the word of God will not be dishonored.

6 Likewise urge the young men to be sensible;

7 in all things show yourself to be an example of good deeds, *with* purity in doctrine, dignified,

8 sound *in* speech which is beyond reproach, so that the opponent will be

LIFE LESSONS

➤ **Titus 2:7 — *Show yourself to be an example of good deeds, with purity in doctrine, dignified.***

*L*eaders must make sure they are worth following, in both conduct and in what they teach. Character and competence are both necessary if the church of God is to successfully fulfill its mission.

WHAT THE BIBLE SAYS ABOUT

The Gift of Teaching

Titus 2:1–6

God has given each believer at least one spiritual gift to build up the body of Christ and to minister in our hurting world. If our gift is prophecy, we will proclaim God's view of right and wrong. If it is service, we will desire to meet others' needs.

The gift of teaching has these characteristics:

- *Organized.* Whether in conversation or in a more formal setting, we will seek to communicate information clearly so the listener can follow. God has wired us to analyze material and present it logically.
- *Thorough.* We want others to understand not simply the conclusion but the steps leading up to it. We also desire to help them think matters through.
- *Accurate.* Our priority is to know the truth, so we ask questions in an attempt to validate the accuracy of what we learn. We will also inquire about the trustworthiness of our source of information.
- *Studious.* We derive great delight from studying and researching and are strongly motivated to share what we learn. Truth

is presented not simply to share knowledge but with the goal that God will transform the hearer's life.

- *Bible-oriented.* With this gift comes a strong desire to know what the Lord has to say. While we may recognize the value of others' experiences, reading about them is not our main concern. Nor are we especially motivated by personal illustrations.

All of the spiritual gifts can be used in the workplace, in our communities, and in our homes. We make effective use of our spiritual gifts when we are filled with the Spirit, but relying on ourselves will get us off track.

A Christian gifted in teaching reaps the fruit of self-control by faithfully absorbing and applying Scripture (Gal. 5:23), whereas shifting to human reasoning leads to self-indulgence. Through one's desire to learn, the Spirit develops dependability and diligence, but unless the believer abides in Christ, he or she can become careless and inconsistent. The fruit of peace and patience grows as studies lead to deeper faith, but anxiety and impatience result if the focus shifts to "self."

As you exercise your God-given gift, pray for the Spirit's leadership—that's how to have the greatest impact for the kingdom. Therefore, allow the Spirit to direct your teaching ability for God's glory and others' gain. ◈

---

put to shame, having nothing bad to say about us.

9 Urge bondslaves to be subject to their own masters in everything, to be well-pleasing, not argumentative,

10 not pilfering, but showing all good faith so that they will adorn the doctrine of God our Savior in every respect.

11 For the grace of God has appeared, bringing salvation to all men,

➤ **12** instructing us to deny ungodliness and worldly desires and to live sensibly, righteously and godly in the present age,

13 looking for the blessed hope and the appearing of the glory of our great God and Savior, Christ Jesus,

➤ **14** who gave Himself for us to redeem us from every lawless deed, and to purify for Himself a people for His own possession, zealous for good deeds.

15 These things speak and exhort and reprove with all authority. Let no one disregard you.

LIFE LESSONS

➤ **Titus 2:12 — *Live sensibly, righteously and godly.***

Just as we laid hold of salvation by grace through faith, so we lay hold of sanctification by grace through faith. By the power of grace we daily crucify our flesh in order to live for God.

➤ **Titus 2:14 — *Who gave Himself for us . . . to purify for Himself a people for His own possession, zealous for good deeds.***

The idea that Christianity is merely a social club and that believers have no responsibility other than believing in God, absolutely contradicts Scripture. We are to be zealously pursuing the work the Lord has called us to do (Eph. 2:10)—motivated by faith and hope in Him and committed to serving others and leading them into a growing relationship with Jesus Christ.

Lamentations 1:1—2:22

1 HOW lonely sits the city
That was full of people!
She has become like a widow
Who was *once* great among the
nations!
She who was a princess among the
provinces
Has become a forced laborer!

2 She weeps bitterly in the night
And her tears are on her cheeks;
She has none to comfort her
Among all her lovers.
All her friends have dealt
treacherously with her;
They have become her enemies.

3 Judah has gone into exile under
affliction
And under harsh servitude;
She dwells among the nations,
But she has found no rest;
All her pursuers have overtaken
her
In the midst of distress.

4 The roads of Zion are in mourning
Because no one comes to the
appointed feasts.
All her gates are desolate;
Her priests are groaning,
Her virgins are afflicted,
And she herself is bitter.

5 Her adversaries have become her
masters,
Her enemies prosper;
For the LORD has caused her grief
Because of the multitude of her
transgressions;
Her little ones have gone away
As captives before the adversary.

6 All her majesty
Has departed from the daughter of
Zion;
Her princes have become like deer
That have found no pasture;
And they have fled without strength
Before the pursuer.

7 In the days of her affliction and
homelessness
Jerusalem remembers all her
precious things
That were from the days of old,
When her people fell into the hand
of the adversary
And no one helped her.
The adversaries saw her,
They mocked at her ruin.

8 Jerusalem sinned greatly,
Therefore she has become an
unclean thing.
All who honored her despise her
Because they have seen her
nakedness;
Even she herself groans and turns
away.

9 Her uncleanness was in her skirts;
She did not consider her future.
Therefore she has fallen
astonishingly;
She has no comforter.
"See, O LORD, my affliction,
For the enemy has magnified
himself!"

10 The adversary has stretched out his
hand
Over all her precious things,
For she has seen the nations enter
her sanctuary,
The ones whom You commanded
That they should not enter into Your
congregation.

11 All her people groan seeking bread;
They have given their precious
things for food
To restore their lives themselves.
"See, O LORD, and look,
For I am despised."

12 "Is it nothing to all you who pass this
way?
Look and see if there is any pain
like my pain
Which was severely dealt out to me,
Which the LORD inflicted on the day
of His fierce anger.

13 "From on high He sent fire into my
bones,

LIFE LESSONS

➢ **Lamentations 1:8** — *Jerusalem sinned
greatly, therefore she has become an
unclean thing.*

*D*espite what the world may suggest,
sin does not make us cool, fashion-
able, sophisticated, or attractive. It only
destroys us and makes us vile. Therefore,
we must stop trying to impress those
who are headed for destruction, and
obey the One who created and saves us.
In Him is all the acceptance and love we
need.

WHAT THE BIBLE SAYS ABOUT ⊕

Barriers to Knowing God's Will

Lamentations 1—2

In Lamentations, the prophet Jeremiah describes the desolation of Jerusalem after the Babylonians carried off the Jews. Yet we may wonder how the people of Judah got to this point—especially after all of Jeremiah's warnings to them. Jeremiah had told them exactly what was going to happen (Jer. 20:4, 5). Of course, they ignored him because of their sinfulness; however, there are some things we should note to avoid their mistakes.

Remember, God is always pleased to reveal His will to us. But at times, we cannot or will not receive the message. Something in our lives is creating a barrier to hearing Him.

Obstacles to the believer include *self-will.* Sometimes, we decide what we're going to do without God's input. We still talk to Him about our plans, even thinking they are so logical that the Lord must agree. But we have stopped listening for His will.

A second obstacle to Christians is *influence.* It's wise to seek godly counsel. But believers must be careful whom they allow to influence them. Many people will say what someone else wants to hear rather than what is actually needed.

A third barrier is *sin.* There are two ways sin hinders our ability to know God's will. First, our spirit is clouded so we cannot determine His mind. Second, the Father may not reveal the next step in His plan because He's waiting for us to repent and become willing to obey.

A fourth obstacle for believers is *distraction.* One of the most subtle obstructions to knowing God's will is busyness. Our hands and our minds are so full we don't have the patience to wait and listen. The Lord does not chase after us, trying to force us to hear Him. Psalm 46:10—"Cease striving and know that I am God"—is His simple solution for clearing the clutter of overbooked lives.

The next time you seem unable to determine the Lord's will, try slowing down so that you can focus on Him. Then, consider whether you might have allowed one of these barriers to be constructed between you and God. Ask, and He will gladly help you to dismantle it. ⊕

And it prevailed *over them.*
He has spread a net for my feet;
He has turned me back;
He has made me desolate,
Faint all day long.
14 "The yoke of my transgressions is
      bound;
By His hand they are knit together.
They have come upon my neck;
He has made my strength fail.
The Lord has given me into the
      hands
Of *those against whom* I am not
      able to stand.
15 "The Lord has rejected all my strong
      men
In my midst;
He has called an appointed time
      against me
To crush my young men;
The Lord has trodden *as in* a wine
      press
The virgin daughter of Judah.
16 "For these things I weep;
My eyes run down with water;
Because far from me is a comforter,
One who restores my soul.

My children are desolate
Because the enemy has prevailed."
17 Zion stretches out her hands;
There is no one to comfort her;
The LORD has commanded
      concerning Jacob
That the ones round about him
      should be his adversaries;
Jerusalem has become an unclean
      thing among them.
18 "The LORD is righteous;
For I have rebelled against His
      command;
Hear now, all peoples,
And behold my pain;
My virgins and my young men
Have gone into captivity.
19 "I called to my lovers, *but* they
      deceived me;
My priests and my elders perished
      in the city
While they sought food to restore
      their strength themselves.
20 "See, O LORD, for I am in distress;
My spirit is greatly troubled;
My heart is overturned within me,
For I have been very rebellious.

In the street the sword slays;
In the house it is like death.
21 "They have heard that I groan;
There is no one to comfort me;
All my enemies have heard of my
calamity;
They are glad that You have done *it.*
Oh, that You would bring the day
which You have proclaimed,
That they may become like me.
22 "Let all their wickedness come
before You;
And deal with them as You have
dealt with me
For all my transgressions;
For my groans are many and my
heart is faint."

2 HOW the Lord has covered the
daughter of Zion
With a cloud in His anger!
He has cast from heaven to earth
The glory of Israel,
And has not remembered His
footstool
In the day of His anger.
2 The Lord has swallowed up; He has
not spared
All the habitations of Jacob.
In His wrath He has thrown down
The strongholds of the daughter of
Judah;
He has brought *them* down to the
ground;
He has profaned the kingdom and
its princes.
3 In fierce anger He has cut off
All the strength of Israel;
He has drawn back His right hand
From before the enemy.
And He has burned in Jacob like a
flaming fire
Consuming round about.
4 He has bent His bow like an enemy;
He has set His right hand like an
adversary
And slain all that were pleasant to
the eye;
In the tent of the daughter of Zion
He has poured out His wrath like
fire.
5 The Lord has become like an enemy.
He has swallowed up Israel;
He has swallowed up all its palaces,
He has destroyed its strongholds
And multiplied in the daughter of
Judah
Mourning and moaning.

6 And He has violently treated His
tabernacle like a garden *booth;*
He has destroyed His appointed
meeting place.
The LORD has caused to be forgotten
The appointed feast and sabbath in
Zion,
And He has despised king and
priest
In the indignation of His anger.
7 The Lord has rejected His altar,
He has abandoned His sanctuary;
He has delivered into the hand of
the enemy
The walls of her palaces.
They have made a noise in the
house of the LORD
As in the day of an appointed feast.
8 The LORD determined to destroy
The wall of the daughter of Zion.
He has stretched out a line,
He has not restrained His hand
from destroying,
And He has caused rampart and
wall to lament;
They have languished together.
9 Her gates have sunk into the
ground,
He has destroyed and broken her
bars.
Her king and her princes are among
the nations;
The law is no more.
Also, her prophets find
No vision from the LORD.
10 The elders of the daughter of Zion
Sit on the ground, they are silent.
They have thrown dust on their
heads;
They have girded themselves with
sackcloth.
The virgins of Jerusalem
Have bowed their heads to the
ground.
11 My eyes fail because of tears,
My spirit is greatly troubled;
My heart is poured out on the earth
Because of the destruction of the
daughter of my people,
When little ones and infants faint
In the streets of the city.
12 They say to their mothers,
"Where is grain and wine?"
As they faint like a wounded man
In the streets of the city,
As their life is poured out
On their mothers' bosom.

13 How shall I admonish you?
    To what shall I compare you,
    O daughter of Jerusalem?
    To what shall I liken you as I
        comfort you,
    O virgin daughter of Zion?
    For your ruin is as vast as the sea;
    Who can heal you?
➤ 14 Your prophets have seen for you
    False and foolish *visions;*
    And they have not exposed your
        iniquity
    So as to restore you from captivity,
    But they have seen for you false and
        misleading oracles.
15 All who pass along the way
    Clap their hands *in derision* at you;
    They hiss and shake their heads
    At the daughter of Jerusalem,
    "Is this the city of which they said,
    'The perfection of beauty,
    A joy to all the earth'?"
16 All your enemies
    Have opened their mouths wide
        against you;
    They hiss and gnash *their* teeth.
    They say, "We have swallowed *her*
        up!
    Surely this is the day for which we
        waited;
    We have reached *it,* we have seen
        it."
➤ 17 The LORD has done what He
    purposed;

LIFE LESSONS

➤ **Lamentations 2:14** — *Your prophets have seen for you false and foolish
visions; and they have not exposed your
iniquity.*

*W*e can trust God's Word, not only
     because it speaks to us of pleasant
things like heaven, grace, and love, but
also because it uncovers our sins, so that
we may turn from them and live.

➤ **Lamentations 2:17** — *The LORD has
done what He purposed; He has accomplished His word which He commanded
from days of old.*

*W*e never have to wonder whether
     the Lord will keep His promises. We
never have to question whether He will
really fulfill His Word. Whatever He says,
He will do (Matt. 5:18).

He has accomplished His word
Which He commanded from days of
    old.
He has thrown down without sparing,
And He has caused the enemy to
    rejoice over you;
He has exalted the might of your
    adversaries.
18 Their heart cried out to the Lord,
    "O wall of the daughter of Zion,
    Let *your* tears run down like a river
        day and night;
    Give yourself no relief,
    Let your eyes have no rest.
19 "Arise, cry aloud in the night
    At the beginning of the night
        watches;
    Pour out your heart like water
    Before the presence of the Lord;
    Lift up your hands to Him
    For the life of your little ones
    Who are faint because of hunger
    At the head of every street."
20 See, O LORD, and look!
    With whom have You dealt thus?
    Should women eat their offspring,
    The little ones who were born
        healthy?
    Should priest and prophet be slain
    In the sanctuary of the Lord?
21 On the ground in the streets
    Lie young and old;
    My virgins and my young men
    Have fallen by the sword.
    You have slain *them* in the day of
        Your anger,
    You have slaughtered, not sparing.
22 You called as in the day of an
        appointed feast
    My terrors on every side;
    And there was no one who escaped
        or survived
    In the day of the LORD'S anger.
    Those whom I bore and reared,
    My enemy annihilated them.

✦ Psalm 119:137–144

צ Tsadhe.

137 Righteous are You, O LORD,
    And upright are Your judgments.
138 You have commanded Your
        testimonies in righteousness
    And exceeding faithfulness.

139 My zeal has consumed me,
    Because my adversaries have
        forgotten Your words.
140 Your word is very pure,
    Therefore Your servant loves it.
141 I am small and despised,
    Yet I do not forget Your precepts.
142 Your righteousness is an everlasting
        righteousness,
    And Your law is truth.
143 Trouble and anguish have come
        upon me,
    Yet Your commandments are my
        delight.
144 Your testimonies are righteous
        forever;
    Give me understanding that I may
        live.

Proverbs 28:9, 10

9   He who turns away his ear from
        listening to the law,
    Even his prayer is an abomination.
10 He who leads the upright astray in
        an evil way
    Will himself fall into his own pit,
    But the blameless will inherit
        good.

Titus 3:1–15

3 REMIND them to be subject to rulers,
  to authorities, to be obedient, to be
ready for every good deed,
2   to malign no one, to be peaceable,
gentle, showing every consideration for
all men.
3   For we also once were foolish ourselves, disobedient, deceived, enslaved
to various lusts and pleasures, spending
our life in malice and envy, hateful, hating one another.
4   But when the kindness of God our
Savior and His love for mankind appeared,
5   He saved us, not on the basis of
deeds which we have done in righteousness, but according to His mercy, by the
washing of regeneration and renewing
by the Holy Spirit,
6   whom He poured out upon us richly
through Jesus Christ our Savior,

7   so that being justified by His grace
we would be made heirs according to the
hope of eternal life.
8   This is a trustworthy statement; and
concerning these things I want you to
speak confidently, so that those who
have believed God will be careful to
engage in good deeds. These things are
good and profitable for men.
9   But avoid foolish controversies
and genealogies and strife and disputes
about the Law, for they are unprofitable
and worthless.
10 Reject a factious man after a first
and second warning,

LIFE LESSONS

➤ Titus 3:2 — *Be peaceable, gentle,
showing every consideration for all men.*

*J*esus had all power, yet He came to
serve, not to be served (Mark 10:45).
Therefore, Paul admonishes, "Do nothing from selfishness or empty conceit,
but with humility of mind regard one
another as more important than yourselves" (Phil. 2:3). We are to resemble
Christ in all ways, especially in the manner we treat others.

➤ Titus 3:8 — *Those who have believed
in God will be careful to engage in good
deeds.*

*A*re we living in a manner that
reflects the purpose and work of
the Lord Jesus? Are we learning to be
helpers, encouragers, and servants—
giving ourselves away? Are we faithfully
reading God's Word, remaining fervent
in prayer, and devotedly worshipping
Him? Are we obeying the Lord no matter
what He asks of us? This is the evidence
that we really believe in God and that
we have truly embraced His salvation
(2 Pet. 1:3–8).

➤ Titus 3:9 — *Avoid foolish controversies and genealogies and strife and
disputes about the Law, for they are
unprofitable and worthless.*

*P*aul admonished Titus to avoid useless discussions because they distracted believers from the Lord's purpose
for their lives. However, when God is in
the center of our conversations, all that
we say and do will reflect His love and
truth.

11 knowing that such a man is perverted and is sinning, being self-condemned.

12 When I send Artemas or Tychicus to you, make every effort to come to me at Nicopolis, for I have decided to spend the winter there.

13 Diligently help Zenas the lawyer and Apollos on their way so that nothing is lacking for them.

14 Our people must also learn to engage in good deeds to meet pressing needs, so that they will not be unfruitful.

15 All who are with me greet you. Greet those who love us in *the* faith.

Grace be with you all.

🧭 Lamentations 3:1—5:22

3 I AM the man who has seen affliction
Because of the rod of His wrath.

2 He has driven me and made me walk
In darkness and not in light.

3 Surely against me He has turned His hand
Repeatedly all the day.

4 He has caused my flesh and my skin to waste away,
He has broken my bones.

5 He has besieged and encompassed me with bitterness and hardship.

6 In dark places He has made me dwell,
Like those who have long been dead.

7 He has walled me in so that I cannot go out;
He has made my chain heavy.

8 Even when I cry out and call for help,
He shuts out my prayer.

9 He has blocked my ways with hewn stone;
He has made my paths crooked.

10 He is to me like a bear lying in wait,
Like a lion in secret places.

11 He has turned aside my ways and torn me to pieces;
He has made me desolate.

12 He bent His bow
And set me as a target for the arrow.

13 He made the arrows of His quiver
To enter into my inward parts.

14 I have become a laughingstock to all my people,
Their *mocking* song all the day.

15 He has filled me with bitterness,

He has made me drunk with wormwood.

16 He has broken my teeth with gravel;
He has made me cower in the dust.

17 My soul has been rejected from peace;
I have forgotten happiness.

18 So I say, "My strength has perished,
And *so has* my hope from the LORD."

19 Remember my affliction and my wandering, the wormwood and bitterness.

20 Surely my soul remembers
And is bowed down within me.

21 This I recall to my mind,
Therefore I have hope.

22 The LORD's lovingkindnesses indeed never cease,
For His compassions never fail.

23 *They* are new every morning;
Great is Your faithfulness.   ✳

24 "The LORD is my portion," says my soul,
"Therefore I have hope in Him."

25 The LORD is good to those who wait ⊰
for Him,
To the person who seeks Him.

LIFE LESSONS

➤ **Lamentations 3:25 —** *The LORD is good to those who wait for Him, to the person who seeks Him.*

*W*aiting upon God isn't passive. We don't sit with folded hands until He acts on our behalf. Instead, we praise and worship Him, we inquire about His ways, we pray, and we obey whatever He tells us to do. We ask, seek, and knock in a prudent fashion with faith and confidence that He will do just as He's promised.

WHAT THE BIBLE SAYS ABOUT ◉

God's Limitations on Adversity

Lamentations 3:33

*T*he Lord uses adversity in the life of the believer for many purposes, all of them ultimately good. He uses adversity to conform us to the image of Christ, and He provides a bridge to a deeper relationship with Himself through it.

Unfortunately, none of these statements can be made on behalf of the unbeliever. The unbeliever stands before God in a position of estrangement and alienation. Still, God loves all men and women and wants each one of us to come to a point of repentance.

The Father is just and righteous. He *must* judge and oppose sin. He allows both the saved and the unsaved person to bear the consequences of their willful sin and acts of transgression. He moves decisively against sin with the desire that all would repent of their sin and seek Him wholeheartedly. That is the message of the Book of Lamentations when Jeremiah concludes that the Lord does not willingly afflict the children of men forever (Lam. 3:31–33). He will show compassion; therefore, we should turn to Him, trust Him, and remember His lovingkindness.

The Lord does not desire adversity for His people. Rather, He responds wisely and appropriately to our actions and works to fulfill His purpose in our lives. Fortunately, the dark moments of our lives will last only so long as is necessary for God to accomplish His purpose in us. ◈

26 *It is* good that he waits silently
　　For the salvation of the LORD.
27 *It is* good for a man that he should bear
　　The yoke in his youth.
28 Let him sit alone and be silent
　　Since He has laid *it* on him.
29 Let him put his mouth in the dust,
　　Perhaps there is hope.
30 Let him give his cheek to the smiter,
　　Let him be filled with reproach.
➤ 31 For the Lord will not reject forever,
32 For if He causes grief,
　　Then He will have compassion
　　According to His abundant lovingkindness.
33 For He does not afflict willingly
　　Or grieve the sons of men.
34 To crush under His feet
　　All the prisoners of the land,

35 To deprive a man of justice
　　In the presence of the Most High,
36 To defraud a man in his lawsuit—
　　Of these things the Lord does not approve.
37 Who is there who speaks and it comes to pass,
　　Unless the Lord has commanded *it*?
38 *Is it* not from the mouth of the Most High
　　That both good and ill go forth?
39 Why should *any* living mortal, or *any* man,
　　Offer complaint in view of his sins?
40 Let us examine and probe our ways,
　　And let us return to the LORD.
41 We lift up our heart and hands
　　Toward God in heaven;
42 We have transgressed and rebelled,
　　You have not pardoned.
43 You have covered *Yourself* with anger
　　And pursued us;
　　You have slain *and* have not spared.
44 You have covered Yourself with a cloud
　　So that no prayer can pass through.
45 *You have made us mere* offscouring and refuse
　　In the midst of the peoples.
46 All our enemies have opened their mouths against us.
47 Panic and pitfall have befallen us,
　　Devastation and destruction;

LIFE LESSONS

➤ **Lamentations 3:31, 32 — *The LORD will not reject forever, for if He causes grief, then He will have compassion.***

*T*he Lord sometimes brings affliction into our lives, not to hurt us, but to shape and mold us increasingly into the image of His Son (Rom. 8:29; Rom. 12:1, 2). Adversity is a bridge to a deeper relationship with God, and it will last only so long as is necessary for Him to accomplish His purpose in us.

That the adversary and the enemy
Could enter the gates of Jerusalem.

13 Because of the sins of her prophets
And the iniquities of her priests,
Who have shed in her midst
The blood of the righteous;

14 They wandered, blind, in the streets;
They were defiled with blood
So that no one could touch their
garments.

15 "Depart! Unclean!" they cried of
themselves.
"Depart, depart, do not touch!"
So they fled and wandered;
Men among the nations said,
"They shall not continue to dwell
with us."

16 The presence of the LORD has
scattered them,
He will not continue to regard them;
They did not honor the priests,
They did not favor the elders.

17 Yet our eyes failed,
Looking for help was useless;
In our watching we have watched
For a nation that could not save.

18 They hunted our steps
So that we could not walk in our
streets;
Our end drew near,
Our days were finished
For our end had come.

19 Our pursuers were swifter
Than the eagles of the sky;
They chased us on the mountains,
They waited in ambush for us in the
wilderness.

20 The breath of our nostrils, the
LORD'S anointed,
Was captured in their pits,
Of whom we had said, "Under his
shadow
We shall live among the nations."

21 Rejoice and be glad, O daughter of
Edom,
Who dwells in the land of Uz;
But the cup will come around to you
as well,
You will become drunk and make
yourself naked.

22 *The punishment* of your iniquity
has been completed, O daughter
of Zion;
He will exile you no longer.
But He will punish your iniquity,
O daughter of Edom;
He will expose your sins!

5 REMEMBER, O LORD, what has
befallen us;
Look, and see our reproach!

2 Our inheritance has been turned
over to strangers,
Our houses to aliens.

3 We have become orphans without a
father,
Our mothers are like widows.

4 We have to pay for our drinking
water,
Our wood comes *to us* at a price.

5 Our pursuers are at our necks;
We are worn out, there is no rest for
us.

6 We have submitted to Egypt *and*
Assyria to get enough bread.

7 Our fathers sinned, *and* are no
more;
It is we who have borne their
iniquities.

8 Slaves rule over us;
There is no one to deliver us from
their hand.

9 We get our bread at the risk of our
lives
Because of the sword in the
wilderness.

10 Our skin has become as hot as an
oven,
Because of the burning heat of
famine.

11 They ravished the women in Zion,
The virgins in the cities of Judah.

12 Princes were hung by their hands;
Elders were not respected.

13 Young men worked at the grinding
mill,
And youths stumbled under *loads* of
wood.

14 Elders are gone from the gate,
Young men from their music.

15 The joy of our hearts has ceased;
Our dancing has been turned into
mourning.

16 The crown has fallen from our
head;
Woe to us, for we have sinned!

17 Because of this our heart is faint,
Because of these things our eyes are
dim;

18 Because of Mount Zion which lies
desolate,
Foxes prowl in it.

19 You, O LORD, rule forever;
Your throne is from generation to
generation.

48 My eyes run down with streams of
water
Because of the destruction of the
daughter of my people.
49 My eyes pour down unceasingly,
Without stopping,
50 Until the LORD looks down
And sees from heaven.
51 My eyes bring pain to my soul
Because of all the daughters of my
city.
52 My enemies without cause
Hunted me down like a bird;
53 They have silenced me in the pit
And have placed a stone on me.
54 Waters flowed over my head;
I said, "I am cut off!"
55 I called on Your name, O LORD,
Out of the lowest pit.
56 You have heard my voice,
"Do not hide Your ear from my
prayer for relief,
From my cry for help."
57 You drew near when I called on
You;
You said, "Do not fear!"
58 O Lord, You have pleaded my soul's
cause;
You have redeemed my life.
59 O LORD, You have seen my
oppression;
Judge my case.
60 You have seen all their vengeance,
All their schemes against me.
61 You have heard their reproach,
O LORD,
All their schemes against me.
62 The lips of my assailants and their
whispering
Are against me all day long.
63 Look on their sitting and their
rising;
I am their mocking song.
64 You will recompense them, O LORD,
According to the work of their
hands.
65 You will give them hardness of
heart,
Your curse will be on them.
66 You will pursue them in anger and
destroy them
From under the heavens of the
LORD!

4 HOW dark the gold has become,
How the pure gold has changed!
The sacred stones are poured out
At the corner of every street.

2 The precious sons of Zion,
Weighed against fine gold,
How they are regarded as earthen
jars,
The work of a potter's hands!
3 Even jackals offer the breast,
They nurse their young;
But the daughter of my people has
become cruel
Like ostriches in the wilderness.
4 The tongue of the infant cleaves
To the roof of its mouth because of
thirst;
The little ones ask for bread,
But no one breaks it for them.
5 Those who ate delicacies
Are desolate in the streets;
Those reared in purple
Embrace ash pits.
6 For the iniquity of the daughter of
my people
Is greater than the sin of Sodom,
Which was overthrown as in a
moment,
And no hands were turned toward
her.
7 Her consecrated ones were purer
than snow,
They were whiter than milk;
They were more ruddy in body than
corals,
Their polishing was like lapis lazuli.
8 Their appearance is blacker than
soot,
They are not recognized in the
streets;
Their skin is shriveled on their bones,
It is withered, it has become like
wood.
9 Better are those slain with the sword
Than those slain with hunger;
For they pine away, being stricken
For lack of the fruits of the field.
10 The hands of compassionate women
Boiled their own children;
They became food for them
Because of the destruction of the
daughter of my people.
11 The LORD has accomplished His
wrath,
He has poured out His fierce anger;
And He has kindled a fire in Zion
Which has consumed its
foundations.
12 The kings of the earth did not believe,
Nor did any of the inhabitants of the
world,

LIFE LESSONS

➤ **Lamentations 5:19** — *You, O LORD, rule forever; Your throne is from generation to generation.*

*W*e live in a time of enormous and rapid change. Yet God remains exactly the same today as He was in the days of Jeremiah—and as He will be forever (Heb. 13:8). The changes do not surprise Him, nor do they hinder Him in any way. Praise Him today!

20 Why do You forget us forever?
Why do You forsake us so long?
21 Restore us to You, O LORD, that we
may be restored;
Renew our days as of old,
22 Unless You have utterly rejected us
And are exceedingly angry with us.

Psalm 119:145–152

פ Qoph.

145 I cried with all my heart; answer
me, O LORD!
I will observe Your statutes.
146 I cried to You; save me
And I shall keep Your testimonies.
147 I rise before dawn and cry for help;
I wait for Your words.
148 My eyes anticipate the night watches,
That I may meditate on Your word.
149 Hear my voice according to Your
lovingkindness;
Revive me, O LORD, according to
Your ordinances.
150 Those who follow after wickedness
draw near;
They are far from Your law.
151 You are near, O LORD,
And all Your commandments are
truth.
152 Of old I have known from Your
testimonies
That You have founded them forever.

Proverbs 28:11

11 The rich man is wise in his own eyes,
But the poor who has understanding
sees through him.

Philemon 1–25

1 PAUL, a prisoner of Christ Jesus, and
Timothy our brother,
To Philemon our beloved *brother*
and fellow worker,
2 and to Apphia our sister, and to
Archippus our fellow soldier, and to the
church in your house:
3 Grace to you and peace from God
our Father and the Lord Jesus Christ.
4 I thank my God always, making
mention of you in my prayers,
5 because I hear of your love and of
the faith which you have toward the
Lord Jesus and toward all the saints;
6 *and I pray* that the fellowship of your
faith may become effective through the
knowledge of every good thing which is
in you for Christ's sake.
7 For I have come to have much joy
and comfort in your love, because the
hearts of the saints have been refreshed
through you, brother.
8 Therefore, though I have enough
confidence in Christ to order you *to do*
what is proper,
9 yet for love's sake I rather appeal *to
you*—since I am such a person as Paul,
the aged, and now also a prisoner of
Christ Jesus—
10 I appeal to you for my child Onesimus, whom I have begotten in my imprisonment,
11 who formerly was useless to you, but
now is useful both to you and to me.
12 I have sent him back to you in person, that is, *sending* my very heart,
13 whom I wished to keep with me,
so that on your behalf he might minister to me in my imprisonment for the
gospel;

LIFE LESSONS

➤ **Philemon 6** — *That the fellowship of
your faith may become effective through
the knowledge of every good thing
which is in you for Christ's sake.*

*P*aul wants his friend Philemon to
know that his testimony to outsiders
about the glories of Jesus will become
strong and powerful as he meditates on
how much Christ has already done for
him.

➤ **Philemon 14 —** *That your goodness would not be, in effect, by compulsion but of your own free will.*

*G*od has the power to compel us to do anything He wants, but He does not normally choose to use that power. Why? Because He wants our willing and joyful obedience, not grudging submission. If we truly believe His way is best, we will have no trouble doing exactly as He says.

➤ **Philemon 15 —** *Perhaps he was for this reason separated from you for a while, that you would have him back forever.*

*P*aul did not know why Onesimus ran away from his master. No doubt his escape caused an economic setback for Philemon. But Paul understood that trusting God in this situation would include looking beyond human reasoning. The Lord undoubtedly had a great purpose for both Onesimus and Philemon, and He would be glorified through the lives of these men.

➤ 14 but without your consent I did not want to do anything, so that your goodness would not be, in effect, by compulsion but of your own free will.

15 For perhaps he was for this reason ◄ separated *from you* for a while, that you would have him back forever,
16 no longer as a slave, but more than a slave, a beloved brother, especially to me, but how much more to you, both in the flesh and in the Lord.
17 If then you regard me a partner, accept him as *you would* me.
18 But if he has wronged you in any way or owes you anything, charge that to my account;
19 I, Paul, am writing this with my own hand, I will repay it (not to mention to you that you owe to me even your own self as well).
20 Yes, brother, let me benefit from you in the Lord; refresh my heart in Christ.
21 Having confidence in your obedience, I write to you, since I know that you will do even more than what I say.
22 At the same time also prepare me a lodging, for I hope that through your prayers I will be given to you.
23 Epaphras, my fellow prisoner in Christ Jesus, greets you,
24 *as do* Mark, Aristarchus, Demas, Luke, my fellow workers.
25 The grace of the Lord Jesus Christ be with your spirit.

NOVEMBER 5

◈ **Ezekiel 1:1—2:10**

➤ **1** NOW it came about in the thirtieth year, on the fifth *day* of the fourth month, while I was by the river Chebar among the exiles, the heavens were opened and I saw visions of God.
2 (On the fifth of the month in the fifth year of King Jehoiachin's exile,
3 the word of the LORD came expressly to Ezekiel the priest, son of Buzi, in the land of the Chaldeans by the river Chebar; and there the hand of the LORD came upon him.)
4 As I looked, behold, a storm wind was coming from the north, a great cloud with fire flashing forth continually and a bright light around it, and in its midst

something like glowing metal in the midst of the fire.
5 Within it there were figures resembling four living beings. And this was their appearance: they had human form.
6 Each of them had four faces and four wings.
7 Their legs were straight and their

➤ **Ezekiel 1:1 —** *I saw visions of God.*

*E*zekiel did not choose to see "visions of God." Rather, the Lord took the initiative and chose him. "No prophecy was ever made by an act of human will, but men moved by the Holy Spirit spoke from God" (2 Pet. 1:21).

feet were like a calf's hoof, and they gleamed like burnished bronze.

8 Under their wings on their four sides *were* human hands. As for the faces and wings of the four of them,

9 their wings touched one another; *their faces* did not turn when they moved, each went straight forward.

10 As for the form of their faces, *each* had the face of a man; all four had the face of a lion on the right and the face of a bull on the left, and all four had the face of an eagle.

11 Such were their faces. Their wings were spread out above; each had two touching another *being*, and two covering their bodies.

12 And each went straight forward; wherever the spirit was about to go, they would go, without turning as they went.

13 In the midst of the living beings there was something that looked like burning coals of fire, like torches darting back and forth among the living beings. The fire was bright, and lightning was flashing from the fire.

14 And the living beings ran to and fro like bolts of lightning.

15 Now as I looked at the living beings, behold, there was one wheel on the earth beside the living beings, for *each of* the four of them.

16 The appearance of the wheels and their workmanship *was* like sparkling beryl, and all four of them had the same form, their appearance and workmanship *being* as if one wheel were within another.

17 Whenever they moved, they moved in any of their four directions without turning as they moved.

18 As for their rims they were lofty and awesome, and the rims of all four of them were full of eyes round about.

19 Whenever the living beings moved, the wheels moved with them. And whenever the living beings rose from the earth, the wheels rose *also*.

20 Wherever the spirit was about to go, they would go in that direction. And the wheels rose close beside them; for the spirit of the living beings *was* in the wheels.

21 Whenever those went, these went; and whenever those stood still, these stood still. And whenever those rose from the earth, the wheels rose close

beside them; for the spirit of the living beings *was* in the wheels.

22 Now over the heads of the living beings *there was* something like an expanse, like the awesome gleam of crystal, spread out over their heads.

23 Under the expanse their wings *were stretched out* straight, one toward the other; each one also had two wings covering its body on the one side and on the other.

24 I also heard the sound of their wings like the sound of abundant waters as they went, like the voice of the Almighty, a sound of tumult like the sound of an army camp; whenever they stood still, they dropped their wings.

25 And there came a voice from above the expanse that was over their heads; whenever they stood still, they dropped their wings.

26 Now above the expanse that was over their heads there was something resembling a throne, like lapis lazuli in appearance; and on that which resembled a throne, high up, *was* a figure with the appearance of a man.

27 Then I noticed from the appearance of His loins and upward something like glowing metal that looked like fire all around within it, and from the appearance of His loins and downward I saw something like fire; and *there was* a radiance around Him.

28 As the appearance of the rainbow in the clouds on a rainy day, so *was* the appearance of the surrounding radiance. Such *was* the appearance of the likeness of the glory of the LORD. And when I saw *it*, I fell on my face and heard a voice speaking.

2 THEN He said to me, "Son of man, stand on your feet that I may speak with you!"

LIFE LESSONS

➤ **Ezekiel 1:28** — *Such was the appearance of the likeness of the glory of the* LORD.

*I*t is impossible to fully describe the splendor of God. The best Ezekiel or the apostle John could do was to compare it to something we've already seen, such as a rainbow or the sunshine (Rev. 1:16). However, God's glory is radically different from everything we know.

➤ 2   As He spoke to me the Spirit entered me and set me on my feet; and I heard *Him* speaking to me.

3   Then He said to me, "Son of man, I am sending you to the sons of Israel, to a rebellious people who have rebelled against Me; they and their fathers have transgressed against Me to this very day.

4   "I am sending you to them who are stubborn and obstinate children, and you shall say to them, 'Thus says the Lord GOD.'

5   "As for them, whether they listen or not—for they are a rebellious house—they will know that a prophet has been among them.

➤ 6   "And you, son of man, neither fear them nor fear their words, though thistles and thorns are with you and you sit on scorpions; neither fear their words nor be dismayed at their presence, for they are a rebellious house.

7   "But you shall speak My words to them whether they listen or not, for they are rebellious.

8   "Now you, son of man, listen to what I am speaking to you; do not be rebellious like that rebellious house. Open your mouth and eat what I am giving you."

9   Then I looked, and behold, a hand was extended to me; and lo, a scroll *was* in it.

10   When He spread it out before me, it was written on the front and back, and written on it were lamentations, mourning and woe.

LIFE LESSONS

➤ **Ezekiel 2:2 —** *As He spoke to me the Spirit entered me and set me on my feet.*

*G*od never gives us a command that He doesn't also give us the ability to fulfill. He never calls us to a task without also enabling us to complete it. He also assumes full responsibility for our needs when we obey Him.

➤ **Ezekiel 2:6 —** *"Neither fear them nor fear their words."*

*G*od sent Ezekiel to speak to a nation He called "rebellious" (Ezek. 2:6) and "stubborn and obstinate" (Ezek. 2:4). It was not an easy task! But since God would be with Ezekiel, the prophet did not have to fear.

Psalm 119:153–160

ר **Resh.**

153 Look upon my affliction and
       rescue me,
    For I do not forget Your law.
154 Plead my cause and redeem me;
    Revive me according to Your
       word.
155 Salvation is far from the wicked,
    For they do not seek Your
       statutes.
156 Great are Your mercies, O LORD;
    Revive me according to Your
       ordinances.
157 Many are my persecutors and my
       adversaries,
    Yet I do not turn aside from Your
       testimonies.
158 I behold the treacherous and loathe
       them,
    Because they do not keep Your
       word.
159 Consider how I love Your
       precepts;
    Revive me, O LORD, according to
       Your lovingkindness.
160 The sum of Your word is truth,
    And every one of Your righteous
       ordinances is everlasting.

Proverbs 28:12

12   When the righteous triumph, there
       is great glory,
    But when the wicked rise, men hide
       themselves.

Hebrews 1:1–14

1 GOD, after He spoke long ago to the fathers in the prophets in many portions and in many ways,

2   in these last days has spoken to us in His Son, whom He appointed heir of all things, through whom also He made the world.

3   And He is the radiance of His glory and the exact representation of His nature, and upholds all things by the word of His power. When He had made

ANSWERS TO LIFE'S QUESTIONS

What if?

HEBREWS 1:1–4

*I*t rises up through your chest like a shudder of electricity. You ponder the devastating "What if?" What if I am not pleasing to God? What if there is something still standing between the two of us? What if I am not really saved?

Israelites surely felt shivers of uncertainty as high priests went before God to make atonement for their sins. Small bells on the hem of the priest's garments indicated whether he had survived being in God's holy presence. When the bells stopped ringing, the people knew that the priest had failed to make acceptable sacrifices to God for them.

For Christians, there is never the uncertainty of being accepted, for we are served by a very different High Priest. Hebrews 1:3 assures us that Jesus "when He had made purification of sins, He sat down at the right hand of the Majesty on high."

Have you ever felt the tremble of uncertainty in your heart? There are no more "What ifs?" for the person who has believed in Jesus Christ because He is the perfect priest.

"He is able also to save forever those who draw near to God through Him, since He always lives to make intercession for them" (Heb. 7:25).

Friend, take heart—your salvation is utterly secure. When you feel the tremble, remind yourself that you can trust Him because He will never fail you.

---

purification of sins, He sat down at the right hand of the Majesty on high,
4   having become as much better than the angels, as He has inherited a more excellent name than they.
5   For to which of the angels did He ever say,
"You are My Son,
    Today I have begotten You"?
And again,
"I will be a Father to Him
    And He shall be a Son to Me"?
6   And when He again brings the firstborn into the world, He says,
"And let all the angels of God
    worship Him."
7   And of the angels He says,
"Who makes His angels winds,
    And His ministers a flame of fire."
➤ 8   But of the Son *He says,*

"Your throne, O God, is forever and ever,
    And the righteous scepter is the scepter of His kingdom.
9   "You have loved righteousness and hated lawlessness;
    Therefore God, Your God, has anointed You
    With the oil of gladness above Your companions."
10   And,
"You, Lord, in the beginning laid the foundation of the earth,
    And the heavens are the works of Your hands;
11   They will perish, but You remain;
    And they all will become old like a garment,
12   And like a mantle You will roll them up;

LIFE LESSONS

➤ **Hebrews 1:8 —** *Of the Son He says, "Your throne, O God, is forever."*

*B*y contrasting how God refers to the angels and how He addresses Jesus, the author shows our Savior's superior and exalted position. Repeatedly, the Lord Himself identifies Christ as an integral Person of the Godhead (Deut. 32:43; Ps. 2:7; 45:6, 7; 102:25–27; 110:1; Is. 61:1–3, etc.). Jesus is God in the flesh (John 10:30; Phil. 2:5–11). He is to be worshiped as the Lord, praised as the Creator, recognized as Ruler, and glorified as our only Savior.

➤ **Hebrews 1:14 —** *Are they not all ministering spirits, sent out to render service for the sake of those who will inherit salvation?*

*W*e may not see most of their activity, but God has given His angels the job of ministering to us—of bringing us His message, grace, and protection. We may never know how often an angel spared us from injury, guided us to safety, or engineered some success. However, we can know that they did so as vessels of God's perfect provision for us (Ps. 103:19–21).

LIKE A GARMENT THEY WILL ALSO BE
  CHANGED.
BUT YOU ARE THE SAME,
AND YOUR YEARS WILL NOT COME TO
  AN END."

13 But to which of the angels has He ever said,

"SIT AT MY RIGHT HAND,
UNTIL I MAKE YOUR ENEMIES
A FOOTSTOOL FOR YOUR FEET"?

14 Are they not all ministering spirits, sent out to render service for the sake of those who will inherit salvation?

NOVEMBER 6

Ezekiel 3:1—4:17

3 THEN He said to me, "Son of man, eat what you find; eat this scroll, and go, speak to the house of Israel."
2 So I opened my mouth, and He fed me this scroll.
3 He said to me, "Son of man, feed your stomach and fill your body with this scroll which I am giving you." Then I ate it, and it was sweet as honey in my mouth.
4 Then He said to me, "Son of man, go to the house of Israel and speak with My words to them.
5 "For you are not being sent to a people of unintelligible speech or difficult language, but to the house of Israel,
6 nor to many peoples of unintelligible speech or difficult language, whose words you cannot understand. But I have sent you to them who should listen to you;
7 yet the house of Israel will not be willing to listen to you, since they are not willing to listen to Me. Surely the whole house of Israel is stubborn and obstinate.
8 "Behold, I have made your face as hard as their faces and your forehead as hard as their foreheads.
9 "Like emery harder than flint I have made your forehead. Do not be afraid of them or be dismayed before them, though they are a rebellious house."
10 Moreover, He said to me, "Son of man, take into your heart all My words which I will speak to you and listen closely.
11 "Go to the exiles, to the sons of your people, and speak to them and tell them, whether they listen or not, 'Thus says the Lord GOD.'"
12 Then the Spirit lifted me up, and I heard a great rumbling sound behind me, "Blessed be the glory of the LORD in His place."
13 And I heard the sound of the wings of the living beings touching one another and the sound of the wheels beside them, even a great rumbling sound.
14 So the Spirit lifted me up and took me away; and I went embittered in the rage of my spirit, and the hand of the LORD was strong on me.
15 Then I came to the exiles who lived beside the river Chebar at Tel-abib, and I sat there seven days where they were living, causing consternation among them.
16 At the end of seven days the word of the LORD came to me, saying,
17 "Son of man, I have appointed you a watchman to the house of Israel; whenever you hear a word from My mouth, warn them from Me.
18 "When I say to the wicked, 'You will surely die,' and you do not warn him or speak out to warn the wicked from his wicked way that he may live, that wicked man shall die in his iniquity, but his blood I will require at your hand.
19 "Yet if you have warned the wicked and he does not turn from his wickedness or from his wicked way, he shall die in his iniquity; but you have delivered yourself.

LIFE LESSONS

➤ **Ezekiel 3:10** — *"Take into your heart all My words which I will speak to you and listen closely."*

Listening to God is essential to walking with God. Listening requires not only paying attention to His voice, but also taking His words so seriously that our greatest desire is to apply His principles to our hearts and lives.

20 "Again, when a righteous man turns away from his righteousness and commits iniquity, and I place an obstacle before him, he will die; since you have not warned him, he shall die in his sin, and his righteous deeds which he has done shall not be remembered; but his blood I will require at your hand.

21 "However, if you have warned the righteous man that the righteous should not sin and he does not sin, he shall surely live because he took warning; and you have delivered yourself."

22 The hand of the LORD was on me there, and He said to me, "Get up, go out to the plain, and there I will speak to you."

23 So I got up and went out to the plain; and behold, the glory of the LORD was standing there, like the glory which I saw by the river Chebar, and I fell on my face.

24 The Spirit then entered me and made me stand on my feet, and He spoke with me and said to me, "Go, shut yourself up in your house.

25 "As for you, son of man, they will put ropes on you and bind you with them so that you cannot go out among them.

26 "Moreover, I will make your tongue stick to the roof of your mouth so that you will be mute and cannot be a man who rebukes them, for they are a rebellious house.

27 "But when I speak to you, I will open your mouth and you will say to them, 'Thus says the Lord GOD.' He who hears, let him hear; and he who refuses, let him refuse; for they are a rebellious house.

4 "NOW you son of man, get yourself a brick, place it before you and inscribe a city on it, Jerusalem.

2 "Then lay siege against it, build a siege wall, raise up a ramp, pitch camps and place battering rams against it all around.

3 "Then get yourself an iron plate and set it up as an iron wall between you and the city, and set your face toward it so that it is under siege, and besiege it. This is a sign to the house of Israel.

4 "As for you, lie down on your left side and lay the iniquity of the house of Israel on it; you shall bear their iniquity for the number of days that you lie on it.

5 "For I have assigned you a number of days corresponding to the years of their iniquity, three hundred and ninety days; thus you shall bear the iniquity of the house of Israel.

6 "When you have completed these, you shall lie down a second time, but on your right side and bear the iniquity of the house of Judah; I have assigned it to you for forty days, a day for each year.

7 "Then you shall set your face toward the siege of Jerusalem with your arm bared and prophesy against it.

8 "Now behold, I will put ropes on you so that you cannot turn from one side to the other until you have completed the days of your siege.

9 "But as for you, take wheat, barley, beans, lentils, millet and spelt, put them in one vessel and make them into bread for yourself; you shall eat it according to the number of the days that you lie on your side, three hundred and ninety days.

10 "Your food which you eat shall be twenty shekels a day by weight; you shall eat it from time to time.

11 "The water you drink shall be the sixth part of a hin by measure; you shall drink it from time to time.

12 "You shall eat it as a barley cake, having baked it in their sight over human dung."

13 Then the LORD said, "Thus will the sons of Israel eat their bread unclean among the nations where I will banish them."

14 But I said, "Ah, Lord GOD! Behold, I have never been defiled; for from my youth until now I have never eaten what died of itself or was torn by beasts, nor has any unclean meat ever entered my mouth."

15 Then He said to me, "See, I will give you cow's dung in place of human dung over which you will prepare your bread."

LIFE LESSONS

➤ **Ezekiel 4:1 —** *"Get yourself a brick, place it before you and inscribe a city on it, Jerusalem."*

Ezekiel was to publicly "lay siege" to his model city to illustrate the coming onslaught against the real Jerusalem. God uses a wild variety of ways to try to help us understand His Word.

16 Moreover, He said to me, "Son of man, behold, I am going to break the staff of bread in Jerusalem, and they will eat bread by weight and with anxiety, and drink water by measure and in horror,
17 because bread and water will be scarce; and they will be appalled with one another and waste away in their iniquity.

Psalm 119:161–168

ש Shin.

161 Princes persecute me without cause,
     But my heart stands in awe of Your words.
162 I rejoice at Your word,
     As one who finds great spoil.
163 I hate and despise falsehood,
     But I love Your law.
164 Seven times a day I praise You,
     Because of Your righteous ordinances.
165 Those who love Your law have great peace,
     And nothing causes them to stumble.
166 I hope for Your salvation, O LORD,
     And do Your commandments.
167 My soul keeps Your testimonies,
     And I love them exceedingly.
168 I keep Your precepts and Your testimonies,
     For all my ways are before You.

Proverbs 28:13

13 He who conceals his transgressions will not prosper,
     But he who confesses and forsakes them will find compassion.

Hebrews 2:1–18

2 FOR this reason we must pay much closer attention to what we have heard, so that we do not drift away from it.
2 For if the word spoken through angels proved unalterable, and every transgression and disobedience received a just penalty,
3 how will we escape if we neglect so great a salvation? After it was at the first spoken through the Lord, it was confirmed to us by those who heard,
4 God also testifying with them, both by signs and wonders and by various miracles and by gifts of the Holy Spirit according to His own will.
5 For He did not subject to angels the world to come, concerning which we are speaking.
6 But one has testified somewhere, saying,

"WHAT IS MAN, THAT YOU REMEMBER HIM?
OR THE SON OF MAN, THAT YOU ARE CONCERNED ABOUT HIM?
7 "YOU HAVE MADE HIM FOR A LITTLE WHILE LOWER THAN THE ANGELS;
YOU HAVE CROWNED HIM WITH GLORY AND HONOR,
AND HAVE APPOINTED HIM OVER THE WORKS OF YOUR HANDS;
8 YOU HAVE PUT ALL THINGS IN SUBJECTION UNDER HIS FEET."

For in subjecting all things to him, He left nothing that is not subject to him. But now we do not yet see all things subjected to him.
9 But we do see Him who was made for a little while lower than the angels,

---

LIFE LESSONS

➤ **Psalm 119:162 —** *I rejoice at Your word, as one who finds great spoil.*

*I*f we think of the Bible as a mysterious book that's hard to understand, we won't value it much and will read it even less. But if we see it as priceless treasure, we'll dive into it often and reap its amazing benefits.

➤ **Proverbs 28:13 —** *He who conceals his transgressions will not prosper, but he who confesses and forsakes them will find compassion.*

*S*ins left covered and in the dark retain their awful power over us, while sins exposed to the light of truth through confession lose their ability to keep us bound. Confession is not beating yourself up over sin, but embracing the freedom Christ offers from its power.

WHAT THE BIBLE SAYS ABOUT ⊕

Our Great Salvation

Hebrews 2:1–4

What has been the greatest moment of your life? For some people, the answer might be their wedding day, the birth of a child, or an important promotion. But for believers, the best experience is salvation, when their eternal destiny was changed. New Christians often have a fervor to share their faith. In time, however, many find their hearts cooling as they focus less on their relationships with Jesus Christ.

Hebrews 2:1 instructs, "We must pay much closer attention to what we have heard, so that we do not drift away from it." Salvation is God's amazing solution to man's sinful condition: it is His gift of rescue—through the death of Jesus—from the penalty for our transgres-

sions. Paul says that before Christ entered our lives, "We too all formerly lived in the lusts of our flesh, indulging the desires of the flesh and of the mind, and were by nature children of wrath" (Eph. 2:3).

No matter how good our behavior may have seemed, we were spiritually dead and separated from God. Receiving Christ's forgiveness breathed life back into our spirits so that we could go before the Father's throne. We must not forget what Jesus did for us. We have the balm to soothe the hurting hearts we come in contact with every day. But if excuses crowd our minds before passion fills our hearts, people will never hear.

Thankfully, we can rediscover the passion of our early Christian days. Take time today to praise God for His salvation, which delivered you from a path toward disaster. Then, commit to carrying out your part in the Great Commission by talking about Jesus with someone in your life (Matt. 28:19). ⊕

---

namely, Jesus, because of the suffering of death crowned with glory and honor, so that by the grace of God He might taste death for everyone.
10 For it was fitting for Him, for whom are all things, and through whom are all things, in bringing many sons to glory, to perfect the author of their salvation through sufferings.
11 For both He who sanctifies and those who are sanctified are all from one *Father*; for which reason He is not ashamed to call them brethren,
12 saying,
"I WILL PROCLAIM YOUR NAME TO MY BRETHREN,
IN THE MIDST OF THE CONGREGATION I WILL SING YOUR PRAISE."
13 And again,
"I WILL PUT MY TRUST IN HIM."
And again,
"BEHOLD, I AND THE CHILDREN WHOM GOD HAS GIVEN ME."
14 Therefore, since the children share in flesh and blood, He Himself likewise also partook of the same, that through death He might render powerless him who had the power of death, that is, the devil,
15 and might free those who through fear of death were subject to slavery all their lives.

LIFE LESSONS

➤ **Hebrews 2:17 —** *He had to be made like His brethren in all things, so that He might become a merciful and faithful high priest.*

Jesus left heaven and became a man not only to become the sacrifice for our sins, but also to experience what we feel and to know exactly what it's like to be one of us. That's what makes Him our great advocate and our absolutely perfect representative on the throne of grace.

➤ **Hebrews 2:18 —** *He Himself was tempted in that which He was suffered, He is able to come to the aid of those who are tempted.*

Jesus knows what it feels like to be tempted. He understands our weaknesses, pains, insecurities, and fears, and He wants to help us break free from them and from the unforgiveness we feel towards ourselves. We can never say to Him, "You don't know what it's like to be me," because He does. In fact, we know less of the pain of temptation than He does because He never gave in to it.

16 For assuredly He does not give help to angels, but He gives help to the descendant of Abraham.

17 Therefore, He had to be made like His brethren in all things, so that He might become a merciful and faithful high priest in things pertaining to God, to make propitiation for the sins of the people.

18 For since He Himself was tempted in that which He has suffered, He is able to come to the aid of those who are tempted.

NOVEMBER 7

Ezekiel 5:1—6:14

5 "AS for you, son of man, take a sharp sword; take and use it *as* a barber's razor on your head and beard. Then take scales for weighing and divide the hair.

2 "One third you shall burn in the fire at the center of the city, when the days of the siege are completed. Then you shall take one third and strike *it* with the sword all around the city, and one third you shall scatter to the wind; and I will unsheathe a sword behind them.

3 "Take also a few in number from them and bind them in the edges of your *robes*.

4 "Take again some of them and throw them into the fire and burn them in the fire; from it a fire will spread to all the house of Israel.

5 "Thus says the Lord GOD, 'This is Jerusalem; I have set her at the center of the nations, with lands around her.

6 'But she has rebelled against My ordinances more wickedly than the nations and against My statutes more than the lands which surround her; for they have rejected My ordinances and have not walked in My statutes.'

7 "Therefore, thus says the Lord GOD, 'Because you have more turmoil than the nations which surround you *and* have not walked in My statutes, nor observed My ordinances, nor observed the ordinances of the nations which surround you,'

8 therefore, thus says the Lord GOD, 'Behold, I, even I, am against you, and I will execute judgments among you in the sight of the nations.

9 'And because of all your abominations, I will do among you what I have not done, and the like of which I will never do again.

10 'Therefore, fathers will eat *their* sons among you, and sons will eat their fa-thers; for I will execute judgments on you and scatter all your remnant to every wind.

11 'So as I live,' declares the Lord GOD, 'surely, because you have defiled My sanctuary with all your detestable idols and with all your abominations, therefore I will also withdraw, and My eye will have no pity and I will not spare.

12 'One third of you will die by plague or be consumed by famine among you, one third will fall by the sword around you, and one third I will scatter to every wind, and I will unsheathe a sword behind them.

13 'Thus My anger will be spent and I will satisfy My wrath on them, and I will be appeased; then they will know that I, the LORD, have spoken in My zeal when I have spent My wrath upon them.

14 'Moreover, I will make you a desolation and a reproach among the nations which surround you, in the sight of all who pass by.

15 'So it will be a reproach, a reviling, a warning and an object of horror to the nations who surround you when I execute judgments against you in anger, wrath and raging rebukes. I, the LORD, have spoken.

16 'When I send against them the deadly arrows of famine which were for the

---

LIFE LESSONS

➤ **Ezekiel 5:15 — *"It will be a reproach, a reviling, a warning and an object of horror to the nations who surround you."***

*A*ll along, God intended for Jerusalem to serve as an example to the nations of the world regarding the goodness and holiness of God (Is. 26:9; Jer. 22:8, 9). Sadly, because the people refused to obey Him, they suffered His judgment instead of receiving His blessings (Deut. 28:25; Ezek. 5:5–9).

destruction of those whom I will send to destroy you, then I will also intensify the famine upon you and break the staff of bread.

17 'Moreover, I will send on you famine and wild beasts, and they will bereave you of children; plague and bloodshed also will pass through you, and I will bring the sword on you. I, the LORD, have spoken.'"

6 AND the word of the LORD came to me saying,

2 "Son of man, set your face toward the mountains of Israel, and prophesy against them

3 and say, 'Mountains of Israel, listen to the word of the Lord GOD! Thus says the Lord GOD to the mountains, the hills, the ravines and the valleys: "Behold, I Myself am going to bring a sword on you, and I will destroy your high places.

4 "So your altars will become desolate and your incense altars will be smashed; and I will make your slain fall in front of your idols.

5 "I will also lay the dead bodies of the sons of Israel in front of their idols; and I will scatter your bones around your altars.

6 "In all your dwellings, cities will become waste and the high places will be desolate, that your altars may become waste and desolate, your idols may be broken and brought to an end, your incense altars may be cut down, and your works may be blotted out.

7 "The slain will fall among you, and you will know that I am the LORD.

8 "However, I will leave a remnant, for you will have those who escaped the sword among the nations when you are scattered among the countries.

➤ 9 "Then those of you who escape will remember Me among the nations to which they will be carried captive, how I have been hurt by their adulterous hearts which turned away from Me, and by their eyes which played the harlot after their idols; and they will loathe themselves in their own sight for the evils which they have committed, for all their abominations.

10 "Then they will know that I am the LORD; I have not said in vain that I would inflict this disaster on them.'"

11 "Thus says the Lord GOD, 'Clap your hand, stamp your foot and say, "Alas, because of all the evil abominations of the house of Israel, which will fall by sword, famine and plague!

12 "He who is far off will die by the plague, and he who is near will fall by the sword, and he who remains and is besieged will die by the famine. Thus will I spend My wrath on them.

13 "Then you will know that I am the LORD, when their slain are among their idols around their altars, on every high hill, on all the tops of the mountains, under every green tree and under every leafy oak—the places where they offered soothing aroma to all their idols.

14 "So throughout all their habitations ➤ I will stretch out My hand against them and make the land more desolate and waste than the wilderness toward Diblah; thus they will know that I am the LORD."'"

✛ Psalm 119:169–176

ת Tav.

169 Let my cry come before You,
    O LORD;
  Give me understanding according to
    Your word.

LIFE LESSONS

➤ **Ezekiel 6:9 — "I have been hurt by their adulterous hearts which turned away from Me."**

The Lord loves us and He has invested Himself in us—even as a husband gives himself freely to his bride (Is. 54:5; 62:4, 5; Rev. 21:2, 9–27). God has given Himself completely to us, and we are to be singular in our devotion to Him (Ex. 20:5; 34:13–16; Song. 8:6; Eph. 5:22–30; Rev. 19:7–9). He created us to connect with Him through an intimate relationship, and when we give our hearts to something else, it grieves Him (Is. 63:9, 10).

➤ **Ezekiel 6:14 — "They will know that I am the LORD."**

This phrase recurs throughout the Book of Ezekiel. Repeatedly, God says that He will execute mighty judgments and secure redemption so that the entire world will know that He alone is God.

WHAT THE BIBLE SAYS ABOUT

Your Identity in Christ

Hebrews 3:1

Hebrews 3:1 tells us, "Therefore, holy brethren, partakers of a heavenly calling, consider Jesus, the Apostle and High Priest of our confession." This verse overflows with hope and assurance for the believer.

First, note that it's addressed to the "holy brethren." This refers to anyone who has trusted Jesus Christ as Lord and Savior. The word *holy* signifies that believers have been set apart for God. Because of who you are in Christ, God loves you. Your profession, salary, appearance, or nationality does not define you. Only your status as a child of God gives you the special identity you enjoy.

As one of the "partakers of a heavenly calling," your destination is heaven. Your heart resides with Christ, where your home is. Knowing where your home is means you aren't searching for earth—this temporary dwelling—to satisfy you. Regardless of what happens around you, you can rejoice because this life does not hold you—God does.

By knowing who you are in Christ, you can deny all the false messages of the world. Many strident voices will try to convince you that you're not pretty enough, smart enough, or successful enough. But your identity in Christ alone completes you! You can add nothing to it, and this world's detractors can take nothing from it.

The final phrase of Hebrews 3:1 reminds us that Jesus is our "Apostle" and "High Priest." The first title signifies that Jesus represents God to us. When we want to know what God is like or how God would act in a given situation, we look to Jesus. The second title signifies that Jesus represents us to God. God looks at His children through the eyes of His blameless and holy Son.

The command in this verse tells believers to "consider Jesus." The word consider means "to observe or think." We are to observe Christ, meditate on His Word, and imitate what we see.

Let the assurance of your identity, home, and Lord inspire you to explore new depths of God and serve Him with all your heart. You won't be disappointed! ◈

---

170 Let my supplication come before
　　You;
　　Deliver me according to Your word.
171 Let my lips utter praise,
　　For You teach me Your statutes.
172 Let my tongue sing of Your word,
　　For all Your commandments are
　　　righteousness.
173 Let Your hand be ready to help me,
　　For I have chosen Your precepts.
174 I long for Your salvation, O LORD,
　　And Your law is my delight.
175 Let my soul live that it may praise
　　You,
　　And let Your ordinances help me.
176 I have gone astray like a lost sheep;
　　seek Your servant,
　　For I do not forget Your
　　　commandments.

◈ Proverbs 28:14

14 How blessed is the man who fears
　　always,

But he who hardens his heart will
　　fall into calamity.

◈ Hebrews 3:1–19

3 THEREFORE, holy brethren, partakers of a heavenly calling, consider Jesus, the Apostle and High Priest of our confession;
2 He was faithful to Him who appointed Him, as Moses also was in all His house.
3 For He has been counted worthy of more glory than Moses, by just so much as the builder of the house has more honor than the house.
4 For every house is built by someone, but the builder of all things is God.
5 Now Moses was faithful in all His house as a servant, for a testimony of those things which were to be spoken later;
6 but Christ *was faithful* as a Son over ◄ His house—whose house we are, if we

hold fast our confidence and the boast of our hope firm until the end.

7 Therefore, just as the Holy Spirit says,

"TODAY IF YOU HEAR HIS VOICE,

8 DO NOT HARDEN YOUR HEARTS AS
     WHEN THEY PROVOKED ME,
     AS IN THE DAY OF TRIAL IN THE
     WILDERNESS,

9 WHERE YOUR FATHERS TRIED *ME* BY
     TESTING *ME*,
     AND SAW MY WORKS FOR FORTY
     YEARS.

10 "THEREFORE I WAS ANGRY WITH THIS
     GENERATION,
     AND SAID, 'THEY ALWAYS GO ASTRAY
     IN THEIR HEART,
     AND THEY DID NOT KNOW MY WAYS';

11 AS I SWORE IN MY WRATH,
     'THEY SHALL NOT ENTER MY REST.'"

12 Take care, brethren, that there not be in any one of you an evil, unbelieving heart that falls away from the living God.
13 But encourage one another day after day, as long as it is *still* called "Today," so that none of you will be hardened by the deceitfulness of sin.
14 For we have become partakers of Christ, if we hold fast the beginning of our assurance firm until the end,
15 while it is said,

"TODAY IF YOU HEAR HIS VOICE,
   DO NOT HARDEN YOUR HEARTS, AS
     WHEN THEY PROVOKED ME."

16 For who provoked *Him* when they had heard? Indeed, did not all those who came out of Egypt *led* by Moses?
17 And with whom was He angry for forty years? Was it not with those who sinned, whose bodies fell in the wilderness?

18 And to whom did He swear that they would not enter His rest, but to those who were disobedient?
19 *So* we see that they were not able to enter because of unbelief.

LIFE LESSONS

➤ **Hebrews 3:6** — *Whose house we are, if we hold fast our confidence and the boast of our hope firm until the end.*

Those who truly accept Jesus Christ as Savior and Lord must persevere in their faith until the end, no matter what happens. One of the hallmarks of a genuine relationship with God is the commitment to remain faithful to Him through everything.

➤ **Hebrews 3:13** — *Encourage one another day after day, as long as it is still called "Today," so that none of you will be hardened by the deceitfulness of sin.*

None of us can progress in our relationship with the Lord or stay true to Him without the help and encouragement of fellow believers. In fact, we need this kind of healthy interaction every day because we require constant reminders of God's unfailing love to us.

➤ **Hebrews 3:18** — *To whom did He swear that they would not enter His rest, but to those who were disobedient?*

There is a direct and clear connection between unbelief and disobedience. When we refuse to submit to God's call, it is always because we do not believe either His promises of blessing or His warnings against rebellion.

Ezekiel 7:1—8:18

7 MOREOVER, the word of the LORD came to me saying,
2 "And you, son of man, thus says the Lord GOD to the land of Israel, 'An end! The end is coming on the four corners of the land.
3 'Now the end is upon you, and I will send My anger against you; I will judge you according to your ways and bring all your abominations upon you.
4 'For My eye will have no pity on you, nor will I spare you, but I will bring your ways upon you, and your abominations will be among you; then you will know that I am the LORD.'
5 "Thus says the Lord GOD, 'A disaster, unique disaster, behold it is coming!

6 'An end is coming; the end has come! It has awakened against you; behold, it has come!

7 'Your doom has come to you, O inhabitant of the land. The time has come, the day is near—tumult rather than joyful shouting on the mountains.

8 'Now I will shortly pour out My wrath on you and spend My anger against you; judge you according to your ways and bring on you all your abominations.

9 'My eye will show no pity nor will I spare. I will repay you according to your ways, while your abominations are in your midst; then you will know that I, the LORD, do the smiting.

10 'Behold, the day! Behold, it is coming! *Your* doom has gone forth; the rod has budded, arrogance has blossomed.

11 'Violence has grown into a rod of wickedness. None of them *shall remain*, none of their people, none of their wealth, nor anything eminent among them.

12 'The time has come, the day has arrived. Let not the buyer rejoice nor the seller mourn; for wrath is against all their multitude.

13 'Indeed, the seller will not regain what he sold as long as they *both* live; for the vision regarding all their multitude will not be averted, nor will any of them maintain his life by his iniquity.

14 'They have blown the trumpet and made everything ready, but no one is going to the battle, for My wrath is against all their multitude.

15 'The sword is outside and the plague and the famine are within. He who is in the field will die by the sword; famine and the plague will also consume those in the city.

16 'Even when their survivors escape, they will be on the mountains like doves of the valleys, all of them mourning, each over his own iniquity.

17 'All hands will hang limp and all knees will become *like* water.

18 'They will gird themselves with sackcloth and shuddering will overwhelm them; and shame *will be* on all faces and baldness on all their heads.

19 'They will fling their silver into the streets and their gold will become an abhorrent thing; their silver and their gold will not be able to deliver them in the day of the wrath of the LORD. They cannot satisfy their appetite nor can they fill their stomachs, for their iniquity has become an occasion of stumbling.

20 'They transformed the beauty of His ornaments into pride, and they made the images of their abominations *and* their detestable things with it; therefore I will make it an abhorrent thing to them.

21 'I will give it into the hands of the foreigners as plunder and to the wicked of the earth as spoil, and they will profane it.

22 'I will also turn My face from them, and they will profane My secret place; then robbers will enter and profane it.

23 'Make the chain, for the land is full of bloody crimes and the city is full of violence.

24 'Therefore, I will bring the worst of the nations, and they will possess their houses. I will also make the pride of the strong ones cease, and their holy places will be profaned.

25 'When anguish comes, they will seek peace, but there will be none.

26 'Disaster will come upon disaster and rumor will be *added* to rumor; then they will seek a vision from a prophet, but the law will be lost from the priest and counsel from the elders.

27 'The king will mourn, the prince will ◄ be clothed with horror, and the hands of the people of the land will tremble. According to their conduct I will deal with them, and by their judgments I will judge them. And they will know that I am the LORD.'"

8 IT came about in the sixth year, on the fifth *day* of the sixth month, as I was sitting in my house with the elders of Judah sitting before me, that the hand of the Lord GOD fell on me there.

2 Then I looked, and behold, a likeness as the appearance of a man; from

---

LIFE LESSONS

➤ **Ezekiel 7:27 —** *"According to their conduct I will deal with them, and by their judgments I will judge them."*

The Bible tells us that God keeps careful records of what we say, do, and even think, to make sure that everyone receives what is due at the final judgment (Dan. 7:10; Rev. 20:12).

His loins and downward *there was* the appearance of fire, and from His loins and upward the appearance of brightness, like the appearance of glowing metal.

➤ 3 He stretched out the form of a hand and caught me by a lock of my head; and the Spirit lifted me up between earth and heaven and brought me in the visions of God to Jerusalem, to the entrance of the north gate of the inner *court*, where the seat of the idol of jealousy, which provokes to jealousy, was *located*.

4 And behold, the glory of the God of Israel *was* there, like the appearance which I saw in the plain.

5 Then He said to me, "Son of man, raise your eyes now toward the north." So I raised my eyes toward the north, and behold, to the north of the altar gate *was* this idol of jealousy at the entrance.

6 And He said to me, "Son of man, do you see what they are doing, the great abominations which the house of Israel are committing here, so that I would be far from My sanctuary? But yet you will see still greater abominations."

7 Then He brought me to the entrance of the court, and when I looked, behold, a hole in the wall.

8 He said to me, "Son of man, now dig through the wall." So I dug through the wall, and behold, an entrance.

9 And He said to me, "Go in and see the wicked abominations that they are committing here."

10 So I entered and looked, and behold, every form of creeping things and beasts *and* detestable things, with all the idols of the house of Israel, were carved on the wall all around.

11 Standing in front of them were seventy elders of the house of Israel, with Jaazaniah the son of Shaphan standing among them, each man with his censer in his hand and the fragrance of the cloud of incense rising.

12 Then He said to me, "Son of man, do you see what the elders of the house of Israel are committing in the dark, each man in the room of his carved images? For they say, 'The LORD does not see us; the LORD has forsaken the land.'"

13 And He said to me, "Yet you will see still greater abominations which they are committing."

14 Then He brought me to the entrance of the gate of the LORD's house which *was* toward the north; and behold, women were sitting there weeping for Tammuz.

15 He said to me, "Do you see *this*, son of man? Yet you will see still greater abominations than these."

16 Then He brought me into the inner court of the LORD's house. And behold, at the entrance to the temple of the LORD, between the porch and the altar, *were* about twenty-five men with their backs to the temple of the LORD and their faces toward the east; and they were prostrating themselves eastward toward the sun.

17 He said to me, "Do you see *this*, son ◄ of man? Is it too light a thing for the house of Judah to commit the abominations which they have committed here, that they have filled the land with violence and provoked Me repeatedly? For behold, they are putting the twig to their nose.

18 "Therefore, I indeed will deal in wrath. My eye will have no pity nor will I spare; and though they cry in My ears with a loud voice, yet I will not listen to them."

LIFE LESSONS

➤ **Ezekiel 8:3** — *The Spirit lifted me up between earth and heaven and brought me in the visions of God to Jerusalem.*

*E*zekiel gives us more vivid descriptions of the prophetic process than almost any other Old Testament prophet. God speaks to us in uncounted ways—sometimes in a manner that is truly amazing (Gen. 32:24–30; Ex. 3:1–10; Num. 22:22–34; Matt. 17:1–6; Rev. 1:9–19). Are you watching and listening for Him?

➤ **Ezekiel 8:17** — *"Is it too light a thing for the house of Judah to commit the abominations which they have committed here?"*

*S*in is *never* a light thing. We may get so used to some offense that it seems harmless and even inconsequential, but God's holy nature never changes. Sin never becomes acceptable to Him.

Psalm 120:1–7

A Song of Ascents.

120 IN my trouble I cried to the LORD,
And He answered me.
2 Deliver my soul, O LORD, from lying lips,
From a deceitful tongue.
3 What shall be given to you, and
what more shall be done to you,
You deceitful tongue?
4 Sharp arrows of the warrior,
With the *burning* coals of the broom tree.
5 Woe is me, for I sojourn in Meshech,
For I dwell among the tents of Kedar!
6 Too long has my soul had its dwelling
With those who hate peace.
7 I am *for* peace, but when I speak,
They are for war.

Proverbs 28:15

15 *Like* a roaring lion and a rushing bear
Is a wicked ruler over a poor people.

Hebrews 4:1–16

4 THEREFORE, let us fear if, while a promise remains of entering His rest, any one of you may seem to have come short of it.
2 For indeed we have had good news preached to us, just as they also; but the word they heard did not profit them, because it was not united by faith in those who heard.
3 For we who have believed enter that rest, just as He has said,
"AS I SWORE IN MY WRATH,
THEY SHALL NOT ENTER MY REST,"
although His works were finished from the foundation of the world.
4 For He has said somewhere concerning the seventh *day:* "AND GOD RESTED ON THE SEVENTH DAY FROM ALL HIS WORKS";

5 and again in this *passage,* "THEY SHALL NOT ENTER MY REST."
6 Therefore, since it remains for some to enter it, and those who formerly had good news preached to them failed to enter because of disobedience,
7 He again fixes a certain day, "Today," saying through David after so long a time just as has been said before,
"TODAY IF YOU HEAR HIS VOICE,
DO NOT HARDEN YOUR HEARTS."
8 For if Joshua had given them rest, He would not have spoken of another day after that.
9 So there remains a Sabbath rest for the people of God.
10 For the one who has entered His rest has himself also rested from his works, as God did from His.
11 Therefore let us be diligent to enter that rest, so that no one will fall, through *following* the same example of disobedience.
12 For the word of God is living and active and sharper than any two-edged sword, and piercing as far as the division of soul and spirit, of both joints and marrow, and able to judge the thoughts and intentions of the heart.

LIFE LESSONS

➤ **Hebrews 4:12 — *The word of God is living and active and sharper than any two-edged sword . . . and able to judge the thoughts and intentions of the heart.***

The Bible lives, both because the Lord brought it into existence and because His Spirit brings its message to life in our hearts. It has His power to transform our lives and to keep us steadfastly anchored to Him when the storms of life strike. No other book in history has the inspiration, truth, and power of the Word of God.

➤ **Hebrews 4:15 — *We do not have a high priest who cannot sympathize with our weaknesses, but One who has been tempted in all things as we are, yet without sin.***

Because Jesus knows what it feels like to be tempted, He is sympathetic toward us—that is, He does not feel annoyed at our failures or exasperated with our struggles. He knows just how to move us on to maturity.

WHAT THE BIBLE SAYS ABOUT
Finding Confidence in God

Hebrews 4:15, 16

God's people have only one way to face life: confidently. After all, He loves us, has saved us from eternal death, and is committed to guiding us through every moment of life. The Father wants us to live confidently—but too often we allow feelings of personal inadequacy and unworthiness to derail our faith.

The apostle Paul lived through horrendous circumstances—rejected by his Jewish peers, stoned, abandoned for dead, ridiculed, ignored, and often beaten and imprisoned for his devotion to Christ. But Paul continued to maintain a confident hope, right up to the very end. How did he manage this?

The apostle recalled one simple truth: "I can do all things through Him who strengthens me" (Phil. 4:13). He focused on his Lord, just as Jeremiah had: "Great is Your faithfulness. 'The LORD is my portion,' says my soul, 'Therefore I have hope in Him'" (Lam. 3:23, 24).

The classic hymn "Great Is Thy Faithfulness" expands on this important idea. Next time you sing it, don't miss its wonderful message: God is faithful and does not change (Heb. 13:8). In this one truth we find our reason for hope and unwavering confidence. The Lord's unchanging nature teaches us that even when we feel unlovely, we remain beautiful to Him. We can do nothing to change His love for us—it is unconditional and flows freely from His throne of grace. He never changes, and He is faithful to keep all of His promises.

Do you trust Him? Have you experienced the strong assurance that comes from placing your faith in His unfailing love? He loved you unconditionally yesterday, and He loves you with the same love today and tomorrow—forever. Therefore, roll the burden of your heart onto Him and you will discover that you too can sing, "Great is Thy faithfulness."

13 And there is no creature hidden from His sight, but all things are open and laid bare to the eyes of Him with whom we have to do.
14 Therefore, since we have a great high priest who has passed through the heavens, Jesus the Son of God, let us hold fast our confession.
15 For we do not have a high priest who cannot sympathize with our weaknesses, but One who has been tempted in all things as *we are,* yet without sin.
16 Therefore let us draw near with confidence to the throne of grace, so that we may receive mercy and find grace to help in time of need.

LIFE LESSONS

➤ *Hebrews 4:16 — Therefore let us draw near with confidence to the throne of grace, so that we may receive mercy and find grace to help in time of need.*

God wants us to come with confidence into His presence—not timidly, anxiously, or in fear of how He might respond. He wants to help us, and He has everything we need to confront any challenge we might face. So never be afraid to approach the Father in prayer. He loves you and wants you to draw near, and because of His great mercy and grace, you can.

 Ezekiel 9:1—10:22

9 THEN He cried out in my hearing with a loud voice saying, "Draw near, O executioners of the city, each with his destroying weapon in his hand."
2 Behold, six men came from the direction of the upper gate which faces north, each with his shattering weapon in his hand; and among them was a certain man clothed in linen with a writing case at his loins. And they went in and stood beside the bronze altar.
3 Then the glory of the God of Israel went up from the cherub on which it had been, to the threshold of the temple. And He called to the man clothed in

linen at whose loins was the writing case.

➤ 4 The LORD said to him, "Go through the midst of the city, even through the midst of Jerusalem, and put a mark on the foreheads of the men who sigh and groan over all the abominations which are being committed in its midst."

5 But to the others He said in my hearing, "Go through the city after him and strike; do not let your eye have pity and do not spare.

6 "Utterly slay old men, young men, maidens, little children, and women, but do not touch any man on whom is the mark; and you shall start from My sanctuary." So they started with the elders who were before the temple.

7 And He said to them, "Defile the temple and fill the courts with the slain. Go out!" Thus they went out and struck down the people in the city.

8 As they were striking the people and I alone was left, I fell on my face and cried out saying, "Alas, Lord GOD! Are You destroying the whole remnant of Israel by pouring out Your wrath on Jerusalem?"

➤ 9 Then He said to me, "The iniquity of the house of Israel and Judah is very, very great, and the land is filled with

---

LIFE LESSONS

➤ **Ezekiel 9:4** — *"Put a mark on the fore-heads of the men who sigh and groan over all the abominations."*

*G*od ordered His angels to distinguish between those who honored Him and those who did not. When it came time for judgment, He would spare His faithful people: "Do not touch any man on whom is the mark" (Ezek. 9:6).

➤ **Ezekiel 9:9** — *"The LORD has forsaken the land."*

*M*ost of God's people made excuses for what happened during the Babylonian invasions. They did not acknowledge them for what they were—a prophesied divine judgment because of their wickedness and idolatry. Rather, they blamed the Lord—believing their destruction was proof that He had abandoned them and did not care about their sin. God considered their perspective deeply evil.

---

blood and the city is full of perversion; for they say, 'The LORD has forsaken the land, and the LORD does not see!'

10 "But as for Me, My eye will have no pity nor will I spare, but I will bring their conduct upon their heads."

11 Then behold, the man clothed in linen at whose loins was the writing case reported, saying, "I have done just as You have commanded me."

10 THEN I looked, and behold, in the expanse that was over the heads of the cherubim something like a sapphire stone, in appearance resembling a throne, appeared above them.

2 And He spoke to the man clothed in linen and said, "Enter between the whirling wheels under the cherubim and fill your hands with coals of fire from between the cherubim and scatter them over the city." And he entered in my sight.

3 Now the cherubim were standing on the right side of the temple when the man entered, and the cloud filled the inner court.

4 Then the glory of the LORD went up from the cherub to the threshold of the temple, and the temple was filled with the cloud and the court was filled with the brightness of the glory of the LORD.

5 Moreover, the sound of the wings of the cherubim was heard as far as the outer court, like the voice of God Almighty when He speaks.

6 It came about when He commanded the man clothed in linen, saying, "Take fire from between the whirling wheels, from between the cherubim," he entered and stood beside a wheel.

7 Then the cherub stretched out his hand from between the cherubim to the fire which was between the cherubim, took some and put it into the hands of the one clothed in linen, who took it and went out.

8 The cherubim appeared to have the form of a man's hand under their wings.

9 Then I looked, and behold, four wheels beside the cherubim, one wheel beside each cherub; and the appearance of the wheels was like the gleam of a Tarshish stone.

10 As for their appearance, all four of them had the same likeness, as if one wheel were within another wheel.

11 When they moved, they went in any of their four directions without turning

as they went; but they followed in the direction which they faced, without turning as they went.

12 Their whole body, their backs, their hands, their wings and the wheels were full of eyes all around, the wheels belonging to all four of them.

13 The wheels were called in my hearing, the whirling wheels.

14 And each one had four faces. The first face *was* the face of a cherub, the second face *was* the face of a man, the third the face of a lion, and the fourth the face of an eagle.

15 Then the cherubim rose up. They are the living beings that I saw by the river Chebar.

16 Now when the cherubim moved, the wheels would go beside them; also when the cherubim lifted up their wings to rise from the ground, the wheels would not turn from beside them.

17 When the cherubim stood still, the wheels would stand still; and when they rose up, the wheels would rise with them, for the spirit of the living beings *was* in them.

➤ 18 Then the glory of the LORD departed from the threshold of the temple and stood over the cherubim.

19 When the cherubim departed, they lifted their wings and rose up from the earth in my sight with the wheels beside them; and they stood still at the entrance of the east gate of the LORD's house, and the glory of the God of Israel hovered over them.

20 These are the living beings that I saw beneath the God of Israel by the river Chebar; so I knew that they *were* cherubim.

21 Each one had four faces and each one four wings, and beneath their wings *was* the form of human hands.

22 As for the likeness of their faces, they were the same faces whose appearance I had seen by the river Chebar. Each one went straight ahead.

✦ Psalm 121:1–8

A Song of Ascents.

✳ **121** I WILL lift up my eyes to the mountains;
From where shall my help come?

2 My help *comes* from the LORD,
Who made heaven and earth.

3 He will not allow your foot to slip;
He who keeps you will not slumber. ◄

4 Behold, He who keeps Israel
Will neither slumber nor sleep.

5 The LORD is your keeper;
The LORD is your shade on your right hand.

6 The sun will not smite you by day,
Nor the moon by night.

7 The LORD will protect you from all evil;
He will keep your soul.

8 The LORD will guard your going out and your coming in
From this time forth and forever.

✦ Proverbs 28:16

16 A leader who is a great oppressor lacks understanding,
But he who hates unjust gain will prolong *his* days.

✦ Hebrews 5:1–14

5 FOR every high priest taken from among men is appointed on behalf of

---

LIFE LESSONS

➤ **Ezekiel 10:18 —** *Then the glory of the LORD departed from the threshold of the temple and stood over the cherubim.*

Many in Israel mistakenly believed Jerusalem would never be destroyed because the temple, God's dwelling place, was located there. They could not imagine He would abandon the temple, even though this is what He warned would happen (1 Kin. 9:6, 7; Jer. 7:9–14).

➤ **Psalm 121:3 —** *He who keeps you will not slumber.*

God never sleeps. He is on guard every moment of every day, watching over you with infinite care. Why worry? The omnipotent Lord of the universe has declared His unending love for you and will never fail in protecting you.

WHAT THE BIBLE SAYS ABOUT

The Importance of Developing a Discerning Spirit

Hebrews 5:13, 14

Many of God's people get into trouble because they lack a discerning spirit. They walk right into Satan's traps and never even know what hit them. "I can't imagine what went wrong," they might say. But a person with a discerning spirit will be quick to explain, "Here's the trap Satan set, and here's how I fell into it."

Each of us needs to develop a discerning spirit, rooted in a strong relationship with the Lord and the knowledge of right and wrong. We must also show our children how to do the same. The time to teach them to listen to and obey God is not when they reach adulthood; rather, we should instruct them from the time they are very young. Moses told the Israelites they must thoroughly train their children in God's commandments:

> These words, which I am commanding you today, shall be on your heart.
> You shall teach them diligently to your sons and shall talk of them when you sit in your house and when you walk by the way and when you lie down and when you rise up. You shall bind them as a sign on your hand and they shall be as frontals on your forehead. You shall write them on the doorposts of your house and on your gates. (Deut. 6:6–9)

We must know right from wrong, not only in theory but in practice. We must also ask God to show us how to apply His truth to our lives so we can live in obedience to His Word. That's why Moses instructed us to teach our children God's commandments throughout the day, not just in a half-hour Sunday school lesson. We are to say plainly to them, "This is right behavior; this is wrong behavior. This is God's command. This is the consequence for disobeying God." However, an education in right and wrong is not just about legalistically following God's rules. Rather, we must teach our children to love God and embrace His principles—always obeying the initial promptings of His Spirit so as to keep in step with Him.

A child thoroughly committed to God, who knows how to seek and obey Him, has little trouble discerning what God's will is in each situation. That child quickly understands when the Holy Spirit signals that things are askew; his conscience remains alive and sensitive. So he avoids becoming an easy target for the enemy. ◈

---

men in things pertaining to God, in order to offer both gifts and sacrifices for sins; 2 he can deal gently with the ignorant and misguided, since he himself also is beset with weakness; 3 and because of it he is obligated to offer *sacrifices* for sins, as for the people, so also for himself. 4 And no one takes the honor to himself, but *receives it* when he is called by God, even as Aaron was. 5 So also Christ did not glorify Himself so as to become a high priest, but He who said to Him,

> "YOU ARE MY SON,
> TODAY I HAVE BEGOTTEN YOU";

6 just as He says also in another *passage,*

> "YOU ARE A PRIEST FOREVER
> ACCORDING TO THE ORDER OF
> MELCHIZEDEK."

7 In the days of His flesh, He offered ✳ up both prayers and supplications with loud crying and tears to the One able to save Him from death, and He was heard because of His piety. 8 Although He was a Son, He learned ◄

LIFE LESSONS

➤ **Hebrews 5:8 — *Although He was a Son, He learned obedience from the things which He suffered.***

Being obedient is not difficult when it is not costly. However, when it requires the sacrifice of all we have and are—when it requires our very lives—that is a different story altogether. In heaven, as part of the Godhead, Jesus never experienced any lack—there was no reason for Him to suffer or fear because everything existed for His pleasure. But when He "emptied Himself, taking the form of a bond-servant, and being made in the likeness of men" (Phil. 2:7), He accepted all the pain, affliction, and neediness that we experience. This was when His obedience was perfected.

obedience from the things which He suffered.

➤ 9 And having been made perfect, He became to all those who obey Him the source of eternal salvation,

10 being designated by God as a high

LIFE LESSONS

➤ **Hebrews 5:9 —** *Having been made perfect, He became to all those who obey Him the source of eternal salvation.*

*D*oes our obedience gain us a Savior? No. *Nothing* we do can ever earn our salvation. Yet all those who truly believe in Him will obey His leadership.

---

priest according to the order of Melchizedek.

11 Concerning him we have much to say, and *it is* hard to explain, since you have become dull of hearing.

12 For though by this time you ought to be teachers, you have need again for someone to teach you the elementary principles of the oracles of God, and you have come to need milk and not solid food.

13 For everyone who partakes *only* of milk is not accustomed to the word of righteousness, for he is an infant.

14 But solid food is for the mature, who because of practice have their senses trained to discern good and evil.

✦ Ezekiel 11:1—12:28

11 MOREOVER, the Spirit lifted me up and brought me to the east gate of the Lord's house which faced eastward. And behold, *there were* twenty-five men at the entrance of the gate, and among them I saw Jaazaniah son of Azzur and Pelatiah son of Benaiah, leaders of the people.

2 He said to me, "Son of man, these are the men who devise iniquity and give evil advice in this city,

3 who say, 'The time is not near to build houses. This *city* is the pot and we are the flesh.'

4 "Therefore, prophesy against them, son of man, prophesy!"

➤ 5 Then the Spirit of the Lord fell upon me, and He said to me, "Say, 'Thus says the Lord, "So you think, house of Israel, for I know your thoughts.

LIFE LESSONS

➤ **Ezekiel 11:5 —** *"I know your thoughts."*

*T*he Lord knows us completely—our thoughts, our plans, our hopes, our feelings. We can hide nothing from Him, and we can never surprise Him. He knows us better than we know ourselves; that is why we can trust Him.

---

6 "You have multiplied your slain in this city, filling its streets with them."

7 'Therefore, thus says the Lord God, "Your slain whom you have laid in the midst of the city are the flesh and this *city* is the pot; but I will bring you out of it.

8 "You have feared a sword; so I will bring a sword upon you," the Lord God declares.

9 "And I will bring you out of the midst of the city and deliver you into the hands of strangers and execute judgments against you.

10 "You will fall by the sword. I will judge you to the border of Israel; so you shall know that I am the Lord.

11 "This *city* will not be a pot for you, nor will you be flesh in the midst of it, *but* I will judge you to the border of Israel.

12 "Thus you will know that I am the Lord; for you have not walked in My statutes nor have you executed My ordinances, but have acted according to the ordinances of the nations around you."'"

13 Now it came about as I prophesied, that Pelatiah son of Benaiah died. Then I fell on my face and cried out with a loud voice and said, "Alas, Lord God! Will You bring the remnant of Israel to a complete end?"

14 Then the word of the Lord came to me, saying,

15 "Son of man, your brothers, your relatives, your fellow exiles and the whole house of Israel, all of them, *are those* to whom the inhabitants of Jerusalem have said, 'Go far from the LORD; this land has been given us as a possession.'

16 "Therefore say, 'Thus says the Lord GOD, "Though I had removed them far away among the nations and though I had scattered them among the countries, yet I was a sanctuary for them a little while in the countries where they had gone."'

17 "Therefore say, 'Thus says the Lord GOD, "I will gather you from the peoples and assemble you out of the countries among which you have been scattered, and I will give you the land of Israel."'

18 "When they come there, they will remove all its detestable things and all its abominations from it.

19 "And I will give them one heart, and put a new spirit within them. And I will take the heart of stone out of their flesh and give them a heart of flesh,

20 that they may walk in My statutes and keep My ordinances and do them. Then they will be My people, and I shall be their God.

21 "But as for those whose hearts go after their detestable things and abominations, I will bring their conduct down on their heads," declares the Lord GOD.

22 Then the cherubim lifted up their wings with the wheels beside them, and the glory of the God of Israel hovered over them.

23 The glory of the LORD went up from the midst of the city and stood over the mountain which is east of the city.

24 And the Spirit lifted me up and brought me in a vision by the Spirit of God to the exiles in Chaldea. So the vision that I had seen left me.

25 Then I told the exiles all the things that the LORD had shown me.

12 THEN the word of the LORD came to me, saying,

2 "Son of man, you live in the midst of the rebellious house, who have eyes to see but do not see, ears to hear but do not hear; for they are a rebellious house.

3 "Therefore, son of man, prepare for yourself baggage for exile and go into exile by day in their sight; even go into exile from your place to another place in their sight. Perhaps they will understand though they are a rebellious house.

4 "Bring your baggage out by day in their sight, as baggage for exile. Then you will go out at evening in their sight, as those going into exile.

5 "Dig a hole through the wall in their sight and go out through it.

6 "Load *the baggage* on your shoulder in their sight *and* carry *it* out in the dark. You shall cover your face so that you cannot see the land, for I have set you as a sign to the house of Israel."

7 I did so, as I had been commanded. By day I brought out my baggage like the baggage of an exile. Then in the evening I dug through the wall with my hands; I went out in the dark *and* carried *the baggage* on my shoulder in their sight.

8 In the morning the word of the LORD came to me, saying,

9 "Son of man, has not the house of Israel, the rebellious house, said to you, 'What are you doing?'

10 "Say to them, 'Thus says the Lord GOD, "This burden *concerns* the prince in Jerusalem as well as all the house of Israel who are in it."'

11 "Say, 'I am a sign to you. As I have done, so it will be done to them; they will go into exile, into captivity.'

12 "The prince who is among them will

load *his baggage* on *his* shoulder in the dark and go out. They will dig a hole through the wall to bring *it* out. He will cover his face so that he can not see the land with *his* eyes.

13 "I will also spread My net over him, and he will be caught in My snare. And I will bring him to Babylon in the land of the Chaldeans; yet he will not see it, though he will die there.

14 "I will scatter to every wind all who are around him, his helpers and all his troops; and I will draw out a sword after them.

15 "So they will know that I am the LORD when I scatter them among the nations and spread them among the countries.

16 "But I will spare a few of them from the sword, the famine and the pestilence that they may tell all their abominations among the nations where they go, and may know that I am the LORD."

17 Moreover, the word of the LORD came to me saying,

18 "Son of man, eat your bread with trembling and drink your water with quivering and anxiety.

19 "Then say to the people of the land, 'Thus says the Lord GOD concerning the inhabitants of Jerusalem in the land of Israel, "They will eat their bread with anxiety and drink their water with horror, because their land will be stripped of its fullness on account of the violence of all who live in it.

20 "The inhabited cities will be laid waste and the land will be a desolation. So you will know that I am the LORD."'"

21 Then the word of the LORD came to me, saying,

22 "Son of man, what is this proverb you *people* have concerning the land of Israel, saying, 'The days are long and every vision fails'?

23 "Therefore say to them, 'Thus says the Lord GOD, "I will make this proverb cease so that they will no longer use it as a proverb in Israel." But tell them, "The days draw near as well as the fulfillment of every vision.

24 "For there will no longer be any false vision or flattering divination within the house of Israel.

➤ 25 "For I the LORD will speak, and whatever word I speak will be performed. It will no longer be delayed, for in your days, O rebellious house, I will speak the word and perform it," declares the Lord GOD.'"

26 Furthermore, the word of the LORD came to me, saying,

27 "Son of man, behold, the house of Israel is saying, 'The vision that he sees is for many years *from now*, and he prophesies of times far off.'

28 "Therefore say to them, 'Thus says the Lord GOD, "None of My words will be delayed any longer. Whatever word I speak will be performed,"'" declares the Lord GOD.

✦ Psalm 122:1–5

A Song of Ascents, of David.

122 I WAS glad when they said to me,
"Let us go to the house of the LORD." ✳

2 Our feet are standing
Within your gates, O Jerusalem,

3 Jerusalem, that is built
As a city that is compact together;

4 To which the tribes go up, even the tribes of the LORD—
An ordinance for Israel—
To give thanks to the name of the LORD.

5 For there thrones were set for judgment,
The thrones of the house of David.

✦ Proverbs 28:17, 18

17 A man who is laden with the guilt of human blood
Will be a fugitive until death; let no one support him.

18 He who walks blamelessly will be
    delivered,
    But he who is crooked will fall all at
    once.

Hebrews 6:1–20

6 THEREFORE leaving the elementary
    teaching about the Christ, let us press
on to maturity, not laying again a foundation of repentance from dead works
and of faith toward God,
2 of instruction about washings and
laying on of hands, and the resurrection
of the dead and eternal judgment,
3 And this we will do, if God permits.

4 For in the case of those who have
once been enlightened and have tasted
of the heavenly gift and have been made
partakers of the Holy Spirit,
5 and have tasted the good word of
God and the powers of the age to come,
6 and then have fallen away, it is impossible to renew them again to repentance,
since they again crucify to themselves the
Son of God and put Him to open shame.
7 For ground that drinks the rain
which often falls on it and brings forth
vegetation useful to those for whose sake
it is also tilled, receives a blessing from
God;
8 but if it yields thorns and thistles, it
is worthless and close to being cursed,
and it ends up being burned.

ANSWERS TO LIFE'S QUESTIONS

How can I be the kind of faithful person God honors?

HEBREWS 6:11, 12

Do you want to see the favor of God blossom in your life? If you do, the writer of Hebrews has some advice for you: "Show the same diligence so as to realize the full assurance of hope until the end, so that you will not be sluggish, but imitators of those who through faith and patience inherit the promises" (Heb. 6:11, 12).

He has in mind someone like the Old Testament saint Abraham, who displayed great faith and patience. When God called Abraham (Abram's) to leave his homeland for a place unknown, he left and followed the Lord. He did not know where he was going. He only knew that he was committed to obeying the One who called him. Genesis 12:4 displays his diligence: "So Abram went forth as the Lord had spoken to him."

God told Abraham he would have a son, even though his wife Sarah was already 90 years old (Gen. 17:17–19). Nothing is too dif-ficult for the Lord! A year later, God faithfully fulfilled His promise, and Sarah bore Abraham a son.

When the boy was only a young lad, God directed Abraham to sacrifice the son for whom he had waited 25 years. What a heart-breaking command this must have been. Had Abraham heard the Lord correctly? He loved his son more than any earthly thing or being, but he knew that the greater test was the level of his devotion to God. Abraham was determined to obey the Lord. But God stopped him before

he could make the sacrifice and provided a ram instead. This was a defining test of faith, and Abraham passed with flying colors. As a result, God blessed him for his devotion (Gen. 22:1–18).

We are to mirror Abraham's faithfulness. In our attempts to pursue God with diligence, we need to take stock of everything we do:

- Set clear goals. Olympic athletes don't begin with a vague dream of becoming an Olympian. Each step of the way requires them to work for a faster time, a higher jump, or an improved technique.
- Be patient. When Pablo Casals reached age 95, a young reporter asked him, "Mr. Casals, you are 95 and the greatest cellist that ever lived. Why do you still practice six hours a day?" Casals answered, "Because I think I'm making progress." He never stopped practicing or reaching for even greater goals.
- Be willing to take risks. God asks that we trust Him, despite our limited understanding. As the saying goes, a turtle makes progress only when he sticks his neck out.
- Be persistent. If God has given you a clearly defined goal and you sincerely believe it to be His will, don't let doubt or discouragement defeat you. Keep trusting and believing. Never give up!
- Be flexible. Remember that the process is the greatest learning experience we have. Learn from your mistakes and move on. Flexibility enables you to change as God changes you.

If you want God to honor you, then be the kind of person who honors Him by consistently acting on your faith.

9 But, beloved, we are convinced of better things concerning you, and things that accompany salvation, though we are speaking in this way.

10 For God is not unjust so as to forget your work and the love which you have shown toward His name, in having ministered and in still ministering to the saints.

11 And we desire that each one of you show the same diligence so as to realize the full assurance of hope until the end,

12 so that you will not be sluggish, but imitators of those who through faith and patience inherit the promises.

13 For when God made the promise to Abraham, since He could swear by no one greater, He swore by Himself,

14 saying, "I WILL SURELY BLESS YOU AND I WILL SURELY MULTIPLY YOU."

15 And so, having patiently waited, he obtained the promise.

16 For men swear by one greater *than themselves*, and with them an oath *given* as confirmation is an end of every dispute.

17 In the same way God, desiring even more to show to the heirs of the promise the unchangeableness of His purpose, interposed with an oath,

18 so that by two unchangeable things in which it is impossible for God to lie, we who have taken refuge would have strong encouragement to take hold of the hope set before us.

19 This hope we have as an anchor of the soul, a *hope* both sure and steadfast and one which enters within the veil,

20 where Jesus has entered as a forerunner for us, having become a high priest forever according to the order of Melchizedek.

LIFE LESSONS

➤ **Hebrews 6:12** — *Imitators of those who through faith and patience inherit the promises.*

*Y*our inheritance is the same as those faithful saints of old, but you must trust God to take you through every obstacle in your path, just as they did. Like the biblical believers who have preceded you, you'll find that no challenge is a match for the amazing power of God. There are great blessings ahead if you'll diligently do what He says.

➤ **Hebrews 6:19** — *This hope we have as an anchor of the soul, a hope both sure and steadfast and one which enters within the veil.*

*O*ur hope in Christ gives us the firm and rock-solid confidence that nothing life throws at us can ultimately move us. This hope reaches to the very throne of God Himself to bring us comfort and assurance.

Ezekiel 13:1—14:23

13 THEN the word of the LORD came to me saying,

2 "Son of man, prophesy against the prophets of Israel who prophesy, and say to those who prophesy from their own inspiration, 'Listen to the word of the LORD!

3 'Thus says the Lord GOD, "Woe to the foolish prophets who are following their own spirit and have seen nothing.

4 "O Israel, your prophets have been like foxes among ruins.

5 "You have not gone up into the breaches, nor did you build the wall around the house of Israel to stand in the battle on the day of the LORD.

6 "They see falsehood and lying divination who are saying, 'The LORD declares,' when the LORD has not sent them; yet they hope for the fulfillment of *their* word.

7 "Did you not see a false vision and speak a lying divination when you said, 'The LORD declares,' but it is not I who have spoken?"'"

8 Therefore, thus says the Lord GOD, "Because you have spoken falsehood and seen a lie, therefore behold, I am against you," declares the Lord GOD.

9 "So My hand will be against the prophets who see false visions and utter

lying divinations. They will have no place in the council of My people, nor will they be written down in the register of the house of Israel, nor will they enter the land of Israel, that you may know that I am the Lord God.

10 "It is definitely because they have misled My people by saying, 'Peace!' when there is no peace. And when anyone builds a wall, behold, they plaster it over with whitewash;

11 so tell those who plaster it over with whitewash, that it will fall. A flooding rain will come, and you, O hailstones, will fall; and a violent wind will break out.

12 "Behold, when the wall has fallen, will you not be asked, 'Where is the plaster with which you plastered it?'"

13 Therefore, thus says the Lord God, "I will make a violent wind break out in My wrath. There will also be in My anger a flooding rain and hailstones to consume it in wrath.

14 "So I will tear down the wall which you plastered over with whitewash and bring it down to the ground, so that its foundation is laid bare; and when it falls, you will be consumed in its midst. And you will know that I am the Lord.

15 "Thus I will spend My wrath on the wall and on those who have plastered it over with whitewash; and I will say to you, 'The wall is gone and its plasterers are gone,

16 along with the prophets of Israel who prophesy to Jerusalem, and who see visions of peace for her when there is no peace,' declares the Lord God.

17 "Now you, son of man, set your face against the daughters of your people who are prophesying from their own inspiration. Prophesy against them

18 and say, 'Thus says the Lord God, "Woe to the women who sew magic bands on all wrists and make veils for the heads of persons of every stature to hunt down lives! Will you hunt down the lives of My people, but preserve the lives of others for yourselves?

➤ 19 "For handfuls of barley and fragments of bread, you have profaned Me to My people to put to death some who should not die and to keep others alive who should not live, by your lying to My people who listen to lies."'"

20 Therefore, thus says the Lord God,

"Behold, I am against your magic bands by which you hunt lives there as birds and I will tear them from your arms; and I will let them go, even those lives whom you hunt as birds.

21 "I will also tear off your veils and deliver My people from your hands, and they will no longer be in your hands to be hunted; and you will know that I am the Lord.

22 "Because you disheartened the right- ◄ eous with falsehood when I did not cause him grief, but have encouraged the wicked not to turn from his wicked way and preserve his life,

23 therefore, you women will no longer see false visions or practice divination, and I will deliver My people out of your hand. Thus you will know that I am the Lord."

14 THEN some elders of Israel came to me and sat down before me.

2 And the word of the Lord came to me, saying,

3 "Son of man, these men have set up ◄ their idols in their hearts and have put right before their faces the stumbling block of their iniquity. Should I be consulted by them at all?

4 "Therefore speak to them and tell them, 'Thus says the Lord God, "Any man of the house of Israel who sets up

---

LIFE LESSONS

➤ **Ezekiel 13:19 —** *"For handfuls of barley and fragments of bread, you have profaned Me to My people."*

*W*hen we stray from God's truth, we usually end up committing a series of terrible transgressions: blasphemy, bribery, perjury, and worse. One sin opens the way for many more—for lusts that do not satisfy and pleasures that do not last. Yet our obedience to Him always brings blessing.

➤ **Ezekiel 13:22 —** *"You . . . have encouraged the wicked not to turn from his wicked way and preserve his life."*

*W*e must be very careful how we represent God's message, neither adding to it nor taking away from it. Any true word from the Lord will encourage His people and urge the wicked to turn from evil.

his idols in his heart, puts right before his face the stumbling block of his iniquity, and *then* comes to the prophet, I the LORD will be brought to give him an answer in the matter in view of the multitude of his idols,

5 in order to lay hold of the hearts of the house of Israel who are estranged from Me through all their idols."'

6 "Therefore say to the house of Israel, 'Thus says the Lord GOD, "Repent and turn away from your idols and turn your faces away from all your abominations.

7 "For anyone of the house of Israel or of the immigrants who stay in Israel who separates himself from Me, sets up his idols in his heart, puts right before his face the stumbling block of his iniquity, and *then* comes to the prophet to inquire of Me for himself, I the LORD will be brought to answer him in My own person.

8 "I will set My face against that man and make him a sign and a proverb, and I will cut him off from among My people. So you will know that I am the LORD.

9 "But if the prophet is prevailed upon to speak a word, it is I, the LORD, who have prevailed upon that prophet, and I will stretch out My hand against him and destroy him from among My people Israel.

10 "They will bear *the punishment of* their iniquity; as the iniquity of the inquirer is, so the iniquity of the prophet will be,

11 in order that the house of Israel may no longer stray from Me and no longer defile themselves with all their transgressions. Thus they will be My people, and I shall be their God,"' declares the Lord GOD."

12 Then the word of the LORD came to me saying,

13 "Son of man, if a country sins against

Me by committing unfaithfulness, and I stretch out My hand against it, destroy its supply of bread, send famine against it and cut off from it both man and beast,

14 even *though* these three men, Noah, Daniel and Job were in its midst, by their *own* righteousness they could *only* deliver themselves," declares the Lord GOD.

15 "If I were to cause wild beasts to pass through the land and they depopulated it, and it became desolate so that no one would pass through it because of the beasts,

16 *though* these three men were in its midst, as I live," declares the Lord GOD, "they could not deliver either *their* sons or *their* daughters. They alone would be delivered, but the country would be desolate.

17 "Or *if* I should bring a sword on that country and say, 'Let the sword pass through the country and cut off man and beast from it,'

18 even *though* these three men were in its midst, as I live," declares the Lord GOD, "they could not deliver either *their* sons or *their* daughters, but they alone would be delivered.

19 "Or *if* I should send a plague against that country and pour out My wrath in blood on it to cut off man and beast from it,

20 even *though* Noah, Daniel and Job were in its midst, as I live," declares the Lord GOD, "they could not deliver either *their* son or *their* daughter. They would deliver only themselves by their righteousness."

21 For thus says the Lord GOD, "How much more when I send My four severe judgments against Jerusalem: sword, famine, wild beasts and plague to cut off man and beast from it!

22 "Yet, behold, survivors will be left in it who will be brought out, *both* sons and daughters. Behold, they are going to come forth to you and you will see their conduct and actions; then you will be comforted for the calamity which I have brought against Jerusalem for everything which I have brought upon it.

23 "Then they will comfort you when you see their conduct and actions, for you will know that I have not done in vain whatever I did to it," declares the Lord GOD.

Psalm 122:6–9

ע Ayin.

6   Pray for the peace of Jerusalem:
     "May they prosper who love you.
7   "May peace be within your walls,
     And prosperity within your
       palaces."
8   For the sake of my brothers and my
       friends,
     I will now say, "May peace be within
       you."
9   For the sake of the house of the
       LORD our God,
     I will seek your good.

Proverbs 28:19

19   He who tills his land will have
       plenty of food,
     But he who follows empty *pursuits*
       will have poverty in plenty.

Hebrews 7:1–28

7 FOR this Melchizedek, king of Salem,
   priest of the Most High God, who met
Abraham as he was returning from the
slaughter of the kings and blessed him,
2   to whom also Abraham apportioned
a tenth part of all *the spoils*, was first of
all, by the translation *of his name*, king
of righteousness, and then also king of
Salem, which is king of peace.
3   Without father, without mother,
without genealogy, having neither beginning of days nor end of life, but made
like the Son of God, he remains a priest
perpetually.
4   Now observe how great this man
was to whom Abraham, the patriarch,
gave a tenth of the choicest spoils.
5   And those indeed of the sons of Levi
who receive the priest's office have commandment in the Law to collect a tenth
from the people, that is, from their brethren, although these are descended from
Abraham.
6   But the one whose genealogy is not
traced from them collected a tenth from

Abraham and blessed the one who had
the promises.
7   But without any dispute the lesser is
blessed by the greater.
8   In this case mortal men receive
tithes, but in that case one *receives them*,
of whom it is witnessed that he lives on.
9   And, so to speak, through Abraham
even Levi, who received tithes, paid
tithes,
10   for he was still in the loins of his
father when Melchizedek met him.
11   Now if perfection was through the
Levitical priesthood (for on the basis of
it the people received the Law), what further need *was there* for another priest to
arise according to the order of Melchizedek, and not be designated according to
the order of Aaron?
12   For when the priesthood is changed,
of necessity there takes place a change of
law also.
13   For the one concerning whom these
things are spoken belongs to another
tribe, from which no one has officiated
at the altar.
14   For it is evident that our Lord was
descended from Judah, a tribe with reference to which Moses spoke nothing
concerning priests.
15   And this is clearer still, if another
priest arises according to the likeness of
Melchizedek,
16   who has become *such* not on the
basis of a law of physical requirement,
but according to the power of an inde-
structible life.
17   For it is attested *of Him*,
   "YOU ARE A PRIEST FOREVER
     ACCORDING TO THE ORDER OF
       MELCHIZEDEK."
18   For, on the one hand, there is a setting

LIFE LESSONS

➤ **Hebrews 7:19 — *There is a bringing
in of a better hope, through which we
draw near to God.***

The law can show us God's righteous
   demands, but it has no power to
help us comply with His holy standard
(Rom. 7:7). Our only hope of salvation is
through faith in Christ, who fulfills the
law on our behalf and cleanses us from
all unrighteousness.

aside of a former commandment because of its weakness and uselessness

➤ 19 (for the Law made nothing perfect), and on the other hand there is a bringing in of a better hope, through which we draw near to God.

20 And inasmuch as *it was* not without an oath

➤ 21 (for they indeed became priests without an oath, but He with an oath through the One who said to Him,

"THE LORD HAS SWORN
AND WILL NOT CHANGE HIS MIND,
'YOU ARE A PRIEST FOREVER'");

22 so much the more also Jesus has become the guarantee of a better covenant.

23 The *former* priests, on the one hand, existed in greater numbers because they were prevented by death from continuing,

24 but Jesus, on the other hand, because He continues forever, holds His priesthood permanently.

25 Therefore He is able also to save forever those who draw near to God through Him, since He always lives to make intercession for them.

➤ 26 For it was fitting for us to have such a high priest, holy, innocent, undefiled, separated from sinners and exalted above the heavens;

27 who does not need daily, like those

high priests, to offer up sacrifices, first for His own sins and then for the *sins* of the people, because this He did once for all when He offered up Himself.

28 For the Law appoints men as high priests who are weak, but the word of the oath, which came after the Law, *appoints* a Son, made perfect forever.

WHAT THE BIBLE SAYS ABOUT

The Grace of God

Hebrews 7:25–27

*G*race is God's goodness and kindness to those who do not deserve it and cannot earn it. Its benefits are available to everyone. Each day God causes hearts to beat, bodies to heal, and love to be given and received. And it all happens, regardless of peoples' opinions of Him.

He offers forgiveness to the rebellious, freedom to sinners, and intimacy with Himself to all who trust Christ as Savior. Through Jesus, He offers access to the throne of grace (Heb. 4:16). That's where the Savior serves as high priest, interceding for His own (Heb. 7:25).

We know we can approach God confidently because there is no condemnation for those

who belong to Him (Rom. 8:1). What amazing grace! It was not always so. Israel, God's chosen people, lived under the Law, not under grace. They, like us, were a disobedient people. God in His mercy established the sacrificial system to symbolically provide a way for them to be forgiven of their wrongdoing.

Jesus gives us permanent forgiveness because He died once for all sins (Heb. 7:27). It was humanly impossible to obey every aspect of all 613 commandments God handed down through Moses. But Jesus fulfilled the Law for us, and grace makes it count on our behalf. Because our Savior sacrificed His life for us, we can approach God's throne.

As believers, we stand upon the immovable foundation of God's grace. It's over us like a canopy and surrounds us like a protective wall. As the truth of it penetrates our hearts and minds, we become expressions of the Lord's love, kindness, and goodness to others. ◉

Ezekiel 15:1—16:63

15 THEN the word of the LORD came to me, saying,

2 "Son of man, how is the wood of the vine *better* than any wood of a branch which is among the trees of the forest?

3 "Can wood be taken from it to make anything, or can *men* take a peg from it on which to hang any vessel?

4 "If it has been put into the fire for fuel, *and* the fire has consumed both of its ends and its middle part has been charred, is it *then* useful for anything?

5 "Behold, while it is intact, it is not made into anything. How much less, when the fire has consumed it and it is charred, can it still be made into anything!

6 "Therefore, thus says the Lord GOD, 'As the wood of the vine among the trees of the forest, which I have given to the fire for fuel, so have I given up the inhabitants of Jerusalem;

7 and I set My face against them. *Though* they have come out of the fire, yet the fire will consume them. Then you will know that I am the LORD, when I set My face against them.

8 'Thus I will make the land desolate, because they have acted unfaithfully,'" declares the Lord GOD.

16 THEN the word of the LORD came to me, saying,

2 "Son of man, make known to Jerusalem her abominations

3 and say, 'Thus says the Lord GOD to Jerusalem, "Your origin and your birth are from the land of the Canaanite, your father was an Amorite and your mother a Hittite.

4 "As for your birth, on the day you were born your navel cord was not cut, nor were you washed with water for cleansing; you were not rubbed with salt or even wrapped in cloths.

5 "No eye looked with pity on you to do any of these things for you, to have compassion on you. Rather you were thrown out into the open field, for you were abhorred on the day you were born.

➤ 6 "When I passed by you and saw you squirming in your blood, I said to you *while you were* in your blood, 'Live!'

Yes, I said to you *while you were* in your blood, 'Live!'

7 "I made you numerous like plants of the field. Then you grew up, became tall and reached the age for fine ornaments; *your* breasts were formed and your hair had grown. Yet you were naked and bare.

8 "Then I passed by you and saw you, and behold, you were at the time for love; so I spread My skirt over you and covered your nakedness. I also swore to you and entered into a covenant with you so that you became Mine," declares the Lord GOD.

9 "Then I bathed you with water, washed off your blood from you and anointed you with oil.

10 "I also clothed you with embroidered cloth and put sandals of porpoise skin on your feet; and I wrapped you with fine linen and covered you with silk.

11 "I adorned you with ornaments, put bracelets on your hands and a necklace around your neck.

12 "I also put a ring in your nostril, earrings in your ears and a beautiful crown on your head.

13 "Thus you were adorned with gold and silver, and your dress was of fine linen, silk and embroidered cloth. You ate fine flour, honey and oil; so you were exceedingly beautiful and advanced to royalty.

14 "Then your fame went forth among ◄

LIFE LESSONS

➤ **Ezekiel 16:6 — *"I said to you while you were in your blood, 'Live!'"***

*W*e owe our very lives to God. Without Him, we are a mess. Without Him, we wallow in our own blood, unable to grow and thrive. He sees us in our moral ugliness and yet says to us, "Live!"

➤ **Ezekiel 16:14 — *"It was perfect because of My splendor which I bestowed on you."***

*J*udah forgot that any good thing she had, she had received from God. That is why we must remember any success, talent, ability, insight, or strength comes from Him, and we should use it all for His glory.

ANSWERS TO LIFE'S QUESTIONS

How can I confront a believer who has fallen spiritually?

EZEKIEL 16:2

God gave Ezekiel a tremendous task: he was to confront the people about their sin. "Son of man," He told the prophet, "make known to Jerusalem her abominations" (Ezek. 16:2; also 20:4; 22:2; 23:36). This was a difficult assignment. Even so, at times He will likewise call us to confront someone who is sinning unrepentantly. How can one be an effective and godly minister in such circumstances?

First, we must watch the spirit in which we address the fallen believer. We must be firm but gentle (Gal. 6:1). Hurting people can be fragile; they don't need our condemnation. We should not go to them out of anger or to vent our hurt; rather, we must go to them with kindness, sensitive to their pain, and with the desire to restore them to fellowship.

Second, we are to confront the person in the spirit of humility: "If anyone thinks he is something when he is nothing, he deceives himself" (Gal. 6:3). We can't go with a haughty attitude, as if we could never commit such sin. That kind of mindset deeply offends God (Matt. 7:1–5; 1 John 1:10). If we go to hurting people with the attitude that we are above them, they certainly won't respond to our efforts. In fact, we only build a wall that will obstruct the restoration process, which is the goal of our confrontation. Rather, we must remember that we are *all* vulnerable to temptation, and that it is only by His grace that we are not enslaved by the same iniquity. We must also realize that we do not convict anyone of his sin—the Holy Spirit does that (John 16:8). We are there simply to urge the person to do whatever God says and receive His grace.

Third, we are to go to the person in love, doing and saying whatever God requires of us so that he or she will repent. We should not automatically interpret their inability to express grief for their actions as a lack of remorse or repentance. They may suffer greatly and fear releasing their tears. Still, we must remain firm in our efforts to encourage them to obey God and to agree with Him by confessing their sin to Him. This must all be done in love, because if we do not go with the right spirit—honoring Him and caring for them—we may as well not go at all.

Those who walk with the Father are to gently, humbly, and lovingly confront the straying person, in the hope that they will experience "the sorrow that is according to the will of God" which "produces a repentance without regret, leading to salvation" (2 Cor. 7:10). Confrontation is never easy, but it is often a prerequisite to restoration, the real goal.

---

the nations on account of your beauty, for it was perfect because of My splendor which I bestowed on you," declares the Lord GOD.

15 "But you trusted in your beauty and played the harlot because of your fame, and you poured out your harlotries on every passer-by who might be *willing*.

16 "You took some of your clothes, made for yourself high places of various colors and played the harlot on them, which should never come about nor happen.

17 "You also took your beautiful jewels *made* of My gold and of My silver, which I had given you, and made for yourself male images that you might play the harlot with them.

18 "Then you took your embroidered cloth and covered them, and offered My oil and My incense before them.

19 "Also My bread which I gave you, fine flour, oil and honey with which I fed you, you would offer before them for a sooth-ing aroma; so it happened," declares the Lord GOD.

20 "Moreover, you took your sons and daughters whom you had borne to Me and sacrificed them to idols to be devoured. Were your harlotries so small a matter?

21 "You slaughtered My children and offered them up to idols by causing them to pass through *the fire*.

22 "Besides all your abominations and harlotries you did not remember the days of your youth, when you were naked and bare and squirming in your blood.

23 "Then it came about after all your wickedness ('Woe, woe to you!' declares the Lord GOD),

24 that you built yourself a shrine and made yourself a high place in every square.

25 "You built yourself a high place at the top of every street and made your

beauty abominable, and you spread your legs to every passer-by to multiply your harlotry.

26 "You also played the harlot with the Egyptians, your lustful neighbors, and multiplied your harlotry to make Me angry.

27 "Behold now, I have stretched out My hand against you and diminished your rations. And I delivered you up to the desire of those who hate you, the daughters of the Philistines, who are ashamed of your lewd conduct.

28 "Moreover, you played the harlot with the Assyrians because you were not satisfied; you played the harlot with them and still were not satisfied.

29 "You also multiplied your harlotry with the land of merchants, Chaldea, yet even with this you were not satisfied."'"

30 "How languishing is your heart," declares the Lord GOD, "while you do all these things, the actions of a bold-faced harlot.

31 "When you built your shrine at the beginning of every street and made your high place in every square, in disdaining money, you were not like a harlot.

32 "You adulteress wife, who takes strangers instead of her husband!

33 "Men give gifts to all harlots, but you give your gifts to all your lovers to bribe them to come to you from every direction for your harlotries.

34 "Thus you are different from those women in your harlotries, in that no one plays the harlot as you do, because you give money and no money is given you; thus you are different."

35 Therefore, O harlot, hear the word of the LORD.

36 Thus says the Lord GOD, "Because your lewdness was poured out and your nakedness uncovered through your harlotries with your lovers and with all your detestable idols, and because of the blood of your sons which you gave to idols,

37 therefore, behold, I will gather all your lovers with whom you took pleasure, even all those whom you loved and all those whom you hated. So I will gather them against you from every direction and expose your nakedness to them that they may see all your nakedness.

38 "Thus I will judge you like women

who commit adultery or shed blood are judged; and I will bring on you the blood of wrath and jealousy.

39 "I will also give you into the hands of your lovers, and they will tear down your shrines, demolish your high places, strip you of your clothing, take away your jewels, and will leave you naked and bare.

40 "They will incite a crowd against you and they will stone you and cut you to pieces with their swords.

41 "They will burn your houses with fire and execute judgments on you in the sight of many women. Then I will stop you from playing the harlot, and you will also no longer pay your lovers.

42 "So I will calm My fury against you and My jealousy will depart from you, and I will be pacified and angry no more.

43 "Because you have not remembered the days of your youth but have enraged Me by all these things, behold, I in turn will bring your conduct down on your own head," declares the Lord GOD, "so that you will not commit this lewdness on top of all your other abominations.

44 "Behold, everyone who quotes proverbs will quote this proverb concerning you, saying, 'Like mother, like daughter.'

45 "You are the daughter of your mother, who loathed her husband and children. You are also the sister of your sisters, who loathed their husbands and children. Your mother was a Hittite and your father an Amorite.

46 "Now your older sister is Samaria, who lives north of you with her daughters; and your younger sister, who lives south of you, is Sodom with her daughters.

47 "Yet you have not merely walked in their ways or done according to their abominations; but, as if that were too little, you acted more corruptly in all your conduct than they.

48 "As I live," declares the Lord GOD, "Sodom, your sister and her daughters have not done as you and your daughters have done.

49 "Behold, this was the guilt of your sister Sodom: she and her daughters had arrogance, abundant food and careless ease, but she did not help the poor and needy.

50 "Thus they were haughty and committed abominations before Me. Therefore I removed them when I saw *it*.
51 "Furthermore, Samaria did not commit half of your sins, for you have multiplied your abominations more than they. Thus you have made your sisters appear righteous by all your abominations which you have committed.
52 "Also bear your disgrace in that you have made judgment favorable for your sisters. Because of your sins in which you acted more abominably than they, they are more in the right than you. Yes, be also ashamed and bear your disgrace, in that you made your sisters appear righteous.
53 "Nevertheless, I will restore their captivity, the captivity of Sodom and her daughters, the captivity of Samaria and her daughters, and along with them your own captivity,
54 in order that you may bear your humiliation and feel ashamed for all that you have done when you become a consolation to them.
55 "Your sisters, Sodom with her daughters and Samaria with her daughters, will return to their former state, and you with your daughters will *also* return to your former state.
56 "As *the name of* your sister Sodom was not heard from your lips in your day of pride,
57 before your wickedness was uncovered, so now you have become the reproach of the daughters of Edom and of all who are around her, of the daughters of the Philistines—those surrounding you who despise you.
58 "You have borne *the penalty of* your lewdness and abominations," the LORD declares.
59 For thus says the Lord GOD, "I will also do with you as you have done, you who have despised the oath by breaking the covenant.
60 "Nevertheless, I will remember My covenant with you in the days of your youth, and I will establish an everlasting covenant with you.
61 "Then you will remember your ways and be ashamed when you receive your sisters, *both* your older and your younger; and I will give them to you as daughters, but not because of your covenant.

62 "Thus I will establish My covenant with you, and you shall know that I am the LORD,
63 so that you may remember and be ashamed and never open your mouth anymore because of your humiliation, when I have forgiven you for all that you have done," the Lord GOD declares.

Psalm 123:1–4

A Song of Ascents.

123 TO You I lift up my eyes,
O You who are enthroned in the heavens!
2 Behold, as the eyes of servants *look* to the hand of their master,
As the eyes of a maid to the hand of her mistress,
So our eyes *look* to the LORD our God,
Until He is gracious to us.
3 Be gracious to us, O LORD, be gracious to us,
For we are greatly filled with contempt.
4 Our soul is greatly filled
With the scoffing of those who are at ease,
And with the contempt of the proud.

Proverbs 28:20

20 A faithful man will abound with blessings,
But he who makes haste to be rich will not go unpunished.

LIFE LESSONS

➤ **Psalm 123:2** — *Our eyes look to the* LORD *our God, until He is gracious to us.*

There may be many reasons why God does not immediately answer our prayers for help and mercy—He has a better plan, greater blessings, or knows something we do not know. One thing is sure: He instructs us to keep on asking until He responds (Luke 18:1–8). Then He sends His blessings.

Hebrews 8:1–13

8 NOW the main point in what has been said *is this*: we have such a high priest, who has taken His seat at the right hand of the throne of the Majesty in the heavens,

2 a minister in the sanctuary and in the true tabernacle, which the Lord pitched, not man.

3 For every high priest is appointed to offer both gifts and sacrifices; so it is necessary that this *high priest* also have something to offer.

4 Now if He were on earth, He would not be a priest at all, since there are those who offer the gifts according to the Law;

5 who serve a copy and shadow of the heavenly things, just as Moses was warned *by God* when he was about to erect the tabernacle; for, "SEE," He says, "THAT YOU MAKE all things ACCORDING TO THE PATTERN WHICH WAS SHOWN YOU ON THE MOUNTAIN."

6 But now He has obtained a more excellent ministry, by as much as He is also the mediator of a better covenant, which has been enacted on better promises.

7 For if that first *covenant* had been faultless, there would have been no occasion sought for a second.

8 For finding fault with them, He says, "BEHOLD, DAYS ARE COMING, SAYS THE LORD,
WHEN I WILL EFFECT A NEW COVENANT WITH THE HOUSE OF ISRAEL AND WITH THE HOUSE OF JUDAH;

9 NOT LIKE THE COVENANT WHICH I MADE WITH THEIR FATHERS
ON THE DAY WHEN I TOOK THEM BY THE HAND
TO LEAD THEM OUT OF THE LAND OF EGYPT;
FOR THEY DID NOT CONTINUE IN MY COVENANT,
AND I DID NOT CARE FOR THEM, SAYS THE LORD.

10 "FOR THIS IS THE COVENANT THAT I WILL MAKE WITH THE HOUSE OF ISRAEL AFTER THOSE DAYS, SAYS THE LORD:
I WILL PUT MY LAWS INTO THEIR MINDS,
AND I WILL WRITE THEM ON THEIR HEARTS.
AND I WILL BE THEIR GOD,

AND THEY SHALL BE MY PEOPLE.

11 "AND THEY SHALL NOT TEACH EVERYONE HIS FELLOW CITIZEN,
AND EVERYONE HIS BROTHER, SAYING, 'KNOW THE LORD,'
FOR ALL WILL KNOW ME,
FROM THE LEAST TO THE GREATEST OF THEM.

12 "FOR I WILL BE MERCIFUL TO THEIR INIQUITIES,
AND I WILL REMEMBER THEIR SINS NO MORE."

13 When He said, "A new *covenant*," He has made the first obsolete. But whatever is becoming obsolete and growing old is ready to disappear.

LIFE LESSONS

Hebrews 8:1 — *We have such a high priest, who has taken His seat at the right hand of the throne of the Majesty in the heavens.*

To be seated at "the right hand of the throne of the Majesty in the heavens" is to occupy the most powerful position anywhere—it is the place of absolute honor. Jesus intercedes for us as our Savior, Lord, Friend, and fellow heir, and He ministers to us perfectly forever.

Hebrews 8:6 — *He is also the mediator of a better covenant, which has been enacted on better promises.*

The Old Covenant, which was received by Moses on Mount Sinai (Ex. 19:1—24:3), was conditional. In order to receive God's promises, the people would have to obey the Lord and keep His commands (Deut. 28). However, the Lord established a New Covenant and wrote His laws upon the hearts of those who accepted His Son as Savior. Jesus enacted this new, better covenant through His death on the Cross and resurrection.

Hebrews 8:13 — *When He said, "A new covenant," He has made the first obsolete . . . ready to disappear.*

At the time Hebrews was written, the temple in Jerusalem apparently still existed. In A.D. 70, however, the Romans destroyed Jerusalem and the temple, which meant the Jews could no longer comply with the requirements of the old system (Deut. 12:5–9; 16:6).

17 NOW the word of the LORD came to me saying,

2 "Son of man, propound a riddle and speak a parable to the house of Israel,

3 saying, 'Thus says the Lord GOD, "A great eagle with great wings, long pinions and a full plumage of many colors came to Lebanon and took away the top of the cedar.

4 "He plucked off the topmost of its young twigs and brought it to a land of merchants; he set it in a city of traders.

5 "He also took some of the seed of the land and planted it in fertile soil. He placed *it* beside abundant waters; he set it *like* a willow.

6 "Then it sprouted and became a low, spreading vine with its branches turned toward him, but its roots remained under it. So it became a vine and yielded shoots and sent out branches.

7 "But there was another great eagle with great wings and much plumage; and behold, this vine bent its roots toward him and sent out its branches toward him from the beds where it was planted, that he might water it.

8 "It was planted in good soil beside abundant waters, that it might yield branches and bear fruit *and* become a splendid vine."'

9 "Say, 'Thus says the Lord GOD, "Will it thrive? Will he not pull up its roots and cut off its fruit, so that it withers—so that all its sprouting leaves wither? And neither by great strength nor by many people can it be raised from its roots *again*.

10 "Behold, though it is planted, will it thrive? Will it not completely wither as soon as the east wind strikes it—wither on the beds where it grew?"'"

11 Moreover, the word of the LORD came to me, saying,

12 "Say now to the rebellious house, 'Do you not know what these things *mean*?' Say, 'Behold, the king of Babylon came to Jerusalem, took its king and princes and brought them to him in Babylon.

13 'He took one of the royal family and made a covenant with him, putting him under oath. He also took away the mighty of the land,

14 that the kingdom might be in subjection, not exalting itself, *but* keeping his covenant that it might continue.

15 'But he rebelled against him by sending his envoys to Egypt that they might give him horses and many troops. Will he succeed? Will he who does such things escape? Can he indeed break the covenant and escape?

16 'As I live,' declares the Lord GOD, 'Surely in the country of the king who put him on the throne, whose oath he despised and whose covenant he broke, in Babylon he shall die.

17 'Pharaoh with *his* mighty army and great company will not help him in the war, when they cast up ramps and build siege walls to cut off many lives.

18 'Now he despised the oath by breaking the covenant, and behold, he pledged his allegiance, yet did all these things; he shall not escape.'"

19 Therefore, thus says the Lord GOD, "As I live, surely My oath which he despised and My covenant which he broke, I will inflict on his head.

20 "I will spread My net over him, and he will be caught in My snare. Then I will bring him to Babylon and enter into judgment with him there *regarding* the unfaithful act which he has committed against Me.

21 "All the choice men in all his troops will fall by the sword, and the survivors will be scattered to every wind; and you will know that I, the LORD, have spoken."

22 Thus says the Lord GOD, "I will also take *a* sprig from the lofty top of the cedar and set *it* out; I will pluck from the topmost of its young twigs a tender one and I will plant *it* on a high and lofty mountain.

23 "On the high mountain of Israel I will plant it, that it may bring forth boughs and bear fruit and become a stately cedar. And birds of every kind will nest under it; they will nest in the shade of its branches.

24 "All the trees of the field will know that I am the LORD; I bring down the high tree, exalt the low tree, dry up the green tree and make the dry tree flourish. I am

1417

---

the Lord; I have spoken, and I will perform *it*."

18 THEN the word of the Lord came to me, saying,

2 "What do you mean by using this proverb concerning the land of Israel, saying,

'The fathers eat the sour grapes,
But the children's teeth are set on edge'?

3 "As I live," declares the Lord God, "you are surely not going to use this proverb in Israel anymore.

➤ 4 "Behold, all souls are Mine; the soul of the father as well as the soul of the son is Mine. The soul who sins will die.

5 "But if a man is righteous and practices justice and righteousness,

6 and does not eat at the mountain *shrines* or lift up his eyes to the idols of the house of Israel, or defile his neighbor's wife or approach a woman during her menstrual period—

7 if a man does not oppress anyone, but restores to the debtor his pledge, does not commit robbery, *but* gives his bread to the hungry and covers the naked with clothing,

8 if he does not lend *money* on interest or take increase, *if* he keeps his hand

from iniquity *and* executes true justice between man and man,

9 *if* he walks in My statutes and My ordinances so as to deal faithfully—he is righteous *and* will surely live," declares the Lord God.

10 "Then he may have a violent son who sheds blood and who does any of these things to a brother

11 (though he himself did not do any of these things), that is, he even eats at the mountain *shrines*, and defiles his neighbor's wife,

12 oppresses the poor and needy, commits robbery, does not restore a pledge, but lifts up his eyes to the idols *and* commits abomination,

13 he lends *money* on interest and takes increase; will he live? He will not live! He has committed all these abominations, he will surely be put to death; his blood will be on his own head.

14 "Now behold, he has a son who has observed all his father's sins which he committed, and observing does not do likewise.

15 "He does not eat at the mountain *shrines* or lift up his eyes to the idols of the house of Israel, or defile his neighbor's wife,

16 or oppress anyone, or retain a pledge, or commit robbery, *but* he gives his bread to the hungry and covers the naked with clothing,

17 he keeps his hand from the poor, does not take interest or increase, *but* executes My ordinances, and walks in My statutes; he will not die for his father's iniquity, he will surely live.

18 "As for his father, because he practiced extortion, robbed *his* brother and did what was not good among his people, behold, he will die for his iniquity.

19 "Yet you say, 'Why should the son not bear the punishment for the father's iniquity?' When the son has practiced justice and righteousness and has observed all My statutes and has done them, he shall surely live.

20 "The person who sins will die. The son will not bear the punishment for the father's iniquity, nor will the father bear the punishment for the son's iniquity; the righteousness of the righteous will be upon himself, and the wickedness of the wicked will be upon himself. ✴

21 "But if the wicked man turns from all his sins which he has committed and observes all My statutes and practices justice and righteousness, he shall surely live; he shall not die.

22 "All his transgressions which he has committed will not be remembered against him; because of his righteousness which he has practiced, he will live.

23 "Do I have any pleasure in the death of the wicked," declares the Lord GOD, "rather than that he should turn from his ways and live?

24 "But when a righteous man turns away from his righteousness, commits iniquity and does according to all the abominations that a wicked man does, will he live? All his righteous deeds which he has done will not be remembered for his treachery which he has committed and his sin which he has committed; for them he will die.

25 "Yet you say, 'The way of the Lord is not right.' Hear now, O house of Israel! Is My way not right? Is it not your ways that are not right?

26 "When a righteous man turns away from his righteousness, commits iniquity and dies because of it, for his iniquity which he has committed he will die.

27 "Again, when a wicked man turns away from his wickedness which he has committed and practices justice and righteousness, he will save his life.

28 "Because he considered and turned away from all his transgressions which he had committed, he shall surely live; he shall not die.

29 "But the house of Israel says, 'The way of the Lord is not right.' Are My ways not right, O house of Israel? Is it not your ways that are not right?

30 "Therefore I will judge you, O house of Israel, each according to his conduct," declares the Lord GOD. "Repent and turn away from all your transgressions, so that iniquity may not become a stumbling block to you.

31 "Cast away from you all your transgressions which you have committed and make yourselves a new heart and a new spirit! For why will you die, O house of Israel?

32 "For I have no pleasure in the death of anyone who dies," declares the Lord GOD. "Therefore, repent and live."

Psalm 124:1–8

A Song of Ascents, of David.

124 "HAD it not been the LORD who was on our side,"
Let Israel now say,
2   "Had it not been the LORD who was on our side
When men rose up against us,
3   Then they would have swallowed us alive,
When their anger was kindled against us;
4   Then the waters would have engulfed us,
The stream would have swept over our soul;
5   Then the raging waters would have swept over our soul."
6   Blessed be the LORD,
Who has not given us to be torn by their teeth.
7   Our soul has escaped as a bird out of the snare of the trapper;
The snare is broken and we have escaped.
8   Our help is in the name of the LORD, ✳
Who made heaven and earth.

Proverbs 28:21

21   To show partiality is not good,
Because for a piece of bread a man will transgress.

LIFE LESSONS

➤ **Ezekiel 18:32 — "I have no pleasure in the death of anyone who dies . . . Therefore, repent and live."**

Romans 6:23 tells us, "The wages of sin is death, but the free gift of God is eternal life in Christ Jesus our Lord." The Father's desire is that we repent and receive the free gift of eternal life that He offers to us (2 Pet. 3:9). He has already paid the penalty of our sin through the sacrificial, substitutionary, all-sufficient death of His Son. Therefore, we must simply accept His gift and come to Him on His terms.

WHAT THE BIBLE SAYS ABOUT

Giving Thanks to God

Psalm 124:8

Our prayers are often more self-centered than we realize. As we talk to God, we tend to forget the many ways that He has helped us. Instead, we focus on the things that we want from Him. However, we should continually give thanks to our LORD and Savior. This is one of the most important priorities in the life of the believer. We're taught, "It is good to give thanks to the Lord and to sing praises to Your name, O Most High; to declare Your lovingkindness in the morning and Your faithfulness by night" (Ps. 92:1, 2).

Why is it so important that we express gratitude to God? Because He deserves the glory—and giving thanks honors Him. We act in obedience by giving Him the credit and praise to the One who should receive it. He is the author of every good thing, and should receive every honor.

Giving thanks to God refocuses our attention. What better way to bring our focus back to Him than to think of how He's delivered us? Doing so releases us from anxiety. Psalm 124:8 declares, "Our help is in the name of the LORD, who made heaven and earth." Because He is our help, we have nothing to fear.

Our gratefulness refreshes our relationship with Him and reinforces our faith. As we declare His lovingkindness and faithfulness, our spirits are rejuvenated. We feel closer to Him because He draws near to us when we thank Him and praise Him, and we have more joy in lives.

Therefore, how can we express our thanks to God?

- We express our thanks in words.
- We express our thanks by singing.
- We express our thanks by living obediently.
- We express our thanks through public worship.
- We give thanks by giving generously.

Have you counted your blessings lately? Have you stopped to think of the many things that God has done, not only for you, but for this world?

Giving thanks is something you can do at any time and in any place. Why not take a few moments to reflect upon the greatness of God and the ways He's helped you? Why not begin each morning and end every day with songs of praise and gratitude? If you do that, you're going to feel more joy in your life. You're going to feel closer to Him and be more eager to serve Him. Therefore, give thanks to God! ✸

✸ Hebrews 9:1–28

9 NOW even the first *covenant* had regulations of divine worship and the earthly sanctuary.

2 For there was a tabernacle prepared, the outer one, in which *were* the lampstand and the table and the sacred bread; this is called the holy place.

3 Behind the second veil there was a tabernacle which is called the Holy of Holies,

4 having a golden altar of incense and the ark of the covenant covered on all sides with gold, in which was a golden jar holding the manna, and Aaron's rod which budded, and the tables of the covenant;

5 and above it *were* the cherubim of glory overshadowing the mercy seat; but of these things we cannot now speak in detail.

6 Now when these things have been so prepared, the priests are continually entering the outer tabernacle performing the divine worship,

7 but into the second, only the high priest *enters* once a year, not without *taking* blood, which he offers for himself and for the sins of the people committed in ignorance.

8 The Holy Spirit *is* signifying this, that the way into the holy place has not yet been disclosed while the outer tabernacle is still standing,

9 which *is* a symbol for the present time. Accordingly both gifts and sacrifices are offered which cannot make the worshiper perfect in conscience,

10 since they *relate* only to food and drink and various washings, regulations for the body imposed until a time of reformation.

11 But when Christ appeared *as* a high

priest of the good things to come, *He entered* through the greater and more perfect tabernacle, not made with hands, that is to say, not of this creation;

12 and not through the blood of goats and calves, but through His own blood, He entered the holy place once for all, having obtained eternal redemption.

13 For if the blood of goats and bulls and the ashes of a heifer sprinkling those who have been defiled sanctify for the cleansing of the flesh,

14 how much more will the blood of Christ, who through the eternal Spirit offered Himself without blemish to God, cleanse your conscience from dead works to serve the living God?

15 For this reason He is the mediator of a new covenant, so that, since a death has taken place for the redemption of the transgressions that were *committed* under the first covenant, those who have been called may receive the promise of the eternal inheritance.

16 For where a covenant is, there must of necessity be the death of the one who made it.

17 For a covenant is valid *only* when men are dead, for it is never in force while the one who made it lives.

18 Therefore even the first *covenant* was not inaugurated without blood.

19 For when every commandment had been spoken by Moses to all the people according to the Law, he took the blood of the calves and the goats, with water and scarlet wool and hyssop, and sprinkled both the book itself and all the people,

20 saying, "THIS IS THE BLOOD OF THE COVENANT WHICH GOD COMMANDED YOU."

21 And in the same way he sprinkled both the tabernacle and all the vessels of the ministry with the blood.

22 And according to the Law, *one may* almost *say*, all things are cleansed with blood, and without shedding of blood there is no forgiveness.

23 Therefore it was necessary for the copies of the things in the heavens to be cleansed with these, but the heavenly things themselves with better sacrifices than these.

24 For Christ did not enter a holy place made with hands, a *mere* copy of the true one, but into heaven itself, now to appear in the presence of God for us;

25 nor was it that He would offer Himself often, as the high priest enters the holy place year by year with blood that is not his own.

26 Otherwise, He would have needed to suffer often since the foundation of the world; but now once at the consummation of the ages He has been manifested to put away sin by the sacrifice of Himself.

27 And inasmuch as it is appointed for men to die once and after this *comes* judgment,

28 so Christ also, having been offered once to bear the sins of many, will appear a second time for salvation without *reference to* sin, to those who eagerly await Him.

LIFE LESSONS

➤ **Hebrews 9:14 —** *The blood of Christ . . . cleanse your conscience from dead works to serve the living God.*

*N*one of us have to live with unresolved guilt. Jesus wants to take our accusing consciences and wipe them clean with His blood, enabling us to serve Him with joy and without the slightest bit of shame.

➤ **Hebrews 9:26 —** *He has been manifested to put away sin by the sacrifice of Himself.*

*N*o longer is it necessary for someone to make sacrifices for our sins year after year. Now we are completely forgiven of the penalty of our offenses through the sufficient, substitutionary death of Jesus Christ. Because of His love for us, Jesus lifts this burden of our transgressions off of us and takes them on Himself—completely annulling the shackles of sin and the sting of death.

➤ **Hebrews 9:27 —** *It is appointed for men to die once and after this comes judgment.*

*N*one of us can avoid death and judgment. Unless we're alive when the Lord returns, all of us will die, and every person in history will answer to God for how he or she lived.

19 "AS for you, take up a lamentation for the princes of Israel

2 and say,

'What was your mother?
A lioness among lions!
She lay down among young lions,
She reared her cubs.

3 'When she brought up one of her cubs,
He became a lion,
And he learned to tear *his* prey;
He devoured men.

4 'Then nations heard about him;
He was captured in their pit,
And they brought him with hooks
To the land of Egypt.

5 'When she saw, as she waited,
That her hope was lost,
She took another of her cubs
And made him a young lion.

6 'And he walked about among the lions;
He became a young lion,
He learned to tear *his* prey;
He devoured men.

7 'He destroyed their fortified towers
And laid waste their cities;
And the land and its fullness were appalled
Because of the sound of his roaring.

8 'Then nations set against him
On every side from *their* provinces,
And they spread their net over him;
He was captured in their pit.

9 'They put him in a cage with hooks
And brought him to the king of Babylon;
They brought him in hunting nets
So that his voice would be heard no more
On the mountains of Israel.

10 'Your mother was like a vine in your vineyard,
Planted by the waters;
It was fruitful and full of branches
Because of abundant waters.

11 'And it had strong branches *fit* for scepters of rulers,
And its height was raised above the clouds
So that it was seen in its height with the mass of its branches.

12 'But it was plucked up in fury;
It was cast down to the ground;
And the east wind dried up its fruit.
Its strong branch was torn off
So that it withered;
The fire consumed it.

13 'And now it is planted in the wilderness,
In a dry and thirsty land.

14 'And fire has gone out from *its* branch;
It has consumed its shoots *and* fruit,
So that there is not in it a strong branch,
A scepter to rule.'"

This is a lamentation, and has become a lamentation.

20 NOW in the seventh year, in the fifth *month*, on the tenth of the month, certain of the elders of Israel came to inquire of the LORD, and sat before me.

2 And the word of the LORD came to me saying,

3 "Son of man, speak to the elders of Israel and say to them, 'Thus says the Lord GOD, "Do you come to inquire of Me? As I live," declares the Lord GOD, "I will not be inquired of by you."'

4 "Will you judge them, will you judge them, son of man? Make them know the abominations of their fathers;

5 and say to them, 'Thus says the Lord GOD, "On the day when I chose Israel and swore to the descendants of the house of Jacob and made Myself known to them in the land of Egypt, when I swore to them, saying, I am the LORD your God,

6 on that day I swore to them, to bring them out from the land of Egypt into a land that I had selected for them, flowing with milk and honey, which is the glory of all lands.

7 "I said to them, 'Cast away, each of you, the detestable things of his eyes, and do not defile yourselves with the idols of Egypt; I am the LORD your God.'

8 "But they rebelled against Me and were not willing to listen to Me; they did not cast away the detestable things of their eyes, nor did they forsake the idols of Egypt.

Then I resolved to pour out My wrath on them, to accomplish My anger against them in the midst of the land of Egypt.

9 "But I acted for the sake of My name,

that it should not be profaned in the sight of the nations among whom they *lived,* in whose sight I made Myself known to them by bringing them out of the land of Egypt.

10 "So I took them out of the land of Egypt and brought them into the wilderness.

11 "I gave them My statutes and informed them of My ordinances, by which, if a man observes them, he will live.

12 "Also I gave them My sabbaths to be a sign between Me and them, that they might know that I am the LORD who sanctifies them.

13 "But the house of Israel rebelled against Me in the wilderness. They did not walk in My statutes and they rejected My ordinances, by which, if a man observes them, he will live; and My sabbaths they greatly profaned. Then I resolved to pour out My wrath on them in the wilderness, to annihilate them.

14 "But I acted for the sake of My name, that it should not be profaned in the sight of the nations, before whose sight I had brought them out.

15 "Also I swore to them in the wilderness that I would not bring them into the land which I had given them, flowing with milk and honey, which is the glory of all lands,

16 because they rejected My ordinances, and as for My statutes, they did not walk in them; they even profaned My sabbaths, for their heart continually went after their idols.

17 "Yet My eye spared them rather than destroying them, and I did not cause their annihilation in the wilderness.

18 "I said to their children in the wilderness, 'Do not walk in the statutes of your fathers or keep their ordinances or defile yourselves with their idols.

19 'I am the LORD your God; walk in My statutes and keep My ordinances and observe them.

20 'Sanctify My sabbaths; and they shall be a sign between Me and you, that you may know that I am the LORD your God.'

21 "But the children rebelled against Me; they did not walk in My statutes, nor were they careful to observe My ordinances, by which, *if* a man observes them, he will live; they profaned My sabbaths. So I resolved to pour out My

wrath on them, to accomplish My anger against them in the wilderness.

22 "But I withdrew My hand and acted for the sake of My name, that it should not be profaned in the sight of the nations in whose sight I had brought them out.

23 "Also I swore to them in the wilderness that I would scatter them among the nations and disperse them among the lands,

24 because they had not observed My ordinances, but had rejected My statutes and had profaned My sabbaths, and their eyes were on the idols of their fathers.

25 "I also gave them statutes that were not good and ordinances by which they could not live;

26 and I pronounced them unclean because of their gifts, in that they caused all their firstborn to pass through *the fire* so that I might make them desolate, in order that they might know that I am the LORD."'

27 "Therefore, son of man, speak to the house of Israel and say to them, 'Thus says the Lord GOD, "Yet in this your fathers have blasphemed Me by acting treacherously against Me.

28 "When I had brought them into the

LIFE LESSONS

➤ **Ezekiel 20:14 —** *"I acted for the sake of My name, that it should not be profaned in the sight of the nations."*

God rescued the stiff-necked Israelites out of Egyptian slavery, not because they deserved it, but as a demonstration of His grace and mercy. He wants the world to both see and enjoy His love and goodness.

➤ **Ezekiel 20:25 —** *"I also gave them statutes that were not good and ordinances by which they could not live."*

If we refuse to live by God's wisdom, He will give us over to our own (Ps. 81:11, 12; Rom. 1:24–26)—which is sure to lead to destruction (Prov. 14:12). In this instance, the people of Israel were so intent on serving other deities that they willingly sacrificed their firstborn (Ezek. 20:26)—imposing a greater penalty on themselves than God ever required of them.

land which I swore to give to them, then they saw every high hill and every leafy tree, and they offered there their sacrifices and there they presented the provocation of their offering. There also they made their soothing aroma and there they poured out their drink offerings.

29 "Then I said to them, 'What is the high place to which you go?' So its name is called Bamah to this day.'"

30 "Therefore, say to the house of Israel, 'Thus says the Lord GOD, "Will you defile yourselves after the manner of your fathers and play the harlot after their detestable things?

31 "When you offer your gifts, when you cause your sons to pass through the fire, you are defiling yourselves with all your idols to this day. And shall I be inquired of by you, O house of Israel? As I live," declares the Lord GOD, "I will not be inquired of by you.

32 "What comes into your mind will not come about, when you say: 'We will be like the nations, like the tribes of the lands, serving wood and stone.'

33 "As I live," declares the Lord GOD, "surely with a mighty hand and with an outstretched arm and with wrath poured out, I shall be king over you.

34 "I will bring you out from the peoples and gather you from the lands where you are scattered, with a mighty hand and with an outstretched arm and with wrath poured out;

35 and I will bring you into the wilderness of the peoples, and there I will enter into judgment with you face to face.

36 "As I entered into judgment with your fathers in the wilderness of the land of Egypt, so I will enter into judgment with you," declares the Lord GOD.

37 "I will make you pass under the rod, and I will bring you into the bond of the covenant;

38 and I will purge from you the rebels and those who transgress against Me; I will bring them out of the land where they sojourn, but they will not enter the land of Israel. Thus you will know that I am the LORD.

39 "As for you, O house of Israel," thus says the Lord GOD, "Go, serve everyone his idols; but later you will surely listen to Me, and My holy name you will profane no longer with your gifts and with your idols.

40 "For on My holy mountain, on the high mountain of Israel," declares the Lord GOD, "there the whole house of Israel, all of them, will serve Me in the land; there I will accept them and there I will seek your contributions and the choicest of your gifts, with all your holy things.

41 "As a soothing aroma I will accept you when I bring you out from the peoples and gather you from the lands where you are scattered; and I will prove Myself holy among you in the sight of the nations.

42 "And you will know that I am the LORD, when I bring you into the land of Israel, into the land which I swore to give to your forefathers.

43 "There you will remember your ways and all your deeds with which you have defiled yourselves; and you will loathe yourselves in your own sight for all the evil things that you have done.

44 "Then you will know that I am the LORD when I have dealt with you for My name's sake, not according to your evil ways or according to your corrupt deeds, O house of Israel," declares the Lord GOD.'"

45 Now the word of the LORD came to me, saying,

46 "Son of man, set your face toward Teman, and speak out against the south and prophesy against the forest land of the Negev,

47 and say to the forest of the Negev, 'Hear the word of the LORD: thus says the Lord GOD, "Behold, I am about to kindle a fire in you, and it will consume every green tree in you, as well as every dry tree; the blazing flame will not be quenched and the whole surface from south to north will be burned by it.

LIFE LESSONS

➤ **Ezekiel 20:44 —** *"I have dealt with you for My name's sake."*

*I*f God did not deal with us on the basis of His mercy and grace, none of us would have any hope for the future. But because He acts according to His loving nature, and has provided salvation for us through Jesus Christ, we have the brightest future imaginable.

48 "All flesh will see that I, the LORD, have kindled it; it shall not be quenched."'"
49 Then I said, "Ah Lord GOD! They are saying of me, 'Is he not *just* speaking parables?'"

Psalm 125:1–5

A Song of Ascents.

125 THOSE who trust in the LORD Are as Mount Zion, which cannot be moved but abides forever.
2 As the mountains surround Jerusalem,
So the LORD surrounds His people
From this time forth and forever.
3 For the scepter of wickedness shall not rest upon the land of the righteous,
So that the righteous will not put forth their hands to do wrong.
4 Do good, O LORD, to those who are good
And to those who are upright in their hearts.
5 But as for those who turn aside to their crooked ways,
The LORD will lead them away with the doers of iniquity.
Peace be upon Israel.

Proverbs 28:22

22 A man with an evil eye hastens after wealth
And does not know that want will come upon him.

Hebrews 10:1–18

10 FOR the Law, since it has *only* a shadow of the good things to come *and* not the very form of things, can never, by the same sacrifices which they offer continually year by year, make perfect those who draw near.
2 Otherwise, would they not have ceased to be offered, because the worshipers, having once been cleansed,

would no longer have had consciousness of sins?
3 But in those *sacrifices* there is a reminder of sins year by year.
4 For it is impossible for the blood of bulls and goats to take away sins.
5 Therefore, when He comes into the world, He says,
"SACRIFICE AND OFFERING YOU HAVE NOT DESIRED,
BUT A BODY YOU HAVE PREPARED FOR ME;
6 IN WHOLE BURNT OFFERINGS AND *sacrifices* FOR SIN YOU HAVE TAKEN NO PLEASURE.
7 "THEN I SAID, 'BEHOLD, I HAVE COME (IN THE SCROLL OF THE BOOK IT IS WRITTEN OF ME)
TO DO YOUR WILL, O GOD.'"
8 After saying above, "SACRIFICES AND OFFERINGS AND WHOLE BURNT OFFERINGS AND *sacrifices* FOR SIN YOU HAVE NOT DESIRED, NOR HAVE YOU TAKEN PLEASURE *in them*" (which are offered according to the Law),
9 then He said, "BEHOLD, I HAVE COME TO DO YOUR WILL." He takes away the first in order to establish the second.
10 By this will we have been sanctified

LIFE LESSONS

➤ **Psalm 125:2** — *As the mountains surround Jerusalem, so the LORD surrounds His people from this time forth and forever.*

*D*uring the psalmist's time, Jerusalem was virtually inaccessible to invading armies because of Mounts Olivet and Scopus, and the valleys of Hinnom, Tyropoeon, and Kidron. Likewise, God surrounds His people as an impenetrable defense. He covers us on every side so that nothing can reach us without first passing through His loving hands.

➤ **Hebrews 10:4** — *It is impossible for the blood of bulls and goats to take away sins.*

*T*hrough the shedding of blood, God in His graciousness provided soft animal pelts to cover them (Gen. 3). Before Jesus came, innumerable animals were slain in sacrifice for people's sins. But only His death as the unblemished Lamb of God provided an eternal covering.

WHAT THE BIBLE SAYS ABOUT

What Happened at the Cross

Hebrews 10:1–14

$\mathcal{H}$oly God is absolutely uncompromising and unrelenting in His attitude toward all forms of evil. His justice requires payment for every sin.

Under the Old Testament sacrificial system established by God, priests made daily offerings for the nation's sins (Ex. 29:38, 39). People also brought sacrifices of lambs and other animals to the temple as payment for their wrongdoings (Lev. 5:5–7). Sacrifices were repeated day after day because an animal's blood could never take away sin.

But when God's chosen Lamb laid down His life as a substitute for all men, payment for sin was complete. Jesus bore in His body the full penalty for our disobedience—past, present, and future (1 Pet. 2:24). No further sacrifice is required (Heb. 7:27).

At the Cross, God revealed His wrath against all unrighteousness (Rom. 1:18, 19). Judgment against sin was carried out. One man—the virgin-born, sinless, incarnate Son of God—voluntarily offered Himself to stand in our place and receive God's judgment for our sin.

Jesus took on the divine condemnation and wrath that we deserve. This is good news. When we receive Jesus as our personal Savior, we are no longer under a death sentence. We are proclaimed "not guilty" because He took our place.

The mercy of God in not punishing us is ours forever. The riches of His grace give us life, even though we deserve to die. The Cross brought death to One so that many might live. Have you thanked Jesus today for life?

---

through the offering of the body of Jesus Christ once for all.

11 Every priest stands daily ministering and offering time after time the same sacrifices, which can never take away sins;

12 but He, having offered one sacrifice for sins for all time, SAT DOWN AT THE RIGHT HAND OF GOD,

LIFE LESSONS

> **Hebrews 10:14 — *By one offering He has perfected for all time those who are sanctified.***

$\mathcal{O}$ur salvation is both a completed fact and an ongoing process. Through faith in Jesus, we are *justified*—or in right relationship with Him having been forgiven of our sin (Rom. 5:1). And by the power of His Spirit, He enables us to become more like Him, whose righteousness we received (Rom. 8:29).

13 waiting from that time onward UNTIL HIS ENEMIES BE MADE A FOOTSTOOL FOR HIS FEET.

14 For by one offering He has perfected for all time those who are sanctified.

15 And the Holy Spirit also testifies to us; for after saying,

16 "THIS IS THE COVENANT THAT I WILL
     MAKE WITH THEM
     AFTER THOSE DAYS, SAYS THE
     LORD:
     I WILL PUT MY LAWS UPON THEIR
     HEART,
     AND ON THEIR MIND I WILL WRITE
     THEM,"

He then says,

17 "AND THEIR SINS AND THEIR LAWLESS
     DEEDS
     I WILL REMEMBER NO MORE."

18 Now where there is forgiveness of these things, there is no longer *any* offering for sin.

 Ezekiel 21:1—22:31

21 AND the word of the LORD came to me saying,

2 "Son of man, set your face toward Jerusalem, and speak against the sanctuaries and prophesy against the land of Israel;

3 and say to the land of Israel, 'Thus says the LORD, "Behold, I am against you; and I will draw My sword out of its

sheath and cut off from you the righteous and the wicked.

4 "Because I will cut off from you the righteous and the wicked, therefore My sword will go forth from its sheath against all flesh from south to north.

5 "Thus all flesh will know that I, the LORD, have drawn My sword out of its sheath. It will not return to its sheath again."

6 "As for you, son of man, groan with breaking heart and bitter grief, groan in their sight.

7 "And when they say to you, 'Why do you groan?' you shall say, 'Because of the news that is coming; and every heart will melt, all hands will be feeble, every spirit will faint and all knees will be weak as water. Behold, it comes and it will happen,' declares the Lord GOD."

8 Again the word of the LORD came to me, saying,

9 "Son of man, prophesy and say, 'Thus says the LORD.' Say,

'A sword, a sword sharpened
And also polished!

10 'Sharpened to make a slaughter,
Polished to flash like lightning!'

Or shall we rejoice, the rod of My son despising every tree?

11 "It is given to be polished, that it may be handled; the sword is sharpened and polished, to give it into the hand of the slayer.

12 "Cry out and wail, son of man; for it is against My people, it is against all the officials of Israel. They are delivered over to the sword with My people, therefore strike your thigh.

13 "For there is a testing; and what if even the rod which despises will be no more?" declares the Lord GOD.

14 "You therefore, son of man, prophesy and clap your hands together; and let the sword be doubled the third time, the sword for the slain. It is the sword for the great one slain, which surrounds them,

15 that their hearts may melt, and many fall at all their gates. I have given the glittering sword. Ah! It is made for striking like lightning, it is wrapped up in readiness for slaughter.

16 "Show yourself sharp, go to the right; set yourself; go to the left, wherever your edge is appointed.

17 "I will also clap My hands together, and I will appease My wrath; I, the LORD, have spoken."

18 The word of the LORD came to me saying,

19 "As for you, son of man, make two ways for the sword of the king of Babylon to come; both of them will go out of one land. And make a signpost; make it at the head of the way to the city.

20 "You shall mark a way for the sword to come to Rabbah of the sons of Ammon, and to Judah into fortified Jerusalem.

21 "For the king of Babylon stands at the parting of the way, at the head of the two ways, to use divination; he shakes the arrows, he consults the household idols, he looks at the liver.

22 "Into his right hand came the divination, 'Jerusalem,' to set battering rams, to open the mouth for slaughter, to lift up the voice with a battle cry, to set battering rams against the gates, to cast up ramps, to build a siege wall.

23 "And it will be to them like a false divination in their eyes; they have sworn solemn oaths. But he brings iniquity to remembrance, that they may be seized.

24 "Therefore, thus says the Lord GOD, 'Because you have made your iniquity to be remembered, in that your transgressions are uncovered, so that in all your deeds your sins appear—because you have come to remembrance, you will be seized with the hand.

25 'And you, O slain, wicked one, the prince of Israel, whose day has come, in the time of the punishment of the end,'

26 thus says the Lord GOD, 'Remove the turban and take off the crown; this will no longer be the same. Exalt that which is low and abase that which is high.

27 'A ruin, a ruin, a ruin, I will make it. ◁

LIFE LESSONS

➤ Ezekiel 21:27 — *"This also will be no more until He comes whose right it is, and I will give it to Him."*

With the destruction of Jerusalem by the Babylonians, the line of David ceased to rule on Judah's throne (the line of David had not ruled in the northern kingdom of Israel from the time the nation was divided in two. See 1 Kings 12.) According to this prophecy, no other Davidic king would rule until the Messiah—who we know to be Jesus Christ—established His reign. And His rule will last forever.

This also will be no more until He comes whose right it is, and I will give it *to Him.*'

28 "And you, son of man, prophesy and say, 'Thus says the Lord GOD concerning the sons of Ammon and concerning their reproach,' and say: 'A sword, a sword is drawn, polished for the slaughter, to cause it to consume, that it may be like lightning—

29 while they see for you false visions, while they divine lies for you—to place you on the necks of the wicked who are slain, whose day has come, in the time of the punishment of the end.

30 'Return *it* to its sheath. In the place where you were created, in the land of your origin, I will judge you.

31 'I will pour out My indignation on you; I will blow on you with the fire of My wrath, and I will give you into the hand of brutal men, skilled in destruction.

32 'You will be fuel for the fire; your blood will be in the midst of the land. You will not be remembered, for I, the LORD, have spoken.'"

22 THEN the word of the LORD came to me, saying,

2 "And you, son of man, will you judge, will you judge the bloody city? Then cause her to know all her abominations.

3 "You shall say, 'Thus says the Lord GOD, "A city shedding blood in her midst, so that her time will come, and that makes idols, contrary to her *interest,* for defilement!

4 "You have become guilty by the blood which you have shed, and defiled by your idols which you have made. Thus you have brought your day near and have come to your years; therefore I have made you a reproach to the nations and a mocking to all the lands.

5 "Those who are near and those who are far from you will mock you, you of ill repute, full of turmoil.

6 "Behold, the rulers of Israel, each according to his power, have been in you for the purpose of shedding blood.

7 "They have treated father and mother lightly within you. The alien they have oppressed in your midst; the fatherless and the widow they have wronged in you.

8 "You have despised My holy things and profaned My sabbaths.

9 "Slanderous men have been in you for the purpose of shedding blood, and in you they have eaten at the mountain *shrines.* In your midst they have committed acts of lewdness.

10 "In you they have uncovered *their* fathers' nakedness; in you they have humbled her who was unclean in her menstrual impurity.

11 "One has committed abomination with his neighbor's wife and another has lewdly defiled his daughter-in-law. And another in you has humbled his sister, his father's daughter.

12 "In you they have taken bribes to shed blood; you have taken interest and profits, and you have injured your neighbors for gain by oppression, and you have forgotten Me," declares the Lord GOD.

13 "Behold, then, I smite My hand at your dishonest gain which you have acquired and at the bloodshed which is among you.

14 "Can your heart endure, or can your hands be strong in the days that I will deal with you? I, the LORD, have spoken and will act.

15 "I will scatter you among the nations and I will disperse you through the lands, and I will consume your uncleanness from you.

16 "You will profane yourself in the sight of the nations, and you will know that I am the LORD."'"

17 And the word of the LORD came to me, saying,

LIFE LESSONS

➤ **Ezekiel 22:14 —** *"Can your heart endure, or can your hands be strong in the days that I will deal with you?"*

Some believe that at the Great White Throne Judgment, they will be able to air their complaints and excuses to God. However, that is not the case. If the judgment He sent to Jerusalem was too terrible for the people to endure, "How much severer punishment do you think he will deserve who has trampled under foot the Son of God?" (Heb. 10:29). As believers, our names are written in the Lamb's Book of Life, and we have absolutely no reason to fear. We are assured that we will enjoy heaven with Him forever.

18 "Son of man, the house of Israel has become dross to Me; all of them are bronze and tin and iron and lead in the furnace; they are the dross of silver.
19 "Therefore, thus says the Lord GOD, 'Because all of you have become dross, therefore, behold, I am going to gather you into the midst of Jerusalem.
20 'As they gather silver and bronze and iron and lead and tin into the furnace to blow fire on it in order to melt *it*, so I will gather *you* in My anger and in My wrath and I will lay you *there* and melt you.
21 'I will gather you and blow on you with the fire of My wrath, and you will be melted in the midst of it.
22 'As silver is melted in the furnace, so you will be melted in the midst of it; and you will know that I, the LORD, have poured out My wrath on you.'"
23 And the word of the LORD came to me, saying,
24 "Son of man, say to her, 'You are a land that is not cleansed or rained on in the day of indignation.'
25 "There is a conspiracy of her prophets in her midst like a roaring lion tearing the prey. They have devoured lives; they have taken treasure and precious things; they have made many widows in the midst of her.
26 "Her priests have done violence to My law and have profaned My holy things; they have made no distinction between the holy and the profane, and they have not taught the difference between the unclean and the clean; and they hide their eyes from My sabbaths, and I am profaned among them.
27 "Her princes within her are like wolves tearing the prey, by shedding blood *and* destroying lives in order to get dishonest gain.
28 "Her prophets have smeared whitewash for them, seeing false visions and divining lies for them, saying, 'Thus says the Lord GOD,' when the LORD has not spoken.
29 "The people of the land have practiced oppression and committed robbery, and they have wronged the poor and needy and have oppressed the sojourner without justice.
30 "I searched for a man among them who would build up the wall and stand in the gap before Me for the land, so that I would not destroy it; but I found no one.

31 "Thus I have poured out My indignation on them; I have consumed them with the fire of My wrath; their way I have brought upon their heads," declares the Lord GOD.

Psalm 126:1–6

A Song of Ascents.

126 WHEN the LORD brought back the captive ones of Zion,
We were like those who dream.
2 Then our mouth was filled with laughter
And our tongue with joyful shouting;
Then they said among the nations,
"The LORD has done great things for them."
3 The LORD has done great things for us;
We are glad.
4 Restore our captivity, O LORD,
As the streams in the South.
5 Those who sow in tears shall reap with joyful shouting.
6 He who goes to and fro weeping, carrying *his* bag of seed,
Shall indeed come again with a shout of joy, bringing his sheaves *with him.*

LIFE LESSONS

➤ **Ezekiel 22:30 — *"I searched for a man among them who would build up the wall and stand in the gap before Me for the land, so that I would not destroy it; but I found no one."***

God calls us, His people, to "stand in the gap" and call those around us to repentance and new life in Christ. Who do you know that needs to hear the Good News? Whose heart needs your prayers and faithful witness?

➤ **Psalm 126:5 — *Those who sow in tears shall reap with joyful shouting.***

God never pretends that this life will be free of hardship or pain, but He insists that, for those who know and love Him, our tears are seeds that will one day bloom into enormous joy.

LIFE PRINCIPLE 28

NO CHRISTIAN HAS EVER BEEN CALLED TO
"GO IT ALONE" IN HIS OR HER WALK OF FAITH.

HEBREWS 10:24, 25

*T*he writer of Hebrews knew that his audience, made up mainly of Jewish believers who had just come to faith, was struggling with how to incorporate their Jewish heritage into their walk with Christ. The author therefore spends a great deal of time explaining that Jesus Christ prepared the way for uninterrupted fellowship with the Father. He is our great High Priest. His death provided the way for individuals to have personal access to God without going through a human agent.

At times, this principle was difficult for the Jewish Christians to accept. They were accustomed to participating in a variety of ceremonial washings and offerings to be cleansed from their sins; immediate access to God apart from those things was something new. But the writer assured them that since Christ died for their sins and rose from the dead, they could now go directly to the Father with their prayers and needs. The author also knew the challenge facing these converts to remain faithful to their new faith. So he exhorted them to "hold fast ... without wavering" (Heb. 10:23).

He instructed his readers to *help one another* hold fast to their faith in God. He knew they would be tempted by trial and persecution to drift from the truth that God had plans for their lives. So he said, "Let us consider how to stimulate one another to love and good deeds" (Heb. 10:24). The Greek term translated "stimulate" literally means "to irritate" or to pressure one another to consider what the Lord has done in the past. He is faithful and does not abandon the work of His hands. We are His creations, and when we encounter difficulty, sorrow, rejection or any other distress, we can know without doubt that God will provide the wisdom and resources we need. Even in times of joy, He is blessed by happiness and contentment. In essence, the author was instructing his readers to spur one another along, to refuse to become ensnared by negativity, and to take responsibility for their lives in Christ as well as one another.

With this backdrop, he made it clear that they should not stop meeting together (Heb. 10:25). They needed one another, just as we need other believers. To give up meeting together would spell disaster because it would provide Satan an opportunity to draw them away from the Lord. In meeting together, they found the mutual encouragement to keep going. The same is true for us.

God wants us to regularly meet with other believers. He wants His people in church! Many believers don't take this admonition seriously because they don't know the reason behind it. I have often heard this refrain: "I can worship God at home. I don't need to go to church." Many believers believe the sole reason we meet together is to worship—and understandably so. After all, we call it a worship service.

If worship were the only reason we are commanded to meet, then those who claim they can worship at home would have a strong argument. But worship is not the sole reason. Nor is it so that we can be taught God's truth. We can turn on our radios and televisions and hear good Bible teaching. On the surface, it seems that anything we can do at church we can do just as well at home, alone.

So why are we commanded to meet? Why go to church?

The writer of Hebrews says it is to safeguard against drifting. We are the body of Christ, and when we are with other believers, we are doing what comes naturally and what we will do for eternity—being together in His presence. We make up the church, and together we provide strength for one another through prayer, fellowship, and encouragement.

Enemy forces are always at work around us, seeking to blow us off course. Sheer individual commitment is really not enough to keep us in line. We need the presence and accountability of other believers who love us and are willing to laugh, cry, and check on us. At times, when we feel as if our faith makes no difference—or we see no fruit in our lives, and we don't think our testimony makes a difference—it does. When we surrender our lives to Christ, He uses us in countless ways, ways we may never know.

In the atmosphere, worship, and fellowship in God's house, we discover that we are not alone. We hear others talk about how the Lord has miraculously provided for them. One may describe the pain he has suffered as a result of a loss. A new believer may tell her story of redemption, rejoicing in God's grace. As we listen to others recount God's work in their lives, something happens inside of us. We are spurred on to faithfulness and to praising God for His goodness.

The accountability and encouragement found in church anchor us against the tides that work to sweep us away. To neglect the regular assembly of fellow Christians is to miss out on this essential element in the development of our faith.

Throughout the Bible, we find that one of God's principle desires is to have a close relationship with each one of us. By becoming active in a local church, you safeguard yourself against missing out on all that God has for you. Your participation in a body of other believers safeguards your personal fellowship with God. Remember, when you drift away from the family of God, it is only a matter of time until you drift away from fellowship with God.

Regular church attendance should never be viewed as something you do to gain God's merit. We are not saved by good works. Instead, it should provide the catalyst for spiritual growth. Make sure the church you attend teaches the Word of God without compromising His truth. If yours doesn't, I recommend you visit another church. Find one that accurately teaches the principles in Scripture while demonstrating God's love, forgiveness, and grace. Remember that you also have a responsibility to actively use your spiritual gifts for the benefit of other believers. ◈

Proverbs 28:23

23 He who rebukes a man will
afterward find *more* favor
Than he who flatters with the tongue.

Hebrews 10:19–39

19 Therefore, brethren, since we have confidence to enter the holy place by the blood of Jesus,
20 by a new and living way which He inaugurated for us through the veil, that is, His flesh,
21 and since *we have* a great priest over the house of God,
22 let us draw near with a sincere heart in full assurance of faith, having our hearts sprinkled *clean* from an evil conscience and our bodies washed with pure water.
23 Let us hold fast the confession of our hope without wavering, for He who promised is faithful;
24 and let us consider how to stimulate one another to love and good deeds,
25 not forsaking our own assembling together, as is the habit of some, but encouraging *one another*; and all the more as you see the day drawing near.
26 For if we go on sinning willfully after receiving the knowledge of the truth, there no longer remains a sacrifice for sins,
27 but a terrifying expectation of judgment and THE FURY OF A FIRE WHICH WILL CONSUME THE ADVERSARIES.
28 Anyone who has set aside the Law of Moses dies without mercy on *the testimony of* two or three witnesses.
29 How much severer punishment do you think he will deserve who has trampled under foot the Son of God, and has regarded as unclean the blood of the

covenant by which he was sanctified, and has insulted the Spirit of grace?
30 For we know Him who said, "VENGEANCE IS MINE, I WILL REPAY." And again, "THE LORD WILL JUDGE HIS PEOPLE."
31 It is a terrifying thing to fall into the hands of the living God.
32 But remember the former days, when, after being enlightened, you endured a great conflict of sufferings,
33 partly by being made a public spectacle through reproaches and tribulations, and partly by becoming sharers with those who were so treated.
34 For you showed sympathy to the prisoners and accepted joyfully the seizure of your property, knowing that you have for yourselves a better possession and a lasting one.
35 Therefore, do not throw away your confidence, which has a great reward.
36 For you have need of endurance, so that when you have done the will of God, you may receive what was promised.
37 FOR YET IN A VERY LITTLE WHILE,
HE WHO IS COMING WILL COME, AND
WILL NOT DELAY.
38 BUT MY RIGHTEOUS ONE SHALL LIVE BY
FAITH;
AND IF HE SHRINKS BACK, MY SOUL
HAS NO PLEASURE IN HIM.
39 But we are not of those who shrink back to destruction, but of those who have faith to the preserving of the soul.

LIFE LESSONS

➤ **Hebrews 10:31 —** *It is a terrifying thing to fall into the hands of the living God.*

The "hands" the writer has in mind here are not the hands of divine grace but those of divine judgment. Can a gracious God also dispense "terrifying" discipline? The writer of Hebrews thought so.

Ezekiel 23:1—24:27

23 THE word of the LORD came to me again, saying,

2 "Son of man, there were two women, the daughters of one mother;
3 and they played the harlot in Egypt. They played the harlot in their youth; there their breasts were pressed and there their virgin bosom was handled.

4 "Their names were Oholah the elder and Oholibah her sister. And they became Mine, and they bore sons and daughters. And *as for* their names, Samaria is Oholah and Jerusalem is Oholibah.

5 "Oholah played the harlot while she was Mine; and she lusted after her lovers, after the Assyrians, *her* neighbors,

6 who were clothed in purple, governors and officials, all of them desirable young men, horsemen riding on horses.

7 "She bestowed her harlotries on them, all of whom *were* the choicest men of Assyria; and with all whom she lusted after, with all their idols she defiled herself.

8 "She did not forsake her harlotries from *the time in* Egypt; for in her youth men had lain with her, and they handled her virgin bosom and poured out their lust on her.

9 "Therefore, I gave her into the hand of her lovers, into the hand of the Assyrians, after whom she lusted.

10 "They uncovered her nakedness; they took her sons and her daughters, but they slew her with the sword. Thus she became a byword among women, and they executed judgments on her.

11 "Now her sister Oholibah saw *this*, yet she was more corrupt in her lust than she, and her harlotries were more than the harlotries of her sister.

12 "She lusted after the Assyrians, governors and officials, the ones near, magnificently dressed, horsemen riding on horses, all of them desirable young men.

13 "I saw that she had defiled herself; they both took the same way.

14 "So she increased her harlotries. And she saw men portrayed on the wall, images of the Chaldeans portrayed with vermilion,

15 girded with belts on their loins, with flowing turbans on their heads, all of them looking like officers, like the Babylonians *in* Chaldea, the land of their birth.

16 "When she saw them she lusted after them and sent messengers to them in Chaldea.

17 "The Babylonians came to her to the bed of love and defiled her with their harlotry. And when she had been defiled by them, she became disgusted with them.

18 "She uncovered her harlotries and uncovered her nakedness; then I became disgusted with her, as I had become disgusted with her sister.

19 "Yet she multiplied her harlotries, remembering the days of her youth, when she played the harlot in the land of Egypt.

20 "She lusted after their paramours, whose flesh is *like* the flesh of donkeys and whose issue is *like* the issue of horses.

21 "Thus you longed for the lewdness of your youth, when the Egyptians handled your bosom because of the breasts of your youth.

22 "Therefore, O Oholibah, thus says the Lord GOD, 'Behold I will arouse your lovers against you, from whom you were alienated, and I will bring them against you from every side:

23 the Babylonians and all the Chaldeans, Pekod and Shoa and Koa, *and* all the Assyrians with them; desirable young men, governors and officials all of them, officers and men of renown, all of them riding on horses.

24 'They will come against you with weapons, chariots and wagons, and with a company of peoples. They will set themselves against you on every side with buckler and shield and helmet; and I will commit the judgment to them, and they will judge you according to their customs.

25 'I will set My jealousy against you, that they may deal with you in wrath. They will remove your nose and your ears; and your survivors will fall by the sword. They will take your sons and your daughters; and your survivors will be consumed by the fire.

26 'They will also strip you of your clothes and take away your beautiful jewels.

27 'Thus I will make your lewdness and your harlotry *brought* from the land of Egypt to cease from you, so that you will not lift up your eyes to them or remember Egypt anymore.'

28 "For thus says the Lord GOD, 'Behold, I will give you into the hand of those whom you hate, into the hand of those from whom you were alienated.

29 'They will deal with you in hatred, take all your property, and leave you naked and bare. And the nakedness of

your harlotries will be uncovered, both your lewdness and your harlotries.

30 'These things will be done to you because you have played the harlot with the nations, because you have defiled yourself with their idols.

31 'You have walked in the way of your sister; therefore I will give her cup into your hand.'

32 "Thus says the Lord GOD,

'You will drink your sister's cup,
Which is deep and wide.
You will be laughed at and held in
    derision;
It contains much.

33 'You will be filled with drunkenness
    and sorrow,
The cup of horror and desolation,
The cup of your sister Samaria.

34 'You will drink it and drain it.
Then you will gnaw its fragments
    And tear your breasts;

for I have spoken,' declares the Lord GOD.

35 "Therefore, thus says the Lord GOD, 'Because you have forgotten Me and cast Me behind your back, bear now the *punishment* of your lewdness and your harlotries.'"

36 Moreover, the LORD said to me, "Son of man, will you judge Oholah and Oholibah? Then declare to them their abominations.

37 "For they have committed adultery, and blood is on their hands. Thus they have committed adultery with their idols and even caused their sons, whom they bore to Me, to pass through *the fire* to them as food.

38 "Again, they have done this to Me: they have defiled My sanctuary on the same day and have profaned My sabbaths.

39 "For when they had slaughtered their children for their idols, they entered My sanctuary on the same day to profane it; and lo, thus they did within My house.

40 "Furthermore, they have even sent for men who come from afar, to whom a messenger was sent; and lo, they came— for whom you bathed, painted your eyes and decorated yourselves with ornaments;

41 and you sat on a splendid couch with a table arranged before it on which you had set My incense and My oil.

42 "The sound of a carefree multitude was with her; and drunkards were brought from the wilderness with men of the common sort. And they put bracelets on the hands of the women and beautiful crowns on their heads.

43 "Then I said concerning her who was worn out by adulteries, 'Will they now commit adultery with her when she is *thus?*'

44 "But they went in to her as they would go in to a harlot. Thus they went in to Oholah and to Oholibah, the lewd women.

45 "But they, righteous men, will judge them with the judgment of adulteresses and with the judgment of women who shed blood, because they are adulteresses and blood is on their hands.

46 "For thus says the Lord GOD, 'Bring up a company against them and give them over to terror and plunder.

47 'The company will stone them with stones and cut them down with their swords; they will slay their sons and their daughters and burn their houses with fire.

48 'Thus I will make lewdness cease from the land, that all women may be admonished and not commit lewdness as you have done.

49 'Your lewdness will be requited upon you, and you will bear the penalty of *worshiping* your idols; thus you will know that I am the Lord GOD.'"

24 AND the word of the LORD came to me in the ninth year, in the tenth month, on the tenth of the month, saying,

2 "Son of man, write the name of the day, this very day. The king of Babylon has laid siege to Jerusalem this very day.

3 "Speak a parable to the rebellious house and say to them, 'Thus says the Lord GOD,

"Put on the pot, put *it* on and also
    pour water in it;

4 Put in it the pieces,
Every good piece, the thigh and the
    shoulder;
Fill *it* with choice bones.

5 "Take the choicest of the flock,
And also pile wood under the pot.
Make it boil vigorously.
Also seethe its bones in it."

6 'Therefore, thus says the Lord GOD,
"Woe to the bloody city,
To the pot in which there is rust

And whose rust has not gone out of
it!
Take out of it piece after piece,
Without making a choice.

7 "For her blood is in her midst;
She placed it on the bare rock;
She did not pour it on the ground
To cover it with dust.

8 "That it may cause wrath to come up
to take vengeance,
I have put her blood on the bare
rock,
That it may not be covered."

9 'Therefore, thus says the Lord GOD,
"Woe to the bloody city!
I also will make the pile great.

10 "Heap on the wood, kindle the fire,
Boil the flesh well
And mix in the spices,
And let the bones be burned.

11 "Then set it empty on its coals
So that it may be hot
And its bronze may glow
And its filthiness may be melted in
it,
Its rust consumed.

12 "She has wearied Me with toil,
Yet her great rust has not gone
from her;
Let her rust be in the fire!

13 "In your filthiness is lewdness.
Because I would have cleansed you,
Yet you are not clean,
You will not be cleansed from your
filthiness again
Until I have spent My wrath on you.

14 "I, the LORD, have spoken; it is coming
and I will act. I will not relent, and I will
not pity and I will not be sorry; according to your ways and according to your
deeds I will judge you," declares the Lord
GOD.'"

15 And the word of the LORD came to
me saying,

➤ 16 "Son of man, behold, I am about to
take from you the desire of your eyes
with a blow; but you shall not mourn and
you shall not weep, and your tears shall
not come.

17 "Groan silently; make no mourning
for the dead. Bind on your turban and
put your shoes on your feet, and do not
cover your mustache and do not eat the
bread of men."

18 So I spoke to the people in the morning, and in the evening my wife died.

And in the morning I did as I was commanded.

19 The people said to me, "Will you not
tell us what these things that you are
doing mean for us?"

20 Then I said to them, "The word of the
LORD came to me saying,

21 'Speak to the house of Israel, "Thus
says the Lord GOD, 'Behold, I am about
to profane My sanctuary, the pride of
your power, the desire of your eyes and
the delight of your soul; and your sons
and your daughters whom you have left
behind will fall by the sword.

22 'You will do as I have done; you will
not cover your mustache and you will not
eat the bread of men.

23 'Your turbans will be on your heads
and your shoes on your feet. You will not
mourn and you will not weep, but you
will rot away in your iniquities and you
will groan to one another.

24 'Thus Ezekiel will be a sign to you; ◄
according to all that he has done you will
do; when it comes, then you will know
that I am the Lord GOD.'"

25 'As for you, son of man, will it not
be on the day when I take from them

LIFE LESSONS

➤ **Ezekiel 24:16 — "You shall not mourn
and you shall not weep, and your tears
shall not come."**

God required some difficult things
of His servants the prophets. He
told Ezekiel not to weep or exhibit the
customary signs of mourning when his
beloved wife died in order to show the
people of Israel that they would soon
lose the desire of their eyes—the temple
in Jerusalem and the loved ones they
had left behind in the city (Ezek. 24:20,
21). This is exactly what happened. God
will use the most extraordinary measures
to awaken His sleeping people to their
imminent danger.

➤ **Ezekiel 24:24 — "According to all that
he has done you will do; when it comes,
then you will know that I am the Lord
GOD."**

God made Ezekiel's entire life into a
living message to Israel and Judah.
He will move heaven and earth, if necessary, to show us His will. Our job is to
obey it through the power of the Spirit.

their stronghold, the joy of their pride, the desire of their eyes and their heart's delight, their sons and their daughters,
26 that on that day he who escapes will come to you with information for *your* ears?
27 'On that day your mouth will be opened to him who escaped, and you will speak and be mute no longer. Thus you will be a sign to them, and they will know that I am the LORD.'"

Psalm 127:1–5

A Song of Ascents, of Solomon.

127 UNLESS the LORD builds the
house,
They labor in vain who build it;
Unless the LORD guards the city,
The watchman keeps awake in vain.
2 It is vain for you to rise up early,
To retire late,
To eat the bread of painful labors;
For He gives to His beloved *even in his* sleep.
3 Behold, children are a gift of the
LORD,
The fruit of the womb is a reward.
4 Like arrows in the hand of a
warrior,
So are the children of one's youth.
5 How blessed is the man whose
quiver is full of them;
They will not be ashamed
When they speak with their enemies
in the gate.

Proverbs 28:24

24 He who robs his father or his
mother
And says, "It is not a transgression,"
Is the companion of a man who
destroys.

Hebrews 11:1–12

11 NOW faith is the assurance of
things hoped for, the conviction of
things not seen.

2 For by it the men of old gained approval.
3 By faith we understand that the worlds were prepared by the word of God, so that what is seen was not made out of things which are visible.
4 By faith Abel offered to God a better sacrifice than Cain, through which he obtained the testimony that he was righteous, God testifying about his gifts, and through faith, though he is dead, he still speaks.
5 By faith Enoch was taken up so that he would not see death; AND HE WAS NOT FOUND BECAUSE GOD TOOK HIM UP; for he obtained the witness that before his being taken up he was pleasing to God.
6 And without faith it is impossible to please *Him*, for he who comes to God must believe that He is and *that* He is a rewarder of those who seek Him.
7 By faith Noah, being warned *by* God about things not yet seen, in reverence prepared an ark for the salvation of his household, by which he condemned the world, and became an heir of the righteousness which is according to faith.
8 By faith Abraham, when he was called, obeyed by going out to a place

LIFE LESSONS

➤ **Psalm 127:1 —** *Unless the LORD builds the house, they labor in vain who build it.*

*A*ll our efforts are useless and futile if we do not partner with God in what He wants, and in the time and manner He desires to accomplish it. The blessing of the Lord spells the difference between success and failure, satisfaction and regret.

➤ **Hebrews 11:6 —** *Without faith it is impossible to please Him.*

*W*hy is faith necessary to please God? Because we cannot serve Him unless we are convinced that He not only exists, but also that His plans for us are "good and acceptable and perfect" (Rom. 12:2). We must trust the Lord enough to walk in the center of His will, even if His commands seem unreasonable, impossible, or don't make any sense to us. Like the biblical heroes of old, we bring even the smallest decisions to Him, knowing He will lead us in the best way.

WHAT THE BIBLE SAYS ABOUT

Faith Is Assurance and Action

Hebrews 11:1–10

I have had the privilege of flying in several single-engine airplanes and seeing beautiful sights like the glaciers of Alaska and the jungles of Peru. But on none of those trips did I once think to ask the pilot what his qualifications were, whether the wings were sturdy, or if the engine was in good working order. I expect the pilot and his aircraft to carry me safely. Why is it that people can rely on a plane or automobile without question, but we sometimes fail to trust almighty God?

Christians have the capacity to believe God for far more than we are typically willing to ask Him to do. We have a foundation of assurance built from both Scripture and our experiences of His trustworthiness. Therefore, we have no cause for anxiety or uncertainty because we have complete access to a heavenly Father who is personally interested in our lives. We know the Lord of the universe is available to meet every need and that He will act on our behalf.

However, instead of demonstrating a solid conviction of His faithfulness, we often act out of a weak, halfhearted belief. Of course,

to put effective faith to work, we must go beyond simply thinking that He *can* do all things. We must *know* that He *will* do whatever He says. Faith is like a spiritual eye for believers: though our physical eyesight may not detect evidence that God is answering our prayers, we are confident He has already begun to fulfill every promise He's made to us.

Exercising faith cannot be passive. Notice that an action word follows every mention of faith in Hebrews 11 (*prepared, obeyed,* and *lived*). Instead of folding hands and waiting for God to do something, believers must trust Him enough to step out and obey Him. Our first responsibility is to go before the Lord with our petition. Then, we must consciously trust Him for an answer and wait with assurance and anticipation that He will follow through on His promises.

God did amazing feats through the lives of the men and women in Hebrews 11. As believers, we have the same potential for Him to work powerfully in and through us. Like an under-used muscle, faith might at times become flabby, but by putting it into action, believers can build a strong, tough trust that mirrors those in the roll call of faith. As our assurance builds, we believe the Lord for progressively greater things. In return, He will use us in ways we never imagined.

---

which he was to receive for an inheritance; and he went out, not knowing where he was going.
9   By faith he lived as an alien in the land of promise, as in a foreign *land*, dwelling in tents with Isaac and Jacob, fellow heirs of the same promise;
10 for he was looking for the city which has foundations, whose architect and builder is God.

11 By faith even Sarah herself received ability to conceive, even beyond the proper time of life, since she considered Him faithful who had promised.
12 Therefore there was born even of one man, and him as good as dead at that, *as many descendants* AS THE STARS OF HEAVEN IN NUMBER, AND INNUMERABLE AS THE SAND WHICH IS BY THE SEASHORE.

NOVEMBER 17

✦ Ezekiel 25:1—26:21

25 AND the word of the LORD came to me saying,
2   "Son of man, set your face toward the sons of Ammon and prophesy against them,

3   and say to the sons of Ammon, 'Hear the word of the Lord GOD! Thus says the Lord GOD, "Because you said, 'Aha!' against My sanctuary when it was profaned, and against the land of Israel when it was made desolate, and against the house of Judah when they went into exile,

4 therefore, behold, I am going to give you to the sons of the east for a possession, and they will set their encampments among you and make their dwellings among you; they will eat your fruit and drink your milk.

5 "I will make Rabbah a pasture for camels and the sons of Ammon a resting place for flocks. Thus you will know that I am the LORD."

6 'For thus says the Lord GOD, "Because you have clapped your hands and stamped your feet and rejoiced with all the scorn of your soul against the land of Israel,

7 therefore, behold, I have stretched out My hand against you and I will give you for spoil to the nations. And I will cut you off from the peoples and make you perish from the lands; I will destroy you. Thus you will know that I am the LORD."

8 'Thus says the Lord GOD, "Because Moab and Seir say, 'Behold, the house of Judah is like all the nations,'

9 therefore, behold, I am going to deprive the flank of Moab of its cities, of its cities which are on its frontiers, the glory of the land, Beth-jeshimoth, Baal-meon and Kiriathaim,

10 and I will give it for a possession along with the sons of Ammon to the sons of the east, so that the sons of Ammon will not be remembered among the nations.

11 "Thus I will execute judgments on Moab, and they will know that I am the LORD."

12 'Thus says the Lord GOD, "Because Edom has acted against the house of Judah by taking vengeance, and has incurred grievous guilt, and avenged themselves upon them,"

13 therefore thus says the Lord GOD, "I will also stretch out My hand against Edom and cut off man and beast from it. And I will lay it waste; from Teman even to Dedan they will fall by the sword.

14 "I will lay My vengeance on Edom by the hand of My people Israel. Therefore, they will act in Edom according to My anger and according to My wrath; thus they will know My vengeance," declares the Lord GOD.

15 'Thus says the Lord GOD, "Because the Philistines have acted in revenge and have taken vengeance with scorn of soul to destroy with everlasting enmity,"

16 therefore thus says the Lord GOD, "Behold, I will stretch out My hand against the Philistines, even cut off the Cherethites and destroy the remnant of the seacoast.

17 "I will execute great vengeance on them with wrathful rebukes; and they will know that I am the LORD when I lay My vengeance on them."'"

26 NOW in the eleventh year, on the first of the month, the word of the LORD came to me saying,

2 "Son of man, because Tyre has said concerning Jerusalem, 'Aha, the gateway of the peoples is broken; it has opened to me. I shall be filled, now that she is laid waste,'

3 therefore thus says the Lord GOD, 'Behold, I am against you, O Tyre, and I will bring up many nations against you, as the sea brings up its waves.

4 'They will destroy the walls of Tyre and break down her towers; and I will scrape her debris from her and make her a bare rock.

5 'She will be a place for the spreading ◄ of nets in the midst of the sea, for I have spoken,' declares the Lord GOD, 'and she will become spoil for the nations.

6 'Also her daughters who are on the mainland will be slain by the sword, and they will know that I am the LORD.'"

7 For thus says the Lord GOD, "Behold, I will bring upon Tyre from the north Nebuchadnezzar king of Babylon, king of kings, with horses, chariots, cavalry and a great army.

8 "He will slay your daughters on the mainland with the sword; and he will

---

LIFE LESSONS

➤ **Ezekiel 26:5** — *"She will be a place for the spreading of nets."*

*A*lthough Tyre was at the height of her power during Ezekiel's time, he predicted she would become a place to dry fishing nets, which history shows occurred through the conquests of Nebuchadnezzar (Ezek. 26:7–11; 586–571 B.C.) and Alexander the Great (Ezek. 26:12–14; 332 B.C.). Ezekiel's prophecy about the fate of Tyre—now located in modern day Lebanon—is a remarkable example of how God faithfully fulfills His Word.

LIFE PRINCIPLE 16

WHATEVER YOU ACQUIRE OUTSIDE OF GOD'S WILL EVENTUALLY TURNS TO ASHES.

EZEKIEL 25:6, 7

Some people think that God's refusal to grant them some cherished wish would be the worst thing that could ever happen to them. They believe they will be truly disappointed and devastated if that deep desire continues unmet.

So they pursue their desire, either in opposition to God's will or in disregard of it—and end up *truly* disappointed, even if they get what they thought they wanted. They are like the Israelites in Moses' day, who complained to God and insisted on having meat (Num. 11:4, 31–34; Ps. 78:27–31). Psalm 106:15 tells us, "He gave them their request, but sent a wasting disease among them." The desire becomes a curse.

G. K. Chesterton said, "There are two ways to get enough: One is to accumulate more and more, the other is to desire less." While you can always collect additional possessions, relationships, success, etc.—there will always be room for more. And when there's room for more, there's room for *wanting* more. The cycle never ends.

If you choose the second route of Chesterton's advice, "to desire less," the likelihood of living a fulfilling life increases. But how does one want less?

By going back to the deepest desire present in every human heart—the one thing we're truly longing for: to know God. Once we satisfy ourselves with His presence, we require far less of what the world has to offer.

You may not understand the longing within you to be a desire for God—in fact, you may simply feel dissatisfaction with your life. Maybe the relationship you wanted and attained isn't everything you thought it would be. Perhaps you have everything you'd ever wanted and yet still go through periods of longing, sadness, and loneliness.

Dissatisfaction, unfulfilled expectations, and feelings of dejection and isolation originate from the same place: a raging hunger for God. Centuries ago Augustine wrote, "You made us for Yourself, and our heart is restless until it rests in You."

There is always more we can learn about God—we will never fully know Him while we live here on earth (1 Cor. 13:12). But once we enter into a relationship with the Lord, He promises to reveal more of Himself to us as we fellowship with Him. Hosea 2:19, 20 says, "I will betroth you to Me forever; yes, I will betroth you to Me in righteousness and in justice, in lovingkindness and in compassion, and I will betroth you to Me in faithfulness. Then you will know the LORD."

To fellowship with God—to talk to Him and listen to Him as you study the Bible, pray, and worship Him—is to get to know Him better. He has "betrothed" (or engaged) His people to Himself for one reason: to let Himself be known.

When you develop your relationship with God and discover more about His holy character, He illuminates your heart and mind, giving you a greater desire to know Him more intimately—leaving your fleshly desires behind in the process. Your worldly desires simply cannot compare to the deep comfort, joy, and fulfillment that God offers you. Rather, you see the things that you acquire outside of His will turning to ashes, while the blessings He gives you endure and satisfy your soul.

This process deepens:

- *Our humility.* As we see God's sovereignty unveiled, we more deeply understand our need for Him.
- *Our gratitude.* Knowing that God's lovingkindness motivates His forgiveness, deliverance, and guidance, gives us a thankful heart. Instead of coming to God with complaints about our unfulfilled, selfish desires, we come to Him with adoration and praise.
- *Our purpose.* As the Holy Spirit sheds new light on verses we've read many times before, our quest for a relationship with Him becomes stronger, deeper, and more personal. Our appreciation of God's Word gives us a more profound delight in studying and applying His truth.
- *Our reverence.* Learning something new about our Creator reminds us that we don't know everything about Him. As we come to terms with the depths and heights of God's love, power, and wisdom, our awe of Him grows.
- *Our desire to please God.* When we have a holy, respectful fear of the Lord, our desire changes from satisfying ourselves to serving our God. Pleasing Him is not a chore; rather, it becomes a joy done out of humility and thankfulness.

Amazingly, as we pursue our desire for God, He fulfills the other desires He has given us (Ps. 37:4). And so we learn afresh that while acquiring *anything* outside of His will ultimately disappoint us, He fills us with truly satisfying "pleasures forever" (Ps. 16:11). ◈

make siege walls against you, cast up a ramp against you and raise up a large shield against you.

9 "The blow of his battering rams he will direct against your walls, and with his axes he will break down your towers.

10 "Because of the multitude of his horses, the dust *raised by* them will cover you; your walls will shake at the noise of cavalry and wagons and chariots when he enters your gates as men enter a city that is breached.

11 "With the hoofs of his horses he will trample all your streets. He will slay your people with the sword; and your strong pillars will come down to the ground.

12 "Also they will make a spoil of your riches and a prey of your merchandise, break down your walls and destroy your pleasant houses, and throw your stones and your timbers and your debris into the water.

13 "So I will silence the sound of your songs, and the sound of your harps will be heard no more.

14 "I will make you a bare rock; you will be a place for the spreading of nets. You will be built no more, for I the LORD have spoken," declares the Lord GOD.

15 Thus says the Lord GOD to Tyre, "Shall not the coastlands shake at the sound of your fall when the wounded groan, when the slaughter occurs in your midst?

16 "Then all the princes of the sea will go down from their thrones, remove their robes and strip off their embroidered garments. They will clothe themselves with trembling; they will sit on the ground, tremble every moment and be appalled at you.

17 "They will take up a lamentation over you and say to you,

'How you have perished, O inhabited one,
From the seas, O renowned city,
Which was mighty on the sea,
She and her inhabitants,
Who imposed her terror
On all her inhabitants!

18 'Now the coastlands will tremble
On the day of your fall;
Yes, the coastlands which are by the sea
Will be terrified at your passing.'"

19 For thus says the Lord GOD, "When I make you a desolate city, like the cities which are not inhabited, when I bring up the deep over you and the great waters cover you,

20 then I will bring you down with those who go down to the pit, to the people of old, and I will make you dwell in the lower parts of the earth, like the ancient waste places, with those who go down to the pit, so that you will not be inhabited; but I will set glory in the land of the living.

21 "I will bring terrors on you and you will be no more; though you will be sought, you will never be found again," declares the Lord GOD.

Psalm 128:1–6

A Song of Ascents.

128 HOW blessed is everyone who fears the LORD,
Who walks in His ways.
2 When you shall eat of the fruit of your hands,
You will be happy and it will be well with you.
3 Your wife shall be like a fruitful vine
Within your house,
Your children like olive plants
Around your table.
4 Behold, for thus shall the man be blessed
Who fears the LORD.
5 The LORD bless you from Zion,
And may you see the prosperity of Jerusalem all the days of your life.
6 Indeed, may you see your children's children.
Peace be upon Israel!

Proverbs 28:25

25 An arrogant man stirs up strife,
But he who trusts in the LORD will prosper.

Hebrews 11:13–40

13 All these died in faith, without receiving the promises, but having seen

LIFE LESSONS

> Hebrews 11:13 — *These died in faith, without receiving the promises, but having seen them and having welcomed them from a distance.*

*A*braham died having seen some, but not all, of God's promises fulfilled. He received the son the Lord had promised in Isaac (Gen. 15:4; 21:1–5), but he was not able to see the accomplishment of God's pledge: "In your seed all the nations of the earth shall be blessed" (Gen. 22:18). This covenant was realized through Jesus (Acts 3:25, 26; Rev. 5:9; 7:9, 10). Because of Christ, every person on earth has the blessing of being able to know God. Like Abraham, we must look beyond what we can see to what the Lord sees because He will certainly fulfill all His promises to us as well.

them and having welcomed them from a distance, and having confessed that they were strangers and exiles on the earth.
14 For those who say such things make it clear that they are seeking a country of their own.
15 And indeed if they had been thinking of that *country* from which they went out, they would have had opportunity to return.
16 But as it is, they desire a better *country*, that is, a heavenly one. Therefore God is not ashamed to be called their God; for He has prepared a city for them.
17 By faith Abraham, when he was tested, offered up Isaac, and he who had received the promises was offering up his only begotten *son*;
18 *it was he* to whom it was said, "IN ISAAC YOUR DESCENDANTS SHALL BE CALLED."
19 He considered that God is able to raise *people* even from the dead, from which he also received him back as a type.
20 By faith Isaac blessed Jacob and Esau, even regarding things to come.
21 By faith Jacob, as he was dying, blessed each of the sons of Joseph, and worshiped, *leaning* on the top of his staff.
22 By faith Joseph, when he was dying, made mention of the exodus of the sons of Israel, and gave orders concerning his bones.
23 By faith Moses, when he was born,

was hidden for three months by his parents, because they saw he was a beautiful child; and they were not afraid of the king's edict.
24 By faith Moses, when he had grown up, refused to be called the son of Pharaoh's daughter,
25 choosing rather to endure ill-treatment with the people of God than to enjoy the passing pleasures of sin,
26 considering the reproach of Christ greater riches than the treasures of Egypt; for he was looking to the reward.
27 By faith he left Egypt, not fearing the wrath of the king; for he endured, as seeing Him who is unseen.
28 By faith he kept the Passover and the sprinkling of the blood, so that he who destroyed the firstborn would not touch them.
29 By faith they passed through the Red Sea as though *they were passing* through dry land; and the Egyptians, when they attempted it, were drowned.
30 By faith the walls of Jericho fell down after they had been encircled for seven days.
31 By faith Rahab the harlot did not perish along with those who were disobedient, after she had welcomed the spies in peace.
32 And what more shall I say? For time will fail me if I tell of Gideon, Barak, Samson, Jephthah, of David and Samuel and the prophets,
33 who by faith conquered kingdoms, performed *acts of* righteousness, obtained promises, shut the mouths of lions,
34 quenched the power of fire, escaped

LIFE LESSONS

> Hebrews 11:25, 26 — *Choosing rather to endure ill-treatment with the people of God . . . for he was looking to the reward.*

*T*he Bible acknowledges that there is some pleasure in sin, even though it quickly passes and leaves the sinner feeling more empty and unsatisfied than before. The Bible also acknowledges that there is some affliction in godliness, even though that quickly passes too. Yet the reward for godliness far outstrips any pleasure in sin.

the edge of the sword, from weakness were made strong, became mighty in war, put foreign armies to flight.
35 Women received *back* their dead by resurrection; and others were tortured, not accepting their release, so that they might obtain a better resurrection;
36 and others experienced mockings and scourgings, yes, also chains and imprisonment.
37 They were stoned, they were sawn in two, they were tempted, they were put to death with the sword; they went about in sheepskins, in goatskins, being destitute, afflicted, ill-treated
38 (*men* of whom the world was not worthy), wandering in deserts and mountains and caves and holes in the ground.
39 And all these, having gained approval through their faith, did not receive what was promised,
40 because God had provided something better for us, so that apart from us they would not be made perfect.

Ezekiel 27:1—28:26

27 MOREOVER, the word of the LORD came to me saying,
2 "And you, son of man, take up a lamentation over Tyre;
3 and say to Tyre, who dwells at the entrance to the sea, merchant of the peoples to many coastlands, 'Thus says the Lord GOD,
"O Tyre, you have said, 'I am perfect in beauty.'
4 "Your borders are in the heart of the seas;
Your builders have perfected your beauty.
5 "They have made all *your* planks of fir trees from Senir;
They have taken a cedar from Lebanon to make a mast for you.
6 "Of oaks from Bashan they have made your oars;
With ivory they have inlaid your deck of boxwood from the coastlands of Cyprus.
7 "Your sail was of fine embroidered linen from Egypt
So that it became your distinguishing mark;
Your awning was blue and purple from the coastlands of Elishah.
8 "The inhabitants of Sidon and Arvad were your rowers;
Your wise men, O Tyre, were aboard; they were your pilots.
9 "The elders of Gebal and her wise men were with you repairing your seams;

All the ships of the sea and their sailors were with you in order to deal in your merchandise.
10 "Persia and Lud and Put were in your army, your men of war. They hung shield and helmet in you; they set forth your splendor.
11 "The sons of Arvad and your army were on your walls, *all* around, and the Gammadim were in your towers. They hung their shields on your walls *all* around; they perfected your beauty.
12 "Tarshish was your customer because of the abundance of all *kinds* of wealth; with silver, iron, tin and lead they paid for your wares.
13 "Javan, Tubal and Meshech, they were your traders; with the lives of men and vessels of bronze they paid for your merchandise.
14 "Those from Beth-togarmah gave horses and war horses and mules for your wares.
15 "The sons of Dedan were your traders. Many coastlands were your market; ivory tusks and ebony they brought as your payment.
16 "Aram was your customer because of the abundance of your goods; they paid for your wares with emeralds, purple, embroidered work, fine linen, coral and rubies.
17 "Judah and the land of Israel, they were your traders; with the wheat of Minnith, cakes, honey, oil and balm they paid for your merchandise.
18 "Damascus was your customer because of the abundance of your goods, because of the abundance of all *kinds* of

wealth, because of the wine of Helbon and white wool.

19 "Vedan and Javan paid for your wares from Uzal; wrought iron, cassia and sweet cane were among your merchandise.

20 "Dedan traded with you in saddlecloths for riding.

21 "Arabia and all the princes of Kedar, they were your customers for lambs, rams and goats; for these they were your customers.

22 "The traders of Sheba and Raamah, they traded with you; they paid for your wares with the best of all *kinds* of spices, and with all *kinds* of precious stones and gold.

23 "Haran, Canneh, Eden, the traders of Sheba, Asshur *and* Chilmad traded with you.

24 "They traded with you in choice garments, in clothes of blue and embroidered work, and in carpets of many colors *and* tightly wound cords, *which were* among your merchandise.

25 "The ships of Tarshish were the carriers for your merchandise.

And you were filled and were very glorious
In the heart of the seas.

26 "Your rowers have brought you
Into great waters;
The east wind has broken you
In the heart of the seas.

27 "Your wealth, your wares, your merchandise,
Your sailors and your pilots,
Your repairers of seams, your dealers in merchandise
And all your men of war who are in you,
With all your company that is in your midst,
Will fall into the heart of the seas
On the day of your overthrow.

28 "At the sound of the cry of your pilots
The pasture lands will shake.

29 "All who handle the oar,
The sailors *and* all the pilots of the sea
Will come down from their ships;
They will stand on the land,

30 And they will make their voice heard over you
And will cry bitterly.

They will cast dust on their heads,
They will wallow in ashes.

31 "Also they will make themselves bald for you
And gird themselves with sackcloth;
And they will weep for you in bitterness of soul
With bitter mourning.

32 "Moreover, in their wailing they will take up a lamentation for you
And lament over you:
'Who is like Tyre,
Like her who is silent in the midst of the sea?

33 'When your wares went out from the seas,
You satisfied many peoples;
With the abundance of your wealth and your merchandise
You enriched the kings of earth.

34 'Now that you are broken by the seas
In the depths of the waters,
Your merchandise and all your company
Have fallen in the midst of you.

35 'All the inhabitants of the coastlands
Are appalled at you,
And their kings are horribly afraid;
They are troubled in countenance.

36 'The merchants among the peoples hiss at you;
You have become terrified
And you will cease to be forever.'"'"

28 THE word of the LORD came again to me, saying,

2 "Son of man, say to the leader of Tyre, 'Thus says the Lord GOD,
"Because your heart is lifted up
And you have said, 'I am a god,
I sit in the seat of gods
In the heart of the seas';
Yet you are a man and not God,

LIFE LESSONS

➤ **Ezekiel 27:36** — *"The merchants among the peoples hiss at you; you have become terrified and you will cease to be forever."*

Despite a fabulous location and plenty of fresh water available, God foretold that Tyre would cease to be a city and remain a desolation forever. So He spoke, and so it has been even to this day.

Although you make your heart like
the heart of God—
3 Behold, you are wiser than
Daniel;
There is no secret that is a match for
you.
4 "By your wisdom and understanding
You have acquired riches for
yourself
And have acquired gold and silver
for your treasuries.
5 "By your great wisdom, by your
trade
You have increased your riches
And your heart is lifted up because
of your riches—
6 Therefore thus says the Lord GOD,
'Because you have made your heart
Like the heart of God,
7 Therefore, behold, I will bring
strangers upon you,
The most ruthless of the nations.
And they will draw their swords
Against the beauty of your wisdom
And defile your splendor.
8 'They will bring you down to the pit,
And you will die the death of those
who are slain
In the heart of the seas.
9 'Will you still say, "I am a god,"
In the presence of your slayer,
Though you are a man and not God,
In the hands of those who wound
you?
10 'You will die the death of the
uncircumcised
By the hand of strangers,
For I have spoken!' declares the
Lord GOD!"'"

11 Again the word of the LORD came to
me saying,
➤ 12 "Son of man, take up a lamentation
over the king of Tyre and say to him,
'Thus says the Lord GOD,

LIFE LESSONS

➤ **Ezekiel 28:12 —** *"You had the seal of
perfection, full of wisdom and perfect in
beauty."*

*M*any scholars believe this passage
speaks of Satan and how through
his rebellion he lost his privileged place
in heaven and became the devil. As a
fallen angel, he possesses power, but not
all power.

"You had the seal of perfection,
Full of wisdom and perfect in
beauty.
13 "You were in Eden, the garden of
God;
Every precious stone was your
covering:
The ruby, the topaz and the
diamond;
The beryl, the onyx and the
jasper;
The lapis lazuli, the turquoise and
the emerald;
And the gold, the workmanship of
your settings and sockets,
Was in you.
On the day that you were created
They were prepared.
14 "You were the anointed cherub who
covers,
And I placed you *there*.
You were on the holy mountain of
God;
You walked in the midst of the
stones of fire.
15 "You were blameless in your
ways
From the day you were created
Until unrighteousness was found in
you.
16 "By the abundance of your trade
You were internally filled with
violence,

LIFE LESSONS

➤ **Ezekiel 28:16, 17 —** *". . . I have cast
you as profane from the mountain
of God. And I have destroyed you,
O covering cherub . . . Your heart was
lifted up because of your beauty; you
corrupted your wisdom by reason of
your splendor . . . ."*

*M*any scholars believe this passage speaks of Satan and how
through his rebellion he was expelled
from heaven (Ezek. 28:12–17). The devil
fell from his lofty position because he
wanted to be "like the Most High" (Is.
14:14). Pride always places an overemphasis on self—we get to the point
where we think we don't need God.
Both Satan and the king of Tyre forgot
that any power, wisdom, beauty or
splendor they had came as a gift from
God. We must be careful not to make
the same deadly mistake.

WHAT THE BIBLE SAYS ABOUT

The Origin, Work, and Destiny of Satan

Ezekiel 28:12–19

*E*zekiel 28:12–19 tells us that God created Satan as a beautiful and eminent angel, a being as real as any of us. Yet the devil arrogantly lusted to make himself "like the Most High" (Is. 14:14) and rebelled against the Creator, who subsequently cast him and his co-conspirators to earth. Here he set up a counterfeit kingdom in order that he might reign as the god of this world.

Satan uses deception and division to ensnare believers. He works tirelessly to tempt us, hoping that we will fall into sin, thereby damaging our relationship with God and ruining our witness for Christ. He also desires to keep unbelievers away from the saving grace of Jesus Christ, thereby destroying them. Jesus called him a murderer and the father of lies (John 8:44), and as such, his goal is to instigate pain, sorrow, and death throughout the world. Satan accuses and deceives—condemning, antagonizing, and confusing us in an attempt to fill us with doubt and despair.

But Christians have no cause to fear Satan. This is true for two reasons.

First, "Greater is He who is in you than he who is in the world" (1 John 4:4). We live under the protection of the Holy Spirit; nothing can happen to us that God does not allow, and we know that whatever He permits—no matter how bad it may seem—He can turn for our good (Rom. 8:28).

Second, all of us who have read Scripture understand Satan's end. Revelation 12:10, 11 tell us, "The salvation, and the power, and the kingdom of our God and the authority of His Christ have come, for the accuser of our brethren has been thrown down, he who accuses them before our God day and night. And they overcame him because of the blood of the Lamb and because of the word of their testimony." The enemy will be thrown into the lake of fire and eternally punished for his rebellion against almighty God (Rev. 20:10). And he will never bother us again.

The apostle Peter refers to Satan as "a roaring lion, seeking someone to devour" (1 Pet. 5:8). Yet even though the devil is as dangerous as a lion, he's on a short leash. His eternal destination is certain. While he may be able to harass us, tempt us, and prompt us to stumble, our ultimate victory over him and his work was secured for us when Jesus Christ defeated sin once and for all on the Cross. ◉

And you sinned;
Therefore I have cast you as
   profane
From the mountain of God.
And I have destroyed you,
   O covering cherub,
From the midst of the stones of
   fire.
17 "Your heart was lifted up because of
   your beauty;
You corrupted your wisdom by
   reason of your splendor.
I cast you to the ground;
I put you before kings,
That they may see you.
18 "By the multitude of your iniquities,
In the unrighteousness of your
   trade
You profaned your sanctuaries.
Therefore I have brought fire from
   the midst of you;
It has consumed you,

And I have turned you to ashes on
   the earth
In the eyes of all who see you.
19 "All who know you among the
   peoples
Are appalled at you;
You have become terrified
And you will cease to be forever."'"
20 And the word of the LORD came to
me saying,
21 "Son of man, set your face toward
Sidon, prophesy against her
22 and say, 'Thus says the Lord GOD,
"Behold, I am against you, O Sidon,
And I will be glorified in your
   midst.
Then they will know that I am the
   LORD when I execute judgments
   in her,
And I will manifest My holiness in
   her.
23 "For I will send pestilence to her

And blood to her streets,
And the wounded will fall in her
    midst
By the sword upon her on every
    side;
Then they will know that I am the
    LORD.
24 "And there will be no more for the house of Israel a prickling brier or a painful thorn from any round about them who scorned them; then they will know that I am the Lord GOD."
25 'Thus says the Lord GOD, "When I gather the house of Israel from the peoples among whom they are scattered, and will manifest My holiness in them in the sight of the nations, then they will live in their land which I gave to My servant Jacob.
26 "They will live in it securely; and they will build houses, plant vineyards and live securely when I execute judgments upon all who scorn them round about them. Then they will know that I am the LORD their God."'"

Psalm 129:1–4

A Song of Ascents.

129 "MANY times they have
        persecuted me from my
        youth up,"
Let Israel now say,
2 "Many times they have persecuted
    me from my youth up;
Yet they have not prevailed against
    me.
3 "The plowers plowed upon my
    back;
They lengthened their furrows."
4 The LORD is righteous;
He has cut in two the cords of the
    wicked.

Proverbs 28:26

26 He who trusts in his own heart is a
    fool,
But he who walks wisely will be
    delivered.

Hebrews 12:1–29

12 THEREFORE, since we have so great a cloud of witnesses surrounding us, let us also lay aside every encumbrance and the sin which so easily entangles us, and let us run with endurance the race that is set before us,
2   fixing our eyes on Jesus, the author and perfecter of faith, who for the joy set before Him endured the cross, despising the shame, and has sat down at the right hand of the throne of God.
3   For consider Him who has endured such hostility by sinners against Himself, so that you will not grow weary and lose heart.
4   You have not yet resisted to the point of shedding blood in your striving against sin;
5   and you have forgotten the exhortation which is addressed to you as sons,
    "MY SON, DO NOT REGARD LIGHTLY THE
        DISCIPLINE OF THE LORD,
    NOR FAINT WHEN YOU ARE REPROVED
        BY HIM;
6   FOR THOSE WHOM THE LORD LOVES HE
        DISCIPLINES,
    AND HE SCOURGES EVERY SON WHOM
        HE RECEIVES."
7   It is for discipline that you endure; God deals with you as with sons; for what son is there whom *his* father does not discipline?
8   But if you are without discipline, of which all have become partakers, then you are illegitimate children and not sons.
9   Furthermore, we had earthly fathers

LIFE LESSONS

➤ **Hebrews 12:2 —** *Fixing our eyes on Jesus, the author and perfecter of faith, who for the joy set before Him endured the Cross, despising the shame.*

*J*esus endured the pain, scorn, sorrow, rejection, and betrayal of the Cross for the joy set before Him. It was enough to keep Him focused and stop Him from answering His accusers. What was this overcoming joy? Us. Jesus looked forward to fulfilling the purpose for which He came, which was to restore our relationship with Himself.

to discipline us, and we respected them; shall we not much rather be subject to the Father of spirits, and live?

10 For they disciplined us for a short time as seemed best to them, but He *disciplines us* for *our* good, so that we may share His holiness.

➤ 11 All discipline for the moment seems not to be joyful, but sorrowful; yet to those who have been trained by it, afterwards it yields the peaceful fruit of righteousness.

12 Therefore, strengthen the hands that are weak and the knees that are feeble,

13 and make straight paths for your feet, so that *the limb* which is lame may not be put out of joint, but rather be healed.

14 Pursue peace with all men, and the sanctification without which no one will see the Lord.

15 See to it that no one comes short of the grace of God; that no root of bitterness springing up causes trouble, and by it many be defiled;

16 that *there be* no immoral or godless person like Esau, who sold his own birthright for a *single* meal.

17 For you know that even afterwards, when he desired to inherit the blessing, he was rejected, for he found no place for repentance, though he sought for it with tears.

18 For you have not come to *a mountain* that can be touched and to a blazing fire, and to darkness and gloom and whirlwind,

19 and to the blast of a trumpet and the sound of words which *sound was such that* those who heard begged that no further word be spoken to them.

20 For they could not bear the command, "IF EVEN A BEAST TOUCHES THE MOUNTAIN, IT WILL BE STONED."

21 And so terrible was the sight, *that* Moses said, "I AM FULL OF FEAR and trembling."

22 But you have come to Mount Zion and to the city of the living God, the heavenly Jerusalem, and to myriads of angels,

23 to the general assembly and church of the firstborn who are enrolled in heaven, and to God, the Judge of all, and to the spirits of *the* righteous made perfect,

24 and to Jesus, the mediator of a new covenant, and to the sprinkled blood, which speaks better than *the blood* of Abel.

25 See to it that you do not refuse Him who is speaking. For if those did not escape when they refused him who warned *them* on earth, much less *will* we *escape* who turn away from Him who *warns* from heaven.

26 And His voice shook the earth then, but now He has promised, saying, "YET ONCE MORE I WILL SHAKE NOT ONLY THE EARTH, BUT ALSO THE HEAVEN."

27 This *expression,* "Yet once more," denotes the removing of those things which can be shaken, as of created things, so that those things which cannot be shaken may remain.

28 Therefore, since we receive a kingdom which cannot be shaken, let us ➤ show gratitude, by which we may offer to God an acceptable service with reverence and awe;

29 for our God is a consuming fire.

LIFE LESSONS

➤ **Hebrews 12:11** — *All discipline for the moment seems not to be joyful, but sorrowful; yet to those who have been trained by it, afterwards it yields the peaceful fruit of righteousness.*

*N*o one likes to be disciplined. It is never pleasant because it requires a change in our perspectives, goals, behaviors, and attitudes. Deeply entrenched sinfulness and destructive habits are rooted out, and our earthly sources of security are destroyed. This is all very painful and difficult. But if we cooperate with God when He corrects us, we will become more like Him, and great blessings will result.

➤ **Hebrews 12:28** — *We receive a kingdom which cannot be shaken, let us show gratitude, by which we may offer to God an acceptable service with reverence and awe.*

*D*ivine grace never encourages us to live in ungodly ways, but instead motivates us to fear and obey God in a healthy and reverent way. Grace enables us to serve, not to sin.

29IN the tenth year, in the tenth *month*, on the twelfth of the month, the word of the LORD came to me saying,
2 "Son of man, set your face against Pharaoh king of Egypt and prophesy against him and against all Egypt.
3 "Speak and say, 'Thus says the Lord GOD,

"Behold, I am against you, Pharaoh
    king of Egypt,
The great monster that lies in the
    midst of his rivers,
That has said, 'My Nile is mine, and
    I myself have made *it*.'
4 "I will put hooks in your jaws
    And make the fish of your rivers
        cling to your scales.
    And I will bring you up out of the
        midst of your rivers,
    And all the fish of your rivers will
        cling to your scales.
5 "I will abandon you to the wilderness,
    you and all the fish of your rivers;
    You will fall on the open field; you
        will not be brought together or
        gathered.
    I have given you for food to the
        beasts of the earth and to the
        birds of the sky.
6 "Then all the inhabitants of Egypt
    will know that I am the LORD,
    Because they have been *only* a staff
    made of reed to the house of Israel.
7 "When they took hold of you with
    the hand,
    You broke and tore all their hands;
    And when they leaned on you,
    You broke and made all their loins
        quake."

8 'Therefore thus says the Lord GOD, "Behold, I will bring upon you a sword and I will cut off from you man and beast.
9 "The land of Egypt will become a desolation and waste. Then they will know that I am the LORD.

Because you said, 'The Nile is mine, and I have made *it*,'
10 therefore, behold, I am against you and against your rivers, and I will make the land of Egypt an utter waste and desolation, from Migdol *to* Syene and even to the border of Ethiopia.
11 "A man's foot will not pass through it, and the foot of a beast will not pass through it, and it will not be inhabited for forty years.
12 "So I will make the land of Egypt a desolation in the midst of desolated lands. And her cities, in the midst of cities that are laid waste, will be desolate forty years; and I will scatter the Egyptians among the nations and disperse them among the lands."
13 'For thus says the Lord GOD, "At the end of forty years I will gather the Egyptians from the peoples among whom they were scattered.
14 "I will turn the fortunes of Egypt and make them return to the land of Pathros, to the land of their origin, and there they will be a lowly kingdom.
15 "It will be the lowest of the kingdoms, ≺ and it will never again lift itself up above the nations. And I will make them so small that they will not rule over the nations.
16 "And it will never again be the confidence of the house of Israel, bringing to mind the iniquity of their having turned to Egypt. Then they will know that I am the Lord GOD."'"
17 Now in the twenty-seventh year, in the first *month*, on the first of the month, the word of the LORD came to me saying,
18 "Son of man, Nebuchadnezzar king of Babylon made his army labor hard against Tyre; every head was made bald and every shoulder was rubbed bare. But he and his army had no wages from Tyre for the labor that he had performed against it."
19 Therefore thus says the Lord GOD, "Behold, I will give the land of Egypt to Nebuchadnezzar king of Babylon. And he will carry off her wealth and capture her spoil and seize her plunder; and it will be wages for his army.
20 "I have given him the land of Egypt *for* his labor which he performed, because

---

LIFE LESSONS

➤ **Ezekiel 29:15 — *"I will make them so small that they will not rule over the nations."***

*W*ho but God could have declared that Egypt, the ancient ruler of nations, would fall so completely from its heights? No one at the time could have—except God.

they acted for Me," declares the Lord GOD.

21 "On that day I will make a horn sprout for the house of Israel, and I will open your mouth in their midst. Then they will know that I am the LORD."

30 THE word of the LORD came again to me saying,

2 "Son of man, prophesy and say, 'Thus says the Lord GOD,
"Wail, 'Alas for the day!'

3 "For the day is near,
Even the day of the LORD is near;
It will be a day of clouds,
A time of doom for the nations.

4 "A sword will come upon Egypt,
And anguish will be in Ethiopia;
When the slain fall in Egypt,
They take away her wealth,
And her foundations are torn down.

5 "Ethiopia, Put, Lud, all Arabia, Libya and the people of the land that is in league will fall with them by the sword."

6 'Thus says the LORD,
"Indeed, those who support Egypt will fall
And the pride of her power will come down;
From Migdol to Syene
They will fall within her by the sword,"
Declares the Lord GOD.

7 "They will be desolate
In the midst of the desolated lands;
And her cities will be
In the midst of the devastated cities.

8 "And they will know that I am the LORD,
When I set a fire in Egypt
And all her helpers are broken.

9 "On that day messengers will go forth from Me in ships to frighten secure Ethiopia; and anguish will be on them as on the day of Egypt; for behold, it comes!"

10 'Thus says the Lord GOD,
"I will also make the hordes of Egypt cease
By the hand of Nebuchadnezzar king of Babylon.

11 "He and his people with him,
The most ruthless of the nations,
Will be brought in to destroy the land;
And they will draw their swords against Egypt
And fill the land with the slain.

12 "Moreover, I will make the Nile canals dry

And sell the land into the hands of evil men.
And I will make the land desolate
And all that is in it,
By the hand of strangers; I the LORD have spoken."

13 'Thus says the Lord GOD,
"I will also destroy the idols
And make the images cease from Memphis.
And there will no longer be a prince in the land of Egypt;
And I will put fear in the land of Egypt.

14 "I will make Pathros desolate,
Set a fire in Zoan
And execute judgments on Thebes.

15 "I will pour out My wrath on Sin,
The stronghold of Egypt;
I will also cut off the hordes of Thebes.

16 "I will set a fire in Egypt;
Sin will writhe in anguish,
Thebes will be breached
And Memphis will have distresses daily.

17 "The young men of On and of Pi-beseth
Will fall by the sword,
And the women will go into captivity.

18 "In Tehaphnehes the day will be dark
When I break there the yoke bars of Egypt.
Then the pride of her power will cease in her;
A cloud will cover her,
And her daughters will go into captivity.

19 "Thus I will execute judgments on Egypt,
And they will know that I am the LORD."'"

20 In the eleventh year, in the first month, on the seventh of the month, the word of the LORD came to me saying,

21 "Son of man, I have broken the arm of Pharaoh king of Egypt; and, behold, it has not been bound up for healing or wrapped with a bandage, that it may be strong to hold the sword.

22 "Therefore thus says the Lord GOD, 'Behold, I am against Pharaoh king of Egypt and will break his arms, both the strong and the broken; and I will make the sword fall from his hand.

23 'I will scatter the Egyptians among

the nations and disperse them among the lands.

24 'For I will strengthen the arms of the king of Babylon and put My sword in his hand; and I will break the arms of Pharaoh, so that he will groan before him with the groanings of a wounded man.

25 'Thus I will strengthen the arms of the king of Babylon, but the arms of Pharaoh will fall. Then they will know that I am the LORD, when I put My sword into the hand of the king of Babylon and he stretches it out against the land of Egypt.

26 'When I scatter the Egyptians among the nations and disperse them among the lands, then they will know that I am the LORD.'"

Psalm 129:5–8

5   May all who hate Zion
      Be put to shame and turned
         backward;
6   Let them be like grass upon the
         housetops,
      Which withers before it grows up;
7   With which the reaper does not fill
         his hand,
      Or the binder of sheaves his bosom;
8   Nor do those who pass by say,
      "The blessing of the LORD be upon you;
      We bless you in the name of the
         LORD."

Proverbs 28:27

27 He who gives to the poor will never
         want,
      But he who shuts his eyes will have
         many curses.

Hebrews 13:1–25

13 LET love of the brethren continue.
2   Do not neglect to show hospitality to strangers, for by this some have entertained angels without knowing it.
✻ 3   Remember the prisoners, as though in prison with them, *and* those who are ill-treated, since you yourselves also are in the body.
4   Marriage *is to be held* in honor among all, and the *marriage* bed *is to be* undefiled; for fornicators and adulterers God will judge.

5   *Make sure that* your character is free from the love of money, being content with what you have; for He Himself has said, "I WILL NEVER DESERT YOU, NOR WILL I EVER FORSAKE YOU,"
6   so that we confidently say,
      "THE LORD IS MY HELPER, I WILL NOT
         BE AFRAID.
      WHAT WILL MAN DO TO ME?"
7   Remember those who led you, who spoke the word of God to you; and considering the result of their conduct, imitate their faith.
8   Jesus Christ *is* the same yesterday ◄ and today and forever.
9   Do not be carried away by varied and strange teachings; for it is good for the heart to be strengthened by grace, not by foods, through which those who were so occupied were not benefited.
10 We have an altar from which those who serve the tabernacle have no right to eat.
11 For the bodies of those animals whose blood is brought into the holy place by the high priest *as an offering* for sin, are burned outside the camp.
12 Therefore Jesus also, that He might sanctify the people through His own blood, suffered outside the gate.
13 So, let us go out to Him outside the ◄ camp, bearing His reproach.
14 For here we do not have a lasting city, but we are seeking *the city* which is to come.

LIFE LESSONS

➤ **Hebrews 13:8 — *Jesus Christ is the same yesterday and today and forever.***

*J*ust like His Father, "the Everlasting God" (Gen. 21:33), whose "ways are everlasting" (Hab. 3:6) and who says, "I ... do not change" (Mal. 3:6), so Jesus remains the same forever.

➤ **Hebrews 13:13 — *Let us go out to Him outside the camp, bearing His reproach.***

*I*dentification with Jesus brings undeniable blessings, but it can also bring reproach and persecution. This is not something to be avoided at all costs, but rather is something to be embraced when it occurs.

ANSWERS TO LIFE'S QUESTIONS

How can I claim God's promises?

HEBREWS 13:5

*B*y some counts, God has issued more than 40 thousand promises in the Bible. That's *a lot* of promises! But sometimes it can be difficult to determine how to properly respond to His awesome assurances.

The first thing to keep in mind is that the Bible contains two kinds of divine promises.

1. *Limited promises*

God has made many promises to specific people living in particular circumstances for explicit purposes. These promises are definitely *not* "one size fits all." If you try to "claim" these promises for yourself, you're headed for trouble.

For example, the resurrected Jesus told His disciples to wait in Jerusalem "for what the Father had promised," and that as they did, they would "be baptized with the Holy Spirit" (Acts 1:4, 5). It would be foolish for you to travel to Jerusalem and wait there to receive this promise, since Jesus already fulfilled it that first Pentecost. Today, the Spirit baptizes every believer into the body of Christ and takes up residence within us at the very moment we trust in Christ. Jesus gave this promise to a specific group of people at a particular time for an explicit purpose—it isn't for anyone else to claim.

2. *General promises*

God has made many universal promises, applicable to all His children throughout all of history. For example, He has promised to never leave us nor forsake us (Heb. 13:5). He also promised many times to return for us (John 14:3). These promises pertain to all believers across all of time. Yet general promises can also be of two types.

(a) *Conditional promises.* Texts like Psalm 37:4, Philippians 4:19, and others contain conditional promises; to receive the benefit offered, you must meet some condition. Conditional promises require something of the believer.

In Philippians 4:19, the condition is that we be in Christ; the believer must be living for Him and in total submission to His will. The same holds true for "delighting" in the Lord, as stated in Psalm 37:4. Clearly a relationship comes before a request.

(b) *Unconditional promises.* Unconditional promises require nothing of the believer. The promises mentioned above in Hebrews 13:5 and John 14:3 are of this type. God will fulfill these promises because He has pledged to fulfill them. Nothing anyone does can alter His commitment or change His plans. He will keep these promises, not because of anything we do, but because of His own faithfulness.

---

15 Through Him then, let us continually offer up a sacrifice of praise to God, that is, the fruit of lips that give thanks to His name.

16 And do not neglect doing good and sharing, for with such sacrifices God is pleased.

17 Obey your leaders and submit *to them*, for they keep watch over your souls as those who will give an account. Let them do this with joy and not with grief, for this would be unprofitable for you.

18 Pray for us, for we are sure that we have a good conscience, desiring to conduct ourselves honorably in all things.

19 And I urge *you* all the more to do this, so that I may be restored to you the sooner.

➤ 20 Now the God of peace, who brought up from the dead the great Shepherd of the sheep through the blood of the eternal covenant, *even* Jesus our Lord,

21 equip you in every good thing to do His will, working in us that which is pleasing in His sight, through Jesus Christ, to whom *be* the glory forever and ever. Amen.

22 But I urge you, brethren, bear with this word of exhortation, for I have written to you briefly.

23 Take notice that our brother Timothy has been released, with whom, if he comes soon, I will see you.

24 Greet all of your leaders and all the saints. Those from Italy greet you.

25 Grace be with you all.

LIFE LESSONS

➤ Hebrews 13:20, 21 — *God . . . equip you in every good thing to do His will, working in us that which is pleasing in His sight.*

*I*t is *God* working *in us* that enables us to do anything worthwhile for His kingdom. We obey the Lord, submit to His will and purpose, rely on His Holy Spirit who dwells within us for our every need, and please Him by giving Him all the honor and glory.

31 IN the eleventh year, in the third *month,* on the first of the month, the word of the LORD came to me saying,
2   "Son of man, say to Pharaoh king of Egypt and to his hordes,
'Whom are you like in your greatness?
3   'Behold, Assyria *was* a cedar in Lebanon
With beautiful branches and forest shade,
And very high,
And its top was among the clouds.
4   'The waters made it grow, the deep made it high.
With its rivers it continually extended all around its planting place,
And sent out its channels to all the trees of the field.
5   'Therefore its height was loftier than all the trees of the field
And its boughs became many and its branches long
Because of many waters as it spread them out.
6   'All the birds of the heavens nested in its boughs,
And under its branches all the beasts of the field gave birth,
And all great nations lived under its shade.
7   'So it was beautiful in its greatness, in the length of its branches;
For its roots extended to many waters.
8   'The cedars in God's garden could not match it;
The cypresses could not compare with its boughs,
And the plane trees could not match its branches.
No tree in God's garden could compare with it in its beauty.
9   'I made it beautiful with the multitude of its branches,
And all the trees of Eden, which were in the garden of God, were jealous of it.
10   'Therefore thus says the Lord GOD, "Because it is high in stature and has set its top among the clouds, and its heart is haughty in its loftiness,
11   therefore I will give it into the hand of a despot of the nations; he will thoroughly deal with it. According to its wickedness I have driven it away.
12   "Alien tyrants of the nations have cut it down and left it; on the mountains and in all the valleys its branches have fallen and its boughs have been broken in all the ravines of the land. And all the peoples of the earth have gone down from its shade and left it.
13   "On its ruin all the birds of the heavens will dwell, and all the beasts of the field will be on its *fallen* branches
14   so that all the trees by the waters may not be exalted in their stature, nor set their top among the clouds, nor their well-watered mighty ones stand *erect* in their height. For they have all been given over to death, to the earth beneath, among the sons of men, with those who go down to the pit."
15   'Thus says the Lord GOD, "On the day when it went down to Sheol I caused lamentations; I closed the deep over it and held back its rivers. And *its* many waters were stopped up, and I made Lebanon mourn for it, and all the trees of the field wilted away on account of it.
16   "I made the nations quake at the sound of its fall when I made it go down to Sheol with those who go down to the pit; and all the well-watered trees of Eden, the choicest and best of Lebanon, were comforted in the earth beneath.
17   "They also went down with it to Sheol to those who were slain by the sword; and those who were its strength lived under its shade among the nations.
18   "To which among the trees of Eden are you thus equal in glory and greatness? Yet you will be brought down with the trees of Eden to the earth beneath; you will lie in the midst of the uncircumcised, with those who were slain by the sword. So is Pharaoh and all his hordes!"' declares the Lord GOD."

32 IN the twelfth year, in the twelfth *month,* on the first of the month, the word of the LORD came to me saying,
2   "Son of man, take up a lamentation over Pharaoh king of Egypt and say to him,
'You compared yourself to a young lion of the nations,
Yet you are like the monster in the seas;

And you burst forth in your rivers
And muddied the waters with your
feet
And fouled their rivers.'"

3   Thus says the Lord GOD,
"Now I will spread My net over you
With a company of many peoples,
And they shall lift you up in My net.

4   "I will leave you on the land;
I will cast you on the open field.
And I will cause all the birds of the
heavens to dwell on you,
And I will satisfy the beasts of the
whole earth with you.

5   "I will lay your flesh on the
mountains
And fill the valleys with your
refuse.

6   "I will also make the land drink the
discharge of your blood
As far as the mountains,
And the ravines will be full of you.

7   "And when I extinguish you,
I will cover the heavens and darken
their stars;
I will cover the sun with a cloud
And the moon will not give its light.

8   "All the shining lights in the heavens
I will darken over you
And will set darkness on your
land,"
Declares the Lord GOD.

9   "I will also trouble the hearts of many
peoples when I bring your destruction
among the nations, into lands which you
have not known.

10   "I will make many peoples appalled
at you, and their kings will be horribly
afraid of you when I brandish My sword
before them; and they will tremble every
moment, every man for his own life, on
the day of your fall."

11   For thus says the Lord GOD, "The
sword of the king of Babylon will come
upon you.

12   "By the swords of the mighty ones I
will cause your hordes to fall; all of them
are tyrants of the nations,
And they will devastate the pride of
Egypt,
And all its hordes will be destroyed.

13   "I will also destroy all its cattle from
beside many waters;
And the foot of man will not muddy
them anymore
And the hoofs of beasts will not
muddy them.

14   "Then I will make their waters settle
And will cause their rivers to run
like oil,"
Declares the Lord GOD.

15   "When I make the land of Egypt a
desolation,
And the land is destitute of that
which filled it,
When I smite all those who live in
it,
Then they shall know that I am the
LORD.

16   "This is a lamentation and they shall
chant it. The daughters of the nations
shall chant it. Over Egypt and over all
her hordes they shall chant it," declares
the Lord GOD.

17   In the twelfth year, on the fifteenth
of the month, the word of the LORD came
to me saying,

18   "Son of man, wail for the hordes of
Egypt and bring it down, her and the
daughters of the powerful nations, to the
nether world, with those who go down to
the pit;

19   'Whom do you surpass in beauty?
Go down and make your bed with
the uncircumcised.'

20   "They shall fall in the midst of those
who are slain by the sword. She is given
over to the sword; they have drawn her
and all her hordes away.

21   "The strong among the mighty ones
shall speak of him and his helpers from
the midst of Sheol, 'They have gone
down, they lie still, the uncircumcised,
slain by the sword.'

22   "Assyria is there and all her company; her graves are round about her. All
of them are slain, fallen by the sword,

23   whose graves are set in the remotest
parts of the pit and her company is round
about her grave. All of them are slain,
fallen by the sword, who spread terror in
the land of the living.

24   "Elam is there and all her hordes
around her grave; all of them slain, fallen
by the sword, who went down uncircumcised to the lower parts of the earth, who
instilled their terror in the land of the
living and bore their disgrace with those
who went down to the pit.

25   "They have made a bed for her among
the slain with all her hordes. Her graves
are around it, they are all uncircumcised,
slain by the sword (although their terror
was instilled in the land of the living),

and they bore their disgrace with those who go down to the pit; they were put in the midst of the slain.

26 "Meshech, Tubal and all their hordes are there; their graves surround them. All of them were slain by the sword uncircumcised, though they instilled their terror in the land of the living.

27 "Nor do they lie beside the fallen heroes of the uncircumcised, who went down to Sheol with their weapons of war and whose swords were laid under their heads; but the punishment for their iniquity rested on their bones, though the terror of *these* heroes *was once* in the land of the living.

28 "But in the midst of the uncircumcised you will be broken and lie with those slain by the sword.

29 "There also is Edom, its kings and all its princes, who for *all* their might are laid with those slain by the sword; they will lie with the uncircumcised and with those who go down to the pit.

30 "There also are the chiefs of the north, all of them, and all the Sidonians, who in spite of the terror resulting from their might, in shame went down with the slain. So they lay down uncircumcised with those slain by the sword and bore their disgrace with those who go down to the pit.

31 "These Pharaoh will see, and he will be comforted for all his hordes slain by the sword, *even* Pharaoh and all his army," declares the Lord GOD.

32 "Though I instilled a terror of him in the land of the living, yet he will be made to lie down among *the* uncircumcised *along* with those slain by the sword, *even* Pharaoh and all his hordes," declares the Lord GOD.

Psalm 130:1–4

A Song of Ascents.

130 OUT of the depths I have cried to You, O LORD.

2 Lord, hear my voice!
Let Your ears be attentive
To the voice of my supplications.

3 If You, LORD, should mark iniquities,
O Lord, who could stand?

4 But there is forgiveness with You,
That You may be feared.

Proverbs 28:28

28 When the wicked rise, men hide themselves;
But when they perish, the righteous increase.

James 1:1–27

1 JAMES, a bond-servant of God and of the Lord Jesus Christ,
To the twelve tribes who are dispersed abroad: Greetings.

2 Consider it all joy, my brethren, when you encounter various trials,

3 knowing that the testing of your faith produces endurance.

4 And let endurance have *its* perfect result, so that you may be perfect and complete, lacking in nothing.

5 But if any of you lacks wisdom, let him ask of God, who gives to all generously and without reproach, and it will be given to him.

6 But he must ask in faith without any doubting, for the one who doubts is like the surf of the sea, driven and tossed by the wind.

7 For that man ought not to expect that he will receive anything from the Lord,

8 *being* a double-minded man, unstable in all his ways.

9 But the brother of humble circumstances is to glory in his high position;

LIFE LESSONS

➤ **James 1:2, 3 — *Consider it all joy, my brethren, when you encounter various trials, knowing that the testing of your faith produces endurance.***

There is nothing joyful about trials, in and of themselves. There is no value in suffering for its own sake. God uses both trials and suffering to test and strengthen our faith so that we may learn to patiently endure all that comes against us.

ANSWERS TO LIFE'S QUESTIONS

How does God teach me perseverance?

JAMES 1:2, 3

*P*erseverance has been defined as accepting difficult situations as from God without giving Him a deadline for their removal. We know we need to learn endurance, but we generally shun the process by which it takes root in our lives.

Ours is the "now" generation—we want everything immediately. We refuse to wait for the Lord's direction or provision, so we either give in to discouragement or move ahead on our own initiative. However, rejecting God because we do not get our own way or running ahead of His timing are costly and disappointing courses of action.

Psalm 27:14 admonishes, "Wait for the LORD; be strong and let your heart take courage; yes, wait for the LORD." The Thessalonians were doing this successfully, and Paul commended them for staying firm in the faith, even though they faced terrible opposition. He wrote, "Your faith is greatly enlarged, and the love of each one of you toward one another grows ever greater; therefore, we ourselves speak proudly of you among the churches of God for your perseverance and faith in the midst of all your persecutions and afflictions which you endure . . . . so that you will be considered worthy of the kingdom of God, for which indeed you are suffering" (2 Thess. 1:3–5).

Their troubles were not causing them to fall away. Rather, the Thessalonians were trusting the Lord and maturing in their relationship with Him. And through their difficulties, God was teaching them abiding hope and perseverance that nothing could destroy.

Likewise, He may allow us to experience difficulties or to wait for relief from some situation or obstacle for several reasons:

- The Lord is teaching us discipline and endurance through waiting.
- God is using the adversity to reveal hidden sin in our lives.
- The Lord wants to teach us to depend on Him, not on ourselves or others.
- God is molding our character so we will honor Him with our lives.
- God wants to teach us to trust His ways and timing, and to learn that they are best.

Yet James 1:2–4 encourages us, "Consider it all joy, my brethren, when you encounter various trials, knowing that the testing of your faith produces endurance. And let endurance have its perfect result, so that you may be perfect and complete, lacking in nothing." In times of difficulty, we learn to persevere, and to keep holding to the Lord as our hope and our victory. Our troubles may not be pleasant, but they are profitable in our relationship with Him and our character because they teach us to trust Him, to wait for Him, and to have confidence in His provision.

Therefore, when you face adversity, do not despair. Cling to God and trust Him no matter what happens. He is teaching you to persevere, and it is a lesson worth learning.

---

10 and the rich man *is to glory* in his humiliation, because like flowering grass he will pass away.

11 For the sun rises with a scorching wind and withers the grass; and its flower falls off and the beauty of its appearance is destroyed; so too the rich man in the midst of his pursuits will fade away.

12 Blessed is a man who perseveres under trial; for once he has been approved, he will receive the crown of life which *the Lord* has promised to those who love Him.

➤ 13 Let no one say when he is tempted, "I am being tempted by God"; for God cannot be tempted by evil, and He Himself does not tempt anyone.

14 But each one is tempted when he is carried away and enticed by his own lust.

15 Then when lust has conceived, it gives birth to sin; and when sin is accomplished, it brings forth death.

16 Do not be deceived, my beloved brethren.

17 Every good thing given and every ◄ perfect gift is from above, coming down

LIFE LESSONS

➤ **James 1:13 — *God cannot be tempted by evil, and He Himself does not tempt anyone.***

*A*lthough the Lord *tests* us to strengthen our faith, He will not lead us to do anything that is counter to His will. God is holy and would never tempt anyone to do evil because that is completely inconsistent with His character.

LIFE LESSONS

➤ **James 1:17 — *Every good thing given and every perfect gift is from above, coming down from the Father of lights.***

*G*od is the source of every good thing we have. When we acknowledge His role in our blessings, we develop the best defense against pride and fear— and that's humble dependence on Him.

➤ **James 1:22 — *Prove yourselves doers of the word, and not merely hearers who delude themselves.***

*O*beying God's Word is not always easy. Many of His commands require sacrifice and even suffering. The Lord understands the difficulty in submitting ourselves to Him, but He still calls us to obey Him and allow Him to handle the consequences. We must apply His principles to our lives because that is the only way we will find true victory over sin and death—in Him.

from the Father of lights, with whom there is no variation or shifting shadow.
18   In the exercise of His will He brought us forth by the word of truth, so that we would be a kind of first fruits among His creatures.

19   *This* you know, my beloved brethren. But everyone must be quick to hear, slow to speak *and* slow to anger;
20   for the anger of man does not achieve the righteousness of God.
21   Therefore, putting aside all filthiness and *all* that remains of wickedness, in humility receive the word implanted, which is able to save your souls.
22   But prove yourselves doers of the word, and not merely hearers who delude themselves.
23   For if anyone is a hearer of the word and not a doer, he is like a man who looks at his natural face in a mirror;
24   for *once* he has looked at himself and gone away, he has immediately forgotten what kind of person he was.
25   But one who looks intently at the perfect law, the *law* of liberty, and abides by it, not having become a forgetful hearer but an effectual doer, this man will be blessed in what he does.
26   If anyone thinks himself to be religious, and yet does not bridle his tongue but deceives his *own* heart, this man's religion is worthless.
27   Pure and undefiled religion in the sight of *our* God and Father is this: to visit orphans and widows in their distress, *and* to keep oneself unstained by the world.

Ezekiel 33:1—34:31

33 AND the word of the LORD came to me, saying,
2   "Son of man, speak to the sons of your people and say to them, 'If I bring a sword upon a land, and the people of the land take one man from among them and make him their watchman,
3   and he sees the sword coming upon the land and blows on the trumpet and warns the people,
4   then he who hears the sound of the trumpet and does not take warning, and a sword comes and takes him away, his blood will be on his *own* head.
5   'He heard the sound of the trumpet but did not take warning; his blood will

be on himself. But had he taken warning, he would have delivered his life.
6   'But if the watchman sees the sword coming and does not blow the trumpet and the people are not warned, and a sword comes and takes a person from them, he is taken away in his iniquity; but his blood I will require from the watchman's hand.'
7   "Now as for you, son of man, I have appointed you a watchman for the house of Israel; so you will hear a message from My mouth and give them warning from Me.
8   "When I say to the wicked, 'O wicked man, you will surely die,' and you do not speak to warn the wicked from his way, that wicked man shall die in his iniquity, but his blood I will require from your hand.

9 "But if you on your part warn a wicked man to turn from his way and he does not turn from his way, he will die in his iniquity, but you have delivered your life.

10 "Now as for you, son of man, say to the house of Israel, 'Thus you have spoken, saying, "Surely our transgressions and our sins are upon us, and we are rotting away in them; how then can we survive?"'

➤ 11 "Say to them, 'As I live!' declares the Lord GOD, 'I take no pleasure in the death of the wicked, but rather that the wicked turn from his way and live. Turn back, turn back from your evil ways! Why then will you die, O house of Israel?'

12 "And you, son of man, say to your fellow citizens, 'The righteousness of a righteous man will not deliver him in the day of his transgression, and as for the wickedness of the wicked, he will not stumble because of it in the day when he turns from his wickedness; whereas a righteous man will not be able to live by his righteousness on the day when he commits sin.'

13 "When I say to the righteous he will surely live, and he so trusts in his righteousness that he commits iniquity, none of his righteous deeds will be remembered; but in that same iniquity of his which he has committed he will die.

14 "But when I say to the wicked, 'You will surely die,' and he turns from his sin and practices justice and righteousness,

15 if a wicked man restores a pledge, pays back what he has taken by robbery, walks by the statutes which ensure life without committing iniquity, he shall surely live; he shall not die.

16 "None of his sins that he has committed will be remembered against him. He has practiced justice and righteousness; he shall surely live.

17 "Yet your fellow citizens say, 'The way of the Lord is not right,' when it is their own way that is not right.

18 "When the righteous turns from his righteousness and commits iniquity, then he shall die in it.

19 "But when the wicked turns from his wickedness and practices justice and righteousness, he will live by them.

20 "Yet you say, 'The way of the Lord is not right.' O house of Israel, I will judge each of you according to his ways."

21 Now in the twelfth year of our exile, on the fifth of the tenth month, the refugees from Jerusalem came to me, saying, "The city has been taken."

22 Now the hand of the LORD had been upon me in the evening, before the refugees came. And He opened my mouth at the time they came to me in the morning; so my mouth was opened and I was no longer speechless.

23 Then the word of the LORD came to me saying,

24 "Son of man, they who live in these waste places in the land of Israel are saying, 'Abraham was only one, yet he possessed the land; so to us who are many the land has been given as a possession.'

25 "Therefore say to them, 'Thus says the Lord GOD, "You eat meat with the blood in it, lift up your eyes to your idols as you shed blood. Should you then possess the land?

26 "You rely on your sword, you commit abominations and each of you defiles his neighbor's wife. Should you then possess the land?"'

27 "Thus you shall say to them, 'Thus says the Lord GOD, "As I live, surely those who are in the waste places will fall by the sword, and whoever is in the open field I will give to the beasts to be devoured, and those who are in the strongholds and in the caves will die of pestilence.

28 "I will make the land a desolation and a waste, and the pride of her power will cease; and the mountains of Israel will be desolate so that no one will pass through.

29 "Then they will know that I am the LORD, when I make the land a desolation and a waste because of all their abominations which they have committed."'

30 "But as for you, son of man, your

LIFE LESSONS

➤ **Ezekiel 33:11** — *"I take no pleasure in the death of the wicked, but rather that the wicked turn from his way and live."*

*G*od does not want to condemn us, which is why He pleads with us to turn from our wicked ways and to return to Him with all our hearts and all our souls. The Lord will never reject anyone with a truly repentant heart.

fellow citizens who talk about you by the walls and in the doorways of the houses, speak to one another, each to his brother, saying, 'Come now and hear what the message is which comes forth from the LORD.'

31 "They come to you as people come, and sit before you *as* My people and hear your words, but they do not do them, for they do the lustful desires *expressed* by their mouth, *and* their heart goes after their gain.

➤ 32 "Behold, you are to them like a sensual song by one who has a beautiful voice and plays well on an instrument; for they hear your words but they do not practice them.

33 "So when it comes to pass—as surely it will—then they will know that a prophet has been in their midst."

34 THEN the word of the LORD came to me saying,

2 "Son of man, prophesy against the shepherds of Israel. Prophesy and say to those shepherds, 'Thus says the Lord GOD, "Woe, shepherds of Israel who have been feeding themselves! Should not the shepherds feed the flock?

3 "You eat the fat and clothe yourselves with the wool, you slaughter the fat *sheep* without feeding the flock.

4 "Those who are sickly you have not strengthened, the diseased you have not healed, the broken you have not bound up, the scattered you have not brought back, nor have you sought for the lost; but with force and with severity you have dominated them.

5 "They were scattered for lack of a

LIFE LESSONS

➤ **Ezekiel 33:32 — *"They hear your words but they do not practice them."***

*T*he New Testament tells us that—like the people in this passage—King Herod was afraid of John the Baptist, "but he used to enjoy listening to him" (Mark 6:20); that is, until Herod killed him. Many people have their favorite preachers and listen to them because they are entertaining. The point, however, is not merely hearing the Word of God, but embracing and doing it wholeheartedly in obedience to the Lord (James 1:22).

---

shepherd, and they became food for every beast of the field and were scattered.

6 "My flock wandered through all the mountains and on every high hill; My flock was scattered over all the surface of the earth, and there was no one to search or seek *for them*."'"

7 Therefore, you shepherds, hear the word of the LORD:

8 "As I live," declares the Lord GOD, "surely because My flock has become a prey, My flock has even become food for all the beasts of the field for lack of a shepherd, and My shepherds did not search for My flock, but *rather* the shepherds fed themselves and did not feed My flock;

9 therefore, you shepherds, hear the word of the LORD:

10 'Thus says the Lord GOD, "Behold, I am against the shepherds, and I will demand My sheep from them and make them cease from feeding sheep. So the shepherds will not feed themselves anymore, but I will deliver My flock from their mouth, so that they will not be food for them."'"

11 For thus says the Lord GOD, "Behold, I Myself will search for My sheep and seek them out.

12 "As a shepherd cares for his herd in the day when he is among his scattered sheep, so I will care for My sheep and will deliver them from all the places to which they were scattered on a cloudy and gloomy day.

13 "I will bring them out from the peoples and gather them from the countries and bring them to their own land; and I will feed them on the mountains of Israel, by the streams, and in all the inhabited places of the land.

14 "I will feed them in a good pasture, and their grazing ground will be on the mountain heights of Israel. There they will lie down on good grazing ground and feed in rich pasture on the mountains of Israel.

15 "I will feed My flock and I will lead them to rest," declares the Lord GOD.

16 "I will seek the lost, bring back the scattered, bind up the broken and strengthen the sick; but the fat and the strong I will destroy. I will feed them with judgment.

17 "As for you, My flock, thus says the Lord GOD, 'Behold, I will judge between

one sheep and another, between the rams and the male goats.

18 'Is it too slight a thing for you that you should feed in the good pasture, that you must tread down with your feet the rest of your pastures? Or that you should drink of the clear waters, that you must foul the rest with your feet?

19 'As for My flock, they must eat what you tread down with your feet and drink what you foul with your feet!'"

20 Therefore, thus says the Lord GOD to them, "Behold, I, even I, will judge between the fat sheep and the lean sheep.

21 "Because you push with side and with shoulder, and thrust at all the weak with your horns until you have scattered them abroad,

22 therefore, I will deliver My flock, and they will no longer be a prey; and I will judge between one sheep and another.

23 "Then I will set over them one shepherd, My servant David, and he will feed them; he will feed them himself and be ✳ their shepherd.

24 "And I, the LORD, will be their God, and My servant David will be prince among them; I the LORD have spoken.

25 "I will make a covenant of peace with them and eliminate harmful beasts from the land so that they may live securely in the wilderness and sleep in the woods.

26 "I will make them and the places around My hill a blessing. And I will cause showers to come down in their season; they will be showers of blessing.

27 "Also the tree of the field will yield its fruit and the earth will yield its increase, and they will be secure on their land. Then they will know that I am the LORD, when I have broken the bars of their yoke and have delivered them from the hand of those who enslaved them.

28 "They will no longer be a prey to the nations, and the beasts of the earth will not devour them; but they will live securely, and no one will make them afraid.

29 "I will establish for them a renowned planting place, and they will not again be victims of famine in the land, and they will not endure the insults of the nations anymore.

30 "Then they will know that I, the LORD their God, am with them, and that they, the house of Israel, are My people," declares the Lord GOD.

31 "As for you, My sheep, the sheep of ◄ My pasture, you are men, and I am your God," declares the Lord GOD.

✦ Psalm 130:5–8

5 I wait for the LORD, my soul does ◄
   wait,
   And in His word do I hope.
6 My soul *waits* for the Lord   ✳
   More than the watchmen for the
   morning;
   Indeed, more than the watchmen for
   the morning.
7 O Israel, hope in the LORD;
   For with the LORD there is
   lovingkindness,
   And with Him is abundant
   redemption.
8 And He will redeem Israel
   From all his iniquities.

✦ Proverbs 29:1

29 A MAN who hardens *his* neck
   after much reproof
   Will suddenly be broken beyond
   remedy.

LIFE LESSONS

➤ **Ezekiel 34:31 —** *"As for you, My sheep, the sheep of My pasture, you are men, and I am your God," says the Lord GOD.*

*I*n both testaments, God calls His people His "flock" (Ps. 80:1; Is. 40:11; Micah 5:4; Luke 12:32; 1 Pet. 5:2). Why? For one thing, it's a term of endearment and a picture of close, personal connection. For another, it reveals our total dependence upon Him. Third, it honors Him as our Shepherd.

➤ **Psalm 130:5 —** *I wait for the LORD, my soul does wait, and in His word do I hope.*

*G*od does not spring into action on our timetable. In fact, He waits until the very best moment to intervene. Why? Waiting is the Lord's training ground for building strong faith. As we wait, we learn to trust Him.

ANSWERS **TO LIFE'S QUESTIONS**

How can I enrich my time alone with God?

PSALM 130:6

*H*ave you ever sat down in a quiet place with your Bible, ready to have a devotional time with the Lord—but you felt aimless? Maybe you flipped through the pages and finally settled on a psalm. But then you remembered another appointment, so you said a quick prayer and told yourself you would take more time to pray later—but it never happened.

You're not alone if you feel frustrated with the quality of your quiet times. As much as you may desire real intimacy with your personal Savior, He longs for this even more. James 4:8 promises, "Draw near to God and He will draw near to you."

It helps many people to receive some direction on how to develop a close walk with Christ. Here are four easy steps to help you begin.

First, set a goal to spend time with God every day. Regardless of tight schedules, we cannot afford to do otherwise. The Father knows everything. He knows what we will face today, tomorrow, and in the future. He is loving, kind, gentle, caring, omniscient, holy, and worthy of all our worship and praise (Psalm 18:3). He is our best friend and our living Lord. Starting the day without acknowledging His goodness and love should be the last thing we do. Before our feet hit the floor in the morning, we need to thank Him for His protective care, for loving us, and for being the sovereign God of the universe.

Also, we need to pray along with the apostle Paul and take on the "whole" armor of God each day (Ephesians 6). We are living in a time of extreme spiritual warfare when Satan is seeking to draw us away from God's truth. We won't fall for his deceptive and wicked schemes as long as we hide the Word of God in our hearts. Jesus spent time alone in prayer, and His pattern is the one we need to follow and not the one established by the world.

Second, make a commitment to pray and to read His Word daily. Even when you don't feel like it, take time to express your heart to the Lord. Then ask Him to show you certain passages in His Word that would help you see your situation from His perspective. We need to pray when times are good and when they are bad. We also need to pray without ceasing, knowing that the One person who holds the answer to all of life's problems loves us unconditionally and has a wonderful plan for our lives.

If you had the opportunity to experience the greatest level of peace and security, would you turn away from it? None of us would. Then why do so many people turn away from God and never take time to pray? When we bypass spending time with Him, we are only hurting ourselves. In the process, we miss His blessings—one after another. If there is a need for wisdom, He has promised to provide it. If there is a need for encouragement, hope, guidance, and provision, He provides each one of these. But if we fail to spend time with Him, we will never know the benefits that are ours.

Third, keep a journal of your spiritual trek. Keep a notebook and pen ready to write down the insight God provides. Some people record their daily prayers, leaving a space to describe how God answered them. You may prefer a format in which you write down a special verse and describe why it impacted you. If you have kept a journal before, you know what a treat it is to see a reminder of your spiritual journey.

Fourth, make a commitment to obey the Lord. Obedience always leads to blessing. It reveals our level of trust in Him and our willingness to do what He requires. Micah wrote, "He has told you, O man, what is good; and what does the LORD require of you but to do justice, to love kindness, and to walk humbly with your God?" (Micah 6:8). We cannot walk with God unless we agree with Him, and there is no agreement apart from obedience. Likewise, there can be no peace or lasting joy when we are in opposition to Him.

Are you ready for a relationship with Jesus that knows no boundaries? Then open your time, your life, and your heart—and know without a doubt that He will meet with you.

James 2:1–26

2 MY brethren, do not hold your faith in our glorious Lord Jesus Christ with *an attitude of* personal favoritism.

2   For if a man comes into your assembly with a gold ring and dressed in fine clothes, and there also comes in a poor man in dirty clothes,

3   and you pay special attention to the one who is wearing the fine clothes, and say, "You sit here in a good place," and you say to the poor man, "You stand over there, or sit down by my footstool,"

4   have you not made distinctions

among yourselves, and become judges with evil motives?

➤ 5   Listen, my beloved brethren: did not God choose the poor of this world *to be* rich in faith and heirs of the kingdom which He promised to those who love Him?

6   But you have dishonored the poor man. Is it not the rich who oppress you and personally drag you into court?

7   Do they not blaspheme the fair name by which you have been called?

8   If, however, you are fulfilling the royal law according to the Scripture, "YOU SHALL LOVE YOUR NEIGHBOR AS YOUR-SELF," you are doing well.

9   But if you show partiality, you are committing sin *and* are convicted by the law as transgressors.

➤ 10   For whoever keeps the whole law and yet stumbles in one *point*, he has become guilty of all.

11   For He who said, "DO NOT COMMIT ADULTERY," also said, "DO NOT COMMIT MURDER." Now if you do not commit adultery, but do commit murder, you have become a transgressor of the law.

12   So speak and so act as those who are to be judged by *the* law of liberty.

13   For judgment *will be* merciless to one who has shown no mercy; mercy triumphs over judgment.

14   What use is it, my brethren, if someone says he has faith but he has no works? Can that faith save him?

15   If a brother or sister is without clothing and in need of daily food,

16   and one of you says to them, "Go in peace, be warmed and be filled," and yet you do not give them what is necessary for *their* body, what use is that?

17   Even so faith, if it has no works, is dead, *being* by itself.

➤ 18   But someone may *well* say, "You have faith and I have works; show me your faith without the works, and I will show you my faith by my works."

19   You believe that God is one. You do well; the demons also believe, and shudder.

✳ 20   But are you willing to recognize, you foolish fellow, that faith without works is useless?

21   Was not Abraham our father justified by works when he offered up Isaac his son on the altar?

22   You see that faith was working with his works, and as a result of the works, faith was perfected;

23   and the Scripture was fulfilled which says, "AND ABRAHAM BELIEVED GOD, AND IT WAS RECKONED TO HIM AS RIGHTEOUSNESS," and he was called the friend of God.

24   You see that a man is justified by works and not by faith alone.

25   In the same way, was not Rahab the harlot also justified by works when she received the messengers and sent them out by another way?

26   For just as the body without *the* spirit is dead, so also faith without works is dead.

LIFE LESSONS

➤ **James 2:5 — *Did not God choose the poor of this world to be rich in faith and heirs of the kingdom?***

*E*arthly riches do not equal spiritual wealth, any more than economic destitution indicates spiritual poverty. Those who love God, regardless of their earthly financial positions, are rich in faith and heirs of the kingdom because of their relationships with Him.

➤ **James 2:10 — *Whoever keeps the whole law and yet stumbles in one point, he has become guilty of all.***

*J*ames warned Jewish believers that if they renounced Christ, they would once again be enslaved by the law, which had no true power in their lives. Even if they kept every command, they could not rid themselves of the sins they had already committed. This is true for us. We can never be "good enough" to earn salvation or the grace that God gives so freely. We are either completely obedient to God by accepting Christ—who fulfills the law completely—or we are disobedient. We cannot have it both ways.

➤ **James 2:18 — *Show me your faith without the works, and I will show you my faith by my works.***

*G*ood works done in obedience to God are the *evidence* of our faith. They do not earn or purchase our salvation. If a person says they know Jesus Christ as their Savior, there must be proof of it—there must be confirmation that the Holy Spirit is molding that individual into the likeness of Christ. This does not mean an artificial change in behavior, but one that stems from the transformation of their very character.

35 MOREOVER, the word of the LORD came to me saying,

2 "Son of man, set your face against Mount Seir, and prophesy against it

3 and say to it, 'Thus says the Lord GOD,
"Behold, I am against you, Mount Seir,
And I will stretch out My hand
against you
And make you a desolation and a
waste.

4 "I will lay waste your cities
And you will become a desolation.
Then you will know that I am the
LORD.

5 "Because you have had everlasting enmity and have delivered the sons of Israel to the power of the sword at the time of their calamity, at the time of the punishment of the end,

6 therefore as I live," declares the Lord GOD, "I will give you over to bloodshed, and bloodshed will pursue you; since you have not hated bloodshed, therefore bloodshed will pursue you.

7 "I will make Mount Seir a waste and a desolation and I will cut off from it the one who passes through and returns.

8 "I will fill its mountains with its slain; on your hills and in your valleys and in all your ravines those slain by the sword will fall.

9 "I will make you an everlasting desolation and your cities will not be inhabited. Then you will know that I am the LORD.

10 "Because you have said, 'These two nations and these two lands will be mine, and we will possess them,' although the LORD was there,

11 therefore as I live," declares the Lord GOD, "I will deal *with you* according to your anger and according to your envy which you showed because of your hatred against them; so I will make Myself known among them when I judge you.

12 "Then you will know that I, the LORD, have heard all your revilings which you have spoken against the mountains of Israel saying, 'They are laid desolate; they are given to us for food.'

13 "And you have spoken arrogantly against Me and have multiplied your words against Me; I have heard *it*."

14 'Thus says the Lord GOD, "As all the earth rejoices, I will make you a desolation.

15 "As you rejoiced over the inheritance of the house of Israel because it was desolate, so I will do to you. You will be a desolation, O Mount Seir, and all Edom, all of it. Then they will know that I am the LORD."'

36 "AND you, son of man, prophesy to the mountains of Israel and say, 'O mountains of Israel, hear the word of the LORD.

2 'Thus says the Lord GOD, "Because the enemy has spoken against you, 'Aha!' and, 'The everlasting heights have become our possession,'

3 therefore prophesy and say, 'Thus says the Lord GOD, "For good reason they have made you desolate and crushed you from every side, that you would become a possession of the rest of the nations and you have been taken up in the talk and the whispering of the people."'"

4 'Therefore, O mountains of Israel, hear the word of the Lord GOD. Thus says the Lord GOD to the mountains and to the hills, to the ravines and to the valleys, to the desolate wastes and to the forsaken cities which have become a prey and a derision to the rest of the nations which are round about,

5 therefore thus says the Lord GOD, "Surely in the fire of My jealousy I have spoken against the rest of the nations, and against all Edom, who appropriated My land for themselves as a possession with wholehearted joy *and* with scorn of soul, to drive it out for a prey."

6 'Therefore prophesy concerning the land of Israel and say to the mountains and to the hills, to the ravines and to the valleys, "Thus says the Lord GOD, 'Behold, I have spoken in My jealousy and in My wrath because you have endured the insults of the nations.'

7 "Therefore thus says the Lord GOD, 'I have sworn that surely the nations which are around you will themselves endure their insults.

8 'But you, O mountains of Israel, you will put forth your branches and bear your fruit for My people Israel; for they will soon come.

9 'For, behold, I am for you, and I will turn to you, and you will be cultivated and sown.

10 'I will multiply men on you, all the house of Israel, all of it; and the cities will be inhabited and the waste places will be rebuilt.

11 'I will multiply on you man and beast; and they will increase and be fruitful; and I will cause you to be inhabited as you were formerly and will treat you better than at the first. Thus you will know that I am the LORD.

12 'Yes, I will cause men—My people Israel—to walk on you and possess you, so that you will become their inheritance and never again bereave them of children.'

13 "Thus says the Lord GOD, 'Because they say to you, "You are a devourer of men and have bereaved your nation of children,"

14 therefore you will no longer devour men and no longer bereave your nation of children,' declares the Lord GOD.

15 "I will not let you hear insults from the nations anymore, nor will you bear disgrace from the peoples any longer, nor will you cause your nation to stumble any longer," declares the Lord GOD.'"

16 Then the word of the LORD came to me saying,

17 "Son of man, when the house of Israel was living in their own land, they defiled it by their ways and their deeds; their way before Me was like the uncleanness of a woman in her impurity.

18 "Therefore I poured out My wrath on them for the blood which they had shed on the land, because they had defiled it with their idols.

19 "Also I scattered them among the nations and they were dispersed throughout the lands. According to their ways and their deeds I judged them.

20 "When they came to the nations where they went, they profaned My holy name, because it was said of them, 'These are the people of the LORD; yet they have come out of His land.'

21 "But I had concern for My holy name, ◄ which the house of Israel had profaned among the nations where they went.

22 "Therefore say to the house of Israel, 'Thus says the Lord GOD, "It is not for your sake, O house of Israel, that I am about to act, but for My holy name,

ANSWERS TO LIFE'S QUESTIONS

How can I help to restore someone to fellowship with God?

EZEKIEL 36:16–38

*T*he term "restore" is an interesting one. In ancient Greek, it means to set a broken bone back in place. In restoring someone we do not place bandages on small cuts, but instead we set broken spiritual bones. Therefore, the work is often long and painful. The steps to restoration are as follows:

1. *Lead the person to recognize his failure.* Help him see the nature of the problem and call it by its right name: sin. As long as a person can rationalize his behavior, he will never accept responsibility for it.

2. *Lead the person to acknowledge responsibility for his sin.* Blaming others will do no good. Others may have been involved, but the person chose to sin—and claiming proper responsibility is essential to restoration.

3. *Lead the fallen saint to repent.* Pray that the Holy Spirit will convict the person to feel remorse, regret, and grief. Repentance means a change of mind leading to a change

of conduct. Paul taught that our thinking must change first; then our actions will follow (Rom. 12:2).

4. *Lead the person to receive the message God wants to teach him.* Sometimes a person is stubborn and reluctant to learn. But failure is especially unprofitable when we refuse to be taught by the experience and change our ways. However, if we take the opportunity to learn from our mistakes, we will grow in our understanding about ourselves and about God.

5. *Lead the sinful believer to respond to God's chastisement with gratitude.* The one leading might point out two helpful verses: "Before I was afflicted I went astray, but now I keep Your word," and, "It is good for me that I was afflicted, that I may learn Your statutes" (Ps. 119:67, 71). Gently remind the person how wonderful it is that God loves us enough to chastise us and mend us.

The goal of all spiritual restoration is to help our sinning brothers and sisters "come to their senses and escape from the snare of the devil, having been held captive by him to do his will" (2 Tim. 2:26). What a joy is ours when we see God put a new heart and a new spirit in them, causing them to walk joyfully and willingly in His ways and to keep His commandments for their own good (Ezek. 36:26, 27)!

which you have profaned among the nations where you went.

23 "I will vindicate the holiness of My great name which has been profaned among the nations, which you have profaned in their midst. Then the nations will know that I am the LORD," declares the Lord GOD, "when I prove Myself holy among you in their sight.

24 "For I will take you from the nations, gather you from all the lands and bring you into your own land.

25 "Then I will sprinkle clean water on you, and you will be clean; I will cleanse you from all your filthiness and from all your idols.

26 "Moreover, I will give you a new heart and put a new spirit within you; and I will remove the heart of stone from your flesh and give you a heart of flesh.

27 "I will put My Spirit within you and cause you to walk in My statutes, and you will be careful to observe My ordinances.

28 "You will live in the land that I gave to your forefathers; so you will be My people, and I will be your God.

29 "Moreover, I will save you from all your uncleanness; and I will call for the grain and multiply it, and I will not bring a famine on you.

30 "I will multiply the fruit of the tree and the produce of the field, so that you will not receive again the disgrace of famine among the nations.

31 "Then you will remember your evil ways and your deeds that were not good, and you will loathe yourselves in your own sight for your iniquities and your abominations.

32 "I am not doing *this* for your sake," declares the Lord GOD, "let it be known to you. Be ashamed and confounded for your ways, O house of Israel!"

33 'Thus says the Lord GOD, "On the day that I cleanse you from all your iniquities, I will cause the cities to be inhabited, and the waste places will be rebuilt.

34 "The desolate land will be cultivated instead of being a desolation in the sight of everyone who passes by.

35 "They will say, 'This desolate land has become like the garden of Eden; and the waste, desolate and ruined cities are fortified *and* inhabited.'

36 "Then the nations that are left round about you will know that I, the LORD, have rebuilt the ruined places *and* planted that which was desolate; I, the LORD, have spoken and will do it."

37 'Thus says the Lord GOD, "This also I will let the house of Israel ask Me to do for them: I will increase their men like a flock.

38 "Like the flock for sacrifices, like the flock at Jerusalem during her appointed feasts, so will the waste cities be filled with flocks of men. Then they will know that I am the LORD."'"

Psalm 131:1–3

A Song of Ascents, of David.

131 O LORD, my heart is not proud, nor my eyes haughty;

LIFE LESSONS

➤ **Ezekiel 36:21 —** *"I had concern for My holy name, which the house of Israel had profaned among the nations."*

*O*ur behavior not only reflects how much or little we love God (John 14:15; 1 John 5:3), but it also either attracts or repels those who do not yet know Him. Our relationships with the Lord should draw others to Him.

➤ **Ezekiel 36:26 —** *"I will give you a new heart and put a new spirit within you."*

*G*od does not want remodeled hearts, but brand new ones. He doesn't want a reform in character, but a new spirit that loves to do His will. He wants transformation, not mere accommodation. This is why Christ came—to completely change our lives (Rom. 12:1, 2; 2 Cor. 5:17).

➤ **Psalm 131:1 —** *O LORD, my heart is not proud, nor my eyes haughty.*

*I*t takes humility to admit that some things are bigger than we are or just plain beyond us. Even the great David called himself a "flea" and a "dead dog" (1 Sam. 24:14). And we are told, "Moses was very humble, more than any man who was on the face of the earth" (Num. 12:3). Thus we see that it is true that "a humble spirit will obtain honor" (Prov. 29:23).

Nor do I involve myself in great
matters,
Or in things too difficult for me.
2 Surely I have composed and quieted
my soul;
Like a weaned child *rests* against
his mother,
My soul is like a weaned child within
me.
3 O Israel, hope in the LORD
From this time forth and forever.

Proverbs 29:2, 3

2 When the righteous increase, the
people rejoice,
But when a wicked man rules,
people groan.
3 A man who loves wisdom makes his
father glad,
But he who keeps company with
harlots wastes *his* wealth.

James 3:1–18

3 LET not many *of you* become teachers, my brethren, knowing that as
such we will incur a stricter judgment.
2 For we all stumble in many *ways*.
If anyone does not stumble in what he
says, he is a perfect man, able to bridle
the whole body as well.
3 Now if we put the bits into the
horses' mouths so that they will obey us,
we direct their entire body as well.
4 Look at the ships also, though they
are so great and are driven by strong
winds, are still directed by a very small
rudder wherever the inclination of the
pilot desires.
5 So also the tongue is a small part
of the body, and *yet* it boasts of great
things.
See how great a forest is set aflame
by such a small fire!
6 And the tongue is a fire, the *very*
world of iniquity; the tongue is set among
our members as that which defiles the
entire body, and sets on fire the course
of *our* life, and is set on fire by hell.
7 For every species of beasts and
birds, of reptiles and creatures of the
sea, is tamed and has been tamed by the
human race.
8 But no one can tame the tongue;
it is a restless evil *and* full of deadly
poison.
9 With it we bless *our* Lord and Father, and with it we curse men, who have
been made in the likeness of God;
10 from the same mouth come *both*
blessing and cursing. My brethren, these
things ought not to be this way.
11 Does a fountain send out from the
same opening *both* fresh and bitter
water?
12 Can a fig tree, my brethren, produce
olives, or a vine produce figs? Nor *can*
salt water produce fresh.
13 Who among you is wise and understanding? Let him show by his good

LIFE LESSONS

➤ **James 3:2 — *We all stumble in many ways.***

N o one is perfect (Phil. 3:12). Not one
of us does everything right. And
certainly no one is so wise that he always
speaks the right words or always does
the right thing. Remembering this keeps
us humble.

➤ **James 3:5 — *The tongue is a small part of the body, and yet it boasts of great things.***

A person may do seemingly selfless, good works, and yet their
words betray the true intentions of
their hearts—pride, lust, and dishonesty.
The tongue and the spoken word are
powerful and can set the course of your
life. Though you try to suppress the sinfulness and hide the selfish ambitions
within, these often are revealed by what
you say. This is why you need Jesus to
sanctify—or transform—you from the
inside out.

➤ **James 3:17 — *The wisdom from above is first pure, then peaceable.***

G od's wisdom leads to harmony and
peace, while human reasoning leads
to arrogance and dissension. Which of
these characterizes your life? You can
answer this question by evaluating your
relationships. When you fail to seek the
Lord, it shows.

behavior his deeds in the gentleness of wisdom.

14 But if you have bitter jealousy and selfish ambition in your heart, do not be arrogant and *so* lie against the truth.

15 This wisdom is not that which comes down from above, but is earthly, natural, demonic.

16 For where jealousy and selfish ambi-

tion exist, there is disorder and every evil thing.

17 But the wisdom from above is first pure, then peaceable, gentle, reasonable, full of mercy and good fruits, unwavering, without hypocrisy.

18 And the seed whose fruit is righteousness is sown in peace by those who make peace.

Ezekiel 37:1—38:23

37 THE hand of the LORD was upon me, and He brought me out by the Spirit of the LORD and set me down in the middle of the valley; and it was full of bones.

2 He caused me to pass among them round about, and behold, *there were* very many on the surface of the valley; and lo, *they were* very dry.

3 He said to me, "Son of man, can these bones live?" And I answered, "O Lord GOD, You know."

4 Again He said to me, "Prophesy over these bones and say to them, 'O dry bones, hear the word of the LORD.'

5 "Thus says the Lord GOD to these bones, 'Behold, I will cause breath to enter you that you may come to life.

6 'I will put sinews on you, make flesh grow back on you, cover you with skin and put breath in you that you may come

alive; and you will know that I am the LORD.'"

7 So I prophesied as I was commanded; and as I prophesied, there was a noise, and behold, a rattling; and the bones came together, bone to its bone.

8 And I looked, and behold, sinews were on them, and flesh grew and skin covered them; but there was no breath in them.

9 Then He said to me, "Prophesy to the breath, prophesy, son of man, and say to the breath, 'Thus says the Lord GOD, "Come from the four winds, O breath, and breathe on these slain, that they come to life."'"

10 So I prophesied as He commanded me, and the breath came into them, and they came to life and stood on their feet, an exceedingly great army.

11 Then He said to me, "Son of man, these bones are the whole house of Israel; behold, they say, 'Our bones are dried up and our hope has perished. We are completely cut off.'

12 "Therefore prophesy and say to them, 'Thus says the Lord GOD, "Behold, I will open your graves and cause you to come up out of your graves, My people; and I will bring you into the land of Israel.

13 "Then you will know that I am the LORD, when I have opened your graves and caused you to come up out of your graves, My people.

14 "I will put My Spirit within you and you will come to life, and I will place you on your own land. Then you will know that I, the LORD, have spoken and done it," declares the LORD.'"

15 The word of the LORD came again to me saying,

16 "And you, son of man, take for your-

LIFE LESSONS

➤ **Ezekiel 37:6 — "I will . . . put breath in you that you may come alive; and you will know that I am the LORD."**

*T*his passage looked forward to a day when God would gather the remnant of His people to Israel again, which happened during the reign of Persian king Cyrus (2 Chr. 36:22, 23; Ezra 1:1–3). However, it was not until 1948 that Israel was reestablished as a nation and was acknowledged to have a right to the Promised Land. God breathed new life into them in such a way that the entire world was compelled to recognize their existence.

Life Examples:

EZEKIEL: Watching Dead Bones Come Alive

EZEKIEL 37:14

In his day, hope had become a rare commodity. A captive in the land of Babylon, Ezekiel must have felt as desolate and useless as the piles of bones that he had seen in the startling vision God had given him (Ezek. 37:1–10). He knew that only a miracle could bring the decimated and scattered people of Judah back together again in the Promised Land.

Yet as Ezekiel sat in the valley and watched the Lord's mighty work, a miracle unfolded before him. Where before only dry bones had littered the landscape, the Lord added muscles, tendons, and tissue. And into those restored, silent bodies, God breathed new life. It was a testimony that He would do the same for Judah—He would take the spiritually dead, dispersed nation, and, by His might, bring it back to life.

Maybe you feel dry, defeated, and emotionally scattered. Perhaps your valley of dry bones is a great loss, a failed relationship, an illness that consumes you, or a circumstance, which is absolutely beyond your control and requires a miracle. But do not despair! The same God who breathed life into the old, dry bones, sustains you today, and He is able to infuse you with new purpose and hope. Just as He provided the victory to Ezekiel and Judah, God is near to you and can make you triumphant. Just one breath from Him and your life will never be the same.

---

self one stick and write on it, 'For Judah and for the sons of Israel, his companions'; then take another stick and write on it, 'For Joseph, the stick of Ephraim and all the house of Israel, his companions.'
17 "Then join them for yourself one to another into one stick, that they may become one in your hand.
18 "When the sons of your people speak to you saying, 'Will you not declare to us what you mean by these?'
19 say to them, 'Thus says the Lord GOD, "Behold, I will take the stick of Joseph, which is in the hand of Ephraim, and the tribes of Israel, his companions; and I will put them with it, with the stick of Judah, and make them one stick, and they will be one in My hand."'
20 "The sticks on which you write will be in your hand before their eyes.
21 "Say to them, 'Thus says the Lord GOD, "Behold, I will take the sons of Israel from among the nations where they have gone, and I will gather them from every side and bring them into their own land;
22 and I will make them one nation in the land, on the mountains of Israel; and one king will be king for all of them; and they will no longer be two nations and no longer be divided into two kingdoms.
23 "They will no longer defile themselves with their idols, or with their detestable things, or with any of their transgressions; but I will deliver them from all their dwelling places in which they have sinned, and will cleanse them.

And they will be My people, and I will be their God.
24 "My servant David will be king over them, and they will all have one shepherd; and they will walk in My ordinances and keep My statutes and observe them.
25 "They will live on the land that I gave to Jacob My servant, in which your fathers lived; and they will live on it, they, and their sons and their sons' sons, forever; and David My servant will be their prince forever.
26 "I will make a covenant of peace with them; it will be an everlasting covenant with them. And I will place them and multiply them, and will set My sanctuary in their midst forever.
27 "My dwelling place also will be with them; and I will be their God, and they will be My people.
28 "And the nations will know that I am the LORD who sanctifies Israel, when My sanctuary is in their midst forever."'"

38 AND the word of the LORD came to me saying,
2 "Son of man, set your face toward Gog of the land of Magog, the prince of Rosh, Meshech and Tubal, and prophesy against him
3 and say, 'Thus says the Lord GOD, "Behold, I am against you, O Gog, prince of Rosh, Meshech and Tubal.
4 "I will turn you about and put hooks into your jaws, and I will bring you out, and all your army, horses and horsemen,

all of them splendidly attired, a great company *with* buckler and shield, all of them wielding swords;

5 Persia, Ethiopia and Put with them, all of them *with* shield and helmet;

6 Gomer with all its troops; Beth-togarmah *from* the remote parts of the north with all its troops—many peoples with you.

7 "Be prepared, and prepare yourself, you and all your companies that are assembled about you, and be a guard for them.

8 "After many days you will be summoned; in the latter years you will come into the land that is restored from the sword, *whose inhabitants* have been gathered from many nations to the mountains of Israel which had been a continual waste; but its people were brought out from the nations, and they are living securely, all of them.

9 "You will go up, you will come like a storm; you will be like a cloud covering the land, you and all your troops, and many peoples with you."

10 'Thus says the Lord GOD, "It will come about on that day, that thoughts will come into your mind and you will devise an evil plan,

11 and you will say, 'I will go up against the land of unwalled villages. I will go against those who are at rest, that live securely, all of them living without walls and having no bars or gates,

12 to capture spoil and to seize plunder, to turn your hand against the waste places which are *now* inhabited, and against the people who are gathered from the nations, who have acquired cattle and goods, who live at the center of the world.'

13 "Sheba and Dedan and the merchants of Tarshish with all its villages will say to you, 'Have you come to capture spoil? Have you assembled your company to seize plunder, to carry away silver and gold, to take away cattle and goods, to capture great spoil?'"

14 "Therefore prophesy, son of man, and say to Gog, 'Thus says the Lord GOD, "On that day when My people Israel are living securely, will you not know *it?*

15 "You will come from your place out of the remote parts of the north, you and many peoples with you, all of them rid-

ing on horses, a great assembly and a mighty army;

16 and you will come up against My ◄ people Israel like a cloud to cover the land. It shall come about in the last days that I will bring you against My land, so that the nations may know Me when I am sanctified through you before their eyes, O Gog."

17 'Thus says the Lord GOD, "Are you the one of whom I spoke in former days through My servants the prophets of Israel, who prophesied in those days for *many* years that I would bring you against them?

18 "It will come about on that day, when Gog comes against the land of Israel," declares the Lord GOD, "that My fury will mount up in My anger.

19 "In My zeal and in My blazing wrath I declare *that* on that day there will surely be a great earthquake in the land of Israel.

20 "The fish of the sea, the birds of the heavens, the beasts of the field, all the creeping things that creep on the earth, and all the men who are on the face of the earth will shake at My presence; the mountains also will be thrown down, the steep pathways will collapse and every wall will fall to the ground.

21 "I will call for a sword against him on all My mountains," declares the Lord GOD. "Every man's sword will be against his brother.

22 "With pestilence and with blood I will enter into judgment with him; and I will rain on him and on his troops, and on the many peoples who are with him, a torrential rain, with hailstones, fire and brimstone.

23 "I will magnify Myself, sanctify My- ◄ self, and make Myself known in the sight

---

LIFE LESSONS

➤ **Ezekiel 38:16** — *"I will bring you against My land, so that the nations may know Me when I am sanctified through you before their eyes, O Gog."*

*J*ust as God used stubborn Pharaoh to gain glory for Himself in the eyes of the watching nations (Josh. 2:10; 9:9), so will He use Gog one day to again gain glory for Himself on the world stage.

➤ **Ezekiel 38:23 —** *"I will . . . make Myself known in the sight of many nations."*

*D*uring the time of judgment, God will show the entire earth His power and might. No army, nation, or coalition will be able to stand against Him. By striking Israel's enemies with terrible calamities, all the nations will know that He is the Lord (Zech. 14:1–9).

of many nations; and they will know that I am the LORD."'

Psalm 132:1–9

A Song of Ascents.

132 REMEMBER, O LORD, on David's behalf,
All his affliction;
2 How he swore to the LORD
And vowed to the Mighty One of Jacob,
3 "Surely I will not enter my house,
Nor lie on my bed;
4 I will not give sleep to my eyes
Or slumber to my eyelids,
5 Until I find a place for the LORD,
A dwelling place for the Mighty One of Jacob."
6 Behold, we heard of it in Ephrathah,
We found it in the field of Jaar.
7 Let us go into His dwelling place;
Let us worship at His footstool.
8 Arise, O LORD, to Your resting place,
You and the ark of Your strength.
9 Let Your priests be clothed with righteousness,
And let Your godly ones sing for joy.

Proverbs 29:4

4 The king gives stability to the land by justice,
But a man who takes bribes overthrows it.

James 4:1–17

4 WHAT is the source of quarrels and conflicts among you? Is not the source your pleasures that wage war in your members?
2 You lust and do not have; so you commit murder. You are envious and cannot obtain; so you fight and quarrel. You do not have because you do not ask.
3 You ask and do not receive, because you ask with wrong motives, so that you may spend *it* on your pleasures.
4 You adulteresses, do you not know that friendship with the world is hostility toward God? Therefore whoever wishes to be a friend of the world makes himself an enemy of God.
5 Or do you think that the Scripture speaks to no purpose: "He jealously desires the Spirit which He has made to dwell in us"?
6 But He gives a greater grace. Therefore *it* says, "GOD IS OPPOSED TO THE PROUD, BUT GIVES GRACE TO THE HUMBLE."
7 Submit therefore to God. Resist the devil and he will flee from you.
8 Draw near to God and He will draw near to you. Cleanse your hands, you sinners; and purify your hearts, you doubleminded.
9 Be miserable and mourn and weep; let your laughter be turned into mourning and your joy to gloom.
10 Humble yourselves in the presence of the Lord, and He will exalt you.
11 Do not speak against one another,

➤ **James 4:2 —** *You do not have because you do not ask.*

*W*hen we try to reach our goals in our own strength, we often find ourselves at odds with God and others. This is the result of pride in our lives and is why we do not ask God to help us—we want to achieve it all on our own. We also realize that if we ask Him to give us what we want, He may say no because it is not His best for us; and that, we feel, is unacceptable. Remember, whatever we acquire outside of His will eventually turns to ashes.

brethren. He who speaks against a brother or judges his brother, speaks against the law and judges the law; but if you judge the law, you are not a doer of the law but a judge *of it.*

12 There is *only* one Lawgiver and Judge, the One who is able to save and to destroy; but who are you who judge your neighbor?

13 Come now, you who say, "Today or tomorrow we will go to such and such a city, and spend a year there and engage in business and make a profit."

14 Yet you do not know what your life will be like tomorrow. You are *just* a vapor that appears for a little while and then vanishes away.

15 Instead, *you ought* to say, "If the Lord wills, we will live and also do this or that."

16 But as it is, you boast in your arrogance; all such boasting is evil.

➤ 17 Therefore, to one who knows *the* right thing to do and does not do it, to him it is sin.

LIFE LESSONS

➤ **James 4:10 — *Humble yourselves in the presence of the Lord, and He will exalt you.***

*T*his is another way of saying, as God spoke through Samuel the prophet, "Those who honor Me I will honor, and those who despise Me will be lightly esteemed" (1 Sam. 2:30). When we submit ourselves fully to the Lord, He works through us to achieve His will. It is then that His glory shines through us, and we are able to achieve things that would never be possible through our own wisdom and strength.

➤ **James 4:17 — *Therefore, to one who knows the right thing to do and does not do it, to him it is sin.***

*W*hen God puts a burden on our hearts for someone, we dare not shove the inclination to the back of our minds. If we do such a wicked thing, John asks, "how does the love of God abide in" us (1 John 3:17)?

Ezekiel 39:1—40:49

39 "AND you, son of man, prophesy against Gog and say, 'Thus says the Lord God, "Behold, I am against you, O Gog, prince of Rosh, Meshech and Tubal;

2 and I will turn you around, drive you on, take you up from the remotest parts of the north and bring you against the mountains of Israel.

3 "I will strike your bow from your left hand and dash down your arrows from your right hand.

4 "You will fall on the mountains of Israel, you and all your troops and the peoples who are with you; I will give you as food to every kind of predatory bird and beast of the field.

5 "You will fall on the open field; for it is I who have spoken," declares the Lord God.

6 "And I will send fire upon Magog and those who inhabit the coastlands in safety; and they will know that I am the Lord.

7 "My holy name I will make known in the midst of My people Israel; and I will not let My holy name be profaned anymore. And the nations will know that I am the Lord, the Holy One in Israel.

8 "Behold, it is coming and it shall be done," declares the Lord God. "That is the day of which I have spoken.

9 "Then those who inhabit the cities of Israel will go out and make fires with the weapons and burn *them,* both shields and bucklers, bows and arrows, war clubs and spears, and for seven years they will make fires of them.

10 "They will not take wood from the field or gather firewood from the forests, for they will make fires with the weapons; and they will take the spoil of those who despoiled them and seize the plunder of those who plundered them," declares the Lord God.

11 "On that day I will give Gog a burial ground there in Israel, the valley of those

who pass by east of the sea, and it will block off those who would pass by. So they will bury Gog there with all his horde, and they will call it the valley of Hamon-gog.

12 "For seven months the house of Israel will be burying them in order to cleanse the land.

13 "Even all the people of the land will bury them; and it will be to their renown on the day that I glorify Myself," declares the Lord GOD.

14 "They will set apart men who will constantly pass through the land, burying those who were passing through, even those who left on the surface of the ground, in order to cleanse it. At the end of seven months they will make a search.

15 "As those who pass through the land pass through and anyone sees a man's bone, then he will set up a marker by it until the buriers have buried it in the valley of Hamon-gog.

16 "And even the name of the city will be Hamonah. So they will cleanse the land."'

17 "As for you, son of man, thus says the Lord GOD, 'Speak to every kind of bird and to every beast of the field, "Assemble and come, gather from every side to My sacrifice which I am going to sacrifice for you, as a great sacrifice on the mountains of Israel, that you may eat flesh and drink blood.

18 "You will eat the flesh of mighty men and drink the blood of the princes of the earth, as though they were rams, lambs, goats and bulls, all of them fatlings of Bashan.

19 "So you will eat fat until you are glutted, and drink blood until you are drunk, from My sacrifice which I have sacrificed for you.

20 "You will be glutted at My table with horses and charioteers, with mighty men and all the men of war," declares the Lord GOD.

21 "And I will set My glory among the nations; and all the nations will see My judgment which I have executed and My hand which I have laid on them.

➤ 22 "And the house of Israel will know that I am the LORD their God from that day onward.

23 "The nations will know that the house of Israel went into exile for their iniquity because they acted treacherously against

Me, and I hid My face from them; so I gave them into the hand of their adversaries, and all of them fell by the sword.

24 "According to their uncleanness and according to their transgressions I dealt with them, and I hid My face from them."'"

25 Therefore thus says the Lord GOD, "Now I will restore the fortunes of Jacob and have mercy on the whole house of Israel; and I will be jealous for My holy name.

26 "They will forget their disgrace and all their treachery which they perpetrated against Me, when they live securely on their own land with no one to make them afraid.

27 "When I bring them back from the peoples and gather them from the lands of their enemies, then I shall be sanctified through them in the sight of the many nations. ✳

28 "Then they will know that I am the LORD their God because I made them go into exile among the nations, and then gathered them again to their own land; and I will leave none of them there any longer.

29 "I will not hide My face from them any longer, for I will have poured out My Spirit on the house of Israel," declares the Lord GOD.

40 IN the twenty-fifth year of our exile, at the beginning of the year, on the tenth of the month, in the fourteenth year after the city was taken, on that same day the hand of the LORD was upon me and He brought me there.

2 In the visions of God He brought me into the land of Israel and set me on a very high mountain, and on it to the south there was a structure like a city.

3 So He brought me there; and behold, there was a man whose appearance was

---

LIFE LESSONS

➤ **Ezekiel 39:22** — *"The house of Israel will know that I am the LORD their God from that day onward."*

We do not know why God waits to do some of the good things He has promised to do, but we can have total confidence that He will bring all of them about in His perfect time. He calls us to wait and to trust.

like the appearance of bronze, with a line of flax and a measuring rod in his hand; and he was standing in the gateway.

4 The man said to me, "Son of man, see with your eyes, hear with your ears, and give attention to all that I am going to show you; for you have been brought here in order to show *it* to you. Declare to the house of Israel all that you see."

5 And behold, there was a wall on the outside of the temple all around, and in the man's hand was a measuring rod of six cubits, *each of which was* a cubit and a handbreadth. So he measured the thickness of the wall, one rod; and the height, one rod.

6 Then he went to the gate which faced east, went up its steps and measured the threshold of the gate, one rod in width; and the other threshold *was* one rod in width.

7 The guardroom *was* one rod long and one rod wide; and *there were* five cubits between the guardrooms. And the threshold of the gate by the porch of the gate facing inward *was* one rod.

8 Then he measured the porch of the gate facing inward, one rod.

9 He measured the porch of the gate, eight cubits; and its side pillars, two cubits. And the porch of the gate was faced inward.

10 The guardrooms of the gate toward the east *numbered* three on each side; the three of them had the same measurement. The side pillars also had the same measurement on each side.

11 And he measured the width of the gateway, ten cubits, and the length of the gate, thirteen cubits.

12 *There was* a barrier *wall* one cubit *wide* in front of the guardrooms on each side; and the guardrooms *were* six cubits *square* on each side.

13 He measured the gate from the roof of the one guardroom to the roof of the other, a width of twenty-five cubits from *one* door to *the* door opposite.

14 He made the side pillars sixty cubits *high;* the gate *extended* round about to the side pillar of the courtyard.

15 *From* the front of the entrance gate to the front of the inner porch of the gate *was* fifty cubits.

16 *There were* shuttered windows *looking* toward the guardrooms, and toward their side pillars within the gate all around, and likewise for the porches. And *there were* windows all around inside; and on *each* side pillar *were* palm tree ornaments.

17 Then he brought me into the outer court, and behold, *there were* chambers and a pavement made for the court all around; thirty chambers faced the pavement.

18 The pavement (*that is,* the lower pavement) *was* by the side of the gates, corresponding to the length of the gates.

19 Then he measured the width from the front of the lower gate to the front of the exterior of the inner court, a hundred cubits on the east and on the north.

20 *As for* the gate of the outer court which faced the north, he measured its length and its width.

21 It had three guardrooms on each side; and its side pillars and its porches had the same measurement as the first gate. Its length *was* fifty cubits and the width twenty-five cubits.

22 Its windows and its porches and its palm tree ornaments *had* the same measurements as the gate which faced toward the east; and it was reached by seven steps, and its porch *was* in front of them.

23 The inner court had a gate opposite the gate on the north as well as *the gate* on the east; and he measured a hundred cubits from gate to gate.

24 Then he led me toward the south, and behold, there was a gate toward the south; and he measured its side pillars and its porches according to those same measurements.

25 The gate and its porches had windows all around like those other windows; the length *was* fifty cubits and the width twenty-five cubits.

26 *There were* seven steps going up to it, and its porches *were* in front of them; and it had palm tree ornaments on its side pillars, one on each side.

27 The inner court had a gate toward the south; and he measured from gate to gate toward the south, a hundred cubits.

28 Then he brought me to the inner court by the south gate; and he measured the south gate according to those same measurements.

29 Its guardrooms also, its side pillars and its porches *were* according to those same measurements. And the gate and

its porches had windows all around; it *was* fifty cubits long and twenty-five cubits wide.

30 *There were* porches all around, twenty-five cubits long and five cubits wide.

31 Its porches *were* toward the outer court; and palm tree ornaments *were* on its side pillars, and its stairway *had* eight steps.

32 He brought me into the inner court toward the east. And he measured the gate according to those same measurements.

33 Its guardrooms also, its side pillars and its porches *were* according to those same measurements. And the gate and its porches had windows all around; it *was* fifty cubits long and twenty-five cubits wide.

34 Its porches *were* toward the outer court; and palm tree ornaments *were* on its side pillars, on each side, and its stairway *had* eight steps.

35 Then he brought me to the north gate; and he measured *it* according to those same measurements,

36 *with* its guardrooms, its side pillars and its porches. And the gate had windows all around; the length *was* fifty cubits and the width twenty-five cubits.

37 Its side pillars *were* toward the outer court; and palm tree ornaments *were* on its side pillars on each side, and its stairway had eight steps.

38 A chamber with its doorway was by the side pillars at the gates; there they rinse the burnt offering.

39 In the porch of the gate *were* two tables on each side, on which to slaughter the burnt offering, the sin offering and the guilt offering.

40 On the outer side, as one went up to the gateway toward the north, *were* two tables; and on the other side of the porch of the gate *were* two tables.

41 Four tables *were* on each side next to the gate; *or*, eight tables on which they slaughter *sacrifices*.

42 For the burnt offering *there were* four tables of hewn stone, a cubit and a half long, a cubit and a half wide and one cubit high, on which they lay the instruments with which they slaughter the burnt offering and the sacrifice.

43 The double hooks, one handbreadth in length, were installed in the house all around; and on the tables *was* the flesh of the offering.

44 From the outside to the inner gate were chambers for the singers in the inner court, *one of* which was at the side of the north gate, with its front toward the south, and one at the side of the south gate facing toward the north.

45 He said to me, "This is the chamber which faces toward the south, *intended* for the priests who keep charge of the temple;

46 but the chamber which faces toward the north is for the priests who keep charge of the altar. These are the sons of Zadok, who from the sons of Levi come near to the LORD to minister to Him."

47 He measured the court, a *perfect* square, a hundred cubits long and a hundred cubits wide; and the altar was in front of the temple.

48 Then he brought me to the porch of the temple and measured *each* side pillar of the porch, five cubits on each side; and the width of the gate was three cubits on each side.

49 The length of the porch *was* twenty cubits and the width eleven cubits; and at the stairway by which it was ascended *were* columns belonging to the side pillars, one on each side.

Psalm 132:10–18

10 For the sake of David Your servant,
   Do not turn away the face of Your
   anointed.

11 The LORD has sworn to David
   A truth from which He will not turn
   back:
   "Of the fruit of your body I will set
   upon your throne.

12 "If your sons will keep My covenant
   And My testimony which I will
   teach them,
   Their sons also shall sit upon your
   throne forever."

13 For the LORD has chosen Zion;
   He has desired it for His
   habitation.

14 "This is My resting place forever;
   Here I will dwell, for I have desired
   it.

15 "I will abundantly bless her
   provision;

I will satisfy her needy with
bread.
16 "Her priests also I will clothe with
salvation,
And her godly ones will sing aloud
for joy.
17 "There I will cause the horn of David
to spring forth;
I have prepared a lamp for Mine
anointed.
18 "His enemies I will clothe with
shame,
But upon himself his crown shall
shine."

Proverbs 29:5

5   A man who flatters his neighbor
Is spreading a net for his steps.

James 5:1–20

5 COME now, you rich, weep and howl
for your miseries which are coming
upon you.
2   Your riches have rotted and your
garments have become moth-eaten.
3   Your gold and your silver have
rusted; and their rust will be a witness
against you and will consume your flesh
like fire. It is in the last days that you
have stored up your treasure!
4   Behold, the pay of the laborers who
mowed your fields, *and* which has been
withheld by you, cries out *against you;*
and the outcry of those who did the harvesting has reached the ears of the Lord
of Sabaoth.
5   You have lived luxuriously on the
earth and led a life of wanton pleasure;
you have fattened your hearts in a day of
slaughter.
6   You have condemned and put to
death the righteous *man;* he does not
resist you.
➤ 7   Therefore be patient, brethren, until
the coming of the Lord. The farmer waits
for the precious produce of the soil,
being patient about it, until it gets the
early and late rains.
8   You too be patient; strengthen your
hearts, for the coming of the Lord is
near.

9   Do not complain, brethren, against
one another, so that you yourselves may
not be judged; behold, the Judge is standing right at the door.
10   As an example, brethren, of suffering and patience, take the prophets who
spoke in the name of the Lord.
11   We count those blessed who en- ≺
dured. You have heard of the endurance
of Job and have seen the outcome of the
Lord's dealings, that the Lord is full of
compassion and *is* merciful.
12   But above all, my brethren, do not
swear, either by heaven or by earth or
with any other oath; but your yes is to be
yes, and your no, no, so that you may not
fall under judgment.
13   Is anyone among you suffering?
Then he must pray. Is anyone cheerful?
He is to sing praises.
14   Is anyone among you sick? *Then* he
must call for the elders of the church and
they are to pray over him, anointing him
with oil in the name of the Lord;
15   and the prayer offered in faith will
restore the one who is sick, and the Lord ✳
will raise him up, and if he has committed sins, they will be forgiven him.
16   Therefore, confess your sins to one ≺
another, and pray for one another so
that you may be healed. The effective
prayer of a righteous man can accomplish much.
17   Elijah was a man with a nature like
ours, and he prayed earnestly that it

LIFE LESSONS

➤ **James 5:7 — *Be patient, brethren,
until the coming of the Lord.***

*W*e do not know when the Lord will
return to reward His faithful people and to set right the world, but we
know that He will. His promise gives us
hope—but we must remain patient until
He fulfills it.

➤ **James 5:11 — *You have heard of the
endurance of Job and have seen the outcome of the Lord's dealings, that the Lord
is full of compassion and is merciful.***

*J*ob had to go through some very
dark, excruciating days, but God
never abandoned Him. It always helps to
remember the Lord's unchanging compassion and mercy when we suffer.

LIFE PRINCIPLE 29

WE LEARN MORE IN OUR VALLEY EXPERIENCES
THAN ON OUR MOUNTAINTOPS.

JAMES 5:10

*A*dversity, anguish, trials, tribulations, and heartaches operate as lessons in the school of experience. They bring us to a place of new insight and understanding. They can alter our perception of the world, our view of God, and lead us to change our behavior. The Lord, of course, is the ultimate Teacher. He is the One to whom we must look for the meaning of any lesson related to adversity.

God allows adversity for at least three reasons:

1. God uses adversity to get our attention.

The Lord uses a wide variety of methods to gain our attention when necessary—adversity is one of them. One of the best responses I know to adversity that strikes us suddenly (and yet obviously) with a God-intended message is to turn to Psalm 25 and make it our personal prayer:

To You, O LORD, I lift up my soul. O my God, in You I trust, do not let me be ashamed; do not let my enemies exult over me. Indeed, none of those who wait for You will be ashamed; those who deal treacherously without cause will be ashamed. Make me know Your ways, O LORD; teach me Your paths. Lead me in Your truth and teach me, for You are the God of my salvation; for You I wait all the day. Remember, O LORD, Your compassion and Your lovingkindnesses, for they have been from of old. Do not remember the sins of my youth or my transgressions; according to Your lovingkindness remember me, for Your goodness' sake, O LORD. (vv. 1–7)

Don't delay in responding to the Lord when He moves to get your attention. Respond quickly and humbly. Hear what He has to say to you.

2. Adversity leads to examination.

At times, God allows adversity to motivate us to self-examination. The winds of adversity blow away the surface issues and force us to cope with things on a deeper level. Nothing has the ability to drive us closer to God than tribulation. It removes the cloak of denial and reveals who we really are, as well as what we believe about God, His deity, and faithfulness.

We need to examine both our faith and our levels of discipline. Are we committed to standing firm in our trust in Christ, or are we blown off course by every ill wind that blows our way? Paul encouraged the Corinthians, "But a man must examine himself" (1 Cor. 11:28). In other words, "Take a straight

forward look inside and discover what is driving you, motivating you, and enticing you." If it is anything but God, then it is not right. He needs to be your motivating factor at every turn in life.

Those who have accepted Christ as Savior are the temples of the Holy Spirit, and He wants us to be clean and usable vessels. We have no reason to allow the rubbish of the world or our past failures to remain in the forefront of our lives. The Lord desires that we free ourselves of anything that might keep us in inner bondage, whether mentally, emotionally, psychologically, or spiritually. When we become complacent and accept the hurts of the past as a part of who we are, we have accepted the wrong view, the wrong definition, and the wrong game plan. We are new creations in Christ. There is never a point where we are separated from Him. He has sealed us with His Spirit. The old is gone; the new has come. And that newness of life is the very thing that gives us hope in hopeless times.

3. The effective lesson leads to change in behavior.

When we act like Christ, our true identity emerges. Teachers often prepare behavioral objectives for their classroom lectures. These objectives list in concrete and measurable form the behaviors that the teacher desires for a student to display as proof that the student has learned the lesson. The lessons that the Lord teaches us through adversity are ultimately for that very purpose: a change in behavior, including a change in the belief that prompted the behavior.

It isn't enough that God desires to get our attention or that we take time to look truthfully at our lives. We must allow His Spirit to have free access to every area. We learn to watch, listen, and look for His guidance and direction. We can see a problem or feel a flush of anger and think: How should I respond? We may make the wrong choice, say the wrong word, or ignore what we know He is telling us to do. Unless we change our response and behavior, we will never benefit from adversity or grow as a result of it. God provides a challenge, and we have an opportunity to obey or disobey Him. The choice is ours, and the consequences that come belong to us, as well.

Jesus came to bear the burdens that plague our lives. He will help us carry our burdens to the cross and deal with them there, once and for all. He always has our best interests in mind. He alone knows that pain paves the path to complete spiritual healing and restoration.

If you are willing to allow God to surface the inner rubbish of your life, and if you are willing to change what needs to be changed, you will emerge from adversity closer to Christ, more mature as His child, and with far greater potential to reflect the love of God to the world around you. ◈

would not rain, and it did not rain on the earth for three years and six months.

18 Then he prayed again, and the sky poured rain and the earth produced its fruit.

19 My brethren, if any among you strays from the truth and one turns him back,

20 let him know that he who turns a sinner from the error of his way will save his soul from death and will cover a multitude of sins.

LIFE LESSONS

➤ **James 5:16 — *Confess your sins to one another, and pray for one another so that you may be healed.***

*N*o Christian has ever been called to "go it alone" in his or her walk of faith. We cannot obey God without being in regular, close fellowship with other believers. He has designed us so that many of our needs can only be met through mutual interdependence.

Ezekiel 41:1—42:20

41 THEN he brought me to the nave and measured the side pillars; six cubits wide on each side *was* the width of the side pillar.

2 The width of the entrance *was* ten cubits and the sides of the entrance *were* five cubits on each side. And he measured the length of the nave, forty cubits, and the width, twenty cubits.

3 Then he went inside and measured each side pillar of the doorway, two cubits, and the doorway, six cubits *high;* and the width of the doorway, seven cubits.

4 He measured its length, twenty cubits, and the width, twenty cubits, before the nave; and he said to me, "This is the most holy *place.*"

5 Then he measured the wall of the temple, six cubits; and the width of the side chambers, four cubits, all around about the house on every side.

6 The side chambers were in three stories, one above another, and thirty in each story; and the side chambers extended to the wall which *stood* on their inward side all around, that they might be fastened, and not be fastened into the wall of the temple *itself.*

7 The side chambers surrounding the temple were wider at each successive story. Because the structure surrounding the temple went upward by stages on all sides of the temple, therefore the width of the temple *increased* as it went higher;

and thus one went up from the lowest *story* to the highest by way of the second *story.*

8 I saw also that the house had a raised platform all around; the foundations of the side chambers were a full rod of six long cubits *in height.*

9 The thickness of the outer wall of the side chambers *was* five cubits. But the free space between the side chambers belonging to the temple

10 and the *outer* chambers *was* twenty cubits in width all around the temple on every side.

11 The doorways of the side chambers toward the free space *consisted of* one doorway toward the north and another doorway toward the south; and the width of the free space *was* five cubits all around.

12 The building that *was* in front of the separate area at the side toward the west *was* seventy cubits wide; and the wall of the building *was* five cubits thick all around, and its length *was* ninety cubits.

13 Then he measured the temple, a hundred cubits long; the separate area with the building and its walls *were* also a hundred cubits long.

14 Also the width of the front of the temple and *that of* the separate areas along the east *side totaled* a hundred cubits.

15 He measured the length of the building along the front of the separate area behind it, with a gallery on each side, a hundred cubits; *he* also *measured* the inner nave and the porches of the court.

16 The thresholds, the latticed windows

and the galleries round about their three stories, opposite the threshold, were paneled with wood all around, and *from* the ground to the windows (but the windows were covered),

17 over the entrance, and to the inner house, and on the outside, and on all the wall all around inside and outside, by measurement.

18 It was carved with cherubim and palm trees; and a palm tree was between cherub and cherub, and every cherub had two faces,

19 a man's face toward the palm tree on one side and a young lion's face toward the palm tree on the other side; they were carved on all the house all around.

20 From the ground to above the entrance cherubim and palm trees were carved, as well as *on* the wall of the nave.

21 The doorposts of the nave were square; as for the front of the sanctuary, the appearance of one doorpost was like that of the other.

22 The altar *was* of wood, three cubits high and its length two cubits; its corners, its base and its sides *were* of wood. And he said to me, "This is the table that is before the LORD."

23 The nave and the sanctuary each had a double door.

24 Each of the doors had two leaves, two swinging leaves; two *leaves* for one door and two leaves for the other.

25 Also there were carved on them, on the doors of the nave, cherubim and palm trees like those carved on the walls; and *there was* a threshold of wood on the front of the porch outside.

26 *There were* latticed windows and palm trees on one side and on the other, on the sides of the porch; thus *were* the side chambers of the house and the thresholds.

42 THEN he brought me out into the outer court, the way toward the north; and he brought me to the chamber which *was* opposite the separate area and opposite the building toward the north.

2 Along the length, *which was* a hundred cubits, *was* the north door; the width *was* fifty cubits.

3 Opposite the twenty *cubits* which belonged to the inner court, and opposite the pavement which belonged to the outer court, *was* gallery corresponding to gallery in three stories.

4 Before the chambers *was* an inner walk ten cubits wide, a way of one *hundred* cubits; and their openings *were* on the north.

5 Now the upper chambers *were* smaller because the galleries took more space away from them than from the lower and middle ones in the building.

6 For they *were* in three stories and had no pillars like the pillars of the courts; therefore *the upper chambers* were set back from the ground upward, more than the lower and middle ones.

7 As for the outer wall by the side of the chambers, toward the outer court facing the chambers, its length *was* fifty cubits.

8 For the length of the chambers which *were* in the outer court *was* fifty cubits; and behold, *the length of those* facing the temple *was* a hundred cubits.

9 Below these chambers *was* the entrance on the east side, as one enters them from the outer court.

10 In the thickness of the wall of the court toward the east, facing the separate area and facing the building, *there were* chambers.

11 The way in front of them *was* like the appearance of the chambers which *were* on the north, according to their length so was their width, and all their exits *were* both according to their arrangements and openings.

12 Corresponding to the openings of the chambers which were toward the south was an opening at the head of the way, the way in front of the wall toward the east, as one enters them.

13 Then he said to me, "The north chambers *and* the south chambers, which are opposite the separate area, they are the holy chambers where the priests who are near to the LORD shall eat the most holy things. There they shall lay the most holy things, the grain offering, the sin offering and the guilt offering; for the place is holy.

14 "When the priests enter, then they shall not go out into the outer court from the sanctuary without laying there their garments in which they minister, for they are holy. They shall put on other garments; then they shall approach that which is for the people."

15 Now when he had finished measuring the inner house, he brought me out by the way of the gate which faced toward the east and measured it all around.

16 He measured on the east side with the measuring reed five hundred reeds by the measuring reed.

17 He measured on the north side five hundred reeds by the measuring reed.

18 On the south side he measured five hundred reeds with the measuring reed.

19 He turned to the west side *and* measured five hundred reeds with the measuring reed.

20 He measured it on the four sides; it had a wall all around, the length five hundred and the width five hundred, to divide between the holy and the profane.

✦ Psalm 133:1–3

A Song of Ascents, of David.

133 BEHOLD, how good and how pleasant it is
For brothers to dwell together in unity!

2 It is like the precious oil upon the head,
Coming down upon the beard,
Even Aaron's beard,
Coming down upon the edge of his robes.

3 It is like the dew of Hermon
Coming down upon the mountains of Zion;
For there the LORD commanded the blessing—life forever.

✦ Proverbs 29:6

6 By transgression an evil man is ensnared,
But the righteous sings and rejoices.

✦ 1 Peter 1:1–25

1 PETER, an apostle of Jesus Christ,
To those who reside as aliens, scattered throughout Pontus, Galatia, Cappadocia, Asia, and Bithynia, who are chosen

2 according to the foreknowledge of God the Father, by the sanctifying work of the Spirit, to obey Jesus Christ and be sprinkled with His blood: May grace and peace be yours in the fullest measure.

3 Blessed be the God and Father of our Lord Jesus Christ, who according to His great mercy has caused us to be born again to a living hope through the resurrection of Jesus Christ from the dead,

4 to *obtain* an inheritance *which is* imperishable and undefiled and will not fade away, reserved in heaven for you,

5 who are protected by the power of God through faith for a salvation ready to be revealed in the last time.

6 In this you greatly rejoice, even though now for a little while, if necessary, you have been distressed by various trials,

7 so that the proof of your faith, *being* more precious than gold which is perishable, even though tested by fire, may be found to result in praise and glory and honor at the revelation of Jesus Christ;

8 and though you have not seen Him, you love Him, and though you do not see Him now, but believe in Him, you greatly rejoice with joy inexpressible and full of glory,

---

LIFE LESSONS

➤ **Psalm 133:1 —** *How good and how pleasant it is for brothers to dwell together in unity!*

*I*f as believers we all serve the One True God, then why shouldn't His love express itself in us through unity (Eph. 4:1–16)? It really should. Therefore, "be like-minded, live in peace" (2 Cor. 13:11).

➤ **1 Peter 1:3 —** *According to His great mercy has caused us to be born again to a living hope through the resurrection of Jesus Christ from the dead.*

*B*ecause our Savior is alive, we have a living hope. The resurrection of Jesus guarantees that God will honor all His promises to His faithful children. And the knowledge that He is with us and will never forsake us can encourage us and keep us going—even in the darkest times.

ANSWERS TO LIFE'S QUESTIONS

How do I handle a difficult trial not of my own doing?

1 PETER 1:6, 7

*E*ven those who maintain close, intimate fellowship with the Lord are not immune to disappointments, obstacles, challenges, struggles, and feelings of hopelessness. In fact at times, God allows us to face impossible circumstances in order to test and try our faith. It is the adversity that motivates us to seek Him, and when we do, He faithfully strengthens and refreshes us.

God knows every emotion, need, and desire we have. He cares when we face difficult situations and grow weary. He hears our cries and understands exactly what it will take to bring us into a more intimate relationship with Him.

The apostle Peter addressed his two letters to "those who reside as aliens, scattered throughout Pontus, Galatia, Cappadocia, Asia, and Bithynia" (1 Pet. 1:1; 2 Pet. 3:1). If he were choosing a modern title for his letters, he might consider "Encouragement for Times of Suffering," or "Hope for the Hurting," because encouragement and hope are exactly what Peter conveyed to these distressed believers.

These Christians faced all kinds of persecution. They were beaten, slandered, assaulted, and in many cases lost their lives for their faith in Jesus Christ. Peter called them "aliens" because their citizenship was not of this world but of the kingdom of God. Still, they faced times of great discouragement and loss, and needed the courage only available through Christ. Peter explained that they could rejoice even in times of trial because Jesus—their risen Savior and Lord—would always be the living hope within them (1 Pet. 1:3). So long as we have the Lord Jesus Christ, no situation is hopeless.

Would you like to have eternal hope? Then focus your heart on Jesus (1 Tim. 4:6). He wants to bring His will and good pleasure to fruition in your life. Even if you find yourself in a seemingly impossible situation, remember that He has an entirely different view of the details. And if you will let Him, He will take your life, no matter how bruised and broken, and make something beautiful out of it.

Isn't this what hope is all about—beauty for ashes, gladness instead of sorrow, and a coat of praise instead of fainting (Is. 61:1–3)? *This* is the ongoing ministry of Jesus Christ in your life. Therefore bring to Him your afflictions and disappointments. Tell Him your sorrows, and He will restore your hope.

LIFE LESSONS

➤ **1 Peter 1:8 —** *Though you do not see Him now, but believe in Him, you greatly rejoice with joy inexpressible and full of glory.*

*T*he Christian life should be characterized by joy because of the unassailable power, love, and wisdom of our Savior Jesus Christ. Although we face adversity and cannot see Him in it, we know He can redeem any situation. He uses everything that touches our lives for our good and His glory.

➤ **1 Peter 1:13 —** *Fix your hope completely on the grace to be brought to you at the revelation of Jesus Christ.*

*T*he Christian life is both a joyful experience and serious business. It takes conscious, deliberate, Spirit-filled action to ponder God's grace and Jesus' return in such a way that it positively shapes how we live.

---

9 obtaining as the outcome of your faith the salvation of your souls.

10 As to this salvation, the prophets who prophesied of the grace that *would come* to you made careful searches and inquiries,

11 seeking to know what person or time the Spirit of Christ within them was indicating as He predicted the sufferings of Christ and the glories to follow.

12 It was revealed to them that they were not serving themselves, but you, in these things which now have been announced to you through those who preached the gospel to you by the Holy Spirit sent from heaven—things into which angels long to look.

13 Therefore, prepare your minds for action, keep sober *in spirit*, fix your hope completely on the grace to be brought to you at the revelation of Jesus Christ.

14 As obedient children, do not be conformed to the former lusts *which were yours* in your ignorance,

➢ **1 Peter 1:15 — *Like the Holy One who called you, be holy yourselves also in all your behavior.***

*I*t takes a godly, deliberate, Spirit-filled walk to honor God and glorify Him. This does not mean we adopt a dour, grim-faced determination to do the pious, religious rituals that drain all enjoyment out of life. Rather, we live out the holiness that Christ has given us by obeying Him and imitating His ways.

➢ 15 but like the Holy One who called you, be holy yourselves also in all *your* behavior;
16 because it is written, "YOU SHALL BE HOLY, FOR I AM HOLY."
17 If you address as Father the One who impartially judges according to each one's work, conduct yourselves in fear during the time of your stay *on earth*;
18 knowing that you were not redeemed with perishable things like silver or gold from your futile way of life inherited from your forefathers,

19 but with precious blood, as of a lamb unblemished and spotless, *the blood* of Christ.
20 For He was foreknown before the foundation of the world, but has appeared in these last times for the sake of you
21 who through Him are believers in God, who raised Him from the dead and gave Him glory, so that your faith and hope are in God.
22 Since you have in obedience to the truth purified your souls for a sincere love of the brethren, fervently love one another from the heart,
23 for you have been born again not of seed which is perishable but imperishable, *that is,* through the living and enduring word of God.
24 For,

> "ALL FLESH IS LIKE GRASS,
>   AND ALL ITS GLORY LIKE THE FLOWER
>   OF GRASS.
>   THE GRASS WITHERS,
>   AND THE FLOWER FALLS OFF,
25   BUT THE WORD OF THE LORD ENDURES
>   FOREVER."

And this is the word which was preached to you.

◉ **Ezekiel 43:1—44:31**

43 THEN he led me to the gate, the gate facing toward the east;
➢ 2 and behold, the glory of the God of Israel was coming from the way of the
✳ east. And His voice was like the sound of many waters; and the earth shone with His glory.
3 And *it was* like the appearance of the vision which I saw, like the vision which I saw when He came to destroy the city. And the visions *were* like the vision which I saw by the river Chebar; and I fell on my face.
4 And the glory of the LORD came into the house by the way of the gate facing toward the east.
5 And the Spirit lifted me up and brought me into the inner court; and behold, the glory of the LORD filled the house.

6 Then I heard one speaking to me from the house, while a man was standing beside me.
7 He said to me, "Son of man, *this is* the place of My throne and the place of

➢ **Ezekiel 43:2 — *The glory of the God of Israel was coming from the way of the east.***

*E*zekiel foresaw the glory of the Lord departing from the temple (Ezek. 10). Yet he also anticipated the day when the *Shekinah*—or majestic presence—of the Lord would return in joy and triumph (Ezek. 43:4, 5). Today, as darkness and sinfulness increase in the world, it may be difficult to catch glimpses of His glory. But one day He will come to redeem His people, His radiance will illuminate all that exists, and He will reign forever and ever (Rev. 21:23–26; 22:5).

the soles of My feet, where I will dwell among the sons of Israel forever. And the house of Israel will not again defile My holy name, neither they nor their kings, by their harlotry and by the corpses of their kings when they die,

8   by setting their threshold by My threshold and their door post beside My door post, with *only* the wall between Me and them. And they have defiled My holy name by their abominations which they have committed. So I have consumed them in My anger.

9   "Now let them put away their harlotry and the corpses of their kings far from Me; and I will dwell among them forever.

10   "As for you, son of man, describe the temple to the house of Israel, that they may be ashamed of their iniquities; and let them measure the plan.

11   "If they are ashamed of all that they have done, make known to them the design of the house, its structure, its exits, its entrances, all its designs, all its statutes, and all its laws. And write *it* in their sight, so that they may observe its whole design and all its statutes and do them.

12   "This is the law of the house: its entire area on the top of the mountain all around *shall be* most holy. Behold, this is the law of the house.

13   "And these are the measurements of the altar by cubits (the cubit being a cubit and a handbreadth): the base *shall be* a cubit and the width a cubit, and its border on its edge round about one span; and this *shall be* the *height* of the base of the altar.

14   "From the base on the ground to the lower ledge *shall be* two cubits and the width one cubit; and from the smaller ledge to the larger ledge *shall be* four cubits and the width one cubit.

15   "The altar hearth *shall be* four cubits; and from the altar hearth shall extend upwards four horns.

16   "Now the altar hearth *shall be* twelve *cubits* long by twelve wide, square in its four sides.

17   "The ledge *shall be* fourteen *cubits* long by fourteen wide in its four sides, the border around it *shall be* half a cubit and its base *shall be* a cubit round about; and its steps shall face the east."

18   And He said to me, "Son of man, thus says the Lord God, 'These are the statutes for the altar on the day it is built, to offer burnt offerings on it and to sprinkle blood on it.

19   'You shall give to the Levitical priests who are from the offspring of Zadok, who draw near to Me to minister to Me,' declares the Lord God, 'a young bull for a sin offering.

20   'You shall take some of its blood and put it on its four horns and on the four corners of the ledge and on the border round about; thus you shall cleanse it and make atonement for it.

21   'You shall also take the bull for the sin offering, and it *shall be* burned in the appointed place of the house, outside the sanctuary.

22   'On the second day you shall offer a male goat without blemish for a sin offering, and they shall cleanse the altar as they cleansed *it* with the bull.

23   'When you have finished cleansing *it*, you shall present a young bull without blemish and a ram without blemish from the flock.

24   'You shall present them before the Lord, and the priests shall throw salt on them, and they shall offer them up as a burnt offering to the Lord.

25   'For seven days you shall prepare daily a goat for a sin offering; also a young bull and a ram from the flock, without blemish, shall be prepared.

26   'For seven days they shall make atonement for the altar and purify it; so shall they consecrate it.

27   'When they have completed the days, it shall be that on the eighth day and onward, the priests shall offer your burnt offerings on the altar, and your peace offerings; and I will accept you,' declares the Lord God."

44 THEN He brought me back by the way of the outer gate of the sanctuary, which faces the east; and it was shut.

2   The Lord said to me, "This gate shall be shut; it shall not be opened, and no one shall enter by it, for the Lord God of Israel has entered by it; therefore it shall be shut.

3   "As for the prince, he shall sit in it as prince to eat bread before the Lord; he shall enter by way of the porch of the gate and shall go out by the same way."

4   Then He brought me by way of the north gate to the front of the house; and I looked, and behold, the glory of the Lord

filled the house of the LORD, and I fell on my face.

5 The LORD said to me, "Son of man, mark well, see with your eyes and hear with your ears all that I say to you concerning all the statutes of the house of the LORD and concerning all its laws; and mark well the entrance of the house, with all exits of the sanctuary.

6 "You shall say to the rebellious ones, to the house of Israel, 'Thus says the Lord GOD, "Enough of all your abominations, O house of Israel,

7 when you brought in foreigners, uncircumcised in heart and uncircumcised in flesh, to be in My sanctuary to profane it, *even* My house, when you offered My food, the fat and the blood; for they made My covenant void—*this* in addition to all your abominations.

8 "And you have not kept charge of My holy things yourselves, but you have set *foreigners* to keep charge of My sanctuary."

9 'Thus says the Lord GOD, "No foreigner uncircumcised in heart and uncircumcised in flesh, of all the foreigners who are among the sons of Israel, shall enter My sanctuary.

10 "But the Levites who went far from Me when Israel went astray, who went astray from Me after their idols, shall bear the punishment for their iniquity.

11 "Yet they shall be ministers in My sanctuary, having oversight at the gates of the house and ministering in the house; they shall slaughter the burnt offering and the sacrifice for the people, and they shall stand before them to minister to them.

12 "Because they ministered to them before their idols and became a stumbling block of iniquity to the house of Israel, therefore I have sworn against them," declares the Lord GOD, "that they shall bear *the punishment for* their iniquity.

13 "And they shall not come near to Me to serve as a priest to Me, nor come near to any of My holy things, to the things that are most holy; but they will bear their shame and their abominations which they have committed.

14 "Yet I will appoint them to keep charge of the house, of all its service and of all that shall be done in it.

15 "But the Levitical priests, the sons of Zadok, who kept charge of My sanctuary when the sons of Israel went astray from Me, shall come near to Me to minister to Me; and they shall stand before Me to offer Me the fat and the blood," declares the Lord GOD.

16 "They shall enter My sanctuary; they shall come near to My table to minister to Me and keep My charge.

17 "It shall be that when they enter at the gates of the inner court, they shall be clothed with linen garments; and wool shall not be on them while they are ministering in the gates of the inner court and in the house.

18 "Linen turbans shall be on their heads and linen undergarments shall be on their loins; they shall not gird themselves with *anything which makes them* sweat.

19 "When they go out into the outer court, into the outer court to the people, they shall put off their garments in which they have been ministering and lay them in the holy chambers; then they shall put on other garments so that they will not transmit holiness to the people with their garments.

20 "Also they shall not shave their heads, yet they shall not let their locks grow long; they shall only trim *the hair of* their heads.

21 "Nor shall any of the priests drink wine when they enter the inner court.

22 "And they shall not marry a widow or a divorced woman but shall take virgins from the offspring of the house of Israel, or a widow who is the widow of a priest.

23 "Moreover, they shall teach My people *the difference* between the holy and the profane, and cause them to discern between the unclean and the clean.

24 "In a dispute they shall take their stand to judge; they shall judge it according to My ordinances. They shall also keep My laws and My statutes in all My appointed feasts and sanctify My sabbaths.

25 "They shall not go to a dead person to defile *themselves;* however, for father, for mother, for son, for daughter, for brother, or for a sister who has not had a husband, they may defile themselves.

26 "After he is cleansed, seven days shall elapse for him.

27 "On the day that he goes into the sanctuary, into the inner court to minister in the sanctuary, he shall offer his sin offering," declares the Lord GOD.

28 "And it shall be with regard to an inheritance for them, *that* I am their

Life Examples:

PETER: Willing to Change

1 PETER 2:1–12

*W*e have heard people say, "What's in a name?" The answer to this famous question is very important from God's perspective. Names often reflect something about us, and Jesus chose the names He gave His disciples wisely. Peter's original name was Simon Bar-Jona (or son of Jonah). The name Peter comes from the Greek *Petros*, meaning "rock" or "stone." He was faithful and steady, and though he was also impetuous, impulsive, brash, outspoken, loud, self-confident, and even arrogant—he was rock-solid in his love for Jesus.

Why would the Savior pick a man who at one point denied knowing Him (Matt. 26:69–75)? For the same reason He picks us. He sees potential in our lives. Though we fail, He knows what our lives contain, and He wants to transform our brokenness and faults for His use (1 Cor. 1: 26–31; 2 Cor. 12:9, 10).

We can learn an awesome lesson about faithfulness by studying the life of Peter. What we will find is this: his most compelling characteristic wasn't impulsiveness or outspokenness, but his willingness to change and, in Jesus' hands, to become a person mightily used by God.

What's in a name? Today it isn't so important what we are called—just that we hear and obey when God calls us.

---

inheritance; and you shall give them no possession in Israel—I am their possession.

29 "They shall eat the grain offering, the sin offering and the guilt offering; and every devoted thing in Israel shall be theirs.

30 "The first of all the first fruits of every kind and every contribution of every kind, from all your contributions, shall be for the priests; you shall also give to the priest the first of your dough to cause a blessing to rest on your house.

31 "The priests shall not eat any bird or beast that has died a natural death or has been torn to pieces.

Psalm 134:1–3

A Song of Ascents.

134 BEHOLD, bless the LORD, all servants of the LORD,
Who serve by night in the house of the LORD!

2 Lift up your hands to the sanctuary
And bless the LORD.

3 May the LORD bless you from Zion,
He who made heaven and earth.

Proverbs 29:7

7 The righteous is concerned for the rights of the poor,
The wicked does not understand *such* concern.

1 Peter 2:1–25

2 THEREFORE, putting aside all malice and all deceit and hypocrisy and envy and all slander,

2 like newborn babies, long for the pure milk of the word, so that by it you may grow in respect to salvation,

3 if you have tasted the kindness of the Lord.

4 And coming to Him as to a living stone which has been rejected by men, but is choice and precious in the sight of God,

5 you also, as living stones, are being built up as a spiritual house for a holy priesthood, to offer up spiritual sacrifices acceptable to God through Jesus Christ.

6 For *this* is contained in Scripture:
"BEHOLD, I LAY IN ZION A CHOICE STONE, A PRECIOUS CORNER *stone*, AND HE WHO BELIEVES IN HIM WILL NOT BE DISAPPOINTED."

LIFE LESSONS

➤ **1 Peter 2:2** — *Like newborn babies, long for the pure milk of the word, so that by it you may grow.*

*A*s infants crave their mothers' nutritious milk, so we are to yearn for the life-giving Word of God. Growing in Christ requires that we spend time in His Word—learning His ways and being transformed into His image through the work of the Holy Spirit.

7 This precious value, then, is for you who believe; but for those who disbelieve,

"THE STONE WHICH THE BUILDERS REJECTED,
THIS BECAME THE VERY CORNER stone,"

8 and,

"A STONE OF STUMBLING AND A ROCK OF OFFENSE";

for they stumble because they are disobedient to the word, and to this *doom* they were also appointed.

➤ 9 But you are A CHOSEN RACE, A royal PRIESTHOOD, A HOLY NATION, A PEOPLE FOR *God's* OWN POSSESSION, so that you may proclaim the excellencies of Him who has called you out of darkness into His marvelous light;

✱ 10 for you once were NOT A PEOPLE, but now you are THE PEOPLE OF GOD; you had NOT RECEIVED MERCY, but now you have RECEIVED MERCY.

➤ 11 Beloved, I urge you as aliens and strangers to abstain from fleshly lusts which wage war against the soul.

12 Keep your behavior excellent among the Gentiles, so that in the thing in which they slander you as evildoers, they may because of your good deeds, as they observe *them*, glorify God in the day of visitation.

13 Submit yourselves for the Lord's sake to every human institution, whether to a king as the one in authority,

14 or to governors as sent by him for the punishment of evildoers and the praise of those who do right.

15 For such is the will of God that by doing right you may silence the ignorance of foolish men.

16 *Act* as free men, and do not use your freedom as a covering for evil, but *use it* as bondslaves of God.

17 Honor all people, love the brotherhood, fear God, honor the king.

18 Servants, be submissive to your masters with all respect, not only to those who are good and gentle, but also to those who are unreasonable.

19 For this *finds* favor, if for the sake of conscience toward God a person bears up under sorrows when suffering unjustly.

20 For what credit is there if, when you sin and are harshly treated, you endure it with patience? But if when you do what is right and suffer *for it* you patiently endure it, this *finds* favor with God.

21 For you have been called for this ◄ purpose, since Christ also suffered for you, leaving you an example for you to follow in His steps,

22 WHO COMMITTED NO SIN, NOR WAS ANY DECEIT FOUND IN HIS MOUTH;

23 and while being reviled, He did not revile in return; while suffering, He uttered no threats, but kept entrusting *Himself* to Him who judges righteously;

24 and He Himself bore our sins in His body on the cross, so that we might die to sin and live to righteousness; for by His wounds you were healed.

25 For you were continually straying like sheep, but now you have returned to the Shepherd and Guardian of your souls.

LIFE LESSONS

➤ **1 Peter 2:9 — *You are a chosen race, a royal priesthood, a holy nation, a people for God's own possession.***

*P*eter uses the wonderful descriptions that were originally applied to Israel to portray the position we enjoy as believers in Christ (Ex. 19: 5, 6). As the church, we do not replace Israel as God's people. Rather, we have been "grafted in" to His family through Christ (Rom. 11:17). Just as Israel was called to be a blessing to the nations (Gen. 28:14), we are, too.

➤ **1 Peter 2:11 — *Abstain from fleshly lusts which wage war against the soul.***

*T*rouble comes when we forget that this world is not our home. Therefore, we must have an eternal perspective and remember we are only aliens and strangers here. Our real home is in heaven with God but even here He is in control of everything that concerns us.

➤ **1 Peter 2:21 — *Christ also suffered for you, leaving you an example for you to follow in His steps.***

*J*esus is our example in all things, even in suffering. He did not willingly suffer merely for suffering's sake (John 18:23), but He eagerly accepted it when He saw it as God's will for Him (Luke 22:42).

45 "AND when you divide by lot the land for inheritance, you shall offer an allotment to the LORD, a holy portion of the land; the length shall be the length of 25,000 *cubits,* and the width shall be 20,000. It shall be holy within all its boundary round about.

2 "Out of this there shall be for the holy place a square round about five hundred by five hundred *cubits,* and fifty cubits for its open space round about.

3 "From this area you shall measure a length of 25,000 *cubits* and a width of 10,000 *cubits;* and in it shall be the sanctuary, the most holy place.

4 "It shall be the holy portion of the land; it shall be for the priests, the ministers of the sanctuary, who come near to minister to the LORD, and it shall be a place for their houses and a holy place for the sanctuary.

5 "*An area* 25,000 *cubits* in length and 10,000 in width shall be for the Levites, the ministers of the house, *and* for their possession cities to dwell in.

6 "You shall give the city possession of *an area* 5,000 *cubits* wide and 25,000 *cubits* long, alongside the allotment of the holy portion; it shall be for the whole house of Israel.

7 "The prince shall have *land* on either side of the holy allotment and the property of the city, adjacent to the holy allotment and the property of the city, on the west side toward the west and on the east side toward the east, and in length comparable to one of the portions, from the west border to the east border.

8 "This shall be his land for a possession in Israel; so My princes shall no longer oppress My people, but they shall give *the rest of* the land to the house of Israel according to their tribes."

9 'Thus says the Lord GOD, "Enough, you princes of Israel; put away violence and destruction, and practice justice and righteousness. Stop your expropriations from My people," declares the Lord GOD.

10 "You shall have just balances, a just ephah and a just bath.

11 "The ephah and the bath shall be the same quantity, so that the bath will contain a tenth of a homer and the ephah a tenth of a homer; their standard shall be according to the homer.

12 "The shekel shall be twenty gerahs; twenty shekels, twenty-five shekels, *and* fifteen shekels shall be your maneh.

13 "This is the offering that you shall offer: a sixth of an ephah from a homer of wheat; a sixth of an ephah from a homer of barley;

14 and the prescribed portion of oil (*namely,* the bath of oil), a tenth of a bath from *each* kor (*which is* ten baths *or a* homer, for ten baths are a homer);

15 and one sheep from *each* flock of two hundred from the watering places of Israel—for a grain offering, for a burnt offering and for peace offerings, to make atonement for them," declares the Lord GOD.

16 "All the people of the land shall give to this offering for the prince in Israel.

17 "It shall be the prince's part *to provide* the burnt offerings, the grain offerings and the drink offerings, at the feasts, on the new moons and on the sabbaths, at all the appointed feasts of the house of Israel; he shall provide the sin offering, the grain offering, the burnt offering and the peace offerings, to make atonement for the house of Israel."

18 'Thus says the Lord GOD, "In the first *month,* on the first of the month, you shall take a young bull without blemish and cleanse the sanctuary.

19 "The priest shall take some of the blood from the sin offering and put *it* on the door posts of the house, on the four corners of the ledge of the altar and on the posts of the gate of the inner court.

20 "Thus you shall do on the seventh *day* of the month for everyone who goes astray or is naive; so you shall make atonement for the house.

21 "In the first *month,* on the fourteenth day of the month, you shall have the Passover, a feast of seven days; unleavened bread shall be eaten.

22 "On that day the prince shall provide for himself and all the people of the land a bull for a sin offering.

23 "*During* the seven days of the feast he shall provide as a burnt offering to the LORD seven bulls and seven rams without blemish on every day of the seven days, and a male goat daily for a sin offering.

24 "He shall provide as a grain offering

an ephah with a bull, an ephah with a ram and a hin of oil with an ephah.

25 "In the seventh *month*, on the fifteenth day of the month, at the feast, he shall provide like this, seven days for the sin offering, the burnt offering, the grain offering and the oil."

46 THUS says the Lord GOD, "The gate of the inner court facing east shall be shut the six working days; but it shall be opened on the sabbath day and opened on the day of the new moon.

2 "The prince shall enter by way of the porch of the gate from outside and stand by the post of the gate. Then the priests shall provide his burnt offering and his peace offerings, and he shall worship at the threshold of the gate and then go out; but the gate shall not be shut until the evening.

3 "The people of the land shall also worship at the doorway of that gate before the LORD on the sabbaths and on the new moons.

4 "The burnt offering which the prince shall offer to the LORD on the sabbath day shall be six lambs without blemish and a ram without blemish;

5 and the grain offering shall be an ephah with the ram, and the grain offering with the lambs as much as he is able to give, and a hin of oil with an ephah.

6 "On the day of the new moon *he shall offer* a young bull without blemish, also six lambs and a ram, *which* shall be without blemish.

7 "And he shall provide a grain offering, an ephah with the bull and an ephah with the ram, and with the lambs as much as he is able, and a hin of oil with an ephah.

8 "When the prince enters, he shall go in by way of the porch of the gate and go out by the same way.

9 "But when the people of the land come before the LORD at the appointed feasts, he who enters by way of the north gate to worship shall go out by way of the south gate. And he who enters by way of the south gate shall go out by way of the north gate. No one shall return by way of the gate by which he entered but shall go straight out.

10 "When they go in, the prince shall go in among them; and when they go out, he shall go out.

11 "At the festivals and the appointed feasts the grain offering shall be an ephah with a bull and an ephah with a ram, and with the lambs as much as one is able to give, and a hin of oil with an ephah.

12 "When the prince provides a freewill offering, a burnt offering, or peace offerings *as* a freewill offering to the LORD, the gate facing east shall be opened for him. And he shall provide his burnt offering and his peace offerings as he does on the sabbath day. Then he shall go out, and the gate shall be shut after he goes out.

13 "And you shall provide a lamb a year old without blemish for a burnt offering to the LORD daily; morning by morning you shall provide it.

14 "Also you shall provide a grain offering with it morning by morning, a sixth of an ephah and a third of a hin of oil to moisten the fine flour, a grain offering to the LORD continually by a perpetual ordinance.

15 "Thus they shall provide the lamb, the grain offering and the oil, morning by morning, for a continual burnt offering."

16 Thus says the Lord GOD, "If the prince gives a gift *out of* his inheritance to any of his sons, it shall belong to his sons; it is their possession by inheritance.

17 "But if he gives a gift from his inheritance to one of his servants, it shall be his until the year of liberty; then it shall return to the prince. His inheritance *shall be* only his sons'; it shall belong to them.

18 "The prince shall not take from the people's inheritance, thrusting them out of their possession; he shall give his sons inheritance from his own possession so that My people will not be scattered, anyone from his possession."'"

19 Then he brought me through the entrance, which *was* at the side of the gate, into the holy chambers for the priests, which faced north; and behold, there *was* a place at the extreme rear toward the west.

20 He said to me, "This is the place where the priests shall boil the guilt offering and the sin offering *and* where they shall bake the grain offering, in order that they may not bring *them* out into the outer court to transmit holiness to the people."

21 Then he brought me out into the outer

court and led me across to the four corners of the court; and behold, in every corner of the court *there was a small* court.
22 In the four corners of the court *there were* enclosed courts, forty *cubits* long and thirty wide; these four in the corners *were* the same size.
23 *There was* a row *of masonry* round about in them, around the four of them, and boiling places were made under the rows round about.
24 Then he said to me, "These are the boiling places where the ministers of the house shall boil the sacrifices of the people."

Psalm 135:1–7

135 PRAISE the LORD!
Praise the name of the LORD;
Praise *Him,* O servants of the LORD,
2 You who stand in the house of the
LORD,
In the courts of the house of our God!
3 Praise the LORD, for the LORD is good;
Sing praises to His name, for it is
lovely.
4 For the LORD has chosen Jacob for
Himself,
Israel for His own possession.
5 For I know that the LORD is great
And that our Lord is above all gods.
6 Whatever the LORD pleases, He does,
In heaven and in earth, in the seas
and in all deeps.
7 He causes the vapors to ascend
from the ends of the earth;
Who makes lightnings for the rain,
Who brings forth the wind from His
treasuries.

Proverbs 29:8

8 Scorners set a city aflame,
But wise men turn away anger.

1 Peter 3:1–22

3 IN the same way, you wives, be submissive to your own husbands so that even if any *of them* are disobedient to the word, they may be won without a word by the behavior of their wives,
2 as they observe your chaste and respectful behavior.
3 Your adornment must not be *merely* external—braiding the hair, and wearing gold jewelry, or putting on dresses;
4 but *let it be* the hidden person of the heart, with the imperishable quality of a gentle and quiet spirit, which is precious in the sight of God.
5 For in this way in former times the holy women also, who hoped in God, used to adorn themselves, being submissive to their own husbands;
6 just as Sarah obeyed Abraham, calling him lord, and you have become her children if you do what is right without being frightened by any fear.
7 You husbands in the same way, live with *your wives* in an understanding way, as with someone weaker, since she is a woman; and show her honor as a fel-

---

LIFE LESSONS

➤ **Psalm 135:6 —** *Whatever the LORD pleases, He does, in heaven and in earth, in the seas and in all deeps.*

*W*hat does God *want* to do? It pleases the Lord to do good, to show mercy, to bestow grace—and nothing can stop Him. Yet, as is also His right, He will judge the unrepentantly wicked.

➤ **1 Peter 3:4 —** *Let it be the hidden person of the heart, with the imperishable quality of a gentle and quiet spirit, which is precious in the sight of God.*

*W*hat would happen in our spiritual lives if we spent as much time working on our souls as we do on our bodies? Our bodies are not unimportant, but they will die; our spirits, however, will live forever.

➤ **1 Peter 3:7 —** *You husbands in the same way, live with your wives in an understanding way . . . and show her honor . . . that your prayers will not be hindered.*

*W*hy would failing to make the effort to understand and honor his wife hinder a husband's prayers? All believers are co-heirs of God's promises, and He wants us to treat one another as we would treat Him.

low heir of the grace of life, so that your prayers will not be hindered.

8   To sum up, all of you be harmonious, sympathetic, brotherly, kindhearted, and humble in spirit;

9   not returning evil for evil or insult for insult, but giving a blessing instead; for you were called for the very purpose that you might inherit a blessing.

10   For,

"THE ONE WHO DESIRES LIFE, TO LOVE
AND SEE GOOD DAYS,
MUST KEEP HIS TONGUE FROM EVIL AND
HIS LIPS FROM SPEAKING DECEIT.

11   "HE MUST TURN AWAY FROM EVIL AND
DO GOOD;
HE MUST SEEK PEACE AND PURSUE IT.

12   "FOR THE EYES OF THE LORD ARE
TOWARD THE RIGHTEOUS,

AND HIS EARS ATTEND TO THEIR
PRAYER,
BUT THE FACE OF THE LORD IS AGAINST
THOSE WHO DO EVIL."

13   Who is there to harm you if you prove zealous for what is good?

14   But even if you should suffer for the sake of righteousness, you are blessed. AND DO NOT FEAR THEIR INTIMIDATION, AND DO NOT BE TROUBLED,

15   but sanctify Christ as Lord in your hearts, always being ready to make a defense to everyone who asks you to give an account for the hope that is in you, yet with gentleness and reverence;

16   and keep a good conscience so that in the thing in which you are slandered, those who revile your good behavior in Christ will be put to shame.

ANSWERS TO LIFE'S QUESTIONS

Does it matter what you believe?

1 PETER 3:13–16

*W*hen the apostle Peter wrote to the believers scattered throughout Asia Minor, the persecution of Christians was intensifying. He realized that believers needed to stand strong in their faith, so he instructed them, "Do not fear their intimidation, and do not be troubled, but sanctify Christ as Lord in your hearts, always being ready to make a defense to everyone who asks you to give an account for the hope that is in you, yet with gentleness and reverence" (1 Pet. 3:14, 15).

Everyone needs faith during times of adversity and hardship. Whether the trouble is persecution from a political body, a natural disaster, or interpersonal conflict, it is important to know what you believe so that you can remain strong.

When you trust in Christ, you have placed your faith in the very One who has overcome the world. Yet if you do not have confidence that Christ's salvation is sure, what guarantee do you have?

Malcolm Muggeridge wrote, "It is often supposed that when people stop believing in God, they believe in nothing. Alas, it is worse than that. When they stop believing in God, they believe in anything."

It is important to know what you believe about Jesus so that you can stand firm in adversity. But it is also important because belief in Christ keeps you from placing your faith in that which does not satisfy and cannot save.

As the early believers trusted Christ through the persecutions, so can you. And together with them you will find the reward of your faith (Heb. 11:40).

In prison and in chains, the apostle Paul faced the possibility that he would not live to see one more day, yet his faith remained strong. Though his future appeared bleak, Paul knew that he had a guarantee in Christ which was the hope of heaven.

In 2 Timothy 1:12 Paul courageously proclaims, "I am not ashamed; for I know whom I have believed and I am convinced that He is able to guard what I have entrusted to Him until that day."

When you know in Whom you have placed your faith, you realize that He never forsakes you. Rather, He prepares that which is greater than you can conceive. He has made a covenant with all who believe in Jesus Christ. The covenant is that Jesus is your eternal priest and the Holy Spirit is your enduring guarantee of your inheritance in heaven.

Hebrews 10:23 admonishes, "Let us hold fast the confession of our hope without wavering, for He who promised is faithful."

How easy is it to throw away your faith when it seems like God has abandoned you and your circumstances are more than you can bear? Yet it is precisely in the darkest moments of your life when faith in God is crucial.

The next time you face devastating difficulties, remember that Christ will never forget the promise He made to save you. Clutch your faith in Him with both hands. He is faithful, and you will not be disappointed.

17 For it is better, if God should will it so, that you suffer for doing what is right rather than for doing what is wrong.
18 For Christ also died for sins once for all, *the* just for *the* unjust, so that He might bring us to God, having been put to death in the flesh, but made alive in the spirit;
19 in which also He went and made proclamation to the spirits *now* in prison,
20 who once were disobedient, when the patience of God kept waiting in the days of Noah, during the construction of the ark, in which a few, that is, eight persons, were brought safely through *the* water.
21 Corresponding to that, baptism now saves you—not the removal of dirt from the flesh, but an appeal to God for a good conscience—through the resurrection of Jesus Christ,
22 who is at the right hand of God, having gone into heaven, after angels and authorities and powers had been subjected to Him.

NOVEMBER 28

✣ Ezekiel 47:1—48:35

47 THEN he brought me back to the door of the house; and behold, water was flowing from under the threshold of the house toward the east, for the house faced east. And the water was flowing down from under, from the right side of the house, from south of the altar.
2 He brought me out by way of the north gate and led me around on the outside of the house to the outer gate by way of *the gate* that faces east. And behold, water was trickling from the south side.
3 When the man went out toward the east with a line in his hand, he measured a thousand cubits, and he led me through the water, water *reaching* the ankles.
4 Again he measured a thousand and led me through the water, water *reaching* the knees. Again he measured a thousand and led me through *the water*, water *reaching* the loins.
5 Again he measured a thousand; *and it was* a river that I could not ford, for the water had risen, *enough* water to swim in, a river that could not be forded.
6 He said to me, "Son of man, have you seen *this*?" Then he brought me back to the bank of the river.
7 Now when I had returned, behold, on the bank of the river there *were* very many trees on the one side and on the other.
8 Then he said to me, "These waters go out toward the eastern region and go down into the Arabah; then they go toward the sea, being made to flow into the sea, and the waters *of the sea* become fresh.
9 "It will come about that every living ◄ creature which swarms in every place where the river goes, will live. And there will be very many fish, for these waters

go there and *the others* become fresh; so everything will live where the river goes.

10 "And it will come about that fishermen will stand beside it; from Engedi to Eneglaim there will be a place for the spreading of nets. Their fish will be according to their kinds, like the fish of the Great Sea, very many.

11 "But its swamps and marshes will not become fresh; they will be left for salt.

12 "By the river on its bank, on one side and on the other, will grow all *kinds of* trees for food. Their leaves will not wither and their fruit will not fail. They will bear every month because their water flows from the sanctuary, and their fruit will be for food and their leaves for healing."

13 Thus says the Lord GOD, "This *shall be* the boundary by which you shall divide the land for an inheritance among the twelve tribes of Israel; Joseph *shall have* two portions.

14 "You shall divide it for an inheritance, each one equally with the other; for I swore to give it to your forefathers, and this land shall fall to you as an inheritance.

15 "This *shall be* the boundary of the land: on the north side, from the Great Sea *by* the way of Hethlon, to the entrance of Zedad;

16 Hamath, Berothah, Sibraim, which is between the border of Damascus and the border of Hamath; Hazer-hatticon, which is by the border of Hauran.

17 "The boundary shall extend from the sea *to* Hazar-enan *at* the border of Damascus, and on the north toward the north is the border of Hamath. This is the north side.

18 "The east side, from between Hauran, Damascus, Gilead and the land of Israel, *shall be* the Jordan; from the *north* border to the eastern sea you shall measure. This is the east side.

19 "The south side toward the south *shall extend* from Tamar as far as the waters of Meribath-kadesh, to the brook *of Egypt and* to the Great Sea. This is the south side toward the south.

20 "The west side *shall be* the Great Sea, from the *south* border to a point opposite Lebo-hamath. This is the west side.

21 "So you shall divide this land among yourselves according to the tribes of Israel.

22 "You shall divide it by lot for an inheritance among yourselves and among the aliens who stay in your midst, who bring forth sons in your midst. And they shall be to you as the native-born among the sons of Israel; they shall be allotted an inheritance with you among the tribes of Israel.

23 "And in the tribe with which the alien stays, there you shall give *him* his inheritance," declares the Lord GOD.

48 "NOW these are the names of the tribes: from the northern extremity, beside the way of Hethlon to Lebo-hamath, *as far as* Hazar-enan *at* the border of Damascus, toward the north beside Hamath, running from east to west, Dan, one *portion.*

2 "Beside the border of Dan, from the east side to the west side, Asher, one *portion.*

3 "Beside the border of Asher, from the east side to the west side, Naphtali, one *portion.*

4 "Beside the border of Naphtali, from the east side to the west side, Manasseh, one *portion.*

5 "Beside the border of Manasseh, from the east side to the west side, Ephraim, one *portion.*

6 "Beside the border of Ephraim, from the east side to the west side, Reuben, one *portion.*

7 "Beside the border of Reuben, from the east side to the west side, Judah, one *portion.*

8 "And beside the border of Judah, from the east side to the west side, shall be the allotment which you shall set apart, 25,000 *cubits* in width, and in length like one of the portions, from the east side to the west side; and the sanctuary shall be in the middle of it.

9 "The allotment that you shall set apart to the LORD *shall be* 25,000 *cubits* in length and 10,000 in width.

10 "The holy allotment shall be for these, *namely* for the priests, toward the north 25,000 *cubits in length,* toward the west 10,000 in width, toward the east 10,000 in width, and toward the south 25,000 in length; and the sanctuary of the LORD shall be in its midst.

11 "*It shall be* for the priests who are sanctified of the sons of Zadok, who have kept My charge, who did not go astray when the sons of Israel went astray as the Levites went astray.

12 "It shall be an allotment to them from the allotment of the land, a most holy place, by the border of the Levites.

13 "Alongside the border of the priests the Levites *shall have* 25,000 *cubits* in length and 10,000 in width. The whole length *shall be* 25,000 *cubits* and the width 10,000.

14 "Moreover, they shall not sell or exchange any of it, or alienate this choice *portion* of land; for it is holy to the LORD.

15 "The remainder, 5,000 *cubits* in width and 25,000 in length, shall be for common use for the city, for dwellings and for open spaces; and the city shall be in its midst.

16 "These *shall be* its measurements: the north side 4,500 *cubits*, the south side 4,500 *cubits*, the east side 4,500 *cubits*, and the west side 4,500 *cubits*.

17 "The city shall have open spaces: on the north 250 *cubits*, on the south 250 *cubits*, on the east 250 *cubits*, and on the west 250 *cubits*.

18 "The remainder of the length alongside the holy allotment shall be 10,000 *cubits* toward the east and 10,000 toward the west; and it shall be alongside the holy allotment. And its produce shall be food for the workers of the city.

19 "The workers of the city, out of all the tribes of Israel, shall cultivate it.

20 "The whole allotment *shall be* 25,000 by 25,000 *cubits*; you shall set apart the holy allotment, a square, with the property of the city.

21 "The remainder *shall be* for the prince, on the one side and on the other of the holy allotment and of the property of the city; in front of the 25,000 *cubits* of the allotment toward the east border and westward in front of the 25,000 toward the west border, alongside the portions, *it shall be* for the prince. And the holy allotment and the sanctuary of the house shall be in the middle of it.

22 "Exclusive of the property of the Levites and the property of the city, *which* are in the middle of that which belongs to the prince, *everything* between the border of Judah and the border of Benjamin shall be for the prince.

23 "As for the rest of the tribes: from the east side to the west side, Benjamin, one *portion.*

24 "Beside the border of Benjamin, from the east side to the west side, Simeon, one *portion.*

25 "Beside the border of Simeon, from the east side to the west side, Issachar, one *portion.*

26 "Beside the border of Issachar, from the east side to the west side, Zebulun, one *portion.*

27 "Beside the border of Zebulun, from the east side to the west side, Gad, one *portion.*

28 "And beside the border of Gad, at the south side toward the south, the border shall be from Tamar to the waters of Meribath-kadesh, to the brook *of Egypt,* to the Great Sea.

29 "This is the land which you shall divide by lot to the tribes of Israel for an inheritance, and these are their *several* portions," declares the Lord GOD.

30 "These are the exits of the city: on the north side, 4,500 *cubits* by measurement,

31 shall be the gates of the city, named for the tribes of Israel, three gates toward the north: the gate of Reuben, one; the gate of Judah, one; the gate of Levi, one.

32 "On the east side, 4,500 *cubits,* shall be three gates: the gate of Joseph, one; the gate of Benjamin, one; the gate of Dan, one.

33 "On the south side, 4,500 *cubits* by measurement, shall be three gates: the gate of Simeon, one; the gate of Issachar, one; the gate of Zebulun, one.

34 "On the west side, 4,500 *cubits, shall be* three gates: the gate of Gad, one; the gate of Asher, one; the gate of Naphtali, one.

35 "*The city shall be* 18,000 *cubits* round about; and the name of the city from *that* day *shall be,* 'The LORD is there.'"

◈ Psalm 135:8–14

8 He smote the firstborn of Egypt,
Both of man and beast.

9 He sent signs and wonders into your midst, O Egypt,
Upon Pharaoh and all his servants.

10 He smote many nations
And slew mighty kings,

11 Sihon, king of the Amorites,
And Og, king of Bashan,

And all the kingdoms of Canaan;
12 And He gave their land as a
    heritage,
    A heritage to Israel His people.
13 Your name, O LORD, is everlasting,
    Your remembrance, O LORD,
        throughout all generations.
14 For the LORD will judge His people
    And will have compassion on His
        servants.

Proverbs 29:9

9 When a wise man has a controversy
      with a foolish man,
    The foolish man either rages or
      laughs, and there is no rest.

1 Peter 4:1–19

4 THEREFORE, since Christ has suffered in the flesh, arm yourselves also
with the same purpose, because he who
has suffered in the flesh has ceased from
sin,
2   so as to live the rest of the time in the
flesh no longer for the lusts of men, but
for the will of God.
3   For the time already past is sufficient
for you to have carried out the desire of
the Gentiles, having pursued a course of
sensuality, lusts, drunkenness, carousing, drinking parties and abominable
idolatries.
4   In *all* this, they are surprised that you
do not run with *them* into the same excesses of dissipation, and they malign you;
5   but they will give account to Him
who is ready to judge the living and the
dead.
6   For the gospel has for this purpose
been preached even to those who are
dead, that though they are judged in the
flesh as men, they may live in the spirit
according to *the will of* God.
7   The end of all things is near; therefore, be of sound judgment and sober
spirit for the purpose of prayer.
8   Above all, keep fervent in your love
for one another, because love covers a
multitude of sins.
9   Be hospitable to one another without
complaint.

10   As each one has received a *special*
gift, employ it in serving one another as
good stewards of the manifold grace of
God.
11   Whoever speaks, *is to do so* as one
who is speaking the utterances of God;
whoever serves *is to do so* as one who is
serving by the strength which God supplies; so that in all things God may be
glorified through Jesus Christ, to whom
belongs the glory and dominion forever
and ever. Amen.
12   Beloved, do not be surprised at the
fiery ordeal among you, which comes
upon you for your testing, as though some
strange thing were happening to you;
13   but to the degree that you share the
sufferings of Christ, keep on rejoicing,

LIFE LESSONS

➤ **1 Peter 4:2 —** *So as to live the rest of
the time in the flesh no longer for the
lusts of men, but for the will of God.*

*H*ad He chosen to do so, God could
have taken us immediately to
heaven when we placed our faith in
Christ. But He didn't. Why not? He wants
us reach others for Him by showing them
how His power has changed our lives.

➤ **1 Peter 4:4 —** *They are surprised that
you do not run with them in the same
excesses of dissipation, and they malign
you.*

*P*eople who knew us before we
placed our faith in Christ sometimes
do not understand why we no longer
want to participate in the ungodly activities we engaged in before we accepted
God's love. But we should not give in
to their taunts or entreaties to return
to that sinful behavior. We now have
the unique opportunity to be a light to
them, and we do that by allowing Christ
to shine through us, not by returning to
the bondage that once held us captive.

➤ **1 Peter 4:8 —** *Above all, keep fervent
in your love for one another, because
love covers a multitude of sins."*

*E*ven in the best of churches and the
most godly of homes, things go
wrong. What do we do then? The place
to start (and end) is to choose to imitate
God's love to us, and bear with one
another (Col. 3:13).

How does God use suffering in our lives?

1 PETER 4:12–19

Suffering is not new to the Christian life—or to the Lord Jesus Christ, the apostle Paul, or any other saint who's lived down through the ages (Phil. 3:8–11; 1 Pet. 4:12–19). When we think about why God allows trials into our lives, we know that He uses our suffering in several ways.

1. *God uses suffering to get our attention.*

Affliction helps us to refocus on the Lord (Ps. 119:67, 71). When He sees that we are moving toward sin and disobedience, He allows us to experience pressure so that we will return to Him.

2. *God uses suffering to develop personal righteousness and maturity.*

As Christians, we are often unaware of the sinful activities that remain in our lives. God develops maturity in us and reveals lingering issues that He wants us to resolve through trials. We learn perseverance and steadfastness in our trials. Even though we suffer, we know that the Creator is developing His awesome character in our lives (Rom. 5:1–5).

3. *God uses suffering for the purpose of pruning.*

Pruning is God's process of cutting back the useless parts of our lives that will never be productive for His kingdom. He cuts away our attitudes and actions so that godly ones may grow, thus maximizing our potential as children of God.

4. *God uses suffering to teach us obedience.*

Even Jesus had to learn obedience (Heb. 5:8). He was always perfect, yet always learning obedience. That's why we must focus on what the Lord is teaching us. We must accept His discipline because it is transforming us into the likeness of our Savior.

5. *God uses suffering to teach us to trust Him.*

Faith, when tested by fire, is more precious than gold, which is perishable (1 Pet. 1:6, 7). God loves us so much that He's willing to do whatever it takes to teach us to trust Him.

6. *God uses suffering to bring about continuous dependence upon His grace.*

Paul wrote about the incredible lesson he learned—when he was at his weakest in human strength, he was at his strongest in Christ (2 Cor. 12:9, 10). God is glorified most in our weakness because we must rely on Him. Christ uses all of us to demonstrate His power to the world.

7. *God allows suffering to purify the heart and to make us holy.*

We share in the holiness of Christ. Therefore, God's goal for us is that we be like Jesus—that we manifest Christ's life in our bodies. Through our suffering, God purifies our hearts, allowing His holiness to shine through our character.

8. *God allows suffering to teach us to give thanks in everything.*

Being thankful for suffering isn't easy. We may not feel thankful, but we should have gratitude knowing that God uses our suffering (Rom 8:28; 1 Thess. 5:18). We also give thanks knowing that no matter what happens to us here on earth, in the end, we will be with our Savior in heaven, and He will wipe the tears from our eyes (Is. 25:8).

---

so that also at the revelation of His glory you may rejoice with exultation.
14 If you are reviled for the name of Christ, you are blessed, because the Spirit of glory and of God rests on you.
15 Make sure that none of you suffers as a murderer, or thief, or evildoer, or a troublesome meddler;
16 but if *anyone suffers* as a Christian, he is not to be ashamed, but is to glorify God in this name.
17 For *it is* time for judgment to begin with the household of God; and if *it begins* with us first, what *will be* the outcome for those who do not obey the gospel of God?
18 AND IF IT IS WITH DIFFICULTY THAT THE RIGHTEOUS IS SAVED, WHAT WILL BECOME OF THE GODLESS MAN AND THE SINNER?
19 Therefore, those also who suffer according to the will of God shall entrust their souls to a faithful Creator in doing what is right.

LIFE LESSONS

➤ **1 Peter 4:19 — *Therefore, those who suffer according to the will of God shall entrust their souls to a faithful Creator in doing what is right.***

Did you realize that it is God's will for us to suffer at some points along the way of life's journey? We are "destined" to it (1 Thess. 3:3) and are to "exult" in it (Rom. 5:3). Only trust in God enables us to endure.

Daniel 1:1—2:49

1 IN the third year of the reign of Jehoiakim king of Judah, Nebuchadnezzar king of Babylon came to Jerusalem and besieged it.
2 The Lord gave Jehoiakim king of Judah into his hand, along with some of the vessels of the house of God; and he brought them to the land of Shinar, to the house of his god, and he brought the vessels into the treasury of his god.
3 Then the king ordered Ashpenaz, the chief of his officials, to bring in some of the sons of Israel, including some of the royal family and of the nobles,
4 youths in whom was no defect, who were good-looking, showing intelligence in every branch of wisdom, endowed with understanding and discerning knowledge, and who had ability for serving in the king's court; and he ordered him to teach them the literature and language of the Chaldeans.

5 The king appointed for them a daily ration from the king's choice food and from the wine which he drank, and appointed that they should be educated three years, at the end of which they were to enter the king's personal service.
6 Now among them from the sons of Judah were Daniel, Hananiah, Mishael and Azariah.
7 Then the commander of the officials assigned new names to them; and to Daniel he assigned the name Belteshazzar, to Hananiah Shadrach, to Mishael Meshach and to Azariah Abed-nego.
8 But Daniel made up his mind that he would not defile himself with the king's choice food or with the wine which he drank; so he sought permission from the commander of the officials that he might not defile himself.
9 Now God granted Daniel favor and compassion in the sight of the commander of the officials,
10 and the commander of the officials said to Daniel, "I am afraid of my lord

---

ANSWERS TO LIFE'S QUESTIONS

How can I become a more obedient Christian?

DANIEL 1:4–16

*O*bedience is the bottom line in the Christian life. This means compliance to God's plan and pattern, observance of His commands, adherence to His standard, and submission to His will.

If we want to obey the Lord, we need to know what action God wants us to take, what attitude would most please Him, and what He requires of us. So how do we get ourselves to that point of obedience?

First, we have to know what God's commands are. We cannot obey what we do not know or understand—and we begin to understand God's perspective by becoming familiar with His Word.

However, simply knowing God's Word isn't enough. We must also tap into His power by submitting to the promptings of the Holy Spirit, who helps us relate His commands to our own situation and who assists us in determining the wisest course of action.

Once we decide to obey, we can expect a challenge to compromise. Since Satan doesn't want us to follow God, he will offer temptation after temptation to divert us or to weaken our

devotion to the Lord through small steps of disobedience. Yet remember, partial obedience is disobedience.

It takes commitment and courage to obey God in the face of these challenges: courage to give up what we like in order to do what He asks; courage to do things that may bring unwelcome results; courage to rearrange our schedule to match His plan; courage to love the unlovely, to forgive the seemingly unforgivable, and to give when we want to keep. How can we counter his challenge to compromise? By renewing our resolve to obey.

When Jesus neared the end of forty days of fasting and prayer following His baptism, Satan tempted Him to compromise His calling (Matt. 4:1–11). But Jesus stood up to Satan with courage, answering temptation after temptation with the Word of God. If we desire to have such resolute commitment to Him, we must love God above all else, be obedient in our actions, have a determined attitude, and be willing to suffer any consequences that result.

Whenever you feel tempted to disobey God, remember that your faithfulness and devotion to Christ are at stake. Ask yourself: "Is my understanding of Scripture increasing? Am I able to hold to God's plan without compromise? How committed am I to obeying God? If I love Him, I'll obey Him—so how much do I really love Him?"

the king, who has appointed your food and your drink; for why should he see your faces looking more haggard than the youths who are your own age? Then you would make me forfeit my head to the king."

11 But Daniel said to the overseer whom the commander of the officials had appointed over Daniel, Hananiah, Mishael and Azariah,

12 "Please test your servants for ten days, and let us be given some vegetables to eat and water to drink.

13 "Then let our appearance be observed in your presence and the appearance of the youths who are eating the king's choice food; and deal with your servants according to what you see."

14 So he listened to them in this matter and tested them for ten days.

15 At the end of ten days their appearance seemed better and they were fatter than all the youths who had been eating the king's choice food.

16 So the overseer continued to withhold their choice food and the wine they were to drink, and kept giving them vegetables.

➤ 17 As for these four youths, God gave them knowledge and intelligence in every *branch of* literature and wisdom; Daniel even understood all *kinds of* visions and dreams.

18 Then at the end of the days which the king had specified for presenting them, the commander of the officials presented them before Nebuchadnezzar.

19 The king talked with them, and out of them all not one was found like Daniel, Hananiah, Mishael and Azariah; so they entered the king's personal service.

20 As for every matter of wisdom and understanding about which the king consulted them, he found them ten times better than all the magicians *and* conjurers who *were* in all his realm.

21 And Daniel continued until the first year of Cyrus the king.

2 NOW in the second year of the reign of Nebuchadnezzar, Nebuchadnezzar had dreams; and his spirit was troubled and his sleep left him.

2 Then the king gave orders to call in the magicians, the conjurers, the sorcerers and the Chaldeans to tell the king his dreams. So they came in and stood before the king.

3 The king said to them, "I had a dream and my spirit is anxious to understand the dream."

4 Then the Chaldeans spoke to the king in Aramaic: "O king, live forever! Tell the dream to your servants, and we will declare the interpretation."

5 The king replied to the Chaldeans, "The command from me is firm: if you do not make known to me the dream and its interpretation, you will be torn limb from limb and your houses will be made a rubbish heap.

6 "But if you declare the dream and its interpretation, you will receive from me gifts and a reward and great honor; therefore declare to me the dream and its interpretation."

7 They answered a second time and said, "Let the king tell the dream to his servants, and we will declare the interpretation."

8 The king replied, "I know for certain that you are bargaining for time, inasmuch as you have seen that the command from me is firm,

9 that if you do not make the dream known to me, there is only one decree for you. For you have agreed together to speak lying and corrupt words before me until the situation is changed; therefore tell me the dream, that I may know that you can declare to me its interpretation."

10 The Chaldeans answered the king and said, "There is not a man on earth who could declare the matter for the king, inasmuch as no great king or ruler has *ever* asked anything like this of any magician, conjurer or Chaldean.

11 "Moreover, the thing which the king demands is difficult, and there is no one else who could declare it to the king ex-

---

LIFE LESSONS

➤ **Daniel 1:17** — *God gave them knowledge and intelligence in every branch of literature and wisdom; Daniel even understood all kinds of visions and dreams.*

God has the power, wisdom, and resolve to equip you fully for whatever task or position He wants you to tackle. We will never fail in a God-given task because He failed to give us what we need.

cept gods, whose dwelling place is not with *mortal* flesh.''

12 Because of this the king became indignant and very furious and gave orders to destroy all the wise men of Babylon.

13 So the decree went forth that the wise men should be slain; and they looked for Daniel and his friends to kill *them.*

14 Then Daniel replied with discretion and discernment to Arioch, the captain of the king's bodyguard, who had gone forth to slay the wise men of Babylon;

15 he said to Arioch, the king's commander, ''For what reason is the decree from the king *so* urgent?'' Then Arioch informed Daniel about the matter.

➤ 16 So Daniel went in and requested of the king that he would give him time, in order that he might declare the interpretation to the king.

17 Then Daniel went to his house and informed his friends, Hananiah, Mishael and Azariah, about the matter,

18 so that they might request compassion from the God of heaven concerning this mystery, so that Daniel and his friends would not be destroyed with the rest of the wise men of Babylon.

19 Then the mystery was revealed to Daniel in a night vision. Then Daniel blessed the God of heaven;

20 Daniel said,
''Let the name of God be blessed forever and ever,

✳   For wisdom and power belong to Him.

21 ''It is He who changes the times and the epochs;
He removes kings and establishes kings;
He gives wisdom to wise men

And knowledge to men of understanding.

22 ''It is He who reveals the profound and hidden things;
He knows what is in the darkness, And the light dwells with Him.

23 ''To You, O God of my fathers, I give thanks and praise,
For You have given me wisdom and power;
Even now You have made known to me what we requested of You,
For You have made known to us the king's matter.''

24 Therefore, Daniel went in to Arioch, whom the king had appointed to destroy the wise men of Babylon; he went and spoke to him as follows: ''Do not destroy the wise men of Babylon! Take me into the king's presence, and I will declare the interpretation to the king.''

25 Then Arioch hurriedly brought Daniel into the king's presence and spoke to him as follows: ''I have found a man among the exiles from Judah who can make the interpretation known to the king!''

26 The king said to Daniel, whose name was Belteshazzar, ''Are you able to make known to me the dream which I have seen and its interpretation?''

27 Daniel answered before the king and said, ''As for the mystery about which the king has inquired, neither wise men, conjurers, magicians *nor* diviners are able to declare *it* to the king.

28 ''However, there is a God in heaven who reveals mysteries, and He has made known to King Nebuchadnezzar what will take place in the latter days. This was your dream and the visions in your mind *while* on your bed.

29 ''As for you, O king, *while* on your bed your thoughts turned to what would take place in the future; and He who reveals mysteries has made known to you what will take place.

30 ''But as for me, this mystery has not been revealed to me for any wisdom residing in me more than in any *other* living man, but for the purpose of making the interpretation known to the king, and that you may understand the thoughts of your mind.

31 ''You, O king, were looking and behold, there was a single great statue; that statue, which was large and of extraordinary

---

LIFE LESSONS

➤ **Daniel 2:16** — *Daniel went in and requested of the king that he would give him time, in order that he might declare the interpretation to the king.*

*B*efore Daniel ever brought his urgent request to God, he demonstrated his trust that the Lord would interpret the dream for the king. Trusting God means looking beyond what we can see to what God sees.

splendor, was standing in front of you, and its appearance was awesome.

32 "The head of that statue *was made* of fine gold, its breast and its arms of silver, its belly and its thighs of bronze,

33 its legs of iron, its feet partly of iron and partly of clay.

34 "You continued looking until a stone was cut out without hands, and it struck the statue on its feet of iron and clay and crushed them.

35 "Then the iron, the clay, the bronze, the silver and the gold were crushed all at the same time and became like chaff from the summer threshing floors; and the wind carried them away so that not a trace of them was found. But the stone that struck the statue became a great mountain and filled the whole earth.

36 "This *was* the dream; now we will tell its interpretation before the king.

37 "You, O king, are the king of kings, to whom the God of heaven has given the kingdom, the power, the strength and the glory;

38 and wherever the sons of men dwell, *or* the beasts of the field, or the birds of the sky, He has given *them* into your hand and has caused you to rule over them all. You are the head of gold.

39 "After you there will arise another kingdom inferior to you, then another third kingdom of bronze, which will rule over all the earth.

40 "Then there will be a fourth kingdom as strong as iron; inasmuch as iron crushes and shatters all things, so, like iron that breaks in pieces, it will crush and break all these in pieces.

41 "In that you saw the feet and toes, partly of potter's clay and partly of iron, it will be a divided kingdom; but it will have in it the toughness of iron, inasmuch as you saw the iron mixed with common clay.

42 "As the toes of the feet *were* partly of iron and partly of pottery, *so* some of the kingdom will be strong and part of it will be brittle.

43 "And in that you saw the iron mixed with common clay, they will combine with one another in the seed of men; but they will not adhere to one another, even as iron does not combine with pottery.

➤ 44 "In the days of those kings the God of heaven will set up a kingdom which will never be destroyed, and *that* kingdom will not be left for another people; it will crush and put an end to all these kingdoms, but it will itself endure forever.

45 "Inasmuch as you saw that a stone was cut out of the mountain without hands and that it crushed the iron, the bronze, the clay, the silver and the gold, the great God has made known to the king what will take place in the future; so the dream is true and its interpretation is trustworthy."

46 Then King Nebuchadnezzar fell on his face and did homage to Daniel, and gave orders to present to him an offering and fragrant incense.

47 The king answered Daniel and said, "Surely your God is a God of gods and a Lord of kings and a revealer of mysteries, since you have been able to reveal this mystery."

48 Then the king promoted Daniel and gave him many great gifts, and he made him ruler over the whole province of Babylon and chief prefect over all the wise men of Babylon.

49 And Daniel made request of the king, and he appointed Shadrach, Meshach and Abed-nego over the administration of the province of Babylon, while Daniel *was* at the king's court.

✦ Psalm 135:15–21

15 The idols of the nations are *but* silver and gold,
   The work of man's hands.

16 They have mouths, but they do not speak;
   They have eyes, but they do not see;

17 They have ears, but they do not hear,
   Nor is there any breath at all in their mouths.

LIFE LESSONS

➤ **Daniel 2:44 — *The God of heaven will set up a kingdom which will never be destroyed.***

*W*hen we face various difficulties and challenges, it can give us great hope to remember that, whatever happens, we are intimately connected to the One who is always victorious.

18 Those who make them will be like
      them,
      Yes, everyone who trusts in them.
19 O house of Israel, bless the LORD;
      O house of Aaron, bless the LORD;
20 O house of Levi, bless the LORD;
      You who revere the LORD, bless the
      LORD.
21 Blessed be the LORD from Zion,
      Who dwells in Jerusalem.
      Praise the LORD!

✦ Proverbs 29:10

10 Men of bloodshed hate the
      blameless,
      But the upright are concerned for
      his life.

✦ 1 Peter 5:1–14

5 THEREFORE, I exhort the elders
among you, as *your* fellow elder and
witness of the sufferings of Christ, and
a partaker also of the glory that is to be
revealed,
➤ 2   shepherd the flock of God among
you, exercising oversight not under compulsion, but voluntarily, according to *the
will of* God; and not for sordid gain, but
with eagerness;
3   nor yet as lording it over those allotted to your charge, but proving to be
examples to the flock.
4   And when the Chief Shepherd appears, you will receive the unfading
crown of glory.
5   You younger men, likewise, be subject to *your* elders; and all of you, clothe
yourselves with humility toward one another, for GOD IS OPPOSED TO THE PROUD,
BUT GIVES GRACE TO THE HUMBLE.
6   Therefore humble yourselves under
the mighty hand of God, that He may
exalt you at the proper time,
➤ 7   casting all your anxiety on Him, because He cares for you.
➤ 8   Be of sober *spirit,* be on the alert.
✳ Your adversary, the devil, prowls around
like a roaring lion, seeking someone to
devour.
9   But resist him, firm in *your* faith,
knowing that the same experiences of

suffering are being accomplished by
your brethren who are in the world.
10 After you have suffered for a little
while, the God of all grace, who called
you to His eternal glory in Christ, will
Himself perfect, confirm, strengthen *and*
establish you.
11 To Him *be* dominion forever and
ever. Amen.
12 Through Silvanus, our faithful
brother (for so I regard *him*), I have
written to you briefly, exhorting and testifying that this is the true grace of God.
Stand firm in it!
13 She who is in Babylon, chosen together with you, sends you greetings,
and *so does* my son, Mark.
14 Greet one another with a kiss of
love.
      Peace be to you all who are in Christ.

LIFE LESSONS

➤ **1 Peter 5:2** — *Shepherd the flock of
God among you, exercising oversight not
under compulsion, but voluntarily.*

*G*od delights in willing service, not in
grudging compliance—as if we were
doing Him a favor by submitting to His
instructions. Eager obedience reveals a
heart in love with the One who gave the
command.

➤ **1 Peter 5:7** — *Casting all your anxiety
on Him, because He cares for you.*

*R*egardless of the concern or worry,
God wants us to bring everything
to Him. He always has our best interests
at heart and will use His infinite power
to help us become the people we are
meant to be.

➤ **1 Peter 5:8** — *Your adversary, the
devil, prowls around like a roaring lion,
seeking someone to devour.*

*W*e must never forget that we are in
a spiritual war with an enemy who
is looking for weaknesses. We should
never give him a foothold. Regardless of
how well things may seem to be going
for us, we must always keep our hearts
and minds focused on Christ—obedient
to His commands and faithful to His purposes (Eph. 6:10–17).

Daniel 3:1—4:37

3 NEBUCHADNEZZAR the king made an image of gold, the height of which *was* sixty cubits *and* its width six cubits; he set it up on the plain of Dura in the province of Babylon.

2 Then Nebuchadnezzar the king sent *word* to assemble the satraps, the prefects and the governors, the counselors, the treasurers, the judges, the magistrates and all the rulers of the provinces to come to the dedication of the image that Nebuchadnezzar the king had set up.

3 Then the satraps, the prefects and the governors, the counselors, the treasurers, the judges, the magistrates and all the rulers of the provinces were assembled for the dedication of the image that Nebuchadnezzar the king had set up; and they stood before the image that Nebuchadnezzar had set up.

4 Then the herald loudly proclaimed: "To you the command is given, O peoples, nations and *men of every* language,

5 that at the moment you hear the sound of the horn, flute, lyre, trigon, psaltery, bagpipe and all kinds of music, you are to fall down and worship the golden image that Nebuchadnezzar the king has set up.

6 "But whoever does not fall down and worship shall immediately be cast into the midst of a furnace of blazing fire."

7 Therefore at that time, when all the peoples heard the sound of the horn, flute, lyre, trigon, psaltery, bagpipe and all kinds of music, all the peoples, nations and *men of every* language fell down *and* worshiped the golden image that Nebuchadnezzar the king had set up.

8 For this reason at that time certain Chaldeans came forward and brought charges against the Jews.

9 They responded and said to Nebuchadnezzar the king: "O king, live forever!

10 "You, O king, have made a decree that every man who hears the sound of the horn, flute, lyre, trigon, psaltery, and bagpipe and all kinds of music, is to fall down and worship the golden image.

11 "But whoever does not fall down and worship shall be cast into the midst of a furnace of blazing fire.

12 "There are certain Jews whom you have appointed over the administration of the province of Babylon, *namely* Shadrach, Meshach and Abed-nego. These men, O king, have disregarded you; they do not serve your gods or worship the golden image which you have set up."

13 Then Nebuchadnezzar in rage and anger gave orders to bring Shadrach, Meshach and Abed-nego; then these men were brought before the king.

14 Nebuchadnezzar responded and said to them, "Is it true, Shadrach, Meshach and Abed-nego, that you do not serve my gods or worship the golden image that I have set up?

15 "Now if you are ready, at the moment you hear the sound of the horn, flute, lyre, trigon, psaltery and bagpipe and all kinds of music, to fall down and worship the image that I have made, *very well.* But if you do not worship, you will immediately be cast into the midst of a furnace of blazing fire; and what god is there who can deliver you out of my hands?"

16 Shadrach, Meshach and Abed-nego replied to the king, "O Nebuchadnezzar, we do not need to give you an answer concerning this matter.

17 "If it be *so,* our God whom we serve is able to deliver us from the furnace of blazing fire; and He will deliver us out of your hand, O king.

18 "But *even* if He *does* not, let it be known to you, O king, that we are not going to serve your gods or worship the golden image that you have set up."

19 Then Nebuchadnezzar was filled with wrath, and his facial expression was altered toward Shadrach, Meshach and Abed-nego. He answered by giving

---

LIFE LESSONS

➤ **Daniel 3:15 — *"What god is there who can deliver you out of my hands?"***

Nebuchadnezzar could not conceive of a deity with the power to frustrate his wishes. Hadn't he already destroyed Jerusalem, where the temple of the Lord had been? God would not let his arrogant challenge stand.

Life Examples:

SHADRACH, MESHACH, AND ABEDNEGO:
Facing the Fire

DANIEL 3:19–29

*A*s Nebuchadnezzar scanned the horizon, he saw people of many nationalities bowing down to the image he had made. He had declared that when the music began, everyone was to fall in worship before the immense gold statue he had set up. As far as he could see, people were obeying.

But then the king received word that three Hebrews—Shadrach, Meshach, and Abed-nego—refused to bow. Nebuchadnezzar flew into a rage and threatened to throw the three men into a raging furnace. They faced a decision: obey God and face the fire, or pay homage to Nebuchadnezzar and dishonor God.

They chose the former—and God delivered them.

The Lord is just as able to deliver you from whatever fire you face. Therefore, trust Him, for He is able and willing to help you today, regardless of your struggle.

orders to heat the furnace seven times more than it was usually heated.
20 He commanded certain valiant warriors who *were* in his army to tie up Shadrach, Meshach and Abed-nego in order to cast *them* into the furnace of blazing fire.
21 Then these men were tied up in their trousers, their coats, their caps and their *other* clothes, and were cast into the midst of the furnace of blazing fire.
22 For this reason, because the king's command *was* urgent and the furnace had been made extremely hot, the flame of the fire slew those men who carried up Shadrach, Meshach and Abed-nego.
23 But these three men, Shadrach, Meshach and Abed-nego, fell into the midst of the furnace of blazing fire *still* tied up.
24 Then Nebuchadnezzar the king was astounded and stood up in haste; he said to his high officials, "Was it not three men we cast bound into the midst of the fire?" They replied to the king, "Certainly, O king."
25 He said, "Look! I see four men loosed *and* walking *about* in the midst of the fire without harm, and the appearance of the fourth is like a son of *the* gods!"
26 Then Nebuchadnezzar came near to the door of the furnace of blazing fire; he responded and said, "Shadrach, Meshach and Abed-nego, come out, you servants of the Most High God, and come here!" Then Shadrach, Meshach and Abed-nego came out of the midst of the fire.
27 The satraps, the prefects, the governors and the king's high officials gathered around *and* saw in regard to these men that the fire had no effect on the

bodies of these men nor was the hair of their head singed, nor were their trousers damaged, nor had the smell of fire *even* come upon them.
28 Nebuchadnezzar responded and ◄ said, "Blessed be the God of Shadrach, Meshach and Abed-nego, who has sent His angel and delivered His servants who put their trust in Him, violating the king's command, and yielded up their bodies so as not to serve or worship any god except their own God.
29 "Therefore I make a decree that any people, nation or tongue that speaks anything offensive against the God of Shadrach, Meshach and Abed-nego shall be torn limb from limb and their houses reduced to a rubbish heap, inasmuch as there is no other god who is able to deliver in this way."
30 Then the king caused Shadrach, Meshach and Abed-nego to prosper in the province of Babylon.

LIFE LESSONS

➤ **Daniel 3:28 — "God . . . sent His Angel and delivered His servants who put their trust in Him."**

*N*ebuchadnezzar could not conceive of a deity with the power to frustrate his wishes. Hadn't he already destroyed Jerusalem, where the temple of the Lord had been? Yet God would not let his arrogant challenge stand. Shadrach, Meshach and Abed-nego remained faithful to the Lord—regardless of whether or not He saved them—because they acknowledged His right to their lives (Dan. 3:16–17). You should do so as well.

4 NEBUCHADNEZZAR the king to all the peoples, nations, and *men of every* language that live in all the earth: "May your peace abound!

2 "It has seemed good to me to declare the signs and wonders which the Most High God has done for me.

3 "How great are His signs
And how mighty are His wonders!
His kingdom is an everlasting
  kingdom
And His dominion is from
  generation to generation.

4 "I, Nebuchadnezzar, was at ease in my house and flourishing in my palace.

5 "I saw a dream and it made me fearful; and *these* fantasies *as I lay* on my bed and the visions in my mind kept alarming me.

6 "So I gave orders to bring into my presence all the wise men of Babylon, that they might make known to me the interpretation of the dream.

7 "Then the magicians, the conjurers, the Chaldeans and the diviners came in and I related the dream to them, but they could not make its interpretation known to me.

8 "But finally Daniel came in before me, whose name is Belteshazzar according to the name of my god, and in whom is a spirit of the holy gods; and I related the dream to him, *saying,*

9 'O Belteshazzar, chief of the magicians, since I know that a spirit of the holy gods is in you and no mystery baffles you, tell *me* the visions of my dream which I have seen, along with its interpretation.

10 'Now *these were* the visions in my mind *as I lay* on my bed: I was looking, and behold, *there was* a tree in the midst of the earth and its height *was* great.

11 'The tree grew large and became
    strong
And its height reached to the sky,
And it *was* visible to the end of the
    whole earth.

12 'Its foliage *was* beautiful and its fruit
    abundant,
And in it *was* food for all.
The beasts of the field found shade
    under it,
And the birds of the sky dwelt in its
    branches,
And all living creatures fed
    themselves from it.

13 'I was looking in the visions in my mind *as I lay* on my bed, and behold, an *angelic* watcher, a holy one, descended from heaven.

14 'He shouted out and spoke as
    follows:
"Chop down the tree and cut off its
    branches,
Strip off its foliage and scatter its
    fruit;
Let the beasts flee from under it
And the birds from its branches.

15 "Yet leave the stump with its roots in
    the ground,
But with a band of iron and bronze
    around it
In the new grass of the field;
And let him be drenched with the
    dew of heaven,
And let him share with the beasts in
    the grass of the earth.

16 "Let his mind be changed from *that*
    of a man
And let a beast's mind be given to
    him,
And let seven periods of time pass
    over him.

17 "This sentence is by the decree of the
    angelic watchers
And the decision is a command of
    the holy ones,
In order that the living may know
That the Most High is ruler over the
    realm of mankind,
And bestows it on whom He wishes
And sets over it the lowliest of
    men."

18 'This is the dream *which* I, King Nebuchadnezzar, have seen. Now you, Belteshazzar, tell *me* its interpretation, inasmuch as none of the wise men of my kingdom is able to make known to me the interpretation; but you are able, for a spirit of the holy gods is in you.'

19 "Then Daniel, whose name is Belteshazzar, was appalled for a while as his thoughts alarmed him. The king responded and said, 'Belteshazzar, do not let the dream or its interpretation alarm you.' Belteshazzar replied, 'My lord, *if only* the dream applied to those who hate you and its interpretation to your adversaries!

20 'The tree that you saw, which became large and grew strong, whose height reached to the sky and was visible to all the earth

21 and whose foliage *was* beautiful and its fruit abundant, and in which *was* food for all, under which the beasts of the field dwelt and in whose branches the birds of the sky lodged—

22 it is you, O king; for you have become great and grown strong, and your majesty has become great and reached to the sky and your dominion to the end of the earth.

23 'In that the king saw an *angelic* watcher, a holy one, descending from heaven and saying, "Chop down the tree and destroy it; yet leave the stump with its roots in the ground, but with a band of iron and bronze *around it* in the new grass of the field, and let him be drenched with the dew of heaven, and let him share with the beasts of the field until seven periods of time pass over him,"

24 this is the interpretation, O king, and this is the decree of the Most High, which has come upon my lord the king:

25 that you be driven away from mankind and your dwelling place be with the beasts of the field, and you be given grass to eat like cattle and be drenched with the dew of heaven; and seven periods of time will pass over you, until you recognize that the Most High is ruler over the realm of mankind and bestows it on whomever He wishes.

➤ 26 'And in that it was commanded to leave the stump with the roots of the tree, your kingdom will be assured to you after you recognize that *it is* Heaven *that* rules.

27 'Therefore, O king, may my advice be pleasing to you: break away now from

---

---

your sins by *doing* righteousness and from your iniquities by showing mercy to *the* poor, in case there may be a prolonging of your prosperity.'

28 "All *this* happened to Nebuchadnezzar the king.

29 "Twelve months later he was walking on the *roof of* the royal palace of Babylon.

30 "The king reflected and said, 'Is this not Babylon the great, which I myself have built as a royal residence by the might of my power and for the glory of my majesty?'

31 "While the word *was* in the king's mouth, a voice came from heaven, *saying,* 'King Nebuchadnezzar, to you it is declared: sovereignty has been removed from you,

32 and you will be driven away from mankind, and your dwelling place *will be* with the beasts of the field. You will be given grass to eat like cattle, and seven periods of time will pass over you until you recognize that the Most High is ruler over the realm of mankind and bestows it on whomever He wishes.'

33 "Immediately the word concerning Nebuchadnezzar was fulfilled; and he was driven away from mankind and began eating grass like cattle, and his body was drenched with the dew of heaven until his hair had grown like eagles' *feathers* and his nails like birds' *claws.*

34 "But at the end of that period, I, Nebuchadnezzar, raised my eyes toward heaven and my reason returned to me, and I blessed the Most High and praised and honored Him who lives forever;

> For His dominion is an everlasting dominion,
> And His kingdom *endures* from generation to generation.

35 "All the inhabitants of the earth are accounted as nothing,
> But He does according to His will in the host of heaven
> And *among* the inhabitants of earth;
> And no one can ward off His hand
> Or say to Him, 'What have You done?'

36 "At that time my reason returned to me. And my majesty and splendor were restored to me for the glory of my kingdom, and my counselors and my nobles

➤ **Daniel 4:37** — *"He is able to humble those who walk in pride."*

*G*od opposes human pride wherever He finds it, and He always will. He declares, "I will also put an end to the arrogance of the proud and abase the haughtiness of the ruthless" (Is. 13:11).

began seeking me out; so I was reestablished in my sovereignty, and surpassing greatness was added to me.
➤ 37 "Now I, Nebuchadnezzar, praise, exalt and honor the King of heaven, for all His works are true and His ways just, and He is able to humble those who walk in pride."

Psalm 136:1–9

136 GIVE thanks to the LORD, for He is good,
For His lovingkindness is everlasting.
2   Give thanks to the God of gods,
For His lovingkindness is everlasting.
3   Give thanks to the Lord of lords,
For His lovingkindness is everlasting.
✳4   To Him who alone does great wonders,
For His lovingkindness is everlasting;
5   To Him who made the heavens with skill,
For His lovingkindness is everlasting;
6   To Him who spread out the earth above the waters,
For His lovingkindness is everlasting;
7   To Him who made the great lights,
For His lovingkindness is everlasting:
8   The sun to rule by day,
For His lovingkindness is everlasting,
9   The moon and stars to rule by night,
For His lovingkindness is everlasting.

Proverbs 29:11

11   A fool always loses his temper,
But a wise man holds it back.

2 Peter 1:1–21

1 SIMON PETER, a bond-servant and apostle of Jesus Christ,
To those who have received a faith of the same kind as ours, by the righteousness of our God and Savior, Jesus Christ:
2   Grace and peace be multiplied to you in the knowledge of God and of Jesus our Lord;
3   seeing that His divine power has granted to us everything pertaining to life and godliness, through the true knowledge of Him who called us by His own glory and excellence.
4   For by these He has granted to us His precious and magnificent promises, so that by them you may become partakers of *the* divine nature, having escaped the corruption that is in the world by lust.
5   Now for this very reason also, applying all diligence, in your faith supply moral excellence, and in *your* moral excellence, knowledge,
6   and in *your* knowledge, self-control, and in *your* self-control, perseverance, and in *your* perseverance, godliness,
7   and in *your* godliness, brotherly kindness, and in *your* brotherly kindness, love.
8   For if these *qualities* are yours and are increasing, they render you neither useless nor unfruitful in the true knowledge of our Lord Jesus Christ.
9   For he who lacks these *qualities* is blind *or* short-sighted, having forgotten *his* purification from his former sins.
10   Therefore, brethren, be all the more diligent to make certain about His calling and choosing you; for as long as you practice these things, you will never stumble;
11   for in this way the entrance into the eternal kingdom of our Lord and Savior Jesus Christ will be abundantly supplied to you.

LIFE LESSONS

➤ **2 Peter 1:8** — *If these qualities are yours and are increasing, they render you neither useless nor unfruitful in the true knowledge of our Lord Jesus Christ.*

*E*verything we need to become more like Christ, God has already given us. We do not need some new experience or fresh revelation to help us draw close to the Lord; we simply have to appropriate what He's already given. Jesus wants our spiritual lives to become both lush and fruitful, for He knows that such a fertile life greatly pleases God and gives us enormous satisfaction. How do we become fruitful? By abiding in Christ.

➤ **2 Peter 1:20, 21** — *No prophecy of Scripture is a matter of one's own interpretation, for no prophecy was ever made by an act of human will, but men moved by the Holy Spirit spoke from God.*

*A*t one time, Peter thought Christ's mission was to free Israel from the grasp of the Romans (Matt. 16:13–23; John 18:10, 11). Yet Jesus' purpose was far greater than that—He came to free mankind from sin and death. Just as no one could have predicted the way by which God would save the world, so we should not presume to know how He will fulfill His promises to us.

12 Therefore, I will always be ready to remind you of these things, even though you *already* know *them*, and have been established in the truth which is present with *you*.

13 I consider it right, as long as I am in this *earthly* dwelling, to stir you up by way of reminder,

14 knowing that the laying aside of my *earthly* dwelling is imminent, as also our Lord Jesus Christ has made clear to me.

15 And I will also be diligent that at any time after my departure you will be able to call these things to mind.

16 For we did not follow cleverly devised tales when we made known to you the power and coming of our Lord Jesus Christ, but we were eyewitnesses of His majesty.

17 For when He received honor and glory from God the Father, such an utterance as this was made to Him by the Majestic Glory, "This is My beloved Son with whom I am well-pleased"—

18 and we ourselves heard this utterance made from heaven when we were with Him on the holy mountain.

19 *So* we have the prophetic word *made* more sure, to which you do well to pay attention as to a lamp shining in a dark place, until the day dawns and the morning star arises in your hearts.

20 But know this first of all, that no ≺ prophecy of Scripture is *a matter* of one's own interpretation,

21 for no prophecy was ever made by an act of human will, but men moved by the Holy Spirit spoke from God.

Daniel 5:1—6:28

5 BELSHAZZAR the king held a great feast for a thousand of his nobles, and he was drinking wine in the presence of the thousand.

2 When Belshazzar tasted the wine, he gave orders to bring the gold and silver vessels which Nebuchadnezzar his father had taken out of the temple which *was* in Jerusalem, so that the king and his nobles, his wives and his concubines might drink from them.

3 Then they brought the gold vessels that had been taken out of the temple, the house of God which *was* in Jerusalem; and the king and his nobles, his wives and his concubines drank from them.

4 They drank the wine and praised the gods of gold and silver, of bronze, iron, wood and stone.

5 Suddenly the fingers of a man's hand emerged and began writing opposite the lampstand on the plaster of the wall of the king's palace, and the king saw the back of the hand that did the writing.

6 Then the king's face grew pale and his thoughts alarmed him, and his hip joints went slack and his knees began knocking together.

7 The king called aloud to bring in the conjurers, the Chaldeans and the diviners. The king spoke and said to the wise men of Babylon, "Any man who can read this inscription and explain its interpretation to me shall be clothed with purple and *have* a necklace of gold around his neck, and have authority as third *ruler* in the kingdom."

8 Then all the king's wise men came in, but they could not read the inscription or make known its interpretation to the king.

9 Then King Belshazzar was greatly alarmed, his face grew *even* paler, and his nobles were perplexed.

10 The queen entered the banquet hall because of the words of the king and his nobles; the queen spoke and said, "O king, live forever! Do not let your thoughts alarm you or your face be pale.

11 "There is a man in your kingdom in whom is a spirit of the holy gods; and in the days of your father, illumination, insight and wisdom like the wisdom of the gods were found in him. And King Nebuchadnezzar, your father, your father the king, appointed him chief of the magicians, conjurers, Chaldeans *and* diviners.

12 "This *was* because an extraordinary spirit, knowledge and insight, interpretation of dreams, explanation of enigmas and solving of difficult problems were found in this Daniel, whom the king named Belteshazzar. Let Daniel now be summoned and he will declare the interpretation."

13 Then Daniel was brought in before the king. The king spoke and said to Daniel, "Are you that Daniel who is one of the exiles from Judah, whom my father the king brought from Judah?

14 "Now I have heard about you that a spirit of the gods is in you, and that illumination, insight and extraordinary wisdom have been found in you.

15 "Just now the wise men *and* the conjurers were brought in before me that they might read this inscription and make its interpretation known to me, but they could not declare the interpretation of the message.

16 "But I personally have heard about you, that you are able to give interpretations and solve difficult problems. Now if you are able to read the inscription and make its interpretation known to me, you will be clothed with purple and *wear* a necklace of gold around your neck, and you will have authority as the third *ruler* in the kingdom."

17 Then Daniel answered and said before the king, "Keep your gifts for yourself or give your rewards to someone else; however, I will read the inscription to the king and make the interpretation known to him.

18 "O king, the Most High God granted

LIFE LESSONS

➤ **Daniel 5:17 —** *"Keep your gifts for yourself or give your rewards to someone else."*

Like Abraham long before him, Daniel had no interest in being made rich by a wicked ruler (Gen. 14:23). He also had no fear of the Babylonian king, for he feared the Lord above all (Is. 51:12, 13).

sovereignty, grandeur, glory and majesty to Nebuchadnezzar your father.

19 "Because of the grandeur which He bestowed on him, all the peoples, nations and *men of every* language feared and trembled before him; whomever he wished he killed and whomever he wished he spared alive; and whomever he wished he elevated and whomever he wished he humbled.

20 "But when his heart was lifted up and his spirit became so proud that he behaved arrogantly, he was deposed from his royal throne and *his* glory was taken away from him.

21 "He was also driven away from mankind, and his heart was made like *that of* beasts, and his dwelling place *was* with the wild donkeys. He was given grass to eat like cattle, and his body was drenched with the dew of heaven until he recognized that the Most High God is ruler over the realm of mankind and *that* He sets over it whomever He wishes.

22 "Yet you, his son, Belshazzar, have not humbled your heart, even though you knew all this,

23 but you have exalted yourself against the Lord of heaven; and they have brought the vessels of His house before you, and you and your nobles, your wives and your concubines have been drinking wine from them; and you have praised the gods of silver and gold, of bronze, iron, wood and stone, which do not see, hear or understand. But the God in whose hand are your life-breath and all your ways, you have not glorified.

24 "Then the hand was sent from Him and this inscription was written out.

25 "Now this is the inscription that was written out: 'MENĒ, MENĒ, TEKĒL, UPHARSIN.'

26 "This is the interpretation of the message: 'MENĒ'—God has numbered your kingdom and put an end to it.

27 "'TEKĒL'—you have been weighed on the scales and found deficient.

28 "'PERĒS'—your kingdom has been divided and given over to the Medes and Persians."

29 Then Belshazzar gave orders, and they clothed Daniel with purple and *put* a necklace of gold around his neck, and issued a proclamation concerning him that he *now* had authority as the third *ruler* in the kingdom.

30 That same night Belshazzar the Chaldean king was slain.

31 So Darius the Mede received the kingdom at about the age of sixty-two.

6 IT seemed good to Darius to appoint 120 satraps over the kingdom, that they would be in charge of the whole kingdom,

2 and over them three commissioners (of whom Daniel was one), that these satraps might be accountable to them, and that the king might not suffer loss.

3 Then this Daniel began distinguishing himself among the commissioners and satraps because he possessed an extraordinary spirit, and the king planned to appoint him over the entire kingdom.

4 Then the commissioners and satraps began trying to find a ground of accusation against Daniel in regard to government affairs; but they could find no ground of accusation or *evidence of* corruption, inasmuch as he was faithful, and no negligence or corruption was *to be* found in him.

5 Then these men said, "We will not find any ground of accusation against this Daniel unless we find *it* against him with regard to the law of his God."

6 Then these commissioners and satraps came by agreement to the king and spoke to him as follows: "King Darius, live forever!

7 "All the commissioners of the kingdom, the prefects and the satraps, the high officials and the governors have consulted together that the king should establish a statute and enforce an injunction that anyone who makes a petition to any god or man besides you, O king, for thirty days, shall be cast into the lions' den.

8 "Now, O king, establish the injunction and sign the document so that it may not be changed, according to the law of the Medes and Persians, which may not be revoked."

9 Therefore King Darius signed the document, that is, the injunction.

10 Now when Daniel knew that the document was signed, he entered his house (now in his roof chamber he had windows open toward Jerusalem); and he continued kneeling on his knees three times a day, praying and giving thanks before his God, as he had been doing previously.

LIFE PRINCIPLE **17**

WE STAND TALLEST AND STRONGEST ON OUR KNEES.

DANIEL 6:10, 11

*A*n older pastor got into the habit of challenging his congregation by quoting Jeremiah 33:3: "Call to Me and I will answer you, and I will tell you great and mighty things, which you do not know." Leveling his eyes at those gathered before him, he would say, "Try it. It works!"

This is a simple thought, but it carries a tremendous truth: God wants us to call to Him. In fact, many times He allows disappointments and difficulties into our lives so that we will draw closer to Him in intimate communion.

Prayer is a very powerful tool for believers—through it the Lord blesses us and frees us from bondage. In prayer we profess our need of Christ and ask for His solution to our problems. We also learn to worship Him and grow spiritually in His loving presence.

As we spend time with Him, God lovingly teaches us how to communicate with Him and listen for His still, small voice. Through it all, we grow deeper in our relationship with Him

Several things are essential to establishing a powerful prayer life:

1. *Choose a definite time to spend with the Lord in prayer.* Setting a time, whether early in the morning or late in the evening, is not the issue. Rather, consistency is the key. Ask God to show you the perfect time when you can be alone with Him.

2. *Select a place where you can be alone with Him.* Although, you may be limited as to where you can go to have time alone with the Lord, He will provide the perfect place for you to seek Him.

3. *Make the commitment to pray daily.* This alone tells God that your heart is open to Him and that you want to learn more about Him and what He has planned for you.

4. *Keep a journal that contains your requests*

and how God answers your prayers as a continuing testimony of God's work in your life. Remember to write down the specific verses that He applies to your situation and the promises He gives you from His Word.

God honors the prayers of His people. If you go to Him—seeking Him earnestly and obeying His commands—He will provide all you need. So don't worry about what to say; the Holy Spirit will show you. At times, tears are just as effective as words, and God is sensitive to every tear you cry. Just as He understands the hurt you feel, so He knows how to deal with and guide you through any trial you must endure.

Therefore, whenever a trial strikes, turn to Him immediately in prayer. His presence will fill you with hope, and He will give you the strength and wisdom you need to face the situation with confidence. Throughout your lifetime, you may face many difficult situations. Some will be very exciting, while others may feel as though they will break your heart. No matter what challenges come, you can be sure God is in the difficulty with you. He enjoys seeing you rejoice over His blessings, but He also mourns with you when tragedy strikes.

Always remember that God is bigger than any problem you face, and the distance between your success and failure or your victory and defeat is the distance between your knees and the floor as you kneel before your wondrous Lord and Savior in surrendered prayer. You are never taller or stronger than while on your knees! Why? Because He knows the way before you, and He can guide you through the difficulty if you will trust Him. And when you submit to Him in obedience, He applies His unlimited resources, wisdom, and power to help you.

My challenge to you is simple: Whatever you're facing, trust God with it. Ask Him to take away the anxiety, fear, and feelings of frustration. Have faith in the Lord and rest in His care. You will never feel more accepted or secure than you do in the presence of God. Victory awaits, so come to Him. ◈

11 Then these men came by agreement and found Daniel making petition and supplication before his God.

12 Then they approached and spoke before the king about the king's injunction, "Did you not sign an injunction that any man who makes a petition to any god or man besides you, O king, for thirty days, is to be cast into the lions' den?" The king replied, "The statement is true, according to the law of the Medes and Persians, which may not be revoked."

13 Then they answered and spoke before the king, "Daniel, who is one of the exiles from Judah, pays no attention to you, O king, or to the injunction which you signed, but keeps making his petition three times a day."

14 Then, as soon as the king heard this statement, he was deeply distressed and set *his* mind on delivering Daniel; and even until sunset he kept exerting himself to rescue him.

15 Then these men came by agreement to the king and said to the king, "Recognize, O king, that it is a law of the Medes and Persians that no injunction or statute which the king establishes may be changed."

16 Then the king gave orders, and Daniel was brought in and cast into the lions' den. The king spoke and said to Daniel, "Your God whom you constantly serve will Himself deliver you."

17 A stone was brought and laid over the mouth of the den; and the king sealed it with his own signet ring and with the signet rings of his nobles, so that nothing would be changed in regard to Daniel.

18 Then the king went off to his palace and spent the night fasting, and no entertainment was brought before him; and his sleep fled from him.

19 Then the king arose at dawn, at the break of day, and went in haste to the lions' den.

20 When he had come near the den to Daniel, he cried out with a troubled voice. The king spoke and said to Daniel, "Daniel, servant of the living God, has your God, whom you constantly serve, been able to deliver you from the lions?"

21 Then Daniel spoke to the king, "O king, live forever!

22 "My God sent His angel and shut the lions' mouths and they have not harmed me, inasmuch as I was found innocent before Him; and also toward you, O king, I have committed no crime."

23 Then the king was very pleased and gave orders for Daniel to be taken up out of the den. So Daniel was taken up out of the den and no injury whatever was found on him, because he had trusted in his God.

24 The king then gave orders, and they brought those men who had maliciously accused Daniel, and they cast them, their children and their wives into the lions' den; and they had not reached the bottom of the den before the lions overpowered them and crushed all their bones.

25 Then Darius the king wrote to all the peoples, nations and *men of every* language who were living in all the land: "May your peace abound!

26 "I make a decree that in all the dominion of my kingdom men are to fear and tremble before the God of Daniel;

> For He is the living God and
> enduring forever,
> And His kingdom is one which will
> not be destroyed,
> And His dominion *will be* forever.

27 "He delivers and rescues and
> performs signs and wonders
> In heaven and on earth,
> Who has *also* delivered Daniel from
> the power of the lions."

28 So this Daniel enjoyed success in the reign of Darius and in the reign of Cyrus the Persian.

✦ Psalm 136:10–26

10 To Him who smote the Egyptians in
> their firstborn,
> For His lovingkindness is
> everlasting,

LIFE LESSONS

➤ **Daniel 6:28 —** *So this Daniel enjoyed success in the reign of Darius and in the reign of Cyrus the Persian.*

*G*od desires for you to flourish, regardless of your circumstances. Daniel lived well and achieved great success in the midst of his situation—and he did so by honoring the Lord above all else. We are called to do the same.

11 And brought Israel out from their
midst,
For His lovingkindness is
everlasting,

12 With a strong hand and an
outstretched arm,
For His lovingkindness is
everlasting.

13 To Him who divided the Red Sea
asunder,
For His lovingkindness is
everlasting,

14 And made Israel pass through the
midst of it,
For His lovingkindness is
everlasting;

15 But He overthrew Pharaoh and his
army in the Red Sea,
For His lovingkindness is
everlasting.

16 To Him who led His people through
the wilderness,
For His lovingkindness is
everlasting;

17 To Him who smote great kings,
For His lovingkindness is
everlasting,

18 And slew mighty kings,
For His lovingkindness is
everlasting:

19 Sihon, king of the Amorites,
For His lovingkindness is
everlasting,

20 And Og, king of Bashan,
For His lovingkindness is
everlasting,

21 And gave their land as a heritage,
For His lovingkindness is
everlasting,

22 Even a heritage to Israel His
servant,
For His lovingkindness is
everlasting.

23 Who remembered us in our low
estate,
For His lovingkindness is
everlasting,

24 And has rescued us from our
adversaries,
For His lovingkindness is
everlasting;

25 Who gives food to all flesh,
For His lovingkindness is
everlasting.

26 Give thanks to the God of heaven,
For His lovingkindness is
everlasting.

Proverbs 29:12, 13

12 If a ruler pays attention to
falsehood,
All his ministers become wicked.

13 The poor man and the oppressor
have this in common:
The LORD gives light to the eyes of
both.

2 Peter 2:1–22

2 BUT false prophets also arose among
the people, just as there will also
be false teachers among you, who will
secretly introduce destructive heresies,
even denying the Master who bought
them, bringing swift destruction upon
themselves.
2 Many will follow their sensuality,
and because of them the way of the truth
will be maligned;
3 and in their greed they will exploit
you with false words; their judgment from
long ago is not idle, and their destruction
is asleep.
4 For if God did not spare angels when
they sinned, but cast them into hell and
committed them to pits of darkness, reserved for judgment;
5 and did not spare the ancient world,
but preserved Noah, a preacher of righteousness, with seven others, when He
brought a flood upon the world of the
ungodly;
6 and if He condemned the cities of
Sodom and Gomorrah to destruction by
reducing them to ashes, having made
them an example to those who would live
ungodly lives thereafter;

LIFE LESSONS

➤ **2 Peter 2:1 — But false prophets also
arose among the people . . . who will
secretly introduce destructive heresies.**

The best way to recognize counterfeit
doctrine is to become thoroughly
familiar with the truth. Someone who
walks daily with the Lord and has been
trained in the Word by His Holy Spirit
will not easily be led astray by false
teaching.

7   and *if* He rescued righteous Lot, oppressed by the sensual conduct of unprincipled men

8   (for by what he saw and heard *that* righteous man, while living among them, felt *his* righteous soul tormented day after day by *their* lawless deeds),

9   *then* the Lord knows how to rescue the godly from temptation, and to keep the unrighteous under punishment for the day of judgment,

10   and especially those who indulge the flesh in *its* corrupt desires and despise authority.

Daring, self-willed, they do not tremble when they revile angelic majesties,

11   whereas angels who are greater in might and power do not bring a reviling judgment against them before the Lord.

12   But these, like unreasoning animals, born as creatures of instinct to be captured and killed, reviling where they have no knowledge, will in the destruction of those creatures also be destroyed,

13   suffering wrong as the wages of doing wrong. They count it a pleasure to revel in the daytime. They are stains and blemishes, reveling in their deceptions, as they carouse with you,

14   having eyes full of adultery that never cease from sin, enticing unstable souls, having a heart trained in greed, accursed children;

15   forsaking the right way, they have gone astray, having followed the way of Balaam, the *son* of Beor, who loved the wages of unrighteousness;

16   but he received a rebuke for his own transgression, *for* a mute donkey, speaking with a voice of a man, restrained the madness of the prophet.

17   These are springs without water and mists driven by a storm, for whom the black darkness has been reserved.

18   For speaking out arrogant *words* of vanity they entice by fleshly desires, by sensuality, those who barely escape from the ones who live in error,

19   promising them freedom while they ◄ themselves are slaves of corruption; for by what a man is overcome, by this he is enslaved.

20   For if, after they have escaped the defilements of the world by the knowledge of the Lord and Savior Jesus Christ, they are again entangled in them and are overcome, the last state has become worse for them than the first.

21   For it would be better for them not to have known the way of righteousness, than having known it, to turn away from the holy commandment handed on to them.

22   It has happened to them according to the true proverb, "A DOG RETURNS TO ITS OWN VOMIT," and, "A sow, after washing, *returns* to wallowing in the mire."

LIFE LESSONS

➤ **2 Peter 2:19 — *They themselves are slaves of corruption.***

People will often encourage us to join them in sin. We don't have to yield to temptation or become ensnared in a destructive lifestyle. We must remember that only Jesus offers true freedom (John 8:36).

 Daniel 7:1—8:27

7 IN the first year of Belshazzar king of Babylon Daniel saw a dream and visions in his mind *as he lay* on his bed; then he wrote the dream down *and* related the *following* summary of it.

2   Daniel said, "I was looking in my vision by night, and behold, the four winds of heaven were stirring up the great sea.

3   "And four great beasts were coming up from the sea, different from one another.

4   "The first *was* like a lion and had *the* wings of an eagle. I kept looking until its wings were plucked, and it was lifted up from the ground and made to stand on two feet like a man; a human mind also was given to it.

5   "And behold, another beast, a second one, resembling a bear. And it was raised

up on one side, and three ribs *were* in its mouth between its teeth; and thus they said to it, 'Arise, devour much meat!'

6 "After this I kept looking, and behold, another one, like a leopard, which had on its back four wings of a bird; the beast also had four heads, and dominion was given to it.

7 "After this I kept looking in the night visions, and behold, a fourth beast, dreadful and terrifying and extremely strong; and it had large iron teeth. It devoured and crushed and trampled down the remainder with its feet; and it was different from all the beasts that were before it, and it had ten horns.

8 "While I was contemplating the horns, behold, another horn, a little one, came up among them, and three of the first horns were pulled out by the roots before it; and behold, this horn possessed eyes like the eyes of a man and a mouth uttering great *boasts*.

9 "I kept looking
Until thrones were set up,
And the Ancient of Days took *His* seat;
His vesture *was* like white snow
And the hair of His head like pure wool.
His throne *was* ablaze with flames,
Its wheels *were* a burning fire.

10 "A river of fire was flowing
And coming out from before Him;
Thousands upon thousands were attending Him,
And myriads upon myriads were standing before Him;
The court sat,
And the books were opened.

11 "Then I kept looking because of the sound of the boastful words which the horn was speaking; I kept looking until the beast was slain, and its body was destroyed and given to the burning fire.

12 "As for the rest of the beasts, their dominion was taken away, but an extension of life was granted to them for an appointed period of time.

13 "I kept looking in the night visions,
And behold, with the clouds of heaven
One like a Son of Man was coming,
And He came up to the Ancient of Days
And was presented before Him.

14 "And to Him was given dominion,

Glory and a kingdom,
That all the peoples, nations and men *of every* language
Might serve Him.
His dominion is an everlasting dominion
Which will not pass away;
And His kingdom is one
Which will not be destroyed.

15 "As for me, Daniel, my spirit was distressed within me, and the visions in my mind kept alarming me.

16 "I approached one of those who were standing by and began asking him the exact meaning of all this. So he told me and made known to me the interpretation of these things:

17 'These great beasts, which are four *in number*, are four kings *who* will arise from the earth.

18 'But the saints of the Highest One will receive the kingdom and possess the kingdom forever, for all ages to come.'

19 "Then I desired to know the exact meaning of the fourth beast, which was different from all the others, exceedingly dreadful, with its teeth of iron and its claws of bronze, *and which* devoured, crushed and trampled down the remainder with its feet,

20 and *the meaning* of the ten horns that *were* on its head and the other *horn* which came up, and before which three *of them* fell, namely, that horn which had eyes and a mouth uttering great *boasts* and which was larger in appearance than its associates.

21 "I kept looking, and that horn was waging war with the saints and overpowering them

22 until the Ancient of Days came and judgment was passed in favor of the

---

LIFE LESSONS

> **Daniel 7:13** — *"I kept looking in the night visions, and behold, with the clouds of heaven One like a Son of Man was coming."*

*I*n Matthew 26:64, Jesus explained that Daniel's vision applied to His Second Coming, causing an uproar in the Sanhedrin. They considered it blasphemy—but the only blasphemy committed that day was theirs for not recognizing that the Messiah was standing in front of them.

saints of the Highest One, and the time arrived when the saints took possession of the kingdom.

23 "Thus he said: 'The fourth beast will be a fourth kingdom on the earth, which will be different from all the *other* kingdoms and will devour the whole earth and tread it down and crush it.

24 'As for the ten horns, out of this kingdom ten kings will arise; and another will arise after them, and he will be different from the previous ones and will subdue three kings.

➤ 25 'He will speak out against the Most High and wear down the saints of the Highest One, and he will intend to make alterations in times and in law; and they will be given into his hand for a time, times, and half a time.

26 'But the court will sit *for judgment*, and his dominion will be taken away, annihilated and destroyed forever.

27 'Then the sovereignty, the dominion and the greatness of *all* the kingdoms under the whole heaven will be given to the people of the saints of the Highest One; His kingdom *will be* an everlasting kingdom, and all the dominions will serve and obey Him.'

28 "At this point the revelation ended. As for me, Daniel, my thoughts were greatly alarming me and my face grew pale, but I kept the matter to myself."

8 IN the third year of the reign of Belshazzar the king a vision appeared to me, Daniel, subsequent to the one which appeared to me previously.

2 I looked in the vision, and while I was looking I was in the citadel of Susa, which is in the province of Elam; and I looked in the vision and I myself was beside the Ulai Canal.

3 Then I lifted my eyes and looked, and behold, a ram which had two horns was standing in front of the canal. Now the two horns *were* long, but one *was* longer than the other, with the longer one coming up last.

4 I saw the ram butting westward, northward, and southward, and no *other* beasts could stand before him nor was there anyone to rescue from his power, but he did as he pleased and magnified *himself.*

5 While I was observing, behold, a male goat was coming from the west over the surface of the whole earth without

touching the ground; and the goat *had* a conspicuous horn between his eyes.

6 He came up to the ram that had the two horns, which I had seen standing in front of the canal, and rushed at him in his mighty wrath.

7 I saw him come beside the ram, and he was enraged at him; and he struck the ram and shattered his two horns, and the ram had no strength to withstand him. So he hurled him to the ground and trampled on him, and there was none to rescue the ram from his power.

8 Then the male goat magnified *himself* exceedingly. But as soon as he was mighty, the large horn was broken; and in its place there came up four conspicuous *horns* toward the four winds of heaven.

9 Out of one of them came forth a rather small horn which grew exceedingly great toward the south, toward the east, and toward the Beautiful *Land.*

10 It grew up to the host of heaven and caused some of the host and some of the stars to fall to the earth, and it trampled them down.

11 It even magnified *itself* to be equal with the Commander of the host; and it removed the regular sacrifice from Him, and the place of His sanctuary was thrown down.

12 And on account of transgression the host will be given over *to the horn* along with the regular sacrifice; and it will fling truth to the ground and perform *its will* and prosper.

13 Then I heard a holy one speaking, and another holy one said to that particular one who was speaking, "How long will the vision *about* the regular sacrifice apply, while the transgression causes horror, so as to allow both the holy place and the host to be trampled?"

14 He said to me, "For 2,300 evenings *and* mornings; then the holy place will be properly restored."

15 When I, Daniel, had seen the vision, I sought to understand it; and behold, standing before me was one who looked like a man.

16 And I heard the voice of a man between *the banks of* Ulai, and he called out and said, "Gabriel, give this *man* an understanding of the vision."

17 So he came near to where I was standing, and when he came I was frightened and fell on my face; but he said to me, "Son of man, understand that the vision pertains to the time of the end."

18 Now while he was talking with me, I sank into a deep sleep with my face to the ground; but he touched me and made me stand upright.

19 He said, "Behold, I am going to let you know what will occur at the final period of the indignation, for *it* pertains to the appointed time of the end.

20 "The ram which you saw with the two horns represents the kings of Media and Persia.

➤ 21 "The shaggy goat *represents* the kingdom of Greece, and the large horn that is between his eyes is the first king.

22 "The broken *horn* and the four *horns that* arose in its place *represent* four kingdoms *which* will arise from *his* nation, although not with his power.

23 "In the latter period of their rule,
When the transgressors have run
    their course,
A king will arise,
Insolent and skilled in intrigue.

24 "His power will be mighty, but not
    by his *own* power,
And he will destroy to an
    extraordinary degree
And prosper and perform *his* will;

He will destroy mighty men and the
    holy people.

25 "And through his shrewdness
He will cause deceit to succeed by
    his influence;
And he will magnify *himself* in his
    heart,
And he will destroy many while
    they are at ease.
He will even oppose the Prince of
    princes,
But he will be broken without
    human agency.

26 "The vision of the evenings and
    mornings
Which has been told is true;
But keep the vision secret,
For *it* pertains to many days *in the
    future."*

27 Then I, Daniel, was exhausted and sick for days. Then I got up *again* and carried on the king's business; but I was astounded at the vision, and there was none to explain *it.*

✦ Psalm 137:1–6

137 BY the rivers of Babylon,
    There we sat down and wept,
When we remembered Zion.

2 Upon the willows in the midst of it
We hung our harps.

3 For there our captors demanded of
    us songs,
And our tormentors mirth, *saying,*
"Sing us one of the songs of Zion."

4 How can we sing the LORD'S song   ◄
In a foreign land?

5 If I forget you, O Jerusalem,
May my right hand forget *her* skill.

6 May my tongue cling to the roof of
    my mouth

LIFE LESSONS

➤ **Daniel 8:21 — *"The shaggy goat represents the kingdom of Greece, and the large horn that is between his eyes is the first king."***

This prophecy about Alexander the Great is so precise and clear that critics have tried to claim that it was written after the fact. God gives prophecies like this to build our trust in the truth and accuracy of His Word.

➤ **Psalm 137:4 — *How can we sing the LORD's song in a foreign land?***

While our surroundings and circumstances can greatly influence our natural ability to worship God, true worship has less to do with outward conditions than with a decision of the will to draw on the inward resources of the Spirit.

If I do not remember you,
If I do not exalt Jerusalem
Above my chief joy.

Proverbs 29:14

14 If a king judges the poor with truth,
His throne will be established
forever.

2 Peter 3:1–18

3 THIS is now, beloved, the second letter I am writing to you in which I am

WHAT THE BIBLE SAYS ABOUT

Spiritual Growth

2 Peter 3:18

*N*ot many people can say that on
the day they were saved, someone
explained the steps to spiritual growth. Unfortunately, some believers *never* hear how to
develop in their relationship with the Lord.
Since none of us matures as a Christian without taking action, Peter instructs believers,
"Grow in the grace and knowledge of our
Lord and Savior Jesus Christ" (2 Pet. 3:18).

Then how are we to grow? Second Peter 1:3
promises, "His divine power has granted to us
everything pertaining to life and godliness." It
is God that transforms us into His image, but
it is our responsibility to implement all that
He teaches us. Second Peter 1:5–7 continues,
"For this very reason also, applying all diligence, in your faith supply moral excellence,
and in your moral excellence, knowledge,
and in your knowledge, self-control, and in
your self-control, perseverance, and in your
perseverance, godliness, and in your godliness,
brotherly kindness, and in your brotherly kindness, love."

The Bible gives us powerful principles about
how to do so:

*First, we are responsible for renewing our
mind (Rom. 12:2).* Though God saves us and
gives us a new spirit, it is our duty to control
our thoughts and focus our minds on what

stirring up your sincere mind by way of
reminder,
2 that you should remember the words
spoken beforehand by the holy prophets
and the commandment of the Lord and
Savior *spoken* by your apostles.
3 Know this first of all, that in the last
days mockers will come with *their* mocking, following after their own lusts,
4 and saying, "Where is the promise
of His coming? For *ever* since the fathers
fell asleep, all continues just as it was
from the beginning of creation."
5 For when they maintain this, it escapes their notice that by the word of
God *the* heavens existed long ago and
the earth was formed out of water and
by water,

honors Him so that our minds can be transformed. Therefore, we must meditate on the
Word, considering what it means and applying
the truth we discover to our lives—because
that is how the Holy Spirit changes us and we
obtain "the mind of Christ" (1 Cor. 2:16).

*Second, we must be ready to admit our
failures and assume responsibility for them.*
When we deny our sins, we delay our spiritual
growth. But when we confess our transgressions, the opposite happens—we mature
because we admit our dependence upon God.
John tells us, "If we confess our sins, He is
faithful and righteous to forgive us our sins
and to cleanse us from all unrighteousness"
(James 5:16).

*The third step naturally follows the sec-
ond—after confession should come repentance.* This is more than acknowledging
wrongdoing or promising to try harder.
Repentance means that we commit to making
an about-face and heading in the opposite
direction from our sin. Paul taught, "Repent
and turn to God, performing deeds appropriate to repentance" (Acts 26:20). Instead of
behavior that is unbecoming to a believer, the
fruit of the Spirit is produced in us—"love, joy,
peace, patience, kindness, goodness, faithfulness, gentleness, self-control" (Gal. 5:22, 23).

God's ultimate goal is for all believers to
become more Christlike. That happens only
when, through faith, we obey His commands
and implement His principles. And soon our
relationship with Him begins to deepen in
ways we never thought possible. ◈

6 through which the world at that time was destroyed, being flooded with water.
7 But by His word the present heavens and earth are being reserved for fire, kept for the day of judgment and destruction of ungodly men.
➤ 8 But do not let this one *fact* escape your notice, beloved, that with the Lord one day is like a thousand years, and a thousand years like one day.
✳ 9 The Lord is not slow about His promise, as some count slowness, but is patient toward you, not wishing for any to perish but for all to come to repentance.
10 But the day of the Lord will come like a thief, in which the heavens will pass away with a roar and the elements will be destroyed with intense heat, and the earth and its works will be burned up.
11 Since all these things are to be destroyed in this way, what sort of people ought you to be in holy conduct and godliness,
➤ 12 looking for and hastening the coming of the day of God, because of which the heavens will be destroyed by burning, and the elements will melt with intense heat!
13 But according to His promise we are looking for new heavens and a new earth, in which righteousness dwells.
14 Therefore, beloved, since you look for these things, be diligent to be found by Him in peace, spotless and blameless,
15 and regard the patience of our Lord *as* salvation; just as also our beloved brother Paul, according to the wisdom given him, wrote to you,
16 as also in all *his* letters, speaking in

LIFE LESSONS

➤ **2 Peter 3:8 — *With the Lord one day is like a thousand years, and a thousand years like one day.***

*G*od simply does not run this world by our timetable—His view of time is inherently different than ours. What feels like a delay to us is right on schedule by His calendar. He often makes us wait, not to frustrate us, but to deepen our trust in Him.

➤ **2 Peter 3:12 — *Looking for . . . the coming of the day of God.***

*I*n Peter's day, believers experiencing persecution were eager for Christ to return to free them from suffering and oppression. However, this prophecy was not given merely for their relief but to spur them to live in a godly manner. An eager anticipation of the Lord's return should keep us living productively. Knowing what lies ahead should move us to please God, before Whom we will stand for judgment (1 Cor. 3:11–15).

them of these things, in which are some things hard to understand, which the untaught and unstable distort, as *they do* also the rest of the Scriptures, to their own destruction.
17 You therefore, beloved, knowing this beforehand, be on your guard so that you are not carried away by the error of unprincipled men and fall from your own steadfastness,
18 but grow in the grace and knowledge of our Lord and Savior Jesus Christ. To Him *be* the glory, both now and to the day of eternity. Amen.

DECEMBER 3

◈ Daniel 9:1—10:21

9 IN the first year of Darius the son of Ahasuerus, of Median descent, who was made king over the kingdom of the Chaldeans—
2 in the first year of his reign, I, Daniel, observed in the books the number of the years which was *revealed as* the word of the LORD to Jeremiah the prophet for the

completion of the desolations of Jerusalem, *namely,* seventy years.
3 So I gave my attention to the Lord God to seek *Him by* prayer and supplications, with fasting, sackcloth and ashes.
4 I prayed to the LORD my God and confessed and said, "Alas, O Lord, the great and awesome God, who keeps His covenant and lovingkindness for those who love Him and keep His commandments,

ANSWERS TO LIFE'S QUESTIONS

How can I learn to pray effectively?

DANIEL 9:2

Daniel demonstrates how to pray with both power and confidence. When he discovered that Jeremiah had prophesied that the Babylonian captivity would last seventy years and was almost over (Dan. 9:2), he fell to his knees and began interceding for his people (Dan. 9:4–19).

In Daniel 9, we see a great example of what prayer should be. Its focus is on almighty God and His character. It includes sincere confession, unselfishness, and dependence on the Word of God.

Such prayer has great power. In Daniel's case, God sent the angel Gabriel with His answer even before the prophet had completed his supplication.

To seek God during your own hardship, assume the humble stance that Daniel did—go to your knees. Model your prayer after Daniel's. As he said in Daniel 11:32: "The people who know their God will display strength and take action."

The Bible tells us, "The effective prayer of a righteous man can accomplish much" (James 5:16). *Effective*—that is exactly what we want our prayers to be, especially in a crisis. When we are obedient to God and are seeking Him in sincerity and truth, we can feel confident that He will answer our earnest prayers. What are His requirements for us?

Requirement 1: Fervent prayer.

Fervent prayers are filled with passion and the acknowledgement of personal helplessness. They also have a narrow focus on some specific difficulty. Scripture calls this type of prayer "laboring earnestly" (Col. 4:12).

Requirement 2: Righteousness.

At salvation, we become rightly related to God as His children. He permanently seals us with the Holy Spirit and declares us righteous forever because of our position in Jesus Christ. But the Bible also uses the word "righteous" to describe a believer's conduct. This means that to be called a "righteous person," we must be found in Christ (Phil. 3:9) *and* make it a habit to obey God (Eph. 4:1; Col. 1:10). This also means that as we pray, we listen intently and submit ourselves wholeheartedly to Him—confessing our sin and obeying all He tells us to do. If we willingly and knowingly engage in sin, then we do not live righteously and our prayers will lack power.

When the Lord hears the impassioned prayer of a righteous person whose life reflects God's ways, Scripture promises that the Holy Spirit will begin His divine work (Rom. 8:26, 27; 1 Cor. 2:12, 13). God responds with great power to the prayers of even one righteous person. Friend, that person can be *you!*

---

5   we have sinned, committed iniquity, acted wickedly and rebelled, even turning aside from Your commandments and ordinances.

6   "Moreover, we have not listened to Your servants the prophets, who spoke in Your name to our kings, our princes, our fathers and all the people of the land.

7   "Righteousness belongs to You, O Lord, but to us open shame, as it is this day—to the men of Judah, the inhabitants of Jerusalem and all Israel, those who are nearby and those who are far away in all the countries to which You have driven them, because of their unfaithful deeds which they have committed against You.

8   "Open shame belongs to us, O Lord, to our kings, our princes and our fathers, because we have sinned against You.

9   "To the Lord our God *belong* compassion and forgiveness, for we have rebelled against Him;

10 nor have we obeyed the voice of the LORD our God, to walk in His teachings which He set before us through His servants the prophets.

11 "Indeed all Israel has transgressed Your law and turned aside, not obeying Your voice; so the curse has been poured out on us, along with the oath which is written in the law of Moses the servant of God, for we have sinned against Him.

12 "Thus He has confirmed His words which He had spoken against us and against our rulers who ruled us, to bring on us great calamity; for under the whole heaven there has not been done *anything* like what was done to Jerusalem.

13 "As it is written in the law of Moses, all this calamity has come on us; yet we have not sought the favor of the LORD our God by turning from our iniquity and giving attention to Your truth.

14 "Therefore the LORD has kept the calamity in store and brought it on us; for the LORD our God is righteous with respect to all His deeds which He has done, but we have not obeyed His voice.

15 "And now, O Lord our God, who have brought Your people out of the land of Egypt with a mighty hand and have made a name for Yourself, as it is this day—we have sinned, we have been wicked.
16 "O Lord, in accordance with all Your righteous acts, let now Your anger and Your wrath turn away from Your city Jerusalem, Your holy mountain; for because of our sins and the iniquities of our fathers, Jerusalem and Your people *have become* a reproach to all those around us.
17 "So now, our God, listen to the prayer of Your servant and to his supplications, and for Your sake, O Lord, let Your face shine on Your desolate sanctuary.
18 "O my God, incline Your ear and hear! Open Your eyes and see our desolations and the city which is called by Your name; for we are not presenting our supplications before You on account of any merits of our own, but on account of Your great compassion.
19 "O Lord, hear! O Lord, forgive! O Lord, listen and take action! For Your own sake, O my God, do not delay, because Your city and Your people are called by Your name."
20 Now while I was speaking and praying, and confessing my sin and the sin of my people Israel, and presenting my supplication before the LORD my God in behalf of the holy mountain of my God,
21 while I was still speaking in prayer, then the man Gabriel, whom I had seen in the vision previously, came to me in *my* extreme weariness about the time of the evening offering.
22 He gave *me* instruction and talked with me and said, "O Daniel, I have now come forth to give you insight with understanding.
23 "At the beginning of your supplications the command was issued, and I have come to tell *you*, for you are highly esteemed; so give heed to the message and gain understanding of the vision.
24 "Seventy weeks have been decreed for your people and your holy city, to finish the transgression, to make an end of sin, to make atonement for iniquity, to bring in everlasting righteousness, to seal up vision and prophecy and to anoint the most holy *place.*
25 "So you are to know and discern *that* from the issuing of a decree to restore and rebuild Jerusalem until Messiah the Prince

there will be seven weeks and sixty-two weeks; it will be built again, with plaza and moat, even in times of distress.
26 "Then after the sixty-two weeks the Messiah will be cut off and have nothing, and the people of the prince who is to come will destroy the city and the sanctuary. And its end *will come* with a flood; even to the end there will be war; desolations are determined.
27 "And he will make a firm covenant with the many for one week, but in the middle of the week he will put a stop to sacrifice and grain offering; and on the wing of abominations *will come* one who makes desolate, even until a complete destruction, one that is decreed, is poured out on the one who makes desolate."

10 IN the third year of Cyrus king of Persia a message was revealed to Daniel, who was named Belteshazzar; and the message was true and *one of* great conflict, but he understood the message and had an understanding of the vision.
2 In those days, I, Daniel, had been mourning for three entire weeks.
3 I did not eat any tasty food, nor did meat or wine enter my mouth, nor did I use any ointment at all until the entire three weeks were completed.
4 On the twenty-fourth day of the first month, while I was by the bank of the great river, that is, the Tigris,
5 I lifted my eyes and looked, and behold, there was a certain man dressed in linen, whose waist was girded with *a belt of* pure gold of Uphaz.
6 His body also *was* like beryl, his face had the appearance of lightning, his eyes were like flaming torches, his arms and feet like the gleam of polished bronze, and the sound of his words like the sound of a tumult.

➤ 7 Now I, Daniel, alone saw the vision, while the men who were with me did not see the vision; nevertheless, a great dread fell on them, and they ran away to hide themselves.

8 So I was left alone and saw this great vision; yet no strength was left in me, for my natural color turned to a deathly pallor, and I retained no strength.

9 But I heard the sound of his words; and as soon as I heard the sound of his words, I fell into a deep sleep on my face, with my face to the ground.

10 Then behold, a hand touched me and set me trembling on my hands and knees.

11 He said to me, "O Daniel, man of high esteem, understand the words that I am about to tell you and stand upright, for I have now been sent to you." And when he had spoken this word to me, I stood up trembling.

✳ 12 Then he said to me, "Do not be afraid, Daniel, for from the first day that you set your heart on understanding *this* and on humbling yourself before your God, your words were heard, and I have come in response to your words.

➤ 13 "But the prince of the kingdom of Persia was withstanding me for twenty-one days; then behold, Michael, one of the chief princes, came to help me, for I had been left there with the kings of Persia.

14 "Now I have come to give you an understanding of what will happen to your people in the latter days, for the vision pertains to the days yet *future*."

15 When he had spoken to me according to these words, I turned my face toward the ground and became speechless.

16 And behold, one who resembled a human being was touching my lips; then I opened my mouth and spoke and said to him who was standing before me, "O my lord, as a result of the vision anguish has come upon me, and I have retained no strength.

17 "For how can such a servant of my lord talk with such as my lord? As for me, there remains just now no strength in me, nor has any breath been left in me."

18 Then *this* one with human appearance touched me again and strengthened me.

19 He said, "O man of high esteem, do not be afraid. Peace be with you; take courage and be courageous!" Now as soon as he spoke to me, I received strength and said, "May my lord speak, for you have strengthened me."

20 Then he said, "Do you understand why I came to you? But I shall now return to fight against the prince of Persia; so I am going forth, and behold, the prince of Greece is about to come.

21 "However, I will tell you what is inscribed in the writing of truth. Yet there is no one who stands firmly with me against these *forces* except Michael your prince.

✦ Psalm 137:7–9

7 Remember, O LORD, against the
    sons of Edom
  The day of Jerusalem,
  Who said, "Raze it, raze it
  To its very foundation."

8 O daughter of Babylon, you
    devastated one,
  How blessed will be the one who
    repays you
  With the recompense with which
    you have repaid us.

LIFE LESSONS

➤ **Daniel 10:7 — "I, Daniel, alone saw the vision, while the men who were with me did not see the vision; nevertheless, a great dread fell on them."**

𝒯he Lord told Moses, "No man can see Me and live" (Ex. 33:20). Paul said God dwells "in unapproachable light, whom no man has seen or can see" (1 Tim. 6:16). And yet even God's invisible presence makes men tremble.

➤ **Daniel 10:13 — "The prince of the kingdom of Persia was withstanding me twenty-one days."**

𝒲e get a small glimpse here of the spiritual realities of unseen warfare that take place around the prayers of God's people. Although our prayers are heard at once in heaven (Dan. 10:12), God's answer may delay in coming for reasons that are unknown and imperceptible to us—but they are still coming (2 Cor. 4:18; Heb 11:1).

9   How blessed will be the one who
         seizes and dashes your little ones
     Against the rock.

Proverbs 29:15

15   The rod and reproof give wisdom,
     But a child who gets his own way
         brings shame to his mother.

1 John 1:1–10

1 WHAT was from the beginning, what
  we have heard, what we have seen
with our eyes, what we have looked at
and touched with our hands, concerning
the Word of Life—
2   and the life was manifested, and we
have seen and testify and proclaim to
you the eternal life, which was with the
Father and was manifested to us—
➤ 3   what we have seen and heard we
proclaim to you also, so that you too may
have fellowship with us; and indeed our
fellowship is with the Father, and with
His Son Jesus Christ.
➤ 4   These things we write, so that our
joy may be made complete.
5   This is the message we have heard
from Him and announce to you, that God
is Light, and in Him there is no darkness
at all.
➤ 6   If we say that we have fellowship
with Him and yet walk in the darkness,
we lie and do not practice the truth;
7   but if we walk in the Light as He
Himself is in the Light, we have fellowship with one another, and the blood of
Jesus His Son cleanses us from all sin.
8   If we say that we have no sin, we are
deceiving ourselves and the truth is not
in us.

9   If we confess our sins, He is faithful
and righteous to forgive us our sins and
to cleanse us from all unrighteousness.
10   If we say that we have not sinned, we
make Him a liar and His word is not in us.

LIFE LESSONS

➤ **1 John 1:3 —** *Our fellowship is with
the Father and with His Son Jesus Christ.*

*E*verything in the Bible has been given
 to us to help us and enable us to
enjoy an intimate relationship with God
(Rom. 15:4). The Lord's top priority for
your life is to walk in close fellowship
with Him, and He makes sure we have
everything we need for "life and godliness" (2 Pet. 1:3).

➤ **1 John 1:4 —** *These things we write,
so that our joy may be made complete.*

*F*alse teachers were luring believers away from the faith, so John
reminded them of Jesus' words, "These
things I have spoken to you so that My
joy may be in you, and that your joy
may be made full" (John 15:11). When
we obey the Lord, His joy abides in us
regardless of circumstances. This is one
of the many blessings of obedience,
which cannot be found anywhere else.

➤ **1 John 1:6 —** *If we say that we have
fellowship with Him and yet walk in the
darkness, we lie and do not practice the
truth.*

*W*henever there is light, the darkness
 scatters. Likewise, when we have
a relationship with the Lord, sin cannot
continue in our lives (Is. 6:5–7). We are
reconciled to Him by the cleansing blood
of Jesus, and we continue in our fellowship with Him when we acknowledge
our transgressions, turn from our sin,
and follow Him in righteousness (Gal. 5).

Daniel 11:1—12:13

11 "IN the first year of Darius the
   Mede, I arose to be an encouragement and a protection for him.
2   "And now I will tell you the truth.

Behold, three more kings are going to
arise in Persia. Then a fourth will gain
far more riches than all *of them*; as soon
as he becomes strong through his riches,
he will arouse the whole *empire* against
the realm of Greece.
3   "And a mighty king will arise, and he

will rule with great authority and do as he pleases.

4 "But as soon as he has arisen, his kingdom will be broken up and parceled out toward the four points of the compass, though not to his *own* descendants, nor according to his authority which he wielded, for his sovereignty will be uprooted and *given* to others besides them.

5 "Then the king of the South will grow strong, along with *one* of his princes who will gain ascendancy over him and obtain dominion; his domain *will be* a great dominion *indeed*.

6 "After some years they will form an alliance, and the daughter of the king of the South will come to the king of the North to carry out a peaceful arrangement. But she will not retain her position of power, nor will he remain with his power, but she will be given up, along with those who brought her in and the one who sired her as well as he who supported her in *those* times.

7 "But one of the descendants of her line will arise in his place, and he will come against *their* army and enter the fortress of the king of the North, and he will deal with them and display *great* strength.

8 "Also their gods with their metal images *and* their precious vessels of silver and gold he will take into captivity to Egypt, and he on his part will refrain from *attacking* the king of the North for *some* years.

9 "Then the latter will enter the realm of the king of the South, but will return to his *own* land.

10 "His sons will mobilize and assemble a multitude of great forces; and one of them will keep on coming and overflow and pass through, that he may again wage war up to his *very* fortress.

11 "The king of the South will be enraged and go forth and fight with the king of the North. Then the latter will raise a great multitude, but *that* multitude will be given into the hand of the *former*.

12 "When the multitude is carried away, his heart will be lifted up, and he will cause tens of thousands to fall; yet he will not prevail.

13 "For the king of the North will again raise a greater multitude than the former, and after an interval of some years

he will press on with a great army and much equipment.

14 "Now in those times many will rise up against the king of the South; the violent ones among your people will also lift themselves up in order to fulfill the vision, but they will fall down.

15 "Then the king of the North will come, cast up a siege ramp and capture a well-fortified city; and the forces of the South will not stand *their ground,* not even their choicest troops, for there will be no strength to make a stand.

16 "But he who comes against him will do as he pleases, and no one will *be able to* withstand him; he will also stay *for a time* in the Beautiful Land, with destruction in his hand.

17 "He will set his face to come with the power of his whole kingdom, bringing with him a proposal of peace which he will put into effect; he will also give him the daughter of women to ruin it. But she will not take a stand *for him* or be on his side.

18 "Then he will turn his face to the coastlands and capture many. But a commander will put a stop to his scorn against him; moreover, he will repay him for his scorn.

19 "So he will turn his face toward the fortresses of his own land, but he will stumble and fall and be found no more.

20 "Then in his place one will arise who will send an oppressor through the Jewel of *his* kingdom; yet within a few days he will be shattered, though not in anger nor in battle.

21 "In his place a despicable person will arise, on whom the honor of kingship has not been conferred, but he will come in a time of tranquility and seize the kingdom by intrigue.

22 "The overflowing forces will be flooded away before him and shattered, and also the prince of the covenant.

23 "After an alliance is made with him he will practice deception, and he will go up and gain power with a small *force of* people.

24 "In a time of tranquility he will enter the richest *parts* of the realm, and he will accomplish what his fathers never did, nor his ancestors; he will distribute plunder, booty and possessions among them, and he will devise his schemes against strongholds, but *only* for a time.

25 "He will stir up his strength and courage against the king of the South with a large army; so the king of the South will mobilize an extremely large and mighty army for war; but he will not stand, for schemes will be devised against him.

26 "Those who eat his choice food will destroy him, and his army will overflow, but many will fall down slain.

27 "As for both kings, their hearts will be *intent* on evil, and they will speak lies *to each other* at the same table; but it will not succeed, for the end is still *to come* at the appointed time.

28 "Then he will return to his land with much plunder; but his heart will be *set* against the holy covenant, and he will take action and *then* return to his *own* land.

29 "At the appointed time he will return and come into the South, but this last time it will not turn out the way it did before.

30 "For ships of Kittim will come against him; therefore he will be disheartened and will return and become enraged at the holy covenant and take action; so he will come back and show regard for those who forsake the holy covenant.

31 "Forces from him will arise, desecrate the sanctuary fortress, and do away with the regular sacrifice. And they will set up the abomination of desolation.

➤ 32 "By smooth *words* he will turn to godlessness those who act wickedly toward the covenant, but the people who know their God will display strength and take action.

33 "Those who have insight among the people will give understanding to the many; yet they will fall by sword and by flame, by captivity and by plunder for *many* days.

34 "Now when they fall they will be

LIFE LESSONS

➤ **Daniel 11:32 — *"The people who know their God will display strength and take action."***

*O*ur intimacy with God—his highest priority for our lives—determines the impact of our lives. The better we know and love Him, the more "action" we take—not in our own power, but in His.

---

granted a little help, and many will join with them in hypocrisy.

35 "Some of those who have insight will fall, in order to refine, purge and make them pure until the end time; because *it is* still *to come* at the appointed time.

36 "Then the king will do as he pleases, and he will exalt and magnify himself above every god and will speak monstrous things against the God of gods; and he will prosper until the indignation is finished, for that which is decreed will be done.

37 "He will show no regard for the gods of his fathers or for the desire of women, nor will he show regard for any *other* god; for he will magnify himself above *them* all.

38 "But instead he will honor a god of fortresses, a god whom his fathers did not know; he will honor *him* with gold, silver, costly stones and treasures.

39 "He will take action against the strongest of fortresses with *the help of* a foreign god; he will give great honor to those who acknowledge *him* and will cause them to rule over the many, and will parcel out land for a price.

40 "At the end time the king of the South will collide with him, and the king of the North will storm against him with chariots, with horsemen and with many ships; and he will enter countries, overflow *them* and pass through.

41 "He will also enter the Beautiful Land, and many *countries* will fall; but these will be rescued out of his hand: Edom, Moab and the foremost of the sons of Ammon.

42 "Then he will stretch out his hand against *other* countries, and the land of Egypt will not escape.

43 "But he will gain control over the hidden treasures of gold and silver and over all the precious things of Egypt; and Libyans and Ethiopians *will follow* at his heels.

44 "But rumors from the East and from the North will disturb him, and he will go forth with great wrath to destroy and annihilate many.

45 "He will pitch the tents of his royal pavilion between the seas and the beautiful Holy Mountain; yet he will come to his end, and no one will help him.

12 "NOW at that time Michael, the great prince who stands *guard* over the sons of your people, will arise. And there will be a time of distress such as never occurred since there was a nation until that time; and at that time your people, everyone who is found written in the book, will be rescued.

➤ 2 "Many of those who sleep in the dust of the ground will awake, these to everlasting life, but the others to disgrace *and* everlasting contempt.

3 "Those who have insight will shine brightly like the brightness of the expanse of heaven, and those who lead the many to righteousness, like the stars forever and ever.

4 "But as for you, Daniel, conceal these words and seal up the book until the end of time; many will go back and forth, and knowledge will increase."

5 Then I, Daniel, looked and behold, two others were standing, one on this bank of the river and the other on that bank of the river.

6 And one said to the man dressed in linen, who was above the waters of the river, "How long *will it be* until the end of *these* wonders?"

7 I heard the man dressed in linen, who was above the waters of the river, as he raised his right hand and his left toward heaven, and swore by Him who lives forever that it would be for a time, times, and half *a time*; and as soon as they finish shattering the power of the holy people, all these *events* will be completed.

➤ 8 As for me, I heard but could not understand; so I said, "My lord, what *will be* the outcome of these *events*?"

9 He said, "Go *your way*, Daniel, for *these* words are concealed and sealed up until the end time.

10 "Many will be purged, purified and refined, but the wicked will act wickedly; and none of the wicked will understand, but those who have insight will understand.

11 "From the time that the regular sacrifice is abolished and the abomination of desolation is set up, *there will be* 1,290 days.

12 "How blessed is he who keeps waiting and attains to the 1,335 days!

13 "But as for you, go *your way* to the end; then you will enter into rest and rise *again* for your allotted portion at the end of the age."

Psalm 138:1–3

A Psalm of David.

138 I WILL give You thanks with all my heart;
I will sing praises to You before the gods.

2 I will bow down toward Your holy temple
And give thanks to Your name for Your lovingkindness and Your truth;
For You have magnified Your word according to all Your name.

3 On the day I called, You answered me;
You made me bold with strength in my soul.

LIFE LESSONS

➤ **Daniel 12:2 — *"Many of those who sleep in the dust of the ground will awake, these to everlasting life, but the others to disgrace and everlasting contempt."***

*A*ny hardships that God asks us to endure for His sake will one day seem like nothing in comparison to His reward (Rom. 8:18). However, if we fail to believe in Christ or choose anything in His place, a terrible judgment awaits (Rev. 20:11–15). As Jesus said in Mark 8:35, "Whoever wishes to save his life will lose it, but whoever loses his life for My sake and the gospel's will save it."

➤ **Daniel 12:8 — *"I heard but could not understand."***

*A*re there some Bible passages that confuse you? Take heart. Even the great prophet Daniel couldn't understand some of the visions given to Him because they were for a time yet to come. God will help us understand whatever we need to know through His Spirit and in His time (1 Cor. 2:10–13).

➤ **Psalm 138:2 — *You have magnified Your word according to all Your name.***

*T*he Bible is not merely one holy book among several; it is God's holy revelation to humanity. There is nothing else like it.

Proverbs 29:16

16 When the wicked increase,
      transgression increases;
      But the righteous will see their fall.

1 John 2:1–29

2 MY little children, I am writing these things to you so that you may not sin. And if anyone sins, we have an Advocate with the Father, Jesus Christ the righteous;
2 and He Himself is the propitiation for our sins; and not for ours only, but also for *those* of the whole world.
3 By this we know that we have come to know Him, if we keep His commandments.
4 The one who says, "I have come to know Him," and does not keep His commandments, is a liar, and the truth is not in him;
5 but whoever keeps His word, in him the love of God has truly been perfected. By this we know that we are in Him:
6 the one who says he abides in Him ought himself to walk in the same manner as He walked.
7 Beloved, I am not writing a new commandment to you, but an old commandment which you have had from the beginning; the old commandment is the word which you have heard.
8 On the other hand, I am writing a new commandment to you, which is true in Him and in you, because the darkness is passing away and the true Light is already shining.
9 The one who says he is in the Light and *yet* hates his brother is in the darkness until now.
10 The one who loves his brother abides in the Light and there is no cause for stumbling in him.
11 But the one who hates his brother is in the darkness and walks in the darkness, and does not know where he is going because the darkness has blinded his eyes.
12 I am writing to you, little children, because your sins have been forgiven you for His name's sake.

13 I am writing to you, fathers, because you know Him who has been from the beginning. I am writing to you, young men, because you have overcome the evil one. I have written to you, children, because you know the Father.
14 I have written to you, fathers, because you know Him who has been from the beginning. I have written to you, young men, because you are strong, and the word of God abides in you, and you have overcome the evil one.
15 Do not love the world nor the things in the world. If anyone loves the world, the love of the Father is not in him.
16 For all that is in the world, the lust of the flesh and the lust of the eyes and the boastful pride of life, is not from the Father, but is from the world.
17 The world is passing away, and *also* its lusts; but the one who does the will of God lives forever.
18 Children, it is the last hour; and just as you heard that antichrist is coming, even now many antichrists have appeared; from this we know that it is the last hour.
19 They went out from us, but they were not *really* of us; for if they had been

---

LIFE LESSONS

➤ 1 John 2:3 — *By this we know that we have come to know Him, if we keep His commandments.*

*W*hen we obey God by the power of His Spirit, we not only please God and make it possible for us to enjoy close fellowship with Him, we also build confidence in our hearts that we truly belong to Him. An intimate relationship with Christ makes it both possible and appealing for us to obey God, just as Jesus did. If we think of salvation as an invitation to sin—"He'll forgive me anyway"— we're on the wrong track.

➤ 1 John 2:19 — *If they had been of us, they would have remained with us.*

*N*ot even John the apostle knew what was in the hearts of those who comprised his local church. He did not know that some members of his congregation did not truly know Jesus, until they abandoned the faith.

The Spirit of the Antichrist

1 John 2:15–24

*M*any people have the philosophy that "it doesn't matter what you believe as long as you're sincere." However, it does matter what you believe because your beliefs determine your relationship with the Father, how you relate to others, and what eternal destiny is in store for you. One day we will stand before almighty God to give an account of how we've lived. Therefore, now is the time to be certain about what we believe and where those beliefs lead us.

What really matters is if our beliefs measure up to God's Word, or whether we've been taken in by the spirit of the age—which the Bible calls "the spirit of antichrist." Although *Antichrist* is the Bible's name for a specific individual who will someday lead the earth to rebel against almighty God, *antichrist* also means the spirit underlying our culture as it opposes the lordship of Jesus Christ.

It is as old as the garden of Eden: When Eve chose to rebel against the command of God, the spirit of antichrist appeared in our world. It's the willful determination to usurp the place of God by making our own decisions and ignoring His wisdom and sovereignty. Unfortunately, this lawless spirit has penetrated every part of the world we live in—it fills our universities, our businesses, and even our pulpits.

Therefore, it's vitally important that we know what we believe and why we believe it. We must believe that the Bible is the Word of God. We must believe Jesus is the Son of God, deity in human flesh, and that He is the only way to salvation. We must believe that He died on the Cross as the full payment for our sins and experienced a bodily resurrection so that we may be forgiven and have eternal life. We must believe that the Holy Spirit indwells every believer and has sealed us as children of God. Finally, we must believe that Jesus Christ is coming again and will take us to the eternal home He has prepared.

John writes, "Every spirit that confesses that Jesus Christ has come in the flesh is from God; and every spirit that does not confess Jesus is not from God; this is the spirit of the antichrist, which you have heard that it is coming, and now it is already in the world" (1 John 4:2, 3).

Antichrist denies Christ's deity, atoning death, and the truth of God's Word. However, the Lord has given every believer the presence of the Holy Spirit and the Word of God to help us discern truth from error.

If we don't have Jesus Christ, we have nothing. All else is vain and empty philosophy and offers us only death. The truth is that we need not surrender to this deception, for Christ the Lord has risen. He is real, He is God, and He has the victory over the spirit of this age. Jesus said, "The world is passing away, and also its lusts; but the one who does the will of God lives forever" (1 John 2:17).

The opposition may seem powerful today, and it may seem to have won the war for our culture. Yet Christ is still Lord of all creation, and He will have the final word. In the meantime, you and I must know our beliefs and know them well so that we can communicate them to a world hungry for truth. ◉

---

of us, they would have remained with us; but *they went out*, so that it would be shown that they all are not of us.
20 But you have an anointing from the Holy One, and you all know.
21 I have not written to you because you do not know the truth, but because you do know it, and because no lie is of the truth.
22 Who is the liar but the one who denies that Jesus is the Christ? This is the antichrist, the one who denies the Father and the Son.
23 Whoever denies the Son does not have the Father; the one who confesses the Son has the Father also.
24 As for you, let that abide in you which you heard from the beginning. If what you heard from the beginning abides in you, you also will abide in the Son and in the Father.
25 This is the promise which He Himself made to us: eternal life.
26 These things I have written to you concerning those who are trying to deceive you.
27 As for you, the anointing which you received from Him abides in you, and

you have no need for anyone to teach you; but as His anointing teaches you about all things, and is true and is not a lie, and just as it has taught you, you abide in Him.

28 Now, little children, abide in Him, so that when He appears, we may have confidence and not shrink away from Him in shame at His coming.

29 If you know that He is righteous, you know that everyone also who practices righteousness is born of Him.

DECEMBER 5

◈ Hosea 1:1—2:23

1 THE word of the LORD which came to Hosea the son of Beeri, during the days of Uzziah, Jotham, Ahaz *and* Hezekiah, kings of Judah, and during the days of Jeroboam the son of Joash, king of Israel.

2 When the LORD first spoke through Hosea, the LORD said to Hosea, "Go, take to yourself a wife of harlotry and *have* children of harlotry; for the land commits flagrant harlotry, forsaking the LORD."

3 So he went and took Gomer the daughter of Diblaim, and she conceived and bore him a son.

4 And the LORD said to him, "Name him Jezreel; for yet a little while, and I will punish the house of Jehu for the bloodshed of Jezreel, and I will put an end to the kingdom of the house of Israel.

5 "On that day I will break the bow of Israel in the valley of Jezreel."

6 Then she conceived again and gave birth to a daughter. And the LORD said to him, "Name her Lo-ruhamah, for I will no longer have compassion on the house of Israel, that I would ever forgive them.

7 "But I will have compassion on the house of Judah and deliver them by the LORD their God, and will not deliver them by bow, sword, battle, horses or horsemen."

8 When she had weaned Lo-ruhamah, she conceived and gave birth to a son.

9 And the LORD said, "Name him Lo-ammi, for you are not My people and I am not your God."

➤ **10** Yet the number of the sons of Israel
        Will be like the sand of the sea,
        Which cannot be measured or
            numbered;
        And in the place

Where it is said to them,
"You are not My people,"
It will be said to them,
"*You are* the sons of the living God."

11 And the sons of Judah and the sons
        of Israel will be gathered together,
        And they will appoint for
            themselves one leader,
        And they will go up from the land,
        For great will be the day of Jezreel.

2 SAY to your brothers, "Ammi," and to your sisters, "Ruhamah."

2 "Contend with your mother, contend,
        For she is not my wife, and I am not
            her husband;
        And let her put away her harlotry
            from her face
        And her adultery from between her
            breasts,

3 Or I will strip her naked
        And expose her as on the day when
            she was born.
        I will also make her like a
            wilderness,
        Make her like desert land
        And slay her with thirst.

4 "Also, I will have no compassion on
        her children,
        Because they are children of
            harlotry.

5 "For their mother has played the
        harlot;

LIFE LESSONS

➤ **Hosea 1:10** — *In the place where it is said to them, 'You are not my people,' it will be said to them, 'You are sons of the living God.'*

*E*ven in judgment, the Lord shows mercy. Throughout the prophets, declarations of terrible judgment are intertwined with promises of restoration and mercy. We owe everything to God's grace.

She who conceived them has acted
shamefully.
For she said, 'I will go after my lovers,
Who give *me* my bread and my water,
My wool and my flax, my oil and
my drink.'

6 "Therefore, behold, I will hedge up
her way with thorns,
And I will build a wall against her
so that she cannot find her paths.

7 "She will pursue her lovers, but she
will not overtake them;
And she will seek them, but will not
find *them*.
Then she will say, 'I will go back to
my first husband,
For it was better for me then than
now!'

8 "For she does not know that it was I
who gave her the grain, the new
wine and the oil,
And lavished on her silver and gold,
Which they used for Baal.

9 "Therefore, I will take back My grain
at harvest time
And My new wine in its season.
I will also take away My wool and
My flax
Given to cover her nakedness.

10 "And then I will uncover her lewdness
In the sight of her lovers,
And no one will rescue her out of
My hand.

11 "I will also put an end to all her
gaiety,
Her feasts, her new moons, her
sabbaths
And all her festal assemblies.

12 "I will destroy her vines and fig
trees,
Of which she said, 'These are my
wages
Which my lovers have given me.'
And I will make them a forest,
And the beasts of the field will
devour them.

13 "I will punish her for the days of the
Baals
When she used to offer sacrifices to
them
And adorn herself with her earrings
and jewelry,
And follow her lovers, so that she
forgot Me," declares the LORD.

14 "Therefore, behold, I will allure her,
Bring her into the wilderness
And speak kindly to her.

15 "Then I will give her her vineyards
from there,
And the valley of Achor as a door of
hope.
And she will sing there as in the
days of her youth,
As in the day when she came up
from the land of Egypt.

16 "It will come about in that day,"
declares the LORD,
"That you will call Me Ishi
And will no longer call Me Baali.

17 "For I will remove the names of the
Baals from her mouth,
So that they will be mentioned by
their names no more.

18 "In that day I will also make a
covenant for them
With the beasts of the field,
The birds of the sky
And the creeping things of the
ground.
And I will abolish the bow, the
sword and war from the land,
And will make them lie down in
safety.

19 "I will betroth you to Me forever;
Yes, I will betroth you to Me in
righteousness and in justice,
In lovingkindness and in
compassion,

20 And I will betroth you to Me in
faithfulness.
Then you will know the LORD.

LIFE LESSONS

➤ **Hosea 2:16 —** *"You will call Me Ishi and will no longer call Me Baali."*

The Hebrew word *ishi* means "husband," while *baali* means "owner." The first word expresses the deepest desire of God's heart for us ... that we would know Him intimately as a wife knows her mate.

➤ **Hosea 2:20 —** *"I will betroth you to Me in faithfulness. Then you will know the LORD."*

God extends His lovingkindness to us, even when we stray from Him. As we test the waters of worldly desire, only to find ourselves drowning in them, God remains loyal to us, rescuing us and restoring our desire for Him alone.

WHAT THE BIBLE SAYS ABOUT

Knowing All of God

Hosea 2:19, 20

In order to know someone intimately, you can't just know what they do—you must know their character and heart. You have to know what motivates them. The same is true for God. In Hosea 2:19, 20, He says, "I will betroth you to Me forever; yes, I will betroth you to Me in righteousness and in justice, in lovingkindness and in compassion, and I will betroth you to Me in faithfulness. Then you will know the LORD." He has "betrothed" (or engaged) His people to Himself for one reason: to let Himself be known.

Unfortunately, sometimes we know *about* God, but we really don't know *Him*. Yet God wants us to love Him in a deep, intimate relationship. Here are six reasons we should know God's ways.

1. *We should know the ways of God because they are essential in knowing Him.* By learning the ways God works, we become acquainted with His heart—and life's greatest joy is knowing Him personally and intimately (Ps. 25:4, 5).

2. *We should know the ways of God because He requires that we know them.* The Lord desires for us to go beyond a surface relationship with Him, so He has given us commands to follow to facilitate it. We learn not merely to see Him as our Master but also as our Beloved (Deut. 10:12).

3. *We should know the ways of God because it is the yearning of His heart for us to do so.* The Lord desires our fellowship—for us to seek and to worship Him wholeheartedly (Jer. 33:3). This fact alone should motivate us to pursue a deep, meaningful relationship with Him.

4. *We should know the ways of God because He loves us.* Our heavenly Father desires the very best for us, and He wants each of us to realize that His plans for us will always be above and beyond all we could ask or imagine (Jer. 31:3; 1 Cor. 2:9; Eph. 3:20).

5. *We should know the ways of God because they are the best way.* No matter what situation we must endure or how difficult a choice we have to make, we can be certain that God's way is the best way to face it. He will guide us and will give us the strength and wisdom to handle our circumstances in a godly manner (Jer. 29:11).

6. *We should know the ways of God because they are the pathway to success.* Although the world's definition of achievement involves wealth and power, to the Lord true success lies in obedience to His will (1 John 2:17). Ultimately, no one can thwart the plans of God—He will succeed and achieve the victory (Job 42:2). And when we submit to Him, we share in His triumph.

Therefore, set your heart to know all of God—His works, His ways, and His will for your life. Because He promises, "You will seek Me and find Me when you search for Me with all your heart" (Jer. 29:13). ◈

---

21 "It will come about in that day that I will respond," declares the LORD. "I will respond to the heavens, and they will respond to the earth,

22 And the earth will respond to the grain, to the new wine and to the oil, And they will respond to Jezreel.

23 "I will sow her for Myself in the land. I will also have compassion on her who had not obtained compassion, And I will say to those who were not My people, 'You are My people!' And they will say, '*You are* my God!'"

◈ Psalm 138:4–6

4 All the kings of the earth will give thanks to You, O LORD, When they have heard the words of Your mouth.

5 And they will sing of the ways of the LORD, For great is the glory of the LORD.

6 For though the LORD is exalted, Yet He regards the lowly, But the haughty He knows from afar.

Proverbs 29:17

17 Correct your son, and he will give
    you comfort;
    He will also delight your soul.

1 John 3:1–24

3 SEE how great a love the Father has
bestowed on us, that we would be
called children of God; and *such* we are.
For this reason the world does not know
us, because it did not know Him.
2   Beloved, now we are children of
God, and it has not appeared as yet what
we will be. We know that when He appears, we will be like Him, because we
will see Him just as He is.
3   And everyone who has this hope
fixed on Him purifies himself, just as He
is pure.
4   Everyone who practices sin also
practices lawlessness; and sin is lawlessness.
5   You know that He appeared in order
to take away sins; and in Him there is no
sin.
6   No one who abides in Him sins; no
one who sins has seen Him or knows
Him.
7   Little children, make sure no one
deceives you; the one who practices
righteousness is righteous, just as He is
righteous;
8   the one who practices sin is of the
devil; for the devil has sinned from the
beginning. The Son of God appeared for
this purpose, to destroy the works of the
devil.
9   No one who is born of God practices
sin, because His seed abides in him; and
he cannot sin, because he is born of God.
10   By this the children of God and the
children of the devil are obvious: anyone who does not practice righteousness is not of God, nor the one who does
not love his brother.
11   For this is the message which you
have heard from the beginning, that we
should love one another;
12   not as Cain, *who* was of the evil one
and slew his brother. And for what reason did he slay him? Because his deeds

were evil, and his brother's were righteous.
13   Do not be surprised, brethren, if the
world hates you.
14   We know that we have passed out
of death into life, because we love the
brethren. He who does not love abides in
death.
15   Everyone who hates his brother is
a murderer; and you know that no murderer has eternal life abiding in him.
16   We know love by this, that He laid
down His life for us; and we ought to lay
down our lives for the brethren.
17   But whoever has the world's goods,
and sees his brother in need and closes
his heart against him, how does the love
of God abide in him?
18   Little children, let us not love with
word or with tongue, but in deed and
truth.
19   We will know by this that we are of
the truth, and will assure our heart before Him
20   in whatever our heart condemns us;
for God is greater than our heart and
knows all things.

LIFE LESSONS

**1 John 3:2 — *We know that when He
appears, we will be like Him, because we
will see Him just as He is.***

One day we will exchange our worn-
out, sin-prone, weak bodies for new
models patterned after Jesus' resurrection body—strong, ageless, free from all
sin, and completely at home in the holy
presence of God (1 Cor. 13:12; 15:42–57).

**1 John 3:20 — *In whatever our heart
condemns us; for God is greater than our
heart and knows all things.***

This is the reason many people do not
pray—they know when they kneel
before holy God, the sin in their lives
will be brought to light (Is. 6:5). The Holy
Spirit will convict them of any sin they've
been hiding. As believers we should
want to obey and please the Lord, and
because of that, we should be glad
when our consciences are sensitive to
Him. Although the Spirit may pierce our
heart with "sorrow that . . . produces a
repentance" (2 Cor. 7:10), we take joy
because He also "testifies . . . . that we
are children of God" (Rom. 8:16).

21 Beloved, if our heart does not condemn us, we have confidence before God; 22 and whatever we ask we receive from Him, because we keep His commandments and do the things that are pleasing in His sight. 23 This is His commandment, that we believe in the name of His Son Jesus Christ, and love one another, just as He commanded us.

24 The one who keeps His commandments abides in Him, and He in him. We know by this that He abides in us, by the Spirit whom He has given us.

DECEMBER 6

Hosea 3:1—4:19

3 THEN the LORD said to me, "Go again, love a woman *who* is loved by *her* husband, yet an adulteress, even as the LORD loves the sons of Israel, though they turn to other gods and love raisin cakes."

2 So I bought her for myself for fifteen *shekels* of silver and a homer and a half of barley.

3 Then I said to her, "You shall stay with me for many days. You shall not play the harlot, nor shall you have a man; so I will also be toward you."

4 For the sons of Israel will remain for many days without king or prince, without sacrifice or *sacred* pillar and without ephod or household idols.

➤ 5 Afterward the sons of Israel will return and seek the LORD their God and David their king; and they will come trembling to the LORD and to His goodness in the last days.

4 LISTEN to the word of the LORD,
O sons of Israel,
For the LORD has a case against the
inhabitants of the land,
Because there is no faithfulness or
kindness
Or knowledge of God in the land.

2 *There is* swearing, deception,
murder, stealing and adultery.
They employ violence, so that
bloodshed follows bloodshed.
3 Therefore the land mourns,
And everyone who lives in it
languishes
Along with the beasts of the field
and the birds of the sky,
And also the fish of the sea
disappear.
4 Yet let no one find fault, and let
none offer reproof;
For your people are like those who
contend with the priest.
5 So you will stumble by day,
And the prophet also will stumble
with you by night;
And I will destroy your mother.
6 My people are destroyed for lack of ◄
knowledge.
Because you have rejected
knowledge,
I also will reject you from being My
priest.
Since you have forgotten the law of
your God,
I also will forget your children.
7 The more they multiplied, the more
they sinned against Me;
I will change their glory into shame.
8 They feed on the sin of My people

LIFE LESSONS

➤ **Hosea 3:5 — *They will come trembling to the LORD and to His goodness in the last days.***

*W*e may know what it means to "come trembling to the Lord"—but what does it mean to fear "His goodness"? Hosea means that the goodness of God to us is so great and undeserved that it ought to make us tremble.

➤ **Hosea 4:6 — *"My people are destroyed for lack of knowledge."***

*I*f only in the Lord do we find life, then we had better make it a priority to learn as much about Him and His ways as possible—and that means spending prayerful and extended time in His Word.

⊕ LIFE PRINCIPLE 18

AS CHILDREN OF A SOVEREIGN GOD, WE ARE
NEVER VICTIMS OF OUR CIRCUMSTANCES.

HOSEA 3:4, 5

*L*ife is not simple. We face many bumps
and turns along the way. The race is real;
the battle continuous, and the painful experiences
may pierce our heart. However, our circumstances should not define who we are or how we
react. Rather, as believers our behavior in every
situation should honor the Lord Jesus, and our
identity should always be based on the salvation
He has provided for us.

Chapter 11 of Hebrews is populated with
men and women who endured despite adverse
circumstances. You may say, "Of course they
persevered—God worked so powerfully in their
situation. Look how their story turned out!"
Yet understand, just like you, the saints of old
did not know how their story would end, nor
whether God would keep His promises to them.
Yet 1 Kings 8:56 reports, "Not one word has
failed of all His good promise."

So how did they demonstrate such strong faith
in God? They did so because they trusted in the
fact that the Lord was able to help them and
work everything out for their good (Rom. 8:28;
Heb. 11:1). Even when nothing else made sense
to them, they placed their hope in their sovereign
Lord—and He rewarded them for their confidence (Heb. 11:6).

In the fifth grade, a young man, who is now
a pastor, had to memorize the inspiring list of
godly people in Hebrews 11—the faithful servants of the Lord who persevered in their great
trials by trusting God. It was one of the most
transformative lessons of his life. When he went
through a rough time in the ministry, the Lord
reminded him of these great people of faith and
gave him the confidence to endure as they did.

When thinking about the Bible's unseen
cloud of witnesses (Heb. 12:1), we should likewise be encouraged by their testimonies. We
should be heartened by the story of Joseph,
who endured though life seemed so unfair (Gen.
45:4–8; 50:20). Or David, who obeyed God
even though, at times, everything seemed to
work against him becoming king of Israel as the
Lord had promised (1 Sam. 23:14). Or Moses,
who "endured as seeing Him who is unseen"
(Heb. 11:27) and led the people of Israel to

the Promised Land. Or the disciples, who were
desolated at the crucifixion of Christ, only to be
strengthened, heartened, and filled with purpose
at His resurrection.

Had any of them considered themselves victims of their circumstances, they would have
begun their journey with God in defeat and
discouragement. Instead, they focused on the
almighty hand of the Lord and triumphed with
Him.

Likewise, we can say, "God, if they endured,
so can I, because You are sovereign just as You
were then, and You love me as You loved them.
Therefore, I will not consider myself a victim of
my circumstances. Rather, I will view every situation as an opportunity for Your glory to shine
forth in victory."

God knows the Christian life is not easy. When
you received the Lord Jesus as your Savior, He
set you on your course. As your sovereign Lord,
He mapped out all the bumps, turns, detours,
hills, and valleys. He knew all the difficulties
you would face. He understood that you would
continually clash with the world, the flesh, and
the devil until you were home with Him. Yet He
didn't merely set you on the path, hoping you
would find your way. He sent the Holy Spirit
to indwell you, guide you, and encourage you.
Endurance requires something that doesn't come
easily—and that is trust in your unseen, sovereign
God. However, with the Holy Spirit to remind
you of His faithfulness and power (John 14:26),
you can remain committed to Him.

When the going gets rough—and it will—you
can't run away. You can't quit. The longer you
faithfully obey the Lord, regardless of the circumstances, the stronger your faith becomes.
You become prepared for greater service and
expanded ministry. You become strong, stalwart,
and steadfast.

The One who endured the Cross lives in you,
so that you are fully equipped for anything He
calls you to do. If you stumble, He is there to
pick you up. Just remember to always keep your
eyes on Jesus. Don't quit. Persevere.

You aren't alone—your sovereign Lord is with
you in every situation. Therefore, call upon Him
to infuse you with His power and wisdom, and
obey anything He calls you to do. And remember that you are *never* a victim of your circumstances, for your sovereign God can use everything that happens to you for your blessing and
His glory. ⊕

And direct their desire toward their
　　iniquity.
9　And it will be, like people, like
　　priest;
　　So I will punish them for their ways
　　And repay them for their deeds.
10　They will eat, but not have enough;
　　They will play the harlot, but not
　　　increase,
　　Because they have stopped giving
　　　heed to the LORD.
11　Harlotry, wine and new wine take
　　away the understanding.
12　My people consult their wooden
　　idol, and their *diviner's* wand
　　informs them;
　　For a spirit of harlotry has led *them*
　　　astray,
　　And they have played the harlot,
　　departing from their God.
13　They offer sacrifices on the tops of
　　the mountains
　　And burn incense on the hills,
　　Under oak, poplar and terebinth,
　　Because their shade is pleasant.
　　Therefore your daughters play the
　　　harlot
　　And your brides commit adultery.
14　I will not punish your daughters
　　　when they play the harlot
　　Or your brides when they commit
　　　adultery,
　　For *the men* themselves go apart
　　　with harlots
　　And offer sacrifices with temple
　　　prostitutes;
　　So the people without
　　　understanding are ruined.
15　Though you, Israel, play the harlot,
　　Do not let Judah become guilty;
　　Also do not go to Gilgal,
　　Or go up to Beth-aven
　　And take the oath:
　　"As the LORD lives!"
16　Since Israel is stubborn

Like a stubborn heifer,
Can the LORD now pasture them
Like a lamb in a large field?
17　Ephraim is joined to idols;
　　Let him alone.
18　Their liquor gone,
　　They play the harlot continually;
　　Their rulers dearly love shame.
19　The wind wraps them in its wings,
　　And they will be ashamed because
　　　of their sacrifices.

Psalm 138:7, 8

7　Though I walk in the midst of
　　trouble, You will revive me;
　　You will stretch forth Your hand
　　　against the wrath of my enemies,
　　And Your right hand will save me.
8　The LORD will accomplish what
　　concerns me;
　　Your lovingkindness, O LORD, is
　　everlasting;
　　Do not forsake the works of Your
　　hands.

Proverbs 29:18

18　Where there is no vision, the people
　　are unrestrained,
　　But happy is he who keeps the law.

1 John 4:1–21

4 BELOVED, do not believe every spirit,
but test the spirits to see whether
they are from God, because many false
prophets have gone out into the world.
2　By this you know the Spirit of God:

LIFE LESSONS

**Hosea 4:10 — *"They will eat, but not
have enough . . . because they have
stopped giving heed to the LORD."***

*W*hen we obey the Lord, He can take a
little and make it stretch a long way
(2 Kin. 4:2–7). But when we disobey, He
can take a lot and make it seem like nothing (Eccl. 6:3–6). The choice is up to us.

**Proverbs 29:18 — *Where there is no
vision, the people are unrestrained.***

*W*hat happens when a society rejects
God's revelation and everyone does
as he sees fit? You get a culture that looks
a lot like the perverted one described in
the Book of Judges (17:6; 21:25). And this
type of society never works.

every spirit that confesses that Jesus Christ has come in the flesh is from God; 3 and every spirit that does not confess Jesus is not from God; this is the *spirit* of the antichrist, of which you have heard that it is coming, and now it is already in the world.

4 You are from God, little children, and have overcome them; because greater is He who is in you than he who is in the world.

5 They are from the world; therefore they speak *as* from the world, and the world listens to them.

6 We are from God; he who knows God listens to us; he who is not from God does not listen to us. By this we know the spirit of truth and the spirit of error.

7 Beloved, let us love one another, for love is from God; and everyone who loves is born of God and knows God.

8 The one who does not love does not know God, for God is love.

9 By this the love of God was manifested in us, that God has sent His only begotten Son into the world so that we might live through Him.

10 In this is love, not that we loved God, but that He loved us and sent His Son *to be* the propitiation for our sins.

11 Beloved, if God so loved us, we also ought to love one another.

12 No one has seen God at any time; if we love one another, God abides in us, and His love is perfected in us.

13 By this we know that we abide in Him and He in us, because He has given us of His Spirit.

14 We have seen and testify that the Father has sent the Son *to be* the Savior of the world.

15 Whoever confesses that Jesus is the Son of God, God abides in him, and he in God.

16 We have come to know and have be-

LIFE LESSONS

➤ **1 John 4:4 — *Greater is He who is in you than he who is in the world.***

*T*he Holy Spirit is within us from the moment of salvation and enables us to say no to temptation. So anytime we resist some temptation, overcome some spiritual challenge, or triumph in a contest of faith, we do so because God's Spirit lives in us. We move ahead in our walks with the Lord by relying on His power, not ours.

➤ **1 John 4:8 — *The one who does not love does not know God, for God is love.***

*T*o be transformed into the image of Christ means to increasingly reflect His loving character in our behaviors and attitudes. Therefore, if we are not becoming more loving, we have taken a wrong turn somewhere—either by neglecting our relationships with Him or by disobeying His commands.

---

lieved the love which God has for us. God is love, and the one who abides in love abides in God, and God abides in him.

17 By this, love is perfected with us, so that we may have confidence in the day of judgment; because as He is, so also are we in this world.

18 There is no fear in love; but perfect love casts out fear, because fear involves punishment, and the one who fears is not perfected in love.

19 We love, because He first loved us.

20 If someone says, "I love God," and hates his brother, he is a liar; for the one who does not love his brother whom he has seen, cannot love God whom he has not seen.

21 And this commandment we have from Him, that the one who loves God should love his brother also.

 Hosea 5:1—6:11

5 HEAR this, O priests! Give heed, O house of Israel! Listen, O house of the king!

For the judgment applies to you, For you have been a snare at Mizpah And a net spread out on Tabor.

2 The revolters have gone deep in depravity, But I will chastise all of them.

3   I know Ephraim, and Israel is not
     hidden from Me;
     For now, O Ephraim, you have
     played the harlot,
     Israel has defiled itself.
4   Their deeds will not allow them
     To return to their God.
     For a spirit of harlotry is within
     them,
     And they do not know the LORD.
5   Moreover, the pride of Israel
     testifies against him,
     And Israel and Ephraim stumble in
     their iniquity;
     Judah also has stumbled with them.
6   They will go with their flocks and
     herds
     To seek the LORD, but they will not
     find *Him;*
     He has withdrawn from them.
7   They have dealt treacherously
     against the LORD,
     For they have borne illegitimate
     children.
     Now the new moon will devour
     them with their land.
8   Blow the horn in Gibeah,
     The trumpet in Ramah.
     Sound an alarm at Beth-aven:
     "Behind you, Benjamin!"
9   Ephraim will become a desolation
     in the day of rebuke;
     Among the tribes of Israel I declare
     what is sure.
10   The princes of Judah have become
     like those who move a boundary;
     On them I will pour out My wrath
     like water.
11   Ephraim is oppressed, crushed in
     judgment,
     Because he was determined to
     follow *man's* command.
12   Therefore I am like a moth to
     Ephraim
     And like rottenness to the house of
     Judah.
13   When Ephraim saw his sickness,
     And Judah his wound,
     Then Ephraim went to Assyria
     And sent to King Jareb.
     But he is unable to heal you,
     Or to cure you of your wound.
14   For I *will be* like a lion to Ephraim
     And like a young lion to the house
     of Judah.
     I, even I, will tear to pieces and go
     away,

I will carry away, and there will be
none to deliver.
15   I will go away *and* return to My
     place
     Until they acknowledge their guilt
     and seek My face;
     In their affliction they will earnestly
     seek Me.

6   "COME, let us return to the LORD.
     For He has torn *us,* but He will heal
     us;
     He has wounded *us,* but He will
     bandage us.
2   "He will revive us after two days;
     He will raise us up on the third day,
     That we may live before Him.
3   "So let us know, let us press on to
     know the LORD.
     His going forth is as certain as the
     dawn;
     And He will come to us like the
     rain,
     Like the spring rain watering the
     earth."
4   What shall I do with you,
     O Ephraim?
     What shall I do with you, O Judah?
     For your loyalty is like a morning
     cloud
     And like the dew which goes away
     early.
5   Therefore I have hewn *them* in
     pieces by the prophets;
     I have slain them by the words of
     My mouth;
     And the judgments on you are *like*
     the light that goes forth.

LIFE LESSONS

➢ **Hosea 5:15 — *"In their affliction they
will earnestly seek Me."***

*G*od does not use affliction because He
enjoys it; He uses affliction because
sometimes that is the only language we
understand, the only warning we will
heed.

➢ **Hosea 6:3 — *"Let us know, let us press
on to know the LORD."***

*O*ur highest pursuit in life is to get
to know the Lord for who He really
is. While we can do much of this on
our own, God directs us to pursue Him
together with other believers who also
love Him.

WHAT THE BIBLE SAYS ABOUT ⊕

God's Desire to Communicate with Us

Psalm 139:1–24

*H*ow many times have we heard some-one say, "Why would God want to speak to *me?* I am not a preacher or in full-time Christian service. Why in the world would He want to communicate with me?"

The truth is, we are all saved by His grace (Eph. 2:8). When we know Christ as our Savior, we are all washed and sanctified (1 Cor. 6:11) and are all children of the living God (John 1:12). As our Heavenly Father, God naturally wants to fellowship with us.

Many times, we may see ourselves in an unworthy light—and when we do, we wonder why our great, magnificent God would ever want to speak to us. In that case, the Lord could scream into our ears, but we would have a difficult time hearing Him.

We must see ourselves as the Lord sees us: that is, as children who need Him to speak, who need to listen, and who need His guidance every day of their lives. If we have a pauper-like image of ourselves, wondering why the God who created the heavens and the earth would engage in meaningful conversation with insignificant us, then communication shuts down.

It all depends on our relationship with Him. We are children of God, and we can be sure that our Father eagerly seeks to speak to us! Psalm 139 provides us with marvelous insight into the Father's perfect knowledge of us and His abundant love for us, just the way we are. He knows how we are made. He knows our weaknesses. He knows our sinful desires, and our transgressions are not hidden from Him. He knows our innermost hurts, fears, and frustrations—and yet He longs to gain intimacy with us.

Jesus has chosen to put His unmatched presence into these scarred, earthen vessels. He is at home in these tattered earthly tents. We need not be ill at ease, but instead we can relax and enjoy His fellowship, knowing that He died for us while we were hopeless sinners (Rom. 5:6–8). He has permanently accepted us into His family, with *all* our undesirable baggage. We are His—lock, stock, and barrel.

So listen for Him and embrace all the wonderful things He wants to share! ⊕

---

6   For I delight in loyalty rather than
       sacrifice,
     And in the knowledge of God rather
       than burnt offerings.
7   But like Adam they have
       transgressed the covenant;
     There they have dealt treacherously
       against Me.
8   Gilead is a city of wrongdoers,
     Tracked with bloody *footprints.*
9   And as raiders wait for a man,
     So a band of priests murder on the
       way to Shechem;

Surely they have committed
       crime.
10 In the house of Israel I have seen a
       horrible thing;
     Ephraim's harlotry is there, Israel
       has defiled itself.
11 Also, O Judah, there is a harvest
       appointed for you,
     When I restore the fortunes of My
       people.

⊕   **Psalm 139:1–6**

LIFE LESSONS

➤ **Hosea 6:6 — *"I delight in loyalty rather than sacrifice, and in the knowledge of God rather than burnt offerings."***

*R*epeatedly in Scripture the Lord tells us that while He has no desire for half-hearted religious ritual, He greatly desires hearts on fire for Him—those who will joyfully love God and love others.

For the choir director.
A Psalm of David.

139 O LORD, You have searched me
          and known *me.*
2   You know when I sit down and
       when I rise up;
     You understand my thought from
       afar.
3   You scrutinize my path and my
       lying down,

And are intimately acquainted with
all my ways.
4   Even before there is a word on my
tongue,
Behold, O LORD, You know it all.
5   You have enclosed me behind and
before,
And laid Your hand upon me.
6   *Such* knowledge is too wonderful
for me;
It is *too* high, I cannot attain to it.

Proverbs 29:19

19   A slave will not be instructed by
words *alone*;
For though he understands, there
will be no response.

1 John 5:1–21

5 WHOEVER believes that Jesus is the
Christ is born of God, and whoever
loves the Father loves the *child* born of
Him.
2   By this we know that we love the
children of God, when we love God and
observe His commandments.
3   For this is the love of God, that we
keep His commandments; and His commandments are not burdensome.
4   For whatever is born of God overcomes the world; and this is the victory that has overcome the world—our
faith.
5   Who is the one who overcomes the
world, but he who believes that Jesus is
the Son of God?
6   This is the One who came by water
and blood, Jesus Christ; not with the
water only, but with the water and with

the blood. It is the Spirit who testifies,
because the Spirit is the truth.
7   For there are three that testify:
8   the Spirit and the water and the
blood; and the three are in agreement.
9   If we receive the testimony of men,
the testimony of God is greater; for the
testimony of God is this, that He has testified concerning His Son.
10   The one who believes in the Son of
God has the testimony in himself; the
one who does not believe God has made
Him a liar, because he has not believed
in the testimony that God has given concerning His Son.
11   And the testimony is this, that God
has given us eternal life, and this life is
in His Son.
12   He who has the Son has the life; he
who does not have the Son of God does
not have the life.
13   These things I have written to you
who believe in the name of the Son of
God, so that you may know that you
have eternal life.
14   This is the confidence which we
have before Him, that, if we ask anything
according to His will, He hears us.
15   And if we know that He hears us *in*
whatever we ask, we know that we have
the requests which we have asked from
Him.
16   If anyone sees his brother committing a sin not *leading* to death, he shall
ask and *God* will for him give life to
those who commit sin not *leading* to
death. There is a sin *leading* to death; I
do not say that he should make request
for this.
17   All unrighteousness is sin, and there
is a sin not *leading* to death.
18   We know that no one who is born of
God sins; but He who was born of God
keeps him, and the evil one does not
touch him.

LIFE LESSONS

➤ **1 John 5:3** — *This is the love of God,
that we keep His commandments; and His
commandments are not burdensome.*

*O*nly when we try to obey God through
our own power do His commandments feel burdensome. When we rely
on His Spirit to enable us to do what we
can't, we find great joy in obedience.

➤ **1 John 5:12** — *He who has the Son has
the life.*

*H*ave you asked the Lord Jesus Christ
to come into your heart through
faith, forgive you of your sins, and give
you an eternal home in heaven? If you
have, you have life; if you haven't, you
don't (Mark 8:35).

19 We know that we are of God, and that the whole world lies in *the power of* the evil one.

➤ 20 And we know that the Son of God has come, and has given us understanding so that we may know Him who is true; and we are in Him who is true, in His Son Jesus Christ. This is the true God and eternal life.

21 Little children, guard yourselves from idols.

LIFE LESSONS

➤ *1 John 5:20 — The Son of God has come, and has given us understanding so that we may know Him who is true.*

God helps us to grasp His Word, not merely so we can amass an impressive body of religious knowledge, but so that we can know, love, obey, and enjoy the Lord of the universe who created us and has a wonderful purpose for our lives.

✵ Hosea 7:1—8:14

7 WHEN I would heal Israel,
The iniquity of Ephraim is uncovered,
And the evil deeds of Samaria,
For they deal falsely;
The thief enters in,
Bandits raid outside,

2 And they do not consider in their hearts
That I remember all their wickedness.
Now their deeds are all around them;
They are before My face.

3 With their wickedness they make the king glad,
And the princes with their lies.

4 They are all adulterers,
Like an oven heated by the baker
Who ceases to stir up *the fire*
From the kneading of the dough until it is leavened.

5 On the day of our king, the princes became sick with the heat of wine;
He stretched out his hand with scoffers.

6 For their hearts are like an oven
As they approach their plotting;
Their anger smolders all night,
In the morning it burns like a flaming fire.

7 All of them are hot like an oven,
And they consume their rulers;
All their kings have fallen.
None of them calls on Me.

8 Ephraim mixes himself with the nations;

Ephraim has become a cake not turned.

9 Strangers devour his strength,
Yet he does not know *it;*
Gray hairs also are sprinkled on him,
Yet he does not know *it.*

10 Though the pride of Israel testifies against him,
Yet they have not returned to the LORD their God,
Nor have they sought Him, for all this.

11 So Ephraim has become like a silly dove, without sense;
They call to Egypt, they go to Assyria.

12 When they go, I will spread My net over them;
I will bring them down like the birds of the sky,
I will chastise them in accordance with the proclamation to their assembly.

13 Woe to them, for they have strayed from Me!
Destruction is theirs, for they have rebelled against Me!
I would redeem them, but they speak lies against Me.

14 And they do not cry to Me from their heart
When they wail on their beds;
For the sake of grain and new wine they assemble themselves,
They turn away from Me.

15 Although I trained *and* strengthened their arms,
Yet they devise evil against Me.

16 They turn, *but* not upward,
They are like a deceitful bow;
Their princes will fall by the sword
Because of the insolence of their
tongue.
This *will be* their derision in the
land of Egypt.

8 PUT the trumpet to your lips!
Like an eagle the enemy comes
against the house of the LORD,
Because they have transgressed My
covenant
And rebelled against My law.
2 They cry out to Me,
"My God, we of Israel know You!"
3 Israel has rejected the good;
The enemy will pursue him.
4 They have set up kings, but not by
Me;
They have appointed princes, but I
did not know *it*.
With their silver and gold they have
made idols for themselves,
That they might be cut off.
5 He has rejected your calf,
O Samaria, *saying*,
"My anger burns against them!"
How long will they be incapable of
innocence?
6 For from Israel is even this!
A craftsman made it, so it is not
God;
Surely the calf of Samaria will be
broken to pieces.
➤ 7 For they sow the wind
And they reap the whirlwind.
The standing grain has no heads;
It yields no grain.
Should it yield, strangers would
swallow it up.

8 Israel is swallowed up;
They are now among the nations
Like a vessel in which no one
delights.
9 For they have gone up to Assyria,
Like a wild donkey all alone;
Ephraim has hired lovers.
10 Even though they hire *allies* among
the nations,
Now I will gather them up;
And they will begin to diminish
Because of the burden of the king of
princes.
11 Since Ephraim has multiplied altars
for sin,
They have become altars of sinning
for him.
12 Though I wrote for him ten
thousand *precepts* of My law,
They are regarded as a strange
thing.
13 As for My sacrificial gifts,
They sacrifice the flesh and eat *it*,
But the LORD has taken no delight
in them.
Now He will remember their
iniquity,
And punish *them* for their sins;
They will return to Egypt.
14 For Israel has forgotten his Maker
and built palaces;
And Judah has multiplied fortified
cities,
But I will send a fire on its cities
that it may consume its palatial
dwellings.

◈ **Psalm 139:7–12**

7 Where can I go from Your Spirit?
Or where can I flee from Your
presence?

WHAT THE BIBLE SAYS ABOUT ◉

Everywhere You Go

Psalm 139:7–12

*I*f you so desired, you could go to where there is not enough oxygen to sustain breathing. You could go where there is no food to fuel the body. You could travel to where there is not sufficient water to maintain life. You could find a place of utter darkness, and journey to lands that are barren.

Although you could find places lacking all these things, you could never find a place devoid of God. Wherever you go, He is with you.

You can conceal your thoughts, actions, and emotions from your family, friends, colleagues, acquaintances, and strangers. Some psychologists say you can even hide things from yourself.

But you can conceal nothing from God.

You can run and hide, but He is with you. You can pretend you are someone or something else, but He knows exactly what is going on. He knows what you need and what you desire. He knows what plagues your thoughts and touches your heart.

God knows you.

In Psalm 139:7–10, David wrote, "Where can I go from Your Spirit? Or where can I flee from Your presence? If I ascend to heaven, You are there; if I make my bed in Sheol, behold, You are there. If I take the wings of the dawn, if I dwell in the remotest part of the sea, even there Your hand will lead me, and Your right hand will lay hold of me."

God created you and knows best about how you function. And as you stand before Him, you don't have to be ashamed of anything because He accepts you completely. Therefore, take comfort that the Lord God loves every bit of you, and He is with you wherever you go and whatever you go through. You never have to feel alone again. ◉

---

8 If I ascend to heaven, You are there;
   If I make my bed in Sheol, behold, You are there.
9 If I take the wings of the dawn,
   If I dwell in the remotest part of the sea,
10 Even there Your hand will lead me,
   And Your right hand will lay hold of me.
11 If I say, "Surely the darkness will overwhelm me,
   And the light around me will be night,"
12 Even the darkness is not dark to You,
   And the night is as bright as the day.
   Darkness and light are alike *to You.*

◉ Proverbs 29:20

20 Do you see a man who is hasty in his words?
   There is more hope for a fool than for him.

◉ 2 John 1–13

1 THE elder to the chosen lady and her children, whom I love in truth; and not only I, but also all who know the truth,
2 for the sake of the truth which abides ◄ in us and will be with us forever:
3 Grace, mercy *and* peace will be with us, from God the Father and from Jesus Christ, the Son of the Father, in truth and love.
4 I was very glad to find *some* of your children walking in truth, just as we have received commandment *to do* from the Father.
5 Now I ask you, lady, not as though *I* ◄

LIFE LESSONS

➣ *2 John 2 — For the sake of the truth which abides in us and will be with us forever.*

*N*either the Word of God which we have received, nor the Savior and Lord who inspired it and lives in us, will ever change or abandon us (Heb. 13:8). God's truth does not alter from age to age, nor does He.

LIFE LESSONS

> **2 John 5 — Love one another.**

*T*o love God and to love others as we love ourselves—the core commandment of heaven—has remained the same from Old Testament times (Lev. 19:18; Deut. 6:5; 10:12), to the days of the New Testament (Matt. 22:36–40; John 13:34, 35; 15:9–17), and on to today.

were writing to you a new commandment, but the one which we have had from the beginning, that we love one another.
6　And this is love, that we walk according to His commandments. This is the commandment, just as you have heard from the beginning, that you should walk in it.
7　For many deceivers have gone out into the world, those who do not acknowledge Jesus Christ *as* coming in the flesh. This is the deceiver and the antichrist.
8　Watch yourselves, that you do not lose what we have accomplished, but that you may receive a full reward.
9　Anyone who goes too far and does not abide in the teaching of Christ, does not have God; the one who abides in the teaching, he has both the Father and the Son.
10　If anyone comes to you and does not bring this teaching, do not receive him into *your* house, and do not give him a greeting;
11　for the one who gives him a greeting participates in his evil deeds.
12　Though I have many things to write to you, I do not want to *do so* with paper and ink; but I hope to come to you and speak face to face, so that your joy may be made full.
13　The children of your chosen sister greet you.

DECEMBER 9

Hosea 9:1—10:15

9DO not rejoice, O Israel, with exultation like the nations!
For you have played the harlot,
　forsaking your God.
You have loved *harlots'* earnings on
　every threshing floor.
2　Threshing floor and wine press will
　not feed them,
And the new wine will fail them.
3　They will not remain in the LORD's
　land,
But Ephraim will return to Egypt,
And in Assyria they will eat unclean
　food.
4　They will not pour out drink
　offerings of wine to the LORD,
Their sacrifices will not please Him.
Their bread will be like mourners'
　bread;
All who eat of it will be defiled,
For their bread will be for
　themselves *alone;*
It will not enter the house of the
　LORD.

5　What will you do on the day of the
　appointed festival
And on the day of the feast of the
　LORD?
6　For behold, they will go because of
　destruction;
Egypt will gather them up, Memphis
　will bury them.
Weeds will take over their treasures
　of silver;
Thorns *will be* in their tents.
7　The days of punishment have come,
The days of retribution have come;
Let Israel know *this!*
The prophet is a fool,

LIFE LESSONS

> **Hosea 9:5 — What will you do on the day of the appointed festival and on the day of the feast of the LORD?**

*N*ever mistake the Lord's great patience for acceptance of evil. When we knowingly step out of His will, He gives us chance after chance to turn back to Him. But if we never turn back, that road will eventually end.

The inspired man is demented,
Because of the grossness of your
    iniquity,
And *because* your hostility is *so*
    great.

8   Ephraim *was* a watchman with my
    God, a prophet;
    Yet the snare of a bird catcher is in
        all his ways,
    And there is *only* hostility in the
        house of his God.

9   They have gone deep in depravity
    As in the days of Gibeah;
    He will remember their iniquity,
    He will punish their sins.

10 I found Israel like grapes in the
        wilderness;
    I saw your forefathers as the
        earliest fruit on the fig tree in its
        first *season.*
    But they came to Baal-peor and
        devoted themselves to shame,
    And they became as detestable as
        that which they loved.

11 As for Ephraim, their glory will fly
        away like a bird—
    No birth, no pregnancy and no
        conception!

12 Though they bring up their
        children,
    Yet I will bereave them until not a
        man is left.
    Yes, woe to them indeed when I
        depart from them!

13 Ephraim, as I have seen,
    Is planted in a pleasant meadow like
        Tyre;
    But Ephraim will bring out his
        children for slaughter.

14 Give them, O LORD—what will You
        give?
    Give them a miscarrying womb and
        dry breasts.

15 All their evil is at Gilgal;
    Indeed, I came to hate them there!
    Because of the wickedness of their
        deeds
    I will drive them out of My house!
    I will love them no more;
    All their princes are rebels.

16 Ephraim is stricken, their root is
        dried up,
    They will bear no fruit.
    Even though they bear children,
    I will slay the precious ones of their
        womb.

➤ 17 My God will cast them away

Because they have not listened to
    Him;
And they will be wanderers among
    the nations.

10 ISRAEL is a luxuriant vine;
    He produces fruit for himself.
    The more his fruit,
    The more altars he made;
    The richer his land,
    The better he made the *sacred*
        pillars.

2   Their heart is faithless;
    Now they must bear their guilt.
    The LORD will break down their
        altars
    And destroy their *sacred* pillars.

3   Surely now they will say, "We have
        no king,
    For we do not revere the LORD.
    As for the king, what can he do for
        us?"

4   They speak *mere* words,
    With worthless oaths they make
        covenants;
    And judgment sprouts like
        poisonous weeds in the furrows
        of the field.

5   The inhabitants of Samaria will fear
    For the calf of Beth-aven.
    Indeed, its people will mourn for it,
    And its idolatrous priests will cry
        out over it,
    Over its glory, since it has departed
        from it.

6   The thing itself will be carried to
        Assyria
    As tribute to King Jareb;
    Ephraim will be seized with shame
    And Israel will be ashamed of its
        own counsel.

7   Samaria will be cut off *with* her
        king
    Like a stick on the surface of the
        water.

➤ 8　Also the high places of Aven, the
　　　sin of Israel, will be destroyed;
　　　Thorn and thistle will grow on their
　　　　altars;
　　　Then they will say to the mountains,
　　　　"Cover us!" And to the hills, "Fall on
　　　　us!"
9　From the days of Gibeah you have
　　　sinned, O Israel;
　　　There they stand!
　　　Will not the battle against the sons
　　　　of iniquity overtake them in
　　　　Gibeah?
10　When it is My desire, I will chastise
　　　them;
　　　And the peoples will be gathered
　　　　against them
　　　When they are bound for their
　　　　double guilt.
11　Ephraim is a trained heifer that
　　　loves to thresh,
　　　But I will come over her fair neck
　　　　with a yoke;
　　　I will harness Ephraim,
　　　Judah will plow, Jacob will harrow
　　　　for himself.
12　Sow with a view to righteousness,
　　　Reap in accordance with kindness;
　　　Break up your fallow ground,
　　　For it is time to seek the LORD
　　　Until He comes to rain
　　　　righteousness on you.
➤ 13　You have plowed wickedness, you
　　　have reaped injustice,
　　　You have eaten the fruit of lies.

LIFE LESSONS

➤ **Hosea 10:8 — *They will say to the
mountains, "Cover us!" And to the hills,
"Fall on us!"***

*J*esus quoted this verse as the Romans
led Him away to be crucified (Luke
23:30); John alludes to it in a future
scene of divine judgment (Rev. 6:16).
How much better to call on God than on
the tools of His judgment!

➤ **Hosea 10:13 — *You have eaten the
fruit of lies. Because you have trusted in
your way, in your numerous warriors.***

*G*od wants us to develop both our
minds and our relationships, but He
never wants us to put our hope for the
future in either one. "A warrior is not
delivered by great strength" (Ps. 33:16).

　　Because you have trusted in your
　　　way, in your numerous warriors,
14　Therefore a tumult will arise among
　　　your people,
　　And all your fortresses will be
　　　destroyed,
　　As Shalman destroyed Beth-arbel
　　　on the day of battle,
　　When mothers were dashed in
　　　pieces with *their* children.
15　Thus it will be done to you at
　　　Bethel because of your great
　　　wickedness.
　　At dawn the king of Israel will be
　　　completely cut off.

◈ Psalm 139:13–16

13　For You formed my inward parts;
　　You wove me in my mother's
　　　womb.
14　I will give thanks to You, for I am
　　　fearfully and wonderfully made;
　　Wonderful are Your works,
　　And my soul knows it very well.
15　My frame was not hidden from
　　　You,
　　When I was made in secret,
　　And skillfully wrought in the depths
　　　of the earth;
16　Your eyes have seen my unformed
　　　substance;
　　And in Your book were all written
　　The days that were ordained *for me,*
　　When as yet there was not one of
　　　them.

◈ Proverbs 29:21

21　He who pampers his slave from
　　　childhood
　　Will in the end find him to be a
　　　son.

◈ 3 John 1–15

1　THE elder to the beloved Gaius, whom
　I love in truth.
2　Beloved, I pray that in all respects
you may prosper and be in good health,
just as your soul prospers.

WHAT THE BIBLE SAYS ABOUT ✦

Living in the Center of God's Will

Psalm 139:13–16

Psalm 139:16 reveals, "Your eyes have seen my unformed substance; and in Your book were all written the days that were ordained for me, when as yet there was not one of them." Our three-in-one God has the right to plan our lives because of who He is and what He has done. As Creator, He has fashioned us in the womb (Ps. 139:13). As Sustainer, He causes our hearts to beat and our bodies to function.

Jesus is our Redeemer who released us from bondage to sin. He purchased our freedom with His shed blood. He is the Savior who rescued us from an eternity of punishment. He is also our Counselor, from whom we receive wisdom and understanding. Jesus is also our Guide who directs us perfectly since He sees all (Heb. 4:13). As our Provider, He knows what is best for us in every situation and gives us just what we need (James 1:17).

Yet throughout history, many have chosen to resist His will. For example, the unbelieving and fearful Israelites turned away from entering the Promised Land (Num. 14:1–4). King Solomon disregarded God's instructions about marriage. And Jonah refused to witness to Nineveh. God allowed them to rebel, but He also let them suffer the consequences. Then, the Lord pressured them to return to Him.

Israel made a 40-year detour before arriving back where they started. King Solomon found life meaningless apart from God and was attacked by enemies. And, Jonah landed in the fish's belly before repenting and obeying the Lord.

A life that brings honor and glory to God is a surrendered life. It is one which operates in the center of His will. Ephesians 2:10 tells us, "We are His workmanship, created in Christ Jesus for good works, which God prepared beforehand that we would walk in them." Won't you spend your remaining days discovering the good works God has for you to do and walking in His will for you? You'll certainly never regret it. ✦

---

3   For I was very glad when brethren came and testified to your truth, *that is,* how you are walking in truth.

➤ 4   I have no greater joy than this, to hear of my children walking in the truth.

5   Beloved, you are acting faithfully in whatever you accomplish for the brethren, and especially *when they are* strangers;

6   and they have testified to your love before the church. You will do well to send them on their way in a manner worthy of God.

7   For they went out for the sake of the Name, accepting nothing from the Gentiles.

8   Therefore we ought to support such men, so that we may be fellow workers with the truth.

9   I wrote something to the church; but Diotrephes, who loves to be first among them, does not accept what we say.

10 For this reason, if I come, I will call attention to his deeds which he does, unjustly accusing us with wicked words; and not satisfied with this, he himself

---

LIFE LESSONS

➤ **3 John 2 — *I pray that in all respects you may prosper and be in good health, just as your soul prospers.***

Prayers for our physical well-being are just as legitimate as prayers for our spiritual health (James 5:13–16). God wants us to flourish in all the spiritual disciplines that will draw our hearts closer to Him and to our fellow believers in Christ.

➤ **3 John 4 — *I have no greater joy than this, to hear of my children walking in truth.***

To walk in truth means to believe the Word of God and to gladly obey the Lord's instruction by drawing on the power of the Holy Spirit. This kind of life brings great joy both to us and to those who follow after and learn from our example.

does not receive the brethren, either, and he forbids those who desire *to do so* and puts *them* out of the church.

11 Beloved, do not imitate what is evil, but what is good. The one who does good is of God; the one who does evil has not seen God.

12 Demetrius has received a *good* testimony from everyone, and from the truth itself; and we add our testimony, and you know that our testimony is true.

13 I had many things to write to you, but I am not willing to write *them* to you with pen and ink;

14 but I hope to see you shortly, and we will speak face to face.

15 Peace *be* to you. The friends greet you. Greet the friends by name.

DECEMBER 10

◈ Hosea 11:1—12:14

11 WHEN Israel *was* a youth I loved him,
And out of Egypt I called My son.
2 The more they called them,
The more they went from them;
They kept sacrificing to the Baals
And burning incense to idols.
3 Yet it is I who taught Ephraim to walk,
I took them in My arms;
But they did not know that I healed them.
4 I led them with cords of a man, with bonds of love,
And I became to them as one who lifts the yoke from their jaws;
And I bent down *and* fed them.
5 They will not return to the land of Egypt;
But Assyria—he will be their king
Because they refused to return *to Me.*
6 The sword will whirl against their cities,
And will demolish their gate bars
And consume *them* because of their counsels.

7 So My people are bent on turning from Me.
Though they call them to *the One* on high,
None at all exalts *Him.*
8 How can I give you up, O Ephraim?
How can I surrender you, O Israel?
How can I make you like Admah?
How can I treat you like Zeboiim?
My heart is turned over within Me,
All My compassions are kindled.
9 I will not execute My fierce anger;
I will not destroy Ephraim again.
For I am God and not man, the Holy One in your midst,
And I will not come in wrath.
10 They will walk after the LORD,
He will roar like a lion;
Indeed He will roar
And *His* sons will come trembling from the west.
11 They will come trembling like birds from Egypt
And like doves from the land of Assyria;
And I will settle them in their houses, declares the LORD.
12 Ephraim surrounds Me with lies
And the house of Israel with deceit;

LIFE LESSONS

➤ **Hosea 11:3** — *"It is I who taught Ephraim to walk, I took them in My arms; but they did not know that I healed them."*

*G*od healed Ephraim over and over again, even when His people disobeyed and lacked the sense to recognize His loving hand. How has God healed you? Where do you recognize His hand in *your* life?

➤ **Hosea 11:4** — *"I led them with the cords of a man, with bonds of love, and I became to them as one who lifts the yoke from their jaws."*

*G*od prefers to deal with His people in love and grace, not in anger and judgment. Sometimes, however, it is that very tenderness that allows us to forget how seriously God takes our relationships with Him.

* * * * * * * * * * * * * *
Life Examples:

HOSEA: A Longing for Intimacy

HOSEA 11:8, 9

*W*ithout questioning God, Hosea obeyed Him and took the prostitute Gomer to be his wife. Though she wandered and repeatedly slipped into unfaithfulness, Hosea obeyed the Lord and did not cast her away.

The moving poetry of Hosea reveals the longing of God for uninterrupted intimacy with His people. Can you sense the agony in His words?

"How can I give you up, O Ephraim? How can I surrender you, O Israel? . . . My heart is turned over within Me, all My compassions are kindled" (Hos.11:8).

God longs for an intimate relationship with you. And in the most dramatic display of love for all time, He provided His Son, Jesus Christ, as the means to make such fellowship possible. God is the passionate and faithful Lover of your soul.

Judah is also unruly against God,
Even against the Holy One who is faithful.

12 EPHRAIM feeds on wind,
And pursues the east wind continually;
He multiplies lies and violence.
Moreover, he makes a covenant with Assyria,
And oil is carried to Egypt.

2 The LORD also has a dispute with Judah,
And will punish Jacob according to his ways;
He will repay him according to his deeds.

3 In the womb he took his brother by the heel,
And in his maturity he contended with God.

4 Yes, he wrestled with the angel and prevailed;
He wept and sought His favor.
He found Him at Bethel
And there He spoke with us,

5 Even the LORD, the God of hosts,
The LORD is His name.

6 Therefore, return to your God,
Observe kindness and justice,
And wait for your God continually.

7 A merchant, in whose hands are false balances,
He loves to oppress.

8 And Ephraim said, "Surely I have become rich,
I have found wealth for myself;
In all my labors they will find in me
No iniquity, which *would be* sin."

9 But I *have been* the LORD your God since the land of Egypt;
I will make you live in tents again,
As in the days of the appointed festival.

10 I have also spoken to the prophets,
And I gave numerous visions,
And through the prophets I gave parables.

11 Is there iniquity *in* Gilead?
Surely they are worthless.
In Gilgal they sacrifice bulls,
Yes, their altars are like the stone heaps
Beside the furrows of the field.

12 Now Jacob fled to the land of Aram,
And Israel worked for a wife,
And for a wife he kept *sheep.*

13 But by a prophet the LORD brought Israel from Egypt,
And by a prophet he was kept.

14 Ephraim has provoked to bitter anger;
So his Lord will leave his bloodguilt on him
And bring back his reproach to him.

LIFE LESSONS

➤ **Hosea 12:6 — "Therefore, return to your God; observe kindness and justice, and wait for your God continually."**

*G*od wants to partner with us in *everything,* including those times when we need to repent. He actually helps us return to Him! Without His help, we could not show mercy or provide justice, or even wait for Him.

✦ Psalm 139:17–24

17 How precious also are Your thoughts to me, O God!
How vast is the sum of them!

18 If I should count them, they would
    outnumber the sand.
    When I awake, I am still with You.
19 O that You would slay the wicked,
    O God;
    Depart from me, therefore, men of
    bloodshed.
20 For they speak against You
    wickedly,
    And Your enemies take *Your name*
    in vain.
21 Do I not hate those who hate You,
    O LORD?
    And do I not loathe those who rise
    up against You?
22 I hate them with the utmost hatred;
    They have become my enemies.
23 Search me, O God, and know my
    heart;
    Try me and know my anxious
    thoughts;
24 And see if there be any hurtful way
    in me,
    And lead me in the everlasting way.

Proverbs 29:22

22 An angry man stirs up strife,
    And a hot-tempered man abounds
    in transgression.

Jude 1–25

1 JUDE, a bond-servant of Jesus Christ,
  and brother of James,
    To those who are the called, beloved
    in God the Father, and kept for Jesus
    Christ:
2   May mercy and peace and love be
    multiplied to you.
3   Beloved, while I was making every
    effort to write you about our common
    salvation, I felt the necessity to write
    to you appealing that you contend ear-
    nestly for the faith which was once for
    all handed down to the saints.
4   For certain persons have crept in
    unnoticed, those who were long before-
    hand marked out for this condemnation,
    ungodly persons who turn the grace of
    our God into licentiousness and deny our
    only Master and Lord, Jesus Christ.
5   Now I desire to remind you, though

you know all things once for all, that the
Lord, after saving a people out of the
land of Egypt, subsequently destroyed
those who did not believe.
6   And angels who did not keep their
own domain, but abandoned their proper
abode, He has kept in eternal bonds
under darkness for the judgment of the
great day,
7   just as Sodom and Gomorrah and
the cities around them, since they in the
same way as these indulged in gross immorality and went after strange flesh,
are exhibited as an example in undergo-
ing the punishment of eternal fire.
8   Yet in the same way these men, also
by dreaming, defile the flesh, and reject
authority, and revile angelic majesties.
9   But Michael the archangel, when he
disputed with the devil and argued about
the body of Moses, did not dare pronounce against him a railing judgment,
but said, "The Lord rebuke you!"
10 But these men revile the things
which they do not understand; and the
things which they know by instinct, like
unreasoning animals, by these things
they are destroyed.
11 Woe to them! For they have gone
the way of Cain, and for pay they have
rushed headlong into the error of Balaam,
and perished in the rebellion of Korah.

LIFE LESSONS

➤ **Jude 3 — *Contend earnestly for the
faith which was once for all handed
down to the saints.***

*T*he gospel of Jesus Christ does not
change. He is the same yesterday,
today, and forever (Heb. 13:8), and His
salvation remains eternally secure for
those who believe. It is worth fighting
for, so we must contend for the faith, no
matter what challenge we face.

➤ **Jude 5 — *The Lord, after saving a
people out of the land of Egypt, subsequently destroyed those who did not
believe.***

*H*ere we see both the love and justice
of God. The Lord showed His goodness in rescuing the Israelites from Egyptian slavery, but we also see His holiness
in punishing their stubborn unbelief and
disobedience.

12　These are the men who are hidden reefs in your love feasts when they feast with you without fear, caring for themselves; clouds without water, carried along by winds; autumn trees without fruit, doubly dead, uprooted;
13　wild waves of the sea, casting up their own shame like foam; wandering stars, for whom the black darkness has been reserved forever.
14　*It was* also about these men *that* Enoch, *in* the seventh *generation* from Adam, prophesied, saying, "Behold, the Lord came with many thousands of His holy ones,
15　to execute judgment upon all, and to convict all the ungodly of all their ungodly deeds which they have done in an ungodly way, and of all the harsh things which ungodly sinners have spoken against Him."
16　These are grumblers, finding fault, following after their *own* lusts; they speak arrogantly, flattering people for the sake of *gaining an* advantage.
17　But you, beloved, ought to remember the words that were spoken beforehand by the apostles of our Lord Jesus Christ,
18　that they were saying to you, "In the last time there will be mockers, following after their own ungodly lusts."
19　These are the ones who cause divisions, worldly-minded, devoid of the Spirit.

20　But you, beloved, building yourselves up on your most holy faith, praying in the Holy Spirit,
21　keep yourselves in the love of God, waiting anxiously for the mercy of our Lord Jesus Christ to eternal life.
22　And have mercy on some, who are doubting;
23　save others, snatching them out of the fire; and on some have mercy with fear, hating even the garment polluted by the flesh.
24　Now to Him who is able to keep you from stumbling, and to make you stand in the presence of His glory blameless with great joy,
25　to the only God our Savior, through Jesus Christ our Lord, *be* glory, majesty, dominion and authority, before all time and now and forever. Amen.

LIFE LESSONS

➤ **Jude 24 —** *To Him who is able to keep you from stumbling, and to make you stand in the presence of His glory blameless with great joy.*

While God asks us to cooperate with Him in the process of sanctification, it is He who conforms us to the image of Jesus by His power and infinite wisdom. He is the One Who makes us holy and perfect forever, which is why we can joyfully anticipate our total transformation.

Hosea 13:1—14:9

13 WHEN Ephraim spoke, *there was* trembling.
　　He exalted himself in Israel,
　　　But through Baal he did wrong and died.
2　And now they sin more and more,
　　And make for themselves molten images,
　　Idols skillfully made from their silver,
　　All of them the work of craftsmen.
　　They say of them, "Let the men who sacrifice kiss the calves!"

3　Therefore they will be like the morning cloud
　　And like dew which soon disappears,
　　Like chaff which is blown away from the threshing floor
　　And like smoke from a chimney.
4　Yet I *have been* the LORD your God
　　Since the land of Egypt;
　　And you were not to know any god except Me,
　　For there is no savior besides Me.
5　I cared for you in the wilderness,
　　In the land of drought.
6　As *they had* their pasture, they became satisfied,

LIFE LESSONS

> Hosea 13:4 — *"You were not to know any god except Me, for there is no savior besides Me."*

*P*assages like these show us the truth of the Trinity. There is only one God, and He is our only Savior; yet Scripture plainly calls Jesus our Savior (Acts 13:23; Phil. 3:20; 2 Pet. 1:11). Therefore, Jesus and the Father are one (John 10:30).

And being satisfied, their heart
    became proud;
Therefore they forgot Me.
7 So I will be like a lion to them;
Like a leopard I will lie in wait by
    the wayside.
8 I will encounter them like a bear
    robbed of her cubs,
And I will tear open their chests;
There I will also devour them like a
    lioness,
As a wild beast would tear them.
9 *It is* your destruction, O Israel,
That *you are* against Me, against
    your help.
10 Where now is your king
That he may save you in all your
    cities,
And your judges of whom you
    requested,
"Give me a king and princes"?
11 I gave you a king in My anger
And took him away in My wrath.
12 The iniquity of Ephraim is bound up;
His sin is stored up.
13 The pains of childbirth come upon
    him;
He is not a wise son,
For it is not the time that he should
    delay at the opening of the womb.
14 Shall I ransom them from the power
    of Sheol?
Shall I redeem them from death?
O Death, where are your thorns?
O Sheol, where is your sting?
Compassion will be hidden from My
    sight.
15 Though he flourishes among the
    reeds,
An east wind will come,
The wind of the LORD coming up
    from the wilderness;
And his fountain will become dry
And his spring will be dried up;

It will plunder *his* treasury of every
    precious article.
16 Samaria will be held guilty,
For she has rebelled against her God.
They will fall by the sword,
Their little ones will be dashed in
    pieces,
And their pregnant women will be
    ripped open.

14 RETURN, O Israel, to the LORD
    your God,
For you have stumbled because of
    your iniquity.
2 Take words with you and return to
    the LORD.
Say to Him, "Take away all iniquity
And receive *us* graciously,
That we may present the fruit of our
    lips.
3 "Assyria will not save us,
We will not ride on horses;
Nor will we say again, 'Our god,'
To the work of our hands;
For in You the orphan finds mercy."
4 I will heal their apostasy,
I will love them freely,
For My anger has turned away from
    them.
5 I will be like the dew to Israel;
He will blossom like the lily,
And he will take root like *the*
    cedars of Lebanon.
6 His shoots will sprout,
And his beauty will be like the olive
    tree
And his fragrance like *the cedars of*
    Lebanon.
7 Those who live in his shadow
Will again raise grain,
And they will blossom like the vine.
His renown *will be* like the wine of
    Lebanon.

LIFE LESSONS

> Hosea 14:2 — *Take words with you and return to the LORD.*

*W*hy does God insist that we confess our sins to Him (Ps. 32:5; 1 John 1:9)? Why should we "take words" with us when we return to the Lord? Confession breaks the power that sin wields over us when it is hidden. Jesus died not only to save us from the penalty of sin, but also from its power. His grace enables us to walk in His righteous ways.

---

8   O Ephraim, what more have I to do
    with idols?
    It is I who answer and look after you.
    I am like a luxuriant cypress;
    From Me comes your fruit.
9   Whoever is wise, let him understand
        these things;
    Whoever is discerning, let him
        know them.
    For the ways of the LORD are right,
    And the righteous will walk in
        them,
    But transgressors will stumble in
        them.

Psalm 140:1–5

For the choir director. A Psalm of David.

140 RESCUE me, O LORD, from evil
        men;
    Preserve me from violent men
2   Who devise evil things in their hearts;
    They continually stir up wars.
3   They sharpen their tongues as a
        serpent;
    Poison of a viper is under their lips.
                                    Selah.
4   Keep me, O LORD, from the hands of
        the wicked;
    Preserve me from violent men
    Who have purposed to trip up my
        feet.
5   The proud have hidden a trap for
        me, and cords;
    They have spread a net by the
        wayside;
    They have set snares for me. Selah.

Proverbs 29:23

23 A man's pride will bring him low,
    But a humble spirit will obtain honor.

Revelation 1:1–20

1 THE Revelation of Jesus Christ, which
    God gave Him to show to His bond-
servants, the things which must soon take
place; and He sent and communicated it
by His angel to His bond-servant John,
2   who testified to the word of God and

to the testimony of Jesus Christ, even to
all that he saw.
3   Blessed is he who reads and those
who hear the words of the prophecy, and
heed the things which are written in it;
for the time is near.
4   John to the seven churches that are
in Asia: Grace to you and peace, from
Him who is and who was and who is to
come, and from the seven Spirits who
are before His throne,
5   and from Jesus Christ, the faithful
witness, the firstborn of the dead, and
the ruler of the kings of the earth. To
Him who loves us and released us from
our sins by His blood—
6   and He has made us to be a kingdom, priests to His God and Father—to
Him be the glory and the dominion for
ever and ever. Amen.
7   BEHOLD, HE IS COMING WITH THE CLOUDS,
and every eye will see Him, even those who
pierced Him; and all the tribes of the earth
will mourn over Him. So it is to be. Amen.
8   "I am the Alpha and the Omega,"
says the Lord God, "who is and who was
and who is to come, the Almighty."
9   I, John, your brother and fellow partaker in the tribulation and kingdom and
perseverance which are in Jesus, was on
the island called Patmos because of the
word of God and the testimony of Jesus.
10 I was in the Spirit on the Lord's day,
and I heard behind me a loud voice like
the sound of a trumpet,

LIFE LESSONS

➤ **Revelation 1:4 — Grace to you and
peace.**

Grace was a typical Greek greeting of
the first century, while peace served as
the typical Hebrew greeting. The author
thus lets his readers know that this book
is for everyone, Jew and Gentile alike.

➤ **Revelation 1:5 — Jesus Christ . . . the
firstborn of the dead.**

Several individuals in the Bible (before
Jesus) had been raised from the
dead. But all of them—the Shunammite's
son (2 Kin. 4:35), Jairus' daughter (Mark
5:42), and Lazarus (John 11:44)—all
died a second time. Jesus, however, conquered death for all eternity, and everyone who believes in Him will live forever.

WHAT THE BIBLE SAYS ABOUT

The Holy Spirit and the Trinity

Revelation 1

*L*ook closely at Genesis 1:1, 2, and you'll notice the Bible refers to "God" and "the Spirit of God" without making the slightest distinction between the two. It uses the two terms interchangeably. Have you ever wondered why?

It's because the two are one! This is the first allusion to the doctrine of the Trinity in Scripture.

A little later in the creation story we find a second reference to the Trinity: "Then God said, 'Let Us make man in Our image, according to Our likeness' " (Gen. 1:26). Now, to whom was God speaking? Whomever He meant, He (or They) clearly played a crucial part in the creation process: "Let *Us* make man." So who was this mysterious "Us"? The only other beings then alive were animals and angels, and the Bible gives no indication that either group played any role in the creation process.

Fortunately, in the very next verse God clarifies who He meant: "God created man in His own image, in the image of God He created him; male and female He created them" (Gen. 1:27). God did not create Adam and Eve in the image of animals or angels; He created them in His own image. Therefore, the "Us" in Genesis 1:26 could only refer to God Himself— that is, to God the Father, God the Son, and God the Spirit. There is only one God, but He expresses Himself through the three persons of the Trinity.

Within the eternal fellowship of the Trinity, the members of the Godhead have always enjoyed a deep and rich and unbroken relationship of love with one another. When God created us, He wanted us to share in some measure of that fellowship; that's why He created us in His image. By creating us to reflect His own nature, He made it possible for us to develop a deep and intimate relationship with Himself.

In this truth we come to the heart of who God made us to be. Our intimacy with God— His highest priority for our lives—determines the impact of our lives! So the closer we grow to Him, the more positive and lasting impact we can have on this world. ◈

---

11 saying, "Write in a book what you see, and send *it* to the seven churches: to Ephesus and to Smyrna and to Pergamum and to Thyatira and to Sardis and to Philadelphia and to Laodicea."
12 Then I turned to see the voice that was speaking with me. And having turned I saw seven golden lampstands;
13 and in the middle of the lampstands I *saw* one like a son of man, clothed in a robe reaching to the feet, and girded across His chest with a golden sash.
14 His head and His hair were white like white wool, like snow; and His eyes were like a flame of fire.
15 His feet *were* like burnished bronze, when it has been made to glow in a furnace, and His voice *was* like the sound of many waters.
16 In His right hand He held seven stars, and out of His mouth came a sharp two-edged sword; and His face was like the sun shining in its strength.
➤ 17 When I saw Him, I fell at His feet
✳ like a dead man. And He placed His right

hand on me, saying, "Do not be afraid; I am the first and the last,
18 and the living One; and I was dead, and behold, I am alive forevermore, and I have the keys of death and of Hades.
19 "Therefore write the things which you have seen, and the things which are, and the things which will take place after these things.
20 "As for the mystery of the seven stars which you saw in My right hand, and the seven golden lampstands: the seven stars are the angels of the seven churches, and the seven lampstands are the seven churches.

LIFE LESSONS

➤ **Revelation 1:17 —** *When I saw Him, I fell at His feet like a dead man.*

*T*he majestic, glorious appearance of the unveiled Christ so overwhelmed John that he fainted. We must never forget that our Savior and Friend is also our Lord, Master, King, and Sovereign.

1 THE word of the LORD that came to Joel, the son of Pethuel:

2 Hear this, O elders,
And listen, all inhabitants of the land.
Has *anything like* this happened in your days
Or in your fathers' days?

3 Tell your sons about it,
And *let* your sons *tell* their sons,
And their sons the next generation.

4 What the gnawing locust has left,
the swarming locust has eaten;
And what the swarming locust has left, the creeping locust has eaten;
And what the creeping locust has left, the stripping locust has eaten.

5 Awake, drunkards, and weep;
And wail, all you wine drinkers,
On account of the sweet wine
That is cut off from your mouth.

6 For a nation has invaded my land,
Mighty and without number;
Its teeth are the teeth of a lion,
And it has the fangs of a lioness.

7 It has made my vine a waste
And my fig tree splinters.
It has stripped them bare and cast *them* away;
Their branches have become white.

8 Wail like a virgin girded with sackcloth
For the bridegroom of her youth.

9 The grain offering and the drink offering are cut off
From the house of the LORD.
The priests mourn,
The ministers of the LORD.

10 The field is ruined,
The land mourns;
For the grain is ruined,
The new wine dries up,
Fresh oil fails.

11 Be ashamed, O farmers,
Wail, O vinedressers,
For the wheat and the barley;
Because the harvest of the field is destroyed.

12 The vine dries up
And the fig tree fails;
The pomegranate, the palm also, and the apple tree,
All the trees of the field dry up.

Indeed, rejoicing dries up
From the sons of men.

13 Gird yourselves *with sackcloth*
And lament, O priests;
Wail, O ministers of the altar!
Come, spend the night in sackcloth
O ministers of my God,
For the grain offering and the drink offering
Are withheld from the house of your God.

14 Consecrate a fast,
Proclaim a solemn assembly;
Gather the elders
And all the inhabitants of the land
To the house of the LORD your God,
And cry out to the LORD.

15 Alas for the day!
For the day of the LORD is near,
And it will come as destruction from the Almighty.

16 Has not food been cut off before our eyes,
Gladness and joy from the house of our God?

17 The seeds shrivel under their clods;
The storehouses are desolate,
The barns are torn down,
For the grain is dried up.

18 How the beasts groan!
The herds of cattle wander aimlessly
Because there is no pasture for them;
Even the flocks of sheep suffer.

19 To You, O LORD, I cry;
For fire has devoured the pastures of the wilderness
And the flame has burned up all the trees of the field.

20 Even the beasts of the field pant for You;
For the water brooks are dried up
And fire has devoured the pastures of the wilderness.

2 BLOW a trumpet in Zion,
And sound an alarm on My holy mountain!
Let all the inhabitants of the land tremble,
For the day of the LORD is coming;
Surely it is near,

2 A day of darkness and gloom,
A day of clouds and thick darkness.
As the dawn is spread over the mountains,

WHAT THE BIBLE SAYS ABOUT

Brokenness, the Way to Blessing

Joel 2:12–20

No one enjoys experiencing emotional, physical, or spiritual afflictions. And it is difficult to understand how strength and blessing can result from adversity, even though they often do. Yet we seldom recognize the benefit of brokenness in the midst of our pain.

The apostle Paul faced discouragement and many intense trials, but he believed God was in control. Therefore, he placed his hope and faith in Jesus Christ. In Second Corinthians he wrote, "We are afflicted in every way, but not crushed; perplexed, but not despairing; persecuted, but not forsaken; struck down, but not destroyed; always carrying about in the body the dying of Jesus, so that the life of Jesus also may be manifested in our body" (4:8–10).

Paul believed the trials in his life came with a purpose. He considered them tools in the hand of God, who reshaped, refined, and refocused his life so that it could better reflect the life of Christ, full of purpose and blessing.

Just like us, Paul fought with emotional and physical difficulties. He was forthright in his epistles about the trials he was enduring, but he also filled his letters with words of hope and the certainty of divine intervention. Paul often encouraged those who faced the agony of brokenness with reminders of God's unfailing faithfulness and purpose (Rom. 8:18; 2 Cor. 1:3–10; 4:16–18; 12:7–10; Phil. 1:29, 30; 2:12–18; 3:7–12; 4:12, 13; Col. 1:24; 2 Tim. 1:8–10; 2:3; 3:10–12; 4:5–8). God's work in your life may not appear to make sense in the beginning, but He knows what lies ahead in your life. He disciplines, guides, and directs, not to hem you in, but to place you in a better position to live a free and blessed life.

Understand that clinging to what you desire and think is right for your life can prolong the brokenness process. As a Christian, you must focus your heart on Christ and obey Him implicitly, which often means giving up what you think you want. Yet, He knows what your heart truly needs. And although you may feel as though you are coming apart at the seams as you release your grip on certain goals and behaviors, if you will transfer your fear and anxiety to Jesus, then something amazing will happen. Not only will you begin the process of transformation into the image of God's Son, but you will sense a greater strength growing within you. ◈

So there is a great and mighty people;
There has never been *anything* like it,
Nor will there be again after it
To the years of many generations.

3　A fire consumes before them
And behind them a flame burns.
The land is like the garden of Eden before them
But a desolate wilderness behind them,
And nothing at all escapes them.

4　Their appearance is like the appearance of horses;
And like war horses, so they run.

5　With a noise as of chariots
They leap on the tops of the mountains,
Like the crackling of a flame of fire consuming the stubble,
Like a mighty people arranged for battle.

6　Before them the people are in anguish;
All faces turn pale.

7　They run like mighty men,
They climb the wall like soldiers;
And they each march in line,
Nor do they deviate from their paths.

8　They do not crowd each other,
They march everyone in his path;
When they burst through the defenses,
They do not break ranks.

9　They rush on the city,
They run on the wall;
They climb into the houses,
They enter through the windows like a thief.

10　Before them the earth quakes,
The heavens tremble,
The sun and the moon grow dark
And the stars lose their brightness.

11　The LORD utters His voice before His army;
Surely His camp is very great,
For strong is he who carries out His word.

The day of the Lord is indeed great
and very awesome,
And who can endure it?

12 "Yet even now," declares the Lord,
"Return to Me with all your heart,
And with fasting, weeping and
mourning;

➤ 13 And rend your heart and not your
garments."
Now return to the Lord your God,
For He is gracious and
compassionate,
Slow to anger, abounding in
lovingkindness
And relenting of evil.

14 Who knows whether He will *not*
turn and relent
And leave a blessing behind Him,
Even a grain offering and a drink
offering
For the Lord your God?

15 Blow a trumpet in Zion,
Consecrate a fast, proclaim a
solemn assembly,

16 Gather the people, sanctify the
congregation,
Assemble the elders,
Gather the children and the nursing
infants.
Let the bridegroom come out of his
room
And the bride out of her *bridal*
chamber.

17 Let the priests, the Lord's ministers,
Weep between the porch and the
altar,

And let them say, "Spare Your
people, O Lord,
And do not make Your inheritance a
reproach,
A byword among the nations.
Why should they among the peoples
say,
'Where is their God?'"

18 Then the Lord will be zealous for
His land
And will have pity on His people.

19 The Lord will answer and say to
His people,
"Behold, I am going to send you
grain, new wine and oil,
And you will be satisfied *in full* with
them;
And I will never again make you a
reproach among the nations.

20 "But I will remove the northern *army*
far from you,
And I will drive it into a parched
and desolate land,
And its vanguard into the eastern
sea,
And its rear guard into the western
sea.
And its stench will arise and its foul
smell will come up,
For it has done great things."

21 Do not fear, O land, rejoice and be
glad,
For the Lord has done great things.

22 Do not fear, beasts of the field,
For the pastures of the wilderness
have turned green,
For the tree has borne its fruit,
The fig tree and the vine have
yielded in full.

23 So rejoice, O sons of Zion,
And be glad in the Lord your God;
For He has given you the early rain
for *your* vindication.
And He has poured down for you the
rain,
The early and latter rain as before.

24 The threshing floors will be full of
grain,
And the vats will overflow with the
new wine and oil.

25 "Then I will make up to you for the
years
That the swarming locust has eaten,
The creeping locust, the stripping
locust and the gnawing locust,
My great army which I sent among
you.

LIFE LESSONS

➤ **Joel 2:11** — *Strong is he who carries
out His word.*

*O*ur omnipotent Lord will use all of
His power to fulfill every one of His
promises. Not one of them can or will
fail. That is why we can build our lives
on His every word.

➤ **Joel 2:13** — *Rend your heart and not
your garments.*

*G*od is always after the heart, not
mere outward religious expression.
He wants heartfelt prayer, not impressive
oratory (Matt. 6:7). He wants genuine
devotion, not smug declarations (Matt.
15:8). He wants your heart.

✳

26 "You will have plenty to eat and be
    satisfied
    And praise the name of the LORD
    your God,
    Who has dealt wondrously with
    you;
    Then My people will never be put to
    shame.
27 "Thus you will know that I am in the
    midst of Israel,
    And that I am the LORD your God,
    And there is no other;
    And My people will never be put to
    shame.
28 "It will come about after this
    That I will pour out My Spirit on all
    mankind;
    And your sons and daughters will
    prophesy,
    Your old men will dream dreams,
    Your young men will see visions.
➤ 29 "Even on the male and female
    servants
    I will pour out My Spirit in those
    days.
30 "I will display wonders in the sky
    and on the earth,
    Blood, fire and columns of smoke.
31 "The sun will be turned into
    darkness
    And the moon into blood
    Before the great and awesome day
    of the LORD comes.
32 "And it will come about that whoever
    calls on the name of the LORD
    Will be delivered;
    For on Mount Zion and in
    Jerusalem
    There will be those who escape,
    As the LORD has said,
    Even among the survivors whom
    the LORD calls.

3 "FOR behold, in those days and at
    that time,

When I restore the fortunes of
    Judah and Jerusalem,
2   I will gather all the nations
    And bring them down to the valley
    of Jehoshaphat.
    Then I will enter into judgment with
    them there
    On behalf of My people and My
    inheritance, Israel,
    Whom they have scattered among
    the nations;
    And they have divided up My land.
3 "They have also cast lots for My
    people,
    Traded a boy for a harlot
    And sold a girl for wine that they
    may drink.
4 "Moreover, what are you to Me, O
Tyre, Sidon and all the regions of Philistia? Are you rendering Me a recompense? But if you do recompense Me,
swiftly and speedily I will return your
recompense on your head.
5 "Since you have taken My silver and
My gold, brought My precious treasures
to your temples,
6   and sold the sons of Judah and Jerusalem to the Greeks in order to remove
them far from their territory,
7   behold, I am going to arouse them
from the place where you have sold
them, and return your recompense on
your head.
8 "Also I will sell your sons and your
daughters into the hand of the sons of
Judah, and they will sell them to the Sabeans, to a distant nation," for the LORD
has spoken.
9   Proclaim this among the nations:
    Prepare a war; rouse the mighty men!
    Let all the soldiers draw near, let
    them come up!
10   Beat your plowshares into swords
    And your pruning hooks into
    spears;
    Let the weak say, "I am a mighty
    man."
11   Hasten and come, all you
    surrounding nations,
    And gather yourselves there.
    Bring down, O LORD, Your mighty
    ones.
12   Let the nations be aroused
    And come up to the valley of
    Jehoshaphat,
    For there I will sit to judge
    All the surrounding nations.

LIFE LESSONS

➤ **Joel 2:29 — "Even on the male and
female servants I will pour out My Spirit
in those days."**

*W*e live in the great day when God is
    pouring out His Spirit on all believ-
ers in Christ, filling them and empowering them to serve Him in holiness and
great joy. Have you asked the Lord to fill
you today?

13　Put in the sickle, for the harvest is
　　ripe.
　　Come, tread, for the wine press is
　　full;
　　The vats overflow, for their
　　wickedness is great.
14　Multitudes, multitudes in the valley
　　of decision!
　　For the day of the LORD is near in
　　the valley of decision.
15　The sun and moon grow dark
　　And the stars lose their brightness.
16　The LORD roars from Zion
　　And utters His voice from
　　Jerusalem,
　　And the heavens and the earth
　　tremble.
　　But the LORD is a refuge for His
　　people
　　And a stronghold to the sons of
　　Israel.
17　Then you will know that I am the
　　LORD your God,
　　Dwelling in Zion, My holy
　　mountain.
　　So Jerusalem will be holy,
　　And strangers will pass through it
　　no more.
18　And in that day
　　The mountains will drip with sweet
　　wine,
　　And the hills will flow with milk,
　　And all the brooks of Judah will
　　flow with water;
　　And a spring will go out from the
　　house of the LORD
　　To water the valley of Shittim.
19　Egypt will become a waste,
　　And Edom will become a desolate
　　wilderness,
　　Because of the violence done to the
　　sons of Judah,
　　In whose land they have shed
　　innocent blood.
20　But Judah will be inhabited forever
　　And Jerusalem for all generations.
21　And I will avenge their blood which
　　I have not avenged,
　　For the LORD dwells in Zion.

Psalm 140:6–13

6　I said to the LORD, "You are my God;
　　Give ear, O LORD, to the voice of my
　　supplications.

7　"O GOD the Lord, the strength of my
　　salvation,
　　You have covered my head in the
　　day of battle.
8　"Do not grant, O LORD, the desires of
　　the wicked;
　　Do not promote his *evil* device, *that*
　　they *not* be exalted.　　Selah.
9　"As for the head of those who
　　surround me,
　　May the mischief of their lips cover
　　them.
10　"May burning coals fall upon them;
　　May they be cast into the fire,
　　Into deep pits from which they
　　cannot rise.
11　"May a slanderer not be established
　　in the earth;
　　May evil hunt the violent man
　　speedily."
12　I know that the LORD will maintain
　　the cause of the afflicted
　　And justice for the poor.
13　Surely the righteous will give
　　thanks to Your name;
　　The upright will dwell in Your
　　presence.

Proverbs 29:24

24　He who is a partner with a thief
　　hates his own life;
　　He hears the oath but tells
　　nothing.

Revelation 2:1–29

2 "TO the angel of the church in Ephe-
　sus write:
　　The One who holds the seven stars
in His right hand, the One who walks
among the seven golden lampstands,
says this:
2　'I know your deeds and your toil and
perseverance, and that you cannot tolerate evil men, and you put to the test those
who call themselves apostles, and they
are not, and you found them *to be* false;
3　and you have perseverance and have
endured for My name's sake, and have
not grown weary.
4　'But I have *this* against you, that you
have left your first love.

➤ **Revelation 2:2 — "I know your deeds and your toil and perseverance."**

*W*e may sometimes feel as though we toil in anonymity and that our labors go unnoticed and unappreciated. However, first we must remember that we do not exist to glorify ourselves but the One who has redeemed us so that others will be saved (Matt. 5:16; John 12:32). Second, we must recall that Jesus notices everything. He sees both our work and the love and obedience we express for Him as we serve (Heb. 6:10). He remembers it all faithfully, and He rewards us when the time is right (1 Cor. 3:11–15; 2 Cor. 5:9, 10; Heb. 11:6).

5 'Therefore remember from where you have fallen, and repent and do the deeds you did at first; or else I am coming to you and will remove your lampstand out of its place—unless you repent.
6 'Yet this you do have, that you hate the deeds of the Nicolaitans, which I also hate.
7 'He who has an ear, let him hear what the Spirit says to the churches. To him who overcomes, I will grant to eat of the tree of life which is in the Paradise of God.'
8 "And to the angel of the church in Smyrna write:

The first and the last, who was dead, and has come to life, says this:
9 'I know your tribulation and your poverty (but you are rich), and the blasphemy by those who say they are Jews and are not, but are a synagogue of Satan.
➤ 10 'Do not fear what you are about to suffer. Behold, the devil is about to cast some of you into prison, so that you will be tested, and you will have tribulation for ten days. Be faithful until death, and I will give you the crown of life.
11 'He who has an ear, let him hear what the Spirit says to the churches. He who overcomes will not be hurt by the second death.'
12 "And to the angel of the church in Pergamum write:

The One who has the sharp two-edged sword says this:
13 'I know where you dwell, where Satan's throne is; and you hold fast My name, and did not deny My faith even in the days of Antipas, My witness, My faithful one, who was killed among you, where Satan dwells.
14 'But I have a few things against you, because you have there some who hold the teaching of Balaam, who kept teaching Balak to put a stumbling block before the sons of Israel, to eat things sacrificed to idols and to commit *acts of* immorality.
15 'So you also have some who in the same way hold the teaching of the Nicolaitans.
16 'Therefore repent; or else I am coming to you quickly, and I will make war against them with the sword of My mouth.
17 'He who has an ear, let him hear what the Spirit says to the churches. To him who overcomes, to him I will give *some* of the hidden manna, and I will give him a white stone, and a new name written on the stone which no one knows but he who receives it.'
18 "And to the angel of the church in Thyatira write:

The Son of God, who has eyes like a flame of fire, and His feet are like burnished bronze, says this:
19 'I know your deeds, and your love and faith and service and perseverance, and that your deeds of late are greater than at first.

➤ **Revelation 2:10 — "Do not fear what you are about to suffer."**

*O*bedience may bring suffering, but this is because brokenness is God's requirement for maximum usefulness. Sorrows and trials keep us close to the Lord where we can serve Him.

➤ **Revelation 2:16 — "Repent; or else I am coming to you quickly, and I will make war against them with the sword of My mouth."**

*N*o one should ever imagine that because of His unconditional love for us, God will not discipline our unrepentant sinfulness. Jesus uses strong language against those at Pergamum to remind us that He expects us to represent Him well.

20 'But I have *this* against you, that you tolerate the woman Jezebel, who calls herself a prophetess, and she teaches and leads My bond-servants astray so that they commit *acts of* immorality and eat things sacrificed to idols.

21 'I gave her time to repent, and she does not want to repent of her immorality.

22 'Behold, I will throw her on a bed *of sickness*, and those who commit adultery with her into great tribulation, unless they repent of her deeds.

23 'And I will kill her children with pestilence, and all the churches will know that I am He who searches the minds and hearts; and I will give to each one of you according to your deeds.

24 'But I say to you, the rest who are in Thyatira, who do not hold this teaching, who have not known the deep things of Satan, as they call them—I place no other burden on you.

25 'Nevertheless what you have, hold fast until I come.

26 'He who overcomes, and he who keeps My deeds until the end, TO HIM I WILL GIVE AUTHORITY OVER THE NATIONS;

27 AND HE SHALL RULE THEM WITH A ROD OF IRON, AS THE VESSELS OF THE POTTER ARE BROKEN TO PIECES, as I also have received *authority* from My Father;

28 and I will give him the morning star.

29 'He who has an ear, let him hear what the Spirit says to the churches.'

Amos 1:1—3:15

1 THE words of Amos, who was among the sheepherders from Tekoa, which he envisioned in visions concerning Israel in the days of Uzziah king of Judah, and in the days of Jeroboam son of Joash, king of Israel, two years before the earthquake.

2 He said,
"The LORD roars from Zion
And from Jerusalem He utters His voice;
And the shepherds' pasture grounds mourn,

And the summit of Carmel dries up."

3 Thus says the LORD,
"For three transgressions of Damascus and for four
I will not revoke its *punishment*,
Because they threshed Gilead with *implements* of sharp iron.

4 "So I will send fire upon the house of Hazael
And it will consume the citadels of Ben-hadad.

5 "I will also break the *gate* bar of Damascus,
And cut off the inhabitant from the valley of Aven,

Life Examples:

AMOS: Obedient Without Compromise

AMOS 1:1

God called Amos from his flocks and groves in Judah to prophesy to the northern kingdom of Israel. Although King Jeroboam II had expanded Israel's territory and the nation was enjoying a time of prosperity, the people were corrupt, immoral, and idolatrous. Without hesitation or argument, the shepherd complied with God's command and declared the Lord's judgment upon Israel and the surrounding nations.

Amos knew he would be fighting an uphill battle. During this economic golden era, the people did not welcome his words of warning. Yet he understood that for the people to be saved from God's wrath, they would have to repent—turning from their wicked ways and serving the Lord wholeheartedly. And so the shepherd proclaimed God's call to repentance, "Hate evil, love good, and establish justice in the gate! Perhaps the LORD God of hosts may be gracious to the remnant of Joseph" (Amos 5:15).

How many of us today have the mighty spirit of Amos? How many boldly face a hostile world and faithfully proclaim the truth of the Lord? How many obey, regardless of the repercussions? How many absorb blow after blow from the enemy, only to turn and take the next obedient step in their walk of faith?

And him who holds the scepter,
   from Beth-eden;
So the people of Aram will go exiled
   to Kir,"
   Says the LORD.

6   Thus says the LORD,
"For three transgressions of Gaza
   and for four
I will not revoke its *punishment*,
Because they deported an entire
   population
To deliver *it* up to Edom.

7   "So I will send fire upon the wall of
   Gaza
And it will consume her citadels.

8   "I will also cut off the inhabitant
   from Ashdod,
And him who holds the scepter,
   from Ashkelon;
I will even unleash My power upon
   Ekron,
And the remnant of the Philistines
   will perish,"
   Says the Lord GOD.

9   Thus says the LORD,
"For three transgressions of Tyre and
   for four
I will not revoke its *punishment*,
Because they delivered up an entire
   population to Edom
And did not remember *the* covenant
   of brotherhood.

10 "So I will send fire upon the wall of
   Tyre
And it will consume her citadels."

11 Thus says the LORD,
"For three transgressions of Edom
   and for four
I will not revoke its *punishment*,
Because he pursued his brother
   with the sword,
While he stifled his compassion;
His anger also tore continually,
And he maintained his fury forever.

12 "So I will send fire upon Teman
And it will consume the citadels of
   Bozrah."

13 Thus says the LORD,
"For three transgressions of the sons
   of Ammon and for four
I will not revoke its *punishment*,
Because they ripped open the
   pregnant women of Gilead
In order to enlarge their borders.

14 "So I will kindle a fire on the wall of
   Rabbah
And it will consume her citadels

Amid war cries on the day of battle,
And a storm on the day of tempest.

15 "Their king will go into exile,
He and his princes together," says
   the LORD.

2 THUS says the LORD,
"For three transgressions of Moab
   and for four
I will not revoke its *punishment*,
Because he burned the bones of the
   king of Edom to lime.

2   "So I will send fire upon Moab
And it will consume the citadels of
   Kerioth;
And Moab will die amid tumult,
With war cries and the sound of a
   trumpet.

3   "I will also cut off the judge from her
   midst
And slay all her princes with him,"
   says the LORD.

4   Thus says the LORD,
"For three transgressions of Judah
   and for four
I will not revoke its *punishment*,
Because they rejected the law of the
   LORD
And have not kept His statutes;
Their lies also have led them astray,
Those after which their fathers
   walked.

5   "So I will send fire upon Judah
And it will consume the citadels of
   Jerusalem."

6   Thus says the LORD,
"For three transgressions of Israel
   and for four
I will not revoke its *punishment*,
Because they sell the righteous for
   money
And the needy for a pair of sandals.

7   "These who pant after the *very* dust
   of the earth on the head of the
   helpless
Also turn aside the way of the humble;
And a man and his father resort to
   the same girl
In order to profane My holy name.

8   "On garments taken as pledges they
   stretch out beside every altar,
And in the house of their God they
   drink the wine of those who have
   been fined.

9   "Yet it was I who destroyed the
   Amorite before them,
Though his height *was* like the
   height of cedars

And he *was* strong as the oaks;
I even destroyed his fruit above and
his root below.

➤ 10 "It was I who brought you up from
the land of Egypt,
And I led you in the wilderness
forty years
That you might take possession of
the land of the Amorite.

11 "Then I raised up some of your sons
to be prophets
And some of your young men to be
Nazirites.
Is this not so, O sons of Israel?"
declares the LORD.

12 "But you made the Nazirites drink
wine,
And you commanded the prophets
saying, 'You shall not prophesy!'

13 "Behold, I am weighted down
beneath you
As a wagon is weighted down when
filled with sheaves.

14 "Flight will perish from the swift,
And the stalwart will not strengthen
his power,
Nor the mighty man save his life.

15 "He who grasps the bow will not
stand *his* ground,
The swift of foot will not escape,
Nor will he who rides the horse
save his life.

16 "Even the bravest among the
warriors will flee naked in that
day," declares the LORD.

3 HEAR this word which the LORD
has spoken against you, sons of Israel, against the entire family which He
brought up from the land of Egypt:

➤ 2 "You only have I chosen among all
the families of the earth;
Therefore I will punish you for all
your iniquities."

3 Do two men walk together unless
they have made an appointment?

4 Does a lion roar in the forest when
he has no prey?
Does a young lion growl from
his den unless he has captured
something?

5 Does a bird fall into a trap on the
ground when there is no bait in
it?
Does a trap spring up from the earth
when it captures nothing at all?

6 If a trumpet is blown in a city will
not the people tremble?

If a calamity occurs in a city has not
the LORD done it?

7 Surely the Lord GOD does nothing
Unless He reveals His secret counsel
To His servants the prophets.

8 A lion has roared! Who will not fear?
The Lord GOD has spoken! Who can
but prophesy?

9 Proclaim on the citadels in Ashdod
and on the citadels in the land of Egypt
and say, "Assemble yourselves on the
mountains of Samaria and see *the* great
tumults within her and *the* oppressions
in her midst.

10 "But they do not know how to do
what is right," declares the LORD, "these
who hoard up violence and devastation
in their citadels."

11 Therefore, thus says the Lord GOD,
"An enemy, even one surrounding
the land,
Will pull down your strength from
you
And your citadels will be looted."

12 Thus says the LORD,
"Just as the shepherd snatches from
the lion's mouth a couple of legs
or a piece of an ear,
So will the sons of Israel dwelling in
Samaria be snatched away—

LIFE LESSONS

➤ **Amos 2:10 —** *"It was I who brought
you up from the land of Egypt, and I led
you in the wilderness forty years."*

*I*t is good to regularly remind ourselves how the Lord has helped and
delivered us in the past, otherwise we
tend to either forget His goodness to us
or we begin to imagine that we have
blessed ourselves. If we do not immerse
ourselves in the truth of God's Word, the
lies that flourish all around us can easily take hold in our minds and lead us
astray, to our own destruction.

➤ **Amos 3:2 —** *"You only have I chosen among all the families of the earth;
therefore I will punish you for all your
iniquities."*

A relationship with God is not only a
phenomenal privilege, it is also a
great responsibility. "It is time for judgment to begin with the household of
God" (1 Pet. 4:17).

With *the* corner of a bed and *the* cover of a couch!

13 "Hear and testify against the house of Jacob,"

Declares the Lord GOD, the God of hosts.

14 "For on the day that I punish Israel's transgressions,

I will also punish the altars of Bethel;
The horns of the altar will be cut off
And they will fall to the ground.

➤ 15 "I will also smite the winter house together with the summer house;
The houses of ivory will also perish
And the great houses will come to an end,"
Declares the LORD.

❂ Psalm 141:1–4

A Psalm of David.

141 O LORD, I call upon You; hasten to me!
Give ear to my voice when I call to You!

2 May my prayer be counted as incense before You;
The lifting up of my hands as the evening offering.

3 Set a guard, O LORD, over my mouth;
Keep watch over the door of my lips.

4 Do not incline my heart to any evil thing,
To practice deeds of wickedness
With men who do iniquity;
And do not let me eat of their delicacies.

❂ Proverbs 29:25

25 The fear of man brings a snare,
But he who trusts in the LORD will be exalted.

❂ Revelation 3:1–22

3 "TO the angel of the church in Sardis write:
He who has the seven Spirits of God and the seven stars, says this: 'I know

your deeds, that you have a name that you are alive, but you are dead.

2 'Wake up, and strengthen the things that remain, which were about to die; for I have not found your deeds completed in the sight of My God.

3 'So remember what you have received and heard; and keep *it*, and repent. Therefore if you do not wake up, I will come like a thief, and you will not know at what hour I will come to you.

4 'But you have a few people in Sardis who have not soiled their garments; and they will walk with Me in white, for they are worthy.

5 'He who overcomes will thus be clothed in white garments; and I will not erase his name from the book of life, and I will confess his name before My Father and before His angels.

6 'He who has an ear, let him hear what the Spirit says to the churches.'

7 "And to the angel of the church in Philadelphia write:

He who is holy, who is true, who has the key of David, who opens and no one will shut, and who shuts and no one opens, says this:

8 'I know your deeds. Behold, I have ◄ put before you an open door which no one can shut, because you have a little power, and have kept My word, and have not denied My name.

LIFE LESSONS

➤ **Amos 3:15 — "I will also smite the winter house together with the summer house."**

The ancient Israelites had allowed their pursuit of material abundance to eclipse their commitment to God—and He will never allow anything or anyone to take the place that belongs to Him alone.

➤ **Revelation 3:8 — "I have put before you an open door which no one can shut, because you have a little power, and have kept My word, and have not denied My name."**

We do not have to be mighty conquerors or giant-killers to take advantage of the open doors of opportunity that God sets before us; a "little power" is plenty when we obey His Word and honor His Son.

9 'Behold, I will cause *those* of the synagogue of Satan, who say that they are Jews and are not, but lie—I will make them come and bow down at your feet, and *make them* know that I have loved you.

10 'Because you have kept the word of My perseverance, I also will keep you from the hour of testing, that *hour* which is about to come upon the whole world, to test those who dwell on the earth.

11 'I am coming quickly; hold fast what you have, so that no one will take your crown.

12 'He who overcomes, I will make him a pillar in the temple of My God, and he will not go out from it anymore; and I will write on him the name of My God, and the name of the city of My God, the new Jerusalem, which comes down out of heaven from My God, and My new name.

13 'He who has an ear, let him hear what the Spirit says to the churches.'

14 "To the angel of the church in Laodicea write:

The Amen, the faithful and true Witness, the Beginning of the creation of God, says this:

15 'I know your deeds, that you are neither cold nor hot; I wish that you were cold or hot.

16 'So because you are lukewarm, and neither hot nor cold, I will spit you out of My mouth.

17 'Because you say, "I am rich, and have become wealthy, and have need of nothing," and you do not know that you are wretched and miserable and poor and blind and naked,

18 I advise you to buy from Me gold refined by fire so that you may become rich, and white garments so that you may clothe yourself, and *that* the shame of your nakedness will not be revealed; and eye salve to anoint your eyes so that you may see.

19 'Those whom I love, I reprove and discipline; therefore be zealous and repent.

20 'Behold, I stand at the door and knock; if anyone hears My voice and opens the door, I will come in to him and will dine with him, and he with Me.

21 'He who overcomes, I will grant to him to sit down with Me on My throne, as I also overcame and sat down with My Father on His throne.

22 'He who has an ear, let him hear what the Spirit says to the churches.'"

LIFE LESSONS

➤ **Revelation 3:15 —** *"I know your deeds, that you are neither cold nor hot."*

Laodicea was known for its exceptional black wool, medical school, and banking. It was also the picture of ungodly compromise. To illustrate the church's indifferent commitment to Him, Jesus referred to the two sources of water available to them—the icy streams of the Hierapolis and the hot mineral springs to the south. However, once the water reached the city through the six-mile Roman aqueduct, they were tepid and undrinkable. Lukewarm believers who had accommodated secular society had become likewise repellent.

➤ **Revelation 3:19 —** *"Those whom I love, I reprove and discipline."*

No one likes to be disciplined because it requires a change in our perspectives, goals, behaviors, and attitudes. Deeply entrenched sinfulness, compromise, and destructive habits are rooted out, and our earthly sources of security are destroyed. This is all very painful and difficult. But if we cooperate with God when He corrects us, we will become more like Him, and great blessings will always result.

DECEMBER 14

Amos 4:1—5:27

4 HEAR this word, you cows of Bashan who are on the mountain of Samaria,

Who oppress the poor, who crush the needy,

Who say to your husbands, "Bring now, that we may drink!"

2 The Lord GOD has sworn by His holiness,

"Behold, the days are coming upon you
When they will take you away with meat hooks,
And the last of you with fish hooks.
3 "You will go out *through* breaches *in the walls,*
Each one straight before her,
And you will be cast to Harmon,"
declares the LORD.
4 "Enter Bethel and transgress;
In Gilgal multiply transgression!
Bring your sacrifices every morning,
Your tithes every three days.
5 "Offer a thank offering also from that which is leavened,
And proclaim freewill offerings, make them known.
For so you love *to do,* you sons of Israel,"
Declares the Lord GOD.
6 "But I gave you also cleanness of teeth in all your cities
And lack of bread in all your places,
Yet you have not returned to Me,"
declares the LORD.
7 "Furthermore, I withheld the rain from you
While *there were* still three months until harvest.
Then I would send rain on one city
And on another city I would not send rain;
One part would be rained on,
While the part not rained on would dry up.
8 "So two or three cities would stagger to another city to drink water,
But would not be satisfied;
Yet you have not returned to Me,"
declares the LORD.
9 "I smote you with scorching *wind* and mildew;
And the caterpillar was devouring
Your many gardens and vineyards, fig trees and olive trees;
Yet you have not returned to Me,"
declares the LORD.
10 "I sent a plague among you after the manner of Egypt;
I slew your young men by the sword along with your captured horses,
And I made the stench of your camp rise up in your nostrils;
Yet you have not returned to Me,"
declares the LORD.
11 "I overthrew you, as God overthrew Sodom and Gomorrah,
And you were like a firebrand snatched from a blaze;
Yet you have not returned to Me,"
declares the LORD.
12 "Therefore thus I will do to you, O Israel;
Because I will do this to you,
Prepare to meet your God, O Israel."
13 For behold, He who forms mountains and creates the wind
And declares to man what are His thoughts,
He who makes dawn into darkness
And treads on the high places of the earth,
The LORD God of hosts is His name.

5 HEAR this word which I take up for you as a dirge, O house of Israel:
2 She has fallen, she will not rise again—
The virgin Israel.
She *lies* neglected on her land;
There is none to raise her up.
3 For thus says the Lord GOD,
"The city which goes forth a thousand *strong*
Will have a hundred left,
And the one which goes forth a hundred *strong*
Will have ten left to the house of Israel."

4   For thus says the LORD to the house
of Israel,
"Seek Me that you may live.

5   "But do not resort to Bethel
And do not come to Gilgal,
Nor cross over to Beersheba;
For Gilgal will certainly go into
captivity
And Bethel will come to trouble.

6   "Seek the LORD that you may live,
Or He will break forth like a fire,
O house of Joseph,
And it will consume with none to
quench it for Bethel,

7   For those who turn justice into
wormwood
And cast righteousness down to the
earth."

8   He who made the Pleiades and
Orion
And changes deep darkness into
morning,
Who also darkens day into night,
Who calls for the waters of the sea
And pours them out on the surface
of the earth,
The LORD is His name.

9   It is He who flashes forth with
destruction upon the strong,
So that destruction comes upon the
fortress.

10 They hate him who reproves in the
gate,
And they abhor him who speaks
with integrity.

11 Therefore because you impose
heavy rent on the poor
And exact a tribute of grain from
them,
Though you have built houses of
well-hewn stone,
Yet you will not live in them;
You have planted pleasant
vineyards, yet you will not drink
their wine.

12 For I know your transgressions are
many and your sins are great,
You who distress the righteous and
accept bribes
And turn aside the poor in the
gate.

13 Therefore at such a time the
prudent person keeps silent, for it
is an evil time.

14 Seek good and not evil, that you
may live;

And thus may the LORD God of
hosts be with you,
Just as you have said!

15 Hate evil, love good,
And establish justice in the gate!
Perhaps the LORD God of hosts
May be gracious to the remnant of
Joseph.

16 Therefore thus says the LORD God
of hosts, the Lord,
"There is wailing in all the
plazas,
And in all the streets they say,
'Alas! Alas!'
They also call the farmer to
mourning
And professional mourners to
lamentation.

17 "And in all the vineyards there is
wailing,
Because I will pass through the
midst of you," says the LORD.

18 Alas, you who are longing for the
day of the LORD,
For what purpose will the day of the
LORD be to you?
It will be darkness and not light;

19 As when a man flees from a lion
And a bear meets him,
Or goes home, leans his hand
against the wall
And a snake bites him.

20 Will not the day of the LORD be
darkness instead of light,
Even gloom with no brightness
in it?

LIFE LESSONS

➤ **Amos 5:14 —** *Seek good and not evil,
that you may live; and thus may the* LORD
God of hosts will be with you.

*W*e find life when we find the Lord,
and we seek good when we seek
God. Christ delivers us from our sins so
we can joyfully live free of them.

➤ **Amos 5:24 —** *"Let justice roll down
like waters and righteousness like an
ever-flowing stream."*

*G*od intends for our personal righteousness to prompt us to actions
of community justice. John said, "If
someone says, 'I love God,' and hates his
brother, he is a liar" (1 John 4:20).

21 "I hate, I reject your festivals,
   Nor do I delight in your solemn
     assemblies.
22 "Even though you offer up to Me
     burnt offerings and your grain
     offerings,
   I will not accept *them*;
   And I will not *even* look at the
     peace offerings of your fatlings.
23 "Take away from Me the noise of
     your songs;
   I will not even listen to the sound of
     your harps.
➤ 24 "But let justice roll down like waters
   And righteousness like an ever-
     flowing stream.
25 "Did you present Me with sacrifices
and grain offerings in the wilderness for
forty years, O house of Israel?
26 "You also carried along Sikkuth your
king and Kiyyun, your images, the star
of your gods which you made for yourselves.
27 "Therefore, I will make you go into
exile beyond Damascus," says the LORD,
whose name is the God of hosts.

Psalm 141:5–10

➤ 5   Let the righteous smite me in
        kindness and reprove me;
     It is oil upon the head;
     Do not let my head refuse it,
     For still my prayer is against their
        wicked deeds.
6   Their judges are thrown down by
        the sides of the rock,
     And they hear my words, for they
        are pleasant.
7   As when one plows and breaks
        open the earth,
     Our bones have been scattered at
        the mouth of Sheol.
8   For my eyes are toward You, O GOD,
        the Lord;
     In You I take refuge; do not leave me
        defenseless.
9   Keep me from the jaws of the trap
        which they have set for me,
     And from the snares of those who
        do iniquity.
10   Let the wicked fall into their own
        nets,
     While I pass by safely.

Proverbs 29:26

26   Many seek the ruler's favor,
     But justice for man *comes* from the
       LORD.

Revelation 4:1–11

4 AFTER these things I looked, and behold, a door *standing* open in heaven,
and the first *voice* which I had heard,
like *the sound* of a trumpet speaking
with me, said, "Come up here, and I will
show you what must take place after
these things."
2   Immediately I was in the Spirit; and
behold, a throne was standing in heaven,
and One sitting on the throne.
3   And He who was sitting *was* like
a jasper stone and a sardius in appearance; and *there was* a rainbow around
the throne, like an emerald in appearance.
4   Around the throne *were* twenty-four
thrones; and upon the thrones *I saw*
twenty-four elders sitting, clothed in
white garments, and golden crowns on
their heads.
5   Out from the throne come flashes of
lightning and sounds and peals of thunder. And *there were* seven lamps of fire

---

LIFE LESSONS

➤ **Psalm 141:5 — *Let the righteous smite
me in kindness reprove me.***

*W*hen the righteous "smite" us
   through a stern rebuke or painful
correction, they do so for our own good.

➤ **Revelation 4:8 — *"Holy, holy, holy is
the Lord God, the Almighty, who was
and who is and who is to come."***

*T*his is the theme of the Book of
   Revelation: God rules the earth and
every individual in it on the basis of His
eternal holiness and perfect judgment.
He evaluates every situation and can tell
us what is coming because He inhabits
eternity—existing from the infinite past
and forever without end. No one is like
Him, and only He is worthy of praise.

WHAT THE BIBLE SAYS ABOUT ⊕

A Glimpse of Heavenly Praise

Revelation 4

*W*hy do believers spend so little time praising God? It's because we have an inadequate understanding of Him. We use words like majestic, righteous, and holy. But do we know what they really mean? God is above all earthly things and deserves more than the occasional "Hallelujah."

When the disciple John was exiled to Patmos, he received a glimpse of heavenly praise. Within the limits of language and his own experience, he did his best to describe the Holy Spirit's revelations. In that divine vision, John saw a throne with the radiance of God's Spirit shining like precious gems. This is a description of the Lord's purity and His holiness in poetic form.

From John's description in Revelation 4, we can see that God is clearly set apart from humanity. He's greater than any created being or thing. But the same magnificent God who is praised by heaven hears your prayers. He is not out of reach.

Elders were seated around the throne, representing the redeemed throughout history. There were also four creatures, all bowing to the Father and constantly praising Him. These creatures, which were created by God to worship Him, probably represent His attributes. The lion is most likely majesty. The ox may represent patience and toil. Man probably symbolizes God's intelligence and reason. And the eagle could signify His sovereignty and supremacy. The elders have cast their crowns—their heavenly rewards—at God's feet. All of heaven worships the Lord for who He is.

The only way to adequately worship Him is to praise God for who He is. This kind of praise focuses on Him and recognizes that He transcends all earthly things. Spend time studying and meditating on God's Word. That way, you'll have accurate perceptions of the Lord and be able to worship in a way that brings Him honor.

God has done so much for you. He created, loved, saved, and sealed you for eternity. He asks for very little in return. But what He does desire is personal and unashamed praise. Does He receive that kind of worship from you? ⊕

---

burning before the throne, which are the seven Spirits of God;

6 and before the throne *there was something* like a sea of glass, like crystal; and in the center and around the throne, four living creatures full of eyes in front and behind.

7 The first creature *was* like a lion, and the second creature like a calf, and the third creature had a face like that of a man, and the fourth creature *was* like a flying eagle.

8 And the four living creatures, each one of them having six wings, are full of eyes around and within; and day and night they do not cease to say,

"HOLY, HOLY, HOLY *is* THE LORD GOD, THE ALMIGHTY, WHO WAS AND WHO IS AND WHO IS TO COME."

9 And when the living creatures give glory and honor and thanks to Him who sits on the throne, to Him who lives forever and ever,

10 the twenty-four elders will fall down before Him who sits on the throne, and will worship Him who lives forever and

ever, and will cast their crowns before the throne, saying,

11 "Worthy are You, our Lord and our God, to receive glory and honor and power; for You created all things, and because of Your will they existed, and were created."

LIFE LESSONS

➤ **Revelation 4:11 — *"Worthy are You, our Lord and our God, to receive glory and honor and power; for You created all things, and because of Your will they existed, and were created."***

*A*s our Creator, God is worthy of all praise and adoration. We are merely a reflection of His glory. This will be abundantly clear when we reach heaven. All who know the Lord—who have seen Him in all of His beauty, holiness, power, and majesty—will worship Him and lay our crowns at His feet in thankfulness, giving Him the glory and honor He deserves.

6 WOE to those who are at ease in
Zion
And to those who *feel* secure in the
mountain of Samaria,
The distinguished men of the
foremost of nations,
To whom the house of Israel comes.

2 Go over to Calneh and look,
And go from there to Hamath the
great,
Then go down to Gath of the
Philistines.
Are they better than these kingdoms,
Or is their territory greater than
yours?

3 Do you put off the day of calamity,
And would you bring near the seat
of violence?

4 Those who recline on beds of ivory
And sprawl on their couches,
And eat lambs from the flock
And calves from the midst of the stall,

5 Who improvise to the sound of the
harp,
And like David have composed
songs for themselves,

6 Who drink wine from sacrificial
bowls
While they anoint themselves with
the finest of oils,
Yet they have not grieved over the
ruin of Joseph.

7 Therefore, they will now go into
exile at the head of the exiles,
And the sprawlers' banqueting will
pass away.

8 The Lord GOD has sworn by
Himself, the LORD God of hosts
has declared:
"I loathe the arrogance of Jacob,
And detest his citadels;
Therefore I will deliver up *the* city
and all it contains."

9 And it will be, if ten men are left in
one house, they will die.
10 Then one's uncle, or his undertaker,
will lift him up to carry out *his* bones
from the house, and he will say to the
one who is in the innermost part of the
house, "Is anyone else with you?" And
that one will say, "No one." Then he will
answer, "Keep quiet. For the name of the
LORD is not to be mentioned."

11 For behold, the LORD is going to command that the great house be smashed to
pieces and the small house to fragments.
12 Do horses run on rocks?
Or does one plow them with oxen?
Yet you have turned justice into
poison
And the fruit of righteousness into
wormwood,

13 You who rejoice in Lodebar,
And say, "Have we not by our *own*
strength taken Karnaim for
ourselves?"

14 "For behold, I am going to raise up a
nation against you,
O house of Israel," declares the
LORD God of hosts,
"And they will afflict you from the
entrance of Hamath
To the brook of the Arabah."

7 THUS the Lord GOD showed me, and
behold, He was forming a locust-
swarm when the spring crop began to
sprout. And behold, the spring crop *was*
after the king's mowing.
2 And it came about, when it had finished eating the vegetation of the land,
that I said,
"Lord GOD, please pardon!
How can Jacob stand,
For he is small?"
3 The LORD changed His mind about
this.
"It shall not be," said the LORD.
4 Thus the Lord GOD showed me, and
behold, the Lord GOD was calling to contend *with them* by fire, and it consumed
the great deep and began to consume the
farm land.
5 Then I said,
"Lord GOD, please stop!
How can Jacob stand, for he is small?"
6 The LORD changed His mind about
this.
"This too shall not be," said the Lord
GOD.
7 Thus He showed me, and behold, the
Lord was standing by a vertical wall with
a plumb line in His hand.
8 The LORD said to me, "What do you ◄
see, Amos?" And I said, "A plumb line."
Then the Lord said,
"Behold I am about to put a plumb line
In the midst of My people Israel.
I will spare them no longer.
9 "The high places of Isaac will be
desolated

ANYTHING YOU HOLD TOO TIGHTLY, YOU
WILL LOSE.

AMOS 6:6, 7

*I*n seventeenth century France, a humble
church leader named François Fénelon
wrote a letter of encouragement to believers
who sought spiritual perspective during some
discouraging trials. He said,

Do not worry about the future. It makes
no sense to worry if God loves you and has
taken care of you. However, when God
blesses you, remember to keep your eyes on
Him and not the blessing. Enjoy your blessings day by day, just as the Israelites enjoyed
their manna; but do not try to store the blessings for the future. . . .
Sometimes in this life of faith God will
remove His blessings from you. But remember that He knows how and when to replace
them, either through the ministry of others or
by Himself. He can raise up children from the
very stones.
Eat then your daily bread without worrying about tomorrow. There is time enough
tomorrow to think about the things tomorrow will bring. The same God who feeds
you today is the very God who will feed you
tomorrow. God will see to it that manna falls
again from Heaven in the midst of the desert,
before His children lack any good thing.

If we lived with faith of this kind, we would
stop being so anxious and fretting about all
our troubles. Will we humbly depend on God
to provide?
Admit it—in a tough situation, your first
emotional response is to take control. We
all want control. We want to live with the
assurance that everything will be okay, and
the things that aren't right can be fixed with
concentrated effort. Secretly, we often think,
"If I plan carefully and labor enough, I can
overcome any difficulty."
The problem comes when your efforts
aren't enough—the problem you face is
greater than all of your resources or completely outside your scope of influence. God

allows those trials for an important reason—
He wants you to recognize that *He* is in control. Yet, the Lord does not want merely to be
the resource you call on when you're in trouble. God wants to be your all-sufficient Lord
and Master, Savior and Friend. He knows
you intimately; He formed your very cells and
fibers (Ps. 139:13–16); He has a good plan
for every day of your life (Eph. 2:10), and He
knows how to fulfill His purpose for you (Ps.
138:8).
When you face circumstances that rapidly
deplete your spiritual, emotional, and physical
reserves, you may want to cling to something
strong out of fear. The question you must
consider is whether your worries drive you to
the arms of God or to your own resources.
Are you hanging on to something other
than the Lord? Are you gripping some form
of earthly security instead of trusting Him to
help you? Remember, whatever you hold too
tightly, you will lose. Whatever you are clutch-
ing for safety has become an idol to you—
regardless of whether it is wealth, your giftedness, a relationship, religious rituals, or what
have you—and God is not going to allow
you to keep it as your source of confidence—
a role that rightly belongs to Him. Rather, He
will allow it to fail you so you can see that He
truly is your sovereign and unfailing Lord.
God longs for you to release yourself into
His control and eternal support. He will takes
care of all that concerns you in the best way
possible, and He will also sustain you in the
process (Phil. 4:6, 7).
When you feel ready to yield wholly to the
Lord, Psalm 56 provides a wonderful model
prayer: "When I am afraid, I will put My
trust in You. In God, whose word I praise, in
God I have put my trust; I shall not be afraid.
What can mere man do to me?" (vv. 3, 4).
Maybe to this point in your relationship
with the Lord you have not experienced a trial
so extreme that it caused you to assess the true
foundation of your trust. God has blessed you
with a time of quiet strengthening.
But understand that He loves you too
much to allow you any notions of self-
sufficiency. He will test you in time, but
always with the purpose of demonstrating
His never-ending love. ◈

And the sanctuaries of Israel laid
waste.
Then I will rise up against the house
of Jeroboam with the sword."
10 Then Amaziah, the priest of Bethel,
sent *word* to Jeroboam king of Israel,
saying, "Amos has conspired against you
in the midst of the house of Israel; the
land is unable to endure all his words.
11 "For thus Amos says, 'Jeroboam will
die by the sword and Israel will certainly
go from its land into exile.'"
12 Then Amaziah said to Amos, "Go,
you seer, flee away to the land of Judah
and there eat bread and there do your
prophesying!
13 "But no longer prophesy at Bethel, for
it is a sanctuary of the king and a royal
residence."
14 Then Amos replied to Amaziah, "I
am not a prophet, nor am I the son of
a prophet; for I am a herdsman and a
grower of sycamore figs.
15 "But the LORD took me from following
the flock and the LORD said to me, 'Go
prophesy to My people Israel.'
16 "Now hear the word of the LORD:
you are saying, 'You shall not prophesy against Israel nor shall you speak
against the house of Isaac.'
17 "Therefore, thus says the LORD, 'Your
wife will become a harlot in the city, your
sons and your daughters will fall by the
sword, your land will be parceled up by a
measuring line and you yourself will die
upon unclean soil. Moreover, Israel will
certainly go from its land into exile.'"

Psalm 142:1–7

Maskil of David, when he was in the cave.
A Prayer.

142 I CRY aloud with my voice to
the LORD;
I make supplication with my voice
to the LORD.
2   I pour out my complaint before Him;
I declare my trouble before Him.
3   When my spirit was overwhelmed
within me,
You knew my path.
In the way where I walk
They have hidden a trap for me.
4   Look to the right and see;

For there is no one who regards me;
There is no escape for me;
No one cares for my soul.
5   I cried out to You, O LORD;
I said, "You are my refuge,
My portion in the land of the living.
6   "Give heed to my cry,
For I am brought very low;
Deliver me from my persecutors,
For they are too strong for me.
7   "Bring my soul out of prison,
So that I may give thanks to Your
name;
The righteous will surround me,
For You will deal bountifully with me."

Proverbs 29:27

27 An unjust man is abominable to the
righteous,

LIFE LESSONS

Amos 7:8 — *"I am about to put a
plumb line in the midst of My people
Israel. I will spare them no longer."*

A plumb line pictures God's careful evaluation of the hearts and
behaviors of His people. Sometimes He
delivers His defiant people up "to Satan
for the destruction of his flesh, so that
his spirit may be saved" (1 Cor. 5:5).

Amos 7:14 — *"I am not a prophet,
nor am I the son of a prophet; for I am
a herdsman and a grower of sycamore
figs."*

R egardless of who you are or what
you do for a living, God wants to
use you to bring the Good News to those
around you, and ultimately to the entire
world. If you love Christ, *you* are God's
ambassador (2 Cor. 5:20).

Psalm 142:7 — *Bring my soul out of
prison, so that I may give thanks to Your
name.*

O ur souls get imprisoned in many
ways. Sometimes we put ourselves
there through sin. Sometimes enemies
put us there. Sometimes we are just at
the wrong place at the wrong time. But
our God is a specialist at setting captives
free!

And he who is upright in the way is abominable to the wicked.

✦ Revelation 5:1–14

5 I SAW in the right hand of Him who sat on the throne a book written inside and on the back, sealed up with seven seals.

2   And I saw a strong angel proclaiming with a loud voice, "Who is worthy to open the book and to break its seals?"

3   And no one in heaven or on the earth or under the earth was able to open the book or to look into it.

4   Then I *began* to weep greatly because no one was found worthy to open the book or to look into it;

➤ 5   and one of the elders *said to me, "Stop weeping; behold, the Lion that is from the tribe of Judah, the Root of David, has overcome so as to open the book and its seven seals."

6   And I saw between the throne (with the four living creatures) and the elders a Lamb standing, as if slain, having seven horns and seven eyes, which are the seven Spirits of God, sent out into all the earth.

7   And He came and took the book out of the right hand of Him who sat on the throne.

8   When He had taken the book, the four living creatures and the twenty-four elders fell down before the Lamb, each one holding a harp and golden bowls full of incense, which are the prayers of the saints.

➤ 9   And they *sang a new song, saying, "Worthy are You to take the book and to break its seals; for You were slain, and purchased for God with Your blood *men* from every tribe and tongue and people and nation.

10   "You have made them *to be* a kingdom and priests to our God; and they will reign upon the earth."

✳ 11   Then I looked, and I heard the voice of many angels around the throne and the living creatures and the elders; and the number of them was myriads of myriads, and thousands of thousands,

12   saying with a loud voice, "Worthy is the Lamb that was slain to receive power and riches and wisdom and might and honor and glory and blessing."

13   And every created thing which is in ◄ heaven and on the earth and under the earth and on the sea, and all things in them, I heard saying, "To Him who sits on the throne, and to the Lamb, *be* blessing and honor and glory and dominion forever and ever."

14   And the four living creatures kept saying, "Amen." And the elders fell down and worshiped.

LIFE LESSONS

➤ **Revelation 5:5 — "Stop weeping; behold, the Lion that is from the tribe of Judah, the Root of David, has overcome."**

*J*esus prevails when no one else can. As the Lamb of God (1 Cor. 5:7), He took our sins upon Himself, giving His life on the Cross so we could be saved. As the Lion of Judah (Gen. 49:9, 10; Hos. 5:14, 15), He is coming as the conquering warrior and Messiah who will bring justice to the earth. Finally, as the Root of David (Is. 11:1–10; Rom. 15:12; Rev. 22:16, 17), Jesus fulfills the promises made to King David and ushers in His everlasting kingdom (2 Sam. 7:10–16).

➤ **Revelation 5:9 — "You were slain, and purchased for God with Your blood men from every tribe and tongue and people and nation."**

*G*od does not play favorites. He offers His gift of salvation to people from every ethnic group, race, and language from throughout the world. He is truly the God of all the earth. And in heaven, there will be people from every tribe, tongue, and nation as evidence of this.

➤ **Revelation 5:13 — "To Him who sits on the throne, and to the Lamb, be blessing and honor and glory and dominion forever and ever."**

*A*s the moment nears for the Lamb to break open the seven seals of the judgment, all creation worships Him (Is. 45:23; Rom. 14:11; Phil. 2:10, 11). Here we can see the unity of the Godhead—both the Father and Son are worshiped as One. He is the sovereign King of the universe. He is our Creator and deserves all our praise.

Amos 8:1—9:15

8 THUS the Lord GOD showed me, and behold, *there was* a basket of summer fruit.

2 He said, "What do you see, Amos?" And I said, "A basket of summer fruit." Then the LORD said to me, "The end has come for My people Israel. I will spare them no longer.

3 "The songs of the palace will turn to wailing in that day," declares the Lord GOD. "Many *will be* the corpses; in every place they will cast them forth in silence."

4 Hear this, you who trample the needy, to do away with the humble of the land,

5 saying,

"When will the new moon be over,
So that we may sell grain,
And the sabbath, that we may open
the wheat *market*,
To make the bushel smaller and the
shekel bigger,
And to cheat with dishonest scales,

6 So as to buy the helpless for money
And the needy for a pair of sandals,
And *that* we may sell the refuse of
the wheat?"

7 The LORD has sworn by the pride of
Jacob,
"Indeed, I will never forget any of
their deeds.

8 "Because of this will not the land
quake
And everyone who dwells in it
mourn?
Indeed, all of it will rise up like the
Nile,
And it will be tossed about
And subside like the Nile of Egypt.

9 "It will come about in that day,"
declares the Lord GOD,

"That I will make the sun go down at
noon
And make the earth dark in broad
daylight.

10 "Then I will turn your festivals into
mourning
And all your songs into lamentation;
And I will bring sackcloth on
everyone's loins
And baldness on every head.
And I will make it like *a time of*
mourning for an only son,
And the end of it will be like a bitter
day.

11 "Behold, days are coming," declares
the Lord GOD,
"When I will send a famine on the
land,
Not a famine for bread or a thirst
for water,
But rather for hearing the words of
the LORD.

12 "People will stagger from sea to sea
And from the north even to the east;
They will go to and fro to seek the
word of the LORD,
But they will not find *it.*

13 "In that day the beautiful virgins
And the young men will faint from
thirst.

14 "*As for* those who swear by the guilt
of Samaria,
Who say, 'As your god lives, O Dan,'
And, 'As the way of Beersheba lives,'
They will fall and not rise again."

9 I SAW the Lord standing beside the
altar, and He said,
"Smite the capitals so that the
thresholds will shake,
And break them on the heads of
them all!
Then I will slay the rest of them
with the sword;

LIFE LESSONS

➤ **Amos 8:5** — *"When will the new moon be over, so that we may sell grain, and the sabbath, that we may open the wheat market."*

Something has gone seriously wrong in our hearts when we see God's commandments and regular, corporate worship as a burden to get through rather than as a privilege to savor and enjoy.

➤ **Amos 8:11** — *"I will send a famine on the land, not a famine for bread or a thirst for water, but rather for hearing the words of the LORD."*

From the time of the prophet Malachi to the time of John the Baptist— a period of almost 500 years—this drought of God's Word withered the land. Let us daily feast on God's Word and so avoid a similar drought in our souls.

They will not have a fugitive who
    will flee,
Or a refugee who will escape.

➤ 2 "Though they dig into Sheol,
    From there will My hand take them;
    And though they ascend to heaven,
    From there will I bring them down.

3 "Though they hide on the summit of
    Carmel,
    I will search them out and take
      them from there;
    And though they conceal
      themselves from My sight on the
      floor of the sea,
    From there I will command the
      serpent and it will bite them.

4 "And though they go into captivity
    before their enemies,
    From there I will command the
      sword that it slay them,
    And I will set My eyes against them
      for evil and not for good."

5 The Lord GOD of hosts,
    The One who touches the land so
      that it melts,
    And all those who dwell in it mourn,
    And all of it rises up like the Nile
    And subsides like the Nile of Egypt;

6 The One who builds His upper
    chambers in the heavens
    And has founded His vaulted dome
      over the earth,
    He who calls for the waters of the
      sea
    And pours them out on the face of
      the earth,
    The LORD is His name.

7 "Are you not as the sons of Ethiopia
    to Me,
    O sons of Israel?" declares the LORD.
    "Have I not brought up Israel from
      the land of Egypt,
    And the Philistines from Caphtor
      and the Arameans from Kir?

LIFE LESSONS

➤ **Amos 9:2 —** *"Though they ascend to heaven, from there will I bring them down."*

*N*o one can prevent the Lord from doing all He has decided to do, whether for judgment or blessing. Since we serve a sovereign God, we should never think of ourselves as victims of our circumstances.

---

8 "Behold, the eyes of the Lord GOD
    are on the sinful kingdom,
    And I will destroy it from the face
      of the earth;
    Nevertheless, I will not totally
      destroy the house of Jacob,"
    Declares the LORD.

9 "For behold, I am commanding,
    And I will shake the house of Israel
      among all nations
    As *grain* is shaken in a sieve,
    But not a kernel will fall to the
      ground.

10 "All the sinners of My people will die
    by the sword,
    Those who say, 'The calamity will
      not overtake or confront us.'

11 "In that day I will raise up the fallen
    booth of David,
    And wall up its breaches;
    I will also raise up its ruins
    And rebuild it as in the days of old;

12 That they may possess the remnant
    of Edom
    And all the nations who are called
      by My name,"
    Declares the LORD who does this.

13 "Behold, days are coming," declares
    the LORD,
    "When the plowman will overtake
      the reaper
    And the treader of grapes him who
      sows seed;
    When the mountains will drip sweet
      wine
    And all the hills will be dissolved.

14 "Also I will restore the captivity of
    My people Israel,
    And they will rebuild the ruined
      cities and live *in them*;
    They will also plant vineyards and
      drink their wine,
    And make gardens and eat their fruit.

15 "I will also plant them on their land,
    And they will not again be rooted
      out from their land
    Which I have given them,"
    Says the LORD your God.

✳

◈   **Psalm 143:1–6**

A Psalm of David.

143 HEAR my prayer, O LORD,
    Give ear to my supplications!

WHAT THE BIBLE SAYS ABOUT

Set Apart for Victory

Revelation 6

The four horsemen of the Apocalypse: creatures that characterize the wrath of God. The thought of them inspires fear and trembling.

The white horse conquers, taking power from all on the earth. The red horse brings war, destroying all hope of peace. The black horse ushers in a famine so dreadful that bread is rationed out on his terrible scales. The ashen horse comes to bring death and pestilence, tearing life away from the people left on earth.

Revelation 6 depicts the horror that the unbelieving world will face when learning of the judgment. "The kings of the earth and the great men and the commanders and the rich and the strong and every slave and free man hid themselves in the caves and among the rocks of the mountains; and they said to the mountains and to the rocks, 'Fall on us and hide us from the presence of Him who sits on the throne, and from the wrath of the Lamb'" (Rev. 6:15, 16).

However, whereas the pagan are deprived of all their hope, the saints are set apart. Revelation 6:11 says, "And there was given to each of them a white robe; and they were told that they should rest a little while longer, until the number of their fellow servants and their brethren who were to be killed even as they had been, would be completed also."

Even though every aspect of worldly security is stripped from the earth, as a believer you are clothed with the heavenly security of Christ. You will never lack hope because you will never have to fear the presence of the King upon His throne. You have been clothed with God's promise, so rejoice in your confidence and security. ◈

Answer me in Your faithfulness, in Your righteousness!
2 And do not enter into judgment with Your servant,
For in Your sight no man living is righteous.
3 For the enemy has persecuted my soul;
He has crushed my life to the ground;
He has made me dwell in dark places, like those who have long been dead.
4 Therefore my spirit is overwhelmed within me;
My heart is appalled within me.
**5 I remember the days of old;
I meditate on all Your doings;
I muse on the work of Your hands.**
6 I stretch out my hands to You;
My soul *longs* for You, as a parched land.   Selah.

◈   Proverbs 30:1–4

30 THE words of Agur the son of Jakeh, the oracle.
The man declares to Ithiel, to Ithiel and Ucal:

2 Surely I am more stupid than any man,
And I do not have the understanding of a man.
3 Neither have I learned wisdom,
Nor do I have the knowledge of the Holy One.
4 Who has ascended into heaven and descended?
Who has gathered the wind in His fists?
Who has wrapped the waters in His garment?
Who has established all the ends of the earth?
What is His name or His son's name? Surely you know!

◈   Revelation 6:1–17

6 THEN I saw when the Lamb broke one of the seven seals, and I heard one of the four living creatures saying as with a voice of thunder, "Come."
2 I looked, and behold, a white horse, and he who sat on it had a bow; and a crown was given to him, and he went out conquering and to conquer.
3 When He broke the second seal, I

heard the second living creature saying, "Come."

➤ 4   And another, a red horse, went out; and to him who sat on it, it was granted to take peace from the earth, and that *men* would slay one another; and a great sword was given to him.

5   When He broke the third seal, I heard the third living creature saying, "Come." I looked, and behold, a black horse; and he who sat on it had a pair of scales in his hand.

6   And I heard *something* like a voice in the center of the four living creatures saying, "A quart of wheat for a denarius, and three quarts of barley for a denarius; and do not damage the oil and the wine."

7   When the Lamb broke the fourth seal, I heard the voice of the fourth living creature saying, "Come."

8   I looked, and behold, an ashen horse; and he who sat on it had the name Death; and Hades was following with him. Authority was given to them over a fourth of the earth, to kill with sword and with famine and with pestilence and by the wild beasts of the earth.

➤ 9   When the Lamb broke the fifth seal, I saw underneath the altar the souls of those who had been slain because of the word of God, and because of the testimony which they had maintained;

10   and they cried out with a loud voice, saying, "How long, O Lord, holy and true, will You refrain from judging and avenging our blood on those who dwell on the earth?"

11   And there was given to each of them a white robe; and they were told that they should rest for a little while longer,
✳ until *the number of* their fellow servants and their brethren who were to be killed even as they had been, would be completed also.

12   I looked when He broke the sixth seal, and there was a great earthquake; and the sun became black as sackcloth *made* of hair, and the whole moon became like blood;

13   and the stars of the sky fell to the earth, as a fig tree casts its unripe figs when shaken by a great wind.

14   The sky was split apart like a scroll when it is rolled up, and every mountain and island were moved out of their places.

15   Then the kings of the earth and the great men and the commanders and the rich and the strong and every slave and free man hid themselves in the caves and among the rocks of the mountains;

16   and they *said to the mountains and to the rocks, "Fall on us and hide us from the presence of Him who sits on the throne, and from the wrath of the Lamb;

17   for the great day of their wrath has ➤ come, and who is able to stand?"

LIFE LESSONS

➤ **Revelation 6:4 — *A red horse, went out; and to him who sat on it, it was granted to take peace from the earth.***

*W*hen the red horse is released, war will break out in ways that we have never seen before. War is seen as an instrument of God's judgment throughout the Old Testament (Ezek. 21). Romans 1:28, 29 explains, "Just as they did not see fit to acknowledge God any longer, God gave them over to a depraved mind ... being filled with all unrighteousness, wickedness, greed, evil; full of envy, murder, strife, deceit."

➤ **Revelation 6:9 — *I saw underneath the altar the souls of those who had been slain because of the word of God, and because of the testimony which they had maintained.***

*T*his is not a reference to the church, but to *tribulation saints*. After the rapture, there will be those who realize that believers were right—Jesus Christ *is* the only Savior—and they will accept His salvation. They will preach the gospel, and many people will be saved because of their testimony. However, they will also face great persecution. God will not forget them, but He will wait until everything He has promised is complete before He honors them.

➤ **Revelation 6:17 — *"The great day of their wrath has come, and who is able to stand?"***

*N*ote that it is the ungodly who make this statement. They recognize God's hand in their circumstances, and yet they refuse to repent. Judgment always results when people refuse to humble themselves before the Lord. Yet they will find in that day that neither wealth, nor power, nor social connections will be able to save them. Though they cling to these things for safety, in the Day of the Lord, all will turn to ashes.

Obadiah 1–21

1 THE vision of Obadiah.
Thus says the Lord GOD concerning
Edom—
> We have heard a report from the
> LORD,
> And an envoy has been sent among
> the nations *saying*,
> "Arise and let us go against her for
> battle"—
2 "Behold, I will make you small
> among the nations;
> You are greatly despised.
3 "The arrogance of your heart has
> deceived you,
> You who live in the clefts of the
> rock,
> In the loftiness of your dwelling
> place,
> Who say in your heart,
> 'Who will bring me down to earth?'
4 "Though you build high like the
> eagle,
> Though you set your nest among
> the stars,
> From there I will bring you down,"
> declares the LORD.
5 "If thieves came to you,
> If robbers by night—
> O how you will be ruined!—
> Would they not steal *only* until they
> had enough?
> If grape gatherers came to you,
> Would they not leave *some*
> gleanings?
6 "O how Esau will be ransacked,
> *And* his hidden treasures searched
> out!
7 "All the men allied with you
> Will send you forth to the border,
> And the men at peace with you
> Will deceive you and overpower you.
> *They who eat* your bread
> Will set an ambush for you.
> (There is no understanding in him.)
8 "Will I not on that day," declares the
> LORD,
> "Destroy wise men from Edom
> And understanding from the
> mountain of Esau?
9 "Then your mighty men will be
> dismayed, O Teman,
> So that everyone may be cut off

from the mountain of Esau by
slaughter.
10 "Because of violence to your brother
> Jacob,
> You will be covered *with* shame,
> And you will be cut off forever.
11 "On the day that you stood aloof,
> On the day that strangers carried
> off his wealth,
> And foreigners entered his gate
> And cast lots for Jerusalem—
> You too were as one of them.
12 "Do not gloat over your brother's
> day,
> The day of his misfortune.
> And do not rejoice over the sons of
> Judah
> In the day of their destruction;
> Yes, do not boast
> In the day of *their* distress.
13 "Do not enter the gate of My people
> In the day of their disaster.
> Yes, you, do not gloat over their
> calamity
> In the day of their disaster.
> And do not loot their wealth
> In the day of their disaster.
14 "Do not stand at the fork of the road
> To cut down their fugitives;
> And do not imprison their survivors
> In the day of their distress.
15 "For the day of the LORD draws near
> on all the nations.
> As you have done, it will be done to
> you.
> Your dealings will return on your
> own head.
16 "Because just as you drank on My
> holy mountain,
> All the nations will drink
> continually.
> They will drink and swallow

LIFE LESSONS

> Obadiah 3 — *"The arrogance of your
heart has deceived you."*

God hates pride (Prov. 8:13; James 4:6)
because it is an overemphasis on self.
We believe the lie, as the Edomites did,
that we know better than the Lord. Yet
in such arrogance is sure destruction
(Prov. 16:18). Always remember, whatever you acquire outside of God's will
eventually turns to ashes.

And become as if they had never existed.

17 "But on Mount Zion there will be those who escape,
And it will be holy.
And the house of Jacob will possess their possessions.

18 "Then the house of Jacob will be a fire
And the house of Joseph a flame;
But the house of Esau *will be* as stubble.
And they will set them on fire and consume them,
So that there will be no survivor of the house of Esau,"
For the LORD has spoken.

19 Then *those of* the Negev will possess the mountain of Esau,
And *those of* the Shephelah the Philistine *plain;*
Also, possess the territory of Ephraim and the territory of Samaria,
And Benjamin *will possess* Gilead.

20 And the exiles of this host of the sons of Israel,
Who are *among* the Canaanites as far as Zarephath,
And the exiles of Jerusalem who are in Sepharad
Will possess the cities of the Negev.

21 The deliverers will ascend Mount Zion
To judge the mountain of Esau,
And the kingdom will be the LORD's.

⊛ Psalm 143:7–12

7 Answer me quickly, O LORD, my spirit fails;
Do not hide Your face from me,

Or I will become like those who go down to the pit.

8 Let me hear Your lovingkindness in the morning;
For I trust in You;
Teach me the way in which I should walk;
For to You I lift up my soul.

9 Deliver me, O LORD, from my enemies;
I take refuge in You.

10 Teach me to do Your will,
For You are my God;
Let Your good Spirit lead me on level ground.

11 For the sake of Your name, O LORD, revive me.
In Your righteousness bring my soul out of trouble.

12 And in Your lovingkindness, cut off my enemies
And destroy all those who afflict my soul,
For I am Your servant.

⊛ Proverbs 30:5

5 Every word of God is tested;
He is a shield to those who take refuge in Him.

⊛ Revelation 7:1–17

*7*AFTER this I saw four angels standing at the four corners of the earth, holding back the four winds of the earth, so that no wind would blow on the earth or on the sea or on any tree.

2   And I saw another angel ascending from the rising of the sun, having the seal of the living God; and he cried out with a loud voice to the four angels to whom it was granted to harm the earth and the sea,

➤ 3   saying, "Do not harm the earth or the sea or the trees until we have sealed the bond-servants of our God on their foreheads."

4   And I heard the number of those who were sealed, one hundred and forty-four thousand sealed from every tribe of the sons of Israel:

5   from the tribe of Judah, twelve thousand *were* sealed, from the tribe of Reuben twelve thousand, from the tribe of Gad twelve thousand,

6   from the tribe of Asher twelve thousand, from the tribe of Naphtali twelve thousand, from the tribe of Manasseh twelve thousand,

7:   from the tribe of Simeon twelve thousand, from the tribe of Levi twelve thousand, from the tribe of Issachar twelve thousand,

8   from the tribe of Zebulun twelve thousand, from the tribe of Joseph twelve thousand, from the tribe of Benjamin, twelve thousand *were* sealed.

➤ 9   After these things I looked, and behold, a great multitude which no one could count, from every nation and *all* tribes and peoples and tongues, standing before the throne and before the Lamb, clothed in white robes, and palm branches *were* in their hands;

10   and they cry out with a loud voice, saying,

"Salvation to our God who sits on the throne, and to the Lamb."

11   And all the angels were standing around the throne and *around* the elders and the four living creatures; and they fell on their faces before the throne and worshiped God,

12   saying,

"Amen, blessing and glory and wisdom and thanksgiving and honor and power and might, *be* to our God forever and ever. Amen."

13   Then one of the elders answered, saying to me, "These who are clothed in the white robes, who are they, and where have they come from?"

14   I said to him, "My lord, you know." And he said to me, "These are the ones who come out of the great tribulation, and they have washed their robes and made them white in the blood of the Lamb.

15   "For this reason, they are before the throne of God; and they serve Him day and night in His temple; and He who sits on the throne will spread His tabernacle ✳ over them.

16   "They will hunger no longer, nor thirst anymore; nor will the sun beat down on them, nor any heat;

17   for the Lamb in the center of the ◄ throne will be their shepherd, and will guide them to springs of the water of life; and God will wipe every tear from their eyes."

LIFE LESSONS

➤ **Revelation 7:3 — *"We have sealed the bond-servants of our God on their foreheads."***

God marks His children with a permanent seal that shows we belong to Him (Ezek. 9:4–6; 2 Cor. 1:22; Eph. 1:13; 4:30). During the last days, this will be revealed by a mark on the forehead, which distinguishes believers from those who have completely rejected the Lord and those who worship the Antichrist (Rev. 13:15–17; 14:1–5).

➤ **Revelation 7:9 — *A great multitude … from every nation and all tribes and peoples and tongues, standing before the throne and before the Lamb, clothed in white robes.***

God redeems multitudes of people from every nation, culture, and background (Matt. 24:14). His grace reaches into every corner of the world, and His salvation is offered to everyone (2 Pet. 3:9).

➤ **Revelation 7:17 — *"God will wipe away every tear from their eyes."***

This line is repeated later in Revelation (Rev. 21:4). It is as if God wants us to remember that though our tears will flow, He will personally comfort us. He will delegate this task to no one else.

WHAT THE BIBLE SAYS ABOUT

A Good Shepherd to the End

Revelation 7:16, 17

As a young man, David devoted his days to the nurturing of his sheep. Carefully he would watch them, ably defend them, tenderly heal them, and abundantly provide for their every need.

As a shepherd, he had to be aware of dangers and opportunities that the sheep were not able to perceive. When he called, they knew his voice. Wherever he directed, they went, for they depended upon the comfort and sustenance that David provided.

In Psalm 23:1 David proclaimed, "The LORD is my shepherd." David knew that the Lord was caring for him with the great care and love of one tending to a beloved flock.

In this self-sufficient world, it is often difficult to admit the need for a Shepherd. Yet having the Lord care for our needs is a great gift. Calling God "my Shepherd" signifies identity and privilege. He is my shepherd, my protector. I bear His name and am the recipient of all His benefits.

In Revelation 7:16, 17, believers are informed of the wonderful promises of the Good Shepherd. "They will hunger no longer, nor thirst anymore; nor will the sun not beat down on them, nor any heat; for the Lamb in the center of the throne will be their shepherd, and will guide them to springs of the water of life; and God will wipe away every tear from their eyes."

God is a good and kind Shepherd, who tends to your needs, hurts, joys, and desires with love and compassion. Trust Him—you shall never be in want. ◈

◈ Jonah 1:1—4:11

1 THE word of the LORD came to Jonah the son of Amittai saying,

2 "Arise, go to Nineveh the great city and cry against it, for their wickedness has come up before Me."

3 But Jonah rose up to flee to Tarshish from the presence of the LORD. So he went down to Joppa, found a ship which was going to Tarshish, paid the fare and went down into it to go with them to Tarshish from the presence of the LORD.

4 The LORD hurled a great wind on the sea and there was a great storm on the sea so that the ship was about to break up.

5 Then the sailors became afraid and every man cried to his god, and they threw the cargo which was in the ship into the sea to lighten *it* for them. But Jonah had gone below into the hold of the ship, lain down and fallen sound asleep.

6 So the captain approached him and said, "How is it that you are sleeping? Get up, call on your god. Perhaps *your* god will be concerned about us so that we will not perish."

7 Each man said to his mate, "Come, let us cast lots so we may learn on whose account this calamity *has struck* us." So they cast lots and the lot fell on Jonah.

8 Then they said to him, "Tell us, now! On whose account *has* this calamity *struck* us? What is your occupation? And where do you come from? What is your country? From what people are you?"

9 He said to them, "I am a Hebrew, and I fear the LORD God of heaven who made the sea and the dry land."

10 Then the men became extremely frightened and they said to him, "How could you do this?" For the men knew that he was fleeing from the presence of the LORD, because he had told them.

11 So they said to him, "What should we do to you that the sea may become calm for us?"—for the sea was becoming increasingly stormy.

12 He said to them, "Pick me up and ≺ throw me into the sea. Then the sea will become calm for you, for I know that on

account of me this great storm *has come upon you.*"

13 However, the men rowed *desperately* to return to land but they could not, for the sea was becoming *even* stormier against them.

14 Then they called on the LORD and said, "We earnestly pray, O LORD, do not let us perish on account of this man's life and do not put innocent blood on us; for You, O LORD, have done as You have pleased."

15 So they picked up Jonah, threw him into the sea, and the sea stopped its raging.

➤ 16 Then the men feared the LORD greatly, and they offered a sacrifice to the LORD and made vows.

17 And the LORD appointed a great fish to swallow Jonah, and Jonah was in the stomach of the fish three days and three nights.

2 THEN Jonah prayed to the LORD his God from the stomach of the fish,

2 and he said,
"I called out of my distress to the
        LORD,
    And He answered me.
    I cried for help from the depth of
        Sheol;
    You heard my voice.

3 "For You had cast me into the deep,
    Into the heart of the seas,
    And the current engulfed me.
    All Your breakers and billows
        passed over me.

4 "So I said, 'I have been expelled from
        Your sight.
    Nevertheless I will look again
        toward Your holy temple.'

5 "Water encompassed me to the point
        of death.
    The great deep engulfed me,
    Weeds were wrapped around my
        head.

6 "I descended to the roots of the
        mountains.
    The earth with its bars *was* around
        me forever,
    But You have brought up my life
        from the pit, O LORD my God.

7 "While I was fainting away,
    I remembered the LORD,
    And my prayer came to You,
    Into Your holy temple.

8 "Those who regard vain idols
    Forsake their faithfulness,

9 But I will sacrifice to You
    With the voice of thanksgiving.
    That which I have vowed I will pay.
    Salvation is from the LORD."

10 Then the LORD commanded the fish, and it vomited Jonah up onto the dry land.

3 NOW the word of the LORD came to Jonah the second time, saying,

2 "Arise, go to Nineveh the great city and proclaim to it the proclamation which I am going to tell you."

3 So Jonah arose and went to Nineveh according to the word of the LORD. Now Nineveh was an exceedingly great city, a three days' walk.

4 Then Jonah began to go through the city one day's walk; and he cried out and said, "Yet forty days and Nineveh will be overthrown."

5 Then the people of Nineveh believed in God; and they called a fast and put on sackcloth from the greatest to the least of them.

6 When the word reached the king of Nineveh, he arose from his throne, laid aside his robe from him, covered *himself* with sackcloth and sat on the ashes.

7 He issued a proclamation and it said, "In Nineveh by the decree of the king and his nobles: Do not let man, beast, herd, or flock taste a thing. Do not let them eat or drink water.

LIFE LESSONS

➤ **Jonah 1:12 —** *"Pick me up and throw me into the sea. Then the sea will become calm for you, for I know that on account of me this great storm has come upon you."*

*J*onah knew that his own disobedience had put the ship in peril; yet he would rather die than return to land and obey God's command. But the Lord does not give up so easily on us, and He had a fish ready to prove it.

➤ **Jonah 1:16 —** *Then the men feared the LORD greatly, and they offered a sacrifice to the LORD and made vows.*

*G*od inspires prophecy not to satisfy our curiosity, but to prompt faith in His grace and glory. He tells us about the future so that we might live well in the present and ready ourselves for what's to come.

How does God deal with our disobedience?

JONAH 3:1

*I*n the light of God's omniscience and omnipresence, it's easy to wonder why Christians still attempt to run from the Lord. Jonah certainly demonstrated that it could not be done, and yet many people still insist on trying. Why?

Sometimes we act out of pure selfishness. We believe we know what is best for us, regardless of what God says. Sometimes we balk out of simple fear. We worry that we might not succeed, or that others will criticize our efforts, or that our obedience will cost us too much. What we fail to recognize, however, is the much higher price of fleeing from the Lord.

Jonah paid dearly for his rebellion. Not only did he suffer embarrassment, terror, and guilt, but he also jeopardized the lives of men whom God wanted to save. Jonah overlooked two essentials that we should all keep in mind.

First, he incorrectly assumed that fleeing from God would release him from having to obey God. He never imagined how persistent the Lord could be when He called him to duty. Eventually Jonah found that God will pursue us in love, even to the depths of the sea, in order to conform us to His will and His plan for our lives. God simply will not be deterred by our disobedience.

Second, Jonah forgot that disobedience to the Lord leads only to destruction—our own and those whom God wants to bless through us. How many people say, "I can do what I want. It's my life"? No, it's not. If you are a Christian, God tells you, "You are not your own." In fact, "you have been bought with a price," and both your body and your life belong to God (1 Cor. 6:19, 20). You cannot sin against the Lord without paying a terrible price and hurting others in the process.

Despite these awful realities, it is also true that God is willing to forgive. He kept after Jonah as long as it was necessary for the prophet to respond in obedience so the people of Nineveh could hear God's warning and repent. And He will do the same with you. Therefore, obey God and leave all the consequences of your obedience to Him. Any other course just isn't worth it.

---

8 "But both man and beast must be covered with sackcloth; and let men call on God earnestly that each may turn from his wicked way and from the violence which is in his hands.

9 "Who knows, God may turn and relent and withdraw His burning anger so that we will not perish."

➤ 10 When God saw their deeds, that they turned from their wicked way, then God relented concerning the calamity which He had declared He would bring upon them. And He did not do *it*.

4 BUT it greatly displeased Jonah and he became angry.

2 He prayed to the LORD and said, "Please LORD, was not this what I said while I was still in my *own* country? Therefore in order to forestall this I fled to Tarshish, for I knew that You are a gracious and compassionate God, slow to anger and abundant in lovingkindness, and one who relents concerning calamity.

3 "Therefore now, O LORD, please take my life from me, for death is better to me than life."

4 The LORD said, "Do you have good reason to be angry?"

5 Then Jonah went out from the city and sat east of it. There he made a shelter for himself and sat under it in the shade until he could see what would happen in the city.

6 So the LORD God appointed a plant and it grew up over Jonah to be a shade over his head to deliver him from his discomfort. And Jonah was extremely happy about the plant.

LIFE LESSONS

➤ *Jonah 3:10 — When God saw their deeds, that they turned from their wicked way, then God relented concerning their calamity which He had declared He would bring upon them.*

*O*ver and over again in Scripture, we see that God does not want to bring calamity or judgment upon anyone. So He pleads with us and urges us to repent. Only when no other option remains does judgment fall. God will never turn away from a truly repentant heart, even if that heart beats in a man who tried to run away from Him. The Lord often uses affliction, not to punish us, but to bring us back to Him.

7 But God appointed a worm when dawn came the next day and it attacked the plant and it withered.
8 When the sun came up God appointed a scorching east wind, and the sun beat down on Jonah's head so that he became faint and begged with *all* his soul to die, saying, "Death is better to me than life."
9 Then God said to Jonah, "Do you have good reason to be angry about the plant?" And he said, "I have good reason to be angry, even to death."
10 Then the LORD said, "You had compassion on the plant for which you did not work and *which* you did not cause to grow, which came up overnight and perished overnight.
11 "Should I not have compassion on Nineveh, the great city in which there are more than 120,000 persons who do not know *the difference* between their right and left hand, as well as many animals?"

Psalm 144:1–8

A Psalm of David.

144 BLESSED be the LORD, my rock,
Who trains my hands for war,
And my fingers for battle;
2 My lovingkindness and my fortress,
My stronghold and my deliverer,
My shield and He in whom I take refuge,
Who subdues my people under me.
3 O LORD, what is man, that You take knowledge of him?
Or the son of man, that You think of him?
4 Man is like a mere breath;
His days are like a passing shadow.
5 Bow Your heavens, O LORD, and come down;
Touch the mountains, that they may smoke.
6 Flash forth lightning and scatter them;
Send out Your arrows and confuse them.
7 Stretch forth Your hand from on high;
Rescue me and deliver me out of great waters,

Out of the hand of aliens
8 Whose mouths speak deceit,
And whose right hand is a right hand of falsehood.

Proverbs 30:6–9

6 Do not add to His words
Or He will reprove you, and you will be proved a liar.
7 Two things I asked of You,
Do not refuse me before I die:
8 Keep deception and lies far from me,
Give me neither poverty nor riches;
Feed me with the food that is my portion,
9 That I not be full and deny You and say, "Who is the LORD?"
Or that I not be in want and steal,
And profane the name of my God.

Revelation 8:1–13

8 WHEN the Lamb broke the seventh seal, there was silence in heaven for about half an hour.
2 And I saw the seven angels who stand before God, and seven trumpets were given to them.
3 Another angel came and stood at the altar, holding a golden censer; and much incense was given to him, so that he might add it to the prayers of all the saints on the golden altar which was before the throne.
4 And the smoke of the incense, with the prayers of the saints, went up before God out of the angel's hand.
5 Then the angel took the censer and

LIFE LESSONS

➤ **Proverbs 30:6 —** *Do not add to His words or He will reprove you, and you will be proved a liar.*

*W*e must be careful to distinguish between our own opinions and interpretations of Scripture, and what God actually says in His Word. Paul says we are "not to exceed what is written" (1 Cor. 4:6).

filled it with the fire of the altar, and threw it to the earth; and there followed peals of thunder and sounds and flashes of lightning and an earthquake.

6 And the seven angels who had the seven trumpets prepared themselves to sound them.

7 The first sounded, and there came hail and fire, mixed with blood, and they were thrown to the earth; and a third of the earth was burned up, and a third of the trees were burned up, and all the green grass was burned up.

8 The second angel sounded, and *something* like a great mountain burning with fire was thrown into the sea; and a third of the sea became blood,

9 and a third of the creatures which were in the sea and had life, died; and a third of the ships were destroyed.

10 The third angel sounded, and a great star fell from heaven, burning like a torch, and it fell on a third of the rivers and on the springs of waters.

11 The name of the star is called Wormwood; and a third of the waters became wormwood, and many men died from the waters, because they were made bitter.

12 The fourth angel sounded, and a third of the sun and a third of the moon and a third of the stars were struck, so that a third of them would be darkened and the day would not shine for a third of it, and the night in the same way.

13 Then I looked, and I heard an eagle flying in midheaven, saying with a loud voice, "Woe, woe, woe to those who dwell on the earth, because of the remaining blasts of the trumpet of the three angels who are about to sound!"

DECEMBER 19

Micah 1:1—3:12

1 THE word of the LORD which came to Micah of Moresheth in the days of Jotham, Ahaz *and* Hezekiah, kings of Judah, which he saw concerning Samaria and Jerusalem.

2 Hear, O peoples, all of you;
Listen, O earth and all it contains,
And let the Lord GOD be a witness against you,
The Lord from His holy temple.

3 For behold, the LORD is coming forth from His place.

He will come down and tread on the high places of the earth.

4 The mountains will melt under Him
And the valleys will be split,
Like wax before the fire,
Like water poured down a steep place.

5 All this is for the rebellion of Jacob
And for the sins of the house of Israel.
What is the rebellion of Jacob?
Is it not Samaria?
What is the high place of Judah?
Is it not Jerusalem?

6 For I will make Samaria a heap of ruins in the open country,

Planting places for a vineyard.
I will pour her stones down into the valley
And will lay bare her foundations.

7 All of her idols will be smashed,
All of her earnings will be burned with fire
And all of her images I will make desolate,
For she collected *them* from a harlot's earnings,
And to the earnings of a harlot they will return.

8 Because of this I must lament and wail,
I must go barefoot and naked;
I must make a lament like the jackals
And a mourning like the ostriches.

9 For her wound is incurable,
For it has come to Judah;
It has reached the gate of my people,
Even to Jerusalem.

10 Tell it not in Gath,
Weep not at all.
At Beth-le-aphrah roll yourself in the dust.

11 Go on your way, inhabitant of Shaphir, in shameful nakedness.
The inhabitant of Zaanan does not escape.
The lamentation of Beth-ezel: "He will take from you its support."

12 For the inhabitant of Maroth
Becomes weak waiting for good,
Because a calamity has come down from the Lord
To the gate of Jerusalem.

13 Harness the chariot to the team of horses,
O inhabitant of Lachish—
She was the beginning of sin
To the daughter of Zion—
Because in you were found
The rebellious acts of Israel.

14 Therefore you will give parting gifts
On behalf of Moresheth-gath;
The houses of Achzib *will* become a deception
To the kings of Israel.

15 Moreover, I will bring on you
The one who takes possession,
O inhabitant of Mareshah.
The glory of Israel will enter Adullam.

16 Make yourself bald and cut off your hair,
Because of the children of your delight;

Extend your baldness like the eagle,
For they will go from you into exile.

2 WOE to those who scheme iniquity,
Who work out evil on their beds!
When morning comes, they do it,
For it is in the power of their hands.

2 They covet fields and then seize *them*,
And houses, and take *them* away.
They rob a man and his house,
A man and his inheritance.

3 Therefore thus says the Lord,
"Behold, I am planning against this family a calamity
From which you cannot remove your necks;
And you will not walk haughtily,
For it will be an evil time.

4 "On that day they will take up against you a taunt
And utter a bitter lamentation *and* say,
'We are completely destroyed!
He exchanges the portion of my people;
How He removes it from me!
To the apostate He apportions our fields.'

5 "Therefore you will have no one stretching a measuring line
For you by lot in the assembly of the Lord.

6 'Do not speak out,' so they speak out.
But if they do not speak out concerning these things,
Reproaches will not be turned back.

7 "Is it being said, O house of Jacob: ◄
'Is the Spirit of the Lord impatient?
Are these His doings?'
Do not My words do good
To the one walking uprightly?

8 "Recently My people have arisen as an enemy—
You strip the robe off the garment
From unsuspecting passers-by,

LIFE LESSONS

➤ **Micah 2:7 — *"Do not My words do good to the one walking uprightly?"***

*G*od desires to bless us, not punish us, so even His words of rebuke and correction are good for us. "Let the righteous . . . reprove me; it is oil upon the head; do not let my head refuse it" (Ps. 141:5).

From those returned from war.

9 "The women of My people you evict,
Each one from her pleasant house.
From her children you take My
splendor forever.

10 "Arise and go,
For this is no place of rest
Because of the uncleanness that
brings on destruction,
A painful destruction.

11 "If a man walking after wind and
falsehood
Had told lies and said,
'I will speak out to you concerning
wine and liquor,'
He would be spokesman to this
people.

12 "I will surely assemble all of you,
Jacob,
I will surely gather the remnant of
Israel.
I will put them together like sheep
in the fold;
Like a flock in the midst of its
pasture
They will be noisy with men.

13 "The breaker goes up before them;
They break out, pass through the
gate and go out by it.
So their king goes on before them,
And the LORD at their head."

3 AND I said,
"Hear now, heads of Jacob
And rulers of the house of Israel.
Is it not for you to know justice?

2 "You who hate good and love evil,
Who tear off their skin from them
And their flesh from their bones,

3 Who eat the flesh of my people,
Strip off their skin from them,
Break their bones
And chop them up as for the pot
And as meat in a kettle."

4 Then they will cry out to the LORD,
But He will not answer them.
Instead, He will hide His face from
them at that time
Because they have practiced evil
deeds.

5 Thus says the LORD concerning the
prophets who lead my people astray;
When they have something to bite
with their teeth,
They cry, "Peace,"
But against him who puts nothing in
their mouths
They declare holy war.

6 Therefore it will be night for you—
without vision,
And darkness for you—without
divination.
The sun will go down on the
prophets,
And the day will become dark over
them.

7 The seers will be ashamed
And the diviners will be
embarrassed.
Indeed, they will all cover their
mouths
Because there is no answer from
God.

8 On the other hand I am filled with
power—
With the Spirit of the LORD—
And with justice and courage
To make known to Jacob his
rebellious act,
Even to Israel his sin.

9 Now hear this, heads of the house
of Jacob
And rulers of the house of Israel,
Who abhor justice
And twist everything that is
straight,

10 Who build Zion with bloodshed
And Jerusalem with violent
injustice.

11 Her leaders pronounce judgment for
a bribe,
Her priests instruct for a price
And her prophets divine for
money.
Yet they lean on the LORD saying,
"Is not the LORD in our midst?
Calamity will not come upon us."

12 Therefore, on account of you
Zion will be plowed as a field,
Jerusalem will become a heap of
ruins,
And the mountain of the temple will
become high places of a forest.

LIFE LESSONS

➤ **Micah 3:8** — *I am filled with power—
with the Spirit of the LORD.*

God has given us, not a spirit of fear,
but of power (2 Tim. 1:7), and that
power comes from His Spirit: "But you
will receive power when the Holy Spirit
has come upon you" (Acts 1:8; see also
Eph. 3:16).

Psalm 144:9–15

➤ 9   I will sing a new song to You,
          O God;
        Upon a harp of ten strings I will
          sing praises to You,
10   Who gives salvation to kings,
        Who rescues David His servant
          from the evil sword.
11   Rescue me and deliver me out of the
          hand of aliens,
        Whose mouth speaks deceit
        And whose right hand is a right
          hand of falsehood.
12   Let our sons in their youth be as
          grown-up plants,
        And our daughters as corner pillars
          fashioned as for a palace;
13   Let our garners be full, furnishing
          every kind of produce,
        And our flocks bring forth
          thousands and ten thousands in
          our fields;
14   Let our cattle bear
        Without mishap and without loss,
        Let there be no outcry in our
          streets!
15   How blessed are the people who are
          so situated;
        How blessed are the people whose
          God is the LORD!

Proverbs 30:10

10   Do not slander a slave to his master,
        Or he will curse you and you will be
          found guilty.

Revelation 9:1–21

9 THEN the fifth angel sounded, and
    I saw a star from heaven which had
fallen to the earth; and the key of the bottomless pit was given to him.
2   He opened the bottomless pit, and
smoke went up out of the pit, like the
smoke of a great furnace; and the sun
and the air were darkened by the smoke
of the pit.
3   Then out of the smoke came locusts
upon the earth, and power was given

them, as the scorpions of the earth have
power.
4   They were told not to hurt the grass
of the earth, nor any green thing, nor any
tree, but only the men who do not have
the seal of God on their foreheads.
5   And they were not permitted to kill
anyone, but to torment for five months;
and their torment was like the torment
of a scorpion when it stings a man.
6   And in those days men will seek ◄
death and will not find it; they will long
to die, and death flees from them.
7   The appearance of the locusts was
like horses prepared for battle; and on
their heads appeared to be crowns like
gold, and their faces were like the faces
of men.
8   They had hair like the hair of women,
and their teeth were like *the teeth* of
lions.
9   They had breastplates like breastplates of iron; and the sound of their
wings was like the sound of chariots, of
many horses rushing to battle.
10   They have tails like scorpions, and
stings; and in their tails is their power to
hurt men for five months.
11   They have as king over them, the
angel of the abyss; his name in Hebrew

LIFE LESSONS

➤ **Psalm 144:9 —** *I will sing a new song
to You, O God; upon a harp of ten strings
I will sing praises to You.*

If we have instrumental abilities, the
Lord invites us to use them to praise
Him. If we have only a mediocre voice,
He invites us to use that to praise Him.
The key is to praise Him with all we
have.

➤ **Revelation 9:6 —** *Men will seek death
and will not find it.*

Jesus said, "Whoever wishes to save
his life will lose it; but whoever loses
his life for My sake will find it" (Matt.
16:25). Many people refuse to believe in
Christ because they do not want to give
up control of their lives. However, anything we hold too tightly, we will lose. In
the end times, people will despair of the
lives they've fought so hard to keep. God
does not desire for anyone to perish, so
He will use even severe pain to get our
attention and urge us back to Him.

WHAT THE BIBLE SAYS ABOUT

Softening Hard Hearts

Revelation 9

Revelation 9 describes the woes which come from the trumpet judgments. Certainly, the terrors described there would make even the bravest person faint with fear.

You might imagine that after all the wrath that God rains down, people will eventually acknowledge Him and repent. However, that is not the case. Revelation 9:20 reports, "The rest of mankind, who were not killed by these plagues, did not repent of the works of their hands."

By the time the trumpet judgments sound, there is a hardness of heart that has overcome people in the world. It is a truly sorrowful sight: people who are so steeped in their own sin that they will not acknowledge the living God—no matter what the evidence. The thought that those people will face the final judgment should move Christians to proclaim the gospel openly now while hearts are still receptive.

Hebrews 3:13 admonishes, "Encourage one another day after day, as long as it is still called 'Today,' so that none of you will be hardened by the deceitfulness of sin."

Encouragement and expressions of God's grace can soften hearts before the Day of Judgment. Today, show someone the love of God in a genuine way so that their hearts might be softened and they may repent. You may be instrumental in changing their eternal destination! ◈

---

is Abaddon, and in the Greek he has the name Apollyon.

12 The first woe is past; behold, two woes are still coming after these things.

13 Then the sixth angel sounded, and I heard a voice from the four horns of the golden altar which is before God,

14 one saying to the sixth angel who had the trumpet, "Release the four angels who are bound at the great river Euphrates."

➤ **15** And the four angels, who had been prepared for the hour and day and month and year, were released, so that they would kill a third of mankind.

16 The number of the armies of the horsemen was two hundred million; I heard the number of them.

17 And this is how I saw in the vision the horses and those who sat on them: *the riders* had breastplates *the color* of fire and of hyacinth and of brimstone; and the heads of the horses are like the heads of lions; and out of their mouths proceed fire and smoke and brimstone.

18 A third of mankind was killed by these three plagues, by the fire and the smoke and the brimstone which proceeded out of their mouths.

19 For the power of the horses is in their mouths and in their tails; for their tails are like serpents and have heads, and with them they do harm.

➤ **20** The rest of mankind, who were not killed by these plagues, did not repent of the works of their hands, so as not to worship demons, and the idols of gold and of silver and of brass and of stone and of wood, which can neither see nor hear nor walk;

21 and they did not repent of their murders nor of their sorceries nor of their immorality nor of their thefts.

LIFE LESSONS

➤ **Revelation 9:15 —** *The four angels, who had been prepared for the hour and day and month and year, were released.*

Despite the chaos on earth that the Book of Revelation describes, God remains completely in control (Ps. 103:19). The Lord has prepared these angels for this specific work at this precise time. Likewise, God has chosen the particular circumstances, era, location, and giftedness with which you exist for the purpose of serving Him.

➤ **Revelation 9:20 —** *The rest of mankind, who were not killed by these plagues, did not repent of the works of their hands.*

Why does the Book of Revelation repeatedly tell us that the wicked did not repent? First, because it shows the necessity of God's judgment. Second, because it shows God's desire that they repent and live (Ezek. 18:32; 2 Pet. 3:9).

Micah 4:1—5:15

4 AND it will come about in the last days
> That the mountain of the house of the LORD
> Will be established as the chief of the mountains.
> It will be raised above the hills,
> And the peoples will stream to it.
2 Many nations will come and say,
> "Come and let us go up to the mountain of the LORD
> And to the house of the God of Jacob,
> That He may teach us about His ways
> And that we may walk in His paths."
> For from Zion will go forth the law,
> Even the word of the LORD from Jerusalem.
3 And He will judge between many peoples
> And render decisions for mighty, distant nations.
> Then they will hammer their swords into plowshares
> And their spears into pruning hooks;
> Nation will not lift up sword against nation,
> And never again will they train for war.
4 Each of them will sit under his vine
> And under his fig tree,
> With no one to make *them* afraid,
> For the mouth of the LORD of hosts has spoken.
5 Though all the peoples walk
> Each in the name of his god,
> As for us, we will walk
> In the name of the LORD our God forever and ever.

LIFE LESSONS

> **Micah 4:2 — "He may teach us about His ways and that we may walk in His paths."**

*G*od does not leave us in the dark about His nature and will, and through His Spirit He enables us to reflect His nature and do His will. We walk in His paths when we allow Jesus to live through us.

---

6 "In that day," declares the LORD,
> "I will assemble the lame
> And gather the outcasts,
> Even those whom I have afflicted.
7 "I will make the lame a remnant
> And the outcasts a strong nation,
> And the LORD will reign over them in Mount Zion
> From now on and forever.
8 "As for you, tower of the flock,
> Hill of the daughter of Zion,
> To you it will come—
> Even the former dominion will come,
> The kingdom of the daughter of Jerusalem.
9 "Now, why do you cry out loudly?
> Is there no king among you,
> Or has your counselor perished,
> That agony has gripped you like a woman in childbirth?
10 "Writhe and labor to give birth,
> Daughter of Zion,
> Like a woman in childbirth;
> For now you will go out of the city,
> Dwell in the field,
> And go to Babylon.
> There you will be rescued;
> There the LORD will redeem you
> From the hand of your enemies.
11 "And now many nations have been assembled against you
> Who say, 'Let her be polluted,
> And let our eyes gloat over Zion.'
12 "But they do not know the thoughts of the LORD,
> And they do not understand His purpose;
> For He has gathered them like sheaves to the threshing floor.
13 "Arise and thresh, daughter of Zion,
> For your horn I will make iron
> And your hoofs I will make bronze,
> That you may pulverize many peoples,
> That you may devote to the LORD their unjust gain
> And their wealth to the Lord of all the earth.

5 "NOW muster yourselves in troops, daughter of troops;
> They have laid siege against us;
> With a rod they will smite the judge of Israel on the cheek.
2 "But as for you, Bethlehem Ephrathah,

WHAT THE BIBLE SAYS ABOUT ◉

The Meaning of Christmas

Micah 5:2–4

Christmas's true meaning is waning in many hearts and minds. The evidence is a growing use of "Season's Greetings!" or "Happy Holidays!" rather than "Merry Christmas!" Businesses and individuals who prefer not to mention Christmas claim they don't want to offend anyone. I say that if the traditional words containing Christ's name offend, then so be it. People who understand the authentic meaning of Christmas will not worry about displeasing others—they will simply be thankful that they have a Savior to share.

Christmas is a celebration of the historic moment when God came to earth in the person of Jesus Christ for the purpose of redeeming sinful man. This story begins not in a manger, but rather in Adam and Eve's garden. There, the Lord initiated a genealogical line that would remain unbroken throughout centuries of slavery, famine, and turbulence, ultimately leading to the Messiah.

Meanwhile, God prepared the world for Christ's arrival and impact. Roman conquests placed men like Caesar Augustus in charge—his call for a census served God's purposes by leading Joseph and Mary to Bethlehem, where the prophesied Messiah was to be born (see Micah 5:2–4). Rome's influence also led to a network of roads, which would eventually enable Paul and others to spread the Good News.

God arranged all of this so that at just the right time, Jesus Christ could arrive on earth as a baby who would grow to be our Savior, dying for mankind's sins. We should be truly thankful for Christmas! ◉

Too little to be among the clans of Judah,
From you One will go forth for Me to be ruler in Israel.
His goings forth are from long ago, From the days of eternity."

3   Therefore He will give them *up* until the time
When she who is in labor has borne a child.
Then the remainder of His brethren Will return to the sons of Israel.

4   And He will arise and shepherd *His* flock
In the strength of the LORD,
In the majesty of the name of the LORD His God.
And they will remain,
Because at that time He will be great
To the ends of the earth.

5   This One will be *our* peace.
When the Assyrian invades our land,
When he tramples on our citadels,
Then we will raise against him
Seven shepherds and eight leaders of men.

6   They will shepherd the land of Assyria with the sword,
The land of Nimrod at its entrances;
And He will deliver *us* from the Assyrian
When he attacks our land
And when he tramples our territory.

7   Then the remnant of Jacob
Will be among many peoples
Like dew from the LORD,
Like showers on vegetation
Which do not wait for man
Or delay for the sons of men.

8   The remnant of Jacob

LIFE LESSONS

➤ **Micah 5:2 — "One will go forth for Me to be ruler in Israel. His goings forth are from long ago, from the days of eternity."**

When Jesus told the Pharisees, "Before Abraham was born, I am" (John 8:58), He was simply restating what Micah said here—that the Messiah would be the eternal God who would come to earth in the flesh.

➤ **Micah 5:4 — He will arise and shepherd His flock . . . in the majesty of the name of the Lord His God.**

During His earthly ministry, Jesus practically made this verse His motto when He said, "I am the good shepherd; the good shepherd lays down His life for the sheep . . . I am the good shepherd" (John 10:11, 14).

Will be among the nations,
Among many peoples
Like a lion among the beasts of the
forest,
Like a young lion among flocks of
sheep,
Which, if he passes through,
Tramples down and tears,
And there is none to rescue.
9 Your hand will be lifted up against
your adversaries,
And all your enemies will be cut
off.
10 "It will be in that day," declares the
LORD,
"That I will cut off your horses from
among you
And destroy your chariots.
11 "I will also cut off the cities of your
land
And tear down all your
fortifications.
12 "I will cut off sorceries from your
hand,
And you will have fortune-tellers no
more.
13 "I will cut off your carved images
And your *sacred* pillars from among
you,
So that you will no longer bow
down
To the work of your hands.
14 "I will root out your Asherim from
among you
And destroy your cities.
15 "And I will execute vengeance in
anger and wrath
On the nations which have not
obeyed."

Psalm 145:1–9

A Psalm of Praise, of David.

145 I WILL extol You, my God,
      O King,
And I will bless Your name forever
and ever.
2 Every day I will bless You,
And I will praise Your name forever
and ever.
3 Great is the LORD, and highly to be
praised,
And His greatness is
unsearchable.

4 One generation shall praise Your
works to another,
And shall declare Your mighty acts.
5 On the glorious splendor of Your
majesty
And on Your wonderful works, I will
meditate.
6 Men shall speak of the power of
Your awesome acts,
And I will tell of Your greatness.
7 They shall eagerly utter the memory
of Your abundant goodness
And will shout joyfully of Your
righteousness.
8 The LORD is gracious and merciful;
Slow to anger and great in
lovingkindness.
9 The LORD is good to all,
And His mercies are over all His
works.

Proverbs 30:11–14

11 There is a kind of *man* who curses
his father
And does not bless his mother.
12 There is a kind who is pure in his
own eyes,
Yet is not washed from his
filthiness.
13 There is a kind—oh how lofty are
his eyes!
And his eyelids are raised in
arrogance.
14 There is a kind of *man* whose teeth
are *like* swords
And his jaw teeth *like* knives,
To devour the afflicted from the
earth
And the needy from among men.

Revelation 10:1–11

10 I SAW another strong angel coming down out of heaven, clothed
with a cloud; and the rainbow was upon
his head, and his face was like the sun,
and his feet like pillars of fire;
2 and he had in his hand a little book
which was open. He placed his right foot
on the sea and his left on the land;
3 and he cried out with a loud voice, as
when a lion roars; and when he had cried

out, the seven peals of thunder uttered their voices.

➤ 4   When the seven peals of thunder had spoken, I was about to write; and I heard a voice from heaven saying, "Seal up the things which the seven peals of thunder have spoken and do not write them."

5   Then the angel whom I saw standing on the sea and on the land lifted up his right hand to heaven,

6   and swore by Him who lives forever and ever, WHO CREATED HEAVEN AND THE THINGS IN IT, AND THE EARTH AND THE THINGS IN IT, AND THE SEA AND THE THINGS IN IT, that there will be delay no longer,

➤ 7   but in the days of the voice of the seventh angel, when he is about to sound, then the mystery of God is finished, as He preached to His servants the prophets.

8   Then the voice which I heard from heaven, *I heard* again speaking with me, and saying, "Go, take the book which is open in the hand of the angel who stands on the sea and on the land."

➤ 9   So I went to the angel, telling him to give me the little book. And he *said to me, "Take it and eat it; it will make your stomach bitter, but in your mouth it will be sweet as honey."

10   I took the little book out of the angel's hand and ate it, and in my mouth it was sweet as honey; and when I had eaten it, my stomach was made bitter.

11   And they *said to me, "You must prophesy again concerning many peoples and nations and tongues and kings."

LIFE LESSONS

➤ **Revelation 10:4 — *"Seal up the things which the seven peals of thunder have spoken and do not write them."***

*G*od reveals to us the things He wants us to know. He does not disclose details about the future to satisfy our curiosity but to motivate and equip us to live for Him today with passion, holiness, and joy. He also leaves some particulars unknown so we will cling to Him and seek Him for wisdom and direction.

➤ **Revelation 10:7 — *The mystery of God is finished, as He preached to His servants the prophets.***

*G*od will move heaven and earth to show us His will, and throughout history, He has spoken to us about what will take place through His prophets (1 Pet. 1:10–13). However, we may not fully understand it all until it is fulfilled, just as the disciples did not comprehend all the prophesies concerning Jesus until they saw Him as the resurrected Messiah (John 2:19–22; 12:12–16).

➤ **Revelation 10:9 — *"Take it and eat it; it will make your stomach bitter, but in your mouth it will be as honey."***

*I*t is always a joy to read and proclaim the Word of God. Yet some parts of Scripture—like these passages describing catastrophic divine judgment—give no pleasure either to the prophets or to the Lord (Jer. 15:16, 17, 19; Ezek. 2:8–3:15).

DECEMBER 21

◈ **Micah 6:1—7:20**

6 Hear now what the Lord is saying,
    "Arise, plead your case before the
       mountains,
    And let the hills hear your voice.
2   "Listen, you mountains, to the
       indictment of the LORD,
    And you enduring foundations of
       the earth,
    Because the LORD has a case against
       His people;
    Even with Israel He will dispute.
3   "My people, what have I done to you,

And how have I wearied you?
    Answer Me.
4   "Indeed, I brought you up from the
       land of Egypt
    And ransomed you from the house
       of slavery,
    And I sent before you Moses, Aaron
       and Miriam.
5   "My people, remember now
    What Balak king of Moab counseled
    And what Balaam son of Beor
       answered him,
    And from Shittim to Gilgal,
    So that you might know the
       righteous acts of the LORD."

6   With what shall I come to the LORD
And bow myself before the God on
high?
Shall I come to Him with burnt
offerings,
With yearling calves?
7   Does the LORD take delight in
thousands of rams,
In ten thousand rivers of oil?
Shall I present my firstborn *for* my
rebellious acts,
The fruit of my body for the sin of
my soul?
8   He has told you, O man, what is
good;
And what does the LORD require of
you
But to do justice, to love kindness,
And to walk humbly with your God?
9   The voice of the LORD will call to
the city—
And it is sound wisdom to fear Your
name:
"Hear, O tribe. Who has appointed
its time?
10 "Is there yet a man in the wicked
house,
Along with treasures of wickedness
And a short measure *that is* cursed?
11 "Can I justify wicked scales
And a bag of deceptive weights?
12 "For the rich men of *the* city are full
of violence,
Her residents speak lies,
And their tongue is deceitful in their
mouth.
13 "So also I will make *you* sick,
striking you down,
Desolating *you* because of your sins.
14 "You will eat, but you will not be
satisfied,
And your vileness will be in your
midst.
You will *try to* remove *for*
safekeeping,
But you will not preserve *anything,*
And what you do preserve I will
give to the sword.
15 "You will sow but you will not reap.
You will tread the olive but will not
anoint yourself with oil;
And the grapes, but you will not
drink wine.
16 "The statutes of Omri
And all the works of the house of
Ahab are observed;
And in their devices you walk.

Therefore I will give you up for
destruction
And your inhabitants for derision,
And you will bear the reproach of
My people."

7   WOE is me! For I am
Like the fruit pickers, like the grape
gatherers.
There is not a cluster of grapes to eat,
Or a first-ripe fig *which* I crave.
2   The godly person has perished from
the land,
And there is no upright *person*
among men.
All of them lie in wait for bloodshed;
Each of them hunts the other with a
net.
3   Concerning evil, both hands do it
well.
The prince asks, also the judge, for
a bribe,
And a great man speaks the desire
of his soul;
So they weave it together.
4   The best of them is like a briar,
The most upright like a thorn hedge.
The day when you post your
watchmen,
Your punishment will come.
Then their confusion will occur.
5   Do not trust in a neighbor;
Do not have confidence in a friend.
From her who lies in your bosom
Guard your lips.
6   For son treats father contemptuously,
Daughter rises up against her mother,
Daughter-in-law against her mother-
in-law;
A man's enemies are the men of his
own household.
7   But as for me, I will watch
expectantly for the LORD;
I will wait for the God of my
salvation.
My God will hear me.
8   Do not rejoice over me, O my
enemy.
Though I fall I will rise;
Though I dwell in darkness, the
LORD is a light for me.
9   I will bear the indignation of the
LORD
Because I have sinned against Him,
Until He pleads my case and
executes justice for me.
He will bring me out to the light,
And I will see His righteousness.

WHAT THE BIBLE SAYS ABOUT ◈

True Religion

Micah 6:8

What a tragedy that we have lost our ability to function in society the way God originally intended. He left us here to be a light to our world. People should be able to look at us and see something wonderfully different about us. The good things God places on the inside of us should show up in practical ways on the outside.

The prophet Micah said it like this: "He has told you, O man, what is good; and what does the LORD require of you but to do justice, to love kindness, and to walk humbly with your God?" (Mic. 6:8). And don't think Micah gave an exclusively Old Testament perspective! The New Testament tells us, "Pure and undefiled religion in the sight of our God and Father is this: to visit orphans and widows in their distress, and to keep oneself unstained by the world" (James 1:27).

This means there should be something different in the way we do business. There should be some clear differences in the way we raise our children. Our marriages should testify to the love of Christ. Those outside the church should feel powerfully attracted to the unity and love they see among believers.

Unfortunately, this rarely happens today. Consequently, our society has a warped view of the person and work of Christ. It is no wonder that so many non-Christians want nothing to do with Christ or His church.

We cannot expect anyone to embrace a Savior they know nothing about. We certainly cannot expect them to surrender to a Lord whose servants can't even get along with each other. As ambassadors for Christ, believers have the God-given responsibility to live in such a way that others see Christ in us. As the body of Christ, *we* are His hands and His feet. *We* are His mouth piece. ◈

---

10 Then my enemy will see,
    And shame will cover her who said
      to me,
  "Where is the LORD your God?"
    My eyes will look on her;
    At that time she will be trampled
      down
    Like mire of the streets.
11 *It will be* a day for building your
    walls.
    On that day will your boundary be
      extended.
12 It *will be* a day when they will come
      to you
    From Assyria and the cities of Egypt,

From Egypt even to the Euphrates,
    Even from sea to sea and mountain
      to mountain.
13 And the earth will become desolate
      because of her inhabitants,
    On account of the fruit of their
      deeds.
14 Shepherd Your people with Your
      scepter,
    The flock of Your possession
    Which dwells by itself in the
      woodland,
    In the midst of a fruitful field.
    Let them feed in Bashan and Gilead
    As in the days of old.
15 "As in the days when you came out
      from the land of Egypt,
    I will show you miracles."
16 Nations will see and be ashamed
    Of all their might.
    They will put *their* hand on *their*
      mouth,
    Their ears will be deaf.
17 They will lick the dust like a serpent,
    Like reptiles of the earth.
    They will come trembling out of
      their fortresses;
    To the LORD our God they will come
      in dread
    And they will be afraid before You.

LIFE LESSONS

➤ **Micah 7:8** — *Though I dwell in darkness, the LORD is a light for me.*

All of us will go through difficult times. Whether we like it or not, waiting on God is a big part in our walks of faith. When we do all that we can, in faith, and then wait for God to do the rest, we demonstrate our trust and proclaim His faithfulness. The dark moments of our lives will last only so long as is necessary for God to accomplish His purpose in us.

18 Who is a God like You, who
      pardons iniquity
   And passes over the rebellious act
      of the remnant of His possession?
   He does not retain His anger
      forever,
   Because He delights in unchanging
      love.
19 He will again have compassion on
      us;
   He will tread our iniquities under
      foot.
   Yes, You will cast all their sins
   Into the depths of the sea.
20 You will give truth to Jacob
   And unchanging love to Abraham,
   Which You swore to our forefathers
   From the days of old.

◈ Psalm 145:10–16

10 All Your works shall give thanks to
      You, O LORD,
   And Your godly ones shall bless
      You.
11 They shall speak of the glory of
      Your kingdom
   And talk of Your power;
12 To make known to the sons of men
      Your mighty acts
   And the glory of the majesty of Your
      kingdom.
13 Your kingdom is an everlasting
      kingdom,
   And Your dominion *endures*
      throughout all generations.
14 The LORD sustains all who fall
   And raises up all who are bowed
      down.
15 The eyes of all look to You,
   And You give them their food in due
      time.
16 You open Your hand
   And satisfy the desire of every
      living thing.

◈ Proverbs 30:15

15 The leech has two daughters,
   "Give," "Give."
   There are three things that will not
      be satisfied,
   Four that will not say, "Enough":

◈ Revelation 11:1–19

11 THEN there was given me a measuring rod like a staff; and someone
said, "Get up and measure the temple of
God and the altar, and those who worship in it.
2 "Leave out the court which is outside
the temple and do not measure it, for it
has been given to the nations; and they
will tread under foot the holy city for
forty-two months.
3 "And I will grant *authority* to my two
witnesses, and they will prophesy for
twelve hundred and sixty days, clothed
in sackcloth."
4 These are the two olive trees and
the two lampstands that stand before the
Lord of the earth.
5 And if anyone wants to harm them,
fire flows out of their mouth and devours
their enemies; so if anyone wants to
harm them, he must be killed in this way.
6 These have the power to shut up the
sky, so that rain will not fall during the
days of their prophesying; and they have
power over the waters to turn them into
blood, and to strike the earth with every
plague, as often as they desire.

LIFE LESSONS

➤ Micah 7:18 — *Who is a God like You,
who pardons iniquity?*

When God forgives us in Christ, He
   does not merely turn His back on
our sins or force Himself to overlook
them. He deals with them radically and
once-and-for-all, removing them from us
forever. But understand, God was never
under any obligation to forgive our
sins or pardon our iniquities. We do not
deserve His mercy. But He loves us and
so sent His Son to die for our sins. Who,
indeed, is a God like that?

➤ Psalm 145:15 — *The eyes of all look
to You, and You give them their food in
due time.*

God is the great Provider. As Paul said,
   "He Himself gives to all people life
and breath and all things" (Acts 17:25).
We do not look to God presumptuously
for what we need, but expectantly, for
we put our hope in His great love.

7   When they have finished their testimony, the beast that comes up out of the abyss will make war with them, and overcome them and kill them.

8   And their dead bodies *will lie* in the street of the great city which mystically is called Sodom and Egypt, where also their Lord was crucified.

9   Those from the peoples and tribes and tongues and nations *will* look at their dead bodies for three and a half days, and will not permit their dead bodies to be laid in a tomb.

10   And those who dwell on the earth *will* rejoice over them and celebrate; and they will send gifts to one another, because these two prophets tormented those who dwell on the earth.

11   But after the three and a half days, the breath of life from God came into them, and they stood on their feet; and great fear fell upon those who were watching them.

12   And they heard a loud voice from heaven saying to them, "Come up here." Then they went up into heaven in the cloud, and their enemies watched them.

➤ 13   And in that hour there was a great earthquake, and a tenth of the city fell; seven thousand people were killed in the earthquake, and the rest were terrified and gave glory to the God of heaven.

14   The second woe is past; behold, the third woe is coming quickly.

15   Then the seventh angel sounded; and there were loud voices in heaven, saying,

"The kingdom of the world has become *the kingdom* of our Lord and of His Christ; and He will reign forever and ever."

16   And the twenty-four elders, who sit on their thrones before God, fell on their faces and worshiped God,

17   saying,

"We give You thanks, O Lord God, the Almighty, who are and who were, because You have taken Your great power and have begun to reign.

18   "And the nations were enraged, and Your wrath came, and the time *came* for the dead to be judged, and *the time* to reward Your bond-servants the prophets and the saints and those who fear Your name, the small and the great, and to destroy those who destroy the earth."

19   And the temple of God which is in heaven was opened; and the ark of His covenant appeared in His temple, and there were flashes of lightning and sounds and peals of thunder and an earthquake and a great hailstorm.

LIFE LESSONS

➤ **Revelation 11:6 —** *They have power over the waters to turn them into blood, and to strike the earth with every plague, as often as they desire.*

The miracles described here may remind us of the wonders performed through Elijah (1 Kin. 17:1) and Moses (Ex. 7:14—12:42). The same God who empowered them will demonstrate His power once again so that many can be saved.

➤ **Revelation 11:13 —** *Seven thousand people were killed in the earthquake, and the rest were terrified and gave glory to the God of heaven.*

This is the only time in Revelation that a tragedy prompts those who survive to give glory to God. Tragedies such as this devastating earthquake are terrible, but the Lord can use them to show people their great need for His grace and redemption.

 Nahum 1:1—3:19

1 THE oracle of Nineveh. The book of the vision of Nahum the Elkoshite.

2   A jealous and avenging God is the Lord; ◄
    The Lord is avenging and wrathful.
    The Lord takes vengeance on His adversaries,

And He reserves wrath for His
  enemies.
3 The LORD is slow to anger and great
    in power,
  And the LORD will by no means
    leave *the guilty* unpunished.
  In whirlwind and storm is His way,
  And clouds are the dust beneath His
    feet.
4 He rebukes the sea and makes it
    dry;
  He dries up all the rivers.
  Bashan and Carmel wither;
  The blossoms of Lebanon wither.
5 Mountains quake because of Him
  And the hills dissolve;
  Indeed the earth is upheaved by His
    presence,
  The world and all the inhabitants in
    it.
6 Who can stand before His
    indignation?
  Who can endure the burning of His
    anger?
  His wrath is poured out like fire
  And the rocks are broken up by
    Him.
7 The LORD is good,
  A stronghold in the day of trouble,
  And He knows those who take
    refuge in Him.
8 But with an overflowing flood
  He will make a complete end of its
    site,
  And will pursue His enemies into
    darkness.
9 Whatever you devise against the
    LORD,
  He will make a complete end of it.
  Distress will not rise up twice.
10 Like tangled thorns,
  And like those who are drunken
    with their drink,
  They are consumed
  As stubble completely withered.

11 From you has gone forth
  One who plotted evil against the
    LORD,
  A wicked counselor.
12 Thus says the LORD,
  "Though they are at full *strength* and
    likewise many,
  Even so, they will be cut off and
    pass away.
  Though I have afflicted you,
  I will afflict you no longer.
13 "So now, I will break his yoke bar
    from upon you,
  And I will tear off your shackles."
14 The LORD has issued a command
    concerning you:
  "Your name will no longer be
    perpetuated.
  I will cut off idol and image
  From the house of your gods.
  I will prepare your grave,
  For you are contemptible."
15 Behold, on the mountains the feet of
    him who brings good news,
  Who announces peace!
  Celebrate your feasts, O Judah;
  Pay your vows.
  For never again will the wicked one
    pass through you;
  He is cut off completely.

2 THE one who scatters has come up
    against you.
  Man the fortress, watch the road;
  Strengthen your back, summon all
    your strength.
2 For the LORD will restore the
    splendor of Jacob
  Like the splendor of Israel,
  Even though devastators have
    devastated them
  And destroyed their vine branches.
3 The shields of his mighty men are
    colored red,
  The warriors are dressed in scarlet,
  The chariots are *enveloped* in
    flashing steel
  When he is prepared *to march*,
  And the cypress *spears* are
    brandished.
4 The chariots race madly in the
    streets,
  They rush wildly in the squares,
  Their appearance is like torches,
  They dash to and fro like lightning
    flashes.
5 He remembers his nobles;
  They stumble in their march,

They hurry to her wall,
And the mantelet is set up.

6 The gates of the rivers are opened
And the palace is dissolved.

7 It is fixed:
She is stripped, she is carried away,
And her handmaids are moaning
    like the sound of doves,
Beating on their breasts.

8 Though Nineveh *was* like a pool of
    water throughout her days,
Now they are fleeing;
"Stop, stop,"
But no one turns back.

9 Plunder the silver!
Plunder the gold!
For there is no limit to the
    treasure—
Wealth from every kind of desirable
    object.

10 She is emptied! Yes, she is desolate
    and waste!
Hearts are melting and knees
    knocking!
Also anguish is in the whole body
And all their faces are grown pale!

11 Where is the den of the lions
And the feeding place of the young
    lions,
Where the lion, lioness and lion's
    cub prowled,
With nothing to disturb *them*?

12 The lion tore enough for his cubs,
Killed *enough* for his lionesses,
And filled his lairs with prey
And his dens with torn flesh.

➤ 13 "Behold, I am against you," declares
the Lord of hosts. "I will burn up her
chariots in smoke, a sword will devour
your young lions; I will cut off your prey

---

from the land, and no longer will the
voice of your messengers be heard."

3 WOE to the bloody city, completely
    full of lies *and* pillage;
Her prey never departs.

2 The noise of the whip,
The noise of the rattling of the
    wheel,
Galloping horses
And bounding chariots!

3 Horsemen charging,
Swords flashing, spears gleaming,
Many slain, a mass of corpses,
And countless dead bodies—
They stumble over the dead
    bodies!

4 *All* because of the many harlotries
    of the harlot,
The charming one, the mistress of
    sorceries,
Who sells nations by her harlotries
And families by her sorceries.

5 "Behold, I am against you," declares
    the Lord of hosts;
"And I will lift up your skirts over
    your face,
And show to the nations your
    nakedness
And to the kingdoms your
    disgrace.

6 "I will throw filth on you
And make you vile,
And set you up as a spectacle.

7 "And it will come about that all who
    see you
Will shrink from you and say,
'Nineveh is devastated!
Who will grieve for her?'
Where will I seek comforters for
    you?"

8 Are you better than No-amon,
Which was situated by the waters of
    the Nile,
With water surrounding her,
Whose rampart *was* the sea,
Whose wall *consisted* of the sea?

9 Ethiopia was *her* might,
And Egypt too, without limits.
Put and Lubim were among her
    helpers.

10 Yet she became an exile,
She went into captivity;
Also her small children were
    dashed to pieces
At the head of every street;
They cast lots for her honorable
    men,

And all her great men were bound
with fetters.

11 You too will become drunk,
You will be hidden.
You too will search for a refuge
from the enemy.

12 All your fortifications are fig trees
with ripe fruit—
When shaken, they fall into the
eater's mouth.

13 Behold, your people are women in
your midst!
The gates of your land are opened
wide to your enemies;
Fire consumes your gate bars.

➤ 14 Draw for yourself water for the
siege!
Strengthen your fortifications!
Go into the clay and tread the
mortar!
Take hold of the brick mold!

15 There fire will consume you,
The sword will cut you down;
It will consume you as the locust
does.
Multiply yourself like the creeping
locust,
Multiply yourself like the swarming
locust.

16 You have increased your traders
more than the stars of heaven—
The creeping locust strips and flies
away.

17 Your guardsmen are like the
swarming locust.
Your marshals are like hordes of
grasshoppers
Settling in the stone walls on a cold
day.
The sun rises and they flee,
And the place where they are is not
known.

18 Your shepherds are sleeping,
O king of Assyria;
Your nobles are lying down.
Your people are scattered on the
mountains
And there is no one to regather
them.

➤ 19 There is no relief for your
breakdown,
Your wound is incurable.
All who hear about you
Will clap *their* hands over you,
For on whom has not your evil
passed continually?

Psalm 145:17–21

17 The LORD is righteous in all His
ways
And kind in all His deeds.

18 The LORD is near to all who call
upon Him,
To all who call upon Him in truth.

19 He will fulfill the desire of those
who fear Him;
He will also hear their cry and will
save them.

20 The LORD keeps all who love Him,
But all the wicked He will destroy.

21 My mouth will speak the praise of
the LORD,
And all flesh will bless His holy
name forever and ever.

Proverbs 30:16

16 Sheol, and the barren womb,
Earth that is never satisfied with
water,
And fire that never says, "Enough."

Revelation 12:1–17

12 A GREAT sign appeared in heaven:
a woman clothed with the sun, and

LIFE LESSONS

➤ **Nahum 3:14 — *Strengthen your fortifications!***

*G*od does not always plead with rebels
to repent. The time comes when they
reach a point of no return. Pharaoh did
this (Ex. 9:12). Assyria did this. And some
still do it (1 John 5:16).

➤ **Nahum 3:19 — *There is no relief for
your breakdown, your wound is incurable.***

*T*hose who refuse to come to the Lord
for their spiritual healing will never
be healed. We were made for intimacy
with God, and to seek a cure for spiritual
wounds apart from Him is to seek poison, not medicine.

the moon under her feet, and on her head a crown of twelve stars;

2   and she was with child; and she *cried out, being in labor and in pain to give birth.

3   Then another sign appeared in heaven: and behold, a great red dragon having seven heads and ten horns, and on his heads *were* seven diadems.

4   And his tail *swept away a third of the stars of heaven and threw them to the earth. And the dragon stood before the woman who was about to give birth, so that when she gave birth he might devour her child.

5   And she gave birth to a son, a male *child,* who is to rule all the nations with a rod of iron; and her child was caught up to God and to His throne.

6   Then the woman fled into the wilderness where she *had a place prepared by God, so that there she would be nourished for one thousand two hundred and sixty days.

7   And there was war in heaven, Michael and his angels waging war with the dragon. The dragon and his angels waged war,

8   and they were not strong enough, and there was no longer a place found for them in heaven.

9   And the great dragon was thrown down, the serpent of old who is called the devil and Satan, who deceives the whole world; he was thrown down to the earth, and his angels were thrown down with him.

10   Then I heard a loud voice in heaven, saying,

"Now the salvation, and the power,

Why doesn't God keep us from tests and trials?

REVELATION 12:11

*W*e live in a fallen world—all of us will face times of suffering and heartache. Sometimes God keeps us from certain tests and trials, but at other times He allows them, knowing that the testing strengthens and perfects our faith in Him.

God wants us to have an unshakable faith—and if trials, tests, and suffering are what it takes for us to have it, then He'll allow them. Even the strongest faith in God does not mean we will be spared life's trials.

Daniel's faith was severely tested, but he emerged victorious. We're told that because Daniel was very successful and favored by King Darius, the other commissioners and satraps became jealous and decided to set a trap for him. Daniel 6:7 reports that the conspirators told the king, "All the commissioners of the kingdom . . . have consulted together that the king should establish a statute and enforce an injunction that anyone who makes a petition to any god or man besides you, O king, for thirty days, shall (be cast into the lions' den."

As they knew he would, Daniel refused to compromise his love for God by worshiping King Darius, even though he understood that his obedience to the Lord would jeopardize his life (Dan. 6:16). He chose the path of other faithful believers who "did not love their life even when faced with death" (Rev. 12:11).

And the conspirators caught him in the act of praying to the Lord and condemned him to the lion's den (Dan. 6:10–13).

Many of God's greatest saints—those in the Bible and others throughout Christian history—faced varying degrees of suffering. All of them, however, developed an unshakable faith that provided the inner strength they needed to face every difficulty with hope and blessed assurance.

Do you have an unshakable faith? Are you in an extreme place of testing?

If so, do not be afraid. God has planned this very moment, and He will teach you how to trust Him perfectly.

A person with an unshakable faith never judges God's faithfulness by his or her feelings. Instead, he or she believes and trusts the Lord through every season of life, knowing that in the end, God's plan will emerge as perfect.

At times in your walk with God, He may require you to do something that, from a human perspective, seems unreasonable. From His viewpoint, however, it will be in perfect alignment with His Word and will turn out for your ultimate benefit.

Therefore, open your heart to His love and give Him the opportunity to prove His faithfulness. That is what Daniel did, and God made it possible for him to walk away from the lion's den with a song of victory on his lips (Dan. 6:19–28).

What is your level of faith in God? Do you believe that He will do exactly what He has promised? Are you convinced that He has already moved heaven and earth for you, and all you have to do is move toward His blessing?

and the kingdom of our God and the authority of His Christ have come, for the accuser of our brethren has been thrown down, he who accuses them before our God day and night.

➤ 11 "And they overcame him because of the blood of the Lamb and because of the word of their testimony, and they did not love their life even when faced with death.

12 "For this reason, rejoice, O heavens and you who dwell in them. Woe to the earth and the sea, because the devil has come down to you, having great wrath, knowing that he has *only* a short time."

13 And when the dragon saw that he was thrown down to the earth, he persecuted the woman who gave birth to the male *child*.

14 But the two wings of the great eagle were given to the woman, so that she could fly into the wilderness to her place, where she *was nourished for a time and times and half a time, from the presence of the serpent.

15 And the serpent poured water like a river out of his mouth after the woman, so that he might cause her to be swept away with the flood.

16 But the earth helped the woman, and the earth opened its mouth and drank up the river which the dragon poured out of his mouth.

17 So the dragon was enraged with the woman, and went off to make war with the rest of her children, who keep the commandments of God and hold to the testimony of Jesus.

LIFE LESSONS

➤ **Revelation 12:11 — *"They overcame him because of the blood of the Lamb and because of the word of their testimony."***

*W*e cannot win our battles against Satan with swords, bullets, or bombs. Rather, our invincible weapons are salvation through Christ and the Word of God. These weapons are "divinely powerful for the destruction of fortresses" (2 Cor. 10:4).

➤ **Revelation 12:17 — *So the dragon was enraged with the woman, and went off to make war with the rest of her children, who keep the commandments of God and hold to the testimony of Jesus.***

*S*atan has a particular hatred for Christians who obey God and who work to represent Jesus to the best of their abilities.

DECEMBER 23

Habakkuk 1:1—3:19

1 THE oracle which Habakkuk the prophet saw.

2 How long, O LORD, will I call for help,
And You will not hear?
I cry out to You, "Violence!"
Yet You do not save.

3 Why do You make me see iniquity,
And cause *me* to look on wickedness?
Yes, destruction and violence are before me;
Strife exists and contention arises.

4 Therefore the law is ignored
And justice is never upheld.

For the wicked surround the righteous;
Therefore justice comes out perverted.

5 "Look among the nations! Observe!
Be astonished! Wonder!
Because *I am* doing something in your days—
You would not believe if you were told.

6 "For behold, I am raising up the Chaldeans,
That fierce and impetuous people
Who march throughout the earth
To seize dwelling places which are not theirs.

7 "They are dreaded and feared;
Their justice and authority originate with themselves.

8   "Their horses are swifter than
      leopards
    And keener than wolves in the
      evening.
    Their horsemen come galloping,
    Their horsemen come from afar;
    They fly like an eagle swooping
      down to devour.

9   "All of them come for violence.
    Their horde of faces *moves*
      forward.
    They collect captives like sand.

10   "They mock at kings
    And rulers are a laughing matter to
      them.
    They laugh at every fortress
    And heap up rubble to capture it.

11   "Then they will sweep through *like*
      the wind and pass on.
    But they will be held guilty,
    They whose strength is their god."

12   Are You not from everlasting,
    O Lord, my God, my Holy One?
    We will not die.
    You, O Lord, have appointed them
      to judge;
    And You, O Rock, have established
      them to correct.

13   *Your* eyes are too pure to approve
      evil,
    And You can not look on
      wickedness *with favor.*
    Why do You look with favor
    On those who deal treacherously?
    Why are You silent when the wicked
      swallow up
    Those more righteous than they?

14   *Why* have You made men like the
      fish of the sea,
    Like creeping things without a ruler
      over them?

15   *The Chaldeans* bring all of them up
      with a hook,
    Drag them away with their net,
    And gather them together in their
      fishing net.
    Therefore they rejoice and are glad.

16   Therefore they offer a sacrifice to
      their net
    And burn incense to their fishing
      net;
    Because through these things their
      catch is large,
    And their food is plentiful.

17   Will they therefore empty their net
    And continually slay nations
      without sparing?

2 I WILL stand on my guard post
    And station myself on the rampart;
    And I will keep watch to see what
      He will speak to me,
    And how I may reply when I am
      reproved.

2   Then the Lord answered me and
      said,
    "Record the vision
    And inscribe *it* on tablets,
    That the one who reads it may run.

3   "For the vision is yet for the
      appointed time;
    It hastens toward the goal and it
      will not fail.
    Though it tarries, wait for it;
    For it will certainly come, it will not
      delay.

4   "Behold, as for the proud one,
    His soul is not right within him;
    But the righteous will live by his
      faith.

5   "Furthermore, wine betrays the
      haughty man,
    So that he does not stay at home.
    He enlarges his appetite like Sheol,

LIFE LESSONS

➤ **Habakkuk 1:13 —** *Why are You silent when the wicked swallow up those more righteous than they?*

*W*e might prefer a world where God instantly judges every wrong, but that is not the world we have. Yet in His time, He will certainly judge all evil and reward all good.

➤ **Habakkuk 2:2 —** *"Record the vision and inscribe it on tablets, that the one who reads it may run."*

*G*od told Jeremiah, "Write all the words which I have spoken to you in a book" (Jer. 30:2). He also instructed Israel's kings to copy His Word (Deut. 17:18). Why? It is simple: We remember what we write.

➤ **Habakkuk 2:4 —** *"The righteous will live by his faith."*

*W*hy does God contrast pride with faith? Because pride stems from the belief that we know better than God, while faith understands we are completely dependent upon Him (Ps. 75:5–7; Heb. 11:1, 6).

And he is like death, never satisfied.
He also gathers to himself all nations
And collects to himself all peoples.

6 "Will not all of these take up a taunt-
song against him,
Even mockery *and* insinuations
against him
And say, 'Woe to him who increases
what is not his—
For how long—
And makes himself rich with loans?'

7 "Will not your creditors rise up
suddenly,
And those who collect from you
awaken?
Indeed, you will become plunder for
them.

8 "Because you have looted many
nations,
All the remainder of the peoples
will loot you—
Because of human bloodshed and
violence done to the land,
To the town and all its inhabitants.

9 "Woe to him who gets evil gain for
his house
To put his nest on high,
To be delivered from the hand of
calamity!

10 "You have devised a shameful thing
for your house
By cutting off many peoples;
So you are sinning against yourself.

11 "Surely the stone will cry out from
the wall,
And the rafter will answer it from
the framework.

12 "Woe to him who builds a city with
bloodshed
And founds a town with violence!

13 "Is it not indeed from the LORD of
hosts
That peoples toil for fire,
And nations grow weary for nothing?

14 "For the earth will be filled
With the knowledge of the glory of
the LORD,
As the waters cover the sea.

15 "Woe to you who make your
neighbors drink,
Who mix in your venom even to
make *them* drunk
So as to look on their nakedness!

16 "You will be filled with disgrace
rather than honor.
Now you yourself drink and expose
your *own* nakedness.

The cup in the LORD's right hand
will come around to you,
And utter disgrace *will come* upon
your glory.

17 "For the violence done to Lebanon
will overwhelm you,
And the devastation of *its* beasts by
which you terrified them,
Because of human bloodshed and
violence done to the land,
To the town and all its inhabitants.

18 "What profit is the idol when its
maker has carved it,
Or an image, a teacher of
falsehood?
For *its* maker trusts in his *own*
handiwork
When he fashions speechless idols.

19 "Woe to him who says to a *piece of*
wood, 'Awake!'
To a mute stone, 'Arise!'
And that is *your* teacher?
Behold, it is overlaid with gold and
silver,
And there is no breath at all inside it.

20 "But the LORD is in His holy temple.
Let all the earth be silent before
Him."

3 A PRAYER of Habakkuk the prophet,
according to Shigionoth.

2   LORD, I have heard the report about
You *and* I fear.
O LORD, revive Your work in the
midst of the years,
In the midst of the years make it
known;
In wrath remember mercy.

3   God comes from Teman,
And the Holy One from Mount
Paran.   Selah.
His splendor covers the heavens,
And the earth is full of His praise.

4   *His* radiance is like the sunlight;
He has rays *flashing* from His hand,
And there is the hiding of His
power.

5   Before Him goes pestilence,
And plague comes after Him.

6   He stood and surveyed the earth;
He looked and startled the nations.
Yes, the perpetual mountains were
shattered,
The ancient hills collapsed.
His ways are everlasting.

7   I saw the tents of Cushan under
distress,

LIFE PRINCIPLE 20

DISAPPOINTMENTS ARE INEVITABLE; DISCOURAGEMENT IS A CHOICE.

HABAKKUK 3:17–19

*E*veryone has known the ache of sadness that comes when life moves in an unanticipated, undesired direction. Disappointment may come as a result of a negative change in circumstances, a sudden reversal of plans, or a frustrating personal issue. If someone close to you behaves in a manner that lets you down, you may experience deep sensations of loss. For example if someone works spitefully to thwart your plans, you may be tempted to lash out against them. Yet, regardless of what has caused your disappointment, the dream you once cherished seems to be in ruins. You may not know how to respond because it is difficult to sort through your emotions.

Perhaps that was the case for Joseph, the Nazarene carpenter who was betrothed to the godly young woman named Mary. Like any Jewish man, he looked forward to the day when he would take a wife and start a family.

Then the news came.

Imagine the emotions of Joseph's heart when he heard that Mary was pregnant. What a devastating blow to his hopes and plans, for, according to the Law, "If there is a girl who is a virgin engaged to a man, and another man finds her in the city and lies with her, then you shall bring them both out to the gate of that city and you shall stone them to death; the girl, because she did not cry out in the city, and the man, because he has violated his neighbor's wife. Thus you shall purge the evil from among you" (Deut. 22:23, 24). Not only would he have no bride, but his betrothed would be put to death. The disappointment must have been overwhelming.

Matthew 1:19 shows that Joseph pondered a different course of action, perhaps trying to diffuse some of the terrible anguish of the situation: "Joseph her [betrothed] husband, being a righteous man and not wanting to disgrace her, planned to send her away secretly."

Yet, as we know, Mary had by no means violated the Law; and, in fact, God had very special plans for that pregnancy (Is. 7:14; Matt. 1:18; Luke 1:26–38). The Lord's angel told Mary, "You will conceive in your womb and bear a son, and you shall name Him Jesus. He will be great and will be called the Son of the Most High" (Luke 1:31, 32).

The Lord sent an angel to confirm His extraordinary plan to Joseph. He said, "Joseph, son of David, do not be afraid to take Mary as your wife; for the Child who has been conceived in her is of the Holy Spirit. She will bear a Son; and you shall call His name Jesus, for He will save His people from their sins" (Matt. 1:20, 21). Joseph did not allow his initial disappointment to give way to discouragement. Rather, he accepted God's will, obeyed the Lord, and brought Mary home to live with him, as a virgin, until the birth of Jesus (Matt. 1:24, 25).

The Lord has a unique plan for your life, too—one that does not change according to unexpected circumstances. When you confront a situation that does not line up with your understanding of how God wants your life to proceed, you must stop and look to Him for direction. Sometimes He allows disappointments to occur so that you will learn to rely on Him more fully—to walk by faith and not by sight. But never forget this: while disappointments are inevitable, discouragement is a choice. You should not allow the challenges that arise to steal your enthusiasm or confidence in Him.

In the daily disappointments that threaten to consume your emotional resources and deflect your attention away from the Lord, you have real hope and a real choice for joy and abundant living in Christ. Circumstances do not control you; Jesus does. You never have to be the victim of your feelings. You can choose to look to God, listen, learn, and move ahead. As you do, the wounded, dejected places in your heart and the scars of old disappointments will melt away in God's restoring love.

God does have blessings for you—more than you can imagine. Let go of disappointments and the fear of hoping and trusting again. God holds your future in His hands, and you will never lose by looking forward to what He has in store. ❖

The tent curtains of the land of
    Midian were trembling.
8 Did the LORD rage against the rivers,
    Or *was* Your anger against the
      rivers,
    Or *was* Your wrath against the sea,
    That You rode on Your horses,
    On Your chariots of salvation?
9 Your bow was made bare,
    The rods of chastisement were
      sworn.   Selah.
    You cleaved the earth with rivers.
10 The mountains saw You *and*
      quaked;
    The downpour of waters swept by.
    The deep uttered forth its voice,
    It lifted high its hands.
11 Sun *and* moon stood in their
      places;
    They went away at the light of Your
      arrows,
    At the radiance of Your gleaming
      spear.
12 In indignation You marched
      through the earth;
    In anger You trampled the nations.
13 You went forth for the salvation of
      Your people,
    For the salvation of Your anointed.
    You struck the head of the house of
      the evil
    To lay him open from thigh to neck.
               Selah.
14 You pierced with his own spears
    The head of his throngs.
    They stormed in to scatter us;
    Their exultation *was* like those
    Who devour the oppressed in
      secret.
15 You trampled on the sea with Your
      horses,
    On the surge of many waters.
16 I heard and my inward parts
      trembled,
    At the sound my lips quivered.
    Decay enters my bones,
    And in my place I tremble.
    Because I must wait quietly for the
      day of distress,
    For the people to arise *who* will
      invade us.
17 Though the fig tree should not
      blossom
    And there be no fruit on the vines,
    Though the yield of the olive should
      fail
    And the fields produce no food,

Though the flock should be cut off
    from the fold
    And there be no cattle in the stalls,
18 Yet I will exult in the LORD,
    I will rejoice in the God of my
      salvation.
19 The Lord GOD is my strength,
    And He has made my feet like
      hinds' *feet,*
    And makes me walk on my high
      places.
For the choir director, on my stringed
instruments.

Psalm 146:1–10

146 PRAISE the LORD!
      Praise the LORD, O my soul!
2 I will praise the LORD while I live;
    I will sing praises to my God while I
      have my being.
3 Do not trust in princes,
    In mortal man, in whom there is no
      salvation.
4 His spirit departs, he returns to the
      earth;
    In that very day his thoughts
      perish.
5 How blessed is he whose help is the
      God of Jacob,
    Whose hope is in the LORD his
      God,
6 Who made heaven and earth,
    The sea and all that is in them;
    Who keeps faith forever;
7 Who executes justice for the
      oppressed;
    Who gives food to the hungry.

LIFE LESSONS

➢ **Habakkuk 3:18** — *I will exult in the
LORD, I will rejoice in the God of my salvation.*

*H*ow should we respond when our
situations seems dire, even hopeless? What should we do when God
appears silent or allows us to endure
suffering? Trusting God means looking
beyond what we can see to what God
sees. If we want to honor Him as God,
we must continue to have faith in Him
and glorify Him in all we say and do,
regardless of the circumstances.

The LORD sets the prisoners free.
8   The LORD opens *the eyes of* the
      blind;
      The LORD raises up those who are
      bowed down;
      The LORD loves the righteous;
9   The LORD protects the strangers;
      He supports the fatherless and the
      widow,
      But He thwarts the way of the
      wicked.
10   The LORD will reign forever,
      Your God, O Zion, to all generations.
      Praise the LORD!

Proverbs 30:17

17   The eye that mocks a father
      And scorns a mother,
      The ravens of the valley will pick it
      out,
      And the young eagles will eat it.

Revelation 13:1–18

13 AND the dragon stood on the sand of the seashore.
Then I saw a beast coming up out of the sea, having ten horns and seven heads, and on his horns *were* ten diadems, and on his heads *were* blasphemous names.
2   And the beast which I saw was like a leopard, and his feet were like *those* of a bear, and his mouth like the mouth of a lion. And the dragon gave him his power and his throne and great authority.
3   *I saw* one of his heads as if it had been slain, and his fatal wound was healed. And the whole earth was amazed *and followed* after the beast;
4   they worshiped the dragon because he gave his authority to the beast; and they worshiped the beast, saying, "Who is like the beast, and who is able to wage war with him?"
5   There was given to him a mouth speaking arrogant words and blasphemies, and authority to act for forty-two months was given to him.
6   And he opened his mouth in blasphemies against God, to blaspheme His name and His tabernacle, *that is*, those who dwell in heaven.
7   It was also given to him to make war with the saints and to overcome them, and authority over every tribe and people and tongue and nation was given to him.
8   All who dwell on the earth will worship him, *everyone* whose name has not been written from the foundation of the world in the book of life of the Lamb who has been slain.
9   If anyone has an ear, let him hear.
10   If anyone *is destined* for captivity, to captivity he goes; if anyone kills with the sword, with the sword he must be killed. Here is the perseverance and the faith of the saints.
11   Then I saw another beast coming up out of the earth; and he had two horns like a lamb and he spoke as a dragon.
12   He exercises all the authority of the first beast in his presence. And he makes the earth and those who dwell in it to worship the first beast, whose fatal wound was healed.
13   He performs great signs, so that he even makes fire come down out of heaven to the earth in the presence of men.

LIFE LESSONS

➢ **Revelation 13:3 — *His fatal wound was healed. And the whole earth was amazed and followed after the beast.***

The beast—or Antichrist—will attempt to deceive the world by staging a false resurrection. However, only the Lord Jesus Christ can give eternal life. Though the enemy will counterfeit Christ's work, he will never be able to escape the everlasting condemnation that awaits him (Rev. 20:10). Neither will *anyone* who rejects Jesus (Rev. 20:11–15).

➢ **Revelation 13:5 — *There was given to him a mouth speaking arrogant words and blasphemies, and authority to act for forty-two months was given to him.***

The beast opposes the Lord and tries to destroy all that He loves, and no horror in history will compare with the Antichrist's reign of terror. However, the beast's time is short—God will strictly control the length of his rule—even what he can do. The Lord remains sovereign, regardless of all the enemy does.

14 And he deceives those who dwell on the earth because of the signs which it was given him to perform in the presence of the beast, telling those who dwell on the earth to make an image to the beast who *had the wound of the sword and has come to life.
15 And it was given to him to give breath to the image of the beast, so that the image of the beast would even speak and cause as many as do not worship the image of the beast to be killed.
16 And he causes all, the small and the great, and the rich and the poor, and the free men and the slaves, to be given a mark on their right hand or on their forehead,
17 and *he provides* that no one will be able to buy or to sell, except the one who has the mark, *either* the name of the beast or the number of his name.
18 Here is wisdom. Let him who has understanding calculate the number of the beast, for the number is that of a man; and his number is six hundred and sixty-six.

DECEMBER 24

◈ Zephaniah 1:1—3:20

1 THE word of the LORD which came to Zephaniah son of Cushi, son of Gedaliah, son of Amariah, son of Hezekiah, in the days of Josiah son of Amon, king of Judah:
2 "I will completely remove all *things* From the face of the earth," declares the LORD.
3 "I will remove man and beast;
I will remove the birds of the sky And the fish of the sea,
And the ruins along with the wicked;
And I will cut off man from the face of the earth," declares the LORD.
4 "So I will stretch out My hand against Judah
And against all the inhabitants of Jerusalem.
And I will cut off the remnant of Baal from this place,
And the names of the idolatrous priests along with the priests.
5 "And those who bow down on the housetops to the host of heaven,
And those who bow down *and* swear to the LORD and *yet* swear by Milcom,
6 And those who have turned back from following the LORD,
And those who have not sought the LORD or inquired of Him."
➤ 7 Be silent before the Lord GOD!
For the day of the LORD is near,

For the LORD has prepared a sacrifice,
He has consecrated His guests.
8 "Then it will come about on the day of the LORD's sacrifice
That I will punish the princes, the king's sons
And all who clothe themselves with foreign garments.
9 "And I will punish on that day all who leap on the *temple* threshold,
Who fill the house of their lord with violence and deceit.
10 "On that day," declares the LORD,
"There will be the sound of a cry from the Fish Gate,
A wail from the Second Quarter,
And a loud crash from the hills.
11 "Wail, O inhabitants of the Mortar,
For all the people of Canaan will be silenced;
All who weigh out silver will be cut off.
12 "It will come about at that time
That I will search Jerusalem with lamps,

LIFE LESSONS

➤ **Zephaniah 1:7 — *Be silent before the Lord GOD!***

*G*od calls us to silence before Him for many reasons. His awesome power and glory surpass all words. To hear His voice, we need to remain quiet and carefully listen. Anticipating His mighty work stills our mouths.

And I will punish the men
Who are stagnant in spirit,
Who say in their hearts,
'The LORD will not do good or evil!'
13 "Moreover, their wealth will become
   plunder
   And their houses desolate;
   Yes, they will build houses but not
      inhabit *them,*
   And plant vineyards but not drink
      their wine."
14 Near is the great day of the LORD,
   Near and coming very quickly;
   Listen, the day of the LORD!
   In it the warrior cries out bitterly.
15 A day of wrath is that day,
   A day of trouble and distress,
   A day of destruction and desolation,
   A day of darkness and gloom,
   A day of clouds and thick darkness,
16 A day of trumpet and battle cry
   Against the fortified cities
   And the high corner towers.
17 I will bring distress on men
   So that they will walk like the blind,
   Because they have sinned against
      the LORD;
   And their blood will be poured out
      like dust
   And their flesh like dung.
18 Neither their silver nor their gold
   Will be able to deliver them
   On the day of the LORD'S wrath;
   And all the earth will be devoured
   In the fire of His jealousy,
   For He will make a complete end,
   Indeed a terrifying one,
   Of all the inhabitants of the earth.

2 GATHER yourselves together, yes,
   gather,
   O nation without shame,
2 Before the decree takes effect—
   The day passes like the chaff—
   Before the burning anger of the
      LORD comes upon you,
   Before the day of the LORD'S anger
      comes upon you.
➤ 3 Seek the LORD,
   All you humble of the earth
   Who have carried out His ordinances;
   Seek righteousness, seek humility.
   Perhaps you will be hidden
   In the day of the LORD'S anger.
4 For Gaza will be abandoned
   And Ashkelon a desolation;
   Ashdod will be driven out at noon
   And Ekron will be uprooted.

5 Woe to the inhabitants of the
   seacoast,
   The nation of the Cherethites!
   The word of the LORD is against
      you,
   O Canaan, land of the Philistines;
   And I will destroy you
   So that there will be no inhabitant.
6 So the seacoast will be pastures,
   With caves for shepherds and folds
      for flocks.
7 And the coast will be
   For the remnant of the house of
      Judah,
   They will pasture on it.
   In the houses of Ashkelon they will
      lie down at evening;
   For the LORD their God will care for
      them
   And restore their fortune.
8 "I have heard the taunting of Moab
   And the revilings of the sons of
      Ammon,
   With which they have taunted My
      people
   And become arrogant against their
      territory.
9 "Therefore, as I live," declares the
   LORD of hosts,
   The God of Israel,

"Surely Moab will be like Sodom
And the sons of Ammon like
Gomorrah—
A place possessed by nettles and
salt pits,
And a perpetual desolation.
The remnant of My people will
plunder them
And the remainder of My nation
will inherit them."
10 This they will have in return for their
pride, because they have taunted and become arrogant against the people of the
LORD of hosts.
➤ 11 The LORD will be terrifying to them,
for He will starve all the gods of the
earth; and all the coastlands of the nations will bow down to Him, everyone
from his own place.
12 "You also, O Ethiopians, will be slain
by My sword."
13 And He will stretch out His hand
against the north
And destroy Assyria,
And He will make Nineveh a
desolation,
Parched like the wilderness.
14 Flocks will lie down in her midst,
All beasts which range in herds;
Both the pelican and the hedgehog
Will lodge in the tops of her pillars;
Birds will sing in the window,
Desolation will be on the threshold;
For He has laid bare the cedar work.
15 This is the exultant city
Which dwells securely,
Who says in her heart,
"I am, and there is no one besides
me."
How she has become a desolation,

LIFE LESSONS

➤ **Zephaniah 2:11** — *The LORD will be terrifying to them . . . and all the coastlands of the nations will bow down to Him, everyone from his own place.*

*T*he Lord wants the entire world to know Him, serve Him, worship Him, and love Him. One day it will be obvious to everyone everywhere that there is only one true God—there is no other (Is. 45:22–24; Rom. 14:7–11; Phil. 2:5–11). The gospel is for every kingdom, tribe, nation, and tongue on earth, and God commissions us to be His ambassadors (2 Cor. 5:20).

A resting place for beasts!
Everyone who passes by her will
hiss
And wave his hand *in contempt.*

3 WOE to her who is rebellious and
defiled,
The tyrannical city!
2 She heeded no voice,
She accepted no instruction.
She did not trust in the LORD,
She did not draw near to her God.
3 Her princes within her are roaring
lions,
Her judges are wolves at evening;
They leave nothing for the morning.
4 Her prophets are reckless,
treacherous men;
Her priests have profaned the
sanctuary.
They have done violence to the law.
5 The LORD is righteous within her;
He will do no injustice.
Every morning He brings His justice
to light;
He does not fail.
But the unjust knows no shame.
6 "I have cut off nations;
Their corner towers are in ruins.
I have made their streets desolate,
With no one passing by;
Their cities are laid waste,
Without a man, without an
inhabitant.
7 "I said, 'Surely you will revere Me,
Accept instruction.'
So her dwelling will not be cut off
According to all that I have
appointed concerning her.
But they were eager to corrupt all
their deeds.
8 "Therefore wait for Me," declares the
LORD,
"For the day when I rise up as a
witness.
Indeed, My decision is to gather
nations,
To assemble kingdoms,
To pour out on them My
indignation,
All My burning anger;
For all the earth will be devoured
By the fire of My zeal.
9 "For then I will give to the peoples
purified lips,
That all of them may call on the
name of the LORD,
To serve Him shoulder to shoulder.

How can I endure in my faith during hard times?

ZEPHANIAH 3:17

*Y*ou are God's masterpiece, and He has given you His Word as a testimony to the love and joy He has for you. Zephaniah 3:17 says, "The LORD your God is in your midst, a victorious warrior. He will exult over you with joy, He will be quiet in His love, He will rejoice over you with shouts of joy."

God rejoices over you and is transforming your life to reflect His goodness to others. He has an awesome plan for your life. You are not yet what you will be when you step into the eternal presence of God (1 Cor. 13:12; 1 John 3:2). Until that time, God is patiently molding and shaping you into the image of His Son. Therefore, you never have a reason to give up (Gal. 6:9). You are not alone! Jesus is with you, cheering you on to victory. He is at your side to strengthen and encourage you. When you fix your eyes on Him and not on your circumstances, you will begin to see life differently. Instead of thinking negatively, the Holy Spirit will teach you to think about the things of God—pure thoughts that honor Jesus Christ.

God also makes it clear that He loves you with an everlasting love and has pledged to never leave or forsake you (Deut. 31:6, 8; John 14:18; Heb. 13:5). He walks with you through disappointment and when you confess your sins, "He is faithful and righteous to forgive [your] sins and to cleanse [you] from all unrighteousness" (1 John 1:9). He has seen the finished portrait! While on your own you can do nothing, He knows that through Christ you can and will succeed (Phil. 1:6; 4:13). This does not mean that you won't suffer or feel pain. Jesus endured both, and yet He did not give up. He knew that in order to complete His mission He would have to endure until the end, and He wanted more than anything else to accomplish the Father's will.

How could He possibly bear the weight of all our sins and still remain victorious? Because He had an eternal perspective (Heb. 12:2). Long before it happened, Jesus saw the resurrection as a completed fact (Matt. 20:18, 19)—that after three days, He would rise from the grave to walk in victory over sin and death (1 Cor. 15:55–57). You can walk in confidence and triumph because Jesus is your example and His Spirit lives in you (Prov. 3:5–6). Like colors on an artist's palette, God can work through every situation in your life—even the one you are facing right now—to bring you closer to Himself (Jer. 29:11–13; Rom. 8:28).

10 "From beyond the rivers of Ethiopia
    My worshipers, My dispersed ones,
    Will bring My offerings.
11 "In that day you will feel no shame
    Because of all your deeds
    By which you have rebelled against
        Me;
    For then I will remove from your
        midst
    Your proud, exulting ones,
    And you will never again be
        haughty
    On My holy mountain.
12 "But I will leave among you
    A humble and lowly people,
    And they will take refuge in the
        name of the LORD.
13 "The remnant of Israel will do no
        wrong
    And tell no lies,
    Nor will a deceitful tongue
    Be found in their mouths;
    For they will feed and lie down
    With no one to make them tremble."
14 Shout for joy, O daughter of Zion!
    Shout *in triumph*, O Israel!

    Rejoice and exult with all *your*
        heart,
    O daughter of Jerusalem!
15 The LORD has taken away *His*
        judgments against you,
    He has cleared away your enemies.
    The King of Israel, the LORD, is in
        your midst;
    You will fear disaster no more.
16 In that day it will be said to
        Jerusalem:
    "Do not be afraid, O Zion;
    Do not let your hands fall limp.
17 "The LORD your God is in your midst,
    A victorious warrior.
    He will exult over you with joy,
    He will be quiet in His love,
    He will rejoice over you with shouts
        of joy.
18 "I will gather those who grieve about
        the appointed feasts—
    They came from you, O Zion;
    The reproach *of exile* is a burden on
        them.
19 "Behold, I am going to deal at that
        time

With all your oppressors,
I will save the lame
And gather the outcast,
And I will turn their shame into
     praise and renown
In all the earth.
20 "At that time I will bring you in,
Even at the time when I gather you
     together;
Indeed, I will give you renown and
     praise
Among all the peoples of the earth,
When I restore your fortunes before
     your eyes,"
Says the LORD.

✦ Psalm 147:1–6

147 PRAISE the LORD!
For it is good to sing praises to
our God;
For it is pleasant *and* praise is
     becoming.
2 The LORD builds up Jerusalem;
He gathers the outcasts of Israel.
3 He heals the brokenhearted
And binds up their wounds.
4 He counts the number of the stars;
He gives names to all of them.
5 Great is our Lord and abundant in
     strength;
His understanding is infinite.
6 The LORD supports the afflicted;
He brings down the wicked to the
     ground.

✦ Proverbs 30:18, 19

18 There are three things which are
     too wonderful for me,
Four which I do not understand:
19 The way of an eagle in the sky,
The way of a serpent on a rock,
The way of a ship in the middle of
     the sea,
And the way of a man with a maid.

✦ Revelation 14:1–20

14 THEN I looked, and behold, the
Lamb *was* standing on Mount Zion,

and with Him one hundred and forty-
four thousand, having His name and
the name of His Father written on their
foreheads.
2 And I heard a voice from heaven,
like the sound of many waters and like
the sound of loud thunder, and the voice
which I heard *was* like *the sound* of
harpists playing on their harps.
3 And they *sang a new song before
the throne and before the four living
creatures and the elders; and no one
could learn the song except the one hundred and forty-four thousand who had
been purchased from the earth.
4 These are the ones who have not
been defiled with women, for they have
kept themselves chaste. These *are* the
ones who follow the Lamb wherever He
goes. These have been purchased from
among men as first fruits to God and to
the Lamb.
5 And no lie was found in their mouth;
they are blameless.
6 And I saw another angel flying in
midheaven, having an eternal gospel to
preach to those who live on the earth,
and to every nation and tribe and tongue
and people;
7 and he said with a loud voice, "Fear
God, and give Him glory, because the
hour of His judgment has come; worship
Him who made the heaven and the earth
and sea and springs of waters."
8 And another angel, a second one,
followed, saying, "Fallen, fallen is Babylon the great, she who has made all the
nations drink of the wine of the passion
of her immorality."
9 Then another angel, a third one, followed them, saying with a loud voice,
"If anyone worships the beast and his
image, and receives a mark on his forehead or on his hand,

LIFE LESSONS

➢ **Revelation 14:7 — "Fear God, and give
Him glory, because the hour of His judgment has come."**

*M*odern believers do not often connect divine judgment with glory,
but the Bible does (Ex. 14:4, 17, 18; Ezek.
28:22; 39:21; John 8:50). God reveals His
majesty not only in loving acts of mercy,
but also in holy acts of vengeance.

10 he also will drink of the wine of the wrath of God, which is mixed in full strength in the cup of His anger; and he will be tormented with fire and brimstone in the presence of the holy angels and in the presence of the Lamb.

➤ 11 "And the smoke of their torment goes up forever and ever; they have no rest day and night, those who worship the beast and his image, and whoever receives the mark of his name."

12 Here is the perseverance of the saints who keep the commandments of God and their faith in Jesus.

13 And I heard a voice from heaven, saying, "Write, 'Blessed are the dead who die in the Lord from now on!'" "Yes," says the Spirit, "so that they may rest from their labors, for their deeds follow with them."

LIFE LESSONS

➤ **Revelation 14:11 —** *"The smoke of their torment goes up forever and ever; they have no rest day and night."*

*H*ell is a place of eternal suffering—the unredeemed souls of the lost are forever separated from God, the only One who could have made them whole (Rev. 20:15). "'There is no peace for the wicked,' says the LORD" (Is. 48:22).

---

14 Then I looked, and behold, a white cloud, and sitting on the cloud *was* one like a son of man, having a golden crown on His head and a sharp sickle in His hand.

15 And another angel came out of the temple, crying out with a loud voice to Him who sat on the cloud, "Put in your sickle and reap, for the hour to reap has come, because the harvest of the earth is ripe."

16 Then He who sat on the cloud swung His sickle over the earth, and the earth was reaped.

17 And another angel came out of the temple which is in heaven, and he also had a sharp sickle.

18 Then another angel, the one who has power over fire, came out from the altar; and he called with a loud voice to him who had the sharp sickle, saying, "Put in your sharp sickle and gather the clusters from the vine of the earth, because her grapes are ripe."

19 So the angel swung his sickle to the earth and gathered *the clusters from* the vine of the earth, and threw them into the great wine press of the wrath of God.

20 And the wine press was trodden outside the city, and blood came out from the wine press, up to the horses' bridles, for a distance of two hundred miles.

DECEMBER 25

Haggai 1:1—2:23

1 IN the second year of Darius the king, on the first day of the sixth month, the word of the LORD came by the prophet Haggai to Zerubbabel the son of Shealtiel, governor of Judah, and to Joshua the son of Jehozadak, the high priest, saying,

2 "Thus says the LORD of hosts, 'This people says, "The time has not come, *even* the time for the house of the LORD to be rebuilt."'"

3 Then the word of the LORD came by Haggai the prophet, saying,

4 "Is it time for you yourselves to dwell in your paneled houses while this house *lies* desolate?"

5 Now therefore, thus says the LORD of hosts, "Consider your ways!

6 "You have sown much, but harvest little; *you* eat, but *there is* not *enough* to be satisfied; *you* drink, but *there is* not *enough* to become drunk; *you* put on clothing, but no one is warm *enough*; and he who earns, earns wages *to put* into a purse with holes."

7 Thus says the LORD of hosts, "Consider your ways!

8 "Go up to the mountains, bring wood and rebuild the temple, that I may be pleased with it and be glorified," says the LORD.

9 "*You* look for much, but behold, *it comes* to little; when you bring *it* home, I blow it *away*. Why?" declares the LORD of hosts, "Because of My house which

LIFE LESSONS

➤ Haggai 1:7 — *"Consider your ways!"*

*W*e ought to stop and periodically review our lives in light of God's Word. Very often this is all it would take to alert us to a dangerous trend or to confirm that we are heading in the right direction.

lies desolate, while each of you runs to his own house.

10 "Therefore, because of you the sky has withheld its dew and the earth has withheld its produce.

11 "I called for a drought on the land, on the mountains, on the grain, on the new wine, on the oil, on what the ground produces, on men, on cattle, and on all the labor of your hands."

12 Then Zerubbabel the son of Shealtiel, and Joshua the son of Jehozadak, the high priest, with all the remnant of the people, obeyed the voice of the LORD their God and the words of Haggai the prophet, as the LORD their God had sent him. And the people showed reverence for the LORD.

➤ 13 Then Haggai, the messenger of the LORD, spoke by the commission of the LORD to the people saying, "'I am with you,' declares the LORD."

14 So the LORD stirred up the spirit of Zerubbabel the son of Shealtiel, governor of Judah, and the spirit of Joshua the son of Jehozadak, the high priest, and the spirit of all the remnant of the people; and they came and worked on the house of the LORD of hosts, their God,

15 on the twenty-fourth day of the sixth month in the second year of Darius the king.

2 ON the twenty-first of the seventh month, the word of the LORD came by Haggai the prophet saying,

2 "Speak now to Zerubbabel the son of Shealtiel, governor of Judah, and to Joshua the son of Jehozadak, the high priest, and to the remnant of the people saying,

3 'Who is left among you who saw this temple in its former glory? And how do you see it now? Does it not seem to you like nothing in comparison?

➤ 4 'But now take courage, Zerubbabel,' declares the LORD, 'take courage also,

Joshua son of Jehozadak, the high priest, and all you people of the land take courage,' declares the LORD, 'and work; for I am with you,' declares the LORD of hosts.

5 'As for the promise which I made you when you came out of Egypt, My Spirit is abiding in your midst; do not fear!'

6 "For thus says the LORD of hosts, 'Once more in a little while, I am going to shake the heavens and the earth, the sea also and the dry land.

7 'I will shake all the nations; and they will come with the wealth of all nations, and I will fill this house with glory,' says the LORD of hosts.

8 'The silver is Mine and the gold is Mine,' declares the LORD of hosts.

9 'The latter glory of this house will be greater than the former,' says the LORD of hosts, 'and in this place I will give peace,' declares the LORD of hosts."

10 On the twenty-fourth of the ninth *month,* in the second year of Darius, the word of the LORD came to Haggai the prophet, saying,

11 "Thus says the LORD of hosts, 'Ask now the priests *for* a ruling:

12 'If a man carries holy meat in the fold of his garment, and touches bread with this fold, or cooked food, wine, oil, or any *other* food, will it become holy?'" And the priests answered, "No."

LIFE LESSONS

➤ Haggai 1:13 — *" 'I am with you,' declares the LORD."*

*T*he Holy Spirit empowers us to carry out God's commands. He gives us the courage, strength, and ability we need. Do not hesitate to obey God in the midst of your trouble. He will equip you to carry out His commands.

➤ Haggai 2:4 — *"Take courage . . . and work; for I am with you."*

*G*od knows we tend to compare our current circumstances with what went before and to long for "the good old days." But He wants us to fix our eyes on Him and the still greater things He has planned for us. We can work hard and effectively for the Lord when we remember that He has promised to be with us. The awareness of God's presence energizes us for our work.

WHAT THE BIBLE SAYS ABOUT ⊚

Unexpected Glory

Haggai 2:6, 7

*I*t passes like a red, green, and gold blur of lights, wrapping paper, and familiar carols. Bombarded by gift requests, holiday programming, church pageants, and relatives, it seems that the most blessed of seasons may hit as hard and fast as a Texas tornado.

Christmas has commenced, yet instead of joy, peace, and glory to God, it produces physical, emotional, and financial overload. With all the activity and sensory stimulation, it is no surprise that we often become "thrill junkies." What a strange response to Christ's humble birth.

Yet something that we desperately need is to be quiet and observant instead of continually seeking the blast of overwhelming images. We need to learn that tranquility is to be cherished as a time to seek God. It is amazing how much we can miss when we don't take the time to be still and see how the Lord is moving.

Who would have expected that an ordinary young shepherd boy could defeat a mighty warrior like Goliath? And who would have guessed he would make a great king? Yet David was able to accomplish great things through God's provision (1 Sam. 17).

It was not through the spectacular and pretentious great wind, earthquake, or fire that God spoke to Elijah. When God spoke to Elijah, He did so in a gentle whisper (1 Kings 19).

When Christ chose the disciples that would take His message to the world, He did not choose those who graduated first in their class at rabbinical school. Instead, He chose ordinary, uneducated fishermen who were willing to follow Him and become fishers of men (Acts 4:13).

And no one in Israel would have anticipated how God would send the Messiah. After all, God had told the prophet Haggai, "I will shake all the nations; and they will come with the wealth of all nations, and I will fill this house with glory" (Hag. 2:6, 7). Who could have guessed that meant the birth of the Christ child would take place in a barn or that God's salvation would be accomplished on a cross? These were completely unexpected places to find God's phenomenal glory displayed. Truly, God works through the common to exhibit His great power.

Stopping in the midst of a hectic schedule and looking for ways God is working in our lives is an immensely valuable practice. It's in the simple things that the Father chooses to display His glory, and by looking for Him in the everyday occurrences of life, we learn that nothing in our lives is beyond His care.

The unimpressive shepherd boy became Israel's great king. Burly, unschooled fishermen became the great disciples of the faith. Elijah heard God in a whisper. And the Messiah was born in a manger. Ordinary things are used to display God's power, and He is still at work all around you, in the humble matters of life. Who knows what amazing things He can do through you?

Therefore, this Christmas, enjoy moments of silence and meditate upon God's character and Word. Learn to look for Him and to anticipate His glory in the most unexpected places. In doing so, you will strengthen the foundation of your growing relationship with Christ. ⊚

---

13 Then Haggai said, "If one who is unclean from a corpse touches any of these, will *the latter* become unclean?" And the priests answered, "It will become unclean."

14 Then Haggai said, "'So is this people. And so is this nation before Me,' declares the LORD, 'and so is every work of their hands; and what they offer there is unclean.

15 'But now, do consider from this day onward: before one stone was placed on another in the temple of the LORD,

16 from that time *when* one came to a *grain* heap of twenty *measures*, there would be only ten; and *when* one came to the wine vat to draw fifty measures, there would be *only* twenty.

17 'I smote you *and* every work of your hands with blasting wind, mildew and hail; yet you *did* not *come* back to Me,' declares the LORD.

18 'Do consider from this day onward, from the twenty-fourth day of the ninth *month;* from the day when the temple of the LORD was founded, consider:

LIFE LESSONS

➤ **Haggai 2:19 —** *"Is the seed still in the barn?"*

God asks for our obedience today so that He may bless us tomorrow. The Lord's blessings for obedience usually do not appear as soon as we obey; but He truly works for those who wait for Him.

➤ 19 'Is the seed still in the barn? Even including the vine, the fig tree, the pomegranate and the olive tree, it has not borne *fruit*. Yet from this day on I will bless *you*.'"
20 Then the word of the LORD came a second time to Haggai on the twenty-fourth *day* of the month, saying,
21 "Speak to Zerubbabel governor of Judah, saying, 'I am going to shake the heavens and the earth.
22 'I will overthrow the thrones of kingdoms and destroy the power of the kingdoms of the nations; and I will overthrow the chariots and their riders, and the horses and their riders will go down, everyone by the sword of another.'
23 'On that day,' declares the LORD of hosts, 'I will take you, Zerubbabel, son of Shealtiel, My servant,' declares the LORD, 'and I will make you like a signet *ring*, for I have chosen you,'" declares the LORD of hosts.

Psalm 147:7–11

7   Sing to the LORD with thanksgiving;
      Sing praises to our God on the lyre,
8   Who covers the heavens with clouds,
      Who provides rain for the earth,
      Who makes grass to grow on the mountains.
9   He gives to the beast its food,
      And to the young ravens which cry.
10   He does not delight in the strength of the horse;
      He does not take pleasure in the legs of a man.
✱ 11   The LORD favors those who fear Him,

Those who wait for His lovingkindness.

Proverbs 30:20

20   This is the way of an adulterous woman:
      She eats and wipes her mouth,
      And says, "I have done no wrong."

Revelation 15:1–8

15THEN I saw another sign in heaven, great and marvelous, seven angels who had seven plagues, *which are* the last, because in them the wrath of God is finished.
2   And I saw something like a sea of glass mixed with fire, and those who had been victorious over the beast and his image and the number of his name, standing on the sea of glass, holding harps of God.
3   And they *sang the song of Moses, the bond-servant of God, and the song of the Lamb, saying,
      "Great and marvelous are Your works,
      O Lord God, the Almighty;
      Righteous and true are Your ways, King of the nations!
4   "Who will not fear, O Lord, and glorify Your name?
      For You alone are holy;
      For ALL THE NATIONS WILL COME AND WORSHIP BEFORE YOU,
      FOR YOUR RIGHTEOUS ACTS HAVE BEEN REVEALED."

LIFE LESSONS

➤ **Revelation 15:4 —** *"Who will not fear, O Lord, and glorify Your name? For You alone are holy."*

One day, every knee shall bow and every tongue confess that Jesus is Lord (Rom. 14:11; Phil. 2:10). Some will prostrate themselves willingly before Him out of love, joy, worship, and respect. Others will bend their knees to Him out of dread. But everyone *will* bow.

5   After these things I looked, and the temple of the tabernacle of testimony in heaven was opened,
6   and the seven angels who had the seven plagues came out of the temple, clothed in linen, clean *and* bright, and girded around their chests with golden sashes.
7   Then one of the four living creatures gave to the seven angels seven golden bowls full of the wrath of God, who lives forever and ever.
8   And the temple was filled with smoke from the glory of God and from His power; and no one was able to enter the temple until the seven plagues of the seven angels were finished.

Zechariah 1:1—3:10

1 IN the eighth month of the second year of Darius, the word of the LORD came to Zechariah the prophet, the son of Berechiah, the son of Iddo saying,
2   "The LORD was very angry with your fathers.
3   "Therefore say to them, 'Thus says the LORD of hosts, "Return to Me," declares the LORD of hosts, "that I may return to you," says the LORD of hosts.
4   "Do not be like your fathers, to whom the former prophets proclaimed, saying, 'Thus says the LORD of hosts, "Return now from your evil ways and from your evil deeds."' But they did not listen or give heed to Me," declares the LORD.

5   "Your fathers, where are they? And the prophets, do they live forever?
6   "But did not My words and My statutes, which I commanded My servants the prophets, overtake your fathers? Then they repented and said, 'As the LORD of hosts purposed to do to us in accordance with our ways and our deeds, so He has dealt with us.'"'"
7   On the twenty-fourth day of the eleventh month, which is the month Shebat, in the second year of Darius, the word of the LORD came to Zechariah the prophet, the son of Berechiah, the son of Iddo, as follows:
8   I saw at night, and behold, a man was riding on a red horse, and he was standing among the myrtle trees which were in the ravine, with red, sorrel and white horses behind him.
9   Then I said, "My lord, what are these?" And the angel who was speaking with me said to me, "I will show you what these are."
10   And the man who was standing among the myrtle trees answered and said, "These are those whom the LORD has sent to patrol the earth."
11   So they answered the angel of the LORD who was standing among the myrtle trees and said, "We have patrolled the earth, and behold, all the earth is peaceful and quiet."
12   Then the angel of the LORD said, "O

LORD of hosts, how long will You have no compassion for Jerusalem and the cities of Judah, with which You have been indignant these seventy years?"

13 The LORD answered the angel who was speaking with me with gracious words, comforting words.

14 So the angel who was speaking with me said to me, "Proclaim, saying, 'Thus says the LORD of hosts, "I am exceedingly jealous for Jerusalem and Zion.

15 "But I am very angry with the nations who are at ease; for while I was only a little angry, they furthered the disaster."

16 'Therefore thus says the LORD, "I will return to Jerusalem with compassion; My house will be built in it," declares the LORD of hosts, "and a measuring line will be stretched over Jerusalem."'

17 "Again, proclaim, saying, 'Thus says the LORD of hosts, "My cities will again overflow with prosperity, and the LORD will again comfort Zion and again choose Jerusalem."'"

18 Then I lifted up my eyes and looked, and behold, *there were* four horns.

19 So I said to the angel who was speaking with me, "What are these?" And he answered me, "These are the horns which have scattered Judah, Israel and Jerusalem."

20 Then the LORD showed me four craftsmen.

21 I said, "What are these coming to do?" And he said, "These are the horns which have scattered Judah so that no man lifts up his head; but these *craftsmen* have come to terrify them, to throw down the horns of the nations who have lifted up *their* horns against the land of Judah in order to scatter it."

2 THEN I lifted up my eyes and looked, and behold, *there was* a man with a measuring line in his hand.

2 So I said, "Where are you going?" And he said to me, "To measure Jerusalem, to see how wide it is and how long it is."

3 And behold, the angel who was speaking with me was going out, and another angel was coming out to meet him,

4 and said to him, "Run, speak to that young man, saying, 'Jerusalem will be inhabited without walls because of the multitude of men and cattle within it.

5 'For I,' declares the LORD, 'will be a wall of fire around her, and I will be the glory in her midst.'"

6 "Ho there! Flee from the land of the north," declares the LORD, "for I have dispersed you as the four winds of the heavens," declares the LORD.

7 "Ho, Zion! Escape, you who are living with the daughter of Babylon."

8 For thus says the LORD of hosts, "After glory He has sent me against the nations which plunder you, for he who touches you, touches the apple of His eye.

9 "For behold, I will wave My hand over them so that they will be plunder for their slaves. Then you will know that the LORD of hosts has sent Me.

10 "Sing for joy and be glad, O daughter of Zion; for behold I am coming and I will dwell in your midst," declares the LORD.

11 "Many nations will join themselves to the LORD in that day and will become My people. Then I will dwell in your midst, and you will know that the LORD of hosts has sent Me to you.

12 "The LORD will possess Judah as His portion in the holy land, and will again choose Jerusalem.

13 "Be silent, all flesh, before the LORD; for He is aroused from His holy habitation."

3 THEN he showed me Joshua the high priest standing before the angel of the LORD, and Satan standing at his right hand to accuse him.

LIFE LESSONS

➤ Zechariah 2:10 — *"Sing for joy and be glad, O daughter of Zion; for behold I am coming and I will dwell in your midst."*

*W*hen we know that God is with us and that He desires to enjoy intimate fellowship with us, how can we not break out in song and rejoice with all our hearts? He loves us, and we can trust His promises because He puts His heart and infinite power into making sure they come to pass, just as He promised.

➤ Zechariah 2:11 — *"Many nations will join themselves to the LORD in that day and will become My people."*

*I*t has always been the Lord's plan to redeem people by the blood of Christ from "every tribe and tongue and people and nation" (Rev. 5:9). His love covers the world!

2 The LORD said to Satan, "The LORD rebuke you, Satan! Indeed, the LORD who has chosen Jerusalem rebuke you! Is this not a brand plucked from the fire?"

3 Now Joshua was clothed with filthy garments and standing before the angel.

4 He spoke and said to those who were standing before him, saying, "Remove the filthy garments from him." Again he said to him, "See, I have taken your iniquity away from you and will clothe you with festal robes."

5 Then I said, "Let them put a clean turban on his head." So they put a clean turban on his head and clothed him with garments, while the angel of the LORD was standing by.

6 And the angel of the LORD admonished Joshua, saying,

7 "Thus says the LORD of hosts, 'If you will walk in My ways and if you will perform My service, then you will also govern My house and also have charge of My courts, and I will grant you free access among these who are standing here.

8 'Now listen, Joshua the high priest, you and your friends who are sitting in front of you—indeed they are men who are a symbol, for behold, I am going to bring in My servant the Branch.

9 'For behold, the stone that I have set before Joshua; on one stone are seven eyes. Behold, I will engrave an inscription on it,' declares the LORD of hosts, 'and I will remove the iniquity of that land in one day.

10 'In that day,' declares the LORD of hosts, 'every one of you will invite his neighbor to sit under his vine and under his fig tree.'"

LIFE LESSONS

> **Zechariah 3:4 — "I have taken your iniquity away from you and I will clothe you with festal robes."**

*G*od says, "Since you laid aside the old self with its evil practices, and have put on the new self who is being renewed to a true knowledge according to the image of the One who created him" (Col. 3:9, 10). We must "clothe" ourselves with Jesus as we would a garment.

Psalm 147:12–20

12 Praise the LORD, O Jerusalem!
Praise your God, O Zion!
13 For He has strengthened the bars of your gates;
He has blessed your sons within you.
14 He makes peace in your borders;
He satisfies you with the finest of the wheat.
15 He sends forth His command to the earth;
His word runs very swiftly.
16 He gives snow like wool;
He scatters the frost like ashes.
17 He casts forth His ice as fragments;
Who can stand before His cold?
18 He sends forth His word and melts them;
He causes His wind to blow and the waters to flow.
19 He declares His words to Jacob,
His statutes and His ordinances to Israel.
20 He has not dealt thus with any nation;
And as for His ordinances, they have not known them.
Praise the LORD!

Proverbs 30:21–23

21 Under three things the earth quakes,
And under four, it cannot bear up:
22 Under a slave when he becomes king,
And a fool when he is satisfied with food,
23 Under an unloved woman when she gets a husband,
And a maidservant when she supplants her mistress.

Revelation 16:1–21

16 THEN I heard a loud voice from the temple, saying to the seven angels, "Go and pour out on the earth the seven bowls of the wrath of God."

WHAT THE BIBLE SAYS ABOUT ◉

Never Give Up

Psalm 147:12–18

*W*inston Churchill, the United Kingdom's Prime Minister during World War II, included a now-famous quote in a speech to students of his former school: "Never give in—never, never, never, never, in nothing great or small, large or petty . . . Never yield to force; never yield to the apparently overwhelming might of the enemy."

As Christians, we are called to wait on God until He acts on our behalf. In order to resist the urge to give up, we must not focus on our circumstances; rather we must focus on the power of the very One who protects us.

Speaking about Moses, Hebrews 11:27 says, "He endured, as seeing Him who is unseen." Moses consistently looked for God and His will. Standing on the shore of the Red Sea while the Egyptians prepared an attack, Moses clung to God's promise of protection and called out, "Do not fear! Stand by and see the salvation of the LORD" (Ex. 14:13). God parted the sea and the Israelites escaped what seemed to be an impossible situation. Moses triumphed

over many dangerous and difficult situations because he was committed to doing God's work and was focused on the Lord.

Psalm 147:12–15 tells us, "Praise the LORD, O Jerusalem . . . He has strengthened the bars of your gates; He has blessed your sons within you. He makes peace in your borders; He satisfies you with the finest of the wheat. He sends forth His command to the earth; His word runs very swiftly." God strengthens us, protects us, and provides whatever we need to serve Him—no matter how dire the situation may appear or how vulnerable we feel.

Too often, believers are distracted by their circumstances. When the Lord's will calls us to step out in faith, we sometimes falter. But a genuine commitment to God with no exceptions means nothing can induce us to give up.

Our unchanging Lord never deserts His children; He encourages us to cast our cares on Him (Heb. 13:5, 8; 1 Pet. 5:7) and to remember that although we may not see Him, He is continually working out His will (2 Cor. 4:16–18).

Even now He is answering you. Even now He is sending out His command, and His word is running very swiftly on your behalf. Therefore, remember His power and faithfulness whenever you are tempted to quit. Put your faith in Him, cling to His promises, and commit to His way. Never give up! ◉

---

2 So the first *angel* went and poured out his bowl on the earth; and it became a loathsome and malignant sore on the people who had the mark of the beast and who worshiped his image.

3 The second *angel* poured out his bowl into the sea, and it became blood like *that* of a dead man; and every living thing in the sea died.

4 Then the third *angel* poured out his bowl into the rivers and the springs of waters; and they became blood.

5 And I heard the angel of the waters saying, "Righteous are You, who are and who were, O Holy One, because You judged these things;

6 for they poured out the blood of saints and prophets, and You have given them blood to drink. They deserve it."

7 And I heard the altar saying, "Yes, O Lord God, the Almighty, true and righteous are Your judgments."

8 The fourth *angel* poured out his bowl

upon the sun, and it was given to it to scorch men with fire.

9 Men were scorched with fierce heat; and they blasphemed the name of God who has the power over these plagues, and they did not repent so as to give Him glory.

10 Then the fifth *angel* poured out his bowl on the throne of the beast, and his kingdom became darkened; and they gnawed their tongues because of pain,

11 and they blasphemed the God of heaven because of their pains and their sores; and they did not repent of their deeds.

12 The sixth *angel* poured out his bowl on the great river, the Euphrates; and its water was dried up, so that the way would be prepared for the kings from the east.

13 And I saw *coming* out of the mouth of the dragon and out of the mouth of the beast and out of the mouth of the false prophet, three unclean spirits like frogs;

14 for they are spirits of demons, performing signs, which go out to the kings of the whole world, to gather them together for the war of the great day of God, the Almighty.

> 15 ("Behold, I am coming like a thief. Blessed is the one who stays awake and keeps his clothes, so that he will not walk about naked and men will not see his shame.")

16 And they gathered them together to the place which in Hebrew is called Har-Magedon.

17 Then the seventh *angel* poured out his bowl upon the air, and a loud voice came out of the temple from the throne, saying, "It is done."

18 And there were flashes of lightning and sounds and peals of thunder; and there was a great earthquake, such as there had not been since man came to be upon the earth, so great an earthquake *was it, and* so mighty.

19 The great city was split into three parts, and the cities of the nations fell.

Babylon the great was remembered before God, to give her the cup of the wine of His fierce wrath.

20 And every island fled away, and the mountains were not found.

21 And huge hailstones, about one hundred pounds each, *came down from heaven upon men; and men blasphemed God because of the plague of the hail, because its plague *was extremely severe.

Zechariah 4:1—6:15

4 THEN the angel who was speaking with me returned and roused me, as a man who is awakened from his sleep.

2 He said to me, "What do you see?" And I said, "I see, and behold, a lampstand all of gold with its bowl on the top of it, and its seven lamps on it with seven spouts belonging to each of the lamps which are on the top of it;

3 also two olive trees by it, one on the right side of the bowl and the other on its left side."

4 Then I said to the angel who was speaking with me saying, "What are these, my lord?"

> 5 So the angel who was speaking with me answered and said to me, "Do you not know what these are?" And I said, "No, my lord."

6 Then he said to me, "This is the word of the LORD to Zerubbabel saying, 'Not by might nor by power, but by My Spirit,' says the LORD of hosts.

7 'What are you, O great mountain? Before Zerubbabel *you will become* a plain; and he will bring forth the top stone with shouts of "Grace, grace to it!"' "

8 Also the word of the LORD came to me, saying,

9 "The hands of Zerubbabel have laid the foundation of this house, and his hands will finish *it*. Then you will know that the LORD of hosts has sent me to you.

10 "For who has despised the day of small things? But these seven will be glad when they see the plumb line in the hand of Zerubbabel—*these are* the

➤ **Zechariah 4:10 —** *"Who has despised the day of small things?"*

*N*ever despise the small things God asks you to do, for a basic principle of spiritual growth is that God gives bigger and greater things and responsibilities to those who faithfully handle the small things (Luke 16:10).

---

eyes of the LORD which range to and fro throughout the earth."

11　Then I said to him, "What are these two olive trees on the right of the lampstand and on its left?"

12　And I answered the second time and said to him, "What are the two olive branches which are beside the two golden pipes, which empty the golden *oil* from themselves?"

13　So he answered me, saying, "Do you

ANSWERS TO LIFE'S QUESTIONS

How can I avoid burnout in doing God's work?

ZECHARIAH 4:6, 7

*F*or decades, the Jews that were held in Babylonian captivity prayed for God to allow them to return to Jerusalem so they could rebuild the temple and restore the land they had once called home (Ps. 137:1–6). God answered by sending King Cyrus of Persia to overthrow the Babylonians and send the Jews back to the Promised Land. In Ezra 1:2, 3, Cyrus declared, "The LORD, the God of heaven, has given me all the kingdoms of the earth and He has appointed me to build Him a house in Jerusalem, which is in Judah. Whoever there is among you of all His people, may his God be with him! Let him go up to Jerusalem which is in Judah and rebuild the house of the LORD, the God of Israel."

Many took the opportunity and returned to Jerusalem to accomplish the monumental task of restoration. Unfortunately, the work was very challenging and the people became disheartened. When they ran into opposition, they abandoned the project altogether. For sixteen years the work stood at a standstill.

Do you ever wonder how people serving the living God could become so discouraged or distracted that they would walk away from the important task God had called them to do? In most cases, it seems to make little sense. Sure, there are pressures, but stress is a normal part of life, especially when you are in a position of responsibility. Yet, there is a common reason why many of God's servants are unsuccessful, and it is this: they do not do His work in His way. Consequently, they become easily stressed, distracted, disappointed and face failure.

God knew the people, like their predecessors, would face opposition. To prepare them

for what lay ahead, He encouraged them through the prophet Zechariah, who spoke these memorial words: "'Not by might nor by power, but by My Spirit,' says the LORD of hosts" (Zech. 4:6). He encouraged them that He did not expect them to accomplish the work on their own. On the contrary, the construction of the temple could only be completed if they would trust and obey Him.

There are two ways to approach God's work. First, you can do it in the flesh, depending on your own influence, personality, gifts, resources, education, and experience. Or second, you can accomplish the task God's way—through the direction of and in the power of the Holy Spirit. What is the difference? First Corinthians 3:13–15 explains, "Each man's work will become evident; for the day will show it because it is *to be* revealed with fire, and the fire itself will test the quality of each man's work. If any man's work which he has built on it remains, he will receive a reward. If any man's work is burned up, he will suffer loss." What is the work that will be consumed? Anything we do according to the flesh—for ourselves and not in keeping with God's plans and commandments. In the end, the only things that will remain are those things that have been done in obedience to Him.

As believers, we have been commissioned to be involved in what He is doing throughout the world (Matt. 28:19, 20; Acts 1:8). We can be confident that there is no immovable obstacle or unconquerable challenge. When God's Spirit is at work through us, we will accomplish the goals He helps us to set. When we submit to His plan, we gain fresh strength and courage. No matter how overwhelming, complicated, or impossible the task may seem, God provides exactly what we need. He also assumes full responsibility for helping us reach these goals. When we obey Him, He does mighty things. We will never go wrong trusting the Savior.

not know what these are?" And I said, "No, my lord."

14 Then he said, "These are the two anointed ones who are standing by the Lord of the whole earth."

5 THEN I lifted up my eyes again and looked, and behold, *there was* a flying scroll.

2 And he said to me, "What do you see?" And I answered, "I see a flying scroll; its length is twenty cubits and its width ten cubits."

3 Then he said to me, "This is the curse that is going forth over the face of the whole land; surely everyone who steals will be purged away according to the writing on one side, and everyone who swears will be purged away according to the writing on the other side.

4 "I will make it go forth," declares the LORD of hosts, "and it will enter the house of the thief and the house of the one who swears falsely by My name; and it will spend the night within that house and consume it with its timber and stones."

5 Then the angel who was speaking with me went out and said to me, "Lift up now your eyes and see what this is going forth."

6 I said, "What is it?" And he said, "This is the ephah going forth." Again he said, "This is their appearance in all the land

7 (and behold, a lead cover was lifted up); and this is a woman sitting inside the ephah."

8 Then he said, "This is Wickedness!" And he threw her down into the middle of the ephah and cast the lead weight on its opening.

9 Then I lifted up my eyes and looked, and there two women were coming out with the wind in their wings; and they had wings like the wings of a stork, and they lifted up the ephah between the earth and the heavens.

10 I said to the angel who was speaking with me, "Where are they taking the ephah?"

11 Then he said to me, "To build a temple for her in the land of Shinar; and when it is prepared, she will be set there on her own pedestal."

6 NOW I lifted up my eyes again and looked, and behold, four chariots were coming forth from between the two mountains; and the mountains *were* bronze mountains.

2 With the first chariot *were* red horses, with the second chariot black horses,

3 with the third chariot white horses, and with the fourth chariot strong dappled horses.

4 Then I spoke and said to the angel who was speaking with me, "What are these, my lord?"

5 The angel replied to me, "These are the four spirits of heaven, going forth after standing before the Lord of all the earth,

6 with one of which the black horses are going forth to the north country; and the white ones go forth after them, while the dappled ones go forth to the south country.

7 "When the strong ones went out, they were eager to go to patrol the earth." And He said, "Go, patrol the earth." So they patrolled the earth.

8 Then He cried out to me and spoke to me saying, "See, those who are going to the land of the north have appeased My wrath in the land of the north."

9 The word of the LORD also came to me, saying,

10 "Take *an offering* from the exiles, from Heldai, Tobijah and Jedaiah; and you go the same day and enter the house of Josiah the son of Zephaniah, where they have arrived from Babylon.

11 "Take silver and gold, make an *ornate* crown and set *it* on the head of Joshua the son of Jehozadak, the high priest.

12 "Then say to him, 'Thus says the LORD of hosts, "Behold, a man whose name is Branch, for He will branch out from where He is; and He will build the temple of the LORD.

13 "Yes, it is He who will build the temple of the LORD, and He who will bear the honor and sit and rule on His throne. Thus, He will be a priest on His throne, and the counsel of peace will be between the two offices."'

14 "Now the crown will become a reminder in the temple of the LORD to Helem, Tobijah, Jedaiah and Hen the son of Zephaniah.

15 "Those who are far off will come and build the temple of the LORD." Then you will know that the LORD of hosts has sent

me to you. And it will take place if you completely obey the LORD your God.

Psalm 148:1–6

148 PRAISE the LORD!
Praise the LORD from the heavens;
Praise Him in the heights!

2 Praise Him, all His angels;
Praise Him, all His hosts!

3 Praise Him, sun and moon;
Praise Him, all stars of light!

4 Praise Him, highest heavens,
And the waters that are above the heavens!

5 Let them praise the name of the LORD,
For He commanded and they were created.

6 He has also established them forever and ever;
He has made a decree which will not pass away.

Proverbs 30:24–28

24 Four things are small on the earth,
But they are exceedingly wise:

25 The ants are not a strong people,
But they prepare their food in the summer;

26 The shephanim are not mighty people,
Yet they make their houses in the rocks;

27 The locusts have no king,
Yet all of them go out in ranks;

28 The lizard you may grasp with the hands,
Yet it is in kings' palaces.

Revelation 17:1–18

17 THEN one of the seven angels who had the seven bowls came and spoke with me, saying, "Come here, I will show you the judgment of the great harlot who sits on many waters,

2 with whom the kings of the earth committed *acts of* immorality, and those who dwell on the earth were made drunk with the wine of her immorality."

3 And he carried me away in the Spirit into a wilderness; and I saw a woman sitting on a scarlet beast, full of blasphemous names, having seven heads and ten horns.

4 The woman was clothed in purple and scarlet, and adorned with gold and precious stones and pearls, having in her hand a gold cup full of abominations and of the unclean things of her immorality,

5 and on her forehead a name *was* written, a mystery, "BABYLON THE GREAT, THE MOTHER OF HARLOTS AND OF THE ABOMINATIONS OF THE EARTH."

6 And I saw the woman drunk with the blood of the saints, and with the blood of the witnesses of Jesus. When I saw her, I wondered greatly.

7 And the angel said to me, "Why do you wonder? I will tell you the mystery of the woman and of the beast that carries her, which has the seven heads and the ten horns.

8 "The beast that you saw was, and is not, and is about to come up out of the abyss and go to destruction. And those who dwell on the earth, whose name has not been written in the book of life from the foundation of the world, will wonder

when they see the beast, that he was and is not and will come.

9 "Here is the mind which has wisdom. The seven heads are seven mountains on which the woman sits,

10 and they are seven kings; five have fallen, one is, the other has not yet come; and when he comes, he must remain a little while.

11 "The beast which was and is not, is himself also an eighth and is *one* of the seven, and he goes to destruction.

12 "The ten horns which you saw are ten kings who have not yet received a kingdom, but they receive authority as kings with the beast for one hour.

13 "These have one purpose, and they give their power and authority to the beast.

14 "These will wage war against the Lamb, and the Lamb will overcome them, because He is Lord of lords and King of kings, and those who are with Him *are the* called and chosen and faithful."

15 And he *said to me, "The waters which you saw where the harlot sits, are peoples and multitudes and nations and tongues.

16 "And the ten horns which you saw, and the beast, these will hate the harlot and will make her desolate and naked, and will eat her flesh and will burn her up with fire.

17 "For God has put it in their hearts to execute His purpose by having a common purpose, and by giving their kingdom to the beast, until the words of God will be fulfilled.

18 "The woman whom you saw is the great city, which reigns over the kings of the earth."

LIFE LESSONS

➤ Revelation 17:14 — "These will wage war against the Lamb, and the Lamb will overcome them, because He is Lord of lords and King of kings, and those who are with Him are the called and chosen and faithful."

*T*hese kings will ultimately do battle with the Lord at His Second Coming (Rev. 19:19–21). It is always foolish for anyone to think that they can openly oppose the sovereign Lord of the universe or those He loves. However, this is exactly what the kings who follow the beast will do. And they will be soundly defeated for all eternity (Rev. 20:10–15).

➤ Revelation 17:17 — "God has put it in their hearts to execute His purpose by having a common purpose, and by giving their kingdom to the beast, until the words of God will be fulfilled."

*A*lthough the Lord will give the wicked "over to a depraved mind, to do those things which are not proper" (Rom. 1:28), it does not mean He relinquishes all control over them. Ultimately, no one can do anything outside of God's permissive will, and He can even use the alliance of evil rulers to serve His eternal purposes and glorify Himself.

Zechariah 7:1—9:17

DECEMBER 28

7 IN the fourth year of King Darius, the word of the LORD came to Zechariah on the fourth *day* of the ninth month, *which is* Chislev.

2 Now *the town of* Bethel had sent Sharezer and Regemmelech and their men to seek the favor of the LORD,

3 speaking to the priests who belong to the house of the LORD of hosts, and to the prophets, saying, "Shall I weep in the fifth month and abstain, as I have done these many years?"

4 Then the word of the LORD of hosts came to me, saying,

5 "Say to all the people of the land and to the priests, 'When you fasted and mourned in the fifth and seventh months these seventy years, was it actually for Me that you fasted?

6 'When you eat and drink, do you not eat for yourselves and do you not drink for yourselves?

7 'Are not *these* the words which the

LORD proclaimed by the former prophets, when Jerusalem was inhabited and prosperous along with its cities around it, and the Negev and the foothills were inhabited?'"

8 Then the word of the LORD came to Zechariah saying,

➤ 9 "Thus has the LORD of hosts said, 'Dispense true justice and practice kindness and compassion each to his brother;

10 and do not oppress the widow or the orphan, the stranger or the poor; and do not devise evil in your hearts against one another.'

11 "But they refused to pay attention and turned a stubborn shoulder and stopped their ears from hearing.

12 "They made their hearts *like* flint so that they could not hear the law and the words which the LORD of hosts had sent by His Spirit through the former prophets; therefore great wrath came from the LORD of hosts.

13 "And just as He called and they would not listen, so they called and I would not listen," says the LORD of hosts;

14 "but I scattered them with a storm wind among all the nations whom they have not known. Thus the land is desolated behind them so that no one went back and forth, for they made the pleasant land desolate."

8 THEN the word of the LORD of hosts came, saying,

2 "Thus says the LORD of hosts, 'I am exceedingly jealous for Zion, yes, with great wrath I am jealous for her.'

3 "Thus says the LORD, 'I will return to Zion and will dwell in the midst of Jerusalem. Then Jerusalem will be called the City of Truth, and the mountain of the LORD of hosts *will be called* the Holy Mountain.'

4 "Thus says the LORD of hosts, 'Old men and old women will again sit in the streets of Jerusalem, each man with his staff in his hand because of age.

5 'And the streets of the city will be filled with boys and girls playing in its streets.'

6 "Thus says the LORD of hosts, 'If it is too difficult in the sight of the remnant of this people in those days, will it also be too difficult in My sight?' declares the LORD of hosts.

7 "Thus says the LORD of hosts, 'Behold, I am going to save My people from the land of the east and from the land of the west;

8 and I will bring them *back* and they will live in the midst of Jerusalem; and they shall be My people, and I will be their God in truth and righteousness.'

9 "Thus says the LORD of hosts, 'Let ◄ your hands be strong, you who are listening in these days to these words from the mouth of the prophets, *those* who *spoke* in the day that the foundation of the house of the LORD of hosts was laid, to the end that the temple might be built.

10 'For before those days there was no wage for man or any wage for animal; and for him who went out or came in there was no peace because of his enemies, and I set all men one against another.

11 'But now I will not treat the remnant of this people as in the former days,' declares the LORD of hosts.

12 'For *there will be* peace for the seed: the vine will yield its fruit, the land will yield its produce and the heavens will give their dew; and I will cause the remnant of this people to inherit all these *things*.

13 'It will come about that just as you were a curse among the nations, O house

---

LIFE LESSONS

➤ **Zechariah 7:9** — *"Dispense true justice and practice kindness and compassion each to his brother."*

*G*od is not interested in religious observance or sacred ritual apart from a genuine, heart-felt, intimate relationship with Him. A genuine and dynamic relationship with the Lord leads naturally to genuine and dynamic relationships with others in which you seek their best and treat them as you would like to be treated.

➤ **Zechariah 8:9** — *"Let your hands be strong, you who are listening in these days to these words by the mouth of the prophets."*

*I*f you feel weak and need spiritual strength, determine right now to spend some extended time in the Word of God. The Father delights to give us strength through His Word—but we have to be taking it in and meditating on it.

of Judah and house of Israel, so I will save you that you may become a blessing. Do not fear; let your hands be strong.'

14 "For thus says the LORD of hosts, 'Just as I purposed to do harm to you when your fathers provoked Me to wrath,' says the LORD of hosts, 'and I have not relented,

15 so I have again purposed in these days to do good to Jerusalem and to the house of Judah. Do not fear!

16 'These are the things which you should do: speak the truth to one another; judge with truth and judgment for peace in your gates.

17 'Also let none of you devise evil in your heart against another, and do not love perjury; for all these are what I hate,' declares the LORD."

18 Then the word of the LORD of hosts came to me, saying,

19 "Thus says the LORD of hosts, 'The fast of the fourth, the fast of the fifth, the fast of the seventh and the fast of the tenth *months* will become joy, gladness, and cheerful feasts for the house of Judah; so love truth and peace.'

20 "Thus says the LORD of hosts, '*It will* yet *be* that peoples will come, even the inhabitants of many cities.

➤ 21 'The inhabitants of one will go to another, saying, "Let us go at once to entreat the favor of the LORD, and to seek the LORD of hosts; I will also go."

22 'So many peoples and mighty nations will come to seek the LORD of hosts in Jerusalem and to entreat the favor of the LORD.'

23 "Thus says the LORD of hosts, 'In those days ten men from all the nations will grasp the garment of a Jew, saying, "Let us go with you, for we have heard that God is with you."'"

9 THE burden of the word of the LORD is against the land of Hadrach, with Damascus as its resting place (for the eyes of men, especially of all the tribes of Israel, are toward the LORD),

2 And Hamath also, which borders on it;
Tyre and Sidon, though they are very wise.

3 For Tyre built herself a fortress
And piled up silver like dust,
And gold like the mire of the streets.

4 Behold, the Lord will dispossess her
And cast her wealth into the sea;
And she will be consumed with fire.

5 Ashkelon will see *it* and be afraid.
Gaza too will writhe in great pain;
Also Ekron, for her expectation has been confounded.
Moreover, the king will perish from Gaza,
And Ashkelon will not be inhabited.

6 And a mongrel race will dwell in Ashdod,
And I will cut off the pride of the Philistines.

7 And I will remove their blood from their mouth
And their detestable things from between their teeth.
Then they also will be a remnant for our God,
And be like a clan in Judah,
And Ekron like a Jebusite.

8 But I will camp around My house because of an army,
Because of him who passes by and returns;
And no oppressor will pass over them anymore,
For now I have seen with My eyes.

LIFE LESSONS

➤ **Zechariah 8:21 —** *"Let us go at once to entreat the favor of the LORD."*

*P*rayer needs to be continual, God-centered, and personal. Occasional prayers will not cut it. Mere ritual will not cut it. Rote prayers will not cut it. We must daily seek the Lord through our heart-felt prayers.

➤ **Zechariah 9:9 —** *"Your king is coming to you; He is just and endowed with salvation, humble, and mounted on a donkey."*

*W*e serve a just, humble Savior who doesn't wait for us to make our way to Him but who willingly comes to us. How could we not praise, worship, and gladly welcome such a glorious King?

➤ 9 Rejoice greatly, O daughter of Zion!
    Shout *in triumph*, O daughter of
    Jerusalem!
✳   Behold, your king is coming to you;
    He is just and endowed with
      salvation,
    Humble, and mounted on a donkey,
    Even on a colt, the foal of a donkey.
10 I will cut off the chariot from
      Ephraim
    And the horse from Jerusalem;
    And the bow of war will be cut off.
    And He will speak peace to the
      nations;
    And His dominion will be from sea
      to sea,
    And from the River to the ends of
      the earth.
11 As for you also, because of the
      blood of *My* covenant with you,
    I have set your prisoners free from
      the waterless pit.
12 Return to the stronghold,
      O prisoners who have the hope;
    This very day I am declaring that I
      will restore double to you.
13 For I will bend Judah as My bow,
    I will fill the bow with Ephraim.
    And I will stir up your sons, O Zion,
      against your sons, O Greece;
    And I will make you like a warrior's
      sword.
14 Then the Lord will appear over
      them,
    And His arrow will go forth like
      lightning;
    And the Lord God will blow the
      trumpet,
    And will march in the storm winds
      of the south.
15 The Lord of hosts will defend them.
    And they will devour and trample
      on the sling stones;
    And they will drink *and* be
      boisterous as with wine;
    And they will be filled like a
      sacrificial basin,
    Drenched like the corners of the
      altar.
16 And the Lord their God will save
      them in that day
    As the flock of His people;
    For *they are as* the stones of a
      crown,
    Sparkling in His land.
17 For what comeliness and beauty
      will be theirs!

    Grain will make the young men
      flourish, and new wine the virgins.

◈ Psalm 148:7–14

7 Praise the Lord from the earth,
    Sea monsters and all deeps;
8 Fire and hail, snow and clouds;
    Stormy wind, fulfilling His word;
9 Mountains and all hills;
    Fruit trees and all cedars;
10 Beasts and all cattle;
    Creeping things and winged fowl;
11 Kings of the earth and all peoples;
    Princes and all judges of the earth;
12 Both young men and virgins;
    Old men and children.
13 Let them praise the name of the
      Lord,
    For His name alone is exalted;   ✳
    His glory is above earth and heaven.
14 And He has lifted up a horn for His
      people,
    Praise for all His godly ones;
    Even for the sons of Israel, a people
      near to Him.
    Praise the Lord!

◈ Proverbs 30:29–31

29 There are three things which are
      stately in *their* march,
    Even four which are stately when
      they walk:
30 The lion *which* is mighty among
      beasts
    And does not retreat before any,
31 The strutting rooster, the male goat
      also,
    And a king *when his* army is with
      him.

◈ Revelation 18:1–24

18 AFTER these things I saw another
angel coming down from heaven,
having great authority, and the earth
was illumined with his glory.
2   And he cried out with a mighty
voice, saying, "Fallen, fallen is Babylon
the great! She has become a dwelling

place of demons and a prison of every unclean spirit, and a prison of every unclean and hateful bird.

3 "For all the nations have drunk of the wine of the passion of her immorality, and the kings of the earth have committed *acts of* immorality with her, and the merchants of the earth have become rich by the wealth of her sensuality."

➤ 4 I heard another voice from heaven, saying, "Come out of her, my people, so that you will not participate in her sins and receive of her plagues;

5 for her sins have piled up as high as heaven, and God has remembered her iniquities.

6 "Pay her back even as she has paid, and give back *to her* double according to her deeds; in the cup which she has mixed, mix twice as much for her.

7 "To the degree that she glorified herself and lived sensuously, to the same degree give her torment and mourning; for she says in her heart, 'I SIT *as* A QUEEN AND I AM NOT A WIDOW, and will never see mourning.'

➤ 8 "For this reason in one day her plagues will come, pestilence and mourning and famine, and she will be burned up with fire; for the Lord God who judges her is strong.

9 "And the kings of the earth, who committed *acts of* immorality and lived

---

LIFE LESSONS

➤ **Revelation 18:4 —** *"Come out of her, my people, so that you will not participate in her sins and receive of her plagues."*

*G*od does not want His people entwined with evil because He wants to bless them, not judge them. " 'Come out from their midst and be separate,' says the Lord. 'And do not touch what is unclean' " (2 Cor. 6:17).

➤ **Revelation 18:8 —** *"She will be burned up with fire; for the Lord God who judges her is strong."*

*J*ust as God wiped out Sodom and Gomorrah with a hail of fire, so He promises to destroy the evil world system, "Babylon the great," at the time of the end. No one can restrain the Lord's hand of judgment.

---

sensuously with her, will weep and lament over her when they see the smoke of her burning,

10 standing at a distance because of the fear of her torment, saying, 'Woe, woe, the great city, Babylon, the strong city! For in one hour your judgment has come.'

11 "And the merchants of the earth weep and mourn over her, because no one buys their cargoes any more—

12 cargoes of gold and silver and precious stones and pearls and fine linen and purple and silk and scarlet, and every *kind of* citron wood and every article of ivory and every article *made* from very costly wood and bronze and iron and marble,

13 and cinnamon and spice and incense and perfume and frankincense and wine and olive oil and fine flour and wheat and cattle and sheep, and *cargoes* of horses and chariots and slaves and human lives.

14 "The fruit you long for has gone from you, and all things that were luxurious and splendid have passed away from you and *men* will no longer find them.

15 "The merchants of these things, who became rich from her, will stand at a distance because of the fear of her torment, weeping and mourning,

16 saying, 'Woe, woe, the great city, she who was clothed in fine linen and purple and scarlet, and adorned with gold and precious stones and pearls;

17 for in one hour such great wealth has been laid waste!' And every shipmaster and every passenger and sailor, and as many as make their living by the sea, stood at a distance,

18 and were crying out as they saw the smoke of her burning, saying, 'What *city* is like the great city?'

19 "And they threw dust on their heads and were crying out, weeping and mourning, saying, 'Woe, woe, the great city, in which all who had ships at sea became rich by her wealth, for in one hour she has been laid waste!'

20 "Rejoice over her, O heaven, and you saints and apostles and prophets, because God has pronounced judgment for you against her." ✳

21 Then a strong angel took up a stone like a great millstone and threw it into the sea, saying, "So will Babylon, the

---

Can the devil really make me do something?

REVELATION 18:23

*T*he late comedian Flip Wilson may have popularized the catchphrase, "The devil made me do it," but this excuse has always been around. We blame Satan since we know he has something to do with the temptation process.

But in fact, the devil cannot *make* us do anything. The Bible calls Satan a deceiver (Gen. 3:13; 2 Cor. 11:3; Rev. 18:23) and the "father of lies" (John 8:44). Satan's only power over us is through manipulation and deceit.

If the devil could actually *make* us do things, then he wouldn't need to go to all the trouble of deceiving us. When he dangles the right bait in front of us at the right time, our fleshly desires make it seem as though something is relentlessly drawing us toward sin; but this power does not control us. In each case we *choose* to disobey.

Think of it this way. Imagine yourself standing at the edge of a cliff that drops off into a deep, rocky gorge. Now suppose I walked up to you and said, "We have kidnapped a member of your family. If you refuse to jump, your relative will be brutally beaten and then killed." Have I made you jump? If you believed my story and you believed that by jumping you could save your family member, I may have made you *willing* to jump or even *anxious* to jump. But I have not *caused* you to jump. Even if you jumped and you found out on the way to the bottom that I had lied about the whole thing, I still did not *make* you jump. I simply tricked you into jumping. On the other hand, if I walked up behind you and pushed you, then I made you do something contrary to what you wanted to do, felt like doing, or even thought about doing.

Now think about the last time you felt tempted to sin. Did you suddenly discover that you were sinning or had sinned? Were you in the process before you ever thought about it? Or did it begin with a thought; then a feeling; then maybe a little struggle; then the actual sin?

Just as no one held Eve and forced her to bite the fruit, no one holds you down and forces you to sin. Satan cannot *make* you do anything, but he will do all he can to deceive you into dishonoring God.

---

great city, be thrown down with violence, and will not be found any longer.
22 "And the sound of harpists and musicians and flute-players and trumpeters will not be heard in you any longer; and no craftsman of any craft will be found in you any longer; and the sound of a mill will not be heard in you any longer;
23 and the light of a lamp will not shine in you any longer; and the voice of the bridegroom and bride will not be heard in you any longer; for your merchants were the great men of the earth, because all the nations were deceived by your sorcery.
24 "And in her was found the blood of prophets and of saints and of all who have been slain on the earth."

DECEMBER 29

 Zechariah 10:1—12:14

10 ASK rain from the LORD at the time of the spring rain—
The LORD who makes the storm clouds;
And He will give them showers of rain, vegetation in the field to *each* man.
2 For the teraphim speak iniquity,
And the diviners see lying visions
And tell false dreams;
They comfort in vain.
Therefore *the people* wander like sheep,
They are afflicted, because there is no shepherd.
3 "My anger is kindled against the shepherds,
And I will punish the male goats;
For the LORD of hosts has visited His flock, the house of Judah,
And will make them like His majestic horse in battle.

4 "From them will come the
      cornerstone,
   From them the tent peg,
   From them the bow of battle,
   From them every ruler, *all* of them
      together.
5 "They will be as mighty men,
   Treading down *the enemy* in the
      mire of the streets in battle;
   And they will fight, for the LORD
      will be with them;
   And the riders on horses will be put
      to shame.
6 "I will strengthen the house of
      Judah,
   And I will save the house of Joseph,
   And I will bring them back,
   Because I have had compassion on
      them;
   And they will be as though I had
      not rejected them,
   For I am the LORD their God and I
      will answer them.
7 "Ephraim will be like a mighty man,
   And their heart will be glad as if
      from wine;
   Indeed, their children will see *it* and
      be glad,
   Their heart will rejoice in the LORD.
8 "I will whistle for them to gather
      them together,
   For I have redeemed them;
   And they will be as numerous as
      they were before.
9 "When I scatter them among the
      peoples,
   They will remember Me in far
      countries,
   And they with their children will
      live and come back.
10 "I will bring them back from the land
      of Egypt
   And gather them from Assyria;
   And I will bring them into the land
      of Gilead and Lebanon
   Until no *room* can be found for
      them.
11 "And they will pass through the sea
      of distress
   And He will strike the waves in the
      sea,
   So that all the depths of the Nile
      will dry up;
   And the pride of Assyria will be
      brought down
   And the scepter of Egypt will
      depart.

12 "And I will strengthen them in the
      LORD,
   And in His name they will walk,"
      declares the LORD.

11 OPEN your doors, O Lebanon,
      That a fire may feed on your
         cedars.
2   Wail, O cypress, for the cedar has
      fallen,
   Because the glorious *trees* have
      been destroyed;
   Wail, O oaks of Bashan,
   For the impenetrable forest has
      come down.
3   There is a sound of the shepherds'
      wail,
   For their glory is ruined;
   There is a sound of the young lions'
      roar,
   For the pride of the Jordan is ruined.
4   Thus says the LORD my God, "Pasture the flock *doomed* to slaughter.
5   "Those who buy them slay them and go unpunished, and *each of* those who sell them says, 'Blessed be the LORD, for I have become rich!' And their own shepherds have no pity on them.
6   "For I will no longer have pity on the inhabitants of the land," declares the LORD; "but behold, I will cause the men to fall, each into another's power and into the power of his king; and they will strike the land, and I will not deliver *them* from their power."
7   So I pastured the flock *doomed* to slaughter, hence the afflicted of the flock. And I took for myself two staffs: the one I called Favor and the other I called Union; so I pastured the flock.
8   Then I annihilated the three shepherds in one month, for my soul was impatient with them, and their soul also was weary of me.
9   Then I said, "I will not pasture you. What is to die, let it die, and what is to be annihilated, let it be annihilated; and let those who are left eat one another's flesh."
10 I took my staff Favor and cut it in pieces, to break my covenant which I had made with all the peoples.
11 So it was broken on that day, and thus the afflicted of the flock who were watching me realized that it was the word of the LORD.
12 I said to them, "If it is good in your sight, give *me* my wages; but if not, never

mind!" So they weighed out thirty *shekels* of silver as my wages.

➤ 13 Then the LORD said to me, "Throw it to the potter, *that* magnificent price at which I was valued by them." So I took the thirty *shekels* of silver and threw them to the potter in the house of the LORD.

14 Then I cut in pieces my second staff Union, to break the brotherhood between Judah and Israel.

15 The LORD said to me, "Take again for yourself the equipment of a foolish shepherd.

16 "For behold, I am going to raise up a shepherd in the land who will not care for the perishing, seek the scattered, heal the broken, or sustain the one standing, but will devour the flesh of the fat *sheep* and tear off their hoofs.

17 "Woe to the worthless shepherd
Who leaves the flock!
A sword will be on his arm
And on his right eye!
His arm will be totally withered
And his right eye will be blind."

➤ **12** THE burden of the word of the LORD concerning Israel.

Thus declares the LORD who stretches out the heavens, lays the foundation of the earth, and forms the spirit of man within him,

2 "Behold, I am going to make Jerusalem a cup that causes reeling to all the peoples around; and when the siege is against Jerusalem, it will also be against Judah.

3 "It will come about in that day that I will make Jerusalem a heavy stone for all the peoples; all who lift it will be severely injured. And all the nations of the earth will be gathered against it.

4 "In that day," declares the LORD, "I will strike every horse with bewilderment and his rider with madness. But I will watch over the house of Judah, while I strike every horse of the peoples with blindness.

5 "Then the clans of Judah will say in their hearts, 'A strong support for us are the inhabitants of Jerusalem through the LORD of hosts, their God.'

6 "In that day I will make the clans of Judah like a firepot among pieces of wood and a flaming torch among sheaves, so they will consume on the right hand and on the left all the surrounding peoples, while the inhabitants

of Jerusalem again dwell on their own sites in Jerusalem.

7 "The LORD also will save the tents of Judah first, so that the glory of the house of David and the glory of the inhabitants of Jerusalem will not be magnified above Judah.

8 "In that day the LORD will defend the inhabitants of Jerusalem, and the one who is feeble among them in that day will be like David, and the house of David *will be* like God, like the angel of the LORD before them.

9 "And in that day I will set about to destroy all the nations that come against Jerusalem.

10 "I will pour out on the house of ◀ David and on the inhabitants of Jerusalem, the Spirit of grace and of supplication, so that they will look on Me whom they have pierced; and they will mourn for Him, as one mourns for an only son, and they will weep bitterly over Him like the bitter weeping over a firstborn.

11 "In that day there will be great mourn-

LIFE LESSONS

➤ **Zechariah 11:13** — *"Throw it to the potter, that magnificent price at which I was valued by them."*

*J*udas Iscariot fulfilled this prophecy when he betrayed the Lord Jesus for thirty pieces of silver (Matt. 27:3–10). How many of us have betrayed Him for less by choosing trinkets over Him?

➤ **Zechariah 12:1** — *The LORD . . . stretches out the heavens, lays the foundation of the earth, and forms the spirit of man within him.*

*T*he same God who designed and created the vast universe around you— who devised and fashioned the earth you live on—also molded and shaped your very spirit. He knows you inside and out—and He wants you to know Him.

➤ **Zechariah 12:10** — *"They will look on Me whom they have pierced."*

*T*he day will come when the resurrected Jesus will return to this earth to bring God's covenant people back into a close, warm, intimate relationship with Himself (Rom. 11:25–32). What a day that will be!

ing in Jerusalem, like the mourning of Hadadrimmon in the plain of Megiddo.
12 "The land will mourn, every family by itself; the family of the house of David by itself and their wives by themselves; the family of the house of Nathan by itself and their wives by themselves;
13 the family of the house of Levi by itself and their wives by themselves; the family of the Shimeites by itself and their wives by themselves;
14 all the families that remain, every family by itself and their wives by themselves.

Psalm 149:1–4

149 PRAISE the LORD!
Sing to the LORD a new song,
And His praise in the congregation of the godly ones.
2 Let Israel be glad in his Maker;
Let the sons of Zion rejoice in their King.
3 Let them praise His name with dancing;
Let them sing praises to Him with timbrel and lyre.
4 For the LORD takes pleasure in His people;
He will beautify the afflicted ones with salvation.

Proverbs 30:32, 33

32 If you have been foolish in exalting yourself
Or if you have plotted *evil, put your* hand on your mouth.
33 For the churning of milk produces butter,
And pressing the nose brings forth blood;
So the churning of anger produces strife.

Revelation 19:1–21

19 AFTER these things I heard something like a loud voice of a great multitude in heaven, saying,

"Hallelujah! Salvation and glory and power belong to our God;
2 BECAUSE HIS JUDGMENTS ARE TRUE AND RIGHTEOUS; for He has judged the great harlot who was corrupting the earth with her immorality, and HE HAS AVENGED THE BLOOD OF HIS BOND-SERVANTS ON HER."
3 And a second time they said, "Hallelujah! HER SMOKE RISES UP FOREVER AND EVER."
4 And the twenty-four elders and the four living creatures fell down and worshiped God who sits on the throne saying, "Amen. Hallelujah!"
5 And a voice came from the throne, saying,

"Give praise to our God, all you His bond-servants, you who fear Him, the small and the great."
6 Then I heard *something* like the voice of a great multitude and like the sound of many waters and like the sound of mighty peals of thunder, saying,

"Hallelujah! For the Lord our God, the Almighty, reigns.
7 "Let us rejoice and be glad and give the glory to Him, for the marriage of the Lamb has come and His bride has made herself ready."
8 It was given to her to clothe herself in fine linen, bright *and* clean; for the fine linen is the righteous acts of the saints.
9 Then he *said to me, "Write, 'Blessed are those who are invited to the marriage supper of the Lamb.'" And he *said to me, "These are true words of God."
10 Then I fell at his feet to worship him. But he *said to me, "Do not do that; I am a fellow servant of yours and your brethren who hold the testimony of Jesus; worship God. For the testimony of Jesus is the spirit of prophecy."
11 And I saw heaven opened, and behold, a white horse, and He who sat on

LIFE LESSONS

➤ **Revelation 19:10 —** *"Do not do that; I am a fellow servant . . . worship God."*

*A*ngels have such majesty and power that human beings sometimes feel tempted to worship them—even someone as mature and godly as John. But angels know their place. God alone deserves our worship!

WHAT THE BIBLE SAYS ABOUT

God's Determined Will

Revelation 19

God's determined will includes His unchangeable plans for the world. As the sovereign ruler, He is in total control—no government rises to power and no physical ailment occurs unless He allows it. He is determined to carry out the plan that He developed before Creation.

God reveals very little of His determined will to mankind. We can anticipate only those events He has disclosed, such as Christ's return and the White Throne Judgment (Rev. 19:11; 20:11–15). Much of our knowledge comes from our experience and Bible reading. We know, for example, that the Lord has given us limited free will and that He has a plan for redeeming us from the sin we choose.

Yet God's ultimate purpose is His glory—and we know He will ultimately attain it. As the multitudes sing out in Revelation 19:6,

7, "Hallelujah! For the Lord our God, the Almighty, reigns. Let us rejoice and be glad and give the glory to Him."

Of course, because of a limited human perspective that sees only the evil, people often wonder how He can allow crime, disease, or war. However, we must keep this in mind: "We know that God causes all things to work together for good to those who love God, to those who are the called according to His purpose" (Rom. 8:28). Look at the Cross—that device of torturous death is the greatest expression of good and glory in Christianity! And we know that the One who died and rose again as the perfect, sinless Lamb of God, will return as the victorious "KING OF KINGS, AND LORD OF LORDS" (Rev. 19:16).

The Father will have His way, whether we believe in His sovereignty or not. His plan is far bigger than we can grasp, and it is designed to highlight our need for Him.

You may not know how He has determined to unroll your future, but you know what the ultimate outcome will be. Therefore, always remember that as one of God's children, triumph awaits you. ◉

it *is* called Faithful and True, and in righteousness He judges and wages war.
12 His eyes *are* a flame of fire, and on His head *are* many diadems; and He has a name written *on Him* which no one knows except Himself.
13 *He is* clothed with a robe dipped in blood, and His name is called The Word of God.
14 And the armies which are in heaven, clothed in fine linen, white *and* clean, were following Him on white horses.
15 From His mouth comes a sharp sword, so that with it He may strike down the nations, and He will rule them with a rod of iron; and He treads the wine press of the fierce wrath of God, the Almighty.
➤ 16 And on His robe and on His thigh He has a name written, "KING OF KINGS, AND LORD OF LORDS."
17 Then I saw an angel standing in the sun, and he cried out with a loud voice, saying to all the birds which fly in midheaven, "Come, assemble for the great supper of God,

LIFE LESSONS

➤ **Revelation 19:11 —** *He . . . is called Faithful and True, and in righteousness He judges and wages war.*

When Jesus returns, He is not coming back as the gentle Lamb. He will appear as the reigning King, our Mighty Warrior, and as the righteous Judge of the living and the dead. Jesus will return with His forces to accomplish all the remaining prophesies and covenants of His Word—establishing His kingdom on earth and destroying evil. He is called Faithful and True because not one of His promises will go unfulfilled.

➤ **Revelation 19:16 —** *On His thigh He has a name written, "KING OF KINGS AND LORD OF LORDS."*

The Lord veiled His royal majesty during His years of earthly ministry, but God will spotlight His glory upon His return so that no one could possibly miss it: "He is coming with the clouds, and every eye will see Him" (Rev. 1:7).

18 so that you may eat the flesh of kings and the flesh of commanders and the flesh of mighty men and the flesh of horses and of those who sit on them and the flesh of all men, both free men and slaves, and small and great."

19 And I saw the beast and the kings of the earth and their armies assembled to make war against Him who sat on the horse and against His army.

20 And the beast was seized, and with him the false prophet who performed the signs in his presence, by which he deceived those who had received the mark of the beast and those who worshiped his image; these two were thrown alive into the lake of fire which burns with brimstone.

21 And the rest were killed with the sword which came from the mouth of Him who sat on the horse, and all the birds were filled with their flesh.

Zechariah 13:1—14:21

13 "IN that day a fountain will be opened for the house of David and for the inhabitants of Jerusalem, for sin and for impurity.

2 "It will come about in that day," declares the LORD of hosts, "that I will cut off the names of the idols from the land, and they will no longer be remembered; and I will also remove the prophets and the unclean spirit from the land.

3 "And if anyone still prophesies, then his father and mother who gave birth to him will say to him, 'You shall not live, for you have spoken falsely in the name of the LORD'; and his father and mother who gave birth to him will pierce him through when he prophesies.

4 "Also it will come about in that day that the prophets will each be ashamed of his vision when he prophesies, and they will not put on a hairy robe in order to deceive;

5 but he will say, 'I am not a prophet; I am a tiller of the ground, for a man sold me as a slave in my youth.'

6 "And one will say to him, 'What are these wounds between your arms?' Then he will say, 'Those with which I was wounded in the house of my friends.'

7 "Awake, O sword, against My Shepherd,
And against the man, My Associate,"
Declares the LORD of hosts.
"Strike the Shepherd that the sheep may be scattered;
And I will turn My hand against the little ones.

8 "It will come about in all the land,"
Declares the LORD,
"That two parts in it will be cut off
and perish;
But the third will be left in it.

9 "And I will bring the third part through the fire,
Refine them as silver is refined,
And test them as gold is tested.
They will call on My name,
And I will answer them;
I will say, 'They are My people,'
And they will say, 'The LORD is my God.'"

LIFE LESSONS

Zechariah 13:1 — *"In that day a fountain will be opened for the house of David and for the inhabitants of Jerusalem, for sin and for impurity."*

God often uses a fountain to picture Himself as our source of salvation. As a fountain, He overflows with mercy and grace. As a fountain, He refreshes. And as a fountain, His love must be individually taken in. Water brings life, and living water brings eternal life. God calls Himself our spring of living water (Jer. 2:13); the Spirit is a stream of living water in us (John 7:38, 39); and His living water is ours forever (Rev. 7:17).

Zechariah 13:7 — *"Awake, O sword, against My Shepherd."*

Think of it: *the Lord* called for the sword against His Son, Jesus Christ. He planned the events of the Cross; He willingly bruised His only Son (Is. 53:10; Acts 4:27, 28). And He did it *for you.*

14 BEHOLD, a day is coming for the LORD when the spoil taken from you will be divided among you.

2   For I will gather all the nations against Jerusalem to battle, and the city will be captured, the houses plundered, the women ravished and half of the city exiled, but the rest of the people will not be cut off from the city.

3   Then the LORD will go forth and fight against those nations, as when He fights on a day of battle.

4   In that day His feet will stand on the Mount of Olives, which is in front of Jerusalem on the east; and the Mount of Olives will be split in its middle from east to west by a very large valley, so that half of the mountain will move toward the north and the other half toward the south.

5   You will flee by the valley of My mountains, for the valley of the mountains will reach to Azel; yes, you will flee just as you fled before the earthquake in the days of Uzziah king of Judah. Then the LORD, my God, will come, *and* all the holy ones with Him!

6   In that day there will be no light; the luminaries will dwindle.

7   For it will be a unique day which is known to the LORD, neither day nor night, but it will come about that at evening time there will be light.

8   And in that day living waters will flow out of Jerusalem, half of them toward the eastern sea and the other half toward the western sea; it will be in summer as well as in winter.

9   And the LORD will be king over all the earth; in that day the LORD will be *the only* one, and His name *the only* one.

10   All the land will be changed into a plain from Geba to Rimmon south of Jerusalem; but Jerusalem will rise and remain on its site from Benjamin's Gate as far as the place of the First Gate to the Corner Gate, and from the Tower of Hananel to the king's wine presses.

11   People will live in it, and there will no longer be a curse, for Jerusalem will dwell in security.

12   Now this will be the plague with which the LORD will strike all the peoples who have gone to war against Jerusalem; their flesh will rot while they stand on their feet, and their eyes will rot in their sockets, and their tongue will rot in their mouth.

13   It will come about in that day that a great panic from the LORD will fall on them; and they will seize one another's hand, and the hand of one will be lifted against the hand of another.

14   Judah also will fight at Jerusalem; and the wealth of all the surrounding nations will be gathered, gold and silver and garments in great abundance.

15   So also like this plague will be the plague on the horse, the mule, the camel, the donkey and all the cattle that will be in those camps.

16   Then it will come about that any who are left of all the nations that went against Jerusalem will go up from year to year to worship the King, the LORD of hosts, and to celebrate the Feast of Booths.

17   And it will be that whichever of the families of the earth does not go up to Jerusalem to worship the King, the LORD of hosts, there will be no rain on them.

18   If the family of Egypt does not go up or enter, then no *rain will fall* on them; it will be the plague with which the LORD smites the nations who do not go up to celebrate the Feast of Booths.

19   This will be the punishment of Egypt, and the punishment of all the nations who do not go up to celebrate the Feast of Booths.

20   In that day there will be *inscribed* on the bells of the horses, "HOLY TO THE LORD." And the cooking pots in the LORD's house will be like the bowls before the altar.

21   Every cooking pot in Jerusalem and in Judah will be holy to the LORD of hosts; and all who sacrifice will come

---

LIFE LESSONS

➤ **Zechariah 14:5 — *Then the LORD, my God, will come, and all the holy ones with Him!***

*D*id you know that the Bible contains almost three times as many predictions of the second coming of Christ as it has for His first coming? He is coming again! And He wants us to be ready (Matt. 24:44).

and take of them and boil in them. And there will no longer be a Canaanite in the house of the LORD of hosts in that day.

Psalm 149:5–9

5 Let the godly ones exult in glory;
Let them sing for joy on their beds.
6 *Let* the high praises of God *be* in
their mouth,
And a two-edged sword in their
hand,
7 To execute vengeance on the
nations
And punishment on the peoples,
8 To bind their kings with chains
And their nobles with fetters of
iron,
9 To execute on them the judgment
written;
This is an honor for all His godly
ones.
Praise the LORD!

Proverbs 31:1–9

31 THE words of King Lemuel, the oracle which his mother taught him:
2 What, O my son?
And what, O son of my womb?
And what, O son of my vows?
3 Do not give your strength to
women,
Or your ways to that which destroys
kings.
4 It is not for kings, O Lemuel,
It is not for kings to drink wine,
Or for rulers to desire strong
drink,
5 For they will drink and forget what
is decreed,
And pervert the rights of all the
afflicted.
6 Give strong drink to him who is
perishing,
And wine to him whose life is
bitter.
7 Let him drink and forget his
poverty
And remember his trouble no
more.

8 Open your mouth for the mute,
For the rights of all the unfortunate.
9 Open your mouth, judge
righteously,
And defend the rights of the
afflicted and needy.

Revelation 20:1–15

20 THEN I saw an angel coming down
from heaven, holding the key of the abyss and a great chain in his hand.
2 And he laid hold of the dragon, the serpent of old, who is the devil and Satan, and bound him for a thousand years;
3 and he threw him into the abyss, and shut *it* and sealed *it* over him, so that he would not deceive the nations any longer, until the thousand years were completed; after these things he must be released for a short time.
4 Then I saw thrones, and they sat on them, and judgment was given to them. And I *saw* the souls of those who had been beheaded because of their testimony of Jesus and because of the word of God, and those who had not worshiped the beast or his image, and had not received the mark on their forehead and on their hand; and they came to life and reigned with Christ for a thousand years.
5 The rest of the dead did not come to life until the thousand years were completed. This is the first resurrection.
6 Blessed and holy is the one who has a part in the first resurrection; over these the second death has no power, but they will be priests of God and of Christ and will reign with Him for a thousand years.

LIFE LESSONS

➤ **Revelation 20:3 — *After these things
he must be released for a short time.***

*W*hy must Satan be released after his long imprisonment? Why doesn't God judge him immediately? Through the enemy's rebellion, the hearts of those who only pretend to love the Lord are revealed (Rev. 20:7–9). And then the devil meets his final judgment.

What role does Satan play in our adversity?

REVELATION 20:10

Several biblical accounts illustrate Satan's role in adversity. We find the clearest example in the story of Job. Those who attribute all adversity to sin or to a lack of faith sometimes have a difficult time with this narrative. Though some may speculate that Job's problems are due to pride or the sin of his children, there is no real evidence for this. The Book of Job is the story of one man's faith under trial. Job faced the fires of hopelessness, rejection, intense physical pain, and deep emotional sorrow and he passed the test. He was a man who "was blameless, upright, fearing God and turning away from evil." Later in the same chapter, the Lord Himself says of Job, "There is no one like him on the earth, a blameless and upright man, fearing God and turning away from evil" (Job 1:8).

Job was a righteous man whose adversity did *not* come as a result of sin. In fact, an ensuing discussion between God and Satan spells out why Job suffered the way he did. Satan accused Job of following God only because the Lord had blessed him and protected him. Take away that protection, Satan challenged, and Job would curse God to His face.

So Satan set out to destroy all Job had. Yet Job continued to serve God and walk in His ways. Satan then made another request of God, asking Him permission to afflict Job's body (Job 2:4–7).

Clearly, Satan, who asked God for permission to send trouble into Job's life, initiated Job's adversity. God, in turn, allowed the enemy to afflict Job in a limited way. Permission for the trial came from God; but adversity came from the devil.

Peter reminded his readers that Satan "roams" around like a lion, seeking those he can destroy (1 Pet. 5:8). We may think Peter's words refer only to Satan's involvement in our temptations. However, the enemy is crafty and he wants to use suffering of any kind to destroy us. He roams the earth, looking for opportunities to bring adversity into our lives in an all out attempt to harm the body of Christ. However, he is a defeated foe. Jesus Christ won the ultimate victory on the Cross and because He lives within us, we can have this same victory. We may have to face serious threats at times, but like Job, we can respond to the trial by holding firm in our faith.

Not only does adversity train us to trust God, it also can be a bridge to a deeper relationship with Him. At the end of his season of suffering, Job praised the Lord, saying, "I have heard of You by the hearing of the ear; but now my eye sees You" (Job 42:5).

7 When the thousand years are completed, Satan will be released from his prison,
8 and will come out to deceive the nations which are in the four corners of the earth, Gog and Magog, to gather them together for the war; the number of them is like the sand of the seashore.
9 And they came up on the broad plain of the earth and surrounded the camp of the saints and the beloved city, and fire came down from heaven and devoured them.
10 And the devil who deceived them was thrown into the lake of fire and brimstone, where the beast and the false prophet are also; and they will be tormented day and night forever and ever.
11 Then I saw a great white throne and Him who sat upon it, from whose presence earth and heaven fled away, and no place was found for them.

12 And I saw the dead, the great and the small, standing before the throne,

LIFE LESSONS

➤ **Revelation 20:12 — *I saw the dead, the great and the small, standing before the throne, and books were opened . . . and the dead were judged . . . according to their deeds.***

At the Great White Throne everyone is judged according to whether or not he has accepted Christ as his Savior and his name is written in the Lamb's Book of Life. Those who have been redeemed are welcomed into heaven. Those who refuse to believe in Christ must bear the penalty of their sin and are cast into the lake of fire (John 3:18; Rom. 6:23). There is no board of appeals in heaven. Once we appear before Christ, our character and eternal destination are fixed.

and books were opened; and another book was opened, which is *the book* of life; and the dead were judged from the things which were written in the books, according to their deeds.

13   And the sea gave up the dead which were in it, and death and Hades gave up the dead which were in them; and they were judged, every one *of them* according to their deeds.

14   Then death and Hades were thrown into the lake of fire. This is the second death, the lake of fire.

> 15   And if anyone's name was not found written in the book of life, he was thrown into the lake of fire.

✦ Malachi 1:1—4:6

1 THE oracle of the word of the LORD to Israel through Malachi.

2   "I have loved you," says the LORD. But you say, "How have You loved us?" "*Was* not Esau Jacob's brother?" declares the LORD. "Yet I have loved Jacob;

3   but I have hated Esau, and I have made his mountains a desolation and *appointed* his inheritance for the jackals of the wilderness."

4   Though Edom says, "We have been beaten down, but we will return and build up the ruins"; thus says the LORD of hosts, "They may build, but I will tear down; and *men* will call them the wicked territory, and the people toward whom the LORD is indignant forever."

5   Your eyes will see this and you will say, "The LORD be magnified beyond the border of Israel!"

6   "'A son honors *his* father, and a servant his master. Then if I am a father, where is My honor? And if I am a master, where is My respect?' says the LORD of hosts to you, O priests who despise My name. But you say, 'How have we despised Your name?'

7   "*You* are presenting defiled food upon My altar. But you say, 'How have we defiled You?' In that you say, 'The table of the LORD is to be despised.'

8   "But when you present the blind for sacrifice, is it not evil? And when you present the lame and sick, is it not evil? Why not offer it to your governor? Would he be pleased with you? Or would he receive you kindly?" says the LORD of hosts.

9   "But now will you not entreat God's favor, that He may be gracious to us? With such an offering on your part, will He receive any of you kindly?" says the LORD of hosts.

10 "Oh that there were one among you who would shut the gates, that you might not uselessly kindle *fire on* My altar! I am not pleased with you," says the LORD of hosts, "nor will I accept an offering from you.

11 "For from the rising of the sun even to its setting, My name *will be* great among the nations, and in every place incense is going to be offered to My name, and a grain offering *that is* pure; for My name *will be* great among the nations," says the LORD of hosts.

12 "But you are profaning it, in that you say, 'The table of the Lord is defiled, and as for its fruit, its food is to be despised.'

13 "You also say, 'My, how tiresome it is!' And you disdainfully sniff at it," says

the LORD of hosts, "and you bring what was taken by robbery and *what is* lame or sick; so you bring the offering! Should I receive that from your hand?" says the LORD.

14 "But cursed be the swindler who has a male in his flock and vows it, but sacrifices a blemished animal to the Lord, for I am a great King," says the LORD of hosts, "and My name is feared among the nations."

2 "AND now this commandment is for you, O priests.

2 "If you do not listen, and if you do not take it to heart to give honor to My name," says the LORD of hosts, "then I will send the curse upon you and I will curse your blessings; and indeed, I have cursed them *already*, because you are not taking *it* to heart.

3 "Behold, I am going to rebuke your offspring, and I will spread refuse on your faces, the refuse of your feasts; and you will be taken away with it.

4 "Then you will know that I have sent this commandment to you, that My covenant may continue with Levi," says the LORD of hosts.

➤ 5 "My covenant with him was *one of* life and peace, and I gave them to him *as an object of* reverence; so he revered Me and stood in awe of My name.

6 "True instruction was in his mouth and unrighteousness was not found on his lips; he walked with Me in peace and uprightness, and he turned many back from iniquity.

7 "For the lips of a priest should preserve knowledge, and men should seek instruction from his mouth; for he is the messenger of the LORD of hosts.

8 "But as for you, you have turned aside

from the way; you have caused many to stumble by the instruction; you have corrupted the covenant of Levi," says the LORD of hosts.

9 "So I also have made you despised and abased before all the people, just as you are not keeping My ways but are showing partiality in the instruction.

10 "Do we not all have one father? Has not one God created us? Why do we deal treacherously each against his brother so as to profane the covenant of our fathers?

11 "Judah has dealt treacherously, and an abomination has been committed in Israel and in Jerusalem; for Judah has profaned the sanctuary of the LORD which He loves and has married the daughter of a foreign god.

12 "*As* for the man who does this, may the LORD cut off from the tents of Jacob *everyone* who awakes and answers, or who presents an offering to the LORD of hosts.

13 "This is another thing you do: you cover the altar of the LORD with tears, with weeping and with groaning, because He no longer regards the offering or accepts *it with* favor from your hand.

14 "Yet you say, 'For what reason?' Because the LORD has been a witness between you and the wife of your youth, against whom you have dealt treacherously, though she is your companion and your wife by covenant.

15 "But not one has done *so* who has a remnant of the Spirit. And what did *that* one *do* while he was seeking a godly offspring? Take heed then to your spirit, and let no one deal treacherously against the wife of your youth.

16 "For I hate divorce," says the LORD, the God of Israel, "and him who covers his garment with wrong," says the LORD of hosts. "So take heed to your spirit, that you do not deal treacherously."

17 You have wearied the LORD with your words. Yet you say, "How have we wearied *Him?*" In that you say, "Everyone who does evil is good in the sight of the LORD, and He delights in them," or, "Where is the God of justice?"

3 "BEHOLD, I am going to send My messenger, and he will clear the way before Me. And the Lord, whom you seek, will suddenly come to His temple;

and the messenger of the covenant, in whom you delight, behold, He is coming," says the LORD of hosts.

2 "But who can endure the day of His coming? And who can stand when He appears? For He is like a refiner's fire and like fullers' soap.

3 "He will sit as a smelter and purifier of silver, and He will purify the sons of Levi and refine them like gold and silver, so that they may present to the LORD offerings in righteousness.

4 "Then the offering of Judah and Jerusalem will be pleasing to the LORD as in the days of old and as in former years.

5 "Then I will draw near to you for judgment; and I will be a swift witness against the sorcerers and against the adulterers and against those who swear falsely, and against those who oppress the wage earner in his wages, the widow and the orphan, and those who turn aside the alien and do not fear Me," says the LORD of hosts.

6 "For I, the LORD, do not change; therefore you, O sons of Jacob, are not consumed.

7 "From the days of your fathers you have turned aside from My statutes and have not kept *them*. Return to Me, and I will return to you," says the LORD of hosts. "But you say, 'How shall we return?'

8 "Will a man rob God? Yet you are robbing Me! But you say, 'How have we robbed You?' In tithes and offerings.

9 "You are cursed with a curse, for you are robbing Me, the whole nation *of you!*

10 "Bring the whole tithe into the storehouse, so that there may be food in My house, and test Me now in this," says the LORD of hosts, "if I will not open for you the windows of heaven and pour out for you a blessing until it overflows.

11 "Then I will rebuke the devourer for you, so that it will not destroy the fruits of the ground; nor will your vine in the field cast *its grapes*," says the LORD of hosts.

12 "All the nations will call you blessed, for you shall be a delightful land," says the LORD of hosts.

13 "Your words have been arrogant against Me," says the LORD. "Yet you say, 'What have we spoken against You?'

14 "You have said, 'It is vain to serve God; and what profit is it that we have kept His charge, and that we have walked in mourning before the LORD of hosts?

15 'So now we call the arrogant blessed; not only are the doers of wickedness built up but they also test God and escape.'"

16 Then those who feared the LORD spoke to one another, and the LORD gave attention and heard *it,* and a book of remembrance was written before Him for those who fear the LORD and who esteem His name.

17 "They will be Mine," says the LORD of hosts, "on the day that I prepare *My* own possession, and I will spare them as a man spares his own son who serves him."

18 So you will again distinguish between the righteous and the wicked, between one who serves God and one who does not serve Him.

4 "FOR behold, the day is coming, burning like a furnace; and all the arrogant and every evildoer will be chaff; and the day that is coming will set them ablaze," says the LORD of hosts, "so that it will leave them neither root nor branch."

2 "But for you who fear My name, the sun of righteousness will rise with healing in its wings; and you will go forth and skip about like calves from the stall.

3 "You will tread down the wicked, for they will be ashes under the soles of your feet on the day which I am preparing," says the LORD of hosts.

4 "Remember the law of Moses My servant, *even the* statutes and ordinances

---

LIFE LESSONS

➤ **Malachi 3:16** — *Then those who feared the LORD spoke to one another, and the LORD gave attention and heard it.*

*N*one of us are in this walk of faith on our own. We need to encourage one another to "love and good deeds" (Heb. 10:24). Best of all, the Lord promises to reward such healthy obedience. Of course, the closest mission field we have is our own family. God says that He "was seeking a godly offspring" (Mal. 2:15), but children have to be trained to be godly—and that's the job of parents.

which I commanded him in Horeb for all Israel.

5 "Behold, I am going to send you Elijah the prophet before the coming of the great and terrible day of the LORD.

6 "He will restore the hearts of the fathers to *their* children and the hearts of the children to their fathers, so that I will not come and smite the land with a curse."

◈ Psalm 150:1–6

150 PRAISE the LORD!
Praise God in His sanctuary;
Praise Him in His mighty
expanse.

2 Praise Him for His mighty deeds;
Praise Him according to His
excellent greatness.

3 Praise Him with trumpet sound;
Praise Him with harp and lyre.

4 Praise Him with timbrel and
dancing;
Praise Him with stringed
instruments and pipe.

5 Praise Him with loud cymbals;
Praise Him with resounding
cymbals.

 6 Let everything that has breath
praise the LORD.
Praise the LORD!

◈ Proverbs 31:10–31

10 An excellent wife, who can find?
For her worth is far above jewels.

11 The heart of her husband trusts in
her,
And he will have no lack of gain.

12 She does him good and not evil
All the days of her life.

13 She looks for wool and flax
And works with her hands in
delight.

14 She is like merchant ships;
She brings her food from afar.

15 She rises also while it is still night
And gives food to her household
And portions to her maidens.

16 She considers a field and buys it;

From her earnings she plants a
vineyard.

17 She girds herself with strength
And makes her arms strong.

18 She senses that her gain is good;
Her lamp does not go out at night.

19 She stretches out her hands to the
distaff,
And her hands grasp the spindle.

20 She extends her hand to the poor,
And she stretches out her hands to
the needy.

21 She is not afraid of the snow for her
household,
For all her household are clothed
with scarlet.

22 She makes coverings for herself;
Her clothing is fine linen and
purple.

23 Her husband is known in the
gates,
When he sits among the elders of
the land.

24 She makes linen garments and
sells *them*,
And supplies belts to the
tradesmen.

25 Strength and dignity are her
clothing,
And she smiles at the future.

26 She opens her mouth in wisdom,
And the teaching of kindness is on
her tongue.

27 She looks well to the ways of her
household,
And does not eat the bread of
idleness.

28 Her children rise up and bless her;
Her husband *also*, and he praises
her, *saying:*

29 "Many daughters have done nobly,
But you excel them all."

30 Charm is deceitful and beauty is
vain,

LIFE LESSONS

➢ **Proverbs 31:30** — *Charm is deceitful and beauty is vain, but a woman who fears the LORD, she shall be praised.*

*T*he Book of Proverbs ends where it begins, with a focus on the fear of the Lord (Prov. 1:7). Those who know and worship God for who He really is find both success in life and praise after it.

But a woman who fears the LORD,
   she shall be praised.
31 Give her the product of her
   hands,
   And let her works praise her in
    the gates.

❖ Revelation 21:1—22:21

21 THEN I saw a new heaven and a new earth; for the first heaven and the first earth passed away, and there is no longer *any* sea.

2 And I saw the holy city, new Jerusalem, coming down out of heaven from God, made ready as a bride adorned for her husband.

3 And I heard a loud voice from the throne, saying, "Behold, the tabernacle of God is among men, and He will dwell among them, and they shall be His people, and God Himself will be among them,

4 and He will wipe away every tear from their eyes; and there will no longer be *any* death; there will no longer be *any* mourning, or crying, or pain; the first things have passed away."

5 And He who sits on the throne said, "Behold, I am making all things new." And He *said, "Write, for these words are faithful and true."

6 Then He said to me, "It is done. I am the Alpha and the Omega, the beginning and the end. I will give to the one who thirsts from the spring of the water of life without cost.

7 "He who overcomes will inherit these things, and I will be his God and he will be My son.

8 "But for the cowardly and unbelieving and abominable and murderers and immoral persons and sorcerers and idolaters and all liars, their part *will be* in the lake that burns with fire and brimstone, which is the second death."

9 Then one of the seven angels who had the seven bowls full of the seven last plagues came and spoke with me, saying, "Come here, I will show you the bride, the wife of the Lamb."

10 And he carried me away in the Spirit to a great and high mountain, and showed me the holy city, Jerusalem, coming down out of heaven from God,

11 having the glory of God. Her brilliance was like a very costly stone, as a stone of crystal-clear jasper.

12 It had a great and high wall, with twelve gates, and at the gates twelve angels; and names *were* written on them, which are *the names* of the twelve tribes of the sons of Israel.

13 *There were* three gates on the east and three gates on the north and three gates on the south and three gates on the west.

14 And the wall of the city had twelve foundation stones, and on them *were* the twelve names of the twelve apostles of the Lamb.

15 The one who spoke with me had a gold measuring rod to measure the city, and its gates and its wall.

16 The city is laid out as a square, and its length is as great as the width; and he measured the city with the rod, fifteen hundred miles; its length and width and height are equal.

17 And he measured its wall, seventy-two yards, *according to* human measurements, which are *also* angelic *measurements.*

18 The material of the wall was jasper; and the city was pure gold, like clear glass.

19 The foundation stones of the city wall were adorned with every kind of precious stone. The first foundation stone was jasper; the second, sapphire; the third, chalcedony; the fourth, emerald;

LIFE LESSONS

➢ **Revelation 21:23 —** *The city has no need of the sun or of the moon to shine in it, for the glory of God has illumined it, and its lamp is the Lamb.*

*G*enesis 1:3 tells us there was light in this world long before the sun, moon, and stars existed (Gen. 1:16). Likewise, 1 John 1:5 tells us, "God is Light, and in Him there is no darkness at all." Believers will again enjoy the Lord's pure, uninterrupted light in the Holy City, the New Jerusalem, because He will be with us always, and we will never be separated from Him again.

LIFE PRINCIPLE 30

AN EAGER ANTICIPATION OF THE LORD'S
RETURN KEEPS US LIVING PRODUCTIVELY.

REVELATION 22:12

*T*hroughout Scripture we find three
admonitions given to us about the
Lord's return:

❶ **Watch faithfully.**

❷ **Work diligently.**

❸ **Wait peacefully.**

1. We are to watch. The Lord said repeatedly
that we are to watch for His coming because
we do not know the day or hour of His return
(Matt. 24:42; 25:13). In Luke 21:36, Jesus
gave this specific instruction: "Keep on the
alert at all times, praying that you may have
strength to escape all these things that are
about to take place, and to stand before the
Son of Man."

We are to do more than pray as we watch.
We are to stand fast in the faith with courage
and strength (1 Cor. 16:13). We are to watch
soberly, arming ourselves with faith, love, and
salvation (1 Thess. 5:8). As we watch, we are
to remain especially aware of false prophets. We
are to discern the spirits and to reject soundly
all who do not confess that Jesus Christ is God
in the flesh (2 Peter 2:1; 1 John 4:1–2).

Jesus spoke to John in a vision and gave this
great promise to those who remain watchful:
"Behold, I am coming like a thief. Blessed is
the one who stays awake" (Rev. 16:15).

2. We are to work. Why does Jesus leave us
here on earth after He saves us? Why aren't we
born again, then immediately taken into the
Lord's presence? Because we still have work
to do!

First, God calls us to win souls. We are to
be the Lord's witnesses—telling of the love
of God and the atoning death of Jesus Christ.
We are to testify about what He has done in
our own lives, both with our words and by our
example. So long as there remains a soul on
earth who hasn't heard the gospel of our Lord
Jesus Christ, we have work to do!

Second, we are to grow spiritually, developing an ever-increasing intimacy with the
Lord. None of us fully lives up to our spiritual
potential. We all have room to grow. In those

areas where we discover we are unlike Christ,
we must work with the Spirit to become conformed to His likeness. Our minds must be
renewed (Rom. 12:1). Our inner hurts and
emotions must be healed. We must grow in
spiritual discernment and in the wisdom of
God. Our faith must be strengthened and used
so that our prayers and our actions more effectively build up the Lord's kingdom.

3. We are to wait. Waiting isn't easy.
Impatience often leads to frustration. Waiting
can also cause a buildup of fear. The longer
something anticipated doesn't happen, the
greater our concern grows with what will happen, which can degenerate into worry over
what might happen. And fear is only a step
away.

The angels spoke peace to the earth at Jesus'
first coming (Luke 2:14). More than four
hundred times in Scripture, the Lord says that
we are not to fear, but to enjoy peace. The
prophet Isaiah referred to Jesus as the Prince of
Peace (Is. 9:6). Throughout His ministry, the
Lord Jesus spoke peace. To the woman with
an issue of blood He said, "Go in peace;" to a
stormy sea He said, "Peace be still;" and to His
disciples He said, "My peace I give you." The
Lord calls us to peace as we await His return.

Apart from Jesus, there is no peace—not
within a human heart and not among human
beings or nations. With Jesus, we can experience peace that surpasses our rational capacity
and settles deep within (Phil. 4:7). We are to
seek and find this peace as we await the Lord's
return.

When the Lord comes, will He find you
among those who love Him and call Him
Savior and Lord?

When the Lord comes, will He find you
doing what He has commanded you to do?

When the Lord comes, will He find you
eager to see Him?

When the Lord comes, will He find you
ready for His appearing?

When the Lord calls with a shout from
heaven, will you instantly rise to be with Him?

When the Lord appears in the clouds, will
your heart rejoice with exceedingly great joy?

You have it within your grasp to positively
answer these questions. How will you choose
to respond to the Lord's challenges upon your
life?

The fact is: He is coming again! ◈

20 the fifth, sardonyx; the sixth, sardius; the seventh, chrysolite; the eighth, beryl; the ninth, topaz; the tenth, chrysoprase; the eleventh, jacinth; the twelfth, amethyst.

21 And the twelve gates were twelve pearls; each one of the gates was a single pearl. And the street of the city was pure gold, like transparent glass.

22 I saw no temple in it, for the Lord God the Almighty and the Lamb are its temple.

➤ 23 And the city has no need of the sun or of the moon to shine on it, for the glory of God has illumined it, and its lamp *is* the Lamb.

24 The nations will walk by its light, and the kings of the earth will bring their glory into it.

25 In the daytime (for there will be no night there) its gates will never be closed;

26 and they will bring the glory and the honor of the nations into it;

27 and nothing unclean, and no one who practices abomination and lying, shall ever come into it, but only those whose names are written in the Lamb's book of life.

22 THEN he showed me a river of the water of life, clear as crystal, coming from the throne of God and of the Lamb,

2 in the middle of its street. On either side of the river was the tree of life, bearing twelve *kinds of* fruit, yielding its fruit every month; and the leaves of the tree were for the healing of the nations.

3 There will no longer be any curse; and the throne of God and of the Lamb will be in it, and His bond-servants will serve Him;

4 they will see His face, and His name *will be* on their foreheads.

5 And there will no longer be *any* night; and they will not have need of the light of a lamp nor the light of the sun, because the Lord God will illumine them; and they will reign forever and ever.

6 And he said to me, "These words are faithful and true"; and the Lord, the God of the spirits of the prophets, sent His angel to show to His bond-servants the things which must soon take place.

7 "And behold, I am coming quickly. Blessed is he who heeds the words of the prophecy of this book."

8 I, John, am the one who heard and saw these things. And when I heard and saw, I fell down to worship at the feet of the angel who showed me these things.

9 But he *said to me, "Do not do that. I am a fellow servant of yours and of your brethren the prophets and of those who heed the words of this book. Worship God."

10 And he *said to me, "Do not seal up the words of the prophecy of this book, for the time is near.

11 "Let the one who does wrong, still do wrong; and the one who is filthy, still be filthy; and let the one who is righteous, still practice righteousness; and the one who is holy, still keep himself holy."

12 "Behold, I am coming quickly, and My reward *is* with Me, to render to every man according to what he has done.

13 "I am the Alpha and the Omega, the first and the last, the beginning and the end." ✴

14 Blessed are those who wash their ◁ robes, so that they may have the right to the tree of life, and may enter by the gates into the city.

15 Outside are the dogs and the sorcerers and the immoral persons and the murderers and the idolaters, and everyone who loves and practices lying.

16 "I, Jesus, have sent My angel to testify to you these things for the churches. I am the root and the descendant of David, the bright morning star."

17 The Spirit and the bride say, "Come." And let the one who hears say, "Come." And let the one who is thirsty come; let

---

LIFE LESSONS

➤ **Revelation 22:14** — *Blessed are those who wash their robes, so that they may have the right to the tree of life, and may enter by the gates into the city.*

*A*ll the way through the Bible, from Genesis to Revelation, we learn that obedience to God's commands brings great blessing. We have washed our robes in the blood of the Lamb and because we have submitted ourselves to the Lord in this, we are invited to eat of the tree of life—the very tree Adam and Eve were prevented from partaking of after they sinned (Gen. 3:22–24).

the one who wishes take the water of life without cost.

18 I testify to everyone who hears the words of the prophecy of this book: if anyone adds to them, God will add to him the plagues which are written in this book;

19 and if anyone takes away from the words of the book of this prophecy, God will take away his part from the tree of life and from the holy city, which are written in this book.

➤ **20** He who testifies to these things says, "Yes, I am coming quickly." Amen. Come, Lord Jesus.

21 The grace of the Lord Jesus be with all. Amen.